ROTHMANS FOOTBALL YEARBOOK 1989–90

EDITOR: JACK ROLLIN

QUEEN ANNE PRESS
MACDONALD & CO
LONDON and SYDNEY

A Queen Anne Press BOOK

First published in Great Britain in 1989 by
Queen Anne Press, a division of
Macdonald & Co (Publishers) Ltd
66–73 Shoe Lane
London EC4P 4AB

A member of Maxwell Pergamon Publishing Corporation plc

Cover photograph: (by *Steve Bacon*) West Ham United v Norwich City

Other photographic acknowledgements
All-Sport Photographic Ltd: Pages 9, 657, 859, 869, 975
Associated Sports Photography: Pages 8 (3), 9 (4), 654, 859
Colorsport: Pages 8 (2), 9 (5), 32, 35, 593, 742, 882, 885, 888, 941
Doug Poole: Pages 8, 9, 940
Syndication International: Page 944
Norman Barrett: Page 944

British Library Cataloguing in Publication Data
Rothmans football yearbook.—1989–90
1. Association football – Serials
796.334′05

ISBN 0-356-17921-4
ISBN 0-356-17910-9 Pbk

Typeset, printed and bound in Great Britain by
BPCC Hazell Books Ltd
Member of BPCC Ltd
Aylesbury, Bucks, England

CONTENTS

FOREWORD FROM ROTHMANS PUBLICATIONS LTD

The pages of this, the 20th edition of the *Rothmans Football Yearbook*, reflect all aspects of the past season which was overshadowed by the tragedy at Hillsborough.

This year the Rothmans Awards feature The Best British International Players of the last 20 years to commemorate this milestone edition.

Moreover, Rothmans are pleased to have been able to extend their involvement with football further than the Yearbook, by way of supporting the National Federation of Football Supporters Clubs, team and individual football quizzes, known as *The Rothmans Football Quiz* and *The Rothmans Football Mastermind* respectively, for which all the questions are based on information contained in the Yearbook.

In addition, we have linked with the Football League in a new sponsorship initiative. The *Rothmans Football League Bursary* is the first sponsorship of this type in British Soccer, which will enable one of the League's Commercial Managers to visit a top American NFL team, to study their way of handling the business aspect of football.

INTRODUCTION

To mark the 20th edition of *Rothmans Football Yearbook*, there are several exciting innovations as well as an increase in the number of pages. Every one of the 92 Football League clubs has a full page photograph of the 1988–89 squad and there are now six pages devoted to each team with extended information in an easier-to-read style of presentation. Throughout the book the emphasis is focused on a comprehensive study of the previous season while retaining a balance with vital historical material for reference purposes. Increased coverage of the GM Vauxhall Conference, a new International Section and special articles on Sport and the Law, the All-Party Football Committee at the House of Commons and the Football Trust are also featured.

All international matches involving the four home countries and the Republic of Ireland are also dealt with, together with coverage of Welsh and Northern Irish League football. More familiar items are a list of transfers during the season, important addresses, the Laws of the Game and Football League managers for each League club over the years.

The Editor would like to thank Maurice Golesworthy for historical notes on the clubs and the diary, as well as Alan Elliott for the Scottish section and Norman Barrett for picture research. Thanks are also due to Melanie Georgi, whose painstaking and conscientious reading of the proofs has been of invaluable assistance in the preparation of the book.

The Editor would also like to pay tribute to the various organisations who have helped to make this edition complete, especially Mike Foster of the Football League, Mike McNamara of The Football Association, and the secretaries of all the Football League and Scottish League clubs for their kind co-operation. The ready availability of Football League secretary David Dent and his staff to answer queries was as usual most appreciated, and thanks are due in equal measure to Jim Farry, the Scottish Football League secretary, and his staff.

ACKNOWLEDGEMENTS

The Editor would like to express his appreciation of the following individuals and organisations for their co-operation: Glynis Firth, Sandra Whiteside, Sheila Murphy and Debbie Birch (all from The Football League), David Barber and Steve Clark (The Football Assoc-iation), David C. Thompson of The Scottish Football League, Brian Turner (FA of Wales), Alan Dick, Malcolm Brodie, C. S. Allatt (English Schools FA), W. P. Goss (AFA), Ken Scott for GM Vauxhall Conference information, C. Ashridge, Rev. Nigel Sands, Edward Grayson, Andy Howland, Don Aldridge and former *Rothmans Football Yearbook* editor Peter Dunk.

Finally, thanks to Celia Kent, Editorial Director at Queen Anne Press, for her support and encouragement during the year, and to Jo O'Neill (Celia Kent's assistant), not forgetting Ian McFarlane and the staff at BPCC Hazell Books for their enthusiasm and commitment in the production of this book. This was much appreciated in the final stages.

EDITORIAL

Heysel and Hillsborough were horrific tragedies. At each event the victims were the innocent. Yet in the most simplistic of terms, the prime causes could be attributed to the low standard of behaviour to which so-called civilisation has sunk. One one side, the aggressive nature of the human being carried beyond acceptable levels, on the other hand the total neglect of normal functions of duty.

By an irony of fate, the Heysel verdict on accused Liverpool followers came in the aftermath of the death toll which finally numbered 95 at Hillsborough, all of them supporters of the Anfield club. The game cannot afford to witness anything approaching either catastrophe again.

All-seater stadiums seem certain to become the norm in the future. Already FIFA has ruled such for its next World Cup series. And in this edition of the Yearbook, the Football League has produced an interesting set of projected figures for all-seater grounds among the 92 League clubs. Seating will not eliminate the hooligan, but it may help towards deterring him. The real answer is to attract a better behaved type of spectator and this may take some time.

People who have been driven away from attending games but retain an interest, must be encouraged to return. They will only do so when the atmosphere at grounds improves. The game needs strong leadership. There can be no acceptable levels of pitch invasion, no mere token attempts to ban obscene and racial chants.

None of us can escape criticism for the situation in which football finds itself. Blaming society for soccer's ills is merely a cop-out. The game cannot disown those travelling to and from matches any more than science can escape blame for its destruction of the ozone layer. The media must take full responsibility for encouraging the win-at-all-costs attitude which leads the simple-minded towards tribal warfare. The well-behaved spectator must not be naive enough to imagine his or her needs should take precedence over the priority to eradicate the hooligan.

Fences were originally erected because opposing fans could not be trusted to mingle with each other without fighting. Outside grounds they must also be separated for the same reasons. Policing costs may be crippling but withdrawing present levels would surely destroy any theory that trouble is exaggerated.

The hooligan can be either the premeditated troublemaker or the susceptible, usually the worse for drink. According to RSL Leisure Monitor's annual survey sample, the group which has the highest proportion of attendance at matches is the 15–24 age group. The same section also consumes more alcohol than any other. Another survey actually produced figures to say that 77% of 15 year olds are drinking up to half the acceptable level of alcohol per week considered wise on health grounds.

Not all these youngsters attend matches, though there must be a fair proportion of them. Alcohol abuse is the gravest danger facing the community next to drug addiction. To many people, drink and the hooligan would seem to be synonymous. Agan those advocating sensible drinking habits must be given greater publicity.

The Government's identity scheme may not solve the problem. It will certainly cost clubs financially. Politicians in general must be treated with caution. The Opposition has u-turned on its principles to such a degree that the game would be at the mercy of whatever current whim possessed it, should it gain office itself. As far as the vitriolic attacks from all quarters on Sports Minister Colin Moynihan, one suspects that had the incumbent not been a boat race cox but a boxing blue built like Frank Bruno, he would not have been subjected to the same abuse – "know wot I mean, 'arry."

Naturally the good in the game is submerged by its continuing malaise. The work of the Football Trust and the involvement of football in the community is documented in this Yearbook. The government benefits mightily from its taxation of the game, but also renders excellent practical service to it through the Trainee scheme.

Attendances rose at Barclays League games for the third successive season to the level of six years ago. Family membership schemes have proved popular and must be encouraged, especially as the long term scenario will be for teenagers and young people to diminish as the birth rate drops.

The close season saw the British transfer market stunned by Chris Waddle's transfer from Tottenham Hotspur to Marseille for a record £4.5 million. Waddle's colleague in the England side Gary Lineker arrived from Barcelona to replace him at a more modest £1.5 million. A similar fee bought Mo Johnston to Rangers from Nantes. In this move, Rangers manager Graeme Souness and the club's board challenged Glasgow to show that religion has no part in sport. Johnston seemed set to return to his old club Celtic when Rangers bid for him, the first leading Catholic to join Protestant Rangers.

The Scottish Cup is to be sponsored by Tennents. The FA Cup is up for grabs itself. There seems to be no lack of sponsorship interest and with the transfer market booming, little substance for the game to complain that it cannot afford to improve its facilities or its image.

JACK ROLLIN

Rothmans Football Awards 1989

Selecting a team which will never be expected to prove itself on the field of play, might seem a comparatively easy task. But to achieve a list of the best international players from Britain over the last two decades, to mark the 20th edition of Rothmans Football Yearbook, requires as much thought and care – if not more – than a practical exercise.

Rothmans Publications Ltd in conjunction with Paragaon Communications arranged for a panel of judges to choose the Rothmans Football Allstars. A distinguished quintet under the chairmanship of Ted Croker, former secretary of the Football Association, met at the Grosvenor House Hotel, Park Lane, London on March 29. The other members of the selecting panel were: Brian Roach (Rothmans Publications Ltd), Ken Montgomery (Chief Football Correspondent, *Sunday Mirror* and Football Writers Association Chairman), Ian St John (London Weekend Television) and Alan Samson (Pubishing Director, Queen Anne Press), the latter being a late replacement for the withdrawal of Gordon Taylor (Chief Executive, Professional Footballers Association).

The criterion for selection of the team was that all players and the manager must have represented their country (England, Scotland, Wales or Northern Ireland) between January 1, 1969 and March 29, 1989. The squad had to be made up of 11 players, five substitutes and one manager with each player/manager considered at the 'peak' of his career within the specified time.

It was also designed to provide the best individual for each position, rather than players who might fit into any overall system in the side as a whole. Though players from all the four home countries were considered, there was no attempt to reprsent all of them in the final selection.

Each position was to be taken in isolation, no particular team pattern would be pre-ordained, but once judging began, it soon became evident that the selection would be easier to obtain by splitting the team into attack, midfield, defence and goalkeeper. Again, once the lively discussions began on individual players, it was agreed that entertainment value was to be a prime objective and to this end the attack and midfield areas were dovetailed to some degree.

Shortlists were voted on by members of the panel with the chairman having the casting vote on split decisions. At the end of a fascinating debate, liberally sprinkled with anecdotes about the characters proposed and with David Brain (Paragon Communications) and Jack Rollin (Editor, Rothmans Football Yearbook) holding a watching brief, the strength of the final selection is probably best judged by those players mentioned during the discussions who did not make the side or the substitutes bench.

Gary Lineker, Trevor Francis, and John Toshack wre among the strikers, Jimmy Johnstone as a winger, Alan Ball, Colin Bell, Trevor Brooking, Billy Bremner and Glenn Hoddle in midfield. In defence Phil Neal, Gary Stevens, Richard Gough and Mick Mills all had strong claims put forward for them.

Goalkeepers who also came under the spotlight were Peter Shilton, Neville Southall and Ray Clemence. Then for the managerial spot, the late Jock Stein, Billy Bingham and Bobby Robson were those who entered the list of possibilities. Only international managers were considered.

The argument was constructive and thoroughly enjoyed by all present, the final selection of the panellists being a tribute to their expertise, personal preference and collective compromise.

THE BEST BRITISH INTERNATIONAL PLAYERS OF THE LAST 20 YEARS

THE ROTHMANS ALLSTARS SQUAD

1970–71

Manager: SIR ALF RAMSEY

1989–90

GORDON BANKS
(England)

DANNY McGRAIN
(Scotland)

BOBBY MOORE
(England)

ALAN HANSEN
(Scotland)

KENNY SANSOM
(England)

GRAEME SOUNESS
(Scotland)

BOBBY CHARLTON
(England)

BRYAN ROBSON
(England)

KENNY DALGLISH
(Scotland)

IAN RUSH
(Wales)

GEORGE BEST
(Northern Ireland)

Substitutes:

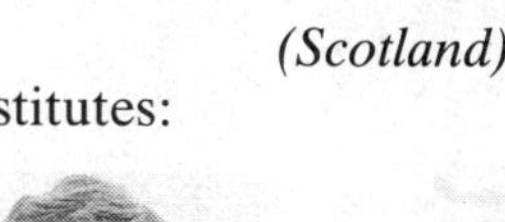

PAT JENNINGS
(Northern Ireland)

KEVIN RATCLIFFE
(Wales)

STEVE NICOL
(Scotland)

KEVIN KEEGAN
(England)

DENIS LAW
(Scotland).

MILESTONES DIARY 1988-89

July 1988

4 At the **FIFA conference** in Zurich the **United States** get the vote to stage the **1994 World Cup. Rochdale** appoint Uruguayan **Danny Bergara** as manager – the **first foreign manager** in the Football League.

5 **Everton** not only sign **Pat Nevin** from **Chelsea** at a fee to be settled by a tribunal but increase their offer to **West Ham** for **Tony Cottee** to **£2m.**

6 At a **Downing Street** meeting on soccer **hooliganism,** figures from the Association of **Police Officers** reveal that **arrests** at **Football League** matches in **England** last season were **10%** up on the previous year. **Tottenham Hotspur** appear to have beaten a counter bid from **Manchester United** and expect to sign **Newcastle's England U-21** midfielder **Paul Gascoigne** for a record **British transfer fee** of **£2m. Plymouth Argyle** appoint **Ken Brown** as **manager** with a three-year contract.

10 There is a threat of a split in the Football League as **ITV** offer **£33m** over four years to screen **League** and **Littlewoods Cup** games. This amount to be shared among 10 clubs. The top five of these – **Liverpool, Everton, Manchester United, Arsenal** and **Tottenham Hotspur** being guaranteed **£600,000** a year plus **£150,000** per game. The second five – **Aston Villa, Newcastle United, Nottingham Forest, Sheffield Wednesday** and **West Ham United** are guaranteed **£400,000** a year plus **£150,000** per game. **BBC** and **British Satellite Broadcasting** are offering **£39m** or maybe up to **£47m** over four years to be divided between the **League** and the **F.A.**

11 **Jim McLean,** 17 years **Dundee United's** manager, threatens to quit the game following the **SFA's £4,000 fine** and three-year touchline ban over his confrontation with **Aberdeen** skipper **Willie Miller.**

12 The **Football League** obtain an injunction in the **High Court** preventing the big five clubs signing a separate deal with **ITV. Peterborough United** promote **assistant-manager Mick Jones** to **manager** while **Noel Cantwell** becomes **General Manager. Swansea City** manager **Terry Yorath** is appointed part-time **Wales** team-manager.

13 The threat of a breakaway **Super-League** remains a possibility as **ITV** increase their offer to **£52m** for four years. However, after a meeting of the 10 big clubs at Old Trafford, League president **Philip Carter** says that the increased offer will be of overall benefit to all clubs. **Chelsea** are fined a record **£75,000** plus costs by the **FA** for failing to control spectators after their play-off against **Middlesbrough** on **May 28.** Other restrictions are imposed on the club. **Everton** are advised that the fee for **Chelsea's Pat Nevin** will be **£925,000.** This is the **largest fee** ever fixed by a **tribunal. Everton** had bid **400,000** while **Chelsea** were asking **£1.7m. Everton** manager **Colin Harvey** calls for a change in the tribunal system.

15 At today's meetings of the **Football League Management committee** and the full members (**eight** of the **10** rebel clubs do not attend) there is an agreement that the **EGM** will consider both **TV** bids. The tone of the meetings indicate that there is now **less chance** of a **split.** However, the **League** will return to **Court** on Tuesday asking for an extension to the **injunction** if the **10 big clubs** do not agree to forget about a unilateral deal with **ITV.**

16 Busy **Everton** sign **Neil McDonald – Newcastle's** right-back as replacement for **Gary Stevens** who has joined **Glasgow Rangers** for **£1m.**

19 The **High Court** extend the **Football League's injunction.** At a meeting at **Villa Park, First Division** clubs decide to recommend acceptance of a revised **ITV** offer at the **League's EGM** on August 8. This **offer** will **heal** the **split** as the money will be **shared 80%** to the **First Division** and **20%** to the **remainder. Manchester United** manager **Alex Ferguson** is surprised at the lack of interest shown by leading clubs in transfer-listed **Norman Whiteside** and **Paul McGrath.**

20 There is a **move** afoot to **unseat League** president **Philip Carter** following criticism of his involvement with the big five's threat to break away from the League over the deal with **ITV.**

22 In the **High Court** the **League drop** their **injunction** as the **rebel clubs agree** that no matches can be televised without the League's consent.

25 **Tony Cottee,** who has had talks with **Everton** and **Arsenal,** decides to join the former from **West Ham.** The fee at **£2.2m** is a **British record.**

26 **Andy Thorn** moves from **Wimbledon** to **Newcastle** for **£850,000.**

28 **West Ham United** defender **Billy Bonds** decides to retire less than two months short of his **42nd** birthday after a total of **758 League appearances** including **95** for his first club **Charlton Athletic.**

August 1988

5 **Chelsea** sign Welsh international **Peter Nicholas** from **Aberdeen** for **£350,000.**

8 The **£44m ITV** deal is saved by **Players' Union** boss **Gordon Taylor** agreeing to accept only **5%** of the money on offer. After the **League's** extraordinary general meeting's **discussion** about the **TV** deal, **Sports Minister Colin Moynihan** warns that he still wants a **membership scheme** within a **year** to combat soccer **hooliganism. Player-manager Graeme Souness** agrees to allow unhappy **Graham Roberts** to leave **Ibrox** and return to London to join **Chelsea** for **£475,000**

9 Former **Tottenham** and **Barcelona** star **Steve Archibald** signs for **Hibernian.** In a part-exchange deal, experienced **Trevor Hebberd** joins **Derby** who pay **Oxford United £200,000** plus **Mickey Lewis.**

10 Steve Hodge, whom **Brian Clough** sold to **Aston Villa,** returns to **Nottingham Forest** from **Tottenham Hotspur** for a fee of **£550,000,** but only after some hard bargaining between Clough and the player. Honest **Steve Wicks** owns up to having back trouble and his proposed move from **Chelsea** to **Spurs** falls through.

12 **Chelsea's** appeal against the record **£75,000 fine** for crowd trouble **fails.**
13 The **B & Q League** kicks off in **Scotland** with **low scoring** and no surprises except for **Montrose's 6-2** win at **Cowdenbeath** with **Gary Murray** getting the season's first hat-trick. In the **international tournament** at Wembley, **Arsenal** thrash **Spurs 4-0.**
14 **Arsenal** win the **Wembley** tournament by beating **Bayern Munich 3-0. Vinny Jones'** reputation as a hard man gains publicity as he is **sent off** in **Wimbledon's** friendly on the **Isle of Wight** after a **Shanklin** defender is knocked out.
15 **Wimbledon** fine **Vinny Jones £1000** and he will not play in Saturday's **Charity Shield** game.
16 Recently warned about his future behaviour by **Villa** manager **Graham Taylor, Warren Aspinall** is transferred to **Portsmouth** for **£315,000. Paul McGrath** settles his differences with **Manchester United.**
17 **Wimbledon** begin rebuilding their side by signing former **Spurs** and **Norwich** midfielder **Garry Brooke** from Dutch club **Groningen** for **£100,000.**
18 Transfer sensation brings **Ian Rush** back to **Liverpool** from **Juventus** in **£2.8m** deal, 15 months after he left Anfield for **£3.2m.** There is immediate speculation about the future of last season's leading **Liverpool** scorer **John Aldridge. PFA** boss **Gordon Taylor** is widely considered favourite to become **chief executive** of the **Football League. Swindon Town** postpone their opening game for safety reasons. **John O'Neill,** who was **injured** on his debut for **Norwich** last December following his transfer from **QPR** is forced to quit the game.
20 **John Aldridge** scores both of **Liverpool's goals** as they avenge last season's **FA Cup** final defeat by beating **Wimbledon 2-1** in the **FA Charity Shield** game in front of a crowd of **54,887** at **Wembley.**
21 Expensive **Spurs** suffer their fourth defeat in five pre-season games going down **2-0** at **West Ham. George Best** fails to turn up for **Kevin Moran's testimonial** game at Old Trafford. **QPR** return to grass with a friendly against **Al Ahly** from **Egypt.**
22 **Walsall** shareholders agree to plans to **sell Fellows Park** and build a new stadium.
23 The **FA International Committee** accept manager **Bobby Robson's report** on **England's dismal display** in the **European Championship** and also set up a three-man committee to investigate allegations about skipper **Bryan Robson's** night club drinking three days before leaving for the championships. Another **Englishman** leaves **Glasgow Rangers** – full-back **Jimmy Phillips** joins **Oxford United** for **£150,000.**
25 **PFA** boss **Gordon Taylor** is angered by the campaign to depose **Bryan Robson** as **England** captain.
27 **Tony Cottee, Everton's £2.2m** summer signing from **West Ham,** hits the **fastest goal** as the Football League season gets under way. He scores after **34 seconds** and goes on to complete a hat-trick in a 4-0 win over **Newcastle.** Other first day **hat-tricks** come from **John Aldridge** in **Liverpool's 3-0** away win against **Charlton** and **Arsenal's Alan Smith** as the Gunners win **5-1** at **Wimbledon. Spurs** have to **postpone** their opening game against **Coventry City** because continuing building work means that **safety regulations** cannot be met. **Peterborough,** who draw **2-2** at **Carlisle** in the Fourth Division, have **gone longer** than any other Football League side **without defeat** in the season's opening game – **12 years. Dave Cowling** scores the first goal at **Scunthorpe's new Glanford Road** ground as they beat **Hereford United 3-1.** In Scotland, **Rangers** with **six Englishmen** in the side, rock **Celtic 5-1** at Ibrox to **equal** their **highest-ever League** score against their keenest rivals.
29 The **Scottish FA** agree **£1m** deal to screen **Scottish Cup** and **World Cup** Games. In the Second Division, **Oldham** win **4-1** at **Manchester City** with a **Roger Palmer hat-trick.**
30 **Notts County** beat **Mansfield Town 5-0** in a First Round (1st leg) **Littlewoods Cup** tie as **Ian McParland** scores a **hat-trick.**
31 Fourth Division **Peterborough** gain an easy **3-0 Littlewoods Cup** victory at **West Bromwich.**

September 1988

1 Malicious gossip about the threat to **Bryan Robson's England captaincy** ends as manager **Bobby Robson** names him for the squad to meet **Denmark** at Wembley. **David Bulstrode,** chairman of **QPR** dies suddenly aged 48. **Falkirk** part company with **manager Dave Clarke.**
3 Newly promoted **Aston Villa** win **3-2** at **Arsenal** – only their second victory in the past 15 years at Highbury. A crowd of nearly **33,000** at **Newcastle** for the return of **Paul Gascoigne** with **Spurs** watch a **2-2** draw. **Liverpool** nail their **Manchester United** bogey **1-0** with a **Jan Molby penalty** – their first win over United in a run of **13 League games.** After only four games there are **no 100%** records in the **Scottish League** which is headed by **Rangers** who register their fifth successive League victory at **Motherwell.**
6 **Bobby Robson** introduces a number of uncapped players into his squad for the game with **Denmark** while discarding six with a total of **216** caps between them. The most senior to be dropped are **Kenny Sansom** and **Glenn Hoddle.** In the **European Cup Winners' Cup, Dundee United** can only gain a goalless draw away to Maltese part-timers **Floriana.** Any hopes of relegated **Reading** being able to defend the **Simod Cup** are officially **dashed.** The competition is only for First and Second Division clubs.
7 **Rangers** scrape a **1-0** home victory over Polish side **Katowice** in the First Round (1st leg) of **UEFA Cup,** while **Aberdeen** are held to a **goalless draw** at home to **Dynamo Dresden. Celtic** are beaten **1-0** by **Honved** in Hungary in the **European Cup** in front of a crowd of only **7,000. West Bromwich** are knocked out of the **Littlewoods Cup 3-2** on aggregate despite a fighting come-back and a **2-0** win at **Peterborough.**
8 The **FA's six-match ban** on **Chelsea** selling tickets on match days is **relaxed** for Saturday **games because of the postal strike. The Football League** tribunal cut **Portsmouth's £60,000** valuation of striker **Andy Perry** to **£5,000** plus 50% of any future profits from transfers. **Gillingham** had valued him at **£2,000** when they signed him. **Richard Thompson** becomes the League's **youngest chairman** at **24** when he takes over at **QPR.**

10 **Southampton** make it three wins in a row (their best start for 31 years) by beating **Luton 2-1** and lead the First Division with **Norwich** who have also collected maximum points after beating **QPR 1-0. Burnley** hit the first "six" of the season beating **York City 6-0** in the Fourth Division. After three games, only **Middlesbrough** (Div. 1) and **Brighton** and **Birmingham** (Div. 2) are pointless. **Brighton** goalkeeper **Perry Digweed** fails to turn up for their game with **Bournemouth** because nobody had advised him he was playing. Because of next week's **World Cup** game in **Norway** the Scottish Premier Division has a day off, but in the Second Division **Berwick** make it five defeats in a row.

12 **Dumbarton,** next to bottom in the Second Division, dismiss **manager Bertie Auld.**

13 **Enland** manager **Bobby Robson** annoys his critics by not including new youngsters into tomorrow's team to meet **Denmark** at Wembley. **England U-21** use all of their players, including three substitutes, but are held to a **goalless draw** by **Denmark U-21.**

14 A crowd of only **25,837** at **Wembley** watch **England** beat **Denmark** by a **single goal** in their friendly with **Neil Webb** the scorer. In the **World Cup** qualifying games **N. Ireland** survive an early **Eire** onslaught and goal claim to fight out a **goalless draw** amid tight security at Windsor Park. Injury hit **Scotland** win **2-1** in **Norway** while **Wales** hold out until the 83rd minute, thanks to great goalkeeping by **Neville Southall,** before **Ruud Gullit** scores **Holland's** winner in Amsterdam.

16 A number of Football League clubs want to sign **Lee Chapman** who seeks a return home after only three months with French club **Niort** following his **£290,000** transfer from **Sheffield Wednesday.**

17 **QPR** end the worst start in their history as veteran **Trevor Francis** scores their first goals of the season in a **2-0** win over **Sheffield Wednesday. Norwich** march on with their **fourth successive victory – a club record start**– beating **Newcastle 2-0** at St. James' Park. **Southampton's** run of victories ends in a **2-2** draw at Highbury although **Arsenal's equaliser** is scored in the seventh minute of injury time. **Southampton's Glenn Cockerill** suffers a **broken jaw** in being floored by **Paul Davis. Middlesbrough** and **Birmingham** get off the mark and only **Brighton** are still without a point after four games. In the Third Division **Sheffield United** produce the season's **first double hat-trick – Brian Deane** and **Tony Agana** sharing the goals between them in a **6-1** victory over **Chester. Rangers** continue to lead the Premier Division extending their unbeaten run at **Hearts** to five games with a **2-1** victory, but **Celtic** slump to seventh position after losing 3-1 at home to **Aberdeen** – the Dons first win in 11 League visits to Parkhead.

19 Found guilty of "poaching", **Derby County** are fined **£5,000** by the Football League. **Wolves** had complained about **Derby** signing **16-year-old Kris Sleeuwenhoek. Gordon Taylor,** who has been strongly tipped to succeed **Graham Kelly** as secretary of the **Football League** decides to remain **chief executive** of the **Professional Footballers' Association. Bobby Saxton** resigns as manager of bottom-of-the-League **York City.**

20 **Derby County** agree a fee of **£300,000** with French club **Niort** for **Lee Chapman** but the player may prefer to join **Nottingham Forest.** Injury-hit **Liverpool** go down **2-1** to **Arsenal** at Highbury in the semi-finals of the **Mercantile Credit Centenary Trophy.** In the Second Division, **Walsall** slam neighbours **Birmingham 5-0. Southampton's Glenn Cockerill** decides not to take a private action against **Arsenal's Paul Davis** following the incident on Saturday which left Cockerill with a broken jaw.

21 **Brighton** suffer their seventh successive defeat losing **1-0** at home to **West Bromwich Albion** after their goalkeeper went off injured.

22 **Glasgow Rangers** are fined the equivalent of **£3,800** and full-back **John Brown** is suspended for **two European matches** following an incident in their **UEFA Cup** match against **Katowice** at Ibrox.

24 Considering the amount of **crowd trouble** there has been at this fixture, the **FA** and **Scottish FA** decide that there will be no more **England v Scotland** games on a **Saturday** at Wembley, but they will be played in **mid-week.** Despite being without some of their star players, **Liverpool** win **3-1** at **Southampton** and move into second place behind **Norwich,** who drop their first points of the season in a **2-2** draw with another undefeated side, **Millwall,** at Carrow Road. **Brighton** are the only club still **without a point** after six games. **Celtic** suffer their fourth League defeat of the season going down **1-0** at **Dundee** where **Tommy Coyne** scores his first of the season. **Four defeats** after only six games is one more than **Celtic** suffered all last season.

27 Following trouble at last week's First Round (2nd leg) **Littlewoods Cup** tie at **Swansea, Cardiff City** fans are **banned** for tonight's Littlewoods Cup game at **QPR** and other away games until further notice.

28 **Liverpool** can only beat **Walsall 1-0** at Anfield in the 1st leg of their Second Round **Littlewoods Cup** tie. Full-back **Gary Gillespie** gets the winner a minute before the interval and **Kenny Dalglish** comes on for a rare appearance after 65 minutes. Veteran **Trevor Francis** continues to please **QPR** who beat **Cardiff 3-0** in another **Littlewoods Cup** tie, while **Nottingham Forest** show better form than of late by thrashing **Chester 6-0. Leeds United** sack **manager Billy Bremner** after only one win in their first six Second Division games.

29 **Arsenal's Paul Davis** receives a **nine-game ban** and a **£3,000** fine for throwing the punch which broke **Glenn Cockerill's jaw** nearly two weeks ago. This is the **longest ban** for a single offence since the **present disciplinary points system** was introduced. Struggling **Brighton** sign **Sheffield Wednesday's** central defender **Larry May** for **£200,000. Sports Minister Colin Moynihan** re-iterates the Government's insistance on a **national membership scheme** for football supporters to commence next season and be **financed** by the **League.**

30 There is speculation about **Derby** manager **Arthur Cox** returning to **Newcastle** to displace **Willie McFaul. Chelsea** want **West Bromwich** goalkeeper **Stuart Naylor** but he is priced at **£750,000. Hibernian** are going public (like Tottenham Hotspur) and are floating **£2m** worth of shares onto the market.

October 1988

1 **Russia** win the **Olympic gold** by beating **Brazil 2-1** after extra time in front of a crowd of **73,675** in **Seoul. Newcastle,** without a win in their opening five games, shock **Liverpool** with a **2-1** win at Anfield – **Liverpool's first home defeat** in the League **since** losing to **Wimbledon** in **March 1987.** It was also the Geordies' **first League win** at Anfield for **37 years**. One of **Newcastle's** heroes is goalkeeper **Dave Beasant** who also figured in that **Wimbledon** shock win on this ground. Undefeated **Millwall** lead the First Division after beating **QPR 3-2.** A **hat-trick** is scored for both sides in **Middlesbrough's 4-3** win at **Coventry** – **Bernie Slaven** and **David Speedie** achieving this distinction. At the bottom of the Second Division, **Brighton** gain their first points of the season by beating managerless **Leeds 2-1. Rangers** hold their lead with a **2-0** victory over **Dundee,** while **Celtic's** slack defence brings them their fifth defeat in eight games – going down **3-1** to unbeaten **Hibernian.**

3 **Millionaire John Hall** doubles his previous offer for **Newcastle United shares** to **£1,000** each in his bid to gain control.

4 Bottom of the Second Division **Birmingham City,** suffer their fifth successive defeat losing **1-0** at home to **Plymouth Argyle.**

5 **Jimmy Gilligan** scores a hat-trick as **Cardiff City** beat **Derry 4-0** at home and go through to the next round of the **European Cup Winners' Cup. Celtic** get back on the winning trail by thrashing **Honved 4-0** (winning 4-1 on aggregate) in the First Round of the **European Cup. Terry Butcher** stars in **Rangers'** outstanding **4-2** victory in Poland against League leaders **Katowice** by heading two goals. Rangers win this **UEFA** tie **5-2** on aggregate. **Footballers' wages** have **doubled** in the past **eight years** but their Union's chief executive **Gordon Taylor** says that they should get **more** when **wages** are related to **gate money.**

6 **Ken Wheldon,** chairman of struggling **Birmingham,** says he will back manager **Garry Pendrey** at least until the end of the season. **England** cancel friendly in **Morocco** and will play **Saudi Arabia** instead.

7 The transfer of **Lee Chapman** from French club **Niort** to **Nottingham Forest** is **held up** by the Football League because **Sheffield Wednesday** have not yet received the balance of their **£290,000** fee for the player.

8 **Norwich** return to the top of the First Division after winning by an "own goal" at **Derby** where the scorer, **Mark Wright,** and **Norwich** winger **Trevor Putney** are sent off. **Nottingham Forest** get their first win of the season – 2-1 at **QPR. Liverpool** lose for the second time in succession – this time **1-0** at **Luton** where **Mick Harford** gets the winner. **Spurs** are held up in a traffic jam and arrive late for their game against **Charlton** but draw **2-2.** In the Second Division, **Manchester City** again fail to score at **Ipswich** losing **1-0.** They have **not scored** in over **nine hours** of League football at **Portman Road.** Police disperse an angry crowd of demonstrating fans after **Leeds United's fourth successive defeat – 1-0** by **Watford.** At this early stage, **Shrewsbury** in the Second Division and **Carlisle** and **Darlington** in Division 4 remain the only sides **without a win. Celtic's** poor start to the season is brightened up with a **7-1** beating of **St. Mirren,** including a **hat-trick** by **Mark McGhee. Rangers** suffer their first defeat of the season going down **2-1** in a bad tempered game at **Aberdeen** where police are reported to have interviewed **Terry Butcher** for an incident under the stand after the game. This leaves the **Dons** as the **only unbeaten** side in the **Scottish League.**

9 **Arsenal** beat **Manchester United** 2-1 in final of the **Mercantile Credit Centenary Trophy** at **Villa Park.** One of Tyneside's greatest players **Jackie Milburn, dies** of cancer at the age of **64.**

10 **Newcastle United,** next to bottom of the First Division, sack **manager Willie McFaul** and want **Derby manager Arthur Cox** to succeed him. **Howard Wilkinson** moves from **Sheffield Wednesday** to become **manager** of **Leeds United** with a four-year contract. **Trevor Senior** returns to **Reading** for **£150,000** from **Middlesbrough** 14 months after leaving for **Watford.** He has scored only **nine goals** during his absence from **Reading** for whom he scored over a **century of goals.**

11 **Derby manager Arthur Cox** seeks talks about his future with **chairman Robert Maxwell. Leeds** sack coach **Norman Hunter.** An appeal by **Paul Davis** against his **£3,000** fine is rejected.

12 **West Bromwich manager Ron Atkinson** accepts the managership of **Atletico Madrid.** The job is said to be worth around **£525,000** over two years. He will take his assistant **Colin Addison** with him. **Aston Villa** hammer local rivals **Birmingham 5-0** to go through to the Third Round of the **Littlewoods Cup 7-0** on aggregate. In another tie, a crowd of only **5,814** at **Stamford Bridge** see **Chelsea** held to a **2-2** draw by **Scunthorpe** and go out of the competition **6-3** on aggregate.

13 **Lee Chapman** makes his first appearance for **Nottingham Forest** in their **reserve** team at **Leeds** and must wait until next week for his registration to be accepted by the Football League.

14 **Ron Atkinson** returns from Spain in order to take charge of **West Bromwich** for the last time in their local derby at **Birmingham City,** but is persuaded to stay away by the players who fear an angry demonstration. **Aston Villa's Doug Ellis** is elected to fill the vacancy on the **Football League management committee** left by the death of **David Bulstrode.**

15 Because of next week's **World Cup** qualifying games, there are only **three matches** in the **Football League First Division** and **none** in the **Premier Division** of the **Scottish League. Millwall** are now the League's only remaining **unbeaten side** after playing out a drab **goalless draw** at **Coventry. Mansfield,** the only other unbeaten side before today **lose** by a **solitary goal** at **Reading.** A goal down at **Oldham, Chelsea** fight back to win **4-1** and climb to sixth place in the Second Division. **Oxford** end their run of **20 away games** without a win by beating **Ipswich 2-1** at Portman Road. In the Fourth Division, **Leyton Orient** put **eight** past **Colchester** without reply. **Leyton** previously shared with **Reading** the record for **Colchester's biggest defeat** which had stood at **7-0.**

16 After eight defeats in 10 games, **Chesterfield** sack **manager Kevin Randall.**

17 **Arthur Cox** ends speculation about taking over at **Newcastle** by swearing allegiance to **Derby County. Sheffield Wednesday** receive the **£290,000** owed them by French club **Niort** for striker **Lee Chapman** and his registration with **Nottingham Forest** should now be completed. The **Football**

League deduct two points from **Tottenham Hotspur's** total for calling off their opening game of the season at such short notice. Already in trouble this sends them down to next to bottom in the table. **Liverpool's Jan Molby**gets a three months prison sentence for a driving offence. **Liverpool** are now reduced to 13 fit players with First Division experience.

18 **Everton** chairman **Philip Carter** becomes the first **President** of the **Football League** to be **voted out** of office. **Arsenal** vice-chairman **David Dein** is also removed from the League Management Committee. They have been accused of **showing bias** towards the top clubs during recent TV negotiations which threatened a **breakaway Super League. Colchester** manager **Roger Brown** resigns following last Saturday's **8-0** defeat at **Leyton Orient.**

19 **England's** lack of goalscoring ability is in evidence again as they can only manage a **goalless draw** with **Sweden** at **Wembley** in the World Cup qualifying game. **Wales** miss a **penalty** and disappoint with a **2-2** draw against **Finland** at **Swansea.** In **Hungary, N. Ireland** go down to a **solitary goal** scored five minutes from time, while **Scotland** dismay their fans in a **1-1** draw with **Yugoslavia** at **Hampden** after taking the lead. **Athletic Bilbao manager Howard Kendall** declines the **Newcastle** job.

20 **Liverpool** sign **West Bromwich** defender **David Burrows** for **£500,000.**

21 **Manchester United** are considering **Middlesbrough's £750,000** bid for striker **Peter Davenport.**

22 **Coventry** halt a run of **12 League defeats** at **Anfield** and continue their current run of 10 away League games without defeat by holding **Liverpool** to a **goalless draw. Three Wallace brothers – Danny, Rodney and Ray** – appear in **Southampton's** First Division side beaten **2-1** at home by **Sheffield Wednesday.** It is the first time for **68 years** that three brothers appear in the same First Division side. That is since the **Carr brothers – William, John and George** – with **Middlesbrough. Norwich** open up a three-point lead at the top of the First Division and put **Spurs** under further pressure by beating the Londoners **3-1** at Carrow Road. **Celtic** gain their first away win of the season **2-0** at **Hearts.**

23 **Derby** sign **Oxford's** Welsh international striker **Dean Saunders** for **£1m. Derby** chairman **Robert Maxwell** clinches the deal with his son **Kevin, chairman of Oxford. Rangers** win the **Skol Cup** for the third season in a row beating **Aberdeen 3-2** in a thriller at **Hampden.**

24 **Oxford United manager Mark Lawrenson** threatens to quit over the transfer of **Dean Saunders** – a deal completed without his involvement. **Aston Villa** match **Middlesbrough's £750,000** bid for **Manchester United's Peter Davenport.** In the Fourth Division, **Tranmere Rovers** beat **Lincoln City 1-0** despite being reduced to nine men.

25 **Alan Smith** equals **52-year-old Arsenal record** created by **Ted Drake** by scoring in his **eighth consecutive League game** – a **1-1** draw at **Luton. Oxford** dismiss **manager Mark Lawrenson** following his complaint about the transfer of **Dean Saunders.** He had only been in the job eight months. Assistant **Brian Horton** takes over.

26 **Celtic** are beaten **1-0** at home by **Werder Bremen** in the European Cup Second Round (1st leg) while **Rangers** also lose – **2-0** away to **Cologne** in the **UEFA Cup.** In this latter competition, **Hearts** can only draw **0-0** at home to **Austria Vienna**- both **Cardiff City** and **Dundee United** are beaten at home in the **Cup Winners' Cup** by Aarhus and **Dinamo Bucharest** respectively. League leaders **Norwich** win **2-1** at Old Trafford against **Manchester United,** both of their goals coming in the last five minutes. Following their fifth defeat in six home games, **Gillingham** sack **manager Paul Taylor.**

27 First Division clubs cause widespread annoyance by **snubbing Bobby Charlton's bid** to become a member of the **Football League Management Committee.** They elect **John Smith** (Liverpool) and **Robert Chase** (Norwich) to fill the vacancies.

28 **Sheffield Wednesday** promote assistant-manager **Peter Eustace** to **manager** in succession to **Howard Wilkinson. Manchester United** sign **Luton's** N. Ireland defender **Mal Donaghy** for **£650,000. Wigan's 2-1** win at **Southend** is their first away victory since last January. The **Government** shock the football hierarchy by proposing to impose a **levy on transfer fees** to finance the **identity card scheme.**

29 **Norwich** increase their First Division lead to six points with a **1-1** home draw against **Southampton,** but the crowd at Carrow Road numbers only **14,808,** the third lowest in the First Division which is disappointing for a team going so well. Terry Fenwick scores for both sides as **Spurs** lose **2-1** at Aston Villa. **Fenwick** nets **Spurs'** goal from the **penalty** spot. This defeat puts **Tottenham's £5m** side on the **bottom** of the table – the first time for eight years they have sunk so low. **Millwall,** the League's only remaining undefeated side, go down **4-2** at **Middlesbrough** and drop to third place. For the first time this season **Arsenal's Alan Smith** fails to score but the Gunners beat **Coventry 2-0** to move into second position. **Celtic** suffer their second home defeat of the season **3-2** to **Dundee** who so end a run of 13 away League games without a win. **Middlesbrough** agree to pay **Manchester United £700,000** for **Peter Davenport.**

30 Soccer makes a return to **live TV** at Goodison today when **Everton** draw **1-1** with **Manchester United.** However, the **TV presentation** is **criticised** and **United's manager Alex Ferguson** accuses the **referee** of playing to the cameras.

31 Today's **FA Cup** First Round draw includes **10 former winners** of the trophy. Bottom of the table **Spurs** are said to be prepared to pay **QPR £1m** for goalkeeper **David Seaman.** After nine defeats in a row **Gillingham** appoint **Keith Burkinshaw as manager.**

November 1988

1 Without nearly **£2m** worth of talent in cup-tied **Dean Saunders** and suspended **Mark Wright, Derby** are knocked out of the **Littlewoods Cup 5-0** at West Ham – the Londoners' biggest win for over two years.

2 **Manchester United** go out of the **Littlewoods Cup** losing their Third Round tie **2-1** at **Wimbledon.** Most dramatic moment here is an incident in the tunnel involving **Viv Anderson** and **John Fashanu**

with the **Wimbledon** player allegedly punching Anderson who needed three stitches in his gashed face. In another **Littlewoods Cup** tie **Norwich** suffer only their second defeat of the season losing **2-0** at **Leicester.** The **managers' merry-go-round** continues apace. **PFA** chief **Brian Talbot** is appointed **player-manager** of **West Bromwich Albion; Newcastle** coach **Colin Suggett** is now their temporary team manager; **Chesterfield** new **player-manager** is **Paul Hart** from **Notts County** and **Hartlepools** give their **manager's job** to **Bobby Moncur** two weeks after he had taken the position on a part-time basis.

3 **Trevor Francis** signs a new one and half year contract with **QPR** which will take him past his 36th birthday. **FIFA** place **international ban** on **Chile** because they fail to comply with directions concerning a player's transfer.

5 **Spurs** suffer their fourth consecutive First Division defeat a **3-1** home beating by **Derby. Norwich** open up a seven-point lead by winning **2-0** at **Wimbledon** – their fifth away win in succession. For the first time, both **John Aldridge** and **Ian Rush** score in the same game for **Liverpool** who beat **Middlesbrough 3-0. Plymouth Argyle** veteran **Tommy Tynan scores all his side's goals** as they beat **Blackburn Rovers 4-3** in the Second Division. After losing **3-1** at home to **Doncaster Rovers, Darlington** are still the only club **without a win** this season. Both **Frank McAvennie** and **Mark McGhee score hat-tricks** in **Celtic's 8-0** win over luckless **Hamilton** at Douglas Park. This is **Celtic's biggest win** in the League since beating **Clyde 9-1** just over **17 year ago** and equals the **Premier Division's record** win by **Aberdeen** over **Motherwell** in 1979. Chile reinstated by FIFA.

6 **Arsenal** show themselves as serious Championship contenders by displaying real class in beating **Nottingham Forest 4-1 – Forest's first home defeat** since losing to **Newcastle 10 months** earlier.

7 The **Scottish FA** fine **Rangers** and **England** defender **Terry Butcher £500** for bringing the game into disrepute by kicking the referee's door following the ill-tempered game at **Aberdeen.**

8 **Celtic** give it all they have in their **European Cup** tie in Germany and earn a goalless draw with **Werder Bremen** but even this cannot prevent them losing **1-0** on aggregate.

9 A total of over **94,000** fans watch two key games, one either side of the border. **Arsenal** and **Liverpool** battle out a **goalless draw** at **Highbury** in front of a crowd of more than **54,000** in a **Littlewoods Cup** Third Round replay with around **6,000** more fans unable to gain admission. At Ibrox over **44,000** see **Rangers** knocked out of the **UEFA Cup 3-1** on aggregate after drawing **1-1**. But in the same competition **Hearts** gain a memorable **1-0** victory away to **Austria Vienna** to go through to the Third Round as **Britain's only survivor** in Europe. **Spurs** gain their third win of the season in extra time beating **Blackburn Rovers 2-1** at Ewood Park to win through to the Fourth Round of the **Littlewoods Cup**. **Cardiff City** are knocked out of the **Cup Winners' Cup** being well beaten **4-0** by **Aarhus** in Denmark. Lack of interest in the **Simod Cup** is evident at **Stamford Bridge** where one of **Chelsea's smallest-ever crowds – 4767 – see the Blues beat Plymouth Argyle 6-2**. Having already beaten **Birmingham 5-0** in the **Littlewoods Cup**, **Villa** now make it **6-0** in the **Simod Cup**. The **Government publishes** its proposed legislation to cover **membership cards** for football fans.

11 **Hamilton manager John Lambie** is replaced by **Jimmy Dempsey**. **Eire** international **Liam O'Brien** moves from **Manchester United** to **Newcastle** in **£350,000** transfer.

12 Suffering **Spurs** have **Gary Stevens** stretchered off and probably out for the rest of the season after a tackle by **Wimbledon's Vinny Jones** but they still manage to win **3-2**. The **referee vindicates Jones** by confirming that his first contact was with the ball. Critics who still believe that newly promoted **Millwall** are out of place near the top of the First Division are shocked by the Lions' **1-1** draw at **Liverpool**. With leaders **Norwich** held to a **1-1** draw by **Sheffield Wednesday** at Carrow Road, **Arsenal** close the gap on them with a **1-0** win at **Newcastle** – the Gunners' third League win in a row on this ground. Bottom-of-the-League **Darlington** gain their first victory of the season beating fellow stragglers **Carlisle United 2-1** at Brunton Park. The Old Firm's game at Parkhead draws a crowd of over **60,000** and see **Celtic** win **3-1**. This means that **Rangers** have gone 16 League games without a win on this ground. **Oxford** fans have a petition with around **4,000** names calling for the resignation of **chairman Kevin Maxwell**.

14 In his newly published biography, **Manchester United**'s **Viv Anderson** shocks true-blue sportsmen by strongly supporting the so-called professional foul.

15 **Bobby Robson** includes three newcomers in his side to meet **Saudi Arabia – David Seaman**, **Michael Thomas** and **Mel Sterland**. The **Referees' Association** demand action against **Viv Anderson** for the statement in his biography about cheating on the field.

16 A 54th minute equaliser by **Tony Adams** spares **England's** blushes as they draw **1-1** in **Saudi Arabia**. Including subs, there were no less than **five Arsenal players** in the side and the disappointing result revives the media's recent strong **criticism** of **Robson's England management**. Depleted by injuries, **Eire** are beaten **2-0** in **Spain** in the qualifying competition of the **World Cup**. **Manchester United's Jesper Olsen** will join former **Tottenham** striker **Clive Allen** with **Bordeaux**. The fee: **£400,000**.

18 Former **Hearts** director Douglas Park is fined **£1,000** by the **Scottish League** after the referee and his two linesmen were locked in their dressing room for 45 minutes following **Hearts' 2-1** home defeat by **Rangers** on September 17. The missing key was in Mr. Park's pocket.

19 **Arsenal** narrow the gap at the top to only two points by stretching their unbeaten run to 12 games, with a **3-0** victory over a **Middlesbrough** side that has a generous defence, while **Norwich** draw **1-1** at **Everton**. Third placed **Millwall** are still the First Division's only unbeaten side at home after gaining a decisive **4-0** victory over **Newcastle United**. A run of eight games without defeat takes **Portsmouth** to the top of the Second Division on goal difference over **Watford** and **Blackburn Rovers**. In the First round of the **FA Cup two non-League clubs** beat League sides – **Altrincham** and **Bognor** knocking out **Lincoln** and **Exeter** respectively. **Woking** enjoy the distinction of including **two pairs** of **brothers** in their side but are beaten **4-1** at home by **Cambridge United**. Undefeated **Aberdeen** are only two points behind leaders **Rangers** after beating **Motherwell 2-1**. In the First Division **Gerry McCoy** scores after only **10 seconds** for **Partick** who go on to win **3-1** at **Ayr**.

20 In their **3-0 FA Cup** victory over non-League **Fisher Athletic**, **Bristol Rover**'s defender **Ian Alexander** is saved from death through the prompt action of **physio Roy Dolling** when the player was choking on two swallowed false teeth. **David Webb**, who resigned the managership of **Southend United** 19 months ago, returns as **general manager**. For the first time in over 11 months, **Spurs** register successive League victories. Their **3-2** win over **Wimbledon** eight days ago is followed by a **2-0** victory at **Sheffield Wednesday** where £1.7m Paul Stewart scores both of their goals.

21 **Notts County** director **Jack Dunnett** becomes the **first man** to be elected **president** of the **Football League** for a **second time**. He was president **1981–86**. He pledges himself to fight the Government's membership scheme for the fans. A group of shareholders of unhappy **Birmingham City** fail in their bid to oust chairman **Ken Wheldon**.

22 **FA** charge **Viv Anderson** with bringing the game into disrepute following his remarks about professional fouls. They also **fine Graeme Hogg £2,000** after his criticism of **Manchester United** in a Sunday newspaper. At least **eight First Division clubs** have enthusiastically backed a scheme whereby their **away games** will be beamed to their home ground and shown on **large TV screens**. **Crewe Alexandra** break their run of six seasons without surviving the **FA Cup** First Round by beating **Stafford 3-2** in a replay. But in another replay **Wrexham** lose **3-2** at home to **Runcorn**. the **FA** decide to revive **England B internationals**.

23 Following a takeover of **Glasgow Rangers**, the new company headed by multi-millionaire **David Murray** appoints player-manager **Graeme Souness** to the Board of Directors with a **10%** stake worth **£600,000**. **David Holmes** remains as **chairman**. The **FA** have included **Viv Anderson** in a charge of bringing the game into disrepute for the incident in the tunnel at **Wimbledon** involving **John Fashanu** who has been already charged. **Liverpool** emerge **2-1** winners over **Arsenal** in the second replacy of their Third Round **Littlewoods Cup** tie. **John Aldridge** scores the winner. **Hearts** beat **Velez Moster 3-0** at home in the **UEFA Cup** Third Round (1st leg). **Barcelona** boss **Johan Cruyff** has offered striker **Gary Lineker** to **Manchester United** for £2.5m.

24 The **BBC** and **BSB** complete a five-year **£30m** deal with the **FA** to screen **FA Cup** ties and **England internationals**. **Manchester United** cannot afford to sign **Lineker** and **Arsenal** are not interested. **Glasgow Rangers** are reported as favourites. Viewing figures for **Independent Television**'s first two weeks of live coverage are disappointing.

25 Thirty-nine-year-old **Peter Shilton** signs new two-year contract with **Derby County**. **Brian Clough** expresses his interest in managing the revived **England B** team.

26 None of the League's top five clubs can manage a win. **Derby** who beat **Arsenal 2–1** at the Baseball Ground and **Coventry** with a **2-1** victory over **Aston Villa** are the highest placed winners. **Coventry's** victory is the **first** over **Aston Villa** in the League since **February 1937**. All **12 Second Division** games end in **home wins**. **Barnsley's David Currie** celebrates his **26th birthday** by scoring **four goals** in his side's **5-2** win over **Bournemouth**. **Steve Bull**, last season's leading scorer, is back at the top again as he helps **Wolves** maintain their lead in the Third Division by scoring **four goals** in their **6-0** thrashing of **Preston North End**. This is **Wolves'** highest League score for **12 years** and their **eighth successive victory**. **Aberdeen** suffer their first League defeat of the season going down **1-0** at Ibrox where **Rangers** scored their first goal in a run of four home games against the Dons. **Motherwell** register their first League win of the season **2-0** at home to **Hearts**.

27 The televised **Newcastle – Manchester United** game is criticised as a **bore**. It ends in a **goalless draw** – the fifth successive game in which **Newcastle** have failed to score and **Manchester United's sixth draw** in a row.

28 It is reported that **Barcelona** have told **Aston Villa** that **Gary Lineker** would want **£1m** to return to England. This is the balance of his contract with **Barcelona** which would be in addition to their **£2m** transfer fee. **John Fashanu** wants to leave **Wimbledon**. **Garth Crooks** succeeds **Brian Talbot** as **PFA** chairman. Non-League **Enfield** beat **Leyton Orient 1-0** in the second replay of their **FA Cup** First Round tie. This is the first time for **40 years** that **Orient** have been eliminated from this competition by a **non-League** side. Former **N. Ireland** international **George Best** collects **£75,708** from his August testimonial.

29 **Littlewoods Cup** holders **Luton Town** come from behind to beat **Manchester City 3-1**, while **Tottenham Hotspur** are defeated **2-1** by **Southampton**. **Luther Blissett**, signed from **Watford** last week for **£60,000**, scores **four** of **Bournemouth's goals** in their **5-1** Second Division defeat of **Hull City**. All six goals are scored in the second half. **Shrewsbury Town** are **expelled** from the **Welsh Cup** for fielding an ineligible player in their **2-0** win over **Caernarfon**.

30 The **Appeal board** give **Spurs back** the **two points** deducted for late postponement of their season's opening game, but fine them **£15,000**, instead. In the **Littlewoods Cup** Fourth Round, **Aston Villa** turn on the power to slam **Ipswich Town 6-2** at Villa Park with **Dave Platt** scoring **four goals** in an 18-minute spell, including a **hat-trick** in 12 minutes. In another tie **Liverpool** are beaten **4-1** at Upton Park by lowly placed **West Ham**.

December 1988

1 **Graham Kelly**, the Football Association's chief executive designate, criticises **Sports Minister Colin Moynihan's** allegations about the **FA** breaching new rules on **drug testing**.

2 **Notts County** sack manager **John Barnwell** after only 18 months in the job. They have won only one of their last eight Third Diviion games. **Davy Wilson** resigns as manager of **Queen of the South**, bottom of the Scottish First Division with only one win in 16 games.

3 Leaders **Norwich** are beaten away for the first time this season going down **3-1** in an entertaining game at **Aston Villa**, while **Millwall** suffer their first home defeat against an apparently revitalised **West Ham United**. **Paul Ince** gets the only goal of this game. **Tony Cottee's 100th League goal** gives **Everton** a hotly disputed home win over **Spurs** – even Cottee thought he might have been offside.

Newcastle fail to score for the sixth successive game but earn a point in their **goalless draw** at **Luton. Manchester United** break a run of six draws in succession by beating **Charlton 3-0**. In Scotland **Rangers** suffer their first home defeat of the season **1-0** to **Dundee United**.

4 **Arsenal** and **Liverpool** apparently provide much better **TV** viewing. Their fourth meeting in a month produces a **1-1** draw which puts **Arsenal** only two points behind leaders **Norwich** and keeps **Liverpool** in fourth place. Third Division leaders **Wolves** end their run of eight wins in succession in a **3-1** defeat at **Northampton**. **Jim Smith** quits **QPR** to take over as manager of **Newcastle United**.

7 **Hearts** reach the **quarter-finals** of the **UEFA Cup** for the first time, their **3-0** home victory over **Velez Mostar** carrying them through despite today's **2-1** defeat in Yugoslavia where the home fans give the visitors a hard time. **Newcastle** sell **John Robertson** back to **Hearts** where he was leading goalscorer for the past three seasons before moving to St. Jame's Park where he has failed to score a single goal. The fee is **£625,000**. At the same time **Newcastle** complete the deal which brought manager **Jim Smith** from **QPR** by signing their midfielder **Kevin Brock**, paying **£350,000** for the player and **£150,000 compensation** for the **manager**.

8 **Ipswich Town** sign **Russian Sergei Baltacha** from **Dynamo Kiev** for **£200,000** but may have to wait two months before he can play for them. **Club secretaries** and other executives belonging to the **Football League Executive Staff Association** want to persuade the **Government** either to abandon their **membership card scheme** or make some drastic alterations.

9 **Mark Dennis (QPR)** is charged for the sixth time with bringing the game into **disrepute** following an alleged spitting incident.

10 The shock of the **F.A. Cup** Second Round is the defeat of **Bristol Rovers 2-1** at **Kettering**. **Crewe** reach the Third Round for the first time in 16 years with a **3-0** win at **Runcorn**. The clash between the League's top two clubs **Norwich** and **Arsenal** results in a **goalless draw** – the first time the Gunners have failed to score in the First Division this season. Not surprisingly the attendance of **23,069** is the biggest at **Norwich** for a League game since **December 1983** when neighbours **Ipswich** drew over **25,000**. **Spurs** show better form in beating **Millwall 2-0** but remain five places off the bottom of the table. **Manchester City** take over the lead from **Watford** in the Second Division by beating **Bradford City 4-0** – their sixth successive victory. Scottish League leaders **Rangers** suffer their second successive defeat without scoring. This time it is **2-0** at **Hearts**, Rangers first League defeat on this ground in a run of six visits. **Aberdeen** make it seven Premier Division visits in a row to **Celtic** without defeat by holding them to a **goalless draw**.

11 **Liverpool** fail to win at home for the sixth time in eight First Division games being held to a **1-1** draw by **Everton**, who equalise from the penalty spot. At **42,372** the attendance for the live TV game is marginally the **second lowest** since the war for a **Merseyside** derby at **Anfield**.

12 As **Spain** pull out of the **Rous Cup** in May, **England** try to persuade **Chile** to join in.

13 The **Football League** have signed a contract in the **USA** for American manufacturers of **soccer kit** to use the **League logo**. The deal could eventually be worth **£3m** a year. The **FA** of **Ireland** have bought **Dalymount Park** from the **Bohemians** for **£600,000**. **Steve Bull** scores **four goals** in a game for the **second time** this season as **Wolves** beat **Port Vale 5-1** in the preliminary round of the **Sherpa Van Trophy**. **Police** enter the dressing room at **Southampton** to interview **Crystal Palace** striker **Ian Wright** for allegedly using bad language during this Second Round **Simod Cup** game which **Palace** won **2-1**. **Coventry** strip **Brian Kilcline** of the captaincy after he is breathalysed in the early hours of the morning and will appear in Court on Tuesday.

14 **Bradford City** cause a major upset in the **Littlewoods Cup** Fourth Round by beating **Everton 3-1** at Valley Parade. **Derby** are confident of signing two Czechoslovakian internationals who have defected and are at present in hiding somewhere in Spain. They are **Lubos Kubik** and **Ivo Knoflicek**. Speculation at **QPR** is finally ended late this evening when it is announced that **Trevor Francis** is appointed **player-manager**. Disappointed caretaker **Peter Shreeve** will be his assistant.

15 Following a six-hour meeting of the League Management Committee **Graham Kelly**, the Football Association's chief executive designate, describes the Government's compulsory **membership scheme** as **"horrendous"**. **Chile** accept invitation to take part in the **Rous Cup**.

16 At the end of a two-day meeting, **Football League** president **Jack Dunnett** scares League clubs by announcing that the Government's **membership scheme** could cost up to £34m. **Chelsea** take over the lead in the Second Division with a **4-1** win at **Birmingham** and their two-goal hero **Gordon Durie** is now wanted by **Graeme Souness** who offers **£1m** to take the player to **Rangers**. **Hearts** bring former Scotland keeper **Peter McCloy** out of retirement at the age of 42.

17 **Norwich** critics are shaken as the East Anglian club win **1-0** at Anfield – the third successive game in which **Liverpool** have failed to score against the Canaries. After two defeats in a row, **Millwall** move up into third place with a **1-0** home win over **Sheffield Wednesday**. At the foot of the Second Division **Walsall's** 10th defeat in a row (**2-1** at **Bournemouth**) puts manager **Tommy Coakley** under greater pressure. **Luther Blissett** scores his eighth goal in five games for **Bournemouth**. **Steve Bull** nets his **third hat-trick** in **three successive games** at **Molineux** as **Wolves** beat **Mansfield 6-2**. **Celtic** lose for the seventh time this season – **2-0** at **Dundee United**.

18 There are six League games played this Sunday. **Wimbledon** climb out of the First Division's bottom three places with **Lawrie Sanchez** getting his first goal of the season in a **1-0** win at **Nottingham Forest**. **Brian Clough's** side has won only one of eight home League games so far this season. **West Bromwich** move up to third place in the Second Division by beating **Stoke 6-0** – their **highest** League score for **10 years**. Sports Minister **Colin Moynihan** has no sympathy with **Football League** claims about the high cost of the **membership card scheme**. He says that the League has **rejected overtures** from companies willing to do it **free**.

19 **Tottenham Hotspur** have signed for the next three years with their sponsors **Holsten's Lager** and will receive **£1.1m** over this period. This is the **biggest club sponsorship** deal in British football **history**.

20 A five-man **FA commission** annoy a lot of critics of football's lack of discipline by choosing not to be harsh on **John Fashanu** and **Viv Anderson** following the incident in the player's tunnel at **Wimbledon** on November 2. **Fashanu** is banned for **three matches** and fined **£2,000**, while **Anderson** is banned for **one match** and fined **£750**. Sports minister **Colin Moynihan** releases a list showing the number of **arrests** in and around Football League grounds **last season**. **Aston Villa** top this list with **308 arrests** followed by **Portsmouth** with **282**. The only club with a clean sheet is **Colchester**. Worst in relation to attendance aggregates is **Scarborough**. As well as manager and director, **Jim McLean** becomes chairman of **Dundee United**. Only **3,703** turn up at **Goodison Park** to see **Everton** beat **Millwall 2-0** in Third Round of **Simod Cup**. This is believed to be **Everton's lowest-ever first team attendance**.

21 Harrassed **Newcastle** agree terms with **Arsenal** for **Kenny Samson** and also with **Birmingham** for their right-back **Ray Ranson**. In the **World Cup** qualifying competition **Spain** head Group VI after beating defensive-minded **N. Ireland 4-0** in **Seville**. It is announced that the **European Championship** in June made a record **profit** of about **£9.5M. Bristol City's John Bailey** is sommonsed to appear in Court after allegedly using bad language at Tuesday night's **FA Cup replay** at **Aldershot**. **Gordon Taylor**, secretary of the **PFA** announces that there are now **958 trainees** with professional clubs compared with **300** five years ago.

22 The **FA** again annoy critics of their disciplinary system as they fine **QPR** defender **Mark Dennis £1,000** after he is found guilty of his sixth charge of bringing the game into disrepute. He is also **banned** for the statutory **three matches**. The **FA** formally approve **Spurs' £350,000** signing of **Norwegian** international goalkeeper **Erik Thorstvedt** from **IFK Gothenburg**. Weakened by injuries, **Scotland** lose a friendly international **2-0** in **Italy**. It is claimed that **Marler Estates**, owners of **Stamford Bridge**, have lost their application to build on the **Chelsea** ground. **Chelsea chairman Ken Bates** declares the Bridge **saved for football**. Some **top clubs** contemplating end of season tours are **angry** that **England manager Bobby Robson** has arranged a friendly with **Denmark** only four days after **England** play **Poland** at Wembley in a **World Cup** qualifying game.

23 **Arsenal** manager **George Graham** has banned **ITN** and **BBC news** cameras from any of his club's games following the provision of film by **ITN** to the **FA** as evidence of the incident which resulted in a nine-match ban for Paul Davis. **Marler Estates** admit their planning application for **Stamford Bridge** has expired but say it is merely a **technicality** and not the end of the line. **Aston Villa** centre-forward **Garry Thompson** moves to **Watford** for **£325,000** bringing the total fees for his four transfers in six years to £1.5m.

26 With the **Norwich v West Ham** game postponed until tomorrow, **Arsenal** take over the lead with a **3-2** win away to **Charlton**. **Liverpool** move into third place with a **1-0** victory at **Derby** where **Ian Rush** scores his fourth League goal of the season. It is **Liverpool's** first victory in five League games. In the Second Division, luckless **Walsall** suffer a **5-1** defeat at home to **Oxford United** for whom **Richard Hill** scores **four goals** in a 16-minute spell. Fourth Division **Darlington** are still without a home win after losing **2-0** at home to **Halifax Town**. **Eight players** are **sent off** in the Football League today and there is serious incident at **Southampton's 2-2** draw with **Coventry City**, a large number of players becoming involved in a melee before **Gary Bannister** and **Russell Osman** are sent off. **Attendances** this **Boxing Day** show a 17% increase on last year.

27 **Norwich City** are top again after beating **West Ham 2-1** in an interesting TV spectacle which silenced yet more critics who still do not appreciate the true quality of this East Anglian side. After a run of **11 successive defeats Walsall** sack manager **Tommy Coakley** and assistant **Gerry Sweeney**. **Spurs** offer Iceland international defender **Gudni Bergsson** a long term contract following his debut against **Luton** on **Boxing Day**. **Brian Clough** is reported to have refused to meet **Neil Webb's** agent to discuss a new contract for the player whom **Clough** values at **£2m**. He insists on dealing with the player only. **Justin Fashanu** is training with **Manchester City** three years after being forced to give up with a knee injury. **Brighton** still hold his registration.

29 Currently in their reserves, **Southampton** price **N. Ireland** striker **Colin Clarke** at £1m in response to an enquiry from **Manchester City**. Frustrated **Clarke** has been on loan to **Bournemouth**. **Brian Kilcline** (Coventry City) is fined **£260** and banned from driving for 18 months for failing a breath test.

30 **Derby County** are told by the **FA** that they must pay **£65,000** for teenagers **Jason Kavanagh** from **Birmingham City** and **Kris Sleeuwenhoek** from **Wolves**. **Derby** have been found guilty of poaching these players. Additional payments for appearances and internationals could bring the total payments to **£170,000. Chelsea** sign **David Mitchell**, Australian World Cup striker from **Feyenoord**, for **£200,000**.

31 **Arsenal** end the year leading the table on goal difference and are favourites for the championship after winning **3-0** at **Aston Villa**, while **Norwich** play a **goalless draw** at home to **Middlesbrough**. **Tottenham** have not conceded a goal in four games after beating **Newcastle 3-0** and are the First Division's most improved side of recent weeks. **Chelsea** head the Second Division on goal difference above **West Bromwich** with whom they draw **1-1**. **Watford** have the same number of points in third position. **Steve Bull** scores his **100th goal** for Third Division leaders **Wolves** who draw **2-2** at **Brentford**, while **Wrexham** take over as Fourth Division leaders with a **1-0** win at **Leyton Orient**, stretching their unbeaten run to nine games and climbing from 10th position in two months. **Rangers** continue to lead the Scottish League while **Dunfermline** head the First Division and **Albion Rovers** the Second Division.

January 1989

2 **Arsenal** head the **First Division** after beating **Spurs 2-0** at Highbury. **Everton's 10-game** unbeaten run ends in a **2-0** defeat at **Nottingham Forest**. **Peter Davenport** scores his first goal in 12 games for **Middlesbrough** since his transfer from **Manchester United**. Appropriately enough it's the winner

against his old club. **David Speedie** scores a **hat-trick** of **headed goals** as **Coventry** beat **Sheffield Wednesday 5-0**. This was **Coventry's 900th First Division** game. **Mark Atkins (Blackburn Rovers)** scores for both sides in their 4-3 victory over **Stoke City**. **Away wins** by **Cardiff City** and **Leyton Orient** leave **Walsall** as the only side **without** an **away League success** this season. **Celtic** suffer another notable defeat at **Ibrox** against **Rangers** going down **4-1** after opening the scoring in the second minute. They also lose **Frank McAvennie** with a broken arm. **Bobby Robson** makes another plea for more time with his **England** players before an international.

3 Teenager **Dion Dublin** scores his first League hat-trick as **Cambridge** beat **Peterborough 5-1**.

5 **Luton Town** report a **loss** of **£327,000** for last season which was one of the club's most successful from a results point of view. Their club membership scheme and ban on visiting supporters are blamed. Five days after leaving **Scarborough**, **Neil Warnock** becomes manager of **Notts County**.

6 **Derby County's** new **Czech** internationals **Lubos Kubic** and **Ivo Knoflicek** have been granted political asylum in Britain but FIFA rules prevent them from playing competitive football for 12 months because they have quit Czech football without permission. Many **League clubs** are **angry** about the figures of arrests recently released by **Sports Minister Colin Moynihan** and claim they give a misleading impression.

7 There are the usual crop of **FA Cup** third round shock results. **Sutton United** perform one of the biggest giant-killing acts by beating First Division **Coventry City 2-1** at Gander Green Lane. The League's bottom club **Colchester United** win **2-0** at **Shrewsbury** while **Grimsby Town** (5th from bottom of Division 4) beat **Middlesbrough 2-1** at Ayrsome Park – both goals by **Marc North**. **Tottenham** go out **1-0** at **Bradford City** while **Huddersfield**, **Leicester** and **Oldham** lose in this round for the fourth successive season. **Kettering** survive with a **1-1** draw at home to **Halifax**, but the other remaining non-League side, **Welling** are beaten **1-0** at home by **Blackburn Rovers**. Knocked unconscious, England captain **Bryan Robson** is saved from **choking to death** by club physio **Jim McGregor**. As **Rangers** suffer their first defeat in a run of six League visits to **Motherwell**, **Dundee United** close the gap at the top of the table to one point by winning **1-0** in a hard game with **Dundee**. This was the fifth League game in a row that Dundee have failed to find the net against United.

8 **West Ham** gain a two-goal lead over **Arsenal** in their third round Cup tie but **Paul Merson** scores twice to force a replay.

9 The **Scottish FA** decide to settle their drawn **Cup Finals** by **penalty shoot-outs** from **1990**. There will also be only one replay in earlier rounds with **extra time** and **penalty shoot-outs** where necessary. They also **ban two referees**, **Kenny Hope** and **Louis Thow** from handling **Scottish Cup** ties for the remainder of this season because they have been too lenient in recent League matches between **Rangers** and **Aberdeen**. The Scottish League are taking no action. The **Referees' Association** have written to the **Sports Minister** rejecting the proposed identity card scheme. In a match to raise money for the **Lockerbie air disaster**, **Rangers'** first team lose **2-1** at **Gretna**.

10 **Brentford** reach the **FA Cup fourth round** for the first time in **18 years** by winning their replay **1-0** against luckless **Walsall**. Non-league **Kettering** win their replay **3-2** at **Halifax** with two goals by **Robbie Cooke**.

11 **Arsenal** are surprisingly beaten **1-0** by **West Ham** at Highbury in their third round replay while **WBA** go down **1-0** at **Everton**. It is the fifth season in succession that the **Albion** have been knocked out at this stage of the competition.

12 **Chelsea** sign goalkeeper **Dave Beasant** for **£750,000** from **Newcastle** whom he joined last summer. Former **Leicester** and **Glasgow Rangers** manager **Jock Wallace** comes out of retirement in Spain to manage **Colchester United**, the League's bottom club.

13 **Soviet** international **Sergei Baltatcha** arrives in England with his wife and two children to join **Ipswich Town**.

14 Two goals by **Speedie** enable **Coventry** to beat **Norwich 2-1** at Carrow Road and move into second place as **Millwall** lose **3-0 at Old Trafford**. **Arsenal** extend their lead to five points winning **3-1** at **Everton** – their third win in a row on this ground and one which earns them a standing ovation from the discerning Everton supporters. Second Division leaders **WBA** lose for the first time in nine League games **2-0** at **Watford** as **Chelsea** take the lead in this division by beating **Crystal Palace 1-0** with goalkeeper Beasant making some fine saves. **Celtic** move up to third place behind Rangers and Dundee United by beating **St. Mirren 2-1**, but luckless **Hamilton** go down **5-0** at home to **Dundee United** – their fifth defeat in a row without scoring.

16 The **Newcastle-Watford F.A. Cup** third round, second replay, ends in a goalless draw with **Watford** goalkeeper **Tony Coton** outstanding. With seven players anxious to leave the club, **Walsall** hold a **crisis** meeting after **15 defeats** in **16 games**.

17 Portsmouth sack manager (officially chief coach) **Alan Ball** after **five defeats** in a run of **six games**. He is succeeded by his deputy **John Gregory**. **Ron Atkinson** loses his **£250,000** a year job as manager of **Atletico Madrid** after only 96 days during which he lifted them to third place. **Assistant Colin Addison** is expected to take over. Crisis club Walsall confirm appointment of **John Barnwell** as manager. **Justin Fashanu** is forced to abandon his attempted comeback with **Manchester City** and is returning to the **USA.** for further treatment to his injured knee.

18 **Bristol City** win through to the semi-finals of the **Littlewoods Cup** with a **1-0** win at **Bradford**, **Alan Walsh** scoring in the first minute, while **Nottingham Forest** swamp **QPR 5-2** with **Lee Chapman** hitting **four** goals. **Forest** fans invade the pitch and millions of TV viewers see manager **Brian Clough** react violently with two of the fans. Only **2477** turn up at **Wimbledon** to see **Everton** win **2-1** in the **quarter-finals** of the **Simod Cup**. **Lewisham Council** plan a new ground for **Millwall** at Deptford. The Den will be used for low cost housing.

19 As **Brian Clough** comes under fire he admits that his violent actions were regrettable but done with the right motives. **Middlesbrough** are ordered to hand over a **£1m** bond to their biggest creditors. This bond was set aside when they escaped bankruptcy in July 1986. **Millwall** chairman **Reg Burr** states that stories about their impending move are exaggerated.

20 **Clough** obtains apologies from two fans he struck two nights ago. They apologise for invading the pitch and he apologises for his involvement. A miscalculation in the **QPR** office kept **Alan McDonald** out of last Saturday's game with **Wimbledon** which they lost **1-0**. His disciplinary points total actually meant that his ban began two days later. **Dave Smith resigns** after only seven months as manager of **Dundee**.

21 **Nottingham Forest** fans give **Clough** a standing ovation before the team goes on to thrash **Aston Villa 4-0** – their seventh League and Cup victory in a row. **Peter Shilton saves** a **penalty** for **Derby** who win **1-0** at **QPR**. Russian **Sergei Baltatcha** scores on his debut for **Ipswich** who beat **Stoke 5-1** at Portman Road. With Danish striker **Frank Pingel** making his debut for **Newcastle**, they lose **2-0** at home to **Charlton** and drop to the bottom of the table. Leading a tight Second Division promotion race, **Chelsea's 1-1** draw at **Blackburn** extends their unbeaten run to **13 League** games. **Watford** retain second place with a **3-2** win at **Birmingham** who have now gone eight games without a win. **Walsall**'s new manager **John Barnwell** is left in no doubt about the amount of hard work necessary to save Walsall from dropping into the Third Division as they lose **2-0** at **Plymouth** – Walsall's **14th defeat** in a row. **Hamilton Academical** go down **1-0** at **St. Mirren** and have played nine hours without scoring. **Aberdeen's £300,000 6ft 5in Dutchman**, **Willem van der Ark** scores on his debut as the Dons win **2-0** at **Motherwell**. **Dundee United** extend their unbeaten run to **14 games** in a **goalless draw** at home to **Hearts** – the only such result in either the Scottish or Football Leagues this Saturday.

22 **Millwall's** first appearance on live television provides good entertainment with **Norwich** winning **3-2** as **Robert Fleck** scores in injury time.

23 **Portsmouth** have opened talks which may lead to them leaving Fratton Park and building a new stadium alongside in **Goldsmith Avenue**.

24 **Steve Bull** passes his century for **Wolves** by scoring another **hat-trick** in their **3-0** home **Sherpa Van Trophy** victory over **Bristol City**. **Malcolm Allison** returns to management in Portugal by taking over struggling First Division side **Farense**.

25 **Littlewoods Cup**-holders **Luton Town** win their quarter-final replay **2-1** a **Southampton** with all the goals being scored in extra time.

27 The **FA** charge **Brian Clough** with bringing the game into **disrepute** following last week's incident when **Forest** fans invaded the pitch.

28 In the day's **FA Cup** ties, Third Division **Brentford** win through to the **fifth round** for the **first time** in **18 years** by beating **Manchester City 3-1** thanks largely to two goals by **Gary Blissett**. Bottom-of-the-League **Colchester** shake **Sheffield United** by taking a two-goal lead at Bramall Lane where the game ends in a **3-3** draw. **Aston Villa**, **Sheffield Wednesday** and **Derby County** are the First Division clubs eliminated by **Wimbledon**, **Blackburn Rovers** and **Watford** respectively. The remaining non-League sides are disposed of as **Kettering** go down **2-1** to **Charlton** and **Sutton United** prove no match for **Norwich City** who win **8-0** with late replacement **Malcolm Allen** hitting **four** and **Robert Fleck three goals**. This was the **highest score** for **30 years** at this stage of the competition. In the third round of the **Scottish Cup**, **Rangers** are held to a **1-1** draw at **Raith Rovers**. **David Narey** makes his **57th Scottish Cup** appearance for **Dundee United** (a club record) and they win **2-1** at neighbouring **Dundee**.

29 For the second game in succession **Rush** and **Aldridge** produce the goals for **Liverpool** to jolt the critics who are constantly questioning the wisdom of playing two brilliant strikers in the same side. This time their goals knock out **Millwall 2-0** at the Den and help the Reds through to the fifth round of the FA Cup for the **8th time** in the last **11 seasons**.

30 **Bradford City** sack manager **Terry Dolan** exactly two years after his appointment.

31 Following five defeats in their last seven League matches, **Aston Villa** agree deals worth nearly £1m for **Bradford City** striker **Ian Ormondroyd** and Austrian defender **Alex Sperr** of **SK Voest Linz**. **QPR** sign midfielder **Nigel Spackman** from **Liverpool** for **£500,000** and forward **Andy Gray** from **Aston Villa**. **Colchester** lose their Cup replay **2-0** at **Sheffield United**.

February 1989

1 **Grimsby Town** win through to the **fifth round** of the **FA Cup** for the second time since the war by beating **Reading 2-1** in their replay at Elm Park. **Rangers** win their replay **3-0** against **Raith Rovers**. **Mechelen** of Belgium beat **PSV Eindhoven** (Holland) **3-0** in the first leg of the **European Super Cup**. **Swansea City** refuse to allow **Bradford City** permission to interview **Terry Yorath** for the managership.

2 **Yorath** quits **Swansea** to take over at **Bradford City** but Swansea issue a High Court injunction preventing this move and also stopping Yorath from taking charge of the Welsh team in their friendly in Israel next week.

3 **Swansea City** win High Court temporary injunction preventing manager Yorath from becoming manager of Bradford City less than one and a half hours after he is introduced in this position at Valley Parade. However, **Swansea** drop the injunction preventing **Yorath** from managing the **Welsh international team**.

4 **Rush** and **Aldridge** provide the goals for the third successive game and enable **Liverpool** to draw **2-2** at **Newcastle**. **Nottingham Forest** register their **10th successive League** victory by beating **Luton 3-2**. The dismal situation at **Walsall** is highlighted with a **7-0** home defeat by **Chelsea**. **Gordon Durie** is the first **Chelsea** player to score five goals since **Bobby Tambling** over 22 years ago. **Port Vale** and **Wolverhampton**, the top two teams in the Third Division, attract a crowd of **16,362** who watch a goalless draw. This was **Port Vale's** biggest crowd for 20 years. Because of **Scotland's** forthcoming World Cup qualifier in **Cyprus** there are no big games north of the border but there is a shock in the Second Division where bottom club **Berwick Rangers** beat top club **Albion Rovers** at Shielfield Park.

6 **Ian Greaves** ends his six-year reign at **Mansfield Town** where club captain **George Foster** becomes **player-manager**. **Newport County** are given **three days** to pay debts of over **£126,000** or face closure.

7 **England** manager **Bobby Robson** breaks the **Beardsley-Lineker** partnership by dropping **Beardsley** and bringing in Arsenal's **Alan Smith** for the friendly in **Greece**. The **Department of Employment** refuse to issue a work permit and **Southampton's Yugoslavian** defender **Milos Drizic** must go home as must **Villa's Sperr**. The decision was taken on advice from the FA who had apparently changed their minds about allowing the player to stay but were too late in confirming this. The Belgian side **Mechelen** lose 1-0 in **Holland** but beat **PSV Eindhoven 3-1** on aggregate in the **European Super Cup**.

8 **England** struggle to gain a welcome **2-1** win against **Greece** in a friendly in Athens with **Bryan Robson** scoring the winner in the 79th minute. In **Cyprus**, **Scotland** win their World Cup Qualifying game **3-2** with the winner coming from **Richard Gough** five minutes into injury time. The crowd **rioted** after the referee added on **seven minutes** largely because of the home side's time wasting tactics. **Wales** find it hard going in **Israel** where they draw **3-3** in a friendly with **Malcolm Allen** getting their equaliser with only two minutes to spare. **Northern Ireland**'s hopes of reaching the World Cup finals are shaken by a **2-0** home defeat against **Spain** who play quality football in Belfast.

9 **Brian Clough** is fined **£5000** by the **FA** and **banned** from the **touchline** for the remaining League games of the season following his televised fracas with pitch-invading fans.

10 **Wimbledon** manager **Bobby Gould** is involved in a **skirmish** with a **TV film crew** who were trying to interview **Vinny Jones** at the club's training ground. A High Court judge frees **Swansea** manager **Terry Yorath** from an injunction which had prevented him taking over at **Bradford City**. Swansea will sue for damages in a civil action. **Ted Croker** retires today after nearly **16 years** as **secretary** of the **FA**.

11 **Clough** is given another standing ovation before the start of a home game, but this time **QPR** end his side's run of **10 consecutive victories** with a **goalless draw**. **Manchester United** register their fourth consecutive League victory – a **2-0** win at **Sheffield Wednesday** which takes them to third place behind **Arsenal** and **Norwich**. **United** have climbed from **11th** position in **six matches**. At Stamford Bridge, **Chelsea** stretch their unbeaten run to **15 games** beating **Swindon 3-2** with the aid of two "own goals". A **Stuart Rimmer** hat-trick gives bottom-of-the-table **Walsall** their first away win of the season in a **3-0** victory at **Sunderland**. This also ended a run of **15 consecutive League defeats** since beating **Sunderland 2-0** in October. In the Third Division, **Cambridge United** gain the second **6-0** win of their League career. Their victims were **Hartlepools** who had been disorganised following a car crash involving three of their players and their coach going first to **Cambridge City's** ground in error. Without a home win this season, **Darlington** sack manager **Dave Booth**. Scotland's League leaders **Rangers** and **Dundee United** battle out a **1-1** draw at Tannadice where United's deserved equaliser is an own goal by **Gary Stevens** in injury time. **Celtic** retain third place behind these two sides despite a disastrous **2-1** home defeat by **Motherwell** – the visitors' first victory at Parkhead in a run of **13 League games**.

12 **Littlewoods Cup**-holders **Luton** look set for a Wembley return after a fine **3-0** win at **West Ham** in the first leg of their **semi-final**. Following the riot by local fans at the Cyprus-Scotland World Cup tie, **FIFA** order the **closure** of Tsirion Stadium in **Limassol** for an indefinite period.

13 **Darlington** appoint former **Wolves** manager **Brian Little** to succeed David Booth.

14 **Ron Atkinson** returns to the Football League following his 90-day spell in charge of Atletico Madrid and replaces **Peter Eustace** at relegation threatened **Sheffield Wednesday**. Eustace had been manager for only a little over three months during which **Wednesday** won **two** of their **19 League and Cup** games. **Arsenal** beat the French national team **2-0** at Highbury. **John Mortimore** is sacked as manager of Portuguese club **Belenenses**.

15 **Bristol City** shake **Nottingham Forest** with a **1-1 Littlewoods Cup**, **semi-final** first leg draw at Nottingham, Forest equalising with an "**own goal**" five minutes from time. After pleading guilty to causing actual bodily harm to a spectator at a Brighton reserve game last month, **Gerry Armstrong** is conditionally discharged; ordered to pay £100 compensation and £20 costs. He has already quit Brighton.

18 **Brentford's** best **FA Cup** run for **40 years** continues with a **2-0** fifth round victory at **Blackburn**, **Gary Blissett** getting both goals in the last 10 minutes. All the First Division clubs involved in today's Cup ties survive, but **Manchester United** are held to a **1-1** draw at **Bournemouth**. The 38-year-old **West Ham** goalkeeper **Phil Parkes** is recalled for their fifth round tie at **Charlton** which the Hammers win **1-0**. In the Football League **Birmingham** fans stage a protest following their **2-0** defeat at home to **Manchester City** and a brick is thrown through a dressing room window. Bottom-of-the-League **Colchester** under new manager **Jock Wallace** win **3-2** at **Scunthorpe** – their first victory in a run of **20 Fourth Division games**. There are no major upsets in the fourth round of the **Scottish Cup** where **Rangers** enjoy an **8-0** victory over Second Division **Stranraer**.

19 **Nottingham Forest** maintain their three-pronged attack on Wembley by winning **3-0** at **Watford** to reach the **sixth round** of the **FA Cup**. They are still in both the **Littlewoods** and **Simod Cup** competitions.

20 **Newport County** are given another stay of execution with a **week** to find the money needed to avoid **bankruptcy**. **Dundee United** coach **Gordon Wallace** is appointed manager of **Dundee**.

21 The Championship race remains open as the two leading clubs both lose – **Coventry City** halt **Arsenal**'s run of **11 League** games without defeat with a **1-0** victory at Highfield Road and **Norwich City** go down **2-1** at **Spurs**.

22 **Old Trafford** has its biggest crowd of the season (**54,222**) for **United's fifth round FA Cup** replay with **Bournemouth** and **Brian McClair** takes advantage of a poorly judged back-pass to score the only goal. **Nottingham Forest** book a place at Wembley with their **3-1** win over **Crystal Palace** in the semi-finals of the **Simod Cup**. **Newcastle City Council**, who owns St. James's Park, offer to mediate in the current battle for control of the club which they believe is blocking further development of the ground. **Walsall** have agreed to sell their ground to **Gateway Supermarkets** for **£6m**.

23 Furious **Cardiff City** chairman **Tony Clemo** seeks compensation from the Welsh FA who have arranged to play their World Cup qualifying game against **West Germany** at the Welsh Rugby home of **Cardiff Arms Park** instead of **Ninian Park**. **Bryan Robson** could miss the FA Cup quarter-finals because of an automatic two-match ban which the FA insist on being imposed despite his total of points including a caution in the **Mercantile Centenary Cup**. **Manchester United** and the Football League believe that this competition should not be included in any disciplinary points. **Sheffield Wednesday** capture **WBA** midfielder **Carlton Palmer** in a deal which includes striker **Colin West** in part exchange and is said to be worth **£850,000**. **Wembley Stadium** is spending another **£20m** on improvements which will include an **Executive perimeter area**.

24 The **FA**'s new Chief Executive **Graham Kelly** has made a formal written request to make a personal plea for **England**'s return to European club competition at **UEFA**'s meeting on April 11. League President **Jack Dunnett** takes over as their Chief Executive in a temporary unpaid capacity.

25 **Manchester United** slip to fifth position after losing **2-1** at **Norwich** who retain second position behind **Arsenal**. **Peter Shilton** celebrates his **850th** Football League game in **Derby County's 3-2** win over **Everton**. **Manchester City** regain the lead in the Second Division with their sixth successive League victory – **2-0** over Plymouth Argyle. In the Third Division, **Preston** hit **Chesterfield** for **six** without reply.

26 **Brian Clough** books a second visit to **Wembley** as **Nottingham Forest** win **1-0** at **Bristol City** after **extra time** in the second leg of their **Littlewoods Cup** Semi-final.

27 **Newcastle** chairman **Gordon McKeag** is suffering a hate campaign through the mail and by telephone and police launch an investigation as even **death threats** are made. **Ian Evans**, assistant manager of **Crystal Palace** succeeds **Terry Yorath** as manager of **Swansea City**. **GM Vauxhall Conference** club **Newport County** is **wound up** nearly **77 years** after their formation. A three-man Football League commission meets a delegation from **Wimbledon** to examine a charge of making **illegal payments** to players. **Dundee United** are through to the quarter-finals of the Scottish Cup after beating **Aberdeen 1-0** in their second replay.

28 Understrength **Hearts** beat **Bayern Munich** with a 55th minute goal from **Iain Ferguson** in the first leg of their UEFA Cup quarter-finals in Edinburgh. Only **7072** turn up at **Goodison Park** in pouring rain to see **Everton** reach the Final of the **Simod Cup** by beating **QPR** with a **Pat Nevin** header in the 68th minute. **Swansea City**'s Third Division game with **Huddersfield** is abandoned through floodlight failure with **Huddersfield** leading **1-0** and **Robbie James** making his **600th** League appearance. Sports Minister **Colin Moynihan** re-iterates the Government's position in not supporting the FA's application for a **return** to **Europe** until the **anti-hooligan** measures are established.

March 1989

1 **Luton Town** extend their unbeaten run in the **Littlewoods Cup** to **16 games** and reach the Final for the second successive year with a comfortable **2-0** (5-0 aggregate) win over **West Ham**. One of the First Division's lowest post-war attendances – **4,207** – is recorded at **Wimbledon** where stand-in striker **Paul Miller** scores his first League hat-trick in a **4-0** victory over **Derby County**. The Second Division local derby between **Leeds United** and **Bradford**, which ends in a **3-3** draw, attracts this division's biggest crowd of the season – **33,325**. The **FA back down** on their decision over disciplinary points collected in the **Mercantile Credit** tournament so reducing **Bryan Robson**'s total and freeing him for **Manchester United's FA Cup** clash with **Nottingham Forest**. There is a break through in **Women's football** as highlights of their **FA Cup final** at **Old Trafford** on **April 22** will be **televised** for showing on Channel 4 the following evening.

2 The **Football League** fine **Wimbledon £10,000** for making unauthorised loans to three players but the club is **cleared** of making illegal payments.

3 **Wales** confirm that their World Cup qualifier with **West Germany** on May 31 wll be played at **Cardiff Arms Park**. **Sheffield Wednesday** sell **England** full-back **Mel Sterland** to **Glasgow Rangers** for **£800,000** – the **13th English player** signed by **Graeme Souness** although only seven (with Sterland) are still at the club. Leading **GM Vauxhall Conference** club **Maidstone United** pay **Fisher Athletic £35,000** for **Ken Charlery** – a **record** fee between non-League clubs.

4 In this Saturday's only First Division game, **Sheffield Wednesday** register their first home League win for **five months** and push **Charlton** closer to relegation by beating them **3-1**. Struggling **Birmingham** (only four wins in 32 games) have another brick thrown through their dressing-room window after being held to a **goalless draw** at home to **Oxford United**. **Wolves** increase their Third Division lead to nine points by beating **Bolton 1-0** with **Steve Bull** getting his **36th** goal of the season. **Darlington** break their 11-month home duck by beating **Lincoln City 2-1** and stop one short of the all-time record of **16 home games** without a win.

5 **England** manager **Bobby Robson** is increasingly annoyed by the clash of interest between his **England World Cup** qualifying campaign and **ITV** who still insist on screening **Liverpool**'s home game with **Arsenal** three days before **England**'s return match with **Albania**.

6 **Greg Dyke**, chairman of **ITV Sport** is angry at remarks about the screening of the **Liverpool-Arsenal** game on **April 23** and points out that the **Football League** refused an offer to screen this vital game a day earlier with a 5.30 pm kick-off.

9 **QPR** sign **Colin Clarke** from Southampton in an £800,000 deal.

10 **David Oldfield**, **Luton**'s Australian-born striker, rejects a move to **West Ham** and joins **Manchester City** for a fee of **£600,000**. **Terry Yorath** buys out the five remaining months of his contract with **Swansea City** at a cost of **£18,000** to settle the dispute over his move to **Bradford**.

11 **Arsenal** appear to be feeling the strain of leading the First Division as they are beaten **3-1** by **Nottingham Forest** in a thriller at Highbury and have now won only one of their last five games. In addition to **Forest**, **Arsenal**'s three other closest Championship rivals, **Norwich**, **Liverpool** and **Millwall** all win – **Liverpool's 4-0** victory at **Middlesbrough** stretching their unbeaten run to nine

games. **Manchester City** regain the Second Division leadership from **Chelsea** by beating **Leicester 4-2** with **Trevor Morley** scoring their first hat-trick of the season. An "own goal" by veteran **Dundee United** defender **Paul Hegarty** in 50 seconds heralded one of the season's shock results as **St. Mirren** go on to win **4-1** at Tannadice Park.

13 **QPR** fine **Martin Allen** two weeks wages for failing to play on Saturday when, despite a warning from Manager **Trevor Francis**, he returned to London to attend the birth of his son. **Atletico Madrid** appoint new manager **Javier Clemente** for next season and so mark the end of **Colin Addison**'s brief reign.

14 **Liverpool** relentlessly pursue the League championshp demolishing **Luton 5-0** at Anfield with **John Aldridge** scoring a hat-trick. **Manchester City** increase their lead over **Chelsea** to four points at the top of the Second Division with a **4-2** victory at **Sunderland**. **Wolves** again emphasise their superiority in the Third Division by beating bottom club **Gillingham 6-1**. This was their third "six" of the season in the Third Division. **Hearts** fight a brave rearguard action but go out of the **UEFA Cup** by losing **2-0** (2-1 on aggregate) to **Bayern Munich** in Germany. Football League President **Jack Dunnett** confirms that the **Liverpool-Arsenal** game will be **televised** only three days before **England** meet **Albania** at Wembley but denies the suggestion that **Bobby Robson** is angry about this arrangement.

15 The row between **Robson** and the Football League goes on despite **Dunnett's** remarks. **Nottingham Forest** slip out of the championship race when they are surprisingly held to a **1-1** draw at home to struggling **Newcastle United**. **Wigan Athletic** sack manager **Ray Mathias** and **Bryan Hamilton** takes over in a temporary capacity.

16 **Charlton Athletic** will be returning to their old ground at **The Valley** next season. Part of the ground will be sold for housing but the stadium will have a **20,000** capacity. **Luton Town** sell their ground to the **local council** for **£3.25m** and have a **seven-year** tenancy.

17 After only three victories in their last **16 League games Doncaster Rovers** manager **Dave Mackay** resigns.

18 **Liverpool** end Third Division **Brentford**'s fine cup run by beating them **4-0** in the sixth round at Anfield while **Nottingham Forest** stay on course for three Wembley finals with a **1-0** win at **Manchester United**. **United** claim that a shot by **Brian McClair** earned them a replay but as it was hooked out of the goalmouth by **Steve Hodge** the referee rules that it was not wholly over the line. **Chelsea** are back on top of the Second Division after beating closest rivals **Manchester City 3-2** at Maine Road where the visitors were **3-0** up at one stage. **Steve Bull** scores his **sixth hat-trick** of the season as **Wolves** beat Bury **4-0** – their 16th consecutive victory. North of the border there are no **Cup** shocks as in the two games played today **Celtic** and **Hibernian** win through to the semi-finals against **Hearts** and **Alloa** respectively. There were fireworks at Parkhead where one **Celtic** and two **Hearts** players are sent off after some punches were exchanged. Having failed to complete their **GM Vauxhall Conference** fixture **Newport County** are **expelled** from the competition.

19 **FA Cup**-holders **Wimbledon** lose to a solitary goal by **Everton's £850,000** midfielder **Stuart McCall** in their sixth round tie at Goodison.

21 League-leaders **Arsenal** show further signs of nerves as they can only draw **2-2** at home to relegation candidates **Charlton Athletic**. After 18 games without a victory, **Southampton** sign Welsh international midfielder **Barry Horne** from **Portsmouth** for **£700,000**. **Rangers** and **Dundee United** draw their postponed Fifth Round tie **2-2** at Ibrox. **Graeme Souness** is fined **£100** and banned from the touchline in his role as manager for the rest of the season. **Malcolm Allison** is **sacked** after less than two months in charge of Portuguese Second Division club **Farense**.

22 **Norwich** keep up their hopes of a **League and Cup double** by beating **West Ham 3-1** in their **FA Cup Sixth round replay** with **Malcolm Allen** getting both goals. **Liverpool**, however, continue their strong run for the Championship by demolishing **Coventry 3-1** at Highfield Road – their fourth League win in a row with a goals tally of **14-1**. **Nottingham Forest** suffer their first defeat in **19 games** going down **2-1** at home to **Spurs**. **West Ham** – the First Division's bottom club – beat the transfer deadline to get **Frank McAvennie** back from **Celtic** for a fee of **£1.25m**.

23 Over **1000 Littlewoods Cup Final** tickets earmarked for the sponsors are sent in error by **Wembley Stadium** to the finalists involved. Those sent to **Luton** are returned but **Nottingham Forest** have already sold the others.

24 A number of clubs want the **First Division** returned to **22 clubs** instead of **20**. They are missing the extra income. **Hearts** are fined **£36,000** for allowing the first leg of their **UEFA Cup** quarter-final to be **screened** by a cable company in **West Germany**.

25 **Newcastle United**, who beat **Everton 2-0** at St. James's Park in mid-week, now win by the **same scoree** at **Norwich**. It's the first time this season that **United** have managed to string two consecutive victories together. **Mirandinha** and **Liam O'Brien** were the scorers in both games. **West Ham** cause fellow stragglers **Aston Villa** more problems by winning **1-0** at **Villa Park** – the Midland club's **seventh game** without a victory.

26 **Liverpool** extend their unbeaten run to **13 games** as **Peter Beardsley** scores a classic winner in their **2-1** victory at **White Hart Lane**. This takes them up into third place above **Millwall**.

27 Referee **Kelvin Morton** creates a Football League record by awarding **five penalties** (including **three in five minutes) as Crystal Palace** beat **Brighton 2-1** in the Second Division. He also **sends off one player** and **books another five**. While **Brighton** convert their penalty, **Palace** miss three of their four. On this Easter Monday the attendance at **Wolverhampton** is nearly **21,000** but the Third Division leaders lose **1-0** to **Bristol Rovers** – their first home defeat in over 12 months.

28 **Chelsea's 1-0** win at **Ipswich** puts the Londoners seven points clear at the top of the Second Division. **England** fans have been virtually banned from the game with **Scotland** at Hampden in May because the **FA** in London have told their Scottish counterparts they do not want any tickets and the Scots have agreed not to sell any south of the border.

29 **Liverpool** stretch their winning run to six with a victory over **Derby County**. About to slip into the

Third Division for the first time in their history, **Birmingham**'s chairman **Ken Wheldon** announces that he expects to **sell the club** within a week. **Rangers** announce plans for a new **£11m** two-tier stand which will increase the Ibrox capacity to **52,000**. The **FA** of **Wales** are so **hard-up** that they cannot afford to give each player a **cap** for representing them in the recent non-League international with England but the players can **keep their jerseys**.

30 A **Football League** commission agrees that **QPR** were justified in fining **Martin Allen** for walking out on the club before their game at **Newcastle** to attend the birth of his son, but the fine of **£1200** was excessive. It is halved. **FA** Chief Executive **Graham Kelly** admits that he has failed to persuade the League to bring forward **Liverpool**'s game with **Arsenal** which is only three days before **England** meet **Albania**.

31 The **FA** release figures which show that the number of **Football League** players **sent off** this season up to **16th March** is down on the same period of last year – **147** against **174**. Although well placed in the Third Division, **Bury** part company with manager **Martin Dobson**.

April 1989

1 **Liverpool** move into second place with a **1-0** victory at **Norwich**. As relegation threatens some clubs are fighting back and **Southampton**, who have slipped from eighth to 18th since Christmas, manage their first win in nearly four months, beating **Newcastle United 1-0** at The Dell. In the Second Division, bottom club **Birmingham** steal a point in a **2-2** draw at **Sunderland**, while **Kerry Dixon** hits **four goals** in **Chelsea's 5-3** win over **Barnsley**. **Gillingham** climb off the bottom of the Third Division by beating **Northampton 1-0**. Managerless **Bury** are hammered **6-0** at home by **Huddersfield Town**. **Rangers** register their first win at **Celtic** in a run of **17 League** visits. In front of a crowd of **59,745** they win **2-1**. With six games to play, **Hamilton Academical** are already booked for relegation from the Premier Division, following their **1-0** defeat at **Motherwell**. This was their **11th defeat** in a row while scoring only one goal.

2 **Arsenal** skipper **Tony Adams** heads his side into the lead at **Manchester United** but slices an attempted clearance to give the home side their **equaliser**.

3 **Spurs** manager **Terry Venables** is reported to be in **Spain** trying to sign **Moroccan-born Nayim** on loan from **Barcelona**, but he is also pursuing the transfer of **Gary Lineker** whom he signed from **Everton** when he was manager of the **Spanish** club. **Lineker**'s position is in doubt as manager **Johan Cruyff** left him out of last Saturday's important game with **Real Madrid**.

4 **Arsenal's** title hopes receive a set-back when striker **Alan Smith fractures a cheekbone** in training. **Liverpool** and **Celtic** draw **1-1** in Dubai before **Celtic** win **4-2** on **penalties**. In a Third Division game, **Tony Sealy** scores after **12 seconds** and they go on to beat **Bristol City 3-0**. **Roger Palmer** breaks **Eric Gemmell's 35-year-old Oldham Athletic** scoring record by taking his aggregate past the **110** mark as the Latics beat **Ipswich Town 4-0**.

5 In one of the top two League positions all season so far, **Norwich City** now shows signs of losing their way as they suffer their **third defeat** in **four games**, this time **2-0** at **Nottingham Forest**. **Chester** beat **Fulham 7-0** in the Third Division with **Carl Dale** scoring a second half hat-trick. The **FA** reject **Newport County's** appeal against expulsion from the **GM Vauxhall Conference**.

6 Last season's **League centenary** celebrations suffered a **loss** of **£191,000** despite an input of **£300,000** in sponsorship from **Mercantile Credit**.

8 Hammering **Sheffield Wednesday 5-1** in a morning kick-of to beat the **Grand National**, **Liverpool** take over the League **leadership** for the **first time** this season, although only for a few hours. In the afternoon, **Arsenal** return to the top spot by beating **Everton 2-0** at Highbury. **Chelsea** make it **eight wins** in a row in an unbeaten run of **27 games** with a **3-2** victory at **West Bromwich** who had gone **10 games** without defeat. After **leading** the **Fourth Division** for a long spell, **Crewe** have now **slipped** to **fourth place** after only one win in their last five games. **Rangers** beat **Motherwell 1-0** – their **fifth League win** in a row and are four points ahead of **Aberdeen** who make it **seven successive victories** with a **2-1** win at **Hibernian**. There's a sensation at **Hamilton** where the Accies beat **Celtic 2-0** with **Stuart Gordon** scoring both goals. **Gordon** with a total of **three** goals is the only Hamilton player to score in their last **13 League and Cup** games. **Berwick Rangers**, third from bottom of the Second Division, create a club record by taking their **unbeaten run** to **17 League games** with a **4-0** win at **Dumbarton**.

9 **Nottingham Forest** are *en route* for a Cup treble by beating **Luton Town 3-1** in the **Littlewoods Cup Final** with "Man of the Match" **Nigel Clough** scoring twice and making another. It was the third season in succession that the **Littlewoods Cup** holders have **lost** in the **final**.

10 In a sporting gesture, **Brian Clough** gives his **Littlewoods Cup trophy** (a replica of the trophy) to **assistant manager Ronnie Fenton**. **Walsall** sign the contract for the building of their new stadium at **Bescot** only a quarter of a mile from **Fellows Park**.

11 The **UEFA** executive committee lift the ban on **English** clubs for the beginning of **1990–91** providing the **British Government** give their backing. **Liverpool** are due for an **additional three years ban** but Minister for Sport **Colin Moynihan** will appeal personally for them to be allowed back at the same time as other English clubs. **Liverpool** return to top place in the **League** on goal difference by beating **Millwall 2-1**. **Keith Burkinshaw** quits the managership of **Gillingham** after less than six months in the job.

12 It is reported that **Dave Mackay**, who left **Doncaster Rovers** last month, will succeed **Garry Pendrey** as **Birmingham's** manager at the end of this season. In the World Cup, **Hungary** are held to a surprise **1-1** draw by **Malta**, a result which improves **Republic of Ireland's** chances of qualifying.

13 **Peterborough** dispense with the services of **Noel Cantwell** as **General Manager** and commercial chief **Ellis Stafford**.

15 The day's events are entirely overshadowed by a disaster of sickening proportions at Hillsborough where the FA Cup semi-final between **Liverpool** and **Nottingham Forest** is abandoned after **six**

minutes when a crush of fans trapped behind the safety fencing at the **Leppings Lane** end leaves many dead and dying. This was the **Liverpool supporters'** end and before the day is out it is reported that **94** fans had **died** and at least **200 injured** thus making it Britain's worst sporting disaster. At the top of the Second Division, **Chelsea's** unbeaten run of **27 League games** ends with a **2-0** defeat at **Leicester**, while at the bottom of this division **Birmingham** are relegated to the Third Division for the first time in their history after a **goalless draw** at **Barnsley** and with six games still to play.

16 The **Prime Minister** announces that there will be a public enquiry into the **Hillsborough disaster**. The FA give the go ahead for the **Cup Final** to be played on **May 20** – a week later than arranged. **Liverpool FC** contribute **£100,000** to a fund for the families of the victims and the **FA** give **£250,000**. Liverpool suspend their games for the immediate future. Messages of condolence flood in from around the world as thousands of fans make pilgrimages to Anfield leaving bouquets of flowers, scarves, caps, etc. The **14-ton master bell** of **Liverpool's Anglican Cathedral** is rung **94 times**.

17 The **Hillsborough** death toll rises to **95**. The Scottish FA announce that nett gate receipts from next week's **World Cup** game with **Cyprus** will be donated to the **Hillsborough** disaster fund. **Arsenal** defy the League and **postpone** tomorrow's game against **Wimbledon** as a mark of respect for victims of Hillsborough. The League agrees to call off games involving **Everton** and **Liverpool**. Shocked **Liverpool players** may not wish to replay the semi-final on **May 7** as arranged by the **FA**. **Derby County** and **Spurs** decide to remove their 15ft high safety fences.

18 **Liverpool** announce that they will wait another week before deciding whether to play their semi-final against **Nottingham Forest**. Chairman **John Smith** believes it was insensitive of the **FA** to move so quickly in fixing a date for this replay. The **Football League** is criticised for not postponing all of their games for a week. **Walsall** will join **Birmingham** in the Third Division next season after today's **5-0** thrashing at **Watford**. In the Third Division, **Bristol City** beat **Huddersfield Town 6-1** with **Bob Taylor** getting a first-half hat-trick – the first "six" for **Bristol City** in the **Football League** since **1969**. **Glasgow Rangers** make amends for last Saturday's poor display by beating **St. Johnstone 4-0** in their semi-final replay. Football League President **Jack Dunnett** reveals that **Liverpool**, **Everton** and **Tranmere Rovers** have been given permission to postpone matches for as long as they like. **QPR** postpone their game with **Manchester United**.

19 **Liverpool** manager **Keny Dalglish** refutes accusations by the **South Yorkshire Police** that some **Liverpool** fans were drunk and disorderly at Hillsborough on Saturday. The club is to spend more than **£6m** to make Anfield a **40,000** capacity all-seated stadium. The **Kop** will be **all seats** for the start of **1990–91**. The **Football League** now give permission for any clubs to postpone Saturday's matches. **One minute's silence** is observed at the semi-finals of all three major European Cup matches played today. **AC Milan** slam Real Madrid 5-0 to win **6-1** on aggregate in the **European Cup** semi-finals.

20 **Kenny Dalglish** and four **Liverpool** players attend the first funeral of a **Hillsborough disaster** victim. All **Football League** clubs meet to discuss the lessons of Hillsborough and agree to donate at least **£1m** to the disaster fund and also call on the Government to help finance ground improvements by releasing some of the **£240m** it collects each year from **football pools**.

21 **Lord Justice Taylor** visits Anfield as he leads the inquiry into the Hillsborough disaster. **UEFA** donate **£70,000** to the disaster fund.

22 All **Football League** games played today kicked off at **3.06pm** – the time of abandonment at **Hillsborough** last Saturday and the games are preceeded by a **minute's silence**. **Chelsea** win the Second Division championship with four games in hand by beating **Leeds United 1-0**. Better still, their fans at this all-ticket game remain behind the fences. **QPR** register a rare victory at **Coventry** winning **3-0** – their first in a run of **10 League visits**. **Rotherham** return to the top of the Fourth Division with a **3-1** success against **Burnley**. While **Rangers** march on towards the Scottish League championship with their **sixth League win** in a row (**2-0** at **St. Mirren**) their nearest rivals **Aberdeen** go down **1-0** at **Hearts** – the Dons' first defeat in a run of **nine League** games. There is jubilation at Second Division **Albion Rovers** as they beat **Dumbarton 2-0** to win promotion for the first time in over 40 years.

25 The takeover of **Marler Estates** by **Conrad Holdings** means that **Loftus Road** is saved for **QPR**. **Conrad Holdings** have agreed to sell QPR and Loftus Road to a firm connected with **QPR** chairman **Richard Thompson**. The future of **Fulham** and **Chelsea** is less certain. **Steve Bull** marks his international debut with a goal as **England U-21** beat **Albania U-21** 2-0 at **Portman Road**.

26 **England** restore something of a smile to the mourning football community as they beat **Albania 5-0** at Wembley. **Gary Lineker** scores his first England goal in a run of eight internationals and **Paul Gascoigne** is outstanding. In other **World Cup** qualifying games, **Scotland** beat **Cyprus 2-1** at Hampden, **Northern Ireland** win comfortably **2-0** in **Malta** and **Republic of Ireland** surprisingly beat **Spain 1-0** in Dublin – one of the most important victories in their history. In a friendly at **Wrexham**, **Wales** go down **2-0** to **Sweden**. **Birmingham's** new owners appoint **Dave Mackay** as General Manager and offer manager **Garry Pendrey** the position of coack on his present salary. However, **Pendry** prefers to leave. For breaching an existing touchline ban, **Rangers'** manager **Graeme Souness** is banned from the dug-out area for the whole of next season and fined **£2000** by the **Scottish FA**.

27 **Rangers'** defender **Richard Gough** is elected **Player of the Year** by the **Scottish Football Writers' Association**. Former **Brighton** manager **Chris Cattlin** has ended his legal battle for the remaining 17 months outstanding salary of his contract as the club agree to pay him **£60,000**.

28 **Fourteen** of the **24 Liverpool fans** on trial in Brussels for their part in the **Heysel** Stadium riot are found **guilty of manslaughter** and given **three years' imprisonment** with **half of each term suspended**. In addition, the guilty 14 are each fined **£1000** with a further three months' imprisonment in default. All but one must forfeit **£2000** bail. The cases against the other **10** are **dismissed** for insufficient evidence. The guilty were given a fortnight to appeal and allowed to go home!

29 The season's most improved First Division side **Tottenham Hotspur** in fifth place beat **Millwall 5-0**. In their desperate bid to avoid relegation, **Luton Town** halt a run of **10 games** without a win by

beating **Derby 3-0**. But in even more serious trouble, **Newcastle** lose **4-0** at **Wimbledon**. At a critical stage of the struggle to remain in the Football League, **Colchester** win **2-1** at **Darlington** in front of the Quakers' biggest crowd for over two years – **7126**. **Rotherham** consolidate their position at the top of the Fourth Division with a **6-0** victory over **Hereford**. This was the **latter's record League defeat. Rangers** win their **39th Scottish League** championship with three games in hand in a ruthless **4-0** beating of **Hearts** at Ibrox. **Steve Kirk** scores all **Motherwell's** goals in their **4-0 win** over **St. Mirren**. **St. Johnstone** disappointingly lose their last game at **Muirton Park**, going down **1-0** to **Ayr United**. Next season they move to their new **£4.5m** all-seater stadium.

30 **Brian Clough** becomes the **first manager** to win a **domestic cup** double as **Nottingham Forest** beat **Everton 4-3** in a thrilling **Simod Cup Final** which went into extra time in front of a Wembley crowd of **46,604**. **Liverpool** turn out to play for the first time since **Hillsborough** and prove too good for **Celtic** whom they beat **4-0** in this **Hillsborough Testimonial** in front of a crowd of **60,437** at Parkhead. This adds **£300,000** to the appeal fund.

May 1989

1 After the period of mourning, **Arsenal** resume their race for the championship in grand style easily beating third placed **Norwich 5-0** at Highbury. This was **Norwich's** sixth First Division game without a win and their biggest defeat for over eight years. As **Wolves** earn promotion to the Second Division with a **2-0** win over **Bristol City**, **Steve Bull** nets both goals to take his total to **48**. Having scored **52** last season he becomes the **first Football League** player to score a **century of goals** in **two successive seasons** since **George Camsell** with **101** for **Middlesbrough 1926–28**. **Shrewsbury's 1-0** defeat at **Swindon** sends them down to the Third Division along with **Birmingham** and **Walsall**. **Gillingham** will accompany **Aldershot** down to the Fourth Division after losing **4-1** at **Blackpool** who are still fighting desperately to avoid the drop. **Maidstone United**, occupied in winning the Kent Senior Cup **1-0** against **Welling**, gain **promotion** to the **Football League** as nearest **GM Vauxhall Conference** rivals **Kettering** lose **1-0** at home to lowly placed **Enfield**.

2 **Manchester United** halt their slide down the table with their first victory in seven games beating **Wimbledon 1-0** at Old Trafford in front of a crowd of **23,368** – their **lowest** for over **17 years**. It was in the last minute that **Brian McClair** scores the **first goal** by a United player in nearly **12 hours** of First Division football. **Liverpool's** utility player **Steve Nicol** is voted **Footballer of the Year** by the **Football Writers' Association**. **Rangers'** player-manager **Graeme Souness** beats his touchline ban by naming himself substitute for this evening's **2-0** home win over **Dundee**.

3 **Liverpool** get back to the business of winning the Championship with their usual professionalism but **fail to score** for the **third time** in succession at Goodison where they earn a **goalless draw**. **Nottingham Forest** climb into third place with a **4-1** victory over a sad **Millwall** who have slid from **third** to **eighth** position in a little over a month. **Newcatle** are condemned to relegation through a **2-1** home defeat by bottom-of-the-table **West Ham** in front of a crowd of only **14,202**.

4 With five First Division games still to play, plus the **FA Cup semi-final** and possibly a Final, **Liverpool** are **angry** at the **League's decision** that they must finish by **May 25**. **Gillingham** appoint **Damien Richardson** as manager.

5 The **FA** decide that if tomorrow's replayed **FA Cup semi-final** between **Liverpool** and **Nottingham Forest** is drawn after extra time, it will be decided with a **penalty shoot-out.**

6 **Bournemouth** prevent **Manchester City** from clinching promotion at this stage by drawing **3-3** at Maine Road after being **3-0** down. **Extra time** fails to break the dead-lock as **Sudbury** and **Tamworth** draw 1-1 in an entertaining **FA Vase** final at **Wembley**. Veteran **Andy Gray** scores both of **Rangers** goals in their **2-1** victory at **Dundee**, the town (though not the club) where his first-class career began more than **15 years** ago. **Falkirk**, still in with a chance of pipping **Dunfermline** to the First Division championship, destroy luckless **Queen of the South 7-1** at Brockville Park.

7 Talented **Liverpool** make way for the second all-Merseyside FA Cup Final in four years and wreck **Brian Clough's** hopes of a unique Cup treble, by beating **Nottingham Forest 3-1** in their postponed semi-final. **John Aldridge** gets two brilliant goals.

8 **Liverpool** are now left with the task of playing six games in 16 days in their quest for the double.

9 **West Ham** make it four wins in a row by beating **Sheffield Wednesday 2-0** at Hillsborough but they are still not certain of escaping relegation. The **FA** now agree that the **Cup Final** will be replayed if necessary abandoning thoughts of a **penalty shoot-out**. Some First Division clubs are campaigning for **ITV's £11m** to be shared out according to each club's position in the competition. They also want to **ban plastic pitches** in the top two divisions from **1991–92**. The satellite broadcasting company **BSB** agree to pay the **Scottish FA £6.25m** and the League **£6m** over the next three seasons. **Real Madrid** appoint **John Toshack** manager with a two-year contract worth **£500,000** a season. **Real** will pay **Toshack's** present club, **Real Sociedad**, **£200,000** compensation.

10 **Liverpool** continue their race for the double with another win over **Nottingham Forest**, this time **1-0** in the First Division with **John Aldridge** converting a **late penalty**. **Manchester United's** nightmare ending to the season continues as **Everton** win **2-1** before an Old Trafford crowd of only **26,722**. **Barcelona** beat **Sampdoria 2-0** in the **European Cup-Winners' Cup final**. **Tamworth** beat **Sudbury Town 3-0** in the **FA Vase** final replay. **Japanese sportswear** giants **Asics** will sponsor **Norwich City** to the tune of up to **£1.5m** over the next three years depending on the club's success.

11 **Gordon McQueen** resigns as manager of **Airdrie**.

12 **Celtic** are reported to have agreed to pay **Nantes £1.2m** for the return of **Maurice Johnston** after two years in France. **Ernie Walker** resigns as **secretary** of the **Scottish FA** saying that it is time for younger blood. His parting message is that football in Scotland is getting too rough.

13 The last Saturday of the **Football League** season ends with the championship as well as relegation from the **First Division** undecided. The champions will be either **Arsenal** or **Liverpool**, while either **West Ham** or **Aston Villa** will accompany **Middlesbrough** and **Newcastle United** down into the

Second Division. The **Gunners** failed to clinch the title in a surprising **2-1** home defeat by **Derby County** while **Liverpool** extend their unbeaten League and Cup run to **21 games** by winning **2-1** at **Wimbledon**. **Middlesbrough** drop into the Second Division after a **1-0** defeat at **Sheffield Wednesday**. **Trevor Morley** earns **Manchester City** promotion to the First Division in a **1-1** draw at **Bradford City**. For the first time on record, **Spurs** make it **three defeats** in a row at **QPR** where they go down **1-0**. Serious crowd problems delay **Crystal Palace's** game for **26 minutes** before they beat **Birmingham 4-1**, while at **Bristol City play** is also **halted** to enable the police to clear the pitch of fighting fans before **Sheffield United** are beaten **2-0**. Despite this defeat, **United** are promoted on goal difference. **Crewe** climb out of the **Fourth Division** for the first time in **20 years** gaining the promotion-winning point with an equaliser by **Paul Clayton** in a **1-1** draw at **Tranmere** who also win promotion. Scottish League champions **Rangers** get no points for effort against **Aberdeen** as they go down **3-0** – making it **four times** in the last **five League** clashes with the **Dons** at **Ibrox** that **Rangers** have failed to score. **Dunfermline** are back in the Premier Division after only one season. **Willie Watters** scores the first "five" in the Scottish League for more than three years as **Kilmarnock** beat **Queen of the South 6-0**. Despite this runaway victory, the Killies are still relegated to the Second Division on goal difference, while **Alloa** accompany **Albion Rovers** up into **Division I**. **Telford** beat **Macclesfield** with a solitary goal scored in extra time to win the **FA Trophy** for the second time in six years.

16 **Martin Edwards** denies rumours that he is selling his majority interest in **Manchester United**. **Liverpool** remain favourites to carry off the double as they beat **QPR 2-0**. **England 'B'** enjoy a comfortable **2-0** win in **Switzerland** with **Paul Gascoigne** scoring from a brilliant solo effort. **Dundee United** coach **Jimmy Bone** becomes manager of **Airdrie**.

17 **Arsenal** appear to have blown their chance of the League championship as they are held to a **2-2** draw by **Wimbledon** at Highbury. **Napoli** and **Stuttgart** draw **3-3** giving the Italians victory in the **UEFA Cup Final 5-4** on aggregate. **FA** chairman **Bert Millichip** shakes the fooball fraternity by suggesting that all away supporters should be baned from "high risk" matches.

18 **Leroy Rosenoir** scores one of the season's fastest goals (**in 19 seconds**) for **West Ham** at **Nottingham Forest** in the Londoners desperate bid to avoid relegation. The same player scores again to give the **Hammers** an amazing **2-1** victory. Former **Birmingham** manager **Garry Pendrey** is reported to be suing the club over a two-year contract worth around **£75,000. John Still**, **Maidstone's part-time manager**, resigns because the club will not give him the security of a three-year contract to enable him to give up his full-time job.

19 **England 'B'** win **2-0** in **Iceland**.

20 Two extra-time goals by substitute **Ian Rush** help **Liverpool** to win the **FA Cup** against **Merseyside** rivals Everton. **Liverpool** took a fourth minute lead but then went into a long first-half spell of complacency, before the game developed into one of the most dramatic finals of recent years with Everton substitute **Stuart McCall** getting a last-minute equaliser. **McCall** scored another equaliser after **Rush** put Liverpool ahead in extra time. Then **Rush** hits the **winner** in the **104th minute**. The **Scottish Cup Final** is not so exciting but holders **Celtic** beat **Rangers** with a solitary goal by little **Joe Miller** just before the interval. **Hull City** dismiss manager **Eddie Gray**, while caretaker manager **Jimmy Mullen** gets the job at **Blackpool**.

21 The pitch invasion by jubilant **Liverpool** fans at Wembley yesterday has persuaded the authorities that lowering the fences for this game was a one-off and they will be up again for **England v Chile**. Big attendance **increases** are reported in the **Scottish League** including an amazing **83%** in the First Division. **Rangers** manager **Graeme Souness** announces his retirement as a player.

22 A small fire started on the terraces holds up **Preston's play-off** match with **Port Vale** for eight minutes. No one is injured. **Colin Appleton** returns to **Hull City** for a second spell as manager. **Maidstone United** appoint **Keith Peacock manager**.

23 A new look **England** side with **John Fashanu** and **Nigel Clough** making their debuts, is held to a **goalless** draw by **Chile** in their **Rous Cup** at Wembley before a crowd of only **15,628**. The **attendance** was undoubtedly affected by an **underground train strike**. Former Hammer, **Ray Houghton** scores twice in **Liverpool's 5-1** victory over **West Ham** condemning the Londoners to relegation. **Liverpool** now need only one point to land the double against **Arsenal** in three days time.

24 In **Barcelona**, **AC Milan** beat **Steaua Bucharest** 4-0 to win the **European Cup** for the third time.

26 **Arsenal** pull off a remarkable **2-0** victory at **Anfield** to **win** the **Championship** and destroy **Liverpool's** hopes of their second double in four seasons. It was one of the finest wins ever recorded by **Arsenal** who had lost their previous **seven First Division visits** to **Anfield**, and it ended **Liverpool's** run of **24 games without defeat**.

27 After leading **Wolves** to promotion, the prolific scoring **Steve Bull** scores on his full international debut as **England** beat a lack-lustre **Scotland 2-0** at Hampden where **Chris Waddle** scores the other goal. This was **England's fourth** win in their last **seven visits** to Hampden.

28 **Republic of Ireland** have a great chance of reaching the **World Cup** finals for the first time following their **2-0** home win over **Malta**. **Bolton Wanderers** prove too strong for Fourth Division **Torquay United** whom they beat **4-1** in the **Sherpa Van Trophy** final which attracts **46,513** to Wembley.

29 The **£1.2m** return of **Mo Johnston** from **Nantes** to **Celtic** agreed two weeks ago, has fallen through despite strong **Celtic** protests and the player is expected to play out his contract with **Nantes** which expires in **June 1990**.

30 There is bound to be some **re-thinking** about the end-of-season **Rous Cup** after only **9006** turn up at Hampden Park to see **Scotland** beat **Chile 2-0**.

31 **Wales** are superior to a disappointing **West German** side at **Cardiff Arms Park** but are denied a penalty and cannot find the net in a **goalless draw** which appears to have ended the home country's chance of reaching the **World Cup** Finals. This was the **first soccer international** in **Britain** to be played in an **all-seater** stadium.

June 1989

2 **England U-21** beat **Poland U-21, 2-1** at **Plymouth** with skipper **Michael Thomas** hitting the winner.

3 **England** earn a well deserved **3-0** win over **Poland** at **Wembley** with **Gary Lineker** scoring the first goal and helping to set up the others scored by **John Barnes** and **Neil Webb**. This puts England well in line for the Finals. **Peter Shilton** equalled **Bobby Moore's record** of **108** internationals in his **1200th** first-class game. **Crystal Palace** earn promotion to the **First Division** by beating **Blackburn Rovers 2-0** (4-3 on aggregate) in the **play-offs**. **Port Vale** return to the Second Division for the first time in **32 years** with a **1-0** win over **Bristol Rovers** – the goal scored by **Robbie Earle**, and **Leyton Orient** are promoted to the Third Division with a **2-1** win over **Wrexham** – **Mark Cooper** getting the vital winner in the 82nd minute.

4 **Republic of Ireland** win again in the **World Cup** qualifying competition, this time beating **Hungary 2-0** in Dublin.

5 Relegated **West Ham** sack **John Lyall** the Football League's **longest serving manager** who was appointed **15 years ago**.

7 In a game held in Copenhagen to celebrate **100 years of Danish football**, **Gary Lineker** puts **England** ahead with his **29th goal in 38 internationals** but Denmark equalise early in the second half. This was the first goal conceded by **Peter Shilton** in **six matches** as he celebrated a new **England record** of **109** appearances. The **International Board** decide to make it compulsory for all players to **wear shinguards** from season **1990–91**. **UEFA** more than double the fine inflicted on **Hearts** for allowing the home leg of their **UEFA Cup tie** with **Bayern Munich** to be televised live in West Germany. The fine is now **£93,000**.

9 **Leeds United's** signing of hard man **Vinny Jones** from **Wimbledon** at a fee of **£650,000** causes some raised eyebrows and ex-Leeds star **Johnny Giles** is bold enough to say that the late lamented Don Revie "would not have let him through the door, let alone put on a Leeds shirt." At the **Football League's annual meeting Jack Dunnett** announces that he has **quit** as **League president**; resigned as a director of **Notts County** and joined the **Portsmouth** board. Proposals for "fairer shares" of **TV fees** are dropped but the First Division clubs will discuss this matter further. It was agreed that clubs may field **three foreign players** instead of **two**.

12 **Atletico Madrid** part company with **Colin Addison**.

13 **Aston Villa** manager **Graham Taylor** is annoyed at what he claims to have been an illegal approach by **Bayern Munich** for Scottish striker **Alan McInally** and ups his price to squeeze a total of **£1.1m** out of them for the player's signature. He is also selling **Martin Keown** to **Everton** for **£750,000**.

14 After what was by their own standards a poor season, **Manchester United** complete the signing of **Mike Phelan** at **£750,000** from **Norwich City** and **£2m** rated **Neil Webb** from **Nottingham Forest**. A **tribunal** will decide on the fee for **Webb**.

15 **West Ham** want their former winger **Harry Redknapp** to succeed sacked **John Lyall** but his present club **Bournemouth** accuse **West Ham** of making an illegal approach. **Everton** sign **Mike Newell** from **Leicester City** in a deal worth **£1.1m** and which takes **Wayne Clarke** to Filbert Street.

16 Assuming they win their fight for ownership, **Chelsea** show that they have big plans for **Stamford Bridge** costing **£40m**.

19 **Malcolm Allison** becomes manager of **Fisher Athletic** the **London dockland club** and is confident of achieving Football League status. **Brewers Bass** take over the sponsorship of the **Charity Shield** with a **four-year £600,000** deal.

20 After rejecting a more lucrative move to **Monaco**, **Gary Lineker** joins **Tottenham Hotspur** in a **£1.5m** deal which includes **Nayim** (Mohammed Ali Amar) who has been on loan at White Hart Lane during the past season. **Lineker** will be paid **£5000**-a-week.

21 By coincidence, the **Football League's** fixtures for the coming season have **Sheffield Wednesday** at home to **Liverpool** a year and a day after the **Hillsborough disaster**.

22 **Northampton** magistrates fine **Aldershot** manager **Len Walker £100** with **£100 costs** for using **bad language** when admonishing two of his players within the hearing of spectators during last October's **6-0** defeat at **Northampton**.

23 After concern had been expressed about the distribution of tickets in this country for the **1990 World Cup Finals** in **Italy**, the Italian authorities assure the FA that checks on recipients will be made before vouchers are exchanged for tickets.

24 **Saudi Arabia** beat **Scotland 5-4** on **penalties** after drawing **2-2** to win the **FIFA U-16 World Tournament** for the **JVC Cup** at Hampden Park. A crowd of **51,674** saw this game which ended a tournament which had brought nothing but credit to the game. The **Mo Johnston** transfer saga is re-opened as **FIFA General Secretary Sepp Blatter** tells a Hampden Park press conference that he has studied the documents and Johnston should be a **Celtic** player from **July 1** because there is a binding contract between the Scottish club and **Nantes**. Only a mutual agreement to rescind could change this. However, **Johnston** declares that he has signed no contract.

27 **Everton** secure **Swedish international** midfielder **Stefan Rehn** from **Djurgaarden**.

INDEX OF SOME OF THE MORE INTERESTING DIARY ITEMS

FOOTBALL LEAGUE MATCHES
1888–1989

	P	W	D	L	Goals F	Goals A
Aberdare Athletic	252	78	59	115	334	413
Accrington Stanley*	1542	544	298	700	2441	2954
Aldershot	2254	767	580	907	3107	3462
Arsenal	3406	1476	834	1096	5636	4625
Ashington	328	109	71	148	489	650
Aston Villa	3542	1510	795	1237	6096	5316
Barnsley	3366	1224	848	1294	4837	5100
Barrow	1924	624	414	886	2606	3349
Birmingham City	3440	1283	825	1332	5122	5114
Blackburn Rovers	3562	1388	852	1322	5617	5493
Blackpool	3334	1234	819	1281	4892	4967
Bolton Wanderers	3568	1386	820	1362	5425	5262
Bootle	22	8	3	11	49	63
AFC Bournemouth	2632	995	688	949	3678	3549
Bradford (Park Avenue)	2190	837	476	877	3516	3582
Bradford City	3238	1210	821	1207	4739	4663
Brentford	2744	1046	692	1006	4030	3924
Brighton & Hove Albion	2700	1089	682	929	4074	3702
Bristol City	3234	1254	815	1165	4740	4531
Bristol Rovers	2696	1009	672	1015	4054	4066
Burnley	3568	1389	842	1337	5434	5402
Burton United[1]	484	147	80	257	657	994
Burton Wanderers	90	42	13	35	167	146
Bury	3484	1304	811	1369	5185	5242
Cambridge United	850	291	234	325	1066	1172
Cardiff City	2628	956	647	1025	3669	3983
Carlisle United	2356	859	561	936	3463	3677
Charlton Athletic	2572	936	634	1002	3874	4108
Chelsea	3028	1169	785	1074	4596	4462
Chester City	2294	812	577	905	3309	3440
Chesterfield	3060	1189	713	1158	4504	4356
Colchester United	1792	664	475	653	2799	2604
Coventry City	2688	989	683	1016	3989	3989
Crewe Alexandra	2816	941	658	1217	3872	4658
Crystal Palace	2678	983	713	982	3828	3817
Darlington	2706	925	643	1138	3902	4412
Darwen	232	75	27	130	401	619
Derby County	3546	1413	845	1288	5725	5362
Doncaster Rovers	2700	978	668	1054	3876	4191
Durham City	286	95	54	137	394	529
Everton	3530	1494	850	1186	5859	5058
Exeter City	2757	929	713	1115	3793	4275
Fulham	2978	1114	721	1143	4497	4433
Gainsborough Trinity	564	175	118	271	718	1029
Gateshead	1466	559	361	546	2292	2335
Gillingham	2548	896	658	994	3425	3770
Glossop North End	618	197	136	285	829	1026
Grimsby Town	3492	1351	763	1378	5266	5386
Halifax Town	2708	872	703	1133	3499	4265
Hartlepool United	2706	898	599	1209	3643	4538
Hereford United	778	258	223	297	945	1023
Huddersfield Town	2882	1117	735	1030	4203	3945
Hull City	3094	1204	799	1091	4606	4292
Ipswich Town	1878	775	447	656	2866	2631
Leeds United[2]	2998	1219	750	1029	4543	4152
Leicester City	3390	1261	854	1275	5256	5323
Leyton Orient	3094	1035	794	1265	3991	4565
Lincoln City	3380	1235	777	1368	5144	5391
Liverpool	3406	1588	818	1000	5869	4410
Loughborough Town	158	34	20	104	170	410
Luton Town	2724	1071	672	981	4329	3997
Manchester City	3440	1414	817	1209	5761	5161
Manchester United	3438	1518	836	1084	5789	4716
Mansfield Town	2292	847	590	855	3481	3440

	P	W	D	L	Goals F	A
Merthyr Town	420	115	106	199	524	779
Middlesbrough	3236	1231	774	1231	5012	4874
Middlesbrough Ironopolis	28	8	4	16	37	72
Millwall	2692	1072	698	922	3962	3652
Nelson	412	154	73	185	668	796
New Brighton	884	287	187	410	1191	1527
New Brighton Tower	102	48	24	30	194	148
Newcastle United	3406	1394	771	1241	5466	4979
Newport County	2672	888	625	1159	3700	4557
Northampton Town	2744	1079	619	1046	4279	4135
Northwich Victoria	50	12	5	33	72	156
Norwich City	2638	975	704	959	3856	3857
Nottingham Forest	3442	1293	847	1302	5095	5070
Notts County	3610	1344	874	1392	5316	5438
Oldham Athletic	3046	1133	763	1150	4455	4537
Oxford United	1192	412	348	432	1516	1542
Peterborough United	1334	526	366	442	2004	1774
Plymouth Argyle	2694	1057	686	951	4134	3815
Portsmouth	2638	980	679	979	3956	3943
Port Vale[3]	3206	1148	822	1236	4435	4683
Preston North End	3588	1387	890	1311	5449	5191
Queen's Park Rangers	2658	1068	660	930	4039	3699
Reading	2754	1110	670	974	4270	3948
Rochdale	2706	883	673	1150	3711	4392
Rotherham United[4]	2812	1062	640	1110	4234	4412
Scarborough	92	38	28	26	123	100
Scunthorpe United	1769	620	495	654	2421	2512
Sheffield United	3462	1390	820	1252	5498	5209
Sheffield Wednesday	3458	1368	842	1248	5380	5083
Shrewsbury Town	1760	620	479	661	2437	2519
Southampton	2626	1025	675	926	4079	3818
Southend United	2760	1036	678	1046	4083	4066
Southport	2200	723	568	909	2961	3488
Stalybridge Celtic	76	33	11	32	104	110
Stockport County	3310	1201	788	1321	4650	4900
Stoke City	3254	1180	784	1290	4556	4803
Sunderland	3500	1447	835	1218	5756	5147
Swansea City	2680	994	636	1050	3927	4153
Swindon Town	2730	1039	701	990	4073	3948
Thames	84	20	17	47	107	202
Torquay United	2466	875	620	971	3482	3833
Tottenham Hotspur	2906	1230	706	970	4897	4132
Tranmere Rovers	2706	1026	638	1042	4121	4076
Walsall	2942	1041	695	1206	4410	4702
Watford	2710	1029	688	993	3976	3836
West Bromwich Albion	3542	1399	843	1300	5661	5339
West Ham United	2640	1007	640	993	4127	4045
Wigan Athletic	506	214	136	156	726	624
Wigan Borough[5]	412	145	94	173	635	706
Wimbledon	526	225	137	164	808	691
Wolverhampton W	3552	1455	782	1315	5964	5492
Workington	1194	385	310	499	1525	1810
Wrexham	2690	1023	656	1011	4109	3972
York City	2370	843	575	952	3530	3656

The above figures do not include games played at the start of season 1939–40 before the competition was abandoned because of the outbreak of World War II, nor do they include the old end-of-season Test matches or the modern Play-offs.

* Includes the original club known simply as Accrington but none of the games played during season 1961–62 when they resigned from the League.

[1] Includes Burton Swifts who amalgamated with Burton Wanderers to form Burton United in 1901.

[2] Includes Leeds City and the eight games played 1919–20.

[3] Includes only 34 games played 1919–20 when took over from Leeds City.

[4] Including Rotherham County who amalgamated with Rotherham Town to form Rotherham United in 1925.

[5] Games played in season 1931–32 prior to their resignation on 26 October were expunged from the record and therefore not included in these figures.

FOOTBALL AND PARLIAMENT

This season has been one of the most hectic ever for football. There has also never been a time when soccer has been as high on the political agenda as now. The legacy of the European Championships, the proposed identity card scheme for supporters, the attempt to return to UEFA club competitions, the Hillsborough disaster and now the Taylor Inquiry have all been debated at some length in the Houses of Parliament.

With all this activity, the role for the All-Party Football Committee has developed apace. This Committee, formed by Jim Lester MP and myself in 1979, brings together MPs and Peers from all parties who support our national game and who help it whenever Parliament appears to impinge upon it. It has grown into one of the largest backbench committees with over 120 members. The Committee works closely with the football world for the benefit of the game. Regular speaker meetings and visits to grounds take place throughout the year.

In recent seasons the Committee has used its influence to make the Government see a little sense as regards the affect of alcohol legislation on football, to help Fulham FC and other clubs with their difficulties, to give evidence to the Popplewell Inquiry and to seek better tax concessions for football to name but a few. It may seem surprising but dozens of MPs attend matches week in, week out and the soccer lobby within Parliament is potentially very strong indeed.

All the improvements being made in football – and there have been many – have been overshadowed this season. The development of community schemes at 50+ clubs, the rise in attendances and the fall in arrests have been largely forgotten in the aftermath of Hillsborough.

No simple solution to the games' problems will be found by the Taylor Inquiry into the events of April 15th. It should, however, point to better safety standards, stadium improvements and will raise questions about the proposed identity card scheme.

The majority of the Committee oppose the imposition of identity cards. An all-party delegation was unanimously sent to see the Ministers concerned with the Football Spectators Bill after Hillsborough to press for it to be 'put on ice' until the lessons of the tragedy had been learnt. Unfortunately the Government is pressing on with this contentious Bill rather than listen to MPs on all sides of the House who wish to see it postponed.

The coming months will see bitter debate over identity cards at a time when politicians should unite to help football. Consensus has already been reached on the legislation which seeks to ban convicted hooligans from travelling abroad: that should be introduced as soon as possible. A large injection of money will be needed for safety work, seats and other improvements in the coming months. The Government cannot stand aside from playing its part in financing football, particularly as it takes £279m each year as tax on the pools industry. I hope that a genuine debate can be held to determine the best way to help football into the twenty-first century. Parliament's involvement will be crucial for the healthy future of our national game.

Tom Pendry MP, *Chairman of the All-Party Football Committee.*

Liverpool fans help others as the crush begins at Hillsborough on the fateful day of the FA Cup semi-final.

THE FOOTBALL LEAGUE

Featuring full details of each of the 92 clubs in the Football League.

Officials, statistics, 1988–89 team photo, full 1988–89 League record and career details of the players.

THE FOOTBALL LEAGUE OFFICIALS

President

Life Vice-Presidents

L. C. Cearns
H. E. McGee
Sir Arthur South
R. Wragg

Management Committee

R. I. Burr (*Millwall*)
R. T. Chase (*Norwich City*)
H. D. Ellis (*Aston Villa*)
W. Fox (*Blackburn Rovers*)
W. G. McKeag (*Newcastle United*)
M. D. B. Sinclair (*York City*)
J. W. Smith (*Liverpool*)
I. H. Stott (*Oldham Athletic*)

Life Members

Sir Matt Busby CBE, KCSG
E. M. Gliksten
L. T. Shipman CBE
The Rt Hon Lord Westwood JP, FCIS
J. F. Wiseman
F. A. Would
R. Wragg

Secretary

David Dent

REVIEW OF THE SEASON

Criticising George Graham, manager of Arsenal, the League Champions, is really like putting the boot into Wellington after Waterloo. He made mistakes, but ultimately the Napoleonic strategy of the shrewd Kenny Dalglish erred more crucially in the Anfield clash of these two Scots, which yielded the most dramatic title decision in the League's history.

The fateful tragedy of Hillsborough had ironically left the confrontation between champions and challengers until the last fixture of the season. Liverpool had emerged from their lengthy mourning to commendably recapture their most incisive form, adding Everton to their list of victims in the FA Cup Final six days earlier and ending a gallant effort by West Ham to avoid relegation just three days previously.

Liverpool had not lost in 18 League games. Their last defeat had been on New Year's Day at Old Trafford where Manchester United beat them 3-1. Earlier on December 17, when Arsenal had beaten United 2-1 at Highbury, Liverpool's 1-0 home defeat at the hands of Norwich City had left them eight points adrift of the Gunners who had a game in hand.

But having hit the top on Boxing Day, Arsenal saw their commanding lead slip away in the last two home games from which they derived just one point. Graham who had shored up a suspect defence by introducing a sweeper on April 2, ironically at Old Trafford in a 1-1 draw with Manchester United, subsequently enjoyed four wins without conceding a goal.

Then, however, he and his team found themselves frustrated by England goalkeeper Peter Shilton in the match with Derby County on a fated May 13. He abandoned his new system during the game, but the Rams still won 2-1. In the following match with Wimbledon he decided to revert to the pre-sweeper idea, only to see the side struggle to a 2-2 draw.

With nine more days in which to reflect on this change of fortune which had cost five points, he watched as Liverpool went to the head of the League for the first time in the season. Liverpool's 5–1 win over West Ham appeared to seal the prospect of a second League and Cup double in three years for the Anfield club.

Arsenal's task was formidable enough. They had to win by two goals to take the title by virtue of scoring more goals than Liverpool, as both teams were level on goal difference. Liverpool had not lost at home by such a margin for three years when Everton had beaten them. It was to be the closest race for the championship since Arsenal had gone to Old Trafford in 1952 faced with the unlikely prospect of winning by seven goals to deprive Manchester United of the title.

In that event, Arsenal lost 6-1 and while a similar score seemed remote this time, the odds seemed as heavily stacked against them as they had been 37 years earlier.

Despite the desperate need for goals, Graham decided to revert to using a sweeper with Steve Bould and Tony Adams marking John Aldridge and Ian Rush, leaving David O'Leary to tidy up behind them. Indeed Arsenal looked slightly the more relaxed side and might have gone ahead from Bould's header in the ninth minute.

Yet the game probably turned Arsenal's way as early as the 32nd minute when Ian Rush suffered a slight groin strain and was replaced by Peter Beardsley. Arsenal were still finding the lack of bodies up front something of a handicap, but as the game wore on, Liverpool, understandably perhaps, appeared more and more willing to settle for what they already had, a goalless draw which would have given them the championship.

The half-time whistle arrived with still no score, but the Gunners resumed with the same line-up. Yet the breakthrough came unexpectedly after seven minutes from a free-kick awarded against Steve Nicol, just outside the area on the left side of Liverpool's defence.

Without the injured dead-ball expert Brian Marwood, it was left to Nigel Winterburn to curl the ball to the far post with his left foot, into the crowded penalty area. The ball sailed over, O'Leary stumbled and fell into a Liverpool defender, a linesman flagged but Alan Smith stole in to nudge the ball with his head inside Bruce Grobbelaar's right-hand post and the referee signalled a goal. He was immediately surrounded by protesting Liverpool players who persuaded him to consult the linesman. After an agonisingly lengthy dialogue, the referee confirmed the goal.

Liverpool – unwisely perhaps – retreated, deciding it was enough, reverting to the possession game to rely on breakaways to stretch the opposition and shrink time. Graham sent on Martin Hayes but only for Paul Merson. Then in the 74th minute Michael Thomas found himself in front of goal ten yards out only to mis-hit his shot. Arsenal's best chance appeared to have sped away. On came Perry Groves for Bould and at last Arsenal had three more attackers.

Time was running out. A prolonged repair job carried out on Kevin Richardson which

Michael Thomas (far right) scores Arsenal's second goal against Liverpool at Anfield in the last minute of the final League game of the 1988–89 season to clinch the championship.

took the game into injury time, might well have inadvertently aided Arsenal's cause. With the seconds ticking away and the Gunners' continually pumping the ball into the Liverpool box, it was villain Thomas who assumed the mantle of hero.

Receiving the ball in a similar position, but with defenders closing on both sides, he coolly swept the ball past the advancing goalkeeper. There was time only for the decency of a token restart before the final whistle heralded this improbable victory for Arsenal.

Whatever arguments can be put forward for Liverpool's undisputed qualities as a first-class club, highly efficient and probably the outstanding team in England on its day, Arsenal must be given unrestrained credit for achieving exactly the result they required at Anfield.

Dalglish referred afterwards to the manner in which Arsenal had played. It was not the Liverpool way. But he might have been haunted by his own words after the cup semi-final victory over Nottingham Forest when he said that only one team had wanted to win on the day.

There were other facets to appreciate in the term, not the least of them the rise in attendances for a third successive season, something never achieved in the post-war period. The final figures showed an increase of half a million, putting the aggregate at 18.4 million, the highest level for six years.

All four divisions benefited. The First Division reduced to its lowest complement in modern times, revealed the biggest increase on average followed by the Third Division. Liverpool was again the best supported team, with Manchester United runners-up. At the other end of the League, there were no attendances of three figures.

The performances of the so-called ten 'Super-League' teams was interesting. Two of them, West Ham and Newcastle were relegated. True with Arsenal, Liverpool and Nottingham Forest finishing 1-2-3, they held the key positions at the top, but at no time in the season did they manage on a full day's programme, to have more than five teams in the top half of the table and once towards the end of the season, they could only scrape four!

However for the attractiveness of their play, Nottingham Forest at their best had the purists purring. So did Norwich who championed the cause of the 'other First Division teams', heading the table for three months in the first half of the campaign and even winning at Anfield.

Tottenham rocketed up the table after finding their most effective form late on, to transform themselves from rock bottom on November 5 into a top six outfit. Aston Villa had to wait ten days before West Ham's bubble finally burst at Liverpool to relieve them of the fear of relegation, but Charlton, with far more practice of playing on their nerve ends, pulled themselves clear with two wins from their last three games.

Coventry, in third place by the middle of January, held up reasonably well to finish seventh, while Derby with that man Shilton conceded just a goal a game on average, were as high as fourth after beating Coventry on December 17 and ended the season one place lower.

It was a disappointing season for Everton, despite being runners-up to their Merseyside neighbours in the FA Cup, though three wins in the last three outings improved their rating to eighth. Luton became favourites for Division Two on April 1, after losing 2-1 at Villa Park having taken one point from a possible 24, but survived after a revival which was completed on May 13 with a penalty kick win over Norwich.

Manchester United in third place on February 11 won only three more games and saw attendances shrivel as a consequence of a miserly 11 goals in 14 matches. For newly promoted Middlesbrough, it was a short sojourn in the top flight, winning only one of their last 15 games. They went down with north-east neighbours Newcastle, who only managed to be out of the bottom three once and then after the opening two games with a solitary point. Newcastle used 35 different players, more than any other team in the four divisions.

Millwall surprised everyone except themselves by remaining unbeaten in their opening eight games and even topped the division on October 1. They clung on well in third place until March before their long ball game found short shrift in the last ten games, in which they picked up only three points to leave them tenth.

Fourth placed Norwich assumed first place after beating Newcastle 2–0 in the middle of September and had still only lost three times by the middle of February. But when Newcastle avenged the score at Carrow Road in March, City won only two more games. Forest's largely youthful side performed poorly at home winning only one game at the City Ground in the opening half of the season, yet threatened to overtake the leaders in the final run-up before running out of steam.

Ninth placed Queen's Park Rangers hauled themselves to safety from a mid-season crisis and though Ron Atkinson's arrival at Sheffield Wednesday was immediately rewarded by only two points from a possible 15, saved the day with a victory over Middlesbrough, toppled 1-0 on May 13.

Southampton, briefly top on September 10, skidded 17 games without a win before braking to a respectable 13th, while Wimbledon, those ace exponents of the short route to opposing territory, threatened to cause more general problems with only two defeats in 15 games to early April before they eased out to 12th.

Chelsea ultimately shook off the attentions of Manchester City to emerge as worthy Second Division champions, returning to Division One after one season. Ironically Graham Roberts 12 penalty goals was just one short of City's Francis Lee record 13 spot kicks more than a decade earlier. Gordon Durie with five goals in the 7-0 win at Walsall on February 4 and Kerry Dixon with one 'four' in a total of 25 goals, rendered outfield scoring respectability as well. Chelsea's 2-0 defeat at Leicester on April 15 prevented them equalling a club record 28 League games without defeat. City, erratic at Maine Road, accompanied them in promotion.

Birmingham, who spent most of the season in the bottom two, went down with Walsall, who occupied the same two positions from the end of November. They were joined by Shrewsbury, to make it a midlands relegation trio.

But there was more joy in the Black Country at Wolverhampton, never headed in Division Three from the first week in November. Steve Bull left many opponents on the horns of a defensive dilemma with 37 goals among his total of 50 for the season in League and Cup games.

Sheffield United, who clung to their tails with Tony Agana and Brian Deane, vying with Bull and Andy Mutch for the twin strikers medals, just edged out Port Vale. At the other end, Aldershot, Chesterfield and Southend who only just escaped last season, succumbed this time along with Gillingham, but Rotherham, unbeaten in their last eight games, made it back first time along with Tranmere and Crewe who had looked completely secure until a late wobble. Rovers for their part had just one reverse in their last 14 games.

Colchester's attendances doubled after they hit the bottom of Division Four in December. No win in 18 games mattered little to their supporters. They were rewarded with the team winning their last five games, including a 2-1 victory at Darlington who found themselves consigned to the GM Vauxhall Conference.

JACK ROLLIN

INTRODUCTION TO THE CLUB SECTION

The full page team photographs which appear on the first of each club's six pages in this section of the yearbook were taken at the beginning of the 1988–89 season, and therefore relate to the season covered by this edition's statistics.

The third and fourth pages of each club's section give a complete record of the League season for the club concerned, including date, venue, opponents, result, half-time score, League position, goalscorers, attendance and complete line-ups, including substitutes where used, for every League game in the 1988–89 season. These two pages also include consolidated lists of goalscorers for the club in League, Littlewoods Cup and FA Cup matches and a summary of results in the two main domestic cups. The full League history of the club, a full list of major honours won and best placings achieved, and a note of the team's first and second choice colours appear on the second page of this section. The colours are checked with the clubs, but please note that second choice colours may vary during the season.

Note also that the League position shown after each League result is re-calculated as at every Saturday night plus full holiday programmes, but the position after mid-week fixtures will not normally be up-dated. Please be advised that the attendance figures quoted for each League game are those which appeared in the Press at the time, whereas the attendance statistics published on pages 439 and 440 are those issued officially by the Football League after the season has been completed. However, the figures for each League game are those used by the Football League in their weekly bulletin, in conjunction with the *Sunday Telegraph* and Jack Rollin's column in that newspaper.

On the fourth page of each club's section, the total League appearances for the season are listed at the foot of each player's column. Substitutes are inserted as numbers 12 and 14 where they actually came on to play. The players taken off are respectively given an asterisk (*) and a dagger (†). But in order to give the chart a uniform appearance, where only one substitute has played the number 12 will have been used. Some clubs, Aston Villa for example, have used 13 as their second substitute number, but again for purposes of uniformity, they appear as 14.

In the totals at the foot of each column, substitute appearances are listed separately below the '+' sign, but have been amalgamated in the totals which feature in the player's historical section on the final page for each club.

The final pages for each club lists all the players included on the Football League's 'Retained' list, which is published at the end of May. Here you will find each player's height and weight, where known plus birthplace, birthdate and source, together with total League appearances and goals for each club he has represented. Full names of all other players retained including trainees, non-contract players and schoolboys are also given. In addition more club information is added on these pages with a potted history of the club's foundation and a full list of managers over the years since entering the League.

Any transfers which take place between the publication of the League's Retained list and this book going to press will be included in the transfer section between pages 605 and 613, but the player's details will remain under the club which retained him at the end of the season. An asterisk * by a player's name on the fifth and sixth pages mean that he was given a free transfer at the end of the 1988–89 season, a dagger † against a name means that he is a non-contract player, and a double dagger ‡ indicates that the player's registration was cancelled during the season. An § indicates either a Trainee or an Associated Schoolboy who has made Football League appearances.

The play-offs in the Football League are listed separately on pages 592 and 593. Appearances made by players in these play-offs will *not* be included in their career totals on 'page four'.

Two pages have been included for Maidstone United, newcomers to the League.

Editor's note: In the Scottish League, two substitutes have been allowed for several seasons. Substitutes where used are listed as 12 and 14. The second player to be taken off is also picked out with a dagger.

ALDERSHOT 1988–89 *Back row (left to right):* Glen Burvill, David Barnes, Tony Lange, Mike Ring, Steve Wignall.
Centre row: Darren Anderson, Colin Smith, Giorgic Mazzon, Steve Berry, Ian Chandler, James Devereux, Ian Gillard (Coach).
Front row: Jim Lange (Physiotherapist), Glyn Riley, Peter Leebrook, Ian McDonald, Daren Hewitt, Ian Phillips, Steve Wilkes, Len Walker (Manager).

Division 4 **ALDERSHOT**

Recreation Ground, High St., Aldershot GU11 1TW. Telephone Aldershot (0252) 20211. Club call 0898 12 16 30

Record attendance: 19,138 v Carlisle U, FA Cup 4th rd replay, 28 January 1970.

Record receipts: £21,275.30 v Norwich C, Milk Cup 3rd rd, 6 November, 1984.

Ground capacity: 12,000 (10,000 under cover).

Pitch measurements: 116yd × 76yd.

President: Arthur English.

Chairman:

Directors: C. Hancock BDS (Lon).

Team Manager: Len Walker.

Secretary: Jon Pollard.

Team coach: Ian Gillard. ***Physio:*** Jim Lange, Grad. Phys. Dip. MCSP, SRP. ***Youth team coach:*** Ian McDonald.***Marketing and Commercial Manager:*** Mike Twiss.
Year Formed: 1926. ***Turned Professional:*** 1927. ***Ltd Co.:*** 1927.

Club Nickname: 'Shots'.***Record League Victory:*** 8-1 v Gateshead, Division 4, 13 September 1958 – Marshall; Henry, Jackson; Mundy, Price, Gough; Walters, Stepney (3), Lacey (3), Matthews (2), Tyrer.

Record Cup Victory: 7-0 v Chelmsford, FA Cup, 1st rd, 28 November 1931 – Robb; Twine, McDougall (1); Norman Wilson, Gardiner, Middleton (1); Blackbourne, Stevenson (1), Thorn (3), Hopkins (1), Edgar. 7-0 v Newport (I of W)., FA Cup, 2nd rd, 8 December 1945 – Reynolds; Horton, Sheppard; Ray, White, Summerbee; Sinclair, Hold (1), Brooks (5), Fitzgerald, Hobbs (1).

Record Defeat: 0-9 v Bristol C, Division 3(S), 28 December 1946.

Most League Points (2 for a win): 57, Division 4, 1978–9.

Most League Points (3 for a win): 75, Division 4, 1983–84.

Most League Goals: 83, Division 4, 1963–64.

Highest League Scorer in Season: John Dungworth, 26, Division 4, 1978–79.

Most League Goals in Total Aggregate: Jack Howarth, 171, 1965–71 and 1972–77.

Most Capped Player: Peter Scott, 1 (10), Northern Ireland.

Most League Appearances: Murray Brodie, 461, 1970–83.

Record Transfer Fee Received: £150,000 from Wolverhampton W for Tony Lange, July 1989.

Record Transfer Fee Paid: £54,000 to Portsmouth for Colin Garwood, February 1980.

Football League Record: 1932 Elected to Division 3(S); 1958–73 Division 4; 1973–76 Division 3; 1976–87 Division 4; 1987-89 Division 3;1989 Division 4.

Honours: *Football League:* best season: 8th, Division 3, 1973–74. *FA Cup:* best season: 5th rd, 1932–33, 5th rd replay, 1978–79. *Football League Cup:* best season: 3rd rd replay 1984–85.

Colours: Red shirts, Royal blue trim, blue shorts red trim, red stockings with Royal blue trim. **Change colours:** White with blue trim

ALDERSHOT 1988–89 LEAGUE RECORD

Match No.	Date	Venue	Opponents	Result	H/T Score	Lg. Pos.	Goalscorers	Atten-dance
1	Aug 27	A	Chesterfield	L 1-2	0-0	—	Wignall	2327
2	Sept 3	H	Gillingham	L 0-2	0-1	22		2477
3	10	A	Bristol R	D 2-2	2-0	23	Reece (og), Burvill	3382
4	17	H	Southend U	D 2-2	0-1	23	McDonald (pen), Anderson	2170
5	20	A	Wolverhampton W	L 0-1	0-1	—		8991
6	24	H	Bolton W	L 0-3	0-1	24		2126
7	Oct 1	A	Northampton T	L 0-6	0-1	24		3477
8	4	H	Wigan Ath	W 3-1	1-0	—	Chandler, Randall, Anderson	1527
9	9	H	Swansea C	L 0-1	0-1	—		2809
10	15	A	Fulham	L 1-5	0-2	24	Mazzon	5101
11	22	H	Huddersfield	L 0-1	0-1	24		2155
12	25	A	Bristol C	D 1-1	1-0	—	Burvill	8685
13	29	H	Chester C	D 1-1	1-1	23	Claridge	1862
14	Nov 8	H	Sheffield U	W 1-0	1-0	—	Claridge	2934
15	12	A	Blackpool	L 0-4	0-2	23		2690
16	26	A	Mansfield T	D 1-1	1-0	23	McDonald	2715
17	Dec 3	H	Notts Co	L 2-3	0-2	23	Burvill, Barnes	2191
18	18	H	Brentford	D 0-0	0-0	—		4012
19	26	A	Reading	L 1-3	0-1	23	Chandler	6350
20	31	A	Bury	W 1-0	0-0	23	Randall	3196
21	Jan 2	H	Cardiff C	L 0-1	0-0	23		2768
22	7	H	Preston NE	W 2-1	0-0	23	Smith, Ring	2135
23	14	A	Gillingham	D 1-1	0-1	24	Burvill	3781
24	21	H	Bristol R	L 1-3	0-2	24	Ring	3101
25	28	A	Southend U	D 1-1	0-0	24	McDonald	3014
26	Feb 4	H	Northampton T	W 5-1	3-1	22	Claridge, Wilson (og), Puckett 3	2244
27	11	A	Wigan Ath	L 1-2	1-0	23	McDonald	2132
28	13	A	Port Vale	L 0-0	0-1	—		5033
29	17	A	Swansea C	L 0-1	0-0	—		4922
30	21	H	Bristol C	L 0-0	0-1	—		1960
31	Mar 4	A	Huddersfield T	L 1-2	1-1	23	Claridge	4709
32	11	H	Port Vale	D 2-2	0-0	23	Puckett, Burvill	2397
33	15	A	Chester C	D 1-1	1-0	—	Claridge	2038
34	18	H	Chesterfield	W 2-0	0-0	23	Puckett, Claridge	1886
35	25	A	Cardiff C	L 2-3	1-1	23	Puckett (pen), McDonald	3251
36	27	H	Reading	D 1-1	0-0	23	Puckett (pen)	4960
37	Apr 1	A	Brentford	L 1-2	0-0	24	Claridge	5200
38	4	A	Preston NE	D 2-2	0-0	—	Puckett, Claridge	5977
39	8	H	Bury	W 4-1	0-1	23	Puckett 2 (1 pen), McDonald, Claridge	1677
40	15	H	Wolverhampton W	L 1-2	0-1	24	Smith	5465
41	22	A	Bolton W	L 0-1	0-0	24		4407
42	25	H	Fulham	L 1-2	0-0	—	Burvill	3841
43	29	H	Blackpool	W 1-0	1-0	24	Puckett	1763
44	May 1	A	Sheffield U	L 0-1	0-0	24		11,737
45	6	A	Notts Co	L 1-4	1-0	24	Burvill	4261
46	13	H	Mansfield T	D 0-0	0-0	24		1549

Final League Position: 24

GOALSCORERS

League (48): Puckett 11 (3 pens), Claridge 9, Burvill 7, McDonald 6 (1 pen), Anderson 2, Chandler 2, Randall 2, Ring 2, Smith 2, Barnes 1, Mazzon 1, Wignall 1, own goals 2.
Littlewoods Cup (0).
FA Cup (4): McDonald 2 (1 pen), Claridge 1, Randall 1.

Littlewoods Cup	First Round	Leyton Orient (a)	0-2
		(h)	0-0
FA Cup	First Round	Hayes (h)	1-0
	Second Round	Bristol C (h)	1-1
		(a)	0-0
		(h)	2-2
		(a)	0-1

Lange	Phillips	Barnes	Burvill	Smith	Wignall	Berry	Riley	Chandler	McDonald	Mazzon	Ring	Anderson	Randall	Claridge	Hewitt	Brown	Holsgrove	Devereux	Stewart	Puckett	Osgood	Coombs	*Match No.*
1	2	3	4	5	6	7	8	9*	10	11	12												1
1	7	3	4	5	6	2	8	9*	10		11	12											2
1	7	3	4	5	6	2	8	9	10		11												3
1	7	3		5	6	2	8	9*	10	4	11	12											4
1	7	3		5	6	2	8		10	4	11		9										5
1	7	3		5	6	2	8	12	10	4†	11*	14	9										6
1	7	3	4	5	6	2	8*	12	10			9	11										7
1	7	3	4	5	6	2		8*	10	12		9	11										8
1	7	3	4*	5	6	2	8	14	10	12		9†	11										9
1	7	3	4	5	6	2	8		10	12			11*	9									10
1	7	3	4†	5	6	2	8		10	12			11*	9	14								11
1	7	3	4	5	6	2	8		10				11	9									12
1	7	3	4*	5	6		8†		10	2	12	14	11	9									13
1		3	4	5	6		8		10	7			11	9		2							14
1	11	3		5	6		8		10	7	4*			9		2	12						15
1		3	4	5	6				10	7		8	11	9		2							16
1		3	4	5	6				10	7*	12	8	11	9		2							17
1	3		4*	5	6				10	7	8	12	11	9		2							18
1		3	4†		6			12	10	7*	8	5	11	9		2		14					19
1		3	4	5	6		8		10*	7		12	11	9		2							20
1		3	4*	5	6		8		10	7	12		11	9		2							21
1		3	4*	5	6		8		10	7†	12	14	11	9		2							22
1		3	4	5	6		8		10	12			11	9		2			7*				23
1		3	4	5			8		10		12	6	11*	9		2			7				24
1		3	4*	5	6		12		10			14	11	9†		2			7	8			25
1		3	4	5	6				10				11	9		2			7	8			26
1		3	4	5	6		12		10†			14	11	9*		2			7	8			27
1		3	4	5	6		12			10*			11	9		2			7	8			28
1		3	4	5	6		12			10†		14	11	9*		2			7	8			29
1		3	4	5	6		12			10			11*	9		2			7	8			30
1	2	3	4	5	6†		12		10			14	11*	9					7	8			31
1	2	3	4	5					10			6	11	9					7	8			32
1	2	3	4	5			12		10			6	11*	9					7	8			33
1	2	3*	4	5					10†	14		6	11	9		12			7	8			34
1	2	3	4	5					10	12		6	11*	9					7	8			35
1	3		4	5					10*	12		6	11	9		2			7	8			36
1	3		4	5					10			6	11	9		2			7	8			37
1	3	11	4	5					10			6		9		2			7	8			38
1	3	11	4	5					10			6		9		2			7	8			39
1	2	3	4	5			11		10			6		9					7	8			40
1	3		4	5			11		10			6		9		2			7	8			41
	2		4	5	14		11*		10	12		6	8	9†		3			7		1		42
1	3		4	5					10	12		6	11*	9		2			7	8			43
1	3	7	4	5	12				10			6	11	9*		2				8			44
1	3	7	4	5					10*			6	11	9		2			12	8			45
1			4*	5					10	3		6	11	9	12	2				8		7	46
45	30	39	42	45	30 + 2s	12	22 + 7s	5 + 4s	43	18 + 10s	8 + 6s	22 + 11s	37	37	— + 2s	27 + 1s	— + 1s	— + 1s	21 + 1s	21	1	1	

ALDERSHOT

Player and Position	Ht	Wt	Birth Date	Birth Place	Source	Clubs	League App	League Gls
Goalkeepers								
Tony Lange	6 0	12 09	10 12 64	London	Apprentice	Charlton Ath	12	—
						Aldershot (loan)	7	—
						Aldershot	125	—
Steve Osgood‡			20 1 62	Surrey	Farnborough	Aldershot	1	—
Defenders								
Darren Anderson	6 1	13 05	6 9 66	Merton	Apprentice	Coventry C	—	—
						Charlton Ath	10	1
						Crewe Alex (loan)	5	—
						Aldershot	82	3
David Barnes	5 10	11 01	16 11 61	London	Apprentice	Coventry C	9	—
						Ipswich T	17	—
						Wolverhampton W	88	4
						Aldershot	69	1
Kevan Brown	5 9	11 08	2 1 66	Andover		Southampton	—	—
						Brighton & HA	53	—
						Aldershot	28	—
Jimmy Devereux	6 4	13 00	20 2 70	Aldershot	Trainee	Aldershot	1	—
Peter Leebrook‡	5 8	11 00	18 9 68	Saltburn	YTS	Burnley	52	—
						Aldershot	—	—
Ian Phillips	5 9	11 12	23 4 59	Kilwinning	Apprentice	Ipswich T	—	—
						Mansfield T	23	—
						Peterborough U	97	3
						Northampton T	42	1
						Colchester U	150	10
						Aldershot	62	—
Colin Smith	6 0	12 10	3 11 58	Ruddington	Local	Nottingham F	—	—
						Norwich C	4	—
					See Bee	Cardiff C	50	3
						Aldershot	165	4
Steve Wignall	5 11	12 01	17 9 54	Liverpool	Amateur	Liverpool	—	—
						Doncaster R	130	1
						Nottingham F (loan)	—	—
						Colchester U	281	22
						Brentford	67	2
						Aldershot	109	3
Midfield								
Glen Burvill	5 9	10 10	26 10 62	Canning Town	Apprentice	West Ham U	—	—
						Aldershot	65	15
						Reading	30	—
						Fulham (loan)	9	2
						Aldershot	121	18
Nigel Costello‡			22 11 68	Catterick		York C	4	—
						Aldershot	—	—
Daren Hewitt†	5 8	11 06	1 9 69	Chichester	Trainee	Aldershot	2	—
Ian McDonald	5 9	11 09	10 5 53	Barrow	Apprentice	Barrow	35	2
						Workington	42	4
						Liverpool	—	—
						Colchester U (loan)	5	2
						Mansfield T	56	4
						York C	175	29
						Aldershot	340	49
Giorgio Mazzon*	5 11	12 02	4 9 60	Waltham Cross	Waltham NT	Tottenham H	2	—
						Aldershot	195	6
Forwards								
Ian Chandler*	6 1	12 05	20 3 68	Sunderland		Barnsley	12	4
						Stockport Co (loan)	5	—
						Aldershot	9	2

ALDERSHOT

Foundation: It was through the initiative of Councillor Jack White, a local newsagent who immediately captured the interest of the Town Clerk D. Llewellyn Griffiths, that Aldershot Town was formed in 1926. Having established a limited liability company under the chairmanship of Norman Clinton, an Aldershot resident and chairman of the Hampshire County FA they rented the Recreation Ground from the Aldershot Borough Council.

Managers (and Secretary-managers)
Angus Seed 1927–37, Bill McCracken 1937–49, Gordon Clark 1950–55, Harry Evans 1955–59, Dave Smith 1959–71 (GM from 1967), Tommy McAnearney 1967–68, Jimmy Melia 1968–72, Tommy McAnearney 1972–81, Len Walker 1981–84, Ron Harris (GM) 1984–85, Len Walker 1985– .

Player and Position	*Ht*	*Wt*	*Birth Date*	*Birth Place*	*Source*	*Clubs*	*League App*	*League Gls*
Steve Claridge	5 11	11 08	10 4 66	Portsmouth	Fareham	Bournemouth	7	1
					Weymouth	Crystal Palace	—	—
						Aldershot	37	9
Paul Coombs§	5 11	12 05	4 9 70	Bristol	QPR	Aldershot	1	—
Paul Holsgrove	6 1	12 00	26 8 69	Wellington	YTS	Aldershot	3	—
						Wimbledon (loan)	—	—
David Puckett	5 7	10 05	29 10 60	Southampton	Apprentice	Southampton	95	14
						Nottingham F (loan)	—	—
						Bournemouth	35	14
						Stoke C (loan)	7	—
						Swansea (loan)	8	3
						Aldershot	21	11
Adrian Randall	5 11	11 00	10 11 68	Amesbury	Apprentice	Bournemouth	3	—
						Aldershot	37	2
Glyn Riley*	5 10	11 11	24 7 58	Barnsley	Apprentice	Barnsley	130	16
						Doncaster R (loan)	8	2
						Bristol C	199	61
						Torquay U (loan)	6	1
						Aldershot	58	5
Mike Ring‡	5 10	10 06	13 2 61	Brighton	Apprentice	Brighton & HA	5	—
						Morton (loan)	4	—
					Ballymena U	Hull C	24	2
						Bolton W (loan)	3	—
						Aldershot	79	16
Ian Stewart	5 7	11 09	10 9 61	Belfast	Juniors	QPR	67	2
						Millwall (loan)	11	3
						Newcastle U	42	3
						Portsmouth	1	—
						Brentford (loan)	7	—
						Aldershot	22	—

Trainees
Barham, David L; Beeks, Stephen J; Cable, Gary; Coombs, Paul A; Dunbuya, Koo J; Jenkinson, Robert R; Kirby, Mark L; Phillips, Lee J; Rickwood, Justin P; Robson, Andrew C; Ryan, Lee; Watts, Darren.

****Non-Contract**
Hewitt, Daren P; Osgood, Stephen.

ARSENAL 1988–89 *Back row (left to right):* Theo Foley (Assistant Manager), Perry Groves, Paul Merson, Tony Adams, Niall Quinn, Steve Bould, Alan Smith, David O'Leary, Gus Caesar, Kenny Sansom, Gary Lewin (Physiotl.erapist).
Front row: Kevin Richardson, Michael Thomas, Nigel Winterburn, Lee Dixon, Rhys Wilmot, George Graham (Manager), John Lukic, Paul Davis, David Rocastle, Martin Hayes, Brian Marwood.

Division 1 **ARSENAL**

Arsenal Stadium, Highbury, London N5. Telephone 01-226 0304. Recorded information on 01-359 0131. Club call 0898 12 11 70

Ground Capacity: 57,000.

Record attendance: 73,295 v Sunderland, Div 1, 9 March, 1935.

Record receipts: £233,595 v Everton, Littlewoods Cup Semi-Final, 24 Feb 1988.

Pitch measurements: 110yd × 71yd.

Chairman: P. D. Hill-Wood. ***Vice-Chairman:*** D. Dein.

Directors: Sir Robert Bellinger CBE, DSC, S. C. McIntyre MBE, FCIS, R. G. Gibbs, C. E. B. L. Carr, R. C. S. Carr.

Managing Director: K. J. Friar.

Manager: George Graham. ***Assistant Manager:*** Theo Foley

Physio: Gary Lewin.

Secretary: K. J. Friar. ***Assistant Secretary:*** David Miles. ***Commercial Manager:*** Jack Kelsey.

Formed: 1886. ***Turned Professional:*** 1891. ***Ltd Co.:*** 1893.

Former Names: 1886 Dial Square; 1886–91, Royal Arsenal; 1891–1914, Woolwich Arsenal.

Club Nickname: 'Gunners'.

Former Grounds: 1886–87, Plumstead Common; 1887–88, Sportsman Ground; 1888–90, Manor Ground; 1890–93, Invicta Ground; 1893–1913, Manor Ground; 1913– Highbury.

Record League Victory: 12-0 v Loughborough T, Division 2, 12 March 1900 – Orr; McNichol, Jackson; Moir, Dick (2), Anderson (1); Hunt, Cottrell (2), Main (2), Gaudie (3), Tennant (2).

Record Cup Victory: 11-1 v Darwen, FA Cup, 3rd rd, 9 January 1932 – Moss; Parker, Hapgood; Jones, Roberts, John; Hulme (2), Jack (3), Lambert (2), James, Bastin (4).

Record Defeat: 0-8 v Loughborough T, Division 2, 12 December, 1896.

Most League Points (2 for a win): 66, Division 1, 1930–31.

Most League Points (3 for a win): 76, Division 1, 1988–89.

Most League Goals: 127. Division 1, 1930–31.

Highest League Scorer in Season: Ted Drake, 42, 1934–35.

Most League Goals in Total Aggregate: Cliff Bastin, 150, 1930–47.

Most Capped Player: Kenny Sansom, 77 (86), England.

Most League Appearances: George Armstrong, 500, 1960–77.

Record Transfer Fee Received: £1,250,000 from Crystal Palace for Clive Allen, August 1980.

Record Transfer Fee Paid: £1,250,000 to QPR for Clive Allen, June 1980.

Football League Record: 1893 Elected to Division 2; 1904–13 Division 1; 1913–19 Division 2; 1919–Division 1.

Honours: *Football League:* Division 1 – Champions 1930–31, 1932–33, 1933–34, 1934–35, 1937–38, 1947–48, 1952–53, 1970–71, 1988–89; Runners-up 1925–26, 1931–32, 1972–73; Division 2 – Runners-up 1903–04, *FA Cup:* Winners 1929–30, 1935–36,1949–50, 1970–71, 1978–79; Runners-up 1926–27, 1931–32, 1951–52, 1971–72, 1977–78, 1979–80. *Double Performed:* 1970–71. *League Cup:* Winners 1986–87; Runners-up 1967–68, 1968–69, 1987–88. **European Competitions:** *Fairs Cup:* 1963–64, 1969–70 (winners), 1970–71; *European Cup:* 1971–72; *UEFA Cup:* 1978–79, 1981–82, 1982–83; *European Cup-Winners' Cup:* 1979–80 (runners-up).

Colours: Red shirts with white sleeves, white shorts, red stockings. **Change colours:** Yellow shirts, navy blue shorts, yellow stockings.

ARSENAL 1988–89 LEAGUE RECORD

Match No.	Date		Venue	Opponents	Result		H/T Score	Lg. Pos.	Goalscorers	Attendance
1	Aug	27	A	Wimbledon	W	5-1	3-1	—	Marwood, Smith 3, Merson	15,710
2	Sept	3	H	Aston Villa	L	2-3	0-1	8	Marwood, Smith	37,417
3		10	A	Tottenham H	W	3-2	3-2	6	Winterburn, Marwood, Smith	32,621
4		17	H	Southampton	D	2-2	0-2	5	Marwood (pen), Smith	31,384
5		24	A	Sheffield W	L	1-2	0-1	7	Smith	17,830
6	Oct	1	A	West Ham U	W	4-1	2-1	6	Smith 2, Thomas, Rocastle	27,658
7		22	H	QPR	W	2-1	0-0	4	Adams, Smith	33,202
8		25	A	Luton	D	1-1	1-0	—	Smith	10,548
9		29	H	Coventry C	W	2-0	1-0	2	Thomas, Adams	31,273
10	Nov	6	A	Nottingham F	W	4-1	1-1	—	Smith, Bould, Adams, Marwood	19,038
11		12	A	Newcastle U	W	1-0	0-0	2	Bould	24,033
12		19	H	Middlesbrough	W	3-0	1-0	2	Merson 2, Rocastle	32,294
13		26	A	Derby Co	L	1-2	0-0	2	Thomas	21,209
14	Dec	4	H	Liverpool	D	1-1	0-0	—	Smith	31,863
15		10	A	Norwich C	D	0-0	0-0	2		23,069
16		17	H	Manchester U	W	2-1	2-0	2	Thomas, Merson	37,422
17		•26	A	Charlton Ath	W	3-2	1-0	1	Marwood 2 (1 pen), Merson	18,439
18		31	A	Aston Villa	W	3-0	2-0	1	Smith, Rocastle, Groves	32,486
19	Jan	2	H	Tottenham H	W	2-0	1-0	1	Merson Thomas	45,129
20		14	A	Everton	W	3-1	0-0	1	Merson, Smith, Richardson	34,825
21		21	H	Sheffield W	D	1-1	0-0	1	Merson	33,490
22	Feb	4	H	West Ham U	W	2-1	0-0	1	Groves, Smith	40,139
23		11	A	Millwall	W	2-1	0-1	1	Marwood, Smith	21,854
24		18	A	QPR	D	0-0	0-0	1		20,543
25		21	A	Coventry C	L	0-1	0-0	—		21,390
26		25	H	Luton T	W	2-0	0-0	1	Groves, Smith	31,012
27		28	H	Millwall	D	0-0	0-0	—		37,524
28	Mar	11	H	Nottingham F	L	1-3	1-3	1	Smith	39,639
29		21	H	Charlton Ath	D	2-2	2-1	—	Rocastle, Davis	30,255
30		25	A	Southampton	W	3-1	1-0	1	Groves, Rocastle, Merson	19,202
31	Apr	2	A	Manchester U	D	1-1	0-0	—	Adams	37,977
32		8	H	Everton	W	2-0	1-0	1	Dixon, Quinn	37,608
33		15	H	Newcastle U	W	1-0	0-0	1	Marwood	38,023
34	May	1	H	Norwich C	W	5-0	2-0	1	Winterburn, Smith 2, Thomas, Rocastle	28,449
35		6	A	Middlesbrough	W	1-0	0-0	1	Hayes	21,803
36		13	H	Derby Co	L	1-2	0-1	1	Smith	41,008
37		17	H	Wimbledon	D	2-2	1-1	—	Winterburn, Merson	39,132
38		26	A	Liverpool	W	2-0	0-0	—	Smith, Thomas	41,783

Final League Position: 1

GOALSCORERS

League (73): Smith 23, Merson 10, Marwood 9 (2 pens), Thomas 7, Rocastle 6, Adams 4, Groves 4, Winterburn 3, Bould 2, Davis 1, Dixon 1, Hayes 1, Quinn 1, Richardson 1.
Littlewoods Cup (7): Merson 2, Smith 2, Marwood 1, Rocastle 1, Winterburn 1.
FA Cup (2): Merson 2.

Littlewoods Cup	Second Round	Hull C (a)	2-1
		(h)	3-0
	Third Round	Liverpool (a)	1-1
		(h)	0-0
		(at Villa Park)	1-2
FA Cup	Third Round	West Ham U (a)	2-2
		(h)	0-1

Lukic	Dixon	Winterburn	Thomas	Bould	Adams	Rocastle	Davis	Smith	Merson	Marwood	O'Leary	Groves	Richardson	Hayes	Caesar	Quinn	*Match No.*
1	2	3	4	5	6	7	8	9	10	11							1
1	2	3	4		6	7*	8	9	10	11	5	12					2
1	2	3	4		6	7†	8	9	10	11*	5	12	14				3
1	2	3	4		6	7	8†	9	10	11*	5		14	12			4
1	2	3	4		6	7	8	9	10*	11	5	12					5
1	2	3	4	5	6	7	8	9		11		10*		12			6
1	2	3	4	5	6	7		9	10*	11		12	8				7
1	2	3	4	5	6	7		9	10	11			8				8
1	2	3	4	5	6	7†		9	10*	11		12	8	14			9
1	2	3	4	5	6	7		9	10*	11			8	12			10
1	2	3	4	5	6	7*		9	12	11			8	10			11
1	2	3	4	5	6	7		9	10	11*			8	12			12
1	2	3	4	5	6	7		9	10			12	8*	11			13
1	2	3	4	5	6	7		9	10	11*			8	12			14
1	2	3	4	5	6	7		9	10*	11			8	12			15
1	2	3	4	5	6	7		9	10	11			8				16
1		3	4	5	6	7		9	10	11	2		8				17
1		3	4	5	6	7		9	10*	11	2	12	8				18
1		3	4	5	6	7	14	9	10	11*	2	12	8†				19
1	2	3	14			7	4	9	10*	11†	5	12	8		6		20
1	2	3	14			7*	4	9	10	11	5	12	8		6†		21
1	2	3	4	14	6	7		9	10*		5†	11	8	12			22
1	2	3	4	12	6	7		9	10	11	5*		8				23
1	2†	3	4	14	6	7		9	10*	11	5		8	12			24
1		3	4	5	6	7		9	10	11*	2		8	12			25
1		3	4	5	6	7*		9	12	11	2	10	8				26
1	14	3	4	5	6	7*		9	12	11	2	10	8†				27
1	14	3	4	5†	6	7		9	12	11	2	10*	8				28
1	2	3	14		6	7	4	9	10*	11	5	12	8†				29
1	2	3			6	7	4	9	12	11	5	10*	8				30
1	2	3	14	10	6	7	4†	9	12	11*	5		8				31
1	2	3	4	10	6	7			12	11*	5		8			9	32
1	2	3	4	10	6	7†			12	11	5*	14	8			9	33
1	2	3	4	10	6	7		9*	11†		5		8	14		12	34
1	2	3	4	10	6	7		9	11*		5		8	12			35
1	2	3	4	10†	6	7		9	11*		5	12	8	14			36
1	2	3	4	14	6	7		9	10†		5	12	8	11*			37
1	2	3	4	10*	6	7		9	11†		5	12	8	14			38
38	31 + 2s	38	33 + 4s	26 + 4s	36	38	11 + 1s	36	29 + 8s	31	26	6 + 15s	32 + 2s	3 + 14s	2	2 + 1s	

ARSENAL

Player and Position	*Ht*	*Wt*	*Birth Date*	*Birth Place*	*Source*	*Clubs*	*League App*	*League Gls*
Goalkeepers								
John Lukic	6 4	13 07	11 12 60	Chesterfield	Apprentice	Leeds U	146	—
						Arsenal	185	—
Andrew Marriott	6 0	12 07	11 10 70	Nottingham	Trainee	Arsenal	—	–
Allan Miller	6 2	13 08	29 3 70	Epping	Trainee	Arsenal	—	—
						Plymouth Arg (loan)	13	–
Rhys Wilmot	6 1	12 00	21 2 62	Newport	Apprentice	Arsenal	8	—
						Hereford U (loan)	9	—
						Orient (loan)	46	—
						Swansea C (loan)	16	—
						Plymouth Arg (loan)	17	—
Defenders								
Tony Adams	6 1	13 03	10 10 66	London	Apprentice	Arsenal	146	12
Steve Bould	6 3	12 08	16 11 62	Stoke	Apprentice	Stoke C	183	6
						Torquay U (loan)	9	—
						Arsenal	30	2
Gus Caesar	6 0	12 00	5 3 66	London	Apprentice	Arsenal	41	—
Jim Carstairs	6 0	12 05	29 1 71	Fife	Trainee	Arsenal	—	—
Lee Dixon	5 9	10 12	17 3 64	Manchester	Local	Burnley	4	—
						Chester C	57	1
						Bury	45	5
						Stoke C	71	5
						Arsenal	39	1
Robert Flanagan‡			18.9.70	Dublin	Trainee	Arsenal	—	—
Lee Francis	5 10	10 11	24 10 69	Walthamstow	Trainee	Arsenal	—	—
Al Hinnigan	6 0	12 04	26 1 71	Islington	Trainee	Arsenal	—	—
Steve Morrow	6 0	11 03	2 7 70	Belfast	Trainee	Arsenal	—	—
David O'Leary	6 1	13 02	2 5 58	London	Apprentice	Arsenal	467	9
Patrick Scully	6 1	12 07	23 6 70	Dublin	Trainee	Arsenal	—	—
Nigel Winterburn	5 10	10 07	11 12 63	Coventry	Local	Birmingham C	—	—
						Oxford U	—	—
						Wimbledon	165	8
						Arsenal	55	3
Midfield								
Steve Ball*	6 0	12 01	2 9 69	Colchester	Trainee	Arsenal	—	—
Dino Connelly	5 9	10 08	6 1 70	Glasgow	Trainee	Arsenal	—	—
Paul Davis	5 10	10 10	9 12 61	London	Apprentice	Arsenal	259	25
David Hillier	5 10	11 06	19 12 69	Blackheath	Trainee	Arsenal	—	—
Raymond Lee	5 8	11 12	19 9 70	Bristol	Trainee	Arsenal	—	—
Gary McKeown	5 10	11 07	19 10 70	Oxford	Trainee	Arsenal	—	—
Brian Marwood	5 7	11 06	5 2 60	Seaham Harbour	Apprentice	Hull C	158	51
						Sheffield W	128	27
						Arsenal	35	10
Russell Milton*	5 8	10 08	12 1 69	Folkestone	YTS	Arsenal	—	—
Andrew Mockler	5 11	11 13	18 11 70	Stockton	Trainee	Arsenal	—	—
Kevin Richardson	5 9	11 02	4 12 62	Newcastle	Apprentice	Everton	109	16
						Watford	39	2
						Arsenal	63	5
David Rocastle	5 9	11 12	2 5 67	Lewisham	Apprentice	Arsenal	130	15
Michael Thomas	5 10	12 04	24 8 67	Lambeth	Apprentice	Arsenal	86	16
						Portsmouth (loan)	3	—

ARSENAL

Foundation: Formed by workers at the Royal Arsenal, Woolwich in 1886 they began as Dial Square (name of one of the workshops) and included two former Nottingham Forest players Fred Beardsley and Morris Bates. Beardsley wrote to his old club seeking help and they provided the new club with a full set of red jerseys and a ball. The club became known as the "Woolwich Reds" although their official title soon after formation was Woolwich Arsenal.

Managers (and Secretary-managers)
Sam Hollis 1894–97, Tom Mitchell 1897–98, George Elcoat 1898–99, Harry Bradshaw 1899–1904, Phil Kelso 1904–08, George Morrell 1908–15, Leslie Knighton 1919–25, Herbert Chapman 1925–34, George Allison 1934–47, Tom Whittaker 1947–56, Jack Crayston 1956–58, George Swindin 1958–62, Billy Wright 1962–66, Bertie Mee 1966–76, Terry Neill 1976–83, Don Howe 1984–86, George Graham 1986– .

Player and Position	*Ht*	*Wt*	*Birth Date*	*Place*	*Source*	*Clubs*	*League App*	*Gls*
Forwards								
Kwame Ampadu	5 10	10 13	20 11 70	Bradford	Trainee	Arsenal	—	—
Kevin Campbell	6 0	13 01	4 2 70	Lambeth	Trainee	Arsenal	1	—
						Leyton Orient (loan)	16	9
Danny Esqulant*	5 7	9 11	28 9 69	London	FA School	Arsenal	—	—
						Charlton Ath (loan)	—	—
Perry Groves	5 11	11 12	19 4 65	London	Apprentice	Colchester U	156	26
						Arsenal	80	13
Martin Hayes	6 0	11 08	21 3 66	Walthamstow	Apprentice	Arsenal	90	23
Paul Merson	5 10	11 09	20 3 68	London	Apprentice	Arsenal	59	18
						Brentford (loan)	7	—
Niall Quinn	6 4	12 04	6 10 66	Dublin	Eire Youth	Arsenal	61	12
Alan Smith	6 3	12 10	21 11 62	Birmingham	Alvechurch	Leicester C	191	73
						Arsenal	75	34
						Leicester C (loan)	9	3
Steve Ward*			10 1 70	London	Trainee	Arsenal	—	—

Trainees
Cole, Andrew A; Dickov, Paul; Donnelly, Jamie; Hartfield, Charles J; Heaney, Neil A; Hoyle, Colin R; Warden, Danny.

Associated Schoolboys
Charlton, John L; Clarke, Adrian J; Clements, Stephen; Faulkner, Mark; Flatts, Mark; Fowler, Kevin; Guppy, Jonathan; Gaunt, Craig; Jordan, Kevin; Joseph, Matthew; Lee, Justin D; Parlour, Raymond; Read, Paul C; Rust, Nicholas C.I; Shaw, Paul; Selley, Ian; Swain, Joel T; Webster, Kenneth; Young, Stuart; Zumrutel, Soner.

ASTON VILLA 1988–89 *Back row (left to right)*: Martin Keown, Mark Lillis, Alan McInally, Nigel Spink, Lee Butler, Gareth Williams, Garry Thompson.
Centre row: Bobby Downes (Youth Team Coach), David Hunt, David Platt, Warren Aspinall, Paul Birch, Andy Blair, Gordon Cowans, Neale Cooper, Derek Mountfield, Steve Sims, Jim Walker (Physiotherapist).
Front row: Tony Daley, Bernard Gallacher, Allan Evans, John Ward (Assistant Manager), Graham Taylor (Manager), Dave Richardson (Assistant Manager), Andy Gray, Chris Price, Stuart Gray.

Division 1 ASTON VILLA

Villa Park, Trinity Rd, Birmingham B6 6HE. Telephone 021-327 6604. Information: 021-328 1722. Commercial Dept. 021-327 5399. Clubcall: 0898 121148.

Ground Capacity: 46,908.

Record attendance: 76,588 v Derby Co, FA Cup 6th rd, 2 March, 1946.

Record Receipts: £385,678 Everton v Norwich C, FA Cup semi-final, 15 April, 1989.

Pitch measurements: 115yd × 75yd.

President: H. J. Musgrove. ***Chairman:*** H. D. Ellis.

Directors: J. A. Alderson, Dr D. H. Targett, P. E. Ellis.

Manager: Graham Taylor. ***Assistant Managers:*** Dave Richardson and John Ward.

Secretary: Steven Stride.***Coach:*** Dennis Booth.

Physio: Jim Walker. ***Youth Coach:*** Bobby Downes.

Commercial Manager: Abdul Rashid.

Year Formed: 1874. ***Turned Professional:*** 1885. ***Ltd Co.:*** 1986.

Previous Grounds: 1874–76, Aston Park; 1876–97, Perry Barr; 1897– Villa Park.

Club Nickname: 'The Villans'.

Record League Victory: 12-2 v Accrington S, Division 1, 12 March 1892 – Warner; Evans. Cox; Harry Devey, Jimmy Cowan, Baird; Athersmith (1), Dickson (2), John Devey (4), Campbell L. (4), Hodgetts (1).

Record Cup Victory: 13-0 v Wednesbury Old Ath, FA Cup 1st rd, 30 October 1886 – Warner; Coulton, Simmonds, Yates, Robertson, Burton (2); R. Davis (1), A. Brown (3), Hunter (3), Loach (2), Hodgetts (2).

Record Defeat: 1-8 v Blackburn R, FA Cup 3rd rd, 16 February, 1889.

Most League Points (2 for a win): 70, Division 3, 1971–72.

Most League Points (3 for a win): 78, Division 2, 1987–88.

Most League Goals: 128, Division 1, 1930–31.

Highest League Scorer in Season: 'Pongo' Waring, 49, Division 1, 1930–31.

Most League Goals in Total Aggregate: Harry Hampton, 213, 1904–20 and Billy Walker, 213, 1919–34.

Most Capped Player: Peter McParland 33 (34), Northern Ireland.

Most League Appearances: Charlie Aitken, 560, 1961–76.

Record Transfer Fee Received: £1,469,000 (£1,175,000 basic fee) from Wolverhampton W for Andy Gray, September 1979.

Record Transfer Fee Paid: £650,000 to Bradford C for Ian Ormondroyd, February 1989.

Football League Record: 1888 Founder Member of the League; 1936–38 Division 2; 1938–59 Division 1; 1959–60 Division 2; 1960–67 Division 1; 1967–70 Division 2; 1970–72 Division 3; 1972–75 Division 2; 1975–87 Division 1; 1987–88 Division 2; 1988– Division 1.

Honours: *Football League:* Division 1 – Champions 1893–94, 1895–96, 1896–97, 1898–99, 1899–1900. 1909–10, 1980–81; Runners-up 1888–89, 1902–03, 1907–08, 1910–11, 1912–13, 1913–14, 1930–31, 1932–33; Division 2 – Champions 1937–38, 1959–60; Runners-up 1974–75, 1987–88; Division 3 – Champions 1971–72. *FA Cup:* Winners 1887, 1895, 1897, 1905, 1913, 1920, 1957 (7 wins stands as the joint record); Runners-up 1892, 1924. *Double Performed:* 1896–97. *Football League Cup:* Winners 1961, 1975, 1977; Runners-up 1963, 1971. **European Competitions:** *European Cup:* 1981–82 (winners). 1982–83; *UEFA Cup:* 1975–76, 1977–78, 1983–84; *World Club Championship:* 1982–83; *European Super Cup:* 1982–83 (winners).

Colours: Claret and blue shirts, white shorts, blue stockings. **Change colours:** White shirts, black shorts, white stockings.

ASTON VILLA 1988–89 LEAGUE RECORD

Match No.	Date	Venue	Opponents	Result	H/T Score	Lg. Pos.	Goalscorers	Attendance
1	Aug 27	H	Millwall	D 2-2	2-2	—	Gray S (pen), McInally	22,449
2	Sept 3	A	Arsenal	W 3-2	1-0	5	McInally 2, Gray A	37,417
3	10	H	Liverpool	D 1-1	1-0	8	McInally	41,409
4	17	A	West Ham U	D 2-2	2-0	10	McInally 2	19,186
5	24	H	Nottingham F	D 1-1	1-0	9	Gage	23,029
6	Oct 1	A	Sheffield W	L 0-1	0-1	11		18,301
7	8	H	Wimbledon	L 0-1	0-0	16		15,416
8	15	A	Charlton Ath	D 2-2	0-1	15	McInally, Platt	7594
9	22	H	Everton	W 2-0	1-0	9	Daley, Platt	26,636
10	29	H	Tottenham H	W 2-1	0-0	9	Fenwick (og), Daley	26,238
11	Nov 5	A	Manchester U	D 1-1	0-1	8	Cowans	44,804
12	12	A	Southampton	L 1-3	1-1	12	Daley	16,007
13	19	H	Derby Co	L 1-2	0-0	13	Mountfield	23,489
14	26	A	Coventry C	L 1-2	0-1	14	McInally	20,104
15	Dec 3	H	Norwich C	W 3-1	1-1	14	Gage 2, Platt	19,653
16	10	A	Middlesbrough	D 3-3	2-1	14	Gray A, McInally 2	18,096
17	17	A	Luton T	D 1-1	0-1	15	Johnson M (og)	8785
18	26	H	QPR	W 2-1	2-0	10	McInally 2	25,106
19	31	H	Arsenal	L 0-3	0-2	13		32,486
20	Jan 3	A	Liverpool	L 0-1	0-0	—		39,014
21	14	H	Newcastle U	W 3-1	1-1	12	Gray A, Daley, McInally	21,010
22	21	A	Nottingham F	L 0-4	0-1	14		22,662
23	Feb 4	H	Sheffield W	W 2-0	2-0	11	Callaghan, Platt	19,334
24	11	A	Wimbledon	L 0-1	0-1	12		6201
25	14	A	Everton	D 1-1	1-1	—	Ormondroyd	20,142
26	25	H	Charlton Ath	L 1-2	1-1	12	Cowans	16,481
27	Mar 1	A	Tottenham H	L 0-2	0-1	—		19,090
28	12	H	Manchester U	D 0-0	0-0	—		28,332
29	18	A	Millwall	L 0-2	0-1	12		13,206
30	25	H	West Ham U	L 0-1	0-1	14		22,471
31	27	A	QPR	L 0-1	0-0	15		11,378
32	Apr 1	H	Luton T	W 2-1	2-1	14	Daley, Olney	15,640
33	8	A	Newcastle U	W 2-1	1-0	13	Gray, Platt	20,329
34	22	A	Norwich C	D 2-2	0-0	13	Olney, McInally	14,550
35	29	H	Middlesbrough	D 1-1	0-0	13	Gray	18,590
36	May 2	H	Southampton	L 1-2	0-2	—	Gray	15,218
37	6	A	Derby Co	L 1-2	1-1	14	Platt	18,112
38	13	H	Coventry C	D 1-1	1-0	17	Platt	29,906

Final League Position: 17

GOALSCORERS

League (45): McInally 14, Platt 7, Daley 5, Gray S 4 (1 pen), Gage 3, Gray A 3, Cowans 2, Olney 2, Callaghan 1, Mountfield 1, Ormondroyd 1, own goals 2.
Littlewoods Cup (17): Platt 6, McInally 4, Gage 3, Daley 1, Gray A 1, Mountfield 1, Olney 1.
FA Cup (3): Gage 1, McInally 1, Platt 1.

Littlewoods Cup	Second Round	Birmingham C (a)	2-0
		(h)	5-0
	Third Round	Millwall (h)	3-1
	Fourth Round	Ipswich T (h)	6-2
	Fifth Round	West Ham U (a)	1-2
FA Cup	Third Round	Crewe Alex (a)	3-2
	Fourth Round	Wimbledon (h)	0-1

Spink	Price	Gage	Gray, A	Evans	Keown	Birch	Platt	McInally	Cowans	Gray, S	Daley	Thompson	Sims	Mountfield	Gallacher	Olney	Callaghan	Ormondroyd	Butler	Williams	Lillis	Duffy	Hunt	Match No.
1	2	3	4†	5	6	7*	8	9	10	11	12	14												1
1	2		4	5	6		8	9	10	11	7		3											2
1	2	3	4	5	6	12	8	9†	10	11	7*	14												3
1	2	12	4	5*	6		8	9	10	11	7			3										4
1	2	3	4		5		8	9*	10	11†	7	12		6	14									5
1	2	5	4		6		8		10	11	7	9		3										6
1	2	5	4	12	6		8		10	11	7	9*		3										7
1	2	5		4	6		8	12	10	11	7			3		9*								8
1	2	5		4	6		8	9	10	11	7			3										9
1	2	3		4	6		8	9	10	11	7			3										10
1	2	5		4	6		8	9	10		7			3	11									11
1	2	5	12	4	6		8	9	10		7*			3	11									12
1	2	5	12	4	6		8	9	10		7			3	11*									13
1	2	4	7		6	12	8	9	10	3	7*			5										14
1	2	4	7	5	6		8	9	10	3	11													15
1	2	4*	7	5	6	12†	8	9	10	3	11			14										16
1	2	4	7	5	6	12	8	9	10	3	11*													17
1	2	4	7	5			8	9	10	3	11			6										18
1	2	4	7*	5	12		8	9	10	3	11			6										19
1	2	4	12	5	6		8	9†	10*	11	7			3		14								20
1	2*	4	7		6		8	9	10	3	11			5		12								21
1		2	4*		6	7	8	9	10	3	12			5		11								22
1	2	4			6		8	9	10	3				5			7	11						23
1	2	4		6		12	8	9	10*	3				5			7	11						24
	2	4		6			8	9	10	3				5			7	11	1					25
1	2	4		6*	12		8		10	3	9			5			7	11						26
1	2	4			6	7	8		10	3				5			11	9						27
	2	4			6	7	8	9		3			5			12	11	10*	1					28
	2	4†			6	7*	8	9	14	3			5			12	11	10	1					29
	2				6		4	9*	10†	3	8		5	14		12	7		1	11				30
1	2			4*	6		8			3	14		5	7		9	12	10			11†			31
1	2			4	6		8	9	10	3	11*		5			12	7							32
1	2			4	6		8	9	10	3			5			11	7							33
1	2			4	6		8	9	10*	3			5			11	7	12						34
1	2			4	6		8	9		3	10*		5			11	7	12						35
1	2			4	6		8	9*		3	12		5			11	7	10						36
1						14	8	9		3	10*		5			11	7†	12			4	2	6	37
1	2			4	6	7	8	9*	10	3			5			12	11							38
34	36	27	15	26	32	6	38	32	32	35	25	2	12	22	3	8	15	9	4	1	2	1	1	
		+ 1s	+ 3s	+ 1s	+ 2s	+ 6s		+ 1s	+ 1s		+ 4s	+ 3s		+ 2s	+ 1s	+ 7s	+ 1s	+ 3s						

ASTON VILLA

Player and Position	Ht	Wt	Birth Date	Birth Place	Source	Clubs	League App	League Gls
Goalkeepers								
Lee Butler	6 2	14 02	30 5 66	Sheffield	Haworth Coll	Lincoln C	30	—
						Aston Villa	4	—
Nigel Spink	6 1	14 06	8 8 58	Chelmsford	Chelmsford C	Aston Villa	211	—
Defenders								
Eamonn Deacy‡	5 8	10 09	1 10 58	Galway	Galway R	Aston Villa	33	1
						Derby Co (loan)	5	—
Darrell Duffy§			17 1 71	Birmingham	Trainee	Aston Villa	1	—
Allan Evans*	6 1	12 13	12 10 56	Dunfermline	Dunfermline U	Dunfermline Ath	98	14
						Aston Villa	380	51
Kevin Gage	5 9	11 02	21 4 64	Chiswick	Apprentice	Wimbledon	168	15
						Aston Villa	72	5
Bernard Gallacher	5 8	11 02	22 3 67	Johnstone	Apprentice	Aston Villa	48	—
Martin Keown	6 1	12 04	24 7 66	Oxford	Apprentice	Arsenal	22	—
						Brighton & HA (loan)	23	1
						Aston Villa	112	3
Derek Mountfield	6 1	12 07	2 11 62	Liverpool	Apprentice	Tranmere R	26	1
						Everton	106	19
						Aston Villa	24	1
Chris Price	5 7	10 02	30 3 60	Hereford	Apprentice	Hereford U	330	27
						Blackburn R	83	11
						Aston Villa	36	—
Steve Sims	6 1	14 04	2 7 57	Lincoln	Apprentice	Leicester C	79	3
						Watford	152	4
						Notts Co	85	5
						Watford	19	1
						Aston Villa	41	—
Mark Williams*	5 9	10 08	11 8 70	Merthyr Tydfil	Trainee	Aston Villa	—	—
Midfield								
Paul Birch	5 6	10 09	20 11 62	West Bromwich	Apprentice	Aston Villa	153	16
Neale Cooper (To Rangers, Oct 1988)	6 1	12 11	24 11 63	Darjeeling	King St	Aberdeen	132	6
						Aston Villa	20	—
Stuart Gray	5 10	11 05	19 4 60	Withernsea	Local	Nottingham F	49	3
						Bolton W (loan)	10	—
						Barnsley	120	23
						Aston Villa	55	9
David Hunt*	5 11	13 09	17 4 59	Leicester	Apprentice	Derby Co	5	—
						Notts Co	336	28
						Aston Villa	13	—
Mark Lillis	6 0	13 06	17 1 60	Manchester	Local	Huddersfield T	206	56
						Manchester C	39	11
						Derby Co	15	1
						Aston Villa	31	4
Gordon Cowans	5 9	10 07	27 10 58	Durham	Apprentice	Aston Villa	286	42
					Bari	Aston Villa	33	2
Carl Morris*	5 9	10 07	10 11 69	Birmingham	Trainee	Aston Villa	—	—

ASTON VILLA

Foundation: Cricketing enthusiasts of Villa Cross Wesleyan Chapel, Aston, Birmingham decided to form a football club during the winter of 1873–74. Football clubs were few and far between in the Birmingham area and in their first game against Aston Brook St. Mary's Rugby team they played one half rugby and the other soccer. In 1876 they were joined by a Scottish soccer enthusiast George Ramsay who was immediately appointed captain and went on to lead Aston Villa from obscurity to one of the country's top clubs in a period of less than 10 years.

Managers (and Secretary-managers)
George Ramsay 1884–1926*, W. J. Smith 1926–34*, Jimmy McMullan 1934–35, Jimmy Hogan 1936–44, Alex Massie 1945–50, George Martin 1950–53, Eric Houghton 1953–58, Joe Mercer 1958–64, Dick Taylor 1965–67, Tommy Cummings 1967–68, Tommy Docherty 1968–70, Vic Crowe 1970–74, Ron Saunders 1974–82, Tony Barton 1982–84, Graham Turner 1984–86, Billy McNeill 1986–87, Graham Taylor 1987– .

Player and Position	*Ht*	*Wt*	*Birth Date*	*Birth Place*	*Source*	*Clubs*	*League App*	*League Gls*
Forwards								
Nigel Callaghan	5 9	10 09	12 9 62	Singapore	Apprentice	Watford	222	41
						Derby Co	76	10
						Aston Villa	16	1
Tony Daley	5 9	10 05	18 10 67	Birmingham	Apprentice	Aston Villa	104	13
Alan McInally	6 1	13 03	10 2 63	Ayr	Ayr U BC	Ayr U	93	32
						Celtic	65	17
						Aston Villa	58	18
Ian Olney	6 1	11 03	17 12 69	Luton	Trainee	Aston Villa	15	2
Ian Ormondroyd	6 4	13 07	22 9 64	Bradford	Thackley	Bradford C	87	20
						Oldham Ath (loan)	10	1
						Aston Villa	12	1
David Platt	5 10	11 12	10 6 66	Chadderton	Chadderton	Manchester U	—	—
						Crewe Alex	134	55
						Aston Villa	49	12
Gareth Williams	5 10	11 08	12 3 67	Isle of Wight	Gosport	Aston Villa	2	—

Trainees
Blake, Mark A; Carruthers, Martin G; Crisp, Richard I; Duffy, Darrell G; Jones, David; Liddle, Craig G; Mooney, Thomas J; Parrott, Mark A; Small, Bryan; Smith, Andrew D.

Associated Schoolboys
Boden, Christopher; Bullivant, Russell P; Boyce, Christopher; Carr, Sean B; Cope, Justin A; Evans, Darren; Fenton, Graham A; Ferry, David L; Froggatt, Stephen J; Goodwin, Craig; Harrison, Gary M; Hoban, Neil A; Hodgson, Shaun D; Hutson, Otis M.F; Ibrahim, Kevin A; King, Ian J; Livingstone, Glen; Norris, Jonathan; Peachey, Wayne T; Pearce, Christopher J; Pearce, Dennis A; Rampton, Adrian P; Thomson, Steven J; Travis, David L; Tyrell, Ian D; Walker, Stephen; Walker, Steven; Watt, David S; Williams, Jamie D; Williams, Lee.

BARNSLEY 1988–89 *Back row (left to right):* Darren Rolph, Paul Futcher, Ian Wardle, John Sidlow, Clive Baker, Paul Cross, Gary Coatsworth.
Centre row: Eric Winstanley (First Team Coach), David Currie, Mark Robinson, Tony Rees, Carl Tiler, Paul McGugan, Andy Duggan, Steve Cooper, Michael Clarke, Jim Dobbin, David Ross, Frank Barlow (Reserve and Youth Team Coach), Mark Nile (Physiotherapist).
Front row: Julian Broddle, John Beresford, John MacDonald, Gwyn Thomas, Colin Marshall, Allan Clarke (Manager), Joe Joyce, Darren Foreman, Steve Agnew, Jonathan Bond, Steve Lowndes.

Division 2 BARNSLEY

Oakwell Ground, Grove St, Barnsley. Telephone Barnsley (0226) 295353; Clubcall: 0898 121152; Commercial Office: 0226 286718.

Ground Capacity: 36,987 (15,000 under cover).

Record attendance: 40,255 v Stoke C, 15 Feb, 1936, FA Cup 5th rd.

Pitch measurements: 110yd × 75yd.

President: Arthur Raynor. ***Vice-Presidents:*** N. W. B. Moody, G. Pallister, J. Steele, C. Williams. ***Chairman:*** G. Buckle LLB.

Directors: C. B. Taylor (Vice-Chairman), R. F. Potter, J. A. Dennis, C. H. Harrison, M. R. Hayselden.

Secretary: Michael Spinks. ***Commercial Manager:*** G. Whewall.

Team Manager: Allan Clarke.

Coach: Eric Winstanley. ***Physio:*** Mark Nile.

Year Formed: 1887. ***Turned Professional:*** 1888. ***Ltd Co.:*** 1899.

Previous Name: Barnsley St Peter's, 1887–89

Club Nickname: 'The Tykes', 'Reds' or 'Colliers'.

Record League Victory: 9-0 v Loughborough T, Division 2, 28 January 1899 – Greaves; McCartney, Nixon; Porteous, Burleigh, Howard; Davis (4), Hepworth (1), Lees (1), McCullough (1), Jones (2). 9-0 v Accrington S, Division 3 (N), 3 February 1934 – Ellis; Cookson, Shotton; Harper, Henderson, Whitworth; Spence (2), Smith (1), Blight (4), Andrews (1), Ashton (1).

Record Cup Victory: 6-0 v Blackpool, FA Cup, 1st rd (replay), 20 January 1910 – Mearns; Downs, Ness; Glendinning, Boyle (1), Utley; Bartrop, Gadsby (1), Lillycrop (2), Tufnell (2), Forman. 6-0 v Peterborough U. League Cup, 1st rd (2nd leg), 15 September 1981 – Horn; Joyce, Chambers, Glavin (2), Banks, McCarthy, Evans, Parker (2), Aylott (1), McHale, Barrowclough (1).

Record Defeat: 0-9 v Notts Co, Division 2, 19 November, 1927.

Most League Points (2 for a win): 67, Division 3 (N), 1938–39.

Most League Points (3 for a win): 74, Division 2, 1988–89.

Most League Goals: 118, Division 3 (N), 1933–34.

Highest League Scorer in Season: Cecil McCormack, 33, Division 2, 1950–51.

Most League Goals in Total Aggregate: Ernest Hine, 123, 1921–26 and 1934–38.

Most Capped Player: Eddie McMorran, 9 (15), Northern Ireland.

Most League Appearances: Barry Murphy, 514, 1962–78.

Record Transfer Fee Received: £300,000 from Portsmouth for John Beresford, March 1989.

Record Transfer Fee Paid: £150,000 to Darlington for David Currie, February 1988.

Football League Record: 1898 Elected to Division 2; 1932–34 Division 3 (N); 1934–38 Division 2; 1938–39 Division 3 (N); 1946–53 Division 2; 1953–55 Division 3 (N); 1955–59 Division 2; 1959–65 Division 3; 1965–68 Division 4; 1968–72 Division 3; 1972–79 Division 4; 1979–81 Division 3; 1981– Division 2.

Honours: *Football League:* best season; 3rd, Division 2, 1914–15, 1921–22; Division 3 (N) – Champions 1933–34, 1938–39, 1954–55; Runners-up 1953–54; Division 3 – Runners-up 1980–81; Division 4 – Runners-up 1967–68; Promoted 1978–79. *FA Cup:* Winners 1912; Runners-up 1910. *Football League Cup:* best season, 5th rd. 1981–82.

Colours: Red shirts white trim, white shorts, red stockings. **Change colours:** All white.

BARNSLEY 1988–89 LEAGUE RECORD

Match No.	Date	Venue	Opponents	Result	H/T Score	Lg. Pos.	Goalscorers	Attendance
1	Aug 27	A	Oldham Ath	D 1-1	0-1	—	Cooper	6551
2	29	H	Swindon T	D 1-1	1-0	—	Lowndes	6034
3	Sept 3	H	Stoke C	W 1-0	0-0	6	Agnew	5682
4	10	A	Hull C	D 0-0	0-0	9		5654
5	17	H	Chelsea	D 1-1	1-1	10	Dobbin	6942
6	21	A	Leeds U	L 0-2	0-0	—		17,390
7	24	H	Manchester C	L 1-2	0-0	16	Shotton	9300
8	Oct 1	A	Birmingham C	W 5-3	2-0	12	Beresford, Broddle, Currie, Rees, Lowndes	4892
9	5	A	Brighton & HA	W 1-0	0-0	—	Currie (pen)	7327
10	8	H	WBA	W 2-1	0-1	5	Currie, Thomas	5674
11	15	A	Blackburn R	L 1-2	1-1	8	Mail (og)	9316
12	22	H	Ipswich T	W 2-0	2-0	7	Cooper 2	6325
13	25	A	Watford	L 0-4	0-2	—		10,356
14	29	H	Plymouth Arg	W 3-1	1-0	7	Cooper, Thomas, Dobbin	5485
15	Nov 5	A	Crystal Palace	D 1-1	0-0	7	Broddle	7768
16	12	H	Bradford C	D 0-0	0-0	8		8838
17	19	A	Portsmouth	L 0-3	0-2	11		10,001
18	26	H	Bournemouth	W 5-2	2-0	7	Currie 4 (1 pen), Dobbin	4937
19	Dec 3	A	Oxford U	L 0-2	0-0	9		4449
20	10	H	Walsall	W 1-0	0-0	7	Broddle	5173
21	17	H	Leicester C	W 3-0	2-0	7	Currie (pen), McGugan, Agnew	6477
22	26	A	Sunderland	L 0-1	0-0	8		21,994
23	31	A	Shrewsbury T	W 3-2	1-1	6	Currie (pen), Lowndes, Moyes (og)	4401
24	Jan 2	H	Hull C	L 0-2	0-2	7		9879
25	14	A	Swindon T	D 0-0	0-0	9		10,201
26	21	H	Oldham Ath	W 4-3	1-0	8	Lowndes, Skipper (og), Currie 2 (1 pen)	7879
27	Feb 4	H	Brighton & HA	D 2-2	1-1	7	Cooper, Agnew	12,498
28	11	A	WBA	D 1-1	1-0	8	Lowndes	12,650
29	21	A	Ipswich T	L 0-2	0-1	—		9995
30	25	H	Blackburn R	L 0-1	0-0	11		8777
31	28	H	Watford	D 2-2	1-0	—	MacDonald, Shotton	6163
32	Mar 4	A	Bradford C	W 2-1	1-0	11	Currie (pen), MacDonald	11,085
33	11	H	Crystal Palace	D 1-1	1-1	10	MacDonald	7055
34	19	H	Leeds U	D 2-2	1-1	—	Agnew, Robinson	11,578
35	25	A	Stoke C	D 1-1	0-1	12	Currie (pen)	10,209
36	27	H	Sunderland	W 3-0	1-0	12	Robinson, Cooper, Dobbin (pen)	8070
3	Apr 1	A	Chelsea	L 3-5	2-2	12	McLaughlin (og), Dobbin, Agnew	16,023
38	8	H	Shrewsbury T	W 1-0	1-0	11	MacDonald	5252
39	11	A	Leicester C	W 1-0	1-0	—	Lowndes	7266
40	15	H	Birmingham C	D 0-0	0-0	9		6464
41	22	A	Manchester C	W 2-1	1-0	8	Cooper (og), Shotton	21,274
42	25	A	Plymouth Arg	W 2-1	1-1	—	Currie, Shotton	5468
43	29	A	Bournemouth	L 2-3	1-1	8	O'Driscoll (og), Shotton	5520
44	May 1	H	Oxford U	W 1-0	0-0	8	Evans (og)	5940
45	6	H	Portsmouth	W 1-0	0-0	7	Currie (pen)	5178
46	13	A	Walsall	W 3-1	1-0	7	MacDonald, Currie, Agnew	3966

Final League Position: 7

GOALSCORERS

League (66): Currie 16 (8 pens), Agnew 6, Cooper 6, Lowndes 6, Dobbin 5 (1 pen), MacDonald 5, Shotton 5, Broddle 3, Robinson 2, Thomas 2, Beresford 1, McGugan 1, Rees 1, own goals 7.
Littlewoods Cup (1): Currie 1.
FA Cup (9): Currie 3, Agnew 2, MacDonald 2, Cooper 1, Thomas 1.

Littlewoods Cup	Second Round	Wimbledon (h)	0-2
		(a)	1-0
FA Cup	Third Round	Chelsea (h)	4-0
	Fourth Round	Stoke C (a)	3-3
		(h)	2-1
	Fifth Round	Everton (h)	0-1

Baker	Joyce	Beresford	Dobbin	McGugan	Futcher	Lowndes	Agnew	Cooper	Currie	Thomas	MacDonald	Clarke	Broddle	Shotton	Foreman	Marshall	Rees	Robinson	Tiler	*Match No.*
1	2	3	4	5	6	7*	8	9	10	11	12									1
1	2	3	4	5	6	7	8	9	10	11										2
1	2	3*	5		6	7	8	9	10	4	12	11†	14							3
1	2	3	11		6	7	8	9	10	4				5						4
1	2	3	11		6	7	8	9		4	10*			5	12					5
1	2	3	11		6	7	8	9	10	4				5						6
1	2	3	11		6	7*	8	9	10	4				5		12				7
1	2	3	12	6		7	8*		10	4			11	5			9			8
1	2	3		6		7	8	12	10	4			11	5			9*			9
1	2	3	14	6†		7*	8	12	10	4			11	5			9			10
1	2	3	14		6	7†	8*	12	10	4			11	5			9			11
1	2	3	8		6	12	14	9	10*	4			11	5			7†			12
1	2	3	8		6	7*	12	9		4			11	5			10			13
1	2	3	8		6			9		4	10		11	5			7			14
1	2	3*	8	12	6			9		4	10		11	5			7			15
1	2		8	3	6			9	10*	4	12		11	5			7			16
1	2		8	3	6	9			10	4			11	5			7			17
1	2		8	3	6				10	4	7		11	5			9*	12		18
1	2		8	3	6	12	14		10	4	7*		11	5			9†			19
1	2	3	8	5*	6		12	9	10	4			11				7†	14		20
1	2	3		5	6	7	8	9	10	4			11							21
1	2	3	12	5	6	7	8*	9†	10	4			11				14			22
1	2	8		5	6	7		9	10	4	12		11	3*						23
1	2	3	12	5	6			9	10	4	8		11				7*			24
1	2	3	8	5	6		7	9	10		11			4						25
1	2	3*	4	5	6	7	8	9	10		11			12						26
1	2	3		5*	6		8	9	10		11		12	4			7			27
1	2	3		5	6	7	8	9			11		10	4						28
1	2	3	4	5*	6	7†	8	9	10		11		14	12						29
1	2	3	4		6		8	9	10		11*		12	5				7		30
1	2		4		6		8		10		11	3	9	5				7		31
1	2	3	4		6		8		10		11		9	5				7		32
1	2		4		6		8		10		11	3*	9	5			12	7		33
1	2		4		6	9	8		10*		11		3		12			7	5	34
1	2		4		6	9	8	12	10		11		3					7*	5	35
1	2		4		6	9	8	12	10*		11		3	5				7		36
1	2		4		6	9	8	12	10		11†		3	5	14			7*		37
1	2		4			6	8	9*	10		11		3	5	12			7		38
1	2		4		6	7	8	9	10		11		3	5						39
1	2		4		6	7	8	9	10*		11		3	5				12		40
1	2		4		6	9	8		10		11		3	5				7		41
1	2		4		6	9	8		10		11		3	5				7		42
1	2		4		6	9	8	12	10		11		3	5				7*		43
1	2		4				8	9	10*		11		3	5	12			7	6	44
1	2		4		6	12	8	9*	10		11		3	5				7		45
1			4		6	9	8		10		11		3	5				7	2	46
46	45	27	36 + 5s	19 + 1s	41	30 + 3s	35 + 4s	28 + 7s	41	24	28 + 4s	3	34 + 4s	35 + 2s	— + 5s	— + 1s	15 + 2s	15 + 3s	4	

BARNSLEY

Player and Position	Ht	Wt	Birth Date	Birth Place	Source	Clubs	League App	League Gls
Goalkeepers								
Clive Baker	5 9	11 00	14 3 59	N Walsham	Amateur	Norwich C	14	—
						Barnsley	208	—
Ian Wardle	5 9	11 00	27 3 70	Doncaster	Schoolboys	Barnsley	—	—
Defenders								
Gary Coatsworth*	6 1	11 06	7 10 68	Sunderland		Barnsley	6	—
Paul Cross	5 7	9 06	31 10 65	Barnsley	Apprentice	Barnsley	77	—
Paul Futcher	6 0	12 03	25 9 56	Chester	Apprentice	Chester	20	—
						Luton T	131	1
						Manchester C	37	—
						Oldham Ath	98	1
						Derby Co	35	—
						Barnsley	201	—
Joe Joyce	5 9	10 05	18 3 61	Consett	Amateur	Barnsley	331	4
Paul McGugan	6 3	13 07	17 7 64	Glasgow	Eastercraigs	Celtic	49	2
						Barnsley	49	2
Darren Rolph	5 8	11 04	19 11 68	Romford		Barnsley	2	—
Malcolm Shotton	6 3	13 12	16 2 57	Newcastle	Apprentice	Leicester C	—	—
						Nuneaton Bor	—	—
						Oxford U	263	12
						Portsmouth	10	—
						Huddersfield T	16	1
						Barnsley	37	5
Carl Tiler	6 2	13 00	11 2 70	Sheffield	Trainee	Barnsley	5	—
Midfield								
Steve Agnew	5 9	10 06	9 11 65	Shipley	Apprentice	Barnsley	110	13
Jim Dobbin	5 10	10 06	17 9 61	Dunfermine	Whitburn BC	Celtic	2	—
						Motherwell (loan)	2	—
						Doncaster R	64	13
						Barnsley	87	11
Colin Marshall	5 5	9 05	1 11 69	Glasgow	Trainee	Barnsley	1	—
Mark Robinson	5 9	11 08	21 11 68	Manchester	YTS	WBA	2	—
						Barnsley	21	2
Gwyn Thomas	5 7	11 05	26 9 57	Swansea	Apprentice	Leeds U	89	3
						Barnsley	198	17
Forwards								
Julian Broddle	5 9	11 03	1 11 64	Laughton	Apprentice	Sheffield U	1	—
						Scunthorpe U	144	32
						Barnsley	57	4
Michael Clarke	5 11	11 05	22 12 67	Birmingham		Barnsley	40	3
Steve Cooper	5 11	10 12	22 6 64	Birmingham		Birmingham C	—	—
						Halifax (loan)	7	1
						Mansfield T (loan)	—	—
						Newport Co	38	11
						Plymouth Arg	73	15
						Barnsley	35	6
David Currie	5 11	12 09	27 11 62	Stockton	Local	Middlesbrough	113	31
						Darlington	76	33
						Barnsley	56	23
Darren Foreman	5 10	10 08	12 2 68	Southampton		Barnsley	30	5

BARNSLEY

Foundation: Many clubs owe their inception to the church and Barnsley are among them, for they were formed in 1887 by the Rev. T. T. Preedy, curate of Barnsley St. Peter's and went under that name until a year after being admitted to the Second Division of the Football League in 1898.

Managers (and Secretary-managers)
Arthur Fairclough 1898–1901*, John McCartney 1901–04*, Arthur Fairclough 1904–12, John Hastie 1912–14, Percy Lewis 1914–19, Peter Sant 1919–26, John Commins 1926–29, Arthur Fairclough 1929–30, Brough Fletcher 1930–37, Angus Seed 1937–53, Tim Ward 1953–60, Johnny Steele 1960–71 (continued as GM), John McSeveney 1971–72, Johnny Steele (GM) 1972–73, Jim Iley 1973–78, Allan Clarke 1978–80, Norman Hunter 1980–84, Bobby Collins 1984–85, Allan Clarke 1985– .

Player and Position	*Ht*	*Wt*	*Birth Date*	*Birth Place*	*Source*	*Clubs*	*League App*	*League Gls*
Steve Lowndes	5 10	10 13	17 6 60	Cwmbran	Amateur	Newport Co	208	39
						Millwall	96	16
						Barnsley	92	16
John MacDonald	5 9	10 08	15 4 61	Glasgow	Clydebank	Rangers	160	44
						Charlton Ath	2	—
						Barnsley	90	19
Tony Rees	5 9	11 13	1 8 64	Merthyr Tydfil	Apprentice	Aston Villa	—	—
						Birmingham C	95	12
						Peterborough U (loan)	5	2
						Shrewsbury T (loan)	2	—
						Barnsley	31	3
David Ross	6 1	10 03	21 11 69	Durham		Barnsley	—	—
Alan Semley‡	6 0	1143 00	21 2 66	Barnsley	Apprentice	Barnsley	4	—

Trainees
Beaumont, Wayne; Cawthorne, Neil B; Drewery, Jason M; Dunphy, Sean; Holmes, Steven; Jarvis, Mark M; Kaye, Stephen; Neal, David; Parker, Lee D; Sanders, Wayne; Winstanley, Mark A.

****Non-Contract**
Bond, Jonathan J.

Associated Schoolboys
Bissett, Andrew G; Bland, Neal A; Brown, Keith D; Cullen, Michael J; Dale, Stephen C; Degnan, Lee A; Drinkwater, Lee R; Driver, Christopher; Duke, Adrian M; Dunford, Paul J; Eaton, Barry; Firth, Lee; Gartland, Paul M; Goodard, Richard C; Hall, Richard I; McNicholas, David A; Morgan, Gregory D; Noble, Dean; Nowell, Martyn; O'Sullivan, David J; Oxley, Lea J; Poskitt, Adrian; Pullan, Richard; Senior, Andrew; Skelton, Ian S; Tate, Nathan K; Tyler, Dean; Warner, Paul C; Watson, David N; Winks, Corrie D.

BIRMINGHAM CITY 1988–89 *Back row (left to right):* Steve Wigley, John Frain, Tony Godden, Tony Elliott, Roger Hansbury, Kevin Ashley, Ian Handysides.
Centre row: Fred Davies, Ian Atkins, Kevin Langley, Vince Overson, Guy Russell, Adrian Bird, John Trewick, Peter Henderson, Tony Brown.
Front row: Ray Ranson, Colin Robinson, Des Bremner, Garry Pendrey (Manager), Steve Whitton, Brian Roberts, Gary Childs.

Division 3 BIRMINGHAM CITY

St Andrews, Birmingham B9 4NH. Telephone 021-772 0101/2689. Lottery office/Souvenir shop 021 772 1245. Clubcall: 0898 121188.

Ground capacity: 38,408.

Record Attendance: 66,844 v Everton, FA Cup 5th rd, 11 Feb, 1939.

Record receipts: £116,372.50 v Nottingham Forest, FA Cup 5th rd, 20 February 1988.

Pitch measurements: 115yd × 75yd.

Match tickets: Bookable three weeks in advance.

Directors: S. Kumar BA (Chairman), R. Kumar BSC (Vice-Chairman), B. Kumar MSC, K. E. Wheldon (Managing Director), B. H. Slater BA (HONS), J. F. Wiseman, T. W. J. Edmonds.

Secretary: H. J. Westmancoat FFA, MBIM.

General Manager: Dave Mackay.

Assistant Manager: Bobby Ferguson. ***Physio:*** Peter Henderson MCSP.

Year Formed: 1875. ***Turned Professional:*** 1885. ***Ltd Co.:*** 1888.

Previous Grounds: Waste ground near Arthur St, 1875; Muntz St. Small Heath, 1877; St Andrews, 1906.

Previous Names: 1875–88, Small Heath Alliance; 1888, dropped 'Alliance'; became Birmingham 1905; became Birmingham City 1945.

Club Nickname: 'Blues'.

Record League Victory: 12-0 v Walsall T Swifts, Division 2, 17 December 1892 – Charnley; Bayley, Jones; Ollis, Jenkyns, Devey; Hallam (2), Walton (3), Mobley (3), Wheldon (2), Hands (2). 12-0 v Doncaster R, Division 2, 11 April 1903 – Dorrington; Goldie, Wassell; Beer, Dougherty (1), Howard; Athersmith (1), Leonard (3), McRoberts (1), Wilcox (4), Field (1). Aston. (1 og).

Record Cup Victory: 9-2 v Burton W, FA Cup, 1st rd, 31 October 1885 – Hedges; Jones, Evetts (1); James (F), Felton, James (A) (1); Davenport (2), Stanley (4), Simms, Figures, Morris (1).

Record Defeat: 1-9 v Sheffield W, Division 1, 13 December, 1930 and v Blackburn R, Division 1, 5 January, 1895.

Most League Points (2 for a win): 59, Division 2, 1947–48.

Most League Points (3 for a win): 82, Division 2, 1984–85.

Most League Goals: 103, Division 2, 1893–94 (only 28 games).

Highest League Scorer in Season: Joe Bradford, 29, Division 1, 1927–28.

Most League Goals in Total Aggregate: Joe Bradford, 249, 1920–35.

Most Capped Player: Malcolm Page, 28, Wales.

Most League Appearances: Gil Merrick, 486, 1946–60.

Record Transfer Fee Received: £975,000 from Nottingham F for Trevor Francis, February 1979.

Record Transfer Fee Paid: £350,000 to Derby Co for David Langan, June 1980.

Football League Record: Division 1: 1894–96; 1901–02, 1903–08; 1921–39; 1948–50; 1955–65; 1972–79; 1980–84; 1985–86. Division 2: 1892–94; 1896–1901; 1902–03; 1908–21; 1946–48; 1950–55; 1965–72; 1979–80, 1984–85; 1986–89; Division 3: 1989–.

Honours: *Football League:* Division 1 best season: 6th, 1955–56; Division 2 – Champions 1892–93, 1920–21, 1947–48, 1954–55; Runners-up 1893–94, 1900–01, 1902–03, 1971–72, 1984–85. *FA Cup:* Runners-up 1931, 1956. *Football League Cup:* Winners 1963. **European Competitions:** *European Fairs Cup:* 1955–58, 1958–60 (runners-up), 1960–61 (runners-up), 1960–62.

Colours: Royal blue shirts, white shorts, blue stockings with white trim. **Change colours:** All yellow.

BIRMINGHAM CITY 1988–89 LEAGUE RECORD

Match No.	Date	Venue	Opponents	Result		H/T Score	Lg. Pos.	Goalscorers	Attendance
1	Aug 27	A	Watford	L	0-1	0-1	—		12,656
2	Sept 3	H	Leicester C	L	2-3	2-2	22	Walsh (og), Robinson	7932
3	10	A	Oldham Ath	L	0-4	0-1	24		5796
4	17	H	Sunderland	W	3-2	1-0	20	Atkins, Childs, Robinson	6871
5	20	A	Walsall	L	0-5	0-0	—		8780
6	24	A	Blackburn R	L	0-3	0-3	23		7562
7	Oct 1	H	Barnsley	L	3-5	0-2	24	Langley, Robinson, Atkins	4892
8	4	H	Plymouth Arg	L	0-1	0-0	—		4921
9	8	A	Bournemouth	W	1-0	1-0	22	Frain	6186
10	15	H	WBA	L	1-4	1-2	22	Bremner	10,453
11	22	A	Manchester C	D	0-0	0-0	24		20,205
12	25	H	Stoke C	L	0-1	0-0	—		6262
13	29	A	Swindon T	L	1-2	0-1	24	Atkins (pen)	6937
14	Nov 5	H	Portsmouth	D	0-0	0-0	24		5866
15	12	A	Oxford U	L	0-3	0-1	24		5589
16	19	A	Hull C	D	1-1	1-0	24	Langley	5134
17	22	H	Leeds U	D	0-0	0-0	—		6168
18	26	H	Ipswich T	W	1-0	1-0	24	Whitton	5932
19	Dec 3	A	Bradford C	D	2-2	1-1	24	Whitton, Richards	9503
20	10	H	Crystal Palace	L	0-1	0-1	24		6523
21	16	H	Chelsea	L	1-4	0-1	—	Whitton	7897
22	26	A	Shrewsbury T	D	0-0	0-0	23		7347
23	31	A	Brighton & HA	L	0-4	0-0	23		9324
24	Jan 2	H	Oldham Ath	D	0-0	0-0	23		5998
17	14	A	Leeds U	L	0-1	0-0	23		5690
26	21	H	Watford	L	2-3	2-2	23	Whitton 2 (1 pen)	6396
27	Feb 4	A	Plymouth Arg	W	1-0	1-0	23	Robinson	7721
28	11	H	Bournemouth	L	0-1	0-0	23		6444
29	18	H	Manchester C	L	0-2	0-1	23		11,707
30	25	A	WBA	D	0-0	0-0	23		16,148
31	28	A	Stoke C	L	0-1	0-1	—		7904
32	Mar 4	H	Oxford U	D	0-0	0-0	24		4954
33	11	A	Portsmouth	L	0-1	0-0	24		8078
34	18	H	Walsall	W	1-0	0-0	23	Wigley	6558
35	25	A	Leicester C	L	0-2	0-1	24		9564
36	27	H	Shrewsbury T	L	1-2	1-0	24	Sturridge	4964
37	Apr 1	A	Sunderland	D	2-2	0-1	24	Yates, Frain	10,969
38	4	A	Chelsea	L	1-3	0-1	—	Richards	14,796
39	8	H	Brighton & HA	L	1-2	1-2	24	Sturridge	4579
40	15	A	Barnsley	D	0-0	0-0	24		6464
41	18	H	Swindon T	L	1-2	0-2	—	Peer	4026
42	22	H	Blackburn R	W	2-0	0-0	24	Robinson, Yates	5813
43	29	A	Ipswich T	L	0-4	0-2	24		9975
44	May 1	H	Bradford C	W	1-0	1-0	23	Frain	4735
45	6	H	Hull C	W	1-0	0-0	23	Yates	4686
46	13	A	Crystal Palace	L	1-4	0-4	23	Sturridge	17,581

Final League Position: 23

GOALSCORERS

League (31): Robinson 5, Whitton 5 (1 pen), Atkins 3 (1 pen), Frain 3, Sturridge 3, Yates 3, Langley 2, Richards 2, Bremner 1, Childs 1, Peer 1, Wigley 1, own goal 1.
Littlewoods Cup (3): Bird 1, Whitton 1, own goal 1.
FA Cup (0).

Littlewoods Cup	First Round	Wolverhampton W (a)	2-3
		(h)	1-0
	Second Round	Aston Villa (h)	0-2
		(a)	0-5
FA Cup	Third Round	Wimbledon (h)	0-1

Godden	Ranson	Roberts	Atkins	Bird	Trewick	Bremner	Langley	Whitton	Robinson	Wigley	Overson	Frain	Childs	Morris	Yates	Clarkson	Tait	Thomas	Peer	Richards	Sturridge	Ashley	Hansbury	Fox	Hopkins	Burton	*Match No.*
1	2	3	4	5	6	7	8	9	10	11																	1
1	2	3	4	6			8	9	10	11	5	7															2
1	2	3	4	6			8†	9	10	11	5	7*	12	14													3
1	2	3	4			7		9	10	11	5	6	8														4
1	2	3	4		8	7		9	10	11	5	6*		12													5
1	2	3	4	6	8*	7		9	10	11	5				12												6
1	2	3†	4			12	8*	9	10	11	5			7		6	14										7
	2	3	4	6*		7	8†	9	10	11	5		12	14				1									8
	2		4	6		7		9*	10	11	5	3			12			1	8								9
			4	6		7			10†	11	5	3	8*	12				1	2	9	14						10
		2	4			7			10	11	5	3	8*					1	6	9	12						11
		2	4	12		7			10†	11	5	3*	8					1	6	9	14						12
	2	3	4			7	8		10†	11			12		14	5*		1	6	9							13
	2	3	4	5		7	6			11			8		9		12	1			10*						14
		3	4			7	6			11	5	8*			9			1		10	12	2					15
	2		4	8		7	6			11	5	3			9			1		10							16
	2	3	4			7	6	9		11	5		8*		12			1		10							17
	2	3	4			7	6	9		11	5		8*				14		12	10†			1				18
	2	3	4	8		7	6	9		11	5									10			1				19
	2	3	4			7	6	9		11	5			8						10			1				20
	2	3	4			7	6	9	14	11	5		12	8*				1		10†							21
		3	4	8*	12	7	6	9		11	5							1		10		2					22
		3	4		8	7	6	9	12	11	5							1		10*		2					23
		2	4		3	7	6	9			5		11				8	1		10							24
		4			3	7	6	9	10	11	5				8*			1	12			2					25
		4			3	7	6	9	10	11	5						8*	1			12	2					26
		7	4		3		6		10	11	5	9					8	1				2					27
		7	4		3		6*	8	10	11	5	9†		14			12	1				2					28
		6	4		3	7		9	10	11	5						8*	1		12		2					29
		6*	4			7		9	10	11		3						1	8		12	2		5			30
			4			7	12	9	10†	11	5	3				6		1	8*		14	2					31
		6	4			7			10	11	5	3		12	9			1			8*	2					32
		6*	4			7	12		10	11	5	3			9			1		8		2					33
			4				8		9	7	6	3	10					1		11*	12	2		5			34
		6	4				7		10		5	3	8*					1			9	2			11	12	35
		6	4				7		9		5	3	8	14				1			10	2*			11†	12	36
		6	4				7				5	3	8		11			1	2	10	9						37
		6	4				7				5	3	8		11			1	2	10	9						38
		6	4				7		9*		5	3	8		2			1			10				11	12	39
		6	4				7		10		5	3	8		11		9	1	2								40
		6	4				7								11	3	9	1	2		10			5	8		41
		6					7		8		5	3			9	2		1	4		10				11		42
		6					7		8		5	3	12		9*	2†		1	4		10				11	14	43
		6					7		8		5	3	9		4	2		1			10				11		44
		6					7		8		5	3	12		4	2*		1	9		10				11		45
		6	4				7				5	3	12		9*	2		1	8		10				11		46
7	17	41	40	11 + 1s	10 + 1s	28 + 1s	34 + 2s	23	31 + 2s	33	41	28	16 + 7s	3 + 7s	16 + 4s	9	6 + 4s	36	15 + 2s	18 + 1s	13 + 8s	15	3	3	9	— + 4s	

BIRMINGHAM CITY

Player and Position	Ht	Wt	Birth Date	Birth Place	Source	Clubs	League App	League Gls
Goalkeepers								
Tony Godden‡	6 0	13 00	2 8 55	Gillingham	Ashford T	WBA	267	—
						Preston NE (loan)	—	—
						Luton T (loan)	12	—
						Walsall (loan)	19	—
						Chelsea (loan)	8	—
						Chelsea	26	—
						Birmingham C	29	—
						Bury (loan)	1	—
						Sheffield W (loan)	—	—
Roger Hansbury	5 11	12 00	26 1 55	Barnsley	Apprentice	Norwich C	78	—
						Bolton W (loan)	—	—
						Cambridge U (loan)	11	—
						Orient (loan)	—	—
					Eastern Ath	Burnley	83	—
						Cambridge U	37	—
						Birmingham C	56	—
						Sheffield U (loan)	5	—
						Wolverhampton W (loan)	3	—
Martin Thomas	6 1	13 00	28 11 59	Senghennydd	Apprentice	Bristol R	162	—
						Cardiff C (loan)	15	—
						Tottenham H (loan)	—	—
						Southend U (loan)	6	—
						Newcastle U (loan)	3	—
						Newcastle U	115	—
						Middlesbrough	4	—
						(loan)	36	—
						Birmingham C		
Defenders								
Kevin Ashley	5 7	10 04	31 12 68	Birmingham	Apprentice	Birmingham C	23	—
Adrian Bird	6 1	11 07	8 7 69	Bristol	School	Birmingham C	27	—
Ian Clarkson			4 12 70	Birmingham	Trainee	Birmingham C	9	—
Matthew Fox§			13 7 71	Birmingham	Trainee	Birmingham C	3	—
Vince Overson	6 0	13 00	15 5 62	Kettering	Apprentice	Burnley	211	6
						Birmingham C	112	1
Dean Peer	6 2	12 00	8 8 69	Dudley	Trainee	Birmingham C	19	1
Brian Roberts	5 8	11 07	6 11 55	Manchester	Apprentice	Coventry C	215	1
						Hereford U (loan)	5	—
						Birmingham C	177	—
Neil Sproston§	6 2	12 03	20 11 70	Dudley	Trainee	Birmingham C	1	—
Midfield								
Ian Atkins	6 0	12 03	16 1 57	Birmingham	Apprentice	Shrewsbury T	278	58
						Sunderland	77	6
						Everton	7	1
						Ipswich T	77	4
						Birmingham C	48	4
Des Bremner*	5 10	11 08	7 9 52	Aberchirder	Deveronvale	Hibernian	199	18
						Aston Villa	174	9
						Birmingham C	168	5
Micky Burton			5 11 69	Birmingham	Trainee	Birmingham C	4	—
Gary Childs	5 7	10 08	19 4 64	Birmingham	Apprentice	WBA	3	—
						Walsall	131	17
						Birmingham C	55	2
John Frain	5 7	11 10	8 10 68	Birmingham	Apprentice	Birmingham C	48	6
Ian Handysides* (Retired)	5 6	10 06	14 12 62	Jarrow	Apprentice	Birmingham C	62	2
						Walsall	66	11
						Birmingham C	56	4
						Wolverhampton W (loan)	11	2

BIRMINGHAM CITY

Foundation: In 1875 cricketing enthusiasts who were largely members of Trinity Church, Bordesley, determined to continue their sporting relationships throughout the year by forming a football club which they called Small Heath Alliance. For their earliest games played on waste land in Arthur Street, the team included three Edden brothers and two James brothers.

Managers (and Secretary-managers)
Alfred Jones 1892–1908*, Alec Watson 1908–1911, Frank Richards 1911–25 (Sec. only 1911–12), R. McRoberts 1912–13, W. J. Steer 1925–27, Leslie Knighton 1928–33, George Liddell 1933–39, Ted Goodier 1939–40, Harry Storer 1945–48, Bob Brocklebank 1949–54, Arthur Turner 1954–58, Pat Beasley 1959–60, Gil Merrick 1960–64, Joe Mallett 1965, Stan Cullis 1965–70, Fred Goodwin 1970–75, Willie Bell 1975–77, Jim Smith 1978–82, Ron Saunders 1982–86, John Bond 1986–87, Garry Pendrey 1987–89, Dave Mackay 1989– .

Player and Position	*Ht*	*Wt*	*Birth Date*	*Place*	*Source*	*Clubs*	*League App*	*Gls*
Robert Hopkins	5 7	10 05	25 10 61	Birmingham	Apprentice	Aston Villa	3	1
						Birmingham C	123	21
						Manchester C	7	1
						WBA	83	11
						Birmingham C	9	—
Kevin Langley	6 1	10 03	24 5 64	St Helens	Apprentice	Wigan Ath	160	6
						Everton	16	2
						Manchester C (loan)	9	—
						Manchester C	—	—
						Chester C (loan)	9	—
						Birmingham C	43	2
Ronnie Morris	6 0	11 08	25 9 70	Birmingham	Trainee	Birmingham C	11	—
John Trewick*	5 10	10 13	3 6 57	Bedlington	Apprentice	WBA	96	11
						Newcastle U	78	8
						Oxford U (loan)	3	—
						Oxford U	111	4
						Birmingham C	37	—
Forwards								
Colin Robinson	5 10	10 12	15 5 60	Birmingham	Mile Oak R	Shrewsbury T	194	41
						Birmingham C	37	6
Guy Russell‡	6 1	12 03	28 9 67	Shirley		Birmingham C	16	—
						Carlisle U (loan)	12	2
Carl Richards	6 0	13 00	12 1 60	Jamaica	Enfield	Bournemouth	71	15
						Birmingham C	19	2
Simon Sturridge			9 12 69	Birmingham	Trainee	Birmingham C	21	3
Paul Tait			31 7 71	Sutton Coldfield	Trainee	Birmingham C	11	—
Mark Yates	5 11	11 09	24 1 70	Birmingham	Trainee	Birmingham C	23	3

Trainees
Cook, Alan A.H; Fox, Matthew C; Francis, Sean R; Harris, Andrew; Larkins, Nigel K; Machin, Jason A; Masefield, Paul D; Rhodes, Jason P; Rutherford, Mark R; Sproston, Neil R; Thorpe, Nicholas S; Williams, Andrew P; Williams, Dean.

Associated Schoolboys
Adams, Carl A; Afford, Andrew B; Aston, David E; Baker, Lewis M; Bigot, Marcus; Brown, Steven M; Casemore, Craig P; Chiles, Lawrence; Coogan, Mark A; Cook, David R; Devery, Brendon J; Duffy, Paul J; Dutton, Matthew J; Elliot, Dean M; Halford, John D; Harris, Richard; Harrison, Mark; Jones, Paul T; Kodua, Derek B; O'Connor, David W.P; Peplow, Warren D; Tafft, Darren J; Wratten, Adam P.

BLACKBURN ROVERS 1988–89 *Back row (left to right):* Mark Atkins, Colin Hendry, Vince O'Keefe, Terry Gennoe, Darren Collier, Andy Kennedy, Keith Hill.
Centre row: Dave Hall (Youth Team Coach), David May, Tony Diamond, Ian Miller, Howard Gayle, Don Mackay (Manager), Lenny Johnrose, John Millar, Ally Dawson, David Mail, Jim Furnell (Reserve Team Manager).
Front row: Tony Parkes (Assistant Manager), Ronnie Hildersley, Sean Curry, Alan Ainscow, Simon Garner, Chris Sulley, Scott Sellars, Tony Finnigan, Jack Cunningham (Physiotherapist).

Division 2 BLACKBURN ROVERS

Ewood Park, Blackburn BB2 4JF. Telephone Blackburn (0254) 55432.

Ground capacity: 21,500.

Record attendance: 61,783 v Bolton W, FA Cup 6th rd, 2 Mar, 1929.

Record receipts: £60,612 v Liverpool, FA Cup 3rd rd, 8 Jan, 1983.

Pitch measurements: 116yd 2ft × 72yd 2ft.

Chairman: W. Fox. ***Vice Chairman:*** R. D. Coar BSC.

Directors: T. W. Ibbotson LLB, K. C. Lee, I. R. Stanners, G. R. Root FCMA

Commercial Manager: Ken Beamish.

Secretary: John W. Howarth FAAI.

Manager: Donald Mackay. ***Asst. Manager:*** Tony Parkes. ***Reserve Team Manager:*** Jim Furnell.

Physio: Jack Cunningham.

Year Formed: 1875. ***Turned Professional:*** 1880. ***Ltd Co.:*** 1897.

Previous Grounds: 1875, Brookhouse Ground; 1876, Alexandra Meadows; 1881, Leamington Road; 1890, Ewood Park.

Previous Name: Blackburn Grammar School OB.

Club Nickname: 'Blue and Whites'.

Record League Victory: 9-0 v Middlesbrough, Division 2, 6 November 1954 – Elvy; Suart, Eckersley; Clayton, Kelly, Bell; Mooney (3), Crossan (2), Briggs, Quigley (3), Langton (1).

Record Cup Victory: 11-0 v Rossendale, RA Cup 1st rd, 13 October 1884 – Arthur; Hopwood, McIntyre; Forrest, Blenkhorn, Lofthouse; Sowerbutts (2), J. Brown (1), Fecitt (4), Barton (3), Birtwistle (1).

Record Defeat: 0-8 v Arsenal, Division 1, 25 February, 1933.

Most League Points (2 for a win): 60, Division 3, 1974–75.

Most League Points (3 for a win): 77, Division 2, 1987–88, 1988–89.

Most League Goals: 114, Division 2, 1954–55.

Highest League Scorer in Season: Ted Harper, 43 Division 1, 1925–26.

Most League Goals in Total Aggregate: Simon Garner, 144, 1978–89.

Most Capped Player: Bob Crompton, 41, England.

Most League Appearances: Derek Fazackerley, 596, 1970–86.

Record Transfer Fee Received: £357,000 from Leeds U for Kevin Hird, February 1979.

Record Transfer Fee Paid: £150,000 to Birmingham C for Andy Kennedy, June 1988.

Football League Record: 1888 Founder Member of the League; 1936–39 Division 2; 1946–47 Division 1; 1947–57 Division 2; 1957–66 Division 1; 1966–71 Division 2; 1971–75 Division 3; 1975-79 Division 2; 1979–80 Division 3; 1980– Division 2.

Honours: *Football League:* Division 1 – Champions 1911–12, 1913–14; Division 2 – Champions 1938–39; Runners-up 1957–58; Division 3 – Champions 1974–75; Runners-up 1979–80; *FA Cup:* Winners 1884, 1885, 1886, 1890, 1891, 1928; Runners-up 1882. 1960. *Football League Cup:* Semi-final 1961–62. *Full Members' Cup:* Winners 1986–87.

Colours: Blue and white halved shirts, white shorts, blue stockings with red tops. **Change colours:** Yellow shirts, blue stripe, yellow shorts, blue stripe, yellow stockings.

BLACKBURN ROVERS 1988–89 LEAGUE RECORD

Match No.	Date	Venue	Opponents	Result	H/T Score	Lg. Pos.	Goalscorers	Attendance
1	Aug 27	A	Chelsea	W 2-1	1-1	—	Gayle 2 (1 pen)	8722
2	Sept 3	H	Oldham Ath	W 3-1	2-0	5	Garner 3	10,082
3	10	A	Stoke C	W 1-0	1-0	3	Hendry	8624
4	17	H	Swindon T	D 0-0	0-0	5		7622
5	20	A	Hull C	W 3-1	3-1	—	Hendry, Garner 2	6681
6	24	H	Birmingham C	W 3-0	3-0	1	Hendry, Garner 2	7562
7	Oct 1	A	Manchester C	L 0-1	0-0	2		22,111
8	5	A	Bradford C	D 1-1	1-0	—	Hendry	13,022
9	8	H	Crystal Palace	W 5-4	1-1	2	Gayle 2 (1 pen), Garner 2, Hendry	8025
10	15	H	Barnsley	W 2-1	1-1	1	Kennedy, Gayle (pen)	9316
11	22	A	Oxford U	D 1-1	1-0	1	Garner	6478
12	25	A	Sunderland	L 0-2	0-2	—		16,601
13	29	H	WBA	L 1-2	1-1	2	Hill	9503
14	Nov 5	A	Plymouth Arg	L 3-4	0-3	4	Reid, Garner, Kennedy	7823
15	12	H	Brighton & HA	W 2-1	2-1	2	Kennedy 2	6980
16	19	A	Walsall	W 2-1	1-0	3	Kennedy 2	5848
17	22	H	Shrewsbury	L 0-1	0-1	—		6895
18	26	H	Portsmouth	W 3-1	1-1	2	Hendry, Gayle 2	8141
19	Dec 3	A	Bournemouth	L 1-2	0-0	3	Garner	8418
20	10	H	Ipswich T	W 1-0	1-0	2	Gayle (pen)	7258
21	17	H	Watford	W 2-1	2-0	1	Hildersley, Gayle	8080
22	26	A	Leeds U	L 0-2	0-2	3		31,622
23	31	A	Leicester C	L 0-4	0-2	5		10,820
24	Jan 2	H	Stoke C	W 4-3	2-3	3	Atkins, Gayle (pen), Kennedy, Hildersley	11,654
25	14	A	Shrewsbury T	D 1-1	0-0	5	Hildersley	3879
26	21	H	Chelsea	D 1-1	0-1	5	Atkins	11,713
27	Feb 4	H	Bradford C	W 2-1	0-1	4	Gayle, Atkins	9571
28	11	A	Crystal Palace	D 2-2	1-1	4	Gayle, Miller	11,270
29	21	H	Oxford U	W 3-1	2-0	—	Hendry, Slatter (og), Diamond	5742
30	25	A	Barnsley	W 1-0	0-0	3	Garner	8777
31	28	H	Sunderland	D 2-2	0-2	—	Atkins, Gray (og)	8288
32	Mar 4	A	Brighton & HA	L 0-3	0-0	3		8075
33	11	H	Plymouth Arg	L 1-2	0-1	3	Hildersley	7462
34	15	A	WBA	L 0-2	0-1	—		12,821
35	18	H	Hull C	W 4-0	1-0	4	Garner, Gayle 2 (1 pen), Kennedy	5864
36	24	A	Oldham Ath	D 1-1	0-1	—	Garner	11,752
37	27	H	Leeds U	W 2-0	0-0	4	Kennedy, Gayle	11,533
38	Apr 1	A	Swindon T	D 1-1	0-0	4	Gayle	8220
39	4	A	Watford	D 2-2	0-0	—	Atkins, Gayle	8667
40	8	H	Leicester C	D 0-0	0-0	3		8080
41	15	H	Manchester C	W 4-0	2-0	3	Kennedy, Garner 3	16,927
42	22	A	Birmingham C	L 0-2	0-0	5		5813
43	29	A	Portsmouth	W 2-1	0-0	5	Gayle 2 (2 pens)	6057
44	May 1	H	Bournemouth	W 2-0	1-0	5	Atkins, Garner	9345
45	6	H	Walsall	W 3-0	0-0	3	Garner, Sellars 2	8236
46	13	A	Ipswich T	L 0-2	0-1	5		10,861

Final League Position: 5

GOALSCORERS

League (74): Garner 20, Gayle 19 (8 pens), Kennedy 10, Hendry 7, Atkins 6, Hildersley 4, Sellars 2, Diamond 1, Hill 1, Miller 1, Reid 1, own goals 2.
Littlewoods Cup (7): Garner 2, Sellars 2, Atkins 1, Gayle 1, own goal 1.
FA Cup (3): Finnigan 1, Garner 1, Hildersley 1.

Littlewoods Cup	Second Round	Brentford (h)	3-1
		(a)	3-4
	Third Round	Tottenham H (a)	0-0
		(h)	1-2
FA Cup	Third Round	Welling (a)	1-0
	Fourth Round	Sheffield W (h)	2-1
	Fifth Round	Brentford (h)	0-2

Gennoe	Atkins	Millar	Finnigan	Hendry	Mail	Miller	Hildersley	Gayle	Garner	Sellars	Ainscow	Dawson	Reid	Curry	Kennedy	Hill	O'Keefe	Sulley	Diamond	Byrne	Collier	May	*Match No.*
1	2	3	4*	5	6	7	8	9	10	11	12												1
1	2	3	4	5	6	7	8*	9	10	11	12												2
1	2	3	4	5	6	7	8*	9	10	11†	12	14											3
1	2	3	4	5	6	7		9	10	11			8										4
1	2	3	4	5	6	7		9	10	11			8										5
1	2	3	4	5	6	7		9*	10	11			8	12									6
1	2	3	4*	5	6	7†		9	10	11	12		8	14									7
1	2	3		5	6	7*		9	10	11	4		8		12								8
1	2	3		5	6			7	10	11	4		8		9								9
1	2	3		5	6	12		7*	10	11	4		8		9								10
1	2	3		5	6	12		7	10	11	4		8		9*								11
1	2	3		5	6	7*		9	10	11	4†	14	8	12									12
1	2	3			6	7		9	10	11	4*		8	12		5							13
1	2	3*			6			7	10	11	12	4	8	9†	14	5							14
1	2	3			6		4	7	10	11			8		9	5							15
1	2	3		5	6		4	7	10	11			8		9								16
1	2	3		5	6		4	7	10	11			8		9								17
1	2†	3		5	6	12	4	7	10	11		14	8		9*								18
1	2	3		5	6	12	8	7*	10	11			4		9								19
1	2			5	6		8	7	10	11		3	4		9								20
1	2	14		5	6	12	8	7	10†	11		3*	4		9								21
	2	3	14	5	6	12	8†	7	10	11			4		9*		1						22
	2	3	4	5	6†	9	8	7*	10	11	12					14	1						23
1	2		4	5	6*		8	7	10	11	12				9			3					24
1	2		4*		6	7	8		10	11	12				9†	5		3	14				25
1	2		4		6	12	8	7	10	11					9*	5		3					26
1	2		4	5	6	9	8	7	10	11								3					27
1	2		4	5	6	9	8	7	10*	11								3	12				28
1	2	3		5	6	9*	8	7	10	11			4						12				29
1	2	3		5	6		8	7	10*	11			4						12	9			30
1	2	3†	14	5	6		8	7	10	11			4						12	9*			31
1	2	3	14	5†			8	7	10*	11			4			6			12	9			32
1	2		14	5			8	7	12	11			4			6†		3	10*	9			33
1	2			5	6†	9	8*	7	10	11			4			14		3	12				34
1	2	8		5				7	10	11			4		9	6		3					35
1	2	8		5*			14	7	10	11†			4		9	6		3	12				36
1	2	8†		5		10	14	7		11			4		9*	6		3	12				37
1	2	8				10		7		11			4		9*	5		3	12			6	38
1	2	8			6	12		7	10*	11			4		9	5		3					39
1	2	8			6	12		7	10*	11			4		9	5		3					40
1	2	8		5	6			7	10	11			4		9			3					41
1	2	8		5	6			7	10	11			4		9			3					42
1	2	8		5	6	12		7	10	11			4		9*			3					43
1	2	8		5	6	9*		7	10	11			4	12				3					44
1	2	8		5	6	9		7*	10	11			4	12				3					45
	2	8		5	6	9		7	10	11	12		4					3*			1		46
43	46	37 + 1s	13 + 4s	38	40	21 + 10s	23 + 2s	45	43 + 1s	46	6 + 9s	3 + 3s	37	1 + 6s	23 + 2s	13 + 2s	2	19	1 + 10s	4	1	1	

BLACKBURN ROVERS

Player and Position	Ht	Wt	Birth Date	Birth Place	Source	Clubs	League App	League Gls
Goalkeepers								
Darren Collier	6 0	12 06	1 12 67	Stockton	Middlesbrough	Blackburn R	1	—
Terry Gennoe	6 2	13 03	16 3 53	Shrewsbury	Bricklayers Sp	Bury	3	—
						Blackburn R (loan)	—	—
						Leeds U (loan)	—	—
						Halifax T	78	—
						Southampton	36	—
						Everton (loan)	—	—
						Crystal Palace (loan	3	—
						Blackburn R	260	—
Vince O'Keefe*	6 2	13 00	2 4 57	Coleshill	Local	Birmingham C	—	—
						Peterborough U (loan)	—	—
						Walsall	—	—
					AP Leamington	Exeter C	53	—
						Torquay U	108	—
						Blackburn R	68	—
						Bury (loan)	2	—
						Blackpool (loan)	7	—
Defenders								
Mark Atkins	6 1	12 00	14 8 68	Doncaster	School	Scunthorpe U	48	2
						Blackburn R	46	6
Ally Dawson	5 10	11 10	25 2 58	Glasgow	School	Rangers	218	6
						Blackburn R	28	—
Tony Finnigan	6 0	12 00	17 10 62	Wimbledon	Fulham	Crystal Palace	105	10
						Blackburn R	17	—
Colin Hendry	6 1	12 02	7 12 65	Keith	Islavale	Dundee	41	2
						Blackburn R	95	22
Keith Hill	6 0	11 03	17 5 69	Bolton	Apprentice	Blackburn R	16	1
David Mail	5 11	11 12	12 9 62	Bristol	Apprentice	Aston Villa	—	—
						Blackburn R	181	2
David May	6 0	12 00	24 6 70	Oldham	Trainee	Blackburn R	1	—
John Millar	5 7	10 00	8 12 66	Lanark		Chelsea	11	—
						Northampton T	1	—
						(loan)	10	—
						Hamilton A (loan)	53	—
						Blackburn R		
Chris Sulley	5 8	10 00	3 12 59	Camberwell	Apprentice	Chelsea	—	—
						Bournemouth	206	3
						Dundee U	7	—
						Blackburn R	66	—
Midfield								
Alan Ainscow*	5 8	11 05	15 7 53	Bolton	Apprentice	Blackpool	192	28
						Birmingham C	108	16
						Everton	28	3
						Barnsley (loan)	2	—
					Eastern	Wolverhampton W	58	5
						Blackburn R	65	5
Lenny Johnrose	5 11	12 00	29 11 69	Preston	Trainee	Blackburn R	1	—
Nicky Reid	5 10	12 04	30 10 60	Ormston	Apprentice	Manchester C	217	2
						Blackburn R	81	2
Scott Sellars	5 7	9 10	27 11 65	Sheffield	Apprentice	Leeds U	76	12
						Blackburn R	120	13
Forwards								
Sean Curry*	5 8	10 11	13 11 66	Liverpool	Apprentice	Liverpool	—	—
						Blackburn R	38	6
Tony Diamond	5 10	10 04	23 8 68	Rochdale	Apprentice	Blackburn R	26	3
						Wigan Ath (loan)	6	3

BLACKBURN ROVERS

Foundation: It was in 1875 that some Public School old boys called a meeting at which the Blackburn Rovers club was formed and the colours blue and white adopted. The leading light was John Lewis, later to become a founder of the Lancashire FA, a famous referee who was in charge of two FA Cup Finals, and a vice-president of both the FA and the Football League.

Managers (and Secretary-managers)
Thomas Mitchell 1884–96*, J. Walmsley 1896–1903*, R. B. Middleton 1903–25, Jack Carr 1922–26 (TM under Middleton to 1925), Bob Crompton 1926–30 (Hon. TM), Arthur Barritt 1930–36 (had been Sec. from 1927), Reg Taylor 1936–38, Bob Crompton 1938–41, Eddie Hapgood 1944–47, Will Scott 1947, Jack Bruton 1947–49, Jackie Bestall 1949–53, Johnny Carey 1953–58, Dally Duncan 1958–60, Jack Marshall 1960–67, Eddie Quigley 1967–70, Johnny Carey 1970–71, Ken Furphy 1971–73, Gordon Lee 1974–75, Jim Smith 1975–78, Jim Iley 1978, John Pickering 1978–79, Howard Kendall 1979–81, Bobby Saxton 1981–86, Don Mackay 1987– .

Player and Position	*Ht*	*Wt*	*Birth Date*	*Birth Place*	*Source*	*Clubs*	*League App*	*League Gls*
Simon Garner	5 9	11 12	23 11 59	Boston	Apprentice	Blackburn R	404	144
Howard Gayle	5 10	10 09	18 5 58	Liverpool	Local	Liverpool	4	1
						Fulham (loan)	14	—
						Birmingham C (loan)	13	1
						Newcastle U (loan)	8	2
						Birmingham C	33	8
						Sunderland	48	4
						Stoke C	6	2
						Blackburn R	58	20
Ron Hildersley	5 4	9 02	6 4 65	Fife	Apprentice	Manchester C	1	—
						Chester (loan)	9	—
						Chester C	9	—
						Rochdale	16	—
						Preston NE	58	3
						Cambridge U (loan)	9	3
						Blackburn R	25	4
Andy Kennedy	6 1	12 00	8 10 64	Stirling	Sauchie Ath	Rangers	15	3
						Birmingham C	76	18
						Sheffield U (loan)	9	1
						Blackburn R	25	10
Ian Miller*	5 8	11 12	13 5 55	Perth		Bury	15	—
						Nottingham F	—	—
						Doncaster R	124	14
						Swindon T	127	9
						Blackburn R	268	16

Trainees
Bolton, Paul D; Cunningham, Malcolm; Dewhurst, Robert M; Donnelly, Darren C; Gillespie, Lee; Hodson, Steven F; Holmes, Stephen A; Latham, Ian D; Lee, Mark J; Mylott, Michael E; Skinner, Craig R; Smalley, Dylan T; Wilcox, Jason M.

Associated Schoolboys
Berry, James S; Burch, Damian P; Gaston, Gary M; Grunshaw, Steven J; Hassall, Andrew R; Isherwood, Mark K; Lindsay, Scott W; McGarry, Ian J; Metcalf, Joshua H; Moss, Lee; Peake, Warren C; Pickup, Jonathan J; Robinson, Mark A; Sweeney, Paul B.

BLACKPOOL 1988–89 *Back row (left to right):* Mike Lester, Ian Gore, Shaun Elliott, Colin Methven, Simon Rooney, Dave Burgess. *Centre row:* Bob Ward, John Deary, Steve Morgan, Richard Powell, Keith Walwyn, Barry Siddall, Tony Cunningham, Mark Bradshaw, Mike Docherty.
Front row: Russell Coughlin, Craig Madden, Mike Walsh, Sam Ellis (Manager), Mark Taylor, Mike Davies, Alan Hughes.

Division 3 **BLACKPOOL**

Bloomfield Rd Ground, Blackpool FY1 6JJ. Telephone Blackpool (0253) 404331.

Ground capacity: 12,696.

Record attendance: 38,098 v Wolverhampton W, Division 1, 17 Sept. 1955.

Record receipts: 35,474.18 v Manchester C, FA Cup 3rd rd, 7 February, 1983.

Pitch measurements: 111yd × 73yd.

President: C. A. Sagar BEM.

Chairman: K. Chadwick LLB. ***Vice Chairman:*** G. Bloor.

Managing Director:

Secretary: David Johnson.

Directors: M. H. Melling, T, White, J. Wilde MBE, O. Oyston, J. Allitt, J. Crowther LLB. Mrs. V. Oyston.

Manager: Jimmy Mullen. ***General Manager:*** F. McGrath.

Commercial Manager: Geoffrey Warburton.

Coach: ***Physio:*** Stephen Redmond.

Year Formed: 1887. Turned Professional: 1887. ***Ltd Co.:*** 1896.

Previous Grounds: 1887, Raikes Hall Gardens; 1897, Athletic Grounds; 1899, Raikes Hall Gardens; 1899, Bloomfield Road.

Previous Name: 'South Shore' combined with Blackpool in 1899, twelve years after the latter had been formed on the breaking up of the old 'Blackpool St John's' club.

Club Nickname: 'The Seasiders'.

Record League Victory: 7-0 v Preston NE (away), Division 1, 1 May 1948 – Robinson; Shimwell, Crosland; Buchan, Hayward, Kelly; Hobson, Munro (1), McIntosh (5), McCall, Rickett (1).

Record Cup Victory: 7-1 v Charlton Ath, League Cup, 2nd rd, 25 September 1963 – Harvey; Armfield, Martin; Crawford, Gratrix, Cranston; Lea, Ball (1), Charnley (4), Durie (1), Oakes (1).

Record Defeat: 1-10 v Small Heath, Division 2, 2 March, 1901 and v Huddersfield T, Division 1, 13 December, 1930.

Most League Points (2 for a win): 58, Division 2, 1929–30.

Most League Points (3 for a win): 86, Division 4, 1984–85.

Most League Goals: 98, Division 2, 1929–30.

Highest League Scorer in Season: Jimmy Hampson, 45, Division 2, 1929–30.

Most League Goals in Total Aggregate: Jimmy Hampson, 247, 1927–38.

Most Capped Player: Jimmy Armfield, 43, England.

Most League Appearances: Jimmy Armfield, 568, 1952–71.

Record Transfer Fee Received: £330,000 from Leeds U for Paul Hart, March 1978.

Record Transfer Fee Paid: £116,666 to Sunderland for Jack Ashurst, October 1979.

Football League Record: 1896 Elected to Division 2; 1899 Failed Re-election; 1900 Re-elected; 1900–20 Division 2; 1930–33 Division 1; 1933–37 Division 2; 1937–67 Division 1; 1967–70 Division 2; 1970–71 Division 1; 1971–78 Division 2; 1978–81 Division 3; 1981–85 Division 4; 1985– Division 3.

Honours: *Football League:* Division 1 – Runners-up 1955–56; Division 2 Champions 1929–30; Runners-up 1936–37, 1969–70; Division 4 – Runners-up 1984–85. *FA Cup:* Winners 1953; Runners-up1948, 1951. *Football League Cup:* Semi-final 1962. *Anglo-Italian Cup:* Winners 1971; Runners-up 1972.

Colours: Tangerine shirts with white trim, tangerine shorts, tangerine stockings with white tops. **Change colours:** All blue.

BLACKPOOL 1988–89 LEAGUE RECORD

Match No.	Date	Venue	Opponents	Result	H/T Score	Lg. Pos.	Goalscorers	Attendance
1	Aug 27	A	Chester C	D 1-1	0-1	—	Cunningham	3496
2	Sept 3	H	Notts Co	L 0-1	0-0	20		4669
3	10	A	Preston NE	L 0-1	0-0	22		8779
4	17	H	Mansfield T	D 1-1	0-1	22	Garner	4012
5	20	H	Bristol C	D 2-2	1-2	—	Davies, Taylor	3412
6	24	A	Chesterfield	W 2-0	0-0	17	Garner, Taylor	2128
7	30	A	Wigan Ath	L 1-2	0-1	—	Taylor	4141
8	Oct 4	H	Northampton T	W 3-1	1-0	—	Thomas (og), Thompson, Deary	3034
9	8	A	Bolton W	D 2-2	1-1	18	Cunningham, Morgan	7106
10	15	H	Sheffield U	L 1-2	1-1	18	Coughlin (pen)	8471
11	22	H	Port Vale	W 3-2	1-2	16	Cunningham, Madden, Coughlin (pen)	7045
12	25	A	Wolverhampton W	L 1-2	0-1	—	Morgan	12,104
13	29	H	Cardiff C	W 1-0	0-0	16	Garner	3849
14	Nov 5	A	Fulham	D 1-1	0-0	16	Garner	4760
15	8	A	Gillingham	L 0-1	0-1	—		3541
16	12	H	Aldershot	W 4-0	2-0	15	Garner 2, Coughlin (pen), Deary	2690
17	26	H	Swansea C	D 0-0	0-0	16		3443
18	Dec 3	A	Huddersfield T	D 1-1	0-0	16	Cunningham	5738
19	17	H	Bristol R	D 1-1	0-0	16	Garner	3240
20	26	A	Brentford	L 0-1	0-0	17		6021
21	30	A	Reading	L 1-2	1-2	—	Cunningham	5554
22	Jan 2	H	Bury	D 2-2	1-0	17	Cunningham, Coughlin (pen)	4199
23	14	A	Notts Co	D 1-1	1-0	17	Morgan	4748
24	21	H	Preston NE	W 1-0	0-0	16	Thompson	8951
25	28	A	Mansfield T	W 1-0	0-0	15	Madden	2738
26	Feb 4	H	Wigan Ath	W 2-0	0-0	12	Deary 2	4221
27	11	A	Northampton T	L 2-4	1-2	15	Thompson 2	3303
28	18	H	Bolton W	W 2-0	0-0	11	Cunningham, Thompson	5552
29	25	A	Sheffield U	L 1-4	0-3	13	Garner	11,017
30	28	H	Wolverhampton W	L 0-2	0-0	—		6482
31	Mar 4	A	Port Vale	L 0-1	0-1	17		6306
32	11	H	Fulham	L 0-1	0-0	18		3014
33	18	H	Chester C	D 1-1	0-0	19	Deary	2795
34	25	A	Bury	D 0-0	0-0	19		3717
35	27	H	Brentford	L 0-3	0-0	19		3053
36	Apr 1	A	Bristol R	L 0-1	0-0	20		5355
37	4	A	Southend U	L 1-2	1-1	—	Methven	2795
38	8	H	Reading	L 2-4	0-1	21	Garner, Davies	2792
39	15	A	Bristol C	W 2-1	0-1	21	Walwyn 2	5090
40	22	H	Chesterfield	L 1-2	0-0	22	Garner	3221
41	29	A	Aldershot	L 0-1	0-1	22		1763
42	May 1	H	Gillingham	W 4-1	1-1	22	Walwyn, Matthews, O'Shea (og), Garner (pen)	2152
43	6	H	Huddersfield T	W 2-1	1-0	22	Thompson, Madden	4070
44	9	H	Southend U	W 3-2	3-0	—	Thompson 2, Madden	3999
45	13	A	Swansea C	W 2-1	1-1	19	Coughlin, Davies (og)	3494
46	16	A	Cardiff C	D 0-0	0-0	—		3246

Final League Position: 19

GOALSCORERS

League (56): Garner 11 (1 pen), Thompson 8, Cunningham 7, Coughlin 5 (4 pens), Deary 5, Madden 4, Morgan 3, Taylor 3, Walwyn 3, Davies 2, Matthews 1, Methven 1, own goals 3.
Littlewoods Cup (7): Garner 2, Coughlin 1, Cunningham 1, Deary 1, Morgan 1, Taylor 1 (pen).
FA Cup (5): Cunningham 2, Garner 2, Deary 1.

Littlewoods Cup	First Round	Carlisle U (a)	1-1
		(h)	3-0
	Second Round	Sheffield W (h)	2-0
		(a)	1-3
	Third Round	Tranmere R (a)	0-1
FA Cup	First Round	Scunthorpe U (h)	2-1
	Second Round	Bury (h)	3-0
	Third Round	Bournemouth (h)	0-1

Siddall	Gore	Burgess	Deary	Methven	Elliott	Davies	Cunningham	Garner	Coughlin	Wright	Walwyn	Morgan	Thompson	Taylor	Matthews	Madden	Kelly	Walsh	O'Keefe	Rooney	*Match No.*
1	2	3	4	5	6	7	8	9*	10	11	12										1
1	2†	3	4	5	6	7	8	9*	10		12	11	14								2
1		2	4	5*	6	7	8	9	10			3	12	11							3
1		2	4	5	6	7	8	9	10†		12	3*	14	11							4
1		2	4	5	6	7	8*	9	10†		12	3	14	11							5
1		2	4	5	6	7	8	9	10		14	3*	12	11†							6
1		2	4	5	6		8	9	10		7*	3		11	12						7
1		2	4	5	6†		8	9	10	11*		3	14		7	12					8
	6	2	4	5			8	9	10			3	11*		7	12	1				9
	6	2	4	5			8	9	10		7	3	11*			12	1				10
	14	2	4	5†	6		8	9	10			3	11		7*	12	1				11
	11	2	4	12	6		8	9	10†			3	14		7*	5	1				12
	7	2	4	5	6		8	9	10		12	3				11*	1				13
1	7	2	4	5	6		8	9	10			3	11								14
1	7	2	4	5	6		8	9	10		12	3†	11*	14							15
1		2	4	5*	6	7	8	9	10	14	12	3		11†							16
1		2	4*	5	6		8	9	10			3		11†	14	12		7			17
1		2	4	5	6		8	9	10			3	14	11†		12		7*			18
1		2	4	5	6	12	8	9	10			3*	11			7					19
1		2	4	5	6	7	8	9	10		12	3†				11*		14			20
1		2		5	6	7	8	9	10	11*	12	3						4			21
1		2	14	5	6	7	8	9	10	11*	12	3						4†			22
1	4	2		5	6	7	8	9	10		11	3									23
1	4	2	10	5*	6	7	8	9			12†	3	14			11					24
1	4	2	5		6	7	8	9				3	10			11					25
1	4	2	5		6	7*	8	9	12			3	10			11					26
1	4†	2	7	5			8	9	6		12	3	10			11*		14			27
	4†	2	7	5		14	8	9	6		12	3	10			11*			1		28
		2	7	5*	6	12	8	9	4		11	3	10†					14	1		29
		2	7	5*	6	11	8	9	4		12	3	10						1		30
		2	7	5*	6	11	8	9	4		12	3	10						1		31
		2	7	5	6	11		9	4	12	8	3	10*						1		32
		2	7	5	6	11		9	4		8	3	10						1		33
1	8	2	7	5	6	11*		9	4			3	12			10					34
1	8*	2	7	5	6	11			4			3	10		12	9					35
1	7*	2		5	6	12		9	4	11		3	10			8					36
1		2	4	5	6	7		9		11		3*	10			8				12	37
1		2	10	5	6	7		9	4	11		3*	12			8					38
1	10	2	4	5	6	7		9	8		12				3*	11					39
1	11	2			6	7		9	10	3	8	12	5*			4					40
1		2		5	6	7		9	10	11*	8†	3	4		12	14					41
1		2		5	6			9	10	11	8	3	4		7						42
1	14	2	12	5	6†				10*	11	8	3	4		7	9					43
1		2		5	6	12			10	11	8	3	4		7*	9					44
1		2		5					10	11	8	3	4		7	9		6			45
1		2			6			12	10	11	8*	3	4		7	9		5			46
35	19 + 2s	46	35 + 2s	41 + 1s	41	25 + 5s	31	41 + 1s	42 + 1s	14 + 2s	13 + 17s	43 + 1s	25 + 11s	8 + 1s	10 + 4s	20 + 7s	5	6 + 3s	6	— + 1s	

BLACKPOOL

Player and Position	Ht	Wt	Birth Date	Birth Place	Source	Clubs	League App	League Gls
Goalkeepers								
Richard Powell*	6 1	13 04	3 9 69	Chesterfield		Blackpool	14	—
Barry Siddall‡	6 1	14 02	12 9 54	Ellesmere Port	Apprentice	Bolton W	137	—
						Sunderland	167	—
						Darlington (loan)	8	—
						Port Vale	81	—
						Blackpool (loan)	7	—
						Stoke City	20	—
						Tranmere R (loan)	12	—
						Manchester C (loan)	6	—
						Blackpool	110	—
Defenders								
Dave Burgess	5 10	11 02	20 1 60	Liverpool	Local	Tranmere R	218	1
						Grimsby T	69	—
						Blackpool	46	—
Steve Burns			28 10 68	Salford	Local	Blackpool	—	—
Shaun Elliott	6 0	11 10	26 1 58	Haltwhistle	Apprentice	Sunderland	321	12
						Norwich C	31	2
						Blackpool	41	—
Neil Matthews	6 0	11 07	3 12 67	Manchester	Apprentice	Blackpool	64	1
Colin Methven‡	6 2	12 07	10 12 55	Kirkcaldy	Leven Royals	East Fife	144	14
						Wigan Ath	296	21
						Blackpool	128	8
Steve Morgan	5 11	13 00	19 9 68	Oldham	Apprentice	Blackpool	106	9
Mick Walsh‡	6 0	12 00	20 6 56	Manchester		Bolton W	177	4
						Everton	20	—
						Norwich C (loan)	5	—
						Burnley (loan)	3	—
					Ft Lauderdale	Manchester C	4	—
						Blackpool	153	5
Midfield								
Mark Bradshaw	5 10	11 05	7 6 69	Ashton	Trainee	Blackpool	20	—
Russell Coughlin	5 8	11 08	15 2 60	Swansea	Apprentice	Manchester C	—	—
						Blackburn R	24	—
						Carlisle U	130	13
						Plymouth Arg	131	18
						Blackpool	67	7
Michael Davies	5 8	10 00	19 1 66	Stretford	Apprentice	Blackpool	166	13
John Deary	5 10	11 11	18 10 62	Ormskirk	Apprentice	Blackpool	303	43
Ian Gore	5 11	12 04	10 1 68	Liverpool		Birmingham C	—	—
					Southport	Blackpool	21	—
Alan Hughes*			1 11 69	Bangor	Trainee	Blackpool	—	—
Mike Lester‡	5 10	11 07	4 8 54	Manchester	Apprentice	Oldham Ath	27	1
						Manchester C	2	—
					Washington D	Stockport Co (loan)	9	1
						Grimsby T	48	10
						Barnsley	64	11
						Exeter C	19	6
						Bradford C	49	2
						Scunthorpe U	106	9
						Hartlepool U (loan)	11	1
						Stockport Co	11	—
						Scarborough	—	—
					Ludvick FK	Blackpool	11	1
Simon Rooney	5 11	11 08	10 7 70	Manchester	Trainee	Blackpool	9	—
Alan Wright			28 9 71	Ashton Under Lyne		Blackpool	17	—

BLACKPOOL

Foundation: Old boys of St. John's School who had formed themselves into a football club decided to establish a club bearing the name of their town and Blackpool FC came into being at a meeting at the Stanley Arms Hotel in the summer of 1887. In their first season playing at Raikes Hall Gardens, the club won both the Lancashire Junior Cup and the Fylde Cup.

Managers (and Secretary-managers)
Tom Barcroft 1903–33* (Hon. Sec.), John Cox 1909–11, Bill Norman 1919–23, Maj. Frank Buckley 1923–27, Sid Beaumont 1927–28, Harry Evans 1928–33 (Hon. TM), Alex "Sandy" Macfarlane 1933–35, Joe Smith 1935–58, Ronnie Suart 1958–67, Stan Mortensen 1967–69, Les Shannon 1969–70, Bob Stokoe 1970–72, Harry Potts 1972–76, Allan Brown 1976–78, Bob Stokoe 1978–79, Stan Ternent 1979–80, Alan Ball 1980–81, Allan Brown 1981–82, Sam Ellis 1982–89, Jimmy Mullen 1989– .

Player and Position	Ht	Wt	Birth Date	Birth Place	Source	Clubs	League App	League Gls
Forwards								
Tony Cunningham	6 2	13 10	12 11 57	Jamaica	Stourbridge	Lincoln C	123	32
						Barnsley	42	11
						Sheffield W	28	5
						Manchester C	18	1
						Newcastle U	47	4
						Blackpool	71	17
Andy Garner	6 0	12 01	8 3 66	Chesterfield	Apprentice	Derby Co	71	17
						Blackpool	42	11
Craig Madden	5 8	11 08	25 9 58	Manchester	Northern Nomads	Bury	297	129
						WBA	12	3
						Blackpool	80	20
Mark Taylor	5 7	10 00	20 11 64	Hartlepool	Local	Hartlepool U	47	4
						Crewe Alex (loan)	3	—
						Blackpool	90	38
Chris Thompson	5 11	12 02	24 1 60	Walsall	Apprentice	Bolton W	73	18
						Lincoln C (loan)	6	—
						Blackburn R	85	24
						Wigan Ath	74	14
						Blackpool	36	8
Keith Walwyn‡	6 1	13 02	17 2 56	Jamaica	Winterton	Chesterfield	3	2
						York C	245	119
						Blackpool	69	16
Dean King‡			4 2 70	Darwen	Local	Blackpool	—	—

Trainees
Bailey, David J; Butcher, Jason J; Gouck, Andrew S; Kay, Dean W; Kellett, Shaun; McCarthy, Michael J.

****Non-Contract**
Dunn, Shaun; James, Ryan.

Associated Schoolboys
Barnes, Terry; Barr, Colin P; Evans, Craig; Horsfield, Damien J; Leach, Colin J; Leitch, Grant J; Marsh, Simon J; Mitchell, Neil; Murphy, James A; Murphy, Sean R; Murphy, Steven A; Murray, Mark; Pollitt, Neil J; Sinclair, Trevor L; Stoddard, John A.

BOLTON WANDERERS 1988–89 *Back row (left to right):* Ian Callaghan, Gary Henshaw, Paul Hughes, David Felgate, Julian Darby, Ian Stevens, Chris O'Brien.
Centre row: Phil Neal (Manager), Steve Carroll (Youth Coach), Nicky Brookman, Gary Brown, Stuart Storer, Trevor Morgan, Dave McKearney, Bob Savage, Jeff Chandler, Mick Brown (Coach), Phil Stock (Physiotherapist).
Front row: John Thomas, Steve Elliott, Phil Brown, Mark Came, Mark Winstanley, Dean Crombie, Barry Cowdrill, Steve Thompson.

Division 3 **BOLTON WANDERERS**

Burnden Park, Bolton BL3 2QR. Telephone Bolton (0204) 389200. Information Service: Bolton 21101. Commercial Dept. 0204 24518

Ground capacity: 29,000.

Record attendance: 69,912 v Manchester C, FA Cup 5th rd, 18 Feb, 1933.

Record receipts: £53,931 v Everton, League Cup semi-final, 2nd leg, 15 Feb, 1977.

Pitch measurements: 113yd × 76yd.

President: Nat Lofthouse.

Chairman: S. Jones.

Directors: P. A. Gartside, G. Ball, G. Hargreaves, G. Seymour, G. Warburton, W. B. Warburton.

Team Manager: Phil Neal. ***Coach:*** Mick Brown.

Secretary: Des McBain. ***Commercial Manager:***

Physio: E. Simpson.

Year Formed: 1874. ***Turned Professional:*** 1880. ***Ltd Co.:*** 1895.

Previous Grounds: Park Recreation Ground and Cockle's Field before moving to Pike's Lane ground 1881; Burnden Park 1895.

Previous Name: 1874–77, Christ Church FC; 1877 became Bolton Wanderers.

Club Nickname: 'The Trotters'.

Record League Victory: 8-0 v Barnsley, Division 2, 6 October 1934 – Jones; Smith, Finney; Goslin, Atkinson, George Taylor; George T. Taylor (2), Eastham, Milsom (1), Westwood (4), Cook. (1 og).

Record Cup Victory: 13-0 v Sheffield U, FA Cup 2nd rd, 1 February 1890 – Parkinson; Robinson (1), Jones; Bullough, Davenport, Roberts; Rushton, Brogan (3), Cassidy (5), McNee, Weir (4).

Record Defeat: 0-7 v Manchester C.., Division 1, 21 March, 1936.

Most League Points (2 for a win): 61, Division 3, 1972–73.

Most League Points (3 for a win): 78, Division 4, 1987–88.

Most League Goals: 96, Division 2, 1934–35.

Highest League Scorer in Season: Joe Smith, 38, Division 1, 1920-21.

Most League Goals in Total Aggregate: Nat Lofthouse, 225, 1946–61.

Most Capped Player: Nat Lofthouse, 33, England.

Most League Appearances: Eddie Hopkinson, 519, 1956–70.

Record Transfer Fee Received: £340,000 from Birmingham C for Neil Whatmore, August 1981.

Record Transfer Fee Paid: £350,000 to WBA for Len Cantello, May 1979.

Football League Record: 1888 Founder Member of the League; 1899–1900 Division 2; 1900–03 Division 1; 1903–05 Division 2; 1905–08 Division 1; 1908–09 Division 2; 1909–10 Division 1; 1910–11Division 2; 1911–33 Division 1; 1933–35 Division 2; 1935–64 Division 1; 1964–71 Division 2; 1971–73 Division 3; 1973–78 Division 2; 1978–80 Division 1; 1980–83 Division 2; 1983–87 Division 3; 1987–88 Division 4; 1988– Division 3.

Honours: *Football League:* Division 1 best season: 3rd, 1891–92, 1920–21, 1924–25. Division 2 – Champions 1908–09, 1977–78; Runners-up 1899–1900, 1904–05, 1910–11, 1934–35, Division 3 – Champions 1972–73. *FA Cup: Winners 1923, 1926, 1929, 1958; Runners-up 1894, 1904, 1953. Football League Cup:* Semi-final 1976–77.*Freight Rover Trophy:* Runners-up 1986. *Sherpa Van Trophy:* Winners 1989.

Colours: White shirts, navy blue shorts, white stockings. **Change colours:** Red shirts, white shorts, red stockings.

BOLTON WANDERERS 1988–89 LEAGUE RECORD

Match No.	Date		Venue	Opponents	Result		H/T Score	Lg. Pos.	Goalscorers	Attendance
1	Aug	27	A	Southend U	L	0-2	0-1	—		4075
2	Sept	3	H	Cardiff C	W	4-0	0-0	9	Thomas, Darby 2, Henshaw	4831
3		10	A	Reading	D	1-1	0-0	10	Thomas	4660
4		17	H	Bristol R	D	1-1	1-0	10	Brown	4821
5		20	H	Fulham	W	3-2	1-1	—	Savage, Thompson, Morgan	4239
6		24	A	Aldershot	W	3-0	1-0	5	Stevens 2, Brookman	2126
7	Oct	1	H	Sheffield U	W	2-0	1-0	3	Thompson 2 (1 pen)	9345
8		4	A	Swansea C	L	0-1	0-0	—		3283
9		8	H	Blackpool	D	2-2	1-1	4	Morgan, Thompson (pen)	7106
10		15	A	Port Vale	L	1-2	1-1	9	Brookman	7985
11		22	H	Wolverhampton W	L	1-2	1-0	14	Morgan	8174
12		25	A	Wigan Ath	D	1-1	0-0	—	Brookman	4438
13		29	H	Chesterfield	W	5-0	2-0	12	Morgan 2, Stevens, Brown 2	4757
14	Nov	5	A	Bristol C	D	1-1	0-1	12	Morgan	8807
15		8	A	Huddersfield T	W	1-0	0-0	—	Morgan	7802
16		12	H	Bury	L	2-4	0-2	12	Brown, Thompson	7897
17		26	H	Northampton T	W	2-1	0-1	9	Stevens, Brookman	4446
18	Dec	3	A	Brentford	L	0-3	0-1	12		4628
19		17	H	Chester C	L	0-1	0-0	13		4318
20		26	A	Preston NE	L	1-3	0-2	15	Savage	12,104
21		31	A	Notts Co	L	0-2	0-2	15		5097
22	Jan	2	H	Mansfield T	D	0-0	0-0	15		4935
23		6	H	Gillingham	W	2-1	1-0	—	Stevens, Thompson (pen)	4187
24		14	A	Cardiff C	L	0-1	0-0	15		4212
25		21	H	Reading	D	1-1	0-0	15	Henshaw	5172
26		28	A	Bristol R	L	0-2	0-1	16		5375
27	Feb	4	A	Sheffield U	L	0-1	0-0	18		11,162
28		11	H	Swansea C	W	1-0	0-0	17	Savage	1179
29		18	A	Blackpool	L	0-2	0-0	17		5552
30	Mar	4	A	Wolverhampton W	L	0-1	0-1	19		13,516
31		11	H	Bristol C	W	2-0	0-0	19	Darby 2	4423
32		14	A	Chesterfield	D	1-1	0-1	—	Thompson	2877
33		18	H	Southend U	D	0-0	0-0	17		3505
34		25	A	Mansfield T	D	1-1	1-1	18	Savage	3253
35		27	H	Preston NE	W	1-0	1-0	17	Thompson	10,281
36	Apr	1	A	Chester C	D	0-0	0-0	16		3225
37		4	A	Gillingham	W	1-0	1-0	—	Thomas	3096
38		8	H	Notts Co	D	3-3	0-3	16	Thomas, Thompson, Morgan	4521
39		15	A	Fulham	D	1-1	0-0	16	Morgan	4950
40		22	H	Aldershot	W	1-0	0-0	15	Savage	4407
41		25	H	Port Vale	D	1-1	1-0	—	Chandler	5296
42		29	A	Bury	D	0-0	0-0	14		4393
43	May	1	H	Huddersfield T	W	3-1	1-0	13	Chandler, Morgan, Thomas	5511
44		6	H	Brentford	W	4-2	3-2	10	Thomas 2, Savage, Darby	4627
45		9	H	Wigan Ath	D	1-1	1-0	10	Storer	6166
46		13	A	Northampton T	W	3-2	0-2	10	Thomas 2, Storer	3655

Final League Position: 10

GOALSCORERS

League (58): Morgan 10, Thomas 9, Thompson 9 (3 pens), Savage 6, Darby 5, Stevens 5, Brookman 4, Brown 4, Chandler 2, Henshaw 2, Storer 2.
Littlewoods Cup (2): Cowdrill 1, Darby 1.
FA Cup (4): Darby 1, Keeley 1, Stevens 1, Storer 1.

Littlewoods Cup	First Round	Chester C (h)	1-0
		(a)	1-3
FA Cup	First Round	Chesterfield (h)	0-0
		(a)	3-2
	Second Round	Port Vale (h)	1-2

Felgate	Brown	Cowdrill	Darby	Came	Winstanley	Brookman	Thompson	Stevens	Elliott	Savage	Henshaw	Thomas	Keeley	Crombie	Morgan	Storer	Neal	Chandler	Jemson	Barnes	Jeffrey	Match No.
1	2	3	4	5	6	7	8	9*	10	11	12											1
1	2	3	11	5	6	4	8		10		7	9										2
1	2	3	11		6		8				4	9	5	7	10							3
1	2	3	11		6		8		10*		4	9	5	14	12	7†						4
1	2	3	11		6		8	12		4	7	9*	5		10							5
1	2	3	11		6	12	8	10		4*	7		5		9							6
1	2		11		6		8	10		4	7		5	3	9							7
1	2		11		6	12	8	10		4	7*		5	3	9							8
1	2		11		6		8	10*		4	7	12	5	3	9							9
1	2		11		6	8				4	7	10	5	3	9							10
1	2		11		6	5	8	12		4	7	10*		3†	9		14					11
1	2		5		6	11	8	10		4	7			3	9							12
1	2	3	11		6†	7	8	10		4*			5	14	9	12						13
1	2	3	11		6	5	8	10		4*				7	9	12						14
1	2	3	11		6	5	8	10*		4				7	9	12						15
1	2	3	11		6†	5	8	10		4*				7	9	12	14					16
1	2	3	11		6	4	8	10			12			5	9	7*						17
1	2	3	11		6	4	8	10		12				5	9*	7†		14				18
1	2	3	11		6	10	8	12		4	7*		5		9							19
1	2	3	11		6	12	8			4	7*		5		9				10			20
1	2	3	11		6		8			4*			5		9	12		7	10			21
1	2	3	11		6		8	12		4†			5		9	7		14	10*			22
1	2	3	4		6		8	10*					5		9	7		11	12			23
1	2	3	4		6	14	8				12		5		9	7*		11	10†			24
1	2	3			6	4	8				7	10	5		9			11*		12		25
1	2	3			6	4		12		8	7†	10	5	14	9*					11		26
1	2	3	7		6	4				8		10	5		9		12			11*		27
1	2	3	11		6	7	8			4		10	5		9							28
1	2	3	11		6	7*	8			4		10	5		9	12						29
1	2	3	11		6	7	8			4†	12	9		5			14				10*	30
1	2	3	11		6	4*	8					9		5		12		7			10	31
1	2	3	11		6		8			4		9		5		7		12			10*	32
1	2	3	11		6	14	8			4†		9		5		7*		12			10	33
1	2	3	11		6		8			4		9		5	12			7			10*	34
1	2	3	11		6		8			4*		9†		5	14	12		7			10	35
1	2	3†	5		6		8			4	7	9			12		14	11			10*	36
1	2		11		6		8	10		4		9		5			3	7				37
1	2		5			11	8	10*		4		9		6	12	14	3†	7				38
1	2	3	11				8			4		9		5	10	12	6	7*				39
1	2	3	11		6		8			4		9		5	10†	12		7*			14	40
1	2	3	11		6		8			4		9		5	10			7				41
1	2	3	11		6		8			4		9†		5	10	12		7*			14	42
1	2	3	11		6		8			4		9		5	10			7				43
1	2	3	11		6		8			4		9		5	10	12		7*				44
1	2	3	11		6		8	12		4		9		5	10*	7						45
1	2	3	11		6		8			4	12	9		5*	10	7						46
46	46	38	44	2	44	20	43	15	3	37	16	28	20	28	34	10	3	16	4	2	7	
						+ 5s		+ 6s		+ 1s	+ 5s	+ 1s		+ 3s	+ 5s	+ 13s	+ 5s	+ 4s	+ 1s	+ 1s	+ 2s	

BOLTON WANDERERS

Player and Position	Ht	Wt	Birth Date	Birth Place	Source	Clubs	League App	League Gls
Goalkeepers								
David Felgate	6 2	13 10	4 3 60	Bl Ffestiniog	Blaenau	Bolton W	—	—
						Rochdale (loan)	35	—
						Bradford C (loan)	—	—
						Crewe Alex (loan)	14	—
						Rochdale (loan)	12	—
						Lincoln C	198	—
						Cardiff C (loan)	4	—
						Grimsby T (loan)	12	—
						Grimsby T	12	—
						Rotherham U (loan)	—	—
						Bolton W	127	—
Gareth Gray	6 0	11 02	24 2 70	Longridge	Darwen	Bolton W	—	—
Defenders								
Phil Brown	5 11	11 06	30 5 59	South Shields	Local	Hartlepool U	217	8
						Halifax T	135	19
						Bolton W	46	4
Mark Came	6 0	12 13	14 9 61	Exeter	Winsford U	Bolton W	146	7
Barry Cowdrill	5 11	11 04	3 1 57	Birmingham	Sutton Coldfield	WBA	131	—
						Rotherham U (loan)	2	—
						Bolton W	38	—
Dean Crombie	6 0	11 12	9 8 57	Lincoln	Ruston Sp	Lincoln C	33	—
						Grimsby T	320	3
						Reading (loan)	4	—
						Bolton W	55	—
Julian Darby	6 0	11 04	3 10 68	Bolton		Bolton W	109	7
Paul Hughes	5 9	11 06	19 12 68	Denton	Trainee	Bolton W	11	—
Glenn Keeley‡	6 2	12 12	1 9 54	Barking	Apprentice	Ipswich T	4	—
						Newcastle U	44	2
						Blackburn R	370	23
						Everton (loan)	1	—
						Oldham Ath	11	—
						Colchester U (loan)	4	—
						Bolton W	20	—
Phil Neal	5 11	12 02	20 2 51	Irchester	Apprentice	Northampton T	186	29
						Liverpool	455	41
						Bolton W	64	3
Chris O'Brien*	5 9	10 08	21 2 70	Manchester	Trainee	Bolton W	—	—
Mark Winstanley	6 1	12 04	22 1 68	St. Helens	Trainee	Bolton W	68	1
Midfield								
Nick Brookman	5 9	10 07	28 10 68	Manchester	Trainee	Bolton W	55	10
Gary Brown	5 10	11 02	3 1 69	Beverley	Blackburn R	Bolton W	—	—
Ian Callaghan*	5 7	10 11	5 8 69	Liverpool	Trainee	Bolton W	1	—
Gary Henshaw	5 9	11 08	18 2 65	Leeds	Apprentice	Grimsby T	50	9
						Bolton W	52	4
Bob Savage	5 7	11 01	8 1 60	Liverpool	Apprentice	Liverpool	—	—
						Wrexham (loan)	27	10
						Stoke C	7	—
						Bournemouth	82	18
						Bradford C	11	—
						Bolton W	77	11
Steve Thompson	5 11	11 10	2 11 64	Oldham	Apprentice	Bolton W	243	38
Forwards								
Peter Bell‡	5 7	11 13	23 12 65	Newcastle	Apprentice	Manchester C	—	—
						Bolton W	—	—

BOLTON WANDERERS

Foundation: In 1874 boys of Christ Church Sunday School, Blackburn Street, led by their master Thomas Ogden, established a football club which went under the name of the school and whose president was Vicar of Christ Church. Membership was 6d (2½p). When their president began to lay down too many rules about the use of church premises, the club broke away and formed Bolton Wanderers in 1877, holding their earliest meetings at the Gladstone Hotel.

Managers (and Secretary-managers)
Tom Rawthorne 1874–85*, J. J. Bentley 1885–86*, W. G. Struthers 1886–87*, Fitzroy Norris 1887*, J. J. Bentley 1887–95*, Harry Downs 1895–96*, Frank Brettell 1896–98*, John Somerville 1898–1910, Will Settle 1910–15, Tom Mather 1915–19, Charles Foweraker 1919–44, Walter Rowley 1944–50, Bill Ridding 1951–68, Nat Lofthouse 1968–70, Jimmy McIlroy 1970, Jimmy Meadows 1971, Nat Lofthouse 1971 (then admin. man. to 1972), Jimmy Armfield 1971–74, Ian Greaves 1974–80, Stan Anderson 1980–81, George Mulhall 1981–82, John McGovern 1982–85, Charlie Wright 1985, Phil Neal 1985– .

Player and Position	*Ht*	*Wt*	*Birth Date*	*Birth Place*	*Source*	*Clubs*	*League App*	*League Gls*
Jeff Chandler	5 7	10 01	19 6 59	Hammersmith	Apprentice	Blackpool	37	7
						Leeds U	26	2
						Bolton W	157	36
						Derby Co	46	10
						Mansfield T (loan)	6	—
						Bolton W	23	4
Mike Jeffrey	5 9	10 06	11 8 71	Liverpool	Trainee	Bolton W	9	–
David McKearney‡	5 10	11 02	20 6 68	Crosby		Bolton W	—	—
Trevor Morgan	6 1	13 01	30 9 56	Forest Gate	Leytonstone	Bournemouth	53	13
						Mansfield T	12	6
						Bournemouth	88	33
						Bristol C	32	8
						Exeter C	30	9
						Bristol R	55	24
						Bristol C	19	8
						Bolton W	77	17
Ian Stevens	5 09	12 00	21 10 66	Malta		Preston NE	11	2
						Stockport Co	2	—
					Lancaster C	Bolton W	38	7
Stuart Storer	5 11	11 08	16 1 67	Harborough		Mansfield T	1	—
						Birmingham C	8	—
						Everton	—	—
						Wigan Ath (loan)	12	—
						Bolton W	38	3
John Thomas	5 8	11 03	5 8 58	Wednesbury		Everton	—	—
						Tranmere R (loan)	11	2
						Halifax T (loan)	5	—
						Bolton W	22	6
						Chester	44	20
						Lincoln C	67	20
						Preston NE	78	38
						Bolton W	73	31

Trainees

Fisher, Neil J; Gaskell, Paul; Halligan, Patrick; Hart, Neil J; Hughes, Keiran M; Jackson, Malcom J; Mason, Darren J; Oliver, Darren; Roberts, David; Sharrock, Simon J; Spooner, Nicholas; Still, Kevin; Stubbs, Alan; Vain, Stephen J; Williams, Shane.

Associated Schoolboys

Bebe, Roberts E; Clark, Christopher; Cowley, Darren; Jones, Andrew; Leedham, Paul; Lewin, Craig; McKay, Andrew S; Mason, Andrew; Randles, Martin; Strange, Anthony M.

A.F.C. BOURNEMOUTH 1988–89 *Back row (left to right):* Brian Gant (Physiotherapist), Tony Pulis, Adrian Randall, Kevin Bond, Gerry Peyton, Trevor Aylott, John Williams, John Smeulders, Carl Richards, Paul Morrell, Mark Whitlock, Jimmy Gabriel (Assistant Manager).
Front row: Sean O'Driscoll, David Coleman, Denny Mundee, Richard Cooke, Mark Newson (Captain), Harry Redknapp (Manager), Shaun Close, Ian Bishop, Shaun Brooks, David Puckett, Mark O'Connor.

Division 2 AFC BOURNEMOUTH

Dean Court Ground, Bournemouth. Telephone Bournemouth (0202) 395381. Fax No: 0202 309797

Ground capacity: 12,708.

Record attendance: 28,799 v Manchester U, FA Cup 6th rd. 2nd March, 1957.

Record receipts: £33,723 v Manchester U, FA Cup 3rd. 7th Jan, 1984.

Pitch measurements: 112yd × 75yd.

Chairman: J. P. Nolan. ***Vice-Chairman:*** P. W. Hayward JP.

Managing Director: B. Tiler. ***Directors:*** E. G. Keep, W. Oakley, G. M. Hayward, B. E. Willis, C. W. Legg.

Secretary: Brian Tiler.

Manager: Harry Redknapp.

Coach: Terry Shanahan. ***Trainer:*** J. Kirk. ***Physio:*** B. Gant, MCSP, SRP, Dip RT.

Asst. Manager: Jimmy Gabriel.

Commercial Manager: B. Tiler.

Club Nickname: 'Cherries'.

Year Formed: 1899. ***Turned Professional:*** 1912. ***Ltd Co.:*** 1914.

Previous Names: Boscombe St Johns, 1890–99; Boscombe FC, 1899–1923; Bournemouth & Boscombe Ath FC, 1923–71.

Previous Grounds: 1899–1910. Castlemain Road, Pokesdown; 1910, Dean Court.

Record League Victory: 7-0 v Swindon T, Division 3 (S), 22 September 1956 – Godwin; Cunningham, Keetley; Clayton, Crosland, Rushworth; Siddall (1), Norris (2), Arnott (1), Newsham (2), Cutler (1). 10-0 win v Northampton T at start of 1939–40 expunged from the records on outbreak of war.

Record Cup Victory: 11-0 v Margate, FA Cup, 1st rd, 20 November 1971 – Davies; Machin (1), Kitchener, Benson, Jones, Powell, Cave (1), Boyer, MacDougall (9 incl. 1p), Miller, Scott (De Garis).

Record Defeat: 0-9 v Lincoln C. Division 3, 18 December, 1982.

Most League Points (2 for a win): 62, Division 3, 1971–72.

Most League Points (3 for a win): 97, Division 3, 1986–87.

Most League Goals: 88, Division 3 (S), 1956–57.

Highest League Scorer in Season: Ted MacDougall, 42, 1970–71.

Most League Goals in Total Aggregate: Ron Eyre, 202, 1924–33.

Most Capped Player: Colin Clarke, 6 (15), Northern Ireland.

Most League Appearances: Ray Bumstead, 412, 1958–70.

Record Transfer Fee Received: £350,000 from Southampton for Colin Clarke, June 1986.

Record Transfer Fee Paid: £110,000 to Swindon Town for Bobby Barnes, March 1989.

Football League Record: Elected to Division 3 (S), 1923. Remained a Third Division Club for record number of years until 1970; 1970–71 Division 4; 1971–75 Division 3; 1975–82 Division 4; 1982–87 Division 3; 1987– Division 2.

Honours: *Football League:* Division 3 – Champions 1986–87; Division 3(S) – Runners-up 1947–48. Promotion from Division 4 1970–71 (2nd), 1981–82 (4th). *FA Cup:* best season: 6th rd, 1956–57. *Football League Cup:* best season: 4th rd, 1962, 1964. *Associate Members' Cup:* Winners 1984.

Colours: All red. **Change colours:** All sky blue.

BOURNEMOUTH 1988–89 LEAGUE RECORD

Match No.	Date	Venue	Opponents	Result	H/T Score	Lg. Pos.	Goalscorers	Attendance
1	Aug 27	A	Sunderland	D 1-1	1-1	—	Close	17,998
2	Sept 3	H	Chelsea	W 1-0	0-0	11	Cooke	8763
3	10	A	Brighton & HA	W 2-1	2-0	8	Newson, Brooks	8247
4	17	H	Leeds U	D 0-0	0-0	7		7922
5	20	A	Swindon T	L 1-3	1-2	—	Bond	8055
6	24	H	Oxford U	W 2-1	1-0	7	Aylott, Newson	6532
7	Oct 1	A	Stoke C	L 1-2	0-1	10	Brooks	7485
8	5	A	WBA	D 0-0	0-0	—		7248
9	8	H	Birmingham C	L 0-1	0-1	15		6186
10	15	A	Portsmouth	L 1-2	0-1	18	Close	12,801
11	21	H	Shrewsbury T	L 0-1	0-1	—		5449
12	25	A	Oldham Ath	L 0-2	0-1	—		4518
13	29	H	Ipswich T	W 1-0	0-0	18	Bishop	6648
14	Nov 15	A	Bradford C	W 1-0	0-0	17	Brooks	9067
15	12	H	Crystal Palace	W 2-0	1-0	13	Aylott, O'Connor	8697
16	19	H	Manchester C	L 0-1	0-1	15		9874
17	26	A	Barnsley	L 2-5	0-2	19	Aylott, Blissett	4937
18	29	H	Hull C	W 5-1	0-0	—	Blissett 4, Aylott	5420
19	Dec 3	H	Blackburn R	W 2-1	0-0	8	Clarke, Blissett	8418
20	10	A	Plymouth Arg	D 1-1	0-0	11	Blissett	10,619
21	17	H	Walsall	W 2-1	1-0	8	Aylott, Blissett	6985
22	26	A	Leicester C	W 1-0	0-0	7	Clarke	13,896
23	31	A	Watford	L 0-1	0-0	9		14,006
24	Jan 2	H	Brighton & HA	W 2-1	0-1	6	Blissett, Newson	10,627
25	14	A	Hull C	L 0-4	0-3	10		5690
26	21	H	Sunderland	L 0-1	0-1	12		8992
27	Feb 4	H	WBA	W 2-1	1-1	11	Cooke, Coleman	11,571
28	11	A	Birmingham C	W 1-0	0-0	0	Newson	6444
29	25	H	Portsmouth	W 1-0	0-0	6	Newson	9995
30	28	H	Oldham Ath	D 2-2	1-1	—	Blissett 2	7783
31	Mar 4	A	Crystal Palace	W 3-2	2-0	5	Williams, O'Connor, Cooke	10,022
32	11	H	Bradford C	W 3-0	1-0	5	Blissett 2 (1 pen), Bishop	8122
33	14	A	Ipswich T	L 1-3	0-3	—	Blissett	10,747
34	18	H	Swindon T	L 2-3	0-2	8	Blissett, Newson	9752
35	25	A	Chelsea	L 0-2	0-0	9		22,467
36	27	H	Leicester C	W 2-1	2-0	6	Blissett, Newell(og)	8913
37	Apr 1	A	Leeds U	L 0-3	0-1	8		21,095
38	4	A	Walsall	D 1-1	1-1	—	Williams	3619
39	8	H	Watford	L 0-1	0-1	9		9766
40	11	A	Shrewsbury T	L 0-1	0-0	—		2457
41	15	H	Stoke City	L 0-1	0-0	12		6834
42	22	A	Oxford U	L 1-3	0-2	12	Aylott	5684
43	29	H	Barnsley	W 3-2	1-1	11	Blissett 2 (1 pen), Newson	5520
44	May 1	A	Blackburn R	L 0-2	0-1	12		9345
45	6	A	Manchester C	D 3-3	0-3	12	Shearer, Holmes, Blissett (pen)	30,564
46	13	H	Plymouth Arg	D 0-0	0-0	12		7230

Final League Position: 12

GOALSCORERS

League (53): Blissett 19 (3 pens), Newson 7, Aylott 6, Brooks 3, Cooke 3, Bishop 2, Clarke 2, Close 2, O'Connor 2, Williams 2, Bond 1, Coleman 1, Holmes 1, Shearer 1, own goal 1.
Littlewoods Cup (2): Aylott 1, Cooke 1.
FA Cup (8): Blissett 2 (1 pen), Aylott 1, Cooke 1, Morrell 1, Newson 1, own goals 2.

Littlewoods Cup	First Round	Bristol R (h)	1-0
		(a)	0-0
	Second Round	Coventry C (h)	0-4
		(a)	1-3
FA Cup	Third Round	Blackpool (a)	1-0
	Fourth Round	Hartlepool U (a)	1-1
		(h)	5-2
	Fifth Round	Manchester U (h)	1-1
		(a)	0-1

Peyton	Newson	Morrell	Bond	Williams	Whitlock	Cooke	Brooks	Aylott	Bishop	Close	O'Driscoll	Richards	O'Connor	Puckett	Pulis	Coleman	Mundee	Blissett	Clarke	Teale	Barnes	Smeulders	Shearer	Holmes	*Match No.*
1	2	3	4	5	6	7	8	9	10	11															1
1	2	3	4	5	6	7*	8	9	10		12	11													2
1	2	3	4	5	6		8	9	10			11	7												3
1	2	3	4	5	6		8	9	10			11	7												4
1	2	3	4	5	6*		8	9	10	14	12	11	7†												5
1	2	3	4	5	6		8	9	10	12		11*	7												6
1	2	3	4	5	6*		8	9	10	12		7	11												7
1	2	3	4	5	6		8	9	10*	14	12	7†	11												8
1		3	4	5	6	12	8		10	11*	2	7		9											9
1	2	3*	4	5†	6		8	9	10	11	7		14	12											10
1	2	3†	4		6*	11	12	9	10		7			8	5	14									11
1			4		6		8*	9†	10	11	2		7	12	5	3	14								12
1	2		4	5				9	10	11	8		7		6	3									13
1	2	3	4	5			8	9	10	11	6		7												14
1	2	3	4	5			8	9	10	11	6		7												15
1	2	3	4*	5		12	8	9	10	11	6		7												16
1	2	3	4	5	12		8*	9	10		6		7					11							17
1	2	3	4	5			8	9	10	12	6*		7					11							18
1	2	3	4	5			8	9*	10		6		7					11	12						19
1		3	4	5			6	9	10		2		7					11	8						20
1		3	4	5			6	9	10		2		7					11	8						21
1		3	4	5			6	9	10		2		7					11	8						22
1	2	3	4	5			8	9	10		6		7					11							23
1	2	3	4	5			8	9	10		6		7					11							24
1	2	3	4*	5		14	8†	9	10	12	6		7					11							25
1	2	3	4	5		14	8†	9	10	12	6		7*					11							26
1	2	3	4	5		7*		9	10		6					8		11		12					27
1	2	3		4		7		10	6		5					8		9		11					28
1	2	3		5		7			10	9	6		8					11		4					29
1	2	3		5		7			10	9	6		8					11		4					30
1	2	3		5		7			10	9	6		8					11		4					31
1	2	3		5		7		9*	10	12	6		8					11		4					32
1	2	3*		5		7†		9	10	12	6		8			14		11		4					33
1	2	3		5		7	12	9	10		6		8*					11		4					34
1	2	3		5			12	14	10	9†	6		8*					11		4	7				35
1	2	3		5				9	10		6				8			11		4	7				36
1	2	3		5				9	10		6*		12		8			11		4	7				37
1	2	3		5*			12	9	10		6				8			11		4	7				38
	2	3					8	9			6		10		5			11		4	7	1			39
		3					8	9			6		12		5	2*		11		4	7	1	10		40
1	2	3					12	9	10		6		14		5			11		4	7†		8*		41
	2	3					8	9	10		6				5			11		4	7	1			42
	2	3		5*			12	9	10		6							11		4	7	1		8	43
	2	3*					12		10	9	6					5		11		4	7	1		8	44
	2	3					8	9†	10	12	6					14		11		4		1	5	7*	45
	2	3					8		10		6						9	11		4		1	5	7	46
39	40	44	27	37	12 + 1s	11 + 4s	29 + 7s	39 + 1s	44	13 + 10s	38 + 3s	8	29 + 4s	2 + 2s	10	6 + 3s	1 + 1s	30	3 + 1s	19 + 1s	10	7	4	4	

BOURNEMOUTH

Player and Position	Ht	Wt	Birth Date	Birth Place	Source	Clubs	League App	League Gls
Goalkeepers								
Gerry Peyton	6 2	13 09	20 5 56	Birmingham	Atherstone T	Burnley	30	—
						Fulham	345	—
						Southend U (loan)	10	—
						Bournemouth	127	—
John Smeulders†	5 11	13 00	28 3 57	Hackney	Apprentice	Orient	—	—
						Bournemouth	14	—
					Trowbridge T	Bournemouth	75	—
						Torquay U	18	—
						Peterborough U (loan)	1	—
						Bournemouth	9	—
						Brentford	8	—
Defenders								
Kevin Bond	6 0	13 07	22 6 57	London	Apprentice	Bournemouth	—	—
						Norwich C	142	12
					Seattle S	Manchester C	110	11
						Southampton	140	6
						Bournemouth	27	1
Paul Morrell	5 11	13 05	23 3 61	Poole	Weymouth	Bournemouth	235	6
Mark Newson	5 10	12 06	7 12 60	Stepney	Apprentice	Charlton Ath	—	—
					Maidstone U	Bournemouth	161	22
Shaun Teale	6 0	13 07	10 3 64	Southport	Weymouth	Bournemouth	20	—
John Williams	6 1	13 12	3 10 60	Liverpool	Amateur	Tranmere R	173	13
						Port Vale	50	2
						Bournemouth	101	7
Midfield								
David Armstrong‡	5 8	11 05	26 12 54	Durham	Apprentice	Middlesbrough	359	59
						Southampton	222	59
						Bournemouth	9	2
Ian Bishop	5 9	10 06	29 5 65	Liverpool	Apprentice	Everton	1	—
						Crewe Alex (loan)	4	—
						Carlisle U	132	14
						Bournemouth	44	2
Shaun Brooks	5 7	11 00	9 10 62	London	Apprentice	Crystal Palace	54	4
						Orient	148	26
						Bournemouth	73	9
David Coleman	5 7	10 08	8 4 67	Salisbury		Bournemouth	16	1
						Colchester U (loan)	6	1
Sean O'Driscoll	5 8	11 03	1 7 57	Wolverhampton	Alvechurch	Fulham	148	13
						Bournemouth (loan)	19	1
						Bournemouth	216	15
Tony Pulis	5 10	11 08	16 1 58	Newport	Apprentice	Bristol R	85	3
					Happy Valley, HK	Bristol R	45	2
						Newport Co	77	—
						Bournemouth	74	3
Forwards								
Trevor Aylott	6 1	14 00	26 11 57	London	Apprentice	Chelsea	29	2
						QPR (loan)	—	–
						Barnsley	96	26
						Millwall	32	5
						Luton T	32	10
						Crystal Palace	53	12
						Barnsley (loan)	9	—
						Bournemouth	120	25
Bobby Barnes	5 7	10 05	17 12 62	Kingston	Apprentice	West Ham U	43	5
						Sounthorpe U (loan)	6	—
						Aldershot	49	26
						Swindon T	45	13
						Bournemouth	10	—

AFC BOURNEMOUTH

Foundation: There was a Bournemouth FC as early as 1875, but the present club arose out of the remnants of the Boscombe St John's club (formed 1890). The meeting at which Boscombe FC came into being was held at a house in Gladstone Road in 1899. They began by playing in the Boscombe and District Junior League.

Managers (and Secretary-managers)
Vincent Kitcher 1914–23*, Harry Kinghorn 1923–25, Leslie Knighton 1925–28, Frank Richards 1928–30, Billy Birrell 1930–35, Bob Crompton 1935–36, Charlie Bell 1936–39, Harry Kinghorn 1939–47, Harry Lowe 1947–50, Jack Bruton 1950–56, Fred Cox 1956–58, Don Welsh 1958–61, Bill McGarry 1961–63, Reg Flewin 1963–65, Fred Cox 1965–70, John Bond 1970–73, Trevor Hartley 1974–78, John Benson 1975–78, Alec Stock 1979–80, David Webb 1980–82, Don Megson 1983, Harry Redknapp 1983– .

Player and Position	*Ht*	*Wt*	*Birth Date*	*Birth Place*	*Source*	*Clubs*	*League App*	*League Gls*
Luther Blissett	5 11	12 00	1 2 58	Jamaica		Watford	246	95
						AC Milan	30	5
						Watford	127	44
						Bournemouth	30	19
Shaun Close	5 8	10 01	8 9 66	Islington	Trainee	Tottenham H	9	—
						Bournemouth	39	8
Brent Goulet‡	5 11	12 00	19 6 64	Tacoma	Portland	Bournemouth	6	—
						Crewe Alex (loan)	3	3
Matt Holmes			1 8 69	Luton		Bournemouth	4	1
						Cardiff C (loan)	1	—
Denny Mundee	5 10	11 00	10 10 68	Swindon	Apprentice	QPR	—	—
						Swindon T	—	—
						Bournemouth	2	—
Mark O'Connor	5 7	10 02	10 3 63	Rochdale	Apprentice	QPR	3	—
						Exeter C (loan)	38	1
						Bristol R	80	10
						Bournemouth	122	12
Peter Shearer	6 0	11 06	4 2 67	Birmingham	Apprentice	Birmingham C	4	—
						Rochdale	1	—
					Cheltenham T	Bournemouth	4	1

Trainees
Butchard, Ian J; Giddings, Dean; Hill, Richard J; Master, Neil B; Mitchell, Paul R; Morris, David K; Rowland, Keith; Spires, Justin J; Taylor, Thomas W.

****Non-Contract**
Smeulders, John.

Associated Schoolboys
Bax, Tobias J; Berry, Trevor J; Elliott, Steven M; Fudge, Paul A; Grace, Gary I; Gray, Andrew; Lovell, Matthew W; Smith, Paul.

BRADFORD CITY 1988–89 *Back row (left to right):* Mark Ellis, Greg Abbott, Micky Kennedy, Andy Thomas, Mark Leonard, Peter Litchfield, Ian Ormondroyd, Paul Tomlinson, Gavin Oliver, Ian Banks, Dave Evans, Lee Sinnott.
Front row: Karl Goddard, Leigh Palin, David Thompson (Financial Director), Jack Tordoff (Chairman), Lord Mayor, Terry Fountain (Vice Chairman), Terry Dolan (Manager), Stan Ternent (Assistant Manager), Brian Mitchell, Paul Jewell.

Division 2 **BRADFORD CITY**

Valley Parade Ground, Bradford BD8 7DY. Telephone Bradford (0274) 306062 (Office); (0274) 307050 (Ticket Office).

Ground capacity: 16,072.

Record attendance: 39,146 v Burnley, FA Cup 4th rd, 11 March, 1911.

Record receipts: £59,250 v Tottenham H, FA Cup 3rd rd, 7 January, 1989.

Pitch measurements: 110yd × 76yd.

Chairman: J. C. Tordoff. ***Vice-Chairman:*** J. T. Fountain.

Director: D. Thompson, FCA. (Finance Director). ***Associate Directors:*** W. McGrath, M. Smith, G. Lee, H. Williams. M. Scott, P. Brearley.

Manager: Terry Yorath.

Youth Coach: Arthur Graham. ***Physiotherapist:*** Brian Edwards. ***Coach:*** Norman Hunter.

Secretary: T. F. Newman. ***Commercial Manager:*** Tony Thornton.

Club Nickname: 'The Bantams'.

Year Formed: 1903. ***Turned Professional:*** 1903. ***Ltd Co.:*** 1908.

Record League Victory: 11-1 v Rotherham U, Division 3 (N), 25 September 1928 – Sherlaw; Russell, Watson; Burkinshaw (1), Summers, Bauld; Harvey (2), Edmunds (3), White (3), Cairns, Scriven (2).

Record Cup Victory: 11-3 v Walker Celtic, FA Cup, 1st rd (replay) – Parker; Rookes, McDermott; Murphy, Mackie, Moore; Bagley (1), Whittingham (1), Deakin (4 incl. 1p), Cooke (1), Bartholomew (4).

Record Defeat: 1-9 v Colchester U, Division 4, 30 December, 1961.

Most League Points (2 for a win): 63, Division 3 (N), 1928–29.

Most League Points (3 for a win): 94, Division 3, 1984–85.

Most League Goals: 128, Division 3 (N), 1928–29.

Highest League Scorer in Season: David Layne, 34, Division 4, 1961–62.

Most League Goals in Total Aggregate: Bobbby Campbell, 121, 1981–84, 1984–86.

Most Capped Player: Harry Hampton, 9, Northern Ireland.

Most League Appearances: Cec Podd, 502, 1970–84.

Record Transfer Fee Received: £850,000 from Everton for Stuart McCall, June 1988.

Record Transfer Fee Paid: £290,000 to Newcastle U for Peter Jackson, October 1988.

Football League Record: 1903 Elected to Division 2; 1908–22 Division 1; 1922–27 Division 2; 1972–29 Division 3 (N); 1929–37 Division 2; 1937–61 Division 3; 1961–69 Division 4; 1969–72 Division 3; 1972–77 Division 4; 1977–78 Division 3; 1978–82 Division 4; 1982–85 Division 3; 1985– Division 2.

Honours: *Football League:* Division 1 best season: 5th, 1910–11; Division 2 – Champions 1907–08; Division 3 – Champions 1984–85; Division 3 (N) – Champions 1928–29; Division 4 – Runners- up 1981–82. *FA Cup:* Winners 1911 (first holders of the present trophy). *Football League Cup* best season: 5th rd, 1965, 1989.

Colours: Claret and amber striped shirts, black shorts, claret stockings. **Change colours:** All white.

BRADFORD CITY 1988–89 LEAGUE RECORD

Match No.	Date	Venue	Opponents	Result	H/T Score	Lg. Pos.	Goalscorers	Attendance
1	Aug 27	A	Brighton & HA	W 3-1	1-1	—	Ormondroyd, Thomas, Banks	10,190
2	29	H	Stoke C	D 0-0	0-0	—		11,918
3	Sept 3	H	Shrewsbury T	W 1-0	1-0	3	Ormondroyd	9765
4	10	A	Sunderland	D 0-0	0-0	4		16,286
5	17	H	Oldham Ath	W 2-0	2-0	2	Thomas 2	12,325
6	20	A	Watford	L 0-2	0-0	—		12,296
7	24	A	Ipswich T	D 1-1	0-0	5	Mitchell	13,074
8	Oct 1	H	Portsmouth	W 2-1	2-1	4	Thomas (pen), Sinnott	11,208
9	5	H	Blackburn R	D 1-1	0-1	—	Thomas	13,022
10	8	A	Plymouth Arg	L 1-3	0-3	6	Jewell	6855
11	15	H	Crystal Palace	L 0-1	0-1	9		11,098
12	22	A	WBA	L 0-1	0-0	12		8989
13	26	H	Leeds U	D 1-1	0-1	—	Abbott (pen)	13,046
14	29	A	Oxford U	W 4-3	1-1	10	Leonard, Kennedy, Jackson, Palin	5303
15	Nov 5	H	Bournemouth	L 0-1	0-0	13		9067
16	12	A	Barnsley	D 0-0	0-0	12		8838
17	19	H	Chelsea	D 2-2	1-0	12	Ormondroyd 2	11,442
18	26	A	Leicester C	L 0-1	0-1	16		9533
19	Dec 3	H	Birmingham C	D 2-2	1-1	19	Leonard, Jewell	9503
20	10	A	Manchester C	L 0-4	0-1	20		20,129
21	17	H	Swindon T	D 2-2	1-2	18	Palin, Jewell	9462
22	26	A	Hull C	D 1-1	0-0	18	Palin (pen)	8791
23	31	A	Walsall	W 1-0	1-0	17	Leonard	5366
24	Jan 2	H	Sunderland	W 1-0	0-0	17	Leonard	12,186
25	14	A	Stoke C	L 1-2	1-2	18	Banks	9919
26	21	H	Brighton & HA	L 0-1	0-1	18		8183
27	Feb 4	A	Blackburn R	L 1-2	1-0	18	Abbott	9571
28	11	H	Plymouth Arg	D 1-1	0-1	19	Costello	8693
29	18	H	WBA	W 2-0	1-0	18	Abbott, Banks	11,047
30	25	A	Crystal Palace	L 0-2	0-1	18		7455
31	Mar 1	A	Leeds U	D 3-3	2-2	—	Jackson, Costello, Sinnott	33,325
32	4	H	Barnsley	L 1-2	0-1	21	Leonard	11,085
33	11	A	Bournemouth	L 0-3	0-1	21		8122
34	15	H	Oxford U	D 0-0	0-0	—		7553
35	18	H	Watford	W 2-1	0-0	19	Leonard, Abbott(pen)	10,003
36	25	A	Shrewsbury T	W 3-1	1-0	16	Quinn 2, Campbell	4575
37	27	H	Hull C	D 1-1	1-1	17	Quinn	11,802
38	Apr 1	A	Oldham Ath	D 1-1	0-0	16	Quinn	8589
39	4	A	Swindon T	L 0-1	0-1	—		6476
40	8	H	Walsall	W 3-1	1-1	18	Jewell, Tinnion(pen), Quinn	8763
41	15	H	Ipswich T	D 2-2	2-1	18	Oliver, Leonard	9691
42	22	A	Portsmouth	W 2-1	1-0	16	Palin, Quinn	6909
43	29	H	Leicester C	W 2-1	0-0	14	Jackson, Quinn	8703
44	May 1	A	Birmingham C	L 0-1	0-1	14		4735
45	6	A	Chelsea	L 1-3	0-1	14	Quinn	18,003
46	13	H	Manchester C	D 1-1	1-0	14	Ellis	12,479

Final League Position: 14

GOALSCORERS

League (52): Quinn 8, Leonard 7, Thomas 5 (1 pen), Abbott 4 (2 pens), Jewell 4, Ormondroyd 4, Palin 4 (1 pen), Banks 3, Jackson 3, Costello 2, Sinnott 2, Campbell 1, Ellis 1, Kennedy 1, Mitchell 1, Oliver 1, Tinnion 1 (pen).
Littlewoods Cup (8): Banks 3, Leonard 2, Jewell 1, Ormondroyd 1, Palin 1.
FA Cup (2): Leonard 1, Mitchell 1.

Littlewoods Cup	Second Round	Reading (a)	1-1
		(h)	2-1
	Third Round	Scunthorpe U (h)	1-1
		(a)	1-0
	Fourth Round	Everton (h)	3-1
	Fifth Round	Bristol C (h)	0-1
FA Cup	Third Round	Tottenham H (h)	1-0
	Fourth Round	Hull C (h)	1-2

Tomlinson	Mitchell	Goddard	Banks	Oliver	Evans, D	Thomas	Sinnott	Ormondroyd	Kennedy	Jewell	Leonard	Jackson	Abbott	Palin	Chapman	Litchfield	Costello	Evans, M	Graham	Tinnion	Quinn	Campbell	Ellis	Duxbury	Match No.
1	2	3	4	5	6	7	8	9	10	11*	12														1
1	2	3	4	5	6	7	8	9	10	11*	12														2
1	2	3	4	5	6	7*	8	9	10	11	12														3
1	2	3	4	5	6	7	8	9	10	11*	12														4
1	2		4	5	6	7	8	9	10		11	3*	12												5
1	2*		4	5	6	7	8	9	10	12	11	3													6
1	2		4	5	6	7	8	9			11	3	10*	12											7
1	2		4	5	6	7	8	9	10	12	11*	3													8
1	2		4	5	6*	7	8	9†	10	12	11	3	14												9
1	2	3	4	5		7*	8	9	10	11		6	12												10
1	2	3*	4		6	7†	8	9	10	11		5	12		14										11
1	2		4†	5	6		8	9	10*	12	11	3	7	14											12
	2			5	6		8	9	10	12	11	3	4		7*	1									13
	2	3			6	12		9*	10	7	11	5	4	8		1									14
	2		14	6		12	3	9	10	7*	11	5	4†	8		1									15
1	14	3	4	5		12	8	9	10		11	6*	2†	7											16
1	2	3	4*	5			8	9	10		11	6	12	7											17
1	2	3	4*	5		12	8	9	10		11	6		7											18
1	2		4*	5			8	9	10	12	11	6		7			3								19
1	2		4	5	3		8	9	10	12	11†	6*		7			14								20
1	2	3*	4	5	6		8	9	10	12	11			7											21
1	2	3*	4	5	6		8	9	10	12	11			7											22
1	2		4	5	6		8	9	10	12	11*	3		7											23
1	2		4		6		8	9	10*	12	11	5	3	7											24
1	2		4*	14	6		8	9	10	12	11	5	3†	7											25
1	2			3	6*	4	8		10	9	11	5		7			12								26
1	2	10†	14	3	6*	12	8			11	9	5	4	7											27
	2	10†	14	3*	6	7	8			11	9	5	4				12	1							28
1	2		11	3	6	7	8			10	9*	5	4				12								29
1	2		4	3	6†	7*	8		10	11	9	5					12		14						30
1	2	14	4	3		12	8		10	11	9	5		6†			7*								31
1	2			3†	14	12	8		10	11	9	5	4	6			7*								32
1	2	12			6*		8		10	11	9	5	4	7						3					33
1	2		12	5*	6		8		10	11	9		4	7						3					34
1	2	12	6*	5			8				9		4	7						3	10	11			35
1	2	11†		5			8			12	9	14	4	7						3	10	6*			36
1	2	11*		5			8			12	9		4	7						3	10	6			37
1	2	11*		5			8			12	9		4	7						3	10	6			38
1	2	11*		5			8			12	9		4	7						3	10	6			39
1	2			5	6		8			11	9		4							3	10	7			40
1	2			5	6		8			11*	9		4							3	10	7	12		41
	2			5*	6					8	9	12		4				1		3	10	7	11		42
	2	12			6					8	9	5		4		1				3	10	7	11*		43
		14			6	12	2			8	9	5		4		1				3	10	7*	11†		44
	2			5	6		8*			12	9		11	4				1		3	10	7			45
1	2				6						9	5	11	4						3	10	7*	8	12	46
38	44 + 1s	18 + 5s	26 + 4s	38 + 1s	33 + 1s	15 + 8s	42	25	30	22 + 17s	40 + 4s	30 + 2s	23 + 5s	28 + 2s	1 + 1s	5	3 + 5s	3	— + 1s	14	12	12	4 + 1s	— + 1s	

BRADFORD CITY

Player and Position	Ht	Wt	Birth Date	Birth Place	Source	Clubs	League App	League Gls
Goalkeepers								
Mark Evans	6 0	11 08	24 8 70	Leeds	Trainee	Bradford C	3	—
Peter Litchfield*	6 1	12 12	27 7 56	Manchester	Droylsden	Preston NE	107	—
						Bradford C	88	—
						Oldham Ath (loan)	3	—
Paul Tomlinson	6 2	12 10	22 2 64	Brierley Hill	Amateur	Sheffield U	37	—
						Birmingham C (loan)	11	—
						Bradford C	80	—
Defenders								
David Evans	5 11	12 05	20 5 58	West Bromwich	Apprentice	Aston Villa	2	—
						Halifax T	218	9
						Bradford C	199	3
Karl Goddard	5 9	10 10	29 12 67	Leeds	Apprentice	Manchester U	—	—
						Bradford C	72	—
Peter Jackson	6 1	12 06	6 4 61	Bradford	Apprentice	Bradford C	278	24
						Newcastle U	60	3
						Bradford C	32	3
Brian Mitchell	6 2	13 00	30 7 63	Stonehaven	King Street	Aberdeen	65	1
						Bradford C	103	7
Gavin Oliver	6 0	12 10	6 9 62	Felling	Apprentice	Sheffield W	20	—
						Tranmere R (loan)	17	1
						Brighton & HA (loan)	16	—
						Bradford C	149	2
Lee Sinnott	6 1	12 07	12 7 65	Aldridge	Apprentice	Walsall	40	2
						Watford	78	2
						Bradford C	84	3
Brian Tinnion	6 0	11 05	23 2 68	Newcastle	Apprentice	Newcastle U	32	2
						Bradford C	14	1
Midfield								
Greg Abbott	5 9	10 07	14 12 63	Coventry	Apprentice	Coventry C	—	—
						Bradford C	220	35
David Campbell	5 9	10 09	2 6 65	Eglington	Oxford BC (NI)	Nottingham F	41	3
						Notts Co (loan)	18	2
						Charlton Ath	30	1
						Plymouth Arg (loan)	1	—
						Bradford C	12	1
Gary Chapman	5 10	12 00	1 5 64	Leeds		Bradford C	2	—
Lee Duxbury	5 10	11 07	7 10 69	Skipton	Trainee	Bradford C	1	—
Jimmy Graham	5 11	11 00	15 11 68	Glasgow	Trainee	Bradford C	1	—
Leigh Palin	5 9	10 03	12 9 65	Worcester	Apprentice	Aston Villa	—	—
						Shrewsbury T (loan)	2	—
						Nottingham F	—	—
						Bradford C	71	10
Forwards								
Mike Allott*			26 12 69	Lower Agbrigg		Bradford C	—	—
Peter Costello	6 0	11 07	31 10 69	Halifax	Trainee	Bradford C	8	2
Mark Ellis	5 9	10 09	6 1 62	Bradford	Trinity Ath	Bradford C	212	30
Paul Jewell	5 8	10 08	28 9 64	Liverpool	Apprentice	Liverpool	—	—
						Wigan Ath	137	35
						Bradford C	39	4
Mark Leonard	5 11	11 10	27 9 62	St Helens	Witton A	Everton	—	—
						Tranmere R (loan)	7	—
						Crewe Alex	54	15
						Stockport Co	73	24
						Bradford C	96	20

BRADFORD CITY

Foundation: Bradford was a rugby stronghold around the turn of the century but after Manningham RFC held an archery contest to help them out of financial difficulties in 1903, they were persuaded to give up the handling code and turn to soccer. So they formed Bradford City and continued at Valley Parade. Recognising this as an opportunity of spreading the dribbling code in this part of Yorkshire, the Football League immediately accepted the new club's first application for membership of the Second Division.

Managers (and Secretary-managers)
Robert Campbell 1903–05, Peter O'Rourke 1905–21, David Menzies 1921–26, Colin Veitch 1926–28, Peter O'Rourke 1928–30, Jack Peart 1930–35, Dick Ray 1935–37, Fred Westgarth 1938–43, Bob Sharp 1943–46, Jack Barker 1946–47, John Milburn 1947–48, David Steele 1948–52, Albert Harris 1952, Ivor Powell 1952–55, Peter Jackson 1955–61, Bob Brocklebank 1961–64, Bill Harris 1965–66, Willie Watson 1966–69, Grenville Hair 1967–68, Jimmy Wheeler 1968–71, Bryan Edwards 1971–75, Bobby Kennedy 1975–78, John Napier 1978, George Mulhall 1978–81, Roy McFarland 1981–82, Trevor Cherry 1982–87, Terry Dolan 1987–89, Terry Yorath 1989– .

Player and Position	*Ht*	*Wt*	*Birth Date*	*Birth Place*	*Source*	*Clubs*	*League App*	*League Gls*
Jimmy Quinn	6 1	12 00	18 11 59	Belfast	Oswestry T	Swindon T	49	10
						Blackburn R	71	17
						Swindon T	64	30
						Leicester C	31	6
						Bradford C	12	8
Andy Thomas	6 0	10 10	16 12 62	Oxford	Apprentice	Oxford U	116	32
						Fulham (loan)	4	2
						Derby Co (loan)	1	—
						Newcastle U	31	6
						Bradford C	23	5
Robbie Whellans*	5 8	10 09	10 12 69	Harrogate	Trainee	Bradford C	—	—
						Hartlepool U (loan)	11	1

Trainees
Bairstow, Scott; Clapham, Lee A; Clarkson, Andrew P; Deery, Eamon C; Hobby, Paul D; Jules, Mark A; Lee, Christopher; Maloney, Kyle; Megson, Kevin C; Pattinson, Martin; Pedder, Craig A; Ryan, Jason; Shanks, Andrew I; Sykes, Darren M; Taylor, Craig; Wroe, Derek.

****Non-Contract**
Bryson, Leslie N.

Associated Schoolboys
Blackmore, Robert; Boardman, Stephen; Clegg, Russell J; Coy, Paul T; Crabtree, Anthony M; Cressey, Matthew A; Dover, Paul N; Gregory, Andrew E; Hillas, Martin P; Horrocks, Andrew L; Howe, Jeremy R; Hutton, Emmot J; Miller, Paul T; Smith, Darren P; Tomkinson, Alan P; Trees, James A.

BRENTFORD 1988–89 *Back row (left to right):* Colin Lee (Youth Development Officer), Roger Stanislaus, Jamie Bates, Keith Millen, Terry Evans, Tony Parks, Bob Booker, Gary Blissett, Paul Birch, Roger Joseph, Roy Clare (Physiotherapist).
Front row: Andy Feeley, Keith Jones, Allan Cockram, Steve Perryman (Manager), Phil Holder (Assistant Manager), Andy Sinton, Richard Cadette, Neil Smillie.

Division 3 BRENTFORD

Griffin Park, Braemar Rd, Brentford, Middlesex TW8 0NT. Telephone 01-847 2511. Commercial Dept: 01-560 6062, Press Office 01-574 3047, Clubcall 0898 12 11 08.

Ground capacity: 12,500.

Record attendance: 39,626 v Preston NE, FA Cup 6th rd, 5 March, 1938.

Record receipts: £55,002 v Liberpool, Milk Cup 2nd rd, 5 Oct, 1983.

Pitch measurements: 111yd × 74yd.

President: W. Wheatley. ***Life Vice-President:*** F. Edwards.

Chief Executive: K. A. Loring.

Chairman: M. M. Lange.

Vice-Chairman: E. J. Radley-Smith MS, FRCS, LRCP.

Directors: R. J. J. Blindell LLB, D. Tana, G. V. Potter.

Manager: Steve Perryman. ***Asst. Manager:*** Phil Holder.

Physiotherapist: Roy Clare.

Youth Development Manager: Colin Lee.

Community Liaison Officer: Martyn Spong.

Secretary: Polly Kates.

Press Officer/Programme Editor: Eric White (01-574 3047).

Year Formed: 1889. ***Turned Professional:*** 1899. ***Ltd Co.:*** 1901.

Club Nickname: 'The Bees'.

Previous Grounds: Clifden Road 1889–91; Benns Fields, Little Ealing 1891–95; Shotters Field 1895–98; Cross Road, S. Ealing 1898–1900; Boston Park 1900–04; Griffin Park 1904.

Record League Victory: 9-0 v Wrexham, Division 3, 15 October 1963 – Cakebread; Coote, Jones; Slater, Scott, Higginson; Summers (1), Brooks (2), McAdams (2), Ward (2), Hales (1). (1 og).

Record Cup Victory: 7-0 v Windsor & Eton (away), FA Cup, 1st rd, 20 November 1982 – Roche; Rowe, Harris (Booker), McNichol (1), Whitehead, Hurlock (2), Kamara, Bowles, Joseph (1), Mahoney (3), Roberts.

Record Defeat: 0-7 v Swansea T, Division 3 (S), 8 November, 1924 and v Walsall, Division 3 (S), 19 January, 1957.

Most League Points (2 for a win): 62, Division 3 (S), 1932–33 and Division 4, 1962–63.

Most League Points (3 for a win): 68, Division 3, 1981–82, 1988–89.

Most League Goals: 98, Division 4, 1962–63.

Highest League Scorer in Season: Jack Holliday, 38, Division 3 (S), 1932–33.

Most League Goals in Total Aggregate: Jim Towers, 153, 1954–61.

Most Capped Player: Dai Hopkins, 12, Wales.

Most League Appearances: Ken Coote, 514, 1949–64.

Record Transfer Fee Received: £350,000 from QPR for Andy Sinton, March 1989.

Record Transfer Fee Paid: £100,000 to Norwich C for Simon Ratcliffe, January 1989.

Football League Record: 1920 Original Member of Division 3; 1921–33 Division 3 (S); 1933–35 Division 2; 1935–47 Division 1; 1947–54 Division 2; 1954–62 Division 3(S); 1962–63 Division 4; 1963–66 Division 3; 1966–72 Division 4; 1972–73 Division 3; 1973–78 Division 4; 1978– Division 3.

Honours: *Football League:* Division 1 best season: 5th, 1935–36; Division 2 – Champions 1934–35; Division 3 (S) – Champions 1932–33; Runners-up 1929–30. 1957–58; Division 4 – Champions 1962–63. *FA Cup* best season: 6th rd, 1938, 1946, 1949, 1989. *Football League Cup* best season: 4th rd, 1982–83. *Freight Rover Trophy* – Runners-up 1985.

Colours: Red and white striped shirts, black shorts, red stockings with white tops. **Change colours:** All blue.

BRENTFORD 1988–89 LEAGUE RECORD

Match No.	Date	Venue	Opponents	Result	H/T Score	Lg. Pos.	Goalscorers	Attendance
1	Aug 27	H	Huddersfield T	W 1-0	0-0	—	Cockram	5632
2	Sept 3	A	Northampton T	L 0-1	0-1	14		4488
3	10	H	Wigan Ath	D 1-1	1-0	13	Blissett	4081
4	17	A	Swansea C	D 1-1	0-0	14	Millen	5015
5	21	A	Bristol R	W 2-1	0-0	—	Cadette 2	3836
6	24	H	Sheffield U	L 1-4	1-1	11	Sinton (pen)	6577
7	Oct 1	H	Gillingham	W 1-0	0-0	8	Sinton (pen)	4839
8	5	A	Chester C	L 2-3	2-3	—	Blissett, Cadette	2004
9	9	H	Southend U	W 4-0	0-0	—	Evans, Sinton 2, Cockram	5016
10	15	A	Bury	L 1-3	1-2	14	Cockram	2359
11	22	H	Preston NE	L 0-2	0-0	15		5584
12	25	A	Chesterfield	D 2-2	0-0	—	Cadette 2	1876
13	29	H	Port Vale	W 2-1	0-0	13	Jones, Holdsworth	5212
14	Nov 5	A	Reading	D 2-2	2-1	15	Phillips (og), Sinton (pen)	7974
15	8	H	Notts Co	W 2-1	1-0	—	Cadette 2	4013
16	12	A	Mansfield T	L 0-1	0-1	14		3181
17	25	A	Cardiff C	L 0-1	0-1	—		3405
18	Dec 3	H	Bolton W	W 3-0	1-0	14	Cadette 2, Evans	4628
19	18	A	Aldershot	D 0-0	0-0	—		4012
20	26	H	Blackpool	W 1-0	0-0	12	Sinton	6021
21	31	H	Wolverhampton W	D 2-2	1-1	12	Godfrey, Jones	8020
22	Jan 2	A	Fulham	D 3-3	2-2	12	Sinton, Godfrey, Cadette	8120
23	14	H	Northampton T	W 2-0	2-0	10	Cadette, Stanislaus	6043
24	21	A	Wigan Ath	D 1-1	1-1	10	Sinton	2514
25	Feb 4	A	Gillingham	D 0-0	0-0	11		4002
26	11	H	Chester C	L 0-1	0-1	12		5748
27	25	H	Bury	D 2-2	1-0	14	Godfrey, Blissett	6077
28	28	H	Chesterfield	W 1-0	0-0	—	Cadette	4192
29	Mar 4	A	Preston NE	L 3-5	2-2	13	Ratcliffe, Bates, Godfrey	8186
30	11	H	Reading	W 3-2	2-1	11	Millen, Evans, Sinton (pen)	6866
31	13	A	Port Vale	L 2-3	0-1	—	Godfrey, Millen	5577
32	24	H	Fulham	L 0-1	0-0	—		10,851
33	27	A	Blackpool	W 3-0	0-0	14	Godfrey, Cockram 2(1 pen)	3053
34	Apr 1	H	Aldershot	W 2-1	0-0	14	Jones, Sealy	5200
35	4	H	Bristol C	W 3-0	2-0	—	Sealy 2, Cockram(pen)	4627
36	8	A	Wolverhampton W	L 0-2	0-1	13		14,196
37	11	A	Bristol C	W 1-0	0-0	—	Evans	4339
38	15	H	Bristol R	W 2-1	0-1	8	Blissett, Smillie	7558
39	18	A	Southend U	D 1-1	0-0	—	Smillie	4119
40	22	A	Sheffield U	D 2-2	0-1	7	Sealy, Godfrey	12,613
41	25	A	Huddersfield T	W 2-1	0-0	—	Godfrey, Blissett	3538
42	29	H	Mansfield T	W 1-0	1-0	7	Cockram	5231
43	May 1	A	Notts Co	L 0-3	0-2	7		4989
44	6	A	Bolton W	L 2-4	2-3	9	Ansah 2	4627
45	9	H	Swansea C	D 1-1	0-1	9	Blissett	4415
46	13	H	Cardiff C	D 1-1	0-1	7	Evans	4865

Final League Position: 7

GOALSCORERS

League (66): Cadette 12, Sinton 9 (4 pens), Godfrey 8, Cockram 7 (2 pens), Blissett 6, Evans 5, Sealy 4, Jones 3, Millen 3, Ansah 2, Smillie 2, Bates 1, Holdsworth 1, Ratcliffe 1, Stanislaus 1, own goal 1.
Littlewoods Cup (8): Blissett 2, Cadette 2, Sinton 2, Jones 1, Stanislaus 1.
FA Cup (12): Blissett 4, Cockram 2, Jones 2, Cadette 1, Evans 1, Sinton 1, Smillie 1.

Littlewoods Cup	First Round	Fulham (a)	2-2
		(h)	1-0
	Second Round	Blackburn R (a)	1-3
		(h)	4-3

Parks	Feeley	Stanislaus	Millen	Evans	Cockram	Jones	Sinton	Cadette	Blissett	Smillie	Birch	Bates	Booker	Perryman	Smeulders	Holdsworth	Gayle	Pearce	Lee	Godfrey	Buttigieg	Roberts	Ratcliffe	Sealy	Ansah	Purdie	Driscoll	*Match No.*
1	2	3	4	5	6	7	8	9*	10	11	12																	1
1		3	4	5	6†	7	8	9*	10	11	12	2	14															2
1	2	3	4	5*	6	7	8	9	10	11		12																3
1		3	4	5		7	8	9	10	11		2	6*	12														4
1		3	4	5		7	8	9	10	11		2	6															5
1		3	4	5		7	8	9	10	11		2	6*	12														6
1	3		4	5	12	7	8	9	10	11		2	6*															7
1	3†	14	4	5	12	7	8	9	10	11		2	6*															8
	12	2*	4	5	6	7	8	9	10	11		3			1													9
	11	2*	4	5	6†	7	8	9	10			3	14		1	12												10
	2*	3	4			7	8	9				5	14	6†	1	10	12	11										11
	12		4	5*		7	8	9	10			3		6†	1	11		2	14									12
	6†	3	4	5		7	8	9	10			2		14	1	12				11*								13
	6	3	4	5		7	8	9	10*			2			1	12		11										14
	6	3		5		7	8	9*	10			2			1	12		11			4							15
	6	3		5*		7	8	9	10			2			1	12		11			4							16
	6	3	4	5	12	7	8	9	10			2*								14	11†	1						17
			4	5	2	7	8*	9	10	12								3		11	6	1						18
1		3	4	5	6	7	8	9		11							12			10*	2							19
1	2	3	4	5	6	7	8	9		11										10								20
1	2	3	4	5	6	7	8	9		11										10								21
1	2	3	4	5	6*	7	8	9		11										10	12							22
1	2	3	4	5	6*	7	8	9		11										10			12					23
1	2*	3	4	5	6	7	8	9	14	11										10†			12					24
1	2	3*	4	5	6		8	9	10	11								12					7					25
1	2*	3	4	5	6		8	9	10	11							12						7					26
	2*	3	4	5	14	7	8	9†	10			12								11		1	6					27
	2	3*	4	5	11	7	8	9				12								10		1	6					28
		3	4	5	11	7	8			12†		2						14		10	9*	1	6					29
1		3	4	5	12	7	8	9	10			2*								11			6					30
1	2	3	4	5	14	7	8	9†	10			12								11			6*					31
1	7	3*		5	6				10			2						9	4	11				8	12			32
1	2	3		5*	6	7			10			4						8		11†	12			9		14		33
1	2†	3		5	6	7			10	12		4								11*	14			8		9		34
1		3†		5	6	7			10	11		4						14		12	2			8		9*		35
1	14	3		5	6†	7			10	11		4								12	2			8		9*		36
1	2	3†		5	6	7			10	11		4						14		12				8		9*		37
1		3†		5	6	7			10	11		4						14		12	2			8		9*		38
1		3		5	6	7			10	11		4								9	2			8*	12			39
1		3	4	5	6	7			10	11		2								9				8				40
1		3	4	5	6†	7			10	11		2						14		9				8*	12			41
1	8	3	4	5	6	7			10	11†		2*						14		9	12							42
1	8	3	4	5	6	7†		9*				2						11		10	14				12			43
1	8*	9	4	5	6							2						3		11	7				10		12	44
1	8	9	4	5	6				10			2*						3		11	12			14	7†			45
1	7†	3	4	5	6			12	10			14								11	2			8	9*			46
33	30 + 3s	42 + 1s	36	45	31 + 6s	40	31	31 + 1s	35 + 1s	25 + 3s	— + 2s	31 + 5s	5 + 3s	2 + 3s	8	2 + 5s	— + 3s	11 + 7s	1 + 1s	24 + 5s	12 + 6s	5	7 + 2s	11 + 1s	3 + 4s	5 + 1s	— + 1s	

FA Cup			
	First Round	Halesowen (h)	2-0
	Second Round	Peterborough U (a)	0-0
		(h)	3-2
	Third Round	Walsall (a)	1-1
		(h)	1-0
	Fourth Round	Manchester C (h)	3-1
	Fifth Round	Blackburn R (a)	2-0
	Sixth Round	Liverpool (a)	0-4

BRENTFORD

Player and Position	Ht	Wt	Birth Date	Birth Place	Source	Clubs	League App	League Gls
Goalkeepers								
Tony Parks	5 11	10 08	26 1 63	Hackney	Apprentice	Tottenham H	37	—
						Oxford U (loan)	5	—
						Gillingham (loan)	2	—
						Brentford	33	—
Jeremy Roberts*	6 0	13 00	24 11 66	Middlesbrough	School	Hartlepool U	1	—
						Leicester C	3	—
						Darlington	29	—
						Brentford	5	—
Defenders								
Jamie Bates	6 1	12 12	24 2 68	London	Trainee	Brentford	83	3
John Buttigieg	6 0	11 3	5 10 63	Sliema	Sliema W	Brentford	18	—
Terry Evans	6 5	15 01	12 4 65	London	Hillingdon B.	Brentford	94	10
Marcus Gayle§			27 9 70	Hammersmith	Trainee	Brentford	3	—
Colin Lee*	6 1	12 10	12 6 56	Plymouth	Apprentice	Bristol C	—	—
						Hereford U (loan)	9	—
						Torquay U	35	14
						Tottenham H	62	18
						Chelsea	185	36
						Brentford	24	1
Keith Millen	6 2	12 04	26 9 66	Croydon	Juniors	Brentford	164	10
Graham Pearce*	5 9	11 00	8 7 59	Hammersmith	Barnet	Brighton & HA	88	2
						Gillingham	65	—
						Brentford	18	—
Steve Perryman†	5 8	10 10	21 12 51	Ealing	Apprentice	Tottenham H	655	31
						Oxford U	17	—
						Brentford	50	—
Simon Ratcliffe	5 11	11 09	8 2 67	Davyhulme	Apprentice	Manchester U	—	—
						Norwich C	9	—
						Brentford	9	1
Roger Stanislaus	5 9	12 11	2 11 68	Hammersmith	Trainee	Arsenal	—	—
						Brentford	80	3
Midfield								
Paul Buckle§			16 12 70	Hatfield	Trainee	Brentford	1	—
Allan Cockram	5 8	10 08	8 10 63	Kensington	Local	Tottenham H	2	—
						Bristol R	1	—
					St Albans	Brentford	44	9
Andy Driscoll§			21 10 71	Staines	Trainee	Brentford	1	—
Andy Feeley	5 10	12 07	30 9 61	Hereford	Apprentice	Hereford U	51	3
						Chelsea (loan)	—	—
					Trowbridge T	Leicester C	76	—
						Brentford	67	—
Matthew Howard§			5 12 70	Watford	Trainee	Brentford	1	—
Keith Jones	5 9	10 11	14 10 65	Dulwich	Apprentice	Chelsea	52	7
						Brentford	76	4
Neil Smillie	5 6	10 07	19 7 58	Barnsley	Apprentice	C Palace	83	7
						Brentford (loan)	3	—
						Brighton & HA	75	2
						Watford	16	3
						Reading	39	—
						Brentford	28	2
Wayne Turner‡	5 9	11 05	9 3 61	Luton	Apprentice	Luton T	84	2
						Lincoln C (loan)	16	—
						Coventry C	15	1
						Brentford	56	2
Forwards								
Andy Ansah	5 10	11 01	19 3 69	Lewisham		Crystal Palace	—	—
						Brentford	7	2

BRENTFORD

Foundation: Formed as a small amateur concern in 1889 they were very successful in local circles. They won the championship of the West London Alliance in 1893 and a year later the West Middlesex Junior Cup before carrying off the Senior Cup in 1895. After winning both the London Senior Amateur Cup and the Middlesex Senior Cup in 1898 they were admitted to the Second Division of the Southern League.

Managers (and Secretary-managers)
Will Lewis 1900–03*, Dick Molyneux 1903–06, W. G. Brown 1906–08, Fred Halliday 1908–26 (only secretary to 1922), Ephraim Rhodes 1912–15, Archie Mitchell 1921–22, Harry Curtis 1926–49, Jackie Gibbons 1949–52, Jimmy Bain 1952–53, Tommy Lawton 1953, Bill Dodgin Snr 1953–57, Malcolm Macdonald 1957–65, Tommy Cavanagh 1965–66, Billy Gray 1966–67, Jimmy Sirrel 1967–69, Frank Blunstone 1969–73, Mike Everitt 1973–75, John Docherty 1975–76, Bill Dodgin Jnr 1976–80, Fred Callaghan 1980–84, Frank McLintock 1984–87, Steve Perryman 1987– .

Player and Position	*Ht*	*Wt*	*Birth Date*	*Birth Place*	*Source*	*Clubs*	*League App*	*League Gls*
Paul Birch	6 0	12 05	3 12 68	Reading	Trainee	Arsenal	—	—
						Portsmouth	—	—
						Brentford	18	2
Gary Blissett	6 1	11 13	29 6 64	Manchester	Altrincham	Crewe Alex	122	39
						Brentford	87	20
Richard Cadette	5 8	11 07	21 3 65	Hammersmith	Wembley	Orient	21	4
						Southend U	90	48
						Sheffield U	28	7
						Brentford	32	12
Kevin Godfrey	5 10	10 11	24 2 60	Kennington	Apprentice	Leyton Orient	285	65
						Plymouth Arg (loan)	7	1
						Brentford	29	8
Jon Purdie*	5 9	11 12	22 2 67	Corby	Apprentice	Arsenal	—	—
						Wolverhampton W	89	12
						Cambridge U (loan)	7	2
						Oxford U	11	—
						Brentford	6	—
Tony Sealy†	5 8	11 08	7 5 59	London	Apprentice	Southampton	7	—
						Crystal Palace	24	5
						Port Vale (loan)	17	6
						QPR	63	18
						Port Vale (loan)	6	4
						Fulham (loan)	5	1
						Fulham	20	9
						Leicester C	39	7
						Bournemouth (loan)	13	2
					Braga	Brentford	12	4

Trainees
Bayes, Ashley J; Buckle, Paul J; Cousins, Jason; Cronk, Brian J; Dale, Paul M; Driscoll, Andrew; Fenton, Jason; Gayle, Marcus A; Haag, Kelly J; Howard, Matthew J; Jones, Colin A; Larkin, Robert P; Moabi, Abraham K; Moore, Fergus; Moyse, Jonathan P; Peter, Robert A.G; Ryder, Nicholas J; Sim, Peter J; Small, Steven E; Tuckerman, Spencer J.

****Non-Contract**
Perryman, Stephen J; Sealy, Anthony J.

Associated Schoolboys
Bone, Guy; Bradley, Jason P; Connor, James; Dixon, Keiran; Ivers, Mark A; Lewis, Junior; Macklin-Day, Robert L; Swift, Darren M; Townend, Dean P; Turner, Mark; Tweed, Darryl A; Wadge, Lee R.

BRIGHTON & HOVE ALBION 1988–89 *Back row (left to right):* Mark Leather (Physiotherapist), Jack Dineen, Geoff Cooper, Robert Isaac, Doug Rougvie, Gerry Armstrong, Grant Horscroft, Gary Chivers, Roy Hales, Mike Trusson, Ted Streeter (Youth Development Officer).
Centre row: Barry Lloyd (Manager), Paul Wood, Kevan Brown, Perry Digweed, Ian Chapman, John Keeley, John Crumplin, David Gipp, Martin Hinshelwood (Coach).
Front row: Alan Curbishley, Keith Dublin, Kevin Bremner, Steve Gatting, Garry Nelson, Dean Wilkins, Steve Penney, Adrian Owers.

Division 2 BRIGHTON & HOVE ALBION

Goldstone Ground, Old Shoreham Rd, Hove, Sussex BN3 7DE. Telephone Brighton (0273) 739535. Commercial Dept: 0273-778230. Recorded information (team & ticket news etc): Seagull Line 0898 800 609.

Ground capacity: 23,000.

Record attendance: 36,747 v Fulham, Division 2, 27 December, 1958.

Pitch measurements: 112yd × 75yd.

Chairman: D. C. Sizen. ***Vice-Chairman:*** J. L. Campbell.

Directors: B. S. Bedson, P. F. Kent, R. A. Bloom, G. Appleby, G. A. Stanley, F. Shannon FCA, B. E. Clarke.

Manager: Barry Lloyd.

Secretary:Steve Rooke. ***Chief Executive:*** Ron Pavey.

Coach: Martin Hinshelwood. ***Physiotherapist:*** Malcolm Stuart.

Marketing Manager: Terry Gill. ***Lottery Manager:*** Dave Treagus.

Year Formed: 1900. ***Turned Professional:*** 1900. ***Ltd Co.:*** 1904.

Previous Name: Brighton & Hove Rangers.***Previous Grounds:*** 1900, Withdean; 1901, County Ground; 1902, Goldstone Ground.

Club Nickname: 'The Seagulls'.

Record League Victory: 9-1 v Newport C, Division 3 (S), 18 April 1951 – Ball; Tennant (1p), Mansell (1p); Willard, McCoy, Wilson; Reed, McNichol (4), Garbutt, Bennett (2), Keene (1). 9-1 v Southend U, Division 3, 27 November 1965 – Powney; Magill, Baxter; Leck, Gall, Turner; Gould (1), Collins (1), Livesey (2), Smith (3), Goodchild (2).

Record Cup Victory: 10-1 v Wisbech, FA Cup, 1st rd, 13 November 1965 – Powney; Magill, Baxter; Collins (1), Gall, Turner; Gould, Smith (2), Livesey (3), Cassidy (2), Goodchild (1). (1 og).

Record Defeat: 0-9 v Middlesbrough, Division 2, 23 August, 1958.

Most League Points (2 for a win): 65, Division 3 (S), 1955–56 and Division 3, 1971–72.

Most League Points (3 for a win): 84, Division 3, 1987–88.

Most League Goals: 112, Division 3 (S), 1955–56.

Highest League Scorer in Season: Peter Ward, 32, Division 3, 1976–77.

Most League Goals in Total Aggregate: Tommy Cook, 113, 1922-29.

Most Capped Player: Steve Penney, 17, Northern Ireland.

Most League Appearances: 'Tug' Wilson, 509, 1922–36.

Record Transfer Fee Received: £900,000 from Liverpool for Mark Lawrenson, August 1981.

Record Transfer Fee Paid: £500,000 to Manchester U for Andy Ritchie,October 1980.

Football League Record: 1920 Original Member of Division 3; 1921–58 Division 3 (S); 1958–62 Division 2; 1962–63 Division 3; 1963–65 Division 4; 1965–72 Division 3; 1972–73 Division 2; 1973–77 Division 3; 1977-79 Division 2; 1979–83 Division 1; 1983–87 Division 2; 1987–88 Division 3; 1988– Division 2.

Honours: *Football League:* Division 1 best season: 16th 1979–80; Division 2 – Runners-up 1978–79; Division 3 (S) – Champions 1957–58; Runners-up 1953–54, 1955–56; Division 3 – Runners-up 1971–72, 1976–77, 1987–88; Division 4 – Champions 1964–65. *FA Cup:* Runners-up 1982–83. *Football League Cup* best season: 5th rd, 1978–79.

Colours: Blue and white striped shirts, blue shorts, blue stockings. **Change colours:** White shirts with red patterned check, red shorts, red stockings with blue and white trim.

BRIGHTON & HOVE ALBION 1988–89 LEAGUE RECORD

Match No.	Date	Venue	Opponents	Result	H/T Score	Lg. Pos.	Goalscorers	Attendance
1	Aug 27	H	Bradford C	L 1-3	1-1	—	Nelson	10,190
2	Sept 3	A	Oxford U	L 2-3	0-2	24	Chivers, Armstrong	6004
3	10	H	Bournemouth	L 1-2	0-2	23	Chivers	8247
4	17	A	Manchester C	L 1-2	0-1	24	Bremner	16,033
5	21	H	WBA	L 0-1	0-0	—		7395
6	24	A	Swindon T	L 0-3	0-1	24		6585
7	Oct 1	H	Leeds U	W 2-1	0-1	22	Nelson, Bremner	7109
8	5	H	Barnsley	L 0-1	0-0	—		7327
9	8	A	Leicester C	L 0-1	0-0	24		9201
10	15	A	Watford	D 1-1	0-0	24	McClelland (og)	12,126
11	22	H	Oldham Ath	W 2-0	2-0	23	Gatting, May	9799
12	26	H	Walsall	D 2-2	1-2	—	Bremner, Curbishley	8311
13	29	A	Chelsea	L 0-2	0-1	23		15,406
14	Nov 5	H	Shrewsbury T	W 3-1	0-0	22	Chivers, Nelson, Wood	7365
15	12	A	Blackburn R	L 1-2	1-2	23	Curbishley (pen)	6980
16	19	A	Ipswich T	W 3-2	1-2	22	Curbishley, May, Bremner	12,386
17	26	H	Sunderland	W 3-0	1-0	21	Chivers, Penney, Bremner	10,039
18	Dec 3	A	Hull C	L 2-5	1-3	21	Bremner, Gatting	5686
19	6	A	Plymouth Arg	L 0-3	0-1	—		8133
20	10	H	Stoke C	D 1-1	0-1	22	Gatting	7443
21	17	A	Portsmouth	L 0-2	0-1	22		12,467
22	26	H	Crystal Palace	W 3-1	2-0	22	Bremner, Chivers, Nelson	13,515
23	31	H	Birmingham C	W 4-0	0-0	20	Chivers, Bremner 3	9324
24	Jan 2	A	Bournemouth	L 1-2	1-0	21	Nelson	10,627
25	14	H	Plymouth Arg	D 2-2	1-1	20	Bremner, May	8504
26	21	A	Bradford C	W 1-0	1-0	20	Owers	8183
27	Feb 4	A	Barnsley	D 2-2	1-1	20	Nelson, Bremner	12,498
28	11	H	Leicester C	D 1-1	0-1	20	Nelson	9572
29	18	A	Oldham Ath	L 1-2	1-2	21	Owers	5010
30	25	H	Watford	W 1-0	1-0	20	Bremner	9522
31	28	A	Walsall	L 0-1	0-0	—		4613
32	Mar 4	H	Blackburn R	W 3-0	0-0	20	Nelson 2, Bremner	8075
33	11	A	Shrewsbury T	D 1-1	1-0	20	Nelson	4029
34	15	H	Chelsea	L 0-1	0-1	—		12,600
35	18	A	WBA	L 0-1	0-0	21		11,586
36	25	H	Oxford U	W 2-1	0-1	21	Curbishley (pen), Nelson	9077
37	27	A	Crystal Palace	L 1-2	0-2	21	Curbishley (pen)	14,384
38	Apr 1	H	Manchester C	W 2-1	1-0	20	Curbishley (pen), Brightwell (og)	12,072
39	5	H	Portsmouth	W 2-1	0-1	—	Bremner, Nelson	10,100
40	8	A	Birmingham C	W 2-1	2-1	17	Nelson 2	4579
41	15	A	Leeds U	L 0-1	0-1	17		14,915
42	22	H	Swindon T	L 0-2	0-0	18		9510
43	29	A	Sunderland	L 0-1	0-1	20		12,856
44	May 1	H	Hull C	D 1-1	0-0	19	Codner	6750
45	6	H	Ipswich T	L 0-1	0-1	20		8616
46	13	A	Stoke C	D 2-2	1-1	19	Nelson, Wilkins	5841

Final League Position: 19

GOALSCORERS

League (57): Bremner 15, Nelson 15, Chivers 6, Curbishley 6 (4 pens), Gatting 3, May 3, Owers 2, Armstrong 1, Codner 1, Penney 1, Wilkins 1, Wood 1, own goals 2.
Littlewoods Cup (0).
FA Cup (1): Curbishley 1 (pen).

Littlewoods Cup	First Round	Southend U (a)	0-2
		(h)	0-1
FA Cup	Third Round	Leeds U (h)	1-2

Keeley	Brown	Chivers	Curbishley	Isaac	Gatting	Nelson	Owers	Wood	Wilkins	Penney	Dublin	Armstrong	Codner	Bremner	Digweed	Crumplin	Fearon	May	Trusson	Chapman	Bissett	Cooper	Coles	Match No.
1	2	3	4	5	6	7	8	9	10	11														1
1		2	4	5	6	7	8	9	10	11*	3	12												2
1		2	4*	5	6	7	8	12	10†	14	3	9	11											3
1		2	4	5	6	7	8	12	10*		3		11	9										4
		2	4	5	6	7	8	12	10		3		11†	9	1*	14								5
	12	2		5	6	7	8*	4	10		3		11	9			1							6
		2		4	6	7	12	10			3		11	9			1	5	8*					7
	3	2	12	4*	6	7		10†	14				11	9			1	5	8					8
		2		4	6	7		10			3	9	11				1	5	8					9
		2			6	7		10	4		3	9	11				1	5	8					10
		2	8		6	7	12	10*	4				11	9			1	5		3				11
		2	8		6	7		10	4		3		11	9			1	5						12
1		2	8		6	7		10*	4		3	12	11	9				5						13
1		2	8		6	7		10	4		3		11	9				5						14
1		2	8		6	7			4		3		11	9		10		5						15
1		2	8		6	7	10		4	11	3			9				5						16
1		2	8		6	7	10		4	11	3			9				5						17
1		2	8*		6	7	10	12	4	11†	3			9		14		5						18
1		2	8		6	7	10†	12	4		3		14	9		11*		5						19
1		2	8		6	7			4		3		11	9		10					5			20
1		2	8		6	7			4	11	3		10	9							5			21
1		2	8		6	7			4	11	3		10*	9							5	12		22
1		2	8		6	7		12	4	10	3			9							5	11*		23
1		2	8		6	7		12	4	10	3			9							5	11*		24
1		2	8		6	7	10*	11†	4		3			9		14		5				12		25
1		2			6	7	10	11	4		3			9				5	8					26
1		2			6	7	10	11	4		3			9				5	8					27
1		2	12		6†	7	10	11	4		3			9				5	8*	14				28
1		2	12			7	10	11	4		3			9				5	8*		6			29
1		2	12			7	10	11	4		3			9					8*	5	6			30
1		2				7	10	11*	4		3			9		12			8	5	6			31
1		2				7	10		4		3			9		11			8	5	6			32
		2				7	10		4		3			9		11		5	8	6			1	33
1		2	12			7	10	14	4		3			9		11*		5	8†	6				34
1		2	10			7			4		3			9		11		5	8	6				35
1		2	10			7		11	4		3		12	9				5	8*	6				36
1		2	10			7		11*	4		3		12	9				5	8	6				37
1		2	10			7		11	4		3		12	9				5*	8	6				38
1		2	10			7		11	4		3		12	9					8*	6	5			39
1		2	10			7		11	4		3		12	9					8*	6	5			40
1		2	10			7	12	11	4†		3		8*	9		14				6	5			41
1		2	10			7	4	11			3		8*	9						6	5	12		42
1		2	10			7		11	4		3		8	9						6	5			43
1		2	10			7		11*	4		3		8	9					12	6	5			44
1		2	10			7			4		3		8	9					11	6	5			45
1		2	10		5	7			4		3		8	9					11	6				46
37	2 + 1s	46	32 + 5s	9	29	46	21 + 3s	27 + 8s	42 + 1s	9 + 1s	43	3 + 2s	22 + 6s	41	1	7 + 5s	7	24	21 + 1s	18 + 1s	16	2 + 3s	1	

BRIGHTON & HOVE ALBION

Player and Position	*Ht*	*Wt*	*Birth Date*	*Birth Place*	*Source*	*Clubs*	*League App*	*League Gls*
Goalkeepers								
Perry Digweed	6 0	11 04	26 10 59	London	Apprentice	Fulham	15	—
						Brighton & HA	102	—
						WBA (loan)	—	—
						Charlton Ath (loan)	—	—
						Newcastle U (loan)	—	—
						Chelsea (loan)	3	—
David Coles‡	5 10	12 00	15 6 64	Wandsworth	Apprentice	Birmingham C	—	—
						Mansfield T	3	—
						Aldershot	120	—
						Newport Co (loan)	14	—
					HJK Helsinki	Crystal Palace	—	—
						Brighton & HA	1	—
John Keeley	6 1	14 02	27 7 61	Plaistow	Apprentice	Southend U	54	—
					Chelmsford	Brighton & HA	103	—
Defenders								
Nicky Bissett	6 2	12 10	5 4 64	Fulham	Barnet	Brighton & HA	16	—
Ian Chapman	5 8	11 05	31 5 70	Brighton		Brighton & HA	24	—
Gary Chivers	5 11	11 05	15 5 60	Stockwell	Apprentice	Chelsea	133	4
						Swansea C	10	—
						QPR	60	—
						Watford	14	—
						Brighton & H A	56	6
Keith Dublin	5 11	11 09	29 1 66	Wycombe	Apprentice	Chelsea	51	—
						Brighton & H A	89	5
Steve Gatting	5 11	11 11	29 5 59	Park Royal	Apprentice	Arsenal	58	5
						Brighton & HA	254	18
Grant Horscroft‡	6 4	14 00	30 7 61	Fletching	Lewes	Brighton & HA	2	—
Robert Isaac	5 11	12 07	30 11 65	Hackney	Apprentice	Chelsea	9	—
						Brighton & HA	30	—
Paul McCarthy			4 8 71	Cork	Trainee	Brighton & HA	—	—
Larry May	6 1	12 00	26 12 58	Sutton Coldfield	Apprentice	Leicester C	187	12
						Barnsley	122	3
						Sheffield W	31	1
						Brighton & HA	24	3
John Robinson			29 8 71	Rhodesia	Trainee	Brighton & HA	—	—
Wayne Stemp	5 11	11 02	9 9 70	Epsom	Trainee	Brighton & HA	—	—
Midfield								
Geoff Cooper*	5 10	11 00	27 12 60	Kingston	Bognor Regis	Brighton & H A	7	—
John Crumplin	5 8	11 10	26 5 67	Bath	Bognor	Brighton & HA	43	2
Alan Curbishley	5 11	11 10	8 11 57	Forest Gate	Apprentice	West Ham U	85	5
						Birmingham C	130	11
						Aston Villa	36	1
						Charlton Ath	63	6
						Brighton & HA	71	12
Jack Dineen	5 7	10 06	23 9 70	Brighton		Brighton & H A	—	—
Adrian Owers	5 8	10 02	26 2 65	Banbury	Apprentice	Southend U	27	—
					Chelmsford C	Brighton & H A	33	4
Steve Penney	5 9	10 04	16 1 64	Ballymena	Ballymena U	Brighton & HA	138	15
Mike Trusson	5 10	12 04	26 5 59	Northolt	Apprentice	Plymouth Arg	73	15
						Stoke C (loan)	—	—
						Sheffield U	126	31
						Rotherham U	124	19
						Brighton & H A	37	2
Dean Wilkins	5 8	11 08	12 7 62	Hillingdon	Apprentice	QPR	6	—
						Brighton & H A	2	—
						Orient (loan)	10	—
					Zwolle	Brighton & H A	87	4

BRIGHTON & HOVE ALBION

Foundation: After barely two seasons in existence, a professional club named Brighton United, consisting mostly of Scotsmen, was forced to disband in 1900. The club's manager John Jackson determined to keep the professional game alive in the town and initiated the movement which led to the formation of Brighton & Hove Rangers that same year.

Managers (and Secretary-managers)
John Jackson 1901–05, Frank Scott-Walford 1905–08, John Robson 1908–14, Charles Webb 1919–47, Tommy Cook 1947, Don Welsh 1947–51, Billy Lane 1951–61, George Curtis 1961–63, Archie Macaulay 1963–68, Fred Goodwin 1968–70, Pat Saward 1970–73, Brian Clough 1973–74, Peter Taylor 1974–76, Alan Mullery 1976–81, Mike Bailey 1981–82, Jimmy Melia 1982–83, Chris Cattlin 1983–86, Alan Mullery 1986–87, Barry Lloyd 1987– .

Player and Position	*Ht*	*Wt*	*Birth Date*	*Birth Place*	*Source*	*Clubs*	*League App*	*League Gls*
Forwards								
Gerry Armstrong‡	5 11	13 02	23 5 54	Belfast	Bangor	Tottenham H	84	10
						Watford	76	12
					Mallorca	WBA	8	—
						Chesterfield	12	1
						Brighton & HA	47	6
						Millwall (loan)	7	—
Kevin Bremner	5 9	12 05	7 10 57	Banff	Keith	Colchester U	95	31
						Birmingham C (loan)	4	1
						Wrexham (loan)	4	1
						Plymouth Arg (loan)	5	1
						Millwall	96	33
						Reading	64	22
						Brighton & H A	85	23
Robert Codner	5 11	11 05	23 1 65	Walthamstow	Dagenham	Leicester C	—	—
					Barnet	Brighton & HA	28	1
David Gipp*	5 7	9 12	13 7 69	Forest Gate	Apprentice	Brighton & HA	5	—
Roy Hales*	5 9	11 00	10 6 70	Chatham		Brighton & HA	—	—
Garry Nelson	5 10	11 04	16 1 61	Southend	Amateur	Southend U	129	17
						Swindon T	79	7
						Plymouth Arg	74	20
						Brighton & H A	88	37
Paul Wood	5 9	10 01	1 11 64	Middlesbrough	Apprentice	Portsmouth	47	6
						Brighton & H A	66	5

Trainees
Alexander, Wayne K; Bown, Matthew R.N; Coldwell, David J; Jones, James H; Lyons, Christian W; McFadden, Sean; McGrath, Derek B.J; Mummery, Jason; O'Dowd, Gregory H; Roberts, David K.

Associated Schoolboys
Astell, Richard C; Baker, Darren R; Danbury, Stuart J; Devlin, Timothy; Gumpright, Mark; Manuel, Wayne P; Micklethwaite, Marc; Munday, Stuart C; Myall, Stuart T; Newman, Zak T; Ngo, Tran H; Nimmo, Andrew K; Oliva, Umberto; Piper, Matthew R; Rhone, Dwayne, B.J; Sapiro, Joel; Sheriff, Mark; Simmonds, Daniel.

BRISTOL CITY 1988–89 *Back row (left to right):-* Carl Shutt, Russell Bromage, Steve McClaren, Tony Caldwell.
Centre row: Jimmy Lumsden (Assistant Manager), Alan Walsh, Rob Newman, Paul Fitzpatrick, Keith Waugh, John Pender, Paul Mardon, Glenn Humphries, Alan Crawford (Youth Team Manager).
Front row: Nigel Hawkins, Ralph Milne, Steve Galliers (Captain), Joe Jordan (Manager), Chris Honor, Andy Llewellyn, Mark Cooper.

BRISTOL CITY

Ashton Gate, Bristol BS3 2EJ. Telephone Bristol 0272) 632812 (5 lines). Clubcall 0898 12 11 76

Ground capacity: 30,868.

Record attendance: 43,335 v Preston NE, FA Cup 5th rd, 16 Feb, 1935.

Record receipts: £97,097 v Nottingham F, Littlewoods Cup semi-final, 26 February, 1989.

Pitch measurements: 115yd × 75yd.

Chairman: D. T. Williams. *Vice-Chairman:* L. J. Kew.

Directors: O. W. Newland, W. I. Williams, P. Manning, M. Fricker, K. Sage. *Commercial Manager:* D. Easton.

Manager: Joe Jordan. *Assistant Manager/Coach:* Jimmy Lumsden.

Physio: Buster Footman. *Football Secretary:* Miss J. Harrison.*Commercial Manager:* John Cox.

Year Formed: 1894. *Turned Professional:* 1897. *Ltd Co.:* 1897. BCFC (1982) PLC.

Previous Grounds: 1894, St John's Lane; 1904, Ashton Gate.

Previous Name: 1894–97, Bristol South End. *Club Nickname:* 'Robins'

Record League Victory: 9-0 v Aldershot, Division 3(S), 28 December 1946 – Eddols; Morgan, Fox; Peacock, Roberts, Jones (1); Chilcott, Thomas, Clark (4 incl 1p), Cyril Williams (1), Hargreaves (3).

Record Cup Victory: 11-0 v Chichester C, FA Cup, 1st rd, 5 November 1960 – Cook; Collinson, Thresher; Connor, Alan Williams, Etheridge; Tait (1), Bobby Williams (1), Atyeo (5), Adrian Williams (3), Derrick. (1 og).

Record Defeat: 0-9 v Coventry C, Division 3(S), 28 April, 1934.

Most League Points (2 for a win): 70, Division 3 (S), 1954–55.

Most League Points (3 for a win): 82, Division 4, 1983–84.

Most League Goals: 104, Division 3(S), 1926–27.

Highest League Scorer in Season: Don Clark, 36, Division 3(S), 1946–47.

Most League Goals in Total Aggregate: John Atyeo, 315, 1951–66.

Most Capped Player: Billy Wedlock, 26, England.

Most League Appearances: John Atyeo, 597, 1951–66

Record Transfer Fee Received: £325,000 from Coventry C for Gary Collier, July 1979.

Record Transfer Fee Paid: £235,000 to St Mirren for Tony Fitzpatrick, July 1979.

Football League Record: 1901 Elected to Division 2; 1906–11 Division 1; 1911–22 Division 2; 1922–23 Division 3 (S); 1923-24 Division 2; 1924–27 Division 3(S); 1927–32 Division 2; 1932–55 Division 3(S); 1955–60 Division 2; 1960–65 Division 3; 1965–76 Division 2; 1976–80 Division 1; 1908–81 Division 2; 1981–82 Division 3; 1982–84 Division 4; 1984–Division 3.

Honours: Football League: Division 1 – Runners-up 1906–07; Division 2 – Champions 1905–06; Runners-up 1975–76; Division 3(S) – Champions 1922–23, 1926–27, 1954–55; Runners-up 1937–38; Division 3 – Runners-up 1964–65. *FA Cup:* Runners-up 1909. *Football League Cup:* Semi-final 1970–71, 1988–89. *Welsh Cup:* Winners 1934. *Anglo-Scottish Cup:* Winners 1977–78. *Freight Rover Trophy:* Winners, 1985–86; Runners-up 1986–87.

Colours: Red shirts, white shorts, red stockings. **Change colours:** Yellow shirts, green shorts, yellow stockings.

BRISTOL CITY 1988–89 LEAGUE RECORD

Match No.	Date	Venue	Opponents	Result	H/T Score	Lg. Pos.	Goalscorers	Attendance
1	Aug 27	A	Notts Co	D 0-0	0-0	—		6280
2	Sept 3	H	Chesterfield	W 4-0	1-0	3	Walsh 2, Newman (pen), Llewellyn	7547
3	10	A	Chester C	L 0-2	0-0	11		2823
4	17	H	Preston NE	D 1-1	1-1	12	Bromage	7913
5	20	A	Blackpool	D 2-2	2-1	—	McGarvey 2	3412
6	24	H	Port Vale	L 0-1	0-1	16		7235
7	Oct 1	H	Swansea C	W 2-0	1-0	12	Walsh, Milne	7786
8	4	A	Gillingham	W 1-0	1-0	—	Gavin	3102
9	8	H	Fulham	L 1-5	0-2	11	Newman (pen)	8160
10	15	A	Huddersfield T	W 1-0	0-0	11	Walsh	5952
11	22	A	Northampton T	W 3-1	0-1	7	Milne, McGarvey 2	3668
12	25	H	Aldershot	D 1-1	0-1	—	McGarvey	8685
13	29	A	Mansfield T	D 2-2	2-1	11	McGarvey, Walsh	3800
14	Nov 5	H	Bolton W	D 1-1	1-0	9	Newman	8807
15	8	H	Wolverhampton W	L 0-1	0-0	—		11,336
16	12	A	Wigan ATh	W 1-0	0-0	10	Gavin	2675
17	26	A	Sheffield U	L 0-3	0-1	12		11,249
18	Dec 3	H	Reading	W 2-1	0-1	10	Walsh, Hawkins	8045
19	17	H	Cardiff C	W 2-0	1-0	7	Newman, Hawkins	7493
20	26	A	Bury	L 1-2	1-1	10	McGarvey	3368
21	31	A	Southend U	W 2-1	1-0	9	McGarvey, Walsh	4012
22	Jan 2	H	Bristol R	L 0-1	0-0	10		23,191
23	14	A	Chesterfield	L 0-1	0-0	11		3488
24	21	H	Chester C	L 0-1	0-0	13		9586
25	28	A	Preston NE	L 0-2	0-0	13		6080
26	Feb 3	A	Swansea C	D 1-1	1-0	—	Turner	6523
27	11	H	Gillingham	W 1-0	0-0	11	Jordan	7319
28	18	A	Fulham	L 1-3	1-1	13	McGarvey	4408
29	21	A	Aldershot	W 1-0	1-0	—	Walsh	1960
30	Mar 4	H	Northampton T	W 3-1	3-0	12	Shutt, Walsh, Turner	7197
31	11	A	Bolton W	L 0-2	0-0	14		4423
32	18	H	Notts Co	L 0-4	0-1	14		6407
33	21	H	Mansfield T	W 2-0	1-0	—	Newman 2(1 pen)	5065
34	25	A	Bristol R	D 1-1	1-1	11	Walsh	8676
35	27	H	Bury	W 3-0	1-0	10	Turner 2, Taylor	8496
36	Apr 1	A	Cardiff C	D 1-1	0-1	11	Taylor	6152
37	4	A	Brentford	L 0-3	0-2	—		4627
38	8	H	Southend U	L 0-2	0-1	14		6213
39	11	H	Brentford	L 0-1	0-0	—		4339
40	15	H	Blackpool	L 1-2	1-0	14	Taylor	5090
41	18	H	Huddersfield T	W 6-1	5-0	—	Taylor 3, Walsh (pen), Gavin, McClaren	4542
42	21	A	Port Vale	W 1-0	0-0	—	Taylor	6923
43	29	H	Wigan Ath	L 0-1	0-0	13		5156
44	May 1	A	Wolverhampton W	L 0-2	0-1	14		17,351
45	5	A	Reading	W 2-1	1-1	—	Turner, Pender	3620
46	13	H	Sheffield U	W 2-0	0-0	11	Turner, Taylor	10,769

Final League Position: 11

GOALSCORERS

League (53): Walsh 11 (1 pen), McGarvey 9, Taylor 8, Newman 6 (3 pens), Turner 6, Gavin 3, Hawkins 2, Milne 2, Bromage 1, Jordan 1, Llewellyn 1, McClaren 1, Pender 1, Shutt 1.
Littlewoods Cup (15): Shutt 4, Walsh 4, Milne 3, Hawkins 1, McClaren 1, Mardon 1, Newman 1 (pen).
FA Cup (7): Shutt 4, McGarvey 1, Newman 1 (pen), Walsh 1.

Littlewoods Cup			
	First Round	Exeter C (h)	1-0
		(a)	1-0
	Second Round	Oxford U (a)	4-2
		(h)	2-0
	Third Round	Crystal Palace (h)	4-1
	Fourth Round	Tranmere R (h)	1-0
	Fifth Round	Bradford C (a)	1-0
	Semi-Final	Nottingham F (a)	1-1
		(h)	0-1

Waugh	Llewellyn	Bromage	Humphries	Pender	McClaren	Milne	Galliers	Newman	Walsh	Caldwell	Honor	Mardon	Shutt	Hawkins	Fitzpatrick	McGarvey	Carter	Leaning	Gavin	Jordan	Bailey	Stanley	Shepherd	Turner	Dolan	Taylor	Eaton	*Match No.*
1	2	3	4	5	6	7*	8	9	10	11	12																	1
1	2	3		5	6*		8	7	10			4	9	11	12													2
1	2	3		5	6	12	8	7	10			4	9*			11												3
	2†	3		5	6	7*	8	9	10		14	4	12			11	1											4
	2	3		5	6	7*	8	4	10				9	12		11	1											5
	2	3		5	6	7	8	4	10				9*	12		11	1											6
	2	3		5	6	7	8	4†	10			14	9*	11		12		1										7
	2	3†		5	6		8	4	10			14		11*		9		1	7	12								8
	2†		14	5	6		8	4	10			3		11		9*		1	7	12								9
	2†		4	5	6		8	7	10			14	9*			12		1		11	3							10
			4	5	6	7	8	2	10							9		1	11*	12	3							11
1			4	5	6	7	8	2	10				12			9				11*	3							12
1			4	5	6	7	8	2	10				12			9*			11		3							13
1	2		4	5	6	7		8	10				9*			12			11		3							14
1	14		4	5	6†	7	8	2	10				9*			12			11		3							15
1	14		4	5			8	2	10				9	12		7*			11		3	6†						16
1			4		6		8	5	10				9	12		7*			11		3	2						17
1			4	5	6		8	2	10				9	12		7*			11		3							18
1	14		4†	5	6			2	10				9*	12		7			11		3	8						19
1				5	6			4	10		2		9*	12		7			11		3	8						20
1				5	6		12	4	10		2		9			7			11		3	8*						21
1				5	6			4	10		2		9	12		7			11*		3	8†	14					22
1				5	6		11	4	10		2					7*			9	12	3		8					23
1				5	6		7	4	10*		2		9			12			11		3		8					24
1				5	6		7	4	10		2		9						11		3			8				25
1				5	12		7	4	10		2	6				9†			14		3	11*		8				26
1				5	11		7	4	10		2	6				9*			14	12	3				8†			27
1				5	8			4	10		2	6				11*			9		3	12			7			28
1				5	8			4	10		2	14	9							12	3	6†		11	7*			29
1	7			5	8			4	10		2	6	9								3*	12		11				30
1	7			5	8			4	10		2*	6	9						12		3			11				31
1				5	8		12	4	10		2	6	9						7*		3			11				32
1			4	5	8†		7	6	10		2	14		9*						12	3			11				33
1			4*	5	8		7†	6	10		2	14		12							3			11		9		34
1			4	5	7			6	10		2	8									3			11		9		35
1			4	5	7			6	10		2	8									3			11		9		36
1			4	5	7		12	6	10		2	8*									3			11		9		37
1		8	4	5	7†			6	10*		2	14		9		12					3			11				38
1		8	4	5	7			2	10										6		3			11		9		39
1		8	4	5	7			2	10					12					6		3			11*		9		40
1				5	7		8	4	10		2								6		3			11		9		41
1				5	7		8	4	10		2								6		3			11		9		42
1			12	5	6		7	4	10		2*								8		3			11†		9	14	43
1			2	5	6		7	4	10					11*					8		3					9	12	44
1		3		5	6		7	4	10		2								8					11		9		45
		3		5	6		7	4	10		2							1	8					11		9		46
37	13 + 3s	13	20 + 2s	45	44 + 1s	10 + 1s	30 + 3s	46	46	1	24 + 2s	13 + 7s	21 + 3s	7 + 10s	— + 1s	20 + 6s	3	6	26 + 3s	2 + 7s	35	8 + 2s	2 + 1s	19	3	12	— + 2s	

FA Cup	First Round	Southend U (h)	3-1
	Second Round	Aldershot (a)	1-1
		(h)	0-0
		(a)	2-2
		(h)	1-0
	Third Round	Hartlepool U (a)	0-1

Tony Shepherd on loan from Celtic.

BRISTOL CITY

Player and Position	*Ht*	*Wt*	*Birth Date*	*Birth Place*	*Source*	*Clubs*	*League App*	*League Gls*
Goalkeepers								
Andy Leaning	6 1	13 07	18 5 62	York	Rowntree M	York C	69	—
						Sheffield U	21	—
						Bristol C	6	—
Keith Waugh	6 1	13 00	27 10 56	Sunderland	Apprentice	Sunderland	—	—
						Peterborough U	195	—
						Sheffield U	99	—
						Cambridge U (loan)	4	—
						Bristol C (loan)	3	—
						Bristol C	167	—
Defenders								
Robert Ainley‡			20 11 69	Bromsgrove		Bristol C	—	—
John Bailey	5 8	11 03	1 4 57	Liverpool	Apprentice	Blackburn R	120	1
						Everton	171	3
						Newcastle U	40	—
						Bristol C	35	—
Russel Bromage	5 11	11 05	9 11 59	Stoke	Apprentice	Port Vale	347	13
						Oldham Ath (loan)	2	—
						Bristol C	43	1
Chris Honor	5 9	10 09	5 6 68	Bristol	Apprentice	Bristol C	46	—
						Torquay U (loan)	3	—
Glenn Humphries	6 0	12 00	11 8 64	Hull	Apprentice	Doncaster R	180	8
						Lincoln C (loan)	9	—
						Bristol C	46	—
Andy Llewellyn	5 7	11 12	26 2 66	Bristol	Apprentice	Bristol C	149	3
Ron McQuilter	6 2	12 01	24 12 70	Glasgow		Bristol C	—	—
Paul Mardon	6 0	11 10	14 9 69	Bristol	Trainee	Bristol C	28	—
Rob Newman	6 2	12 00	13 12 63	London	Apprentice	Bristol C	302	36
John Pender	6 0	12 07	19 11 63	Luton	Apprentice	Wolverhampton W	117	3
						Charlton Ath	41	—
						Bristol C	73	3
Midfield								
Mark Cooper*	5 8	11 04	18 12 68	Wakefield	Trainee	Bristol C	—	—
Steve Galliers	5 6	9 07	21 8 57	Fulwood	Chorley	Wimbledon	155	10
						Crystal Palace	13	—
						Wimbledon	146	5
						Bristol C (loan)	9	—
						Bristol C	68	6
Steve McClaren	5 7	9 08	3 5 61	Fulford	Apprentice	Hull C	178	16
						Derby Co	25	—
						Lincoln C (loan)	8	—
						Bristol C	61	2
Gary Stanley*	5 9	12 02	4 3 54	Burton	Apprentice	Chelsea	109	15
						Everton	52	1
						Swansea C	72	4
						Portsmouth	47	1
					Wichita	Bristol C	10	—
Forwards								
Nick Dent	6 1	12 04	30 12 67	Bristol		Bristol C	—	—
Jason Eaton	5 10	11 00	29 1 69	Bristol		Bristol R	3	—
						Bristol C	2	—
Mark Gavin	5 8	10 07	10 12 63	Bailleston	Apprentice	Leeds U	30	3
						Hartlepool U (loan)	7	—
						Carlisle U	13	1
						Bolton W	49	3
						Rochdale	23	6
						Hearts	9	—
						Bristol C	29	3

BRISTOL CITY

Foundation: The name Bristol City came into being in 1897 when the Bristol South End club, formed three years earlier, decided to adopt professionalism and apply for admission to the Southern League after competing in the Western League. The historic meeting was held at The Albert Hall, Bedminster. Bristol City employed Sam Hollis from Woolwich Arsenal as manager and gave him £40 to buy players. In 1901 they merged with Bedminster, another leading Bristol club.

Managers (and Secretary-managers)
Sam Hollis 1897–99, Bob Campbell 1899–1901, Sam Hollis 1901–05, Harry Thickett 1905–10, Sam Hollis 1911–13, George Hedley 1913–15, Jack Hamilton 1915–19, Joe Palmer 1919–21, Alex Raisbeck 1921–29, Joe Bradshaw 1929–32, Bob Hewison 1932–49 (under suspension 1938–39), Bob Wright 1949–50, Pat Beasley 1950–58, Peter Doherty 1958–60, Fred Ford 1960–67, Alan Dicks 1967–80, Bobby Houghton 1980–82, Roy Hodgson 1982, Terry Cooper 1982–88 (Director from 1983), Joe Jordan 1988– .

Player and Position	*Ht*	*Wt*	*Birth Date*	*Birth Place*	*Source*	*Clubs*	*League App*	*League Gls*
Nigel Hawkins	5 9	10 07	7 9 68	Bristol	Apprentice	Bristol C	18	2
Joe Jordan	6 1	12 01	15 12 51	Carluke		Morton	10	1
						Leeds U	169	35
						Manchester U	109	37
						AC Milan	52	12
						Verona	12	1
						Southampton	48	12
						Bristol C	56	8
Bob Taylor	5 10	11 02	3 2 67	Horden	Horden CW	Leeds U	42	9
						Bristol C	12	8
Rob Turner	6 3	14 01	18 9 66	Easington	Apprentice	Huddersfield T	1	—
						Cardiff C	39	8
						Hartlepool U (loan)	7	1
						Bristol R	26	2
						Wimbledon	10	—
						Bristol C	19	6
Alan Walsh	6 0	11 00	9 12 56	Darlington	Horden CW	Middlesbrough	3	—
						Darlington	251	90
						Bristol C	218	77
Robert Ainley‡			20 11 69	Bromsgrove		Bristol C	—	—

Trainees
Bryant, Matthew; Cousins, Robert P; Gorwill, Wayne J; Hopkins, Anthony; Madge, Mark A; Mellon, Michael; Palfrey, Damon A; Sannachan, Thomas D; Smith, Jason M; Theobald, Alan F; Weaver, Steven A; Wright, Ashley M.

Associated Schoolboys
Allan, Timothy J; Benton, Stephen; Bessell, Wayne; Day, Christian J; Darlaston, Simon; Durbin, Gary; Griffiths, Craig; Gillett, Darren; Harris, Darren; Hayes, Nicholas; Haynes, Gordon; Lewis, Martyn; Mark, Jonathon; Mitchell, Craig A; Mortimer, Paul; O'Brien, Paul; Old, Simon; Palmer, Stuart; Pettifer, Mark; Russe, Jeremy; Smith, Graham; Terry, Paul; Winter, Steven D; Wood, Steven.

BRISTOL ROVERS 1988–89 *Back row (left to right):* Geoff Twentyman, Andy Reece, Steve Yates, Ian Weston, Billy Clark, Devon White, Nigel Martyn, Jeff Meacham, Christian McClean, Richard Dryden, Simon Stapleton, Ian Alexander.
Centre row: Roy Dolling (Physiotherapist), Vaughan Jones, Gary Penrice, Phil Purnell, Kenny Hibbitt, Gerry Francis (Manager), Des Bulpin (Coach), Paul Smith, Ian Holloway, David Mehew, Ray Kendall (Kit Manager).
Front row: Lee Jacobs, Neil Reeves, Marcus Browning, Paul Harrison, Neil James.

Division 3 BRISTOL ROVERS

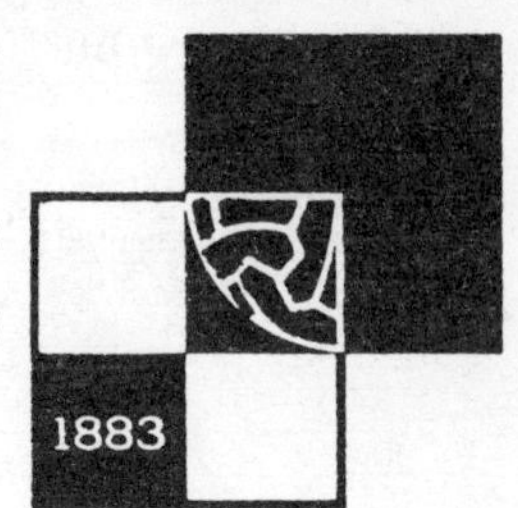

Twerton Park, Twerton, Bath. Telephone: 0272 352508. Training ground: 0272 861743. Match day ticket office: 0225 312327. Offices: 199 Two Mile Road, Kingswood, Bristol BS15 1AZ.

Ground capacity: 9044.

Record attendance: 38,472 v Preston NE, FA Cup 4th rd, 30 Jan, 1960.

Record receipts: £23,275 v Southampton, FA Cup 4th rd, 28 Jan, 1978.

Pitch measurements: 112yd × 75yd.

President: Marquis of Worcester.

Vice-Presidents: Dr W. T. Cussen, A. I. Seager, H. E. L. Brown.

Chairman: D. H. A. Dunford. ***Vice-Chairman:*** R. D. Redman.

Directors: R. Craig, G. M. H. Dunford, V. Stokes. ***Associate Director:*** N. Draper

Manager: Gerry Francis. ***Assistant Manager:*** Ken Hibbitt.

Coach: Des Bulpin. ***Physio:*** Roy Dolling.

Commercial Manager: A. Wood.

Secretary: R. C. Twyford. ***Office Manager:*** Mrs Angela Mann.

Year Formed: 1883. ***Turned Professional:*** 1897.

Ltd Co.: 1896.

Club Nickname: 'Pirates'.

Previous Names: 1883, Black Arabs; 1884, Eastville Rovers; 1897, Bristol Eastville Rovers; 1898, Bristol Rovers.

Previous Grounds: Purdown, Three Acres, Ashley Hill, Rudgeway, Eastville.

Record League Victory: 7-0 v Brighton & HA, Division 3(S), 29 November 1952 – Hoyle; Bamford, Geoff Fox; Pitt, Warren, Sampson; McIlvenny, Roost (2), Lambden (1), Bradford (1), Peterbridge (2). (1 og). 7-0 v Swansea T, Division 2, 2 October 1954 – Radford; Bamford, Watkins; Pitt, Muir, Anderson; Petherbridge, Bradford (2), Meyer, Roost (1), Hooper (2). (2 og). 7-0 v Shrewsbury T, Division 3, 21 March 1964 – Hall, Hillard, Gwyn Jones; Oldfield, Stone (1), Mabbutt; Jarman (2), Brown (1), Biggs (1p), Hamilton, Bobby Jones (2).

Record Cup Victory: 6-0 v Merthyr Tydfil, FA Cup, 1st rd, 14 November 1987 – Martyn; Alexander (Dryden), Tanner, Hibbitt, Twentyman, Jones, Holloway, Meacham (1), White (2), Penrice (3) (Reece), Purnell.

Record Defeat: 0-12 v Luton T, Division 3(S), 13 April, 1936.

Most League Points (2 for a win): 64, Division 3(S), 1952–53.

Most League Points (3 for a win): 79, Division 3, 1983–84.

Most League Goals: 92, Division 3(S), 1952–53.

Highest League Scorer in Season: Geoff Bradford, 33, Division 3(S), 1952–53.

Most League Goals in Total Aggregate: Geoff Bradford, 245, 1949–64.

Most Capped Player: Neil Slatter, 10 (22), Wales.

Most League Appearances: Stuart Taylor, 545, 1966–80.

Record Transfer Fee Received: £200,000 from Luton T for Steve White, December 1979.

Record Transfer Fee Paid: £100,000 to Birmingham C for Stewart Barrowclough, July 1979.

Football League Record: 1920 Original Member of Division 3; 1921–53 Division 3(S); 1953–62 Division 2; 1962–74 Division 3; 1974–81 Division 2; 1981–Division 3.

Honours: *Football League:* Division 2 best season: 6th, 1955–56, 1958–59; Division 3(S) – Champions 1952–53; Division 3 – Runners-up 1973–74. *FA Cup* Best season: 6th rd, 1950–51, 1957–58. *Football League Cup* best season: 5th rd, 1970–71, 1971–72.

Colours: Blue and white quartered shirts, white shorts, blue stockings with two white rings on top. **Change colours:** White shirts, black shorts, white stockings

BRISTOL ROVERS 1988–89 LEAGUE RECORD

Match No.	Date	Venue	Opponents	Result	H/T Score	Lg. Pos.	Goalscorers	Attendance
1	Aug 27	H	Wigan Ath	W 3-2	1-2	—	Penrice 2, White	4080
2	Sept 3	A	Sheffield U	L 1-4	1-2	16	Holloway	9586
3	10	H	Aldershot	D 2-2	0-2	15	White 2	3382
4	17	A	Bolton W	D 1-1	0-1	16	Twentyman	4821
5	21	H	Brentford	L 1-2	0-0	—	Penrice	3836
6	24	A	Northampton T	W 2-1	0-0	10	Smith, Penrice	3886
7	Oct 1	A	Cardiff C	D 2-2	2-0	14	Penrice, Holloway	5038
8	5	H	Preston NE	W 1-0	1-0	—	Penrice	3689
9	8	A	Mansfield T	L 1-2	1-1	12	Penrice	3381
10	15	H	Notts Co	W 2-0	1-0	12	Jones, Penrice	4183
11	22	H	Chester C	W 4-1	2-1	6	Mehew, Reece 2, McClean	3811
12	26	A	Reading	L 1-3	1-2	—	Reece	7150
13	29	H	Huddersfield T	W 5-1	3-1	8	Purnell 2, Holloway, Reece, Penrice	4460
14	Nov 5	A	Chesterfield	W 3-0	1-0	6	Purnell, Mehew 2	2480
15	8	A	Southend U	D 2-2	1-1	—	Purnell, Mehew	2453
16	12	H	Gillingham	W 2-0	0-0	4	Reece, McClean	4826
17	26	H	Bury	L 1-3	0-2	6	Mehew	4251
18	Dec 3	A	Fulham	W 2-0	1-0	4	Mehew, Penrice	4461
19	17	A	Blackpool	D 1-1	0-0	5	Purnell	3240
20	26	H	Wolverhampton W	D 0-0	0-0	6		8480
21	31	H	Swansea C	D 1-1	1-1	6	Purnell	4803
22	Jan 2	A	Bristol C	W 1-0	0-0	5	Penrice	23,191
23	14	H	Sheffield U	D 1-1	0-0	5	Holloway (pen)	6623
24	21	A	Aldershot	W 3-1	2-0	5	Holloway, Penrice 2	3101
25	28	H	Bolton W	W 2-0	1-0	3	Reece, White	5375
26	Feb 4	H	Cardiff C	L 0-1	0-0	6		5815
27	11	A	Preston NE	D 1-1	1-0	5	Penrice	7365
28	18	H	Mansfield T	D 0-0	0-0	7		4669
29	25	A	Notts Co	L 0-1	0-1	7		5176
30	Mar 1	H	Reading	D 1-1	1-0	—	Bailey	4573
31	4	A	Chester C	W 2-0	0-0	6	Purnell, Bailey	3082
32	11	H	Chesterfield	W 2-1	2-0	6	Bailey, Penrice	4686
33	14	A	Huddersfield T	W 3-2	1-2	—	Bailey 2, Jones (pen)	4105
34	25	H	Bristol C	D 1-1	1-1	5	Penrice	8676
35	27	A	Wolverhampton W	W 1-0	1-0	4	Bailey	20,913
36	Apr 1	H	Blackpool	W 1-0	0-0	4	White	5355
37	5	H	Port Vale	D 2-2	1-1	—	Reece, Penrice	6869
38	8	A	Swansea C	W 2-1	1-1	4	Penrice, Bailey	5645
39	15	A	Brentford	L 1-2	1-0	4	Bailey	7558
40	22	H	Northampton T	D 1-1	0-1	4	Bailey	5568
41	28	A	Gillingham	W 3-2	0-1	—	Penrice 2, Holloway (pen)	4044
42	May 1	H	Southend U	D 1-1	0-1	5	Mehew	6250
43	3	A	Wigan Ath	L 0-3	0-1	—		2529
44	6	H	Fulham	D 0-0	0-0	5		7302
45	9	A	Port Vale	L 0-1	0-0	—		6136
46	13	A	Bury	D 0-0	0-0	5		3073

Final League Position: 5

GOALSCORERS

League (67): Penrice 20, Bailey 9, Mehew 7, Purnell 7, Reece 7, Holloway 6 (2 pens), White 5, Jones 2 (1 pen), McClean 2, Smith 1, Twentyman 1.
Littlewoods Cup (0).
FA Cup (4): Holloway 1 (pen), Jones 1, Penrice 1, Reece 1.

Littlewoods Cup	First Round	Bournemouth (a)	0-1
		(h)	0-0
FA Cup	First Round	Fisher Ath (h)	3-0
	Second Round	Kettering (a)	1-2

Martyn	Stapleton	Twentyman	Clark	Mehew	Jones	Holloway	Reece	White	Penrice	Purnell	Alexander	Smith	Dryden	McClean	Viney	Yates	Hazel	Bailey	Hibbitt	Nixon	*Match No.*
1	2	3	4	5	6	7	8	9	10	11											1
1		3	4	5	6*	7	8	9	10	11	2	12									2
1		3	4	5	6	7	8	9	10*	11	2	12									3
1		3	4	5	6	7	8	9		11*	2	10	12								4
1		3	4		6	7	8*	9	10	11	2	5		12							5
1		3			6	7	8	9	10	11	2	5			4						6
1	12	3	6			7	8	9	10	11	2*	5			4						7
1		3	4	5	6	7	8	9	10	11	2										8
1		3	4	5	6	7	8	9	10	11	2										9
1		3		5	6	7	8	9	10	11	2				12	4*					10
1		3	4	5*	6	7	8	9	10	11	2			12							11
1		3	4	5	6	7	8	9*	10	11	2			12							12
1		3		5	6	7	8	9	10	11	2					4					13
1		3		5	6	7	8		10	11	2			9		4					14
1		3		5	6	7	8		10	11	2			9		4					15
1	2	3		5	6	7	8		10	11				9		4					16
1	2	3		5*	6	7	8	9	10	11				12		4					17
1	2	3		5	6	7	8	9	10	11						4					18
1		3		5	6	7	8	9*	10	11	2			12		4					19
1		3			6	7	8	9	10	11	2	5				4					20
1		3			6	7	8	9*	10	11	2	5		12		4					21
1		3			6	7	8	9	10	11	2	5*		12		4					22
1		3			6	7	8	9	10	11	2	5*		12		4					23
1		3			6	7	8	9	10	11	2	5				4					24
1		3	12		6	7	8	9		11	2*	5		10		4					25
1		3			6	7	8	9	10	11	2	5*		12		4					26
1		3			6	7	8	9	10	11	2	5				4					27
1		3			6	7	8	9	10	11	2	5*		12		4					28
1		3		5*	6	7		9	10	11	2	8		12		4					29
1		3			6	7			10	11	2			9		4	5	8			30
1		3			6	7		12	10	11	2			9		4	5	8*			31
1		3		7	6				10	11	2			9		4	5*	8	12		32
1		3		5	6		7		10	11	2			9		4		8			33
1		3			6	7	5	12	10	11*	2			9		4		8			34
1		3		11	6	7	5	12	10		2			9*		4		8			35
1		3		11	6	7	5	12	10		2			9*		4		8			36
1		3		11*	6	7	5	9	10		2			12		4		8			37
1		3		5*	6	7	11	12	10		2			9		4		8			38
1		3		5	6	7	11	12	10		2			9*		4		8			39
1		3		5	6	7	11	9*	10		2					4		8		12	40
1		3		5	6	7	11	9	10		2					4		8			41
1		3		5*	6	7	11	9	10	12	2					4		8			42
1		3		5*	6	7	11	9	10	12	2					4		8			43
1		3		5	6	7	9	12	10		2			11*		4		8			44
1		3		5	6	7	9	12	10		2			11		4		8*			45
1		3		5	6	7	8	12		9	2			11*		4		10			46
46	4 + 1s	46	10 + 1s	31	45	44	42	31 + 9s	43	35 + 2s	42	14 + 2s	— + 1s	16 + 12s	2 + 1s	35	3	17	— + 1s	— + 1s	

BRISTOL ROVERS

Player and Position	Ht	Wt	Birth Date	Birth Place	Source	Clubs	League App	League Gls
Goalkeepers								
Nigel Martyn	6 2	14 00	11 8 66	St Austell	St Blazey	Bristol R	85	—
Defenders								
Billy Clark	6 0	12 03	19 5 67	Christchurch	Local	Bournemouth	4	—
						Bristol R	42	1
Vaughan Jones	5 8	11 11	2 9 59	Tonyrefail	Apprentice	Bristol R	101	3
						Newport Co	68	4
						Cardiff C	11	—
						Bristol R	177	6
Geoff Twentyman	6 1	13 02	10 3 59	Liverpool	Chorley	Preston NE	98	4
						Bristol R	127	2
Ian Willmott	5 10	12 06	10 7 68	Bristol	Weston Super Mare	Bristol R	—	—
Steven Yates	5 11	12 06	29 1 70	Bristol	Trainee	Bristol R	37	—
Midfield								
Ian Alexander	5 8	10 07	26 1 63	Glasgow	Leicester Juv	Rotherham U	11	—
						Motherwell	24	2
						Morton	7	1
					Pezoporikos	Bristol R	109	2
Kenny Hibbitt*	5 11	12 00	3 1 51	Bradford	Apprentice	Bradford PA	15	—
						Wolverhampton	465	88
						Coventry C	47	4
						Bristol R	53	5
Ian Holloway	5 7	9 12	12 3 63	Kingswood	Apprentice	Bristol R	111	14
						Wimbledon	19	2
						Brentford (loan)	13	2
						Brentford	17	—
						Torquay U (loan)	5	—
						Bristol R	87	11
Gary Penrice	5 7	10 00	23 3 64	Bristol	Mangotsfield	Bristol R	176	51
Andy Reece	5 11	12 04	5 9 62	Shrewsbury	Willenhall	Bristol R	82	8
Simon Stapleton	6 0	12 00	10 12 68	Oxford	Trainee	Portsmouth	—	—
						Bristol R	5	—

BRISTOL ROVERS

Foundation: Bristol Rovers were formed at a meeting in Stapleton Road, Eastville, in 1883. However, they first went under the name of the Black Arabs (wearing black shirts). Changing their name to Eastville Rovers in their second season, they won the Gloucestershire Senior Cup in 1888–89. Original members of the Bristol & District League in 1892, this eventually became the Western League and Eastville Rovers adopted professionalism in 1897.

Managers (and Secretary-managers)
Alfred Homer 1899–1920 (continued as secretary to 1928), Ben Hall 1920–21, Andy Wilson 1921–26, Joe Palmer 1926–29, Dave McLean 1929–30, Albert Prince-Cox 1930–36, Percy Smith 1936–37, Brough Fletcher 1938–49, Bert Tann 1950–68 (continued as GM to 1972), Fred Ford 1968–69, Bill Dodgin Snr 1969–72, Don Megson 1972–77, Bobby Campbell 1978–79, Harold Jarman 1979–80, Terry Cooper 1980–81, Bobby Gould 1981–83, David Williams 1983–85, Bobby Gould 1985–87, Gerry Francis 1987– .

Player and Position	*Ht*	*Wt*	*Birth Date*	*Birth Place*	*Source*	*Clubs*	*League App*	*League Gls*
Forwards								
Christian McClean	6 4	14 00	17 10 63	Colchester	Clacton	Bristol R	34	2
Jeff Meacham‡	5 10	11 08	6 2 62	Bristol		Bristol R	26	9
David Mehew	5 11	11 07	29 10 67	Camberley		Leeds U	—	—
						Bristol R	74	25
Paul Nixon	5 10	11 03	23 09 63	Seaham	New Zealand	Bristol R	1	—
Philip Purnell	5 8	10 02	16 9 64	Bristol	Mangotsfield	Bristol R	110	20
Devon White	6 3	14 00	2 3 64	Nottingham	Arnold T	Lincoln C	29	4
					Boston U	Bristol R	79	20

Trainees
Browning, Marcus T; Harrison, Paul M; Jacobs, Lee T; James, Neil; Reeves, Neil R.

****Non-Contract**
Stevens, Mark A; Thomas, Glenn.

Associated Schoolboys
Brain, Kevin L; Chattoe, Richard J; Crossey, Scott; Dampier, Stephen M; Ead, Stephen F; Gurney, Andrew R; Kempster, Paul G; Lock, Simon; Malsom, David; Marsh, Andrew J; Milner, Nicholas J; Perks, Lee J; Robottom, Karl D; Shore, Justin M; Smith, Ian S; Stewart, Andrew W; Tovey, Paul W.

BURNLEY 1988–89 *Back row (left to right):* Arthur Bellamy (Assistant Manager), Neil Grewcock, Peter Daniel, Peter Zelem, Andy Farrell, David Williams, Paul Comstive, Chris Pearce, Steve Davis, Steve Gardner, Paul Atkinson, Leighton James (Youth Team Coach).
Centre row: Jason Hardy, Stewart Hooper, Steve Taylor, Ashley Hoskin, Jason Harris, Ray Deakin, Brendan O'Connell, Gary Rowell, George Oghani, Shaun McGrory, Ian Britton.
Front row: Phillip Clegg, Neil Howarth, Paul McKay, Mark Monington, Stuart Banks, Sean Whorlow, Kurt Whipp, Steve Eyre, Carl Parker, Andy Taylor.

Division 4 BURNLEY

Turf Moor, Burnley BB10 4BX. Telephone: Burnley (0282) 27777; Ticket Office and Shop: Burnely 27777 and 38021.
Ground capacity: 25,000.
Record attendance: 54,775 v Huddersfield T, FA Cup 3rd rd, 23 Feb, 1924.
Record Receipts; £63,988 v Sheffield W, FA Cup 6th rd, 12 March, 1983.
Pitch measurements: 115yd × 73yd.
Chairman: F. J. Teasdale.
Vice-Chairman: Dr R. D. Iven MRCS (Eng), LRCP (Lond), MRCGP.
Directors: B. Dearing Llb, B. Rothwell JP, C. Holt, R. Blakeborough.
Manager: Frank Casper. ***Assistant Manager:*** Mick Docherty.
Secretary: Albert Maddox. ***Youth Team Coach:*** Leighton James.
Marketing Manager: Mrs. Joyce Pickles. ***Physio:*** Jimmy Holland.
Year Formed: 1882. ***Turned Professional:*** 1883.
Ltd. Co.: 1897.
Club Nickname: 'The Clarets'. ***Previous Name:*** 1881–82, Burnley Rovers.
Previous Grounds: 1881, Calder Vale; 1882, Turf Moor.
Record League Victory: 9-0 v Darwen, Division 1, 9th January 1892 – Hillman; Walker, Lang; McFettridge, Matthews, Keene; Nicol (3), Bowes, Espie (1), McLardie (3), Hill (2).
Record Cup Victory: 9-0 v Crystal Palace, FA Cup, 2nd rd, replay, 10 February 1909 – Dawson; Barron, McLean; Cretney (2), Leake, Moffat (1); Morley, Ogden, Smith (3), Abbott (2), Smethams (1). 9-0 v New Brighton, FA Cup, 4th rd, 26 January 1957 – Blacklaw; Angus, Winton; Seith, Adamson, Miller; Newlands (1), McIlroy (3), Lawson (3), Cheesebrough (1), Pilkington (1). 9-0 v Penrith (tie drawn away but played at Burnley) FA Cup, 1st rd, 17 November 1984 – Hansbury; Miller, Hampton, Phelan, Overson (Kennedy), Hird (3 incl 1p), Grewcock (1), Powell (2), Taylor (3), Biggins, Hutchison.
Record Defeat: 0-10 v Aston Villa, Division 1, 29 August, 1925 and v Sheffield U, Division 1, 19 January, 1929.
Most League Points (2 for a win): 62, Division 2, 1972–73.
Most League Points (3 for a win): 80, Division 3, 1981–82.
Most League Goals: 102, Division 1, 1960–61.
Highest League Scorer in Season: George Beel, 35, Division 1, 1927–28.
Most League Goals in Total Aggregate: George Beel, 178, 1923–32.
Most Capped Player: Jimmy McIlroy, 52 (55), Northern Ireland.
Most League Appearances: Jerry Dawson, 530, 1906–29.
Record Transfer Fee Received: £300,000 from Everton for Martin Dobson, August 1974, and from Derby Co for Leighton James, November 1975.
Record Transfer Fee Paid: £165,000 to QPR for Leighton James, September 1978.
Football League Record: 1888 Original Member of the Football League; 1897–98 Division 2; 1898–1900 Division 1; 1900–13 Division 2; 1913–30 Division 1; 1930–47 Division 2; 1947–71 Division 1; 1971–73 Division 2; 1973–76 Division 1; 1976–80 Division 2; 1980–82 Division 3; 1982–83 Division 2; 1983–85 Division 3; 1985– Division 4.
Honours: *Football League:* Division 1 – Champions 1920–21, 1959–60; Runners-up 1919–20, 1961–62; Division 2 – Champions 1897–98, 1972–73; Runners-up 1912–13, 1946–47; Division 3 – Champions 1981–82. Record 30 Consecutive Division 1 games without defeat 1920–21. *FA Cup:* Winners 1913–14; Runners-up 1946–47, 1961–62. *Football League Cup:* semi-final 1960–61, 1968–69, 1982–83. *Anglo Scottish Cup:* Winners 1978–79. *Sherpa Van Trophy:* Runners-up 1988. **European Competitions;** *European Cup:* 1960–61. *European Fairs Cup:* 1966–67.
Colours: Claret shirts with light blue sleeves, white shorts and stockings. **Change colours:** All White with claret facings.

BURNLEY 1988–89 LEAGUE RECORD

Match No.	Date	Venue	Opponents	Result	H/T Score	Lg. Pos.	Goalscorers	Attendance
1	Aug 27	H	Rochdale	W 2-1	1-0	—	Comstive, Farrell	7510
2	Sept 3	A	Halifax T	W 2-1	1-0	3	Comstive, O'Connell	3371
3	10	H	York C	W 6-0	2-0	1	Atkinson, Britton, Comstive 2 (1 pen), O'Connell, Oghani	7239
4	16	A	Stockport Co	D 0-0	0-0	—		6676
5	20	A	Torquay U	L 0-2	0-1	—		3021
6	24	H	Colchester U	W 2-0	1-0	3	Rowell, O'Connell	7177
7	Oct 1	A	Darlington	D 1-1	0-0	4	O'Connell	3409
8	4	H	Rotherham U	W 1-0	0-0	—	Oghani	9283
9	8	H	Exeter C	W 3-0	1-0	1	Oghani, Zelem, O'Connell	7889
10	15	A	Peterborough U	L 0-3	0-1	1		5023
11	22	H	Leyton Orient	D 2-2	0-1	2	Comstive (pen), O'Connell	8503
12	25	A	Carlisle U	D 0-0	0-0	—		4543
13	29	H	Cambridge U	W 2-0	1-0	1	Oghani, O'Connell	8670
14	Nov 5	A	Scunthorpe U	L 1-2	0-0	4	O'Connell	6358
15	8	H	Lincoln C	L 1-4	1-1	—	Comstive (pen)	8742
16	12	A	Scarborough	L 0-1	0-0	5		5258
17	26	A	Doncaster R	L 0-1	0-0	9		2724
18	Dec 3	H	Hartlepool U	D 0-0	0-0	9		6284
19	17	A	Hereford U	D 0-0	0-0	9		2442
20	26	H	Wrexham	L 1-3	1-1	12	O'Connell	9174
21	31	H	Grimsby T	W 1-0	0-0	10	Oghani	7367
22	Jan 2	A	Tranmere R	L 1-2	0-1	13	Britton	7974
23	14	H	Halifax T	W 2-1	1-0	12	Oghani 2	8297
24	21	A	Rochdale	L 1-2	1-0	13	Farrell	5799
25	28	H	Stockport Co	W 1-0	0-0	9	Britton	6942
26	Feb 4	H	Torquay U	W 1-0	0-0	8	O'Connell	6626
27	10	A	Colchester U	D 2-2	2-0	—	White 2 (1 pen)	3809
28	18	A	Exeter C	L 0-3	0-1	10		3672
29	25	H	Peterborough U	D 1-1	0-0	9	Measham	6848
30	Mar 4	A	Leyton Orient	L 0-3	0-0	11		3946
31	11	H	Scunthorpe U	L 0-1	0-1	14		6813
32	14	A	Cambridge U	L 1-2	0-1	—	White	3100
33	18	A	York C	D 0-0	0-0	18		3164
34	21	H	Carlisle U	D 0-0	0-0	—		5258
35	25	H	Tranmere R	D 2-2	0-1	15	Comstive 2	6838
36	27	A	Wrexham	L 2-4	1-3	17	Grewcock, McGrory	3956
37	Apr 1	H	Hereford U	D 3-3	1-1	18	James 2(2 pens), Monington	5534
38	4	H	Crewe Alex	W 1-0	1-0	—	Hardy	5677
39	8	A	Grimsby T	L 0-1	0-0	17		4856
40	15	H	Darlington	L 0-1	0-0	17		5578
41	22	A	Rotherman U	L 1-3	1-3	17	Farrell	5726
42	29	H	Doncaster R	W 3-0	1-0	16	O'Connell 2, Comstive	4211
43	May 1	A	Lincoln C	W 3-2	2-0	16	White 2, O'Connell	3594
44	6	A	Hartlepool U	D 2-2	1-0	16	Farrell, James (pen)	2174
45	9	A	Crewe Alex	L 0-4	0-1	—		2963
46	13	H	Scarborough	L 0-1	0-0	16		6206

Final League Position: 16

GOALSCORERS

League (52): O'Connell 13, Comstive 9 (3 pens), Oghani 7, White 5 (1 pen), Farrell 4, Britton 3, James 3 (3 pens), Atkinson 1, Grewcock 1, Hardy 1, McGrory 1, Measham 1, Monington 1, Rowell 1, Zelem 1.
Littlewoods Cup (6): O'Connell 3, Comstive 2 (2 pens), Oghani 1.
FA Cup (0).

Littlewoods Cup	First Round	Rochdale (a)	3-3
		(h)	2-1
	Second Round	Luton T (a)	1-1
		(h)	0-1
FA Cup	First Round	Chester C (h)	0-2

Pearce	Daniel	Deakin	Farrell	Davis	Gardner	Britton	Oghani	Rowell	Comstive	James	O'Connell	Atkinson	Taylor	Zelem	White	McGrory	Hoskin	Morley	Measham	Miller	Jones	Hardy	Monington	Grewcock	Williams	Hooper	*Match No.*
1	2	3	4	5	6	7	8	9*	10	11	12																1
1	2	3	4	5	6	7	8		10		9	11															2
1	2	3	4	5	6	7	8		10		9	11															3
1	2	3	4	5	6	7	8		10		9	11															4
1	2	3	4	5	6	7	8		10		9	11															5
1	2	3*	4	5	6	7	8	12	10		9	11															6
1	2		3	5	6	7	8	4	10		9	11*	12														7
1	2		3		6	7	8	4	10		9	11		5													8
1	2		3		6	7	8	4	10		9	11		5													9
1	2		3		6	7	8	4	10		9	11		5													10
1	2		4	6	3	11*	8	12	10		9			5	7												11
1	2		4	6			8	11*	10		9			5	7	3	12										12
1	2		4		6		8		10		9			5	7	3		11									13
1	2		4		6		8		10		9			5	7	3		11									14
1			4	6	2		8	12	10		9			5	7	3*		11									15
1			4	5	6		8		10		9				7	3		11	2								16
1			3	5	6	4	8*	12	10		9	11†			14			7	2								17
1			3	5	6	4	8*	14	10		9	11†	12		7				2								18
1			3	5	6	4	8		10		9	11			7				2								19
1			3	5	6	4	8		10		9	11*			7		12		2								20
1			3	5	6	4	8		10		9				7	12	11		2*								21
1			2	5	6	4	8		10		9		12		7	3	11*										22
1			3	5	6	4	8		10*	11	9			12	7				2								23
1			3	5	6	4	8		10	11*	9				7	12			2								24
1			3	5	6	4	8		10	11	9				7				2								25
1			3	5	6	4	8		10	11*	9				7†	14	12		2								26
1		11	3*	5	6	4	8	12	10		9				7				2								27
1		11	12	5		4	8	14	10†		9				7	3*			2	6							28
1		11		5	3	4	8	10*		12	9				7				2	6							29
1			3	5	10	4	8†	12		11					7*				2	6	9	14					30
1			7	5	6	4	8			11		14			12				2	10*	9†	3					31
1				5	6	4	8†	14	10*	12	9				7				2			3	11				32
1				5	6	4	8		10		9				7*				2			3	11	12			33
1					6	4	8*	12	10		9				7				2			3	5	11			34
1					6	4	8		10		9				7				2			3	5	11			35
1					6	4†		8	10	12	9				7*	14			2			3	5	11			36
1					6*	4	8		10†	11	9				12	14			2			3	5	7			37
1				5	6	4	8			11	9					10			2			3		7			38
				5	6	4				11	9				12	10			2		8*	3		7	1		39
				5	6	4				11*	9				12	10			2		8†	3	14	7	1		40
			4	5	6	12				11	9				8	10†			2			3		7*	1	14	41
		11	4	5	6				12		9				8	10*			2			3		7	1		42
		11	4	5	6				10		9				8				2			3		7	1		43
		11	4	5	6				10	9					8				2			3		7	1		44
		11	4†	5	6				10*	12	9				8	14			2			3		7	1		45
1		11	4	5	6	10*				7†	9				8	14			2			3	12				46
39	14	14	35 + 1s	37	44	36 + 1s	37	8 + 10s	37 + 1s	14 + 4s	42 + 1s	13 + 1s	— + 3s	8 + 1s	30 + 5s	12 + 7s	2 + 3s	5	30	4	4	16 + 1s	6 + 2s	12 + 1s	7	— + 1s	

BURNLEY

Player and Position	Ht	Wt	Birth Date	Birth Place	Source	Clubs	League App	League Gls
Goalkeepers								
Chris Pearce	6 0	11 04	7 8 61	Newport	Apprentice	Wolverhampton W	—	—
						Blackburn R	—	—
						Rochdale (loan)	5	—
						Barnsley (loan)	—	—
						Rochdale	36	—
						Port Vale	48	—
						Wrexham	25	—
						Burnley	85	—
David Williams	6 0	12 00	18 9 68	Liverpool	Trainee	Oldham Ath	—	—
						Burnley	7	—
Defenders								
Peter Daniel‡	5 9	11 05	12 12 55	Hull	Amateur	Hull C	113	9
						Wolverhampton W	157	13
						Sunderland	34	—
						Lincoln C	55	2
						Burnley	41	—
Steve Davis	6 0	12 07	26 7 65	Birmingham	Apprentice	Stoke C	—	—
						Crewe Alex	145	1
						Burnley	70	5
Ray Deakin	5 8	11 01	19 6 59	Liverpool	Apprentice	Everton	—	—
						Port Vale	23	6
						Bolton W	105	2
						Burnley	143	6
Steve Gardner	5 9	12 8	3 7 68	Teeside	Apprentice	Manchester U	—	—
						Burnley	86	—
Jim Heggarty	6 2	13 08	4 8 65	Larne		Brighton & HA	—	—
						Burnley	36	1
Leighton James‡	5 9	12 05	16 2 53	Llwchyr	Apprentice	Burnley	181	44
						Derby Co	68	15
						QPR	28	4
						Burnley	76	9
						Swansea C	98	27
						Sunderland	52	4
						Bury	46	5
						Newport Co	28	2
						Burnley	79	13
Shaun McGrory	5 10	12 00	29 2 68	Coventry		Coventry C	—	—
						Burnley	35	2
Ian Measham	5 11	11 08	14 12 64	Barnsley	Apprentice	Huddersfield T	17	—
						Lincoln C (loan)	6	—
						Rochdale (loan)	12	—
						Cambridge U	46	—
						Burnley	30	1
Peter Zelem*	6 0	11 04	13 2 62	Manchester	Apprentice	Chester C	129	15
						Wolverhampton W	45	1
						Preston NE	6	1
						Burnley	19	2
Midfield								
Paul Atkinson	5 10	11 05	14 8 61	Otley	Apprentice	Oldham Ath	143	11
						Watford	11	—
						Oldham Ath	59	2
						Swansea C (loan)	18	3
						Bolton W (loan)	3	—
						Burnley	14	1
Ian Britton*	5 5	9 07	19 5 54	Dundee	Apprentice	Chelsea	263	33
						Dundee U	10	1
						Blackpool	106	15
						Burnley	108	10
Paul Comstive	6 1	12 07	25 11 61	Southport	Amateur	Blackburn R	6	—
						Rochdale (loan)	9	2
						Wigan Ath	35	2
						Wrexham	99	8
						Burnley	82	17

BURNLEY

Foundation: The majority of those responsible for the formation of the Burnley club in 1881 were from the defunct rugby club Burnley Rovers. Indeed, they continued to play rugby for a year before changing to soccer and dropping "Rovers" from their name. The changes were decided at a meeting held in May 1882 at the Bull Hotel.

Managers (and Secretary-managers)
Arthur F. Sutcliffe 1893–96*, Harry Bradshaw 1896–99*, Ernest Magnall 1899–1903*, Spen Whittaker 1903–10, R. H. Wadge 1910–11*, John Haworth 1911–25, Albert Pickles 1925–32, Tom Bromilow 1932–35, Alf Boland 1935–39*, Cliff Britton 1945–48, Frank Hill 1948–54, Alan Brown 1954–57, Billy Dougall 1957–58, Harry Potts 1958–70 (GM to 1972), Jimmy Adamson 1970–76, Joe Brown 1976–77, Harry Potts 1977–79, Brian Miller 1979–83, John Bond 1983–84, John Benson 1984–85, Martin Buchan 1985, Tommy Cavanagh 1985–86, Brian Miller 1986–89, Frank Casper 1989– .

Player and Position	*Ht*	*Wt*	*Birth Date*	*Birth Place*	*Source*	*Clubs*	*League App*	*League Gls*
Andy Farrell	5 11	11 00	7 10 65	Colchester	School	Colchester U	105	5
						Burnley	81	7
Jason Hardy	5 8	10 00	14 12 69		Trainee	Burnley	18	1
Jason Harris	5 7	10 00	26 12 69	Rochdale	Trainee	Burnley	4	—
Stuart Hooper*	5 8	10 06	16 6 70	Lytham St Annes	Trainee	Burnley	1	—
Ashley Hoskin*	5 2	8 05	27 3 68	Accrington	Apprentice	Burnley	88	11
Mark Monington	5 8	11 00	21 10 70	Bilsthorpe	School	Burnley	8	1
Forwards								
Neil Grewcock	5 6	11 03	26 4 62	Leicester		Leicester C	8	1
						Gillingham (loan)	13	1
						Gillingham	21	3
					Shepshed C	Burnley	165	23
David Jones*			3 7 64	Harrow		Chelsea	—	—
						Bury	1	—
						Leyton Orient	2	—
						Burnley	4	—
Brendan O'Connell	5 10	10 09	12 11 66	London		Portsmouth	—	—
						Exeter C	81	19
						Burnley	43	13
George Oghani	5 11	12 03	2 9 60	Manchester	Hyde U	Bolton W	99	27
						Wrexham (loan)	7	—
						Burnley	74	21
Gary Rowell	5 10	11 03	6 6 57	Seaham	Apprentice	Sunderland	254	88
						Norwich C	6	1
						Middlesbrough	27	10
						Brighton & HA	12	—
						Dundee	1	—
						Carlisle U	7	—
						Burnley	18	1
Winston White	5 10	10 12	26 10 58	Leicester	Apprentice	Leicester C	12	1
						Hereford U	175	21
						Chesterfield	1	—
						Port Vale	1	—
						Stockport Co	4	—
						Bury	125	11
						Rochdale (loan)	4	—
						Colchester U	65	8
						Burnley	35	5

Trainees
Clegg, Philip A; Eyre, Steven F; Howarth, Neil; Oliver, John R; Whipp, Kurt M; Whorlow, Sean.

****Non-Contract**
Mercer, Stephen T.

Associated Schoolboys
Bainbridge, Karl J; Isherwood, Alvin L; King, Andrew P; Lawson, Andrew R; McGlory, Richard H; Parry, Christopher M; Rigby, Douglas M; Ryder, Damian M; Wallace, Simon P.

BURY 1988–89 *Back row (left to right):* Peter Valentine, Charlie Bishop, Simon Farnworth, Gary Leonard, Terry Pashley.
Centre row: Wilf McGuinness (Physiotherapist/Coach), Martin Dobson (Manager), Noel Brotherston, Phil Parkinson, Mark Higgins, Jamie Hoyland, Frank Casper (Assistant Manager), Ray Pointer (Youth Coach).
Front row: Craig Brown, David Lee, Liam Robinson, Andy Hill, Kenny Clements, Nigel Greenwood.

Division 3 BURY

Gigg Lane, Bury BL9 9HR. Telephone 061-764 4881/2. Commercial Dept. 061-764 7475/705 2144. Clubcall: 0898 121197. Community Programme: 061-797 5423. Social Club: 061-764 6771.

Ground capacity: 8,000.

Record attendance: 35,000 v Bolton, FA Cup 3rd rd, 9 Jan, 1960.

Record receipts: £22,200 v Nottingham F, League Cup quarter-final, 17 Jan, 1978.

Pitch measurements: 112yd × 72yd.

President:

Chairman: T. Robinson. ***Vice-Chairman:*** Canon J. R. Smith MA.

Directors: C. H. Eaves, I. Pickup, J. Smith, A. Noonan, F. Mason.

Manager: Sam Ellis. ***Assistant Manager:***

Reserve Coach: Ray Pointer. ***Physio:*** Wilf McGuinness.

Secretary: John Heap. ***Commercial Manager:*** Neville Neville.

Year Formed: 1885. ***Turned professional:*** 1885.

Ltd Co.: 1897. **Club Nickname:** 'Shakers'.

Club Sponsors: MacPherson Paints.

Record League Victory: 8-0 v Tranmere R, Division 3, 10 January 1970 – Forrest: Tinney, Saile; Anderson, Turner, McDermott; Hince (1), Arrowsmith (1), Jones (4), Kerr (1), Grundy. (1 og)

Record Cup Victory: 12-1 v Stockton, FA Cup, 1st rd (replay), 2 February 1897 – Montgomery; Darroch, Barbour; Hendry (1), Clegg, Ross (1); Wylie (3), Pangbourn, Millar (4), Henderson (2), Plant. (1 og).

Record Defeat: 0-10 v Blackburn R, FA Cup, preliminary round, 1st October, 1887 and v West Ham U, Milk Cup, 2nd rd, 2nd leg, 25 October, 1983.

Most League Points (2 for a win): 68, Division 3, 1960–61.

Most League Points (3 for a win): 84, Division 4, 1984–85.

Most League Goals: 108, Division 3, 1960–61.

Highest League Scorer in Season: Craig Madden, 35, Division 4, 1981–82.

Most League Goals in Total Aggregate: Craig Madden, 129, 1978–86.

Most Capped Player: Bill Gorman, 11 (13), Eire and (4), Northern Ireland.

Most League Appearances: Norman Bullock, 506, 1920–35.

Record Transfer Fee Received: £150,000 from Chesterfield for Danny Wilson, July 1980 and from Everton for Neville Southall, July 1981.

Record Transfer Fee Paid: £30,000 to Stoke C for David Gregory and to Port Vale for Ken Beamish, September 1978.

Football League Record: 1894 Elected to Division 2; 1895–1912 Division 1; 1912–24 Division 2; 1924–28 Division 1; 1929–57 Division 2; 1957–61 Division 3; 1961–67 Division 2; 1967–68 Division 3; 1968–69 Division 2; 1969–71 Division 3; 1971–74 Division 3; 1980–85 Division 4; 1985– Division 3.

Honours: *Football League:* Division 1 best season: 4th, 1925–26; Division 2 – Champions 1894–95; Runners-up 1923–24; Division 3 – Champions 1960–61; Runners-up 1967–68. *FA Cup:* Winners 1900, 1903. *Football League Cup:* Semi-final 1963.

Colours: White shirts, navy blue shorts, navy stockings. **Change colours:** Red shirts, white shorts, red stockings.

BURY 1988–89 LEAGUE RECORD

Match No.	Date	Venue	Opponents	Result		H/T Score	Lg. Pos.	Goalscorers	Atten-dance
1	Aug 27	H	Wolverhampton W	W	3-1	2-0	—	Hoyland, Robinson, Bishop	4314
2	Sept 3	A	Swansea C	D	1-1	0-1	4	Lee	5141
3	10	H	Port Vale	D	0-0	0-0	8		2978
4	17	A	Fulham	L	0-1	0-1	13		3754
5	24	H	Mansfield T	L	0-1	0-0	20		2412
6	Oct 1	A	Chesterfield	W	2-1	1-1	16	Robinson (pen), Valentine	1837
7	4	H	Reading	W	2-1	1-1	—	Elliott, Lee	2027
8	8	A	Preston NE	L	0-1	0-0	14		5863
9	15	H	Brentford	W	3-1	2-1	13	Robinson (pen), Elliott, McIlroy	2359
10	22	A	Gillingham	W	4-3	3-1	10	Robinson 3 (1 pen), Bishop	2850
11	25	A	Southend U	W	3-1	0-0	—	Robinson 2, Lee	2419
12	29	A	Sheffield U	L	1-2	0-2	9	Robinson	12,348
13	Nov 1	A	Cardiff C	L	0-3	0-0	—		2411
14	5	H	Notts Co	D	1-1	0-1	10	Hoyland	2612
15	8	H	Chester C	W	2-1	1-0	—	Hoyland, Greenwood	2497
16	12	A	Bolton W	W	4-2	2-0	8	Elliott 2, Leonard, Robinson (pen)	7897
17	26	A	Bristol R	W	3-1	2-0	4	Elliott 2, Reece (og)	4251
18	Dec 3	H	Wigan Ath	D	1-1	1-0	5	Robinson (pen)	3121
19	17	A	Huddersfield T	L	2-3	1-2	6	Robinson, Elliott	5150
20	26	H	Bristol C	W	2-1	1-1	4	Hoyland, Robinson (pen)	3368
21	31	H	Aldershot	L	0-1	0-0	8		3196
22	Jan 2	A	Blackpool	D	2-2	0-1	7	Robinson, Elliott	4199
23	7	A	Northampton T	L	0-2	0-1	8		3463
24	14	H	Swansea C	W	1-0	0-0	6	Robinson	2608
25	21	A	Port Vale	W	3-1	1-1	6	Robinson 2, Lee	5783
26	28	H	Fulham	W	3-1	1-0	5	Robinson 2 (1 pen), Hoyland	3582
27	Feb 4	H	Chesterfield	W	2-1	1-1	3	Robinson, McIlroy	3844
28	11	A	Reading	D	1-1	0-1	3	Hoyland	3804
29	18	H	Preston NE	D	1-1	0-0	3	Bishop	0977
30	25	A	Brentford	D	2-2	0-1	3	Hoyland, Elliott	6077
31	28	A	Southend U	D	1-1	0-1	—	Elliott	2479
32	Mar 4	H	Gillingham	W	1-0	1-0	3	Hoyland	4313
33	11	A	Notts Co	L	0-3	0-1	5		5757
34	14	H	Sheffield U	L	1-2	0-1	—	Wassall	5334
35	18	A	Wolverhampton W	L	0-4	0-1	7		14,828
36	25	H	Blackpool	D	0-0	0-0	8		3717
37	27	A	Bristol C	L	0-3	0-1	8		8496
38	Apr 1	H	Huddersfield T	L	0-6	0-2	8		4145
39	4	H	Northampton T	L	0-1	0-1	—		1965
40	8	A	Aldershot	L	1-4	1-0	10	Pashley	1677
41	15	H	Cardiff C	W	1-0	1-0	10	Elliott	2124
42	22	A	Mansfield T	D	1-1	0-1	10	Hoyland	2826
43	29	H	Bolton W	D	0-0	0-0	10		4393
44	May 1	A	Chester C	L	0-2	0-1	10		2110
45	6	A	Wigan Ath	L	0-1	0-0	13		3045
46	13	H	Bristol R	D	0-0	0-0	13		3073

Final League Position: 13

GOALSCORERS

League (55): Robinson 20 (7 pens), Elliott 11, Hoyland 9, Lee 4, Bishop 3, McIlroy 2, Greenwood 1, Leonard 1, Pashley 1, Valentine 1, Wassall 1, own goal 1.
Littlewoods Cup (6): Hoyland 2, Robinson 2 (1 pen), Entwistle 1, Lee 1.
FA Cup (1): Parkinson 1.

Littlewoods Cup	First Round	Wrexham (h)	2-1
		(a)	2-2
	Second Round	Everton (a)	0-3
		(h)	2-2
FA Cup	First Round	Guisborough (at Middlesbrough)	1-0
	Second Round	Blackpool (a)	0-3

Farnworth	Hill	Pashley	Leonard	Valentine	Higgins	Lee	Robinson	Hoyland	McIlroy	Bishop	Clements	Parkinson	Brotherston	Entwistle	Jones	Elliott	Greenwood	Godden	Windridge	Fazackerley	Eli	Wassall	Hulme	Atkin	*Match No.*
1	2	3	4	5	6	7	8	9	10	11															1
1	2	3	4	5*	6	7	8	9	10	11	12														2
1	2				6	7	8	9	10	3	5	4*	11	12											3
1	2				6	7	8	9	10	3	5	4	11*	12											4
1	2	3†	12	5	6	7	8	9	10	11		4*			14										5
1	2	11*		5		7	8	4	10	3	6	12				9									6
1	2	11	12	5		7	8	4	10	3	6*					9									7
1	2	11	8	5		7		4	10*	3	6					9	12								8
1	2	3		5		7	8	4	10		6	11				9									9
1	2	11*		5		7†	8	4	10	3	6	12				9	14								10
1	2			5		7	8	4	10	3	6	11				9									11
1	2			5		7	8	4	10	3	6	11				9									12
1	2*		12	5		7	8	4	10	3	6	11				9†	14								13
1	2			5		7	8	4	10	3	6	11				9									14
1	2		12†	5		7	8	4	10*	3	6	11				9	14								15
1	2		10	5		7	8	4		3	6	11				9									16
1	2			5		7	8	4	10	3	6	11				9									17
1	2			5		7	8*	4	10	3	6	11				9	12								18
	2			5		7	8	4	10		6	11				9		1	3						19
1	2			5		7	8	4	10	3	6	11				9									20
1	2			5†		7	8	4	10	3*	6	11				9	12			14					21
1	2					7	8	4	10	3	6	11				9				5					22
1	2			5		7	8	4	10*	3†	6	11				9	12			14					23
1	2			5		7	8	4	10	3	6	11				9*	12								24
1	2			5		7	8	4	10	3	6	11				9									25
1	2			5*		7	8	4	10	3	6	11				9					12				26
1	2	5†				7	8	4	10	3	6	11				9*	12			14					27
1	2	5†	14			7	8	4	10	3	6	11				9*	12								28
1	2	11				7	8	4	10	3	6					9				5					29
1	2	11*				7	8	4	10	3	6					9				5	12				30
1	2					7	8	4	10	3	6	11				9*	12			5					31
1		3*				7	8	4	10	2	6	11					9			12		5			32
1	2	14				7	8	4	10	3	6	11					9†			12		5*			33
1	2					7	8	4	10	3	6	11				9						5			34
1	2	14				7	8†	4	10	3	6	11				9*				12		5			35
1	2					7		4	10	3	6	11					9					5	8		36
1		2				7	8	4	10†	3	6	11					12					5	9*	14	37
1		2				7	8	4	10	3	6	11					9					5			38
1	2	3				7	8*	4	10		6	11				9	12			5					39
1	2	3		12		7		4	10		6	11				9	8			5*					40
1	2	3		5		7	8	4	10		6	11				9									41
1	2*	3		5		7	8	4	10	11	6						9			12					42
1	2	3		5		7	8	4	10		6	11					9								43
1	2	3		5		7†	8	4	10	12	6	11*					9						14		44
1	2	3		5			8	4	10		6*	12					9			7			11		45
1	2	3		5		7	8	4	10		6	11					9*						12		46
45	43	23	4	29	5	45	43	46	45	37	43	36	2	—	—	31	10	1	1	7	—	7	3	—	
		+	+	+						+	+	+		+	+		+			+	+		+	+	
		2s	5s	1s						1s	1s	3s		2s	1s		13s			7s	2s		2s	1s	

BURY

Player and Position	Ht	Wt	Birth Date	Birth Place	Source	Clubs	League App	League Gls
Goalkeepers								
Peter Cole*			15 9 70	Manchester		Bury	—	—
Simon Farnworth	6 0	11 10	28 10 63	Chorley	Apprentice	Bolton W	113	—
						Stockport Co (loan)	10	—
						Tranmere R (loan)	7	—
						Bury	98	—
Keith Mason‡	6 1	13 09	19 7 58	Leicester		Huddersfield T	30	—
						Bury	—	—
Defenders								
Paul Atkin	6 0	12 04	3 9 69	Nottingham	Trainee	Notts Co	—	—
						Bury	1	—
Charlie Bishop	6 0	12 01	16 2 68	Nottingham	Apprentice	Stoke C	—	—
						Watford	—	—
						Bury	55	3
Kenny Clements	6 1	12 06	9 4 55	Manchester	Amateur	Manchester C	119	—
						Oldham Ath	206	2
						Manchester C (loan)	12	1
						Manchester C	94	—
						Bury	53	1
Roger Eli*	5 10	12 00	11 9 65	Bradford	Apprentice	Leeds U	2	—
						Wolverhampton W	18	—
						Cambridge U	—	—
						Crewe Alex	27	1
						York C	4	1
						Bury	2	—
Derek Fazackerley*	5 11	12 03	5 11 51	Preston	Apprentice	Blackburn R	596	24
						Chester C	66	—
						York C	16	—
						Bury	14	—
Andy Hill	5 11	12 00	20 1 65	Maltby	Apprentice	Manchester U	—	—
						Bury	206	8
Terry Pashley	5 8	12 00	11 10 56	Chesterfield	Apprentice	Burnley	18	—
						Blackpool	201	7
						Bury	217	5
Peter Valentine	5 10	12 00	16 4 63	Huddersfield	Apprentice	Huddersfield T	19	1
						Bolton W	68	1
						Bury	164	8
Andy Walsh*	6 0	11 02	15 2 70	Preston		Bury	1	—
Midfield								
Noel Brotherston	5 7	11 04	18 11 56	Belfast	Apprentice	Tottenham H	1	—
						Blackburn R	317	40
						Bury	38	4
						Scarborough (loan)	5	—
Craig Brown*	5 10	10 09	10 1 70	Chorley	Trainee	Bury	—	—
Steve Holland‡	5 9	10 03	30 4 70	Stockport	Derby Co	Bury	—	—
Jamie Hoyland	6 0	12 08	23 1 66	Sheffield	Apprentice	Manchester C	2	—
						Bury	126	19
Dave Lee	5 8	10 02	5 11 67	Manchester	Schools	Bury	116	11
Sammy McIlroy	5 10	11 08	2 8 54	Belfast	Apprentice	Manchester U	342	57
						Stoke C	133	14
						Manchester C	13	1
						Bury	43	6
					Modling	Bury	45	2
Philip Parkinson	5 10	10 11	1 12 67	Chorley	Apprentice	Southampton	—	—
						Bury	47	1

BURY

Foundation: A meeting at the Waggon & Horses Hotel, attended largely by members of Bury Wesleyans and Bury Unitarians football clubs, decided to form a new Bury club. This was officially formed at a subsequent gathering at the Old White Horse Hotel, Fleet Street, Bury on April 24, 1885.

Managers (and Secretary-managers)
T. Hargreaves 1887*, H. S. Hamer 1887–1907*, Archie Montgomery 1907–15, William Cameron 1919–23, James Hunter Thompson 1923–27, Percy Smith 1927–30, Arthur Paine 1930–34, Norman Bullock 1934–38, Jim Porter 1944–45, Norman Bullock 1945–49, John McNeil 1950–53, Dave Russell 1953–61, Bob Stokoe 1961–65, Bert Head 1965–66, Les Shannon 1966–69, Jack Marshall 1969, Les Hart 1970, Tommy McAnearney 1970–72, Alan Brown 1972–73, Bobby Smith 1973–77, Bob Stokoe 1977–78, David Hatton 1978–79, Dave Connor 1979–80, Jim Iley 1980–84, Martin Dobson 1984–89, Sam Ellis 1989– .

Player and Position	*Ht*	*Wt*	*Birth Date*	*Birth Place*	*Source*	*Clubs*	*League App*	*League Gls*
Forwards								
Steve Elliott	6 0	11 10	15 9 58	Haltwistle	Apprentice	Nottingham F	4	—
						Preston NE	208	70
						Luton T	12	3
						Walsall	69	21
						Bolton W	60	11
						Bury	31	11
Nigel Greenwood	5 11	12 00	27 11 66	Preston	Apprentice	Preston NE	45	14
						Bury	90	20
Kevin Hulme†			2 12 67	Farnworth		Bury	5	—
Liam Robinson	5 6	11 04	29 12 65	Bradford	School	Nottingham F	—	—
						Huddersfield T	21	2
						Tranmere R (loan)	4	3
						Bury	118	52

Trainees
Ashworth, Adam; Bennett, Ian H; Bradley, Patrick; Bridge, Jason; Crossley, Neil J; Faulkner, Antony H; Hurst, Gordon; Miller, Alan; Newberry, Adrian; Robinson, Paul J; Seabrook, Antony R.

****Non-Contract**
Hulme, Kevin.

Associated Schoolboys
Curran, Francis L; Davies, Darren T; Dean, John P; Drake, Peter S; Hartley, Jonathan D; Horridge, Paul M; Hurst, Neil J; Kent, Daniel R.J; McCroray, Christopher R; Motby, Lee A; Phillips, Daniel P; Wolstencroft, Gary.

CAMBRIDGE UNITED 1988–89 *Back row (left to right):* Greg Allen, Paul Turner, Chris Leadbitter, Paul Bastock, Phil Chapple, John Vaughan, Lindsay Smith, Nigel Costello, Laurie Ryan. *Front row:* John Beck (Player/Coach), Gary Clayton, Ian Hamilton, Liam Daish, Colin Bailie, Chris Turner (Manager), Gary Bull, Alan Kimble, Ian Measham, George Reilly, Gary Johnson (Reserve Team Manager).

Division 4 CAMBRIDGE UNITED

Abbey Stadium, Newmarket Rd, Cambridge. Telephone Teversham (0223) 241237. Commercial dept: 0223-241244. Clubcall: 0898 12 11 41

Ground capacity: 10,150.

Record attendance; 14,000 v Chelsea, Friendly, 1 May, 1970.

Record receipts: £51,362.50 v Tottenham H. League Cup 4th Rd, 26 Nov 1986.

Pitch measurements: 110yd × 74yd.

Chairman: D. A. Ruston. ***Vice-Chairman:*** R. H. Smart.

Directors: R. J. Smith, R. Stops, C. Howlett, J. Howard.

Manager: Chris Turner. ***Assistant Manager:*** John Beck.

Physio: Roy Johnson.

Secretary: Terry Coad. ***Sales Manager:*** Gary Johnson.

Year Formed: 1919. ***Turned Professional:*** 1946. ***Ltd Co.:*** 1948.

Club Nickname: 'United'.

Previous Name: Abbey United until 1949.

Record League Victory: 6-0 v Darlington, Division 4, 18 September 1971 – Roberts; Thompson, Akers, Guild, Eades, Foote, Collins (1p), Horrey, Hollett, Greenhalgh (4), Phillips. (1 og). 6-0 v Hartlepool, Division 4, 11 February 1989 – Vaughan; Beck, Kimble, Turner, Chapple (1), Daish, Clayton, Holmes, Taylor (3 incl 1p), Bull (1), Leadbitter (1).

Record Cup Victory: 4-1 v Woking (away), FA Cup, 1st rd, 19 November 1988 – Vaughan; Bailie, Kimble, Smith, Chapple, Beck, Clayton, Ryan, Reilly (2), Hamilton, Croft (2).

Record Defeat: 0-6 v Aldershot, Division 3, 13 April, 1974 and v Darlington, Division 4, 28 September, 1974 and v Chelsea, Division 2, 15 January 1983.

Most League Points (2 for a win): 65, Division 4, 1976–77.

Most League Points (3 for a win): 68, Division 4, 1988–89.

Most League Goals: 87, Division 4, 1976–77.

Highest League Scorer in Season: David Crown, 24, Division 4, 1985–86.

Most League Goals in Total Aggregate: Alan Biley, 74, 1975–80.

Most Capped Player: Tom Finney, 7 (15), Northern Ireland.

Most League Appearances: Steve Spriggs, 416, 1975–87.

Record Transfer Fee Received: £350,000 from Derby Co for Alan Biley, January 1980.

Record Transfer Fee Paid: £140,000 to Northampton T for George Reilly, November 1979.

Football League Record: 1970 Elected to Division 4; 1973–74 Division 3; 1974–77 Division 4; 1977–78 Division 3; 1978–84 Division 2; 1984–85 Division 3; 1985– Division 4.

Honours: *Football League:* Division 2 best season: 8th, 1979–80 Division 3 – Runners-up 1977–78; Division 4 – Champions 1976–77 *FA Cup* season: 5th rd. 1982–83. *Football League Cup:* 4th rd. 1980–81.

Colours: Yellow and black shirts, yellow and black shorts, yellow stockings. **Change colours:** All sky blue with amber and black trim.

CAMBRIDGE UNITED 1988–89 LEAGUE RECORD

Match No.	Date	Venue	Opponents	Result	H/T Score	Lg. Pos.	Goalscorers	Attendance
1	Aug 27	H	Grimsby T	W 4-1	2-1	—	Reilly 2, Ryan 2	2290
2	Sept 3	A	Hereford U	L 2-4	1-3	9	Jones (og), Reilly	1711
3	10	H	Stockport Co	W 1-0	1-0	5	Ryan	1911
4	16	A	Tranmere R	W 2-1	2-1	—	Kimble, Ryan	3248
5	20	H	Lincoln C	L 2-3	0-1	—	Reilly, Smith (pen)	2776
6	24	A	Hartlepool U	L 2-3	1-2	9	Chapple, Taylor	2385
7	30	H	Carlisle U	W 3-2	1-1	—	Reilly, Chapple, Clayton	2043
8	Oct 4	A	Crewe Alex	L 0-2	0-1	—		1588
9	8	H	Halifax T	W 2-1	0-0	6	Smith (pen), Taylor	1800
10	15	A	Scunthorpe U	L 0-1	0-0	8		3514
11	21	A	Colchester U	W 2-1	0-0	—	Anderson 2	2138
12	25	H	Scarborough	D 2-2	1-1	—	Beck, Taylor	2673
13	29	A	Burnley	L 0-2	0-1	8		8670
14	Nov 4	H	Exeter C	W 2-0	0-0	—	Bailie, Croft	2063
15	8	A	Darlington	D 1-1	0-1	—	Smith (pen)	1467
16	12	H	Rotherham U	D 1-1	1-0	8	Croft	2882
17	26	H	Leyton Orient	D 2-2	1-0	11	Reilly 2	2675
18	Dec 2	A	Torquay U	L 1-3	0-3	—	Smith	1992
19	16	A	Wrexham	L 1-3	1-2	—	Ryan	1728
20	26	H	Doncaster R	D 0-0	0-0	17		2673
21	30	H	Rochdale	W 2-0	0-0	—	Ryan, Kimble (pen)	2319
22	Jan 3	A	Peterborough U	W 5-1	3-1	—	Dublin 3, Ryan, Leadbitter	4622
23	14	H	Hereford U	W 2-1	2-1	9	Dublin, Ryan	2193
24	21	A	Grimsby T	L 0-4	0-2	10		3644
25	28	H	Tranmere R	D 1-1	1-0	11	Beck	2239
26	Feb 4	A	Lincoln C	L 0-3	0-0	11		3239
27	11	H	Hartlepool U	W 6-0	2-0	9	Leadbitter, Taylor 3 (1 pen),Bull, Chapple	2300
28	17	A	Halifax T	D 0-0	0-0	—		1531
29	25	H	Scunthorpe U	L 0-3	0-1	10		2563
30	Mar 1	A	Scarborough	L 1-2	0-0	—	Dennis	2011
31	5	H	Colchester U	W 3-1	2-1	—	Taylor, Leadbitter, Ryan	4205
32	11	A	Exeter C	W 3-0	1-0	7	Leadbitter, Beck, Taylor	3180
33	14	H	Burnley	W 2-1	1-0	—	Kimble (pen), Taylor	3100
34	17	A	Stockport Co	D 0-0	0-0	—		2521
35	25	H	Peterborough U	W 2-1	0-0	8	Kimble (pen), Dennis	4215
36	27	A	Doncaster R	D 1-1	0-0	8	Ryan	1937
37	31	H	Wrexham	W 2-0	0-0	—	Taylor, Beck	3072
38	Apr 4	H	York C	D 1-1	0-1	—	Kimble (pen)	2400
39	8	A	Rochdale	L 1-2	1-2	8	Ryan	1314
40	15	A	Carlisle U	D 1-1	0-0	7	Dennis	2579
41	22	H	Crewe Alex	D 1-1	0-1	8	Leadbitter	3512
42	29	A	Leyton Orient	D 1-1	1-1	8	Taylor	5657
43	May 2	H	Darlington	L 1-3	0-1	—	Ryan	3310
44	6	H	Torquay U	W 3-0	1-1	8	Dublin, Leadbitter, Kimble (pen)	2163
45	9	A	York C	W 2-1	2-0	—	Taylor, Dublin	2336
46	13	A	Rotherham U	D 0-0	0-0	8		9567

Final League Position: 8

GOALSCORERS

League (71): Ryan 12, Taylor 12, Reilly 7, Dublin 6, Kimble 6 (5 pens), Leadbitter 6, Beck 4, Smith 4 (3 pens), Chapple 3, Dennis 3, Anderson 2, Croft 2, Bailie 1, Bull 1, Clayton 1, own goal 1.
Littlewoods Cup (2): Clayton 1, Ryan 1.
FA Cup (5): Croft 2, Reilly 2, Chapple 1.

Littlewoods Cup	First Round	Gillingham (h)	1-2
		(a)	1-3
FA Cup	First Round	Woking (a)	4-1
	Second Round	Bognor (a)	1-0
	Third Round	Plymouth Arg (a)	0-2

Bastock	Bailie	Kimble	Smith	Chapple	Allen	Beck	Ryan	Reilly	Hamilton	Leadbitter	Clayton	Taylor	Turner	Bull	Vaughan	Byrne	Anderson	Croft	Dublin	Daish	Poole	Holmes	Dennis	Dearden	Howard	Match No.
1	2	3	4	5	6*	7	8	9	10	11	12															1
1	2	3	4	5		6		9		11	7	8*	10	12												2
	2	3	4	5	10		8	9	12	11	7				1	6*										3
	2	3	4	5	10	12	8	9		11	7				1	6*										4
	2	3	4	5	10	12	8	9		11*	7				1	6										5
	2	3	4	5		12	8	9	10	11†	7	14			1	6*										6
	2	3	4	5		6	8*	9	10		7	12			1		11									7
	2	3	4	5		6	8	9*	10		7	12			1		11									8
	2	3	4	5		6	8*	9	10		7	12			1		11									9
	2	3	4	5		6		9	10		7	8			1		11									10
	2	3	4	5		6		9	10		7	8			1		11									11
	2	3	4	5		6†	9*		10		7	8		12	1		11	14								12
	2	3	4	5		6	12	9	10		7	8*			1		11†	14								13
	2	3	4	5		6	12	9	10		7	8*			1		11†	14								14
	2	3	4	5		6	8	9*	10†		7	12	14		1			11								15
	2	3	4	5		6	8*	9	10		7	12			1			11								16
	2	3	4	5		6	8	9	10		7				1			11								17
	2	3	4	5		6	8*	9	10		7			12	1			11								18
	2	3		5		6*	8	9†			7	10		12	1			11	14	4						19
	2	3		5			8	9*			7	10	6		1			11	12	4						20
	2	3		5			8			12	7	10	6		1			11*	9	4						21
	2	3		5			8			12	7	10	6		1			11*	9	4						22
	2*	3		5			8			12	7	10	6		1			11	9	4						23
		3		5		14	8*				7	10	6	12	1			11†	9	4	2					24
		3		5		2	8†			14	7	10	6	12	1			11*	9	4						25
				5		2	14	9*		3	7	10	6	8	1			11	12†	4						26
		3		5		2				11	7	10	4	9	1					6		8				27
		3		5		2	12			11	7	10	4	9*	1					6		8				28
		3		5		14	12			11	2	10	4	9*	1					6		8†	7			29
		3		5			9*			11	2	10	4		1			12		6		8	7			30
		3		5		8	9			11	2	10	4		1*			12		6			7			31
		3		5		8	9*			11	2	10	4						12	6		14	7†	1		32
		3		5		8	9			11	2	10	4						12	6			7*	1		33
		3		5		8	9*			11	2	10	4						12	6			7	1		34
		3		5		8	9*			11	2	10	4						12	6			7	1		35
		3		5		8	9			11	2	10	4							6			7	1		36
		3		5		8	9*			11	2	10	4						12	6			7	1		37
		3		5		8	9*			11	2	10	4						12	6			7	1		38
		3		5		8	9			11	2	10	4†							6		14	7*	1	12	39
		3		5		8	9			11	2	10							4	6			7	1		40
		3		5		8	9			11	2	10							4*	6		12	7	1		41
		3		5		8	9			11	2	10							4	6			7	1		42
		3		5		8†	9			11*	2	10							4	6		14	7	1	12	43
		3		5		8				11	2	10							4	6		9	7	1		44
		3		5		8				11	2	10							4	6		9	7	1		45
		3		5		8				11	2	10							4	6		9	7	1		46
2	23	45	18	46	4	35 + 5s	34 + 5s	20	14 + 1s	27 + 4s	45 + 1s	34 + 6s	21 + 1s	4 + 6s	29	4	8	12 + 5s	12 + 9s	28	1	7 + 4s	18	15	— + 2s	

CAMBRIDGE UNITED

Player and Position	Ht	Wt	Birth Date	Birth Place	Source	Clubs	League App	League Gls
Goalkeepers								
Paul Bastock*	5 8	10 00	19 5 70	Leamington	Trainee	Coventry C	—	—
						Cambridge U	12	—
John Vaughan	5 10	13 01	26 6 64	Isleworth	Apprentice	West Ham U	—	—
						Charlton Ath (loan)	6	—
						West Ham U	—	—
						Bristol R (loan)	6	—
						Wrexham (loan)	4	—
						Bristol C (loan)	2	—
						Fulham	44	—
						Bristol C (loan)	3	—
						Cambridge U	29	—
Defenders								
Colin Bailie	5 11	10 11	31 3 64	Belfast	Apprentice	Swindon T	107	4
						Reading	84	1
						Cambridge U	23	1
Phil Chapple	6 2	12 07	26 11 66	Norwich	Apprentice	Norwich C	—	—
						Cambridge U	52	4
Mark Crowe‡	5 10	10 10	21 1 65	Southwold	Apprentice	Norwich C	1	—
						Torquay U	57	2
						Cambridge U	51	—
Liam Daish	6 2	13 05	23 9 68	Portsmouth	Apprentice	Portsmouth	1	—
						Cambridge U	28	—
Alan Kimble	5 8	11 00	6 8 66	Poole		Charlton Ath	6	—
						Exeter C (loan)	1	—
						Cambridge U	121	8
Jamie Murray‡	5 9	10 12	27 12 58	Glasgow	Rivet Sports	Cambridge U	229	3
						Sunderland (loan)	1	—
						Brentford	134	3
						Cambridge U	13	—
Gary Poole‡	6 0	11 00	11 9 67	Stratford	School	Tottenham H	—	—
						Cambridge U	43	—
Lindsay Smith†	5 11	12 00	18 9 54	Enfield	Apprentice	Colchester U	212	16
						Charlton Ath (loan)	1	—
						Millwall (loan)	5	—
						Cambridge U	174	7
						Lincoln C (loan)	5	—
						Plymouth Arg	76	5
						Millwall	55	5
						Cambridge U	102	16
Midfield								
John Beck	5 11	11 09	25 5 54	Edmonton	Apprentice	QPR	40	1
						Coventry C	69	6
						Fulham	114	13
						Bournemouth (loan)	4	1
						Bournemouth	133	12
						Cambridge U	110	11
Gary Clayton	5 11	12 08	2 2 63	Sheffield	Apprentice	Rotherham U	—	—
					Burton Alb	Doncaster R	35	5
						Cambridge U	91	6
Paul Turner†	5 10	11 07	13 11 68	Enfield	Trainee	Arsenal	—	—
						Cambridge U	37	—
Forwards								
Greg Allen‡	5 9	11 01	18 10 67	London	Apprentice	Arsenal	—	—
					Dagenham	Cambridge U	4	—
Gary Bull‡	5 9	11 07	12 6 66	West Bromwich		Southampton	—	—
						Cambridge U	19	4
Brian Croft	5 9	10 10	27 9 67	Chester		Chester C	59	3
						Cambridge U	17	2

CAMBRIDGE UNITED

Foundation: The football revival in Cambridge began soon after World War II when the Abbey United club (formed 1919) decided to turn professional and in 1949 changed their name to Cambridge United. They were competing in the United Counties League before graduating to the Eastern Counties League in 1951 and the Southern League in 1958.

Managers (and Secretary-managers)
Bill Whittaker 1949–55, Gerald Williams 1955, Bert Johnson 1955–59, Bill Craig 1959–60, Alan Moore 1960–63, Roy Kirk 1964–66, Bill Leivers 1967–74, Ron Atkinson 1974–78, John Docherty 1978–83, John Ryan 1984–85, Ken Shellito 1985, Chris Turner 1985– .

Player and Position	*Ht*	*Wt*	*Birth Date*	*Birth Place*	*Source*	*Clubs*	*League App*	*League Gls*
Tony Dennis	5 7	10 02	1 12 63	Eton	Slough	Cambridge U	18	3
Dion Dublin	6 0	12 04	22 4 69	Leicester		Norwich C	—	—
						Cambridge U	21	6
Micky Holmes*	5 8	10 12	9 9 65	Blackpool		Bradford C	5	—
						Burnley	—	—
						Wolverhampton W	83	13
						Huddersfield T	7	—
						Cambridge U	11	—
Chris Leadbitter†	5 9	10 07	17 10 67	Middlesbrough	Apprentice	Grimsby T	—	—
						Hereford U	36	1
						Cambridge U	31	6
George Reilly‡	6 3	13 05	14 9 57	Bellshill	Corby T	Northampton T	127	46
						Cambridge U	138	36
						Watford	48	14
						Newcastle U	31	10
						WBA	43	9
						Cambridge U	20	7
Laurie Ryan	5 9	10 12	15 10 63	Watford	Dunstable	Cambridge U	41	12
John Taylor	6 2	11 12	24 10 64	Norwich	Local	Colchester U	—	—
					Sudbury	Cambridge U	40	12

Trainees
Batch, David J; Heard, Stephen J; Kearns, Jamie A; Lewis, Stephen R; Parnwell, Giles T; Pincher, Andrew; Robinson, David J; Vowden, Colin D.

****Non-Contract**
Leadbitter, Christopher J.

Associated Schoolboys
Banthorpe, Alex; Ellis, Steven M; Moir, Simon J; Pope, Neil; Woodcock, Robert.

CARDIFF CITY 1988–89 *Back row (left to right):* Alan Curtis, Jimmy Gilligan, Steve Tupling, John Roberts, Nigel Stevenson, George Wood, Paul Wheeler, Ian Walsh, Phil Bater. *Front row:* Ian Rogerson, Brian McDermott, Paul Wimbleton, Nicky Platnauer, Terry Boyle (Captain), Kevin Bartlett, Steve Lynex, Jason Gummer, Mark Kelly.

Division 3 — CARDIFF CITY

Ninian Park, Cardiff CF1 8SX. Telephone Cardiff (0222) 398636. Commercial Office: 0222 220516.

Ground Capacity: 39,500.

Record attendance: 61,566, Wales v England, 14 Oc, 1961.

Club record: 57,893 v Arsenal, Division 1, 22 April, 1953.

Record receipts: £33,164.01 v Sheffield W, Division 2, 12 May, 1984.

Pitch Measurements: 114yd × 78yd

President: Lord Brooks of Tremorfa.

Chairman: J. A. Clemo.

Directors: D. Proctor, D. Whiteman, L. Clemo.

Secretary: Eddie Harrison.

Team Manager: Frank Burrows. ***Commercial Manager:*** Sue Wynne.

Physio: Jimmy Goodfellow. ***Coach:*** Bobby Smith.

Year Formed: 1899. ***Turned Professional:*** 1910. ***Ltd Co.:*** 1910.

Club Nickname: 'Bluebirds'.

Previous Grounds: Riverside, Sophia Gardens, Old Park and Fir Gardens. Moved to Ninian Park, 1910.

Previous Names: 1899–1902 Riverside; 1902–08, Riverside Albion; 1908, Cardiff City.

Record League Victory: 9-2 v Thames, Division 3(S), 6 February 1932 – Farquharson; E. L. Morris, Roberts; Galbraith, Harris, Ronan; Emmerson (1), Keating (1), Jones (1), McCambridge (1), Robbins (5).

Record Cup Victory: 8-0 v Enfield, FA Cup, 1st rd, 28 November 1931 – Farquharson; Smith, Roberts; Harris (1), Galbraith, Ronan; Emmerson (2), Keating (3); O'Neill (2), Robbins, McCambridge.

Record Defeat: 2-11 v Sheffield U, Division 1, 1 January, 1926.

Most League Points (2 for a win): 66, Division 3(S), 1946–47.

Most League Points (3 for a win): 86, Division 3, 1982–83.

Most League Goals: 93, Division 3(S), 1946–47.

Highest League Scorer in Season: Stan Richards, 30, Division 3(S), 1946–47.

Most League Goals in Total Aggregate: Len Davies, 128, 1920–31.

Most Capped Player: Alf Sherwood, 39(41), Wales.

Most League Appearances: Phil Dwyer, 471, 1972–85.

Record Transfer Fee Received: £150,000 from Oxford U for Mike Ford, June 1988.

Record Transfer Fee Paid: £180,000 to San Jose Earthquakes for Godfrey Ingram, September 1982.

Football League Record: 1920 Elected to Division 2; 1921–29 Division 1; 1929—31 Division 2; 1931–47 Division 3(S); 1947–52 Division 2; 1952–57 Division 1; 1957–60 Division 2; 1960–62 Division 1; 1962–75 Division 2; 1975–76 Division 3; 1976–82 Division 2; 1982–83 Division 3; 1983–85 Division 2; 1985–86 Division 3; 1986–88 Division 4; 1988– Division 3.

Honours: *Football League:* Division 1 – Runners-up 1923–24; Division 2 – Runners-up 1920–21, 1951–52, 1959–60; Division 3(S) – Champions 1946–47; Division 3 – Runners-up 1975–76, 1982–83; Division 4 – Runners-up 1987–88. *FA Cup:* Winners 1926–27 (only occasion the Cup has been won by a club outside England); Runners-up 1925. *Football League Cup:* Semi-final 1965–66. *Welsh Cup:* Winners 20 times. *Charity Shield:* 1927. European Competitions: *European Cup-Winners' Cup:* 1964–65, 1965–66, 1967–68, 1968–69, 1969–70, 1970–71, 1971–72, 1973–74, 1974–75, 1976–77, 1977–78. 1988–89.

Colours: Blue shirts, white shorts, blue stockings with white tops. **Change colours:** All red.

CARDIFF CITY 1988–89 LEAGUE RECORD

Match No.	Date	Venue	Opponents	Result		H/T Score	Lg. Pos.	Goalscorers	Attendance
1	Aug 27	H	Fulham	L	1-2	1-0	—	Walsh	6024
2	Sept 3	A	Bolton W	L	0-4	0-0	24		4831
3	10	H	Huddersfield T	W	3-0	3-0	17	Stevenson, Walsh 2	3891
4	17	A	Port Vale	L	1-6	1-3	20	Gilligan	4280
5	23	A	Southend U	D	0-0	0-0	—		3199
6	Oct 1	H	Bristol R	D	2-2	0-2	22	Gilligan, Bartlett	5038
7	8	H	Reading	L	1-2	1-0	23	Curtis	4057
8	15	A	Chester C	D	0-0	0-0	22		2796
9	22	A	Mansfield T	D	2-2	1-0	22	Ketteridge, McDermott	3566
10	29	A	Blackpool	L	0-1	0-0	21		3849
11	Nov 1	H	Bury	W	3-0	0-0	—	Gilligan, Bartlett, Ketteridge	2411
12	5	H	Gillingham	W	1-0	0-0	20	Bartlett	3658
13	12	H	Northampton T	W	1-0	1-0	17	Bartlett	3280
14	25	H	Brentford	W	1-0	1-0	—	Gilligan	3405
15	Dec 3	A	Preston NE	D	3-3	0-2	17	Gilligan, Bartlett 2	4963
16	17	A	Bristol C	L	0-2	0-1	18		7493
17	26	H	Swansea C	D	2-2	2-2	18	Gilligan 2	10,675
18	30	H	Wigan Ath	D	2-2	0-1	—	Bartlett, Curtis	4621
19	Jan 2	A	Aldershot	W	1-0	0-0	16	Curtis	2768
20	10	A	Wolverhampton W	L	0-2	0-2	—		14,870
21	14	H	Bolton W	W	1-0	0-0	16	Bartlett	4212
22	21	A	Huddersfield T	L	0-1	0-1	17		4869
23	28	H	Port Vale	W	3-0	1-0	17	Gilligan 2, Bartlett	4507
24	Feb 4	A	Bristol R	W	1-0	0-0	13	Gilligan	5815
25	11	H	Sheffield U	D	0-0	0-0	14		5772
26	18	A	Reading	L	1-3	0-2	16	Walsh	4359
27	28	A	Notts Co	L	0-2	0-1	—		4266
28	Mar 4	H	Mansfield T	D	0-0	0-0	18		3217
29	11	A	Gillingham	W	2-1	2-0	16	Boyle, Gilligan	2927
30	18	A	Fulham	L	0-2	0-1	18		4261
31	21	A	Chesterfield	L	0-4	0-2	—		2888
32	25	H	Aldershot	W	3-2	1-1	17	Gilligan (pen), Wheeler, Curtis	3251
33	27	A	Swansea C	D	1-1	1-0	18	Gilligan	9201
35	Apr 1	H	Bristol C	D	1-1	1-0	18	Platnauer	6152
35	4	H	Wolverhampton W	D	1-1	0-1	—	Platnauer	7219
36	7	A	Wigan Ath	L	0-1	0-0	—		2083
37	11	A	Sheffield U	W	1-0	1-0	—	Abraham	11,618
38	15	A	Bury	L	0-1	0-1	17		2124
39	18	H	Notts Co	L	0-1	0-1	—		3079
40	22	H	Southend U	W	2-0	1-0	17	Abraham, Gilligan	3268
41	29	A	Northampton T	L	0-3	0-1	18		3194
42	May 1	H	Chesterfield	L	0-1	0-1	18		3244
43	5	H	Preston NE	D	0-0	0-0	—		3196
44	9	H	Chester C	W	2-0	0-0	16	Boyle, Gilligan	3002
45	13	A	Brentford	D	1-1	1-0	17	Gummer	4865
46	16	H	Blackpool	D	0-0	0-0	—		3246

Final League Position: 16

GOALSCORERS

League (44): Gilligan 15 (1 pen), Bartlett 9, Curtis 4, Walsh 4, Abraham 2, Boyle 2, Ketteridge 2, Platnauer 2, Gummer 1, McDermott 1, Stevenson 1, Wheeler 1.
Littlewoods Cup (3): Bartlett 1, Curtis 1, Wheeler 1.
FA Cup (8): Gilligan 3, Lynex 2, Bartlett 1, Tupling 1, Wimbleton 1 (pen).

Littlewoods Cup	First Round	Swansea C (h)	0-1
		(a)	2-0
	Second Round	QPR (a)	0-3
		(h)	1-4
FA Cup	First Round	Hereford U (h)	3-0
	Second Round	Enfield (a)	4-1
	Third Round	Hull C (h)	1-2

Wood	Bater	Platnauer	Lynex	Stevenson	Boyle	Curtis	Walsh	Gilligan	McDermott	Kelly	Rodgerson	Bartlett	Wimbleton	Gummer	Tupling	Morgan	Wheeler	Abraham	Ketteridge	Holmes	Gibbins	Fry	Roberts	Haig	*Match No.*
1	2	3	4†	5	6	7	8*	9	10	11	14	12													1
1		3*	14	5	6	7	8	9		11	2	12	4	10†											2
1		3	7	5*	6		8	9		11	2		4	10	12										3
1	12	3	11	5	6*	7		9	8		2		4	10											4
1	12	3	7	5	6	8		9		11	2		4	10*											5
1	10†	3	7*	5	6	8		9	14	11	2	12	4												6
1	2	3		5	6	7		9	10	11		8*				4	12								7
1	2		11	5	6			9				8				3	7	4	10						8
1	2		11	5	6			9	7	4	3	8							10						9
1		2	11	5				9	12	4	3	8	7*					6	10						10
1		3	11*	5		7		9		10	2	12	4					6	8						11
1		3		5		7		9		11	2	8	4					6	10						12
1	12	3		5*		7		9		11	2	8	4					6	10						13
1	12	3	11*		6	7		9			2	8	4		10			5							14
1	12	3	11		6	7		9			2	8	4		10*			5							15
1	12	3	11		6	7*		9			2†	8	4	10			14	5							16
1			11	3	6	7		9		12	2	8	4	10*				5							17
1			11	3	6	7		9		10	2	8*	4				12	5							18
1			11	3	6	7		9		10	2	8*	4				12	5							19
1	14		11	3	6	7†		9		10	2	8*	4				12	5							20
1	6		11	3	14	7*		9		10†	2	8	4				12	5							21
1	6	7	11*	3	14			9		10	2	8	4				12	5†							22
1	3	7	11	6	5			9		10*	2	8	4			12									23
1	3	7	11	6†	5			9		10	2	8*	4			14	12								24
1	6	3	11		5			9		10	2	8	4					7							25
1	8*	3	11		5	7†	14	9		12	2		4				10	6							26
1	8	3	11		5	7	12	9			2		4				10	6*							27
1	8	3	11		5	7	14	9		12	2		4*				10†	6							28
1	14	3	11		5	7		9		8	2		4†			12	10*	6							29
1	14	3	11†		5	7		9		8*	2		4			12	10	6							30
1	11†	3	14		5	7		9		12	2		4			8*	10	6							31
1	8	3	11*	6	5	7		9			2		4				10			12					32
1	8	3	11	6	5	7	12	9			2		4				10*								33
1	8	3	11	6	5		12	9			2					4	10*								34
1		3	11	6	5	7	12	9		7	2		4			8†	10*				14				35
1	8	3	11	6	5	7†	10*	9			2		4				12				14				36
1	8	3	11	6				9			2					4	10	5			7				37
1	8	3	11†	6		12		9			2					4	10*	5			7	14			38
1	2	3		6		7		9		11†			8			4	10*	5			12	14			39
1	2	3		6		7	12	9					8			4		5			10	11*			40
1	6	3		12		7		9		11*	2†		8			4		5			10	14			41
1	8	3		6†		7		9			2			14		4	12	5			10	11*			42
1	8	3			6	7		9			2†			14		4	12	5			10	11*			43
1	2	3			6	7		9					14	8		4	12	5†			10	11*			44
		3			6			9					4	8	2	12	7*	5			10	11†	1	14	45
1	8*	3	11		6	7†		9			2			10		12		5			4	14			46
45	27	39	34	31	34	34	4	46	4	24	39	18	35	9	3	13	15	31	6	—	9	5	1	—	
	+		+	+	+	+	+		+	+	+	+	+	+	+	+	+			+	+	+		+	
	9s		2s	1s	2s	1s	7s		2s	4s	1s	4s	1s	2s	1s	6s	12s			1s	3s	4s		1s	

CARDIFF CITY

Player and Position	Ht	Wt	Birth Date	Birth Place	Source	Clubs	League App	League Gls
Goalkeepers								
Graham Moseley‡	6 1	12 12	16 11 53	Manchester	Apprentice	Blackburn R	—	—
						Derby Co	32	—
						Aston Villa (loan)	3	—
						Walsall (loan)	3	—
						Brighton & HA	189	—
						Ipswich T (loan)	—	—
						Cardiff C	38	—
Jonathan Roberts	6 0	12 05	30 12 68	Llwynpia	Trainee	Cardiff C	9	—
George Wood	6 3	14 00	26 9 52	Douglas	East Stirling	East Stirling	44	1
						Blackpool	117	—
						Everton	103	—
						Arsenal	60	—
						Crystal Palace	192	—
						Cardiff C	58	—
Defenders								
Gareth Abraham	6 4	12 11	13 2 69	Merthyr Tydfil	Trainee	Cardiff C	33	3
Phil Bater	5 11	12 12	24 10 53	Cardiff	Apprentice	Bristol R	212	2
						Wrexham	73	1
						Bristol R	98	1
						Brentford	19	2
						Cardiff C	76	—
Terry Boyle	5 10	12 04	29 10 58	Ammanford	Apprentice	Tottenham H	—	—
						Crystal Palace	26	1
						Wimbledon (loan)	5	1
						Bristol C	37	—
						Newport Co	166	11
						Cardiff C	128	7
Jason Perry	5 11	10 04	2 4 70	Newport		Cardiff C	4	—
Nicky Platnauer	5 10	12 12	10 6 61	Leicester	Bedford T	Bristol R	24	7
						Coventry C	44	6
						Birmingham C	28	2
						Reading (loan)	7	—
						Cardiff C	115	6
Ian Rodgerson	5 8	11 05	9 4 66	Hereford	Local	Hereford U	100	6
						Cardiff C	40	—
Nigel Stevenson*	6 2	12 10	2 11 58	Swansea	Apprentice	Swansea C	259	15
						Cardiff C (loan)	14	—
						Reading (loan)	3	—
						Cardiff C	68	2
Midfield								
Roger Gibbins‡	5 10	11 09	6 9 55	Enfield	Apprentice	Tottenham H	—	—
						Oxford U	19	2
						Norwich C	48	12
					N England	Cambridge U	100	12
						CardiffC	139	17
						Swansea C	35	6
						Newport Co	79	9
						Torquay U	33	5
					Newport Co	Cardiff C	12	—
Jason Gummer	5 9	11 00	27 10 67	Tredegar	Apprentice	Cardiff C	33	5
						Torquay U (loan)	7	1
Richard Haig§			29 12 70	Pontypridd	Trainee	Cardiff C	1	—
Mark Kelly	5 8	10 06	7 10 66	Blackpool		Shrewsbury T	—	—
						Cardiff C	64	1
Jon Morgan	5 8	10 01	10 7 70	Cardiff	Trainee	Cardiff C	19	—

CARDIFF CITY

Foundation: Credit for the establishment of a first class professional football club in such a rugby stronghold as Cardiff, is due to members of the Riverside club formed in 1899 out of a cricket club of that name. Cardiff became a city in 1905 and in 1908 the local FA granted Riverside permission to call themselves Cardiff City.

Managers (and Secretary-managers)
Davy McDougall 1910–11, Fred Stewart 1911–33, Bartley Wilson 1933–34, B. Watts-Jones 1934–37, Bill Jennings 1937–39, Cyril Spiers 1939–46, Billy McCandless 1946–48, Cyril Spiers 1948–54, Trevor Morris 1954–58, Bill Jones 1958–62, George Swindin 1962–64, Jimmy Scoular 1964–73, Frank O'Farrell 1973–74, Jimmy Andrews 1974–78, Richie Morgan 1978–82, Len Ashurst 1982–84, Jimmy Goodfellow 1984, Alan Durban 1984–86, Frank Burrows 1986– .

Player and Position	*Ht*	*Wt*	*Birth Date*	*Birth Place*	*Source*	*Clubs*	*League App*	*League Gls*
Steve Tupling	6 0	12 08	11 7 64	Wensleydale	Apprentice	Middlesbrough	—	—
						Carlisle U (loan)	1	—
						Darlington	111	8
						Newport Co	33	2
						Cardiff C	4	—
						Torquay U (loan)	3	—
						Exeter C (loan)	9	1
Paul Wimbleton	5 8	10 06	13 11 64	Havant	Apprentice	Portsmouth	10	—
						Cardiff C	119	17
Forwards								
Alan Curtis	5 11	12 05	16 4 54	Rhondda	Amateur	Swansea C	248	72
						Leeds U	28	5
						Swansea C	90	21
						Southampton	50	5
						Stoke C (loan)	3	—
						Cardiff C	117	10
Chris Fry	5 9	9 06	23 10 69	Cardiff	Trainee	Cardiff C	9	—
Jimmy Gilligan	6 2	11 07	24 1 64	Hammersmith	Apprentice	Watford	27	6
						Lincoln C (loan)	3	—
						Grimsby T	25	4
						Swindon T	17	5
						Lincoln C	11	1
						Newport Co (loan)	5	1
						Cardiff C	92	34
Steve Lynex	5 7	11 10	23 1 58	West Bromwich	Apprentice Shamrock R	WBA	—	—
						Birmingham C	46	10
						Leicester C	213	57
						Birmingham C (loan)	10	2
						WBA	29	3
						Cardiff C	36	—
Ian Walsh	5 9	11 06	4 9 58	St Davids	Apprentice	Crystal Palace	117	23
						Swansea C	37	11
						Barnsley	49	15
						Grimsby T	41	14
						Cardiff C	17	4
Paul Wheeler	5 11	11 03	3 1 65	Caerphilly	Apprentice Aberaman	Bristol R	—	—
						Cardiff C	101	10

Trainees
Denton, Nicholas A; Haig, Richard N; Hookings, Stephen P; Hughes, Barrie R; Jarrett, Paul; Lewis, Allan; O'Hagan, Patrick J; Painter, Robert B; Roberts, Jason L; Scott, Morrys J; Searle, Damon P; Summers, Christopher; Thomas, Paul G; Wynne, Geraint.Leaman, Jason.Baddeley, Lee M; Bellamy, Nicholas M; Bird, Anthony; Breslin, Keiran; Crocker, Matthew; Gorman, Andrew; Gribble, Mark; Janes, Leighton D; Johns, Andrew M; Jones, Stephen; Popham, Philip H;

Semark, Robin; Sime, Leighton R; Walters, Carl M.P; Wilcox, Richard H; Williams, Craig; Williams, Morgan D.

CARLISLE UNITED 1988–89 *Back row (left to right):* Jimmy Robertson, Brent Hetherington, Dean Holdsworth, Mark Prudhoe, Derek Walsh, Richard Sendall, Ian Dalziel.
Centre row: Mark Ogley, Garry Marshall, Jonathan Clark, Nigel Saddington, Paul Gorman, Simon Jeffels, Archie Stephens, Tony Fyfe.
Front row: Peter Hampton (Physiotherapist), John McNamee, Jason Priestley, Clive Middlehass (Manager), Andrew Jenkins (Chairman), Steven Harkness, Ian Wilburn, Aidan McCaffery (Coach).
Kneeling: Eamonn Elliott, Kenneth Beal, Mark Eagling, Martin Heaney.

Division 4 CARLISLE UNITED

Brunton Park, Carlisle CA1 1LL. Telephone Carlisle (0228) 26237. Commercial Dept: (0228) 24014.

Record attendance: 27,500 v Birmingham C, FA Cup 3rd rd, 5 Jan, 1957 and v Middlesbrough, RA Cup 5th rd, 7 Feb, 1970.

Record receipts: £75,988.50 v Liverpool, FA Cup 3rd, 7 January, 1989.

Ground capacity: 18,506.

Pitch measurements: 117yd × 78yd.

President: J. C. Monkhouse. ***Vice-Presidents:*** J. Johnstone JP, T. L. Sibson, Dr. T. Gardner B, CHB.

Chairman: H. A. Jenkins. ***Vice-Chairman:*** J. R. Sheffield.

Directors: R. S. Liddell, T. A. Bingley, C. J. Vasey, J. B. Lloyd, A. Liddell, A. Hodgkinson.

Team Manager: Clive Middlemass. ***Assistant Manager:*** Peter Hampton.

Coach: Aidan McCaffery. ***Physio:*** Peter Hampton.

Match Secretary: N. Irving. ***Commercial Manager:*** Frank Layton.

Club Secretary: Miss Alison Moore.

Club Nickname: 'Cumbrians' or 'The Blues'.

Year Formed: 1903. ***Ltd Co:*** 1921.

Previous Grounds: 1903–5, Milholme Bank; 1905–9, Devonshire Park; 1909– Brunton Park.

Previous name: Shaddowgate United.

Record League Victory: 8-0 v Hartlepools U, Division 3(N), 1 September 1928 – Prout; Smiles, Cook; Robinson (1) Ross. Pigg; Agar (1), Hutchison (1), McConnell (4), Ward (1), Watson, 8-0 v Scunthorpe United, Division 3(N), 25 December 1952 – MacLaren; Hill, Scott; Stokoe, Twentyman, Waters; Harrison (1), Whitehouse (5), Ashman (2), Duffett, Bond.

Record Cup Victory: 6-1 v Billingham Synthonia, FA Cup, 1st rd, 17 November 1956 – Fairley; Hill, Kenny; Johnston, Waters, Thompson; Mooney, Broadis (1), Ackerman (2), Garvie (3), Bond.

Record Defeat: 1-11 v Hull C, Division 3(N), 14 January, 1939.

Most League Points (2 for a win): 62, Division 3(N), 1950–51.

Most League Points (3 for a win): 80, Division 3, 1981–82.

Most League Goals: 113, Division 4, 1963–64.

Highest League Scorer in Season: Jimmy McConnell, 42, Division 3(N), 1928–29.

Most League Goals in Total Aggregate: Jimmy McConnell, 126, 1928–32.

Most Capped Player: Eric Welsh, 4, Northern Ireland.

Most League Appearances: Alan Ross, 466, 1963–79.

Record Transfer Fee Received: £275,000 from Vancouver Whitecaps for Peter Beardsley, April 1981.

Record Transfer Fee Paid: £120,000 to York C for Gordon Staniforth, October 1979.

Football League Record: 1928 Elected to Division 3(N); 1958–62 Division 4; 1962–63 Division 3; 1963–64 Division 4; 1964–65 Division 3; 1965–74 Division 2; 1974–75 Division 1; 1975–77 Division 2; 1977–82 Division 3; 1982–86 Division 2; 1986–87 Division 3; 1987– Division 4.

Honours: *Football League:* Division 1 best season: 22nd, 1974–75; Promoted from Division 2 (3rd) 1973–74; Division 3 – Champions 1964–65; Runners-up 1981–82; Division 4 – Runners-up 1963–64. *FA Cup:* 6th rd 1974–75. *Football League Cup:* Semi-final 1969–70.

Colours: Blue shirts, white shorts, blue stockings. **Change colours:** Red shirts, white shorts, red stockings.

CARLISLE UNITED 1988–89 LEAGUE RECORD

Match No.	Date	Venue	Opponents	Result	H/T Score	Lg. Pos.	Goalscorers	Attendance
1	Aug 27	H	Peterborough U	D 2-2	1-1	—	Hetherington 2	2650
2	Sept 3	A	York C	D 1-1	1-0	15	Walsh	2303
3	10	H	Tranmere R	D 1-1	0-0	15	Clark	2384
4	16	A	Halifax T	D 3-3	3-1	—	Marshall, Hetherington, Sendall	1546
5	20	A	Scunthorpe U	D 1-1	0-1	—	Gorman (pen)	3113
6	24	H	Rotherham U	L 0-2	0-0	19		2862
7	30	A	Cambridge U	L 2-3	1-1	—	Saddington, Walsh	2043
8	Oct 4	H	Colchester U	L 1-2	0-0	—	Sendall	2193
9	8	A	Hereford U	L 1-2	1-1	23	Hetherington	2127
10	15	H	Torquay U	W 2-1	0-0	23	Fyfe, Hetherington	2164
11	22	A	Exeter C	L 0-3	0-1	23		2235
12	25	H	Burnley	D 0-0	0-0	—		4543
13	29	A	Lincoln C	W 2-0	0-0	22	Hetherington 2	3727
14	Nov 5	H	Scarborough	L 0-1	0-1	22		2617
15	8	A	Leyton Orient	L 0-2	0-0	—		2879
16	12	H	Darlington	L 1-2	0-2	23	Dalziel (pen)	2194
17	26	H	Grimsby T	W 2-1	0-1	22	Marshall, Hetherington	2175
18	Dec 3	A	Wrexham	L 1-2	1-2	22	Williams (og)	1892
19	17	A	Hartlepool U	W 2-0	2-0	22	Halpin, Saddington	1974
20	26	H	Rochdale	W 1-0	0-0	22	Stephens	10,013
21	31	H	Stockport Co	D 1-1	1-0	22	Hart (og)	3774
22	Jan 2	A	Crewe Alex	L 0-1	0-1	22		4626
23	10	A	Doncaster R	W 3-1	1-0	—	Gorman 3	2128
24	14	H	York C	D 0-0	0-0	21		3462
25	21	A	Peterborough U	W 4-1	2-0	20	Hetherington 2, Halpin, Graham	2537
26	28	H	Halifax T	W 3-1	0-0	16	Gorman, Halpin 2	3007
27	Feb 4	H	Scunthorpe U	L 0-3	0-1	18		2627
28	11	A	Rotherham U	L 1-2	1-1	19	Graham	4111
29	18	H	Hereford U	W 3-0	1-0	18	Walsh, Fyfe 2	2548
30	Mar 4	H	Exeter C	W 1-0	0-0	17	Sendall	2601
31	11	A	Scarborough	W 1-0	0-0	13	Saddington	2354
32	14	H	Lincoln C	W 2-1	2-0	—	Fyfe, Halpin	2691
33	17	A	Tranmere R	D 0-0	0-0	—		5143
34	21	A	Burnley	D 0-0	0-0	—		5258
35	25	H	Crewe Alex	L 0-1	0-1	12		4866
36	27	A	Rochdale	D 0-0	0-0	14		2145
37	Apr 1	H	Hartlepool U	W 2-1	2-0	11	Halpin 2	3158
38	4	H	Doncaster R	L 0-1	0-1	—		2991
39	7	A	Stockport Co	D 1-1	0-1	—	Saddington	2543
40	15	H	Cambridge U	D 1-1	0-0	14	Sendall	2579
41	21	A	Colchester U	D 1-1	1-0	—	Proudlock	3906
42	29	A	Grimsby T	D 0-0	0-0	14		3833
43	May 1	H	Leyton Orient	W 2-1	2-1	13	Sendall, Hetherington	2410
44	3	A	Torquay U	L 0-1	0-1	—		1603
45	6	H	Wrexham	L 1-2	0-1	14	Sendall	2427
46	13	A	Darlington	W 3-2	3-1	12	Proudlock 2, Gorman	3049

Final League Position: 12

GOALSCORERS

League (53): Hetherington 11, Halpin 7, Gorman 6 (1 pen), Sendall 6, Saddington 4, Fyfe 4, Proudlock 3, Walsh 3, Graham 2, Marshall 2, Clark 1, Dalziel 1 (pen), Stephens 1, own goals 2.
Littlewoods Cup (1): Gorman 1 (pen).
FA Cup (6): Fitzpatrick 1, Gorman 1, Halpin 1, Saddington 1, Walsh 1, own goal 1.

Littlewoods Cup	First Round	Blackpool (h)	1-1
		(a)	0-3
FA Cup	First Round	Telford (a)	1-1
		(h)	4-1
	Second Round	Scarborough (a)	1-0
	Third Round	Liverpool (h)	0-3

Prudhoe	Robertson	Dalziel	Saddington	Ogley	Clark	Marshall	Gorman	Sendall	Hetherington	Halpin	Walsh	Stephens	Graham	Fyfe	Fitzpatrick	McKellar	Nuttell	Jeffels	Butler	Harkness	Proudlock	Stonehouse	*Match No.*
1	2	3	4	5	6	7	8	9	10	11													1
1	2	3	4	5	6	11	8	9	10*		7	12											2
1		3	4	5	6	7	8	9	14	11†	12	10*	2										3
1		3	4	5	6	7	8	9	10*		11		2	12									4
1		3	4	5	6	11	8	9	10		7		2										5
1		3	4	5	6	11	8	9	10		7*		2	12									6
1	12	3*	4	5	6	11	8	9	10		7		2										7
1			4	5	6	11	8	9	7		3		2		10								8
1		3	4	5		11	8	9	7		6		2		10								9
		3	4	5		11	8		10		7		2	9	6	1							10
		3	4	5		11	8	12	10		7		2	9*	6	1							11
		3	4	5		11	8		10		7	9	2		6	1							12
		3	4	5		11	8	12	10		7	9*	2		6	1							13
		3	4	5		11	8	10			7	9*	2		6	1	12						14
		3	4	5		11	8				7	9	2		6	1	10						15
		3	4	5*		11	8†			10	7	9	2		6	1	12	14					16
	14		4			7	8	12	10	11	3	9*	2		6	1		5†					17
		3	4	5		7	8		10	11	6	9*	2	12		1							18
1		3	4	5			8	12	7	11	6	9*	2	10									19
1		3	4				8	12	7	11	6	9	2	10*				5					20
1		3	4				8	10	7	11			2	9	6			5					21
		3	4				8	9	10	11			2		6	1		5	7				22
		3	4				8	12	10	11	7		2	9*	6	1		5					23
		3	4				8	12	10	11	7	9*	2	14	6†	1		5					24
		3	4				8		10	11	7	9*	2	12	6	1		5					25
		3	4				8		10	11	7	9*	2	12	6	1		5					26
		3	4				8		10	11	7	9*	2	12	6	1		5					27
		3	4				8		10	11	7		2	9	6	1		5					28
		3	4			12	8			11	7		2	9	6	1		5*		10			29
		3	4					10		11	7	9*	2	12	6	1		5		8			30
		3	4	7				8†	14	11		12	2	9*	6	1		5		10			31
		3	4				8		10	11			2	9	6	1		5		7			32
		3	4				8		10	11		12	2	9*	6	1		5		7			33
		3	4				8		10	11			2	9	6	1		5		7			34
		3	4				8†		14	11			2	9*	6	1		5		7	10	12	35
		3	4*				8		12	11	7		2	9	6	1		5			10		36
				4			8			11	3		2	9	6	1		5		7	10		37
			4				8		12	11	3		2	9	6*	1		5		7	10		38
		3	4				8	9	12	11			2		6	1		5*		7†	10	14	39
		3	4				8	9†	12	11*	7		2		6	1		5			10	14	40
		3		4			8	9		11	7		2		6	1		5			10		41
	2	3		4			8	10	12	11	7		6*	9		1		5					42
	2	3		4				9	10	11	7		6			1		5		8			43
	2†	3		4		14	8	9	12	11	7*		6			1		5			10		44
		3		4		14	8	9	7*	11			2		6†	1		5		12	10		45
		3	4	6			8	9	12	11			2			1		5		7	10*		46
12	5 + 2s	42	40	26	8	18 + 3s	43	22 + 7s	29 + 10s	33	34 + 1s	15 + 3s	44	17 + 8s	32	34	1 + 2s	28 + 1s	1	12 + 1s	10	— + 3s	

CARLISLE UNITED

Player and Position	Ht	Wt	Birth Date	Birth Place	Source	Clubs	League App	League Gls
Goalkeepers								
David McKellar	6 1	13 06	22 5 56	Irvine	Apprentice	Ipswich T	—	—
						Colchester U (loan)	—	—
						Peterborough U	—	—
					Ardrossan	(loan)	41	—
						Derby Co	84	—
						Brentford	82	—
						Carlisle U	—	—
						Hibernian	—	—
						Manchester C (loan)	10	—
						Newcastle U (loan)	52	—
						Hamilton A	6	—
						Dunfermline Ath	5	—
						Hartlepool U (loan)	34	—
						Carlisle U		
Defenders								
Ian Dalziel	5 8	11 10	24 10 62	South Shields	Apprentice	Derby Co	22	4
						Hereford U	150	8
						Carlisle U	42	1
Mike Graham	5 9	11 07	24 2 59	Lancaster	Apprentice	Bolton W	46	—
						Swindon T	141	1
						Mansfield T	133	1
						Carlisle U	44	2
Peter Hampton	5 7	11 02	12 9 54	Oldham	Apprentice	Leeds U	68	2
						Stoke C	138	4
						Burnley	118	2
						Rochdale	19	1
						Carlisle U	12	—
Simon Jeffels	6 1	11 08	18 1 66	Barnsley	Apprentice	Barnsley	42	—
						Preston NE (loan)	1	—
						Carlisle U	29	—
Mark Ogley	5 10	11 02	10 3 67	Barnsley	Apprentice	Barnsley	19	—
						Aldershot (loan)	8	—
						Carlisle U	29	—
Jimmy Robertson	5 9	11 00	24 11 69	Gateshead	Trainee	Carlisle U	12	—
Andy Robinson‡	5 10	12 04	10 3 66	Oldham	Apprentice	Manchester U	—	—
						Burnley (loan)	5	1
						Bury	19	—
						Carlisle U	46	3
Nigel Saddington	6 1	12 06	9 12 65	Sunderland		Doncaster R	6	—
						Sunderland	3	—
						Carlisle U	53	6
Midfield								
Jonathan Clark‡	5 10	11 10	12 11 58	Swansea	Apprentice	Manchester U	1	—
						Derby Co	53	3
						Preston NE	110	10
						Bury	14	1
						Carlisle U	49	2
Paul Fitzpatrick	6 4	11 10	5 10 65	Liverpool	Local	Tranmere R	—	—
						Liverpool	—	—
						Preston NE	—	—
						Bolton W	14	—
						Bristol C	44	7
						Carlisle U	32	—
						Preston NE (loan)	2	—
Paul Gorman	5 10	11 08	6 8 63	Dublin	Apprentice	Arsenal	6	—
						Birmingham C	6	—
						Carlisle U	146	7
John Halpin	5 10	11 07	15 11 61	Broxburn	Celtic BC	Celtic	7	—
						Sunderland (loan)	—	—
						Carlisle U	115	16

CARLISLE UNITED

Foundation: Carlisle United came into being in 1903 through the amalgamation of Shaddongate United and Carlisle Red Rose. The new club was admitted to the Second Division of the Lancashire Combination in 1905–06, winning promotion the following season.

Managers (and Secretary-managers)
H. Kirkbride 1904–05*, McCumiskey 1905–06*, J. Houston 1906–08*, Bert Stansfield 1908–10, J. Houston 1910–12, D. Graham 1912–13, George Bristow 1913–30, Billy Hampson 1930–33, Bill Clarke 1933–35, Robert Kelly 1935–36, Fred Westgarth 1936–38, David Taylor 1938–40, Howard Harkness 1940–45, Bill Clark 1945–46*, Ivor Broadis 1946–49, Bill Shankly 1949–51, Fred Emery 1951–58, Andy Beattie 1958–60, Ivor Powell 1960–63, Alan Ashman 1963–67, Tim Ward 1967–68, Bob Stokoe 1968–70, Ian MacFarlane 1970–72, Alan Ashman 1972–75, Dick Young 1975–76, Bobby Moncur 1976–80, Martin Harvey 1980, Bob Stokoe 1980–85, Bryan "Pop" Robson 1985, Bob Stokoe 1985–86, Harry Gregg 1986–87, Cliff Middlemass 1987– .

Player and Position	*Ht*	*Wt*	*Birth Date*	*Birth Place*	*Source*	*Clubs*	*League App*	*League Gls*
Steve Harkness	5 9	10 11	27 8 71	Carlisle	Trainee	Carlisle U	13	—
Aiden McCaffery	5 11	11 05	30 8 57	Newcastle	Apprentice	Newcastle U	59	4
						Derby Co	37	4
						Bristol R	184	11
						Bristol C (loan)	6	1
						Torquay U (loan)	6	—
						Exeter C	58	—
						Hartlepool U	6	1
						Carlisle U	14	—
Derek Walsh	5 7	11 05	24 10 67	Hamilton	Apprentice	Everton	1	—
						Hamilton A	2	—
						Carlisle U	35	3
Forwards								
Gary Marshall	5 11	10 10	20 4 64	Bristol	Shepton Mallet	Bristol C	68	7
						Torquay U (loan)	7	1
						Carlisle U	21	2
Tony Fyfe	6 2	12 00	23 2 62	Carlisle		Carlisle U	35	8
Brent Hetherington	5 7	11 10	6 12 61	Carlisle	Penrith, Workington	Carlisle U	76	21
Paul Proudlock	5 10	11 00	25 10 65			Hartlepool U	15	—
						Middlesbrough	5	1
						Carlisle U	10	3
Richard Sendell	5 10	11 06	10 7 67	Stamford	Apprentice	Watford	—	—
						Blackpool	11	—
						Carlisle U	29	6

Trainees
Eagling, Mark; Elliott, Eamonn G; Heaney, Martin W; Middlemass, Scott L; Milburn, Ian J; Priestley, Jason A.

Associated Schoolboys
Ashbridge, Stephen R; Beck, Seth; Bell, Robert G; Caig, Antony; Carruthers, Graham A; Graham, Stephen; Gray, Alan M; Jackson, Michael A; Nugent, Richard; Old, Christopher; Potts, Craig; Rossi, Jason; Short, Robbie; Slee, Simon J; Todd, Simon.

CHARLTON ATHLETIC 1988–89 *Back row (left to right):* Andy Jones, Michael Bennett, David Campbell, Darren Pitcher, Steve Gritt, Mark Stuart, Paul Mortimer.
Centre row: Jimmy Hendrey (Physiotherapist), Bill Gallagher (Kit Manager), Steve MacKenzie, Bob Bolder, Carl Leaburn, Jim McDonagh, Paul Miller, Colin Clarke (Youth Team Coach), Mike Flanagan (First Team Coach).
Front row: Mark Reid, Robert Lee, Colin Walsh, Garth Crooks, Lennie Lawrence (Manager), Peter Shirtliff, John Humphrey, Andy Peake, Paul Williams.

Division 1 — CHARLTON ATHLETIC

Selhurst Park, London SE25 6PH. Telephone 01-771 6321.

Ground capacity: 31,000.

Record attendance: 75,031 v Aston Villa, FA Cup 5th rd, 12 Feb, 1938 (at The Valley).

Record receipts: £114,618.70 v Liverpool (at Selhurst Park), Division 1, 23 Jan. 1988.

Pitch measurements: 110yd × 74yd.

Presidents: R. D. Collins, J. A. E. Fryer, J. B. Sunley.

Chairman: R. N. Alwen. ***Vice-chairman:*** M. J. Norris.

Directors: R. D. Collins, D. G. Ufton, J. B. Sunley.

General Manager: Arnie Warren.

Commercial Manager: Steve Sutherland

Manager: Lennie Lawrence.

Coach: Mike Flanagan. ***Physio:*** Jimmy Hendry.

Secretary: Miss Anne Payne.

Year Formed: 1905. ***Turned professional:*** 1920. ***Ltd Co.:*** 1919.

Club Nickname: 'Haddicks', 'Robins' or 'Valiants'.

Previous Grounds: 1906, Siemen's Meadow; 1907, Woolwich Common; 1909, Pound Park; 1913, Horn Lane; 1920, The Valley; 1923, Catford (The Mount); 1924, The Valley; 1985 Selhurst Park.

Record League Victory: 8-1 v Middlesbrough, Division 1, 12 September 1953 – Bartram; Campbell, Ellis; Fenton, Ufton, Hammond; Hurst (2), O'Linn (2), Leary (1), Firmani (3), Kiernan.

Record Cup Victory: 7-0 v Burton A, FA Cup 3rd rd, 7 January 1956 – Bartram; Campbell, Townsend; Hewie, Ufton, Hammond; Hurst (1), Gauld (1), Leary (3), White, Kiernan (2).

Record Defeat: 1-11 v Aston Villa, Division 2, 14 November, 1959.

Most League Points (2 for a win): 61, Division 3(S), 1934–35.

Most League Points (3 for a win): 77, Division 2, 1985–86.

Most League Goals: 107, Division 2, 1957–58.

Highest League Scorer in Season: Ralph Allen, 32, Division 3(S), 1934–35.

Most League Goals in Total Aggregate: Stuart Leary, 153, 1953–62.

Most Capped Player: John Hewie, 19, Scotland.

Most League Appearances: Sam Bartram, 583, 1934–56.

Record Transfer Fee Received: £650,000 from Crystal Palace for Mike Flanagan, August 1979.

Record Transfer Fee Paid: £430,000 to Chelsea for Colin Pates, October 1988.

Football League Record: 1921 Elected to Division 3(S); 1929–33 Division 2; 1933–35 Division 3(S); 1935–36 Division 2; 1936–57 Division 1; 1957–72 Division 2; 1972–75 Division 3; 1975–80 Division 2; 1980–81 Division 3; 1981–86; Division 2; 1986– Division 1.

Honours: *Football League:* Division 1 – Runners-up 1936–37; Division 2 – Runners-up 1935–36, 1985–86; Division 3(S) – Champions 1928–29, 1934–35; Promoted from Division 3 (3rd) 1974–75, 1980–81. *FA Cup:* Winners 1947; Runners-up 1946. *Football League Cup* best season: 4th rd. 1962–63, 1965–66, 1978–79.*Full Members Cup:* Runners-up 1987.

Colours: Red shirts, white shorts, white stockings. **Change colours:** All blue.

CHARLTON ATHLETIC 1988–89 LEAGUE RECORD

Match No.	*Date*	*Venue*	*Opponents*	*Result*	*H/T Score*	*Lg. Pos.*	*Goalscorers*	*Attendance*
1	Aug 27	H	Liverpool	L 0-3	0-1	—		21,389
2	Sept 3	A	West Ham U	W 3-1	1-0	10	Williams 2, Robson (og)	19,566
3	10	H	Millwall	L 0-3	0-2	12		13,375
4	17	A	Coventry C	L 0-3	0-0	16		11,890
5	24	H	Newcastle U	D 2-2	1-0	16	Williams, Lee	6088
6	Oct 1	A	Norwich C	W 3-1	1-1	13	Williams 2, Mortimer	11,470
7	8	H	Tottenham H	D 2-2	1-0	14	Peake, Jones	14,384
8	15	H	Aston Villa	D 2-2	1-0	12	Gritt, Williams	7594
9	22	A	Derby Co	D 0-0	0-0	13		14,106
10	29	H	Sheffield W	W 2-1	1-0	11	Shirtliff, Williams	5933
11	Nov 5	A	Southampton	L 0-2	0-0	14		12,826
12	12	H	Everton	L 1-2	1-2	15	Williams	8627
13	19	A	Wimbledon	D 1-1	0-0	15	Lee	5631
14	26	H	Nottingham F	L 0-1	0-1	16		6411
15	Dec 3	A	Manchester U	L 0-3	0-1	17		31,173
16	10	H	QPR	D 1-1	0-1	17	Gritt	6012
17	17	A	Middlesbrough	D 0-0	0-0	17		16,065
18	26	H	Arsenal	L 2-3	0-1	19	MacKenzie 2	18,439
19	31	H	West Ham U	D 0-0	0-0	18		11,084
20	Jan 2	A	Millwall	L 0-1	0-0	18		17,025
21	14	H	Luton T	W 3-0	3-0	18	Mortimer, Crooks, Williams	5212
22	21	A	Newcastle U	W 2-0	1-0	17	Lee 2	19,076
23	Feb 4	H	Norwich C	L 1-2	0-0	17	Crooks	7518
24	11	A	Tottenham H	D 1-1	1-0	17	Williams	22,803
25	25	A	Aston Villa	W 2-1	1-1	17	Caton, Leaburn	16,481
26	Mar 1	A	Liverpool	L 0-2	0-1	—		30,283
27	4	A	Sheffield W	L 1-3	1-1	17	Williams	16,081
28	11	H	Southampton	D 2-2	1-0	17	Lee, Williams	6377
29	21	A	Arsenal	D 2-2	1-2	—	Mortimer, MacKenzie	30,259
30	25	H	Coventry C	D 0-0	0-0	15		6728
31	Apr 1	H	Middlesbrough	W 2-0	1-0	15	Humphrey, Mortimer	6696
32	10	A	Everton	L 2-3	1-1	—	Mortimer, Ratcliffe (og)	16,316
33	22	H	Manchester U	W 1-0	1-0	17	Reid (pen)	12,055
34	29	A	QPR	L 0-1	0-1	17		13,452
35	May 2	A	Luton T	L 2-5	0-4	—	Jones 2	10,024
36	6	H	Wimbledon	W 1-0	1-0	15	Leaburn	7230
37	10	H	Derby Co	W 3-0	1-0	—	Jones, Shirtliff, Williams	7448
38	13	A	Nottingham F	L 0-4	0-3	14		17,637

Final League Position: 14

GOALSCORERS

League (44): Williams 13, Lee 5, Mortimer 5, Jones 4, MacKenzie 3, Crooks 2, Gritt 2, Leaburn 2, Shirtliff 2, Caton 1, Humphrey 1, Peake 1, Reid 1 (pen), own goals 2.
Littlewoods Cup (4): Williams 2, Jones 1, Reid 1 (pen).
FA Cup (4): Williams 2, Crooks 1, Lee 1.

Littlewoods Cup	Second Round	Northampton T (a)	1-1
		(h)	2-1
	Third Round	QPR (a)	1-2
FA Cup	Third Round	Oldham Ath (h)	2-1
	Fourth Round	Kettering (h)	2-1
	Fifth Round	West Ham U (h)	0-1

Bolder	Humphrey	Reid	Peake	Shirtliff	Miller	Gritt	Lee	Leaburn	MacKenzie	Walsh	Williams	Stuart	Mortimer	Campbell	Jones	Bennett	Pates	Caton	Crooks	Minto	*Match No.*
1	2	3	4	5	6	7	8	9	10	11											1
1	2	3		5	6	9	7	10	4		8	11									2
1	2	3		5	6	9*	7	10	4		8	11	12								3
1*	2	3	12	5	6	9	7	10	4		8	11†		14							4
1	2	3		5	6	9	7	10*	4		8	11			12						5
1	2	3	6	5		9		10	4		8		11			7					6
1	2	3	6	5		9*		10	4		8		11		12	7					7
1	2	3		5		9*	14	10†	4		8		11		12	7	6				8
1	2	3	9	5				10	4		8		11			7	6				9
1	2	3	9	5			12	10	4		8*		11			7	6				10
1	2	3	9	5			14	10	4		8†		11		12	7*	6				11
1	2	3	9	5		6	14	10*	4		8		11		12	7†					12
1	2	3	9			6	12	10	4		8*		11			7		5			13
1	2	3*	9			6	8	10	4				11	12		7		5			14
1	2	3	9			6		10	4				11	8*		7		5	12		15
1	2	3	9	4		6		10					11	12		7*		5	8†	14	16
1	2	3	9	4		6		10					11	7				5	8		17
1	2	3	9*	4		6	14	10	12				11	7				5	8†		18
1	2	3	14	5		9†	8	10*	4		12		11	7			6				19
1	2	3	9	5			7	10	4		8						6			11	20
1	2		6	4		3†	7	12	9		8		10				5		11*	14	21
1	2		6	4		3	7		9		8		10				5		11		22
1	2	3*	6	4		10†	7	12	9		8		14				5		11		23
1	2	3	6*	4		10	7		9		8		12				5		11		24
1	2	3	6	4			7	12	9		10		8					5	11*		25
1	2	3	6	4			7	11	9*		10		8	12				5			26
1	2	3	6	4				11†	9*		10		8	7			14	5	12		27
1	2	3	6	4			7		9		10		8					5	11		28
1	2	3	6	4			7	11	9		10		8				5				29
1	2	3	6†	4			7	11	9	14	10*		8				5		12		30
1	2	3	6	4			7	11	9		10		8				5				31
1	2	3	6	4			7	11	9		8		10				5				32
1	2	3	6				7	11	9		8		10				5	4			33
1	2	3		14		6*	7	11	9		8		10				5	4†	12		34
1	2	3		6			7		9	8	12		10		14		5	4*	11†		35
1	2	3		4		6	7	11†	9	12	8		10*		14		5				36
1	2	3	6	4			7		9		8		10		11		5				37
1	2	3	6	4			7		9	12	8		10*		11		5				38
38	38	36	29 + 2s	33 + 1s	5	22	25 + 6s	29 + 3s	35 + 1s	2 + 3s	30 + 2s	4	30 + 3s	5 + 4s	2 + 7s	11	20 + 1s	13	10 + 4s	1 + 2s	

CHARLTON ATHLETIC

Player and Position	Ht	Wt	Birth Date	Birth Place	Source	Clubs	League App	League Gls
Goalkeepers								
Nathan Amato‡	6 0	11 07	24 1 70	Kent		Charlton Ath	—	—
Bob Bolder	6 3	14 06	2 10 58	Dover	Dover	Sheffield W	196	—
						Liverpool	—	—
						Sunderland	22	—
						Luton T (loan)	—	—
						Charlton Ath	99	—
Seamus (Jim) McDonagh‡	6 0	13 09	6 10 52	Rotherham	Apprentice	Rotherham U	121	—
						Manchester U (loan)	—	—
						Bolton W	161	—
						Everton	40	—
						Bolton W	81	1
						Notts Co	35	—
						Birmingham C (loan)	1	—
						Gillingham (loan)	10	—
						Sunderland (loan)	7	—
						Scarborough	9	—
						Huddersfield T (loan)	6	—
						Charlton Ath	—	—
Defenders								
Paul Bacon	5 9	10 04	20 12 70	London	Trainee	Charlton Ath	—	—
Tommy Caton	6 2	13 00	6 10 62	Liverpool	Apprentice	Manchester C	165	8
						Arsenal	81	2
						Oxford U	53	3
						Charlton Ath	13	1
Steve Gritt	5 9	10 10	31 10 57	Bournemouth	Apprentice	Bournemouth	6	3
						Charlton Ath	347	24
John Humphrey	5 10	11 01	31 1 61	Paddington	Apprentice	Wolverhampton W	149	3
						Charlton Ath	156	3
Scott Minto	5 10	10 00	6 8 71	Cheshire	Trainee	Charlton Ath	3	—
Colin Pates	5 11	11 00	10 8 61	Mitcham	Apprentice	Chelsea	281	10
						Charlton Ath	21	—
Darren Pitcher	5 9	12 02	12 10 69	London	Trainee	Charlton Ath	—	—
						Galway U (loan)	—	—
Mark Reid	5 8	11 05	15 9 61	Kilwinning	Celtic BC	Celtic	124	5
						Charlton Ath	156	13
Peter Shirtiff	6 2	13 04	6 4 61	Barnsley	Apprentice	Sheffield W	188	4
						Charlton Ath	103	7
Marcus Smart†			14 3 71	Bromley	Trainee	Charlton Ath	—	—
Midfield								
Peter Evans‡	5 8	11 00	21 7 70	London	School	Charlton Ath	—	—
Michael Bennett	5 10	11 11	27 7 69	London	Apprentice	Charlton Ath	29	1
Steve MacKenzie	5 11	12 05	23 11 61	Romford	Apprentice	Crystal Palace	—	—
						Manchester C	58	8
						WBA	148	23
						Charlton Ath	68	5
Paul Mortimer	5 11	11 03	8 5 68	London	Fulham	Charlton Ath	45	5
Paul Murray‡	5 7	9 03	28 12 69	Ireland	Trainee	Charlton Ath	—	—
Andy Peake	5 10	12 00	1 11 61	Market Harborough	Apprentice	Leicester C	147	13
						Grimsby T	39	4
						Charlton Ath	76	1
Colin Walsh	5 9	10 11	22 7 62	Hamilton	Apprentice	Nottingham F	139	32
						Charlton Ath	49	9
						Peterborough U (loan)	5	1

CHARLTON ATHLETIC

Foundation: Although formed in 1905 by members of such clubs as East Street Mission, Blundell Mission, and Charlton Reds, Charlton Athletic did not really make their presence felt until adopting professionalism and joining the Southern League in 1920. Before that, they had played in such competitions as the Lewisham, Southern Suburban and London Leagues.

Managers (and Secretary-managers)
Bill Rayner 1920–25, Alex McFarlane 1925–27, Albert Lindon 1928, Alex McFarlane 1928–32, Jimmy Seed 1933–56, Jimmy Trotter 1956–61, Frank Hill 1961–65, Bob Stokoe 1965–67, Eddie Firmani 1967–70, Theo Foley 1970–74, Andy Nelson 1974–79, Mike Bailey 1979–81, Alan Mullery 1981–82, Ken Craggs 1982, Lennie Lawrence 1982– .

Player and Position	*Ht*	*Wt*	*Birth Date*	*Birth Place*	*Source*	*Clubs*	*League App*	*League Gls*
Forwards								
Garth Crooks	5 8	12 01	10 3 58	Stoke	Apprentice	Stoke C	147	48
						Tottenham H	125	48
						Manchester U (loan)	7	2
						WBA	40	16
						Charlton Ath	49	14
Andy Jones	5 11	13 06	9 1 63	Wrexham	Rhyl	Port Vale	90	49
						Charlton Ath	34	10
						Port Vale (loan)	17	3
Carl Leaburn	6 3	11 02	30 3 69	Lewisham	Apprentice	Charlton Ath	47	3
Robert Lee	5 8	10 12	1 2 66	West Ham	ABTA	Charlton Ath	172	32
Gordon Watson	6 0	12 00	20 3 71	Kent	Trainee	Charlton Ath	—	—
Paul Williams	5 7	10 03	16 8 65	London	Woodford T	Charlton Ath	44	13
						Brentford (loan)	7	3

Trainees
Barham, Spencer J; Brown, Steven B; Bulgen, Christopher; Crane, Steven J; Evans, Jonathan D; Franco, Rosario; Harrison, Lee D; Lee, Jason; Moss, Gary T; Skeet, Andrew F; Tivey, Mark R; Wareham, Daniel; Warner, Roger J.

Associated Schoolboys
Agius, Russel A; Bakes, Sean; Barness, Anthony; Butler, Warren; Gell, Roger A; Grant, Kim T; Granville, Daniel P; Gray, Andrew J; Jordine, Aundrae; Logan, William P; Nelson, Rainbow; Norman, David P; Nguyen, Vinh; O'Brien, Paul J; Oliver, Gavin J; Page, Ricky; Parker, Matthew T; Rodway, Dennis S; Smeeth, Jamie F; Salako, Andrew O.

CHELSEA 1988–89 *Back row (left to right):* Eddie Cunnington, Graeme Le Saux, John Coady, Micky Bodley, Jason Cundy, Stephen Beatty, Billy Dodds, Tommy Byrne.
Centre row: Gwyn Williams (Reserve Team Manager), Eddie Niedzwiecki (Youth Team Manager), Steve Clarke, Kerry Dixon, Joe McLaughlin, Kevin Hitchcock, David Lee, Roger Freestone, Colin Pates, Gareth Hall, Mick Hazard, Norman Medhurst (Physiotherapist), Bobby Campbell (Manager).
Front row: Graham Roberts (Captain), Kevin McAllister, Kevin Wilson, Gordon Durie, Clive Wilson, Tony Dorigo, Darren Wood, Peter Nicholas.

Division 1 CHELSEA

Stamford Bridge, London SW6. Telephone 01-385 5545. Information Service: 01-381 6221. Club call 0898-121159. Lottery office: 01-385-3255.

Ground capacity: 43,900 (21,500 covered).

Record attendance: 82,905 v Arsenal, Division 1, 12 Oct, 1935.

Record receipts: £204,913 v Middlesbrough, Division 1 and 2 play-offs, 28 May, 1988.

Pitch measurements: 114yd × 71yd.

President: G. M. Thomson.

Chairman: K. W. Bates. ***Vice-Chairman:*** R. M. Bates.

Directors: S. S. Tollman, G. W. C. Smith.

Manager: Bobby Campbell. ***Asst. Manager:***Ian Porterfield.

Physio: Bob Ward. ***Chief Executive:*** C. Hutchinson.

Secretary: Janet Wayth. ***Sales Manager:*** John Shaw.

Year formed: 1905. ***Turned Professional:*** 1905. ***Ltd Co.:*** 1905.

Club Nickname: 'The Blues'.

Record League Victory: 9-2 v Glossop N E, Division 2, 1 September 1906 – Byrne; Walton, Miller; Key (1), McRoberts, Henderson; Moran, McDermott (1), Hilsdon (5), Copeland (1), Kirwan (1)

Record Cup Victory: 13-0 v Jeunesse Hautcharage, ECWC, 1st rd (2nd leg), 29 September 1971 – Bonetti; Boyle, Harris (1), Hollins (1p), Webb (1), Hinton, Cooke, Baldwin (3), Osgood (5), Hudson (1), Houseman (1).

Record Defeat: 1-8 v Wolverhampton W, Division 1, 26 September, 1953.

Most League Points (2 for a win): 57, Division 2, 1906–07.

Most League Points (3 for a win): 99, Division 2, 1988-89.

Most League Goals: 98, Division 1, 1960–61.

Highest League Scorer in Season: Jimmy Greaves, 41, 1960–61.

Most League Goals in Total Aggregate: Bobby Tambling, 164, 1958–70.

Most Capped Player: Ray Wilkins, 24 (84), England.

Most League Appearances: Ron Harris, 655, 1962–80.

Record Transfer Fee Received: £925,000 from Everton for Pat Nevin, July 1988.

Record Transfer Fee Paid: £725,000 to Newcastle U for Dave Beasant, January 1989.

Football League Record: 1905 Elected to Division 2; 1907–10 Division 1, 1910–12 Division 2; 1912–24 Division 1; 1924–30 Division 2; 1930–62 Division 1; 1962–63 Division 2; 1963–75 Division 1; 1975–77 Division 2; 1977–79 Division 1; 1979–84 Division 2; 1984–88 Division 1; 1988– Division 2.

Honours: *Football League:* Division 1 – Champions 1954–55; Division 2 – Champions 1983–84, 1988–89; Runners-up 1906–7, 1911–12, 1929–30, 1962–63, 1976–77. *FA Cup:* Winners 1979; Runners-up 1914–15, 1966–67. *Football League Cup:* Winners 1964–65, Runners-up 1971–72. *Full Members' Cup:* Winners 1985–86.
European Competitions: *European Fairs Cup:* 1958–60, 1965–66, 1968–69; *European Cup-Winners' Cup:* 1970–71 (winners), 1971–72.

Colours: All Royal blue. **Change colours:** Red and white shirts, red shorts, red stockings.

CHELSEA 1988–89 LEAGUE RECORD

Match No.	Date	Venue	Opponents	Result	H/T Score	Lg. Pos.	Goalscorers	Attendance
1	Aug 27	H	Blackburn R	L 1-2	1-1	—	Wilson K	8722
2	30	A	Crystal Palace	D 1-1	1-1	—	Wilson K	17,490
3	Sept 3	A	Bournemouth	L 0-1	0-0	16		8763
4	10	H	Oxford U	D 1-1	0-0	15	McAllister	7587
5	17	A	Barnsley	D 1-1	1-1	16	Roberts (pen)	6942
6	20	H	Manchester C	L 1-3	1-1	—	Pates	8858
7	24	A	Leeds U	W 2-0	2-0	17	Bumstead, Durie	26,080
8	Oct 1	H	Leicester C	W 2-1	0-0	13	Lee, Roberts (pen)	7050
9	4	H	Walsall	W 2-0	0-0	—	Dixon, Dorigo	6747
10	9	A	Swindon T	D 1-1	0-0	—	Dixon	11,347
11	15	A	Oldham Ath	W 4-1	2-1	6	Wilson K, Nicholas, McAllister, Wood	7817
12	22	H	Plymouth Arg	W 5-0	4-0	5	Dixon, Durie 2, Roberts (pen), Dorigo	12,658
13	25	A	Hull C	L 0-3	0-1	—		6953
14	29	H	Brighton & HA	W 2-0	1-0	5	Wilson K, Dixon	15,406
15	Nov 5	A	Watford	W 2-1	2-1	3	Durie, Dixon	17,631
16	12	H	Sunderland	D 1-1	0-1	4	Wilson K	19210
17	19	A	Bradford C	D 2-2	0-1	5	Lee, Wilson K	11,442
18	26	H	Shrewsbury T	W 2-0	2-0	4	Dorigo, Dixon	11,595
19	Dec 3	A	Stoke C	W 3-0	1-0	2	Roberts (pen), Wilson C, McAllister	12,288
20	10	H	Portsmouth	D 3-3	2-1	4	Dixon, Durie, Wilson K	20,221
21	16	A	Birmingham C	W 4-1	1-0	—	Durie 2, Dixon 2	7897
22	26	H	Ipswich T	W 3-0	2-0	1	Durie, Lee, Dixon	17,621
23	31	H	WBA	D 1-1	0-1	1	Roberts (pen)	25,906
24	Jan 2	A	Oxford U	W 3-2	2-1	2	Dixon 2, Wilson C	11,427
25	14	H	Crystal Palace	W 1-0	1-0	1	Dorigo	24,184
26	21	A	Blackburn R	D 1-1	1-0	1	Dixon	11,713
27	Feb 4	A	Walsall	W 7-0	4-0	1	Durie 5, Wilson K, Roberts (pen)	6860
28	11	H	Swindon T	W 3-2	3-2	1	Durie, Gittens(og), MacLaren (og)	17,829
29	18	A	Plymouth Arg	W 1-0	1-0	1	Dixon	13,180
30	25	H	Oldham Ath	D 2-2	2-1	2	Roberts 2 (1 pen)	13,261
31	28	H	Hull C	W 2-1	0-0	—	Dixon, Wilson K	11,407
32	Mar 11	H	Watford	D 2-2	2-2	2	Dorigo, Roberts (pen)	22,188
33	15	A	Brighton & HA	W 1-0	1-0	—	Wilson K	12,600
34	18	A	Manchester C	W 3-2	2-0	1	Dixon, Wilson K, Dorigo	40,070
35	21	A	Sunderland	W 2-1	1-1	—	Roberts, Wilson K	14,714
36	25	H	Bournemouth	W 2-0	0-0	1	Durie, Roberts(pen)	22,467
37	28	A	Ipswich T	W 1-0	0-0	—	Durie	22,950
38	Apr 1	H	Barnsley	W 5-3	2-2	1	Dixon 4, Durie	16,023
39	4	H	Birmingham C	W 3-1	1-0	—	Wilson K, Roberts, Dixon	14,796
40	8	A	WBA	W 3-2	3-2	1	Roberts(pen), Lee, McAllister	22,858
41	15	A	Leicester C	L 0-2	0-0	1		19,468
42	22	H	Leeds U	W 1-0	0-0	1	Bumstead	30,332
43	29	A	Shrewsbury T	D 1-1	0-0	1	Dixon	5588
44	May 1	H	Stoke C	W 2-1	1-1	1	Dixon, Roberts (pen)	14,946
45	6	H	Bradford C	W 3-1	1-0	1	Roberts (pen), Dixon 2	18,003
46	13	A	Portsmouth	W 3-2	0-1	1	McAllister 2, Wilson C	12,051

Final League Position: 1

GOALSCORERS

League (96): Dixon 25, Durie 17, Roberts 15 (12 pens), Wilson K 13, Dorigo 6, McAllister 6, Lee 4, Wilson C 3, Bumstead 2, Nicholas 1, Pates 1, Wood 1, own goals 2.
Littlewoods Cup (3): Dixon 1, Wilson K 1, own goal 1.
FA Cup (0).

Littlewoods Cup	Second Round	Scunthorpe U (a)	1-4
		(h)	2-2
FA Cup	Third Round	Barnsley (a)	0-4

Hitchcock	Clarke	Wilson, C	Roberts	McLaughlin	Pates	McAllister	Nicholas	Wilson, K	Durie	Bumstead	Wood	Freestone	Hall	Dodds	Dorigo	Dixon	Lee	Beasant	Mitchell	Hazard	Monkou	Le Saux	*Match No.*
1	2	3	4*	5	6	7	8	9	10	11	12												1
	2	3	4		5		8	9	10	11	6	1	7										2
1	2	3	4		5	11	8	9	10		6		7*	12									3
	2	3	4		5	11	8	9	10		6	1	7*	12									4
	2	3	4		5	7	8	9	10*	11	6	1	12										5
1	2	11	4		5	7	8	12	10	6*					3	9							6
	2	6	4		5	7	8	12	10*	11		1			3	9							7
	2		4		5	7	8†	10		11	6*	1	14		3	9	12						8
	2		4		5	7	8	10		11		1			3	9	6						9
			4		5		8	10		11	7	1	2		3	9	6						10
		11	4	5		7	8	10			6	1	2		3	9							11
	2	12	4	5		7*	8	11	10		6	1			3	9							12
	2	12	4	5		7†	8	11	10		6*	1			3	9	14						13
	2	11	4	5		12	8	7	10		6	1			3	9*							14
	2	11	4	5			8	7	10		6	1			3	9*	12						15
	2†	11	4	5		12	8	7	10		6*	1			3	9	14						16
		11	4			12	8	7	10		6*	1	2		3	9	5						17
		11	4				8	7	10		6	1	2		3	9	5						18
		11	4			10	8	7			6	1	2		3	9	5						19
		11	4			12	8	7	10*		6	1	2		3	9	5						20
		11	4				8	7	10		6	1	2		3	9	5						21
		11	4	5		12		7	10	14	6	1	2		3†	9	8*						22
		11	4	5		12		7	10	8*	6	1	2		3	9							23
		11	4	5		12		7	10*	14	6	1	2		3	9	8†						24
	2	11	4*	5				7			6		12		3	9	10	1	8				25
	2	11	4	5				7					6		3	9	10	1	8				26
	2	3	4	5			8	7	10	6								1	9	11			27
	2		4	5			8	7	10	6					3			1	9	11			28
	2		4	5			8	12	10†	6					3	9	14	1	7	11*			29
	2		4	5		12	8	7		6					3	9		1	10*	11			30
	2	11	4	5		7	8	10		6					3	9		1					31
	2	11	4	5		7	8	10		6					3	9		1					32
	2	11	4	5		7	8	10		6					3	9		1					33
	2	12	4	5		7	8	11	10*	6					3	9		1					34
	2		4	5		7	8	11	10	6					3	9		1					35
	2		4	5		7	8	11	10	6					3	9		1					36
	2		4	5		7	8	11	10	6					3	9		1					37
	2		4*	5		7	8	11	10	6					3	9	12	1					38
	2		4	5*		7	8	11	10	6					3	9	12	1					39
	2		4			7	8*	11	10	6			12		3	9	5	1					40
	2		4	5		7	8	11	10	6*					3	9	12	1					41
	2		4	5		7	8	11	10	6					3	9		1					42
	2	8	4	5		7		11	10*	6			12		3	9		1					43
	2	8	4	5*		7		11		6			10		3	9		1			12		44
	2	10	4	5		7	8	11					6		3	9		1					45
	2†	11	4	5		7	8	10					6		3	9*		1			12	14	46
3	36	29 + 3s	46	31	10	28 + 8s	39	43 + 3s	32	27 + 2s	21 + 1s	21	17 + 5s	— + 2s	40	39	12 + 8s	22	6	4	— + 2s	— + 1s	

CHELSEA

Player and Position	Ht	Wt	Birth Date	Birth Place	Source	Clubs	League App	League Gls
Goalkeepers								
Dave Beasant	6 4	13 00	20 3 59	Willesden	Edgware T	Wimbledon	340	—
						Newcastle U	20	—
						Chelsea	22	—
Roger Freestone	6 2	12 03	19 8 68	Newport		Newport Co	13	—
						Chelsea	42	—
Kevin Hitchcock	6 1	12 02	5 10 62	Custom House	Barking	Nottingham F	—	—
						Mansfield T (loan)	14	—
						Mansfield T	168	—
						Chelsea	11	—
Eddie Niedzwiecki‡ (Retired)	6 0	11 00	3 5 59	Bangor	Amateur	Wrexham	111	—
						Chelsea	136	—
Defenders								
Steve Beatty	6 0	12 10	1 9 69	Larne	Trainee	Chelsea	—	—
Steve Clarke	5 9	11 02	29 8 63	Saltcoats	Beith Jnrs	St Mirren	151	6
						Chelsea	90	1
John Coady (To Derry C Oct 1988)	5 9	10 10	25 8 60	Dublin	Shamrock R	Chelsea	16	2
Jason Cundy	6 1	13 07	12 11 69	Wimbledon	Trainee	Chelsea	—	—
Tony Dorigo	5 10	10 00	31 12 65	Melbourne	Apprentice	Aston Villa	111	1
						Chelsea	80	6
Gareth Hall	5 8	10 07	20 3 69	Croydon		Chelsea	36	—
David Lee	6 3	12 12	26 11 69	Kingswood	Trainee	Chelsea	20	4
Graeme Le Saux	6 0	12 00	17 10 68	Harrow		Chelsea	1	—
Joe McLaughlin	6 1	12 00	2 6 60	Greenock	School	Morton	134	3
						Chelsea	220	5
Kenneth Monkou	6 0	12 00	29 11 64	Surinam	Feyenoord	Chelsea	2	—
Graham Roberts	5 11	13 10	3 7 59	Southampton	School	Southampton	—	—
						Bournemouth	—	—
					Sholing S	Portsmouth	—	—
					Dorchester T, Weymouth	Tottenham H	209	23
						Rangers	55	3
						Chelsea	46	15
Steve Wicks‡	6 2	13 02	3 10 56	Reading	Apprentice	Chelsea	118	5
						Derby Co	24	—
						QPR	73	—
						Crystal Palace	14	1
						QPR	116	6
						Chelsea	32	1
Midfield								
John Bumstead	5 7	10 05	27 11 58	Rotherhithe	Apprentice	Chelsea	297	35
Tommy Byrne‡	5 8	10 04	30 8 69	Dublin	Apprentice	Chelsea	—	—
Edward Cunnington‡	5 8	10 05	12 11 69	Kilbride	Trainee	Chelsea	—	—
Micky Hazard	5 7	10 05	5 2 60	Sunderland	Apprentice	Tottenham H	91	13
						Chelsea	68	9
Peter Nicholas	5 8	11 08	10 11 59	Newport	Apprentice	Crystal Palace	127	7
						Arsenal	60	1
						Crystal Palace	47	7
						Luton T	102	1
						Aberdeen	39	3
						Chelsea	39	1
Clive Wilson	5 7	10 00	13 11 61	Manchester	Local	Manchester C	98	9
						Chester C (loan)	21	2
						Manchester C (loan)	11	—
						Chelsea	63	5

CHELSEA

Foundation: Chelsea may never have existed but for the fact that Fulham rejected an offer to rent the Stamford Bridge ground from Mr. H. A. Mears who had owned it since 1904. Fortunately he was determined to develop it as a football stadium rather than sell it to the Great Western Railway and got together with Frederick Parker, who persuaded Mears of the financial advantages of developing a major sporting venue. Chelsea FC was formed in 1905, and when admission to the Southern League was denied, they immediately gained admission to the Second Division of the Football League.

Managers (and Secretary-managers)
John Tait Robertson 1905–07, David Calderhead 1907–33, A. Leslie Knighton 1933–39, Billy Birrell 1939–52, Ted Drake 1952–61, Tommy Docherty 1962–67, Dave Sexton 1967–74, Ron Suart 1974–75, Eddie McCreadie 1975–77, Ken Shellito 1977–78, Danny Blanchflower 1978–79, Geoff Hurst 1979–81, John Neal 1981–85 (Director to 1986), John Hollins 1985–88, Bobby Campbell 1988– .

Player and Position	*Ht*	*Wt*	*Birth Date*	*Place*	*Source*	*Clubs*	*League App*	*Gls*
Forwards								
Kerry Dixon	6 0	13 00	24 7 61	Luton	Apprentice	Tottenham H	—	—
					Dunstable	Reading	116	51
						Chelsea	229	112
Billy Dodds	5 7	10 00	5 2 69	New Cummock	Apprentice	Chelsea	3	—
						Partick Th (loan)	30	9
Gordon Durie	6 0	12 00	6 12 65	Paisley	Hill O'Beath	East Fife	81	26
						Hibernian	47	14
						Chelsea	84	34
Kevin McAllister	5 5	11 00	8 11 62	Falkirk		Falkirk	64	18
						Chelsea	69	6
						Falkirk (loan)	6	3
David Mitchell	6 1	12 07	13 6 62	Scotland		Rangers	26	6
					Feyenoord	Chelsea	6	—
Colin West	5 7	11 00	19 9 67	Middlesbrough	Apprentice	Chelsea	16	4
						Partick Th (loan)	24	10
						Swansea C (loan)	14	3
Kevin Wilson	5 7	10 10	18 4 61	Banbury	Banbury U	Derby Co	122	30
						Ipswich T	98	34
						Chelsea	71	18

Trainees
Blake, Nathan A; Bryant, Michael F; Burley, Craig W; Davies, Roy M; Hinton, Darren; Jacobs, Giles; Kilpatrick, Ian; Matthew, Damian; Newton, Edward J.I; Phillips, Walter H; Sinclair, Frank M; Stuart, Graham C; Wilkinson, Glenn; Winters, Jason.

Associated Schoolboys
Agius, Steven M.F; Beadle, Roger J; Chatfield, Ian R; Corbett, Scott; Harrison, Paul M; Hutchings, Carl E; James, Andrew; Marsh, Anthony M.E; Mas, Bartolome; Mearns, John F; Mitchell, Justin A.P; Pearce, Ian A; Rowe, Ezekiel; Sell, Richard G.

CHESTER CITY 1988–89 *Back row (left to right):* Stuart Walker, Graham Abel, Barry Butler, Ian Benjamin, Chris Lightfoot, Billy Stewart, Steve Johnson, Joe Hinningan, Gary Bennett, Colin Woodthorpe.
Front row: Carl Dale, David Glenn, Graham Barrow, Harry McNally (Manager), Milton Graham, Joe Jakub, Sean Lundon.

Division 3 CHESTER CITY

The Stadium, Sealand Rd, Chester CH1 4LW. Telephone Chester (0244) 371376. Commercial Dept. (0244) 378162.

Ground capacity: 8250.

Record attendance: 20,500 v Chelsea, FA Cup 3rd rd replay, 16 Jan, 1952.

Record receipts: £30,609 v Sheffield W, FA Cup 4th rd, 31 January, 1987.

Pitch measurements: 114yd × 76yd.

Club Patron: Duke of Westminster.

President: Reg Rowlands.

Chairman: A. E. Barnes JP, FCA. Vice-Chairman: C. Thompson.

Directors: L. Lloyd, R. H. Crofts, F. Summers, H. McNally, D. Cross, D. Barker.

Team Manager: Harry McNally. ***Assistant Manager:*** Graham Barrow.

Secretary: J. A. Eckersley. ***Physio:*** Stuart Walker.

Year Formed: 1884. ***Turned Professional:*** 1902. ***Ltd Co.:*** 1909.

Previous name: Chester until 1983.

Club Nicknames: 'Blues'.

Previous Grounds: Faulkner Street; Old Showground; 1904, Whipcord Lane; 1906, Sealand Road.

Record League Victory: 12-0 v York C, Division 3(N), 1 February 1936 – Middleton; Common, Hall; Wharton, Wilson, Howarth; Horsman (2), Hughes, Wrightson (4), Cresswell (2), Sargeant (4).

Record Cup Victory: 6-1 v Darlington, FA Cup, 1st rd, 25 November 1933 – Burke; Bennett, Little; Pitcairn, Skitt, Duckworth; Armes (3), Whittam, Mantle (2), Cresswell (1), McLachlan.

Record Defeat: 2-11 v Oldham Ath, Division 3(N), 19 January, 1952.

Most League Points (2 for a win): 56, Division 3(N), 1946–47 and Division 4, 1964–65.

Most League Points (3 for a win): 84, Division 4, 1985–86.

Most League Goals: 119, Division 4, 1964, 1964–65.

Highest League Scorer in Season: Dick Yates, 36, Division 3(N), 1946–47.

Most League Goals in Total Aggregate: Gary Talbot, 83, 1963–67 and 1968–70.

Most Capped Player: Bill Lewis, 7 (30), Wales.

Most League Appearances: Ray Gill, 408, 1951–62.

Record Transfer Fee Received: £300,000 from Liverpool for Ian Rush, May 1980.

Record Transfer Fee Paid: £45,000 to Carlisle U for Steve Ludlam, May 1980.

Football League Record: 1931 Elected Division 3(N); 1958–75 Division 4; 1975–82 Division 3; 1982–86 Division 4; 1986– Division 3.

Honours: *Football League:* Division 3 best season; 5th, 1977–78; Division 3(N) – Runners-up 1935–36; Division 4 – Runners-up 1985–86. *FA Cup* best season: 5th rd, 1976–77, 1979–80. *Football League Cup:* Semi-final 1974–75, *Welsh Cup:* Winners 1908, 1933, 1947. *Debenhams Cup:* Winners 1977.

Colours: Royal blue shirts, white shorts, blue stockings white trim. **Change colours:** Gold shirts and stockings, black shorts.

CHESTER CITY 1988–89 LEAGUE RECORD

Match No.	Date	Venue	Opponents	Result	H/T Score	Lg. Pos.	Goalscorers	Attendance
1	Aug 27	H	Blackpool	D 1-1	1-0	—	Johnson	3496
2	Sept 3	A	Port Vale	W 2-1	2-0	6	Woodthorpe, Johnson	4213
3	10	H	Bristol C	W 2-0	0-0	2	Lightfoot, Dale	2823
4	17	A	Sheffield U	L 1-6	0-3	8	Lightfoot	8675
5	20	A	Preston NE	D 3-3	1-1	—	Dale 2, Johnson	5415
6	24	H	Huddersfield T	W 3-0	2-0	6	Newhouse, Johnson (pen), Tucker (og)	3319
7	Oct 1	A	Reading	L 1-3	0-2	7	Woodthorpe	4376
8	5	H	Brentford	W 3-2	3-2	—	Jakub, Barrow, Dale	2004
9	9	A	Notts Co	D 2-2	1-1	—	Benjamin, Barrow	5772
10	15	H	Cardiff C	D 0-0	0-0	8		2796
11	22	A	Bristol R	L 1-4	1-2	13	Benjamin	3811
12	26	H	Mansfield T	D 0-0	0-0	—		1805
13	29	A	Aldershot	D 1-1	1-1	14	Hawtin	1862
14	Nov 5	H	Swansea C	W 3-1	2-0	11	Dale 2, Abel	2263
15	8	A	Bury	L 1-2	0-1	—	Newhouse	2497
16	12	H	Chesterfield	W 3-1	1-1	11	Hewitt (og), Dale 2	2099
17	26	H	Southend U	L 2-4	1-1	13	Johnson 2	2050
18	Dec 3	A	Gillingham	W 2-0	1-0	11	Dale, Johnson	3329
19	17	A	Bolton W	W 1-0	0-0	9	Dale	4318
20	26	H	Wigan Ath	W 1-0	0-0	8	Lightfoot	3262
21	31	H	Northampton T	W 2-1	0-1	4	Dale, Abel	2733
22	Jan 2	A	Wolverhampton W	L 1-3	1-3	6	Johnson	21,901
23	7	A	Fulham	L 1-4	0-3	7	Lightfoot	4196
24	14	H	Port Vale	L 1-2	1-0	9	Dale	4891
25	21	A	Bristol C	W 1-0	0-0	8	Johnson	9586
26	Feb 4	H	Reading	W 3-0	1-0	7	Dale 2, Hinnigan	2354
27	11	A	Brentford	W 1-0	1-0	7	Dale	5748
28	18	H	Notts Co	W 1-0	0-0	5	Johnson	3157
29	28	A	Mansfield T	L 0-2	0-1	—		2796
30	Mar 4	H	Bristol R	L 0-2	0-0	8		3082
31	11	A	Swansea C	D 1-1	1-1	8	Dale	4311
32	15	H	Aldershot	D 1-1	0-1	—	Dale	2038
33	18	A	Blackpool	D 1-1	0-0	8	O'Keefe	2795
34	25	H	Wolverhampton W	D 1-1	1-1	9	Abel	8236
35	27	A	Wigan Ath	L 0-3	0-1	9		3132
36	Apr 1	H	Bolton W	D 0-0	0-0	9		3225
37	5	H	Fulham	W 7-0	2-0	—	Hinnigan, Woodthorpe, O'Keefe (pen), Dale 3, Graham	2121
38	8	A	Northampton T	W 2-0	0-0	7	Lightfoot, O'Keefe (pen)	2845
39	15	A	Huddersfield T	L 1-3	0-1	7	Painter	6109
40	19	H	Sheffield U	L 0-1	0-1	—		4282
41	22	H	Preston NE	L 0-1	0-0	9		4617
42	29	A	Chesterfield	W 2-1	0-0	8	Dale, Lightfoot	3529
43	May 1	H	Bury	W 2-0	1-0	8	Barrow, Lightfoot	2110
44	6	H	Gillingham	W 2-0	1-0	7	Dale, O'Keefe (pen)	2106
45	9	A	Cardiff C	L 0-2	0-0	7		3002
46	13	A	Southend U	L 0-1	0-0	8		4089

Final League Position: 8

GOALSCORERS

League (64): Dale 22, Johnson 10 (1 pen), Lightfoot 7, O'Keefe 4 (3 pens), Abel 3, Barrow 3, Woodthorpe 3, Benjamin 2, Hinnigan 2, Newhouse 2, Graham 1, Hawtin 1, Jakub 1, Painter 1, own goals 2.
Littlewoods Cup (3): Barrow 1, Lightfoot 1, own goal 1.
FA Cup (2): Benjamin 1, Dale 1.

Littlewoods Cup	First Round	Bolton W (a)	0-1
		(h)	3-1
	Second Round	Nottingham F (a)	0-6
		(h)	0-4
FA Cup	First Round	Burnley (a)	2-0
	Second Round	Huddersfield T (a)	0-1

Stewart	Glenn	Woodthorpe	Hinnigan	Abel	Lightfoot	Jakub	Butler	Benjamin	Johnson	Bennett	Dale	Newhouse	Barrow	Lundon	Kelly	Hawtin	Painter	Graham	Lane	O'Keefe	Wynne	*Match No.*
1	2	3	4	5	6	7	8	9*	10	11†	12	14										1
1	2	3	4	5	6	11		10	9			7	8									2
1	2	3	4	5	6	7		9	10		12	11*	8									3
1	2	3	4	5	6*	7		9	10	12		11	8									4
1	2	3	4*	5		7	6	12	10		9		8	11								5
1	2*	3		5	6	7		12	10		9	11	8		4							6
1	2	3		5	6	7		12	10		9*	11	8		4							7
1	2	3		5	6	7			10	12	9	11*	8		4							8
1	2	3	4	5	6	7		9	10				8		11							9
1	2	3		5	6	7		9*	10	12	11		8		4							10
1	2	3†	4	5	6*	7		9	10	12	14		8	11								11
1	2	3		5	6	7	4	9	10		11		8									12
1		3		5	6	7	4	9	10	12	11*		8			2						13
1	2	3	4	5†	6	7	14	9	12	10	11*		8									14
1		3	4		6	7	5	9	10†		11*	12	8	14		2						15
1		3	4	5	6	7	2	9*	12		11	10	8									16
1		3	4		6	7	5	9	10		11		8			2						17
1			4	5	6	7	2	9	10		11		8	3*							12	18
1	2	3	4	5		7	6	9	10		11		8									19
1	2†	3	4	5	14	7	6	9			11	10*	8					12				20
1		3	4	5	6	7	2	12	9		11			8				10*				21
1		3	4	5†	6	7	2	10	9		11	14		8*				12				22
1		3	4*	5	6	7	2	9	12		11		8					10				23
1		3	4	5		7	2		9		11		8					10	6			24
1		3	4	5	12	7	2*		9		11	14	8					10†	6			25
1		3	4	5		7	2		9		11	10*	8					12	6			26
1		3	4	5	12	7	2		9		11	10*	8						6			27
1	12	3	4	5		7	2		9		11	10*	8						6			28
1		3	4	5		7	2		9		11	10	8						6			29
1		3	4*	5		7	2		9		11	12	8					10	6			30
1		3	4	5		7	2		9		11		8					10	6			31
1		3	4*	5		7	2		9		11	12	8					10	6			32
1		3	4	5		7	2		9		11		8					10*	6	12		33
1		3	4†	5	14	7	2		9		11		8					12	6	10*		34
1	2	3	4†	5	14	7			9			11						8	6	10*	12	35
1		3	4		5	7	2				11	10*					12	9	6	8		36
1		3	4	9*	5	7	2				11						12	10	6	8		37
1		3	4		5	7	2				11*	12					9	10	6	8		38
1		3	4		5	7	2†		9*			12					11	10	6	8	14	39
1		3	4	8	5	7	2		9*		11							10	6	12		40
1	2	3	4	9	5						11	14	8				7†	10*	6	12		41
1		3	4*	9	5		2				11		8				12	10	6	7		42
1		3		4	5		2				11		8				9	10	6	7*	12	43
1		3	14	4	5		2				11		8†				9*	10	6	7	12	44
1			4*	6	5	8	2		9		11	12						10	3	7		45
1		3	4		5	8	2†		9*		11	12						10	6	7	14	46
46	17 + 1s	44	38 + 1s	40	31 + 5s	42	34 + 1s	18 + 4s	35 + 3s	2 + 5s	38 + 3s	14 + 11s	35	5 + 1s	5	3	5 + 3s	20 + 4s	23	11 + 3s	— + 6s	

CHESTER CITY

Player and Position	Ht	Wt	Birth Date	Birth Place	Source	Clubs	League App	League Gls
Goalkeepers								
Steve Farrelly	6 3				Knowsley U	Chester C	—	—
Billy Stewart	5 11	11 07	1 1 65	Liverpool	Apprentice	Liverpool	—	—
						Wigan Ath	14	—
						Chester C	102	—
Defenders								
Graham Abel	6 2	13 00	17 9 60	Runcorn	Runcorn	Chester C	149	8
Barry Butler	6 2	13 00	4 6 62	Farnworth	Atherton T	Chester C	109	—
David Glenn*	5 10	10 10	30 11 62	Wigan	Apprentice	Wigan Ath	72	4
						Blackburn R	24	—
						Chester C	73	1
Craig Hawtin*			29 3 70	Buxton	Trainee	Chester C	7	1
Joe Hinnigan	6 0	12 00	3 12 55	Liverpool	S Liverpool	Wigan Ath	66	10
						Sunderland	63	4
						Preston NE	52	8
						Gillingham	103	7
						Wrexham	29	1
						Chester C	39	2
Martin Lane	5 9	11 04	12 4 61	Altrincham	Amateur	Manchester U	—	—
						Chester C	175	3
						Coventry C	3	—
						Wrexham (loan)	6	—
						Chester C	23	—
Sean Lundon	5 10	10 10	7 3 69	Liverpool	Apprentice	Chester C	40	2
Colin Woodthorpe	5 11	11 08	13 1 69	Ellesmere Pt	Apprentice	Chester C	109	5
Midfield								
Graham Barrow	6 2	13 07	13 6 54	Chorley	Altrincham	Wigan Ath	179	36
						Chester C	114	12
Milton Graham	5 10	12 04	2 11 62	Tottenham	Local	Bournemouth	73	12
						Chester C	129	11
Joe Jakub	5 6	9 06	7 12 56	Falkirk	Apprentice	Burnley	42	—
						Bury	265	27
					AZ 67	Chester C	42	1
Chris Lightfoot	5 11	11 00	1 4 70	Wimwick	Trainee	Chester C	52	8
Aiden Newhouse§			23 5 72	Wallasey	Trainee	Chester C	26	2
Peter Painter§			26 1 71	Ince	Trainee	Chester C	10	1
Mark Parry‡			21 5 70	Wrexham	Trainee	Chester C	5	1
Darren Wynne§			12 10 70	St Asaph	Trainee	Chester C	6	—

CHESTER CITY

Foundation: All students of soccer history have read about the medieval games of football in Chester, but the present club was not formed until 1884 through the amalgamation of King's School Old Boys with Chester Rovers. For many years Chester were overshadowed in Cheshire by Northwich Victoria and Crewe Alexandra who had both won the Senior Cup several times before Chester's first success in 1894–95.

Managers (and Secretary-managers)
Charlie Hewitt 1930–36, Alex Raisbeck 1936–38, Frank Brown 1938–53, Louis Page 1953–56, John Harris 1956–59, Stan Pearson 1959–61, Bill Lambton 1962–63, Peter Hauser 1963–68, Ken Roberts 1968–76, Alan Oakes 1976–82, Cliff Sear 1982, John Sainty 1982–83, John McGrath 1984, Harry McNally 1985– .

Player and Position	*Ht*	*Wt*	*Birth Date*	*Birth Place*	*Source*	*Clubs*	*League App*	*League Gls*
Forwards								
Carl Dale			29 4 66	Colwyn Bay	Bangor C	Chester C	41	22
Steve Johnson*	6 0	12 09	23 6 57	Liverpool	Altrincham	Bury	154	52
						Rochdale	19	7
						Wigan Ath	51	18
						Bristol C	21	3
						Rochdale (loan)	6	1
						Chester C (loan)	10	6
						Scunthorpe U	72	20
						Chester C	38	10
Steve Moore‡			17 12 69	Chester	Trainee	Chester C	1	—
Eamon O'Keefe	5 7	11 05	13 10 53	Manchester	Stalybridge C	Plymouth Arg	—	—
						Hyde U	—	—
						Saudi Arabia	—	—
						Mossley	—	—
						Everton	40	6
						Wigan Ath	58	25
						Port Vale	59	17
						Blackpool	36	23
					Cork C	Chester C	14	4

Trainees
Carroll, Michael J; Griffin, Jamie; Hill, Andrew; Hinchliffe, Phillip J; Jones, David L; Milne, Christopher J; Nassari, Derek J; Newhouse, Aidan R; Newland, Raymond J; Painter, Peter R; Pickthall, Stuart; Richards, Francis A; Roberts, Richard M; Wynne, Darren L.Evans, Gary N; Evans, Thomas P; Fletcher, Gary G; Ingman, David J; McQuillan, Matthew M;

Roberts, Joel H; Senior, Carl R; White, David J; Wilson, Nicholas K.

CHESTERFIELD 1988–89 *Back row (left to right):* Craig Shepherd, Gavin McDonald, Jamie Preston, Shane Gibson, Tony Briffa, Nigel Thompson, David Hoole.
Centre row: Jamie Hewitt, Robert Alleyne, Darren Wood, Les Hunter, Jim Brown, Mike Astbury, Andy Morris, Lee Rogers, Pat McGeeney, Dave Perry.
Front row: Reece Simpson, Steve Prindiville, Bob Bloomer, Brian Ferguson (Coach), Mick Henderson (Player/Coach), Kevin Randall (Manager), Dave Waller, Kevin Eley, Scott Chambers.

Division 4 **CHESTERFIELD**

Recreation Ground, Chesterfield S40 4SX. Telephone Chesterfield (0246) 209765. Commercial Dept: (0246) 31535.

Ground capacity: 12,838.

Record attendance: 30,968 v Newcastle U, Division 2, 7 April, 1939.

Record receipts: £32,410 v Sheffield U, Division 3, 25 March, 1989.

Pitch measurements: 112yd × 72yd.

President: His Grace the Duke of Devonshire MC, DL, JP.

Vice-Presidents: P. C. J. T. Kirkman, E. Brocklehurst.

Chairman: B. W. Hubbard. ***Vice-Chairman:*** J. N. Lea.

Directors: K. R. Unwin, B. Watson, J. Croot, J. A. Plant, H. Diffley.

Team Manager: Paul Hart. ***Coach:*** Mick Henderson.

Physio: Dave Rushbury. ***Assistant Manager:*** Chris McMenemy.

Secretary: Bob Pepper. ***Commercial Manager:*** Jim Brown.

Year Formed: 1866. ***Turned Professional:*** 1891. ***Ltd Co:*** 1871.

Club Nickname: 'Blues' or 'Spireites'.

Record League Victory: 10-0 v Glossop, Division 2, 17 January 1903 – Clutterbuck; Thorpe, Lerper; Haig, Banner, Thacker; Tomlinson (2), Newton (1), Milward (3), Munday (2), Steel (2).

Record Cup Victory: 5-0 v Wath Ath (away), FA Cup, 1st rd, 28 November 1925 – Birch; Saxby, Dennis; Wass, Abbott, Thompson; Fisher (1), Roseboom (1), Cookson (2), Whitfield (1), Hopkinson.

Record Defeat: 0-10 v Gillingham, Division 3, 5 September, 1987.

Most League Points (2 for a win): 64, Division 4, 1969–70.

Most League Points (3 for a win): 91, Division 4, 1984–85.

Most League Goals: 102, Division 3(N), 1930–31.

Highest League Scorer in Season: Jimmy Cookson, 44, Division 3(N), 1925–26.

Most League Goals in Total Aggregate: Ernie Moss, 161, 1969–76, 1979–81 and 1984–86.

Most Capped Player: Walter McMillen, 4 (7), Northern Ireland.

Most League Appearances: Dave Blakey, 613, 1948–67.

Record Transfer Fee Received: £200,000 from Wolverhampton W for Alan Birch, August 1981.

Record Transfer Fee Paid: £150,000 to Carlisle U for Phil Bonnyman, March 1980.

Football League Record: 1898 Elected to Division 2; 1909 failed re-election; 1921–31 Division 3(N); 1931–33 Division 2; 1933–36 Division 3(N); 1936–51 Division 2; 1951–58 Division 3(N); 1958–61 Division 3; 1961–70 Division 4; 1970–83 Division 3; 1983–85 Division 4; 1985–89 Division 3; Division 4 1989–.

Honours: *Football League:* Division 2 best seson: 4th, 1946–47; Division 3(N) – Champions 1930–31, 1935–36; Runners-up 1933–34; Division 4 – Champions 1969–70; 1984–85. *FA Cup* best season: 5th rd. 1932–33, 1937–38, 1949–50. *Football League Cup* best season: 4th rd, 1964–65. *Anglo-Scottish Cup:* Winners 1980–81.

Colours: Blue shirts, white shorts, white stockings. **Change colours:** Red shirts, blue shorts, red stockings.

CHESTERFIELD 1988–89 LEAGUE RECORD

Match No.	Date	Venue	Opponents	Result	H/T Score	Lg. Pos.	Goalscorers	Attendance
1	Aug 27	H	Aldershot	W 2-1	0-0	—	Morris, Waller	2327
2	Sept 3	A	Bristol C	L 0-4	0-1	17		7547
3	10	H	Wolverhampton W	L 0-3	0-2	20		4217
4	17	A	Northampton T	L 0-3	0-2	21		4520
5	19	A	Port Vale	L 0-5	0-3	—		4469
6	24	H	Blackpool	L 0-2	0-0	23		2128
7	Oct 1	H	Bury	L 1-2	1-1	23	Alleyne	1837
8	4	A	Notts Co	L 0-4	0-2	—		4519
9	8	A	Gillingham	W 1-0	1-0	22	Prindiville	2901
10	15	H	Preston NE	L 0-3	0-2	23		2813
11	22	A	Southend U	L 1-3	0-3	23	Morris	2662
12	25	H	Brentford	D 2-2	0-0	—	Alleyne 2	1876
13	29	A	Bolton W	L 0-5	0-2	24		4757
14	Nov 5	H	Bristol R	L 0-3	0-1	24		2480
15	12	A	Chester C	L 1-3	1-1	24	Bloomer	2099
16	26	A	Reading	D 0-0	0-0	24		4775
17	Dec 3	H	Mansfield T	L 1-3	1-1	24	Waller	4236
18	17	A	Swansea C	L 0-2	0-1	24		3656
19	26	H	Huddersfield T	D 1-1	1-1	24	Bloomer (pen)	5539
20	31	H	Fulham	W 4-1	2-0	24	Brien, Bloomer 2 (1 pen), McDonald	3086
21	Jan 2	A	Sheffield U	W 3-1	2-1	24	Bloomer, Morris 2	15,769
22	7	A	Wigan Ath	W 2-0	2-0	24	Wood, Atherton (og)	2249
23	14	H	Bristol C	W 1-0	0-0	22	Bloomer	3488
24	21	A	Wolverhampton W	L 0-1	0-0	22		15,049
25	28	H	Northampton T	D 1-1	0-1	22	Waller	3920
26	Feb 4	A	Bury	L 1-2	1-1	23	Morris	3844
27	11	H	Notts Co	W 3-0	2-0	22	Mills(og), Waller, Yates(og)	4943
28	18	H	Gillingham	W 3-1	1-0	22	Waller, Bloomer(pen), Rolph	3432
29	25	A	Preston NE	L 0-6	0-4	22		7074
30	28	A	Brentford	L 0-1	0-0	—		4192
31	Mar 4	H	Southend U	W 2-1	0-1	21	Bloomer(pen), Waller	3261
32	11	A	Bristol R	L 1-2	0-2	21	Shaw	4686
33	14	H	Bolton W	D 1-1	1-0	—	Waller	2877
34	18	A	Aldershot	L 0-2	0-0	21		1886
35	21	H	Cardiff C	W 4-0	2-0	—	Morris 3, Bloomer(pen)	2888
36	25	H	Sheffield U	W 2-1	1-0	20	Waller 2	10,991
37	27	A	Huddersfield T	D 1-1	1-1	20	Hewitt	5819
38	Apr 1	H	Swansea C	W 2-0	0-0	19	Hough(og), Waller	3349
39	4	H	Wigan Ath	D 1-1	0-1	—	Waller (pen)	3179
40	8	A	Fulham	L 1-2	0-0	20	Waller	4252
41	15	H	Port Vale	L 1-2	0-2	20	Waller	5895
42	22	A	Blackpool	W 2-1	0-0	20	Waller 2	3221
43	29	H	Chester C	L 1-2	0-0	21	Waller	3529
44	May 1	A	Cardiff C	W 1-0	1-0	20	Waller	3244
45	6	A	Mansfield T	L 1-3	0-2	21	Waller	4767
46	13	H	Reading	L 2-4	2-0	22	Bloomer (pen), Morris	3107

Final League Position: 22

GOALSCORERS

League (51): Waller 18 (1 pen), Bloomer 10 (6 pens), Morris 9, Alleyne 3, Brien 1, Hewitt 1, Rolph 1, Shaw 1, Prindiville 1, McDonald 1, Wood 1, own goals 4.
Littlewoods Cup (3): Morris 2, Waller 1.
FA Cup (2): Morris 2.

Littlewoods Cup	First Round	Port Vale (a)	2-3
		(h)	1-1
FA Cup	First Round	Bolton W (a)	0-0
		(h)	2-3

Astbury	Hewitt	McGeeney	Henderson	Rogers	Hunter	Eley	Arnott	Waller	Morris	Thompson	Brown	Bloomer	Wood	Alleyne	Prindiville	Slack	Dempsey	McDonald	Hoole	Gormley	Cherry	Brien	Shaw	Rolph	Leonard	*Match No.*
1	2	3	4	5	6	7	8	9	10	11																1
	2	3*	4	5	6†	7	8	9	10	11	1	12	14													2
1	2	3	4	12†	6	7	8	9	10	11*			5	14												3
1	2		4		6	7	8		10			3	5	9	11											4
1	2	6	4			7	8		10			3	5	9	11											5
	2		4			7	8		10		1	11	5	9	3	6										6
	2		4			7*	8		10		1	12	5	9	3	6	11									7
	2	14	4*			7	8†		10		1	12	5	9	3	6	11									8
	2	7					8		10		1	4	5	9	3	6	11									9
	2	7*	11			12	8		10		1	4	5	9	3	6										10
	2	7				11	8		10		1	4	5	9*	3	6		12								11
	2	7				11	8		10		1	4	5	9	3	6										12
	2	7					8		10	11	1	4	5	9	3	6										13
	2†					7	8	12	10	11*	1	4	5	9	3	6			14							14
	2					7	8	11*	10		1	4	5	9	3	6		12								15
					5	7*	8	11	10	12	1	2	6	9	3					4						16
		4*	12		5	7		9	11			2	6	8	3					10	1					17
			4*	2		7		9	11			8	6	12	3					10	1	5				18
				2		12		9	11			8	6	7*	3					10	1	5	4			19
	2			6		7		9	11			10		8*	3			12			1	5	4			20
	2			6		7		9	11			10		12	3			8*			1	5	4			21
1	2			6		7*	12	9	11			10	8		3							5	4			22
	2			6		7*	8	9	11			10			3			12			1	5	4			23
	2			6		7	12	9	11			10			3			8*			1	5	4			24
	2			6		7	12	9	11			10*			3			8†	14		1	5	4			25
	2			6		7	4	9	11			10*			3			12	8		1	5				26
	2			6		7*	4	9	11			10		8	3						1	5		12		27
1	2			6			4	9	11			10		8	3			12				5		7*		28
1	2			6			4	9	11			10*			3			12	14			5	8	7†		29
1	2†			6			4	9	11			10			3			7	14			5	8*	12		30
				6		10	4	9	11			2			3			7*				5	8	12	1	31
	14			6		10*	4	9	11			2		12	3							5	8	7†	1	32
	4			6		7*		9	11			2		10	3							5	8	12	1	33
	2			6		7*		9	11			4		10†	3				14			5	8	12	1	34
	2					7*		9	11			4			3	6			10			5	8	12	1	35
	10			12		7		9	11			4			3	6			2*			5	8		1	36
	10					7*		9	11			4	12		3	6			2			5	8		1	37
	10					7	14	9				4	11*	12	3	6			2†			5	8		1	38
	10					7	4	9				2*		11	3	6			12			5	8		1	39
	10			6		7	4	9				11			3				2*			5	8	12	1	40
	10†			2		7	4	9				11	14		3	6						5	8*	12	1	41
	2					7	4	9	11			10			3	6						5	8		1	42
	2					7*	4	9	11			10		12	3	6						5	8		1	43
	2					7	4	9	11			10		12	3	6						5	8*		1	44
	2					7†	4	9	11			10		8*	3	6			14			5	12		1	45
				2			4	9	11			10		12	3	6						5	8	7*	1	46
8	39	10	10	22	6	38	32	35	42	5	12	41	19	22	43	21	3	5	6	4	10	29	24	4	16	
	+	+	+	+		+	+	+		+		+	+	+				+	+				+	+		
	1s	1s	1s	2s		2s	4s	1s		1s		3s	3s	8s				7s	7s				1s	8s		

CHESTERFIELD

Player and Position	Ht	Wt	Birth Date	Birth Place	Source	Clubs	League App	League Gls
Goalkeepers								
Mike Astbury	5 10	13 08	22 1 64	Leeds	Apprentice	York C	48	—
						Peterborough U (loan)	4	—
						Darlington	38	—
						Chester C	5	—
						Chesterfield	8	—
Jim Brown†	5 10	11 13	11 5 52	Coatbridge	Bargeddie Am	Albion R	79	—
						Chesterfield	47	—
						Sheffield U	170	—
						Detroit Express	—	—
						Washington D	—	—
						Chicago Sting	—	—
						Cardiff C	3	—
						Kettering T	—	—
						Chesterfield	135	1
Mick Leonard	6 1	12 04	9 5 59	Carshalton	Epsom & Ewell	Halifax T	69	—
						Notts Co	204	—
						Chesterfield	16	—
Defenders								
Bob Bloomer	5 10	11 06	21 6 66	Sheffield		Chesterfield	119	14
Tony Brien	6 0	12 00	10 2 69	Dublin	Apprentice	Leicester C	16	1
						Chesterfield	29	1
Jamie Hewitt	5 10	10 08	17 5 68	Chesterfield	School	Chesterfield	127	5
Dave Perry*	5 10	11 05	17 5 67	Sheffield		Chesterfield	17	—
Steve Prindiville	5 9	11 04	26 12 68	Harlow	Apprentice	Leicester C	1	—
						Chesterfield	43	1
Lee Rogers	5 10	12 00	21 10 66	Doncaster	Doncaster R	Chesterfield	103	—
Trevor Slack	6 1	10 02	26 9 62	Peterborough	Apprentice	Peterborough U	202	18
						Rotherham U	15	1
						Grimsby T	21	—
						Northampton T	13	1
						Chesterfield	21	—
Darren Wood	6 1	12 08	22 10 68	Derby	Trainee	Chesterfield	67	3
Midfield								
Kevin Arnott	5 10	11 12	28 9 58	Bensham	Apprentice	Sunderland	133	16
						Blackburn R (loan)	17	2
						Sheffield U	121	11
						Blackburn R (loan)	12	1
						Rotherham U (loan)	9	2
						Chesterfield	55	1
Mick Henderson	5 10	11 04	31 3 56	Gosforth	Apprentice	Sunderland	84	2
						Watford	51	—
						Cardiff C	11	—
						Sheffield U	67	—
						Chesterfield	136	10
David Hoole§	5 6	10 00	16 10 70	Chesterfield	Trainee	Chesterfield	13	—
Gavin McDonald§	5 7	10 06	6 10 70	Salford	Trainee	Chesterfield	12	1
Pat McGeeney‡	5 10	11 00	31 10 66	Sheffield	Apprentice	Sheffield U	16	—
						Rochdale (loan)	3	—
						Chesterfield	49	1
Adrian Shaw	5 10	11 07	13 4 66	Easington	Apprentice	Nottingham F	—	1
						Halifax T	100	1
						York C	5	—
						Chesterfield	25	1
Nigel Thompson	5 7	10 07	1 3 67	Leeds	Apprentice	Leeds U	7	—
						Rochdale (loan)	5	—
						Chesterfield	10	—

CHESTERFIELD

Foundation: Chesterfield are fourth only to Stoke, Notts County and Nottingham Forest in age for they can trace their existence as far back as 1866, although it is fair to say that they were somewhat casual in the first few years of their history playing only a few friendlies a year. However, their rules of 1871 are still in existence showing an annual membership of 2s (10p), but it was not until 1891 that they won a trophy (the Barnes Cup) and followed this a year later by winning the Sheffield Cup, Barnes Cup and the Derbyshire Junior Cup.

Managers (and Secretary-managers)
E. Russell Timmeus 1891–95*, Gilbert Gillies 1895–1901, E. F. Hind 1901–1902, Jack Hoskin 1902–1906, W. Furness 1906–07, George Swift 1907–10, G. H. Jones 1911–13, R. L. Weston 1913–17, T. Callaghan 1919, J. J. Caffrey 1920–22, Harry Hadley 1922, Harry Parkes 1922–27, Alec Campbell 1927, Ted Davison 1927–32, Bill Harvey 1932–38, Norman Bullock 1938–45, Bob Brocklebank 1945–48, Bobby Marshall 1948–52, Ted Davison 1952–58, Duggie Livingstone 1958–62, Tony McShane 1962–67, Jimmy McGuigan 1967–73, Joe Shaw 1973–76, Arthur Cox 1976–80, Frank Barlow 1980–83, John Duncan 1983–87, Kevin Randall 1987–88, Paul Hart 1988– .

Player and Position	*Ht*	*Wt*	*Birth Date*	*Birth Place*	*Source*	*Clubs*	*League App*	*League Gls*
Forwards								
Robert Alleyne	5 9	11 03	27 9 68	Dudley	Apprentice	Leicester C	3	—
						Wrexham (loan)	10	2
						Chesterfield	40	5
Kevin Eley	5 6	9 07	4 3 68	Mexborough	School	Rotherham U	13	—
						Chesterfield	76	2
Andy Morris	6 5	15 07	17 11 67	Sheffield		Rotherham U	7	—
						Chesterfield	52	9
Andy Rolph	5 6	10 00	28 10 69	Birmingham	Trainee	Birmingham C	—	—
						Chesterfield	12	1
Dave Waller	5 10	10 00	20 12 63	Urmston	Local	Crewe Alex	168	55
						Shrewsbury T	11	3
						Chesterfield	76	37

Trainees
Barber, Martin; Chambers, Scott; Hoole, David; MacDonald, Gavin; Preston, Jamie; Sanderson, Sean; Sheppard, Craig; Simpson, Reece.

****Non-Contract**
Brown, James G; Hart, Paul A; Rushberry, David.

Associated Schoolboys
Blackemore, Paul D; Campbell, Stephen M; Coombes, Richard D; Fitzpatrick, Martin P; Goodwin, Robert; Gregory, Paul Z; Hall, Mark J; Hewitt, Paul S; Hickton, Grant C; Holleworth, Craig B; Jones, Alastair D; Massey, Gary M; Pearson, Michael R; Pell, Steven M; Pick, Ashley C; Taylor, Steven; Vernon, Lee C; Wilcockson, Andrew.

COLCHESTER 1988–89 *Back row (left to right):* Colin Hill, Dave Barnett, Dave Swindlehurst, Mark Walton, Scott Daniels, Mark Coombe, Rudi Hedman, Stuart Hicks, Mark Radford.
Centre row: Steve Hetzke (Coach), Stephen Grenfell, Mario Walsh, Lee Hunter, Nick Chatterton, Kevin Bedford, Richard Wilkins, Stuart Bevis (Physiotherapist).
Front row: Rodney Rooke, Tony English, Steve Foley (Assistant Manager), Gary Bennett, Dale Tempest.

Division 4 **COLCHESTER UNITED**

Layer Rd Ground, Colchester.

Telephone (0206) 574042. ***Commercial Dept:*** (0206) 47754.

Ground capacity: 6,500 (subjective to review).

Record attendance: 19,072 v Reading, FA Cup 1st rd, 27 Nov, 1948.

Record receipts: £22,754 v Manchester U, Milk Cup 3rd rd, 8 Nov, 1983.

Pitch measurements: 110yd × 71yd.

President: M. J. Cadman.

Patron: A. Buck QC, MP.

Chairman: J. T. Crisp. ***Deputy-Chairman:*** J. H. Schultz.

Chief Executive: David Barnard.

Directors: H. F. Carson, D. A. Johnson, G. H. Parker, R. Pleydell.

Manager: Jock Wallace. ***Coach:*** Steve Foley.

Consultant Physio: Charlie Simpson. ***Resident Physio:*** Stuart Bevis.

Secretary: Mrs Dee Elwood.

Commercial Director: J. T. Carter. ***Lottery Manager:*** Cyril Harvey. ***Programme Editor:*** Hal Mason.

Year Formed: 1937. ***Turned Professional:*** 1937. ***Ltd Co.:*** 1937.

Club Nickname: 'The U's'.

Record League Victory: 9-1 v Bradford C, Division 4, 30 December 1961 – Ames; Millar, Fowler; Harris, Abrey, Ron Hunt; Foster, Bobby Hunt (4), King (4), Hill (1), Wright.

Record Cup Victory: 7-1 v Yeovil T (away), FA Cup, 2nd rd (replay), 11 December 1958 – Ames; Fisher, Fowler; Parker, Milligan, Hammond; Williams (1), McLeod (2), Langman (4), Evans, Wright.

Record Defeat: 0-8 v Leyton Orient, Division 4, 15 October 1988.

Most League Points (2 for a win): 60, Division 4, 1973–74.

Most League Points (3 for a win): 81, Division 4, 1982–83.

Most League Goals: 104, Division 4, 1961–62.

Highest League Scorer in Season: Bobby Hunt, 37, Division 4, 1961–62.

Most League Goals in Total Aggregate: Martyn King, 131, 1959–65.

Most Capped Player: None.

Most League Appearances: Micky Cook, 613, 1969–84.

Record Transfer Fee Received: £90,000 from Gillingham for Trevor Lee, January 1981.

Record Transfer Fee Paid: £40,000 to Lokeren for Dale Tempest, August 1987.

Football League Record: 1950 Elected to Division 3(S); 1958–61 Division 3; 1961–62 Division 4; 1962–65 Division 3; 1965–66 Division 4; 1966–68 Division 3; 1968–74 Division 4; 1974–76 Division 3, 1976–77 Division 4; 1977–81 Division 3; 1981 – Division 4.

Honours: *Football League:* Division 3(S) best season: 3rd , 1956–57; Division 4 – Runners-up 1961–62. *FA Cup* best season: 1970–71, 6th rd (record for a Fourth Division club shared with Oxford United and Bradford City). *Football League Cup:* best season 5th rd 1974–75.

Colours: Sky blue and white striped shirts, sky blue shorts, sky blue and white striped stockings. **Change colours:** Amber and red shirts, red shorts, amber and red striped stockings.

COLCHESTER UNITED 1988–89 LEAGUE RECORD

Match No.	Date	Venue	Opponents	Result	H/T Score	Lg. Pos.	Goalscorers	Attendance
1	Aug 27	H	York C	W 1-0	0-0	—	Tempest	1644
2	Sept 2	A	Tranmere R	D 0-0	0-0	—		3401
3	9	H	Doncaster R	L 0-1	0-0	—		1726
4	16	A	Wrexham	D 2-2	1-0	—	Swindlehurst 2	2873
5	20	H	Scarborough	W 3-1	1-0	—	Swindlehurst (pen), Tempest, Wilkins	1420
6	24	A	Burnley	L 0-2	0-1	12		7177
7	Oct 1	H	Lincoln C	L 1-3	1-1	16	Swindlehurst	1529
8	4	A	Carlisle U	W 2-1	0-0	—	Tempest, Swindlehurst	2193
9	8	H	Scunthorpe U	L 1-2	1-1	17	Hedman	1299
10	15	A	Leyton Orient	L 0-8	0-4	21		3421
11	21	H	Cambridge U	L 1-2	0-0	—	English	2138
12	25	A	Rotherhan U	L 0-2	0-0	—		4066
13	28	H	Stockport Co	D 1-1	1-0	—	Tempest	1643
14	Nov 4	A	Crewe Alex	L 1-3	1-1	—	Walsh	2787
15	8	A	Halifax T	L 2-3	1-2	—	Kelly, Wilkins	2176
16	11	H	Torquay U	D 2-2	1-0	—	English, Kelly	1926
17	25	H	Darlington	L 1-2	0-1	—	Radford	1550
18	Dec 3	A	Exeter C	L 2-4	1-2	24	Swindlehurst, Tempest	2132
19	16	A	Rochdale	D 1-1	0-1	—	Walsh	1258
20	26	H	Peterborough U	L 1-2	0-1	24	Walsh	2828
21	30	H	Hartlepool U	L 1-2	1-0	—	English	2359
22	Jan 2	A	Grimsby T	D 2-2	1-2	24	Walsh, Allinson	4472
23	13	H	Tranmere R	L 2-3	1-0	—	Walsh 2	3458
24	21	A	York C	L 0-2	0-1	24		2219
25	Feb 4	A	Scarborough	D 0-0	0-0	24		1913
26	10	H	Burnley	D 2-2	0-2	—	Allinson, Walsh	3809
27	10	A	Scunthorpe U	W 3-2	2-0	24	Wilkins, English, Warner	4286
28	24	H	Leyton Orient	W 1-0	1-0	—	Allinson	4200
29	28	H	Rotherham U	D 1-1	0-1	—	Allinson	3671
30	Mar 5	A	Cambridge U	L 1-3	1-2	—	Wilkins	4205
31	10	H	Crewe Alex	W 2-1	1-1	—	English 2	3088
32	13	A	Stockport Co	L 0-1	0-0	—		2027
33	18	A	Doncaster R	L 1-3	1-2	24	Walsh	1237
34	24	H	Grimsby T	D 0-0	0-0	—		4507
35	27	A	Peterborough U	L 0-3	0-1	24		3529
36	31	H	Rochdale	W 3-0	0-0	—	Scott, Bennett, Wilkins	3631
37	Apr 4	H	Hereford U	D 1-1	1-0	—	English	2862
38	8	A	Hartlepool U	L 1-2	0-0	24	Scott	1501
39	12	A	Hereford U	D 1-1	1-0	—	Scott	2015
40	15	A	Lincoln C	D 1-1	0-0	24	Wilkins	3519
41	21	H	Carlisle U	D 1-1	0-1	—	Scott	3906
42	25	H	Wrexham	W 2-1	1-1	—	Allinson, Hetzke	2918
43	29	A	Darlington	W 2-1	1-1	23	Walsh, Scott	7126
44	May 1	H	Halifax T	W 3-2	0-1	23	Wilkins, Warner, Allinson (pen)	5065
45	5	H	Exeter C	W 4-0	2-0	—	Walsh, Allinson, Pollard, English	5256
46	13	A	Torquay U	W 3-1	0-0	22	Warner, Hetzke, Tempest	2066

Final League Position: 22

GOALSCORERS

League (60): Walsh 10, English 8, Allinson 7 (1 pen), Wilkins 7, Swindlehurst 6 (1 pen), Tempest 6, Scott 5, Warner 3, Hetzke 2, Kelly 2, Bennett 1, Hedman 1, Pollard 1, Radford 1.
Littlewoods Cup (0).
FA Cup (12): Walsh 3, Hedman 2, Wilkins 2, Allinson 1 (pen), Hetzke 1, Hicks 1, Hill 1, own goal 1.

Littlewoods Cup	First Round	Northampton T (h)	0-0
		(a)	0-5
FA Cup	First Round	Fulham (a)	1-0
	Second Round	Swansea C (h)	2-2
		(a)	3-1
	Third Round	Shrewsbury T (a)	3-0
	Fourth Round	Sheffield U (a)	3-3
		(h)	0-2

Walton	Hedman	Cartwright	Barnett	Hetzke	Hill	Wilkins	White	Tempest	Swindlehurst	Grenfell	English	Bedford	Radford	Hicks	Hunter	Daniels	Walsh	Bennett	Kelly	Coombe	Chatterton	Allinson	Taylor	Coleman	McAlister	McGee	Warner	Stafford	*Match No.*
1	2	3	4	5	6	7	8	9	10	11																			1
1		3	4	5	6	7	8	9	10	11*	2	12																	2
1		3			6*	7	8	9	10	11†	2	12	4	5	14														3
1	2	3			6	7	8*	9	10			11	4	5	12														4
1	2	3	4*		6	7	8	9	10			11	12	5															5
1	2	3	4		6	7	8	9	10			11*	12	5															6
1	2	3	4		6	11*	8	9	10				12	5	7														7
1	2	3	4		6	11	8	9	10					5	7														8
1	2	3	4		6	11*	8	9	10				12	5	7														9
1	2	3	4*		6	11	8	9	10				12	5	7														10
1	2		4*		6	7		9		11†	8	3	12	5			10	14											11
1	2				6	7		9*	10	11†	8	3	12	5			14		4										12
1	2				6	7		9			8	3	11*	5	12		10		4										13
1	2				6	7		9		12	8	3	11*	5†		14	10		4										14
1	2		11		6*	7		9			8	3		5		12	10		4										15
	2		11*		6	7†		9			8	3	12	5		14	10		4	1									16
	2		11					9			6†	3	7	5		14	10	8*	4	1	12								17
	7			14	2			12	9			3	11†	5		6	10		4	1	8*								18
1	2		8	14	6	9		12			7	3				5	10*		4†			11							19
1			8	6	2	9		12			7*	3		14		5†	10		4			11							20
1			8	6	2†	9		12			7	3	14			5	10		4			11*							21
1			8	6		9†		12			2	3	14	5		7	10		4			11*							22
1			8†	6	12			9			2	3		5*		7	10		4			11	14						23
1				6	12			9*			8	3		5		7	10		4†			11	14	2					24
			7	5	6	9					8	3		2			10					11	4		1				25
			12	5	6	9					8	3		2			10					7	4		1	11*			26
				5	6	9					8	3		2		12	10*					7	4		1	11†	14		27
			8	5	6	9*						3		2				12				7	4		1	11	10		28
				5	6	11		9			8	3		2				12				7	4*		1		10		29
				5†	6	11		10			8		14	2		12		7					4		1		9	3*	30
					6	11		12			8		4	10		5		7						2	1		9*	3	31
					6	10		4			7		11	8		5								2	1		9	3	32
					6	8					7		11*	5			10					9	4	2	1		12	3	33
				5	6						2	11*		8			10					7	4		1		12	3	34
				5	6						7	11*		4		14	10					9		2†	1		12	3	35
				5	6	11*					8		4	14		2	10†	7				12			1			3	36
				5†	6	11					8		4	14		2		7				10			1		12	3	37
					6	12					7		4	2		5		8†				11		14	1		10*	3	38
					6	7		10			8		12	2		5						11	4*	14	1			3	39
					6	7		10†			8		12	2		5						11	4	14	1			3	40
					6	7		12			8			2†	14	5	10					11	4		1			3*	41
				5	6	7		10†			3		8			12	14					11	4	2*	1				42
				5	6	7†					8		14			2	10					11	4		1		12	3	43
				5	6	7					8		2				10					11	4*	14	1		12	3	44
1				5	6	7					8		4†			2	10					11					12	3	45
1				5	6	7		12			8		4†			2	10*					11					9	3	46
23	17	10	19 + 1s	22 + 2s	42 + 2s	39 + 1s	10	25 + 8s	12	5 + 1s	36	24 + 2s	16 + 14s	34 + 3s	4 + 4s	18 + 8s	25 + 2s	6 + 3s	13	3	1 + 1s	24 + 1s	14 + 2s	6 + 4s	20	3	7 + 8s	16	

Scott — Match No. 34(9) 35(8) 36(9) 37(9*) 38(9) 39(9†) 40(9*) 41(9) 42(9) 43(9*) 44(9†) 45(9*)
Pollard — Match No. 45(14) 46(14)

COLCHESTER UNITED

Player and Position	Ht	Wt	Birth Date	Birth Place	Source	Clubs	League App	League Gls
Goalkeepers								
Mark Walton	6 2	13 13	1 6 69	Merthyr	Swansea C	Luton T	—	—
						Colchester U	40	—
Defenders								
Kevin Bedford‡	5 9	11 02	26 12 68	Carshalton	Trainee	Wimbledon	4	—
						Aldershot (loan)	16	—
						Colchester U	26	—
Steve Cartwright‡	6 1	13 00	8 1 65	Tamworth	Tamworth	Colchester U	10	—
Phil Coleman‡	5 11	11 09	8 9 60	Woolwich	Apprentice	Millwall	36	1
						Colchester	86	6
						Wrexham (loan)	17	2
						Exeter C	6	—
						Aldershot	45	5
						Millwall	10	—
						Colchester U	10	—
Steve Hetzke	6 2	13 04	3 6 55	Malborough	Apprentice	Reading	261	23
						Blackpool	140	18
						Sunderland	31	—
						Chester C	14	—
						Colchester U	29	2
Stuart Hicks	6 1	12 06	30 5 67	Peterborough	Apprentice	Peterborough U	—	—
					Wisbech	Colchester U	44	—
Colin Hill	5 11	12 02	12 11 63	Hillingdon	Apprentice	Arsenal	46	1
						Brighton & HA (loan)	—	—
					Maritimo	Colchester U	69	—
Lee Hunter	5 10	10 08	5 10 69	Oldham	Trainee	Colchester U	9	—
Rodney Rooke	5 5	10 03	7 4 70	Orsett	Trainee	Colchester U	—	
Clive Stafford	6 1	12 02	4 4 63	Ipswich	Diss T	Colchester U	16	—
Midfield								
Ian Allinson	5 10	11 00	1 10 57	Hitchin	Apprentice	Colchester U	308	69
						Arsenal	83	16
						Stoke C	9	—
						Luton T	32	3
						Colchester U	25	7
Dave Barnett*	6 1	12 08	16 4 67	London	Windsor & Eton	Colchester U	20	—
Gary Bennett	5 7	9 13	13 11 70	Enfield	Trainee	Colchester U	9	1
Nicky Chatterton*	5 9	11 04	18 5 54	Norwood	Amateur	Crystal Palace	151	31
						Millwall	264	56
						Colchester U	49	8
Scott Daniels	6 1	11 09	22 11 69	Benfleet	Trainee	Colchester U	27	—
Tony English	6 0	11 00	10 10 66	Luton		Colchester U	178	33
Steve Grenfell*	5 9	10 11	27 10 66	Enfield	Apprentice	Tottenham H	—	—
						Colchester U	70	1
Mark Radford	6 1	11 08	20 12 68	Leicester	Trainee	Colchester U	44	1
Les Taylor	5 8	11 07	4 12 56	North Shields	Apprentice	Oxford U	219	15
						Watford	172	13
						Reading	75	3
						Colchester U	16	—
Richard Wilkins	6 0	12 00	28 5 65	London	Haverhill R	Colchester U	109	18
Keith Williams‡	5 9	11 10	12 4 57	Burtwood	Apprentice	Aston Villa	—	—
						Northampton	131	6
						Bournemouth	102	1
						Colchester U	10	—
Forwards								
Tommy Keane‡ (To Galway)	5 6	10 04	16 9 68	Galway	Apprentice	Bournemouth	3	—
						Colchester U	16	—
John Pollard§			17 11 71	Chelmsford	Trainee	Colchester U	2	1

COLCHESTER UNITED

Foundation: Colchester United was formed in 1937 when a number of enthusiasts of the much older Colchester Town club decided to establish a professional concern as a limited liability company. The new club continued at Layer Road which had been the amateur club's home since 1909.

Managers (and Secretary-managers)
Ted Fenton 1946–48, Jimmy Allen 1948–53, Jack Butler 1953–55, Benny Fenton 1955–63, Neil Franklin 1963–68, Dick Graham 1968–72, Jim Smith 1972–75, Bobby Roberts 1975–82, Allan Hunter 1982–83, Cyril Lea 1983–86, Mike Walker 1986–87, Roger Brown 1987–88, Jock Wallace 1989– .

Player and Position	*Ht*	*Wt*	*Birth Date*	*Birth Place*	*Source*	*Clubs*	*League App*	*League Gls*
Robert Scott	5 10	11 07	13 1 64	Broxburn	Whitburn J	Colchester U	12	5
Dave Swindlehurst*	6 2	13 03	6 1 56	Edgware	Apprentice	Crystal Palace	237	73
						Derby Co	110	29
						West Ham U	61	16
						Sunderland	59	11
					Cyprus	Wimbledon	2	—
						Colchester U	12	6
						Peterborough U (loan(	4	1
Dale Tempest*	5 11	12 04	30 12 63	Leeds	Apprentice	Fulham	34	6
						Huddersfield T	65	27
						Gillingham (loan)	9	4
					Lokeren	Colchester U	77	17
Mario Walsh	6 1	11 12	19 1 66	Paddington	Apprentice	Portsmouth	—	—
						Torquay U	100	18
						Colchester U	38	12
John Warner‡	5 10	12 03	20 11 61	Paddington	Burnham	Colchester U	15	3

Trainees
Baker, Karl J; Bruce, Marcelle E; Cooper, Simon; Finch, David J; Grainger, Martin R; Harvey, Luis J; Holmes, Wayne R; Pollard, Kelly J; Restarick, Stephen L.J; Ricciardi, Franco; Roll, Christopher; Wright, James C.

Associated Schoolboys
Cabey, Michael J; Downing, Stuart L; Gardiner, Mark A; Pierce, Steven; Russell, Dean A; Swan, Matthew; Whitly, Simon.

COVENTRY CITY 1988–89 *Back row (left to right):* Mick Kearns (Chief Scout), Neil Sillett (Assistant Physiotherapist), Martin Lane, Brian Borrows, Trevor Peake, Steve Livingstone, Steve Sedgley, Graham Rodger, Keith Houchen, Jake Findlay, Steve Ogrizovic, Dean Kiely, Chris Galley, Tony Dobson, Cyrille Regis, Howard Clark, Chris Greenham, Michael Cook, Terry Paine (Youth Team Coach), Mick Coop (Reserve Team Coach).
Front row: George Dalton (Physiotherapist), Gary Bannister, David Speedie, David Phillips, Michael Gynn, Greg Downs, Brian Kilcline, John Sillett (Manager), Dean Emerson, Lloyd McGrath, David Bennett, David Smith, Dougie McGuire, Paul Shepstone.

Division 1 COVENTRY CITY

Highfield Road Stadium, King Richard Street, Coventry CV2 4FW. Telephone Coventry (0203) 257171.

Telex: 312132, answer back code COV AFC. Fax No. 0203 630318.

Ground capacity; 28,273.

Record attendance: 51,455 v Wolverhampton W, Division 2, 29 April, 1967.

Record receipts: £127,056.70 v Liverpool, Division 1, 22 March, 1989.

Pitch measurements: 112yd × 76yd.

Life President: Derrick H. Robbins.

Chairman: J. Poynton. ***Vice-chairman:*** E. J. Stocker OBE

Directors: M. F. French FCA, J. F. W. Reason, D. W. Richardson.

Managing Director: G. W. Curtis

Secretary: G. P. Hover.

Team Manager: John Sillett. ***Coach:*** ***Physio:*** G. Dalton.

Year Formed: 1883. ***Turned Professional:*** 1893. ***Ltd Co:*** 1907.

Former Names: 1883–98 Singers FC; 1898 Coventry City FC.

Club Nickname: 'Sky Blues'.

Previous Grounds: Binley Rd 1883–87, Stoke Rd 1887–99, Highfield Rd 1899–.

Record League Victory: 9-0 v Bristol C, Division 3(S), 28 April 1934 – Pearson; Brown, Bisby; Perry, Davidson, Frith; White (2), Lauderdale. Bourton (5), Jones (2), Lake.

Record Cup Victory: 7-0 v Scunthorpe U, FA Cup, 1st rd, 24 November 1934 – Pearson; Brown, Bisby; Mason, Davidson, Boileau; Birtley (2), Lauderdale (2), Bourton (1), Jones (1), Liddle (1).

Record Defeat: 2-10 v Norwich C, Division 3(S), 15 March, 1930.

Most League Points (2 for a win): 60, Division 4, 1958–59 and Division 3, 1963–64.

Most League Points (3 for a win): 63, Division 1, 1986–87.

Most League Goals: 108, Division 3(S), 1931–32.

Highest League Scorer in Season: Clarrie Bourton, 49, Division 3(S), 1931–32.

Most League Goals in Total Aggregate: Clarrie Bourton, 171, 1931–37.

Most Capped Player: Dave Clements, 21 (48), Northern Ireland.

Most League Appearances: George Curtis, 486, 1956–70.

Record Transfer Fee Received: £1,250,000 from Nottingham F for Ian Wallace, July 1980.

Record Transfer Fee Paid: £780,000 to Chelsea for David Speedie, July 1987.

Football League Record: 1919 Elected to Division 2; 1925–26 Division 3(N); 1926–36 Division 3(S); 1936–52 Division 2; 1952–58 Division 3(S); 1958–59 Division 4; 1959–64 Division 3; 1964–67 Division 2; 1967– Division 1.

Honours: *Football League:* Division 1 best season: 6th, 1969–70; Division 2 – Champions 1966–67; Division 3 – Champions 1963–64; Division 3(S) – Champions 1935–36; Runners-up 1933–34. Division 4 – Runners-up 1958–58. *FA Cup:* Winners 1986–87. *Football League Cup* best season: Semi-final 1980–81. **European Competitions:** *European Fairs Cup:* 1970–71.

Colours: All sky blue. **Change colours:** All yellow.

COVENTRY CITY 1988–89 LEAGUE RECORD

Match No.	Date	Venue	Opponents	Result		H/T Score	Lg. Pos.	Goalscorers	Attendance
1	Sept 3	H	Everton	L	0-1	0-1	18		18,625
2	10	A	Sheffield W	W	2-1	0-0	11	Regis, Speedie	15,633
3	17	H	Charlton Ath	W	3-0	0-0	9	Smith 2, Bannister	11,890
4	24	A	Wimbledon	W	1-0	1-0	6	Bannister	4474
5	Oct 1	H	Middlesbrough	L	3-4	1-3	8	Speedie 3	14,527
6	8	A	Newcastle U	W	3-0	3-0	3	Regis, Speedie, Gynn	22,896
7	15	H	Millwall	D	0-0	0-0	3		19,369
8	22	A	Liverpool	D	0-0	0-0	3		38,742
9	29	A	Arsenal	L	0-2	0-1	8		31,273
10	Nov 5	H	West Ham U	D	1-1	0-1	7	Thompson	14,651
11	12	H	Luton T	W	1-0	1-0	6	Rodger	12,631
12	19	A	Nottingham F	D	0-0	0-0	7		17,250
13	23	A	Tottenham H	D	1-1	0-1	—	Houchen	21,961
14	26	H	Aston Villa	W	2-1	1-0	5	Regis, Houchen	20,104
15	Dec 3	A	QPR	L	1-2	0-1	6	Speedie	9853
16	10	H	Manchester U	W	1-0	0-0	3	Regis	19,936
17	17	H	Derby Co	L	0-2	0-0	5		17,229
18	26	A	Southampton	D	2-2	2-0	6	Phillips, Bannister	16,008
19	31	A	Everton	L	1-3	1-2	6	Bannister	30,790
20	Jan 2	H	Sheffield W	W	5-0	2-0	4	Sedgley, Speedie 3, Kilcline (pen)	15,191
21	14	A	Norwich C	W	2-1	0-0	3	Speedie 2	14,399
22	21	H	Wimbledon	W	2-1	1-1	3	Kilcline, Speedie	12,472
23	Feb 4	A	Middlesbrough	D	1-1	1-1	3	Regis	17,352
24	11	H	Newcastle U	L	1-2	0-0	5	Pingel (og)	16,577
25	21	H	Arsenal	W	1-0	0-0	—	Kilcline (pen)	21,390
26	25	A	Millwall	L	0-1	0-0	4		13,021
27	Mar 11	A	West Ham U	D	1-1	1-0	6	Kilcline (pen)	15,205
28	18	H	Tottenham H	D	1-1	1-0	6	Bannister	17,156
29	22	H	Liverpool	L	1-3	1-2	—	Bannister	23,807
30	25	A	Charlton Ath	D	0-0	0-0	7		6728
31	27	H	Southampton	W	2-1	1-1	6	Borrows, Speedie	11,734
32	Apr 1	A	Derby Co	L	0-1	0-0	7		15,175
33	8	H	Norwich C	W	2-1	1-1	6	Phillips, Speedie	12,740
34	15	A	Luton T	D	2-2	0-0	7	Regis, Smith	8610
35	22	H	QPR	L	0-3	0-2	8		11,319
36	29	A	Manchester U	W	1-0	0-0	6	Bannister	29,799
37	May 13	A	Aston Villa	D	1-1	0-1	7	Bannister	29,906
38	15	H	Nottingham F	D	2-2	0-0	—	Clark, Regis	14,003

Final League Position: 7

GOALSCORERS

League (47): Speedie 14, Bannister 8, Regis 7, Kilcline 4 (3 pens), Smith 3, Houchen 2, Phillips 2, Borrows 1, Clark 1, Gynn 1, Rodger 1, Sedgley 1, Thompson 1, own goal 1.
Littlewoods Cup (9): Gynn 3, Bannister 2, Downs 1, Kilcline 1 (pen), Sedgley 1, Speedie 1.
FA Cup (1): Phillips 1.

Littlewoods Cup	Second Round	Bournemouth (a)	4-0
		(h)	3-1
	Third Round	Nottingham F (a)	2-3
FA Cup	Third Round	Sutton (a)	1-2

Ogrizovic	Borrows	Downs	Sedgley	Kilcline	Peake	Gynn	Speedie	Regis	Bannister	Smith	Phillips	Rodger	Houchen	Emerson	Thompson	Clark	McGrath	Bennett	Dobson	Livingstone	*Match No.*
1	2	3	4	5	6	7*	8	9	10	11	12										1
1	2	3	4	5	6	7	8	9	10	11											2
1	2	3	4	5	6	7	8	9	10	11											3
1	2	3	4	5	6	7	8	9	10	11											4
1	2	3	4	5*	6	7	8	9	10	11	12										5
1	2	3	4	5	6	7	8	9	10	11											6
1	2	3	4	5	6	7	8	9	10	11											7
1	2	3	4		6	7*	8	9	10	11	12	5									8
1	2	3	4		6		8	9	10		7	5	11								9
1	2	3	4				8	9	10*	11		6	12	5†	14	7					10
1	2	3	4	5			8	9	10	11		6				7					11
1	2	3	4	5	6		8	9		11	12		10			7*					12
1	2	3	4	5	6		8	9		11	7		10								13
1	2	3	4	5	6		8	9*		11	7		10				12				14
1	2	3*	4	5	6		8	9			7	11	10				12				15
1	2	3	4	5	6		8	9		11	7		10								16
1	2	3	4	5*			8	9	12	11	7†	6	10		14						17
1	2	3	4	5			8		10		7		11	6	9						18
1	2	3*	4	5			8		10†	14	7		9	6	9			12			19
1	2		4	5	6		8	9		11	3						10	7			20
1	2		4	5	6		8	9		11	3			7		12	10*				21
1	2		4	5	6		8	9		11	3			7			10				22
1	2		4	5	6			9	8	11				7			10		3		23
1	2		4	5†	6			9	8	11				7	14		10*	12	3		24
1	2		4	5	6		8	9		11				7				10	3		25
1	2		4	5	6		8	9		11				7				10	3		26
1	2			5	6		8	9*	10	11	4					12		7	3		27
1	2			5	6		8		9	11	4					12	10*	7	3		28
1	2			5	6		8	9	10	11*	4†		12	7	14				3		29
1	2			5	6		8	9*	10	11	4†		12	7		14			3		30
1	2		4	5	6		8			11			9	7	12	10*			3		31
1	2		10	5	6		8	9		11*	7			4	12				3		32
1	2		10	5	6		8	9		11	7			4					3		33
1	2	6	10				8	9	12	11	7	5		4*					3		34
1	2	14	4†		6		8	9	10	11*	7	5			12				3		35
1	2			5	6		8	9	10	11	7			4					3		36
1	2			5	6		8	9	10	11	7			4					3		37
1	2	14		5	6†		8	9		11	7*			4		12			3	10	38
38	38	20	31	33	32	8	36	34	22	34	22	8	10	18	2	4	6	5	16	1	
		+ 2s							+ 2s	+ 1s	+ 4s		+ 3s		+ 7s	+ 5s	+ 2s	+ 2s			

COVENTRY CITY

Player and Position	Ht	Wt	Birth Date	Birth Place	Source	Clubs	League App	League Gls
Goalkeepers								
Jake Findlay*	6 1	14 01	13 7 54	Blairgowrie	Apprentice	Aston Villa	14	—
						Luton T	167	—
						Barnsley (loan)	6	—
						Derby Co (loan)	1	—
						Swindon T	4	—
						Peterborough U	—	—
						Portsmouth	—	—
						Coventry C	—	—
Dean Kiely	5 11	11 08	10 10 70	Manchester	WBA School	Coventry C	—	—
Steve Ogrizovic	6 5	15 00	12 9 57	Mansfield	ONRYC	Chesterfield	16	—
						Liverpool	4	—
						Shrewsbury T	84	—
						Coventry C	204	1
Defenders								
Brian Borrows	5 10	10 12	20 12 60	Liverpool	Amateur	Everton	27	—
						Bolton W	95	—
						Coventry C	153	2
Howard Clark	5 11	11 01	19 9 68	Coventry	Apprentice	Coventry C	9	1
Tony Dobson	6 1	12 10	5 2 69	Coventry	Apprentice	Coventry C	18	—
Greg Downs	5 9	10 07	13 12 58	Carlton	Apprentice	Norwich C	169	7
						Torquay U (loan)	1	1
						Coventry C	129	4
Chris Greenman	5 10	11 06	22 12 68	Bristol	School	Coventry C	—	—
Brian Kilcline	6 2	12 00	7 5 62	Nottingham	Apprentice	Notts Co	158	9
						Coventry C	148	24
Trevor Peake	6 0	12 09	6 7 57	Nuneaton	Nuneaton Bor	Lincoln C	171	7
						Coventry C	207	5
Graham Rodger	6 2	11 11	1 4 67	Glasgow	Apprentice	Wolverhampton W	1	—
						Coventry C	36	2
Midfield								
Mike Cook*	5 9	10 2	18 10 68	Coventry	Trainee	Coventry C	—	—
						York C (loan)	6	1
Dean Emerson	5 10	11 07	27 12 62	Salford	Local	Stockport Co	156	7
						Rotherham U	55	8
						Coventry C	57	—
Mick Gynn	5 5	10 10	19 8 61	Peterborough	Apprentice	Peterborough U	156	33
						Coventry C	129	16
Lloyd McGrath	5 9	10 06	24 2 65	Birmingham	Apprentice	Coventry C	111	3
David Phillips	5 10	11 02	29 7 63	Wegberg	Apprentice	Plymouth Arg	73	15
						Manchester C	81	13
						Coventry C	100	8
Steve Sedgley	6 1	12 06	26 5 68	Enfield	Apprentice	Coventry C	84	3
Paul Shepstone*	5 8	10 06	8 11 70	Coventry		Coventry C	—	—
David Smith	5 8	10 02	29 3 68	Gloucester		Coventry C	51	7
Forwards								
Gary Bannister	5 8	11 01	22 7 60	Warrington	Apprentice	Coventry C	22	3
						Sheffield W	118	55
						QPR	136	56
						Coventry C	32	9
Chris Galley*	6 0	12 00	18 8 70	Bristol	Trainee	Coventry C	—	—
Keith Houchen (To Hibs, Mar 89)	6 2	12 08	25 7 60	Middlesbrough	Amateur	Chesterfield	—	—
						Hartlepool U	170	65
						Orient	76	20
						York C	67	19
						Scunthorpe U	9	3
						Coventry C	54	7

COVENTRY CITY

Foundation: Workers at Singer's cycle factory formed a club in 1883. The first success of Singers' FC was to win the Birmingham Junior Cup in 1891 and this led in 1894 to their election to the Birmingham and District League. Four years later they changed their name to Coventry City and joined the Southern League in 1908 at which time they were playing in blue and white quarters.

Managers (and Secretary-managers)
H. R. Buckle 1909–10, Robert Wallace 1910–13*, Frank Scott-Walford 1913–15, William Clayton 1917–19, H. Pollitt 1919–20, Albert Evans 1920–24, Jimmy Kerr 1924–28, James McIntyre 1928–31, Harry Storer 1931–45, Dick Bayliss 1945–47, Billy Frith 1947–48, Harry Storer 1948–53, Jack Fairbrother 1953–54, Charlie Elliott 1954–55, Jesse Carver 1955–56, Harry Warren 1956–57, Billy Frith 1957–61, Jimmy Hill 1961–67, Noel Cantwell 1967–72, Bob Dennison 1972–81 (became GM), Dave Sexton 1981–83, Bobby Gould 1983–84, Don Mackay 1985–86, George Curtis 1986–87 (became MD), John Sillett 1987– .

Player and Position	*Ht*	*Wt*	*Birth Date*	*Birth Place*	*Source*	*Clubs*	*League App*	*League Gls*
Steve Livingstone	6 1	12 07	8 9 69	Middlesbrough	Trainee	Coventry C	8	—
Doug McGuire	5 8	11 00	6 9 67	Bathgate	Celtic BC	Celtic	2	—
						Coventry C	—	—
Cyrille Regis	6 0	13 06	9 2 58	Mariapousoula	Hayes	WBA	237	82
						Coventry C	170	39
David Speedie	5 7	11 00	20 2 60	Glenrothes	Amateur	Barnsley	23	—
						Darlington	88	21
						Chelsea	162	47
						Coventry C	72	20
Keith Thompson	5 9	11 02	24 4 65	Birmingham	Apprentice	Coventry C	12	—
						Wimbledon (loan)	3	—
						Northampton T (loan)	10	1
					Oviedo	Coventry C	9	—

Trainees
Barefield, Trevor P; Booty, Martyn J; Brown, Stephen M; Harwood, Anthony; Hurst, Lee J; Jenkins, Matthew; Middleton, Craig D; Middleton, Lee J; Moore, Lee; Shepherd, Matthew J; Titterton, David S.J.

Associated Schoolboys
Bickley, Jason; Bufton, Warren R; Carr, Gerald J; Davies, Martin L; Davis, Mark J; Dickson, Darren M; Fleming, Terry; French, Alun K; Green, Andrew P; Harris, John V; Jackson, Russell P; Kirk, Nicholas T; Knight, Steven; McGregor, Jamie; O'Brien, Paul W; Upton, Richard M; Ward, Darren; Williams, Darren P; Woodfine, Steven P; Woollaston, Grant A; Young, Boyd.

CREWE ALEXANDRA 1988–89 *Back row (left to right):* Kenny Swain, Phil Blakemore, John Fleet, Horace Masser, Barry Bennell, Paul McCann, Jimmy Dyer, Pat Slack.
Centre row: Aaron Callaghan, Peter Billing, Paul Fishenden, Chris Cutler, Dean Greygoose, Dale Jasper, Andy Sussex, Lee Elliott, Stuart Ritchie.
Front row: Paul Edwards, Wayne Goodison, Aidan Murphy, Dennis Cronin, Dario Gradi (Manager), Ian Macowat, Mark Gardiner.
Sitting: Neil Morton, Maurice Doyle, Neil Harris, Craig Hignett, Rob Edwards, Rob Jones.

Division 3 CREWE ALEXANDRA

Football Ground, Gresty Rd, Crewe. Telephone Crewe (0270) 213014.

Ground capacity: 6000.

Record attendance: 20,000 v Tottenham H, FA Cup 4th rd, 30 Jan, 1960.

Record receipts: £24,469 v Aston Villa, FA Cup 3rd, 7 January, 1989.

Pitch measurements: 112yd × 74yd.

President: D. Godfrey.

Chairman: N. Rowlinson. ***Vice-Chairman:*** J. Bowler.

Directors: K. Potts, H. Smith, D. Rowlinson, R. Clayton, J. McMillan, G. Basnet.

Managing Director: Hamilton Smith.

Manager: Dario Gradi.

Secretary: Mrs Gill Palin.

Physio: Jim Dyer.

Year Formed: 1877. ***Turned Professional:*** 1893. ***Ltd Co.:*** 1892.

Club Nickname: 'Railwaymen'.

Record League Victory: 8-0 v Rotherham U, Division 3 (N), 1st October 1932 – Foster; Pringle, Dawson; Ward, Keenor (1), Turner (1); Gillespie, Swindells (1), McConnell (2), Deacon (2), Weale (1).

Record Cup Victory: 5-0 v Druids, FA Cup, 1st rd, 15 October 1887 – Hicton; Conde, Cope; Bayman, Halfpenny, Osborne (1); Pearson, Payne (1), Price (1), Tinsley, Ellis. (2 scorers unknown.)

Record Defeat: 2-13 v Tottenham H, FA Cup 4th rd replay, 3 February, 1960.

Most League Points (2 for a win): 59, Division 4, 1962–63.

Most League Points (3 for a win): 78, Division 4, 1988–89.

Most League Goals: 95, Division 3 (N), 1931–32.

Highest League Scorer in Season: Terry Harkin, 35, Division 4, 1964–65.

Most League Goals in Total Aggregate: Bert Swindells. 126, 1928–37.

Most Capped Player: Bill Lewis. 12 (30), Wales.

Most League Appearances: Tommy Lowry, 436, 1966–78.

Record Transfer Fee Received: £200,000 from Aston Villa for David Platt, February 1988.

Record Transfer Fee Paid: £16,000 to Leyton Orient for Andy Sussex, June 1988, £16,000 to Oldham Ath for Aaron Callaghan, July 1988 and £16,000 to Darlington for Paul Clayton, January 1989.

Football League Record: 1892 Original Member of Division 2; 1986 Failed re-election; 1921 Re-entered Division 3 (N); 1958–63 Division 4; 1963–64 Division 3; 1964–68 Division 4; 1968–69 Division 3; 1969–89 Division 4; 1989– Division 3.

Honours: *Football League:* Division 2 best season; 10th, 1892–93. *FA Cup* best season: semi-final 1888. *Football League Cup* best season: 3rd rd. 1974–75, 1975–76, 1978–79.

Colours: Red shirts, white trim, white shorts, red stockings. **Change colours:** White shirts, red shorts, white stockings.

CREWE ALEXANDRA 1988–89 LEAGUE RECORD

Match No.	Date	Venue	Opponents	Result	H/T Score	Lg. Pos.	Goalscorers	Attendance
1	Aug 27	A	Leyton Orient	D 0-0	0-0	—		3932
2	Sept 3	H	Scunthorpe U	W 3-2	2-1	7	Cutler 2, Sussex	1514
3	10	A	Lincoln C	D 2-2	1-1	9	Wilkinson, Fishenden	2651
4	17	H	Darlington	W 2-0	1-0	7	Jones, Fishenden	1711
5	21	A	Hereford U	W 1-0	0-0	—	Wilkinson	1981
6	23	H	Stockport Co	D 1-1	1-0	—	Jasper	2975
7	Oct 1	A	Rochdale	L 1-2	1-0	6	Cronin	2227
8	4	H	Cambridge U	W 2-0	1-0	—	Fishenden, Sussex	1588
9	8	A	Wrexham	D 0-0	0-0	5		2689
10	15	H	Doncaster R	L 0-2	0-0	5		2180
11	22	A	Hartlepool U	W 3-0	1-0	5	Murphy, Fishenden, Gardiner	1972
12	25	H	Grimsby T	D 2-2	1-2	—	Murphy, Macowat	2311
13	29	A	Exeter C	W 2-1	2-0	4	Fishenden, Banks (og)	2567
14	Nov 4	H	Colchester U	W 3-1	1-1	—	Gardiner, Edwards, Callaghan	2787
15	8	A	York C	L 0-3	0-0	—		1980
16	12	H	Tranmere R	W 2-1	0-1	3	Callaghan, Gardiner	3293
17	25	H	Peterborough U	D 1-1	1-0	—	Cronin	2645
18	Dec 2	A	Halifax T	W 1-0	0-0	—	Edwards	2026
19	16	H	Torquay U	D 0-0	0-0	—		3269
20	26	A	Rotherham U	W 2-1	1-0	1	Fishenden, Harrison	7164
21	31	A	Scarborough	L 1-2	0-1	4	Richards (og)	3088
22	Jan 2	H	Carlisle U	W 1-0	1-0	1	Fishenden	4626
23	14	A	Scunthorpe U	D 2-2	1-0	2	Gardiner, Fishenden	4032
24	21	H	Leyton Orient	W 2-1	1-0	2	Goodison, Gardiner	2933
25	28	A	Darlington	D 1-1	0-0	1	Fishenden	1902
26	Feb 4	H	Hereford U	W 2-1	2-1	1	Gardiner, Billing	2987
27	10	A	Stockport Co	W 1-0	1-0	—	Gardiner	5015
28	17	H	Wrexham	D 2-2	1-2	—	Clayton, Fishenden	5627
29	24	A	Doncaster R	W 1-0	0-0	—	Edwards PR	1713
30	28	A	Grimsby T	D 0-0	0-0	—		5404
31	Mar 4	H	Hartlepool U	W 3-0	0-0	1	Gardiner, Stokes(og), Walters	3981
32	10	A	Colchester U	L 1-2	1-1	—	Murphy	3088
33	14	H	Exeter C	W 2-1	0-0	—	Fishenden, Murphy	3156
34	18	H	Lincoln C	W 2-0	1-0	1	Fishenden, Callaghan	3106
35	25	A	Carlisle U	W 1-0	1-0	1	Gardiner	4866
36	27	H	Rotherham U	L 1-3	0-0	2	Callaghan	5994
37	31	A	Torquay U	L 1-2	1-0	—	Fishenden	3087
38	Apr 4	A	Burnley	L 0-1	0-1	—		5677
39	8	H	Scarborough	D 1-1	1-1	4	Doyle	3243
40	14	H	Rochdale	W 3-1	1-0	—	Doyle, Fishenden(pen), Sussex	4144
41	22	A	Cambridge U	D 1-1	1-0	2	Fishenden	3512
42	29	A	Peterborough U	L 2-3	1-1	4	Murphy, Sussex	3546
43	May 1	H	York C	L 1-2	0-1	5	Fishenden	3693
44	5	H	Halifax T	D 2-2	1-0	—	Clayton, Gardiner	3476
45	9	H	Burnley	W 4-0	1-0	—	Edwards, Clayton 3	2963
46	13	A	Tranmere R	D 1-1	0-1	3	Clayton	15,286

Final League Position: 3

GOALSCORERS

League (67): Fishenden 16 (1 pen), Gardiner 10, Clayton 6, Murphy 5, Callaghan 4, Edwards 4, Sussex 4, Cronin 2, Cutler 2, Doyle 2, Wilkinson 2, Billing 1, Goodison 1, Harrison 1, Jones 1, Jasper 1, Macowat 1, Walters 1, own goals 3.
Littlewoods Cup (2): Fishenden 1, Sussex 1.
FA Cup (10): Fishenden 3, Gardiner 2, Murphy 2, Cronin 1, Edwards 1, own goal 1.

Littlewoods Cup	First Round	Lincoln C (h)	1-1
		(a)	1-2
FA Cup	First Round	Stafford (a)	2-2
		(h)	3-2
	Second Round	Runcorn (a)	3-0
	Third Round	Aston Villa (h)	2-3

Greygoose	Goodison	Gardiner	Callaghan	Macowat	Billing	Jasper	Murphy	Cutler	Sussex	Fishenden	Cronin	Edwards, P R	Jones	Morton	Wilkinson	Edwards, R	Swain	Hignett	Doyle	Gage	Elliot	Harrison	Wakenshaw	Walters	Clayton	Edwards P	Match No.
1	2	3*	4	5	6	7	8	9	10	11	12																1
1	2		4	5		7	8	9	10	11*		3	6	12													2
1	2		4	5		7	8		10	11		3	6	12	9*												3
1	2†			5	4	7	8		10	11		3	6		9*	12	14										4
1			4	12	5*	7	8		10	11	14	3	6		9†		2										5
1			4*	12	5	7	8		10	11	9†	3	6		14		2										6
1	6		4	5		7	8		10	11*	9	3†	14	12			2										7
1	2		4	5		7			10	11	9	3	8				6										8
1		2	4	5		7			10	11	9*	3	6		12			8									9
1	2†		4	5		7	14		10*	11	9	3	8	12			6										10
1		10	4	5	12	7	8			11	9	3	6*				2										11
1		10	4*	5	6	7	8			11	9	3		12			2										12
1		10	12	5	4	7	8			11	9†	3	6*				2		14								13
1		10	6	5	4	7	8			11	9	3					2										14
1	14	10	6	5	4†	7	8			11	9	3*	12				2										15
1		10	6	5	4	7	8			11	9*	3†	12				2			14							16
1	2	10	7		4		8			11	9	3	12				5			6*							17
1	2	10†	7	12	4		8			11		3*	14				5			6	9						18
1	2	10	7		4		8			11		3	5			12				6		9*					19
1	2†	10	7	5	4		8			11		3				12	6			14		9*					20
1	2	10*	7	5†	4		8			11		3					6			14		9	12				21
1	2	12	7		4		8			11		3					5			6			9*	10			22
1	2	10	7		4		8			11		3				12	5			6				9*			23
1	2†	10	7	6	4	14				11	12	3	8*				5							9			24
1		10	5	6	4	7*	12			11		3					2							8	9		25
1		10	5	12	4	7*	8			11		3					2							6	9		26
1		10*	5		4	7	8	12		11		3					2							6	9		27
1		10		5	4	7	8			11		3					2							6	9		28
		10		5	4	7	8		12	11		3					2							6	9*	1	29
		10†		5	4	7	8		12	11*		3					2			14				6	9	1	30
		10*	14	5	4	7	8†		12	11		3					2							6	9	1	31
		10	5		4	7†	8		12	11		3					2			14				6	9*	1	32
		10	5		4	7	8		12	11		3					2							6*	9	1	33
		10	5		4	7	8		12	11		3					2							6*	9	1	34
	8	10	5	4		7				11		3					2			12				6*	9	1	35
	8	10	5	4		7				11		3	12				2†			14				6*	9	1	36
	8	10	5	4		7			12	11		3					2							6*	9	1	37
	2	10	5	14	4	7†			12	11*		3					8		6						9	1	38
1	2	10	5		4	7				11		3					8		6						9		39
1	2	10	5		4	7			12	11		3					8		6						9*		40
1	2*	10	5		4	7	8		9	11		3					6							12			41
1	2	10	5		4	7	8		9	11		3					6							12			42
1	2	10			4	7†	12*		9	11		3					6*			5				14	8		42
1		10	5		4	7	12		9	11*		3					2							6	8		44
1		10	5		4	7			9	11		3	12				2							6*	8		45
1		10	5		4	7			9	11		3					2			12				6*	8		46
36	24	37	39	25	36	38	31	2	16	46	12	45	12	—	3	—	40	1	3	6	1	3	1	19	20	10	
	+	+	+	+	+	+	+	+	+		+		+	+	+	+	+		+	+			+	+			
	1s	1s	2s	5s	1s	1s	4s	1s	9s		3s		7s	5s	2s	4s	1s		1s	8s			1s	3s			

CREWE ALEXANDRA

Player and Position	Ht	Wt	Birth Date	Birth Place	Source	Clubs	League App	League Gls
Goalkeepers								
Paul Edwards†			22 2 65	Liverpool	St Helens T	Crewe Alex	10	—
Dean Greygoose	5 11	11 05	18 12 64	Thetford	Apprentice	Cambridge U	26	—
						Orient (loan)	—	—
						Lincoln C (loan)	6	—
						Orient	1	—
						Crystal Palace	—	—
						Crewe Alex	79	—
Defenders								
Peter Billing	6 2	12 07	24 10 64	Liverpool	S Liverpool	Everton	1	—
						Crewe Alex	88	1
Aaron Callaghan	5 11	11 02	8 10 66	Dublin	Apprentice	Stoke C	7	—
						Crewe Alex (loan)	8	—
						Oldham Ath	16	2
						Crewe Alex	41	4
Paul R Edwards	5 11	11 00	25 12 63	Birkenhead	Altrincham	Crewe Alex	58	5
Wakeley Gage*	6 4	13 07	5 5 58	Northampton	Desborough T	Northampton T	218	17
						Chester C	17	1
						Peterborough U	73	1
						Crewe Alex	54	1
Wayne Goodison*	5 8	11 07	23 9 64	Wakefield	Apprentice	Barnsley	36	—
						Crewe Alex	94	1
Rob Jones	5 11	11 00	5 11 71	Wrexham	Trainee	Crewe Alex	24	1
Ian Macowat*	5 10	12 04	19 11 65	Liverpool	Apprentice	Everton	—	—
						Gillingham	5	—
						Crewe Alex	72	1
Kenny Swain	5 9	11 07	28 1 52	Birkenhead	Wycombe W	Chelsea C	119	26
						Aston Villa	148	2
						Nottingham F	112	2
						Portsmouth	113	
						WBA (loan)	7	1
						Crewe Alex	41	—
Steve Wright‡	6 0	11 00	16 6 59	Clacton	Local	Colchester U	117	2
					HJK Helsinki	Wrexham	76	—
						Torquay U	33	—
						Crewe Alex	72	3
Midfield								
Neil Harris‡	5 7	10 12	7 11 69	Manchester	Trainee	Crewe Alex	3	—
Craig Hignett†	5 10	10 08	12 1 70	Whiston		Crewe Alex	1	—
Dale Jasper	6 0	11 07	14 1 64	Croydon	Apprentice	Chelsea	10	—
						Brighton & HA	49	6
						Crewe Alex	39	1
Terry Milligan	5 10	9 05	10 1 66	Manchester	Apprentice	Manchester C	—	—
					New Zealand	Oldham Ath	—	—
						Crewe Alex	77	5
Aidan Murphy	5 10	10 10	17 9 67	Manchester	Apprentice	Manchester U	—	—
						Lincoln C (loan)	2	—
						Oldham Ath (loan)	—	—
						Crewe Alex	55	7
Stuart Ritchie‡	5 10	11 00	20 5 68	Southampton	Apprentice	Aston Villa	1	—
						Crewe Alex	18	—
						Waterford (loan)	—	—
Forwards								
John Bottomley‡	5 10	10 10	13 7 68	Manchester	Local	Manchester U	—	—
						Crewe Alex	—	—
Paul Clayton	5 11	11 03	4 1 65	Dunstable	Apprentice	Norwich C	13	—
						Darlington	22	3
						Crewe Alex	20	6

CREWE ALEXANDRA

Foundation: Crewe Alexandra played cricket and probably rugby before they decided to form a football club in 1877. Whether they took the name "Alexandra" from a pub where they held their meetings, or whether it was after Princess Alexandra, is a matter of conjecture. Crewe's first trophy was the Crewe and District Cup in 1887 and it is worth noting that they reached the semi-finals of the FA Cup the following year.

Managers (and Secretary-managers)
W. C. McNeill 1892–94*, J. G. Hall 1895–96*, 1897 R. Roberts* (1st team sec.), J. B. Bromerley 1898–1911* (continued as Hon. Sec. to 1925), Tom Bailey 1925–38, George Lillicrop 1938–44, Frank Hill 1944–48, Arthur Turner 1948–51, Harry Catterick 1951–53, Ralph Ward 1953–55, Maurice Lindley 1955–58, Harry Ware 1958–60, Jimmy McGuigan 1960–64, Ernie Tagg 1964–71 (continued as secretary to 1972), Dennis Viollet 1971, Jimmy Melia 1972–73, Ernie Tagg 1974, Harry Gregg 1975–78, Warwick Rimmer 1978–79, Tony Waddington 1979–81, Arfon Griffiths 1981–82, Peter Morris 1982–83, Dario Gradi 1983– .

Player and Position	*Ht*	*Wt*	*Birth Date*	*Birth Place*	*Source*	*Clubs*	*League App*	*League Gls*
Denis Cronin*	5 6	9 08	30 10 67	Manchester	Apprentice	Manchester U	—	—
						Stockport Co	15	1
						Crewe Alex	15	2
Chris Cutler	5 11	11 00	7 4 64	Manchester	Amateur	Bury	23	3
						Crewe Alex	102	19
Robert Edwards	5 8	11 07	23 2 70	Manchester	Trainee	Crewe Alex	10	1
Lee Elliott*	5 11	12 00	5 5 70	Ormskirk	Everton Trainee	Crewe Alex	1	—
Paul Fishenden	6 0	10 12	2 8 63	Hillingdon	Local	Wimbledon	75	25
						Fulham (loan)	3	—
						Millwall (loan)	3	—
						Orient (loan)	4	—
						Crewe Alex	61	19
Mark Gardiner	5 10	10 07	25 12 66	Cirencester	Apprentice	Swindon T	10	1
						Torquay U	49	4
						Crewe Alex	38	10
Neil Morton†	5 10	11 00	21 12 68	Congleton	Trainee	Crewe Alex	31	1
Andy Sussex	6 0	11 06	23 11 64	Enfield	Apprentice	Leyton Orient	144	17
						Crewe Alex	25	4
Robbie Wakenshaw‡	5 10	11 10	22 12 65	Southshields	Apprentice	Everton	3	1
						Carlisle U	8	2
						Doncaster R (loan)	8	3
						Rochdale	29	5
						Crewe Alex	22	1
Steve Walters	5 10	11 08	9 1 72	Plymouth	Trainee	Crewe Alex	23	1

Trainees
Buckley-Benbow, Simon J; Cullan, Mark; Curran, Christopher P; Evans, Simon J; Fallon, Marcus; Hill, Jonathan; Holman, Philip; Howard, Shane; Johansen, Benjamin R; Jones, Wayne; Kelsey, Andrew; Prince, Stephen E; Rennie, Paul; Rigby, Anthony A; Rose, Colin J; Stewart, Gareth P.M; Williams, Mark S; Willis, Barry R.J; Winrow, Michael A.Edwards, Paul; Hignett, Craig; Morton, Neil.Clare, Kevin D; Congerton, Lee; Cruise, Ian K; Duffy, Christopher J; Ellershaw, Brian; Garvey, Stephen H; Hughes, Antony B; Jackson, Michael J; Keen, Ryan H; Maloney, Michael P; Meeson, Christopher A; Mitchell, Lee; Podmore, Craig D; Sorvel, Neil S; Stephenson, Ashlyn R; Thelwell, Kevin D; Wall, Justin; Whalley, Gareth; Woodward, Andrew S; Williams, Carwyn.

CRYSTAL PALACE 1988–89 *Back row (left to right):* John Pemberton, Geoff Thomas, Gavin Nebbeling, Alan Pardew, David Madden, Phil Barber, Richard Shaw.
Centre row: Ian Evans (Assistant Manager), Alan Smith (Coach), Adam Locke, Mark Harris, Mark Hone, Brian Parkin, Gary O'Reilly, Perry Suckling, Paul Rains, Ricky Newman, Dennis Bailey, Brian Owen (Physiotherapist), Bob White (Youth Development Officer).
Front row: David Burke, Ian Wright, Glenn Pennyfather, Mark Bright, Steve Coppell (Manager), John Salako, Chris Powell, Steve Claridge, Neil Redfearn.
Sitting: Lawrence Doe, Simon Osborn, John Budden, Gareth Southgate, Barry Ellis, Andy Woodman, David Stevens, Simon Line, Jamie Moralee, Gavin Butler, Russell Green.

Division 1 CRYSTAL PALACE

Selhurst Park, London SE25 6PU. Telephone 01-653 4462. Lottery Office: 01-771 9502. Souvenir Shop: 01-653 5584. Recorded Information: 01-771 5311. Clubcall: 0898 121145. Palace Publications: 01-771 8299. Fax No:01-771 5311.

Ground capacity: 31,000.

Record attendance: 51,482 v Burnley, Division 2, 11 May, 1979.

Record receipts: £103,173 v West Ham U, FA Cup 4th rd, 28 Jan, 1984.

Pitch measurements: 110yd × 74yd.

President: S. Stephenson.

Chairman: R. G. Noades.

Directors: B. Coleman, A. S. C. Souza, G. Geraghty, S. Hume-Kendall, M. E. Lee, P. H. N. Norman, K. A. Sinclair, B. O. Umunna.

Team Manager: Steve Coppell. ***Assistant Manager/Coach:*** ***Physio:*** Brian Owen.

Company Secretary: Alan Leather. ***Club Secretary:*** Mike Hurst. ***Assistant Secretary:*** Terry Byfield. ***Club Accountant:*** Douglas Miller.

Year Formed: 1905. ***Turned Professional:*** 1905. ***Ltd Co.:*** 1905.

Club Nickname: 'The Eagles'.

Club Sponsor: Virgin Atlantic.

Commercial Manager: Graham Drew.

Previous Grounds: 1905, Crystal Palace; 1915, Herne Hill; 1918, The Nest; 1924, Selhurst Park.

Record League Victory: 9-0 v Barrow, Division 4, 10 October 1959 – Rouse; Long, Noakes; Truett, Evans, McNichol; Gavin (1), Summersby (4 incl. 1p), Sexton, Byrne (2), Colfar (2).

Record Cup Victory: 7-0 v Luton T, FA Cup, 3rd rd (replay) 16 January 1929 – Callendar; Weatherby, Charlton; Hamilton (1), Wilde (1), Greener; Harry, Havelock (3), Griffiths (1), Butler (1), Clarke. 7-0 v Stockport C, League Cup, 2nd rd (1st leg), 4 September 1979 – Burridge; Hinshelwood, Sansom, Nicholas, Cannon, Gilbert, Murphy (1), Francis (1) (Walsh (2)), Swindlehurst, Flanagan (2), Hilaire (1).

Record Defeat: 4-11 v Manchester C, FA Cup 5th rd, 20 February, 1926.

Most League Points (2 for a win): 64, Division 4, 1960–61.

Most League Points (3 for a win): 81, Division 2, 1988–89.

Most League Goals: 110, Division 4, 1960–61.

Highest League Scorer in Season: Peter Simpson, 46, Division 3 (S), 1930-31.

Most League Goals in Total Aggregate: Peter Simpson, 154, 1930–36.

Most Capped Player: Paddy Mulligan, 14 (50), Eire; Ian Walsh, 14 (18), Wales; Peter Nicholas, 14 (59) Wales.

Most League Appearances: Jim Cannon, 571, 1973–88.

Record Transfer Fee Received: £800,000 (nett) from Arsenal for Kenny Sansom, August 1980.

Record Transfer Fee Paid: £800,000 (nett) to Arsenal for Clive Allen, August 1980.

Football League Record: 1920 Original Members of Division 3; 1921–25 Division 2; 1925–58 Division 3 (S); 1958–61 Division 4; 1961–64 Division 3; 1964–69 Division 2; 1969–73 Division 1; 1973–74 Division 2; 1974–77 Division 3; 1977–79 Division 2; 1979–81 Division 1; 1981–89 Division 2; 1989– Division 1.

Honours: *Football League:* Division 1 best season; 13th 1979–80; Division 2 – Champions 1978–79; Runners-up 1968–69; Division 3 – Runners-up 1963–64; Division 3(s) – Champions 1920–21; Runners-up 1928–29, 1930–31, 1938–39; Division 4 – Runners-up 1960–61. *FA Cup* best season: semi-final 1975–76. *Football League Cup* best season; 5th rd, 1968–69, 1970–71.

Colours: Red and blue shirts, red shorts, red stockings. **Change colours:** White shirts with red and blue diagonal stripe from left shoulder, white shorts with red and blue trimmings, white stockings with red and blue trimmings.

CRYSTAL PALACE 1988–89 LEAGUE RECORD

Match No.	Date	Venue	Opponents	Result		H/T Score	Lg. Pos.	Goalscorers	Attendance
1	Aug 30	H	Chelsea	D	1-1	1-1	—	Redfearn	17,490
2	Sept 3	H	Watford	L	0-2	0-1	18		10,474
3	10	A	Walsall	D	0-0	0-0	16		6525
4	17	H	Shrewsbury T	D	1-1	0-1	18	Wright	7006
5	20	A	Sunderland	D	1-1	1-0	—	O'Reilly	13,150
6	24	A	Portsmouth	D	1-1	0-1	20	Wright	11,249
7	Oct 1	H	Plymouth Arg	W	4-1	3-1	18	Wright, Thomas, Bright, Pardew	8047
8	4	H	Ipswich T	W	2-0	2-0	—	Bright, Wright	10,325
9	8	A	Blackburn R	L	4-5	1-1	17	Thomas, Wright, Bright, O'Reilly	8025
10	15	A	Bradford C	W	1-0	1-0	12	Wright	11,098
11	22	H	Hull C	W	3-1	1-1	8	Wright, Barber 2	8464
12	25	H	Oxford U	W	1-0	0-0	—	Redfearn (pen)	10,114
13	29	A	Stoke C	L	1-2	0-1	8	Bright	9118
14	Nov 5	H	Barnsley	D	1-1	0-0	9	Bright	7768
15	12	A	Bournemouth	L	0-2	0-1	11		8697
16	19	H	Leicester C	W	4-2	1-1	9	Thomas, Barber 2, Bright	8843
17	26	A	WBA	L	3-5	0-1	11	Dyer, Nebbeling, Thomas	11,099
18	Dec 3	H	Manchester C	D	0-0	0-0	13		12,444
19	10	A	Birmingham C	W	1-0	1-0	10	Dyer	6523
20	17	H	Leeds U	D	0-0	0-0	10		9847
21	26	A	Brighton & HA	L	1-3	0-2	14	Wright	13,515
22	30	A	Oldham Ath	W	3-2	1-0	—	Thomas, Wright 2 (1 pen)	6562
23	Jan 2	H	Walsall	W	4-0	3-0	8	Wright, Bright 3	9352
24	14	A	Chelsea	L	0-1	0-1	12		24,184
25	21	H	Swindon T	W	2-1	0-1	9	Bright 2	8109
26	Feb 4	A	Ipswich T	W	2-1	2-1	6	Wright 2 (1 pen)	14,569
27	11	H	Blackburn R	D	2-2	11	7	Wright, Bright	11,270
28	25	H	Bradford C	W	2-0	1-0	7	Bright 2	7455
29	Mar 1	A	Oxford U	L	0-1	0-0	—		6020
30	4	H	Bournemouth	L	2-3	0-2	12	Pemberton, Wright	10,022
31	11	A	Barnsley	D	1-1	1-1	11	Futcher (og)	7055
32	18	H	Sunderland	W	1-0	0-0	10	Bright (pen)	9108
33	24	A	Watford	W	1-0	0-0	—	Barber	15,095
34	27	H	Brighton & HA	W	2-1	2-0	7	Wright, Bright (pen)	14,384
35	Apr 1	A	Shrewsbury T	L	1-2	1-2	9	Madden	4160
36	5	A	Leeds	W	2-1	2-1	—	Wright, Madden (pen)	25,604
37	8	H	Oldham Ath	W	2-0	1-0	5	Barber, Bright	9089
38	11	A	Hull C	W	1-0	1-0	—	Wright	5050
39	15	H	Portsmouth	W	2-0	0-0	4	Wright, Bright	12,358
40	22	A	Plymouth Arg	W	2-0	1-0	4	Bright 2	8492
41	25	A	Swindon T	L	0-1	0-1	—		11,045
42	29	H	WBA	W	1-0	0-0	4	Wright	13,728
43	May 1	A	Manchester C	D	1-1	0-1	4	Wright	33,456
44	6	A	Leicester C	D	2-2	1-1	5	Madden 2 (2 pens)	9917
45	9	H	Stoke C	W	1-0	1-0	—	Madden (pen)	12,159
46	13	H	Birmingham C	W	4-1	4-0	3	Wright 3, Clarkson (og)	17,581

Final League Position: 3

GOALSCORERS

League (71): Wright 24 (2 pens), Bright 20 (2 pens), Barber 6, Madden 5 (4 pens), Thomas 5, Dyer 2, O'Reilly 2, Redfearn 2 (1 pen), Nebbeling 1, Pardew 1, Pemberton 1, own goals 2.
Littlewoods Cup (5): Bright 1, Pardew 1, Thomas 1, Wright 1, own goal 1.
FA Cup (0).

Littlewoods Cup	Second Round	Swindon T (a)	2-1
		(h)	2-0
	Third Round	Bristol C (a)	1-4
FA Cup	Third Round	Stoke C (a)	0-1

Suckling	Pemberton	Burke	Pennyfather	Nebbeling	O'Reilly	Redfearn	Thomas	Bright	Wright	Salako	Pardew	Barber	Madden	Parkin	Hopkins	Hone	Shaw	Powell	Dyer	Hedman	McGoldrick	Harris	*Match No.*
1	2	3	4†	5*	6	7	8	9	10	11	14	12											1
1	2	3	4		6	7*	8	9	10	11	5†	12	14										2
	2	3			6	7	8	9	10		4	11		1	5								3
	2	3			6	7*	8	9	10	12	4	11		1	5								4
	2	3			6	7*	8	9	10	12	4	11		1	5								5
	2	3			6	7	8	9	10		4	11		1	5								6
	2	3			6	7	8	9	10		4	11		1	5								7
		3			6	7	8	9	10*	12	4	11		1	5	2							8
	2	3			6	7	8	9	10	12	4	11*		1	5								9
	2*	3			6	7	8	9	10		4	11		1	5		12						10
	2	3			6	7	8	9	10*	12	4	11		1	5								11
	2	3			6	7	8	9		10	4	11		1	5								12
	2	3*			6	7	8	9		10	4	11		1	5		12						13
	2				6	7	8	9	12	10*	4	11		1	5			3					14
	2				6	7*	8	9	10		4	11		1	5			3	12				15
			3	6			8	9†	10*	12	4	11		1	5		2	14	7				16
	2		3†	6			8	9	10	12	4	11*		1	5		14		7				17
	2	3		6			8	9	10	12	4	11*		1	5				7				18
	2	3		6			8	9	10		4	11		1	5				7				19
	2	3		6			8	9	10		4	11		1	5				7				20
	2	3	12	6			8	9	10		4*	11†		1	5				7	14			21
1	2	3	4	6			8*	9	10	7	12	11			5								22
1	2	3	4	6				9	10*	7	8	11			5					12			23
1	2	3	4	6				9	10	12	8	11*			5						7		24
1	2	3	4	6				9	10		8	11			5						7		25
1	2	3	4		6			9	10		8	11			5						7		26
1	2	3	4		6			9	10	12	8*	11			5						7		27
1	2	3	4		6			9		11	8	10					5				7		28
1	2	3	4*		6			9		11	8	10	12		5						7		29
1	2	3			6			9	10		8	11	4		5						7		30
1	2*		12		6			9	10		8	11	4		5		3				7		31
1	2				6			9	10		8	11	4		5		3				7		32
1	2				6			9	10	12	8	11	4		5		3				7*		33
1	2	12			6			9	10		8	11	4		5		3*				7		34
1	2	3			6			9	10	12	8	11	4*		5						7		35
1	2	3			6			9	10		8	11	4		5						7		36
1	2	3			6			9	10		8*	11	4		5		12				7		37
1	2	3			6			9	10	12	8	11	4		5						7*		38
1	2	3			6			9	10	12	8	11	4		5						7*		39
1	2	3			6			9	10*	7	8	11	4		5		12						40
1	2	3			6			9	10	7	8	11*	4		5							12	41
1	2	3			6*			9	10	7†	8	11	4		5		12				14		42
1	2	3						9	10		8	11	4*		5		6				7	12	43
1		3		6				9	10	12	8	11	4		5		2†			14	7*		44
1		3		6				9	10		8	11	4		5					2	7		45
1	2	3	8*	6				9	10	12		11	4		5†					14	7		46
27	42	38 + 1s	13 + 2s	14	32	15	22	46	41 + 1s	12 + 16s	43 + 2s	44 + 2s	17 + 2s	19	43	1	8 + 6s	2 + 1s	6 + 1s	1 + 4s	20 + 1s	— + 2s	

CRYSTAL PALACE

Player and Position	Ht	Wt	Birth Date	Birth Place	Source	Clubs	League App	League Gls
Goalkeepers								
Brian Parkin	6 3	13 00	12 10 65	Birkenhead	Local	Oldham Ath	6	—
						Crewe Alex (loan)	12	—
						Crewe Alex	86	—
						Crystal Palace (loan)	—	—
						Crystal Palace	19	—
Perry Suckling	6 1	11 02	12 10 55	Leyton	Apprentice	Coventry C	27	—
						Manchester C	39	—
						Crystal Palace	44	—
Defenders								
David Burke	5 10	10 13	6 8 60	Liverpool	Apprentice	Bolton W	69	1
						Huddersfield T	189	3
						Crystal Palace	70	—
Mark Harris	6 1	13 00	15 7 63	Reading	Wokingham	Crystal Palace	2	—
Rudi Hedman	6 3	12 00	16 11 64	London	Local	Colchester U	176	10
						Crystal Palace	5	—
Jeff Hopkins	6 1	11 11	14 4 64	Swansea	Apprentice	Fulham	219	4
						Crystal Palace	43	—
Gavin Nebbeling	6 0	12 04	15 5 63	Johannesburg	Arcadia S	Crystal Palace	151	8
						Northampton T (loan)	11	—
Gary O'Reilly	5 11	12 00	21 3 61	Isleworth	Amateur	Tottenham H	45	—
						Brighton & HA	79	3
						Crystal Palace	49	2
John Pemberton	5 11	12 03	11 11 64	Oldham	Chadderton	Rochdale	1	—
						Crewe Alex	121	1
						Crystal Palace	44	1
Chris Powell	5 8	11 00	8 9 69	Lambeth	Trainee	Crystal Palace	3	—
Richard Shaw	5 9	11 08	11 9 68	Brentford	Apprentice	Crystal Palace	17	—
Gareth Southgate	5 10	11 12	3 9 70	Watford	Trainee	Crystal Palace	—	—
Midfield								
Phil Barber	5 11	12 06	10 6 65	Tring	Aylesbury U	Crystal Palace	185	33
Mark Hone	6 1	12 00	31 3 68	Croydon		Crystal Palace	4	—
Adam Locke	5 10	11 10	20 8 70	Croydon	Trainee	Crystal Palace	—	—
Eddie McGoldrick	5 10	12 00	30 4 65	London	Nuneaton	Northampton T	107	9
						Crystal Palace	21	—
David Madden	6 0	11 03	6 1 63	London	Apprentice	Southampton	—	—
						Bournemouth (loan)	5	—
						Arsenal	2	—
						Charlton Ath	20	1
						Reading	9	1
						Crystal Palace	19	5
Ricky Newman	5 10	11 00	5 8 70	Guildford		Crystal Palace	—	—
Alan Pardew	5 10	11 00	18 7 61	Wimbleson	Yeovil	Crystal Palace	65	1
Glenn Pennyfather	5 8	10 10	11 2 63	Billericay	Apprentice	Southend U	238	36
						Crystal Palace	34	1
David Stevens	5 11	11 00	19 10 70	Plumstead	Trainee	Crystal Palace	—	—
Geoff Thomas	5 10	10 07	5 8 64	Manchester	Local	Rochdale	11	1
						Crewe Alex	125	20
						Crystal Palace	63	11

CRYSTAL PALACE

Foundation: There was a Crystal Palace club as early as 1861 but the present organisation was born in 1905 after the formation of a club by the company that controlled the Crystal Palace (the building that is), had been rejected by the FA who did not like the idea of the Cup Final hosts running their own club. A separate company had to be formed and they had their home on the old Cup Final ground until 1915.

Managers (and Secretary-managers)
John T. Robson 1905–07, Edmund Goodman 1907–25 (had been secretary since 1905 and afterwards continued in this position to 1933). Alec Maley 1925–27, Fred Maven 1927–30, Jack Tresadern 1930–35, Tom Bromilow 1935–36, R. S. Moyes 1936, Tom Bromilow 1936–39, George Irwin 1939–47, Jack Butler 1947–49, Ronnie Rooke 1949–50, Charlie Slade and Fred Dawes (joint managers) 1950–51, Laurie Scott 1951–54, Cyril Spiers 1954–58, George Smith 1958–60, Arthur Rowe 1960–63, Dick Graham 1963–66, Bert Head 1966–72 (continued as GM to 1973), Malcolm Allison 1973–76, Terry Venables 1976–80, Ernie Walley 1980, Malcolm Allison 1980–81, Dario Gradi 1981, Steve Kember 1981–82, Alan Mullery 1982–84, Dave Bassett 1984, Steve Coppell 1984– .

Player and Position	Ht	Wt	Birth Date	Birth Place	Source	Clubs	League App	League Gls
Forwards								
Dennis Bailey	5 10	11 00	13 11 65	Lambeth		Fulham	—	—
					Farnborough	Crystal Palace	5	1
						Bristol R (loan)	17	9
Mark Bright	6 0	11 00	6 2 62	Stoke	Leek T	Port Vale	29	10
						Leicester C	42	6
						Crystal Palace	112	53
Alex Dyer	5 11	11 12	14 11 65	West Ham	Apprentice	Watford	—	—
						Blackpool	108	19
						Hull C	60	14
						Crystal Palace	7	2
John Salako	5 9	11 00	11 2 69	Nigeria	Trainee	Crystal Palace	63	—
Ian Wright	5 11	11 11	3 11 63	Woolwich	Greenwich B	Crystal Palace	153	61
David Whyte			20 4 71	Greenwich		Crystal Palace	—	—

Trainees
Butler, Gavin M; Doe, Lawrence R; Ellis, Barry D; Green, Russell T; Line, Simon J; Moralee, Jamie D; Osborn, Simon E; Roberts, Carl; Woodman, Andrew J.

Associated Schoolboys
Bevers, Gary D; Brazier, Paul D; Clark, Timothy; Cutler, Scott S; Edwards, Russell J; Endacott, Mark A; Fitzgerald, David; Glass, James; Gordon, Dean D; Harding, Benjamin; Holman, Mark B; Langford, Barry; McKay, Paul J; Myatt, John; Oliva, Umberto; Pepper, Mark J; Rollison, Simon A; Tomlin, Darren; Thomas, Scott P; Tuffin, Gareth; Wells, Mark A.

DARLINGTON 1988–89 *Back row (left to right):* Garry Macdonald, Alan Smith, Keith Granger, Neil Smallwood, Jim Willis, David McAughtrie. *Centre row:* Lew Clayton (Physiotherapist), Kevin Stonehouse, Paul Clayton, Gary Hyde, David Moore, Dale Anderson, Paul Emson, Phil Bonnyman (Assistant Manager). *Front row:* Michael Robinson, Gary Morgan, Neil Robinson, David Booth (Manager), Mark Hine, Kevin Caizley, Gary Worthington.

GM Vauxhall Conference **DARLINGTON**

Feethams Ground, Darlington. Telephone Darlington (0325) 465097, 467712. Commercial Dept. (0325) 481212.

Ground capacity: 13,511.

Record attendance: 21,023 v Bolton W, League Cup 3rd rd, 14 Nov, 1960.

Record receipts: £25,016 v Middlesbrough, Division 3, 8 November, 1986

Pitch measurements: 110yd × 74yd.

President: J. L. T. Moore.

Chairman: A. Heaton. *Vice-Chairman:* J. B. Hadley.

Directors: D. Mason, A. Brown, A. Moore, P. Boddy, J. L. Moore, John Cheadle, R. Corden, A. Noble.

Manager: Brian Little. *Assistant Manager:* Phil Bonnyman.

Secretary: Brian Anderson. *Commercial Manager:* Keith Agar.

Coach:/Assistant Manager: John Gidman. *Physio:* Lew Clayton.

Year Formed: 1883. *Turned Professional:* 1908. *Ltd Co.:* 1891.

Club Nickname: 'The Quakers'.

Record League Victory: 9-2 v Lincoln C, Division 3 (N), 7 January 1928 – Archibald; Brooks, Mellen; Kelly, Waugh, McKinnell; Cochrane (1), Gregg (1), Ruddy (3), Lees (3), McGiffen (1).

Record Cup Victory: 7-2 v Evenwood T, FA Cup, 1st rd, 17 November 1956 – Ward; Devlin, Henderson; Bell (1p), Greener, Furphy; Forster (1), Morton (3), Tulip (2), Davis, Moran.

Record Defeat: 0-10 v Doncaster R, Division 4, 25 January, 1964.

Most League Points (2 for a win): 59, Division 4, 1965–66.

Most League Points (3 for a win): 85, Division 4, 1984–85.

Most League Goals: 108, Division 3 (N), 1929–30.

Highest League Scorer in Season: David Brown, 39, Division 3 (N), 1924–25.

Most League Goals in Total Aggregate: Alan Walsh, 90, 1978–84.

Most Capped Player: None.

Most League Appearances: Ron Greener, 442, 1955–68.

Record Transfer Fee Received: £150,000 from Barnsley for David Currie, February 1988.

Record Transfer Fee Paid: £25,000 to Norwich City for Paul Clayton, March 1988.

Football League Record: 1921 Original Member Division 3 (N); 1925–27 Division 2; 1927–58 Division 3 (N); 1958–66 Division 4; 1966–67 Division 3; 1967–85 Division 4; 1985–87 Division 3; 1987–89 Division 4.

Honours: Football League: Division 2 best season: 15th, 1925–26; Division 3 (N) Champions 1924–25; Runners-up 1921–22; Division 4 – Runners-up 1965–66. *FA Cup* best season: 3rd rd, 1910–11, 5th rd. 1957–58. *Football League Cup* best season: 5th rd, 1967–68.

Colours: All white. **Change colours:** All yellow.

DARLINGTON 1988–89 LEAGUE RECORD

Match No.	Date	Venue	Opponents	Result		H/T Score	Lg. Pos.	Goalscorers	Atten-dance
1	Aug 27	H	Stockport Co	L	1-4	0-2	—	Stonehouse	1794
2	Sept 3	A	Hartlepool U	L	1-2	0-0	23	Stonehouse	2843
3	10	H	Peterborough U	D	2-2	1-1	22	Willis, Stonehouse	1521
4	17	A	Crewe Alex	L	0-2	0-1	23		1711
5	20	H	Exeter City	D	2-2	1-0	—	Taylor (og), MacDonald	1216
6	23	A	Leyton Orient	L	0-1	0-0	—		2755
7	Oct 1	H	Burnley	D	1-1	0-0	24	Stonehouse	3409
8	5	A	Scarborough	L	2-3	1-2	—	Hine, Emson	2442
9	8	H	Rotherham U	D	1-1	0-0	24	Stonehouse	1746
10	15	A	York C	L	1-4	0-2	24	Worthington	2851
11	22	A	Lincoln C	L	2-3	0-0	24	MacDonald, Worthington	3705
12	25	H	Torquay U	D	0-0	0-0	—		1374
13	29	A	Rochdale	D	2-2	1-1	24	Worthington, MacDonald	2476
14	Nov 5	H	Doncaster R	L	1-3	0-1	24	Stonehouse (pen)	1625
15	8	H	Cambridge U	D	1-1	1-0	—	Worthington	1467
16	12	A	Carlisle U	W	2-1	2-0	24	Worthington, Emson	2194
17	25	A	Colchester U	W	2-1	1-0	—	Worthington 2 (1 pen)	1550
18	Dec 3	H	Scunthorpe U	D	3-3	1-1	23	Worthington 3	1745
19	16	A	Tranmere R	L	0-2	0-2	—		2981
20	26	H	Halifax T	L	0-2	0-1	23		2131
21	31	H	Hereford U	D	0-0	0-0	23		1755
22	Jan 2	A	Wrexham	D	3-3	1-2	23	Hyde, Hine, Worthington	6016
23	14	H	Hartlepool U	D	0-0	0-0	23		3521
24	20	A	Stockport Co	D	0-0	0-0	—		2889
25	28	H	Crewe Alex	D	1-1	0-0	23	Worthington	1902
26	Feb 4	A	Exeter C	L	1-2	1-0	23	Morgan	2687
27	11	H	Leyton Orient	L	1-3	1-2	23	Moore	1833
28	14	A	Grimsby T	D	0-0	0-0	—		4628
29	18	A	Rotherham U	W	2-1	0-0	23	Hyde, Emson	4228
30	25	H	York C	D	2-2	0-0	23	Hyde, Robinson	2504
311	28	A	Torquay U	L	0-1	0-0	—		1627
32	Mar 4	H	Lincoln C	W	2-1	1-0	23	Willis, Stonehouse	2169
33	10	A	Doncaster R	L	0-1	0-0	—		1538
34	14	H	Rochdale	L	1-2	1-1	—	Gidman	1876
35	18	A	Peterborough U	D	1-1	0-0	23	Emson	2482
36	25	H	Wrexham	W	2-1	1-1	23	McJannet, Emson	2281
37	27	A	Halifax T	L	0-1	0-0	23		1849
38	Apr 1	H	Tranmere R	L	1-2	0-1	23	MacDonald	2492
39	4	H	Grimsby T	D	1-1	0-1	—	MacDonald	1840
40	8	A	Hereford U	D	1-1	0-0	23	Dyson	2009
41	15	A	Burnley	W	1-0	0-0	23	Dyson	5578
42	22	H	Scarborough	W	2-1	1-0	23	Stephens 2	2850
43	29	H	Colchester U	L	1-2	1-1	24	Bonnyman (pen)	7126
44	May 2	A	Cambridge U	W	3-1	1-0	—	Caizley, Stephens, Bonnyman (pen)	3310
45	6	A	Scunthorpe U	L	1-5	0-1	24	Willis P	5296
46	13	H	Carlisle U	L	2-3	1-3	24	Dyson, Stephens	3049

Final League Position: 24

GOALSCORERS

League (53): Worthington 12 (1 pen), Stonehouse 7 (1 pen), Emson 5, MacDonald 5, Stephens 4, Dyson 3, Hyde 3, Bonnyman 2 (2 pens), Hine 2, Willis J 2, Caizley 1, Gidman 1, McJannet 1, Moore 1, Morgan 1, Robinson N 1, Willis P 1, own goal 1.
Littlewoods Cup (5): Clayton 1, Hine 1, Hyde 1, MacDonald 1, Moore 1.
FA Cup (1): Own goal 1.

Littlewoods Cup	First Round	Doncaster R (a)	1-1
		(h)	2-0
	Second Round	Oldham Ath (h)	2-0
		(a)	0-4
FA Cup	First Round	Notts Co (h)	1-2

Smallwood	Robinson, N	Bonnyman	Hine	Moore	McAughtrie	Emson	Caizley	MacDonald	Clayton	Stonehouse	Anderson	Robinson, M	Willis J	Morgan	Hyde	Rodwell	Batch	Worthington	Smith	McAndrew	McJannet	Shearer	Gidman	Prudhoe	Dyson	Stephens	Willis P	*Match No.*
1	2	3	4	5	6	7	8†	9	10*	11	12	14																1
1	8		4	5	6	7*	12	9		11	10†		2	3	14													2
1	8		4	5	6	7	10*	9		11			2	3	12													3
1	8		4	5	6	7		9	10*	11				3	12	2												4
	2		4	5	6	7	10	9	8*	11				3	12		1											5
	8		4	5	6	7		9*		11	12		2	3	10		1											6
	2		4		5*		7	9	10	11	12		6	3	8		1											7
	2		4			7		6	10	11	9*		5	3	8		1	12										8
	2		4	5		7*		9		11	12		6	3	8		1		10									9
	2		4	5				9	12	11	7†		6	3	8		1*	10	14									10
	2		4	5		7*		9		11	12		6	3	8		1	10										11
	2		4	5	7	12		9		11			6	3	8*		1	10										12
	2		4	5	7†	12		9		11*			6	3	8		1	10	14									13
	2		4	5	7†	12		9		11*			6	3	8		1	10	14									14
	2		4	5		12		9		11*			6	3	8		1	10	7									15
	2			5		11			9	7			6	3	8		1	10	4									16
	2	12		5	7	11			9				6	3	8*		1	10		4								17
	2		4	5	7	11			9				6	3			1	10		8								18
	2			5	7	11†	4*	14		12			6	3	9		1	10		8								19
	2			5*	4	11		14	9†	12			6	3	7		1	10		8								20
	7		4			14		9*		12			6	3	11†		1	10	5	8	2							21
	7		4	12						12			6	3	11		1	10	5*	8*	2	9						22
	7†		4	5				8		12			6	3	11*		1	10	14		2	9						23
			4	5				7		12			6	3	11*		1	10		8	2	9						24
			4	5				7		12			6	3	11*		1	10		8	2	9						25
			4	5				7					6	3	11		1	10		8	2	9						26
			4	5				7		11			6	3			1	10		8	2	9						27
			4	8	5			9					6	3	7		1	10*		11	2	12						28
	11		4	8	5	10		9					6	3	7		1				2							29
	11		4		5	10*	12	9		6				3	7		1				2		8					30
	11†		4		5	10	12	9		6*				3	7		1		14		2		8					31
	11		4		5	10				9			6		7		1		3		2		8					32
	11		4			10		5		9*	12		6		7		1		3		2		8					33
	11		4			9		5		12			6		7		1	10*	3		2		8					34
	11*		4		12	9		14					6		7			10†	3		2		8	1	5			35
		10*	4			11		14					6	3	7			12			2		8	1	5	9†		36
		10	4			11		14					6	3†	7			12			2		8*	1	5	9		37
	12		4			11*		14			10†		6	3	7						2		8	1	5	9		38
	7*	8	4	14		12		11					6	3				10			2			1	5	9†		39
	7	8		14		9†	12	11*					6					10	3		2		4	1	5			40
	7	8		12				11*					6	3				10			2		4	1	5	9		41
	7	8	12					11					6	3				10			2		4*	1	5	9		42
	7†	8	12	14				11					6	3				10			2		4*	1	5	9		43
	12	8	4			10	7	11					6	3*							2			1	5	9		44
	3	8	4			10†	7*	11					6					12			2			1	5	9	14	45
		8	4			12	7*	11					6		14			3†			2			1	5	9	10	46
4	36 + 2s	11 + 1s	38 + 2s	25 + 5s	19 + 1s	27 + 7s	8 + 4s	35 + 6s	9 + 1s	21 + 8s	4 + 6s	— + 1s	41	38	31 + 5s	1	30	27 + 4s	10 + 5s	11	26	6 + 1s	13	12	12	10	1	

DARLINGTON

Player and Position	Ht	Wt	Birth Date	Birth Place	Source	Clubs	League App	League Gls
Goalkeepers								
Nigel Batch	5 10	12 07	9 11 57	Huddersfield	Apprentice	Derby Co	—	—
						Grimsby T	348	—
						Lincoln C	—	—
						Darlington	30	—
						Stockport Co (loan)	12	—
Keith Granger	5 10	10 10	5 10 68	Southampton	Apprentice	Southampton	2	—
						Darlington	23	—
Neil Smallwood*	6 1	11 10	3 12 66	York		York C	13	—
						Darlington	4	—
Mark Prudhoe	6 0	12 12	8 11 63	Washington	Apprentice	Sunderland	7	—
						Hartlepool U (loan)	3	—
						Birmingham C	1	—
						Walsall	26	—
						Doncaster R (loan)	5	—
						Sheffield W (loan)	—	—
						Grimsby T (loan)	8	—
						Hartlepool U (loan)	13	—
						Bristol C (loan)	3	—
						Carlisle U	34	—
						Darlington	12	—
Defenders								
Paul Dyson*	6 2	13 06	27 12 59	Birmingham	Apprentice	Coventry C	140	5
						Stoke C	106	5
						WBA	64	5
						Darlington	12	3
John Gidman*	5 11	12 02	10 1 54	Liverpool	Apprentice	Liverpool	—	—
						Aston Villa	197	9
						Everton	64	2
						Manchester U	95	4
						Manchester C	53	1
						Stoke C	10	—
						Darlington	13	1
David McAughtrie*	6 2	12 03	30 1 63	Cumnock	Apprentice	Stoke C	51	1
						Carlisle U	28	1
						York C	64	1
						Darlington	39	—
Les McJannet	5 8	10 04	2 8 61	Cumnock		Mansfield T	74	—
					Matlock T	Scarborough	34	—
						Darlington	26	1
David Moore*	5 10	12 13	17 12 59	Grimsby	Apprentice	Grimsby T	136	2
						Carlisle U	13	1
						Blackpool	115	1
						Grimsby T	4	—
						Darlington	30	1
Gary Morgan*	5 8	12 00	1 4 61	Consett	Consett	Berwick R	67	4
						Darlington	146	3
Mark Outterside‡	5 11	11 08	13 1 67	Hexham	Apprentice	Sunderland	1	—
						Blackburn R (loan)	—	—
						Darlington	38	—
Mike Robinson*	5 10	11 03	30 10 68	Sunderland		Newcastle U	—	—
						Darlington	1	—
James Rodwell§					Trainee	Darlington	1	—
Alan Smith*	6 0	11 02	7 12 66	Sheffield	Apprentice	Sheffield W	—	—
						Darlington	31	1
Jimmy Willis	6 2	12 04	12 7 68	Liverpool	Blackburn R	Halifax T	—	—
						Stockport Co	10	—
						Darlington	50	2
Midfield								
Phil Bonnyman*	5 11	12 04	6 2 54	Glasgow	Anniesland W	Rangers	—	—
						Hamilton A	71	7
						Carlisle U	152	26
						Chesterfield	99	25
						Grimsby T	151	15
						Stoke C (loan)	7	—
						Darlington	50	5

DARLINGTON

Foundation: A football club was formed in Darlington as early as 1861 but the present club began in 1883 and reached the final of the Durham Senior Cup in their first season, losing to Sunderland in a replay after complaining that they had suffered from intimidation in the first. The following season Darlington won this trophy and for many years were one of the leading amateur clubs in their area.

Managers (and Secretary-managers)
Tom McIntosh 1902–11, W. L. Lane 1911–12*, Dick Jackson 1912–19, Jack English 1919–28, Jack Fairless 1928–33, George Collins 1933–36, George Brown 1936–38, Jackie Carr 1938–42, Jack Surtees 1942, Jack English 1945–46, Bill Forrest 1946–50, George Irwin 1950–52, Bob Gurney 1952–57, Dick Duckworth 1957–60, Eddie Carr 1960–64, Lol Morgan 1964–66, Jimmy Greenhalgh 1966–68, Ray Yeoman 1968–70, Len Richley 1970–71, Frank Brennan 1971, Ken Hale 1971–72, Allan Jones 1972, Ralph Brand 1972–73, Dick Conner 1973–74, Billy Horner 1974–76, Peter Madden 1976–78, Len Walker 1978–79, Billy Elliott 1979–83, Cyril Knowles 1983–87, Dave Booth 1987–89, Brian Little 1989– .

Player and Position	*Ht*	*Wt*	*Birth Date*	*Birth Place*	*Source*	*Clubs*	*League App*	*League Gls*
Kevin Caizley*	5 10	11 03	2 12 68	Jarrow		Newcastle U	—	—
						Darlington	12	1
Paul Emson	5 10	11 00	22 10 58	Lincoln	Brigg T	Derby C	127	13
						Grimsby T	97	15
						Wrexham	49	5
						Darlington	34	5
Mark Hine	5 8	9 11	18 5 64	Middlesbrough	Local	Grimsby T	22	1
						Darlington	128	8
Gary Hyde	6 0	9 07	28 12 69	Wolverhampto	Trainee	Darlington	38	3
Neil Robinson	5 8	10 06	20 4 57	Liverpool	Apprentice	Everton	16	1
						Swansea C	123	7
						Grimsby T	109	6
						Darlington	38	1
Paul Willis†	5 11	11 07	24 1 70	Liverpool	Trainee	Halifax T	5	—
						Darlington	2	1
Forwards								
Dale Anderson	6 0	10 07	23 8 70	Darlington	Trainee	Darlington	15	—
Gary MacDonald*	6 0	12 01	26 3 62	Middlesbrough	Apprentice	Middlesbrough	53	5
						Carlisle U	9	—
						Darlington	162	35
David Shearer‡	5 8	12 00	16 10 58	Fort William	Inverness Clach	Middlesbrough	97	23
						Wigan Ath (loan)	11	9
						Grimsby T	4	—
						Gillingham	93	42
						Bournemouth	11	3
						Scunthorpe U	16	7
						Darlington	7	—
Archie Stephens	5 11	12 08	19 5 54	Liverpool	Melksham	Bristol R	127	40
						Middlesbrough	92	24
						Carlisle U	24	3
						Darlington	10	4
Kevin Stonehouse*	5 11	11 01	20 9 59	Bishop Auckland	Shildon	Blackburn R	85	27
						Huddersfield T	22	4
						Blackpool	55	19
						Darlington	72	20
						Carlisle U (loan)	3	—
Gary Worthington	5 10	10 05	10 11 66	Cleethorpes	Apprentice	Manchester U	—	—
						Huddersfield T	—	—
						Darlington	40	15

Trainees
Darby, Ian J; Errington, Christopher J; Gillies, Ian M; O'Ware, Ian R; Powell, Derrick A; Rodwell, James R; Southall, Leslie N.

****Non-Contract**
Willis, Paul E.

Associated Schoolboys
Walton, Charles A.

DERBY COUNTY 1988–89 *Back row (left to right)*: Roy McFarland (Assistant Manager), Trevor Hebberd, Michael Forsyth, Andy Garner, Martin Taylor, Mark Wright, Peter Shilton, Rob Hindmarch, Mark Wallington, Brett Angell, Nick Pickering, Ted McMinn, Gordon Guthrie (Physiotherapist).
Front row: Brian McCord, Mel Sage,Nigel Callaghan, David Penney, Steve Cross, Phil Gee, Arthur Cox (Manager), Paul Blades, Paul Goddard, John Chiedozie, Gary Micklewhite, Geraint Williams, Mark Patterson.

Division 1 DERBY COUNTY

Baseball Ground, Shaftesbury Crescent, Derby DE3 8NB. Telephone Derby (0332) 40105. Ramtique Sports Shop: 0332 292081. Clubcall 0898 12 11 87.

Ground capacity: 26,700 (16,000 seats).

Record attendance: 41,826 v Tottenham H, Division 1, 20 Sept, 1969.

Record receipts: £108,000 v Manchester U, FA Cup 5th rd, 19 Feb, 1983.

Pitch measurements: 110yd × 75yd.

President:

Chairman: I. R. Maxwell, MC. ***Vice-Chairman:*** I. R. C. Maxwell.

Managing Director: A. S. Webb.

Directors: F. W. Fern, J. N. Kirkland, W. Hart, T. J. East, G. Glossop, C. R. Charlton, C. M. McKerrow, B. E. Fearn, M. McGarry.

Manager: Arthur Cox. ***Assistant Manager:*** Roy McFarland.

Physio: Gordon Guthrie.

Secretary: Michael Dunford. ***Marketing Manager:*** C. Tunnicliffe. (Tel. 0332 40105).

Year Formed: 1884. ***Turned Professional:*** 1884. ***Ltd Co.:*** 1896.

Club Nickname: 'The Rams'.

Former Grounds: 1884–95, Racecourse Ground; 1895, Baseball Ground.

Record League Victory: 9-0 v Wolverhampton W, Division 1, 10 January 1891 – Bunyan; Arthur Goodall, Roberts; Walker, Chalmers, Roulston (1); Bakewell, McLachlan, Johnny Goodall (1), Holmes (2), McMillan (5). 9-0 v Sheffield W, Division 1, 21 January 1899 – Fryer; Methven, Staley; Cox, Arthur Goodall, May; Oakden (1), Bloomer (6), Boag, McDonald (1), Allen. (1 og)

Record Cup Victory: 12-0 v Finns Harps, UEFA Cup, 1st rd (1st leg) – Moseley; Thomas, Nish, Rioch (1), McFarland, Todd (King), Macken, Gemmill, Hector (5), George (3), James (3).

Record Defeat: 2-11 v Everton, FA Cup 1st rd, 1889–90.

Most League Points (2 for a win): 63, Division 2, 1968–69 and Division 3 (N). 1955–56 and 1956–57.

Most League Points (3 for a win): 84, Division 3, 1985–86 and Division 3, 1986–87.

Most League Goals: 111, Division 3 (N), 1956–57.

Highest League Scorer in Season: Jack Bowers, 37,Division 1, 1930–31 and Ray Straw, 37 Division 3 (N). 1956–57.

Most League Goals in Total Aggregate: Steve Bloomer, 291, 1892–1906 and 1910–14.

Most Capped Player: Roy McFarland, 28, England.

Most League Appearances: Kevin Hector, 486, 1966–78 and 1980–82.

Record Transfer Fee Received: £500,000 from Aston Villa for Nigel Callaghan, February 1989.

Record Transfer Fee Paid: £1,000,000 to Oxford U for Dean Saunders, October 1988.

Football League Record: 1888 Founder Member of the Football League: 1904–12 Division 2; 1912–14 Division 1; 1914–15 Division 2; 1915–21 Division 1; 1921–26 Division 2; 1926–53 Division 1; 1955–55 Division 2; 1955–57 Division 3 (N); 1957–69 Division 2; 1969–80 Division 1; 1980–84 Division 2; 1984–86 Division 3; 1986–87Division 2 1987– Division 1.

Honours: *Football League:* Division 1 – Champions 1971–72, 1974–75; Runners-up 1895–96, 1929–30, 1935–36; Division 2 – Champions 1911–12, 1914–15, 1968–69, 1986–87; Runners-up 1925–26; Division 3 (N) Champions 1956–57; Runners-up 1955–56. *FA Cup:* Winners 1945–46; Runners-up 1897–98, 1898–99, 1902–03. *Footbal League Cup:* Semi-final 1967–68. *Texaco Cup:* 1971–72. **European Competitions:** *European Cup:* 1972–73, 1975–76; *UEFA Cup:* 1974–75. 1976–77.

Colours: White shirts, black shorts, black stockings. **Change colours:** Red and black striped shirts, red shorts, red and black stockings.

DERBY COUNTY 1988–89 LEAGUE RECORD

Match No.	*Date*	*Venue*	*Opponents*	*Result*	*H/T Score*	*Lg. Pos.*	*Goalscorers*	*Attendance*
1	Aug 27	H	Middlesbrough	W 1-0	0-0	—	Goddard	19,432
2	Sept 3	A	Millwall	L 0-1	0-1	9		13,061
3	10	H	Newcastle U	W 2-0	0-0	7	Hebberd, Goddard	16,014
4	17	A	Nottingham F	D 1-1	0-0	7	Hebberd	24,818
5	24	H	QPR	L 0-1	0-1	10		14,008
6	Oct 1	A	Southampton	D 0-0	0-0	9		13,283
7	8	H	Norwich C	L 0-1	0-0	12		14,117
8	22	H	Charlton Ath	D 0-0	0-0	15		14,106
9	29	H	Wimbledon	W 4-1	1-1	13	Saunders 2, Sage, Micklewhite	15,050
10	Nov 5	A	Tottenham H	W 3-1	1-1	6	McMinn 2, Saunders	22,868
11	12	H	Manchester U	D 2-2	1-1	8	Saunders, Hebberd	24,080
12	19	A	Aston Villa	W 2-1	0-0	6	Saunders, Goddard	23,489
13	26	H	Arsenal	W 2-1	0-0	7	Callaghan, Gee	21,209
14	Dec 3	A	Sheffield W	D 1-1	0-1	5	Callaghan (pen)	20,609
15	10	H	Luton T	L 0-1	0-1	7		15,228
16	17	A	Coventry C	W 2-0	0-0	4	Saunders, McMinn	17,229
17	26	H	Liverpool	L 0-1	0-1	7		25,213
18	31	H	Millwall	L 0-1	0-0	7		16,154
19	Jan 2	A	Newcastle U	W 1-0	0-0	6	Wright	30,555
20	14	H	West Ham U	L 1-2	1-2	8	Saunders	16,796
21	21	A	QPR	W 1-0	0-0	8	Williams	9516
22	Feb 4	H	Southampton	W 3-1	1-0	7	Hebberd, Goddard, Saunders (pen)	13,758
23	11	A	Norwich C	L 0-1	0-0	8		17,227
24	25	H	Everton	W 3-2	1-1	6	Saunders, Goddard 2	17,103
25	Mar 1	A	Wimbledon	L 0-4	0-3	—		4207
26	11	H	Tottenham H	D 1-1	1-0	8	Saunders	18,206
27	18	A	Middlesbrough	W 1-0	1-0	7	McMinn	16,580
28	25	H	Nottingham F	L 0-2	0-1	8		25,174
29	29	A	Liverpool	L 0-1	0-1	—		42,518
30	Apr 1	H	Coventry C	W 1-0	0-0	9	Blades	15,175
31	8	A	West Ham U	D 1-1	1-1	9	Micklewhite	16,560
32	15	A	Manchester U	W 2-0	1-0	8	Micklewhite, Goddard	34,145
33	22	H	Sheffield W	W 1-0	0-0	6	Saunders	17,529
34	29	A	Luton T	L 0-3	0-1	7		8507
35	May 6	H	Aston Villa	W 2-1	1-1	-6	Saunders, Hebberd	18,112
36	10	A	Charlton Ath	L 0-3	0-1	—		7448
37	13	A	Arsenal	W 2-1	1-0	5	Saunders 2 (1 pen)	41,008
38	15	A	Everton	L 0-1	0-1	—		17,826

Final League Position: 5

GOALSCORERS

League (40): Saunders 14 (2 pens), Goddard 7, Hebberd 5, McMinn 4, Micklewhite 3, Callaghan 2 (1 pen), Blades 1, Gee 1, Sage 1, Williams 1, Wright 1.
Littlewoods Cup (3): Hebberd 2, Penney 1.
FA Cup (4): Callaghan 1, Hebberd 1, McMinn 1, Micklewhite 1.

Littlewoods Cup	Second Round	Southend U (h)	1-0
		(a)	2-1
	Third Round	West Ham U (a)	0-5
FA Cup	Third Round	Southampton (h)	1-1
		(a)	2-1
	Fourth Round	Watford (a)	1-2

Shilton	Sage	Forsyth	Williams	Wright	Blades	Micklewhite	Chiedozie	Goddard	Hebberd	Callaghan	Gee	Pickering	McMinn	Cross	Penney	Hindmarch	Saunders	Patterson	*Match No.*
1	2	3	4	5	6	7	8	9	10	11									1
1	2	3	4	5	6	7†	8*	9	10	11	12	14							2
1	2	3	4	5	6			9	10	11	8*	14	7†	12					3
1	2	3	4	5	6			9	10	11	8*		7	12					4
1	2	3	4	5	6	12		9	10	11		14	7*	8†					5
1	2	3	4	5	6			9	10			11	7		8				6
1	2	3	4	5	6			9	10			11	7		8				7
1	2	3	4		6			9	10			11	7		8	5			8
1	2	3	4		6	12		9	10	11*			7			5	8		9
1	2	3		5	6			9	10	11			7	4			8		10
1	2	3	4	5	6	12		9	10	11*			7				8		11
1	2	3	4	5	6	12		9	10	11*			7				8		12
1	2	3	4	5	6				10	11	9		7				8		13
1	2	3	4	5	6	12			10	11	9*		7				8		14
1		3	4	5	6			9*	10	11	12		7				8	2	15
1		3	4	5	2			9	10	11			7			6	8		16
1		3	4	5	2	12		9*	10	11†			7	14		6	8		17
1		3	4	5	2	12		9	10†	11*			7	14		6	8		18
1		3	4	5	2			9	10	11			7			6	8		19
1		3	4	5	2				10	11	9*		7†	14	12	6	8		20
1		3	4	5	2				10	11*	9		7	12		6	8		21
1		3	4		6	11		9	10				7	2		5	8		22
1		3	4	5	2	11		9	10†				7	14	12	6	8*		23
1		3	4	5	2	7		9	10			11				6	8		24
1		3	4	5	2	7†		9	10*			11		14	12	6	8		25
1		3	4	5	2	11		9*	10				7	12		6	8		26
1		3	4	5	2	11					9		7	10		6	8		27
1		3	4	5	2	11			10		9*		7	12		6	8		28
1		3	4	5	2	11			10*				7	9	12	6	8		29
1		3	4	5	2	11		9	10				7			6	8		30
1		3	4	5	2	11		9*	10				7	12		6	8		31
1		3	4	5	2	11		9	10				7			6	8		32
1		3	4	5	2	11		9	10				7			6	8		33
1		3	4	5	2	11		9†	10*		12		7	14		6	8		34
1		3	4	5	2	11		9	10				7			6	8		35
1		3	4	5	2	11		9	10				7*		12	6	8		36
1	2	3	4		5	11		9	10					7		6	8		37
1	2	3	4		5	11*		9†	10		14			7	12	6	8		38
38	16	38	37	33	38	19 + 7s	2	31	37	18	8 + 4s	5 + 3s	32	7 + 12s	3 + 6s	25	30	1	

DERBY COUNTY

Player and Position	Ht	Wt	Birth Date	Birth Place	Source	Clubs	League App	League Gls
Goalkeepers								
Peter Shilton	6 0	14 00	18 9 49	Leicester	Apprentice	Leicester C	286	1
						Stoke C	110	—
						Nottingham F	202	—
						Southampton	188	—
						Derby Co	78	—
Martin Taylor	5 11	12 04	9 12 66	Tamworth	Mile Oak R	Derby Co	—	—
						Carlisle U (loan)	10	—
						Scunthorpe U (loan)	8	—
Defenders								
Paul Blades	6 0	10 12	5 1 65	Peterborough	Apprentice	Derby Co	147	1
Robert Briscoe	5 8	10 13	4 9 69	Derby	Trainee	Derby Co	—	—
Jonathan Davidson			1 3 70	Cheadle	Trainee	Derby Co	—	—
Mike Forsyth	5 11	12 02	20 3 66	Liverpool	Apprentice	WBA	29	—
						Derby Co	118	4
Rob Hindmarch	6 1	13 4	27 4 61	Stannington	Apprentice	Sunderland	115	2
						Portsmouth (loan)	2	—
						Derby Co	138	9
Mark Patterson	5 10	11 05	13 9 68	Leeds	Trainee	Carlisle U	22	—
						Derby Co	1	—
Mel Sage	5 8	10 04	24 3 64	Gillingham	Apprentice	Gillingham	132	5
						Derby Co	55	3
Mark Wright	6 3	12 01	1 8 63	Dorchester	Amateur	Oxford U	10	—
						Southampton	170	7
						Derby Co	71	4
Midfield								
Steve Cross	5 10	11 05	22 12 59	Wolverhampton	Apprentice	Shrewsbury T	262	34
						Derby Co	40	3
John Gregory	6 1	11 00	11 5 54	Scunthorpe	Apprentice	Northampton T	187	8
						Aston Villa	65	10
						Brighton & HA	72	7
						QPR	161	36
						Derby Co	103	22
Steve Hayward	5 10	11 07	8 9 71	Walsall	Trainee	Derby Co	—	—
Trevor Hebberd	6 0	11 04	19 6 58	Winchester	Apprentice	Southampton	97	7
						Bolton W (loan)	6	—
						Leicester C (loan)	4	1
						Oxford U	260	37
						Derby Co	37	5
Jason Kavanagh	5 9	11 00	23 11 71	Birmingham	Birmingham C Schoolboys	Derby Co	—	—
Brian McCord	5 10	11 06	24 8 68	Derby	Apprentice	Derby Co	1	—
Ted McMinn	6 0	12 11	28 9 62	Castle Douglas	Glenafton Ath	Queen of South	62	5
						Rangers	63	4
					Seville	Derby Co	39	5
Gary Micklewhite	5 7	10 04	21 3 61	Southwark	Apprentice	Manchester U	—	—
						QPR	106	11
						Derby Co	149	25
Nick Pickering	6 0	12 02	4 8 63	Newcastle	Apprentice	Sunderland	179	18
						Coventry C	78	9
						Derby Co	8	—
Steve Taylor			10 1 70	Holbrook	Trainee	Derby Co	—	—
Geraint Williams	5 7	10 06	5 1 62	Treorchy	Apprentice	Bristol R	141	8
						Derby Co	169	7

DERBY COUNTY

Foundation: Derby County was formed by members of the Derbyshire County Cricket Club in 1884, when football was booming in the area and the cricketers thought that a football club would help boost finances for the summer game. To begin with, they sported the cricket club's colours of amber, chocolate and pale blue, and went into the game at the top immediately entering the FA Cup.

Managers (and Secretary-managers)
Harry Newbould 1896–1906, Jimmy Methven 1906–22, Cecil Potter 1922–25, George Jobey 1925–41, Ted Magner 1944–46, Stuart McMillan 1946–53, Jack Barker 1953–55, Harry Storer 1955–62, Tim Ward 1962–67, Brian Clough 1967–73, Dave Mackay 1973–76, Colin Murphy 1977, Tommy Docherty 1977–79, Colin Addison 1979–82, Johnny Newman 1982, Peter Taylor 1982–84, Roy McFarland 1984, Arthur Cox 1984– .

Player and Position	*Ht*	*Wt*	*Birth Date*	*Birth Place*	*Source*	*Clubs*	*League App*	*League Gls*
Forwards								
John Chiedozie	5 7	10 10	18 4 60	Nigeria	Apprentice	Orient	145	20
						Notts Co	111	15
						Tottenham H	53	12
						Derby Co	2	—
Kevin Francis	6 7	15 08	6 12 67	Moseley	Mile Oak Rovers	Derby Co	—	—
Phil Gee	5 9	10 04	19 12 64	Pelsall	Gresley R	Derby Co	95	24
Paul Goddard	5 8	12 00	12 10 59	Harlington	Apprentice	QPR	70	23
						West Ham U	170	54
						Newcastle U	61	19
						Derby Co	31	7
Scott Green			15 1 70	Walsall	Trainee	Derby Co	—	—
David Penney	5 8	10 07	17 8 64	Wakefield	Pontefract	Derby Co	19	—
Craig Ramage			30 3 70	Derby	Trainee	Derby Co	—	—
						Wigan Ath (loan)	10	2
Dean Saunders	5 8	10 06	21 6 64	Swansea	Apprentice	Swansea C	49	12
						Cardiff C (loan)	4	—
						Brighton & HA	72	21
						Oxford U	59	22
						Derby Co	30	14
Kris Sleeuwenhoek	5 7	10 00	2 10 71	Oldham	Wolves Schoolboys	Derby Co	—	—
Frank Stapleton (To Le Havre)	6 0	13 01	10 7 56	Dublin	Apprentice	Arsenal	225	75
						Manchester U	223	60
						Ajax	4	—
						Derby Co	10	1

Trainees
Cooksey, Scott A; Ellis, Brent; Grant, Paul S; Holness, Corin J; Phillips, Justin L; Round, Stephen J; Symonds, John J; White, Jason G; Williams, Paul D.

Associated Schoolboys
Allen, Craig; Batey, Darren; Beazeley, Adam; Blount, Mark; Butler, Martin; Clarke, Mark A; Coleman, Ronald; Crisp, Robert; Gilby, David A; Hayes, Joel; Hillyer, Jamie A; Jamson, Scott; Richards, Michael L; Straw, Robert G; Sturridge, Dean; Timmons, Mark; Weston, Kingsley P; Wilkinson, Robert N.

DONCASTER ROVERS 1988–89 *Back row (left to right):* Rufus Brevett, Gerry Daly, Steve Gaughan, Stuart Beattie, Mark Samways, Paul Malcolm, Ronnie Robinson, Lee Turnbull, Colin Douglas, Paul Gorman, Paul Dobson.
Front row: Gerry Delahunt (Physiotherapist), Mark Hall, Paul Raven, Mark Rankine, Steve Raffell, Dave Mackay (Manager), Joe Kinnear (Assistant Manager), Les Robinson, Andy Peckett, Garry Kimble, Steve Beaglehole (Youth/Reserve Coach).

Division 4 DONCASTER ROVERS

Belle Vue Ground, Doncaster. Telephone Doncaster (0302) 539441.

Ground capacity: 4859.

Record attendance: 37,149 v Hull C, Division 3 (N), 2 Oct, 1948.

Record receipts: £22,000 v QPR, FA Cup 3rd rd, 5 Jan, 1985.

Pitch measurements: 111yd × 74½yd.

Vice-Presidents: K. Jackson, R. Jones.

Chairman: B. E. Boldry. ***Vice-Chairman:*** M. J. H. Collett.

Directors: P. Wetzel, J. J. Burke, T. C. Hamilton, K. Chappell, M. O'Horan, W. Turner.
Manager: Billy Bremner. ***Assistant Manager:***
Physio: Gary Delahunt. ***Youth Team Manager:*** Dave Bentley.

Secretary: Mrs. K. J. Oldale.

Year Formed: 1879. ***Turned Professional:*** 1885. ***Ltd Co.:*** 1905 and 1920.

Club Nickname: 'Rovers'.

Previous Grounds: 1880–1916, Intake Ground; 1920–22, Benetthorpe Ground; 1922, Low Pasture, Belle Vue.

Record League Victory: 10-0 v Darlington, Division 4, 25 January 1964 – Potter; Raine, Meadows; Windross (1), White, Ripley (2); Robinson, Book (2), Hale (4), Jeffrey, Broadbent (1).

Record Cup Victory: 7-0 v Blyth Spartans, FA Cup, 1st rd, 27 November 1937 – Imrie; Shaw, Rodgers; McFarlane, Bycroft, Cyril Smith; Burton (1), Kilourhy (4), Morgan (2), Malam, Dutton.

Record Defeat: 0-12 v Small Heath, Division 2, 11 April, 1903.

Most League Points (2 for a win): 72, Division 3(N), 1946-47.

Most League Points (3 for a win): 85, Division 4, 1983-84.

Most League Goals: 123, Division 3 (N), 1946-47.

Highest League Scorer in Season: Clarrie Jordan, 42, Division 3 (N), 1946–47.

Most League Goals in Total Aggregate: Tom Keetley, 180, 1923-29.

Most Capped Player: Len Graham, 14, Northern Ireland.

Most League Appearances: Fred Emery, 406, 1925–36.

Record Transfer Fee Received: £200,000 from Leeds U for Ian Snodin, May 1985.

Record Transfer Fee Paid: £60,000 to Stirling Albion for John Philliben, March 1984.

Football League Record: 1901 Elected to Division 2; 1903 Failed re-election; 1904 Re-elected; 1905 Failed re-election; 1923 Re-elected to Division 3(N); 1935–37 Division 2; 1937–47 Division 3 (N); 1947–48 Division 2; 1948–50 Division 3 (N); 1950-58 Division 2; 1958-59 Division 3; 1959–66 Division 4; 1966–67 Division 3; 1967–69 Division 4; 1969–71 Division 3; 1971–81 Division 4; 1981–83 Division 3; 1983–84 Division 4; 1984–88 Division 3; 1988– Division 4.

Honours: *Football League:* Division 2 best season: 7th, 1901–02; Division 3 (N) Champions 1934–35, 1946–47, 1949–50; Runners-up 1937–38, 1938–39; Division 4 – Champions 1965–66, 1968–69; Runners-up 1983–84. Promoted 1980–81 (3rd). *FA Cup* best season: 5th rd, 1951–52, 1953–54, 1954–55, 1955–56. *Football League Cup* best season: 5th rd, 1975–76.

Colours: White shirts, red collar and cuffs, red shorts, white stockings. **Change colours:** All green.

DONCASTER ROVERS 1988–89 LEAGUE RECORD

Match No.	Date	Venue	Opponents	Result	H/T Score	Lg. Pos.	Goalscorers	Atten-dance
1	Aug 27	A	Rotherham U	L 0-3	0-1	—		4497
2	Sept 3	H	Exeter C	W 2-1	1-1	13	Dobson 2 (1 pen)	1525
3	9	A	Colchester U	W 1-0	0-0	—	Rankine	1726
4	16	H	Torquay U	L 1-2	0-1	—	Robinson R	2220
5	20	A	Rochdale	L 0-2	0-0	—		1645
6	24	H	Wrexham	D 2-2	1-0	15	Beattie, Rankine	1712
7	Oct 1	A	Stockport Co	L 0-2	0-1	18		1959
8	4	H	Hereford U	W 3-2	2-1	—	Rankine, Robinson R, Douglas	1281
9	8	H	Hartlepool U	W 1-0	1-0	11	Rankine	2091
10	15	A	Crewe Alex	W 2-0	0-0	6	Dobson 2	2180
11	21	H	Halifax T	L 1-4	1-4	—	Robinson R	3038
12	25	A	York C	D 1-1	1-1	—	Dobson (pen)	2957
13	29	H	Leyton Orient	W 1-0	0-0	7	Rankine	2182
14	Nov 5	A	Darlington	W 3-1	1-0	6	Daly, Raven, Gorman	1625
15	8	A	Grimsby T	L 0-5	0-2	—		3382
16	12	H	Peterborough U	L 2-3	0-1	13	Dobson 2	2224
17	26	H	Burnley	W 1-0	0-0	8	Douglas	2724
18	Dec 2	A	Tranmere R	D 2-2	2-0	—	Rankine, Dobson (pen)	3412
19	17	H	Scunthorpe U	D 2-2	1-1	8	Dobson (pen), Daly	3381
20	26	A	Cambridge U	D 0-0	0-0	9		2673
21	28	A	Lincoln C	L 1-3	1-1	—	Matthewson (og)	5213
22	Jan 2	H	Scarborough	W 3-1	2-1	9	Robinson L, Robinson R, Rankine	3053
23	10	H	Carlisle U	L 1-3	0-1	—	Dobson	2128
24	14	A	Exeter C	L 0-3	0-2	13		2540
25	21	H	Rotherham U	W 1-0	0-0	11	Gaughan	4432
26	28	A	Torquay U	L 2-3	2-1	12	Ashurst, Gaughan	2103
27	Feb 4	H	Rochdale	D 1-1	0-0	12	Brockie (pen)	1868
28	11	A	Wrexham	D 1-1	1-0	13	Brockie (pen)	3244
29	18	A	Hartlepool U	L 1-2	0-0	14	Jones	1922
30	24	H	Crewe Alex	L 0-1	0-0	—		1713
31	28	H	York C	L 1-2	0-0	—	Turnbull	1526
32	Mar 3	A	Halifax T	L 0-2	0-0	—		1675
33	10	H	Darlington	W 1-0	0-0	—	Daly (pen)	1538
34	14	A	Leyton Orient	L 0-4	0-1	—		2824
35	18	H	Colchester U	W 3-1	2-1	17	Rankine 2, Jones	1237
36	25	A	Scarborough	L 0-2	0-1	18		2792
37	27	H	Cambridge U	D 1-1	0-0	19	Daly	1937
38	Apr 1	A	Scunthorpe U	L 1-2	1-2	19	Rankine	5334
39	4	A	Carlisle U	W 1-0	1-0	—	Rankine	2991
40	8	H	Lincoln C	L 0-1	0-0	18		2124
41	14	H	Stockport Co	D 2-2	0-1	—	Turnbull, Robinson (pen)	1363
42	22	A	Hereford U	L 1-3	0-1	18	Turnbull	1804
43	29	A	Burnley	L 0-3	0-1	21		4211
44	May 1	H	Grimsby T	L 2-3	1-2	22	Turnbull, Robinson (pen)	2183
45	6	H	Tranmere R	D 0-0	0-0	22		2286
46	13	A	Peterborough U	L 0-2	0-1	23		2984

Final League Position: 23

GOALSCORERS

League (49): Rankine 11, Dobson 10 (4 pens), Daly 4 (1 pen), Robinson R 4, Turnbull 4, Robinson L 3 (2 pens), Brockie 2 (2 pens), Gaughan 2, Douglas 2, Jones 2, Ashurst 1, Beattie 1, Gorman 1, Raven 1, own goal 1.
Littlewoods Cup (1): Rankine 1.
FA Cup (3): Dobson 2, Daly 1.

Littlewoods Cup	First Round	Darlington (h)	1-1
		(a)	0-2
FA Cup	First Round	Brandon (h)	0-0
		(a)	2-1
	Second Round	Sheffield U (h)	1-3

Malcolm	Douglas	Robinson, R	Turnbull	Raffell	Raven	Robinson, L	Daly	Rankine	Dobson	Kimble	Gorman	Gaughan	Beattie	Samways	Stewart	Ashurst	Trotter	Brevett	Peckett	Brockie	Ward	Hall	Jones	Powell	*Match No.*
1	2	3	4	5	6	7	8†	9	10*	11	12	14													1
1	2	3	4		6	7	8*	9	10	11		12	5												2
1	2	3		4	6	7		9	10	11		8	5												3
	2	3	8	4*	6	7		9	10	11†	12	14	5	1											4
	2	3		4	6	7		9	10	11	12	8†	5*	1					14						5
	2	3		4	6	7	8	9	10*	11		12	5	1											6
1	2	6		3	4	7	8	9		11	12		5		10*										7
1	10	3	4	2	6	7	8	9		11	12		5*												8
1	2	3	4		6	7	8	9	10	11			5												9
1	2	3	4		6	7	8	9	10	11			5												10
1	2	3	4	14	6	7	8	9	10†	11*	12		5												11
1	2	3	4		6	7	8	9	10	11			5												12
1	2	3	4		6	7	8†	9	10*	11	12	14	5												13
1	2	3	4		6	7	8	9	10*	11	12	14	5†												14
1	2	3	4		6	7	8	9	10	11			5												15
1	10	3	4†		6	7		9	14	11	12	8*	2			5									16
1	11	3			6	7	8*	9	10			12	2			5	4								17
1	11	3			6	7*	8	9	10			12	2			5	4								18
1	11	3			6		8	9	10			7*				5	4	2	12						19
1	11	4			6	7	8	9	12							5		3		2	10*				20
1	4	3			6	7	8	9	10*							5			12	2	11				21
1	11	3			6	7	8	9	10							5				2	4				22
1	11	3			6	7	8†	9	10							5		14	12	2	4*				23
1	5				6	7	8	9	10			11						3	12	4		2*			24
1	2				6	7	8	9	10*			11				5		3	12	4					25
1	2				6	7	8	9	10*			11				5		3		4			12		26
1	2	14	12		6	7	8*	9				11†				5		3		4			10		27
	2		10		6	7	8	9				11		1		5		3		4					28
	2		10		6	7	8*	9				11		1		5		3		4			12		29
	2	14	10		6		8†	9		12		11		1		5		3		4			7*		30
	2	4	10		6		8	9		12		11		1		5		3					7*		31
	2†	4	10		6	7	8*	9		12		11		1		5		3					14		32
	2	4	10		6	7	8	9		3		11		1		5									33
	2	3*	10		6	7	8	9		11		12		1		5				4					34
1	2		10		6	7	8*	9		11		3				5				4			12		35
1	6		10			7		9		11*		12				5		3		4			8	2	36
1	6		4			7	8	9		11		10*				5		3		2			12		37
1	6		10			7	8	9		11*		4				5		3		2			12		38
1	6		10			7	8	9				11				5		3		4				2	39
1	6		10			7	8*	9				11				5		3		4			12	2	40
1	6		10	14		7	8*	9		11		12				5		3					4	2†	41
1	6		10			7	8*	9		11		4				5		3		2			12		42
1	2		8	6		7	12	9		14		11†				5		3		4			10*		43
1*	2		8	6		7	12	9		14		11†				5		3		4			10		44
	2		8	6		7		9		11				1		5		3		4			10		45
	2		8	6		7		9		11*		14		1		5		3	12	4			10†		46
34	46	27	31	11	35	43	37	46	22	26	—	22	17	12	1	30	3	22	—	23	4	1	9	4	
		+	+	+			+		+	+	+	+						+	+				+		
		2s	1s	2s			2s		2s	5s	9s	12s						1s	7s				8s		

DONCASTER ROVERS

Player and Position	Ht	Wt	Birth Date	Birth Place	Source	Clubs	League App	League Gls
Goalkeepers								
Paul Malcolm*	6 4	13 10	11 12 64	Heworth	Apprentice	Newcastle U	—	—
					Durham C	Rochdale	24	—
						Shrewsbury T	—	—
						Barnsley	3	—
						Doncaster R	34	—
Mark Samways	6 0	11 12	11 11 68	Doncaster	Trainee	Doncaster R	23	—
						Leeds U (loan)	—	—
Defenders								
Jack Ashurst	6 0	12 04	12 10 54	Renton	Apprentice	Sunderland	140	4
						Blackpool	53	3
						Carlisle U	194	2
						Leeds U	89	1
						Doncaster R	30	1
Stuart Beattie*	6 2	12 04	10 7 67	Stevenston	Ardeer Rec.	Rangers	5	—
						Doncaster R	26	1
Rufus Brevett	5 8	11 00	24 9 69	Derby	Trainee	Derby Co	—	—
						Doncaster R	40	—
Vincent Brockie	5 8	10 10	2 2 69	Greenock	Trainee	Leeds U	2	—
						Doncaster R	23	2
Colin Douglas	6 1	11 00	9 9 62	Hurtford	Celtic BC	Celtic	—	—
						Doncaster R	212	48
						Rotherham U	83	4
						Doncaster R	46	2
Mark Hall	5 11	11 00	11 5 70	Doncaster	Trainee	Doncaster R	2	—
Steve Raffell	5 11	11 02	27 4 70	Blyth	Trainee	Doncaster R	27	—
Midfield								
Gerry Daly	5 8	11 04	30 4 54	Dublin	Bohemians	Manchester U	111	23
						Derby Co	112	31
						Coventry C	84	19
						Leicester C (loan)	17	1
						Burmingham C	32	1
						Shrewsbury T	55	8
						Stoke C	22	1
						Doncaster R	39	4
Steven Gaughan	5 11	11 02	14 4 70	Doncaster	Trainee	Doncaster R	38	2
Garry Kimble*	5 8	11 00	6 8 66	Poole		Charlton Ath	9	1
						Exeter C (loan)	1	—
						Cambridge U	41	2
						Doncaster R	65	1
Andy Peckett*	5 10	11 00	19 9 69	Sheffield	Trainee	Doncaster R	9	—
Mark Rankine	5 10	11 01	30 9 69	Doncaster	Trainee	Doncaster R	64	13
Leslie Robinson	5 8	11 05	1 3 67	Mansfield		Mansfield T	15	—
						Stockport Co	67	3
						Doncaster R	50	4

DONCASTER ROVERS

Foundation: In 1879 Mr. Albert Jenkins got together a team to play a game against the Yorkshire Institution for the Deaf. The players stuck together as Doncaster Rovers joining the Midland Alliance in 1889 and the Midland Counties League in 1891.

Managers (and Secretary-managers)
Arthur Porter 1920–21*, Harry Tufnell 1921–22, Arthur Porter 1922–23, Dick Ray 1923–27, David Menzies 1928–36, Fred Emery 1936–40, Bill Marsden 1944–46, Jackie Bestall 1946–49, Peter Doherty 1949–58, Jack Hodgson and Sid Bycroft (joint managers) 1958, Jack Crayston 1958–59 (continued as Sec-Man to 1961), Jackie Bestall (TM) 1959–60, Norman Curtis 1960–61, Danny Malloy 1961–62, Oscar Hold 1962–64, Bill Leivers 1964–66, Keith Kettleborough 1966–67, George Raynor 1967–68, Lawrie McMenemy 1968–71, Maurice Setters 1971–74, Stan Anderson 1975–78, Billy Bremner 1978–85, Dave Cusack 1985–87, Dave Mackay 1987–89, Billy Bremner 1989– .

Player and Position	*Ht*	*Wt*	*Birth Date*	*Birth Place*	*Source*	*Clubs*	*League App*	*League Gls*
Forwards								
Paul Gorman*	5 9	12 02	18 9 68	Macclesfield	Trainee	Doncaster R	16	2
Gary Jones†	5 11	11 06	6 4 69	Huddersfield	Rossington Main	Doncaster R	17	2
Robbie Stewart§			14 6 71	West Lothian	Trainee	Doncaster R	1	—
Lee Turnbull	6 0	11 09	27 9 67	Teeside	Local	Middlesbrough	16	4
						Aston Villa	—	—
						Doncaster R	62	5

Trainees
Clarke, Jonathan P; Copley-Dunn, Jason; Cygan, Paul; Gilliver, Andrew; Harrington, Shaun M; Lamont, Lee S; Nicholson, Maximilian; Normanton, Lee M; Redhead, Christopher A; Stewart, Robert A; Veitch, Steven W; Warren, Jason.

****Non-Contract**
Jones, Gary.

Associated Schoolboys
Barker, Paul D; Beswick, David; Carlin, Ian R; Chapman, Craig; Dunn, Wayne; Fox, Paul B; Gorman, Sean R; Horner, Jay; Lockley, Scott A; Limber, Nicholas; McDonagh, Dermot E; McGarry, Neil; Mann, Karl; Marriott, Karl T; Marsh, Jason L; Mitchell, Wayne; Newey, Ian M; Preston, Nicholas A; Raffo, Stephen; Roberts, Dean E; Roberts, Jamie S; Rushton, Wayne J; Smith, Paul; Shillito, Philip; Tomlinson, Andrew R; Whitehead, Scott; Wilkes, Craig S.

EVERTON 1988–89 *Back row (left to right):* Pat Van Den Hauwe, Dave Watson, Mike Stowell, Neville Southall, Neil McDonald, Paul Bracewell.
Centre row: Chris Goodson (Physiotherapist), Graham Smith (Youth Team Manager), Pat Nevin, Stuart McCall, Neil Pointon, Graeme Sharp, Wayne Clarke, Ian Snodin, Neil Adams, Ian Wilson, Mick Lyons (Reserve Team Coach), Terry Darracott (Assistant Manager/Coach), Paul Power (Youth Team Coach).
Front row: Trevor Steven, Adrian Heath, Kevin Ratcliffe, Colin Harvey (Manager), Peter Reid (Player/Coach), Tony Cottee, Kevin Sheedy.

Division 1 **EVERTON**

Goodison Park, Liverpool L4 4EL. Telephone 051-521 2020. Match ticket information: 051-523 6642. Clubcall 0898 12 11 99.

Ground capacity: 50,059 (25,000 seats).

Record attendance: 78,299 v Liverpool, Division 1, 18 Sept, 1948.

Record receipts: £174,945, Liverpool v Manchester U, FA Cup semi-final replay, 4 April 1979.

Pitch measurements: 112yd × 78yd

Chairman: P. D. Carter CBE. ***Vice-Chairman:*** T. H. W. Scott.

Directors: A. W. Waterworth, D. H. Pitcher, K. M. Tamlin, D. A. B. Newton, Dr. D. M. Marsh.

Manager: Colin Harvey. ***Assistant Manager:*** Terry Darracott.

Physio: Chris Goodson.

Chief Executive & Secretary: Jim Greenwood.

Marketing Manager: Derek Johnston. ***Sales Promotion Manager:*** Nigel Coates.

Year Formed: 1878. ***Turned Professional:*** 1885. ***Ltd Co.:*** 1892.

Previous name: St Domingo FC, 1878–79.

Club Nickname: 'The Toffees'.

Former Grounds: 1878, Stanley Park; 1882, Priory Road; 1884, Anfield Road; 1892, Goodison Park.

Record League Victory: 9-1 v Manchester C, Division 1, 3 September 1906 – Scott; Balmer, Crelley; Booth, Taylor (1), Abbott (1); Sharp, Bolton (1), Young (4), Settle (2), George Wilson. 9-1 v Plymouth Arg, Division 2, 27 December 1930 – Coggins; Williams, Cresswell; McPherson, Griffiths, Thomson; Critchley, Dunn, Dean (4), Johnson (1), Stein (4).

Record Cup Victory: 11-2 v Derby Co, FA Cup, 1st rd, 18 January 1889 – Smalley; Hannah, Doyle; Kirkwood (3), Holt, Parry; Latta, Brady (3), Geary (2), Chadwick, Millward (3).

Record Defeat: 4-10 v Tottenham H, Division 1, 11, October, 1958.

Most League Points (2 for a win): 66, Division 1, 1969–70.

Most League Points (3 for a win): 90, Division 1, 1984–85.

Most League Goals: 121, Division 2, 1930–31.

Highest League Scorer in Season: William Ralph 'Dixie' Dean, 60, Division 1, 1927–28 (All-time League record).

Most League Goals in Total Aggregate: William Ralph 'Dixie' Dean, 349, 1925–37.

Most Capped Player: Kevin Ratcliffe, 47, Wales.

Most League Appearances: Ted Sagar, 465, 1929–53.

Record Transfer Fee Received: £2,750,000 from Barcelona for Gary Lineker. July 1986.

Record Transfer Fee Paid: £2,200,000 to West Ham U for Tony Cottee, July 1988.

Football League Record: 1888 Founder Member of the Football League; 1930–31 Division 2; 1931–51 Division 1; 1951–54 Division 2; 1954– Division 1.

Honours: *Football League:* Division 1 – Champions 1890–91, 1914–15, 1927–28, 1931–32, 1938–39, 1962–63, 1969–70, 1984–85, 1986–87; Runners-up 1889–90, 1894–95, 1901–02, 1904–05, 1908–09, 1911–12, 1985–86; Division 2 Champions 1930–31; Runners-up 1953–54. *FA Cup:* Winners 1906, 1933, 1966, 1984; Runners-up 1893, 1897, 1907, 1968, 1985, 1986, 1989. *Football League Cup:* Runners-up 1976–77, 1983–84. *League Super Cup:* Runners-up 1986. *Simod Cup:* Runners-up 1989. **European Competitions:** *European Cup:* 1963–64, 1970–71; *European Cup-Winners' Cup:* 1966–67, 1984–85 (winners). *European Fairs Cup:* 1962-63. 1964–65, 1965–66. *UEFA Cup:* 1975–76, 1978–79, 1979–80.

Colours: Royal blue shirts, white shorts, blue stockings with white turnovers. **Change colours:** Silver and white striped shirts, Royal blue shorts.

EVERTON 1988–89 LEAGUE RECORD

Match No.	Date		Venue	Opponents	Result		H/T Score	Lg. Pos.	Goalscorers	Attendance
1	Aug	27	H	Newcastle U	W	4-0	2-0	—	Cottee 3, Sharp	41,560
2	Sept	3	A	Coventry C	W	1-0	1-0	1	Cottee	18,625
3		10	H	Nottingham F	D	1-1	0-1	3	Heath	34,003
4		17	A	Millwall	L	1-2	0-2	6	McLeary (og)	17,507
5		24	H	Luton T	L	0-2	0-0	8		26,017
6	Oct	1	A	Wimbledon	L	1-2	0-2	10	Heath	6367
7		8	H	Southampton	W	4-1	1-1	8	Cottee 2, Watson, Steven	25,356
8		22	A	Aston Villa	L	0-2	0-1	11		26,636
9		30	H	Manchester U	D	1-1	0-0	—	Cottee	27,005
10	Nov	5	A	Sheffield W	D	1-1	0-0	15	Steven (pen)	21,761
11		12	A	Charlton Ath	W	2-1	2-1	10	Sharp, Reid	8627
12		19	H	Norwich C	D	1-1	0-0	10	Steven (pen)	28,118
13		26	A	West Ham U	W	1-0	0-0	9	Steven	22,176
14	Dec	3	H	Tottenham H	W	1-0	1-0	8	Cottee	29,657
15		11	A	Liverpool	D	1-1	0-1	—	Clarke (pen)	42,372
16		17	A	QPR	D	0-0	0-0	8		10,067
17		26	H	Middlesbrough	W	2-1	2-1	5	Steven, Cottee	32,651
18		31	H	Coventry C	W	3-1	2-1	4	Sheedy 2, Bracewell	30,790
19	Jan	2	A	Nottingham F	L	0-2	0-1	5		26,008
20		14	H	Arsenal	L	1-3	0-0	7	Watson	34,825
21		21	A	Luton T	L	0-1	0-1	9		9013
22	Feb	4	H	Wimbledon	D	1-1	1-1	9	Sharp (pen)	23,365
23		11	A	Southampton	D	1-1	0-1	9	Sheedy	15,845
24		14	H	Aston Villa	D	1-1	1-1	—	Cottee	20,142
25		25	A	Derby Co	L	2-3	1-1	10	Sharp, Clarke	17,103
26	Mar	11	H	Sheffield W	W	1-0	1-0	11	Cottee	22,542
27		22	A	Newcastle U	L	0-2	0-1	—		20,933
28		25	H	Millwall	D	1-1	0-1	11	Sheedy	27,062
29		27	A	Middlesbrough	D	3-3	2-1	11	Cottee, Sheedy, Nevin	21,351
30	Apr	1	H	QPR	W	4-1	2-0	11	Clarke, Sheedy (pen), Cottee, Steven	23,028
31		8	A	Arsenal	L	0-2	0-1	11		37,608
32		10	H	Charlton Ath	W	3-2	1-1	—	Sharp, Sheedy, Nevin	16,316
33		22	A	Tottenham H	L	1-2	0-0	12	McDonald	28,568
34	May	3	H	Liverpool	D	0-0	0-0	—		45,994
35		6	A	Norwich C	L	0-1	0-0	12		13,239
36		10	A	Manchester U	W	2-1	1-1	—	Sharp 2	26,722
37		13	H	West Ham U	W	3-1	1-1	11	Sheedy, Watson, Bracewell	21,694
38		15	H	Derby Co	W	1-0	1-0	—	Wilson	17,826

Final League Position: 8

GOALSCORERS

League (50): Cottee 13, Sheedy 8 (1 pen), Sharp 7 (1 pen), Steven 6 (2 pens), Clarke 3 (1 pen), Watson 3, Bracewell 2, Heath 2, Nevin 2, Reid 1, McDonald 1, Wilson 1, own goal 1.
Littlewoods Cup (9): Cottee 2, Sharp 2, Steven 2 (2 pens), McCall 1, McDonald 1, Watson 1.
FA Cup (12): Sheedy 4 (2 pens), McCall 3, Sharp 3, Nevin 2.

Littlewoods Cup	Second Round	Bury (h)	3-0
		(a)	2-2
	Third Round	Oldham Ath (h)	1-1
		(a)	2-0
	Fourth Round	Bradford C (a)	1-3
FA Cup	Third Round	WBA (a)	1-1
		(h)	1-0
	Fourth Round	Plymouth Arg (a)	1-1
		(h)	4-0
	Fifth Round	Barnsley (a)	1-0
	Sixth Round	Wimbledon (h)	1-0
	Semi-Final	Norwich C (at Villa Park)	1-0
	Final	Liverpool (at Wembley)	2-3

Southall	McDonald	Pointon	Snodin	Watson	Reid	Steven	McCall	Sharp	Cottee	Nevin	Sheedy	Heath	Wilson	Clarke	Van Den Hauwe	Ratcliffe	Bracewell	Ebbrell	*Match No.*
1	2	3	4	5	6	7*	8	9	10	11	12								1
1	2	3	4	5	6		8	9	10	7	11								2
1	2	3	4	5	6		8	9	10	7*	11†	12	14						3
1	2	3	4	5	6		8*	9	10		11†	7		12	14				4
1	2*		4	5	6		8	9	10		11	7	3	12					5
1	2	3	4		6		8	9	10		11	7			5				6
1			2	5	6	11	8	9	10			7			3	4			7
1		12	2	5	6	11†	8	9	10			7	14		3*	4			8
1			2	5	6	11	8	9	10			7*	12		3	4			9
1			2	5	6	7	8	9	10				11		3	4			10
1			2	5	6	7	8	9	10				11		3	4			11
1			2	5	6	7	8	9	10				11		3	4			12
1			2	5	6	7	8	9	10				11		3	4			13
1			2	5		7	8	9*	10				11	12	3	4	6		14
1			2	5	12	7	8		10				11	9	3	4	6*		15
1			2	5		7	8		10	11*	12			9	3	4	6		16
1		3	2	5	14	7	8		10*	9	11†			12	4		6		17
1		12	2	5	8	7			10	9	11				3*	4	6		18
1		3	2	5	8	7			10	9*	11		12			4	6		19
1	14	3	2	5	8*		12		10	7	11†			9		4	6		20
1	14	3	2	5			8†		10	7*	11		12	9		4	6		21
1	2			5		6	8	9	10	7			11*		3	4		12	22
1	2			5		7	8	9	10†	14	11		6*	12	3	4			23
1	2			5		7	8	9	10	12	11				3*	4	6		24
1	2	3	6	5		7	8	9*		12	11			10		4			25
1	14	3	2†	5		7	8		10	12	11*			9		4	6		26
1	2	3				7	8*	9	10†	14	11			12	5	4	6		27
1	2	3				7	14	9	12	8	11†			10*	5	4	6		28
1	2	3				7			10*	8	11		12	9	5	4	6		29
1	2	3		5		7			10	8	11			9		4	6		30
1	2	3				7*	5		10	8	11			9	4		6	12	31
1	2	3					8	9		7*	11			10	5	4	6	12	32
1	2			5		8	14	9	10	7	11†			12	3	4	6*		33
1	2			5		8	12	9	10	7	11*				3	4	6		34
1	2	3		5		8	7		10		11			9		4	6		35
1	2	12		5		8	6	9	10	7			11		3*	4			36
1	2	3		5		8		9	10	7	11*		12			4	6		37
1	2	3		5			6	9*	10	7			11	12		4		8	38
38	22 + 3s	20 + 3s	23	32	16 + 2s	29	29 + 4s	26	35 + 1s	20 + 5s	24 + 2s	6 + 1s	11 + 7s	12 + 8s	24 + 1s	30	20	1 + 3s	

EVERTON

Player and Position	Ht	Wt	Birth Date	Birth Place	Source	Clubs	League App	League Gls
Goalkeepers								
Jason Kearton	6 1	11 10	9 7 69	Ipswich (Australia)	Brisbane Lions	Everton	—	—
Neville Southall	6 1	12 01	16 9 58	Llandudno	Winsford	Bury	39	—
						Everton	253	—
						Port Vale (loan)	9	—
Mike Stowell	6 2	11 10	19 4 65	Preston	Leyland Motors	Preston NE	—	—
						Everton	—	—
						Chester C (loan)	14	—
						York C (loan)	6	—
						Manchester C (loan)	14	—
						Port Vale (loan)	7	—
						Wolverhampton W (loan)	7	—
Defenders								
Neil McDonald	5 11	11 04	2 11 65	Newcastle	Wallsend BC	Newcastle U	180	24
						Everton	25	1
Neil Pointon	5 10	11 00	28 11 64	Warsop Vale	Apprentice	Scunthorpe U	159	2
						Everton	83	4
Kevin Ratcliffe	5 11	12 07	12 11 60	Mancot	Apprentice	Everton	290	2
Gary Stevens (To Rangers, Aug 1988)	5 11	10 11	27 3 63	Barrow	Apprentice	Everton	208	8
Pat Van Den Hauwe	6 0	10 08	16 12 60	Dendermonde	Apprentice	Birmingham C	123	1
						Everton	135	2
Dave Watson	6 0	11 12	20 11 61	Liverpool	Amateur	Liverpool	—	—
						Norwich C	212	11
						Everton	104	11
Edward Youds	5 11	11 01	3 5 70	Liverpool	Trainee	Everton	—	—
Midfield								
Paul Bracewell	5 8	10 09	19 7 62	Stoke	Apprentice	Stoke C	129	5
						Sunderland	38	4
						Everton	95	7
James Carberry*			13 10 60	Liverpool	Trainee	Everton	—	—
John Ebbrell	5 7	9 12	1 10 69	Bromborough	FA School	Everton	4	—
Philip Jones	5 8	10 09	1 12 69	Liverpool	Trainee	Everton	1	—
Stuart McCall	5 6	10 01	10 6 64	Leeds	Apprentice	Bradford C	238	37
						Everton	33	—
Kevin Sheedy	5 9	10 11	21 10 59	Builth Wells	Apprentice	Hereford U	51	4
						Liverpool	3	—
						Everton	199	53
Ian Snodin	5 7	8 12	15 8 63	Rotherham	Apprentice	Doncaster R	188	25
						Leeds U	51	6
						Everton	70	2
Trevor Steven	5 8	10 09	21 9 63	Berwick	Apprentice	Burnley	76	11
						Everton	214	48
Tony Ward‡	5 6	10 02	4 4 70	Warrington	Trainee	Everton	—	—
						Doncaster R (loan)	4	—
Ian Wilson	5 7	10 10	27 3 58	Aberdeen	Elgin C	Leicester C	285	17
						Everton	34	1
Mark Wright	5 9	10 08	29 1 70	Manchester	Trainee	Everton	—	—

EVERTON

Foundation: St. Domingo Church Sunday School formed a football club in 1878 which played at Stanley Park. Enthusiasm was so great that in November 1879 they decided to expand membership and changed the name to Everton playing in black shirts with a white sash and nicknamed the "Black Watch". After wearing several other colours, royal blue was adopted in 1901.

Managers (and Secretary-managers)
W. E. Barclay 1888–89*, Dick Molyneux 1889–1901*, William C. Cuff 1901–18*, W. J. Sawyer 1918–19*, Thomas H. McIntosh 1919–35*, Theo Kelly 1936–48, Cliff Britton 1948–56, Ian Buchan 1956–58, Johnny Carey 1958–61, Harry Catterick 1961–73, Billy Bingham 1973–77, Gordon Lee 1977–81, Howard Kendall 1981–87, Colin Harvey 1987– .

Player and Position	*Ht*	*Wt*	*Birth Date*	*Birth Place*	*Source*	*Clubs*	*League App*	*League Gls*
Forwards								
Neil Adams	5 8	10 08	23 11 65	Stoke	Local	Stoke C	32	4
						Everton	20	—
						Oldham Ath (loan)	9	—
Wayne Clarke	6 0	11 08	28 2 61	Wolverhampton	Apprentice	Wolverhampton W	148	30
						Birmingham C	92	38
						Everton	57	18
Tony Cottee	5 8	11 04	11 7 65	West Ham	Apprentice	West Ham U	212	92
						Everton	36	13
Adrian Heath (To Espanol, Nov 1988)	5 6	10 01	11 1 61	Stoke	Apprentice	Stoke C	95	16
						Everton	226	71
Pat Nevin	5 6	10 00	6 9 63	Glasgow	Gartcosh U	Clyde	73	17
						Chelsea	193	36
						Everton	25	2
Gary Powell	5 10	10 02	2 4 69	Holylake	Trainee	Everton	—	—
Graeme Sharp	6 1	11 08	16 10 60	Glasgow	Eastercraigs	Dumbarton	40	17
						Everton	262	102

Trainees
Barton, Stuart A; Clifton, Joseph M; Conlan, David J; Cowlishaw, Leigh; Darkes, Jason V; Ebdon, Marcus; Feeney, David S; Jones, Stuart; O'Neil, John A.J; Quinlan, Philip E; Reilly, Stephen J; Sang, Neil; Smith, Paul A; Spellman, Carl M; Whalley, David C.

Associated Schoolboys
Appleton, Marc J.W; Barker, Alan M; Bayley, Andrew J; Boyle, Phillip D; Donoghue, Mark P; Earl, Michael G; Emmett, Darren; Grant, Anthony J; Gresham, Mark A; Griffin, Christopher; Holcroft, Robert J; Jones, Terence P; Langton, Edward P; McCullagh, Edward J; McGuirk, Paul M; Mainwaring, Andrew J; Malkeson, Alan G; Murphy, David G; Norris, Barry; Oulton, James; Owen, Phillip G; Reeves, Stephen W; Ruffer, Carl J; Scotton, Alan; Smith, Barry; Unsworth, David G; Williams, Neil W.

EXETER CITY 1988–89 *Back row (left to right):* Terry Cooper (Manager), Carl Harris, Paul Batty, Chris Banks, Darren Rowbotham, Dave Walter, Richard Young, Richard Dryden, Steve Tupling, Steve Harrower, Mike Davenport (Trainer).

Front row: Brian McDermott, Ian Benjamin, Scott Hiley, Shaun Taylor, Chris Vinnicombe, Keith Smith, Lee Rogers.

Division 4 **EXETER CITY**

St James Park, Exeter EX4 6PX. Telephone Exeter (0392) 54073. Commercial Dept: (0392) 59466.

Ground capacity: 17, 086.

Record attendance: 20, 984 v Sunderland, FA Cup 6th rd replay, 4 March, 1931.

Record receipts: £32,007 v Newcastle U, FA Cup 5th rd replay, 18 Feb, 1981.

Pitch measurements: 114yd × 73yd.

President: W. C. Hill.

Chairman: A. I. Doble.

Directors: I. M. Couch, A. Gooch JP. M. Holladay, G. Vece, P. Carter, B. J. Snell.

Manager: Terry Cooper. ***Coach/Assistant Manager:*** Steve Neville.

Secretary M. Holladay.

Commercial Manager: Tony Kellow.

Year Formed: 1904. ***Turned Professional:*** 1908. ***Ltd Co.:*** 1908.

Club Nickname: 'The Grecians'.

Record League Victory: 8-1 v Coventry C, Division 3 (S), 4 December 1926 – Bailey; Pollard, Charlton; Pullen, Pool, Garrett; Purcell (2), McDevitt, Blackmore (2), Dent (2), Compton (2). 8-1 v Aldershot, Division 3 (S), 4 May 1935 – Chesters; Gray, Miller; Risdon, Webb, Angus; Jack Scott (1), Wrightson (1), Poulter (3), McArthur (1), Dryden (1). (1 og)

Record Cup Victory: 9-1 v Aberdare, FA Cup 1st rd, 26 November 1927 – Holland; Pollard, Charlton; Phoenix, Pool, Gee; Purcell (2), McDevitt, Dent (4), Vaughan (2), Compton (1).

Record Defeat: 0-9 v Notts Co, Division 3 (S), 16 October, 1948 and v Northampton T, Division 3 (S), 12 April 1958.

Most League Points (2 for a win): 62, Division 4, 1976–77.

Most League Points (3 for a win): 60, Division 4, 1988–89.

Most League Goals: 88, Division 3 (S), 1932–33.

Highest League Scorer in Season: Fred Whitlow, 33, Division 3 (S), 1932–33.

Most League Goals in Total Aggregate: Tony Kellow, 129, 1976–78, 1980–83, 1985–88.

Most Capped Player: Dermot Curtis, 1 (17) Eire.

Most League Appearances: Arnold Mitchell, 495, 1952–66.

Record Transfer Fee Received: £105,000 from Blackpool for Tony Kellow, November 1978.

Record Transfer Fee Paid: £65,000 to Blackpool for Tony Kellow, March 1980.

Football League Record: 1920 Elected Division 3; 1921–1958 Division 3 (S); 1958–64 Division 4; 1964–66 Division 3; 1966–77 Division 4; 1977–84 Division 3; 1984– Division 4.

Honours: *Football League:* Division 3 best season: 8th. 1979–80; Division 3 (S) – Runners-up 1932–33; Division 4 – Runners-up 1976–77. *FA Cup* best season: 6th rd replay. 1931. *Football League Cup:* never beyond 4th rd. Division 3(S) *Cup:* Winners 1934.

Colours: Red and white striped shirts, black shorts, red stockings white stripes. **Change colours:** Blue and white.

EXETER CITY 1988–89 LEAGUE RECORD

Match No.	*Date*	*Venue*	*Opponents*	*Result*	*H/T Score*	*Lg. Pos.*	*Goalscorers*	*Attendance*
1	Aug 27	H	Wrexham	L 0-2	0-1	—		2504
2	Sept 3	A	Doncaster R	L 1-2	1-1	20	Neville (pen)	1525
3	10	H	Halifax T	W 4-1	1-0	14	Withey 2, Neville, Rowbotham	1725
4	17	A	Rochdale	L 1-2	1-1	18	Hiley	1216
5	20	A	Darlington	D 2-2	0-1	—	Rowbotham, Langley	1216
6	24	H	Scunthorpe U	D 2-2	1-0	18	Neville, Taylor	1876
7	Oct 1	A	Rotherham U	W 1-0	0-0	15	Johnson (og)	4075
8	5	H	Torquay U	W 3-0	0-0	—	Neville, Batty, Rowbotham	4243
9	8	A	Burnley	L 0-3	0-1	15		7889
10	15	H	Grimsby T	W 2-1	1-0	14	Neville (pen), Taylor	2232
11	22	H	Carlisle U	W 3-0	1-0	8	Rowbotham 2, Langley	2235
12	25	A	Leyton Orient	L 0-4	0-1	—		3873
13	29	H	Crewe Alex	L 1-2	0-2	14	Neville (pen)	2567
14	Nov 4	A	Cambridge U	L 0-2	0-0	—		2063
15	9	H	Scarborough	W 1-0	0-0	—	Rowbotham	2351
16	12	A	Lincoln C	L 0-2	0-1	18		3461
17	26	A	Hartlepool U	D 2-2	0-0	18	Rowbotham, Taylor	2125
18	Dec 3	H	Colchester U	W 4-2	2-1	14	Taylor, Neville, Hiley, Rowbotham	2132
19	17	A	Peterborough U	W 1-0	0-0	12	Neville	3149
20	26	H	Hereford U	W 3-1	1-1	7	Taylor, Rowbotham, Cooper	3229
21	31	H	York C	W 2-0	1-0	6	Rowbotham (pen), Neville	3092
22	Jan 2	A	Stockport Co	L 0-4	0-2	7		2936
23	14	H	Doncaster R	W 3-0	2-0	7	Rowbotham 2 (1 pen), Neville	2540
24	21	A	Wrexham	L 0-3	0-0	8		2514
25	28	H	Rochdale	W 5-1	2-1	7	Smith 2, Rowbotham, Neville, Tupling	2428
26	Feb 4	H	Darlington	W 2-1	0-1	6	Rowbotham(pen), Neville	2687
27	11	A	Scunthorpe U	L 0-2	0-1	7		4102
28	18	H	Burnley	W 3-0	1-0	7	Harris C, Benjamin, Neville	3672
29	25	A	Grimsby T	L 1-2	0-1	7	Rowbotham (pen)	4684
30	Mar 1	H	Leyton Orient	D 1-1	0-0	—	Rowbotham (pen)	2890
31	4	A	Carlisle U	L 0-1	0-0	8		2601
32	11	H	Cambridge U	L 0-3	0-1	9		3180
33	14	A	Crewe Alex	L 1-2	0-0	—	Hiley	3156
34	17	A	Halifax T	W 3-0	1-0	—	Rowbotham, Taylor, Young	1473
35	20	A	Tranmere R	L 0-2	0-1	—		3885
36	25	H	Stockport Co	D 2-2	0-2	9	Rowbotham 2 (1 pen)	3058
37	27	A	Hereford U	L 0-1	0-0	9		2735
38	Apr 1	H	Peterborough U	W 3-1	2-0	9	Banks, Neville, Young	2522
39	5	H	Tranmere R	L 0-1	0-1	—		2956
40	8	A	York C	L 1-3	0-1	10	Hiley	2052
41	15	H	Rotherham U	D 0-0	0-0	10		2594
42	22	A	Torquay U	W 4-0	1-0	10	Young 2, Rowbotham, McDermott	2939
43	29	H	Hartlepool U	W 2-1	1-1	10	Hiley, Benjamin	2380
44	May 1	A	Scarborough	L 1-2	1-2	11	Benjamin	2513
45	5	A	Colchester U	I 0-4	0-2	—		5256
46	13	H	Lincoln C	L 0-1	0-1	10		2249

Final League Position: 10

GOALSCORERS

League (65): Rowbotham 20 (6 pens), Neville 14 (3 pens), Taylor 6, Hiley 5, Young 4, Benjamin 3, Langley 2, Smith 2, Withey 2, Banks 1, Batty 1, Cooper 1, Harris C 1, McDermott 1, Tupling 1, own goal 1.
Littlewoods Cup (0).
FA Cup (1): Rowbotham 1.

Littlewoods Cup	First Round	Bristol C (a)	0-1
		(h)	0-1
FA Cup	First Round	Bognor (a)	1-2

Gwinnett	Banks	Viney	Rogers	Taylor	Cooper	Rowbotham	Hiley	Langley	Neville	Harrower	Harris J	Vinnicombe	Withey	Batty	Dryden	Jones	Harris C	Walter	Roberts	Tupling	Smith	Parker	Benjamin	Heath	McDermott	Young	Miller	Match No.
1	2*	3	4	5	6	7	8	9	10	11	12																	1
1	2	3	4	5	6	7	8		10	11*	9	12																2
1	2		4	5	6	7	8		10	11			3	9														3
1	2		4	5	6*	7	8	12	10	11			3	9														4
1	2		4	5	6	7	8	12	10	11			3*	9														5
1	2		4	5	6	7	8	12	10	11				9	3*													6
1	2		4	5	6	7	8		10	11				9	3													7
1	2		4	5	6	7	8		10	11				9	3													8
1	2		4	5	6	7	8*		10	11			12	9	3													9
1	2		4	5	6	7	8*	12	10	11				9	3													10
1	2		4	5	6	7	8*	12	10	11				9	3													11
1	2		4	5	6	7		8	10	11		3		9														12
1	2		4	5	6	7	8	3*	10	11		12		9														13
1	2		4	5	6	7		8	10	11			12	9*		3												14
1	2		4	5		7	8	12	10	11			6*	9		3												15
1	2		4	5		7	8	12	10	11			6*	9		3												16
1	2	9*	4	5	6	7	8	10†		11	12	14				3												17
	2		4	5	6	7	8		10	11	12	9				3*		1										18
	2		4	5	6	7	8	11	10			9		3				1										19
	2		4	5	6	7	8	11	10			9						1	3									20
	2		4	5	6	7	8*	11	10			9					12	1	3									21
	2		4	5	6	7	14	11†	10*		12	9					8	1	3									22
	2		4	5	6	7	8		10			9					11	1		3								23
	2		4	5	6	7	8	11*	10†			9					12	1		3	14							24
	2		4	5	6	7			10			9					11*	1		3	8	12						25
	2		4	5	6	7			10			9					11*	1		3	14		8†	12				26
	2		4	5	12	7			10*			9					11	1		3	14		8	6†				27
	2		4	5	12	7			10			9					11*	1		3			8		6			28
	2		4	5	12	7			10†			9					11*	1		3	14		8		6			29
	2		4	5	12	7			10			9					11	1		3*			8		6			30
	2		4	5	10	7						9					11*	1			3		8	12	6			31
	2		4	5		7	11*					9†			3			1		12	14		8		6	10		32
	2		4	5		7	11					9			3			1			12		8		6	10*		33
	2		4	5		7	11					9*			3			1			12		8		6	10		34
			4	5		7	11	9							3			1					8	2	6	10		35
	2		4	5		7	11	9							3			1			12		8		6*	10		36
	14		4	5		7	11*	9							3			1			12		8	2†	6	10		37
	2		4	5		7	11	9*	10						3			1					8		6	12		38
	2		4	5		7	11*		10						3			1			12		8		6	9		39
	2		4	5		7	11		10						3*			1			12		8		6	9		40
	2		4	5			11		10						3		7*				12		8		6	9	1	41
	2		4	5		7	11		10						3								8		6	9	1	42
	2		4	5		7	11		10			12			3		9*						8		6		1	43
	2			5		7	11*		10†			4			3		12	1			14		8		6	9		44
	14		4	5		7	11		10			2†			3		12	1					8		6*	9		45
	2		4	5		7	11		10			8			3		12	1							6	9*		46
17	43 + 2s	3	45	46	25 + 4s	45	36 + 1s	14 + 7s	38	18	1 + 4s	21 + 4s	5 + 2s	15	21	5	11 + 5s	26	3	8 + 1s	2 + 13s	— + 1s	20	3 + 2s	19	13 + 1s	3	

EXETER CITY

Player and Position	Ht	Wt	Birth Date	Birth Place	Source	Clubs	League App	League Gls
Goalkeepers								
Mel Gwinnett‡	6 1	11 05	14 5 63	Worcester	Stourbridge	Peterborough U	—	—
						Hereford U	1	—
						Bradford C	—	—
						Exeter C	46	—
								—
Kevin Miller‡	6 1	12 10	11 4 70	Falmouth	Newquay	Exeter C	3	—
Richard Smeath*	6 0		6 6 70	Exeter	Trainee	Exeter C	—	—
David Walter	6 3	13 03	3 9 61	Barnstaple	Bideford T	Exeter C	26	—
Defenders								
Chris Banks*	5 8	10 08	12 11 65	Stone	Local	Port Vale	65	1
						Exeter C	45	1
Richard Dryden	6 0	11 02	14 6 69	Stroud		Bristol R	13	—
						Exeter C	21	—
Herbert Heath‡	6 0	12 08	29 3 70	Wolverhampto n	Darlaston	Exeter C	5	—
Lee Rogers	5 11	12 07	8 4 67	Bristol	Apprentice	Bristol C	30	—
						Hereford U (loan)	13	—
						York C (loan)	7	—
						Exeter C	45	—
Chris Small*			4 10 69	Exeter	Trainee	Exeter C	—	—
Shaun Taylor	6 1	13 00	26 3 63	Plymouth	Bideford	Exeter C	110	7
Keith Viney‡	5 11	11 11	26 10 57	Portsmouth	Apprentice	Portsmouth	166	3
						Exeter C	270	8
						Bristol R (loan)	3	—
Midfield								
Paul Batty	5 7	10 07	9 1 64	E Dington	Apprentice	Swindon T	108	7
						Chesterfield	26	—
						Exeter C	80	9
Richard Cooper‡	5 10	10 08	7 5 65	London	Amateur	Sheffield U	6	—
						Lincoln C	61	2
						Exeter C	62	2
Carl Harris*	5 9	11 00	3 11 56	Neath	Apprentice	Leeds U	154	26
						Charlton Ath	76	7
						Leeds U	—	—
						Bury	38	4
						Cardiff C	—	—
						Rochdale	25	3
						Exeter C	16	1
Steven Harrower	5 8	11 01	9 10 61	Exeter	Local	Exeter C	180	10
Scott Hiley	5 9	10 07	27 9 68	Plymouth	Trainee	Exeter C	52	6
Steve Neville	5 9	11 00	18 9 57	Walthamstow	Apprentice	Southampton	5	1
						Exeter C	93	22
						Sheffield U	49	6
						Exeter C (loan)	33	17
						Exeter C	59	10
						Bristol C	134	40
						Exeter C	38	14
Darren Rowbotham	5 10	11 05	22 10 66	Cardiff	Trainee	Plymouth Arg	46	2
						Exeter C	68	22
Chris Vinnicombe§	5 9	10 04	20 10 70	Exeter	Trainee	Exeter C	25	—
Forwards								
Ian Benjamin	5 11	12 00	11 12 61	Nottingham	Apprentice	Sheffield U	5	3
						WBA	2	—
						Notts Co	—	—
						Peterborough U	80	14
						Northampton T	150	59
						Cambridge U	25	2
						Chester C	22	2
						Exeter C	20	3

EXETER CITY

Foundation: Exeter City was formed in 1904 by the amalgamation of St. Sidwell's United and Exeter United. The club first played in the East Devon League and then the Plymouth & District League. After an exhibition match between West Bromwich Albion and Woolwich Arsenal was held to test interest as Exeter was then a rugby stronghold, Exeter City decided at a meeting at the Red Lion Hotel to turn professional in 1908.

Managers (and Secretary-managers)
Arthur Chadwick 1910–22, Fred Mavin 1923–27, Dave Wilson 1928–29, Billy McDevitt 1929–35, Jack English 1935–39, George Roughton 1945–52, Norman Kirkham 1952–53, Norman Dodgin 1953–57, Bill Thompson 1957–58, Frank Broome 1958–60, Glen Wilson 1960–62, Cyril Spiers 1962–63, Jack Edwards 1963–65, Ellis Stuttard 1965–66, Jock Basford 1966–67, Frank Broome 1967–69, Johnny Newman 1969–76, Bobby Saxton 1977–79, Brian Godfrey 1979–83, Gerry Francis 1983–84, Jim Iley 1984–85, Colin Appleton 1985–87, Terry Cooper 1988– .

Player and Position	*Ht*	*Wt*	*Birth Date*	*Birth Place*	*Source*	*Clubs*	*League App*	*League Gls*
Symon Burgher						Exeter C	14	—
Jamie Harris*	5 10	10 12	4 6 69	Exeter	Trainee	Exeter C	14	1
Tommy Langley‡	5 11	11 07	8 2 58	Lambeth	Apprentice	Chelsea	142	40
						QPR	25	8
						Crystal Palace	59	9
					AEK Athens	Coventry C	2	—
						Wolves	23	4
						Aldershot (loan)	16	4
					South China	Aldershot	81	21
						Exeter C	21	2
Brian McDermott	5 8	9 12	8 4 61	Slough	Apprentice	Arsenal	61	12
						Fulham (loan)	3	—
						Oxford U	24	2
						Huddersfield T (loan)	4	1
						Cardiff C	51	8
						Exeter C	19	1
Martin Parker§	6 0	11 06	3 1 70	Exeter	Trainee	Exeter C	1	—
Keith Smith*	5 10	11 07	17 10 63	Sheffield		Exeter C	15	2
Graham Withey‡	6 3	13 01	11 6 60	Bristol	Bath C	Bristol R	22	10
						Coventry C	22	4
						Cardiff C	27	7
						Bristol C	2	—
					Cheltenham T	Exeter C	7	2
Richard Young	6 3	13 07	31 12 68	Nottingham	Apprentice	Notts Co	35	5
						Southend U	9	—
						Exeter C	14	4

Trainees
Dugdale, James A; Hawkins, Jonathan D; Parker, Martin T; Smith, Stuart J; Vinnicombe, Christopher.

Associated Schoolboys
Annunziata, Lee; Braybrook, Steven J; Dunning, Paul A; Frankland, Tony; Garbin, Spencer, J; Murch, Stephen; Redwood, Toby R.B; Reed, Dean; Roddick, David M; Sercombe, Kevin J; Tidiman, Dominic S; Turvey, Mark A.

FULHAM 1988–89 *Back row (left to right):* Glen Thomas, Michael Cole, Jim Stannard, Shaun Gore, Laurence Batty, Jeff Eckhardt, Justin Skinner.
Centre row: Terry Bullivant (Club Coach), Steven Greaves, Kevin Hoddy, John Marshall, Gordon Davies, Peter Scott, Jack Burkett (Assistant Manager).
Front row: Wayne Kerrins, Richard Langley, Robert Wilson, Ray Lewington (Manager), Clive Walker, Gary Barnett, Gary Elkins.

Division 3 FULHAM

Craven Cottage, Stevenage Rd, Fulham, London SW6. Telephone 01-736 6561. Pools Office: 01-736 4634. Clubcall 0898 12 11 98

Ground capacity: 22,260.

Record attendance: 49, 335 v Millwall, Division 2, 8 Oct, 1938.

Record receipts: £80,247 v Chelsea, Division 2, 8 Oct, 1983.

Pitch measurements: 110yd × 75yd.

Chairman: Jimmy Hill.

Directors: Bill Muddyman (Vice-chairman), D. J. Gardner, C. A. Swain, A. Muddyman.

Manager: Ray Lewington. ***General Manager:*** Stuart Dalrymple. ***Assistant Manager:*** Jack Burkett.

Coach: Terry Bullivant. ***Physio:*** Peter Westacott.

Club Secretary: Mrs Yvonne Haines.

Commercial Manager: Steve Adams.

Year Formed: 1879. ***Turned Professional:*** 1898. ***Ltd Co.:*** 1903. ***Reformed:*** 1987.

Club Nickname: 'Cottagers'.

Previous Name: 1879–98, Fulham St Andrew's.

Previous Grounds: Lillie Road, Fulham Cross; Barn Elms, Barnes; Ranelagh House; Stansfield's Field, Fulham Road; Half-Moon Cricket Ground, Putney: 1896. Craven Cottage.

Record League Victory: 10-1 v Ipswich T, Division 1, 26th December 1963 – Macedo; Cohen, Langley; Mullery (1), Keetch, Robson (1); Key, Cook (1), Leggat (4), Haynes, Howfield (3).

Record Cup Victory: 6-0 v Wimbledon (away), FA Cup, 1st rd (replay), 3 December 1930 – Iceton; Gibbon, Lilley; Oliver, Dudley, Barrett; Temple, Hammond (1), Watkins (1), Gibbons (2), Penn (2). 6-0 v Bury, FA Cup, 3rd rd, 7 January 1938 – Turner; Bacuzzi, Keeping; Evans, Dennison, Tompkins; Higgins, Worsley, Rooke (6), O'Callaghan. Arnold.

Record Defeat: 0-10 v Liverpool, League Cup 2nd Rd, 1st leg. 23 September 1986.

Most League Points (2 for a win): 60, Division 2, 1958–59 and Division 3, 1970–71.

Most League Points (3 for a win): 78, Division 3, 1981–82.

Most League Goals: 111, Division 3 (S), 1931-32.

Highest League Scorer in Season: Frank Newton, 43, Division 3 (S), 1931–32.

Most League Goals in Total Aggregate: Bedford Jezzard, 154, 1948–56.

Most Capped Player: Johnny Haynes, 56, England.

Most League Appearances: Johnny Haynes, 594, 1952–70.

Record Transfer Fee Received: £333,333 from Liverpool for Richard Money, May 1980.

Record Transfer Fee Paid: £150,000 to Orient for Peter Kitchen, February 1979, and to Brighton & HA for Teddy Maybank, December 1979.

Football League Record: 1907 Elected to Division 2: 1928–32 Division 3 (S); 1932–49 Division 2; 1949–52 Division 1; 1952–59 Division 2; 1959–68 Division 1; 1968–69 Division 2; 1969–71 Division 3; 1971–80 Division 2; 1980–82 Division 3; 1982–86 Division 2; 1986– Division 3.

Honours: *Football League:* Division 1 best season: 10th. 1959–60; Division 2 – Champions 1948–49; Runners-up 1958–59; Division 3 (S) – Champions 1931–32; Division 3 – Runners-up 1970–71. *FA Cup:* Runners-up 1974–75. *Football League Cup* best season: 5th rd, 1967–68, 1970–71.

Colours: White shirts black trim, black shorts, white stockings black trim. **Change colours:** All red.

FULHAM 1988–89 LEAGUE RECORD

Match No.	Date	Venue	Opponents	Result	H/T Score	Lg. Pos.	Goalscorers	Attendance
1	Aug 27	A	Cardiff C	W 2-1	0-1	—	Sayer, Elkins	6024
2	Sept 3	H	Southend U	W 1-0	0-0	2	Davies	4754
3	10	A	Mansfield T	L 1-3	0-2	7	Sayer	2737
4	17	H	Bury	W 1-0	1-0	3	Cole	3754
5	20	A	Bolton W	L 2-3	1-1	—	Sayer, Peters	4239
6	24	H	Wigan Ath	D 1-1	0-1	7	Sayer	3431
7	Oct 1	A	Huddersfield T	L 0-2	0-0	11		4576
8	5	H	Wolverhampton W	D 2-2	0-1	—	Wilson, Skinner (pen)	4828
9	8	A	Bristol C	W 5-1	2-0	6	Peters, Sayer 2, Eckhardt, Marshall	8160
10	15	H	Aldershot	W 5-1	2-0	4	Sayer 2, Marshall, Barnett, Eckhardt	5101
11	22	A	Swansea C	L 0-2	0-1	9		4737
12	25	H	Northampton T	W 3-2	1-1	—	Skinner (pen), Barnett, Thomas (og)	4644
13	29	A	Notts Co	W 1-0	1-0	4	Walker	5514
14	Nov 5	H	Blackpool	D 1-1	0-0	8	Gordon	4760
15	8	H	Reading	W 2-1	1-1	—	Barnett, Sayer	6934
16	12	A	Sheffield U	L 0-1	0-1	7		11,087
17	26	A	Port Vale	L 0-3	0-1	8		5097
18	Dec 3	H	Bristol R	L 0-2	0-1	9		4461
19	17	H	Preston NE	W 2-1	1-0	8	Skinner (pen), Walker	3858
20	26	A	Gillingham	W 1-0	0-0	7	Davies	5871
21	31	A	Chesterfield	L 1-4	0-2	10	Walker	3086
22	Jan 2	H	Brentford	D 3-3	2-2	9	Scott, Davies 2	8120
23	7	H	Chester C	W 4-1	3-0	6	Scott, Walker, Barnett, Davies	4196
24	13	A	Southend U	D 0-0	0-0	—		4844
25	21	H	Mansfield T	D 1-1	1-1	7	Davies	4148
26	28	A	Bury	L 1-3	0-1	8	Barnett	3582
27	Feb 4	H	Huddersfield T	L 1-2	0-0	10	Walker (pen)	4081
28	11	A	Wolverhampton W	L 2-5	1-4	10	Davies, Rougvie	15,621
29	18	H	Bristol C	W 3-1	1-1	9	Walker, Davies, Marshall	4408
30	28	A	Northampton T	L 1-2	1-2	—	Skinner (pen)	3948
31	Mar 4	H	Swansea C	W 1-0	0-0	9	Marshall	4710
32	11	A	Blackpool	W 1-0	0-0	9	Skinner (pen)	3014
33	14	H	Notts Co	W 2-1	1-0	—	Davies 2	3402
34	18	H	Cardiff C	W 2-0	1-0	6	Marshall, Skinner	4261
35	24	A	Brentford	W 1-0	0-0	—	Cole	10,851
36	27	H	Gillingham	L 1-2	0-0	7	Marshall	6476
37	Apr 1	A	Preston NE	W 4-1	2-1	5	Davies 2, Walker, Gordon	8190
38	5	A	Chester C	L 0-7	0-2	—		2121
39	8	H	Chesterfield	W 2-1	0-0	5	Marshall, Sayer	4252
40	15	H	Bolton W	D 1-1	0-0	5	Skinner	4950
41	22	A	Wigan Ath	W 1-0	0-0	5	Thomas	3056
42	25	A	Aldershot	W 2-1	0-0	—	Walker, Davies	3841
43	29	H	Sheffield U	D 2-2	1-1	5	Scott, Davies	7794
44	May 1	A	Reading	W 1-0	1-0	4	Skinner	5152
45	6	A	Bristol R	D 0-0	0-0	4		7302
46	13	H	Port Vale	L 1-2	1-0	4	Cole	6257

Final League Position: 4

GOALSCORERS

League (69): Davies 14, Sayer 10, Skinner 8 (5 pens), Walker 8 (1 pen), Marshall 7, Barnett 5, Cole 3, Scott 3, Eckhardt 2, Gordon 2, Peters 2, Elkins 1, Rougvie 1, Thomas 1, Wilson 1, own goal 1.
Littlewoods Cup (2): Sayer 1, Skinner 1 (pen).
FA Cup (0).

Littlewoods Cup	First Round	Brentford (h)	2-2
		(a)	0-1
FA Cup	First Round	Colchester U (h)	0-1

Stannard	Langley	Eckhardt	Wilson	Elkins	Thomas	Skinner	Sayer	Barnett	Cole	Walker	Davies	Hoddy	Marshall	Scott	Peters	Mauge	Gore	Gordon	Kerrins	Cawley	Donnellan	Rougvie	Batty	*Match No.*
1	2	3	4	5	6	7	8	9	10	11														1
1	2	3	4	5	6	7	8	9†	10*	11	12	14												2
1	2	5	4	3	6	8	9	7	10	11*		12												3
1	2	5	4	3	6	8	9	7	10	11*			12											4
1	2	5	4	3	6	8*	9	7	10		12			11†	14									5
1	2	5	4	3	6	8	9*	7	10†		12				14	11								6
1		5	4		6	8	9	7	10†		12		14		2	11*	3							7
1		5	4		6	8*	9	7			10		3	12	2	11								8
1	3	5	4		6	8	9	11					7		2	12		10*						9
1	3	5	4		6	8	9	11					7		2			10						10
1	3*	5	4		6	8†	9	11		12			7	14	2			10						11
1	3†	5	4		6	8*	9	11		12			7	14	2			10						12
1		6	4		3		9*	7		11			2	8			5	10	12					13
1		6	4		3		9*	7		11	12		2	8			5	10						14
1		6	4		3		9	7		11			2	8			5	10						15
1		6	4		3	12	9	7*		11			2	8	5			10						16
1		6	4			12	9	7*		11			2	8			5	10	3					17
1		6	4†	14			9	7	12	11			2	8			5	10*	3					18
1		6		3		4		7	9	11	10		2	8						5				19
1		6		3	5	4		7	9	11	10		2	8										20
1		6		3		4	12	7*	9	11	10		2	8						5				21
1		6†		3	14	4*	12	7	9	11	10		2	8						5				22
1		6	4*	3	5			7	9	11	10†		2	8						12	14			23
1		6	4	3	5*			7†	9	11	10		2	8						12	14			24
1	5	6	4	3				7*	9	11	10		2	8							12			25
1		6	4	3	5	12		7*	9†	11	10		2	8				14						26
1		6	4*	3	5	12		7	9†	11	10		2	8				14						27
1			4	3	5			7	9	11	10		2	8								6		28
1	2			3	6	4			9*	11	10		7	8							12	5		29
1	2			3	6	4	12		9†		10		7	8				14	11*			5		30
1	2	6			3	4	11		9		10		7	8								5		31
1	2	6			3	4			9	11	10		7	8								5		32
1	2	6			3	4			9	11	10		7	8								5		33
1	2	6			3	4			9	11	10		7	8								5		34
1	2	6			3	4			9	11	10*		7	8				12				5		35
	2	6	8*		3	4	12		9	11†	10		7					14				5	1	36
1		6				4			9	11	10		7	8		2		3				5		37
1		6	12		14	4*			9	11	10		7	8		2		3†				5		38
1		6		5	3	4	12		9	11	10*		7	8		2								39
1		6			3	4	12		9*	11	10		7	8		2						5		40
1		6			3	4			9	11	10		7	8		2						5		41
1		6	12		3	4	14		9†	11	10*		7	8		2						5		42
1		6			3	4	12		9*	11	10		7	8		2						5		43
1		6			3	4			9	11	10		7	8		2						5		44
1		6		12	3	4			9	11	10*		7	8		2						5		45
1		6		2	3	4	12		9	11	10*		7	8								5		46
45	19	43	25 + 2s	20 + 2s	38 + 2s	34 + 4s	19 + 9s	28	35 + 1s	36 + 2s	29 + 5s	— + 2s	39 + 2s	34 + 3s	7 + 2s	12 + 1s	6	12 + 5s	3 + 1s	3 + 2s	— + 4s	18	1	

FULHAM

Player and Position	Ht	Wt	Birth Date	Birth Place	Source	Clubs	League App	League Gls
Goalkeepers								
Laurence Batty	6 0	13 07	15 2 64	London	Farense	Fulham	5	—
						Crystal Palace (loan)	—	—
Jim Stannard	6 0	13 06	6 10 62	London	Local	Fulham	41	—
						Charlton Ath (loan)	1	—
						Southend U (loan)	17	—
						Southend U	92	—
						Fulham	91	—
Defenders								
Jeff Eckhardt	5 11	11 06	7 10 65	Sheffield		Sheffield U	74	2
						Fulham	72	3
Gary Elkins	5 8	10 10	4 5 66	Wallingford	Apprentice	Fulham	94	1
Shaun Gore	6 4	13 01	21 9 68	London		Fulham	26	—
Richard Langley	5 7	11 05	20 3 65	London	Cor. Cas.	Fulham	35	—
Gary Peters‡	5 11	11 12	3 8 54	Carshalton	Apprentice	Aldershot	—	—
					Guildford C	Reading	156	7
						Fulham	64	2
						Wimbledon	83	7
						Aldershot	17	1
						Reading	100	4
						Fulham	9	2
Doug Rougvie	6 2	13 08	24 5 56	Ballingry		Aberdeen	178	19
						Chelsea	74	3
						Brighton & H A	35	2
						Shrewsbury T	21	3
						Fulham	18	1
Glen Thomas	6 0	11 06	6 10 67	London	Apprentice	Fulham	68	1
Midfield								
Leo Donnellan	5 10	11 05	19 1 65	Brent	Apprentice	Chelsea		
						Orient (loan)	6	—
						Fulham	68	4
Steve Greaves	5 9	11 03	17 1 70	London	Trainee	Fulham	1	—
						Waterford (loan)	—	—
Kevin Hoddy*	5 10	11 01	6 1 68	Essex	Apprentice	Fulham	22	1
Wayne Kerrins*	5 8	11 02	5 8 65	Essex	Apprentice	Fulham	66	1
						Port Vale (loan)	7	—
						Leyton Orient (loan)	3	—
Ray Lewington	5 6	11 08	7 9 56	Lambeth	Apprentice	Chelsea	85	4
					Vancouver W	Wimbledon (loan)	23	—
						Fulham	174	20
						Sheffield U	36	—
						Fulham	56	1
John Marshall	5 10	11 04	18 8 64	Surrey	Apprentice	Fulham	194	17
Peter Scott	5 8	10 10	1 10 63	London	Apprentice	Fulham	174	21
Justin Skinner	6 0	11 03	30 1 69	London	Apprentice	Fulham	73	14
Robert Wilson	5 10	11 11	5 6 61	Kensington	Apprentice	Fulham	175	34
						Millwall	28	12
						Luton T	24	1
						Fulham	47	4
Forwards								
Kenny Achampong	5 9	10 10	26 6 66	London	Apprentice	Fulham	81	15
						West Ham U (loan)	—	—
Gary Barnett	5 5	9 04	11 3 63	Stratford	Apprentice	Coventry C	—	—
						Oxford U	45	9
						Wimbledon (loan)	5	1
						Fulham (loan)	2	1
						Fulham	148	29

FULHAM

Foundation: Churchgoers were responsible for the foundation of Fulham, which first saw the light of day as Fulham St. Andrew's Church Sunday School FC in 1879. They won the West London Amateur Cup in 1887 and the championship of the West London League in its initial season of 1892–93. The name Fulham had been adopted in 1888.

Managers (and Secretary-managers)
Harry Bradshaw 1904–09, Phil Kelso 1909–24, Andy Ducat 1924–26, Joe Bradshaw 1926–29, Ned Liddell 1929–31, Jim MacIntyre 1931–34, Jim Hogan 1934–35, Jack Peart 1935–48, Frank Osborne 1948–64 (was secretary-manager or GM for most of this period), Bill Dodgin Snr 1949–53, Duggie Livingstone 1956–58, Bedford Jezzard 1958–64 (GM for last two months), Vic Buckingham 1965–68, Bobby Robson 1968, Bill Dodgin Jnr 1969–72, Alec Stock 1972–76, Bobby Campbell 1976–80, Malcolm Macdonald 1980–84, Ray Harford 1984–86, Ray Lewington 1986– .

Player and Position	*Ht*	*Wt*	*Birth Date*	*Birth Place*	*Source*	*Clubs*	*League App*	*League Gls*
Michael Cole	5 11	11 04	3 9 66	Stepney	Amateur	Ipswich T	38	3
						Port Vale (loan)	4	1
						Fulham	45	4
Gordon Davies	5 7	10 12	3 8 55	Merthyr	Merthyr T	Fulham	247	113
						Chelsea	13	6
						Manchester C	31	9
						Fulham	94	33
Colin Gordon	6 1	12 12	17 1 63	Stourbridge	Oldbury U	Swindon T	72	33
						Wimbledon	3	—
						Gillingham (loan)	4	2
						Reading	24	9
						Bristol C (loan)	8	4
						Fulham	17	2
Jason Howes	5 8	11 02	24 9 70	London		Fulham	—	—
Ron Mauge			10 3 69	Islington	Trainee	Charlton Ath	—	—
						Fulham	13	—
Chris Pike*	6 2	13 03	19 10 61	Cardiff	Barry T	Fulham	42	4
						Cardiff C (loan)	6	2
Andy Sayer	5 9	10 12	6 6 66	Brent	Apprentice	Wimbledon	58	15
						Cambridge U (loan)	5	—
						Fulham	28	10
Clive Walker	5 8	11 04	26 5 57	Oxford	Apprentice	Chelsea	198	60
						Sunderland	50	10
						QPR	21	1
						Fulham	64	16

Trainees
Blades, Andrew A; Eaton, Nicholas; Ferney, Martin J; French, Gavin; German, Paul N; Kemp, Finlay C; King, Jason; Onwere, Udo A; Power, Mark K; Sutton, David G; Tucker, Mark J; Vertannes, Desmond M.S.

Associated Schoolboys
Armitage, James A; Bryant, James P; Day, Geoffrey A; Gale, Anthony; Harrison, John E; Humphries, Gavin D; Lewis, Leon J; Nguyen, Peter.

GILLINGHAM 1988–89 *Back row (left to right):* Andy Perry, David Smith, George Burley, Mark Weatherly, Ivan Haines, Jason Lillis, Steve Lovell, Ian Docker, Malcolm Smith.
Centre row: Brian Clarke, Gary West, Alan Walker, Ron Hillyard, Phil Kite, Steve O'Brien, Mark Cooper, Jerry Williams.
Front row: George Shipley, Gavin Peacock, Keith Blunt (Assistant Manager), Keith Burkinshaw (Manager), Damien Richardson (Youth Team Manager), Paul Haylock, Trevor Quow.

Division 4 **GILLINGHAM**

Priestfield Stadium, Gillingham. Telephone Medway (0634) 51854/576828. Commercial Office: 51462.

Ground capacity: 19,581.

Record attendance: 23,002 v QPR, FA Cup 3rd rd. 10 Jan, 1948.

Record receipts: £35,070 v Everton, FA Cup 4th rd, 2nd replay, 4 Feb, 1984.

Pitch measurements: 114yd × 75yd.

President: J. W. Leech. ***Vice-Presidents:*** G. B. Goodere, G. V. W. Lukehurst, B. B. Moore.

Chairman: M. G. Lukehurst. ***Vice-Chairman:*** Rt. Hon. Earl Henry Sondes.

Directors: P. H. Giles FCA. ***Managing Director:*** A. Smith.

Manager: Damien Richardson. ***Assistant Manager:***

Coach: ***Physio:*** Javed Mughal.

Club Secretary: Barry Bright. ***Commercial Manager:*** Mrs Kay Carver.

Year Formed: 1893. ***Turned Professional:*** 1894. ***Ltd Co.:*** 1893.

Club Nickname: 'The Gills'.

Previous Name: New Brompton, 1893–1913.

Record League Victory: 10-0 v Chesterfield, Division 3, 5 September 1987 – Kite; Haylock, Pearce, Shipley (2) (Lillis), West, Greenall (1), Pritchard (2), Shearer (2), Lovell, Elsey (2), David Smith (1).

Record Cup Victory: 10-0 v Gorleston, FA Cup, 1st rd, 16 November 1957 – Brodie; Parry, Hannaway; Riggs, Boswell, Laing; Payne, Fletcher (2), Saunders (5), Morgan (1), Clark (2).

Record Defeat: 2-9 v Nottingham F, Division 3 (S), 18 November, 1950.

Most League Points (2 for a win): 62, Division 4, 1973–74.

Most League Points (3 for a win): 83, Division 3, 1984–85.

Most League Goals: 90, Division 4, 1973–74.

Highest League Scorer in Season: Ernie Morgan, 31, Division 3 (S), 1954–55 and Brian Yeo, 31, Division 4, 1973–74.

Most League Goals in Total Aggregate: Brian Yeo. 135, 1963–75.

Most Capped Player: Tony Cascarino, 3 (15), Republic of Ireland.

Most League Appearances: John Simpson, 571, 1957–72.

Record Transfer Fee Received: £235,000 from Oxford U for Colin Greenall, February 1988.

Record Transfer Fee Paid: £102,500 to Tottenham H for Mark Cooper, October 1987.

Football League Record: 1920 Original Member of Division 3; 1921 Division 3 (S); 1938 Failed re-election; Southern League 1938–44; Kent League 1944–46; Southern League 1946–50; 1950 Re-elected to Division 3 (S); 1958–64 Division 4; 1964–71 Division 3; 1971–74 Division 4; 1974–89 Division 3;1989– Division 4.

Honours: *Football League:* Division 3 best season: 4th, 1978–79, 1984–85; Division 4 – Champions 1963–64; Runners-up 1973–74. *FA Cup* best season: 5th rd. 1969–70. *Football League Cup* best season; 4th rd. 1964.

Colours: Royal blue shirts white trim, white shorts blue trim, white stockings. **Change colours:** White shirts blue trim, white shorts blue trim, white stockings.

GILLINGHAM 1988–89 LEAGUE RECORD

Match No.	Date	Venue	Opponents	Result	H/T Score	Lg. Pos.	Goalscorers	Attendance
1	Aug 27	H	Swansea C	L 2-3	1-1	—	Peacock, Lovell	4437
2	Sept 3	A	Aldershot	W 2-0	1-0	10	Shipley, Lovell	2477
3	10	H	Sheffield U	W 2-1	1-1	5	Lovell, Lillis	5041
4	17	A	Huddersfield T	D 1-1	0-0	6	Lovell	4688
5	20	A	Mansfield T	L 1-2	0-0	—	Lovell	3153
6	24	H	Reading	L 0-1	0-1	13		4469
7	Oct 1	A	Brentford	L 0-1	0-0	18		4839
8	4	H	Bristol C	L 0-1	0-1	—		3102
9	8	H	Chesterfield	L 0-1	0-1	20		2901
10	15	A	Southend U	L 1-2	0-1	21	Lovell	3200
11	22	H	Bury	L 3-4	1-3	21	Lillis, Lovell (pen), Cooper	2850
12	25	A	Preston NE	L 0-5	0-2	—		6390
13	29	H	Wolverhampton W	L 1-3	0-1	22	Lovell	5288
14	Nov 5	A	Cardiff C	L 0-1	0-0	22		3658
15	8	H	Blackpool	W 1-0	1-0	—	Burley	3541
16	12	A	Bristol R	L 0-2	0-0	22		4826
17	26	A	Notts Co	W 2-1	1-1	22	Quow, Smith	4611
18	Dec 3	H	Chester C	L 0-2	0-1	22		3329
19	18	A	Northampton T	W 2-1	0-0	—	Lovell 2(1pen)	3829
20	26	H	Fulham	L 0-1	0-0	22		5871
21	30	H	Port Vale	W 1-0	0-0	22	Cooper	4706
22	Jan 2	A	Wigan Ath	L 0-3	0-2	22		3090
23	6	A	Bolton W	L 1-2	0-1	—	Peacock	4187
24	14	H	Aldershot	D 1-1	1-0	23	Peacock	3781
25	21	A	Sheffield U	L 2-4	0-3	23	West, Cooper	9336
26	28	H	Huddersfield T	L 1-2	1-1	23	Peacock (pen)	3530
27	Feb 4	H	Brentford	D 0-0	0-0	24		4002
28	11	A	Bristol C	L 0-1	0-0	24		7319
29	18	A	Chesterfield	L 1-3	0-1	24	Lovell	3432
30	25	H	Southend U	D 1-1	1-0	24	Walker	3574
31	28	H	Preston NE	L 1-3	1-0	—	Burley	3031
32	Mar 4	A	Bury	L 0-1	0-1	24		4313
33	11	H	Cardiff C	L 1-2	0-2	24	Boyle (og)	2927
34	14	A	Wolverhampton W	L 1-6	0-4	—	Gavin	12,574
35	19	A	Swansea C	L 2-3	0-2	—	Gavin, Lillis	4252
36	24	H	Wigan Ath	W 2-1	0-1	—	Gavin, Peacock	3244
37	27	A	Fulham	W 2-1	0-0	24	Peacock 2	6476
38	Apr 1	H	Northampton T	W 1-0	0-0	23	Gavin	3466
39	4	H	Bolton W	L 0-1	0-1	—		3096
40	8	A	Port Vale	L 1-2	0-1	24	Lovell	5358
41	15	H	Mansfield T	W 3-0	0-0	23	Gavin, Peacock, Joseph	2594
42	22	A	Reading	W 2-1	1-0	23	Lovell, Gavin	3511
43	28	H	Bristol R	L 2-3	1-0	—	Lovell (pen), Smith	4044
44	May 1	A	Blackpool	L 1-4	1-1	23	Peacock	2152
45	6	A	Chester C	L 0-2	0-1	23		2106
46	13	H	Notts Co	W 2-1	2-0	23	Gavin, Manuel	2877

Final League Position: 23

GOALSCORERS

League (47): Lovell 14 (3 pens), Peacock 9 (1 pen), Gavin 7, Cooper 3, Lillis 3, Burley 2, Smith 2, Joseph 1, Manuel 1, Quow 1, Shipley 1, Walker 1, West 1, own goal 1.
Littlewoods Cup (6): Lillis 2, Lovell 2, Quow 1 (pen), Walker 1.
FA Cup (3): Lovell 1, Quow 1, Smith 1.

Littlewoods Cup	First Round	Cambridge U (a)	2-1
		(h)	3-1
	Second Round	Millwall (a)	0-3
		(h)	1-3
FA Cup	First Round	Peterborough U (h)	3-3
		(a)	0-1

Hillyard	Burley	Haylock	Peacock	Clarke	Walker	Shipley	Quow	Lovell	Cooper	Smith, D	Lillis	Weatherly	West	Williams	Perry	Docker	Kite	Haines	Walford	Stimson	Eeles	O'Shea	Reeves	Manuel	Joseph	Beadle	Gavin	Guscott	*Match No.*
1	2	3	4	5	6	7	8	9	10*	11	12																		1
1	2	3	4	5*	6	7	8	9	14	11	10†	12																	2
1	2	3	4		6	7†	8	9		11	10*	12	5	14															3
1	2	3	4	6			8	9		11*	10	7	5		12														4
1	2	3	4	6			8	9		11	10	7*	5		12														5
1	2	3	4		6		8	9		11	10*		5		7	12													6
	2	3*	4	5	6		8	9	10	12		11			7		1												7
	2	3	4	5	6		8*	9	12	11		10			7		1												8
	2	3	4	5	6		8†	9		11	12	10			7*	14	1												9
	2	3	4	5	6		8	9	11		12	10			7*		1												10
	2	3	4	5	6		8	9	11		7*	10		12			1												11
	2	3	4		6		8	9	7*	11	12	10†	5	14			1												12
	2	3	4	5	6		12	9		14	8*	10		7		11†	1												13
	2	3	4		6		8*	9		11	7	5†			12	10	1	14											14
	2	3	4		6			9	12	11	7*				8	10	1	5											15
	2	3	4		6	7*		9	12	11	8					10	1	5											16
	2	3	4		6		8	9*	7	11	12					10	1	5											17
	2	3	4		6	10	8	9*	7	11	12					5	1												18
	2	3	4			7		9	8	11						10	1	5	6										19
	2	3	4			7*	12	9	8	11						10	1	5	6										20
	2	3	4			7	12	9	8	11						10*	1	5	6										21
	2	3	4			10	8	9	7*			12		14		11	1	5	6†										22
	2	3	4			8	12	9	7*	11		6	14			10	1	5†											23
	2	3	4			8		9		11		6	5	7		10	1												24
	2	7	4		6			9*	8	11			5		12	10†	1	14		3									25
	2	10	4			12			9	11			5		7		1	6		3	8*								26
	2	14	4*		6	7†		9		11	12		5			10	1			3		8							27
	2				5	12		9		11	10*					8	1			3		7	4	6					28
	2	10	4		5†			9*		11	12					8	1			3		7	6	14					29
	2		4		5			9		11					8	10	1			3		7	6						30
	2		4*		5			9		11	12					10	1			3		8	6		7				31
	2		4					9		11	10*				12	5	1			3			6	8	7				32
	2		4					9*		11						10	1			3	7		6	5	8	12			33
1	2		4†											14		10				3	7*		6	5	8	11	9	12	34
1	2									11	12			7		10				3		4	6	5	8*		9		35
1	2		12							11				7		10				3		4	6	5*	8		9		36
1	2		4							11				7*		10				3		5	6	14	8		9	12†	37
1	2		4							11				7*		10				3		5	6	12	8		9		38
1	2		4							11				7*		10				3		5	6†	12	8		9		39
1	2		4					12		11				14		10				3		5	6	7†	8*		9		40
1	2		4					8		11						10				3		5	6	7	12		9*		41
1	2	14	4					8		11						10				3		5†	6	7	12		9*		42
1	2		7					10		11		4				3*						5	6	8	12		9		43
1	2	3	4					8		11		10†				14						5	6	7	12		9*		44
1	2	14	4					8		11*						3						5†	6	7	12		9		45
1	2		4					8		11						3		6				10		7			9		46
19	46	28 + 3s	43 + 1s	10	22	12 + 2s	16 + 4s	38 + 1s	14 + 4s	40 + 2s	12 + 10s	14 + 3s	9 + 1s	7 + 6s	8 + 5s	32 + 3s	27	10 + 2s	4	18	3	17	18	13 + 4s	10 + 5s	1 + 1s	13	— + 2s	

Pearson — Match No. 39(14) 45(10) 46(5)

GILLINGHAM

Player and Position	Ht	Wt	Birth Date	Birth Place	Source	Clubs	League App	League Gls
Goalkeepers								
Ron Hillyard	5 11	11 04	31 3 53	Rotherham	Amateur	York C	61	—
						Hartlepool U (loan)	23	—
						Bury (loan)	—	—
						Brighton & HA (loan)	—	—
						Gillingham	517	—
Phil Kite	6 1	14 07	26 10 62	Bristol	Apprentice	Bristol R	96	—
						Tottenham H (loan)	—	—
						Southampton	4	—
						Middlesbrough	2	—
						(loan)	70	—
						Gillingham		
Steve O'Brien*	5 8	10 06	18 1 71	Dublin		Gillingham	—	—
Defenders								
Les Berry‡	6 2	11 13	4 5 56	Plumstead	Apprentice	Charlton Ath	358	11
						Brighton & HA	23	—
						Gillingham (loan)	11	—
						Gillingham	20	—
George Burley*	5 9	11 00	3 6 56	Cumnock	Apprentice	Ipswich T	394	5
						Sunderland	54	—
						Gillingham	46	2
Brian Clarke	6 3	13 08	10 10 68	Eastbourne	School	Gillingham	10	—
Ian Docker	5 8	11 02	12 9 69	Gravesend	Trainee	Gillingham	36	—
Paul Haylock	5 8	11 00	24 3 63	Lowestoft	Apprentice	Norwich C	155	3
						Gillingham	108	—
Billy Manuel	5 5	10 00	28 6 69	Hackney	Apprentice	Tottenham H	—	—
						Gillingham	17	1
Tim O'Shea	5 11	11 04	12 11 66	London	School	Tottenham H	3	—
						Newport Co (loan)	10	—
						Leyton Orient	3	1
						Gillingham	17	—
Lee Palmer§			19 9 70	Gillingham	Trainee	Gillingham	1	—
Ricky Pearson§	5 11	10 09	18 10 70	Maidstone	Trainee	Gillingham	3	—
Alan Walker	6 1	12 07	17 12 59	Mossley	Telford U	Lincoln C	75	4
						Millwall	92	8
						Gillingham	29	1
Midfield								
Peter Beadle§			13 5 72	London	Trainee		2	—
Tony Eeles§	5 7	9 12	15 11 70	Chatham	Trainee	Gillingham	3	—
Lindon Guscott§			29 3 72	London	Trainee	Gillingham	2	—
Ivan Haines	5 9	10 12	14 9 68	Chatham		Gillingham	13	—
Jason Lillis‡	5 11	11 10	1 10 69	Chatham	Trainee	Gillingham	29	3
Gavin Peacock	5 7	11 00	18 11 67	Kent		QPR	17	—
						Gillingham	70	11
George Shipley*	5 8	10 08	7 3 59	Newcastle	Apprentice	Southampton	3	—
						Reading (loan)	12	1
						Blackpool (loan)	—	—
						Lincoln C	223	39
						Charlton Ath	61	6
						Gillingham	29	3
Malcolm Smith*	5 7	11 04	3 8 70	Maidstone	Trainee	Gillingham	2	—
Mark Weatherly*	6 0	11 12	18 1 58	Ramsgate	Apprentice	Gillingham	457	47
Jerry Williams	5 11	11 10	24 3 60	Didcot	Apprentice	Reading	309	17
						Gillingham	13	—

GILLINGHAM

Foundation: The success of the pioneering Royal Engineers of Chatham excited the interest of the residents of the Medway Towns and led to the formation of many clubs including Excelsior. After winning the Kent Junior Cup and the Chatham District League in 1893, Excelsior decided to go for bigger things and it was at a meeting in the Napier Arms, Brompton, in 1893 that New Brompton FC came into being as a professional concern, securing the use of a ground in Priestfield Road.

Managers (and Secretary-managers)
W. Ironside Groombridge 1896–1906* (previously financial secretary), Steve Smith 1906–08, W. I. Groombridge 1908–19*, George Collins 1919–20, John McMillan 1920–23, Harry Curtis 1923–26, Albert Hoskins 1926–29, Dick Hendrie 1929–31, Fred Maven 1932–37, Alan Ure 1937–38, Bill Harvey 1938–39, Archie Clark 1939–58, Harry Barratt 1958–62, Freddie Cox 1962–65, Basil Hayward 1966–71, Andy Nelson 1971–74, Len Ashurst 1974–75, Gerry Summers 1975–81, Keith Peacock 1981–87, Paul Taylor 1988, Keith Burkinshaw 1988–89, Damien Richardson 1989– .

Player and Position	*Ht*	*Wt*	*Birth Date*	*Birth Place*	*Source*	*Clubs*	*League App*	*League Gls*
Forwards								
Pat Gavin	6 0	12 00	5 6 67	Hammersmith	Hanwell T	Gillingham	13	7
Francis Joseph	5 10	12 00	6 3 60	Kilburn	Hillingdon B	Wimbledon	51	14
						Brentford	110	44
						Wimbledon (loan)	5	1
						Reading	11	2
						Bristol R (loan)	3	—
						Aldershot (loan)	10	2
						Sheffield U	13	3
						Gillingham	15	1
Steve Lovell	5 9	12 03	16 7 60	Swansea	Apprentice	Crystal Palace	74	3
						Stockport Co (loan)	12	—
						Millwall	146	44
						Swansea C (loan)	2	1
						Gillingham	91	40
Andy Perry	5 8	10 03	28 12 62	Dulwich		Portsmouth	4	—
						Gillingham	13	—
David Smith	6 0	11 00	25 6 61	Sidcup	Welling U	Gillingham	104	10

Trainees
Barlow, Wayne; Beadle, Peter C; Eeles, Anthony G; Guscott, Lindon; Hume, Lloyd; Jones, Mark; Jordan, David C; Norris, Russell; Paddon, Guy J; Palmer, Lee J; Pearson, Richard; Thompson, Steven.

GRIMSBY TOWN 1988–89 *Back row (left to right):* Paul Agnew, Richard O'Kelly, Marc North, Steve Sherwood, Andy Tilson, Paul Reece, Keith Alexander, Tommy Williams, Sean Cunnington.
Front row: Mark Geeson (Physiotherapist), Scott McGarvey, Steve Stoutt, Andy Dixon, Alan Buckley (Manager), Kevin Jobling, John McDermott, Chris Grocock, Arthur Mann (Assistant Manager and Youth Team Coach).

Division 4 GRIMSBY TOWN

Blundell Park, Cleethorpes, South Humberside DN35 7PY. Telephone Cleethorpes (0472) 697111. Clubcall 0898 12 15 76

Ground capacity: 20,865.

Record attendance: 31,651 v Wolverhampton W, FA Cup 5th rd. 20 Feb, 1937.

Record receipts: £44,137 v Norwich C, Milk Cup 5th rd. 16 Jan, 1985.

Pitch measurements: 111yd × 74yd.

Presidents: T. J. Lindley, T. Wilkinson.

Chairman: P. W. Furneaux. ***Vice-Chairman:***

Directors: P. W. Furneaux (Chairman), T. Aspinall (Vice-Chairman), B. G. Glover, W. R. Ramsden, W. H. Carr, G. W. Duffield.

Manager: Alan Buckley. ***Assistant Manager:*** Arthur Mann.

Coach:

Company Secretary: I. Fleming. ***Commercial Director:*** Brian Glover.

Physio: Peter Jellett.

Year Formed. 1878. ***Turned Professional:*** 1890. ***Ltd Co.:*** 1890.

Club Nickname: The Mariners'.

Previous Name: Grimsby Pelham.

Previous Grounds: Clee Park; Abbey Park.

Record League Victory: 9-2 v Darwen, Division 2, 15 April 1899 – Bagshaw; Lockie, Nidd; Griffiths, Bell (1), Nelmes; Jenkinson (3), Richards (1), Cockshutt (3), Robinson, Chadburn (1).

Record Cup Victory: 8-0 v Darlington, FA Cup, 2nd rd, 21 November 1885 – G. Atkinson; J. H. Taylor, H. Taylor; Hall, Kimpson, Hopewell; H. Atkinson (1), Garnham, Seal (3), Sharman, Monument (4).

Record Defeat: 1-9 v Arsenal, Division 1, 28 January, 1931.

Most League Points (2 for a win): 68, Division 3 (N), 1955–56.

Most League Points (3 for a win): 70, Division 2, 1983–84.

Most League Goals: 103, Division 2, 1933–34.

Highest League Scorer in Season: Pat Glover, 42, Division 2, 1933–34.

Most League Goals in Total Aggregate: Pat Glover, 182. 1930–39.

Most Capped Player: Pat Glover, 7, Wales.

Most League Appearances: Keith Jobling, 448, 1953–69.

Record Transfer Fee Received: £300,000 from Everton for Paul Wilkinson, March 1985.

Record Transfer Fee Paid: £110,000 to Watford for James Gilligan, July 1985.

Football League Record: 1892 Original Member Division 2; 1901–03 Division 1; 1903 Division 2; 1910 Failed Re-election; 1911 Re-elected Division 2; 1920–21 Division 3; 1921–26 Division 3 (N); 1926–29 Division 2; 1929–32 Division 1; 1932–34 Division 2; 1934–48 Division 1; 1948–51 Division 2; 1951–56 Division 3 (N); 1956–59 Division 2; 1959–62 Division 3; 1962–64 Division 2; 1964–68 Division 3; 1968–72 Division 4; 1972–77 Division 3; 1977–79 Division 4; 1979–80 Division 3; 1980–87 Division 2; 1987–88 Division 3; 1988– Division 4.

Honours: *Football League:* Division 1 best season: 5th, 1934–35; Division 2 – Champions 1900–01, 1933–34; Runners-up 1928–29; Division 3 (N) – Champions 1925–26, 1955–56. Runners-up 1951–52; Division 3 – Champions 1979–80; Runners-up 1961–62, Division 4 – Champions 1971–72; Runners-up 1978–79. *FA Cup:* Semi-finals, 1936, 1939. *Football League Cup:* best season: 5th rd. 1979–80, 1984–85. *League Group Cup:* Winners. 1981–82.

Colours: Black and white vertical striped shirts, black shorts with white stripe on side, white stockings with red and black band on turnover. **Change colours:** Black and red striped shirts, red with black stripe shorts, red with black and white band on turnover stockings.

GRIMSBY TOWN 1988–89 LEAGUE RECORD

Match No.	Date	Venue	Opponents	Result	H/T Score	Lg. Pos.	Goalscorers	Attendance
1	Aug 27	A	Cambridge U	L 1-4	1-2	—	Stoutt	2290
2	Sept 3	H	Torquay U	W 1-0	0-0	14	North	2889
3	10	A	Scunthorpe U	D 1-1	1-1	13	Alexander	6037
4	17	H	Rotherham U	L 0-4	0-3	17		3697
5	20	A	Wrexham	W 2-1	2-1	—	Jobling, North	2267
6	24	H	Rochdale	L 1-3	1-1	16	North	2939
7	Oct 1	A	Hereford U	L 1-2	1-0	19	O'Kelly	1888
8	4	H	Tranmere R	D 0-0	0-0	—		2288
9	8	H	Peterborough U	D 0-0	0-0	20		2822
10	15	A	Exeter C	L 1-2	0-1	22	Alexander	2232
11	22	H	York C	W 2-0	2-0	21	Cockerill, Alexander	2825
12	25	A	Crewe Alex	D 2-2	2-1	—	Saunders 2	2311
13	29	H	Halifax T	W 3-2	0-1	18	Saunders 2, O'Kelly	3260
14	Nov 5	A	Stockport Co	L 1-3	0-1	19	McDermott	2064
15	8	H	Doncaster R	W 5-0	2-0	—	Watson 2 (1 pen), Cockerill, Alexander, Saunders	3382
16	12	A	Hartlepool U	L 1-2	0-0	20	Watson (pen)	1782
17	26	A	Carlisle U	L 1-2	1-0	20	Cockerill	2175
18	Dec 3	H	Scarborough	W 2-1	1-0	20	Alexander, Cockerill	3887
19	17	H	Leyton Orient	D 2-2	0-0	20	Lever, Saunders	3446
20	26	A	Lincoln C	D 2-2	0-1	19	Watson (pen), Alexander	8038
21	31	A	Burnley	L 0-1	0-0	19		7367
22	Jan 2	H	Colchester U	D 2-2	2-1	20	O'Kelly, Alexander	4472
23	14	A	Torquay U	D 2-2	0-1	20	North, Alexander	2251
24	21	H	Cambridge U	W 4-0	2-0	19	O'Kelly, Saunders, Cunnington, Tillson	3644
25	Feb 4	H	Wrexham	L 0-1	0-1	20		5058
26	11	A	Rochdale	W 2-0	2-0	18	Alexander 2	1621
27	14	H	Darlington	D 0-0	0-0	—		4020
28	25	H	Exeter C	W 2-1	1-0	16	O'Kelly, Lever	4684
29	28	H	Crewe Alex	D 0-0	0-0	—		5404
30	Mar 4	A	York C	W 3-0	1-0	13	Saunders, O'Kelly, North	3481
31	7	A	Rotherham U	L 0-1	0-0	—		4888
32	11	H	Stockport Co	W 2-0	0-0	11	North, Jobling	4685
33	14	A	Halifax T	L 1-2	0-2	—	O'Kelly	1609
34	18	H	Scunthorpe U	D 1-1	0-0	14	O'Kelly	9796
35	24	A	Colchester U	D 0-0	0-0	—		4507
36	27	H	Lincoln C	W 1-0	0-0	12	O'Kelly	8618
37	Apr 1	A	Leyton Orient	L 0-5	0-1	13		4149
38	4	A	Darlington	D 1-1	1-0	—	Jobling	1840
39	8	H	Burnley	W 1-0	0-0	12	Saunders	4856
40	15	H	Hereford U	D 1-1	0-0	11	Gilbert	4036
41	25	A	Peterborough U	W 2-1	0-1	—	Alexander, Jobling (pen)	2937
42	29	H	Carlisle U	D 0-0	0-0	11		3833
43	May 1	A	Doncaster R	W 3-2	2-1	10	Banton, Tillson, O'Kelly	2183
44	6	A	Scarborough	W 3-2	2-1	9	Alexander 2, Saunders	3923
45	9	A	Tranmere R	L 2-3	2-2	—	Cockerill, Gilbert	6938
46	13	H	Hartlepool U	W 3-0	1-0	9	Cockerill, Alexander, Gilbert	3801

Final League Position: 9

GOALSCORERS

League (65): Alexander 14, O'Kelly 10, Saunders 10, Cockerill 6, North 6, Jobling 4 (1 pen), Watson 4 (3 pens), Gilbert 3, Lever 2, Tillson 2, Banton 1, Cunnington 1, McDermott 1, Stoutt 1.
Littlewoods Cup (0).
FA Cup (10): North 4, Cunnington 2, Alexander 1, Cockerill 1, Jobling 1, own goal 1.

Littlewoods Cup	First Round	Rotherham U (h)	0-1
		(a)	0-1
FA Cup	First Round	Wolverhampton W (h)	1-0
	Second Round	Rotherham U (h)	3-2
	Third Round	Middlesbrough (a)	2-1
	Fourth Round	Reading (h)	1-1
		(a)	2-1
	Fifth Round	Wimbledon (a)	1-3

Sherwood	Dixon	Agnew	Williams	Cunnington	Cockerill	Jobling	McDermott	O'Kelly	Stoutt	North	Tillson	Reece	Lever	Alexander	Caldwell	Saunders	Grocock	Watson	Stephenson	Banton	Gilbert	Smaller	*Match No.*
1	2*	3	4	5	6	7	8†	9	10	11	12						14						1
		3	4	6		7	12	8	10	9	5	1	2	11*									2
		3	4	6		7		9		8	5	1	2	11	10*	12							3
		3	4	8	6	7	14	9†			5	1		11	10*	12	2						4
	2	3	4	6		7		9		8	5	1		11			10						5
	2	3	4	6		7		9		8	5	1		11	12		10*						6
1	2*	3	4	6	14	7	10	9		8	5			11†		12							7
1		3		6		7	2	9		8	4		5	11*		10	12						8
1		3		6		7*	2	9		8	4		5	11		10	12						9
1	12	3		6	14	7†	2	9		8*	4		5	11			10						10
1		3	2*	6	10		7	9		12	4		5	11		8							11
1		3		6			2	9		7	4		5	11		8		10					12
1		3	2	6			7	9			4		5	11		8		10					13
1			2*	6	3		7	9			4		5	11		8	12	10					14
1				6	10		2	9			4		5	11		8		7	3				15
1		14		6	10		2	9*			4		5	11		8	12	7	3†				16
		3		6	10		2	9		7	4	1	5	11*		8		12					7
1		3		6	10		2	9		7	4		5	11		8							18
1		3		6	10	12	2	9*		7	4		5	11		8							19
		3				10	2	9		7*	4	1	5	11		8	12	6					20
		3				10	2	9*		7	4	1	5	11		8	12	6					21
		3		6	14	10†	2	9		12	4	1	5	11*		8		7					22
		3		6	10	7*	2			9	4	1	5	11		8		12					23
		3		6	10		2	9		7	4	1	5	11		8							24
		3		6	10	2		9		7	4	1	5*	11		8		12					25
1		3		6	10	7		9		2	4		5	11		8							26
1		3		6	10	7*		9		2	4		5	11		8		12					27
1		3		6	10		2	9		7	4		5	11		8							28
1		3		6		10	2	9		7	4		5	11*		8		12					29
1				6		10	2	9		7	4		5			8		11	3				30
1				6		10	2	9		7	4		5	12		8		11*	3				31
1				6		10	2	9		7	4		5	11		8			3				32
1				6		10	2	9		7	4		5	11		8		12	3*				33
1		12		6		10	2	9		7	4		5	11		8			3*				34
1		3		6	10	7	2	9			4		5	11		8							35
1		3		6	10	2		9			4		5	11		12				7*	8		36
1		3		6	10	7	2	9*			4		5†	11		12			14		8		37
1			5	6	10	7	2				4			11		9			3		8		38
			2	6		10					4	1	5	11		7		12	3	9*	8		39
			2	6	12	10*	9				4	1	5†	11		7			3	14	8		40
1		3	5	6	12	10	2	9*			4			11		7					8		41
1		3	5†	6	10	7*	2	12			4			11		9				14	8		42
1		3*	5	6	10		2	9			4			14		7†		12		11	8		43
1			2	6	10		9				4		5	11		7		12	3*	14	8†		44
1			2	6	10		3				4*		5	11		9		7†	12	14	8		45
1			4	6	10		2						5*	11		9		7†	3	14	8	12	46
32	4 + 1s	32 + 2s	19	44	24 + 5s	31 + 1s	36 + 2s	38 + 1s	2	27 + 2s	44 + 1s	14	37	42 + 2s	2 + 1s	36 + 5s	4 + 7s	12 + 9s	12 + 2s	3 + 5s	11	— + 1s	

GRIMSBY TOWN

Player and Position	Ht	Wt	Birth Date	Birth Place	Source	Clubs	League App	League Gls
Goalkeepers								
Lee Pratt*	5 10	11 07	31 3 70	Cleethorpes		Grimsby T	1	—
Paul Reece	5 11	12 07	16 7 68	Nottingham	Kettering	Grimsby T	14	—
Steve Sherwood	6 4	14 07	10 12 53	Selby	Apprentice	Chelsea	16	—
						Brighton HA (loan)	—	—
						Millwall (loan)	1	—
						Brentford (loan)	62	—
						Watford	211	1
						Grimsby T	78	—
Defenders								
Paul Agnew	5 9	10 04	15 8 65	Lisburn	Cliftonville	Grimsby T	130	1
Andrew Dixon*	6 1	10 11	19 4 68	Louth	Apprentice	Grimsby T	38	—
Mark Lever	6 3	12 05	29 3 70	Beverley	Trainee	Grimsby T	38	2
John McDermott	5 7	10 07	3 2 69	Middlesbrough		Grimsby T	79	1
Geoff Stephenson	5 7	11 00	28 4 70	Tynemouth	Trainee	Grimsby T	14	—
Stephen Stoutt	5 8	11 06	5 4 64	Halifax	Local	Huddersfield T	6	—
						Wolverhampton W	94	5
						Grimsby T	2	1
Andy Tillson	6 2	12 07	30 6 66	Huntingdon	Kettering	Grimsby T	45	2
John Cockerill	6 0	12 07	12 7 61	Cleethorpes	Stafford R	Grimsby T	29	6
Tom Williams*	5 9	11 06	18 12 57	West Lothian	Apprentice	Leicester C	241	10
						Birmingham C	62	1
						Grimsby T	19	—
Midfield								
Shaun Cunnington	5 8	10 04	4 1 66	Bourne	Amateur	Wrexham	199	12
						Grimsby T	59	3
Kevin Jobling	5 9	10 13	1 1 00	Sunderland	Apprentice	Leicester C	9	—
						Grimsby T	47	5
Marcus Newell*	5 9	11 00	19 10 69	Grimsby	Trainee	Grimsby T	—	—
Paul Smaller§			18 9 70	Scunthorpe	Trainee	Grimsby T	1	—
Tommy Watson	5 8	10 10	29 9 69	Liverpool	Trainee	Grimsby T	40	4
Forwards								
Keith Alexander	6 4	13 06	14 11 58	Nottingham	Barnet	Grimsby T	44	14
David Gilbert	5 4	10 04	22 6 63	Lincoln	Apprentice	Lincoln C	30	1
					Boston U	Scunthorpe U	1	—
						Northampton T	120	21
						Grimsby T	11	3

GRIMSBY TOWN

Foundation: Grimsby Pelham FC as they were first known, came into being at a meeting held at the Wellington Arms in September 1878. Pelham is the family name of big landowners in the area, the Earls of Yarborough. The receipts for their first game amounted to 6s. 9d. (approx. 39p). After a year, the club name was changed to Grimsby Town.

Managers (and Secretary-managers)
H. M. Hickson 1903–20*, Haydn Price 1920, George Fraser 1921–24, Wilf Gillow 1924–32, Frank Womack 1932–36, Charles Spencer 1937–51, Bill Shankly 1951–53, Billy Walsh 1954–55, Allenby Chilton 1955–59, Tim Ward 1960–62, Tom Johnston 1962–64, Jimmy McGuigan 1964–67, Don McEvoy 1967–68, Bill Harvey 1968–69, Bobby Kennedy 1969–71, Lawrie McMenemy 1971–73, Ron Ashman 1973–75, Tom Casey 1975–76, Johnny Newman 1976–79, George Kerr 1979–82, David Booth 1982–85, Mike Lyons 1985–87, Bobby Roberts 1987–88, Alan Buckley 1988– .

Player and Position	*Ht*	*Wt*	*Birth Date*	*Birth Place*	*Source*	*Clubs*	*League App*	*League Gls*
Chris Grocock*	5 10	10 05	30 10 68	Grimsby	School	Grimsby T	43	1
Richard O'Kelly	5 10	11 08	8 1 57	West Bromwich	Alvechurch	Walsall	204	56
						Port Vale	28	4
						Walsall	12	1
						Grimsby T	39	10
Steve Saunders	5 7	10 06	21 9 64	Warrington	Apprentice	Bolton W	3	—
						Crewe Alex	22	1
						Preston NE	—	—
						Grimsby T	76	13
Jimmy Shaw‡	5 10	12 00	20 9 69	Cleethorpes	School	Grimsby T	—	—

Trainees
Curtis, Gary A; Davies, Lee S; Gamble, David P; King, Paul; Liversidge, Scott; Smaller, Paul A; Thompson, Robert; Waite, Mark.

****Non-Contract**
Cooper, Alan; Willis, Roger C.

Associated Schoolboys
Atkin, Leighton J; Johnson, Stephen P; Shearman, James C.

HALIFAX 1988–89 *Back row (left to right):* Frank Harrison, Chris Hedworth, John Bramhall, Paddy Roche, Phil Whitehead, Alan Whitehead, Dave Robinson, Bobby Barr.
Centre row: Colin Blain, Dave Logan, Phil Horner, Billy Barr, Neil Matthews, Terry McPhillips, Andy Watson, Gerry Brook (Youth Team Coach).
Front row: Paul Fleming, Wayne Allison, Paul Willis, Bill Ayre (Manager), Mick Matthews, Dean Martin, Lee Richardson.

Division 4 — HALIFAX TOWN

Shay Ground, Halifax HX1 2YS. Offices: 7 Clare Road, Halifax HX1 2HX. Telephone Halifax (0422) 53423/43381. Ground: 0422 361582 (Match day only).

Ground capacity: 5,656.

Record attendance: 36,885 v Tottenham H, FA Cup 5th rd, 15 Feb, 1953.

Record receipts: £14,000 v Manchester C, FA Cup 3rd rd, 5 Jan, 1980.

Pitch measurements: 110yd × 70yd.

President: John S. Crowther. ***Vice-President:*** F. Hinchliffe.

Chairman: S. J. Brown. ***Vice-Chairman:*** J. Haymer.

Directors: B. Dawson, Mrs. P. Burton.

Manager: Bill Ayre. ***Physio:*** Mrs. Jane Appleyard.

Secretary: Mrs A. Pettifor. ***Assistant Secretary:*** Miss J. Magee.

Commercial Manager: Tony Thwaites.

Year Formed; 1911. ***Turned Professional:*** 1911. ***Ltd Co.:*** 1911.

Club Nickname: 'The Shaymen'.

Previous Grounds: Sandhall and Exley.

Record League Victory: 6-0 v Bradford PA, Division 3 (N), 3 December 1955 – Johnson; Griffiths, Ferguson; Watson, Harris, Bell; Hampson (2), Baker (3), Watkinson (1), Capel, Lonsdale. 6-0 v Doncaster R, Division 4, 2 November 1976 – Gennoe; Trainer, Loska (Bradley), McGill, Dunleavy (1), Phelan, Hoy (2), Carroll (1), Bullock (1), Lawson (1), Johnston.

Record Cup Victory: 7-0 v Bishop Auckland, FA Cup 2 rd (replay), 10 January 1967 – White; Russell, Bodell; Smith, Holt, Jeff Lee; Taylor (2), Hutchison (2), Parks (2), Atkins (1), McCarthy.

Record Defeat: 0-13 v Stockport Co, Division 3 (N). 6 January, 1934.

Most League Points (2 for a win): 57, Division 4, 1968–69.

Most League Points (3 for a win): 60, Division 4, 1982–83.

Most League Goals: 83, Division 3 (N), 1957–58.

Highest League Scorer in Season: Albert Valentine. 34, Division 3 (N), 1934–35.

Most League Goals in Total Aggregate: Ernest Dixon, 129, 1922—30.

Most Capped Player: None.

Most League Appearances: John Pickering, 367, 1965–74.

Record Transfer Fee Received: £150,000 from Watford for Rick Holden, March 1988.

Record Transfer Fee Paid: £25,000 to Huddersfield T for Kevin Johnson, August 1978.

Football League Record: 1921 Original Member of Division 3 (N); 1958–63 Division 3; 1963–69 Division 4; 1969–76 Division 3; 1976– Division 4.

Honours: *Football League:* Division 3 best season; 3rd. 1970–71; Division 3(N) – Runners-up 1934–35; Division 4 – Runners-up 1968–69. *FA Cup* best season; 5th rd, 1932–33, 1952–53. *Football League Cup* best season: 4th rd, 1964.

Colours: Blue and white shirts, blue shorts, blue stockings. **Change colours:** Blue and yellow shirts, blue and yellow shorts, yellow stockings.

HALIFAX TOWN 1988–89 LEAGUE RECORD

Match No.	Date	Venue	Opponents	Result	H/T Score	Lg. Pos.	Goalscorers	Attendance
1	Aug 27	A	Torquay U	W 2-0	1-0	—	Bramhall, Allison	2769
2	Sept 3	H	Burnley	L 1-2	0-1	11	McPhillips	3371
3	10	A	Exeter C	L 1-4	0-1	18	Whitehead	1725
4	16	H	Carlisle U	D 3-3	1-3	—	McPhillips 3 (1 pen)	1546
5	19	A	Stockport Co	D 1-1	0-1	—	Martin (pen)	2206
6	23	H	Tranmere R	L 2-3	1-1	—	Barr W, McPhillips	1662
7	Oct 1	A	York C	L 3-5	1-3	21	Allison 2, Horner	2238
8	4	H	Wrexham	W 4-0	3-0	—	Matthews N, Allison, McPhillips, Horner	1199
9	8	A	Cambridge U	L 1-2	0-0	21	McPhillips	1800
10	14	H	Rochdale	W 4-1	2-0	—	McPhillips 2 (1 pen) Barr W, Matthews N	2553
11	21	A	Doncaster R	W 4-1	4-1	—	McPhillips 2, Watson, Matthews N	3038
12	25	H	Peterborough U	W 5-0	0-0	—	Richardson, McPhillips, Watson, Matthews N 2	2248
13	29	A	Grimsby T	L 2-3	1-0	13	Bramhall, Matthews M	3260
14	Nov 4	H	Hartlepool U	W 1-0	1-0	—	Allison	2182
15	8	H	Colchester U	W 3-2	2-1	—	Martin, McPhillips 2 (1 pen)	2176
16	12	A	Hereford U	L 1-3	0-2	10	Horner	1929
17	26	A	Lincoln C	L 1-2	1-1	13	Allison	3379
18	Dec 2	H	Crewe Alex	L 0-1	0-0	—		2026
19	17	H	Scarborough	L 0-2	0-1	18		1890
20	26	A	Darlington	W 2-0	1-0	15	McPhillips, Allison	2131
21	31	A	Rotherham U	L 0-2	0-0	18		5258
22	Jan 2	H	Scunthorpe U	W 5-1	2-0	14	Allison 2, Watson, Matthews, Robinson	2650
23	14	A	Burnley	L 1-2	0-1	16	Allison	8297
24	20	H	Torquay U	W 2-0	2-0	—	Allison 2	1830
25	28	A	Carlisle U	L 1-3	0-0	15	Bramhall	3007
26	Feb 4	H	Stockport Co	D 2-2	1-0	15	Watson, McPhillips	1938
27	10	A	Tranmere R	L 0-2	0-0	—		4674
28	14	H	Leyton Orient	D 2-2	0-0	—	Matthews, Allison	1477
29	17	H	Cambridge U	D 0-0	0-0	—		1531
30	Mar 1	A	Peterborough U	L 1-2	0-0	—	Pullan	2159
31	3	H	Doncaster R	W 2-0	0-0	—	Watson, Broadbent	1675
32	11	A	Hartlepool U	L 0-2	0-1	20		1786
33	14	H	Grimsby T	W 2-1	2-0	—	Allison, McPhillips	1609
34	17	H	Exeter C	L 0-3	0-1	—		1473
35	25	A	Scunthorpe U	D 0-0	0-0	19		4591
36	27	H	Darlington	W 1-0	0-0	13	Barr W	1849
37	Apr 1	A	Scarborough	L 1-3	0-1	17	McPhillips	2365
38	4	A	Leyton Orient	L 0-2	0-0	—		3288
39	7	H	Rotherham U	D 1-1	1-0	—	McPhillips (pen)	2947
40	14	H	York C	D 0-0	0-0	—		1875
41	21	A	Wrexham	L 0-3	0-1	—		1782
42	25	A	Rochdale	D 1-1	0-0	—	Barr W	1388
43	29	H	Lincoln C	L 0-1	0-0	20		1261
44	May 1	A	Colchester U	L 2-3	1-0	21	Hill (og), McPhillips	5065
45	5	A	Crewe Alex	D 2-2	0-1	—	Broadbent, Allison	3476
46	13	H	Hereford U	D 2-2	1-1	21	McPhillips 2 (1 pen)	1082

Final League Position: 21

GOALSCORERS

League (69): McPhillips 22 (5 pens), Allison 15, Matthews N 7, Watson 5, Barr W 4, Bramhall 3, Horner 3, Broadbent 2, Martin 2 (1 pen), Matthews M 1, Pullan 1, Richardson 1, Robinson 1, Whitehead A 1, own goal 1.
Littlewoods Cup (3): Allison 1, McPhillips 1, Watson 1.
FA Cup (7): Barr W 2, Allison 2, Bramhall 1, McPhillips 1, Watson 1.

Littlewoods Cup	First Round	Scarborough (a)	1-1
		(h)	2-2
FA Cup	First Round	York C (h)	1-0
	Second Round	Altrincham (a)	3-0
	Third Round	Kettering (a)	1-1
		(h)	2-3

Roche	Barr, W	Logan	Matthews, M	Bramhall	Whitehead, A	Blain	Horner	Matthews, N	Allison	Richardson L	Willis	Watson	Henry	McPhillips	Martin	Barr, R	Whitehead, P	Smith	Robinson	Hedworth	Sinclair	Fleming P	Richardson N	Pullan	Broadbent	Harrison	Paterson	Donnelly	*Match No.*
1	2	3	4	5	6	7	8	9	10	11																			1
1	2	3	4	5	6		8		10	11	7*	9†	12	14															2
1	2	3†	4	5	6		8		10	11		14	12	9	7*														3
1	2			5	6		8			11		4	10	9	7	3													4
	2				6	3	8		10	11		4	12	9*	7	5	1												5
	2†				6	3*	8		10	11		4	12	9	7	5	1	14											6
	2		4		6	3*	8	12	10	11		14		9	7†		1		5										7
1	3		4				6	11	10*	12		8		9	7				5	2									8
1	3		4	5			6	11		10		8		9	7					2									9
1	3		4	5			6*	11		10	12	8		9	7					2									10
1	3		4	6				11	10	12		8*		9	7				5	2									11
1	3		4	6				11	10	12		8		9	7				5	2*									12
1	3		4	6				11	10	2		8		9	7				5										13
1	3		4	6				11	10	2		8		9	7				5										14
1	3		4	6				11	10	2		8		9	7				5										15
1	3		4	6			14		10	11	12	8		9	7*				5	2†									16
1	12		4	6			3	11	10	7		8*		9					5	2									17
1	9*		4	6			3	11	10	7	12	8							5	2									18
1	9			6			3	11	10	4		8			7				5	2									19
	2			6	12	14	3	11	10	4		8		9	7†				5*		1								20
	2			6		12	3	11	10	4*		8		9	7		1		5										21
	2			6		4*	3	11	10			8		9	7		1		5										22
	2			6		9*	3	11	10	4		8			7		1		5			12							23
	2			6			3	11	10	4		8			7		1		5			9*	12						24
	2			6			3	11	10	4		8		12	7		1		5			9*							25
	2			6			3	11		4		8		9	7				5		1	10							26
	2					10	3	11				8		9	7				5		1	6		4					27
	2					12	3	11*	10			8		9	7				5		1	6		4					28
	2					12	3	11†	10			8		9	7				5		1	6		4*	14				29
	2			6	3	11			10			8		9*					5		1	7		4	12				30
	2			6	3	11			10			8*		9					5		1	7	14	4†	12				31
	2			6	4†	8	3	11	10			14		9*					5		1	7			12				32
	2			6		4		11	10			8		9					5		1	7				3			33
				6		4	14	11*	10			8†		9	7				5		1	2			12	3			34
1	11			6			4		10			8		9	7				5			2				3			35
1	11			6			4		10			8		9	7				5			2				3			36
1	11*			6		5	4		10			8		9	7							2			12	3			37
1	5			6			4	11	10			8		9	7							2				3			38
				6			4	11	10			8		9	7		1		5			2				3			39
1				6			4	11	10			8		9*	7				5			2			12	3			40
1	7†			6			4		10			8		9		5						2	11*		12	3	14		41
1	7			6		5	4	11	10			8		9								2				3			42
1	7			6*		5†	4	11	10			8		9								2	14		12	3			43
1*	7			6			4	11	10			8		12								2	5		9	3			44
	7†			6		3	4	11	10			8		12			1			5		2*	9		14				45
	7			6*			4	12	10			8		9			1			2			5†		11	3		14	46
25	42 + 1s	3	15	39	10 + 1s	16 + 4s	36 + 2s	32 + 2s	41	22 + 3s	1 + 3s	42 + 3s	1 + 4s	37 + 4s	32	4	11	— + 1s	30	11	10	22 + 1s	4 + 3s	5	2 + 10s	13	— + 1s	— + 1s	

Fleming C — Match No. 22(12)

HALIFAX TOWN

Player and Position	*Ht*	*Wt*	*Birth Date*	*Birth Place*	*Source*	*Clubs*	*League App*	*League Gls*
Goalkeepers								
Paddy Roche*	6 1	11 04	4 1 51	Dublin	Shelbourne	Manchester U	46	—
						Brentford	71	—
						Halifax T	184	—
Phil Whitehead	6 3	13 07	17 12 69	Halifax		Halifax T	23	—
Defenders								
Billy Barr	5 11	11 07	21 1 69	Halifax	Trainee	Halifax T	73	4
Bobby Barr*	6 1	13 06	5 12 69	Halifax		Halifax T	5	—
Colin Blain*	5 7	9 10	7 3 70	Urmston	Trainee	Halifax T	23	—
John Bramhall	6 2	13 06	20 11 56	Warrington	Amateur	Tranmere R	170	7
						Bury	167	17
						Chester C (loan)	4	—
						Rochdale	86	13
						Halifax T	39	3
Paul Fleming	5 7	10 00	6 9 67	Halifax		Halifax T	60	—
Frankie Harrison*	6 1	12 06	19 9 63	Middlesbrough		Middlesbrough	—	—
						Lincoln C	1	—
						Halifax T	45	—
Chris Hedworth	6 1	10 11	5 1 64	Newcastle	Apprentice	Newcastle U	9	—
						Barnsley	25	—
						Halifax T	11	—
Philip Horner	6 1	12 07	10 11 66	Leeds	School	Leicester C	10	—
						Rotherham U (loan)	4	—
						Halifax T	38	3
Toby Paterson§			15 5 71	Scotland	Trainee	Halifax T	1	—
David Robinson	6 0	12 03	14 1 65	Cleveland	Billingham	Hartlepool U	66	1
						Halifax T	72	1
Gareth Smith§			9 4 71	Leeds	Trainee	Halifax T	1	—
Alan Whitehead‡	6 1	13 11	20 11 56	Bury	Local	Bury	99	13
						Brentford	102	4
						Scunthorpe U	108	8
						York C	41	1
						Wigan Ath (loan)	2	—
						Halifax T	11	1
Midfield								
Paul Donnelly§			23 12 71	Liverpool	Trainee	Halifax T	1	—
Stewart Ferebee‡	5 10	11 05	6 9 60	Carshalton	Harrogate T	York C	13	—
						Bradford C	—	—
						Darlington	8	—
					Whitley B	Halifax T	12	—
Craig Fleming§			6 10 71	Calder	Trainee	Halifax T	1	—
Dean Martin	5 10	10 02	9 9 67	Halifax	Local	Halifax T	88	6
Nick Richardson	6 0	12 07	11 04 67	Halifax	Local	Halifax T	7	—

HALIFAX TOWN

Foundation: The idea of a soccer club in a Rugby League stronghold was first mooted by a Mr. A. E. Muir who soon interested Joe McClelland (who became secretary-manager of the new club) and Dr. A. H. Muir their first chairman. Following correspondence in *The Halifax Evening Courier* the club was formed at a meeting at the Saddle Hotel in May 1911.

Managers (and Secretary-managers)
A. M. Ricketts 1911–12*, Joe McClelland 1912–30, Alec Raisbeck 1930–36, Jimmy Thomson 1936–47, Jack Breedon 1947–50, William Wootton 1951–52, Gerald Henry 1952–54, Willie Watson 1954–56, Billy Burnikell 1956, Harry Hooper 1957–62, Willie Watson 1964–66, Vic Metcalfe 1966–67, Alan Ball Snr 1967–70, George Kirby 1970–71, Ray Henderson 1971–72, George Mulhall 1972–74, Johnny Quinn 1974–76, Alan Ball Snr 1976–77, Jimmy Lawson 1977–78, George Kirby 1978–81, Mick Bullock 1981–84, Mick Jones 1984–86, Bill Ayre 1986– .

Player and Position	Ht	Wt	Birth Date	Birth Place	Source	Clubs	League App	League Gls
Forwards								
Wayne Allison	6 1	12 06	16 10 68	Huddersfield		Halifax T	84	23
Graham Broadbent†			20 12 58	Halifax		Halifax T	12	2
Terry McPhillips	5 10	11 00	1 10 68	Manchester	Trainee	Liverpool	—	—
						Halifax T	66	25
Neil Matthews	5 11	12 00	19 9 66	Grimsby	Apprentice	Grimsby T	11	1
						Scunthorpe U (loan)	1	—
						Halifax T (loan)	9	2
						Bolton W (loan)	1	—
						Halifax T	66	17
Andy Watson	5 9	11 12	1 4 67	Leeds	Harrogate T	Halifax T	45	5

Trainees
Abbishaw, David S; Audin, Mark D; Condon, Paul S; Cotterill, Darren M; Donnelly, Paul A; Fitzgibbon, Martin J; Fleming, Craig; Gilbertson, Paul A; Gilfillan, Daniel; Gourley, Bryan; Nolan, Gerard A; Paterson, Toby L; Smith, Gareth S; Smoczyk, Marc R.

****Non-Contract**
Broadbent, Graham;

Associated Schoolboys
Armstrong, Leighton J; Bodrozic, Peter G; Higgins, David K; Hook, Steven J; Orlic, Peter; Rancatore, Ricardo P; Smith, Richard J; Whittaker, Scott J; Wood, Sean.

HARTLEPOOL UNITED 1988–89 *Back row (left to right):* Simon Grayson, Wayne Stokes, John Borthwick, David Stokle.
Centre row: Paul Norton, Keith Ncbbs, Tony Smith, Gary Henderson (Physiotherapist), John Craggs (Coach), Bryan Robson (Assistant Manager), Rob McKinnon, Joe Allon, Rob Moverley.
Front row: Russell Doig, Andy Toman, Tony Barratt, Paul Ogden, Bob Moncur (Manager), Paul Baker (Captain), John Tinkler, Brian Honour.

Division 4 **HARTLEPOOL UNITED**

The Victoria Ground, Clarendon Road, Hartlepool. Telephone Hartlepool (0429) 272584. Commercial Dept: (0429) 222077.

Ground capacity: 6,620.

Record attendance: 17,426 v Manchester U, FA Cup 3rd rd, 5 Jan, 1957.

Record receipts: £17,000 v Leeds U, FA Cup 3rd rd, 18 Jan, 1979.

Pitch measurements: 110yd × 75yd

President: E. Leadbitter. ***Executive Vice-Presidents:*** R. Boyes MP, J. C. Thomas, E. Ord.

Chairman: J. W. Smart. ***Vice-Chairman:*** D. Jukes.

Directors: R. Boyes MP, A. Bamford ARICS, G. Lormor, P. Montgomery, W. Southeran, E. Egglestone.

Manager: Bobby Moncur.

Secretary: M. Kirby. ***Commercial Manager:*** Eddie Barnett.

Coach: Bryan Robson. ***Physio:*** Gary Henderson.

Year Formed: 1908. ***Turned Professional:*** 1908. ***Ltd Co.:*** 1908.

Club Nickname: 'The Pool'.

Previous Names: Hartlepools United until 1968; Hartlepool until 1977

Record League Victory: 10-1 v Barrow, Division 4, 4 April 1959 – Oakley; Cameron, Waugh; Johnson, Moore, Anderson; Scott (1), Langland (1), Smith (3), Clark (2), Luke (2). (1 og)

Record Cup Victory: 6-0 v North Shields, FA Cup, 1st rd, 30 November 1946 – Heywood; Brown, Gregory; Spelman, Lambert, Jones; Price, Scott (2), Sloan (4), Moses, McMahon.

Record Defeat: 1-10 v Wrexham, Division 4, 3 March, 1962.

Most League Points (2 for a win): 60, Division 4, 1967–68.

Most League Points (3 for a win): 70, Division 4, 1985–86.

Most League Goals: 90, Division 3 (N), 1956–57.

Highest League Scorer in Season: William Robinson, 28, Division 3 (N), 1927–28.

Most League Goals in Total Aggregate: Ken Johnson, 98, 1949–64.

Most Capped Player: Ambrose Fogarty, 1 (11), Eire.

Most League Appearances: Wattie Moore, 447, 1948–64.

Record Transfer Fee Received: £60,000 from Brighton & HA for Malcolm Poskett, February 1978.

Record Transfer Fee Paid: £17,500 to Chesterfield for Bob Newton, July 1985.

Football League Record: 1921 Original Member of Division 3 (N); 1958–68 Division 4; 1968–69 Division 3; 1969– Division 4.

Honours: *Football League:* Division 3 best season: 22nd, 1968–69; Division 3 (N) – Runners-up 1956–57. *FA Cup* best season: 4th rd. 1954–55, 1977–78, 1988–89. *Football League Cup best season : 4th rd. 1974–75.*

Colours: All blue. **Change colours:** All yellow.

HARTLEPOOL UNITED 1988–89 LEAGUE RECORD

Match No.	Date	Venue	Opponents	Result	H/T Score	Lg. Pos.	Goalscorers	Attendance
1	Aug 27	A	Lincoln C	W 1-0	1-0	—	Toman	3361
2	Sept 3	H	Darlington	W 2-1	0-0	4	Toman, Smith	2843
3	10	A	Torquay U	L 0-2	0-0	6		2027
4	17	H	Leyton Orient	W 1-0	0-0	4	Tinkler	1823
5	20	A	York C	W 3-2	2-1	—	Honour, Doig, Dixon	2611
6	24	H	Cambridge U	W 3-2	2-1	2	Dixon 2 (2 pens), Toman	2385
7	30	A	Tranmere R	L 1-2	1-2	—	Dixon	3624
8	Oct 4	H	Rochdale	L 0-1	0-0	—		2483
9	8	A	Doncaster R	L 0-1	0-1	8		2091
10	15	H	Wrexham	L 1-3	1-2	12	Baker	2235
11	22	H	Crewe Alex	L 0-3	0-1	15		1972
12	24	A	Stockport Co	L 0-3	0-2	—		2098
13	29	H	Hereford U	D 1-1	1-0	19	Barratt	1593
14	Nov 4	A	Halifax T	L 0-1	0-1	—		2182
15	9	A	Peterborough U	W 1-0	0-0	—	Grayson	3148
16	12	H	Grimsby T	W 2-1	0-0	15	Grayson, Toman	1782
17	26	H	Exeter C	D 2-2	0-0	15	Grayson, Smith	2125
18	Dec 3	A	Burnley	D 0-0	0-0	16		6284
19	17	H	Carlisle U	L 0-2	0-2	17		1974
20	26	A	Scunthorpe U	D 1-1	0-0	18	Allon	4595
21	30	A	Colchester U	W 2-1	0-1	—	Borthwick, Stokes	2359
22	Jan 2	H	Rotherham U	D 1-1	0-0	16	Grayson	3337
23	14	A	Darlington	D 0-0	0-0	15		3521
24	21	H	Lincoln C	W 3-2	2-0	14	Atkinson 2, Grayson	2860
25	Feb 4	H	York C	L 0-1	0-0	17		2863
26	11	A	Cambridge U	L 0-6	0-2	17		2300
27	18	H	Doncaster R	W 2-1	0-0	16	Tinkler, Grayson	1922
28	28	H	Stockport Co	D 2-2	1-0	—	Toman, Grayson	1692
29	Mar 4	A	Crewe Alex	L 0-3	0-0	19		3981
30	7	A	Wrexham	L 3-4	2-3	—	Grayson 2, Baker (pen)	2449
31	11	H	Halifax T	W 2-0	1-0	17	Grayson, Toman	1786
32	15	A	Hereford U	L 0-2	0-1	—		2157
33	18	H	Torquay U	L 0-1	0-1	21		1516
34	21	A	Leyton Orient	L 3-4	1-1	—	Baker 2 (1 pen), Atkinson	3406
35	25	A	Rotherham U	L 0-4	0-3	21		4915
36	27	H	Scunthorpe U	L 0-2	0-0	21		1923
37	Apr 1	A	Carlisle U	L 1-2	0-2	21	Grayson	3158
38	5	A	Scarborough	L 0-2	0-2	—		2155
39	8	H	Colchester U	W 2-1	0-0	21	Tinkler, Baker	1501
40	11	H	Scarborough	W 3-1	0-0	—	Allon, Baker (pen), Dalton	1897
41	15	H	Tranmere R	D 2-2	1-0	20	Baker (pen), McKinnon	2496
42	22	A	Rochdale	D 0-0	0-0	19		1406
43	29	A	Exeter C	L 1-2	1-1	22	Allon	2380
44	May 1	H	Peterborough U	W 2-1	0-0	19	Grayson, Dalton	1643
45	6	H	Burnley	D 2-2	0-1	18	Allon, McKinnon	2174
46	13	A	Grimsby T	L 0-3	0-1	19		3801

Final League Position: 19

GOALSCORERS

League (50): Grayson 12, Baker 7 (4 pens), Toman 6, Allon 4, Dixon 4 (2 pens), Atkinson 3, Tinkler 3, Dalton 2, McKinnon 2, Smith 2, Barratt 1, Borthwick 1, Doig 1, Honour 1, Stokes 1.
Littlewoods Cup (2): Dixon 1 (pen), own goal 1.
FA Cup (7): Allon 2, Baker 1 (pen), Borthwick 1, Honour 1, Smith 1, Toman 1.

Littlewoods Cup	First Round	Sheffield U (h)	2-2
		(a)	0-2
FA Cup	First Round	Wigan Ath (h)	2-0
	Second Round	Notts Co (h)	1-0
	Third Round	Bristol C (h)	1-0
	Fourth Round	Bournemouth (h)	1-1
		(a)	2-5

McKellar	Haigh	McKinnon	Tinkler	Smith	Stokes	Honour	Toman	Dixon	Borthwick	Barratt	Grayson	Doig	Atkinson	Tunks	Baker	Ogden	Norton	Muggleton	Allon	Nobbs	Moverley	Dalton	Barrass	Plaskett	McAndrew	Hepple	Locker	*Match No.*
1	2	3	4	5	6	7	8	9	10*	11	12																	1
1	2	3	4	5	6	7	8	9	10*	11	12																	2
1	2	3†	4	5	6	7	8	9*	10	11	12	14																3
1		3	4	5	6	7	8	9		2	10	11																4
1		3	4	5	6	7	8	9	12†	2	10*	11	14															5
		3	4	5	6	7	8	9		2	10	11		1														6
		3	4*	5	6	7	8	9		2	10	11		1	12													7
		3	4		6	7	8	9		2	10	11		1	5													8
	12	3	4		6	7	8	9		2	10*	11†		1	5	14												9
	5	3	4		6	7	8	9		2	12	11*		1	10													10
	2*	3	4	5	6	7	8	9		12		11			10		1											11
	11	3	4	5	6	7	8	9		2					10		1											12
	11	3	4	5	6	7	8			2					10			1	9									13
	11	3	4†	5	6	7	8			2	12	14*			10			1	9									14
	2	3		5		7	8	4*		11	10	12			6			1	9									15
	2	3		5		7	8	4		11	10				6			1	9									16
		3		5		7	8		9	11*	10	4	12		6			1		2								17
		3		5		7	8				10	4			6	11		1	9	2								18
		3			5	7	8		12	4	10		14		6	11†		1	9*	2								19
		3	4		5	7	8*		12	11	10				6			1	9	2								20
		3	4		5	7	8		9	11	10				6					2	1							21
		3	4		5	7	8		9	11	10				6					2	1							22
		3	4		5	7	8			11	10				6				9	2	1							23
		3	4		5	7				2	10		11		6	8			9		1							24
		3	4		5	7	8			2	10		11		6				9		1							25
		3	4		5	7	8			11	10*	12			6				9	2	1							26
		3	4		5	7	8		12	11	10	14			6				9*	2†	1							27
		3	4		5	7	8		9	2	10	12	11*		6						1							28
		3	4		5	7	8		9*	2	10	12	11†		6					14	1							29
		3	4		5	7	8		9	2	10				6						1	11						30
		3	4			7	8		9	2	10				6					5*	1	11	12					31
		3	4		5	7	8		9*	2	10	12			6						1	11						32
		3	4		5	7	8		9	2		10*			6						1	11	12					33
		3	4		5	7*	8		9				12		6						1	11	10	2				34
		3	4†		5		8				10*		7		9	14					1	11		2	6	12		35
		3	4		5		8				10				9	7	1					11		2	6			3
		3	4		5		8				10				9		1		7			11		2	6			3
		3	4		5		8				10				9		1		7			11		2	6			3
		3	4		5		8				10*		12		9				7	6	1	11		2				39
		3	4		5		8				10				9				7	6	1	11		2				40
		3	4		5		8				10				9				7	6	1	11		2				41
		3	4		5*		8				10		12		9				7	6	1	11		2				42
		3	4*	5			8				10				9	12			7	6	1	11		2				43
		3		5			8				10				9	4			7	6	1	11		2				44
		3		5*			8		12		10		14		9	4†			7	6	1	11		2				45
		3*		5			8		6		10		7		9	4					1	11				2	12	46
5	10 + 1s	46	38	19	37	34	45	14	14 + 5s	31 + 1s	36 + 5s	11 + 8s	6 + 7s	5	39 + 1s	7 + 3s	5	8	21	17 + 1s	23	17	1 + 2s	12	4	1 + 1s	— + 1s	

HARTLEPOOL UNITED

Player and Position	*Ht*	*Wt*	*Birth Date*	*Birth Place*	*Source*	*Clubs*	*League App*	*League Gls*
Goalkeepers								
Rob Moverley	6 3	12 00	16 1 69	Batley	Trainee	Bradford C	—	—
						Hartlepool U	23	—
Paul Norton*	5 11	12 10	17 9 69	Mexborough	Trainee	Sheffield U	—	—
						Hartlepool U	5	—
Philip Owers‡			28 4 55	Bishop Auckland		Darlington	45	—
						Gillingham	2	—
						Darlington	69	—
						Hartlepool U	2	—
Defenders								
Paul Haigh‡	5 11	12 06	4 5 58	Scarborough	Apprentice	Hull C	180	8
						Carlisle U	233	4
						Hartlepool U	50	—
Rob McKinnon	5 11	11 01	31 7 66	Glasgow	Rutherglen G	Newcastle U	1	—
						Hartlepool U	133	4
Keith Nobbs	5 10	11 10	19 9 61	Bishop Auckland	Apprentice	Middlesbrough	1	—
						Halifax T	87	1
					Bishop Auckland	Hartlepool U	140	1
Steve Plaskett‡			24 4 71	Newcastle	Trainee	Hartlepool U	12	—
Tony Smith	5 10	12 01	20 2 57	Sunderland	Amateur	Newcastle U	2	—
						Peterborough U	68	5
						Halifax T	83	3
						Hartlepool U	200	8
David Stokle*	6 3	13 00	1 12 69	Hartlepool		Hartlepool U	8	—
Wayne Stokes	6 1	13 00	16 2 65	Birmingham	Apprentice	Coventry C	—	—
						Gillingham	3	—
						Stockport Co	18	1
						Hartlepool U	61	1
Midfield								
Patrick Atkinson			22 5 70	Singapore	Trainee	Sheffield U	—	—
						Hartlepool U	13	3
Kenny Cramman*	5 10	12 00	25 1 70	Newcastle	Trainee	Hartlepool U	—	—
Paul Dalton	5 11	11 07	25 4 67	Middlesbrough	Brandon U	Manchester U	—	—
						Hartlepool U	17	2
Brian Honour	5 7	12 05	16 2 64	Horden	Apprentice	Darlington	74	4
					Peterlee	Hartlepool U	173	11
Steve Locker§			5 11 70	Ashington	Trainee	Hartlepool U	1	—
Tony McAndrew‡	5 10	12 06	11 4 56	Glasgow		Middlesbrough	247	13
						Chelsea	20	4
						Middlesbrough	64	2
						Darlington	11	—
						Hartlepool U	4	—
Paul Ogden	5 10	11 02	19 10 69	Salford	Trainee	Oldham Ath	—	—
						Hartlepool U	10	—
John Tinkler	5 8	11 07	24 8 68	Trimdon		Hartlepool U	60	3
Andy Toman	5 10	11 09	7 3 62	Northallerton	Bishop Auckland	Lincoln C	24	4
						Hartlepool U	112	28
Forwards								
Joe Allon	5 11	11 02	12 11 66	Gateshead		Newcastle U	9	2
						Swansea C	34	11
						Hartlepool U	21	4
Paul Baker	6 1	12 10	5 1 63	Newcastle	Bishop Auckland	Southampton	—	—
						Carlisle U	71	11
						Hartlepool U	79	26
Tony Barrass§			29 3 71	Teesside	Trainee	Hartlepool U	3	—
John Borthwick	6 0	10 12	24 3 64	Hartlepool		Hartlepool U	117	15

HARTLEPOOL UNITED

Foundation: The inspiration for the launching of Hartlepool United was the West Hartlepool club which won the FA Amateur Cup in 1904–05. They had been in existence since 1881 and their Cup success led in 1908 to the formation of the new professional concern which first joined the North-Eastern League. In those days they were Hartlepools United and won the Durham Senior Cup in their first two seasons.

Managers (and Secretary-managers)
Alfred Priest 1908–12, Percy Humphreys 1912–13, Jack Manners 1913–20, Cecil Potter 1920–22, David Gordon 1922–24, Jack Manners 1924–27, Bill Norman 1927–31, Jack Carr 1932–35 (had been player-coach since 1931), Jimmy Hamilton 1935–43, Fred Westgarth 1943–57, Ray Middleton 1957–59, Bill Robinson 1959–62, Allenby Chilton 1962–63, Bob Gurney 1963–64, Alvan Williams 1964–65, Geoff Twentyman 1965, Brian Clough 1965–67, Angus McLean 1967–70, John Simpson 1970–71, Len Ashurst 1971–74, Ken Hale 1974–76, Billy Horner 1976–83, Johnny Duncan 1983, Mike Docherty 1983, Billy Horner 1984–86, John Bird 1986–88, Bobby Moncur 1988– .

Player and Position	*Ht*	*Wt*	*Birth Date*	*Birth Place*	*Source*	*Clubs*	*League App*	*League Gls*
Russell Doig	5 8	10 09	17 1 64	Millport	St. Mirren	E Stirling	109	9
						Leeds U	6	—
						Peterborough U (loan)	7	—
						Hartlepool U	28	1
Simon Grayson	6 1	12 00	21 10 68	Sheffield		Sheffield U	—	—
						Chesterfield (loan)	8	—
						Hartlepool U	42	12
Jonathan McCarthy‡			18 8 70	Middlesbrough		Hartlepool U	1	—

Trainees
Barrass, Anthony; Brown, Steven; Carr, Graham G.J; Clark, Paul J; Cooper, Graham P; Davies, Kenneth F; Fletcher, Steven M; Hanford, Kevin M; Kennedy, Jonathan; Locker, Stephen; Oliver, Scott; Percival, Paul; Plaskett, Stephen C; Todd, Lee; White, Karl A; Wilson, Philip M.

HEREFORD UNITED 1988–89 *Back row (left to right):* Steve Mardenborough, Ian Rock, Ian Bowyer (Manager), Paul Tester, Andy Crane, Kevin Rose, Gary Stevens, Ian Benbow, Paul McLoughlin, Peter Isaac (Physiotherapist).
Centre row: Robbie Williams, Richard Jones, Phil Stant, Mel Pejic, Steve Devine, Paul Maddy, Mark Jones.
Front row: Simon Morgan, Lucas Johnson, Jason Westmancott, Mark Priday, Adam Moore, Ian Gardiner, Lee Thomas.

Division 4 HEREFORD UNITED

*Edgar Street, Hereford.*Telephone Hereford (0432) 276666. Commercial Dept: (0432) 273155.

Ground capacity: 16,119.

Record attendance: 18,114 v Sheffield W, FA Cup 3rd rd, 4 Jan, 1958.

Record receipts: £51,234 v Arsenal, FA Cup 3rd rd, 5 Jan, 1985.

Pitch measurements: 111yd × 74yd.

Chairman: P. S. Hill FRICS. *Vice-Chairman:* M. B. Roberts.

Directors: D. H. Vaughan, A. J. Phillips, G. C. E. Hales, H. A. R. Cotterell, J. Duggan, G. V. Hope.

Manager: Ian Bowyer. *Assistant Manager:*

Physio: Peter Isaac.

Secretary: D. H. Vaughan. *Commercial Manager:*

Year Formed: 1924. *Turned Professional:* 1924. *Ltd Co.:* 1939.

Club Nickname: 'United'.

Record League Victory: 6-0 v Burnley (away), Division 4, 24 January 1987 – Rose; Rodgerson, Devine, Halliday, Pejic, Dalziel, Harvey (1p), Wells, Phillips (3), Kearns (2), Spooner.

Record Cup Victory: 6-1 v QPR, FA Cup, 2nd rd, 7 December 1957 – Sewell; Tomkins, Wade; Masters, Niblett, Horton (2p); Reg Bowen (1), Clayton (1), Fidler, Williams (1), Cyril Beech (1).

Record Defeat: 0-6 v Rotherham U, Division 4, 29 April, 1989.

Most League Points (2 for a win): 63, Division 3, 1975–76.

Most League Points (3 for a win): 77, Division 4, 1984–85.

Most League Goals: 86. Division 3, 1975–76.

Highest League Scorer in Season: Dixie McNeil, 35, 1975–76.

Most League Goals in Total Aggregate: Dixie McNeil, 85, 1974–77.

Most Capped Player: Brian Evans, 1 (7), Wales.

Most League Appearances: Chris Price 330, 1976–86.

Record Transfer Fee Received: £100,000 from Derby Co for Steve Emery, September 1979.

Record Transfer Fee Paid: £27,500 to Shrewsbury T for Jon Narbett, December 1988.

Football League Record: 1972 Elected to Division 4; 1973–76 Division 3; 1976–77 Division 2; 1977–78 Division 3; 1978– Division 4.

Honours: Football League: Division 2 best season: 22nd, 1976–77; Division 3 – Champions 1975–76; Division 4 – Runners-up 1972–73. *FA Cup* best season: 4th rd, 1971–72, 1976–77, 1981–82. *Football League Cup* best season: 3rd rd. 1974–75. *Welsh Cup:* Finalists 3 times.

Colours: White shirts, black shorts, white stockings. **Change colours:** All red.

HEREFORD UNITED 1988–89 LEAGUE RECORD

Match No.	Date	Venue	Opponents	Result	H/T Score	Lg. Pos.	Goalscorers	Attendance
1	Aug 27	A	Scunthorpe U	L 1-3	0-0	—	McLoughlin	3663
2	Sept 3	H	Cambridge U	W 4-2	3-1	12	McLoughlin 2, Maddy, Stant	1711
3	10	A	Leyton Orient	W 3-1	2-0	4	Stant 2, Tester	3087
4	17	H	Scarborough	L 1-3	0-1	9	Stant	2359
5	21	H	Crewe Alex	L 0-1	0-0	—		1981
6	24	A	Lincoln C	L 0-2	0-1	17		2915
7	Oct 1	H	Grimsby T	W 2-1	0-1	14	Tester, Stant (pen)	1888
8	4	A	Doncaster R	L 2-3	1-2	—	Stant 2 (1 pen)	1281
9	8	H	Carlisle U	W 2-1	1-1	13	Pejic, McLoughlin	2127
10	15	A	Stockport Co	W 2-1	1-1	10	Stevens 2	2035
11	22	A	Peterborough U	L 1-2	0-1	13	Stevens (pen)	3460
12	26	H	Rochdale	D 4-4	2-3	—	Stant 3, Tester	2071
13	29	H	Hartlepool U	D 1-1	0-1	15	Narbett	1593
14	Nov 5	H	Wrexham	D 0-0	0-0	14		2372
15	7	A	Tranmere R	L 0-1	0-1	—		3587
16	12	H	Halifax T	W 3-1	2-0	16	Narbett 2, Stant (pen)	1929
17	26	H	Rotherham U	D 1-1	1-0	16	Stant	2058
18	Dec 3	A	York C	L 1-4	0-1	19	Stant	1698
19	17	H	Burnley	D 0-0	0-0	19		2442
20	26	A	Exeter C	L 1-3	1-1	20	Stant	3229
21	31	A	Darlington	D 0-0	0-0	20		1755
22	Jan 2	H	Torquay U	D 1-1	1-0	21	Stant	2356
23	14	A	Cambridge U	L 1-2	1-2	22	Stant	2193
24	21	H	Scunthorpe U	L 1-2	0-0	22	Jones R	2024
25	28	A	Scarborough	W 2-0	0-0	21	Narbett 2	2199
26	Feb 4	A	Crewe Alex	L 1-2	1-2	22	Stant	2987
27	11	H	Lincoln C	W 3-2	1-0	21	Stant, Tester, Pejic	2113
28	18	A	Carlisle U	L 0-3	0-1	21		2548
29	25	H	Stockport Co	W 2-1	2-0	20	McLoughlin, Stant	2015
30	28	A	Rochdale	D 2-2	2-1	—	McLoughlin 2	1060
31	Mar 4	H	Peterborough U	W 4-0	0-0	18	Stant 3, McLoughlin	2094
32	11	A	Wrexham	D 1-1	1-0	19	Tester	2960
33	15	H	Hartlepool U	W 2-0	1-0	—	Tester, Stant (pen)	2157
34	18	H	Leyton Orient	D 1-1	1-0	16	Pejic	2063
35	25	A	Torquay U	L 0-1	0-0	17		2542
36	27	H	Exeter C	W 1-0	0-0	16	Lamb	2735
37	Apr 1	A	Burnley	D 3-3	1-1	16	McLoughlin 2, Lamb	5534
38	4	A	Colchester U	D 1-1	0-1	—	Bradley	2862
39	8	H	Darlington	D 1-1	0-0	16	Stant	2009
40	12	H	Colchester U	D 1-1	0-1	—	McLoughlin	2015
41	15	A	Grimsby T	D 1-1	0-0	15	Benbow	4036
42	22	H	Doncaster R	W 3-1	1-0	11	McLoughlin 2, Stant	1804
43	29	A	Rotherham U	L 0-6	0-2	15		5334
44	May 1	H	Tranmere R	W 2-1	1-1	14	Stant, Narbett	2844
45	6	H	York C	L 1-2	0-1	15	Stant	1819
46	13	A	Halifax T	D 2-2	1-1	15	Stant, Narbett	1082

Final League Position: 15

GOALSCORERS

League (66): Stant 28 (4 pens), McLoughlin 13, Narbett 7, Tester 6, Pejic 3, Stevens 3 (1 pen), Lamb 2, Bradley 1, Benbow 1, Jones R 1, Maddy 1.
Littlewoods Cup (2): Stant 1, Tester 1.
FA Cup (0).

Littlewoods Cup	First Round	Plymouth Arg (h)	0-3
		(a)	2-3
FA Cup	First Round	Cardiff C (a)	0-3

Rose	Jones, M	Crane	Pejic	Stevens	Maddy	Campbell	Jones, R	Stant	Devine	McLoughlin	Bowyer	Benbow	Mardenborough	Tester	Williams	Narbett	Bradley	Elliott	Lamb	Peacock	*Match No.*
1	2	3	4	5	6	7†	8*	9	10	11	14	12									1
1	2	3		4	8			9	5	11	6		7	10							2
1	2	3		4				9	5	11	6	8	7	10							3
1		3		4	8			9	5	11	6		7	10	2						4
1		3		4	8		6	9†	5	11*	14	12	7	10	2						5
1		3		4	8†		6	9	5	11	14	12	7*	10	2						6
1	2	3†	14	4	8*		6	9	5	11		12	7	10							7
1	2	3		4	8		6	9	5			11	7	10							8
1	2		5	4	10		6		3	9			7	11		8					9
1	2	3		5					4	9	6	10	7	11		8					10
1	2	3		5	12				4	9	6	10*	7	11		8					11
1	2	3			6		4	9	5	11			7	10		8					12
1	2	3		5			4	9		11		6	7	10		8					13
1	2	3		12	6		4	9	5	11			7*	10		8					14
1		3		4				9	5	11	12	6*	7	10	2	8					15
1	2	3		4	12		6	9*	5	11			7	10		8					16
1	2	3		4	7		6	9	12	11				10*		8	5				17
1	2	3		4	7*		6	9		11		12		10		8	5				18
1	2	3		4			6	9	7	11				10		8	5				19
1	2	3*		14			6	9	4	11		12	7	10		8†	5				20
1	2	3		5			6	9	4	11		7		10		8					21
1	2	3					6	9	4	11*		7	12	10		8	5				22
	2	3	12	5			6	9	4	11		7*	10			8		1			23
	2	3*	5	4			7	9	6	11			10	12		8		1			24
	2	7	5	4			6	9	3	11				10		8		1			25
		3	5	4			6	9		11		7		10	2	8		1			26
	2		5	4			6	9	3	11		7		10		8		1			27
	2		5	4	6			9	3	11		7*	12	10		8		1			28
	2		5	4			6	9	3	11		7		10		8		1			29
	2		5	4			6	9	3	11		7		10		8		1			30
	2	3	5	14	6			9	4	11		7*	12	10†		8		1			31
	2		4	5	12		6	9*	3	11			7	10		8		1			32
	2		5	4			6	9	3	11		7		10		8		1			33
	2	3	5	4	12		6	9		11		7*		10		8		1			34
	2		5		10		6	9†	3	14		8	12	11*			4	1	7		35
	2		5		8		6	9*	3	11†		7	12	14			4	1	10		36
	2		5*		8		6	9*	3	11		7		14		12	4	1	10		37
	2	3†					6		5	10*		7	12	11		8	4	1	9	14	38
	2	3					6	9	4	11†		7*		12		8	5	1	10	14	39
	2			4*	12		6	9	3	11				7		8	5	1	10		40
	2				12		6	9*	3	7		14		11†		8	5	1	10	4	41
	2				6		5	12	4	11		9*		7		8		1	10	3	42
	2	12			6		5		3	11		9		10*		8		1	7	4	43
	2	12			6		5	9	3*	11		7		10		8		1		4	44
	2	3			6		5	9		11		7*	12	10†		8		1	14	4	45
1	2						5	9	3	11		6	7	10		8				4	46
23	41	30 + 2s	16 + 2s	30 + 3s	21 + 6s	1	38	40 + 1s	40 + 1s	44 + 1s	5 + 4s	27 + 7s	20 + 7s	40 + 4s	5	35 + 1s	12	23	9 + 1s	6 + 2s	

HEREFORD UNITED

Player and Position	Ht	Wt	Birth Date	Birth Place	Source	Clubs	League App	League Gls
Goalkeepers								
Tony Elliott	6 0	12 12	30 11 69	Nuneaton		Birmingham C	—	—
						Hereford U	23	—
Kevin Rose	6 1	13 06	23 11 60	Evesham	Ledbury T	Lincoln C	—	—
					Ledbury T	Hereford U	268	—
Defenders								
Andy Crane*	5 9	11 03	3 1 67	Ipswich	Apprentice	Ipswich T	—	—
						Shrewsbury T	—	—
						Hereford U	32	—
Steve Devine	5 9	10 07	11 12 64	Strabane	Apprentice	Wolverhampton W	—	—
						Derby Co	11	—
						Stockport Co	2	—
						Hereford U	136	2
Mark Jones	5 8	10 12	22 10 61	Warley	Apprentice	Aston Villa	24	—
						Brighton & HA	9	—
						Birmingham C	34	—
						Shrewsbury T	—	—
						Hereford U	69	—
Darren Peacock	6 2	12 06	3 2 68	Bristol	Apprentice	Newport Co	28	—
						Hereford U	8	—
Mel Pejic	5 9	10 08	27 4 59	Chesterton	Local	Stoke C	1	—
						Hereford U	313	7
Gary Stevens*	6 1	12 03	30 8 54	Birmingham	Evesham	Cardiff C	150	44
						Shrewsbury T	150	29
						Brentford	32	10
						Hereford U	88	10
Midfield								
Ian Benbow	5 10	11 00	9 1 69	Hereford	Trainee	Hereford U	55	3
Ian Bowyer	5 10	11 11	6 6 51	Ellesmere Port	Apprentice	Manchester C	50	13
						Orient	78	18
						Nottingham F	239	49
						Sunderland	15	1
						Nottingham F	205	19
						Hereford U	38	1
Mike Campbell‡			19 11 66	Oban		Hereford U	1	—
Richard Jones	5 11	11 01	26 4 69	Pontypool		Newport Co	41	1
						Hereford U	38	1
Paul Maddy*	5 10	9 11	17 8 62	Cwmcarn	Apprentice	Cardiff C	43	3
						Stoke C (loan)	—	—
						Hereford U (loan)	9	1
						Swansea C	20	3
						Hereford U	77	16
						Brentford	31	5
						Chester C	18	1
						Hereford U	35	1
Paul Mallender‡			30 11 69	Norwich	Trainee	Hereford U	1	—
Steve Marden-borough*	5 8	11 00	11 9 64	Birmingham	Apprentice	Coventry C	—	—
						Wolverhampton W	9	1
						Cambridge U (loan)	6	—
						Swansea C	36	7
						Newport Co	64	11
						Cardiff C	32	1
						Hereford U	27	—
Jon Narbett	5 10	10 08	21 11 68	Birmingham	Apprentice	Shrewsbury T	26	3
						Hereford U	36	7
Robbie Williams*	5 9	10 09	9 10 68	Bridgend	Trainee	Oxford U	—	—
						Hereford U	5	—

HEREFORD UNITED

Foundation: A number of local teams amalgamated in 1924 under the chairmanship of Dr. E. W. Maples to form Hereford United and join the Birmingham Combination. They graduated to the Birmingham League four years later.

Managers (and Secretary-managers)
Eric Keen 1939, George Tranter 1948–49, Alex Massie 1952, George Tranter 1953–55, Joe Wade 1956–62, Ray Daniels 1962–63, Bob Dennison 1963–67, John Charles 1967–71, Colin Addison 1971–74, John Sillett 1974–78, Mike Bailey 1978–79, Frank Lord 1979–82, Tommy Hughes 1982–83, Johnny Newman 1983–87, Ian Bowyer 1987– .

Player and Position	*Ht*	*Wt*	*Birth Date*	*Birth Place*	*Source*	*Clubs*	*League App*	*League Gls*
Forwards								
Paul McLoughlin	5 10	10 07	23 12 63	Bristol	Bristol C	Cardiff C	49	4
					Gisborne C	Hereford U	74	14
Phil Stant	6 1	12 07	13 10 62	Bolton	Camberley	Reading	4	2
					Army	Hereford U	89	38
Paul Tester	5 8	10 12	10 3 59	Stroud	Cheltenham T	Shrewsbury T	98	12
						Hereford U (loan)	4	—
						Hereford U	44	6

Trainees
Johnson, Lucas G.R; Priday, Marcus A.

Associated Schoolboys
Cocum, Neil; Roberts, Simon P; Sykes, Alex; Watkins, Andrew.

HUDDERSFIELD TOWN 1988–89 *Back row (left to right):* Paul Kirkham, Simon Trevitt, Michael France, Steve Hardwick, Lee Martin, Graham Mitchell, Ken O'Doherty, Malcolm Brown, Julian Winter.
Centre row: Gordon McAllister (Physiotherapist), David Cork, Chris Marsden, Craig Maskell, Andy May, Peter Withe (Assistant Manager), Vincent Chapman, Kieran O'Regan, Richard Shelton, Junior Bent, Don Mann (Youth Coach).
Front row: Carl Madrick, Chris Hutchings, Gordon Tucker, Peter Ward, Eoin Hand (Manager), Malcolm Shotton, Mark Barham, Ian Bray, Micky Holmes.

Division 3 HUDDERSFIELD TOWN

Leeds Rd, Huddersfield HD1 6PE. Telephone (0484) 420335/6. Commercial Dept: (0484) 534867. Recorded Information: (0484) 515122.

Ground capacity: 32,000.

Record attendance: 67,037 v Arsenal, FA Cup 6th rd, 27 Feb, 1932.

Record receipts: £52,607 v Newcastle U, Division 2,7 May, 1984.

Pitch measurements: 115yd × 75yd.

Chairman: K. S. Longbottom. ***Vice-Chairman:*** D. G. Headey.

Directors: C. Senior, C. Hodgkinson, J. B. Buckley, F. L. Thewlis.

Manager: Eoin Hand. ***Assistant Manager:*** Peter Withe.

Coaches: Jimmy Robson, Steve Smith.

Secretary: G. S. Binns. ***Commercial Manager:*** Tony Flynn. ***Commercial Executive:*** Keith Hanvey.

Physio: Gary Williams.

Year Formed: 1908. ***Turned Professional:*** 1908. ***Ltd Co.:*** 1908.

Club Nickname: 'The Terriers'.

Record League Victory: 10-1 v Blackpool, Division 1, 13 December 1930 – Turner; Goodall, Spencer; Redfern, Wilson, Campbell; Bob Kelly (1), McLean (4), Robson (3), Davies (1), Smailes (1).

Record Cup Victory: 7-1 v Chesterfield (away), FA Cup, 3rd rd, 12 January 1929: Turvey; Goodall, Wadsworth; Evans, Wilson, Naylor: Jackson (1), Kelly, Brown (3), Cumming (2), Smith. (1 o.g)

Record Defeat: 1-10 v Manchester C, Division 2, 7 November, 1987.

Most League Points (2 for a win): 66, Division 4, 1979–80.

Most League Points (3 for a win): 82, Division 3, 1982–83.

Most League Goals: 101, Division 4, 1979–80.

Highest League Scorer in Season: Sam Taylor, 35, Division 2, 1919–20; George Brown, 35, Division 1, 1925–26.

Most League Goals in Total Aggregate: George Brown, 142, 1921–29 and Jimmy Glazzard, 142, 1946–56.

Most Capped Player: Jimmy Nicholson, 31 (41), Northern Ireland.

Most League Appearances: Billy Smith, 520, 1914–34.

Record Transfer Fee Received: £230,000 from Swindon T for Duncan Shearer, June 1988.

Record Transfer Fee Paid: £110,000 to Mansfield T for Terry Austin, December 1980.

Football League Record: 1910 Elected to Division 2; 1920–52 Division 1; 1952–53 Division 2; 1953–56 Division 1; 1956–70 Division 2; 1970–72 Division 1; 1972–73 Division 2; 1973–75Division 3; 1975–80 Division 4; 1980–83 Division 3; 1983–88 Division 2; 1988– Division 3.

Honours: *Football League:* Division 1 – Champions 1923–24, 1924–25, 1925–26; Runners-up 1926–27, 1927–28, 1933–34; Division 2 – Champions 1969–70; Runners-up 1919–20, 1952–53; Division 4 – Champions 1979–80. *FA Cup:* Winners 1922; Runners-up 1920, 1928, 1930, 1938. *Football League Cup:* Semi-final. 1967–68.

Colours: Blue and white striped shirts, white shorts, white stockings. **Change colours:** Yellow and black squared shirts, black shorts, yellow stockings.

HUDDERSFIELD TOWN 1988–89 LEAGUE RECORD

Match No.	Date	Venue	Opponents	Result	H/T Score	Lg. Pos.	Goalscorers	Attendance
1	Aug 27	A	Brentford	L 0-1	0-0	—		5632
2	Sept 3	H	Preston NE	W 2-0	2-0	12	Maskell, Shotton	5622
3	10	A	Cardiff C	L 0-3	0-3	18		3891
4	17	H	Gillingham	D 1-1	0-0	18	Hutchings	4688
5	20	H	Notts Co	W 3-1	1-1	—	Byrne 2, Maskell (pen)	5655
6	24	A	Chester C	L 0-3	0-2	14		3319
7	Oct 1	H	Fulham	W 2-0	0-0	10	Maskell 2	4576
8	3	A	Port Vale	L 0-2	0-2	—		5938
9	8	A	Northampton T	W 3-1	3-0	10	Bent, Hutchings, Maskell (pen)	3975
10	15	H	Bristol C	L 0-1	0-0	16		5952
11	22	A	Aldershot	W 1-0	1-0	12	Hutchings	2155
12	25	H	Swansea C	D 1-1	0-0	—	Hutchings	5711
13	29	A	Bristol R	L 1-5	1-3	15	Hutchings	4460
14	Nov 5	H	Sheffield U	W 3-2	2-1	14	Byrne, Maskell 2	10,400
15	8	H	Bolton W	L 0-1	0-0	—		7802
16	12	A	Wolverhampton W	L 1-4	1-1	16	Maskell	12,697
17	26	A	Wigan Ath	W 2-0	1-0	14	Maskell, Cecere	2779
18	Dec 3	H	Blackpool	D 1-1	0-0	15	Maskell	5738
19	17	H	Bury	W 3-2	2-1	12	Bent, O'Regan, Maskell	5150
20	26	A	Chesterfield	D 1-1	1-1	13	Bent	5539
21	31	A	Mansfield T	L 0-1	0-0	14		4638
22	Jan 2	H	Southend U	W 3-2	1-0	14	Maskell, Bent, Byrne	6403
23	14	A	Preston NE	L 0-1	0-0	14		6959
24	21	H	Cardiff C	W 1-0	1-0	11	Bent	4869
25	28	A	Gillingham	W 2-1	1-1	10	Maskell, O'Regan	3530
26	Feb 4	A	Fulham	W 2-1	0-0	9	O'Doherty, Cecere	4081
27	11	H	Port Vale	D 0-0	0-0	9		8004
28	18	H	Northampton T	L 1-2	1-1	10	Maskell (pen)	5802
29	Mar 4	H	Aldershot	W 2-1	1-1	10	Winter, Byrne	4709
30	7	H	Reading	D 2-2	1-1	—	Duggan, Maskell	4933
31	11	A	Sheffield U	L 1-5	0-1	10	Marsden	13,680
32	14	H	Bristol R	L 2-3	2-1	—	Cecere, Maskell	4105
33	22	A	Swansea C	L 0-1	0-1	—		4075
34	25	A	Southend U	W 4-2	2-0	10	Duggan, Byrne, Maskell 2 (1 pen)	3582
35	27	H	Chesterfield	D 1-1	1-1	11	Maskell	5819
36	Apr 1	A	Bury	W 6-0	2-0	10	Cecere, Maskell 3, Smith, Byrne	4145
37	5	A	Reading	L 1-2	0-1	—	May	3802
38	8	H	Mansfield T	W 2-0	0-0	9	Maskell, McInerney	5327
39	15	H	Chester C	W 3-1	1-0	9	Winter, Smith, May	6109
40	18	A	Bristol C	L 1-6	0-5	—	Maskell	4542
41	22	A	Notts Co	L 0-3	0-1	12		5499
42	25	H	Brentford	L 1-2	0-0	—	Maskell	3538
43	29	H	Wolverhampton W	D 0-0	0-0	12		8757
44	May 1	A	Bolton W	L 1-3	0-1	12	Maskell (pen)	5511
45	6	A	Blackpool	L 1-2	0-1	14	Maskell	4070
46	13	H	Wigan Ath	D 1-1	0-0	14	Maskell	4225

Final League Position: 14

GOALSCORERS

League (63): Maskell 28 (5 pens), Byrne 7, Bent 5, Hutchings 5, Cecere 4, Duggan 2, May 2, O'Regan 2, Smith 2, Winter 2, McInerney 1, Marsden 1, O'Doherty 1, Shotton 1.
Littlewoods Cup (4): Maskell 2, Mitchell 1, Trevitt 1.
FA Cup (6): Bent 1, Maskell 1, May 1, O'Regan 1, Withe 1, own goal 1.

Littlewoods Cup	First Round	Scunthorpe U (a)	2-3
		(h)	2-2
FA Cup	First Round	Rochdale (h)	1-1
		(a)	4-3
	Second Round	Chester C (h)	1-0
	Third Round	Sheffield U (h)	0-1

Hardwick	Trevitt	Hutchings	Holmes	Tucker	Shotton	O'Regan	May	Withe	Maskell	Barham	Mitchell	Ward	O'Doherty	Marsden	Brown	Byrne	McInerney	France	Bent	Winter	Cecere	Smith	Duggan	*Match No.*
1	2	3	4*	5	6	7	8	9	10	11†	12	14												1
1	2	3	4	12	6	8		9	10		7		5*	11										2
1	2	3	12	5		4	8	14	10		6			11	7*	9†								3
1	2	3	12	6		7*	4	9†	10		8		5	11		14								4
1	2	3	12	6		7	4	14	10		8†		5	11*		9								5
1	2	3	12	6		7	4*	14	10		8		5			9	11†							6
1	2		8			3	4		10		7	14	5			9†	11*	6	12					7
1	2	8				3	4		10		7	9	5					6	11					8
1	2	3				7	4	9†	10		6	14	5	12					11*	8				9
1	2	3				7	4	9	10		6		5	12					11*	8				10
1	2	3				7	4	9	10		6		5			12			11*	8				11
1	2	3				7	4	9	10*		6		5			11			12	8				12
1	2	3				7	4	9	10		6*		5			11			12	8				13
1	2	3				7	4	9	10		6		5			11				8				14
1	2	3				7*	4	9	10		6		5			11			12	8				15
1	2	3				7	4*	14	10		6		5			11†			12	8	9			16
1		3				7	4	12	10		6		5			11*			2	8	9			17
1		3				7	4	11*	10		6		5			12			2	8	9			18
1		3				7	4		10		6		5	11		9*			2	8	12			19
1		3				7	4		10		6		5	11*		9			2	8	12			20
1		3				7	4		10		6		5	11*		9			2	8	12			21
1	2	3				7	4		10		6		5			9			8		11			22
1	12	3		5		7	4	14	10		6					11†			2*	8	9			23
1		3				7	4	12	10		6		5			11*			2	8	9			24
1	12	3				7	4	14	10		6		5			11†			2*	8	9			25
1	2	3				7	4	11*	10		6		5			12				8	9			26
1	2	3				7	4	11†	10		6		5			12				8*	9	14		27
1	2	3				7	4	8†	10				5	6		12		14			9	11*		28
1	2					3	4	14	10				5			12			7	8†	9	11*	6	29
1	2					3	4	14	10				5			7*			12	8	9	11†	6	30
1	12	3				7	4	14	10				5	6*						8†	9	11	2	31
1		3				2	4		10				5			7*			12	8	9	11	6	32
1	2	3					4		10				5			7				8	9	11	6	33
1	2	3		5			4		10							7				8	9	11	6	34
1	2	3					4		10				5	14		7			12	8†	9*	11	6	35
1	2	3					4		10				5			7				8	9	11	6	36
1	2	3					4		10				5			7*	12			8	9	11	6	37
1	2	3		6			4†		10				5	14		7	12			8	9*	11		38
1	2	3					4		10				5			7*	12			8	9	11	6	39
1	2						4		10		3		5			7*	12			8	9	11	6	40
1	2						4	12	10		3		5	8		7*					9	11	6	41
1	2	3		5		7	4*		10		6						11			8	9	12		42
1	2	3		5		7	4		10		6						12			8	9*	11		43
1	2	3		5		7*	4		10		6						11			8	9	12		44
1	14	3				2†	4		10		6					12	7			8	9*	11	5	45
1	2	3					4		10		6					7				8	9	11	5	46
46	35 + 4s	41	3 + 4s	11 + 1s	2	36	45	14 + 12s	46	1	33 + 1s	1 + 3s	37	10 + 4s	1	29 + 8s	5 + 5s	2 + 1s	14 + 8s	35	28 + 3s	17 + 3s	14	

HUDDERSFIELD TOWN

Player and Position	Ht	Wt	Birth Date	Birth Place	Source	Clubs	League App	League Gls
Goalkeepers								
Steve Hardwick	5 11	13 00	6 9 56	Mansfield	Amateur	Chesterfield	38	—
						Newcastle U	92	—
						Oxford U	156	—
						Crystal Palace (loan)	3	—
						Sunderland (loan)	6	—
						Huddersfield T	46	—
Lee Martin	5 11	11 08	9 9 68	Huddersfield	Trainee	Huddersfield T	18	—
Defenders								
Ian Bray	5 8	11 05	6 12 62	Neath	Apprentice	Hereford U	108	4
						Huddersfield T	75	1
Vincent Chapman*	5 9	11 00	5 12 67	Newcastle	Tow Law T	Huddersfield T	6	—
						York C (loan)	—	—
Andrew Duggan	6 3	13 00	19 9 67	Bradford	Apprentice	Barnsley	2	1
						Rochdale (loan)	3	—
						Huddersfield T	14	2
Graham Mitchell	6 0	11 05	16 2 68	Shipley	Apprentice	Huddersfield T	80	1
Ken O'Doherty	6 0	12 00	30 3 63	Dublin	UCD	Crystal Palace	42	—
						Huddersfield T	37	1
Simon Trevitt	5 11	11 02	20 12 67	Dewsbury	Apprentice	Huddersfield T	87	1
Gordon Tucker	5 11	11 12	5 1 68	Manchester	Derby Co	Huddersfield T	35	—
Midfield								
Graham Easter‡			26 9 69	Epsom	Trainee	WBA	—	—
						Huddersfield T	—	—
Michael France*	6 1	11 08	10 9 68	Huddersfield	Trainee	Huddersfield T	8	—
						Cobh Ramblers (loan)	—	—
Chris Hutchings	5 10	11 00	5 7 57	Winchester	Harrow Bor	Chelsea	87	0
						Brighton & HA	153	4
						Huddersfield T	64	5
Ian McInerney*	5 10	11 08	26 1 64	Liverpool	Blue Star	Huddersfield T	10	1
Chris Marsden	5 11	10 12	3 1 69	Sheffield	Trainee	Sheffield U	16	1
						Huddersfield T	14	1
Andy May	5 8	11 00	26 2 64	Bury	Apprentice	Manchester C	150	8
						Huddersfield T	73	5
						Bolton W (loan)	10	2
Kieran O'Regan	5 9	10 08	9 11 63	Cork	Tranmore Ath	Brighton & HA	86	2
						Swindon T	26	1
						Huddersfield T	36	2
Richard Shelton	5 8	10 11	8 6 68	Sheffield	Trainee	Huddersfield T	—	—
Julian Winter	6 0	11 02	6 9 65	Huddersfield	Local	Huddersfield T	93	5
						Scunthorpe U (loan)	4	—
Forwards								
Junior Bent	5 5	10 06	1 3 70	Huddersfield	Trainee	Huddersfield T	29	5
Mick Byrne	5 11	12 03	14 1 60	Dublin	Shamrock R	Huddersfield T	37	7
Michele Cecere	6 0	11 04	4 1 68	Chester	Apprentice	Oldham Ath	52	8
						Huddersfield T	31	4
Paul Kirkham	5 11	11 05	5 7 69	Manchester	Manchester U	Huddersfield T	1	—
						Waterford (loan)	—	—
Craig Maskell	5 10	11 04	10 4 68	Aldershot	Apprentice	Southampton	6	1
						Swindon T (loan)	—	—
						Huddersfield T	46	28
Mark Smith	5 11	11 05	19 12 61	Sheffield		Sheffield U	—	—
					Gainsborough Tr	Scunthorpe U	1	—
					Kettering	Rochdale	27	7
						Huddersfield T	20	2
Peter Ward‡	6 0	11 10	15 10 64	Co Durham	Chester-le-Street	Huddersfield T	37	2

HUDDERSFIELD TOWN

Foundation: A meeting, attended largely by members of the Huddersfield & District FA, was held at the Imperial Hotel in 1906 to discuss the feasibility of establishing a football club in this rugby stronghold. However, it was not until a man with both the enthusiasm and the money to back the scheme came on the scene, that real progress was made. This benefactor was Mr. Hilton Crowther and it was at a meeting at the Albert Hotel in 1908, that the club formally came into existence with a capital of £2,000 and joined the North-Eastern League.

Managers (and Secretary-managers)
Frank Walker 1908–10, Richard Pudan 1910–12, Arthur Fairclough 1912–19, Ambrose Langley 1919–21, Herbert Chapman 1921–25, Cecil Potter 1925–26, Jack Chaplin 1926–29, Clem Stephenson 1929–42, David Steele 1943–47, George Stephenson 1947–52, Andy Beattie 1952–56, Bill Shankly 1956–59, Eddie Boot 1960–64, Tom Johnston 1964–68, Ian Greaves 1968–74, Bobby Collins 1974, Tom Johnston 1975–78 (had been GM since 1975), Mike Buxton 1978–86, Steve Smith 1986–87, Malcolm Macdonald 1987–88, Eoin Hand 1988– .

Player and Position	*Ht*	*Wt*	*Birth Date*	*Birth Place*	*Source*	*Clubs*	*League App*	*League Gls*
Peter Withe†	6 1	12 00	30 8 51	Liverpool	Skelmers-dale	Southport	3	—
						Barrow	1	—
					Pt Elizabeth/ Arcadia S	Wolverhampton W	17	3
						Birmingham C	35	9
					Portland T	Nottingham F	75	28
						Newcastle U	76	25
						Aston Villa	182	74
						Sheffield U	74	18
						Birmingham C (loan)	8	2
						Huddersfield T	26	—

Trainees
Boothroyd, Adrian N; Byrne, Brian J; Byrne, Jason M; Charlton, Simon T; Crossley, Richard M; Donald, Steven A; Donovan, Kevin; Haylock, Gary A; Helliwell, Sean C; Hilditch, John; Hirst, Andrew M; McKee, Christopher J; Rainton, Karl; Weatherhead, Shaun; Wraight, Robert.

****Non-Contract**
Gledhill Richard; Withe, Peter.

Associated Schoolboys
Bell, Stephen J; Billy, Christopher A; Castle, Neil C; Chesters, Lee A; Collins, Simon; Dearnley, Robert; Dysart, John; Graley, Marc; Ireland, Simon P; Johnson, Matthew L; Kelly, Kevin; Rayne, Dean E; Stocchero, Daniel M; Tinker, Jonathan; Thomas, Stephen R; Wallace, David A.

HULL CITY 1988–89 *Back row (left to right):* Ken De Mange, Les Thompson Wayne Jacobs, Garreth Roberts, Billy Askew, Tim Hotte, Andy Payton, Ray Daniel.
Centre row: Tom Wilson (Reserve Team Coach), Steve Terry, Nicky Brown, Andy Saville, Tony Norman, Gavin Kelly, Leigh Jenkinson, John Moore, Richard Jobson, Don Robinson (Chairman), Jeff Radcliffe (Physiotherapist).
Front row: Neil Buckley, Charlie Palmer, Dennis Booth (Assistant Manager), Pete Skipper, Eddie Gray (Manager), Alex Dyer, Keith Edwards.

Division 2 HULL CITY

Boothferry Park, Hull HU4 6EU. Telephone Hull (0482) 51119.

Ground capacity: 20,058.

Record attendance: 55,019 v Manchester U, FA Cup 6th rd, 26 Feb, 1949.

Record receipts: £79,604 v Liverpool FA Cup, 5th rd, 18 February, 1989.

Pitch measurements: 112yd × 75yd.

Vice-Presidents: The Rt. Hon. H. Zammit, Toni Dalli, Max Payne MICM.

Chairman: D. Robinson. ***Vice-Chairman:*** T. C. Waite FIM, MIRTE.

Directors: M. W. Fish FCA, J. Johnson BA, DPA, G. H. C. Needler MA,ACA, R. Chetham, C. M. Thorpe LL.B.,, E. Hughes.

Manager: Colin Appleton. ***Assistant Manager/Coach:***

Reserve Team Coach: Tom Wilson. ***Physio:*** Jeff Radcliffe.

Secretary: Frank Boughton. ***Commercial Manager:*** Simon Cawkill. ***Development Executive:***

Year Formed: 1904. ***Turned Professional:*** 1905. ***Ltd Co.: 1905.***

Club Nickname: 'The Tigers'.

Previous Grounds: 1904, Boulevard Ground (Hull RFC); 1905, Anlaby Road (Hull CC); 1944/5 Boulevard Grounds; 1946, Boothferry Park.

Record League Victory: 11-1 v Carlisle U, Division 3 (N), 14 January 1939 – Ellis; Woodhead, Dowen; Robinson (1), Blyth, Hardy; Hubbard (2), Richardson (2), Dickinson (2), Davies (2), Cunliffe (2).

Record Cup Victory: 8-2 v Stalybridge Celtic (away), FA Cup, 1st rd, 26 November 1932 – Maddison; Goldsmith, Woodhead; Gardner, Hill (1), Denby; Forward (1), Duncan, McNaughton (1), Wainscoat (4), Sargeant (1).

Record Defeat: 0-8 v Wolverhampton W, Division 2, 4, November, 1911.

Most League Points (2 for a win): 69, Division 3, 1965–66.

Most League Points (3 for a win): 90, Division 4, 1982–83.

Most League Goals: 109, Division 3, 1965–66.

Highest League Scorer in Season: Bill McNaughton, 39, Division 3 (N), 1932–33.

Most League Goals in Total Aggregate: Chris Chilton, 195, 1960–71.

Most Capped Player: Terry Neill, 15 (59), Northern Ireland.

Most League Appearances: Andy Davidson, 520, 1952–67.

Record Transfer Fee Received: £400,000 from Sunderland for Tony Norman, December 1988.

Record Transfer Fee Paid: £200,000 to Leeds U for Peter Swan, March 1989.

Football League Record: 1905 Elected to Division 2; 1930–33 Division 3 (N); 1933–36 Division 2; 1936–49 Division 3 (N); 1949–56 Division 2; 1956–58 Division 3 (N); 1958–59 Division 3; 1959–60 Division 2; 1960–66 Division 3; 1966–78 Division 2; 1978–81 Division 3; 1981–83 Division 4; 1983–85 Division 3; 1985– Division 2.

Honours: *Football League:* Division 2 best season: 3rd, 1909–10; Division 3 (N) – Champions 1932–33, 1948–49; Division 3 – Champions 1965–66; Runners-up 1958–59; Division 4 – Runners-up 1982–83. *FA Cup* best season: Semi-final, 1930. *Football League Cup* best season: 4th, 1973–74, 1975–76, 1977–78. *Associate Members' Cup:* Runners-up 1984.

Colours: Amber shirts, red and black trim, black shorts, amber stockings. **Change colours:** White shirts,amber and black shorts, white stockings.

HULL CITY 1988–89 LEAGUE RECORD

Match No.	Date	Venue	Opponents	Result	H/T Score	Lg. Pos.	Goalscorers	Attendance
1	Aug 27	H	Manchester C	W 1-0	0-0	—	Edwards	11,653
2	29	A	Oxford U	L 0-1	0-1	—		5772
3	Sept 3	A	Plymouth Arg	L 0-2	0-0	13		8202
4	10	H	Barnsley	D 0-0	0-0	12		5654
5	17	A	Portsmouth	W 3-1	2-0	11	Edwards 2, Dyer	11,599
6	20	H	Blackburn R	L 1-3	1-3	—	Edwards	6681
7	24	A	Oldham Ath	D 2-2	0-2	14	Marshall (og), Terry	6319
8	Oct 1	H	Walsall	D 0-0	0-0	14		4845
9	4	H	Leicester C	D 2-2	1-1	—	Edwards (pen), De Mange	5079
10	8	A	Shrewsbury T	W 3-1	2-0	11	Edwards 2, Roberts	3287
11	15	H	Sunderland	D 0-0	0-0	15		8261
12	22	A	Crystal Palace	L 1-3	1-1	15	Dyer	8464
13	25	H	Chelsea	W 3-0	1-0	—	Edwards 2 (1 pen), Smith	6953
14	29	A	Leeds U	L 1-2	0-1	15	Palmer	17,536
15	Nov 5	H	Swindon T	W 1-0	1-0	12	Moore	5192
16	13	A	Stoke C	L 0-4	0-1	—		10,505
17	19	H	Birmingham C	D 1-1	0-1	16	Edwards	5134
18	26	A	Watford	L 0-2	0-2	18		10,404
19	29	A	Bournemouth	L 1-5	0-0	—	Payton	5420
20	Dec 3	H	Brighton & HA	W 5-2	3-1	17	Payton 2, Saville, Gatting (og), Daniel	5686
21	10	A	WBA	L 0-2	0-0	18		10,094
22	26	H	Bradford C	D 1-1	0-0	19	Payton (pen)	8791
23	31	H	Ipswich T	D 1-1	1-0	19	Whitehurst	7800
24	Jan 2	A	Barnsley	W 2-0	2-0	18	Edwards 2	9879
25	14	H	Bournemouth	W 4-0	3-0	17	Edwards 3 (1 pen), Whitehurst	5690
26	21	A	Manchester C	L 1-4	0-3	17	Edwards (pen)	20,485
27	Feb 4	A	Leicester C	W 2-0	1-0	16	Edwards 2 (1 pen)	9996
28	11	H	Shrewsbury T	W 3-0	2-0	14	Edwards 2, Whitehurst	11,472
29	25	A	Sunderland	L 0-2	0-0	15		14,719
30	28	A	Chelsea	L 1-2	0-0	—	Roberts	11,407
31	Mar 4	H	Stoke C	L 1-4	0-4	17	Whitehurst	5915
32	11	A	Swindon T	L 0-1	0-1	18		7090
33	14	H	Leeds U	L 1-2	1-1	19	Roberts	8887
34	18	A	Blackburn R	L 0-4	0-1	20		5864
35	25	H	Plymouth Arg	W 3-0	2-0	19	Jobson, Edwards 2	5851
36	27	A	Bradford C	D 1-1	1-1	20	Edwards	11,802
37	Apr 1	H	Portsmouth	D 1-1	0-0	21	Edwards	5325
38	4	H	Oxford U	L 1-2	0-2	—	Swan	6260
39	8	A	Ipswich T	D 1-1	0-1	21	Whitehurst	10,191
40	11	H	Crystal Palace	L 0-1	0-1	—		5050
41	15	A	Walsall	D 1-1	0-0	21	Edwards	3935
42	22	H	Oldham Ath	D 1-1	0-1	21	McParland	6748
43	29	H	Watford	L 0-3	0-1	21		5225
44	May 1	A	Brighton & HA	D 1-1	0-0	21	Edwards	6750
45	6	A	Birmingham C	L 0-1	0-0	21		4686
46	13	H	WBA	L 0-1	0-1	21		5217

Final League Position: 21

GOALSCORERS

League (52): Edwards 26 (5 pens), Whitehurst 5, Payton 4 (1 pen), Roberts 3, Dyer 2, Daniel 1, De Mange 1, Jobson 1, McParland 1, Moore 1, Palmer 1, Saville 1, Smith 1, Swan 1, Terry 1, own goals 2.
Littlewoods Cup (1): Edwards 1.
FA Cup (6): Edwards 3, Whitehurst 2, Brown 1.

Littlewoods Cup	Second Round	Arsenal (h)	1-2
		(a)	0-3
FA Cup	Third Round	Cardiff C (a)	2-1
	Fourth Round	Bradford C (a)	2-1
	Fifth Round	Liverpool (h)	2-3

Norman	Jobson	Jacobs	Warren	Skipper	Terry	Dyer	Roberts	Moore	Edwards	Saville	Palmer	Payton	Daniel	De Mange	Thompson	Kelly	Smith	Askew	Hotte	Jenkinson	Buckley	Hesford	Whitehurst	Brown	Calvert	Murray	Swan	McParland	Bell	*Match No.*
1	2	3	4*	5	6	7	8	9	10	11	12																			1
1	2	3	4	5	6	7	8	9	10	11																				2
1	2	3	4	5	6	7	8	9	10	11*		12																		3
1	5	3	4*		6	7	8	9	10		2		11	12																4
1	5	3†	4		6	7	8*		10	14	2	9	11	12																5
1	5		4		6	7	8	12	10		2†	9	11*	14	3															6
	5		4		6	11	8		10		2	9		12	3*	1	7													7
1	5	3†	4		6	11	8	12	10		2	9*		14	7															8
1	5		4		6	11	8	9	10	12	2†		3	14				7*												9
1	5		2		6	11	8	9	10	7			3	4																10
1	5	3	2		6	11	8	9	10			12	7*	4†			14													11
1	5	3	4		6	11			10	9	2		7				8*		12											12
1	5	3*	4		6	11			10	9	2		7	12			8													13
1	5	3	4		6	11			10	9†	2	14	7	12			8*													14
1	5	3	4		6	11	7	9	10		2			8																15
1	5	3	4		6		7*	9	10		2	12		8						11										16
1	5		4†		6		7	9*	10	12	2	11	3	8						14										17
1	5		4		6		7	12	10	9*	2	11	3	8																18
1	5		4		6		7	9*	10	12		11	3	8							2									19
1	5		4		6		8		10	9	2	7	3							11										20
1	5		4		6		8		10	9	2	7	3				12			11*										21
1	5		4				8			9	2	7	3	10			11				6									22
	5		4				8			12	2	7	3	10			11*				6	1	9							23
	5	3	14				8		10	12		7†	11*	4							6	1	9	2						24
	5	3					8		10			7		4				11			6	1	9	2						25
	5	3					8		10			7		4				11			6	1	9	2						26
	5	3					8		10			7		4				11			6	1	9	2						27
	5	3					8		10			7		4				11			6	1	9	2						28
	5	3					8		10			7		4*			12	11			6	1	9	2						29
	5	3					8		10				11	4				7			6	1	9	2						30
	5	3					8		10				11	4				7			6	1	9	2						31
	4	3			5		8		10	9		12						7			6†	1		2	11*	14				32
	4	3			5		8		10*	6		12						7		11		1	9			2				33
	4	3	6		5		8		10*	9		12		14			7			11†		1				2				34
	5	3			6		8*		10			12								14		1	9			2†	4	7	11	35
	5	3			6				10						8							1	9	2			4	7	11	36
	5	3			6				10						8*					12		1	9	2			4	7	11	37
	5	3			6				10									8		12		1	9	2			4	7	11*	38
	5	3			6				10						12		11	8				1	9	2			4*	7		39
	5	3	4		6		11		10*			12						8				1	9			2		7		40
	5	3	6				8		10					12	11							1	9			2	4	7*		41
	5	3	6†				8		10					12				11*		14		1	9			2	4	7		42
	2	3							10				6	12				11			5	1	9		8*		4	7		43
	2	3			5				10			12	6	11		1							9*		8		4	7		44
	2				5				10			9	6	11		1									8		4	7		45
	2				5				10				3	12			7†	6		11		1	9		8*	14	4			46
21	46	33	27 + 1s	3	33	15	35	11 + 3s	44	14 + 6s	17 + 1s	18 + 10s	23	19 + 13s	6 + 1s	3	9 + 3s	16	— + 1s	6 + 5s	13	22	21	13	5	6 + 2s	11	11	4	

Mudd — Match No. 45(3)

HULL CITY

Player and Position	Ht	Wt	Birth Date	Birth Place	Source	Clubs	League App	League Gls
Goalkeepers								
Iain Hesford	6 2	13 12	4 3 60	Zambia	Apprentice	Blackpool	202	—
						Sheffield W	—	—
						Fulham (loan)	3	—
						Notts Co (loan)	—	—
						Sunderland	10	—
						Hull C	97	—
							22	—
Gavin Kelly	6 0	12 13	29 9 68	Beverley		Hull C	3	—
Defenders								
Dennis Booth*	5 7	11 03	9 4 49	Stanley	Apprentice	Charlton Ath	77	5
						Blackpool	12	—
						Southend U	78	1
						Lincoln C	162	9
						Watford	100	2
						Hull C	123	2
Nicky Brown	6 0	12 03	16 10 66	Hull	Local	Hull C	24	—
Neil Buckley	6 2	13 06	25 9 68	Hull	Trainee	Hull C	14	—
Wayne Jacobs	5 9	10 02	3 2 69	Sheffield	Apprentice	Sheffield W	6	—
						Hull C	39	—
Richard Jobson	6 1	12 02	9 5 63	Hull	Burton A	Watford	28	4
						Hull C	174	15
Paul Mudd§			13 11 70	Hull	Trainee	Hull C	1	—
Malcolm Murray	5 11	11 02	26 7 64	Buckie	Buckie T	Hearts	27	—
						Hull C	8	—
Steve Terry	6 1	13 03	14 6 62	Clapton	Apprentice	Watford	160	14
						Hull C	33	1
Midfield								
Billy Askew	5 5	10 10	2 10 59	Lumley	Apprentice	Middlesbrough	12	—
						Blackburn R (loan)	—	—
						Hull C	221	18
Mark Calvert§			11 9 70	Consett	Trainee	Hull C	5	—
Ray Daniel	5 10	11 00	10 12 64	Luton	Apprentice	Luton T	22	4
						Gillingham (loan)	5	—
						Hull C	58	3
Ken De Mange	5 9	11 10	3 9 64	Dublin	Home Farm	Liverpool	—	—
						Scunthorpe U (loan)	3	2
						Leeds U	15	1
						Hull C	41	1
Tim Hotte‡	5 7	11 07	4 10 63	Bradford	Apprentice	Arsenal	—	—
					Finland	Huddersfield T	16	4
					Harrogate T	Halifax T	4	—
					N Ferriby U	Hull C	5	—
						York C (loan)	2	—
Andy Payton	5 9	10 06	23 10 66	Burnley		Hull C	52	6
Garreth Roberts	5 5	10 08	15 11 60	Hull	Apprentice	Hull C	370	47
Peter Swan	6 0	11 12	28 9 66	Leeds	Local	Leeds U	49	11
						Hull C	11	1
Lee Warren	6 0	11 13	28 2 69	Manchester	Trainee	Leeds U	—	—
						Rochdale	31	1
						Hull C	28	—
Forwards								
Keith Edwards	5 8	10 03	16 7 57	Stockton		Sheffield U	70	29
						Hull C	132	57
						Sheffield U	191	114
						Leeds U	38	6
						Aberdeen	9	2
						Hull C	53	29

HULL CITY

Foundation: The enthusiasts who formed Hull City in 1904 were brave men indeed. More than that they were audacious for they immediately put the club on the map in this Rugby League fortress by obtaining a three-year agreement with the Hull Rugby League club to rent their ground! They had obtained quite a number of conversions to the dribbling code, before the Rugby League forbade the use of any of their club grounds by Association Football clubs. By that time, Hull City were well away having entered the FA Cup in their initial season and the Football League, Second Division after only a year.

Managers (and Secretary-managers)
James Ramster 1904–05*, Ambrose Langley 1905–13, Harry Chapman 1913–14, Fred Stringer 1914–16, David Menzies 1916–21, Percy Lewis 1921–23, Bill McCracken 1923–31, Haydn Green 1931–34, John Hill 1934–36, David Menzies 1936, Ernest Blackburn 1936–46, Major Frank Buckley 1946–48, Raich Carter 1948–51, Bob Jackson 1952–55, Bob Brocklebank 1955–61, Cliff Britton 1961–70 (continued as GM to 1971), Terry Neill 1970–74, John Kaye 1974–77, Bobby Collins 1977–78, Ken Houghton 1978–79, Mike Smith 1979–82, Bobby Brown 1982, Colin Appleton 1982–84, Brian Horton 1984–88, Eddie Gray 1988–89, Colin Appleton 1989– .

Player and Position	*Ht*	*Wt*	*Birth Date*	*Birth Place*	*Source*	*Clubs*	*League App*	*League Gls*
Leigh Jenkinson	6 0	12 02	9 7 69	Thorne	Trainee	Hull C	14	1
Ian McParland	5 8	10 08	4 10 61	Edinburgh	Ormiston Pr	Notts Co	221	69
						Hull C	11	1
John Moore	6 0	11 11	1 10 66	Consett	Apprentice	Sunderland	16	1
						St Patricks Ath	—	—
						(loan)	2	—
						Newport Co (loan)	2	1
						Darlington (loan)	5	1
						Mansfield T (loan)	10	2
						Rochdale (loan)	14	1
						Hull C	5	—
						Sheffield U (loan)		
Michael Smith	5 8	10 09	19 12 68	Hull		Hull C	12	1
Les Thompson	5 10	11 00	23 9 68	Cleethorpes		Hull C	14	2
						Scarborough (loan)	3	1
Billy Whitehurst	6 0	13 00	10 6 59	Thurnscoe	Mexborough	Hull C	193	47
						Newcastle U	28	7
						Oxford U	40	4
						Reading	17	8
						Sunderland	17	3
						Hull C	21	5

Trainees
Atkinson, Graeme; Atkinson, Steven F; Ball, Alan; Booth, Grant A; Calvert, Mark R; Carroll, Mark A; Cleminshaw, David C; Cooper, Mark A; Davison, Lee D; Edmondson, Darren S; Gawthorpe, Robert N; Heath, William; Hutchinson, Mark J; Mennell, Simon; Mudd, Paul A; Robinson, Darren P; Waites, Paul; Warhurst, Mark A; Webster, Wayne A; Whitehead, Peter E.

Associated Schoolboys
Allison, Neil J; Endacott, Mark A; Gallagher, Mark; Goldspink, Steven J; Heath, Michael; Holmes, Nicholas J; Hopkin, Matthew C; Horsley, Richard C; Ledingham, Marc L; Malton, David C; Noonan, Lee; Robinson, Dale C; Salter, Alan; Shirtliff, Mark A; Smith, Carl A; Steer, Craig R; Wilson, Stephen L.

IPSWICH TOWN 1988–89 *Back row (left to right):* David Lowe, Graham Harbey, David Hill, Tony Humes, Chris O'Donnell, Neil Woods, Simon Milton.
Centre row: John Duncan (Manager), David Linighan, Ron Fearon, Craig Forrest, Jon Hallworth, Chris Kiwomya, Peter Trevivian (First Team Coach).
Front row: Mick Stockwell, Dalian Atkinson, Mich D'Avray, Romeo Zondervan, Frank Yallop, Jason Dozzell, John Wark.

Division 2 **IPSWICH TOWN**

Portman Road, Ipswich, Suffolk IP1 2DA. Telephone Ipswich (0473) 219211 (4 lines). Sales & Marketing Dept: (0473) 212202.

Ground capacity: 37,000.

Record attendance: 38,010 v Leeds U, FA Cup 6th rd, 8 March, 1975.

Record receipts: £105,950 v AZ 67 Alkmaar, UEFA Cup final 1st leg, 6 May, 1981.

Pitch measurements: 112yd × 70yd.

Chairman: P. M. Cobbold.

Directors: J. Kerr MBE, H. R. Smith, J. M. Sangster, K. H. Brightwell, J. Kerridge, D. Sheepshanks.

Manager: John Duncan. ***Assistant Manager:*** Charlie Woods.

First Team Coach: Peter Trevivian. ***Reserve Coach:***

Physio: D. Bingham. ***Youth Team Coach:***

Secretary: David C. Rose.

Sales & Promotions Manager: M. Noye.

Year Formed: 1878. ***Turned Professional:*** 1936. ***Ltd Co.:*** 1936.

Club Nickname: 'Blues' or 'Town'.

Record League Victory: 7-0 v Portsmouth, Division 2, 7 November 1964 – Thorburn; Smith, McNeil; Baxter, Bolton, Thompson; Broadfoot (1), Hegan (2), Baker (1), Leadbetter, Brogan (3). 7-0 v Southampton Division 1, 2 February 1974 – Sivell; Burley, Mills (1), Morris, Hunter, Beattie (1), Hamilton (2), Viljoen, Johnson, Whymark (2), Lambert (1) (Woods). 7-0 v WBA, Division 1, 6 November 1976 – Sivell; Burley, Mills, Talbot, Hunter, Beattie (1), Osborne, Wark (1), Mariner (1) (Bertschin), Whymark (4), Woods.

Record Cup Victory: 10-0 v Floriana, European Cup, Prel. rd, 25 September 1962 – Bailey; Malcolm, Compton; Baxter, Laurel, Elsworthy (1); Stephenson, Moran (2), Crawford (5), Phillips (2), Blackwood.

Record Defeat: 1-10 v Fulham, Division 1, 26 December, 1963.

Most League Points (2 for a win): 64, Division 3 (S), 1953–54 and 1955–56.

Most League Points (3 for a win): 83, Division 1, 1981–82.

Most League Goals: 106, Division 3 (S), 1955–56.

Highest League Scorer in Season: Ted Phillips, 41, Division 3 (S), 1956–57.

Most League Goals in Total Aggregate: Ray Crawford, 203, 1958–63 and 1966–69.

Most Capped Player: Allan Hunter, 47 (53), Northern Ireland.

Most League Appearances: Mick Mills, 591, 1966–82.

Record Transfer Fee Received: £725,000 from Glasgow Rangers for Terry Butcher, August 1986.

Record Transfer Fee Paid: £300,000 to Shrewsbury T for David Linighan, July 1988.

Football League Record: 1938 Elected to Division 3 (S); 1954–55 Division 2; 1955–57 Division 3 (S); 1957–61 Division 2; 1961–64 Division 1; 1964–68 Division 2; 1968–86 Division 1; 1986– Division 2.

Honours: *Football League:* Division 1 – Champions 1961–62; Runners-up 1980–81, 1981–82; Division 2 – Champions 1960–61, 1967–68; Division 3 (S) – Champions 1953–54, 1956–57. *FA Cup:* Winners 1977–78. *Football League Cup* best season: Semi-final 1981–82, 1984–85, *Texaco Cup:* 1972–73. **European Competitions:** *European Cup:* 1962–63; *European Cup-Winners' Cup:* 1978–79; *UEFA Cup:* 1973–74, 1974–75, 1975–76, 1977–78, 1979–80, 1980–81 (winners), 1981–82, 1982–83.

Colours: Blue shirts, white shorts, blue stockings. **Change colours:** All Orange.

IPSWICH TOWN 1988–89 LEAGUE RECORD

Match No.	*Date*	*Venue*	*Opponents*	*Result*	*H/T Score*	*Lg. Pos.*	*Goalscorers*	*Atten-dance*
1	Aug 27	A	Stoke C	D 1-1	0-1	—	Humes	8639
2	Sept 3	H	Sunderland	W 2-0	1-0	8	Atkinson, Dozzell	12,835
3	10	A	Leicester C	W 1-0	1-0	7	Atkinson	10,816
4	17	H	Watford	W 3-2	1-1	4	Milton, Atkinson, Lowe	14,644
5	20	A	Shrewsbury T	W 5-1	3-1	3-1	Dozzell, Milton 3, Yallop	4154
6	24	H	Bradford C	D 1-1	0-0	3	Atkinson	13,074
7	Oct 1	A	WBA	W 2-1	1-0	1	Lowe, Dozzell	9357
8	4	A	Crystal Palace	L 0-2	0-2	—		10,325
9	8	H	Manchester C	W 1-0	1-0	3	Dozzell	15,521
10	15	H	Oxford U	L 1-2	0-2	3	Dozzell	13,039
11	22	A	Barnsley	L 0-2	0-2	4		6325
12	25	H	Portsmouth	L 0-1	0-0	—		14,796
13	29	A	Bournemouth	L 0-1	0-0	9		6648
14	Nov 5	H	Leeds U	L 0-1	0-1	11		11,755
15	8	H	Walsall	W 3-1	1-0	—	Wark 2 (2 pens), Stockwell	9067
16	12	A	Swindon T	W 3-2	0-1	6	Atkinson, Dozzell, Zondervan	7246
17	19	H	Brighton & HA	L 2-3	2-1	8	Lowe, Stockwell	12,386
18	26	A	Birmingham C	L 0-1	0-1	9		5932
19	Dec 3	H	Plymouth Arg	D 2-2	1-2	7	Lowe, D'Avray	9929
20	10	A	Blackburn R	L 0-1	0-1	13		7258
21	16	H	Oldham Ath	W 2-1	0-1	—	Dozzell, Wark	8982
22	26	A	Chelsea	L 0-3	0-2	13		17,621
23	31	A	Hull C	D 1-1	0-1	14	Redford	7800
24	Jan 2	H	Leicester C	W 2-0	1-0	12	Linighan, Milton	14,037
25	14	A	Walsall	W 4-2	0-0	8	Wark (pen), Dozzell, Kiwomya, Redford	4623
26	21	H	Stoke C	W 5-1	0-0	7	Baltacha, Dozzell 2, Kiwomya, Yallop	14,692
27	Feb 4	H	Crystal Palace	L 1-2	1-2	9	Wark	14,569
28	11	A	Manchester C	L 0-4	0-2	12		22,140
29	21	H	Barnsley	W 2-0	1-0	—	Dozzell, Milton	9995
30	25	A	Oxford U	D 1-1	0-1	9	Linighan	6086
31	28	A	Portsmouth	W 1-0	0-0	—	Milton	7145
32	Mar 4	H	Swindon T	L 1-2	0-0	9	Milton	11,542
33	11	A	Leeds U	W 4-2	1-0	9	Atkinson, Milton, Wark 2 (1 pen)	19,639
34	14	H	Bournemouth	W 3-1	3-0	—	Wark, Atkinson 2	10,747
35	18	H	Shrewsbury T	W 2-0	0-0	5	Atkinson 2	10,913
36	25	A	Sunderland	L 0-4	0-1	5		13,859
37	28	H	Chelsea	L 0-1	0-0	—		22,950
38	Apr 1	A	Watford	L 2-3	0-2	7	Milton, Wark	12,054
39	4	A	Oldham Ath	L 0-4	0-2	—		5182
40	8	H	Hull C	D 1-1	1-0	8	Swan (og)	10,191
41	15	A	Bradford C	D 2-2	1-2	10	D'Avray, Zondervan	9691
42	22	H	WBA	W 2-1	0-0	9	Humes, Wark (pen)	12,047
43	29	H	Birmingham C	W 4-0	2-0	9	Wark, Lowe 2, Zondervan	9975
44	May 1	A	Plymouth Arg	W 1-0	1-0	9	Humes	6484
45	6	A	Brighton & HA	W 1-0	1-0	8	D'Avray	8616
46	13	H	Blackburn R	W 2-0	1-0	8	Wark 2 (2 pens)	10,861

Final League Position: 8

GOALSCORERS

League (71): Wark 13 (7 pens), Dozzell 11, Atkinson 10, Milton 10, Lowe 6, D'Avray 3, Humes 3, Zondervan 3, Kiwomya 2, Linighan 2, Redford 2, Stockwell 2, Yallop 2, Baltacha 1, own goal 1.
Littlewoods Cup (7): Atkinson 3, Stockwell 2, Dozzell 1, Lowe 1.
FA Cup (0).

Littlewoods Cup	Second Round	Port Vale (a)	0-1
		(h)	3-0
	Third Round	Leyton Orient (h)	2-0
	Fourth Round	Aston Villa (a)	2-6
FA Cup	Third Round	Nottingham F (a)	0-3

Forrest	Yallop	Hill	Zondervan	Humes	Linighan	Lowe	Dozzell	D'Avray	Atkinson	Wark	Milton	Stockwell	Woods	Kiwomya	Harbey	Redford	O'Donnell	Gregory	Fearon	Baltacha	Juryeff	Johnson	Cheetham	*Match No.*
1	2	3	4	5	6	7	8	9*	10	11	12													1
1	2	3	4	5*	6	7	8	9	10	11	12													2
1	2	3	4	5	6	7	8	9	10	11														3
1	2	3	4	5	6	7	8	9*	10		11	12												4
1	2	3		5	6	7	8		10	11	9	4												5
1	2	3		5*		7	8	9	10	11		4	12†	14	6									6
1	2	3	4	5		7	8	6	10	11	9													7
1	2	3	4	5*	12	7	8	6	10	11	9													8
1	2	3	4	5	11	7	8	6	10		9													9
1	2	3	4	5	6	7	8		10		9*	11		12										10
1	2	3	4	5		7	8	12	10		9†	6		11*	14									11
1	2	3	4			7	8	5	10	9	12	6		11*										12
1	2	3	4			7	8	5	10*	11	9†	6		12	14									13
1	2		4	5	6	7	8	9†	14	10	12	11*			3									14
1	2		4	5	6	7*	8		10	9		11		12	3									15
1	2		4	5*	6	7	8		10	9	12	11†		14	3									16
1	2		4		6†	7	8		10	9	5*	11			3	12	14							17
1					8	9	5		10	4	6	11			2	7	3							18
1	2	3	4		6	7	8	12	10	9		11				5*								19
1	2	3	4		6	7*	8	12	10	9	14	11				5†								20
1	2	3	4		6	7	8	12		9	14	11		10*		5†								21
1	2		4		6	7	8		10†		9*	11		12	3	5		14						22
	2	10	4		6	7	8			9		11			3	5			1					23
	2	10	4		6		8			9	11			7	3	5			1					24
	2	10	4		6		8	12		9		11†		7	3*	5		14	1					25
	2	10	4		6		8	12		9*				7	3	5			1	11				26
	2	10	4		6		8			9	12			7	3	5*			1	11				27
	2	4			6		8		10	9				7	3	5			1	11*	12			28
	2	4			6		8*		10†	9	7			14		5			1	11	12	3		29
	2	4			6			8	10	9	7					5			1	11		3		30
	2	4			6			8	10	9	7				12	5			1	11		3*		31
	2	4			6			8	10*	9	7			12		5			1	11		3		32
	3	11	4	2	6			8	10	9	7			12					1	5*				33
	3	11	4	2	6			5	10	9	7			8					1					34
	3*	11	4	2	6			5	10	9	7			8					1	12				35
		11	4	3	6	12		5	10	9	7*			8					1	2				36
	2	11	4	3	6				10	9	7			8					1	5				37
	2	11	4	3*	6	14		12	10	9	7			8†					1	5				38
	2	11	4	3	6	7		12	10	9				8		14			1	5*				39
	2	11*	4		6	7			10*	9				8	12	3			1	5				40
1	12		4	3	6	7		5		9	10				11	8				2*				41
1			4	11	6	7		5		9	10†	14		12	3*	8				2				42
1			4	11	6	7		5		9*	10†	14			3	8				2			12	43
1	12		4*	11	6	7		5		9		10			3	8				2				44
1		4		11†	6			5		9	14	10		7*	3	8				2			12	45
1		12	4†		6	7		5*		9	14	11			3	8				2			10	46
28	38 + 2s	35 + 1s	37	26	40 + 1s	30 + 2s	29	24 + 8s	33 + 1s	41	25 + 10s	20 + 3s	— + 1s	16 + 10s	19 + 4s	22 + 2s	1 + 1s	— + 2s	18	19 + 1s	— + 2s	4	1 + 2s	

IPSWICH TOWN

Player and Position	Ht	Wt	Birth Date	Birth Place	Source	Clubs	League App	League Gls
Goalkeepers								
Ron Fearon	6 0	11 12	19 11 60	Romford	Apprentice	QPR	—	—
						Reading	61	—
					Sutton	Ipswich T	28	—
						Brighton & HA (loan)	7	—
Craig Forrest	6 4	12 03	20 9 67	Vancouver	Apprentice	Ipswich T	28	—
						Colchester U (loan)	11	—
Defenders								
Sergei Baltacha†	6 0	12 00	17 2 58	Ukraine	Dynamo Kiev	Ipswich T	20	1
Jason Dozzell	6 2	12 04	9 12 67	Ipswich	School	Ipswich T	170	20
Graham Harbey	5 8	10 08	29 8 64	Chesterfield	Apprentice	Derby Co	40	1
						Ipswich T	58	1
Anthony Humes	5 11	10 10	19 3 66	Blyth	Apprentice	Ipswich T	75	5
Gavin Johnson	6 0	11 01	10 10 70	Ipswich	Trainee	Ipswich T	4	—
David Linighan	6 2	10 12	9 1 65	Hartlepool	Local	Hartlepool U	91	5
						Leeds U (loan)	—	—
						Derby Co	—	—
						Shrewsbury T	65	1
						Ipswich T	41	2
Scott Mills*	5 10	11 03	29 3 70	Sudbury	Trainee	Ipswich T	—	—
Chris O'Donnell*	5 9	12 00	26 5 68	Newcastle	Apprentice	Ipswich T	14	—
						Northampton T (loan)	1	—
Darren Oxbrow*	6 1	12 06	1 9 69	Ipswich	Trainee	Ipswich T	—	—
Frank Yallop	5 11	11 03	4 4 64	Watford	Apprentice	Ipswich T	162	4
Midfield								
Andy Bernal	5 10	12 05	16 7 66	Canberra		Ipswich T	9	—
Michael Cheetham			30 6 67	Amsterdam		Ipswich T	3	—
David Gregory	5 10	11 03	23 1 70	Sudbury	Trainee	Ipswich T	2	—
David Hill	5 9	10 03	6 6 66	Nottingham	Local	Scunthorpe U	140	10
						Ipswich T	36	—
Robert Mayes‡			18 12 67	Ipswich		Ipswich T	—	—
Simon Milton	5 9	11 09	23 8 63	London	Bury St Edmunds	Ipswich T	43	11
						Exeter C (loan)	2	3
						Torquay U (loan)	4	1
Ian Redford	5 10	11 08	5 4 60	Dundee	Errol R	Dundee	85	34
						Rangers	172	23
						Dundee U	101	20
						Ipswich T	24	2
Mike Stockwell	5 6	10 02	14 2 65	Chelmsford	Apprentice	Ipswich T	95	4
John Wark	5 10	11 07	4 8 57	Glasgow	Apprentice	Ipswich T	296	94
						Liverpool	70	28
						Ipswich T	48	13
Romeo Zondervan	5 9	10 02	4 3 59	Surinam	Den Haag	Twente Enschede	—	—
						WBA	84	5
						Ipswich T	182	13
Forwards								
Dalian Atkinson	6 1	12 10	21 3 68	Shrewsbury		Ipswich T	60	18
Mich D'Avray	6 1	13 02	19 2 62	Johannesburg	Apprentice	Ipswich T	199	36
						Leicester C (loan)	3	—

IPSWICH TOWN

Foundation: Considering that Ipswich Town only reached the Football League in 1938, many people outside of East Anglia may be surprised to learn that this club was formed at a meeting held in the Town Hall as far back as 1878 when Mr. T. C. Cobbold, MP, was voted president. Originally it was the Ipswich Association FC to distinguish it from the older Ipswich Football Club which played rugby. These two amalgamated in 1888 and the handling game was dropped in 1893.

Managers (and Secretary-managers)
Mick O'Brien 1936–37, Scott Duncan 1937–55 (continued as secretary), Alf Ramsey 1955–63, Jackie Milburn 1963–64, Bill McGarry 1964–68, Bobby Robson 1969–82, Bobby Ferguson 1982–87, Johnny Duncan 1987– .

Player and Position	*Ht*	*Wt*	*Birth Date*	*Birth Place*	*Source*	*Clubs*	*League App*	*League Gls*
Lee Howey‡	6 1	11 04	1 4 69	Sunderland	Apprentice	Ipswich T	—	—
Chris Kiwomya	5 10	10 05	2 12 69	Huddersfield		Ipswich T	26	2
David Lowe	5 11	11 00	30 8 65	Liverpool	Apprentice	Wigan Ath	188	40
						Ipswich T	73	23
Neil Woods	6 1	12 12	30 7 66	York	Apprentice	Doncaster R	65	16
						Rangers	3	—
						Ipswich T	20	4

Trainees
Banks, Andrew C; Boyle, Lee; Currie, Neil W; Devereux, Robert; Doyle, Graeme M; Durrant, Gary J; Ellis, David S; Gardiner, Aaron R.W; Gray, David B; Grice, Neil T; Honeywood, Lee B; Hooper, Glynn D; Horne, Ian M; Hyde, Stephen; Neville, Christopher W; Pick, Neil J; Swailles, Christopher W.

****Non-Contract**
Baltatcha, Sergei P.

Associated Schoolboys
Bailey, Darren E; Betts, Simon R; Bringloe, Paul D; Cook, Adam; Cotterell, Leo S; Doody, James C; Durrant, Lee R; Flear, Christopher R; Ford, Simon; Gibbs, Paul J; Goodhand, Peter J; Gregory, Neil R; Harrison, Gary D; Hewitson, Mark W.G; Hunter, David S; Melling, Jason L; Nicholls, Darren; Pearn, Steven; Powley, Darren L; Shaw, Marcus; Smedley, Martin; Williams, Shaun; Windard, Richard C; Winter, Darren M.

LEEDS UNITED 1988–89 *Back row (left to right):* Peter Gunby (Coach), John Pearson, Jack Ashurst, Mark Aizlewood, Mervyn Day, Peter Haddock, Peter Swan, Neil Aspin.
Centre row: Norman Hunter (Coach), Alan Sutton (Physiotherapist), David Rennie, Noel Blake, Bobby Davison, Ronnie Sinclair, Gary Williams, Bob Taylor, John Stiles, Dave Blakey, (Chief Scout), Billy Bremner (Manager), Dave Bentley (Assistant Manager).
Front row: Ian Baird, Glynn Snodin, John Sheridan, Brendan Ormsby, Vince Hilaire, David Batty, Micky Adams.

Division 2 LEEDS UNITED

Elland Road, Leeds LS11 0ES. Telephone Leeds (0532) 716037 (4 lines).

Ground capacity: 40,176.

Record attendance: 57,892 v Sunderland, FA Cup 5th rd replay, 15 March, 1967.

Record receipts: £146,483, FA Cup semi-final replay, Everton v West Ham U, 16 April, 1980.

Pitch measurements: 117yd × 76yd.

President: The Right Hon The Earl of Harewood LLD.

Chairman: L. Silver OBE. ***Vice-Chairman:*** P. J. Gilman. ***Deputy Chairman:*** J. W. G. Marjason. ***Managing Director:*** W. J. Fotherby.

Directors: R. Barker MCIT, MBIM, Coun. M. J. Bedford, E. Carlile, Coun. R. D. Feldman, G. M. Holmes BSC (ECON), Coun. A. Hudson, R. P. Ridsdale.

Manager: Howard Wilkinson.

Secretary: D. J. Dowse.

Coaches: Mike Hennigan, Peter Gunby, Dick Bate. ***Physio:*** Alan Sutton.

Commercial Manager: Bob Baldwin.

Year Formed: 1919, as Leeds United after disbandment (by FA order) of Leeds City (formed in 1904). ***Turned Professional:*** 1920. ***Ltd Co.:*** 1920.

Club Nickname: United.

Record League Victory: 8-0 v Leicester C, Division 1, 7 April 1934 – Moore; George Milburn, Jack Milburn; Edwards, Hart, Copping; Mahon (2), Firth (2), Duggan (2), Furness (2), Cochrane.

Record Cup Victory: 10-0 v Lyn (Oslo), European Cup, 1st rd (1st leg), 17 September 1969 – Sprake; Reaney, Cooper, Bremner (2), Charlton, Hunter, Madeley, Clarke (2), Jones (3), Giles (2) (Bates), O'Grady (1).

Record Defeat: 1-8 v Stoke C, Division 1, 27 August, 1934.

Most League Points (2 for a win): 67, Division 1, 1968–69.

Most League Points (3 for a win): 69, Division 2, 1984–85 and Division 2, 1987–88.

Most League Goals: 98, Division 2, 1927–28.

Highest League Scorer in Season: John Charles, 42, Division 2, 1953–54.

Most League Goals in Total Aggregate: Peter Lorimer, 168, 1965–79 and 1983–86.

Most Capped Player: Billy Bremner, 54, Scotland.

Most League Appearances: Jack Charlton, 629, 1953–73.

Record Transfer Fee Received: £800,000 from Everton for Ian Snodin, January 1987.

Record Transfer Fee Paid: £930,000 to WBA for Peter Barnes, August 1981.

Football League Record: 1920 Elected to Division 2; 1924–27 Division 1; 1927–28 Division 2; 1928–31 Division 1; 1931–32 Division 2; 1932–47 Division 1; 1947–56 Division 2; 1956–60 Division 1; 1960–64 Division 2; 1964–82 Division 1; 1982– Division 2.

Honours: *Football League:* Division 1 – Champions 1968–69, 1973–74; Runners-up 1964–65, 1965–66, 1969–70, 1970–71, 1971–72; Division 2 – Champions 1923–24, 1963–64; Runners-up 1927–28, 1931–32, 1955–56. *FA Cup:* Winners 1972, Runners-up 1965, 1970, 1973. *Football League Cup:* Winners 1967-68.**European Competitions:** *European Cup:* 1969–70, 1974–75 (runners-up). *European Cup-Winners' Cup:* 1972–73 (runners-up). *European Fairs Cup:* 1965–66, 1966–67 (runners-up), 1967–68 (winners), 1968–69, 1970–71 (winners). *EUFA Cup:* 1971–72, 1973–74, 1979–80.

Colours: All white. **Change colours:** All yellow.

LEEDS UNITED 1988–89 LEAGUE RECORD

Match No.	*Date*	*Venue*	*Opponents*	*Result*	*H/T Score*	*Lg. Pos.*	*Goalscorers*	*Atten-dance*
1	Aug 27	H	Oxford U	D 1-1	1-1	—	Snodin	20,697
2	Sept 3	A	Portsmouth	L 0-4	0-2	21		15,263
3	10	H	Manchester C	D 1-1	0-0	20	Blake	23,122
4	17	A	Bournemouth	D 0-0	0-0	19		7922
5	21	H	Barnsley	W 2-0	0-0	—	Davison, Hilaire	17,390
6	24	H	Chelsea	L 0-2	0-2	18		26,080
7	Oct 1	A	Brighton & HA	L 1-2	1-0	21	Baird	7109
8	4	A	Sunderland	L 1-2	0-1	—	Davison	12,671
9	8	H	Watford	L 0-1	0-0	21		15,657
10	16	A	Swindon T	D 0-0	0-0	—		9234
11	22	H	Leicester C	D 1-1	1-0	21	Hilaire	17,263
12	26	A	Bradford C	D 1-1	1-0	—	Davison	13,046
13	29	H	Hull C	W 2-1	1-0	21	Sheridan, Baird	17,536
14	Nov 5	A	Ipswich T	W 1-0	1-0	20	Sheridan (pen)	11,755
15	12	H	WBA	W 2-1	2-1	19	Aizlewood, Baird	20,442
16	19	A	Oldham Ath	D 2-2	1-1	20	Davison 2	8824
17	22	A	Birmingham C	D 0-0	0-0	—		6168
18	26	H	Stoke C	W 4-0	2-0	14	Baird 2, Davison, Sheridan (pen)	19,933
19	Dec 3	A	Walsall	W 3-0	1-0	11	Davison 2, Whitlow	6885
20	10	H	Shrewsbury T	L 2-3	0-2	14	Sheridan (pen), Davison	19,967
21	17	A	Crystal Palace	D 0-0	0-0	14		9847
22	26	H	Blackburn R	W 2-0	2-0	11	Baird, Davison	31,622
23	31	H	Plymouth Arg	W 2-0	0-0	11	Baird, Snodin	24,043
24	Jan 2	A	Manchester C	D 0-0	0-0	11		33,034
25	14	H	Birmingham C	W 1-0	0-0	7	Hilaire	21,837
26	21	A	Oxford U	L 2-3	2-2	11	Blake, Hilaire	7926
27	Feb 4	H	Sunderland	W 2-0	1-0	8	Davison, Sheridan (pen)	31,984
28	11	A	Watford	D 1-1	0-1	9	Pearson	13,439
29	18	A	Leicester C	W 2-1	2-1	6	Davison, Snodin	14,151
30	25	H	Swindon T	D 0-0	0-0	8		22,651
31	Mar 1	H	Bradford C	D 3-3	2-2	—	Blake, Hilaire, Baird	33,325
32	5	A	WBA	L 1-2	1-2	—	Adams	15,914
33	11	H	Ipswich T	L 2-4	0-1	12	Hilaire, Blake	19,639
34	14	A	Hull C	W 2-1	1-1	—	Baird, Davison	8887
35	19	A	Barnsley	D 2-2	1-1	—	Aizlewood, Sheridan (pen)	11,578
36	25	H	Portsmouth	W 1-0	0-0	8	Baird	27,049
37	27	A	Blackburn R	L 0-2	0-0	10		11,533
38	Apr 1	H	Bournemouth	W 3-0	1-0	6	Shutt 3	21,095
39	5	H	Crystal Palace	L 1-2	1-2	—	Shutt	25,604
40	9	A	Plymouth Arg	L 0-1	0-0	—		9365
41	15	H	Brighton & HA	W 1-0	1-0	7	Williams	14,915
42	22	A	Chelsea	L 0-1	0-0	10		30,332
43	29	A	Stoke C	W 3-2	1-2	10	Sheridan (pen), Davison, Strachan	9051
44	May 1	H	Walsall	W 1-0	0-0	10	Aizlewood	13,280
45	6	H	Oldham Ath	D 0-0	0-0	10		14,459
46	13	A	Shrewsbury T	D 3-3	2-2	10	Strachan 2 (1 pen), Rennie	4693

Final League Position: 10

GOALSCORERS

League (59): Davison 14, Baird 10, Sheridan 7 (6 pens), Hilaire 6, Blake 4, Shutt 4, Aizlewood 3, Snodin 3, Strachan 3 (1 pen), Adams 1, Pearson 1, Rennie 1, Whitlow 1, Williams A 1.
Littlewoods Cup (5): Baird 1, Davison 1, Hilaire 1, Pearson 1, Sheridan 1 (pen).
FA Cup (2): Baird 2.

Littlewoods Cup	Second Round	Peterborough U (a)	2-1
		(h)	3-1
	Third Round	Luton T (h)	0-2
FA Cup	Third Round	Brighton & HA (a)	2-1
	Fourth Round	Nottingham F (a)	0-2

Day	Haddock	Adams	Aizlewood	Blake	Ashurst	Stiles	Hilaire	Baird	Pearson	Snodin	Davison	Rennie	Taylor	Williams G	Batty	Sheridan	Aspin	Williams A	Whitlow	Andrews	Swan	Fairclough	Strachan	Shutt	Kerr	Speed	Mumby	Ormsby	*Match No.*
1	2	3	4	5	6	7†	8	9	10*	11	12	14																	1
1	2	3	4	5	6	8	11	9	10		12		7*																2
1		3†	4	5	6		11	9	12		10*			2	7	8	14												3
1	14	3	4	5	6		11		12		10		9*	2	7	8†													4
1	12	3	4*	5	6		11	9			10			2	7	8													5
1	4*	3		5	6		11	9†	14	12	10			2	7	8													6
1		3	4*	5			11	9	10	8		6		2	7	12													7
1	2†	3		5		4	11	9*	12		10	6			7	8	14												8
1		3		5		4†	11	9	12	14	10*	6			7	8	2												9
1			4	5	14		11	9	12	3	10*	6			7†	8	2												10
1			4	5		14	11	9	12	3	10*	6			7†	8	2												11
1			4	5		14	11	9*	12	3	10	6			7	8†	2												12
1			4	5		14	11†	9	12	3	10*	6			7	8	2												13
1			4	5		14	11†	9	12	3	10	6			7	8*	2												14
1			4	5			11	9	12	3†	10*	6			7	8	2	14											15
1			4	5			11	9	12	3	10*	6			7†	8	2	14											16
1		12	4	5			11	9		3	10†	6	14			8	2	7*											17
1			4	5			11	9		3	10	6			12	8*	2		7										18
1			4	5			11*	9		3	10	6				8	2	12	7										19
1			4	5			11	9*		3	10	6	12			8	2		7										20
			4	5			11†	9		3	10*	6	12			8	2	14	7	1									21
1			4	5			11†	9	12	3	10*	6				8	2	14	7										22
1			4	5			11	9	12	3	10*	6				8	2		7										23
1			4	5			11†	9*	12	3	10	6			14	8	2		7										24
1			4	5			11	9	12	3	10*	6					2	8	7										25
1			4	5			11	9*	12	3	10	6				8	2	14	7†										26
1		4		5			11	9		3	10	6			7	8	2												27
1		4		5			11	9	12	3	10*	6			7	8	2†	14											28
1		4	14	5			11	9†	12	3	10	6			7	8*	2												29
1		4	14	5			11	9*	12	3†	10	6			7	8	2												30
1		4*	12	5			11	9		3	10	6			7	8	2												31
1		4†	14	5			11	9	12	3	10*	6		2	7	8													32
1			4	5			11	9	12	3	10*	6†		2	7	8			14										33
1			4				11†	9	12	3	10*			2	7	8	6		14		5								34
1	2		4	5			11†		9	3	10*		12			8	6	14	7										35
1			4	5			11	9	12	3	10†					8*	2	14				6	7						36
1			4	5			11†	9	10	3					12	8*	2	14				6	7						37
1			4	5				9		3*						8	2	12	11			6	7	10					38
1			4				11*	9	12	3		5				8	2					6	7	10					39
1				5				9	12	3†		14			8		2	4	11			6	7	10*					40
1	2†		3	5					9		10	14				8		4	11*			6	7		12				41
1			4	5				9	12		10					14	2*	8	11			6	7		3†				42
1	14		4*	5			11	9†			10				12	8		2	3			6	7						43
1	14		4*	5			11	9			10†				12	8		2	3			6	7						44
1	2			5		14	11	9				4†			8				3*			6	7			10	12		45
1	2			5		14	11	9†				10			8				3*			6	7		12			4	46
45	8 + 4s	15 + 1s	34 + 4s	44	6 + 1s	4 + 6s	42	43	6 + 27s	33 + 2s	37 + 2s	30 + 3s	2 + 4s	8	25 + 5s	38 + 2s	31 + 2s	7 + 11s	18 + 2s	1	1	11	11	3	1 + 2s	1	— + 1s	1	

Ian Andrews on loan from Celtic.

LEEDS UNITED

Player and Position	Ht	Wt	Birth Date	Birth Place	Source	Clubs	League App	League Gls
Goalkeepers								
Mervyn Day	6 2	15 01	26 6 55	Chelmsford	Apprentice	West Ham U	194	—
						Orient	170	—
						Aston Villa	30	—
						Leeds U	181	—
Neil Edwards	5 8	11 02	5 12 70	Aberdare	Trainee	Leeds U	—	—
Ron Sinclair	5 10	11 09	19 11 64	Stirling	Apprentice	Nottingham F	—	—
						Wrexham (loan)	11	—
						Sheffield U (loan)	—	—
						Leeds U (loan)	—	—
						Derby Co (loan)	—	—
						Leeds U	8	—
						Halifax T (loan)	14	—
Defenders								
Neil Aspin	6 0	12 03	12 4 65	Gateshead	Apprentice	Leeds U	207	5
Noel Blake	6 0	13 05	12 1 62	Kingston, Jamaica	Sutton C T	Walsall	—	—
						Aston Villa	4	—
						Shrewsbury T (loan)	6	—
						Birmingham C	76	5
						Portsmouth	144	10
						Leeds U	44	4
Chris Fairclough	5 11	11 02	12 4 64	Nottingham	Apprentice	Nottingham F	107	1
						Tottenham H	60	5
						Leeds U	11	—
Peter Haddock	5 11	11 05	9 12 61	Newcastle	Apprentice	Newcastle U	57	—
						Burnley (loan)	7	—
						Leeds U	63	1
Dylan Kerr	5 11	12 05	14 1 67	Valetta	Arcadia Shepherds	Leeds U	3	—
Brendan Ormsby	5 11	11 09	1 10 60	Birmingham	Apprentice	Aston Villa	117	4
						Leeds U	46	5
Neil Parsley	5 10	10 11	25 4 66	Liverpool	Witton Alb	Leeds U	—	—
David Rennie	6 0	12 00	29 8 64	Edinburgh	Apprentice	Leicester C	21	1
						Leeds U	101	5
Gary Williams	5 9	11 01	17 6 60	Wolver-hampton	Apprentice	Aston Villa	240	—
						Walsall (loan)	9	—
						Leeds U	39	3
Midfield								
Mark Aizlewood	6 0	12 08	1 10 59	Newport	Apprentice	Newport Co	38	1
						Luton T	98	3
						Charlton Ath	152	9
						Leeds U	70	3
David Batty	5 7	10 07	2 12 68	Leeds	Trainee	Leeds U	53	1
Simon Grayson	5 11	10 11	16 12 69	Ripon	Trainee	Leeds U	2	—
John Sheridan	5 9	10 08	1 10 64	Stretford	Local	Leeds U	230	47
Glynn Snodin	5 6	9 05	14 2 60	Rotherham	Apprentice	Doncaster R	309	61
						Sheffield W	59	1
						Leeds U	70	10
Gary Speed	5 9	10 06	8 9 69	Hawarden	Trainee	Leeds U	1	—
John Stiles	5 9	10 12	6 5 64	Manchester	Vancouver W	Leeds U	65	2
Gordon Strachan	5 6	10 03	9 2 57	Edinburgh		Dundee	60	13
						Aberdeen	183	55
						Manchester U	160	33
						Leeds U	11	3
Mick Whitlow	5 11	12 01	13 1 68	Northwich	Witton Alb	Leeds U	20	1
Andy Williams	6 0	11 09	29 7 62	Birmingham	Solihull	Coventry C	9	—
						Rotherham U	87	13
						Leeds I	18	1

LEEDS UNITED

Foundation: Immediately the Leeds City club (founded in 1904) was wound up by the FA in October 1919, following allegations of illegal payments to players, a meeting was called by a Leeds solicitor, Mr. Alf Masser, at which Leeds United was formed. They joined the Midland League playing their first game in that competition in November 1919. It was in this same month that the new club had discussions with the directors of a virtually bankrupt Huddersfield Town who wanted to move to Leeds in an amalgamation. But Huddersfield survived even that crisis.

Managers (and Secretary-managers)
Dick Ray 1919–20, Arthur Fairclough 1920–27, Dick Ray 1927–35, Bill Hampson 1935–47, Willis Edwards 1947–48, Major Frank Buckley 1948–53, Raich Carter 1953–58, Bill Lambton 1958–59, Jack Taylor 1959–61, Don Revie 1961–74, Brian Clough 1974, Jimmy Armfield 1974–78, Jock Stein 1978, Jimmy Adamson 1978–80, Allan Clarke 1980–82, Eddie Gray 1982–85, Billy Bremner 1985–88, Howard Wilkinson 1988–

Player and Position	*Ht*	*Wt*	*Birth Date*	*Birth Place*	*Source*	*Clubs*	*League App*	*League Gls*
Forwards								
Ian Baird	6 0	12 09	1 4 64	Southampton	Apprentice	Southampton	17	3
						Cardiff C (loan)	12	6
						Southampton	5	2
						Newcastle U (loan)	5	1
						Leeds U	85	33
						Portsmouth	20	1
						Leeds U	53	13
Bob Davison	5 8	11 08	17 7 59	South Shields	Seaham CW	Huddersfield T	2	—
						Halifax T	63	29
						Derby Co	206	83
						Leeds U	55	19
Vince Hilaire	5 6	10 00	10 10 59	Forest Hill	Apprentice	Crystal Palace	255	29
						Luton T	6	—
						Portsmouth	146	26
						Leeds U	42	6
Peter Maguire	5 8	9 10	11 9 69	Holmfirth	Trainee	Leeds U	2	—
Peter Mumby*	5 9	11 05	22 2 69	Bradford	Trainee	Leeds U	6	—
						Shamrock R (loan)	—	—
Kevin Noteman	5 10	10 09	15 10 69	Preston	Trainee	Leeds U	1	—
John Pearson	6 2	13 02	1 9 63	Sheffield	Apprentice	Sheffield W	105	24
						Charlton Ath	61	15
						Leeds U	79	11
Carl Shutt	5 10	11 10	10 10 61	Sheffield	Spalding U	Sheffield W	40	16
						Bristol C	46	10
						Leeds U	3	4

Trainees
Blunt, Scott R; Edmonds, Darren; Franklin, Darryl; Jackson, Wayne M; Knop, Michael P; Longstaff, Jason A; Nicholson, Steven P; Old, Simon J; Rogan, Scott; Shorte, Grenville J; Smart, Tony G; Smith, Jeremy; Stephens, Lee M; Sumner, Justin T; Wigley, Russell D.C.G.

****Non-Contract**
Smith, Nigel P.

Associated Schoolboys
Anderson, James; Ball, Stephen J; Billy, Marlon K; Brooker, David; Brooker, Simon; Byrne, Alexander M; Cox, Paul W; Crosby, Andrew K; Curley, Paul A; Daly, Kevin T; Fawcett, Mark W; Fitch, Scott; Gott, Christopher P; Greenwood, James E; Hayward, Darren F; Henderson, Damian M; Hepworth, Richard J; McMichael, Stuart D; McNeil, Sean D; Moore, Sean; Morgan, Ross G; Mulrain, Steven F; Nicholls, Ryan; Owen, Alun H; Philpott, Marcus; Preston, Mark R; Stoker, Gareth; Tobin, Steven R; Watson, Paul J.

LEICESTER CITY 1988–89 *Back row (left to right):* Phil Turner, Tony Brien, Peter Weir, Alan Paris, Simon Morgan, Paul Groves, Martin Russell. *Centre row:* Cyril Lea (Youth Team Manager), Bobby Roberts (Coach), Steve Thompson, Jari Rantanen, Carl Muggleton, Steve Walsh, Paul Cooper, Jimmy Quinn, Mike Newell, Gordon Lee (Coach), John McVey (Physiotherapist). *Front row:* Nicky Cross, Gary McAllister, Paul Ramsey, David Pleat (Manager), Ally Mauchlen, Tony Spearing, Paul Reid.

Division 2 **LEICESTER CITY**

City Statium, Filbert St, Leicester LE2 7FL. Telephone Leicester (0533) 555000. Clubcall: 0898 121185.

Ground capacity: 31,000.

Record attendance: 47,298 v Tottenham H, FA Cup 5th rd, 18 Feb, 1928.

Record receipts: £123,695 v Nottingham F, Littlewoods Cup, 4th rd, 30 November 1988.

Pitch measurements: 112yd × 75yd.

President: T. L. Bennett. ***Vice-President:*** K. G. Brigstock.

Chairman: T. W. Shipman. ***Vice-Chairman:*** M. F. George.

Directors: W. G. Page, W. K. Shooter FCA, T. Smeaton, J. M. Elsom FCA.

Manager: David Pleat.***Coach/Assistant Manager:*** Gordon Lee.

Secretary: A. K. Bennet.

Physio: Mark Geeson. ***PRO:*** Alan Birchenall. ***Commercial Manager:*** P. Hill.

Year Formed: 1884.

Club Nickname: 'Fiberts' or 'Foxes'.

Previous Grounds: 1884, Victoria Park; 1887, Belgrave Road; 1888, Victoria Park; 1891, Filbert Street.

Previous Name: 1884–1919, Leicester Fosse.

Record League Victory: 10-0 v Portsmouth, Division 1, 20 October 1928 – McLaren; Black, Brown; Findlay, Carr, Watson; Adcock, Hine (3), Chandler (6), Lochhead, Barry (1).

Record Cup Victory: 8-1 v Coventry C (away), League Cup, 5th rd, 1 December 1964 – Banks; Sjoberg, Norman (2); Roberts, King, McDerment; Hodgson (2), Cross, Goodfellow, Gibson (1), Stringfellow (2). (1 og).

Record Defeat: 0-12 (as Leicester Fosse) v Nottingham F, Division 1, 21 April, 1909.

Most League Points (2 for a win): 51, Division 2, 1956–57.

Most League Points (3 for a win): 70, Division 2, 1982–83.

Most League Goals: 109, Division 2, 1956–57.

Highest League Scorer in Season: Arthur Rowley, 44, Division 2, 1956–57.

Most League Goals in Total Aggregate: Arthur Chandler, 259, 1923–35.

Most Capped Player: Gordon Banks, 37 (73), England.

Most League Appearances: Adam Black, 528, 1920–35.

Record Transfer Fee Received: £1,050,000 from Everton for Gary Lineker, July 1985.

Record Transfer Fee Paid: £350,000 to Luton Town for Mike Newell, September 1987.

Football League Record: 1894 Elected to Division 2; 1908–09 Division 1; 1909–25 Division 2; 1925–35 Division 1; 1935–37 Division 2; 1937–39 Division 1; 1946–54 Division 2; 1954–55 Division 1; 1955–57 Division 2; 1957–69 Division 1; 1969–71 Division 2; 1971–78 Division 1: 1978–80 Division 2; 1980-81 Division 1; 1981–83 Division 2; 1983–87 Division 1; 1987– Division 2.

Honours: *Football League:* Division 1 – Runners-up 1928–29; Division 2 – Champions 1924–25, 1936–37, 1953–54, 1956–57, 1970–71, 1979–80; Runners-up 1907–80. *FA Cup:* Runners-up 1949, 1961, 1963, 1969. *Football League Cup:* Winners 1964; Runners-up 1965. **European Competitions:** *European Cup-Winners' Cup:* 1961–62.

Colours: Blue shirts, white shorts, white stockings. **Change colours:** Red shirts, black shorts, black stockings.

LEICESTER CITY 1988–89 LEAGUE RECORD

Match No.	Date	Venue	Opponents	Result	H/T Score	Lg. Pos.	Goalscorers	Attendance
1	Aug 27	H	WBA	D 1-1	0-0	—	Mauchlen	13,082
2	29	H	Portsmouth	L 0-3	0-1	—		10,737
3	Sept 3	A	Birmingham C	W 3-2	2-2	12	Newell, Cross, Quinn	7932
4	10	H	Ipswich T	L 0-1	0-1	13		10,816
5	17	A	Oxford U	D 1-1	1-0	14	Cross	6610
6	21	H	Plymouth Arg	W 1-0	0-0	—	Newell	9117
7	24	H	Watford	D 2-2	1-1	11	Walsh, Reid	10,957
8	Oct 1	A	Chelsea	L 1-2	0-0	15	Quinn	7050
9	4	A	Hull C	D 2-2	1-1	—	McAllister, Williams	5079
10	8	H	Brighton & HA	W 1-0	0-0	12	Quinn	9021
11	15	H	Stoke C	W 2-0	1-0	10	Newell 2	10,312
12	22	A	Leeds U	D 1-1	0-1	11	Quinn	17,263
13	26	H	Swindon T	D 3-3	0-3	—	McAllister 2 (1 pen), King (og)	9751
14	29	A	Shrewsbury T	L 0-3	0-1	14		5178
15	Nov 5	H	Manchester C	D 0-0	0-0	16		14,080
16	12	A	Walsall	W 1-0	1-0	10	Newell	6895
17	19	A	Crystal Palace	L 2-4	1-1	13	Newell, McAllister	8843
18	26	H	Bradford C	W 1-0	1-0	10	Quinn	9533
19	Dec 3	A	Oldham Ath	D 1-1	0-0	12	Quinn	5789
20	10	H	Sunderland	W 3-1	2-0	9	Newell, Cross, Reid	11,093
21	17	A	Barnsley	L 0-3	0-2	12		6477
22	26	H	Bournemouth	L 0-1	0-0	16		13,896
23	31	H	Blackburn R	W 4-0	2-0	13	Turner, Cross, Newell, McAllister	10,820
24	Jan 2	A	Ipswich T	L 0-2	0-1	15		14,037
25	14	H	Portsmouth	W 2-1	1-1	14	Turner, Reid	10,567
26	21	A	WBA	D 1-1	0-0	14	Reid	15,792
27	Feb 4	H	Hull C	L 0-2	0-1	15		9996
28	11	A	Brighton & HA	D 1-1	1-0	17	McAllister	9572
29	18	H	Leeds U	L 1-2	1-2	17	Cross	14,151
30	25	A	Stoke C	D 2-2	2-2	16	Reid, Walsh	9666
31	28	A	Swindon T	L 1-2	1-0	—	Newell	7456
32	Mar 4	H	Walsall	W 1-0	0-0	15	Cross	9375
33	11	A	Manchester C	L 2-4	0-0	15	McAllister, Newell	22,266
34	15	H	Shrewsbury T	D 1-1	1-1	—	McAllister	7750
35	18	A	Plymouth Arg	D 1-1	0-1	15	Cross	6703
36	25	H	Birmingham C	W 2-0	1-0	15	Mauchlen 2	9564
37	27	A	Bournemouth	L 1-2	0-2	15	McAllister	8913
38	Apr 1	H	Oxford U	W 1-0	1-0	13	McAllister	8187
39	8	A	Blackburn R	D 0-0	0-0	16		8080
40	11	H	Barnsley	L 0-1	0-1	—		7266
41	15	H	Chelsea	W 2-0	0-0	13	Reid, Cross	19,468
42	22	A	Watford	L 1-2	1-1	15	Newell	11,262
43	29	A	Bradford C	L 1-2	0-0	16	Paris	8703
44	May 1	H	Oldham Ath	L 1-2	1-1	16	Newell	7223
45	6	H	Crystal Palace	D 2-2	1-1	16	North, Cross	9917
46	13	A	Sunderland	D 2-2	0-0	15	McAllister, Newell (pen)	15,819

Final League Position: 15

GOALSCORERS

League (56): Newell 13 (1 pen), McAllister 11 (1 pen), Cross 9, Quinn 6, Reid 6, Mauchlen 3, Turner 2, Walsh 2, North 1, Paris 1, Williams 1, own goal 1.
Littlewoods Cup (9): Newell 2, Reid 2, Cross 1, Groves 1, McAllister 1 (pen), Mauchlen 1, Walsh 1.
FA Cup (0).

Littlewoods Cup	Second Round	Watford (h)	4-1
		(a)	2-2
	Third Round	Norwich C (h)	2-0
	Fourth Round	Nottingham F (h)	0-0
		(a)	1-2
FA Cup	Third Round	Manchester C (a)	0-1

Hodge	Mauchlen	Spearing	Ramsey	Walsh	Brown	Reid	Cross	Newell	McAllister	Turner	Quinn	Cooper	Paris	Weir	Morgan	Russell	Williams	Groves	Brien	Muggleton	Mills	Kennedy	Charles	North	Eccles	Puttnam	Wilkinson	*Match No.*
1	2	3	4	5	6	7*	8	9	10	11	12																	1
	2	3	4†	5		14	8*	9	10	7	12	1	6	11														2
	2	3	4	5	6	7	8*	9	10		11	1		12														3
	2*	3	4	5	6	7†	8	9	10	12	11	1		14														4
	2	3	4	5	6	12	8*	9	10		11	1		7														5
	2*	3	4	5	6		8	9	10		11	1		7	12													6
	2		4	5	6	7	8	9	10			1		11	3													7
	2		4	5	6	7	8	9	10		12	1			3	11*												8
	4			5		7	8	9	10		6	1	2		3		11											9
	4			5	6	7	8	9	10		12	1	2*		3		11†	14										10
				5	6	7	8	9	10			1	2	11*	3		12	4										11
		3		5	6	7	8	9	10		12	1	2	11†		14		4*										12
		3		5	6*	7	8	9	10		4	1	2	11		12												13
	4	3†		5		7	8	9	10		12	1	2	11*	6	14												14
	4	3		5		7	8	9	10		12	1	2		6	11*												15
	4	3		5		7	8	9	10		12	1	2		6	11*												16
	4	3				7	8	9	10		11	1	2		6				5									17
	4	3		5		7		9	10		11	1	2		6	8												18
	4					7		9	10	3	11	1	2		6		8	5										19
	4†					7	12	9	10	3	11	1	2		6*	8	14	5										20
		3				7	8	9	10	4*	12	1	2		6	14	11	5†										21
		3	4*	5		7	14	9	10	12	11	1	2		6	8†												22
	2*	3	4	5†		7	8	9	10	11	12	1			6			14										23
	2	3	4*			7	8	9	10	11	12	1	5		6†			14										24
	2	3	4			7	8		10	11	9	1	5		6													25
	2	3	4†			7*	8	9	10	11	12		5		6			14		1								26
	2	3	4			7		9	10	11	8		5		6					1								27
	4	3		5		7		9	10	11	12		2		6			8*		1								28
1	2	3	4	5		7	8	9	10†	11*	12		6					14										29
1	2	3	4†	5		7	8	9	10	11*	12		6					14										30
1	2	3		5		7	8	9	10	11	12		6					4*										31
1	2*	3	4	5		7	8	9	10				6					12			11							32
1	2	3*	4	5		7	8	9	10		12				6						11							33
1	2	3	4	5		7*	8	9	10		12		6								11							34
1	2	3		5		7	8	9	10				6								11	4						35
1	2			5		7	8†	9	10				6*		3						11	4	12	14				36
1	8			5		7	12	9	10				6		3*						11	4†	2	14				37
1	2			5		7	8*	9	10				6								11	4	3	12				38
1		3	4*			7	8	9	10				6		14						11		2	12	5†			39
1	4	3				7*	8	9	10				6		5						11		2†	12		14		40
1	2	3				7	8	9	10				6		5						11	4						41
1	2	3				7	8*	9	10				6		5						11	4†	14	12				42
1	2	3				7	8	9	10				6		5						11	4						43
1	2	3				7	8*	9	10				6		5						11†	4	14	12				44
1		3	4†			7	12	9	10				6		5			14					2	8*		11		45
1		3	4		6	7		9	10				2		5							8				11*	12	46
19	38	36	22	30	12	43 + 2s	37 + 4s	45	46	14 + 2s	13 + 18s	24	37	8 + 2s	30 + 2s	6 + 4s	4 + 2s	7 + 8s	1	3	13	9	5 + 3s	1 + 7s	1	2 + 1s	— + 1s	

LEICESTER CITY

Player and Position	Ht	Wt	Birth Date	Birth Place	Source	Clubs	League App	League Gls
Goalkeepers								
Ian Andrews	6 2	12 02	1 12 64	Nottingham	Apprentice	Leicester C	126	—
(To Celtic, Aug 1988)						Swindon T (loan)	1	—
Martin Hodge	6 2	13 07	4 2 59	Southport	Apprentice	Plymouth Arg	43	—
						Everton	25	—
						Preston NE (loan)	44	—
						Oldham Ath (loan)	4	—
						Gillingham (loan)	4	—
						Sheffield W	197	—
						Leicester C	19	—
Carl Muggleton	6 1	11 13	13 9 68	Leicester	Apprentice	Leicester C	3	—
						Chesterfield (loan)	17	—
						Blackpool (loan)	2	—
						Hartlepool U (loan)	8	—
Paul O'Connor			17 8 71	Easington	Trainee	Leicester C	—	—
Defenders								
Grant Brown	6 0	11 12	19 11 69	Sunderland	Trainee	Leicester C	14	—
Peter Eccles‡	6 2	13 03	24 8 62	Dublin	Dundalk	Leicester C	1	—
Mark Gayle*			21 10 69	Bromsgrove	Trainee	Leicester C	—	—
Ian Hill‡	5 11	11 06	9 5 65	Dublin		Leicester C	—	—
Simon Morgan	5 11	12 07	5 9 66	Birmingham		Leicester C	143	1
Alan Paris	5 11	10 12	15 8 64	Slough	Slough T	Watford	—	—
						Peterborough U	137	2
						Leicester C	37	1
Richard Smith			3 10 70	Leicester	Trainee	Leicester C	—	—
Tony Spearing	5 9	10 12	7 10 64	Romford	Apprentice	Norwich C	69	—
						Stoke C (loan)	9	—
						Oxford U (loan)	5	—
						Leicester C	36	—
Steve Walsh	6 3	14 00	3 11 64	Fulwood	Local	Wigan Ath	126	4
						Leicester C	83	9
Midfield								
John Flanagan‡			11 8 70	Stafford	Trainee	Leicester C	—	—
Paul Groves	5 11	11 05	28 2 66	Derby	Burton Alb	Leicester C	16	1
Mick Kennedy	5 10	10 06	9 4 61	Salford	Apprentice	Halifax T	76	4
						Huddersfield T	81	9
						Middlesbrough	68	5
						Portsmouth	129	4
						Bradford C	45	2
						Leicester C	9	—
Gary McAllister	5 10	9 06	25 12 64	Motherwell	Fir Park BC	Motherwell	59	6
						Leicester C	158	37
Ally Mauchlen	5 7	10 05	29 6 60	Kilwinning	Irvine Meadow	Kilmarnock	120	10
						Motherwell	76	4
						Leicester C	141	8
Gary Mills	5 8	11 05	11 11 61	Northampton	Apprentice	Nottingham F	58	8
					Seattle S	Derby Co	18	1
					Seattle S	Nottingham F	79	4
						Notts Co	75	8
						Leicester C	13	—
Paul Ramsey	5 11	13 00	3 9 62	Derry	Apprentice	Leicester C	231	10
Darren Williams	5 10	10 05	15 12 68	Birmingham	YTS	Leicester C	6	1
Forwards								
Ian Baraclough			4 12 70	Leicester	Trainee	Leicester C	—	—
Dean Bridge‡			11 9 69	Wordsley	Trainee	Leicester C	—	—

LEICESTER CITY

Foundation: In 1884 a number of young footballers who were mostly old boys of Wyggeston School, held a meeting at a house on the Roman Fosse Way and formed Leicester Fosse FC. They collected 9d (less than 4p) towards the cost of a ball, plus the same amount for membership. Their first professional, Harry Webb from Stafford Rangers, was signed in 1888 for 2s 6d (12½p) per week, plus travelling expenses.

Managers (and Secretary-managers)
William Clark 1896–97, George Johnson 1898–1907*, James Blessington 1907–09, Andy Aitken 1909–11, J. W. Bartlett 1912–14, Peter Hodge 1919–26, William Orr 1926–32, Peter Hodge 1932–34, Andy Lochhead 1934–36, Frank Womack 1936–39, Tom Bromilow 1939–45, Tom Mather 1945–46, Johnny Duncan 1946–49, Norman Bullock 1949–55, David Halliday 1955–58, Matt Gillies 1959–68, Frank O'Farrell 1968–71, Jimmy Bloomfield 1971–77, Frank McLintock 1977–78, Jock Wallace 1978–82, Gordon Milne 1982–86, Bryan Hamilton 1986–87, David Pleat 1987–

Player and Position	Ht	Wt	Birth Date	Birth Place	Source	Clubs	League App	League Gls
Nicky Cross	5 9	11 04	7 2 61	Birmingham	Apprentice	WBA	105	15
						Walsall	109	45
						Leicester C	58	15
Jason Garwood‡	5 8	9 11	23 3 69	Birmingham	Apprentice	Leicester C	—	—
						Northampton T (loan)	6	—
Paul Kitson			9 1 71	Co Durham	Trainee	Leicester C	—	—
Mike Newell	6 0	11 00	27 1 65	Liverpool	Amateur	Liverpool	—	—
						Crewe Alex	3	—
						Wigan Ath	72	25
						Luton T	63	18
						Leicester C	81	21
Marc North	5 10	11 00	25 9 66	Ware	Apprentice	Luton T	18	3
						Lincoln C (loan)	4	—
						Scunthorpe U (loan)	5	2
						Birmingham C (loan)	5	1
						Grimsby T	67	17
						Leicester C	8	1
David Puttnam			3 2 67	Leicester	Leicester U	Leicester C	3	—
Jari Rantanen	6 3	15 02	31 12 61	Finland	Gothenburg	Leicester C	13	3
Paul Reid	5 5	10 02	19 1 68	Warley	Apprentice	Leicester C	77	11
Peter Weir (To St Mirren, Nov 1988)	6 0	11 09	18 1 58	Johnstone	Neilston J	St Mirren	60	4
						Aberdeen	160	23
						Leicester C	28	2
Steve Wilkinson	6 0	10 12	1 9 68	Lincoln	Apprentice	Leicester C	7	1
						Rochdale (loan)	—	—
						Crewe Alex (loan)	5	2
Paul Williams‡			11 9 69	Leicester	Trainee	Leicester C	—	—

Trainees
Blencowe, Jonathan P; Duncan, Iain; Fitzpatrick, Gary G; Jeffrey, Andrew S; Linton, Desmond; Littlejohn, Matthew S; Lyttle, Desmond; Oakes, Scott J; O'Boyle, David A; Peake, Jason W; Stephens, Darren J; Weldrick, Alan; Williams, Ian B.

Associated Schoolboys
Bedder, Matthew J; Bunting, Nathan J; Camps, Mark R; Clines, James; Conway, Russell J; Crane, Adrian P; Elliott, Paul J; Foley, Dean; Gallagher, Gordon; Haughton, Warren; Hewitt, Steven J; Holden, Steven A; Hoult, Russell; Hurst, Simon P; Joachim, Julian K; Kane, Liam B.D; Kennedy, Paul; Linnell, John; Madigan, Terrance G; Mallett, Carl; Mogg, Lewis; McConnell, Matthew; Newcombe, Simon; Poulastides, Lee; Thorpe, Anthony; Vassell, Robert A; Woolerton, Neil J.

LEYTON ORIENT 1938–89 *Back row (left to right):* Terry Howard, Ian Juryeff, Steve Castle, John Sitton, Kevin Nugent, Paul Shinners, Michael Marks.
Centre row: Brian Eastick (Assistant Manager), Keith Day, Paul Ward, Peter Wells, David Cass, Lee Harvey, Alan Comfort, Bill Songhurst (Physiotherapist).
Front row: Steve Baker, Kevin Hales, David Corner, Frank Clark (Manager), Tim O'Shea, Steve Ketteridge, Alan Hull, Kevin Dickenson.

Division 3 LEYTON ORIENT

Leyton Stadium, Brisbane Road, Leyton, London E10 5NE. Telephone 01–539 2223/4.

Ground capacity: 26,500 (7,171 seats).

Record attendance: 34,345 v West Ham U, FA Cup 4th rd, 25 Jan, 1964.

Record receipts: £87,867.92 v West Ham U, FA Cup 3rd rd, 10 January 1987.

Pitch measurements: 110yd × 80yd.

Chairman: T. Wood OBE. ***Vice-Chairman:***

Managing Director: Frank Clark.

Directors: A. Pincus, D. L. Weinrabe, H. Linney, M. Pears.

Manager: Frank Clark. ***Coach/Assistant Manager:*** Brian Eastick. ***Physio:*** Bill Songhurst.

Secretary: Miss Carol Stokes. ***Asst. Sec.:*** Mrs Sue Tilling. ***Commercial Manager:*** Frank Woolf.

Year Formed: 1881. ***Turned Professional:*** 1903. ***Ltd Co.:*** 1906.

Club Nickname: 'The O's'.

Previous Names: 1881–86, Glyn Cricket and Football Club; 1886-88, Eagle Football Club; 1888–98, Orient Football Club; 1898–1946, Clapton Orient; 1946–66, Leyton Orient; 1966–87, Orient.

Previous Grounds: Glyn Rd (1884–96), Whittles Athletic Ground (1896–1900). Millfields Rd (1900–30), and Lea Bridge Rd (1930–37).

Record League Victory: 8-0 v Crystal Palace, Division 3 (S), 12 November 1955 – Welton; Lee, Earl; Blizzard, Aldous, McKnight; White (1), Facey (3), Burgess (2), Heckman, Hartburn (2). 8-0 v Colchester U, Division 4, 15 October 1988 – Wells, Howard, Dickenson, Hales (1p), Day (1). Sitton (1), Baker (1), Ward, Hull (3). Juryeff, Comfort (1). 8-0 v Rochdale, Division 4, 20 October 1987 – Wells; Howard, Dickenson, Smalley, Day, Hull, Hales, Castle (Sussex), Shinners, Godfrey (Harvey), Comfort.

Record Cup Victory: 9-2 v Chester, League Cup, 3rd rd, 15 October 1962 – Robertson; Charlton, Taylor; Gibbs, Bishop, Lea; Deeley (1), Waites (3), Dunmore (2), Graham (3), Wedge.

Record Defeat: 0-8 v Aston Villa, FA Cup 4th rd, 30 January, 1929.

Most League Points (2 for a win): 66, Division 3 (S). 1955–56.

Most League Points (3 for a win): 75, Division 4, 1988–89.

Most League Goals: 106, Division 3 (S), 1955–56.

Highest League Scorer in Season: Tom Johnston, 35, Division 2, 1957–58.

Most League Goals in Total Aggregate: Tom Johnston, 121, 1956–58, 1959–61.

Most Capped Player: John Chiedozie, 8 (10), Nigeria.

Most League Appearances: Peter Allen, 432, 1965–78.

Record Transfer Fee Received: £600,000 from Notts Co for John Chiedozie, August 1981.

Record Transfer Fee Paid: £150,000 to Tottenham H for Peter Taylor, November 1980.

Football League Record: 1905 Elected to Division 2; 1929–56 Division 3 (S); 1956–62 Division 2; 1962–63 Division 1; 1963–66 Division 2; 1966–70 Division 3; 1970–82 Division 2; 1982–85 Division 3; 1985–89 Division 4; 1989– Division 3.

Honours: *Football League:* Division 1 best season: 22nd, 1962–63; Division 2 – Runners-up 1961–62; Division 3 – Champions 1969–70; Division 3 (S) – Champions 1955–56; Runners-up 1954–55. *FA Cup:* Semi-final 1977–78. *Football League Cup* best season: 5th rd, 1963.

Colours: Red shirts, white shorts, red stockings. **Change colours:** Yellow shirts, blue shorts, yellow stockings.

LEYTON ORIENT 1988–89 LEAGUE RECORD

Match No.	Date	Venue	Opponents	Result	H/T Score	Lg. Pos.	Goalscorers	Attendance
1	Aug 27	H	Crewe Alex	D 0-0	0-0	—		3932
2	Sept 3	A	Stockport Co	D 0-0	0-0	16		1947
3	10	H	Hereford U	L 1-3	0-2	19	Hull	3087
4	17	A	Hartlepool U	L 0-1	0-0	21		1823
5	20	A	Rotherham U	L 1-4	0-2	—	Ketteridge	4289
6	23	H	Darlington	W 1-0	0-0	—	Juryeff	2755
7	Oct 1	A	Torquay U	L 0-3	0-2	22		2526
8	4	H	York C	W 4-0	2-0	—	Sitton, Comfort, Hales, Juryeff	2467
9	8	A	Scarborough	D 0-0	0-0	19		2376
10	15	H	Colchester U	W 8-0	4-0	17	Hull 3, Sitton, Baker, Comfort, Hales (pen), Day	3421
11	22	A	Burnley	D 2-2	1-0	18	Juryeff, Comfort	8503
12	25	H	Exeter C	W 4-0	1-0	—	Hull, Dickenson, Comfort, Juryeff	3873
13	29	A	Doncaster R	L 0-1	0-0	16		2182
14	Nov 5	H	Peterborough U	L 1-2	0-1	18	Juryeff	3695
15	8	H	Carlisle U	W 2-0	0-0	—	Baker, Comfort	2879
16	12	A	Scunthorpe U	D 2-2	1-1	17	Harvey, Comfort	4239
17	26	A	Cambridge U	D 2-2	0-1	17	Juryeff, Hales	2675
18	Dec 3	H	Lincoln C	W 3-1	2-0	13	Hales, Juryeff, Ward	3093
19	17	A	Grimsby T	D 2-2	0-0	14	Juryeff, Comfort	3446
20	26	H	Tranmere R	W 2-0	0-0	10	Howard, O'Shea	4249
21	31	H	Wrexham	L 0-1	0-0	13		4025
22	Jan 2	A	Rochdale	W 3-0	1-0	10	Harvey 2, Juryeff	2036
23	14	H	Stockport Co	L 1-2	0-1	14	Howard	3828
24	21	A	Crewe Alex	L 1-2	0-1	16	Campbell	2933
25	Feb 4	H	Rotherham U	W 3-1	0-1	14	Campbell 2, Comfort	3290
26	11	A	Darlington	W 3-1	2-1	12	Comfort, Howard, Cooper	1833
27	14	A	Halifax T	D 2-2	0-0	—	Comfort 2	1477
28	18	H	Scarborough	L 2-3	2-0	12	Campbell, Castle	3877
29	24	A	Colchester U	L 0-1	0-1	—		4269
30	Mar 1	A	Exeter C	D 1-1	0-0	—	Campbell	2890
31	4	H	Burnley	W 3-0	0-0	9	Comfort 2, Campbell	3946
32	11	A	Peterborough U	W 1-0	0-0	10	Howard	3306
33	14	H	Doncaster R	W 4-0	1-0	—	Campbell, Harvey, Castle, Comfort	2824
34	18	A	Hereford U	D 1-1	0-1	8	Comfort	2063
35	21	H	Hartlepool U	W 4-3	1-1	—	Howard, Day, Campbell, Sitton	3406
36	25	H	Rochdale	W 3-0	1-0	6	Comfort, Hales, Castle	4591
37	27	A	Tranmere R	L 0-3	0-1	7		6872
38	Apr 1	H	Grimsby T	W 5-0	1-0	6	Harvey 2, Agnew (og), Comfort, Campbell	4149
39	4	H	Halifax T	W 2-0	0-0	—	Hales 2 (1 pen)	3288
40	8	A	Wrexham	W 1-0	1-0	6	Comfort	2437
41	15	H	Torquay U	W 3-1	1-0	6	Hales, Comfort, Baker	4642
42	22	A	York C	D 1-1	1-0	5	Sitton	2744
43	29	H	Cambridge U	D 1-1	1-1	6	Hales (pen)	5657
44	May 1	A	Carlisle U	L 1-2	1-2	6	Castle	2410
45	6	A	Lincoln C	W 1-0	0-0	6	Castle	3579
46	13	H	Scunthorpe U	W 4-1	2-0	6	Cooper 3, Castle	6366

Final League Position: 6

GOALSCORERS

League (86): Comfort 19, Campbell 9, Hales 9 (3 pens), Juryeff 9, Castle 6, Harvey 6, Howard 5, Hull 5, Cooper 4, Sitton 4, Baker 3, Day 2, Dickenson 1, Ketteridge 1, O'Shea 1, Ward 1, own goal 1.
Littlewoods Cup (5): Juryeff 2, Comfort 1, Hales 1 (pen), Hull 1.
FA Cup (3) Juryeff 2, Ward 1.

Littlewoods Cup	First Round	Aldershot (h)	2-0
		(a)	0-0
	Second Round	Stoke C (h)	1-2
		(a)	2-1
	Third Round	Ipswich T (a)	0-2
FA Cup	First Round	Enfield (a)	1-1
		(h)	2-2
		(h)	0-1

Wells	Howard	Corner	Day	Dickenson	Hales	Baker	Ward	Shinners	Juryeff	Comfort	Hull	Ketteridge	Nugent	Harvey	Sitton	O'Shea	Heald	Smalley	Jones	Castle	Campbell	Cooper	Kerrins	Carter	*Match No.*
1	2	3	4	5	6	7	8	9*	10	11	12														1
1	2	3	4	5	6	7	8	12	10*	11	9														2
1	2	3		5	6	4	8		10	11	9	7*	12												3
1	2		5	3	4	7		12	10*	11	9	6		8											4
1	2		5	3	4	7		9	10	11		6		8											5
1	2		5	3	4	7		9	10	11		6		8											6
1	2		5	3	4	7	8		10	11	12		9*		6										7
1	2		5	3	4	7	8	9	10	11					6										8
1	2		5	3	4	7	8		10	11	9				6										9
1	2		5	3	4	7	8		10	11	9				6										10
1	2		5	3		7	8		10	11	9				6	4									11
1	2		5	3	4	7	8		10	11	9				6										12
1	2		5	3	4	7*	8		10	11	9			12	6										13
1	2		5	3	4	7	8*		10	11	9			6		12									14
1	2	6	5		4	7	8		10	11	9					3									15
1	2		5		4	7	8		10	11	9*			12	6	3									16
1	2		5	3	4	11	8		10		9			7	6										17
1	2		5	3	4	9	8		10			11		7	6										18
	2		5	3	4	9	8		10	11				7	6		1								19
	2		5	3	4*	9	8		10	11				7	6	12	1								20
	2		5	3*		9	8		10	11				7		4	1	6	12						21
	2		5			9	8		10*	11				7	6	4	1	3	12						22
	2		5			9*	8		10	11			7		6	4	1	3		12					23
	2		5	3		9	8		10	11					6	4*	1			12	7				24
	2		5	3		7	8		10*	11					6		1			4	9	12			25
	2		5	3		7	8			11					6		1			4	10	9			26
	2		5	3		7	8			11					6		1			4	10	9			27
	2		5	3		7	8			11					6		1			4	10	9			28
	2		5	3		7	8			11	12				6		1			4	10	9*			29
	2		5	3		7	8			11				12	6		1			4	10	9*			30
	2		3		5	7*	8			11				12	4		1			6	10	9			31
	2		5	3	8	7				11				9*	6		1			4	10	12			32
	2		5	3	4	7				11				9	6		1			8	10				33
	2		5	3	4*	7				11				9	6		1			8	10	12			34
	2		5	3	4	7				11				9	6		1			8	10				35
	2		5	3	4	7				11				9	6		1			8	10				36
	2		5	3	4*	7				11				9	6		1			8	10	12			37
	2		5	3	4	7				11	12			9	6		1			8	10*				38
	2		5	3	4	7				11				9	6		1			8	10				39
	2		5	3	4	7				11				9	6		1			8		10			40
	2		5	3*	4	7				11				9	6		1	12		8		10			41
	2		5		4	7			10	11				9	6		1			8			3		42
	2		5		4	7			10	11				9	6		1			8			3		43
	2		5	14	4†	7			10*	11	12			9	6		1			8			3		44
	2		5	3	4	7				11				9	6		1			8		10			45
	2		5	3	4	7			12	11†				9*	6		1			8		10		14	46
18	46	4	45	38 + 1s	35	46	28	4 + 2s	28 + 1s	44	12 + 5s	5	2 + 1s	25 + 4s	37	7 + 2s	28	3 + 1s	— + 2s	22 + 2s	16	10 + 4s	3	— + 1s	

LEYTON ORIENT

Player and Position	Ht	Wt	Birth Date	Birth Place	Source	Clubs	League App	League Gls
Goalkeepers								
David Cass‡	6 0	12 00	27 3 62	Forest Gate	Billericay	Leyton Orient	7	—
Paul Heald	6 2	12 05	20 8 68	Wath on Dearne	Trainee	Sheffield U	—	—
						Leyton Orient	28	—
Peter Wells	6 1	13 00	13 8 56	Nottingham	Apprentice	Nottingham F	27	—
						Southampton	141	—
						Millwall (loan)	18	—
						Millwall	15	—
						Leyton Orient	148	—
Defenders								
David Corner	6 2	12 13	15 5 66	Sunderland	Apprentice	Sunderland	33	1
						Cardiff C (loan)	6	—
						Peterborough U	9	—
						(loan)	4	—
						Leyton Orient		
Keith Day	6 1	11 00	29 11 62	Grays	Aveley	Colchester U	113	12
						Leyton Orient	86	5
Kevin Dickenson	5 6	10 06	24 2 62	London	Apprentice	Tottenham H	—	—
						Charlton Ath	75	1
						Leyton Orient	146	3
Jeremy Gill			8 9 70	Bristol	Trowbridge	Leyton Orient	—	—
Kevin Hales	5 7	10 04	13 1 61	Dartford	Apprentice	Chelsea	20	2
						Leyton Orient	217	20
Lee Harvey	5 11	11 07	21 12 66	Harlow	Local	Leyton Orient	87	10
Terry Howard	6 1	11 07	26 2 66	Stepney	Amateur	Chelsea	6	—
						Crystal Palace (loan)	4	—
						Chester C (loan)	2	—
						Leyton Orient	99	9
John Sitton	6 0	12 02	21 10 59	Hackney	Apprentice	Chelsea	13	—
						Millwall	45	1
						Gillingham	107	5
						Leyton Orient	109	5
Mark Smalley	5 11	11 06	2 1 65	Newark	Apprentice	Nottingham F	3	—
						Birmingham C (loan)	7	—
						Bristol R (loan)	10	—
						Leyton Orient	61	4
Midfield								
Steve Baker	5 5	10 05	2 12 61	Newcastle	Apprentice	Southampton	73	—
						Burnley (loan)	10	—
						Leyton Orient	55	6
Steve Castle	5 11	12 05	17 5 56	Ilford	Apprentice	Leyton Orient	134	26
Hakan Hayrettin*			4 2 70	Enfield	Trainee	Leyton Orient	—	—
Steve Ketteridge	5 9	10 07	7 11 59	Stevenage	Apprentice	Derby Co	–	—
						Wimbledon	237	32
						Crystal Palace	59	6
						Leyton Orient	31	—
						Cardiff C (loan)	6	2
Ian Rawlings*			5 6 70	Essex	Trainee	Leyton Orient	—	—
Paul Ward	5 11	1205	15 9 63	Bedlington	Apprentice	Chelsea	—	—
						Middlesbrough	76	1
						Darlington	124	9
						Leyton Orient	28	1
Forwards								
Danny Carter			29 6 69	Hackney	Billericay	Leyton Orient	1	—
Alan Comfort	5 7	11 02	8 12 64	Aldershot	Apprentice	QPR	—	—
						Cambridge U	63	5
						Leyton Orient	150	47

LEYTON ORIENT

Foundation: There is some doubt about the foundation of Leyton Orient, and, indeed, some confusion with clubs like Leyton and Clapton over their early history. As regards the foundation, the most favoured version is that Leyton Orient was formed originally by members of Homerton Theological College who established Glyn Cricket Club in 1881 and then carried on through the following winter playing football. Eventually many employees of the Orient Shipping Line became involved and so the name Orient was chosen in 1888.

Managers (and Secretary-managers)
Sam Omerod 1905–06, Ike Ivenson 1906, Billy Holmes 1907–22, Peter Proudfoot 1922–29, Arthur Grimsdell 1929–30, Peter Proudfoot 1930–31, Jimmy Seed 1931–33, David Pratt 1933–34, Peter Proudfoot 1935–39, Tom Halsey 1939–40, Billy Wright 1940–45, Billy Hall 1945, Billy Wright 1945–46, Charlie Hewitt 1946–48, Neil McBain 1948–49, Alec Stock 1949–56, 1956–57, 1957–59, Johnny Carey 1961–63, Benny Fenton 1963–64, Dave Sexton 1965, Dick Graham 1966–68, Jimmy Bloomfield 1968–71, George Petchey 1971–77, Jimmy Bloomfield 1977–81, Paul Went 1981, Ken Knighton 1981, Frank Clark 1982– .

Player and Position	*Ht*	*Wt*	*Birth Date*	*Birth Place*	*Source*	*Clubs*	*League App*	*League Gls*
Mark Cooper	6 1	13 00	5 4 67	Watford	Apprentice	Cambridge U	71	17
						Tottenham H	—	—
						Shrewsbury T (loan)	6	2
						Gillingham	49	11
						Leyton Orient	14	4
Alan Hull	5 9	11 00	4 9 62	Rochford	Barking	Leyton Orient	53	10
Ian Juryeff	5 11	12 00	24 11 62	Gosport	Apprentice	Southampton	2	—
						Mansfield T (loan)	12	5
						Reading (loan)	7	1
						Leyton Orient	111	44
						Ipswich T (loan)	2	—
Michael Marks	6 0	12 06	23 3 68	Lambeth		Millwall	36	10
						Mansfield T (loan)	1	—
						Leyton Orient	3	—
Kevin Nugent	6 1	12 04	10 4 69	Edmonton	Trainee	Leyton Orient	14	3
						Cork C (loan)	—	—
Paul Shinners‡	6 0	12 00	8 1 59	Westminster	Fisher Ath	Gillingham	4	—
						Colchester U (loan)	6	1
						Leyton Orient	77	32

Trainees
Burnett, Wayne; Jordan, Dean B; Moncur, Lloyd; Murphy, James; Parker, David M; Sharman, Keith E; Sturt, Paul G; Whitbread, Adrian R.

Associated Schoolboys
Bart-Williams, Christopher; Denny, Neil R; Elliott, Colin E; Howard, Anthony; Lacey, Vernon J; McCarthy, John; Matheson, James M; Okai, Stephen P; Patience, Brett J; Ramage, Andrew; Rayment, Stuart; Read, Mark; Rolls, George E; Sheikh, Azzaz; Singh, Wayne; Smith, Murray H; Stephenson, Andrew; Sweetman, Nicholas E; Thompson, David; Thompson, Glenroy H; Tomlinson, Michael L; Walker, Scott P.

LINCOLN CITY 1988–89 *Back row (left to right):* Paul Casey, Phil Brown, Darren Angell, Graham Bressington, Mark Sertori, Nigel Batch, Chris Scott, Trevor Matthewson, Mark Cook, Paul Smith, Wille Gamble.
Front row: Shane Nicholson, David Clarke, Bobby Cumming, Mr Overton, Mr Davey, Mr Staples, Mr Pryor, Mr Reames, Mr Murphy, Steve Buckley, Clive Evans.

Division 4 LINCOLN CITY

Sincil Bank, Lincoln LN5 8LD. Telephone Lincoln (0522) 22224 and 510263.Fax No. 0522 20564. Social Club 0522 20960.

Ground capacity: 9,500.

Record attendance: 23,196 v Derby Co, League Cup 4th rd, 15 November, 1967.

Record receipts: £34,843.30 v Tottenham H, Milk Cup 2nd rd, 26 October 1983.

Pitch measurements: 110yd × 75yd.

Hon. Life Presidents: V. C. Withers, D. W. L. Bocock.

President: H. Dove.

Chairman: K. J. Reames. ***Vice-Chairman:*** M. B. Pryor.

Directors: G. D. Overton, G. R. Davey (Managing), R. Staples, D. Barron.

Hon. Consultant Surgeon: Mr. Brian Smith.

Secretary: G. R. Davey. ***Club Doctor:*** Malcolm Locker.

Manager: Colin Murphy. ***Assistant Manager:*** Dick Bate.

Physio: Adrian Davies. ***Commercial Manager:*** Wayne Jenner.

Year Formed: 1883. ***Turned Professional:*** 1892. ***Ltd Co.:*** 1892.

Club Nickname: 'The Red Imps'.

Previous Grounds: 1883, John O'Gaunt's; 1894, Sincil Bank.

Record League Victory: 11-1 v Crewe Alex, Division 3(N), 29 September 1951 – Jones; Green (1p), Varney; Wright, Emery, Grummett (1); Troops (1), Garvey, Graver (6), Whittle (1), Johnson (1).

Record Cup Victory: 8-1 v Bromley, FA Cup, 2nd rd, 10 December 1938 – McPhail; Hartshorne, Corbett; Bean, Leach, Whyte (1); Hancock, Wilson (1), Ponting (3), Deacon (1), Clare (2).

Record Defeat: 3-11 v Manchester C, Division 2, 23 March, 1895.

Most League Points (2 for a win): 74, Division 4, 1975–76.

Most League Points (3 for a win): 77, Division 3, 1981–82.

Most League Goals: 121, Division 3(N), 1951–52.

Highest League Scorer in Season: Allan Hall, 42, Division 3(N), 1931–32.

Most League Goals in Total Aggregate: Andy Graver, 144, 1950–55 and 1958–61.

Most Capped Player: David Pugh, 3 (7), Wales and George Moulson, 3, Eire.

Most League Appearances: Tony Emery, 402, 1946–59.

Record Transfer Fee Received: £180,000 from Newcastle U for Mick Harford, December 1980.

Record Transfer Fee Paid: £60,000 to Southampton for Gordon Hobson, September 1988.

Football League Record: 1892 founder member of Division 2. Remained in Division 2 until 1920 when they failed re-election but also missed seasons 1908–09 and 1911–12 when not re-elected. 1921–32 Division 3(N); 1932–34 Division 2; 1934–48 Division 3(N); 1948–49 Division 2; 1949–52 Division 3(N); 1952–61 Division 2; 1961–62 Division 3; 1962–76 Division 4; 1976–79 Division 3; 1979–81 Division 4; 1981–86 Division 3; 1986–87 Division 4; 1987–88 GM Vauxhall Conference; 1988– Division 4.

Honours: *Football League:* Divison 2 best season: 5th, 1901–02; Division 3(N) — Champions 1931–32, 1947–48, 1951–52; Runners-up 1927–28. 1930–31, 1936–37; Division 4 — Champions 1975–76; Runners-up 1980–81. *FA Cup:* best season: 1st rd of Second Series (5th rd equivalent), 1886–87, 2nd rd (5th rd equivalent), 1889–90, 1901–02. *Football League Cup:* best season: 4th rd, 1967–68.

Colours: Red and white striped shirts, black shorts, red stockings with white trim. ***Change colours:*** All blue.

LINCOLN CITY 1988–89 LEAGUE RECORD

Match No.	Date	Venue	Opponents	Result	H/T Score	Lg. Pos.	Goalscorers	Attendance
1	Aug 27	H	Hartlepool U	L 0-1	0-1	—		3361
2	Sept 3	A	Wrexham	L 0-3	0-0	24		2312
3	10	H	Crewe Alex	D 2-2	1-1	23	Evans, Smith	2651
4	17	A	Peterborough U	D 1-1	0-0	22	Smith	4256
5	20	A	Cambridge U	W 3-2	1-0	—	Hobson, Sertori 2	2776
6	24	H	Hereford U	W 2-0	1-0	13	Gamble, Hobson	2915
7	Oct 1	A	Colchester U	W 3-1	1-1	10	Hobson 2, Hill (og)	1529
8	5	H	Scunthorpe U	W 1-0	1-0	—	Gamble	5443
9	8	A	Torquay U	L 0-1	0-1	9		2105
10	15	H	Scarborough	D 2-2	2-1	7	Clarke (pen), Gamble	4535
11	22	H	Darlington	W 3-2	0-0	6	Gamble (pen), Nicholson, Sertori	3705
12	24	H	Tranmere R	L 0-1	0-0	—		3498
13	29	H	Carlisle U	L 0-2	0-0	12		3727
14	Nov 5	A	Rotherham U	L 0-2	0-2	15		4506
15	8	A	Burnley	W 4-1	1-1	—	Hobson 3 (1 pen), Sertori	8742
16	12	H	Exeter C	W 2-0	1-0	7	Hobson 2	3461
17	26	H	Halifax T	W 2-1	1-1	5	Cumming, Matthewson	3379
18	Dec 3	A	Leyton Orient	L 1-3	0-2	6	Cumming	3093
19	17	A	Stockport Co	L 0-1	0-0	11		2355
20	26	H	Grimsby T	D 2-2	1-0	11	Smith, McDermott (og)	8038
21	28	H	Doncaster R	W 3-1	1-1	—	Smith 2, Matthewson	5213
22	Jan 2	A	York C	L 1-2	1-0	11	Smith	3589
23	7	A	Rochdale	D 2-2	1-1	10	Smith, Cumming	1515
24	14	H	Wrexham	W 4-3	2-1	10	Schofield, Hobson 2, Cumming (pen)	3860
25	21	A	Hartlepool U	L 2-3	0-2	9	Brown, McGinley	2860
26	28	H	Peterborough U	D 1-1	0-0	10	Brown	4150
27	Feb 4	H	Cambridge U	W 3-0	0-0	9	Dunkley 2, Hobson	3239
28	11	A	Hereford U	L 2-3	0-1	10	Dunkley, Hobson (pen)	2113
29	18	H	Torquay U	W 1-0	1-0	8	Bressington	3423
30	25	A	Scarborough	D 1-1	0-1	8	Clarke	3293
31	Mar 1	H	Tranmere R	W 2-1	0-0	–	Clarke, Vickers (og)	3580
32	4	A	Darlington	L 1-2	0-1	7	Dunkley	2169
33	11	H	Rotherham U	L 0-1	0-1	8		5186
34	14	A	Carlisle U	L 1-2	0-2	—	Hobson (pen)	2691
35	18	A	Crewe Alex	L 0-2	0-1	10		3106
36	25	H	York C	W 2-1	1-1	10	Smith 2	3710
37	27	A	Grimsby T	L 0-1	0-0	10		8618
38	Apr 1	H	Stockport Co	D 0-0	0-0	12		3400
39	5	H	Rochdale	W 4-1	3-0	—	Clarke, Smith, Schofield, Evans	2033
40	8	A	Doncaster R	W 1-0	0-0	9	Cumming	2124
41	15	H	Colchester U	D 1-1	0-0	9	McGinley	3519
42	22	A	Scunthorpe U	D 0-0	0-0	9		5729
43	29	A	Halifax T	W 1-0	0-0	9	Brown	1261
44	May 1	H	Burnley	L 2-3	0-2	9	Davis, Gamble	3594
45	6	H	Leyton Orient	L 0-1	0-0	10		3579
46	13	A	Exeter C	W 1-0	1-0	10	Davis	2249

Final League Position: 10

GOALSCORERS

League (64): Hobson 14 (3 pens), Smith 10, Cumming 5 (1 pen), Gamble 5 (1 pen), Clarke 4 (1 pen), Dunkley 4, Sertori 4, Brown 3, Davis 2, Evans 2, McGinley 2, Matthewson 2, Schofield 2, Bressington 1, Nicholson 1, own goals 3.
Littlewoods Cup (5): Brown 1, Clarke 1, Gamble 1, Hobson 1, own goal 1.
FA Cup (2): Davis 1, Sertori 1.

Littlewoods Cup	First Round	Crewe Alex (a)	1-1
		(h)	2-1
	Second Round	Southampton (h)	1-1
		(a)	1-3
FA Cup	First Round	Altrincham (a)	2-3

Wallington	Evans	Nicholson	Clarke	Bressington	Matthewson	Davis	Cumming	Brown	Smith	Sertori	Ranshaw	Gamble	James	Hobson	Schofield	Franklin	Casey	McGinley	Scott	Dunkley	Bowling	Cook	*Match No.*
1	2	3	4*	5	6	7	8†	9	10	11	14	12											1
1	2	3	4†	5	6	7	8*	9	10	11		12	14										2
1	2	3		5	6	7		9	10	11		4	8										3
1	2	3		5	6	7		4	10*	11		12	8	9									4
1	2	3		5	6	7	8	4		11		10		9									5
1	2	3	12	5	6	7	8*	4		11		10		9									6
1	2	3*	10	5	6	7	8	4		11			12	9									7
1	2		3	5	6	7	8	4		11		10		9									8
1	2		3	5	6	7		4		11		10	8	9									9
1	2	3	8	5	6	7		4		11		10		9									10
1	2	3	8*	5	6	7		4		11		10	12	9									11
1	2	3	8	5	6	7		4		11		10	9										12
1	2	3	8	5	6	7		4		11		10*	12	9									13
1	2	3	8	5	6	7		4		11		12	10*	9									14
1	2	3	8	5	6*	7		10		11				9	4	12							15
1	2	3	8	5		7		10		11			6	9	4								16
1	2	3		5	6	7	8	10		11				9	4								17
1	2	3	14	5	6	7†	8	10		11		12		9	4*								18
1	2	3			6	7	8	10	9	11		12	5				4*						19
1	2	4			6	3	8	10	7	11			5	9									20
1	2	11		5	6	3	8		10					9	4		7*	12					21
1	2	4†		5	6	3	8	14	10				12	9	7			11*					22
1	2	4		5	6	3	8	14	10*	12				9	7			11†					23
1	2	11		5	6	3	8	7		12				9	4			10*					24
1	2	11	12		6	3*	8	7						9	4			10	5				25
1	2	11	3		6		8	7						9	4			10	5				26
1	2		3	8	6			7					5	9	4			11		10			27
1	2		3	7†	6			11	12				5	9	8		14		4*	10			28
1	2		3	8	6			7	9						4			11	5	10			29
1	2	11*	3	7†	6		8	14	9				5		4			12		10			30
1	2		3		6		8	7	9				5		4			11		10			31
1	2		3		6		8	7	9			12	5		4			11*		10			32
1	2*		3		6		8	12	7				5	9	4			11		10			33
	2		11		6	3	8		7				5	9	4					10	1		34
	2		11*		6	3	8		7	14			5	9	4			12		10†	1		35
1	2	12	11		6*	3	8		10				5	9†	4			7		14			36
1	2	8	11		6	3			10				5	9	4			7*		12			37
1	2	8	11		6	3		7	10				5	9	4								38
1	2	8	11		6	3		7	10	14			5*	9	4†			12					39
1	2	8	3		6	5	11		10			7			4			9					40
	2*	4	11		6	3	8	12	10			7	5					9			1		41
	2*	11	3			6	8		10			7	5		4		12	9			1		42
			3	8	6*	14	11	12	10	9		7	5†		4		2				1		43
		8	3	5		6	11	12	10	9*		7			4		2				1		44
			11	5	6	3	8		10			7*		9	4		2	12			1		45
		12	11	5*	6	3		8	10					9	4		2				1	7	46
38	42	32	33	30	43	37	29	31	27	22	—	15	23	32	29	—	6	15	4	9	8	1	
		+ 2s	+ 3s			+ 1s		+ 7s	+ 1s	+ 4s	+ 1s	+ 7s	+ 5s			+ 1s	+ 2s	+ 5s		+ 2s			

LINCOLN CITY

Player and Position	Ht	Wt	Birth Date	Birth Place	Source	Clubs	League App	League Gls
Goalkeepers								
Ian Bowling	6 3	14 08	27 7 65	Sheffield	Gainsborough T	Lincoln C	8	–
Mark Wallington	6 1	14 11	17 9 52	Grantham	Amateur	Walsall	11	—
						Leicester C	412	—
						Derby Co	67	—
						Lincoln C	38	—
Defenders								
Darren Angell‡	6 2	11 04	19 1 67	Newbury	Amateur	Reading	—	—
						Portsmouth	—	—
						Colchester U (loan)	1	—
						Lincoln C	—	–
Steve Buckley‡	5 11	11 12	16 10 53	Brinsley	Burton A	Luton T	123	9
						Derby Co	323	21
						Lincoln C	36	2
Paul Casey	5 8	10 06	6 10 61	Rinteln	Apprentice	Sheffield U	25	1
					Boston U	Lincoln C	8	—
Darren Davis	6 0	11 00	5 2 67	Sutton Ashfield	Apprentice	Notts Co	92	1
						Lincoln C	38	2
Clive Evans*	5 10	11 05	1 5 57	Birkenhead	Apprentice	Tranmere R	178	27
						Wigan Ath	32	2
						Crewe Alex	28	7
						Stockport Co	160	23
						Lincoln C	42	2
Neil Franklin‡			10 3 69	North Kesteven		Lincoln C	1	—
Tony James	6 3	13 08	27 6 67	Sheffield	Gainsborough T	Lincoln C	28	—
Trevor Matthewson	6 1	12 05	12 2 63	Sheffield	Apprentice	Sheffield W	3	—
						Newport Co	75	—
						Stockport Co	80	—
						Lincoln C	43	2
Shane Nicholson	5 10	11 06	3 6 70	Newark	Trainee	Lincoln C	41	1
Chris Scott*	6 1	13 00	11 9 63	Wallsend	Blyth S	Northampton T	—	—
						Darlington (loan)	—	—
						Lincoln C	4	—
Midfield								
Graham Bressington	6 0	12 06	8 7 66	Eton	Wycombe W	Lincoln C	30	1
Phil Brown	5 8	9 07	16 1 66	Sheffield	Apprentice	Chesterfield	87	19
						Stockport Co	23	1
						Lincoln C	38	3
David Clarke	5 10	11 00	3 12 64	Nottingham	Apprentice	Notts Co	123	7
						Lincoln C	36	4
Mark Cook	6 0	11 11	7 8 70	Boston	Trainee	Lincoln C	1	—
Bob Cumming‡	5 8	10 05	7 12 55	Aidrie	Bailleston Jrs	Grimsby T	365	57
						Lincoln C	29	5
Richard Ranshaw‡			17 4 70	Sleaford		Lincoln C	1	—
Jon Schofield	5 11	11 03	16 5 65	Barnsley	Gainsborough T	Lincoln C	29	2
Forwards								
Malcolm Dunkley	6 6	14 00	12 7 61	Wolverhampton	Bromsgrove R	Lincoln C	11	4
Willie Gamble*	5 9	11 07	5 3 68	Cottam	Apprentice	Lincoln C	64	15
Gordon Hobson	5 9	10 07	27 11 57	Sheffield	Sheffield RGRS	Lincoln C	272	73
						Grimsby T	52	18
						Southampton	33	8
						Lincoln C	32	14

LINCOLN CITY

Foundation: Although there was a Lincoln club as far back as 1861, the present organisation was formed in 1883 winning the Lincolnshire Senior Cup in only their fourth season. They were Founder members of the Midland League in 1889 and that competition's first champions.

Managers (and Secretary-managers)
David Calderhead 1900–07, John Henry Strawson 1907–14 (had been secretary), George Fraser 1919–21, David Calderhead Jnr. 1921–24, Horace Henshall 1924–27, Harry Parkes 1927–36, Joe McClelland 1936–46, Bill Anderson 1946–65 (GM to 1966), Roy Chapman 1965–66, Ron Gray 1966–70, Bert Loxley 1970–71, David Herd 1971–72, Graham Taylor 1972–77, George Kerr 1977–78, Willie Bell 1977–78, Colin Murphy 1978–85, John Pickering 1985, George Kerr 1985–87, Peter Daniel 1987, Colin Murphy 1987–

Player and Position	*Ht*	*Wt*	*Birth Date*	*Birth Place*	*Source*	*Clubs*	*League App*	*League Gls*
John McGinley*	6 2	13 08	11 6 59	Rowlands Gill	Gateshead	Sunderland	3	—
					Charleroi	Lincoln C	71	11
						Rotherham U	3	—
						Lincoln C	21	5
						Hartlepool U (loan)	2	—
						Lincoln C	20	2
Mark Sertori	6 3	12 00	1 9 67	Manchester		Stockport Co	4	—
						Lincoln C	26	4
Paul Smith	5 11	10 09	9 11 64	Rotherham	Apprentice	Sheffield U	36	1
						Stockport Co (loan)	7	5
						Port Vale	44	7
						Lincoln C	28	10
Mick Waitt	6 4	12 00	25 6 60	Hexham	Keyworth U	Notts Co	82	27
						Lincoln C	—	—

Trainees
Butler, Jason; Holmes, Steven P; Kent, Scott R; McGrane, Dermot; McNulty, John.

****Non-Contract**
Briggs, Stephen; Brown, Neil R; French, Richard.

Associated Schoolboys
Blow, Matthew S; Johnson, Craig A; Tindall, Neil D.

LIVERPOOL 1988–89 *Back row (left to right):* Jan Molby, Gary Gillespie, Mike Hooper, Bruce Grobbelaar, Alex Watson, Kevin MacDonald
Centre row: Ronnie Moran (Coach), Ray Houghton, Nigel Spackman, Jim Beglin, Gary Ablett, John Aldridge, Barry Venison, Ray Evans (Trainer).
Front row: John Barnes, Steve Nicol, Alan Hansen (Captain), Kenny Dalglish (Manager), Ronnie Whelan, Steve McMahon, Peter Beardsley.

Division 1 **LIVERPOOL**

Anfield Road, Liverpool 4. Telephone 051-263 2361. Clubcall: 0898-121184.

Ground Capacity: 45,600.

Record attendance: 61,905 v Wolverhampton W, FA Cup 4th rd, 2 Feb, 1952.

Record receipts: £164,000 v Panathinaikos, European Cup Semi-final, 10 April, 1985.

Pitch measurements: 110yd × 75yd.

Chairman: J. W. Smith CBE, DL, JP

Directors: Coun. S. T. Moss JP, S. C. Reakes JP, J. T. Cross, W. D. Corkish FCA, R. Paisley OBE, MSC (HON), G. A. Ensor LLB, N. White.

Vice-Presidents: C. J. Hill, H. E. Roberts.

Team Manager: Kenny Dalglish. ***Coach:*** Ron Moran.

Chief Executive/General Secretary: Peter Robinson.

Commercial Manager: K. Addison.

Year Formed: 1892. ***Turned Professional:*** 1892. ***Ltd Co.:*** 1892.

Club Nickname: 'Reds' or 'Pool'.

Record League Victory: 10-1 v Rotherham T, Division 2, 18 February 1896 – Storer; Goldie, Wilkie; McCarthy, McQueen, Holmes; McVean (3), Ross (2), Allan (4), Becton (1), Bradshaw.

Record Cup Victory: 11-0 v Stomsgodset Drammen, ECWC 1st rd (1st leg), 17 September 1974 – Clemence; Smith (1), Lindsay (1p), Thompson (2), Cormack (1), Hughes (1), Boersma (2), Hall, Heighway (1), Kennedy (1), Callaghan (1).

Record Defeat: 1-9 v Birmingham C, Division 2, 11 December, 1954.

Most League Points (2 for a win): 68, Division 1, 1978–79

Most League Points (3 for a win): 90, Division 1, 1987–88.

Most League Goals: 106, Division 2, 1895–96.

Highest League Scorer in Season: Roger Hunt, 41, Division 2, 1961–62.

Most League Goals in Total Aggregate: Roger Hunt, 245, 1959–69.

Most Capped Player: Emlyn Hughes, 59 (62), England.

Most League Appearances: Ian Callaghan, 640, 1960–78.

Record Transfer Fee Received: £3,200,000 from Juventus for Ian Rush, June 1986.

Record Transfer Fee Paid: £2,800,000 to Juventus for Ian Rush, August 1988.

Football League Record: 1893 Elected to Division 2; 1894–95 Division 1; 1895–96 Division 2; 1896–1904 Division 1; 1904–05 Division 2; 1905–54 Division 1; 1954–62 Division 2; 1962– Division 1.

Honours: *Football League:* Division 1 – Champions 1900–01, 1905–06, 1921–22, 1922–23, 1946–47, 1963–64, 1965–66, 1972–73, 1975–76, 1976–77, 1978–79, 1979–80, 1981–82, 1982–83, 1983–84, 1985–86, 1987–88 (Liverpool have a record number of 17 League Championship wins); Runners-up 1898–99, 1909–10, 1968–69, 1973–74, 1974–75, 1977–78, 1984–85, 1986–87, 1988–89; Division 2 – Champions 1893–94, 1894–95, 1904–05, 1961–62; *FA Cup:* Winners 1965, 1974, 1986, 1989; Runners-up 1914, 1950, 1971, 1977, 1988; *Football League Cup:* Winners 1981, 1982, 1983, 1984. Runners-up 1977–78, 1986–87. *League Super Cup-Winners:* 1985–86. **European Competitions;** *European Cup:* 1964–65, 1966–67, 1973–74, 1976–77 (winners), 1977–78 (winners), 1978–79, 1979–80, 1980–81 (winners), 1981–82, 1982–83, 1983–84 (winners), 1984–85 (runners-up); *European Cup-Winners' Cup:* 1965–66 (runners-up), 1971–72, 1974–75; **European Fairs Cup:** 1967–68, 1968–69, 1969–70, 1970–71; *UEFA Cup:* 1972–73 (winners), 1975–76 (winners);*Super Cup:* 1977 (winners), 1978; *World Club Championship;* 1981 (runners-up).

Colours: All red. **Change colours:** All silver grey.

LIVERPOOL 1988–89 LEAGUE RECORD

Match No.	Date	Venue	Opponents	Result	H/T Score	Lg. Pos.	Goalscorers	Attendance
1	Aug 27	A	Charlton Ath	W 3-0	1-0	—	Aldridge 3	21,389
2	Sept 3	H	Manchester U	W 1-0	1-0	3	Molby (pen)	42,026
3	10	A	Aston Villa	D 1-1	0-1	5	Houghton	41,409
4	17	H	Tottenham H	D 1-1	0-0	4	Beardsley	40,929
5	24	A	Southampton	W 3-1	1-1	2	Aldridge, Beardsley, Molby (pen)	21,046
6	Oct 1	H	Newcastle U	L 1-2	1-1	3	Gillespie	39,139
7	8	A	Luton T	L 0-1	0-1	4		12,117
8	22	H	Coventry C	D 0-0	0-0	6		38,742
9	26	A	Nottingham F	L 1-2	0-0	—	Rush	29,755
10	29	A	West Ham U	W 2-0	0-0	4	Rush, Beardsley	30,198
11	Nov 5	H	Middlesbrough	W 3-0	1-0	3	Rush, Aldridge, Beardsley	39,489
12	12	H	Millwall	D 1-1	1-1	5	Nicol	41,966
13	19	A	QPR	W 1-0	1-0	4	Aldridge	20,063
14	26	H	Wimbledon	D 1-1	0-0	4	Houghton	36,188
15	Dec 4	A	Arsenal	D 1-1	0-0	—	Barnes	31,863
16	11	H	Everton	D 1-1	1-0	—	Houghton	42,372
17	17	H	Norwich C	L 0-1	0-0	6		34,325
18	26	A	Derby Co	W 1-0	1-0	3	Rush	25,213
19	Jan 1	A	Manchester U	L 1-3	0-0	—	Barnes	44,745
20	3	H	Aston Villa	W 1-0	0-0	—	Whelan	39,014
21	14	A	Sheffield W	D 2-2	0-2	5	Nicol, Aldridge	31,524
22	21	H	Southampton	W 2-0	0-0	4	Aldridge, Rush	35,565
23	Feb 4	A	Newcastle U	D 2-2	1-1	5	Rush, Aldridge	30,966
24	Mar 1	H	Charlton Ath	W 2-0	1-0	—	Beardsley, Aldridge (pen)	30,283
25	11	A	Middlesbrough	W 4-0	2-0	4	Beardsley, Houghton, Aldridge, McMahon	25,197
26	14	H	Luton T	W 5-0	2-0	—	Aldridge 3 (1 pen), Beardsley, McMahon	31,447
27	22	A	Coventry C	W 3-1	2-1	—	Barnes, Aldridge, Whelan	23,807
28	26	A	Tottenham H	W 2-1	0-0	—	Aldridge (pen) Beardsley	30,012
29	29	H	Derby Co	W 1-0	1-0	—	Barnes	42,518
30	Apr 1	A	Norwich C	W 1-0	1-0	2	Whelan	26,338
31	8	H	Sheffield W	W 5-1	2-0	2	McMahon, Beardsley 2, Houghton, Barnes	39,672
32	11	A	Millwall	W 2-1	2-1	—	Barnes, Aldridge	22,130
33	May 3	A	Everton	D 0-0	0-0	—		45,994
34	10	H	Nottingham F	W 1-0	0-0	—	Aldridge (pen)	39,793
35	13	A	Wimbledon	W 2-1	0-1	2	Aldridge, Barnes	14,730
36	16	H	QPR	W 2-0	1-0	—	Aldridge, Whelan	38,368
37	23	H	West Ham U	W 5-1	1-1	—	Aldridge, Houghton 2, Rush, Barnes	41,855
38	26	H	Arsenal	L 0-2	0-0	—		41,783

Final League Position: 2

GOALSCORERS

League (65): Aldridge 21 (4 pens), Beardsley 10, Barnes 8, Houghton 7, Rush 7, Whelan 4, McMahon 3, Molby 2 (2 pens), Nicol 2, Gillespie 1.
Littlewoods Cup (8): Aldridge 2 (1 pen), Barnes 2, Gillespie 1, McMahon 1, Molby 1 (pen), Rush 1.
FA Cup (18): Aldridge 6, Barnes 3, McMahon 3, Rush 3, Beardsley 2, own goal 1.

Littlewoods Cup	Second Round	Walsall (h)	1-0
		(a)	3-1
	Third Round	Arsenal (h)	1-1
		(a)	0-0
		(at Villa Park)	2-1
	Fourth Round	West Ham U (a)	1-4
FA Cup	Third Round	Carlisle U (a)	3-0
	Fourth Round	Millwall (a)	2-0
	Fifth Round	Hull C (a)	3-2
	Sixth Round	Brentford (h)	4-0
	Semi-Final	Nottingham F (at Hillsborough) aband.	0-0
		(at Old Trafford)	3-1
	Final	Everton (at Wembley)	3-2

Grobbelaar	Gillespie	Venison	Nicol	Whelan	Molby	Beardsley	Aldridge	Houghton	Barnes	McMahon	Rush	Spackman	Ablett	Staunton	Hooper	MacDonald	Burrows	Marsh	Watson	Hansen	*Match No.*
1	2	3	4	5	6	7*	8	9	10	11	12										1
1	2	3	4	5	6	7	8*	9	10	11†	12	14									2
1	2	3	4	5	6	12	8	7	10*		9	11									3
1	2		4	5	6*	7	8	10			9	11	3	12							4
	2	3*	4	5	10	7	8	9					11	12	1	6					5
	2		4	5	10	7	8	9			12	6	3	11*	1						6
	2*	3	4	5	6	7		8	10		9		12		1	11					7
		3	4	5		7	12	8	10		9		2		1	11*	6				8
		3	4	5		7	12	8	10		9	11*	2		1		6				9
		3	4	5*		7	8	11	10		9	12	2		1		6				10
		3†	4	5		7	8	11	10	12	9*	14	2		1		6				11
			4	5*		7	8	9	10	11		6	2	12	1		3				12
			4	5		7	8*	10		11	9	6	2	12	1		3				13
		3	4	5		7	12	10		11	9*	6	2	8	1						14
			4	5		7	8	9	10	11		6	2	3*	1		12				15
		3	4	5		7	8*	9	10	11	12		2		1		6				16
		3*	4	5		7		8	10	11	9	12	2		1		6				17
			4	5		7		8	10	11	9		2	3	1		6				18
			4	5	12	7	8	9	10	11			2	3*	1		6				19
			4	5	6	7	8	9	10	11			2		1		3				20
			4	5	6	7	12	8	10	11*	9		2		1		3				21
1			4	5	6	7	8	11	10		9		2				3				22
1			4	5	6	12	8	7	10	11*	9		2				3				23
1	5		4		6*	7	8	9	10	11			2				3	12			24
1	6		4	5		7	8	9	10	11			2	3							25
1	6†		4	5		7	8	9	10*	11			2	3			12		14		26
1	6		4	5		7	8	9	10	11			2	3							27
1	6		4	5		7	8	9	10	11			2	3							28
1	6		4	5		7	8	9	10	11			2	3							29
1	6		4	5		7	8	9	10	11			2	3							30
1	6†	14	4	5		7	8	9	10	11			2	3*			12				31
1		6	4	5		7	8	9	10	11			2	3							32
1			4	5		7	8*	9	10	11	12		2	3						6	33
1			4	5		7*	8	9	10	11	12		2				3			6	34
1			4	5			8	9	10	11	12		2	3					7*	6	35
1			4	5		7	8†	9	10	11	14		2	3*			12			6	36
1		3	4	5		12	8*	7	10	11	9		2				14			6†	37
1			4	5		12	8	7	10	11	9*		2	3						6	38
21	15	14 + 1s	38	37	12 + 1s	33 + 4s	31 + 4s	38	33	28 + 1s	16 + 8s	8 + 4s	34 + 1s	17 + 4s	17	3	16 + 5s	— + 1s	1 + 1s	6	

LIVERPOOL

Player and Position	Ht	Wt	Birth Date	Birth Place	Source	Clubs	League App	League Gls
Goalkeepers								
Mark Brack	6 0	12 02	18 9 70	Liverpool	Trainee	Liverpool	—	—
Bruce Grobbelaar	6 1	13 00	6 10 57	Durban	Vancouver W	Crewe Alex	24	1
						Vancouver W	—	—
						Liverpool	300	—
Michael Hooper	6 2	13 05	10 2 64	Bristol	Local	Bristol C	1	—
						Wrexham (loan)	20	—
						Wrexham	14	—
						Liverpool	30	—
Defenders								
Gary Ablett	6 0	11 04	19 11 65	Liverpool	Apprentice	Liverpool	57	1
						Derby Co (loan)	6	—
						Hull C (loan)	5	—
Jim Beglin*	5 11	11 00	29 7 63	Dublin	Shamrock R	Liverpool	64	2
David Burrows	5 8	11 00	25 10 68	Dudley	Apprentice	WBA	46	1
						Liverpool	21	—
John Carroll	6 1	11 08	13 10 71	Dublin	Home Farm	Liverpool	—	—
David Collins	6 1	12 10	30 10 71	Dublin	Trainee	Liverpool	—	—
Gary Gillespie	6 2	12 07	5 7 60	Stirling	School	Falkirk	22	—
						Coventry C	172	6
						Liverpool	113	9
Alan Hansen	6 1	13 00	13 6 55	Alloa	Sauchie BC	Partick Th	86	6
						Liverpool	403	8
Barry Jones	6 0	12 00	30 6 70	Liverpool	Prescot T	Liverpool	—	—
Steve Nicol	5 10	12 00	11 12 61	Irvine	Ayr U BC	Ayr	70	7
						Liverpool	184	25
John Smyth	5 10	11 00	28 4 70	Dundalk	Dundalk	Liverpool	—	—
Steve Staunton	5 11	11 02	19 1 69	Drogheda	Dundalk	Liverpool	21	—
						Bradford C (loan)	8	—
Phil Thompson‡	6 0	11 08	21 1 54	Liverpool	Apprentice	Liverpool	340	7
						Sheffield U	37	—
						Liverpool	—	—
Barry Venison	5 10	11 09	16 8 64	Consett	Apprentice	Sunderland	173	2
						Liverpool	66	—
Alex Watson	6 0	10 12	6 4 68	Liverpool	Apprentice	Liverpool	4	—
John Williams*			12 10 69	Liverpool		Liverpool	—	—
Midfield								
Ray Houghton	5 8	11 04	9 1 62	Glasgow	Amateur	West Ham U	1	—
						Fulham	129	16
						Oxford U	83	10
						Liverpool	66	12
Craig Johnston	5 8	10 13	8 12 60	Johannesburg	Sydney C	Middlesbrough	64	16
						Liverpool	190	30
Kevin MacDonald*	6 1	12 01	22 12 60	Inverness	Inverness Caley	Leicester C	138	8
						Liverpool	40	1
						Leicester C (loan)	3	—
						Rangers (loan)	3	—
Steve McMahon	5 9	11 08	20 8 61	Liverpool	Apprentice	Everton	100	11
						Aston Villa	75	7
						Liverpool	129	23
Jim Magilton	5 10	12 07	6 5 69	Belfast	Apprentice	Liverpool	—	—
Jan Molby	6 1	14 07	4 7 63	Denmark	Ajax	Liverpool	115	24
Nick Tanner	6 1	13 10	24 5 65	Bristol	Mangotsfield	Bristol R	107	3
						Liverpool	—	—
Ronnie Whelan	5 9	10 13	25 9 61	Dublin	Home Farm	Liverpool	264	42

LIVERPOOL

Foundation: But for a dispute between Everton FC and their landlord at Anfield in 1892, there may never have been a Liverpool club. This dispute persuaded the majority of Evertonians to quit Anfield for Goodison Park, leaving the landlord, Mr. John Houlding, to form a new club. He originally tried to retain the name "Everton" but when this failed, he founded Liverpool Association FC on 15 March, 1892.

Managers (and Secretary-managers)
W. E. Barclay 1892–96, Tom Watson 1896–1915, David Ashworth 1920–22, Matt McQueen 1923–28, George Patterson 1928–36 (continued as secretary), George Kay 1936–51, Don Welsh 1951–56, Phil Taylor 1956–59, Bill Shankly 1959–74, Bob Paisley 1974–83, Joe Fagan 1983–85, Kenny Dalglish 1985– .

Player and Position	*Ht*	*Wt*	*Birth Date*	*Birth Place*	*Source*	*Clubs*	*League App*	*League Gls*
Forwards								
John Aldridge	5 11	10 04	18 9 58	Liverpool	South Liverpool	Newport Co	170	69
						Oxford U	114	72
						Liverpool	81	49
John Barnes	5 11	12 00	7 11 63	Jamaica	Sudbury Court	Watford	233	65
						Liverpool	71	23
Peter Beardsley	5 8	11 07	18 1 61	Newcastle	Wallsend BC	Carlisle U	102	22
					Vancouver W	Manchester U	—	—
					Vancouver W	Newcastle U	147	61
						Liverpool	75	25
Charlie Boyd	5 6	9 04	20 9 69	Liverpool	Trainee	Liverpool	—	—
Kenny Dalglish†	5 8	11 13	4 3 51	Glasgow	Cumb'n'ld U	Celtic	204	112
						Liverpool	354	118
Wayne Harrison	5 8	10 07	15 11 67	Stockport	Apprentice	Oldham Ath	5	1
						Liverpool	—	—
						Oldham Ath (loan)	1	—
						Crewe Alex (loan)	3	1
Mike Marsh	5 8	10 14	21 7 69	Liverpool	Kirkby T	Liverpool	1	—
Ian Rush	6 2	12 06	20 10 61	St Asaph	Apprentice	Chester	34	14
						Liverpool	224	139
						Juventus	29	7
						Liverpool	24	7

Trainees
Fagan, John; Hayde, Michael P; Hollis, Stephen J; Levene, Kevin; McManaman, Steven; McVey, Stephen J; McWilliam, Phillip N; Meskell, Vincent W; Murray, Joseph E; Robinson, Jamie; Rubbery, Howard A; Scanlon, Richard T; Sermanni, Peter; Smith, David R; Taylor, Andrew J; Vaughan, Daniel J; Whelan, Spencer R.C.

****Non-Contract**
Dalglish, Kenneth M; Smith, Colin A.

Associated Schoolboys
Agger, David E; Bold, Matthew B; Brough, Steven L; Brownhill, Barry K; Coady, Gary; Ferris, Ian J; Fitzpatrick, Kevin; Flaherty, Paul T; Fox, Michael J; Godfrey, Warren P; Grindley, David E; Hagan, Kevin K; Howard, Andrew P; Kelly, Jonathan J; Lampkin, Kevin; Martin, Alan D; Matthews, Anthony; Neild, Michael C; Smith, Anthony K; Stalker, Mark E; Walsh, Stephen J; White, Scott L; Whittaker, Stuart.

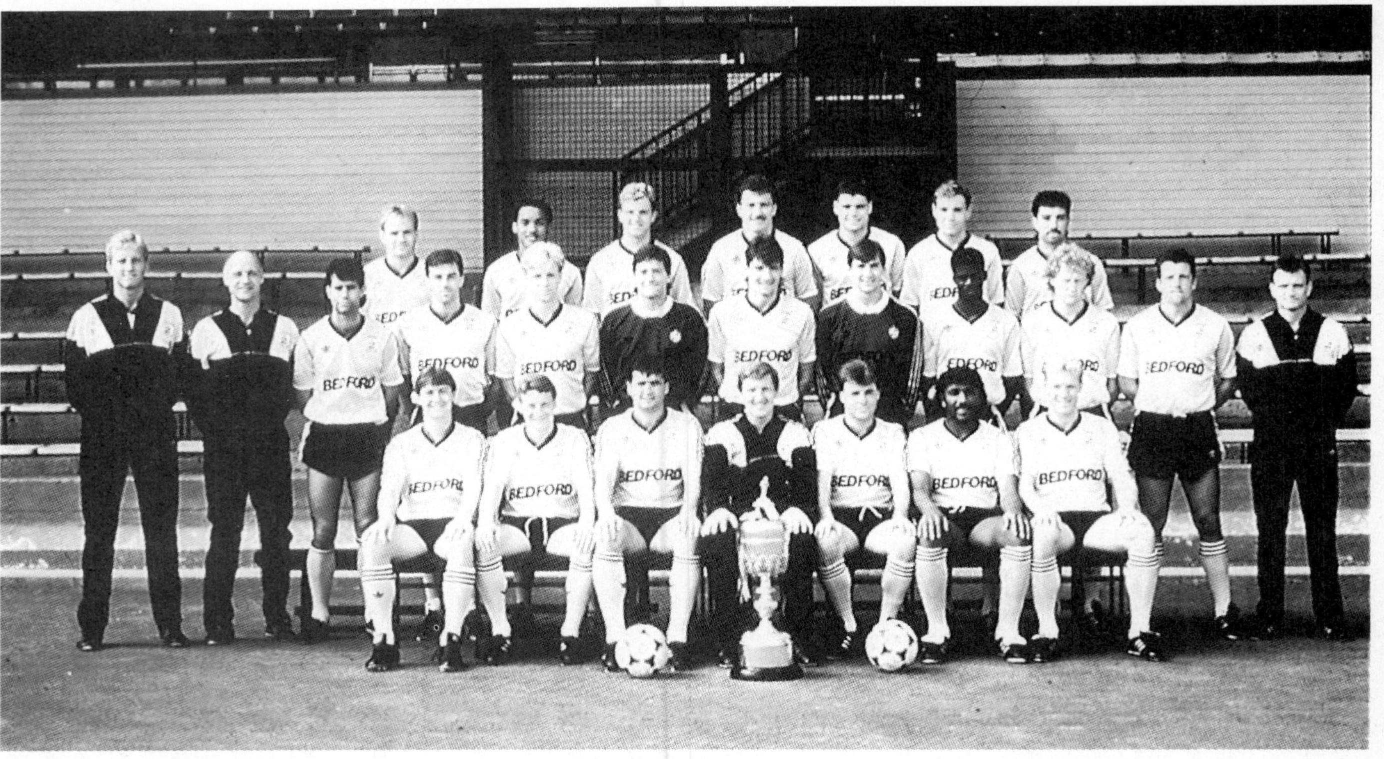

LUTON TOWN 1988–89 *Back row (left to right):* David Preece, Mark Stein, Gary Cobb, Ian Allinson, Richard Harvey, Kingsley Black, Rob Johnson.
Centre row: David Galley (Physiotherapist), John Faulkner (Coach), Roy Wegerle, John Dreyer, David Oldfield, Les Sealey, Mick Harford, Alec Chamberlain, Marvin Johnson, Ashley Grimes, Darron McDonough, Jim Ryan (Coach).
Front row: Steve Williams, Danny Wilson, Steve Foster (Captain), Ray Harford (Manager), Mal Donaghy, Ricky Hill, Tim Breacker.

LUTON TOWN

Kenilworth Road Stadium, 1 Maple Rd, Luton, Beds., LU4 8AW. Telephone, Offices: Luton (0582) 411622; Credit Hotline (0582) 30748 (24 hrs); Banquetting: (0582) 411526.

Ground capacity: 14,000.

Record attendance: 30,069 v Blackpool, FA Cup 6th rd replay, 4 March, 1959.

Record receipts: £77,000 v Oxford U, Littlewoods Cup Semi-final, 28 Feb, 1988.

Pitch measurements: 110yd × 72yd. (Artificial surface).

President: Bert Ward.

Chairman: B. Cole.

Chief Executive/Director: John R. Smith.

General Secretary: William J. Tomlins.

Directors: David Evans, T. W. Bailey, S. Pearson, J. R. Smith, M. Watson Challis, C. J. Hudson.

Marketing Executive: Wendy Greaves.

Team Manager: Ray Harford.

Coaches: Jim Ryan, John Faulkner.

Physio: David Galley.

Year Formed: 1885. ***Turned Professional:*** 1890. ***Ltd Co.:*** 1897.

Club Nickname: 'The Hatters'.

Previous Grounds: 1885, Excelsior, Dallow Lane; 1897, Dunstable Road; 1905, Kenilworth Road.

Record League Victory: 12-0 v Bristol R, Division 3(S), 13 April 1936 – Dolman; Mackey, Smith; Finlayson, Nelson, Godfrey; Rich, Martin (1), Payne (10), Roberts (1), Stephenson.

Record Cup Victory: 9-0 v Clapton, FA Cup, 1st rd (replay after abandoned game), 30 November 1927 – Abbott; Kingham, Graham; Black, Rennie, Fraser; Pointon, Yardley (4), Reid (2), Woods (1), Dennis (2).

Record Defeat: 0-9 v Small Heath, Division 2, 12 November, 1898.

Most League Points (2 for a win): 66, Division 4, 1967–68.

Most League Points (3 for a win): 88, Division 2, 1981–82.

Most League Goals: 103, Division 3(S), 1936–37.

Highest League Scorer in Season: Joe Payne, 55, Division 3(S), 1936–37.

Most League Goals in Total Aggregate: Gordon Turner, 243, 1949–64.

Most Capped Player: Mal Donaghy, 58 (62), Northern Ireland.

Most League Appearances: Bob Morton, 494, 1948–64.

Record Transfer Fee Received: £750,000 from Liverpool for Paul Walsh, May 1984.

Record Transfer Fee Paid: £300,000 to Arsenal for Steve Williams, August 1988.

Football League Record: 1897 Elected to Division 2; 1900 failed re-election; 1920 Division 3; 1921 Division 3(S); 1937–55 Division 2; 1955–60 Division 1; 1960–63 Division 2; 1963–65 Division 3; 1965–68 Division 4; 1968–70 Division 3; 1970–74 Division 2; 1974–75 Division 1; 1975–82 Division 2; 1982– Division 1.

Honours: *Football League:* Division 1 best season : 7th, 1986–87; Division 2 – Champions 1981–82 Runners-up 1954–55, 1973–74; Division 3 – Runners-up 1969–70; Division 4 – Champions 1967–68; Division 3(S) – Champions 1936–37; Runners-up 1935–36. *FA Cup:* Runners-up 1959. *Football League Cup:* Winners 1987–88; Runners-up 1988–89. *Simod Cup:* Runners-up 1988.

Colours: White shirts with navy and orange trim, navy shorts, white stockings. **Change colours:** All royal blue

Special Loupe system for deaf and blind in our handicapped area. New Health Line Club – featuring multi gym, sauna, spa pool, situated beneath our executive boxes. Tel: 41622. SoccerLine, 0898 700 273 for latest news and views about Luton Town.

LUTON TOWN 1988–89 LEAGUE RECORD

Match No.	Date	Venue	Opponents	Result	H/T Score	Lg. Pos.	Goalscorers	Attendance
1	Aug 27	A	Sheffield W	L 0-1	0-0	—		16,433
2	Sept 3	H	Wimbledon	D 2-2	1-1	12	Ryan (og), Black	8067
3	10	A	Southampton	L 1-2	0-1	16	Foster	13,214
4	17	H	Manchester U	L 0-2	0-1	18		11,010
5	24	A	Everton	W 2-0	0-0	15	Oldfield, Black	26,017
6	Oct 1	A	Nottingham F	D 0-0	0-0	17		15,340
7	8	H	Liverpool	W 1-0	1-0	13	Harford	12,117
8	22	A	Middlesbrough	L 1-2	0-2	16	Wilson (pen)	17,792
9	25	H	Arsenal	D 1-1	0-1	—	Black	10,548
10	29	H	QPR	D 0-0	0-0	16		8453
11	Nov 5	A	Millwall	L 1-3	0-3	16	Wilson	12,511
12	12	A	Coventry C	L 0-1	0-1	16		12,631
13	19	H	West Ham U	W 4-1	3-0	16	Black 2, Wegerle, Wilson	9038
14	26	A	Norwich C	D 2-2	1-1	15	Wegerle 2	13,541
15	Dec 3	H	Newcastle U	D 0-0	0-0	15		8338
16	10	A	Derby Co	W 1-0	1-0	15	Harford	15,228
17	17	H	Aston Villa	D 1-1	1-0	16	Wegerle	8785
18	26	A	Tottenham H	D 0-0	0-0	16		27,337
19	31	A	Wimbledon	L 0-4	0-2	17		4899
20	Jan 2	H	Southampton	W 6-1	2-0	15	Harford 2, Black, Wegerle 2, Hill	8637
21	14	A	Charlton Ath	L 0-3	0-3	16		5212
22	21	H	Everton	W 1-0	1-0	13	Wegerle	9013
23	Feb 4	H	Nottingham F	L 2-3	2-2	14	Harford, Black	10,465
24	18	H	Middlesbrough	W 1-0	0-0	13	Foster	8187
25	25	A	Arsenal	L 0-2	0-0	14		31,012
26	Mar 11	H	Millwall	L 1-2	0-2	15	Wilson (pen)	7838
27	14	A	Liverpool	L 0-5	0-2	—		31,447
28	18	H	Sheffield W	L 0-1	0-0	16		7776
29	21	A	QPR	D 1-1	0-0	—	Hill	9372
30	25	A	Manchester U	L 0-2	0-2	20		36,335
31	28	H	Tottenham H	L 1-3	1-0	—	Foster	11,146
32	Apr 1	A	Aston Villa	L 1-2	1-2	18	Hill	15,640
33	15	H	Coventry C	D 2-2	0-0	18	Dreyer, Wilson	8610
34	22	A	Newcastle U	D 0-0	0-0	18		18,493
35	29	H	Derby Co	W 3-0	1-0	18	Wilson (pen), Harford, Black	8507
36	May 2	H	Charlton Ath	W 5-2	4-0	—	Wilson 2, Walsh (og), Harford, Wegerle	10,024
37	6	A	West Ham U	L 0-1	0-1	17		18,686
38	13	H	Norwich C	W 1-0	0-0	15	Wilson (pen)	10,862

Final League Position: 16

GOALSCORERS

League (42): Wilson 9 (4 pens), Black 8, Wegerle 8, Harford 7, Foster 3, Hill 3, Dreyer 1, Oldfield 1, own goals 2.
Littlewoods Cup (16): Harford 4, Wegerle 4, Hill 3, Oldfield 2, Wilson 2 (1 pen), Johnson 1.
FA Cup (2): Black 1, Wilson 1 (pen).

Littlewoods Cup	Second Round	Burnley (h)	1-1
		(a)	1-0
	Third Round	Leeds U (a)	2-0
	Fourth Round	Manchester C (h)	3-1
	Fifth Round	Southampton (h)	1-1
		(a)	2-1
	Semi-Final	West Ham U (a)	3-0
		(h)	2-0
	Final	Nottingham F (at Wembley)	1-3
FA Cup	Third Round	Millwall (a)	2-3

Sealey	Breacker	Dreyer	Williams	Foster	Donaghy	Wilson	Wegerle	Harford	Oldfield	Black	Allinson	Johnson, R	Grimes	Preece	Johnson, M	Hill	McDonough	James	Harvey	Dowie	Beaumont	Meade	Cooke	Chamberlain	*Match No.*
1	2	3	4	5	6	7	8*	9	10	11	12														1
1			4	5	6	7		9	10	11		2	3	8											2
1			4	5	6	7	12	9	8	11		2	3	10*											3
1		3	4	5		7	12	9	8*	11		2			6	10									4
1	12	3	4	5	6	7		9	8†	11	14	2				10*									5
1		3	4	5	6	7		9*	8	11	12	2				10									6
1		3	4	5	6	7	12	9	8*	11		2				10									7
1	14	3		5		7	12	9	8	11		2*			6	10	4†								8
1	3			5		7	8	9	12	11		2			6	10	4*								9
1		3	4	5		7	9		12	11	8*	2			6	10									10
1		3	4	5		7	9		8	11		12			6	10		2*							11
1			4*	5		7	8	9	12	11		2	3		6	10									12
1				5		7	8	9	10	11		2	3	4	6										13
1				5		7	8	9	10	11		2		4	6				3						14
1				5		7	8		9*	11	12	2		4	6	10			3						15
1				5		7	8*	9	12	11		2		4	6	10			3						16
1				5		7	8	9		11		2		4	6	10			3						17
1				5		7	8	9	11			2		4	6	10			3						18
1				5		7	8*	9	11	12		2		4	6	10			3						19
1				5		7	8	9		11		2		4	6	10			3						20
1	12			5		7	8		9†	11		2		4	6	10			3*	14					21
1	2	6		5		7*	8	9		11†		12	3	4		10				14					22
1	2	6		5		7	8	9	12	11			3*	4		10									23
1	2			5		7	8	9		11			3	4		10					6				24
1	2			5		7	8	9	12	11				4*		10			3		6				25
1	2	12				7	8*	9		11			3	4†		10	5			14	6				26
1	2					7		9		11			3	4*	5	10	8			12	6				27
1	2			5		7		9		11			3†	4*		10	8		14	12	6				28
1	2			5		7		9		11						10	4		3	12	6	8*			29
1	2			5		7*		9		11				8†		10	4		3	14	6		12		30
1	2			5				9		11			3	7		10	4			8*	6		12		31
1	2	14		5		7	8	9		11			3†			10	4*				6	12			32
	2	3		5		7	8			11				4		10					6	9*	12	1	33
	2	3		5		7	8*	9		11†				4		10	14				6	12		1	34
	2	3		5		7*	8	9		11				4		10					6		12	1	35
	2	3		5		7	8	9		11*				4		10					6		12	1	36
	2	3		5		7	8	9		11*				4		10					6		12	1	37
	2	3		5		7	8	9		11				4		10					6			1	38
32	19 + 3s	16 + 2s	10	36	6	37	26 + 4s	33	15 + 6s	36 + 1s	1 + 4s	19 + 2s	12	26	16	33	9 + 1s	1	11 + 1s	1 + 7s	15	2 + 2s	— + 6s	6	

LUTON TOWN

Player and Position	Ht	Wt	Birth Date	Birth Place	Source	Clubs	League App	League Gls
Goalkeepers								
Alec Chamberlain	6 2	13 00	20 6 64	March	Ramsey T	Ipswich T	—	—
						Colchester U	184	—
						Everton	—	—
						Tranmere R (loan)	15	—
						Luton T	6	—
Les Sealey	6 1	12 08	29 9 57	Bethnal Green	Apprentice	Coventry C	158	—
						Luton T	207	—
						Plymouth Arg (loan)	6	—
Andy Petterson	6 1	14 12	26 9 69	Freemantle		Luton T	—	—
						Swindon T (loan)	—	—
Defenders								
Dave Beaumont	5 10	11 05	10 12 63	Edinburgh	'S' Form	Dundee U	89	3
						Luton T	15	—
Tim Breacker	6 0	12 06	2 7 65	Bicester		Luton T	164	2
John Dreyer	6 0	11 10	11 6 63	Alnwick	Wallingford T	Oxford U	60	2
						Torquay U (loan)	5	—
						Fulham (loan)	12	2
						Luton T	18	1
Steve Foster	6 0	14 00	24 9 57	Portsmouth	Apprentice	Portsmouth	109	6
						Brighton HA	172	6
						Aston Villa	15	3
						Luton T	163	11
Ken Gillard	5 9	11 08	30 4 72	Dublin	Trainee	Luton T	—	—
Paul Gray	5 9	11 08	28 1 70	Belfast	Trainee	Luton T	—	—
Ashley Grimes*	5 11	11 02	2 8 57	Dublin	Bohemians	Manchester U	90	10
						Coventry C	32	1
						Luton T	87	3
Richard Harvey	5 9	11 10	17 4 69	Letchworth	Apprentice	Luton T	17	—
Marvin Johnson	5 11	11 06	29 10 68	Wembley	Apprentice	Luton T	25	—
Neil Poutch			27 11 69	Dublin	Trainee	Luton T	—	—
Midfield								
Kingsley Black	5 8	10 11	22 6 68	Luton	School	Luton T	50	8
Gary Cobb	5 8	11 05	6 8 68	Luton	Apprentice	Luton T	9	—
						Northampton T (loan)	1	—
Sean Farrell	6 1	12 08	28 2 69	Watford	Apprentice	Luton T	—	—
						Colchester U (loan)	9	1
Ricky Hill	5 11	13 00	5 3 59	London	Apprentice	Luton T	436	54
Julian James	5 10	11 11	22 3 70	Tring	Trainee	Luton T	4	—
Rob Johnson	5 6	9 12	22 2 62	Bedford	Apprentice	Luton T	97	—
						Lincoln C (loan)	4	—
Darron McDonough	5 11	12 06	7 11 62	Antwerp	Apprentice	Oldham Ath	183	14
						Luton T	55	5
Michael O'Brien	5 10	11 04	28 11 70	Dublin	Trainee	Luton T	—	—
Alan O'Sullivan	5 5	10 01	26 8 71	Cork		Luton T	—	—
David Preece	5 5	10 00	28 5 63	Bridgnorth	Apprentice	Walsall	111	5
						Luton T	115	4
Jason Rees	5 5	10 05	22 12 69	Aberdare	Trainee	Luton T	—	—
Ian Scott	5 10	11 05	25 11 68	Luton	Apprentice	Luton T	—	—
Paul Telfer	5 9	10 02	21 10 71	Edinburgh	Trainee	Luton T	—	—
Aaron Tighe	5 9	10 09	11 7 69	Banbury	Apprentice	Luton T	—	—
						Leicester C (loan)	—	—
Steve Williams	5 11	10 11	12 7 58	London	Apprentice	Southampton	278	18
						Arsenal	95	4
						Luton T	10	—

LUTON TOWN

Foundation: Formed by an amalgamation of two leading local clubs, Wanderers and Excelsior a works team, at a meeting in Luton Town Hall in April 1885. The Wanderers had three months earlier changed their name to Luton Town Wanderers and did not take too kindly to the formation of another Town club but were talked around at this meeting. Wanderers had already appeared in the FA Cup and the new club entered in its inaugural season.

Managers (and Secretary-managers)
Charlie Green 1901–28*, George Thomson 1925, John McCartney 1927–29, George Kay 1929–31, Harold Wightman 1931–35, Ted Liddell 1936–38, Neil McBain 1938–39, George Martin 1939–47, Dally Duncan 1947–58, Syd Owen 1959–60, Sam Bartram 1960–62, Bill Harvey 1962–64, George Martin 1965–66, Allan Brown 1966–68, Alec Stock 1968–72, Harry Haslam 1972–78, David Pleat 1978–86, John Moore 1986–87, Ray Harford 1987– .

Player and Position	*Ht*	*Wt*	*Birth Date*	*Birth Place*	*Source*	*Clubs*	*League App*	*League Gls*
Danny Wilson	5 6	11 04	1 1 60	Wigan	Wigan Ath	Bury	90	8
						Chesterfield	100	13
						Nottingham F	10	1
						Scunthorpe U (loan)	6	3
						Brighton & HA	135	33
						Luton T	75	17
Forwards								
Richard Cooke	5 6	9 00	4 9 65	Islington	Apprentice	Tottenham H	11	2
						Birmingham C (loan)	5	—
						Bournemouth	57	13
						Luton T	6	—
Iain Dowie	6 0	13 03	9 1 65		Hendon	Luton T	8	—
Mick Harford	6 2	12 09	12 2 59	Sunderland	Lambton St BC	Lincoln C	115	41
						Newcastle U	19	4
						Bristol C	30	11
						Birmingham C	92	25
						Luton T	135	57
Raphael Meade	5 10	11 09	22 11 62	Islington	Apprentice	Arsenal	41	14
					Sporting Lisbon	Dundee U	11	4
						Luton T	4	—
Roy Wegerle	5 8	10 02	19 3 64	South Africa	Tampa Bay R	Chelsea	23	3
						Swindon T (loan)	7	1
						Luton T	30	8
Darren Salton	6 1	13 08	16 3 72	Edinburgh	Trainee	Luton T	—	—

Trainees
Allpress, Timothy J; Brown, Stuart W; Crawshaw, Gary; Edworthy, Jason S; Hughes, Ceri M; Husband, Jamie; McGonagle, Mark B; Nogan, Kurt; Pembridge, Mark A; Shanley, Kevin J; Watkiss, Richard K.

Associated Schoolboys
Campbell, Jamie; Cooper, David B.E; Denham, Martin; Goodfellow, Scott; Hancock, Paul J; Hazel, Julian E; Heath, Richard J; Jackson, Matthew A; Newman, Paul S; Parfitt, Delme J.R; Williams, Barry J.

MAIDSTONE UNITED 1988–89 *Back row (left to right):* Tony Sorrell, Paul Collins, Andy Beattie, Jesse Roast, Mervyn Cawston, Mark Beeney, Ken Charlery, Malcolm Stewart, Les Berry, Mark Golley.

Centre row: Mike Mercer (Secretary), Barbara Legg (Office Administrator), Bernie Holden (Lottery Manager), Barry Fenn (Kit Man), John Brooks (Senior Vice-President), Frank Brooks (Trainer), Joe Sullivan (Goalkeeper/Coach), George Dudley (Ass. Manager), Jim Dawkins (Vice-Chairman), David Twiddy (Company Secretary), Michael Frank (Club Doctor), Dennis Berry (Director), Geoff Pearson (Director).

Front row: Tony Rogers, Noel Ashford, David Jacques, Steve Butler, Bill Williams (General Manager), Jim Thompson (Chairman), John Still (Team Manager), Tony Pamphlett (Captain), Mark Hill, Mark Gall, Dave Mehmet.

Division 4 MAIDSTONE UNITED

Watling Street, Dartford, Kent DA2 6EN. Telephone (0622) 54403.
Ground capacity: 15,000.
Record Attendance: (at The Stadium, London Road, Maidstone): 10,591 v Charlton Ath., FA Cup 3rd rd replay, 15 Jan 1979.
Manager: Keith Peacock.
Directors: J. C. Thompson (Chairman), J. G. Dawkins, G. Pearson, M. Oldham.
Secretary: Mike Mercer.
Year formed: 1897.
Club Nickname: 'Stones'.
Previous Leagues: East Kent, Thames & Medway Combination, Kent, Corinthian, Athenian, Isthmian, Southern.
Record Transfer fee paid: £35,000 to Fisher Athletic for Ken Charlery, March 1989.
Colours: Amber shirts, black shorts, black stockings with gold trim.

Player and Position	Ht	Wt	Birth Date	Birth Place	Source	Clubs	League App	League Gls
Goalkeepers								
Mark Beeney	6 4	13 00	30 12 67	Pembury		Gillingham	2	—
						Maidstone U	—	—
Mervyn Cawston	6 2	13 04	4 2 52	Norwich	Apprentice	Norwich C	4	—
						Southend U (loan)	10	—
						Newport Co (loan)	—	—
						Gillingham	19	—
					Chicago S	Southend U	198	—
						Stoke C	—	—
						Southend U	—	—
						Maidstone U	—	—
Defenders								
Andy Beattie	6 2	11 06	9 2 64	Liverpool	Apprentice	Cambridge U	97	2
						Maidstone U	—	—
Mark Golley	6 1	13 00	28 10 62	Beckenham	Sutton U	Maidstone U	—	—
Jesse Roast	6 1	12 07	16 3 64	Barking	Barking	Maidstone U	—	—
Midfield								
Noel Ashford			15 2 58	Barking	Barnet	Maidstone U	—	—
Paul Collins			11 8 66	West Ham	Apprentice	Gillingham	37	3
						Maidstone U	—	—
Gary Cooper	5 8	11 03	20 11 65	Edgware	Fisher Ath	Maidstone U	—	—
David Mehmet	5 9	11 09	2 12 60	London	Apprentice	Millwall	114	15
						Tampa Bay R	—	—
						Charlton Ath	29	3
						Gillingham	132	39
						Millwall	18	1
						Maidstone U	—	—
Tony Sorrell	5 10	12 04	17 10 66	Bromchurch	Bishops Stortford	Maidstone U	—	—
Malcolm Stewart			31 7 60	Bishops Stortford	Dartford	Maidstone U	—	—
Forwards								
Steve Butler	6 2	11 01	27 1 62	Birmingham	Army	Brentford	21	3
						Maidstone U	—	—
Ken Charlery	6 1	12 07	28 11 64	London	Fisher Ath	Maidstone U	—	—
Mark Gall	5 10	12 00	14 5 63	Brixton	Greenwich Bor	Maidstone U	—	—
Tony Rogers			10 9 63	Plaistow	Barking	Maidstone	—	—

MANCHESTER CITY 1988–89 *Back row (left to right):* Paul Moulden, Trevor Morely, Wayne Biggins, Nigel Gleghorn, John Deehan, Andy Hinchcliffe, Ian Scott.
Centre row: Mel Machin (Team Manager), Brian Gayle, Dave White, Andy Dibble, Mark Seagraves, Paul Lake, Roy Bailey (Physiotherapist), Jimmy Frizzell (Manager).
Front row: Neil McNab, Paul Simpson, Steve Fedmond (Captain), Ian Brightwell, Jason Beckford.

Division 1 **MANCHESTER CITY**

Maine road, Moss Side, Manchester M14 7WN. Telephone 061-226 1191/2.Ticket Office: 061-226 2224. Development Office: 061-226 3143. Clubcall: 0898 12 11 91.
Ground capacity: 48,500.
Record attendance: 84,569 v Stoke C, FA Cup 6th rd, 3 March, 1934 (British record for any game outside London or Glasgow).
Record receipts: £239,476. Everton v Liverpool, Milk Cup Final replay, 28 March, 1984.
Pitch measurements: 117yd × 76yd.
Chairman: P. J. Swales. ***Vice-Charman:*** F. Pye.
Directors: I. L. G. Niven, C. B. Muir, M. T. Horwich, W. C. Adams, A. Thomas, G. Doyle, W. A. Miles, B. Turnbull, J. Greiback.
Secretary: J. B. Halford.
Commercial Manager: P. Critchley.
General Manager: Jimmy Frizzell. ***Manager:*** Mel Machin.
Coaches: Tony Book, Glyn Pardoe and John Deehan.
Physio: Roy Bailey.
Year formed: 1887 as Ardwick FC; 1894 as Manchester City.
Turned Professional: 1887 as Ardwick FC. ***Ltd Co.:*** 1894.
Nickname: Blues.
Previous Names: 1887–94, Ardwick FC (formed through the amalgamation of West Gorton and Gorton Athletic, the latter having been formed in 1880).
Previous Grounds: 1880–81, Clowes Street; 1881–82, Kirkmanshulme Cricket Ground; 1882–84, Queens Road; 1884–87, Pink Bank Lane; 1887–1923, Hyde Road (1894–1923, as City); 1923, Maine Road.
Record League Victory: 10-1 Huddersfield T, Division 2, 7 November 1987 – Nixon; Gidman, Hinchcliffe, Clements, Lake, Redmond, White (3), Stewart (3), Adcock (3), McNab (1) Simpson.
Record Cup Victory: 10-1 v Swindon T, FA Cup, 4th rd, 29 January 1930 – Barber; Felton, McCloy; Barrass, Cowan, Heinemann; Toseland, Marshall (5), Tait (3), Johnson (1), Brook (1).
Record Defeat: 1-9 v Everton, Division 1, 3 September, 1906.
Most League Points (2 for a win): 62, Division 2, 1946–47.
Most League Points (3 for a win): 82, Division 2, 1988–89.
Most League Goals: 108, Division 2, 1926–27.
Highest League Scorer in Season: Tommy Johnson, 38, Division 1, 1928–29.
Most League Goals in Total Aggregate: Tommy Johnson, 158,1919–30.
Most Capped Player: Colin Bell, 48, England.
Most League Appearances: Alan Oakes, 565, 1959–76.
Record Transfer Fee Received: £1,700,000 from Tottenham H for Paul Stewart, June 1988.
Record Transfer Fee Paid: £1,437,500 to Wolverhampton W for Steve Daley, September 1979 (£1,150,000 basic fee).
Football League Record: 1982 Ardwick elected founder member of Division 2, 1894 Newly-formed Manchester C elected to Division 2; Division 1 1899–1902, 1903–09, 1910–26, 1928–38, 1947–50, 1951–63, 1966–83, 1985–87, 1989–; Division 2 1902–03, 1909–10, 1926–28, 1938–47, 1950–51, 1963–66, 1983–85, 1987–89.
Honours: *Football League:* Division 1 – Champions 1936–37, 1967–68; Runners-up 1903–04, 1920–21, 1976–77; Division 2 – Champions 1898–99, 1902–03, 1909–10, 1927–28, 1946–47, 1965–66; Runners-up 1895–96, 1950–51. *FA Cup:* Winners 1904, 1934, 1956, 1969; Runners-up 1926, 1933, 1955, 1981. *Football League Cup:* Winners 1970, 1976; Runners-up 1973–74. **European Competitions:** *European Cup:* 1968–69. *European Cup-Winners: Cup:* 1969–70 (winners), 1970–71. *UEFA Cup:* 1972–73, 1976–77, 1977–78, 1978–79.
Colours: Sky blue shirts, white shorts, navy blue stockings. **Change colours:** Alternate maroon and white striped shirts with fine blue stripe between, England neckline with button down neck, integral shadow diamond weave, maroooon shorts with 1½″ blue stripe and white stripe, maroon stockings with sky blue diamond on turnover.

MANCHESTER CITY 1988–89 LEAGUE RECORD

Match No.	Date		Venue	Opponents	Result		H/T Score	Lg. Pos.	Goalscorers	Attendance
1	Aug	27	A	Hull C	L	0-1	0-0	—		11,653
2		29	H	Oldham Ath	L	1-4	0-2	—	Lake	22,594
3	Sept	3	H	Walsall	D	2-2	0-1	20	McNab (pen), Morley	17,104
4		10	A	Leeds U	D	1-1	0-0	19	McNab (pen)	23,122
5		17	H	Brighton & HA	W	2-1	1-0	13	Brightwell, Moulden	16,033
6		20	A	Chelsea	W	3-1	1-1	—	Brightwell 2, Moulden	8858
7		24	A	Barnsley	W	2-1	0-0	8	White, Morley	9300
8	Oct	1	H	Blackburn R	W	1-0	0-0	5	Biggins	22,111
9		5	H	Portsmouth	W	4-1	3-1	—	White, Moulden, Biggins, Lake	17,202
10		8	A	Ipswich T	L	0-1	0-1	4		15,521
11		15	A	Plymouth Arg	W	1-0	0-0	4	Gayle	10,158
12		22	H	Birmingham C	D	0-0	0-0	3		20,205
13		26	A	WBA	L	0-1	0-1	—		14,258
14		29	H	Sunderland	D	1-1	1-1	6	Hinchcliffe	22,398
15	Nov	5	A	Leicester C	D	0-0	0-0	6		14,080
16		12	H	Watford	W	3-1	0-1	7	Moulden, Biggins 2	21,142
17		19	A	Bournemouth	W	1-0	1-0	4	Moulden	9874
18		26	H	Oxford U	W	2-1	0-1	3	Morley, Redmond	20,145
19	Dec	3	A	Crystal Palace	D	0-0	0-0	4		12,444
20		10	H	Bradford C	W	4-0	1-0	1	Brightwell 2, Moulden 2	20,129
21		17	H	Shrewsbury T	D	2-2	0-2	3	Hinchcliffe 2 (1 pen)	19,613
22		26	A	Stoke C	L	1-3	1-0	5	Gleghorn	24,056
23		31	A	Swindon T	W	2-1	1-0	4	Gayle, Beckford	10,776
24	Jan	2	H	Leeds U	D	0-0	0-0	5		33,034
25		14	A	Oldham Ath	W	1-0	1-0	4	Megson	19,200
26		21	H	Hull C	W	4-1	3-0	3	Biggins 2, Moulden, White	20,485
27	Feb	4	A	Portsmouth	W	1-0	1-0	2	Gleghorn	13,207
28		11	H	Ipswich T	W	4-0	2-0	2	Gayle, Biggins 2, Morley	22,145
29		18	A	Birmingham C	W	2-0	1-0	2	Gleghorn, McNab	11,707
30		25	H	Plymouth Arg	W	2-0	1-0	1	McNab (pen), Biggins	22,451
31	Mar	1	H	WBA	D	1-1	0-0	—	Moulden	25,109
32		4	A	Watford	L	0-1	0-1	2		15,747
33		11	H	Leicester C	W	4-2	0-0	1	Spearing (og), Morley 3	22,266
34		14	A	Sunderland	W	4-2	3-1	—	White 2, Gleghorn, Morley	16,101
35		18	H	Chelsea	L	2-3	0-2	2	McNab (pen), Taggart	40,070
36		25	A	Walsall	D	3-3	2-2	2	Oldfield, Moulden 2	7562
37		27	H	Stoke C	W	2-1	1-0	2	Oldfield, Hinchcliffe (pen)	28,303
38	Apr	1	A	Brighton & HA	L	1-2	0-1	2	Morley	12,072
39		4	A	Shrewsbury T	W	1-0	0-0	—	Morley	8271
40		8	H	Swindon T	W	2-1	1-1	2	Hinchcliffe (pen), Oldfield	22,663
41		15	A	Blackburn R	L	0-4	0-2	2		16,927
42		22	H	Barnsley	L	1-2	0-1	2	Lake	21,274
43		29	A	Oxford U	W	4-2	0-2	2	Gleghorn, White, Greenall (og), Brightwell	7762
44	May	1	H	Crystal Palace	D	1-1	1-0	2	Gleghorn	33,456
45		6	H	Bournemouth	D	3-3	3-0	2	Moulden 2, Morley	30,564
46		13	A	Bradford C	D	1-1	0-1	2	Morley	12,479

Final League Position: 2

GOALSCORERS

League (77): Moulden 13, Morley 12, Biggins 9, Brightwell 6, Gleghorn 6, White 6, Hinchcliffe 5 (3 pens), McNab 5 (4 pens), Gayle 3, Lake 3, Oldfield 3, Beckford 1, Megson 1, Redmond 1, Taggart 1, own goals 2.
Littlewoods Cup (12): Moulden 4, Gleghorn 2, White 2, Biggins 1, Lake 1, McNab 1 (pen), Morley 1.
FA Cup (2): Gleghorn 1, McNab 1 (pen).

Littlewoods Cup	Second Round	Plymouth Arg (h)	1-0
		(a)	6-3
	Third Round	Sheffield U (h)	4-2
	Fourth Round	Luton T (a)	1-3
FA Cup	Third Round	Leicester C (h)	1-0
	Fourth Round	Brentford (a)	1-3

Dibble	Lake	Hinchcliffe	Gayle	Brightwell	Redmond	White	Biggins	Morley	McNab	Gleghorn	Varadi	Seagraves	Simpson	Moulden	Williams	Hughes	Beckford	Bradshaw	Megson	Taggart	Oldfield	Cooper	Scott	*Match No.*
1	2	3	4	5	6	7	8	9	10*	11	12													1
1	2	3	4	5	6	7†	8	9	10		12	14	11*											2
1	7	3	4	5	6	12		9	10	11†	8*	2		14										3
1	11	3	4	5	6	7		9	10			2		8										4
1	11	3	4	5	6	7		9	10			2		8										5
1	11	3	4	5	6	7		9	10			2		8										6
1	11	3	4	5	6	7		9	10			2		8										7
1	11	3	4		6	7	5	9	10			2		8										8
1	11	3	4		6	7	5	9	10			2		8										9
1	11	3	4		6	7	5	9	10			2*		8	12									10
1		3	4		6	7	5	9	10	2				8		11*	12							11
1	11	3	4	12	6	7	5	9	10	2†		14		8*										12
1		3	4	5	6	7	11	9*	10	2				8				12						13
1		3	4	5	6	7	11*		10	8		2					12	9						14
1		3	4	5	6	7	11	9	10			2		8										15
1		3	4	5	6	7	11	9	10			2		8										16
1		3	4	5	6	7	11	9	10			2		8										17
1	3†		4	5	6	7	11	9	10*	14		2		8			12							18
1	3*		4	5	6	7	11	9	10	14		2		8†				12						19
1	14	3	4	5	6	7*		9	10	11		2†		8			12							20
1	10	3	4	5	6	7	12	9		11*		2		8										21
1	10	3	4	5	6	7†	11*	9		8		2		14			12							22
1	8	3	4	5	6	7	11		10	12		2					9*							23
1	8*	3	4	5	6	7	11	12	10	14		2					9†							24
1	9	3	4	12	6	7	11		10	14		2		8†					5*					25
1	9	3	4		6	7	11		10			2		8					5					26
1	2		4		6	7	11	8	10	9									5	3				27
1	2		4		6	7	11	8	10	9									5	3				28
1	2		4		6	7	11	8	10	9									5	3				29
1	2	12	4		6	7	11†	8	10	9				14					5	3*				30
1	2	12	4		6	7	11	8	10	9†				14					5	3*				31
1	2	3	4		6	7	11	8	10	9*				12					5					32
1	2†	3	4		6		11*	8	10	9				7			12		5	14				33
1		3	4		6	7		8	10	9									5	2	11			34
1	2		4		6	7		8	10	9*				12					5	3	11			35
1*	2		4		6	7			10	9				8				12	5	3	11			36
	2	3	4		6	7		11	10	12				8					5		9*	1		37
	4	3		2*	6	7		11		12				8					5	14	9	1	10†	38
	2	3	4		6	7	11	8		9								12	5		10*	1		39
	2*	3	4		6	7	11	9	10					8					5		12	1		40
		3	4		6	7	11*	8	10					12					5	2	9	1		41
	2	3	4		6	7	12		10	11*				8					5		9	1		42
1	2	3		5	6	7		9	10	11				8					4					43
1*	2	3		5	6	7	14	9	10	11				8†					4		12			44
	2	3		5	6	7		9	10	11				8*					4		12	1		45
	2	3		5	6	7		9	10	11				8					4			1		46
38	37 + 1s	37 + 2s	41	24 + 2s	46	44 + 1s	29 + 3s	39 + 1s	42	25 + 7s	1 + 2s	21 + 2s	1	29 + 7s	— + 1s	1	2 + 6s	1 + 4s	22	9 + 2s	8 + 3s	8	1	

MANCHESTER CITY

Player and Position	Ht	Wt	Birth Date	Birth Place	Source	Clubs	League App	League Gls
Goalkeepers								
Paul Cooper	5 11	13 10	21 12 53	Brierley Hill	Apprentice	Birmingham C	17	—
						Ipswich T	447	—
						Leicester C	56	—
						Manchester C	8	—
Andy Dibble	6 2	13 07	8 5 65	Cwmbran	Apprentice	Cardiff C	62	—
						Luton T	30	—
						Sunderland (loan)	12	—
						Huddersfield T (loan)	5	—
						Manchester C	38	—
Defenders								
Robert Barnes*	5 8	10 08	26 11 69	Stoke	Trainee	Manchester C	—	—
Willie Burns*	5 11	10 10	10 12 69	Motherwell	Trainee	Manchester C	—	—
Brian Gayle	6 1	12 07	6 3 65	London		Wimbledon	83	3
						Manchester C	41	3
Andy Hinchcliffe	5 10	12 10	5 2 69	Manchester	Apprentice	Manchester C	81	6
Neil Lennon§			25 6 71	Lurgan	Trainee	Manchester C	1	—
Steven Macauley‡	5 11	11 06	4 3 69	Lytham St Annes	Trainee	Manchester C	—	—
Steve Redmond	5 11	12 13	2 11 67	Liverpool	Apprentice	Manchester C	129	3
Mark Seagraves	6 1	12 10	22 10 66	Bootle	Local	Liverpool	—	—
						Norwich C (loan)	3	—
						Manchester C	40	—
Gerry Taggart§			18 10 70	Belfast	Trainee	Manchester C	11	1
Darren Wilson			30 9 71	Manchester		Manchester C	—	—
Midfield								
David Brightwell			7 1 71	Lutterworth		Manchester C	—	—
Ian Brightwell	5 10	11 07	9 4 68	Lutterworth	Trainee	Manchester C	75	12
Michael Hughes	5 6	10 08	2 8 71	Larne	School	Manchester C	1	—
Paul Lake	6 0	12 02	28 10 68	Manchester	Trainee	Manchester C	74	7
Gary Megson	5 10	11 06	2 5 59	Manchester	Apprentice	Plymouth Arg	78	10
						Everton	22	2
						Sheffield W	123	13
						Nottingham F	—	—
						Newcastle U	24	1
						Sheffield W	110	12
						Manchester C	22	1
Ian Scott	5 9	11 04	20 9 67	Radcliffe	Apprentice	Manchester C	24	3
Neil McNab	5 7	11 00	4 6 57	Greenock		Morton	14	—
						Tottenham H	72	3
						Bolton W	35	4
						Brighton & HA	103	4
						Leeds U (loan)	5	—
						Portsmouth (loan)	—	—
						Manchester C	209	16
Ian Thompstone§			17 1 71		Trainee	Manchester C	1	1
Forwards								
Jason Beckford	5 9	12 04	14 2 70	Manchester	Trainee	Manchester C	13	1
Wayne Biggins	5 11	11 00	20 11 61	Sheffield	Apprentice	Lincoln C	8	1
					Kings Lynn	Burnley	78	29
						Norwich C	79	16
						Manchester C	32	9
Carl Bradshaw	6 0	11 00	2 10 68	Sheffield	Apprentice	Sheffield W	32	4
						Barnsley (loan)	6	1
						Manchester C	5	—

MANCHESTER CITY

Foundation: Manchester City was formed as a Limited Company in 1894 after their predecessors Ardwick had been forced into bankruptcy. However, many historians like to trace the club's lineage as far back as 1880 when St. Mark's Church, West Gorton added a football section to their cricket club. They amalgamated with Gorton Athletic in 1884 as Gorton FC. Because of a change of ground they became Ardwick in 1887.

Managers (and Secretary-managers)
Joshua Parlby 1894–95*, Sam Omerod 1895–1902, Tom Maley 1902–06, Harry Newbould 1906–12, Ernest Magnall 1912–24, David Ashworth 1924–25, Peter Hodge 1926–32, Wilf Wild 1932–46 (continued as secretary to 1950), Sam Cowan 1946–47, John "Jock" Thomson 1947–50, Leslie McDowall 1950–63, George Poyser 1963–65, Joe Mercer 1965–71 (continued as GM to 1972), Malcolm Allison 1972–73, Johnny Hart 1973, Ron Saunders 1973–74, Tony Book 1974–79, Malcolm Allison 1979–80, John Bond 1980–83, John Benson 1983, Billy McNeill 1983–86, Jimmy Frizzell 1986–87 (continued as GM), Mel Machin 1987– .

Player and Position	*Ht*	*Wt*	*Birth Date*	*Birth Place*	*Source*	*Clubs*	*League App*	*League Gls*
John Deehan	6 0	11 03	8 8 57	Solihull	Apprentice	Aston Villa	110	42
						WBA	47	5
						Norwich C	162	62
						Ipswich T	49	11
						Manchester C	—	—
Nigel Gleghorn	6 0	12 13	12 8 62	Seaham	Seaham Red Star	Ipswich T	66	11
						Manchester C	32	6
Andy Milner	5 11	11 07	10 2 67	Kendal	Netherfield	Manchester C	—	—
Trevor Morley	5 11	12 01	20 3 62	Nottingham	Nuneaton	Northampton T	107	39
						Manchester C	55	16
Paul Moulden	5 10	11 00	6 9 67	Farnworth	Apprentice	Manchester C	64	18
David Oldfield	6 0	12 02	30 5 68	Perth, Aust	Apprentice	Luton T	29	4
						Manchester C	11	3
David White	6 1	12 09	30 10 67	Manchester		Manchester C	113	20

Trainees
Agius, Mark S; Dyer, Simon R; Hasford, Jason; Kelly, Paul; Lennon, Neil F; Margetson, Martyn W; Peters, Mark; Quigley, Michael A; Sheron, Michael N; Small, Colin; Taggart, Gerald P; Thompstone, Ian P; Wallace, Michael; Ward, Ashley S; Williams, Paul J; Wills, John.

****Non-Contract**
White, Martin.

Associated Schoolboys
Beirne, Michael A; Bell, Stephen J; Bibby, Richard; Callaghan, Matthew; Edghill, Richard; Flitcroft, Gary W; Foster, John C; Forster, Nicholas J; Graham, Andrew G; Harkin, Sean C; Ingram, Rae; Jackson, Robert; Lewis, Ian R; Lees, John E; Locke, Stuart J; Lomas, Steven; McCullough, Ronnie; McHugh, Darren R; Mike, Adrian; Mulvey, Eamon; Newsham, Paul J; Roach, David P; Thomas, Scott L; Wood, Timothy.

MANCHESTER UNITED 1988–89 *Back row (left to right):* Nicky Wood, Lee Martin, Steve Bruce, Viv Anderson, Peter Davenport, Paul McGrath, Liam O'Brien, Norman Whiteside.
Centre row: Archie Knox (Assistant Manager), Alex Ferguson (Manager), Clayton Blackmore, Chris Turner, Jim Leighton, Gary Walsh, Billy Garton, Jim McGregor (Physiotherapist), Norman Davies (Kit Manager).
Front row: Kevin Moran, Mike Duxbury, Jesper Olsen, Mark Hughes, Bryan Robson, Brian McClair, Gordon Strachan, Colin Gibson.

Division 1 MANCHESTER UNITED

Old Trafford, Manchester M16 0RA. Telephone 061-872 1661/2. Recorded information: 061-872 0199. Membership enquiries: 061-872 5208. Souvenir shop: 061-872 3398.
Ground capacity: 56,385.
Record attendance: 76,962 Wolverhampton W v Grimsby T. FA Cup semi-final. 25 March, 1939.
Club record: 70,504 v Aston Villa, Division 1, 27 December, 1920.
Record receipts: £232,173.70 v Nottingham F, FA Cup 6th rd, 18 March, 1989.
Pitch measurements: 116yd × 76yd.
President: Sir Matt Busby CBE, KCSG.
Vice-Presidents: J. A. Gibson, W. A. Young, J. G. Gulliver, R. L. Edwards.
Chairman/Chief Executive: C. M. Edwards.
Directors: J. M. Edelson, R. Charlton CBE, E. M. Watkins LL.M., A. M. Midani, N. Burrows, R. L. Olive.
Manager: Alex Ferguson. ***Assistant Manager:*** Archie Knox
Secretary: K. R. Merrett.
Commercial Manager: D. McGregor.
Physio: Jim McGregor.
Year Formed: 1878 as Newton Heath LYR; 1902, Manchester United.
Turned Professional: 1885. ***Ltd Co.:*** 1907.
Previous Name: Newton Heath, 1880–1902. ***Nickname:*** 'Red Devils'.
Previous Grounds: 1880–93, North Road, Monsall Road; 1893, Bank Street; 1910, Old Trafford (played at Main Rd 1941–49).
Record League Victory: 10-1 v Wolverhampton W, Division 2, 15 October 1892 – Warner; Mitchell, Clements; Perrins, Stewart (3), Erentz; Farman (1), Hood (1), Donaldson (3), Carson (1), Hendry (1).
Record Cup Victory: 10-0 v RSC Anderlecht, European Cup, Prel. rd (2nd leg), 26 September 1956 – Wood; Foulkes; Byrne; Colman, Jones, Edwards; Berry (1), Whelan (2), Taylor (3), Viollet (4), Pegg.
Record Defeat: 0-7 v Blackburn R, Division 1, 10 April, 1926 and v Aston Villa, Division 1, 27 December, 1930 and v Wolverhampton W. Division 2, 26 December, 1931.
Most League Points (2 for a win): 64, Division 1, 1956–57.
Most League Points (3 for a win): 81 Division 1, 1987–8.
Most League Goals: 103, Division 1, 1956–57 and 1958–59
Highest League Scorer in Season: Dennis Viollet, 32, 1959–60.
Most League Goals in Total Aggregate: Bobby Charlton, 198, 1956–73.
Most Capped Player: Bobby Charlton, 106, England.
Most League Appearances: Bobby Charlton, 606, 1956–73.
Record Transfer Fee Received: £1,800,000 from Barcelona for Mark Hughes, August 1986.
Record Transfer Fee Paid: £1,500,000 to WBA for Bryan Robson, October 1981 and £1,500,000 to Barcelona for Mark Hughes, June 1988.
Football League Record: 1892 Newton Heath elected to Division 1; 1894–1906 Division 2; 1906–22 Division 1; 1922–25 Division 2; 1925–31 Division 1; 1931–36 Division 2; 1936–37 Division 1; 1937–38 Division 2; 1938–74 Division 1; 1974–75 Division 2; 1975– Division 1.
Honours: *Football League:* Division 1 – Champions 1907–8, 1910–11, 1951–52, 1955–65, 1956–57, 1964–65, 1966–67; Runners-up 1946–47, 1947–48, 1948–49, 1950–51, 1958–59, 1963–64, 1967–68, 1979–80, 1987–88. Division 2 – Champions 1935–36, 1974–75; Runners-up 1896–97, 1905–06, 1924–25, 1937–38. *FA Cup:* Winners 1909, 1948, 1963, 1977, 1983, 1985; Runners-up 1957, 1958, 1976, 1979, *Milk Cup:* 1982–83 (Runners-up). European Competitions: *European Cup:* 1956–57 (s-f), 1957-58 (s-f), 1965–66 (s-f), 1967–68 (winners), 1968–69 (s-f). *European Cup-Winners' Cup:* 1963–64, 1977–78, 1983–84. *European Fairs Cup:* 1964–65. *UEFA Cup:* 1976–77, 1980–81, 1982–83, 1984–85.
Colours: Red shirts, white shorts, with red trim, black stockings. **Change colours:** White shirts, black shorts, white stockings.

MANCHESTER UNITED 1988–89 LEAGUE RECORD

Match No.	Date	Venue	Opponents	Result	H/T Score	Lg. Pos.	Goalscorers	Attendance
1	Aug 27	H	QPR	D 0-0	0-0	—		46,377
2	Sept 3	A	Liverpool	L 0-1	0-1	14		42,026
3	10	H	Middlesbrough	W 1-0	0-0	10	Robson	40,422
4	17	A	Luton T	W 2-0	1-0	8	Davenport, Robson	11,010
5	24	H	West Ham U	W 2-0	1-0	5	Davenport, Hughes	39,941
6	Oct 1	A	Tottenham H	D 2-2	1-1	5	Hughes, McClair	29,318
7	22	A	Wimbledon	D 1-1	1-0	7	Hughes	12,143
8	26	H	Norwich C	L 1-2	0-0	—	Hughes	36,998
9	30	A	Everton	D 1-1	0-0	—	Hughes	27,005
10	Nov 5	H	Aston Villa	D 1-1	1-0	11	Bruce	44,804
11	12	A	Derby Co	D 2-2	1-1	11	Hughes, McClair	24,080
12	19	H	Southampton	D 2-2	1-1	11	Robson, Hughes	37,277
13	23	H	Sheffield W	D 1-1	0-0	—	Hughes	30,867
14	27	A	Newcastle U	D 0-0	0-0	—		20,350
15	Dec 3	H	Charlton Ath	W 3-0	1-0	9	Milne, McClair, Hughes	31,173
16	10	A	Coventry C	L 0-1	0-0	10		19,936
17	17	A	Arsenal	L 1-2	0-2	10	Hughes	37,422
18	26	H	Nottingham F	W 2-0	1-0	9	Milne, Hughes	39,582
19	Jan 1	H	Liverpool	W 3-1	0-0	—	McClair, Hughes, Beardsmore	44,745
20	2	A	Middlesbrough	L 0-1	0-0	9		24,411
21	14	H	Millwall	W 3-0	2-0	6	Blackmore, Gill, Hughes	40,931
22	21	A	West Ham U	W 3-1	1-1	6	Strachan, Martin, McClair	29,822
23	Feb 5	H	Tottenham H	W 1-0	0-0	—	McClair	41,423
24	11	A	Sheffield W	W 2-0	1-0	3	McClair 2	34,820
25	25	A	Norwich C	L 1-2	0-2	5	McGrath	23,155
26	Mar 12	A	Aston Villa	D 0-0	0-0	—		28,332
27	25	H	Luton T	W 2-0	2-0	6	Milne, Blackmore	36,335
28	27	A	Nottingham F	L 0-2	0-1	7		[illegible]
29	Apr 2	H	Arsenal	D 1-1	0-0	—	Adams (og)	37,977
30	8	A	Millwall	D 0-0	0-0	10		17,523
31	15	H	Derby Co	L 0-2	0-1	10		34,145
32	22	A	Charlton Ath	L 0-1	0-1	10		12,055
33	29	H	Coventry C	L 0-1	0-0	11		29,799
34	May 2	H	Wimbledon	W 1-0	0-0	—	McClair	23,368
35	6	A	Southampton	L 1-2	0-1	10	Beardsmore	17,021
36	8	A	QPR	L 2-3	2-1	—	Bruce, Blackmore	10,017
37	10	H	Everton	L 1-2	1-1	—	Hughes	26,722
38	13	H	Newcastle U	W 2-0	0-0	10	McClair, Robson	30,379

Final League Position: 11

GOALSCORERS

League (45): Hughes 14, McClair 10, Robson 4, Blackmore 3, Milne 3, Beardsmore 2, Bruce 2, Davenport 2, Gill 1, McGrath 1, Martin 1, Strachan 1, own goal 1.
Littlewoods Cup (7): McClair 3, Robson 2, Bruce 1, Davenport 1.
FA Cup (11): McClair 3 (1 pen), Hughes 2, Robson 2, Bruce 1, Gill 1, Graham 1, own goal 1.

Littlewoods Cup	Second Round	Rotherham U (a)	1-0
		(h)	5-0
	Third Round	Wimbledon (a)	1-2
FA Cup	Third Round	QPR (h)	0-0
		(a)	2-2
		(h)	3-0
	Fourth Round	Oxford U (h)	4-0
	Fifth Round	Bournemouth (a)	1-1
		(h)	1-0
	Sixth Round	Nottingham F (h)	0-1

Leighton	Blackmore	Martin	Bruce	McGrath	McClair	Robson	Strachan	Davenport	Hughes	Olsen	O'Brien	Anderson	Duxbury	Garton	Sharpe	Beardsmore	Robins	Donaghy	Gibson	Milne	Gill	Wilson	Maiorana	Whiteside	Brazil	Match No.
1	2	3	4	5	6	7	8	9*	10	11	12															1
1	3		4	5*	9	7	8†	14	10	11		2	6	12												2
1	3		4	5	9	7		8	10	11			6	2												3
1	3		4	5	9	7		8	10	11			6	2												4
1	2		4		9	7	8	11	10	12			6	5†	3*	14										5
1			4	5	9	7	8	11*	10	12		14	6	2†	3											6
1	2		4		9	7	8*	11†	10				6	5	3	12	14									7
1	2		4		9	7	8	11*	10	12			6	5	3											8
1	3		4		9	7	8*		10	11	14		5	2				6†	12							9
1	2		4		9	7	8		10	11	5		12					6	3*							10
1	3		4		9	7	8		10	12			5*	2	11			6								11
1	3		4		9	7	8		10					2	11*			6		5	12					12
1	3†		4		9	7	8*		10					2	11			6		5	12	14				13
1	3	12	4		9	7			10					2	11†		14	6		8*	5					14
1	5	3	4		9	7	8		10					2				6		11						15
1	5	3	4		9	7	8		10					2*	11			6		14	12†					16
1	5*	2†	4		9	7	8		10						3	14		6		11	12					17
1		2	4		9	7	8		10						3	5		6		11						18
1		2*	4	12	9	7	8†		10						3	5	14	6		11						19
1			4	5	9	7			10						3	8*	14	6		11	2†	12				20
1	8	2	4		9				10						3	5*		6		11†	7	12	14			21
1	5	3	4		9	7	8*		10						12			6		11	2					22
1	5	2	4	12	9	7	8†		10						3*	14		6		11						23
1	5	3	4	2	9	7	8		10*							12		6		11						24
1	2†	12	4	5	9	7	8		10						3	14		6		11*						25
1	12	3†	4	5	9	7	8		10						11	2*		6		14						26
1	3	2	4	5	9	7			10							8*		6		11			12			27
1	3	12	4	5*	9	7			10			2				8		6		11†	14					28
1	14	12	4	5	9	7			10			2				8†		3					11*	6		29
1		11	4	5*	9	7			10			2				8		3					12	6		30
1		3	4	5	9				10			2†	12			8*	7	6				14	11			31
1			4	5	9	7			10				2			8	12	3		11*				6		32
1		11*	4	5	9	7			10				2			8	12	3						6		33
1		11	4	5	9	7			10				2			8		3					12	6*		34
1		11*	4	5	9	7†			10				2		12	8		3		14				6		35
1	5	11	4		9				10				2		3*	8	12	6		7						36
1	5*	11	4		9				10				2†		3	8	12	6		7					14	37
1	5†	3	4		9	7			10				2		14	8	12	6		11*						38
38	26 + 2s	20 + 4s	38	18 + 2s	38	34	21	7 + 1s	38	6 + 4s	1 + 2s	5 + 1s	16 + 2s	13 + 1s	19 + 3s	17 + 6s	1 + 9s	30	1 + 1s	19 + 3s	4 + 5s	— + 4s	2 + 4s	6	— + 1s	

MANCHESTER UNITED

Player and Position	Ht	Wt	Birth Date	Birth Place	Source	Clubs	League App	League Gls
Goalkeepers								
Jim Leighton	6 1	12 08	24 7 58	Johnstone	Dalry T	Aberdeen	300	—
						Manchester U	38	—
Jim O'Donnell*	5 10	12 01	23 7 69	Manchester		Manchester U	—	—
						Charlton Ath (loan)	—	—
						Swindon T (loan)	—	—
Gary Walsh	6 1	12 12	21 3 68	Wigan		Manchester U	30	—
						Airdrie (loan)	3	—
Defenders								
Viv Anderson	6 0	11 01	29 8 56	Nottingham	Apprentice	Nottingham F	328	15
						Arsenal	120	9
						Manchester U	37	2
Derek Brazil	6 0	12 00	14 12 68	Dublin	Rivermount BC	Manchester U	1	—
Steve Bruce	6 0	12 06	31 12 60	Newcastle	Apprentice	Gillingham	205	29
						Norwich C	141	14
						Manchester U	59	4
Mal Donaghy	5 10	12 07	13 9 57	Belfast	Larne	Luton T	410	16
						Manchester U	30	—
Mike Duxbury	5 9	11 02	1 9 59	Accrington	Apprentice	Manchester U	280	6
Billy Garton	5 11	11 08	15 3 65	Salford	Apprentice	Manchester U	41	—
						Birmingham C (loan)	5	—
Colin Gibson	5 8	10 08	6 4 60	Bridport	Apprentice	Aston Villa	185	10
						Manchester U	73	8
Tony Gill	5 9	10 00	6 3 68	Bradford	Apprentice	Manchester U	10	1
Wayne Heseltine	5 9	11 06	3 12 69	Bradford	Trainee	Manchester U	—	—
Paul McGrath	6 0	13 02	4 12 59	Ealing	St Patrick's Ath	Manchester U	163	12
Lee Martin	5 11	11 05	5 2 68	Hyde		Manchester U	25	1
Midfield								
Russell Beardsmore	5 6	8 10	28 9 68	Wigan	Apprentice	Manchester U	23	2
Clayton Blackmore	5 9	11 03	23 9 64	Neath	Apprentice	Manchester U	76	10
Wayne Bullimore	5 9	10 06	12 9 70	Sutton-in-Ashfield	Trainee	Manchester U	—	—
Simon Hutchinson*	5 10	10 11	24 9 69	Sheffield	Trainee	Manchester U	—	—
						Sheffield W (loan)	—	—
Ralph Milne	5 9	12 04	13 5 61	Dundee	School	Dundee U	179	44
						Charlton Ath	22	—
						Bristol C	30	6
						Manchester U	22	3
Remi Moses (Retired)	5 6	10 09	14 11 60	Manchester	Apprentice	WBA	63	5
						Manchester U	150	7
Bryan Robson	5 11	11 12	11 1 57	Chester-Le-Street	Apprentice	WBA	197	39
						Manchester U	252	65
Lee Sharpe	5 11	11 04	27 5 71	Birmingham	Trainee	Torquay U	14	3
						Manchester U	22	—
Norman Whiteside	6 0	12 08	7 5 65	Belfast	Apprentice	Manchester U	206	47
David Wilson	5 9	10 10	20 3 69	Burnley	Apprentice	Manchester U	4	—
Paul Wratten	5 7	9 13	29 11 70	Middlesbrough	Trainee	Manchester U	—	—

MANCHESTER UNITED

Foundation: Manchester United was formed as comparatively recently as 1902 after their predecessors, Newton Heath, went bankrupt. However, it is usual to give the date of the club's foundation as 1878 when employees of the Lancashire and Yorkshire Railway Company formed Newton Heath L and YR. Cricket and Football Club. They won the Manchester Cup in 1886 and as Newton Heath FC were admitted to the Second Division in 1892.

Managers (and Secretary-managers)
Ernest Magnall 1900–12, John Robson 1914–21, John Chapman 1921–26, Clarence Hildrith 1926–27, Herbert Bamlett 1927–31, Walter Crickmer 1931–32, Scott Duncan 1932–37, Jimmy Porter 1938–44, Walter Crickmer 1944–45*, Matt Busby 1945–69 (continued as GM then Director), Wilf McGuinness 1969–70, Frank O'Farrell 1971–72, Tommy Docherty 1972–77, Dave Sexton 1977–81, Ron Atkinson 1981–86, Alex Ferguson 1986– .

Player and Position	*Ht*	*Wt*	*Birth Date*	*Birth Place*	*Source*	*Clubs*	*League App*	*League Gls*
Forwards								
Simon Andrews*	5 9	11 01	26 9 70	Macclesfield	Trainee	Manchester U	—	—
Shaun Goater			25 2 70	Bermuda		Manchester U	—	—
Deiniol Graham	5 10	10 05	4 10 69	Cannock	Trainee	Manchester U	1	—
Mark Hughes	5 8	12 05	1 11 63	Wrexham	Apprentice	Manchester U	89	37
					Barcelona	Manchester U	38	14
Brian McClair	5 9	12 02	8 12 63	Airdrie	Apprentice	Aston Villa	—	—
						Motherwell	39	15
						Celtic	145	99
						Manchester U	78	34
Giuliano Maiorana	5 9	11 08	18 4 69	Cambridge	Histon	Manchester U	6	—
Jesper Olsen (To Bordeaux, Nov 1988)	5 6	9 09	20 3 61	Fakse, Denmark	Ajax	Manchester U	139	21
Mark Robins	5 7	10 01	22 12 69	Ashton-under-Lyme	Apprentice	Manchester U	10	—
Nicky Wood‡	5 11	10 08	11 1 66	Oldham	School	Manchester U	3	—

Trainees

Baggaley, Phillip J; Carter, Stephen G; Costa, Lee A; Ferguson, Darren; Jackson, Anthony J; Lawton, Craig T; Lydiate, Jason L; McAuley, Sean; Pollitt, Michael F; Sallis, Roger J; Shotton, John M; Sixsmith, Paul; Taylor, Christopher; Toal, Keiran M; Tonge, Alan J.

Associated Schoolboys

Bates, Simon; Brameld, Marcus J; Burke, Raphael E; Davies, Simon I; Doherty, Adrian J; Gordon, Mark; Gough, Paul; Gray, Michael; McShane, Patrick; McReaveie, Alan S; Noone, Andrew C; Potts, Leslie A; Roberts, Joseph; Savage, Roberts W; Sharples, John B; Shields, James J; Smyth, Peter W; Stanger, Jonathan N; Switzer, George; Wilkinson, Ian M; Wilson, Ryan J.

MANSFIELD TOWN 1988–89 *Back row (left to right):* Mark Place, Nicky Andersen, Simon Coleman, Jason Pearcey, Andy Beasley, Brian Cox, Mark Kearney, Tony Kenworthy, David Hodges.
Centre row: Steve Williams, Paul Garner, Steve Chambers, Dennis Pettit (Physiotherapist), Bill Dearden (First Team Coach), Ian Greaves (Manager), John Jarman (Assistant Manager), Steve Charles, Keith Cassells, Paul Brogan.
Front row: Gareth Price, Mike Graham, Tony Lowery, George Foster (Captain), Kevin Kent, Gordon Owen, Ian Stringfellow, John Ryan, Craig McKernon.
Sitting: Gary Bircumshaw, Tony Clarke, Justin Elkington, Kevin Gray, Sean Hood, Ricky Ellerton, Shane Reddish, Jason Milner, David Parker.

Division 3 MANSFIELD TOWN

Field Mill Ground, Quarry Lane, Mansield. Telepone Mansfield (0623) 23567. Commercial Office: 0623 658070.

Ground capacity: 10,468.

Record attendance: 24,467 v Nottingham F, FA Cup 3rd rd, 10 Jan, 1953.

Record receipts: £33,321 v Wimbledon, FA Cup 4th rd, 30 Jan, 1988.

Pitch measurements: 115yd × 72yd.

Chairman: J. W. Pratt. *Vice-Chairman:* J. B. Almond JP

Directors: G. Hall, J. A. Brown.

Player-Manager: George Foster. *Assistant Manager:* John Jarman.

Coach: Bill Dearden. *Physio:* Dennis Pettitt

Secretary: J. D. Eaton. *Commercial Manager:* J.Slater.

Year Formed: 1910. *Turned Professional:* 1910. *ltd Co.:* 1910.

Previous name: Mansfield Wesleyans 1891–1910.

Club Nickname: 'The Stags'.

Record League Victory: 9-2 v Rotherham U, Division 3(N), 27 December 1932 – Wilson; Anthony, England; Davies, Robinson (S), Slack; Prior, Broom, Readman (3), Hoyland (3), Bowater (3)

Record Cup Victory: 8-0 v Scarborough (away), FA Cup, 1st rd, 22 November 1952 – Bramley; Chessell, Bradley; Field, Plummer, Lewis; Scott, Fox (3), Marron (2), Sid Watson (1), Adam (2).

Record Defeat: 1-8 v Walsall, Division 3(N), 19 January, 1933

Most League Points (2 for a win): 68, Division 4, 1974–75.

Most League Points (3 for a win): 81, Division 4, 1985–86.

Most League Goals: 108, Divisin 4, 1962–63.

Highest League Scorer in Season: Ted Harston, 55, Division 3(N), 1936–37.

Most League Goals in Total Aggregate: Harry Johnson, 104, 1931–36.

Most Capped Player: John McClelland, 6 (52), Northern Ireland.

Most League Appearances: Sandy Pate, 413, 1967–78.

Record Transfer Fee Received: £250,000 from Chelsea for Kevin Hitchcock, March 1988.

Record Transfer Fee Paid: £75,000 to Luton T for Steve Taylor, July 1979.

Football League Record: 1931 Elected to Division 3(S); 1932–37 Division 3(N); 1937–47 Division 3(S); 1947–58Division 3(N); 1958–60 Division 3; 1960–63 Division 4; 1963–72 Division 3; 1972–75 Division 4; 1975–77 Division 3; 1977–78 Division 2; 1978–80 Division 3;1980–86 Division 4; 1986 Division 3.

Honours: Football League: Division 2 best season: 21st 1977–78; Division 3 – Champions 1976–77; Division 4 – Champions 1974–75; Division 3(N) – Runners-up 1950–51. *FA Cup* best season: 6th rd, 1968–69. *Football League Cup* Best season: 5th rd, 1975–76. *Freight Rover Trophy* – Winners 1986–87.

Colours: Amber shirts with blue vertical side panels, amber shorts with blue stripe down side, amber stockings with two blue rings on turnover. **Change colours:** All red.

MANSFIELD TOWN 1988–89 LEAGUE RECORD

Match No.	Date	Venue	Opponents	Result	H/T Score	Lg. Pos.	Goalscorers	Attendance
1	Aug 27	H	Northampton T	D 1-1	0-0	—	Charles	4042
2	Sept 3	A	Wigan Ath	D 0-0	0-0	18		2514
3	10	H	Fulham	W 3-1	2-0	9	Cassells 2, Hodges	2737
4	17	A	Blackpool	D 1-1	1-0	9	Owen	4012
5	20	H	Gillingham	W 2-1	0-0	—	Cassells, Stringfellow	3153
6	24	A	Bury	W 1-0	0-0	4	Cassells	2412
7	Oct 1	H	Notts Co	D 1-1	0-0	6	Hodges	5907
8	4	A	Southend U	D 1-1	0-1	—	Hodges	2436
9	8	H	Bristol R	W 2-1	1-1	3	Charles 2 (1 pen)	3381
10	15	A	Reading	L 0-1	0-1	5		6604
11	22	H	Cardiff C	D 2-2	0-1	5	Cassells 2	3566
12	26	A	Chester C	D 0-0	0-0	—		1805
13	29	H	Bristol C	D 2-2	1-2	10	Kent, Charles	3800
14	Nov 5	A	Preston NE	L 0-2	0-1	13		6434
15	8	A	Swansea C	L 1-3	0-0	—	Hodges	3526
16	12	H	Brentford	W 1-0	1-0	13	Charles	3181
17	26	H	Aldershot	D 1-1	0-1	11	Coleman	2715
18	Dec 3	A	Chesterfield	W 3-1	1-1	8	Coleman 2, Hunter (og)	4236
19	17	A	Wolverhampton W	L 2-6	1-4	11	Coleman, Leishman	12,134
20	26	H	Port Vale	L 0-1	0-0	14		5218
21	31	H	Huddersfield T	W 1-0	0-0	13	Owen	4638
22	Jan 2	A	Bolton W	D 0-0	0-0	13		4935
23	14	H	Wigan Ath	L 0-1	0-1	13		2788
24	21	A	Fulham	D 1-1	1-1	14	Cassells	4148
25	28	H	Blackpool	L 0-1	0-0	14		2738
26	Feb 4	A	Notts Co	L 1-2	1-2	16	Cassells	5924
27	11	H	Southend U	W 4-0	2-0	13	Charles, Cassells 2, Kent	2414
28	18	A	Bristol R	D 0-0	0-0	15		4669
29	25	H	Reading	W 2-1	0-0	12	Owen 2	3012
30	28	H	Chester C	W 2-0	1-0	—	Kearney, Charles	2796
31	Mar 4	A	Cardiff C	D 0-0	0-0	11		3217
32	11	H	Preston NE	L 0-3	0-0	13		4706
33	18	A	Northampton T	L 1-2	1-0	13	Berry (og)	2821
34	21	A	Bristol C	L 0-2	0-1	—		5065
35	25	H	Bolton W	D 1-1	1-1	13	Christie	3253
36	27	A	Port Vale	W 2-1	1-1	13	Coleman, Owen	8198
37	Apr 1	H	Wolverhampton W	W 3-1	1-1	13	Kent, Cassells 2	9205
38	4	H	Sheffield U	L 0-1	0-0	—		8524
39	8	A	Huddersfield T	L 0-2	0-0	15		5327
40	15	A	Gillingham	L 0-3	0-0	15		2594
41	22	H	Bury	D 1-1	1-0	16	Kent	2826
42	25	A	Sheffield U	W 2-1	1-0	—	Cassells, Kent	11,638
43	29	A	Brentford	L 0-1	0-1	15		5231
44	May 2	H	Swansea C	D 0-0	0-0	—		2550
45	6	H	Chesterfield	W 3-1	2-0	15	Kearney, Cassells, Hathaway	4767
46	13	A	Aldershot	D 0-0	0-0	15		1549

Final League Position: 15

GOALSCORERS

League (48): Cassells 14, Charles 7 (1 pen), Coleman 5, Kent 5, Owen 5, Hodges 4, Kearney 2, Christie 1, Hathaway 1, Leishman 1, Stringfellow 1, own goals 2.
Littlewoods Cup (1): Hodges 1.
FA Cup (2): Kearney 1, Kent 1.

Littlewoods Cup	First Round	Notts Co (a)	0-5
		(h)	1-0
FA Cup	First Round	Sheffield U (h)	1-1
		(a)	1-2

Cox	Graham	Kenworthy	Lowery	Foster	Coleman	Owen	Kearney	Kent	Cassells	Charles	Ryan	McKernon	Hodges	Chambers	Stringfellow	Place	Garner	Anderson	Leishman	Hathaway	Christie	Williams	Beasley	Gray	Pearcey	Match No.
1	2	3	4*	5	6	7	8	9	10	11	12															1
1		3	4	5	6	7	8		10	11		2	9													2
1		3		5	6	7	8		10	11		2	9	4												3
1		3		5	6	7	8		10	11	4	2	9													4
1		3		5	6	7	8		10	11	4*	2	9		12											5
1		3*	4†	5	6	7	8	14	10	11		2	9		12											6
1		3*	4	5	6	7	8	12	10	11		2	9													7
1			4*	5	6	7	8	12	10	11		2	9			3										8
1				5	6	7	8	10		11		2	9	4		3										9
1				5	6	7	8	10*		11	12	2	9	4†		3	14									10
1				5	6	7	8	4	10	11†	14	2	9*		12		3									11
1				5	6	7	8	4	10	11	3	2	9													12
1				5	6	7	8	4	10*	11	3	2	9		12											13
1		14	4	5	6	7	8†	10		11	3	2	9*		12											14
1			4	5	6	7	8	10†		11	3		9		12	14		2*								15
1		8	4	5	6	7	12	10		11*	3	2	9													16
1		3	4*	5	6	7	11	10		12	8	2	9†		14											17
1		3	4	5	6	7†	11	10		8		2*	9	12	14											18
1		3	4	5	6		11		10	8	9*	2	7†				12		14							19
1		3		5	6		8	7	10	11		2	4			12			9*							20
1		3		5	6	12	8	7	10	11		2	4						9*							21
1		3	12	5	6	7*	8	9	10	11		2	4													22
1		3		5	6	7	8	9*	10	11	12	2	4													23
1		3		5	6	7	8	9	10	11		2	4													24
1				5	6	7*	8	9	10	11	12	2	4						3							25
1				5	6	7	3	9	10	11	12	2	4						8*							26
1				5	6	7*	3	9	10	8	11	2	4						12							27
1				5	6	7*	3	9	10	8	11	2	4						12							28
1				5	6	7	3	9	10	8	11		4			2										29
1		5			6	7*	3	9	10	8	11		4			2			12							30
1		5			6		3	9*	10	8	11	2	4			12			7							31
1		5			6†	7*	3		10	8	11	2	4			9			12	14						32
1				5	6	7	3		10	8	11	2	4						9*	12						33
1				5	6	12	3	9	10	8	11	2	4*							7						34
1				5	6	7	3	4	10*	8	11	2	12								9					35
1				5	6	7	3	4	10	8	11	2									9					36
1				5	6	7*	3	4	10	8	11	2								12	9					37
1				5	6	7	3	4	10*	8	11	2	12								9					38
1				5	6	7		4	10	8		2	3†						12	11*	9	14				39
				5		7	3	4	10	8		2	11*			6				12	9		1			40
				5	6	7	3	4*	10	8		2				11				12	9		1			41
				5	6	7	3	8	10*	11	12	2				4†				14	9		1			42
					6	7	3	4		8	11*	2	10			5				12	9		1			43
				5	6	7	3	4		11	10	2				8*				12	9		1			44
				5	6		3	4	10	8		2								11	9	12	1*	7		45
				5	6		3	4	12	8		2	10	14						11†	9*	7			1	46
39	1	19 + 1s	11 + 1s	42	45	39 + 2s	44 + 1s	36 + 3s	36 + 1s	45 + 1s	23 + 7s	42	37 + 2s	3 + 2s	— + 8s	11 + 3s	1 + 2s	1	6 + 6s	4 + 8s	12	1 + 2s	6	1	1	

MANSFIELD TOWN

Player and Position	Ht	Wt	Birth Date	Birth Place	Source	Clubs	League App	League Gls
Goalkeepers								
Andy Beasley	6 2	12 01	5 2 64	Sedgley	Apprentice	Luton T	—	—
						Mansfield T	17	—
						Gillingham (loan)	—	—
						Peterborough U	7	—
						(loan)	4	—
						Scarborough (loan)		
Brian Cox	6 1	13 10	7 5 61	Sheffield	Apprentice	Sheffield W	22	—
						Huddersfield T	213	—
						Mansfield T	39	—
Jason Pearcey§			23 7 71	Leamington Spa	Trainee	Mansfield T	1	—
Defenders								
Paul Brogan*			7 7 70	Birmingham		Mansfield T	—	—
Simon Coleman	6 0	10 08	13 3 68	Worksop		Mansfield T	91	7
George Foster	5 10	11 02	26 9 56	Plymouth	Apprentice	Plymouth Arg	212	6
						Torquay U (loan)	6	3
						Exeter C (loan)	28	—
						Derby Co	30	—
						Mansfield T	263	—
Mark Kearney	5 10	11 00	12 6 62	Ormskirk	Marine	Everton	—	—
						Mansfield T	189	26
Tony Kenworthy	5 10	10 07	31 10 58	Leeds	Apprentice	Sheffield U	286	34
						Mansfield T (loan)	13	—
						Mansfield T	86	—
Mark Place	5 11	10 08	16 11 69		Trainee	Mansfield T	14	—
Gareth Price*	5 9	10 01	21 2 70	Swindon	Trainee	Mansfield T	—	—
John Ryan	5 10	11 07	18 2 62	Oldham	Apprentice	Oldham Ath	77	8
						Newcastle U	28	1
						Sheffield W	8	1
						Oldham Ath	23	—
						Mansfield T	62	1
Midfield								
Nicky Anderson*	5 10	10 10	29 3 69	Lincoln	Trainee	Mansfield T	20	—
Steve Chambers*	5 10	10 10	20 7 68	Worksop	Apprentice	Sheffield W	—	—
						Mansfield T	18	—
Steve Charles	5 9	10 07	10 5 60	Sheffield	Sheffield Univ	Sheffield U	123	10
						Wrexham	113	37
						Mansfield T	92	19
Paul Garner*	5 9	10 08	1 12 55	Doncaster	Apprentice	Huddersfield T	96	2
						Sheffield U	251	7
						Gillingham (loan)	5	—
						Mansfield T	111	8
Kevin Gray§			7 1 72	Sheffield	Trainee	Mansfield T	1	—
David Hodges	5 9	10 02	17 1 70	Hereford		Mansfield T	64	6
Tony Lowery	5 9	11 01	6 7 61	Wallsend	Ashington	WBA	1	—
						Walsall (loan)	6	1
						Mansfield T	231	19
Craig McKernon	5 9	11 00	23 2 68	Gloucester	Apprentice	Mansfield T	87	—
Steven Williams*	5 11	11 06	18 7 70	Mansfield		Mansfield T	11	—
Forwards								
Keith Cassells	5 10	11 12	10 7 57	London	Wembley T	Watford	12	—
						Peterborough U	8	—
						(loan)	45	13
						Oxford U	19	4
						Southampton	86	28
						Brentford	163	52
						Mansfield T		

MANSFIELD TOWN

Foundation: Many records give the date of Mansfield Town's formation as 1905. But the present club did not come into being until 1910 when the Mansfield Wesleyans (formed 1891) and playing in the Notts and District League, decided to spread their wings and changed their name to Mansfield Town, joining the new Central Alliance in 1911.

Managers (and Secretary-managers)
John Baynes 1922–25, Ted Davison 1926–28, J. Hickling 1928–33, Henry Martin 1933–35, Charlie Bell 1935, Harold Wightman 1936, Harold Parkes 1936–38, Jack Poole 1938–39, Lloyd Barke 1939–45, Roy Goodall 1945–49, Freddie Steele 1949–51, George Jobey 1952–53, Stan Mercer 1953–55, Charlie Mitten 1956–58, Sam Weaver 1958–60, Raich Carter 1960–63, Tommy Cummings 1963–67, Tommy Eggleston 1967–70, Jock Basford 1970–71, Danny Williams 1971–74, Dave Smith 1974–76, Peter Morris 1976–78, Billy Bingham 1978–79, Mick Jones 1979–81, Stuart Boam 1981–83, Ian Greaves 1983–89, George Foster 1989– .

Player and Position	*Ht*	*Wt*	*Birth Date*	*Birth Place*	*Source*	*Clubs*	*League App*	*League Gls*
Trevor Christie	6 2	12 00	28 2 59	Newcastle	Apprentice	Leicester C	31	8
						Notts Co	187	64
						Nottingham F	14	5
						Derby Co	65	22
						Manchester C	9	3
						Walsall	99	22
						Mansfield T	12	1
Ian Hathaway	5 8	10 06	22 8 68	Worsley	Bedworth U	Mansfield T	12	1
Kevin Kent	5 11	11 00	19 3 65	Stoke	Apprentice	WBA	2	—
						Newport Co	33	1
						Mansfield T	164	29
Graham Leishman	5 9	10 07	6 4 68	Manchester	Irlam T	Mansfield T	12	1
Gordon Owen	5 8	10 09	14 6 59	Barnsley	Amateur	Sheffield W	48	5
						Rotherham U (loan)	9	—
						Doncaster R (loan)	9	—
						Chesterfield (loan)	6	2
						Cardiff C	39	14
						Barnsley	68	25
						Bristol C	53	11
						Hull C (loan)	3	—
						Mansfield T	58	8
Ian Stringfellow	5 9	10 02	8 5 69	Nottingham	Apprentice	Mansfield T	63	13

Trainees

Bircumshaw, Gary; Clarke, Anthony D; Elkington, Justin C; Ellerton, Ricky; Gray, Kevin J; Milner, Jason; Pearcey, Jason; Reddish, Shane.

Associated Schoolboys

Brown, Neil V; Doughty, Stephen J; Hall, Geoffrey; Holland, Paul; Jones, Adam; Kerrigan, Jonathan R; Martin, Stephen A; Morgan, Peter C; Mowbray, Scott G; Richardson, Paul S; Sheldon, Mark J; Soar, Mark; Timons, Christopher B; Travis, Steven; Ward, Darren; Wilkinson, Andrew J.

MIDDLESBROUGH 1988–89 *Back row (left to right):* Garry Robinson, Colin Cooper, Kevin Poole, Matthew Coddington, Stephen Pears, Mark Burke, Trevor Senior.
Centre row: Tony Mowbray, Gary Pallister, Stuart Ripley, Alan Kernaghan, Nicky Mohan, Drew Coverdale, Garry Agnew, Owen McGee, Michael Trotter.
Front row: Gary Hamilton, Gary Parkinson, Gary Gill, Paul Kerr, Mark Brennan, Dean Glover, Bernie Slaven.

Division 2 MIDDLESBROUGH

Ayresome Park, Middlesbrough, Cleveland TS1 4PB. Telephone Middlesbrough (0642) 819659/815996. Commercial Dept. 0642 826664. Clubcall, 0898 121181. Special Answering Service available on (0642) 825383.

Ground capacity; 30,000.

Record attendance: 53,596 v Newcastle U, Division 1, 27 Dec, 1979.

£82,835.95 v Everton. FA Cup, 4th rd replay, 3 Feb, 1988.

Pitch measurements: 115yd × 75yd.

Chairman: M. C. Henderson.

Directors: G. Fordy, S. Gibson, R. Corbidge.

Chief Executive: Keith Lamb.

Manager: Bruce Rioch. ***Coach:*** Colin Todd.

Physiotherapist: Tommy Johnson.

Secretary: Tom Hughes.

Commercial Manager: Alan Murray.

Year Formed: 1876. ***Turned Professional:*** 1889; became amateur 1892, and professional again, 1899. ***Ltd Co:*** 1892.

Club Nickname: 'The Boro'.

Previous Grounds: 1877, Old Archery Ground, Linhorpe Rd; 1903, Ayresome Park.

Record League Victory: 9-0 v Brighton & HA, Division 2, 23 August 1958 – Taylor; Bilcliff, Robinson; Harris (2 pens), Phillips, Walley; Day, McLean, Clough (5), Peacock (2), Holliday.

Record Cup Victory: 9-3 v Goole T, FA Cup, 1st rd, 9 January 1915 – Williamson; Haworth, Weir; Davidson, Cook, Malcolm; Wilson, Carr (3), Elliott (3), Tinsley (3), Davies.

Record Defeat: 0-9 v Blackburn R, Division 2, 6 Novmber, 1954.

Most League Points (2 for a win): 65, Division 2, 1973–74.

Most League Points (3 for a win): 94, Division 3, 1986–87.

Most League Goals: 122, Division 2, 1926–27.

Highest League Scorer in Season: George Camsell, 59, Division 2, 1926–27 (Second Division record).

Most League Goals in Total Aggregate: George Camsell, 326, 1925–39.

Most Capped Player: Wilf Mannion, 26, England.

Most League Appearances: Tim Williamson, 563, 1902–23.

Record Transfer Fee Received: £600,000 from Southampton for David Armstrong, August 1981.

Record Transfer Fee Paid: £700,000 to Manchester U for Peter Davenport, November 1988.

Football League Record: 1899 Elected to Division 2; 1902–24 Division 1; 1924–27 Division 2; 1927–28 Division 1; 1928–29 Division 2; 1929–54 Division 1; 1954–66 Division 2; 1966–67 Division 3; 1967–74 Division 2; 1974–82 Division 1; 1982–86 Division 2; 1986–87 Division 3; 1987–88 Division 2; 1988–89 Division 1; 1989– Division 2.

Honours: *Football League:* Division 1 best season : 3rd, 1913–14. Division 2 – Champions 1926–27, 1928–29, 1973–74; Runners-up 1901–02. Division 3 – Runners-up 1966–67, 1986–87. *FA Cup* best season; 6th rd, 1935–36, 1946–47, 1969–70, 1974–75, 1976–77, 1977–78; old last eight 1900–01, 1903–04. *Football League Cup:* Semi-final 1975–76. *Amateure Cup:* Winners 1895, 1898, *Anglo-Scottish Cup:* Winners 1975–76.

Colours: Red shirts, white shorts, red stockings. **Change colours:** All sky blue.

MIDDLESBROUGH 1988–89 LEAGUE RECORD

Match No.	Date		Venue	Opponents	Result		H/T Score	Lg. Pos.	Goalscorers	Attendance
1	Aug	27	A	Derby Co	L	0-1	0-0	—		19,432
2	Sept	3	H	Norwich C	L	2-3	1-2	19	Mowbray, Burke	18,259
3		10	A	Manchester U	L	0-1	0-0	20		40,422
4		17	H	Wimbledon	W	1-0	1-0	15	Hamilton	17,709
5		24	A	Tottenham H	L	2-3	1-1	18	Slaven, Mowbray	23,427
6	Oct	1	A	Coventry C	W	4-3	3-1	15	Slaven 3, Burke	14,527
7		8	H	West Ham U	W	1-0	1-0	10	Pallister	19,608
8		22	H	Luton T	W	2-1	2-0	8	Slaven, Cooper	17,792
9		26	A	Newcastle U	L	0-3	0-1	—		23,927
10		29	H	Millwall	W	4-2	1-2	7	Slaven, Ripley, Burke, Parkinson (pen)	19,788
11	Nov	5	A	Liverpool	L	0-3	0-1	10		39,489
12		12	H	QPR	W	1-0	1-0	7	Brennan	20,565
13		19	A	Arsenal	L	0-3	0-1	8		32,294
14		26	H	Sheffield W	L	0-1	0-1	11		19,310
15	Dec	3	A	Nottingham F	D	2-2	0-0	12	Brennan, Ripley	17,742
16		10	H	Aston Villa	D	3-3	1-2	12	Brennan, Hamilton, Mowbray	18,096
17		17	H	Charlton Ath	D	0-0	0-0	13		16,065
18		26	A	Everton	L	1-2	1-2	14	Glover (pen)	32,651
19		31	A	Norwich C	D	0-0	0-0	15		16,021
20	Jan	2	H	Manchester U	W	1-0	0-0	13	Davenport	24,411
21		14	A	Southampton	W	3-1	0-1	11	Kerr, Slaven, Burke	13,157
22		21	H	Tottenham H	D	2-2	1-1	10	Cooper, Ripley	23,692
23	Feb	4	H	Coventry C	D	1-1	1-1	10	Slaven	17,352
24		18	A	Luton T	L	0-1	0-0	12		8187
25		21	A	Millwall	L	0-2	0-1	—		11,394
26		26	H	Newcastle U	D	1-1	0-1	—	Slaven	24,385
27	Mar	11	H	Liverpool	L	0-4	0-2	12		25,197
28		18	H	Derby Co	L	0-1	0-1	13		16,580
29		25	A	Wimbledon	D	1-1	1-1	13	Slaven	5276
30		27	H	Everton	D	3-3	1-2	13	Slaven, Parkinson (pen), Davenport	21,351
31	Apr	1	A	Charlton Ath	L	0-2	0-1	16		6696
32		8	H	Southampton	D	3-3	1-0	15	Hamilton, Slaven, Burke	16,983
33		11	A	West Ham U	W	2-1	0-1	—	Slaven 2	16,230
34		15	A	QPR	D	0-0	0-0	13		10,347
35		22	H	Nottingham F	L	3-4	1-2	14	Ripley, Slaven, Davenport	20,778
36		29	A	Aston Villa	D	1-1	0-0	14	Davenport	18,590
37	May	6	H	Arsenal	L	0-1	0-0	16		21,803
38		13	A	Sheffield W	L	0-1	0-0	18		20,582

Final League Position: 18

GOALSCORERS

League (44): Slaven 15, Burke 5, Davenport 4, Ripley 4, Brennan 3, Hamilton 3, Mowbray 3, Cooper 2, Parkinson 2 (2 pens), Glover 1 (pen), Kerr 1, Pallister 1.
Littlewoods Cup (0).
FA Cup (1): Slaven 1.

Littlewoods Cup	Second Round	Tranmere R (h)	0-0
		(a)	0-1
FA Cup	Third Round	Grimsby T (h)	1-2

Pears	Parkinson	Cooper	Mowbray	Hamilton	Kernaghan	Slaven	Brennan	Senior	Ripley	Glover	Gill	Burke	Pallister	Kerr	Davenport	Mohan	Poole	Proudlock	Proctor	Barham	*Match No.*
1	2	3	4	5*	6	7	8	9†	10	11	12	14									1
1	2	3	4	5	12	7	8	9*	10			11	6								2
1	2	3	4	5	12	7	8		9			11	6	10*							3
1	2	3	4	5		7	8	9	11				6	10							4
1	2	3	4	5		7	8	9	11				6	10							5
1	2	3		5	4	7	8		11			9	6	10							6
1	2	3	4	5	12	7	8		11	14		9*	6	10†							7
1	2	3	4	5	12	7	8		11			9*	6	10							8
1	2	3	4	5	12	7	8		11†	14		9	6	10*							9
1	2	3	4	5	12	7	8		11			9	6	10*							10
1	2	3	4	5		7	8		11			9	6		10						11
1	2	3	4	5	12	7	8		11	14		9*	6		10†						12
1	2	3	4	5*	12	7	8		11	14		9†	6		10						13
1	2	3	4	5*		7	8		11	9		12	6		10						14
1	2	3	4	5			8		7	9		11	6		10						15
1	2	3	4	5	12	14	8		7†	9		11*	6		10						16
1	2	3	4	5	12	7	8			11		9	6		10*						17
1	2	3	4	5	12	7	8		11*	9†			6	14	10						18
1	2	3	4	5		7	8		11	9			6		10						19
1	2*	3	4	5		7	8		11	9		12	6		10						20
1		3	4	5		7			11		8*	12	6	9	10	2					21
1	2	3	4	5		7	8*		11			12	6	9	10						22
		3	4	5		7	8		11		12	9	6	10*		2	1				23
	2	3	4	5	14	7	8†		11		9*	12	6	10			1				24
	2	3	4	5	8	7			11				6	9	10		1				25
	2	3	4	5		7	8		11			12	6	9*	10		1				26
1	2	3	4	5		7	8*		11				6	9	10			12			27
1	2	3	4	5		7			11			9	6	8	10						28
1	2	3	4			7			9		8		6		10				5	11	29
1	2	3	4		12	7			9*		8		6		10				5	11	30
	2	3	4	12	14	7*			9		8		6		10		1		5	11†	31
	2	3	4	11	14	7			9		8*	12	6		10†		1		5		32
	2	3	4	11	8	7			9*			10	6	12			1		5		33
	2	3	4	11	8	7			9			10	6				1		5		34
	2	3†	4	11*		7			9			10	6	8	12	14	1		5		35
	2		4	9	12	7			8			11*	6		10	3	1		5		36
	2		4	9	12	7			8*			11†	6		10	3	1		5	14	37
	2		4	9	12	7						11*	6	8	10	3	1		5		38
26	36	35	37	35 + 1s	5 + 18s	36 + 1s	25	4	36	8 + 4s	6 + 2s	21 + 8s	37	18 + 2s	23 + 1s	5 + 1s	12	— + 1s	10	3 + 1s	

MIDDLESBROUGH

Player and Position	Ht	Wt	Birth Date	Birth Place	Source	Clubs	League App	League Gls
Goalkeepers								
Matt Coddington	6 1	11 05	17 9 69	Lytham St Annes	Trainee	Middlesbrough	—	—
Stephen Pears	6 0	12 11	22 1 62	Brandon	Apprentice	Manchester U	4	—
						Middlesbrough	12	—
						(loan)	153	—
						Middlesbrough		
Kevin Poole	5 10	11 10	21 7 63	Bromsgrove	Apprentice	Aston Villa	28	—
						Northampton T	3	—
						(loan)	13	—
						Middlesbrough		
Defenders								
Colin Cooper	5 10	10 00	28 2 67	Durham		Middlesbrough	135	4
Drew Coverdale*	5 11	10 06	20 9 69	Teeside	Trainee	Middlesbrough	—	—
Owen McGee	5 7	10 07	20 4 70	Teeside	Trainee	Middlesbrough	—	—
Nicky Mohan	6 2	12 00	6 10 70	Middlesbrough	Trainee	Middlesbrough	6	—
Tony Mowbray	6 1	12 02	22 11 63	Saltburn	Apprentice	Middlesbrough	263	20
Gary Pallister	6 4	13 00	30 6 65	Ramsgate	Billingham	Middlesbrough	153	5
						Darlington (loan)	7	—
Gary Parkinson	5 10	11 11	10 1 68	Middlesbrough	Amateur	Everton	—	—
						Middlesbrough	120	2
Michael Trotter	6 3	12 02	27 10 69	Hartlepool	Trainee	Middlesbrough	—	—
						Doncaster R (loan)	3	—
Midfield								
Gary Agnew	5 11	12 03	27 1 71	Dumfries	Trainee	Middlesbrough	—	—
Mark Barham	5 7	11 00	12 7 62	Folkestone	Apprentice	Norwich C	177	23
						Huddersfield T	27	1
						Middlesbrough	4	—
Mark Brennan	5 10	10 13	4 10 65	Rossendale	Apprentice	Ipswich T	168	19
						Middlesbrough	25	3
Gary Gill	5 10	11 09	28 11 64	Middlesbrough	Apprentice	Middlesbrough	76	2
						Hull C (loan)	1	—
Gary Hamilton	5 8	11 02	27 12 65	Glasgow	Apprentice	Middlesbrough	229	25
Paul Kerr	5 8	11 04	9 6 64	Portsmouth	Apprentice	Aston Villa	24	3
						Middlesbrough	84	6
Mark Proctor	5 10	12 08	30 1 61	Middlesbrough	Apprentice	Middlesbrough	109	12
						Nottingham F	64	5
						Sunderland (loan)	5	—
						Sunderland	112	19
						Sheffield W	59	4
						Middlesbrough	10	—
Garry Robinson*	5 10	11 09	24 4 70	Teeside	Trainee	Middlesbrough	—	—

MIDDLESBROUGH

Foundation: The story of how the idea of a Middlesbrough football club was first mooted at a tripe supper at the Corporation Hotel in 1876 is well known locally. But the club was formally established at a meeting in the Talbot Hotel the following year and is one of the oldest clubs in the North East.

Managers (and Secretary-managers)
John Robson 1899–1905, Alex Massie 1905–06, Andy Aitken 1906–09, J. Gunter 1908–10, Andy Walker 1910–11, Tom McIntosh 1911–19, James Howie 1920–23, Herbert Bamlett 1923–26, Peter McWilliam 1927–34, Wilf Gillow 1934–44, David Jack 1944–52, Walter Rowley 1952–54, Bob Dennison 1954–63, Raich Carter 1963–66, Stan Anderson 1966–73, Jack Charlton 1973–77, John Neal 1977–81, Bobby Murdoch 1981–82, Malcolm Allison 1982–84, Willie Maddren 1984–86, Bruce Rioch 1986– .

Player and Position	*Ht*	*Wt*	*Birth Date*	*Birth Place*	*Source*	*Clubs*	*League App*	*League Gls*
Forwards								
Mark Burke	5 10	11 08	12 2 69	Solihull	Apprentice	Aston Villa	7	—
						Middlesbrough	45	5
Peter Davenport	5 11	11 03	24 3 61	Birkenhead	Amateur	Everton	—	—
					Cammel Laird	Nottingham F	118	54
						Manchester U	92	22
						Middlesbrough	24	4
Andy Fletcher			12 8 71	Cleveland	Trainee	Middlesbrough	—	—
Alan Kernaghan	6 2	12 12	25 4 67	Otley	Apprentice	Middlesbrough	85	7
Stuart Ripley	5 11	12 06	20 11 67	Middlesbrough	Apprentice	Middlesbrough	132	16
						Bolton W (loan)	5	1
Bernie Slaven	5 11	10 10	13 11 60	Paisley		Morton	22	1
						Airdrie	2	—
						Q of S	2	—
						Albion R	42	27
						Middlesbrough	159	61

Trainees
Arnold, Ian; Crosby, Lee D; Dixon, Lee D; Driscoll, Michael E; Geldart, Jason B; Giddings, Mark; Griffiths, Martin S; Hanford, Paul A; Hogg, Geoffrey M.J; Holmes, Daniel G; Lake, Robert M; Little, David A; Roxby, Lee; Rutherford, Neil; Sunley, Mark; Tucker, Lee D; Veart, Craig W.

Associated Schoolboys
Barron, Michael J; Collett, Andrew A; Gibson, Mark; Green, Scott; Jenkins, Paul; Keavney, David G; Martin, Steven; Melling, Paul; Passman, Jonathon L; Peverell, Nicholas J; Pollock, Jamie; Taylor, Mark S; Templeman, Richard J.

MILLWALL 1988–89 *Back row (left to right):* George Lawrence, Keith Stevens, Teddy Sheringham, Steve Anthrobus, Tony Cascarino, David Thompson, Neil Ruddock, Dean Horrix, Steve Wood. *Centre row:* Peter Melville (Physiotherapist), Terry Hurlock, Robbie Cooke, Alan McLeary, Keith Branagan, Brian Horne, Danis Salman, Kevin O'Callaghan, Jimmy Carter, Roger Cross (Coach).
Front row: Wesley Reid, Darren Morgan, Alan Dowson, Les Briley, John Docherty (Manager), Frank McLintock (Assistant Manager), David Bryne, Nicky Coleman, Sean Sparham, Richard Chick.

Division 1 MILLWALL

The Den, Cold Blow Lane, London, SE14 5RH. Telephone 01-639 3143/4, Commercial Dept. 01-639 4590.

Ground capacity: 26,000

Record Attendance: 48,672 v Derby Co, FA Cup 5th rd, 20 Feb, 1937.

Record Receipts: £52,637 v Leicester C, FA Cup 5th rd, 19 Feb, 1985.

Pitch measurements: 112yd × 74yd.

President: Lord Mellish.

Chairman: *Vice-Chairmen:* R. M. Mead, R. I. Burr. ***Directors:*** J. D. Burnige, B. E. Mitchell, P. M. Mead, D. Sullivan.

Chief Executive Secretary: G. I. S. Hortop

Manager: John Docherty. ***Assistant Manager:*** Frank McLintock.

Coach: Roger Cross.

Commercial Manager: W. W. Neil.

Chief Scout: Bob Pearson. ***Physio:*** Peter Melville.

Year Formed: 1885. ***Turned Professional:*** 1893. ***Ltd Co.:*** 1894.

Club Nickname: 'The Lions'.

Previous Grounds: 1885, Glengall Road, Millwall; 1886, Back of 'Lord Nelson'; 1890, East Ferry Road; 1901, North Greenwich; 1910, The Den.

Previous Names: 1885, Millwall Rovers; 1889, Millwall Athletic.

Record League Victory: 9-1 v Torquay U, Division 3(S), 29 August 1927 – Lansdale; Tilling, Hill; Amos, Bryant (3), Graham; Chance, Hawkins (3), Landells (1), Phillips (2), Black. 9-1 v Coventry C, Division 3(S), 19 November 1927 – Lansdale; Fort, Hill; Amos, Collins (1), Graham; Chance, Landells (4), Cock (2), Phillips (2), Black.

Record Cup Victory: 7-0 v Gateshead, FA Cup, 2nd rd, 12 December 1936 – Yuill; Ted Smith, Inns; Brolly, Hancock, Forsyth; Thomas (1), Mangnall (1), Ken Burditt (2), McCartney (2), Thorogood (1).

Record Defeat: 1-9 v Aston Villa, FA Cup 4th rd, 28 January, 1946.

Most League Points (2 for a win): 65, Division 3(S), 1927–28 and Division 3, 1965–66.

Most League Points (3 for a win): 90, Division 3, 1984–85.

Most League Goals: 124, Division 3(S), 1927–28.

Highest League Scorer in Season: Richard Parker, 37, Division 3(S), 1926–27.

Most League Goals in Total Aggregate: Derek Possee, 79, 1967–73.

Most Capped Player: Eamonn Dunphy, 22 (23), Eire.

Most League Appearances: Barry Kitchener, 523, 1967–82.

Record Transfer Fee Received: £250,000 from Ipswich T for Kevin O'Callaghan, January 1980.

Record Transfer Fee Paid: £300,000 to Tottenham H for Neil Ruddock, June 1988.

Football League Record: 1920 Original Members of Division 3; 1921 Division 3(S); 1928–34 Division 2; 1934–38 Division 3(S); 1938–48 Division 2; 1948–58 Division 3(S); 1958–62 Division 4; 1962–64 Division 3; 1964–65 Division 4; 1965–66 Division 3; 1966–75 Division 2; 1975–76 Division 3; 1976–79 Division 2; 1979–85 Division 3; 1985–88 Division 2; 1988– Division 1.

Honours: *Football League:* Division 2 – Champions 1987–88; Division 3(S) – Champions 1927–28, 1937–38; Runners-up 1952–53; Division 3 – Runners-up 1965–66, 1984–85; Division 4 – Champions 1961–62; Runners-up 1964–65. *FA Cup:* Semi-final 1900, 1903, 1937 (first Division 3 side to reach semi-final). *Football League Cup* best season: 5th rd, 1973–74, 1976–77. *Football League Trophy* – Winners 1982–83.

Colours: Blue shirts, white shorts, blue stockings. **Change colours:** Yellow shirts, black shorts, black stockings.

MILLWALL 1988–89 LEAGUE RECORD

Match No.	Date		Venue	Opponents	Result		H/T Score	Lg. Pos.	Goalscorers	Attendance
1	Aug	27	A	Aston Villa	D	2-2	2-2	—	Cascarino 2	22,449
2	Sept	3	H	Derby Co	W	1-0	1-0	6	Sheringham	13,061
3		10	A	Charlton Ath	W	3-0	2-0	4	Sheringham, Cascarino, Briley	13,735
4		17	H	Everton	W	2-1	2-0	3	Cascarino 2	17,507
5		24	A	Norwich C	D	2-2	0-0	3	Cascarino, O'Callaghan	16,616
6	Oct	1	H	QPR	W	3-2	3-1	1	Cascarino 2, Hurlock	14,103
7		15	A	Coventry C	D	0-0	0-0	2		19,369
8		22	H	Nottingham F	D	2-2	0-1	2	Sheringham, Ruddock	16,874
9		29	A	Middlesbrough	L	2-4	2-1	3	Sheringham, Cascarino	19,788
10	Nov	5	H	Luton T	W	3-1	3-0	2	Sheringham, O'Callaghan (pen), Dawes	12,511
11		12	A	Liverpool	D	1-1	1-1	4	Stephenson	41,966
12		19	H	Newcastle U	W	4-0	2-0	3	McLeary, Hurlock, Cascarino, O'Callaghan	15,767
13		26	A	Southampton	D	2-2	1-1	3	O'Callaghan, Sheringham	15,925
14	Dec	3	H	West Ham U	L	0-1	0-1	3		20,105
15		10	A	Tottenham H	L	0-2	0-1	5		27,660
16		17	H	Sheffield W	W	1-0	0-0	3	Sheringham	11,197
17		26	A	Wimbledon	L	0-1	0-0	4		11,398
18		31	A	Derby Co	W	1-0	0-0	3	Sheringham	16,154
19	Jan	2	H	Charlton Ath	W	1-0	0-0	3	Thompson	17,025
20		14	A	Manchester U	L	0-3	0-2	4		40,931
21		22	H	Norwich C	L	2-3	2-2	—	Cascarino, Carter	13,687
22	Feb	4	A	QPR	W	2-1	0-0	6	Carter, Cascarino	12,381
23		11	H	Arsenal	L	1-2	1-0	7	Carter	21,854
24		21	H	Middlesbrough	W	2-0	1-0	—	Briley, Mowbray (og)	11,394
25		25	H	Coventry C	W	1-0	0-0	3	Cascarino	13,021
26		28	A	Arsenal	D	0-0	0-0	—		37,524
27	Mar	11	A	Luton T	W	2-1	2-0	3	Carter 2	7838
28		18	H	Aston Villa	W	2-0	1-0	3	O'Callaghan, Hurlock	13,206
29		25	A	Everton	D	1-1	1-0	3	Sheringham	27,062
30		27	H	Wimbledon	L	0-1	0-0	4		13,679
31	Apr	1	A	Sheffield W	L	0-3	0-1	4		18,358
32		8	H	Manchester U	D	0-0	0-0	5		17,523
33		11	H	Liverpool	L	1-2	1-2	—	Salman	22,130
34		22	A	West Ham U	L	0-3	0-3	7		16,603
35		29	H	Tottenham H	L	0-5	0-2	8		16,551
36	May	3	A	Nottingham F	L	1-4	0-1	—	Laws (og)	15,928
37		6	A	Newcastle U	D	1-1	1-0	8	Sheringham	14,435
38		13	H	Southampton	D	1-1	0-1	9	Sheringham	12,011

Final League Position: 10

GOALSCORERS

League (47): Cascarino 13, Sheringham 11, Carter 5, O'Callaghan 5 (1 pen), Hurlock 3, Briley 2, Dawes 1, McLeary 1, Ruddock 1, Salman 1, Stephenson 1, Thompson 1, own goals 2.
Littlewoods Cup (7): Sheringham 3, Ruddock 2, Ruddock 1, Salman 1.
FA Cup (3): Carter 1, Cascarino 1, Sheringham 1.

Littlewoods Cup	Second Round	Gillingham (h)	3-0
		(a)	3-1
	Third Round	Aston Villa (a)	1-3
FA Cup	Third Round	Luton T (h)	3-2
	Fourth Round	Liverpool (h)	0-2

Horne	Salman	Dawes	Hurlock	Thompson	McLeary	Lawrence	Briley	Sheringham	Cascarino	O'Callaghan	Wood	Carter	Stevens	Morgan	Ruddock	Stephenson	Horrix	Sparham	Treacey	Anthrobus	Reid	Match No.
1	2	3	4	5	6	7	8	9	10	11												1
1	2	3	4		6	7	8	9	10	11*	5	12										2
1	2	3	4		6	7	8	9	10	11	5											3
1	2†	3	4		6	7*	8	9	10	11	5	12	14									4
1		3	4		6	7	8	9	10	11	5		2									5
1		3	4		6	7*		9	10	11	5	12	2	8								6
1	7	3	4		6			9	10	11	5		2	8								7
1	12	3	4		6	7†	8	9	10	11	5*		2		14							8
1	5	3	4		6	7	8	9	10	11*			2		12							9
1		3		5	6	7	8	9	10	11			2	4								10
1	14	3†	4		6		8	9	10	11*	5		2	12		7						11
1		3	4		6		8	9	10	11	5		2			7						12
1		3	4		6		8	9	10	11	5		2			7						13
1		3	4		6		8	9	10	11	5		2			7						14
1	12	3*	4		6		8	9	10	11	5		2			7						15
1		3	4		6		8	9	10	11	5		2			7						16
1		3	4		6		8	9	10	11	5		2			7*	12					17
1		3	4		6		8	9	10	11	5		2			7						18
1	12	3	4	14	6		8	9	10	11	5		2*			7†						19
1	3	14	4*		6			9	10	11	5	7	2†	8		12						20
1	2	3	4		6			9	10	11	5	7		8								21
1		3	4	2	6		8		10	11	5	7					9					22
1		3	4	2	6		8	9	10	11	5	7										23
1	12			2	6		8	9	10	11	5	7		4*				3				24
1	12			2	6		8	9	10	11	5	7		4*				3				25
1			4	2	6		8	9	10	11	5	7						3				26
1			4	2	6		8	9	10	11	5	7						3				27
1			4	5	2		8	9	10	11	6	7						3				28
1			4	5	2		8	9	10	11	6	7						3				29
1	12		4	5	2		8	9	10	11†	6	7*					14	3				30
1	12		4	5	2		8	9	10	11*	6	7†					14	3				31
1	7	3	4		6		8		10	11	5		2				9					32
1	7	3	4		6		8		10	11	5		2*				9	12				33
1	7	3		14	6	12	8*		10	11	5	4†	2				9					34
1		3	4	5	2	7*	8		10		6	11					9	12				35
1		14	4		6			9	10		5	12	2			7*		3	8†	11		36
1		14	4		6			9	10		5	12	2			7*		3	8	11†		37
1		3	4		6			9	10		5	12	2						8	11	7*	38
38	11 + 8s	27 + 3s	34	13 + 2s	38	10 + 1s	31	33	38	34	35	14 + 6s	22 + 1s	7 + 1s	— + 2s	11 + 1s	5 + 3s	10 + 2s	3	3	1	

MILLWALL

Player and Position	Ht	Wt	Birth Date	Birth Place	Source	Clubs	League App	League Gls
Goalkeepers								
Keith Branagan	6 1	13 02	10 7 66	Fulham		Cambridge U	110	—
						Millwall	—	—
Brian Horne	5 11	13 13	5 10 67	Billericay	Apprentice	Millwall	113	—
Defenders								
Nicky Coleman	5 10	11 12	6 5 66	Crayford	Apprentice	Millwall	85	—
						Swindon T (loan)	13	4
Ian Dawes	5 7	11 11	22 2 63	Croyden	Apprentice	QPR	229	3
						Millwall	30	1
Alan Dowson			17 6 70	Gateshead	Trainee	Millwall	—	—
Alan McLeary	5 11	10 08	6 10 64	London	Apprentice	Millwall	200	5
Danis Salman	5 10	11 08	12 3 60	Cyprus	Apprentice	Brentford	325	8
						Millwall	86	4
Sean Sparham	5 7	10 10	4 12 68	Bexley		Millwall	19	—
David Thompson	6 3	12 07	20 11 68	N'humberland	Trainee	Millwall	20	1
Steve Wood	6 0	11 09	2 2 63	Bracknell	Apprentice	Reading	219	9
						Millwall	57	—
Midfield								
Philip Babb			30 11 70		Lambeth	Millwall	—	—
Les Briley	5 6	11 00	2 10 56	Lambeth	Apprentice	Chelsea	—	—
						Hereford U	61	2
						Wimbledon	61	2
						Aldershot	157	3
						Millwall	180	10
Terry Hurlock	5 9	13 02	22 9 58	Hackney	Leytonstone	Brentford	220	18
						Reading	29	—
						Millwall	75	8
Darren Morgan	5 6	9 05	5 11 67	Camberwell	Apprentice	Millwall	33	1
Wesley Reid	5 8	11 03	10 9 68	Lewisham	YTS	Arsenal	—	—
						Millwall	1	—
Keith Stevens	6 0	12 05	21 6 64	Merton	Apprentice	Millwall	218	3
Forwards								
Steve Anthrobus	6 2	12 13	10 11 68	Lewisham		Millwall	6	—
Jimmy Carter	5 10	10 04	9 11 65	London	Apprentice	Crystal Palace	—	—
						QPR	—	—
						Millwall	58	6
Tony Cascarino	6 2	11 10	1 9 62	St Paul's Cray	Crockenhill	Gillingham	219	78
						Millwall	77	33
Richard Chick‡	5 9	11 02	30 9 70	Walthamstow	Trainee	Millwall	—	—
Robbie Cooke‡	5 9	10 08	16 2 57	Rotherham	Apprentice	Mansfield T	15	1
					Grantham T	Peterborough U	115	51
						Luton T (loan)	—	—
						Cambridge U	65	14
						Brentford	124	53
						Millwall	4	1
Dean Horrix	5 11	10 10	21 11 61	Taplow	Apprentice	Millwall	72	19
						Gillingham	14	—
						Reading	158	35
						Cardiff C (loan)	9	3
						Millwall	10	1

MILLWALL

Foundation: Formed in 1885 as Millwall Rovers by employees of Morton & Co, a jam and marmalade factory in West Ferry Road. The founders were predominantly Scotsmen. Their first headquarters was the The Islanders pub in Tooke Street, Millwall. Their first trophy was the East End Cup in 1887.

Managers (and Secretary-managers)
Willie Henderson 1894–95*, John Beveridge 1895–1907* (continued as secretary until 1915), Fred Kidd 1907–08, George Saunders 1908–09, Herbert Lipsham 1913–19, Robert Hunter 1919–33, Bill McCracken 1933–36, Charlie Hewitt 1936–40, Bill Voisey 1940–44, Jack Cock 1944–48, Charlie Hewitt 1948–56, Ron Gray 1956–57, Jimmy Seed 1958–59, Reg Smith 1959–61, Ron Gray 1961–63, Billy Gray 1963–66, Benny Fenton 1966–74, Gordon Jago 1974–77, George Petchey 1978–80, Peter Anderson 1980–82, George Graham 1982–86, John Docherty 1986– .

Player and Position	*Ht*	*Wt*	*Birth Date*	*Birth Place*	*Source*	*Clubs*	*League App*	*League Gls*
George Lawrence	5 10	12 02	14 9 62	London	Apprentice	Southampton	10	1
						Oxford U (loan)	15	4
						Oxford U	63	21
						Southampton	68	11
						Millwall	28	4
Manus Magill			2 8 71	Ballymena		Millwall	—	—
Kevin O'Callaghan	5 8	11 04	19 10 61	London	Apprentice	Millwall	20	3
						Ipswich T	115	3
						Portsmouth	87	16
						Millwall	56	12
Teddy Sheringham	5 8	12 04	2 4 66	Highams Park	Apprentice	Millwall	143	51
						Aldershot (loan)	5	—
Paul Stephenson	5 10	10 09	2 1 68	Newcastle	Apprentice	Newcastle U	61	1
						Millwall	12	1
Stephen Torpey	6 2	12 11	8 12 70	Islington	Trainee	Millwall	—	—
Darren Treacy	5 10	12 09	6 9 70	Lambeth	Trainee	Millwall	3	—

Trainees
Cooper, Nicholas J; Dunwell, Richard K; Hendry, Ansel A; Lewis, Darren; Osborne, Colin A.C; Pope, Barry D; Thompson, Darren.

Associated Schoolboys
Bedford, Roy D; Cooke, David; Foran, Mark J; Lee, Brian R; McCall, Stuart M; Manning, Paul J; Okyere-Darkoh, Joseph; Rogerson, Colin C; Smith, Brett R; Walker, Lee M.D.

NEWCASTLE UNITED 1988–89 *Back row (left to right):* Archie Gourlay, Mark Gill, Graeme Carter, Anth Lormor, David Robinson, David Hallam, David Roche, Craig Chapman, Phil Coxall.
Centre row: Derek Wright (Physiotherapist), Paul Stephenson, Tommy Wright, Dave Beasant, Kevin Scott, John Cornwell, Peter Jackson, Brian Tinnion, Andy Thorn, Martin Thomas, Gary Kelly, John Anderson, John Pickering (Coach).
Front row: Colin Suggett (Coach), Darren Jackson, Michael O'Neill, John Robertson, Ken Wharton, Glenn Roeder, Willie McFaul (Manager), Mirandinha, David McCreery, John Hendrie, Ian Bogie, Albert Craig.

Division 2 NEWCASTLE UNITED

St James' Park, Newcastle-upon-Tyne NE1 4ST. Telephone Tyneside (091) 232 8361. Commercial Managers: (091) 232 2285. Club Shop: (091) 261 6357. Recorded information: (091) 261 1571. Fax: 091-232 9875. Clubcall 0898-121190. Harveys (Restaurant) 2221860

Ground capacity: 37,637.

Record attendance: 68,386 v Chelsea, Division 1, 3 Sept, 1930.

Record receipts: £135,000 v Watford, FA Cup 3rd rd 2nd replay, 16 January, 1989.

Pitch measurements: 115yd × 75yd.

Chairman: W.G. McKeag. **Vice-Chairman:** G. R. Forbes.

Directors: Stan Seymour, J. Rush AFC, Sir George Bowman JP E. Dunn, G. R. Dickson, P. Mallinger.

Manager: Jim Smith. ***Asst. Manager:*** Bobby Saxton.

Coach: Colin Suggett. ***Physio:*** Derek Wright.

General Manager/Secretary: R. Cushing.

Assistant Secretary: K. Slater. ***Commercial Manager:*** G. McDonnell.

Year Formed: 1881. ***Turned Professional:*** 1889. ***Ltd Co.:*** 1890.

Club Nickname: 'Magpies'.

Previous Names: Stanley 1881; Newcastle East End 1882–1892.

Previous Ground: South Byker 1881; Chillingham Road, Heaton, 1886 to 1892.

Record League Victory: 13-0 v Newport Co, Division 2, 5 October 1946 – Garbutt; Cowell, Graham; Harvey, Brennan, Wright; Milburn (2), Bentley (1), Wayman (4), Shackleton (6), Pearson.

Record Cup Victory: 9-0 v Southport (at Hillsborough) FA Cup, 4th rd, 1 February 1932 – McInroy; Nelson, Fairhurst; McKenzie, Davidson, Weaver (1); Boyd (1), Jimmy Richardson (3), Cape (2), McMenemy (1), Lang (1).

Record Defeat: 0-9 v Burton Wanderers, Division 2, 15 April, 1895.

Most League Points (2 for a win): 57, Division 2, 1964–65.

Most League Points (3 for a win): 80, Division 2, 1983–84.

Most League Goals: 98, Division 1, 1951–52.

Highest League Scorer in Season: Hughie Gallacher, 36, Division 1, 1926–27.

Most League Goals in Total Aggregate: Jackie Milburn, 178, 1946–57.

Most Capped Player: Alf McMichael, 40, Northern Ireland.

Most League Appearances: Jim Lawrence. 432, 1904–22.

Record Transfer Fee Received: £2,000,000 from Tottenham H for Paul Gascoigne, July 1988.

Record Transfer Fee Paid: £850,000 to Wimbledon for Dave Beasant, June 1988 and £850,000 to Wimbledon for Andy Thorn, August 1988.

Football League Record: 1893 Elected to Division 2; 1898–1934 Division 1; 1934–48 Division 2; 1948–61 Division 1; 1961–65 Division 2; 1965–78 Division 1; 1978–84 Division 2; 1984–89 Division 1; 1989– Division 2.

Honours: *Football League;* Division 1 – Champions 1904–05, 1906–07, 1908–09, 1926–27; Division 2 – Champions 1964–65; Runners-up 1897–98, 1947–48. *FA Cup:* Winners 1910, 1924, 1932, 1951, 1952, 1955; Runners-up 1905, 1906, 1908, 1911, 1974. *Football League Cup:* Runners-up 1975–76. *Texaco Cup:* Winners 1973–74, 1974–75. **European Competitions;** *European Fairs Cup:* 1968–69 (winners), 1969–70, 1970–71, *UEFA Cup:* 1977–78. *Anglo-Italian Cup:* Winners 1973.

Colours: Black and white striped shirts, black shorts, black stockings. **Change colours:** Yellow and green striped shirts, green shorts, yellow stockings.

NEWCASTLE UNITED 1988–89 LEAGUE RECORD

Match No.	Date	Venue	Opponents	Result	H/T Score	Lg. Pos.	Goalscorers	Attendance
1	Aug 27	A	Everton	L 0-4	0-2	—		41,560
2	Sept 3	H	Tottenham H	D 2-2	2-0	17	Thorn, Jackson D	32,977
3	10	A	Derby Co	L 0-2	0-0	19		16,014
4	17	H	Norwich C	L 0-2	0-1	20		22,801
5	24	A	Charlton Ath	D 2-2	0-1	19	Jackson D, Tinnion	6088
6	Oct 1	A	Liverpool	W 2-1	1-1	18	Hendrie, Mirandinha (pen)	39,139
7	8	H	Coventry C	L 0-3	0-3	19		22,896
8	22	A	West Ham U	L 0-2	0-0	20		17,765
9	26	H	Middlesbrough	W 3-0	1-0	—	Pallister (og), Mirandinha 2	23,927
10	29	H	Nottingham F	L 0-1	0-0	18		24,765
11	Nov 5	A	QPR	L 0-3	0-2	18		11,013
12	12	H	Arsenal	L 0-1	0-0	20		24,033
13	19	A	Millwall	L 0-4	0-2	20		15,767
14	27	H	Manchester U	D 0-0	0-0	—		20,350
15	Dec 3	A	Luton T	D 0-0	0-0	20		8338
16	10	H	Wimbledon	W 2-1	1-0	20	Hendrie 2	20,146
17	17	H	Southampton	D 3-3	1-2	18	Brock, O'Neill 2	19,986
18	26	A	Sheffield W	W 2-1	2-1	18	McDonald, O'Neill	25,573
19	31	A	Tottenham H	L 0-2	0-2	19		27,739
20	Jan 2	H	Derby Co	L 0-1	0-0	19		30,555
21	14	A	Aston Villa	L 1-3	1-1	20	Mirandinha (pen)	21,010
22	21	H	Charlton Ath	L 0-2	0-1	20		19,076
23	Feb 4	H	Liverpool	D 2-2	1-1	19	Mirandinha, Pingel	30,966
24	11	A	Coventry C	W 2-1	0-0	19	Hendrie, Mirandinha (pen)	16,577
25	26	A	Middlesbrough	D 1-1	1-0	—	O'Brien	24,385
26	Mar 11	H	QPR	L 1-2	0-0	19	Ranson	21,577
27	15	A	Nottingham F	D 1-1	0-1	—	Brock	20,800
28	22	H	Everton	W 2-0	1-0	—	Mirandinha, O'Brien	20,933
29	25	A	Norwich C	W 2-0	1-0	19	Mirandinha, O'Brien	22,440
30	27	H	Sheffield W	L 1-3	0-2	19	Mirandinha (pen)	31,040
31	Apr 1	A	Southampton	L 0-1	0-0	19		16,175
32	8	H	Aston Villa	L 1-2	0-1	19	O'Brien	20,329
33	15	A	Arsenal	L 0-1	0-0	19		38,023
34	22	H	Luton T	D 0-0	0-0	19		18,493
35	29	A	Wimbledon	L 0-4	0-1	19		5206
36	May 3	H	West Ham U	L 1-2	1-1	—	Lormor	14,202
37	6	H	Millwall	D 1-1	0-1	20	Anderson	14,435
38	13	A	Manchester U	L 0-2	0-0	20		30,379

Final League Position: 20

GOALSCORERS

League (32): Mirandinha 9 (4 pens), Hendrie 4, O'Brien 4, O'Neill 3, Brock 2, Jackson D 2, Anderson 1, Lormor 1, McDonald 1, Pingel 1, Ranson 1, Thorn 1, Tinnion 1, own goal 1.
Littlewoods Cup (2): Hendrie 1, Mirandinha 1.
FA Cup (2): Brock 1, Mirandinha 1 (pen).

Littlewoods Cup	Second Round	Sheffield U (a)	0-3
		(h)	2-0
FA Cup	Third Round	Watford (h)	0-0
		(a)	2-2
		(h)	0-0
		(a)	0-1

Beasant	Anderson	Tinnion	McCreery	Jackson, P	Thorn	Hendrie	Robertson	Mirandinha	Wharton	O'Neill	Jackson, D	Scott	Bogie	Craig	Stephenson	Cornwell	Payne	Robinson	O'Brien	McDonald	Roeder	Gourlay	Brock	Ranson	Sansom	Wright	Pingel	Brazil	Kelly	*Match No.*
1	2	3	4	5	6	7	8	9*	10	11	12																			1
1	2*		4		6	7	11		3	9	10	5	8	12																2
1	2		4		6	7	11		3	9	10	5	8																	3
1	2	3	4		6	7	11			9*	10	5	8		12															4
1		14	4		6	7	11†	9	3		10	5	12		8	2*														5
1	2		4		6	7	12	9	3	10*	8	5			11															6
1	2		4		6†	7	12	9	3	10*	8	5			11	14														7
1	2	3	4*		6†	8	12	9		11	10	5	14		7															8
1	2	3				8	12	9		10	4	5			7	6	11*													9
1	2	3				8	12	9		10	4	5			7	6	11*													10
1	2	3*	4		6	8	9			11	10	5			7		12													11
1	2	3	4		6	8	7*	9			10					5	11	12												12
1	2	3	4		6	8		12	11*		14					5†			7	9	10									13
1	2	3	4		6	7		10	12							5	11*		8	9										14
1	2	3	4		6	7		10*			9					5	11		8			12								15
1	2	3	4		6	7		10†	14		9*					5			8	12			11							16
1		3†	4		5	7		9*	10	12			14						2	8	6		11							17
1			4†		5	7		12	10	8*									14	9	6		11	2	3					18
1			4†			7		12	10	8*		5							14	9	6		11	2	3					19
1			4			7		9†	10*	12		5							14	8	6		11	2	3					20
			4			7		9	10			5					8*		6				11	2	3	1	12			21
	5		4†			7		12	10*	14									9		6		11	2	3	1	8			22
	5		4			7		9				2							10		6		11		3	1	8			23
	5		4			7		9*		12		2							10		6				3	1	8	11		24
			4			7		9*				5							10		6		11	2	3	1	8	12		25
			4			7*		12		14		5							10†		6		11	2	3	1	8	9		26
			4		6	7			14	12		5							10				11	2	3		8†	9*	1	27
			4		6	7		9†		14		5							10				11	2	3		8*	12	1	28
			4		6	7		9*		14		5							10				11	2	3		8†	12	1	29
			4		6	7		9		14		5							10				11	2†	3		8*	12	1	30
			4			7		9†		12		5							10		6		11	2	3		8*		1	31
			4			7		9*				5							10		6		11	2	3				1	32
			4		9	7				10		5								12	6				3		8*		1	33
			4		9	7		12	14	10*		5									6		11		3				1	34
			4		9					10		5								12	6		11	14	3		7*		1	35
	2†		4		9							5								12	6		11		3	1	10*			36
	2		4		9				8	10		5									6		11			1				37
	2		4		6					10*		5									9		11		3	1				38
20	21	12 + 1s	36	1	26	34	7 + 5s	22 + 6s	14 + 4s	17 + 10s	13 + 2s	29	3 + 3s	— + 1s	7 + 1s	8 + 1s	6 + 1s	— + 1s	17 + 3s	6 + 4s	18	— + 1s	21	13 + 1s	20	9	13 + 1s	3 + 4s	9	

Sweeney — Match No.31(14) 32(12) 33(11†) 34(8) 35(8) 36(8) 37(3) 38(8)
Kristensen — Match No. 32(8) 33(2) 34(2†) 35(2†) 36(14)
Roche — Match No. 33(14) 38(14)
Lormor — Match No. 36(7) 37(7) 38(7†)
Howey — Match No. 38(12)

NEWCASTLE UNITED

Player and Position	Ht	Wt	Birth Date	Birth Place	Source	Clubs	League App	League Gls
Goalkeepers								
Gary Kelly	5 10	12 03	3 8 66	Fulwood	Apprentice	Newcastle U	49	—
						Blackpool (loan)	5	—
Tommy Wright	6 1	13 05	29 8 63	Belfast	Linfield	Newcastle U	9	—
Defenders								
John Anderson	5 11	11 06	7 11 59	Dublin	Apprentice	WBA	—	—
						Preston NE	51	—
						Newcastle U	235	9
Graeme Carter	6 0	12 00	18 11 69	Castle Eden	Trainee	Newcastle U	—	—
Craig Chapman	5 7	10 05	9 12 70	Middlesbrough	Trainee	Newcastle U	—	—
Philip Coxall‡	5 10	11 05	29 1 69	Sunderland		Newcastle U	—	—
Bjorn Kristensen	6 1	12 05	10 10 63	Malling	Aarhus	Newcastle U	5	—
Ray Ranson	5 9	11 12	12 6 60	St Helens	Apprentice	Manchester C	183	1
						Birmingham C	137	—
						Newcastle U	14	1
David Roche	5 11	12 01	13 12 70	Newcastle	Trainee	Newcastle U	2	—
Glenn Roeder*	6 0	12 13	13 12 55	Woodford	Apprentice	Orient	115	4
						QPR	157	17
						Notts Co (loan)	4	—
						Newcastle U	193	8
Kenny Sansom	5 6	11 08	26 9 58	Camberwell	Apprentice	Crystal Palace	172	3
						Arsenal	314	6
						Newcastle U	20	—
Kevin Scott	6 2	11 06	17 12 66	Easington		Newcastle U	36	2
Andy Thorn	6 0	11 05	12 11 66	Carshalton	Apprentice	Wimbledon	107	2
						Newcastle U	26	1
Ken Wharton*	5 7	8 10	28 11 60	Newcastle	Grainger Park BC	Newcastle U	290	26
Midfield								
Kevin Brock	5 9	10 12	9 9 62	Middleton Stoney	Apprentice	Oxford U	246	26
						QPR	40	2
						Newcastle U	21	2
Albert Craig (To Dundee Mar 1989)	5 8	11 03	3 1 62	Glasgow		Dumbarton	138	23
						Hamilton A	16	5
						Newcastle U	10	—
						Hamilton A (loan)	6	1
						Northampton T (loan)	2	1
Archie Gourlay	5 8	10 00	29 6 69	Greenock		Morton	2	—
						Newcastle U	1	—
Darren Jackson (To Dundee U Dec 1988)	5 7	10 00	25 7 66	Edinburgh	Broxburn Am	Meadowbank Th	48	22
						Newcastle U	69	7
David McCreery*	5 6	9 07	16 9 57	Belfast	Apprentice	Manchester U	87	7
						QPR	57	4
					Tulsa R	Newcastle U	243	2
Liam O'Brien	6 1	13 03	5 9 64	Dublin	Shamrock R	Manchester U	31	2
						Newcastle U	20	4
Paul Sweeney	5 7	10 00	10 1 65	Glasgow	St Kentigerns Acad.	Raith R	177	6
						Newcastle U	8	—
Forwards								
Gary Brazil	5 11	9 13	19 9 62	Tunbridge Wells	Apprentice	Crystal Palace	—	—
						Sheffield U	62	9
						Port Vale (loan)	6	3
						Preston NE	166	58
						Mansfield T (loan)	—	—
						Newcastle U	7	—

NEWCASTLE UNITED

Foundation: It stemmed from a newly formed club called Stanley in 1881. In October 1882 they changed their name to Newcastle East End to avoid confusion with Stanley in Co. Durham. Shortly afterwards another club Rosewood merged with them. Newcastle West End had been formed in August 1882 and they played on a ground which is now St. James' Park. In 1889, West End went out of existence after a bad run and the remaining committee men invited East End to move to St. James' Park. They accepted and at a meeting in Bath Lane Hall in 1892, changed their name to Newcastle United.

Managers (and Secretary-managers)
Frank Watt 1895–32 (continued as secretary to 1932), Andy Cunningham 1930–35, Tom Mather 1935–39, Stan Seymour 1939–47 (Hon-manager), George Martin 1947–50, Stan Seymour 1950–54 (Hon-manager), Duggie Livingstone 1954–56, Stan Seymour (Hon-manager 1956–58), Charlie Mitten 1958–61, Norman Smith 1961–62, Joe Harvey 1962–75, Gordon Lee 1975–77, Richard Dinnis 1977, Bill McGarry 1977–80, Arthur Cox 1980–84, Jack Charlton 1984, Willie McFaul 1985–88, Jim Smith 1988– .

Player and Position	*Ht*	*Wt*	*Birth Date*	*Place*	*Source*	*Clubs*	*League App*	*Gls*
Mark Gill	5 9	11 01	6 6 66	Dublin	Home Farm	Newcastle U	—	—
David Hallam‡	6 0	12 00	18 10 69	Newcastle	Trainee	Newcastle U	—	—
John Hendrie	5 7	11 04	24 10 63	Lennoxtown	Apprentice	Coventry C	21	2
						Hereford U (loan)	6	—
						Bradford C	173	46
						Newcastle U	34	4
Steve Howey§	6 1	10 09	26 10 71	Sunderland	Trainee	Newcastle U	1	—
Anth Lormor	6 1	12 03	29 10 70	Ashington	Trainee	Newcastle U	8	3
						Norwich C (loan)	—	—
Rob McDonald	6 2	13 00	22 1 59	Hull	Apprentice	Hull C	25	2
					PSV Eindhoven	Newcastle U	10	1
Mirandinha	5 8	11 00	2 7 59	Sao Paulo	Fluminense	Newcastle U	54	20
Michael O'Neill	5 11	10 10	5 7 69	Portadown	Coleraine	Newcastle U	48	15
Frank Pingel	6 1	13 08	9 5 64	Resskov	Aarhus	Newcastle U	14	1
John Robertson (To Hearts Dec 1988)	5 7	11 06	2 10 64	Edinburgh		Hearts	203	104
						Newcastle U	12	—
David Robinson	6 0	13 02	27 11 69	Newcastle	Trainee	Newcastle U	1	—

Trainees
Appleby, Matthew W; Bishop, Simon T; Cleary, David J; Elliott, John A; Howey, Stephen N; Mason, Philip; Parkinson, Michael; Tinmouth, Paul J.

****Non-Contract**
Bennett, Ian M.

Associated Schoolboys
Cole, Anthony R; Didlick, Stephen M; Elliott, Robert J; English, Michael J; Foster, Gary H; Heron, Thomas; Lewis, Stephen; Makel, Lee R; Milner, John F; Reay, Simon; Thompson, Alan; Watson, John I; Young, Michael S.

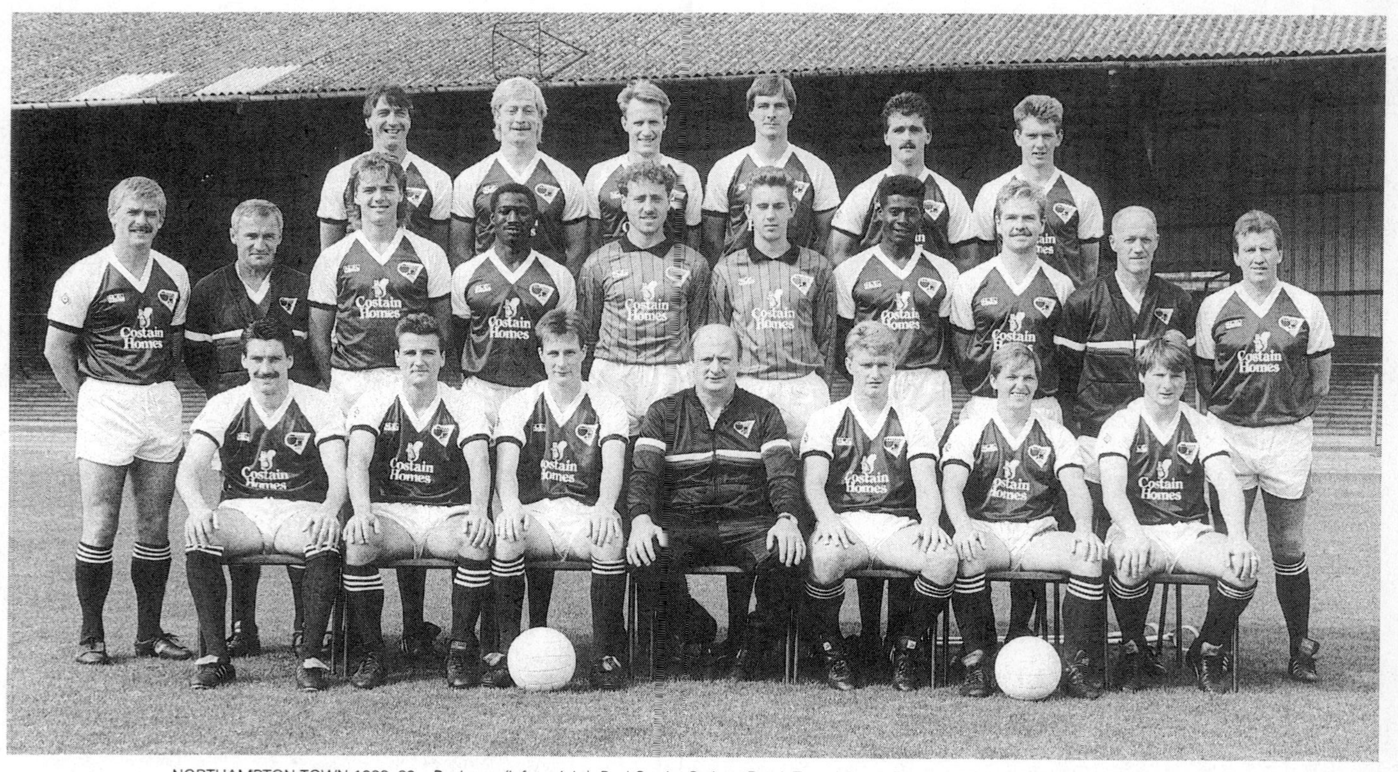

NORTHAMPTON TOWN 1988–89 *Back row (left to right):* Paul Culpin, Graham Reed, Tony Adcock, Trevor Slack, Eddie McGoldrick, Paul Wilson.
Centre row: Jimmy Holmes, Dennis Casey (Physiotherapist), Ian Johnson, Keith McPherson, Peter Gleasure, Gerald Sylvester, Glen Donegal, Russ Wilcox, Clive Walker (Coach and Assistant Manager), Brian Knight.
Front row: Dean Thomas, David Longhurst, Brad Sandeman, Graham Carr (Manager), Martin Singleton, David Gilbert, Warren Donald.

Division 3 NORTHAMPTON TOWN

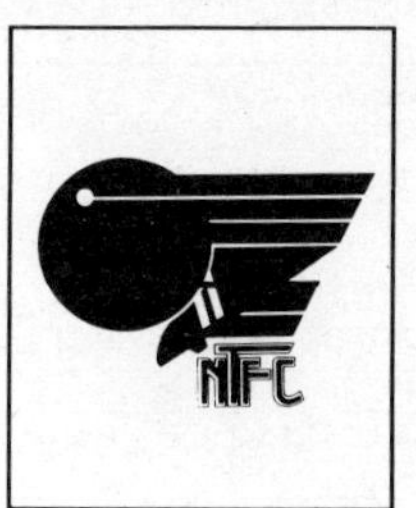

County Ground, Abington Avenue, Northampton NN1 4PS. Telephone Northampton (0604) 234100. Commercial Dept. (0604) 712847. Information Line, 0898 700 275.

Ground capacity: 11,907.

Record attendance: 24,523 v Fulham, Division 1, 23 April, 1966.

Record receipts: £25,763 v Aston Villa, 3rd rd FA Cup, 8 January, 1983.

Pitch measurements: 112yd × 75yd.

Chairman: R. J. Underwood. ***Vice-Chairman:*** B. Stonhill.

Directors: D. Kerr, M. Church, R. Church, M. Deane, B. Hancock.

Secretary: Philip Mark Hough.

Manager: Graham Carr.

Coach: Clive Walker.

Physio: Dennis Casey. ***Commercial Manager:*** Mark Underwood.

Year Formed: 1897. ***Turned Professional:*** 1901. ***Ltd Co.:*** 1901.

Club Nickname: 'The Cobblers'.

Record League Victory: 10-0 v Walsall, Division 3 (S), 5 November 1927 – Hammond; Watson, Jeffs; Allen, Brett, Odell, Daley, Smith (3), Loasby (3), Hoten (1), Wells (3).

Record Cup Victory: 9-1 v Metropolitan Police, FA Cup, 1st rd, 28 November 1931 – Hammond; English, Fred Dawes; Dowsey, O'Dell, Davies; Scott, Riches (1), Bowen (2), Albert Dawes (3), Wells (2). (1 og)

Record Defeat: 0-11 v Southampton, Southern League, 28 December, 1901.

Most League Points (2 for a win): 68, Division 4, 1975–76.

Most League Points (3 for a win): 99, Division 4, 1986–87.

Most League Goals: 109. Division 3, 1962–63 and Division 3 (S), 1952–53.

Highest League Scorer in Season: Cliff Holton, 36, Division 3, 1961–62.

Most League Goals in Total Aggregate: Jack English, 135, 1947–60.

Most Capped Player: E. Lloyd Davies, 12 (16), Wales.

Most League Appearances: Tommy Fowler, 521, 1946–61.

Record Transfer Fee Received: £265,000 from Watford for Richard Hill, July 1987.

Record Transfer Fee Paid: £85,000 to Manchester C for Tony Adcock, January 1988.

Football League Record: 1920 Original Member of Division 3; 1921 Division 3 (S); 1958–61 Division 4; 1961–63 Division 3; 1963–65 Division 2; 1965–66 Division 1; 1966–67 Division 2; 1967–69 Division 3; 1969–76 Division 4; 1976–77 Division 3; 1977–87 Division 4; 1987– Division 3.

Honours: *Football League:* Division 1 best season: 21st. 1965–66; Division 2 – Runners-up 1964–65; Division 3 – Champions 1962–63; Division 3 (S) – Runners-up 1927–28, 1949–50; Division 4 – Champions 1986–87; Runners-up 1975–76. *FA Cup* best season: 5th rd, 1933–34, 1949–50, 1969–70. *Football League Cup* best season: 5th rd, 1964–65, 1966–67.

Colours: Claret shirts white shoulders, white shorts claret triangle, claret stockings white tops. **Change colours:** Dark blue shirts blue trim, dark blue shorts white triangle, dark blue stockings white tops.

NORTHAMPTON TOWN 1988–89 LEAGUE RECORD

Match No.	Date	Venue	Opponents	Result		H/T Score	Lg. Pos.	Goalscorers	Attendance
1	Aug 27	A	Mansfield T	D	1-1	0-0	—	Donegal	4042
2	Sept 3	H	Brentford	W	1-0	1-0	7	Wilson	4488
3	10	A	Notts Co	W	1-0	0-0	3	Culpin	6084
4	17	H	Chesterfield	W	3-0	2-0	1	Adcock 3	4520
5	20	A	Sheffield U	L	0-4	0-2	—		11,904
6	24	H	Bristol R	L	1-2	0-0	8	Adcock	3886
7	Oct 1	H	Aldershot	W	6-0	1-0	5	Culpin 3, Gilbert, Adcock 2	3477
8	4	A	Blackpool	L	1-3	0-1	—	Gilbert	3034
9	8	H	Huddersfield T	L	1-3	0-3	8	Singleton	3975
10	15	A	Swansea C	L	0-1	0-1	15		4583
11	22	H	Bristol C	L	1-3	1-0	17	McGoldrick	3668
12	25	A	Fulham	L	2-3	1-1	—	Sandeman, Adcock	4644
13	29	H	Reading	L	1-3	0-2	18	McGoldrick	4355
14	Nov 5	A	Wigan Ath	W	3-1	2-1	17	Berry, Adcock, Culpin	2472
15	8	H	Port Vale	L	1-3	1-1	—	Culpin	3796
16	12	A	Cardiff C	L	0-1	0-1	18		3280
17	26	A	Bolton W	L	1-2	1-0	19	Culpin	4446
18	Dec 4	H	Wolverhampton W	W	3-1	2-1	—	Williams, Thomas, Adcock	6494
19	18	H	Gillingham	L	1-2	0-0	—	Gilbert	3829
20	26	A	Southend U	L	1-2	1-2	20	Adcock	5034
21	31	A	Chester C	L	1-2	1-0	20	Culpin	2733
22	Jan 2	H	Preston NE	W	1-0	0-0	21	Thomas	4219
23	7	H	Bury	W	2-0	1-0	16	Culpin, Sandeman	3463
24	14	A	Brentford	L	0-2	0-2	19		6043
25	21	H	Notts Co	L	1-3	0-1	20	Adcock	3704
26	28	A	Chesterfield	D	1-1	1-0	20	Craig	3920
27	Feb 4	A	Aldershot	L	1-5	1-3	21	Wignall (og)	2244
28	11	H	Blackpool	W	4-2	2-1	20	Gilbert 2(1 pen), Adcock, Berry	3303
29	18	A	Huddersfield T	W	2-1	1-1	18	Gilbert (pen), Culpin	5802
30	25	H	Swansea C	W	1-0	0-0	17	Thomas	3900
31	28	H	Fulham	W	2-1	2-1	—	Gilbert, Thomas	3948
32	Mar 4	A	Bristol C	L	1-3	0-3	16	Walsh (og)	7197
33	11	H	Wigan Ath	D	1-1	0-0	17	Adcock	3443
34	15	A	Reading	D	1-1	1-1	—	McPherson	3746
35	18	H	Mansfield T	W	2-1	0-1	15	Thomas, Donald	2821
36	25	A	Preston NE	L	2-3	1-1	16	Thomas, Adcock	9137
37	27	H	Southend U	D	2-2	0-0	16	Adcock, Culpin	3707
38	Apr 1	A	Gillingham	L	0-1	0-0	17		3466
39	4	A	Bury	W	1-0	1-0	—	Quow	1965
40	8	H	Chester C	L	0-2	0-0	17		2845
41	15	H	Sheffield U	L	1-2	1-1	19	McPherson	5030
42	22	A	Bristol R	D	1-1	1-0	19	Adcock	5568
43	29	H	Cardiff C	W	3-0	1-0	17	Thomas 2, Berry	3194
44	May 1	A	Port Vale	W	2-1	1-0	16	Culpin, Thomas	6604
45	6	A	Wolverhampton W	L	2-3	0-2	16	Wilcox, Donegal	15,259
46	13	H	Bolton W	L	2-3	2-0	20	Adcock, Culpin	3655

Final League Position: 20

GOALSCORERS

League (66): Adcock 17, Culpin 13, Thomas 9, Gilbert 7 (2 pens), Berry 3, Donegal 2, McGoldrick 2, McPherson 2, Sandeman 2, Craig 1, Donald 1, Quow 1, Singleton 1, Wilcox 1, Williams 1, Wilson 1, own goals 2.
Littlewoods Cup (7): Adcock 2, Culpin 2, Gilbert 1 (pen), Singleton 1, Wilson 1.
FA Cup (1): Berry 1.

Littlewoods Cup	First Round	Colchester U (a)	0-0
		(h)	5-0
	Second Round	Charlton Ath (h)	1-1
		(a)	1-2
FA Cup	First Round	Swansea C (a)	1-3

Gleasure	Reed	Thomas	Donald	McGoldrick	McPherson	Singleton	Longhurst	Gilbert	Adcock	Donegal	Wilson	Sanderman	Flexney	Culpin	Garwood	Cobb	Johnson	Blair	Berry	Williams	Preece	Anderson	Bodley	Quow	Craig	Collins	Wilcox	*Match No.*
1	2	3	4	5	6	7	8†	9*	10	11	12	14																1
1	6	3	4	2		7		9	10	11*	8		5	12														2
1	6	3	4	2		7		9	10				5	8	11													3
1	6	3	4	2		7		9	10				5	8	11													4
1	6	3	4	2		7		9	10	14	12		5*	8	11†													5
1	6	3	4	2		7		9	10	12			5	8*	11													6
1		3	4	2	6	7		9	10		12		5	8	11*													7
1		3	4	2	6	7	12	9	10		11†	14	5	8*														8
1		3	4	2	6	7		9	10	8†	11*	14	5		12													9
1	5*	3	4	2	6	7		9	10	8	12	14				11†												10
1	8†	3	4	2	6	7		9	10		12	11*	5				14											11
1		3	4	2	6			9	10		11	7		8			5											12
1		3	4*	2	6			9	10			12	5	8				7	11									13
1		3	4	2	6*			9	10		11		5	8				12	7									14
1		3	4		6			9	10		11	7		8			5		2									15
1		3	4†	2	6			9	10		11*	14		8				12	7	5								16
1		3	4	11	6			9	10				5	8					7	2								17
1		3	4	5	6			9	10		11			8					7	2								18
1		3	4	5	6			9	10	12	11	7*		8†					2		14							19
1		3		5	6			9	10	12	4	7		8*					2			11						20
1		3	4	5	6			9	10		7			8					2			11						21
1		3	4	5	6			9	10		7			8					2			11						22
1		3	4	5	6			9	10		7	12		8					2			11*						23
1		3	4		6			9†	10		7	12		8*					11	2			5	14				24
1			4		6			9*	10		3			8					11	2		12	5	7				25
1		4			6				10		3*	12		8					11	2			5	9	7			26
1		4			6			8	10		3	12							11	2†			5	9	7*	14		27
1					6			9	10		3	4		8					11	2			5	7				28
1					6			9	10		3	4		8					11	2			5	7				29
1		4			6			9	10		3			8					11	2			5	7				30
1		4			6			9	10		3								11	2			5	7		8		31
1		4			6			9	10		3	14		12					11	2			5†	7		8*		32
1		4			6			9	10		3	5*		12					11	2				7		8		33
1		4	5		6			9	10		3			8					11	2				7				34
1		4	5		6			9	10		3			8*					11	2				7		12		35
1		4	5		6				10		3								11	2			8	7			9	36
1		4	5		6				10		3	14		12					11	2			8	7†			9*	37
1		4	5		6				10		3†	14		7*					11	2			8			12	9	38
1		4	5		6				10					8					11	2			3	7			9	39
1		4	5		6				10					8*					11	2			3	7		12	9	40
1		4	5		6				10		14			12					11	2			3†	7		8*	9	41
1		4	5		6				10		11			12					8	2*			3	7			9	42
1		4	5		6				10		11			8					7	2			3				9	43
1		4	5		6				10		11			8					7	2			3				9	44
1		4	5		6				10	12	11	14		8					7†	2			3*				9	45
1		4	5		6				10		11			8					7	2			3				9	46
46	8	43	37	22	41	11	1 + 1s	34	46	4 + 5s	33 + 6s	8 + 14s	12	33 + 6s	5 + 1s	1	2 + 1s	1 + 2s	34	26	— + 1s	4 + 1s	20	17 + 1s	2	4 + 4s	11	

NORTHAMPTON TOWN

Player and Position	Ht	Wt	Birth Date	Birth Place	Source	Clubs	League App	League Gls
Goalkeepers								
Peter Gleasure	5 11	12 13	8 10 60	Luton	Apprentice	Millwall	55	—
						Northampton T (loan)	11	—
						Northampton T	271	—
Defenders								
Mickey Bodley	5 11	12 00	14 9 67	Hayes	Apprentice	Chelsea	6	1
						Northampton T	20	—
Lee Carter‡	5 10	11 10	22 3 70	Dartford	Trainee	Northampton T	1	—
Paul Flexney (To Kilmarnock Dec 1988)	6 1	11 12	18 1 65	Glasgow	John Bosco School	Clyde	203	13
						Northampton T	12	—
Ian Johnson‡			14 2 69	Newcastle	Gateshead	Northampton T	3	—
Keith McPherson	5 11	10 11	11 9 63	Greenwich	Apprentice	West Ham U	1	—
						Cambridge U (loan)	11	1
						Northampton T	139	7
Graham Reed‡	5 11	12 06	24 6 61	Doncaster	Apprentice	Barnsley	3	—
					Frickley Ath	Northampton T	112	2
Dean Thomas	5 9	11 08	19 12 61	Bedworth	Nuneaton Bor	Wimbledon	57	8
					Dusseldorf	Northampton	43	9
Les Webster*			20 2 66	Newcastle-upon-Tyne		Northampton T	—	—
Russell Wilcox	6 0	11 10	25 3 64	Hemsworth	Apprentice	Doncaster R	1	—
						Cambridge U	—	—
					Frickley	Northampton T	92	6
Wayne Williams	5 11	11 09	17 11 63	Telford	Apprentice	Shrewsbury T	221	7
						Northampton T	26	1
Paul Wilson	5 10	10 12	2 8 68	Bradford	Trainee	Huddersfield T	15	—
						Norwich C	—	—
						Northampton T	54	2
Midfield								
Steve Berry	5 7	11 06	4 4 63	Gosport	Apprentice	Portsmouth	28	2
						Aldershot (loan)	7	—
						Sunderland	35	2
						Newport Co	60	6
						Swindon T	4	—
						Aldershot	48	6
						Northampton T	34	3
Andy Blair‡	5 8	10 06	18 12 59	Kirkcaldy	Apprentice	Coventry C	93	6
						Aston Villa	34	—
						Wolverhampton W (loan)	10	—
						Sheffield W	58	3
						Aston Villa	20	1
						Barnsley (loan)	6	—
						Northampton T	3	—
Warren Donald	5 7	10 01	7 10 64	Uxbridge	Apprentice	West Ham U	2	—
						Northampton T (loan)	11	2
						Northampton T	150	9
Trevor Quow	5 7	10 12	28 9 60	Peterborough	Apprentice	Peterborough U	203	17
						Gillingham	79	3
						Northampton T	18	1
Bradley Sandeman	5 10	10 08	24 2 70	Northampton	Trainee	Northampton T	24	2
Martin Singleton	5 10	11 00	2 8 63	Banbury	Apprentice	Coventry C	23	1
						Bradford C	71	3
						WBA	19	1
						Northampton T	40	4

NORTHAMPTON TOWN

Foundation: Formed in 1897 by school teachers connected with the Northampton and District Elementary Schools' Association, they survived a financial crisis at the end of their first year when they were £675 in the red and became members of the Midland League – a fast move indeed for a new club. They achieved Southern League membership in 1901.

Managers (and Secretary-managers)
Arthur Jones 1897–1907*, Herbert Chapman 1907–12, Walter Bull 1912–13, Fred Lessons 1913–19, Bob Hewison 1920–25, Jack Tresadern 1925–30, Jack English 1931–35, Syd Puddefoot 1935–37, Warney Cresswell 1937–39, Tom Smith 1939–49, Bob Dennison 1949–54, Dave Smith 1954–59, David Bowen 1959–67, Tony Marchi 1967–68, Ron Flowers 1968–69, Dave Bowen 1969–72 (continued as GM and secretary to 1985 when joined the board), Billy Baxter 1972–73, Bill Dodgin Jnr 1973–76, Pat Crerand 1976–77, Bill Dodgin Jnr 1977, John Petts 1977–78, Mike Keen 1978–79, Clive Walker 1979–80, Bill Dodgin Jnr 1980–82, Clive Walker 1982–84, Tony Barton 1984–85, Graham Carr 1985– .

Player and Position	Ht	Wt	Birth Date	Birth Place	Source	Clubs	League App	League Gls
Forwards								
Tony Adcock	5 10	12 04	27 2 63	Bethnal Green	Apprentice	Colchester U	210	98
						Manchester C	15	5
						Northampton T	64	27
Darren Collins			24 5 67	Winchester	Petersfield U	Northampton T	8	—
Paul Culpin	5 10	11 10	8 2 62	Kirby Muxloe		Leicester C	—	—
					Nuneaton	Coventry C	9	2
						Northampton T	59	23
Glenville Donegal	6 2	12 08	20 6 69		Trainee	Northampton T	19	3
Andy Preece‡			27 3 67	Evesham		Northampton T	1	—

Trainees

Barrett, James D.A; Bell, Michael; Bone, Chad; Carlin, Scott; Carlisle, Robert E; Carr, Matthew J; Douglas, Michael J; Downing, Mark J; Graham, Christopher A; Hall, Stephen J; Hays, Gary S; Hogg, Michael A; Peaks, Andrew M; Proud, Andrew J; Shearman, Robert M; Stewart, Richard L; Tarry, Matthew C; Watson, Cameron O.

Associated Schoolboys

Ashdjian, John; Deacon, Jan; Kiernan, Daniel J; Kitching, Lee; Knight, Stuart A; Lamb, Paul D; Scrimshire, John A; Stembridge, Adam D; Willis, Ian.

NORWICH CITY 1988–89 *Back row (left to right):* Alan Reeves, Ian Butterworth, Robert Rosario, Jon Sheffield, Bryan Gunn, Andy Linighan, Mike Phelan, Andy Townsend.
Centre row: Tim Sheppard (Physiotherapist), Malcolm Allen, Jeremy Goss, Dale Gordon, Simon Ratcliffe, Paul Cook, Ian Culverhouse, Andy Fensome, Mark Bowen, Dave Williams (Assistant Manager).
Front row: Mike Walker (Reserve Team Manager), Trevor Putney, Junior Soanes, Robert Fleck, Tony Flanagan, Ruel Fox, Ian Crook, Dave Stringer (Manager).

Division 1 NORWICH CITY

Carrow Road, Norwich NR1 1JE. Telephone Norwich (0603) 612131. Commercial Dept. (0603) 615011. Box Office (0603) 761661 and 616422. Clubcall: 0898 12 11 44.

Ground capacity: 26,408.

Record attendance: 43,984 v Leicester C, FA Cup 6th rd, 30 March, 1963.

Record receipts: £126,395 v West Ham U, FA Cup 6th rd replay, 22 March, 1989.

Pitch measurements: 114yd × 74yd.

President: G. C. Watling.

Chairman: Robert T. Chase JP. *Vice-Chairman:* J. A. Jones.

Directors: F. J. Kennedy, B. W. Lockwood, G. A. Paterson, A. Scholes DMS, IPFA.

Manager: Dave Stringer. *Coach:* Dave Williams.

Commercial Manager: Ray Cossey.

Physio: Tim Sheppard MCSP, SRP.

Secretary: A. R. W. Neville.

Year Formed: 1902. *Turned Professional:* 1905. *Ltd Co.:* 1905.

Club Nickname: 'The Canaries'.

Previous Grounds: 1902, Newmarket Road; 1908–35. The Nest, Rosary Road.

Record League Victory: 10-2 v Coventry C, Division 3 (S), 15 March 1930 – Jarvie; Hannah, Graham; Brown, O'Brien, Lochhead (1); Porter (1), Anderson, Hunt (5), Scott (2), Slicer (1).

Record Cup Victory: 8-0 v Sutton U, FA Cup, 4th rd, 28 January 1989 – Gunn; Culverhouse, Bowen, Butterworth, Linighan, Townsend (Crook), Gordon, Fleck (3), Allen (4), Phelan, Putney (1).

Record Defeat: 2-10 v Swindon T, Southern League, 5, September, 1908.

Most League Points (2 for a win): 64, Division 3 (S), 1950–51.

Most League Points (3 for a win): 84, Division 2, 1985–86.

Most League Goals: 99, Division 3(S), 1952–53.

Highest League Scorer in Season: Ralph Hunt, 31. Division 3 (S), 1955–56.

Most League Goals in Total Aggregate: Johnny Gavin, 122, 1945–54, 1955–58.

Most Capped Player: Martin O'Neill, 18 (64), Northern Ireland.

Most League Appearances: Ron Ashman, 590, 1947–64.

Record Transfer Fee Received: £1,000,000 from Manchester C.for Kevin Reeves, March 1980 and from Nottingham F for Justin Fashanu, August 1981, and from Everton for Dave Watson, August 1986.

Record Transfer Fee Paid: £500,000 to Glasgow Rangers for Robert Fleck, December 1987.

Football League Record: 1920 Original Member of Division 3; 1921 Division 3 (S): 1934–39 Division 2; 1946–60 Division 3; 1960–72 Division 2; 1972–74 Division 1; 1974–75 Division 2; 1975–81 Division 1; 1981–82 Division 2; 1982–85 Division 1; 1985–86 Division 2 1986 Division 1.

Honours: Football League: Division 1 best season: 5th, 1986–87; Division 2 – Champions 1971–72, 1985–86. Division 3 (S) – Champions 1933–34; Division 3 – Runners-up 1959–60. *FA Cup:* Semi-finals 1959, 1989. *Football League Cup:* Winners 1962, 1985; Runners-up 1973, 1975.

Colours: Yellow shirts green trim, green shorts yellow trim, yellow stockings. **Change Colours:** White shirts green trim, white shorts green trim, white stockings.

NORWICH CITY 1988–89 LEAGUE RECORD

Match No.	Date	Venue	Opponents	Result	H/T Score	Lg. Pos.	Goalscorers	Attendance
1	Aug 27	H	Nottingham F	W 2-1	2-0	—	Fleck, Bowen	13,488
2	Sept 3	A	Middlesbrough	W 3-2	2-1	4	Rosario, Fleck 2	18,259
3	10	H	QPR	W 1-0	0-0	2	Phelan	11,174
4	17	A	Newcastle U	W 2-0	1-0	1	Gordon, Fleck	22,801
5	24	H	Millwall	D 2-2	0-0	1	Crook, Rosario	16,616
6	Oct 1	H	Charlton Ath	L 1-3	1-1	2	Linighan	11,470
7	8	A	Derby Co	W 1-0	0-0	1	Wright (og)	14,117
8	22	H	Tottenham H	W 3-1	2-0	1	Rorario, Fleck, Linighan	20,330
9	26	A	Manchester U	W 2-1	0-0	—	Phelan, Townsend	36,998
10	29	H	Southampton	D 1-1	0-0	1	Fleck	14,808
11	Nov 5	A	Wimbledon	W 2-0	1-0	1	Linighan, Allen	5853
12	12	H	Sheffield W	D 1-1	1-0	1	Putney	14,353
13	19	A	Everton	D 1-1	0-0	1	Allen	28,118
14	26	H	Luton T	D 2-2	1-1	1	Johnson (og), Gordon	13,541
15	Dec 3	A	Aston Villa	L 1-3	1-1	1	Putney	19,653
16	10	H	Arsenal	D 0-0	0-0	1		23,069
17	17	A	Liverpool	W 1-0	0-0	1	Townsend	34,325
18	27	H	West Ham U	W 2-1	0-0	—	Gordon, Townsend	17,491
19	31	H	Middlesbrough	D 0-0	0-0	2		16,021
20	Jan 2	A	QPR	D 1-1	0-0	2	Taylor	12,410
21	14	H	Coventry C	L 1-2	0-0	2	Gordon	14,399
22	22	A	Millwall	W 3-2	2-2	—	Butterworth, Bowen, Fleck	13,687
23	Feb 4	A	Charlton Ath	W 2-1	0-0	2	Allen, Townsend	7518
24	11	H	Derby Co	W 1-0	0-0	2	Fleck	17,227
25	21	A	Tottenham H	L 1-2	0-1	—	Putney	19,120
26	25	H	Manchester U	W 2-1	2-0	2	Butterworth, Allen	23,155
27	Mar 11	H	Wimbledon	W 1-0	0-0	2	Putney	15,159
28	25	H	Newcastle U	L 0-2	0-1	2		22,440
29	27	A	West Ham U	W 2-0	0-0	2	Linighan, Allen	27,265
30	Apr 1	H	Liverpool	L 0-1	0-1	3		26,338
31	5	A	Nottingham F	L 0-2	0-2	—		19,872
32	8	A	Coventry C	L 1-2	1-1	3	Fleck	12,740
33	19	A	Southampton	D 0-0	0-0	—		14,403
34	22	H	Aston Villa	D 2-2	0-0	3	Coney, Townsend	14,550
35	May 1	A	Arsenal	L 0-5	0-2	3		28,449
36	6	H	Everton	W 1-0	0-0	3	Gordon	13,239
37	13	A	Luton T	L 0-1	0-0	4		10,862
38	17	A	Sheffield W	D 2-2	0-0	—	Rosario, Fleck	16,238

Final League Position: 4

GOALSCORERS

League (48): Fleck 10, Allen 5, Gordon 5, Townsend 5, Linighan 4, Putney 4, Rosario 4, Bowen 2, Butterworth 2, Phelan 2, Coney 1, Crook 1, Taylor 1, own goals 2.
Littlewoods Cup (5): Rosario 2, Crook 1, Fleck 1, Gordon 1.
FA Cup (17): Allen 7 (1 pen), Fleck 4, Gordon 2, Townsend 2, Putney 1, own goal 1.

Littlewoods Cup	Second Round	Preston NE (h)	2-0
		(a)	3-0
	Third Round	Leicester C (a)	0-2
FA Cup	Third Round	Port Vale (a)	3-1
	Fourth Round	Sutton (h)	8-0
	Fifth Round	Sheffield U (h)	3-2
	Sixth Round	West Ham U (a)	0-0
		(h)	3-1
	Semi-Final	Everton (at Villa Park)	0-1

Gunn	Culverhouse	Bowen	Butterworth	Linighan	Crook	Gordon	Fleck	Rosario	Phelan	Putney	Allen	Townsend	Fox	Taylor	Coney	Cook	Sheffield	*Match No.*
1	2	3	4	5	6	7	8*	9	10	11	12							1
1	2	3	4	5	6	7†	8*	9	10	11	12	14						2
1	2	3	4	5	6*	7	8	9	10	11		12						3
1	2	3	4	5	6	7	8	9*	10	11	12							4
1	2	3	4	5	6	7	8	9	10	11*		12						5
1	2	3†	4	5	6	7	8*	9	10	11	12	14						6
1	2	3	4	5	6†	7	8*	9	10	11	12	14						7
1	2	3	4	5	6	7	8	9	10			11						8
1	2	3	4	5	6*	7	8	9	10			11	12					9
1	2	3	4	5	6	7	8	9	10			11*	12					10
1	2	3	4	5		7	8*	9	10	11	12	6						11
1	2	3	4	5		7	8*		10	11	9	6		12				12
1	2	3	4	5		7	8*		10	11	9	6		12				13
1	2	3	4	5		7	8	12	10	11	9*	6						14
1	2	3	4	5	14	7†	8*	12	10	11	9	6						15
1	2	3	4	5		7	8*	9	10	11	12	6						16
1	2	3		5	4	7	8	9	10	11		6						17
1	2	3	12	5	4	7	8	9	10	11		6*						18
1	2	3	14	5	4	7	8*	9	10	11†		6		12				19
1	2	3	4	5†	6	7	12	9*	10	14		11		8				20
1	2	3	4	5		7	8	9	10	11		6						21
1	2	3	4	5		7	8	9	10	11		6						22
1	2	3	4	5		7	8		10	11	9	6						23
1	2	3*	4	5	12	7	8		10	11	9	6						24
1	2	3	4*	5	12	7		8	10	11	9	6						25
1	2	3	4	5		7		8	10	11	9	6						26
1	2	3	4	5		7		8	10	11	9	6						27
1	2†	3	4	5	14	7	12	8*	10	11	9	6						28
1	2	3	4	5	14	7	8*		10†	11	9	6			12			29
1	2	3	4	5		7	12		10	11	9*	6			8			30
1	2†	3	4	5	14	7	12		10	11	9*	6			8			31
1	2	3	4	5	12	7	9		10*	11		6			8			32
1	2		4	5	10	7			12	3*	9	6	11†		8	14		33
	2	3	4	5	10	7*			11		9	6	12		8		1	34
1	2	3	4	5		7	8		10	11		6			9			35
1	2		4	5*	3	7	8	9	10	12		6				11		36
1	2		4		3	7*	8	9	10†	5	12	6			14	11		37
1	2	3	4	5	10	7	8	9				6				11		38
37	38	35	35 + 2s	37	19 + 7s	38	29 + 4s	25 + 2s	36 + 1s	31 + 2s	15 + 8s	31 + 5s	1 + 3s	1 + 3s	6 + 2s	3 + 1s	1	

NORWICH CITY

Player and Position	Ht	Wt	Birth Date	Birth Place	Source	Clubs	League App	League Gls
Goalkeepers								
Bryan Gunn	6 2	13 13	22 12 63	Thurso	Invergordon BC	Aberdeen	15	—
						Norwich C	104	—
Jon Sheffield	5 11	11 07	1 2 69	Bedworth		Norwich C	1	—
Defenders								
Mark Bowen	5 8	11 13	7 12 63	Neath	Apprentice	Tottenham H	17	2
						Norwich C	59	3
Ian Butterworth	6 1	12 10	25 1 64	Nantwich	Apprentice	Coventry C	90	—
						Nottingham F	27	—
						Norwich C	100	2
Ian Culverhouse	5 10	11 02	22 9 64	B Stortford	Apprentice	Tottenham H	2	—
						Norwich C	126	—
Tony Flanagan*			28 10 69	London	Trainee	Norwich C	—	—
Mike Flynn	6 0	11 00	23 2 69	Oldham	Trainee	Oldham Ath	40	1
						Norwich C	—	—
Andy Linighan	6 3	12 06	18 8 62	Hartlepool	Smiths BC	Hartlepool U	110	4
						Leeds U	66	3
						Oldham Ath	87	6
						Norwich C	49	6
John O'Neill (Retired)	6 0	13 00	11 3 58	Derry	Derry ABC	Leicester C	313	10
						QPR	2	—
						Norwich C	1	—
Alan Reeves	6 0	12 00	19 11 67	Birkenhead		Norwich C	—	—
						Gillingham (loan)	18	—
Midfield								
Paul Cook	5 11	10 10	22 2 67	Liverpool		Wigan Ath	83	14
						Norwich C	4	—
Ian Crook	5 8	10 06	18 1 63	Romford	Apprentice	Tottenham H	20	1
						Norwich C	82	7
Andy Fensome*	5 8	11 02	18 2 69	Northampton	Trainee	Norwich C	—	—
						Newcastle U (loan)	—	—
Dale Gordon	5 10	11 08	9 1 67	Gt Yarmouth	Apprentice	Norwich C	129	17
Jeremy Goss	5 9	10 09	11 5 65	Cyprus	Amateur	Norwich C	29	2
Mike Phelan	5 11	11 01	24 9 62	Nelson	Apprentice	Burnley	168	9
						Norwich C	156	9
Trevor Putney	5 7	10 11	11 2 61	Harold Hill	Brentwood W	Ipswich T	103	8
						Norwich C	82	9
Doug Soanes‡			10 4 70	Ipswich	Trainee	Norwich C	—	—
Andy Townsend	5 11	12 07	23 7 63	Maidstone	Weymouth	Southampton	83	5
						Norwich C	36	5
David Williams†	5 10	11 08	11 3 55	Cardiff	Clifton Ath	Bristol R	352	66
						Norwich C	60	11
Forwards								
Malcolm Allen	5 8	10 06	21 3 67	Deiniolen	Apprentice	Watford	39	5
						Aston Villa (loan)	4	—
						Norwich C	23	5
Dean Coney	6 0	13 04	18 9 63	Dagenham	Apprentice	Fulham	211	56
						QPR	48	7
						Norwich C	8	1
Kevin Drinkell (To Rangers, Aug 1988)	5 11	12 06	18 8 60	Grimsby	Apprentice	Grimsby T	270	89
						Norwich C	121	50

NORWICH CITY

Foundation: Formed in 1902, largely through the initiative of two local schoolmasters who called a meeting at the Criterion Cafe, they were shocked by an FA Commission which in 1904 declared the club professional and ejected them from the FA Amateur Cup. However, this only served to strengthen their determination. New officials were appointed and a professional club established at a meeting in the Agricultural Hall in March 1905.

Managers (and Secretary-managers)
John Bowman 1905–07, James McEwen 1907–08, Arthur Turner 1909–10, Bert Stansfield 1910–15, Major Frank Buckley 1919–20, Charles O'Hagan 1920–21, Albert Gosnell 1921–26, Bert Stansfield 1926, Cecil Potter 1926–29, James Kerr 1929–33, Tom Parker 1933–37, Bob Young 1937–39, Jimmy Jewell 1939, Bob Young 1939–45, Cyril Spiers 1946–47, Duggie Lochhead 1945–50, Norman Low 1950–55, Tom Parker 1955–57, Archie Macaulay 1957–61, Willie Reid 1961–62, George Swindin 1962, Ron Ashman 1962–66, Lol Morgan 1966–69, Ron Saunders 1969–73, John Bond 1973–80, Ken Brown 1980–87, Dave Stringer 1987– .

Player and Position	*Ht*	*Wt*	*Birth Date*	*Birth Place*	*Source*	*Clubs*	*League App*	*League Gls*
Robert Fleck	5 8	11 08	11 8 65	Glasgow	Possil Y M	Partick Th	2	1
						Rangers	85	29
						Norwich C	51	17
Ruel Fox	5 6	10 00	14 1 68	Ipswich	Apprentice	Norwich C	41	2
Robert Rosario	6 3	12 01	4 3 66	Hammersmith	Hillingdon Bor	Norwich C	86	13
						Wolverhampton W (loan)	2	1
Alan Taylor	5 9	10 06	14 11 53	Hinckley	Morecambe	Rochdale	55	7
						West Ham U	98	25
						Norwich C	24	5
					Vancouver W	Cambridge U	8	2
					Vancouver W	Hull C	14	3
						Burnley	64	23
						Bury	62	10
						Norwich C	4	1

Trainees

Batty, Jason A; Carey, Neil; Cochrane, Gary S; Daines, Paul J; Gill, Darren; Hunt, Martin; Ikin, Brian; Ling, Marcus R; May, Adam C; Minett, Jason K; Notton, Simon P; Pauling, Gavin J; Pennock, Adrian B; Power, Lee M; Roberts, Mark G; Rocastle, Stephen O; Smith, David; Sutch, Daryl; Taylor, Robert A; Ullathorne, Robert.

****Non-Contract**

Williams, David M.

Associated Schoolboys

Akinbiyi, Adelola; Bowden, Scott R; Brown, Nicholas J; Cleveland, Darren L; Collins, Sean C; Cousin, Scott; Ewens, David T; Hamilton, John T; Harley, Nathan P; Hayes, Marc G; Hazelwood, Philip; Herd, Stuart A.L; Johnson, Andrew; King, Benjamin; Loss, Colin P; Mortimer, Philip D; Rule, Keith C; Southon, Jamie P; Sinclair, Colin N.

NOTTINGHAM FOREST 1988–89 *Back row (left to right)*: Brian Laws, Gary Fleming, Garry Parker, Stephen Chettle, Darren Wassall, Brian Rice, Stephen Hodge.
Centre row: Liam O'Kane (Coach), Tommy Gaynor, Terry Wilson, Stephen Sutton, Hans Segers, Colin Foster, Neil Webb, Brian Clough (Manager).
Front row: Nigel Clough, Lee Glover, Des Walker, Stuart Pearce (Captain), Franz Carr, Gary Crosby.

Division 1 NOTTINGHAM FOREST

City Ground, Nottingham NG2 5FJ. Telephone Nottingham (0602) 822202. Information Desk: 821122.

Commercial Manager: 820444.

Ground capacity: 35,417 (14,789 seats).

Record attendance:49,945 v Manchester U, Division 1, 28 Oct. 1967.

Record receipts: £163,000 v Bristol C, Littlewoods Cup, Semi-final 1st leg, 15 February, 1989

Pitch measurements: 115 × 78yd.

Chairman: M. Roworth. ***Vice Chairman:*** F. T. C. Pell FCA.

Directors: G. E. Macpherson JP, F. Reacher, J. F. Hickling, I. I. Korn, J. M. Smith, C. Wootton.

Manager: Brian Clough. ***Assistant Manager:*** Ron Fenton.

Secretary: P. White. ***Commercial Manager:*** Dave Pullan.

Coach: Liam O'Kane. ***Physio:*** G. Lyas.

Year Formed: 1865. ***Turned Professional:*** 1889. ***Ltd Co.:*** 1982.

Club Nickname: 'Reds'.

Previous Grounds: 1865, Forest Racecourse: 1879. The Meadows; 1880, Trent Bridge Cricket Ground; 1882, Parkside, Lenton; 1885, Gregory, Lenton; 1890. Town Grown; 1898, City Ground.

Record League Victory: 12-0 v Leicester Fosse, Division 1, 12 April 1909 – Iremonger; Dudley, Maltby; Hughes (1), Needham, Armstrong; Hooper (3), Marrison, West (3), Morris (2), Spouncer (3 incl. 1p).

Record Cup Victory: 14-0 v Clapton (away), FA Cup, 1st rd, 17 January 1891 – Brown: Earp, Scott; Smith (A), Russell, Jeacock; McCallum (2), 'Tich' Smith (1), Higgins (5), Lindley (4), Shaw (2).

Record Defeat: 1-9 v Blackburn R, Division 2, 10 April, 1937.

Most League Points (2 for a win): 70, Division 3 (S), 1950–51.

Most League Points (3 for a win): 74, Division 1, 1983–84.

Most League Goals: 110, Division 3 (S), 1950–51.

Highest League Scorer in Season: Wally Ardron. 36, Division 3(S), 1950–51.

Most League Goals in Total Aggregate: Grenville Morris, 199, 1898–1913.

Most Capped Player: Martin O'Neill, 36 (64), Northern Ireland.

Most League Appearances: Bob McKinlay, 614, 1951–70.

Record Transfer Fee Received: £1,250,000 from Manchester U for Garry Birtles, October 1980.

Record Transfer Fee Paid: £1,250,000 to Coventry C for Ian Wallace, July 1980.

Football League Record: 1892 Elected to Division 1; 1906–07 Division 2; 1907–11 Division 1; 1911–22 Division 2; 1922–25 Division 1; 1925–49 Division 2; 1949–51 Division 3 (S); 1951–57 Division 2; 1957–72 Division 1; 1972–77 Division 2; 1977– Division 1.

Honours: *Football League:* Division 1 – Champions 1977–78; Runners-up 1966–67, 1978–79, Division 2 – Champions 1906–07, 1921–22. Runners-up 1956–57; Division 3 (S) – Champions 1950–51. *FA Cup:* Winners 1898, 1959. *Anglo-Scottish Cup:* Winners 1976–77, *Football League Cup:* Winners 1977–78, 1978–79, 1988–89; Runners-up 1979–80. *Simod Cup:* Winners 1989.**European Competitions:** *Fairs Cup:* 1961–62, 1967–68. *European Cup:* 1978–79 (winners), 1979–80 (winners), 1980–81. *Super Cup:* 1979–80 (winners), 1980–81 (runners-up). *World Club Championship:* 1980–81 (runners-up). *UEFA Cup:* 1983–84, 1984–85.

Colours: Red shirts, white shorts, red stockings. **Change colours:** White shirts, black shorts, white stockings.

NOTTINGHAM FOREST 1988–89 LEAGUE RECORD

Match No.	*Date*	*Venue*	*Opponents*	*Result*		*H/T Score*	*Lg. Pos.*	*Goalscorers*	*Attendance*
1	Aug 27	A	Norwich C	L	1-2	0-2	—	Chettle	13,488
2	Sept 3	H	Sheffield W	D	1-1	1-0	13	Worthington (og)	18,963
3	10	A	Everton	D	1-1	1-0	14	Webb	34,003
4	17	H	Derby Co	D	1-1	0-0	14	Foster	24,818
5	24	A	Aston Villa	D	1-1	0-1	14	Carr	23,029
6	Oct 1	H	Luton T	D	0-0	0-0	16		15,340
7	8	A	QPR	W	2-1	1-1	11	Clough (pen), Foster	11,205
8	22	A	Millwall	D	2-2	1-0	14	Hodge 2	16,874
9	26	H	Liverpool	W	2-1	0-0	—	Rice, Webb	29,755
10	29	A	Newcastle U	W	1-0	0-0	5	Chapman	24,765
11	Nov 6	H	Arsenal	L	1-4	1-1	—	Clough	19,038
12	12	A	West Ham U	D	3-3	3-2	9	Clough 2, Hodge	21,682
13	19	H	Coventry C	D	0-0	0-0	9		17,250
14	26	A	Charlton Ath	W	1-0	1-0	8	Pearce	6411
15	Dec 3	H	Middlesbrough	D	2-2	0-0	10	Chapman 2	17,742
16	10	A	Southampton	D	1-1	0-1	9	Clough	15,259
17	18	H	Wimbledon	L	0-1	0-0	—		16,427
18	26	A	Manchester U	L	0-2	0-1	12		39,582
19	31	A	Sheffield W	W	3-0	3-0	10	Gaynor, Webb, Hodge	20,407
20	Jan 2	H	Everton	W	2-0	1-0	8	Parker, Gaynor	26,008
21	15	A	Tottenham H	W	2-1	2-1	—	Parker, Clough	16,903
22	21	H	Aston Villa	W	4-0	1-0	5	Hodge, Pearce, Parker, Laws	22,662
23	Feb 4	A	Luton T	W	3-2	2-2	4	Parker, Clough 2(1 pen)	10,465
24	11	H	QPR	D	0-0	0-0	4		19,690
25	Mar 11	A	Arsenal	W	3-1	3-1	5	Clough, Carr, Pearce	39,639
26	15	H	Newcastle U	D	1-1	1-0	—	Clough (pen)	20,800
27	22	H	Tottenham H	L	1-2	0-0	—	Parker	23,098
28	25	A	Derby Co	W	2-0	1-0	5	Hodge, Chapman	25,174
29	27	H	Manchester U	W	2-0	1-0	5	Pearce, Chapman	30,092
30	Apr 1	A	Wimbledon	L	1-4	1-2	5	Clough	7867
31	5	H	Norwich C	W	2-0	2-0	—	Clough, Pearce	19,872
32	12	H	Southampton	W	3-0	2-0	—	Clough (pen), Pearce, Gaynor	18,948
33	22	A	Middlesbrough	W	4-3	2-1	4	Webb, Chapman 2, Parker	20,778
34	May 3	H	Millwall	W	4-1	1-0	—	Gaynor, Hodge, Wood (og), Parker	15,928
35	10	A	Liverpool	L	0-1	0-0	—		39,793
36	13	H	Charlton Ath	W	4-0	3-0	3	Carr, Wilson, Webb, Chettle	17,637
37	15	A	Coventry C	D	2-2	0-0	—	Webb, Clough	14,003
38	18	H	West Ham U	L	1-2	1-2	—	Chapman	20,843

Final League Position: 3

GOALSCORERS

League (64): Clough 14 (4 pens), Chapman 8, Hodge 7, Parker 7, Pearce 6, Webb 6, Gaynor 4, Carr 3, Chettle 2, Foster 2, Laws 1, Rice 1, Wilson 1, own goals 2.

Littlewoods Cup (25): Clough 7 (2 pens), Chapman 5, Gaynor 4, Hodge 2, Webb 2, Crosby 1, Foster 1, Parker 1, Pearce 1, own goal 1.

FA Cup (10); Chapman 3, Parker 2, Webb 2, Gaynor 1, Laws 1, own goal 1.

Littlewoods Cup	Second Round	Chester C (h)	6-0
		(a)	4-0
	Third Round	Coventry C (h)	3-2
	Fourth Round	Leicester C (a)	0-0
		(h)	2-1
	Fifth Round	QPR (h)	5-2
	Semi-Final	Bristol C (h)	1-1
		(a)	1-0
	Final	Luton T (at Wembley)	3-1
FA Cup	Third Round	Ipswich T (h)	3-0
	Fourth Round	Leeds U (h)	2-0
	Fifth Round	Watford (a)	3-0
	Sixth Round	Manchester U (a)	1-0
	Semi-Final	Liverpool	
		(at Hillsborough)	
		aband.	0-0
		(at Old Trafford)	1-3

Sutton	Chettle	Pearce	Walker	Foster	Wilson	Crosby	Webb	Clough	Hodge	Rice	Carr	Gaynor	Chapman	Crossley	Charles	Starbuck	Laws	Parker	Williams	*Match No.*
1	2	3	4	5	6	7	8	9	10	11*	12									1
1	2	3	4	5	6	7	8	9	10	11										2
1	2	3	4	5		7*	8	9	6	11	12	10								3
1	2	3	4	5		7	8	9	6	11	12	10*								4
1	2	3	4	5		7	8	9	6	11	12	10*								5
1	2	3	4	5		7	8	9	6	11	12	10*								6
1	2	3	4	5		11	8	9	6		7	10								7
1	2	3	4	5		7	8	9	6			11	10							8
	2	3	4	5		7	8	9	6	11			10	1						9
	2	3	4	5	12	7	8*	9	6	11			10	1						10
1	2	3	4	5	8			9	6	11			10		7*	12				11
1	2	3†	4	5	8	12		9	6	11			10*			7	14			12
1	2	3	4	5	12	7*	8	9	6	11			10							13
1	2	3	4	5	12		8	9	6	11			10*			7				14
1	2	3	4	5			8	9	6	11	7		10							15
1	4	3		5			8	9		11	7		10				2	6		16
1	2†		4	5			8	9	12	11	7		10				14	6*	3	17
1			4		5		8	9*	6	11	7	14	10†			12	2		3	18
1		3	4		5		8		6		7*	9	10			12	2	11		19
1		3	4		5		8		6		7*	9	10			12	2	11		20
1	12	3	4*		5		8	9	6		7		10				2	11		21
1	4	3			5	12	8	9	6		7*		10				2	11		22
1	4	3			5		8	9	6		7		10				2	11		23
1	4	3			5		8	9	6		7		10*			12	2	11		24
1		3	4		5		8	9	6		7		10				2	11		25
1		3	4		5		8	9	6		7		10				2	11		26
1		3	4		5		8	9	6		7		10				2	11		27
1	12	3	4		5		8	9	6			7*	10				2	11		28
1	12	3*	4		5		8	9	6			7	10				2	11		29
1	2	3	4		5		8	9	6			7	10					11		30
1	2	3	4	12	5		8	9	6			7	10*					11		31
1		3	4		5		8	9*	6	12		7	10				2	11		32
1	12	3	4		5		8	9	6			7*	10				2	11		33
1		3	4		5		8	9	6		7	10					2	11		34
1		3	4		5		8	9		6	7*	12	10				2	11		35
1	14	3	4		5		8	9		6	7	12	10*				2	11†		36
1		3	4		5		8	9		6	7		10				2	11		37
1	5	3	4				8	9	6			7	10				2	11		38
36	23 + 5s	36	34	17 + 1s	24 + 3s	11 + 2s	36	36	33 + 1s	19 + 1s	18 + 5s	16 + 3s	30	2	1	2 + 5s	20 + 2s	22	2	

NOTTINGHAM FOREST

Player and Position	*Ht*	*Wt*	*Birth Date*	*Birth Place*	*Source*	*Clubs*	*League App*	*League Gls*
Goalkeepers								
Mark Crossley	6 0	13 09	16 6 69	Barnsley		Nottingham F	2	—
Steve Sutton	6 1	13 07	16 4 61	Hartington	Apprentice	Nottingham F	169	—
						Mansfield T (loan)	8	—
						Derby Co (loan)	14	—
Defenders								
Craig Boardman			30 11 70	Barnsley	Trainee	Nottingham F	—	—
Russell Bradley			28 3 66	Birmingham		Nottingham F	—	—
						Hereford U (loan)	12	—
Gary Charles			13 4 70	London		Nottingham F	1	—
						Leicester C (loan)	8	—
Steve Chettle	6 1	12 00	27 9 68	Nottingham	Apprentice	Nottingham F	58	2
Jim Fleming	5 9	11 01	17 2 67	Londonderry	Apprentice	Nottingham F	74	—
Jason Fletcher†			29 9 69	Nottingham	Trainee	Nottingham F	—	—
Colin Foster	6 4	13 10	16 7 64	Chislehurst	Apprentice	Orient	174	10
						Nottingham F	66	5
Brian Laws	5 10	11 05	14 10 61	Wallsend	Apprentice	Burnley	125	12
						Huddersfield T	56	1
						Middlesbrough	107	12
						Nottingham F	22	1
Stuart Pearce	5 10	12 09	24 4 62	Shepherds Bush	Wealdstone	Coventry C	51	4
						Nottingham F	139	18
Kevin Sharp			1 11 70	Stapleford	Trainee	Nottingham F	—	—
Des Walker	5 11	11 03	26 11 65	Hackney	Apprentice	Nottingham F	156	—
Darren Wassall	5 11	11 09	27 6 68	Edgbaston		Nottingham F	3	—
						Hereford U (loan)	5	—
						Bury (loan)	7	1
Brett Williams	5 10	11 11	19 3 68	Dudley	Apprentice	Nottingham F	20	—
						Stockport Co (loan)	2	—
						Northampton T (loan)	4	—
Midfield								
Anthony Abrahams†			8 12 69	Liverpool	Trainee	Nottingham F	—	—
Martin Clark	5 9	10 11	13 10 68	Uddington	Hamilton A	Clyde	26	—
						Nottingham F	—	—
Gary Crosby			8 5 64	Sleaford	Lincoln U	Lincoln C	7	—
					Grantham	Nottingham F	27	1
Sean Dyche			28 6 71	Kettering	Trainee	Nottingham F	—	—
Steve Hodge	5 7	9 12	25 10 62	Nottingham	Apprentice	Nottingham F	123	30
						Aston Villa	53	12
						Tottenham H	45	7
						Nottingham F	34	7
Garry Parker	5 8	11 00	7 9 65	Oxford	Apprentice	Luton T	42	3
						Hull C	84	8
						Nottingham F	24	7
Brian Rice	6 0	11 10	11 10 63	Glasgow	Whitburn Central	Hibernian	84	11
						Nottingham F	72	7
						Grimsby T (loan)	4	—
						WBA (loan)	3	—
Steven Stone			20 8 71	Gateshead	Trainee	Nottingham F	—	—
Neil Webb	6 0	13 00	30 7 63	Reading	Apprentice	Reading	72	22
						Portsmouth	123	34
						Nottingham F	146	47
Terry Wilson	6 0	10 10	8 2 69	Broxburn	Apprentice	Nottingham F	63	6

NOTTINGHAM FOREST

Foundation: One of the oldest football clubs in the world, Nottingham Forest was formed at a meeting in the Clinton Arms in 1865. Known originally as the Forest Football Club, the game which first drew the founders together was "shinney" a form of hockey. When they determined to change to football in 1865, one of their first moves was to buy a set of red caps to wear on the field.

Managers (and Secretary-managers)
Harry Radford 1889–97*, Harry Haslam 1897–1909*, Fred Earp 1909–12, Bob Masters 1912–25, John Baynes 1925–29, Stan Hardy 1930–31, Noel Watson 1931–36, Harold Wightman 1936–39, Billy Walker 1939–60, Andy Beattie 1960–63, John Carey 1963–68, Matt Gillies 1969–72, Dave Mackay 1972, Allan Brown 1973–75, Brian Clough 1975– .

Player and Position	Ht	Wt	Birth Date	Birth Place	Source	Clubs	League App	League Gls
Forwards								
Franz Carr	5 7	10 12	24 9 66	Preston	Apprentice	Blackburn R	—	—
						Nottingham F	104	14
Lee Chapman	6 3	13 00	5 12 59	Lincoln	Amateur	Stoke C	99	34
						Plymouth Arg (loan)	4	—
						Arsenal	23	4
						Sunderland	15	3
						Sheffield W	149	63
					Niort	Nottingham F	30	8
Nigel Clough	5 9	11 04	19 3 66	Sunderland	AC Hunters	Nottingham F	160	63
Michael Danzey			8 2 71	Widnes	Trainee	Nottingham F	—	—
Tommy Gaynor	6 1	13 02	29 1 63	Limerick	Limerick	Doncaster R	33	7
						Nottingham F	31	7
Lee Glover	5 10	12 01	24 4 70	Kettering	Trainee	Nottingham F	20	3
Mark Hurst			18 8 70	Derby	Trainee	Nottingham F	—	—
Nigel Jemson	5 10	11 10	10 8 69	Preston	Trainee	Preston NE	32	8
						Nottingham F	—	—
						Bolton W (loan)	5	—
						Preston NE (loan)	9	2
Alan Lamb			30 10 70	Gateshead		Nottingham F	—	—
						Hereford U (loan)	10	2
Stephen McLoughlin			21 11 69	Nottingham	Trainee	Nottingham F	—	—
Philip Starbuck	5 10	10 13	24 11 68	Nottingham	Apprentice	Nottingham F	22	2
						Birmingham C (loan)	3	—
Billy Stubbs*	5 11	12 00	1 8 66	Hartlepool		Nottingham F	—	—
						Doncaster R (loan)	9	1
						Grimsby T (loan)	7	2

Trainees
Ainslie, Christopher; Ashby, Nicholas R; Brown, Gary; Browne, Shaun M; Dunn, Colin F; Edwards, Alex D; Gemmill, Scot; Hodder, Steven J; Hope, Stephen F; Jarrett, Justin M; Mountford, Kearon J; Nevitt, Gary J; Stobart, Loy.

****Non-Contract**
Abrahams, Anthony J; Fletcher, Jason L.

Associated Schoolboys
Beale, John N; Bell, Stephen; Daykin, Simon M; Dowell, Wayne A; Drinkall, Gary K; Elliott, Andrew; Elliott, Andrew A; Fancutt, Martin S; Fowkes, Graham L; Hogg, Andrew K; Howe, Stephen; Jeffrey, Paul; Keay, Christopher J; Kilford, Ian A; Lewins, Kevin; McGregor, Paul A; Mitchell, Andrew; Pearce, Dale; Ransom, John P; Saunders, Darren; Simpson, Michael; Storer, Richard; Thomas, Spencer P; Thompson, Paul; Warner, Vance J; Yates, Luke.

NOTTS COUNTY 1988–89 *Back row (left to right):* Scott Machin, Wayne Fairclough, Paul Atkin, Mick Leonard, Aidan Davison, Navid Norton, Mark Draper, Tommy Johnson.
Centre row: John Barnwell (Manager), Mick Walker (Youth Coach), Nicky Law, Dean Yates, Paul Smalley, Gary Lund, Craig Jackson, David Kevan, Paul Hart (Player/Coach), John Newman (Assistant Manager).
Front row: Chris Withe, Ian McParland, Willie McStay, Garry Birtles, Geoff Pike, Donald O'Riordan, Gary Mills, Adrian Thorpe.

Division 3 NOTTS COUNTY

County Ground, Meadow Lane, Nottingham NG2 3HJ. Telephone Nottingham (0602) 861155. Clubcall: 0898 121101.

Ground capacity: 24,071.

Record attendance: 47,310 v York C, FA Cup 6th rd, 12 Mar, 1955.

Record receipts: £63,505 v Everton, FA Cup 6th rd, 10 March, 1984.

Pitch measurements: 114yd × 74yd.

Chairman: D. C. Pavis. ***Vice Chairman:*** J. Mounteney.

Directors: J. J. Dunnett, MA, LLM, W. A. Hopcroft.

Team Manager: Neil Warnock. ***Commerical Manager:*** Fiona Green.

Coach/Assistant Manager: John Newman.

Chief Executive: N. E. Hook, M.INST.M.

Physio: Wayne Jones.

Year Formed: 1862 *(*see Foundation*).

Turned Professional: 1885. ***Ltd Co.:*** 1888.

Previous Grounds: 1862, The Park; 1864, The Meadows; 1877, Beeston Cricket Ground: 1880, Castle Ground; 1883, Trent Bridge; 1910, Meadow Lane.

Club Nickanme: 'Magpies'.

Record League Victory: 11-1 v Newport C, Division 3 (S), 15 January 1949 – Smith; Southwell, Purvis; Gannon, Baxter, Adamson; Houghton (1), Sewell (4), Lawton (4), Pibley, Johnston (2).

Record Cup Victory: 15-0 v Rotherham T (at Trent Bridge), FA Cup, 1st rd, 24 October 1885 – Sherwin; Snook, H. T. Moore; Dobson (1), Emmett (1), Chapman; Gunn (1), Albert Moore (2), Jackson (3), Daft (2), Cursham (4). (1 og)

Record Defeat: 1-9 v Blackburn R, Division 1, 16 November, 1889 and v Aston Villa, Division 1, 29 September, 1888 and v Portsmouth, Division 2, 9 April, 1927.

Most League Points (2 for a win): 69, Division 4, 1970–71.

Most League Points (3 for a win): 81, Division 3, 1987–88.

Most League Goals: 107, Division 4, 1959–60.

Highest League Scorer in Season: Tom Keetley, 39, Division 3 (S), 1930–31.

Most League Goals in Total Aggregate: Les Bradd, 124, 1967–78.

Most Capped Player: Harry Cursham, 8, England.

Most League Appearances: Albert Iremonger, 564, 1904–26.

Record Transfer Fee Received: £350,000 from Tottenham H for John Chiedozie, August 1984.

Record Transfer Fee Paid: £600,000 to Orient for John Chiedozie, August 1981.

Football League Record: 1888 Founder Member of the Football League; 1893–97 Division 2; 1897–1913 Division 1; 1913–14 Division 2; 1914–20 Division 1; 1920–23 Division 2; 1923–26 Division 1; 1926–30 Division 2; 1930–31 Division 3 (S); 1931–35 Division 2; 1935–50 Division 3 (S); 1950–58 Division 2; 1958–59 Division 3; 1959–60 Division 4; 1960–64 Division 3; 1964–71 Division 4; 1971–73 Division 3; 1973–81 Division 2; 1981–84 Division 1; 1984 Division 2; 1985– Division .

Honours: *Football League:* Division 1 best season: 3rd, 1890—91, 1900–01; Division 2 – Champions 1896–97, 1913–14, 1922–23; Runners-up 1894–95, 1980–81; Division 3(S) – Champions 1930–31, 1949–50; Runners-up 1936–37; Division 3 – Runners-up 1972-73; Division 4 – Champions 1970–71; Runners-up 1959–60. *FA Cup:* Winners 1893–94; Runners-up 1890–91. *Football League Cup* best season: 5th rd, 1963–64, 1972–73, 1975–76.

Colours: Black and white broad striped shirts, amber sleeve and neck trim, black shorts, with white side flash, black stockings. **Change colours:** All Gold.

NOTTS COUNTY 1988–89 LEAGUE RECORD

Match No.	Date	Venue	Opponents	Result	H/T Score	Lg. Pos.	Goalscorers	Attendance
1	Aug 27	H	Bristol C	D 0-0	0-0	—		6280
2	Sept 3	A	Blackpool	W 1-0	0-0	8	Mills	4669
3	10	H	Northampton T	L 0-1	0-0	14		6084
4	17	A	Wolverhampton W	D 0-0	0-0	15		10,870
5	20	A	Huddersfield T	L 1-3	1-1	—	Yates	5655
6	24	H	Preston NE	D 0-0	0-0	18		4965
7	Oct 1	A	Mansfield T	D 1-1	0-0	19	McParland	5907
8	4	H	Chesterfield	W 4-0	2-0	—	Thorpe, McStay, Yates, Pike (pen)	4519
9	9	H	Chester C	D 2-2	1-1	—	Birtles 2	5772
10	15	A	Bristol R	L 0-2	0-1	17		4183
11	22	H	Reading	D 3-3	1-3	18	Thorpe, Law, Mills (pen)	5170
12	29	H	Fulham	L 0-1	0-1	19		5514
13	Nov 5	A	Bury	D 1-1	1-0	18	Lund	2612
14	8	A	Brentford	L 1-2	0-1	—	O'Riordan	4013
15	12	H	Southend U	D 1-1	1-0	19	Mills	5037
16	26	H	Gillingham	L 1-2	1-1	20	Rimmer	4611
17	Dec 3	A	Aldershot	W 3-2	2-0	19	Kevan, Lund, Rimmer	2191
18	18	A	Wigan Ath	W 1-0	0-0	—	McParland	3016
19	26	H	Sheffield U	L 1-4	1-0	19	Pike	11,590
20	31	H	Bolton W	W 2-0	2-0	18	Lund, Law	5097
21	Jan 2	A	Port Vale	L 0-1	0-0	19		7084
22	7	A	Swansea C	L 0-2	0-1	20		5808
23	14	H	Blackpool	D 1-1	0-1	21	Lund	4748
24	21	A	Northampton T	W 3-1	1-0	18	McParland 2 (1 pen), Draper	3704
25	29	H	Wolverhampton W	D 1-1	1-0	—	O'Riordan	9058
26	Feb 4	H	Mansfield T	W 2-1	2-1	17	Pike, Coleman(og)	5924
27	11	A	Chesterfield	L 0-3	0-2	18		4943
28	18	A	Chester C	L 0-1	0-0	19		3157
29	25	H	Bristol R	W 1-0	1-0	19	Barnes	5176
30	28	H	Cardiff C	W 2-0	1-0	—	Kevan, Withe	4266
31	Mar 4	A	Reading	W 3-1	1-1	14	Barnes 3	4153
32	11	H	Bury	W 3-0	1-0	12	Lund, Barnes, McParland	5757
33	14	A	Fulham	L 1-2	0-1	—	McParland (pen)	3402
34	18	A	Bristol C	W 4-0	1-0	10	Barnes 2, O'Riordan, Draper	6407
35	25	H	Port Vale	L 1-4	0-2	12	Yates	7328
36	27	A	Sheffield U	D 1-1	1-1	12	Yates	13,039
37	Apr 1	H	Wigan Ath	W 1-0	1-0	12	Thorpe	4929
38	4	H	Swansea C	W 1-0	1-0	—	Lund	3940
39	8	A	Bolton W	D 3-3	3-0	11	Turner, Thorpe, Crombie (og)	4521
40	15	A	Preston NE	L 0-3	0-1	12		6735
41	18	A	Cardiff C	W 1-0	1-0	—	Yates	3079
42	22	H	Huddersfield T	W 3-0	1-0	8	Draper, Johnson 2	5499
43	28	A	Southend U	D 1-1	0-1	—	Johnson	3931
44	May 1	H	Brentford	W 3-0	2-0	9	Lund, Bates (og), Yates	4989
45	6	H	Aldershot	W 4-1	0-1	8	Lund, Turner, Johnson, Law (pen)	4261
46	13	A	Gillingham	L 1-2	0-2	9	Law (pen)	2877

Final League Position: 9

GOALSCORERS

League (64): Lund 8, Barnes 7, McParland 6 (2 pens), Yates 6, Johnson 4, Law 4 (2 pens), Thorpe 4, Draper 3, Mills 3 (1 pen), O'Riordan 3, Pike 3 (1 pen), Birtles 2, Kevan 2, Rimmer 2, Turner 2, McStay 1, Withe 1, own goals 3.
Littlewoods Cup (7): McParland 3, Birtles 1, Mills 1, Pike 1, Thorpe 1.
FA Cup (2): Pike 1, Thorpe 1.

Littlewoods Cup	First Round	Mansfield T (h)	5-0
		(a)	0-1
	Second Round	Tottenham H (h)	1-1
		(a)	1-2
FA Cup	First Round	Darlington (a)	2-1
	Second Round	Hartlepool U (a)	0-1

Leonard	Norton	Withe	O'Riordan	Yates	Law	Mills	McParland	Birtles	Pike	Thorpe	Lund	McStay	Draper	Johnson	Kevan	Fairclough	Barnes	Rimmer	Cherry	Palmer	Turner	Davison	*Match No.*
1	2	3	4	5	6	7	8*	9	10	11	12												1
1	2	3	4	5	6	7	8	9*	10	11	12												2
1	2	3	4	5	6	7	8	9	10	11*		12											3
1	2	3	4	5	6	7	8	9	10			12	11*										4
1	2	3	4	5	6	7	8	9*	10	11	12												5
1	2	3	4*	5	6	7	8			11	9†	10		14	12								6
1		3*		5	6	7	8	9	10	11		2			4	12							7
1		3		5	6	7		9	10	11	8	2			4								8
1		3		5	6	7	8	9	10	11		2			4								9
1		3	14	5	6	7		9	10*	11	12	2			4		8†						10
1		3	14	5	6	7	8*	9	10	11	12				4†	2							11
1	2	3	4	5	6	7		9*	10	11	8						12						12
1	2*	3	4	5	6	7		9	10	11†	8	12					14						13
1		3	4	5	6	7		9	10	11	8	2											14
1		3	4	5		7		6		11	9	2			10			8					15
1		3	2	5	12	7		6*	10	11	9				4			8					16
1		3	6	2	5		12			11*	9	7	8		4			10					17
1		3	4	2	5	7	8	6*	10		9	12				11							18
1		3	4	6†	5*	7	8		10	14	9	2				11		12					19
1		3	4		5	7	8	6	10		9	2				11							20
1		3	4		5	7	8	6	10	12	9	2				11*							21
1		3	4	5	12	7	8	6*	10	14	9	2†				11							22
1		3	4	5	6	7	8		10*	12	9	2				11							23
1		3	4	5		7	8		10*	11	9		12		6	2							24
1		3	4	5	2	7	8		12	11	9		10		6*								25
1		3	4	5	2	7	8†		6	11	9*		10	14			12						26
1		3	4†	5	2	7	8		6	11	9*		10			14	12						27
		3	4	5	6	7			10		9		11				8		1	2			28
		3	5		6	7	12		10		9	2	11				8*		1	4			29
		3	5		6	7*			10	12	9	2			11		8		1	4			30
		3	4	5	6				10	14	9	12			11		8†		1	2*	7		31
		3	4	5	6		12		10		9	2			11		8*		1		7		32
		3	4	5	6		12		10		9	2		14	11†		8*		1		7		33
		3	4	5	6				10†	12	9	2	11			14	8*		1		7		34
		3	4	5	6			12	10†	14	9*	2	11				8		1		7		35
		3	4	5	6					11*	9	2	12			10	8		1		7		36
		3	4	5	6†				12	11	9	2	10*			14	8		1		7		37
		3	4	5	6				10	11	9	2	12			8*			1		7		38
		3*	4	5	6				10	11	9	2	12		8				1		7		39
			5		6				10	11	9	2	8*	12		3				4	7	1	40
		3	12	5	6					11*	9			10	4	8			1	2	7		41
		3	4	5	6						9		8	11		10			1	2	7		42
		3	4	5	6						9	12	8*	11		10			1	2	7		43
		3	4†	5	6					12	9	10	8	11*	14				1	2	7		44
		3*	4	5	6						9	10	8	11		12			1	2	7		45
		3	4*	5	6					12	9	10	8	11		14			1	2†	7		46
27	8	45	40 + 3s	41	42 + 2s	29	19 + 4s	19 + 1s	34 + 2s	26 + 10s	37 + 5s	27 + 6s	16 + 4s	6 + 4s	16 + 2s	14 + 6s	11 + 4s	3 + 1s	18	11	16	1	

NOTTS COUNTY

Player and Position	Ht	Wt	Birth Date	Birth Place	Source	Clubs	League App	League Gls
Goalkeepers								
Steve Cherry	5 11	11 00	5 8 60	Nottingham	Apprentice	Derby Co	77	—
						Port Vale (loan)	4	—
						Walsall	71	—
						Plymouth Arg	73	—
						Chesterfield (loan)	10	—
						Notts Co	18	—
Aidan Davison	6 1	13 02	11 5 68	Sedgefield	Billingham Syn.	Notts Co	1	—
Paul Dolan	6 4	13 05	16 4 66	Ottawa	Vancouver W	Notts Co	—	—
Defenders								
Wayne Fairclough	5 10	9 12	27 4 68	Nottingham	Apprentice	Notts Co	63	—
Craig Jackson‡	6 0	12 01	17 1 69	Rennishaw	Trainee	Notts Co	5	—
Nicky Law	6 0	13 05	8 9 61	Greenwich	Apprentice	Arsenal	—	—
						Barnsley	114	1
						Blackpool	66	1
						Plymouth Arg	38	5
						Notts Co	44	4
David Norton	5 7	11 03	3 3 65	Cannock	Apprentice	Aston Villa	44	2
						Notts Co	8	—
Charlie Palmer	5 11	12 03	10 7 63	Aylesbury	Apprentice	Watford	10	1
						Derby Co	51	2
						Hull C	70	1
						Notts Co	11	—
Chris Withe	5 10	11 03	25 9 62	Liverpool	Apprentice	Newcastle U	2	—
						Bradford C	143	2
						Notts Co	80	3
Dean Yates	6 1	10 04	26 10 67	Leicester	Apprentice	Notts Co	181	21
Midfield								
Mark Draper	5 10	10 00	11 11 70	Derbyshire	Trainee	Notts Co	20	3
David Kevan	5 8	9 10	31 8 68	Wigtown	Apprentice	Notts Co	86	3
Willie McStay	5 10	11 0	26 11 61	Hamilton	Celtic BC	Celtic	68	2
						Huddersfield T	9	—
						Notts Co	42	1
Don O'Riordan	6 0	11 12	14 5 57	Dublin	Apprentice	Derby Co	6	1
						Doncaster R (loan)	2	—
					Tulsa	Preston NE	158	8
						Carlisle U	84	18
						Middlesbrough	41	2
						Grimsby T	86	14
						Notts Co	43	3
Geoff Pike	5 6	11 00	28 9 56	Clapton	Apprentice	West Ham U	291	32
						Notts Co	82	17
Eddie Snook	5 7	10 01	18 10 68	Washington	Apprentice	Notts Co	—	—
Phil Turner	5 8	10 13	12 2 62	Sheffield	Apprentice	Lincoln C	241	19
						Grimsby T	62	8
						Leicester C	24	2
						Notts Co	16	2

NOTTS COUNTY

Foundation: For many years the foundation date of the Football League's oldest club was given as 1862 and the club celebrated its centenary in 1962. However, the researches of Keith Warsop have since shown that the club was on a very haphazard basis at that time, playing little more than practice matches. The meeting which put it on a firm footing was held at the George IV Hotel in December 1864, when they became known as the Notts Football Club.

Managers (and Secretary-managers)
Edwin Browne 1883–93*, Tom Featherstone 1893*, Tom Harris 1893–13*, Albert Fisher 1913–27, Horace Henshall 1927–34, Charlie Jones 1934–35, David Pratt 1935, Percy Smith 1935–36, Jimmy McMullan 1936–37, Harry Parkes 1938–39, Tony Towers 1939–42, Frank Womack 1942–43, Major Frank Buckley 1944–46, Arthur Stollery 1946–49, Eric Houghton 1949–53, George Poyser 1953–57, Tommy Lawton 1957–58, Frank Hill 1958–61, Tim Coleman 1961–63, Eddie Lowe 1963–65, Tim Coleman 1965–66, Jack Burkitt 1966–67, Andy Beattie (GM 1967), Billy Gray 1967–68, Jimmy Sirrel 1969–75, Ron Fenton 1975–77, Jimmy Sirrel 1978–82 (continues as GM to 1984), Howard Wilkinson 1982–83, Larry Lloyd 1983–84, Richie Barker 1984–85, Jimmy Sirrel 1985–87, John Barnwell 1987–88, Neil Warnock 1989– .

Player and Position	*Ht*	*Wt*	*Birth Date*	*Birth Place*	*Source*	*Clubs*	*League App*	*League Gls*
Forwards								
Paul Barnes	5 10	10 02	16 11 67	Leicester	Apprentice	Notts Co	40	13
Garry Birtles*	6 0	12 00	27 7 56	Nottingham	Long Eaton U	Nottingham F	87	32
						Manchester U	58	11
						Nottingham F	125	38
						Notts Co	63	9
Tom Johnson	5 10	10 00	15 1 71	Newcastle	Trainee	Notts Co	10	4
Gary Lund	5 11	11 00	13 9 64	Grimsby	School	Grimsby T	60	24
						Lincoln C	44	13
						Notts Co	82	28
Scott Machin	6 0	12 00	29 9 70	Leicester	Trainee	Notts Co	—	—
Adrian Thorpe	5 6	11 00	20 11 63	Chesterfield	Heanor T	Bradford C	17	1
						Tranmere R (loan)	5	3
						Notts Co	59	9

Trainees
Aldridge, Stephen P; Brown, Warren J; Cox, Paul R; Finch, Craig B; Hearne, Darren J; House, Adam; Telford, Mark A; Thompson, John A; Walls, Matthew J.J; Walker, Richard N; Wells, Mark A.

****Non-Contract**
Eley, James R.

Associated Schoolboys
Barrow, Lee A; Bird, Matthew; Brough, John; Crossland, Daniel; Galloway, Michael A; Harmon, Darren J; Johnson, Michael O; Moore, James W; Patterson, Gary; Rogers, Kevin A; Scott, Wayne P; Sherlock, Paul G; Slawson, Stephen M; Walker, James B; Wells, Iain D; Whitehurst, Nicholas.

OLDHAM ATHLETIC 1988–89 *Back row (left to right):* Neil Edmonds, Gary Hoolickin, Ian Marshall, Glenn Keeley, Mike Flynn, Mike Cecere.
Centre row: Billy Urmson (Coach), Ronnie Evans (Kit Manager), Andy Ritchie, Frank Bunn, Paul Turner, Andy Rhodes, Roger Palmer, Chris Blundell, Willie Donachie (Player/Coach), Ian Liversedge (Physiotherapist).
Front row: Andy Barlow, Gary Williams, Denis Irwin, John Kelly, Joe Royle (Manager), Tommy Wright, Earl Barrett, Tony Philliskirk, Mike Milligan.

Division 2 **OLDHAM ATHLETIC**

Boundary Park, Oldham. Telephone 061-624-4972. Commercial Dept. 061-652-0966. Clubcall, 0898 121142.

Ground capacity: 21,949.

Record attendance: 47,671 v Sheffield W, FA Cup 4th rd. 25 Jan, 1930.

Record receipts: £60,133.50 v Manchester C, Divsion 2, 14 January, 1989.

Pitch measurements: 110yd × 74yd. (Artificial surface).

President: R. Schofield.

Chairman & Chief Executive: I. H. Stott, ***Vice-Chairman:*** D. A. Brierley.

Directors: G. T. Butterworth, R. Adams, D. R. Taylor, P. Chadwick, J. Slevin, N. Holden.

Manager: Joe Royle.

Secretary: Terry Cale. ***Commercial Manager:*** Alan Hardy.

Player-Coach: Willie Donachie. ***Coach:*** Billy Urmson.

Physio: Ian Liversedge.

Year Formed: 1895. ***Turned Professional:*** 1899. ***Ltd Co.:*** 1906.

Club Nickname: 'The Latics'.

Previous Names: 1895, Pine Villa; 1899, Oldham Athletic.

Previous Ground: Sheepfoot Lane; 1905, Boundary Park.

Record League Victory: 11-0 v Southport, Division 4, 26 December 1962 – Hollands; Branagan, Marshall; McCall, Williams, Scott; Ledger (1), Johnstone, Lister (6), Colquhoun (1), Whitaker (3).

Record Cup Victory: 10-1 v Lytham, FA Cup, 1st rd, 28 November 1925 – Gray; Wynne, Grundy; Adlam, Heaton, Naylor (1), Douglas, Pynegar (2), Ormston (2), Barnes (3), Watson (2).

Record Defeat: 4-13 v Tranmere R, Division 3 (N), 26 December, 1935.

Most League Points (2 for a win): 62, Division 3, 1973–74.

Most League Points (3 for a win): 75, Division 2, 1986–87.

Most League Goals: 95, Division 4, 1962–63.

Highest League Scorer in Season: Tom Davis, 33, Division 3 (N), 1936–37.

Most League Goals in Total Aggregate: Roger Palmer, 113, 1980–89.

Most Capped Player: Albert Gray, 9 (24), Wales.

Most League Appearances: Ian Wood, 525, 1966–80.

Record Transfer Fee Received: £350,000 from Norwich City for Andy Linighan, March 1988.

Record Transfer Fee Paid: £200,000 to Manchester C for Kenny Clements, September 1979.

Football League Record: 1907 Elected to Division 2; 1910–23 Division 1; 1923–35 Division 2; 1935–53 Division 3 (N); 1953–54 Division 2; 1954–58 Division 3 (N); 1958–63 Division 4; 1963–69 Division 3; 1969–71 Division 4; 1971–74 Division 3; 1974– Division 2.

Honours: *Football League:* Division 1 – Runners-up 1914–15; Division 2 – Runners-up 1909–10; Division 3 (N) – Champions 1952–53; Division 3 – Champions 1973–74; Division 4 – Runners-up 1962–63. *FA Cup:* Semi-final 1913. *Footbal League Cup:* never past 3rd rd.

Colours: All blue. **Change Colours:** All red.

OLDHAM ATHLETIC 1988–89 LEAGUE RECORD

Match No.	Date	Venue	Opponents	Result	H/T Score	Lg. Pos.	Goalscorers	Attendance
1	Aug 27	H	Barnsley	D 1-1	1-0	—	Bunn	6551
2	29	A	Manchester C	W 4-1	2-0	—	Milligan, Palmer 3	22,594
3	Sept 3	A	Blackburn R	L 1-3	0-2	9	Marshall (pen)	10,082
4	10	H	Birmingham C	W 4-0	1-0	6	Cecere 2, Bunn, Marshall	5796
5	17	A	Bradford C	L 0-2	0-2	8		12,325
6	20	H	Oxford U	W 3-0	2-0	—	Palmer 2, Williams	5847
7	24	H	Hull C	D 2-2	2-0	6	Bunn 2	6319
8	Oct 1	A	Sunderland	L 2-3	2-2	9	Bunn 2	12,529
9	4	A	Watford	L 1-3	0-2	—	Bunn	10,038
10	8	H	Stoke C	D 2-2	2-0	13	Kelly, Bunn	6600
11	15	H	Chelsea	L 1-4	1-2	17	Palmer	7817
12	22	A	Brighton & HA	L 0-2	0-2	19		9799
13	25	H	Bournemouth	W 2-0	1-0	—	Marshall, Bunn	4518
14	29	A	Portsmouth	D 1-1	1-1	17	Bunn	11,310
15	Nov 5	H	Walsall	W 3-0	3-0	14	Palmer, Marshall, Ritchie	5760
16	11	A	Shrewsbury T	D 0-0	0-0	—		4701
17	19	H	Leeds U	D 2-2	1-1	14	Palmer, Bunn	8824
18	26	A	Plymouth Arg	L 0-3	0-2	17		7829
19	Dec 3	H	Leicester C	D 1-1	0-0	20	Ritchie (pen)	5789
20	10	A	Swindon T	D 2-2	0-1	19	Palmer, Kelly	5540
21	16	A	Ipswich T	L 1-2	1-0	—	Kelly	8982
22	26	H	WBA	L 1-3	0-2	20	Philliskirk	9827
23	30	H	Crystal Palace	L 2-3	0-1	—	Skipper, Ritchie (pen)	6562
24	Jan 2	A	Birmingham C	D 0-0	0-0	20		5998
25	14	H	Manchester C	L 0-1	0-1	21		19,200
26	21	A	Barnsley	L 3-4	0-1	21	Palmer, Ritchie 2 (1 pen)	7879
27	Feb 4	H	Watford	W 3-1	2-0	21	Ritchie 2, Irwin	6364
28	11	A	Stoke C	D 0-0	0-0	21		10,992
29	18	H	Brighton & HA	W 2-1	2-1	20	Wright, Holden	5918
30	25	A	Chelsea	D 2-2	1-2	21	Ritchie, Palmer	13,261
31	28	A	Bournemouth	D 2-2	1-1	—	Milligan, Kelly	7783
32	Mar 3	H	Shrewsbury T	W 3-0	1-0	—	Ritchie 2, Palmer	6014
33	11	A	Walsall	D 2-2	0-1	19	Holden, Bunn	5576
34	14	H	Portsmouth	W 5-3	2-0	—	Holden, Wright 2, Milligan, Ritchie	5773
35	18	A	Oxford U	D 1-1	1-1	16	Ritchie	4588
36	24	H	Blackburn R	D 1-1	1-0	—	Kelly	11,752
37	27	A	WBA	L 1-3	0-1	19	Ritchie	13,812
38	Apr 1	H	Bradford C	D 1-1	0-0	19	Milligan	8589
39	4	H	Ipswich T	W 4-0	2-0	—	Ritchie, Palmer 2, Milligan	5182
40	8	A	Crystal Palace	L 0-2	0-1	19		9089
41	15	H	Sunderland	D 2-2	1-2	20	Wright, Milligan	5944
42	22	A	Hull C	D 1-1	1-0	20	Wright	6748
43	29	H	Plymouth Arg	D 2-2	2-1	19	Irwin, Wright	4614
44	May 1	A	Leicester C	W 2-1	1-1	17	Wright, Kelly	33,456
45	6	A	Leeds U	D 0-0	0-0	17		14,459
46	13	H	Swindon T	D 2-2	1-2	16	Palmer, Holden	5676

Final League Position: 16

GOALSCORERS

League (75): Palmer 15, Ritchie 14 (3 pens), Bunn 12, Wright 7, Kelly 6, Milligan 6, Holden 4, Marshall 4 (1 pen), Cecere 2, Irwin 2, Philliskirk 1, Skipper 1, Williams 1.
Littlewoods Cup (5): Ritchie 2, Bunn 1, Philliskirk 1, Williams 1.
FA Cup (1): Milligan 1.

Littlewoods Cup	Second Round	Darlington (a)	0-2
		(h)	4-0
	Third Round	Everton (a)	1-1
		(h)	0-2
FA Cup	Third Round	Charlton Ath (a)	1-2

Rhodes	Barrett	Barlow	Flynn	Marshall	Milligan	Palmer	Kelly J	Cecere	Bunn	Wright	Philliskirk	Donachie	Irwin	Williams	Ritchie	Litchfield	Blundell	Skipper	Warhurst	Henry	Morgan	Kelly N	Holden	Adams	H Hallworth	R Gayle	G Hartford	H Bramwell	*Match No.*
1	2	3	4	5	6	7	8	9	10	11																			1
1	2	3	4	5	6	7	8	9*	10	11	12																		2
1	2	3†	4	5	6	7	8	9*	10	11	12	14																	3
1	2	3	4	5	6	7	8*	9	10	11		12																	4
1	2	3	4*	5	6†	7	8	9	10	11		14	12																5
1	4	3		5	6	7	8	9	10*	11			2	12															6
1	4	3		5	6	7	8	9	10*	11			2		12														7
1	4	3†		5	6	7	8*	12	9	11		14	2		10														8
	4			5	6*	7	8		9	11		14	2†	12	10	1	3												9
	4			5		7	8	12	9	11		2		6*	10	1	3												10
	3			5		7	8	12	9		14	6	2	10†	11*	1		4											11
1	3			5		7*	8	11†	9	10	14	6	2	12				4											12
1	3			5		7	8	12	9	11†	10*	6	2	14				4											13
1	3		12	5		7	8	10†	9	11	14		2					4	6*										14
1	3			5	6	7	8		9	11			2		10			4											15
1	3		5		6	7	8		9	11			2		10			4											16
1	3		5		6	7	8		9	11			2		10			4											17
1	3	9*	5†		6	7	8			11	12		2		10			4	14										18
1	3			5	6	7	8		9	11			2		10			4											19
1	3			5	6	7	8		9*	11	12		2		10			4											20
1	3	10		5	6	7	8			11			2		9			4											21
1	3	14		5	6	7	8			11*	10		2†		9			4		12									22
1	3	6		5		7	8			9*	10†		2		11			4	14	12									23
1	3	6		5		7	8						2					4	10	11	9*	12							24
1	3	6*		9	10	7							2		8			4		12			5	11					25
1	3			9	10	7				12			2		8			4*		6			5	11					26
	3			5	10	7	4			9			2		8					12			6*	11	1				27
	3			5	10	7	4			9			2		8			6						11	1				28
	3			5	10	7	4			9			2		8								6	11	1				29
	3			5	10	7	4			9			2		8								6	11	1				30
				5	10	7	4			9			2		8			3					6	11	1				31
				5	10	7	4		12	9			2		8			3					6	11*	1				32
	3			5	10	7	4		12	9*			2		8								6	11	1				33
	3			5	10	7	4		9	11			2		8								6		1				34
	3				10	7	4		9	11			2		8			6		5					1				35
	3			5	10	7	4			11			2		8			6		9					1				36
	3			5	10	7†	4			11*			2		8			6		9					1		12	14	37
	3			5	10	7				11			2		8			6		9					1		4		38
	3			5	10	7			9	11*			2		8			6		4					1		12		39
	3			5	10	7	14		9	11†			2		8*			6		4					1		12		40
	3			5	10	7	8		9	11			2					6		4					1				41
1	3	5			10	7	8		9	11			2					6		4									42
	3			5	10	7	8		9*	11			2							4			6		1		12		43
1	3			5	10	7	8			11			2							4			6				9		44
1	3			5	10	7	8			11			2							4			6				9		45
1	3			5	10	7	8*			11			2		9					4			6			12			46
27	44	14 + 1s	8 + 1s	41	39	46	41 + 1s	9 + 4s	26 + 2s	42 + 1s	3 + 7s	4 + 5s	40 + 1s	2 + 4s	30 + 1s	3	2	27	2 + 2s	14 + 4s	1	— + 1s	13	9	16	— + 1s	3 + 4s	— + 1s	

OLDHAM ATHLETIC

Player and Position	Ht	Wt	Birth Date	Birth Place	Source	Clubs	League App	League Gls
Goalkeepers								
Winston Dubose‡			28 7 55	Florida	Tampa Bay	Oldham Ath	—	—
Jon Hallworth	6 2	12 10	26 10 65	Stockport	School	Ipswich T	45	—
						Swindon T (loan)	—	—
						Bristol R (loan)	2	—
						Fulham (loan)	—	—
						Oldham Ath	16	—
Andy Rhodes	6 0	12 00	23 8 64	Doncaster	Apprentice	Barnsley	36	—
						Doncaster R	106	—
						Oldham Ath	38	—
Defenders								
Andrew Barlow	5 9	11 01	24 11 65	Oldham		Oldham Ath	129	2
Earl Barrett	5 10	11 00	28 4 67	Rochdale	Apprentice	Manchester C	3	—
						Chester C (loan)	12	—
						Oldham Ath	62	—
Chris Blundell	5 10	10 09	7 12 69	Billinge	Trainee	Oldham Ath	3	—
Willie Donachie	5 9	11 03	5 10 51	Glasgow	Juniors	Manchester C	351	2
					Portland T	Norwich C	11	—
					Portland T	Burnley	60	3
						Oldham Ath	145	3
Andy Holden	6 1	13 00	14 9 62	Flint	Rhyl	Chester C	100	17
						Wigan Ath	49	4
						Oldham Ath	13	4
Gary Hoolickin*	5 11	11 01	29 10 57	Middleton	Apprentice	Oldham Ath	211	
(Retired)								2
Dennis Irwin	5 7	9 07	31 10 65	Cork	Apprentice	Leeds U	72	1
						Oldham Ath	125	3
Ian Marshall	6 1	12 12	20 3 66	Liverpool	Apprentice	Everton	15	1
						Oldham Ath	51	4
Peter Skipper	5 11	12 05	11 4 58	Hull	Local	Hull C	23	2
						Scunthorpe U (loan)	1	—
						Darlington	91	4
						Hull C	265	17
						Oldham Ath	27	1
Paul Warhurst	6 11	14 00	26 9 69	Stockport	Trainee	Manchester C	—	—
						Oldham Ath	4	—
Midfield								
Steve Bramwell§			9 10 70	Stockport	Trainee	Oldham Ath	1	—
Asa Hartford	5 7	11 04	24 10 50	Clydebank	Amateur	WBA	213	18
						Manchester C	185	22
						Nottingham F	3	—
						Everton	81	6
						Manchester C	75	7
						Norwich C	28	2
						Bolton W	81	8
						Stockport Co	45	—
						Oldham Ath	7	—
Nick Henry	5 6	9 08	21 2 69	Liverpool	Trainee	Oldham Ath	23	—
John Kelly	5 10	10 09	20 10 60	Bebbington	Cammellaird	Tranmere R	64	9
						Preston NE	130	27
						Chester C	85	17
						Swindon T	7	1
						Oldham Ath	52	6
Norman Kelly§	5 8	11 00	10 10 70	Belfast	Trainee	Oldham Ath	2	—
Mike Milligan	5 8	11 00	20 2 67	Manchester	Apprentice	Oldham Ath	121	10
Steve Morgan§	5 9	11 05	28 12 70	Wrexham	Trainee	Oldham Ath	2	—
Mark Stewart			26 7 67	Bury		Oldham Ath	—	—

OLDHAM ATHLETIC

Foundation: It was in 1895 that John Garland, the landlord of the Featherstall and Junction Hotel, decided to form a football club. As Pine Villa they played in the Oldham Junior League. In 1899 the local professional club Oldham County, went out of existence and one of the liquidators persuaded Pine Villa to take over their ground at Sheepfoot Lane and change their name to Oldham Athletic.

Managers (and Secretary-managers)
David Ashworth 1906–14, Herbert Bamlett 1914–21, Charlie Roberts 1921–22, David Ashworth 1923–24, Bob Mellor 1924–27, Andy Wilson 1927–32, Jimmy McMullan 1933–34, Bob Mellor 1934–45 (continued as secretary to 1953), Frank Womack 1945–47, Billy Wootton 1947–50, George Hardwick 1950–56, Ted Goodier 1956–58, Norman Dodgin 1958–60, Jack Rowley 1960–63, Les McDowall 1963–65, Gordon Hurst 1965–66, Jimmy McIlroy 1966–68, Jack Rowley 1968–69, Jimmy Frizzell 1970–82, Joe Royle 1982– .

Player and Position	*Ht*	*Wt*	*Birth Date*	*Birth Place*	*Source*	*Clubs*	*League App*	*League Gls*
Forwards								
Frankie Bunn	5 11	10 06	6 11 62	Birmingham	Apprentice	Luton T	59	9
						Hull C	95	23
						Oldham Ath	49	21
Andy Gayle§			17 9 70	Manchester	Trainee	Oldham Ath	1	—
Scott McGarvey	6 0	11 05	22 4 63	Glasgow	Apprentice	Manchester U	25	3
						Wolverhampton W (loan)	13	2
						Portsmouth	23	6
						Carlisle U (loan)	10	3
						Carlisle U	25	8
						Grimsby T	50	7
						Bristol C	26	9
						Oldham Ath	—	—
Roger Palmer	5 10	11 00	30 1 59	Manchester	Apprentice	Manchester C	31	9
						Oldham Ath	349	113
Andy Ritchie	5 9	11 11	28 11 60	Manchester	Apprentice	Manchester U	33	13
						Brighton & HA	89	23
						Leeds U	136	40
						Oldham Ath	67	33
Gary Williams	5 8	10 11	8 6 63	Bristol	Apprentice	Bristol C	100	1
						Portsmouth	—	—
						Swansea C	6	—
						Bristol R	—	—
						Oldham Ath	56	12
Tommy Wright	5 7	9 10	10 1 66	Fife	Apprentice	Leeds U	81	24
						Oldham Ath	112	23
Mark Stewart			26 7 67	Bury		Oldham Ath	—	—
Steve Bramwell§			9 10 70	Stockport	Trainee	Oldham Ath	1	—

Trainees

Allen, Jason R; Barlow, Anthony L; Bennett, Ian M; Bramwell, Steven; Fisk, Jason T; Gayle, Andrew K; Halstead, Christopher; Huyton, Darren J; Kelly, Norman; Leeming, Daniel J; Mooney, Simon G; Morgan, Stephen J; Pye, Matthew J; Raynor, Steven; Wall, David M; Wood, Clark L; Woodcock, Andrew J.

Associated Schoolboys

Bamber, Neil S; Bernard, Paul R.J; Bradshaw, Gary J; Challender, Gregory L; Everingham, Nicholas P; Eyre, John R; Gerrard, Paul W; Hall, David; Hardman, Lee; Hoolickin, Anthony P; Johnson, Bradley M; Jones, Michael C; Kenton, Andrew M; Lockley, Richard J; Makin, Christopher; Mayo, Jonathan P; Miller, Peter D; Nelson, Michael J; Osborne, Julian M.G.E; Petts, Samuel; Price, Robert J; Shard, Anthony; Simmons, Mark S; White, Gary W; Wilson, Gregory J.

OXFORD UNITED 1988–89 *Back row (left to right):* Paul Simpson, Paul Swarmack, Richard Hill, Alan Judge, Jimmy Phillips, Paul Kee, Gary Briggs, Sean Reck, Mike Ford.
Centre row: David Leworthy, Lee Nogan, Jon Purdie, David Fogg (Coach), Mickey Lewis, Maurice Evans (General Manager), Philip Heath, John Clinkard (Physiotherapist), Robbie Mustoe, Garry Smart, Eddie Denton.
Front row: David Bardsley, Gary Shelton, Les Phillips, Colin Greenall, Brian Horton (Manager), Tommy Caton, Martin Foyle, Neil Slatter, Peter Rhoades-Brown.

Division 2 OXFORD UNITED

Manor Ground, Headington, Oxford. Telephone Oxford (0865) 61503. Supporters Club: 0865 63063. Clubcall: 0898 121172. Fax No. 0865 741820.

Ground capacity: 14,374.

Record attendance: 22,730 v Preston NE, FA Cup 6th rd, 29 Feb, 1964.

Record receipts: £71,304 v Aston Villa, Milk Cup semi-final, 12 March, 1986.

Pitch measurements: 110yd × 75yd.

President: The Duke of Marlborough.

Chairman: K. F. T. Maxwell.

Directors: G. E. Coppock, Miss G. N. Maxwell, P. D. McGeough, P. J. Morrissey, P. Reeves.

Manager: Brian Horton. ***Coach:*** David Fogg.

Physio: John Clinkard.

Secretary: Mick Brown ***Commercial Manager:*** Nick Johnson.

Year Formed: 1896. ***Turned Professional:*** 1949. ***Ltd Co.:*** 1949.

Club Nickname: 'The U's'.

Previous Names: 1896, Headington; 1899, Headington United; 1960, Oxford United.

Previous Grounds: Quarry Fields, Wooton's Fields.

Record League Victory: 7-0 v Barrow, Division 4, 19 December 1964 – Fearnley; Beavon, Quartermann; Ron Atkinson (1), Kyle, Jones; Morris, Booth (3), Willey (1), Graham Atkinson (1), Harrington (1).

Record Cup Victory: 6-0 v Gillingham, League Cup, 2nd rd (1st leg), 24 September 1986 – Judge; Langan, Trewick, Phillips (Brock), Briggs, Shotton, Houghton (1), Aldridge (4) incl. 1p), Charles (Leworthy), Hebberd, Slatter. (1 og)

Record Defeat: 0-6 v Liverpool, Division 1, 22 March 1986.

Most League Points (2 for a win): 61, Division 4, 1964–65.

Most League Points (3 for a win): 95, Division 3, 1983–84.

Most League Goals: 91, Division 3, 1983–84.

Highest League Scorer in Season: John Aldridge, 30, Division 2, 1984–85.

Most League Goals in Total Aggregate: Graham Atkinson, 73, 1962–73.

Most Capped Player: Ray Houghton, 12 (26), Eire and Neil Slatter, 12 (22), Wales.

Most League Appearances: John Shuker, 480, 1962–77.

Record Transfer Fee Received: £1,000,000 from Derby Co for Dean Saunders, October 1988.

Record Transfer Fee Paid: £265,000 to Watford for David Bardsley, September 1987.

Football League Record: 1962 Elected to Division 4; 1965–68 Division 3; 1968–76 Division 2; 1976–84 Division 3; 1984–85 Division 2; 1985–88 Division 1; 1988– Division 2.

Honours: *Football League:* Division 1 best season: 18th, 1985–86, 1986–87; Division 2 – Champions 1984–85; Division 3 – Champions 1967–68, 1983–84; Division 4 – Promoted 1964–65 (4th). *FA Cup* best season: 6th rd, 1963-64 (record for 4th Division club), 1981–82. *Football League Cup:* Winners 1985–86.

Colours: Gold, navy blue sleeves, navy blue shorts, navy stockings. **Change Colours:** All red.

OXFORD UNITED 1988–89 LEAGUE RECORD

Match No.	*Date*	*Venue*	*Opponents*	*Result*	*H/T Score*	*Lg. Pos.*	*Goalscorers*	*Attendance*
1	Aug 27	A	Leeds U	D 1-1	1-1	—	Foyle	20,697
2	29	H	Hull C	W 1-0	1-0	—	Saunders	5772
3	Sept 3	H	Brighton & HA	W 3-2	2-0	4	Heath, Saunders, Greenall	6004
4	10	A	Chelsea	D 1-1	0-0	5	Leworthy	7587
5	17	H	Leicester C	D 1-1	0-1	6	Shelton	6610
6	20	A	Oldham Ath	L 0-3	0-2	—		5847
7	24	A	Bournemouth	L 1-2	0-2	12	Mustoe	6532
8	Oct 1	H	Shrewsbury T	W 4-1	2-1	8	Phillips J, Mustoe, Foyle, Saunders	4385
9	5	H	Swindon T	D 1-1	0-0	—	Saunders	9398
10	8	A	Portsmouth	L 1-2	1-1	10	Bardsley	9567
11	15	A	Ipswich T	W 2-1	2-0	7	Foyle, Phillips J	13,039
12	22	H	Blackburn R	D 1-1	0-1	10	Bardsley (pen)	6478
13	25	A	Crystal Palace	L 0-1	0-0	—		10,114
14	29	H	Bradford C	L 3-4	1-1	16	Phillips L, Foyle, Hill	5303
15	Nov 2	H	Sunderland	L 2-4	1-3	—	Foyle 2	6270
16	5	A	WBA	L 2-3	1-1	19	Foyle, Simpson	11,643
17	12	H	Birmingham C	W 3-0	1-0	17	Foyle 2, Bardsley (pen)	5589
18	19	H	Plymouth Arg	L 0-1	0-1	18		5429
19	26	A	Manchester C	L 1-2	1-0	20	Hill	20,145
20	Dec 3	H	Barnsley	W 2-0	0-0	18	Phillips J, Simpson	4449
21	10	A	Watford	D 1-1	1-0	17	Bardsley	10,473
22	26	A	Walsall	W 5-1	0-1	17	Hill 4, Foyle	6332
23	31	A	Stoke C	L 0-1	0-1	18		10,552
24	Jan 2	H	Chelsea	L 2-3	1-2	19	Foyle, Hill	11,427
25	14	A	Sunderland	L 0-1	0-1	19		12,853
26	21	H	Leeds U	W 3-2	2-2	19	Foyle, Phillips J, Simpson	7926
27	Feb 5	A	Swindon T	L 0-3	0-1	—		10,227
28	11	H	Portsmouth	W 1-0	1-0	18	Phillips L	6156
29	21	A	Blackburn R	L 1-3	0-2	—	Simpson	5724
30	25	H	Ipswich T	D 1-1	1-0	19	Hill	6086
31	Mar 1	H	Crystal Palace	W 1-0	0-0	—	Bardsley	6020
32	4	A	Birmingham C	D 0-0	0-0	16		4954
33	11	H	WBA	D 1-1	1-1	17	Foyle	7581
34	15	A	Bradford C	D 0-0	0-0	—		7553
35	18	H	Oldham Ath	D 1-1	1-1	17	Phillips L	4588
36	25	A	Brighton & HA	L 1-2	1-0	18	Foyle	9077
37	27	H	Walsall	W 1-0	1-0	16	Durnin	5101
38	Apr 1	A	Leicester C	L 0-1	0-1	18		8187
39	4	A	Hull C	W 2-1	2-0	—	Durnin, Mustoe	6260
40	8	H	Stoke C	W 3-2	2-1	15	Hill 2, Durnin	5297
41	15	A	Shrewsbury T	D 2-2	1-0	15	Greenall (pen), Briggs	3583
42	22	H	Bournemouth	W 3-1	2-0	14	Simpson 3	5684
43	29	H	Manchester C	L 2-4	2-0	15	Bardsley, Simpson	7762
44	May 1	A	Barnsley	L 0-1	0-0	15		5940
45	6	A	Plymouth Arg	L 1-3	0-0	15	Ford	4989
46	13	H	Watford	L 0-4	0-1	17		6573

Final League Position: 17

GOALSCORERS

League (62): Foyle 14, Hill 10, Simpson 8, Bardsley 6 (2 pens), Phillips J 4, Saunders 4, Durnin 3, Mustoe 3, Phillips L 3, Greenall 2 (1 pen), Briggs 1, Ford 1, Heath 1, Leworthy 1, Shelton 1.
Littlewoods Cup (2): Saunders 2.
FA Cup (3): Hill 3.

Littlewoods Cup	Second Round	Bristol C (h)	2-4
		(a)	0-2
FA Cup	Third Round	Sunderland (a)	1-1
		(h)	2-0
	Fourth Round	Manchester U (a)	0-4

Hucker	Bardsley	Phillips, J	Lewis	Hill	Greenall	Heath	Foyle	Saunders	Mustoe	Rhoades-Brown	Shelton	Purdie	Leworthy	Phillips, L	Smart	Judge	Briggs	Reck	Slatter	Nogan	Simpson	Ford	Durnin	Evans	Beauchamp	*Match No.*
1	2	3	4	5	6	7	8	9	10	11*	12															1
1	2	3	4	5	6	7	8	9	10	11*	12															2
1	2	3	4	5	6	7	8	9	10*		11	12														3
1	2	3*	4	5	6	7	8		10	12	11†	9	14													4
1	2	3	4	5	6	7	8		10		11	12	9*													5
1	2	3	4†	5	6	7	8	9	10*		11	12		14												6
1	2		4†	5	6	7	8	9	14	12	11*			10	3											7
	2	3			6		8	9	10	11		7		4		1	5									8
	2	3		12	6		8	9	10*	11		7		4		1	5									9
	2	3		12	6		8	9	10	11*		7		4		1	5									10
	2	3		12	6		8	9	10					4		1	5*	7	11							11
	2	3			6		8	9	10*			12		4		1	5	7	11							12
	2	3		9	6		8		10*			12		4		1	5	7†	11	14						13
	7	3		10	6	11*	8				12		9	4		1	5		2							14
	7	3		10†	6	12	8		14				9	4		1	5		2*		11					15
	2	3	10†		6	12	8		14					4		1	5	7	11*		9					16
	2	3	10		6		8		11		4	12				1	5	7*			9					17
	2	3	10	14	6	12	8		4			11*				1	5	7†			9					18
	2	3		9	6		8				10			4	7	1	5				11					19
	2	3	5	9	6		8				10			4	7	1					11					20
	2	3	5	9	6		8		12		10			4	7	1					11*					21
	2	3	5	9	6		8				10			4	7	1					11					22
	2	3	5	9	6	12	8				10		14	4*	7	1					11†					23
1	2	3	5	9	6	12	8		4		10		14		7*						11†					24
	2	3	5	9	6		8				10		14		7*	1			4		11†	12				25
	2	3	5	9	6		8				10			4*		1			7		11	12				26
	2	3	5	9	6		8				10*		14	4		1			7		11†	12				27
1	7	3	5	11	6		8							4					2			10	9			28
1	7	3	5	11†			8				12			4	2				6		14	10*	9			29
1	7	3	5	11			8				12			4	2				6			10*	9			30
1	7	3	5	11			8				10			4	2				6				9			31
1	7*	3	5	11	6		8		12		10			4					2				9			32
1		3	5	7	6		8		9					4					2		11		10			33
1		3	5	11	6		8		9					4					2		7		10			34
1		3	5	7	6	12	8		9					4*	14				2†		11		10			35
1		3	5	11	6		8		9		4		12						2		7		10*			36
1		3	5		6		8		9		4								2		7	11	10			37
1		3		12	6		8		9		4								2		7	11*	10	5		38
1		3	5	11	6		8		9		4				2		7						10			39
1		3	5	11	6		8*		9		4		12		2		7						10			40
1		3	5	11*	6				9		4		12				7		2		8		10			41
1	7	3	5		6	12			9*		4				11				2		8		10			42
1	7	3	5		6				9		4		12		11*				2		8		10			43
1	7	3	5	11					9		4								2		8		10	6		44
1	7	3	5	11		12			9†		4								2*	8		14	10	6		45
	7	3	5	12							4				2	1				9†	8	11*	10	6	14	46
26	37	45	36	33 + 6s	40	8 + 8s	40	10	28 + 5s	5 + 2s	28 + 5s	5 + 6s	3 + 9s	25 + 1s	16 + 1s	20	15	6	25	2 + 1s	24 + 1s	6 + 4s	19	4	— + 1s	

OXFORD UNITED

Player and Position	Ht	Wt	Birth Date	Birth Place	Source	Clubs	League App	League Gls
Goalkeepers								
Peter Hucker	6 2	12 12	28 10 59	London	Apprentice	QPR	160	—
						Cambridge U (loan)	—	—
						Oxford U	58	—
						WBA (loan)	7	—
						Manchester U (loan)	—	—
Alan Judge	5 11	11 06	15 5 60	Kingsbury	Amateur	Luton T	11	—
						Reading (loan)	33	—
						Reading	44	—
						Oxford U	57	—
						Lincoln C (loan)	2	—
						Cardiff C (loan)	8	—
Paul Kee	6 3	12 12	8 11 69	Belfast	Ards	Oxford U	—	—
Defenders								
David Bardsley	5 10	10 06	11 9 64	Manchester	Apprentice	Blackpool	45	—
						Watford	100	7
						Oxford U	71	7
Gary Briggs*	6 3	12 10	8 5 58	Leeds	Apprentice	Middlesbrough	—	—
						Oxford U	420	18
Ceri Evans	6 1	14 02	2 10 63	Christchurch	Otaga Univ, Worcester Coll (Oxford)	Oxford U	4	—
Mike Ford	5 11	12 05	9 2 66	Bristol		Leicester C	—	—
					Devizes	Cardiff C	145	13
						Oxford U	10	1
Colin Greenall	5 10	11 06	30 12 63	Billinge	Apprentice	Blackpool	183	9
						Gillingham	62	4
						Oxford U	52	2
Jim Phillips	6 0	12 07	8 2 66	Bolton	Apprentice	Bolton W	108	2
						Rangers	25	—
						Oxford U	45	4
Neil Slatter	5 11	10 09	30 5 64	Cardiff	Apprentice	Bristol R	148	4
						Oxford U	81	6
Gary Smart	5 9	11 03	29 4 64	Totnes	Wokingham	Oxford U	17	—
Midfield								
Edward Denton*			18 5 70	Oxford	Trainee	Oxford U	2	—
Mark Hewitson			27 2 71	Oxford	Trainee	Oxford U	—	—
Richard Hill	6 0	12 04	20 9 63	Hinckley		Leicester C	—	—
					Nuneaton	Northampton T	86	46
						Watford	4	—
						Oxford U	63	13
Mickey Lewis	5 8	12 07	15 2 65	Birmingham	School	WBA	24	—
						Derby Co	43	1
						Oxford U	36	—
Robbie Mustoe	5 10	10 08	28 8 68	Oxford		Oxford U	53	3
Les Phillips	5 8	10 06	7 1 63	London	Apprentice	Birmingham C	44	3
						Oxford U	128	9
Sean Reck	5 10	12 07	5 5 67	Oxford	Apprentice	Oxford U	14	—
						Newport Co (loan)	15	—
						Reading (loan)	1	—
Gary Shelton	5 7	11 03	21 3 58	Nottingham	Apprentice	Walsall	24	—
						Aston Villa	24	7
						Notts Co (loan)	8	—
						Sheffield W	198	18
						Oxford U	65	1
Paul Swannack*	5 9	10 08	10 5 69	Guildford		Oxford U	—	—

OXFORD UNITED

Foundation: There had been an Oxford United club around the time of World War I but only in the Oxfordshire Thursday League and there is no connection with the modern club which began as Headington in 1896, adding "United" three years later. Playing first on Quarry Fields and subsequently Wooton's Fields, they owe much to a Dr. Hitchings for their early development.

Managers (and Secretary-managers)
Harry Thompson 1950–58 (Player coach since 1949), Arthur Turner 1959–69 (continued as GM to 1972), Ron Saunders 1969, George Summers 1969–75, Mike Brown 1975–79, Bill Asprey 1979–80, Ian Greaves 1980–82, Jim Smith 1982–85, Maurice Evans 1985–88, Mark Lawrenson 1988, Brian Horton 1988– .

Player and Position	*Ht*	*Wt*	*Birth Date*	*Birth Place*	*Source*	*Clubs*	*League App*	*League Gls*
Forwards								
Joe Beauchamp	5 11	11 10	13 3 71	Oxford	Trainee	Oxford U	1	—
John Durnin	5 10	11 10	18 8 65	Liverpool	Waterloo Dock	Liverpool	—	—
						WBA (loan)	5	2
						Oxford U	19	3
Martin Foyle	5 10	11 02	2 5 63	Salisbury	Amateur	Southampton	12	1
						Blackburn R (loan)	—	—
						Aldershot	98	35
						Oxford U	77	24
Philip Heath	5 9	12 02	24 11 64	Stoke	Apprentice	Stoke C	156	17
						Oxford U	16	1
David Leworthy*	5 9	12 00	22 10 62	Portsmouth	Apprentice	Portsmouth	1	—
					Fareham T	Tottenham H	11	3
						Oxford U	37	8
						Shrewsbury T (loan)	6	3
Matt McDonnell	5 10	10 10	10 4 71	Reading	Trainee	Oxford U	—	—
Lee Nogan	5 10	11 00	21 5 69	Cardiff	Apprentice	Oxford U	6	—
						Brentford (loan)	11	2
						Southend U (loan)	6	1
Peter Rhoades-Brown	5 9	11 04	2 1 62	Hampton	Apprentice	Chelsea	96	4
						Oxford U	112	13
Paul Simpson	5 6	11 11	26 7 66	Carlisle	Apprentice	Manchester C	118	18
						Oxford U	25	8

Trainees

Byrne, Paul B; Dempsey, Mark A; Didcock, Liam P; Eldridge, Richard; Evans, Paul; Jackson, Darren W; Muttock, Jonathan L; Sorrell, Jason G; Stranks, James R; Waters, Graham J.

Associated Schoolboys

Allen, Christopher A; Bayliss, Gary J; Campbell, Nicholas P; Conneely, Michael; Didcock, Tristan; Dore, Craig A; Druce, Mark A; Fisher, Stuart; Ford, Robert J; Fowler, Jason K.G; Fox, Francis; Harwood, Paul D; Howard, Carl W; Hyatt, Lee C; Jefferd, Kenneth M; Jones, Jason D; Judge, Kevin A; Keeble, Matthew E; Kelly, Leighton; Kennett, Wilson; Lawton, Daniel P; Maisey, Darren; Mclean, Richard G; Mutchell, Robert D; Simpson, Craig G; Tavinor, Stephen J; Wallbridge, Andrew J; Wanless, Paul S; Wild, Robert P; Wright, Andrew L.

PETERBOROUGH UNITED 1988–89 *Back row (left to right):* Gary Butterworth, Adrian Fife, Keith Oakes, Nick Cusack, Gerry McElhinney, Noel Luke, David Langan.
Centre row: Bill Harvey (Physiotherapist), Matthew Sanderson, Bryn Gunn, Paul Crichton, Gary Andrews, Gary Pollard, Joe Neenan, Lee Philpott, Carl Madrick, Tommy Robson (Youth Team Manager).
Front row: Craig Goldsmith, Ashley Carr, David Longhurst, Mick Jones (Manager), Mick Halsall, Steve Collins, Dominic Genovese.

Division 4 **PETERBOROUGH UNITED**

London Road Ground, Peterborough PE2 8AL. Telephone Peterborough (0733) 63947.

Ground capacity: 28,000.

Record attendance: 30,096 v Swansea T, FA Cup 5th rd, 20 Feb, 1965.

Record receipts: £51,315 v Brighton & HA, 5th rd, 15 Feb, 1986.

Pitch measurements: 112yd × 76yd.

President: C. W. Swift OBE.

Chairman: J. F. Devaney. ***Vice-Chairman:*** M. C. Lewis.

Directors: R. D. Bowerman, M. G. Cook, FCA, M. B. Devaney (Mrs), A. Devaney (Miss), J. T. Dykes.

General Manager:

Manager: Mick Jones. ***Coach:*** D. Booth.

General Manager/Secretary: A. V. Blades.

Physio: Bill Harvey.

Commercial Manager: J. Hill.

Year Formed: 1934. ***Turned Professional:*** 1934. ***Ltd Co.:*** 1934.

Club Nickname: 'The Posh'.

Record League Victory: 8-1 v Oldham Ath, Division 4, 26 November 1969 – Drewery; Potts, Noble; Conmy, Wile, Wright; Moss (1), Price (3), Hall (4), Halliday, Robson.

Record Cup Victory: 6–0 v Redditch, FA Cup, 1st rd (replay), 22 November 1971 – Drewery; Carmichael, Brookes; Oakes, Turner, Wright; Conmy, Price (1), Hall (2), Barker (2), Robson (1).

Record Defeat: 1-8 v Northampton T, FA Cup 2nd rd 2nd replay, 18 December, 1946.

Most League Points (2 for a win): 66, Division 4, 1960–61.

Most League Points (3 for a win): 82, Division 4, 1981–82.

Most League Goals: 134, Division 4, 1960–61.

Highest League Scorer in Season: Terry Bly, 52, Division 4, 1960–61.

Most League Goals in Total Aggregate: Jim Hall, 122, 1967–75.

Most Capped Player: Tony Millington, 8 (21), Wales.

Most League Appearances: Tommy Robson, 482, 1968–81.

Record Transfer Fee Received: £110,000 from Blackpool for Bob Doyle, July 1979.

Record Transfer Fee Paid: £100,000 to Halifax T for David Robinson, July 1989.

Football League Record: 1960 Elected to Division 4; 1961–68 Division 3, when they were demoted for financial irregularities; 1968–74 Division 4; 1974–79 Division 3; 1979– Division 4.

Honours: *Football League:* Division 3 best season: 4th, 1977–78. Division 4 – Champions 1960–61, 1973–74, *FA Cup* best season: 6th rd, 1965. *Football League Cup:* Semi-final 1966.

Colours: Royal blue shirts, white shorts, royal blue stockings. **Change Colours:** Yellow shirts, black shorts, yellow stockings.

PETERBOROUGH UNITED 1988–89 LEAGUE RECORD

Match No.	Date	Venue	Opponents	Result	H/T Score	Lg. Pos.	Goalscorers	Attendance
1	Aug 27	A	Carlisle U	D 2-2	1-1	—	Gooding 2 (1 pen)	2650
2	Sept 3	H	Scarborough	L 1-4	1-1	19	Gooding	3916
3	10	A	Darlington	D 2-2	1-1	20	Cusack 2	1521
4	17	H	Lincoln C	D 1-1	0-0	20	Genovese	4256
5	19	A	Tranmere R	L 0-1	0-1	—		2597
6	24	H	York C	L 0-1	0-0	23		2756
7	Oct 1	A	Wrexham	D 1-1	1-0	23	Cusack	1826
8	5	H	Stockport Co	W 1-0	1-0	—	Goldsmith	2572
9	8	A	Grimsby T	D 0-0	0-0	22		2822
10	15	H	Burnley	W 3-0	1-0	20	Goldsmith, Cusack, Oakes	5023
11	22	H	Hereford U	W 2-1	1-0	17	Longhurst, Cusack	3460
12	25	A	Halifax T	L 0-5	0-0	—		2248
13	29	H	Scunthorpe U	L 1-2	1-1	20	Luke	3532
14	Nov 5	A	Leyton Orient	W 2-1	1-0	17	Collins, Longhurst	3695
15	9	H	Hartlepool U	L 0-1	0-0	—		3148
16	12	A	Doncaster R	W 3-2	1-0	19	Cusack, Gunn 2 (1 pen)	2224
17	25	A	Crewe Alex	D 1-1	0-1	—	Cusack	2645
18	Dec 3	H	Rochdale	W 1-0	0-0	15	Oakes	3273
19	17	H	Exeter C	L 0-1	0-0	16		3149
20	26	A	Colchester U	W 2-1	1-0	14	Gunn (pen), McElhinney	2828
21	31	A	Torquay U	L 0-1	0-0	17		2877
22	Jan 3	H	Cambridge U	L 1-5	1-3	—	Swindlehurst	4622
23	7	H	Rotherham U	L 0-3	0-0	18		3368
24	14	A	Scarborough	L 1-2	0-0	19	Cusack	2279
25	21	H	Carlisle U	L 1-4	0-2	21	Halsall	2537
26	28	A	Lincoln C	D 1-1	0-0	22	Goldsmith	4150
27	Feb 4	H	Tranmere R	D 1-1	0-0	21	Oakes	2744
28	11	A	York C	L 1-5	0-2	22	Walsh	2438
29	25	A	Burnley	D 1-1	0-0	22	Gunn (pen)	6848
30	Mar 1	H	Halifax T	W 2-1	0-0	—	Cusack, Oakes	2159
31	4	A	Hereford U	L 0-4	0-0	22		2094
32	11	H	Leyton Orient	L 0-1	0-0	22		3306
33	14	A	Scunthorpe U	L 0-3	0-1	—		3983
34	18	H	Darlington	D 1-1	0-0	22	Longhurst	2482
35	25	A	Cambridge U	L 1-2	0-0	22	Goldsmith	4215
36	27	H	Colchester U	W 3-0	1-0	22	Hetzke (og), Longhurst 2	3529
37	Apr 1	A	Exeter C	L 1-3	0-2	22	Oakes	2522
38	4	A	Rotherham U	D 1-1	1-0	—	Goldsmith	4762
39	8	H	Torquay U	W 3-1	0-0	22	Longhurst 2, Sterling	2614
40	15	H	Wrexham	W 1-0	1-0	22	Cusack	3067
41	21	A	Stockport Co	W 2-1	2-0	—	Luke, Gunn (pen)	2091
42	25	H	Grimsby T	L 1-2	1-0	—	Osborne	2937
43	29	H	Crewe Alex	W 3-2	1-1	18	Gunn (pen), Sterling, Luke	3546
44	May 1	A	Hartlepool U	L 1-2	0-0	20	Gunn (pen)	1643
45	6	A	Rochdale	D 0-0	0-0	20		1430
46	13	H	Doncaster R	W 2-0	1-0	17	Goldsmith, Sterling	2984

Final League Position: 17

GOALSCORERS

League (52): Cusack 10, Gunn 7 (6 pens), Longhurst 7, Goldsmith 6, Oakes 5, Gooding 3 (1 pen), Luke 3, Sterling 3, Collins 1, Genovese 1, Halsall 1, McElhinney 1, Osborne 1, Swindlehurst 1, Walsh 1, own goal 1.
Littlewoods Cup (5): Cusack 1, Genovese 1, Goldsmith 1, Gunn 1 (pen), Oakes 1.
FA Cup (6): Longhurst 3, Cusack 1, Halsall 1, own goal 1.

Littlewoods Cup	First Round	WBA (a)	3-0
		(h)	0-2
	Second Round	Leeds U (h)	1-2
		(a)	1-3
FA Cup	First Round	Gillingham (a)	3-3
		(h)	1-0
	Second Round	Brentford (h)	0-0
		(a)	2-3

Neenan	Langan	Collins	Gooding	McElhinney	Oakes	Genovese	Halsall	Cusack	Gunn	Luke	Goldsmith	Pollard	Andrews	Madrick	Longhurst	Crichton	Carr	Philpott	Butterworth	Swindlehurst	Walsh	Sterling	Harle	Osborne	*Match No.*
1	2	3	4	5	6	7	8	9	10	11															1
1	2	3	4	5	6	7*	8	9	10	11	12														2
1	2	3	4	5	6	7*	8	9	10	11	12														3
1	2			5	6	10*	8	9	3	4	11		7	12											4
1	2			5	6	10*	8	9	3	4	11		7	12											5
1	2	3		5	6		8	9	10	4	11			7											6
1	2†	14		5	6	12	8	9	3	4	11		7	10*											7
1	2*	12		5	6		8	9	3	4	11		7	10											8
1		2		5	6		8	9	3	4	11		7		10										9
1	2			5	6		8	9	3	4	11		7		10										10
1	2			5	6		8	9	3	4	11		7		10										11
1	2			5	6		8	9	3	4	11		7		10										12
1	2*	12		5	6		8	9	3	4	11		7		10										13
		2		5	6		8	9	3	4	11		7		10	1									14
	14*	2†		5	6		8	9	3	4	11		7	12	10	1									15
		2		5	6		8	9	3	4	11		7	12	10*	1									16
		2		5*	6		8	9	3	4	11		7		10	1	12								17
		2		5	6		8	9	3	4	11		7		10	1									18
	4	2		5*	6		8	9	3		11			12	10	1		7†	14						19
	7	2		5	6		8*	9	3	4	11				10	1		12							20
1	7	2		5	6		8		3	4	11				10					9					21
1	7	2		5	6		8		3	4	11				10					9					22
	7	12		5*	6		8	11	3	4	14		2		10†	1				9					23
	2	12		5*	6		8	11	3	4	14		7		10	1				9†					24
		3			6	10	8	9	2	7	11		5			1			4						25
		3			6		8	9	5	2	11		7		10	1			4						26
		3			6		8	9	2	7	11		5		10	1					4				27
		3*				12	8	9	5†	2	11	6	7		10	1			14		4				28
					6	12	8	9	3	2		5	7		10*	1			4		11				29
					6		8	9	3	2		5	7		10	1			4		11				30
					6		8	9	3	2		5	7		10	1			4		11				31
					6	12	8	9	3	2	11*	5	7		10	1		14	4†						32
		11			6	4	8	9	3	2		5	7		10	1									33
		4			6	12	8	9	3	2	11	5	7*		10	1									34
		4			6		8	9	3	2	11	5			10	1						7			35
				5	6		8	9*	3	2	11				10	1						7	4	12	36
		8		5	6	14		9	3	2	11†				10*	1						7	4	12	37
		8		5				9	3	2	11		6		10	1						7	4		38
		8		5		14		9*	3	2	11†		6		10	1						7	4	12	39
		8		5	6	14		9	3	2	11†		4*		10	1						7		12	40
				5	6		8	9	3	2	11				10	1						7	4		41
				5*	6		8	9	3	2	11				10	1						7	4	12	42
		12			6		8	9	3	2			5		10	1						7	4*	11	43
		4			6		8	9	3	2	12		5*		10	1						7		11	44
		4		6			8	9	3	2	12		5		10	1						7		11*	45
		4		5			8	9	3	2	11		6*		10	1						7		12	46
15	18 + 1s	28 + 6s	3	33	41	7 + 8s	42	44	46	45	34 + 6s	8	33	3 + 5s	37	31	— + 1s	1 + 2s	6 + 2s	4	5	12	7	3 + 6s	

PETERBOROUGH UNITED

Player and Position	Ht	Wt	Birth Date	Birth Place	Source	Clubs	League App	League Gls
Goalkeepers								
Paul Crichton	6 1	12 05	3 10 68	Pontefract	Apprentice	Nottingham F	—	—
						Notts Co (loan)	5	—
						Darlington (loan)	5	—
						Peterborough U	4	—
						(loan)	3	—
						Darlington (loan)	4	—
						Swindon T (loan)	6	—
						Rotherham U (loan)	13	—
						Torquay U (loan)	31	—
						Peterborough U		
Joe Neenan‡	6 2	12 13	17 3 59	Manchester	Apprentice	York C	56	—
						Scunthorpe U	191	—
						Burnley (loan)	9	—
						Burnley	81	—
						Peterborough U	55	—
						Scarborough (loan)	6	—
Defenders								
Gary Andrews	5 11	12 01	12 5 68	Nottingham		Nottingham F	—	—
						Peterborough U	33	—
Steve Collins	5 8	12 04	21 3 62	Stamford	Apprentice	Peterborough U	94	1
						Southend U	51	—
						Lincoln C (loan)	13	—
						Lincoln C	11	—
						Peterborough U	122	2
Bryn Gunn	6 2	13 07	21 8 58	Kettering	Apprentice	Nottingham F	131	1
						Shrewsbury T (loan)	9	—
						Walsall (loan)	6	—
						Mansfield T (loan)	5	—
						Peterborough U	131	14
David Langan‡	5 10	11 02	12 2 57	Dublin	Apprentice	Derby Co	143	1
						Birmingham C	92	3
						Oxford U	114	2
						Leicester C (loan)	5	—
						Bournemouth	20	—
						Peterborough U	19	—
Gerry McElhinney	6 1	13 10	19 9 56	Londonderry	Distillery	Bolton W	109	2
						Rochdale (loan)	20	1
						Plymouth Arg	91	2
						Peterborough U	33	1
Keith Oakes	5 10	12 02	3 7 56	Bedworth	Apprentice	Peterborough U	62	2
						Newport Co	232	27
						Gillingham	86	7
						Fulham	76	3
						Peterborough U	41	5
Gary Pollard‡	6 1	11 10	22 5 54	Staveley	Amateur	Chesterfield	87	1
						Port Vale	18	—
						Mansfield T	67	1
						Peterborough U	20	—
Midfield								
Garry Butterworth			8 9 69	Peterborough	Trainee	Peterborough U	20	—
Ashley Carr‡	5 9	10 03	15 8 68	Crowland		Peterborough U	15	—
Adrian Fife‡			13 9 69	Peterborough	Trainee	Peterborough U	2	—
Mick Halsall	5 10	11 04	21 7 61	Bootle	Apprentice	Liverpool	—	—
						Birmingham C	36	3
						Carlisle U	92	11
						Grimsby T	12	—
						Peterborough U	87	5

PETERBOROUGH UNITED

Foundation: The old Peterborough & Fletton club, founded in 1923, was suspended by the FA during season 1932–33 and disbanded. Local enthusiasts determined to carry on and in 1934 a new professional club Peterborough United was formed and entered the Midland League the following year.

Managers (and Secretary-managers)
Jock Porter 1934–36, Fred Taylor 1936–37, Vic Poulter 1937–38, Sam Madden 1938–48, Jack Blood 1948–50, Bob Gurney 1950–52, Jack Fairbrother 1952–54, George Swindin 1954–58, Jimmy Hagan 1958–62, Jack Fairbrother 1962–64, Gordon Clark 1964–67, Norman Rigby 1967–69, Jim Iley 1969–72, Noel Cantwell 1972–77, John Barnwell 1977–78, Billy Hails 1978–79, Peter Morris 1979–82, Martin Wilkinson 1982–83, John Wile 1983–86, Noel Cantwell 1986–88 (continued as GM), Mick Jones 1988– .

Player and Position	*Ht*	*Wt*	*Birth Date*	*Birth Place*	*Source*	*Clubs*	*League App*	*League Gls*
David Harle	5 9	10 07	15 8 63	Denaby	Apprentice	Doncaster R	61	3
						Exeter C	43	6
						Doncaster R	83	17
						Leeds U	3	—
						Bristol C (loan)	8	—
						Bristol C	15	2
						Scunthorpe U	89	10
						Peterborough U	7	—
Noel Luke	5 11	10 11	28 12 64	Birmingham	School	WBA	9	1
						Mansfield T	50	9
						Peterborough U	118	20
Carl Madrick‡	5 9	9 11	20 9 68	Bolton	Trainee	Huddersfield T	8	1
						Peterborough U	8	—
Lee Philpott‡			21 2 70	Barnet	Trainee	Peterborough U	4	—
Matt Sanderson‡			30 4 70	Peterborough	Trainee	Peterborough U	—	—
Forwards								
Nicky Cusack	6 00	11 13	24 12 65	Rotherham	Alvechurch	Leicester C	16	1
						Peterborough U	44	10
Domenico Genovese*			2 2 61	Peterborough	Cambridge C	Peterborough U	16	1
Craig Goldsmith			27 8 63	Peterborough	Blackstones	Peterborough U	40	6
David Longhurst	5 8	10 12	15 1 65	Northampton	Apprentice	Nottingham F	—	—
						Halifax T	85	24
						Northampton T	37	7
						Peterborough U	37	7
Mike Nuttell	6 1	12 00	22 11 68	Boston	Trainee	Peterborough U	21	—
						Crewe Alex (loan)	3	1
						Carlisle U (loan)	3	—
Steve Osborne			3 3 69	Middlesbrough	South Bank	Peterborough U	9	1
Worrell Sterling	5 8	10 08	8 6 65	Bethnal Green	Apprentice	Watford	94	14
						Peterborough U	12	3

Trainees
Atkin, Robert; Bradley, Martin P; Burrows, Lee M; Cheyne, James W; Clarke, Darrin W; Cooper, Darren; Facer, Jon; Heal, David J; Islam, Rezaul; Mackintosh, Stuart; Marshall, Trevor J; Speed, Adrian C; Sullivan, Robert; Tuffs, Andrew G; Wick, Jason P; Wills, Shaun D.

PLYMOUTH ARGYLE 1988–89 *Back row (left to right):* John Brimacombe, Nicky Marker, Stewart Evans, Garry Penhaligon, Geoff Crudgington, Steve Cherry, Mark Smith, Andrew Morrison. *Centre row:* Stuart Casey, Owen Pickard, Tommy Tynan, John Uzzell, Adrian Burrows, Doug Anderson, Kevin Summerfield. *Front row:* Kevin Hodges, Leigh Cooper, John Matthews, Malcolm Musgrove (Physiotherapist), Ken Brown (Manager), Martin Harvey (Coach), Sean McCarthy, Kenny Brown, Jason Rowbotham.

Division 2 PLYMOUTH ARGYLE

Home Park, Plymouth, Devon PL2 3DQ. Telephone Plymouth (0752) 562561-2-3. Lottery Shop: 561041.

Ground capacity: 26,000.

Record attendance: 43,596 v Aston Villa, Division 2. 10 Oct, 1936.

Record receipts: £96,989.57 v Derby Co, FA Cup 6th rd. 10 March, 1984.

Pitch measurements: 112yd × 75yd.

President: G. H. Gillin.

Chairman: P. D. Bloom.

Directors: B. L. Hooper, R. Burroughs ARICS. G. E. Jasper, J. E. C. Kent, D. Forshaw, C. Hartley.

Team Manager: Ken Brown. ***Coach:*** Martin Harvey.

Secretary: Graham Little. ***Commercial Manager:*** D. Botham.

Physio: Malcolm Musgrove.

Year Formed: 1886. ***Turned Professional:*** 1903. ***Ltd Co.:*** 1903.

Club Nickname: 'The Pilgrims'.

Previous Name: 1886–1903. Argyle Athletic Club.

Record League Victory: 8-1 v Millwall, Division 2, 16 January 1932 – Harper; Roberts, Titmuss; Mackay, Pullan, Reed; Grozier, Bowden (2), Vidler (3), Leslie (1), Black (1). (1 og)

Record Cup Victory: 6-0 v Corby T, FA Cup, 3rd rd, 22 January 1966 – Leiper; Book, Baird; Williams, Nelson, Newman; Jones (1), Jackson (1), Bickle (3), Piper (1), Jennings.

Record Defeat: 0-9 v Stoke C, Division 2, 17 December, 1960.

Most League Points (2 for a win): 68, Division 3 (S), 1929–30.

Most League Points (3 for a win): 87, Division 3, 1985–86.

Most League Goals: 107, Division 3 (S), 1925–26 and 1951–52.

Highest League Scorer in Season: Jack Cock, 32, Division 3 (S), 1925–26.

Most League Goals in Total Aggregate: Sammy Black, 180, 1924–38.

Most Capped Player: Moses Russell, 20 (23), Wales.

Most League Appearances: Sammy Black, 470, 1924–38.

Record Transfer Fee Received: £250,000 from Everton for Gary Megson, February 1980.

Record Transfer Fee Paid: £170,000 to Sheffield W for Mark Smith, January 1987.

Football League Record: 1920 Original Member of Division 3; 1921–30 Division 3 (S); 1930–50 Division 2; 1950–52 Division 3 (S); 1952–56 Division 2; 1956–58 Division 3 (S); 1958–59 Division 3; 1959–68 Division 2; 1968–75 Division 3; 1975–77 Division 2; 1977–86 Division 3; 1986– Division 2.

Honours: *Football League:* Division 2 best season: 4th, 1931–32, 1952–53; Division 3 (S) – Champions 1929–30, 1951–52; Runners-up 1921–22, 1922–23, 1923–24, 1924–25, 1925–26, 1926–27 (record of six consecutive years); Division 3 – Champions 1958–59; Runners-up 1974–75, 1985–86. *FA Cup* best season: semi-final 1983–84. *Football League Cup:* Semi-final, 1965, 1974.

Colours: Green shirts, black shorts, white stockings green tops. **Change Colours:** White shirts, white shorts, white stockings green tops.

PLYMOUTH ARGYLE 1988–89 LEAGUE RECORD

Match No.	Date	Venue	Opponents	Result	H/T Score	Lg. Pos.	Goalscorers	Attendance
1	Aug 27	A	Walsall	D 2-2	2-0	—	Tynan, Marker	6178
2	Sept 3	H	Hull C	W 2-0	0-0	7	Tynan, Skipper (og)	8202
3	10	A	Watford	L 0-3	0-1	11		12,040
4	17	H	Stoke C	W 4-0	2-0	9	Tynan 3, Marker	7823
5	21	A	Leicester C	L 0-1	0-0	—		9117
6	24	H	WBA	D 1-1	0-0	13	Tynan	8539
7	Oct 1	A	Crystal Palace	L 1-4	1-3	19	Brimacombe	8047
8	4	A	Birmingham C	W 1-0	0-0	—	Tynan	4921
9	8	H	Bradford C	W 3-1	3-0	8	Tynan 2, McCarthy	6855
10	15	H	Manchester C	L 0-1	0-0	14		10,158
11	22	A	Chelsea	L 0-5	0-4	16		12,658
12	25	H	Shrewsbury T	D 0-0	0-0	—		6298
13	29	A	Barnsley	L 1-3	0-1	19	Marker	5485
14	Nov 5	H	Blackburn R	W 4-3	3-0	18	Tynan 4	7823
15	12	A	Portsmouth	L 0-2	0-2	20		11,572
16	19	A	Oxford U	W 1-0	1-0	17	Tynan	5429
17	26	H	Oldham Ath	W 3-0	2-0	13	Tynan, Campbell, Hodges	7829
18	Dec 3	A	Ipswich T	D 2-2	2-1	16	Campbell, Stuart	9929
19	6	H	Brighton & HA	W 3-0	1-0	—	Tynan 2 (1 pen), Plummer	8133
20	10	H	Bournemouth	D 1-1	0-0	8	Summerfield	10,619
21	18	H	Sunderland	L 1-4	0-2	—	Tynan (pen)	13,498
22	26	A	Swindon T	L 0-1	0-1	15		7883
23	31	A	Leeds U	L 0-2	0-0	16		24,043
24	Jan 2	H	Watford	W 1-0	0-0	16	Summerfield	12,142
25	14	A	Brighton & HA	D 2-2	1-1	16	Tynan, Stuart	8504
26	21	H	Walsall	W 2-0	0-0	15	Tynan, Marker	11,505
27	Feb 4	H	Birmingham C	L 0-1	0-1	14		7721
28	11	A	Bradford C	D 1-1	1-0	16	McCarthy	8693
29	18	H	Chelsea	L 0-1	0-1	16		13,180
30	25	A	Manchester C	L 0-2	0-1	17		22,451
31	28	A	Shrewsbury T	L 0-2	0-1	—		2978
32	Mar 4	H	Portsmouth	L 0-1	0-0	18		8131
33	11	A	Blackburn R	W 2-1	1-0	16	Stuart, Tynan	7462
34	18	H	Leicester C	D 1-1	1-0	18	Stuart	6703
35	25	A	Hull C	L 0-3	0-2	20		5851
36	27	H	Swindon T	W 4-1	3-0	18	Marker, Tynan (pen), McCarthy 2	8487
37	Apr 1	A	Stoke C	D 2-2	0-2	17	Tynan (pen), McCarthy	8363
38	4	A	Sunderland	L 1-2	0-2	—	Tynan	8003
39	9	H	Leeds U	W 1-0	0-0	—	McCarthy	9365
40	15	A	WBA	D 2-2	0-1	19	Brown, McCarthy	11,358
41	22	H	Crystal Palace	L 0-2	0-1	19		8492
42	25	H	Barnsley	L 1-2	1-1	—	Byrne	5468
43	29	A	Oldham Ath	D 2-2	1-2	18	Marker, Campbell	4614
44	May 1	H	Ipswich T	L 0-1	0-1	20		6484
45	6	H	Oxford U	W 3-1	0-0	18	Burrows, McCarthy, Stuart	4989
46	13	A	Bournemouth	D 0-0	0-0	18		7230

Final League Position: 18

GOALSCORERS

League (55): Tynan 24 (4 pens), McCarthy 8, Marker 6, Stuart 5, Campbell 3, Summerfield 2, Brimacombe 1, Brown 1, Burrows 1, Byrne 1, Hodges 1, Plummer 1, own goal 1.
Littlewoods Cup (9): McCarthy 4, Marker 2, Smith 1, Summerfield 1, Tynan 1.
FA Cup (3): McCarthy 1, Summerfield 1, Tynan 1.

Littlewoods Cup	First Round	Hereford U (a)	3-0
		(h)	3-2
	Second Round	Manchester C (a)	0-1
		(h)	3-6
FA Cup	Third Round	Cambridge U (h)	2-0
	Fourth Round	Everton (h)	1-1
		(a)	0-4

Cherry	Brimacombe	Cooper	Burrows	Marker	Smith	Hodges	Matthews	Tynan	McCarthy	Summerfield	Evans	Uzzell	Plummer	Brown	Penhaligon	Stuart	Campbell G	Miller	Rowbotham	Wilmot	Pickard	Byrne	Morrison	Garner	Barlow	Whiston	Campbell D	*Match No.*
1	2	3	4	5	6	7	8	9*	10	11	12																	1
1	2	3	4	5	6		8	9	10*	11	7	12																2
1	2	3	4	5	6		8	9	10	11			7															3
1	11	3	4	5	6		8	9	10				7	2														4
1	11	3	4*	5	6		8	9	10	12			7	2														5
1	11	3	4	5	6		8	9	10				7	2														6
1	11	3	4	5	6		8*	9†	10	12	14		7	2														7
	11	3	4	5	6		8	9	10				7	2	1													8
1	11	3	4	5	6		8	9	10				7	2														9
1	11	3	4	5			8*	9	10	12		6	7	2														10
1	11	3	4	5	6	14	8*	9	10			12	7†	2														11
1	11	3	4	5	6	7		9	10	8				2														12
1	11*	3	4	5	6	7		9	10	8		12		2														13
1		3	4	5				9	10	8		6	7	2		11												14
1	6	3*	4			8	12	9	10†			5	7	2		11	14											15
1	5		4			7	8	9		6		3	10	2		11												16
	5		4			8		9		6		3	7	2		11	10	1										17
	5		4	12		8		9		6		3	7*	2		11	10	1										18
	4			5		8		9		6		3	7	2		11	10	1										19
	4			5		8		9	12	6		3	7	2		11	10*	1										20
	4			5		8		9		6		3	7	2		11	10	1										21
			4	5	7	8		9	10	6		3		2		11		1										22
			4	5	7	8		9	10	6		3		2		11		1										23
			4	5	6	8		9	10	7		3		2		11		1										24
			4	5	6	8		9	10*	7		3				11	12	1	2									25
			4	5	6	8		9	10*	7		3				11	12	1	2									26
			4	5	6	10*	7	9	8			3		2		11	12	1										27
			4	5	6	10	7†	9*	8			3	14	2		11	12	1										28
			4	5	6	10	7*	9	8			3	12	2		11		1										29
			4	5	6	10	7	9	8*			3	12	2		11				1								30
			4	5	6	10	7*	9	8			3	12	2		11				1								31
			4	5	6	10	7*	9	8†				12	2		11			3	1	14							32
			4	5	6		7	9	8			3		2		11				1							10	33
			4	5	6	12	7*	9				3				11			2	1	10	8						34
			4	5	6		7	9	8			3				11			2	1		10						35
			4	5	6		7	9*	8			3		2		11	12			1		10						36
			4	5	6	12	10	9	8			3		2		11				1		7*						37
			4	5	6	12	10*	9	8			3		2		11				1		7						38
			4	5	6	12	10*	9	8			3		2		11				1		7						39
			4	5	6	11	10	9	8			3		2						1		7						40
			4	5	6	12	10*	9	8			3		2		11				1		7						41
			4	5	6		10	9	8			3		2		11				1		7						42
	8		4	5	6	12	10*	9				3†		2		11	14			1		7						43
	3		4	5	6	10		9	8					2		11				1		7						44
	3		4	5				9	8					2		11				1		7*	6	10†	12	14		45
	3		4	5		12		9					14	2		11	8			1		7†	6			10*		46
15	24	15	43	42 + 1s	35	23 + 8s	29 + 1s	46	37 + 1s	17 + 3s	1 + 2s	30 + 3s	17 + 6s	39	1	32	6 + 7s	13	5	17	1 + 1s	13	2	1	— + 1s	1 + 1s	1	

PLYMOUTH ARGYLE

Player and Position	Ht	Wt	Birth Date	Birth Place	Source	Clubs	League App	League Gls
Goalkeepers								
Geoff Crudgington*	6 0	12 12	14 2 52	Wolverhampton	Amateur	Aston Villa	4	—
						Bradford C (loan)	1	—
						Crewe Alex	250	—
						Preston NE (loan)	—	—
						Swansea C	52	—
						Plymouth Arg	326	—
Garry Penhaligon	6 0	12 01	13 5 70	St Austell	Trainee	Plymouth Arg	1	—
Defenders								
John Brimacombe	5 11	11 10	25 11 58	Plymouth	Liskeard/ Saltash	Plymouth Arg	78	3
Kenny Brown	5 8	11 06	11 7 67	Barking	Apprentice	Norwich C	25	—
						Plymouth Arg	39	1
Adrian Burrows	5 11	11 12	16 1 59	Sutton	Local	Mansfield T	78	5
						Northampton T	88	4
						Plymouth Arg	129	5
						Southend U (loan)	6	—
Leigh Cooper	5 8	10 09	7 5 61	Reading	Apprentice	Plymouth Arg	321	15
Nick Marker	6 1	13 00	3 5 65	Exeter	Apprentice	Exeter C	202	3
						Plymouth Arg	69	7
Andy Morrison			30 7 70	Inverness	Trainee	Plymouth Arg	3	—
Jason Rowbotham			3 1 69	Cardiff	Trainee	Plymouth Arg	9	—
Mark Smith	6 0	12 10	21 3 60	Sheffield	Apprentice	Sheffield W	282	16
						Plymouth Arg	76	6
John Uzzell	5 10	11 03	31 3 59	Plymouth	Apprentice	Plymouth Arg	302	6
Midfield								
Dougie Anderson	6 0	10 05	29 8 63	Hong Kong	Port Glasgow	Oldham Ath	9	—
						Tranmere R	120	15
						Plymouth Arg	19	1
						Cambridge U (loan)	8	2
						Northampton T (loan)	5	—
Martin Barlow§			25 6 71	Barnstable	Trainee	Plymouth Arg	1	—
Stuart Casey	5 7	10 07	5 9 69	Plymouth	Trainee	Plymouth Arg	—	—
Darren Garner	5 6	11 01	10 12 71	Plymouth	Trainee	Plymouth Arg	1	—
Kevin Hodges	5 8	10 00	12 6 60	Bridport	Apprentice	Plymouth Arg	426	74
John Matthews‡	6 0	12 06	1 11 55	London	Apprentice	Arsenal	45	2
						Sheffield U	103	14
						Mansfield T	72	6
						Chesterfield	38	1
						Plymouth Arg	135	4
Kevin Summerfield	5 11	11 00	7 1 59	Walsall	Apprentice	WBA	9	4
						Birmingham C	5	1
						Walsall	54	17
						Cardiff C	10	1
						Plymouth Arg	128	25
Forwards								
David Byrne	5 8	11 00	5 3 61	London	Kingstonian	Gillingham	63,	6
						Millwall	4	—
						Cambridge U (loan)	4	—
						Blackburn R (loan)	13	1
						Plymouth Arg		
Greg Campbell	5 11	11 05	13 7 65	Portsmouth	Apprentice	West Ham U	5	—
						Brighton & HA (loan)	2	—
						Plymouth Arg	13	3
John Clayton (To Fortuna Sittard)	5 11	11 07	20 8 61	Elgin	Apprentice Bulova	Derby Co	24	4
						Chesterfield	33	5
						Tranmere R	47	35
						Plymouth Arg	77	22

PLYMOUTH ARGYLE

Foundation: The Plymouth Argyle Association Football Club developed out of the Argyle Athletic club which was formed in 1886 at a meeting in Argyle Terrace, Mutley. Plymouth was a rugby stronghold, but servicemen brought soccer to the town and it spread quickly. At first Argyle Athletic Club played both soccer and rugby in colours of green and black. The rugby section was eventually disbanded, and after a number of exhibition games had satisfied the locals of the feasibility of running a professional club, Plymouth Argyle was formed in 1903.

Managers (and Secretary-managers)
Frank Brettell 1903–05, Bob Jack 1905–06, Bill Fullerton 1906–07, Bob Jack 1910–38, Jack Tresadern 1938–47, Jimmy Rae 1948–55, Jack Rowley 1955–60, Neil Dougall 1961, Ellis Stuttard 1961–63, Andy Beattie 1963–64, Malcolm Allison 1964–65, Derek Ufton 1965–68, Billy Bingham 1968–70, Ellis Stuttard 1970–72, Tony Waiters 1972–77, Mike Kelly 1977–78, Malcolm Allison 1978-79, Bobby Saxton 1979–81, Bobby Moncur 1981–83, Johnny Hore 1983–84, Dave Smith 1984–88, Ken Brown 1988– .

Player and Position	*Ht*	*Wt*	*Birth Date*	*Place*	*Source*	*Clubs*	*League App*	*Gls*
Sean McCarthy	6 0	12 02	12 9 67	Bridgend	Bridgend	Swansea C	91	25
						Plymouth Arg	38	8
Owen Pickard	5 10	1 03	18 11 69	Barnstaple	Trainee	Plymouth Arg	2	—
Calvin Plummer	5 8	10 07	14 2 63	Nottingham	Apprentice	Nottingham F	12	2
						Chesterfield	28	7
						Derby Co	27	3
						Barnsley	54	6
						Nottingham F	8	2
						Derry C (loan)	—	—
						Plymouth Arg	23	1
Mark Stuart	5 8	11 02	15 12 66	Hammersmith	QPR schoolboy	Charlton Ath	107	28
						Plymouth Arg	32	5
Tommy Tynan	5 10	12 09	17 11 55	Liverpool	Apprentice	Liverpool	—	—
						Swansea C (loan)	6	2
						Sheffield W	91	31
						Lincoln C	9	1
						Newport Co	183	66
						Plymouth Arg	80	43
						Rotherham U	32	13
						Plymouth Arg (loan)	9	9
						Plymouth Arg	129	58
Peter Whiston			4 1 68	Widnes		Plymouth Arg	2	—

Trainees
Adcock, Paul M; Barlow, Martin D; Browne, Martyn A; Cansfield, Lee; Casey, Robert N; Davey, Damien S; Evans, Anthony D; Goddard, Scott; Jones, Jason S; Pethick, Robert J; Rowe, Paul D; Smith, Paul A; Tallon, Darren J.B.

****Non-Contract**
Nute, Stephen L.R.

Associated Schoolboys
Bagnall, William J.D; Bull, Leighton J; Crocker, Marcus; Hajiyianni, John; Jones, Stephen A; Kendall, Lee; Mead, Paul A; Roberts, Kevan P; Smith, Damian B; Widger, Andy; Williams, Keith R; Wotton, Garry L.

PORTSMOUTH 1988–89 *Back row (left to right):* Eamonn Collins, Mark Chamberlain, Gavin Maguire, Clive Whitehead, Warren Neill, Terry Connor, Paul Hardyman, Mark Kelly.
Centre row: John Dickens (Physiotherapist), Kevin Dillon, Lee Sandford, Kit Symons, Alan Knight, Andy Gosney, Graeme Hogg, Billy Gilbert, Mick Fillery, Gordon Neave (Kitman).
Front row: Warren Aspinall, Barry Horne, Graham Paddon (Youth Coach), Kevin Ball, John Gregory (Manager), Mick Quinn, Martin Kuhl.

Division 2 PORTSMOUTH

Fratton Park, Frogmore Rd, Portsmouth PO4 8RA. Telephone Portsmouth (0705) 731204. Commercial Dept: 0705-827111. Ticket Office: 0705-750825. Lottery Office: 0705 825016. Clubcall: 0898 121182.

Ground capacity: 28,000.

Record attendance: 51,385 v Derby Co, FA Cup 6th rd, 26 Feb, 1949.

Record receipts: £122,000 v Southampton, FA Cup 4th rd, 28 Jan, 1984.

Pitch measurements: 116yd × 73yd.

President: B. J. Deacon CBE. ***Vice-Presidents:*** Sir A. L. Blake MC, LLB, KCVO, Mrs J. Deacon.

Chairman: J. A. Gregory. ***Vice-Chairman:*** D. K. Deacon.

Directors: M. H. Gregory, R. Stainton, J. W. Slaon, J. P. R. Prevost FCA., M. Murphy, R. Jones, D. Deacon, B. Henson, J. Dunnett.

Team Manager: John Gregory. ***Coach:*** Steve Wicks.

Chief Executive/Company Secretary: P. Weld. ***Commercial Manager:*** Ray Stainton.

Physio: John Dickens. ***Youth Team Coach:*** Graham Paddon.

Year Formed: 1898. ***Turned Professional:*** 1898. ***Ltd Co.:*** 1898.

Club Nickname: 'Pompey'.

Record League Victory: 9-1 v Notts Co, Division 2, 9 April 1927 – McPhail; Clifford, Ted Smith; Reg Davies (1), Foxall, Moffat; Forward (1), Mackie (2), Haines (3), Watson, Cook (2).

Record Cup Victory: 7-0 v Stockport Co, FA Cup, 3rd rd, 8 January 1949 – Butler; Rookes, Ferrier; Scoular, Flewin, Dickinson; Harris (3), Barlow, Clarke (2), Phillips (2), Froggatt.

Record Defeat: 0-10 v Leicester C, Division 1, 20 October, 1928.

Most League Points (2 for a win): 65, Division 3, 1961–62.

Most League Points (3 for a win): 91, Division 3, 1982–83.

Most League Goals: 91, Division 4, 1979–80.

Highest League Scorer in Season: Billy Haines, 40. Division 2, 1926–27.

Most League Goals in Total Aggregate: Peter Harris, 194, 1946–60.

Most Capped Player: Jimmy Dickinson, 48, England.

Most League Appearances: Jimmy Dickinson, 764, 1946–65.

Record Transfer Fee Received: £915,000 from AC Milan for Mark Hateley, June 1984.

Record Transfer Fee Paid: £315,000 to Aston Villa for Warren Aspinall, August 1988.

Football League Record: 1920 Original Member of Division 3; 1921 Division 3 (S); 1924–27 Division 2; 1927–59 Division 1; 1959–61 Division 2; 1961–62 Division 3; 1962–76 Division 2; 1976–78 Division 3; 1978–80 Division 4; 1980–83 Division 3; 1983–87 Division 2; 1987–88 Division 1; 1988– Division 2.

Honours: *Football League:* Division 1 – Champions 1948–49, 1949–50; Division 2 – Runners-up 1926–27, 1986–87; Division 3 (S) – Champions 1923–24; Division 3 – Champions 1961–62, 1982–83. *FA Cup:* Winners 1939; Runners-up 1929, 1934. *Football League Cup* best season: 5th rd, 1960–61. 1985–86.

Colours: Blue shirts, white shorts, red stockings. **Change Colours:** Yellow shirts, blue shorts, black stockings.

PORTSMOUTH 1988–89 LEAGUE RECORD

Match No.	Date	Venue	Opponents	Result	H/T Score	Lg. Pos.	Goalscorers	Attendance
1	Aug 27	A	Shrewsbury T	W 2-1	1-1	—	Connor, Kelly	5333
2	29	H	Leicester C	W 3-0	1-0	—	Connor 2, Quinn (pen)	10,737
3	Sept 3	H	Leeds U	W 4-0	2-0	1	Taylor (og), Quinn, Connor, Chamberlain	15,263
4	11	A	Swindon T	D 1-1	1-0	—	Chamberlain	11,443
5	17	H	Hull C	L 1-3	0-2	3	Connor	11,599
6	20	A	Stoke C	D 2-2	1-1	—	Horne, Aspinall	7025
7	24	H	Crystal Palace	D 1-1	1-0	4	Aspinall (pen)	11,249
8	Oct 1	A	Bradford C	L 1-2	1-2	6	Aspinall (pen)	11,208
9	5	A	Manchester C	L 1-4	1-3	—	Aspinall	17,202
10	8	H	Oxford U	W 2-1	1-1	7	Aspinall (pen), Quinn	9567
11	15	H	Bournemouth	W 2-1	1-0	5	Chamberlain, Quinn	12,801
12	22	A	Walsall	D 1-1	1-0	6	Quinn	5626
13	25	A	Ipswich T	W 1-0	0-0	—	Horne	14,796
14	29	H	Oldham Ath	D 1-1	1-1	4	Aspinall (pen)	11,310
15	Nov 5	A	Birmingham C	D 0-0	0-0	5		5866
16	12	H	Plymouth Arg	W 2-0	2-0	3	Chamberlain, Quinn	11,572
17	19	H	Barnsley	W 3-0	2-0	1	Quinn, Horne 2	10,001
18	26	A	Blackburn R	L 1-3	1-1	5	Chamberlain	8141
19	Dec 3	H	WBA	D 0-0	0-0	5		12,779
20	10	A	Chelsea	D 3-3	1-2	6	Quinn, Kuhl, Ball	20,221
21	17	H	Brighton & HA	W 2-0	1-0	5	Aspinall, Hardyman	12,467
22	26	A	Watford	L 0-1	0-0	6		15,224
23	31	A	Sunderland	L 0-4	0-2	7		21,566
24	Jan 2	H	Swindon T	L 0-2	0-1	9		11,681
25	14	A	Leicester C	L 1-2	1-1	13	Quinn	10,567
26	21	H	Shrewsbury T	W 2-0	1-0	10	Aspinall (pen), Hogg	8446
27	Feb 4	H	Manchester C	L 0-1	0-1	13		13,207
28	11	A	Oxford U	L 0-1	0-1	13		6150
29	18	H	Walsall	D 1-1	0-1	14	Quinn	7310
30	25	A	Bournemouth	L 0-1	0-0	14		9995
31	28	H	Ipswich T	L 0-1	0-0	—		7145
32	Mar 4	A	Plymouth Arg	W 1-0	0-0	14	Quinn	8131
33	11	H	Birmingham C	W 1-0	0-0	13	Chamberlain	8078
34	14	A	Oldham Ath	L 3-5	0-2	—	Aspinall, Quinn 2	5773
35	18	H	Stoke C	D 0-0	0-0	13		7624
36	25	A	Leeds U	L 0-1	0-0	14		27,049
37	27	H	Watford	D 2-2	2-0	13	Quinn, Aspinall	9364
38	Apr 1	A	Hull C	D 1-1	0-0	14	Quinn	5325
39	5	A	Brighton & HA	L 1-2	1-0	—	Fillery	10,100
40	8	H	Sunderland	W 2-0	1-0	13	Quinn 2	7724
41	15	A	Crystal Palace	L 0-2	0-0	16		12,358
42	22	H	Bradford C	L 1-2	0-1	17	Aspinall	6909
43	29	H	Blackburn R	L 1-2	0-0	17	Fillery	6057
44	May 1	A	WBA	L 0-3	0-1	18		9586
45	6	A	Barnsley	L 0-1	0-0	19		5178
46	13	H	Chelsea	L 2-3	1-0	20	Roberts (og), Quinn (pen)	12,051

Final League Position: 20

GOALSCORERS

League (53): Quinn 18 (2 pens), Aspinall 11 (5 pens), Chamberlain 6, Connor 5, Horne 4, Fillery 2, Ball 1, Hardyman 1, Hogg 1, Kelly 1, Kuhl 1, own goals 2.
Littlewoods Cup (3): Aspinall 1, Connor 1, Quinn 1.
FA Cup (1): Quinn 1.

Littlewoods Cup	Second Round	Scarborough (h)	2-2
		(a)	1-3
FA Cup	Third Round	Swindon T (h)	1-1
		(a)	0-2

Knight	Neill	Hardyman	Dillon	Hogg	Gilbert	Whitehead	Horne	Quinn	Connor	Sandford	Kelly	Chamberlain	Aspinall	Russell	Kuhl	Ball	Powell	Maguire	Symons	Moran	Fillery	Ross	Gosney	Moncur	Wigley	Beresford	Awford	*Match No.*
1	2	3	4	5	6	7*	8	9	10	11	12																	1
1	2	3	4	5	6	7	8	9	10	11																		2
1	2	3	4	5	6†	14	8*	9	10	11	12	7																3
1	2	3	4	5	6		8	9*	10	11		7	12															4
1	2†	3	4	5	6	14	8	9	10	11		7*	12															5
1		3	4	5		6	8		10	2	11	7	9															6
1		3*	4	5		6	2	9	8		11	7	10	12														7
1	2†	3		5	4	6	8	12	10	14	11*		9		7													8
1	2	3		5	6		8	12	10*		11	7	9		4													9
1	2	3	12	5		6	8	10	7*		11		9		4													10
1	2	3		5			8	12	10*		11	7	9		4	6												11
1	2	3*			5	14	8	10		12	11†	7	9		4	6												12
1	2			5			8	10		3	11	7	9		4	6												13
1	2			5			8	10		3	11	7	9		4	6												14
1	2			5		12	8	10		3	11*	7	9		4	6												15
1	2	11		5			8	10		3*	12	7	9		4	6												16
1	2		14	5		12	8	10		3	11†	7	9*		4	6												17
1	2	11*	12	5			8	10		3		7	9		4	6												18
1	2		12	5			8	10		3	11*	7	9		4	6												19
1	2	11	8	5				10		3		7	9		4	6												20
1	2	11	8	5	4			10		3		7	9			6												21
1	2	11*	8			5	14	10		3	12	7†	9		4	6												22
1	2	14	11	5			8	10		3†	12	7*	9		4	6												23
1	2	11	7	5			8	10		3*	12		9†		4	6	14											24
1	2			5		3	8	9			12				10			4	6	7	11*							25
1	2	3		5			8	9			12		10		11			4	6	7*								26
1	2	3†	8	5		6		9			12		10		11			4		7*	14							27
1	2		8†	5		3		9		14	12	7	10		11			4			6*							28
1	2			5		3	8	9				7	10		11			4			6							29
1	2		12	5		3	8		10†	11		7			4*		9	6				14						30
	2		4	5		3	8		10	11	12	7					9*	6					1					31
	2		4	5		3	8	9	10*		11	7	12					6					1					32
	2		4	5		3	8	9			11	7	10					6					1					33
		2	4	5		3	8	9			11*	7	10					6			12		1					34
	2		4†	5		3	8	9			12	7	10		14			6			11*		1					35
	2			5		3*		9				7†	10		4			6			14		1	8	11	12		36
	2			5				9					10		4			6			7		1	8	11	3		37
	2			5		6		9		3			10		4						7		1	8	11			38
	2	12		5		3		9					10		4			6			7		1	8*	11			39
	2					3		9		5			10		4			6			7		1	8	11			40
	2	9				3				5	12		10		4						7		1	8*	11		6	41
	2	9*	4			3				5			10	12							7		1	8	11		6	42
	2		4	5	12	3		9*		8			10								7		1		11		6	43
	2		4	5	12	3				8			10†		9			6			7		1*		11		14	44
1	2		4	5		3				8			10		9			6			7				11			45
1	2		10	5	14	3		9		8*			12		4			6			7				11†			46
32	43	23	24	41	9	27	30	36	14	28	15	28	36	—	31	14	2	18	2	3	14	—	14	7	11	1	3	
		+	+		+	+	+	+		+	+		+	+	+		+				+	+				+	+	
		2s	5s		3s	5s	1s	3s		3s	13s		4s	2s	1s		1s				3s	1s				1s	1s	

PORTSMOUTH

Player and Position	Ht	Wt	Birth Date	Birth Place	Source	Clubs	League App	League Gls
Goalkeepers								
Andy Gosney	6 4	13 05	8 11 63	Southampton	Apprentice	Portsmouth	23	—
Alan Knight	6 1	13 02	3 7 61	Ballham	Apprentice	Portsmouth	333	—
Defenders								
Andy Awford§			14 7 72	Worcester	Trainee	Portsmouth	4	—
Kevin Ball	5 9	11 06	12 11 64	Hastings	Amateur	Coventry C	—	—
						Portsmouth	69	2
Shaun Gale	6 0	11 06	8 10 69	Reading	Trainee	Portsmouth	—	—
Billy Gilbert*	5 11	12 00	10 11 59	Lewisham	Apprentice	Crystal Palace	237	3
						Portsmouth	140	—
Paul Hardyman	5 8	11 04	11 3 64	Portsmouth	Fareham	Portsmouth	117	3
Graeme Hogg	6 1	12 12	17 6 64	Aberdeen	Apprentice	Manchester U	83	1
						WBA (loan)	7	—
						Portsmouth	41	1
Gavin Maguire	5 10	11 08	24 11 67	Hammersmith	Apprentice	QPR	40	—
						Portsmouth	18	—
Warren Neill	5 8	11 10	21 11 62	Acton	Apprentice	QPR	181	3
						Portsmouth	43	—
Lee Sandford	6 1	12 02	22 4 68	Basingstoke	Apprentice	Portsmouth	59	1
Kit Symons	6 1	11 09	5 3 71	Basingstoke	Trainee	Portsmouth	2	—
Clive Whitehead*	5 11	11 06	24 11 55	Birmingham	Northfield J	Bristol C	229	10
						WBA	168	6
						Wolverhampton W (loan)	2	—
						Portsmouth	65	2
Midfield								
John Beresford	5 5	10 04	4 9 66	Sheffield	Apprentice	Manchester C	—	—
						Barnsley	88	5
						Portsmouth	2	—
Mark Chamberlain	5 8	10 07	19 11 61	Stoke	Apprentice	Port Vale	96	17
						Stoke C	112	17
						Sheffield W	66	8
						Portsmouth	28	6
Eamonn Collins*	5 6	8 13	22 10 65	Dublin	Apprentice	Blackpool	—	—
						Southampton	3	—
						Portsmouth	5	—
						Exeter C (loan)	9	—
						Gillingham (loan)	—	—
Lee Darby	6 0	11 06	20 9 69	Salford		Portsmouth	1	—
Kevin Dillon*	6 0	12 07	18 12 59	Sunderland	Apprentice	Birmingham C	186	15
						Portsmouth	215	45
Mike Fillery	5 11	13 00	17 9 60	Mitcham	Apprentice	Chelsea	161	32
						QPR	97	9
						Portsmouth	35	2
Lee Gosling	5 10	11 07	5 3 70	Basingstoke	Trainee	Portsmouth	—	—
Martin Kuhl	5 11	11 13	10 1 65	Frimley	Apprentice	Birmingham C	111	5
						Sheffield U	38	4
						Watford	4	—
						Portsmouth	32	1
Lee Russell			3 9 69	Southampton	Trainee	Portsmouth	2	—
Forwards								
Warren Aspinall	5 9	12 05	13 9 67	Wigan	Apprentice	Wigan Ath	51	22
						Everton	7	—
						Aston Villa	44	14
						Portsmouth	40	11
Philip Carroll‡			27 11 69	London	Trainee	Portsmouth	—	—

PORTSMOUTH

Foundation: At a meeting held in his High Street, Portsmouth offices in 1898, solicitor Alderman J. E. Pink and five other business and professional men agreed to buy some ground close to Goldsmith Avenue for £4,950 which they developed into Fratton Park in record breaking time. A team of professionals was signed up by manager Frank Brettell and entry to the Southern League obtained for the new club's September 1899 kick-off.

Managers (and Secretary-managers)
Frank Brettell 1898–1901, Bob Blyth 1901–04, Richard Bonney 1905–08, Bob Brown 1911–20, John McCartney 1920–27, Jack Tinn 1927–47, Bob Jackson 1947–52, Eddie Lever 1952–58, Freddie Cox 1958–61, George Smith 1961–70, Ron Tindall 1970–73 (GM to 1974), John Mortimore 1973–74, Ian St. John 1974–77, Jimmy Dickinson 1977–79, Frank Burrows 1979–82, Bobby Campbell 1982–84, Alan Ball 1984–89, John Gregory 1989– .

Player and Position	*Ht*	*Wt*	*Birth Date*	*Birth Place*	*Source*	*Clubs*	*League App*	*League Gls*
Terry Connor	5 9	11 08	9 11 62	Leeds	Apprentice	Leeds U	96	19
						Brighton & HA	156	51
						Portsmouth	33	9
Mark Kelly	5 8	9 10	27 11 69	Sutton		Portsmouth	31	1
Darryl Powell	6 0	12 03	15 11 71	London	Trainee	Portsmouth	3	—
Mick Quinn	5 10	13 04	2 5 62	Liverpool	Apprentice	Derby Co	—	—
						Wigan Ath	69	19
						Stockport Co	63	39
						Oldham Ath	80	34
						Portsmouth	121	54
Mike Ross	5 6		2 9 71	Southampton	Trainee	Portsmouth	1	—
Steve Wigley	5 9	10 05	15 10 61	Ashton	Curzon Ashton	Nottingham F	82	2
						Sheffield U	28	1
						Birmingham C	87	4
						Portsmouth	11	—

Trainees
Anderton, Darren R; Awford, Andrew T; Beare, Ian; Bishop, Clive A; Davies, Shaun; Male, Christopher; Meek, John C; Pettican, David J; Robbins, Ian; Smith, Lee A; Stanley, Christie J; Turner, Michael G; White, Christoper J.

****Non-Contract**
Gough, Alan T.

Associated Schoolboys
Askham, Paul N; Bines, Jonathan A; Bluck, Lee; Burton, Nicholas J; Coleman, Stephen M.J; Draddy, Johnathan S; Ellis, Neil J; Green, BJay; Hayes, Simon J; Laxton, Wayne G; Martin, Adam D.A; Merry, Kai; Miles, Graeme D; O'Brien, Simon; Ogburn, Mark; O'Mahoney, Sean S; Owen, Christian P; Pattison, Marc D; Price, Benjamin; Russell, Paul M; Sutton, Graham W; Tyndall, Paul F; Watts, Christian J; Wiseman, Simon L; Young, Roy E.

PORT VALE 1988–89 *Back row (left to right):* Darren Beckford, Ron Futcher, Phil Sproson, Mark Grew, Bob Hazell (Captain), Trevor Wood, Simon Mills, Robbie Earle, Kevin Finney.
Centre row: John Rudge (Manager), Wayne Simpson, Steve Davies, Alan Webb, Darren Hughes, Ray Walker, Mike Pejic (Coach).
Front row: Simon Lomax, David Riley, Paul Atkinson, Gary Ford, Steven Harper, Andy Porter.

Division 2 PORT VALE

Vale Park, Burslem, Stoke-on-Trent. Telephone Stoke-on-Trent (0782) 814134. Commercial Dept. 0782-835524. Clubcall 0898 12 16 36.

Ground capacity: 19,800.

Record attendance: 50,000 v Aston Villa, FA Cup 5th rd, 20 Feb, 1960.

Record receipts: £87,699 v Watford, FA Cup 5th rd, 20 Feb 1988.

Pitch measurements: 116yd × 76yd.

President: J. Burgess.

Chairman: W. T. Bell Tech. Eng. MIMI.

Vice-Chairman: M. J. Thompstone. ***Executive Director:*** J. Cooper.

Directors: D. P. McGrath, N. C. Tizley, I. McPherson, A. Belfield.

Manager: John Rudge.

Secretary: D. E. Barber JP. AMITD. ***Commercial Manager:*** Mrs M. Moran-Smith.

Coach: Mike Pejic. ***Physio:*** Martin Copeland.

Year Formed: 1876. ***Turned Professional:*** 1885. ***Ltd Co.:*** 1911.

Club Nickname: 'Valiants'.

Previous Name: Burslem Port Vale; became Port Vale, 1913.

Previous Grounds: 1876, Limekin Lane, Longport; 1881, Westport; 1884, Moorland Road, Burslem; 1886, Athletic Ground, Cobridge; 1913, Recreation Ground, Hanley; 1950, Vale Park.

Record League Victory: 9-1 v Chesterfield, Division 2, 24 September 1932 – Leckie; Shenton, Poyser; Sherlock, Round, Jones; McGrath, Mills, Littlewood (6), Kirkham (2), Morton (1).

Record Cup Victory: 7-1 v Irthlingborough (away), FA Cup, 1st rd, 12 January 1907 – Matthews; Dunn, Hamilton; Eardley, Baddeley, Holyhead; Carter, Dodds (2), Beats, Mountford (2), Coxon (3).

Record Defeat: 0-10 v Sheffield U, Division 2, 10 December, 1892 and v Notts Co, Division 2, 26 February, 1895.

Most League Points (2 for a win): 69, Division 3 (N), 1953–54.

Most League Points (3 for a win): 88, Division 4, 1982–83.

Most League Goals: 110, Division 4, 1958–59.

Highest League Scorer in Season: Wilf Kirkham 38, Division 2, 1926–27.

Most League Goals in Total Aggregate: Wilf Kirkham, 154, 1923–29, 1931–33.

Most Capped Player: Sammy Morgan, 7 (18), Northern Ireland.

Most League Appearances: Roy Sproson, 761, 1950–72.

Record Transfer Fee Received: £300,000 from Charlton Ath for Andy Jones, September 1987.

Record Transfer Fee Paid: £200,000 to Middlesbrough for Dean Glover, February 1989.

Football League Record: Original Member of Division 2, 1892–96; Failed re-election in 1896; Re-elected 1898; Resigned 1907; Returned in Oct, 1919, when they took over the fixtures of Leeds City; 1929–30 Division 3 (N); 1930–36 Division 2; 1936–38 Division 3 (N); 1938–52 Division 3 (S); 1952–54 Division 3 (N); 1954–57 Division 2; 1957–58 Division 3(S); 1958–59 Division 4; 1959–65 Division 3; 1965–70 Division 4; 1970–78 Division 3; 1978–83 Division 4; 1983–84 Division 3; 1984–86 Division 4; 1986–89 Division 3; 1989– Division 2.

Honours: *Football League:* Division 2 best season: 5th, 1930–31; Division 3 (N) – Champions 1929–30, 1953–54; Runners-up 1952–53; Division 4 – Champions 1958–59; Promoted 1969–70 (4th). *FA Cup:* Semi-final 1954, when in Division 3. *Football League Cup:* never past 2nd rd.

Colours: White shirts with black trim, black shorts, white stockings black rings. **Change Colours:** All yellow.

PORT VALE 1988–89 LEAGUE RECORD

Match No.	Date	Venue	Opponents	Result	H/T Score	Lg. Pos.	Goalscorers	Attendance
1	Aug 27	A	Preston NE	W 3-1	1-0	—	Atkinson 2 (1 pen), Beckford	6718
2	Sept 3	H	Chester C	L 1-2	0-2	11	Futcher	4213
3	10	A	Bury	D 0-0	0-0	12		2978
4	17	H	Cardiff C	W 6-1	3-1	5	Beckford, Futcher 2, Riley, Earle, Walker	4280
5	19	H	Chesterfield	W 5-0	3-0	—	Beckford 3, Ford 2	4469
6	24	A	Bristol C	W 1-0	1-0	2	Walker	7235
7	Oct 1	A	Wolverhampton W	D 3-3	2-1	2	Earle, Futcher, Sproson	14,108
8	3	H	Huddersfield T	W 2-0	2-0	—	Ford, Futcher	5938
9	8	A	Wigan Ath	W 2-0	0-0	1	Earle, Beckford	3976
10	15	H	Bolton W	W 2-1	1-1	1	Riley, Walker	7985
11	22	A	Blackpool	L 2-3	2-1	2	Futcher 2	7045
12	24	H	Sheffield U	D 3-3	0-1	—	Ford 2, Futcher (pen)	13,246
13	29	A	Brentford	L 1-2	0-0	3	Earle	5212
14	Nov 8	A	Northampton T	W 3-1	1-1	—	Beckford, Earle, Futcher	3796
15	12	H	Swansea C	W 2-1	2-1	3	Futcher, Beckford	6248
16	26	H	Fulham	W 3-0	1-0	3	Atkinson (pen), Beckford 2	5097
17	Dec 2	A	Southend U	D 1-1	1-1	—	Sproson	3245
18	17	H	Reading	W 3-0	1-0	2	Hicks (og), Beckford, Riley	4779
19	26	A	Mansfield T	W 1-0	0-0	2	Earle	5218
20	30	A	Gillingham	L 0-1	0-0	—		4706
21	Jan 2	H	Notts Co	W 1-0	0-0	2	Beckford	7084
22	14	A	Chester C	W 2-1	0-1	2	Earle, Beckford	4891
23	21	H	Bury	L 1-3	1-1	2	Futcher	5783
24	28	A	Cardiff C	L 0-3	0-1	2		4507
25	Feb 4	H	Wolverhampton W	D 0-0	0-0	2		16,362
26	11	A	Huddersfield T	D 0-0	0-0	2		8004
27	13	H	Aldershot	W 3-0	1-0	—	Jones, Beckford 2	5033
28	18	H	Wigan Ath	W 2-1	1-0	2	Earle, Futcher	6100
29	28	A	Sheffield U	D 0-0	0-0	—		18,787
30	Mar 4	H	Blackpool	W 1-0	1-0	2	Futcher (pen)	6306
31	11	A	Aldershot	D 2-2	0-0	2	Futcher (pen), Earle	2397
32	13	H	Brentford	W 3-2	1-0	—	Futcher, Ford, Jones	5577
33	18	H	Preston NE	D 1-1	0-1	2	Ford	8584
34	25	A	Notts Co	W 4-1	2-0	2	Walker, Beckford 3 (1 pen)	7328
35	27	H	Mansfield T	L 1-2	1-1	2	Earle	8198
36	Apr 1	A	Reading	L 0-3	0-1	2		4501
37	5	A	Bristol R	D 2-2	1-1	—	Jones, Earle	6869
38	8	H	Gillingham	W 2-1	1-0	2	Reeves (og), Walker	5358
39	15	A	Chesterfield	W 2-1	2-0	2	Beckford 2	5895
40	21	H	Bristol C	L 0-1	0-0	—		6923
41	25	A	Bolton W	D 1-1	0-1	—	Earle	5296
42	29	A	Swansea C	D 0-0	0-0	3		4229
43	May 1	H	Northampton T	L 1-2	0-1	3	Futcher	6604
44	6	H	Southend U	W 2-0	2-0	3	Futcher, Porter	4516
45	9	H	Bristol R	W 1-0	0-0	—	Earle	6136
46	13	A	Fulham	W 2-1	0-1	3	Finney, West	6257

Final League Position: 3

GOALSCORERS

League (78): Beckford 20 (1 pen), Futcher 17 (3 pens), Earle 13, Ford 7, Walker 5, Atkinson 3 (2 pens), Jones 3, Riley 3, Sproson 2, Finney 1, Porter 1, West 1, own goals 2.
Littlewoods Cup (5): Earle 2, Sproson 2, Futcher 1 (pen).
FA Cup (5): Earle 1, Futcher 1, Riley 1, Sproson 1, Webb 1.

Littlewoods Cup	First Round	Chesterfield (h)	3-2
		(a)	1-1
	Second Round	Ipswich T (h)	1-0
		(a)	0-3
FA Cup	First Round	Southport (a)	2-0
	Second Round	Bolton W (a)	2-1
	Third Round	Norwich C (h)	1-3

Grew	Mills	Webb	Walker	Hazell	Sproson	Ford	Earle	Futcher	Beckford	Atkinson	Finney	Riley	Hughes	Harper	Wood	Stowell	Porter	Jeffers	Glover	Jones	West	Jepson	*Match No.*
1	2	3	4	5	6	7	8	9	10	11*	12												1
1	2	3*	4	5	6	7	8	9	10	11		12											2
1		2	4	5	6	7	8	9	10			11	3										3
1		2	4	5	6	7†	8*	9	10		12	11	3	14									4
1	5	2	4		6	7	8*	9	10		12	11†	3	14									5
1	5	2	4		6	7	8	9	10			11	3										6
1	5	2			6	7	8	9	10		4	11	3										7
	5	2			6	7	8	9	10		4	11	3		1								8
1	5	2	4		6	7	8	9	10			11	3										9
1	2		4	5	6	7	8	9	10			11	3										10
	6	2	4	5		7		9	10		12	11	3			1	8*						11
	2		4	5	6	7		9	10		8	11	3			1							12
	2	6	4*	5		7	8	9	10		12	11	3			1							13
	2	6	4	5		7*	8	9	10†		12	11	3	14		1							14
	7	2	4	5	6		8	9	10		12	11*	3			1							15
	7	2	4	5	6		8		10	11*		9	3	12		1							16
	7	2	4	5	6		8*		10	11	12	9	3			1							17
1	2		4	5	6	7	8	9	10			11	3										18
1	2	7	4	5	6		8	9	10			11	3										19
1	2*	7	4	5	6		8	9	10			11	3					12					20
1		2	4	5	6		8	9	10			11	3					7					21
1	4	2		5	6		8	9	10			11	3					7					22
1	5	2	4		6		8	9	10			11	3				12	7*					23
1	5	2	4				8	9	10*			11	3	12			6	7					24
1	2	5	4				8	9				11	3				7		6	10			25
1	2	5	4			7*	8		10			11	3	14			12		6	9†			26
1	2	5	4				8		10			11	3	12			7		6	9*			27
1	2	5	4				8	9	10			11	3				7		6				28
1	2	5	4				8	9	10			11*	3						6	12	7		29
1	2		4				8	9*	10			11	3				7		6	12	5		30
1	2*	5	4			12	8	9	10†			11	3						6	14	7		31
1	2		4			7*	8	9	10			11	3						6	12	5		32
1	2		4			7	8	9	10			11*	3						6	12	5		33
1	2		4			7	8	9*	10			11	3						6	12	5		34
1	2†	14	4			7*	8	9	10			11	3						6	12	5		35
1	2	14	4			7†	8	9	10*			11	3						6	12	5		36
1	2	5	4				8	9				11	3				7*	12	6	10			37
1	2	5	4				8	9	12			11	3				7†	14	6	10*			38
1	2	6	4				8		10			11	3					7	5	9*		12	39
1	2	5	4				8	12	10			11	3					7	6	9*			40
1	2	5	4				8	9	10			11*	3					7†	6	12	14		41
1	2	5	4				8	9	10*				3					12	6	11	7		42
1	2	5	4				8	9	10				3				11	7*	6		12		43
1	2	5*	4				8	9	10†		14		3				11	7	6		12		44
1	2		4				8	9			10		3				11	7	6		5		45
	2		4				8	12			10		3		1		11	7	6		5	9*	46
37	43	35	43	17	20	21	44	39	41	4	5	39	44	—	2	7	12	11	22	8	11	1	
		+				+		+	+		+	+		+			+	+		+	+	+	
		2s				1s		2s	1s		9s	1s		7s			2s	4s		9s	3s	1s	

PORT VALE

Player and Position	Ht	Wt	Birth Date	Birth Place	Source	Clubs	League App	League Gls
Goalkeepers								
Mark Grew	5 11	12 08	15 2 58	Bilston	Amateur	WBA	33	—
						Wigan Ath (loan)	4	—
						Notts Co (loan)	—	—
						Leicester C	5	—
						Oldham Ath (loan)	5	—
						Ipswich T	6	—
						Fulham (loan)	4	—
						WBA (loan)	1	—
						Derby Co (loan)	—	—
						Port Vale	81	—
Trevor Wood	6 0	12 06	3 11 68	Jersey	Apprentice	Brighton & HA	—	—
						Port Vale	2	—
Defenders								
Dean Glover	5 10	11 11	29 12 63	Birmingham	Apprentice	Aston Villa	28	—
						Sheffield U (loan)	5	—
						Middlesbrough	50	5
						Port Vale	22	—
Bob Hazell*	6 1	15 07	14 6 59	Kingston, Jamaica	Apprentice	Wolverhampton W	33	1
						QPR	106	8
						Leicester C	41	2
						Wolverhampton W (loan)	1	—
						Leeds U	—	—
						Reading	4	1
						Port Vale	81	1
Darren Hughes	5 11	10 11	6 10 65	Prescot	Apprentice	Everton	3	—
						Shrewsbury T	37	1
						Brighton & HA	26	2
						Port Vale	87	1
Wayne Simpson	5 9	11 00	19 9 68	Stoke	Trainee	Port Vale	—	—
Phil Sproson‡ (Retired)	6 0	12 00	13 10 59	Trent Vale	Amateur	Port Vale	426	33
Alan Webb	5 10	12 00	1 1 63	Wellington	Apprentice	WBA	24	—
						Lincoln C (loan)	11	—
						Port Vale	169	2
Gary West	6 2	12 07	25 8 64	Scunthorpe	Apprentice	Sheffield U	75	1
						Lincoln C	83	4
						Gillingham	52	3
						Port Vale	14	1
Midfield								
Robbie Earle	5 9	10 10	27 1 65	Newcastle, Staffs	Amateur	Stoke C	—	—
						Port Vale	216	54
Kevin Finney	6 0	12 00	19 10 69	Newcastle-U-Lyne	Apprentice	Port Vale	29	1
Gary Ford	5 8	11 10	8 2 61	York	Apprentice	York C	366	52
						Leicester C	16	2
						Port Vale	45	10
Simon Mills	5 8	11 04	16 8 64	Sheffield	Apprentice	Sheffield W	5	—
						York C	99	5
						Port Vale	62	5
Andy Porter	5 9	11 02	17 9 68	Manchester	Trainee	Port Vale	21	1
Ray Walker	5 10	12 00	6 7 81	North Shields	Apprentice	Aston Villa	23	—
						Port Vale (loan)	15	1
						Port Vale	130	15
Forwards								
Paul Atkinson	5 9	10 02	19 1 66	Chester-Le-Street	Apprentice	Sunderland	60	5
						Port Vale	4	3

PORT VALE

Foundation: Formed in 1876 in the Longport area of Burslem, it is said that the name Burslem Port Vale was taken from Port Vale House, Alexandra Road, Longport, where the club made its first headquarters. The name Burslem was not dropped until the club moved to Hanley in 1913.

Managers (and Secretary-managers)
Sam Gleaves 1896–1905*, Tom Clare 1905–11, A. S. Walker 1911–12, H. Myatt 1912–14, Tom Holford 1919–24 (continued as trainer), Joe Schofield 1924–30, Tom Morgan 1930–32, Tom Holford 1932–35, Warney Cresswell 1936–37, Tom Morgan 1937–38, Billy Frith 1945–46, Gordon Hodgson 1946–51, Ivor Powell 1951, Freddie Steele 1951–57, Norman Low 1957–62, Freddie Steele 1962–65, Jackie Mudie 1965–67, Sir Stanley Matthews (GM) 1965–68, Gordon Lee 1968–74, Roy Sproson 1974–77, Colin Harper 1977, Bobby Smith 1977–78, Dennis Butler 1978–79, Alan Bloor 1979, John McGrath 1980–83, John Rudge 1983– .

Player and Position	*Ht*	*Wt*	*Birth Date*	*Birth Place*	*Source*	*Clubs*	*League App*	*League Gls*
Darren Beckford	6 1	11 01	12 5 67	Manchester	Apprentice	Manchester C	11	—
						Bury (loan)	12	5
						Port Vale (loan)	11	4
						Port Vale	82	29
Steve Davies	6 0	11 09	16 7 60	Liverpool	Congleton	Port Vale	6	—
Ron Futcher	6 0	12 10	25 9 56	Chester	Apprentice	Chester	4	—
						Luton T	120	40
						Manchester C	17	7
					Minnesota	Barnsley	19	6
					Portland	Oldham Ath	65	30
					NAC Breda	Bradford C	42	18
					Tulsa	Port Vale	41	17
John Jeffers	5 10	11 10	5 10 68	Liverpool	Trainee	Liverpool	—	—
						Port Vale	15	—
Ron Jepson†			12 5 63	Stoke	Nantwich	Port Vale	2	—
Simon Lomax*	5 7	10 08	29 12 69	Salford	Trainee	Port Vale	—	—
Paul Millar			16 11 66	Belfast	Portadown	Port Vale	—	—
David Riley	5 7	10 10	8 12 60	Northampton	Keyworth U	Nottingham F	12	2
						Darlington (loan)	6	2
						Peterborough U	12	2
						(loan)	74	11
						Port Vale		
Glen Shepherd			4 1 71	Dudley	Trainee	Port Vale	—	—

Trainees
Booth, Matthew; Burrows, Michael J; Dawson, Jason; Johnston, John; Kidd, Ryan A; Knight, Matthew S; Leech, Philip; Llewellyn, Paul; Lowe, David E; Mills, Brian; Moore, Paul C; Mulliner, Andrew W; Myatt, Robert J; Owen, Steven L; Slater, Steven L.

****Non-Contract**
Jepson, Ronald.

Associated Schoolboys
Banks, Ian; Bedson, Nicholas S; Beeby, Matthew; Boswell, Christopher W; Brown, Timothy D; Craig, Nikolas; Dyass, Mark W; Gillard, Christopher; Harrison, Michael; Lovatt, Gregory; Mitchell, Richard D; Royall, Adam; Rushton, David; Shea, Gareth D; Stirk, Mark A; Stutcinskas, Keith D; Tweats, Timothy A.

PRESTON NORTH END 1988–89 *Back row (left to right):* Warren Joyce, Michael Bennett, Gary Brazil, Gary Swann, David Brown, Alan Kelly, Andrew McAteer, Michael Rathbone, Les Chapman, Mark Patterson.
Front row: Oshor Williams, Neil Williams, Gary Walker, Jeff Wrightson, Alex Jones, Sam Allardyce, Bob Atkins, Tony Ellis, David Miller, Brian Mooney.

Division 3 PRESTON NORTH END

Deepdale, Preston PR1 6RU. Telephone Preston (0772) 795919. Ansaphone (0772) 709170. Commercial Dept. (0772) 795465/795156. Pitch Hire: (0772) 705468. Community Office: (0772) 704275.

Ground capacity: 17,000.

Record attendance: 42, 684 v Arsenal, Division 1, 23 Apr, 1938.

Record receipts: £54,000 v Burnley, Sherpa Van Trophy, Northern Final, second leg, 19 April, 1988.

Pitch measurements: 110yd × 72yd. (artificial surface.)

President: Tom Finney, OBE, JP.

Vice President: T. C. Nicholson JP, FCIOB.

Chairman: Keith W. Leeming.

Vice-Chairmen: J. T. Garratt, M. J. Woodhouse.

Directors: B. J. Campbell, J. Francis, E. Griffith BVSC, MRCVS (Company Secretary), J. E. Wignall, J. W. Wilding, J. T. Worden.

Manager: John McGrath. ***Asst. Manager:*** Les Chapman.

Physio: Andy Jones.

Secretary: D. J. Allan. ***Promotions Manager:*** Wayne Dore.

Year Formed: 1881. ***Turned Professional:*** 1885. ***Ltd Co.:*** 1893.

Club Nickname: 'The Lilywhites' or 'North End'.

Record League Victory: 10-0 v Stoke, Division 1, 14 September 1889 – Trainer; Howarth, Holmes; Kelso, Russell (1), Graham; Gordon, Jimmy Ross (2), Nick Ross (3), Thomson (2), Drummond (2).

Record Cup Victory: 26-0 v Hyde, FA Cup, 1st rd, 15 October 1887 – Addision; Howarth, Nick Ross; Russell (1), Thomson (5), Graham (1); Gordon (5), Jimmy Ross (8), John Goodall (1), Dewhurst (3), Drummond (2).

Record Defeat: 0-7 v Blackool, Division 1, 1 May, 1948.

Most League Points (2 for a win): 61, Division 3, 1970–71.

Most League Points (3 for a win): 90, Division 4, 1986–87.

Most League Goals: 100, Division 2, 1927–28 and Division 1, 1957–58.

Highest League Scorer in Season: Ted Harper, 37, Division 2, 1932–33.

Most League Goals in Total Aggregate: Tom Finney, 1946–60.

Most Capped Player: Tom Finney, 76, England.

Most League Appearances: Alan Kelly, 447, 1961–75.

Record Transfer Fee Received: £765,000 from Manchester C for Michael Robinson, June 1979.

Record Transfer Fee Paid: £100,000 to Newcastle U for Ian Bogie, February 1989.

Football League Record: 1888 Founder Member of League; 1901–04 Division 2; 1904–12 Division 1; 1912–13 Division 2; 1913–14 Division 1; 1914–15 Division 2 1919–25 Division 2; 1919–25 Division 1; 1925–34 Division 2; 1934–49 Division 1; 1949–51 Division 2; 1951–61 Division 1; 1961–70 Division 2; 1970–71 Division 3; 1971–74 Division 2; 1974–78 Division 3; 1978–81 Division 2, 1981–85 Division 3; 1985–87 Division 4; 1987– Division 3.

Honours: *Football League;* Division 1 – Champions 1888–89 (first champions, 1889–90; Runners-up 1890–91, 1891–92, 1892–93, 1905–06, 1952–53, 1957–58; Division 2 – Champions 1903–04, 1912–13, 1950–51; Runners-up 1914–15, 1933–34; Division 3 – Champions 1970–71; Division 4 Runners-up 1986–87. *FA Cup:* Winners 1889, 1938; Runners-up 1888, 1922, 1937, 1954, 1964. *Double Performed:* 1888–89. *Football League Cup* best season: 4th rd, 1963, 1966, 1972, 1981.

Colours: All white. **Change Colours:** All yellow.

PRESTON NORTH END 1988–89 LEAGUE RECORD

Match No.	Date	Venue	Opponents	Result	H/T Score	Lg. Pos.	Goalscorers	Attendance
1	Aug 27	H	Port Vale	L 1-3	0-1	—	Williams N	6718
2	Sept 3	A	Huddersfield T	L 0-2	0-2	23		5622
3	10	H	Blackpool	W 1-0	0-0	19	Patterson	8779
4	17	A	Bristol C	D 1-1	1-1	19	Rathbone	7913
5	20	H	Chester C	D 3-3	1-1	—	Patterson 2, Ellis	5415
6	24	A	Notts Co	D 0-0	0-0	19		4965
7	Oct 1	H	Southend U	W 3-2	0-2	15	McAteer, Brazil 2 (1 pen)	5348
8	5	A	Bristol R	L 0-1	0-1	—		3689
9	8	H	Bury	W 1-0	0-0	13	Ellis	5863
10	15	A	Chesterfield	W 3-0	2-0	10	Swann, Mooney, Ellis	2813
11	22	A	Brentford	W 2-0	0-0	8	Brazil 2	5584
12	25	H	Gillingham	W 5-0	2-0	—	Brazil 3 (1 pen), Ellis, Joyce	6390
13	29	A	Swansea C	D 1-1	1-0	6	Ellis	5370
14	Nov 5	H	Mansfield T	W 2-0	1-0	3	Mooney, Rathbone	6434
15	8	H	Wigan Ath	D 2-2	1-2	—	Brazil (pen), Patterson	8396
16	12	A	Reading	D 2-2	1-1	6	Ellis, Patterson	6225
17	26	A	Wolverhampton W	L 0-6	0-3	7		13,180
18	Dec 3	H	Cardiff C	D 3-3	2-0	7	Brazil, Ellis 2	4963
19	17	A	Fulham	L 1-2	0-1	10	Patterson	3858
20	26	H	Bolton W	W 3-1	2-0	9	Hughes, Ellis, Joyce	12,104
21	31	H	Sheffield U	W 2-0	0-0	7	Patterson, Joyce	11,005
22	Jan 2	A	Northampton T	L 0-1	0-0	8		4219
23	7	A	Aldershot	L 1-2	0-0	9	Joyce	2135
24	14	H	Huddersfield T	W 1-0	0-0	8	Patterson	6959
25	21	A	Blackpool	L 0-1	0-0	9		8951
26	28	H	Bristol C	W 2-0	0-0	7	Mooney 2	6080
27	Feb 3	A	Southend U	L 1-2	0-2	—	Mooney	2948
28	11	H	Bristol R	D 1-1	0-1	8	Mooney	7365
29	18	A	Bury	D 1-1	0-0	8	Williams N	6977
30	25	H	Chesterfield	W 6-0	4-0	8	Philliskirk 2, Bloomer (og), Patterson (pen), Ellis 2	7074
31	28	A	Gillingham	W 3-1	0-1	—	Patterson (pen), Ellis 2	3031
32	Mar 4	H	Brentford	W 5-3	2-2	5	Philliskirk, Patterson, Joyce 2, Ellis	8186
33	11	A	Mansfield T	W 3-0	0-0	4	Coleman (og), Philliskirk, Ellis	4706
34	14	H	Swansea C	D 1-1	1-0	—	James (og)	8975
35	18	A	Port Vale	D 1-1	1-0	4	Ellis	8584
36	25	H	Northampton T	W 3-2	1-1	4	Joyce 2, Patterson (pen)	9137
37	27	A	Bolton W	L 0-1	0-1	5		10,281
38	Apr 1	H	Fulham	L 1-4	1-2	6	Philliskirk	8190
39	4	H	Aldershot	D 2-2	0-0	—	Bogie, Philliskirk	5977
40	8	A	Sheffield U	L 1-3	0-0	6	Stancliffe (og)	12,718
41	15	H	Notts Co	W 3-0	1-0	6	Swann, Joyce, Ellis	6735
42	22	A	Chester C	W 1-0	0-0	6	Jemson	4617
43	29	H	Reading	W 2-1	2-0	6	Patterson 2 (1 pen)	7003
44	May 1	A	Wigan Ath	D 1-1	1-0	6	Jemson	5671
45	5	A	Cardiff C	D 0-0	0-0	—		3196
46	13	H	Wolverhampton W	D 3-3	1-1	6	Ellis 2, Patterson	14,126

Final League Position: 6

GOALSCORERS

League (79): Ellis 19, Patterson 15 (4 pens), Brazil 9 (3 pens), Joyce 9, Mooney 6, Philliskirk 6, Jemson 2, Rathbone 2, Swann 2, Williams N 2, Bogie 1, Hughes 1, McAteer 1, own goals 4.
Littlewoods Cup (1): Brazil 1.
FA Cup (1): Atkins 1.

Littlewoods Cup	First Round	Wigan Ath (a)	0-0
		(h)	1-0
	Second Round	Norwich C (a)	0-2
		(h)	0-3
FA Cup	First Round	Tranmere R (h)	1-1
		(a)	0-3

Brown	Miller	McAteer	Atkins	Jones	Wrightson	Williams, N	Swann	Ellis	Brazil	Patterson	Rathbone	Allardyce	Mooney	Joyce	Hughes	Tunks	Fitzpatrick	Bogie	Philliskirk	Jemson	Harper	*Match No.*
1	2	3	4	5	6	7	8	9	10	11*	12											1
1	2		4	5		9†	8*	14	10	11	3	6	7	12								2
1	7	3	4	5	6			9	10	11	2			8								3
1	7	3	4	5				9	10	11	2	6		8								4
1	7*	3	4	5			12	9	10	11	2	6		8								5
1	7*	3	4	5			8	9	10	11	2	6	12									6
1	12	3	4	5			8	9*	10	11	2	6	7									7
1	2		4	5*	12	14	8†	9	10	11	3	6	7									8
1	2*		4		5	8	12	9		11	3		7	10	6							9
1			4		5	2	10	9		11	3		7	8	6							10
1			4		5	2	10*	9	12	11	3	14	7	8	6†							11
1	11		4	12	5	2		9	10		3	6*	7	8								12
1	12		4		5	2		9	10	11*	3		7	8	6							13
1			4		5	2		9	10	11	3		7	8	6							14
1			4		5	2		9	10	11	3		7	8	6							15
1			4		5	2		9	10	11	3	6	7	8								16
1			4		5*	2		9	10	11	3	6	7	8	12							17
			4			2		9	7	11	3	6		8	5	1	10					18
		3		4	6	2			9	11			7	8	5	1	10					19
		3		4	5	2		9	10	11			7	8	6	1						20
		3		4	5	2		9	10	11			7	8	6	1						21
	12	3†		4	5	2		9*	10	11	14		7	8	6	1						22
		14		4	12	2		9	10	11	3†	5*	7	8	6	1						23
				4	5	2		9	10	11	3		7	8	6	1						24
		12		4	5	2		9	10	11	3*		7	8	6	1						25
			6	4	5	2		9	10	11	3		7	8		1						26
		10*	6	4	5	2		9	12	11	3		7	8		1						27
			6	4	5	2		12		11	3		7	8*		1		9	10			28
			6	4	5	2		8		11	3		7	12		1		9	10*			29
			6	4	5	2		8		11	3		7*	12		1		9	10			30
			6	4	5	2		8		11	3		7			1		9	10			31
			6	4	5	2		8		11	3		7	12		1		9	10*			32
			6	4	5	2		8		11	3		7			1		9	10			33
			6	4	5	2		8		11	3		7	12		1		9*	10			34
			6	4	5	2		8		11	3		7	9		1		12	10*			35
			6	4	5	2		8		11	3		7	9		1			10			36
			6	4	5	2		8		11	3*		7	9		1		12	10†	14		37
			6	4	5	2	11†	8				3	7*	9		1		12	10		14	38
			6	4		2	3	8*		11				7	5	1		9†	10	12	14	39
			6			2	3	8				4	12	9	5	1		7		10*	11	40
1			4		5	2	3	8		11			7	9	6					10		41
1			4		5	2	3	8					7	9	6			12		10	11*	42
1			4		5	2	3	8		11			7	9	6					10		43
1			4		5	2	3	8		11			7	9	6					10*	12	44
1			4		5	2	3	8		11			7	9	6				10*	12		45
1			4		5	2	3	8		11			7	9	6				12	10*		46
23	9 + 3s	11 + 2s	39	29 + 1s	36 + 2s	40 + 1s	16 + 2s	43 + 2s	23 + 2s	42	32 + 2s	13 + 1s	38 + 2s	35 + 5s	22 + 1s	23	2	9 + 4s	13 + 1s	6 + 3s	2 + 3s	

PRESTON NORTH END

Player and Position	Ht	Wt	Birth Date	Birth Place	Source	Clubs	League App	League Gls
Goalkeepers								
David Brown*	6 1	12 08	28 1 57	Hartlepool	Horden CW	Middlesbrough	10	—
						Plymouth Arg (loan)	5	—
						Oxford U	21	—
						Bury	146	—
						Preston NE	74	—
						Scunthorpe U (loan)	5	—
Alan Kelly	6 2	12 05	11 8 68	Preston		Preston NE	54	—
Roy Tunks	6 1	13 11	21 1 51	Wuppertal	Apprentice	Rotherham U	138	—
						York C (loan)	4	—
						Ipswich T (loan)	—	—
						Newcastle U (loan)	—	—
						Preston NE	277	—
						Wigan Ath	245	—
						Hartlepool U	5	—
						Preston NE	23	—
Defenders								
Sam Allardyce*	6 1	14 00	19 10 54	Dudley	Apprentice	Bolton W	184	21
						Sunderland	25	2
						Millwall	63	2
						Coventry C	28	1
						Hudersfield T	37	—
						Bolton W	14	—
						Preston NE	90	2
Shaun Allen	5 11	12 05	28 2 69	Preston	Trainee	Preston NE	—	—
Bob Atkins	6 0	12 02	16 10 62	Leicester	Local	Sheffield U	40	3
						Preston NE	172	4
Michael Bennett	5 7	10 00	24 12 62	Bolton	Apprentice	Bolton W	65	1
						Wolverhampton W	6	—
						Cambridge U	76	—
						Bradford C	—	—
						Preston NE	76	1
Les Chapman	5 7	10 04	27 9 48	Oldham	High Barn	Oldham Ath	76	9
						Huddersfield T	133	8
						Oldham Ath	187	11
						Stockport Co	32	1
						Bradford C	139	3
						Rochdale	88	—
						Stockport Co	38	3
						Preston NE	53	1
Adrian Hughes			19 12 70	Billinge	Trainee	Preston NE	24	1
Alex Jones	6 2	12 08	27 11 64	Blackburn	Apprentice	Oldham Ath	9	—
						Stockport Co (loan)	3	—
						Preston NE	98	3
Andy McAteer	5 10	11 10	24 4 61	Preston	Apprentice	Preston NE	238	8
						Blackpool	41	—
						Preston NE	13	1
David Miller	5 11	11 02	8 1 64	Burnley	Apprentice	Burnley	32	3
						Crewe Alex (loan)	3	—
					Colne D	Tranmere R	29	1
						Preston NE	55	2
						Burnley (loan)	4	—
Mike Rathbone	5 10	11 12	6 11 58	Birmingham	Apprentice	Birmingham C	20	—
						Blackburn R	273	2
						Preston NE	70	3
Gary Walker	6 1	12 05	12 9 69	Billinge	Trainee	Preston NE	—	—
Steven Wilkes†	5 6	10 04	30 6 67	Preston	Apprentice	Wigan Ath	—	—
						Preston NE	3	—
						Aldershot	—	—
						Preston NE	—	—
Jeff Wrightson	5 11	11 00	18 5 68	Newcastle	Apprentice	Newcastle U	4	—
						Preston NE	63	—

PRESTON NORTH END

Foundation: North End Cricket and Rugby Club which was formed in 1863, indulged in most sports before taking up soccer in about 1879. In 1881 they decided to stick to football to the exclusion of other sports and even a 16–0 drubbing by Blackburn Rovers in an invitation game at Deepdale, a few weeks after taking this decision, did not deter them for they immediately became affiliated to the Lancashire FA.

Managers (and Secretary-managers)
Charlie Parker 1906–15, Vincent Hayes 1919–23, Jim Lawrence 1923–25, Frank Richards 1925–27, Alex Gibson 1927–31, Lincoln Hayes 1931–1932 (run by committee 1932–36), Tommy Muirhead 1936–37, (run by committee 1937–49), Will Scott 1949–53, Scot Symon 1953–54, Frank Hill 1954–56, Cliff Britton 1956–61, Jimmy Milne 1961–68, Bobby Seith 1968–70, Alan Ball Sr 1970–73, Bobby Charlton 1970–75, Harry Catterick 1975–77, Nobby Stiles 1977–81, Tommy Docherty 1981, Gordon Lee 1981–83, Alan Kelly 1983–85, Tommy Booth 1985–86, Brian Kidd 1986, John McGrath 1986– .

Player and Position	*Ht*	*Wt*	*Birth Date*	*Birth Place*	*Source*	*Clubs*	*League App*	*League Gls*
Midfield								
Ian Bogie	5 7	10 02	6 12 67	Newcastle	Apprentice	Newcastle U	14	—
						Preston NE	13	1
Warren Joyce	5 9	11 11	20 1 65	Oldham	Local	Bolton W	184	17
						Preston NE	62	9
Paul Maloney	5 6	9 10	10 11 69	St Helens	Trainee	Preston NE	—	—
Brian Mooney	5 11	11 02	2 2 66	Dublin	Home Farm	Liverpool	—	—
						Wrexham (loan)	9	2
						Preston NE	74	9
Mark Patterson	5 6	10 10	24 5 65	Darwen	Apprentice	Blackburn R	101	20
						Preston NE	42	15
Gary Swann	5 9	11 02	11 4 62	York	Apprentice	Hull C	186	9
						Preston NE	94	19
Stuart Todhunter*	5 8	10 07	5 3 70	Workington	Trainee	Preston NE	—	—
Neil Williams	5 11	11 04	23 10 64	Waltham Abbey	Apprentice	Watford	—	—
						Hull C	91	10
						Preston NE	41	2
Forwards								
Tony Ellis	5 11	11 00	20 10 64	Salford	Northwich V	Oldham Ath	8	—
						Preston NE	69	23
Steve Harper	5 10	11 05	3 2 69	Stoke	Trainee	Port Vale	28	2
						Preston NE	5	—
Tony Philliskirk	6 1	11 03	10 2 65	Sunderland	Amateur	Sheffield U	80	20
						Rotherham U (loan)	6	1
						Oldham Ath	10	1
						Preston NE	14	6
Oshor Williams*	5 9	11 07	21 4 58	Stockton	Apprentice	Middlesbrough	—	—
						Manchester U	—	—
					Gateshead	Southampton	—	—
						Exeter C (loan)	6	—
						Stockport Co	3	—
						Port Vale	193	26
						Preston NE	49	7
							39	12

Trainees
Clark, Martin A; Cunningham, Richard A; Doody, Lee M; Gallagher, Lee; Gill, Andrew D; Greenway, Julian C; Hollis, Christopher P; James, Martin J; Lambert, Matthew R; O'Reilly, Stephen J; Peel, Nathan J; Raynor, Kevin B.C; Simms, Mark W.

****Non-Contract**
Evans, Keith; Keighley, John P; Nolan, Ian R; Wilkes, Stephen B.

Associated Schoolboys
Ashcroft, Lee; Bagnall, John A; Burrow, David; Burton, Simon P; Carruthers, Neil R; Cartwright, Lee; Christie, David; Critchley, Adam D; Eaves, David M.C; Finney, Stephen K; Flitcroft, David J; Heavey, Paul A; Hindle, Paul J; Kellett, Ian; Kerfoot, Jason J; McCullough, Gary; Medling, Andrew; Moore, Darren E; Morris, Darren A; Morris, Paul I; Moylon, Craig; Rapsey, Jason A; Rimmer, David J; Schofield, Christopher; Siddall, Adam M; Simpson, Mark A; Singleton, Jason R; Taylor, Nicholas John; Williams, Christopher.

QUEENS PARK RANGERS 1988–89 *Back row (left to right):* Mark Dennis, David Kerslake, David Pizanti, Martin Allen, Brian Law, Alan McDonald, Gavin Maguire, Justin Channing, Simon Barker.
Centre row: Danny Maddix, Keith Peacock (Reserve Team Manager), Ron Berry (Kit Manager), Tony Roberts, Peter Shreeves (Assistant Manager), Nicky Johns, Frank Sibley (Youth Team Manager), Dave Butler (Physiotherapist), Wayne Fereday.
Front row: Kevin Brock, Ian Dawes, Mark Falco, David Seaman (Captain), Jim Smith (Manager), Dean Coney, Trevor Francis, Paul Parker.

Division 1 QUEEN'S PARK RANGERS

South Africa Road, W12 7PA. Telephone 01-743 0262 (Marketing, 740 8737) (Box Office, 749 5744).
Ground capacity: 27,500 (23,000 covered).
Record attendance: 35,353 v Leeds U, Division 1, 27 April, 1974.
Record receipts: £114,743 v Tottenham H, Division 1, 12 January, 1985.
Pitch measurements: 112yd × 72yd.
Chairman: R. C. Thompson. ***Vice-Chairman:*** R. P. B. Noonan.
Directors: C. B. Berlin (Managing), P. D. Ellis, A. Ingham, A. Chandler, M. R. Turner, B. Evans (Sponsor).
Player-Manager: Trevor Francis.
Secretary: R. J. Phillips. ***Head of Marketing:*** B. Rowe.
Coach: Frank Sibley. ***Assistant Team Manager:*** Don Howe.
Physio: C. Speight.
Year Formed: 1885 *(*see Foundation*). ***Turned Professional;*** 1898. ***Ltd Co.:*** 1899.
Club Nickname: 'Rangers' or 'Rs'. ***Previous Name:*** 1885–87, St Jude's.
Previous Grounds: 1885 *(*see Foundation*), Welford's Fields; 1888–89: London Scottish Ground, Brondesbury, Home Farm, Kensal Rise Green, Gun Club Wormwood Scrubs, Kilburn Cricket Ground; 1899, Kensal Rise Athletic Ground; 1901, Latimer Road, Notting Hill; 1904, Agricultural Society, Park Royal; 1907, Park Royal Ground; 1917, Loftus Road; 1931, White City; 1933, Loftus Road; 1962, White City; 1963, Loftus Road.
Record League Victory: 9-2 v Tranmere R, Division 3, 3 December 1960 – Drinkwater; Woods, Ingham; Keen, Rutter, Angell; Lazarus (2), Bedford (2), Evans (2), Andrews (1), Clark (2).
Record Cup Victory: 8-1 (away) v Bristol R (away), FA Cup, 1st rd, 27 November 1937 – Gilfillan; Smith, Jefferson; Lowe, James, March; Cape, Mallett, Cheetham (3), Fitzgerald (3) Bott (2). 8-1 v Crewe Alex, Milk Cup, 1st rd, 3 October 1983 – Hucker; Neill, Dawes, Waddock (1), McDonald (1), Fenwick, Micklewhite (1), Stewart (1), Allen (1), Stainrod (3), Gregory.
Record Defeat: 1-8 v Mansfield T, Division 3, 15 March, 1965 and v Manchester U, Division 1, 19 March, 1969.
Most League Points (2 for a win): 67, Division 3, 1966–67.
Most League Points (3 for a win): 85, Division 2, 1982–83.
Most League Goals: 111, Division 3, 1961–62.
Highest League Scorer in Season: George Goddard, 37, Division 3(S), 1929–30.
Most League Goals in Total Aggregate: George Goddard, 172, 1926–34.
Most Capped Player: Don Givens, 26 (56), Eire.
Most League Appearances: Tony Ingham, 519, 1950–63.
Record Transfer Fee Received: £1,250,000 from Arsenal for Clive Allen, June 1980.
Record Transfer Fee Paid: £800,000 to to Southampton for Colin Clarke, March 1989.
Football League Record: 1920 Original Members of Division 3; 1921 Division 3(S); 1948–52 Division 2; 1952–58 Division 3(S); 1958–67 Division 3; 1967–68 Division 2; 1968–69 Division 1; 1969–73 Division 2; 1973–79 Division 1; 1979–83 Division 2; 1983– Division 1.
Honours: *Football League:* Division 1 – Runners-up 1975–76; Division 2 – Champions 1982–83; Runners-up 1967–68, 1972–73; Division 3(S) – Champions 1947–48; Runners-up 1946–47; Division 3 – Champions 1966–67. *FA Cup:* Runners-up 1982. *Football League Cup:* Winners 1966–67. Runners-up 1985–86. (In 1966–67 won Division 3 and Football League Cup.) **European Competiton:** *UEFA Cup:* 1976–77, 1984–85.
Colours: Blue and white hooped shirts, white shorts, white stockings with 3 blue hands at top. **Change Colours:** Red and black hooped shirts, black shorts, black stockings with 4 red bands at top.

QUEEN'S PARK RANGERS 1988–89 LEAGUE RECORD

Match No.	Date	Venue	Opponents	Result	H/T Score	Lg. Pos.	Goalscorers	Attendance
1	Aug 27	A	Manchester U	D 0-0	0-0	—		46,377
2	Sept 3	H	Southampton	L 0-1	0-1	15		9053
3	10	A	Norwich C	L 0-1	0-0	17		11,174
4	17	H	Sheffield W	W 2-0	1-0	11	Francis 2 (1 pen)	8011
5	24	A	Derby Co	W 1-0	1-0	11	Stein	14,008
6	Oct 1	A	Millwall	L 2-3	1-3	12	Francis, Allen	14,103
7	8	H	Nottingham F	L 1-2	1-1	17	Stein	11,205
8	15	H	West Ham U	W 2-1	0-1	9	Stein, Maddix	14,566
9	22	A	Arsenal	L 1-2	0-0	12	Falco	33,202
10	29	A	Luton T	D 0-0	0-0	14		8453
11	Nov 5	H	Newcastle U	W 3-0	2-0	12	Maddix, Allen, Falco	11,013
12	12	A	Middlesbrough	L 0-1	0-1	14		20,565
13	19	H	Liverpool	L 0-1	0-1	14		20,063
14	26	A	Tottenham U	D 2-2	2-0	13	Falco, Francis	26,698
15	Dec 3	H	Coventry C	W 2-1	1-0	13	Francis, Falco	9853
16	10	A	Charlton Ath	D 1-1	1-0	13	Francis	6012
17	17	H	Evertpm	D 0-0	0-0	14		10,067
18	26	A	Aston Villa	L 1-2	0-2	15	Francis	25,106
19	31	A	Southampton	W 4-1	0-2	12	Allen, Barker, Falco 2	15,086
20	Jan 2	H	Norwich C	D 1-1	0-0	14	Falco	12,410
21	14	A	Wimbledon	L 0-1	0-1	15		7118
22	21	H	Derby Co	L 0-1	0-0	16		9516
23	Feb 4	H	Millwall	L 1-2	0-0	16	Falco (pen)	12,381
24	11	A	Nottingham F	D 0-0	0-0	16		19,690
25	18	H	Arsenal	D 0-0	0-0	16		20,543
26	25	A	West Ham U	D 0-0	0-0	16		17,371
27	Mar 11	A	Newcastle U	W 2-1	0-0	13	Clarke, Stein	21,577
28	21	H	Luton T	D 1-1	0-0	—	Clarke	9372
29	25	A	Sheffield W	W 2-0	0-0	12	Falco, Allen	18,804
30	27	H	Aston Villa	W 1-0	0-0	12	Sinton	11,378
31	Apr 1	A	Everton	L 1-4	0-2	12	Falco (pen)	23,028
32	8	H	Wimbledon	W 4-3	3-1	12	Clarke, Spackman, Falco, Reid	9056
33	15	H	Middlesbrough	D 0-0	0-0	12		10,347
34	22	A	Coventry C	W 3-0	2-0	11	Channing, Clarke 2	11,319
35	29	H	Charlton Ath	W 1-0	1-0	10	Sinton	13,452
36	May 8	H	Manchester U	W 3-2	1-2	—	Sinton, Gray 2	10,017
37	13	H	Tottenham H	W 1-0	0-0	8	Falco	21,873
38	16	A	Liverpool	L 0-2	0-1	—		38,368

Final League Position: 9

GOALSCORERS

League (43): Falco 12 (2 pens), Francis 7 (1 pen), Clarke 5, Allen M 4, Stein 4, Sinton 3, Gray 2, Maddix 2, Barker 1, Channing 1, Reid 1, Spackman 1.
Littlewoods Cup (12): Francis 3, Stein 3, Falco 2, Allen M 1, Fereday 1, Kerslake 1, Maddix 1.
FA Cup (2): McDonald 1, Stein 1.

Littlewoods Cup	Second Round	Cardiff C (h)	3-0
		(a)	4-1
	Third Round	Charlton Ath (h)	2-1
	Fourth Round	Wimbledon (h)	0-0
		(a)	1-0
	Fifth Round	Nottingham F (a)	2-5
FA Cup	Third Round	Manchester U (a)	0-0
		(h)	2-2
		(a)	0-3

Seaman	Fereday	Dennis	Parker	McDonald	Ardiles	Allen M	Brock	Falco	Francis	Barker	Stein	Maddix	Coney	Law	Kerslake	Johns	Maguire	Pizanti	Herrera	Fleming	Gray	Spackman	Channing	Reid	Clarke	Sinton	Allen B	*Match No.*
1	2	3	4	5	6	7	8	9	10*	11	12																	1
1	2	3	4	5	6	7	8†	9	10*	11	12	14																2
1	2	3	4	5	14	7	11*	12		8†	10	6	9															3
1	9	3	4	5		7	11		8		10	6		2														4
1	9	3	4	5		7			8	11	10*	6	12		2													5
	9	3*	4	5		7	11†	12	8	14	10				2	1	6											6
	9	3*	4	5		7	11		8		12	2	10			1	6											7
	9		4	5		3	11†	7	8	2	10*	6	12		14	1												8
1	9		4	5		3	11	7	8*	2	10	6			12													9
1	9		4	5		3	11	7	8†	2*	10	6	12		14													10
1	9		4	5		3	12	7	8	2*	10†	6			14		11											11
1	9		4	5	14	3*	12	7	8	2	10†	6					11											12
1	9		4	5	14	3	11	7	8*	2†		6			12			10										13
1	9		4		5†	3	11	7	8	2*		6			12		14	10										14
1	9	12	4*			3	11	7	8			6	2				5	10										15
1	9		4	2		3		7	8			6			11		5	10										16
1	9	3*	4	2				7	8	11†	12	6	10		14			5										17
1	9*		4	2				7	8	11	12	14	10		6		3†	5										18
1			4	2	14	11		7	8	12	9†	6	10	5				3*										19
1			4	2		11		7	8	10	9*	6		5	12			3										20
1	9		4		2					8	7	6	10	5	11†			3*	14								12	21
1	9*		4							8	7	6	10	5	11			3	12	2								22
1	3*		4	2				9		12	7	6	10	5†				14			8	11						23
1			4							9	7	5	10		12			3			8*	6	2	11				24
1		3*						9		7†	12	5	10		14			11			8	6	2	4				25
1		3†		5				9*		7	11	10	12					14			8	6	2	4				26
1	2	3	4	5							8	14	12					11*			7†	6		10	9			27
1	2		4	5		11				12	8	3									7*	6		10	9			28
1	2	3	4	5		11		12			8*	14										6		10	9†	7		29
1	2	3	4	5		11†		8*			12	14										6		10	9	7		30
1	2	3	4	5		11*		8			12											6		10	9	7		31
1	14	3	4	5		7		8*			12											6	2†	10	9	11		32
1	14	3	4	5†		7		8*			12											6	2	10	9	11		33
1	3		4			12						5			8						7*	6	2	10	9	11		34
1	3		4			14					12	5			8						7†	6	2	10*	9	11		35
1	3†		4	14							12	5			8						7	6	2	10*	9	11		36
1			4	14		3		12		10		5			8†						7	6	2*		9	11		37
1			4	14		3		12		2		5			8						7*	6		10†	9	11		38
35	29 + 2s	16 + 1s	36	27 + 3s	4 + 4s	26 + 2s	12 + 2s	22 + 5s	19	21 + 4s	19 + 12s	28 + 5s	11 + 5s	6	11 + 10s	3	7 + 1s	13 + 2s	— + 2s	1	11	16	9	14	12	10	— + 1s	

QUEEN'S PARK RANGERS

Player and Position	Ht	Wt	Birth Date	Birth Place	Source	Clubs	League App	League Gls
Goalkeepers								
Nicky Johns	6 2	11 05	8 6 57	Bristol	Minehead	Millwall	50	—
						Tampa Bay R	—	—
						Sheffield U (loan)	1	—
						Charlton Ath	288	—
						QPR	10	—
Antony Roberts	6 0		4 8 69	Bangor	Trainee	QPR	1	—
David Seaman	6 3	13 00	19 9 63	Rotherham	Apprentice	Leeds U	—	—
						Peterborough U	91	—
						Birmingham C	75	—
						QPR	108	—
Defenders								
Justin Channing	5 10		19 11 68	Reading	Apprentice	QPR	25	2
Mark Dennis	5 9	10 08	2 5 61	Streatham	Apprentice	Birmingham C	130	1
						Southampton	95	2
						QPR	28	—
Mark Fleming*			11 8 69	Hammersmith	Trainee	QPR	3	—
Roberto Herrera			12 6 70	Torbay	Trainee	QPR	2	—
Brian Law			1 1 70	Merthyr	Apprentice	QPR	7	—
Alan McDonald	6 2	12 07	12 10 63	Belfast	Apprentice	QPR	168	8
						Charlton Ath (loan)	9	—
Danny Maddix	5 11	11 00	11 10 67	Ashford	Apprentice	Tottenham H	—	—
						Southend U (loan)	2	—
						QPR	42	2
David Pizanti	5 10	11 00	27 5 62	Israel	Cologne	QPR	22	—
Midfield								
Martin Allen	5 10	11 00	14 8 65	Reading	School	QPR	134	16
Ossie Ardiles‡	5 6	9 10	3 8 52	Cordoba	Huracan	Tottenham H	140	13
						Paris St Germain	14	1
						Tottenham H	98	3
						Blackburn R (loan)	5	—
						QPR	8	—
Simon Barker	5 9	11 00	4 11 64	Farnworth	Apprentice	Blackburn R	182	35
						QPR	25	1
Greg Costello			5 4 70	Dublin	Apprentice	QPR	—	—
Gary Eaton*	5 8	11 07	22 9 69	Paddington		QPR	—	—
Wayne Fereday	5 9	11 0	16 6 63	Warley	Apprentice	QPR	197	21
Andy Gray	5 11	13 03	22 2 64	Lambeth	Dulwich H	Crystal Palace	98	27
						Aston Villa	37	4
						QPR	11	2
David Kerslake	5 8	11 04	19 6 66	London	Apprentice	QPR	57	6
Paul Parker	5 7	10 09	4 4 64	Essex	Apprentice	Fulham	153	2
						QPR	76	—
Peter Reid	5 8	10 07	20 6 56	Huyton	Apprentice	Bolton W	225	23
						Everton	159	8
						QPR	14	1
Andy Sinton	5 7	10 07	19 3 66	Newcastle	Apprentice	Cambridge U	93	13
						Brentford	149	28
						QPR	10	3
Nigel Spackman	6 1	12 04	2 12 60	Romsey	Andover	Bournemouth	119	10
						Chelsea	141	12
						Liverpool	51	—
						QPR	16	1
Forwards								
Bradley Allen	5 7	10 00	13 9 71	Harold Wood	Schoolboys	QPR	1	—
John Byrne	6 0	12 04	1 2 61	Manchester	Apprentice	York C	175	55
(To Le Havre)						QPR	126	30

QUEEN'S PARK RANGERS

Foundation: There is an element of doubt about the date of the foundation of this club, but it is believed that in either 1885 or 1886 it was formed through the amalgamation of Christchurch Rangers and St. Jude's Institute FC. The leading light was George Wodehouse, whose family maintained a connection with the club until comparatively recent times. Most of the players came from the Queen's Park district so this name was adopted after a year as St. Jude's Institute.

Managers (and Secretary-managers)
James Cowan 1906–13, James Howie 1913–20, Ted Liddell 1920–24, Will Wood 1924–25 (had been secretary since 1903), Bob Hewison 1925–30, John Bowman 1930–31, Archie Mitchell 1931–33, Mick O'Brien 1933–35, Billy Birrell 1935–39, Ted Vizard 1939–44, Dave Mangnall 1944–52, Jack Taylor 1952–59, Alec Stock 1959–65 (GM to 1968), Jimmy Andrews 1965, Bill Dodgin Jnr 1968, Tommy Docherty 1968, Les Allen 1969–70, Gordon Jago 1971–74, Dave Sexton 1974–77, Frank Sibley 1977–78, Steve Burtenshaw 1978–79, Tommy Docherty 1979–80, Terry Venables 1980–84, Gordon Jago 1984, Alan Mullery 1984, Frank Sibley 1984–85, Jim Smith 1985–88, Trevor Francis 1988– .

Player and Position	*Ht*	*Wt*	*Birth Date*	*Birth Place*	*Source*	*Clubs*	*League App*	*League Gls*
Colin Clarke	5 11	12 10	30 10 62	Newry	Apprentice	Ipswich T	—	—
						Peterborough U	82	18
						Gillingham (loan)	8	1
						Tranmere R	45	22
						Bournemouth	46	26
						Southampton	82	36
						Bournemouth (loan)	4	2
						QPR	12	5
Maurice Doyle	5 8	10 07	17 10 69	Ellesmere Port	Trainee	Crewe Alex	8	2
						QPR	—	—
Mark Falco	6 0	12 00	22 10 60	Hackney	Apprentice	Tottenham H	174	67
						Chelsea (loan)	3	—
						Watford	33	14
						Rangers	14	5
						QPR	46	17
Les Ferdinand	5 11	13 05	18 12 66	London	Hayes	QPR	3	—
						Brentford (loan)	3	—
						Besiktas (loan)	—	—
Trevor Francis	5 10	11 07	19 4 54	Plymouth	Apprentice	Birmingham C	280	118
						Nottingham F	70	28
						Manchester C	26	12
						Sampdoria	68	17
						Rangers	18	—
						QPR	28	7
Kevin Kingsmore	5 7	11 02	14 10 70	Belfast	Trainee	QPR	—	—
Steve Lynch			25 9 69	Belfast	Trainee	QPR	—	—
Mark Stein	5 3	9 02	28 1 66	Capetown, SA		Luton T	54	19
						Aldershot (loan)	2	1
						QPR	31	4

Trainees
Allosp, Justin P; Caldwell, Peter J; Crocker, Steven; Flower, Simon F.N; Hunt, Richard A; Joyce, Anthony J; McCarthy, Alan J; Macciohi, David A; Meaker, Michael J; Rutherford, Michael A; Vowles, Paul.

****Non-Contract**
McEnroe, David J; Parker, Thomas G.

Associated Schoolboys
Acton, Philip D; Bixby, Michael E; Bromage, Raymond P; Brookes, Steffan L; Dichio, Daniele; Dickinson, Steven D; Duong, Vinh-Tam; Finlay, Darren J; Graham, Mark R; Hubbard, Kevin; Hurrell, Paul C; Jackson, Stephen; Jones, Michael S; McGivern, Allan J; Millard, Martyn L; Ready, Karl; Schonberger, David P; Wilkinson, Gary R.

READING 1988–89 *Back row (left to right):* Keith Knight, Mick Tait, Andy King, Gary Phillips, Mike Conroy, Martin Hicks, Trevor Senior, Adrian Chatterley, Paul Franklin, Ivan Gernon, Linden Jones.

Front row: Michael Gilkes, Les Taylor, Stuart Beavon, Naseem Bashir, Russell Goodenough, Colin Mitchell, Karl Elsey,Steve Richardson, Jason Walkington.

Division 3 READING

Elm Park, Norfolk Road, Reading. Telephone Reading (0734) 507878. Royals Social Club 0734 596958.*Ground capacity:* 17,500.

Record attendance: 33,042 v Brentford, FA Cup 5th rd, 19 Feb, 1927.

Record receipts: £70,693.79 v Arsenal, FA Cup 3 rd, 10 January 1987.

Pitch measurements: 112yd × 77yd.

Life President: J. H. Brooks.

Chairman: Roger Smee. *Vice-Chairman:* J. H. Brooks.

Financial Controller/Secretary: C. R. Winter.

Directors: J. Campbell, C. M. Brooks.

Manager: Ian Branfoot. *Assistant Manager:* Lew Chatterley. *Coach:* Stewart Henderson.

Physio: John Hasleden.

Sales/Marketing Manager: Vivienne Ball.

Secretary:

Year Formed: 1871. *Turned Professional:* 1895 *Ltd Co.:* 1895.

Club Nickname: 'The Royals'.

Previous Grounds: 1871, Reading Recreation; Reading Cricket Ground; 1882, Coley Park; 1889, Caversham Cricket Ground; 1896, Elm Park.

Record League Victory: 10-2 v Crystal Palace, Division 3(S), 4 September 1946 – Groves; Glidden, Gulliver; McKenna, Ratcliffe, Young; Chitty, Maurice Edelston (3), McPhee (4), Barney (1), Deverell (2).

Record Cup Victory: 6-0 v Leyton, FA Cup, 2nd rd, 12 December 1925 – Duckworth; Eggo, McConnell; Wilson, Messer, Evans; Smith (2), Braithwaite (1), Davey (1), Tinsley, Robson (2).

Record Defeat: 0-18 v Preston NE, FA Cup 1st rd, 1893–94.

Most League Points (2 for a win): 65, Division 4, 1978–79.

Most League Points (3 for a win): 94, Division 3, 1985–86.

Most League Goals: 112, Division 3(S), 1951–52.

Highest League Scorer in Season: Ronnie Blackman, 39, Division 3(S), 1951,52.

Most League Goals in Total Aggregate: Ronnie Blackman, 156, 1947–54

Most Capped Player: Billy McConnell, 8, Northern Ireland.

Most League Appearances: Steve Death, 471, 1969–82.

Record Transfer Fee Received: £325,000 from Watford for Trevor Senior, July 1987.

Record Transfer Fee Paid: £250,000 to Leicester C for Steve Moran, November 1987.

Football League Record: 1920 Original Member of Division 3; 1921–26 Division 3(S); 1926–31 Division 2; 1931–58 Division 3(S); 1958–71 Division 3; 1971–76 Division 4; 1976–77 Division 3; 1977–79 Division 4; 1979–83 Division 3; 1983–84 Division 4; 1984–86 Division 3; 1986–88 Division 2; 1988– Division 3.

Honours: Football League: Division 2 best season: 13th 1986–87; Division 3 – Champions 1985–86. Division 3(S) – Champions 1925–26; Runners-up 1931–32, 1934–35, 1948–49, 1951–52; Division 4 – Champions 1978–79. *FA Cup;* Semi-final 1927. *Football League Cup* best season: 4th rd, 1965, 1966, 1978. *Simod Cup:* Winners 1987–88.

Colours: Sky blue shirts with white centre panel, sky blue shorts, navy stockings. **Change Colours:** All yellow.

READING 1988–89 LEAGUE RECORD

Match No.	Date	Venue	Opponents	Result		H/T Score	Lg. Pos.	Goalscorers	Attendance
1	Aug 27	H	Sheffield U	L	1-3	0-2	—	Gilkes	5512
2	Sept 3	A	Wolverhampton W	L	1-2	1-0	21	Whitehurst	10,513
3	10	H	Bolton W	D	1-1	0-0	24	Whitehurst	4660
4	17	A	Wigan Ath	L	0-3	0-1	24		2534
5	21	H	Southend U	W	4-0	2-0	—	Knight, Beavon (pen), Gordon, Hicks	4062
6	24	A	Gillingham	W	1-0	1-0	12	Moran	4469
7	Oct 1	H	Chester C	W	3-1	2-0	9	Tait, Knight 2	4376
8	4	A	Bury	L	1-2	1-1	—	Tait	2027
9	8	A	Cardiff C	W	2-1	0-1	9	Conroy, Gilkes	4057
10	15	H	Mansfield T	W	1-0	1-0	7	Beavon (pen)	6604
11	22	A	Notts Co	D	3-3	3-1	11	Elsey, Senior, Gilkes	5170
12	26	H	Bristol R	W	3-1	2-1	—	Conroy 2, Knight	7150
13	29	A	Northampton T	W	3-1	2-0	5	Gilkes, Conroy, Jones	4355
14	Nov 5	H	Brentford	D	2-2	1-2	7	Jones, Knight	7974
15	8	A	Fulham	L	1-2	1-1	—	Senior	6934
16	12	H	Preston NE	D	2-2	1-1	9	Moran, Senior	6225
17	26	H	Chesterfield	D	0-0	0-0	10		4775
18	Dec 3	A	Bristol C	L	1-2	1-0	13	Senior	8045
19	17	A	Port Vale	L	0-3	0-1	14		4779
20	26	H	Aldershot	W	3-1	1-0	11	Knight, Tait 2	6350
21	30	H	Blackpool	W	2-1	2-1	—	Senior (pen), Knight	5554
22	Jan 2	A	Swansea C	L	0-2	0-0	11		6772
23	14	H	Wolverhampton W	L	0-2	0-2	12		9353
24	21	A	Bolton W	D	1-1	0-0	12	Hicks	5172
25	Feb 4	A	Chester C	L	0-3	0-1	15		2354
26	11	H	Bury	D	1-1	1-0	16	Moran	3804
27	18	H	Cardiff C	W	3-1	2-0	12	Gilkes, Moran, Senior	4359
28	25	A	Mansfield T	L	1-2	0-0	15	Senior	3012
29	Mar 1	A	Bristol R	D	1-1	0-1	—	Elsey	4573
30	4	H	Notts Co	L	1-3	1-1	15	Beavon	4153
31	7	A	Huddersfield T	D	2-2	1-1	—	Senior 2	4933
32	11	A	Brentford	L	2-3	1-2	15	Senior, Jones	6866
33	15	H	Northampton T	D	1-1	1-1	—	Payne	3746
34	18	A	Sheffield U	L	0-1	0-0	16		11,867
35	25	H	Swansea C	W	2-0	1-0	15	Senior 2	4367
36	27	A	Aldershot	D	1-1	0-0	15	Beavon (pen)	4960
37	Apr 1	H	Port Vale	W	3-0	1-0	15	Beavon, Gilkes, Senior	4501
38	5	H	Huddersfield T	W	2-1	1-0	—	Senior 2	3802
39	8	A	Blackpool	W	4-2	1-0	12	Elsey, Gilkes, Payne, Beavon	2792
40	14	A	Southend U	L	1-2	0-1	—	Gilkes	4623
41	19	H	Wigan Ath	L	0-3	0-2	—		3821
42	22	H	Gillingham	L	1-2	0-1	14	Gilkes	3511
43	29	A	Preston NE	L	1-2	0-2	16	Beavon (pen)	7003
44	May 1	H	Fulham	L	0-1	0-1	17		5152
45	5	H	Bristol C	L	1-2	1-1	—	Hicks	3620
46	13	A	Chesterfield	W	4-2	0-2	16	Senior, Payne, Beavon 2 (2 pens)	3107

Final League Position: 18

GOALSCORERS

League (68): Senior 16 (1 pen), Beavon 9 (6 pens), Gilkes 9, Knight 7, Conroy 4, Moran 4, Tait 4, Elsey 3, Hicks 3, Jones 3, Payne 3, Whitehurst 2, Gordon 1.
Littlewoods Cup (6): Moran 2, Tait 2, Beavon 1 (pen), Jones 1.
FA Cup (12): Senior 4, Elsey 2, Taylor 2, Franklin 1, Gernon 1, Moran 1, own goal 1.

Littlewoods Cup	First Round	Torquay U (a)	1-0
		(h)	3-1
	Second Round	Bradford C (h)	1-1
		(a)	1-2

Francis	Curle	Richardson	Beavon	Hicks	Franklin	Jones	Taylor, L	Tait	Moran	Gilkes	Gordon	Elsey	Whitehurst	Taylor, S	King	Gernon	Knight	Conroy	Senior	Williams	Phillips	Whitlock	Payne	*Match No.*
1	2	3	4	5	6	7†	8	9	10*	11	12	14												1
1	6	3		5		7	8	4	10	11		2	9											2
1	6	3	8	5		7		4	10	11		2	9											3
1	6	3	4	5	7		8*		10†	11	9	2		12	14									4
1	6	2†	4	5	14				10	11	9	8		12		3	7*							5
1	6		4	5	2				10	11	9	8				3	7							6
1	6		4	5	2			9	10	11		8				3	7							7
1	6		4	5	2	12		9	10†	11		8				3	7*	14						8
1	6		4		2	12		5	10	11		8				3	7*	9						9
1	6	3	4*	5	2†	7		10	12	11		8				14			9					10
1		3		5			4			11		8				6	7	10	9	2				11
1*		2		5		7	4	6		11		8				3	12	10	9					12
		2	4	5		7	8			11		3				6		10	9		1			13
			4	5	2	7†	8		12	11		3				6	14	10*	9		1			14
			4	5		7†	8	6	12	11		2				3	14	10*	9		1			15
		3	4*	5	2	7	12	6	10	11		8							9		1			16
		2		5	12		8	6	10*	11		4				3	7		9		1			17
		3		5	2		12	8*	10	11		4					7		9		1	6		18
		3		5	2			8		11		4				6	7	10	9		1			19
		2		5			8	10		11		4				3	7		9		1	6		20
			14	5	2		8	10*		11		4†				3	7	12	9		1	6		21
		12	14	5	2		8			11		4*				3	7†	10	9		1	6		22
		2	4	5				8†	12	11		14				3	7	10*	9		1	6		23
		3	4	5		7			10	11		8				12			9	2	1	6*		24
		3	4	5		2		7	10*	11		8				6		12	9		1			25
		3	4	5		2		7	10	11		8							9		1	6		26
		3	4	5		2		7	10	11		8							9		1	6		27
		3	4	5		2		7	10	11		8							9		1	6		28
		3	4	5		2		7	10*	11		8						12	9		1	6		29
		3	4	5		2		7	10	11		8*							9	12	1	6		30
		3	4	5		7		8	10	11		12							9	2*	1	6		31
		2	4	5		7		8	10	3									9		1	6	11	32
		2	4	5		7*		8	10	3							12		9		1	6	11	33
		3	4	5		2		6		10		8					7		9		1		11	34
		3	4	5		2		6	12	10		8					7†		9		1	14	11*	35
		3	4	5		2		6	12	10		8					7*		9		1		11	36
1		3	4	5		2		6	12	10		8					7*		9				11	37
1		3	4	5		2		6	12	10		8					7*		9				11	38
1		3	4	5		2				10		8				12	7*		9			6	11	39
1		3	4	5		2		6	12	10		8					7*		9				11	40
1		3	4	5				6		10		8					7		9	2			11	41
1		2	4	5				6	10*	3		8				12	7		9				11	42
1		3	4	5				6		10		8					7		9	2			11	43
1		2	4	5				6†	12	10		8		14		3	7*		9				11	44
1		3	4	5		2†			12	10		8					7*		9	14		6	11	45
1		3	4	5	2			6		10		8							9	7			11	46
22	10	38 + 1s	37 + 2s	45	14 + 2s	27 + 2s	12 + 2s	36	23 + 11s	46	3 + 1s	41 + 3s	2	— + 3s	— + 1s	18 + 4s	25 + 4s	9 + 4s	37	6 + 2s	24	16 + 1s	15	

FA Cup	First Round	Hendon (h)	4-2
	Second Round	Maidstone (h)	1-1
		(a)	2-1
	Third Round	Tranmere R (a)	1-1
		(h)	2-1
	Fourth Round	Grimsby T (a)	1-1
		(h)	1-2

READING

Player and Position	Ht	Wt	Birth Date	Place	Source	Clubs	League App	Gls
Goalkeepers								
Phil Burns			18 12 66	Stockport	Army	Reading	—	—
Steve Francis	5 11	11 05	29 5 64	Billericay	Apprentice	Chelsea	71	—
						Reading	70	—
Gary Phillips	6 0	14 00	20 9 61	St Albans	Barnet	WBA	—	—
						Brentford	143	—
						Reading	24	—
Gary Westwood‡	6 0	13 12	3 4 63	Barrow	Apprentice	Ipswich T	—	—
						Charlton Ath (loan)	—	—
						Crystal Palace (loan)	—	—
						Reading (loan)	5	—
						Peterborough U (loan)	—	—
						Reading	123	—
Defenders								
Adrian Chatterley	6 1	12 09	29 6 70	Walsall		Reading	—	—
Paul Franklin*	6 0	11 08	5 10 63	Ilford	Apprentice	Watford	32	—
						Shrewsbury T (loan)	6	—
						Swindon T (loan)	5	1
						Reading	20	—
Irving Gernon	6 2	12 01	30 12 62	Birmingham	Apprentice	Ipswich T	76	—
						Northampton T	9	—
						(loan)	35	1
						Gillingham	22	—
						Reading		
Russell Goodenough‡	5 8	11 01	25 1 70	Slough		Reading	—	—
Steve Head†			11 9 63	Reading		Reading	—	—
Martin Hicks	6 3	13 06	27 2 57	Stratford on Avon	Stratford T	Charlton Ath	—	—
						Reading	412	21
Linden Jones	5 6	10 08	5 3 61	Tredegar	Apprentice	Cardiff C	145	2
						Newport Co	142	5
						Reading	57	6
Domenyk Newman						Reading	—	—
Steve Richardson	5 5	10 03	11 2 62	Slough	Apprentice	Southampton	—	—
						Reading	252	2
Mark Whitlock	6 0	12 02	14 3 61	Portsmouth	Apprentice	Southampton	61	1
						Grimsby T (loan)	8	—
						Aldershot (loan)	14	—
						Bournemouth	99	1
						Reading	17	—
Adrian Williams			16 8 71	Reading	Trainee	Reading	8	—
Midfield								
Naseem Bashir	5 6	10 06	12 9 69	Amersham		Reading	—	—
Stuart Beavon	5 6	10 04	30 11 58	Wolverhampton	Apprentice	Tottenham H	4	—
						Notts Co (loan)	6	—
						Reading	364	41
Karl Elsey	5 10	12 00	20 11 58	Swansea	Pembroke B	QPR	7	—
						Newport Co	123	15
						Cardiff C	59	5
						Gillingham	128	13
						Reading	44	3
Colin Mitchell	5 6	9 03	24 3 71	Reading		Reading	—	—
Mick Tait	5 11	12 05	30 9 56	Wallsend	Apprentice	Oxford U	64	23
						Carlisle U	106	20
						Hull C	33	3
						Portsmouth	240	30
						Reading	71	6
Scott Taylor§			28 11 70	Portsmouth	Trainee	Reading	3	—
Jason Walkington*						Reading	—	—

READING

Foundation: Reading was formed as far back as 1871 at a public meeting held at the Bridge Street Rooms. They first entered the FA Cup as early as 1877 when they amalgamated with the Reading Hornets. The club was further strengthened in 1889 when Earley FC joined them. They were the first winners of the Berks and Bucks Cup in 1878–79.

Managers (and Secretary-managers)
Thomas Sefton 1897–1901*, James Sharp 1901–02, Harry Matthews 1902–20, Harry Marshall 1920–22, Arthur Chadwick 1923–25, H. S. Bray 1925–26 (secretary only since 1922 and 26–35), Andrew Wylie 1926–31, Joe Smith 1931–35, Billy Butler 1935–39, John Cochrane 1939, Joe Edelston 1939–47, Ted Drake 1947–52, Jack Smith 1952–55, Harry Johnston 1955–63, Roy Bentley 1963–69, Jack Mansell 1969–71, Charlie Hurley 1972–77, Maurice Evans 1977–84, Ian Branfoot 1984– .

Player and Position	*Ht*	*Wt*	*Birth Date*	*Birth Place*	*Source*	*Clubs*	*League App*	*League Gls*
Forwards								
Mike Conroy	6 0	11 00	31 12 65	Glasgow	Apprentice	Coventry C	—	—
						Clyde Bank	114	38
						St Mirren	10	1
						Reading	13	4
Michael Gilkes	5 8	10 02	20 7 65	Hackney		Reading	117	17
Andy King	6 0	11 07	30 3 70	Newbury		Reading	1	—
Keith Knight			16 2 69	Cheltenham	Cheltenham T	Reading	29	7
Steve Moran	5 8	11 00	10 1 61	Croydon	Amateur	Southampton	180	78
						Leicester C	43	14
						Reading	62	11
Lee Payne	5 10	11 05	12 12 66	Luton	Barnet	Newcastle U	7	—
						Reading	15	3
Trevor Senior	6 1	12 08	28 11 61	Dorchester	Dorchester T	Portsmouth	11	2
						Aldershot (loan)	10	7
						Reading	164	102
						Watford	24	1
						Middlesbrough	10	2
						Reading	37	16

Trainees
Butler, Steven J; Cox, Richard A; Friel, George P; Hodgson, David N; Lovell, Stuart A; Saunders, Paul B; Seymour, Christopher D; Shaw, Wayne G; Stevens, Gary; Taylor, Scott D.

****Non-Contract**
Head, Stephen J; Luck, Paul A.

Associated Schoolboys
Barkus, Lea P; Bass, David; Emery, Barry; Ferguson, Gary; Gardner, Dudley J; Gregory, Paul; Harvey, Michael; Haveron, Jason J; Henry, Mark C; Honey, Daniel W; Horner, Duncan R; Jordan, Ben; Liney, Paul; Mills, Ryan; McCance, Darren; McGuigan, Gareth J; Moore, Daniel P; Silvey, Paul S.

ROCHDALE 1988–89 *Back row (left to right):* Dean Walling, Andy Armitage, Stuart Mellish, Mark Smith, Jason Smart, Keith Welch, Steve O'Shaughnessy, Simon Copeland, David Mycock, Chris Beaumont, Tom Jones (Trainer).
Centre row: Carl Harris, Lyndon Simmonds, Geoff Lomax, Danny Bergara (Manager), Dave Sutton, Shaun Reid, David Frain.
Front row: Chris Lucketti, John Worsley, Paul Hancox, Paul Buckley, Jason Appleby, Zac Hughes, Jamie Hedderman, Dave Allen.

Division 4 ROCHDALE

Spotland, Willbutts Lane, Rochdale OL11 5DA. Telephone Rochdale (0706) 44648-9.

Ground capacity: 12,001.

Record attendance: 24,231 v Notts Co, FA Cup 2nd rd, 10 Dec, 1949.

Record receipts: £16,483 v Burnley, Div 4, 21 January 1989.

Pitch measurements: 113yd × 75yd.

President: Mrs L. Stoney.

Chairman: J. Marsh. ***Vice-Chairman:*** C. D. Walkden.

Directors: D. F. Kilpatrick, G. Morris, W. A. C. Dronsfield, E. Lord, L. Hilton, G. R. Brierley.

Manager: Terry Dolan.

Secretary: Bill Kenyon JP. ***Asst. Manager:*** Dave Sutton.

Commercial Manager: Sheila Hodgkinson. ***Lottery Manager:*** B. Johnson.

Physio:

Year Formed: 1907. ***Turned Professional:*** 1907. ***Ltd Co.:*** 1910.

Club Nickname: 'The Dale'.

Record League Victory: 8-1 v Chesterfield, Division 3(N), 18 December 1926 – Hill; Brown, Ward; Hillhouse, Parkes, Braidwood; Hughes, Bertram, Whitehurst (5), Schofield (2), Martin (1).

Record Cup Victory: 8-2 v Crook T, FA Cup, 1st rd, 26 November 1927 – Moody; Hopkins, Ward; Braidwood, Parkes, Barker; Tompkinson, Clennell (3) Whitehurst (4), Hall, Martin (1).

Record Defeat: 0-8 v Wrexham, Division 3(N), 28 December, 1929, 0-8 v Leyton Orient, Division 4, 20 October, 1987, and 1-9 v Tranmere R, Division 3(N), 25 December, 1931.

Most League Points (2 for a win): 65, Division 4, 1978–79.

Most League Points (3 for a win): 55, Division 4, 1985–86.

Most League Goals: 105, Division 3(N), 1926–27.

Highest League Scorer in Season: Albert Whitehurst, 44, Division 3(N), 1926–27.

Most League Goals in Total Aggregate: Reg Jenkins, 119, 1964–73.

Most Capped Player: None.

Most League Appearances: Graham Smith, 317, 1966–74.

Record Transfer Fee Received: £50,000 from Huddersfield T for Mark Smith, January 1989.

Record Transfer Fee Paid: £25,000 to Bolton W for Mark Gavin, October 1987.

Football League Record: 1921 Elected to Division 3(N); 1958–59 Division 3; 1959–69 Division 4; 1969–74 Division 3; 1974– Division 4.

Honours: *Football League: Division 3 best season: 9th, 1969–70; Division 3(N) – Runners-up 1923–24, 1926–27. FA Cup* best season: 4th rd, 1970–71. *Football League Cup:* Runners-up 1962 (record for 4th Division club).

Colours: All Royal blue. **Change Colours:** All yellow.

ROCHDALE 1988–89 LEAGUE RECORD

Match No.	Date	Venue	Opponents	Result	H/T Score	Lg. Pos.	Goalscorers	Attendance
1	Aug 27	A	Burnley	L 1-2	0-1	—	Frain	7510
2	Sept 3	H	Rotherham U	L 0-2	0-2	21		2107
3	10	A	Scarborough	D 3-3	1-0	21	Harris, Sutton, O'Shaughnessy	2456
4	17	H	Exeter C	W 2-1	1-1	16	Smith, Frain	1216
5	20	H	Doncaster R	W 2-0	0-0	—	Edmonds, Frain (pen)	1645
6	24	A	Grimsby T	W 3-1	1-1	6	Smith 2, Mellish	2939
7	Oct 1	H	Crewe Alex	W 2-1	0-1	5	Edmonds, Smith	2227
8	4	A	Hartlepool U	W 1-0	0-0	—	Toman (og)	2483
9	8	H	Stockport Co	D 1-1	1-1	4	Reid	3021
10	14	A	Halifax T	L 1-4	0-2	—	Smith	2553
11	22	H	Scunthorpe U	W 1-0	0-0	4	Edmonds	2250
12	26	A	Hereford U	D 4-4	3-2	—	Frain 2, Beaumont, Sutton	2071
13	29	H	Darlington	D 2-2	1-1	5	Edmonds 2	2476
14	Nov 4	A	Tranmere R	L 0-2	0-1	—		3740
15	8	A	Torquay U	L 0-1	0-1	—		1931
16	12	H	Wrexham	D 3-3	0-1	12	Reid, Beaumont, Frain	280
17	26	H	York C	W 2-0	0-0	7	Smith, Beaumont	1880
18	Dec 3	A	Peterborough U	L 0-1	0-0	11		3273
19	16	H	Colchester U	D 1-1	1-0	—	O'Shaughnessy	1258
20	26	A	Carlisle U	L 0-1	0-0	13		10,013
21	30	A	Cambridge U	L 0-2	0-0	—		2319
22	Jan 2	H	Leyton Orient	L 0-3	0-1	18		2036
23	7	H	Lincoln C	D 2-2	1-1	17	Smith, Walling	1515
24	14	A	Rotherham U	L 1-3	1-2	17	Frain	4541
25	21	H	Burnley	W 2-1	0-1	17	Frain(pen), Beaumont	5799
26	28	A	Exeter C	L 1-5	1-2	18	Beaumont	2428
27	Feb 4	A	Doncaster R	D 1-1	0-0	19	Beaumont	1868
28	11	H	Grimsby T	L 0-2	0-2	20		1621
29	17	A	Stockport Co	L 0-3	0-2	—		2858
30	28	H	Hereford U	D 2-2	1-2	—	O'Shaughnessy, Taylor	1060
31	Mar 4	A	Scunthorpe U	L 0-4	0-2	21		4098
32	11	H	Tranmere R	W 3-1	0-1	21	Beaumont, O'Shaughnessy 2	2158
33	14	A	Darlington	W 2-1	1-1	—	Taylor, Walling	1876
34	18	H	Scarborough	W 2-1	2-0	19	Jones 2	1636
35	25	A	Leyton Orient	L 0-3	0-1	20		4591
36	27	H	Carlisle U	D 0-0	0-0	20		2145
37	31	A	Colchester U	L 0-3	0-0	—		3631
38	Apr 5	A	Lincoln C	L 1-4	0-3	—	Edmonds	2033
39	8	H	Cambridge U	W 2-1	2-1	20	Frain, Edmonds	1314
40	14	A	Crewe Alex	L 1-3	0-1	—	Frain	4144
41	22	H	Hartlepool U	D 0-0	0-0	22		1406
42	25	H	Halifax T	D 1-1	0-0	—	Frain	1388
43	29	A	York C	D 3-3	1-2	19	Walling, Edmonds, O'Shaughnessy	1920
44	May 1	H	Torquay U	W 2-1	1-0	17	Taylor, Frain (pen)	1239
45	6	H	Peterborough U	D 0-0	0-0	17		1430
46	13	A	Wrexham	L 1-2	0-1	18	Taylor	3125

Final League Position: 18

GOALSCORERS

League (56): Frain 12 (3 pens), Edmonds 8, Beaumont 7, Smith 7, O'Shaughnessy 6, Taylor 4, Walling 3, Jones 2, Reid 2, Sutton 2, Harris 1, Mellish 1, own goal 1.
Littlewoods Cup (4): O'Shaughnessy 2, Beaumont 1, Reid 1 (pen).
FA Cup (4): Beaumont 1, Edmonds 1, Frain 1, Reid (1 pen).

Littlewoods Cup	First Round	Burnley (h)	3-3
		(a)	1-2
FA Cup	First Round	Huddersfield T (a)	1-1
		(h)	3-4

Welch	Copeland	Armitage	Lomax	Sutton	Smart	Harris	Reid	Smith	O'Shaughnessy	Frain	Walling	Beaumont	Mellish	Mycock	Edmonds	Wood	Windridge	Alford	Fothergill	Roberts	Brown	Taylor	McIntyre	Jones	Lucketti	*Match No.*
1	2*	3	4	5	6	7	8	9	10	11	12															1
1	2	3	4	5	14	7†	6	8	10	11	12	9*														2
1	2	3		5	4	7	6	8*	10	11	9		12													3
1	2			5	4	7*	6	8	10	11	12			3	9											4
1	2		6	5	4			8	10	11	9			3	7											5
1	2		6†	5	4		14	8	10	11*	9		12	3	7											6
1	2	3		5	4		6	8	10		9		11		7											7
1	2	3		5	4		6	8	10	11	9				7											8
1	2	3		5	4	12	6	8	10*	11	9				7											9
1	2	3		5	4	7*	6	8	10	11	9†	14			12											10
1		3	2	5	4	7	6	8	10	11					9											11
1			2	5	4	7*	6	8	10	11	12	9			3											12
1		3	2	5	4	7	6	8		11		10			9											13
1	2		3	5	4	11*	6	10		7	12	9			8											14
1	2		3	5	4		6	8	12	11	9*	10			7											15
1	2	14	3	5	4		6	12	7†	11	8*	10			9											16
1	2	4	3*	5			6	8	7	11		10			9	12										17
1	2	12		5			6	8	4	11		10	9*	3		7										18
1	6	3	2	5			4	8	7	11	12	9*			10											19
1		3	7	5	6			8	4	11*		9	2		10	12										20
1		3	6	5	2			8	4	11	9	7			10*	12										21
1	14		3†	5	2			8	4	11	9	12	6		10	7*										22
1	2	3	6	5	4			8		11	9		7		10											23
1	2*	3		5	4			8	6	11	9	12	7		10											24
1	2	3		5	4			8	6	11		9			7		10									25
1	2	3	12	5	4			8	6*	11		9			7		10†	14								26
1	2	3	6	5*	4			8		11		9	12		7		10									27
1	2	3		5*	4				12	11	8†	9	6		7		10	14								28
1	2		5		4				6	11		9		3	12		10		7	8*						29
1	2		5		6				10			9		3					7		4	8	11			30
1	2	3	5		4				6		12	9	7						10			8	11*			31
1		12	3*		4				6	11	9	7†			10				2			8	14	5		32
1		3			4				6	11	9	7			10				2			8		5		33
1		3			4				6	11	9	7			10				2			8		5		34
1		3			4				6	11	9	7			10				2			8		5		35
1		3			4				6	11	9	7*			10						2	8	12	5		36
1		3	6		4					11	9	7			10						2	8		5		37
1		3	6		4				12	11		7	8*		10						2	9		5		38
1		3	6						4	11		7	8		10						2	9		5		39
1		3	10		4				6	11	12		8		7						2*	9		5		40
1		3	10†		4				6		9	7	8		11*				14		2	12			5	41
1	6	3†			4				8	11	10	7		14	12				2*			9		5		42
1	6*				4				8	11	9	7		3	12						2	10		5		43
1		3			4				8	11	10	7*		6	12						2	9		5		44
1		3			4				8	11	10			6	7*			12			2	9		5		45
1		3			4				8	11	10	7		6*				12			2	9		5		46
46	27 + 1s	33 + 3s	26 + 1s	28	41 + 1s	9 + 1s	17 + 1s	26 + 1s	38 + 3s	42	26 + 8s	31 + 3s	12 + 3s	10 + 1s	34 + 5s	2 + 3s	5	— + 4s	8 + 1s	1	11	16	2 + 2s	14	1	

ROCHDALE

Player and Position	Ht	Wt	Birth Date	Birth Place	Source	Clubs	League App	League Gls
Goalkeepers								
Keith Welch	6 0	12 00	3 10 68	Bolton	Trainee	Bolton W	—	—
						Rochdale	116	—
Defenders								
Andy Armitage*			17 10 68	Leds		Leeds U	—	—
						Rochdale	36	—
Malcolm Brown†	6 2	12 06	13 12 56	Salford	Apprentice	Bury	11	—
						Huddersfield T	256	16
						Newcastle U	39	—
						Huddersfield T	96	1
						Rochdale	11	—
Simon Copeland*	6 1	11 08	10 10 68	Sheffield U	Trainee	Sheffield U	—	—
						Rochdale	28	—
Neil Edmonds	5 8	10 08	18 10 68	Accrington	Trainee	Oldham Ath	5	—
						Rochdale	39	8
Zacari Hughes§			6 6 71	Bentley	Trainee	Rochdale	2	—
Paul Jones‡	6 1	12 09	13 5 53	Ellesmere Pt.	Apprentice	Bolton W	444	37
						Huddersfield T	73	8
						Oldham Ath	32	1
						Blackpool	37	—
					Galway	Wigan Ath	—	—
						Rochdale		
							14	2
Geoff Lomax*	5 9	11 08	6 7 64	Manchester	Local	Manchester C	25	1
						Carlisle U	37	—
						Wolverhampton W (loan)	5	—
						Rochdale	71	—
Chris Lucketti§			28 9 71	Littleborough	Trainee	Rochdale	1	—
David Mycock*	5 10	11 12	18 9 69	Todmorden	Trainee	Rochdale	22	—
Steve O'Shaughnessy	6 2	13 00	13 10 67		Wrexham	Leeds U	—	—
						Bradford C	1	—
						Rochdale	41	6
Jason Smart	6 0	12 00	15 2 69	Rochdale	Trainee	Rochdale	117	4
Dave Sutton*	6 1	12 07	21 1 57	Tarleton	Apprentice	Plymouth Arg	61	—
						Reading (loan)	9	—
						Huddersfield T	242	11
						Bolton W	98	4
						Rochdale	28	2
Midfield								
Carl Alford§			11 2 72	Manchester	Trainee	Rochdale	4	—
Ashley Fothergill*			3 10 69	Harrogate	Middlebrough Trainee	Rochdale	9	—
Paul Hancox†			22 7 70	Manchester	Trainee	Rochdale	2	—
Joe McIntyre§			19 6 71	Manchester	Port Vale§	Rochdale	4	—
Stuart Mellish*	5 10	11 03	19 11 69	Hyde	Trainee	Blackpool	—	—
						Rochdale	27	1
David Windridge‡	5 9	11 00	7 12 61	Atherstone	Amateur	Sheffield U	—	—
						Chesterfield	78	14
						Blackpool	101	18
					Cork C	Bury	1	—
						Rochdale	5	—

ROCHDALE

Foundation: Considering the love of rugby in their area, it is not surprising that Rochdale had difficulty in establishing an Association Football club. The earlier Rochdale Town club formed in 1900 went out of existence in 1907 when the present club was immediately established and joined the Manchester League, before graduating to the Lancashire Combination in 1908.

Managers (and Secretary-managers)
Billy Bradshaw 1920, (run by committee 1920–22), Tom Wilson 1922–23, Jack Peart 1923–30, Will Cameron 1930–31, Herbert Hopkinson 1932–34, Billy Smith 1934–35, Ernest Nixon 1935–37, Sam Jennings 1937–38, Ted Goodier 1938–52, Jack Warner 1952–53, Harry Catterick 1953–58, Jack Marshall 1958–60, Tony Collins 1960–68, Bob Stokoe 1967–68, Len Richley 1968–70, Dick Conner 1970–73, Walter Joyce 1973–76, Brian Green 1976–77, Mike Ferguson 1977–78, Doug Collins 1979, Bob Stokoe 1979–80, Peter Madden 1980–83, Jimmy Greenhoff 1983–84, Vic Halom 1984–86, Eddie Gray 1986–88, Danny Bergara 1988–89.

Player and Position	*Ht*	*Wt*	*Birth Date*	*Birth Place*	*Source*	*Clubs*	*League App*	*League Gls*
Forwards								
Chris Beaumont			5 12 65	Sheffield	Denaby	Rochdale	34	7
David Frain	5 8	10 05	11 10 62	Sheffield	Rowlinson YC	Sheffield U	44	6
						Rochdale	42	12
Mark Hunt‡			5 10 69	Farnworth	Trainee	Rochdale	2	1
Bill Roberts‡			9 4 63	Bradford		Rochdale	1	—
Lyndon Simmonds*	5 5	10 07	11 11 66	Pontypool	Apprentice	Leeds U	9	3
						Swansea C (loan)	8	1
						Rochdale (loan)	22	10
						Rochdale	43	12
Steve Taylor	5 10	10 09	18 10 55	Royton	Apprentice	Bolton W	40	16
						Port Vale (loan)	4	2
						Oldham Ath	47	25
						Luton T	20	1
						Mansfield T	37	7
						Burnley	86	37
						Wigan Ath	30	7
						Stockport Co	26	8
						Rochdale	84	42
						Preston NE	5	2
						Burnley	45	6
						Rochdale	17	4
Dean Walling	6 0	10 08	17 4 69	Leeds		Leeds U	—	—
						Rochdale	46	5

Trainees
Alford, Carl P; Buckley, Paul K; Cramer, Stuart; Dutton, Lee; Hedderman, Jamie T; Hughes, Zacari D; Lucketti, Christopher J; McIntyre, Joseph G; Worsley, John.

****Non-Contract**
Brown, Malcolm.

ROTHERHAM 1988–89 *Back row (left to right):* Ian Clarke, Nigel Pepper, Giles Newcombe, Andy Williams, Nigel Johnson, Ray Warburton, Kelham O'Hanlon, Paul Haycock, John Green.
Centre row: John Breckin (Youth Coach), Mark Ash, John Buckley, David Tomlinson, Phil Henson (Assistant Manager), Billy Russell, Simon Thompson, Martin Scott, Ian Bailey (Physiotherapist).
Front row: Pat Heard, Bobby Williamson, Shaun Goodwin, Billy McEwan (Manager), Tony Grealish, Phil Crosby, Des Hazel.

Division 3 **ROTHERHAM UNITED**

Millmoor Ground, Rotherham. Telephone Rotherham (0709) 562434.

Ground Capacity: 18,500.

Record attendance: 25,000 v Sheffield U, Division 2, 13 Dec, 1952 and v Sheffield W, Division 2, 26 Jan, 1952.

Record receipts: £44,091 v Manchester U, Littlewoods Cup, 2nd rd, 1st leg, 28 September, 1989.

Pitch measurements. 115yd × 75yd.

President: Sir J. Layden.

Chairman: K. F. Booth.

Directors: R. Hull (Vice-Chairman), B. J. Peacock, C. A. Luckock, D. J. Batty, J. A. Webb.

Manager: Billy McEwan. ***Asst. Manager:*** Phil Henson. ***Physio:*** Ian Bailey.

Secretary: N. Darnill.

Commercial Manager: D. Nicholls.

Year Formed: 1884. ***Turned Professional:*** 1905. ***Ltd Co.:*** 1920.

Club Nickname: 'The Merry Millers'.

Previous Names: 1884, Thornhill United; 1905, Rotherham County; 1925, amalgamated with Rotherham Town under Rotherham United.

Previous Grounds: Red House Ground; 1907, Millmoor.

Record League Victory: 8-0 v Oldham Ath, Division 3(N), 26 May 1947 – Warnes; Selkirk, Ibbotson; Edwards, Horace Williams, Danny Williams; Wilson (2), Shaw (1), Ardron (3), Guest (1), Hainsworth (1).

Record Cup Victory: 6-0 v Spennymoor U, FA Cup 2nd rd, 17 December 1977 – McAlister; Forrest, Breckin, Womble, Stancliffe, Green, Finney, Phillips (3), Gwyther (2) (Smith), Goodfellow, Crawford (1). 6-0 v Wolverhampton W. FA Cup, 1st rd, 16 November 1985 – O'Hanlon, Forrest, Dungworth, Gooding (1), Smith (1), Pickering, Birch (2), Emerson, Tynan (1), Simmons (1), Pugh.

Record Defeat: 1-11 v Bradford C, Division 3(N), 25 August, 1928.

Most League Points (2 for a win): 71, Division 3(N), 1950–1.

Most League Points (3 for a win): 82, Division 4, 1988–89.

Most League Goals: 114, Division 3(N), 1946–47.

Highest League Scorer in Season: Wally Ardron, 38, Division 3(N), 1946–47.

Most League Goals in Total Aggregate: Gladstone Guest, 130, 1946–56.

Most Capped Player: Harold Millership, 6, Wales.

Most League Appearances: Danny Williams, 459, 1946–62.

Record Transfer Fee Received: £180,000 from Everton for Bobby Mimms, May 1985.

Record Transfer Fee Paid: £100,000 to Cardiff C for Ronnie Moore, August 1980.

Football League Record: 1893 Rotherham Town elected to Division 2; 1986 failed re-election; 1919 Rotherham County elected to Division 2; 1923–51 Division 3(N); 1951–68 Division 2; 1968–73 Division 3; 1973–75 Division 4; 1975–81 Division 3; 1981–83 Division 2; 1983–88 Division 3; 1988–89 Division 4; 1989– Division 3.

Honours: *Football League:* Division 2 best season: 3rd, 1954–55 (equal points with champions and runners-up); Division 3 – Champions 1980–81; Division 3(N) – Champions 1950–51; Runners-up 1946–47, 1947–48, 1948–49; Division 4 – Champioins 1988–89. *FA Cup* best season: 5th rd, 1953, 1968. *Football League Cup:* Runners-up 1961.

Colours: Red shirts, white shorts, red stockings. **Change colours:** Yellow shirts, blue shorts, yellow stockings.

ROTHERHAM UNITED 1988–89 LEAGUE RECORD

Match No.	Date	Venue	Opponents	Result	H/T Score	Lg. Pos.	Goalscorers	Attendance
1	Aug 27	H	Doncaster R	W 3-0	1-0	—	Williamson (pen), Heard, Russell	4497
2	Sept 3	A	Rochdale	W 2-0	2-0	1	Williamson, Johnson	2107
3	10	H	Wrexham	D 2-2	1-1	2	Williamson 2	4367
4	17	A	Grimsby T	W 4-0	3-0	1	Heard, Williamson 2 (1 pen), Williams	3697
5	20	H	Leyton Orient	W 4-1	2-0	—	Buckley, Williams, Grealish, Heard	4289
6	24	A	Carlisle U	W 2-0	0-0	1	Haycock, Williamson	2862
7	Oct 1	H	Exeter C	L 0-1	0-0	1		4075
8	4	A	Burnley	L 0-1	0-0	—		9283
9	8	A	Darlington	D 1-1	0-0	3	Grealish	1746
10	15	H	Tranmere R	D 0-0	0-0	3		4133
11	22	A	Torquay U	W 2-1	2-0	1	Goodwin, Crosby	2228
12	25	H	Colchester U	W 2-0	0-0	—	Green, Williamson	4066
13	29	A	Scarborough	L 0-1	0-1	2		4106
14	Nov 5	H	Lincoln C	W 2-0	2-0	1	Mendonca, Williams	4506
15	8	H	Scunthorpe U	D 3-3	2-1	—	Lister (og), Goodwin, Hazel	5923
16	12	A	Cambridge U	D 1-1	0-1	2	Dempsey	2882
17	26	A	Hereford U	D 1-1	0-1	1	Bradley (og)	2058
18	Dec 3	H	Stockport Co	W 2-1	1-1	1	Haycock, Hazel	4105
19	16	A	York C	D 1-1	0-0	—	Buckley	2656
20	26	H	Crewe Alex	L 1-2	0-1	3	Williamson	7164
21	31	H	Halifax T	W 2-0	0-0	2	Russell, Buckley	5258
22	Jan 2	A	Hartlepool U	D 1-1	0-0	3	Williamson	3337
23	7	A	Peterborough U	W 3-0	0-0	1	Evans 2, Williamson	3368
24	14	H	Rochdale	W 3-1	2-1	1	Crosby, Williamson 2 (1 pen)	4541
25	21	A	Doncaster R	L 0-1	0-0	1		4432
26	Feb 4	A	Leyton Orient	L 1-3	1-0	4	Williamson (pen)	3290
27	11	H	Carlisle U	W 2-1	1-1	3	Heard, Haycock	4111
28	18	H	Darlington	L 1-2	0-0	4	Williamson	4228
29	25	A	Tranmere R	D 0-0	0-0	4		6509
30	28	A	Colchester U	D 1-1	1-0	—	Grealish	3671
31	Mar 4	H	Torquay U	W 1-0	1-0	4	Williamson	3791
32	7	H	Grimsby T	W 1-0	0-0	—	Johnson	4888
33	11	A	Lincoln C	W 1-0	1-0	2	Clarke (og)	5186
34	14	H	Scarborough	D 1-1	1-1	—	Hazel	6010
35	18	A	Wrexham	W 4-1	1-1	2	Williamson 2 (1 pen), Evans 2	2929
36	25	H	Hartlepool U	W 4-0	3-0	2	Stokes (og), Evans 2, Williamson (pen)	4915
37	27	A	Crewe Alex	W 3-1	0-0	1	Williamson 3 (1 pen)	5994
38	Apr 1	H	York C	L 0-1	0-0	1		5929
39	4	H	Peterborough U	D 1-1	0-1	—	Williamson	4762
40	7	A	Halifax T	D 1-1	0-1	—	Williamson	2947
41	15	A	Exeter C	D 0-0	0-0	3		2594
42	22	H	Burnley	W 3-1	3-1	1	Scott, Williamson 2	5726
43	29	H	Hereford U	W 6-0	2-0	1	Haycock, Williamson, Buckley 2, Hazel Goodwin	5334
44	May 1	A	Scunthorpe U	D 0-0	0-0	1		8775
45	6	A	Stockport Co	W 3-1	1-1	1	Hazel 2, Goodwin	4313
46	13	H	Cambridge U	D 0-0	0-0	1		9567

Final League Position: 1

GOALSCORERS

League (76): Williamson 27 (7 pens), Evans 6, Hazel 6, Buckley 5, Goodwin 4, Haycock 4, Heard 4, Grealish 3, Williams 3, Crosby 2, Johnson 2, Russell 2, Dempsey 1, Green 1, Mendonca 1, Scott 1, own goals 4.
Littlewoods Cup (2): Grealish 1, own goal 1.
FA Cup (5): Dempsey 1 (pen), Grealish 1, Green 1, Williamson 1 (pen), own goal 1.

Littlewoods Cup	First Round	Grimsby T (a)	1-0
		(h)	1-0
	Second Round	Manchester U (h)	0-1
		(a)	0-5
FA Cup	First Round	Barrow (h)	3-1
	Second Round	Grimsby T (a)	2-3

O'Hanlon	Russell	Crosby	Grealish	Johnson	Green	Hazel	Williams	Williamson	Haycock	Heard	Goodwin	Mendonca	Buckley	Dempsey	Pepper	Evans	Thompson	Barnsley	Scott	Ash	*Match No.*
1	2	3	4*	5	6	7	8	9	10†	11	12	14									1
1	2	3	4	5	6	7*	8	9	10	11	12										2
1	2	3	4	5	6		8	9	10	11			7								3
1	2	3*	4	5	6		8	9	10†	11	12	14	7								4
1	2	3	4*	5	6		8	9	10	11	12		7								5
1	2	3	4	5	6		8	9	10	11			7								6
1	2	3		5	6	12	8	9	10†	11	4	14	7*								7
1	2	3	4	5	6	7*	8	9	10	11			12								8
1	2	3*	8	5	6	10	4	9		7	14	11†	12								9
1	2	5			6	11	8	9	10	3	4		7								10
1	2	6			5	11	8	9	10	3	4		7								11
1	2	6	12		5	11*	8	9	10	3	4		7								12
1	2		12	5	6	11	8	9	10*	3	4		7								13
1	2		4	5	6	11*	8	9		3	7	10		12							14
1	2		4*	5	6	11	8	9		3	7	10		12							15
1	2	6	4		5	11		9		3	7*			8	12	10					16
1	2	6	4		5	7				3		9*		8	11	10	12				17
1	2	6	4		5	7			9	3	11		12	8*		10					18
1	2	6*	4		5	7			9	3			12	8		10		11			19
1	2		4		5†	7		12	9*	6	3		14	8		10		11			20
1	2	6	4			12		9		3	11	14	7	8*		10†		5			21
1	2	6	4			7		9		3	8	10	11					5			22
1	2	6	4			11		9†		3	12	14	7*	8		10		5			23
1	2	6	4			11		9		4	12		7*	8		10		5			24
1	2	6	4			11		9	14	3	12		7	8*		10†		5			25
1		6	4		2	12		9	14	7*	8		11			10†		5	3		26
1		6	4			7			9	11*	8		12			10		2	3	5	28
1	2	6	4*			11		9	14	12	8		7			10†		5	3		28
1	2	6	4			11		9	10		8			7				5	3		29
1	2	6	4			11		9	10		8*		12	7				5	3		30
1	2	6	4			11		9	10		8*		12	7				5	3		31
1	2	6	4	5		11		9†		14	8*		12	7		10		3			32
1	2	6	4	5		11		9			8			7		10		3			33
1	2	6		5		11		9		4*	8		12	7		10		3†	14		34
1	2	3	4	5		11†		9	10*		8		14	7		12			6		35
1	2	3		5		11†		9	14		8*		12	7		10		4	6		36
1	2	3		5		11		9			8			7		10		4	6		37
1	2	3		5		11		9†	14		8		12	7*		10		4	6		38
1	2	3	7*	5		11		9	14		8		12			10†		4	6		39
1	2	6	4			11		9	10		8		12	7*				5	3		40
1	2		4	5		11		9	10		8		12	7*				6	3		41
1	2	14	4	5		11		9	10*		8		7			12		6†	3		42
1	2		4†	5		11*		9	10		8		7	14		12		6	3		43
1	2		4	5		11		9	10*		8			7		12		6	3		44
1	2		4†	5		11		9	10*		8		14	7		12		6	3		45
1	2		14	5		11		9	10*		8†		4	7		12		6	3		46
46	44	36 + 1s	36 + 3s	26	21	39 + 3s	15	41 + 1s	27 + 6s	28 + 2s	33 + 8s	5 + 5s	19 + 17s	24 + 3s	1 + 1s	19 + 6s	— + 1s	27	18 + 1s	1	

ROTHERHAM UNITED

Player and Position	Ht	Wt	Birth Date	Birth Place	Source	Clubs	League App	League Gls
Goalkeepers								
Billy Mercer	6 1	11 00	22 5 69	Liverpool	Trainee	Liverpool	—	—
						Rotherham U	—	—
Giles Newcombe‡	6 0	12 12	9 7 68	Doncaster	Trainee	Rotherham U	6	—
Kelham O'Hanlon	6 1	13 03	16 5 62	Saltburn	Apprentice	Middlesbrough	87	—
						Rotherham U	172	—
Defenders								
Mark Ash*	5 9	11 04	22 1 68	Sheffield	Apprentice	Rotherham U	20	—
Andy Barnsley	6 0	11 11	9 6 62	Sheffield	Denaby U	Rotherham U	28	—
						Sheffield U	77	1
						Rotherham U	27	—
Phil Crosby	5 9	10 08	9 11 62	Leeds	Apprentice	Grimsby T	39	1
						Rotherham U	183	2
John Green*	5 11	12 12	7 8 58	Rotherham	Apprentice	Rotherham U	248	8
						Scunthorpe U	100	4
						Darlington	45	2
						Rotherham U	85	3
Pat Heard	5 9	11 05	17 3 60	Hull	Apprentice	Everton	11	—
						Aston Villa	24	2
						Sheffield W	25	3
						Newcastle U	34	2
						Middlesbrough	25	2
						Hull C	80	5
						Rotherham U	30	4
Nigel Johnson	6 2	12 08	23 6 64	Rotherham	Apprentice	Rotherham U	54	1
						Nottingham F (loan)	—	—
						Rotherham U	35	—
						Manchester C	4	—
						Rotherham U	49	2
Billy Russell	5 10	11 04	14 9 59	Glasgow	Apprentice	Everton	—	—
						Celtic	—	—
						Doncaster R	244	15
						Scunthorpe U	117	7
						Rotherham U	44	2
Martin Scott	5 8	9 10	7 1 68	Sheffield	Apprentice	Rotherham U	53	1
						Nottingham F (loan)	—	—
Ray Warburton*	6 0	11 05	7 10 67	Rotherham	Apprentice	Rotherham U	4	—
Midfield								
Mark Dempsey	5 8	10 04	14 1 64	Manchester	Apprentice	Manchester U	1	—
						Swindon T (loan)	5	—
						Sheffield U	63	9
						Chesterfield (loan)	3	—
						Rotherham U	27	1
Shaun Goodwin	5 7	8 10	14 6 69	Rotherham	Trainee	Rotherham U	44	4
Tony Grealish	5 7	11 08	21 9 56	Paddington	Apprentice	Orient	171	10
						Luton T	78	2
						Brighton & HA	100	6
						WBA	65	5
						Manchester C	11	—
						Rotherham U	77	6
Lee Hunter	5 10	10 08	5 10 69	Oldham	Trainee	Colchester U	9	—
Nigel Pepper	5 10	10 03	25 4 68	Rotherham	Apprentice	Rotherham U	26	—
Simon Thompson			27 2 70	Sheffield	Trainee	Rotherham U	1	—

ROTHERHAM UNITED

Foundation: This club traces its history back to the formation of Thornhill United in 1878 (reformed 1884). They changed their name to Rotherham County in 1905. Confusion exists because of the existence of the Rotherham Town club (founded c. 1885) and in the Football League as early as 1893 but this club was not the one previously mentioned. The Town amalgamated with Rotherham County to form Rotherham United in 1925.

Managers (and Secretary-managers)
Billy Heald 1925–29 (secretary only for long spell), Stanley Davies 1929–30, Billy Heald 1930–33, Reg Freeman 1934–52, Andy Smailes 1952–58, Tom Johnston 1958–62, Danny Williams 1962–65, Jack Mansell 1965–67, Tommy Docherty 1967–68, Jimmy McAnearney 1968–73, Jimmy McGuigan 1973–79, Ian Porterfield 1979–81, Emlyn Hughes 1981–83, George Kerr 1983–85, Norman Hunter 1985–87, Dave Cusack 1987–88, Billy McEwan 1988– .

Player and Position	*Ht*	*Wt*	*Birth Date*	*Birth Place*	*Source*	*Clubs*	*League App*	*League Gls*
Forwards								
John Buckley	5 9	10 07	10 5 62	Glasgow	Queen's Park	Partick Th	45	5
						Doncaster R	84	11
						Leeds U	10	1
						Leicester C (loan)	5	—
						Doncaster R (loan)	6	—
						Rotherham U	62	5
Ian Clarke‡			3 1 70	Maltby	Trainee	Rotherham U	—	—
Stewart Evans	6 4	11 05	15 11 60	Maltby	Apprentice	Rotherham U	—	—
					Gainsborough T	Sheffield U	—	—
						Wimbledon	175	50
						WBA	14	1
						Plymouth Arg	45	10
						Rotherham U	25	6
Paul Haycock	6 1	12 00	8 7 62	Sheffield	Burton Alb	Rotherham U	94	22
Desmond Hazel	5 10	10 04	15 7 67	Bradford	Apprentice	Sheffield W	6	—
						Grimsby T (loan)	9	2
						Rotherham U	42	6
Clive Mendonca	5 10	11 07	9 9 68	Tullington	Apprentice	Sheffield U	13	4
						Doncaster R (loan)	2	—
						Rotherham U	18	3
Bobby Williamson	5 10	11 00	13 8 61	Glasgow	Auchengill	Clydebank	70	28
						Rangers	41	12
						WBA	53	11
						Rotherham U	42	27

Trainees
Barker, Fraser; Booker, Neil G; Brooks, Christopher; Ford, Stuart T; Foster, Fraser P; Hodges, Mark; Howard, Jonathan; Jarvis, Craig E; Liversidge, Michael; Middleton, Gary L; Roberts, Mark A; Saunders, Anthony; Saunders, Paul; Staniforth, Andrew J; Struggles, Nicholas D; Tomlinson, Michael J; Wilson, Mark.

Associated Schoolboys
Barnfield, Paul; Bennett, Paul S; Clark, Matthew; Cox, Darren J; Curtis, Andrew; Day, Paul E; Dolby, Christopher J; Gibson, Martin M; Hardwick, Matthew; Hurst, Paul; Hutchinson, Robert L; Lawlor, Shane; Mason, Scott A; Mellows, Dean J; Newton, Mark A; Pearson, Jamie S; Pickstone, Lee M; Reddish, Lee; Seddons, Darren; Sheldon, Neil; Smith, Lee; Talbot, Kyle; Taylor, Andrew; Tesh, John A; Tomkins, David A; Walker, David M; Wasden, Lee D.

SCARBOROUGH 1988–89 *Back row (left to right):* Tommy Graham, Mitch Cook, Ian Bennyworth, Steve Richards (Captain), Ian Ironside, Craig Short, Neil Thompson, Christian Short. *Front row:* Paul Olsson, Paul Dobson, Gary Brook, Ray McHale, (Assistant Manager), Colin Morris (Player/Manager), Steve Norris, Alan Kamara, Martin Russell.

Division 4 SCARBOROUGH

The Athletic Ground, Seamer Road, Scarborough YO12 4HF. Telephone 0723-375094. Club shop 0723-379211.

Ground capacity: 10,000.

Record Attendance: 11,130 v Luton T, FA Cup 3rd rd, 8 January 1938. Football League: 7,314 v Wolverhampton W, Division 4, 15 August, 1987.

Record receipts: £19,754 v Wolverhampton W, Division 4, 15 August, 1987.

Pitch measurements: 120yd × 75yd.

President: John Birley.

Vice-Presidents: Jim Crawford, John Fawcett, Walter Hunter, Robert Luff.

Chairman: G. Richmond, ***Vice-Chairman:*** P. Gargett, FCBSI, MBIM..

Directors: D. Fordham, Tim Farrant (BA, Law), M. L. Jones FCA, A Scott, A. Peers.

Manager: Colin Morris. ***Assistant Manager:*** Ray McHale.

General Manager/Secretary:

Commercial Manager: Gordon Butterfield. ***Physio:*** D. Wilson.

Year Formed: 1879. ***Turned Professional:*** 1926. ***Ltd Co.:*** 1933.

Club Nickname: 'The Boro'.

Previous Grounds: 1879–87, Scarborough Cricket Ground; 1887—98, Recreation Ground; 1898– Athletic Ground.

Record League Victory: 4-0 v Bolton W, Division 4, 29 August 1987 – Blackwell; McJannet, Thompson, Bennyworth (Walker), Richards (1) (Cook), Kendall, Hamill (1), Moss, McHale, Mell (1), Graham. (log). 4-0 v Newport C, Division 4, 12 April 1988 – Ironside; McJannet, Thompson, Kamara, Richards (1), Short (1), Adams (Cook 1), Brook, Outhart (1), Russell, Graham.

Record Cup Victory: 6-0 v Rhyl Ath, FA Cup, 1st rd, 29 November 1930 – Turner; Severn, Belton; Maskell, Robinson, Wallis; Small (1), Rand (2), Palfreman (2), Hill A. D. (1), Mickman.

Record Defeat: 1-16 v Southbank, Northern League, 15 November, 1919.

Most League Points (3 for a win): 77, Division 4, 1988–89.

Most League Goals: 67, Division 4, 1988–89

Highest League Scorer in Season: Gary Brook, 12, Division 4, 1988–89.

Record Transfer Fee Received: £100,000 from Ipswich for Neil Thompson, June 1989.

Record Transfer Fee Paid: £102,000 to Leicester C for Martin Russell, March 1989.

Football League Record: Promoted to Division 4 1987.

Honours: *Football League:* Division 4 best season: 5th, 1988–89. *FA Cup:* best seasons: 3rd rd, 1931, 1938, 1976, 1978. *Football League Cup:* best season: 3rd rd 1989.

Colours: All red. **Change colours:** All white.

SCARBOROUGH 1988–89 LEAGUE RECORD

Match No.	Date	Venue	Opponents	Result	H/T Score	Lg. Pos.	Goalscorers	Attendance
1	Aug 27	H	Tranmere R	D 0-0	0-0	—		2893
2	Sept 3	A	Peterborough U	W 4-1	1-1	5	Norris, Thompson, Bennyworth, Cook	3916
3	10	H	Rochdale	D 3-3	0-1	8	Cook (pen), Brook, Morris	2456
4	17	A	Hereford U	W 3-1	1-0	5	Richards, Norris, Cook	2359
5	20	A	Colchester U	L 1-3	0-1	—	Cook (pen)	1420
6	24	H	Torquay U	W 5-2	2-1	5	Brook, Thompson 2, Morris, Adams	1986
7	Oct 1	A	Scunthorpe U	W 3-0	1-0	3	Adams, Thompson, Norris	4167
8	5	H	Darlington	W 3-2	2-1	—	Short, Norris 2	2442
9	8	H	Leyton Orient	D 0-0	0-0	2		2376
10	15	A	Lincoln C	D 2-2	1-2	2	Short, Thompson	4535
11	22	H	Stockport Co	D 1-1	1-1	3	Bennyworth	2449
12	25	A	Cambridge U	D 2-2	1-1	—	Olsson, Short	2673
13	29	H	Rotherham U	W 1-0	1-0	3	Norris	4106
14	Nov 5	A	Carlisle U	W 1-0	1-0	2	Graham	2617
15	9	A	Exeter C	L 0-1	0-0	—		2351
16	12	H	Burnley	W 1-0	0-0	1	Brook	5258
17	26	H	Wrexham	L 0-3	0-1	2		3489
18	Dec 3	A	Grimsby T	L 1-2	0-1	3	Brook	3887
19	17	A	Halifax T	W 2-0	1-0	3	Matthews, Norris	1890
20	26	H	York C	D 0-0	0-0	4		5057
21	31	H	Crewe Alex	W 2-1	1-0	3	Thompson L, Graham	3088
22	Jan 2	A	Doncaster R	L 1-3	1-2	4	Adams	3053
23	14	H	Peterborough U	W 2-1	0-0	3	Cook, Morris	2279
24	21	A	Tranmere R	D 1-1	1-0	4	Kamara	4538
25	28	H	Hereford U	L 0-2	0-0	5		2199
26	Feb 4	H	Colchester U	D 0-0	0-0	5		1913
27	11	A	Torquay U	W 1-0	0-0	5	Russell	2442
28	18	A	Leyton Orient	W 3-2	0-2	2	Dobson, Brook, Olsson	3877
29	25	H	Lincoln C	D 1-1	1-0	3	Brook	3293
30	Mar 1	H	Cambridge U	W 2-1	0-0	—	Brook, Russell	2011
31	4	A	Stockport Co	D 2-2	0-2	3	Brook, Dobson	2648
32	11	H	Carlisle U	L 0-1	0-0	5		2354
33	14	A	Rotherham U	D 1-1	1-1	—	Thompson	6010
34	18	A	Rochdale	L 1-2	0-2	6	Dobson	1636
35	25	H	Doncaster R	W 2-0	1-0	5	Olsson, Brook	2792
36	27	A	York C	D 0-0	0-0	5		4872
37	Apr 1	H	Halifax T	W 3-1	1-0	5	Thompson (pen), Norris, Brook	2365
38	5	H	Hartlepool U	W 2-0	2-0	—	Brook, Thompson	2155
39	8	A	Crewe Alex	D 1-1	1-1	5	Dobson	3243
40	11	A	Hartlepool U	L 1-3	0-0	—	Dobson	1897
41	15	H	Scunthorpe U	W 1-0	0-0	5	Olsson	4456
42	22	A	Darlington	L 1-2	0-1	6	Short	2850
43	29	A	Wrexham	W 1-0	0-0	5	Brook	1948
44	May 1	H	Exeter C	W 2-1	2-1	4	Short, Graham	2513
45	6	H	Grimsby T	L 2-3	1-2	5	Norris, Thompson (pen)	3923
46	13	A	Burnley	W 1-0	0-0	5	Graham	6206

Final League Position: 5

GOALSCORERS

League (67): Brook 12, Norris 9, Thompson N 9 (2 pens), Cook 5 (2 pens), Dobson 5, Short (Craig) 5, Graham 4, Olsson 4, Adams 3, Morris 3, Bennyworth 2, Russell 2, Kamara 1, Matthews 1, Richards 1, Thompson L 1.
Littlewoods Cup (10): Cooke 4 (2 pens), Norris 2, Brook 1, Graham 1, Richards 1, Thompson 1.
FA Cup (2): Brook 1, Cook 1.

Littlewoods Cup	First Round	Halifax T (h)	1-1
		(a)	2-2
	Second Round	Portsmouth (a)	2-2
		(h)	3-1
	Third Round	Southampton (h)	2-2
		(a)	0-1
FA Cup	First Round	Stockport Co (h)	2-1
	Second Round	Carlisle U (h)	0-1

Blackwell	Kamara	Thompson N	Short Craig	Richards	Bennyworth	Morris	Norris	Brook	Cook	Graham	Adams	Mell	Charlton	Olsson	Outhart	McJannet	Brotherston	Ironside	Matthews	Thompson L	Dobson	Russell	Short Chris	*Match No.*
1	2	3	4	5	6	7	8	9	10	11														1
1	2	3	4	5	6	7	8	9	10	11														2
1	2	3	4	5	6	7	9*	10	8	11	12													3
1	2	3	4	5	6	7	9*	10	8	11		12												4
1	2	3	4	5	6	7	9	10*	8	11		12												5
	2	3	4	5	6	7	9*	10	8	11	12		1											6
	2	3	4	5	6		9	10	8	11	7*		1	12										7
	2	3	4	5	6		9	10	8	11	7*		1	12										8
1	2	3	4	5	6	7*	9	10	8	11	12													9
1	2	3	4	5	6		9	10	8	11				7										10
1	2	3	4	5	6*		9	10	8	11				7	12									11
1	2	3	4	5*	6		9	10	8	11		14		7†		12								12
1	2*	3	4	5	6		9	10	8	11						12	7							13
1	2	3	4	5	6		9	10	8	11				12			7*							14
1	2	3	4	5	6		9	10	8	11				12			7*							15
1	2	3	4	5	6		9	10	8	11				12			7*							16
1	2*	3	4	5	6		9	10	8	11				14		12	7†							17
1	2	3	4	5	6		9	10	8	11	12			7*										18
	2	3	4	5	6	7*	9†	10		11	12			14				1	8					19
	2	3	4	5	6			10	12	11	7*	9†						1	8	14				20
	2	3	4	5	6			10		11	7							1	8	9				21
	2	3	4	5	6*			10	12	11	7	14						1	8	9†				22
	2	3	4	5	6	12		10	9	11	7*							1	8					23
	2	3	4	5	6	7		10	9	11*	12							1	8					24
	2	3	4	5	6	7		10	9	11	12							1	8*					25
	2	3	4	5	6*	7		10	8	11	12			9				1						26
	2	3		5	6	7		10	8					4				1			9	11		27
	2	3		5	6	7		10	8					4				1			9	11		28
	2	3		5	6	7		10	8					4				1			9*	11		29
	2	3		5	6	7		10	8	12				4				1			9	11		30
	2	3	14	5*	6†	7		10	8	12				4				1			9	11		31
	2	3	5		6		12		8	10	7*			4				1			9	11		32
	2	3	5		6	7			8	10				4				1			9	11		33
	2*	3	5		6	7†		10	8	12	14			4				1			9	11		34
	2	3	6	5			14	10	12	8*	7†			4				1			9	11		35
	2	3	6	5*			7†	10	12	8	14			4				1			9	11		36
	2	3	6	5			7	10	12	8*	14			4				1			9†	11		37
	2	3	6	5			7	10	12	8				4				1			9*	11		38
	2	3	6	5			9*	10	12	8	14			4				1			7†	11		39
	2	3	6	5		14	9†	10*	12	8				4				1			7	11		40
	2	3	6	5				10	9	8				4				1			7	11		41
	2	3	6	5			12	10	9	8				4				1			7*	11		42
		3	6	5		9	12	10*	14	8				4				1			7†	11	2	43
		3	6	5		12	9*	10	14	8				4				1			7†	11	2	44
	2	3	6	5		7	9	10		8				4				1				11		45
	2	3	6		5		9	10	7	8				4				1				11		46
15	44	46	41 + 1s	42	35	20 + 3s	27 + 4s	44	33 + 10s	40 + 3s	8 + 12s	1 + 4s	3	25 + 7s	— + 1s	— + 3s	5	28	7	2 + 1s	18	20	2	

SCARBOROUGH

Player and Position	*Ht*	*Wt*	*Birth Date*	*Birth Place*	*Source*	*Clubs*	*League App*	*League Gls*
Goalkeepers								
Kevin Blackwell	5 11	12 10	21 12 58	Luton	Boston U	Barnet	—	—
						Scarborough	36	—
Kevin Charlton†			12 9 54	Atherstone	Apprentice	Wolverhampton W	—	—
						Bournemouth	21	—
						Hereford U	52	—
					Telford U	Scarborough	—	—
							3	—
Paul Evans‡			24 2 49	Sheffield		Sheffield W	—	—
						Mansfield T	6	—
						Scarborough	—	—
Ian Ironside	6 2	13 00	8 3 64	Sheffield	Apprentice	Barnsley	—	—
					N Ferriby U	Scarborough	34	—
Defenders								
Ian Bennyworth	6 0	12 07	15 1 62	Hull	Apprentice	Hull C	1	—
					Gainsborough Tr, Nuneaton Bor	Scarborough	74	3
Alan Kamara	5 9	10 12	15 7 58	Sheffield	Kiveton Park	York C	10	—
						Darlington	134	1
					Burton Alb	Scarborough	73	1
Steve Richards	6 0	12 00	24 10 61	Dundee	Apprentice	Hull C	58	2
					Gains-borough T	York C	7	—
						Lincoln C	21	—
						Cambridge U	4	2
						Scarborough	84	6
Chris Short			9 5 70	Munster		Scarborough	2	—
Craig Short	6 0	11 04	25 6 68	Bridlington	Pickering T	Scarborough	63	7
Neil Thompson	6 0	13 07	2 10 63	Beverley	Apprentice	Nottingham F	—	—
						Hull C	—	—
						Scarborough	87	15
Midfield								
Andy Barkway‡			1 7 66			Scarborough	—	—
Mitch Cook	5 10	12 00	15 10 61	Scarborough	Scarborough	Darlington	34	4
						Middlesbrough	6	—
						Scarborough	81	10
Tommy Graham	5 9	11 09	31 3 58	Glasgow	Arthurlie	Aston Villa	—	—
						Barnsley	38	13
						Halifax T	71	17
						Doncaster R	11	2
						Scunthorpe U	109	21
						Scarborough	87	11
Stewart Hamill‡	5 9	10 08	22 1 60	Glasgow	Pullock	Leicester C	10	2
						Scunthorpe U (loan)	4	—
					Local	Northampton T	3	1
						Scarborough	28	3
Ken Lowe‡	5 10	11 04	6 11 61	Sedgefield		Hartlepool U	54	3
					Barrow	Scarborough	4	—
Ray McHale‡	5 8	12 06	12 8 50	Sheffield	Local	Chesterfield	124	27
						Halifax T	86	21
						Swindon T	173	33
						Brighton & HA	11	—
						Barnsley	53	1
						Sheffield U	67	2
						Bury (loan)	6	—
						Swansea C	47	1
						Rochdale T	7	—
						Scarborough	25	3
Doug Newton‡			16 1 59	Newcastle	Altrincham	Scarborough	5	—

SCARBOROUGH

Foundation: Scarborough came into being as early as 1879 when they were formed by members of the town's cricket club and went under the name of Scarborough Cricketers' FC with home games played on the North Marine Road Cricket Ground.

Managers (and Secretary-managers)
B. Chapman 1945–47*, George Hall 1946–47, Harold Taylor 1947–48, Frank Taylor 1948–50, A. C. Bell (Director & Hon. TM) 1950–53, Reg Halton 1953–54, Charles Robson (Hon. TM) 1954–57, George Higgins 1957–58, Andy Smailes 1959–61, Eddie Brown 1961–64, Albert Franks 1964–65, Stuart Myers 1965–66, Graham Shaw 1968–69, Colin Appleton 1969–73, Ken Houghton 1974–75, Colin Appleton 1975–81, Jimmy McAnearney 1981–82, John Cottam 1982–84, Harry Dunn 1984–86, Neil Warnock 1986–88, Colin Morris 1989– .

Player and Position	*Ht*	*Wt*	*Birth Date*	*Birth Place*	*Source*	*Clubs*	*League App*	*League Gls*
Paul Olsson	5 8	10 11	24 12 65	Hull	Apprentice	Hull C	—	—
						Exeter C (loan)	8	—
						Exeter C	35	2
						Scarborough	32	4
Martin Russell	5 9	10 05	27 4 67	Dublin	Apprentice	Manchester U	—	—
						Birmingham C (loan)	5	—
						Leicester C	20	—
						Norwich C (loan)	—	—
						Scarborough	20	2
Forwards								
Steve Adams	5 8	10 12	7 5 59	Sheffield	Worksop T	Scarborough	48	5
David Bowman‡			16 12 60	Scarborough		Scarborough	4	2
Gary Brook	5 10	12 04	9 5 64	Dewsbury	Frickley Ath	Newport Co	14	2
						Scarborough	49	12
Paul Dobson	5 9	10 06	17 12 62	Hartlepool	Amateur	Newcastle U	—	—
						Hartlepool U	31	8
					Horden	Hartlepool U	80	24
						Torquay U	77	38
						Doncaster R	24	10
						Scarborough	18	5
Simon Lowe‡	5 11	12 03	26 12 62	London	Apprentice	Barnsley	2	—
						Halifax T	77	19
						Hartlepool U	14	1
						Colchester U	36	8
						Scarborough	16	3
Stewart Mell‡	5 10	11 07	15 10 57	Doncaster	Appley F	Doncaster R	76	14
						Halifax T	30	8
						Burton Alb	—	—
						Scarborough	39	8
Colin Morris	5 7	10 06	22 8 53	Blyth	Apprentice	Burnley	10	—
						Southend U	133	25
						Blackpool	87	26
						Sheffield U	240	68
						Scarborough	23	3
Steve Norris			22 9 61	Coventry	Telford	Scarborough	31	9
Tony Outhart‡			17 9 63	Scarborough	Bridlington Tr	Scarborough	6	1
Richard Preston‡			10 6 67	Nottingham	Stanton T	Scarborough	4	—

Trainees
Browning, Timothy; Glenister, Andrew A; Heblich, Kieron; Hird, Paul R; Hull, Martin; Lycett, Christopher; McCrorie, Craig D; Mackness, Paul D; Meyer, Adrian M; Milthorpe, Anthony; Needler, Peter J; Wright, Dean B.

Associated Schoolboys
Brackstone, Lee; Brooks, Duncan S; Foster, Grant; Hill, Philip; Johnson, David; O'Neill, James B; Pratt, Jeremy; Swales, Stephen C; Ward, Richard; Wignall, Adrian.

SCUNTHORPE UNITED 1988–89 *Back row (left to right):* Richard Money, Mick Buxton (Manager), Darren Mountain, Andrew Stevenson, Mike Thompson, Paul Musselwhite, Paul Nicol, Steve Lister, Tony Brown, David Shearer, Bill Green, Phil McLoughlin.
Front row: Andy Flounders, David Cowling, Paul Longden, Tony Daws, David Harle, Ian Richardson, Kevin Taylor.

Division 4 SCUNTHORPE UNITED

Glanford Park, Scunthorpe, South Humberside. Telephone Scunthorpe (0724) 848077.

Ground capacity: 10,800.

Record attendance: Old Showground: 23,935 v Portsmouth, FA Cup 4th rd, 30 Jan, 1954. Glanford Park: 6358 v Burnley, Division 4, 5 May 1989.

Record receipts: £28,612 v Leeds U, FA Cup 3rd rd replay, 16 Jan, 1984.

Pitch measurements: 111yd × 73yd.

President: Sir Reginald Sheffield, Bt.

Vice-Presidents: I. T. Botham, G. Johnson.

Chairman: G. Pearson. ***Vice-Chairman:*** ***Deputy Chairman:*** T. E. Belton.

Directors: R. Garton, G. Pearson, D. M. Fletton, J. B. Borrill.

Manager: Mick Buxton. ***Asst. Manager:*** W. Green.

Secretary: A. D. Rowing. ***Commercial Manager:*** A. D. Rowing.

Year Formed:1899. ***Turned Professional:*** 1912. ***Ltd Co.:*** 1912.

Club Nickname: 'The Iron'.

Previous Names: Amalgamated with Brumby Hall: North Lindsey United to become Scunthorpe & Lindsey United, 1910; dropped '& Lindsey' in 1958.

Record League Victory: 8-1 v Luton T, Division 3, 24 April 1965 – Sidebottom; Horstead, Hemstead; Smith, Neale, Lindsey; Bramley (1), Scott, Thomas (5), Mahy (1), Wilson (1).

Record Cup Victory: 9-0 v Boston U, FA Cup, 1st rd, 21 November 1953 – Malan; Hubbard, Brownsword; Sharpe, White, Bushby; Mosby (1), Haigh (3), Whitfield (2), Gregory (1), Mervyn Jones (2).

Record Defeat: 0-8 v Carlisle U, Division 3(N), 25 December, 1952.

Most League Points (2 for a win): 66, Division 3(N), 1957, 1957–58.

Most League Points (3 for a win): 83, Division 4, 1982–83.

Most League Goals: 88, Division 3(N), 1957–58.

Highest League Scorer in Season: Barrie Thomas, 31, Division 2, 1961–62.

Most League Goals in Total Aggregate: Steve Cammack, 110, 1979–81, 1981–86.

Most Capped Player: None.

Most League Appearances: Jack Brownsword, 600, 1950–65.

Record Transfer Fee Received: £90,000 from Ipswich T for Dave Hill, July 1988.

Record Transfer Fee Paid: £34,000 to Brentford for Alan Whitehead, March 1984.

Football League Record: 1950 Elected to Division 3(N); 1958–64 Division 2; 1964–68 Division 3; 1968–72 Division 4; 1972–73 Division 3; 1973–83 Division 4; 1983–84 Division 3; 1984– Division 4.

Honours: *Football League:* Division 2 best season: 4th, 1961–62; Division 3(N) – Champions 1957–58. *FA Cup* best season; 5th rd. 1957–58, 1969–70. *Football League Cup:* never past 3rd rd.

Colours: Claret and blue striped shirts, blue shorts claret band, blue stockings claret band. **Change colours:** White shirts, claret and blue trim, claret shorts blue band, white stockings claret band.

SCUNTHORPE UNITED 1988–89 LEAGUE RECORD

Match No.	Date	Venue	Opponents	Result		H/T Score	Lg. Pos.	Goalscorers	Attendance
1	Aug 27	H	Hereford U	W	3-1	0-0	—	Cowling, Daws, Taylor	3663
2	Sept 3	A	Crewe Alex	L	2-3	1-2	10	Flounders, Lister (pen)	1514
3	10	H	Grimsby T	D	1-1	1-1	11	Lister	6037
4	17	A	York C	W	2-1	1-0	8	Daws 2	2735
5	20	H	Carlisle U	D	1-1	1-0	—	Flounders	3113
6	24	A	Exeter C	D	2-2	0-1	8	Daws, Rumble	1876
7	Oct 1	H	Scarborough	L	0-3	0-1	13		4167
8	5	A	Lincoln C	L	0-1	0-1	—		5443
9	8	A	Colchester U	W	2-1	1-1	12	Flounders, Richardson	1299
10	15	H	Cambridge U	W	1-0	0-0	9	Taylor	3514
11	22	A	Rochdale	L	0-1	0-0	12		2250
12	25	H	Wrexham	W	3-1	1-1	—	Daws, Hodkinson, Flounders	2999
13	29	A	Peterborough U	W	2-1	1-1	6	Hodkinson, Harle (pen)	3532
14	Nov 5	H	Burnley	W	2-1	0-0	5	Flounders, Lister	6358
15	8	A	Rotherham U	D	3-3	1-2	—	Flounders, Lister, Hodkinson	5923
16	12	H	Leyton Orient	D	2-2	1-1	4	Daws 2	4239
17	26	H	Torquay U	W	1-0	1-0	4	Daws	3359
18	Dec 3	A	Darlington	D	3-3	1-1	4	Smalley, Daws, Lister	1745
19	17	A	Doncaster R	D	2-2	1-1	5	Hodkinson, Flounders	3381
20	26	H	Hartlepool U	D	1-1	0-0	5	Harle (pen)	4595
21	31	H	Tranmere R	L	0-1	0-1	8		4154
22	Jan 2	A	Halifax T	L	1-5	0-2	8	Hamilton	2650
23	7	A	Stockport Co	W	2-1	1-0	7	Flounders, Daws	2656
24	14	H	Crewe Alex	D	2-2	0-1	8	Daws 2	4032
25	21	A	Hereford U	W	2-1	0-0	6	Hodkinson, Daws	2024
26	28	H	York C	W	4-2	3-1	4	Smith (og), Brown, Daws 2	4196
27	Feb 4	A	Carlisle U	W	3-0	1-0	3	Lister, Taylor (pen), Flounders	2627
28	11	H	Exeter C	W	2-0	1-0	2	Lister, Cowling	4102
29	18	H	Colchester U	L	2-3	0-2	3	Lister, Nicol	4286
30	25	A	Cambridge U	W	3-0	1-0	2	Taylor, Flounders, Daws	2563
31	28	A	Wrexham	L	0-2	0-2	—		2609
32	Mar 4	H	Rochdale	W	4-0	2-0	2	Daws 2, Brown, Hodkinson	4098
33	11	A	Burnley	W	1-0	1-0	3	Lister	6813
34	14	H	Peterborough U	W	3-0	1-0	—	Flounders 3	3983
35	18	A	Grimsby T	D	1-1	0-0	3	Flounders	9796
36	25	H	Halifax T	D	0-0	0-0	3		4591
37	27	A	Hartlepool U	W	2-0	0-0	3	Flounders, Daws	1923
38	Apr 1	H	Doncaster R	W	2-1	2-1	2	Taylor (pen), Hodkinson	5334
39	4	H	Stockport Co	D	1-1	0-0	—	Taylor (pen)	3958
40	7	A	Tranmere R	L	1-2	0-2	—	Daws	10,465
41	15	A	Scarborough	L	0-1	0-0	4		4456
42	22	H	Lincoln C	D	0-0	0-0	4		5729
43	28	A	Torquay U	W	2-0	0-0	—	Daws, Hodkinson	2544
44	May 1	H	Rotherham U	D	0-0	0-0	3		8775
45	6	H	Darlington	W	5-1	1-0	2	Daws 3, Taylor, Flounders	5296
46	13	A	Leyton Orient	L	1-4	0-2	4	Taylor	6366

Final League Position: 4

GOALSCORERS

League (77): Daws 24, Flounders 16, Lister 9 (1 pen), Hodkinson 8, Taylor 8 (3 pens), Brown 2, Cowling 2, Harle 2 (2 pens), Hamilton 1, Nicol 1, Richardson 1, Rumble 1, Smalley 1, own goal 1.
Littlewoods Cup (12): Flounders 4, Daws 3, Harle 1 (pen), Hodkinson 1, Lister 1, Stevenson 1, Taylor 1.
FA Cup (1): Harle 1 (pen).

Littlewoods Cup	First Round	Huddersfield T (h)	3-2
		(a)	2-2
	Second Round	Chelsea (h)	4-1
		(a)	2-2
	Third Round	Bradford C (a)	1-1
		(h)	0-1
FA Cup	First Round	Blackpool (a)	1-2

Musselwhite	Longden	Rumble	Taylor	Lister	Brown T	Hodkinson	Winter	Shearer	Flounders	Cowling	Daws	Stevenson	Richardson	Money	Smalley	Harle	Hamilton	Brown D	Nicol	Cork	Cotton	Match No.
1	2	3	4	5	6	7	8	9*	10	11	12											1
1	2*		4	5	6	7	8		10	11	9	3	12									2
1	2	3	4	5	6	7	8		10	11	9											3
1	2	3	4	5		7	8		10	11	9	6										4
1	2	3	4	5	6†	7			10	11*	9	8	12	14								5
1	2	3	4	5	6	7			10	11*	9	8	12									6
1		3	4	5	6	7			10		9		11		2	8						7
1		3	4	5	12	7			10		9	6	11*		2	8						8
1	12	3*	4	5	11	7			10†		9	6	14		2	8						9
1	3		4	5	11	7			10		9	6			2	8						10
1	3		4	5	6	7			10	11	9				2	8						11
1	3		4	5		7			10	11	9	6			2	8						12
1	3			5		7			10	11	9	6		4	2	8						13
1	3			5		7			10	11	9	6		4	2	8						14
1	3			5		7			10	11	9	6		4	2	8						15
1	3		14	5		7*			10	11	9	6	12	4†	2	8						16
1	3		4	5	12	7			10*	11	9	6			2	8						17
1	3		4	5	11	7			10		9	6			2	8						18
1	3		4	5	6	7			10	11*	9	2	12			8						19
1	3		4	5	6	7*			10	11†	9	12			2	8	14					20
1	3		4	5	6	7			10	11	9*	12			2†	8	14					21
1	3		4	5	6	7			12		9*	11			2	8	10					22
	3		4	5		7*			10	12	9	6†			2	8	11	1	14			23
	14		4	5	12	7			10	3†	9	6			2	8*	11	1				24
	3		4		6	7			10	8	9				2		11	1	5			25
	3		4		6	7			10	8	9				2		11	1	5			26
	3		4	7	6				10	8	9				2		11	1	5			27
1			4	7	6				10	8	9	3			2		11		5			28
1			4	7	6	12			10†	8	9	3*			2		11		5	14		29
1			4	7	6	3			10	8	9				2		11		5			30
1	3		4	7	6	5*			10	8	9				2		11		12			31
1	3*		4	7	6	5			10	8†	9				2		11		12	14		32
1	3			7	6				10	7	9				2		11		5	4		33
1	3			7	6				10	8	9				2		11		5	4		34
1	3		12	7	6				10	8	9				2		11		5	4*		35
1	3		4	7	6	12			10	8	9				2		11*		5			36
1	3		4*		6	7			10	8	9				2		11		5	12		37
1	3		4		6	7*			10	8	9				2		11		5	12		38
1	3		4			7†			10	8	9	6			2*		11		5	12	14	39
1	3		4			14			10	8	9	6		7*	2†		11		5	12		40
1	3		4		6	7*			10	8	9				2		11		5	12		41
1	3		4			7			10	8	9				2		11		5	6		42
1	3		4			7			10	8*	9	12			2		11		5	6		43
1	3		4			7			10		9	8	12		2		11		5	6*		44
1	3		4			7			10	8	9				2		11		5	6		45
1	3		4			7			10	8	9				2		11		5	6		46
41	39 + 2s	8	39 + 2s	34	29 + 3s	38 + 3s	4	1	45 + 1s	38 + 1s	45 + 1s	23 + 3s	2 + 7s	5 + 1s	39	18	25 + 2s	5	20 + 3s	8 + 7s	— + 1s	

SCUNTHORPE UNITED

Player and Position	Ht	Wt	Birth Date	Birth Place	Source	Clubs	League App	League Gls
Goalkeepers								
Paul Johnson‡	5 11	11 01	10 5 63	Scunthorpe	Apprentice	Scunthorpe U	14	—
Paul Musselwhite	6 2	12 07	22 12 68	Portsmouth	Portsmouth†	Scunthorpe U	41	—
Barry Richardson*	6 0	12 00	5 8 69	Willington Key	Trainee	Sunderland	—	—
						Scunthorpe U	—	—
Defenders								
Tony Brown*	6 2	12 07	17 9 58	Bradford	Thackley	Leeds U	24	1
						Doncaster (loan)	14	—
						Doncaster R	73	2
						Scunthorpe U	54	2
Steve Lister	6 1	11 00	18 11 61	Doncaster	Apprentice	Doncaster R	237	30
						Scunthorpe U	150	28
Paul Longden	5 9	11 00	28 9 62	Wakefield	Apprentice	Barnsley	5	—
						Scunthorpe U	215	—
Richard Money*	5 11	11 07	13 10 55	Lowestoft	Lowestoft T	Scunthorpe U	173	4
						Fulham	106	3
						Liverpool	14	—
						Derby Co (loan)	5	—
						Luton T	44	1
						Portsmouth	17	—
						Scunthorpe U	105	—
Darren Mountain*	5 9	10 09	16 8 70	Sheffield	Trainee	Scunthorpe U	—	—
Paul Nicol	6 1	12 00	31 10 67	Scunthorpe		Scunthorpe U	57	1
Paul Smalley	5 11	11 00	17 11 66	Nottingham	Apprentice	Notts Co	118	—
						Scunthorpe U	39	1
Mike Thompson*	6 1	12 00	25 1 70	Barnsley	Trainee	Scunthorpe U	—	—
Midfield								
David Cowling	5 7	11 04	27 11 58	Doncaster	Apprentice	Mansfield T	—	—
						Huddersfield T	340	43
						Scunthorpe U (loan)	1	—
						Reading	10	1
						Scunthorpe U	39	2
Perry Cotton†			11 11 65	Chislehurst		Scunthorpe U	1	—
Ian Hamilton	5 9	11 03	14 12 67	Stevenage	Apprentice	Southampton	—	—
						Cambridge U	24	1
						Scunthorpe U	27	1
Andy Stevenson	6 0	12 03	29 9 67	Scunthorpe	School	Scunthorpe U	43	—
Kevin Taylor	5 10	11 00	22 1 61	Sheffield	Apprentice	Sheffield W	125	21
						Derby Co	22	2
						Crystal Palace	87	14
						Scunthorpe U	76	13

SCUNTHORPE UNITED

Foundation: The year of foundation for Scunthorpe United has often been quoted as 1910, but the club can trace its history back to 1899 when Brumby Hall FC, who played on the Old Showground, consolidated their position by amalgamating with some other clubs and changing their name to Scunthorpe United. The year 1910 was when that club amalgamated with North Lindsey United as Scunthorpe and Lindsey United. The link is Mr. W. T. Lockwood whose chairmanship covers both years.

Managers (and Secretary-managers)
Harry Allcock 1915–53*, Tom Crilly 1936–37, Bernard Harper 1946–48, Leslie Jones 1950–51, Bill Corkhill 1952–56, Ron Suart 1956–58, Tony McShane 1959, Bill Lambton 1959, Frank Soo 1959–60, Dick Duckworth 1960–64, Fred Goodwin 1964–66, Ron Ashman 1967–73, Ron Bradley 1973–74, Dick Rooks 1974–76, Ron Ashman 1976–81, John Duncan 1981–83, Allan Clarke 1983–84, Frank Barlow 1984–87, Mick Buxton 1987– .

Player and Position	*Ht*	*Wt*	*Birth Date*	*Birth Place*	*Source*	*Clubs*	*League App*	*League Gls*
Forwards								
David Cork‡	5 9	11 08	28 10 62	Doncaster	Apprentice	Arsenal	7	1
						Huddersfield T	110	25
						WBA (loan)	4	—
						Scunthorpe U	15	—
Tony Daws	5 9	10 02	10 9 66	Sheffield		Notts Co	8	1
						Sheffield U	11	3
						Scunthorpe U	56	27
Andy Flounders	5 11	11 06	13 12 63	Hull	Apprentice	Hull C	159	54
						Scunthorpe U	106	46
Andrew Hodkinson	5 6	10 10	4 11 65	Ashton	Apprentice	Bolton W	—	—
						Oldham Ath	5	1
						Stockport Co	118	18
						Scunthorpe U	41	8
Ian Richardson*	5 8	10 02	9 5 64	Ely	Apprentice	Watford	8	2
						Blackpool (loan)	5	2
						Rotherham U (loan)	5	2
						Chester C	35	10
						Scunthorpe U	18	4

Trainees
Alexander, Graham; Barbrook, Matthew A; Brooks, Peter; Cox, Neil J; Creaton, Sean T; Dunnill, Nicholas J; Hall, Richard A; Hancock, Lee A; McGlinchey, Lee J; Sykes, Wayne.

****Non-Contract**
Cotton, Perry.

Associated Schoolboys
Brown, Paul J; Deer, Brendan; Hall, James M; Holland, Gavin M; McCullagh, Paul A; Metcalf, Stuart; Talbot, David.

SHEFFIELD UNITED 1988–89 *Back row (left to right):* Andy Barnsley, Cliff Powell, Simon Webster, Paul Williams, Andy Leaning, Brian Deane, Darren Carr, Paul Stancliffe, Tony Agana.
Centre row: Derek French (Physiotherapist), Chris Wilder, Martin Dickinson, Paul Heald, Graham Benstead, Martin Pike, Francis Joseph, Keith Mincher (Youth Team Coach), Geoff Taylor (Coach).
Front row: Peter Duffield, Mark Todd, Wally Downes, Dave Bassett (Manager), Brian Smith, Chris Downes, Alan Roberts.

Division 2 SHEFFIELD UNITED

Bramall Lane Ground, Sheffield, S2 4SU. Telephone Sheffield (0742) 738955/6/7. Bladesline (recorded message), 0898 888 650.

Ground capacity: 44,010 (13,600 seats).

Record attendance: 68,287 v Leeds U, FA Cup 5th rd, 15 Feb, 1936.

Record receipts: £65,092 v Sheffield W, Division 3, 5 Apr, 1980.

Pitch measurements: 117yd × 75yd.

President: R. Wragg M. INST. BM.

Chairman: R. J. Brealey.

Directors: A. H. Laver, M. Wragg, D. Dooley.

Manager: Dave Bassett. ***Coach:*** Geoff Taylor.

Assistant Manager: ***Physio:*** Derek French.

Secretary: D. Capper. ***Commercial Manager:*** Andy R. Daykin.

Year Formed: 1889. ***Turned Professional:*** 1889. ***Ltd Co.:*** 1899.

Club Nickname: 'The Blades'.

Record League Victory: 10-0 v Burslem Port Vale, 10 December 1892 – Howlett; Witham, Lilley; Howell, Hendry, Needham; Drummond (1), Wallace (1), Hammond (4), Davies (2), Watson (2).

Record Cup Victory: 5-0 v Newcastle U (away), FA Cup, 1st rd, 10 January 1914 – Gough; Cook, English; Brelsford, Howley, Sturgess; Simmons (2), Gillespie (1), Kitchen (1), Fazackerley, Revill (1). 5-0 v Corinthians, FA Cup, 1st rd, 10 January 1925 – Sutcliffe; Cook, Milton; Longworth, King, Green; Partridge, Boyle (1), Johnson 4), Gillespie, Tunstall. 5-0 v Barrow, FA Cup, 3rd rd, 7 January 1956 – Burgin; Coldwell, Mason; Fountain, Johnson, Iley; Hawksworth (1), Hoyland (2), Howitt, Wragg (1), Grainger (1).

Record Defeat: 0-13 v Bolton W, FA Cup 2nd rd, 1 February, 1890.

Most League Points (2 for a win): 60, Division 2, 1952–53.

Most League Points (3 for a win): 96, Division 4, 1981–82.

Most League Goals: 102, Division 1, 1925–26.

Highest League Scorer in Season: Jimmy Dunne, 41, Division 1, 1930–31.

Most League Goals in Total Aggregate: Harry Johnson, 205, 1919–30.

Most Capped Player: Billy Gillespie, 25, Northern Ireland.

Most League Appearances: Joe Shaw, 629, 1948–66.

Record Transfer Fee Received: £400,000 from Leeds U for Alex Sabella, May 1980.

Record Transfer Fee Paid: £160,000 to River Plate for Alex Sabella, July 1978 and to Leicester C for Alan Young, August 1982.

Football League Record: 1982 Elected to Division 2; 1983–1934 Division 1; 1934–39 Division 2; 1946–49 Division 1; 1949–53 Division 2; 1953–56 Division 1; 1956–61 Division 2; 1961–68 Division 1; 1968–71 Division 2; 1971–76 Division 1; 1976–79 Division 2; 1979–81 Division 3; 1981–82 Division 4; 1982–84 Division 3; 1984–88 Division 2; 1988–89 Division 3; 1989– Division 2.

Honours: *Football League:* Division 1 – Champions 1897–98; Runners-up 1896–97, 1899–1900; Division 2 – Champions 1952–53; Runners-up 1892–93, 1938–39, 1960–61, 1970–71; Division 4 – Champions 1981–82. *FA Cup:* Winners 1899, 1902, 1915, 1925; Runners-up 1901, 1936. *Football League Cup* best season: 5th rd, 1961–62, 1966–67, 1971–72.

Colours: Red (broader) and white striped shirts, red and white trim, black shorts red and white flash, black stockings red trim. **Change colours:** Yellow shadow striped shirts, yellow shorts red and white flash, yellow stockings red trim.

SHEFFIELD UNITED 1988–89 LEAGUE RECORD

Match No.	*Date*	*Venue*	*Opponents*	*Result*	*H/T Score*	*Lg. Pos.*	*Goalscorers*	*Attendance*
1	Aug 27	A	Reading	W 3-1	2-0	—	Stancliffe, Joseph, Deane	5512
2	Sept 3	H	Bristol R	W 4-1	2-1	1	Bryson 2, Roberts, Agana	9586
3	10	A	Gillingham	L 1-2	1-1	4	Bryson	5041
4	17	H	Chester C	W 6-1	3-0	2	Deane 3, Agana 3	8675
5	20	H	Northampton T	W 4-0	2-0	—	Agana, Bryson 2, Deane	11,904
6	24	A	Brentford	W 4-1	1-1	1	Todd, Agana 2, Roberts	6577
7	Oct 1	A	Bolton W	L 0-2	0-1	1		9345
8	8	H	Wolverhampton W	W 2-0	1-0	2	Deane, Agana	14,272
9	15	A	Blackpool	W 2-1	1-1	2	Pike, Webster	8471
10	22	H	Wigan Ath	W 2-1	1-0	1	Deane, Webster	11,363
11	24	A	Port Vale	D 3-3	1-0	—	Joseph, Duffield, Deane	13,246
12	29	H	Bury	W 2-1	2-0	1	Wilder, Deane	12,348
13	Nov 5	A	Huddersfield T	L 2-3	1-2	2	Agana 2	10,400
14	8	A	Aldershot	L 0-1	0-1	—		2934
15	12	H	Fulham	W 1-0	1-0	2	Deane	11,087
16	26	H	Bristol C	W 3-0	1-0	2	Deane 2, Agana	11,249
17	Dec 3	A	Swansea C	D 2-2	1-0	2	Agana, Deane	5676
18	17	H	Southend U	L 1-2	0-0	3	Francis	9556
19	26	A	Notts Co	W 4-1	0-1	3	Pike 2, Duffield, Todd	11,590
20	31	A	Preston NE	L 0-2	0-0	3		11,005
21	Jan 2	H	Chesterfield	L 1-3	1-2	3	Agana	15,769
22	14	A	Bristol R	D 1-1	0-0	4	Agana	6623
23	21	H	Gillingham	W 4-2	3-0	4	Joseph, Booker, Carr, Duffield (pen)	9336
24	Feb 4	H	Bolton W	W 4-0	0-0	4	Agana, Winstanley (og), Duffield 2 (2 pen)	11,162
25	11	A	Cardiff C	D 0-0	0-0	4		5772
26	25	H	Blackpool	W 4-1	3-0	4	Pike, Todd, Duffield, Gannon	11,317
27	28	H	Port Vale	D 0-0	0-0	—		18,787
28	Mar 4	A	Wigan Ath	W 2-1	1-1	4	Deane 2	3966
29	11	H	Huddersfield T	W 5-1	1-0	3	Duffield 2 (1 pen), May (og), Bryson, Deane	13,680
30	14	A	Bury	W 2-1	1-0	—	Todd, Deane	5334
31	18	H	Reading	W 1-0	0-0	3	Deane	11,867
32	25	A	Chesterfield	L 1-2	0-1	3	Bryson	10,991
33	27	H	Notts Co	D 1-1	1-1	3	Deane	13,039
34	31	A	Southend U	L 1-2	1-1	—	Booker	4584
35	Apr 4	A	Mansfield T	W 1-0	0-0	—	Duffield (pen)	8524
36	8	H	Preston NE	W 3-1	0-0	3	Deane, Agana, Duffield	12,718
37	11	H	Cardiff C	L 0-1	0-1	—		11,618
38	15	A	Northampton T	W 2-1	1-1	3	Thompson, Deane	5030
39	19	A	Chester C	W 1-0	1-0	—	Agana	4282
40	22	H	Brentford	D 2-2	1-0	2	Agana, Duffield	12,613
41	25	H	Mansfield T	L 1-2	0-1	—	Agana	11,638
42	29	A	Fulham	D 2-2	1-1	2	Agana, Bryson	7794
43	May 1	H	Aldershot	W 1-0	0-0	2	Deane	11,737
44	6	H	Swansea C	W 5-1	2-0	2	Agana 3, Pike, Stancliffe	15,383
45	9	A	Wolverhampton W	D 2-2	0-1	—	Stancliffe, Agana	24,321
46	13	A	Bristol C	L 0-2	0-0	2		10,769

Final League Position: 2

GOALSCORERS

League (93): Agana 24, Deane 22, Duffield 11 (5 pens), Bryson 8, Pike 5, Todd 4, Joseph 3, Stancliffe 3, Booker 2, Roberts 2, Webster 2, Carr 1, Francis 1, Gannon 1, Thompson 1, Wilder 1, own goals 2.
Littlewoods Cup (9): Deane 3, Agana 2, Duffield 2, Bryson 1, Stancliffe 1.
FA Cup (14): Deane 5, Agana 3, Bryson 2, Duffield 1, Stancliffe 1, Todd 1, own goal 1.

Littlewoods Cup	First Round	Hartlepool U (a)	2-2
		(h)	2-0
	Second Round	Newcastle U (h)	3-0
		(a)	0-2
	Third Round	Manchester C (a)	2-4

Benstead	Powell	Pike	Webster	Stancliffe	Smith	Roberts	Todd	Joseph	Deane	Bryson	Agana	Wilder	Duffield	Barnsley	Williams	Francis	Dickinson	Whitehouse	Downes C	Carr	Booker	Ryan	Thompson	Gannon	Tracey	Moore	*Match No.*
1	2	3	4	5	6	7	8	9*	10	11	12																1
1		3	4*	5	6	7	8		10	11	9	2	12														2
1		3	4	5	6		8		10	11	9		7	2*	12												3
1		3	4	5	6		8		10*	11	9	2	7			12											4
1		3	4	5	6	7*	8		10	11	9	2	12														5
1		3	4	5*	6	7	8		10	11	9	2					12										6
1		3	4	5	6	7*	8	14	10	11†	9	2	12														7
1		3	4	5	6	7*	8		10		9	2	11			12											8
1		3	4	5	6	7*	8	14	10		9	2	12					11†									9
1		3	4	5	6	7*	8	14	10		9	2	12					11†									10
1		3	4	5	6	7*	8†	11	10		9	2	12			14											11
1		3	4	5	6	7	8	11*	10		9	2	12														12
1		3			6		8	14	10	11*	9	2	7	12					4†	5							13
1		3		5	6	12	8	11*	10		9	2	7						4								14
1		3		5	6	7*	8	12	10		9	2	4			11											15
1		3		5	6	7	8		10	11	9	2									4						16
1		3		5	6	7†	8		10	11	9	2*	14	12							4						17
1		3		5	6	12	8*	14		11†	9	2	7			10					4						18
1		3		5	6		8		10	11	9	2	7								4						19
1		3		5	6	12	8*	14	10	11†	9	2	7								4						20
1		3		5	6	7	8*		10	11	9†	2	12			14					4						21
1				5		7†	8	12		11	9		14		10*			3		6	4	2					22
1		3			12		8	10†		11	9		7			14				6	4*	2	5				23
1		3		5	2	7			10*	11	9		8			12				6			4				24
1		3		5	2	7*			10	11	9		8							6		12	4				25
1		3		5	2		8		10	11*	9†		7			14					4		6	12			26
1		3		5	2		8		10	11	9*		7			12				14	4†		6				27
1		3		5	2		8		10	11†	9		7*			12					4		6	14			28
		3		5	2		8		10	11	9		7*			12					4		6		1		29
1		3		5	2		8		10	11*	9		7								4		6	12			30
1		3		5*	2		8		10	11	9		7†			14					4		6	12			31
1		3		5	2		8		10	11	9		7*			12					4		6				32
1		3		5	2	7†	8		10	11*	9					14					4		6	12			33
1		3		5	2		8		10	11*	12		7			9					4		6†	14			34
1		3		5	2		8		10	11*	9		7			12					4		6				35
1		3		5	2†		8		10	11*	9		7			12					4		6	14			36
1		3		5			8		10	11*	9	2	7			12					4		6†	14			37
1		3		5		14	8†		10		9	2	7			12					4		6	11*			38
1		3		5		7			10		9	2								8	4		6	11			39
1		3		5		7	8*		10	14	9	2	12							4			6†	11			40
		3		5					10	11	9	2	7*			12					4		6†	8	1	14	41
		3				7	4*		10	11	9	2	12†					14			6		5	8	1		42
	5	3				7*			10	11†	9	2	12					14			6			8	1	4	43
	14	3		5		7*			10	11	9	2				12					4†			8	1	6	44
		3		5		7			10	11	9	2								6				8	1	4	45
	12	3		5		7	8*		10	11	9	2								6					1	4	46
39	2 + 2s	45	12	42	34 + 1s	25 + 4s	39	5 + 8s	43	36 + 1s	44 + 2s	29	25 + 13s	1 + 2s	1 + 1s	3 + 19s	— + 1s	3 + 2s	2	9 + 1s	26	2 + 1s	20	8 + 8s	7	4 + 1s	

FA Cup			
	First Round	Mansfield T (a)	1-1
		(h)	2-1
	Second Round	Doncaster R (a)	3-1
	Third Round	Huddersfield T (a)	1-0
	Fourth Round	Colchester U (h)	3-3
		(a)	2-0
	Fifth Round	Norwich C (a)	2-3

SHEFFIELD UNITED

Player and Position	Ht	Wt	Birth Date	Birth Place	Source	Clubs	League App	League Gls
Goalkeepers								
Graham Benstead	6 1	13 07	20 8 63	Aldershot	Apprentice	QPR	—	—
						Norwich C (loan)	1	—
						Norwich C	15	—
						Colchester U (loan)	18	—
						Sheffield U (loan)	8	—
						Sheffield U	39	—
Simon Tracey	6 0	13 00	9 12 67	Woolwich	Apprentice	Wimbledon	1	—
						Sheffield U	7	—
Defenders								
Darren Carr	6 0	12 07	4 9 68	Bristol		Bristol R	30	—
						Newport Co	9	—
						Sheffield U	13	1
Martin Dickinson	5 10	12 03	14 3 63	Leeds	Apprentice	Leeds U	103	2
						WBA	50	2
						Sheffield U	1	—
Chris Downes	5 10	10 08	17 1 69	Sheffield	Trainee	Sheffield U	2	—
						Scarborough (loan)	2	—
Jim Gannon			7 9 68	London	Dundalk	Sheffield U	—	—
Martin Pike	5 9	11 04	21 10 64	South Shields	Apprentice	WBA	—	—
						Peterborough U	126	8
						Sheffield U	126	5
Cliff Powell	6 0	12 00	21 2 68	Watford	Apprentice	Watford	—	—
						Hereford U (loan)	7	—
						Sheffield U	10	—
						Doncaster R (loan)	4	—
Brian Smith	5 9	11 02	27 10 66	Sheffield	Local	Sheffield U	84	—
						Scunthorpe U (loan)	6	1
Paul Stancliffe	6 2	12 13	5 5 58	Sheffield	Apprentice	Rotherham U	285	8
						Sheffield U	235	11
Steve Thompson	6 1	14 04	28 7 55	Sheffield	Boston U	Lincoln C	154	8
						Charlton Ath	95	—
						Leicester C	—	—
						Sheffield U	20	1
Simon Webster	6 0	11 07	20 1 64	Earl Shilton	Apprentice	Tottenham H	3	—
						Exeter C (loan)	26	—
						Norwich C (loan)	—	—
						Huddersfield T	118	4
						Sheffield U	17	3
Chris Wilder	5 10	10 08	23 9 67	Wortley	Apprentice	Southampton	—	—
						Sheffield U	65	1
Paul Williams‡	6 2	12 09	8 9 63	Sheffield	Nuneaton	Preston NE	1	—
						Newport Co	26	3
						Sheffield U	8	—
Midfield								
Bob Booker	6 2	12 04	25 1 58	Watford	Bedmond Sp	Brentford	251	42
						Sheffield U	26	2
Ian Bryson	5 11	11 11	26 11 62	Kilmarnock		Kilmarnock	215	40
						Sheffield U	37	8
Wally Downes‡	5 10	10 11	9 6 61	London	Apprentice	Wimbledon	208	15
						Newport Co (loan)	4	2
						Sheffield U	9	1
Peter Hetherston (To Falkirk Aug 1988)	5 10	11 05	6 11 64	Glasgow	Bargeddie U	Falkirk	71	8
						Watford	5	—
						Sheffield U	11	—
Alan Roberts	5 9	10 00	8 12 64	Newcastle	Apprentice	Middlesbrough	38	2
						Darlington	119	19
						Sheffield U	29	2

SHEFFIELD UNITED

Foundation: In March 1889, Yorkshire County Cricket Club formed Sheffield United six days after an FA Cup semi-final between Preston North End and West Bromwich Albion had finally convinced Charles Stokes, a member of the cricket club, that the formation of a professional football club would prove successful at Bramall Lane. The United's first secretary, Mr. J. B. Wostinholm was also secretary of the cricket club.

Managers (and Secretary-managers)
J. B. Wostinholm 1889–1899*, John Nicholson 1899–1932, Ted Davison 1932–52, Reg Freeman 1952–55, Joe Mercer 1955–58, Johnny Harris 1959–68 (continued as GM to 1970), Arthur Rowley 1968–69, Johnny Harris (GM resumed TM duties) 1969–73, Ken Furphy 1973–75, Jimmy Sirrel 1975–77, Harry Haslam 1978–81, Martin Peters 1981, Ian Porterfield 1981–86, Billy McEwan 1986–88, Dave Bassett 1988– .

Player and Position	*Ht*	*Wt*	*Birth Date*	*Birth Place*	*Source*	*Clubs*	*League App*	*League Gls*
Mark Todd	5 7	10 00	4 12 67	Belfast	Trainee	Manchester U	—	—
						Sheffield U	51	4
Dane Whitehouse§	5 8	10 12	14 10 70	Sheffield	Trainee	Sheffield U	5	—
Paul Wood‡			20 3 70	Saddleworth	Trainee	Sheffield U	1	—
						Rochdale (loan)	5	—
Forwards								
Tony Agana	5 11	12 02	2 10 63	London	Weymouth	Watford	15	1
						Sheffield U	58	26
Brian Deane	6 3	12 07	7 2 68	Leeds	Apprentice	Doncaster R	66	12
						Sheffield U	43	22
Peter Duffield	5 6	10 07	4 2 69	Middlesbrough		Middlesbrough	—	—
						Sheffield U	49	12
						Halifax T (loan)	12	6
John Francis	5 8	11 02	21 11 63	Dewsbury	Emley	Sheffield U	22	1

Trainees
Bothwell, Brian; Circuit, Steven; Dickens, Matthew J; Fenwick, Ashley J.C; Ford, Reece; Harrison, Richard; Knowles, Darren T; Lucas, Richard; Reed, John P; Wagstaff, Russell J; Ward, Mitchum D; Watkins, Dale A; Whitehouse, Dane L.

Associated Schoolboys
Archbold, John D; Atkinson, Timothy; Beal, Nicholas P; Brocklehurst, David; Butterfield, Timothy; Camacho, Luiz M.C; Cherrill, Matthew G; Clarke, Simon J; Dickerson, Ian; Evans, James D; Fickling, Ashley D.S; Foreman, Matthew B; Godwin, Jon B; Heywood, Colin L.J; Ingram, Stephen; Jacques, John W; Johnson, Andrew P; Morris, Lee; Myhill, Craig S; Reaney, Andrew; Ridsdale, Scott; Stevens, Paul J; Wainwright, Daniel J; Wainwright, Lee; Ward, Timothy M.J; Watts, Gregory.

SHEFFIELD WEDNESDAY 1988–89 *Back row (left to right):* Nigel Pearson, Larry May, Colin West, Kevin Pressman, Martin Hodge, Ian Knight, Ian Cranson, Lawrie Madden.
Centre row: Peter Eustace (Assistant Manager), Michael Hennigan (Youth Team Coach), Tony Galvin, David Hirst, Greg Fee, Siggi Jonsson, David Hodgson, Carl Bradshaw, Alan Smith (Physiotherapist), Clive Baker (Chief Scout).
Front row: Gary Megson, Alan Harper, Mel Sterland, Howard Wilkinson (Manager), Nigel Worthington, Mark Proctor, Steve McCall.

Division 1 SHEFFIELD WEDNESDAY

Hillsborough, Sheffield, S6 1SW. Telephone (Sheffield (0742) 343122. Box Office: Sheffield 337233. Clubcall: 0898-121186.

Ground capacity: 54,101.

Record attendance: 72,841 v Manchester C, FA Cup 5th rd, 17 Feb, 1934.

Record receipts: £398,134, Liverpool v Notingham F, FA Cup semi-final, 9 April, 1988.

Pitch measurements: 115yd × 75yd.

Chairman: H. E. McGee. *Vice-Chairman:* M. Sheppard JP, FCA.

Directors: S. L. Speight OBE, C. Woodward, K. T. Addy, E. Barron, G. K. Hulley.

Manager: Ron Atkinson. *Assistant Manager:* Richie Barker.

Physio: A. Smith.

Secretary: G. H. Mackrell FCCA. *Commercial Manager:* R. Gorrill (Tel. 0742-337235).

Club Nickname: 'The Owls'.

Year Formed: 1867 (fifth oldest League Club).

Turned Profesional: 1887. *Ltd Co.:* 1899.

Previous Grounds: 1867, Highfield; 1869, Myrtle Road; 1877, Sheaf House; 1887, Olive Grove; 1899, Owlerton (since 1912 known as Hillsborough). Some games were played at Endcliffe in the 1880s. Until 1895 Bramall Lane was used for some games.

Record League Victory: 9-1 v Birmingham, Division 1, 13 December 1930 – Brown; Walker, Blenkinsop; Strange, Leach, Wilson; Hooper (3), Seed (2), Ball (2), Burgess (1), Rimmer (1).

Record Cup Victory: 12-0 v Halliwell, FA Cup, 1st rd, 17 January 1891 – Smith; Thompson, Brayshaw; Harry Brandon (1), Betts, Cawley (2); Winterbottom, Mumford (2), Bob Brandon (1), Woolhouse (5), Ingram (1).

Record Defeat: 0-10 v Aston Villa, Division 1, 5 October, 1912.

Most League Points (2 for a win): 62, Division 2, 1958–59.

Most League Points (3 for a win): 88, Division 2, 1983–84.

Most League Goals: 106, Division 2, 1958–58.

Highest League Scorer in Season: Derek Dooley, 46, Division 2, 1951–52.

Most League Goals in Total Aggregate: Andy Wilson, 199, 1900–20.

Most Capped Player: Ron Springett, 33, England.

Most League Appearances: Andy Wilson, 502, 1900–20.

Record Transfer Fee Received: £800,000 from Rangers for Mel Sterland, March 1989.

Record Transfer Fee Paid: £750,000 to WBA for Carlton Palmer, February 1989.

Football League Record: 1892 Elected to Division 1; 1899–1900 Division 2; 1900–20 Division 1; 1920–26 Division 2; 1926–37 Division 1; 1937–50 Division 2; 1950–51 Division 1; 1951–52 Division 2; 1952–55 Division 1; 1955–56 Division 2; 1956–58 Division 1; 1958–59 Division 2; 1959–70 Division 1; 1970–75 Division 2; 1975–80 Division 3; 1980–84 Division 2; 1984– Division 1.

Honours: Football League: Division 1 – Champions 1902–03, 1903–04, 1928–29, 1929–30; Runners-up 1960–61; Division 2 – Champions 1899–1900, 1925–26, 1951–52, 1955–56, 1958–59; Runners-up 1949–50, 1983–84. *FA Cup:* Winners 1896, 1907, 1935; Runners-up 1890, 1966. *Football League Cup* best season: 5th rd, 1982–83, 1983–84, 1984–85. **European Competitions:** *Fairs Cup:* 1961–62, 1963–64.

Colours: Blue and white striped shirts, black shorts, white stockings. **Change colours:** Green and white hooped shirts, green shorts, green stockings.

SHEFFIELD WEDNESDAY 1988–89 LEAGUE RECORD

Match No.	*Date*	*Venue*	*Opponents*	*Result*	*H/T Score*	*Lg. Pos.*	*Goalscorers*	*Attendance*
1	Aug 27	H	Luton T	W 1-0	0-0	—	Sterland	16,433
2	Sept 3	A	Nottingham F	D 1-1	0-1	7	Sterland	18,963
3	10	H	Coventry C	L 1-2	0-0	9	Hirst	15,633
4	17	A	QPR	L 0-2	0-1	12		8011
5	24	H	Arsenal	W 2-1	1-0	12	Megson, Pearson	17,830
6	Oct 1	H	Aston Villa	W 1-0	1-0	7	Hirst	18,301
7	22	A	Southampton	W 2-1	1-1	5	Varadi, Reeves	12,725
8	29	A	Charlton Ath	L 1-2	0-1	10	Hodgson	5933
9	Nov 5	H	Everton	D 1-1	0-0	13	Sterland	21,761
10	12	A	Norwich C	D 1-1	0-1	13	Sterland	14,353
11	20	H	Tottenham H	L 0-2	0-0	—		15,386
12	23	A	Manchester U	D 1-1	0-0	10	West	30,867
13	26	A	Middlesbrough	W 1-0	1-0	10	Sterland	19,310
14	Dec 3	H	Derby Co	D 1-1	1-0	11	Sterland	20,609
15	10	A	West Ham U	D 0-0	0-0	11		16,676
16	17	A	Millwall	L 0-1	0-0	12		11,197
17	26	H	Newcastle U	L 1-2	1-2	13	Hirst	25,573
18	31	H	Nottingham F	L 0-3	0-3	16		20,407
19	Jan 2	A	Coventry C	L 0-5	0-2	17		15,191
20	14	H	Liverpool	D 2-2	2-0	17	Proctor, Varadi	31,524
21	21	A	Arsenal	D 1-1	0-0	18	Varadi	33,490
22	Feb 4	A	Aston Villa	L 0-2	0-2	18		19,334
23	11	H	Manchester U	L 0-2	0-1	18		34,820
24	18	H	Southampton	D 1-1	0-0	18	Proctor	16,677
25	25	A	Wimbledon	L 0-1	0-1	18		4384
26	Mar 4	H	Charlton Ath	W 3-1	1-1	18	Hirst, Jonsson, Galvin	16,081
27	11	A	Everton	L 0-1	0-1	18		22,542
28	18	A	Luton T	W 1-0	0-0	15	Hirst	7776
29	25	H	QPR	L 0-2	0-0	17		18,804
30	27	A	Newcastle U	W 3-1	2-0	14	Barrick, Pearson, Hirst	31,040
31	Apr 1	H	Millwall	W 3-0	1-0	13	Palmer, Whitton 2	18,358
32	5	H	Wimbledon	D 1-1	0-0	—	Hirst	15,777
33	8	A	Liverpool	L 1-5	0-2	14	Barrick	39,672
34	12	A	Tottenham H	D 0-0	0-0	—		17,270
35	22	A	Derby Co	L 0-1	0-0	16		17,529
36	May 9	H	West Ham U	L 0-2	0-0	—		19,905
37	13	H	Midddlesbrough	W 1-0	0-0	16	Whitton	20,582
38	17	H	Norwich C	D 2-2	0-0	—	Linighan (og), Reeves	16,238

Final League Position: 15

GOALSCORERS

League (34): Hirst 7, Sterland 6, Varadi 3, Whitton 3, Barrick 2, Pearson 2, Proctor 2, Reeves 2, Galvin 1, Hodgson 1, Jonsson 1, Megson 1, Palmer 1, West 1, own goal 1.
Littlewoods Cup (3): Hirst 1, Reeves 1, Varadi 1.
FA Cup (6): Varadi 2, Hirst 1, Hodgson 1, Jonsson 1, Proctor 1.

Littlewoods Cup	Second Round	Blackpool (a)	0-2
		(h)	3-1
FA Cup	Third Round	Torquay U (h)	5-1
	Fourth Round	Blackburn R (a)	1-2

Pressman	Sterland	Worthington	Pearson	Madden	Harper	Megson	Proctor	West	Jonsson	Galvin	Hirst	Bradshaw	Cranson	Reeves	Varadi	Turner	Hodgson	Gregory	Knight	Rostron	Wood	Palmer	Whitton	McCall	Bennett	Fee	Barrick	*Match No.*
1	2	3	4	5	6	7	8	9	10	11*	12																	1
1	2	3	4	5	6	7	8*	9	10	11	12																	2
1	2	3	4	5	6†	7		9	10	11*	8	12	14															3
1	2	3	4	5		7		9	10	11*	8	12	6															4
1	2	3	4	5		7		12	10	14	8	11†	6	9*														5
1	2	3	4	5		7		12	10†	14	8*		6	9	11													6
	2	3	4	5		7	11	10					6	8*	9	1	12											7
	2	3	4	5		7	11	10					6	8*	9	1	12											8
	2	3	4	5		7†	11	8	14				6	12	9*	1	10											9
	2	3	5			7	8	9	6		12		4	10		1	11*											10
	2	3	5	6			8	9	7		12		4	10		1	11*											11
	2	3	5	6		12	8	9	7		10*		4		14	1	11†											12
	2†	3	5	6		11	8	9	7		10*		4		12	1	14											13
	2	3	5	6	14	7	11	9	8†		10*		4	12		1												14
1	2*	3	5		10	7	11		6		8		4		12		9											15
1		3	5	6	10	7*	2		11		8		4		9†		14	12										16
1	2	3	5	6		7	8	12	11		10		4		9*													17
		3†	5	6		14	2	8	11		10*		4	12	9	1		7										18
			5*	6	2	7	3	10	11	14					9†	1	8	12	4									19
	2		5	6			7	9	11	12			4	8	10*	1				3								20
	2*		5		11		7	9†					4	8	10	1	14		6	3	12							21
	2		5	6	11		7	9*	8		10		4		12	1				3								22
	2		5	6	11		7		8		10		4	12	9*	1				3								23
	2		5		11		6		9	7	8*		4	12	10	1				3								24
	2		5	3			7			11	10		4	12	9*	1					8	4						25
		3	5		6		7		8	11	10		4		12	1					2		9*					26
		3	5	6	2		7		8	11*	10			12		1						4	9					27
		3	5	6*	2		7			14	10				12	1				11†		4	9	8				28
		3	5		2				11	12	10		6			1						4	9	8*	7			29
			5		2					12	10		6			1					3	4	9		7*	8	11	30
		3	5		2				12		10		6*			1						4	9		7	8	11	31
		3	5		2				6		10					1						4	9		7	8	11	32
		3			2				6		10					1				5		4	9		7	8	11	33
		3	5		2						10					1					6	4	9		7	8	11	34
		3	5	8	2						10				9	1					6	4			7		11	35
		3†	5	6	2					14	10			12		1						4	9		7*	8	11	36
			5	6	2				12	14	10†					1					3	4	9		7*	8	11	37
			5	6	2					11*	10			12		1					3	4	9		7	8		38
9	22	28	37	27	23 + 1s	16 + 2s	24	17 + 3s	25 + 3s	9 + 9s	28 + 4s	1 + 2s	25 + 1s	8 + 9s	14 + 6s	29	6 + 5s	1 + 2s	2	7	7 + 1s	13	12	2	10	8	8	

SHEFFIELD WEDNESDAY

Player and Position	Ht	Wt	Birth Date	Birth Place	Source	Clubs	League App	League Gls
Goalkeepers								
Marlon Beresford	6 1	10 11	2 9 69	Lincoln	Trainee	Sheffield W	—	—
Kevin Pressman	6 1	13 00	6 11 67	Fareham	Apprentice	Sheffield W	20	—
Chris Turner	6 0	12 04	15 9 58	Sheffield	Apprentice	Sheffield W	91	—
						Lincoln C (loan)	5	—
						Sunderland	195	—
						Manchester U	64	—
						Sheffield W	29	—
Defenders								
Scott Cam	5 9	10 00	3 5 70	Sheffield	Trainee	Sheffield W	—	—
Ian Cranson	5 11	12 04	2 7 64	Easington	Apprentice	Ipswich T	131	5
						Sheffield W	30	—
Greg Fee	6 1	12 00	24 6 64	Halifax		Bradford C	7	—
					Boston U	Sheffield W	24	—
Ian Knight	6 2	12 04	26 10 66	Hartlepool	Apprentice	Barnsley	—	—
						Sheffield W	21	—
Steve McCall	5 11	11 03	15 10 60	Carlisle	Apprentice	Ipswich T	257	7
						Sheffield W	7	—
Lawrie Madden	5 11	13 01	28 9 55	London	Amateur	Arsenal	—	—
					Manchester Univ	Mansfield T	10	—
						Charlton Ath	113	7
						Millwall	47	2
						Sheffield W	182	2
Carlton Palmer	5 10	11 00	5 12 65	West Bromwich	Trainee	WBA	121	4
						Sheffield W	13	1
Nigel Pearson	6 1	13 07	21 8 63	Nottingham	Heanor T	Shrewsbury T	153	5
						Sheffield W	56	4
Wilf Rostron	5 7	11 11	29 9 56	Sunderland	Apprentice	Arsenal	17	2
						Sunderland	76	17
						Watford	317	22
						Sheffield W	7	—
Mel Sterland (To Rangers March 1989)	5 10	12 10	1 10 61	Sheffield	Apprentice	Sheffield W	279	37
Darren Wood	5 10	11 08	9 6 64	Scarborough	Apprentice	Middlesbrough	101	6
						Chelsea	144	3
						Sheffield W	8	—
Nigel Worthington	5 10	12 06	4 11 61	Ballymena	Ballymena U	Notts Co	67	4
						Sheffield W	168	2
Midfield								
Dean Barrick	5 9	11 04	30 9 69	Hemsworth	Trainee	Sheffield W	8	2
Robert Beaumont‡			9 12 69	Sheffield	Trainee	Sheffield W	—	—
Tony Gregory	5 8	10 10	21 3 68	Doncaster	Apprentice	Sheffield W	18	1
Alan Harper	5 8	10 09	1 11 60	Liverpool	Apprentice	Liverpool	—	—
						Everton	127	4
						Sheffield W	24	—
Graham Hyde	5 7	11 07	10 11 70	Doncaster	Trainee	Sheffield W	—	—
Siggi Jonsson	5 11	11 11	27 9 66	Akranes, Iceland	Akranes FC	Sheffield W	67	4
						Barnsley (loan)	5	—
Forwards								
Dave Bennett	5 9	10 07	11 7 59	Manchester	Amateur	Manchester C	52	9
						Cardiff C	77	18
						Coventry C	172	25
						Sheffield W	10	—
Tony Galvin	5 9	11 05	12 7 56	Huddersfield	Goole T	Tottenham H	201	20
						Sheffield W	36	1
Kevin Haigh	5 6	10 00	16 7 70	Sheffield	Local	Sheffield W	—	—

SHEFFIELD WEDNESDAY

Foundation: Sheffield, being one of the principal centres of early Association Football, this club was formed as long ago as 1867 by the Sheffield Wednesday Cricket Club (formed 1825) and their colours from the start were blue and white. The inaugural meeting was held at the Adelphi Hotel and the original committee included Charles Stokes who was subsequently a founder member of Sheffield United.

Managers (and Secretary-managers)
Arthur Dickinson 1891–1920*, Robert Brown 1920–33, Billy Walker 1933–37, Jimmy McMullan 1937–42, Eric Taylor 1942–58 (continued as GM to 1974), Harry Catterick 1958–61, Vic Buckingham 1961–64, Alan Brown 1964–68, Jack Marshall 1968–69, Danny Williams 1969–71, Derek Dooley 1971–73, Steve Burtenshaw 1974–75, Len Ashurst 1975–77, Jackie Charlton 1977–83, Howard Wilkinson 1983–88, Peter Eustace 1988–89, Ron Atkinson 1989– .

Player and Position	*Ht*	*Wt*	*Birth Date*	*Birth Place*	*Source*	*Clubs*	*League App*	*League Gls*
David Hirst	5 11	12 05	7 12 67	Barnsley	Apprentice	Barnsley	28	9
						Sheffield W	77	16
David Hodgson	5 9	12 02	1 11 60	Gateshead	Amateur	Middlesbrough	125	16
						Liverpool	28	4
						Sunderland	50	5
						Norwich C	6	2
						Middlesbrough (loan)	2	—
					Jerez	Sheffield W	11	1
David Reeves	6 0	11 05	19 11 67	Birkenhead	Heswell	Sheffield W	17	2
						Scunthorpe U (loan)	4	2
						Scunthorpe U (loan)	6	4
						Burnley (loan)	16	8
Imre Varadi	5 8	11 01	8 7 59	Paddington	Letchworth GC	Sheffield U	10	4
						Everton	26	6
						Newcastle U	81	39
						Sheffield W	76	33
						WBA	32	9
						Manchester C	65	26
						Sheffield W	20	3
Steve Whitton	6 0	12 07	4 12 60	East Ham	Apprentice	Coventry C	74	21
						West Ham U	39	6
						Birmingham C (loan)	8	2
						Birmingham C	95	28
						Sheffield W	12	3

Trainees

Curry, Ian; Dickinson, Mark A; Downing, Nigel; Elshaw, Kevin W; Hawley, Marcus J; Holmshaw, Richard J; Johnson, David A; Kiddy, Steven R; Lycett, David R; Newsome, Jon; Nightingale, Mark J; Swan, Jason W.

Associated Schoolboys

Bean, Nigel; Bekisz, Paul D; Brookfield, Nicholas; Brown, Stephen M; Burton, Paul; Chambers, Leroy D; Dunn, Gareth T; Flint, Jonathan A; Frank, Ian D; Fuller, Simon M; German, David; Goodacre, Samuel D; Holmes, Darren P; Jones, Ryan A; Linighan, Brian; Linighan, John; Mitchell, Graham P; Nankivell, Lee M; Newton, Paul; Robinson, Nicholas; Robinson, Paul; Roden, Andrew P; Rowntree, Michael C; Simpson, Ronald J; Smith, Mark A; Wetherall, David; Wright, Jeremy H.

SHREWSBURY TOWN 1988–89 *Back row (left to right):* Richard Pratley, Alan Finley, Ken Hughes, Steve Perks, Richard Green, Dougie Bell.
Centre row: Paul Tester, David Geddis, Neil Smith, David Moyes, Alan Irvine, Wayne Williams, Phil Priest.
Front row: Colin Griffin (Coach), Bernard McNally, Jim Melrose, Victor Kasule, Ian McNeill (Manager), Brian Williams, Mickey Brown, Les Helm (Physiotherapist).
Sitting: Micky Thomas, Tim Steele, Jon Narbett, Garry Osbourne.

Division 3 **SHREWSBURY TOWN**

Gay Meadow, Shrewsbury. Telephone Shrewsbury (0743) 60111. Commercial Dept. 56316.

Match information: 8040.

Ground capacity:16,000

Record attendance: 18,917 v Walsall, Division 3, 26 Apr, 1961.

Record receipts: £36,240 v Ipswich T, FA Cup 5th rd, 13 Feb, 1982.

Pitch measurements: 116yd × 76yd.

President: ***Vice-President:*** Dr. J. Millard Bryson.

Chairman: K. R. Woodhouse.

Directors: A. C. Williams, F. C. G. Fry, R. Bailey, M. J. Starkey, G. W. Nelson, W. H. Richards.

Manager: Ian McNeill. ***Commercial Manager:*** M. Thomas.

Physio: L. Helm. ***Coach:*** Asa Hartford.

Secretary: M. J. Starkey.

Club Nickname: 'Town' or 'Shrews'.

Year Formed: 1886. ***Turned Professional:*** 1905 (approx). ***Ltd Co.:*** 1936.

Previous Ground: Old Shrewsbury Racecourse.

Record League Victory: 7-0, v Swindon T, Division 3(S), 6 May 1955 – McBride; Bannister, Keech; Wallace, Maloney, Candlin; Price, O'Donnell (1), Weigh (4), Russell, McCue (2).

Record Cup Victory: 7-1 v Banbury Spencer, FA Cup, 1st rd, 4 November 1961 – Gibson; Walters, Skeech; Wallace, Pountney, Harley; Kenning (2), Pragg, Starkey (1), Rowley (2), McLaughlin (2).

Record Defeat: 1-8 v Norwich C, Division 3(S), 1952–53 and v Coventry C, Division 3, 22 October, 1963.

Most League Points (2 for a win): 62, Division 4, 1974–75.

Most League Points (3 for a win): 70, Division 2, 1981–82.

Most League Goals: 101, Division 4, 1958–59.

Highest League Scorer in Season: Arthur Rowley, 38, Division 4, 1958–59.

Most League Goals in Total Aggregate: Arthur Rowley, 152, 1958–65 (thus completing his League record of 434 goals).

Most Capped Player: Jimmy McLaughlin, 5 (12), Northern Ireland.

Most League Appearances: Colin Griffin, 406, 1975–89.

Record Transfer Fee Received: £300,000 from Ipswich T for David Linighan, June 1988.

Record Transfer Fee Paid: £100,000 to Aldershot for John Dungworth, November 1979.

Football League Record: 1950 Elected to Division 3(N); 1951–58 Division 3(S); 1958–59 Division 4; 1959–74 Division 3; 1974–75 Division 4; 1975–79 Division 3; 1979–89 Division 2; 1989– Division 3.

Honours: *Football League:* Division 2 best season: 8th, 1983–84, 1984–85; Division 3 – Champions 1978–79; Division 4 – Runners-up 1974–5. *FA Cup* best season: 6th rd, 1978–79, 1981–82. *Football League Cup:* Semi-final 1961. *Welsh Cup:* Winners 1891, 1938, 1977, 1979, 1984, 1985; Runners-up 1931, 1948, 1980.

Colours: White shirts, blue trim, blue shorts, white stockings, blue and gold trim. **Change colours:** Red Shirts, white shorts, red stockings.

SHREWSBURY TOWN 1988–89 LEAGUE RECORD

Match No.	Date	Venue	Opponents	Result	H/T Score	Lg. Pos.	Goalscorers	Attendance
1	Aug 27	H	Portsmouth	L 1-2	1-1	—	McNally (pen)	5333
2	Sept 3	A	Bradford C	L 0-1	0-1	23		9765
3	10	H	WBA	D 1-1	0-0	22	Geddis	5851
4	17	A	Crystal Palace	D 1-1	1-0	21	Rougvie	7006
5	20	H	Ipswich T	L 1-5	1-3	—	Rougvie	4154
6	24	H	Sunderland	D 0-0	0-0	22		4195
7	Oct 1	A	Oxford U	L 1-4	1-2	23	Moyes	4385
8	4	A	Stoke C	D 0-0	0-0	—		8075
9	8	H	Hull C	L 1-3	0-2	23	Green (Richard)	3287
10	15	H	Walsall	D 0-0	0-0	23		5026
11	21	A	Bournemouth	W 1-0	1-0	—	Irvine	5449
12	25	A	Plymouth Arg	D 0-0	0-0	—		6298
13	29	H	Leicester C	W 3-0	1-0	22	Finley, Irvine 2	5178
14	Nov 5	A	Brighton & HA	L 1-3	0-0	22	Green (Richard)	7365
15	11	H	Oldham Ath	D 0-0	0-0	—		4701
16	19	H	Watford	D 1-1	1-0	23	Steele	4621
17	22	A	Blackburn R	W 1-0	1-0	—	Irvine	6895
18	26	A	Chelsea	L 0-2	0-2	22		11,595
19	Dec 3	H	Swindon T	L 0-1	0-1	22		3524
20	10	A	Leeds U	W 3-2	2-0	21	Rougvie, Griffiths 2	19,967
21	17	A	Manchester C	D 2-2	2-0	21	Griffiths 2	19,613
22	26	H	Birmingham C	D 0-0	0-0	21		7347
23	31	H	Barnsley	L 2-3	1-1	22	Bell (pen), Irvine	4401
24	Jan 2	A	WBA	L 0-4	0-0	22		18,411
25	14	H	Blackburn R	D 1-1	0-0	22	Kasule	3879
26	21	A	Portsmouth	L 0-2	0-1	22		8446
27	Feb 4	H	Stoke C	L 1-2	1-0	22	Priest	6646
28	11	A	Hull C	L 0-3	0-2	22		11,472
29	25	A	Walsall	D 1-1	1-1	22	Green (Richard)	5871
30	28	H	Plymouth Arg	W 2-0	1-0	—	Kelly, McGinlay	2978
31	Mar 3	A	Oldham Ath	L 0-3	0-1	—		6014
32	11	H	Brighton & HA	D 1-1	0-1	22	Kelly	4029
33	15	A	Leicester C	D 1-1	1-1	—	Williams	7750
34	18	A	Ipswich T	L 0-2	0-0	22		10,913
35	25	H	Bradford C	L 1-3	0-1	22	Kelly (pen)	4575
36	27	A	Birmingham C	W 2-1	0-1	22	Thomas, Kelly	4964
37	Apr 1	H	Crystal Palace	W 2-1	2-1	22	Kelly, McGinlay	4160
38	4	H	Manchester C	L 0-1	0-0	—		8271
39	8	A	Barnsley	L 0-1	0-1	22		5252
40	11	H	Bournemouth	W 1-0	0-0	—	Melrose	2457
41	15	H	Oxford U	D 2-2	0-1	22	McGinlay, Melrose	3583
42	22	A	Sunderland	L 1-2	0-1	22	McGinlay	9427
43	29	H	Chelsea	D 1-1	0-0	22	McGinlay	5588
44	May 1	A	Swindon T	L 0-1	0-1	22		8698
45	6	A	Watford	D 0-0	0-0	22		10,052
46	13	H	Leeds U	D 3-3	2-2	22	McNally, Griffiths 2	4693

Final League Position: 22

GOALSCORERS

League (40): Griffiths 6, Irvine 5, Kelly 5 (1 pen), McGinlay 5, Green (Richard) 3, Rougvie 3, McInally 2 (1 pen), Melrose 2, Bell 1 (pen), Finley 1, Geddis 1, Kasule 1, Moyes 1, Priest 1, Steele 1, Thomas 1, Williams B 1.
Littlewoods Cup (2): Brown 1, Melrose 1.
FA Cup (0).

Littlewoods Cup	First Round	Walsall (h)	2-2
		(a)	0-3
FA Cup	Third Round	Colchester U (h)	0-3

Perks	Williams, W	Williams, B	Priest	Green, Richard	Finley	Kasule	McNally	Irvine	Thomas	Brown	Melrose	Griffin	Rougvie	Geddis	Bell	Steele	Moyes	Green, Ron	Griffiths	Osbourne	Pratley	Hughes	Kelly	McGinlay	Pittman	Worsley	*Match No.*
1	2	3	4*	5	6	7	8	9	10†	11	12	14															1
1	2	3		5	6	12†	8	10	11	7	9		4*	14													2
1	2	3	7*	5	6	14	8	10†		11	12		4	9													3
1	2	3		5	6	7*	8	10		11	9†		4	12	14												4
1	2			3	6	11	8	9	10†	7	12		5		4*	14											5
1	2			3	6	7	8*	9†	11	10			5	4		12	14										6
	2*	12		3	6	7†		10	11				5	9	8		4	1	14								7
	2			3	6		8		11	12			5	9	7		4	1	10*								8
	2*			3	6			14	11	12			5	9	7	8	4†	1	10								9
		3	8	2	6			10	11	7*			5	9	4	12		1									10
		3	8	2	6			10*	11†	7	12			9	4		5	1	14								11
		3	8*	2	6			10	11	7	9		12		4†		5	1	14								12
		12	4	2	6	14		10	11*	7	9†		3				5	1	8								13
			4	2	6	12		10	11	7†	9*		3		8		5	1	14								14
			4*	2	6			10	11	12			3		8	7	5	1	9								15
			4*	2	6			10	11	9			3		8	7	5	1		12							16
			4	2	6			10	11	9*			3		8	7	5	1		12							17
			4*	2	6	9		10	11				3		8	7†	5	1	14		12						18
			4	2		9*			11	12	10†		3		8	7	5	1	14		6						19
			4*	2				10	11†	12			3		8	14	5	1	9	7	6						20
			4*	2				10	11				3		8	12	5	1	9	7	6						21
			4*	2	12			10	11				3		8†	14	5	1	9	7	6						22
		4		2	6			10	11	7			3		8		5	1	9								23
	3	4		2*	6	14		10	11	7					8		5		9†		12	1					24
		3	4	2		8		10	11	7							5		9		6	1					25
		3	4	2	12	8		10	11†	7*						14	5		9		6	1					26
		3	4†	2*		8		10		7					11	14	5		9		6	1	12				27
		3	4*		2	8†				7	9				11	12	5		14		6	1	10				28
		3	4	2	6				11	7	9*								8		5	1	10	12			29
1		3		2	6				11	7					4				10	12	5		8	9*			30
1		3	14	2	6				11†	7					4				10	12	5		8	9*			31
1		3	2		6	14	12	10	11	7					4*						5		8	9†			32
1		3	2		6		8	10	11	7									12		5		4	9*			33
1		3	2		6		8	10*	11†	7							14		12		5		4	9			34
1		3	12	2			8	10*	11	7							6		9†		5		4		14		35
1				2		12	8		11	7	10						6				5		4	9*	3		36
1				2	6		8		11	7	10						14		12		5		4†	9*	3		37
1				2	6	12	8		11*	7	10										5		4	9	3		38
			11	2	6	14	8	12		7	10*										5	1	4	9†	3		39
1			10		6	11†	8	9*		7	12						14				5		4		3	2	40
1			10*		6†		8		11	7	9						14				5		4	12	3	2	41
1		12					8		11		9				7		6				5		4	10	3*	2	42
1				14			8		11†	12	9				7*		6				5		4	10	3	2	43
1				12			8		11	7	9*						6				5		4	10	3	2	44
1				9			8		11	7							6		12		5		4	10	3*	2	45
1				2			8		11	7							6		9		5		4	10	3		46
22	10	20 + 3s	26 + 2s	37 + 2s	32 + 2s	12 + 9s	21 + 1s	29 + 2s	40	35 + 6s	16 + 5s	— + 1s	20 + 1s	7 + 2s	25 + 1s	6 + 9s	28 + 5s	17	17 + 11s	3 + 4s	26 + 2s	7	19 + 1s	14 + 2s	11 + 1s	6	

SHREWSBURY TOWN

Player and Position	Ht	Wt	Birth Date	Birth Place	Source	Clubs	League App	League Gls
Goalkeepers								
Ken Hughes	6 0	11 08	9 1 66	Barmouth		Crystal Palace	—	—
						Shrewsbury T	15	—
Steve Perks	6 0	12 02	19 4 63	Shrewsbury	Apprentice	Shrewsbury T	165	—
Gavin Ward*	6 2	12 12	30 6 70	Sutton Coldfield		Shrewsbury T	—	—
Defenders								
Alan Finley	6 3	14 03	10 12 67	Liverpool	Marine	Shrewsbury T	34	1
Richard Green	6 0	11 08	22 11 67	Wolverhampton		Shrewsbury T	85	5
Colin Griffin‡	6 0	11 10	8 1 56	Dudley	Apprentice	Derby Co	—	—
						Shrewsbury T	406	7
David Moyes	6 1	11 05	25 4 63	Blythswood	Drumchapel A	Celtic	24	—
						Cambridge U	79	1
						Bristol C	83	6
						Shrewsbury T	50	3
Steve Pittman	5 9	12 05	18 7 67	Livingstone		East Fife	43	2
						Shrewsbury T	12	—
Richard Pratley	6 2	14 02	12 1 63	Banbury	Banbury U	Derby Co	31	1
						Scunthorpe U (loan)	10	—
						Shrewsbury T	39	—
Brian Williams	5 9	12 1	5 11 55	Salford	Apprentice	Bury	159	19
						QPR	19	—
						Swindon T	99	8
						Bristol R	172	20
						Bristol C	77	3
						Shrewsbury T	65	1
Graeme Worsley	5 10	11 02	4 1 69	Liverpool	Bootle	Shrewsbury T	6	—
Midfield								
Doug Bell	5 11	12 01	5 9 59	Paisley	Cumbernauld	St Mirren	2	1
						Aberdeen	108	6
						Rangers	35	1
						Hibernian	32	3
						Shrewsbury T	41	3
						Hull C (loan)	4	—
Tony Kelly	5 10	11 09	1 10 64	Liverpool	Apprentice	Liverpool	—	—
						Derby Co	—	—
						Wigan Ath	101	15
						Stoke C	36	4
						WBA	26	1
						Chester C (loan)	5	—
						Colchester U :(loan)	13	2
						Shrewsbury T	20	5
Bernard McNally	5 7	10 11	17 2 63	Shrewsbury	Apprentice	Shrewsbury T	282	23
Cal Osbourne*	5 7	11 00	22 10 69	Wolverhampton	Trainee	Shrewsbury T	7	—
Philip Priest	5 7	10 06	9 9 66	Warley	School	Chelsea	—	—
						Blackpool (loan)	1	—
						Brentford (loan)	5	1
						Shrewsbury T	49	3
Neil Smith*	5 10	10 12	10 2 70	Warley	Trainee	Shrewsbury T	1	—
Mickey Thomas	5 6	10 07	7 7 54	Mochdre	Amateur	Wrexham	230	33
						Manchester U	90	11
						Everton	10	—
						Brighton & HA	20	—
						Stoke C	57	14
						Chelsea	44	9
						WBA	20	—
						Derby Co (loan)	9	—
					Wichita W	Shrewsbury T	40	1

SHREWSBURY TOWN

Foundation: Shrewsbury School having provided a number of the early England and Wales internationals it is not surprising that there was a Town club as early as 1876 which won the Birmingham Senior Cup in 1879. However, the present Shrewsbury Town club was formed in 1886 and won the Welsh FA Cup as early as 1891.

Managers (and Secretary-managers)
W. Adams 1905–12*, A. Weston 1912–34*, Jack Roscamp 1934–35, Sam Ramsey 1935–36, Ted Bousted 1936–40, Leslie Knighton 1945–49, Harry Chapman 1949–50, Sammy Crooks 1950–54, Walter Rowley 1955–57, Harry Potts 1957–58, Johnny Spuhler 1958, Arthur Rowley 1958–68, Harry Gregg 1968–72, Maurice Evans 1972–73, Alan Durban 1974–78, Richie Barker 1978, Graham Turner 1978–84, Chic Bates 1984–87, Ian McNeill 1987– .

Player and Position	Ht	Wt	Birth Date	Birth Place	Source	Clubs	League App	League Gls
Forwards								
Michael Brown	5 9	10 12	8 2 68	Birmingham		Shrewsbury T	104	7
Carl Griffiths	5 9	10 06	15 7 71	Oswestry	Trainee	Shrewsbury T	28	6
Alan Irvine	6 2	11 06	29 11 62	Broxburn		Hibernian	—	—
						Falkirk	110	17
						Liverpool	2	—
						Dundee U	7	—
						Shrewsbury T	37	6
Vic Kasule	5 10	10 03	28 5 65	Glasgow	Motherwell M	Albion R	132	18
						Meadowbank Th	35	7
						Shrewsbury T	35	4
John McGinlay	5 9	11 06	8 4 64	Inverness	Elgin C	Shrewsbury T	16	5
Jim Melrose	5 9	10 01	7 10 58	Glasgow	Eastercraigs	Partick Th	122	31
						Leicester C	72	21
						Coventry C	24	8
						Celtic	29	7
						Wolverhampton W (loan)	7	2
						Manchester C	34	8
						Charlton Ath	48	19
						Leeds U	4	—
						Shrewsbury T	30	3

Trainees
Baxter, David; Bywater, Paul R; Copeland, Stephen; Copson, Darren J; Evans, Paul A; Hay, John; Jarvis, Robert; Jones, Dale; McClean, Wayne R; Renshaw, Matthew J; Roberts, Mark A; Ryan, Darren T; Thomson, Scott M.

Associated Schoolboys
Bailey, Stephen P; Evans, Jason S; Evans, Paul S; Haner, Gareth C; Hodgin, Christopher; Malpass, Jody; Yates, Jason.

SOUTHAMPTON 1988–89 *Back row (left to right):* Rodney Wallace, Barrie Wilson, Jamie Webb, Neil Maddison, Matt Le Tissier, Steve Davis, Russell Osman, Colin Clarke, Paul Rideout, Francis Benali, Ray Wallace.

Centre row: Gordon Hobson, Graham Baker, Phil Underhill, Andy Townsend, Glenn Cockerill, Tim Flowers, Mark Blake, John Burridge, Danny Wallace, Derek Statham, Andy Cook, Gerry Forrest, Alan Shearer.

Front row: Dave Merrington (Youth Manager), Don Taylor (Physiotherapist), Dennis Rofe (First Team Coach), Kevin Moore, Chris Nicholl (Manager), Jimmy Case, Nick Holmes (Coach), Bob Higgins (Youth Development Officer), George Horsfall (Reserve Team Coach).

Division 1 **SOUTHAMPTON**

The Dell, Milton Road, Southampton SO9 4XX. Telephone Southampton (0703) 220505. Ticket enquiries 0703-228575.

Ground capacity: 25,175.

Record attendance: 31,044 v Manchester U, Division 1, 8 Oct, 1969.

Record receipts: £106,145 v Liverpool, Division 1, 24 September, 1988.

Pitch measurements: 110yd × 72yd.

Chairman: F. G. L. Askham FCA.

Vice-Chairman: K. St. J. Wiseman.

Directors: J. Corbett, E. T. Bates, I. L. Gordon, B. H. D. Hunt.

Manager: Chris Nicholl. *Asst. Manager:*

Coach: Dennis Rofe. *Physio:* Don Taylor.

Secretary: Brian Truscott. *Commercial Manager:* Bob Russell.

Club Nickname: 'The Saints'.

Year Formed: 1885. *Turned Professional:* 1894. *Ltd Co.:* 1897.

Previous Name: Southampton St Mary's until 1885.

Previous Grounds: 1885, Antelope Ground; 1897, County Cricket Ground: 1898, The Dell.

Record League Victory: 9-3 v Wolverhampton W, Division 2, 18 September 1965 – Godfrey; Jones, Williams; Walker, Knapp, Huxford; Paine (2), O'Brien (1), Melia, Chivers (4), Sydenham (2).

Record Cup Victory: 7-1 v Ipswich T, FA Cup, 3rd rd, 7 January 1961 – Reynolds; Davies, Traynor; Conner, Page, Huxford; Paine (1), O'Brien (3 incl. 1p), Reeves, Mulgrew (2), Penk (1).

Record Defeat: 0-8 v Tottenham H, Division 2, 28 March, 1936 and v Everton, Division 1, 20 November, 1971.

Most League Points (2 for a win): 61, Division 3 (S), 1921–22 and Division 3, 1959–60.

Most League Points (3 for a win): 77, Division 1, 1983–84.

Most League Goals: 112, Division 3 (S), 1957–58.

Highest League Scorer in Season: Derek Reeves, 39, Division 3, 1959–60.

Most League Goals in Total Aggregate: Mike Channon, 182, 1966–77, 1979–82.

Most Capped Player: Peter Shilton 49 (109), England.

Most League Appearances: Terry Paine, 713, 1956–74.

Record Transfer Fee Received: £800,000 from QPR for Colin Clarke, February 1989.

Record Transfer Fee Paid: £700,000 to Portsmouth for Barry Horne, March 1989.

Football League Record: 1920 Original Member of Division 3; 1921 Division 3 (S); 1922–53 Division 2; 1953–58 Division 3(S); 1958–60 Division 3; 1960–66 Division 2; 1966–74 Division 1; 1974–78 Division 2; 1978– Division 1.

Honours: Football League: Division 1 – Runners-up 1983–84; Division 2 – Runners-up 1965–66, 1977–78; Division 3 (S) – Champions 1921–22; Runners-up 1920–21; Division 3 – Champions 1959–60. *FA Cup:* Winners 1975–76; Runners-up 1900, 1902. *Football League Cup:* Runners-up 1978–79. **European Competitions:** *European Fairs Cup:* 1969–70, *UEFA Cup:* 1971–72, 1981–82, 1982–83, 1984–85; *European Cup-Winners' Cup:* 1976–77.

Colours: Red and white striped shirts, black shorts, white stockings, red trim. **Change Colours:** White shirts, Solent green trim, white shorts, white stockings, Solent green trim.

SOUTHAMPTON 1988–89 LEAGUE RECORD

Match No.	Date	Venue	Opponents	Result	H/T Score	Lg. Pos.	Goalscorers	Attendance
1	Aug 27	H	West Ham U	W 4-0	2-0	—	Rideout 2, Cockerill, Le Tissier	18,407
2	Sept 3	A	QPR	W 1-0	1-0	2	Le Tissier	9053
3	10	H	Luton T	W 2-1	1-0	1	Rideout, Wallace Rod	13,214
4	17	A	Arsenal	D 2-2	2-0	2	Le Tissier, Wallace Rod	31,384
5	24	H	Liverpool	L 1-3	1-1	4	Statham (pen)	21,046
6	Oct 1	H	Derby Co	D 0-0	0-0	4		13,283
7	8	A	Everton	L 1-4	1-1	6	Wallace D	25,356
8	22	H	Sheffield W	L 1-2	1-1	10	Statham (pen)	12,725
9	25	A	Tottenham H	W 2-1	0-1	—	Cockerill 2	19,517
10	29	A	Norwich C	D 1-1	0-0	6	Wallace D	14,808
11	Nov 5	H	Charlton Ath	W 2-0	0-0	4	Baker, Wallace D	12,826
12	12	H	Aston Villa	W 3-1	1-1	3	Le Tissier 2, Wallace Rod	16,007
13	19	A	Manchester U	D 2-2	1-1	5	Baker, Le Tissier	37,277
14	26	H	Millwall	D 2-2	1-1	6	Baker 2	15,925
15	Dec 3	A	Wimbledon	L 1-2	1-1	7	Maddison	6040
16	10	H	Nottingham F	D 1-1	1-0	6	Maddison	15,259
17	17	A	Newcastle U	D 3-3	2-1	7	Le Tissier 2, Wallace Rod	19,986
18	26	H	Coventry C	D 2-2	0-2	8	Wallace Rod, Moore	16,008
19	31	H	QPR	L 1-4	0-0	8	Le Tissier	15,086
20	Jan 2	A	Luton T	L 1-6	0-2	10	Wallace Rod	8637
21	14	H	Middlesbrough	L 1-3	1-0	13	Moore	13,157
22	21	A	Liverpool	L 0-2	0-0	15		35,565
23	Feb 4	A	Derby Co	L 1-3	0-1	15	Wallace D	13,758
24	11	H	Everton	D 1-1	1-0	14	Moore	15,845
25	18	A	Sheffield W	D 1-1	0-0	14	Wallace Rod	16,677
26	25	H	Tottenham H	L 0-2	0-1	15		16,702
27	Mar 11	A	Charlton Ath	D 2-2	0-1	16	Wallace Rod, Rideout	6377
28	25	H	Arsenal	L 1-3	0-1	18	Cockerill	19,202
29	27	A	Coventry C	L 1-2	1-1	18	Wallace D	11,734
30	Apr 1	H	Newcastle U	W 1-0	0-0	17	Ruddock (pen)	16,175
31	8	A	Middlesbrough	D 3-3	0-1	17	Wallace Rod, Ruddock 2	16,983
32	12	A	Nottingham F	L 0-3	0-2	—		18,948
33	15	A	West Ham U	W 2-1	1-1	16	Wallace Rod, Rideout	14,766
34	19	H	Norwich C	D 0-0	0-0	—		14,403
35	22	H	Wimbledon	D 0-0	0-0	15		13,805
36	May 2	A	Aston Villa	W 2-1	2-0	—	Wallace Rod, Rideout	15,218
37	6	H	Manchester U	W 2-1	1-0	13	Cockerill, Wallace Rod	17,021
38	13	A	Millwall	D 1-1	1-0	13	Cockerill	12,011

Final League Position: 13

GOALSCORERS

League (52): Wallace (Rod) 12, Le Tissier 9, Cockerill 6, Rideout 6, Wallace D 5, Baker 4, Moore 3, Ruddock 3 (1 pen), Maddison 2, Statham 2 (2 pens).
Littlewoods Cup (11): Baker 2, Cockerill 2, Le Tissier 2, Wallace (Rod) 2, Case 1, Moore 1, Rideout 1.
FA Cup (2): Forrest 1, Statham 1 (pen).

Littlewoods Cup	Second Round	Lincoln C (a)	1-1
		(h)	3-1
	Third Round	Scarborough (a)	2-2
		(h)	1-0
	Fourth Round	Tottenham H (h)	2-1
	Fifth Round	Luton T (a)	1-1
		(h)	1-2
FA Cup	Third Round	Derby Co (a)	1-1
		(h)	1-2

Burridge	Forrest	Statham	Case	Moore	Osman	Wallace, Rod	Cockerill	Clarke	Rideout	Wallace, D	Le Tissier	Shearer	Baker	Benali	Blake	Wallace, Ray	Maddison	Flowers	Cook	Ruddock	Adams	Horne	*Match No.*
1	2	3	4	5	6	7	8	9	10	11*	12												1
1	2	3	4	5	6	7	8	9	10*		11	12											2
1	2	3	4	5	6	7	8	9	10	12	11*												3
1	2	3	4	5	6	7	8	9	10	12	11*												4
1	2	3	4	5	6	7		9	10*	11		12	8										5
1	2	3	4	5†	6	7*		9	10	11	12		8	14									6
1	2	3	4		6	7*		9	10	11†	12		8	14	5								7
1		3		5	6	7	4	9	10	11*	12		8†	14		2							8
1		3		5	6	7	8	9*		11	12†		4	10		2	14						9
1		3		5	6	7	8			11	9*		4	10		2	12						10
1		3	4	5	6	7	8			11	9		10			2							11
1		3	4	5	6	7	8			11	9		10			2							12
1		3	4	5	6	7	8			11	9		10			2							13
1		3	4	5	6	7	8			11	9		10			2							14
1		3	4	5	6	7	8			11	9					2	10						15
		3	4	5	6	7	8			11	9					2	10	1					16
		3	4	5	6	7	8		12	11	9*		10			2		1					17
		3	4	5	6	7	8*		12	11	9		10			2		1					18
	2	3	4	5	6	7	8†		12	11	9		10*			14		1					19
1	2	3	4	5	6	7				11	9		10				8						20
1	2	3†	8	5		11	12		9		7		10*		4	6			14				21
1			8	5	6	11	7		9	12			10		4*	2			3				22
1			4	5	6	11	8		10	9	7*		2	12					3				23
1	2	3	4	5	6	7	10			11		9	8										24
1	2	3	4		6	7	10			11		9	8							5			25
1	2	3	4		6	7	10		12	11		9	8*							5			26
		3	4		6	7	8		10	12		9		11*		2		1		5			27
	14				6†	7	8		10*	11		9	12			2		1		5	3	4	28
			10	6		7	8			11		9				2		1		5	3	4	29
1			10		6	7	8			11		9				2				5	3	4	30
1			4		6	7*	8			11	12	9				2				5	3	10	31
1	14		4		6	7	8		9*	11	12					2				5	3	10†	32
1			4	5	6	8	8		9	11						2					3	10	33
1			4		6	7	8		9		11					2				5	3	10	34
1			4		6	7	8		9		11					2				5	3	10	35
1	3		4		6	7	8		9		11					2				5		10	36
1	3		4		6	7	8		9		11					2				5		10	37
1		3	4		6	7	8		9		11					2				5		10	38
31	15 + 2s	26	34	25	36	38	33 + 1s	9	20 + 4s	27 + 4s	21 + 7s	8 + 2s	20 + 1s	3 + 4s	3	25 + 1s	3 + 2s	7	2 + 1s	13	8	11	

SOUTHAMPTON

Player and Position	Ht	Wt	Birth Date	Birth Place	Source	Clubs	League App	League Gls
Goalkeepers								
John Burridge	5 11	12 11	3 12 51	Workington	Apprentice	Workington	27	—
						Blackpool	134	—
						Aston Villa	65	—
						Southend U (loan)	6	—
						Crystal Palace	88	—
						QPR	39	—
						Wolverhampton W	74	—
						Derby Co (loan)	6	—
						Sheffield U	109	—
						Southampton	62	—
Tim Flowers	6 2	13 04	3 2 67	Kenilworth	Apprentice	Wolverhampton W	63	—
						Southampton (loan)	—	—
						Southampton	25	—
						Swindon T (loan)	2	—
						Swindon T (loan)	5	—
Defenders								
Mick Adams	5 7	10 10	8 11 61	Sheffield	Apprentice	Gillingham	92	5
						Coventry C	90	9
						Leeds U	73	2
						Southampton	8	—
Mark Blake	6 0	12 04	19 12 67	Portsmouth	Apprentice	Southampton	18	2
Andy Cook	5 9	10 12	10 8 69	Romsey	Apprentice	Southampton	5	—
Steve Davis	6 2	12 08	30 10 68	Hexham	Trainee	Southampton	—	—
Jason Dodd	5 10	11 10	2 11 70	Bath		Southampton	—	—
Gerry Forrest	5 10	10 11	21 1 57	Stockton	South Bank	Rotherham U	357	7
						Southampton	114	—
Jeff Kenna	5 11	11 07		Dublin	Trainee	Southampton	—	—
Kevin Moore	5 11	12 02	29 4 58	Grimsby	Local	Grimsby T	400	27
						Oldham Ath	13	1
						Southampton	60	6
Russell Osman	6 0	11 10	14 2 59	Repton	Apprentice	Ipswich T	294	17
						Leicester C	108	8
						Southampton	36	—
Dean Radford	5 11	11 05		London	Trainee	Southampton	—	—
Neil Ruddock	6 2	12 06	9 5 68	London	Apprentice	Millwall	—	—
						Tottenham H	9	—
						Millwall	2	1
						Southampton	13	3
Derek Statham	5 5	11 05	24 3 59	Wolverhampton	Apprentice	WBA	299	8
						Southampton	64	2
Ray Wallace	5 6	10 02	2 10 69	Lewisham	Trainee	Southampton	26	—
Midfield								
Graham Baker	5 9	10 08	3 12 58	Southampton	Apprentice	Southampton	113	22
						Manchester C	117	19
						Southampton	57	9
Jimmy Case	5 9	12 07	18 5 54	Liverpool	S Liverpool	Liverpool	186	23
						Brighton & HA	127	10
						Southampton	157	6
Glenn Cockerill	6 0	12 04	26 8 50	Grimsby	Louth U	Lincoln C	71	10
						Swindon T	26	1
						Lincoln C	115	25
						Sheffield U	62	10
						Southampton	145	22
Barry Horne	5 10	11 06	18 5 62	St Asaph	Rhyl	Wrexham	136	17
						Portsmouth	70	7
						Southampton	11	—
Neil Maddison	5 9	11 08	2 10 69	Darlington	Trainee	Southampton	5	2

SOUTHAMPTON

Foundation: Formed largely by players from the Deanery FC, which had been established by school teachers in 1880. Most of the founders were connected with the young men's association of St. Mary's Church. At the inaugural meeting held in November 1885 the club was named Southampton St. Mary's and the church's curate was elected president.

Managers (and Secretary-managers)
Cecil Knight 1894–95*, Charles Robson 1895–97, E. Arnfield 1897–1911* (continued as secretary), George Swift 1911–12, E. Arnfield 1912–19, Jimmy McIntyre 1919–24, Arthur Chadwick 1925–31, George Kay 1931–36, George Gross 1936–37, Tom Parker 1937–43, J. R. Sarjantson stepped down from the board to act as secretary-manager 1943–47 with the next two listed being team managers during this period), Arthur Dominy 1943–46, Bill Dodgin Snr 1946–49, Sid Cann 1949–51, George Roughton 1952–55, Ted Bates 1955–73, Lawrie McMenemy 1973–85, Chris Nicholl 1985– .

Player and Position	*Ht*	*Wt*	*Birth Date*	*Place*	*Source*	*Clubs*	*League App*	*Gls*
Paul Masters	5 6	10 07		Southampton	Trainee	Southampton	—	—
Jamie Webb	5 8	10 06	7 12 69	Portsmouth	Trainee	Southampton	—	—
Forwards								
Nicky Banger	5 8	10 06	25 2 71	Southampton	Trainee	Southampton	—	—
Francis Benali	5 9	11 01	30 12 68	Southampton	Apprentice	Southampton	7	—
Matthew Le Tissier	6 0	11 06	14 10 68	Guernsey	Vale Recreation	Southampton	71	15
Lee Luscombe	6 0	11 10		Guernsey	Trainee	Southampton	—	—
Paul Rideout	5 11	12 01	14 8 64	Bournemouth	Apprentice	Swindon T	95	38
						Aston Villa	54	19
						Bari	99	23
						Southampton	24	6
Alan Shearer	5 11	11 03	13 8 70	Newcastle	Trainee	Southampton	15	3
Danny Wallace	5 4	9 13	21 1 64	London	Apprentice	Southampton	250	62
Rodney Wallace	5 7	10 01	2 10 69	Lewisham	Trainee	Southampton	53	13
Barrie Wilson‡	5 8	10 02	19 1 70	Newcastle	Trainee	Southampton	—	—

Trainees
Allsopp, Daniel; Burnett, Darren D; Cormack, Lee D; French, Gary R; O'Driscoll, Paul M; Tate, Michael J; Wheeler, Shane; Widdrington, Thomas.

Associated Schoolboys
Adams, Andrew; Andrews, Matthew J; Atkinson, Neil C; Cleeve, Anthony G; Crowley, Thomas; Frost, Neil; Hellings, Wayne; Jones, Stephen; Kamara, Abdul S; Lapointe, Conrad R; McKhuen, Dean R; Morgan, Alan M; Reed, Adam M; Savage, Ian; Selby, Neil S; Smith, Justin M.F; Snelgrove, Wayne A; Taylor, Craig; Thomas, Martin; Thorne, Kevin M; Tisdale, Paul R; Watson, Paul D; Whitman, Nathan; Wright, Scott.

SOUTHEND UNITED 1988–89 *Back row (left to right):* Martin Robinson, Danny Schneider, Danny O'Shea, Paul Brush, David Crown, Russel Short, Peter Johnson, Kevin Lock (Youth Team Manager).
Centre row: Buster Footman (Physiotherapist), Justin Edinburgh, Roy McDonough, Paul Sansome, Shane Westley, Paul Newell, Richard Young, Dave Martin, Frank Banks (Assistant Manager).
Front row: Nicky Thurston, Peter Butler, Derek Hall, Paul Clark (Player/Manager), Nicky Smith, Martin Ling, David Matthews.

Division 4 SOUTHEND UNITED

Roots Hall Football Ground, Victoria Avenue, Southend-on-Sea SS2 6NQ. Telephone Southend (0702) 340707. Commercial Dept: (0702) 332113. Soccerline: 0898 700 279.

Ground capacity: 11,863.

Record attendance: 31,090 v Liverpool FA Cup 3rd rd, 10 Jan, 1979.

Record receipts: £36,599 v Liverpool, FA Cup 3rd rd, 10 Jan, 1979.

Pitch measurements: 110yd × 74yd.

President: N. J. Woodcock.

Chairman: V. T. Jobson. ***Vice-Chairman/Company Secretary:*** R. J. Osborne.

Secretary: J. W. Adams.

Directors: R. F. Moore OBE, M. Markscheffel, J. Foster, W. E. Parsons, R. J. Osborne.

Manager: David Webb ***Assistant Manager:*** Kevin Lock.

Commercial Manager: Harry Stobart. ***Physio:*** Ken Steggles.

Club Nickname: 'The Shrimpers'.

Year Formed: 1906. ***Turned Professional:*** 1906. ***Ltd Co.:*** 1919.

Previous Grounds: 1906, Roots Hall, Prittlewell; 1920, Kursaal; 1934, Southend Stadium; 1955, Roots Hall Football Ground.

Record League Victory: 9-2 v Newport Co, Division 3 (S), 5 September 1936 – McKenzie; Nelson, Everest (1); Deacon, Turner, Carr; Bolan, Lane (1), Goddard (4), Dickinson (2), Oswald (1).

Record Cup Victory: 10-1 v Golders Green, FA Cup, 1st rd, 24 November 1934 – Moore; Morfitt, Kelly; Mackay, Joe Wilson, Carr (1); Lane (1), Johnson (5), Cheesmuir (2), Deacon (1), Oswald. 10-1 v Brentwood, FA Cup, 2nd rd, 7 December 1968 – Roberts; Bentley, Birks; McMillan (1) Beesley, Kurila; Clayton, Chisnall, Moore (4), Best (5), Hamilton.

Record Defeat: 1-9 v Brighton & HA, Division 3, 27 November, 1965.

Most League Points (2 for a win): 67, Division 4, 1980–81.

Most League Points (3 for a win): 80, Division 4, 1986–87.

Most League Goals: 92, Division 3 (S), 1950–51.

Highest League Scorer in Season: Jim Shankly, 31, 1928–29 and Sammy McCrory, 1957–58, both in Division 3 (S).

Most League Goals in Total Aggregate: Roy Hollis, 122, 1953–60.

Most Capped Player: George Mackenzie, 9, Eire.

Most League Appearances: Sandy Anderson, 451, 1950–63.

Record Transfer Fee Received: £150,000 from Crystal Palace for Glenn Pennyfather, November 1987.

Record Transfer Fee Paid: £111,111 to Blackpool for Derek Spence, December 1979.

Football League Record: 1920 Original Member of Division 3; 1921 Division 3 (S); 1958–66 Division 3; 1966–72 Division 4; 1972–76 Division 3; 1976–78 Division 4; 1978–80 Division 3; 1980–81 Division 4; 1981–84 Division 3; 1984–87 Division 4; 1987–89 Division 3; 1989– Division 4.

Honours: *Football League:* Division 3 (S) best season; 3rd, 1931–32, 1949–50; Division 4 – Champions 1980–81; Runners-up 1971–72, 1977–78. *FA Cup* best season: old 3rd rd, 1920–21, 5th rd, 1925-26, 1951-52, 1975-76. *Football League Cup:* never past 3rd rd.

Colours: Blue shirts yellow trim, yellow shorts blue trim, blue stockings. **Change Colours:** All yellow.

SOUTHEND UNITED 1988–89 LEAGUE RECORD

Match No.	Date	Venue	Opponents	Result	H/T Score	Lg. Pos.	Goalscorers	Attendance
1	Aug 27	H	Bolton W	W 2-0	1-0	—	O'Shea, Crown	4075
2	Sept 3	A	Fulham	L 0-1	0-0	13		4754
3	9	H	Swansea C	L 0-2	0-1	—		4357
4	17	A	Aldershot	D 2-2	1-0	17	Crown, Ling	2170
5	21	A	Reading	L 0-4	0-2	—		4062
6	23	H	Cardiff C	D 0-0	0-0	—		3199
7	Oct 1	A	Preston NE	L 2-3	2-0	21	Crown, Hall	5348
8	4	H	Mansfield T	D 1-1	1-0	—	Ling	2436
9	9	A	Brentford	L 0-4	0-0	—		5016
10	15	H	Gillingham	W 2-1	1-0	20	Ling, Crown (pen)	3200
11	22	H	Chesterfield	W 3-1	3-0	19	Crown 2 (1 pen), McDonough	2662
12	25	A	Bury	L 1-3	0-0	—	Crown (pen)	2419
13	28	H	Wigan Ath	L 1-2	0-1	—	Robinson	3120
14	Nov 5	A	Wolverhampton W	L 0-3	0-2	21		10,432
15	8	H	Bristol R	D 2-2	1-1	—	Crown 2	2453
16	12	A	Notts Co	D 1-1	0-1	21	Crown (pen)	5037
17	26	A	Chester C	W 4-2	1-1	18	Ling, Crown, Robinson, Bennett	2050
18	Dec 2	H	Port Vale	D 1-1	1-1	—	Robinson	3245
19	10	A	Wigan Ath	L 0-3	0-1	20		2027
20	17	A	Sheffield U	W 2-1	0-0	17	Robinson, Pike (og)	9556
21	26	H	Northampton T	W 2-1	2-1	16	Martin, McDonough	5034
22	31	H	Bristol C	L 1-2	0-1	16	Bennett	4012
23	Jan 2	A	Huddersfield T	L 2-3	0-1	18	Crown, McDonough	6403
24	13	H	Fulham	D 0-0	0-0	—		4844
25	21	A	Swansea C	L 0-2	0-1	21		3388
26	28	H	Aldershot	D 1-1	0-0	21	Crown	3014
27	Feb 3	H	Preston NE	W 2-1	2-0	—	Crown, Hall	2948
28	11	A	Mansfield T	L 0-4	0-2	21		2414
29	25	A	Gillingham	D 1-1	0-1	20	Crown	3574
30	28	H	Bury	D 1-1	1-0	—	Crown	2479
31	Mar 4	A	Chesterfield	L 1-2	1-0	20	Butler	3261
32	10	H	Wolverhampton W	W 3-1	2-0	—	Crown 2 (1 pen), Tilson	5924
33	18	A	Bolton W	D 0-0	0-0	20		3505
34	25	H	Huddersfield T	L 2-4	0-2	21	Crown 2	3582
35	27	A	Northampton T	D 2-2	0-0	21	Crown, Robinson	3707
36	31	H	Sheffield U	W 2-1	1-1	—	McDonough, Thompson (og)	4584
37	Apr 4	H	Blackpool	W 2-1	1-1	—	Hall, McDonough	2795
38	8	A	Bristol C	W 2-0	1-0	19	Ling 2	6213
39	14	H	Reading	W 2-1	1-0	—	Crown 2	4623
40	18	H	Brentford	D 1-1	0-0	—	Tilson	4119
41	22	A	Cardiff C	L 0-2	0-1	18		3268
42	28	H	Notts Co	D 1-1	1-0	—	Crown	3931
43	May 1	A	Bristol R	D 1-1	1-0	19	Robinson	6250
44	6	A	Port Vale	L 0-2	0-2	20		6250
45	9	A	Blackpool	L 2-3	0-3	—	Butler, Crown	3999
46	13	H	Chester C	W 1-0	0-0	21	Prior	4089

Final League Position: 21

GOALSCORERS

League (56): Crown 25 (5 pens), Ling 6, Robinson 6, McDonough 5, Hall 3, Bennett 2, Butler 2, Tilson 2, Martin 1, O'Shea 1, Prior 1, own goals 2.
Littlewoods Cup (4): Ling 2, Crown 1, own goal 1.
FA Cup (1): Ling 1.

Littlewoods Cup	First Round	Brighton & HA (h)	2-0
		(a)	1-0
	Second Round	Derby Co (a)	0-1
		(h)	1-2
FA Cup	First Round	Bristol C (a)	1-3

Sansome	O'Shea	Johnson	Martin	Westley	Brush	Butler	Hall	Crown	McDonough	Ling	Young	Smith	Matthews	Edinburgh	Clark	Robinson	Jones	Bennett	Edwards	Newell	Roberts	Tilson	Prior	*Match No.*
1	2	3	4	5	6	7	8	9	10*	11	12													1
1	2	3	4	5	6	7	8	9	10	11														2
1	2	3	4	5	6†	7	8*	9	10	11		12	14											3
1	2	3	4	5	6	7	8	9*	10	11			12											4
1	2	3	4	5	6	7	8	9	10*	11			12											5
1	6	3	4		5	7	8	9	10†	11*		12	14	2										6
1	6	3	4		5	7	8	9	10	11				2										7
1		3	4		5	7	8	9	10	11		6		2										8
1	12	3	4		5	7	8	9	10	11		6†	14	2*										9
1	2	3		5	6	4	8	9	10	11					7									10
1	2	3		5	6	4	8	9	10	11					7									11
1	2	3	12	5	6	4	8	9	10†	11					7*	14								12
1	2	3		5	6		8*	9	10	11		4			7	12								13
1		3	4	5	6*		12	9	14	11			8†	2	7	10								14
1		3	4	5			6	9	10†	11		12		2	7*	8	14							15
1		3	4	5			6	9		11				2	7	8		10						16
1	6	3	4	5				9		11		7		2		8		10						17
1	6	3	4	5				9		11		7		2		8		10						18
1	6	3			5			9	12	11		7		2		8*		10	4					19
1	2	3			6	4	12	9	5	11		7				8*		10						20
1	2	3	4†	5	6	7	8		9*	11	12			14				10						21
1		3	2	5	6	4	7	9	12	11				8*				10						22
1		3	2	5	6	4	7	9	8	11								10						23
		3	4	5		6	8	9		11					7			10		1	2			24
1		3	4	5		6	8	9*	10	11					7	12					2			25
1		3	4	5		6	8	9		11					7			10			2			26
1		3	4	5			8	9	12	11					7	6		10*			2			27
1			4		6		7	9	5	11		12		3		8*		10†			2	14		28
1	6		4				7	9	10	11				3							2	8	5	29
1	6		4			12	7*	9	10	11				3							2	8	5	30
1	6	3	4			7		9	10	11											2	8	5	31
1		3		5		4	8	9	10						7			11			2	6		32
1		3		5		4	8	9		10					7			11			2	6		33
1		3	12	5		4	8	9	10	14					7			11†			2	6*		34
1		3	12	5		4	8	9	10	11					7*	14					2	6†		35
1		3	7	5		4	8	9	10	11											2		6	36
1		3	7	5			8	9	10	11								4*			2	12	6	37
1		3	7		6	4	8	9	10	11											2		5	38
1		3	7		6	4	8	9	10	11											2		5	39
1		3	7		6	4	8*	9†	10	11						14					2	12	5	40
1		3	7		6	4	8†		10	11*						14		12			2	9	5	41
1		3	7		6	4	8†	9	10	11*						14					2	12	5	42
1		3	7		6	4	8	9	10							11*					2	12	5	43
1		3	7		6	4†	8	9	10*	14						11					2	12	5	44
		3		6		4		9	10	7						11				1	2	8	5	45
1		3			6	4		9	10	11					7						2	8	5	46
44	19 + 1s	43	34 + 3s	28	28	34 + 1s	38 + 2s	44	36 + 4s	42 + 2s	— + 2s	7 + 4s	1 + 5s	14 + 1s	16	12 + 7s	— + 1s	16 + 1s	1	2	23	10 + 6s	14	

SOUTHEND UNITED

Player and Position	Ht	Wt	Birth Date	Birth Place	Source	Clubs	League App	League Gls
Goalkeepers								
Paul Newell	6 1	11 05	23 2 69	Greenwich	Trainee	Southend U	15	—
Paul Sansome	6 0	12 00	6 10 61	N. Addington	Apprentice	Crystal Palace	—	—
						Milwall	156	—
						Southend U	50	—
Defenders								
Paul Brush	5 11	12 02	22 2 58	Plaistow	Apprentice	West Ham U	151	1
						Crystal Palace	50	3
						Southend U	42	1
Justin Edinburgh	5 9	11 06	18 12 69	Brentwood	Trainee	Southend U	15	—
Peter Johnson	5 9	11 00	5 10 58	Harrogate	Apprentice	Middlesbrough	43	—
						Newcastle U	16	—
						Bristol C (loan)	20	—
						Doncaster R	12	—
						Darlington	89	2
						Crewe Alex	8	—
						Exeter C	5	—
						Southend U	126	3
David Martin	6 1	11 08	25 4 63	East Ham	Apprentice	Millwall	140	6
						Wimbledon	35	3
						Southend U	110	3
Danny O'Shea*	6 0	12 08	26 3 63	Kennington	Apprentice	Arsenal	6	—
						Charlton Ath (loan)	9	—
						Exeter C	45	2
						Southend U	118	12
Spencer Prior§			22 4 71	Rochford	Trainee	Southend U	14	1
Chris Ramsey‡	5 9	10 12	28 4 62	Birmingham	Amateur	Bristol C	—	—
						Brighton HA	30	—
						Swindon T	100	5
						Southend U	13	—
Paul Roberts	5 9	11 13	27 4 62	London	Apprentice	Millwall	146	—
						Brentford	62	—
						Swindon T	27	—
						Southend U	38	—
						Aldershot	39	—
						Exeter C	3	—
						Southend U	23	—
Danny Schneider‡			30 3 70	Rochford	Trainee	Southend U	—	—
Russell Short‡	5 9	10 07	4 9 68	Ilford	Trainee	Southend U	1	—
Shane Westley	6 2	12 10	16 6 65	Canterbury	Apprentice	Charlton Ath	8	—
						Southend U	144	10
						Norwich C (loan)	—	—
Midfield								
Peter Butler	5 9	11 01	27 8 66	Halifax	Apprentice	Huddersfield T	5	—
						Cambridge U (loan)	14	1
						Bury	11	—
						Cambridge U	55	9
						Southend U	50	5
Paul Clark	5 10	12 12	14 9 58	Benfleet	Apprentice	Southend U	33	1
						Brighton HA	79	9
						Reading (loan)	2	—
						Southend U	211	3
Andy Edwards§			17 9 71	Epping	Trainee	Southend U	1	—
Derek Hall*	5 8	11 02	5 1 65	Manchester	Apprentice	Coventry C	1	—
						Torquay U (loan)	10	2
						Torquay U	45	4
						Swindon T	10	—
						Southend U	123	15
Matthew Jones§			9 10 70	Chiswick	Trainee	Southend U	1	—

SOUTHEND UNITED

Foundation: The leading club in Southend around the turn of the century was Southend Athletic, but they were an amateur concern. Southend United was a more ambitious professional club when they were founded in 1906, employing Bob Jack as secretary-manager and immediately joining the Second Division of the Southern League.

Managers (and Secretary-managers)
Bob Jack 1906–10, George Molyneux 1910–11, O. M. Howard 1911–12, Joe Bradshaw 1912–19, Ned Liddell 1919–20, Tom Mather 1920–21, Ted Birnie 1921–34, David Jack 1934–40, Harry Warren 1946–56, Eddie Perry 1956–60, Frank Broome 1960, Ted Fenton 1961–65, Alvan Williams 1965–67, Ernie Shepherd 1967–69, Geoff Hudson 1969–70, Arthur Rowley 1970–76, Dave Smith 1976–83, Peter Morris 1983–84, Bobby Moore 1984–86, Dave Webb 1986–87, Dick Bate 1987, Paul Clark 1987–88, Dave Webb (GM) 1988– .

Player and Position	*Ht*	*Wt*	*Birth Date*	*Place*	*Source*	*Clubs*	*League App*	*Gls*
Martin Ling	5 7	9 12	15 7 66	West Ham	Apprentice	Exeter C	116	14
						Swindon T	2	—
						Southend U	110	21
Nick Smith	5 8	10 00	28 1 69	Berkley		Southend U	46	5
Nick Thurston‡			13 12 69	Chelmsford	Trainee	Southend U	—	—
Forwards								
Gary Bennett	6 1	12 06	20 9 63	Liverpool		Wigan Ath	20	3
						Chester C	126	36
						Southend U	17	2
David Crown	5 10	11 04	16 2 58	Enfield	Walthamstow A	Brentford	46	8
						Portsmouth	28	2
						Exeter C (loan)	7	3
						Reading	88	15
						Cambridge U	106	45
						Southend U	72	42
Roy McDonough	6 1	11 11	16 10 58	Solihull	Apprentice	Birmingham C	2	1
						Walsall	82	15
						Chelsea	—	—
						Colchester U	93	24
						Southend U	22	4
						Exeter C	20	1
						Cambridge U	32	5
						Southend U	153	25
David Matthews‡			20 11 65	Hackney	Apprentice	West Ham U	—	—
					Basildon U	Walsall	—	—
						Southend U	6	—
Martin Robinson*	5 8	11 02	17 7 57	Ilford	Apprentice	Tottenham H	6	2
						Charlton Ath	228	58
						Reading (loan)	6	2
						Gillingham	96	24
						Southend U	56	14
Steve Tilson			27 7 66	Essex	Burnham	Southend U	16	2

Trainees
Edwards, Andrew D; Heffer, John E; Hyslop, Christian T; Jones, Matthew L; Lawrence, Martyn; Newell, Michael W; O'Connell, Iain A; Prior, Spencer, J; Smith, Paul W; Taylor, Paul M; West, Adrian P.

****Non-Contract**
Greaves, Daniel T; Webb, David J.

Associated Schoolboys
Anderson, John R; Ashenden, Scott; Brown, Stephen R.M; Jones, Shane N.

STOCKPORT COUNTY 1988–89 *Back row (left to right):* Bill Williams, Andy Thorpe, Bob Colville, Andy Gorton, Ian McKenzie, Steve Bullock.
Centre row: Dave Hindley (Physiotherapist), Mike Pickering, Nigel Hart, Rodger Wylde, Ian Scott, Mark Payne, Neil Bailey (Youth Coach).
Front row: Craig Farnaby, Andy Hodkinson, Paul Hendrie, Len Cantello (Assistant Manager), Asa Hartford (Manager), Mark Howard, John Cooke, Brian Butler.

Division 4 STOCKPORT COUNTY

Edgeley Park, Hardcastle Road, Stockport, Cheshire SK3 9DD. Telephone 061-480-8888. Clubcall: 0898 12 16 38. Promotions Office: 061-480-1247.

Ground capacity: 8,050.

Record attendance: 27,833 v Liverpool, FA Cup 5th rd, 11 Feb, 1950.

Record receipts: £23,515 v Liverpool, Milk Cup 2nd rd, 1st leg, 24 Sept, 1984.

Pitch measurements: 110yd × 71yd.

Hon. Vice-Presidents: Mike Yarwood OBE, Freddie Pye, Andrew Barlow.

Chairman: B. Elwood. ***Vice-Chairman:*** G. White.

Directors: J. N. Lewis. M. Baker, B. Taylor, M. H. Rains, H. T. Stephenson.

Chief Executive/Secretary: J. D. Simpson.

Manager: Danny Bergara. ***Asst. Manager:***

Coach: Paul Jones. ***Physio:*** Rodger Wylde.

Assistant Secretary/Commercial Manager: Graham Blakey.

General Manager: John Higgins. ***Programme Editors:*** Steve Bellis and Todd White.

Year Formed: 1883. ***Turned Professional:*** 1891. ***Ltd Co.:*** 1908.

Club Nickname: 'County' or 'Hatters'.

Previous Names: Heaton Norris Rovers 1883–88, Heaton Norris 1888–90.

Previous Grounds: 1883 Heaton Norris Recreation Ground; 1884 Heaton Norris Wanderers Cricket Ground; 1885 Chorlton's Farm, Chorlton's Lane; 1886 Heaton Norris Cricket Ground; 1887 Wilkes' Field, Belmont Street; 1889 Nursery Inn, Green Lane; 1902 Edgeley Park.

Record League Victory: 13-0 v Halifax T, Division 3 (N), 6 January 1934 – McGann; Vincent (1p), Jenkinson; Robinson, Stevens, Len Jones; Foulkes (1), Hill (3), Lythgoe (2), Stevenson (2), Downes (4).

Record Cup Victory: 6-2 v West Auckland T (away), FA Cup, 1st rd, 14th November 1959 – Lea; Betts (1), Webb; Murray, Hodder, Porteous; Wilson (1), Holland, Guy (2), Ritchie (1), Davock (1).

Record Defeat: 1-8 v Chesterfield, Division 2, 19 April, 1902.

Most League Points (2 for a win): 64, Division 4, 1966–67.

Most League Points (3 for a win): 64, Division 4, 1985–86.

Most League Goals: 115, Division 3 (N), 1933–34.

Highest League Scorer in Season: Alf Lythgoe, 46, Division 3 (N), 1933–34.

Most League Goals in Total Aggregate: Jack Connor, 132, 1951–56.

Most Capped Player: Harry Hardy, 1, England.

Most League Appearances: Bob Murray, 465, 1952–63.

Record Transfer Fee Received: £80,000 from Manchester C for Stuart Lee, September 1979.

Record Transfer Fee Paid: £50,000 to Rochdale for David Frain, July 1989.

Football League Record: 1900 Elected to Division 2; 1904 failed re-election; 1905–21 Division 2; 1921-22 Division 3 (N); 1922–26 Division 2; 1926–37 Division 3 (N); 1937–38 Division 2; 1938-58 Division 3 (N); 1958–59 Division 3; 1959–67 Division 4; 1967–70 Division 3; 1970– Division 4.

Honours: *Football League:* Division 2 best season: 10th, 1905–06; Division 3 (N) – Champions 1921–22, 1936–37; Runners-up 1928–29, 1929-30; Division 4 – Champions 1966–67. *FA Cup* best season: 5th rd. 1935, 1950. *Football League Cup* best season: 4th rd, 1972–73.

Colours: White shirts, royal blue shorts, white stockings. **Change Colours:** All red.

STOCKPORT COUNTY 1988–89 LEAGUE RECORD

Match No.	Date	Venue	Opponents	Result	H/T Score	Lg. Pos.	Goalscorers	Attendance
1	Aug 27	A	Darlington	W 4-1	2-0	—	Payne, Wylde, Coyle, Howard	1794
2	Sept 3	H	Leyton Orient	D 0-0	0-0	6		1947
3	10	A	Cambridge U	L 0-1	0-1	10		1911
4	16	H	Burnley	D 0-0	0-0	—		6676
5	19	H	Halifax T	D 1-1	1-0	—	Wylde	2206
6	23	A	Crewe Alex	D 1-1	0-1	—	Butler	2975
7	Oct 1	H	Doncaster R	W 2-0	1-0	12	Cooke, Wylde	1959
8	5	A	Peterborough U	L 0-1	0-1	—		2572
9	8	A	Rochdale	D 1-1	1-1	14	Wylde	3021
10	15	H	Hereford U	L 1-2	1-1	18	Wylde	2035
11	22	A	Scarborough	D 1-1	1-1	20	Hart	2449
12	24	H	Hartlepool U	W 3-0	2-0	—	Angell, Cooke, Wylde	2098
13	28	A	Colchester U	D 1-1	0-1	—	Hill (og)	1643
14	Nov 5	H	Grimsby T	W 3-1	1-0	12	Coyle, Caldwell, Wylde	2064
15	8	A	Wrexham	L 0-2	0-1	—		1865
16	11	H	York C	W 3-2	2-2	—	Colville, Hart, Angell	2477
17	25	H	Tranmere R	D 1-1	0-1	—	Wylde	2952
18	Dec 3	A	Rotherham U	L 1-2	1-1	18	Wylde	4105
19	17	H	Lincoln C	W 1-0	0-0	13	Williams (pen)	2355
20	26	A	Torquay U	L 1-2	0-1	16	Colville	2838
21	31	A	Carlisle U	D 1-1	0-1	15	Colville	3774
22	Jan 2	H	Exeter C	W 4-0	2-0	12	Caldwell, Colville, Cooke (pen), Hancock	2936
23	7	H	Scunthorpe U	L 1-2	0-1	13	Hancock	2656
24	14	A	Leyton Orient	W 2-1	1-0	11	Colville, Howard	3828
25	20	H	Darlington	D 0-0	0-0	—		2889
26	28	A	Burnley	L 0-1	0-0	13		6942
27	Feb 4	A	Halifax T	D 2-2	0-1	13	Cooke, Caldwell (pen)	1938
28	10	H	Crewe Alex	L 0-1	0-1	—		5015
29	17	H	Rochdale	W 3-0	2-0	—	Angell 2, Wylde	2858
30	25	A	Hereford U	L 1-2	0-2	13	Butler	2015
31	28	A	Hartlepool U	D 2-2	0-1	—	Caldwell, Hancock	1892
32	Mar 4	H	Scarborough	D 2-2	2-0	12	Colville, Hancock	2648
33	11	A	Grimsby T	L 0-2	0-0	15		4685
34	13	H	Colchester U	W 1-0	0-0	—	Cooke	2027
35	17	H	Cambridge U	D 0-0	0-0	—		2521
36	25	A	Exeter C	D 2-2	2-0	13	Coyle, Wylde	3058
37	27	H	Torquay U	D 0-0	0-0	15		2808
38	Apr 1	A	Lincoln C	D 0-0	0-0	15		3400
39	4	A	Scunthorpe U	D 1-1	1-0	—	Cooke	3958
40	7	H	Carlisle U	D 1-1	1-0	—	Wylde (pen)	2543
41	14	A	Doncaster R	D 2-2	1-0	—	Hancock, Caldwell	1363
42	21	H	Peterborough U	L 1-2	0-2	—	Williams	2091
43	28	A	Tranmere R	L 0-1	0-0	—		6270
44	May 1	H	Wrexham	D 2-2	0-1	18	Matthews, Angell	2118
45	6	H	Rotherham U	L 1-3	1-1	19	Leonard	4313
46	13	A	York C	L 0-2	0-1	20		2327

Final League Position: 20

GOALSCORERS

League (54): Wylde 12 (1 pen), Colville 6, Cooke 6 (1 pen), Angell 5, Caldwell 5 (1 pen), Hancock 5, Coyle 3, Butler 2, Hart 2, Howard 2, Williams 2 (1 pen), Leonard 1, Matthews 1, Payne 1, own goal 1.
Littlewoods Cup (1): Wylde 1 (pen).
FA Cup (1): Colville 1.

Littlewoods Cup	First Round	Tranmere R (h)	0-1
		(a)	1-1
FA Cup	First Round	Scarborough (a)	1-2

Gorton	Butler	Hart	Coyle	Thorpe	Williams	Wylde	Hendrie	Payne	Hartford	Howard	Scott	Colville	Bullock	Stapleton	Cooke	McKenzie	Caldwell	Logan	Angell	Pickering	Hancock	Matthews	Batch	Leonard	Dooner	*Match No.*
1	2	3	4	5	6	7	8	9	10*	11	12															1
1	2	3	4	5	6	7	10			11		8	9													2
1	2	3		5	6	7	8	9		11			12	4*	10											3
1	2	3*		5	6	7	4	9		11		8	12		10											4
1	2	3		5	6	7	8	9		11*			12		10	4										5
1	2	3	11	5	6	7	8	9*					12		10	4										6
1	2	3	4*	5	6	7	8	9		12					10	11										7
1	2	3	4	5		7	8			11*	6		12		10	9										8
1	2	3	4	5		7	8				6*		12		10	11	9									9
1	2	3	4	5		7		6*		12	8				10	11	9									10
1	2	3		5		7			10*		6				11	12	9	4	8							11
1	2	3		5		7			10*	14	6				11†	12	9	4	8							12
1	2	3	9	5		7*		14	10†	11	6	12						4	8							13
1	2	3	4	5		7			10	14	6†					12	9	11*	8							14
1	2	3	4	5		7			10	14	6†	12					9	11	8*							15
1	2*	3	4	5		7			10†	6		8	12			14		11	9							16
1	2	3	4*	5		7	10	6		14		8	12					11	9†							17
1	2	3		5	6	7	10*					8	4					11	9	12						18
1	2	3			6			7				8	4		10			11	9	5						19
1	2*	3			6			7				8	4		10		12	11	9†	5	14					20
1		3			6			7	10*			8	2		4		9	11		5	12					21
1	2	3		7	6							8*	4		10		9†	11	12	5	14					22
1	2	3*		7	6			12				8	4		10		9	11		5†	14					23
1				5	6			7	10*	2		8	4		11	3	9				12					24
1				5	6			7	10*	2†		8	4		11		9	3	12		14					25
1	2			5	6			7				8	4		11	14	9	3†	12		10*					26
1	2*			5	6			7†				8			11	14	9	3	12		10	4				27
1	2			5	6			7				8			11		10	3			9	4				28
1	11			2	6	12		7*				8					10	3	9	5		4				29
1	11	14		2	6	12		7*				8					10	3	9	5†		4				30
1	2			5	6				10*			8			11	12	7	3			9	4				31
1	2			5	6				10			8			11		7	3			9	4				32
1		5		2	6							8			11	10*	7	3	12		9	4				33
1		5	7		6				14			8			11†	2	10	3	12		9*	4				34
		5	7		6				14			8			11†	2	10*	3	12		9	4	1			35
		5	7	2	6	9						8*						3	10		12	4	1	11		36
		5	7	2	6	9						8			12			3			10*	4	1	11		37
		5	7	2	6	9						8			10			3				4	1	11		38
		5	7	2	6	9						8			10			3				4	1	11		39
	4	5	7	2	6	9						8			10			3					1	11		40
	7	5	11*	2	6												9	3	12		10	4	1	8		41
	7	5	11*	2	6										12		9†	3	14		10	4	1	8		42
		5	11	2		7							6		12			3	9		10*	4	1	8		43
		5	11	7	6							12	2†		10			3	9		14	4	1	8*		4
		5		7	6			11*				12	2		10			3	9		14	4	1	8†		4
		5		2	6			7*					12		10			3	9		14	4†	1	8	11	46
34	32	37 + 1s	23	41	35	24 + 2s	11	20 + 2s	12 + 2s	10 + 6s	8 + 1s	27 + 4s	13 + 9s	1	31 + 3s	10 + 7s	23 + 1s	35	17 + 9s	7 + 1s	12 + 10s	19	12	11	1	

STOCKPORT COUNTY

Player and Position	Ht	Wt	Birth Date	Birth Place	Source	Clubs	League App	League Gls
Goalkeepers								
Steve Crompton‡			20 4 68	Manchester		Manchester C	—	—
						Carlisle U	10	—
						Stockport Co	2	—
Andy Gorton	5 11	11 04	23 9 66	Salford		Oldham Ath	26	—
						Stockport Co (loan)	14	—
						Tranmere R (loan)	1	—
						Stockport Co	34	—
Defenders								
Neil Bailey‡	5 9	11 00	26 9 58	Wigan	Apprentice	Burnley	—	—
						Newport Co	134	7
						Wigan Ath	41	2
						Stockport Co	51	—
						Newport Co (loan)	9	1
Steven Bullock	5 8	11 01	5 10 66	Stockport	Apprentice	Oldham Ath	18	—
						Tranmere R	30	1
						Stockport Co	63	—
Brian Butler	5 6	10 08	4 7 66	Salford	Apprentice	Blackpool	74	5
						Stockport Co	32	2
Craig Farnaby*	6 1	12 00	8 8 67	Hartlepool		Hartlepool U	5	—
						Middlesbrough	—	—
						Halifax T	10	1
						Stockport Co	22	1
Nigel Hart	6 0	12 03	1 10 58	Golborne	Local	Wigan Ath	1	—
						Leicester C	—	—
						Blackpool	37	—
						Crewe Alex	142	10
						Bury	45	2
						Stockport Co	38	2
Mark Howard			21 10 64	Kings Lynn		Norwich C	—	—
						Stockport Co	18	2
						Cambridge U (loan)	2	—
David Logan	5 9	10 11	5 12 63	Middlesbrough	Whitby	Mansfield T	67	1
						Northampton T	41	1
						Halifax T	3	—
						Stockport Co	35	—
Ian McKenzie*	5 11	10 08	22 8 66	Wallsend	Apprentice	Barnsley	1	—
						Stockport Co	59	—
Mike Pickering*	5 11	12 06	29 9 56	Huddersfield	Local	Barnsley	100	1
						Southampton	44	—
						Sheffield W	110	1
						Norwich C (loan)	1	—
						Bradford C (loan)	4	—
						Barnsley (loan)	3	—
						Rotherham U	102	1
						York C	32	1
						Stockport Co	16	—
Ian Scott‡	5 11	12 01	4 3 69	Wharfedale	Apprentice	Manchester U	—	—
						Stockport Co	25	—
Andy Thorpe	5 11	12 00	15 9 60	Stockport	Amateur	Stockport Co	314	3
						Tranmere R	53	—
						Stockport Co	61	—
Bill Williams	6 1	12 11	7 10 60	Rochdale	Local	Rochdale	95	2
						Stockport Co	104	1
						Manchester C	1	—
						Stockport Co	28	2
Midfield								
Tony Coyle*	5 10	11 12	17 1 60	Glasgow	Avoco Amats	Albion R	46	5
						Stockport Co	219	28
						Chesterfield	76	4
						Stockport Co	23	3
Gary Dooner§			14 9 70	St Helens	Trainee	Stockport Co	1	—

STOCKPORT COUNTY

Foundation: Formed at a meeting held at Wellington Road South by members of Wycliffe Congregational Chapel in 1883, they called themselves Heaton Norris Rovers until changing to Stockport County in 1890, a year before joining the Football Combination.

Managers (and Secretary-managers)
Fred Stewart 1894–1911, Harry Lewis 1911–14, David Ashworth 1914–19, Albert Williams 1919–24, Fred Scotchbrook 1924–26, Lincoln Hyde 1926–31, Andrew Wilson 1932–33, Fred Westgarth 1934–36, Bob Kelly 1936–38, George Hunt 1938–39, Bob Marshall 1939–49, Andy Beattie 1949–52, Dick Duckworth 1952–56, Billy Moir 1956–60, Reg Flewin 1960–63, Trevor Porteous 1963–65, Bert Trautmann (GM) 1965–66, Eddie Quigley (TM) 1965–66, Jimmy Meadows 1966–69, Wally Galbraith 1969–70, Matt Woods 1970–71, Brian Doyle 1972–74, Jimmy Meadows 1974–75, Roy Chapman 1975–76, Eddie Quigley 1976–77, Alan Thompson 1977–78, Mike Summerbee 1978–79, Jimmy McGuigan 1979–82, Eric Webster 1982–85, Colin Murphy 1985, Les Chapman 1985–86, Jimmy Melia 1986, Colin Murphy 1986–87, Asa Hartford 1987–89, Danny Bergara 1989– .

Player and Position	Ht	Wt	Birth Date	Birth Place	Source	Clubs	League App	League Gls
Paul Hendrie‡	5 6	10 03	27 3 54	Glasgow	School	Birmingham C	23	1
					Portland T	Bristol R	30	1
						Halifax T	187	12
						Stockport Co	121	6
Gary Leonard	5 9	10 12	28 11 65	Newcastle	Apprentice	WBA	—	—
						Shrewsbury T	67	1
						Hereford U (loan)	11	1
						Bury	9	1
						Stockport Co	11	1
Mike Matthews	5 8	11 03	25 9 60	Hull	Apprentice	Wolverhampton W	76	7
						Scunthorpe U	58	5
						Halifax T	99	8
						Scarborough	7	1
						Stockport Co	19	1
Mark Payne			3 8 60	Cheltenham	Cambuur	Stockport Co	22	1
John Stapleton‡			30 9 69	Manchester		Stockport Co	1	—
Forwards								
Brett Angell	6 1	12 03	20 8 68	Marlborough		Portsmouth	—	—
					Cheltenham T	Derby Co	—	—
						Stockport Co	26	5
Tony Caldwell	5 9	11 07	21 3 58	Salford	Horwich RMI	Bolton W	139	58
						Bristol C	17	3
						Chester C (loan)	4	—
						Grimsby T	3	—
						Stockport Co	24	5
Bob Colville	5 10	12 00	27 4 63	Nuneaton	Rhos U	Oldham Ath	32	4
						Bury	11	1
						Stockport Co	71	20
John Cooke	5 8	11 00	25 4 62	Salford	Apprentice	Sunderland	55	4
						Carlisle U (loan)	6	2
						Sheffield W	—	—
						Carlisle U	106	11
						Stockport Co	34	6
Tony Hancock			31 1 67	Manchester	Stockport Georgians	Stockport Co	22	5
Roger Wylde*	6 1	12 00	8 3 54	Sheffield	Apprentice	Sheffield W	169	54
						Oldham Ath	113	51
						Sporting Lisbon	2	1
						Sunderland	11	3
						Barnsley	52	19
						Rotherham U (loan)	6	1
						Stockport Co	26	12

Trainees
Barrett, Lee S; Brabin, Gary; Burnside, Scott; Dooner, Gary J; Faulkner, Martin B; Fieldsend, Shaun M; Grimshaw, Scott A; Hibbert, Andrew L; Kelly, Neil; Lomas, Craig; Mannion, John P; Morton, Michael W; Parker, Philip; Shepherd, Wayne D.

STOKE CITY 1988–89 *Back row (left to right):* Lee Fowler, Carl Beeston, John Gidman, Tony Henry, Nicky Morgan, Graham Shaw, Garry Hackett.
Centre row: Keith Rowley (Physiotherapist), Simon Stainrod, Andy Holmes, Peter Fox, Scott Barrett, Chris Hemming, Cliff Carr, Sammy Chung (Coach).
Front row: Carl Saunders, Tony Ford, Peter Beagrie, Mick Mills (Manager), George Berry, Steve Parkin, Chris Kamara.

Division 2 STOKE CITY

Victoria Ground, Stoke-on-Trent. Telephone Stoke-on-Trent (0782) 413511. Commercial Dept. 0782 45840. Soccerline Information: 0898 700278.

Ground capacity: 35,812.

Record attendance: 51,380 v Arsenal, Division 1, 29 Mar, 1937.

Record receipts: £97,000 v Liverpool, FA Cup 3rd rd, 9 January 1988.

Pitch measurements: 116yd × 75yd.

Vice-President: J. A. M. Humphries.

Chairman: P. Coates. ***Vice-Chairman:*** T. E. Weetman.

Directors: G. L. Manning, M. Nield, K. A. Humphreys, J. M. Loftus.

Manager: Mick Mills.

Coach: Sammy Chung. ***Physio:*** Keith Rowley.

Secretary: M. J. Potts.

Sales & Marketing Manager: M. J. Cullerton.

Year Formed: 1863 *(*see Foundation*).

Turned Professional: 1885. ***Ltd Co.:*** 1908.

Club Nickname: 'The Potters'.

Previous Grounds: 1875, Sweeting's Field; 1878, Victoria Ground (previously known as the Athletic Club Ground).

Record League Victory: 10-3 v WBA, Division 1, 4 February 1937 – Doug Westland; Brigham, Harbot; Tutin, Turner (1p), Kirton; Matthews, Antonio (2), Fred Steele (5), Jimmy Westland, Johnson (2).

Record Cup Victory: 7–1 v Burnley, FA Cup, 2nd rd (replay), 20 February 1896 – Clawley; Clare, Eccles; Turner, Grewe, Robertson; Willie Maxwell, Dickson, Maxwell (A) (3), Hyslop (4), Schofield.

Record Defeat: 0–10 v Preston NE, Division 1, 14 September, 1889.

Most League Points (2 for a win): 63, Division 3 (N), 1926–27.

Most League Points (3 for a win): 62, Division 2, 1987–88.

Most League Goals: 92, Division 3 (N), 1926–27.

Highest League Scorer in Season: Freddie Steele, 33, Division 1, 1936–37.

Most League Goals in Total Aggregate: Freddie Steele, 142, 1934–49.

Most Capped Player: Gordon Banks, 36, (73), England.

Most League Appearances: Eric Skeels, 506, 1958–76.

Record Transfer Fee Received: £700,000 from Everton for Adrian Heath, January 1982.

Record Transfer Fee Paid: £350,000 to Manchester U for Sammy McIlroy, February 1982.

Football League Record: 1888 Founder Member of Football League; 1890 Not re-elected; 1891 Re-elected; Relegated in 1907, and after one year in Division 2, resigned for financial reasons; Re-elected to Division 2 in 1919; 1922–23 Division 1; 1923–26 Division 2; 1926–27 Division 3(N); 1927–33 Division 2; 1933–53 Division 1; 1953–63 Division 2; 1963–77 Division 1; 1977–79 Division 2; 1978–85 Division 1; 1985– Division 2.

Honours: *Football League:* Division 1 best season: 4th, 1935–36, 1946–47; Division 2 – Champions 1932–33, 1962–63; Runners-up 1921–22; Promoted 1978–79 (3rd); Division 3 (N) – Champions 1926–27. *FA Cup:* Semi-finals 1899, 1971, 1972. *Football League Cup:* Winners 1971–72. **European Competitions:** *UEFA Cup:* 1972–73, 1974–75.

Colours: Red and white striped shirts, white shorts, white stockings. **Change Colours:** Yellow shirts, black shorts, yellow stockings.

STOKE CITY 1988–89 LEAGUE RECORD

Match No.	Date	Venue	Opponents	Result	H/T Score	Lg. Pos.	Goalscorers	Attendance
1	Aug 27	H	Ipswich T	D 1-1	1-0	—	Kamara	8639
2	29	A	Bradford C	D 0-0	0-0	—		11,918
3	Sept 3	A	Barnsley	L 0-1	0-0	15		5682
4	10	H	Blackburn R	L 0-1	0-1	17		8624
5	17	A	Plymouth Arg	L 0-4	0-2	23		7823
6	20	H	Portsmouth	D 2-2	1-1	—	Stainrod, Hackett	7025
7	24	A	Walsall	W 2-1	1-1	19	Morgan, Stainrod	7795
8	Oct 1	H	Bournemouth	W 2-1	1-0	16	Shaw, Beagrie	7485
9	4	H	Shrewsbury T	D 0-0	0-0	—		8075
10	8	A	Oldham Ath	D 2-2	0-2	19	Kamara, Stainrod	6600
11	15	A	Leicester C	L 0-2	0-1	20		10,312
12	22	H	Watford	W 2-0	1-0	17	Coton (og), Beagrie	7878
13	25	A	Birmingham C	W 1-0	0-0	—	Stainrod	6262
14	29	H	Crystal Palace	W 2-1	1-0	11	Shaw, Henry	9118
15	Nov 5	A	Sunderland	D 1-1	1-0	10	Shaw	17,923
16	13	H	Hull C	W 4-0	1-0	—	Henry, Beagrie, Hackett, Carr	10,505
17	19	H	Swindon T	W 2-1	0-0	7	Berry (pen), Shaw	9339
18	26	A	Leeds U	L 0-4	0-2	8		19,933
19	Dec 3	H	Chelsea	L 0-3	0-1	10		12,288
20	10	A	Brighton & HA	D 1-1	1-0	12	Beagrie	7443
21	18	A	WBA	L 0-6	0-2	—		17,634
22	26	H	Manchester C	W 3-1	0-1	10	Kamara 2, Berry (pen)	24,056
23	31	H	Oxford U	W 1-0	1-0	10	Henry	10,552
24	Jan 2	A	Blackburn R	L 3-4	3-2	13	Saunders 2, Atkins (og)	11,654
25	14	H	Bradford C	W 2-1	2-1	11	Hackett, Henry	9919
26	21	A	Ipswich T	L 1-5	0-0	13	Bamber	14,692
27	Feb 4	A	Shrewsbury T	W 2-1	0-1	12	Moyes (og), Shaw	6646
28	11	H	Oldham Ath	D 0-0	0-0	10		10,992
29	25	H	Leicester C	D 2-2	2-2	12	Beagrie, Bamber	9666
30	28	H	Birmingham C	W 1-0	1-0	—	Berry	7904
31	Mar 4	A	Hull C	W 4-1	4-0	7	Hackett, Morgan, Beeston 2	5915
32	11	H	Sunderland	W 2-0	1-0	7	Hackett, Beagrie	12,489
33	18	A	Portsmouth	D 0-0	0-0	9		7624
34	25	H	Barnsley	D 1-1	1-0	10	Berry (pen)	10,209
35	27	A	Manchester C	L 1-2	0-1	11	Butler	28,303
36	Apr 1	H	Plymouth Arg	D 2-2	2-0	11	Bamber, Henry	8363
37	4	H	WBA	D 0-0	0-0	—		11,151
38	8	A	Oxford U	L 2-3	1-2	12	Bamber, Henry	5297
39	11	A	Watford	L 2-3	1-2	—	Morgan 2	9086
40	15	A	Bournemouth	W 1-0	0-0	11	Ware	6834
41	22	H	Walsall	L 0-3	0-2	11		8132
42	29	H	Leeds U	L 2-3	2-1	13	Bamber 2	9051
43	May 1	A	Chelsea	L 1-2	1-1	13	Higgins	14,946
44	6	A	Swindon T	L 0-3	0-0	13		9543
45	9	A	Crystal Palace	L 0-1	0-1	—		12,159
46	13	H	Brighton & HA	D 2-2	1-1	13	Morgan, Beagrie	5841

Final League Position: 13

GOALSCORERS

League (57): Beagrie 7, Bamber 6, Henry 6, Hackett 5, Morgan 5, Shaw 5, Berry 4 (3 pens), Kamara 4, Stainrod 4, Beeston 2, Saunders 2, Butler 1, Carr 1, Higgins 1, Ware 1, own goals 3.
Littlewoods Cup (3): Kamara 1, Morgan 1, Stainrod 1 (pen).
FA Cup (5): Bamber 2, Beagrie 1, Berry 1, Shaw 1.

Littlewoods Cup	Second Round	Leyton Orient (a)	2-1
		(h)	1-2
FA Cup	Third Round	Crystal Palace (h)	1-0
	Fourth Round	Barnsley (h)	3-3
		(a)	1-2

Fox	Gidman	Parkin	Kamara	Beeston	Henry	Hackett	Ford	Shaw	Saunders	Beagrie	Morgan	Ware	Carr	Stainrod	Hemming	Higgins	Barrett	Berry	Butler	Bamber	*Match No.*
1	2	3	4	5	6	7*	8	9	10	11	12										1
1	2	3	4*	5†	6	7		14	10	11	9	8	12								2
1	5	2	4		6	7	8		10	11	9		3								3
1	2		4	5	6	7	8	9	10	11			3								4
1	2†		4	5	6	7	8	12	10	11	14		3	9*							5
1			4		6	7	2		8	11	9		3	10	5						6
1			4		6	7	2		8	11	9		3	10	5						7
1			4		6	7	2	12	8	11	9*			10	3	5					8
1			4	3	6	7	2	9	8	11				10		5					9
1	12		4	3	6	7	2	9*	8	11				10		5					10
					4	7	2	12	9	11		8*	3	10		5	1	6			11
1			4		8	7	2		9	11			3	10		5		6			12
1			4		8	7	2	9		11			3	10		5		6			13
1	12		4		8	7	2	9		11*			3	10		5		6			14
1	12		4		8	7	2	9		11			3	10*		5		6			15
1			4		8	7	2	12	9	11			3	10*		5		6			16
1			4		8	7	2	12	9*	11			3	10		5		6			17
1			4		8	7*	2	12	9	11			3	10		5		6			18
1			4	14	8	7	2	9	12	11			3*	10		5		6*			19
1	2		4	5		11	7		8	9			3	10				6			20
1	2		4		5	7	10	9		11		8	3					6			21
1			4	6	12	7	10			11		8*	3					5	2	9	22
1			4	6	8	7	10			11			3					5	2	9	23
1			4		8	7			10	11			3			5		6	2	9	24
1			4		8	7			10	11			3			5		6	2	9	25
1		3	4		8	12	7		10*	11						5		6	2	9	26
			4		8*	7	9	10	12	11			3			5	1	6	2		27
			4		14	7	8*	10†	12	11			3			5	1	6	2	9	28
						7	4	10*	8	11	12		3			5	1	6	2	9	29
					4	7	8	10		11			3			5	1	6	2	9	30
				4		7		9	8	11	10		3			5	1	6	2		31
			4	5		7		10	8	11			3				1	6	2	9	32
			4	8		7		10*	12	11			3			5	1	6	2	9	33
				4		7		10	8	11	12		3			5	1	6	2	9*	34
			4	8†	14	7		10*	12	11			3			5	1	6	2	9	35
			4	8	11	7		14	10		12		3			5†	1	6	2	9*	36
			4		8	7		10	11				3			5	1	6	2	9	37
			4	11	8	7		12	10*				3		6	5	1		2	9	38
			4	11	8	7					10		3			5	1	6	2	9	39
			4	8	6	7					10	11	3			5	1		2	9	40
			4	5	8	7				11	10	12	3				1	6	2	9*	41
			4	10	8*	7				11		12	3			5	1	6	2	9	42
1			4	6	8	7			12	11	14	10*	3			5			2	9†	43
1				6*	8	7			10	11	14	4	3†			5		12	2	9	44
1					8	7				11	10	4	3			5		6	2	9	45
1					8	7				11	10	4	3			5		6	2	9	46
29	7 + 3s	4	38	22 + 1s	37 + 3s	45 + 1s	27	19 + 9s	27 + 6s	41	11 + 7s	9 + 2s	40 + 1s	16	4	33	17	32 + 1s	25	23	

STOKE CITY

Player and Position	Ht	Wt	Birth Date	Birth Place	Source	Clubs	League App	League Gls
Goalkeepers								
Scott Barrett	6 0	12 11	2 4 63	Ilkeston	Amateur	Wolverhampton W	30	—
						Stoke C	44	—
Peter Fox	5 11	12 10	5 7 57	Scunthorpe	Apprentice	Sheffield W	49	—
						West Ham U (loan)	—	—
						Barnsley (loan)	1	—
						Stoke City	317	—
Defenders								
George Berry	6 0	13 04	19 11 57	Rostrup, W Germ	Apprentice	Wolverhampton W	124	4
						Stoke C	221	26
						Doncaster R (loan)	1	—
John Butler	5 11	11 07	7 2 62	Liverpool	Prescot Cables	Wigan Ath	245	15
						Stoke C	25	1
Cliff Carr	5 5	10 04	19 6 64	London	Apprentice	Fulham	145	14
						Stoke C	82	1
Lee Fowler	5 7	11 11	26 1 69	Nottingham	Trainee	Stoke C	1	—
Chris Hemming	5 11	11 02	13 4 66	Newcastle	School	Stoke C	93	2
						Wigan Ath (loan)	4	—
Mark Higgins	6 1	13 05	29 9 58	Buxton	Apprentice	Everton	152	6
						Manchester U	6	—
						Bury	68	—
						Stoke C	33	1
Andrew Holmes	6 1	12 12	7 1 69	Stoke	Apprentice	Stoke C	2	—
Mick Mills‡	5 7	11 11	4 1 49	Godalming	Apprentice	Portsmouth	—	—
						Ipswich T	591	22
						Southampton	103	3
						Stoke C	38	—
Steve Parkin	5 6	10 07	7 11 65	Mansfield	Apprentice	Stoke C	113	5
Midfield								
Carl Beeston	5 9	10 03	30 6 67	Stoke	Apprentice	Stoke C	41	2
Ian Gibbons‡			8 2 70	Stoke	Trainee	Stoke C	1	—
Tony Henry	5 11	12 00	26 11 57	Sunderland	Apprentice	Manchester C	79	6
						Bolton W	70	22
						Oldham Ath	190	25
						Stoke C	62	11
Chris Kamara	6 1	12 00	25 12 57	Middlesbrough	Apprentice	Portsmouth	63	7
						Swindon T	147	21
						Portsmouth	11	—
						Brentford	152	28
						Swindon T	87	6
						Stoke C	38	4
Kevin Lewis§			17 10 70	Hull	Trainee	Stoke C	1	—
Paul Ware	5 8	11 02	7 11 70	Congleton	Trainee	Stoke C	12	1
Forwards								
Dave Bamber	6 3	13 10	1 2 59	St Helens	Manchester Univ	Blackpool	86	29
						Coventry C	19	3
						Walsall	20	7
						Portsmouth	4	1
						Swindon T	106	31
						Watford	18	3
						Stoke C	23	6
Peter Beagrie	5 8	9 10	28 11 65	Middlesbrough	Local	Middlesbrough	33	2
						Sheffield U	84	11
						Stoke C	41	7
Gary Hackett	5 8	10 13	11 10 62	Stourbridge	Bromsgrove R	Shrewsbury T	150	17
						Aberdeen	15	—
						Stoke C	47	5

STOKE CITY

Foundation: The date of the formation of this club has long been in doubt. The year 1863 was claimed, but more recent research by Wade Martin has uncovered nothing earlier than 1868, when a couple of Old Carthusians, who were apprentices at the local works of the old North Staffordshire Railway Company, met with some others from that works, to form Stoke Ramblers. It should also be noted that the old Stoke club went bankrupt in 1908 when a new club was formed.

Managers (and Secretary-managers)
Tom Slaney 1874–83*, Walter Cox 1883–84*, Harry Lockett 1884–90, Joseph Bradshaw 1890–92, Arthur Reeves 1892–95, William Rowley 1895–97, H. D. Austerberry 1897–1908, A. J. Barker 1908–14, Peter Hodge 1914–15, Joe Schofield 1915–19, Arthur Shallcross 1919–23, John "Jock" Rutherford 1923, Tom Mather 1923–35, Bob McGrory 1935–52, Frank Taylor 1952–60, Tony Waddington 1960–77, George Eastham 1977–78, Alan A'Court 1978, Alan Durban 1978–81, Richie Barker 1981–83, Bill Asprey 1984–85, Mick Mills 1985– .

Player and Position	*Ht*	*Wt*	*Birth Date*	*Place*	*Source*	*Clubs*	*League App*	*Gls*
Nicky Morgan	5 10	12 08	30 10 59	East Ham	Apprentice	West Ham U	21	2
						Portsmouth	95	32
						Stoke C	75	20
Carl Saunders	5 8	10 12	25 11 64	Marston Green	Local	Stoke C	142	22
Graham Shaw	5 8	10 01	7 6 67	Newcastle	Apprentice	Stoke C	99	18
Simon Stainrod	5 10	12 09	1 2 59	Sheffield	Apprentice	Sheffield U	67	14
						Oldham Ath	69	21
						QPR	145	48
						Sheffield W	15	2
						Aston Villa	63	16
						Stoke C	28	6
						Strasbourg (loan)	—	—

Trainees
Baines, Paul; Boughey, Darren J; Duncan, Mark A; Gallimore, Anthony M; Hope, Darren; Jones, Stephen R; Lewis, Kevin; McGinley, Mark P; Morris, Christopher S; Noble, Daniel W.T; Reaney, Scott; Ritchie, David M; Sale, Mark D; Venables, Craig T; Venning, Ryan P; Wilson, Robert J; Wright, Ian M.

Associated Schoolboys
Amesbury, Martin P; Bright, David; Coker, Jonathan P; Davies, Andrew; Hanson, Jonathan M; Lees, Ian W; Martin, Daniel; Percival, Jason C; Wileman, Matthew L.

SUNDERLAND 1988–89 *Back row (left to right):* Colin Pascoe, John Cornforth, Gary Owers, Gary Bennett, John MacPhail, Gordon Armstrong, Richard Ord, Ricardo Gabbiadini. *Centre row:* Steve Smelt, Malcolm Crosby, Frank Gray, Tom Lynch, Michael Heathcote, Ian Hesford, Tim Carter, Barry Richardson, Sean Wharton, Paul McKenzie, John Hepple, Chris McMenemy, Jim Morrow.
Front row: John Kay, Paul Lemon, Marco Gabbiadini, Steve Doyle, Viv Busby, Denis Smith (Manager), Gary Ogilvie, Reuben Agboola, Anthony Cullen, Eric Gates.

Division 2 SUNDERLAND

Roker Park Ground, Sunderland. Telephone Sunderland 091 5140332. Commercial Dept: 091-5672275.

Ground capacity: 37,787.

Record attendance: 75,118 v Derby Co, FA Cup 6th rd replay, 8 Mar, 1933.

Record receipts: £111,165 v Chelsea, Milk Cup Semi-final 1st leg, 13 Feb, 1985.

Pitch measurements: 113yd × 74yd.

Chairman: R. S. Murray FCCA.

Director: G. Davidson FCA., G. W. Hodgson.

Associate Directors: J. Donnolly, G. S. Wood.

Manager: Denis Smith.

General Manager/Secretary: G. Davidson FCA.

Chief Coach: Viv Busby. ***Coach:***

Physio: Steve Smelt. ***Reserve Coach:*** R. Jones. ***Youth Coach:*** Malcolm Crosby.

Commercial Manager: Alec King.

Year Formed: 1879. ***Turned Professional:*** 1886. ***Ltd Co.:*** 1906.

Club Nickname: Rokermen.

Previous Grounds: 1879, Blue House Field, Hendon; 1882, Groves Field, Ashbrooke; 1883, Horatio Street; 1884, Abbs Field, Fulwell; 1886, Newcastle Road; 1898, Roker Park.

Previous Name: 1879–80, Sunderland and District Teacher's AFC.

Record League Victory: 9-1 v Newcastle U, Division 1, 5 December 1908 – Roose; Forster, Melton; Daykin, Thomson, Low; Mordue, Hogg (4), Brown, Holley (3), Bridgett (2).

Record Cup Victory: 11-1 v Fairfield, FA Cup, 1st rd, 2 February 1895 – Doig; McNeill, Johnston; Dunlop, McCreadie (1), Wilson; Gillespie (1), Millar (5), Campbell, Hannah (3), Scott (1).

Record Defeat: 0-8 v West Ham U, Division 1, 19 October, 1968 and v Watford, Division 1, 25 September, 1982.

Most League Points (2 for a win): 63, Division 3 (N), 1926–27.

Most League Points (3 for a win): 93, Division 3, 1987–88.

Most League Goals: 109, Division 1, 1935–36.

Highest League Scorer in Season: Dave Halliday, 43, Division 1, 1928–29.

Most League Goals in Total Aggregate: Charlie Buchan, 209, 1911–25.

Most Capped Player: Martin Harvey, 34, Northern Ireland.

Most League Appearances: Jim Montgomery, 537, 1962–77.

Record Transfer Fee Received: £275,000 from Manchester C for Dennis Tueart, March 1974, from Manchester U for Chris Turner, August 1985 and from Sheffield W for Mark Proctor, September 1987.

Record Transfer Fee Paid: £450,000 to Hull C for Tony Norman, December 1988.

Football League Record: 1890 Elected to Division 1; 1958–64 Division 2; 1964–70 Division 1; 1970–76 Division 2; 1976–77 Division 1; 1977–80 Division 2; 1980–85 Division 1; 1985–87 Division 2; 1987–88 Division 3; 1988– Division 2.

Honours: *Football League:* Division 1 – Champions 1891–92, 1892–93, 1894–95, 1901–02, 1912–13, 1935–36; Runners-up 1893–94; 1897–98, 1900–01, 1922–23, 1934–35; Division 2 – Champions 1975–76; Runners-up 1963–64, 1979–80; Division 3 – Champions 1987–88. *FA Cup:* Winners 1937 1973; Runners-up 1913. *Football League Cup:* Runners-up 1984–85. **European Competitions:** *Cup-Winners' Cup:* 1973–74.

Colours: Red and white striped shirts, black shorts, red stockings white turnover. **Change Colours:** Blue shirts, white shorts, blue stockings white turnover.

Largest non-season ticket membership scheme in Football League over 35,000 members.

SUNDERLAND 1988–89 LEAGUE RECORD

Match No.	Date	Venue	Opponents	Result	H/T Score	Lg. Pos.	Goalscorers	Attendance
1	Aug 27	H	Bournemouth	D 1-1	1-1	—	Bennett	17,998
2	Sept 3	A	Ipswich T	L 0-2	0-1	19		12,835
3	10	H	Bradford C	D 0-0	0-0	18		16,286
4	17	A	Birmingham C	L 2-3	0-1	22	Pascoe 2	6871
5	20	H	Crystal Palace	D 1-1	0-1	—	Pascoe	13,150
6	24	A	Shrewsbury T	D 0-0	0-0	21		4,195
7	Oct 1	H	Oldham Ath	W 3-2	2-2	20	Gabbiadini, MacPhail (pen), Pascoe	12,529
8	4	H	Leeds U	W 2-1	1-0	—	Gabbiadini, Whitehurst	12,671
9	8	A	Walsall	L 0-2	0-0	20		6150
10	15	A	Hull C	D 0-0	0-0	19		8261
11	22	H	Swindon T	W 4-0	2-0	14	Owers, Gabbiadini 2, Whitehurst	13,520
12	25	H	Blackburn R	W 2-0	2-0	—	Gabbiadini, Hendry (og)	16,601
13	29	A	Manchester C	D 1-1	1-1	13	Armstrong	22,398
14	Nov 2	A	Oxford U	W 4-2	3-1	—	Whitehurst, Armstrong, Gabbiadini, MacPhail (pen)	6270
15	5	H	Stoke C	D 1-1	0-1	8	Doyle	17,923
16	12	A	Chelsea	D 1-1	1-0	9	Gabbiadini	19,210
17	19	H	WBA	D 1-1	0-1	10	Bennett	18,141
18	26	A	Brighton & HA	L 0-3	0-1	12		10,039
19	Dec 3	H	Watford	D 1-1	0-1	14	MacPhail (pen)	16,330
20	10	A	Leicester C	L 1-3	0-2	16	Pascoe	11,093
21	18	A	Plymouth Arg	W 4-1	2-0	—	Armstrong, Pascoe, Gabbiadini, Gates	13,498
22	26	H	Barnsley	W 1-0	0-0	9	Dobbin (og)	21,994
23	31	H	Portsmouth	W 4-0	2-0	8	Gates, Ord, Armstrong, Pascoe	21,566
24	Jan 2	A	Bradford C	L 0-1	0-0	10		12,186
25	14	H	Oxford U	W 1-0	1-0	6	Owers	12,853
26	21	A	Bournemouth	W 1-0	1-0	6	Gates	8992
27	Feb 4	A	Leeds U	L 0-2	0-1	10		31,984
28	11	H	Walsall	L 0-3	0-1	11		14,203
29	18	A	Swindon T	L 1-4	1-3	13	Armstrong	7432
30	25	H	Hull C	W 2-0	0-0	10	Pascoe, Gabbiadini	14,719
31	28	A	Blackburn R	D 2-2	2-0	—	Gabbiadini 2 (1 pen)	8288
32	Mar 11	A	Stoke C	L 0-2	0-1	14		12,489
33	14	H	Manchester C	L 2-4	1-3	—	Gabbiadini, Gates	16,101
34	18	A	Crystal Palace	L 0-1	0-0	14		9108
35	21	H	Chelsea	L 1-2	1-1	—	Gabbiadini	14,714
36	25	H	Ipswich T	W 4-0	1-0	13	Gabbiadini 3 (1 pen), Owers	13,859
37	27	A	Barnsley	L 0-3	0-1	14		8070
38	Apr 1	H	Birmingham C	D 2-2	1-0	15	Lemon, Gabbiadini	10,969
39	4	H	Plymouth Arg	W 2-1	2-0	—	Armstrong 2	8003
40	8	A	Portsmouth	L 0-2	0-1	14		7724
41	15	A	Oldham Ath	D 2-2	2-1	14	MacPhail, Hauser	5944
42	22	H	Shrewsbury T	W 2-1	1-0	13	Hauser, Armstrong	9427
43	29	H	Brighton & HA	W 1-0	1-0	12	Pascoe	12,856
44	May 1	A	Watford	W 1-0	1-0	11	Gabbiadini	13,499
45	6	A	WBA	D 0-0	0-0	11		10,451
46	13	H	Leicester C	D 2-2	0-0	11	Bennett, Pascoe	15,819

Final League Position: 11

GOALSCORERS

League (60): Gabbiadini 18 (2 pens), Pascoe 10, Armstrong 8, Gates 4, MacPhail 4 (3 pens), Bennett 3, Owers 3, Whitehurst 3, Hauser 2, Doyle 1, Lemon 1, Ord 1, own goals 2.
Littlewoods Cup (5): Gabbiadini 3, Pascoe 2.
FA Cup (1): Ord 1.

Littlewoods Cup	First Round	York C (a)	0-0
		(h)	4-0
	Second Round	West Ham U (h)	0-3
		(a)	1-2
FA Cup	Third Round	Oxford U (h)	1-1
		(a)	0-2

Hesford	Kay	Agboola	Bennett	MacPhail	Doyle	Lemon	Armstrong	Gates	Gabbiadini	Pascoe	Owers	Ord	Gray	Cornforth	Whitehurst	Lynch	Carter	Norman	Cullen	Barnes	Hauser	Hay	Atkinson	Williams	Wharton	Hawke	Ogilvie	*Match No.*
1	2	3	4	5	6	7	8	9*	10	11	12																	1
1	2	3	4	5*	6	7†	8	9	10	11		12	14															2
1	2		4	5	6		8	9	10*	11	7		3	12														3
1	2		4	5	6		8*	9		11	7		3	12	10													4
1	2	3	4	5	6		8	9*	12	11	7†		14		10													5
1	2	3	4	5	6		8	9*		11	7			12	10													6
1		3		5	6		8		9	11	7	4	2		10													7
1		3		5	6		8		9	11	7	4	2		10													8
1		3		5	6		8	12	9	11	7	4	2		10*													9
1		3		5	6		8	12	9	11	7	4	2		10*													10
1		3	12	5	6		8		9	11	7	4	2*		10													11
1		3		5	6		8		9	11	7	4	2		10													12
1		3		5	6		8		9	11	7	4	2		10													13
1		3	12	5	6		8		9	11	7	4*	2		10													14
1		3*	12	5	6		8		9	11	7	4	2		10													15
1	7		4	5	6†		8	12	9*	11			2		10	3											14	16
1			4	5	6*		8	12	9	11	7		2		10	3												17
1		3	4	5	6*		8	12	9	11	7	14	2†		10													18
1		3	4	5	6		8		9	11	7		2		10													19
1		3	4†	5	6		8	12	9	11	7	14	2		10*													20
			2	5	6		8	9	10	11	7	4	3				1											21
			2	5	6		8	9	10	11	7	4	3				1											22
		14	2	5	6*		8	9	10	11	7	4	3†	12				1										23
			2	5	6	7	8	9	10		11	4	3					1										24
		12	2	5*		7	8	9		11	6	4	3	10				1										25
		12	2	5			8	9	10	11	7	4	3	6*				1										26
			2	5	6	12	8	9		11	7*	4	3	10				1										27
		7*	2	5	6		8	9		11		4	3	10				1	12									28
		12	2	5	6		8	9		11		4*	3	10				1	14	7†								29
		4	2	5	6		8	9*	10†	11			3	12				1	7		14							30
		4	2	5	6		8	9*	10	11			3					1	7		12							31
		4	2	5	6		8	9*	10	11	14		3					1	7†		12							32
		4	2	5	6*		8	9	10	11	7		3†					1	14		12							33
		4†	2	5	6	14	8	9*	10		7	11	3					1			12							34
			2	5		11	8		10		7	6	3			4		1			9							35
			2	5		14	8	12	10	11	7	6	3					1			9*	4†						36
			2	5	4†	14	8	12	10	11	7	6	3					1			9*							37
	2		5			4	8	9	10	11*	7	6	3					1	12†		14							38
			2	5		4	8	9	10		7	6	3					1					11*	12				39
	3		2	5	7	4*	8	10				6	12					1					11		9†	14		40
			2	5		7		10			8	6	3	4		11*		1			9		12					41
	3		2	5		7	8	10*			11	6		4				1			9					12		42
	3†		2	5		4	8	12		11	7	6	14	10				1								9*		43
		3	2	5		14	8	10*	9	11	7	6		4†				1								12		44
		3	2	5	8	4	11	9*	10	7		6						1			12							45
		3	2	5		14	11	12	10	7	4	6†		8*				1			9							46
20	11	25 + 4s	37 + 3s	45	35	12 + 6s	45	27 + 10s	35 + 1s	39	36 + 2s	31 + 3s	36 + 4s	10 + 5s	17	4	2	24	3 + 4s	1	6 + 7s	1	2 + 1s	— + 1s	1	1 + 3s	— + 1s	

SUNDERLAND

Player and Position	Ht	Wt	Birth Date	Birth Place	Source	Clubs	League App	League Gls
Goalkeepers								
Tim Carter	6 1	12 00	5 10 67	Bristol	Apprentice	Bristol R	47	—
						Newport Co (loan)	1	—
						Sunderland	3	—
						Carlisle U (loan)	4	—
						Bristol C (loan)	3	—
Tony Norman	6 2	12 08	24 2 58	Mancot	Amateur	Burnley	—	—
						Hull C	372	—
						Sunderland	24	—
Defenders								
Reuben Agboola	5 9	11 02	30 5 62	London	Apprentice	Southampton	90	—
						Sunderland	98	—
						Charlton Ath (loan)	1	—
Gary Bennett	6 1	12 01	4 12 61	Manchester	Amateur	Manchester C	—	—
						Cardiff C	87	11
						Sunderland	184	15
Frankie Gray‡	5 10	11 10	27 10 54	Glasgow	Apprentice	Leeds U	193	17
						Nottingham F	81	5
						Leeds U	142	10
						Sunderland	146	8
Alan Hay	6 0	12 06	28 11 58	Dunfermine	Amateur	Bolton W	—	—
						Bristol C	74	1
						St Mirren (loan)	—	—
						York C	150	3
						Tranmere R	28	—
						York C	1	—
						Sunderland	1	—
Mike Heathcote	6 2	12 05	10 9 65	Durham		Middlesbrough	—	—
					Spennymoor U	Sunderland	1	—
						Halifax T (loan)	7	1
John Hepple*	5 7	9 05	12 3 70	Cleveland	Trainee	Sunderland	—	—
						Hartlepool U (loan)	2	—
John Kay	5 10	11 06	29 1 64	Sunderland	Apprentice	Arsenal	14	—
						Wimbledon	63	2
						Middlesbrough	8	—
						(loan)	57	—
						Sunderland		
John MacPhail	6 0	12 03	7 12 55	Dundee	St Columba's	Dundee	68	—
						Sheffield U	135	7
						York C	142	24
						Bristol C	26	1
						Sunderland	91	20
Gary Ogilvie‡	5 10	12 02	16 11 67	Dundee	Dundee	Sunderland	1	—
Richard Ord	6 2	12 08	3 3 70	Easington	Trainee	Sunderland	42	1
Midfield								
Gordon Armstrong	6 0	11 02	15 7 67	Newcastle	Apprentice	Sunderland	141	20
Brian Atkinson§			19 1 71	Darlington	Trainee	Sunderland	3	—
Peter Barnes‡	5 10	11 00	10 6 57	Manchester	Apprentice	Manchester C	115	15
						WBA	77	23
						Leeds U	30	1
					Betis	Leeds	27	4
						Manchester U (loan)	—	—
						Coventry	18	2
						Manchester U	20	2
						Manchester C	8	—
						Hull C	11	—
						Port Vale (loan)	3	—
						Bolton W (loan)	2	—
						Bolton W	3	—
						Sunderland	1	—

SUNDERLAND

Foundation: A Scottish schoolmaster named James Allan, working at Hendon Boarding School, took the initiative in the foundation of Sunderland in 1879 when they were formed as The Sunderland and District Teachers' Association FC at a meeting in the Adults School, Norfolk Street. Because of financial difficulties, they quickly allowed members from outside the teaching profession and so became Sunderland AFC in October 1880.

Managers (and Secretary-managers)
Tom Watson 1888–96, Bob Campbell 1896–99, Alex Mackie 1899–1905, Bob Kyle 1905–28, Johnny Cochrane 1928–39, Bill Murray 1939–57, Alan Brown 1957–64, George Hardwick 1964–65, Ian McColl 1965–68, Alan Brown 1968–72, Bob Stokoe 1972–76, Jimmy Adamson 1976–78, Ken Knighton 1979–81, Alan Durban 1981–84, Len Ashurst 1984–85, Lawrie McMenemy 1985–87, Denis Smith 1987– .

Player and Position	*Ht*	*Wt*	*Birth Date*	*Birth Place*	*Source*	*Clubs*	*League App*	*League Gls*
John Cornforth	6 1	11 05	7 10 67	Whitley Bay	Apprentice	Sunderland	28	2
						Doncaster R (loan)	7	3
Steve Doyle	5 9	11 09	2 6 58	Port Talbot	Apprentice	Preston NE	197	8
						Huddersfield T	161	6
						Sunderland	100	2
Ricardo Gabbiadini			11 3 70	Newport	Trainee	York C	1	—
						Sunderland	—	—
Tommy Lynch	6 0	12 06	10 10 64	Limerick	Limerick	Sunderland	4	—
Gary Owers	5 10	11 10	3 10 68	Newcastle	Apprentice	Sunderland	75	7
Paul Williams§			25 9 70	Liverpool	Trainee	Sunderland	1	—
Forwards								
Tony Cullen	5 6	11 07	30 9 69	Newcastle		Sunderland	7	—
Marco Gabbiadini	5 10	11 02	20 1 68	Nottingham	Apprentice	York C	60	14
						Sunderland	71	39
Eric Gates	5 6	10 08	28 6 55	Ferryhill	Apprentice	Ipswich T	296	73
						Sunderland	145	37
Thomas Hauser	6 3	12 06	10 4 65	West Germany	Berne OB	Sunderland	13	2
Warren Hawke			20 9 70	Durham	Trainee	Sunderland	4	—
Paul Lemon	5 10	11 07	3 6 66	Middles-brough	Apprentice	Sunderland	107	15
						Carlisle U (loan)	2	—
Paul McKenzie*	5 9	11 08	4 10 69	Aberdeen	Apprentice	Sunderland	—	—
						Preston NE (loan)	—	—
Colin Pascoe	5 9	10 00	9 4 65	Bridgend	Apprentice	Swansea C	174	39
						Sunderland	48	14
Sean Wharton‡	5 10	11 04	31 10 68	Newport	Trainee	Sunderland	1	—

Trainees
Armstrong, Andrew; Atkinson, Brian; Bone, William; Brady, Keiron; Bramwell, Derek J; Callender, Anthony D; Cuggy, Michael S; Fox, Andrew G; Gray, Martin; Guthrie, Simon; Morton, Lee; Rush, David; Sams, Andrew G; Smith, Anthony; Snowball, David; Trigg, Jonathan M; Walls, Wayne M; Williams, Paul L.

Associated Schoolboys
Atkinson, Jonathan; Barrass, Keith D; Brodie, Stephen; Egen, Jonathan; Gooding, Robert; Hails, Stuart A; Harwood, Paul; Johnson, Neil; Lawson, Ian D; Maskell, Stuart; Morson, David; Redman, Stephen; Robinson, Anthony; Russell, Craig S; Scothern, Andrew; Smith, Anthony; Smith, Martin; Wales, David J.

SWANSEA CITY 1988–89 *Back row (left to right):* Ron Walton, Joe Allon, David Hough, Ian Love, Andrew Melville, Lee Jones, Alan Knill, Chris Coleman, Dudley Lewis, David D'Auria, Ken Davey (Physiotherapist).

Front row: Alan Davies, Bryan Wade, Steve Thornber, Tommy Hutchison, Robbie James, Terry Yorath (Manager), Peter Bodak, Paul Raynor, Ian Marsh.

Division 3 **SWANSEA CITY**

Vetch Field, Swansea. Telephone Swansea (0792) 474114. Club shop and Commercial Office 0792 462584

Ground capacity: 26,237.

Record attendance: 32,796 v Arsenal, FA Cup 4th rd, 17 Feb, 1968.

Record receipts: £36,477.42 v Liverpool, Division 1, 18 Sept, 1982.

Pitch measurements: 112yd × 74yd.

President: I. C. Pursey MBE.

Chairman: D. J. Sharpe.

Directors: D. G. Hammond, M. Griffiths, H. Hyde F.INST.D.

Manager: Ian Evans. ***Assistant Manager:***

Player-Coach: Tommy Hutchison. ***Physio:*** Ken Davey.

Commercial and Marketing Manager: David Easton.

Year Formed: 1912. ***Turned Professional:*** 1912. ***Ltd Co.:*** 1912.

Club Nickname: 'The Swans'.

Secretary: George Taylor.

Previous Name: Swansea Town until Feb 1970.

Record League Victory: 8-0 v Hartlepool U, Division 4, 1 April 1978 – Barber; Evans, Bartley, Lally (1) (Morris), May, Bruton, Kevin Moore, Robbie James (3 incl. 1p), Curtis (3), Toshack (1), Chappell.

Record Cup Victory: 12-0 v Sliema W (Malta), ECWC 1st rd (1st leg). 15 September 1982 – Davies; Marustik, Hadziabdic (1), Irwin (1), Kennedy, Rajkovic (1), Loveridge (2) (Leighton James), Robbie James, Charles (2), Stevenson (1), Latchford (1) (Walsh (3)).

Record Defeat: 1-8 v Fulham, Division 2, 22 January, 1938.

Most League Points (2 for a win): 62, Division 3 (S), 1948–49.

Most League Points (3 for a win): 70, Division 4, 1987–88.

Most League Goals: 90, Division 2, 1956–57.

Highest League Scorer in Season: Cyril Pearce, 35, Division 2, 1931–32.

Most League Goals in Total Aggregate: Ivor Allchurch, 166, 1949–58, 1965–68.

Most Capped Player: Ivor Allchurch, 42 (68), Wales.

Most League Appearances: Wilfred Milne, 585, 1919–37.

Record Transfer Fee Received: £370,000 from Leeds U for Alan Curtis, May 1979.

Record Transfer Fee Paid: £340,000 to Liverpool for Colin Irwin, August 1981.

Football League Record: 1920 Original Member of Division 3; 1921–25 Division 3 (S); 1925–47 Division 2; 1947–49 Division 3 (S); 1949–65 Division 2; 1965–67 Division 3; 1967–70 Division 4; 1970–73 Division 3; 1973–78 Division 4; 1978–79 Division 3; 1979–81 Division 2; 1981–83 Division 1; 1983–84 Division 2; 1984–86 Division 3; 1986–88 Division 4; 1988– Division 3.

Honours: *Football League:* Division 1 best season: 6th 1981–82; Division 2 – Promoted 1980–81 (3rd); Division 3 (S) – Champions 1924–25, 1948–49; Division 3 – Promoted 1978–79 (3rd); Division 4 – Promoted 1969–70 (3rd), 1977–78 (3rd). *FA Cup:* Semi-finals 1926, 1964. *Football League Cup* best season; 4th rd, 1964–65, 1976–77. *Welsh Cup:* Winners 8 times: Runners-up 8 times. **European Competitions:** *European Cup-Winners' Cup:* 1961–62, 1966–67, 1981–82, 1982–83, 1983–84.

Colours: White shirts, white shorts, black stockings. **Change Colours:** All red.

SWANSEA CITY 1988–89 LEAGUE RECORD

Match No.	Date	Venue	Opponents	Result	H/T Score	Lg. Pos.	Goalscorers	Attendance
1	Aug 27	A	Gillingham	W 3-2	1-1	—	Knill, James 2 (1 pen)	4437
2	Sept 3	H	Bury	D 1-1	1-0	5	James	5141
3	10	A	Southend U	W 2-0	1-0	—	Raynor, Melville	4357
4	17	H	Brentford	D 1-1	0-0	4	Melville	5015
5	24	H	Wolverhampton W	L 2-5	1-3	9	Holdsworth, Melville	5240
6	Oct 1	A	Bristol C	L 0-2	0-1	17		7786
7	4	H	Bolton W	W 1-0	0-0	—	James	3283
8	9	A	Aldershot	W 1-0	1-0	—	D'Auria	2809
9	15	H	Northampton T	W 1-0	1-0	6	D'Auria	4583
10	22	H	Fulham	W 2-0	1-0	4	Davies, Hutchison	4737
11	25	A	Huddersfield T	D 1-1	0-0	—	Davies	5711
12	29	H	Preston NE	D 1-1	0-1	7	Melville	5370
13	Nov 1	A	Wigan Ath	W 2-1	1-1	—	Melville, Hutchison	2432
14	5	A	Chester C	L 1-3	0-2	4	Melville	2263
15	8	H	Mansfield T	W 3-1	0-0	—	Wade, Bodak, Davies	3526
16	12	A	Port Vale	L 1-2	1-2	5	Melville	6248
17	26	A	Blackpool	D 0-0	0-0	5		3443
18	Dec 3	H	Sheffield U	D 2-2	0-1	6	Wade, Melville	5676
19	17	H	Chesterfield	W 2-0	1-0	4	Davies, Bodak	3656
20	26	A	Cardiff C	D 2-2	2-2	5	Puckett, Davies	10,675
21	31	A	Bristol R	D 1-1	1-1	5	Puckett	4803
22	Jan 2	H	Reading	W 2-0	0-0	4	Wade, James	6772
23	7	H	Notts Co	W 2-0	1-0	3	James, Wade	5808
24	14	A	Bury	L 0-1	0-0	3		2608
25	21	H	Southend U	W 2-0	1-0	3	Puckett, Raynor	3388
26	Feb 3	H	Bristol C	D 1-1	0-1	—	James (pen)	6523
27	11	A	Bolton W	L 0-1	0-0	6		4178
28	17	H	Aldershot	W 1-0	0-0	—	Bodak	4922
29	25	A	Northampton T	L 0-1	0-0	5		3900
30	Mar 4	A	Fulham	L 0-1	0-0	7		4710
31	11	H	Chester C	D 1-1	1-1	7	Melville	4311
32	14	A	Preston NE	D 1-1	0-1	—	Knill	8975
33	19	H	Gillingham	W 3-2	2-0	—	West, Bodak, Raynor	4252
34	22	H	Huddersfield T	W 1-0	1-0	—	James (pen)	4075
35	25	A	Reading	L 0-2	0-1	7		4367
36	27	H	Cardiff C	D 1-1	0-1	6	Raynor	9201
37	Apr 1	A	Chesterfield	L 0-2	0-0	7		3349
38	4	A	Notts Co	L 0-1	0-1	—		3940
39	8	H	Bristol R	L 1-2	1-1	9	Melville	5645
40	15	H	Wigan Ath	L 1-2	0-1	11	West	3719
41	22	A	Wolverhampton W	D 1-1	0-1	11	West	13,921
42	29	H	Port Vale	D 0-0	0-0	11		4229
43	May 2	A	Mansfield T	D 0-0	0-0	—		2550
44	6	A	Sheffield U	L 1-5	0-2	11	James (pen)	15,383
45	9	A	Brentford	D 1-1	1-0	—	Hutchison	4415
46	13	H	Blackpool	L 1-2	1-1	12	Raynor	3494

Final League Position: 12

GOALSCORERS

League (51): Melville 10, James 9 (4 pens), Davies 5, Raynor 5, Bodak 4, Wade 4, Hutchison 3, Puckett 3, West 3, D'Auria 2, Knill 2, Holdsworth 1.
Littlewoods Cup (1): Thornber 1.
FA Cup (6): Melville 2, Wade 2, Coleman 1, Hutchison 1.

Littlewoods Cup	First Round	Cardiff C (a)	1-0
		(h)	0-2
FA Cup	First Round	Northampton T (h)	3-1
	Second Round	Colchester U (a)	2-2
		(h)	1-3

Wilmot	Hough	Coleman	Melville	Knill	James	Thornber	Wade	Love	Davies	Raynor	Holdsworth	Hutchison	Allon	D'Auria	Legg	Bodak	Lewis	Davey	Bracey	Puckett	Phillips	West	Match No.
1	2	3	4	5	6	7	8*	9	10	11	12												1
1	2	3	4	5	6	7		9	10	11*	8	12											2
1	2	3	4	5	6	7			10	11	8	9											3
1	2	3	4	5	6	7*			10	8	9	11†	12	14									4
1	2	3	4	5	6	7	10		8*		9	12		11									5
1	2		4†	5	6	7		12		8			9*	14	3	10	11						6
1	2	3		5	6		12	8				9		4		10	11	7*					7
1	2	3	12	5	6			8				9		4		10*	11	7					8
1		3	2	5	6		12	8				9		4		10	11	7*					9
1		3	2	5	6	7			8			9		4		10	11						10
1	12	3	2	5	6	7	14		8			9		4*		10†	11						11
1	12	3	2	5		7	10	8*	6			9		4†		14	11						12
1	4	3	2	5	8	7	10		6			9					11						13
1	4†	3	2	5	6	7*	8	12	10			9				14	11						14
1	4*	3	2	5	6		8	12	10			9				7	11						15
1	4*	3	2	5	8	14	10	12	6			9				7†	11						16
	4	3	2		8	7	10*	12	6			9					11		1	5			17
	4	3	2		8	7	10		6			9					11		1	5			18
	4	3	2	5	8	7		12	6*			9				10	11		1				19
	4	3	2	5	8	7			6			9					11		1	10			20
	4	3	2	5	8	7			6			9					11		1	10			21
	4	3	2	5	8	7*	12		6			9					11		1	10			22
	4		2	5	8	12	3		6			10					11		1	7*	9		23
	4		2	5	8	7†	3*		6			10		14			11		1	12	9		24
	4	3	2	5	6			11	8	12		10		14		7†			1	9*			25
	14*	3	4	5	6	7†	10		8	12		11					2		1		9		26
	2*	3	9	5	6		10		8	12		11		7†			4		1		14		27
	2	3	5		6		10		8			11				7	4		1		9		28
	2	3	10	5	6			12	8	9		11		7*			4		1				29
	2	3	10	5	6		7†		8	9		11*		14		12	4		1				30
		3	2	5	6		10		8	9		11				7	4		1				31
		3	2	5	6		7		8	9		11				10	4		1				32
	12	3	2	5	6				8	9		11*				7	4		1			10	33
	12	3	2	5	6				8	9		11				7*	4		1			10	34
	12	3	2	5	6		14		8	9		11†				7*	4		1			10	35
	7	3*	2	5	6	12	14		8	9		11					4		1			10†	36
	7*	3	2	5	6	12	14		8†	9		11					4		1			10	37
	7	3	2	5		6	12		8	9		11					4		1			10*	38
	12	3	2	5	7	6			8	9*		11					4		1		14	10†	39
	7	3	2	5	6				8	9		11				12	4		1			10*	40
	7*	3	2	5		6			8	9		11				12	4		1			10	41
		3	2	5		6			8	9		11			7		4		1			10	42
		3	2	5		6			8	9		11			7	12	4		1			10*	43
	14	3	2	5	12	6			8	9†		11			7*		4		1			10	44
	14	3†	2	5	12	6			8	9		11			7*		4		1			10	45
	14	3†	2	5	12	6			8	9		11*			7		4		1			10	46
16	30 + 10s	43	44 + 1s	43	38 + 3s	27 + 4s	17 + 8s	7 + 7s	42	23 + 3s	4 + 1s	42 + 2s	1 + 1s	9 + 5s	6	16 + 6s	40	3	30	7 + 1s	4 + 2s	14	

SWANSEA CITY

Player and Position	Ht	Wt	Birth Date	Birth Place	Source	Clubs	League App	League Gls
Goalkeepers								
Lee Bracey	6 1	12 08	11 9 68	Ashford	Trainee	West Ham U	—	—
						Swansea C	30	—
Lee Jones	6 2	12 10	9 8 70	Pontypridd	Trainee	Swansea C	—	—
Defenders								
Chris Coleman	6 2	12 10	10 6 70	Swansea	Apprentice	Swansea C	73	—
Alan Knill	6 2	10 09	8 10 64	Slough	Apprentice	Southampton	—	—
						Halifax T	118	6
						Swansea C	89	3
John Lewis‡	5 9	11 03	15 10 55	Tredegar	Pontlanfraith	Cardiff C	140	9
						Newport Co	153	8
						Swansea C	25	—
Dudley Lewis	5 10	10 09	17 11 62	Swansea	Apprentice	Swansea C	230	2
Andy Melville	6 1	12 06	29 11 68	Swansea	School	Swansea C	129	17
Des Trick	6 0	12 00	7 11 69	Swansea	Trainee	Swansea C	—	—
Midfield								
Peter Bodak*	5 8	9 10	12 8 61	Birmingham	Apprentice	Coventry C	32	5
						Manchester U	—	—
						Manchester C	14	1
						Walsall	—	—
						Crewe Alex	53	7
						Swansea C	31	4
Alan Davies	5 8	11 04	5 12 61	Manchester	Apprentice	Manchester U	7	—
						Newcastle U	21	1
						Charlton Ath (loan)	1	—
						Carlisle U (loan)	4	1
						Swansea C	84	8
David D'Auria	5 8	11 00	26 3 70	Swansea	Trainee	Swansea C	18	2
David Hough	5 11	11 02	20 2 66	Crewe	Apprentice	Swansea C	149	8
Tommy Hutchison†	5 11	11 02	22 9 47	Cardenden	Dundonald B	Alloa	68	4
						Blackpool	165	10
						Coventry C	314	24
					Bulova	Manchester C	46	4
						Burnley	92	4
						Swansea C	133	7
Martyn James*	5 10	10 08	22 2 69	Swansea	Trainee	Swansea C	—	—
Andy Legg	5 8	10 07	28 7 66	Neath	Briton Ferry	Swansea	6	—
Ian Marsh*	5 7	9 09	27 10 69	Swansea	Trainee	Swansea C	1	—
Steve Thornber	5 10	11 02	11 10 65	Dewsbury	Local	Halifax T	104	4
						Swansea C	31	—
Forwards								
Simon Davey§			1 10 70	Swansea	Trainee	Swansea C	8	—
Robbie James	5 11	13 00	23 3 57	Swansea	Apprentice	Swansea C	394	99
						Stoke C	48	6
						QPR	87	4
						Leicester C	23	—
						Swansea C	60	12

SWANSEA CITY

Foundation: The earliest Association Football in Wales was played in the Northern part of the country and no international took place in the South until 1894, when a local paper still thought it necessary to publish an outline of the rules and an illustration of the pitch markings. There had been an earlier Swansea club, but this has no connection with Swansea Town (now City) formed at a public meeting in June 1912.

Managers (and Secretary-managers)
Walter Whittaker 1912–14, William Bartlett 1914–15, Joe Bradshaw 1919–26, Jimmy Thomson 1927–31, Neil Harris 1934–39, Haydn Green 1939–47, Bill McCandless 1947–55, Ron Burgess 1955–58, Trevor Morris 1958–65, Glyn Davies 1965–66, Billy Lucas 1967–69, Roy Bentley 1969–72, Harry Gregg 1972–75, Harry Griffiths 1975–77, John Toshack 1978–83 (resigned October re-appointed in December) 1983–84, Colin Appleton 1984, John Bond 1984–85, Tommy Hutchison 1985–86, Terry Yorath 1986–89, Ian Evans 1989– .

Player and Position	*Ht*	*Wt*	*Birth Date*	*Birth Place*	*Source*	*Clubs*	*League App*	*League Gls*
Ray Pennock*	5 10	10 08	21 12 69	Swansea	Trainee	Swansea C	—	—
Stewart Phillips	6 0	11 07	30 12 61	Halifax	Amateur	Hereford U	293	83
						WBA	15	4
						Swansea C	6	—
Paul Raynor	6 0	11 04	29 4 66	Nottingham	Apprentice	Nottingham F	3	—
						Bristol R (loan)	8	—
						Huddersfield T	50	9
						Swansea C	82	14
						Wrexham (loan)	6	—
Cameron Toshack	6 2	12 00	2 3 70	Cardiff	Trainee	Swansea C	—	—
Bryan Wade	5 8	11 05	25 6 63	Bath	Trowbridge T	Swindon T	60	19
						Swansea C	25	4

Trainees
Baldwin, Nicholas; Bowen, Jason; Corcoran, Glen; Davey, Simon; Davies, Wayne; Evans, Philip; Heeps, James; Jenkins, Stephen; Johnson, Alec; Lloyd, Peter; Owen, Julian; Prew, Jason; Thomas, Jason.

****Non-Contract**
Hutchinson, Thomas.

Associated Schoolboys
Brown, Lee J; Morris, Ceri L.

SWINDON TOWN 1988–89 *Back row (left to right):* Liam Dixon, Gavin Sandrey, Charlie Henry, Fraser Digby, Nicky Hammond, Tim Parkin, Adrian Viveash, Dean Casserly.
Third row: Dave Barnett, Dave Hockaday, Phil King, Duncan Shearer, Jon Gittens, Ross MacLaren, Steve White, Leigh Barnard, Fitzroy Simpson.
Second row: Neil Tomlinson, Bobby Barnes, Peter Coyne, Paul Bodin, Colin Calderwood, Steve Foley, Alan McLouglin, Mark Jones, Gary Marshall.
Front row: Paul Hunt, Richard Morgan, Richard Walker, Tony Hammersley, Paul Thompson, Mark Lea, Nicky Summerbee, Paul Trollope, Alex Graham.

Division 2 **SWINDON TOWN**

County Ground, Swindon, Wiltshire. Telephone Swindon (0793) 642984. Fax: 642984 (9am–5pm) or 36170 x35 (after 5pm).

Ground capacity: 19,652.

Record attendance: 32,000 v Arsenal, FA Cup 3rd rd, 15 Jan, 1972.

Record receipts: £56,024 v Tottenham H, FA Cup 4th rd, 26 Jan, 1980.

Pitch measurements: 114yd × 72yd.

President:

Chairman: B. Hillier.

Directors: G. Herbert (Vice-Chairman), T. J. R. Kearsey, L. Smart, N. Arkell, R. Mattick, C. J. Green, C. Howard, D. Alderton.

Company Secretary: P. I. Jones.

Manager: ***Asst. Manager:***

Coaches: Andy Rowland and P. Bates. ***Physio:*** Kevin Morris.

Admin Mangager/Secretary: D. G. King. ***Youth Team Manager:*** John Trollope.

Commercial Manager: Doug Buswell.

Club Nickname: 'Robins'.

Year Formed: 1881 *(*see Foundation*). ***Turned Professional:*** 1894. ***Ltd Co.:*** 1894.

Previous Ground: 1881–96, The Croft.

Record League Victory: 9-1 v Luton T, Division 3 (S), 28 August 1920 – Nash; Kay, Macconachie; Langford, Hawley, Wareing; Jefferson (1), Fleming (4), Rogers, Batty (2), Davies (1), (1og)

Record Cup Victory: 10-1 v Farnham U Breweries (away), FA Cup, 1st rd (replay), 28 November 1925 – Nash; Dickenson, Weston: Archer, Bew, Adey; Denyer (2), Wall (1), Richardson (4), Johnson (3), Davies.

Record Defeat: 1-10 v Manchester C, FA Cup 4th rd replay, 25 January, 1930.

Most League Points (2 for a win): 64, Division 3, 1968–69.

Most League Points (3 for a win): 102, Division 4, 1985–86 (League record).

Most League Goals: 100, Division 3 (S), 1926–27.

Highest League Scorer in Season: Harry Morris, 47, Division 3 (S), 1926–27.

Most League Goals in Total Aggregate: Harry Morris, 216, 1926–33.

Most Capped Player: Rod Thomas, 30 (50), Wales.

Most League Appearances: John Trollope, 770, 1960–80.

Record Transfer Fee Received: £250,000 from Aston Villa for Paul Rideout, May 1983.

Record Transfer Fee Paid: £230,000 to Huddersfield T for Duncan Shearer, June 1988.

Football League Record: 1920 Original Member of Division 3; 1921–58 Division 3 (S); 1958–63 Division 3; 1963–65 Division 2; 1965–69 Division 3; 1969–74 Division 2; 1974–82 Division 3; 1982–86 Division 4; 1986–87 Division 3; 1987– Division 2.

Honours: *Football League:* Division 2 best season; 5th, 1969–70; Division 3 – Runners-up 1962–63, 1968–69; Division 4 – Champions 1985–86 (with record 102 points). *FA Cup:* Semi-finals 1910, 1912. *Football League Cup:* Winners 1968–69. *Anglo-Italian Cup:* Winners 1970.

Colours: All red. **Change Colours:** White with black trim.

SWINDON TOWN 1988–89 LEAGUE RECORD

Match No.	Date	Venue	Opponents	Result	H/T Score	Lg. Pos.	Goalscorers	Atten-dance
1	Aug 29	A	Barnsley	D 1-1	0-1	—	White	6034
2	Sept 3	A	WBA	L 1-3	1-3	17	White	7518
3	11	H	Portsmouth	D 1-1	0-1	—	Foley	11,443
4	17	A	Blackburn R	D 0-0	0-0	17		7622
5	20	H	Bournemouth	W 3-1	2-1	—	Calderwood, MacLaren (pen), Barnes	8055
6	24	H	Brighton & HA	W 3-0	1-0	10	Barnes, White, Calderwood	6585
7	Oct 1	A	Watford	W 3-2	2-1	7	Shearer, Barnes, Jones	11,657
8	5	A	Oxford U	D 1-1	0-0	—	Parkin	9398
9	9	H	Chelsea	D 1-1	0-0	—	Shearer	11,347
10	16	H	Leeds U	D 0-0	0-0	—		9234
11	22	A	Sunderland	L 0-4	0-2	13		13,520
12	26	A	Leicester C	D 3-3	3-0	—	King, White, Henry	9751
13	29	H	Birmingham C	W 2-1	1-0	12	White 2	6937
14	Nov 5	A	Hull C	L 0-1	0-1	15		5192
15	12	H	Ipswich T	L 2-3	1-0	18	Gittens, Henry	7246
16	19	A	Stoke C	L 1-2	0-0	19	Jones	9339
17	26	H	Walsall	W 1-0	0-0	15	Foley	5328
18	Dec 3	A	Shrewsbury T	W 1-0	1-0	15	Geddis	3524
19	10	H	Oldham Ath	D 2-2	1-0	15	Henry, Marshall (og)	5540
20	17	A	Bradford C	D 2-2	2-1	15	Geddis, Shearer	9462
21	26	H	Plymouth Arg	W 1-0	1-0	12	Shearer	7883
22	31	H	Manchester C	L 1-2	0-1	15	White	10,776
23	Jan 2	A	Portsmouth	W 2-0	1-0	14	Geddis, Shearer	11,681
24	14	H	Barnsley	D 0-0	0-0	15		10,201
25	21	A	Crystal Palace	L 1-2	1-0	16	Foley	8109
26	Feb 5	H	Oxford U	W 3-0	1-0	—	McLoughlin, MacLaren, Calderwood	10,227
27	11	A	Chelsea	L 2-3	2-3	15	McLaughlin (og), Bodin	17,829
28	18	H	Sunderland	W 4-1	3-1	11	Shearer 2, McLoughlin, White	7432
29	25	A	Leeds U	D 0-0	0-0	13		22,651
30	28	H	Leicester C	W 2-1	0-1	—	Shearer, Jones (pen)	7456
31	Mar 4	A	Ipswich T	W 2-1	0-0	8	White 2	11,542
32	11	H	Hull C	W 1-0	1-0	8	Shearer	7090
33	18	A	Bournemouth	W 3-2	2-0	7	Foley 2, Jones	9752
34	25	H	WBA	D 0-0	0-0	6		12,240
35	27	A	Plymouth Arg	L 1-4	0-3	9	Jones	8487
36	Apr 1	H	Blackburn R	D 1-1	0-0	10	Foley	8220
37	4	H	Bradford C	W 1-0	1-0	—	Shearer	6476
38	8	A	Manchester C	L 1-2	1-1	7	Shearer	22,663
39	15	H	Watford	D 1-1	1-0	8	White	9828
40	18	A	Birmingham C	W 2-1	2-0	—	MacLaren 2 (1 pen)	4026
41	22	A	Brighton & HA	W 2-0	0-0	7	Foley 2	9510
42	25	H	Crystal Palace	W 1-0	1-0	—	White	11,045
43	29	A	Walsall	D 2-2	1-1	6	Shearer, Calderwood	5288
44	May 1	H	Shrewsbury T	W 1-0	1-0	6	King	8698
45	6	H	Stoke C	W 3-0	0-0	6	Shearer 2, Jones	9543
46	13	A	Oldham Ath	D 2-2	2-1	6	McLoughlin, White	5676

Final League Position: 6

GOALSCORERS

League (68): Shearer 14, White 13, Foley 8, Jones 6 (1 pen), Calderwood 4, MacLaren 4 (2 pens), Barnes 3, Geddis 3, Henry 3, McLoughlin 3, King 2, Bodin 1, Gittens 1, Parkin 1, own goals 2.
Littlewoods Cup (1): Shearer 1.
FA Cup (3): Foley 2, Shearer 1.

Littlewoods Cup	Second Round	Crystal Palace (h)	1-2
		(a)	0-2
FA Cup	Third Round	Portsmouth (a)	1-1
		(h)	2-0
	Fourth Round	West Ham U (h)	0-0
		(a)	0-1

Digby	Hockaday	King	MacLaren	Parkin	Gittens	McLoughlin	Calderwood	Shearer	White	Barnes	Henry	Bodin	Coyne	Foley	Jones	Barnard	Geddis	Simpson	Cornwell	*Match No.*
1	2	3	4	5	6	7*	8	9	10	11	12									1
1	2	3	4	5†	6		8	9*	10	11	12	7	14							2
1	2	3	4		6		5	9	10	11	12	8*		7						3
1	2	3	4	5	6		8	9	10	11				7						4
1	2	3	4	8	6		5	9†	10*	11	12	14		7						5
1	2	3	4	5	6		8	9	10	11				7						6
1	2	3		5	6		8	9	10*	11	12			7	4					7
1	2	3		5	6		8	9	10	11				7	4					8
1	2	3			6	5	8	9	10	11*				7	4	12				9
1	2	3		5	6		8	9*	10	11	12			7	4					10
1	2	3		5	6		8*		10	11	12			7	4	9				11
1	2	3		5	6	12	8		10	11*	9			7	4					12
1	2	3		5	6		8		10	11	9*			7	4		12			13
1	2	3		5	6		8	12	10*	11	9			7	4					14
1	2	3	8	5	6				10	11	9			7	4					15
1	2	3		5	6		8	12	10	11*	9			7	4					16
1	2	3	10	5			6		8		9			7	4		11			17
1	2	3	10	5			6	12	8†		9*			7	4		11	14		18
1	2	3	8	5			6		12	10	9			7	4*		11			19
1	2	3	10	5			6	8			9			7	4		11			20
1	2	3	10	5	6			8			9			7	4		11			21
1	2	3	10	5	6*			11	8		9			7	4				12	22
1	2	3	10	5†			6	8	12		14			7*	4		9		11	23
1			6			2	5		8		9*	3		7	4		11	12	10	24
1			10		8	2	5				9	3		7	4		11		6	25
1	2		10		6	9	5		8			3		7	4				11	26
1	2		10		6	9	5		8			3		7	4		12		11*	27
1	2		10		6	8	5	7	9		12	3			4			11*		28
1	2	11	10		6	8	5	7	9			3			4					29
1	2	12	10*		6	8	5	9	11			3		7	4					30
1	2	12	10	6		8*	5	7	9			3		11	4					31
1	2		10	5		8	6	9	11			3		7	4					32
1	2		10	5		8	6	9	11			3		7	4					33
1	2	12	10	5*		8	6	9	11			3		7	4					34
1	2		10		5	8	6	9	11			3		7	4					35
1	2		10		6	9	5	8	11			3*		7	4			12		36
1	2	3	10		6	9	5	8	11					7	4					37
1	2	3	10		6	9	5	8	11					7	4					38
1	2	3	10	6		9	5	8	11					7	4					39
1	2	3	10	6		9	5	8	11						4			7		40
1	2	3	10	6		9	5	8	11					7*	4			12		41
1	2	3	10	6		9	5	8	11					7	4					42
1	2	3	10	6		9	5	8	11					7	4					43
1	2	3	10	6		9	5	8	11					7	4					44
1	2	3	10	6		9	5	8	11					7	4					45
1	2	3	10		5	9	6	8	11						4			7		46
46	44	34 + 3s	37	32	29	25 + 1s	43	33 + 3s	41 + 2s	17	13 + 9s	15 + 1s	— + 1s	40	40	1 + 1s	8 + 2s	3 + 4s	5 + 1s	

SWINDON TOWN

Player and Position	*Ht*	*Wt*	*Birth Date*	*Birth Place*	*Source*	*Clubs*	*League App*	*League Gls*
Goalkeepers								
Fraser Digby	6 1	12 12	23 4 67	Sheffield	Apprentice	Manchester U	—	—
						Oldham Ath (loan)	—	—
						Swindon T (loan)	—	—
						Swindon T	116	—
Nicky Hammond	6 0	11 13	7 9 67	Hornchurch	Apprentice	Arsenal	—	—
						Bristol R (loan)	3	—
						Peterborough U	—	—
						(loan)	—	—
						Aberdeen (loan)	4	—
						Swindon T		
Defenders								
David Barnett			20 11 69	Swindon	Trainee	Swindon T	—	—
Colin Calderwood	6 0	11 09	20 1 65	Stranraer	Amateur	Mansfield T	169	1
						Swindon T	179	8
Dean Casserly			9 10 69	Wiltshire	Trainee	Swindon T	—	—
Curtis Fleming	5 8	11 04	8 0 68	Manchester	St Patrick's Ath	Swindon T	—	—
Jon Gittens	5 11	12 06	22 1 64	Moseley	Paget R	Southampton	18	—
						Swindon T	58	1
David Hockaday	5 10	10 09	9 11 57	Billingham	Amateur	Blackpool	147	24
						Swindon T	222	6
Phillip King	5 10	12 00	28 12 67	Bristol		Exeter C	27	—
						Torquay U	24	3
						Swindon T	102	3
Ross MacLaren	5 10	12 12	14 4 62	Edinburgh	Rangers	Shrewsbury T	161	18
						Derby Co	122	4
						Swindon T	37	4
Gary Marshall*	5 8	10 00	9 8 69	Stroud	Coventry C	Swindon T	—	—
Tim Parkin	6 2	13 03	31 12 57	Penrith	Apprentice	Blackburn R	13	—
					Malmo,	Bristol R	206	12
					Almondsbury G	Swindon T	104	5
Midfield								
Leigh Barnard	5 8	11 07	29 10 58	Worsley	Apprentice	Portsmouth	79	8
						Peterborough U	4	—
						(loan)	212	21
						Swindon T	6	2
						Exeter C (loan)		
Paul Bodin	6 0	12 01	13 9 64	Cardiff	Chelsea	Newport Co	—	—
						Cardiff C	57	3
					Bath C	Newport Co	6	1
						Swindon T	21	2
John Cornwell	6 0	12 00	13 10 64	Bethnal Green	Apprentice	Orient	202	35
						Newcastle U	33	1
						Swindon T	6	—
Peter Coyne	5 9	10 07	13 11 58	Manchester	Apprentice	Manchester U	2	1
					Ashton U	Crewe Alex	134	47
					Hyde U	Swindon T	110	30
Steve Foley	5 7	10 12	4 10 62	Liverpool	Apprentice	Liverpool	—	—
						Fulham (loan)	3	—
						Grimsby T	31	2
						Sheffield U	66	14
						Swindon T	75	12
Charlie Henry	5 11	12 08	13 2 62	Acton	Apprentice	Swindon T	223	26
						Torquay U (loan)	6	1
						Northampton T	4	1
						(loan)		
Mark Jones	5 8	9 12	26 9 61	Berinsfield	Apprentice	Oxford U	129	7
						Swindon T	40	9
Tommy Jones	5 10	11 07	7 10 64	Aldershot	Weymouth	Aberdeen	28	3
						Swindon T	40	6

SWINDON TOWN

Foundation: It is generally accepted that Swindon Town came into being in 1881, although there is no firm evidence that the club's founder, Rev. William Pitt, captain of the Spartans (an offshoot of a cricket club) changed his club's name to Swindon Town before 1883, when the Spartans amalgamated with St. Mark's Young Men's Friendly Society.

Managers (and Secretary-managers)
Sam Allen 1902–33, Ted Vizard 1933–39, Neil Harris 1939–41, Louis Page 1945–53, Maurice Lindley 1953–55, Bert Head 1956–65, Danny Williams 1965–69, Fred Ford 1969–71, Dave Mackay 1971–72, Les Allen 1972–74, Danny Williams 1974–78, Bobby Smith 1978–80, John Trollope 1980–83, Ken Beamish 1983–84, Lou Macari 1984–89, Ossie Ardiles 1989– .

Player and Position	*Ht*	*Wt*	*Birth Date*	*Birth Place*	*Source*	*Clubs*	*League App*	*League Gls*
Alan McLoughlin	5 8	10 00	20 4 67	Manchester	Local	Manchester U	—	—
						Swindon T	9	—
						Torquay U	24	4
						Swindon T	34	3
Jim Reynolds	5 9	10 10	27 10 67	Swindon	Apprentice	Swindon T	2	—
Fitzroy Simpson	5 8	10 07	26 2 70	Trowbridge	Trainee	Swindon T	7	—
Forwards								
David Geddis	6 0	11 08	12 3 58	Carlisle	Apprentice	Ipswich T	43	5
						Luton T (loan)	13	4
						Aston Villa	47	12
						Luton T (loan	4	—
						Barnsley	45	24
						Birmingham C	46	18
						Brentford (loan)	4	—
						Shrewsbury T	39	11
						Swindon T	10	3
Duncan Shearer	5 10	10 09	28 8 62	Fort William	Inverness Clach	Chelsea	2	1
						Huddersfield T	83	38
						Swindon T	36	14
Neil Tomlinson	5 11	12 00	14 10 69	Birmingham	Shrewsbury T	Swindon T	—	—
Adrian Viveash	6 1	11 12	30 9 69	Swindon	Trainee	Swindon T	—	—
Steve White	5 11	11 04	2 1 59	Chipping Sodbury	Mangotsfield U	Bristol R	50	20
						Luton T	72	25
						Charlton Ath	29	12
						Lincoln C (loan)	3	—
						Luton T (loan)	4	—
						Bristol R	101	24
						Swindon T	103	39

Trainees
Dixon, Liam J; Graham, Alex; Hammersley, Anthony J; Hunt, Paul C; Lea, Mark J; Morgan, Richard B; Sandrey, Gavin V; Spalding, Lee A; Summerbee, Nicholas J; Thompson, Paul S; Trollope, Paul J; Walker, Richard D.

Associated Schoolboys
Braidwood, Jason P; Fishlock, Murray E; Goble, Casey C; Griffiths, Andrew G; Lovegrove, Ryan B; Maudling, Paul; Mitchinson, Steven; Murray, Edwin J; O'Driscoll, Mark A; O'Sullivan, Wayne S; Pearce, Robert L; Phillips, Marcus S; Sly, Simon J; Thomson, Andrew J; Wolsey, Mark N.

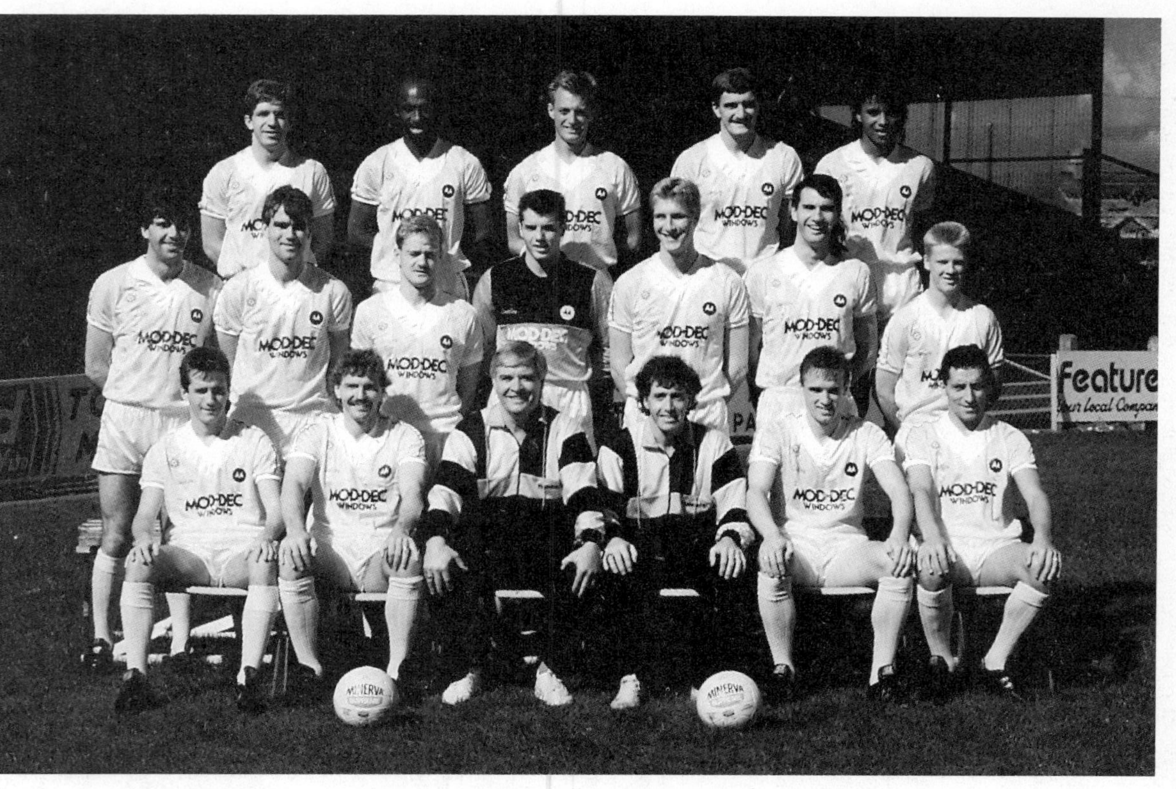

TORQUAY UNITED 1988–89 *Back row (left to right)*: Daral Pugh, Derek Dawkins, Dean Edwards, Phil Lloyd, Darren Leyden.
Centre row: Mark Loram, Jim McNichol, Sean Joyce, Kenny Veysey, David Cole, Richard Thompson, John Morrison.
Front row: Jim Smith, Roger Gibbins, Cyril Knowles (Manager), Sean Haslegrave (Assistant Manager), Paul Holmes, Tom Kelly.

Division 4 **TORQUAY UNITED**

Plainmoor Ground, Torquay, Devon TQ1 3PS. Telephone Torquay (0803) 38666/7. Clubcall 0898 12 16 41.

Ground capacity: 4999.

Record attendance: 21,908 v Huddersfield T, FA Cup 4th rd, 29 Jan, 1955.

Record receipts: £17,771.50 v Tottenham H, Littlewoods Cup, 2nd rd, 1st leg, 23, September 1987.

Pitch measurements: 112 yd × 74yd.

President: A. J. Boyce.

Chairman: L. W. Pope. ***Vice-Chairman:*** G. J. Harvey.

Directors: W. W. Rogers, R. Harvey, F. M. Mosley TD, R. Mildon.

Team Manager: Cyril Knowles. ***Coach:*** Sean Haslegrave.

Physio: Norman Medhurst.

Secretary: D. F. Turner. ***Lottery Administrators:*** C. Munslow and A. Sandford.

Nickname: 'The Gulls'.

Year Formed: 1910. ***Turned Professional:*** 1921. ***Ltd Co.:*** 1921.

Previous Name: 1910, Torquay Town; 1921, Torquay United,

Previous Grounds: 1898, Teignmouth Road; 1901, Torquay Recreation Ground; 1905, Cricket Field Road; 1907–10, Torquay Cricket Ground.

Record League Victory: 9-0 v Swindon T, Division 3 (S), 8 March 1952 – George Webber; Topping, Ralph Calland; Brown, Eric Webber, Towers; Shaw (1), Marchant (1), Northcott (2), Collins (3), Edds (2).

Record Cup Victory: 7-1 v Northampton T, FA Cup, 1st rd, 14 November 1959 – Gill; Penford, Downs; Bettany, George Northcott, Rawson; Baxter, Cox, Tommy Northcott (1), Bond (3), Pym (3).

Record Defeat: 2-10 v Fulham, Division 3 (S), 7 September, 1931 and v Luton T, Division 3 (S), 2 September, 1933.

Most League Points (2 for a win): 60, Division 4, 1959–60.

Most League Points (3 for a win): 77, Division 4, 1987–88.

Most League Goals: 89, Division 3 (S), 1956–57.

Highest League Scorer in Season: Sammy Collins, 40, Division 3 (S), 1955–56.

Most League Goals in Total Aggregate: Sammy Collins, 204, 1948–58.

Most Capped Player: None.

Most League Appearances: Dennis Lewis, 443, 1947–59.

Record Transfer Fee Received: £125,000 from Manchester U for Lee Sharpe, May 1988.

Record Transfer Fee Paid: £25,000 to Exeter C for Vince O'Keefe, March 1980.

Football League Record: 1927 Elected to Division 3 (S); 1958–60 Division 4; 1960–62 Division 3; 1962–66 Division 4; 1966–72 Division 3; 1972– Division 4.

Honours: *Football League:* Division 3 best season: 4th, 1967–68, Division 3(S) – Runners-up 1956–57; Division 4 – Promoted 1959–60 (3rd), 1965–66 (3rd). *FA Cup* best season: 4th rd, 1949, 1955, 1971, 1983. *Football League Cup:* never past 3rd rd.*Sherpa Van Trophy:* Runners-up 1989.

Colours: All white with yellow and blue trim. **Change Colours:** All yellow with blue trim.

TORQUAY UNITED 1988–89 LEAGUE RECORD

Match No.	Date	Venue	Opponents	Result	H/T Score	Lg. Pos.	Goalscorers	Attendance
1	Aug 27	H	Halifax T	L 0-2	0-1	—		2769
2	Sept 3	A	Grimsby T	L 0-1	0-0	22		2889
3	10	H	Hartlepool U	W 2-0	0-0	17	Lloyd, McNichol	2027
4	16	A	Doncaster R	W 2-1	1-0	—	Joyce, Gibbins	2220
5	20	H	Burnley	W 2-0	1-0	—	Edwards 2	3021
6	24	A	Scarborough	L 2-5	1-2	11	McNichol, Edwards	1986
7	Oct 1	H	Leyton Orient	W 3-0	2-0	8	Edwards, Lloyd, Joyce	2526
8	5	A	Exeter C	L 0-3	0-0	—		4243
9	8	H	Lincoln C	W 1-0	1-0	7	Cole	2105
10	15	A	Carlisle U	L 1-2	0-0	11	Lloyd	2164
11	22	H	Rotherham U	L 1-2	0-2	14	Weston	2228
12	25	A	Darlington	D 0-0	0-0	—		1374
13	29	H	Tranmere R	W 3-2	1-1	9	Gibbins, Smith, Lloyd	2038
14	Nov 5	A	York C	D 1-1	0-0	11	Smith (pen)	2007
15	8	H	Rochdale	W 1-0	1-0	—	Thompson	1931
16	11	A	Colchester U	D 2-2	0-1	—	Loram, Thompson	1926
17	26	A	Scunthorpe U	L 0-1	0-1	12		3359
18	Dec 2	H	Cambridge U	W 3-1	3-0	—	Thompson 2, Smith	1992
19	16	A	Crewe Alex	D 0-0	0-0	—		3269
20	26	H	Stockport Co	W 2-1	1-0	6	Loram, NcNichol	2838
21	31	H	Peterborough U	W 1-0	0-0	5	Edwards	2877
22	Jan 2	A	Hereford U	D 1-1	0-1	6	Loram	2356
23	14	H	Grimsby T	D 2-2	1-0	6	Gibbins, McNichol	2251
24	20	A	Halifax T	L 0-2	0-2	—		1830
25	28	H	Doncaster R	W 3-2	1-2	8	Edwards, Weston, Joyce	2103
26	Feb 4	A	Burnley	L 0-1	0-0	10		6626
27	11	H	Scarborough	L 0-1	0-0	11		2442
28	18	A	Lincoln C	L 0-1	0-1	11		3423
29	28	H	Darlington	W 1-0	0-0	—	Edwards	1627
30	Mar 4	A	Rotherham U	L 0-1	0-1	10		3791
31	13	A	Tranmere R	L 0-3	0-1	—		3559
32	18	A	Hartlepool U	W 1-0	1-0	12	Edwards	1516
33	25	H	Hereford U	W 1-0	0-0	11	Smith P	2542
34	27	A	Stockport Co	D 0-0	0-0	11		2808
35	31	H	Crewe Alex	W 2-1	0-1	—	Airey, Gummer	3087
36	Apr 4	H	Wrexham	D 0-0	0-0	—		2421
37	8	A	Peterborough U	L 1-3	0-0	11	Airey	2614
38	15	A	Leyton Orient	L 1-3	0-1	13	Smith J	4642
39	22	H	Exeter C	L 0-4	0-1	15		2939
40	25	H	York C	W 2-0	1-0	—	Airey, Elliott	2015
41	28	H	Scunthorpe U	L 0-2	0-0	—		2544
42	May 1	A	Rochdale	L 1-2	0-1	15	Loram	1239
43	3	H	Carlisle U	W 1-0	1-0	—	Elliott	1603
44	6	A	Cambridge U	L 0-3	0-1	13		2163
45	9	A	Wrexham	L 0-1	0-0	—		2056
46	13	H	Colchester U	L 1-3	0-0	14	Allinson (og)	2066

Final League Position: 14

GOALSCORERS

League (45): Edwards 8, Lloyd 4, Loram 4, McNichol 4, Smith J 4 (1 pen), Thompson 4, Airey 3, Gibbins 3, Joyce 3, Elliott 2, Weston 2, Cole 1, Gummer 1, Smith P 1, own goal 1.
Littlewoods Cup (1): Dawkins 1.
FA Cup (8): Loram 2, Smith J 2, Edwards 1, Joyce 1, McNichol 1, Thompson 1.

Littlewoods Cup	First Round	Reading (h)	0-1
		(a)	1-3
FA Cup	First Round	Fareham (h)	2-2
		(a)	3-2
	Second Round	Yeovil (a)	1-1
		(h)	1-0
	Third Round	Sheffield W (a)	1-5

Crichton	Holmes	Kelly	McNichol	Cole	Joyce	Pugh	Lloyd	Edwards	Loram	Gibbins	Thompson	Morrison	Dawkins	Haslegrave	Smith J	Weston	Tupling	Veysey	Leyden	Airey	Hirons	Gummer	Smith P	Love	Elliott	Davies	Bastow	Coombe	*Match No.*
1	2	3	4*	5	6	7	8	9	10	11	12†	14																	1
1	2	3	4		6*	7	8	9†	5	11			10	12	14														2
1	2	3	4	5	6*	7	8	9		11†			10		14	12													3
1	2	3	4	5	6	7	8	9		11			10																4
1	2	3	4	5	6*	7	8	9		11			10			12													5
1	2	3	4	5†	6	7	8	9		11					14	12	10*												6
1	2	3	4	5	6	7	8	9†		11					14	10*	12												7
1	2	3	4	5†	6*	7	8	9		11					14	10	12												8
1		3	4	5	6	7	8	9	12	11*			14		2	10†													9
1	2	3	4	5	6	7	8	9		11*			14		12	10†													10
1	2	3		5	6	7	8	9*	12	11			14		4†	10													11
1	2	3		5	12	7	8	14	6†	11	9		4			10*													12
1		3		5	6	7	8	9	12	11	10*		14		2	4†													13
	14	3	4	5	6	7†	8	9	12		10*				2	11		1											14
		3	4	5	6		8	12	9	7†	10*		14		2	11		1											15
	2	3	4	5	6		8	9*	10		12		14		7	11†		1											16
		3	4	5	6		8	12	10	14			2	9*	7†	11		1											17
	14	3	4	5		2	8	12	6†	10	9*				7	11		1											18
	9	3	4	5	14	2	8	12	6	10					7*	11†		1											19
		3	4	5	11	2	8	12	6	10	9*				7			1											20
		3	4	5	11	2	8	12	6	10	9				7*			1											21
	14	3	4	5	11	2†	8	7	6	10*	9	12						1											22
	14	3	4	5†	11	2	8	12	6	10	9*				7			1											23
	2*	3	4		11		8	9	6			14			7	10†		1	5	12									24
		3	4		11		8	2	6		9*				7	10		1	5	12									25
	2	3		4	11		8*	9	6			14			7	10†		1	5	12									26
		3	4	5*	11		8	2	6						7	10		1	12	9†	14								27
			4	5	11	12	8*		6		9†	3			14	10		1	2	7									28
		3	4	5	11*		8	9	6			2			7†	10		1	14	12									29
	4	3		5			8	9	6		12	2			7*	10		1		11									30
	4	3		5			8		6		12	2				10*		1		11		9	7						31
	5	3	4	14			8	9†	6			2			12			1		10		11	7*						32
	2	3	4	14			8		6							10		1		9†	12	11	7*	5					33
		3	4				8		6			2				10		1		12		11	7*	9	5				34
	12	3	4			2*	8		6							10		1		12		11	7	9	5				35
	12	3	4				8	9†	6							10*		1		2	14	11	7		5				36
		3	4			2	8		6							10*		1		14		11	7	9†	5				37
		3	4	6			8	9*				2			11	10		1†		7	12				5		14		38
		3*	4				8	9	6			2				10				7	11		12		5			1	39
		3	4	11			8	12	6			2			10					7*				9	5			1	40
		3	4	11†		14	8	7*	6			2			10	12								9	5			1	41
		3		11		14	8	12	6			2			7	10			4					9*	5†			1	42
		14				3	8	9	6						11	12			2†				7		5	4	10*	1	43
				14	6*	3	8	9†				12			7	10			2					11	5	4		1	44
		3				2	8	9	6			11			7*	10							12	14	5	4†		1	45
		3	4		14	2	8	9	6			11†			7*	10							12		5			1	46
13	19 + 6s	43 + 1s	36	32 + 3s	27 + 3s	26 + 3s	46	30 + 10s	33 + 4s	20 + 1s	11 + 4s	13 + 5s	6 + 6s	1 + 1s	26 + 8s	32 + 5s	1 + 2s	25	7 + 2s	10 + 7s	1 + 4s	7	8 + 3s	8 + 1s	13	3	1 + 1s	8	

TORQUAY UNITED

Player and Position	Ht	Wt	Birth Date	Birth Place	Source	Clubs	League App	League Gls
Goalkeepers								
Kenny Allen*	6 4	13 08	12 1 52	Thornaby	Bath C	Bournemouth	152	—
						Bury	—	—
						Peterborough U	—	—
						Torquay U	58	—
						Swindon T	45	—
						Torquay U	74	—
Mark Coombe	6 1	12 06	17 9 68	Torquay	Trainee	Bournemouth	—	—
						Bristol C	—	—
						Carlisle U (loan)	—	—
						Colchester U	3	—
						Torquay U	8	—
Ken Veysey	5 11		8 6 67	Hackney		Torquay U	25	—
Defenders								
David Cole*	6 0	11 10	28 9 62	Barnsley		Sunderland	—	—
						Swansea C	8	—
						Swindon T	69	3
						Torquay U	110	6
Andy Davis§			6 6 72	Wolverhampton	Trainee	Torquay U	3	—
Matthew Elliott	6 3	13 06	1 11 68	Surrey	Epsom & Ewell	Charlton Ath	—	—
						Torquay U	13	2
Paul Holmes	5 10	11 00	18 2 68	Sheffield	Apprentice	Doncaster R	47	1
						Torquay U	25	—
Tom Kelly*	5 10	11 10	28 3 64	Bellshill	Hibernian	Hartlepool U	15	—
						Torquay U	120	—
Darren Layden*	5 11	11 06	20 3 70	Warley	Trainee	Torquay U	9	—
Philip Lloyd	5 11	11 11	26 12 64	Hemsworth	Apprentice	Middlesbrough	—	—
						Barnsley	—	—
						Darlington	127	3
						Torquay U	92	6
Jim McNichol	6 0	12 10	9 6 58	Glasgow	Apprentice	Ipswich T	—	—
						Luton T	15	—
						Brentford	155	22
						Exeter C	87	10
						Torquay U	124	13
John Morrison	5 6	10 04	27 7 70	Kettering	Trainee	Torquay U	18	—
Phil Underhill	5 6	9 09	26 10 69	Bristol	Trainee	Southampton	—	—
						Torquay U	—	—
Midfield								
Ian Bastow	5 8	9 02	12 8 71	Torquay	Trainee	Torquay U	2	—
Derek Dawkins‡	5 10	11 01	29 11 59	Edmonton	Apprentice	Leicester C	3	—
						Mansfield T	73	—
						Bournemouth	8	—
						Torquay U	175	7
Sean Haslegrave*	5 8	10 07	7 6 51	Stoke	Amateur	Stoke C	113	5
						Nottingham F	7	1
						Preston NE	113	2
						Crewe Alex	82	1
						York C	142	—
						Torquay U	36	1
Sean Joyce	5 8	10 05	15 2 67	Doncaster		Doncaster R	41	2
						Exeter C (loan)	1	—
						Torquay U	30	3
Alan Pearce‡	5 8	10 09	25 10 65	Middlesbrough	Apprentice	York C	78	9
						Torquay U	27	2
Daral Pugh	5 8	10 03	5 6 61	Crynant	Apprentice	Doncaster R	154	15
						Huddersfield T	84	7
						Rotherham U	112	6
						Cambridge U (loan)	6	1
						Torquay U	29	—

TORQUAY UNITED

Foundation: The idea of establishing a Torquay club was agreed by old boys of Torquay College and Torbay College, while sitting in Princess Gardens listening to the band. A proper meeting was subsequently held at Tor Abbey Hotel at which officers were elected. This was in 1898 and the club's first competition was the Eastern League (later known as the East Devon League).

Managers (and Secretary-managers)
Percy Mackrill 1927–29, A. H. Hoskins 1929*, Frank Womack 1929–32, Frank Brown 1932–38, Alf Steward 1938–40, Billy Butler 1945–46, Jack Butler 1946–47, John McNeil 1947–50, Bob John 1950, Alex Massie 1950–51, Eric Webber 1951–65, Frank O'Farrell 1965–68, Alan Brown 1969–71, Jack Edwards 1971–73, Malcolm Musgrove 1973–76, Mike Green 1977–81, Frank O'Farrell 1981–82 (continued as GM to 1983), Bruch Rioch 1982–84, Dave Webb 1984–85, John Sims 1985, Stuart Morgan 1985–87, Cyril Knowles 1987– .

Player and Position	*Ht*	*Wt*	*Birth Date*	*Birth Place*	*Source*	*Clubs*	*League App*	*League Gls*
Jim Smith	5 9	10 07	22 11 69	Johnstone	Trainee	Torquay U	35	4
Ian Weston	5 10	11 10	6 5 68			Bristol R	16	—
						Torquay U	37	2
Ian Weston	5 10	11 10	6 5 68			Bristol R	16	—
						Torquay U	37	2
Forwards								
Carl Airey	6 0	12 06	6 2 65	Wakefield	Apprentice	Barnsley	38	5
						Bradford C (loan)	5	—
						Darlington	75	28
					Charleroi	Chesterfield	26	4
						Rotherham U	32	11
						Torquay U	17	3
Dave Caldwell (To Belgium Aug 1988)	5 10	10 08	31 7 60	Aberdeen	Inverness Caley	Mansfield T	157	57
						Carlisle U (loan)	4	—
						Swindon T (loan)	5	—
						Chesterfield	68	17
						Torquay U	24	4
Dean Edwards	5 11	11 07	25 2 62	Wolverhampton	Apprentice	Shrewsbury T	13	1
					Telford U	Wolverhampton W	31	9
						Exeter C	54	17
						Torquay U	40	8
Paul Hirons	5 11	11 00	6 3 71	Bristol	Bristol C§	Torquay U	5	—
Mark Loram	6 0	12 00	13 8 67	Paignton	Brixham	Torquay U	52	8
						QPR (loan)	—	—
						QPR	—	—
						Torquay U (loan)	13	4
						Torquay U	82	12
Ian Love	5 11	11 04	1 3 58	Cardiff	Eastern	Swansea C	41	9
						Torquay U	9	—
Paul Smith	5 8	9 09	5 10 67	London	Apprentice	Arsenal	—	—
						Brentford	17	1
						Bristol R	16	1
						Torquay U	11	1
Richard Thompson	6 2	12 01	11 4 69	Bristol	Watford	Newport Co	13	2
						Torquay U	15	4

Trainees

Davies, Andrew J; Davis, Aaron; Edwards, Fraser L; Evans, Martyn; Ford, Richard J; Hall, Paul A; Kidd, Steven R; McBean, Maurice A.O; Pope, Russel; Taylor, Scott R; Williams, Mark L.G.

Associated Schoolboys

Birrell, Duncan K; Khadaroo, Saleem D; Poblocki, Dean; Stephenson, Matthew; Withycombe, Dean.

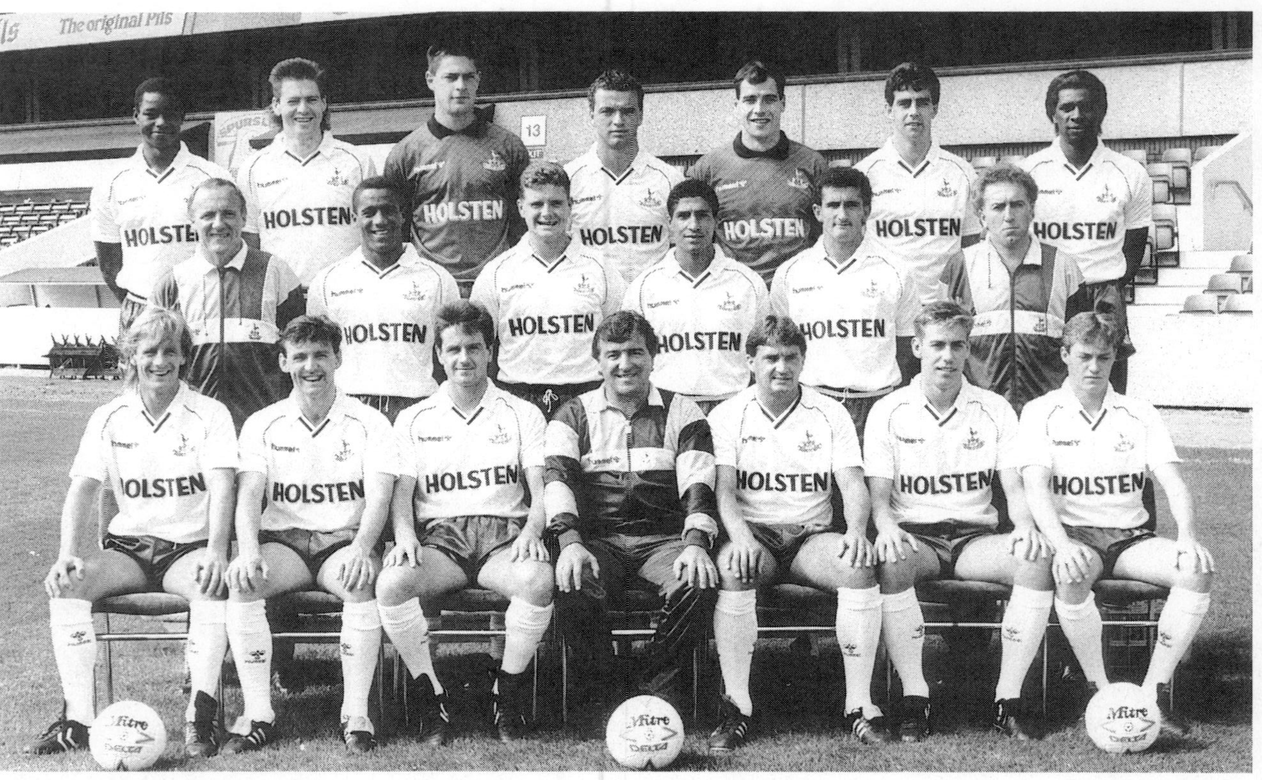

TOTTENHAM HOTSPUR 1988–89 *Back row (left to right):* Chris Fairclough, Chris Waddle, Bobby Mimms, Paul Stewart, Peter Guthrie, Gary Stevens, Mitchell Thomas.
Centre row: Allan Harris (Assistant Manager), Brian Statham, Paul Gascoigne, Chris Hughton, Vinny Samways, Doug Livermore (Reserve Team Manager).
Front row: Paul Walsh, Paul Allen, Terry Fenwick, Terry Venables (Manager), Gary Mabbutt, John Polston, Paul Moran.

Division 1 **TOTTENHAM HOTSPUR**

748 High Rd, Tottenham, London, N17. Telephone 01–808 8080. Commercial Dept: 01-808 0281. Recorded information: 01-808 1020. Dial-a-seat: 01-808 3030. Telex: 24739 and 295261. Spurs Line: 0898 100 500. Fax: 01-885 1951.

Ground Capacity: 38,082.

Record attendance: 75,038 v Sunderland, FA Cup 6th rd, 5 March, 1938.

Record receipts: £245,632.10 v Anderlecht, UEFA Cup Final 2nd leg, 23 May, 1984.

Pitch measurements: 110yd × 73yd.

Chairman: I. A. Scholar. ***Vice-Chairman:*** D. A. Alexiou.

Directors: F. P. Sinclair, P. A. Bobroff, A. G. Berry.

Chief Executive: R. Holt. ***Financial Director:*** D. R. Peter.

Manager: Terry Venables.

Assistant Manager: Doug Livermore. ***Physio:*** John Sheridan.

Secretary: Peter Barnes. ***Commercial Manager:*** Mike Rollo. ***PRO:*** John Fennelly.

Year Formed: 1882. ***Turned Professional:*** 1895. ***Ltd Co.:*** 1898.

Club Nickname: 'Spurs'.

Previous Grounds: 1882, Tottenham Marshes; 1885, Northumberland Park; 1898, White Hart Lane.

Previous Name: 1882–85, Hotspur Football Club.

Record League Victory: 9-0 v Bristol R, Division 2, 22 October 1977 – Davies; Naylor, Holmes, Hoddle (1), McAllister, Perryman, Pratt, McNab, Morris (3), Lee (4), Taylor (1).

Record Cup Victory: 13-2 v Crewe Alex, FA Cup, 4th rd (replay), 3 February 1960 – Brown; Hills, Henry; Blanchflower, Norman, Mackay; White, Harmer (1), Smith (4), Allen (5), Jones (3 incl. 1p).

Record Defeat: 0-7 v Liverpool, Division 1, 2 September, 1978.

Most League Points (2 for a win): 70, Division 2, 1919–20.

Most League Points (3 for a win): 77, Division 1, 1984–85.

Most League Goals: 115, Division 1, 1960-61.

Highest League Scorer in Season: Jimmy Greaves, 37, Division 1, 1962–63.

Most League Goals in Total Aggregate: Jimmy Greaves, 220, 1961–70.

Most Capped Player: Pat Jennings, 75 (119), Northern Ireland.

Most League Appearances: Steve Perryman, 655, 1969–86.

Record Transfer Fee Received: £4,500,000 from Marseille for Chris Waddle, July 1989.

Record Transfer Fee Paid: £2,000,000 to Newcastle U for Paul Gascoigne, July 1988.

Football League Record: 1908 Elected to Division 2; 1909–15 Division 1; 1919–20 Division 2; 1920–28 Division 1; 1928–33 Division 2; 1933–35 Division 1; 1935–50 Division 2; 1950–77 Division 1; 1977–78 Division 2; 1978— Division 1.

Honours: *Football League:* Division 1 – Champions 1950–51, 1960–61; Runners-up 1921–22, 1951–52, 1956–57, 1962–63; Division 2 – Champions 1919–20, 1949–50; Runners-up 1908–09, 1932–33; Promoted 1977–78 (3rd). *FA Cup:* Winners 1901 (as non; League club). 1921, 1961, 1962, 1967, 1981, 1982 (7 wins stands as the joint record): Runners-up 1986—87. *Football League Cup:* Winners 1970–71, 1972–73; Runners-up 1981–82. **European Competitions:** *European Cup:* 1961–62; *European Cup-Winners' Cup:* 1962–63 (winners), 1963–64, 1967–68, 1981–82 (runners-up), 1982–83); *UEFA Cup:* 1971–72 (winners), 1973–74 (runners-up), 1983–84 (winners), 1984–85.

Colours: White shirts, navy blue shorts, white stockings. **Change Colours:** All yellow.

TOTTENHAM HOTSPUR 1988–89 LEAGUE RECORD

Match No.	Date	Venue	Opponents	Result		H/T Score	Lg. Pos.	Goalscorers	Attendance
1	Sept 3	A	Newcastle U	D	2-2	0-2	11	Waddle, Fenwick	32,977
2	10	H	Arsenal	L	2-3	2-3	15	Waddle, Gascoigne	32,621
3	17	A	Liverpool	D	1-1	0-0	17	Fenwick	40,929
4	24	H	Middlesbrough	W	3-2	1-1	13	Waddle, Howells, Fenwick (pen)	23,427
5	Oct 1	H	Manchester U	D	2-2	1-1	14	Waddle, Walsh	29,318
6	8	A	Charlton Ath	D	2-2	0-1	15	Fenwick (pen), Allen	14,384
7	22	A	Norwich C	L	1-3	0-2	19	Fairclough	20,330
8	25	H	Southampton	L	1-2	1-0	—	Wallace Ray (og)	19,517
9	29	A	Aston Villa	L	1-2	0-0	20	Fenwick (pen)	26,238
10	Nov 5	H	Derby Co	L	1-3	1-1	20	Stewart	22,868
11	12	H	Wimbledon	W	3-2	1-1	18	Fenwick (pen), Butters, Samways	23,589
12	20	A	Sheffield W	W	2-0	0-0	—	Stewart 2	15,386
13	23	H	Coventry C	D	1-1	1-0	—	Stewart	21,961
14	26	H	QPR	D	2-2	0-2	17	Gascoigne, Waddle	26,698
15	Dec 3	A	Everton	L	0-1	0-1	16		29,657
16	10	H	Millwall	W	2-0	1-0	16	Waddle, Gascoigne	27,660
17	17	A	West Ham U	W	2-0	1-0	11	Mabbutt, Thomas	28,379
18	26	H	Luton T	D	0-0	0-0	11		27,337
19	31	H	Newcastle U	W	2-0	2-0	9	Walsh, Waddle	27,739
20	Jan 2	A	Arsenal	L	0-2	0-1	11		45,129
21	15	H	Nottingham F	L	1-2	1-2	—	Waddle	16,903
22	21	A	Middlesbrough	D	2-2	1-1	12	Stewart 2	23,692
23	Feb 5	A	Manchester U	L	0-1	0-0	—		41,423
24	11	H	Charlton Ath	D	1-1	0-1	13	Stewart	22,803
25	21	H	Norwich C	W	2-1	1-0	—	Gascoigne, Waddle	19,120
26	25	A	Southampton	W	2-0	1-0	11	Waddle, Nayim	16,702
27	Mar 1	H	Aston Villa	W	2-0	1-0	—	Waddle 2	19,090
28	11	A	Derby C	D	1-1	0-1	10	Gascoigne	18,206
29	18	A	Coventry C	D	1-1	0-1	9	Waddle	17,156
30	22	A	Nottingham F	W	2-1	0-0	—	Howells, Samways	23,098
31	26	H	Liverpool	L	1-2	0-0	—	Fenwick (pen)	30,012
32	28	A	Luton T	W	3-1	0-1	—	Howells, Walsh, Gascoigne	11,146
33	Apr 1	H	West Ham U	W	3-0	1-0	6	Nayim, Fenwick (pen), Stewart	28,375
34	12	H	Sheffield W	D	0-0	0-0	—		17,270
35	15	A	Wimbledon	W	2-1	1-0	5	Stewart, Waddle	12,366
36	22	H	Everton	W	2-1	0-0	5	Walsh 2	28,568
37	29	A	Millwall	W	5-0	2-0	5	Walsh, Stewart 3, Samways	16,551
38	May 13	A	QPR	L	0-1	0-0	6		21,873

Final League Position: 6

GOALSCORERS

League (60): Waddle 14, Stewart 12, Fenwick 8 (6 pens), Gascoigne 6, Walsh 6, Howells 3, Samways 3, Nayim 2, Allen 1, Butters 1, Fairclough 1, Mabbutt 1, Thomas 1, own goal 1.
Littlewoods Cup (6): Fenwick 1 (pen), Gascoigne 1, Samways 1, Stewart 1, Thomas 1, own goal 1.
FA Cup (0).

Littlewoods Cup	Second Round	Notts Co (a)	1-1
		(h)	2-1
	Third Round	Blackburn R (h)	0-0
		(a)	2-1
	Fourth Round	Southampton (a)	1-2
FA Cup	Third Round	Bradford C (a)	0-1

Mimms	Statham	Hughton	Fenwick	Fairclough	Mabbutt	Walsh	Gascoigne	Waddle	Thomas	Allen	Moran	Howells	Samways	Stewart	Stevens	Stimson	Moncur	Butters	Gray	Robson	Polston	Bergsson	Thorstvedt	Nayim	*Match No.*
1	2	3	4	5	6	7*	8†	9	10	11	12	14													1
1	2*		4	5	6	7	8	9	3	11	12	14	10†												2
1	2	12	4	5	6	7*	8	9†	3	11		14	10												3
1	2†		4	5	6	7*	8	9	3	11	12	14	10												4
1	2	5	4		6	7	8†	9*	3	11		14	10	12											5
1	2		4		6	7*	8	9	3	5		12	10	11											6
1			4	5	6		8	9	3	11		12	10*	7	2										7
1			4	5	6	7	8	9	3	11				10	2										8
1			4	5	6		8	9	3	11†		7*		10	2	12	14								9
1			4	5	6		8	9	3	11†	7*	14	12	10	2										10
1			4	5	6		8	9	3		7		11	10	2*			12							11
1			4	5	6		8*	9	3	12	7†	14	11	10				2							12
1			4	5	6	12	8	9	3	14	7*		11†	10				2							13
1			4	5	6	7*	8	9	3†	11			12	10				2	14						14
1			4	5	6	12	8	9	3	11			7*	10				2							15
1			4	5	6	7	8	9	3	11				10				2							16
1			4	5	6	7*	8†	9	3	11				10				2		12	14				17
1			4		6	7*	8†	9	3	11	12		14	10				2				5			18
1			4	5	6	7*		9	3	11		12		10				2				8			19
1			4	5	6	7		9	3	11				10				2				8			20
		3*	4	5	6	7†	12	9		11		14		10				2				8	1		21
		3	4		6	12	8†	9	14	11		7*		10				2				5	1		22
		3	4		6	12	8	9	14	11		7*		10				2				5†	1		23
		3	4		6	12	8	9		11		7*		10				2				5	1		24
		5			6	7	8	9	3	11		12						2		10*			1	4	25
		3		5	6	7		9	8	11		12						2		10*			1	4	26
		3	4	5	6	7		9		11								2		10			1	8	27
		3	4		6	7*	8	9	14	11				10				2		12			1	5†	28
		3	4		6	7	8*	9		11		12		10				2					1	5	29
		3	4		6	7		9		11		8	12	10				2					1	5*	30
		3	4		6	7*		9		11		8	12	10				2			14		1	5†	31
		3	4		6	7	8	9		11		5		10				2					1		32
		3	4		6	7	8	9		11		12		10				2					1	5*	33
		3			6	7	8	9		11		5	10					2				4	1		34
		3	4		6	7	8	9		11		5		10				2					1		35
		3	4		6	7	8†	9		11*		5	14	10				2					1	12	36
		3	4†		6	7	8	9*		11		5	14	10				2					1	12	37
		3			6	7	8*	9		11†		5	4	10				2			14		1	12	38
20	6	20 + 1s	34	20	38	28 + 5s	31 + 1s	38	22 + 3s	35 + 2s	4 + 4s	12 + 15s	12 + 7s	29 + 1s	5	— + 1s	— + 1s	27 + 1s	— + 1s	3 + 2s	— + 3s	8	18	8 + 3s	

TOTTENHAM HOTSPUR

Player and Position	Ht	Wt	Birth Date	Birth Place	Source	Clubs	League App	League Gls
Goalkeepers								
Kevin Dearden	5 11	12 08	8 3 70	Luton	Trainee	Tottenham H	—	—
						Cambridge U (loan)	15	—
Peter Guthrie	6 1	12 13	10 10 61	Newcastle	Weymouth	Tottenham H	—	—
						Swansea C (loan)	14	—
						Charlton Ath (loan)	—	—
Gareth Howells	6 1	12 08	13 6 70	Guildford	Trainee	Tottenham H	—	—
Bobby Mimms	6 2	12 13	12 10 63	York	Apprentice	Halifax T	—	—
						Rotherham U	83	—
						Everton	29	—
						Notts Co (loan)	2	—
						Sunderland (loan)	4	—
						Blackburn R (loan)	6	—
						Manchester C (loan)	3	—
						Tottenham H	33	—
Erik Thorstvedt	6 3	14 04	28 10 62	Stavanger	IFK Gothenburg	Tottenham H	18	—
Defenders								
Gudni Bergsson	5 10	10 07	21 7 65	Iceland	Valur	Tottenham H	8	—
Guy Butters	6 3	13 00	30 10 69	Hillingdon	Trainee	Tottenham H	28	1
Terry Fenwick	5 11	11 01	17 11 59	Camden, Co. Durham	Apprentice	Crystal Palace	70	—
						QPR	256	33
						Tottenham H	51	8
Chris Hughton	5 7	11 05	11 12 58	West Ham	Amateur	Tottenham H	289	12
David McDonald	5 10	11 00	2 1 71	Dublin	Trainee	Tottenham H	—	—
Gary Mabbutt	5 9	10 10	23 8 61	Bristol	Apprentice	Bristol R	131	10
						Tottenham H	228	21
John Moncur	5 7	9 10	22 9 66	Stepney	Apprentice	Tottenham H	7	—
						Doncaster R (loan)	4	—
						Cambridge U (loan)	4	—
						Portsmouth (loan)	7	—
Andy Polston	5 10	11 00	26 7 70	Walthamstow	Trainee	Tottenham H	—	—
John Polston	5 11	11 00	10 6 68	London	Apprentice	Tottenham H	11	—
Brian Statham	5 11	11 00	21 5 69	Zimbabwe	Apprentice	Tottenham H	24	—
Gary Stevens	6 0	12 00	30 3 62	Hillingdon	Apprentice	Brighton HA	133	2
						Tottenham H	140	6
Mark Stimson	5 11	11 00	27 12 67	Plaistow		Tottenham H	2	—
						Leyton Orient (loan)	10	—
						Gillingham (loan)	18	—
Mitchell Thomas	6 0	12 00	2 10 64	Luton	Apprentice	Luton T	107	1
						Tottenham H	100	5
Midfield								
Paul Allen	5 7	10 10	28 8 62	Aveley	Apprentice	West Ham U	152	6
						Tottenham H	146	8
Jason Cook*	5 7	10 06	29 12 69	Edmonton	Trainee	Tottenham H	—	—
Paul Gascoigne	5 10	11 07	27 5 67	Gateshead	Apprentice	Newcastle U	92	21
						Tottenham H	32	6
Eddie Gormley	5 7	10 07	23 10 68	Dublin	Bray W	Tottenham H	—	—
						Chesterfield (loan)	4	—
						Motherwell (loan)	—	—
Johnny Metgod (To Feyenoord, Aug 1988)	6 3	12 06	27 2 58	Amsterdam	Real Madrid	Nottingham F	116	15
						Tottenham H	12	—
Nayim	5 8	11 04	5 11 6 6	Ceuta	Barcelona	Tottenham H	11	2
Vinny Samways	5 8	9 00	27 10 68	Bethnal Green	Apprentice	Tottenham H	47	3
Steve Smart*	5 8	10 11	13 8 70	Enfield	Trainee	Tottenham H	—	—

TOTTENHAM HOTSPUR

Foundation: The Hotspur Football Club was formed from an older cricket club in 1882. Most of the founders were old boys St. John's Presbyterian School and Tottenham Grammar School. The Casey brothers were well to the fore as the family provided the club's first goalposts (painted blue and white) and their first ball. They soon adopted the local YMCA as their meeing place, but after a couple of moves settled at the Red House, which is still their headquarters, although now known simply as 748 High Road.

Managers (and Secretary-managers)
Frank Brettell 1897–98, John Cameron 1901–12, Peter McWilliam 1913–27, Billy Minter 1927–30, Percy Smith 1935, Jack Tresadern 1935–38, Peter McWilliam 1938–42, Joe Hulme 1945–49, Arthur Rowe 1949–55, Jimmy Anderson 1955–58, Bill Nicholson 1958–74, Terry Neill 1974–76, Keith Burtenshaw 1976–84, Peter Shreeves 1984–86, David Pleat 1986–87, Terry Venables 1987– .

Player and Position	*Ht*	*Wt*	*Birth Date*	*Birth Place*	*Source*	*Clubs*	*League App*	*League Gls*
Forwards								
Clive Allen (To Bordeaux, Aug 1988)	5 10	12 03	20 5 61	London	Apprentice	QPR	49	32
						Arsenal	—	—
						Crystal Palace	25	9
						QPR	87	40
						Tottenham H	105	60
Nico Claesen (To Antwerp, Aug 1988)	5 8	10 00	1 10 62	Leut	Standard Liege	Tottenham H	50	18
Tommy Fitzgerald*	5 8	10 07	2 1 70	Dublin	Trainee	Tottenham H	—	—
Ian Gilzean	6 1	12 08	10 12 69	Enfield	Trainee	Tottenham H	—	—
Philip Gray	5 10	11 07	2 10 68	Belfast	Apprentice	Tottenham H	3	—
David Howells	5 11	11 01	15 12 67	Guildford	Trainee	Tottenham H	40	4
Richard Johnston	5 9	10 10	15 10 69	Portadown	Trainee	Tottenham H	—	—
Paul Moran	5 10	11 00	22 5 68	Enfield	Trainee	Tottenham H	22	1
						Portsmouth (loan)	3	—
Shaun Murray	5 8	11 02	7 2 70	Newcastle	Trainee	Tottenham H	—	—
Mark Robson	5 7	10 05	22 5 69	Newham	Trainee	Exeter C	26	7
						Tottenham H	5	—
						Reading (loan)	7	—
Paul Stewart	5 11	11 10	7 10 64	Manchester	Apprentice	Blackpool	201	56
						Manchester C	51	26
						Tottenham H	30	12
Chris Waddle	6 0	11 05	14 12 60	Hepworth	Tow Law T	Newcastle U	170	46
						Tottenham H	138	33
Paul Walsh	5 7	10 08	1 10 62	Plumstead	Apprentice	Charlton Ath	87	24
						Luton T	80	24
						Liverpool	77	25
						Tottenham H	44	7

Trainees

Anton, Robert J; Carney, Steven J; Dang, Hung Q; Edwards, Matthew D; Fulling, Lee; Garland, Peter J; Hackett, Warren J; Hall, Jason M; Hardwicke, Victor; Hendon, Ian M; Houghton, Scott A; Morris, Raymond; Smith, Kevin; Smith, Neil J; Theodosiou, Andrew; Tuttle, David P; Walker, Ian M.

Associated Schoolboys

Binks, Spencer C; Burgess, Christopher; Campbell, Sulzeer; Caskey, Darren M; Culverhouse, David P; Deanus, Del; Flain, Stephen T; Flewin, Jake; Hackett, Benjamin; Hardy, Danny P; Hickles, Peter R; Hill, Daniel R.L; Hodges, Lee L; Kinnear, Colin B.T; Marlowe, Andrew D; Morah, Olisa, H; Price, Paul J; Redknapp, Jamie F; Small, Keith P.D; Smart, Lee; Theodorou, Theodoros S; Thompson-Minton, Jeffrey S; Watson, Kevin E; Winyard, Alfred P.

TRANMERE ROVERS 1988–89 *Back row (left to right):* Kenny McKenna, Gary Williams, Paul Collings, Eric Nixon, Dave Higgins, Eddie Murray.
Centre row: Kenny Jones (Trainer), Ronnie Moore, Mark Hughes, Jim Steele, Steve Vickers, Chris Malkin, Warwick Rimmer, Norman Wilson.
Front row: Shaun Garnett, Johnny Morrissey, Dave Martindale, Mark McCarrick, John King (Manager), Ian Muir, Jim Harvey, Steve Mungall, Eddie Bishop.

Division 3 **TRANMERE ROVERS**

Prenton Park, Prenton Road West, Birkenhead. Telephone 051-608 3677/4194. Commercial Dept. 051-608 0371. Cashline 051-608 0372. Shop 051-608 0438.

Ground capacity: 18,000.

Record attendance: 24,424 v Stoke C, FA Cup 4th rd, 5 Feb, 1972.

Record receipts: £16,392.90 v Wolverhampton W, FA Cup 3rd rd, 8 Jan, 1983.

Pitch measurements: 112yd × 71yd.

President: H. B. Thomas.

Chairman: P. R. Johnson. ***Vice-Chairman and Chief Executive:*** F. D. Corfe.

Directors: A. J. Adams BDS, G. E. H. Jones LLB, F. J. Williams, J. J. Holsgrove, FCA, G. A. Higham MSC TECH LRSC, M INST PI.

Secretary: Norman Wilson FAAI. ***Commercial Manager:*** Janet Watts.

Manager: John King. ***Assistant Manager:*** Kenny Jones.

Player-Coach: Ronnie Moore. ***Physio:*** Alec McClelland.

Year Formed: 1883. ***Turned Professional:*** 1912. ***Ltd Co.:*** 1920.

Previous name: Belmont AFC 1883–84.

Previous grounds: 1883 Steeles Field, 1885 South Road, 1887 Old Prenton Park (Temple Rd), 1912 – Prenton Park.

Club Nickname: 'The Rovers'.

Record League Victory: 13-4 v Oldham Ath, Division 3 (N), 26 December 1935 – Gray; Platt, Fairhurst; McLaren, Newton, Spencer; Eden, MacDonald (1), Bell (9), Woodward (2), Urmson (1).

Record Cup Victory: 9-0 v AP Leamington, FA Cup, 1st rd, 24 November 1979 – Johnson; Mathias, Flood (Mungall), Bramhall, Edwards, Evans (2), O'Neil (2 incl 1p), Parry, Peplow, Lumby (3), Beamish (1). (1 og)

Record Defeat: 1-9 v Tottenham H, FA Cup 3rd rd replay, 14 January, 1953.

Most League Points (2 for a win): 60, Division 4, 1964–65.

Most League Points (3 for a win): 80, Division 4, 1988–89.

Most League Goals: 111, Division 3 (N), 1930–31.

Highest League Scorer in Season: Bunny Bell, 35, Division 3(N), 1933–34.

Most League Goals in Total Aggregate: Bunny Bell, 104, 1931–36.

Most Capped Player: Albert Gray, 3 (24), Wales.

Most League Appearances: Harold Bell, 595, 1946–64 (inc. League record 401 consecutive appearances).

Record Transfer Fee Received: £120,000 from Cardiff C for Ronnie Moore, February 1979.

Record Transfer Fee Paid: £60,000 to Manchester C for Eric Nixon, July 1988.

Football League Record: 1921 Original Member of Division 3 (N): 1938–39 Division 2; 1946–58 Division 3 (N); 1958–61 Division 3; 1961–67 Division 4; 1967–75 Division 3; 1975–76 Division 4; 1976–79 Division 3; 1979–89 Division 4;1989– Division 3.

Honours: *Football League* Division 2 best season: 22nd, 1938–39; Division 3 (N) – Champions 1937–38; Promotion to 3rd Division: 1966–67, 1975–76; Division 4 – Runners-up 1988–89. *FA Cup* best season: 5th rd, 1967–68. *Football League Cup* best season: 4th rd, 1961, 1982, 1989. *Welsh Cup:* Winners 1935. Runners-up 1934.

Colours: All white. **Change Colours:** Claret shirts sky blue sleeves, sky blue shorts, sky blue stockings.

TRANMERE ROVERS 1988–89 LEAGUE RECORD

Match No.	Date	Venue	Opponents	Result	H/T Score	Lg. Pos.	Goalscorers	Attendance
1	Aug 27	A	Scarborough	D 0-0	0-0	—		2893
2	Sept 2	H	Colchester U	D 0-0	0-0	—		3401
3	10	A	Carlisle U	D 1-1	0-0	16	Steel	2384
4	16	H	Cambridge U	L 1-2	1-2	—	Muir (pen)	3248
5	19	H	Peterborough U	W 1-0	1-0	—	Bishop	2597
6	23	A	Halifax T	W 3-2	1-1	—	Muir 2, Higgins	1662
7	30	H	Hartlepool U	W 2-1	2-1	—	Steel, Muir	3624
8	Oct 4	A	Grimsby T	D 0-0	0-0	—		2288
9	7	H	York C	L 0-1	0-1	—		3054
10	15	A	Rotherham U	D 0-0	0-0	15		4133
11	22	A	Wrexham	D 3-3	0-2	11	Harvey 2, Bishop	3334
12	24	H	Lincoln C	W 1-0	0-0	—	Muir	3498
13	29	A	Torquay U	L 2-3	1-1	11	Muir, Steel	2038
14	Nov 4	H	Rochdale	W 2-0	1-0	—	Bishop, Morrissey	3740
15	7	H	Hereford U	W 1-0	1-0	—	Muir	3587
16	12	A	Crew Alex	L 1-2	1-0	6	Bishop	3293
17	25	A	Stockport Co	D 1-1	1-0	—	Muir	2952
18	Dec 2	H	Doncaster R	D 2-2	0-2	—	McCarrick, Morrissey	3412
19	16	H	Darlington	W 2-0	2-0	—	Muir 2 (2 pens)	2981
20	26	A	Leyton Orient	L 0-2	0-0	8		4249
21	31	A	Scunthorpe U	W 1-0	1-0	7	Lister (og)	4154
22	Jan 2	H	Burnley	W 2-1	1-0	5	Steel, Martindale	7974
23	13	A	Colcheste U	W 3-2	0-1	—	McCarrick, Harvey, Vickers	3458
24	21	H	Scarborough	D 1-1	0-1	5	Bishop	4538
25	28	A	Cambridge U	D 1-1	0-1	6	Morrissey	2239
26	Feb 4	A	Peterborough U	D 1-1	0-0	7	Malkin	2744
27	10	H	Halifax T	W 2-0	0-0	—	Vickers, Bishop	4674
28	18	A	York C	W 1-0	1-0	6	Muir	2923
29	25	H	Rotherham U	D 0-0	0-0	5		6509
30	Mar 1	A	Lincoln C	L 1-2	0-0	—	Muir	3560
31	3	H	Wrexham	W 2-1	0-1	—	Muir, Steel	7353
32	11	A	Rochdale	L 1-3	1-0	6	Malkin	2158
33	13	H	Torquay U	W 3-0	1-0	—	Malkin 2, Thompson (og)	3559
34	17	H	Carlisle U	D 0-0	0-0	—		5143
35	20	H	Exeter C	W 2-0	1-0	—	Muir 2	3885
36	25	A	Burnley	D 2-2	1-0	4	Bishop 2	6838
37	27	H	Leyton Orient	W 3-0	1-0	4	Mungall, Steel, Harvey	6872
38	Apr 1	A	Darlington	W 2-1	1-0	4	Thomas, Vickers	2492
39	5	A	Exeter C	W 1-0	1-0	—	Thomas	2956
40	7	H	Scunthorpe U	W 2-1	2-0	—	Morrissey, Muir	10,465
41	15	A	Hartlepool U	D 2-2	0-1	1	Muir, Steel	2496
42	28	H	Stockport Co	W 1-0	0-0	—	Muir	6270
43	May 1	A	Hereford U	L 1-2	1-1	2	Muir (pen)	2844
44	6	A	Doncaster R	D 0-0	0-0	3		2286
45	9	H	Grimsby T	W 3-2	2-2	—	Muir, Hughes, McCarrick	6938
46	13	H	Crewe Alex	D 1-1	1-0	2	Muir	15,286

Final League Position: 2

GOALSCORERS

League (62): Muir 21 (4 pens), Bishop 8, Steel 7, Harvey 4, Malkin 4, Morrissey 4, McCarrick 3, Vickers 3, Thomas 2, Higgins 1, Hughes 1, Martindale 1, Mungall 1, own goals 2.
Littlewoods Cup (4): Muir 2, Bishop 1, Hughes 1.
FA Cup (8): Muir 5 (1 pen), Steel 1, Vickers 1, own goal 1.

Littlewoods Cup	First Round	Stockport Co (a)	1-0
		(h)	1-1
	Second Round	Middlesbrough (a)	0-0
		(h)	1-0
	Third Round	Blackpool (h)	1-0
	Fourth Round	Bristol C (a)	0-1

Nixon	Higgins	Williams	Martindale	Moore	Vickers	Morrissey	Harvey	Steel	Muir	Mungall	Hughes	McCarrick	McKenna	Bishop	Smith	Malkin	Murray	Collings	Thomas	*Match No.*
1	2	3	4	5	6	7	8	9	10	11										1
1	2	3	4	5	6	7	8	9	10	11										2
1	2	3	4		6	7	8	9	10	11	5									3
1	2	14	4†		6	7	8	9	10	11	5*	3	12							4
1	2				6	7	8	9	10	11	5	3		4*	12					5
1	2		12		6	7	8	9	10	11	5	3		4*						6
1	2		12		6	7	8*	9	10	11	5	3		4						7
1	2*				6	7	8	9	10	11	5	3		4		12				8
1	2		12		6	7†	8	9	10	11	5	3		4*		14				9
1	2				6	7*	8	9	10	11	5	3		4			12			10
1	2				6	7	8	9	10	11	5	3		4						11
1	2				6	7	8	9	10	11	5	3		4						12
1	2		12		6	7†	8	9	10	11	5	3		4*			14			13
1	2		12		6	7	8	9	10	11	5	3*		4						14
1	2		12	5	6	7	8*	9	10	11				4	3					15
1	2		8	5	6	7		9	10	11		3		4						16
	2	14	4	5	6	7*	8†	9	10	11		3				12		1		17
1	2	12	4	5*	6	7		9	10	11		3		8						18
1			4	5	6	7	8*	9	10	11	2	3		12						19
1	2		4*	5†	6	7	8	9	10	11		3		12		14				20
1	2*		4	5	6	7	8	9	10	11		3				12				21
1	2		4	5	6	7	8	9	10	11		3								22
1	2		4		6		8	9	10	11	5*	3		12		7				23
1	2		4*		6	7	8	9	10	11	5	3		12						24
1	2		4		6	7	8	9*	10	11	5	3				12				25
1		2	4*		6	7	8		10	11	5†	3		12		9			14	26
1		2			6	7	8	9	10	11	5*	3		4		12				27
1	2		12		6	7	8*	9	10	11	5	3		4						28
1	2				6	7	8	9	10	11	5*	3		4		12				29
1	2				6	7	8	9	10	11	5*	3		4		14				30
1	2				6	7	8	9	10	11	5	3		4						31
1	2		12		6		8	9	10	11	5†	3		4*		7	14			32
1	2				6		8	9	10	11	5	3		4		7				33
1	2		8		6			9	10	11	5*	3		4		7	12			34
1	2		4†		6	7*	8	9	10	11	5	3		14		12				35
1	2				6	7	8	9	10	11	5	3		4						36
1	2				6	7	8	9	10	11	5	3							4	37
1	2				6	7*	8	9	10	11	5	3					12		4	38
1	2		12		6	7	8	9	10	11	5	3							4*	39
1	2				6	7	8†	9	10	11*	5	3		14		12			4	40
1	2		4		6	7*		9	10		5†	3		8		12	14		11	41
1	2		12		6	7	8*	9	10		5	3		4					11	42
1	2		12		6	7†	8	9	10		5	3		4*		14			11	43
1	2		12		6	7	8*		10		5†	3		4		9	14		11	44
1	2		4†		6	7	8	9*	10	11	5	3		14		12				45
1	2		4*		6	7	8	9	10	11	5	3		12						46
45	43	5 + 3s	20 + 12s	10	46	42	42	44	46	42	37	42	— + 1s	26 + 9s	1 + 1s	6 + 14s	— + 7s	1	8 + 1s	

FA Cup	First Round	Preston NE (a)	1-1
		(h)	3-0
	Second Round	Northwich (a)	2-1
	Third Round	Reading (h)	1-1
		(a)	1-2

TRANMERE ROVERS

Player and Position	Ht	Wt	Birth Date	Birth Place	Source	Clubs	League App	League Gls
Goalkeepers								
Paul Collings	6 2	12 00	30 9 68	Liverpool		Tranmere R	1	—
Eric Nixon	6 2	14 03	4 10 62	Manchester	Curzon Ashton	Manchester C	58	—
						Wolverhampton W (loan)	16	—
						Bradford C (loan)	3	—
						Southampton (loan)	4	—
						Carlisle U (loan)	16	—
						Tranmere R (loan)	8	—
						Tranmere R	45	—
Defenders								
Dave Higgins	6 0	11 00	19 8 61	Liverpool	Eagle	Tranmere R	28	—
					Caernarfon	Tranmere R	76	2
Mark Hughes	6 1	12 10	3 2 62	Morriston	Apprentice	Bristol R	74	3
						Torquay U (loan)	9	1
						Swansea C	12	—
						Bristol C	22	—
						Tranmere R	127	2
Mark McCarrick	5 8	10 08	4 2 62	Liverpool	Witton A	Birmingham C	15	—
						Lincoln C	44	—
						Crewe Alex	11	—
					Runcorn	Tranmere R	82	8
Ronnie Moore‡	6 2	13 12	29 1 53	Liverpool	Amateur	Tranmere R	249	72
						Cardiff C	56	6
						Rotherham U	125	51
						Charlton Ath	62	13
						Rochdale	43	9
						Tranmere R	75	6
Steve Mungall	5 8	11 02	22 5 58	Bellshill		Motherwell	20	—
						Tranmere R	365	7
Tony Thomas	5 11	12 05	12 7 71	Liverpool	Trainee	Tranmere R	9	2
Stephen Vickers	6 2	12 00	13 10 67	B Auckland	Spennymoor U	Tranmere R	131	6
Midfield								
Eddie Bishop	5 8	11 07	28 11 62	Liverpool	Runcorn	Tranmere R	40	9
Shaun Garnett	6 2	11 00	22 11 69	Wallasey	Trainee	Tranmere R	1	—
Jimmy Harvey	5 9	11 04	2 5 58	Lurgan	Glenavon	Arsenal	3	—
						Hereford U (loan)	11	—
						Hereford U	267	39
						Bristol C	3	—
						Wrexham (loan)	6	—
						Tranmere R	75	7
Dave Martindale	5 11	11 10	9 4 64	Liverpool	Apprentice	Liverpool	—	—
					Caernarfon	Tranmere R	66	5
John Smith	5 7	10 12	23 7 70	Liverpool		Tranmere R	2	—
Gary Williams‡	5 9	11 05	14 5 59	Nantwich	Amateur	Tranmere R	1	—
					Djurgaarden	Blackpool	31	2
						Swindon T	38	3
						Tranmere R	174	18
Forwards								
Ken McKenna	5 10	12 00	2 7 60	Birkenhead	Local	Tranmere R	4	—
					Telford U	Tranmere R	15	3
Chris Malkin	6 0	10 12	4 6 67	Bebington	Overpool	Tranmere R	25	4
John Morrissey	5 8	11 04	8 3 65	Liverpool	Apprentice	Everton	1	—
						Wolverhampton W	10	1
						Tranmere R	151	20

TRANMERE ROVERS

Foundation: Formed in 1883 as Belmont AFC they adopted their present title the following year although details of their early history are rather sketchy. Most of their early successes were in the Wirral Cup and they played in the Liverpool District League before undergoing a major reorganisation in 1899.

Managers (and Secretary-managers)
Bert Cooke 1921–35, Jackie Carr 1935–36, Jim Knowles 1936–39, Bill Ridding 1939–45, Ernie Blackburn 1946–55, Noel Kelly 1955–57, Peter Farrell 1957–60, Walter Galbraith 1961, Dave Russell 1961–69, Jackie Wright 1969–72, Ron Yeats 1972–75, John King 1975–80, Bryan Hamilton 1980–85, Frank Worthington 1985–87, Ronnie Moore 1987, John King 1987– .

Player and Position	*Ht*	*Wt*	*Birth Date*	*Birth Place*	*Source*	*Clubs*	*League App*	*League Gls*
Ian Muir	5 7	10 10	5 5 63	Coventry	Apprentice	QPR	2	2
						Burnley (loan)	2	1
						Birmingham C	1	—
						Brighton & HA	4	—
						Swindon T (loan)	2	—
						Tranmere R	167	81
Eddie Murray*	5 10	11 08	10 7 62	Liverpool	Stork	Tranmere R	27	1
Jim Steel	6 3	14 00	4 12 59	Dumfries	Apprentice	Oldham Ath	108	24
						Wigan Ath (loan)	2	2
						Wrexham (loan)	9	6
						Port Vale	28	6
						Wrexham	164	51
						Tranmere R	73	14

Trainees
Brady, Mark J; Brannon, Gerard D; Irons, Kenneth; Kearns, Stephen; Kelly, Kevin J; McGreal, John; Norman, John; Pullen, Phillip P.C; Taylor, Scott C; Young, Neil

Associated Schoolboys
Mitchell, Raymond E; Rigby, Neil J; Shalliker, Robert E; Walsh, Steven W.

WALSALL 1988–89 *Back row (left to right):* Paul Jones, Kenny Mower, Willie Naughton, Martin Goldsmith, Stephen McIlhargey, Graeme Forbes, Howard Pritchard, Fred Barber, Phil Hawker, Chris Marsh, Peter Hart, Trevor Christie.
Front row: Mark Rees, Mark Goodwin, Stuart Rimmer, Mark Taylor, Andy Dornan, Mark Jones, Craig Shakespeare, Dale Banton, Keith Bertschin.

Division 3 WALSALL

Fellows Park, Walsall. Telephone Walsall (0922) 22791. Commercial Dept. (0922) 30696. Clubcall: 0898 121104.

Ground capacity: 15,250.

Record attendance: 25,453 v Newcastle U, Division 2, 29 Aug, 1961.

Record receipts: £50,926.50 v Watford, FA Cup 5th rd, 2nd replay, 2 March, 1987.

Pitch measurements: 113yd × 73yd.

President: T. P. Ramsden.

Chairman: B. S. Blower.

Managing Director: R. Dox.

Directors: J. Bowser, R. Clift, T. F. Hargreaves, M. Miller, K. R. Whalley.

Manager: John Barnwell. ***Assistant Manager:*** P. Taylor.

Physio: T. Bradley.

Secretary/Commercial Manager: K. R. Whalley.

Year Formed: 1888. ***Turned Professional:*** 1888. ***Ltd Co.:*** 1921.

Club Nickname: 'The Saddlers'.

Previous Names: Walsall Swifts (founded 1877) and Walsall Town (founded 1879) amalgamated in 1888 and were known as Walsall Town Swifts until 1895.

Record League Victory: 10-0 v Darwen, Division 2, 4 March 1899 – Tennent; Peers (E) (1), Davies; Hickinbotham, Jenkyns, Taggart; Dean (3), Vail (2), Aston (4), Martin, Griffin.

Record Cup Victory: 6-1 v Leytonstone (away). FA Cup, 1st rd, 30 November 1946 – Lewis, Netley, Skidmore; Crutchley, Foulkes, Newman; Maund (1), Talbot, Darby (1), Wilshaw (2), Davies (2). 6–1 v Margate, FA Cup, 1st rd (replay), 24 November 1955 – Davies; Haddington, Vinall; Dorman, McPherson, Crook; Morris, Walsh (3), RIchards (2), McLaren (1), Moore.

Record Defeat: 0-12 v Small Heath, 17 December, 1892 and v Darwen, 26 December, 1896, both Division 2.

Most League Points (2 for a win): 65, Division 4, 1959–60.

Most League Points (3 for a win): 82, Division 3, 1987–88.

Most League Goals: 102, Division 4, 159–60.

Highest League Scorer in Season: Gilbert Alsop, 40, Division 3 (N), 1933–34 and 1934–35.

Most League Goals in Total Aggregate: Tony Richards, 184, 1954–63, and Colin Taylor, 184, 1958–63, 1964–68, 1969–73.

Most Capped Player: Mick Kearns, 15 (18), Eire.

Most League Appearances: Colin Harrison, 467, 1964–82.

Record Transfer Fee Received: £600,000 from West Ham U for David Kelly, July 1988.

Record Transfer Fee Paid: £175,000 to Birmingham C for Alan Buckley, June 1979.

Football League Record: 1892 Elected to Division 2; 1895 failed re-election; 1896–1901 Division 2; 1901 failed re-election; 1921 Original Member of Division 3 (N); 1927–31 Division 3 (S); 1931–36 Division 3 (N); 1936–58 Division 3 (S); 1958–60 Division 4; 1960–61 Division 3; 1961–63 Division 2; 1963–79 Division 3; 1979–80 Division 4; 1980–88 Division 3; 1988–89 Division 2; 1989– Division 3.

Honours: *Football League:* Division 2 best season: 6th,1898–99; Division 3 – Runners-up 1960–61; Division 4 – Champions 1959–60; Runners-up 1979–80. *FA Cup* best season: 5th rd, 1939, 1975, 1978, and last 16 1888–89. *Football League Cup:* Semi-final 1983–84.

Colours: Red shirts, white shorts, white stockings.**Change Colours:** All yellow.

WALSALL 1988–89 LEAGUE RECORD

Match No.	Date	Venue	Opponents	Result		H/T Score	Lg. Pos.	Goalscorers	Atten-dance
1	Aug 27	H	Plymouth Arg	D	2-2	0-2	—	Taylor A 2	6178
2	Sept 3	A	Manchester C	D	2-2	1-0	14	Naughton 2	17,104
3	10	H	Crystal Palace	D	0-0	0-0	16		6525
4	17	A	WBA	D	0-0	0-0	15		13,977
5	20	H	Birmingham C	W	5-0	0-0	—	Forbes, Shakespeare, Taylor A, Naughton, Rees	8780
6	24	H	Stoke C	L	1-2	1-1	15	Callaghan	7795
7	Oct 1	A	Hull C	D	0-0	0-0	17		4845
8	4	A	Chelsea	L	0-2	0-0	—		6747
9	8	H	Sunderland	W	2-0	0-0	16	Christie, Pritchard	6150
10	15	A	Shrewsbury T	D	0-0	0-0	16		5026
11	22	H	Portsmouth	D	1-1	0-1	18	Hawker	5626
12	26	A	Brighton & HA	D	2-2	2-1	—	Pritchard, Naughton	8311
13	29	H	Watford	L	0-1	0-0	20		6682
14	Nov 5	A	Oldham Ath	L	0-3	0-3	21		5760
15	8	A	Ipswich T	L	1-3	0-1	—	Christie (pen)	9067
16	12	H	Leicester C	L	0-1	0-1	21		6895
17	19	H	Blackburn R	L	1-2	0-1	21	Sellars (og)	5848
18	26	A	Swindon T	L	0-1	0-0	23		5328
19	Dec 3	H	Leeds U	L	0-3	0-1	23		6885
20	10	A	Barnsley	L	0-1	0-0	23		5173
21	17	A	Bournemouth	L	1-2	0-1	23	Shakespeare	6985
22	26	H	Oxford U	L	1-5	1-0	24	Naughton (pen)	6332
23	31	H	Bradford C	L	0-1	0-1	24		5366
24	Jan 2	A	Crystal Palace	L	0-4	0-3	24		9352
25	14	H	Ipswich T	L	2-4	0-0	24	Taylor M, Pritchard	4623
26	21	A	Plymouth Arg	L	0-2	0-0	24		11,505
27	Feb 4	H	Chelsea	L	0-7	0-4	24		6860
28	11	A	Sunderland	W	3-0	1-0	24	Rimmer 3	14,203
29	18	A	Portsmouth	D	1-1	1-0	24	Rimmer	7310
30	25	H	Shrewsbury T	D	1-1	1-1	24	Pritchard	5871
31	28	H	Brighton & HA	W	1-0	0-0	—	Naughton(pen)	4613
32	Mar 4	A	Leicester C	L	0-1	0-0	23		9375
33	11	H	Oldham Ath	D	2-2	1-0	23	Milligan(og), Hawker	5576
34	18	A	Birmingham C	L	0-1	0-0	24		6558
35	25	H	Manchester C	D	3-3	2-2	23	Saville 2, Rimmer	7562
36	27	A	Oxford U	L	0-1	0-1	23		5101
37	Apr 1	H	WBA	D	0-0	0-0	23		9520
38	4	H	Bournemouth	D	1-1	1-1	—	Shakespeare	3619
39	8	A	Bradford C	L	1-3	1-1	23	Naughton (pen)	8763
40	15	H	Hull C	D	1-1	0-0	23	Rimmer	3935
41	18	A	Watford	L	0-5	0-4	—		9777
42	22	A	Stoke C	W	3-0	2-0	23	Rimmer, Saville 2	8132
43	29	H	Swindon T	D	2-2	1-1	23	Rimmer, Pritchard	5288
44	May 1	A	Leeds U	L	0-1	0-0	24		13,280
45	6	A	Blackburn R	L	0-3	0-0	24		8236
46	13	H	Barnsley	L	1-3	0-1	24	Pritchard	3966

Final League Position: 24

GOALSCORERS

League (41): Rimmer 8, Naughton 7 (3 pens), Pritchard 6, Saville 4, Sheakespeare 3, Taylor A 3, Christie 2 (1 pen), Hawker 2, Callaghan 1, Forbes 1, Rees 1, Taylor M 1, own goals 2.
Littlewoods Cup (6): Shakespeare 2, Forbes 1, Goodwin 1, Hawker 1, Taylor A 1.
FA Cup (1): Pritchard 1.

Littlewoods Cup	First Round	Shrewsbury T (a)	2-2
		(h)	3-0
	Second Round	Liverpool (a)	0-1
		(h)	1-3
FA Cup	Third Round	Brentford (h)	1-1
		(a)	0-1

Barber	Dornan	Taylor, M	Shakespeare	Forbes	Hart	Pritchard	Goodwin	Taylor, A	Christie	Naughton	Hawker	Marsh	Mower	Callaghan	Rees	Bertschin	Jones, P	Banton	Goldsmith	Rimmer	Smith	Saville	Green	*Match No.*
1	2	3	4*	5	6	7	8	9	10	11	12													1
1	2	3	4	5	6	7*	8	9	10	11	12													2
1	2	3	4	5	6		8*	9	10	11	7	12												3
1	2	3	4	5	6		8	9	10	11		7												4
1	2	3	4	5	6		8	9		11			7	10*	12									5
1	2	3	4*	5	6	14	8†	9		11			7	10	12									6
1	2	3	4	5	6	10*		9		11	7	12				8								7
1		2	4	5	6	11		9†	10	14	7		3			8*	12							8
1		2	4	5	6	14		9	10†	11	7		3			12	8*							9
1		2	4	5	6	8*		9	10	12	7		3			11								10
1		2	4	5	6	14		8	9	11†	7		3			10*	12							11
1		2	4	5	6	8*		9	10	11	7	12	3											12
1		2	4	5	6			9	8	11*	7	12	3					10						13
1		2	4	5	6	7			8	11*		12	3				9	10						14
1		2	4	5	6	12			9	11†		7*	3			14	8	10						15
1		2	4	5	6	11†			9		7	12	3			14	8	10*						16
1	7	2	4	5	6	11			9				3*		12	14	8	10†						17
1	2	3	4	5	6	11*							7		12	9	8	10						18
1	2	3	4	5	14	12	8		10		6†		7*			9	11							19
1	2	3	4	5	6	7	8†		10	14					12	9*	11							20
1	2	3	4	5	6	7	8		10			12				9*	11							21
1	2	3	4	5	6	7	8		10	11							9							22
1	2	3	4	5	6	7†	8		10*	11		14					9	12						23
1	2	3	4	5	6	7	8			11		12	9					10*						24
1	2	4		5	6	7	8		10*			11†	3		12	9			14					25
1	2		4	5	6		8†		12		11		3		7	10	14	9*						26
1	2		4	5	6*	7	14		9		11†		3		12		10			8				27
1	2		4	5		7	8		12				3		11	10*				9	6			28
1	2	12	4	5		7	8						3*		11			10†	14	9	6			29
1	2		4	5		7	10		9				3		11					8	6			30
1	2		4	5		7	10		9	11			3							8	6			31
1	2		4	5		7	10		9	12	14		3†		11*					8	6			32
1	2		4	5		7	10		9	11	3									8	6			33
1	2		4	5		7*	10		9	11	3				12					8	6			34
1	2		4	5		7*	10			11	3				12					8	6	9		35
1		12	4	5		7	10			11*	3		6		2					8		9		36
1		3	4			7	10			11	6				2					8	5	9		37
1		3	4	5		7	10			11	6				2					8		9		38
1		3	4	5		7	10			11	6				2					8		9		39
1		3	4	5		7	10*			11	6				2	12				8		9		40
1			4	5		7	10*			11	3		12		2					8	6	9		41
1			4	5		7				11	10		3		2	12				8*	6	9		42
1			4	5		7	12			11	10*		3		2					8	6	9		43
1		12	4	5		7	10			11*			3		2	14				8	6	9†		44
		12	4	5		7	10			11†			3*		2	14				8	6	9	1	45
		3	4	5		7				11*		14			2	12	10			8†	6	9	1	46
44	26	30 + 4s	45	45	26 + 1s	36 + 5s	30 + 2s	13	26 + 2s	31 + 4s	23 + 3s	3 + 10s	28 + 1s	2	16 + 9s	11 + 9s	13 + 3s	9 + 1s	— + 2s	20	15	12	2	

WALSALL

Player and Position	Ht	Wt	Birth Date	Birth Place	Source	Clubs	League App	League Gls
Goalkeepers								
Fred Barber	5 11	11 07	28 8 63	Ferryhill	Apprentice	Darlington	135	—
						Everton	—	—
						Walsall	126	—
Ron Green	6 2	14 00	3 10 56	Birmingham	Alvechurch	Walsall	163	—
						WBA (loan)	—	—
						Shrewsbury T	19	—
						Bristol R (loan)	18	—
						Bristol R	38	—
						Scunthorpe U	78	—
						Wimbledon	4	—
						Shrewsbury T (loan)	17	—
						Manchester C (loan)	—	—
						Walsall	2	—
Steve McIlhargey	6 0	11 07	28 8 63	Ferryhill	Blantyre Celtic	Walsall	—	—
Defenders								
Andy Dornan	5 9	11 03	19 8 61	Aberdeen	King St	Aberdeen	2	—
						Motherwell	92	3
						Walsall	100	—
Graeme Forbes	6 0	12 00	29 7 58	Forfar	Lochee U	Motherwell	185	16
						Nottingham F (loan)	—	—
						Walsall	129	7
Peter Hart	5 11	12 07	14 8 57	Mexborough	Apprentice	Huddersfield T	210	7
						Walsall	380	12
Mark Jones	5 8	10 01	4 1 68	Brownhills	Apprentice	Walsall	8	—
						Exeter C (loan)	5	—
Ken Mower	6 1	12 04	1 12 60	Walsall	Apprentice	Walsall	368	8
Dean Smith§	6 0	12 01	19 3 71	West Bromwich	Trainee	Walsall	15	—
Mark Taylor	5 10	11 00	22 2 66	Walsall	Local	Walsall	113	4
Midfield								
Mark Goodwin	5 10	10 09	23 2 60	Sheffield	Apprentice	Leicester C	91	8
						Notts Co	237	24
						Walsall	68	2
Phil Hawker	6 1	11 07	7 12 62	Solihull	Apprentice	Birmingham C	35	1
						Walsall	147	9
Paul Jones	5 9	10 04	6 9 65	Walsall	Apprentice	Walsall	140	15
						Wrexham (loan)	5	—
Craig Shakespeare	5 10	11 05	26 10 63	Birmingham	Apprentice	Walsall	284	45
Alex Taylor	5 7	10 11	13 6 62	Bailleston	Blantyre St. J	Dundee U	33	6
						Hamilton A	66	5
						Walsall	13	3
Ray Train‡	5 6	10 04	10 2 51	Nuneaton	Apprentice	Walsall	73	11
						Carlisle U	155	8
						Sunderland	32	1
						Bolton W	51	—
						Watford	92	3
						Oxford U	50	—
						Bournemouth (loan)	7	—
						Northampton T	—	—
						(loan)	46	1
						Northampton T	36	—
						Tranmere R	16	—
						Walsall		
Forwards								
Dale Banton	5 8	11 00	15 5 61	Kensington	Apprentice	West Ham U	5	—
						Aldershot	106	47
						York C	138	48
						Walsall	10	—
						Grimsby T (loan)	8	1

WALSALL

Foundation: Two of the leading clubs around Walsall in the 1880s were Walsall Swifts (formed 1877) and Walsall Town (formed 1879). The Swifts were winners of the Birmingham Senior Cup in 1881, while the Town reached the 4th round (5th round modern equivalent) of the FA Cup in 1883. These clubs amalgamated as Walsall Town Swifts in 1888, becoming simply Walsall in 1895.

Managers (and Secretary-managers)
H. Smallwood 1888–91*, A. G. Burton 1891–93, J. H. Robinson 1893–95, C. H. Ailso 1895–96*, A. E. Parsloe 1896–97*, L. Ford 1897–98*, G. Hughes 1898–99*, L. Ford 1899–1901*, J. E. Shutt 1908–13*, Haydn Price 1914–20, Joe Burchell 1920–26, David Ashworth 1926–27, Jack Torrance 1927–28, James Kerr 1928–29, S. Scholey 1929–30, Peter O'Rourke 1930–32, G. W. Slade 1932–34, Andy Wilson 1934–37, Tommy Lowes 1937–44, Harry Hibbs 1944–51, Tony McPhee 1951, Brough Fletcher 1952–53, Major Frank Buckley 1953–55, John Love 1955–57, Billy Moore 1957–64, Alf Wood 1964, Reg Shaw 1964–68, Dick Graham 1968, Ron Lewin 1968–69, Billy Moore 1969–72, John Smith 1972–73, Doug Fraser 1973–77, Dave Mackay 1977–78, Alan Ashman 1978, Frank Sibley 1979, Alan Buckley 1979–86, Neil Martin (joint manager with Buckley) 1981–82, Tommy Coakley 1986–88, John Barnwell 1989– .

Player and Position	*Ht*	*Wt*	*Birth Date*	*Birth Place*	*Source*	*Clubs*	*League App*	*League Gls*
Keith Bertschin	6 1	11 08	25 8 56	Enfield	Barnet	Ipswich T	32	8
						Birmingham C	118	29
						Norwich C	114	29
						Stoke City	88	29
						Sunderland	36	7
						Walsall	20	—
Martin Goldsmith	6 0	11 11	4 11 69	Walsall	Trainee	Walsall	2	—
Bobby Hutchinson‡	5 9	11 04	19 6 53	Glasgow	Aberdeen LCu	Montrose	41	8
						Dundee	88	25
						Hibernian	67	13
						Wigan Ath	35	3
						Tranmere R	35	6
						Mansfield T	35	3
						Tranmere R	21	4
						Bristol C	92	10
						Walsall	16	—
						Blackpool (loan)	6	—
						Carlisle U (loan)	13	2
Chris Marsh	5 10	12 11	14 1 70	Dudley	Trainee	Walsall	16	—
Willie Naughton	6 0	12 08	20 3 62	Catrine	Apprentice	Preston NE	162	10
						Walsall	151	16
Howard Pritchard	5 10	12 07	18 10 58	Cardiff	Apprentice	Bristol C	38	2
						Swindon T	65	11
						Bristol C	119	22
						Gillingham	88	20
						Walsall	41	6
Mark Rees	5 10	11 10	13 10 61	Smethwick	Apprentice	Walsall	230	36
						Rochdale (loan)	3	—
Stuart Rimmer	5 7	9 04	12 10 64	Southport	Apprentice	Everton	3	—
						Chester C	114	67
						Watford	10	1
						Notts Co	4	2
						Walsall	20	8
Paul Sanderson‡	6 1	12 00	16 12 66	Blackpool	Fleetwood T	Manchester C	—	—
						Chester C	24	3
						Halifax T	104	5
						Cardiff C	21	1
						Walsall	3	—
Andy Saville	6 0	12 00	12 12 64	Hull	Local	Hull C	100	18
						Walsall	12	4

Trainees
Baddams, Adrian A; Beckett, Mark D; Dykes, Alan J; Evason, Paul J; Knight, Craig; Millen, William F; O'Hara, Stephen; Preece, John B; Riley, Darren S; Sadler, Stuart R; Smith, Dean; Sweeney, David; Williams, James A.

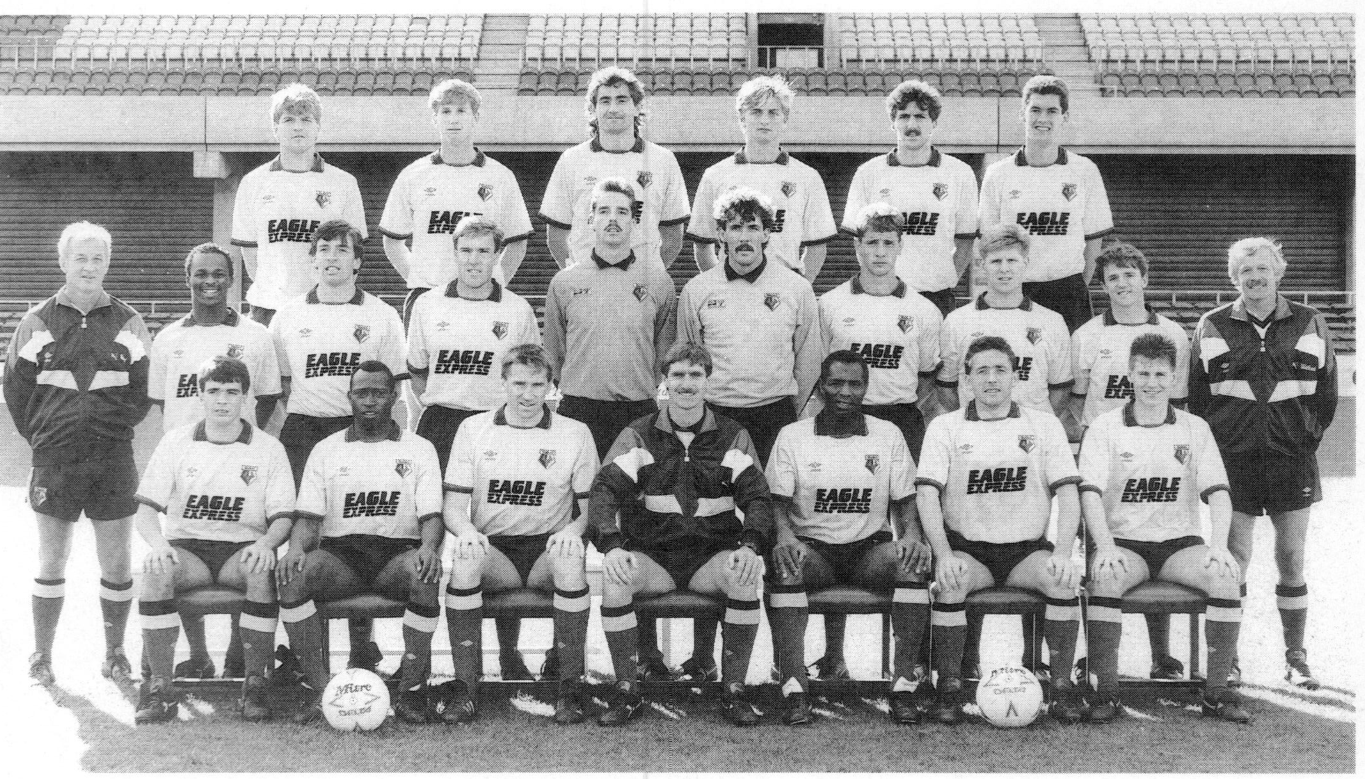

WATFORD 1988–89 *Back row (left to right):* Glyn Hodges, Iwan Roberts, Dave Bamber, Tim Sherwood, Paul Wilkinson, Willie Falconer.
Centre row: Tom Walley (First Team Coach), Roderick Thomas, Rick Holden, Kenny Jackett, Mel Rees, Tony Coton, David Holdsworth, Chris Pullan, Gary Porter, Billy Hails (Physiotherapist).
Front row: Stuart Rimmer, Worrell Sterling, John McClelland (Club Captain), Steve Harrison (Manager), Luther Blissett, Wilf Rostron, Nigel Gibbs.

Division 2 **WATFORD**

Vicarage Road Stadium, Watford WD1 8ER. Telephone Watford (0923) 30933. Answerphone Service: Watford 35133 for information. 0898 700 272 – The 'Hornet Hotline' 24-hour club news service. Ticket Office: 220393. Club shop: 220847. Catering: 221457. Junior Hornets Club: 53836. Marketing: 225761.

Ground capacity: 26,996.

Record attendance: 34,099 v Manchester U, FA Cup 4th rd replay, 3 Feb, 1969.

Record receipts: £104,347 v Liverpool, FA Cup 6th rd replay. 17 March, 1986.

Pitch measurements: 115yd × 75yd.

Chairman: Elton John. ***Vice-Chairman:*** G. A. Smith.

Directors: J. Harrowell, Bertie Mee OBE, J. Reid. H. M. Stratford JP, M. Winwood.

Chief Executive: Eddie Plumley FAAI.

Manager: Steve Harrison.

Coach: Tom Walley. ***Physio:*** Billy Hails.

Marketing Manager: Chris Childs. ***Public Relations Manager:*** Ed Coan.

Year Formed: 1891*(*see Foundation*). ***Turned Professional:*** 1897. ***Ltd Co.:*** 1909.

Club Nickname: 'The Hornets'.

Previous Name: West Herts.

Previous Grounds: 1899, Cassio Road; 1922, Vicarage Road.

Record League Victory: 8-0 v Sunderland, Division 1, 25 September 1982 – Sherwood; Rice, Rostron, Taylor, Terry, Bolton, Callaghan (2), Blissett (4), Jenkins (2), Jackett, Barnes.

Record Cup Victory: 10–1 v Lowestoft T, FA Cup, 1st rd, 27 November 1926 – Yates; Prior, Fletcher (1); Smith (F), 'Bert' Smith, Strain; Stephenson, Warner (3), Edmonds (2), Swan (2), Daniels (1). (1 og)

Record Defeat: 0-10 v Wolverhampton W, FA Cup 1st rd replay, 13 January, 1912.

Most League Points (2 for a win): 71, Division 4, 1977–78.

Most League Points (3 for a win): 80, Division 2, 1981–82.

Most League Goals: 92, Division 4, 1959–60.

Highest League Scorer in Season: Cliff Holton, 42, Division 4, 1959–60.

Most League Goals in Total Aggregate: Tommy Barnett, 144, 1928–39.

Most Capped Player: John Barnes, 31 (47), England and Kenny Jackett, 31, Wales.

Most League Appearances: Duncan Welbourne, 411, 1963–74.

Record Transfer Fee Received: £1,000,000 from AC Milan for Luther Blissett, July 1983.

Record Transfer Fee Paid: £550,000 to AC Milan for Luther Blissett, August 1984.

Football League Record: 1920 Original Member of Division 3; 1921–58 Division 3 (S), 1958–60 Division 4; 1960–69 Division 3; 1969–72 Division 2; 1972–75 Division 3; 1976–78 Division 4; 1978–79 Division 3; 1979–82 Division 2; 1982–88 Division 1; 1988– Division 2.

Honours: *Football League:* Division 1 – Runners-up 1982–83; Division 2 – Runners-up 1981–82; Division 3 – Champions 1968–69, Runners-up 1978–79; Division 4 – Champions 1977–78; Promoted 1959–60 (4th). *FA Cup:* Runners-up 1984. *Football League Cup:* Semi;-final 1978–79. **European Competitions:** *UEFA Cup:* 1983–84.

Colours: Yellow shirts (black /red piping), black shorts, red stockings (yellow/black tops). **Change Colours:** White shirts (black/red piping), white shorts, white stockings.

WATFORD 1988–89 LEAGUE RECORD

Match No.	Date	Venue	Opponents	Result	H/T Score	Lg. Pos.	Goalscorers	Attendance
1	Aug 27	H	Birmingham C	W 1-0	1-0	—	Bamber	12,656
2	29	A	WBA	W 1-0	1-0	—	Gibbs	10,242
3	Sept 3	A	Crystal Palace	W 2-0	1-0	2	Porter, Wilkinson	10,474
4	10	H	Plymouth Arg	W 3-0	1-0	1	Wilkinson, Bamber, Porter (pen)	12,040
5	17	A	Ipswich T	L 2-3	1-1	1	Roberts 2	14,644
6	20	H	Bradford C	W 2-0	0-0	—	Holden 2	12,296
7	24	A	Leicester C	D 2-2	1-1	2	Porter, Wilkinson	10,957
8	Oct 1	H	Swindon T	L 2-3	1-2	3	Holden, Porter	11,657
9	4	H	Oldham Ath	W 3-1	2-0	—	Blissett, Wilkinson 2	10,038
10	8	A	Leeds U	W 1-0	0-0	1	Hodges	15,657
11	15	H	Brighton & HA	D 1-1	0-0	2	Porter (pen)	12,126
12	22	A	Stoke C	L 0-2	0-1	2		7878
13	25	H	Barnsley	W 4-0	2-0	—	Wilkinson, Holden, Roberts, Falconer	10,356
14	29	A	Walsall	W 1-0	0-0	1	Wilkinson	6682
15	Nov 5	H	Chelsea	L 1-2	1-2	1	Wilkinson	17,631
16	12	A	Manchester C	L 1-3	1-0	1	Porter	21,142
17	19	A	Shrewsbury T	D 1-1	0-1	2	Bamber	4621
18	26	H	Hull C	W 2-0	2-0	1	Sherwood, Wilkinson	10,404
19	Dec 3	A	Sunderland	D 1-1	1-0	1	Sherwood	16,330
20	10	H	Oxford U	D 1-1	0-1	3	Wilkinson	10,473
21	17	A	Blackburn R	L 1-2	0-2	4	Holdsworth Dean	8080
22	26	H	Portsmouth	W 1-0	0-0	4	Redfearn	15,224
23	31	H	Bournemouth	W 1-0	0-0	3	Holden	14,006
24	Jan 2	A	Plymouth Arg	L 0-1	0-0	4		12,142
25	14	H	WBA	W 2-0	1-0	3	Holden, Thompson	15,168
26	21	A	Birmingham C	W 3-2	2-2	2	Wilkinson, Thompson 2	6396
27	Feb 4	A	Oldham Ath	L 1-3	0-2	3	Redfearn	6364
28	11	H	Leeds U	D 1-1	1-0	3	Wilkinson	13,439
29	25	A	Brighton & HA	L 0-1	0-1	4		9522
30	28	A	Barnsley	D 2-2	0-1	—	Hodges, Holdsworth David	6163
31	Mar 4	H	Manchester C	W 1-0	1-0	4	Roberts	15,747
32	11	A	Chelsea	D 2-2	2-2	4	Wilkinson, Roberts	22,188
33	18	A	Bradford C	L 1-2	0–0	6	Wilkinson	10,003
34	24	H	Crystal Palace	L 0-1	0-0	—		15,095
35	27	A	Portsmouth	D 2-2	0-2	8	Hodges, Kuhl (og)	9364
36	Apr 1	H	Ipswich T	W 3-2	2-0	5	Wilkinson, Porter, Hodges	12,054
37	4	H	Blackburn R	D 2-2	0-0	—	Thompson, Thomas	8667
38	8	A	Bournemouth	W 1-0	1-0	6	Thompson	9766
39	11	H	Stoke C	W 3-2	2-1	—	Porter, Falconer, Hodges	9086
40	15	A	Swindon T	D 1-1	0-1	6	Miller	9828
41	18	H	Walsall	W 5-0	4-0	—	Wilkinson, Thomas, Thompson, Porter 2 (1 pen)	9777
42	22	H	Leicester C	W 2-1	1-1	3	Wilkinson, Holdsworth Dean	11,262
43	29	A	Hull C	W 3-0	1-0	3	Falconer, Wilkinson, Thompson	5225
44	May 1	H	Sunderland	L 0-1	0-1	3		13,499
45	6	H	Shrewsbury T	D 0-0	0-0	4		10,052
46	13	A	Oxford U	W 4-0	1-0	4	Falconer 2, Wilkinson, Roberts	6573

Final League Position: 4

GOALSCORERS

League (74): Wilkinson 19, Porter 10 (3 pens), Thompson 7, Holden 6, Roberts 6, Falconer 5, Hodges 5, Bamber 3, Holdsworth (Dean) 2, Redfearn 2, Sherwood 2, Thomas 2, Blissett 1, Gibbs 1, Holdsworth (David) 1, Miller 1, own goal 1.
Littlewoods Cup (3): Bamber 1, Rimmer 1, Wilkinson 1.
FA Cup (5): Redfearn 3 (1 pen), Holden 1, own goal 1.

Littlewoods Cup	Second Round	Leicester C (a)	1-4
		(h)	2-2
FA Cup	Third Round	Newcastle U (a)	0-0
		(h)	2-2
		(a)	0-0
		(h)	1-0
	Fourth Round	Derby Co (h)	2-1
	Fifth Round	Nottingham F (h)	0-3

Coton	Gibbs	Falconer	Jackett	Morris	McClelland	Hodges	Wilkinson	Bamber	Porter	Holden	Thomas	Rostron	Sherwood	Holdsworth, David	Roberts	Sterling	Blissett	Rimmer	Miller	Redfearn	Holdsworth, Dean	Thompson	Richardson	Pullan	Henry	*Match No.*
1	2	3	4	5*	6	7	8	9	10	11	12															1
1	2		4		6	7	8	9	10	11		3		5												2
1	2		3		6	7	8	9	10	11			4	5												3
1	2	3	4		6	7*	8	9	10	11	12			5												4
1	2	3	4		6		8	9	10	11	12			5	7*											5
1	2	3	4		6		8	9	10	11				5	7											6
1	2	3	4		6		8	9*	10	11				5	12	7										7
1	2	3	4		6	12	8	9	10	11				5	7*											8
1	2		4		6	7	8		10	11		3		5			9									9
1	2		4		6	7	8	12	10	11†		3*	14	5			9									10
1	2		4		6		8	12	10	11†		3	14	5		7		9*								11
1	2		4		6		8		10	11		3		5	12	7*	9									12
1	2	3	4				8	9*	10	11	7			5	12				6							13
1	2	3	4				8	9*	10	11	7		12	5					6							14
1	2	3	4				8	9	10*	11	7			5	12				6							15
1	2	3	4*		6	7	8	9	10	11			12	14					5†							16
1	2	3	4		6	12	8	9	10	11*			7†	5	14											17
1	2		3		6	11	8	9	10				4	5						7						18
1	2		3		6	11	8	9	10				4	5						7						19
1	2	14	3		6	11	8	9*	10†				4	5	12					7						20
1	2		3		6	11	8*		10				4		9				5	7	12					21
1	2		3		6				10	11			4		8				5	7		9				22
1	2	10			6		8*		14	11		3	4		12				5	7†		9				23
1	2	10			6		8		14	11†		3	4*	12					5	7		9				24
1	2	10	3		6		8			11			4						5	7		9				25
1	2	10	3		6		8			11			4	5	12					7		9*				26
1	2	10	3		6		8			11*			4	5	12					7		9				27
1	2	10	3		6		8			11*			4	5	12					7		9				28
1	2		3		6	11	12		10	7				5	8							9*	4			29
1	2	12	3		6	11	8		10	7				5	9								4*			30
1	2	3			6	11	8*		10	7				5	9							12	4			31
1	2	3	14		6	11	8		10	7				5	9*							12	4†			32
1	2	3	12		6	11	8		10	7*				5	9								4			33
1	2	3†	14		6	11	8		10	7*				5	9							12	4			34
1	2			5†	6	11	8		10		7			14							12	9*	4	3		35
1	2		3		6	11	8		10		7								5		9		4			36
1	2	14	3		6	11	8*		10		7								5		9	12	4†			37
1	2	4	3		6	11	8		10		7*								5		12	9				38
1	2	4	3		6	11	8†		10		7*			14					5		12	9				39
1	2	4	3		6	11	8		10		7*								5		12	9				40
1	2	4	3		6	11	8		10		7*								5		12	9				41
1	2	4	3		6	11†	8		10		7			14					5		12				9*	42
1	2	4	3		6		8		19	11	7								5			9				43
1	2	4	3		6		8		10	11*	7		12	14					5†			9				44
1	2	4	3		6		8		10		7		11						5		12	9*				45
1	2	4	3		6		8		10		7				12				5	11		9*				46
46	46	30 + 3s	39 + 3s	2	43	25 + 2s	44 + 1s	16 + 2s	40 + 2s	32	15 + 3s	7	14 + 5s	27 + 6s	11 + 11s	3	3	1	20	12	2 + 8s	17 + 4s	9	1	1	

WATFORD

Player and Position	Ht	Wt	Birth Date	Birth Place	Source	Clubs	League App	League Gls
Goalkeepers								
Tony Coton	6 1	11 08	19 5 61	Tamworth	Mile Oak	Birmingham C	94	—
						Hereford U (loan)	—	—
						Watford	187	—
David James	6 4	14 07	1 8 70	Welwyn	Trainee	Watford	—	—
Melvyn Rees	6 2	12 12	25 1 67	Cardiff	YTS	Cardiff C	31	—
						Watford	3	—
Defenders								
Barry Ashby	6 2	12 03	21 11 70	London	Trainee	Watford	—	—
Jason Drysdale	5 10	10 07	17 11 70	Bristol	Trainee	Watford	—	—
Willie Falconer	6 1	12 10	5 4 66	Aberdeen	Lewis Utd	Aberdeen	77	13
						Watford	33	5
Martin Gardener	5 11	12 00	29 10 69	Tredegar	School	Watford	—	—
Nigel Gibbs	5 7	10 02	20 11 65	St Albans	Apprentice	Watford	146	2
David Holdsworth	5 11	11 04	8 11 68	London	Trainee	Watford	33	1
John McClelland	6 2	13 05	7 12 55	Belfast	Portadown	Cardiff C	4	1
					Bangor	Mansfield	125	8
						Rangers	96	4
						Watford	184	3
Paul Miller	6 1	12 02	11 10 59	London	Apprentice	Tottenham H	208	7
						Charlton Ath	42	2
						Watford	20	1
Mark Morris	6 0	11 10	26 9 62	Morden	Apprentice	Wimbledon	168	9
						Aldershot (loan)	14	—
						Watford	41	1
Paul Rumble*	5 11	11 05	14 3 69	Hemel Hempstead	Trainee	Watford	—	—
						Scunthorpe U (loan)	8	1
Jason Soloman	6 1	11 09	6 10 70	Welwyn	Trainee	Watford	—	—
Midfield								
Kenny Jackett	5 11	11 13	5 1 62	Watford	Apprentice	Watford	318	26
Dominic Naylor	5 9	11 07	12 8 62	Watford	Trainee	Watford	—	—
Gary Porter	5 5	9 10	6 3 66	Sunderland	Apprentice	Watford	127	18
Chris Pullan	5 8	10 12	14 12 67	Durham	School	Watford	6	—
						Halifax T (loan)	5	1
Neil Redfearn	5 10	12 04	20 6 65	Dewsbury	Apprentice	Nottingham F	—	—
						Bolton W	35	1
						Lincoln C (loan)	10	1
						Lincoln C	90	12
						Doncaster R	46	14
						Crystal Palace	57	10
						Watford	12	2
Lee Richardson	5 11	11 00	12 3 69	Halifax	School	Halifax T	56	2
						Watford	9	—
Tim Sherwood	6 1	11 04	6 2 69	St Albans	Trainee	Watford	32	2
Forwards								
Andrew Gunn	6 0	12 01	2 2 71	Barking	Trainee	Watford	—	—
Liburd Henry	5 11	11 00	29 8 67	Dominica	Leytonstone/ Ilford	Watford	1	—
						Halifax T (loan)	5	—
Glyn Hodges	6 0	12 03	30 4 63	Streatham	Apprentice	Wimbledon	232	49
						Newcastle U	7	—
						Watford	51	8
Ricky Holden	5 11	12 07	9 9 64	Skipton		Burnley	1	—
						Halifax T	67	12
						Watford	42	8

WATFORD

Foundation: Tracing this club's foundation proves difficult. Nowadays it is suggested that Watford was formed as Watford Rovers in 1891. Another version is that Watford Rovers were not forerunners of the present club whose history began in 1898 with the amalgamation of West Herts and Watford St. Mary's.

Managers (and Secretary-managers)
John Goodall 1903–10, Harry Kent 1910–26, Fred Pagnam 1926–29, Neil McBain 1929–37, Bill Findlay 1938–47, Jack Bray 1947–48, Eddie Hapgood 1948–50, Ron Gray 1950–51, Haydn Green 1951–52, Len Goulden 1952–55 (GM to 1956), Johnny Paton 1955–56, Neil McBain 1956–59, Ron Burgess 1959–63, Bill McGarry 1963–64, Ken Furphy 1964–71, George Kirby 1971–73, Mike Keen 1973–77, Graham Taylor 1977–87, Dave Bassett 1987–88, Steve Harrison 1988– .

Player and Position	*Ht*	*Wt*	*Birth Date*	*Birth Place*	*Source*	*Clubs*	*League App*	*League Gls*
Dean Holdsworth	5 11	11 04	8 11 68	London	Trainee	Watford	12	2
						Carlisle U (loan)	4	1
						Port Vale (loan)	6	2
						Swansea C (loan)	5	1
						Brentford (loan)	7	1
Kevin Richardson‡	5 5	8 12	14 8 69	Waltham Abbey	School	Watford	—	—
Iwan Roberts	6 3	12 05	26 6 68	Banour		Watford	54	9
Rod Thomas	5 6	10 03	10 10 70	London	Trainee	Watford	22	2
Garry Thompson	6 1	14 00	7 10 59	Birmingham	Apprentice	Coventry C	134	38
						WBA	91	39
						Sheffield W	36	7
						Aston Villa	55	17
						Watford	21	7
Paul Wilkinson	6 0	11 00	30 10 64	Louth	Apprentice	Grimsby T	71	27
						Everton	31	7
						Nottingham F	34	5
						Watford	45	19

Trainees
Bennett, Warren J; Evans, David W; Price, Jonathan; Rice, Marc G; Smith, Osborn J; Towler, Paul A.

Associated Schoolboys
Abrahams, Paul; Alsford, Julian; Bartholomew, Ian; Bazeley, Darren S; Boachie, Nana; Dalli, Marc J; Durrant, Kevin J; Edgar, Nicholas; Flowers, Paul A; Fuller, Adrian J; Gallen, Joseph; Harrison, Gerald R; Inglethorpe, Alex M; Kendall, Stuart J; Lavin, Gerrard; Meara, James S; Nwaokolo, Daniel; Page, Robert J; Porter, Gareth; Proctor, Neil S.C; Pugh, Stephen; Renford, Richard; Riddick, Alexander G; Sheppard, Simon; Snowdon, Trevor; Somers, Shane P; Wild, Matthew.

WEST BROMWICH ALBION 1988–89 *Back row (left to right):* John Paskin, Stacey North, Chris Whyte, Martyn Bennett, Stuart Naylor, Paul Bradshaw, Paul Dyson, Carlton Palmer, Darren Bradley, Colin Anderson.
Front row: Graham Doig (Physiotherapist), Wayne Dobbins, Gary Robson, Don Goodman, Brian Talbot (Player/Manager), Robert Hopkins, Simeon Hodson, Arthur Albiston, Stewart Phillips, Stuart Pearson (Coach).

Division 2 WEST BROMWICH ALBION

The Hawthorns, West Bromwich B71 4LF. Telephone 021-525 8888 (all Depts).

Ground capacity: 36,159 (10,865 seats).

Record attendance: 64,815 v Arsenal, FA Cup 6th rd, 6 March 1937.

Record receipts: £79,494.76 v Tottenham H, League Cup semi-final, 3 February, 1982.

Pitch measurements: 115yd × 75yd.

President: F. A. Millichip. ***Vice-President:*** C. E. Edwards.

Chairman: J. G. Silk. ***Vice-Chairman:*** D. B. Boundy.

Directors: J. W. Brandrick, J. S. Lucas, M. C. McGinnity, T. Summers, A. B. Hale.

Player-Manager: Brian Talbot. ***Assistant Manager:***

Coach: Stuart Pearson. ***Physio:*** John MacGowan NCSP, SRP. ***Secretary:*** Dr. J. J. Evans.

Club Statistician: Tony Matthews. ***Commercial Manager:*** Alan Stevenson.

Year Formed: 1879. ***Turned Professional:*** 1885. ***Ltd Co.:*** 1892.

Club Nicknames: 'Throstles', 'Baggies', 'Albion'.

Previous Grounds: 1879, Coopers Hill; 1879, Dartmouth Park; 1881, Bunns Field, Walsall Street; 1882, Four Acres (Dartmouth Cricket Club); 1885, Stoney Lane; 1900, The Hawthorns.

Previous Name: 1879–81, West Bromwich Strollers.

Record League Victory: 12-0 v Darwen, Division 1, 4 April 1892 – Reader; Horton, McCulloch; Reynolds (2), Perry, Groves; Bassett (3), McLeod, Nicholls (1), Pearson (4), Geddes (1). (1 og).

Record Cup Victory: 10-1 v Chatham (away), FA Cup, 3rd rd, 2 March 1889 – Roberts; Horton, Green; Timmins (1), Charles Perry, Horton; Bassett (2), Perry (1), Bayliss (2), Pearson, Wilson (3). (1 og)

Record Defeat: 3-10 v Stoke C, Division 1, 4 February, 1937.

Most League Points (2 for a win): 60, Division 1, 1919–20.

Most League Points (3 for a win): 72, Division 2, 1988–89.

Most League Goals: 105, Division 2, 1929–30.

Highest League Scorer in Season: William 'Ginger' Richardson, 39, Division 1, 1935–36.

Most League Goals in Total Aggregate: Tony Brown, 218, 1963–79.

Most Capped Player: Stuart Williams, 33 (43), Wales.

Most League Appearances: Tony Brown, 574, 1963–80.

Record Transfer Fee Received: £1,500,000 from Manchester U for Bryan Robson, October 1981.

Record Transfer Fee Paid: £748,000 to Manchester C for Peter Barnes, July 1979.

Football League Record: 1888 Founder Member of Football League; 1901–02 Division 2; 1902–04 Division 1; 1904–11 Division 2; 1911–27 Division 1; 1927–31 Division 2; 1931–38 Division 1; 1938–49 Division 2; 1949–73 Division 1; 1973–76 Division 2; 1976–86 Division 1; 1986– Division 2.

Honours: *Football League:* Division 1 – Champions 1919–20; Runners-up 1924–25, 1953–54, Division 2 – Champions 1901–02, 1910–11; Runners-up 1930–31, 1948–49; Promoted to Division 1 1975–76 (3rd). *FA Cup:* Winners 1888, 1892, 1931, 1954, 1968; Runners-up 1886, 1887, 1895, 1912, 1935. *Football League Cup:* Winners 1965–66; Runners-up 1966–67, 1969–70. **European Competitions:** *European Cup-Winners' Cup:* 1968–69; *European Fairs Cup:* 1966–67; *UEFA Cup:* 1978–79, 1979–80, 1981–82.

Colours: Navy blue and white striped shirts, navy blue shorts, white stockings. **Change Colours:** Green and yellow striped shirts, green shorts, yellow stockings.

WEST BROMWICH ALBION 1988–89 LEAGUE RECORD

Match No.	Date	Venue	Opponents	Result	H/T Score	Lg. Pos.	Goalscorers	Attendance
1	Aug 27	A	Leicester C	D 1-1	0-0	—	Paskin	13,082
2	29	H	Watford	L 0-1	0-1	—		10,242
3	Sept 3	H	Swindon T	W 3-1	3-1	10	Dyson, Goodman, Paskin	7518
4	10	A	Shrewsbury T	D 1-1	0-0	10	Robson	5851
5	17	H	Walsall	D 0-0	0-0	12		13,977
6	21	A	Brighton & HA	W 1-0	0-0	—	Goodman	7395
7	24	A	Plymouth Arg	D 1-1	0-0	9	Phillips	8539
8	Oct 1	H	Ipswich T	L 1-2	0-1	11	Whyte	9357
9	5	H	Bournemouth	D 0-0	0-0	—		7248
10	8	A	Barnsley	L 1-2	1-0	18	Talbot	5674
11	15	A	Birmingham C	W 4-1	2-1	13	Hopkins 2, Phillips, Robson	10,453
12	22	H	Bradford C	W 1-0	0-0	9	Talbot	8989
13	26	H	Manchester C	W 1-0	1-0	—	Durnin	14,258
14	29	A	Blackburn R	W 2-1	1-1	3	Whyte, Anderson	9503
15	Nov 5	H	Oxford U	W 3-2	1-1	2	Anderson, Hopkins, Goodman	11,643
16	12	A	Leeds U	L 1-2	1-2	5	Durnin	20,442
17	19	A	Sunderland	D 1-1	1-0	6	Robson	18,141
18	26	H	Crystal Palace	W 5-3	1-0	6	Goodman 3, Hopkins, Paskin	11,099
19	Dec 3	A	Portsmouth	D 0-0	0-0	6		12,779
20	10	H	Hull C	W 2-0	0-0	5	Goodman 2	10,094
21	18	H	Stoke C	W 6-0	2-0	—	Robson 2, Goodman 2, Paskin 2	17,634
22	26	A	Oldham Ath	W 3-1	2-0	2	Goodman, Hopkins, Robson	9827
23	31	A	Chelsea	D 1-1	1-0	2	Anderson	25,906
24	Jan 2	H	Shrewsbury T	W 4-0	0-0	1	Goodman, Moyes (og), Albiston, Robson	18,411
25	14	A	Watford	L 0-2	0-1	2		15,168
26	21	H	Leicester C	D 1-1	0-0	4	Robson	15,792
27	Feb 4	A	Bournemouth	L 1-2	1-1	5	Albiston	11,571
28	11	H	Barnsley	D 1-1	0-1	5	Goodman	12,650
29	18	A	Bradford C	L 0-2	0-1	5		11,047
30	25	H	Birmingham C	D 0-0	0-0	5		16,148
31	Mar 1	A	Manchester C	D 1-1	0-0	—	Whyte	25,109
32	5	H	Leeds U	W 2-1	2-1	—	Goodman 2	15,914
33	11	A	Oxford U	D 1-1	1-1	6	West	7581
34	15	H	Blackburn R	W 2-0	1-0	—	West 2	12,821
35	18	H	Brighton & HA	W 1-0	0-0	3	Bartlett	11,586
36	25	A	Swindon T	D 0-0	0-0	3		12,240
37	27	H	Oldham Ath	W 3-1	1-0	3	West, Bartlett, Anderson (pen)	13,812
38	Apr 1	A	Walsall	D 0-0	0-0	3		9520
39	4	A	Stoke C	D 0-0	0-0	—		11,151
40	8	H	Chelsea	L 2-3	2-3	4	Anderson, Ford	22,858
41	15	H	Plymouth Arg	D 2-2	1-0	5	Brown (og), West	11,358
42	22	A	Ipswich T	L 1-2	0-0	6	West	12,047
43	29	A	Crystal Palace	L 0-1	0-0	7		13,728
44	May 1	H	Portsmouth	W 3-0	1-0	7	Anderson (pen), West 2	9586
45	6	H	Sunderland	D 0-0	0-0	9		10,451
46	13	A	Hull C	W 1-0	1-0	9	Bartlett	5217

Final League Position: 9

GOALSCORERS

League (65): Goodman 15, Robson 8, West 8, Anderson 6 (2 pens), Hopkins 5, Paskin 5, Bartlett 3, Whyte 3, Albiston 2, Durnin 2, Phillips 2, Talbot 2, Dyson 1, Ford 1, own goals 2.
Littlewoods Cup (2): Gray 1 (pen), Palmer 1.
FA Cup (1): Anderson 1.

Littlewoods Cup	First Round	Peterborough U (h)	0-3
		(a)	2-0
FA Cup	Third Round	Everton (h)	1-1
		(a)	0-1

Naylor	Bradley	Albiston	Talbot	Dyson	North	Hopkins	Goodman	Paskin	Palmer	Anderson	Gray	Hodson	Burrows	Robson	Whyte	Cork	Phillips	Durnin	Dobbins	Bradshaw	Rice	Cartwright	Bartlett	West	Walford	Ford	Banks	Raven	*Match No.*
1	2	3	4	5	6	7	8	9	10	11																			1
1	2	3	4	5	6	7		9	10	11	8																		2
1	4	3		6†	5	7	8	9*	10	11	12	2	14																3
1	12†	3			6	7	8		10	11	9*	2	14	4	5														4
1			4		6	7	8	9†	10	11		2*	3	12	5	14													5
1		2	4		6	7	8	9*	10	11			3		5	12													6
1		2	4		6	7	8		10*	11			3		5	12	9												7
1		2	4		6	7	8		10	11			3		5		9												8
1		2	4		6	7	8		10	11			3		5		9												9
1	12	2	4		6	7*			10	11			3	14	5	8†	9												10
1	12	2	4		6	7*			10	11			3	8	5		9												11
1	2	3	4		6	7			10	11				8	5			9											12
1		3	4		6	7			10	11				8	5			9	2										13
1		3	4		6	7	12		10	11				8	5			9*	2										14
1		3	4		6	7	12		10	11				8	5			9*	2										15
1	2	3	4		6	7	11	12	10					8*	5			9											16
1	2	3	4		6	7	8	12	10	11				9*	5														17
1	2	3	4*		6	7	8	12	10	11				9	5														18
1	7	3	4		6		8	12	10	11		2		9*	5														19
1	7*	3	4		6		8	12	10	11		2		9	5														20
1		3	4		6		8	10		11		2		9	5				7										21
1		3			6	7	8	10		11		2		9	5				4										22
1		3	4		6	7	8	10		11		2		9	5														23
		3	4		6	7	8	12	10	11		2†		9*	5				14	1									24
	11	3	4		6	7		8	10					9	5				2*	1	12								25
1	2†	3	4		6	7		8*	10					9	5				14		11	12							26
1		3	4		6	7		8	10					9	5				2		11								27
1		3	4*		6	7	8	12	10	11				9	5				2										28
1		3	4		6	7	8		10	11				2	5								9						29
1	2	3	4		6	7	8*			11				10	5								12	9					30
1	2	3*			6	7	8			11				4	5				12				10	9					31
1	7	3*			6		8	12		11				4†	5				2				10	9	14				32
1	7				6		8			11				4	5				2				10	9	3				33
1	2	3	4		6		8			11				7	5								10	9					34
1	2	3	4		6	12	8			11				7*	5								10	9					35
1	2	3	4		6		8*			11				10									12	9	5	7			36
1	2	3	4†		6		8*			11				10	5								12	9		7	14		37
1	2	3	4		6					11				10									8	9	5	7			38
1	2	3	4		6			12		11				10†	5*								8	9		7	14		39
1	6	3	4		5		8*			11									2				12	9		7	10		40
1	2*	3	4		6		8			11				10	5								12	9		7			41
1		3			6		8*	12		11				10	5				14				7†	9		2	4		42
1		3	4		6		12	8		11*				10	5				2					9		7			43
1		3	4		6		14	8†		11				10	5								12	9*		7		2	44
1		3	4		6		14	8*		11				10†	5								12	9		7		2	45
1			4†		6		14	12		11				10	5								8*	9		7		2	46
44	23	43	39	3	46	28	30	14	26	42	2	9	7	36	40	1	5	5	12	2	2	—	10	17	3	11	2	3	
	+					+	+	+			+		+	+		+			+		+	+	+		+		+		
	3s					1s	6s	11s			1s		2s	2s		3s			4s		1s	1s	7s		1s		2s		

Robinson — Match No. 46(3)

WEST BROMWICH ALBION

Player and Position	Ht	Wt	Birth Date	Birth Place	Source	Clubs	League App	League Gls
Goalkeepers								
Paul Bradshaw	6 3	13 04	28 4 56	Altrincham	Apprentice	Blackburn R	78	—
						Wolverhampton W	200	—
					Vancouver W	WBA	8	—
						Bristol R	5	—
						Newport Co	23	—
						WBA	2	—
Gary Leake‡			30 1 70	Hucknall	Trainee	WBA	—	—
						Chester C (loan)	—	—
Stuart Naylor	6 4	12 10	6 12 62	Wetherby	Yorkshire A	Lincoln C	49	—
						Peterborough U (loan)	8	—
						Crewe Alex (loan)	55	—
						WBA	133	—
Defenders								
Arthur Albiston	5 7	11 05	14 7 57	Edinburgh	Apprentice	Manchester U	379	6
						WBA	43	2
Martyn Bennett	6 0	12 12	4 8 61	Birmingham	Apprentice	WBA	181	9
Simeon Hodson	5 9	10 02	5 3 66	Lincoln	Apprentice	Notts Co	27	—
						Charlton Ath	5	—
						Lincoln C	56	—
						Newport Co	34	1
						WBA	16	—
Stacey North	6 2	12 06	25 11 64	Luton	Apprentice	Luton T	25	—
						Wolverhampton W (loan)	3	—
						WBA	64	—
Ronnie Robinson	5 9	11 00	22 10 66	Sunderland	Vaux Breweries	Ipswich T	—	—
						Leeds U	27	—
						Doncaster R	78	5
						WBA	1	—
Darren Rogers			9 4 70	Birmingham	Trainee	WBA	—	—
Chris Whyte	6 1	11 10	2 9 61	London	Amateur	Arsenal	90	8
						Cyrstal Palace (loan)	13	—
					Los Angeles R	WBA	40	3
Midfield								
Colin Anderson	5 9	10 07	26 4 62	Newcastle	Apprentice	Burnley	6	—
						Torquay U	109	11
						QPR (loan)	—	—
						WBA	104	8
Ian Banks	5 11	12 12	9 1 61	Mexborough	Apprentice	Barnsley	164	37
						Leicester C	93	14
						Huddersfield T	88	17
						Bradford C	30	3
						WBA	4	—
Darren Bradley	5 10	11 04	24 11 65	Birmingham	Apprentice	Aston Villa	20	—
						WBA	69	1
Neil Cartwright§			20 2 71	Stourbridge	Trainee	WBA	1	—
Wayne Dobbins	5 7	10 08	30 8 68	Bromsgrove	Apprentice	WBA	32	—
Darren Lloyd‡			30 8 69	Bristol		WBA	—	—
Paul Raven			28 7 70	Salisbury	Schools	Doncaster R	52	4
						WBA	3	—
Gary Robson	5 5	10 10	6 7 65	Co Durham	Apprentice	WBA	108	10
Brian Talbot	5 10	12 00	21 7 53	Ipswich	Apprentice	Ipswich T	177	25
						Arsenal	254	40
						Watford	48	8
						Stoke C	54	5
						WBA	54	4

WEST BROMWICH ALBION

Foundation: There is a well known story that when employees of Salter's Spring Works in West Bromwich decided to form a football club in 1879, they had to send someone to the nearby Association Football stronghold of Wednesbury to purchase a football. A weekly subscription of 2d (less than 1p) was imposed and the name of the new club was West Bromwich Strollers.

Managers (and Secretary-managers)
Louis Ford 1890–92*, Henry Jackson 1892–94*, Edward Stephenson 1894–95*, Clement Keys 1895–96*, Frank Heaven 1896–1902*, Fred Everiss 1902–48, Jack Smith 1948–52, Jesse Carver 1952, Vic Buckingham 1953–59, Gordon Clark 1959–61, Archie Macaulay 1961–63, Jimmy Hagan 1963–67, Alan Ashman 1967–71, Don Howe 1971–75, Johnny Giles 1975–77, Ronnie Allen 1977, Ron Atkinson 1978–81, Ronnie Allen 1981–82, Ron Wylie 1982–84, Johnny Giles 1984–85, Ron Saunders 1986–87, Ron Atkinson 1987–88, Brian Talbot 1988– .

Player and Position	*Ht*	*Wt*	*Birth Date*	*Birth Place*	*Source*	*Clubs*	*League App*	*League Gls*
Forwards								
Kevin Bartlett	5 9	10 12	12 10 62	Portsmouth	Apprentice	Portsmouth	3	—
					Fareham	Cardiff C	82	25
						WBA	17	3
Tony Ford	5 9	12 08	14 5 59	Grimsby	Apprentice	Grimsby T	354	54
						Sunderland (loan)	9	1
						Stoke C	112	13
						WBA	11	1
Donald Goodman	5 10	11 00	9 5 66	Leeds		Bradford C	70	14
						WBA	86	24
Andy Gray (To Rangers Sept 1988)	5 11	11 10	30 11 55	Glasgow	Clydebanks	Dundee U	62	36
						Aston Villa	113	54
						Wolverhampton W	133	38
						Everton	49	14
						Aston Villa	54	5
						Notts Co (loan)	4	—
						WBA	35	10
Cory Johnson‡			22 11 69	Stoke	Trainee	WBA	—	—
Tony Morley‡	5 8	11 06	26 8 54	Ormskirk	Apprentice	Preston NE	84	15
						Burnley	91	5
						Aston Villa	137	25
						WBA	33	4
						Birmingham C (loan)	4	3
					Den Haag	WBA	28	7
						Burnley (loan)	5	—
John Paskin			1 2 6 2	Capetown	Seiko	WBA	25	5
Colin West	6 2	13 11	13 11 62	Wallsend	Apprentice	Sunderland	102	21
						Watford	45	20
						Rangers	10	2
						Sheffield W	45	8
						WBA	17	8

Trainees
Ashton, Mark A; Birch, Matthew J; Burgess, Daryl; Cartwright, Neil A; Colcombe, Scott; Foster, Adrian M; Goodall, Darren T; Hesson, Neil J; Littlejohn, Adrian S; Love, Craig; Mahoney, Timothy M; Palmer, Leslie J; Pritchard, David M; Sheppard, Matthew; Stavrou, Stavros C; Sweeney, Paul A; Whalley, David; Whitehouse, Philip; Withe, Jason L.

****Non-Contract**
Bodell, Tony; Churchill, Lance.

Associated Schoolboys
Ball, Steven G; Coldicott, Stacy; Davies, Nicholas J; Donovan, John D; Dunphy, Steve; Dwyer, James C; Evans, Lee J; Harper, Marcus J; Hicks, Daniel; Hinett, Gregory J; Hollier, Nigel T; Johnson, Jonathan J; Jones, Mark; Mansell, Craig E; Moore, Anthony; Morris, Simon R.J; Nelson, Matthew J; Patterson, Matthew; Price, Lyndon P; Spill, Steven A; Warner, Michael J; Wright, Dean T.J.;

WEST HAM UNITED 1988–89 *Back row (left to right):* Julian Dicks, Alan Dickens, Gary Strodder, Tom McAlister, Phil Parkes, Allen McKnight, Alvin Martin, Tony Gale, Steve Walford.
Centre row: Paul Hilton, Chris Harwood, Paul Ince, Ray Stewart, Alan Devonshire, George Parris, Simon Livett, David Kelly, Leroy Rosenior, Andrew Pearson, Adam King.
Front row: Kevin Keen, Paul Kelly, Steve Potts, Tommy McQueen, Mark Ward, Liam Brady, Stuart Slater, Stewart Robson, Eamonn Dolan.

Division 2 WEST HAM UNITED

Boleyn Ground, Green Street, Upton Park, London E13. Telephone 01-472 2740. Commercial Dept. 01-472 5756. Answerphone 01-470 1325. Hammer Line: 01-475 0555. Dial-a-seat: 01-472 3322.

Ground capacity: 35,510.

Record attendance: 42,322 v Tottenham H, Division 1, 17 Oct, 1970.

Record receipts: £146,074 v Tottenham H, League Cup 5th rd, 27 January 1987.

Pitch measurements: 112yd × 72yd.

Chairman: L. C. Cearns. ***Vice-Chairman:*** W. F. Cearns.

Directors: J. Petchey, M. W. Cearns AIB., C. J. WARNER MA

Manager: Lou Macari.

Secretary: T. M. Finn. ***Commercial Manager:*** Brian Blower.

Year Formed: 1895. ***Turned Professional:*** 1900. ***Ltd Co.:*** 1900.

Previous names: Thames Ironworks FC 1895–1900.

Previous Grounds: Memorial Recreation Ground, Canning Town: 1904 Boleyn Ground.

Club Nickname: 'The Hammers'.

Record League Victory: 8-0 v Rotherham U, Division 2, 8 March 1958 – Gregory; Bond, Wright; Malcolm, Brown, Lansdowne, Grice, Smith (2), Keeble (2), Dick (4), Musgrove. 8-0 v Sunderland, Division 1, 19 October 1968 – Ferguson; Bonds, Charles; Peters, Stephenson, Moore (1); Redknapp, Boyce, Brooking (1), Hurst (6), Sissons.

Record Cup Victory: 10-0 v Bury, League Cup, 2nd rd (2nd leg), 25 October 1980 – Parkes; Stewart (1), Walford, Bonds (Orr), Martin (1), Devonshire (2), Allen, Cottee (4), Swindlehurst, Brooking (2), Pike.

Record Defeat: 2-8 v Blackburn R, Division 1, 26 December, 1963.

Most League Points (2 for a win): 66, Division 2, 1980–81.

Most League Points (3 for a win): 84, Division 1, 1985–86.

Most League Goals: 101, Division 2, 1957–58.

Highest League Scorer in Season: Vic Watson, 41 Division 1, 1929–30.

Most League Goals in Total Aggregate: Vic Watson, 306, 1920–35.

Most Capped Player: Bobby Moore, 108, England.

Most League Appearances: Billy Bonds, 663, 1967–88.

Record Transfer Fee Received: £2,200,000 from Everton for Tony Cottee, July 1988.

Record Transfer Fee Paid: £1,250,000 to Celtic for Frank McAvennie, March 1989.

Football League Record: 1919 Elected to Division 2; 1923–32 Division 1; 1932–58 Division 2; 1958–78 Division 1; 1978–81 Division 2; 1981–89 Division 1; 1989– Division 2.

Honours: *Football League:* Division 1 best season: 3rd, 1985–86, Division 2 – Champions 1957–58, 1980–81; Runners-up 1922–23. *FA Cup:* Winners 1964, 1975, 1980; Runners-up 1922–23. *Football League Cup:* Runners-up 1966, 1981. **European Competitions:** *European Cup-Winner's Cup:* 1964–65 (winners), 1965–66, 1975–76 (runners-up), 1980–81.

Colours: Claret and blue shirts, white shorts, white stockings. **Change colours:** White shirts, blue shorts, blue stockings.

WEST HAM UNITED 1988–89 LEAGUE RECORD

Match No.	Date	Venue	Opponents	Result	H/T Score	Lg. Pos.	Goalscorers	Attendance
1	Aug 27	A	Southampton	L 0-4	0-2	—		18,407
2	Sept 3	H	Charlton Ath	L 1-3	0-1	20	Keen (pen)	19,566
3	10	A	Wimbledon	W 1-0	1-0	13	Ward	7730
4	17	H	Aston Villa	D 2-2	0-2	13	Mountfield (og), Kelly	19,186
5	24	A	Manchester U	L 0-2	0-1	17		39,941
6	Oct 1	H	Arsenal	L 1-4	1-2	20	Dickens	27,658
7	8	A	Middlesbrough	L 0-1	0-1	20		19,608
8	15	A	QPR	L 1-2	1-0	20	Kelly	14,566
9	22	H	Newcastle U	W 2-0	0-0	18	Dickens, Stewart (pen)	17,765
10	29	H	Liverpool	L 0-2	0-0	19		30,198
11	Nov 5	A	Coventry C	D 1-1	1-0	19	Kelly	14,651
12	12	H	Nottingham F	D 3-3	2-3	17	Kelly 2, Rosenior	21,682
13	19	A	Luton T	L 1-4	0-3	18	Martin	9308
14	26	H	Everton	L 0-1	0-0	19		22,176
15	Dec 3	A	Millwall	W 1-0	1-0	19	Ince	20,105
16	10	H	Sheffield W	D 0-0	0-0	19		16,676
17	17	H	Tottenham H	L 0-2	0-1	20		28,379
18	27	A	Norwich C	L 1-2	0-0	—	Stewart (pen)	17,491
19	31	A	Charlton Ath	D 0-0	0-0	20		11,084
20	Jan 2	H	Wimbledon	L 1-2	1-1	20	Rosenior	18,346
21	14	A	Derby Co	W 2-1	2-1	19	Kelly, Brady	16,796
22	21	H	Manchester U	L 1-3	1-1	19	Brady (pen)	29,822
23	Feb 4	A	Arsenal	L 1-2	0-0	20	Dicks	40,139
24	25	H	QPR	D 0-0	0-0	20		17,371
25	Mar 11	H	Coventry C	D 1-1	0-1	20	Ince	15,205
26	25	A	Aston Villa	W 1-0	1-0	20	Ince	22,471
27	27	H	Norwich C	L 0-2	0-0	20		27,265
28	Apr 1	A	Tottenham H	L 0-3	0-1	20		28,375
29	8	H	Derby Co	D 1-1	1-1	20	Rosenior	16,560
30	11	H	Middlesbrough	L 1-2	1-0	—	Keen	16,230
31	15	H	Southampton	L 1-2	1-1	20	Brady (pen)	14,766
32	22	H	Millwall	W 3-0	3-0	20	Dicks,Dickens, Parris	16,603
33	May 3	A	Newcastle U	W 2-1	1-1	—	Keen, Ward	14,202
34	6	H	Luton T	W 1-0	1-0	19	Dickens	18,686
35	9	A	Sheffield W	W 2-0	0-0	—	Dickens, Rosenior	19,905
36	13	A	Everton	L 1-3	1-1	19	Slater	21,694
37	18	A	Nottingham F	W 2-1	2-1	—	Rosenior 2	20,843
38	23	A	Liverpool	L 1-5	1-1	—	Rosenior	41,855

Final League Position: 19

GOALSCORERS

League (37): Rosenior 7, Kelly 6, Dickens 5, Brady 3 (2 pens), Ince 3, Keen 3 (1 pen), Dicks 2, Stewart 2 (2 pens), Ward 2, Martin 1, Parris 1, Slater 1, own goal 1.
Littlewoods Cup (16): Kelly 4, Ince 3, Martin 2, Rosenior 2, Dickens 1, Gale 1, Keen 1, Stewart 1 (pen), own goal 1.
FA Cup (6): Rosenior 2, Dickens 1, Ince 1, Slater 1, own goal 1.

Littlewoods Cup	Second Round	Sunderland (a)	3-0
		(h)	2-1
	Third Round	Derby Co (a)	5-0
	Fourth Round	Liverpool (h)	4-1
	Fifth Round	Aston Villa (h)	2-1
	Semi-Final	Luton T (h)	0-3
		(a)	0-2
FA Cup	Third Round	Arsenal (h)	2-2
		(a)	1-0
	Fourth Round	Swindon T (a)	0-0
		(h)	1-0
	Fifth Round	Charlton Ath (a)	1-0
	Sixth Round	Norwich C (h)	0-0
		(a)	1-3

McAlister	Potts	Dicks	Gale	Martin	Keen	Ward	Parris	Slater	Kelly	Robson	Hilton	Dickens	Ince	Devonshire	McKnight	Rosenior	Strodder	Stewart	Brady	Parkes	McAvennie	McQueen	*Match No.*
1	2	3	4*	5	6	7	8	9†	10	11	12	14											1
1	2*	3		5	6†	7	8	9	10	11		4	12	14									2
		3		5		7	2		8*	11	4	10	6	12	1	9							3
		3		5		7	2		8	11		10	6	12	1	9	4*						4
		3				7	2		8	11	5	10	6	12	1	9	4*						5
		3		5		7	2†		8	11	4	10	6	12	1	9*	14						6
	2*	3	4		12	7	9		8		5	10	11	6	1								7
	2	3	4		12	7			8		5	10	11	6*	1	9							8
		3	4	5	12	7		9	8			10	11	6*	1			2					9
		3	4	5		7		9	8*			10	11	6	1	12		2					10
	2	3	4	5	6	7			8			10	11		1	9							11
	2	3	4	5	6	7	12		8†			10	11*		1	9			14				12
	2	3	4	5	6*	7	12				14	10†	11		1	9			8				13
	2	3	4	5	6	7*						10	11	12	1	9			8				14
	2	3	4	5					8			10	11	6	1	9			7				15
	2		4	5			3		8			10	11	6	1	9			7				16
	2		4	5	12		3		8			10	11	6*	1	9			7				17
	2		4	5*	14		3		8			10†	11	6	1	9		12	7				18
	11	3	4	5	6		12		8			10			1	9		2	7*				19
	11	3	4	5	6				8			10			1	9		2	7				20
	5	3	4		12				8			10	11	6	1	9	14	2†	7*				21
	2	3	4	5	12	10			8†				11	6*	1	9	14		7				22
	2	3	4			7			12			8	11	6*	1	9	5		10				23
	2	3	4	5		7	12	9				8*	11	6					10	1			24
	2	3	4	5				9	8			10	11	6					7	1			25
		3	4			7	2	9			5	12	11	6*					10	1	8		26
		3	4			7	2	9			5	10	11			12			6*	1	8		27
	6	3	4			7	2	9				12	11				5*		10	1	8		28
	14	3	4†	5		7	2	12				6	11			9			10*	1	8		29
	4	3			11	7	2				5	6				9			10	1	8		30
	4				3	7	2	12			5	6*	11			9			10†	1	8	14	31
	5	3	4		10	7	2	9				6	11*							1	8	12	32
		3	4	5	10	7	2	9	12			6	11							1	8*		33
	14	3	4†	5	10	7	2	8	12			6	11			9*				1			34
	12	3	4*	5	10	7	2	8				6	11			9				1			35
	12	3	4	5	10†	7	2	8	14			6	11*			9				1			36
	12	3	4	5	10	7	2	8				6			1	9			11*				37
		3	4	5	14	7	2	8				6	11†		1	9			10*		12		38
2	23 + 5s	34	31	27	16 + 8s	30	23 + 4s	16 + 2s	21 + 4s	6	9 + 2s	34 + 3s	32 + 1s	14 + 6s	23	26 + 2s	4 + 3s	5 + 1s	21 + 1s	13	8 + 1s	— + 2s	

WEST HAM UNITED

Player and Position	Ht	Wt	Birth Date	Birth Place	Source	Clubs	League App	League Gls
Goalkeepers								
Tom McAlister*	6 1	12 13	10 12 52	Clydebank	Apprentice	Sheffield U	63	—
						Rotherham U	159	—
						Blackpool	16	—
						Swindon T	1	—
						Bristol R (loan)	13	—
						West Ham U	85	—
						Colchester U (loan)	20	—
Allen McKnight	6 1	13 07	27 1 64	Antrim	Distillery	Celtic	12	—
						Albion R (loan)	36	—
						West Ham U	23	—
Phil Parkes	6 3	15 01	8 8 50	Sedgeley	Amateur	Walsall	52	—
						QPR	344	—
						West Ham U	322	—
Defenders								
Billy Bonds‡	6 0	13 07	17 9 46	Woolwich	Apprentice	Charlton Ath	95	1
						West Ham U	663	48
Julian Dicks	57	10 08	8 8 68	Bristol	Apprentice	Birmingham C	89	1
						West Ham U	42	2
Tony Gale	6 1	13 10	19 11 59	London	Apprentice	Fulham	277	19
						West Ham U	160	2
Chris Harwood	5 11	12 00	19 4 70	Hendon	Trainee	West Ham U	—	—
Paul Hilton	6 1	11 06	8 10 59	Oldham	Amateur	Bury	148	39
						West Ham U	60	7
Tommy McQueen	5 7	11 01	1 4 63	Bellshill	Gartcosh U	Clyde	112	1
						Aberdeen	53	4
						West Ham U	23	—
Alvin Martin	6 1	13 03	29 7 58	Bootle	Apprentice	West Ham U	343	23
George Parris	5 9	12 00	11 9 64	Ilford	Apprentice	West Ham U	120	5
Andy Pearson	5 7	10 06	27 11 69	London	Trainee	West Ham U	—	—
Steven Potts	5 7	10 04	7 5 67	Hartford, USA	Apprentice	West Ham U	46	—
Ray Stewart	5 11	11 11	7 9 59	Perth	Errol Rovers	Dundee U	44	5
						West Ham U	340	62
John Strain‡			21 9 68	Stenhousemuir	Trainee	West Ham U	—	—
						Falkirk (loan)	—	—
Gary Strodder	6 1	11 04	1 4 65	Leeds	Apprentice	Lincoln C	132	6
						West Ham U	49	1
Steve Walford*	6 1	11 07	5 1 58	Highgate	Apprentice	Tottenham H	2	—
						Arsenal	77	3
						Norwich C	93	2
						West Ham U	115	2
						Huddersfield T (loan)	12	—
						Gillingham (loan)	4	—
						WBA (loan)	4	—
Midfield								
Liam Brady	5 9	11 02	13 2 56	Dublin	Apprentice	Arsenal	235	43
						Juventus	57	13
						Sampdoria	57	6
						Internazionale	58	5
						Ascoli	17	—
						West Ham U	56	7
Alan Devonshire*	5 11	11 00	13 4 56	London	Southall & Ealing	West Ham U	351	29
Alan Dickens	5 11	12 01	3 9 64	Plaistow	Apprentice	West Ham U	192	23
Paul Ince	5 10	11 07	21 10 67	Ilford	Trainee	West Ham U	71	7
Kevin Keen	5 6	9 08	25 2 67	Amersham	Apprentice	West Ham U	60	4
Paul Kelly	5 7	10 13	12 10 69	Bexley	Trainee	West Ham U	—	—
Simon Livett	5 10	12 02	8 1 69	Newham	YTS	West Ham U	—	—

WEST HAM UNITED

Foundation: Thames Ironworks FC was formed by employees of this shipbuilding yard in 1895 and entered the FA Cup in their initial season at Chatham and the London League in their second. Short of funds, the club was wound up in June 1900 and relaunched a month later as West Ham United. Connection with the Ironworks was not finally broken until four years later.

Managers (and Secretary-managers)
Syd King 1902–32, Charlie Paynter 1932–50, Ted Fenton 1950–61, Ron Greenwood 1961–74 (continued as GM to 1977), John Lyall 1974–89, Lou Macari 1989– .

Player and Position	Ht	Wt	Birth Date	Birth Place	Source	Clubs	League App	League Gls
Stewart Robson	5 11	11 13	6 11 64	Billericay	Apprentice	Arsenal	151	16
						West Ham U	61	3
Mark Ward	5 6	9 12	10 10 62	Prescot	Apprentice	Everton	—	—
					Northwich V	Oldham Ath	84	12
						West Ham U	146	7
Forwards								
Eamonn Dolan	5 10	12 03	20 9 67	Essex	Apprentice	West Ham U	5	—
						Bristol C (loan)	3	—
David Kelly	5 11	10 10	25 11 65	Birmingham	Alvechurch	Walsall	147	63
						West Ham U	25	6
Adam King	5 11	12 12	4 10 69	Hillingdon	Trainee	West Ham U	—	—
Frank McAvennie	5 9	11 00	22 11 59	Glasgow	Johnstone B	St Mirren	135	50
						West Ham U	85	33
						Celtic	55	25
						West Ham U	9	—
Paul McMenemy	5 10	11 12	5 11 66	Farnborough	Apprentice	West Ham U	—	—
						Aldershot (loan)	10	5
						Northampton T (loan)	4	2
Leroy Rosenior	6 1	11 10	24 3 64	London	School	Fulham	54	16
						QPR	38	7
						Fulham	34	20
						West Ham U	37	12
Stuart Slater	5 9	10 04	27 3 69	Sudbury	Apprentice	West Ham U	20	1

Trainees

Banks, Steven; Clarke, Simon N; Gibbons, Anthony G; Macklin, Anthony C; Pask, Andrew S; Rush, Matthew J.

Associated Schoolboys

Basham, Michael; Bradbrook, Dean M; Canham, Scott; Comerford, Anthony M; Fletcher, Paul A; Gore, Kevin E; Hancock, Darren J; Harriott, Marvin; Heffer, Steven P; Horlock, Kevin; Johnson, Roy J; Knight, Jason G; Lowe, John; Miller, Simon R; Paddington, John P; Purdie, John D; Reed, Peter M; Reeves, Steven T; Richardson, James A; Savage, James E; Taylor, Darren R; White, David T; White, Stephen A; Williamson, Daniel A.

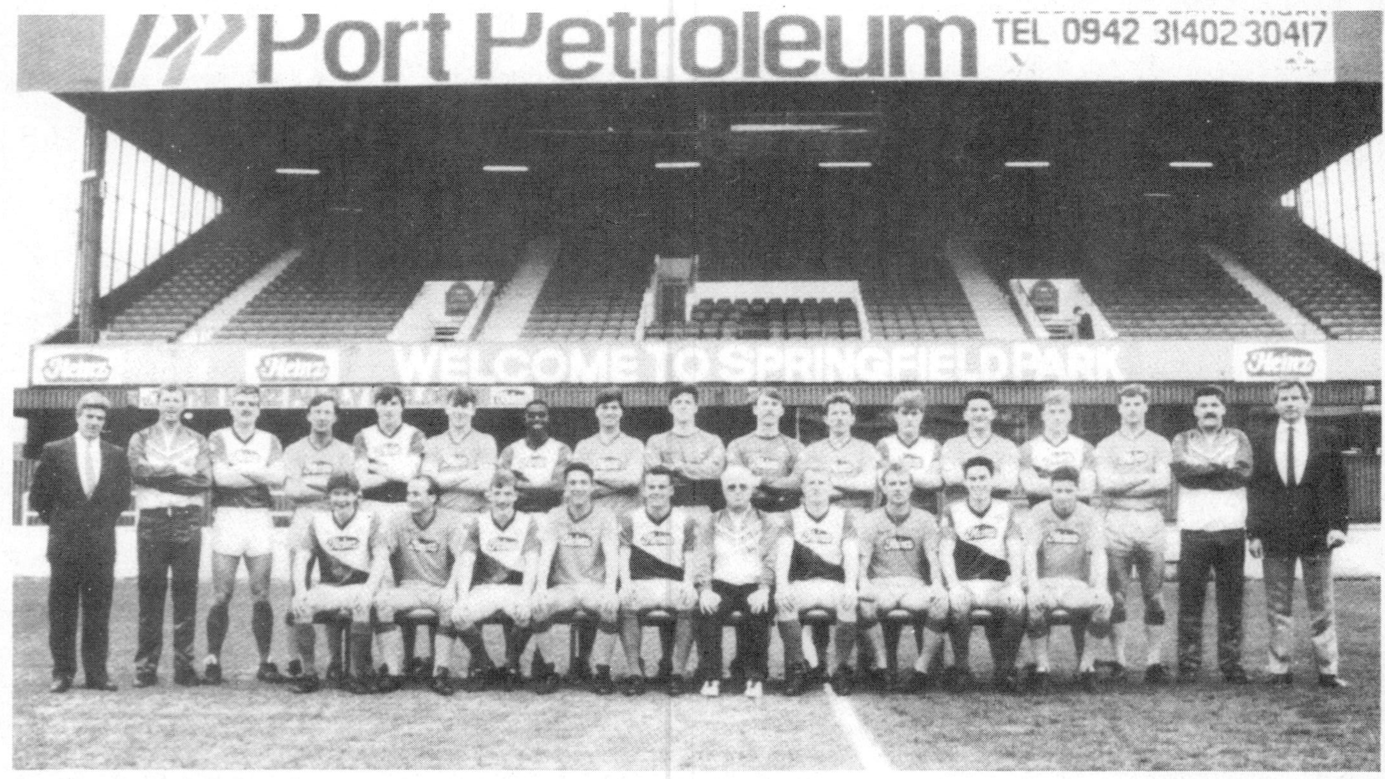

WIGAN ATHLETIC 1988–89 *Back row (left to right):* Bryan Hamilton (Manager), Dave Philpotts (Assistant Manager), Mark Hilditch, Andy Ainscow, Paul Beesley, Darren Patterson, Don Page, Stan McEwan, Phil Hughes, Nigel Adkins, Ray Woods, Craig Ramage, Alan Johnson, Peter Atherton, Joe Parkinson, Alex Cribley (Physiotherapist), John James (Sponsor).
Front row: Neill Rimmer, David Hamilton, Bryan Griffiths, Andy Pilling, Steve Senior, Tommy Cavanagh (Coach), Dave Thompson, Wayne Entwistle, Allen Tankard, Jonathon Crompton.

Division 3 WIGAN ATHLETIC

Springfield Park, Wigan. Telephone Wigan (0942) 44433. Commercial Dept: (0942) 43067.

Ground capacity: 12,500.

Record attendance: 27,500 v Hereford U, 12 Dec, 1953.

Record receipts: £40,577 v Leeds U, FA Cup 6th rd, 15 Mar, 1987.

Pitch measurements: 117yd × 72yd.

Chairman: W. Kenyon. ***Vice-Chairman:***

Directors: J. A. Bennett, J. D. Fillingham, T. Hitchen, W. Howard, S. Jackson, W. Pearce.

Chief Executive: Bryan Hamilton. ***Vice-President:*** J. H. Farrimond.

Secretary: R. A. Allan. ***Commercial Manager:*** John Crossley.

Manager: Brian Hamilton. ***Assistant Manager:***

Coaches: Dave Philpotts and Tommy Cavanagh. ***Physio:*** Alex Cribley.

Year Formed: 1932.

Club Nickname: The Latics'.

Record League Victory: 7-2 v Scunthorpe U (away), Division 4, 12 March 1982 – Tunks; McMahon, Glenn, Wignall, Cribley, Methven (1), O'Keefe, Barrow (1), Bradd (3), Houghton (2), Evans.

Record Cup Victory: 6-0 v Carlisle U (away), FA Cup, 1st rd, 24 November 1934 – Caunce; Robinson, Talbot; Paterson, Watson, Tufnell; Armes (2), Robson (1), Roberts (2), Felton, Scott (1).

Record Defeat: 0-5 v Bristol R, Division 3, 26 February, 1983 and 0-5 v Chelsea, FA Cup 3rd rd replay, 26 January, 1985.

Most League Points (2 for a win): 55, Division 4, 1978–79 and 1979–80.

Most League Points (3 for a win): 91, Division 4, 1981–82.

Most League Goals: 80, Division 4, 1981–82.

Highest League Scorer in Season: Les Bradd, 19, Division 4, 1981–82.

Most League Goals in Total Aggregate: Peter Houghton, 62, 1978–84.

Most Capped Player: None.

Most League Appearances: Colin Methven, 296, 1979–86.

Record Transfer Fee Received: £135,000 from Sunderland for Joe Hinnigan, February 1980.

Record Transfer Fee Paid: £65,000 to Everton for Eamon O'Keefe, January 1982.

Football League Record: 1978 elected to Division 4; 1982 – Division 3.

Honours: Best season in Division 3; 4th, 1985–86, 1986–87; Division 4 – Promoted (3rd) 1981–82. *FA Cup:* 4th rd 1979–80, 1985–86. *Football League Cup* best season: 4th rd, 1981–82. *Freight Rover Trophy:* Winners 1984–85.

Colours: All blue. **Change Colours:** All white.

WIGAN ATHLETIC 1988–89 LEAGUE RECORD

Match No.	Date	Venue	Opponents	Result		H/T Score	Lg. Pos.	Goalscorers	Attendance
1	Aug 27	A	Bristol R	L	2-3	2-1	—	Rimmer, Russell	4080
2	Sept 3	H	Mansfield T	D	0-0	0-0	19		2514
3	10	A	Brentford	D	1-1	0-1	21	Rimmer	4081
4	17	H	Reading	W	3-0	1-0	11	Russell 2, Hilditch	2534
5	24	A	Fulham	D	1-1	1-0	15	Butler	3431
6	30	H	Blackpool	W	2-1	1-0	—	Rimmer (pen), Butler	4141
7	Oct 4	A	Aldershot	L	1-3	0-1	—	Phillips (og)	1527
8	8	H	Port Vale	L	0-2	0-0	19		3976
9	15	A	Wolverhampton W	L	1-2	1-2	19	Hilditch	10,320
10	22	A	Sheffield U	L	1-2	0-1	20	Atherton	11,363
11	25	H	Bolton W	D	1-1	0-0	—	Entwistle	4438
12	28	A	Southend U	W	2-1	1-0	—	Hamilton, Butler	3120
13	Nov 1	H	Swansea C	L	1-2	1-1	—	Diamond	2432
14	5	H	Northampton T	L	1-3	1-2	19	Entwistle	2472
15	8	A	Preston NE	D	2-2	2-1	—	Thompson, Diamond	8396
16	12	H	Bristol C	L	0-1	0-0	20		2675
17	26	H	Huddersfield T	L	0-2	0-1	21		2779
18	Dec 3	A	Bury	D	1-1	0-1	21	Entwistle	3121
19	10	H	Southend U	W	3-0	1-0	19	Thompson, Griffiths, Holden	2027
20	18	H	Notts Co	L	0-1	0-0	—		3016
21	26	A	Chester C	L	0-1	0-0	21		3262
22	30	A	Cardiff C	D	2-2	1-0	—	Entwistle, Griffiths	4621
23	Jan 2	H	Gillingham	W	3-0	2-0	20	Hamilton, Entwistle, Hilditch	3090
24	7	H	Chesterfield	L	0-2	0-2	21		2249
25	14	A	Mansfield T	W	1-0	1-0	18	Parkinson	2788
26	21	H	Brentford	D	1-1	1-1	19	Thompson	2514
27	Feb 4	A	Blackpool	L	0-2	0-0	20		4221
28	11	H	Aldershot	W	2-1	0-1	19	Thompson, Griffiths	2132
29	18	A	Port Vale	L	1-2	0-1	20	Griffiths	6100
30	Mar 4	H	Sheffield U	L	1-2	1-1	22	Senior	3966
31	11	A	Northampton T	D	1-1	0-0	22	Pilling	3443
32	24	A	Gillingham	L	1-2	1-0	—	Griffiths	3244
33	27	H	Chester C	W	3-0	1-0	22	Senior, Griffiths, Ramage	3132
34	Apr 1	A	Notts C	L	0-1	0-1	22		4929
35	4	A	Chesterfield	D	1-1	1-0	—	Beesley	3179
36	7	H	Cardiff C	W	1-0	0-0	—	Ramage	2083
37	15	A	Swansea C	W	2-1	1-0	22	Knill (og), Page	3719
38	19	A	Reading	W	3-0	2-0	—	Thompson, Elsey (og), Page	3821
39	22	H	Fulham	L	0-1	0-0	21		3056
40	29	A	Bristol C	W	1-0	0-0	20	Tankard	5156
41	May 1	H	Preston NE	D	1-1	0-1	21	Beesley	5671
42	3	H	Bristol R	W	3-0	1-0	—	Griffiths, Thompson, Pilling	2529
43	6	H	Bury	W	1-0	0-0	17	Johnson	3045
44	9	A	Bolton W	D	1-1	0-1	—	Thompson	6166
45	13	A	Huddersfield T	D	1-1	0-0	18	Entwistle	4225
46	16	H	Wolverhampton W	D	1-1	0-1	—	Griffiths (pen)	5531

Final League Position: 17

GOALSCORERS

League (55): Griffiths 8 (1 pen), Thompson 7, Entwistle 6, Butler 3, Hilditch 3, Rimmer 3 (1 pen), Russell 3, Beesley 2, Diamond 2, Hamilton 2, Page 2, Pilling 2, Ramage 2, Senior 2, Atherton 1, Holden 1, Johnson 1, Parkinson 1, Tankard 1, own goals 3.
Littlewoods Cup (0).
FA Cup (0).

Littlewoods Cup	First Round	Preston NE (h)	0-0
		(a)	0-1
FA Cup	First Round	Hartlepool U (a)	0-2

Hughes	Atherton	Tankard	Butler	Beesley	Holden	Pilling	Senior	Hilditch	Russell	Rimmer	Thompson	Hamilton	Parkinson	McEwan	Adkins	Entwistle	Diamond	Griffiths	Wilson	Ainscow	Johnson	Hemming	Woods	Ramage	Page	Fallon	*Match No.*
1	2	3	4	5	6	7	8	9	10	11																	1
1		3	4	5	6	8	2	9	10	11	7																2
1		3	4	5	6	8	2	9	10	11	7																3
1		3	4	5	6	8	2	9	10	11	7																4
1		3	4	5	6	8	2	9	10*	11	7	12															5
1	2	3	4	5	6	8		9*		11	7	10	12														6
1	2	3	4	5	6	8	9		7	11		10															7
1	2	3	4	5*	6	8	9		7	11		10		12													8
1	12		2	5	6	8	3	9*	10	11	7	4															9
	12		2	5	6	8	3	9*		11	7	4			1	10											10
	2		9	5	6	8	3			11	7	4			1	10											11
	2		8	5	6	12	3			11	7	4*			1	9	10										12
	2	12	8	5	6	4	3			11*	7				1	9	10										13
	2		8	5	6	4	3			14	7			12	1	9*	10	11†									14
		3	8	5	6	4	2			11	7				1	9	10										15
		3	8	5			2			11	7	4		6	1	9	10										16
	4		8	3	5	7*	2							6	1	9	10		12	11							17
	2		3	5	6	8	4	10			7				1	9				11							18
	2		3	5	6	8	4				7				1	9		11		10							19
	2		3	5	6	8*	4	14			7	12			1	9†		11		10							20
	2			5	6		3	8			7	4			1	9		11		10							21
	2*	12		5	6	8	3	10			7	4			1	9		11									22
	2			5	6	8	3	10			7	4			1	9		11									23
	2	3		5	6	8		10			7	4			1	9*		11		12							24
	2	3				8	6	10			7		4		1	9		11			5						25
	2	3		6		8	10				7		4		1	9		11				5					26
	2†	3		6		8	10				7	12	4*		1	9		11			14	5					27
	2	3*		6		8	10				7	12	4		1	9		11				5					28
	2	3		6		8	10				7	4*	12		1	9†		11			14	5					29
	2	3		6		8	10	12			7		4		1	9†		11			5*		14				30
1	2	3		5		8	10	6			7		4					11						9			31
1	2	3		5		8	4	6			7							11					12	9*	10		32
1	2	3		5		8	4	6			7		12					11*						9	10		33
1	2	3		5		8	4	6			7		14			12		11						9*	10†		34
1	4			5			3	6		8	7		2			12		11						9*	10		35
1	4			5			3	6		8	7		2					11						9	10		36
1	4	3					2	6		8	7					12		11*			5			9	10		37
	4	3		5			2	6		8	7				1			11						9	10		38
	4	3		5			2	6		8	7				1	12		11						9*	10		39
	4	3		5		6	2			8	7				1	9		11							10		40
	4	3		5		6	2			8	7				1			11					12	9*	10		41
	4	3		5		6	2			8	7				1			11					9		10		42
	4	3		5		6	2			8†	7				1			11*		12	14		9		10		43
	4	3		5		6†	2				7			14	1	12		11			8		9		10*		44
	4	3		5		6	2				7			8	1	10		11*					9		12		45
	4	3		5		6	2				7				1	10		11			14		9*		12	8†	46
16	38 + 2s	31 + 2s	20	44	23	38 + 1s	44	23 + 2s	8	24 + 1s	42	13 + 4s	8 + 4s	3 + 3s	30	24 + 5s	6	29	— + 1s	5 + 2s	4 + 4s	4	5 + 3s	10	13 + 2s	1	

WIGAN ATHLETIC

Player and Position	Ht	Wt	Birth Date	Birth Place	Source	Clubs	League App	League Gls
Goalkeepers								
Nigel Adkins	5 11	12 07	11 3 65	Birkenhead	Apprentice	Tranmere R	86	—
						Wigan Ath	40	—
Philip Hughes	5 11	12 07	19 11 64	Manchester	Apprentice	Manchester U	—	—
						Leeds U	6	—
						Bury	80	—
						Wigan Ath	47	—
Peter Atherton	5 11	12 03	6 4 70	Orrell	Trainee	Wigan Ath	56	1
Paul Beesley	6 1	11 05	21 7 65	Wigan		Wigan Ath	144	3
Alex Cribley‡	5 11	12 09	1 4 57	Liverpool	Local	Liverpool	—	—
						Wigan Ath	271	16
Stan McEwan*	6 0	12 07	8 6 57	Cambusrethan	Apprentice	Blackpool	214	24
						Exeter C	65	15
						Hull C	113	25
						Wigan Ath	29	4
Darren Patterson	6 1	12 00	15 10 69	Belfast	Trainee	WBA	—	—
						Wigan Ath	—	—
Steve Senior	5 8	11 04	15 5 64	Sheffield	Apprentice	York C	168	6
						Darlington (loan)	5	—
						Northampton T	4	—
						Wigan Ath	66	3
Allen Tankard	5 10	11 07	21 5 69	Fleet	Apprentice	Southampton	5	—
						Wigan Ath	33	1
Andy Wilson*			7 1 65			Wigan Ath	2	—
Midfield								
Paul Crompton‡	5 9	1007	25 1 70	Orrell		Wigan Ath	—	—
Shaun Fallon§	5 9	10 12	10 9 70	Widnes	Trainee	Wigan Ath	1	—
David Hamilton*	5 6	10 00	7 11 60	South Shields	Apprentice	Sunderland	—	—
						Blackburn R	114	7
						Cardiff C (loan)	10	—
						Wigan Ath	103	7
Alan Johnson			19 2 71	Ince	Trainee	Wigan Ath	8	1
Joe Parkinson			11 6 71	Eccles	Trainee	Wigan Ath	12	1
Andy Pilling			30 6 69	Wigan	Trainee	Preston NE	1	—
						Wigan Ath	59	5
Neill Rimmer	5 6	10 03	13 11 67	Liverpool	Apprentice	Everton	1	—
						Ipswich T	22	3
						Wigan Ath	25	3
Barry Smith‡			21 9 69	Ince	Trainee	Wigan Ath	1	—
David Thompson	5 11	12 04	27 5 62	Manchester	Local	Rochdale	155	13
						Manchester U (loan)	—	—
						Notts Co	55	8
						Wigan Ath	69	9
Forwards								
Andy Ainscow	5 10	10 11	1 10 68	Orrell	Trainee	Wigan Ath	22	4
Jonathan Crompton					Trainee	Wigan Ath	—	—
Wayne Entwistle‡	5 11	11 08	6 8 58		Apprentice	Bury	31	7
						Sunderland	45	12
						Leeds U	11	2
						Blackpool	32	6
						Crewe Alex	11	—
						Wimbledon	9	3
					Grays Ath	Bury	83	32
						Carlisle U	9	2
						Bolton W	8	—
						Burnley (loan)	8	2
						Stockport Co	49	8
						Bury	2	—
						Wigan Ath	29	6

WIGAN ATHLETIC

Foundation: Following the demise of Wigan Borough and their resignation from the Football League in 1931, a public meeting was called in Wigan at the Queen's Hall in May 1932 at which a new club Wigan Athletic, was founded in the hope of carrying on in the Football League. With this in mind, they bought Springfield Park for £2,250, but failed to gain admission to the Football League until 46 years later.

Managers (and Secretary-managers)
Charlie Spencer 1932–37, Jimmy Milne 1946–47, Bob Pryde 1949–52, Ted Goodier 1952–54, Walter Crook 1954–55, Ron Suart 1955–56, Billy Cooke 1956, Sam Barkas 1957, Trevor Hitchen 1957–58, Malcolm Barrass 1958–59, Jimmy Shirley 1959, Pat Murphy 1959–60, Allenby Chilton 1960, Johnny Ball 1961–63, Allan Brown 1963–66, Alf Craig 1966–67, Harry Leyland 1967–68, Alan Saunders 1968, Ian McNeill 1968–70, Gordon Milne 1970–72, Les Rigby 1972–74, Brian Tiler 1974–76, Ian McNeill 1976–81, Larry Lloyd 1981–83, Harry McNally 1983–85, Bryan Hamilton 1985–86, Ray Mathias 1986–89, Bryan Hamilton 1989– .

Player and Position	*Ht*	*Wt*	*Birth Date*	*Birth Place*	*Source*	*Clubs*	*League App*	*League Gls*
Bryan Griffiths			26 1 65	Prescot	St Helens T	Wigan Ath	29	8
Mark Hilditch	6 0	12 01	20 8 60	Royton	Amateur	Rochdale	197	40
						Tranmere R	49	12
						Wigan Ath	82	19
Don Page	5 10	11 04	18 1 64	Manchester	Runcorn	Wigan Ath	15	2
Colin Russell‡	5 7	11 07	21 1 61	Liverpool	Apprentice	Liverpool	1	—
						Huddersfield T	66	23
						Stoke C (loan)	11	2
						Bournemouth	68	14
						Doncaster R	43	5
						Scarborough	13	2
						Wigan Ath	8	3
Ray Woods	5 11	11 00	7 6 65	Birkenhead	Apprentice	Tranmere R	7	2
					Colne	Wigan Ath	8	—

Trainees

Banford, Ian E; Blakemore, Colin; Cannon, Stephen M; Fallon, Shaun; Litherland, Roy I; Maddox, Daniel W; Musker, Paul H; Phoenix, Stuart G; Smith, John R; Sonner, Daniel J; Whitney, John D; Whitworth, Neil A; Wilson, Adam J.

Associated Schoolboys

Appleton, Stephen; Anderson, Mark; Barker, Paul A; Bourne, Michael G; Bradley, Sean; Brown, David; Chamberlain, Stuart; Cunliffe, Lee Jason; Cunliffe, Lee John; Dykes, Stephen; Edwardson, Barry J; Fleming, Daniel; Gossage, Paul; Gwinnett, Martin; Harrison, Anthony; Hulme, Gary B; Hunt, Mark; Kirwin, Paul; Lewis, Gary; Leyland, Neil T; Little, Wayne; Nugent, Stephen; Roberts, Andrew; Robertson, John; Thomas, Craig; Williamson, Colin; Woodward, Chris J.

WIMBLEDON 1988–89 *Back row (left to right):* Terry Burton, John Scales, Lawrie Sanchez, Robbie Turner, Eric Young, Peter Cawley, Vinny Jones, Carlton Fairweather, Alan Cork, Clive Goodyear, David Kemp.
Centre row: Sid Neal, Mark Quamina, Mark Fiore, Ian Hazel, Dean Blackwell, Simon Tracey, Neil Sullivan, Paul Miller, John Gannon, Andy Clement, Andy Sayer, Garry Brooke, Ron Suart.
Front row: Dennis Wise, Vaughan Ryan, Bobby Gould (Manager), Sam Hammam, John Lelliott, Stanley Reed, Peter Cork, Steve Allen, Terry Phelan, Terry Gibson.

Division 1 WIMBLEDON

Plough Lane Ground, Durnsford Road, Wimbledon, London SW19 (first used in 1912. Telephone 01-946 6311. Commercial Manager: 01-947 0867.

Ground capacity: 16,000.

Record attendance: 18,000 v HMS Victory in FA Amateur Cup 3rd rd, 1934–35.

Record receipts: £75,244 v Arsenal, Division 1, 27 August 1988.

Pitch measurements: 110yd × 73yd.

President: Rt Hon Lord Michael Havers of Bury St Edmunds.

Chairman: S. G. Reed. ***Vice-Chairman:*** J. Lelliott.

Managing Director: S. Hammam.

Directors: P. Cork, P. R. Cooper, N. N. Namman.

Manager: Bobby Gould.

Coach: ***Physio:*** Steve Allen.

Secretary: Adrian Cook. ***Commercial Manager:*** Reg Davis.

Year Formed: 1889. ***Turned Professional:*** 1964. ***Ltd Co.:*** 1964.

Previous Name: Wimbledon Old Centrals 1899–1905.

Club Nickname: 'The Dons'.

Record League Victory: 6-0 v Newport C, Division 3, 3 September 1983 – Beasant; Peters, Winterburn, Galliers, Morris, Hatter, Evans (2), Ketteridge (1), Cork (3 incl. 1p), Downes, Hodges (Driver).

Record Cup Victory: 7-2 v Windsor & Eton, FA Cup, 1st rd, 22 November 1980 – Beasant; Jones, Armstrong, Galliers, Mick Smith (2), Cunningham (1), Ketteridge, Hodges, Leslie, Cork (1), Hubbick (3).

Record Defeat: 0-8 v Everton, League Cup 2nd rd, 29 August, 1978.

Most League Points (2 for a win): 61, Division 4, 1978–79.

Most League Points (3 for a win): 98, Division 4, 1982–83.

Most League Goals: 97, Division 3, 1983–84.

Highest League Scorer in Season: Alan Cork, 29, 1983–84.

Most League Goals in Total Aggregate: Alan Cork, 133, 1977–89.

Most Capped Player: Glyn Hodges 5 (11), Wales.

Most League Appearances: Alan Cork, 355, 1977–89.

Record Transfer Fee Received: £850,000 from Newcastle U for Dave Beasant, June 1988 and £850,000 from Newcastle U for Andy Thorn, August 1988.

Record Transfer Fee Paid: £500,000 to Reading for Keith Curle, October 1988.

Football League Record: 1977 Elected to Division 4; 1979–80 Division 3; 1980–81 Division 4; 1981–82 Division 3; 1982–83 Division 4; 1983–84 Division 3; 1984–86 Division 2; 1986 Division 1.

Honours: *Football League:* Division 1 best season 6th, 1986–87, Division 3 – Runners-up 1983–84; Division 4 – Champions 1982–83. *FA Cup:* Winners 1987–88. *Football League Cup* best season: 4th rd, 1979–80, 1983–84, 1988–89. *League Group Cup:* runners-up 1981–82.

Colours: Blue shirts yellow trim, blue shorts yellow trim, blue stockings yellow trim. **Change Colours:** Red shirts green trim, red shorts green trim, red stockings green trim.

WIMBLEDON 1988–89 LEAGUE RECORD

Match No.	Date	Venue	Opponents	Result	H/T Score	Lg. Pos.	Goalscorers	Atten-dance
1	Aug 27	H	Arsenal	L 1-5	1-3	—	Fashanu	15,710
2	Sept 3	A	Luton T	D 2-2	1-1	16	Fashanu (pen), Fairweather	8067
3	10	H	West Ham U	L 0-1	0-1	18		7730
4	17	A	Middlesbrough	L 0-1	0-1	19		17,709
5	24	H	Coventry C	L 0-1	0-1	20		4474
6	Oct 1	H	Everton	W 2-1	2-0	19	Fashanu, Cork	6367
7	8	A	Aston Villa	W 1-0	0-0	18	Scales	15,416
8	22	H	Manchester U	D 1-1	0-1	17	Wise	12,143
9	29	A	Derby Co	L 1-4	1-1	17	Jones	15,050
10	Nov 5	H	Norwich C	L 0-2	0-1	17		5853
11	12	A	Tottenham H	L 2-3	1-1	19	Gibson 2	23,589
12	19	H	Charlton Ath	D 1-1	0-0	17	Fashanu	5631
13	26	A	Liverpool	D 1-1	0-0	18	Nicol (og)	36,188
14	Dec 3	H	Southamptohn	W 2-1	1-1	18	Gibson, Fairweather	6040
15	10	A	Newcastle U	L 1-2	0-1	18	Gibson	20,146
16	18	A	Nottingham F	W 1-0	0-0	—	Sanchez	16,427
17	26	H	Millwall	W 1-0	0-0	21	Fairweather	11,398
18	31	H	Luton T	W 4-0	2-0	14	Jones, Gibson, Scales, Fashanu	4899
19	Jan 2	A	West Ham U	W 2-1	1-1	12	Wise 2	18,346
20	14	H	QPR	W 1-0	1-0	10	Scales	7118
21	21	A	Coventry C	L 1-2	1-1	11	Scales	12,472
22	Feb 4	A	Everton	D 1-1	1-1	12	Sanchez	23,365
23	11	H	Aston Villa	W 1-0	1-0	10	Fashanu	6201
24	25	H	Sheffield W	W 1-0	1-0	9	Fashanu	4384
25	Mar 1	H	Derby Co	W 4-0	3-0	—	Fashanu, Miller 3 (1 pen)	4207
26	11	A	Norwich C	L 0-1	0-0	9		15,159
27	25	H	Middlesbrough	D 1-1	1-1	10	Scales	5276
28	27	A	Millwall	W 1-0	0-0	9	Fashanu (pen)	13,679
29	Apr 1	H	Nottingham F	W 4-1	2-1	8	Sanchez 2, Miller, Fashanu	7867
30	5	A	Sheffield W	D 1-1	0-0	—	Fashanu (pen)	15,777
31	8	A	QPR	L 3-4	1-3	8	Fashanu (pen), Sanchez, Wise	9056
32	15	H	Tottenham H	L 1-2	0-1	9	Young	12,366
33	22	A	Southampton	D 0-0	0-0	9		13,805
34	29	H	Newcastle U	W 4-0	1-0	9	Wise (pen), Miller, Jones, Cotterill	5206
35	May 2	A	Manchester U	L 0-1	0-0	—		23,386
36	6	A	Charlton Ath	L 0-1	0-1	9		7230
37	13	H	Liverpool	L 1-2	1-0	12	Hansen (og)	14,730
38	17	A	Arsenal	D 2-2	1-1	—	Cork, McGee	39,132

Final League Position: 12

GOALSCORERS

League (50): Fashanu 12 (4 pens), Gibson 5, Miller 5 (1 pen), Sanchez 5, Scales 5, Wise 5 (1 pen), Fairweather 3, Jones 3, Cork 2, Cotterill 1, McGee 1, Young 1, own goals 2.
Littlewoods Cup (4): Fashanu 2, Fairweather 1, Gibson 1.
FA Cup (5): Fashanu 1, Gibson 1, Jones 1, Phelan 1, Wise 1.

Littlewoods Cup	Second Round	Barnsley (a)	2-0
		(h)	0-1
	Third Round	Manchester U (h)	2-1
	Fourth Round	QPR (a)	0-0
		(h)	0-1
FA Cup	Third Round	Birmingham C (a)	1-0
	Fourth Round	Aston Villa (h)	1-0
	Fifth Round	Grimsby T (h)	3-1
	Sixth Round	Everton (a)	0-1

Tracey	Joseph	Phelan	Ryan	Young	Cawley	Gibson	Fairweather	Fashanu	Sanchez	Wise	Cork	Scales	Green	Turner	Brooke	Hazel	Clement	Jones	Segers	Curle	Miller	Kruszynski	Cotterill	Fiore	Gayle	Quamina	McGee	*Match No.*
1	2	3	4	5	6†	7	8	9*	10	11	12	14																1
	2	3	4	5		7*	8	9	10†	11		6	1	12	14													2
	2	3	4*	5		7	8	9		11	10	6	1		12													3
	2	3		5		7	8	9	10		12	6	1		11*	4												4
	2			5		7*	8†	9	10	11	12	6	1	14			3	4										5
	2			5				9	10	11	8	6			7		3	4	1									6
	2			5				9*	10	11	8	6		12	7		3	4	1									7
	2			5			14		10	11	8	6		9†	7*		3	4	1	12								8
	2			5			7	9	10	11	8*	6			12		3	4	1									9
	2	3		5		8	11*	9	10	7†	12	6						4	1	14								10
	2	3		5		8	14	9*	10	11†	12	6						4	1	7								11
	2*	3		5			7	9	10	11	8†	12			14			4	1	6								12
	2			5		8*	7†	9	10	11	12	3					14	4	1	6								13
	2†	14	10	5		8	7			11	12	3		9*				4	1	6								14
		2	12	5		8	7		10	11		3						4*	1	6	9							15
		2		5		8*	7	9	10	11	12	3						4	1	6								16
		3		5		8	7	9	10	11		2						4	1	6								17
		3		5		8	7	9	10	11		2						4	1	6								18
		3		5		8*	7	9	10	11†	12	2						4	1	6		14						19
	14	3		5†		8	7*		10	11	9	2		12				4	1	6								20
		3		5		8	7		10	11		2						4	1	6	9							21
		3		5		8*	7	9	10	11		2						4	1	6		12						22
	5	3					7	9	10	11	12	2						4	1	6	8*							23
	5	3					7†	9	10	11	12	2					14		1	6	8*	4						24
	5	3		12			7	9	10*	11		2							1	6	8	4						25
	5	3		12			7	9	10	11		2							1	6*	8	4						26
	5	3		6				9	10	11		2						4	1		8	7						27
	5	3		6				9	10	11	12	2						4	1		8*	7						28
	5			6				9	10	11		2					3	4	1		8	7						29
	6			5*				9	10	11	12	2					3	4	1		8	7						30
	6†	14		5				9	10	11		2			12		3	4	1		8	7*						31
	2	3		5			12	9	10	11		6			7*			4	1		8							32
	2	3		5				9	10	11		6						4	1		8*	7	12					33
	2	3							10	11	12	6						4	1		8	7	14	5†	9*			34
	2			5					10	11	12	6					3	4	1		8†	7	14		9*			35
	2	3		5			8†		10*	11	9	6						4	1		7	12	14					36
	2*	3		5				9	14	11	12	6						4	1		8	7				10†		37
	2	3†		5				9	14	11	8*	6						4	1		12	7					10	38
1	30 + 1s	27 + 2s	4 + 1s	33 + 2s	1	17	23 + 3s	30	34 + 2s	37	9 + 16s	36 + 2s	4	2 + 4s	5 + 5s	1	9 + 2s	31	33	16 + 2s	17 + 1s	13 + 3s	— + 4s	1	2	1	1	

WIMBLEDON

Player and Position	Ht	Wt	Birth Date	Birth Place	Source	Clubs	League App	League Gls
Goalkeepers								
Hans Segers	5 11	12 07	30 10 61	Eindhoven	PSV Eindhoven	Nottingham F	58	—
						Stoke C (loan)	1	—
						Sheffield U (loan)	10	—
						Dunfermline Ath	4	—
						(loan)	33	—
						Wimbledon		
Neil Sullivan	6 0	12 01	24 2 70	Sutton	Trainee	Wimbledon	—	—
Defenders								
Dean Blackwell	6 1	12 10	5 12 69	London	Trainee	Wimbledon	—	—
Peter Cawley*	6 4	13 00	15 9 65	London	Chertsey	Wimbledon	1	—
						Bristol R (loan)	10	—
						Fulham (loan)	5	—
Andy Clement	5 8	11 00	12 11 67	Cardiff	Apprentice	Wimbledon	26	—
						Bristol R (loan)	6	—
						Newport Co (loan)	5	1
Keith Curle	6 0	11 09	14 11 63	Bristol	Bristol	Bristol R	32	4
						Torquay U	16	5
						Bristol C	121	1
						Reading	40	—
						Wimbledon	18	—
Clive Goodyear	6 0	11 04	15 1 61	Lincoln	Local	Luton T	90	4
						Plymouth Arg	106	5
						Wimbledon	22	—
Roger Joseph	5 11	11 13	24 12 65	Paddington	Juniors	Brentford	104	2
						Wimbledon	31	—
Brian McAllister	5 11	12 05	30 11 70	Glasgow	Trainee	Wimbledon	—	—
Terry Phelan	5 8	10 00	16 3 67	Manchester		Leeds U	14	—
						Swansea C	45	—
						Wimbledon	59	—
John Scales	6 0	12 02	4 7 66	Harrogate		Leeds U	—	—
						Bristol R	72	2
						Wimbledon	63	6
Eric Young	6 2	13 00	25 3 60	Singapore	Slough T	Brighton & HA	126	10
						Wimbledon	64	4
Midfield								
Mark Fiore	5 10	11 10	18 11 69	Southwark	Trainee	Wimbledon	1	—
John Gannon*	5 8	10 10	18 12 66	Wimbledon	Apprentice	Wimbledon	16	2
						Crewe Alex (loan)	15	—
						Sheffield U (loan)	16	1
Ian Hazel*	5 10	10 04	1 12 67	London	Apprentice	Wimbledon	7	—
						Bristol R (loan)	3	—
Detsi Kruszynski	6 0	12 12	14 10 61	Divschav	Homburg	Wimbledon	16	—
Vinny Jones	5 11	11 10	5 1 65	Watford	Wealdstone	Wimbledon	77	9
Paul McGee	5 6	9 10	17 5 68	Dublin	Bohemians	Colchester U	3	—
						Wimbledon	1	1
Terry Merriman*	5 7	10 12	10 7 68	Oxford	Apprentice	Coventry C	—	—
						Swindon T	—	—
						Wimbledon	—	—
Vaughan Ryan	5 8	10 12	2 9 68	Westminster		Wimbledon	28	1
						Sheffield U (loan)	3	—
Lawrie Sanchez	5 11	11 07	22 10 59	Lambeth	Amateur	Reading	262	28
						Wimbledon	165	23
Dennis Wise	5 6	9 05	15 12 66	Kensington		Wimbledon	100	19
Forwards								
Garry Brooke	5 7	11 00	24 11 60	Bethnal Green	Apprentice	Tottenham H	73	15
						Norwich C	14	2
					Groningen	Wimbledon	10	—

WIMBLEDON

Foundation: Old boys from Central School formed this club as Wimbledon Old Centrals in 1889. Their earliest successes were in the Clapham League before switching to the Southern Suburban League in 1902.

Managers (and Secretary-managers)
Les Henley 1955–71, Mike Everitt 1971–73, Dick Graham 1973–74, Allen Batsford 1974–78, Dario Gradi 1978–81, Dave Bassett 1981–87, Bobby Gould 1987– .

Player and Position	*Ht*	*Wt*	*Birth Date*	*Place*	*Source*	*Clubs*	*League App*	*Gls*
Alan Cork	6 0	12 00	4 3 59	Derby	Amateur	Derby Co	—	—
						Lincoln C (loan)	5	—
						Wimbledon	355	133
Steve Cotterill	6 1	12 05	20 7 64	Cheltenham	Burton Albion	Wimbledon	4	1
Carlton Fairweather	5 11	11 00	22 9 61	London	Tooting	Wimbledon	106	24
John Fashanu	6 1	11 12	18 9 62	Kensington	Amateur	Cambridge U	—	—
						Norwich C	7	1
						C Palace (loan)	1	—
						Lincoln C	36	10
						Millwall	50	12
						Wimbledon	114	41
John Gayle	6 4	13 01	30 7 64	Birmingham	Burton Albion	Wimbledon	2	—
Terry Gibson	5 5	10 00	23 12 62	Walthamstow	Apprentice	Tottenham H	18	4
						Coventry C	98	43
						Manchester U	23	1
						Wimbledon	34	11
Paul Miller	6 0	11 00	31 1 68	Bisley	Trainee	Wimbledon	23	5
						Newport Co (loan)	6	2
Mark Quamina			25 11 69	St Helier	Trainee	Wimbledon	1	—

Trainees
Alexander, Matthew J; Cooper, David A; Cooper, Keith B; Dobbs, Gerald F; Hudson, David P; Pearson, Matthew J; Rowe, Jeffery; Watson, James G.

Associated Schoolboys
Allen, Daniel J; Andrews, Lee R; Ardley, Neal C; Bowdery, David J; Carney, Michael; Castledine, Stewart M; Diamond, Stuart J; Fear, Peter S; Hughes, Jeremy S; Laker, Barry, J; Marchant, Giles R; McCarthy, Jamie; McCormack, David R; Oatway, Charlie A; Orriss, Craig J; Pane, Grant; Perry, Christopher J; Swift, Keiron; Taylor, Geoffrey J; Tyson, Leon P.

WOLVERHAMPTON WANDERERS 1988–89 *Back row (left to right):* Jackie Gallagher, Andy Mutch, Steve Bull, Philip Robinson, Robert Kelly, Robbie Dennison, Tom Bennett, Phil Chard.
Centre row: Mark Venus, Nick Clarke, Mark Kendall, Alistair Robertson, Chris Brindley, Vince Bartram, Floyd Streete, Gary Bellamy.
Front row: Paul Grainger, Andy Thompson, Paul Darby, Graham Turner (Manager), Barry Powell, Nigel Vaughan, Keith Downing.

Division 2 **WOLVERHAMPTON WANDERERS**

Molineux Grounds, Wolverhampton WV1 4QR. Telephone Admin office: Wolverhampton (0902) 712181; lottery shop: 0902-27524.
Ground capacity: 28,051.
Record attendance: 61,315 v Liverpool, FA Cup 5th rd, 11 Feb, 1939.
Record receipts: £91,137 v Torquay U, Sherpa Van Trophy, Southern Area Final, 18 April 1989.
Pitch measurements: 115yd × 72yd.
President: Sir Jack Haywood.
Chairman: J. Harris.
Directors: A. C. Gallagher, D. M. Gallagher, H. P. D. Glaister (Company Secretary).
Team Manager: Graham Turner.
Coach: Barry Powell. ***Physio:*** Paul Darby.
Chief Executive:
Secretary: Keither Pearson ACIS. ***Commercial Manager:*** Keith Butler.
Year Formed: 1877*(*see Foundation*). ***Turned Professional:*** 1888. ***Ltd Co.:*** 1982.
Previous Grounds: 1877, Goldthorn Hill; 1884, Dudley Road; 1889, Molineux.
Club Nickname: 'Wolves'.
Previous Name: 1880, St Luke's, Blakenhall combined with The Wanderers to become Wolverhampton Wanderers (1923) Ltd until 1982.
Record League Victory: 10-1 v Leicester C, Division 1, 15 April 1938 – Sidlow; Morris, Dowen; Galley, Cullis, Gardiner; Maguire (1), Horace Wright, Westcott (4), Jones (1), Dorsett (4).
Record Cup Victory: 14-0 v Cresswell's Brewery, FA Cup, 2nd rd, 13 November 1886 – I. Griffiths; Baugh, Mason; Pearson, Allen (1), Lowder; Hunter (4), Knight (2), Brodie (4), B. Griffiths (2), Wood. Plus one goal 'scrambled through'.
Record Defeat: 1-10 v Newton Heath, Division 1, 15 October, 1892.
Most League Points (2 for a win): 64, Division 1, 1957–58.
Most League Points (3 for a win): 92, Division 4, 1988–89.
Most League Goals: 115, Division 2, 1931–32.
Highest League Scorer in Season: Dennis Westcott, 38, Division 1, 1946–47.
Most League Goals in Total Aggregate: Bill Hartill, 164, 1928–35.
Most Capped Player: Billy Wright, 105, England (70 consecutive).

Most League Appearances: Derek Parkin, 501, 1967–82.
Record Transfer Fee Received: £1,150,000 from Manchester C for Steve Daley, September 1979.
Record Transfer Fee Paid: £1,175,000 to Aston Villa for Andy Gray, September 1979.
Football League Record: 1888 Founder Member of Football League: 1906–23 Division 2; 1923–24 Division 3 (N); 1924–32 Division 2; 1932–65 Division 1; 1965–67 Division 2; 1967–76 Division 1; 1976–77 Division 2; 1977–82 Division 1; 1982–83 Division 2; 1983–84 Division 1; 1984–85 Division 2; 1985–86 Division 3; 1986–88 Division 4; 1988–89 Division 3; 1989– Division 2.
Honours: *Football League:* Division 1 – Champions 1953–54, 1957–58, 1958–59; Runners-up 1937–38, 1938–39, 1949–50, 1954–55, 1959–60; Division 2 – Champions 1931–32, 1976–77; Runners-up 1966–67, 1982–83; Division 3 (N) – Champions 1923–24; Division 3– Champions 1988–89; Division 4 – Champions 1987–88. *FA Cup:* Winners 1893, 1908, 1949, 1960; Runners-up 1889, 1896, 1921, 1939. *Football League Cup:* Winners 1973–74, 1979–80. *Texaco Cup:* 1970–71; *Sherpa Van Trophy:* Winners 1988. **European Competitions:** *European Cup:* 1958–59, 1959–60. *European Cup-Winners' Cup:* 1960–61. *UEFA Cup:* 1971–72 (runners-up), 1973-74, 1974—75, 1980–81.
Colours: Gold shirts, black shorts, gold stockings. **Change Colours:** All white.

WOLVERHAMPTON WANDERERS 1988–89 LEAGUE RECORD

Match No.	Date	Venue	Opponents	Result	H/T Score	Lg. Pos.	Goalscorers	Attendance
1	Aug 27	A	Bury	L 1-3	0-2	—	Streete	4314
2	Sept 3	H	Reading	W 2-1	0-1	15	Dennison, Chard (pen)	10,513
3	10	A	Chesterfield	W 3-0	2-0	6	Dennison, Robinson, Chard	4217
4	17	H	Notts Co	D 0-0	0-0	7		10,870
5	20	H	Aldershot	W 1-0	1-0	—	Bull	8991
6	24	A	Swansea C	W 5-2	3-1	3	Dennison, Robinson, Bull 2, Chard	5240
7	Oct 1	H	Port Vale	D 3-3	1-2	4	Bull 2, Thompson (pen)	14,108
8	5	A	Fulham	D 2-2	1-0	—	Mutch, Gooding	4828
9	8	A	Sheffield U	L 0-2	0-1	5		14,272
10	15	H	Wigan Ath	W 2-1	2-1	3	Gallagher, Bull	10,320
11	22	A	Bolton W	W 2-1	0-1	3	Dennison, Bull	8,174
12	25	H	Blackpool	W 2-1	1-0	—	Mutch 2	12,104
13	29	A	Gillingham	W 3-1	1-0	2	Mutch, Robinson, Bull	5288
14	Nov 5	H	Southend U	W 3-0	2-0	1	Streete, Downing, Bull	10,432
15	8	A	Bristol C	W 1-0	0-0	—	Mutch	11,336
16	12	H	Huddersfield T	W 4-1	1-1	1	Mutch, Streete, Bull 2	12,697
17	26	H	Preston NE	W 6-0	3-0	1	Bull 4, Mutch, Vaughan	13,180
18	Dec 4	A	Northampton T	L 1-3	1-2	—	Dennison	6494
19	17	H	Mansfield T	W 6-2	4-1	1	Bull 3, Mutch, Gooding, Thompson	12,134
20	26	A	Bristol R	D 0-0	0-0	1		8480
21	31	A	Brentford	D 2-2	1-1	1	Mutch, Bull	8020
22	Jan 2	H	Chester C	W 3-1	3-1	1	Gooding, Bull, Mutch	21,901
23	10	H	Cardiff C	W 2-0	2-0	—	Mutch, Bull	14,870
24	14	A	Reading	W 2-0	2-0	1	Mutch 2	9353
25	21	H	Chesterfield	W 1-0	0-0	1	Vaughan	15,049
26	29	A	Notts Co	D 1-1	0-1	—	Mutch	9058
27	Feb 4	A	Port Vale	D 0-0	0-0	1		16,362
28	11	H	Fulham	W 5-2	4-1	1	Bull 3, Thomas (og), Thompson (pen)	15,621
29	28	A	Blackpool	W 2-0	0-0	—	Bull, Vaughan	6482
30	Mar 4	H	Bolton W	W 1-0	1-0	1	Bull	13,516
31	10	A	Southend U	L 1-3	0-2	—	Streete	5924
32	14	H	Gillingham	W 6-1	4-0	—	Thompson (pen), Dennison, Steele, Mutch 2, Bull	12,574
33	18	H	Bury	W 4-0	1-0	1	Bull 3, Mutch	14,828
34	25	A	Chester C	D 1-1	1-1	1	Mutch	8236
35	27	H	Bristol R	L 0-1	0-1	1		20,913
36	Apr 1	A	Mansfield T	L 1-3	1-1	1	Bull	9205
37	4	A	Cardiff C	D 1-1	1-0	—	Thompson (pen)	7219
38	8	H	Brentford	W 2-0	1-0	1	Streete, Bull	14,196
39	15	A	Aldershot	W 2-1	1-0	1	Bull, Dennison	5465
40	22	H	Swansea C	D 1-1	1-0	1	Vaughan	13,921
41	29	A	Huddersfield T	D 0-0	0-0	1		8757
42	May 1	H	Bristol C	W 2-0	1-0	1	Bull 2	17,351
43	6	H	Northampton T	W 3-2	2-0	1	Bull, Thompson (pen), Mutch	15,529
44	9	H	Sheffield U	D 2-2	1-0	—	Bull, Dennison	24,321
45	13	A	Preston NE	D 3-3	1-1	1	Mutch 2, Bellamy	14,126
46	16	A	Wigan Ath	D 1-1	1-0	—	Gooding	5531

Final League Position: 1

GOALSCORERS

League (96): Bull 37, Mutch 21, Dennison 8, Thompson 6 (5 pens), Streete 5, Gooding 4, Vaughan 4, Chard 3 (1 pen), Robinson 3, Bellamy 1, Downing 1, Gallagher 1, Steele 1, own goal 1.
Littlewoods Cup (3): Bull 2, Dennison 1.
FA Cup (0).

Littlewoods Cup	First Round	Birmingham C (h)	3-2
		(a)	0-1
FA Cup	First Round	Grimsby T (a)	0-1

Kendall	Bellamy	Thompson	Streete	Robertson	Robinson	Chard	Vaughan	Bull	Mutch	Dennison	Venus	Clarke	Gooding	Gallagher	Downing	Bennett	Kelly	Steele	Stowell	Hansbury	*Match No.*
1	2	3	4	5	6	7	8	9	10	11											1
1	2	3	4	5	6	7	8	9	10	11											2
1	2	3	4	5	6	7	8	9	10	11*				12							3
1	2	3	4*	5	6	7	8	9	10	11	12										4
1	2	3		5	6	8		9	10	11		4	7								5
1	2	3			6	8		9	10	11	4	5	7								6
1	2	3		5	6	8		9	10	11		4	7								7
1	2	3		5*	6	8		9	10	11	12	4	7								8
1	2	3			6	8*		9	10	11	5	4	7	12							9
1	2	3	4		6	8		9	10	11	5			7							10
1	2	3	4*		6	8		9	10	11	5			7	12						11
1	2	3		4	6	8*		9	10	11	5			7	12						12
1	2	3		4	6			9	10	11	5			7	8						13
1	2	7	4†	5*	6			9	10	11	3			12	8	14					14
1	2	7	4	5	6			9	10	11	3				8						15
1	2	7	4	5	6			9	10	11	3				8						16
1	2	7	4	5			6†	9	10	11	3			12	8*	14					17
1	2	7*	4	5	6			9	10	11	3		12		8						18
1	2	7	4	5*	6		14	9	10	11†	3		8		12						19
1	2	7	4		6			9	10		3	5	8		11						20
1	2	7	4		6*		12	9	10		3	5	8		11						21
1	2	7	4	5			6	9	10		3		8		11						22
1	2	7	4	5			6	9	10	12	3		8†		11*		14				23
1	2	7	4	5			6	9	10	12	3		8*		11						24
1	2	7	4	5			6	9	10	11	3		8								25
1	2	7	4				6	9	10	11	3		8		5						26
1	2	7	4				6	9	10	11	3		8		5						27
1	2	7	4		12		6*	9	10†	11	3		8		5		14				28
1	2	7	4				6	9	10	11	3		8		5						29
1	2	7	4				6	9	10	11*	3		8		5			12			30
1	2	7*	4			12	6	9	10	11†	3		8		5			14			31
1	2	7	4		12	3†	6	9	10	11	14		8*					5			32
	2	7	4		14		6*	9	10	11†	3		8		12			5	1		33
	2	7	4				6	9	10	11	3		8					5	1		34
	2	7	4				6	9	10	11	3		8*		12			5	1		35
	2	7	4	3	8*		6	9	10	11	14				12			5†	1		36
		2	4	5	8*		6	9	10	11	3				12			7	1		37
		2	4	5	14	12	6	9	10*	11	3				8†			7	1		38
		2		5	14	12	6†	9	10	11*	3	4	7		8				1		39
	2	3	4	5			6	9	10	11			8*		7			12		1	40
	2	3	4	5	14	12	6	9	10	11			8*		7†					1	41
1	2	3	4	5			6	9	10	11			8		7					1	42
	2	3	4	5	14	12	6†	9	10	11			8*		7						43
1	2	3	4	5			6	9	10	11			7		8						44
1	2	3	4	5			6	9	10	11			7		8						45
1	2	3	4	5	8	9	6*			11	10		7					12			46
36	43	46	38	30	23 + 7s	14 + 5s	30 + 2s	45	45	41 + 2s	31 + 4s	8	30 + 1s	4 + 4s	25 + 7s	— + 2s	— + 2s	7 + 4s	7	3	

WOLVERHAMPTON WANDERERS

Player and Position	*Ht*	*Wt*	*Birth Date*	*Birth Place*	*Source*	*Clubs*	*League App*	*League Gls*
Goalkeepers								
Vincent Bartram	6 2	13 04	7 8 68	Birmingham	Amateur	Wolverhampton W	1	—
Mark Kendall	6 0	12 04	20 9 58	Blackwood	Apprentice	Tottenham H	29	—
						Chesterfield (loan)	9	—
						Newport Co	272	—
						Wolverhampton W	106	—
Eric Steele‡	6 0	12 09	14 5 54	Newcastle	Amateur	Newcastle U	—	—
						Peterborough U	124	—
						Brighton HA	87	—
						Watford	51	—
						Cardiff C (loan)	7	—
						Derby Co	47	—
						Southend U	27	—
						Mansfield T (loan)	5	—
						Notts Co	—	—
						Wolverhampton W	—	—
Defenders								
Gary Bellamy	6 2	11 05	4 7 62	Worksop	Apprentice	Chesterfield	184	7
						Wolverhampton W	67	3
Tom Bennett	5 11	11 08	12 12 69	Falkirk	Trainee	Aston Villa	—	—
						Wolverhampton W	2	—
Chris Brindley‡	6 1	12 08	5 7 69	Stoke	Hednesford	Wolverhampton W	7	—
Nicky Clarke	5 11	12 00	20 8 67	Walsall	Apprentice	Wolverhampton W	63	1
Alistair Robertson	5 9	12 04	9 9 52	Philipstoun	Apprentice	WBA	506	8
						Wolverhampton W	102	—
Floyd Streete	5 11	14 00	5 5 59	Jamaica	Rivet S	Cambridge U	125	19
					Utrecht	Derby Co	35	—
						Wolverhampton W	142	6
Mark Venus	6 0	11 08	6 4 67	Hartlepool		Hartlepool U	4	—
						Leicester C	61	1
						Wolverhampton W	39	—
Midfield								
Philip Chard	5 8	11 03	16 10 60	Corby	Nottingham F	Peterborough U	172	18
						Northampton T	115	27
						Wolverhampton W	28	5
Robert Dennison	5 7	11 00	30 4 63	Banbridge	Glenavon	WBA	16	1
						Wolverhampton W	96	14
Keith Downing	5 8	11 00	23 7 65	Oldbury	Mile Oak	Notts Co	23	1
						Wolverhampton W	66	2
Paul Grainger‡	5 8	11 00	28 1 68	Bloxwich	Mile Oak	Wolverhampton W	—	—
Robert Kelly	5 9	10 13	21 12 64	Birmingham	Apprentice	Leicester C	24	1
						Tranmere R (loan)	5	2
						Wolverhampton W	16	2
Barry Powell‡	5 8	11 00	29 1 54	Kenilworth	Apprentice	Wolverhampton W	64	7
						Coventry C	164	48
						Derby Co	84	7
					Hong Kong	Burnley	11	—
						Swansea C	8	—
					South China	Wolverhampton W	14	—
Philip Robinson	5 9	10 10	6 1 67	Stafford	Apprentice	Aston Villa	3	1
						Wolverhampton W	71	8
Andy Thompson	5 4	10 06	9 11 67	Carnock	Apprentice	WBA	24	1
						Wolverhampton W	117	16
Nigel Vaughan	5 5	8 10	20 5 59	Caerleon	Apprentice	Newport Co	224	32
						Cardiff C	149	42
						Reading (loan)	5	1
						Wolverhampton W	68	10

WOLVERHAMPTON WANDERERS

Foundation: Another club where precise details of information are confused, due in part to the existence of an earlier Wolverhampton club which played rugby. However, it is now considered likely that it came into being in 1879 when players from St. Luke's (founded 1877) and Goldthorn (founded 1876) broke away to form Wolverhampton Wanderers Association FC.

Managers (and Secretary-managers)
George Worrall 1877–85*, John Addenbrooke 1885–1922, George Jobey 1922–24, Albert Hoskins 1924–26 (had been secretary since 1922), Fred Scotchbrook 1926–27, Major Frank Buckley 1927–48, Stan Cullis 1948–64, Andy Beattie 1964–65, Ronnie Allen 1966–68, Bill McGarry 1968–76, Sammy Chung 1976–78, John Barnwell 1978–82, Ian Greaves 1982, Graham Hawkins 1982–84, Tommy Docherty 1984–85, Bill McGarry 1985, Sammy Chapman 1985–86, Brian Little 1986, Graham Turner 1986– .

Player and Position	*Ht*	*Wt*	*Birth Date*	*Birth Place*	*Source*	*Clubs*	*League App*	*League Gls*
Mick Gooding	5 7	10 08	12 4 59	Newcastle	B Auckland	Rotherham U	102	10
						Chesterfield	12	—
						Rotherham U	156	33
						Peterborough U	47	21
						Wolverhampton W	31	4
Forwards								
Ioan Bebb*	5 8	11 00	2 9 70	Aberystwyth	Aberystwyth	Wolverhampton W	—	—
Steve Bull	5 11	11 04	28 3 65	Tipton	Apprentice	WBA	4	2
						Wolverhampton W	119	85
Jackie Gallagher*	5 10	12 09	6 4 58	Wisbech	March T	Lincoln C	1	—
					Kings Lynn	Peterborough U	13	1
					Wisbech	Torquay U	42	7
					Wisbech	Peterborough U	82	19
						Wolverhampton W	27	4
Kevin Morrison*			10 2 66	Banff	Aberystwyth	Wolverhampton W	—	—
Andy Mutch	5 10	11 00	28 12 63	Liverpool	Southport	Wolverhampton W	147	59
Tim Steele	5 9	11 00	1 2 67	Coventry	Apprentice	Shrewsbury T	61	5
						Wolverhampton W	11	1

Trainees
Briggs, Martyn B; Butler, David J; Colleymore, Stanley V; Fennel, Neville R; Gibbs, David; Green, Matthew; Hartigan, Richard C; Keough, Lee A; Leeding, Stuart; Marsden, David T; Millington, Chad A; Owen, Steven J; Taylor, Colin D; Taylor, Dominic J; Urbicki, Stephen; Wilson, Justin A.

Associated Schoolboys
Beardshaw, Richard N; Briggs, Steven N; Caldicott, Russell J; Colenso, Thomas S; Colley, Nicholas S; Dunn, Steven P; Evans, Stuart P; Fereday, Michael; Fletcher, Mark; Ireson, Matthew; Noakes, Craig; Robbins, Simon; Russell, Keith; Simpson, Jermaine; Smith, Jason J; Voice, Scott H; Woodbine, Kevin.

WREXHAM 1988–89 *Back row (left to right)*: George Showell (Assistant Manager/Physiotherapist), Kevin Russell, Nigel Beaumont, Mike Williams, Mike Salmon, Jon Bowden, Mark Morris, Darren Wright, Ollie Kearns, Tony Lee, Dixie McNeil (Manager).
Front row: Steve Buxton, Roger Preece, Andy Thackeray, Joey Jones (Captain), Graham Cooper, Geoff Hunter, Neil Salathiel, Mike Carter.

Division 4 WREXHAM

Racecourse Ground, Mold Road, Wrexham. Telephone Wrexham (0978) 262129. Commercial Dept: (0978) 352536. Fax No. 0978 357821. Clubcall 0898 12 16 42.

Ground capacity: 22,500 (18,000 covered).

Record attendance: 34,445 v Manchester U, FA Cup 4th rd, 26 Jan, 1957.

Record receipts: £49,761.70 v AS Roma, European Cup-Winners' Cup, 2nd rd 2nd leg, 7 Nov, 1984.

Pitch measurements: 111yd × 71yd.

President: F. Wellum.

Chairman: W. P. Griffiths. ***Vice-Chairman:*** D. Rhodes.

Directors: G. Mytton, F. J. Tomlinson, C. Griffiths, N. Dickens, G. Dickens, J. Scott.

Manager: Dixie McNeil. ***Assistant Manager:*** George Showell.

Secretary: ***General Manager:*** A. E. Rawce. ***Commercial Manager:*** S. R. Slater.

Year Formed: 1873 (oldest Club in Wales).

Turned Professional: 1912. ***Ltd Co.:*** 1912.

Previous Ground: Acton Park.

Club Nickname: 'Robins'.

Record League Victory: 10-1 v Hartlepools, Division 4, 3 March 1962 – Keelan; Peter Jones, McGavan; Tecwyn Jones, Fox, Ken Barnes; Ron Barnes (3), Bennion (1), Davies (3), Ambler (3), Ron Roberts.

Record Cup Victory: 6-0 v Gateshead, FA Cup, 1st rd, 20 November 1976 – Lloyd; Evans, Whittle, Davis, Roberts, Thomas (Hill), Shinton (3 incl. 1p), Sutton, Ashcroft (2), Lee (1), Griffiths. 6-0 v Charlton Ath, FA Cup, 3rd rd, 5 January 1980 – Davies; Darracott, Kenworthy, Davis, Jones (Hill), Fox, Vinter (3), Sutton, Edwards (1), McNeil (2), Carrodus.

Record Defeat: 0-9 v Brentford, Division 3, 15 October, 1963.

Most League Points (2 for a win): 61, Division 4, 1969–70 and Division 3, 1977–78.

Most League Points (3 for a win): 71, Division 4, 1988–89.

Most League Goals: 106, Division 3 (N), 1932–33.

Highest League Scorer in Season: Tom Bamford, 44, Division 3 (N), 1933–34.

Most League Goals in Total Aggregate: Tom Bamford, 175, 1928–34.

Most Capped Player: Dai Davies, 28 (51), Wales.

Most League Appearances: Arfon Griffiths, 592, 1959–61, 1962–79.

Record Transfer Fee Received: £300,000 from Manchester U for Mickey Thomas, November 1978 and from Manchester C for Bobby Shinton, July 1979.

Record Transfer Fee Paid: £210,000 to Liverpool for Joey Jones, October 1978.

Football League Record: 1921 Original Member of Division 3 (N); 1958–60 Division 3; 1960–62 Division 4; 1962–64 Division 3; 1964–70 Division 4; 1970–78 Division 3; 1978–82 Division 2; 1982–83 Division 3; 1983– Division 4.

Honours: *Football League:* Division 2 best season: 15th, 1978–79; Division 3 – Champions 1977–78; Division 3 (N) – Runners-up 1932–33; Division 4 – Runners-up 1969–70. *FA Cup* best season: 6th rd, 1973–74, 1977–78. *Football League Cup* best season: 5th rd, 1961, 1978. *Welsh Cup:* Winners 21 times. Runners-up 19 times. Record number of victories and appearances in finals. **European Competition:** *European Cup-Winners' Cup:* 1972-73, 1975–76, 1978–79, 1979–80, 1984–85.

Colours: Red shirts, white shorts, red stockings. **Change Colours:** Green shirts, green shorts, green stockings.

WREXHAM 1988–89 LEAGUE RECORD

Match No.	Date	Venue	Opponents	Result	H/T Score	Lg. Pos.	Goalscorers	Attendance
1	Aug 27	A	Exeter C	W 2-0	1-0	—	Cooper, Russell	2504
2	Sept 3	H	Lincoln C	W 3-0	0-0	2	Cooper 2, Russell (pen)	2312
3	10	A	Rotherham U	D 2-2	1-1	3	Wright, Jones	4367
4	16	H	Colchester U	D 2-2	0-1	—	Hunter, Cooper	2873
5	20	H	Grimsby T	L 1-2	1-2	—	Hunter	2267
6	24	A	Doncaster R	D 2-2	0-1	7	Russell, Hunter	1712
7	Oct 1	H	Peterborough U	D 1-1	0-1	11	Russell	1826
8	4	A	Halifax T	L 0-4	0-3	—		1199
9	8	H	Crewe Alex	D 0-0	0-0	16		2689
10	15	A	Hartlepool U	W 3-1	2-1	13	Jones, Preece, Cooper	2235
11	22	H	Tranmere R	D 3-3	2-0	10	Cooper 2, Preece	3334
12	25	A	Scunthorpe U	L 1-3	1-1	—	Stevenson (og)	2999
13	29	H	York C	W 2-1	1-1	10	Bowden, Russell	2014
14	Nov 5	A	Hereford U	D 0-0	0-0	13		2372
15	8	H	Stockport Co	W 2-0	1-0	—	Thackeray, Bowden	1865
16	12	A	Rochdale	D 3-3	1-0	11	Jones 2, Preece	2280
17	26	A	Scarborough	W 3-0	1-0	6	Kearns, Bowden 2	3489
18	Dec 3	H	Carlisle U	W 2-1	2-1	5	Jones 2	1892
19	16	H	Cambridge U	W 3-1	2-1	—	Russell, Buxton, Flynn	1728
20	26	A	Burnley	W 3-1	1-1	2	Bowden, Hunter, Kearns	9174
21	31	A	Leyton Orient	W 1-0	0-0	1	Russell	4025
22	Jan 2	H	Darlington	D 3-3	2-1	2	Russell 2 (1 pen), Preece	6016
23	14	A	Lincoln	L 3-4	1-2	4	Jones, Russell (pen), Cooper	3860
24	21	H	Exeter C	W 3-0	0-0	3	Bowden, Russell, Taylor (og)	2514
25	Feb 4	A	Grimsby T	W 1-0	1-0	2	Bowden	5058
26	11	H	Doncaster R	D 1-1	0-1	4	Wright	3244
27	17	A	Crewe Alex	D 2-2	2-1	—	Bowden, Russell	5627
28	28	H	Scunthorpe U	W 2-0	2-0	—	Jones, Russell (pen)	2609
29	Mar 3	A	Tranmere R	L 1-2	1-0	—	Cooper	7353
30	7	H	Hartlepool U	W 4-3	3-2	—	Carter, Cooper, Russell 2 (1 pen)	2449
31	11	H	Hereford U	D 1-1	0-1	4	Cooper	2960
32	14	A	York C	L 0-1	0-0	—		2006
33	18	H	Rotherham U	L 1-4	1-1	5	Russell	2929
34	25	A	Darlington	L 1-2	1-1	7	Bowden	2281
35	27	H	Burnley	W 4-2	3-1	6	Russell 3, Kearns	3956
36	31	A	Cambridge U	L 0-2	0-0	—		3072
37	Apr 4	A	Torquay U	D 0-0	0-0	—		2421
38	8	H	Leyton Orient	L 0-1	0-1	7		2437
39	15	A	Peterborough U	L 0-1	0-1	8		3067
40	21	H	Halifax T	W 3-0	1-0	—	Buxton 2, Preece	1782
41	25	A	Colchester U	L 1-2	1-1	—	Russell	2918
42	29	H	Scarborough	L 0-1	0-0	7		1948
43	May 1	A	Stockport Co	D 2-2	1-0	7	Russell, Wright	2118
44	6	A	Carlisle U	W 2-1	1-0	7	Thackeray, Russell	2427
45	9	H	Torquay U	W 1-0	0-0	—	Buxton	2056
46	13	H	Rochdale	W 2-1	1-0	7	Kearns, Bowden	3125

Final League Position: 7

GOALSCORERS

League (77): Russell 22 (5 pens), Cooper 11, Bowden 10, Jones 8, Preece 5, Buxton 4, Hunter 4, Kearns 4, Wright 3, Thackeray 2, Carter 1, Flynn 1, own goals 2.
Littlewoods Cup (3): Buxton 2, Cooper 1.
FA Cup (4): Kearns 2, Bowden 1, Cooper 1.

Littlewoods Cup	First Round	Bury (a)	1-2
		(h)	2-2
FA Cup	First Round	Runcorn (a)	2-2
		(h)	2-3

Salmon	Salathiel	Wright	Bowden	Beaumont	Jones J	Preece	Thackeray	Kearns	Russell	Cooper	Flynn	Buxton	Carter	Hunter	Taylor	Wrench	Lane	Raynor	Williams	Morris	Jones P	Filson	*Match No.*
1	2	3	4	5	6	7	8*	9†	10	11	12	14											1
1	2	3	4	5	6		8		10	11	7*	9	12										2
1	2	3	4	5	6		8†		10	11	7*	9	12	14									3
1	2	3†	4*	5	6	12	8		10	11	7	9		14									4
1	3		4	5	6	2†	14		10	11	7*	9	12	8									5
1	2		4*	5†	6	7	3		10	11		9		8	12	14							6
1	2†		4	5	6	7*	14		10	11	12	9		8		3							7
1	2		4	5	6	7			10	11	12	9		8*		3							8
1		3	4*		6	7	2		10	14	11	9†	12	8			5						9
1		3			6	7	2		10	11*	4	9	12	8			5						10
1		3	12		6	7	2		10	11	4*			8			5	9					11
1		3			6	7	2		10	11	4*	12		8			5	9					12
1		3	4		6	7	2		10	11	8						5	9					13
1	2	3	11		6	7	4	12	10		8						5	9*					14
1	2	3	11		6	7	4		10		8							9	5				15
1	2	3	11		6	7	4†		10*	14	8	12						9	5				16
1	2	3	11		6	7		9	10		8			4					5				17
1	2	3	11		6	7		9*	10		8	12		4					5				18
1	2	3	11		6	7	12		10		8	9		4					5*				19
1	2	3	11		6	7*		12	10		8	9		4					5				20
1	2	3	11*		6	7			10	12	8	9		4					5				21
1	2	3	11		6	7		12	10		8	9		4*					5				22
	2	3			6	12	14	9*	10	11	8†	7		4					5	1			23
1	2	3	7*		6				10	11	8	9	12	4					5				24
1	2	3	7		6		4		10	11	8	9							5				25
1	2	3	7		6		4		10	11*	8	9	12						5				26
1	2	3	7		6				10	11	8	9		4					5				27
1	2		7	3	6	12			10	11	8	9*		4					5				28
1	2		11	3	6	7			10	9	8			4					5				29
1	2	3	9	5	6		12		10	11	8		7	4*									30
1	2		11	3	6		12		10	9	8*		7	4					5				31
1	2		11	6					10	9	8		7	4		3			5				32
1	3		11	12	6		2	14	10	9	8		7†	4					5*				33
1	2	3	11	6			12	14	10	9	8†		7*	4					5				34
	2*	3	11		6	14	12	9	10	7†				4					5	1	8		35
		3	11		6	12	2	9	10	7*				4					5	1	8		36
1		3	11		6	12	2	9	10*	7				4					5		8		37
1		3	11		6	12	2	9	10	7*				4					5		8		38
1		3	11		6		2	9*	10	14	7	12		4					5		8†		39
1		3	11		6	7	2		10		8	9		4					5				40
1		3	11*	6		7	2		10	12	8	9		4					5				41
1	12	3	11	6		7†	2		10	14	8	9		4					5*				42
1	5	3	11	6			2	12	10	7*	8	9†		4								14	43
1	2	3	11*	5	6	12	7		10		8	9		4									44
1	2	3		5	6		7*	12	10		8	9	11	4									45
1	2	3	11	5	6		7*	9	10	12	8			4									46
43	34 + 1s	37	41 + 1s	20 + 1s	41	23 + 8s	27 + 8s	10 + 7s	46	29 + 7s	38 + 3s	25 + 5s	6 + 7s	36 + 2s	— + 1s	3 + 1s	6	6	27	3	5	— + 1s	

WREXHAM

Player and Position	Ht	Wt	Birth Date	Birth Place	Source	Clubs	League App	League Gls
Goalkeepers								
Mark Morris	5 11	12 00	1 8 68	Chester		Wrexham	12	—
Mick Salmon	6 2	12 12	14 7 64	Leyland	Local	Blackburn R	1	—
						Chester C (loan)	16	—
						Stockport Co	118	—
						Bolton W	26	—
						Wrexham (loan)	17	—
						Wrexham	83	—
Defenders								
Nigel Beaumont	6 1	12 07	11 2 67	Pontefract		Bradford C	2	—
						Wrexham	21	—
Robert Filson†			25 6 68	St Helens	Everton†	Preston†	—	—
						Wrexham	1	—
Joey Jones	5 10	11 07	4 3 55	Llandudno	Amateur	Wrexham	98	2
						Liverpool	72	3
						Wrexham	146	6
						Chelsea	78	2
						Huddersfield T	68	3
						Wrexham	76	8
Neil Salathiel	5 7	12 00	19 11 62	Wrexham	Amateur	Sheffield W	—	—
						Wrexham	4	—
						Crewe Alex	65	—
					South Africa	Wrexham	211	3
Mike Williams	5 10	10 12	6 2 65	Mancot	Apprentice	Chester C	34	4
						Wrexham	165	3
Mark Wrench	5 10	11 00	27 9 69	Warrington	Trainee	Wrexham	4	—
Darren Wright	5 10	11 04	14 3 68	West Bromwich	Apprentice	Wolverhampton W	1	—
						Wrexham	86	3
Midfield								
John Bowden	6 0	11 07	21 1 63	Stockport	Local	Oldham Ath	82	5
						Port Vale	70	7
						Wrexham	68	11
Mike Carter*	5 9	10 07	18 4 60	Warrington	Apprentice	Bolton W	49	8
						Mansfield T (loan)	18	4
						Swindon T (loan)	5	—
						Plymouth Arg	12	1
						Hereford U (loan)	10	—
						Hereford U	87	11
						Wrexham	34	7
Graham Cooper	5 10	10 09	18 11 65	Huddersfield	Local	Huddersfield T	74	13
						Wrexham	36	11
Brian Flynn	5 4	12 00	12 10 55	Pt Talbot		Burnley	120	8
						Leeds U	154	11
						Burnley (loan)	2	—
						Burnley	80	11
						Cardiff C	32	—
						Doncaster R	27	—
					Limerick	Bury	19	—
						Doncaster R	24	1
						Wrexham	58	2
Geoff Hunter	5 10	10 12	27 10 59	Hull	Apprentice	Manchester U	—	—
						Crewe Alex	87	8
						Port Vale	221	15
						Wrexham	77	8
Roger Preece	5 9	10 12	9 6 69	Much Wenlock	Apprentice	Coventry C	—	—
						Wrexham	78	11
Andy Thackeray	5 9	11 00	13 2 68	Huddersfield		Manchester C	—	—
						Huddersfield T	2	—
						Newport Co	54	4
						Wrexham	35	2

WREXHAM

Foundation: The oldest club still in existence in Wales, Wrexham was founded in 1873 by a group of local businessmen initially to play a 17-a-side game against the Provincial Insurance team. By 1875 their team formation was reduced to 11 men and a year later they were among the founders of the Welsh FA.

Managers (and Secretary-managers)
Ted Robinson 1912–25* (continued as secretary to 1930), Charlie Hewitt 1925–29, Jack Baynes 1929–31, Ernest Blackburn 1932–36, Jimmy Logan 1937–38, Arthur Cowell 1938, Tom Morgan 1938–40, Tom Williams 1940–49, Les McDowall 1949–50, Peter Jackson 1951–54, Cliff Lloyd 1954–57, John Love 1957–59, Billy Morris 1960–61, Ken Barnes 1961–65, Billy Morris 1965, Jack Rowley 1966–67, Alvan Williams 1967–68, John Neal 1968–77, Arfon Griffiths 1977–81, Mel Sutton 1981–82, Bobby Roberts 1982–85, Dixie McNeil 1985– .

Player and Position	*Ht*	*Wt*	*Birth Date*	*Birth Place*	*Source*	*Clubs*	*League App*	*League Gls*
Forwards								
Chris Armstrong	6 0	11 00	19 6 71	Newcastle	Local	Wrexham	—	—
Steve Buxton	5 5	11 02	13 3 60	Birmingham	Amateur	Wrexham	109	21
						Stockport Co	18	1
						Torquay U	—	—
						Wrexham	100	21
Ollie Kearns	6 0	12 00	12 6 56	Banbury	Banbury U	Reading	86	40
						Oxford U	18	4
						Walsall	38	11
						Hereford U	170	58
						Wrexham	34	12
Tony Lee	5 7	10 07	2 3 70	Wirral	Trainee	Wrexham	—	—
Kevin Russell	5 8	10 10	6 12 66	Portsmouth	Apprentice	Brighton & HA	—	—
						Portsmouth	4	1
						Wrexham	84	43
Jason Taylor§			29 8 70	Wrexham	Aston Villa§	Wrexham	1	—

Trainees
Barker, Paul; Jones, Robert S; O'Gormon, David J; Owen, Gareth; Phillips, Wayne; Rawling, Gareth D; Taylor, Jason S; Weaver, Stephen.

****Non-Contract**
Filson, Robert M; Hughes, Michael J; Parrish, Carl; Rowlands, Aled.

Associated Schoolboys
Brammer, David; Burke, Damian P.W; Darracott, Neale; Douglas, Iain S; Durkan, Kieron J; Johnson, Stuart M; Lunt, Robert J; Watkin, Stephen.

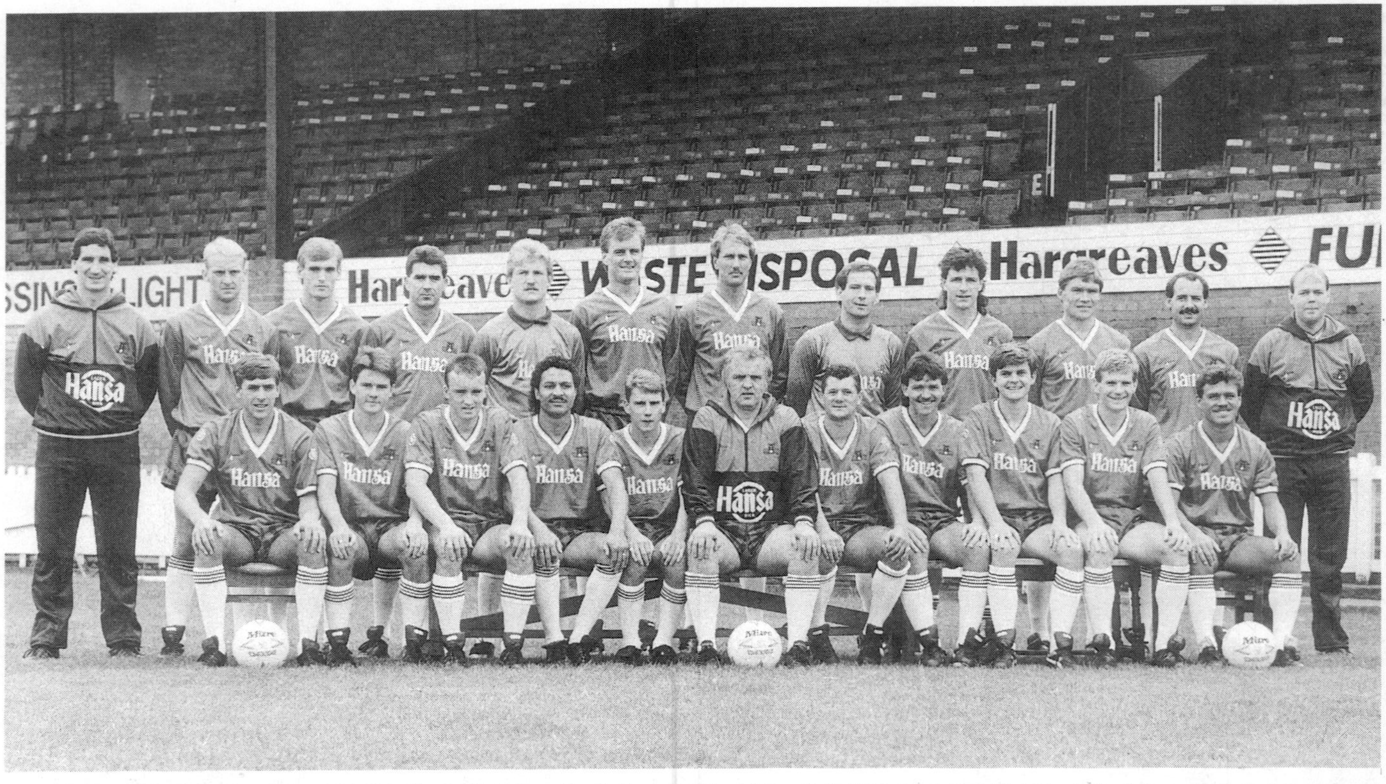

YORK CITY 1988–89 *Back row (left to right):* Ricky Sbragia (Youth Team Coach), Darren Bradshaw, Steven Tutill, Jim Branagan, Chris Martel, Ian Helliwell, Kevan Smith, Scott Endersby, Tony Clegg, Derek Fazackerley (Player/Coach), Paul Johnson, Jeff Miller (Physiotherapist).
Front row: Stuart McKenzie, Andy McMillan, Iain Dunn, Dale Banton, Gary Himsworth, Bob Saxton (Manager), Martin Butler, Tony Canham, Gary Howlett, Steve Spooner. Phil Wilson.

Division 4 YORK CITY

Bootham Crescent, York. Telephone York (0904) 624447.

Ground capacity: 14,109.

Record attendance: 28,123 v Huddersfield T, FA Cup 6th rd, 5 Mar, 1938.

Record receipts: £38,054 v Liverpool, FA Cup 5th rd, 15 Feb, 1986.

Pitch measurements: 115yd × 75yd.

Chairman: M. D. B. Sinclair.

Directors: D. M. Craig OBE, JP, BSC, FICE, FI, MUN E, FCI ARB, M CONS E, B. A. Houghton, R. B. Strachan MA, LLB, FCIS, C. Webb, E. B. Swallow, J. E. H. Quickfall FCA.

Manager: John Bird. *Assistant Manager:* Alan Little.

Secretary: Keith Usher. *Commercial Manager:* Mrs. Sheila Smith.

Physio: Jeff Miller.

Hon. Orthopaedic Surgeon: Mr Peter De Boer, MA, FRCS. *Medical Officer:* Dr A. I. MacLeod.

Year Formed: 1922. *Turned Professional:* 1922. *Ltd Co.:* 1922.

Club Nickname: 'Minstermen'.

Previous Grounds: 1922, Fulfordgate; 1932, Bootham Crescent.

Record League Victory: 9-1 v Southport, Division 3 (N), 2 February 1957 – Forgan; Phillips, Howe; Brown (1), Cairney, Mollatt; Hill, Bottom (4 incl. 1p), Wilkinson (2), Wragg (1), Fenton (1).

Record Cup Victory: 6-0 v South Shields (away), FA Cup, 1st rd, 16 November 1968 – Widdowson; Baker (1p), Richardson; Carr, Jackson, Burrows; Taylor, Ross (3), MacDougall (2), Hodgson, Boyer.

Record Defeat: 0-12 v Chester, Division 3 (N), 1 February, 1936.

Most League Points (2 for a win): 62, Division 4, 1964–65.

Most League Points (3 for a win): 101, Division 4, 1983–84.

Most League Goals: 96, Division 4, 1983–84.

Highest League Scorer in Season: Bill Fenton, 31, Division 3 (N), 1951-52; Arthur Bottom, 31, Division 3 (N), 1954–55 and 1955–56.

Most League Goals in Total Aggregate: Norman Wilkinson, 125, 1954–66.

Most Capped Player: Peter Scott, 7 (10), Northern Ireland.

Most League Appearances: Barry Jackson, 481, 1958–70.

Record Transfer Fee Received: £100,000 from Carlisle U for Gordon Staniforth, October 1979, and from QPR for John Byrne, October 1985.

Record Transfer Fee Paid: £50,000 to Aldershot for Dale Banton, November 1984.

Football League Record: 1929 Elected to Division 3 (N); 1958–59 Division 4; 1959–60 Division 3; 1960–65 Division 4; 1965–66 Division 3; 1966–71 Division 4; 1971–74 Division 3; 1974–76 Division 2; 1976–77 Division 3; 1977–84 Division 4; 1984–88 Division 3; 1988– Division 4.

Honours: Football League: Division 2 best season: 15th, 1974–75; Division 3 – Promoted 1973–74 (3rd); Division 4 – Champions 1983–84. *FA Cup:* Semi-finals 1955, when in Division 3. *Football League Cup* best season: 5th rd, 1962.

Colours: Red shirts, blue shorts, white stockings. **Change Colours:** White shirts, blue shorts, red stockings.

YORK CITY 1988–89 LEAGUE RECORD

Match No.	Date	Venue	Opponents	Result	H/T Score	Lg. Pos.	Goalscorers	Attendance
1	Aug 27	A	Colchester U	L 0-1	0-0	—		1644
2	Sept 3	H	Carlisle U	D 1-1	0-1	18	Banton (pen)	2303
3	10	A	Burnley	L 0-6	0-2	24		7239
4	17	H	Scunthorpe U	L 1-2	0-1	24	Howlett	2735
5	20	H	Hartlepool U	L 2-3	1-2	—	Bradshaw, Banton	2611
6	24	A	Peterborough U	W 1-0	0-0	22	Helliwell	2756
7	Oct 1	H	Halifax T	W 5-3	3-1	17	Butler, Bradshaw, Canham, Howlett, Banton (pen)	2238
8	4	A	Leyton Orient	L 0-4	0-2	—		2467
9	7	A	Tranmere R	W 1-0	1-0	—	Canham	3054
10	15	H	Darlington	W 4-1	2-0	16	Butler 2, Canhan, Banton	2851
11	22	A	Grimsby T	L 0-2	0-2	19		2825
12	25	H	Doncaster R	D 1-1	1-1	—	Dunn	2957
13	29	A	Wrexham	L 1-2	1-1	21	Smith	2014
14	Nov 5	H	Torquay U	D 1-1	0-0	21	Eli	2007
15	8	H	Crewe Alex	W 3-0	0-0	—	Dunn, Johnson, Wilson	1980
16	11	A	Stockport Co	L 2-3	2-2	—	Dunn, Smith	2477
17	26	A	Rochdale	L 0-2	0-0	21		1880
18	Dec 3	H	Hereford U	W 4-1	1-0	21	Helliwell 2, Canham, Himsworth	1698
19	16	H	Rotherham U	D 1-1	0-0	—	Spooner	2656
20	26	A	Scarborough	D 0-0	0-0	21		5057
21	31	A	Exeter C	L 0-2	0-1	21		3092
22	Jan 2	H	Lincoln C	W 2-1	0-1	19	Smith, Dixon	3589
23	14	A	Carlisle U	D 0-0	0-0	18		3462
24	21	H	Colchester U	W 2-0	1-0	18	Dixon, Howlett	2219
25	28	A	Scunthorpe U	L 2-4	1-3	19	Canham 2	4196
26	Feb 4	A	Hartlepool U	W 1-0	0-0	16	Helliwell	2863
27	11	H	Peterborough U	W 5-1	2-0	14	Helliwell 2, Spooner, Canham, Dixon	2438
28	18	H	Tranmere R	L 0-1	0-1	15		2923
29	25	A	Darlington	D 2-2	0-0	14	Dixon, Helliwell	2504
30	28	A	Doncaster R	W 2-1	0-0	—	Greenough, Smith	1526
31	Mar 4	H	Grimsby T	L 0-3	0-1	15		3481
32	14	H	Wrexham	W 1-0	0-0	—	Spooner (pen)	2006
33	18	H	Burnley	D 0-0	0-0	15		3164
34	25	A	Lincoln C	L 1-2	1-1	16	Himsworth	3710
35	27	H	Scarborough	D 0-0	0-0	18		4872
36	Apr 1	A	Rotherham U	W 1-0	0-0	14	Canham	5929
37	4	A	Cambridge U	D 1-1	1-0	—	Reid	2400
38	8	H	Exeter C	W 3-1	1-0	13	Spooner, Dunn, Helliwell	2052
39	14	A	Halifax T	D 0-0	0-0	—		1875
40	22	H	Leyton Orient	D 1-1	0-1	12	Dunn	2744
41	25	A	Torquay U	L 0-2	0-1	—		2015
42	29	H	Rochdale	D 3-3	2-1	13	Canham, Tutill, Dunn	1920
43	May 1	A	Crewe Alex	W 2-1	1-0	12	Reid, Helliwell	3693
44	6	A	Hereford U	W 2-1	1-0	11	Smith, Howlett	1819
45	9	H	Cambridge U	L 1-2	0-2	—	Spooner (pen)	2336
46	13	H	Stockport Co	W 2-0	1-0	11	Helliwell 2	2327

Final League Position: 11

GOALSCORERS

League (62): Helliwell 11, Canham 9, Dunn 6, Smith 5, Spooner 5 (2 pens), Banton 4 (2 pens), Dixon 4, Howlett 4, Butler 3, Bradshaw 2, Himsworth 2, Reid 2, Eli 1, Greenough 1, Johnson 1, Tutill 1, Wilson 1.
Littlewoods Cup (0).
FA Cup (0).

Littlewoods Cup	First Round	Sunderland (h)	0-0
		(a)	0-4
FA Cup	First Round	Halifax T (a)	0-1

Marples	Bradshaw	Johnson	Wilson	Fazackerley	Smith	Howlett	Spooner	Helliwell	Banton	Himsworth	Canham	Branagan	Clegg	Tutill	Butler	Hotte	Dunn	McMillan	Shaw	Morris	Eli	Greenough	Dixon	Hay	Reid	Endersby	Hurlstone	Barratt	*Match No.*
1	2	3	4*	5	6	7	8	9	10	11	12																		1
1				6		7	8	9	10	11*	4	2	3	5	12														2
1	4	3	14	6	5	7		9	10*	11		2	8†		12														3
1	4	3		6		7		9	10*	11		2		5	12	8													4
1	2	4		6		8		9	10		11	3	12	5*	7														5
1	2	4		6	5	8		9	10		11	3			7														6
1	2	4		6		8		9	10		11*	3		5	7	12													7
1	2	4		6	12	8		9	10		11	3		5*	7														8
1	2	4		6		8		9	10		11	3		5	7														9
1	2	4	12	6		8		9†	10		11	3		5*	7		14												10
1	2	4	12	6		8*		9†	10		11	3	5		7		14												11
1	2	4†	12	6	5					10*	11	3			7		9	14	8										12
1	2	4	12	6	5					10*	11	3			7†		9	14	8										13
1	2	3	8	6	5					7*	11						10		4	9	12								14
1	2	3	8	6	5						11						10		4	9	7								15
1	2	3	8	6	5*					14	11	12					10		4	9	7†								16
1		3	4		5			9		11	7			6						12	8	2	10*						17
1	4	3			5		8	9		7	11			6								2	10						18
1	4				6		8	9		7	11	2										5	10	3					19
1	2	3			6		8	9		7	11											5	10		4				20
1	2	3			6		8	9		7	11											5	10		4				21
1	2	3			6		8	9		7*	11						12					5	10		4				22
1	2	3			6		8	9			11						7					5	10		4				23
1	2	3			6	12	8	9			11						7*					5	10		4				24
1	2	3			6	7*	8	9		12	11											5	10		4				25
1	2	3			6		8	9		7	11											5	10		4				2
1	2	3			4	6	8	9		7	11											5	10						27
1	2	3			6	4	8	9		7*	11						12					5	10						28
1	2	3			6	4	8	9		7	11											5	10						29
1	2	3			6		8	9		7	11											5	10		4				30
1	2	3			6	11	8	9		7†				14			12					5	10*		4				31
	2	3			6		8	9		7							11					5	10*		4	1	12		32
1	2	3			6		8	9		7							12					5	10		4		11*		33
1	2	3			6		8	9		7	11											5	10		4				34
1	2	3					8	9		10	11*			6			12					5			4			7	35
1	2	3					8	9		10*	11			6			12					5			4			7	36
1		3					8	9		10	11			6*			7					5	12		4			2	37
1		3					8	9		10	11			6			7					5			4			2	38
1		3					8	9		10	11			6			7					5			4			2	39
1		3					8	9		10	11			6			7					5			4			2	40
1		3				12	8	9		10	11			6			7*					5			4			2	41
1		3				12	8	9		10*	11			6			7					5			4			2	42
1		3			5	10	8	9			11			6			7								4			2	43
1		3			5	10	8	9			11			6			7								4			2	44
1		3			5	10	8	9			11			6			7*								4			2	45
1		3			5	10*	8	9			11			6			7								4			2	46
45	34	44	5 + 5s	16	30 + 1s	20 + 3s	31	41	11	30 + 2s	40 + 1s	13 + 1s	3 + 1s	21 + 1s	9 + 3s	1 + 1s	18 + 8s	— + 2s	5	3 + 1s	3 + 1s	26	18 + 1s	1	24	1	1 + 1s	12	

Hall — Match No. 45(12) 46(12)

YORK CITY

Player and Position	Ht	Wt	Birth Date	Birth Place	Source	Clubs	League App	League Gls
Goalkeepers								
Scott Endersby	5 10	12 04	24 2 62	Lewisham	Kettering T	Ipswich T	—	—
						Tranmere R	79	—
						Swindon T	85	—
						Carlisle U	52	—
						York C	35	—
						Cardiff C (loan)	4	—
						Rochdale (loan	—	—
Chris Marples	5 11	11 12	3 8 64	Chesterfield		Chesterfield	84	—
						Stockport Co	57	—
						York C	45	—
Defenders								
Tony Barratt	5 8	10 02	18 10 65	Salford	Billingham T	Grimsby T	22	—
						Hartlepool U	98	4
						York C	12	—
Jim Branagan‡	5 10	11 07	3 7 55	Daveyhulme	Amateur	Oldham Ath	27	—
					Cape Town C	Huddersfield T	38	—
						Blackburn R	294	5
						Preston NE	3	—
						York C	42	1
Tony Clegg‡	6 0	11 05	8 11 65	Keighley	Apprentice	Bradford C	48	2
						York C	41	3
Ricky Greenough	6 1	13 06	30 5 61	Mexborough	Alfreton T	Chester C	132	15
						Scarborough	—	—
						York C	26	1
Paul Johnson*	5 10	12 05	25 5 59	Stoke	Apprentice	Stoke C	34	—
						Shrewsbury T	180	3
						York C	83	1
Stuart McKenzie‡	5 11	11 00	19 9 67	Hull	Local	York C	32	—
Andy McMillan	5 10	10 13	22 6 68	South Africa		York C	24	—
Kevan Smith	6 3	12 02	13 12 59	Yarm	Stockton	Darlington	245	11
						Rotherham U	59	4
						Coventry C	6	—
						York C	31	5
Steve Tutill	6 0	11 10	1 10 69	Derwent	Trainee	York C	43	1
Phil Wilson‡	5 6	11 13	16 10 60	Hemsworth	Apprentice	Bolton W	39	4
						Huddersfield T	233	16
						York C	46	2
Midfield								
Darren Bradshaw	5 11	11 04	19 3 67	Sheffield	Matlock T	Chesterfield	18	—
						York C	59	3
David Downing‡			6 10 68	Bideford	Trainee	York C	1	—
Wayne Hall‡			25 10 68	Rotherham	Darlington†	York C	2	—
Gary Howlett	5 8	10 04	2 4 63	Dublin	Home Farm	Coventry C	—	—
						Brighton HA	32	2
						Bournemouth	60	7
						Aldershot (loan)	1	—
						Chester C (loan)	6	1
						York C	41	6
Shaun Reid	5 8	11 08	13 10 65	Huyton	Local	Rochdale	133	4
						Preston NE (loan)	3	—
						York C	24	2
Steve Spooner	5 10	12 00	25 1 61	Sutton	Apprentice	Derby Co	8	—
						Halifax T	72	13
						Chesterfield	93	14
						Hereford U	84	19
						York C	31	5

YORK CITY

Foundation: Although there was a York City club formed in 1903 by a soccer enthusiast from Darlington, this has no connection with the modern club because it went out of existence during World War I. Unlike many others of that period who restarted in 1919, York City did not re-form until 1922 and the tendency now is to ignore the modern club's pre-1922 existence.

Managers (and Secretary-managers)
Bill Sherrington 1924–60 (was secretary for most of this time but virtually secretary-manager for a long pre-war spell), John Collier 1929–36, Tom Mitchell 1936–50, Dick Duckworth 1950–52, Charlie Spencer 1952–53, Jimmy McCormick 1953–54, Sam Bartram 1956–60, Tom Lockie 1960–67, Joe Shaw 1967–68, Tom Johnston 1968–75, Wilf McGuinness 1975–77, Charlie Wright 1977–80, Barry Lyons 1980–81, Denis Smith 1982–87, Bobby Saxton 1987–88, John Bird 1988– .

Player and Position	*Ht*	*Wt*	*Birth Date*	*Birth Place*	*Source*	*Clubs*	*League App*	*League Gls*
Forwards								
Martin Butler‡	5 8	10 09	3 3 66	Hull		York C	65	9
						Aldershot (loan)	2	1
						Exeter C (loan)	4	1
						Carlisle U (loan)	1	—
Tony Canham	5 8	10 07	8 6 60	Leeds	Harrogate R	York C	141	34
Kevin Dixon	5 10	10 06	27 7 60	Blackhill	Tow Law T	Carlisle U	9	—
						Hartlepool U (loan)	6	3
						Hartlepool U	107	26
						Scunthorpe U (loan)	14	2
						Scunthorpe U	41	4
						Hartlepool U	14	4
						York C	19	4
Iain Dunn			1 4 70	Derwent	School	York C	26	6
Ian Helliwell	6 3	13 12	7 12 62	Rotherham	Matlock T	York C	73	19
Gary Himsworth	5 7	9 08	19 12 69	Appleton	Trainee	York C	63	4
Gary Hurlstone‡			25 4 63	Mexborough		York C	2	—
Neil Morris‡			3 5 70	Sheffield	Doncaster R§	York C	4	—
Dave Tomlinson‡	5 7	11 00	13 12 68	Rotherham	Apprentice	Sheffield W	1	—
						Rotherham U	9	—
						York C	—	—

Trainees
Alker, Simon; Brown, Andrew; Dean, Alan F; Ede, Stuart; Healey, Scott; Molloy, Christopher S; Naylor, Glenn; Robertson, Paul; Thompson, Warren C; Walsh, Matthew J; Wood, Mark.

****Non-Contract**
Ashworth, Christopher J; Berry, Jason G.L.

Associated Schoolboys
Bridges, Damian J; Crowther, Nicky A; Ellis, Robert; Hall, Craig; Higgins, Neil F; Jones, Andrew; Pollitt, Michael; Robinson, Lee A; Skelton, Peter R; Smith, Andrew; Smith, Michael J; Vause, Adam.

END OF SEASON PLAY-OFFS 1988–89

With the relegation-threatened teams being spared the trauma of facing a play-off situation this season, the ordeal was confined to those seeking promotion. It was therefore somewhat appropriate that Crystal Palace, who missed out on promotion by just one point in the Second Division and Port Vale edged out on goal difference in Division Three, succeeded in elevating themselves.

But again it was in the Fourth Division that the rogue card was once more played in the form of Leyton Orient. They had finished sixth, yet as Swansea City the season before and Aldershot the one previous to that, they contrived to emerge as the fourth promoted side.

Without one relegation-haunted team being involved, there were increased opportunities for promotion-seeking sides, four in each of the three lower divisions having a chance for the remaining place.

Blackburn Rovers were held to a goalless draw at home by Watford but scraped through after extra time in the return at Vicarage Road following a 1-1 draw. But in the Second Division final they were to rue a missed penalty by Howard Gayle in the Ewood Park leg against Palace. However, Gayle did score twice in their 3-1 win. It took the Londoners until the extra period themselves to wipe out the deficit at 3-0, watched by a 30,000 crowd.

Palace, who had also lost their semi-final away leg at Swindon, clearly felt happier playing in the surrounds of Selhurst Park.

Bristol Rovers made short work of Fulham in Division Three, winning 1-0 at Bath and 4-0 at Craven Cottage, but Port Vale had to work slightly harder against Preston, drawing 1-1 at Deepdale and Darren Beckford scoring twice in the second half for a hat-trick in a 3-1 success at Vale Park.

Robbie Earle became Vale's hero against Bristol Rovers scoring in both games as the Potteries side won 2-1 on aggregate, his decisive effort coming in the 51st minute of the second leg.

Wrexham had comfortable victories over Scunthorpe, 3-1 at home, 2-0 away but Leyton Orient's 2-0 lead over Scarborough shrunk to a 2-1 aggregate on their trip north. But Orient fared better at Wrexham, drawing 0-0 and hitting a late winner through Mark Cooper in the 2-1 success at Brisbane Road.

DIVISION 2, Semi-final, First Leg

21 MAY

Blackburn R (0) 0

Watford (0) 0 14,008

Blackburn R: Gennoe; Atkins, Sulley, Reid, Hendry, Mail, Gayle, Millar, Miller, Garner, Sellers.
Watford: Coton; Gibbs, Jackett (Holdsworth David), Falconer, Miller, McClelland, Thomas, Wilkinson, Roberts (Holdsworth Dean), Porter, Redfearn.

Swindon T (0) 1 *(Hopkins (og))*

Crystal Palace (0) 0 16,656

Swindon T: Digby; Hockaday, King, Jones, Parkin, Calderwood, Foley, Shearer, McLoughlin, MacLaren, White.
Crystal Palace: Suckling; Pemberton, Burke, Madden, Hopkins, Hedman, McGoldrick, Pardew, Bright, Wright, Barber (Pennyfather).

DIVISION 3, Semi-final, First Leg

Bristol R (0) 1 *(Penrice)*

Fulham (0) 0 9029

Bristol R: Martyn; Alexander, Clark, Yates, White, Jones, Holloway, Bailey (Mehew), Reece, Penrice, Purnell.
Fulham: Stannard; Mauge, Thomas, Skinner, Rougvie, Eckhardt, Marshall, Scott, Cole, Davies, Walker (Elkins).

DIVISION 4, Semi-final, First Leg

Leyton Orient (1) 2 *(Cooper 2)*

Scarborough (0) 0 9298

Leyton Orient: Heald; Howard, Dickenson, Hales (Carter), Day, Sitton, Baker, Castle, Harvey, Cooper, Comfort.
Scarborough: Ironside; Kamara, Thompson, Olsson, Richards, Short Craig, Cook, Graham, Norris (Dobson), Brook, Russell (Morris).

Wrexham (3) 3 *(Wright, Kearns 2)*

Scunthorpe U (1) 1 *(Cowling)* 5449

Wrexham: Salmon; Salathiel, Wright, Hunter, Beaumont, Jones, Thackeray (Carter), Flynn (Cooper), Kearns, Russell, Bowden.
Scunthorpe U: Musselwhite; Smalley, Longden, Taylor, Nicol, Cork, Hodkinson, Cowling, Daws (Cotton), Flounders, Hamilton.

DIVISION 3, Semi-final, First Leg

22 MAY

Preston NE (1) 1 *(Jemson)*

Port Vale (0) 1 *(Earle)* 14,280

Preston NE: Brown; Williams N, Swann, Atkins, Wrightson, Hughes, Mooney, Ellis, Joyce, Jemson, Patterson.
Port Vale: Grew; Mills, Hughes, Walker, Webb, Glover, Jeffers, Earle, Futcher, Beckford, Porter.

DIVISION 2, Semi-final, Second Leg

24 MAY

Crystal Palace (2) 2 *(Bright, Wright)*

Swindon T (0) 0 23,677

Crystal Palace: Suckling; Pemberton, Burke, Madden, Hopkins, Hedman, McGoldrick, Pardew, Bright, Wright, Barber.
Swindon T: Digby; Hockaday, King, Jones, Parkin (Gittens), Calderwood, Foley (Henry), Shearer, McLoughlin, MacLaren, White.

Watford (1) 1 *(Redfearn)*

Blackburn R (1) 1 *(Garner)* 13,854

Watford: Coton; Gibbs, Jackett, Falconer, Miller, McClelland (Holdsworth David), Thomas, Roberts (Holdsworth Dean), Wilkinson, Porter, Redfearn.
Blackburn R: Gennoe; Atkins, Sulley, Reid, Hendry, Mail, Gayle, Millar, Miller (Curry), Garner, Sellars (Ainscow).
aet; Blackburn R won on away goals.

DIVISION 4, Semi-final, Second Leg

Scarborough (0) 1 *(Russell)*

Leyton Orient (0) 0 4377

Scarborough: Ironside; Kamara, Richards, Short Craig, Thompson, Olsson, Cook (Norris), Russell, Graham, Brook, Dobson.
Leyton Orient: Heald; Baker, Dickenson, Hales, Day, Sitton, Howard, Castle, Harvey, Cooper, Comfort (Ward).

Scunthorpe U (0) 0

Wrexham (2) 2 *(Russell 2)* 5516

Scunthorpe U: Musselwhite; Smalley, Longden, Taylor, Nicol (Money), Cork, Hodkinson, Cowling (Richardson), Daws, Flouders, Hamilton.
Wrexham: Salmon; Salathiel, Wright, Hunter, Beaumont, Jones, Thackeray, Flynn, Kearns (Cooper), Russell, Bowden (Carter).

DIVISION 3, Semi-final, Second Leg

25 MAY

Fulham (0) 0

Bristol R (0) 4 *(Clark, Holloway, Bailey, Reece)* 10,668

Fulham: Stannard; Mague (Sayer), Thomas, Skinner (Wilson), Rougvie, Eckhardt, Marshall, Scott, Cole, Davies, Walker.
Bristol R: Martyn; Alexander, Clark, Yates, White (McClean), Jones, Holloway, Mehew, Reece, Penrice (Bailey), Purnell.

Port Vale (1) 3 *(Beckford 3)*

Preston NE (1) 1 *(Patterson)* 13,416

Port Vale: Grew; Mills, Hughes, Walker, Webb (West), Glover, Jeffers, Earle, Futcher, Beckford, Porter.
Preston NE: Brown; Williams N, Swann, Atkins, Wrightson, Hughes, Mooney (Miller), Ellis, Joyce, Jemson (Rathbone), Patterson.

DIVISION 4, Final, First Leg

30 MAY

Wrexham (0) 0

Leyton Orient (0) 0 7915

Wrexham: Salmon; Salathiel, Wright, Hunter, Beaumont, Jones, Thackeray (Buxton), Flynn, Kearns, Russell, Bowden.
Leyton Orient: Heald; Howard, Dickenson, Hales, Day, Sitton, Baker (Ward), Castle, Harvey, Cooper, Comfort.

DIVISION 2, Final, First Leg

31 MAY

Blackburn R (2) 3 *(Gayle 2, Garner)*

Crystal Palace (0) 1 *(McGoldrick)* 16,421

Blackburn R: Gennoe; Atkins, Sulley, Reid, Hendry, Mail, Gayle, Millar, Miller, Garner, Sellars.
Crystal Palace: Suckling; Pemberton, Burke, Madden (Pennyfather), Hopkins, Hedman, McGoldrick, Pardew, Bright, Wright, Barber.

DIVISION 3, Final, First Leg

Bristol R (1) 1 *(Penrice)*

Port Vale (0) 1 *(Earle)* 9042

Bristol R: Martyn; Alexander, Clark, Yates, White, Jones, Holloway (McClean), Mehew, Reece, Penrice, Purnell.
Port Vale: Grew; Mills, Hughes, Walker, West, Glover, Jeffers, Earle, Futcher, Beckford, Porter.

DIVISION 2, Final, Second Leg

3 JUNE

Crystal Palace (1) 3 *(Wright 2, Madden (pen))*

Blackburn R (0) 0 *aet* 30,000

Crystal Palace: Suckling; Pemberton, Burke, Madden, Hopkins, O'Reilly, McGoldrick, Pardew, Bright, Wright, Barber.
Blackburn R: Gennoe; Atkins, Sulley, Reid, Hendry, Mail, Gayle (Ainscow), Millar, Miller (Curry), Garner, Sellars.

DIVISION 3, Final, Second Leg

Port Vale (0) 1 *(Earle)*

Bristol R (0) 0 17,353

Port Vale: Grew; Mills, Hughes, Walker, West, Glover, Jeffers, Earle, Futcher, Beckford, Porter (Finney).
Bristol R: Martyn; Alexander, Clark, Yates, White, Jones, Holloway, Mehew, Reece, Penrice, Purnell.

DIVISION 4, Final, Second Leg

Leyton Orient (1) 2 *(Harvey, Cooper)*

Wrexham (1) 1 *(Bowden)* 13,355

Leyton Orient: Heald; Howard, Dickenson (Ward), Hales, Day, Sitton, Baker, Castle, Harvey, Cooper, Comfort.
Wrexham: Salmon; Salathiel, Wright, Hunter, Beaumont, Jones, Thackeray (Buxton), Flynn, Kearns, Russell, Bowden.

Ian Wright heads Crystal Palace goal No. 3 in the play-off with Blackburn Rovers.

BARCLAYS LEAGUE FINAL TABLES 1988–89

DIVISION 1

			Home			Goals		Away			Goals			
		P	W	D	L	F	A	W	D	L	F	A	GD	Pts
1	Arsenal	38	10	6	3	35	19	12	4	3	38	17	+37	76
2	Liverpool	38	11	5	3	33	11	11	5	3	32	17	+37	76
3	Nottingham Forest	38	8	7	4	31	16	9	6	4	33	27	+21	64
4	Norwich C	38	8	7	4	23	20	9	4	6	25	25	+3	62
5	Derby Co	38	9	3	7	23	18	8	4	7	17	20	+2	58
6	Tottenham H	38	8	6	5	31	24	7	6	6	29	22	+14	57
7	Coventry C	38	9	4	6	28	23	5	9	5	19	19	+5	55
8	Everton	38	10	7	2	33	18	4	5	10	17	27	+5	54
9	QPR	38	9	5	5	23	16	5	6	8	20	21	+6	53
10	Millwall	38	10	3	6	27	21	4	8	7	20	31	−5	53
11	Manchester U	38	10	5	4	27	13	3	7	9	18	22	+10	51
12	Wimbledon	38	10	3	6	30	19	4	6	9	20	27	+4	51
13	Southampton	38	6	7	6	25	26	4	8	7	27	40	−14	45
14	Charlton Ath	38	6	7	6	25	24	4	5	10	19	34	−14	42
15	Sheffield W	38	6	6	7	21	25	4	6	9	13	26	−17	42
16	Luton T	38	8	6	5	32	21	2	5	12	10	31	−10	41
17	Aston Villa	38	7	6	6	25	22	2	7	10	20	34	−11	40
18	Middlesbrough	38	6	7	6	28	30	3	5	11	16	31	−17	39
19	West Ham U	38	3	6	10	19	30	7	2	10	18	32	−25	38
20	Newcastle U	38	3	6	10	19	28	4	4	11	13	35	−31	31

DIVISION 2

			Home			Goals		Away			Goals			
		P	W	D	L	F	A	W	D	L	F	A	GD	Pts
1	Chelsea	46	15	6	2	50	25	14	6	3	46	25	+46	99
2	Manchester C	46	12	8	3	48	28	11	5	7	29	25	+24	82
3	Crystal Palace	46	15	6	2	42	17	8	6	9	29	32	+22	81
4	Watford	46	14	5	4	41	18	8	7	8	33	30	+26	78
5	Blackburn R	46	16	4	3	50	22	6	7	10	24	37	+15	77
6	Swindon T	46	13	8	2	35	15	7	8	8	33	38	+15	76
7	Barnsley	46	12	8	3	37	21	8	6	9	29	37	+8	74
8	Ipswich T	46	13	3	7	42	23	9	4	10	29	38	+10	73
9	WBA	46	13	7	3	43	18	5	11	7	22	23	+24	72
10	Leeds U	46	12	6	5	34	20	5	10	8	25	30	+9	67
11	Sunderland	46	12	8	3	40	23	4	7	12	20	37	0	63
12	Bournemouth	46	13	3	7	32	20	5	5	13	21	42	−9	62
13	Stoke C	46	10	9	4	33	25	5	5	13	24	47	−15	59
14	Bradford C	46	8	11	4	29	22	5	6	12	23	37	−7	56
15	Leicester C	46	11	6	6	31	20	2	10	11	25	43	−7	55
16	Oldham Ath	46	9	10	4	49	32	2	11	10	26	40	+3	54
17	Oxford U	46	11	6	6	40	34	3	6	14	22	36	−8	54
18	Plymouth Arg	46	11	4	8	35	22	3	8	12	20	44	−11	54
19	Brighton & HA	46	11	5	7	36	24	3	4	16	21	42	−9	51
20	Portsmouth	46	10	6	7	33	21	3	6	14	20	41	−9	51
21	Hull C	46	7	9	7	31	25	4	5	14	21	43	−16	47
22	Shrewsbury	46	4	11	8	25	31	4	7	12	15	36	−27	42
23	Birmingham C	46	6	4	13	21	33	2	7	14	10	43	−45	35
24	Walsall	46	3	10	10	27	42	2	6	15	14	38	−39	31

DIVISION 3

			Home			Goals		Away			Goals			
		P	W	D	L	F	A	W	D	L	F	A	GD	Pts
1	Wolverhampton W	46	18	4	1	61	19	8	10	5	35	30	+47	92
2	Sheffield U	46	16	3	4	57	21	9	6	8	36	33	+39	84
3	Port Vale	46	15	3	5	46	21	9	9	5	32	27	+30	84
4	Fulham	46	12	7	4	42	28	10	2	11	27	39	+2	75
5	Bristol R	46	9	11	3	34	21	10	6	7	33	30	+16	74
6	Preston NE	46	14	7	2	56	31	5	8	10	23	29	+19	72
7	Brentford	46	14	5	4	36	21	4	9	10	30	40	+5	68
8	Chester C	46	12	6	5	38	18	7	5	11	26	43	+3	68
9	Notts Co	46	11	7	5	37	22	7	6	10	27	32	+10	67
10	Bolton W	46	12	8	3	42	23	4	8	11	16	31	+4	64
11	Bristol C	46	10	3	10	32	25	8	6	9	21	30	−2	63
12	Swansea C	46	11	8	4	33	22	4	8	11	18	31	−2	61
13	Bury	46	11	7	5	27	22	5	6	12	28	45	−12	61
14	Huddersfield T	46	10	8	5	35	25	7	1	15	28	48	−10	60
15	Mansfield T	46	10	8	5	32	22	4	9	10	16	30	−4	59
16	Cardiff C	46	10	9	4	30	16	4	6	13	14	40	−12	57
17	Wigan Ath	46	9	5	9	28	22	5	9	9	27	31	+2	56
18	Reading	46	10	6	7	37	29	5	5	13	31	43	−4	56
19	Blackpool	46	10	6	7	36	29	4	7	12	20	30	−3	54
20	Northampton T	46	11	2	10	41	34	5	4	14	25	42	−10	54
21	Southend U	46	10	9	4	33	26	3	6	14	23	49	−19	54
22	Chesterfield	46	9	5	9	35	35	5	2	16	16	51	−35	49
23	Gillingham	46	7	3	13	25	32	5	1	17	22	49	−34	40
24	Aldershot	46	7	6	10	29	29	1	7	15	19	49	−30	37

DIVISION 4

			Home			Goals		Away			Goals			
		P	W	D	L	F	A	W	D	L	F	A	GD	Pts
1	Rotherham U	46	13	6	4	44	18	9	10	4	32	17	+41	82
2	Tranmere R	46	15	6	2	34	13	6	11	6	28	30	+19	80
3	Crewe Alex	46	13	7	3	42	24	8	8	7	25	24	+19	78
4	Scunthorpe U	46	11	9	3	40	22	10	5	8	37	35	+20	77
5	Scarborough	46	12	7	4	33	23	9	7	7	34	29	+15	77
6	Leyton Orient	46	16	2	5	61	19	5	10	8	25	31	+36	75
7	Wrexham	46	12	7	4	44	28	7	7	9	33	35	+14	71
8	Cambridge U	46	13	7	3	45	25	5	7	11	26	37	+9	68
9	Grimsby T	46	11	9	3	33	18	6	6	11	32	41	+6	66
10	Lincoln C	46	12	6	5	39	26	6	4	13	25	34	+4	64
11	York C	46	10	8	5	43	27	7	5	11	19	36	−1	64
12	Carlisle U	46	9	6	8	26	25	6	9	8	27	27	+1	60
13	Exeter C	46	14	4	5	46	23	4	2	17	19	45	−3	60
14	Torquay U	46	15	2	6	32	23	2	6	15	13	37	−15	59
15	Hereford U	46	11	8	4	40	27	3	8	12	26	45	−6	58
16	Burnley	46	12	6	5	35	20	2	7	14	17	41	−9	55
17	Peterborough U	46	10	3	10	29	32	4	9	10	23	42	−22	54
18	Rochdale	46	10	10	3	32	26	3	4	16	24	56	−26	53
19	Hartlepool U	46	10	6	7	33	33	4	4	15	17	45	−28	52
20	Stockport Co	46	8	10	5	31	20	2	11	10	23	32	+2	51
21	Halifax T	46	10	7	6	42	27	3	4	16	27	48	−6	50
22	Colchester U	46	8	7	8	35	30	4	7	12	25	48	−18	50
23	Doncaster R	46	9	6	8	32	32	4	4	15	17	46	−29	49
24	Darlington	46	3	12	8	28	38	5	6	12	25	38	−23	42

FOOTBALL LEAGUE 1888–89 to 1987–89

FOOTBALL LEAGUE

	First	*Pts*	*Second*	*Pts*	*Third*	*Pts*
1888–89*a*	Preston NE	40	Aston Villa	29	Wolverhampton W	28
1889–90*a*	Preston NE	33	Everton	31	Blackburn R	27
1890–91*a*	Everton	29	Preston NE	27	Notts Co	26
1891–92*b*	Sunderland	42	Preston NE	37	Bolton W	36

FIRST DIVISION

Maximum points: a 44; *b* 52; *c* 60; *d* 68; *e* 76; *f* 84; *g* 126; *h* 120; *k* 114

1892–93*c*	Sunderland	48	Preston NE	37	Everton	36
1893–94*c*	Aston Villa	44	Sunderland	38	Derby Co	36
1894–95*c*	Sunderland	47	Everton	42	Aston Villa	39
1895–96*c*	Aston Villa	45	Derby Co	41	Everton	39
1896–97*c*	Aston Villa	47	Sheffield U	36	Derby Co	36
1897–98*c*	Sheffield U	42	Sunderland	37	Wolverhampton W	35
1898–99*d*	Aston Villa	45	Liverpool	43	Burnley	39
1899–1900*d*	Aston Villa	50	Sheffield U	48	Sunderland	41
1900–01*d*	Liverpool	45	Sunderland	43	Notts Co	40
1901–02*d*	Sunderland	44	Everton	41	Newcastle U	37
1902–03*d*	The Wednesday	42	Aston Villa	41	Sunderland	41
1903–04*d*	The Wednesday	47	Manchester C	44	Everton	43
1904–05*d*	Newcastle U	48	Everton	47	Manchester C	46
1905–06*e*	Liverpool	51	Preston NE	47	The Wednesday	44
1906–07*e*	Newcastle U	51	Bristol C	48	Everton	45
1907–08*e*	Manchester U	52	Aston Villa	43	Manchester C	43
1908–09*e*	Newcastle U	53	Everton	46	Sunderland	44
1909–10*e*	Aston Villa	53	Liverpool	48	Blackburn R	45
1910–11*e*	Manchester U	52	Aston Villa	51	Sunderland	45
1911–12*e*	Blackburn R	49	Everton	46	Newcastle U	44
1912–13*e*	Sunderland	54	Aston Villa	50	Sheffield W	49
1913–14*e*	Blackburn R	51	Aston Villa	44	Middlesbrough	43
1914–15*e*	Everton	46	Oldham Ath	45	Blackburn R	43
1919–20*f*	WBA	60	Burnley	51	Chelsea	49
1920–21*f*	Burnley	59	Manchester C	54	Bolton W	52
1921–22*f*	Liverpool	57	Tottenham H	51	Burnley	49
1922-23*f*	Liverpool	60	Sunderland	54	Huddersfield T	53
1923–24*f*	Huddersfield T*	57	Cardiff C	57	Sunderland	53
1924–25*f*	Huddersfield T	58	WBA	56	Bolton W	55
1925–26*f*	Huddersfield T	57	Arsenal	52	Sunderland	48
1926–27*f*	Newcastle U	56	Huddersfield T	51	Sunderland	49
1927–28*f*	Everton	53	Huddersfield T	51	Leicester C	48
1928–29*f*	Sheffield W	52	Leicester C	51	Aston Villa	50
1929–30*f*	Sheffield W	60	Derby Co	50	Manchester C	47
1930–31*f*	Arsenal	66	Aston Villa	59	Sheffield W	52
1931–32*f*	Everton	56	Arsenal	54	Sheffield W	50
1932–33*f*	Arsenal	58	Aston Villa	54	Sheffield W	51
1933–34*f*	Arsenal	59	Huddersfield T	56	Tottenham H	49
1934–35*f*	Arsenal	58	Sunderland	54	Sheffield W	49
1935–36*f*	Sunderland	56	Derby Co	48	Huddersfield T	48
1936–37*f*	Manchester C	57	Charlton Ath	54	Arsenal	52
1937–38*f*	Arsenal	52	Wolverhampton W	51	Preston NE	49
1938–39*f*	Everton	59	Wolverhampton W	55	Charlton Ath	50
1946–47*f*	Liverpool	57	Manchester U	56	Wolverhampton W	56
1947–48*f*	Arsenal	59	Manchester U	52	Burnley	52
1948–49*f*	Portsmouth	58	Manchester U	53	Derby Co	53
1949–50*f*	Portsmouth*	53	Wolverhampton W	53	Sunderland	52
1950–51*f*	Tottenham H	60	Manchester U	56	Blackpool	50
1951–52*f*	Manchester U	57	Tottenham H	53	Arsenal	53
1952–53*f*	Arsenal*	54	Preston NE	54	Wolverhampton W	51
1953–54*f*	Wolverhampton W	57	WBA	53	Huddersfield T	51
1954–55*f*	Chelsea	52	Wolverhampton W	48	Portsmouth	48
1955–56*f*	Manchester U	60	Blackpool	49	Wolverhampton W	49
1956–57*f*	Manchester U	64	Tottenham H	56	Preston NE	56
1957–58*f*	Wolverhampton W	64	Preston NE	59	Tottenham H	51
1958–59*f*	Wolverhampton W	61	Manchester U	55	Arsenal	50
1959–60*f*	Burnley	55	Wolverhampton W	54	Tottenham H	53
1960–61*f*	Tottenham H	66	Sheffield W	58	Wolverhampton W	57
1961–62*f*	Ipswich T	56	Burnley	53	Tottenham H	52

* *Won on goal average.*

	First	Pts	Second	Pts	Third	Pts
1962–63*f*	Everton	61	Tottenham H	55	Burnley	54
1963–64*f*	Liverpool	57	Manchester U	53	Everton	52
1964–65*f*	Manchester U*	61	Leeds U	61	Chelsea	56
1965–66*f*	Liverpool	61	Leeds U	55	Burnley	55
1966–67*f*	Manchester U	60	Nottingham F	56	Tottenham H	56
1967–68*f*	Manchester C	58	Manchester U	56	Liverpool	55
1968–69*f*	Leeds U	67	Liverpool	61	Everton	57
1969–70*f*	Everton	66	Leeds U	57	Chelsea	55
1970–71*f*	Arsenal	65	Leeds U	64	Tottenham H	52
1971–72*f*	Derby Co	58	Leeds U	57	Liverpool	57
1972–73*f*	Liverpool	60	Arsenal	57	Leeds U	53
1973–74*f*	Leeds U	62	Liverpool	57	Derby Co	48
1974–75*f*	Derby Co	53	Liverpool	51	Ipswich T	51
1975–76*f*	Liverpool	60	QPR	59	Manchester U	56
1976–77*f*	Liverpool	57	Manchester C	56	Ipswich T	52
1977–78*f*	Nottingham F	64	Liverpool	57	Everton	55
1978–79*f*	Liverpool	68	Nottingham F	60	WBA	59
1979–80*f*	Liverpool	60	Manchester U	58	Ipswich T	53
1980–81*f*	Aston Villa	60	Ipswich T	56	Arsenal	53
1981–82*g*	Liverpool	87	Ipswich T	83	Manchester U	78
1982–83*g*	Liverpool	82	Watford	71	Manchester U	70
1983–84*g*	Liverpool	80	Southampton	77	Nottingham F	74
1984–85*g*	Everton	90	Liverpool	77	Tottenham H	77
1985–86*g*	Liverpool	88	Everton	86	West Ham	84
1986–87*g*	Everton	86	Liverpool	77	Tottenham H	71
1987–88*h*	Liverpool	90	Manchester U	81	Nottingham F	73
1988–89*k*	Arsenal*	76	Liverpool	76	Nottingham F	64

No official competition during 1915–19 and 1939–46.

SECOND DIVISION

Maximum points: a 44; *b* 56; *c* 60; *d* 68; *e* 76; *f* 84; *g* 126; *h* 132; *k* 138.

	First	Pts	Second	Pts	Third	Pts
1892–93*a*	Small Heath	36	Sheffield U	35	Darwen	30
1893–94*b*	Liverpool	50	Small Heath	42	Notts Co	39
1894–95*c*	Bury	48	Notts Co	39	Newton Heath	38
1895–96*c*	Liverpool*	46	Manchester C	46	Grimsby T	42
1896–97*c*	Notts Co	42	Newton Heath	39	Grimsby T	38
1897–98*c*	Burnley	48	Newcastle U	45	Manchester C	39
1898–99*d*	Manchester C	52	Glossop NE	46	Leicester Fosse	45
1899–1900*d*	The Wednesday	54	Bolton W	52	Small Heath	46
1900–01*d*	Grimsby T	49	Small Heath	48	Burnley	44
1901–02*d*	WBA	55	Middlesbrough	51	Preston NE	42
1902–03*d*	Manchester C	54	Small Heath	51	Woolwich A	48
1903–04*d*	Preston NE	50	Woolwich A	49	Manchester U	48
1904–05*d*	Liverpool	58	Bolton W	56	Manchester U	53
1905–06*e*	Bristol C	66	Manchester U	62	Chelsea	53
1906–07*e*	Nottingham F	60	Chelsea	57	Leicester Fosse	48
1907–08*e*	Bradford C	54	Leicester Fosse	52	Oldham Ath	50
1908–09*e*	Bolton W	52	Tottenham H*	51	WBA	51
1909–10*e*	Manchester C	54	Oldham Ath*	53	Hull C	53
1910–11*e*	WBA	53	Bolton W	51	Chelsea	49
1911–12*e*	Derby Co*	54	Chelsea	54	Burnley	52
1912–13*e*	Preston NE	53	Burnley	50	Birmingham	46
1913–14*e*	Notts Co	53	Bradford PA	49	Woolwich A	49
1914–15*e*	Derby Co	53	Preston NE	50	Barnsley	47
1919–20*f*	Tottenham H	70	Huddersfield T	64	Birmingham	56
1920–21*f*	Birmingham*	58	Cardiff C	58	Bristol C	51
1921–22*f*	Nottingham F	56	Stoke C	52	Barnsley	52
1922–23*f*	Notts Co	53	West Ham U*	51	Leicester C	51
1923–24*f*	Leeds U	54	Bury*	51	Derby Co	51
1924–25*f*	Leicester C	59	Manchester U	57	Derby Co	55
1925–26*f*	Sheffield W	60	Derby Co	57	Chelsea	52
1926–27*f*	Middlesbrough	62	Portsmouth*	54	Manchester C	54
1927–28*f*	Manchester C	59	Leeds U	57	Chelsea	54
1928–29*f*	Middlesbrough	55	Grimsby T	53	Bradford	48
1929–30*f*	Blackpool	58	Chelsea	55	Oldham Ath	53
1930–31*f*	Everton	61	WBA	54	Tottenham H	51
1931–32*f*	Wolverhampton W	56	Leeds U	54	Stoke C	52
1932–33*f*	Stoke C	56	Tottenham H	55	Fulham	50
1933–34*f*	Grimsby T	59	Preston NE	52	Bolton W	51
1934–35*f*	Brentford	61	Bolton W*	56	West Ham U	56
1935–36*f*	Manchester U	56	Charlton Ath	55	Sheffield U	52
1936–37*f*	Leicester C	56	Blackpool	55	Bury	52

* *Won on goal average/goal difference.*

	First	Pts	Second	Pts	Third	Pts
1937–38*f*	Aston Villa	57	Manchester U*	53	Sheffield U	53
1938–39*f*	Blackburn R	55	Sheffield U	54	Sheffield W	53
1946–47*f*	Manchester C	62	Burnley	58	Birmingham C	55
1947–48*f*	Birmingham C	59	Newcastle U	56	Southampton	52
1948–49*f*	Fulham	57	WBA	56	Southampton	55
1949–50*f*	Tottenham H	61	Sheffield W*	52	Sheffield U	52
1950–51*f*	Preston NE	57	Manchester C	52	Cardiff C	50
1951–52*f*	Sheffield W	53	Cardiff C*	51	Birmingham C	51
1952–53*f*	Sheffield U	60	Huddersfield T	58	Luton T	52
1953–54*f*	Leicester C*	56	Everton	56	Blackburn R	55
1954–55*f*	Birmingham C*	54	Luton T*	54	Rotherham U	54
1955–56*f*	Sheffield W	55	Leeds U	52	Liverpool	48
1956–57*f*	Leicester C	61	Nottingham F	54	Liverpool	53
1957–58*f*	West Ham U	57	Blackburn R	56	Charlton Ath	55
1958–59*f*	Sheffield W	62	Fulham	60	Sheffield U	53
1959–60*f*	Aston Villa	59	Cardiff C	58	Liverpool	50
1960–61*f*	Ipswich T	59	Sheffield U	58	Liverpool	52
1961–62*f*	Liverpool	62	Leyton O	54	Sunderland	53
1962–63*f*	Stoke C	53	Chelsea*	52	Sunderland	52
1963–64*f*	Leeds U	63	Sunderland	61	Preston NE	56
1964–65*f*	Newcastle U	57	Northampton T	56	Bolton W	50
1965–66*f*	Manchester C	59	Southampton	54	Coventry C	53
1966–67*f*	Coventry C	59	Wolverhampton W	58	Carlisle U	52
1967–68*f*	Ipswich T	59	QPR*	58	Blackpool	58
1968–69*f*	Derby Co	63	Crystal Palace	56	Charlton Ath	50
1969–70*f*	Huddersfield T	60	Blackpool	53	Leicester C	51
1970–71*f*	Leicester C	59	Sheffield U	56	Cardiff C	53
1971–72*f*	Norwich C	57	Birmingham C	56	Millwall	55
1972–73*f*	Burnley	62	QPR	61	Aston Villa	50
1973–74*f*	Middlesbrough	65	Luton T	50	Carlisle U	49
1974–75*f*	Manchester U	61	Aston Villa	58	Norwich C	53
1975–76*f*	Sunderland	56	Bristol C	53	WBA	53
1976–77*f*	Wolverhampton W	57	Chelsea	55	Nottingham F	52
1977–78*f*	Bolton W	58	Southampton	57	Tottenham H	56
1978–79*f*	Crystal Palace	57	Brighton	56	Stoke C	56
1979–80*f*	Leicester C	55	Sunderland	54	Birmingham C	53
1980–81*f*	West Ham U	66	Notts Co	53	Swansea C*	50
1981–82*g*	Luton T	88	Watford	80	Norwich C	71
1982–83*g*	QPR	85	Wolverhampton W	75	Leicester C	70
1983–84*g*	Chelsea*	88	Sheffield W	88	Newcastle U	80
1984–85*g*	Oxford U	84	Birmingham C	82	Manchester C	74
1985–86*g*	Norwich C	84	Charlton Ath	77	Wimbledon	76
1986–87*g*	Derby Co	84	Portsmouth	78	Oldham Ath††	75
1987–88*h*	Millwall	82	Aston Villa	78	Middlesbrough	78
1988–89*k*	Chelsea	99	Manchester C	82	Crystal Palace	81

No competition during 1915–19 and 1939–46.
††Not promoted after play-offs

THIRD DIVISION

Maximum points: 92; 138 from 1981–82

1958–59	Plymouth Arg	62	Hull C	61	Brentford	57
1959–60	Southampton	61	Norwich C	59	Shrewsbury T	52
1960–61	Bury	68	Walsall	62	QPR	60
1961–62	Portsmouth	65	Grimsby T	62	Bournemouth	59
1962–63	Northampton T	62	Swindon T	58	Port Vale	54
1963–64	Coventry C*	60	Crystal Palace	60	Watford	58
1964–65	Carlisle U	60	Bristol C*	59	Mansfield T	59
1965–66	Hull C	69	Millwall	65	QPR	57
1966–67	QPR	67	Middlesbrough	55	Watford	54
1967–68	Oxford U	57	Bury	56	Shrewsbury T	55
1968–69	Watford*	64	Swindon T	64	Luton T	61
1969–70	Orient	62	Luton T	60	Bristol R	56
1970–71	Preston NE	61	Fulham	60	Halifax T	56
1971–72	Aston Villa	70	Brighton	65	Bournemouth	62
1972–73	Bolton W	61	Notts Co	57	Blackburn R	55
1973–74	Oldham Ath	62	Bristol R	61	York C	61
1974–75	Blackburn R	60	Plymouth Arg	59	Charlton Ath	55
1975–76	Hereford U	63	Cardiff C	57	Millwall	56
1976–77	Mansfield T	64	Brighton & HA	61	Crystal Palace	59
1977–78	Wrexham	61	Cambridge U	58	Preston NE	56
1978–79	Shrewsbury T	61	Watford	60	Swansea C	60
1979–80	Grimsby T	62	Blackburn R	59	Sheffield W	58
1980–81	Rotherham U	61	Barnsley*	59	Charlton Ath	59

**Won on goal average/goal difference.*

1981–82	Burnley*	80	Carlisle U	80	Fulham	78
1982–83	Portsmouth	91	Cardiff C	86	Huddersfield T	82
1983–84	Oxford U	95	Wimbledon	87	Sheffield U*	83
1984–85	Bradford C	94	Millwall	90	Hull C	87
1985–86	Reading	94	Plymouth Arg	87	Derby Co	84
1986–87	Bournemouth	97	Middlesbrough	94	Swindon T	87
1987–88	Sunderland	93	Brighton & HA	84	Walsall	82
1988–89	Wolverhampton W	92	Sheffield U	84	Port Vale	84

FOURTH DIVISION

Maximum points: 92; 138 from 1981–82

	First	*Pts*	*Second*	*Pts*	*Third*	*Pts*	*Fourth*	*Pts*
1958–59	Port Vale	64	Coventry C	60	York C	60	Shrewsbury T	58
1959–60	Walsall	65	Notts Co	60	Torquay U	60	Watford	57
1960–61	Peterborough U	66	Crystal Palace	64	Northampton T	60	Bradford PA	60
1961–62†	Millwall	56	Colchester U	55	Wrexham	53	Carlisle U	52
1962–63	Brentford	62	Oldham Ath	59	Crewe Alex	59	Mansfield T	57
1963–64	Gillingham*	60	Carlisle U	60	Workington T	59	Exeter C	58
1964–65	Brighton	63	Millwall	62	York C	62	Oxford U	61
1965–66	Doncaster R*	59	Darlington	59	Torquay U	58	Colchester U	56
1966–67	Stockport Co	64	Southport	59	Barrow	59	Tranmere R	58
1967–68	Luton T	66	Barnsley	61	Hartlepools U	60	Crewe Alex	58
1968–69	Doncaster R	59	Halifax T	57	Rochdale	56	Bradford C	56
1969–70	Chesterfield	64	Wrexham	61	Swansea C	60	Port Vale	59
1970–71	Notts Co	69	Bournemouth	60	Oldham Ath	59	York C	56
1971–72	Grimsby T	63	Southend U	60	Brentford	59	Scunthorpe U	57
1972–73	Southport	62	Hereford U	58	Cambridge U	57	Aldershot*	56
1973–74	Peterborough U	65	Gillingham	62	Colchester U	60	Bury	59
1974–75	Mansfield T	68	Shrewsbury T	62	Rotherham U	59	Chester	57
1975–76	Lincoln C	74	Northampton T	68	Reading	60	Tranmere R	58
1976–77	Cambridge U	65	Exeter C	62	Colchester U	59	Bradford C	59
1977–78	Watford	71	Southend U	60	Swansea C	56	Brentford	56
1978–79	Reading	65	Grimsby T	61	Wimbledon	61	Barnsley	61
1979–80	Huddersfield T	66	Walsall	64	Newport Co	61	Portsmouth	60
1980–81	Southend U	67	Lincoln C	65	Doncaster R	56	Wimbledon	55
1981–82	Sheffield U	96	Bradford C*	91	Wigan Ath	91	AFC Bournemouth	88
1982–83	Wimbledon	98	Hull C	90	Port Vale	88	Scunthorpe U	83
1983–84	York C	101	Doncaster R	85	Reading*	82	Bristol C	82
1984–85	Chesterfield	91	Blackpool	86	Darlington	85	Bury	84
1985–86	Swindon T	102	Chester C	84	Mansfield T	81	Port Vale	79
1986–87	Northampton T	99	Preston NE	90	Southend U	80	Wolverhampton W††	79
1987–88	Wolverhampton W	90	Cardiff C	85	Bolton W	78	Scunthorpe U††	77
1988–89	Rotherham U	82	Tranmere R	80	Crewe Alex	78	Scunthorpe U	77

†*Maximum points:* 88 owing to Accrington Stanley's resignation. ††*Not promoted after play-offs.*

THIRD DIVISION—SOUTH (1921–1958)

Maximum points: a 84; *b* 76; *c* 80; *d* 92.

	First	*Pts*	*Second*	*Pts*	*Third*	*Pts*
1920–21*a*	Crystal Palace	59	Southampton	54	QPR	53
1921–22*a*	Southampton*	61	Plymouth Arg	61	Portsmouth	53
1922–23*a*	Bristol C	59	Plymouth Arg	53	Swansea T	53
1923–24*a*	Portsmouth	59	Plymouth Arg	55	Millwall	54
1924–25*a*	Swansea T	57	Plymouth Arg	56	Bristol C	53
1925–26*a*	Reading	57	Plymouth Arg	56	Millwall	53
1926–27*a*	Bristol C	62	Plymouth Arg	60	Millwall	56
1927–28*a*	Millwall	65	Northampton T	55	Plymouth Arg	53
1928–29*a*	Charlton Ath*	54	Crystal Palace	54	Northampton T	52
1929–30*a*	Plymouth Arg	68	Brentford	61	QPR	51
1930–31*a*	Notts Co	59	Crystal Palace	51	Brentford	50
1931–32*a*	Fulham	57	Reading	55	Southend U	53
1932–33*a*	Brentford	62	Exeter C	58	Norwich C	57
1933–34*a*	Norwich C	61	Coventry C	54	Reading	54
1934–35*a*	Charlton Ath	61	Reading	53	Coventry C	51
1935–36*a*	Coventry C	57	Luton T	56	Reading	54
1936–37*a*	Luton T	58	Notts Co	56	Brighton	53
1937–38*a*	Millwall	56	Bristol C	55	QPR	53
1938–39*a*	Newport Co	55	Crystal Palace	52	Brighton	49
1939–46	Competition cancelled owing to war.					
1946–47*a*	Cardiff C	66	QPR	57	Bristol C	51
1947–48*a*	QPR	61	Bournemouth	57	Walsall	51
1948–49*a*	Swansea T	62	Reading	55	Bournemouth	52

**Won on goal average/goal difference.*

	First	Pts	Second	Pts	Third	Pts
1949–50*a*	Notts Co	58	Northampton T	51	Southend U	51
1950–51*d*	Nottingham F	70	Norwich C	64	Reading	57
1951–52*d*	Plymouth Arg	66	Reading	61	Norwich C	61
1952–53*d*	Bristol R	64	Millwall	62	Northampton T	62
1953–54*d*	Ipswich T	64	Brighton	61	Bristol C	56
1954–55*d*	Bristol C	70	Leyton O	61	Southampton	59
1955–56*d*	Leyton O	66	Brighton	65	Ipswich T	64
1956–57*d*	Ipswich T*	59	Torquay U	59	Colchester U	58
1957–58*d*	Brighton	60	Brentford	58	Plymouth Arg	58

THIRD DIVISION—NORTH (1921–1958)

Maximum points: a 84; *b* 76; *c* 80; *d* 92.

	First	Pts	Second	Pts	Third	Pts
1921–22*b*	Stockport Co	56	Darlington	50	Grimsby T	50
1922–23*b*	Nelson	51	Bradford PA	47	Walsall	46
1923–24*a*	Wolverhampton W	63	Rochdale	62	Chesterfield	54
1924–25*a*	Darlington	58	Nelson	53	New Brighton	53
1925–26*a*	Grimsby T	61	Bradford PA	60	Rochdale	59
1926–27*a*	Stoke C	63	Rochdale	58	Bradford PA	55
1927–28*a*	Bradford PA	63	Lincoln C	55	Stockport Co	54
1928–29*a*	Bradford C	63	Stockport Co	62	Wrexham	52
1929–30*a*	Port Vale	67	Stockport Co	63	Darlington	50
1930–31*a*	Chesterfield	58	Lincoln C	57	Wrexham	54
1931–32*c*	Lincoln C*	57	Gateshead	57	Chester	50
1932–33*a*	Hull C	59	Wrexham	57	Stockport Co	54
1933–34*a*	Barnsley	62	Chesterfield	61	Stockport Co	59
1934–35*a*	Doncaster R	57	Halifax T	55	Chester	54
1935–36*a*	Chesterfield	60	Chester	55	Tranmere R	55
1936–37*a*	Stockport Co	60	Lincoln C	57	Chester	53
1937–38*a*	Tranmere R	56	Doncaster R	54	Hull C	53
1938–39*a*	Barnsley	67	Doncaster R	56	Bradford C	52
1939–46	Competition cancelled owing to war.					
1946–47*a*	Doncaster R	72	Rotherham U	64	Chester	56
1947–48*a*	Lincoln C	60	Rotherham U	59	Wrexham	50
1948–49*a*	Hull C	65	Rotherham U	62	Doncaster R	50
1949–50*a*	Doncaster R	55	Gateshead	53	Rochdale	51
1950–51*d*	Rotherham U	71	Mansfield T	64	Carlisle U	62
1951–52*d*	Lincoln C	69	Grimsby T	66	Stockport Co	59
1952–53*d*	Oldham Ath	59	Port Vale	58	Wrexham	56
1953–54*d*	Port Vale	69	Barnsley	58	Scunthorpe U	57
1954–55*d*	Barnsley	65	Accrington S	61	Scunthorpe U	58
1955–56*d*	Grimsby T	68	Derby Co	63	Accrington S	59
1956–57*d*	Derby Co	63	Hartlepools U	59	Accrington S	58
1957–58*d*	Scunthorpe U	66	Accrington S	59	Bradford C	57

* *Won on goal average.*

PROMOTED AFTER PLAY-OFFS
(Not accounted for in previous section)

1986–87 Aldershot to Division 3.
1987–88 Swansea C to Divison 3.

LEAGUE TITLE WINS

LEAGUE DIVISION 1 – Liverpool 17, Arsenal 9, Everton 9, Manchester U 7, Aston Villa 7, Sunderland 6, Newcastle U 4, Sheffield W 4, Huddersfield T 3, Wolverhampton W 3, Blackburn R 2, Portsmouth 2, Preston NE 2, Burnley 2, Manchester C 2, Tottenham H 2, Leeds U 2, Derby Co 2, Chelsea 1, Sheffield U 1, WBA 1, Ipswich T 1, Nottingham F 1 each.

LEAGUE DIVISION 2 – Leicester C 6, Manchester C 6, Sheffield W 5, Birmingham C (one as Small Heath) 4, Derby Co 4, Liverpool 4, Notts Co 3, Preston NE 3, Middlesbrough 3, Grimsby T 2, Norwich C 2, Nottingham F 2, Tottenham H 2, WBA 2, Aston Villa 2, Stoke C 2, Leeds U 2, Ipswich T 2, Burnley 2, Chelsea 2, Manchester U 2, West Ham U 2, Wolverhampton W 2, Bolton W 2, Huddersfield T, Bristol C, Brentford, Bury, Bradford C, Everton, Fulham, Sheffield U, Newcastle U, Coventry C, Blackpool, Blackburn R, Sunderland, Crystal Palace, Luton T, QPR, Oxford U, Millwall 1 each.

LEAGUE DIVISION 3 – Portsmouth 2, Oxford U 2, Plymouth Arg, Southampton, Bury, Northampton T, Coventry C, Carlisle U, Hull C, QPR, Watford, Leyton O, Preston NE, Aston Villa, Bolton W, Oldham Ath, Blackburn R, Hereford U, Mansfield T, Wrexham, Shrewsbury T, Grimsby T, Rotherham U, Burnley, Bradford C, Bournemouth, Reading, Sunderland, Wolverhampton W 1 each.

LEAGUE DIVISION 4 – Chesterfield 2, Doncaster R 2, Peterborough U 2, Port Vale, Walsall, Millwall, Brentford, Gillingham, Brighton, Stockport Co, Luton T, Notts Co, Grimsby T, Southport, Mansfield T, Lincoln C, Cambridge U, Watford, Reading, Huddersfield T, Southend U, Sheffield U, Wimbledon, York C, Swindon T, Northampton T, Rotherham U, Wolverhampton W 1 each.

To 1957–58

DIVISION 3 (South) – Bristol C 3; Charlton Ath, Ipswich T, Millwall, Notts Co, Plymouth Arg, Swansea T 2 each; Brentford, Bristol R, Cardiff C, Crystal Palace, Coventry C, Fulham, Leyton O, Luton T, Newport Co, Nottingham F, Norwich C, Portsmouth, QPR, Reading, Southampton, Brighton 1 each.

DIVISION 3 (North) – Barnsley, Doncaster R, Lincoln C 3 each; Chesterfield, Grimsby T, Hull C, Port Vale, Stockport Co 2 each; Bradford PA, Bradford C, Darlington, Derby Co, Nelson, Oldham Ath, Rotherham U, Stoke C, Tranmere R, Wolverhampton W, Scunthorpe U 1 each.

RELEGATED CLUBS

1891–92 League extended. Newton Heath, Sheffield W and Nottingham F admitted. *Second Division formed* including Darwen.
1892–93 In Test matches, Sheffield U and Darwen won promotion in place of Notts Co and Accrington S.
1893–94 In Tests, Liverpool and Small Heath won promotion. Newton Heath and Darwen relegated.
1894–95 After Tests, Bury promoted, Liverpool relegated.
1895–96 After Tests, Liverpool promoted, Small Heath relegated.
1896–97 After Tests, Notts Co promoted, Burnley relegated.
1897–98 Test system abolished after success of Stoke C and Burnley. League extended. Blackburn R and Newcastle U elected to First Division. *Automatic promotion and relegation introduced.*

DIVISION 1 TO DIVISION 2

1898–99 Bolton W and Sheffield W
1899–1900 Burnley and Glossop
1900–01 Preston NE and WBA
1901–02 Small Heath and Manchester C
1902–03 Grimsby T and Bolton W
1903–04 Liverpool and WBA
1904–05 League extended. Bury and Notts Co, two bottom clubs in First Division, re-elected.
1905–06 Nottingham F and Wolverhampton W
1906–07 Derby Co and Stoke C
1907–08 Bolton W and Birmingham C
1908–09 Manchester C and Leicester Fosse
1909–10 Bolton W and Chelsea
1910–11 Bristol C and Nottingham F
1911–12 Preston NE and Bury
1912–13 Notts Co and Woolwich Arsenal
1913–14 Preston NE and Derby Co
1914–15 Tottenham H and Chelsea*
1919–20 Notts Co and Sheffield W
1920–21 Derby Co and Bradford
1921–22 Bradford C and Manchester U
1922–23 Stoke C and Oldham Ath
1923–24 Chelsea and Middlesbrough
1924–25 Preston NE and Nottingham F
1925–26 Manchester C and Notts Co
1926–27 Leeds U and WBA
1927–28 Tottenham H and Middlesbrough
1928–29 Bury and Cardiff C
1929–30 Burnley and Everton
1930–31 Leeds U and Manchester U
1931–32 Grimsby T and West Ham U
1932–33 Bolton W and Blackpool
1933–34 Newcastle U and Sheffield U
1934–35 Leicester C and Tottenham H
1935–36 Aston Villa and Blackburn R
1936–37 Manchester U and Sheffield W
1937–38 Manchester C and WBA
1938–39 Birmingham C and Leicester C
1946–47 Brentford and Leeds U
1947–48 Blackburn R and Grimsby T
1948–49 Preston NE and Sheffield U
1949–50 Manchester C and Birmingham C
1950–51 Sheffield W and Everton
1951–52 Huddersfield and Fulham
1952–53 Stoke C and Derby Co
1953–54 Middlesbrough and Liverpool
1954–55 Leicester C and Sheffield W
1955–56 Huddersfield and Sheffield U
1956–57 Charlton Ath and Cardiff C
1957–58 Sheffield W and Sunderland
1958–59 Portsmouth and Aston Villa
1959–60 Luton T and Leeds U
1960–61 Preston NE and Newcastle U
1961–62 Chelsea and Cardiff C
1962–63 Manchester C and Leyton O
1963–64 Bolton W and Ipswich T
1964–65 Wolverhampton W and Birmingham C
1965–66 Northampton T and Blackburn R
1966–67 Aston Villa and Blackpool
1967–68 Fulham and Sheffield U
1968–69 Leicester C and QPR
1969–70 Sunderland and Sheffield W
1970–71 Burnley and Blackpool
1971–72 Huddersfield T and Nottingham F
1972–73 Crystal Palace and WBA
1973–74 Southampton, Manchester U, Norwich C
1974–75 Luton T, Chelsea, Carlisle U
1975–76 Wolverhampton W, Burnley, Sheffield U
1976–77 Sunderland, Stoke C, Tottenham H
1977–78 West Ham U, Newcastle U, Leicester C
1978–79 QPR, Birmingham C, Chelsea
1979–80 Bristol C, Derby Co, Bolton W
1980–81 Norwich C, Leicester C, Crystal Palace
1981–82 Leeds U, Wolverhampton W, Middlesbrough
1982–83 Manchester C, Swansea C, Brighton & HA
1983–84 Birmingham C, Notts Co, Wolverhampton W
1984–85 Norwich C, Sunderland, Stoke C
1985–86 Ipswich T, Birmingham C, WBA
1986–87 Leicester C, Manchester C, Aston Villa
1987–88 Oxford U, Watford, Portsmouth, Chelsea**
1988–89 Middlesbrough, West Ham U, Newcastle U

*Subsequently re-elected to Division 1 when League was extended after the War.

DIVISION 2 TO DIVISION 3

1920–21 Stockport Co
1921–22 Bradford and Bristol C
1922–23 Rotherham C and Wolverhampton W
1923–24 Nelson and Bristol C
1924–25 Crystal Palace and Coventry C
1925–26 Stoke C and Stockport Co
1926–27 Darlington and Bradford C
1927–28 Fulham and South Shields
1928–29 Port Vale and Clapton O
1929–30 Hull C and Notts Co
1930–31 Reading and Cardiff C
1931–32 Barnsley and Bristol C
1932–33 Chesterfield and Charlton Ath
1933–34 Millwall and Lincoln C
1934–35 Oldham Ath and Notts Co
1935–36 Port Vale and Hull C
1936–37 Doncaster R and Bradford C
1937–38 Barnsley and Stockport Co
1938–39 Norwich C and Tranmere R
1946–47 Swansea T and Newport Co
1947–48 Doncaster R and Millwall
1948–49 Nottingham F and Lincoln C
1949–50 Plymouth Arg and Bradford
1950–51 Grimsby T and Chesterfield
1951–52 Coventry C and QPR
1952–53 Southampton and Barnsley
1953–54 Brentford and Oldham Ath
1954–55 Ipswich T and Derby Co
1955–56 Plymouth Arg and Hull C
1956–57 Port Vale and Bury

1957–58 Doncaster R and Notts Co
1958–59 Barnsley and Grimsby T
1959–60 Bristol C and Hull C
1960–61 Lincoln C and Portsmouth
1961–62 Brighton and Bristol R
1962–63 Walsall and Luton T
1963–64 Grimsby T and Scunthorpe U
1964–65 Swindon T and Swansea T
1965–66 Middlesbrough and Leyton O
1966–67 Northampton T and Bury
1967–68 Plymouth Arg and Rotherham U
1968–69 Fulham and Bury
1969–70 Preston NE and Aston Villa
1970–71 Blackburn R and Bolton W
1971–72 Charlton Ath and Watford
1972–73 Huddersfield T and Brighton
1973–74 Crystal Palace, Preston NE, Swindon T
1974–75 Millwall, Cardiff C, Sheffield W
1975–76 Oxford U, York C, Portsmouth
1976–77 Carlisle U, Plymouth Arg, Hereford U
1977–78 Blackpool, Mansfield T, Hull C
1978–79 Sheffield U, Millwall, Blackburn R
1979–80 Fulham, Burnley, Charlton Ath
1980–81 Preston NE, Bristol C, Bristol R
1981–82 Cardiff C, Wrexham, Orient
1982–83 Rotherham U, Burnley, Bolton W
1983–84 Derby Co, Swansea C, Cambridge U
1984–85 Notts Co, Cardiff C, Wolverhampton W
1985–86 Carlisle U, Middlesbrough, Fulham
1986–87 Sunderland**, Grimsby T, Brighton & HA
1987–88 Huddersfield T, Reading, Sheffield U**
1988–89 Shrewsbury T, Birmingham C, Walsall

DIVISION 3 TO DIVISION 4

1958–59 Rochdale, Notts Co, Doncaster R and Stockport Co
1959–60 Accrington S, Wrexham, Mansfield T and York C
1960–61 Chesterfield, Colchester U, Bradford C and Tranmere R
1961–62 Newport Co, Brentford, Lincoln C and Torquay U
1962–63 Bradford, Brighton, Carlisle U and Halifax T
1963–64 Millwall, Crewe Alex, Wrexham and Notts Co
1964–65 Luton T, Port Vale, Colchester U and Barnsley
1965–66 Southend U, Exeter C, Brentford and York C
1966–67 Doncaster R, Workington T, Darlington and Swansea T
1967–68 Scunthorpe U, Colchester U, Grimsby T and Peterborough U (demoted)
1968–69 Oldham Ath, Crewe Alex, Hartlepool and Northampton T
1969–70 Bournemouth, Southport, Barrow, Stockport Co
1970–71 Reading, Bury, Doncaster R, Gillingham
1971–72 Mansfield T, Barnsley, Torquay U, Bradford C
1972–73 Rotherham U, Brentford, Swansea C, Scunthorpe U
1973–74 Cambridge U, Shrewsbury T, Southport, Rochdale
1974–75 AFC Bournemouth, Tranmere R, Watford, Huddersfield T
1975–76 Aldershot, Colchester U, Southend U, Halifax T
1976–77 Reading, Northampton T, Grimsby T, York C
1977–78 Port Vale, Bradford C, Hereford U, Portsmouth
1978–79 Peterborough U, Walsall, Tranmere R, Lincoln C
1979–80 Bury, Southend U, Mansfield T, Wimbledon
1980–81 Sheffield U, Colchester U, Blackpool, Hull C
1981–82 Wimbledon, Swindon T, Bristol C, Chester
1982–83 Reading, Wrexham, Doncaster R, Chesterfield
1983–84 Scunthorpe U, Southend U, Port Vale, Exeter C
1984–85 Burnley, Orient, Preston NE, Cambridge U
1985–86 Lincoln C, Cardiff C, Wolverhampton W, Swansea C
1986–87 Bolton W**, Carlisle U, Darlington, Newport Co
1987–88 Doncaster R, York C, Grimsby T, Rotherham U**
1988–89 Southend U, Chesterfield, Gillingham, Aldershot

***Relegated after play-offs*

APPLICATIONS FOR RE-ELECTION
FOURTH DIVISION

Eleven: Hartlepool U.
Seven: Crewe Alex
Six: Barrow (lost League place to Hereford U 1972), Halifax T, Rochdale, Southport (lost League place to Wigan Ath 1978), York C
Five: Chester C, Darlington, Lincoln C, Stockport Co, Workington (lost League place to Wimbledon 1977)
Four: Bradford PA (lost League place to Cambridge U 1970), Newport Co, Northampton T
Three: Doncaster R, Northampton T, Hereford U
Two: Bradford C, Exeter C, Oldham Ath, Scunthorpe U, Torquay U
One: Aldershot, Colchester U, Gateshead (lost League place to Peterborough U 1960), Grimsby T, Swansea C, Tranmere R, Wrexham, Blackpool, Cambridge U, Preston NE
Accrington S resigned and Oxford U were elected 1962.
Port Vale were forced to re-apply following expulsion in 1968.

THIRD DIVISIONS NORTH & SOUTH

Seven: Walsall.
Six: Exeter C, Halifax T, Newport Co.
Five: Accrington S, Barrow, Gillingham, New Brighton, Southport.
Four: Rochdale, Norwich C.
Three: Crystal Palace, Crewe Alex, Darlington, Hartlepool, Merthyr T, Swindon T.
Two: Aberdare Ath, Aldershot, Ashington, Bournemouth, Brentford, Chester, Colchester U, Durham C, Millwall, Nelson, QPR, Rotherham U, Southend U, Tranmere R, Watford, Workington
One: Bradford C, Bradford PA, Brighton, Bristol R, Cardiff C, Carlisle U, Charlton Ath, Gateshead, Grimsby T, Mansfield T, Shrewsbury T, Torquay U, York C.

LEAGUE STATUS FROM 1986–87

	RELEGATED FROM LEAGUE	PROMOTED TO LEAGUE
1986–87	Lincoln C	Scarborough
1987–88	Newport Co	Lincoln C
1988–89	Darlington	Maidstone U

LEADING SCORERS 1988–89

Listed in order of League goals

DIVISION 1	League	Littlewoods Cup	FA Cup	Total
Alan Smith *(Arsenal)*	23	2	0	**25**
John Aldridge *(Liverpool)*	21	2	5	**28**
Dean Saunders *(Derby Co)*	18	2	0	**20**
(Including 4 League, 2 Littlewoods Cup for Oxford U)				
Bernie Slaven *(Middlesbrough)*	15	0	1	**16**
Nigel Clough *(Nottingham F)*	14	7	0	**21**
Mark Hughes *(Manchester U)*	14	0	2	**16**
Alan McInally *(Aston Villa)*	14	4	1	**19**
David Speedie *(Coventry C)*	14	1	0	**15**
Chris Waddle *(Tottenham H)*	14	0	0	**14**
Tony Cascarino *(Millwall)*	13	0	1	**14**
Tony Cottee *(Everton)*	13	2	0	**15**
Paul Williams *(Charlton Ath)*	13	2	2	**17**
Mark Falco *(QPR)*	12	3	0	**15**
John Fashanu *(Wimbledon)*	12	2	1	**15**
Teddy Sheringham *(Millwall)*	11	3	1	**15**
Rod Wallace *(Southampton)*	11	2	0	**13**
Peter Beardsley *(Liverpool)*	10	2	0	**12**
Robert Fleck *(Norwich C)*	10	1	4	**15**
Brian McClair *(Manchester U)*	10	3	3	**16**
Paul Merson *(Arsenal)*	10	2	2	**14**
DIVISION 2				
Keith Edwards *(Hull C)*	26	1	3	**29**
Kerry Dixon *(Chelsea)*	25	1	0	**26**
Tommy Tynan *(Plymouth Arg)*	24	1	1	**26**
Ian Wright *(Crystal Palace)*	24	1	0	**25**
Mark Bright *(Crystal Palace)*	20	1	0	**21**
Luther Blissett *(Bournemouth)*	20	2	0	**22**
(Including 1 League for Watford)				
Simon Garner *(Blackburn R)*	20	2	1	**23**
Howard Gayle *(Blackburn R)*	19	1	0	**20**
Paul Wilkinson *(Watford)*	19	0	0	**19**
Marco Gabbiadini *(Sunderland)*	18	3	0	**21**
Mike Quinn *(Portsmouth)*	18	1	1	**20**
Gordon Durie *(Chelsea)*	17	0	0	**17**
David Currie *(Barnsley)*	16	1	3	**20**
Kevin Bremner *(Brighton & HA)*	15	0	0	**15**
Don Goodman *(WBA)*	15	0	0	**15**
Garry Nelson *(Brighton & HA)*	15	0	0	**15**
Roger Palmer *(Oldham Ath)*	15	0	0	**15**
Graham Roberts *(Chelsea)*	15	0	0	**15**
DIVISION 3				
Steve Bull *(Wolverhampton W)*	37	2	0	**39**
Craig Maskell *(Huddersfield T)*	28	2	1	**31**
David Crown *(Southend U)*	25	1	0	**26**
Tony Agana *(Sheffield U)*	23	2	3	**28**
Carl Dale *(Chester C)*	22	0	1	**23**
Brian Deane *(Sheffield U)*	22	3	5	**30**
Andy Mutch *(Wolverhampton W)*	21	0	0	**21**
Darren Beckford *(Port Vale)*	20	0	0	**20**
Gary Penrice *(Bristol R)*	20	0	1	**21**
Liam Robinson *(Bury)*	20	1	0	**21**
Tony Ellis *(Preston NE)*	19	0	0	**19**
David Waller *(Chesterfield)*	18	1	0	**19**
Ron Futcher *(Port Vale)*	17	1	1	**19**
David Gilbert *(Northampton T)*	17	1	0	**18**
Trevor Senior *(Reading)*	16	0	4	**20**
Jimmy Gilligan *(Cardiff C)*	15	0	4	**19**
Mark Patterson *(Preston NE)*	15	0	0	**15**
DIVISION 4				
Phil Stant *(Hereford U)*	28	1	0	**29**
Tony Daws *(Scunthorpe U)*	24	3	0	**27**
Terry McPhillips *(Halifax T)*	22	1	1	**24**
Kevin Russell *(Wrexham)*	22	0	0	**22**
Ian Muir *(Tranmere R)*	21	2	5	**28**
Darran Rowbotham *(Exeter C)*	20	0	1	**21**
Alan Comfort *(Leyton Orient)*	19	1	0	**20**
Paul Fishenden *(Crewe Alex)*	16	1	3	**20**
Wayne Allison *(Halifax T)*	15	1	2	**18**
Andy Flounders *(Scunthorpe U)*	15	4	0	**19**
Keith Alexander *(Grimsby T)*	14	0	1	**15**
Gordon Hobson *(Lincoln C)*	14	1	0	**15**
Steve Neville *(Exeter C)*	14	0	0	**14**
Paul McLoughlin *(Hereford U)*	13	0	0	**13**
Brendan O'Connell *(Burnley)*	13	3	0	**16**

N.B. Overall leading goalscorer in all competitive matches was Steve Bull with 50 (37 League, 11 Sherpa Van, 2 Littlewoods Cup)

MERCANTILE CENTENARY CREDIT TROPHY

Quarter-finals

29 AUG

Liverpool (0) 4 *(Venison, Molby (pen), Houghton, Barnes)*

Nottingham F (0) 1 *(Webb)* 20,141

Liverpool: Grobbelaar; Gillespie, Venison, Nicol, Whelan, Molby, Beardsley, Houghton, Rush, Barnes, McMahon.
Nottingham F: Sutton; Chettle, Pearce, Walker, Foster, Wilson, Crosby, Webb, Clough, Hodge, Rice (Carr).

Manchester U (0) 1 *(Strachan)*

Everton (0) 0 16,439

Manchester U: Leighton; Anderson (Martin), Blackmore, Bruce, Garton, Duxbury, Robson, Strachan, McClair, Hughes, Olsen (Davenport).
Everton: Southall; McDonald, Pointon, Snodin, Sheedy (Bracewell), Reid, Wilson, McCall, Sharp (Heath), Cottee, Nevin.

Newcastle U (0) 1 *(O'Neill)*

Wimbledon (0) 0 17,141

Newcastle U: Beasant; Jackson D, Tinnion, McCreery, Jackson P, Thorn, Hendrie, Robertson, O'Neill, Wharton, Cornwell.
Wimbledon: Green; Joseph, Phelan, Ryan, Young, Scales, Gibson, Fairweather, Fashanu, Sanchez, Wise.

31 AUG

QPR (0) 0

Arsenal (1) 2 *(Adams, Marwood)* 10,019

QPR: Seaman; Fereday, Dennis, Parker, McDonald, Ardiles (Stein), Allen, Brock, Falco, Francis, Barker (Maddix).
Arsenal: Lukic; Richardson, Winterburn, Thomas, O'Leary, Adams, Rocastle, Davis, Smith, Merson (Hayes), Marwood.

Semi-finals

20 SEPT

Arsenal (1) 2 *(Groves, Marwood)*

Liverpool (0) 1 *(Staunton)* 29,135

Arsenal: Lukic; Dixon, Winterburn, Thomas, O'Leary, Adams, Rocastle (Hayes), Richardson, Smith, Groves, Marwood.
Liverpool: Hooper; Gillespie, Ablett, Nicol, Whelan, MacDonald, Beardsley, Houghton, Rush, Staunton, Durnin (Dalglish).

21 SEPT

Manchester U (0) 2 *(Bruce, McClair)*

Newcastle U (0) 0 *aet* 14,968

Manchester U: Leighton; Blackmore, Sharpe, Bruce, Garton, Duxbury, Robson, Davenport (O'Brien), McClair, Hughes, Olsen (Beardsmore).
Newcastle U: Beasant; Cornwell, Wharton, McCreery (Mirandinha), Scott, Thorn, Hendrie, Bogie, Stephenson (Tinnion), Jackson D, Robertson.

9 OCT

Final (at Villa Park)

Arsenal (2) 2 *(Davis, Thomas)*

Manchester U (0) 1 *(Blackmore)* 22,182

Arsenal: Lukic; Dixon, Winterburn, Thomas, Bould, Adams, Rocastle, Davis, Smith, Groves (Merson), Marwood.
Manchester U: Leighton; Blackmore, Sharpe, Bruce, Garton, Duxbury, Robson, Davenport (Beardsmore), McClair, Hughes, Olsen (Strachan).
Referee: G. Courtney (Spennymoor).

FA CHARITY SHIELD

20 AUG (at Wembley)

Liverpool (1) 2 *(Aldridge 2)*

Wimbledon (0) 0 54,000

Liverpool: Grobbelaar; Gillespie, Venison, Ablett, Whelan, Watson, Beardsley, Aldridge, Houghton, Barnes, McMahon.
Wimbledon: Tracey; Scales (Clement), Phelan, Ryan, Young, Cawley, Gibson, Fairweather, Fashanu (Turner), Sanchez, Wise.
Referee: J. Martin (Alton).

FOOTBALL LEAGUE – At home and abroad

The Barclays League drew 2-2 with the Skol Northern League in a Centenary Challenge Match at Croft Park, Blyth on 16 May 1989. The team was: Barber; Anderson, Wharton, Bennett, Linighan D, Robson B, Gleghorn, Robson G, Slaven, Currie, Waddle. Subs: Gabbiadini, Prudhoe, Owers, Armstrong, Dalton.

In the Guinness Soccer Six final in Manchester, Charlton Athletic beat Nottingham Forest 2-1.

A Football League Under-18 team beat a Soviet Under-18 side 2-1 in Moscow on 22 April, 1989. The team comprised: Marriott; Noble, Whitehouse, Round, Rowland, Tonge, Mooney, Stevens, Boughey, Hayward, Garner, Beauchamp, Griffiths, Baraclough, Kitson. Kitson and Stevens were the scorers. The team was managed by Lawrie McMenemy and Alan Ball.

TRANSFERS 1988–89

		From	*To*
May 1988			
23	Callaghan, Aaron J.	Oldham Athletic	Crewe Alexandra
23	Cook, Paul A.	Wigan Athletic	Norwich City
31	Maskell, Craig D.	Southampton	Huddersfield Town
June 1988			
16	Atkins, Mark N.	Scunthorpe United	Blackburn Rovers
21	Atkinson, Paul	Sunderland	Port Vale
28	Bamber, John D.	Swindon Town	Watford
29	Bengrie, Peter S.	Sheffield United	Stoke City
13	Beasant, David	Wimbledon	Newcastle United
13	Bould, Steven A.	Stoke City	Arsenal
23	Brown, Philip	Halifax Town	Bolton Wanderers
20	Dixon, Kevin I.	Scunthorpe United	Hartlepool United
27	Dreyer, John B.	Oxford United	Luton Town
17	Falconer, William	Aberdeen	Watford
10	Ford, Michael P.	Cardiff City	Oxford United
15	Heath, Phillip A.	Stoke City	Oxford United
17	Hendrie, John G.	Bradford City	Newcastle United
1	Kee, Paul V.	Ards	Oxford United
2	Kennedy, Andrew J.	Birmingham City	Blackburn Rovers
17	Law, Nicholas	Plymouth Argyle	Notts. County
1	Leighton, James	Aberdeen	Manchester United
23	Linighan, David	Shrewsbury Town	Ipswich Town
15	McCall, Stuart M.	Bradford City	Everton
29	Moore, John	Sunderland	Hull City
6	Mountfield, Derek N.	Everton	Aston Villa
17	Osman, Russell C	Leicester City	Southampton
15	Patterson, Mark A	Blackburn Rovers	Preston North End
1	Price, Christopher J.	Blackburn Rovers	Aston Villa
20	Quinn, James M.	Swindon Town	Leicester City
29	Ruddock, Neil	Tottenham Hotspur	Millwall
10	Sharpe, Lee S.	Torquay United	Manchester United
22	Shearer, Duncan N.	Huddersfield Town	Swindon Town
21	Stewart, Paul A.	Manchester City	Tottenham Hotspur
23	Sussex, Andrew R.	Leyton Orient	Crewe Alexandra
8	Terry, Steve G.	Watford	Hull City
23	Thomas, Andrew M.	Newcastle United	Bradford City
22	Thompson, Richard	Newport County	Torquay United
6	Williams, Paul A.	Newport County	Sheffield United
Temporary Transfer			
13	Neal, Dean J.	Southend United	Queens Park Rangers
July 1988			
26	Andrews, Ian E.	Leicester City	Celtic F.C.
28	Astbury, Michael J.	Chester City	Chesterfield
21	Bank, Ian F.	Huddersfield Town	Bradford City
20	Barker, Simon	Blackburn Rovers	Queens Park Rangers
28	Benjamin, Ian T.	Cambridge United	Chester City
19	Benstead, Graham M.	Norwich City	Sheffield United
15	Biggins, Wayne	Norwich City	Manchester City
14	Bishop, Ian W.	Carlisle United	A.F.C. Bournemouth
7	Burgess, David J.	Grimsby Town	Blackpool
12	Butler, Brian F.	Blackpool	Stockport County
22	Cadette, Richard R.	Sheffield United	Brentford
27	Chamberlain, Alec F. R.	Everton	Luton Town
28	Cooper, Stephen B.	Plymouth Argyle	Barnsley
27	Corner, David E.	Sunderland	Leyton Orient
29	Cusack, Nicholas J.	Leicester City	Peterborough United
19	Deane, Brian C.	Doncaster Rovers	Sheffield United
28	Deehan, John M.	Ipswich Town	Manchester City
1	Dibble, Andrew	Luton Town	Manchester City
25	Dobson, Paul	Torquay United	Doncaster Rovers
5	Drinkell, Kevin S.	Norwich City	Rangers F.C.
29	Finnigan, Anthony	Crystal Palace	Blackburn Rovers
18	Gascoigne, Paul J.	Newcastle United	Tottenham Hotspur
6	Gayle, Brian W.	Wimbledon	Manchester City
27	Greenough, Richard A.	Chester City	Scarborough
6	Harper, Alan	Everton	Sheffield Wednesday
15	Hart, Nigel	Bury	Stockport County
13	Hazel, Desmond L.	Sheffield Wednesday	Rotherham United
28	Hetherston, Peter	Sheffield United	Falkirk F.C.
25	Hilaire, Vincent M.	Portsmouth	Leeds United
18	Hildersley, Ronald	Preston North End	Blackburn Rovers
29	Hill, David M.	Scunthorpe United	Ipswich Town
21	Jewell, Paul	Wigan Athletic	Bradford City
4	Kamara, Christopher	Swindon Town	Stoke City
7	Laws, Brian	Middlesbrough	Nottingham Forest

		From	To
26	McKnight, Allen	Celtic	West Ham United
12	Marples, Christopher	Stockport County	York City
15	Marsden, Christopher	Sheffield United	Huddersfield Town
13	Marshall, Gary	Bristol City	Carlisle United
28	Neil, Warren A.	Queens Park Rangers	Portsmouth
26	Neville, Steven F.	Bristol City	Exeter City
13	Nevin, Patrick K. F.	Chelsea	Everton
26	Nixon, Eric W.	Manchester City	Tranmere Rovers
13	O'Riordan, Donald J.	Grimsby Town	Notts County
29	Paris, Alan D.	Peterborough United	Leicester City
13	-Philliskirk, Anthony	Sheffield United	Oldham Athletic
11	Pritchard, Howard K.	Gillingham	Walsall
15	Roberts, Alan	Darlington	Sheffield United
12	Spearing, Anthony	Norwich City	Leicester City
12	Spooner, Stephen A.	Hereford United	York City
19	Stevens, Michael G.	Everton	Rangers
8	Tanner, Nicholas	Bristol Rovers	Liverpool
14	Thompson, Steven P.	Charlton Athletic	Leicester City
6	Ward, Paul T.	Darlington	Leyton Orient
27	Wegerle, Roy C.	Chelsea	Luton Town

August 1988

		From	To
12	Allen, Malcolm	Watford	Norwich City
26	Aspinall, Warren	Aston Villa	Portsmouth
24	Bailie, Colin J.	Reading	Cambridge United
1	Bertschin, Keith E.	Sunderland	Walsall
16	Bond, Kevin J.	Southampton	A.F.C. Bournemouth
24	Bryson, James I. C.	Kilmarnock	Sheffield United
2	Chamberlain, Mark V.	Sheffield Wednesday	Portsmouth
3	Cooper, Graham	Huddersfield Town	Wrexham
2	Cottee, Antony R.	West Ham United	Everton
5	Cox, Brian R.	Huddersfield Town	Mansfield Town
25	Davis, Darren J.	Notts. County	Lincoln City
26	Dawes, Ian R.	Queen's Park Rangers	Millwall
3	Douglas, Colin F.	Rotherham United	Doncaster Rovers
12	Edwards, Dean S.	Exeter City	Torquay United
22	Flexney, Paul	Clyde	Northampton Town
5	Futcher, Ronald	Bradford City	Port Vale
26	Garner, Andrew	Derby County	Blackpool
4	Gleghorn, Nigel W.	Ipswich Town	Manchester City
2	Goddard, Paul	Newcastle United	Derby County
17	Hebberd, Trevor N.	Oxford United	Derby County
15	Hedworth, Christopher	Barnsley	Halifax Town
13	Hinnigan, Joseph P.	Wrexham	Chester City
31	Hodge, Martin J.	Sheffield Wednesday	Leicester City
17	Hodge, Stephen B.	Tottenham Hotspur	Nottingham Forest
25	Hodkinson, Andrew J.	Stockport County	Scunthorpe United
25	Hogg, Graeme J.	Manchester United	Portsmouth
12	Holmes, Paul	Doncaster Rovers	Torquay United
17	Hopkins, Jeffrey	Fulham	Crystal Palace
25	Joseph, Roger	Brentford	Wimbledon
1	Kelly, David T.	Walsall	West Ham United
3	Langan, David	A.F.C. Bournemouth	Peterborough United
25	Lewis, Michael	Derby County	Oxford United
11	Lynch, Thomas	Limerick	Sunderland
18	McCarthy, Sean C.	Swansea City	Plymouth Argyle
3	McDonald, Neil R.	Newcastle United	Everton
19	McGuire, Douglas J.	Celtic	Coventry City
4	Maclaren, Ross	Derby County	Swindon Town
15	Nicholas, Peter	Aberdeen	Chelsea
24	Norton, David W.	Aston Villa	Notts County
11	Oakes, Keith B.	Fulham	Peterborough United
4	O'Regan, Kieran	Swindon Town	Huddersfield Town
15	O'Shaughnessy, Stephen	Bradford City	Rochdale
24	Parks, Anthony	Tottenham Hotspur	Brentford
25	Phillips, Gary C.	Brentford	Reading
26	Phillips, James N.	Rangers	Oxford United
15	Pickering, Nicholas	Coventry City	Derby County
15	Roberts, Graham P.	Rangers	Chelsea
3	Rodgerson, Ian	Hereford United	Cardiff City
11	Russell, William M.	Scunthorpe United	Rotherham United
25	Sayer, Andrew C.	Wimbledon	Fulham
15	Smillie, Neil	Reading	Brentford
26	Stein, Earl M. S.	Luton Town	Queen's Park Rangers
19	Taylor, Alexander	Hamilton Academical	Walsall
31	Tester, Paul L.	Shrewsbury Town	Hereford United
1	Thorn, Andrew	Wimbledon	Newcastle United
23	Thornber, Stephen J.	Halifax Town	Swansea City
31	Townsend, Andrew D.	Southampton	Norwich City
24	Wade, Bryan A.	Swindon Town	Swansea City
25	Wallington, Francis M.	Derby County	Lincoln City
25	Warren, Lee A.	Rochdale	Hull City
16	Wilkinson, Paul	Nottingham Forest	Watford
5	Williams, Steven C.	Arsenal	Luton Town

		From	To
Temporary Transfers			
25	Crichton, Paul A.	Nottingham Forest	Torquay United
26	Hodge, Martin J.	Sheffield Wednesday	Leicester City
25	Holdsworth, Dean C.	Watford	Swansea City
27	McElhinney, Gerard	Plymouth Argyle	Peterborough United
26	McKellar, David	Dunfermline	Hartlepool United
24	Rumble, Paul	Watford	Scunthorpe United
24	Strain, John E.	West Ham United	Falkirk
11	Walsh, Gary	Manchester United	Airdrieonians
31	Walsh, Gary	Airdrieonians	Manchester United (Tr. Back)
9	Wilkinson, Stephen J.	Leicester City	Rochdale
26	Wilmot, Rhys.	Arsenal	Swansea City
23	Winter, Julian	Huddersfield Town	Scunthorpe United
September 1988			
30	Bradshaw, Carl	Sheffield Wednesday	Manchester City
6	Byrne, Michael	Shamrock Rovers	Huddersfield Town
8	Caldwell, Anthony	Bristol City	Grimsby Town
27	Conroy, Michael K.	St. Mirren	Reading
8	Duggan, Andrew J.	Barnsley	Huddersfield Town
29	Elliott, Stephen B.	Bolton Wanderers	Bury
21	Gernon, Frederick A. J.	Gillingham	Reading
20	Gooding, Michael C.	Peterborough United	Wolverhampton Wanderers
8	Graham, Michael A.	Mansfield Town	Carlisle United
20	Gray, Andrew M.	West Bromwich Albion	Glasgow Rangers
29	Higgins, Mark N.	Bury	Stoke City
15	Hobson, Gordon	Southampton	Lincoln City
15	Jackson, Peter A.	Newcastle United	Bradford City
27	Jones, Tom	Aberdeen	Swindon Town
9	Keeley, Glenn M.	Oldham Athletic	Bolton Wanderers
30	Kuhl, Martin	Watford	Portsmouth
27	McElhinney, Gerard	Plymouth Argyle	Peterborough United
8	McGarvey, Scott T.	Grimsby Town	Bristol City
30	May, Lawrence C.	Sheffield Wednesday	Brighton & Hove Albion
9	Perry, Andrew	Portsmouth	Gillingham
1	Rougvie, Douglas	Brighton & Hove Albion	Shrewsbury Town
28	Segers, Johannes, C. A.	Nottingham Forest	Wimbledon
9	Shotton, Malcolm	Huddersfield Town	Barnsley
29	Smalley, Paul T.	Notts. County	Scunthorpe United
12	Turner, Christopher R.	Manchester United	Sheffield Wednesday
30	Varardi, Imre	Manchester City	Sheffield Wednesday
8	Weston, Ian P.	Bristol Rovers	Torquay United
16	Whitehurst, William	Reading	Sunderland
Temporary Transfers			
28	Anderson, Douglas E.	Plymouth Argyle	Cambridge United
19	Batch, Nigel A.	Lincoln City	Darlington
8	Byrne, David S.	Millwall	Cambridge United
15	Carter, Timothy D.	Sunderland	Bristol City
27	Carter, Timothy D.	Bristol City	Sunderland (Tr. Back)
16	Callaghan, William T.	Dunfermline Athletic	Walsall
15	Cork, David	Huddersfield Town	West Bromwich Albion
29	Crichton, Paul A.	Nottingham Forest	Torquay United
29	Dempsey, Mark J.	Sheffield United	Chesterfield
22	Dryden, Richard	Bristol Rovers	Exeter City
15	Edmonds, Neil A.	Oldham Athletic	Rochdale
23	Fearon, Ronald T.	Ipswich Town	Brighton & Hove Albion
8	Garwood, Jason	Leicester City	Northampton Town
30	Green, Ronald R.	Wimbledon	Shrewsbury Town
1	Henry, Liburd A.	Watford	Halifax Town
15	Hotte, Timothy A.	Hull City	York City
22	Kelly, Anthony G.	West Bromwich Albion	Chester City
27	Leaning, Andrew J.	Sheffield United	Bristol City
8	Plummer, Calvin A.	Nottingham Forest	Plymouth Argyle
15	Randall, Adrian J.	A.F.C. Bournemouth	Aldershot
22	Slack, Trevor C.	Northampton Town	Chesterfield
23	Tupling, Stephen	Cardiff City	Torquay United
22	Viney, Keith	Exeter City	Bristol Rovers
8	Wilkinson, Stephen	Leicester City	Crewe Alexandra
October 1988			
20	Angell, Brett	Derby County	Stockport County
27	Banton, Dale C.	York City	Walsall
27	Berry, Stephen A.	Aldershot	Northampton Town
20	Burrows, David	West Bromwich Albion	Liverpool
7	Caldwell, Anthony	Grimsby Town	Stockport County
6	Coady, John	Chelsea	Derry City
6	Cooper, Neale J.	Aston Villa	Rangers
21	Curle, Keith	Reading	Wimbledon
19	Dempsey, Mark J.	Sheffield United	Rotherham United
28	Donaghy, Malachy	Luton Town	Manchester United
1	Fitzpatrick, Paul J.	Bristol City	Carlisle United
4	Gavin, Mark W.	Heart of Midlothian	Bristol City
28	Geddis, David	Shrewsbury Town	Swindon Town

		From	*To*
7	Gordon, Colin K.	Reading	Fulham
21	Keane, Thomas J.	Colchester United	Galway
7	Longhurst, David J.	Northampton Town	Peterborough United
13	Miller, Paul R.	Charlton Athletic	Watford
26	Pates, Colin G.	Chelsea	Charlton Athletic
20	Plummer, Calvin A.	Nottingham Forest	Plymouth Argyle
13	Richards, Carrol L.	A.F.C. Bournemouth	Birmingham City
28	Saunders, Dean N.	Oxford United	Derby County
14	Senior, Trevor	Middlesbrough	Reading
31	Simpson, Paul D.	Manchester City	Oxford United
14	Skipper, Peter D.	Hull City	Oldham Athletic
20	Slack, Trevor C.	Northampton Town	Chesterfield
19	Tracey, Simon P.	Wimbledon	Sheffield United
27	Warhurst, Paul	Manchester City	Oldham Athletic
21	White, Eric W.	Colchester United	Burnley
7	Williams, William R.	Stockport County	Manchester City

November 1988

29	Allon, Joseph B.	Swansea City	Hartlepool United
11	Ashurst, Jack	Leeds United	Doncaster Rovers
2	Barham, Mark	Huddersfield Town	Middlesbrough
11	Bennett, Gary M.	Chester City	Southend United
25	Blissett, Luther L.	Watford	A.F.C. Bournemouth
24	Booker, Robert	Brentford	Sheffield United
3	Brown, Kevan	Brighton & Hove Albion	Aldershot
18	Caton,Thomas	Oxford United	Charlton Athletic
11	Cecere, Michele J.	Oldham Athletic	Huddersfield Town
25	Claridge, Stephen E.	Crystal Palace	Aldershot
3	Crichton, Paul A.	Nottingham Forest	Peterborough United
18	Croft, Brian G. A.	Chester City	Cambridge United
3	Davenport, Peter	Manchester United	Middlesbrough
21	Dixon, Kevin L.	Hartlepool United	York City
11	Dyer, Alexander C.	Hull City	Crystal Palace
3	Eccles, Peter	Dundalk	Leicester City
10	Edmonds, Neil A.	Oldham Athletic	Rochdale
11	Evans, Stewart J.	Plymouth Argyle	Rotherham United
21	Greenough, Richard A.	Scarborough	York City
9	Leaning, Andrew J.	Sheffield United	Bristol City
21	Logan, David	Halifax Town	Stockport County
11	McKellar, David	Dunfermline Athletic	Carlisle United
17	Milne, Ralph	Bristol City	Manchester United
15	O'Brien, Liam F.	Manchester United	Newcastle United
21	Redfearn, Neil D.	Crystal Palace	Watford
18	Redford, Ian P.	Dundee United	Ipswich Town
10	Rimmer, Stuart A.	Watford	Notts County
10	Stephenson, Paul	Newcastle United	Millwall
4	Stuart, Mark R.	Charlton Athletic	Plymouth Argyle
2	Thomas, Martin R.	Newcastle United	Birmingham City
15	Thompson, Steven P.	Leicester City	Sheffield United
3	Weir, Peter R.	Leicester City	St. Mirren
11	Williams, Andrew	Rotherham United	Leeds United

Temporary Transfers

14	Anderson, Douglas E.	Cambridge United	Plymouth Argyle (Tr. Back)
13	Bradley, Russell	Nottingham Forest	Hereford United
19	Collins, Eamonn A. S.	Portsmouth	Gillingham
1	Fearon, Ronald T.	Brighton & Hove Albion	Ipswich Town (Tr. Back)
14	Fensome, Andrew B.	Norwich City	Newcastle United
24	Gormley, Edward J.	Tottenham Hotspur	Chesterfield
1	Jones, Mark	Walsall	Exeter City
24	Ketteridge, Stephen J.	Cardiff City	Leyton Orient (Tr. Back)
14	Lormor, Anthony	Newcastle United	Norwich City
25	MacDonald, Kevin D.	Liverpool	Rangers
24	Miller, Alan J.	Arsenal	Plymouth Argyle
3	Nuttell, Michael J.	Peterborough United	Carlisle United
23	Puckett, David C.	A.F.C. Bournemouth	Swansea City
4	Richie, Stuart A.	Crewe Alexandra	Waterford United
24	Samways, Mark	Doncaster Rovers	Leeds United
19	Trotter, Michael	Middlesbrough	Doncaster Rovers
10	Williams, Wayne	Shrewsbury Town	Northampton Town
26	Wood, Paul A.	Sheffield United	Rochdale

December 1988

14	Allinson, Ian J. R.	Luton Town	Colchester United
21	Bamber, John D.	Watford	Stoke City
15	Barnsely, Andrew	Sheffield United	Rotherham United
20	Batch, Nigel A.	Lincoln City	Darlington
16	Brien, Anthony J.	Leicester City	Chesterfield
8	Brock, Kevin S.	Queens Park Rangers	Newcastle United
23	Butler, John E.	Wigan Athletic	Stoke City
31	Cornwell, John A.	Newcastle United	Swindon Town
16	Flexney, Paul	Northampton Town	Kilmarnock
22	Flynn, Michael A.	Oldham Athletic	Norwich City

		From	To
23	Hamilton, Ian R.	Cambridge United	Scunthorpe United
2	Heald, Paul A.	Sheffield United	Leyton Orient
23	Hedman, Rudolph G.	Colchester United	Crystal Palace
29	Hesford, Iain	Sunderland	Hull City
16	Jackson, Darren	Newcastle United	Dundee United
14	Matthews, Michael	Halifax Town	Scarborough
29	Millar, Paul	Portadown	Port Vale
15	Narbett, Jonathan V.	Shrewsbury Town	Hereford United
29	Norman, Anthony J.	Hull City	Sunderland
22	Randall, Adrian J.	A.F.C. Bournemouth	Aldershot
23	Ranson, Raymond	Birmingham City	Newcastle United
23	Reid, Shaun	Rochdale	York City
9	Robertson, John G.	Newcastle United	Heart of Midlothian
24	Sansom, Kenneth G.	Arsenal	Newcastle United
30	Shearer, David J.	Scunthorpe United	Darlington
24	Thompson, Garry L.	Aston Villa	Watford
29	Whitehurst, William	Sunderland	Hull City
2	Whitlock, Mark	A.F.C. Bournemouth	Reading
2	Williams, William R.	Manchester City	Stockport County

Temporary Transfers

19	Anderson, Douglas E.	Plymouth Argyle	Northampton Town
15	Andrews, Ian E.	Glasgow Celtic	Leeds United
23	Brockie, Vincent	Leeds United	Doncaster Rovers
31	Butler, Martin	York City	Carlisle United
14	Cawley, Peter	Wimbledon	Fulham
1	Cherry, Steven R.	Plymouth Argyle	Chesterfield
1	Clarke, Colin J.	Southampton	A.F.C. Bournemouth
2	Fitzpatrick, Paul J.	Carlisle United	Preston North End
12	Godden, Anthony L.	Birmingham City	Bury
23	Guthrie, Peter J.	Tottenham Hotspur	Charlton Athletic
9	Harrison, Wayne	Liverpool	Crewe Alexandra
11	Jeffers, John J.	Liverpool	Port Vale
23	Jemson, Nigel B.	Nottingham Forest	Bolton Wanderers
15	Jones, Mark	Exeter City	Walsall (Tr. Back)
29	McJannet, William L.	Scarborough	Darlington
29	Moverley, Robert	Bradford City	Hartlepool United
6	O'Donnell, James A.	Manchester United	Charlton Athletic
30	Petterson, Andrew K.	Luton Town	Swindon Town
30	Shepherd, Anthony	Glasgow Celtic	Bristol City
23	Sinclair, Ronald M.	Leeds United	Halifax Town
14	Stowell, Michael	Port Vale	Everton (Tr. Back)
29	Swindlehurst, David	Colchester United	Peterborough United
24	Thompson, Leslie	Hull City	Scarborough
7	Walford, Stephen J.	West Ham United	Gillingham
24	Ward, Anthony	Everton	Doncaster Rovers

January 1989

14	Beasant, David	Newcastle United	Chelsea
20	Beaumont, David A.	Dundee United	Luton Town
12	Bodley, Michael J.	Chelsea	Northampton Town
26	Clayton, Paul S.	Darlington	Crewe Alexandra
12	Holden, Andrew I.	Wigan Athletic	Oldham Athletic
13	Lane, Martin J.	Coventry City	Chester City
10	McGoldrick, Eddie J. P.	Northampton Town	Crystal Palace
4	Maguire, Gavin T.	Queens Park Rangers	Portsmouth
12	Megson, Gary J.	Sheffield Wednesday	Manchester City
6	Phillips, Stewart G.	West Bromwich Albion	Swansea City
12	Quow, Trevor	Gillingham	Northampton Town
13	Ratcliffe, Simon	Norwich	Brentford
13	Rostron, John W.	Watford	Sheffield Wednesday
13	Taylor, Leslie	Reading	Colchester United
27	Turner, Robert P.	Wimbledon	Bristol City
12	Williams, Wayne	Shrewsbury Town	Northampton Town
20	Wood, Darren T.	Chelsea	Sheffield Wednesday

Temporary Transfers

14	Achampong, Kenneth	Fulham	West Ham United
11	Adams, Neil J.	Everton	Oldham Athletic
6	Brown, David J.	Preston North End	Scunthorpe United
16	Campbell, Kevin	Arsenal	Leyton Orient
12	Cherry, Steven R.	Plymouth Argyle	Chesterfield
26	Craig, Albert H.	Newcastle United	Northampton Town
5	Endersby, Scott A. G.	York City	Rochdale
13	Ferguson, Eric	Raith Rovers	Birmingham City
13	Hemming, Christopher A. J.	Stoke City	Wigan Athletic
10	Holsgrove, Paul	Aldershot	Wimbledon
28	Kelly, Anthony G.	West Bromwich Albion	Shrewsbury Town
11	Moran, Paul	Tottenham Hotspur	Portsmouth
27	Mumby, Peter	Leeds United	Shamrock Rovers
13	Pitcher, Darren E. J.	Charlton Athletic	Galway United
26	Puckett, David C.	A.F.C. Bournemouth	Aldershot
12	Rice, Brian	Nottingham Forest	West Bromwich Albion

		From	To
11	Ryan, Vaughan W.	Wimbledon	Sheffield United
19	Stimson, Mark	Tottenham Hotspur	Gillingham
23	Thompson, Leslie	Scarborough	Hull City (Tr. Back)
12	Tupling, Stephen	Cardiff City	Exeter City

February 1989

16	Bartlett, Kevin F.	Cardiff City	West Bromwich Albion
2	Benjamin, Ian T.	Chester City	Exeter City
9	Bogie, Ian	Newcastle United	Preston North End
9	Brazil, Gary N.	Preston North End	Newcastle United
2	Callaghan, Nigel	Derby County	Aston Villa
16	Cherry, Steven R.	Plymouth Argyle	Notts County
20	Clark, Martin J.	Clyde	Nottingham Forest
13	Cooper, Mark D.	Gillingham	Leyton Orient
9	Dobson, Paul	Doncaster Rovers	Scarborough
10	Durnin, John	Liverpool	Oxford United
3	Glover, Dean V.	Middlesbrough	Port Vale
2	Gray, Andrew A.	Aston Villa	Queens Park Rangers
27	Hallworth, Jonathan G.	Ipswich Town	Oldham Athletic
28	Joseph, Francis	Sheffield United	Gillingham
2	McJannet, William L.	Scarborough	Darlington
10	Manuel, William A. J.	Tottenham Hotspur	Gillingham
2	Matthews, Michael	Scarborough	Stockport County
10	Ogilvie, Gary F.	Sunderland	Airdieonians
2	Ormondroyd, Ian	Bradford City	Aston Villa
10	O'Shea, Timothy J.	Leyton Orient	Gillingham
23	Palmer, Carlton L.	West Bromwich Albion	Sheffield Wednesday
10	Philliskirk, Anthony	Oldham Athletic	Preston North End
9	Reid, Peter	Everton	Queens Park Rangers
9	Richardson, Lee J.	Halifax Town	Watford
2	Rimmer, Stuart A.	Notts. County	Walsall
10	Rougvie, Douglas	Shrewsbury Town	Fulham
13	Ruddock, Neil	Millwall	Southampton
9	Russell, Martin	Leicester City	Scarborough
10	Smith, Mark C.	Rochdale	Huddersfield Town
2	Spackman, Nigel J.	Liverpool	Queens Park Rangers
22	Steele, Timothy W.	Shrewsbury Town	Wolverhampton Wanderers
24	West, Colin	Sheffield Wednesday	West Bromwich Albion
13	West, Gary	Gillingham	Port Vale

Temporary Transfers

27	Bailey, Dennis L.	Crystal Palace	Bristol Rovers
23	Byrne, David S.	Millwall	Blackburn Rovers
16	Cherry, Steven R.	Chesterfield	Plymouth Argyle (Tr. Back)
2	Cooper, Mark D.	Gillingham	Leyton Orient
9	Dolan, Eamonn J.	West Ham United	Bristol City
23	Gannon, John S.	Wimbledon	Sheffield United
15	Gormley, Edward J.	Tottenham Hotspur	Motherwell
3	Greaves, Steven R.	Fulham	Waterford
16	Green, Ronald R.	Wimbledon	Manchester City
3	Hallworth, Jonathon G.	Ipswich Town	Oldham Athletic
27	Hazel, Ian	Wimbledon	Bristol Rovers
1	Hucker, Peter I.	Oxford United	Manchester United
9	Hucker, Peter I.	Manchester United	Oxford United (Tr. Back)
3	Jeffers, John	Port Vale	Liverpool (Tr. Back)
2	Jones, Andrew M.	Charlton Athletic	Port Vale
9	Juryeff, Ian M.	Leyton Orient	Ipswich Town
1	McAlister, Thomas G.	West Ham United	Colchester United
16	McDermott, Brian J.	Cardiff City	Exeter City
16	Mercer, William	Liverpool	Rotherham United
20	Miller, Alan J.	Plymouth Argyle	Arsenal (Tr. Back)
16	Miller, David B.	Preston North End	Burnley
21	Nugent, Kevin P.	Leyton Orient	Cork City
17	O'Keefe, James V.	Blackburn Rovers	Blackpool
2	O'Shea, Timothy J.	Leyton Orient	Gillingham
15	Palmer, Charles A.	Hull City	Notts. County
22	Porteous, Ian	Aberdeen	Swansea City
8	Pullan, Christopher J.	Watford	Halifax Town
16	Ramage, Craig D.	Derby County	Wigan Athletic
9	Reeves, Alan	Norwich City	Gillingham
23	Taylor, Steven J.	Burnley	Rochdale
20	Tighe, Aaron P.	Luton Town	Leicester City
2	Walsh, Colin D.	Charlton Athletic	Peterborough United
23	Wilmot, Rhys J.	Arsenal	Plymouth Argyle
3	Young, Richard A.	Southend United	Wimbledon

March 1989

14	Adams, Michael R.	Leeds United	Southampton
22	Atkin, Paul A.	Notts. County	Bury
24	Banks, Ian F.	Bradford City	West Bromwich Albion
23	Barnes, David O.	Swindon Town	A.F.C. Bournemouth
23	Barratt, Anthony	Hartlepool United	York City

		From	To
23	Bennett, David	Coventry City	Sheffield Wednesday
23	Beresford, John	Barnsley	Portsmouth
23	Brockie, Vincent	Leeds United	Doncaster Rovers
16	Byrne, David S.	Millwall	Plymouth Argyle
17	Campbell, David A.	Charlton Athletic	Bradford City
24	Christie, Trevor	Walsall	Mansfield Town
9	Clarke, Colin J.	Southampton	Queens Park Rangers
20	Coney, Dean H.	Queens Park Rangers	Norwich City
23	Cooke, Richard E.	A.F.C. Bournemouth	Luton Town
23	Cooper, Paul D.	Leicester City	Manchester City
8	Dryden, Richard A.	Bristol Rovers	Exeter City
23	Fleming, Curtis	St. Patricks Athletic	Swindon Town
24	Ford, Tony	Stoke City	West Bromwich Albion
23	Gilbert, David J.	Northampton Town	Grimsby Town
23	Green, Ronald R.	Wimbledon	Walsall
23	Harle, David	Scunthorpe United	Peterborough United
23	Harper, Steven J.	Port Vale	Preston North End
31	Hopkins, Robert	West Bromwich Albion	Birmingham City
22	Horne, Barry	Portsmouth	Southampton
29	Houchen, Keith M.	Coventry City	Hibernian
23	Jeffers, John J.	Liverpool	Port Vale
10	Kelly, Anthony G.	West Bromwich Albion	Shrewsbury Town
17	Kennedy, Michael F.	Bradford City	Leicester City
23	Leondard, Gary A.	Bury	Stockport County
6	Leonard, Michael C.	Notts. County	Chesterfield
23	Love, Ian J.	Swansea City	Torquay United
23	McAvennie, Francis	Celtic	West Ham United
16	McDermott, Brian J.	Cardiff City	Exeter City
3	McGee, Paul	Colchester United	Wimbledon
23	McParland, Ian J.	Notts. County	Hull City
21	Meade, Raphael J.	Dundee United	Luton Town
24	Mercer, William	Liverpool	Rotherham United
2	Mills, Gary R.	Notts. County	Leicester City
2	Moverley, Robert	Bradford City	Hartlepool United
24	North, Mark V.	Grimsby Town	Leicester City
14	Oldfield, David C.	Luton Town	Manchester City
23	Palmer, Charles A.	Hull City	Notts. County
10	Payne, Lee J.	Newcastle United	Reading
23	Pittman, Stephen	East Fife	Shrewsbury Town
23	Proctor, Mark G.	Sheffield Wednesday	Middlesbrough
23	Proudlock, Paul	Middlesbrough	Carlisle United
16	Prudhoe, Mark	Carlisle United	Darlington
17	Quinn, James M.	Leicester City	Bradford City
23	Raven, Paul	Doncaster Rovers	West Bromwich Albion
21	Richardson, Barry	Sunderland	Scunthorpe United
22	Robinson, Ronald	Doncaster Rovers	West Bromwich Albion
23	Saville, Andrew V.	Hull City	Walsall
23	Shutt, Carl S.	Bristol City	Leeds United
23	Sinton, Andrew	Brentford	Queens Park Rangers
8	Smith, Paul S.	Bristol Rovers	Torquay United
3	Sterland, Melvyn	Sheffield Wednesday	Rangers
23	Sterling, Worrell R.	Watford	Peterborough United
23	Strachan, Gordon D.	Manchester United	Lees United
23	Swan, Peter H.	Leeds United	Hull City
22	Sweeney, Paul	Raith Rovers	Newcastle United
23	Taylor Robert	Leeds United	Bristol City
23	Taylor, Steven J.	Burnley	Rochdale
9	Tinnion, Brian	Newcastle United	Bradford City
3	Turner, Philip	Leicester City	Notts. County
3	Whitton, Stephen P.	Birmingham City	Sheffield Wednesday
23	Wigley, Steven	Birmingham City	Portsmouth
9	Young, Richard A.	Southend United	Exeter City

Temporary Transfers

		From	To
23	Banton, Dale C.	Walsall	Grimsby Town
16	Batch, Nigel A.	Darlington	Stockport County
23	Bell, Douglas	Shrewsbury Town	Hull City
21	Bradley, Russell	Nottingham Forest	Hereford United
15	Byrne, David S.	Blackburn Rovers	Millwall (Tr. Back)
9	Campbell, David A.	Charlton Athletic	Plymouth Argyle
17	Campbell, David A.	Plymouth Argyle	Charlton Athletic (Tr. Back)
23	Chapman, Vincent J.	Huddersfield Town	York City
16	Charles, Gary A.	Nottingham Forest	Leicester City
4	Dalton, Paul	Manchester United	Hartlepool United
9	Dearden, Kevin C.	Tottenham Hotspur	Cambridge United
10	Dixon, Andrew	Grimsby Town	Shrewsbury Town
23	Elliott, Matthew S.	Charlton Athletic	Torquay United
23	Fairclough, Courtney H.	Tottenham Hotspur	Leeds United
23	Godden, Anthony L.	Birmingham City	Sheffield Wednesday
16	Gormley, Edward J.	Motherwell	Tottenham Hotspur (Tr. Back)
8	Gummer, Jason C.	Cardiff City	Torquay United
22	Hamilton, Lindsay	Rangers	Charlton Athletic
21	Hansbury, Roger	Birmingham City	Wolverhampton Wanderers
23	Hepple, John A.	Sunderland	Hartlepool United

		From	To
23	Holmes, Matthew J.	A.F.C. Bournemouth	Cardiff City
23	Hopkins, Robert	West Bromwich Albion	Birmingham City
20	Howard, Mark E.	Stockport County	Cambridge United
15	Jemson, Nigel B.	Nottingham Forest	Preston North End
23	Jones, Paul A.	Walsall	Wrexham
16	Kerrins, Wayne M.	Fulham	Leyton Orient
21	Lamb, Alan	Nottingham Forest	Hereford United
23	Leake, Gary J.	West Bromwich Albion	Chester City
3	Leonard, Michael C.	Notts. County	Chesterfield
23	McIlhargey, Stephen	Walsall	Rotherham United
23	McKenzie, Paul	Sunderland	Preston North End
22	Moncur, John F.	Tottenham Hotspur	Portsmouth
7	Moore, John	Hull City	Sheffield United
9	Murray, Malcolm	Heart of Midlothian	Hull City
21	O'Donnell, James A.	Manchester United	Swindon Town
23	Powell, Clifford G.	Sheffield United	Doncaster Rovers
23	Purdie, Jon	Oxford United	Brentford
22	Stephens, Arthur	Carlisle United	Darlington
23	Stonehouse, Kevin	Darlington	Carlisle United
17	Stowell, Michael	Everton	Wolverhampton Wanderers
3	Walford, Stephen J.	West Ham United	West Bromwich Albion
2	Wassall, Darren P.	Nottingham Forest	Bury
17	West, Colin W.	Chelsea	Swansea City

April 1989

21	Doyle, Maurice	Crewe Alexandra	Queens Park Rangers
18	Elliott, Matthew S.	Charlton Athletic	Torquay United
4	Fairclough, Courtney H.	Tottenham Hotspur	Leeds United
27	Gannon, James P.	Dundalk	Sheffield United
10	Murray, Malcolm	Heart of Midlothian	Hull City
7	Puckett, David C.	A.F.C. Bournemouth	Aldershot
27	Stephens, Arthur	Carlisle United	Darlington

Temporary Transfers

13	Hutchinson, Simon	Manchester United	Sheffield Wednesday
28	Leake, Gary	Chester City	West Bromwich Albion (Tr. Back)
6	O'Keefe, James V.	Blackpool	Blackburn Rovers (Tr. Back)
21	Stowell, Michael	Wovlerhampton Wanderers	Everton (Tr. Back)

May 1989

1	Purdie, Jon	Oxford U	Brentford
5	Dalton, Paul	Manchester U	Hartlepool U
2	Fleming, Curtis	St. Patrick's	Swindon T

Summer moves . . .
Tony Hancock, Stockport Co to Burnley; Neil Thompson, Scarborough to Ipswich T; Paul Wimbleton, Cardiff C to Bristol C; Wayne Fereday, QPR to Newcastle U; Shaun Murray, Tottenham H to Portsmouth; Kenny Sansom, Newcastle U to QPR; Steve Parkin, Stoke C to WBA; Mickey Thomas, Shrewsbury T to Leeds U; Mark Stimson, Tottenham H to Newcastle U; John Gallacher, Falkirk to Newcastle U; John McClelland, Watford to Leeds U; Andy Marriott, Arsenal to Nottingham F; Kevin Russell, Wrexham to Leicester C; Shane Westley, Southend U to Wolverhampton W; Craig Shakespeare, Walsall to Sheffield W; Vinny Jones, Wimbledon to Leeds U; Steven Prindiville, Chesterfield to Mansfield T; Tony Philliskirk, Preston NE to Bolton W; Mark Taylor, Walsall to Sheffield W; David Penney, Derby Co to Oxford U; John Paskin, WBA to Wolverhampton W; Peter Billing, Crewe Alex to Coventry C; John Ryan, Mansfield T to Chesterfield; Nicky Cross, Leicester C to Port Vale; Alan Davies, Swansea C to Bradford C; Mike Phelan, Norwich C to Manchester U; Owen Archdeacon, Celtic to Barnsley; Dudley Lewis, Swansea C to Huddersfield T; Kevin Rose, Hereford U to Bolton W; Peter Skipper, Oldham Ath to Walsall; Ian Scott, Manchester C to Stoke C; Julian Winter, Huddersfield T to Sheffield U; David Barnes, Aldershot to Sheffield U; Steve Foster, Luton T to Oxford U; Paul McLoughlin, Hereford U to Wolverhampton W; Tony Lange, Aldershot to Wolverhampton W; Mark Morris, Watford to Sheffield U; Mike Salmon, Wrexham to Charlton Ath; Jason Smart, Rochdale to Crewe Alex; Carl Richards, Birmingham C to Peterborough U; Steve Harkness, Carlisle U to Liverpool; Tim Sherwood, Watford to Norwich C; John Deary, Blackpool to Burnley; Mario Walsh, Colchester U to Southend U; Malcolm Brown, Rochdale to Stockport Co; Phil Stant, Hereford U to Notts Co; Sean Reck, Oxford U to Wrexham; John Hendrie, Newcastle U to Leeds U; Gordon Tucker, Huddersfield T to Scunthorpe U; Rhys Wilmot, Arsenal to Plymouth Arg; Gary Marshall, Carlisle U to Scunthorpe U; Andy Thomas, Bradford C to Plymouth Arg; Chris Beaumont, Rochdale to Stockport Co; David Frain, Rochdale to Stockport Co; Colin Gordon, Fulham to Birmingham C; Tony Shepherd, Celtic to Carlisle U; Russell Bradley, Nottingham F to Hereford U; Peter Shirtliff, Charlton Ath to Sheffield W; Joe Jakub, Chester C to Burnley; Wayne Allison, Halifax T to Watford; Karl Elsey, Reading to Maidstone U; Bryn Gunn, Peterborough U to Chesterfield; Graham Shaw, Stoke C to Preston NE; Robert Wilson, Fulham to Huddersfield T; Ian Cranson, Sheffield W to Stoke C; Neil Webb, Nottingham F to Manchester U; Eddie May, Hibernian to Brentford; Craig Short, Scarborough to Notts Co; Jim Beglin, Liverpool to Leeds U; David Robinson, Halifax T to Peterborough U; Calvin Plummer, Plymouth Arg to Chesterfield; Darren Wood, Chesterfield to Reading; Kenny Black, Hearts to Portsmouth; Bernard McNally, Shrewsbury T to WBA; Martin Keown, Aston Villa to Everton; Tony Cunningham, Blackpool to Bury; Michael Clarke, Barnsley to Scarborough; Norman Whiteside, Manchester U to Everton; John Sheridan, Leeds U to Nottingham F; John Gregory, Derby Co to Portsmouth; Neil Aspin, Leeds U to Port Vale; Colin Hill, Colchester U to Sheffield U; Steve Sedgley, Coventry C to Tottenham H; Gary Nebbeling, Crystal Palace to Fulham; Phil Kite, Gillingham to Bournemouth; Chris Withe, Notts Co to Bury; Steve Thompson, Sheffield U to Lincoln C; Paul McGrath, Manchester U to Aston Villa; Gavin Peacock, Gillingham to Bournemouth; Dale Banton, Walsall to Aldershot; Brian Butler, Stockport Co to Halifax T; Andy Feeley, Brentford to Bury; Gordon Owen, Mansfield T to Blackpool; Trevor Putney, Norwich C to Middlesbrough; Mitch Cook, Scarborough to Halifax T; Milton Graham, Chester C to Peterborough U; Nicky Cusack, Peterborough U to Motherwell; Chris Downes, Sheffield U to Stockport Co; Paul Hardyman, Portsmouth to Sunderland; Siggi Jonsson, Sheffield W to Arsenal; Chris Waddle, Tottenham H to Marseille; Gary Lineker, Barcelona to Tottenham H; Glenn Hysen, Fiorentina to Liverpool; Frank Stapleton, Le Havre to Blackburn R; Clive Allen, Bordeaux to Manchester C; Trevor Steven, Everton to Rangers; Alan McInally, Aston Villa to Bayern Munich.

The Football Trust: Review of Season 1988–89

MILLWALL AND PRESTON SHARE FOOTBALL TRUST COMMUNITY AWARD

Millwall and Preston North End are the joint winners of the inaugural Football Trust Community Club of the Year Award. The two, deemed by the Trust to have contributed most to their local communities, were each presented with a cheque for £30,000 during a ceremony held at the Waldorf Hotel in London. The money will be used to introduce further community initiatives at The Den and Deepdale.

The panel of judges were unable to separate the two clubs and unanimously agreed to divide the award. Millwall, strongly commended for their extensive work with the elderly and women supporters, received particular praise for their positive endeavours to combat racism. Preston North End, who have approached their community role in a different but equally effective manner, gained high praise for the extensive use of their artificial playing surface at Deepdale.

Prize-money totalling £100,000 was pledged by The Football Trust in recognition of efforts made by professional clubs to strengthen links with their local community and to mark the Football League's Centenary. The awards were presented on a divisional basis by Lord Aberdare KBE, Chairman of The Football Trust.

Millwall and Preston North End, joint winners of the Community Club of the Year Award, won their respective Divisions, promotion challengers Manchester City and Watford shared the award in the Second and Crewe Alexandra collected the Fourth Division title.

Prizes of £30,000 went to Millwall and Preston North End, £20,000 to Crewe Alexandra and £10,000 each to Manchester City and Watford. All prize-money will be spent by the clubs on further community initiatives. Millwall and Preston were also awarded a special illuminated address and the divisional winners and commended clubs received commemorative plaques.

Lord Aberdare commented: "There was an excellent response from the four divisions of the Football League. The submissions, all of which were extremely professional, have highlighted a more enlightened attitude within the game and one which deserves far greater recognition."

A total of 57 Football League clubs tendered applications for the Trust's Community Award Scheme displaying a varied range of initiatives. These include the introduction of creches, programmes to counter racism and sexism and the extensive provision of facilities for spectators with disabilities.

Clubs commended for their efforts were Arsenal (a Special Commendation), Aston Villa, Bradford City, Brentford, Colchester United, Derby County, Doncaster Rovers, Grimsby Town, Leeds United, Oldham Athletic, Reading, Sheffield United, Sheffield Wednesday, Southampton and Tranmere Rovers.

Since 1979, The Football Trust, which is funded entirely by Littlewoods, Vernons and Zetters from their Spotting-the-Ball competition, has worked extensively to support and fund community initiatives in the professional and semi-professional game.

Almost £2.5 million is invested every year by the organisation in football and the community schemes throughout the United Kingdom. Initiatives include the allocation of funds for the PFA's Community Programme in Professional Football, the provisioni of hard surface play areas, full-sized artificial pitches, the development of women's football, the funding of Soccer As Family Entertainment, the building of numerous indoor sports facilities and an extensive programme of pitch and changing accommodation improvements in conjunction with local authorities.

FOOTBALL TRUST COMMUNITY CLUB OF THE YEAR: JOINT WINNERS: MILLWALL: Undertaken close co-operation with the local council in this deprived area of South London to improve the image of the club within its community. Programme demonstrates a strong commitment and hard work mixed with flair and imagination. Particular reference given to efforts to develop relationship between club and local young supporters.

PRESTON NORTH END: Ethos of community involvement runs throughout club. Range of projects vast and supported by all levels of staff. Advantage of synthetic pitch served to strengthen community programme at Deepdale. *TRUST AWARD £30,000 EACH.*

DIVISION ONE: WINNER: MILLWALL: SPECIAL COMMENDATION: ARSENAL: Club's work with The Sports Council and local borough, especially with women's football, a model for their competitors.

COMMENDATIONS: ASTON VILLA: Special mention given to exciting new educational initiatives and family club and match day activities.

DERBY COUNTY, SHEFFIELD WEDNESDAY, SOUTHAMPTON: All three clubs impressed with their range of local activities and imagination of their schemes. Number of applications: 16 (80%).

DIVISION TWO: JOINT WINNERS: MANCHESTER CITY and WATFORD: City's work on Moss Side is well documented with their Junior Blues Scheme and player involvement second to none. Watford have a long established reputation for their work in the local community which has been generated from within the club itself. *TRUST AWARD £10,000 EACH.*

COMMENDATIONS: BRADFORD CITY: Excellent supportive work with local women's team. *LEEDS UNITED:* Creche facility and spectator involvement at Board level highly valued. *OLDHAM ATHLETIC:* Artificial pitch has become centre of community activities. Appplication received substantial local support. Number of applications: 17 (70%)

DIVISION THREE: WINNER: PRESTON NORTH END: COMMENDATIONS: BRENTFORD: Range of activities for unemployed, veterans and coaching clinics. Additional non-football projects. *READING:* Community care campaign has a membership of 1,500 providing anti-crime and safety education. *SHEFFIELD UNITED:* Club employs both full-time and part-time liaison officers. Heavily involved in fund-raising initiatives in the city and visits to hospitals and schools. Number of applications: 12 (50%).

Continued on Page 750

BARCLAYS LEAGUE ATTENDANCES 1988–89

	TOTAL ATTENDANCES	AVERAGE ATTENDANCES
TOTAL	18,464,192	9068
DIVISION 1	7,809,993	20,552
DIVISION 2	5,887,805	10,666
DIVISION 3	3,035,327	5837
DIVISION 4	1,791,067	3244

ALL-SEATER STADIA PROJECTION

DIVISION ONE (1989–90)

Club Name	*Current Capacity*	*Present Standing Capacity*	*Present Seated Capacity*	*Projected All-Seated Capacity*	*Average Attendance Season 1988/89*	*No. of times Attendance Exceeded Average*	*No. of times Attendance Exceeded Projected All-Seated Capacity*
Arsenal	57,000	39,800	17,200	38,925	35,595	10	5
Aston Villa	48,100	32,095	16,005	33,657	23,310	8	1
Charlton Ath	38,366	26,858	11,508	26,280	9398	6	0
Chelsea	43,900	23,300	20,600	33,415	15,731	11	0
Coventry C	29,800	11,304	18,496	24,713	16,040	9	0
Crystal Palace	38,366	26,858	11,508	26,280	10,655	8	0
Derby Co	26,500	16,278	10,222	19,175	17,536	7	5
Everton	50,271	23,800	26,471	39,561	27,765	8	2
Liverpool	45,628	23,100	22,528	35,233	38,574	12	16
Luton T	14,470	7660	6810	11,023	9504	8	2
Manchester C	51,993	26,155	25,838	40,223	23,500	6	0
Manchester U	56,385	30,699	25,686	42,570	36,488	11	3
Millwall	25,850	22,650	3200	15,675	15,416	8	9
Norwich C	26,812	15,587	11,225	19,798	16,785	7	5
Nottingham F	35,367	20,358	15,009	26,206	20,785	8	1
QPR	27,330	12,000	15,330	21,930	12,281	6	0
Sheffield W	54,324	31,000	23,324	40,374	20,037	7	0
Southampton	25,175	16,000	9175	17,975	15,590	10	3
Tottenham H	34,258	18,650	15,608	25,866	24,467	9	9
Wimbledon	16,000	14,000	2000	9700	7824	7	5
Total	745,895			548,579			

DIVISION TWO (1989–90)

Club Name	*Current Capacity*	*Present Standing Capacity*	*Present Seated Capacity*	*Projected All-Seated Capacity*	*Average Attendance Season 1988/89*	*No. of times Attendance Exceeded Average*	*No. of times Attendance Exceeded Projected All-Seated Capacity*
AFC Bournemouth	12,038	8000	4038	8438	8087	12	10
Barnsley	36,987	34,700	2287	21,372	7215	8	0
Blackburn R	21,956	19,300	2656	13,271	8891	9	1
Bradford C	15,519	10,937	4582	10,597	10,524	12	12
Brighton & HA	29,026	24,272	4754	18,104	9048	11	0
Hull C	19,797	13,757	6040	13,606	6666	9	0
Ipswich T	37,345	23,177	14,168	26,915	15,333	2	0
Leeds U	39,133	21,244	17,889	29,573	21,811	11	3
Leicester C	31,057	15,200	15,857	24,217	10,694	9	0
Middlesbrough	30,647	21,080	9567	21,161	19,999	8	6
Newcastle U	37,703	26,290	11,413	25,873	22,921	7	4
Oldham Ath	21,949	18,950	2999	10,423	7204	6	2
Oxford U	14,006	8063	5943	10,378	6352	9	0
Plymouth Arg	28,000	24,741	3259	16,867	8628	7	0
Portsmouth	29,664	22,988	6676	19,319	10,201	12	0
Port Vale	18,640	14,340	4300	12,187	6731	6	5
Sheffield U	44,010	30,413	13,597	30,324	12,222	9	0
Stoke C	35,812	24,500	11,312	24,787	9817	9	0
Sunderland	37,775	28,750	9025	24,837	14,878	10	0
Swindon T	19,652	14,590	5062	13,088	8687	11	0
Watford	26,956	20,050	6906	17,932	12,292	10	0
WBA	35,000	23,000	12,000	24,650	12,757	10	0
West Ham U	35,556	26,816	8740	23,488	20,738	7	5
Wolverhampton W	28,051	18,551	9500	19,703	14,392	10	3
Total	686,279			460,480			

DIVISION THREE (1989–90)

Club Name	*Current Capacity*	*Present Standing Capacity*	*Present Seated Capacity*	*Projected All-Seated Capacity*	*Average Attendance Season 1988/89*	*No. of times Attendance Exceeded Average*	*No. of times Attendance Exceeded Projected All-Seated Capacity*
Birmingham C	38,408	29,040	9368	25,340	6265	9	0
Blackpool	12,696	9500	3196	8421	4276	6	0
Bolton Wanderers	29,000	21,000	8000	19,550	5528	7	0
Brentford	12,100	9183	2917	7968	5681	9	2
Bristol C	30,868	23,452	7416	20,315	8120	8	0
Bristol R	8844	8186	658	5160	5259	10	10
Bury	8000	5300	2700	5615	3367	9	1
Cardiff C	39,545	34,000	5545	24,245	4384	8	0
Chester C	8474	5640	2834	5936	3055	10	0
Crewe Alex	5900	4800	1100	3740	3296	8	6
Fulham	19,400	11,860	7540	14,063	4938	7	0
Huddersfield T	31,010	25,221	5789	19,660	5821	7	0
Leyton Orient	26,500	19,328	7172	17,802	3793	12	0
Mansfield T	12,298	8850	3448	8316	4005	8	2
Northampton T	11,000	10,658	342	6204	3918	8	1
Notts Co	24,077	20,200	3877	14,987	5675	8	0
Preston NE	16,500	13,200	3300	10,560	7737	9	3
Reading	13,500	11,547	1953	8304	5105	9	1
Rotherham U	17,913	14,506	3407	11,385	5063	9	0
Shrewsbury T	16,000	12,000	4000	10,600	4706	7	0
Swansea C	18,165	15,000	3165	11,415	4896	9	0
Tranmere R	18,500	14,700	3800	11,885	5331	8	1
Walsall	16,018	14,660	1358	9421	6108	12	1
Wigan Ath	12,500	11,400	1100	7370	3151	6	0
Total	447,216			288,262			

DIVISION FOUR (1989–90)

Club Name	*Current Capacity*	*Present Standing Capacity*	*Present Seated Capacity*	*Projected All-Seated Capacity*	*Average Attendance Season 1988/89*	*No. of times Attendance Exceeded Average*	*No. of times Attendance Exceeded Projected All-Seated Capacity*
Aldershot	12,000	11,200	1800	7960	2609	8	0
Burnley	20,961	14,200	6761	14,571	7062	11	0
Cambridge U	12,500	9104	3396	8403	2653	11	0
Carlisle U	18,506	16,344	2162	11,151	3176	5	0
Chesterfield	12,838	10,200	2638	8248	3717	7	1
Colchester U	6500	5416	1084	4063	2893	11	4
Doncaster R	8259	7000	1259	5109	2158	10	0
Exeter C	9230	7622	1608	5800	2679	9	0
Gillingham	10,482	9257	1225	6316	3675	9	0
Grimsby T	20,865	15,844	5021	13,735	4302	9	0
Halifax T	5675	3930	1745	3906	1946	9	1
Hartlepool U	6650	5150	1500	4332	2048	9	0
Hereford U	16,119	13,815	2304	9902	2132	7	0
Lincoln C	9477	7448	2029	6125	3887	6	1
Maidstone U	4948	4228	720	3045	1037	10	0
Peterborough U	17,440	14,000	3440	11,140	3264	11	0
Rochdale	12,000	11,350	650	6892	1968	10	0
Scarborough	11,000	10,200	800	6410	2961	8	0
Scunthorpe U	11,266	6466	4800	8356	4547	8	1
Southend U	12,753	10,102	2651	7708	3699	11	0
Stockport Co	7200	4700	2500	5085	2792	8	1
Torquay U	4999	3549	1450	3402	2349	11	0
Wrexham	22,426	17,400	5026	14,596	2636	9	0
York C	14,109	11,050	3059	9135	2613	10	0
Total	276,215			185,390			

N.B. Current capacity refers to safety limit information correct at the end of the 1988–89 season. Subsequent variations appear under respective club pages 38 to 589. Tables courtesy of Football League.

LEAGUE ATTENDANCES SINCE 1946–47

Season	*Matches*	*Total*	*Div. 1*	*Div. 2*	*Div. 3 (S)*	*Div. 3 (N)*
1946–47	1848	35,604,606	15,005,316	11,071,572	5,664,004	3,863,714
1947–48	1848	40,259,130	16,732,341	12,286,350	6,653,610	4,586,829
1948–49	1848	41,271,414	17,914,667	11,353,237	6,998,429	5,005,081
1949–50	1848	40,517,865	17,278,625	11,694,158	7,104,155	4,440,927
1950–51	2028	39,584,967	16,679,454	10,780,580	7,367,884	4,757,109
1951–52	2028	39,015,866	16,110,322	11,066,189	6,958,927	4,880,428
1952–53	2028	37,149,966	16,050,278	9,686,654	6,704,299	4,708,735
1953–54	2028	36,174,590	16,154,915	9,510,053	6,311,508	4,198,114
1954–55	2028	34,133,103	15,087,221	8,988,794	5,996,017	4,051,071
1955–56	2028	33,150,809	14,108,961	9,080,002	5,692,479	4,269,367
1956–57	2028	32,744,405	13,803,037	8,718,162	5,622,189	4,601,017
1957–58	2028	33,562,208	14,468,652	8,663,712	6,097,183	4,332,661
					Div. 3	*Div. 4*
1958–59	2028	33,610,985	14,727,691	8,641,997	5,946,600	4,276,697
1959–60	2028	32,538,611	14,391,227	8,399,627	5,739,707	4,008,050
1960–61	2028	28,619,754	12,926,948	7,033,936	4,784,256	3,874,614
1961–62	2015	27,979,902	12,061,194	7,453,089	5,199,106	3,266,513
1962–63	2028	28,885,852	12,490,239	7,792,770	5,341,362	3,261,481
1963–64	2028	28,535,022	12,486,626	7,594,158	5,419,157	3,035,081
1964–65	2028	27,641,168	12,708,752	6,984,104	4,436,245	3,512,067
1965–66	2028	27,206,980	12,480,644	6,914,757	4,779,150	3,032,429
1966–67	2028	28,902,596	14,242,957	7,253,819	4,421,172	2,984,648
1967–68	2028	30,107,298	15,289,410	7,450,410	4,013,087	3,354,391
1968–69	2028	29,382,172	14,584,851	7,382,390	4,339,656	3,075,275
1969–70	2028	29,600,972	14,868,754	7,581,728	4,223,761	2,926,729
1970–71	2028	28,194,146	13,954,337	7,098,265	4,377,213	2,764,331
1971–72	2028	28,700,729	14,484,603	6,769,308	4,697,392	2,749,426
1972–73	2028	25,448,642	13,998,154	5,631,730	3,737,252	2,081,506
1973–74	2027	24,982,203	13,070,991	6,326,108	3,421,624	2,163,480
1974–75	2028	25,577,977	12,613,178	6,955,970	4,086,145	1,992,684
1975–76	2028	24,896,053	13,089,861	5,798,405	3,948,449	2,059,338
1976–77	2028	26,182,800	13,647,585	6,250,597	4,152,218	2,132,400
1977–78	2028	25,392,872	13,255,677	6,474,763	3,332,042	2,330,390
1978–79	2028	24,540,627	12,704,549	6,153,223	3,374,558	2,308,297
1979–80	2028	24,623,975	12,163,002	6,112,025	3,999,328	2,349,620
1980–81	2028	21,907,569	11,392,894	5,175,442	3,637,854	1,701,379
1981–82	2028	20,006,961	10,420,793	4,750,463	2,836,915	1,998,790
1982–83	2028	18,766,158	9,295,613	4,974,937	2,943,568	1,552,040
1983–84	2028	18,358,631	8,711,448	5,359,757	2,729,942	1,557,484
1984–85	2028	17,849,835	9,761,404	4,030,823	2,667,008	1,390,600
1985–86	2028	16,488,577	9,037,854	3,551,968	2,490,481	1,408,274
1986–87	2028	17,379,218	9,144,676	4,168,131	2,350,970	1,715,441
1987–88	2030	17,959,732	8,094,571	5,341,599	2,751,275	1,772,287
1988–89	2036	18,464,192	7,809,993	5,887,805	3,035,327	1,791,067

This is the first time since the war that attendances have risen for three consecutive seasons.

THE LITTLEWOODS/MILK LEAGUE CUP and OTHER FOOTBALL LEAGUE COMPETITIONS:

SIMOD CUP

SHERPA VAN TROPHY

LEAGUE CUP FINALISTS 1961–89

Played as a two-leg final until 1966. All subsequent finals at Wembley.

Year	*Winners*	*Runners-up*	*Score*
1961	Aston Villa	Rotherham U	0-2, 3-0 (aet)
1962	Norwich C	Rochdale	3-0, 1-0
1963	Birmingham C	Aston Villa	3-1, 0-0
1964	Leicester C	Stoke C	1-1, 3-2
1965	Chelsea	Leicester C	3-2, 0-0
1966	WBA	West Ham U	1-2, 4-1
1967	QPR	WBA	3-2
1968	Leeds U	Arsenal	1-0
1969	Swindon T	Arsenal	3-1 (aet)
1970	Manchester C	WBA	2-1 (aet)
1971	Tottenham H	Aston Villa	2-0
1972	Stoke C	Chelsea	2-1
1973	Tottenham H	Norwich C	1-0
1974	Wolverhampton W	Manchester C	2-1
1975	Aston Villa	Norwich C	1-0
1976	Manchester C	Newcastle U	2-1
1977	Aston Villa	Everton	0-0, 1-1 (aet), 3-2 (aet)
1978	Nottingham F	Liverpool	0-0 (aet), 1-0
1979	Nottingham F	Southampton	3-2
1980	Wolverhampton W	Nottingham F	1-0
1981	Liverpool	West Ham U	1-1 (aet), 2-1
MILK CUP			
1982	Liverpool	Tottenham H	3-1 (aet)
1983	Liverpool	Manchester U	2-1 (aet)
1984	Liverpool	Everton	0-0 (aet), 1-0
1985	Norwich C	Sunderland	1-0
1986	Oxford U	QPR	3-0
LITTLEWOODS CUP			
1987	Arsenal	Liverpool	2-1
1988	Luton T	Arsenal	3-2
1989	Nottingham F	Luton T	3-1

LEAGUE CUP WINS
Liverpool 4, Aston Villa 3, Nottingham F 3, Manchester C 2, Norwich C 2, Tottenham H 2, Wolverhampton W 2, Arsenal 1, Birmingham C 1, Chelsea 1, Leeds U 1, Leicester C 1, Luton T 1, Oxford U 1, QPR 1, Stoke C 1, Swindon T 1, WBA 1.

APPEARANCES IN FINALS
Liverpool 6, Aston Villa 5, Arsenal 4, Norwich C 4, Nottingham F 4, Manchester C 3, Tottenham H 3, WBA 3, Chelsea 2, Everton 2, Leicester C 2, Luton T 2, QPR 2, Stoke C 2, West Ham U 2, Wolverhampton W 2, Birmingham C 1, Leeds U 1, Manchester U 1, Newcastle U 1, Oxford U 1, Rochdale 1, Rotherham U 1, Southampton 1, Sunderland 1, Swindon T 1.

APPEARANCES IN SEMI-FINALS
Aston Villa 8, Liverpool 8, Tottenham H 7, Arsenal 6, West Ham U 6, Manchester C 5, Norwich C 5, Chelsea 4, Manchester U 4, Nottingham F 4, WBA 4, Burnley 3, Everton 3, Leeds U 3, QPR 3, Wolverhampton W 3, Birmingham C 2, Bristol C 2, Ipswich T 2, Leicester C 2, Luton T 2, Oxford U 2, Plymouth Arg 2, Southampton 2, Stoke C 2, Sunderland 2, Swindon T 2, Blackburn R 1, Blackpool 1, Bolton W 1, Bury 1, Cardiff C 1, Carlisle U 1, Chester C 1, Coventry C 1, Derby Co 1, Huddersfield T 1, Middlesbrough 1, Newcastle U 1, Peterborough U 1, Rochdale 1, Rotherham U 1, Shrewsbury T 1, Walsall 1, Watford 1.

LITTLEWOODS CUP 1988–89

FIRST ROUND FIRST LEG
29 AUG

Hereford U (0) 0

Plymouth Arg (2) 3 *(Summerfield, Marker, McCarthy)* 2353

Hereford U: Rose; Jones M, Crane, Stevens, Devine, Bowyer, Mardenborough, Maddy, Stant, Benbow (Williams), McLoughlin.
Plymouth Arg: Cherry; Brimacombe, Cooper, Burrows, Marker, Smith, Hodges, Matthews, Tynan, McCarthy, Summerfield.

Stockport Co (0) 0

Tranmere R (1) 1 *(Muir)* 2602

Stockport Co: Gorton; Butler, Hart, Coyle (Cooke), Thorpe, Williams, Wylde, Hendrie, Payne (Scott), Hartford, Howard.
Tranmere R: Nixon; Higgins, Williams, Martindale (McKenna), Moore, Vickers, Morrissey, Harvey, Steel, Muir, Mungall.

Wigan Ath (0) 0

Preston NE (0) 0 4035

Wigan Ath: Hughes; Atherton, Tankard, Butler, Beesley, Holden, Pilling (Crompton), Senior, Hilditch, Russell, Rimmer.
Preston NE: Brown; Miller, Rathbone, Atkins, Jones, Allardyce, Williams O (Williams N), Swann, Patterson, Brazil, McAteer.

30 AUG

Bolton W (1) 1 *(Darby)*

Chester C (0) 0 3535

Bolton W: Felgate; Brown, Cowdrill, Savage, Came, Winstanley, Henshaw, Thompson, Thomas, Elliott, Darby.
Chester C: Stewart; Glenn, Woodthorpe, Hinnigan, Abel, Lightfoot, Jakub, Butler (Lundon), Benjamin, Johnson, Bennett (Newhouse).

Bournemouth (0) 1 *(Aylott)*

Bristol R (0) 0 4601

Bournemouth: Peyton; Newson, Morrell, Bond, Williams, Whitlock, Cooke, Brooks, Aylott, Bishop, Close (Richards).
Bristol R: Martyn; Stapleton, Twentyman, Clark, Mehew (Smith), Jones, Holloway, Reece, White, Penrice, Purnell (Dryden).

Bristol C (1) 1 *(Newman (pen))*

Exeter C (0) 0 6005

Bristol C: Waugh; Llewellyn, Bromage, Humphries (Honor), Pender, McClaren, Milne, Galliers, Newman, Walsh, Caldwell (Hawkins).
Exeter C: Gwinnett; Banks, Viney, Rogers, Taylor, Cooper, Rowbotham, Hiley, Langley, Neville, Harrower.

Bury (1) 2 *(Robinson, Hoyland)*

Wrexham (0) 1 *(Buxton)* 1809

Bury: Farnworth; Hill (Clements), Pashley, Leonard (Brotherston), Valentine, Higgins, Lee, Robinson, Hoyland, McIlroy, Bishop.
Wrexham: Salmon; Salathiel, Wright (Hunter), Bowden, Beaumont, Jones, Flynn, Thackeray, Buxton, Russell, Cooper.

Cambridge U (0) 1 *(Ryan)*

Gillingham (0) 2 *(Walker, Lovell)* 2296

Cambridge U: Bastock; Bailie, Kimble, Smith, Chapple, Beck (Taylor), Clayton, Ryan, Reilly, Turner, Leadbitter.
Gillingham: Hillyard; Burley, Haylock, Peacock, Clarke, Walker, Shipley, Quow, Lovell (Cooper), Lillis, Smith D.

Cardiff C (0) 0

Swansea C (1) 1 *(Thornber)* 6241

Cardiff C: Wood; Rodgerson, Platnauer, Gummer (Walsh), Stevenson, Boyle, Curtis, Bartlett, Gilligan, McDermott (Lynex), Kelly.
Swansea C: Bracey; Hough, Coleman, Melville, Knill, Davies, Thornber, Wade (Hutchison), Love, James, Raynor.

Carlisle U (0) 1 *(Gorman (pen))*

Blackpool (1) 1 *(Deary)* 2336

Carlisle U: Prudhoe; Robertson, Dalziel, Ogley, Saddington, Clark, Marshall, Gorman, Sendall (Fyfe), Hetherington, Halpin.
Blackpool: Siddall; Gore, Burgess, Deary, Methven, Elliott, Davies, Garner, Cunningham, Coughlin, Wright (Thompson).

Colchester U (0) 0

Northampton T (0) 0 1678

Colchester U: Walton; Hedman, Cartwright, Barnett, Hetzke, Hill, Wilkins, White, Tempest, Swindlehurst, Grenfell.
Northampton T: Gleasure; McGoldrick, Thomas, Donald, Flexney, Reed, Singleton, Culpin, Gilbert, Adcock, Donegal.

Crewe Alex (0) 1 *(Sussex)*

Lincoln C (0) 1 *(Brown)* 1860

Crewe Alex: Greygoose; Goodison, Edwards (Ritchie), Callgahan, Macowat, Jones, Jasper, Murphy, Cutler, Sussex, Fishenden (Cronin).
Lincoln C: Wallington; Evans, Nicholson, Clarke, Bressington, James, Davis, Cumming, Brown, Smith, Sertori.

Doncaster R (1) 1 *(Rankine)*

Darlington (1) 1 *(Hine)* 1504

Doncaster R: Malcolm; Douglas, Robinson R, Turnbull, Raffell, Raven, Robinson L, Daly, Rankine, Dobson, Kimble (Gaughan).
Darlington: Granger (Caizley); Robinson M, Morgan, Hine, Moore, McAughtrie, Emson, Robinson N, Macdonald, Anderson (Hyde), Stonehouse.

Fulham (1) 2 *(Skinner (pen), Sayer)*

Brentford (1) 2 *(Sinton, Stanislaus)* 5489

Fulham: Stannard; Langley, Eckhardt, Wilson, Elkins, Thomas, Skinner, Sayer, Barnett, Cole, Walker (Hoddy).
Brentford: Parks; Feeley, Stanislaus, Millen, Evans, Cockram, Jones, Sinton, Cadette, Blissett, Smillie

Grimsby T (0) 0

Rotherham U (0) 1 *(Stoutt (og))* 2517

Grimsby T: Reece; Dixon (McGarvey), Agnew, Williams, Tillson, Cunnington, Jobling, McDermott, O'Kelly, Stoutt, North.
Rotherham U: O'Hanlon; Russell, Crosby, Grealish, Johnson, Green, Hazel, Williams, Williamson, Haycock (Mendonca), Heard.

Hartlepool U (1) 2 *(Powell (og), Dixon (pen))*

Sheffield U (2) 2 *(Agana, Deane)* 2480

Hartlepool U: McKellar; Haigh, McKinnon, Tinkler (Nobbs), Smith, Stokes, Honour, Toman, Dixon, Borthwick, Barratt (Grayson).
Sheffield U: Benstead; Powell, Pike, Webster, Stancliffe, Smith, Roberts (Duffield), Todd, Agana, Deane, Bryson (Wilder).

Leyton Orient (1) 2 *(Hull, Juryeff)*

Aldershot (0) 0 2331

Leyton Orient: Wells; Howard, Dickenson, Hales, Corner, Harvey (Ketteridge), Baker, Ward, Hull, Juryeff (Nugent), Comfort.
Aldershot: Lange; Berry, Barnes, Burvill, Smith, Wignall, Phillips, Riley, Chandler (Ring), McDonald, Mazzon (Anderson).

Notts Co (2) 5 *(McParland 3, Pike, Mills)*

Mansfield T (0) 0 4428

Notts Co: Leonard; Norton, Withe, O'Riordan, Yates, Law, Mills, McParland, Birtles (Lund), Pike, Thorpe.
Mansfield T: Cox; Graham, Kenworthy, Lowery, Foster, Coleman, Owen, Kearney (Ryan), Stringfellow, Cassells, Charles.

Port Vale (1) 3 *(Futcher (pen), Sproson, Earle)*

Chesterfield (1) 2 *(Morris 2)* 3492

Port Vale: Grew; Mills, Webb, Walker, Hazell, Sproson, Ford, Earle, Futcher, Beckford, Finney (Harper).
Chesterfield: Astbury; Hewitt, McGeeney (Wood), Henderson, Rogers, Hunter, Eley, Arnott, Waller, Morris, Thompson (Bloomer).

Rochdale (1) 3 *(O'Shaughnessy, Reid (pen), Beaumont)*

Burnley (1) 3 *(O'Connell, Comstive (pen), Oghani)* 3669

Rochdale: Welch; Copeland, Armitage, Lomax, Sutton, Smart (Beaumont), Harris, Reid, Smith, O'Shaughnessy, Frain.
Burnley: Pearce; Daniel, Deakin, Farrell, Davis, Gardner, Britton, Oghani, O'Connell, Comstive, James.

Scunthorpe U (0) 3 *(Flounders, Lister, Hodkinson)*

Huddersfield T (1) 2 *(Maskell, Mitchell)* 3820

Scunthorpe U: Musselwhite; Longden, Stevenson, Taylor, Lister, Brown, Hodkinson, Money (Richardson), Daws, Flounders, Cowling.
Huddersfield T: Hardwick; Trevitt, Hutchings, Mitchell, O'Doherty, Shotton, O'Regan, May (Tucker), Withe (Ward), Maskell, Marsden.

Shrewsbury T (1) 2 *(Melrose, Brown)*

Walsall (0) 2 *(Forbes, Shakespeare)* 4579

Shrewsbury T: Perks; Williams W, Williams B, Priest, Green, Finley, Kasule (Steele), McNally, Melrose, Irvine, Brown.
Walsall: Barber; Dornan, Taylor M, Shakespeare, Forbes, Hart, Pritchard, Goodwin, Taylor A, Christie, Naughton.

Southend U (1) 2 *(Gatting (og), Crown)*

Brighton & HA (0) 0 3072

Southend U: Sansome; O'Shea, Johnson, Martin, Westley, Brush, Butler, Hall, Crown, McDonough, Ling.
Brighton & HA: Keeley; Brown, Chivers, Trusson, Isaac, Gatting, Nelson, Owers, Wood, Wilkins, Penney.

Torquay U (0) 0

Reading (0) 1 *(Moran)* 2182

Torquay U: Crichton; Holmes, Kelly (Loram), McNichol, Cole, Joyce, Pugh, Lloyd, Edwards, Dawkins (Haslegrave), Gibbins.
Reading: Francis; Elsey, Richardson, Tait, Hicks, Curle, Jones, Taylor L, Whitehurst, Moran, Gilkes.

Wolverhampton W (0) 3 *(Bull 2, Dennison)*

Birmingham C (1) 2 *(Thompson (og), Bird)* 11,007

Wolverhampton W: Kendall; Bellamy, Thompson, Streete, Robertson, Robinson, Chard, Vaughan, Bull, Mutch, Dennison.
Birmingham C: Godden; Ranson, Roberts, Atkins, Bird, Trewick, Frain, Langley (Bremner), Whitton, Robinson, Wigley.

York C (0) 0

Sunderland (0) 0 4204

York C: Marples; Bradshaw, Johnson, Branagan, Tutill, Fazackerley, Howlett, Spooner, Helliwell, Banton, Himsworth.
Sunderland: Hesford; Kay, Agboola, Bennett, MacPhail, Doyle, Lemon (Owers), Armstrong, Gates, Gabbiadini, Pascoe.

31 AUG

Scarborough (0) 1 *(Brook)*

Halifax T (0) 1 *(Watson)* 2196

Scarborough: Blackwell; Kamara, Thompson (McJannett), Short, Richards, Bennyworth, Morris, Cook, Norris, Brook, Graham.
Halifax T: Roche; Barr W, Logan, Willis, Barr R, Whitehead, Watson, Horner, Matthews N (McPhillips), Allison, Richardson.

WBA (0) 0

Peterborough U (1) 3 *(Oakes, Cusack, Genovese)* 4264

WBA: Naylor; Bradley, Albiston, Gray, Dyson, North, Hopkins, Goodman (Robson), Paskin, Palmer, Anderson.
Peterborough U: Neenan; Langan, Collins, Gooding, McElhinney, Oakes, Genovese, Halsall, Cusack, Gunn, Luke.

FIRST ROUND SECOND LEG
5 SEPT

Tranmere R (0) 1 *(Muir)*

Stockport Co (0) 1 *(Wylde (pen))* 3335

Tranmere R: Nixon; Higgins (McCarrick), Williams, Martindale, Moore (McKenna), Vickers, Morrissey, Harvey, Steel, Muir, Mungall.
Stockport Co: Gorton; Butler, Hart, Coyle, Thorpe, Williams, Wylde, Colville, Bullock (Cook), Hendrie, Howard.
Tranmere R won 2-1 on aggregate

6 SEPT

Aldershot (0) 0

Leyton Orient (0) 0 1785

Aldershot: Lange; Berry, Barnes (Mazzon), Burvill, Smith, Wignall, Phillips, Riley (Anderson), Chandler, McDonald, Ring.
Leyton Orient: Wells; Howard, Dickenson, Hales, Corner, Day (Ketteridge), Baker, Ward, Hull, Juryeff (Shinners), Comfort.
Leyton Orient won 2-0 on aggregate

Birmingham C (0) 1 *(Whitton)*

Wolverhampton W (0) 0 8981

Birmingham C: Godden; Ranson, Roberts, Atkins, Overson, Bird, Frain (Morris), Langley, Whitton (Russell), Robinson, Wigley.
Wolverhampton W: Kendall; Bellamy, Thompson, Streete, Robertson, Robinson (Venus), Vaughan, Chard, Bull, Mutch, Dennison (Gallagher).
aet; Birmingham C won on away goals

Blackpool (1) 3 *(Garner 2, Taylor (pen))*

Carlisle U (0) 0 2955

Blackpool: Siddall; Burgess, Morgan, Deary (Madden), Methven, Elliott, Davies, Cunningham, Garner, Coughlin (Thompson), Taylor.
Carlisle U: Prudhoe (Jeffels); Robertson, Dalziel, Saddington, Ogley, Clark, Walsh, Gorman, Sendall, Hetherington (Stephens), Marshall.
Blackpool won 4-1 on aggregate

Brentford (0) 1 *(Blissett)*

Fulham (0) 0 7707

Brentford: Parks; Feeley, Stanislaus (Bates), Millen, Evans, Cockram, Jones, Sinton, Cadette (Birch), Blissett, Smillie.
Fulham: Stannard; Langley, Elkins, Wilson, Eckhardt, Thomas, Skinner, Sayer, Barnett, Cole, Walker (Davies) (Gore).
aet; Brentford won 3-2 on aggregate

Burnley (1) 2 *(O'Connell 2)*

Rochdale (0) 1 *(O'Shaughnessy)* 6673

Burnley: Pearce; Daniel, Deakin, Farrell, Davis, Gardner, Britton, Oghani, O'Connell, Comstive, Atkinson.
Rochdale: Welch; Copeland, Armitage, Hughes (Smart), Sutton, Reid, Harris, Walling, Smith, O'Shaughnessy, Frain.
Burnley won 5-4 on aggregate

Chesterfield (1) 1 *(Waller)*

Port Vale (1) 1 *(Earle)* 2709

Chesterfield: Astbury; Hewitt, McGeeney, Henderson, Wood, Hunter, Eley, Arnott, Waller, Morris, Thompson (Alleyne).
Port Vale: Grew; Webb, Hughes, Walker, Hazell, Sproson, Ford, Earle, Futcher, Beckford, Atkinson (Riley).
Port Vale won 4-3 on aggregate

Darlington (2) 2 *(Moore, Macdonald)*

Doncaster R (0) 0 1366

Darlington: Smallwood; Willis, Morgan, Hine, Moore, McAughtrie, Emson, Robinson N, Macdonald, Caizley, Stonehouse.
Doncaster R: Malcolm; Douglas R, Raffell, Beattie, Raven (Peckett) (Gorman), Robinson L, Gaughan, Rankine, Dobson, Kimble.
Darlington won 3-1 on aggregate

Gillingham (2) 3 *(Lovell, Lillis 2)*

Cambridge U (0) 1 *(Clayton)* 3066

Gillingham: Hillyard; Haylock, Gernon, Peacock, Weatherly, Walker, Shipley, Quow, Lovell, Lillis (West), Smith D.
Cambridge U: Vaughan; Bailie, Kimble (Allen), Daish, Chapple, Hamilton, Clayton, Ryan, Taylor (Bull), Turner, Leadbitter.
Gillingham won 5-2 on aggregate

Halifax T (1) 2 *(Allison, McPhillips)*

Scarborough (2) 2 *(Richards, Cook (pen))* 1713

Halifax T: Roche; Barr W, Logan, Matthews M, Bramhall, Whitehead, Martin (Watson), Horner, McPhillips, Allison, Richardson.
Scarborough: Blackwell; Kamara, Thompson, Short, Richards, Bennyworth, Morris (Adams), Cook, Norris, Brook, Graham.
aet; Scarborough won on away goals

Huddersfield T (0) 2 *(Maskell, Trevitt)*

Scunthorpe U (1) 2 *(Flounders 2)* 4237

Huddersfield T: Hardwick; Trevitt, Hutchings, Holmes (Byrne), Tucker, Shotton, Mitchell, O'Regan (Brown), Withe, Maskell, Marsden.
Scunthorpe U: Musselwhite; Longden, Stevenson, Taylor, Lister, Brown, Hodkinson, Money, Daws, Flounders, Cowling.
aet; Scunthorpe U won 5-4 on aggregate

Mansfield T (0) 1 *(Hodges)*

Notts Co (0) 0 2695

Mansfield T: Cox; McKernon, Kenworthy, Lowery, Foster, Coleman, Stringfellow, Kearney, Hodges, Cassells, Charles.
Notts Co: Leonard; Norton, Withe, O'Riordan, Yates, Law, Mills (Lund), McParland, Birtles, Pike (McStay), Draper.
Notts Co won 5-1 on aggregate

Northampton T (3) 5 *(Singleton, Culpin, Adcock 2, Gilbert (pen))*

Colchester U (0) 0 3957

Northampton T: Gleasure; McGoldrick, Thomas, Donald, Flexney, Reed, Singleton (Slack), Culpin, Gilbert, Adcock, Wilson.
Colchester U: Walton; English, Cartwright, Barnett, Hetzke (Bedford), Hill, Wilkins, White, Tempest, Swindlehurst, Grenfell (Radford).
Northampton T won 5-0 on aggregate

Plymouth Arg (2) 3 *(McCarthy 2, Marker)*

Hereford U (1) 2 *(Stant, Tester)* 4772

Plymouth Arg: Cherry; Brimacombe, Cooper, Burrows, Marker, Smith, Uzzell, Matthews, Tynan, McCarthy, Summerfield.
Hereford U: Rose; Williams, Crane, Stevens, Devine, Maddy, Mardenborough, Benbow, Stant, Tester, McLoughlin.
Plymouth Arg won 6-2 on aggregate

Preston NE (1) 1 *(Brazil)*

Wigan Ath (0) 0 4945

Preston NE: Brown; Rathbone, McAteer, Atkins, Jones, Allardyce, Mooney (Swann), Joyce, Ellis, Brazil, Patterson.
Wigan Ath: Hughes; Senior, Tankard, Butler, Beesley, Holden, Thompson, Pilling, Hilditch, Russell (McEwan), Rimmer.
Preston NE won 1-0 on aggregate

Rotherham U (1) 1 *(Grealish)*

Grimsby T (0) 0 3381

Rotherham U: O'Hanlon; Russell, Crosby, Grealish, Johnson, Green, Buckley, Williams, Williamson, Haycock (Mendonca), Heard (Goodwin).
Grimsby T: Reece; Lever, Agnew, Williams, Tillson, Cunnington, Jobling, North, O'Kelly, Stoutt (McDermott), Alexander (Saunders).
Rotherham U won 2-0 on aggregate

Sheffield U (0) 2 *(Agana, Duffield)*

Hartlepool U (0) 0 6577

Sheffield U: Benstead; Wilder, Pike, Webster, Stancliffe, Smith, Roberts (Duffield), Todd, Agana, Deane, Bryson.
Hartlepool U: McKellar; Haigh, McKinnon, Dixon, Smith, Stokes, Honour, Toman, Grayson, Borthwick (Atkinson), Barratt (Ogden).
aet; Sheffield U won 4-2 on aggregate

Sunderland (2) 4 *(Gabbiadini 2, Pascoe 2)*

York C (0) 0 9388

Sunderland: Hesford; Kay, Gray, Bennett (Ord), MacPhail, Doyle, Owers, Armstrong, Gates (Cornforth), Gabbiadini, Pascoe.
York C: Marples; Bradshaw, Branagan, Clegg, Fazackerley, Butler, Howlett, Spooner, Helliwell, Banton, Himsworth.
Sunderland won 4-0 on aggregate

Walsall (0) 3 *(Goodwin, Hawker, Taylor A)*

Shrewsbury T (0) 0 5552

Walsall: Barber; Dornan, Taylor M, Shakespeare, Forbes, Hart, Hawker (Bertschin), Goodwin, Taylor A, Christie, Naughton.
Shrewsbury T: Perks; Williams W, Williams B, Priest (Melrose), Green, Finley, Brown, McNally, Geddis, Irvine, Thomas (Kasule).
Walsall won 5-2 on aggregate

Wrexham (2) 2 *(Buxton, Cooper)*

Bury (0) 2 *(Robinson (pen), Entwistle)* 2634

Wrexham: Salmon; Salathiel, Wright, Bowden, Jones, Beaumont, Flynn (Hunter), Thackeray, Buxton (Carter), Russell, Cooper.
Bury: Farnworth; Hill, Bishop, Parkinson, Clements, Higgins, Lee, Robinson (Entwistle), Hoyland, McIlroy, Pashley.
aet; Bury won 4-3 on aggregate

7 SEPT

Brighton & HA (0) 0

Southend U (0) 1 *(Ling)* 4614

Brighton & HA: Keeley; Chivers, Dublin, Curbishley, Isaac, Gatting, Nelson, Owers, Wood (Armstrong), Wilkins, Penney.
Southend U: Sansome; O'Shea, Johnson, Martin, Westley, Brush, Butler, Hall, Crown, McDonough, Ling.
Southend U won 3-0 on aggregate

Bristol R (0) 0

Bournemouth (0) 0 4057

Bristol R: Martyn; Alexander, Twentyman, Clark, Mehew (Smith), Jones, Holloway, Reece (McClean), White, Penrice, Purnell.
Bournemouth: Peyton; Newson, Morrell, Bond, Williams, Whitlock, O'Driscoll, Brooks, Aylott, Bishop, Richards.
Bournemouth won 1-0 on aggregate

Chester C (2) 3 *(Lightfoot, Winstanley (og), Barrow)*

Bolton W (0) 1 *(Cowdrill)* 3784

Chester C: Stewart; Glenn, Woodthorpe, Hinnigan, Abel, Lightfoot, Jakub, Barrow, Benjamin (Bennett), Johnson, Newhouse.
Bolton W: Felgate; Brown, Cowdrill, Brookman, Came (Crombie), Winstanley, Henshaw, Thompson, Thomas, Elliott (Stevens), Darby.
Chester C won 3-2 on aggregate

Exeter C (0) 0

Bristol C (0) 1 *(Walsh)* 2749

Exeter C: Gwinnett; Banks, Viney, Rogers, Taylor, Cooper, Rowbotham, Hiley, Batty, Neville, Harrower.
Bristol C: Waugh; Llewellyn, Bromage, Mardon, Pender, McClaren, Newman, Galliers, Shutt, Walsh, Jordan (Milne).
Bristol C won 2-0 on aggregate

Lincoln C (1) 2 *(Macowat (og), Gamble)*

Crewe Alex (0) 1 *(Fishenden)* 2616

Lincoln C: Wallington; Evans, Nicholson, Clarke (Gamble), Bressington, Matthewson, Davis, James, Brown, Smith, Sertori.
Crewe Alex: Greygoose; Goodison (Walters), Edwards, Callaghan, Macowat, Jones, Jasper, Murphy, Cutler (Morton), Sussex, Fishenden.
Lincoln C won 3-2 on aggregate

Peterborough U (0) 0

WBA (2) 2 *(Gray (pen), Palmer)* 4216

Peterborough U: Neenan; Langan, Collins, Gooding, McElhinney, Oakes, Genovese, Halsall, Cusack, Gunn, Luke.
WBA: Naylor; Hodson, Burrows, Robson, Whyte, North, Hopkins, Goodman, Gray (Easter), Palmer, Anderson.
Peterborough U won 3-2 on aggregate

Reading (0) 3 *(Tait, Beavon (pen), Moran)*

Torquay U (1) 1 *(Dawkins)* 3883

Reading: Francis; Elsey, Richardson, Tait, Hicks, Curle, Jones, Taylor (Beavon), Whitehurst, Moran, Gilkes.
Torquay U: Crichton; Holmes, Kelly, McNichol, Cole, Joyce, Pugh, Lloyd, Edwards (Smith), Dawkins, Gibbins.
Reading won 4-1 on aggregate

20 SEPT

Swansea C (0)

Cardiff C (0) 2 *(Wheeler, Boyle)* 6987

Swansea C: Bracey; Hough, Coleman, Melville, Knill, James, Thornber, Hutchison (D'Auria), Love, Davies, Raynor.
Cardiff C: Wood; Rodgerson, Platnauer, Wimbleton, Stevenson, Boyle, Lynex, Curtis (Wheeler), Gilligan, Gummer, Kelly.
Cardiff won 2-1 on aggregate

SECOND ROUND FIRST LEG

26 SEPT

Port Vale (1) 1 *(Sproson)*

Ipswich T (0) 0 6545

Port Vale: Grew; Webb, Hughes, Walker (Finney), Mills, Sproson, Ford, Earle, Futcher, Beckford, Riley.
Ipswich T: Forrest; Yallop, Hill, Stockwell, D'Avray, Harbey, Lowe, Dozzell, Milton, Atkinson, Wark.

27 SEPT

Barnsley (0) 0

Wimbledon (1) 2 *(Fashanu 2)* 5194

Barnsley: Baker; Joyce, Beresford, Thomas, McGugan, Futcher, Lowndes, Agnew, Rees, Currie, Broddle.
Wimbledon: Green; Joseph, Clement, Jones, Young, Scales, Brooke, Cork (Turner), Fashanu, Sanchez, Wise.

Birmingham C (0) 0

Aston Villa (2) 2 *(Gage, Gray A)* 21,177

Birmingham C: Godden; Ranson (Bremner), Roberts, Atkins, Overson, Clarkson, Morris, Langley, Yates, Robinson (Whitton), Wigley.
Aston Villa: Spink; Price, Mountfield, Gray A, Gage, Keown, Daley, Platt, Thompson, Cowans, Gallacher.

Blackburn R (2) 3 *(Gayle, Sellars, Garner)*

Brentford (1) 1 *(Blissett)* 4606

Blackburn R: O'Keefe; Atkins, Millar, Finnigan, Hendry, Mail, Miller, Reid, Gayle (Curry), Garner, Sellars.
Brentford: Parks; Bakes, Stanislaus, Millen, Evans, Booker (Perryman), Jones, Sinton, Cadette, Blissett, Smillie.

Blackpool (2) 2 *(Coughlin, Cunningham)*

Sheffield W (0) 0 5492

Blackpool: Siddall; Burgess, Morgan, Deary, Methven, Elliott, Davies (Walwyn), Cunningham, Garner, Coughlin, Taylor.
Sheffield W: Pressman; Sterland, Worthington, Pearson, Madden, Cranson, Megson, Hirst, Reeves, Jonsson, Bradshaw (Galvin).

Bournemouth (0) 0

Coventry C (2) 4 *(Downs, Gynn 2, Bannister)* 6543

Bournemouth: Peyton; Newson, Morrell, Bond, Williams, Whitlock (Richards), Cooke, Brooks (O'Driscoll), Aylott, Bishop, Close.
Coventry C: Ogrizovic; Borrows, Downs, Sedgley, Kilcline, Peake, Gynn, Speedie, Regis, Bannister, Smith.

Darlington (2) 2 *(Hyde, Clayton)*

Oldham Ath (0) 0 1655

Darlington: Batch; Robinson N, Morgan, Hine, Moore (Anderson), Willis, Caizley, Hyde, MacDonald, Clayton, Stonehouse.
Oldham Ath: Rhodes; Irwin, Barlow, Barrett, Marshall, Donachie (Williams), Palmer, Kelly, Cecere, Ritchie (Philliskirk), Wright.

Everton (0) 3 *(Sharp, McDonald (pen), McCall)*

Bury (0) 0 11,071

Everton: Southall; McDonald, Wilson, Snodin, Van Den Hauwe, Reid (Clarke), Heath, McCall, Sharp, Cottee, Sheedy.
Bury: Farnworth; Hill, Bishop, Valentine, Clements (Brotherston), Higgins, Lee, Robinson, Hoyland, McIlroy, Greenwood (Pashley).

Leyton Orient (1) 1 *(Juryeff)*

Stoke C (0) 2 *(Morgan, Kamara)* 3154

Leyton Orient: Wells; Howard, Dickenson, Hales, Day, Ward, Baker, Harvey (Ketteridge), Shinners, Juryeff, Comfort.
Stoke C: Fox; Ford, Beeston (Gidman), Kamara, Hemming, Henry, Hackett, Saunders, Morgan, Stainrod, Beagrie.

Luton T (1) 1 *(Johnson R)*

Burnley (1) 1 *(Comstive)* 6282

Luton T: Sealey; Johnson R (Breacker), Dreyer, Williams, Foster, Donaghy, Wilson, Oldfield, Harford, Hill, Black.
Burnley: Pearce; Daniel, Farrell, Rowell, Davis, Gardner, Britton, Oghani, O'Connell, Comstive, Atkinson.

Millwall (1) 3 *(Sheringham, Ruddock 2)*

Gillingham (0) 0 6518

Millwall: Horne; Stevens, Dawes, Hurlock, Wood, McLeary, Lawrence, Ruddock, Sheringham, Cascarino, O'Callaghan.
Gillingham: Hillyard; Burley, Haylock, Peacock, West (Docker), Walker, Perry, Quow, Lovell, Cooper, Weatherly.

Northampton T (1) 1 *(Culpin)*

Charlton Ath (0) 1 *(Williams)* 5290

Northampton T: Gleasure; McGoldrick, Thomas, Donald, Flexney, Reed, Singleton, Culpin, Gilbert, Adcock, Garwood.
Charlton Ath: Bolder; Humphrey, Reid, Campbell (Mortimer), Shirtliff, Pitcher, Bennett, Williams, Peake, Leaburn, Stuart (Jones).

Notts Co (0) 1 *(Birtles)*

Tottenham H (0) 1 *(Samways)* 9279

Notts Co: Leonard; McStay, Withe, Kevan, Yates, Law, Mills, McParland, Birtles (Johnson), Pike, Thorpe.
Tottenham H: Mimms; Statham, Thomas, Fenwick, Fairclough, Mabbutt, Walsh, Gascoigne, Waddle, Samways, Allen.

Peterborough U (1) *(Goldsmith)*

Leeds U (2) 2 *(Pearson, Baird)* 4979

Peterborough U: Neenan; Langan, Gunn, Luke, McElhinney (Collins), Oakes, Andrews, Halsall, Cusack, Madrick (Genovese), Goldsmith.
Leeds U: Day; Williams (Haddock), Adams, Aizlewood, Blake, Rennie, Batty, Snodin, Baird, Pearson, Hilaire.

Portsmouth (1) 2 *(Quinn, Connor)*

Scarborough (0) 2 *(Thompson, Cooke (pen))* 4742

Portsmouth: Knight; Sandford, Russell, Dillon, Hogg, Whitehead, Aspinall, Fillery (Darby), Quinn, Connor, Kelly.
Scarborough: Charlton; Kamara, Thompson, Short, Richards, Bennyworth, Morris, Cook, Norris, Brook (Adams), Graham.

Scunthorpe U (1) 4 *(Daws 2, Stevenson, Taylor)*

Chelsea (1) 1 *(Lister (og))* 5061

Scunthorpe U: Musselwhite; Longden, Stevenson, Taylor, Lister, Brown, Hodkinson, Harle, Daws, Flounders, Richardson.
Chelsea: Freestone; Clarke, Dorigo, Roberts, Pates, Wilson C, McAllister, Nicholas, Dixon, Wilson K, Bumstead.

Sheffield U (2) 3 *(Deane 2, Stancliffe)*

Newcastle U (0) 0 17,900

Sheffield U: Benstead; Wilder, Pike, Webster, Stancliffe, Smith, Roberts, Todd, Agana, Deane, Bryson.
Newcastle U: Beasant; Anderson, Wharton, Jackson, Scott, Thorn, Hendrie, Cornwell, O'Neill (Robertson), Mirandinha, Tinnion.

Sunderland (0) 0

West Ham U (1) 3 *(Kelly 2, Rosenior)* 13,691

Sunderland: Hesford; Kay, Agboola, Bennett (Gray), MacPhail, Doyle, Owers, Armstrong, Gates, Gabbiadini, Pascoe.
West Ham U: McKnight; Parris, Dicks, Hilton, Martin (Potts), Ince, Ward, Kelly, Rosenior, Dickens, Robson.

Swindon T (1) 1 *(Shearer)*

Crystal Palace (1) 2 *(Bright, Wright)* 7084

Swindon T: Digby; Hockaday, King, MacLaren, Parkin, Gittens, Foley, Calderwood (Jones), Shearer, White, Barnes.
Crystal Palace: Parkin; Pemberton, Burke, Pardew, Hopkins, Hone, Redfearn, Thomas, Bright, Wright, Barber.

28 SEPT

Derby Co (1) 1 *(Hebberd)*

Southend U (0) 0 9703

Derby Co: Shilton; Sage, Forsyth, Williams, Wright, Blades, McMinn, Penney (Micklewhite), Goddard, Hebberd, Pickering.
Southend U: Sansome; Edinburgh, Johnson, Martin, Brush, O'Shea, Butler, Hall, Crown, McDonough, Ling.

Hull C (1) 1 *(Edwards)*

Arsenal (1) 2 *(Winterburn, Marwood)* 11,450

Hull C: Norman; Palmer, Thompson, Warren, Jobson, Terry, Smith (Moore), Roberts, Payton, Edwards, Dyer.
Arsenal: Lukic; Dixon, Winterburn, Thomas (Richardson), Bould, Adams, Rocastle (Hayes), Davis, Smith, Groves, Marwood.

Leicester C (2) 4 *(Reid, Walsh, Cross, McAllister (pen))*

Watford (1) 1 *(Wilkinson)* 9512

Leicester C: Cooper; Mauchlen, Morgan, Ramsey (Paris), Walsh, Brown, Reid, Cross, Newell, McAllister, Weir (Quinn).
Watford: Coton; Pullan (Sherwood), Falconer, Jackett, Holdsworth David, McClelland, Sterling, Wilkinson, Bamber (Roberts), Porter, Holden.

Lincoln C (0) 1 *(Clarke)*

Southampton (1) 1 *(Rideout)* 5404

Lincoln C: Wallington; Evans, Nicholson, Brown, Bressington, Matthewson, Davis, Cumming, Hobson, Gamble (Clarke), Sertori.
Southampton: Burridge; Forrest, Statham, Case, Moore, Osman, Wallace Rodney, Baker, Clarke, Rideout, Wallace D.

Liverpool (1) 1 *(Gillespie)*

Walsall (0) 0 18,084

Liverpool: Hooper; Gillespie, Ablett, Nicol, Whelan, Molby, Beardsley, Aldridge (Dalglish), Rush, Houghton, Staunton (MacDonald).
Walsall: Barber; Taylor M, Mower, Shakespeare, Forbes, Hart, Hawker, Bertschin, Taylor A, Pritchard, Naughton.

Manchester C (1) 1 *(White)*

Plymouth Arg (0) 0 9454

Manchester C: Dibble; Biggins (Simpson), Hinchcliffe, Gayle, Brightwell, Redmond, White, Moulden (Beckford), Morley, McNab, Lake.
Plymouth Arg: Cherry; Brown, Cooper, Burrows, Marker, Smith, Plummer, Matthews, Tynan, McCarthy, Brimacombe.

Middlesbrough (0) 0

Tranmere R (0) 0 12,084

Middlesbrough: Pears; Parkinson, Cooper, Mowbray, Hamilton, Pallister, Slaven, Brennan, Senior (Kernaghan), Kerr, Ripley (Gill).
Tranmere R: Nixon; Higgins, McGarrick, Bishop, Hughes, Vickers, Morrissey, Harvey, Steel, Muir, Mungall.

Norwich C (1) 2 *(Rosario, Crook)*

Preston NE (0) 0 7484

Norwich C: Gunn; Culverhouse, Bowen, Butterworth, Linighan, Crook (Townsend), Gordon, Fleck (Allen), Rosario, Phelan, Putney.
Preston NE: Brown; Rathbone, McAteer, Atkins, Jones, Allardyce, Miller (Mooney), Swann, Ellis, Brazil, Patterson.

Nottingham F (3) 6 *(Pearce, Clough 2, Webb, Hodge, Gaynor)*

Chester C (0) 0 11,958

Nottingham F: Sutton; Chettle (Fleming), Pearce, Walker, Foster, Hodge, Crosby, Webb, Clough, Gaynor, Rice.
Chester C: Stewart; Glenn, Woodthorpe, Kelly, Abel, Lightfoot, Jakub, Barrow, Dale (Bennett), Johnson, Newhouse.

Oxford U (1) 2 *(Saunders 2)*

Bristol C (2) 4 *(Walsh, Hawkins, Shutt, Milne)* 3705

Oxford U: Hucker; Bardsley, Smart, Phillips L, Hill, Greenall, Heath (Purdie), Foyle, Saunders, Mustoe, Rhoades-Brown.
Bristol C: Leaning; Llewellyn, Bromage, Newman, Pender, McClaren, Milne, Galliers, Shutt (Mardon), Walsh, Hawkins.

QPR (2) 3 *(Francis, Fereday, Allen)*

Cardiff C (0) 0 6078

QPR: Johns; Kerslake, Dennis, Parker, McDonald, Maddix, Allen, Francis, Fereday (Barker), Stein (Maguire), Brock.
Cardiff C: Wood; Rodgerson, Platnauer, Wimbleton, Stevenson, Boyle, Lynex (Wheeler) (Morgan), Curtis, Gilligan, Bater, Kelly.

Reading (0) 1 *(Tait)*

Bradford C (0) 1 *(Ormondroyd)* 4013

Reading: Francis; Franklin, Elsey, Beavon, Hicks, Curle, Knight (Jones), Tait, Gordon (Conroy), Moran, Gilkes.
Bradford C: Tomlinson; Mitchell, Jackson, Banks, Oliver, Evans, Thomas, Sinnott, Ormondroyd, Kennedy, Leonard.

Rotherham U (0) 0

Manchester U (0) 1 *(Davenport)* 12,592

Rotherham U: O'Hanlon; Russell, Crosby, Grealish (Goodwin), Johnson, Green, Buckley, Williams, Williamson, Haycock, Heard.
Manchester U: Leighton; Blackmore, Sharpe (Beardsmore), Bruce, McGrath, Duxbury, Robson, Stachan (Olsen), McClair, Hughes, Davenport.

SECOND ROUND SECOND LEG
11 OCT

Bristol C (1) 2 *(Shutt, McClaren)*

Oxford U (0) 0 6255

Bristol C: Leaning; Llewellyn, Humphries, Newman,

Pender, McClaren, Gavin (Mardon), Galliers, Shutt, Walsh, Jordan (Hawkins).
Oxford U: Judge; Bardsley, Phillips J, Phillips L, Briggs, Greenall, Purdie, Foyle, Saunders, Mustoe (Hill), Rhoades-Brown (Heath).
Bristol C won 6-2 on aggregate.

Burnley (0) 0

Luton T (0) 1 *(Hill)* 14,021

Burnley: Pearce; Daniel, Farrell, Rowell, Zelem, Gardner, Britton, Oghani, O'Connell, Comstive, Atkinson.
Luton T: Sealey; Johnson R (Breacker), Dreyer, Williams, Foster, Donaghy, Wilson, Oldfield (Allinson), Harford, Hill, Black.
Luton T won 2-1 on aggregate.

Bury (0) 2 *(Lee, Hoyland)*

Everton (2) 2 *(Steven (pen), Sharp)* 4592

Bury: Farnworth; Hill, Bishop, Hoyland, Valentine, Clements, Lee, Robinson, Greenwood (Brotherston), McIlroy, Pashley (Parkinson).
Everton: Southall; Snodin, Van Den Hauwe (Pointon), Ratcliffe, Watson, Reid, Heath, Wilson, Sharp, Cottee, Steven.
Everton won 5-2 on aggegate.

Cardiff C (1) 1 *(Curtis)*

QPR (1) 4 *(Stein, Falco 2, Maddix)* 2692

Cardiff C: Wood; Perry, Abrahams, Morgan, Stevenson, Boyle, Curtis (Lewis), Bartlett, Gilligan, Wheeler, Fry.
QPR: Johns; Barker, Maguire, Parker, McDonald, Maddix, Falco, Francis (Coney), Fereday, Stein, Brock (Kerslake).
QPR won 7-1 on aggregate.

Charlton Ath (2) 2 *(Reid (pen), Jones)*

Northampton T (1) 1 *(Wilson)* 2782

Charlton Ath: Bolder; Humphrey, Reid, MacKenzie, Shirtliff, Elliott, Bennett, Williams, Jones, Campbell (Stuart), Mortimer.
Northampton T: Gleasure; McGoldrick, Thomas, Donald, Flexney, McPherson, Singleton, Sandeman (Preece), Gilbert, Adcock, Wilson.
Charlton Ath won 3-2 on aggegate.

Coventry C (1) 3 *(Sedgley, Speedie, Gynn)*

Bournemouth (0) 1 *(Cooke)* 7212

Coventry C: Ogrizovic; Borrows, Downs (Dobson), Sedgley, Kilcline, Peake, Gynn, Speedie (Thompson), Regis, Bannister, Smith.
Bournemouth: Peyton; O'Driscoll, Morrell, Bond, Williams, Pulis, Close, Brooks, Puckett (O'Connor), Bishop (Cooke), Coleman.
Coventry C won 7-1 on aggregate.

Gillingham (1) 1 *(Quow (pen))*

Millwall (1) 3 *(Sheringham 2, Salman)* 5729

Gillingham: Kite; Burley, Haylock, Peacock, Clarke (Lillis), Walker, Perry, Quow, Cooper, Weatherly, Docker (Haines).
Millwall: Horne; Stevens, Dawes, Hurlock, Wood, McLeary, Horrix (Sparham), Morgan, Sheringham, Cascarino, Salman.
Millwall won 6-2 on aggregate.

Ipswich T (1) 3 *(Lowe, Atkinson 2)*

Port Vale (0) 0 8869

Ipswich T: Forrest; Yallop, Harbey, Zondervan, Humes, Linighan, Lowe, Stockwell, Milton, Atkinson, Kiwomya.
Port Vale: Grew; Webb, Hughes, Walker, Mills. Sproson, Ford, Earle, Futcher, Beckford, Riley.
Ipswich T won 3-1 on aggregate.

Oldham Ath (0) 4 *(Ritchie, Williams, Philliskirk, Bunn)*

Darlington (0) 0 4543

Oldham Ath: Dubose; Donachie, Blundell (Philliskirk), Barrett, Marshall, Williams, Palmer, Kelly, Bunn, Wright (Cecere), Ritchie.
Darlington: Batch; Robinson N, Morgan, Hine, Moore, Willis (Anderson), Caizley (Worthington), Hyde, MacDonald, Smith, Stonehouse.
aet; Oldham Ath won 4-2 on aggregate.

Preston NE (0) 0

Norwich C (1) 3 *(Fleck, Gordon, Rosario)* 7002

Preston NE: Brown; Williams N, Rathbone, Atkins, Wrightson, Hughes (Jones), Mooney, Joyce, Ellis, Swann, Patterson.
Norwich C: Gunn; Culverhouse, Bowen, Butterworth, Linighan, Crook, Gordon, Fleck, Rosario, Phelan, Putney.
Norwich C won 5-0 on aggregate.

Southampton (1) 3 *(Wallace R, Baker 2)*

Lincoln C (1) 1 *(Hobson)* 6401

Southampton: Burridge; Forrest, Statham, Case (Benali), Blake, Osman, Wallace Rodney, Baker, Clarke, Rideout, Wallace D.
Lincoln C: Wallington; Evans, Nicholson, Brown, Bressington, Matthewson, Davis, Clarke, Hobson, Gamble, Sertori.
Southampton won 4-2 on aggregate.

Southend U (1) 1 *(Ling)*

Derby Co (2) 2 *(Penney, Hebberd)* 4422

Southend U: Sansome; Edinburgh (Clark), Johnson, O'Shea, Westley, Brush, Butler, Hall (McDonough), Crown, Martin, Ling.
Derby Co: Shilton; Sage, Forsyth, Williams, Wright, Blades, McMinn, Penney, Goddard, Hebberd, Pickering.
Derby Co won 3-1 on aggregate.

Stoke C (0) 1 *(Stainrod (pen))*

Leyton Orient (1) 2 *(Hales (pen), Comfort)* 5756

Stoke C: Barrett; Gidman (Carr), Beeston, Kamara, Hemming, Henry, Hackett (Ware), Ford, Shaw, Stainrod, Beagrie.
Leyton Orient: Wells; Howard, Dickenson, Hales, Day, Sitton, Baker (Harvey), Ward, Hull, Juryeff, Comfort.
aet; Leyton Orient won 3-2 on penalties after 3-3 on aggregate.

Tottenham H (0) 2 *(Fenwick (pen), Gascoigne)*

Notts Co (0) 1 *(Thorpe)* 14,953

Tottenham H: Mimms; Statham, Thomas, Fenwick, Allen, Mabbutt, Walsh, Gascoigne, Waddle, Samways, Stewart (Howells).
Notts Co: Leonard; McStay, Withe, Kevan, Yates, Law, Mills, McParland, Birtles, Pike, Thorpe.
Tottenham H won 3-2 on aggregate.

Tranmere R (1) 1 *(Hughes)*

Middlesbrough (0) 0 8617

Tranmere R: Nixon; Higgins, McCarrick, Bishop, Hughes, Vickers, Murray, Harvey, Steel, Muir, Mungall.
Middlesbrough: Pears; Parkinson, Cooper, Mowbray, Hamilton, Pallister, Slaven, Brennan, Burke, Kerr, Ripley (Kernaghan).
Tranmere R won 1-0 on aggregate.

Watford (1) 2 *(Bamber, Rimmer)*

Leicester C (0) 2 *(Mauchlen, Newell)* 9087

Watford: Coton; Gibbs, Rostron, Sherwood, Holdsworth David, Falconer, Sterling, Bamber, Blissett (Rimmer), Porter, Holden (Thomas).
Leicester C: Cooper; Paris, Morgan, Mauchlen, Walsh, Brown, Reid, Cross, Newell, McAllister, Williams.
Leicester C won 6-3 on aggregate.

12 OCT

Arsenal (1) 3 *(Merson, Smith 2)*

Hull C (0) 0 17,885

Arsenal: Lukic; Dixon, Winterburn, Thomas, Bould, Adams, Rocastle, Davis (Richardson), Smith, Merson (Hayes), Marwood.
Hull C: Norman; Warren, Jacobs, De Mange, Jobson, Terry, Saville, Roberts, Moore (Payton), Edwards, Dyer.
Arsenal won 5-1 on aggregate.

Aston Villa (4) 5 *(Mountfield, Gage 2, Olney, Daley)*

Birmingham C (0) 0 19,753

Aston Villa: Spink; Price, Mountfield, Evans, Gage, Sims, Daley, Platt, Olney, Cowans, Gray S (Gallacher).
Birmingham C: Elliott; Ranson (Surridge), Frain, Atkins, Overson, Clarkson, Bremner, Peer, Morris (Childs), Robinson, Wigley.
Aston Villa won 7-0 on aggregate.

Bradford C (0) 2 *(Banks 2)*

Reading (0) 1 *(Jones)* 6256

Bradford C: Tomlinson; Mitchell, Goddard, Banks, Oliver, Jackson, Thomas (Palin), Sinnott, Ormondroyd, Kennedy (Abbott), Jewell.
Reading: Francis; Franklin, Richardson, Beavon, Hicks, Curle, Jones, Elsey, Tait, Moran, Gilkes.
aet; Bradford C won 3-2 on aggregate.

Brentford (1) 4 *(Cadette 2, Sinton, Jones)*

Blackburn R (1) 3 *(Garner, Atkins, Sellars)* 3844

Brentford: Smeulders; Bates, Stanislaus, Millen, Evans, Cockram (Feeley), Jones, Sinton, Cadette, Blissett, Smillie (Booker).
Blackburn R: Gennoe; Atkins, Millar, Ainscow, Hendry, Mail, Gayle, Reid, Kennedy, Garner, Sellars.
Blackburn R won 6-5 on aggregate.

Chelsea (1) 2 *(Wilson K, Dixon)*

Scunthorpe U (1) 2 *(Harle (pen), Flounders)* 5814

Chelsea: Freestone; Hall, Dorigo, Roberts, Pates, Wilson K, McAllister (Wilson C), Nicholas, Dixon, Durie, Bumstead.
Scunthorpe U: Musselwhite; Smalley, Longden, Taylor, Lister, Stevenson, Hodkinson, Harle, Daws, Flounders (Richardson), Brown.
Scunthorpe U won 6-3 on aggregate.

Chester C (0) 0

Nottingham F (1) 4 *(Gaynor 3, Crosby)* 4747

Chester C: Stewart; Glenn, Woodthorpe, Hinnigan (Bennett), Abel, Lightfoot, Jakub, Barrow, Newhouse (Dale), Johnson, Kelly.
Nottingham F: Sutton; Fleming, Pearce, Walker, Foster, Hodge, Carr, Webb (Parker), Gaynor, Crosby (Laws), Rice.
Nottingham F won 10-0 on aggregate.

Crystal Palace (1) 2 *(Henry (og), Thomas)*

Swindon T (0)0 6015

Crystal Palace: Parkin; Pemberton, Burke, Pardew (Shaw), Hopkins, O'Reilly, Redfearn, Thomas, Bright, Wright, Barber (Salako).
Swindon T: Digby; Hockaday, King, Gittens, Henry, Jones, Foley, Calderwood, Shearer, White, Barnes.
Crystal Palace won 4-1 on aggregate.

Leeds U (1) 3 *(Davison, Hilaire, Sheridan (pen))*

Peterborough U (0) 1 *(Gunne (pen))* 8894

Leeds U: Day; Aspin, Snodin, Aizlewood, Blake, Rennie, Batty, Sheridan, Baird, Davison (Pearson), Hilaire.
Peterborough U: Neenan; Collins, Gunn, Luke, McElhinney, Oakes, Andrews, Halsall, Cusack, Longhurst, Goldsmith.
Leeds U won 5-2 on aggregate.

Manchester U (3) 5 *(McClair 3, Robson, Bruce)*

Rotherham U (0) 0 20,597

Manchester U: Leighton; Beardsmore, Blackmore, Bruce, Garton, Duxbury (Robins), Robson (Davenport), Strachan, McClair, Hughes, Sharpe.
Rotherham U: O'Hanlon; Russell, Crosby, Goodwin, Johnson, Buckley, Hazel, Williams, Williamson, Mendonca (Haycock), Heard.
Manchester U won 6-0 on aggregate.

Newcastle U (1) 2 *(Hendrie, Mirandinha)*

Sheffield U (0) 0 14,520

Newcastle U: Beasant; Anderson, Tinnion, Jackson (Bogie), Scott, Thorn, Stephenson (Robertson), Hendrie, Mirandinha, Wharton, O'Neill.
Sheffield U: Benstead; Wilder, Pike, Webster, Stancliffe, Smith, Roberts, Todd, Agana, Deane, Duffield (Joseph).
Sheffield U won 3-2 on aggregate.

Plymouth Arg (2) 3 *(Smith, McCarthy, Tynan)*

Manchester C (2) 6 *(Biggins, Gleghorn 2, Moulden, McNab (pen), Lake)* 8794

Plymouth Arg: Cherry; Brown, Cooper, Burrows, Marker, Smith, Plummer (Hodges), Matthews (Summerfield), Tynan, McCarthy, Brimacombe.
Manchester C: Dibble; Gleghorn, Hinchcliffe, Gayle, Biggins (Beckford), Redmond, White, Moulden, Morley, McNab, Lake.
Manchester C won 7-3 on aggregate.

Scarborough (1) 3 *(Norris, Cook, Graham)*

Portsmouth (0) 1 *(Aspinall)* 3802

Scarborough: Blackwell; Kamara, Thompson, Short, Richards, Bennyworth, Olsson, Cook, Norris, Brook, Graham.
Portsmouth: Knight; Neill, Hardyman (Dillon), Kuhl, Hogg, Whitehead, Connor, Horne, Aspinall, Quinn, Sandford.
Scarborough won 5-3 on aggregate.

Sheffield W (1) 3 *(Varadi, Reeves, Hirst)*

Blackpool (1) 1 *(Morgan)* 12,237

Sheffield W: Turner; Sterland, Worthington, Pearson, Madden, Cranson, Megson, Hirst (Galvin), Varadi (Reeves), West, Proctor.
Blackpool: Siddall; Burgess, Morgan, Deary, Methven, Walsh (Gore), Matthews, Cunningham, Garner, Coughlin, Walwyn (Madden).
aet; Blackpool won on away goals.

Walsall (0) 1 *(Shakespeare)*

Liverpool (1) 3 *(Barnes, Rush, Molby (pen))* 12,015

Walsall: Barber; Taylor M, Mower, Shakespeare, Forbes, Hart, Hawker, Pritchard, Taylor A (Jones P), Christie, Naughton (Bertschin).
Liverpool: Hooper; Ablett, Venison, Nicol, Whelan, Molby, Beardsley, Houghton, Rush, Barnes, MacDonald.
Liverpool won 4-1 on aggregate.

West Ham U (1) 2 *(Kelly, Dickens)*

Sunderland (0) 1 *(Gabbiadini)* 10,558

West Ham U: McKnight; Potts, Dicks, Gale, Hilton, Devonshire (Keen), Ward, Kelly, Parris, Dickens, Ince.
Sunderland: Hesford; Gray, Agboola, Ord, MacPhail, Doyle (Lemon), Owers, Armstrong, Gates, Gabbiadini, Pascoe (Ogilvie).
West Ham U won 5-1 on aggregate.

Wimbledon (0) 0

Barnsley (1) 1 *(Currie)* 2259

Wimbledon: Segers; Joseph, Clement, Jones, Young, Scales, Brooke (Phelan), Cork, Turner, Sanchez, Wise.
Barnsley: Baker; Joyce, Beresford, McGugan, Futcher, Thomas, Rees, Currie, Broddle, Dobbin, Lowndes.
Wimbledon won 2-1 on aggregate.

THIRD ROUND
1 NOV

Bristol C (3) 4 *(Shutt, Milne 2, Walsh)*

Crystal Palace (0) 1 *(Pardew)* 12,167

Bristol C: Waugh; Newman, Bailey, Humphries, Pender, McClaren, Milne, Galliers, Shutt, Walsh, Gavin.
Crystal Palace: Parkin; Pemberton, Hone, Pardew, Hopkins, O'Reilly, Redfearn, Thomas, Bright, Salako, Barber.

Ipswich T (0) 2 *(Dozzell, Stockwell)*

Leyton Orient (0) 0 9751

Ipswich T: Forrest; Yallop, Hill, Zondervan, Humes, Linighan, Lowe, Dozzell, D'Avray, Wark (Harbey), Stockwell.
Leyton Orient: Wells, Howard, Dickenson, Hales, Day, Sitton (Harvey), Baker, Ward, Hull, Juryeff, Comfort.

Tottenham H (0) 0

Blackburn R (0) 0 18,814

Tottenham H: Mimms; Stevens, Thomas, Fenwick, Fairclough, Mabbutt, Moran, Gascoigne (Samways), Waddle, Stewart, Allen.
Blackburn R: Gennoe; Atkins, Millar, Dawson, Hendry, Mail, Gayle, Reid, Curry, Garner, Sellars.

Tranmere R (0) 1 *(Bishop)*

Blackpool (0) 0 9454

Tranmere R: Nixon; Higgins, McCarrick, Bishop, Hughes, Vickers, Morrissey, Harvey, Steel, Muir, Mungall.
Blackpool: Siddall; Burgess, Morgan, Deary (Thompson), Methven, Elliott, Gore, Cunningham, Garner, Coughlin, Walwyn.

West Ham U (1) 5 *(Martin 2, Stewart (pen), Rosenior, Keen)*

Derby Co (0) 0 14,226

West Ham U: McKnight; Stewart, Dicks, Gale, Martin, Keen, Ward, Kelly, Rosenior, Dickens (Brady), Ince.
Derby Co: Shilton; Sage, Forsyth, Williams, Hindmarch, Blades, McMinn, Gee (Micklewhite), Goddard, Hebberd (Cross), Callaghan.

2 NOV

Aston Villa (2) 3 *(McInally 2, Platt)*

Millwall (1) 1 *(Ruddock)* 17,648

Aston Villa: Spink; Price, Mountfield, Evans, Gage, Keown, Daley, Platt, McInally, Cowans, Gallacher.
Millwall: Horne; Stevens (O'Callaghan), Dawes, Morgan, Thompson, McLeary, Salman, Briley, Sheringham, Cascarino, Ruddock.

Bradford C (1) 1 *(Jewell)*

Scunthorpe U (0) 1 *(Daws)* 8011

Bradford C: Litchfield; Mitchell, Sinnott, Abbott (Thomas), Jackson, Evans, Jewell, Palin, Ormondroyd (Chapman), Kennedy, Leonard.
Scunthorpe U: Musselwhite; Smalley, Longden, Money, Lister, Stevenson, Hodkinson, Harle, Daws, Flounders, Cowling.

Leeds U (0) 0

Luton T (1) 2 *(Wilson, Oldfield)* 19,447

Leeds U: Day; Aspin, Snodin, Aizlewood, Blake, Rennie, Batty, Sheridan, Baird, Davison, Hilaire.
Luton T: Sealey; James, Dreyer, Williams, Foster, Johnson M, Wilson, Oldfield, Wegerle, Hill, Black.

Leicester C (1) 2 *(Newell, Reid)*

Norwich C (0) 0 14,586

Leicester C: Cooper; Paris, Spearing, Mauchlen, Walsh, Morgan, Reid, Cross, Newell, McAllister, Russell.
Norwich C: Gunn; Culverhouse, Bowen (Allen), Butterworth, Linighan, Crook (Fox), Gordon, Fleck, Rosario, Phelan, Putney.

Liverpool (0) 1 *(Barnes)*

Arsenal (0) 1 *(Rocastle)* 31,961

Liverpool: Hooper; Ablett, Venison, Nicol, Whelan, Spackman, Beardsley, Aldridge, Rush, Barnes, Houghton.
Arsenal: Lukic; Dixon, Winterburn, Thomas, Bould, Adams, Rocastle, Richardson, Smith, Merson (Groves), Marwood.

Manchester C (2) 4 *(Moulden 3, Morley)*

Sheffield U (1) 2 *(Bryson, Duffield)* 16,609

Manchester C: Dibble; Seagraves, Hinchcliffe, Gayle, Brightwell, Redmond, Beckford (Scott), Moulden, Morley, McNab, Biggins.
Sheffield U: Benstead; Wilder, Pike, Webster (Duffield), Carr, Smith, Roberts, Todd, Agana, Deane, Bryson (Joseph).

Nottingham F (1) 3 *(Foster, Hodge, Clough)*

Coventry C (2) 2 *(Bannister, Kilcline (pen))* 21,201

Nottingham F: Crossley; Chettle, Pearce, Walker, Foster, Hodge, Charles, Wilson, Clough, Chapman, Rice.
Coventry C: Ogrizovic; Borrows, Downs, Sedgley, Kilcline (Houchen), Rodger, Phillips (Emerson), Speedie, Regis, Bannister, Smith.

QPR (0) 2 *(Francis 2)*

Charlton Ath (1) 1 *(Williams)* 8701

QPR: Seaman; Barker, Allen, Parker, McDonald, Maddix, Falco (Kerslake), Francis, Fereday, Stein, Brock.
Charlton Ath: Bolder; Humphrey, Reid, Peake, Shirtliff, Bennett (Jones), MacKenzie, Gritt, Leaburn (Lee), Mortimer, Williams.

Scarborough (1) 2 *(Norris, Cook)*

Southampton (2) 2 *(Case, Le Tissier)* 5877

Scarborough: Blackwell; Kamara, Thompson, Short, Richards, Bennyworth, Olsson, Cook, Norris, Brook, Graham.

Southampton: Burridge; Wallace Ray, Statham, Case, Moore, Osman, Wallace Rod, Cockerill, Le Tissier, Baker, Wallace D.

Wimbledon (1) 2 *(Gibson 2)*

Manchester U (1) 1 *(Robson)* 10,864

Wimbledon: Segers; Joseph, Phelan, Jones, Young, Scales, Wise, Gibson (Cork), Fashanu, Sanchez, Fairweather.
Manchester U: Leighton; Blackmore, Gibson, Bruce, Garton, Duxbury (Strachan), Robson, O'Brien, McClair, Hughes, Olsen (Anderson).

8 NOV

Everton (1) 1 *(Steven (pen))*

Oldham Ath (0) 1 *(Ritchie)* 17,230

Everton: Southall; Snodin, Van Den Hauwe, Ratcliffe, Watson, Reid, Steven, McCall, Sharp, Cottee, Wilson (Adams).
Oldham Ath: Rhodes; Irwin, Barrett, Skipper, Marshall (Flynn), Milligan, Palmer, Kelly, Bunn, Ritchie, Wright.

THIRD ROUND REPLAYS
9 NOV

Arsenal (0) 0

Liverpool (0) 0 *aet* 54,029

Arsenal: Lukic; Dixon, Winterburn, Thomas, Bould, Adams, Rocastle, Richardson, Smith, Merson (Hayes), Marwood.
Liverpool: Hooper; Ablett, Staunton, Nicol, Whelan, Spackman, Beardsley, Aldridge, Houghton, Barnes, McMahon.

Blackburn R (0) 1 *(Butters (og))*

Tottenham H (0) 2 *(Thomas, Stewart) aet* 12,965

Blackburn R: Gennoe; Atkins, Millar, Dawson, Hill, Mail, Gayle (Curry), Reid, Kennedy, Garner, Sellars.
Tottenham H: Mimms; Stevens, Thomas, Fenwick, Fairclough (Butters), Mabbutt, Walsh, Gascoigne, Waddle (Samways), Stewart, Allen.

22 NOV

Scunthorpe U (0) 0

Bradford C (0) 1 *(Leonard)* 5793

Scunthorpe U: Musselwhite; Smalley, Longden (Brown), Taylor, Lister, Stevenson, Hodkinson, Harle, Daws, Flounders, Cowling.
Bradford C: Tomlinson; Mitchell, Goddard, Banks, Oliver, Jackson, Palin, Sinnott, Ormondroyd, Kennedy, Leonard.

Southampton (0) 1 *(Le Tissier)*

Scarborough (0) 0 9398

Southampton: Burridge; Wallace Ray, Statham, Case, Moore, Osman, Wallace Rod, Cockerill, Le Tissier, Baker, Wallace D.
Scarborough: Blackwell; Kamara, Thompson, Short, Richards, Bennyworth, Olsson, Cook, Norris, Brook, Graham.

THIRD ROUND SECOND REPLAY *(at Villa Park)*
23 NOV

Arsenal (1) 1 *(Merson)*

Liverpool (0) 2 *(McMahon, Aldridge)* 21,708

Arsenal: Lukic; Dixon, Winterburn, Thomas, Bould, Adams, Rocastle, Richardson, Smith, Merson, Marwood (Hayes).
Liverpool: Hooper; Ablett, Venison, Nicol, Whelan, Spackman, Beardsley, Staunton, Rush (Aldridge), Houghton, McMahon.

THIRD ROUND REPLAY
29 NOV

Oldham Ath (0) 0

Everton (0) 2 *(Cottee 2)* 14,573

Oldham Ath: Rhodes; Irwin, Barrett, Skipper, Marshall, Milligan, Palmer, Kelly, Bunn, Ritchie, Wright.
Everton: Southall; Snodin, Van Den Hauwe, Ratcliffe, Watson, Reid, Steven, Cottee, Sharp, McCall, Wilson.

FOURTH ROUND

Bristol C (1) 1 *(Shutt)*

Tranmere R (0) 0 11,110

Bristol C: Waugh; Stanley, Bailey, Newman, Pender, McClaren, Hawkins, Galliers, Shutt (Jordan), Walsh, Gavin.
Tranmere R: Nixon; Higgins, McCarrick, Martindale, Moore (Malkin), Vickers, Murray (Williams), Bishop, Steel, Muir, Mungall.

Luton T (2) 3 *(Oldfield, Wegerle 2)*

Manchester C (1) 1 *(White)* 10,178

Luton T: Sealey; Johnson R, Harvey, Preece, Foster, Johnson M, Wilson, Wegerle, Harford (Hill), Oldfield, Black.
Manchester C: Dibble; Seagraves, Gleghorn, Gayle, Scott (Beckford), Redmond, White, Moulden, Morley, McNab, Biggins.

Southampton (0) 2 *(Cockerill, Moore)*

Tottenham H (0) 1 *(Osman (og))* 17,375

Southampton: Burridge; Wallace Ray, Statham, Case, Moore, Osman, Wallace Rod, Cockerill, Le Tissier, Baker (Maddison), Wallace D.
Tottenham H: Mimms; Butters, Thomas, Fenwick, Fairclough, Mabbutt, Samways (Moran), Gascoigne, Waddle, Stewart, Allen.

30 NOV

Aston Villa (2) 6 *(McInally 2, Platt 4)*

Ipswich T (0) 2 *(Stockwell, Atkinson)* 16,284

Aston Villa: Spink; Price, Gray S, Gage, Mountfield, Keown, Gray A (Williams), Platt, McInally, Cowans, Daley.
Ipswich T: Forrest; O'Donnell, Harbey (Hill), Redford, Milton, Linighan, Lowe, Dozzell, Wark, Atkinson, Stockwell.

Leicester C (0) 0

Nottingham F (0) 0 26,704

Leicester C: Cooper; Paris, Spearing, Mauchlen, Walsh, Morgan, Reid (Cross), Russell (Turner), Newell, McAllister, Quinn.
Nottingham F: Sutton; Chettle, Pearce, Walker, Wassall, Hodge, Starbuck (Wilson), Webb, Clough, Chapman (Carr), Rice.

QPR (0) 0

Wimbledon (0) 0 10,504

QPR: Seaman; Coney, Allen, Parker, Ardiles (Maguire), Maddix, Falco, Francis, Fereday, Pizanti, Brock.
Wimbledon: Segers; Joseph, Clement, Jones, Young, Scales, Fairweather, Gibson (Cork), Fashanu, Sanchez (Phelan), Wise.

West Ham U (2) 4 *(Ince 2, Staunton (og), Gale)*

Liverpool (1) 1 *(Aldridge (pen))* 26,971

West Ham U: McKnight; Potts, Dicks, Gale, Martin, Devonshire, Brady, Kelly, Rosenior, Dickens, Ince.
Liverpool: Hooper; Ablett, Venison, Nicol (Watson), Whelan, Spackman, Beardsley, Aldridge, Staunton, Houghton, McMahon (Durnin).

14 DEC

Bradford C (2) 3 *(Leonard, Banks, Palin)*

Everton (0) 1 *(Watson)* 15,055

Bradford C: Tomlinson; Mitchell, Evans, Banks, Oliver, Jackson, Palin, Sinnott, Ormondroyd, Kennedy, Leonard.
Everton: Southall; Snodin, Van Den Hauwe, Ratcliffe, Watson, Bracewell (Reid), Steven, McCall, Nevin, Cottee, Wilson (Sheedy).

FOURTH ROUND REPLAYS

Nottingham F (1) 2 *(Clough, Chapman)*

Leicester C (1) 1 *(Groves)* 26,676

Nottingham F: Sutton; Laws, Williams, Chettle, Foster, Parker, Carr, Webb, Clough, Chapman (Hodge), Rice.
Leicester C: Cooper; Paris, Turner, Mauchlen (Cross), Groves (Russell), Morgan, Reid, Williams, Newell, McAllister, Quinn.

Wimbledon (0) 0

QPR (0) 1 *(Falco)* 6585

Wimbledon: Segers; Joseph (Miller), Phelan, Jones, Young, Scales, Fairweather (Kruszyynski), Gibson, Fashanu, Sanchez, Wise.
QPR: Seaman; McDonald, Allen, Parker, Dennis, Maddix, Falco, Francis, Fereday, Coney, Kerslake (Pizanti).

QUARTER-FINALS

18 JAN

Bradford C (0) 0

Bristol C (1) 1 *(Walsh)* 15,330

Bradford C: Tomlinson; Mitchell, Abbott (Jewell), Banks (Oliver), Jackson, Evans, Palin, Sinnott, Ormondroyd, Kennedy, Leonard.
Bristol C: Waugh; Honor, Bailey, Newman, Pender, McClaren, Galliers, Shepherd, Jordan (Shutt), Walsh, Gavin.

Luton T (0) 1 (Hill)

Southampton (0) 1 *(Cockerill)* 11,785

Luton T: Sealey; Breaker, Grimes, Preece, Foster, Dreyer, Wilson, Wegerle, Dowie, Hill, Black.
Southampton: Burridge; Wallace Ray, Cook, Blake, Moore, Cockerill, Wallace Rod, Case, Rideout, Baker, Wallace D.

Nottingham F (4) 5 *(Chapman 4, Clough (pen))*

QPR (1) 2 *(Stein, Kerslake)* 24,065

Nottingham F: Sutton; Laws, Pearce, Chettle, Wilson, Hodge, Carr, Webb, Clough, Chapman, Parker (Crosby)
QPR: Seaman; Ardiles (Allen), Pizanti, Parker, Law (Herrera), Maddix, Stein, Barker, Fereday, Coney, Kerslake.

West Ham U (1) 2 (Ince, Kelly)

Aston Villa (0) 1 *(Platt)* 30,110

West Ham U: McKnight; Potts, Dicks, Gale, Strodder, Devonshire, Brady, Kelly, Rosenior, Dickens (Ward), Ince.
Aston Villa: Spink; Price, Gray S, Gage, Mountfield, Keown, Gray A, Platt, McInally, Cowans, Daley (Olney).

QUARTER-FINAL REPLAY
25 JAN

Southampton (0) 1 *(Wallace Rod)*

Luton T (0) 2 *(Harford, Hill) aet* 18,872

Southampton: Burridge; Wallace Ray, Cook, Case, (Benali), Moore, Osman, Wallace Rod, Baker, Rideout (Le Tissier), Cockerill, Wallace D.
Luton T: Sealey; Breacker, Grimes, Preece, Foster, Dreyer, Wilson, Wegerle, Harford (Oldfield), Hill, Black.

SEMI-FINALS FIRST LEG
12 FEB

West Ham U (0) 0

Luton T (1) 3 (Harford, Wegerle, Wilson (pen)) 24,602

West Ham U: McKnight; Potts, Dicks, Gale, Martin, Devonshire, Ward, Dickens, Rosenior, Brady (Kelly), Ince.
Luton T: Sealey; Breacker, Grimes, Preece, Foster, Beaumont, Wilson, Wegerle, Harford, Hill, Black.

15 FEB

Nottingham F (0) 1 (Pender (og))

Bristol C (0) 1 *(Mardon)* 30,060

Nottingham F: Sutton; Laws, Pearce, Chettle, Wilson, Hodge, Carr, Webb, Clough, Chapman, Parker.
Bristol C: Waugh; Honor, Bailey, Newman, Pender, Mardon, Galliers, McClaren, Gavin, Walsh, Jordan.

SEMI-FINALS SECOND LEG
26 FEB

Bristol C (0) 0

Nottingham F (0) 1 *(Parker) aet* 28,084

Bristol C: Waugh; Honor, Bailey, Newman, Pender, McClaren, Mardon, Galliers, Jordan, Walsh, Gavin (Shutt).
Nottingham F: Sutton; Laws, Pearce, Walker, Wilson, Hodge, Carr, Webb, Clough, Chapman, Parker.
Nottingham F won 2-1 on aggregate

1 MAR

Luton T (1) 2 (Harford, Wegerle)

West Ham U (0) 0 12,020

Luton T: Sealey; Breacker, Grimes, Preece, Foster, Beaumont, Wilson, Wegerle, Harford, Hill, Black.
West Ham U: Parkes; Potts, Dicks, Gale, Martin, Kelly, Ward, Parris, Slater, Brady, Ince.
Luton T won 5-0 on aggregate.

FINAL at Wembley
9 APRIL

Nottingham F (0) 3 *(Clough 2 (1 pen), Webb)*

Luton T (1) 1 *(Harford)* 76,130

Nottingham F: Sutton; Laws, Pearce, Walker, Wilson, Hodge, Gaynor, Webb, Clough, Chapman, Parker.
Luton T: Sealey; Breacker, Grimes (McDonough), Preece, Foster, Beaumont, Wilson, Wegerle, Harford, Hill, Black.
Referee: R. Milford (Bristol)

SIMOD CUP 1988–89

FIRST ROUND

8 NOV

Charlton Ath (0) 0

Sunderland (1) 1 *(Gabbiadini)* 1666

Charlton Ath: Bolder; Humphrey, Reid, MacKenzie, Shirtliff, Gritt, Bennett, Lee R (Lee J), Jones, Campbell, Minto.
Sunderland: Carter; Gray, Lynch, Bennett, MacPhail, Doyle, Kay, Armstrong, Gabbiadini, Gates, Pascoe.

Portsmouth (1) 2 *(Quinn, Hardyman)*

Hull C (1) 1 *(Warren)* 2784

Portsmouth: Gosney; Neill, Sandford, Dillon, Hogg, Gilbert (Symons), Chamberlain, Kuhl, Quinn, Ross, Hardyman.
Hull C: Norman; Palmer, Jacobs, Warren, Jobson, Terry, Roberts, De Mange, Moore, Edwards, Jenkinson.

Southampton (0) 3 *(Wallace D 3)*

Stoke C (0) 0 4627

Southampton: Burridge; Wallace Ray, Statham, Case, Moore, Osman, Wallace Rod, Cockerill, Le Tissier, Baker, Wallace D.
Stoke C: Barrett; Ford, Carr, Kamara, Higgins (Gidman), Berry, Ware, Henry, Shaw (Hemming), Saunders, Hackett.

Watford (0) 2 *(Hodges, Porter [pen])*

Leicester C (0) 0 *aet* 3626

Watford: Coton; Gibbs, Falconer, Jackett, Holdsworth David (McClelland), Miller, Hodges, Wilkinson (Sherwood), Bamber, Porter, Holden,
Leicester C: Cooper; Paris, Spearing, Mauchlen, Walsh (Groves), Morgan, Reid, Cross (Quinn), Newell, McAllister, Russell.

9 NOV

Aston Villa (5) 6 *(Platt, Gallacher, Mountfield, McInally 2, Evans)*

Birmingham C (0) 0 8324

Aston Villa: Butler; Price, Mountfield, Evans, Gage (Gray A), Keown, Daley, Platt, McInally, Cowans (Gray S), Gallacher.
Birmingham C: Thomas; Frain, Roberts, Atkins, Bird, Langley, Bremner, Childs, Yates, Sturridge (Morris), Wigley.

Bradford C (0) 3 *(Leonard 2, Palin)*

Brighton & HA (0) 1 *(Nelson)* 3145

Bradford C: Litchfield; Abbott, Goddard, Banks, Oliver, Jackson, Palin (Thomas), Sinnott, Ormondroyd, Kennedy, Leonard.
Brighton & HA: Keeley; Chivers, Dublin, Wilkins, Bissett, Gatting, Nelson, Curbishley (Owers), Armstrong, Wood, Codner.

Chelsea (1) 6 *(Wilson K, McAllister 2, Clarke, Roberts, McLaughlin)*

Plymouth Arg (0) 2 *(Stuart, McCarthy [pen])* 4767

Chelsea: Freestone; Clarke (Hall), Dorigo, Roberts, McLaughlin, Wood, Wilson K (Dodds), Lee, McAllister, Durie, Wilson C.
Plymouth Arg: Penhaligon; Brown, Cooper, Burrows, Marker, Uzzell, Brimacombe (Matthews), Tynan (McCarthy), Campbell, Plummer, Stuart.

Derby Co (1) 1 *(Saunders)*

Bournemouth (0) 0 7847

Derby Co: Shilton; Patterson, Forsyth, Williams, Wright, Blades (Cross), McMinn, Saunders, Goddard, Hebberd, Callaghan.
Bournemouth: Peyton; Whitlock, Morrell, Bond, Williams, O'Driscoll, (Cooke), O'Connor, Holmes, Aylott, Bishop, Close.

Leeds U (1) 3 *(Aizlewood, Davison 2)*

Shrewsbury T (1) *(Priest [pen])* 3220

Leeds U: Day; Aspin, Whitlow, Aizlewood, Blake, Rennie, Batty, Sheridan, Baird (Taylor), Davison, Hilaire.
Shrewsbury T: Green; Rougvie, Osbourne (Steele), Priest, Moyes, Finley, Griffiths, Bell, Brown, Irvine, Kasule (Melrose).

Millwall (0) 1 *(Horrix)*

Barnsley (0) 1 *(Broddle)* 3330

Millwall: Horne; Stevens, Salman, Morgan (Briley), Thompson, McLeary, Lawrence, Hurlock (Sparham), Horrix, Ruddock, Carter.
Barnsley: Baker; Joyce, McGugan, Thomas (Agnew), Shotton, Futcher, Rees, Dobbin (Robinson), Lowndes, MacDonald, Broddle.
aet; Millwall won 3-0 on penalties

Norwich C (0) 2 *(Goss, Culverhouse)*

Swindon T (0) 1 *(White)* 5014

Norwich C: Gunn; Culverhouse, Putney, Butterworth, Linighan, Goss, Gordon, Allen, Fox (Taylor), Phelan, Cook.
Swindon T: Digby; Hockaday, King, MacLaren, Parkin, Gittens, McLoughlin, Calderwood, Henry, White, Barnes (Shearer).

West Ham U (1) 5 *(Rosenior 4, Kelly)*

WBA (2) 2 *(Goodman, Robson)* 5960

West Ham U: McKnight; Potts, Dicks, Gale, Hilton, Keen, Ward, Kelly, Rosenior, Brady (Parris), Ince.
WBA: Naylor; Dobbins (Goodhall), Albiston, Talbot, Whyte, North, Hopkins, Goodman, Robson (Phillips), Palmer, Bradley.

22 NOV

Crystal Palace (1) 4 *(Barber, Dyer 2, Wright)*

Walsall (2) 2 *(Pritchard, Bertschin)* 2893

Crystal Palace: Parkin; Shaw, Pennyfather, Pardew (Powell), Hopkins, Nebbeling, Dyer, Thomas, Bright, Salako (Wright), Barber.
Walsall: Barber; Dornan, Taylor, Shakespeare, Forbes, Hart, Naughton (Rees), Jones, Christie (Bertschin), Banton, Pritchard.

SECOND ROUND

Watford (0) 1 *(Wilkinson)*

West Ham U (1) 1 *(Ince)* 6468

Watford: Coton; Gibbs, Jackett, Sherwood, Holdsworth David, McClelland, Redfearn (Falconer), Wilkinson, Bamber, Porter, Hodges (Holden).

West Ham U: McKnight; Potts, Dicks, Gale, Martin (Hilton), Keen, Ward, Brady, Rosenior, Dickens, Ince.

23 NOV
FIRST ROUND

Oxford U (0) 2 *(Foyle, Hill)*

Ipswich T (1) 3 *(Zondervan, Lowe 2)* 1560

Oxford U: Judge; Bardsley, Phillips J, Mustoe (Smart), Briggs, Greenall, Heath (Hill), Foyle, Leworthy, Lewis, Simpson.
Ipswich T: Forrest; Yallop (Mayes), Harbey, Zondervan (Cheetham), Milton, O'Donnell, Lowe, Dozzell, Wark, Atkinson, Stockwell.

SECOND ROUND

Derby Co (1) 2 *(Micklewhite 2)*

Aston Villa (1) 1 *(McInally)* 10,056

Derby Co: Shilton; Sage, Forsyth, Williams, Wright, Blades, McMinn, Saunders, Goddard (Cross), Hebberd, Micklewhite.
Aston Villa: Spink; Price, Mountfield, Evans (Gray A), Gage, Keown, Platt, Thompson, McInally, Cowans, Gallacher (Daley).

29 NOV

Millwall (1) 2 *(Briley, Cascarino)*

Leeds U (0) 0 4242

Millwall: Horne; Stevens, Dawes, Hurlock, Thompson, McLeary, Stephenson, Briley, Sheringham, Cascarino, O'Callaghan.
Leeds U: Day; Aspin, Snodin, Aizlewood, Blake, Rennie, Whitlow (Haddock), Sheridan, Baird, Davison, Hilaire (Pearson).

30 NOV

Bradford C (0) 2 *(Thomas, Palin [pen])*

Chelsea (2) 3 *(Dixon, Roberts (pen), Wood)* 5341

Bradford C: Tomlinson; Mitchell, Goddard, Thomas (Abbott), Oliver, Pattison (Leonard), Palin, Sinnott, Ormondroyd, Kennedy, Costello.
Chelsea: Freestone; Hall, Dorigo, Roberts, Lee, Wood, Wilson K, Nicholas, Dixon, Durie (McAllister), Wilson C.

13 DEC
FIRST ROUND

Blackburn R (1) 3 *(Atkins, Kennedy 2 [1 pen])*

Manchester C (1) 2 *(Hendry (og), Gleghorn) aet* 5763

Blackburn R: O'Keefe; Atkins, Dawson, Reid, Hendry, Mail, Finnigan (Miller), Hildersley, Kennedy, Garner, Sellars.
Manchester C: Dibble; Lake, Hinchcliffe, Seagraves, Brightwell, Redmond, White, Moulden, Morley, McNab (Bradshaw), Gleghorn.

SECOND ROUND

Southampton (0) 1 *(Wallace Rod)*

Crystal Palace (1) 2 *(Wright, Dyer)* 4914

Southampton: Flowers; Wallace Ray, Statham, Case, Moore, Osman, Wallace Rod, Cockerill, Le Tissier, Maddison, Wallace D.
Crystal Palace: Parkin; Pemberton, Burke, Pardew, Hopkins, Nebbeling, Dyer, Thomas, Bright, Wright, Barber.

THIRD ROUND

Watford (0) 2 *(Holden, Wilkinson)*

Newcastle U (0) 1 *(McDonald)* 6186

Watford: Coton; Gibbs, Jackett, Sherwood, Holdsworth David, Miller, Redfearn, Wilkinson, Roberts, Porter (Falconer), Holden (Hodges).
Newcastle U: Beasant; Anderson (Cornwell), Wharton, O'Brien, Thorn, Roeder, Hendrie (Scott), McDonald, Mirandinha, Jackson, Brock.

14 DEC
FIRST ROUND

Middlesbrough (0) 1 *(Glover [pen])*

Oldham Ath (0) 0 7439

Middlesbrough: Pears; Parkinson, Cooper, Mowbray, Hamilton, Pallister, Slaven, Brennan, Glover, Davenport, Burke.
Oldham Ath: Rhodes; Irwin, Barrett, Flynn, Marshall, Milligan, Henry, Warhurst (Mooney), Ritchie (Palmer), Philliskirk, Barlow.

20 DEC
SECOND ROUND

Ipswich T (0) 1 *(Milton)*

Norwich C (0) 0 *aet* 18,024

Ipswich T: Forrest; Yallop, Harbey, Hill, Redford, Linighan, (D'Avray), Lowe, Dozzell, Wark, Atkinson, Stockwell (Milton).
Norwich C: Gunn; Culverhouse, Bowen, Crook, Linighan, Townsend, Gordon, Allen, Rosario (Cook), Phelan, Putney (Fox).

THIRD ROUND

Everton (2) 2 *(Hurlock (og), Cottee)*

Millwall (0) 0 3703

Everton: Stowell; McDonald, Pointon, Ratcliffe (Ebbrell), Watson, Bracewell, Steven, Reid, Nevin, Cottee, Sheedy.
Millwall: Horne; Stevens, Dawes, Hurlock, Wood, McLeary, Stephenson (Salman), Briley, Sheringham, Cascarino, O'Callaghan (Ruddock).

21 DEC
SECOND ROUND

Middlesbrough (1) 2 *(Glover (pen), Slaven)*

Portsmouth (1) 1 *(Powell) aet* 6853

Middlesbrough: Pears; Parkinson, Cooper, Mowbray, Hamilton, Pallister, Slaven, Brennan, Glover, Davenport, Ripley (Kerr).
Portsmouth: Gosney; Sandford, Hardyman, Collins, Symons, Whitehead, Chamberlain, Ross (Gale), Powell (Russell), Fillery, Kelly.

THIRD ROUND

Wimbledon (0) 0

Derby Co (0) 0 1386

Wimbledon: Segers; Scales, Joseph, Jones, Young, Curle, Wise (Cork), Gibson, Turner, Kruszynski (Ryan), Fairweather.
Derby Co: Shilton; Blades, Forsyth, Williams, Wright, Hindmarch, McMinn, Saunders, Goddard (Cross), Hebberd, Callaghan.
aet; Wimbledon won 4-3 on penalties.

22 DEC
SECOND ROUND

Blackburn R (1) 2 *(Gayle (pen), Finnigan)*

Sunderland (0) 1 *(Gabbiadini)* 4457

Blackburn R: Gennoe; Atkins, Millar, Reid, Hendry, Mail, Gayle, Hildersley, Kennedy (Curry), Finnigan, Sellars.
Sunderland: Carter; Bennet, Gray (Ogilvie), Ord, Agboola, Lemon, Owers, Armstrong (Cornforth), Whitehurst, Gabbiadini, Pascoe.

10 JAN
THIRD ROUND

Chelsea (0) 1 *(Dixon)*

Nottingham F (0) 4 *(Chapman, Gaynor, Pearce, Parker)* 8475

Chelsea: Freestone; Clarke, Dorigo, Roberts, McLaughlin, Wood, McAllister, Mitchell (Wilson K), Dixon, Durie (Lee), Wilson C.
Nottingham F: Sutton; Laws, Pearce, Walker, Wilson, Hodge (Clough), Carr (Starbuck), Webb, Gaynor, Chapman, Parker.

Crystal Palace (3) 4 *(Bright 3, Wright)*

Luton T (1) 1 *(Dowie)* 5842

Crystal Palace: Suckling; Pemberton, Burke, Pennyfather, Hopkins, Nebbeling, Salako (McGoldrick), Pardew, Bright, Wright, Barber.
Luton T: Chamberlain; Breacker, Dreyer, Hill, James, Johnson M, Williams (Wegerle), Dowie, Harford, Oldfield, Preece.

Ipswich T (1) 1 *(Stockwell)*

Blackburn R (0) 0 8155

Ipswich T: Fearon; Yallop, Harbey, D'Avray, Redford, Linighan, Kiwomya, Dozzell, Wark, Hill, Stockwell (Gregory).
Blackburn R: Gennoe; Atkins (Ainscow), Sulley, Finnigan, Hendry Hill, Gayle, Hildersley, Kennedy, Garner (Miller), Sellars.

11 JAN
Middlesbrough (1) 1 *(Davenport)*

Coventry C (0) 0 9938

Middlesbrough: Pears; Mohan, Cooper, Mowbray, Hamilton, Pallister, Slaven, Gill, Kerr, Davenport, Ripley.
Coventry C: Ogrizovic: Burrows, Phillips, Sedgley, Kilcline, Peake, Bennett, Speedie, Houchen, McGrath, Smith.

18 JAN
QUARTER-FINALS

Wimbledon (1) 1 *(Scales)*

Everton (0) 2 *(Clarke 2)* 2477

Wimbledon: Segers; Scales, Phelan, Jones, Joseph, Curle, Fairweather, Gibson, Turner, Sanchez, Wise.
Everton: Southall; McDonald, Pointon, Ratcliffe, Watson, Steven (Wilson), Nevin, McCall, Clarke, Cottee, Sheedy.

24 JAN
Ipswich T (1) 1 *(Dozzell)*

Nottingham F (2) 3 *(Hodge, Pearce, Crosby)* 16,498

Ipswich T: Fearon; Yallop, Harbey, Zondervan, Redford, Linighan, Kiwomya (Lowe), Dozzell, Wark, Hill (D'Avray), Baltacha.
Nottingham F: Sutton; Laws, Pearce, Chettle, Wilson, Hodge, Carr, Webb, Clough, Chapman (Crosby), Parker.

28 JAN
Middlesbrough (1) 2 *(Slaven, Cooper)*

Crystal Palace (1) 3 *(Pardew, Barber, Wright)* 16,314

Middlesbrough: Pears; Parkinson, Cooper, Mowbray, Hamilton, Pallister, Slaven, Brennan, Burke, Kernaghan, Ripley.
Crystal Palace: Suckling; Pemberton, Burke, Pennyfather, Hopkins, Nebbeling, McGoldrick, Pardew, Bright, Wright, Barber.

THIRD ROUND
1 FEB
Sheffield W (0) 0

QPR (0) 1 (Coney) *aet* 3957

Sheffield W: Turner; Sterland, Rostron, Cranson, Pearson, Madden, Proctor, Hirst (Reeves), West, Varadi, Harper (Galvin).
QPR: Seaman; Channing, Pizanti, Parker, McDonald, Fereday, Stein, Barker, Falco (Kerslake), Coney, Dennis (Maddix).

14 FEB
QUARTER-FINALS

Watford (0) 1 *(Porter [pen])*

QPR (1) 1 *(Coney)* 8103

Watford: Coton; Gibbs, Jackett, Sherwood, Holdsworth David, Miller, Redfearn, Wilkinson (Holdsworth Dean), Roberts, Porter (Falconer), Holden.
QPR: Seaman; Channing, Pizanti, McCarthy (Fleming), Maddix, Spackman, Stein, Kerslake, Barker, Coney, Herrera.
aet; QPR won 2-1 on penalties.

SEMI-FINALS
22 FEB
Nottingham F (1) 3 *(Webb 2, Pearce)*

Crystal Palace (0) 1 *(Wright)* 20,374

Nottingham F: Sutton; Laws, Pearce, Chettle, Wilson, Hodge, Carr, Webb, Clough, Chapman, Parker.
Crystal Palace: Suckling; Pemberton, Burke, Pennyfather, Nebbeling (Shaw), O'Reilly, McGoldrick (Salako), Pardew, Bright, Wright, Barber.

28 FEB
Everton (0) 1 *(Nevin)*

QPR (0) 0 7072

Everton: Southall; McDonald (Bracewell), Pointon, Ratcliffe, Watson, Snodin, Nevin, McCall, Clarke, Cottee, Sheedy.
QPR: Seaman; Channing (Maddix), Dennis, Parker, McDonald, Spackman, Barker, Kerslake, Stein, Coney, Pizanti (Herrera).

FINAL at Wembley
30 APRIL
Everton (1) 3 *(Cottee 2, Sharp)*

Nottingham F (1) 4 *(Parker 2, Chapman 2)* 46,606
aet; 90 mins 2-2

Everton: Southall; McDonald, Van Den Hauwe, Ratcliffe, Watson, Bracewell (McCall), Steven, Nevin, Sharp, Cottee, Sheedy.
Nottingham F: Sutton; Laws, Pearce, Walker, Wilson, Hodge (Chettle), Gaynor (Carr), Webb, Clough, Chapman, Parker.
Referee: A. Gunn (South Challey).

SHERPA VAN TROPHY 1988–89

PRELIMINARY ROUND

Southern Area

21 NOV

Port Vale (1) 1 *(Walker)*

Hereford U (0) 1 *(Stevens)* 1893

Port Vale: Stowell; Webb, Hughes, Walker, Hazell, Sproson, Atkinson (Mills), Earle, Futcher, Beckford, Riley.
Hereford U: Rose; Jones M, Crane, Stevens, Bradley, Jones R, Maddy, Narbett, Stant (Benbow), Tester, McLoughlin.

22 NOV

Fulham (0) 0

Brentford (2) 2 *(Blissett, Cadette)* 2376

Fulham: Batty; Marshall, Kerrins, Wilson (Skinner), Gore, Eckhardt, Barnett, Scott, Sayer, Davies, Walker.
Brentford: Roberts; Bates, Pearce (Lee), Millen, Evans, Feeley, Jones, Sinton, Cadette (Cockram), Blissett, Godfrey.

Northampton T (0) 1 *(McGoldrick)*

Cambridge U (1) 1 *(Ryan)* 1806

Northampton T: Gleasure; Williams, Thomas, Donald, Flexney, McPherson, Berry, Culpin, Gilbert, Adcock, McGoldrick.
Cambridge U: Vaughan; Bailie, Kimble, Daish, Chapple, Beck, Clayton, Ryan (Bull), Reilly, Hamilton, Croft.

Southend U (1) 2 *(Crown 2)*

Lincoln C (1) 1 *(Cumming)* 1176

Southend U: Sansome; Edinburgh, Johnson, Schneider, Westley, O'Shea, Smith, Robinson, Crown, Bennet, Ling.
Lincoln C: Wallington; Evans, Nicholson, Schofield, Bressington, Matthewson (James), Davis, Cumming, Hobson, Clarke, Sertori (McGinley).

Northern Area

Wigan Ath (1) 1 *(Diamond)*

Blackpool (2) 2 *(Cunningham, Morgan)* 1217

Wigan Ath: Adkins; Senior, Beesley, Hamilton, Holden, McEwan, Pilling, Butler, Entwistle (Ainscow), Diamond, Rimmer (Atherton).
Blackpool: Siddall; Burgess, Morgan, Deary (Madden), Methven, Elliott, Matthews (Gore), Cunningham, Garner, Coughlin, Taylor.

York C (0) 0

Burnley (1) 2 *(O'Connell, Comstive [pen])* 1648

York C: Marples; Greenough, Tutill, Fazackerley, Johnson, Eli, Wilson, Shaw (Himsworth), Helliwell, Dixon, Canham.
Burnley: Pearce; Measham, Farrell, Britton, Davis, Gardner, Morley, Oghani, O'Connell, Comstive, Atkinson.

23 NOV
Southern Area

Bristol R (1) 1 *(Reece)*

Bristol C (0) 0 3940

Bristol R: Martyn; Stapleton, Twentyman, Yates, Mehew, Jones, Holloway, Reece, White, Penrice, Purnell.
Bristol C: Waugh; Llewellyn (Stanley), Bailey, Humphries, Pender (McClaren), Newman, McGarvey, Galliers, Shutt, Walsh, Gavin.

28 NOV
Northern Area

Stockport Co (1) 1 *(Wylde)*

Crewe Alex (1) 1 *(Fishenden)* 1328

Stockport Co: Gorton; Butler, Hart, Bullock, Thorpe (Scott), Howard, Wylde, Colville, Angell, Caldwell, Logan (McKenzie).
Crewe Alex: Greygoose; Goodison, Edwards, Billing, Swain, Jones (Gage), Callaghan, Murphy, Cronin, Gardiner (Macowat), Fishenden.

29 NOV

Burnley (1) 3 *(Davis, White, O'Connell)*

Hartlepool U (0) 0 3478

Burnley: Pearce; Measham, Farrell, Britton, Davis, Gardner, White, Oghani, O'Connell, Comstive, Atkinson.
Hartlepool U: Muggleton; Nobbs, McKinnon, Doig, Smith, Baker, Honour, Toman, Allon, Grayson, Atkinson (Ogden).

Carlisle U (0) 1 *(Walsh)*

Scarborough (1) 1 *(Brook)* 1437

Carlisle U: McKellar; Graham, Walsh, Saddington, Ogley, Fitzpatrick (Dalziel), Marshall, Gorman, Stephens, Hetherington, Halpin.
Scarborough: Ironside; Kamara, Thompson, Short Chris, Short Craig, Bennyworth, Outhart, Cook, Mell, Brook, Olsson.

Grimsby T (0) 1 *(Saunders)*

Rotherham U (0) 0 1194

Grimsby T: Reece; McDermott (Jobling), Agnew, Tillson, Lever, Cunnington, North, Saunders, O'Kelly, Cockerill, Alexander.
Rotherham U: O'Hanlon; Russell, Heard, Goodwin, Evans, Dempsey, Green, Crosby, Hazel, Haycock, Pepper (Thompson).

Southern Area

Brentford (0) 2 *(Blissett, Cockram)*

Gillingham (0) 0 3713

Brentford: Roberts; Feeley, Perryman, Millen, Evans, Cockram, Jones, Sinton, Cadette, Blissett, Godfrey.
Gillingham: Hillyard; Burley, Haylock, Peacock, Haines, Cooper, Collins, Quow, Lovell, Lillis (Williams), Smith.

Cambridge U (0) 2 *(Beck, Dublin)*

Peterborough U (2) 2 *(Oakes, Longhurst)* 1296

Cambridge U: Vaughan; Bailie, Kimble, Daish, Chapple, Beck, Clayton, Ryan (Bull), Taylor (Dublin), Hamilton, Croft.
Peterborough U: Crichton; Collins, Gunn, Langan, Carr (Philpott), Oakes, Andrews, Halsall, Cusack, Longhurst, Goldsmith.

Mansfield T (0) 1 *(Kearney)*

Notts Co (1) 1 *(Yates)* 2477

Mansfield T: Cox; McKernon, Kenworthy, Lowery, Foster, Coleman, Owen (Charles), Ryan (Hodges), Stringfellow, Kent, Kearney.
Notts Co: Leonard; McStay, Withe, Kevan, Yates, Law, Draper (Fairclough), Rimmer, Lund, O'Riordan, Thorpe (Barnes).

Swansea C (0) 1 *(Wade)*

Torquay U (0) 0 1409

Swansea C: Bracey; Lewis, Coleman, Hough, Trick, James (D'Auria), Thornber, Love, Hutchison (Wade), Davies, Puckett.
Torquay U: Veysey: Dawkins, Kelly, McNichol, Cole, Leyden, Smith, Lloyd, Edwards, Gibbins, Weston (Loram) (Morrison).

30 NOV

Hereford U (2) 2 *(Jones R, Tester)*

Wolverhampton W (0) 2 *(Thompson (pen), Bull)* 4215

Hereford U: Rose; Jones M, Crane, Stevens, Bradley, Jones R, Devine, Narbett, Stant (Mardenborough), Tester, McLoughlin.
Wolverhampton W: Kendall; Bellamy, Venus, Streete, Robertson, Vaughan, Thompson, Downing, Bull, Mutch, Dennison.

Lincoln C (0) 1 *(Gamble [pen])*

Colchester U (0) 2 *(Walsh 2)* 1448

Lincoln C: Wallington; Evans, Clarke, Schofield, Bressington, Matthewson, Davis, Nicholson, McGinley (Gamble), Brown, Sertori.
Colchester U: Coombe; Hedman, Bedford, Kelly, Hicks, Daniels, Barnett, Chatterton, Swindlehurst, Walsh, Radford.

Reading (3) 5 *(Senior 2, Knight, Moran)*

Aldershot (1) 2 *(Anderson, Mazzon)* 2837

Reading: Phillips; Franklin, Richardson, Elsey, Hicks, Tait, Knight, Taylor L, Senior, Moran, Gilkes.
Aldershot: Lange; Brown, Barnes, Burvill, Smith (Phillips), Wignall, Mazzon (Ring), Anderson, Claridge, McDonald, Randall.

Northern Area
5 DEC

Tranmere R (1) 2 *(Steel, Mungall)*

Stockport Co (1) 1 *(Bullock)* 1494

Tranmere R: Nixon; Higgins, McCarrick, Martindale, Moore, Hughes (Harvey), Morrissey, Bishop, Steel, Muir, Mungall.
Stockport Co: Crompton; Butler, Hart, Pickering, Thorpe, Williams, Wylde (Howard), Colville, Angell, Bullock, Logan.

Wrexham (0) 1 *(Kearns)*

Sheffield U (0) 1 *(Agana)* 1510

Wrexham: Salmon; Salathiel, Wright, Hunter, Williams, Jones, Preece, Flynn, Kearns, Russell, Bowden.
Sheffield U: Tracey; Barnsley, Pike, Booker, Stancliffe, Smith, Roberts (Downes C), Duffield, Agana, Francis, Bryson (Williams).

6 DEC

Blackpool (1) 2 *(Madden 2)*

Rochdale (0) 0 1228

Blackpool: Siddall; Burgess, Wright, Deary, Methven, Elliott (Rooney), Gore (Garner), Cunningham, Madden, Coughlin, Thompson.
Rochdale: Welch; Copeland, Armitage, Smart, Sutton, Reid, Edmonds, Smith (Wood), O'Shaughnessy, Beaumont, Frain.

Bolton W (0) 1 *(Thompson [pen])*

Preston NE (0) 0 2690

Bolton W: Felgate; Brown, Cowdrill, Brookman, Crombie, Winstanley, Henshaw, Thompson, Storer (Jeffrey), Stevens, Darby.
Preston NE: Tunks; Williams N, McAteer, Atkins (Allardyce), Jones, Hughes, Brazil, Joyce, Ellis (Mooney), Patterson, Swann.

Darlington (0) 3 *(Robinson N, Clayton, Hyde)*

Carlisle U (0) 2 *(Gorman (pen), Hetherington)* 867

Darlington: Batch; Robinson N, Morgan, Hine, Moore, Willis, McAughtrie, McAndrew, Clayton (Hyde), Worthington, Emson.
Carlisle U: McKellar; Graham, Dalziel, Saddington, Ogley, Walsh, Marshall, Gorman, Fyfe, Hetherington, Halpin.

Doncaster R (0) 1 *(Ashurst)*

Grimsby T (0) 1 *(Saunders)* 681

Doncaster R: Malcolm; Douglas, Hall (Stewart), Trotter, Ashurst, Raven, Gorman (Peckett), Daly, Rankine, Dobson, Gaughan.
Grimsby T: Sherwood; McDermott, Agnew, Watson, Lever, Cunnington (Jobling), North, Saunders, O'Kelly, Cockerill, Alexander.

Scunthorpe U (0) 1 *(Harle [pen])*

Halifax T (2) 2 *(Matthews N, Allison)* 1547

Scunthorpe U: Musslewhite; Money (Alexander), Longden, Taylor, Lister, Stevenson, Hodkinson, Harle, Daws, Flounders, Brown.
Halifax T: Roche; Hedworth, Horner, Richardson, Robinson, Bramhall, Barr W, Watson, Willis (Blain), Allison, Matthews N.

Southern Area

Bristol C (1) 2 *(Newman (pen), McGarvey)*

Exeter C (0) 0 3642

Bristol C: Waugh; Newman, Bailey, Humphries, Pender, McClaren, Galliers, McGarvey, Shutt, Walsh (Stanley), Gavin.
Exeter C: Gwinnet; Banks, Hawkins, Rogers, Taylor, Cooper, Rowbotham, Hiley (Harris), Vinnicombe, Neville, Harrower.

Cardiff C (0) 2 *(Curtis, Gilligan)*

Swansea C (0) 0 2986

Cardiff C: Wood; Rodgerson, Platnauer, Wimbleton, Abrahams, Boyle, Curtis, Bartlett, Gilligan, Gummer (Bater), Lynex.
Swansea C: Bracey; Puckett, Marsh, Hough, Knill, James, Thornber, Wade (Love), Hutchison (Bodak), Davies, Lewis.

Leyton Orient (1) 1 *(Hales)*

Reading (1) 1 *(Senior)* 1174

Leyton Orient: Wells; Howard, Dickenson (Hull), Hales, Day, Sitton, Harvey, Ward, Jones (Marks), Smalley, Baker.
Reading: Phillips; Franklin, Richardson, Elsey, Hicks, Whitlock, Knight, Taylor L (Beavon), Senior, Moran, Gilkes.

Notts Co (1) 1 *(Yates)*

Chesterfield (0) 1 *(Waller)* 2005

Notts Co: Leonard; Yates, Withe, Kevan (McStay), Law, O'Riordan, Fairclough, Draper, Lund, Rimmer (Barnes), Johnson.
Chesterfield: Cherry; Bloomer, Prindiville, McGeeney (Hewitt), Slack, Wood, Eley, Thompson (Rogers), Waller, Gormley, Morris.

10 DEC

Chesterfield (2) 2 *(Bloomer, Waller)*

Mansfield T (1) 1 *(Coleman)* 2640

Chesterfield: Cherry; Rogers, Prindiville, Bloomer, Slack, Wood, Eley, Henderson, Waller, Gormley, Morris.
Mansfield T: Cox; Anderson, Kenworthy, Lowery, Foster, Coleman, Kent (Ryan), Charles, Hodges, Stringfellow (Leishman), Kearney.

Gillingham (1) 2 *(Lillis, Peacock)*

Fulham (1) 1 *(Walker)* 1970

Gillingham: Kite; Burley, Haylock, Peacock, Haines, Walford, Cooper, Lillis (Williams), Shipley, Docker, Smith.
Fulham: Batty; Marshall, Elkins, Skinner, Gore (Donnellan), Eckhardt, Barnett, Scott, Sayer, Davies, Walker.

13 DEC

Wolverhapton W (2) 5 *Bull 4, Mutch)*

Port Vale (1) 1 *(Ford)* 9734

Wolverhampton W: Kendall; Bellamy, Venus, Streete, Robertson, Robinson (Downing), Thompson (Vaughan), Gooding, Bull, Mutch, Dennison.
Port Vale: Grew; Mills, Hughes, Walker, Hazell, Sproson, Ford, Earle, Futcher, Riley (Beckford), Jeffers.

Northern Area

Crewe Alex (1) 1 *(Murphy)*

Tranmere R (1) 1 *(Muir [pen])* 1460

Crewe Alex: Greygoose; Goodison, Edwards P, Billing, Jones, Gage, Callaghan, Murphy, Harrison (Edwards R), Gardiner, Fishenden.
Tranmere R: Nixon; Hughes, McCarrick, Martindale, Moore, Vickers, Morrissey (Malkin), Harvey, Steel, Muir, Mungall.

Hartlepool U (0) 0

York C (1) 2 *(Dixon 2)* 1396

Hartlepool U: Muggleton; Barratt, McKinnon, Doig (Atkinson), Stokes, Baker, Honour, Toman, Allon, Grayson (Borthwick), Ogden.
York C: Marples; Branagan, Johnson, Bradshaw, Smith, Greenough, Himsworth, Spooner, Helliwell, Dixon, Canham.

Huddersfield T (1) 1 *(Byrne)*

Scunthorpe U (0) 0 2216

Huddersfield T: Hardwick; Byrne, Hutchings, May, O'Doherty, Mitchell, O'Regan, Winter, Cecere, Maskell, Marsden.
Scunthorpe U: Musselwhite; Money (Shearer), Longden, Brown, Lister, Stevenson, Hodkinson, Harle, Daws, Flounders, Richardson.

Preston NE (1) 4 *(Patterson, Mooney, Brazil, Joyce)*

Bury (0) 0 2900

Preston NE: Tunks; Williams N, McAteer, Jones, Hughes, Allardyce, Mooney, Joyce, Patterson, Brazil, Swann (Rathbone).
Bury: Gooden; Hill, Bishop, (Holland), Leonard, Windridge, Clements, Lee, Greenwood, Elliott, McIlroy, Parkinson (Brotherston).

Rochdale (0) 0

Wigan Ath (0) 2 *(Griffiths, Entwistle)* 1134

Rochdale: Welch; Fothergill (Lomax), Mycock (Wood), O'Shaughnessy, Sutton, Copeland, Edmonds, Smith, Beaumont, Reid, Frain.
Wigan Ath: Adkins; Atherton, Butler, Senior, Beesley, Holden, Thompson, Pilling, Entwistle, Ainscow, Griffiths.

Rotherham U (0) 2 *(Hazel, Haycock)*

Doncaster R (0) 1 *(Dobson)* 1790

Rotherham U: O'Hanlon; Russell, Heard, Grealish, Green, Crosby, Hazel, Dempsey, Haycock, Evans (Goodwin), Buckley.
Doncaster R: Malcolm; Beattie (Gorman), Robinson R, Trotter, Ashurst, Raven, Gaughan (Brevett), Daly, Rankine, Dobson, Douglas.

Sheffield U (1) 2 *(Duffield, Bryson)*

Chester C (1) 2 *(Benjamin, Dale)* 2981

Sheffield U: Benstead; Wilder, Pike, Booker, Stancliffe, Barnsley, Duffield, Todd, Agana, Francis, Bryson (Roberts).
Chester C: Stewart; Glenn, Woodthorpe, Hinnigan, Abel, Butler, Jakub, Barrow, Benjamin (Painter), Johnson, Dale.

14 DEC

Scarborough (0) 4 *(Short Craig, Brook, Norris, Richards)*

Darlington (0) 0 1257

Scarborough: Ironside; Kamara, Thompson, Short Craig, Richards, Short Chris, Olsson (Graham), Mathews, Norris, Brook, Adams.
Darlington: Batch; Robinson N, Smith, Hine (Caizley), Moor, Willis, McAughtrie, McAndrew, MacDonald (Hyde), Worthington, Stonehouse.

Southern Area

Exeter C (1) 1 *(Rowbotham)*

Bristol R (0) 1 *(Mehew)* 1609

Exeter C: Walter; Banks, Jones, Rogers, Taylor, Cooper, Rowbotham, Hiley, Vinnicombe, Neville, Harrower (Langley).
Bristol R: Martyn; Alexander, Twentyman, Yates, Mehew, Jones, Holloway, Reece, White, Penrice, Purnell.

20 DEC

Colchester U (1) 2 *(Tempest, Swindlehurst)*

Southend U (1) 1 *(Young)* 993

Colchester U: Walton; Coleman, Hedman, Kelly, Hicks, Hetzke, Allinson, Barnett (Chatterton), Swindlehurst, Tempest, Grenfull.
Southend U: Sansome; O'Shea, Johnson, Butler, McDonough, Brush (Edinburgh), Smith, Hall, Young, Matthews (Jones), Ling.

Torquay U (0) 3 *(Gibbins 2, Smith)*

Cardiff C (1) 1 *(Wimbleton [pen])* 1187

Torquay: Veysey; Pugh, Kelly, McNichol, Cole, Loram, Smith, Lloyd, Thompson (Edwards), Gibbins, Weston (Joyce).
Cardiff C: Wood; Rodgerson, Platnauer, Wimbleton, Abrahams (Bater), Boyle, Curtis, Bartlett, Gilligan, Gummer, Lynex.

Northern Area

Bury (0) 1 *(Robinson)*

Bolton W (0) 0 2032

Bury: Farnworth; Hill, Windridge, Hoyland, Valentine, Clements, Lee, Robinson, Elliott, McIlroy, Leonard.
Bolton W: Felgate; Brown, Cowdrill, Savage, Keeley, Winstanley, Brookman, Thompson, Morgan, Stevens, Darby.

Halifax T (0) 1 *(Watson)*

Huddersfield T (0) 0 2437

Halifax T: Whitehead; Hedworth, Horner, Richardson, Robinson, Bramhall, Martin, Watson, Barr W, Allison, Matthews.
Huddersfield T: Martin; Bent, Hutchings, May, O'Doherty (Tucker), Mitchell, O'Regan, Winter, Cecere (McInerney), Maskell, Marsden.

21 DEC

Chester C (0) 1 *(Hinnigan)*

Wrexham (1) 2 *(Bowden, Preece)* 3887

Chester C: Stewart; Glenn (Lightfoot), Woodthorpe, Hinnigan, Abel, Butler, Jakub, Barrow, Benjamin (Newhouse), Johnson, Dale.
Wrexham: Salmon; Salathiel, Wright, Hunter (Cooper), Williams, Jones, Preece, Flynn, Buxton, Russell, Bowden.

Southern Area

Peterborough U (0) 0

Northampton T (1) 2 *(Adcock, Culpin)* 1754

Peterborough U: Crichton; Collins, Gunn, Luke, McElhinney, Oakes, Andrews (Philpott), Halsall, Cusack, Longhurst, Goldsmith.
Northampton T: Gleasure; Johnson, Thomas, Donald (Wilson), McGoldrick, McPherson, Berry, Culpin, Gilbert, Adcock, Anderson.

FIRST ROUND
Northern Area
7 JAN

Scarborough (1) 3 *(Adams, Thompson N, Richards)*

York C (0) 1 *(Canham)* 2779

Scarborough: Ironside; Kamara, Thompson N, Short Craig, Richards, Bennyworth, Adams, Matthews, Cook, Brook, Graham.
York C: Marples; Bradshaw, Johnson, Wilson, Greenough, Smith, Himsworth (Dunn), Spooner, Helliwell, Dixon, Canham.

PRELIMINARY ROUND
Southern Area
10 JAN

Aldershot (0) 1 *(Stewart)*

Leyton Orient (2) 3 *(O'Shea, Ward, Jones)* 1310

Aldershot: Lange; Brown, Barnes, Stewart, Smith, Wignall, Mazzon (Ring), Riley, Claridge, McDonald, Randall.
Leyton Orient: Heald; Howard, Smalley, O'Shea, Day, Sitton, Harvey (Jones), Ward, Baker, Juryeff, Comfort.

FIRST ROUND
Northern Area
17 JAN

Blackpool (1) 4 *(Davies, Cunningham, Thompson, Madden)*

Rotherham U (1) 3 *(Grealish, Buckley, Hazel)* 1620

Blackpool: Siddall; Burgess, Morgan, Gore (Thomson), Methven, Walsh, Davies, Cunningham, Garner, Coughlin, Walwyn (Madden).
Rotherham U: O'Hanlon; Russell, Heard, Grealish, Green, Crosby, Buckley (Goodwin), Dempsey, Williamson, Evans, Hazel.

Burnley (0) 1 *(Macowat (og))*

Crewe Alex (1) 1 *(Edwards)* 6392

Burnley: Pearce; Measham, Farrell, Britton, Davis, Gardner, White, (Taylor), Oghani, O'Connell, Comstive, James (Zelem).
Crewe Alex: Greygoose; Goodison, Edwards P, Billing, Swain, Gage (Macowat), Callaghan, Murphy, Walters, Gardiner, Fishenden.
aet; Crewe Alex won 4-2 on penalties

Grimsby T (0) 1 *(North)*

Huddersfield T (1) 3 *(Cecere, Maskell, Withe)* 2116

Grimsby T: Reece: McDermott, Agnew, Tillson, Lever (Jobling), Cunnington, Watson (O'Kelly), Saunders, North, Cockerill, Alexander.
Huddersfield T: Hardwick; Bent (Withe), Hutchings, May, Tucker, Mitchell, O'Regan, Winter, Cecere, Maskell, Byrne.

Halifax T (1) 3 *(Allison, Bramhall, Martin)*

Darlington (0) 0 1421

Halifax T: Whitehead P; Barr W, Horner, Richardson, Robinson, Bramhall, Martin, Watson, Fleming, Allison, Matthews N.
Darlington: Batch; Robinson N, Morgan, Hine, Moore, Willis, Stonehouse, MacDonald, Clayton, Worthington, Hyde.

Preston NE (0) 0

Bolton W (0) 1 *(Darby)* 5569

Preston NE: Tunks; Williams N, Rathbone, Jones,

Continued on Pages 938 and 939

THE FA CUP

THE FOOTBALL ASSOCIATION OFFICIALS

Patron: HER MAJESTY THE QUEEN

President: HRH THE DUKE OF KENT

Honorary Vice-Presidents

His Grace the Duke of Marlborough; The Rt Hon The Earl of Derby MC; Air Marshall Michael Simmons KCB, AFC, RAF; General Sir John Stibbon KCB, OBE; Admiral of the Fleet Sir John Fieldhouse GCB, GBE, ADC; Right Hon Earl of Harewood KBE, LLD; Sir Walter Winterbottom CBE; Rt Hon Lord Westwood FCIS, JP; E. A. Croker CBE

Chairman of the Council

F. A. Millichip (West Bromwich Albion FC)

Vice-Chairman of the Council

A. D. McMullen (Bedfordshire FA)

Life Vice-Presidents

A. D. McMullen MBE (Bedfordshire FA);
E. D. Smith MBE JP (Cumberland FA);
L. G. Webb (Somerset and Avon South FA);
R. Wragg F.Inst.B.M. (Sheffield United FC);
R. H. Speake (Kent Co FA);
B. W. Mulrenan (Universities Athletic Union);
Sq/Ldr G. A. Hadley (Royal Air Force);
L. T. Shipman (Leicester City FC);
Dr J. O'Hara MB, ChB, AMRCGP (Sussex Co. FA);
S. A. Rudd (Liverpool Co FA);
E. A. Brown (Suffolk FA)

Vice-Presidents

F. A. Millichip (West Bromwich Albion FC);
E. G. Powell FIBA (Herefordshire FA);
Sir Leonard Smith CBE (Commonwealth Caribbean);
W. T. Annable (Nottinghamshire FA);
L. Smart (Swindon Town FC)

Secretary

R. H. G. Kelly, FCIS, 16 Lancaster Gate, London W2 3LW

FA Challenge Cup Committee

E. A. Brown (Chairman),
W. T. Annable, W. Fox, W. G. Halsey,
W. G. McKeag, Dr. J. O'Hara, P. Rushton,
I. A. Scholar, S. Seymour, T. W. Shipman,
L. Smart, A. L. Smith, J. W. Smith

FA CUP FINALS 1872–1989

1872 and 1874–92	Kennington Oval	1911	Replay at Old Trafford
1873	Lillie Bridge	1912	Replay at Bramall Lane
1893	Fallowfield, Manchester	1915	Old Trafford, Manchester
1894	Everton	1920–22	Stamford Bridge
1895–1914	Crystal Palace	1923 to date	Wembley
1901	Replay at Bolton	1970	Replay at Old Trafford
1910	Replay at Everton	1981	Replay at Wembley

Year	*Winners*	*Runners-up*	*Score*
1872	Wanderers	Royal Engineers	1-0
1873	Wanderers	Oxford University	2-0
1874	Oxford University	Royal Engineers	2-0
1875	Royal Engineers	Old Etonians	2-0 (after 1-1 draw aet)
1876	Wanderers	Old Etonians	3-0 (after 1-1 draw aet)
1877	Wanderers	Oxford University	2-1 (aet)
1878	Wanderers*	Royal Engineers	3-1
1879	Old Etonians	Clapham R	1-0
1880	Clapham R	Oxford University	1-0
1881	Old Carthusians	Old Etonians	3-0
1882	Old Etonians	Blackburn R	1-0
1883	Blackburn Olympic	Old Etonians	2-1 (aet)
1884	Blackburn R	Queen's Park, Glasgow	2-1
1885	Blackburn R	Queen's Park, Glasgow	2-0
1886	Blackburn R†	WBA	2-0 (after 0-0 draw)
1887	Aston Villa	WBA	2-0
1888	WBA	Preston NE	2-1
1889	Preston NE	Wolverhampton W	3-0
1890	Blackburn R	Sheffield W	6-1
1891	Blackburn R	Notts Co	3-1
1892	WBA	Aston Villa	3-0
1893	Wolverhampton W	Everton	1-0
1894	Notts Co	Bolton W	4-1
1895	Aston Villa	WBA	1-0
1896	Sheffield W	Wolverhampton W	2-1
1897	Aston Villa	Everton	3-2
1898	Nottingham F	Derby Co	3-1
1899	Sheffield U	Derby Co	4-1
1900	Bury	Southampton	4-0
1901	Tottenham H	Sheffield U	3-1 (after 2-2 draw)
1902	Sheffield U	Southampton	2-1 (after 1-1 draw)
1903	Bury	Derby Co	6-0
1904	Manchester C	Bolton W	1-0
1905	Aston Villa	Newcastle U	2-0
1906	Everton	Newcastle U	1-0
1907	Sheffield W	Everton	2-1
1908	Wolverhampton W	Newcastle U	3-1
1909	Manchester U	Bristol C	1-0
1910	Newcastle U	Barnsley	2-0 (after 1-1 draw)
1911	Bradford C	Newcastle U	1-0 (after 0-0 draw)
1912	Barnsley	WBA	1-0 (aet, after 0-0 draw)
1913	Aston Villa	Sunderland	1-0
1914	Burnley	Liverpool	1-0
1915	Sheffield U	Chelsea	3-0
1920	Aston Villa	Huddersfield T	1-0 (aet)
1921	Tottenham H	Wolverhampton W	1-0
1922	Huddersfield T	Preston NE	1-0
1923	Bolton W	West Ham U	2-0
1924	Newcastle U	Aston Villa	2-0
1925	Sheffield U	Cardiff C	1-0
1926	Bolton W	Manchester C	1-0
1927	Cardiff C	Arsenal	1-0
1928	Blackburn R	Huddersfield T	3-1
1929	Bolton W	Portsmouth	2-0
1930	Arsenal	Huddersfield T	2-0
1931	WBA	Birmingham	2-1
1932	Newcastle U	Arsenal	2-1
1933	Everton	Manchester C	3-0
1934	Manchester C	Portsmouth	2-1
1935	Sheffield W	WBA	4-2
1936	Arsenal	Sheffield U	1-0
1937	Sunderland	Preston NE	3-1
1938	Preston NE	Huddersfield T	1-0 (aet)
1939	Portsmouth	Wolverhampton W	4-1
1946	Derby Co	Charlton Ath	4-1 (aet)
1947	Charlton Ath	Burnley	1-0 (aet)
1948	Manchester U	Blackpool	4-2
1949	Wolverhampton W	Leicester C	3-1
1950	Arsenal	Liverpool	2-0
1951	Newcastle U	Blackpool	2-0
1952	Newcastle U	Arsenal	1-0

Year	Winners	Runners-up	Score
1953	Blackpool	Bolton W	4-3
1954	WBA	Preston NE	3-2
1955	Newcastle U	Manchester C	3-1
1956	Manchester C	Birmingham C	3-1
1957	Aston Villa	Manchester U	2-1
1958	Bolton W	Manchester U	2-0
1959	Nottingham F	Luton T	2-1
1960	Wolverhampton W	Blackburn R	3-0
1961	Tottenham H	Leicester C	2-0
1962	Tottenham H	Burnley	3-1
1963	Manchester U	Leicester C	3-1
1964	West Ham U	Preston NE	3-2
1965	Liverpool	Leeds U	2-1 (aet)
1966	Everton	Sheffield W	3-2
1967	Tottenham H	Chelsea	2-1
1968	WBA	Everton	1-0 (aet)
1969	Manchester C	Leicester C	1-0
1970	Chelsea	Leeds U	2-1 (aet)
	(after 2-2 draw, after extra time, at Wembley)		
1971	Arsenal	Liverpool	2-1 (aet)
1972	Leeds U	Arsenal	1-0
1973	Sunderland	Leeds U	1-0
1974	Liverpool	Newcastle U	3-0
1975	West Ham U	Fulham	2-0
1976	Southampton	Manchester U	1-0
1977	Manchester U	Liverpool	2-1
1978	Ipswich T	Arsenal	1-0
1979	Arsenal	Manchester U	3-2
1980	West Ham U	Arsenal	1-0
1981	Tottenham H	Manchester C	3-2
	(after 1-1 draw, after extra time, at Wembley)		
1982	Tottenham H	QPR	1-0
	(after 1-1 draw, after extra time, at Wembley)		
1983	Manchester U	Brighton & HA	4-0
	(after 2-2 draw, after extra time, at Wembley)		
1984	Everton	Watford	2-0
1985	Manchester U	Everton	1-0 (aet)
1986	Liverpool	Everton	3-1
1987	Coventry C	Tottenham H	3-2 (aet)
1988	Wimbledon	Liverpool	1-0
1989	Liverpool	Everton	3-2 (aet)

* *Won outright, but restored to the Football Association.*

† *A special trophy was awarded for third consecutive win.*

FA CUP WINS

Aston Villa 7, Tottenham H 7, Blackburn R 6, Manchester U 6, Newcastle U 6, Arsenal 5, The Wanderers 5, WBA 5, Sheffield U 4, Bolton W 4, Everton 4, Liverpool 4, Wolverhampton W 4, Manchester C 4, Sheffield W 3, West Ham U 3, Bury 2, Old Etonians 2, Preston NE 2, Nottingham F 2, Sunderland 2, Barnsley 1, Blackburn Olympic 1, Blackpool 1, Bradford C 1, Burnley 1, Cardiff C 1, Charlton Ath 1, Chelsea 1, Clapham R 1, Coventry C 1, Derby Co 1, Huddersfield T 1, Notts Co 1, Old Carthusians 1, Oxford University 1, Portsmouth 1, Royal Engineers 1, Leeds U 1, Southampton 1, Ipswich T 1, Wimbledon 1.

APPEARANCES IN FINALS

Arsenal 11, Everton 11, Newcastle U 11, Manchester U 10, WBA 10, Aston Villa 9, Liverpool 9, Blackburn R 8, Manchester C 8, Tottenham H 8, Wolverhampton W 8, Bolton W 7, Preston NE 7, Old Etonians 6, Sheffield U 6, Huddersfield T 5, *The Wanderers 5, Sheffield W 5, Derby Co 4, Oxford University 4, Royal Engineers 4, Leeds U 4, Leicester C 4, West Ham U 4, Blackpool 3, Burnley 3, Chelsea 3, Portsmouth 3, Sunderland 3, Southampton 3, Barnsley 2, Birmingham C 2, *Bury 2, Cardiff C 2, Charlton Ath 2, Clapham R 2, Notts Co 2, Queen's Park (Glasgow) 2, *Nottingham F 2, *Blackburn Olympic 1, *Bradford C 1, Bristol C 1, Coventry C 1, *Old Carthusians 1, Luton T 1, Fulham 1, *Ipswich T 1, QPR 1, Brighton & HA 1, Watford 1, *Wimbledon 1.

* *Denotes undefeated.*

APPEARANCES IN SEMI-FINALS

Everton 22, WBA 19, Aston Villa 17, Liverpool 17, Manchester U 17, Blackburn R 16, Arsenal 16, Sheffield W 15, Derby Co 13, Newcastle U 13, Wolverhampton W 13, Bolton W 12, Tottenham H 12, Nottingham F 11, Southampton 10, Sunderland 10, Preston NE 10, Manchester C 10, Sheffield U 10, Chelsea 10, Birmingham C 9, Southampton 9, Burnley 8, Leeds U 8, Huddersfield T 7, Leicester C 7, Old Etonians 6, Oxford University 6, The Wanderers 5, Notts Co 5, Fulham 5, West Ham U 5, Portsmouth 4, Queen's Park (Glasgow) 4, Royal Engineers 4, Blackpool 3, Cardiff C 3, Clapham R 3, Millwall 3, Old Carthusians 3, The Swifts 3, Stoke C 3, Ipswich T 3, Luton T 3, Watford 3, Barnsley 2, Blackburn Olympic 2, Bristol C 2, Bury 2, Charlton Ath 2, Grimsby T 2, Norwich C 2, Swansea T 2, Swindon T 2, Crystal Palace 2, Bradford C 1, Cambridge University 1, Coventry C 1, Crewe Alex 1, Darwen 1, Derby Junction 1, Glasgow R 1, Hull C 1, Marlow 1, Old Harrovians 1, Oldham Ath 1, Port Vale 1, Reading 1, Shropshire W 1, York C 1, Orient 1, QPR 1, Brighton & HA 1, Plymouth Arg 1, Wimbledon 1.

FA CUP 1988–89

PRELIMINARY AND QUALIFYING ROUNDS

Clubs in the Football League Divisions Three and Four are exempted to the First Round Proper, as are last season's FA Trophy finalists (Enfield and Telford United) and two other non-League clubs (Bath City and Maidstone United) at the discretion of the FA. Clubs in the Football League Divisions One and Two are exempted to the Third Round Proper. The following 20 clubs were exempted to the Fourth Round Qualifying: Altrincham, Aylesbury United, Bognor Regis Town, Burton Albion, Caernarfon Town, Chelmsford City, Chorley, Dagenham, Farnborough Town, Halesowen Town, Kidderminster Harriers, Macclesfield Town, Newport County, Runcorn, Slough Town, Sutton United, VS Rugby, Welling United, Whitby Town, Yeovil Town.

Preliminary Round

Esh Winning v Ryhope CA 1-1, 3-2
Cleator Moor Celtic v Bridlington Town 0-0, 1-4
Evenwood Town v Bedlington Terriers 2-0
Farsley Celtic v Netherfield 2-2, 3-0
Workington v Murton 1-1, 4-2
Crook Town v Ferryhill Athletic 0-4
Leyland Motors v Bridlington Trinity 0-1
Stockton v Harrogate Town 1-1, 1-2
(both at Harrogate Town)
Durham City v Guiseley 1-2
Norton & Stockton Ancients v Darwen 1-0
Shildon v Willington 6-2
Annfield Plain v Denaby United 1-0
Ashington v Rossendale United 2-4
Wren Rovers v Whitley Bay 0-3
Ossett Albion v Northallerton Town 2-2, 1-2
West Auckland Town v South Bank 0-0, 0-2
Clitheroe v Lancaster City 2-2, 0-1
Armthorpe Welfare v Darlington CB 3-1
Emley v Langley Park Welfare 4-1
Peterlee Newtown v Droylsden 1-2
Formby v Congleton Town 0-7
St Helens Town v Ashton United 0-1
Irlam Town v Oakham United 3-1
Harworth CI v Belper Town 0-0, 5-1
Radcliffe Borough v Ilkeston Town 2-1
Glossop v Prescot Cables 0-0, 0-1
Arnold v Bootle *(at Bootle)* 1-0
Bilston Town v Alfreton Town 4-0
Leek Town v Heanor Town 3-0
Long Eaton United v Bridgnorth Town 0-5
Warrington Town v Curzon Ashton 3-2
Hinckley Athletic v Winsford United 3-0
Grantham v Borrowash Victoria 2-1
Boston v Sutton Town 2-0
Hednesford Town v Eastwood Town 1-3
Harrisons v Dudley Town 0-2
Walsall Wood v Louth United 0-0, 3-1
Rothwell Town v Mile Oak Rovers & Youth 1-5
Hinckley Town v Stourbridge 2-0
Gresley Rovers v Paget Rangers 2-0
Brackley Town v Spalding United 1-0
Highgate United v Rushden Town 0-4
Desborough Town v Witney Town 2-2, 0-1
Tividale v Rushall Olympic 1-4
Northampton Spencer v Irthlingboro Diamond 0-1
Wednesfield Social v Chasetown 2-3
Chatteris Town v Racing Club Warwick 2-2, 0-6
Leighton Town v Wolverton Town (MK) 2-0
Evesham United v Kings Lynn 3-0
Histon v Wisbech Town 0-1
Holbeach United v Banbury United 1-4
Berkhamsted Town v March Town United 2-2, 2-4
Saffron Walden Town v Ely City 2-0
Bourne Town v Baker Perkins 1-1, 1-0
Ware v Lowestoft Town 2-0
Edgware Town v Hitchin Town 1-4
Wivenhoe Town v Clacton Town 3-0
Basildon United v Braintree Town 2-4
Soham Town Rangers v Watton United 0-1
Heybridge Swifts v Gorleston 3-1
Barkingside v Uxbridge 1-2
Thetford Town v Harlow Town 2-2, 1-4
Potton United v Welwyn Garden City 2-0
Aveley v Halstead Town 2-2, 3-3, 1-4
(First replay abandoned in extra time)
Leatherhead v Hounslow 1-1, 2-1
Tiptree United v Dunstable 1-1, 1-1, 0-0, 1-0
Kempston Rovers v Beckhenham Town 0-1
Canvey Island v Stowmarket Town 2-3
Staines Town v Newmarket Town 3-0
Finchley v Wootton Blue Cross 1-0
Billericay Town v Haverhill Rovers 0-1
Purfleet v Metropolitan Police 0-1
Felixstowe Town v Baldock Town 1-1, 0-4
Chesham United v Hornchurch 1-1, 6-5
Arlesey Town v Hoddesdon Town 1-1, 3-1
Merstham v Clapton 3-3, 1-2
Corinthian Casuals v Hanwell Town 0-4
(at Hanwell Town)
Burgess Hill Town v Harefield United 2-1
Gravesend & Northfleet v Tunbridge Wells 2-1
Flackwell Heath v Camberley Town 3-2
Redhill v Malden Vale 0-1
Darenth Heathside v Hertford Town 0-1
Ruislip v Crockenhill 2-0
Stevenage Borough v Rayners Lane 6-1
Collier Row v Rainham Town 0-3
Sheppey United v Maidenhead United 1-1, 1-0
Cray Wanderers v Tilbury 1-4
Hailsham Town v Ruislip Manor 0-0, 2-0
Yeading v Haywards Heath 2-3
Chatham Town v Dorking 1-5
Sittingbourne v Hastings Town 2-3
Shoreham v Eastbourne United 1-3
Peacehaven & Telscombe v Ramsgate 0-1
Feltham v Hythe Town 1-1, 5-2
Folkestone v Ringmer 2-0
Whyteleafe v Arundel 6-0
Molesey v Herne Bay 7-0
Tonbridge AFC v Canterbury City 2-3
Horndean v Banstead Athletic 2-3
Corinthian v Wick 2-1
Whitehawk v Lancing 2-0
Salisbury v Newbury Town 4-2
Chichester City v Petersfield United 2-1
Abingdon Town v Havant Town 4-2
Oxford City v Pagham *(walkover for Pagham)*
Calne Town v Thatcham Town 0-1
Hungerford Town v Eastleigh 0-0, 1-0
Chippenham Town v Andover 4-0
Trowbridge Town v Romsey Town 2-0
Taunton Town v Poole Town 1-1, 0-1
Devizes Town v Sholing Sports 3-2
Cwmbran Town v Radstock Town 2-2, 0-1
(both games at Radstock)
Tiverton Town v Bridgend Town 7-2
Minehead v Sharpness 0-4

Bristol Manor Farm v Barry Town 0-1
Bideford v Shortwood United 1-1, 1-2
Frome Town v St Blazey 4-1
Paulton Rovers v Barnstable Town 2-1
Clandown v Yate Town 0-2
Welton Rovers v Exmouth Town 0-5

First Round Qualifying

North Shields v Bridlington Town 1-1, 1-1, 1-2
Bishop Auckland v Evenwood Town 4-0
Guisborough Town v Alnwick Town 3-0
Esh Winning v Farsley Celtic 1-1, 1-2
Horden CW v Ferryhill Athletic 0-2
Spennymoor United v Bridlington Trinity 3-0
Tow Law Town v Consett 2-0
Workington v Gateshead 0-0, 0-1
Billingham Town v Guiseley 1-0
Newcastle BS v Norton & Stockton Ancients 4-0
Seaham Red Star v Accrington Stanley 0-0, 1-2
Harrogate Town v Billingham Synthonia 1-3
Brandon United v Annfield Plain 2-0
Blyth Spartans v Rossendale United 1-0
Gretna v Chester-le-Street Town 5-0
Shildon v Whitley Bay 1-5
Shotton Comrades v South Bank 1-1, 1-3
Barrow v Lancaster City 3-1
Morecambe v Skelmersdale United 3-3, 2-1
Northallerton Town v Easington Colliery 2-0
Burscough v Emley 0-1
Horwich RMI v Droylsden 3-3, 2-1
Marine v Thackley 5-0
Armthorpe Welfare v Fleetwood Town 2-2, 0-5
Colwyn Bay v Ashton United 0-0, 1-2
Bangor City v Irlam Town 2-2, 4-1
Southport v Penrith 1-0
Congleton Town v Harworth CI 1-1, 0-1
Eastwood Hanley v Prescot Cables 2-0
Northwich Victoria v Arnold 5-0
Stalybridge Celtic v Chadderton 1-4
Radcliffe Borough v Hyde United 0-2
South Liverpool v Leek Town 1-1, 1-2
Mossley v Bridgnorth Town *(at Curzon Ashton)* 2-0
Rhyl v Ashtree Highfield 4-1
Bilston Town v Warrington Town 0-0, 2-3
North Ferriby United v Grantham 3-2
Witton Albion v Boston 0-0, 2-0
Frickley Athletic v Boldmere St Michaels 2-1
Hinckley Athletic v Buxton 1-3
Oldbury United v Dudley Town 2-3
Matlock Town v Walsall Wood 2-3
Worksop Town v Sutton Coldfield Town 1-2
Eastwood Town v Brigg Town 3-1
Lye Town v Hinckley Town 0-3
Gainsborough Trinity v Gresley Rovers 2-2, 1-3
Boston United v Coventry Sporing 8-1
Mile Oak Rovers & Youth v Goole Town 3-1
Leicester United v Rushden Town 4-1
Shepshed Charterhouse v Witney Town 3-2
Stafford Rangers v Halesowen Harriers 2-0
Brackley Town v Rushall Olympic 1-2
Wellingborough Town v Chasetown 1-2
Tamworth v Racing Club Warwick 3-0
Willenhall Town v Malvern Town 3-3, 0-0, 0-2
Irthlingborough Diamonds v Moor Green 1-1, 3-4
Redditch United v Evesham United 2-1
Atherstone United v Wisbech Town 4-0
Nuneaton Borough v Stamford 2-0
Leighton Town v Banbury United 0-0, 1-2
Barton Rovers v Saffron Walden Town 1-0
Bedworth United v Bourne Town 1-1, 4-3
Bromsgrove Rovers v Chalfont St Peter 1-1, 3-0
March Town United v Alvechurch 1-2
Boreham Wood v Hitchin Town 2-0
Bury Town v Wivenhoe Town 0-0, 2-0
Great Yarmouth Town v Milton Keynes Boro 3-0
Ware v Kettering Town 0-3
Witham Town v Watton United 2-1
Bishops Stortford v Heybridge Swifts 3-1
Hendon v Harwich & Parkeston 5-1
Braintree Town v Corby Town 2-0
Sudbury Town v Harlow Town 3-1
Cambridge City v Potton United 5-1
Leyton-Wingate v Hampton 1-1, 1-0
Uxbridge v Halstead Town 0-2
Grays Athletic v Tiptree United 5-0
Barking v Beckenham Town 0-0, 1-0
Barnet v Epsom & Ewell 7-0
Leatherhead v Stowmarket Town 1-0
Buckingham Town v Finchley 0-3
Wycombe Wanderers v Haverhill Rovers 4-1
Letchworth Garden City v Cheshunt 1-2
Staines Town v Harrow Borough 2-0
Hemel Hempstead v Baldock Town 5-1
Hayes v Chesham United 1-0
Wealdstone v Vauxhall Motors (Beds) 2-1
Metropolitan Police v Arlesey Town 1-1, 0-2
Erith & Belvedere v Hanwell Town 0-1
Wembley v Burgess Hill Town 3-1
Horsham v Walton & Hersham 1-5
Clapton v Leytonstone Ilford 0-1
Dartford v Flackwell Heath 7-1
St Albans City v Malden Vale 1-0
Wokingham Town v Kingsbury Town 2-1
Gravesend & Northfleet v Hertford Town 1-3
Royston Town v Stevenage Borough 0-1
Burnham v Rainham Town 2-2, 1-1, 3-1
Dulwich Hamlet v Three Bridges 1-0
Ruislip v Marlow 1-1, 0-3
Tring Town v Tilbury 2-1
Crawley Town v Hailsham Town 2-1
Carshalton Athletic v Lewes 3-1
Sheppey United v Bromley 1-4
Ashford Town v Dorking 2-1
Croydon v Hastings Town 1-2
Dover Athletic v Egham Town 2-0
Haywards Heath v Eastbourne United 3-2
Chertsey Town v Feltham 0-0, 0-1
Kingstonian v Folkestone 4-1
Thanet United v Portfield 1-0
Ramsgate v Fisher Athletic 0-2
Horsham YMCA v Molesey 1-2
Woking v Canterbury City 3-0
Southwick v Littlehampton Town 5-0
Whyteleafe v Tooting & Mitcham United 2-1
Steyning Town v Corinthian 5-1
Bracknell Town v Whitehawk 1-2
Worthing v AFC Totton 3-2
Banstead Athletic v Windsor & Eton 0-2
Fareham Town v Chichester City 3-0
Basingstoke Town v Abingdon Town 3-1
Newport IOW v Bashley 1-1, 0-1
Salisbury v Pagham 2-3
Abingdon United v Hungerford Town 1-2
Waterlooville v Chippenham Town 2-0
Thame United v Westbury United 3-1
Thatcham Town v Gosport Borough 1-3
Chard Town v Poole Town 0-3
Forest Green Rovers v Devizes Town 5-0
Wimborne Town v Weston-super-Mare 3-5
Trowbridge Town v Weymouth 1-2
Clevedon Town v Tiverton Town 1-2
Merthyr Tydfil v Sharpness 3-0
Melksham Town v Gloucester City 0-5
Radstock Town v Cheltenham Town 0-2
Maesteg Park v Shortwood United 1-0
Dorchester Town v Frome Town 3-1
Mangotsfield United v Torrington 6-0

Barry Town v Worcester City	0-2
Swanage Town & Herston v Yate Town	2-1
Ton Pentre v Exmouth Town	0-1
Falmouth Town v Glastonbury	3-0
Paulton Rovers v Saltash United	1-4

Second Round Qualifying

Guisborough Town v Farsley Celtic	0-0, 1-0
Bridlington Town v Bishop Auckland	2-1
Tow Law Town v Gateshead	3-2
Ferryhill Athletic v Spennymoor United	0-2
Accrington Stanley v Billingham Synthonia	1-1, 1-5
Billingham Town v Newcastle Blue Star	2-1
Gretna v Whitley Bay	1-1, 0-1
Brandon United v Blyth Spartans	4-2
Morecambe v Northallerton Town	3-2
South Bank v Barrow	0-0, 0-1
Marin v Fleetwood Town	2-4
Emley v Horwich RMI	5-0
Southport v Harworth CI	2-0
Ashton United v Bangor City	1-3
Chadderton v Hyde United	1-5
Eastwood Hanley v Northwich Victoria	0-1
Rhyl v Warrington Town	1-1, 0-2
Leek Town v Mossley	2-0
Frickley Athletic v Buxton	1-0
North Ferriby United v Witton Albion	2-2, 1-3
Sutton Coldfield Town v Eastwood Town	1-0
Dudley Town v Walsall Wood	2-1
Boston United v Mile Oak Rovers & Youth	5-0
Hinckley Town v Gresley Rovers	1-0
Stafford Rangers v Rushall Olympic	1-0
Leicester United v Shepshed Charterhouse	1-0
Malvern Town v Moor Green	0-2
Chasetown v Tamworth	0-1
Nuneaton Borough v Banbury United	1-1, 0-1
Redditch United v Atherstone United	2-1
Bromsgrove Rovers v Alvechurch	2-2, 3-3, 2-0
Barton Rovers v Bedworth United	1-3
Great Yarmouth Town v Kettering Town	0-3
Boreham Wood v Bury Town	0-0, 4-1
Hendon v Braintree Town	3-1
Witham Town v Bishops Stortford	2-3
Leyton-Wingate v Halstead Town	7-1
Sudbury Town v Cambridge City	2-1
Barnet v Leatherhead	4-3
Grays Athletic v Barking	1-1, 3-0
Cheshunt v Staines Town	1-2
Finchley v Wycombe Wanderers	0-3
Wealdstone v Arlesey Town	1-0
Hemel Hempstead v Hayes	2-3
Walton & Hersham v Leytonstone Ilford	3-2
Hanwell Town v Wembley	0-1
Wokingham Town v Hertford Town	3-1
Dartford v St Albans City	1-1, 4-2
Dulwich Hamlet v Marlow	1-0
Stevenage Borough v Burnham*	3-2
Carshalton Athletic v Bromley	1-1, 2-4
Tring Town v Crawley Town	1-2
Dover Athletic v Haywards Heath	5-2
Ashford Town v Hastings Town	2-1
Thanet United v Fisher Athletic	1-3
Feltham v Kingstonian	0-0, 0-3
Southwick v Whyteleafe	0-1
Molesey v Woking	1-1, 0-1
Worthing v Windsor & Eton	0-4
Steyning Town v Whitehawk	1-3
Bashley v Pagham	4-3
Fareham Town v Basingstoke Town	3-0
Thame United v Gosport Borough	1-3
Hungerford Town v Waterlooville	0-2
Weston-super-Mare v Weymouth	0-1
Poole Town v Forest Green Rovers	2-4
Gloucester City v Cheltenham Town	3-0
Tiverton Town v Merthyr Tydfil	0-1
Mangotsfield United v Worcester City	0-1
Maesteg Park v Dorchester Town	0-2
Falmouth Town v Saltash United	2-2, 0-5
Swanage Town & Herston v Exmouth Town	1-1, 0-3

Third Round Qualifying

Guisborough Town v Bridlington Town	1-1, 1-0
Tow Law Town v Spennymoor United	2-2, 2-2, 2-1
Billingham Synthonia v Billingham Town	3-0
Whitley Bay v Brandon United	0-1
Morecambe v Barrow	0-0, 1-5
Fleetwood Town v Emley	2-2, 2-2, 3-1
Southport v Bangor City	3-0
Hyde United v Northwich Victoria	1-1, 0-3
Warrington Town v Leek Town	1-2
Frickley Athletic v Witton Albion	3-1
Sutton Coldfield Town v Dudley Town	0-1
Boston United v Hinckley Town	3-4
Stafford Rangers v Leicester United	1-1, 3-2
Moor Green v Tamworth	1-1, 6-4
Banbury United v Redditch United	2-3
Bromsgrove Rovers v Bedworth United	3-1
Kettering Town v Boreham Wood	4-0
Hendon v Bishops Stortford	5-3
Leyton-Wingate v Sudbury Town	1-2
Barnet v Grays Athletic	0-1
Staines Town v Wycombe Wanderers	0-1
Wealdstone v Hayes	1-2
Walton & Hersham v Wembley	2-1
Wokingham Town v Dartford	1-2
Dulwich Hamlet v Burnham	1-1, 3-2
Bromley v Crawley Town	2-2, 0-1
Dover Athletic v Ashford Town	3-0
Fisher Athletic v Kingstonian	1-1, 4-1
Whyteleafe v Woking	0-2
Windsor & Eton v Whitehawk	1-1, 0-1
Bashley v Fareham Town	1-2
Gosport Borough v Waterlooville	0-1
Weymouth v Forest Green Rovers	3-0
Gloucester City v Merthyr Tydfil	0-1
Worcester City v Dorchester Town	1-1, 2-1
Saltash United v Exmouth Town	2-2, 3-4

Fourth Round Qualifying

Frickley Athletic v Chorley	1-1, 1-0
Southport v Tow Law Town	2-1
Barrow v Whitby Town	1-1, 3-1
Fleetwood Town v Runcorn	1-3
Caernarfon Town v Brandon United	1-1, 0-2
Northwich Victoria v Billingham Synthonia	2-0
Leek Town v Guisborough Town	0-0, 0-0, 0-1
Macclesfield Town v Altrincham	0-0, 0-4
Chelmsford City v Halesowen Town	1-3
Dagenham v Burton Albion	2-0
Welling United v Hinckley Town	1-1, 3-0
Dudley Town v Grays Athletic	3-3, 0-2
Bromsgrove Rovers v Moor Green	2-0
Aylesbury United v Sudbury Town	1-1, 1-0
Hayes v Redditch United	1-0
Stafford Rangers v Kidderminster Harriers	2-1
Wycombe Wanderers v Kettering Town	1-2
VS Rugby v Hendon	1-1, 0-2
Slough Town v Dartford	1-2
Sutton United v Walton & Hersham	1-1, 3-0
Fareham Town v Dover Athletic	1-1, 1-0
Crawley Town v Merthyr Tydfil	3-3, 1-3
Bognor Regis Town v Whitehawk	2-2, 2-0
Newport County v Weymouth	2-1
Exmouth Town v Woking	1-5
Fisher Athletic v Dulwich Hamlet	3-3, 3-0
Worcester City v Yeovil Town	1-2
Farnborough Town v Waterlooville	2-3

*tie awarded to Burnham; Stevenage fielded ineligible player

FA CUP 1988–89

FIRST ROUND

19 NOV

Aldershot (0) 1 *(McDonald)*

Hayes (0) 0 2830

Aldershot: Lange; Brown, Barnes, Burvill, Smith, Wignall, Mazzon, Riley (Ring), Claridge, McDonald, Randall.
Hayes: Hyde; Kelly W, Churchouse, Hayward, Leather, Court, Payne, Benning (Graves), Kelly T, Whiskey, Walton (Kuhne).

Altrincham (1) 3 *(Timmons, Ellis 2)*

Lincoln C (2) 2 *(Davis, Sertori)* 2169

Altrincham: Wealands; Johnson, Knowles, Cuddy, Farrelly, Ellis, Cook, Daws, Stewart, Timmons, Kilner.
Lincoln C: Wallington; Franklin, Clarke (Gamble), Nicholson, Bressington, Matthewson, Davis, Cumming, Hobson, Brown, Sertori.

Bath C (0) 2 *(Singleton 2)*

Grays Ath (0) 0 995

Bath C: Preston; Stevens, Palmer, Ricketts, Smith, Smart, Halliday, Keen, Freegard, Payne, Singleton (Dodd).
Grays Ath: Delf; Fox, Timson, Stratford, Brown, Gardey, Sheringham, Sammons, Leslie (Mahoney), Whettell, Boorman (Welch).

Blackpool (1) 2 *(Cunningham, Garner)*

Scunthorpe U (0) 1 *(Harle (pen))* 3976

Blackpool: Siddall; Burgess, Morgan, Deary, Methven, Elliott, Davies, Cunningham, Garner, Coughlin, Taylor.
Scunthorpe U: Musselwhite; Smalley, Longden (Richardson), Taylor (Brown), Lister, Stevenson, Hodkinson, Harle, Daws, Flounders, Cowling.

Bognor R (1) 2 *(Pullen P, Guille)*

Exeter C (0) 1 *(Rowbotham)* 2100

Bognor R: Steele; Cox, Pullen M, Pullen P, Price, Marriner, Burkenshaw, Poole, Fozbury, Guille, Bird.
Exeter C: Gwinnett; Banks, Viney, Rogers, Taylor, Langley, Rowbotham, Hiley (Withey), Batty, Neville, Harrower.

Bolton W (0) 0

Chesterfield (0) 0 4840

Bolton W: Felgate; Brown, Cowdrill, Brookman, Cormbie, Winstanley (Neal), Storer, Thompson, Morgan, Stevens (Henshaw), Darby.
Chesterfield: Brown; Hewitt (Henderson), Prindiville, Bloomer, Hunter, Wood, Eley, Alleyne, Morris, Arnott, Waller.

Brentford (2) 2 *(Evans, Sinton)*

Halesowen (0) 0 4514

Brentford: Roberts; Bates, Pearce, Millen, Evans, Feeley, Jones, Sinton, Cadette (Cockram), Blissett, Godfrey (Buttigieg).
Halesowen: Hughes; Penn, Cash, Gust, Smith, Rose, Hazlewood, Flynn (Joinson L), Spinks, Joinson P, Sturgiss.

Bristol C (2) 3 *(Walsh, McGarvey, Shutt)*

Southend U (0) 1 *(Ling)* 7026

Bristol C: Waugh; Honor; Bailey, Humphries, Pender, Newman, McGarvey, Galliers, Shutt, Walsh, Gavin.
Southend U: Sansome; Edinburgh, Johnson, Martin (Smith), Westley, Hall, Clark (Ramsey), Robinson, Crown, Bennett, Ling.

Burnley (0) 0

Chester C (0) 2 *(Dale, Benjamin)* 8475

Burnley: Pearce; Measham, McGrory, Farrell (Britton), Davis, Gardner, White, Oghani, O'Connell, Comstive, Atkinson.
Chester C: Stewart; Butler, Woodthorpe, Hinnigan, Abel (Hawtin), Lightfoot, Jakub, Barrow, Benjamin, Johnson, Dale.

Cardiff C (0) 3 *(Bartlett, Tupling, Gilligan)*

Hereford U (0) 0 4341

Cardiff C: Wood; Rodgerson, Platnauer, Wimbleton, Abrahams, Boyle, Curtis, Bartlett, Gilligan, Tupling, Lynex.
Hereford U: Rose; Jones M, Crane, Stevens, Bradley, Jones R, Mardenborough, Narbett, Stant, Tester, McLoughlin.

Dagenham (0) 0

Sutton U (0) 4 *(McKinnon 2, Dennis, Rogers)* 1249

Dagenham: Scott; Donovan, Keyes, Horan (Martin), Day, Simpson, Woodruff, Seymour, Neal (Cooper), Staunton, Fitt.
Sutton U: Roffey; Jones, Rains T, Golley, Hemsley, Rogers, Horner, Dawson, Dennis (Stephens), McKinnon, Hanlan.

Darlington (0) 1 *(Leonard (og))*

Notts Co (1) 2 *(Thorpe, Pike)* 2110

Darlington: Batch; Robinson N, McAughtrie, Smith (Caizley), Moore, Willis, Stonehouse, Hyde (Anderson), Clayton, Worthington, Emson.
Notts Co: Leonard; O'Riordan, White, Kevan, Yates, Birtles, Mills, Rimmer, Lund, Pike, Thorpe.

Doncaster R (0) 0

Brandon (0) 0 2139

Doncaster R: Malcolm; Beattie, Hall, Robinson R, Ashurst, Raven, Robinson L, Gorman (Hewitt), Rankine, Dobson, Gaughan.
Brandon: Ward; Bartliff, Wheatley, Lees, Richardson, Herczeg, Lynn, Johnson, Gorman (Calvert), Jennings, Butler.

Enfield (0) 1 *(Furlong)*

Leyton Orient (0) 1 *(Ward)* 4031

Enfield: Pape; Cottington, Smith, Howell, Cooper, Sparrow (Hayzelden), Parkyn, Reeves, Francis, Lewis, Furlong.

Leyton Orient: Wells; Howard, Dickenson, Hales, Day, Sitton, Harvey, Ward, O'Shea (Hull), Juryeff, Comfort.

Frickley Ath (0) 0

Northwich V (1) 2 *(O'Connor, Howey (og))* 1292

Frickley Ath: Weighill; Dungworth, Daniels, Heaney (Myles), Mallywright, Birch, Bishop, Howey, Woodhead, Mallender, Spotswood (Downing).
Northwich V: Ryan; Young, Jones, Maguire, Parker J, McNellis, Nolan, Sayer, Parker D, O'Connor, Danskin.

Fulham (0) 0

Colchester U (1) 1 *(Walsh)* 4481

Fulham: Stannard; Marshall, Thomas, Wilson, Peters (Gore), Eckhardt, Barnett, Scott, Sayer, Gordon (Davies), Walker.
Colchester U: Coombe; Hedman, Bedford, Kelly, Hicks, Hill, Radford, English, Tempest, Walsh, Barnett.

Gillingham (0) 3 *(Lovell, Quow, Smith)*

Peterborough U (1) 3 *(Longhurst 3)* 4509

Gillingham: Kite; Burley, Haylock, Peacock, Haines, Walker, Williams (Quow), Lillis (Cooper), Lovell, Docker, Smith.
Peterborough U: Crichton; Collins, Gunn, Luke, McElhinney, Oakes, Andrews, Halsall, Cusack, Longhurst, Goldsmith.

Grimsby T (1) 1 *(Cockerill)*

Wolverhampton W (0) 0 7922

Grimsby T: Sherwood; McDermott, Agnew, Lever, Tillson, Cunnington, North, Saunders, O'Kelly, Cockerill, Alexander.
Wolverhampton W: Kendall; Bellamy, Venus, Clarke, Robertson, Robinson (Bennett), Thompson, Downing, Bull, Mutch, Dennison (Gallagher).

Guisborough (0) 0

Bury (1) 1 *(Parkinson) (at Middlesbrough)* 5990

Guisborough: Toth; Lovatt, Taylor K, Hodgson (Kennedy), Harland, Smith, Robinson, Omoni, Hankin, Lawrence, Davis.
Bury: Farnworth; Hill, Bishop, Hoyland, Valentine, Clements, Lee, Robinson (Greenwood), Elliott, McIlroy, Parkinson.

Halifax T (0) 1 *(McPhillips)*

York C (0) 0 2894

Halifax T: Roche; Hedworth, Horner, Matthews M, Robinson, Bramhall, Richardson, Watson, McPhillips, Allison, Matthews N.
York C: Marples; Branagan, Johnson, Eli, Tutill, Fazackerley, Butler, Wilson, Helliwell, Dunn (Howlett), Canham.

Hartlepool U (2) 2 *(Smith, Borthwick)*

Wigan Ath (0) 0 2476

Hartlepool U: Norton; Haigh, McKinnon, Dixon, Smith, Baker, Honour, Toman, Borthwick, Grayson, Barratt.
Wigan Ath: Adkins; Senior, Beesley, Hamilton, Holden, McEwan, Thompson, Butler, Entwistle, Pilling, Rimmer (Ainscow).

Huddersfield T (1) 1 *(May)*

Rochdale (1) 1 *(Edmonds)* 6178

Huddersfield T: Hardwick; Trevitt, Hutchings, May, O'Doherty, Mitchell, O'Regan, Winter, Cecere (Withe), Maskell, Byrne.
Rochdale: Welch; Copeland, Lomax, Armitage, Sutton, Reid, O'Shaughnessy, Smith, Edmonds, Beaumont, Frain.

Kettering T (2) 2 *(Lewis, Griffith)*

Dartford (0) 1 *(Taylor (pen))* 3024

Kettering T: Shoemake; Nightingale, Heywood, Fuccillo, Lewis, Brown, Keast, Wright, Moss, Cooke, Griffith.
Dartford: McCutcheon; Myers, Johnson, Keen, Robinson, Connor, Hessenphaler, Britnell (Davidson), Cannon, Sowerby, Taylor.

Mansfield T (1) 1 *(Kent)*

Sheffield U (1) 1 *(Deane)* 9101

Mansfield T: Cox; McKernon, Kenworthy, Lowery, Foster, Coleman, Owen, Ryan, Hodges, Kent, Charles (Kearney).
Sheffield U: Benstead; Wilder, Pike, Webster (Duffield), Stancliffe, Smith, Roberts (Joseph), Todd, Agana, Deane, Bryson.

Newport Co (0) 1 *(Sugrue)*

Maidstone U (0) 2 *(Hill, Gall)* 2148

Newport Co: Bird; Richards, Sherlock, Marustik, Thompson (Banks), Withers, Foley, Sugrue, Sanderson, Williams, Ford.
Maidstone U: Beeney; Berry, Hill, Pamphlett, Roast, Goyette (Jacques), Golley, Stewart (Rogers), Sorrell, Butler, Gall.

Preston NE (0) 1 *(Atkins)*

Tranmere R (0) 1 *(Atkins (og))* 7734

Preston NE: Brown; Williams N, Rathbone, Atkins, Wrightson, Allardyce, Mooney, Joyce, Ellis, Brazil, Patterson.
Tranmere R: Nixon; Higgins, McCarrick, Martindale, Moore (Malkin), Vickers, Morrissey, Harvey, Steel, Muir, Mungall.

Reading (2) 4 *(Taylor L 2, Elsey, Senior)*

Hendon (0) 2 *(Keen, Dowie)* 5096

Reading: Phillips; Richardson, Gernon, Beavon (Knight), Hicks, Tait, Elsey, Taylor L, Senior, Moran, Gilkes.
Hendon: Root; Smart, Furneaux, Duffield, Campbell (Hardey), Gridelet, Drunny, Scott, Dowie, Tate (Smith), Keen.

Rotherham U (1) 3 *(Williamson (pen), Gordon (og), Green)*

Barrow (0) 1 *(Carroll)* 5495

Rotherham U: O'Hanlon; Russell, Heard, Grealish, Green, Crosby, Hazel, Dempsey, Williamson (Mendonca), Evans, Scott (Pepper).
Barrow: McDonnell; Higgins, Hulse, Capstick, Gordon, Gill (Chilton), Carroll, Gilmour (Skivington), Cowperthwaite, Lowe, Burgess.

Runcorn (1) 2 *(Page, Anderson)*

Wrexham (1) 2 *(Bowden, Cooper)* 1910

Runcorn: McBride; Byrne, Densmore, Carroll, Miller, McMahon, Rodwell, Reid, Carter, Page, Anderson.
Wrexham: Salmon; Salathiel, Wright, Hunter, Williams, Jones, Preece, Flynn (Cooper), Kearns, Russell, Bowden.

Scarborough (0) 2 *(Brook, Cook (pen))*

Stockport Co (1) 1 *(Colville)* 2939

Scarborough: Blackwell; Kamara, Thompson, Short, Richards, Bennyworth, Mell, Cook, Norris, Brook, Graham.
Stockport Co: Gorton; Butler, Hart, Coyle, Thorpe, Howard (Payne), Wylde, Colville, Angell, Hendrie (McKenzie), Logan.

Southport (0) 0

Port Vale (0) 2 *(Sproson, Riley)* 3434

Southport: Evans; Lancashire (Oldroyd), Rowlands, Byron, Sturgeon, Wilkes (Shirley), Marsden, Mitchell, Thomson, Quinn, Gamble.
Port Vale: Grew; Webb, Hughes, Walker, Hazell, Sproson, Mills, Earle, Futcher, Beckford, Riley.

Stafford R (1) 2 *(Camden 2)*

Crewe Alex (2) 2 *(Fishenden, Cronin)* 4348

Stafford R: Price; Wood, Upton, Marsh, Thacker, Jones, Newton, Griffiths (Turley), Cavell, Camden, Greaves.
Crewe Alex: Greygoose; Swain, Edwards, Billinge, Macowat (Gage), Callaghan, Jasper, Murphy, Cronin (Jones), Gardiner, Fishenden.

Swansea C (1) 3 *(Melville, Hutchison, Wade)*

Northampton T (0) 1 *(Berry)* 4521

Swansea C: Bracey; Melville, Coleman, Hough, Knill, James, Thornber, Wade, Hutchison, Davies, Lewis.
Northampton T: Gleasure; McGoldrick, Thomas, Wilson, Flexney, McPherson, Sandeman (Donegal), Culpin (Donald), Gilbert, Adcock, Berry.

Telford U (0) 1 *(Lloyd)*

Carlisle U (0) 1 *(Walsh)* 2163

Telford U: Charlton; McGinty, Wiggins, Hancock (Lloyd), Nelson, Storton, Lee, Hanchard, Cunningham, Griffiths, Alcock (Meredith).
Carlisle U: McKellar; Graham, Walsh, Saddington, Jeffels, Fitzpatrick, Marshall, Gorman, Stephens (Sendall), Hetherington, Halpin.

Torquay U (0) 2 *(Joyce, Smith)*

Fareham (2) 2 *(Maddock, Carroll)* 2432

Torquay U: Veysey; Holmes (Gibbins), Kelly, McNichol, Cole, Joyce, Smith, Lloyd, Edwards (Dawkins), Loram, Weston.
Fareham: Grant; Day, Samways, Newman, Bailey, Long, Rutherford, Gowans, Carroll, Maddock, Brady.

Waterlooville (0) 1 *(Whittingham)*

Aylesbury U (1) 4 *(Hercules 2, Boyland 2)* 1196

Waterlooville: Hards; Burns, Jenkins (Pope), Holland, Gill, Cole, Hore, Arnold, Moody, Whittingham, Clements.
Aylesbury U: Garner; Coy, Phillips, Hackett, Hutter, Essex (Alterner), Harthill, O'Dowd, Hercules, Boyland, Lissaman.

Welling (1) 3 *(Booker, Robbins, White)*

Bromsgrove (0) 0 1555

Welling: Barron; MacDonald, Horton, Glover, Ransom, Reynolds, White, Handford, Booker, Robbins, Clements.
Bromsgrove: Atwood; Coniss, Brighton (Jones), O'Connell, Ford, Cooper, Kershaw, Parmenter (Webb), Hanks, Rosegreen, Cunningham.

Woking (1) 1 *(Wye S)*

Cambridge U (2) 4 *(Reilly 2, Croft 2)* 3000

Woking: Jones; Shrubb (Richardson), Cowler, Wye L, Baron, Cassidy, Wye S, Biggins, Davis, Buzaglo T (Moss), Buzaglo R.
Cambridge U: Vaughan; Bailie, Kimble, Smith, Chapple, Beck, Clayton, Ryan, Reilly, Hamilton, Croft.

Yeovil (2) 3 *(Wallace 2, Doherty)*

Merthyr T (0) 2 *(Rogers, Webley)* 4079

Yeovil: Bond; Sherwood, Lowe, Cordice, Rutter, Donnellan, Pearson, Wallace, Mundee (Grimshaw), Doherty, Randall.
Merthyr T: Wager; Tong, Jones, Mullen, Holvey (Hamer), Rogers, Giles (Williams Chris), Webley, Williams S, Beattie, Williams Ceri.

20 NOV

Bristol R (1) 3 *(Jones, Penrice, Holloway (pen))*

Fisher Ath (0) 0 5161

Bristol R: Martyn; Alexander (Clark), Twentyman, Yates, Mehew, Jones, Holloway, Reece, White, Penrice (McClean), Purnell.
Fisher Ath: Richardson; Stead, Little, Collins, Nutton (McClure), Mehmet, Towner, Norman, Neal, Charlery, Ambrose (Cooper).

FIRST ROUND REPLAYS

22 NOV

Brandon (0) 1 *(Calvert)*

Doncaster R (2) 2 *(Dobson 2) (at Doncaster)* 1832

Brandon: Ward; Bartliff, Wheatley, Lees, Richardson, Herczeg, Lynn (Hardman), Calvert, Gorman (Jennings), Johnston, Butler.
Doncaster R: Malcolm; Beattie, Hall (Gorman), Robinson R, Ashurst, Raven, Robinson L, Douglas, Rankine, Dobson, Gaughan.

Carlisle U (1) 4 *(Saddington, Fitzpatrick, Gorman (pen), Halpin)*

Telford U (1) 1 *(Hanchard)* 2833

Carlisle U: McKellar; Graham, Walsh, Saddington, Jeffels, Fitzpatrick, Marshall, Gorman, Stephens, Hetherington, Halpin.
Telford U: Charlton; McGinty (Mayman), Wiggins, Cunningham, Nelson, Storton, Lee, Hanchard (Sankey), Lloyd, Griffiths, Alcock.

Crewe Alex (1) 3 *(Murphy 2, Fishenden)*

Stafford R (2) 2 *(Cavell, Thacker)* 4492

Crewe Alex: Greygoose; Goodison (Jones), Edwards, Billing, Swain, Gage, Jasper (Callaghan), Murphy, Cronin, Gardiner, Fishenden.
Stafford R: Price; Wood, Upton, Marsh, Thacker, Jones, Newton, Turley (Brown), Cavell, Camden (Salmon), Greaves.

Sheffield U (1) 2 *(Bryson, Kenworthy (og))*

Mansfield T (0) 1 *(Kearney)* 12,879

Sheffield U: Benstead; Wilder, Pike, Barnsley, Stancliffe, Smith, Roberts (Duffield), Todd, Agana, Deane, Bryson.
Mansfield T: Cox; McKernon, Kenworthy, Lowery, Foster, Coleman, Owen, Ryan (Kearney), Hodges (Stringfellow), Kent, Charles.

Tranmere R (2) 3 *(Muir 3)*

Preston NE (0) 0 7676

Tranmere R: Nixon; Higgins, McCarrick, Martindale, Moore, Vickers, Morrissey, Harvey, Steel, Muir, Mungall.
Preston NE: Brown; Williams N, Rathbone (McAteer), Atkins, Wrightson, Allardyce, Mooney, Joyce, Ellis, Brazil, Patterson.

Wrexham (2) 2 *(Kearns 2)*

Runcorn (1) 3 *(Reid, Pugh, Rodwell)* 2705

Wrexham: Salmon; Salathiel, Wright, Hunter, Williams, Jones, Priest, Cooper, Kearns, Russell, Bowden.
Runcorn: McBride; Burne, Densmore, Carroll, Miller, McMahon, Rodwell, Reid (Pugh), Carter, Page, Anderson.

23 NOV

Fareham (1) 2 *(Carroll, Maddock)*

Torquay U (1) 3 *(McNichol, Smith, Loram)* 1418

Fareham: Grant; Day, Samways, Newman, Bailey, Long, Rugerford (Brown), Gowans, Carroll, Maddock, Brady (Marks).
Torquay U: Veysey; Dawkins, Kelly, McNichol, Cole, Joyce, Smith, Lloyd (Gibbins), Edwards, Loram, Weston.

Leyton Orient (2) 2 *(Juryeff 2)*

Enfield (1) 2 *(Lewis, Howell) (aet)* 4826

Leyton Orient: Wells; Howard, Baker, Hales (Hull), Day, Sitton, Harvey, Ward, O'Shea, Juryeff, Comfort.
Enfield: Pope; Cottington, Smith, Howell, Cooper (Hayzleden), Sparrow, Parkin, Reeves, Francis, Lewis, Furlong.

Peterborough U (0) 1 *(Haines (og))*

Gillingham (0) 0 *(aet)* 4494

Peterborough U: Crichton; Collins, Gunn, Luke, McElhinney, Oakes, Andrews, Halsall, Cusack, Longhurst, Goldsmith.
Gillingham: Kite; Burley, Haylock, Shipley, Haines, Walker, Cooper, Quow, Lovell, Docker, Smith.

28 NOV

Chesterfield (1) 2 *(Morris 2)*

Bolton W (0) 3 *(Stevens, Storer, Darby)* 4168

Chesterfield: Brown; Bloomer, Prindiville, Henderson (Hewitt), Hunter, Wood, Eley (Thompson), Alleyne, Waller, Arnott, Morris.
Bolton W: Felgate; Brown, Cowdrill, Brookman, Crombie, Winstanley, Neal (Storer), Thompson, Morgan, Stevens, Darby.

Rochdale (1) 3 *(Beaumont, Reid (pen), Frain)*

Huddersfield T (2) 4 *(Withe, O'Shaughnessy (og), Maskell, Bent)* 5645

Rochdale: Welch; Copeland, Mycock, Armitage (Mellish), Sutton, Reid, O'Shaughnessy, Smith, Edmonds, Beaumont, Frain.
Huddersfield T: Hardwick; Bent, Hutchings, May, O'Doherty, Mitchell, O'Regan, Winter, Cecere (Marsden), Maskell, Withe.

FIRST ROUND SECOND REPLAY

Leyton Orient (0) 0

Enfield (0) 1 *(Lewis)* 5944

Leyton Orient: Wells; Howard, Dickenson, Hales, Day, Sitton, Harvey, Ward, Hull, Juryeff, Comfort.
Enfield: Pape; Cottington, Smith, Howell, Cooper, Sparrow, Parkin, Hayzelden, Schiavi (Tionisiou), Lewis (Benstock), Furlong.

SECOND ROUND

10 DEC

Aldershot (0) 1 *(McDonald (pen))*

Bristol C (0) 1 *(Shutt)* 3793

Aldershot: Lange; Brown, Phillips, Burvill, Smith, Wignall, Mazzon (Ring), Anderson, Claridge, McDonald, Randall.
Bristol C: Waugh; Newman, Bailey, Humphries, Pender, McClaren, Galliers (Stanley), Shutt, McGarvey, Walsh, Gavin.

Altrincham (0) 0

Halifax T (2) 3 *(Barr W, Allison, 2)* 3967

Altrincham: Wealands; Johnson, Knowles, Cuddy, Farrelly, Ellis, Cook, Phillips (Daws), Stewart, Timmons, Kilner (Heesom).
Halifax T: Roche; Hedworth, Horner, Richardson, Robinson, Bramhall, Martin, Watson, Barr W, Allison, Matthews N.

Aylesbury (0) 0

Sutton U (0) 1 *(Dennis)* 2135

Aylesbury: Garner; Coy, James (Mann), Hackett, Hutter, Phillips, Harthill, O'Dowd, Hercules, Boyland, Lissaman.
Sutton U: Roffey; Jones, Rains, Golley, Hemsley, Rogers, Stephens, Dawson, Dennis, McKinnon, Hanlan.

Bath C (0) 0

Welling (0) 0 1361

Bath C: Preston; Stevens, Palmer, Ricketts, Smith, Smart (Fulbrook), Halliday, Wiffill, Johns, Singleton, Payne.
Welling: Barron; MacDonald, Horton, Glover, Burgess, Reynolds, White, Handford, Booker, Robbins, Clemmence.

Blackpool (2) 3 *(Cunningham, Garner, Deary)*

Bury (0) 0 5324

Blackpool: Siddall; Burgess, Morgan, Deary, Methven, Elliott, Madden, Cunningham, Garner, Coughlin (Walsh), Thompson.
Bury: Farnworth; Hill, Bishop, Hoyland (Windridge), Valentine, Clements, Lee, Robinson, Elliott, McIlroy, Parkinson.

Bognor (0) 0

Cambridge U (0) 1 *(Chapple)* 3800

Bognor: Steele; Cox, Pullen M, Pullen P, Heggarty, Marriner, Burkenshaw, Wakefield, Fosbury, Guille, Bird.
Cambridge U: Vaughan; Bailie, Kimble, Smith, Chapple, Beck, Clayton, Ryan, Reilly, Hamilton, Croft.

Bolton W (1) 1 *(Keeley)*

Port Vale (0) 2 *(Futcher, Earle)* 7499

Bolton W: Felgate; Brown, Cowdrill, Savage (Barnes), Keeley, Winstanley, Brookman, Thompson, Morgan, Stevens, Darby.
Port Vale: Grew; Mills (Webb), Hughes, Walker, Hazell, Sproson, Ford, Earle, Futcher, Beckford, Riley.

Colchester U (1) 2 *(Hedman, Wilkins)*

Swansea C (1) 2 *(Coleman, Melville)* 2715

Colchester U: Walton; Hedman, Bedford, Kelly, Hicks, Hill, Daniels, English, Swindlehurst (Radford), Walsh, Wilkins.
Swansea C: Bracey; Melville, Coleman, Hough, Knill, Davies, Thornber, James, Hutchison (Bodak), Wade, Lewis.

Grimsby T (1) 3 *(North, Cunnington, Russell (og))*

Rotherham U (1) 2 *(Grealish, Dempsey (pen))* 5676

Grimsby T: Sherwood; McDermott, Agnew, Tillson, Lever, Cunnington, North, Saunders, O'Kelly, Cockerill, Alexander.
Rotherham U: O'Hanlon; Russell, Heard, Grealish, Green, Crosby, Hazel, Dempsey, Haycock, Evans, Buckley.

Hartlepool U (0) 1 *(Allon)*

Notts Co (0) 0 3182

Hartlepool U: Norton; Nobbs, McKinnon, Barratt, Smith, Baker, Honour, Toman, Allon, Grayson, Ogden.
Notts Co: Leonard, Yates, Withe, O'Riordan, Law, Birtles, Mills, Rimmer, Lund, Pike, Fairclough (McParland).

Huddersfield T (0) 1 *(O'Regan)*

Chester C (0) 0 6295

Huddersfield T: Hardwick; Bent, Hutchings, May, O'Doherty, Mitchell, O'Regan, Winter, Cecere, Maskell, Withe (Byrne).
Chester C: Stewart; Glenn, Woodthorpe, Hinnigan, Abel, Butler, Jakub, Barrow, Benjamin, Johnson, Dale.

Kettering (0) 2 *(Cooke 2)*

Bristol R (0) 1 *(Reece)* 4950

Kettering: Shoemake; Nightingale, Heywood, Fuccillo, Lewis, Brown, Keast, Wright, Moss, Cooke, Griffith.
Bristol R: Martyn; Stapleton, Twentyman, Yates, Mehew, Jones, Holloway, Reece, White, Penrice, Purnell.

Northwich V (0) 1 *(O'Connor)*

Tranmere R (1) 2 *(Muir (pen), Steel)* 2594

Northwich V: Ryan; Young, Jones, Maguire, Parker J, McNelis, Nolan (Heeley), Crompton (Sayer), Parker D, O'Connor, Danskin.
Tranmere R: Nixon; Higgins, McCarrick, Martindale, Moore, Vickers, Morrissey, Harvey (Bishop), Steel, Muir, Mungall.

Peterborough U (0) 0

Brentford (0) 0 5609

Peterborough U: Crichton; Collins, Gunn, Luke, McElhinney, Oakes, Andrews (Philpott), Halsall, Cusack, Longhurst, Goldmith.
Brentford: Parks; Feeley, Pearce (Perryman), Millen, Evans, Cockram, Jones, Sinton (Godfrey), Cadette, Blissett, Smillie.

Reading (1) 1 *(Senior)*

Maidstone (0) 1 *(Sorrell)* 5249

Reading: Phillips; Franklin, Richardson, Elsey, Hicks, Gernon, Knight, Taylor L, Senior, Moran, Gilkes.
Maidstone: Beeney; Berry, Hill, Pamphlett, Roast, Jacques, Golley, Stewart, Sorrell, Butler, Gall.

Runcorn (0) 0

Crewe Alex (0) 3 *(Gardiner, Fishenden, Edwards R)* 3509

Runcorn: McBride; Byrne, Densmore (Pugh), Carroll, Miller, McMahon, Rodwell, Reid, Carter, Page, Anderson.
Crewe Alex: Greygoose; Goodison, Edwards P, Billing, Swain (Jones), Gage, Callaghan, Murphy, Edwards R, Gardiner, Fishenden.

Scarborough (0) 0

Carlisle U (0) 1 *(Richards (og))* 2849

Scarborough: Blackwell; Kamara, Thompson, Short, Richards, Bennyworth (Adams), Olsson, Cook, Morris, Brook, Graham.
Carlisle U: McKellar; Graham, Dalziel, Saddington, Ogley, Walsh, Marshall (Hetherington), Gorman, Stephens, Fyfe, Halpin.

Yeovil (1) 1 *(Randall)*

Torquay U (1) 1 *(Loram)* 5612

Yeovil: Bond; Sherwood, Lowe, Cordice, Rutter, Quinn, Pearson (Tong), Wallace, Randall, Mundee, Donnellan.
Torquay U: Veysey; Pugh, Kelly, McNichol, Cole, Loram, Smith, Lloyd, Thompson (Edwards), Gibbins, Weston.

11 DEC

Doncaster R (0) 1 *(Daly)*

Sheffield U (2) 3 *(Stancliffe, Duffield, Agana)* 6556

Doncaster R: Malcolm; Beattie, Robinson R, Trotter, Ashurst, Raven, Robinson L (Gaughan), Daly, Rankine, Dobson, Douglas.
Sheffield U: Benstead; Wilder, Pike, Booker, Stancliffe, Smith, Duffield, Todd, Agana, Deane (Barnsley), Bryson.

Enfield (0) 1 *(Bate)*

Cardiff C (1) 4 *(Wimbleton (pen), Lynex, Gilligan 2)* 3604

Enfield: Pape; Cottington, Smith, Howell, Cooper (Hayzelden), Wilkinson, Parkin (Bate), Reeves, Francis, Lewis, Furlong.

Cardiff C: Wood; Rodgerson, Platnauer, Wimbleton, Abrahams, Boyle, Curtis, Bartlett, Gilligan, Gummer (Bater), Lynex.

SECOND ROUND REPLAYS

13 DEC

Bristol C (0) 0

Aldershot (0) 0 *aet* 7299

Bristol C: Waugh; Newman, Bailey, Humphries, Pender, McClaren, Gavin, Galliers (Stanley), Shutt, Walsh, McGarvey.
Aldershot: Lange; Brown, Phillips, Burvill (Barnes), Smith, Wignall, Mazzon, Ring, Claridge, Randall, McDonald.

Swansea C (0) 1 *(Wade)*

Colchester U (2) 3 *(Hedman, Walsh, Wilkins)* 4045

Swansea C: Bracey; Melville, Coleman, Hough, Knill, Davies, Thornber (Bodak), James, Hutchison, Wade (Puckett), Lewis.
Colchester U: Walton; Hedman, Bedford, Kelly, Daniels, Hill, English, Barnett, Wilkins (Tempest), Walsh, Radford.

14 DEC

Brentford (1) 3 *(Cadette, Corkram, Smillie)*

Peterborough U (1) 2 *(Halsall, Cusack)* 5605

Brentford: Parks; Feeley (Perryman), Stanislaus, Millen, Evans, Cockram, Jones, Godfrey, Cadette, Blissett, Smillie.
Peterborough U; Crichton; Collins, Gunn, Luke, McElhinney, Oakes, Langan, Halsall, Cusack, Longhurst, Goldsmith.

Maidstone (0) 1 *(Gall)*

Reading (1) 2 *(Gernon, Senior)* 2821

Maidstone: Beeney; Berry, Hill, Pamphlett, Roast, Jacques, Golley, Stewart (Rogers), Sorrell, Butler, Gall.
Reading: Phillips; Franklin, Richardson, Elsey, Hicks, Gernon, Knight, Taylor L, Senior, Conroy, Gilkes.

Torquay U (1) 1 *(Thompson)*

Yeovil (0) 0 3246

Torquay U: Veysey; Pugh, Kelly, McNichol, Cole, Loram, Smith (Edwards), Lloyd, Thompson (Holmes), Gibbins, Weston.
Yeovil: Bond; Sherwood, Lowe (Thorpe), Cordice, Rutter, Quinn, Pearson (Tong), Wallace, Randall, Mundee, Donnellan.

Welling (1) 3 *(Robbins, Burgess, Handford)*

Bath C (2) 2 *(Payne, Smith)* 3117

Welling: Barron; MacDonald, Horton, Glover, Burgess, Reynolds, White, Handford, Booker, Robbins, Clemmence.
Bath C: Preston; Stevens (Retford), Fulbrook, Ricketts, Smith, Smart, Halliday (Keen), Wiffill, Freeguard, Singleton, Payne.

SECOND ROUND SECOND REPLAY

20 DEC

Aldershot (1) 2 *(Randall, Claridge)*

Bristol C (0) 2 *(Shutt, Newman (pen)) aet* 3801

Aldershot: Lange; Brown, Phillips (Barnes), Ring, Smith, Wignall, Mazzon, Anderson (Chandler), Claridge, McDonald, Randall.
Bristol C: Waugh; Llewellyn (Honor), Bailey, Newman, Pender, Stanley, McGarvey, Galliers, Hawkins (Shutt), Walsh, Gavin.

SECOND ROUND THIRD REPLAY

22 DEC

Bristol C (1) 1 *(Shutt)*

Aldershot (0) 0 6246

Bristol C: Waugh; Honor, Bailey, Newman, Pender, McClaren, McGarvey, Stanley (Galliers), Shutt, Walsh, Gavin.
Aldershot: Lange; Brown, Barnes, Ring (Chandler), Smith, Wignall, Mazzon, Anderson, Claridge, McDonald, Randall.

THIRD ROUND

7 JAN

Barnsley (3) 4 *(Thomas, Agnew 2, Currie)*

Chelsea (0) 0 13,241

Barnsley: Baker; Joyce, Beresford, Thomas (Foreman), McGugan, Futcher, Agnew (Clarke), Dobbin, Cooper, Currie, MacDonald.
Chelsea: Freestone; Hall (McAllister), Dorigo, Roberts, McLaughlin, Wood, Wilson K, Nicholas, Dixon, Durie, Wilson C (Lee).

Birmingham C (0) 0

Wimbledon (1) 1 *(Gibson)* 10,431

Birmingham C: Hansbury; Ashley, Trewick, Roberts, Overson, Langley, Bremner, Tait, Whitton, Robinson (Yates), Wigley.
Wimbledon: Segers; Scales, Phelan, Jones, Young, Curle, Fairweather, Gibson, Fashanu, Sanchez, Cork.

Blackpool (0) 0

Bournemouth (0) 1 *(Blissett)* 5317

Blackpool: Siddall; Burgess, Morgan, Deary, Methven, Elliott, Davies, Cunningham, Garner, Coughlin, Rooney (Walwyn).
Bournemouth: Peyton; Newson, Morrell, Bond, Williams, O'Driscoll, O'Connor, Brooks, Aylott, Bishop, Blissett.

Bradford C (1) 1 *(Mitchell)*

Tottenham H (0) 0 15,917

Bradford C: Tomlinson; Mitchell, Abbott, Banks, Jackson, Evans, Palin, Sinnott, Ormondroyd (Jewell), Kennedy, Leonard.
Tottenham H: Mimms; Butters, Thomas (Moran), Fenwick, Fairclough, Mabbutt, Walsh, Bergsson (Hughton), Waddle, Stewart, Allen.

Brighton & HA (0) 1 *(Curbishley (pen))*

Leeds U (0) 2 *(Baird 2)* 10,900

Brighton & HA: Keeley; Chivers, Dublin, Wilkins, May, Gatting, Nelson, Curbishley, Bremner, Wood, Cooper.
Leeds U: Day; Aspin, Snodin, Aizlewood, Blake, Rennie, Williams (Haddock), Sheridan, Baird, Davison (Pearson), Hilaire.

Cardiff C (1) 1 *(Gilligan)*

Hull C (1) 2 *(Brown, Edwards)* 7128

Cardiff C: Wood; Rodgerson, Stevenson, Wimbleton (Wheeler), Abrahams, Boyle, Curtis, Bartlett (Tupling), Gilligan, Kelly, Lynex.
Hull C: Hesford; Brown, Jacobs, De Mange, Jobson, Buckley, Payton, Roberts, Whitehurst, Edwards, Daniel.

Carlisle U (0) 0

Liverpool (1) 3 *(Barnes, McMahon 2)* 18,556

Carlisle U: McKellar; Graham, Dalziel, Saddington, Jeffels, Fitzpatrick, Robertson (Sendall), Gorman, Stephens (Fyfe), Hetherington, Halpin. *Liverpool:* Hooper; Ablett, Burrows, Nicol, Whelan, Molby, Beardsley, Aldridge, Houghton, Barnes, McMahon.

Charlton Ath (1) 2 *(Crooks, Williams)*

Oldham Ath (1) 1 *(Milligan)* 5060

Charlton Ath: Bolder; Humphrey, Reid, Shirtliff, Pates, Peake, Lee, Williams, MacKenzie, Mortimer (Gritt), Crooks.
Oldham Ath: Rhodes; Irwin, Barrett, Skipper, Marshall, Barlow, Palmer, Kelly J, Warhurst (Kelly N), Milligan, Henry.

Crewe Alex (2) 2 *(Gardiner, Keown (og))*

Aston Villa (0) 3 *(Platt, Gage, McInally)* 5500

Crewe Alex: Greygoose; Goodison (Edwards R), Edwards P, Billing, Swain, Gage, Callaghan, Murphy, Walters, Gardiner, Fishenden.
Aston Villa: Spink; Price, Mountfield, Gage, Evans (Gray A), Keown, Daley (Olney), Platt, McInally, Cowans, Gray S.

Derby Co (0) 1 *(Hebberd)*

Southampton (0) 1 *(Statham (pen))* 17,178

Derby Co: Shilton; Blades, Forsyth (Micklewhite), Williams, Wright, Hindmarch, McMinn, Saunders, Goddard (Cross), Hebberd, Callaghan.
Southampton: Burridge; Forrest, Statham, Blake, Moore, Osman, Le Tissier (Rideout), Case, Wallace D, Baker, Wallace Rodney.

Hartlepool U (0) 1 *(Baker (pen))*

Bristol C (0) 0 4033

Hartlepool U: Moverley; Nobbs McKinnon, Tinkler, Stokes, Baker, Honour, Toman, Borthwick (Allon), Grayson, Barratt.
Bristol C: Waugh; Honor, Bailey, Newman, Pender, McClaren, McGarvey (Jordan), Shepherd, Shutt, Walsh, Gavin.

Huddersfield T (0) 0

Sheffield U (1) 1 *(Agana)* 15,543

Huddersfield T: Hardwick; Bent, Hutchings, May, O'Doherty, Mitchell, O'Regan, Winter, Cecere, Maskell (Tucker), Byrne (Marsden).
Sheffield U: Benstead; Smith, Pike, Booker, Stancliffe, Carr, Roberts, Todd, Agana, Deane, Bryson.

Kettering (0) 1 *(Griffith)*

Halifax T (1) 1 *(Watson)* 5800

Kettering: Lim; Nightingale, Heywood, Fuccillo, Lewis, Brown, Keast, Cooke, Moss, Wright (Richardson), Griffith.
Halifax T: Whitehead P; Barr W, Horner, Richardson, Bramhall, Robinson, Martin, Watson, McPhillips, Allison, Matthews N.

Manchester C (1) 1 *(McNab (pen))*

Leicester (0) 0 23,838

Manchester C: Dibble; Seagraves (Scott), Hinchcliffe, Gayle, Brightwell, Redmond, White, Moulden, Lake, McNab, Biggins.
Leicester C: Cooper; Mauchlen, Spearing, Ramsey (Groves), Paris, Morgan, Reid, Cross, Newell, McAllister, Turner (Quinn).

Manchester U (0) 0

QPR (0) 0 36,222

Manchester U: Leighton; Gill, Martin, Bruce, Beardsmore, Donaghy, Robson (Wilson), Robins, McClair, Hughes, Milne.
QPR: Seaman; McDonald, Pizanti, Parker, Law, Maddix, Falco (Stein), Francis (Barker), Fereday, Coney, Allen.

Middlesbrough (1) 1 *(Slaven)*

Grimsby T (0) 2 *(North 2)* 19,190

Middlesbrough: Pears; Burke, Cooper, Mowbray, Hamilton, Pallister, Slaven (Mohan), Brennan, Glover, Davenport, Ripley.
Grimsby T: Reece; McDermott, Agnew, Tillson, Lever, Cunnington, Jobling, Saunders, O'Kelly (North), Cockerill, Alexander.

Millwall (2) 3 *(Cascarino, Carter, Sheringham)*

Luton T (1) 2 *(Black, Wilson (pen))* 12,504

Millwall: Horne; Stevens, Salman, Morgan, Wood, McLeary, Carter, Briley, Sheringham, Cascarino, O'Callaghan.
Luton T: Sealey; Johnson R (James), Harvey, Preece, Foster, Johnson M, Wilson, Wegerle, Harford, Hill, Black (Oldfield).

Newcastle U (0) 0

Watford (0) 0 24,086

Newcastle U: Beasant; Ranson, Sansom, McCreery, Scott, O'Brien, Hendrie (Mirandinha), McDonald, O'Neill (Bogie), Wharton, Brock.
Watford: Coton; Gibbs, Porter, Sherwood, Miller, McClelland, Redfearn, Wilkinson, Thompson, Falconer, Holden.

Nottingham F (2) 3 *(Yallop (og), Gaynor, Chapman)*

Ipswich T (0) 0 20,743

Nottingham F: Sutton; Laws, Pearce, Walker, Wilson, Hodge, Carr, Webb, Gaynor, Chapman, Parker.
Ipswich T: Fearon; Yallop, Harbey (O'Donnell), Zondervan, Redford, Linighan, Kiwomya, Dozzell, Wark, Hill, Stockwell.

Plymouth Arg (0) 2 *(Tynan, Summerfield)*

Cambridge U (0) 0 8648

Plymouth Arg: Cherry; Brown, Uzzell, Burrows, Marker, Smith, Summerfield, Hodges, Tynan, McCarthy, Stuart.
Cambridge U: Vaughan; Bailie, Kimble, Daish, Chapple, Turner, Clayton, Ryan, Dublin (Reilly), Taylor, Croft (Leadbitter).

Portsmouth (1) 1 *(Quinn*

Swindon T (0) 1 *(Foley)* 10,582

Portsmouth: Knight; Neill, Sandford (Kelly), Maguire, Hogg, Ball, Dillon, Horne, Quinn, Kuhl, Hardyman (Whitehead).
Swindon T: Digby; Hockaday, King, Jones, Cornwell, Calderwood, Foley, Shearer, Geddis, MacLaren, Henry (White).

Sheffield W (2) 5 *(Jonsson, Hodgson, Varadi 2, Proctor)*

Torquay U (1) 1 *(Edwards)* 11,384

Sheffield W: Turner; Sterland, Cranson, Knight, Pearson, Madden, Proctor, Hodgson, West (Reeves), Varadi, Jonsson.
Torquay U: Veysey; Pugh, Kelly, McNichol, Cole, Loram, Edwards, Lloyd, Thompson (Holmes), Gibbins, Joyce (Morrison).

Shrewsbury T (0) 0

Colchester U (1) 3 *(Walsh, Pratley (og), Allinson (pen))* 3982

Shrewsbury T: Hughes; Green, Rougvie, Williams W, Pratley, Finley, Brown, Bell (Priest), Griffiths (Kasule), Irvine, Thomas.
Colchester U: Walton; English, Bedford, Kelly, Hicks, Hetzke, Daniels, Barnett, Tempest, Walsh, Allinson.

Stoke C (0) 1 *(Shaw)*

Crystal Palace (0) 0 12,294

Stoke C: Fox; Ware, Carr, Kamara, Higgins, Berry, Hackett, Henry, Bamber, Saunders (Shaw), Beagrie.
Crystal Palace: Suckling; Pemberton, Burke, Pennyfather, Hopkins, Nebbeling, Salako, Thomas, Bright, Wright, Barber.

Sunderland (1) 1 *(Ord)*

Oxford U (0) 1 *(Hill)* 17,074

Sunderland: Norman; Bennett, Gray, Ord, McPhail, Doyle, Owers, (Lemon), Armstrong, Gates, Gabbiadini, Pascoe.
Oxford U: Judge; Bardsley, Phillips J, Mustoe, Lewis, Slatter, Smart, Foyle, Hill, Shelton, Simpson.

Sutton U (1) 2 *(Rains, Hanlan)*

Coventry C (0) 1 *(Phillips)* 8000

Sutton U: Roffey; Jones, Rains, Golley, Pratt, Rogers, Stephens, Dawson, Dennis, McKinnin, Hanlan.
Coventry C: Ogrizovic; Borrows, Phillips, Sedgley, Kilcline, Peake, Bennett, Speedie, Regis (Houchen), McGrath, Smith.

Tranmere R (0) 1 *(Vickers)*

Reading (0) 1 *(Elsey)* 7799

Tranmere R: Nixon; Higgins, McCarrick, Martindale, Moore, Vickers, Morrissey, Harvey, Steel (Malkin), Muir, Mungall.
Reading: Phillips; Franklin, Richardson, Beavon, Hicks, Whitlock, Tait, Elsey, Senior, Conroy (Moran), Gilkes.

Walsall (0) 1 *(Pritchard)*

Brentford (0) 1 *(Jones)* 5375

Walsall: Barber; Dornan (Taylor M), Shakespeare, Forbes, Hart, Pritchard, Goodwin, Christie, Banton (Bertschin), Marsh, Mower.
Brentford: Parks; Feeley, Stanislaus, Millen, Evans, Cockram (Pearce), Jones, Sinton, Cadette, Godfrey, Smillie.

Welling (0) 0

Blackburn R (1) 1 *(Hildersley)* 3850

Welling: Barron; McDonald (Ransom), Horton, Glover, Burgess, Reynolds (Lindsay), White, Handford, Booker, Robbins, Clemmence.
Blackburn R: Gennoe; Atkins, Sulley, Finnigan, Hendry, Hill, Gayle, Hildersley, Kenney, Garner, Sellars.

WBA (1) 1 *(Anderson)*

Everton (1) 1 *(Sheedy (pen))* 31,186

WBA: Bradshaw; Dobbins, Albiston, Talbot, Whyte, North, Hopkins, Goodman, Robson, Palmer, Anderson (Paskin).
Everton: Southall; Snodin, Pointon, Ratcliffe, Van Den Hauwe, Bracewell, Steven, Reid, Nevin, Cottee, Sheedy (Clarke).

8 JAN

Port Vale (1) 1 *(Webb)*

Norwich C (0) 3 *(Townsend 2, Fleck)* 15,697

Port Vale: Grew; Webb, Hughes, Walker, Hazell, Sproson, Mills, Earle, Fucher, Beckford, Riley.
Norwich C: Gunn; Culverhouse, Bowen, Butterworth, Linighan, Townsend, Gordon, Taylor (Fleck), Rosario, Phelan, Putney.

West Ham U (2) 2 *(Dickens, Bould (og))*

Arsenal (1) 2 *(Merson 2)* 22,017

West Ham U: McKnight; Stewart, Dicks, Potts, Martin, Devonshire, (Keen), Brady, Kelly, Rosenior, Dickens, Ince.
Arsenal: Lukic; O'Leary, Winterburn, Thomas, Bould (Davis), Adams, Rocastle, Richardson, Smith, Merson, Marwood (Groves).

THIRD ROUND REPLAYS

10 JAN

Brentford (0) 1 *(Cockram)*

Walsall (0) 0 8163

Brentford: Parks; Feeley, Stanislaus, Millen, Evans, Cockram, Jones, Sinton, Cadette, Godfrey, Smillie.
Walsall: Barber; Dornan, Mower (Taylor M), Shakespeare, Forbes, Hart, Pritchard, Goodwin, Banton, Christie, Marsh (Rees).

Halifax T (2) 2 *(Bramhall, Barr W)*

Kettering (2) 3 *(Lewis, Cooke 2)* 5632

Halifax T: Whitehead P: Barr W, Horner, Richardson, Robinson, Bramhall, Martin, Watson, McPhillips, Allison, Matthews N.
Kettering: Lim; Nightingale, Richardson, Fuccillo, Lewis, Brown, Keast, Wright, Moss, Cooke (Edwards), Griffith.

Southampton (0) 1 *(Forrest)*

Derby Co (0) 2 *(McMinn, Callaghan) aet* 16,323

Southampton: Burridge; Forrest (Rideout), Statham,

Blake, Moore, Wallace Ray, Le Tissier, Case (Cockerill), Wallace D, Baker, Wallace Rodney.
Derby Co: Shilton; Blades, Forsyth, Williams, Wright, Hindmarch, McMinn, Saunders, Gee, Hebberd, Callaghan.

Swindon T (0) 2 *(Foley, Shearer)*

Portsmouth (0) 0 11,457

Swindon T: Digby; Hockaday (McLoughlin), King, Jones, Calderwood, White, Foley, Cornwell, Shearer (Henry), McLaren, Geddis.
Portsmouth: Knight; Neill, Sandford (Kelly), Maguire, Hogg, Ball (Whitehead), Dillon, Horne, Quinn, Kuhl, Fillery.

Watford (1) 2 *(Redfearn 2 (1 pen))*

Newcastle U (1) 2 *(Brock, Mirandinha (pen)) aet* 16,431

Watford: Coton; Gibbs, Sherwood, Porter (Roberts), Miller (Jackett), McClelland, Redfearn, Wilkinson, Thompson, Falconer, Holden.
Newcastle U: Beasant; Ranson, Sansom, McCreery, Scott, Roeder, Hendrie, O'Brien, Mirandinha (McDonald), Wharton, Brock.

11 JAN

Arsenal (0) 0

West Ham U (0) 1 *(Rosenior)* 44,124

Arsenal: Lukic; Dixon, Winterburn, Thomas, O'Leary, Adams, Rocastle (Groves), Richardson, Smith, Merson, Marwood (Davis).
West Ham U: McKnight; Stewart, Dicks, Potts, Martin (Strodder), Devonshire, Brady (Keen), Kelly, Rosenior, Dickens, Ince.

Everton (0) 1 *(Sheedy)*

WBA (0) 0 31,697

Everton: Southall; Snodin, Van Den Hauwe (Pointon), Ratcliffe, Watson, Bracewell, Nevin, Reid, Clarke, Cottee, Sheedy.
WBA: Bradshaw; Dobbins, Albiston, Talbot, Whyte, North, Hopkins, Goodman (Paskin), Robson, Palmer, Bradley.

Oxford U (1) 2 *(Hill 2)*

Sunderland (0) 0 7236

Oxford U: Judge; Bardsley, Phillips J, Mustoe, Lewis, Slatter, Smart, Foyle, Hill, Shelton, Simpson.
Sunderland: Norman; Bennett, Gray, Ord (Owers), McPhail, Doyle, Lemon (Agboola), Armstrong, Gates, Gabbiadini, Pascoe.

QPR (0) 2 *(Stein, McDonald)*

Manchester U (0) 2 *(Gill, Graham) aet* 22, 236

QPR: Seaman; McDonald, Pizanti (Ardiles), Parker, Law (Dennis), Maddix, Stein, Barker, Fereday, Coney, Kerslake.
Manchester U: Leighton; Martin, Sharpe (Graham), Bruce, Beardsmore, Donaghy, Gill, Blackmore (Wilson), McClair, Hughes, Milne.

Reading (1) 2 *(Senior, Franklin)*

Tranmere R (0) 1 *(Muir)* 6574

Reading: Phillips, Richardson, Elsey (Beavon), Hicks, Whitlock, Knight, Tait, Senior, Conroy, Gilkes.
Tranmere R Nixon; Higgins, McCarrick, Martindale, Moore (Hughes), Vickers, Morrissey (Bishop), Harvey, Malkin, Muir, Mungall.

THIRD ROUND SECOND REPLAY

16 JAN

Newcastle U (0) 0

Watford (0) 0 *aet* 28,370

Newcastle U: Wright; Ranson, Sansom, McCreery, Scott, Roeder, Hendrie, O'Brien, Bogie (McDonald), Wharton (O'Neill), Brock.
Watford: Coton; Gibbs, Jackett, Sherwood, Miller, McClelland, Redfearn, Wilkinson, Thompson (Roberts), Falconer, Holden.

THIRD ROUND THIRD REPLAY

18 JAN

Watford (0) 1 *(Roeder (og))*

Newcastle U (0) 0 *aet* 15,115

Watford: Coton; Gibbs, Jackett, Sherwood, Miller (Holdsworth David), McClelland, Redfearn, Wilkinson (Roberts), Thompson, Falconer, Holden.
Newcastle U: Wright; Ranson, Sansom, McCreery, Scott, Roeder, Hendrie, O'Brien, Mirandinha (McDonald), Wharton, Brock (Bogie).

THIRD ROUND SECOND REPLAY

23 JAN

Manchester U (0) 3 *(McClair 2 (1 pen), Robson)*

QPR (0) 0 46,257

Manchester U: Leighton; Martin, Sharpe, Bruce, Blackmore (Beardsmore), Donaghy, Robson, Strachan, McClair, Hughes, Milne (McGrath).
QPR: Seaman; McDonald, Pizanti, Parker, Law, Maddix (Allen B), Stein, Barker, Kerslake (Fleming), Coney, Channing.

FOURTH ROUND

28 JAN

Aston Villa (0))

Wimbledon (0) 1 *(Jones)* 25,043

Aston Villa: Spink; Gage, Gray S, Evans, Mountfield, Keown, Gray A, Platt, McInally, Cowans, Daley.
Wimbledon: Segers; Scales, Phelan, Jones, Young, Curle, Fairweather, Gibson, Fashanu, Sanchez, Wise.

Blackburn R (0) 2 *(Garners, Finnigan)*

Sheffield W (0) 1 *(Hirst)* 16,235

Blackburn R: Gennoe; Atkins, Sulley, Finnigan, Hendry (Hill), Mail, Gayle, Hildersley, Miller, Garner, Sellars.
Sheffield W: Turner; Sterland, Rostron, Cranson, Pearson, Knight (Madden), Proctor, Reeves, West, Varadi (Hirst), Harper.

Bradford C (0) 1 *(Leonard)*

Hull C (1) 2 *(Whitehurst, Edwards)* 13,748

Bradford C: Tomlinson; Mitchell, Oliver, Costello (Abbott), Jackson, Evans (Leonard), Palin, Sinnott, Ormondroyd, Kennedy, Jewell.

Hull C: Hesford; Brown, Jacobs, De Mange, Jobson, Buckley, Payton, Roberts, Whitehurst, Edwards, Askew.

Brentford (2) 3 *(Blissett 2, Jones)*

Manchester C (0) 1 *(Gleghorn)* 12,100

Brentford: Parks; Feeley, Stanislaus, Millen, Evans, Cockram (Ratcliffe), Jones, Sinton, Cadette, Blissett, Smillie.
Manchester C: Dibble; Seagraves (Gleghorn), Hinchcliffe, Gayle, Megson, Redmond, White, Morley, Lake, McNab (Bradshaw), Biggins.

Charlton Ath (2) 2 *(Williams, Lee)*

Kettering (0) 1 *(Cooke)* 16,001

Charlton Ath: Bolder; Humphrey, Gritt, Shirtliff, Pates, Peake, Lee, Williams, MacKenzie, Mortimer, Crooks.
Kettering: Lim; Nightingale, Keast, Richardson, Lewis, Brown (Edwards), Wright, Fuccillo, Moss, Cooke, Griffiths.

Grimsby T (0) 1 *(North)*

Reading (0) 1 *(Saunders (og))* 9401

Grimsby T: Reece; McDermott, Agnew, Tillson, Lever, Cunnington, North, Saunders, O'Kelly, Cockerill, Alexander.
Reading: Phillips; Williams, Richardson, Beavon, Hicks, Gernon, Jones, Elsey, Senior, Moran, Tait.

Hartlepool U (1) 1 *(Honour)*

Bournemouth (1) 1 *(Blissett (pen))* 6240

Hartlepool U: Moverley; Barratt, McKinnon, Tinkler, Stokes, Baker, Honour, Toman, Allon, Grayson, Atkinson (Doig)
Bournemouth: Peyton; Newson, Morrell, Bond, Williams, O'Driscoll, O'Connor (Cooke), Pulis, Aylott, Bishop, Blissett.

Manchester U (1) 4 *(Hughes, Bruce, Phillips J (og), Robson)*

Oxford U (0) 0 47,754

Manchester U: Leighton; Blackmore, Sharpe (Beardsmore), Bruce, McGrath (Gill), Donaghy, Robson, Strachan, McClair, Hughes, Milne.
Oxford U: Judge; Bardsley, Phillips J, Phillips L, Lewis, Greenall, Slatter, Purdie (Heath), Hill, Shelton, Simpson (Ford).

Norwich C (3) 8 *(Putney, Allen 4, Fleck 3)*

Sutton (0) 0 23,073

Norwich C: Gunn; Culverhouse, Bowen, Butterworth, Linighan, Townsend (Crook), Gordon, Fleck, Allen, Phelan, Putney
Sutton: Roffey; Jones, Rains, Golley, Pratt, Rogers, Stephens, Dawson, Dennis, McKinnon, Hanlon.

Nottingham F (1) 2 *(Chapman, Parker)*

Leeds U (0) 0 28,107

Nottingham F: Sutton; Laws, Pearce, Chettle, Wilson, Hodge (Starbuck), Carr, Webb, Clough, Chapman, Parker.
Leeds U: Day; Aspin (Williams), Snodin, Swan, Blake,Rennie (Davison), Batty, Sheridan, Baird, Adams, Hilaire.

Plymouth Arg (0) 1 *(McCarthy)*

Everton (0) 1 *(Sheedy (pen))* 27,566

Plymouth Arg: Miller; Brown, Uzzell, Burrows, Marker, Smith, Summerfield, McCarthy, Tynan, Hodges, Stuart.
Everton: Southall; Snodin, Van Den Hauwe, Ratcliffe, Watson, Bracewell, Steven, McCall, Sharp, Cottee, Sheedy.

Sheffield U (1) 3 *(Todd, Deane, Bryson)*

Colchester U (2) 3 *(Hicks, Hill, Hetzke)* 14,406

Sheffield U: Benstead; Smith, Pike, Booker, Stancliffe, Carr, Duffield, Todd, Agana, Deane, Bryson.
Colchester U: Walton; Coleman, Bedford, Hill, Hicks (Barnett), Hetzke, Daniels, English, Tempest, Walsh (Radford), Allinson.

Stoke C (1) 3 *(Bamber, Berry, Beagrie)*

Barnsley (3) 3 *(Currie 2, MacDonald)* 18,592

Stoke C: Fox; Ford, Carr, Kamara, Higgins, Berry, Hackett, Henry, Bamber, Saunders (Shaw), Beagrie.
Barnsley: Baker; Joyce, Beresford, Dobbin, McGugan, Futcher, Lowndes, Agnew, Cooper, Currie, MacDonald.

Swindon T (0) 0

West Ham U (0) 0 18,627

Swindon T: Digby; McLoughlin, Bodin, Jones, Calderwood, Gittens, Foley, Cornwell, Henry, MacLaren, Geddis (Hockaday).
West Ham U: McKnight; Potts, Dicks, Gale, Martin, Devonshire (Dickens), Ward, Kelly, Rosenior, Brady, Ince.

Watford (1) *(Holden, Redfearn)*

Derby Co (0) 1 *(Micklewhite)* 20,078

Watford: Coton; Gibbs, Jackett, Sherwood, Holdsworth David, McClelland, Redfearn, Wilkinson (Roberts), Thompson, Falconer, Holden.
Derby Co: Shilton; Blades, Forsyth, Williams, Cross, Hindmarch, McMinn, Saunders, Gee (Goddard), Hebberd, Callaghan (Micklewhite).

29 JAN

Millwall (0) 0

Liverpool (0) 2 *(Aldridge, Rush)* 23,615

Millwall: Horne; Thompson, Dawes, Hurlock, Wood, McLeary, Carter, Briley, Sheringham, Cascarino, O'Callaghan.
Liverpool: Grobbelaar; Ablett, Burrows, Nicol, Whelan, Molby, Watson, Aldridge, Rush, Barnes, McMahon.

FOURTH ROUND REPLAYS

31 JAN

Barnsley (1) 2 *(MacDonald, Cooper)*

Stoke C (0) 1 *(Bamber)* 21,086

Barnsley: Baker; Joyce, Beresford, Dobbin, McGugan, Futcher, Lowdnes (Rees) (Shotton), Agnew, Cooper, Currie, MacDonald.
Stoke C: Barrett; Ford, Carr, Kamara, Higgins, Berry, Hackett, Henry, Bamber, Shaw (Ware), Beagrie.

Bournemouth (3) 5 *(Baker (og), Stokes (og), Newson, Morrell, Cooke)*

Hartlepool U (1) 2 *(Allon, Toman)* 10,142

Bournemouth: Peyton; Newson, Morrell, Bond, Williams, O'Driscoll, Cooke, Coleman, Aylott, Bishop, Blissett.
Hartlepool: Moverley; Barratt, McKinnon, Tinkler, Stokes, Baker, Honour, Toman, Allon, Grayson, Atkinson.

Colchester U (0) 0

Sheffield U (1) 2 *(Deane 2)* 7638

Colchester U: Walton; Coleman, Bedford, Hill, Hicks, Hetzke, Daniels, English, Swindlehurst (Williams), Walsh (Barnett), Allinson.
Sheffield U: Benstead; Smith, Pike, Thompson, Stancliffe, Carr, Duffield, Roberts, Agana, Deane, Bryson.

Everton (2) 4 *(Sharp 2, Nevin, Sheedy)*

Plymouth Arg (0) 0 28,542

Everton: Southall; Snodin (Wilson), Van Den Hauwe, Ratcliffe, Watson, Steven, Nevin (Clarke), McCall, Sharp, Cottee, Sheedy.
Plymouth Arg: Miller; Brown, Uzzell, Burrows, Marker, Smith, Summerfield (Matthews), McCarthy, Tynan, Hodges (Campbell), Stuart.

1 FEB

Reading (0) 1 *(Moran)*

Grimsby T (0) 2 *(Cunnington, Jobling)* 8541

Reading: Phillips; Williams, Richardson, Beavon, Hicks, Gernon, Jones (Moran),Elsey, Senior, Tait, Gilkes.
Grimsby T: Reece; McDermott (Jobling), Agnew, Tillson, Lever, Cunnington, North, Saunders, O'Kelly, Cockerill, Alexander.

West Ham U (0) 1 *(Rosenior)*

Swindon T (0) 0 24,723

West Ham U: McKnight; Potts, Dicks, Gale, Martin (Strodder), Devonshire, Ward, Kelly (Dickens), Rosenior, Brady, Ince.
Swindon T: Digby; McLoughlin, Bodin, Jones, Calderwood, Gittens, Foley, Cornwell, Hockday (Henry), MacLaren, Geddis.

FIFTH ROUND
18 FEB

Barnsley (0) 0

Everton (1) 1 *(Sharp)* 32,551

Barnsley: Baker; Joyce, Beresford, Dobbin, McGugan, Futcher, Lowndes, Agnew, Cooper, Currie, MacDonald (Broddle).
Everton: Southall; McDonald, Pointon, Ratcliffe, Watson, Snodin (Nevin), Steven, McCall, Sharp, Cottee, Sheedy.

Blackburn R (0))

Brentford (0) 2 *(Blissett 2)* 15,280

Blackburn R: Gennoe; Atkins, Sulley (Reid), Finnigan, Hendry, Mail, Gayle, Hildersley, Miller, Garner, Sellars.
Brentford: Parks; Feeley, Stanislaus, Millen, Evans, Ratcliffe, Jones, Sinton, Cadette (Godfrey), Blissett, Smillie.

Bournemouth (0) 1 *(Aylott)*

Manchester U (0) 1 *(Hughes)* 12,500

Bournemouth: Peyton; Newson, Morrell, Bond, Williams, O'Driscoll, Cooke, O'Connor, Aylott, Bishop, Blissett.
Manchester U: Leighton; Blackmore, Martin (Sharpe), Bruce, McGrath, Donaghy, Robson, Strachan, McClair, Hughes, Milne.

Charlton Ath (0) 0

West Ham U (0) 1 *(Slater)* 18,785

Charlton Ath: Bolder; Humphrey, Reid, Shirtliff, Pates, Peake (Leaburn), Lee (Campbell), Mortimer, MacKenzie, Williams, Crooks.
West Ham U: Parkes; Potts, Parris, Gale, Martin, Devonshire (Keen), Ward, Dickens, Slater, Brady, Ince.

Hull C (2) 2 *(Whitehurst, Edwards)*

Liverpool (1) 3 *(Barnes, Aldridge 2)* 20,058

Hull C: Hesford; Brown, Jacobs, De Mange, Jobson, Buckley, Payton (Saville), Roberts, Whitehurst, Edwards, Askew.
Liverpool: Grobbelaar; Ablett, Burrows, Nicol, Gillespie (Watson), Molby, Beardsley, Aldridge, Houghton, Barnes, McMahon.

Norwich C (1) 3 *(Thompson (og), Allen (pen), Gordon)*

Sheffield U (1) 2 *(Deane, Agana)* 24,139

Norwich: Gunn; Culverhouse, Bowen, Butterworth, Linighan, Townsend, Gordon, Fleck (Rosario), Allen, Phelan, Putney.
Sheffield U: Benstead; Smith, Pike, Booker, Stancliffe, Thompson, Duffield, Todd, Agana, Deane, Bryson.

Wimbledon (0) 3 *(Fashanu, Phelan, Wise)*

Grimsby (1) 1 *(Alexander)* 12,517

Wimbledon: Segers; Scales, Phelan, Kruszynski, Joseph, Curle, Fairweather, Miller, Fashanu, Sanchez, Wise.
Grimsby T: Sherwood; North, Agnew, Tillson, Lever, Cunnington, Jobling, Saunders, O'Kelly (Dixon),Cockerill, Alexander.

19 FEB

Watford (0) 0

Nottingham F (1) 3 *(Webb, Chapman, Laws)* 18,044

Watford: Coton; Gibbs, Jackett, Sherwood, Holdsworth David, Miller, Redfearn (Roberts), Wilkinson, Thompson, Porter, Holden.
Nottingham F: Sutton; Laws, Pearce, Walker, Wilson, Hodge, Carr, Webb, Clough, Chapman, Parker.

FIFTH ROUND REPLAY

22 FEB

Manchester U (1) 1 *(McClair)*

Bournemouth (0) 0 52,422

Manchester U: Leighton; Blackmore, Sharpe, Bruce, McGrath, Donaghy, Robson, Strachan, McClair, Hughes, Milne (Gill).
Bournemouth: Peyton; Newson, Morrell, Bond, Williams, O'Driscoll, Cooke, O'Connor (Close), Aylott, Bishop, Blissett.

SIXTH ROUND
18 MAR
Liverpool (1) 4 *(McMahon, Barnes, Beardsley 2)*

Brentford (0) 0 42,376

Liverpool: Grobbelaar; Ablett, Staunton, Nicol, Whelan, Gillespie, Beardsley, Aldridge, Houghton, Barnes, McMahon.
Brentford: Parks; Feeley (Bates), Stanislaus, Millen, Evans, Cockram, Jones, Sinton, Cadette, Blissett, Godfrey (Sealy).

Manchester U (0) 0

Nottingham F (1) 1 *(Parker)* 55,052

Manchester U: Leighton; Beardsmore, Sharpe (Martin), Bruce, McGrath, Donaghy, Robson, Strachan, McClair, Hughes, Milne (Blackmore).
Nottingham F: Sutton; Laws, Pearce, Walker, Wilson, Hodge, Carr, Webb, Clough, Chapman, Parker.

West Ham U (0) 0

Norwich C (0) 0 29,119

West Ham U: Parkes; Potts, Dicks, Gale, Strodder, Devonshire (Keen), Kelly, Dickens, Slater, Brady, Ince.
Norwich C: Gunn; Culverhouse, Bowen, Butterworth, Linighan, Townsend, Gordon, Rosario, Allen (Fox), Phelan, Putney.

19 MAR
Everton (0) 1 *(McCall)*

Wimbledon (0) 0 24,562

Everton: Southall; McDonald, Pointon, Ratcliffe, Watson, Bracewell, Steven, McCall, Sharp, Cottee, Sheedy.
Wimbledon: Segers; Scales, Phelan, Kruszynski (Jones), Young, Joseph, Fairweather, Miller (Cork), Fashanu, Sanchez, Wise.

SIXTH ROUND REPLAY
22 MAR
Norwich C (2) 3 *(Allen 2, Gordon)*

West Ham U (0) 1 *(Ince)* 25,785

Norwich C: Gunn; Culverhouse, Bowen, Butterworth, Linighan, Townsend (Crook), Gordon, Rosario, Allen, Phelan, Putney.
West Ham U: Parkes; Potts, Dicks, Gale, Strodder, Devonshire (Keen), Kelly (Hilton), Dickens, Slater, Brady, Ince.

SEMI-FINALS
15 APRIL

Everton (1) 1 *(Nevin)*

Norwich (0) 0 *(at Villa Park)* 46,553

Everton: Southall; McDonald, Van Den Hauwe, Ratcliffe, Watson, Bracewell, Nevin, Steven, Sharp, Cottee, Sheedy.
Norwich C: Gunn; Culverhouse, Bowen, Butterworth, Linighan, Townsend, Gordon, Allen (Fox), Rosario, Crook, Putney.

Liverpool (0) 0 *(at Hillsborough)*

Nottingham F (0) 0 *(abandoned after 6 minutes)* 53,000

7 MAY

Liverpool (1) 3 *(Aldridge 2, Laws (og))*

Nottingham F (1) 1 *(Webb)* 38,000

Liverpool: Grobbelaar; Ablett, Staunton, Nicol, Whelan, Hansen, Beardsley, Aldridge, Houghton, Barnes, McMahon.
Nottingham F: Sutton; Laws, Pearce, Walker, Wilson, Hodge, Gaynor (Starbuck), Webb, Clough, Chapman, Parker (Glover).

FINAL at Wembley
20 MAY

Everton (0) 2 *(McCall 2)*

Liverpool (1) 3 *(Aldridge, Rush 2) aet* 82,800

90 mins 1-1; receipts £1.6 Million
Everton: Southall; McDonald, Van Den Hauwe, Ratcliffe, Watson, Bracewell (McCall), Nevin, Steven, Sharp, Cottee, Sheedy (Wilson).
Liverpool: Grobbelaar; Ablett, Staunton (Venison), Nicol, Whelan, Hansen,Beardsley, Aldridge (Rush), Houghton, Barnes, McMahon,
Referee: J. Worrall (Warrington).

Sub. Ian Rush makes it 2-1 to Liverpool in the FA Cup Final.

SCOTTISH FOOTBALL

THE LEAGUE OFFICIALS

Management Committee

I. R. G. Gellatly, CA (President)
J. S. Steedman (Vice-President)
J. Y. Craig, JP, CA (Treasurer)

Premier Division Representatives

J. Y. Craig, JP, CA
G. M. Grant
J. C. McGinn
I. R. Donald
A. O. Fletcher

First Division Representatives

R. H. Davidson
J. Baxter
R. Laughlan

Second Division Representatives

E. Mitchell
P. I. McKay, MA, LL.B, NP

Secretary

James Farry

THE SCOTTISH SEASON 1988–89

The Skol Cup was a good curtain-raiser for the season. There is no doubt that the public wants instant results in all sport nowadays, and the knowledge that there is bound to be a result attracts the supporters. In general there were few upsets, and bigger teams took their due place above the smaller; but plenty of matches went to extra time, and several to penalty shoot-outs: Falkirk finally disposed of Raith Rovers 9-8 after the penalties. In the later stages, Dundee U defeated Celtic to reach the semi-finals, where they lost to Aberdeen; the other beaten semi-finalists were Hearts, and another Rangers-Aberdeen final proved an exciting context, the Dons twice drawing level before Ally McCoist settled the issue a couple of minutes from the end.

In the Premier Division it was not long before Hamilton Academical lost the place, and by Christmas they were well adrift at the foot of the table. This meant that the next group up were clear of the threat of relegation. The top four – Rangers, Aberdeen, Celtic, Dundee U – were soon, realistically, the only teams likely to produce the champions. Dundee U had a poor home record, Aberdeen had too many draws, Celtic made a hash of the early season; that left Rangers in the driving seat, and although everyone talked about "taking nothing for granted" and "we still have a chance", to the unbiased there was only one team in it short of a series of major upsets. None occurred, and Rangers duly took the title. They did have their injuries, but their expensive squad was more or less limitless, and they coped. At their best, they were a joy to watch; at their worst – occasionally – they still usually managed to do enough to gain points. It was not until late on that Hibernian clinched the 5th European place. Hearts, who had a wonderful run in Europe, did not find form in the League, and though for a moment they looked capable of mounting a challenge to Hibs, it fizzled out. St Mirren had their moments, but they were far too inconsistent.

There was interest in the First and Second Divisions right to the end of the season – in fact, in the First Division the issue was not finally settled until the last minutes being added on when a penalty was awarded: on that penalty depended the fates of Clyde and Kilmarnock: Colin McGlashan bravely converted the penalty against St Johnstone for Clyde (incidentally, the fourth he had scored in the last five matches) and down went Kilmarnock; they had scored six at Palmerston Park, but Clyde had the better goal difference – by one.

At the top of the division there was only one place to play for. Dunfermline made the early running, but other teams were ready to make their move. When Dunfermline faltered, Falkirk, Airdrie and Morton were there; St Johnstone and Clydebank, too, were not far off. The interest was kept up and on the last Saturday Falkirk could still have displaced Dunfermline, the leaders: they failed, and were thus left in the First Division for at least another year. There is continued stirring to try to increase the size of the Premier Division, and in truth one place is not much to aim at. The larger Premier Division was not really a success for the top clubs. Forty-four league games was too many when you add to that the Cup and Skol Cup games, perhaps a few in Europe, and other commitments. Two up, two down with a ten-club Premier Division really means a lack of security for the lower clubs in the Premier Division where a drop to the First Division means a very serious loss of income. What is the answer? A play-off has been suggested, with no. 2 in the First Division challenging no. 9 in the Premier Division; but this would mean everything depending upon two games at the end of a long season, where almost anything can happen. Is this really satisfactory? There is no simple answer – different sections of the division have different priorities, different requirements: there is no place for a compromise.

The Second Division was very competitive: Albion Rovers took a useful lead at the halfway stage, and maintained it – partly because of the cut-throat play amongst the teams below. The Wee Rovers confirmed their position as champions, for the first time since 1934. There was a scramble to join them in promotion. A month before the end, there were still six teams in with a good chance; and when the last game was played, three clubs had equal points, with one only a point adrift of them. Of the three, Alloa won their game and maintained their second position to gain promotion; Brechin defeated rivals East Fife, but had an inferior goal difference to Alloa; Stirling Albion, once again, were there or therabouts. Perhaps the most remarkable achievement in the Second Division came from Berwick Rangers: with only three points, they were firmly anchored at the bottom of the division at the beginning of December; they then had a run of twenty-one games without defeat, easily their best ever – and moved just one place up the table! Indeed, after thirteen of these twenty-one games they were still bottom – surely a record for all time.

In the Scottish Cup there were few flutters; no non-League clubs reached the third round, and about the only minor upset was the defeat of St Mirren by Partick after a replay; the

Roy Aitken holds the Scottish Cup aloft after Celtic's triumph in the 1989 final.

Buddies have not had a happy time in cup games since they won the Cup two seasons ago. Stranraer continued their visits to the top spots: last year they had only just lost at Celtic Park; this year they were trounced at Ibrox, but even so, they gave a good account of themselves. St Johnstone, after several encounters with First and Second Division opposition reached the semi-finals, where they lost to Rangers only after a replay. Hibs were the other losing semi-finalists. Rangers and Celtic, managing to keep clear of each other in the usual skilful way, eventually met in the final. Rangers were chasing the treble; Celtic were desperate to avoid a bare trophy cabinet. There was much to play for. There were, said the pundits, all the ingredients for a classic encounter. Well, of course, that is the recipe for just the opposite, and in truth, it was not a great game; but it remained good-tempered both amongst the players and the crowd. Celtic were delighted with Joe Miller's goal and the ribbons on the cup were the green and white ones: Rangers went home disappointed, but not dissatisfied with the season as a whole.

Our record in Europe was undistinguished. Aberdeen went out at the first hurdle, and Celtic, Dundee United and Rangers at the second, though all the results were close. It was left to Hearts to cover themselves with glory, reaching the quarter-finals and very nearly shocking Bayern Munich.

On the international front, Andy Roxburgh and his team enjoyed a magnificent start to their World Cup qualifying campaign. With Mo Johnston regularly scoring goals (there have been problems in this department before now) and with the squad doing well together, and turning in some excellent performances – notably against France, Scotland has reached a commanding position in the group, and we must now be hopeful of reaching the final stages. It is not a time for relaxing or over-confidence: but there seems little chance of that with the competent and thoughtful leadership, and with a great deal of planning and commitment from the management and players. The senior season ended with two somewhat irrelevant games, though doubtless useful in the way of experience. Against England a pretty weak Scottish side, which contained players who barely looked of international class on the occasion, lost to a weakened England side; this performance was redeemed by a good win against Chile, where the attendance was an all time low for an international fixture.

As a final curtain to the season came the FIFA Under 16 World Cup. This proved to be very popular with the fans – not least because of the magnificent achievement of our youngsters in reaching the final. Fancied teams came from the Middle East and Africa, as well as the recent finalists from the European competition, Portugal and East Germany. Brazil, too, could never be counted out. Scotland went from strength to strength: in a memorable final, they were leading 2-0 at half-time; but they had given their all, and the Saudi Arabians were able to level the score, and in the end win on penalties 5-4. The standard of play throughout the tournament was high, and the level of skill indicates the shape of things to come. A crowd of nearly 30,000 saw Scotland's semi-final win at Tynecastle; Motherwell, who hosted one of the groups and who had drawn substantial and enthusiastic crowds, were rewarded when FIFA moved the other semi-final there from Hampden. There were over 50,000 at Hampden for the final: there was a crowd limit, and it was a real family day. In addition to a high standard of play and sportsmanship, it was pleasant for both the SFA and the police to receive glowing compliments from FIFA for the organisation, crowd behaviour and crowd control. Congratulations to all concerned, and in particular to Craig Brown and his youth team who all did so well.

Alan Elliott

ABERDEEN Premier Division

Year Formed: 1903. *Ground & Address:* Pittodrie Stadium, Pittodrie St, Aberdeen AB2 1QH. *Telephone:* 0224 632328.
Ground Capacity: total: 22,568 seated: All. *Size of Pitch:* 110yd×72yd.
Chairman: Richard M. Donald. *Secretary:* Ian J. Taggart. *Commercial Manager:* —.
Managers: Alex Smith and Jocky Scott. *Assist. Manager:* Drew Jarvie. *Physio:* David Wylie. *Coach:* Teddy Scott.
Managers since 1975: Ally MacLeod; Billy McNeill; Alex Ferguson; Ian Porterfield; Alex Smith and Jocky Scott.
Club Nickname(s): The Dons. *Previous Grounds:* None.
Record Attendance: 45,061 v Hearts, Scottish Cup 4th rd; 13 Mar, 1954.
Record Transfer Fee received: £800,000 for Steve Archibald to Tottenham Hotspur (1980).
Record Transfer Fee paid: £500,000 for Charlie Nicholas from Arsenal, Jan , 1988.
Record Victory: 13-0 v Peterhead, Scottish Cup; 9 Feb, 1923.
Record Defeat: 0-8 v Celtic, Division I; 30 Jan, 1965.

1988–89 LEAGUE RECORD

Match No.	Date	Venue	Opponents	Result	H/T Score	Lg. Pos.	Goalscorers	Attendance
1	Aug 13	A	Dundee	D 1-1	0-0	—	Dodds	12,222
2	20	H	St Mirren	D 1-1	0-0	5	Connor	12,046
3	27	A	Dundee U	D 2-2	0-1	4	Bett (pen), Hewitt	14,735
4	Sept 3	H	Hibernian	D 0-0	0-0	4		13,583
5	17	A	Celtic	W 3-1	2-1	3	Grant, Bett (pen), Dodds	37,769
6	24	H	Hearts	W 1-0	1-0	3	Nicholas	14,000
7	27	A	Hamilton A	W 1-0	0-0	—	Connor	3634
8	Oct 1	A	Motherwell	D 1-1	1-1	4	Miller	4225
9	8	H	Rangers	W 2-1	0-1	3	Bett (pen), Nicholas	22,370
10	12	A	St Mirren	D 1-1	0-1	—	Dodds	4284
11	29	A	Hearts	D 1-1	1-0	3	Whittaker (og)	12,644
12	Nov 2	H	Celtic	D 2-2	2-1	—	Dodds, Nicholas	22,000
13	5	A	Hibernian	W 2-1	0-1	2	Nicholas 2	11,500
14	12	H	Dundee U	D 1-1	1-0	2	Mason	15,184
15	16	H	Dundee	W 1-0	0-0	—	Wright	11,181
16	19	H	Motherwell	W 2-1	2-0	2	Hewitt, Nicholas	10,028
17	26	A	Rangers	L 0-1	0-1	2		42,239
18	Dec 3	H	Hamilton A	D 1-1	0-0	2	Nicholas	8324
19	10	A	Celtic	D 0-0	0-0	3		42,437
20	17	H	St Mirren	W 3-1	1-0	3	Robertson C, Irvine, Hewitt	8500
21	31	A	Dundee	L 0-2	0-1	3		9828
22	Jan 3	A	Dundee U	D 1-1	1-1	—	Nicholas	17,952
23	7	H	Hibernian	W 2-0	0-0	3	Nicholas 2	13,500
24	14	H	Rangers	L 1-2	1-2	4	Nicholas	22,000
25	21	A	Motherwell	W 2-0	2-0	4	Van Der Ark, Connor	5906
26	Feb 14	A	Hamilton A	W 2-0	1-0	—	Connor, Wright	2016
27	25	H	Hearts	W 3-0	3-0	3	Irvine, McPherson (og), Wright	15,000
28	Mar 11	H	Dundee	W 2-0	1-0	2	Nicholas, Wright	11,800
29	25	A	St Mirren	W 3-1	1-1	2	Wright, Nicholas, Mason	7541
30	Apr 1	H	Dundee U	W 1-0	0-0	2	Nicholas	16,700
31	8	A	Hibernian	W 2-1	1-1	2	Mason, Bett	11,000
32	15	H	Hamilton A	W 3-0	1-0	2	Mason, Nicholas 2	9712
33	22	A	Hearts	L 0-1	0-1	2		13,367
34	29	H	Celtic	D 0-0	0-0	2		21,500
35	May 6	H	Motherwell	D 0-0	0-0	2		6500
36	13	A	Rangers	W 3-0	1-0	2	Wright, Bett, Van Der Ark	42,480

Final League Position: 2

GOALSCORERS

League: (51): Nicholas 16, Wright 6, Bett 5 (4 pens), Connor 4, Dodds 4, Mason 4, Hewitt 3, Irvine 2, Van Der Ark 2, Grant 1, Miller 1, Robertson C 1, own goals 2.
League Cup: (12): Bett 3, Dodds 3, Hewitt 2, Miller 2, Grant 1, Nicholas 1.
Scottish Cup: (5): Wright 2, Connor 1, Grant 1, Nicholas 1.

Most Capped Players: Alex McLeish and Willie Miller, 63, Scotland.
Most League Appearances: 543: Willie Miller, 1973–89.
Most League Goals in Season (Individual): 38: Benny Yorston, Division I; 1929–30.
Most Goals Overall (Individual): 199: Joe Harper.

Honours
League Champions: Division I 1954–55. Premier Division 1979–80, 1983–84, 1984–85; *Runners-up:* Division I 1910–11, 1936–37, 1955–56, 1970–71, 1971–72. Premier Division 1977–78, 1980–81, 1981–82.
Scottish Cup Winners: 1947, 1970, 1982, 1983, 1984, 1986; *Runners-up:* 1937, 1953, 1954, 1959, 1967, 1978.
League Cup Winners: 1955–56, 1976–77, 1985–86; *Runners-up:* 1946–47, 1978–79, 1979–80, 1987–88.
Drybrough Cup Winners: 1971, 1980.
European: *European Cup* 12 matches (1980–81, 1984–85, 1985–86); *Cup Winners Cup Winners:* 1982–83. Semi-finals 1983–84. 31 matches (1967–68, 1970–71, 1978–79, 1982–83, 1983–84, 1986–87); *UEFA Cup* 28 matches (1968–69 *Fairs Cup;* 1971–72, 1972–73, 1973–74, 1977–78, 1979–80, 1981–82, 1987–88).
Club colours: Shirt, Shorts, Stockings: Red with white trim.

Snelders, T	McKimmie, S	Robertson, D	Simpson, N	McLeish, A	Miller, W	Gray, S	Bett, J	Nicholas, C	Connor, R	Hewitt, J	Dodds, D	Irvine, B	Mason, P	Wright, P	Grant, B	MacLeod, A	Robertson, I	Robertson, C	Van Der Ark, W	Watson Gregg	Jess, E	*Match No.*
1	2	3	4	5	6	7	8	9*	10†	11	12	14										1
1	2	3	4	5	6		8		10	11			7*	9	12							2
1	2	3	4	5	6		8		10	11	9			7								3
1	2	3	4	5	6			12	10	11	9				8	7*						4
1	2	3		5	6		8	7	10	11*	9		12		4							5
1	2		4	5	6		8	7	10	11	9*		12		3							6
1	2		4*	5	6		8	7	10	11		3	12		9							7
1		3		5	6		8	7	10	11	9†	12	2*	14	4							8
1	2	3	4*	5	6		8	7	10	11	9	12										9
1	2	3	4	5	6		8	7*	10	11	9	12										10
1	2	3		5			8	7	10	12	9	6	4*		11							11
1	2	3		5			8	7	10	11†	9*	6	12	14	4							12
1	2	3		5			8	7	10		9	6	11		4							13
1	2	3			6		8	7*	10	12	9	5	11		4							14
1	2	3		5	6		8		10	7	9		11	12	4*							15
1	2	3		5	6		8	7	10	11*	9		4	12								16
1	2	3		5	6		8	7	10	11†	9	4*		14	12							17
1	2	3*	4	5	6		8	7	10	12	9†		11	14								18
1	2	3	4*	5		9		7	10	11		6	8		12							19
1	2	3		5		7			10	11	14	6	12	9*	4			8†				20
1	2	3*	4			7†			10	11	9	5	8	12	6			14				21
1	2		4	5			8	7*	10		14	6	11	9†	12		3					22
1	2		4	5			8	7	10	12		6	11*	9			3					23
1	2		4	5			8	7	10		12	6	11	9			3*					24
1	2		4	5			8	7	10		9†	6	12	14			3		11*			25
1	2		4	5			8	7	10	11		6		9			3					26
1	2	3*		5					10	11†	14	6	7	9	8			4		12		27
1	2			5	6		8	7	10	11				9	4		3					28
1	2*			5	6		8	7	10			12	11	9†	4		3		14			29
1	2			5	6		8	7	10	11†	14	12	3		4				9*			30
1	2			5	6		8*	7†	10	14		3	11	9	4			12				31
1	2			5	6		8	7	10			3	11	9	4*				12			32
1	2†			5	6		8	7	10	12		3	11*	9	4				14			33
1	2	3		5			8	7	10*			6	11	9†	4				14	12		34
1	2	3†		5			8	7	10			6	12		4				9	14	11*	35
1	2	3		5			8		10			6	11*	9†	4				7	12	14	36
36	35	23	16	34	21	4	31	28 + 1s	36	21 + 6s	17 + 6s	21 + 6s	21 + 7s	15 + 8s	22 + 4s	1	7	2 + 2s	4 + 4s	— + 4s	1 + 1s	

AIRDRIEONIANS First Division

Year Formed: 1878. *Ground & Address:* Broomfield Park, Gartlea Rd, Airdrie ML6 9JL. *Telephone:* 0236 62067.
Ground Capacity: total: 11,830 seated: 1350. *Size of Pitch:* 112yd×68yd.
Chairman: Robert H. Davidson. *Secretary:* George W. Peat CA. *Commercial Manager:* —.
Manager: Jim Bone. *Assistant Manager:* —. *Physio:* —. *Coach:* Ian Bird.
Managers since 1975: I. McMillan; J. Stewart; R. Watson; W. Munro; A. MacLeod; D. Whiteford; G. McQueen; J. Bone.
Club Nickname(s): The Diamonds or The Waysiders. *Previous Grounds:* Mavisbank.
Record Attendance: 24,000 v Hearts, Scottish Cup; 8 Mar, 1952.
Record Transfer Fee received: £200,000 for Sandy Clark to West Ham U, May 1982.
Record Transfer Fee paid: £60,000 for Blair Millar from Clydebank, June 1982.

1988–89 LEAGUE RECORD

Match No.	Date	Venue	Opponents	Result	H/T Score	Lg. Pos.	Goalscorers	Attendance
1	Aug 13	A	Falkirk	D 0-0	0-0	—		3500
2	20	H	Morton	D 1-1	1-0	8	Conn	1200
3	27	H	Queen of the S	W 3-0	2-0	3	Macdonald K, Docherty (og), Black	1100
4	Sept 3	A	St Johnstone	L 1-2	0-0	6	Macdonald K	2222
5	10	H	Kilmarnock	W 5-1	2-0	2	Black, MacDonald I, Campbell, Macdonald K, 2 (1 pen)	1500
6	17	A	Raith R	W 2-1	2-0	1	Conn, Macdonald K	2551
7	24	H	Partick T	W 5-1	1-1	1	Conn 2, Grant, Macdonald K, Campbell	2200
8	Oct 1	H	Meadowbank T	D 0-0	0-0	2		1400
9	8	A	Dunfermline Ath	L 0-1	0-0	4		5616
10	15	H	Clyde	D 1-1	0-1	4	Campbell	2500
11	22	A	Clydebank	D 3-3	3-3	4	Macdonald K 2, Campbell	1321
12	29	A	Forfar Ath	D 1-1	1-0	4	Macdonald K	907
13	Nov 5	H	Ayr U	W 2-1	0-0	4	Macdonald K 2 (2 pens)	2430
14	12	A	Kilmarnock	W 3-0	1-0	3	Campbell 2, MacKinnon	1958
15	19	H	Raith R	W 3-1	2-0	2	Campbell 2, Grant	2000
16	26	A	Partick T	W 2-0	2-0	2	Macdonald K (pen), Campbell	2847
17	Dec 3	A	Morton	W 2-0	0-0	2	Macdonald K (pen), Lawrie	2500
18	10	H	Forfar Ath	L 0-3	0-1	2		1500
19	17	H	Clydebank	D 1-1	0-1	2	Campbell	1800
20	27	A	Clyde	D 0-0	0-0	—		1400
21	31	H	St Johnstone	W 1-0	0-0	2	Cherry (og)	2400
22	Jan 3	A	Queen of the S	W 4-2	2-1	—	Macdonald K (pen), Campbell 2, Conn	1350
23	7	A	Ayr U	W 4-1	1-1	1	Lawrie, Macdonald K 2 (1 pen), MacDonald I	3815
24	14	H	Falkirk	W 2-0	1-0	1	Macdonald K, McLeod	6300
25	21	H	Dunfermline Ath	L 0-2	0-0	2		9100
26	Feb 4	A	Meadowbank T	L 2-3	0-3	2	Macdonald K 2 (1 pen)	900
27	11	H	Forfar Ath	W 2-1	1-1	2	Macdonald K 2 (1 pen)	1121
28	Mar 1	A	Raith R	D 1-1	0-0	—	Conn	1683
29	4	A	Kilmarnock	D 1-1	1-0	2	Black	2376
30	11	H	Clyde	D 1-1	1-0	2	Black	1100
31	18	A	Partick T	L 0-1	0-0	2		2793
32	25	H	Morton	W 2-1	1-0	2	Curran, Campbell	1000
33	Apr 1	H	Queen of the S	W 3-0	2-0	2	McPhee, Lawrence, Campbell	900
34	8	A	Dunfermline Ath	D 1-1	0-1	3	Macdonald K	8303
35	22	A	Meadowbank T	L 1-3	0-1	4	MacDonald I	800
36	24	H	St Johnstone	D 1-1	0-1	—	Conn	800
37	29	H	Falkirk	W 3-0	1-0	3	Holmes (og), Lawrence, Conn	4400
38	May 6	A	Ayr U	L 1-3	1-2	3	McPhee	2970
39	13	A	Clydebank	L 1-4	0-3	4	McPhee	1143

Final League Position: 4

GOALSCORERS

League: (66): Macdonald K 22 (9 pens), Campbell 14, Conn 8, Black 4, MacDonald I 3, McPhee 3, Grant 2, Lawrence 2, Lawrie 2, Curran 1, MacKinnon 1, McLeod 1, own goals 3.
League Cup: (0).
Scottish Cup: (0).

Record Victory: 15-1 v Dundee Wanderers, Division II; 1 Dec, 1894.
Record Defeat: 1-11 v Hibernian, Division I; 24 Oct, 1959.
Most Capped Player: Jimmy Crapnell, 9, Scotland.
Most League Appearances: 523: Paul Jonquin, 1962–79.
Most League Goals in Season (Individual): 39: Bert Yarnall, Division I; 1916–17.
Most Goals Overall (Individual): —.

Honours
League Champions: Division II 1902–03, 1954–55, 1973–74; *Runners-up:* Division I 1922–23, 1923–24, 1924–25, 1925–26. First Division 1979–80. Division II 1900–01, 1946–47, 1949–50, 1965–66.
Scottish Cup Winners: 1924; *Runners-up:* 1975.
League Cup:—.
Club colours: Shirt: White with Red diamond. Shorts: White. Stockings: Red with white diamond tops.

Walsh, G	MacKinnon, D	Black, I	McKeown, B	Grant, D	Nelson, M	Butler, J	Conn, S	MacCabe, D	Macdonald, K	MacDonald, I	Lawrie, D	Campbell, C	Thomson, W	Moore, V	Lindsay, C	Martin, J	Shirkie, S	McPhee, I	McLeod, G	McKenna, T	Ogilvie, G	Balfour, E	Curran, P	Lawrence, A	McKeown, D	Match No.
1	2	3	4	5	6*	7	8†	9	10	11	12	14														1
1	2	3	4	5	6	7†	8*	9	10	11	12	14														2
1	2	3	4	5	6	7†		9*	10	11		12	8	14												3
	2	3	4	5	6	7*		9	10	11		12	8†	14		1										4
		3	4	5	6			9	10*	11	2	8	12	7†	14	1										5
	2	3	4	5	6		8*		10	11	12	9			7	1										6
	2	3	4	5	6*	12	8		10	11†		9	14		7	1										7
	2	3	4	5	6		8		10	11		9	12		7*	1										8
	2	3	4	5	6†		8		10	11	12	9		7*	14	1										9
	2	3	4	5	6		8		10		14	9	12	7†	11*	1										10
	2	3	4	5	6		8		10	11		9		7		1										11
	2	3	4	5	6*		8		10	11		9		7	12	1										12
	2	3	4	5	6		7		10	11		9				1		8								13
	2	3	4	5	6		7†		10	11*		9	12	14		1		8								14
	2	3	4	5	12	10*	7			11†		9				1	14	8	6							15
		3	4	5	12		7		10	11*	2	9				1		8	6							16
	2	3	4	5			7		10	11*	12	9				1		8	6							17
		3	4	5	12		7*		10	11	2	9				1		8	6							18
	2	3	4	5		14	7*		10†	11	12	9				1		8	6							19
	2	3	4	5	7				10	11		9				1		8	6							20
	2	3	4	5	7	12			10	11		9				1		8	6*							21
	2	3	4	5	7*	12	6†		10	11	14	9				1		8								22
	2	3		5	6	12	7*		10	11	4	9				1		8								23
	2	3	4	5			7		10	11		9				1		8	6							24
	2	3	4	5		12	7		10	11		9				1		8	6*							25
		3		5	4*	12	7		10	11	2	9		6†		1		8		14						26
		3	4	5			7		10		6	9			11	1		8			2					27
		3	4	5			7		10	11	6*	9			12	1		8			2					28
		3	4	5			7		10	11		9			6	1		8			2					29
		3	4	5			7		10	11		9			6*	1		8			2	12				30
		3	4	5					10	11	7	9			6	1		8			2					31
		3	4	5		12			10		7*	9			6	1		8			2		11			32
		3*	4	5		12	7		10	11		9				1		8			2			6		33
		3	4	5			7		10	11	2	9				1		8						6		34
	6†	3*	4	5	14	9				11	7					1		8			2			10	12	35
	2	3	4	5		12	6			11	9					1		8						10	7*	36
	2	3*	4	5			7		10	11	9					1		8						6	12	37
	2		4	5			7		10	11	3	9				1		8						6*	12	38
	2		4	5			7		10	11*	3†	9				1	12	8						6	14	39
3	27	37	37	39	19 + 4s	6 + 10s	31	5	36	36	15 + 8s	32 + 4s	2 + 5s	6 + 3s	9 + 4s	36	— + 2s	27	9	— + 1s	8	— + 1s	1	7	1 + 4s	

ALBION ROVERS First Division

Year Formed: 1882. *Ground & Address:* Cliftonhill Stadium, Main St, Coatbridge ML5 9XX. *Telephone:* 0236 32350.
Ground Capacity: total: 8780 seated: 474. *Size of Pitch:* 110yd×74yd.
Chairman: David Forrester C.A.. *Secretary:* D. Forrester C.A.. *Commercial Manager:* Robin W. Marwick J.P., R.I.B.A..
Manager: David Provan. *Assistant Manager:* —. *Physio:* Frank Ness. *Coach:* Joe Baker.
Managers since 1975: G. Caldwell; S. Goodwin; D. Whiteford; W. Wilson; T. Gemmell; D. Provan.
Club Nickname(s): The Wee Rovers. *Previous Grounds:* Meadow Park, Whifflet.
Record Attendance: 27,381 v Rangers, Scottish Cup 2nd rd; 8 Feb, 1936.
Record Transfer Fee received: £40,000 for Bruce Cleland to Motherwell.

1988–89 LEAGUE RECORD

Match No.	Date	Venue	Opponents	Result	H/T Score	Lg. Pos.	Goalscorers	Attendance
1	Aug 13	H	East Stirling	W 1-0	1-0	—	Teevan	350
2	20	A	East Fife	W 2-1	0-0	3	Chapman, Cadden	556
3	27	A	Stranraer	L 1-3	1-1	6	Chapman (pen)	550
4	Sept 3	H	Dumbarton	W 2-1	1-1	4	Cougan, Graham	300
5	10	H	Brechin C	D 1-1	1-0	4	Graham	431
6	17	A	Cowdenbeath	D 1-1	0-1	5	Chapman	200
7	24	H	Queen's Park	D 1-1	0-0	5	Chapman (pen)	571
8	Oct 1	A	Alloa	L 1-3	1-1	7	Teevan	377
9	8	H	Berwick R	W 3-1	0-0	5	Chapman, Graham, Teevan	250
10	15	H	Arbroath	W 3-1	0-1	3	Chapman, Teevan, Graham	727
11	22	A	Stirling Albion	L 2-4	0-1	5	Graham, Chapman (pen)	962
12	29	H	Montrose	W 2-1	1-1	4	Cougan, Teevan	520
13	Nov 5	A	Stenhousemuir	W 3-2	2-0	3	Teevan, Cadden 2	300
14	12	H	East Fife	W 2-0	0-0	2	Granger, Graham	465
15	19	A	East Stirling	W 4-3	2-2	2	Cougan, Chapman 2 (1 pen), Watson	200
16	26	A	Brechin C	W 2-0	0-0	1	McGowan, Brown (og)	500
17	Dec 10	H	Cowdenbeath	W 3-1	2-1	1	Teevan 2, Chapman (pen)	521
18	17	A	Queen's Park	D 0-0	0-0	1		820
19	24	H	Stenhousemuir	W 1-0	0-0	1	Graham	663
20	31	A	Montrose	L 0-1	0-1	1		500
21	Jan 3	H	Stranraer	W 3-0	1-0	—	Teevan 2, Graham	845
22	21	A	Arbroath	W 3-0	1-0	1	Bishop 2, Diver	436
23	31	H	Stirling Albion	W 1-0	0-0	—	Graham	756
24	Feb 4	A	Berwick R	L 1-2	0-1	1	McGowan	639
25	11	H	Alloa	W 3-2	1-0	1	Diver, Cadden, McGowan	610
26	18	A	Queen's Park	L 2-3	0-2	1	Chapman, Graham	947
27	Mar 4	H	East Fife	L 1-2	0-1	1	Graham	621
28	7	H	Montrose	D 2-2	1-1	—	McKenzie, Graham	402
29	11	A	East Sterling	W 1-0	0-0	1	McKenzie (pen)	300
30	18	H	Stranraer	D 2-2	1-2	1	Chapman, Granger	634
31	25	A	Stenhousemuir	W 2-1	0-1	1	Bishop, Graham	700
32	Apr 1	A	Brechin C	L 1-2	0-1	1	Diver	485
33	4	A	Dumbarton	L 0-1	0-0	—		600
34	8	H	Cowdenbeath	W 2-1	0-0	1	Teevan, Cadden	452
35	15	A	Stirling Albion	D 0-0	0-0	1		861
36	22	H	Dumbarton	W 2-0	1-0	1	Graham, Chapman	840
37	29	A	Alloa	L 0-2	0-0	1		993
38	May 6	H	Arbroath	D 2-2	1-1	1	Chapman 2 (1 pen)	665
39	13	H	Berwick R	W 2-1	2-0	1	Graham, Granger	600

Final League Position: 1

GOALSCORERS

League: (65): Chapman 15 (6 pens), Graham 15, Teevan 11, Cadden 5, Bishop 3, Cougan 3, Diver 3, Granger 3, McGowan 3, McKenzie 2 (1 pen), Watson 1, own goal 1.
League Cup: (2): Chapman 1 (pen), Rodgers 1.
Scottish Cup: (3): Diver 1, McDonald 1, McGowan 1.

Record Victory: 12-0 v Airdriehill, Scottish Cup; 3 Sept, 1887.
Record Defeat: 1-9 v Motherwell, Division I; 2 Jan, 1937.
Most Capped Player: Jock White, 1 (2), Scotland.
Most League Appearances: —.
Most League Goals in Season (Individual): 41: Jim Renwick, Division II; 1932–33.
Most Goals Overall (Individual): 105: Bunty Weir, 1928–31.

Honours
League Champions: Division II 1933–34; *Runners-up:* Division II 1913–14, 1937–38, 1947–48. Second Division 1988–89.
Scottish Cup Runners-up: 1920.
League Cup:—.
Club colours: Shirt: Yellow with red & white trim. Shorts: Red with yellow stripes. Stockings: Yellow with red band.

McCulloch, R	Edgar, D	McGowan, M	Cadden, S	Oliver, M	Clark, R	Houston, D	Chapman, J	Graham, A	Rodgers, A	Teevan, P	Cougan, C	McDonald, D	Granger, C	Verlaque, D	Fairlie, B	Watson, E	Bishop, J	Diver, D	McKenzie, P	Ashcroft, I	Cormack, D	*Match No.*
1	2	3	4	5	6	7*	8	9	10	11	12											1
1	2	3	4	5	6	7†	8	9	10*	11	14	12										2
1	2	3	4	5	6	7*	8	9	10†	11	12	14										3
1	2	3	4	5	6		8	9		7	11*	12	10									4
1	2	3	4	5	6		8	9	14	11	7*	12	10†									5
1	2	3	4	5	6		8	9		11	7*	14	10†	12								6
1	2	3	4	5	6		8	9		11*	12	7	10†	14								7
1	2	3	4	5	6		8	9		11		7	10*		12							8
1	12	3	4	5	6		8	14		11	7*	2	10		9†							9
1	14	3	4	5	6		8	9		11*		2	10	7†	12							10
1	12	3*	4	5	6		8	9		11	7	2	10†	14								11
1	12	3	4	5	6		8	9		7	11	2*	10									12
1		3	4	5	6		8	9		11	7*	2	10			12						13
1		3	4	5	6		8	9		11	7	2	10									14
1		3	4	5	6		8	9		11	7	2	10*			12						15
1		3	8	5	6			9		11	12	2	10			4	7*					16
1		3	4	5	6		8	9		11		2	10				7					17
1		3	4	5	6		8	9		11	12	2	10				7*					18
1		3	4	5	6		8	9		11		2	10				12	7*				19
1	2	3	4	5			8	9		11		6	10*				12	7				20
1		3	4	5			8	9		11*	12	6	10			2	7					21
1		3	8	5	6			9*		11		2	10†			14	7	12	4			22
1		3	4	5	6			9		11			10			2	7		8			23
1		3	4	5	6		14	9		11			10*			2	7†	12	8			24
1		3	7	5	6		8	9				12	10†			2*	14	11	4			25
1		3	8	5	6		10	9				12	14			2*	7	11†	4			26
1		3		5	6		8	9		11*		2	10				7	12	4			27
1		3		5*	6		8	9		7		2	10				11	12	4			28
1		3	8	5	6		10†	9		7		2	14				12		4	11*		29
1		3	8	5	6		11	9		7*		2	14				12		4	10†		30
1			8	5	3			9		11†		2	10			12	7*	14	4	6		31
1			8	5	3		12	9		11		2†	10				7*	14	4	6		32
1			8	5	3		7	9				2	10*				12	11	4	6		33
1		3	10	5	6		8	9		11*	7†		14					12	4	2		34
1		3	8	5	6		10	9		11†	12	2				14	7*		4			35
1		3	8	5	6		10	9		11		2					7		4			36
		3	4†	5	6		11*	9		12	7	2	10			14			8		1	37
		3		5	6		10	9		11	7†	2*	12			4	14		8		1	38
1		3	8*	5	6		11	7		14		2	10			12	9†		4			39
37	9 + 4s	36	36	39	37	3	33 + 2s	38 + 1s	3 + 1s	34 + 2s	12 + 8s	28 + 7s	29 + 5s	1 + 3s	1 + 2s	7 + 7s	15 + 7s	5 + 7s	18	6	2	

ALLOA

First Division

Year Formed: 1883. *Ground & Address:* Recreation Park, Clackmannan Rd, Alloa FK10 1RR. *Telephone:* 0259 722695.
Ground Capacity: total: 3100 seated: 180. *Size of Pitch:* 110yd×75yd.
Chairman: George Ormiston. *Secretary:* E. G. Cameron. *Commercial Manager:* William McKie.
Manager: George Abel. *Assistant Manager:* —. *Physio:* F. Rae. *Coach:* Billy Little.
Managers since 1975: H. Wilson; A Totten; W. Garner; J. Thomson; D. Sullivan; G. Abel.
Club Nickname(s): The Wasps. *Previous Grounds:* None.
Record Attendance: 13,000 v Dunfermline Athletic, Scottish Cup 3rd rd replay; 26 Feb, 1939.
Record Transfer Fee received: £30,000 for Martin Nelson to Hamilton A (1988).
Record Transfer Fee paid: —.

1988–89 LEAGUE RECORD

Match No.	Date	Venue	Opponents	Result	H/T Score	Lg. Pos.	Goalscorers	Atten-dance
1	Aug 13	A	Brechin C	L 1-2	1-0	—	Lytwyn	558
2	20	H	Cowdenbeath	W 2-1	0-1	7	Lytwyn, Smith A	421
3	27	A	Arbroath	D 2-2	2-0	7	Ramsay, Bateman	406
4	Sept 3	H	Stenhousemuir	L 1-2	1-0	11	Lytwyn	672
5	10	A	East Fife	L 0-2	0-2	11		675
6	17	H	East Stirling	D 2-2	2-1	11	Bateman, Gibson	440
7	24	A	Dumbarton	D 1-1	0-0	12	Rutherford	500
8	Oct 1	H	Albion R	W 3-1	1-1	12	Lamont, Lytwyn, Ramsay	377
9	8	A	Stirling Albion	L 1-3	0-1	12	Smith A	730
10	15	H	Berwick R	W 2-1	2-0	11	Lytwyn, Gibson	408
11	22	A	Montrose	L 0-1	0-1	11		350
12	29	A	Queen's Park	W 2-0	1-0	11	Lytwyn, Smith A	610
13	Nov 5	H	Stranraer	D 1-1	0-0	11	Lee I	418
14	12	A	Cowdenbeath	D 1-1	0-1	11	Lamont	454
15	19	H	Brechin C	D 2-2	2-2	10	Lytwyn, Smith S	398
16	26	H	East Fife	W 2-1	1-1	9	Lytwyn, Gibson	428
17	Dec 10	A	East Stirling	L 1-2	1-1	10	Lytwyn	300
18	17	H	Dumbarton	W 2-0	0-0	9	Blackie, Lytwyn	563
19	24	A	Stranraer	D 2-2	2-0	9	Blackie, Lytwyn	550
20	31	H	Queen's Park	D 0-0	0-0	9		633
21	Jan 3	H	Arbroath	D 3-3	1-1	—	Blackie, Lamont 2	565
22	21	A	Berwick R	D 1-1	0-1	8	Millen	410
23	24	A	Stenhousemuir	L 0-2	0-1	—		460
24	31	H	Montrose	W 1-0	0-0	—	McCallum	600
25	Feb 4	H	Stirling Albion	W 3-2	1-0	7	McCulloch 2, Lee I	895
26	11	A	Albion R	L 2-3	0-1	8	Millen (pen), Lytwyn	610
27	Mar 1	H	Arbroath	W 3-0	2-0	—	Lytwyn 2 (1 pen), McCallum	548
28	4	H	Stenhousemuir	W 4-0	1-0	5	McCallum, Lytwyn, Miller, Smith A	726
29	7	A	Brechin C	W 2-1	1-1	—	McCallum, Lamont	400
30	11	A	East Fife	L 0-1	0-1	5		550
31	22	A	Berwick R	L 0-1	0-0	—		450
32	25	H	Cowdenbeath	W 2-1	0-0	6	McCallum 2	488
33	Apr 1	A	Stranraer	W 4-1	2-1	4	Lytwyn 3 (1 pen), McCallum	850
34	8	H	Stirling Albion	W 4-0	0-0	3	Blackie, Lamont 2, Rodgers	1357
35	15	A	East Stirling	L 0-2	0-0	3		300
36	22	H	Montrose	D 3-3	2-1	3	Lytwyn (pen), Lamont 2	638
37	29	H	Albion R	W 2-0	0-0	2	Lytwyn, McCulloch	993
38	May 6	A	Queen's Park	W 2-0	2-0	2	Lytwyn 2	757
39	13	A	Dumbarton	W 2-0	0-0	2	Lytwyn, Gibson	800

Final League Position: 2

GOALSCORERS

League: (66): Lytwyn 23 (2 pens), Lamont 9, McCallum 7, Blackie 4, Gibson 4, Smith A 4, McCulloch 3, Millen 3 (1 pen), Bateman 2, Lee I 2, Ramsay 2, Rodgers 1, Rutherford 1, Smith S 1.
League Cup: (2): Lytwyn 1, Rutherford 1 (pen).
Scottish Cup: (13): Smith A 5, Lytwyn 3, Gibson 2, Lamont 2, Ramsay 1.

Record Victory: 9-2 v Forfar Ath, Division II; 18 Mar, 1933.
Record Defeat: 0-10 v Dundee, Division II; 8 Mar, 1947: v Third Lanark, League Cup, 8 Aug, 1953.
Most Capped Player: Jock Hepburn, 1, Scotland.
Most League Appearances: —.
Most League Goals in Season (Individual): 49: William 'Wee' Crilley, Division II; 1921–22.
Most Goals Overall (Individual): —.

Honours
League Champions: Division II 1921–22; *Runners-up:* Division II 1938–39. Second Division 1976–77, 1981–82, 1984–85, 1988–89.
Scottish Cup:—.
League Cup:—.
Club colours: Shirt: Gold with black trim. Shorts: Black. Stockings: Gold.

Lowrie, R	Robertson, R	Lee, R	Spence, T	McCulloch, K	Ramsay, S	Shiels, M	Gibson, J	Rutherford, P	Bateman, A	Lytwyn, C	Lamont, P	Millen, A	Smith, A	Haggart, L	McGurn, J	Rodgers, A	Lee, I	Smith, S	Henderson, A	Blackie, W	Conlin, L	McCallum, M	Match No.
1	2	3	4	5	6	7	8*	9	10	11	12												1
1	2	3		5	10	7*	8	9†	6	11	12	4	14										2
1	2	3		5	7		8	9	6	11	10*	4		12									3
1	2	3		5	10*		8	9	6	11	14	4	7†	12									4
1	2	6*		5	14		7	9†	8	11	12	4		3	10								5
1	2	14		5	6†		8	9	10	11	7*	4	12	3									6
1	2	12		5			8	9	10	11	14	4	7†	3*	6								7
1	2	3		5	14		8		10*	9	11†	4	7	12	6								8
1	2	3		5	7		8		10†		14	4	9	11	6*	12							9
1	2*	3		5	6		8†			9	11	4	7	12	14		10						10
1		3		5	6		8*		12	9	11	4	7†	2			10	14					11
1		3		5	6*		8			9	14	4	7†	2		12	10		11				12
1	2			5	12		8			9	14	4	7	3		6*	10		11†				13
1	2			5	14		8†			9	11	4	12	3		6	10		7*				14
1	2			5			6		14	9*	11	4		3		8	10	7†	12				15
1	2	5					6†		12	9	11*	4		3		8	10	14		7			16
1	2	5			6*				12	9	11†	4	14	3		8	10			7			17
1	2	14		5			6		12	9	11†	4		3		8	10*			7			18
1	2	12		5			6		11*	9	14	4		3		8	10			7†			19
1	2	14		5			6		11*	9	12	4		3		8†	10			7			20
1	2†	14		5			6		12	9	11*	4		3		8	10			7			21
1	2	3		5	11		6		8	9		4					10			7			22
1	2	3		5	8†		6		14	9		4	12				10				7*	11	23
1		3		5	8		6		14	9*		4	11†	2			10				7	12	24
1		3		5	8		6		14			4	7†	2			10			11*	12	9	25
1		3		5	8†		6		14	12		4	11*	2			10			7		9	26
1	2†			5	8		6			11*		4	12	3		14	10			7		9	27
1		3		5	8†		6			11		4	12	2		14	10			7		9*	28
1		3		5	8†		6			11	12	4	7*	2		14	10					9	29
1		3		5	8†		6			11		4	12	2		14	10			7		9*	30
1		3		5	8*		6			11	12	4	7	2			10					9	31
1		3		5			6			11*	7†	4	12	2		8	10				14	9	32
1		3		5	7		6			11	12	4		2		8	10					9*	33
1		3		5	8		6			11*	14	4		2		12	10			7		9†	34
1		3		5	8		6			11	12	4		2			10			7*		9	35
1		3		5	8		6			11†	7	4		2		14	10			12		9*	36
1		3		5	8		6			11*	7	4		2			10			12		9	37
1		3		5	8*		6			11		4	14	2		12	10			7		9†	38
1	12	3		5	8		6*			11	7	4		2			10			9†		14	39
39	22	29	1	37	27	2	38	7	12	36	15	38	13	31	4	11	30	1	3	16	2	15	
	+	+			+				+	+	+		+	+	+	+		+	+	+	+	+	
	1s	6s			4s				10s	1s	15s		10s	4s	1s	9s		2s	1s	2s	2s	2s	

ARBROATH

Second Division

Year Formed: 1878. *Ground & Address:* Gayfield Park, Arbroath DD11 1QB. *Telephone:* 0241 72157.
Ground Capacity: total: 10,000 seated: 896. *Size of Pitch:* 115yd×71yd.
Chairman: H. B. Crockatt (President). *Secretary:* Ronald McLeish. *Commercial Manager:* David Kean.
Manager: John Young. *Assistant Manager:* George Mackie.
Physio: William Shearer. *Coach:* James Cant.
Managers since 1975: A. Henderson; I. J. Stewart; G. Fleming; J. Bone; J Young.
Club Nickname(s): The Red Lichties. *Previous Grounds:* None.
Record Attendance: 13,510 v Rangers, Scottish Cup 3rd rd; 23 Feb, 1952.
Record Transfer Fee received: £50,000 for Mark McWalter to St Mirren (June 1987).

1988–89 LEAGUE RECORD

Match No.	Date	Venue	Opponents	Result	H/T Score	Lg. Pos.	Goalscorers	Atten-dance
1	Aug 13	A	Stranraer	W 1-0	1-0	—	Richardson	714
2	20	H	Brechin C	L 1-2	1-1	9	Brand	585
3	27	H	Alloa	D 2-2	0-2	8	Jack, Richardson (pen)	406
4	Sept 3	A	Berwick R	W 3-0	1-0	5	Brand 3	250
5	10	A	Montrose	W 1-0	1-0	2	Richardson	650
6	17	H	Stenhousemuir	W 5-1	3-0	1	Stewart 2, Jack, Richardson (pen), Forrest	470
7	24	A	East Fife	D 0-0	0-0	1		656
8	Oct 1	H	Stirling Albion	W 2-1	0-0	1	Mitchell, Forrest	849
9	8	A	Dumbarton	W 4-1	2-1	1	Fotheringham 2, Anderson P, Cairsty (og)	350
10	15	A	Albion R	L 1-3	1-0	1	Fotheringham	727
11	22	H	East Stirling	D 3-3	2-2	1	Fotheringham 2, Kerr	695
12	29	A	Cowdenbeath	D 1-1	0-1	2	Mitchell	450
13	Nov 5	H	Queen's Park	D 2-2	0-0	2	Anderson P, Forrest	624
14	12	A	Brechin C	L 0-1	0-0	3		500
15	19	H	Stranraer	W 1-0	0-0	3	Kerr	550
16	26	H	Montrose	D 0-0	0-0	4		650
17	Dec 10	A	Stenhousemuir	D 0-0	0-0	2		300
18	17	H	East Fife	L 1-3	1-1	5	Forrest	422
19	24	A	Queen's Park	L 0-2	0-1	7		434
20	31	H	Cowdenbeath	L 0-1	0-0	7		541
21	Jan 3	A	Alloa	D 3-3	1-1	—	Dewar, Brand, Bennett	565
22	14	H	Berwick R	L 1-2	0-1	7	Bennett	374
23	21	H	Albion R	L 0-3	0-1	9		436
24	28	A	East Stirling	W 3-0	0-0	7	Bennett, Forrest 2	200
25	Feb 4	H	Dumbarton	D 1-1	0-0	8	Stewart	404
26	11	A	Stirling Albion	D 1-1	1-0	7	Fotheringham	447
27	25	H	Berwick R	L 0-3	0-0	8		350
28	Mar 1	A	Alloa	L 0-3	0-2	—		548
29	11	H	Stranraer	W 4-3	2-0	10	Fotheringham, Stewart, Mitchell, Dewar	296
30	15	A	Brechin C	W 4-3	1-3	—	Fotheringham,Kerr, Stewart, Forrest	497
31	18	H	East Fife	L 1-3	0-1	10	Kerr	532
32	25	A	Queen's Park	D 1-1	1-0	9	Mitchell	523
33	Apr 1	A	Cowdenbeath	D 1-1	0-1	8	Dewar	205
34	8	H	Stenhousemuir	W 2-1	1-0	8	Fotheringham, Bennett	280
35	15	A	Montrose	D 1-1	1-0	8	Fotheringham	450
36	22	H	East Stirling	D 2-2	0-2	8	Jack 2	300
37	29	H	Dumbarton	L 1-3	0-1	9	Stewart	347
38	May 6	A	Albion R	D 2-2	1-1	9	Fotheringham, Jack (pen)	665
39	13	H	Stirling Albion	L 0-4	0-1	10		400

Final League Position: 10

GOALSCORERS

League: (56): Fotheringham 11, Forrest 7, Stewart 6, Brand 5, Jack 5 (1 pen), Bennett 4, Kerr 4, Mitchell 4, Richardson 4 (2 pens), Dewar 3, Anderson P 2, own goal 1.
League Cup: (1): Forrest 1.
Scottish Cup: (0).

Record Transfer Fee paid: £20,000 for Douglas Robb from Montrose (1981).
Record Victory: 36-0 v Bon Accord, Scottish Cup 1st rd; 12 Sept, 1885.
Record Defeat: 0-8 v Kilmarnock, Division II; 3 Jan, 1949.
Most Capped Player: Ned Doig, 2 (5), Scotland.
Most League Appearances: 445: Tom Cargill, 1966–81.
Most League Goals in Season (Individual): 45: Dave Easson, Division II; 1958–59.
Most Goals Overall (Individual): 120: Jimmy Jack; 1966–71.

Honours
League Champions Runners-up: Division II 1934–35, 1958–59, 1967–68, 1971–72.
Scottish Cup:—.
League Cup:—.
Club colours: Shirt: Maroon with white neck & cuffs. Shorts: White. Stockings: Maroon with white hoop tops.

McAlpine, H	Mitchell, B	Tindal, K	McEwan, G	Anderson, P	Jack, P	Forrest, R	Stewart, I	Brand, R	Fotheringham, J	Richardson, A	McKenna, A	Kerr, B	Anderson, R	Logan, A	Todd, D	Dewar, G	Balfour, D	Fleming, J	Cosgrove, R	McGuinness, S	Smith, R	Jackson, D	Farnan, C	Bennett, M	Hamilton J	Florence, S	O'Brian, J	*Match No.*
1	2	3	4	5	6*	7	8	9	10†	11	12	14																1
1	2	3*	4		6	7		11†	9	8			5	10	12	14												2
1	2	3†	4	5	6	7	8	9*	10	11	12					14												3
	2	3	4	5	6		8	9	10	11						7	1											4
1	2	3	4	5			8	9	10	11	12	14*			6†	7												5
1	2	3	4		6†	12	8	9*	10	11	5	14				7												6
1	2	3	4	5	6	12	8	9*	10	11						7												7
1	2	3	4	5		12	8	9*	10	11						7		6										8
1	2	3	4	5		9	8		10	11		6*				7		12										9
1	2	3	4			9	8		10	11						7		6	5									10
1	2	6	4			9	8		10	11		5				7			3									11
	2	8	6	4		7		9	10			5				11			3	1								12
	2*	8	6	4	7	9	5		10			12				11		3		1								13
		2	4	5	6	9	8	12	10*			11				7		3		1								14
		2	4	5	6	7†	8	9*	10			12				11		3		1	14							15
		2	4	5	6†	12	8	9*	10	11		14				7		3		1								16
		2	4	5	14	12	8	9		11		6				7†		3			10*	1						17
		2*	4	5	12	7	8		10	11		6			14			3			9†	1						18
				5*	2	9	8	12	10	11		6				7†		4	3			1	14					19
			4	5	2	10	8	12	9	11						7*		3				1		6				20
				5	2	10	8	14	9	11*					12	7†		3	4			1		6				21
			4*	5	2	10	8†		9	12		14			11	7			3			1		6				22
		14				7		10	9	11		8*			12				3†			1	5	6	2	4		23
						10	8		9	11						7		4	3			1	5	6	2			24
						10	8		9	11					6	7		4	3			1	5		2			25
						10	8	12	9	11					6	7*		4	3			1	5		2			26
		14				10			9	11*		12			8	7		4	3			1	5		2		6†	27
	6	7		5	10†			14	9			11*			8	12		3				1			2	4		28
	4			5*	10	7	8	14	9	6		12				11†		3				1			2			29
	4			5		7	8	12	9	6		10*				11		3				1			2			30
	4			5		7	8	12	9	6*		10				11		3				1			2			31
	6		4	5	8	14	7		12			10				11*		3		1	9				2†			32
	8		4*	5	7		12	14	9			10				11†		3				1		6	2			33
	4			5			7	8*	9			10				11		3			12	1		6	2			34
	4	12		5	10		7*		9			8				11		3				1		6	2			35
	4				10		7		9			8*				11		3			12	1	5	6	2			36
	4			5	10		7	12†	9	8*						11		3			14	1		6	2			37
	4	12		5	7			10	9	8						11		3*				1		6	2			38
	5	14			10†			9	12	8		7				11*	1	3						6	2	4		39
10	25	19 + 5s	22	28	23 + 2s	23 + 6s	31 + 1s	16 + 11s	36 + 2s	28 + 1s	1 + 3s	17 + 9s	1	1	6 + 4s	33 + 3s	2	27 + 1s	11	6	3 + 4s	21	6 + 1s	12	17	3	1	

AYR UNITED First Division

Year Formed: 1910. *Ground & Address:* Somerset Park, Tryfield Place, Ayr KA8 9NB. *Telephone:* 0292 263435.
Ground Capacity: total: 18,500 seated: 1200. *Size of Pitch:* 111yd×72yd.
Chairman: George H. Smith. *Secretary:* David Quayle. *Commercial Manager:* Mike James.
Manager: Alistair R. MacLeod. *Assistant Manager:* David Wells. *Physio:* Robert Pender. *Coach:* David Wells.
Managers since 1975: Alex Stuart; Ally MacLeod; WIllie McLean; George Caldwell; Ally MacLeod.
Club Nickname(s): The Honest Men. *Previous Grounds:* None.
Record Attendance: 25,225 v Rangers, Division I; 13 Sept, 1969.
Record Transfer Fee received: £300,000 for Steven Nicol to Liverpool (Oct 1981).
Record Transfer Fee paid: £40,000 for Jim Kean from Clyde (1981).
Record Victory: 11-1 v Dumbarton, League Cup; 13 Aug, 1952.

1988–89 LEAGUE RECORD

Match No.	Date	Venue	Opponents	Result	H/T Score	Lg. Pos.	Goalscorers	Attendance
1	Aug 13	H	Clydebank	E 3-2	1-1	—	Templeton, Walker, Sludden	3151
2	20	A	Meadowbank T	W 2-1	1-0	1	Walker, Templeton	1100
3	27	A	Kilmarnock	L 0-2	0-1	5		5387
4	Sept 3	H	Forfar Ath	W 2-1	1-0	3	Love, Sludden	2628
5	10	H	Falkirk	L 3-4	1-1	8	Walker 2, Wilson	4300
6	17	A	Partick T	D 2-2	0-1	7	Sludden, Walker	2551
7	24	H	St Johnstone	W 2-1	2-0	4	Templeton, Sludden	3543
8	Oct 1	A	Raith R	D 0-0	0-0	5		2000
9	8	H	Queen of the S	D 1-1	1-1	6	McIntyre	3019
10	15	H	Dunfermline Ath	D 2-2	2-0	5	Walker, Sludden	5875
11	22	A	Morton	L 0-2	0-2	9		2900
12	29	H	Clyde	D 1-1	0-1	9	Templeton	3105
13	Nov 5	A	Airdrieonians	L 1-2	0-0	9	McIntyre	2430
14	12	A	Falkirk	L 0-1	0-0	9		4000
15	19	H	Partick T	L 1-3	1-3	9	McIntyre	3158
16	26	A	St Johnstone	L 0-2	0-2	11		2813
17	Dec 3	H	Meadowbank T	D 2-2	1-1	10	Walker, Sludden	1849
18	10	A	Clyde	L 2-4	1-2	11	Templeton, Sludden	600
19	17	H	Morton	W 3-1	1-0	10	Walker, Templeton 2	2440
20	24	A	Dunfermline Ath	L 1-5	1-2	11	Templeton (pen)	5871
21	31	A	Forfar Ath	W 2-1	1-1	10	Kennedy, Cowell	891
22	Jan 3	H	Kilmarnock	W 4-1	2-0	—	Walker, Templeton 2, Sludden	8585
23	7	H	Airdrieonians	L 1-4	1-1	9	Sludden	3815
24	18	A	Clydebank	L 1-5	1-2	—	Sludden	1433
25	21	A	Queen of the S	W 2-0	0-0	9	Cowell, Sludden	1240
26	Feb 4	H	Raith R	D 1-1	0-1	10	Walker	2375
27	14	A	Partick T	L 1-4	1-1	—	Walker	1772
28	25	H	Meadowbank T	W 3-2	0-1	9	Templeton 2 (1 pen), Love	2320
29	Mar 4	A	Clyde	L 0-1	0-0	10		1100
30	11	H	Kilmarnock	W 2-1	1-1	9	Sludden, McAllister	5476
31	25	H	Raith R	D 2-2	2-1	10	Templeton 2 (1 pen)	2774
32	28	A	Falkirk	L 0-2	0-2	—		4354
33	Apr 1	A	Forfar Ath	D 0-0	0-0	12		661
34	8	H	Clydebank	L 2-4	1-3	12	Walker, Sludden	2308
35	15	A	Queen of the S	W 2-1	1-1	11	Evans, Templeton (pen)	600
36	22	H	Dunfermline Ath	L 1-2	1-1	11	Sludden	4313
37	29	A	St Johnstone	W 1-0	1-0	11	Sludden	6728
38	May 6	H	Airdrieonians	W 3-1	2-1	11	Templeton 2, Walker	2970
39	13	H	Morton	L 0-1	0-0	11		2824

Final League Position: 11

GOALSCORERS

League: (56): Templeton 17 (5 pen), Sludden 15, Walker 13, McIntyre 3 (1 pen), Cowell 2, Love 2, Evans 1, Kennedy 1, McAllister 1, Wilson 1.
League Cup: (1): Templeton 1.
Scottish Cup: (1): Templeton 1.

Record Defeat: 0-9 in Division I v Rangers (1929); v Hearts (1931); v Third Lanark (1954).
Most Capped Player: Jim Nisbet, 3, Scotland.
Most League Appearances: 340: Ian McAllister, 1977–89.
Most League Goals in Season (Individual): 66: Jimmy Smith, 1927–28.
Most Goals Overall (Individual): —.

Honours
League Champions: Division II 1911–12, 1912–13, 1927–78, 1936–37, 1958–59, 1965–66. Second Division 1987–88; *Runners-up:* Division II 1910–11, 1955–56, 1968–69.
Scottish Cup:—.
League Cup:—.
Club colours: Shirt: White with broad black chest panel and pinstripe. Shorts: Black. Stockings: White with black diamond tops.

Watson, G	McIntyre, S	Love, J	Furphy, W	McAllister, I	Evans, S	Templeton, H	Wilson, K	Walker, T	Sludden, J	Cowell, J	Ross, B	McCracken, D	McKenzie, P	McCann, J	Welsh, P	Brown, B	Hughes, J	Kennedy, D	Tracey, K	Gilmour, G	Scott, R	Shaw, G	McCattrie, N	*Match No.*
1	2*	3	4	5	6	7	8	9	10	11	12													1
1	2	3	4	5	6	7	8	9	10	11*		12												2
1	2*	3	4	5	6	7	8	9	10	11†	12		14											3
1		11	4	5	6		8	9	10*		3		12	2	7									4
1	14	11†	4	5*	6	7	8	9	10	12	3			2										5
1		11	4	5	6		8	9	10	7†	3			2	12									6
1	12	11†	4	5	6	7	8	9	10	14*	3			2										7
1	12	11†	4*	5	6	7	8	9	10	14	3			2										8
1	2	12		5	6	7	8	9	10	11*	3			4†		14								9
1	2	11	4	5†	6	7	8*	9	10		3					12	14							10
1	2†	11*			6	7	8	9	10	12	3		14			5	4							11
1	12	3	4		6	7	8	9	10	11*	2					5								12
1	7	3			6		8	9	10	11*	2					5			4	12				13
1	8	3	4		6		7	9	10	11	2					5								14
1	2	3	4		6		8	9*	10	11						5					7	12		15
1	7	3	5		6		12	9	10*						8†	4	2	14			11			16
1		3	5		6	7	11	9	10							4	2				8			17
1		3	5		6	7	8	9	10					4			2	11						18
1		11*	4		6	7	12	9	10					2			3	5			8			19
1	14	11*	4†		6	7	12	9	10					2			3	5			8			20
1	2		4		6	7	8	9	10	11							3	5						21
1	2		4		6	7	8	9	10	11							3	5						22
1	2		4		6	7	8	9	10	11							3						5	23
1	2		4		6	7	8		10	11*							3				12	9	5	24
1	2	12	4		6	7	8		10	11							3	5			9*			25
1		12	4		6	7	11*	9	10					2			3	5			8			26
1	14		4		6†	7		9	10	12				2			3	5	11*		8			27
1	12	11		5		7		9†	10	14	2*			6		4		3			8			28
1	2	11†		5	12	9	7		10	14				8		4		3			6*			29
1	9		4	5	6	7			10					2			3	11			8			30
1	9		4	5	6	7			10	12				2			3	11*			8			31
1	9†		4	5	6	7			10	12				2		14	3	11			8*			32
1			4	5	6	9	8		10	11				2		7	3							33
1			4	5	6	7	8*	9	10	11				2			3				12			34
1			4	5	6	7		9	10	11				2			3				8			35
1			4	5	6	7		9	10	11				2			3				8			36
1			4	5	6	7		9	10	11				2*			3	12			8			37
1			4	5	6	7		9	10*	11				2			3	12			8			38
1			4	5	6	7	12	9	10*	11				2			3				8			39
39	19 + 7s	21 + 3s	34	22	37 + 1s	33	26 + 4s	32	39	21 + 9s	12 + 2s	— + 1s	— + 3s	23	2 + 1s	10 + 3s	23 + 1s	13 + 3s	2	— + 1s	18 + 2s	1 + 1s	2	

BERWICK RANGERS Second Division

Year Formed: 1881. *Ground & Address:* Shielfield Park, Tweedmouth, Berwick-upon-Tweed TD15 2EF. *Telephone:* 0289 307424.
Ground Capacity: total: 10,673 seated: 1473. *Size of Pitch:* 112yd×76yd.
Chairman: M. G. Elliott. *Secretary:* —. *Commercial Manager:* —.
Manager: Jim Jefferies. *Assistant Manager:* —. *Physio:* Gordon Roberts. *Coach:* R. Johnson, I Oliver.
Managers since 1975: H. Melrose; G. Haig; D. Smith; F. Connor; J. McSherry; E Tait; J. Thomson; J. Jefferies.
Club Nickname(s): The Borderers. *Previous Grounds:* Bull Stot Close, Pier Field, Meadow Field, Union Park, Old Shielfield.
Record Attendance: 13,365 v Rangers, Scottish Cup 1st rd; 28 Jan, 1967.
Record Transfer Fee received: —.

1988–89 LEAGUE RECORD

Match No.	Date	Venue	Opponents	Result	H/T Score	Lg. Pos.	Goalscorers	Atten-dance
1	Aug 13	A	Queen's Park	L 0-2	0-1	—		437
2	20	H	Stranraer	L 0-1	0-0	13		406
3	27	A	Stirling Albion	L 1-2	1-1	13	Porteous	476
4	Sept 3	H	Arbroath	L 0-3	0-1	14		250
5	10	A	East Stirling	L 2-3	1-0	14	Douglas, Bickmore	200
6	17	H	Montrose	L 1-2	0-2	14	Thorpe	330
7	24	A	Stenhousemuir	L 2-3	1-1	14	Ainslie 2	200
8	Oct 1	H	Dumbarton	W 1-0	1-0	14	Douglas	320
9	8	A	Albion R	L 1-3	0-0	14	Callachan	250
10	15	A	Alloa	L 1-2	0-2	14	Porteous	408
11	22	H	East Fife	L 1-2	1-1	14	Porteous	300
12	29	A	Brechin C	L 0-2	0-0	14		320
13	Nov 5	H	Cowdenbeath	L 0-1	0-0	14		252
14	12	A	Stranraer	D 2-2	1-0	14	Leetion, Porteous	750
15	19	H	Queen's Park	L 0-2	0-1	14		275
16	26	H	East Stirling	L 0-5	0-2	14		225
17	Dec 10	A	Montrose	L 1-2	0-1	14	Locke	200
18	17	H	Stenhousemuir	W 1-0	0-0	14	Hughes	278
19	24	A	Cowdenbeath	D 3-3	2-2	14	Hughes, Callachan (pen), Sloan	250
20	31	H	Brechin C	D 4-4	2-0	14	Hughes 2, Cass, Porteous	537
21	Jan 7	H	Stirling Albion	D 0-0	0-0	14		530
22	14	A	Arbroath	W 2-1	1-0	14	Thorpe 2	374
23	21	H	Alloa	D 1-1	1-0	14	Cass	410
24	28	A	East Fife	D 2-2	1-1	14	Thorpe 2 (1 pen)	410
25	Feb 4	H	Albion R	W 2-1	1-0	14	Cass, Sloan	420
26	18	H	Stirling Albion	D 2-2	1-1	14	Hughes 2	506
27	25	A	Arbroath	W 3-0	0-0	14	Cass, Thorpe 2 (1 pen)	350
28	Mar 4	H	East Stirling	W 2-0	1-0	14	Callachan, Marshall	464
29	7	A	Dumbarton	D 2-2	1-1	—	Tait, Hughes	341
30	11	A	Stenhousemuir	D 0-0	0-0	14		350
31	22	H	Alloa	W 1-0	0-0	—	Hughes	450
32	25	A	Stranraer	W 2-1	2-1	12	Cass 2	600
33	Apr 1	H	Queen's Park	D 1-1	1-0	13	Thorpe	681
34	8	A	Dumbarton	W 4-0	1-0	12	Porteous 2, Callachan, Hughes	550
35	15	H	Cowdenbeath	D 0-0	0-0	13		376
36	22	A	Brechin C	W 2-0	1-0	12	Hughes, Sloan	400
37	29	A	East Fife	D 1-1	0-0	12	Sloan	1614
38	May 6	H	Montrose	D 1-1	0-1	13	Graham	696
39	13	A	Albion R	L 1-2	0-2	13	Cass	600

Final League Position: 13

GOALSCORERS

League: (50): Hughes 10, Thorpe 8 (2 pens), Cass 7, Porteous 7, Callachan 4 (1 pen), Sloan 4, Ainslie 2, Douglas 2, Bickmore 1, Graham 1, Leetion 1, Locke 1, Marshall 1, Tait 1.
League Cup: (0).
Scottish Cup: (2): Hughes 1, Sloan 1.

Record Transfer Fee paid: —.
Record Victory: 8-1 v Forfar Ath, Division II; 25 Dec, 1965: v Vale of Leithen, Scottish Cup; Dec, 1966.
Record Defeat: 1-9 v Hamilton A, First Division; 9 Aug, 1980.
Most Capped Player: —.
Most League Appearances: 435: Eric Tait, 1970–87.
Most League Goals in Season (Individual): 38: Ken Bowron, Division II; 1963–64.
Most Goals Overall (Individual): 115: Eric Tait, 1970–87.

Honours
League Champions: Second Division 1978–79.
Scottish Cup:—.
League Cup: Semi-final 1963–64.
Club colours: Shirt: Black and gold shadow pinstripe. Shorts: Black. Stockings: Black.

Donaldson, B	Oliver, N	Fleming, J	Douglas, H	Wood, K	Marshall, B	Leitch, G	Shell, K	Bickmore, S	Porteous, S	Graham, T	Cameron, M	Neil, M	Muir, L	Thorpe, B	Callachan, R	Smith, G	Ainslie, G	McLaren, P	Cairns, M	Renton, P	Hughes, J	Leetion, P	Sloan, S	Watson, S	Locke, S	Cass, M	Davidson, G	Neilson, D	Tait, G	Match No.
1	2	3	4	5	6†	7	8	9	10	11*	12	14																		1
1	2	3	4		5	6	8	9	10	11	7																			2
1	2	3*	4		5	6	8	9	10	11	7	12																		3
1	2	12	4†	14	5	3	6	9	10	11	8*	7																		4
1	2	3	4		5	7	8*	9		11		12	6	10																5
1	2	3	4		5	7*	8†	9	14		12		6	10	11															6
1	2	3	5		4		7†	12				14	6	8	10	9	11*													7
1	2		5		12	4	7	9		11*			6	8	10			3												8
	2		5			7		9		12			6	8	10	11		4*	1	3										9
	2				5	4	7†	9	14				6	8	10	11			1	12	3*									10
	2					7			11	12			6	8	10	9		4*	1	3	5									11
	2					3	12		7				6	8	11*			4	1		5	9	10							12
	2						10*	9	11	14		12	6†	8				4			5	7		1	3					13
	2					3		12	7*					8	11			4			5	9	10	1	6					14
	2					3			7*	14				8	11					4†	5	9	10	1	6	12				15
	2								14	7			3	8	11		9	12			5	4†	10*	1	6					16
1	3†					14		9*	12				4	8	11						10		7		6	5	2			17
1	3					14			9	12			4	8	11						10†		7*		6	5	2			18
1	3					9*			12				4	8	11						10		7		6	5	2			19
1	3				6	9			12				4	8	11						10		7			5*	2			20
	3					9*			12				4	8	11						10		7		6	5	2	1		21
	3								9*				4	8	11						10		7		6	5	2	1	12	22
	3					14		12	9*				4	8	11								7		6	5†	2	1	10	23
	3					12							4	8	11						10*		7		6	5	2	1	9	24
	3												4	8	11						10		7		6	5	2	1	9	25
	3					11							4	8							10		7		6	5	2	1	9	26
	3					12			14				4	8	11*						10		7		6	5	2	1	9†	27
	3				14	2			9†				4	8	11			12			10		7		6	5*		1		28
	3				12	2							4	8	11						10		7	1	6	5			9*	29
	3					2			12				4	8	11						10		7*	1	6	5			9	30
	3					2			12				4		11						10		7†		6	5	8*	1	9	31
	3					2*			12				4	8	11						10		7		6	5	14	1	9†	32
	3					2*				12			4	8	11						10		7		6	5	9	1		33
	3					2		12	9				4	8	11						10				6	5		1		34
	3				14			12	9*				4	8	11			2			10		7†		6	5		1		35
	3				14			12	9*	11			4	8				2†			10		7		6	5		1		36
	3					14			9†	12			4	8	11			2			10		7		6	5*		1		37
	3				10	9†				12		14	4	8*	11			2					7		6	5		1		38
	3				10	2		14	9			8*	4		11			12					7†		6	5		1		39
12	39	6 + 1s	9	1 + 1s	11 + 5s	26 + 6s	10 + 1s	11 + 7s	18 + 11s	8 + 8s	3 + 2s	2 + 6s	33	33	31	4	2	10 + 3s	4	3 + 1s	27	5	26	6	26	23 + 1s	13 + 1s	17	9 + 1s	

Also played: Cavanagh P – Match 31 (14), 34 (7*)

BRECHIN CITY

Second Division

Year Formed: 1906. *Ground & Address:* Glebe Park, Trinity Rd, Brechin, Angus DD9 6BJ. *Telephone:* 03562 2856.
Ground Capacity: total: 3491 seated: 291. *Size of Pitch:* 110yd×67yd.
Chairman: David H. Will. *Secretary:* George C. Johnston. *Commercial Manager:* —.
Manager: John Ritchie. *Assistant Manager:* Dick Campbell. *Physio:* Jack Sunter. *Coach:* Brian Reid; Eric Martin.
Managers since 1975: Charlie Dunn; Ian Stewart; Doug Houston; Ian Fleming; John Ritchie.
Club Nickname(s): The City. *Previous Grounds:* Nursery Park.
Record Attendance: 8122 v Aberdeen, Scottish Cup 3rd rd; 3 Feb, 1973.
Record Transfer Fee received: £46,000 for Ken Eadie to Falkirk (1986).
Record Transfer Fee paid: £15,000 for Gerry Lesslie from Dundee U.

1988–89 LEAGUE RECORD

Match No.	Date	Venue	Opponents	Result	H/T Score	Lg. Pos.	Goalscorers	Attendance
1	Aug 13	H	Alloa	W 2-1	0-1	—	Inglis, Adam	558
2	20	A	Arbroath	W 2-1	1-1	2	Adam 2	585
3	27	A	Montrose	W 2-0	1-0	1	Adam, Scott	600
4	Sept 3	H	Stirling Albion	L 2-3	0-2	3	Adam 2 (1 pen)	600
5	10	A	Albion R	D 1-1	0-1	3	Lees	431
6	17	H	Dumbarton	D 1-1	0-0	4	Frith	430
7	24	A	East Stirling	L 3-4	3-3	7	Paterson IA 2, Adam	360
8	Oct 1	A	Queen's Park	D 1-1	0-0	5	Paterson IA	550
9	8	H	Cowdenbeath	L 0-1	0-0	8		300
10	15	H	Stranraer	D 2-2	0-1	10	Paterson IA, Lees	400
11	22	A	Stenhousemuir	W 2-0	0-0	8	Lees, Wardell	250
12	29	H	Berwick R	W 2-0	0-0	5	Wardell, Paterson IA	320
13	Nov 5	A	East Fife	L 0-1	0-1	7		488
14	12	H	Arbroath	W 1-0	0-0	6	Paterson IA	500
15	19	A	Alloa	D 2-2	2-2	5	Lees, Adam	398
16	26	H	Albion R	L 0-2	0-0	7		500
17	Dec 13	A	Dumbarton	W 2-0	2-0	—	Paterson IA 2	570
18	17	H	East Stirling	D 2-2	1-1	7	Adam 2	250
19	24	H	East Fife	W 1-0	0-0	6	Wardell	550
20	31	A	Berwick R	D 4-4	0-2	6	Candlish, Wardell, Paterson IA, Adam	537
21	Jan 3	H	Montrose	D 1-1	1-1	—	Adam	644
22	18	A	Stirling Albion	D 2-2	0-1	—	Adam 2	476
23	21	A	Stranraer	W 1-0	0-0	3	Lees	850
24	Feb 1	H	Stenhousemuir	W 3-1	1-1	—	Brown, Lees 2	429
25	8	A	Cowdenbeath	D 3-3	2-1	—	Brown, Ritchie, Paterson IA	440
26	11	H	Queen's Park	W 2-0	2-0	2	Adam (pen), Ritchie	500
27	18	A	East Stirling	D 1-1	0-1	2	Ritchie	250
28	Mar 7	H	Alloa	L 1-2	1-1	—	Brown	400
29	11	A	Stirling Albion	D 0-0	0-0	2		547
30	15	H	Arbroath	L 3-4	3-1	—	Lees 2, Ritchie	497
31	18	H	Stenhousemuir	D 1-1	0-0	2	Paterson IG	350
32	25	A	Montrose	L 0-1	0-1	2		500
33	Apr 1	H	Albion R	W 2-1	1-0	2	Sexton, Ritchie	485
34	8	A	Queen's Park	W 2-1	2-1	2	Ritchie, Buckley	559
35	15	A	Dumbarton	L 0-1	0-1	2		500
36	22	H	Berwick R	L 0-2	0-1	4		400
37	29	A	Cowdenbeath	W 2-0	1-0	3	Ritchie, Lees	200
38	May 6	H	East Fife	W 1-0	1-0	3	Candlish (pen)	850
39	13	A	Stranraer	L 1-2	0-1	3	Buckley	788

Final League Position: 3

GOALSCORERS

League: (58): Adam 15 (2 pens), Lees 10, Paterson IA 10, Ritchie 7, Wardell 4, Brown 3, Buckley 2, Candlish 2 (1 pen), Frith 1, Inglis 1, Paterson IG 1, Scott 1, Sexton 1.
League Cup: (3): Adam 1, Buckley 1, Lees 1.
Scottish Cup: (3): Adam 2, Scott 1.

Record Victory: 12-1 v Thornhill, Scottish Cup 1st rd; 28 Jan, 1926.
Record Defeat: 0-10 v Airdrieonians, Albion R and Cowdenbeath, all in Division II, 1937–38.
Most Capped Player: —.
Most League Appearances: 459: David Watt, 1975–89.
Most League Goals in Season (Individual): 26: W. McIntosh, Division II; 1959–60.
Most Goals Overall (Individual): —.

Honours
League Champions: Second Division 1982–83. C Division 1953–54; *Runners-up:*—
Scottish Cup:—.
League Cup:—.
Club colours: Shirt, Shorts, Stockings: Red with white trimmings.

Lawrie, D	Hamilton, R	Watt, D	Inglis, J	Taylor, K	Adam, C	Wardell, S	Gallacher, W	Lees, G	Hill, H	Buckley, G	Paterson, IA	Brown, R	Scott, D	Stevens, G	Wilkie, S	Frith, J	Candlish, C	Kennedy, A	Healey, C	Gillespie, S	Paterson, IG	Ritchie, P	Brash, A	Sexton, P	*Match No.*
1	2	3	4†	5	6	7	8	9*	10	11	12	14													1
1	2	3	5	12	6*		7	14	8	11	9†	4	10												2
1	2	3	5*	12	6		7†	14	8	11	9	4	10												3
1	2	3		8*	6		7†	9		11	12	4	10	5	14										4
1	2†	3	8	12	6			14			9	4	10	5	7*	11									5
1	14	3	2		8	7*		9			12	4	10	5	6†	11									6
1		2	12		10		8	7		14	9†	4	6	5		11*	3								7
1	14	2†	5		6		8	7		12	9	4	10			11*	3								8
1	12		2		6		9†	7	8	11*		4	10	5			3	14							9
1			2		10	12		7	8	11	9*	4	6	5			3								10
1	12		2		8	14		7	6*	11†	9	4	10	5			3								11
1	8		2		6	11		7*		12	9	4	10	5			3								12
1	8		2†		6	11		7*	14	12	9	4	10	5			3								13
1	6				8	11*		7†	14	12	9	4	10	5			3		2						14
1	6				10	7		11	8		9	4		5			3		2						15
1	6				10†	7		11	8	12	9*	4		5	14		3		2						16
1					10	11		7*	8	12	9	5			3		4		2	6					17
1					8	7		11	6	12	9*	5			3		4		2	10					18
1	12				8	7		14	10		9†	4		5	6		3				2*	11			19
1	14				8	7		12	10		9	4		5	6		3			2†		11*			20
1					10	7*		12	8		9	4		5	6		3				2	11			21
1	3				8	7†		11		12	9*	4	10	5	2					14	6				22
1	3†				8	7		11		12	9*	4	10	5	2					14	6				23
1								7		11	9	4	10*	5	6		3		12		8	2			24
1						12		7		11*	9	4	10	5	2†		3		14		6	8			25
1					8	7		12			9	4	10	5*			3		2		6	11			26
1					8	7*		12			9	4	10		5		3		2		6	11			27
1					8	7*		12	6		9	4	10	5			3				2	11			28
1					8	7		12		11*	9	4	10		5		3				2	6			29
1					8	12		7	6		9	4	10		5		3				2	11			30
1					8	12		7			9*	4	10		2		3				6	11	5		31
1						7*		10	8	12	9	4	3		11†				2	14	6		5		32
1								12	6	11	9*	4	10				3				2	7	5	8	33
1								12	6	11	9*	4	10				3			14	2†	7	5	8	34
1								12	6*	11	9	4	10		14		3†			2		7	5	8	35
1								14	12	11	9	4	3		6		2*				8	7†	5	10	36
1						11*		9	6	12	14	4	10†		2		3				8	7	5		37
1						9*		7	8	14	12	4	10		2†		3				6	11	5		38
1						12		7†	8	11	14	4	10				3			6*	2	9	5		39
39	12 + 6s	8	11 + 1s	2 + 3s	29	21 + 6s	7	25 + 14s	22 + 3s	15 + 13s	32 + 6s	38 + 1s	31	21	19 + 3s	4	30	— + 1s	8 + 2s	5 + 4s	19	18	9	4	

CELTIC

Premier Division

Year Formed: 1888. *Ground & Address:* Celtic Park, 95 Kerrydale St, Glasgow G40 3RE. *Telephone:* 041 554 2710/ 556 2611.
Ground Capacity: total: 60,800 seated: 9000. *Size of Pitch:* 115yd×75yd.
Chairman: John C. McGinn. *Secretary:* Desmond White & Co. *Commercial Manager:* John C. McGinn.
Manager: Billy McNeill. *Assistant Manager:* Tommy Craig. *Physio:* Brian Scott. *Coach:* Bobby Lennox.
Managers since 1975: Jock Stein; Billy McNeill; David Hay; Billy McNeill.
Club Nickname(s): The Bhoys. *Previous Grounds:* None.
Record Attendance: 92,000 v Rangers, Division I; 1 Jan, 1938.
Record Transfer Fee received: £850,000 for Brian McClair to Manchester United (1987).
Record Transfer Fee paid: £725,000 for Frank McAvennie from West Ham United (1987).
Record Victory: 11-0 v Dundee, Division I; 26 Oct, 1895.
Record Defeat: 0-8 v Motherwell, Division I; 30 Apr, 1937.
Most Capped Player: Danny McGrain, 62, Scotland.
Most League Appearances: 486: Billy McNeill, 1957–75.

1988–89 LEAGUE RECORD

Match No.	*Date*	*Venue*	*Opponents*	*Result*	*H/T Score*	*Lg. Pos.*	*Goalscorers*	*Attendance*
1	Aug 13	H	Hearts	W 1-0	0-0	—	McAvennie	46,845
2	20	A	Dundee U	L 0-1	0-1	7		18,769
3	27	A	Rangers	L 1-5	1-2	9	McAvennie	42,858
4	Sept 3	H	Hamilton A	W 2-1	1-0	6	Miller, McAvennie	24,084
5	17	H	Aberdeen	L 1-3	1-2	7	Miller (pen)	37,769
6	24	A	Dundee	L 0-1	0-1	8		15,515
7	28	H	Motherwell	W 3-1	1-1	—	Walker, McAvennie 2	20,187
8	Oct 1	A	Hibernian	L 1-3	0-3	7	Walker	24,000
9	8	H	St Mirren	W 7-1	4-1	5	McStay, McGhee 3, Stark 2, Miller	26,091
10	12	H	Dundee U	W 1-0	1-0	—	Miller	36,760
11	22	A	Hearts	W 2-0	0-0	5	McGhee, McAvennie	24,017
12	29	H	Dundee	L 2-3	2-3	5	Stark, Morris	23,843
13	Nov 2	A	Aberdeen	D 2-2	1-2	—	Stark 2 (1 pen)	22,000
14	5	A	Hamilton A	W 8-0	2-0	5	McAvennie 3 (1 pen), Stark, McGhee 3, Miller	10,500
15	12	H	Rangers	W 3-1	3-1	5	Butcher (og), McGhee, Stark	60,113
16	19	H	Hibernian	W 1-0	0-0	3	McAvennie	35,251
17	26	A	St Mirren	W 3-2	1-0	3	Burns 2, McAvennie	21,266
18	Dec 3	A	Motherwell	W 3-1	2-1	3	McGhee, McStay, McAvennie	16,392
19	10	H	Aberdeen	D 0-0	0-0	4		42,437
20	17	A	Dundee U	L 0-2	0-0	4		18,745
21	31	H	Hearts	W 4-2	2-1	4	Stark 2, McGhee 2	44,646
22	Jan 3	A	Rangers	L 1-4	1-3	—	Morris	42,515
23	7	H	Hamilton A	W 2-0	1-0	4	Walker, Miller	18,679
24	14	H	St Mirren	W 2-1	2-0	3	Morris, Walker (pen)	26,796
25	21	A	Hibernian	W 3-1	2-1	3	McGhee, McStay, Walker	23,500
26	Feb 11	H	Motherwell	L 1-2	0-1	3	Walker	21,445
27	25	A	Dundee	W 3-0	1-0	4	Walker, McStay, McCarrison	14,559
28	Mar 11	A	Hearts	W 1-0	0-0	3	McGhee	23,087
29	25	H	Dundee U	W 1-0	1-0	3	McGhee	32,589
30	Apr 1	H	Rangers	L 1-2	0-2	3	Walker	60,800
31	8	A	Hamilton A	L 0-2	0-1	4		9301
32	12	A	Motherwell	D 2-2	0-1	—	McGhee, McStay	10,507
33	22	H	Dundee	W 2-1	0-1	3	Rogan, McGhee	16,000
34	29	A	Aberdeen	D 0-0	0-0	4		21,500
35	May 6	H	Hibernian	W 1-0	0-0	3	Miller	18,316
36	13	A	St Mirren	W 1-0	0-0	3	Miller	13,057

Final League Position: 3

GOALSCORERS

League: (66): McGhee 16, McAvennie 12, Stark 9, Miller 8 (1 pen), Walker 8 (1 pen), McStay 5, Morris 3, Burns 2, McCarrison 1, Rogan 1, own goal 1.
League Cup: (11): Walker 4, McAvennie 3, Burns 2, Archdeacon 1, Stark 1.
Scottish Cup: (12): Burns 3, McGhee 2, Walker 2, Aitken 1 (1 pen), McAvennie 1, McCarthy 1, Miller 1, Stark 1.

Most League Goals in Season (Individual): 50: James McGrory, Division I; 1935–36.
Most Goals Overall (Individual): 397: James McGrory; 1922–39.

Honours
League Champions: (35 times) Division I 1892–93, 1893–94, 1895–96, 1897–98, 1904–05, 1905–06, 1906–07, 1907–08, 1908–09, 1909–10, 1913–14, 1914–15, 1915–16, 1916–17, 1918–19, 1921–22, 1925–26, 1935–36, 1937–38, 1953–54, 1965–66, 1966–67, 1967–68, 1968–69, 1969–70, 1970–71, 1971–72, 1972–73, 1973–74. Premier Division 1976–77, 1978–79, 1980–81, 1981–82, 1985–86, 1987–88; *Runners-up:* 21 times.
Scottish Cup Winners: (27 times) 1892, 1899, 1900, 1904, 1907, 1908, 1911, 1912, 1914, 1923, 1925, 1927, 1931, 1933, 1937, 1951, 1954, 1965, 1967, 1969, 1971, 1972, 1974, 1975, 1977, 1980, 1985, 1988, 1989; *Runners-up:* 15 times.
League Cup Winners: (9 times) 1956–57, 1957–58, 1965–66, 1966–67, 1967–68, 1968–69, 1969–70, 1974–75, 1982–83; *Runners-up:* 8 times.
European: *European Cup Winners:* 1966–67. 74 matches (1966–67 winners, 1967–68, 1968–69, 1969–70 runners-up, 1970–71, 1971–72 semi-finals, 1972–73, 1973–74 semi-finals, 1974–75, 1977–78, 1979–80, 1981–82, 1982–83, 1986–87); *Cup Winners Cup:* 33 matches (1963–64 semi-finals, 1965–66 semi-finals, 1975–76, 1980–81, 1984–85, 1985–86); *UEFA Cup:* 16 matches (1962–63, 1964–65 *Fairs Cup;* 1976–77, 1983–84, 1987–88).
Club colours: Shirt: Green and white hoops. Shorts: White. Stockings: White

Andrews, I	Morris, C	Rogan, A	Whyte, D	McCarthy, M	Grant, P	Miller, J	McStay, P	McAvennie, F	Walker, A	Burns, T	Stark, W	McGhee, M	Aitken, R	Archdeacon, O	Rough, A	Baillie, A	Traynor, J	Fulton, S	Bonner, P	McCarrison, D	Elliot, D	Mathie, A	McCahill, S	Coyne, T	*Match No.*
1	2	3	4	5	6	7	8	9	10	11															1
1	2	3	6	5*	7	14	8	9	10	12		11†	4												2
1	2	3	12	5	6	14	8	9	10	11*	7†		4												3
1	2	3		5	6	7*	8	9	10	11			4	12											4
1	2	3	6*	5		7	8	9	10†	11	12		4	14											5
	2	3	6			7*	8	9	10	11	14		4	12	1	5†									6
	2	3					8	9	10	11			4	7	1	5	6								7
	2	3	14			12	8	9	10	11†			4	7*	1	5	6								8
	2	3	6	5†		11*	8	9			7	10	4	12	1			14							9
	2	3	6	5		11	8	9			7	10	4		1										10
	2	3	6	5				9	10	11	7	8	4						1						11
	2	3	5*			11	8	9		6	7†	10	4	14		12			1						12
	2	3	6	5			8	9		11	7	10	4						1						13
	2	3	6	5		12	8	9*		11†	7	10	4	14					1						14
	2	3	6	5			8	9		11	7	10	4						1						15
	2	3	6	5			8	9		11	7	10	4						1						16
	2	3	6	5			8	9		11	7	10	4						1						17
	2	3*	6	5			8	9		11	7	10	4	12					1						18
	2	3	6				8	9		11	7	10	4			5			1						19
	2	3	6		7†	12	8	9	14	11*		10	4			5			1						20
	2	3	6	5	12		8*	9		11	7	10	4						1						21
	2	3		5	8			9*	12	11	7†	10	4	14		6			1						22
	2	3		5	6	8			9	11	7*	10	4						1		12				23
	2	3		5	6	7	8*		9	11		10	4				12		1						24
	2	3	4	5	6	7	8		9	11		10							1						25
	2	3		5	6		8	9	7	11	12	10†				4*			1			14			26
	2	3		5	6		8		9†	11	7*	10	4						1	14			12		27
	2			5	6		8		9	3	7	10	4						1					11	28
	2	3			6		8		10*	11	7	9	4						1				5	12	29
	2	3			6	14	8		9*	11	7†	10	4						1				5	12	30
	2	3			6	7	8		9*			12				5		11	1				4	10	31
					6	11*	8		12	3	7	9	4				2	14	1				5†	10	32
		3		5	2	11	8			6	7	10	4						1					9	33
		3		5	2	11	8		9*	6	7	10	4						1		12				34
	2	3	6	5	7	9	8					10	4						1		11				35
	2†	3	6	5	7	9	8			14		10*	4						1		11			12	36
5	33	34	20 + 2s	26	20 + 1s	16 + 6s	33	23	19 + 3s	30 + 2s	22 + 3s	28 + 1s	32	2 + 8s	5	8 + 1s	3 + 1s	1 + 2s	26	— + 1s	2 + 2s	— + 1s	4 + 1s	4 + 3s	

CLYDE — First Division

Year Formed: 1878. *Ground & Address:* Firhill Park, 90 Firhill Rd, Glasgow G20 7AL. *Telephone:* 041 946 9000.
Ground Capacity: total: 20,600 seated: 3264. *Size of Pitch:* 106yd×72yd.
Chairman: John F. McBeth F.R.I.C.S.. *Secretary:* John D. Taylor. *Commercial Manager:* John Donnelly.
Manager: John Clark. *Assistant Manager:* John Cushley. *Physio:* J. Watson. *Coach:* —.
Managers since 1975: S. Anderson; C. Brown; J. Clark.
Club Nickname(s): The Bully Wee. *Previous Grounds:* None.
Record Attendance: 52,000 v Rangers, Division I; 21 Nov, 1908.
Record Transfer Fee received: £95,000 for Pat Nevin to Chelsea (July 1983).
Record Transfer Fee paid: £14,000 for Harry Hood from Sunderland (1966).

1988–89 LEAGUE RECORD

Match No.	Date	Venue	Opponents	Result	H/T Score	Lg. Pos.	Goalscorers	Attendance
1	Aug 13	A	Morton	W 2-0	2-0	—	Mailer 2	2300
2	20	H	Forfar Ath	D 1-1	0-0	3	Donnelly	650
3	27	H	Partick T	W 1-0	1-0	2	McGlashan (pen)	2725
4	Sept 3	A	Raith R	D 0-0	0-0	1		1484
5	10	H	Clydebank	L 0-5	0-3	9		1200
6	17	A	Kilmarnock	W 2-1	1-1	4	Mailer, McGlashan	1745
7	24	H	Falkirk	L 1-2	0-2	8	Mailer	1600
8	Oct 1	H	Dunfermline Ath	D 1-1	1-0	9	Feenie (og)	2000
9	8	A	Meadowbank T	L 2-3	0-2	10	Donnelly, McGlashan	600
10	15	A	Airdrieonians	D 1-1	1-0	10	Cowan	2500
11	22	H	St Johnstone	L 2-4	0-2	10	Cowan, McGlashan	1050
12	29	A	Ayr U	D 1-1	1-0	10	Tait	3105
13	Nov 5	H	Queen of the S	W 3-1	1-1	10	Knox, Clark, McGlashan	600
14	12	A	Clydebank	L 2-3	1-2	10	McGlashan 2	911
15	19	H	Kilmarnock	L 0-2	0-2	10		1050
16	26	A	Falkirk	D 0-0	0-0	9		3500
17	Dec 3	A	Forfar Ath	L 1-2	1-0	11	McGlashan (pen)	559
18	10	H	Ayr U	W 4-2	2-1	9	McGlashan, Tait 2, Clark	600
19	17	A	St Johnstone	D 0-0	0-0	8		1959
20	27	H	Airdrieonians	D 0-0	0-0	—		1400
21	31	H	Raith R	L 0-1	0-1	8		720
22	Jan 3	A	Partick T	D 0-0	0-0	—		2952
23	7	A	Queen of the S	D 3-3	1-1	8	Mailer, McGlashan 2 (1 pen)	900
24	17	H	Morton	L 0-1	0-0	—		800
25	21	H	Meadowbank T	L 1-2	1-0	12	Willock	600
26	Feb 4	A	Dunfermline Ath	L 0-3	0-1	12		4733
27	18	A	Kilmarnock	D 0-0	0-0	13		1953
28	28	H	Clydebank	D 1-1	1-0	—	Fairlie	700
29	Mar 4	H	Ayr U	W 1-0	0-0	12	McGlashan	1100
30	11	A	Airdrieonians	D 1-1	0-1	12	McCabe	1100
31	18	A	Meadowbank T	L 0-2	0-1	13		500
32	28	H	Partick T	D 0-0	0-0	—		3185
33	Apr 1	A	Raith R	L 0-2	0-1	13		1500
34	8	H	Forfar Ath	D 1-1	0-1	13	Speirs	500
35	15	A	Falkirk	L 1-3	0-1	13	McGlashan (pen)	3377
36	22	H	Queen of the S	W 2-1	1-1	13	Miller, McGlashan (pen)	600
37	29	H	Morton	W 2-1	0-0	13	McGuinness, McGlashan (pen)	500
38	May 6	A	Dunfermline Ath	D 1-1	0-1	12	Rooney	9695
39	13	H	St Johnstone	W 2-0	0-0	12	McCabe, McGlashan (pen)	1381

Final League Position: 12

GOALSCORERS

League: (40): McGlashan 16 (6 pens), Mailer 5, Tait 3, Clark 2, Cowan 2, Donnelly 2, McCabe 2, Fairlie 1, Knox 1, McGuiness 1, Millar 1, Rooney 1, Speirs 1, Willock 1, own goal 1.
League Cup: (0).
Scottish Cup: (1): Mailer 1.

Record Victory: 11-1 v Cowdenbeath, Division II; 6 Oct, 1951.
Record Defeat: 0-11 v Dumbarton, Scottish Cup 4th rd, 22 Nov, 1879; v Rangers, Scottish Cup 4th rd, 13 Nov, 1880.
Most Capped Player: Tommy Ring, 12, Scotland.
Most League Appearances: 428: Brian Ahern.
Most League Goals in Season (Individual): 32: Bill Boyd, 1932–33.
Most Goals Overall (Individual): —.

Honours
League Champions: Division II 1904–05, 1951–52, 1956–57, 1961–62, 1972–73. Second Division 1977–78, 1981–82; *Runners-up:* Division II 1903–04, 1905–06, 1925–26, 1963–64.
Scottish Cup Winners: 1939, 1955, 1958; *Runners-up:* 1910, 1912, 1949.
League Cup:—.
Club colours: Shirt: White with red and black trim. Shorts: Black. Stockings: White.

Ross, S	McFarlane, R	Napier, C	Anderson, N	Donnelly, R	Clark, M	Willock, A	Knox, K	McGlashan, C	Rooney, J	Mailer, J	Millar, S	Tait, T	Quinn, P	Atkins, D	Nolan, M	McCabe, G	Cowan, T	Quinn, S	McGuiness, B	Devlin, J	Speirs, C	Mackin, A	Fairlie, J	Reid, W	Callaghan, W	Tracey, P	*Match No.*
1	2	3	4†	5	6	7*	8	9	10	11	12	14															1
1	2	3	4	5	6	7†	8*	9	10	11	12		14														2
1	2	3	4	5	6	7	8	9	10	11																	3
1	2	3	4	5	6	7	8	9	10	11																	4
1	2	3	4*	5	6	7	8	9	10	11	12																5
	2	3	4	5	6	7*	8	9	10	11	12			1													6
	2	3	4	5	6	7†	8*	9	10	11		14		1				12									7
	2	3	4	5	6	7†		9	10*	11	8			1	14			12									8
	2	3	4	5	6	7		9	10	11*	8†	14		1				12									9
	2	3		5	6			9	8	11*		4		1		7	10	12									10
	2	3		5*	6		14	9	8*	11		4		1		7	10	12									11
1	2	3			6		8	9				4	11			7	10		5								12
1	2*	3			6		8	9		12		4	11			7	10		5								13
1	2	3			6			9	8*	12		4	11			7	10		5								14
1	2				6	11	8	9	4*				12			7	10			3	5						15
	2				6	7	8	9		11		4		1	12	10*	3				5						16
	2				6	7	8	9		11*		4		1	12	10	3				5						17
	2				6	7*	8	9		11		4		1	12	10	3				5						18
	2				6	7	8	9		11		4		1	5	10	3*			12							19
	2				6	7	8	9		11		4		1		10	3					5					20
	2				6	12		9		11†	8	4		1	14	7	10			3*		5					21
	2†				6	12	8	9	10	11		4		1	14	7*	3					5					22
					6†	7*	8	9	14	11		4	12	1	2	10	3					5					23
	2				6		8	9	10*	11†		4		1	12	7	3	14			5						24
1	2				6	7	8*	9				4	14		12	10	3	11†			5						25
	2					14	8	9		12		4†		1	10	11				3*	5	6	7				26
	2						8	9			7	4		1	6	10				3	5		11				27
	2						8	9		14	7*	4		1	6	10		12		3	5		11†				28
	2						8	9			7	4		1	6	10				3	5		11				29
	2						8	9		12	7*	4		1	6	10				3	5		11				30
	2			12		14	8	9		11		4		1	6	10				3†	5		7*				31
	2†			14		12	8	9				4		1	6					3		5	7*	10	11		32
				2*		7	10			12	14	4		1	6			11		3		5†		8	9		33
						7	2			11*	12	4		1	6	10				3	5			8	9		34
						7	3	9		14	12	4		1	6	10					5			8	11†	2*	35
						7	2	9			8	6		1		10*			12	3	5			4	11		36
						7	10	9			12	4		1	6				2	3	5			8	11*		37
						7	10	9	4	12	11*	14		1	6				2	3	5†			8			38
						7	10	9	4		11*			1	6	12			2	3	5			8			39
10	31	14	9	12 + 2s	25	24 + 5s	33 + 1s	37	17 + 1s	22 + 8s	10 + 8s	27 + 4s	3 + 4s	29	15 + 8s	25 + 1s	16	2 + 7s	6 + 1s	15 + 1s	18	7	7	8	6	1	

CLYDEBANK

First Division

Year Formed: 1965. *Ground & Address:* Kilbowie Park, Arran Place, Clydebank G81 2PB. *Telephone:* 041 952 2887.
Ground Capacity: total: 9900 seated: All. *Size of Pitch:* 110yd×68yd.
Chairman: C. A. Steedman. *Secretary:* I. C. Steedman. *Commercial Manager:* David Curwood.
Manager: J. S. Steedman. *Assistant Manager:* —. *Physio:* John Jolly. *Coach:* Sam Henderson.
Managers since 1975: William Munro; J. S. Steedman.
Club Nickname(s): The Bankies. *Previous Grounds:* None.
Record Attendance: 14,900 v Hibernian, Scottish Cup 1st rd; 10 Feb, 1965.
Record Transfer Fee received: £150,000 for Frank McDougall to St Mirren.
Record Transfer Fee paid: £50,000 for Gerry McCabe from Clyde.

1988–89 LEAGUE RECORD

Match No.	Date	Venue	Opponents	Result	H/T Score	Lg. Pos.	Goalscorers	Attendance
1	Aug 13	A	Ayr U	L 2-3	1-1	—	Bryce, Eadie	3151
2	20	H	Falkirk	D 2-2	0-1	10	Charnley, Eadie	1627
3	27	A	Morton	L 0-1	0-1	13		1200
4	Sept 3	H	Kilmarnock	D 2-2	1-1	12	Coyle, Eadie	1418
5	10	A	Clyde	W 5-0	3-0	10	Wright, Coyle, Auld, Rodger, Bryce	1200
6	17	H	Dunfermline Ath	W 2-1	0-1	8	Eadie, Riddell (og)	2370
7	24	A	Meadowbank T	D 0-0	0-0	9		400
8	Oct 1	H	Forfar Ath	D 2-2	1-2	10	Coyle, Eadie	657
9	8	A	Partick T	D 1-1	0-0	8	Coyle	2059
10	15	A	Raith R	W 3-1	0-0	6	Eadie, Coyle 2	3364
11	22	H	Airdrieonians	D 3-3	3-3	7	Auld, Bryce, Spence	1321
12	29	A	Queen of the S	W 3-0	1-0	5	Bryce, Treanor (pen), Eadie	900
13	Nov 5	H	St Johnstone	W 2-0	2-0	3	Spence, Coyle	1278
14	12	H	Clyde	W 3-2	2-1	4	Coyle, Rodger, Eadie	911
15	19	A	Dunfermline Ath	D 2-2	1-2	4	Rodger, Eadie	5122
16	26	H	Meadowbank T	W 2-1	0-1	4	Spence, Wright	702
17	Dec 3	A	Falkirk	L 1-3	0-2	4	Bryce	3500
18	10	H	Queen of the S	W 4-2	2-1	3	Spence (pen), Eadie 2, Coyle	752
19	17	A	Airdrieonians	D 1-1	1-0	4	Eadie	1800
20	24	H	Raith R	W 3-1	2-1	3	Auld, Caffrey, Treanor (pen)	1143
21	31	A	Kilmarnock	L 0-1	0-1	4		2760
22	Jan 3	H	Morton	D 1-1	1-1	—	Eadie	1661
23	7	A	St Johnstone	L 0-2	0-1	5		2338
24	18	H	Ayr U	W 5-1	2-1	—	Bryce 3, Eadie, Davies	1433
25	21	H	Partick T	W 3-2	2-2	4	Auld, Treanor (pen), Bryce	2038
26	Feb 4	A	Forfar Ath	W 4-2	3-1	3	Eadie, Coyle, Lindsay, Davies	670
27	14	H	Queen of the S	W 3-0	1-0	—	Treanor (pen), Eadie, Bryce	500
28	28	A	Clyde	D 1-1	0-1	—	Treanor	700
29	Mar 4	H	Dunfermline Ath	L 0-1	0-1	3		4802
30	11	A	Meadowbank T	D 1-1	0-0	4	Eadie	400
31	25	H	Falkirk	L 0-1	0-0	4		2607
32	Apr 1	H	St Johnstone	D 2-2	1-1	4	Coyle 2 (1 pen)	1332
33	4	A	Morton	L 0-1	0-0	—		1200
34	8	A	Ayr U	W 4-2	3-1	4	Bryce 3, Coyle	2308
35	15	A	Forfar Ath	W 2-1	1-0	4	Bryce, Coyle	557
36	22	H	Partick T	W 4-2	1-2	3	Coyle, Harvey, Davies, Hughes	1989
37	29	A	Raith R	L 0-3	0-1	4		1032
38	May 6	H	Kilmarnock	W 3-2	1-2	4	Eadie 2, Coyle	1311
39	13	H	Airdrieonians	W 4-1	3-0	3	Eadie 2 (1 pen), Bryce 2	1143

Final League Position: 3

GOALSCORERS

League: (80): Eadie 21 (1 pen), Bryce 16, Coyle 16 (1 pen), Treanor 5 (4 pens), Auld 4, Spence 4 (1 pen), Davies 3, Rodger 3, Wright 2, Caffrey 1, Charnley 1, Harvey 1, Hughes 1, Lindsay 1, own goal 1.
League Cup: (2): Charnley 1, Eadie 1.
Scottish Cup: (3): Coyle 1, Eadie 1, Treanor 1 (pen).

Record Victory: 8-1 v Arbroath, First Division; 3 Jan, 1977.
Record Defeat: 1-9 v Gala Fairydean, Scottish Cup qual. rd; 15 Sept, 1965.
Most Capped Player: —.
Most League Appearances:
Most League Goals in Season (Individual): 28: Blair Millar, First Division; 1978–79.
Most Goals Overall (Individual): —.

Honours
League Champions: Second Division 1975–76; *Runners-up:* First Division 1976–77, 1984–85.
Scottish Cup:—.
League Cup:—.
Club colours: Shirt: White with red zig-zag band. Shorts: White. Stockings: White with red hooped tops.

Gallacher, J	Treanor, M	Rodger, J	Maher, J	Auld, S	McGurn, G	Davies, J	Wright, B	Eadie, K	Bryce, T	Charnley, J	Dickson, J	Harvey, P	Brodie, C	Caffrey, H	Murdoch, S	Coyle, O	Spence, T	Sweeney, S	Lindsay, C	Hughes, J	Campbell, K	*Match No.*
1	2*	3	4	5	6	7	8	9	10	11†	12	14										1
	4	3	6	5		7	8	9	10	11	2*		1	12								2
	4	3		5	2†	7	8	9*	10	11		12	1	14	6							3
	4	3		5		7	8	9	10*		2†	12	1	14	6	11						4
	2	3		5		7	10	9	8		12		1		4*	11	6					5
	2	3		5		7	8	9	10		4		1			11	6					6
	2	3		5		7	8	9	10		4		1			11	6					7
1	2	3		5		7	8	9	10*		4	12				11	6					8
1	2	3		5		7	8	9	10		4	6				11						9
1	2	3		5		7	8	9	10		4	12				11	6*					10
1	2	3		5		7	8	9	10		4					11	6					11
1	2	3		5		7		9	10		4	8				11	6					12
1	2	3		5		7	8	9	10*		4	12				11	6					13
1	2	3		5		7	8	9	10		4					11	6					14
1		3*		5		7	8	9	10		4	14			12	11	6†	2				15
1		3		5		7	8	9	10		4				12	11	6	2*				16
1				5		7	8	9	10		2	12			4*	11	6	3				17
1				5		7	8	9	10		2	6			4	11	3					18
1	2			5		7	8	9	10		4	6				11	3					19
1	2	14		5		7	8		10*		4	6		9†		11	3	12				20
1	2					7	8	9*	10		4	6		12		11	3	5				21
1	2			5		7	8	9	10*		4	6		12		11	3					22
1	2*		4	5		7	8		10					14		11	6	12	3†	9		23
1	2*		4	5		7	8	9†	10			6				11	3	12		14		24
1	2		4	5		7	8	9	10			6*				11	3			12		25
1	2			5		7	8	9	10		4					11	3*	12	6			26
1	2*			5		7		9†	10		4	6				11	3	12		14	8	27
1	2			5		7	8	9	10		4	6				11	3					28
1	2			5		7	8	9	10		4*	6				11	3			12		29
1	2			5		7	8	9	6*		4	14		11†	12	10		3				30
1	2			5		7	8	9	10		4*	12				11		3		6		31
1				5		7	8	9	10		2			12	3	11		4		6*		32
1				5	3	7		9	6		2	8		11*		10		4		12		33
1			4	5	3*	7			9		2	10			12	11		6		8		34
1			4		6	7*	12		9		2	8				11	3	5		10		35
1			4		2	7	8		9			10				11	3	5		6		36
1			4		12	7	2	9*	10†			8		14		11	3	5		6		37
1			4		2	7	10	9				8				11	3	5		6		38
1			4		2		8	9	10*			7		12		11	3	5		6		39
33	27	16	11	33	8	38	34	34	38	3	29	19	6	3	6	36	29	14	2	9	1	
		+ 1s			+ 1s		+ 1s				+ 2s	+ 10s		+ 9s	+ 4s			+ 5s		+ 5s		

COWDENBEATH

Second Division

Year Formed: 1881. *Ground & Address:* Central Park, Cowdenbeath KY4 9EY. *Telephone:* 0383 511205.
Ground Capacity: total: 7250 seated: 2750. *Size of Pitch:* 110yd×70yd.
Chairman: Thomas Currie. *Secretary:* J. Ronald Fairbairn. *Commercial Manager:* James Colvin.
Manager: John Brownlie. *Assistant Manager:* —. *Physio:* James Reekie. *Coach:* John Brownlie.
Managers since 1975: D. McLindon; F. Connor; P. Wilson; A Rolland; H. Wilson; W. McCulloch; J. Clark; J. Craig; R. Campbell; J. Blackley; J. Brownlie.
Club Nickname(s): Cowden. *Previous Grounds:* North End Park, Cowdenbeath.
Record Attendance: 25,586 v Rangers, League Cup quarter final; 21 Sept, 1949.
Record Transfer Fee received: —.
Record Transfer Fee paid: —.

1988–89 LEAGUE RECORD

Match No.	Date	Venue	Opponents	Result	H/T Score	Lg. Pos.	Goalscorers	Attendance
1	Aug 13	H	Montrose	L 2-6	2-3	—	Grant, McGonigal	250
2	20	A	Alloa	L 1-2	1-0	14	McGovern	421
3	27	A	East Fife	L 1-4	0-2	14	Yardley M	566
4	Sept 3	H	Stranraer	W 1-0	1-0	13	McGonigal (pen)	150
5	10	A	Stenhousemuir	D 0-0	0-0	12		200
6	17	H	Albion R	D 1-1	1-0	12	McGonigal	200
7	24	A	Stirling Albion	W 3-2	1-1	11	Grant, Redpath, Malone	691
8	Oct 1	H	East Stirling	W 2-1	2-0	10	Redpath 2	165
9	8	A	Brechin C	W 1-0	0-0	7	Taylor	300
10	15	A	Queen's Park	D 1-1	0-1	8	Reid	730
11	22	H	Dumbarton	W 2-0	1-0	6	McGonigal, Hoggan	350
12	29	H	Arbroath	D 1-1	1-0	6	McGonigal (pen)	450
13	Nov 5	A	Berwick R	W 1-0	0-0	5	Mackenzie	252
14	12	H	Alloa	D 1-1	1-0	5	McGovern	454
15	19	A	Montrose	W 2-0	1-0	4	McGovern, Malone	280
16	26	H	Stenhousemuir	W 2-0	1-0	3	Young, McGonigal	450
17	Dec 10	A	Albion R	L 1-3	1-2	4	Reid	521
18	17	H	Stirling Albion	D 1-1	0-0	4	Redpath	450
19	24	H	Berwick R	D 3-3	2-2	4	Mackenzie, Reid, Hoggan	250
20	31	A	Arbroath	W 1-0	0-0	3	Mackenzie	541
21	Jan 3	H	East Fife	D 1-1	1-0	—	Reid	625
22	21	H	Queen's Park	D 2-2	1-1	5	McGonigal, Reid	300
23	25	A	Stranraer	L 0-2	0-0	—		600
24	31	A	Dumbarton	L 0-3	0-1	—		470
25	Feb 8	H	Brechin C	D 3-3	1-2	—	Malone (pen), Callaghan, Mackenzie	440
26	18	H	Stenhousemuir	W 2-1	0-1	6	Callaghan 2	300
27	25	A	East Fife	L 0-1	0-1	6		564
28	Mar 4	H	Dumbarton	D 1-1	1-0	8	McGonigal	300
29	11	A	Montrose	L 1-2	1-1	9	Ferguson	275
30	15	A	East Stirling	L 0-1	0-0	—		252
31	18	H	Queen's Park	W 3-1	1-0	8	Malone 2, Ferguson	250
32	25	A	Alloa	L 1-2	0-0	10	Ferguson	488
33	Apr 1	H	Arbroath	D 1-1	1-0	9	Ferguson	205
34	8	A	Albion R	L 1-2	0-0	9	Ferguson	452
35	15	A	Berwick R	D 0-0	0-0	10		376
36	22	H	Stranraer	D 1-1	0-0	10	Docherty	200
37	29	H	Brechin C	L 0-2	0-1	10		200
38	May 6	A	Stirling Albion	W 1-0	1-0	10	McGovern	394
39	13	A	East Stirling	W 2-0	2-0	8	Mackenzie 2	300

Final League Position: 8

GOALSCORERS

League: (48): McGonigal 8 (2 pens), Mackenzie 6, Ferguson 5, Malone 5 (1 pen), Reid 5, McGovern 4, Redpath 4, Callaghan 3, Grant 2, Hoggan 2, Docherty 1, Taylor 1, Yardley M 1, Young 1.
League Cup: (0).
Scottish Cup: (3): Kerr 1, Mackenzie 1, Young 1.

Record Victory: 12-0 v St Johnstone, Scottish Cup 1st rd; 21 Jan, 1928.
Record Defeat: 1-11 v Clyde, Division II; 6 Oct, 1951.
Most Capped Player: Jim Paterson, 3, Scotland.
Most League Appearances: —.
Most League Goals in Season (Individual): 40: Willie Devlin, Division II; 1925–26.
Most Goals Overall (Individual): —.

Honours
League Champions: Division II 1913–14, 1914–15, 1938–39; *Runners-up:* Division II 1921–22, 1923–24, 1969–70.
Scottish Cup:—.
League Cup:—.
Club colours: Shirt: Royal blue shadow vertical stripe with white chest band. Shorts: White with blue side stripe. Stockings: Royal blue.

Allan, R	Redpath, A	Taylor, D	McGovern, D	Young, D	Muir, L	Malone, G	Herd, W	Grant, R	McGonigal, A	Kerr, G	Watt, D	Yardley, M	Baillie, R	Leetion, P	Main, A	Hoggan, K	Burnside, S	Reid, J	Mackenzie, A	Douglas, H	Rae, J	Wright, J	Callaghan, W	Ferguson, E	Yardley, K	McConville, J	McElwee, K	Docherty, S	Scott, C	Match No.
1	2	3	4*	5	6	7†	8	9	10	11	12	14																		1
	2*	11	4	5		7	8	9	10†	6	3		12	14	1															2
	2	11*	4	5	6	7†	8	14	10		12	9			1															3
	8		4	5				9	7*	6	2	10†	3	14	1															4
1	8*		4	5		7		9	10	6	2	11†	3																	5
1	8	3	4	5		7		9	10	6	2			12		11*														6
1	4	3	8	5*		7		9	10	6	2	14	12			11†														7
1	4	3	8	5		7*		9	10	6	2			12		11														8
1	4	11	8	5		7			10	6	2		3			9														9
1	4	11*	8	5		7†			10		2		3			9	6	14												10
1	4		8	5		7*			10	6	2		3	12		9	11													11
1	8	3†	4	5		7			10	6	2		14			11		9*	12											12
1	8*		4	5		7			10	6	2		3			11†	12	9	14											13
1	8†		4	5		7			10	6	2		3			11	14	9*	12											14
1	12	3	4	5		7			10	6			2				11	9†	14	8*										15
1	12	3	4	5		7			10	6			2				11	9†	14	8*										16
1	8		4*	5†		7				6	2	14	3			11		10	9	12										17
1	4	3	11			7				6	2					8		10	9	5										18
1	4†	3	11	5		7				6	2*					8	12	10	9	14										19
1	12	3†	4			7			14	6	2					11	8	10	9	5*										20
1	12		8			4			7	6			2			11	3	10	9*	5										21
1	14		8*	5					7	6	2		12			4	11	10	9†		3									22
1	4		8*	5					7	6	2					9	11	10	12		3									23
1	11		8	5					7*	6	2		14			9	3	10	12			4†								24
1			4	5		7			11								2	12	10*	6	3	8	9							25
1	14		8	5		7			11*								2	12	10	6	3†	4	9							26
1			8	5		7			9	12			2					10	11	6	3*	4								27
1	11		8			7*			10	6			2			14	3		12	5		4†		9						28
1	11†			5		8			10*	7	2		12			14	3			6		4		9						29
1				4		7				6	2*		3			8	11		9	5		12		10						30
1			8*			7				6	2		3			12	11			5		4		10	9					31
1			8	12		7				6	2		3*			14	11			5		4		10	9†					32
1			8			7				6	2									5		4†		10	9*	3	11	12	14	33
1			8			7				6	2									5		4		10	9	3		11		34
1			8			7				6	2		12							5		4		10†	14	3*		9	11	35
1			8			4				6	2		3					14		5		7*		10†	12			9	11	36
1						4				6	2							12		5		7		10	9	3		8	11*	37
1			10			4				6	2		14					12		5		7			9*	3		8	11†	38
1			8			4				6	2		3†					11*	12	5		7			9	14			10	39
36	21 + 6s	14	36	26 + 1s	2	35	3	7 + 1s	25 + 1s	34 + 1s	30 + 2s	3 + 3s	18 + 8s	— + 5s	3	18 + 4s	16 + 3s	15 + 6s	10 + 9s	20 + 2s	5	15 + 1s	2	10	7 + 2s	5 + 1s	1	5 + 1s	5 + 1s	

Also played: Spence T – Match 3 (3), 4 (11); Hepburn K – Match 4 (12), 5 (14); Muir S – Match 5 (12), 10 (12).

DUMBARTON

Second Division

Year Formed: 1872. *Ground & Address:* Boghead Park, Miller St, Dumbarton G82 2JA. *Telephone:* 0389 62569/67864.
Ground Capacity: total: 10,700 seated: 700. *Size of Pitch:* 110yd×72yd.
Chairman: George Crozier. *Secretary:* C. Cleary & Co.. *Commercial Manager:* —.
Manager: James George. *Assistant Manager:* —. *Physio:* Robert McCallum. *Coach:* —.
Managers since 1975: A. Wright; D. Wilson; S. Fallon; W. Lamont; D. Wilson; D. Whiteford; A. Totten; M. Clougherty; R. Auld.
Club Nickname(s): The Sons. *Previous Grounds:* None.
Record Attendance: 18,000 v Raith Rovers, Scottish Cup; 2 Mar, 1957.
Record Transfer Fee received: £125,000 for Graeme Sharp to Everton (March 1982).
Record Transfer Fee paid: £20,000 for Mark Clougherty from Clyde (Aug 1980); £20,000 for Jim Muir from Motherwell.

1988–89 LEAGUE RECORD

Match No.	Date	Venue	Opponents	Result	H/T Score	Lg. Pos.	Goalscorers	Atten-dance
1	Aug 13	H	East Fife	W 3-1	2-0	—	Docherty 2, McQuade J	493
2	20	A	Stenhousemuir	L 1-3	1-0	6	Duncan	477
3	27	H	Queen's Park	L 0-3	0-2	12		500
4	Sept 3	A	Albion R	L 1-2	1-1	12	McQuade J	300
5	10	H	Stranraer	L 0-2	0-1	13		450
6	17	A	Brechin C	D 1-1	0-0	13	Rooney	430
7	24	H	Alloa	D 1-1	0-0	13	Rooney	500
8	Oct 1	A	Berwick R	L 0-1	0-1	13		320
9	8	H	Arbroath	L 1-4	1-2	13	McGowan	350
10	15	H	Stirling Albion	L 1-2	1-0	13	MacIver	700
11	22	A	Cowdenbeath	L 0-2	0-1	13		350
12	29	H	East Stirling	W 3-0	1-0	13	Docherty 2 (1 pen), Duncan	400
13	Nov 5	A	Montrose	D 1-1	0-1	13	MacIver	350
14	12	H	Stenhousemuir	L 0-2	0-1	13		500
15	19	A	East Fife	D 1-1	1-0	13	MacIver	558
16	26	A	Stranraer	D 2-2	1-1	13	MacIver, McCahill	850
17	Dec 13	H	Brechin C	L 0-2	0-2	—		570
18	17	A	Alloa	L 0-2	0-0	13		563
19	24	H	Montrose	W 3-2	1-2	13	Spence, McQuade J, Doyle J (pen)	400
20	31	A	East Stirling	W 1-0	0-0	13	McQuade J	250
21	Jan 3	A	Queen's Park	L 1-2	1-1	—	Robertson	832
22	21	A	Stirling Albion	D 1-1	0-1	13	Cairney	620
23	31	H	Cowdenbeath	W 3-0	1-0	—	McQuade J, MacIver, Docherty (pen)	470
24	Feb 4	A	Arbroath	D 1-1	0-0	13	Docherty (pen)	404
25	18	H	East Fife	W 4-0	1-0	12	McQuade J, MacIver 2, Docherty (pen)	400
26	25	A	Stranraer	D 1-1	0-1	12	Quinn	850
27	Mar 4	A	Cowdenbeath	D 1-1	0-1	12	MacIver	300
28	7	H	Berwick R	D 2-2	1-1	—	MacIver 2	341
29	11	H	Queen's Park	W 1-0	1-0	12	Spence	600
30	25	A	East Stirling	L 0-1	0-0	13		300
31	28	H	Montrose	W 2-0	1-0	—	Wharton, MacIver	400
32	Apr 1	A	Stirling Albion	L 1-3	0-3	12	Spence	634
33	4	H	Albion R	W 1-0	0-0	—	Robertson	600
34	8	H	Berwick R	L 0-4	0-1	13		550
35	15	H	Brechin C	W 1-0	1-0	12	Quinn	500
36	22	A	Albion R	L 0-2	0-1	13		840
37	29	A	Arbroath	W 3-1	1-0	13	MacIver, Quinn 2	347
38	May 6	H	Stenhousemuir	W 2-0	1-0	12	MacIver, Douglas	600
39	13	H	Alloa	L 0-2	0-0	12		800

Final League Position: 12

GOALSCORERS

League: (45): MacIver 13, Docherty 7 (4 pens), McQuade J 5, Quinn 4, Spence 3, Duncan 2, Robertson 2, Rooney 2, Cairney 1, Douglas 1, Doyle J 1 (pen), McCahill 1, McGowan 1, McQuade A 1, Wharton 1.
League Cup: (1): McQuade J 1.
Scottish Cup: (8): MacIver 3, Cairney 2, McQuade J 2, McGowan 1.

Record Victory: 13-1 v Kirkintilloch Cl.
Record Defeat: **1-11 v Albion Rovers, Division II; 30 Jan, 1926: v Ayr United, League Cup; 13 Aug, 1952.**
Most Capped Player: John Lindsay, 8, Scotland; James McAulay, 8, Scotland.
Most League Appearances: —.
Most League Goals in Season (Individual): 38: Kenny Wilson, Division II; 1971–72.
Most Goals Overall (Individual): —.

Honours
League Champions: Division I 1890–91 (shared with Rangers), 1891–92. Division II 1910–11, 1971–72; *Runners-up:* First Division 1983–84. Division II 1907–08.
Scottish Cup Winners: 1883; *Runners-up:* 1881, 1882, 1887, 1891, 1897.
League Cup:—.
Club colours: Shirt: Gold with white chest band. Shorts: Black. Stockings: Gold and black.

Stevenson, H	Callan, D	Cranmer, C	Doyle, G	McCahill, S	Martin, D	Blackie, W	Fulton, D	Coyle, O	Docherty, R	Cairns, W	McQuade, J	Duncan, G	McGowan, P	McDougall, I	Gow, S	Rooney, B	Cairney, P	MacIver, S	Elliott, G	Douglas, C	Robertson, S	McKinlay, P	Doyle, J	Strachan, H	Spence, C	Wharton, P	McQuade, A	Quinn, P	Dickie, G	*Match No.*
1	2	3	4	5	6	7*	8	9	10	11	12																			1
1	2	3		5	6		11	9	10	14	12	7*	4	8†																2
1	2	3*		5	6	7†	4	9	10	14	12		11	8																3
1		3*		5	6		4		9	8	10	11†	2	7	14															4
1	12	3		5	4	9	8		7	6*	11		2			10														5
1			4	5		12	8		7	3	11	9*	6		2	10														6
1			4	5	8	12			7	3	11	9	6		2*	10														7
1			4	5		7	6		8	2*	11	9	3	14	12	10†														8
1		3	2	5	8	12			10		11		6	7			4	9*												9
1				6	4				10	8*	11	9	3		2		5	7†	12	14										10
1	2			6		12			10		11†	9*	3		4		5	7	8	14										11
1			2	4					11		8	9	6		3		5	7			10									12
1				4					11		8*	9	2		3			7	6	12	10	5								13
1			2	4					11		12	9	6		3		5	7†	8*	14	10									14
1			2	4		8*			11		14	9	6†		3		5	7		12	10									15
1			2	4					11		12	9	6		3		5	7			10*		8							16
			2	4					11*	6	9				3		5†	7	14	12	10		8	1						17
		3							11	4	9*		6		2		5	7		12	10		8	1						18
			2	4							11		6		3*		5	10	7		8		12	1	9					19
			2	4					14		11	12	3				5	7	6†		10		8*	1	9					20
			2*	4					11		9	12	8				5	7	6†		10		14	1		3				21
			2*	4					10		11		8				5		12				6	1	9	3	7			22
									10		11	12	8		4†			9	2*	14	6			1	5	3	7			23
									8		11*	12	2		4		5	10			6			1	9	3	7			24
			14						11		8†		2		4*		5	10			12			1	6	3	7	9		25
									11		8*		2		4		5	10			12			1	6	3	7	9		26
			4						11		8*		2				5	10			12			1	6	3	7	9		27
			4						11				2				5	10			8			1	6	3	7	9		28
									11		12		2				5	10*			8			1	6	3	7	9	4	29
									11		7						5	10			8			1	6	3	2	9	4	30
									11				2				5	10			8			1	6	3	7	9	4	31
									11*		14		2				5	10			8		12	1	6	3	7	9†	4	32
									11*		7	10			14				12		8		6†	1	5	3	2	9	4	33
			12								11	10†			14		5		7*		8			1	6	3	2	9	4	34
											11		2				5				10		8	1	6	3	7	9	4	35
											11		2				5	10			8		6	1		3	7	9	4	36
			12										2				5	11†		14	10*		8	1	6	3	7	9	4	37
			12										2				5	11†		14	10		8	1	6*	3	7	9	4	38
			12										2				5	11†		14	10		8	1	6*	3	7	9	4	39
16	4	7	16	21	8	5	7	3	31	9	26	14	34	4	16	4	28	27	8	—	24	1	11	23	19	19	18	15	11	
	+ 1s		+ 5s			+ 4s			+ 1s	+ 2s	+ 8s	+ 4s		+ 1s	+ 4s				+ 4s	+ 11s	+ 3s		+ 3s							

Also played: English D – Match 4 (12).

DUNDEE

Premier Division

Year Formed: 1893. *Ground & Address:* Dens Park, Sandeman St, Dundee DD3 7JY. *Telephone:* 0382 826104.
Ground Capacity: total: 22,381 seated: 12,130. *Size of Pitch:* 113yd×73yd.
Chairman: Angus Cook. *Secretary:* John Campbell. *Commercial Manager:* —.
Manager: Gordon Wallace. *Assistant Manager:* John Blackley. *Physio:* Eric Ferguson. *Coach:* Bert Slater.
Managers since 1975: David Whyte; Tommy Gemmell; Donald Mackay; Archie Knox; Jocky Scott; Gordon Wallace.
Club Nickname(s): The Dark Blues or The Dee. *Previous Grounds:* Carolina Port 1893–98.
Record Attendance: 43,024 v Rangers, Scottish Cup; 1953.
Record Transfer Fee received: £350,000 for Robert Connor to Aberdeen.
Record Transfer Fee paid: £90,000 for Albert Kidd from Motherwell.
Record Victory: 10–0 Division II v Alloa; 9 Mar, 1947 and v Dunfermline Ath; 22 Mar, 1947.

1988–89 LEAGUE RECORD

Match No.	*Date*	*Venue*	*Opponents*	*Result*		*H/T Score*	*Lg. Pos.*	*Goalscorers*	*Attendance*
1	Aug 13	H	Aberdeen	D	1-1	0-0	—	Chisholm	12,222
2	20	A	Motherwell	D	1-1	1-0	6	Wright	3803
3	27	A	St Mirren	D	0-0	0-0	6		3801
4	Sept 3	H	Dundee U	L	0-3	0-2	8		14,927
5	17	A	Hamilton A	L	0-1	0-0	9		2194
6	24	H	Celtic	W	1-0	1-0	6	Coyne	15,515
7	28	A	Hearts	D	1-1	0-0	—	Shannon	8392
8	Oct 1	A	Rangers	L	0-2	0-1	6		40,768
9	8	H	Hibernian	W	2-1	2-1	6	Chisholm, Coyne	8127
10	12	H	Motherwell	D	1-1	0-0	—	Wright	4161
11	29	A	Celtic	W	3-2	3-2	7	Frail, Harvey, Rafferty	23,843
12	Nov 2	H	Hamilton A	W	5-2	2-0	—	Harvey, Wright, Coyne 3	3857
13	5	A	Dundee U	L	0-2	0-2	7		14,882
14	12	H	St Mirren	L	0-1	0-1	7		4657
15	16	A	Aberdeen	L	0-1	0-0	—		11,181
16	19	H	Rangers	D	0-0	0-0	7		16,514
17	26	A	Hibernian	D	1-1	1-1	7	Coyne	9000
18	Dec 3	H	Hearts	D	1-1	0-0	7	Harvey	6902
19	10	A	Hamilton A	L	0-1	0-0	7		2083
20	17	A	Motherwell	L	0-1	0-1	8		4560
21	31	H	Aberdeen	W	2-0	1-0	7	Coyne 2	9828
22	Jan 3	A	St Mirren	D	1-1	1-1	—	Wright	4920
23	7	H	Dundee U	L	0-1	0-1	7		16,332
24	14	H	Hibernian	L	1-2	0-1	8	McBride	7261
25	21	A	Rangers	L	1-3	1-1	8	Wright	43,202
26	Feb 11	A	Hearts	L	1-3	1-2	8	Coyne	10,432
27	25	H	Celtic	L	0-3	0-1	8		14,559
28	Mar 11	A	Aberdeen	L	0-2	0-1	9		11,800
29	25	H	Motherwell	W	2-1	1-1	8	McBride, Chisholm	3718
30	Apr 1	H	St Mirren	W	2-1	0-1	8	Craig, Campbell D	3824
31	8	A	Dundee U	L	1-2	0-2	8	Saunders	11,910
32	15	H	Hearts	W	2-1	0-1	8	Chisholm, Wright	6993
33	22	A	Celtic	L	1-2	1-0	8	Harvey (pen)	16,000
34	29	H	Hamilton A	W	1-0	0-0	8	Craig	4042
35	May 6	H	Rangers	L	1-2	1-0	8	Wright	14,889
36	13	A	Hibernian	D	1-1	0-0	8	Wright	7675

Final League Position: 8

GOALSCORERS

League: (34): Coyne 9, Wright 8, Chisholm 4, Harvey 4 (1 pen), Craig 2, McBride 2, Campbell D 1, Frail 1, Rafferty 1, Saunders 1, Shannon 1.
League Cup: (8): Harvey 3, Wright 2, Lawrence 1, McGeachie 1, Rafferty 1.
Scottish Cup: (1): Angus 1.

Record Defeat: 0-11 v Celtic, Division I; 26 Oct, 1895.
Most Capped Player: Alex Hamilton, 24, Scotland.
Most League Appearances: 341: Doug Cowie 1945–61.
Most League Goals in Season (Individual): 38: Dave Halliday, Division I; 1923–24.
Most Goals Overall (Individual): 113: Alan Gilzean.

Honours
League Champions: Division I 1961–62. First Division 1978–79. Division II 1946–47; *Runners-up:* Division I 1902–03, 1906–07, 1908–09, 1948–49, 1980–81.
Scottish Cup Winners: 1910; *Runners-up:* 1925, 1952, 1964.
League Cup Winners: 1951–52, 1952–53, 1973–74; *Runners-up:* 1967–68, 1980–81.
European: *European Cup:* 1962–63 (semi-final). *Cup Winners Cup:* 1964–65.
UEFA Cup: (*Fairs Cup* 1967–68 semi-final), 1971–72, 1974–75.
Club colours: Shirt: Dark blue with red and white trim. Shorts: White. Stockings: Red.

Geddes, R	Forsyth, S	McKinlay, T	Chisholm, G	Smith, J	Saunders, W	Lawrence, A	Angus, I	Wright, K	Harvey, G	Campbell, S	Rafferty, S	Mennie, V	Kirkwood, W	Coyne, T	Shannon, R	Hendry, J	Frail, S	Holt, J	McBride, J	McGeachie, G	Campbell, D	Craib, M	Craig, A	Carson, T	*Match No.*
1	2	3	4	5	6†	7	8*	9	10	11	12	14													1
1	2	3	4	5	6			11	10	7		12	8	9*											2
1	2	3	4	5	6	11*		9	7	12			8	10											3
1	2	3	4		5			9	11†	12	8		6	10*	7	14									4
1	2	3	4		6			9	14	11†	7*		5	10	8		12								5
1	5	3	4		6			9		11	7		2	10	8										6
1	5	3	4		6			9		11	7		2	10	8										7
1	5	3	4		6			9		11	7		2	10	8										8
1	5	3	4		6		12	9		11	7		2	10	8*										9
1	5	3	4		6			9		11	7*		2	10	8	12									10
1	5	3	4			11*		9	8		7	12		10	2		6								11
1		3	4	5	6†	12		9	8		7*	14		10	2		11								12
1		3	4	5	6			9	8	12	7*			10	2		11								13
1	2	3		5	6			·9	12	11	7*			10	4		8								14
1	5	3			6	7*		9	14	11†	8		12	10	2		4								15
1	5	3	12		6	7*		9		11	8			10	2		4								16
1	5	3	4		6			9		11	8			10	2		7								17
1	5	3	4		6			9	12	11	8			10	2		7*								18
1	5		4		3	14*		9	7	11	8		12	10	2		6†								19
1	5		4		6		12	9†	14	7*	8		2	10				3	11						20
1	5		4		6			9			8			10	2		7	3	11						21
1	5		4		6			9			8			10	2		7	3	11						22
1	5		4		6			9			8			10	2		7	3	11						23
1	5		4		6		12	9		14	8			10	2		7†	3*	11						24
1	5		4	2	6†		3	9	14	12	8			10			7*		11						25
1			4			7	3	9		11	8			10	2		6*	5	12						26
1	4		5			9†	8			14	6			10	2		7	3	11*			12			27
1	2		4		6	9†		10		11*	12						7	3	14	8		5			28
1	2		5		6		8	9			14				3		7†	12	11	4*	10				29
1	2		5		6		8	9							3			4	11		10		7		30
1	2		5		6		8	9	12		14				3*		4		11		10		7†		31
	6		5				8	9	14		7				3		12	4*	11	2	10†			1	32
	6		5		4		8	9	10†		12				3				11	2*	14		7	1	33
1	6		5				3	9	10		12				2		8*		14	4	11†		7		34
1	6		5		4		3	9	14		7†				2				11		10	12	8*		35
1	2		5†				3	9	10*	11							8		14	4	12	6	7		36
34	33	18	33 + 1s	7	30	8 + 2s	12 + 3s	35	11 + 9s	18 + 6s	26 + 6s	— + 4s	10 + 2s	26	29	— + 2s	21 + 2s	10 + 1s	13 + 4s	6	6 + 2s	2 + 2s	6	2	

DUNDEE UNITED Premier Division

Year Formed: 1909 (1923). *Ground & Address:* Tannadice Park, Tannadice St, Dundee DD3 7JW. *Telephone:* 0382 826289.
Ground Capacity: total: 22,310 seated: 2252. *Size of Pitch:* 110×74yd.
Chairman: George F. Fox. *Secretary:* Mrs Ann Diamond. *Commercial Manager:* James Connor.
Manager: James Y. McLean. *Assistant Manager:* —. *Physio:* James Joyce. *Coach:* G. Wallace.
Managers since 1975: J. McLean.
Club Nickname(s): The Terrors. *Previous Grounds:* None.
Record Attendance: 28,000 v Barcelona, Fairs Cup; 16 Nov, 1966.
Record Transfer Fee received: £750,000 for Richard Gough to Tottenham Hotspur (Aug 1986).
Record Transfer Fee paid: £165,000 for Eamonn Bannon from Chelsea (Oct, 1979).
Record Victory: 14-0 v Nithsdale Wanderers, Scottish Cup 1st rd; 17 Jan, 1931.
Record Defeat: 1-12 v Motherwell, Division II; 23 Jan, 1954.

1988–89 LEAGUE RECORD

Match No.	Date	Venue	Opponents	Result	H/T Score	Lg. Pos.	Goalscorers	Attendance
1	Aug 13	A	St Mirren	W 1-0	0-0	—	Clark	5852
2	20	H	Celtic	W 1-0	1-0	1	Gallacher	18,769
3	27	H	Aberdeen	D 2-2	1-0	2	Meade, Clark	14,735
4	Sept 3	A	Dundee	W 3-0	2-0	2	Paatelainan 2, Gallacher	14,927
5	17	H	Hibernian	D 1-1	0-1	2	Paatelainan (pen)	11,017
6	24	A	Motherwell	W 2-1	1-1	2	Redford 2	3559
7	27	H	Rangers	L 0-1	0-0	—		20,071
8	Oct 1	H	Hearts	D 0-0	0-0	3		10,838
9	8	A	Hamilton A	W 4-0	2-0	2	Paatelainan 2, Meade, McPhee	3538
10	12	A	Celtic	L 0-1	0-1	—		36,760
11	22	H	St Mirren	L 0-1	0-1	3		7618
12	29	H	Motherwell	D 1-1	0-0	4	Paatelainan	6266
13	Nov 2	A	Hibernian	D 1-1	0-1	—	Meade	9247
14	5	H	Dundee	W 2-0	2-0	3	Meade, Paatelainan	14,882
15	12	A	Aberdeen	D 1-1	0-1	3	Preston	15,184
16	19	A	Hearts	D 0-0	0-0	4		10,124
17	26	H	Hamilton A	W 1-0	0-0	4	Bowman	6357
18	Dec 3	A	Rangers	W 1-0	0-0	4	Beaumont	39,123
19	10	H	Hibernian	W 4-1	2-0	2	French, Mitchell (og), McKinley, Gallacher	9963
20	17	H	Celtic	W 2-0	0-0	2	Paatelainan (pen), Baillie (og)	18,745
21	31	A	St Mirren	W 1-0	1-0	2	Gallacher	7768
22	Jan 3	H	Aberdeen	D 1-1	1-1	—	French	17,952
23	7	A	Dundee	W 1-0	1-0	2	French	16,332
24	14	A	Hamilton A	W 5-0	3-0	2	Paatelainan, Gallagher3, McInally	3792
25	21	H	Hearts	D 0-0	0-0	2		13,674
26	Feb 11	H	Rangers	D 1-1	0-1	2	Stevens (og)	22,019
27	Mar 11	H	St Mirren	L 1-4	1-1	4	Malpas	8320
28	14	A	Motherwell	W 2-1	1-0	—	Krivokapic, Gallacher	3545
29	25	A	Celtic	L 0-1	0-1	4		32,589
30	Apr 1	A	Aberdeen	L 0-1	0-0	4		16,700
31	8	H	Dundee	W 2-1	2-0	3	Sturrock, Gallacher	11,910
32	22	H	Motherwell	D 1-1	0-0	4	Hegarty	6301
33	29	A	Hibernian	W 2-1	1-1	3	Irvine, Paatelainan	7300
34	May 2	A	Rangers	L 0-2	0-2	—		39,058
35	6	A	Hearts	D 0-0	0-0	4		8613
36	13	H	Hamilton A	L 0-1	0-1	4		11,503

Final League Position: 4

GOALSCORERS

League: (44): Paatelainan 10 (2 pens), Gallacher 9, Meade 4, French 3, Clark 2, Redford 2, Beaumont 1, Bowman 1, Hegarty 1, Irvine 1, Krivokapic 1, McInally 1, McKinlay 1, McPhee 1, Malpas 1, Preston 1, Sturrock 1, own goals 3.
League Cup: (7): Paatelainan 3, Gallacher 2, Meade 1, Redford 1.
Scottish Cup: (7): Paatelainan 4 (2 pens), Bowman 1, Gallacher 1, Meade 1.

Most Capped Player: David Narey, 35, Scotland.
Most League Appearances: 625: **Hamish McAlpine; 1969–85.**
Most League Goals in Season (Individual): 41: John Coyle, Division II; 1955–56.
Most Goals Overall (Individual): 202: Peter McKay.

Honours
League Champions: Premier Division 1982–83. Division II 1924–25, 1928–29; *Runners-up:* Division II 1930–31, 1959–60.
Scottish Cup Runners-up: 1974, 1981, 1985, 1987, 1988.
League Cup Winners: 1979–80, 1980–81; *Runners-up:* 1981–82, 1984–85.
Summer Cup Runners-up: 1964–65.
Scottish War Cup Runners-up: 1939–40.
European: *European Cup:* 8 matches 1983–84 (semi-finals); *Cup Winners Cup:* 4 matches 1974–75; *UEFA Cup Runners-up:* 1986–87. 70 matches (1966–67, 1969–70, 1970–71 *Fairs Cup;* 1971–72, 1975–76, 1977–78, 1978–79, 1979–80, 1980–81, 1981–82, 1982–83, 1984–85, 1985–86, 1986–87, 1987–88).
Club colours: Tangerine jersey, black shorts. Change colours: all white.

Thomson, W	Bowman, D	Malpas, M	Cleland, A	Clark, J	Narey, D	Irvine, JA	McKinlay, W	Paatelainan, M	Gallacher, K	Redford, I	French, H	Beaumont, D	McGinnis, G	McInally, J	Hegarty, P	McLeod, J	Meade, R	Krivokapic, M	McLeod, G	Preston, A	McPhee, I	Curran, H	Jackson, D	Sturrock, P	Welsh, B	O'Neil, J	Adam, C	McKinnon, R	Connolly, P	*Match No.*
1	2	3	4†	5	6	7	8	9	10	11*	12	14																		1
1	12	3		7	6		8	9†	10	11			2	4	5*	14														2
1	2	3	12	5	6		8	9	10	11		4					7*													3
1	2	3	9*		6		8	7	10	11	14	12		4†	5															4
1	2	3	12	9†	6		8	11	10		14			4	5		7*													5
1	12	3	7*	5	6		8	9	10	11				4				2												6
1	12	3		8	6			9†	10	11	7		2	4*	5		14													7
1	2	3	9*	6			8†		10	11	7	12			5		14	4												8
1	2	3		5	6			9†				8				14	7	4	10*	11	12									9
1	2	3		5	6			9	10	11		8					7*	4		12										10
1	2	3		5	6			9	7	10*	14	8			12			4†		11										11
1	2	3		7	6			9†	8					4	5	14		12		11	10*									12
1		3		2	6		8*	11			14	12		4	5		7†	10		9										13
1	12	3		2			8*	11				6		4	5		7	10		9										14
1	12	3			6		8	11			14	2		4*	5		7†	10		9										15
1	12	3			6		8	11	14			2		4	5		7*	10		9†										16
1	12	3			6		2*	11†	8		7	14		4	5			10		9										17
1	2	3			6		10	11*	9		7	8		4	5			12												18
1	2	3			6		10*	11†	9		7	8		4	5			12				14								19
1	2*	3			6		10	11	9		7	14		4	5			12					8†							20
1	12	3			6		10	11	9		7	2		4	5*			8												21
1	2*	3			6		10	11	9		7	8	12	4				5												22
1	2	3			6		10*	11	9		7	8	5	4										12						23
1	2	3			6		10	11*	9		7			4	5			8						12						24
1	2	3	10†		6			11*	9		7		12	4	5			8						14						25
1	2*	3		12	6		10†	11	9		7			4	5		14	8												26
1		3	2*		6		9†	11	7					4	5			12						10	8	14				27
1	2	3					11	9	10				6	4	5			8				7								28
1	2	3			6	7	10	9	11				5*	4	12							8†		14						29
1	9*	3	2		6	7†	8		11				12	4	5									10			14			30
1		3		2	6	14	8		11				12	4	5									10			9†	7*		31
1		3		2	6	7	9	11	14					4†	5							12		10*			8			32
1		3		2	6	7	10	11	9				4		5							12					8*			33
1		3		2†	6	7*	10	11	9				4	8	5			12									14			34
1	2	3		12	6		10	11	9					4	5			8*						14					7†	35
1		3		14	6		12	11						4	5			2				9†		10			8*		7	36
36	21 + 8s	36	7 + 2s	17 + 3s	33	6 + 1s	29 + 1s	33	29 + 2s	9	12 + 6s	12 + 6s	7 + 4s	29	27 + 2s	— + 3s	8 + 3s	18 + 6s	1	8 + 1s	1 + 1s	3 + 3s	1	5 + 5s	1	— + 1s	4 + 2s	1	2	

DUNFERMLINE ATHLETIC Premier Division

Year Formed: 1885. *Ground & Address:* East End Park, Halbeath Rd, Dunfermline KY12 7RB. *Telephone:* 0383 724295.
Ground Capacity: total: 27,500 seated: 3000. *Size of Pitch:* 114yd×72yd.
Chairman: William M. Rennie. *Secretary:* James McConville J.P.. *General and Commercial Manager:* Jack E. Kyle.
Manager: Jim Leishman. *Assistant Manager:* —. *Physio:* Philip Yeates, M.C.S.P.. *Coach:* Iain Munro.
Managers since 1975: A. Miller; H. Melrose; P. Stanton; T. Forsyth; J. Leishman.
Club Nickname(s): The Pars. *Previous Grounds:* None.
Record Attendance: 27,816 v Celtic, Division I; 1968.
Record Transfer Fee received: £200,000 for Ian McCall to Rangers (Aug 1987).
Record Transfer Fee paid: —.
Record Victory: 11-2 v Stenhousemuir, Division II; 27 Sept, 1930.

1988–89 LEAGUE RECORD

Match No.	Date	Venue	Opponents	Result	H/T Score	Lg. Pos.	Goalscorers	Attendance
1	Aug 13	A	Partick T	W 2-1	1-1	—	Robertson G, Jack	3941
2	20	H	St Johnstone	W 1-0	1-0	2	Robertson C	5534
3	27	H	Raith R	W 2-1	1-0	1	Robertson C, Smith T	5602
4	Sept 3	A	Falkirk	L 1-2	1-1	2	Robertson C	5000
5	10	H	Queen of the S	W 4-2	3-1	1	Robertson C, Jack, Watson, Smith T	4883
6	17	A	Clydebank	L 1-2	1-0	2	Smith R	2370
7	24	H	Kilmarnock	W 3-0	1-0	2	Watson 2, Smith M	5379
8	Oct 1 1	A	Clyde	D 1-1	0-1	3	Smith P	2000
9	8	H	Airdrieonians	W 1-0	0-0	1	Watson	5616
10	15	A	Ayr U	D 2-2	0-2	2	Smith T, Watson	5875
11	22	H	Meadowbank T	L 1-3	0-3	3	Holt	4761
12	29	A	Morton	L 0-1	0-0	6		4500
13	Nov 5	H	Forfar Ath	W 2-1	2-1	5	Jack 2	4942
14	12	A	Queen of the S	D 0-0	0-0	6		1340
15	19	H	Clydebank	D 2-2	2-1	6	Davies (og), Jack	5122
16	26	A	Kilmarnock	D 2-2	2-0	6	Jack 2	2961
17	Dec 3	A	St Johnstone	W 1-0	1-0	5	Beedie	4146
18	10	H	Morton	W 2-1	2-1	4	Jack, Robertson C	5454
19	17	A	Meadowbank T	W 1-0	1-0	3	Watson	2000
20	24	H	Ayr U	W 5-1	2-1	2	Tierney, Watson 2, Smith P, Jack	5871
21	31	H	Falkirk	W 3-0	2-0	1	Jack 2 (1 pen), Watson	12,889
22	Jan 3	A	Raith R	W 3-1	1-1	—	Jack, Smith P, Smith T	8981
23	7	A	Forfar Ath	L 1-2	0-2	3	Jack	2596
24	14	H	Partick T	W 3-2	2-1	2	Watson, Smith T, Jack	5476
25	21	A	Airdrieonians	W 2-0	0-0	1	Jack, McCathie	9100
26	Feb 4	H	Clyde	W 3-0	1-0	1	Jack, Smith P, Beedie	4733
27	11	H	St Johnstone	W 1-0	0-0	1	Jack	6902
28	Mar 4	A	Clydebank	W 1-0	1-0	1	Dickson (og)	4802
29	7	A	Falkirk	L 0-4	0-3	—		9216
30	11	H	Raith R	L 0-1	0-0	1		6814
31	21	A	Queen of the S	W 2-0	2-0	—	Gallagher, Irons	1550
32	25	H	Kilmarnock	D 0-0	0-0	1		5906
33	Apr 1	A	Partick T	D 0-0	0-0	1		5103
34	8	H	Airdrieonians	D 1-1	1-0	1	Watson	8303
35	15	H	Morton	W 1-0	0-0	1	Jack	5622
36	22	A	Ayr U	W 2-1	1-1	1	Watson, Smith P	4313
37	29	A	Forfar Ath	W 1-0	0-0	1	Irons	3301
38	May 6	H	Clyde	D 1-1	1-0	1	Watson	9695
39	13	H	Meadowbank T	D 1-1	0-0	1	Watson	12,976

Final League Position: 1

GOALSCORERS

League: (60): Jack 18 (1 pen), Watson 14, Robertson C 5, Smith P 5, Smith T 5, Beedie 2, Irons 2, Gallagher 1, Holt 1, McCathie 1, Robertson G 1, Smith M 1, Smith R 1, Tierney 1, own goals 2.
League Cup: (4): Watson 2, Irons 1, Smith T 1.
Scottish Cup: (1): Smith T 1.

Record Defeat: 0-10 v Dundee, Division II; 22 Mar, 1947.
Most Capped Player: Andy Wilson, 6 (12), Scotland.
Most League Appearances: 360: Bobby Robertson; 1977–88.
Most League Goals in Season (Individual): 55: Bobby Skinner, Division II; 1925–26.
Most Goals Overall (Individual): 154: Charles Dickson.

Honours
League Champions: First Division 1988–89. Division II 1925–26. Second Division 1985–86; *Runners-up:* First Division 1986–87. Division II 1912–13, 1933–34, 1954–55, 1957–58, 1972–73. Second Division 1978–79.
Scottish Cup Winners: 1961, 1968; *Runners-up:* 1965.
League Cup Runners-up: 1949–50.
European: *European Cup:*—. *Cup Winners Cup:* 1961–62, 1968–69 (semi-finals). *UEFA Cup:* 1962–63, 1964–65, 1965–66, 1966–67, 1969–70 (*Fairs Cup*).
Club colours: Shirt: Broad black and white vertical stripes. Shorts: Black. Stockings: Black with red diamond tops.

Westwater, I	Robertson, G	Smith, R	Riddell, G	Williamson, A	Irons, D	Smith, M	Morrison, S	Jack, R	Robertson, C	Smith, T	Davidson, G	Callaghan, W	Beedie, S	Watson, J	Holt, J	Smith, P	Feenie, M	McCathie, N	Burns, H	Tierney, G	Farningham, R	Gallagher, E	Sharp, R	Speirs, G	*Match No.*
1	2	3	4	5	6	7*	8	9	10	11		12													1
1	2	3	4	5	6	7†	8		10	9*		14	11	12											2
1	2	3	4	5	6	7†	14	12	10	8			11	9*											3
1	2	3		5	6	7	12		10	8			11*	9	4										4
1	2	3	5		6	7†	12	10	4*	11	14			9		8									5
1	2	3	4	5	6		7	10		11				9		8									6
1		3	4		6	7	12	10*		11				9	5	8	2								7
1		3	4		6	7	10			11				9	5	8	2								8
1	12	3	4			7	6	10		11*				9	2	8		5							9
1		3	4			7	12	10		11			6*	9	2	8		5							10
1	14	3	4				12	10†	7*	11			6	9	2	8		5							11
1	2	3			6		7	14	8	11*			10†	5	4	9		12							12
1	2	3			11	7*		9	10	12			6	5	4	8									13
1	2	3			11	7		9*	10	12			6	5	4	8									14
1	2	3			11	7		9	10				6	5	4	8									15
1		3			11	7*		9	10	12			6	5	4	8			2						16
1		3			11			9	10				6	5	7	8		4	2						17
1		3*	12		11	7		9	10				6	5	4	8			2						18
1	3		4†	14	11	7*		9		12			10	6		8			2	5					19
1	2	3	4		11		14	9		12			6†	10		8			7*	5					20
1	2	3	4		11		12	9		7*		14	6	10†		8				5					21
1		3	4		11			9		7			6	10		8			2	5					22
1	2	3	4		11		12	9		7*		14	6	10		8†				5					23
1	2	3	4		11		12	9		7				10		8			6*	5					24
1	2	3			11			9					6	10		8		4		5	7				25
1	2	3	4		11	12		9		7*			6			8		5			10				26
1	2	3			11			9		10*			6			8		4	12	5	7				27
1	2	3			11	12		9								8		4	6	5	7	10*			28
1	2	3			11	7†		9						10		8*		4	14	5	6	12			29
1		3			11	14		9						10*		8		4	2	5	7	12	6†		30
1		3			11			9*						12		8		4	2	5	7	10		6	31
1		3			11*			9						12		8		4	2	5	7	10	14	6†	32
1	3				11			9*						12		8		4	2	5	7	10	6		33
1	3†				11			9						10		8		4	2	5	7*	14	6	12	34
1	2		5		11	7		9						10		8		4			6		3		35
1	2	14	5		11*	7		9						10		8†		4			6		3	12	36
1	2		6		11			9					12	10		8		4		5	7*		3		37
1	2		6*		11	12		9					7	10		8		4		5			3		38
1	2	3			11	12		9					7	10		8		4		5			6*		39
39	27 + 2s	32 + 1s	21 + 1s	5 + 1s	36	18 + 5s	6 + 10s	34 + 2s	13	18 + 5s	— + 1s	— + 4s	22 + 1s	31 + 4s	13	35	2	19 + 1s	13 + 2s	18	13	4 + 3s	8 + 1s	2 + 2s	

EAST FIFE

Second Division

Year Formed: 1903. *Ground & Address:* Bayview Park, Methil Fife KY8 3AG. *Telephone:* 0333 26323.
Ground Capacity: total: 14,200 seated: 800. *Size of Pitch:* 110yd×71yd.
Chairman: James Baxter. *Secretary:* Mrs I. McCammon. *Commercial Manager:* James Bonthrone.
Manager: Gavin Murray. *Assistant Manager:* —. *Physio:* Bud Porteous. *Coach:* David Gorman.
Managers since 1975: Frank Christie; Roy Barry; David Clarke; Gavin Murray.
Club Nickname(s): The Fifers. *Previous Grounds:* None.
Record Attendance: 22,515 v Raith Rovers, Division I; 2 Jan, 1950.
Record Transfer Fee received: £65,000 for Gordon Marshall to Falkirk (1987).
Record Transfer Fee paid: £29,000 for Ray Charles from Montrose (1987).

1988–89 LEAGUE RECORD

Match No.	Date	Venue	Opponents	Result		H/T Score	Lg. Pos.	Goalscorers	Attendance
1	Aug 13	A	Dumbarton	L	1-3	0-2	—	Pittman	493
2	20	H	Albion R	L	1-2	0-0	12	Harrow	556
3	27	H	Cowdenbeath	W	4-1	2-0	11	McNaughton 2, Pittman 2	566
4	Sept 3	A	East Stirling	D	2-2	2-0	10	McNaughton 2	200
5	10	H	Alloa	W	2-0	2-0	9	Pittman, Hunter	675
6	17	A	Queen's Park	L	0-1	0-0	10		577
7	24	H	Arbroath	D	0-0	0-0	10		656
8	Oct 1	A	Stranraer	D	2-2	1-1	11	McNaughton, Hope	700
9	8	H	Montrose	D	1-1	1-1	11	Harrow	561
10	15	H	Stenhousemuir	W	2-1	0-0	9	Perry, McNaughton	502
11	22	A	Berwick R	W	2-1	1-1	9	Mitchell, Deas	300
12	29	A	Stirling Albion	L	1-3	0-2	9	Fairley	837
13	Nov 5	H	Brechin C	W	1-0	1-0	8	Pittman (pen)	488
14	12	A	Albion R	L	0-2	0-0	9		465
15	19	H	Dumbarton	D	1-1	0-1	8	Mitchell	558
16	26	A	Alloa	L	1-2	1-1	11	Deas	428
17	Dec 10	H	Queen's Park	D	2-2	0-1	11	Pittman (pen), Hunter	650
18	17	A	Arbroath	W	3-1	1-1	10	Bardsley, Hunter, McEwan (og)	422
19	24	A	Brechin C	L	0-1	0-0	10		550
20	31	H	Stirling Albion	W	2-0	1-0	8	Graham (og), Mitchell	886
21	Jan 3	A	Cowdenbeath	D	1-1	0-1	—	Bardsley	625
22	14	H	East Stirling	D	2-2	2-0	8	Kirkwood 2	491
23	21	A	Stenhousemuir	D	1-1	1-1	7	Pittman	300
24	28	H	Berwick R	D	2-2	1-1	8	Hope, Gallacher	410
25	Feb 4	A	Montrose	D	2-2	2-1	9	McNaughton, Gallacher	350
26	11	H	Stranraer	L	1-2	0-1	9	Gallacher (pen)	434
27	18	A	Dumbarton	L	0-4	0-1	10		400
28	25	H	Cowdenbeath	W	1-0	1-0	7	Hunter	564
29	Mar 4	A	Albion R	W	2-1	1-0	7	Connor, Brown	621
30	11	H	Alloa	W	1-0	1-0	6	Hope	550
31	18	A	Arbroath	W	3-1	1-0	5	Pittman (pen), Hope, Hunter	532
32	25	H	Stirling Albion	W	3-0	0-0	4	Hunter, Hope, McGonigal	1041
33	Apr 1	A	East Stirling	L	2-4	0-2	6	McGonigal 2	350
34	8	H	Stranraer	W	2-1	1-0	4	Hunter, Connor	498
35	15	H	Stenhousemuir	D	1-1	0-0	4	Hunter	547
36	22	A	Queen's Park	W	2-1	0-1	2	Mitchell, Hunter	674
37	29	H	Berwick R	D	1-1	0-0	4	Gallacher (pen)	1614
38	May 6	A	Brechin C	L	0-1	0-1	4		850
39	13	H	Montrose	L	1-4	0-3	5	Connor	300

Final League Position: 5

GOALSCORERS

League: (56): Hunter 9, Pittman 8 (3 pens), McNaughton 7, Hope 5, Gallacher 4 (2 pens), Mitchell 4, Connor 3, McGonigal 3, Bardsley 2, Deas 2, Harrow 2, Kirkwood 2, Brown 1, Fairley 1, Perry 1, own goals 2.
League Cup: (1): Hunter 1.
Scottish Cup: (5): Bardsley 1, Hope 1, Hunter 1, Mitchell 1, Pittman 1.

Record Victory: 13-2 v Edinburgh City, Division II; 11 Dec, 1937.
Record Defeat: 0-9 v Hearts, Division I; 5 Oct, 1957.
Most Capped Player: George Aitken, 5 (8), Scotland.
Most League Appearances: 517: David Clarke, 1968–87.
Most League Goals in Season (Individual): 41: Jimmy Wood, Division II; 1926–27 and Henry Morris, Division II; 1947–48.
Most Goals Overall (Individual): 196: George Dewar (149 in League).

Honours
League Champions: Division II 1947–48; *Runners-up:* Division II 1929–30, 1970–71. Second Division 1983–84.
Scottish Cup Winners: 1938; *Runners-up:* 1927, 1950.
League Cup Winners: 1947–48, 1949–50, 1953–54.
Club colours: Shirt: Black and gold stripes. Shorts: Black with gold flashes. Stockings: Black with gold and white tops.

Banner, A	Connor, T	Pittman, S	McCafferty, T	Reid, G	McLaren, J	Graham, D	Scott, C	Hunter, P	McNaughton, B	Hope, D	Ogston, F	Thorpe, J	Harrow, A	Fairley, G	McIlhone, S	Hall, A	Perry, J	Bardsley, A	Deas, B	Charles, R	Mitchell, A	Gallacher, W	Kirkwood, D	Bell, G	Collins, N	Brown, W	McGonigal, A	Match No.
1	2	3	4	5	6	7†	8	9	10	11*	12	14																1
1	2	3	4	5	6	12	11*	9	10†	7		14	8															2
1	2	3		5	6		10	9*	7	11†		12	8	4	14													3
1	2	3	8	5	6		12	9	10	7†		14	4*			11												4
1	2	3	4	5	6		14	9	10*	11			7	8†	12													5
1	2	3*	4	5	6		10		7	11	12		8			14	9†											6
1	2	3	7	5	6		8		10*	11			12				4	9										7
1	2	3	8	5	6		11		10	7			9†		14	4*			12									8
	2	3	4	5	6		10		7	11*			9		12	14	8†			1								9
	2	3	8	5	6		10		11	12			9*				4			1	7							10
	2		10	5	6				11	14			3			8	4*	9†	12	1	7							11
	2		10	5	6			9		11†			3	14		8*	4		12	1	7							12
	2	3	8	5	6		10*	11					9	12					4	1	7							13
	2	3	4	5	6		11	9	10				12	7						1	8*							14
	2	3		5			8†	9	11*	12			10	14		4			6	1	7							15
	2	3	4*	5			11	9					10	12		8			6	1	7							16
	2	3	4	5			11*	9		7						8		10	6	1		12						17
	2	3	4	5				9*		12			14			8		11†	6	1	7	10						18
	2	3		5				9	10†	14			12			8			6	1	7*	11	4					19
	2	3	4	5				9		12						6		10		1	7*	11	8					20
	2	3	4	5				9	12	7*						6		11		1		10	8					21
	2	3		5				9	12				14			4		11*	6	1†	7	10	8					22
	2	3			6			9†	14				12			8		10*	5	1	7	11	4					23
	2	3			6		4†	9	11*	7						5		12	8	1		10		14				24
	2		8	5	6		12	9	10	11*						4			3	1		7						25
	2		4	5	6		11	9	10†	12			14			8*			3	1		7						26
	2*		4	5	6		3	9		11†			7			14			8	1		10		12				27
	14	3†	4	5				9		12			11*			6				1	7	10		2	8			28
	4			5				9		12			3			6			8	1	7*	11		2		10		29
	4	3*	8	5				9		7			12			6				1		11		2		10		30
	4	3	8	5				9		7						6				1		11		2		10		31
	4		8	5				9		7			3		14	6				1		11		2*		10†	12	32
1	4		8	5	6			9		7†			3		14							11		2*		10	12	33
	4		8	5				9		7*			3		12	6				1		11†		2	14		10	34
	4		8	5				9		11*			3		12	6				1		10		2			7	35
	4		8	5				9		11			3			6				1	7	10		2				36
	4		8	5				9		11*			3		12	6				1	7	10		2				37
	4		8	5				9		14			3			6				1	7†	10*		2		11	12	38
	4		8†	5				11		12			3			6				1	7	10		2*		9	14	39
9	38 + 1s	25	32	37	20	1 + 1s	16 + 3s	33	17 + 3s	23 + 11s	— + 2s	— + 4s	24 + 8s	3 + 4s	— + 9s	27 + 3s	6	8 + 1s	13 + 3s	30	18	22 + 1s	5	12 + 2s	1 + 1s	7	2 + 4s	

EAST STIRLINGSHIRE Second Division

Year Formed: 1881. *Ground & Address:* Firs Park, Firs St, Falkirk FK2 7AY. *Telephone:* 0324 23583.
Ground Capacity: total: 6000 seated: 2000. *Size of Pitch:* 112yd×72yd.
Chairman: John P. Turnbull. *Secretary:* Peter I. McKay. *Commercial Manager:* —.
Manager: J. David Connell. *Assistant Manager:* —. *Physio:* Angus Williamson. *Coach:* Hugh McCann.
Managers since 1975: I. Ure; D. McLinden; W. P. Lamont; M. Ferguson; W. Little; D. Whiteford; D. Lawson; J. D. Connell.
Club Nickname(s): The Shire. *Previous Grounds:* Burnhouse, Randyford Park, Merchiston Park, New Kilbowie Park.
Record Attendance: 11,500 v Hibernian, Scottish Cup; 10 Feb, 1969.
Record Transfer Fee received: £35,000 for Jim Docherty to Chelsea (1978).

1988–89 LEAGUE RECORD

Match No.	Date	Venue	Opponents	Result	H/T Score	Lg. Pos.	Goalscorers	Attendance
1	Aug 13	A	Albion R	L 0-1	0-1	—		350
2	20	H	Queen's Park	W 2-1	0-1	10	Wilcox D (pen), Irvine	250
3	27	A	Stenhousemuir	D 1-1	1-0	10	Harvey	350
4	Sept 3	H	East Fife	D 2-2	0-2	9	Ward, Wilcox D	200
5	10	H	Berwick R	W 3-2	0-1	7	Wilson, McNeill 2	200
6	17	A	Alloa	D 2-2	1-2	7	Irvine, Lauchlan	440
7	24	H	Brechin C	W 4-3	3-3	4	Harvey, McNeill 2, Wilcox D (pen)	360
8	Oct 1	A	Cowdenbeath	L 1-2	0-2	6	Scott	165
9	8	H	Stranraer	L 1-2	1-1	9	Irvine	250
10	15	H	Montrose	W 1-0	0-0	7	Irvine	200
11	22	A	Arbroath	D 3-3	2-2	10	Woods, Wilson, Grant	695
12	29	A	Dumbarton	L 0-3	0-1	10		400
13	Nov 5	H	Stirling Albion	D 2-2	1-0	10	Wilson, O'Brien	462
14	12	A	Queen's Park	D 0-0	0-0	10		470
15	19	H	Albion R	L 3-4	2-2	11	Grant A, Wilcox G, McNeill	200
16	26	A	Berwick R	W 5-0	2-0	8	Feeney, McNeill 2, Grant A, Lauchlan	225
17	Dec 10	H	Alloa	W 2-1	1-1	7	McNeill 2	300
18	17	A	Brechin C	D 2-2	1-1	8	Feeney, Lauchlan	250
19	24	A	Stirling Albion	L 0-1	0-0	8		750
20	31	H	Dumbarton	L 0-1	0-0	10		250
21	Jan 3	H	Stenhousemuir	L 0-3	0-0	—		200
22	14	A	East Fife	D 2-2	0-2	11	McNeill 2	491
23	21	A	Montrose	W 1-0	1-0	10	Scott	250
24	28	H	Arbroath	L 0-3	0-0	10		200
25	Feb 4	A	Stranraer	W 2-1	0-0	10	McNeill 2	750
26	18	H	Brechin C	D 1-1	1-0	9	McNeill	250
27	Mar 4	A	Berwick R	L 0-2	0-1	11		464
28	6	A	Stenhousemuir	L 0-1	0-1	—		350
29	11	H	Albion R	L 0-1	0-0	11		300
30	15	H	Cowdenbeath	W 1-0	0-0	—	Yardley	252
31	18	A	Stirling Albion	L 1-2	0-2	11	Grant A	497
32	25	H	Dumbarton	W 1-0	0-0	11	Feeney	300
33	Apr 1	H	East Fife	W 4-2	2-0	11	McEntegart 2, Wilcox D, Wilson	350
34	8	A	Montrose	L 1-2	0-1	11	McNeill	365
35	15	H	Alloa	W 2-0	0-0	9	Feeney, McNeill	300
36	22	A	Arbroath	D 2-2	2-0	9	Wilcox D, Feeney	300
37	29	H	Queen's Park	W 2-1	1-0	8	McEntegart, Wilson	300
38	May 6	A	Stranraer	D 0-0	0-0	8		450
39	13	H	Cowdenbeath	L 0-2	0-2	9		300

Final League Position: 9

GOALSCORERS

League: (54): McNeill 16, Feeney 5, Wilcox D 5 (2 pens), Wilson 5, Grant A 4, Irvine 4, Lauchlan 3, McEntegart 3, Harvey 2, Scott 2, O'Brien 1, Ward 1, Wilcox G 1, Woods 1, Yardley 1.
League Cup: (0).
Scottish Cup: (2): Wilcox D 1, Wilson 1.

Record Transfer Fee paid: —.
Record Victory: 10–1 v Stenhousemuir, Scottish Cup 1st rd; 1 Sept, 1888.
Record Defeat: 1-12 v Dundee United, Division II; 13 Apr, 1936.
Most Capped Player: Humphrey Jones, 5 (14), Wales.
Most League Appearances: Gordon Simpson, 1967–79.
Most League Goals in Season (Individual): 36: Malcolm Morrison, Division II; 1938–39.
Most Goals Overall (Individual): —.

Honours
League Champions: Division II 1931–32; *Runners-up:* Division II 1962–63. Second Division 1979–80.
Scottish Cup:—.
League Cup:—.
Club colours: Shirt: White with black band across chest. Shorts: Black with white and orange trim. Stockings: Black.

Kelly, C	Gilchrist, A	Russell, G	Wilcox, D	Kelly, P	Woods, J	Grant, A	Wilson, C	Ward, T	McNeill, W	Feeney, P	Irvine, J	Lauchlan, G	Harvey, G	O'Brien, P	McLeod, B	Scott, R	Wilcox, G	Main, A	McCann, H	McGraw, A	Kelly, K	Purdie, B	Drew, D	McEntegart, T	McIntosh, G	Yardley, K	Peters, A	*Match No.*
1	2	3	4	5	6	7*	8	9	10	11†	12	14																1
1	2	3	4		6	7	8	9	5†	12	11*		10	14														2
1	2		4	12	6*	7	8	9	14	3	11		10†	5														3
1	2	3	4			7	8	9	12	14	11		10	5†	6*													4
1	2*	3	4	14		7†	8	9	12	5	11		10		6													5
1	2	3	4	5		7	8†	9	10		11	14	12		6*													6
1	2	3	4	12	6	7	8*		9		11	14	10			5†												7
1	2	3	4	12	6	7	8†	14	9		11		10			5*												8
1	2	3	4	5	6	7			9†	12	11	14	10			8*												9
1	2	3	4	5	6	7*	8		9†	12	11	14				10												10
1	2	3	4	5	6	7	8		9	11						10												11
1	2	3	4	5*	6	7	8		11	9				12		10												12
1	2	3	4		6	7*	5		9	14	11	12	10	8†														13
	2	3	4		6	7*	5		9	14	11†	12	10	8														14
	2	3	4		6	7			11	14		9		5		12	8*	1										15
		2	4		6	7†			9	11		10					3	1	5	8*	12							16
1		2	4		6	7	11		9	3		10*		8		5					12							17
1		2	4			7	11†		9	3		10		8		6	12					5						18
1		2	4	3		7	11					9		10		5	12				8*	6						19
1	12	2	4	8		7	11		9	3		10				5*						6						20
1	5	2	4			7	11		9	3*		10				12	8†				14	6						21
1		2	4			7	11		9	3		10				5				12		6	8*					22
1		3	4			7	11†		9	2		10				5*	14			12		6	8					23
1		2	4				11		9	3*		10	12	7			5†				14	6	8					24
1		3	4†		5	7	11		9			12		10			14			2*		6	8					25
1		3	4		5	7†	11		9			14		10			12			2*		6	8					26
1		3	4				11†		9			10	14				12		2			6	8	5	7*			27
1		2*	4						9	3†		10		7			14				11	6	8	5	12			28
1		3	4			7			9					11			12				2	6	8	5*		10		29
1		3	4			7	11*		9					14			12					6	8	5		10	2†	30
1		3	4			7	11*		9			14		12			10					6	8†	5			2	31
1		3	4			7	11		9	10				12			14					6	8*	5†			2	32
1		3	4			7	11		9*	10		12										6	8	5			2	33
1		3	4			7	11		9	10*		12										6	8	5			2	34
1		3	4			7	11*		9	10						12						6	8	5			2	35
1		3	4			7	11†		9	10*		12				14						6	8	5			2	36
1	6	3	4			7	11		9*	10				12									8	5			2	37
1	6	3	4			7	11			10*		12	14	9									8†	5			2	38
1	6	3	4			7				14		9	12	10						11*			8†	5			2	39
36	19 + 1s	38	39	8 + 4s	16	36	33	6 + 1s	33 + 3s	21 + 8s	11 + 1s	13 + 14s	9 + 5s	15 + 6s	3	12 + 4s	5 + 10s	2	2	4 + 2s	3 + 4s	19	18	13	1 + 1s	2	10	

Also played: Hamilton L – Match 14 (1); Walker P 15 (10†); Hammil K 16 (14).

FALKIRK

First Division

Year Formed: 1876. *Ground & Address:* Brockville Park, Hope St, Falkirk FK1 5AX. *Telephone:* 0324 24121.
Ground Capacity: total: 18,000 seated: 2661. *Size of Pitch:* 110yd×70yd.
Chairman: Edward M. Moffat. *Secretary:* W. Barrie Scott, C.A.. *Commercial Manager:* Robert Shaw.
Manager: Jim Duffy. *Assistant Manager:* —. *Physio:* B. Cairney. *Coach:* —.
Managers since 1975: J. Prentice; G. Miller; W. Little; J. Hagart; A. Totten; G. Abel; W. Lamont; D. Clarke; J. Duffy.
Club Nickname(s): The Bairns. *Previous Grounds:* None.
Record Attendance: 23,100 v Celtic, Scottish Cup 3rd rd; 21 Feb, 1953.
Record Transfer Fee received: —.
Record Transfer Fee paid: —.

1988–89 LEAGUE RECORD

Match No.	Date	Venue	Opponents	Result	H/T Score	Lg. Pos.	Goalscorers	Attendance
1	Aug 13	H	Airdrieonians	D 0-0	0-0	—		3500
2	20	A	Clydebank	D 2-2	1-0	6	Burgess 2 (2 pens)	1627
3	27	A	Meadowbank T	L 1-2	0-1	9	Manley	960
4	Sept 3	H	Dunfermline Ath	W 2-1	1-1	8	Baptie, McGivern	5000
5	10	A	Ayr U	W 4-3	1-1	5	McWilliams 3, Rae	4300
6	17	H	Morton	L 0-1	0-0	9		4000
7	24	A	Clyde	W 2-1	2-0	5	McWilliams, Burgess	1600
8	Oct 1	A	Queen of the S	W 3-0	0-0	4	Burgess 2 (1 pen), Rae	1397
9	8	H	St Johnstone	W 2-1	0-0	2	Rae 2	3779
10	15	A	Partick T	W 3-1	1-0	1	Rutherford 2, McGivern	3369
11	22	H	Forfar Ath	L 1-2	1-1	2	Rae	3500
12	29	H	Raith R	W 3-1	2-1	2	McNair, Rae, Houston	3000
13	Nov 5	A	Kilmarnock	W 2-0	1-0	2	Baptie, McWilliams	2561
14	12	H	Ayr U	W 1-0	0-0	1	McWilliams	4000
15	19	A	Morton	W 5-1	2-0	1	McGivern, Rutherford 2, Houston, Burgess (pen)	3500
16	26	H	Clyde	D 0-0	0-0	1		3500
17	Dec 3	H	Clydebank	W [illegible]	2-0	1	Rutherford, McNair, Hetherston	3500
18	10	A	Raith R	W 3-1	2-0	1	Hetherston, Burgess, Rae	3000
19	17	A	Forfar Ath	D 0-0	0-0	1		1693
20	24	H	Partick T	L 0-1	0-0	1		3500
21	31	A	Dunfermline Ath	L 0-3	0-2	3		12,889
22	Jan 3	H	Meadowbank T	W 3-0	1-0	—	Rutherford, Rae, Burgess (pen)	2300
23	7	H	Kilmarnock	W 2-0	2-0	2	Rutherford, McNair	2814
24	14	A	Airdrieonians	L 0-2	0-1	3		6300
25	21	A	St Johnstone	L 1-2	0-1	3	Mennie	5091
26	Feb 7	H	Queen of the S	W 2-0	1-0	—	Gray (og), McNair	2900
27	21	A	Morton	D 2-2	0-2	—	Rutherford, Rae	2401
28	Mar 4	H	Meadowbank T	D 0-0	0-0	4		3014
29	7	H	Dunfermline Ath	W 4-0	3-0	—	Burgess (pen), Rutherford, McWilliams, McGivern	9216
30	11	A	Partick T	L 1-2	1-1	3	McGivern	2461
31	25	A	Clydebank	W 1-0	0-0	3	Burgess	2607
32	28	H	Ayr U	W 2-0	2-0	—	McWilliams 2	4354
33	Apr 1	A	Kilmarnock	D 0-0	0-0	3		3670
34	8	H	Raith R	W 3-0	2-0	2	Gallacher 2, Houston	3600
35	15	H	Clyde	W 3-1	1-0	2	Nolan (og), Rae, Gallacher	3377
36	22	A	St Johnstone	W 1-0	0-0	2	McGivern	4611
37	29	A	Airdrieonians	L 0-3	0-1	2		4400
38	May 6	H	Queen of the S	W 7-1	3-1		Hetherston, McWilliams (pen), Rae, Gallacher 2, McGivern 2	3000
39	13	A	Forfar Ath	D 2-2	1-0	2	Rae, McWilliams	2904

Final League Position: 2

GOALSCORERS

League: (71): Rae 12, McWilliams 11 (1 pen), Burgess 10 (6 pens), Rutherford 9, McGivern 8, Gallacher 5, McNair 4, Hetherston 3, Houston 3, Baptie 2, Manley 1, Mennie 1, own goals 2.
League Cup: (2): Burgess 1 (pen), Rae 1.
Scottish Cup: (2): Burgess 1 (pen), Rutherford 1.

Record Victory: 21-1 v Laurieston, Scottish Cup 2nd rd; 23 Mar, 1893.
Record Defeat: 1-11 v Airdrieonians, Division I; 28 Apr, 1951.
Most Capped Player: Alex Parker, 14 (15), Scotland.
Most League Appearances: —.
Most League Goals in Season (Individual): 43: Evelyn Morrison, Division I; 1928–29.
Most Goals Overall (Individual): —.

Honours
League Champions: Division II 1935–36, 1969–70, 1974–75. Second Division 1979–80; *Runners-up:* Division I 1907–08, 1909–10. First Division 1985–86. Division II 1904–05, 1951–52, 1960–61.
Scottish Cup Winners: 1913, 1957.
League Cup Runners-up: 1947–48.
Club colours: Shirt: Dark blue with white flashings. Shorts: White. Stockings: Red.

Marshall, G	McIntyre, B	Holmes, J	Manley, R	Burgess, S	Hetherston, P	Romaines, S	Nicol, A	Rae, A	McGivern, S	Houston, P	McNair, C	McVeigh, J	McWilliams, D	Baptie, C	McCall, A	Rutherford, P	Mooney, M	Gallacher, J	Stewart, R	Smith, G	McLarty, W	Mennie, V	Brannigan, K	Melvin, M	Match No.
1	2	3	4	5	6	7	8	9	10	11															1
1	2	3	4	5		7	8	12	10†	11	14	6	9*												2
1	2†	3	4	5		12	6	11	7	9	14	8*	10												3
1		3	4	5		12	6	10	9	8*	2		11	7											4
1		3	4	5	8*		6	9	11	12	2	14	7	10†											5
1		3	4	5	10		6†	8	9	12	2*		11	7	14										6
1		3	4	5	11*		6	9	10	12	2		7	8											7
1		3	4	5	11		6	9	10	12	2*		7	8†		14									8
1		3	4	5	7		6	10	9		2		11	8*		12									9
1			4	5	8		6	11†	10	3	2		9	12		7*	14								10
1		3†	4	5	7*		6	8	9	14	2		11	12		10									11
1		3	4	5			6	10		7	2		11	8		9									12
1		3	4	5	12		6	10	14	7	2		11	8*		9†									13
1		3	4	5			6	10	9		2		11	8		7									14
1		3	4	5	12		6	11	10	8	2*		9†			7		14							15
1		3	4	5	12		6*	11	10†	8	2		9			7		14							16
1		3	4	5	12		6	8†	9	10	2		11*			7			14						17
1		3	4†	5	8*		6	11	9	10	2			14		7			12						18
1		3		5	8		6	10		7	2			4		11	12	9*							19
1		3	4	5	12		6	9		7*	2			8		10†		11			14				20
1		3*	4†	5	7		6	8	11	12	2			9		10		14							21
1		3		5	11		6	10	9	12	2*			8		7				4					22
1		3	4	5	10*		6	11	9†	12	2					7		14				8			23
1		3	4	5	10		6	11	9	12	2					7*		14				8†			24
1		3	4	5	10		6	11	9	12	2*					14		7†				8			25
1		3	4				6	9	10	12	2*		11			7		14		5		8†			26
1		3	4				6	10	11*	14	2		8	9†		7						12	5		27
1		3	4	5			6	11†	10	14	2		9	8		7*						12			28
1		3	4	5	10*		6		11	2†			9	8		7		14					12		29
1		3	4	5	10		6		11	2			9	8		7*						12			30
1		3	4	5	8			12	11		2		10	9*		7							6		31
1		3	4	5	10		6	9*	12		2		11	14		7†							8		32
1		3	4	5	10		6	12	9†		2*		11	8		7							14		33
1		3		5*	10		6	9		2			11	8			14	7†		12			4		34
1		3†		5	10		6	9	12	2			11*	8				7					4	14	35
1		3	4	5	10		6	11	8	2				9		12		7*							36
1		3	4	5	10		6	11		2†	12			8		7*	14	9							37
1		3	4	5	8		6	9	12	14	2		11*				10†	7							38
1		3	4	5	10*		6	8	9		12		11	2			14	7†							39
39	3	38	35	37	26	2	38	34	30	19	29	2	28	24	—	24	1	9	—	2	—	4	5	—	
					+	+		+	+	+	+	+		+	+	+	+	+	+	+	+	+	+	+	
					5s	2s		3s	4s	14s	4s	1s		4s	1s	4s	5s	7s	2s	1s	1s	3s	2s	1s	

FORFAR ATHLETIC — First Division

Year Formed: 1885. *Ground & Address:* Station Park, Carseview Road, Forfar. *Telephone:* 0307 63576.
Ground Capacity: total: — seated: —. *Size of Pitch:* 115yd×69yd.
Chairman: Gordon Webster. *Secretary:* David McGregor. *Commercial Manager:* —.
Manager: Henry Hall. *Assistant Manager:* Ian Fleming. *Physio:* Andy Dickson. *Coach:* David Jack.
Managers since 1975: Jerry Kerr; Archie Knox; Alex Rae; Doug Houston; Henry Hall.
Club Nickname(s): Sky Blues. *Previous Grounds:* None.
Record Attendance: 10,780 v Rangers, Scottish Cup 2nd rd, 2 Feb, 1970.
Record Transfer Fee received: £43,000 for Ian McPhee to Dundee U (1987).
Record Transfer Fee paid: £15,000 for Jim Liddle from Cowdenbeath.

1988–89 LEAGUE RECORD

Match No.	Date	Venue	Opponents	Result		H/T Score	Lg. Pos.	Goalscorers	Attendance
1	Aug 13	H	Meadowbank T	W	1-0	1-0	—	Clark J	599
2	20	A	Clyde	D	1-1	0-0	4	Bennett W	650
3	27	H	St Johnstone	D	1-1	0-0	4	Ward	1321
4	Sept 3	A	Ayr U	L	1-2	0-1	9	Brewster	2628
5	10	H	Partick T	W	3-2	0-2	6	Ward 2 (1 pen), Clarke S	974
6	17	A	Queen of the S	L	1-2	1-1	10	Brown	867
7	24	H	Raith R	W	1-0	1-0	6	Clark J	816
8	Oct 1	A	Clydebank	D	2-2	2-1	7	Clark J, Ward	657
9	8	H	Kilmarnock	D	2-2	1-1	7	Ormond 2	685
10	15	H	Morton	L	0-1	0-0	9		958
11	22	A	Falkirk	W	2-1	1-1	8	Ormond, Ward	3500
12	29	H	Airdrieonians	D	1-1	0-1	8	Morton	907
13	Nov 5	A	Dunfermline Ath	L	1-2	1-2	8	Brewster	4942
14	12	A	Partick T	W	2-1	1-1	7	Brewster, Hamill	1849
15	19	H	Queen of the S	D	2-2	0-0	7	Brewster, Brown	558
16	26	A	Raith R	L	1-2	0-1	7	Ward	1247
17	Dec 3	H	Clyde	W	2-1	0-1	7	Ward, Clark J.	559
18	10	A	Airdrieonians	W	3-0	1-0	7	Ward, Brewster, Lorimer	1500
19	17	H	Falkirk	D	0-0	0-0	7		1693
20	24	A	Morton	D	1-1	1-0	7	Brown	1400
21	31	H	Ayr U	L	1-2	1-1	7	Ward	891
22	Jan 2	A	St Johnstone	L	1-2	0-1	—	Whyte	1400
23	7	H	Dunfermline Ath	W	2-1	2-0	7	Lorimer, Ormond	2596
24	14	A	Meadowbank T	D	1-1	1-0	7	Ward	400
25	21	A	Kilmarnock	L	1-2	1-1	7	Ward	1813
26	Feb 4	H	Clydebank	L	2-3	1-3	7	Whyte, Brown	670
27	11	A	Airdrieonians	L	1-2	1-1	7	Brown	1121
28	25	H	Morton	D	0-0	0--0	7		627
29	Mar 4	H	St Johnstone	D	1-1	0-1	8	Brewster	1350
30	11	A	Queen of the S	D	2-2	0-1	8	Clarke S, McNaughton	484
31	18	A	Kilmarnock	D	2-2	2-2	8	Ormond, McNaughton	1586
32	25	H	Meadowbank T	W	2-1	2-1	7	Lorimer, Brewster	621
33	Apr 1	H	Ayr U	D	0-0	0-0	8		661
34	8	A	Clyde	D	1-1	1-0	7	Brewster	500
35	15	H	Clydebank	L	1-2	0-1	8	Bryce (og)	557
36	22	A	Raith R	W	3-2	1-1	7	McNaughton 2, Ward	1587
37	29	H	Dunfermline Ath	L	0-1	0-0	8		3301
38	May 6	A	Partick T	L	1-4	0-3	9	Brewster	3033
39	13	H	Falkirk	D	2-2	0-1	9	Grant 2	2904

Final League Position: 9

GOALSCORERS

League: (52): Ward 12 (1 pen), Brewster 9, Brown 5, Ormond 5, Clark J 4, McNaughton 4, Lorimer 3, Clarke S 2, Grant 2, Whyte 2, Bennett W 1, Hamill 1, Morton 1, own goal.
League Cup: (0)
Scottish Cup: (3): Brewster 1, Clark J 1, Ward 1.

Record Victory: 14-1 v Lindertis, Scottish Cup 1st rd; 1 Sept 1988.
Record Defeat: 2-12 v King's Park, Division II; 2 Jan, 1930.
Most Capped Player: —.
Most League Appearances: 376: Alex Brash, 1974–86.
Most League Goals in Season (Individual): 45: Dave Kilgour, Division II; 1929–30.
Most Goals Overall (Individual): —.

Honours
League Champions: Second Division 1983–84. C Division 1948–49.
Scottish Cup: Semi-finals 1982.
League Cup: Semi-finals 1977–78.
Club colours: Shirt: Sky blue. Shorts: White. Stockings: Sky blue.

Kennedy, S	Lorimer, R	Hamill, A	Morris, R	Smith, P	Morton, J	Grant, B	Clark, J	Brown, W	Brewster, C	Taylor, S	Brazil, A	Bennett, W	Ormond, J	Clarke, S	Ward, K	Moffat, J	Whyte, G	Bennett M	McNaughton B	Hutton G	Winter G	*Match No.*
1	2	3	4	5	6	7	8	9	10	11*	12											1
1	8	3	4	5	6		14	9	10	7*		2	11†	12								2
1	8	3	4	5	6*		9		10	14	12	2	11†		7							3
1	8	3	4	5	6	11*	12	9	10	7†		2	14									4
1	8	3	4	5		12	6	9	10	14	2			11*	7†							5
1	8	3	4	5	6		12	9	10		2			11*	7							6
	8	3	4	5	6	10	11	9				2	12		7*	1						7
	8	3	4	5	6	10*	11	9	12			2			7	1						8
	8	3	4	5	6			9	10	12		2	11		7*	1						9
	8	3	4	5	6	12	9		10			2	11		7*	1						10
	8	3	4	5	6		10					2	11		7	1	9					11
	8*	3	4	5	6		10		12	14		2	11†		7	1	9					12
		3	4		6		8	12	10		5	2	11*		7	1	9					13
1	12	3	4		6		8*	14	10		5	2	11†		7		9					14
1	2*	3	4		6		8	11	10		5	12	14		7		9†					15
1		3	4*	12	6		8	14	10		5	2	11†		7		9					16
1	8	3	4	5	6		11	9	10			2			7							17
1	8	3	4	5	6		11*	9	10			2	14		7†		12					18
1	8	3	4	5	6		11	9	10			2	12		7*							19
1	8	3	4	5	6		11	9	10			2			7*		12					20
1	8	3		5	6		12	9	10		4	2		11*	7							21
1	8	3		5†	6		14	9	10		4	2*		11	7		12					22
1	7	3			6	12	5		10		4	2	11*	8			9					23
1	8	3			6		5		10		4	2		11	7		9					24
1	8	3		12	6		5	14	10		4	2		11	7†		9*					25
1	8	3		5	6		14	9	10		4	2†		7*	12		11					26
1	8†	3	12	5	6		14	9	10		4	2*			7		11					27
1	2	3	4	5	6		11		10				14	8*	7		9†	12				28
1	2	3	4	5	6	14	11		10					8	7†		9*		12			29
1	2	3	4	5	6	14	11		10					8	7†		9*		12			30
1	2	3	4	5	6		11		10*				7	8	12				9			31
1	2	3	4	5	6		11		10				7*	8	12		14		9†			32
1	7	3	4	5	6		11		10			2		8	12				9*			33
1	2	3	4	5	6		14		10			12	7*	8	11				9†			34
1	2	12	4	5	3		6		10					8	7		9*		11			35
1	8		4		3		9		10		5	2*			11				7	6	12	36
1	8	3	4				9		10		5	2		12	11*				7	6		37
	8	3	4	12	6	9	11		10			2			14	1			7†	5*		38
1	8	3	4	5	6*	11			10			2	14		7†		9			12		39
31	36 + 1s	37 + 1s	32 + 1s	29 + 3s	37	6 + 5s	29 + 8s	17 + 4s	35 + 2s	3 + 4s	15 + 2s	28 + 2s	13 + 7s	16 + 2s	30 + 5s	8	16 + 4s	— + 1s	8 + 2s	3 + 1s	— + 1s	

HAMILTON ACADEMICAL First Division

Year Formed: 1875. *Ground & Address:* Douglas Park, Douglas Park Lane, Hamilton ML3 0DF. *Telephone:* 0698 286103.
Ground Capacity: total: 14,505 seated: 1505. *Size of Pitch:* 110yd×68yd.
Chairman: James W. Watson. *Secretary:* David S. Morrison. *Commercial Manager:* George Miller.
Manager: Jim Dempsey. *Assistant Manager:* —. *Physio:* John Hart. *Coach:* —.
Managers since 1975: J. Eric Smith; Dave McParland; John Blackley; Bertie Auld; John Lambie; Jim Dempsey.
Club Nickname(s): The Accies. *Previous Grounds:* Bent Farm, South Avenue, South Haugh.
Record Attendance: 28,690 v Hearts, Scottish Cup 3rd rd, 3 Mar, 1937.
Record Transfer Fee received: £95,000 for Albert Craig to Newcastle U (Feb 1987).
Record Transfer Fee paid: £50,000 for John McNaught from Partick Th (March 1988).

1988–89 LEAGUE RECORD

Match No.	Date	Venue	Opponents	Result	H/T Score	Lg. Pos.	Goalscorers	Attendance
1	Aug 13	H	Rangers	L 0-2	0-1	—		10,500
2	20	A	Hearts	L 2-3	1-1	10	Fairlie, McNaught	12,032
3	27	H	Motherwell	W 1-0	0-0	8	Fairlie	4338
4	Sept 3	A	Celtic	L 1-2	0-1	9	Harris (pen)	24,084
5	17	H	Dundee	W 1-0	0-0	6	Harris	2194
6	24	A	Hibernian	L 0-1	0-0	7		7910
7	27	H	Aberdeen	L 0-1	0-0	—		3634
8	Oct 1	A	St Mirren	L 0-2	0-1	9		3349
9	8	H	Dundee U	L 0-4	0-2	9		3538
10	11	H	Hearts	L 0-4	0-2	—		4764
11	29	H	Hibernian	L 0-3	0-1	10		4569
12	Nov 2	A	Dundee	L 2-5	0-2	—	Harris, Fairlie	3857
13	5	H	Celtic	L 0-8	0-2	10		10,500
14	12	A	Motherwell	D 1-1	0-1	10	Gallagher	5657
15	16	A	Rangers	L 1-3	1-1	—	Jamieson	33,864
16	19	H	St Mirren	L 2-4	1-2	10	Harris, Gallagher	3710
17	26	A	Dundee U	L 0-1	0-0	10		6372
18	Dec 3	A	Aberdeen	D 1-1	0-0	10	Gallagher	8324
19	10	H	Dundee	W 1-0	0-0	10	Gordon	2083
20	17	A	Hearts	L 0-2	0-1	10		11,490
21	31	H	Rangers	L 0-1	0-0	10		10,500
22	Jan 3	H	Motherwell	L 0-2	0-0	—		5704
23	7	A	Celtic	L 0-2	0-1	10		18,679
24	14	H	Dundee U	L 0-5	0-3	10		3792
25	21	A	St Mirren	L 0-1	0-1	10		3330
26	Feb 14	H	Aberdeen	L 0-2	0-1	10		2016
27	Mar 1	A	Hibernian	L 1-2	1-0	—	Gordon	6500
28	11	A	Rangers	L 0-3	0-0	10		34,112
29	25	H	Hearts	L 0-2	0-1	10		3854
30	Apr 1	A	Motherwell	L 0-1	0-0	10		4683
31	8	H	Celtic	W 2-0	1-0	10	Gordon 2	9301
32	15	A	Aberdeen	L 0-3	0-1	10		9712
33	22	H	Hibernian	L 0-3	0-2	10		2975
34	29	A	Dundee	L 0-1	0-0	10		4042
35	May 6	H	St Mirren	W 2-1	1-1	10	Archer, Gordon	1643
36	13	A	Dundee U	W 1-0	1-0	10	Harris (pen)	11,503

Final League Position: 10

GOALSCORERS

League: (19): Gordon 5, Harris 5 (2 pens), Fairlie 3, Gallagher 3, Archer 1, Jamieson 1, McNaught 1.
League Cup: (6): Fairlie 2, Collins 1, McDonald 1, McNaught 1, own goal 1.
Scottish Cup: (0).

Record Victory: 10-2 v Cowdenbeath, Division I, 15 Oct, 1932.
Record Defeat: 1-11 v Hibernian, Division I, 6 Nov, 1965.
Most Capped Players: Colin Miller, 3, Canada.
Most League Appearances: 447: Rikki Ferguson, 1974–8.
Most League Goals in Season (Individual): 34: David Wilson, Division I; 1936–37.
Most Goals Overall (Individual): 246: David Wilson, 1928–39.

Honours
League Champions: First Division 1985–86, 1987–88. Division II 1903–04; *Runners-up:* Division II 1952–53, 1964–65.
Scottish Cup Runners-up: 1911, 1935.
League Cup:—.
Club colours: Shirt: Red and white hoops. Shorts: White. Stockings: White.

Ferguson, A	McKee, K	Kerr, J	McNaught, J	Jamieson, W	Collins, G	Fairlie, J	Gordon, S	Harris, C	Roseburgh, D	McDonald, P	Scott, G	Speirs, C	McCabe, G	Weir, J	Charnley, J	Nelson, M	Miller, CF	Martin, P	Gallagher, E	Napier, C	Fraser, A	Rough, A	Archer, S	Frith, J	Morrison, S	Prentice, A	Andrews, G	*Match No.*
1	2	3	4	5	6	7	8	9	10*	11†	12	14																1
1	2	3	4	5	12	7		9	10†	11	8	6*	14															2
1	2	3	4*	5	6	7		9	10	11			8	12														3
1	2	3		5	6	7†		9	10*	11	14		8	4	12													4
1	2	3		5	6	7		9	10	11			8	4														5
1	2	3		5	6	7		9	10*	11†	14		8	4	12													6
1	2	3		5	6	7		9	14	11†	10		8*	4	12													7
1	8	12		5	6			7	3	11	9		10	2			4*											8
1	4	10		5	6	7	14		3*	11	9		8†	2	12													9
1	4			5		7	9	8	3	11*	12	6		2	10													10
1	4			5		8		9*	3	11	12				10		2	6	7									11
1	8*			5		7		9	3	12		4		14	11		2	6	10†									12
1	4			5		7		9	3	11		12			10*		2	6	8									13
1	8			4	6	7		9	3					10	12		2	5*	11									14
1	2			5	4	7		9	6	14		12		8†	11		3*		10									15
1	2			4		7†	12	10	6	11*				8		14		5	9	3								16
1	2			4			9*	7	6	14				8	12	10		5	11	3†								17
1	2			4			10*	7	6					8†	11	14		5	9	3	12							18
1	2			4			10	7†	6	12				8	11*	14		5	9	3								19
1	2			4		7*	9		6	12				8	11			5	10	3								20
	2			4		7	9		6	8				10				5	11*	3	12	1						21
	2*			4		7†	9		6	8				10			12	5	11	3	14	1						22
	2			4		7†	9*		10	11				8			6	5	12	3	14	1						23
	2			4		7*	9		10	11				8		14	6†	5		3	12	1						24
	2			5			14	11†	10	8				7		6	4		12	3	9*	1						25
1	2			5			9		10	11				4			8			3	7		6					26
1	2			4			10		8	9				7		14	11†	5		6*	12		3					27
1	2			4			9	7		12				10			6	5					3		8	11*		28
1	2			4			9†	7*		11							6	5		12			3	14	8	10		29
1	2			4			9	12		11				7			6	5		3†				14	8	10*		30
1	2			4			9	7		11							6	5		3					8	10		31
1	2						9	7*		11				4			6	5		3			12		8	10†	14	32
1	2						9	7		11				4			6	5		3					8	10		33
1	2			4			9	10*		14				7†			5	12		6			3		8	11		34
1	2			4			9	7		11							5			3			6		8	10		35
1	2			4			9	7		11				8			5			3			6*		12	10		36
31	36	8 + 1s	3	34	10 + 1s	20	21 + 3s	27 + 1s	26 + 1s	27 + 7s	4 + 5s	3 + 3s	7 + 1s	27 + 2s	8 + 6s	2 + 5s	20 + 1s	20 + 1s	12 + 2s	19 + 1s	2 + 6s	5	7 + 1s	— + 2s	8 + 1s	9	— + 1s	

HEART OF MIDLOTHIAN Premier Division

Year Formed: 1874. *Ground & Address:* Tynecastle Park, Gorgie Rd, Edinburgh EH11 2NL. *Telephone:* 031 337 6132.
Ground Capacity: total: 29,000 seated: 9000. *Size of Pitch:* 110yd×76yd.
Chairman: A. Wallace Mercer. *Secretary:* L. W. Porteous. *Commercial Manager:* Charles Burnett.
Manager: Alex MacDonald. *Assistant Manager:* —. *Physio:* Alan Rae. *Coach:* (1) Walter Borthwick, (2) John Binnie.
Managers since 1975: J. Hagart; W. Ormond; R. Moncur; A. MacDonald; A. MacDonald & W. Jardine; A. MacDonald.
Club Nickname(s): Jam Tarts. *Previous Grounds:* The Meadows 1873, Powderhall 1878, Tyneside 1881, (Tynecastle Park, 1886).
Record Attendance: 53,496 v Rangers, Scottish Cup 3rd rd; 13 Feb, 1932.
Record Transfer Fee received: £700,000 for John Robertson to Newcastle U (April 1988).
Record Transfer Fee paid: £350,000 for Dave McPherson from Rangers (July 1987).

1988–89 LEAGUE RECORD

Match No.	Date	Venue	Opponents	Result	H/T Score	Lg. Pos.	Goalscorers	Attendance
1	Aug 13	A	Celtic	L 0-1	0-0	—		46,845
2	20	H	Hamilton A	W 3-2	1-1	4	Ferguson, Clark, Colquhoun	12,032
3	27	A	Hibernian	D 0-0	0-0	5		25,000
4	Sept 3	H	St Mirren	L 1-2	0-2	7	Foster	11,386
5	17	H	Rangers	L 1-2	0-0	8	Butcher (og)	25,401
6	24	A	Aberdeen	L 0-1	0-1	9		14,000
7	28	H	Dundee	D 1-1	0-0	—	Ferguson	8392
8	Oct 1	A	Dundee U	D 0-0	0-0	8		10,838
9	8	H	Motherwell	D 2-2	1-0	8	Moore 2	8809
10	11	A	Hamilton A	W 4-0	2-0	—	Ferguson 2, Black, Colquhoun	4764
11	22	H	Celtic	L 0-2	0-0	8		24,017
12	29	H	Aberdeen	D 1-1	0-1	8	Jardine	12,644
13	Nov 1	A	Rangers	L 0-3	0-0	—		36,505
14	5	A	St Mirren	D 1-1	0-0	8	Godfrey (og)	7563
15	12	H	Hibernian	L 1-2	0-1	8	McPherson	23,002
16	19	H	Dundee U	D 0-0	0-0	8		10,124
17	26	A	Motherwell	L 0-2	0-1	8		6208
18	Dec 3	A	Dundee	D 1-1	0-0	8	Colquhoun	6902
19	10	H	Rangers	W 2-0	1-0	8	Galloway, Ferguson	26,424
20	17	H	Hamilton A	W 2-0	1-0	7	McLaren, McPherson	11,490
21	31	A	Celtic	L 2-4	1-2	8	Robertson 2 (1 pen)	44,646
22	Jan 4	A	Hibernian	L 0-1	0-1	—		25,500
23	7	H	St Mirren	W 2-0	1-0	8	Colquhoun, McKinlay	11,961
24	14	H	Motherwell	D 0-0	0-0	7		13,283
25	21	A	Dundee U	D 0-0	0-0	7		13,674
26	Feb 11	H	Dundee	W 3-1	2-1	7	Colquhoun, Bannon, Mackay	10,432
27	25	A	Aberdeen	L 0-3	0-3	7		15,000
28	Mar 11	H	Celtic	L 0-1	0-0	7		23,087
29	25	A	Hamilton A	W 2-0	1-0	7	Mackay, McPherson	3854
30	Apr 1	H	Hibernian	W 2-1	1-1	7	Bannon, Robertson	22,090
31	8	A	St Mirren	D 1-1	0-1	7	Robertson	6970
32	15	A	Dundee	L 1-2	1-0	7	McPherson	6993
33	22	H	Aberdeen	W 1-0	1-0	6	Galloway	13,367
34	29	A	Rangers	L 0-4	0-2	6		42,856
35	May 6	H	Dundee U	D 0-0	0-0	6		8613
36	13	A	Motherwell	D 1-1	0-0	6	Berry	4587

Final League Position: 6

GOALSCORERS

League: (35): Colquhoun 5, Ferguson 5, McPherson 4, Robertson 4 (1 pen), Bannon 2, Galloway 2, Mackay 2, Moore 2, Berry 1, Black 1, Clark 1, Foster 1 (pen), Jardine 1, McKinlay 1, McLaren 1, own goals 2.
League Cup: (11): Ferguson 5 (1 pen), Mackay 2, Black 1, Colquhoun 1, Jardine 1, Murray 1.
Scottish Cup: (7): Bannon 2, Colquhoun 2, Galloway 1, McPherson 1, own goal 1.

Record Victory: 18-0 v Vale of Lothian, Edinburgh Shield; 17 Sept, 1887.
Record Defeat: 0-7 v Hibernian, Division I; 1 Jan, 1973.
Most Capped Player: Bobby Walker, 29, Scotland.
Most League Appearances: —.
Most League Goals in Season (Individual): 44: Barney Battles.
Most Goals Overall (Individual): 206: Jimmy Wardhaugh, 1946–59.

Honours
League Champions: Division I 1894–85, 1896–97, 1957–58, 1959–60. First Division 1979–80; *Runners-up:* Division I 1893–94, 1898–99, 1903–04, 1905–06, 1914–15, 1937–38, 1953–54, 1956–57, 1958–59, 1964–65. Premier Division 1985–86. First Division 1977–78, 1982–83.
Scottish Cup Winners: 1891, 1896, 1901, 1906, 1956; *Runners-up:* 1903, 1907, 1968, 1976, 1986.
League Cup Winners: 1954–55, 1958–59, 1959–60, 1962–63; *Runners-up:* 1961–62.
European: *European Cup* 4 matches (1958–59, 1960–61). *Cup Winners Cup* 4 matches (1976–77). *UEFA Cup:* 15 matches (1961–62, 1963–64, 1965–66 *Fairs Cup*; 1984–85, 1986-87).
Club colours: Shirt: Maroon. Shorts: White. Stockings: Maroon with white tops.

Smith, H	Murray, M	Black, K	Whittaker, B	Galloway, M	McPherson, D	Colquhoun, J	Berry, N	Ferguson, I	Mackay, G	Bannon, E	Jardine, I	Clark, A	Gavin, M	Foster, W	Kidd, W	Moore, A	Crabbe, S	Sandison, J	McLaren, A	McKinlay, T	Robertson, J	Levein, C	*Match No.*
1	2	3	4	5	6	7	8	9	10*	11		12											1
1	3	11*	4	2	6	7†	5	10	8	12		9	14										2
1	2	10	4	5	6	9	3	8	7*	12				11									3
1	3*	5	4		6	7	2	9	8	11			12	10									4
1		10	4	5	6	7†	2	9*	8	12				11	3	14							5
1	6	10†	4	5		7*	3	12	8	11	14			9	2								6
1		10*	4	5	6	7	3	9	8	11	12				2†	14							7
1		10	4	5	6	7	3	9*	8	11					2	12							8
1		10	4	5	6	7	3	12	8*		14			9†	2	11							9
1	3	10	4		6	7	5	9	8						2	11							10
1	3	10	4	14	6	7	5*	9	8†	12					2	11							11
1		10	3	5	6	14	4*	9†	8	11	12				2	7							12
1	3	10	4	5	6	7†			8	11	12			9	2*	14							13
1		10	5	8	6*	12			7	11	4			9	2			3					14
1		10	5	7	4	9	3		8	11	6*				2†	14		12					15
1		10	5		4	7	6	9	8	11	12				2*			3					16
1		10	5		4	7	6	9	11†		14				2	12	8*	3					17
1		10	5	7		9	4	11*	8	6†	12				2			3	14				18
1		10	5	7	4	9*	6	14	8	12					2					3	11†		19
1		10	5		4	9*		7	8	12	14				2				6†	3	11		20
1		10	5	7	6	9			8		12				2*			4		3	11		21
1		10	5	7	6	9	4		8					12	2					3*	11		22
1		10	5	7	4	9	6	12	8										2	3	11*		23
1		10	5	7	4	9*	6	11	8	12									2	3			24
1				7*	4	9	5	12	8	11									2	3	10	6	25
1				7	4	9	5		8	11								6	2	3	10		26
1		10		7	4	9*	5	14		11								12	2	3	8†	6	27
1				7	4	9	5	10	8	11*									2	3	12	6	28
1		3		9	6†	7	5	10	8	11*					2			14			12	4	29
1		6		9*		7	5	10	8†	11	14							2		3	12	4	30
1		6		9		11	5	8		10				7*				2		3	12	4	31
1		10		7	4	11	5	9		8					2*			6		3	12		32
1		10		7	4	9	5	8*		11†	14							6	2	3	12		33
1		10		8*	4	7	5	9		11								6	2†	3	12	14	34
1		10		9*	4	7	5	8		11						12			2	3		6	35
1		10		8	6	9	5			11*	12					7			2	3		4	36
36	8	33	24	30 + 1s	32	34 + 2s	32	23 + 6s	29	23 + 7s	2 + 13s	1 + 1s	— + 2s	8 + 1s	20	5 + 7s	1	11 + 3s	11 + 1s	17	8 + 7s	8 + 1s	

HIBERNIAN Premier Division

Year Formed: 1875. *Ground & Address:* Easter Road Stadium, Albion Rd, Edinburgh EH7 5QG. *Telephone:* 031 661 2159.
Ground Capacity: total: 23,353 seated: 5853. *Size of Pitch:* 112yd×74yd.
Chairman: David F. Duff. *Secretary:* Cecil F. Graham, F.A.A.I., M.Inst. C.M.. *Commercial Manager:* Raymond Sparkes.
Manager: Alex Miller. *Assistant Manager:* Peter Cormack. *Physio:* Stewart Collie. *Coach:* —.
Managers since 1975: Eddie Turnbull; Willie Ormond; Bertie Auld; Pat Stanton; John Blackley; Alex Miller.
Club Nickname(s): Hibees. *Previous Grounds:* Meadows 1875–78, Powderhall 1878–79, Mayfield 1875–80, First Easter Road 1880–92, Second Easter Road 1892–.
Record Attendance: 65,860 v Hearts, Division I; 2 Jan, 1950.
Record Transfer Fee received: £382,000 for Gordon Durie to Chelsea (May 1986).
Record Transfer Fee paid: £325,000 for Andy Goram from Oldham Ath.

1988–89 LEAGUE RECORD

Match No.	Date	Venue	Opponents	Result	H/T Score	Lg. Pos.	Goalscorers	Attendance
1	Aug 13	H	Motherwell	W 1-0	0-0	—	McIntyre	10,000
2	20	A	Rangers	D 0-0	0-0	3		41,955
3	27	H	Hearts	D 0-0	0-0	3		25,000
4	Sept 3	A	Aberdeen	D 0-0	0-0	3		13,583
5	17	A	Dundee U	D 1-1	1-0	5	Rae	11,017
6	24	H	Hamilton A	W 1-0	0-0	4	Evans	7910
7	28	A	St Mirren	W 1-0	1-0	—	Evans	5384
8	Oct 1	H	Celtic	W 3-1	3-0	2	Archibald 2, Evans	24,000
9	8	A	Dundee	L 1-2	1-2	4	Archibald	8127
10	12	H	Rangers	L 0-1	0-1	—		25,000
11	22	A	Motherwell	D 1-1	0-0	4	McIntyre	5904
12	29	A	Hamilton A	W 3-0	1-0	2	Archibald, McCluskey (pen), Collins	4567
13	Nov 2	H	Dundee U	D 1-1	1-0	—	McCluskey	9247
14	5	H	Aberdeen	L 1-2	1-0	4	Archibald	11,500
15	12	A	Hearts	W 2-1	1-0	4	Kane, Archibald	23,062
16	19	A	Celtic	L 0-1	0-0	6		35,251
17	26	H	Dundee	D 1-1	1-1	5	Archibald	9000
18	Dec 3	H	St Mirren	W 2-0	1-0	5	Archibald, Hunter	8500
19	10	A	Dundee U	L 1-4	0-2	5	Archibald	9963
20	17	A	Rangers	L 0-1	0-0	5		36,472
21	31	H	Motherwell	W 2-0	1-0	5	Kane, May	9000
22	Jan 4	H	Hearts	W 1-0	1-0	—	May	25,500
23	7	A	Aberdeen	L 0-2	0-0	5		13,500
24	14	A	Dundee	W 2-1	1-0	5	Evans, Archibald	7261
25	21	H	Celtic	L 1-3	1-2	5	Kane	23,500
26	Feb 21	A	St Mirren	L 1-3	1-1	—	Kane	4960
27	Mar 1	H	Hamilton A	W 2-1	0-1	—	Collins, Evans	6500
28	11	A	Motherwell	D 0-0	0-0	5		5027
29	25	H	Rangers	L 0-1	0-1	5		22,000
30	Apr 1	A	Hearts	L 1-2	1-1	5	Houchen	22,090
31	8	H	Aberdeen	L 1-2	1-1	5	Houchen	11,000
32	19	H	St Mirren	W 1-0	1-0	—	Archibald	7500
33	22	A	Hamilton A	W 3-0	2-0	5	Archibald 2, Kane	2975
34	29	H	Dundee U	L 1-2	1-1	5	McCluskey	7300
35	May 6	A	Celtic	L 0-1	0-0	5		18,316
36	13	H	Dundee	D 1-1	0-0	5	Findlay	7675

Final League Position: 5

GOALSCORERS

League: (37): Archibald 13, Evans 5, Kane 5, McCluskey 3 (1 pen), Collins 2, Houchen 2, McIntyre 2, May 2, Findlay 1, Hunter 1, Rae 1.
League Cup: (6): Kane 3, Archibald 2, Evans 1.
Scottish Cup: (5): Collins 2, Archibald 1, Kane 1, May 1.

Record Victory: 22-1 v 42nd Highlanders; 3 Sept, 1881.
Record Defeat: 0-10 v Rangers; 24 Dec, 1898.
Most Capped Player: Lawrie Reilly, 38, Scotland.
Most League Appearances: 446: Arthur Duncan.
Most League Goals in Season (Individual): 42: Joe Baker.
Most Goals Overall (Individual): 364: Gordon Smith.

Honours
League Champions: Division I 1902–03, 1947–48, 1950–51, 1951–52. First Division 1980–81. Division II 1893–94, 1894–95, 1932–33; *Runners-up:* Division I 1896–97, 1946–47, 1949–50, 1952–53, 1973–74.
Scottish Cup Winners: 1887, 1902; *Runners-up:* 1896, 1914, 1923, 1924, 1947, 1958, 1972, 1979.
League Cup Winners: 1972–73; *Runners-up:* 1950–51, 1968–69, 1974–75.
European: *European Cup* 6 matches (1955–56 semi-finals). *Cup Winners Cup* 6 matches (1972–73). *UEFA Cup* 54 matches (1960–61 semi-finals, 1961–62, 1962–63, 1965–66, 1967–68, 1968–69, 1970–71 *Fairs Cup*; 1973–74, 1974–75, 1975–76, 1976–77, 1978–79).
Club colours: Shirt: Green with white sleeves. Shorts: White. Stockings: Green with white trim.

Goram, A	Hunter, G	Sneddon, A	Orr, N	Rae, G	McIntyre, T	Weir, M	Kane, P	McCluskey, G	Collins, J	Tortolano, J	Evans, G	May, E	Archibald, S	McGinlay, P	Milne, C	Watson, A	McBride, J	Mitchell, G	Findlay, W	Houchen, K	Fellenger, D	Lennon, D	Match No.
1	2	3	4	5	6	7	8	9*	10	11†	12	14											1
1	2	3	4	5	6	7	9	14	10	12	11*		8†										2
1	2	3	4	5	6		9		10	12	11*	7	8†	14									3
1	2	3	4	5			9	14	10	7	11*	12	8†		6								4
1	2	3	4	5			9	12	10	7	11*		8		6								5
1	2	3	4	5			9	14	10	7†	11	12	8*		6								6
1	2	3	7	5			9		10	12	11	4*	8		6								7
1	2	3	7	5			9		10	12	11	4	8*		6								8
1	2	3	7*	5			9	14	10		11	4†	8		6	12							9
1	2	3	7	5†	14		9*		10	12	11	4	8		6								10
1	2	3	4		5		9	14	10	7*	11	12	8†		6								11
1	2	3	4		5		9	14	10	7*	11	12	8†		6								12
1	2	3	4	5	6		8	9	10	7*	11	12											13
1	2	3*	7	5	4		9		10		11	12	8		6								14
1	6	2	7	5	3		9		10		11		8		4								15
1	2	3			5		9		10	12	11*		8		4		7	6					16
1	2		4	5	3†		9	11	10			12	8		14		7*	6					17
1	2		4	5			9	11*	10		12		8		3		7	6					18
1	2		4	5		12	9		10		11*		8		3		7	6					19
1	2	3	4	5		7*	9	14	10		11†	12	8					6					20
1	2		6	5		7*	9		10	11	12	4	8					3					21
1	2		10	5	3		9			11	7	4	8					6					22
1	2		7	5	3	14	9		10	12	11*	4†	8					6					23
1	2			5	7	12	9		10	14	11	4†	8*		3			6					24
1	2			5	4*		9		10	7	11	12	8		3			6					25
1	2		7		5		9		10	3	11*	4	8					6	12				26
1	2		7	5			9	12	10	3	11	4*	8		6								27
1	2	3	7	5					10		11	4	8		9			6					28
1	2	3	4	5			9*	14	10	7†	11	12	8					6					29
1	2	3	7	5			9		10	12	11	4*						6		8			30
1		3*	4	5	2		9		10	12	11		8					6		7			31
1		2	4	5			9		10	3	11		8					6		7			32
1		2	4	5			9	14	10	3	11*	12	8					6		7†			33
1	2	3	4	5			9	12	10		11		8*					6		7			34
1	2	3	4*	5			9		10		11			12				6	8†	7	14		35
1	2	3	4	5			9*		10		11†							6	8	7	14	12	36
36	33	26	33	32	16 + 1s	4 + 3s	35	4 + 12s	35	15 + 10s	32 + 3s	13 + 12s	31	— + 2s	18 + 1s	— + 1s	4	20	2 + 1s	7	— + 2s	— + 1s	

KILMARNOCK Second Division

Year Formed: 1869. *Ground & Address:* Rugby Park, Kilmarnock KA1 2DP. *Telephone:* 0563 25184.
Ground Capacity: total: 17,528 seated: 4011. *Size of Pitch:* 115yd×75yd.
Chairman: R. Lauchlan. *Secretary and General Manager:* Walter W. McCrae. *Commercial Manager:* —.
Manager: Jim Fleeting. *Assistant Manager:* —. *Physio:* Hugh Allan. *Coaches:* R. Stewart, J. Clark.
Managers since 1975: W. Fernie; D. Sneddon; J. Clunie; E. Morrison; J. Fleeting.
Club Nickname(s): Killie. *Previous Grounds:* None.
Record Attendance: 34,246 v Rangers, League Cup, Aug, 1963.
Record Transfer Fee received: —.
Record Transfer Fee paid: —.
Record Victory: 13-2 v Saltcoats Victoria, Scottish Cup 2nd rd; 12 Sept, 1896.

1988–89 LEAGUE RECORD

Match No.	Date	Venue	Opponents	Result		H/T Score	Lg. Pos.	Goalscorers	Attendance
1	Aug 13	A	Queen of the S	D	2-2	0-0	—	McGuire, Gilmour	1587
2	20	H	Partick T	L	0-1	0-0	12		2760
3	27	H	Ayr U	W	2-0	1-0	6	McGuire, Marshall	5387
4	Sept 3	A	Clydebank	D	2-2	1-1	7	McGuire, Cuthbertson	1418
5	10	A	Airdrieonians	L	1-5	0-2	11	Cook	1500
6	17	H	Clyde	L	1-1	1-1	11	McDonald	1745
7	24	A	Dunfermline Ath	L	0-3	0-1	11		5379
8	Oct 1	H	Morton	L	3-4	1-3	12	Cook, Martin, McInnes	1865
9	8	A	Forfar Ath	D	2-2	1-1	12	McGuire, Gilmour	685
10	15	A	Meadowbank T	W	2-0	0-0	11	Montgomerie, Cook	1800
11	22	H	Raith R	D	1-1	1-1	11	Wylde	2102
12	29	A	St Johnstone	L	0-2	0-0	11		2328
13	Nov 5	H	Falkirk	L	0-2	0-1	12		2561
14	12	H	Airdrieonians	L	0-3	0-1	12		1958
15	19	A	Clyde	W	2-0	2-0	12	MacFarlane 2	1050
16	26	H	Dunfermline Ath	D	2-2	0-2	12	Gilmour (pen), Brannigan	2961
17	Dec 3	A	Partick T	W	1-0	1-0	12	MacFarlane	2624
18	10	H	St Johnstone	L	0-3	0-1	12		2601
19	17	A	Raith R	D	0-0	0-0	12		1436
20	24	H	Meadowbank T	W	1-0	1-0	12	Walters	1650
21	31	H	Clydebank	W	1-0	1-0	11	McLaughlin	2760
22	Jan 3	A	Ayr U	L	1-4	0-2	—	Faulds	8585
23	7	A	Falkirk	L	0-2	0-2	12		2814
24	14	H	Queen of the S	W	2-1	1-1	11	Derek Walker, Watters	2264
25	21	H	Forfar Ath	W	2-1	1-1	10	Watters 2	1813
26	Feb 18	H	Clyde	D	0-0	0-0	10		1953
27	25	A	St Johnstone	D	2-2	0-1	10	Reilly, Watters	2993
28	Mar 1	A	Morton	D	2-2	0-1	—	Watters, Harkness	1750
29	4	H	Airdrieonians	D	1-1	0-1	9	McLaughlin	2376
30	11	A	Ayr U	L	1-2	1-1	11	Montgomerie	5476
31	18	H	Forfar Ath	D	2-2	2-2	12	Harkness, Faulds	1586
32	25	A	Dunfermline Ath	D	0-0	0-0	11		5906
33	Apr 1	H	Falkirk	D	0-0	0-0	11		3670
34	8	A	Meadowbank T	W	2-1	1-0	10	Harkness, Watters	750
35	15	H	Raith R	L	1-2	1-0	10	Harkness	2216
36	22	A	Morton	L	0-3	0-1	12		1600
37	29	H	Partick T	D	0-0	0-0	12		3040
38	May 6	A	Clydebank	L	2-3	2-1	13	Harkness, Stewart	1311
39	13	A	Queen of the S	W	6-0	1-0	13	Watters 5, Reilly	1200

Final League Position: 13

GOALSCORERS

League: (47): Watters 12, Harkness 5, McGuire 4, Cook 4, Gilmour 3 (1 pen), MacFarlane 3, Faulds 2, McLaughlin 2, Montgomerie 2, Reilly 2, Brannigan 1, Cuthbertson 1, McDonald 1, McInnes 1, Marshall 1, Martin 1, Stewart 1, Derek Walker 1, Wylde 1.
League Cup: (1): Gilmour 1 (pen).
Scottish Cup: (2): Davidson 1, Speirs 1.

Record Defeat: 0-8 v Hibernian, Division I; 22 Aug, 1925: v Rangers, Division I; 27 Feb, 1937.
Most Capped Player: Joe Nibloe, 11, Scotland.
Most League Appearances: 478: Alan Robertson, 1972–89.
Most League Goals in Season (Individual): 35: Peerie Cunningham, Division I; 1927–28.
Most Goals Overall (Individual): 148: W. Culley; 1912–23.

Honours
League Champions: Division I 1964–65. Division II 1897–98, 1898–99; *Runners-up:* Division I 1959–60, 1960–61, 1962–63, 1963–64. First Division 1975–76, 1978–79, 1981–82. Division II 1953–54, 1973–74.
Scottish Cup Winners: 1920, 1929; *Runners-up:* 1898, 1932, 1938, 1957, 1960.
League Cup Runners-up: 1952–53, 1960–61, 1962–63.
European: *European Cup —. Cup Winners Cup —. UEFA Cup Fairs Cup:* 1966–67 (semi-finals), 1969–70.
Club colours: Shirt: Blue and white hoops. Shorts: Blue. Stockings: Blue.

McCulloch, A	Montgomerie, R	Robertson, A	Davidson, F	Martin, P	Marshall, S	McConville, R	Gilmour, J	McDonald, T	McGuire, J	Cook, D	Harkness, C	McLean, S	Hughes, M	Wylde, G	Brannigan, K	MacFarlane, D	McQueen, E	Millar, G	McLaughlin, M	Reilly, R	Walker, Derek	Flexney, P	Watters, W	Walker, David	Lindsay, A	Speirs, G	Faulds, G	Callaghan, T	Stewart, A	*Match No.*
1	2	3	4	5	6	7	8	10	11																					1
1	2	3	4	5	6*	7	8	10	11	12																				2
1	2	3	4	5	6	7	8	10†	11	12	9*	14																		3
1		3	4	5	6	7	8	10	11*		9	2																		4
1	2	3	4	5	6*	7	8	10	11	14	9†	12																		5
1	2	3	4	5			8	10*	11	9	14	12	6	7†																6
1	2	3	4	5	8†	12		10	11*		9	6		7																7
1	2	4		5		12	8	11†		9	10	3	6*	7																8
1	2	4		5		7	10		11	9	12	3	6	8*																9
1	2	4		5	8*	12	11	10		9		3		7	6															10
1	2	4		5			11	10		9*	12	3		7	6	8														11
1	2	4			12	10*	8		11	9		3		7	5	6														12
1	2		4		12		8	10*	11		9	3			5	6	7													13
1			4				11	14		9	12	3		8	5	6	7†	2	10*											14
1			4					12			9	3		8	5	6	7	2	10*	11										15
1	3		4				12	10*	14		9	2		8	5	6	7†			11										16
1	2		4				11		12	8	9	3		10*	6	5†		14		7										17
1	2		4				12		11†	14	9*	3			6	5		10		8	7									18
1	2				14						9	3			4	5		10†			8	6	7	11*	12					19
1											9*	3			5	4†		2	11		7	6	8	14	12	10				20
1			6								12	3			5	4		2	11		7		8*		14	10†	9			21
1			6								12	3			5	4		2	11*		7		8		14	10†	9			22
1			10								9				5	2†		3	11		4*	6	7	14	12		8			23
1			4									3			5	14			11*	7	10	6†	8	12	2		9			24
1	4		6									3				5			11*	7	10		8†	14	2	12	9			25
1	2				5						12	3				14			11*	7	10†	6	8			4	9			26
1	2				5						9	3				10*			12	7		6	8		14		11†	4		27
1	2				5						9	3†						14	10	7		6	8		12		11*	4		28
1	2				5						9					7*		3	10		12	6	8		14		11†	4		29
1	2		7		5†						9							3	10*		12	6	8	14			11	4		30
1	2		7†		5						9					14		3	10*		12	6	8				11	4		31
1	2		7		5						9	3							12	10		6	8				11*	4		32
1	2		7		5						9†	3							14	10	12	6	8					4	11*	33
1	2				5						9	3							11*	10	12	6	8					4	7	34
1	2				5						9	3*				14			12	10		6	8				11†	4	7	35
1	2		10		5						9†							3*	12	7	14	6	8					4	11	36
1	2		8		5						9	3				4				11		6					12	10*	7	37
1	2		7		5						9	3				4				10		6	8						11	38
1	2		7		5						9†	3				4*			14	10	12	6	8						11	39
39	31	12	26	11	21	7	14	12	11	8	26	29	3	11	15	19	4	12	14	17	9	18	20	1	2	4	13	11	7	
					+ 3s	+ 3s	+ 2s	+ 2s	+ 2s	+ 4s	+ 7s	+ 3s				+ 4s		+ 2s	+ 6s		+ 7s			+ 5s	+ 8s	+ 1s	+ 1s			

Also played: Bourke J – Match 1-2 (9); Cuthbertson S – Match 4 (12); McInnes I – Match 7-8 (14).

MEADOWBANK THISTLE First Division

Year Formed: 1974. *Ground & Address:* Meadowbank Stadium, London Rd, Edinburgh EH7 6AE.
Ground Capacity: total: 16,500 seated: 16,500. *Size of Pitch:* 105yd×72yd.
Chairman: John P. Blacklaw. *Secretary:* William L. Mill. *Commercial Manager:* Sean Pinkman.
Manager: Terence Christie. *Assistant Manager:* Lawrie Glasson. *Physio:* Arthur Duncan. *Coach:* Tam McLaren.
Managers since 1975: John Bain; Alec Ness; Willie MacFarlane; Terry Christie.
Club Nickname(s): Thistle; Wee Jags. *Previous Grounds:* None.
Record Attendance: 4000 v Albion Rovers, League Cup 1st rd; 9 Sept, 1974.
Record Transfer Fee received: £70,000 for Darren Jackson to Newcastle U (1986).
Record Transfer Fee paid: £28,000 for Victor Kasule from Albion Rovers (1987).

1988–89 LEAGUE RECORD

Match No.	Date	Venue	Opponents	Result	H/T Score	Lg. Pos.	Goalscorers	Attendance
1	Aug 13	A	Forfar Ath	L 0-1	0-1	—		599
2	20	H	Ayr U	L 1-2	0-1	14	McGachie	1100
3	27	H	Falkirk	W 2-1	1-0	10	Sprott, Park	960
4	Sept 3	A	Queen of the S	W 1-0	1-0	10	Park	1000
5	10	H	Raith R	W 2-1	1-0	7	Reilly, Sprott	1268
6	17	A	St Johnstone	D 0-0	0-0	6		1694
7	24	H	Clydebank	D 0-0	0-0	7		400
8	Oct 1	A	Airdrieonians	D 0-0	0-0	8		1400
9	8	H	Clyde	W 3-2	2-0	5	Boyd, Armstrong, Prentice	600
10	15	H	Kilmarnock	L 0-2	0-0	8		1800
11	22	A	Dunfermline Ath	W 3-1	3-0	6	Sprott, Logan, Prentice	4761
12	29	A	Partick T	D 1-1	1-0	7	Sprott	1843
13	Nov 5	A	Morton	L 0-2	0-1	7		1800
14	12	A	Raith R	L 0-1	0-0	8		1495
15	19	H	St Johnstone	D 1-1	1-0	8	Armstrong (pen)	750
16	26	A	Clydebank	L 1-2	1-0	8	Scott	702
17	Dec 3	A	Ayr U	D 2-2	1-1	8	McGachie, Logan	1849
18	10	H	Partick T	L 0-2	0-1	8		800
19	17	H	Dunfermline Ath	L 0-1	0-1	9		2000
20	24	A	Kilmarnock	L 0-1	0-1	9		1650
21	31	H	Queen of the S	L 1-2	1-2	12	Scott	367
22	Jan 3	A	Falkirk	L 0-3	0-1	—		2300
23	7	H	Morton	W 2-1	0-0	11	Lawrence, Williamson	624
24	14	H	Forfar Ath	D 1-1	0-1	12	McGachie	400
25	21	A	Clyde	W 2-1	0-1	11	Sprott, McGachie	600
26	Feb 4	H	Airdrieonians	W 3-2	3-0	8	Lawrence 3	900
27	11	H	Raith R	L 1-3	0-2	9	Armstrong	900
28	25	A	Ayr U	L 2-3	1-0	12	Scott, Perry	2320
29	Mar 4	A	Falkirk	D 0-0	0-0	13		3014
30	11	H	Clydebank	D 1-1	0-0	13	Inglis	400
31	18	H	Clyde	W 2-0	1-0	10	Perry, Roseburgh	500
32	25	A	Forfar Ath	L 1-2	1-2	12	McGachie	621
33	Apr 1	A	Morton	W 2-0	0-0	10	Logan, McCormack	1500
34	8	H	Kilmarnock	L 1-2	0-1	11	Roseburgh	750
35	15	A	Partick T	L 1-2	0-2	12	Roseburgh	2511
36	22	H	Airdrieonians	W 3-1	1-0	10	Roseburgh, Boyd, Forrest	800
37	29	A	Queen of the S	W 2-1	0-1	10	Roseburgh 2	420
38	May 6	H	St Johnstone	W 2-1	0-0	10	Armstrong (pen), Forrest	800
39	13	A	Dunfermline Ath	D 1-1	0-0	10	Scott	12,976

Final League Position: 10

GOALSCORERS

League: (45): Roseburgh 6, McGachie 5, Sprott 5, Armstrong 4 (2 pens), Lawrence 4, Scott 4, Logan 3, Boyd 2, Forrest 2, Park 2, Perry 2, Prentice 2, Inglis 1, McCormack 1, Reilly 1, Williamson 1.
League Cup: (2): Irvine 1, Prentice 1.
Scottish Cup: (2): Lawrence 1, Logan 1.

Record Victory: 6-0 v Raith R, Second Division; 9 Nov, 1985.
Record Defeat: 0-8 v Hamilton A, Division II; 14 Dec, 1974.
Most Capped Player: —.
Most League Appearances: 446: Walter Boyd, 1979–89.
Most League Goals in Season (Individual): 21: John McGachie, 1986–87. *(Team):* 69; Second Division, 1986–87.
Most Goals Overall (Individual): 63: Adrian Sprott, 1980–85.

Honours
League Champions: Second Division 1986-87; *Runners-up:* Second Division 1982–83. First Division 1987–88.
Scottish Cup: —.
League Cup: Semi-finals 1984–85.
Club colours: Shirt: Amber with black trim. Shorts: Black. Stockings: Amber.

McQueen, J	McCormack, J	Armstrong, G	Boyd, W	Tierney, G	Prentice, A	Logan, S	Irvine, N	Walker, D	Sprott, A	McGachie, J	Reilly, R	Hendrie, T	Park, D	Conroy, D	Williamson, S	Scott, G	Perry, J	Inglis, J	Lawrence, A	Roseburgh, D	Forrest, R	Match No.
1	2†	3	4	5	6	7	8	9*	10	11	12	14										1
1	10	3	4	5	6	7*	8†	9		11	12	2	14									2
1	6	3	4	5		7		9	10		11	2	8									3
1	6	3	4	5	12	7		9	10*		11	2	8									4
1	2	3	4	5	6	7	8	9	10		11											5
1		3	4	5	6	7	8†		10	11*	9	14	12		2							6
1		3	4	5	6	7	8	11*	10		9	2			12							7
1		3	4	5	6	7	8		10		9	2			11							8
1		3	4	5	6	7	8		10		9	2			11							9
1		3	4	5	6	7		12	10		9	2	8*		11							10
1	11	3	4	5	6	9	8		10			2			7							11
1		3	4	5	6	9*	8	12	10			2		11	7							12
1	11†	3	4	5	6	9	8	14	10*		12	2			7							13
1		3	4	5	6	7	8		10	11*	12				2	9						14
1		3	4	5		7	12		10	11		2			6	9*	8					15
1		3	4	5	6*	7		14	10	11		2			12	9†	8					16
1		3	4	5		7	14	12	10*	11		2			6	9†	8					17
1		3	4	5	6	7			10	11		2	14		12	9†	8*					18
1		3	4			7	8†		10	12		2	14		6	9*	11	5				19
1	2	3	4			7			10					6	8	9	11	5				20
1		3	4			7			10	12		2	14	6	8	9†	11	5*				21
1	2	3				7	4		10					6	8	9	11	5				22
1	2	3	4		6*	7	5		10	14			12		8		11†		9			23
1	2	3	4		6*	7	5		10	11			12		8				9			24
1	2	3	4		6	7	8		10	11		9*	12		5							25
1	2	3	4		6	7	8		10				11		5				9			26
1	2†	3	4		6	7	8		10			14	12		5	9*	11					27
1	2	3	4		6	7			10						5	9	11	8				28
1	8	3	4		6	7	14		10				12		5	9*	11	2†				29
1	8	3	4			7*	12		10			14	9†		5		11	2		6		30
1	8	3	4			7			10						5	9	11	2		6		31
1	8	3	4			7	12		10†	11		14			5		9*	2		6		32
1	8	3	4			7			10	11		2			5					6	9	33
1	8	3	4			7			10	11		2*			5	12				6	9	34
1	8	3	4			7	14		10	11*					5	12		2†		6	9	35
1	2	3	4			7	8		10	11†					5*	14		12		6	9	36
1	2*	3	4			7	8		10						5	11		12		6	9	37
1	2	3	4			7	8		10				12		5	11				6	9*	38
1	2	3	4			7	8		10				12		5	11*				6	9	39
39	26	39	38	18	21 + 1s	39	22 + 6s	6 + 5s	38	15 + 3s	8 + 4s	19 + 5s	5 + 12s	4	31 + 3s	16 + 3s	15	10 + 2s	3	10	7	

MONTROSE

Second Division

Year Formed: 1879. *Ground & Address:* Links Park, Wellington St, Montrose DD10 8QD. *Telephone:* 0674 73200.
Ground Capacity: total: 6500 seated: 324. *Size of Pitch:* 113yd×70yd.
Chairman: Forbes W. Inglis. *Secretary:* Malcolm J. Watters. *Commercial Manager:* John Archbold.
Manager: Ian Stewart. *Assistant Manager:* John Smith. *Physio:* Andy Bell. *Coach:* Chic McLelland.
Managers since 1975: A. Stuart; K. Cameron; R. Livingstone; S. Murray; D. D'Arcy; I. Stewart.
Club Nickname(s): The Gable Endies. *Previous Grounds:* None.
Record Attendance: 8983 v Dundee, Scottish Cup 3rd rd; 17 Mar, 1973.
Record Transfer Fee received: £50,000 for Gary Murray to Hibernian (Dec, 1980).
Record Transfer Fee paid: —.

1988–89 LEAGUE RECORD

Match No.	Date	Venue	Opponents	Result	H/T Score	Lg. Pos.	Goalscorers	Atten-dance
1	Aug 13	A	Cowdenbeath	W 6-2	3-2	—	Mackay 2, Maver, Murray 3	250
2	20	H	Stirling Albion	W 3-2	1-2	1	Maver, Lyons (pen), Powell	450
3	27	H	Brechin C	L 0-2	0-1	3		600
4	Sept 3	A	Queen's Park	L 0-2	0-2	7		541
5	10	H	Arbroath	L 0-1	0-1	10		650
6	17	A	Berwick R	W 2-1	2-0	8	Lyons (pen), Brown S	330
7	24	H	Stranraer	W 4-2	3-1	6	Maver, Murray, Duffy, Mackay	312
8	Oct 1	H	Stenhousemuir	W 3-1	0-0	3	Murray 2 Paterson	479
9	8	A	East Fife	D 1-1	1-1	3	Maver	561
10	15	A	East Stirling	L 0-1	0-0	5		200
11	22	H	Alloa	W 1-0	1-0	3	Murray	350
12	29	A	Albion R	L 1-2	1-1	7	Maver	520
13	Nov 5	H	Dumbarton	D 1-1	1-0	6	Murray	350
14	12	A	Stirling Albion	L 0-2	0-0	7		741
15	19	H	Cowdenbeath	L 0-2	0-1	9		280
16	26	A	Arbroath	D 0-0	0-0	10		650
17	Dec 10	H	Berwick R	W 2-1	1-0	9	Mackay, Murray	200
18	17	A	Stranraer	L 0-1	0-0	11		750
19	24	A	Dumbarton	L 2-3	2-1	11	McGlashan, Maver	400
20	31	H	Albion R	W 1-0	1-0	—	Forbes	500
21	Jan 3	A	Brechin C	D 1-1	1-1	—	Murray	644
22	14	H	Queen's Park	D 1-1	1-0	10	Murray	350
23	21	H	East Stirling	L 0-1	0-1	11		250
24	31	A	Alloa	L 0-1	0-0	—		600
25	Feb 4	H	East Fife	D 2-2	1-2	11	Maver, Hall (og)	350
26	22	H	Stranraer	W 1-0	0-0	—	Mackay	250
27	Mar 1	A	Stenhousemuir	W 1-0	1-0	—	McGlashan	200
28	4	A	Queen's Park	D 2-2	1-0	9	Murray, Lyons	685
29	7	A	Albion R	D 2-2	1-1	—	Murray, Maver	402
30	11	H	Cowdenbeath	W 2-1	1-1	8	Morrison, Lyons (pen)	275
31	25	H	Brechin C	W 1-0	1-0	7	Murray	500
32	28	A	Dumbarton	L 0-2	0-1	—		400
33	Apr 1	A	Stenhousemuir	W 3-2	1-1	7	Murray 3	300
34	8	H	East Stirling	W 2-1	1-0	7	Murray, Lyons (pen)	365
35	15	H	Arbroath	D 1-1	0-1	7	Lyons (pen)	450
36	22	A	Alloa	D 3-3	1-2	5	Lyons 2 (1 pen), Mackay	638
37	29	H	Stirling Albion	L 0-6	0-4	6		409
38	May 6	A	Berwick R	D 1-1	1-0	6	Forbes	696
39	13	A	East Fife	W 4-1	3-0	6	Murray 3, Maver	300

Final League Position: 6

GOALSCORERS

League: (54): Murray 21, Maver 9, Lyons 8 (6 pens), Mackay 6, Forbes 2, McGlashan 2, Brown S 1, Duffy 1, Morrison 1, Paterson 1, Powell 1, own goal 1.
League Cup: (1): Paterson 1.
Scottish Cup: (5): Murray 2, Lyons 1, Mackay 1, Maver 1.

Record Victory: 12-0 v Vale of Leithen, Scottish Cup 2nd rd; 4 Jan, 1975.
Record Defeat: 0-13 v Aberdeen; 17 Mar, 1951.
Most Capped Player: Alexander Keillor, 2 (6), Scotland.
Most League Appearances: —.
Most League Goals in Season (Individual): 28: Brian Third, Division II; 1972–73.
Most Goals Overall (Individual): —.

Honours
League Champions: Second Division 1984–85.
Scottish Cup: Quarter-finals 1973, 1976.
League Cup: Semi-finals 1975–76.
Club colours: Shirt: Blue with white pin stripe. Shorts: White. Stockings: Red.

Larter, D	Barr, L	King, S	Paterson, D	Brown, K	Forbes, N	Maver, C	Lyons, A	Mackay, H	McGlashan, J	Murray, G	Robertson, G	Powell, D	Duffy, A	Halley, K	Brown, S	Wright, F	Morrison, B	Allan, M	McLelland, C	Wrack, P	Lees, D	Match No.
1	2	3	4	5	6*	7†	8	9	10	11	12	14										1
1	2	3	4	5	6	7	8	9†	10*	11	12	14										2
1	2		4		6	7	8*	9†	10	11	12	14	3	5								3
1	2		4		6†	7	8*	9	10	11	12	14	3	5								4
1			4	2	6	7	8	9*	10	11			3	5	12							5
1			4	3	14	7†	8	12	6	11	10			5	9*	2						6
1			4	2	14	7	8†	12	6	11	10		3	5	9*							7
1			4	2	6	7	8*	14	10	11		12	3	5	9†							8
1			4	2†	6	7	8	12	10	11	14		3	5	9*							9
1	2		4		6†	7	8	9	10	11	14		3*	5	12							10
1	2		4		6	7	8	9†	10	11*		14	3	5	12							11
1		14	4		6*	7	8	9†	10	11		12	3	5			2					12
1			4	6*	12	7	8		10	11†		9	3	5	14		2					13
1			4		6	7*	8	9	10			11	3	5	12		2					14
1			5	4	6*	7	8	12	10	11		9	3				2					15
1		3	5	4	14	7*	8	9	10	12		11	6†				2					16
1		3	5	4	6	7	8	9†		12		11	10*				2	14				17
1			5	4	6	7	8*	9	10	12		11	3†				2	14				18
1		3	5	4	6	7		9	10	11*		8†	14				2	12				19
1		3*	5	4	6	11	8	9†	10	14		12					2	7				20
1			5	4	6	9	8		10	11					12		2	7*	3			21
1	10*		5	4	6	7	8	9		11							2		3	12		22
1	14		5	4	6†	9	8	12	10	11*							2	7	3			23
1	14		5	4	6	11	8	12	10	9							2	7*	3†			24
1	14		5	4	6	8†		9*	10	11					12		2	7	3			25
1	14		5	4	6†			9	10	11					12		2	7*	3	8		26
1	14		5	4	6		8	9*	10	11							2	12	3	7†		27
1	9†		5	4	6	14	8	12	10	11							2	7*	3			28
1	9†		5	4	6	12	8	14	10	11							2	7*	3			29
1	14		5	4	6	9†	8	12	10	11							2	7*	3			30
1	14			4	6	9†	8	12	10*	11				5			2	7	3			31
1	10†	14		4	6	9	8	12		11				5			2	7*	3			32
1	14	10†	5	4	6	9*	8			11					12		2	7	3			33
1		10†	5	4	6*	9	8	12	14	11							2	7	3			34
1		6†	5	4	14	9	8	12	10	11							2	7*	3			35
1		3	5†	4	6*	9	8	12	10	11					14		2	7				36
1			5	4	6	9	8	12†	10	11					14		2	7	3*			37
1		3	5	4	6	9†	8		10	11*					12		2	7			14	38
1		3	5	4	6	9*	8	12	10	11					14		2	7†				39
39	10 + 8s	12 + 2s	37	33	34 + 5s	35 + 2s	36	18 + 17s	34 + 1s	34 + 4s	2 + 6s	7 + 8s	15 + 1s	14	4 + 13s	1	28	18 + 4s	16	2 + 1s	— + 1s	

MORTON

First Division

Year Formed: 1874. *Ground & Address:* Cappielow Park, Sinclair St, Greenock. *Telephone:* 0475 23511.
Ground Capacity: total: 16,000 seated: 5500. *Size of Pitch:* 110yd×71yd.
Chairman: John L. Macpherson. *Secretary:* Mrs Jane Rankin. *Commercial Manager:* —.
Manager: Allan McGraw. *Assistant Manager:* Jackie McNamara. *Physio:* Gerry McElhill. *Coach:* Jackie McNamara.
Managers since 1975: Joe Gilroy; Benny Rooney; Alex Miller; Tommy McLean; Willie McLean; Allan McGraw.
Club Nickname(s): The Ton. *Previous Grounds:* Grant Street 1874, Garvel Park 1875, Cappielow Park 1879, Ladyburn Park 1882, (Cappielow Park 1883).
Record Attendance: 23,000 v Celtic; 1922.
Record Transfer Fee received: £350,000 for Neil Orr to West Ham U.

1988–89 LEAGUE RECORD

Match No.	Date	Venue	Opponents	Result	H/T Score	Lg. Pos.	Goalscorers	Attendance
1	Aug 13	H	Clyde	L 0-2	0-2	—		2300
2	20	A	Airdrieonians	D 1-1	0-1	13	Turner	1200
3	27	H	Clydebank	W 1-0	1-0	8	Roberts	1200
4	Sept 3	A	Partick T	W 4-1	3-1	4	Roberts, Alexander, MacDonald, Clinging	2367
5	10	H	St Johnstone	D 1-1	1-0	3	Alexander	2500
6	17	A	Falkirk	W 1-0	0-0	3	Roberts	4000
7	24	H	Queen of the S	W 1-0	1-0	3	Alexander	1500
8	Oct 1	A	Kilmarnock	W 4-3	3-1	1	Clinging, Robertson J, Alexander 2	1865
9	8	H	Raith R	L 0-1	0-0	3		1422
10	15	A	Forfar Ath	W 1-0	0-0	3	Clinging	958
11	22	H	Ayr U	W 2-0	2-0	1	Turner (pen), Alexander	2900
12	29	H	Dunfermline Ath	W 1-0	0-0	1	Turner (pen)	4500
13	Nov 5	H	Meadowbank	W 2-0	1-0	1	Pickering, Alexander	1800
14	12	A	St Johnstone	L 2-4	0-2	2	Turner, Alexander	3469
15	19	H	Falkirk	L 1-5	0-2	3	Robertson D	3500
16	26	A	Queen of the S	W 3-2	1-1	3	Robertson J, Alexander, MacDonald	850
17	Oct 3	H	Airdrieonians	L 0-2	0-0	3		2500
18	10	A	Dunfermline Ath	L 1-2	1-2	6	Robertson J	5454
19	17	A	Ayr U	L 1-3	0-1	6	Fowler	2440
20	24	H	Forfar Ath	D 1-1	0-1	6	Alexander	1400
21	31	H	Partick T	W 1-0	0-0	5	Robertson D	2500
22	Jan 3	A	Clydebank	D 1-1	1-1	—	Turner (pen)	1661
23	7	A	Meadowbank T	L 1-2	0-0	6	Turner (pen)	624
24	17	A	Clyde	W 1-0	0-0	—	Clinging	800
25	21	A	Raith R	L 0-1	0-0	6		1772
26	Feb 21	H	Falkirk	D 2-2	2-0	—	McInnes, Turner	2401
27	25	A	Forfar Ath	D 0-0	0-0	6		627
28	Mar 1	H	Kilmarnock	D 2-2	1-0	—	Clinging, Ronald	1750
29	4	H	Partick T	D 1-1	0-0	6	McNeil	2050
30	11	A	St Johnstone	W 1-0	0-0	5	Deeney	2525
31	25	A	Airdrieonians	L 1-2	0-1	6	Spencer	1000
32	Apr 1	H	Meadowbank T	L 0-2	0-0	6		1500
33	4	H	Clydebank	W 1-0	0-0	—	Turner	1200
34	8	A	Queen of the S	D 1-1	1-0	6	Turner	500
35	15	A	Dunfermline Ath	L 0-1	0-0	6		5622
36	22	H	Kilmarnock	W 3-0	1-0	6	Collins, Clinging, Alexander	1600
37	29	A	Clyde	L 1-2	0-0	6	Turner	500
38	May 6	H	Raith R	L 0-1	0-1	6		1200
39	13	A	Ayr U	W 1-0	0-0	5	Clinging	2824

Final League Position: 5

GOALSCORERS

League: (46): Alexander 11, Turner 10 (4 pen), Clinging 7, Roberts 3, Robertson J 3, MacDonald 2, Robertson D 2, Collins 1, Deeney 1, Fowler 1, McInnes 1, McNeil 1, Pickering 1, Ronald 1, Spencer 1.
League Cup: (3): Alexander 2, McNeil 1.
Scottish Cup: (6): Robertson D 2, Turner 2, Alexander 1, John Boag 1.

Record Transfer Fee paid: £35,000 for Roddy MacDonald from Hearts.
Record Victory: 11-0 v Carfin Shamrock, Scottish Cup 1st rd; 13 Nov, 1886.
Record Defeat: 1-10 v Port Glasgow Ath, Division II; 5 May, 1894: v St Bernards, Division II; 14 Oct, 1933.
Most Capped Player: Jimmy Cowan, 25, Scotland.
Most League Appearances: 358: David Hayes, 1969–84.
Most League Goals in Season (Individual): 58: Allan McGraw, Division II; 1963–64.
Most Goals Overall (Individual): —.

Honours
League Champions: First Division 1977–78, 1983–84, 1986–87. Division II 1949–50, 1963–64, 1966–67.
Scottish Cup Winners: 1922; *Runners-up:* 1948.
League Cup Runners-up: 1963–64.
European: *European Cup —. Cup Winners Cup —. UEFA Cup (Fairs):* 1968–69.
Club colours: Shirt: Blue and white hoops. Shorts: White. Stockings: Blue.

Wylie, D	Collins, D	Pickering, M	Hunter, J	Boag, John	Clinging, I	Robertson, D	Turner, T	McNeil, J	McInnes, D	Ronald, G	Robertson, J	Fowler, J	MacDonald, R	Roberts, P	Alexander, R	O'Hara, A	Boag, James	Deeney, M	Reid, B	McGeachy, A	Strain, B	Spencer, J	Kelly, G	McGraw, M	Brown, C	Mahood, A	*Match No.*
1	2	3	4	5	6	7	8	9†	10	11*	12	14															1
1	2		3	4	6	12	10	11*	8	7			5	9													2
1	2		3	4	6*		10		8	7		12	5	11	9												3
1	2		3	4	6		10	12	8*	7†		14	5	11	9												4
1	2		3	4	6	12	10		8	7			5	11*	9												5
1	2		4	3	6				8	7		10	5	11*	9		12										6
1	2		4	3†	6				8	7		10*	5	11	9	12	14										7
1	2		4	3*	6		12		8	7	11		5	10†	9			14									8
1	2		4		6		12	14	8	7	11*		5	10†	9	3											9
1	2		4	8	6		10		12	7†	14		5	11*	9	3											10
1	2		4	8	6		10		12	7	14		5*	11†	9	3											11
1	2	5	4	3	6		10			7*	12			11†	9	8	14										12
1	2	5	4	3	6		10			7				11*	9	8	12										13
1	2	3	4		6	11†	10			7	12		5		9	8*	14										14
1	2	14	4	3†	6	7	10				11		5		9	8*	12										15
1	2		4	3	6	12	7				11		5	10*	9	8											16
1	2	14	4	3†	6			12	8				5	11*	9	10	7										17
1	2	3	4		6				8	7	11		5*		9	12			10								18
1	2	3	4	5	6				8	7	11	10			9												19
1	2	3	4	5		7			8	10	11	6			9												20
1	2	3	4	5	12	7†	8			10*	11	6			9					14							21
1	2	3	4	5	6†	7*	8		14		11	10			9					12							22
1		3	4	5	2	7*	8		10		11	6			9					12							23
1	2	3	4	5	6	12	10			14		8			9			11†		7*							24
1	2	3	4	5	6*	12	10		14	7		8			9					11†							25
1	2	3	4		14	7	11		8†	9*		10	5			6				12							26
1	2	3	4		14	7*	11		8	9		10†	5			6				12							27
1	2	3	4*		8	12	11		10	9	14		5			6				7†							28
1	2	3		5	8	14	11	10†		9*						4		12			6	7					29
1	2†	3		5	6	12		14	10			8			9*	4		11				7					30
1		3	4		6	12	11†	14	7			10*	5		9	2						8					31
1		3*		2	6	7			8	12		11	5		9	4						10					32
1	2		4	3	6	7*	8	10	12	11†		14	5		9												33
1	2		4		6		11	10	8*	7†		12	5		9					14	3						34
1		3	4		6		11	10	8*			7	5	12	9	2											35
1	8	3	4		6		11	10				7	5		9	2											36
1	8	3	4		6		11	10*				7	5		9	2		12									37
1	10*				6		11	9	8†			3	5			2		7					4	12	14		38
1	10		4	3	6		11	9	8					12		2			5*	7†						14	39
39	35	22 + 2s	35	27	35 + 3s	11 + 9s	29 + 2s	10 + 5s	24 + 5s	25 + 2s	10 + 6s	18 + 5s	26	14 + 2s	31	21 + 2s	1 + 6s	3 + 3s	2	4 + 6s	2	4	1	— + 1s	— + 1s	— + 1s	

MOTHERWELL

Premier Division

Year Formed: 1886. *Ground & Address:* Fir Park, Motherwell ML1 2QN. *Telephone:* 0698 61437.
Ground Capacity: total: 23,500 seated: 3500. *Size of Pitch:* 110yd×75yd.
Chairman: John C. Chapman. *Secretary:* Alan C. Dick. *Commercial Manager:* John Swinburne.
Manager: Tommy McLean. *Assistant Manager:* Tom Forsyth. *Physio:* Jim Maitland. *Coach:* Cameron Murray.
Managers since 1975: Ian St John; Willie McLean; Rodger Hynd; Ally MacLeod; David Hay; Jock Wallace; Bobby Watson; Tommy McLean.
Club Nickname(s): The 'Well. *Previous Grounds:* Roman Road (1886–95).
Record Attendance: 35,632 v Rangers, Scottish Cup 4th rd replay; 12 Mar, 1952.
Record Transfer Fee received: £375,000 for Andy Walker to Celtic (1987).
Record Transfer Fee paid: £100,000 for Mike Larnach from Newcastle U.

1988–89 LEAGUE RECORD

Match No.	Date	Venue	Opponents	Result	H/T Score	Lg. Pos.	Goalscorers	Attendance
1	Aug 13	A	Hibernian	L 0-1	0-0	—		10,000
2	20	H	Dundee	D 1-1	0-1	8	McBride	3803
3	27	A	Hamilton A	L 0-1	0-0	10		4338
4	Sept 3	H	Rangers	L 0-2	0-2	10		20,112
5	17	A	St Mirren	L 0-1	0-0	10		4045
6	24	H	Dundee U	L 1-2	1-1	10	Kirk	3559
7	28	A	Celtic	L 1-3	1-1	—	Kirk	20,187
8	Oct 1	H	Aberdeen	D 1-1	1-1	10	Farningham	4225
9	8	A	Hearts	D 2-2	0-1	10	Farningham, Paterson	8809
10	12	A	Dundee	D 1-1	0-0	—	Boyd	4161
11	22	H	Hibernian	D 1-1	0-0	9	Cowan	5904
12	29	A	Dundee U	D 1-1	0-0	9	Farningham	6266
13	Nov 1	H	St Mirren	L 1-2	0-1	—	Kirk	3773
14	5	A	Rangers	L 1-2	1-1	9	Russell	35,060
15	12	H	Hamilton A	D 1-1	1-0	9	McAdam	5657
16	19	A	Aberdeen	L 1-2	0-2	9	Russell	10,028
17	26	H	Hearts	W 2-0	1-0	9	Kirk, Cowan	6208
18	Dec 3	H	Celtic	L 1-3	1-2	9	Kirk	16,392
19	10	A	St Mirren	L 1-2	1-0	9	Russell	4496
20	17	H	Dundee	W 1-0	1-0	9	Kirk	4560
21	31	A	Hibernian	L 0-2	0-1	9		9000
22	Jan 3	A	Hamilton A	W 2-0	0-0	—	Kirk, Russell	5704
23	7	H	Rangers	W 2-1	0-1	9	Wishart, Gough (og)	19,275
24	14	A	Hearts	D 0-0	0-0	9		13,283
25	21	H	Aberdeen	L 0-2	0-2	9		5906
26	Feb 11	A	Celtic	W 2-1	1-0	9	Gahagan, Russell	21,445
27	Mar 11	H	Hibernian	D 0-0	0-0	8		5027
28	14	H	Dundee U	L 1-2	0-1	—	O'Neill (pen)	3545
29	25	A	Dundee	L 1-2	1-1	9	Kirk	3718
30	Apr 1	H	Hamilton A	W 1-0	0-0	9	Kirk	4683
31	8	A	Rangers	L 0-1	0-0	9		37,782
32	12	H	Celtic	D 2-2	1-0	—	Gahagan, Arnott	10,507
33	22	A	Dundee U	D 1-1	0-0	9	Kirk	6301
34	29	H	St Mirren	W 4-0	2-0	9	Kirk 4 (1 pen)	2702
35	May 6	A	Aberdeen	D 0-0	0-0	9		6500
36	13	H	Hearts	D 1-1	0-0	9	O'Neill (pen)	4587

Final League Position: 9

GOALSCORERS

League: (35): Kirk 14 (1 pen), Russell 5, Farningham 3, Cowan 2, Gahagan 2, O'Neill 2 (2 pens), Arnott 1, Boyd 1, McAdam 1, McBride 1, Paterson 1, Wishart 1, own goal 1.
League Cup: (2): Farningham 1, Kirk 1 (pen).
Scottish Cup: (4): Kirk 3 (1 pen), Bryce 1.

Record Victory: 12-1 v Dundee U, Division II; 23 Jan, 1954.
Record Defeat: 0-8 v Aberdeen, Premier Division; 26 Mar, 1979.
Most Capped Player: George Stevenson, 12, Scotland.
Most League Appearances: Bobby Ferrier.
Most League Goals in Season (Individual): 52: Willie McFadyen, Division I; 1931–32.
Most Goals Overall (Individual): 283: Hugh Ferguson, 1916–25.

Honours
League Champions: Division I 1931–32. First Division 1981–82, 1984–85. Division II 1953–54, 1968–69; *Runners-up:* Division I 1926–27, 1929–30, 1932–33, 1933–34. Division II 1894–95, 1902–03.
Scottish Cup: 1952; *Runners-up:* 1931, 1933, 1939, 1951.
League Cup: 1950–51; *Runners-up:* 1954–55.
Club colours: Shirt: Amber with claret band. Shorts: Claret. Stockings: Amber.

Duncan, C	Wishart, F	Philliben, J	Paterson, C	McCart, C	Boyd, T	Farningham, R	Russell, R	Smith, P	Kirk, S	Kinnaird, P	Cowan, S	McKeown, K	McBride, M	McAdam, T	Arnott, D	Shanks, D	Mair, G	Griffin, J	Gahagan, J	MacCabe, D	Bryce, S	Kennedy, A	O'Neill, C	Dolan, J	Maxwell, A	*Match No.*
1	2	3	4	5	6	7	8	9*	10	11	12															1
	2	3	4	5†	6	8	10*	12	14	11	9	1	7													2
1	2†	3	4		6		10	11	8		9*		7	5	12	14										3
1		3*	4		6	7	10	9	8	11				5		12		2								4
1	2	14	4		3	8	10		6	11			7†	5*	12					9						5
1	2	3	4		6*	7	12		10	11	8			5						9						6
1	2	3	4		6	8			10	11	12			5					7*	9						7
1	2	3	4	5	6	7	8†		10	11					14				12	9*						8
1*	2	3	4	5	6	7	8		10	11	12									9						9
	2	3	4	5	6	7			10	11	8	1	12							9*						10
1	2	3	4	5*	6	7	12		10	11	8								14	9†						11
1	2	3	4	5	6	7	8†		10	11*	9				12		14									12
1	2	5	4		3*	7	10		6	11	8				9						12					13
1	2	3			6	7	8*		10	9	12			5			14		11†			4				14
1	2	3	4		12	7	8			11	9			5			10†				14		6*			15
1	2	3	4*		12	7	8				9			5		10†			14	11			6			16
1	2	3	4*		12		8		10	11	9		7	5									6			17
1	2	3†		4	14	8*	12		10	11	9		7	5									6			18
1	2			4	3	12	8†		10	11	9*		7	5									6	14		19
	2	14	4†	6	3	8			10	9			7	5					11*	12					1	20
	2		4	6	3		8		10	11†	14		7*	5					12				9		1	21
	2		4	6	3		7*		10	11	12			5						9			8		1	22
	2		4	6	3		7			11	14		12	5		10†				9*			8		1	23
	2		4	6	3		7		10	11				5						9			8		1	24
	2		4	6	3				10	11*			12	5			7			9			8		1	25
	2		4	6	3		7		10	9†				5			12		11*		14		8		1	26
	2		4	6	3		7		10					5*	12		11				9		8		1	27
	2		4	3	12		8		10*				7	5	9†		11				14		6		1	28
	2		4	6	3		7		10				12	5*			11				9		8		1	29
	2		4	12	3				10				7†	5	14		11				9*		8	6	1	30
	2		4	6	3		7		10				12	5	9				11*				8		1	31
	2		4	6	3		7*		10				12	5	9				11				8		1	32
	2		4	6	3		7		10†					5	9*		14		11		12			8	1	33
	2		4	6	3*		7		10†					5	9		14		11		12			8	1	34
	2		4	6	3*		7		10					5	9				11				8	12	1	35
	2		4	6	3		7		10					5	9		12		11*				8		1	36
17	35	17 + 2s	33	25 + 1s	31 + 5s	17 + 1s	28 + 3s	3 + 1s	32 + 1s	24	12 + 7s	2	10 + 6s	28	8 + 6s	2 + 2s	6 + 6s	1	10 + 4s	12 + 1s	3 + 6s	1	19	3 + 2s	17	

PARTICK THISTLE First Division

Year Formed: 1876. *Ground & Address:* Firhill Park, 90 Firhill Rd, Glasgow G20 7AL. *Telephone:* 041 946 2673.
Ground Capacity: total: 20,600 seated: 3264. *Size of Pitch:* 106yd×72yd.
Chairman: T. Miller Reid. *Secretary:* Campbell Gillan. *Commercial Manager:* James Brown.
Manager: John Lambie. *Assistant Manager:* —. *Physio:* Donnie McKinnon. *Coach:* W. McLaren, W. Simpson.
Managers since 1975: R. Auld; P. Cormack; B. Rooney; R. Auld; D. Johnstone; W. Lamont; J. Lambie.
Club Nickname(s): The Jags. *Previous Grounds:* None.
Record Attendance: 49,838 v Rangers, Division I; 18 Feb, 1922.
Record Transfer Fee received: —.
Record Transfer Fee paid: —.

1988–89 LEAGUE RECORD

Match No.	Date	Venue	Opponents	Result	H/T Score	Lg. Pos.	Goalscorers	Attendance
1	Aug 13	H	Dunfermline Ath	L 1-2	1-1	—	Mitchell	3941
2	20	A	Kilmarnock	W 1-0	0-0	7	McGuire	2760
3	27	A	Clyde	L 0-1	0-1	11		2725
4	Sept 3	H	Morton	L 1-4	1-3	13	McCoy	2367
5	10	A	Forfar Ath	L 2-3	2-0	13	Flood, Kelly	974
6	17	H	Ayr U	D 2-2	1-0	13	Gallagher E (pen), Purdie	2551
7	24	A	Airdrieonians	L 1-5	1-1	14	Mitchell	2200
8	Oct 1	A	St Johnstone	L 1-2	0-1	13	Gallagher E	1961
9	8	H	Clydebank	D 1-1	0-0	13	McCoy	2059
10	15	H	Falkirk	L 1-3	0-1	13	McCoy	3369
11	22	A	Queen of the S	W 4-1	2-0	13	Thomson 2, McCoy, Flood	1000
12	29	H	Meadowbank T	D 1-1	0-1	13	McCoy	1843
13	Nov 5	A	Raith R	L 3-5	1-2	13	McCoy, Kelly, Mitchell	1800
14	12	H	Forfar Ath	L 1-2	1-1	13	Kelly	1849
15	19	A	Ayr U	W 3-1	3-1	13	McCoy 2, Kelly	3158
16	26	H	Airdrieonians	L 0-2	0-2	13		2847
17	Dec 3	H	Kilmarnock	L 0-1	0-1	13		2624
18	10	A	Meadowbank T	W 2-0	1-0	13	Kerr, McCoy (pen)	800
19	17	H	Queen of the S	W 2-1	0-1	13	Kerr (pen), Doherty (og)	1826
20	24	A	Falkirk	W 1-0	0-0	13	Kelly	3500
21	31	A	Morton	L 0-1	0-0	13		2500
22	Jan 3	H	Clyde	D 0-0	0-0	—		2952
23	7	H	Raith R	D 1-1	1-1	13	Flood	1999
24	14	A	Dunfermline Ath	L 2-3	1-2	13	Burns (og), McCoy	5476
25	21	A	Clydebank	L 2-3	2-2	13	Flood 2	2038
26	Feb 8	H	St Johnstone	W 2-0	1-0	—	McCoy 2	2131
27	14	H	Ayr U	W 4-1	1-1	—	Charnley (pen), McCoy 3	1772
28	25	A	Queen of the S	W 4-2	2-1	11	Mitchell, Flood 2, Collins	750
29	Mar 4	A	Morton	D 1-1	0-0	11	Dempsey	2050
30	11	H	Falkirk	W 2-1	1-1	10	Charnley, McCoy	3461
31	18	H	Airdrieonians	W 1-0	0-0	9	Charnley	2793
32	28	A	Clyde	D 0-0	0-0	—		3185
33	Apr 1	H	Dunfermline Ath	D 0-0	0-0	9		5103
34	8	A	St Johnstone	D 1-1	1-1	9	Flood	3788
35	15	H	Meadowbank T	W 2-1	2-0	9	McCoy, Grant	2511
36	22	A	Clydebank	L 2-4	2-1	9	McCoy, Charnley	1989
37	29	A	Kilmarnock	D 0-0	0-0	9		3042
38	May 6	H	Forfar Ath	W 4-1	3-0	8	Gallagher B, McCoy, Mitchell, Dinnie	3033
39	13	A	Raith R	D 1-1	1-0	8	Peebles	1750

Final League Position: 8

GOALSCORERS

League: (57): McCoy 19 (1 pen), Flood 8, Kelly 5, Mitchell 5, Charnley 4 (1 pen), Gallagher E 2 (1 pen), Kerr 2 (1 pen), Thomson 2, Collins 1, Dempsey 1, Dinnie 1, Gallagher B 1, Grant 1, McGuire 1, Peebles 1, Purdie 1, own goals 2.
League Cup: (0).
Scottish Cup: (3): McCoy 2, Mitchell 1.

Record Victory: 16-0 v Royal Albert, Scottish Cup 1st rd; 17 Jan, 1931.
Record Defeat: 0-10 v Queen's Park, Scottish Cup; 3 Dec, 1881.
Most Capped Player: Alan Rough, 51 (53), Scotland.
Most League Appearances: 410: Alan Rough, 1969–82.
Most League Goals in Season (Individual): 41: Alec Hair, Division I; 1926–27.
Most Goals Overall (Individual): —.

Honours
League Champions: First Division 1975–76. Division II 1896–97, 1899–1900, 1970–71; *Runners-up:* Division II 1901–02.
Scottish Cup Winners: 1921; *Runners-up:* 1930.
League Cup Winners: 1971–72; *Runners-up:* 1953–54, 1956–57, 1958–59.
European: *European Cup —. Cup Winners Cup —. UEFA Cup* 6 matches (1963–64 *Fairs Cup*; 1972–73).
Club colours: Shirts: Amber with red shoulders and sleeves. Shorts: Red with amber stripe. Stockings: Red.

MacLean, A	Dinnie, A	Workman, J	Purdie, B	McGhie, W	Dempsey, J	Kelly, P	Docherty, P	Flood, J	Mitchell J,	Thomson, I	McGinley, J	Grant, A	McGuire, W	Law, R	McCoy, G	Spittal, J	Brough, J	Gallagher, E	McDonald, I	Kerr, J	Collins, G	Elliott, T	Maher, P	Gallagher, B	Abercromby, W	Charnley, J	Murdoch, A	Peebles, G	McGee, B	*Match No.*
1	2	3	4	5*	6	7†	8	9	10	11	14																			1
1	2†	3	4	5	6		11	9	8*	12	14	7	10																	2
1		3	4	5	6	14	2*	9†	11	12			7	8	10															3
1		3	4		5	9*	6	12		11		8†	7	2	10	14														4
		14	4	5	6	7†	8	9	3*	11			12	2	10		1													5
			4	5	6†	7	8		3	11		12		2	10	14	1	9*												6
		14	4		5	12	6	11	8†	10		7*		3		2	1	9												7
1		3	4		5	7		12		11	8			6		2		9	10*											8
1	2	3		5	6	7		9*	8	11†	14	12		4	10															9
1	2	3		5	4	9			6	11	12	7*		8	10															10
1	2				12	7*	4	9†	8	11				6	10					3	5	14								11
1	2					7	4	9*	8	11				6	10					3	5	12								12
1	2				12	7	4	9	8	11				6*	10					3	5									13
	2				4	7	5	9	6	11*				8†	10		1		12	3			14							14
	2				5	9	4	7	8	11				6	10		1			3										15
	2				5	9	4	7	8	11*				6	10		1			3				12						16
	2				14	10	4	7	11*					8	12		1			3†	5			9	6					17
	2				5†	12	4	7	11	14				8	10		1			3	6			9*						18
	2					12	4	7	11					8	10		1			3	5			9	6*					19
	2	3			5	14	4	7	11†	12					10		1			8				9	6*					20
	2	3†			5	12	4	7	11	14					10		1			8				9	6*					21
	2	3		5		11*	4	7	8			12					1			10				9	6					22
	2			6	5	12	4	7	10					8			1			3				9*		11				23
	2						4	7	8					10	12		1			3	5			9	6*	11				24
	2†						4	7	10					3	12					14	5			9*	6	11	1	8		25
	2	3			5			9	7					8	10		1				6					11		4		26
	2				5			9	7					4	10		1			3	6					11		8		27
	2				5			9	7			12		4	10†					3	6					11	1	8*	14	28
	2				5			9	7					4	10					3	6					11	1	8		29
	2				5			9	7					4	10					3	6					11	1	8		30
	2				5			9	7					4	10					3	6					11	1	8		31
	2				5			9	7†			12		4	10*					3	6				14	11	1	8		32
	2*				5			9		12				4	10					3	6				7	11	1	8		33
					5			9	4			7		2	10					3	6					11	1	8		34
					5			9	4	12		7		2	10						6					11	1	8	3*	35
	2				5			9	8	11		7		3	10						6					4	1			36
	2				5			8*	7	11		9		4	10					3	6			12			1			37
	2				5				7	12				8	10				11*	3	6			9			1		4	38
	2				12					6		14			10				7	4	5			9	11*		1	8†	3	39
10	31	11 + 2s	8	9	30 + 4s	15 + 7s	22	33 + 2s	35	17 + 8s	1 + 4s	8 + 6s	3 + 1s	33	30 + 3s	2 + 2s	16	3	3 + 1s	25 + 1s	22	— + 2s	— + 1s	11 + 2s	9 + 1s	14	13	12	3 + 1s	

Also played: Watson K – Match 1 (12).

QUEEN OF THE SOUTH Second Division

Year Formed: 1919. *Ground & Address:* Palmerston Park, Terregles St, Dumfries DG2 9BA. *Telephone:* 0387 54853.
Ground Capacity: total: 13,000 seated: 1300. *Size of Pitch:* 125yd×72yd.
Chairman: W. J. Harkness C.B.E.. *Secretary:* Mrs Doreen Alcorn. *Commercial Manager:* J. Anderson.
Manager: William McLaren. *Assistant Manager:* —. *Physio:* —. *Coach:* I. McChesney.
Managers since 1975: M. Jackson; G. Herd; A. Busby; R. Clark; M. Jackson; D. Wilson; W. McLaren.
Club Nickname(s): The Doonhamers. *Previous Grounds:* None.
Record Attendance: 24,500 v Hearts, Scottish Cup 3rd rd; 23 Feb, 1952.
Record Transfer Fee received: —.
Record Transfer Fee paid: —.

1988–89 LEAGUE RECORD

Match No.	Date	Venue	Opponents	Result	H/T Score	Lg. Pos.	Goalscorers	Attendance
1	Aug 13	H	Kilmarnock	D 2-2	0-0	—	Moore, Robertson	1587
2	20	A	Raith R	L 1-2	1-1	11	Moore (pen)	1700
3	27	A	Airdrieonians	L 0-3	0-2	14		1100
4	Sept 3	H	Meadowbank T	L 0-1	0-1	14		1000
5	10	A	Dunfermline Ath	L 2-4	1-3	14	Hughes, Doherty	4883
6	17	H	Forfar Ath	W 2-1	1-1	14	Moore, Doherty	867
7	24	A	Morton	L 0-1	0-1	13		1500
8	Oct 1	H	Falkirk	L 0-3	0-0	14		1397
9	8	A	Ayr U	D 1-1	1-1	14	Moore	3019
10	15	A	St Johnstone	L 1-3	0-2	14	Fraser	1689
11	22	H	Partick T	L 1-4	0-2	14	Mills	1000
12	29	H	Clydebank	L 0-3	0-1	14		900
13	Nov 5	A	Clyde	L 1-3	1-1	14	Bain	600
14	12	H	Dunfermline Ath	D 0-0	0-0	14		1340
15	19	A	Forfar Ath	D 2-2	0-0	14	Reid 2 (1 pen)	558
16	26	H	Morton	L 2-3	1-1	14	Olabode 2	850
17	Dec 3	H	Raith R	L 0-1	0-1	14		600
18	10	A	Clydebank	L 2-4	1-2	14	Reid (pen), Mills	752
19	17	A	Partick T	L 1-2	1-0	14	Fraser	1826
20	24	H	St Johnstone	D 1-1	1-0	14	Hetherington	1200
21	31	A	Meadowbank T	W 2-1	2-1	14	Reid (pen), Cook	367
22	Jan 3	H	Airdrieonians	L 2-4	1-2	—	Cook, Gamble	1350
23	7	H	Clyde	D 3-3	1-1	14	Reid (pen), Telfer, Mills	900
24	14	A	Kilmarnock	L 1-2	1-1	14	Fraser	2264
25	21	H	Ayr U	L 0-2	0-0	14		1240
26	Feb 7	A	Falkirk	L 0-2	0-1	—		2900
27	14	A	Clydebank	L 0-3	0-1	—		500
28	25	H	Partick T	L 2-4	1-2	14	Sloan, Cook	750
29	Mar 4	A	Raith R	L 1-4	0-3	14	McGuire	1525
30	11	H	Forfar Ath	D 2-2	1-0	14	Gamble, Sloan	484
31	21	H	Dunfermline Ath	L 0-2	0-2	—		1550
32	25	A	St Johnstone	L 1-3	0-3	14	Telfer	1575
33	Apr 1	A	Airdrieonians	L 0-3	0-2	14		900
34	8	H	Morton	D 1-1	0-1	14	Fraser (pen)	500
35	15	H	Ayr U	L 1-2	1-1	14	Sloan	600
36	22	A	Clyde	L 1-2	1-1	14	Fraser	600
37	29	H	Meadowbank T	L 1-2	1-0	14	Fraser (pen)	420
38	May 6	A	Falkirk	L 1-7	1-3	14	Fraser	3000
39	13	H	Kilmarnock	L 0-6	0-1	14		1200

Final League Position: 14

GOALSCORERS

League: (38): Fraser 7 (2 pens), Reid 5 (4 pens), Moore 4 (1 pen), Cook 3, Mills 3, Sloan 3, Doherty 2, Gamble 2, Olabode 2, Telfer 2, Bain 1, Hetherington 1, Hughes 1, McGuire 1, Robertson 1.
League Cup: (1): Doherty 1.
Scottish Cup: (5): McGuire 2, Hetherington 1, McDonald 1, Sloan 1.

Record Victory: 11-1 v Stranraer, Scottish Cup 1st rd; 16 Jan, 1932.
Record Defeat: 2-10 v Dundee, Division I; 1 Dec, 1962.
Most Capped Player: Billy Houliston, 3, Scotland.
Most League Appearances: Allan Ball; 1962–83.
Most League Goals in Season (Individual): 33: Jimmy Gray, Division II; 1927–28.
Most Goals Overall (Individual): —.

Honours
League Champions: Division II 1950–51; *Runners-up:* Division II 1932–33, 1961–62, 1974–75. Second Division 1980–81, 1985–86.
Scottish Cup:—.
League Cup:—.
Club colours: Shirt: Royal blue. Shorts: White. Stockings: Royal blue with white tops.

Cunningham, W	Sinclair, J	Gray, W	Johnston, G	Mackin, A	Mills, D	Robertson, S	Hughes, J	Moore, S	Hetherington, K	Telfer, G	Shanks, M	Doherty, J	Sim, W	Ferguson, R	Docherty, D	Reid, W	Fraser, G	Martin, D	Bain, A	Olabode, J	Cook, D	McGuire, J	McDonald, T	Gamble, J	Sloan, T	Holland, B	McQueen, A	McCulloch, J	Stewart, R	Match No.
1	2	3	4	5	6	7	8	9	10	11																				1
1	2		12	5	6	7*	8	9	10	14	4	11†	3																	2
	2		12	5	6		8	9	10	14	3	11†		1	4*	7														3
	3	14	2		5	6†	9		10	12	8*	11		1	4	7														4
	3	12	2	5*	6		8		10	14	11	9		1	4†	7														5
	6	3	2		5			9	10	14	8†	11	12	1	4*	7														6
	6	3*	2		5		8	9	10	12		11		1		7	4													7
	6		2				8	9	10	12		11	3	1		7	4													8
	6		2		5	8*		9	10		12	11	3	1		7	4													9
	6		2		5	14		9	10	12	8†	11*	3	1		7	4													10
	8†	3	2	5	6			9	10*	14		12		1		7	4	11												11
	3		2	5	6*			9	10			11	12	1	14	7	4	8†												12
			2	5	6		8	9		12	10			1		7	4*	3	11											13
	6		2	5					10	11*	8	12	3	1		7	4†		9											14
	6		2	5					11	10	8		3	1		7	4*		9											15
	6		2	5				12	10		8		3	1		7	4		11	9*										16
	3	14		5	4			11†	10	12	2			1	8	6	7			9†										17
	12		2		5			11	10		6*	14	3	1		7	4†		8	9										18
		3	2		5		7		10			12		1			4*		8		9	11								19
		5							10	6*	3	4		1		7	8		2		9	11								20
		5							10		2	12		1		7	6*		8		9	11	3	4						21
		5			14				10		2	12		1		7	6		8*		9	11†	3	4						22
		5			14				10	12	2		8*	1		7	6				9	11	3†	4						23
		5							10		2			1		7	6		4		9	11	3	12	8*					24
			12		5				10	8*	2			1		7	6		9			11	3							25
		3	14						10†	11*	2		12	1		7	4		9				6	5	8					26
		4	2†						10	12			3			7*	6				9		11	5	8	1	14			27
			2		5				10	14	7		6			12			4*		9	11	3†		8	1				28
			2		5			4†	10	8							6				9	11	3*	12	7	1	14			29
1			2		4			14		7	12		3				10				9*	11	6	5†	8					30
			2		5						8		3	1			6				9*	11		4	12			7	10	31
					8			10		14	2		3	1			6					11	5*	7	12			4	9†	32
					4			10†			14		3	1	2		7				9*	11		5	8			6	12	33
1			2		5			12	10				7		4		6					11*	3†		8			14	9	34
1			2		5			11	10				7		4		6						3*		8			12	9	35
			2		5				10		3		7	1	4		6					9			8				11	36
1					5						3*		8		2		6		4		12	11			9			7	10	37
1			12		6					2	3		4		7†		9*		8				14	5	11				10	38
1					4					12	2		3		7		6				10		8	5	11				9*	39
8	16 + 1s	12 + 3s	24 + 5s	11	28 + 2s	4 + 1s	9	17 + 3s	31	9 + 16s	26 + 3s	11 + 6s	21 + 3s	28	12 + 1s	24 + 1s	32	3	15	3	13 + 1s	16	14 + 1s	11 + 2s	13 + 2s	3	— + 2s	4 + 2s	8 + 1s	

Also played: Dawson L – Match 8 (5*), 14 (14), 20 (12); Clark G – Match 15 (12); McBride J – Match 19 (6), 25 (4)

QUEEN'S PARK Second Division

Year Formed: 1867. *Ground & Address:* Hampden Park, Mount Florida, Glasgow G42 9BA.
Ground Capacity: total: 74,730 seated: 10,000. *Size of Pitch:* 115yd×75yd.
Chairman: W. G. N. Geddes C.B.E. (President). *Secretary:* James C. Rutherford. *Commercial Manager:* —.
Manager: —. *Assistant Manager:* —. *Physio:* A. P. McEwan. *Coach:* Edward Hunter.
Managers since 1975: —.
Club Nickname(s): The Spiders. *Previous Grounds:* 1st Hampden (Titwood Park), 2nd Hampden, 3rd Hampden.
Record Attendance: 95,772 v Rangers, Scottish Cup; 18 Jan, 1930.
Record for ground: 149,547, Scotland v England, 1937.
Record Transfer Fee received: —.
Record Transfer Fee paid: —.

1988–89 LEAGUE RECORD

Match No.	Date	Venue	Opponents	Result	H/T Score	Lg. Pos.	Goalscorers	Attendance
1	Aug 13	H	Berwick R	W 2-0	1-0	—	Rodden, Caven	437
2	20	A	East Stirling	L 1-2	1-0	5	Rodden	250
3	27	A	Dumbarton	W 3-0	2-0	2	Crooks 2, Armstrong	500
4	Sept 3	H	Montrose	W 2-0	2-0	1	Caven, McNamee	541
5	10	A	Stirling Albion	L 2-3	0-1	5	Rodden, Lennox (pen)	1208
6	17	H	East Fife	W 1-0	0-0	3	Rodden	577
7	24	A	Albion R	D 1-1	0-0	2	Lennox (pen)	571
8	Oct 1	H	Brechin C	D 1-1	0-0	2	O'Brien	550
9	8	A	Stenhousemuir	D 0-0	0-0	2		400
10	15	H	Cowdenbeath	D 1-1	1-0	4	Hendry	730
11	22	A	Stranraer	L 1-3	1-0	7	Boyle (pen)	800
12	29	H	Alloa	L 0-2	0-1	8		610
13	Nov 5	A	Arbroath	D 2-2	0-0	9	Hendry, Armstrong	624
14	12	H	East Stirling	D 0-0	0-0	8		470
15	19	A	Berwick R	W 2-0	1-0	7	Hendry, McNamee	275
16	26	H	Stirling Albion	W 2-0	0-0	5	McLaughlin, Brown	710
17	Dec 10	A	East Fife	D 2-2	1-0	5	Crooks, Brown	650
18	17	H	Albion R	D 0-0	0-0	6		820
19	24	H	Arbroath	W 2-0	1-0	5	Crooks, O'Brien	434
20	31	A	Alloa	D 0-0	0-0	5		633
21	Jan 3	H	Dumbarton	W 2-1	1-1	—	Crooks, Caven	832
22	14	A	Montrose	D 1-1	0-1	2	Hendry	350
23	21	A	Cowdenbeath	D 2-2	1-1	2	Boyle (pen), O'Brien	300
24	Feb 4	H	Stenhousemuir	D 1-1	1-0	3	McLean P	705
25	7	H	Stranraer	W 4-3	2-1	—	Boyle (pen), Elliot, Crooks 2	623
26	11	A	Brechin C	L 0-2	0-2	3		500
27	18	H	Albion R	W 3-2	2-0	3	McNamee, O'Brien, Crooks	947
28	27	A	Stirling Albion	D 0-0	0-0	—		419
29	Mar 4	H	Montrose	D 2-2	0-1	2	Elliot, McLean P	685
30	11	A	Dumbarton	L 0-1	0-1	3		600
31	18	A	Cowdenbeath	L 1-3	0-1	4	Rodden	250
32	25	H	Arbroath	D 1-1	0-1	3	Hendry	523
33	Apr 1	A	Berwick R	D 1-1	0-1	5	Boyle	681
34	8	H	Brechin C	L 1-2	1-2	6	Hendry	559
35	15	A	Stranraer	D 3-3	2-2	6	Hendry 2, Caven	750
36	22	H	East Fife	L 1-2	1-0	7	Hendry	674
37	29	A	East Stirling	L 1-2	0-1	7	McEntegart (pen)	300
38	May 6	H	Alloa	L 0-2	0-2	7		757
39	13	A	Stenhousemuir	D 1-1	1-0	7	Caven	386

Final League Position: 7

GOALSCORERS

League: (50): Hendry 9, Crooks 8, Caven 5, Rodden 5, Boyle 4 (3 pens), O'Brien 4, McNamee 3, Armstrong 2, Brown 2, Elliot 2, Lennox (2 pens), McLean P 2, McEntegart 1 (pen), McLaughlin 1.
League Cup: (1): Lennox 1.
Scottish Cup: (5): Brown 2, Elliot 2, McLaughlin 1.

Record Victory: 16-0 v St Peters, Scottish Cup 1st rd; 29 Aug, 1885.
Record Defeat: 0-9 v Motherwell, Division I; 26 Apr, 1930.
Most Capped Player: Walter Arnott, 14, Scotland.
Most League Appearances: 473: J. B. McAlpine.
Most League Goals in Season (Individual): 30: William Martin, Division 1; 1937–38.
Most Goals Overall (Individual): 163: J. B. McAlpine.

Honours
League Champions: Division II 1922–23. B Division 1955–56. Second Division 1980–81.
Scottish Cup Winners: 1874, 1875, 1876, 1880, 1881, 1882, 1884, 1886, 1890, 1893; *Runners-up:* 1892, 1900.
League Cup:—.
FA Cup runners-up: 1884, 1885
Club colours: Shirt: White and black hoops. Shorts: White. Stockings: White with black hoops.

Monaghan, M	Boyle, J	McLaughlin, P	McNamee, P	McLean, S	Lennox, G	McLean, P	Morton, C	Rodden, J	Caven, R	Crooks, G	Hendry, M	Armstrong, P	Elder, G	McEntegart, S	O'Brien, P	Brown, I	Elliot, D	Jack, S	Flannigan, M	McGregor, S	*Match No.*
1	2	3	4	5	6	7	8	9	10	11											1
1	2	3	4	5	6	7	8*	9	10	11		12									2
1	2	3*	4		6†	12	14	9	7	11	10	8	5								3
1	2	3	4		6*	12		9	7	11	10	8	5								4
1	2	3	4		6	12		9	7*	11	10	8	5								5
1	2	3	4		6*	7	12	9		11	10†	8	5	14							6
1	2		4		6	7	3	9		11	10*	8†	5	14	12						7
1	2	3	4		6	7	12	9*		11		8	5		10						8
1	2	3	4		6	7		11		12	10	8	5		9*						9
1	2	3	4		12	7	14	9		11†	10*	8	5		6						10
1	2	3	4		14	6		11*	7	12	10	8†	5		9						11
1	2	3	4		14	6		11*	7	12	10†	8	5		9						12
1	2	3	4		6*	7		9	10	11†	14	8	5		12						13
1	2	3	4			6	12	9†	7	11	10*	8	5		14						14
1	2	3	4†			6		12	7	11	10	8	5		9*	14					15
1	2	3	4			6		9	7	11	10*	8	5			12					16
1	2	3			6†	4	8	9*	7	11	10		5		12	14					17
1	2	3		4	6*	7	8	9†	10	11			5		12	14					18
1	2	3			6	4	8		7	11	10*		5		12		9				19
1	2	3			6	4	8†		7	11	10*	14	5		12		9				20
1	2	3			6	4	8†		7*	11		14	5		12	10	9				21
1	2	3	5		12	4			7	11	6	8				10	9*				22
1	2	3	5			4	14		7	10	6*	8†			9	11	12				23
1	2	3	4			6			7	11*	10†	8	5		9	14	12				24
1	2	3	4			7	12		10	11		8	5		9*		6				25
1	2	3	4			7	14		10	11†	6	8	5		12		9*				26
1	2		7		9	4	8*	14		11	12	3	5		10		6†				27
1	2		7		9*	4	8	12		11		3	5		10		6				28
1	2					4	8	10*		11	7	3	5		9	12	6				29
1	2	3				4	14	12	7	11†	10*	8	5		9		6				30
1	2				6	4	8*	10	7	11†	14	3	5		9		12				31
1	2	3	4†		6	7		10		11*	14	8	5		9		12				32
1	2	3	4		6	7		12			10	8†	5		11*	14	9				33
1	2	3			7	4	12	14		11*	10	8	5		6		9†				34
1	2	3			8	4		11	7	9	10		5		6						35
1	2	3			7	4			8	11*	10		5		6	9	12				36
1	2	3			6†	7	8*			11	10		4	14	9	12		5			37
1	2	3				4			7	11*	10†	14	5	8	6		12		9		38
1	2	3				4			7		10*	8	5	6†	9		14		11	12	39
39	39	34	25	3	24	36	13	21	27	34	28	28	35	2	22	4	12	1	2	—	
					+	+	+	+		+	+	+		+	+	+	+			+	
					4s	3s	10s	6s		3s	4s	4s		3s	9s	8s	7s			1s	

RAITH ROVERS First Division

Year Formed: 1883. *Ground & Address:* Stark's Park, Pratt St, Kirkcaldy KY1 1SA. *Telephone:* 0592 263514.
Ground Capacity: total: 9500 seated: 3075. *Size of Pitch:* 113yd×67yd.
Chairman: John Urquhart. *Secretary:* P. J. Campsie. *Commercial Manager:* Alex Kilgour.
Manager: Frank Connor. *Assistant Manager:* —. *Physio:* David Campbell. *Coach:* Alex Kinninmouth.
Managers since 1975: A. Matthews; R. Paton; W. McLean; G. Wallace; R. Wilson; F. Connor.
Club Nickname(s): Rovers. *Previous Grounds:* Robbie's Park.
Record Attendance: 31,306 v Hearts, Scottish Cup 2nd rd; 7 Feb, 1953.
Record Transfer Fee received: £85,000 for Andy Harrow to Luton T (Oct 1980).
Record Transfer Fee paid: £35,000 for Willie Gibson from Partick Th (Oct 1981).
Record Victory: 10-1 v Coldstream, Scottish Cup 2nd rd; 13 Feb, 1954.

1988–89 LEAGUE RECORD

Match No.	Date	Venue	Opponents	Result		H/T Score	Lg. Pos.	Goalscorers	Attendance
1	Aug 13	A	St Johnstone	L	1-3	1-2	—	Sweeney	2635
2	20	H	Queen of the S	W	2-1	1-1	9	Wright, Mills (og)	1700
3	27	A	Dunfermline Ath	L	1-2	0-1	12	Simpson	5602
4	Sept 3	H	Clyde	D	0-0	0-0	11		1484
5	10	A	Meadowbank T	L	1-2	0-1	12	Murray	1268
6	17	H	Airdrieonians	L	1-2	0-2	12	McStay (pen)	1502
7	24	A	Forfar Ath	L	0-1	0-1	12		816
8	Oct 1	H	Ayr U	D	0-0	0-0	11		2000
9	8	A	Morton	W	1-0	0-0	11	Simpson	1422
10	15	H	Clydebank	L	1-3	0-0	12	McStay (pen)	1655
11	22	A	Kilmarnock	D	1-1	1-1	12	Gibson	2102
12	29	A	Falkirk	L	1-3	1-2	12	Gibson	3000
13	Nov 5	H	Partick T	W	5-3	2-1	11	Ferguson I 2, Gibson, Fraser 2	1800
14	12	H	Meadowbank T	W	1-0	0-0	11	Ferguson I	1495
15	19	A	Airdrieonians	L	1-3	0-2	11	Murray	2000
16	26	H	Forfar Ath	W	2-1	1-0	10	Dalziel, Logan	1247
17	Dec 3	A	Queen of the S	W	1-0	1-0	9	Logan	600
18	10	H	Falkirk	L	1-3	0-2	10	Gibson	3000
19	17	H	Kilmarnock	D	0-0	0-0	11		1436
20	24	A	Clydebank	L	1-3	1-2	10	Logan	1143
21	31	A	Clyde	W	1-0	1-0	9	Dalziel	720
22	Jan 3	H	Dunfermline Ath	L	1-3	1-1	—	Dalziel	8981
23	7	A	Partick T	D	1-1	1-1	10	Strachan	1999
24	14	H	St Johnstone	D	1-1	1-1	10	McStay (pen)	4500
25	21	H	Morton	W	1-0	0-0	8	Ferguson I	1772
26	Feb 4	A	Ayr U	D	1-1	1-0	9	Dalziel	2375
27	11	A	Meadowbank T	W	3-1	2-0	8	Dalziel 2, Logan	900
28	Mar 1	H	Airdrieonians	D	1-1	0-0	—	Logan	1683
29	4	H	Queen of the S	W	4-1	3-0	7	Brash 2, Logan, Sweeney	1525
30	11	A	Dunfermline Ath	W	1-0	0-0	7	Dalziel	6814
31	25	A	Ayr U	D	2-2	1-2	8	Dalziel, McStay (pen)	2774
32	Apr 1	H	Clyde	W	2-0	1-0	7	Dalziel, McStay (pen)	1500
33	5	H	St Johnstone	L	0-2	0-1	—		1550
34	8	A	Falkirk	L	0-3	0-2	8		3600
35	15	A	Kilmarnock	W	2-1	0-1	7	Simpson, Dalziel	2216
36	22	H	Forfar Ath	L	2-3	1-1	8	Gibson, Dalziel	1587
37	29	H	Clydebank	W	3-0	1-0	7	Nelson, Coyle, Fraser (pen)	1032
38	May 6	A	Morton	W	1-0	1-0	7	Nelson	1200
39	13	H	Partick T	D	1-1	0-1	7	Marshall	1750

Final League Position: 7

GOALSCORERS

League: (50): Dalziel 11, Logan 6, Gibson 5, McStay 5 (5 pens), Ferguson I 4, Fraser 3 (1 pen), Simpson 3, Brash 2, Murray 2, Nelson 2, Sweeney 2, Coyle 1, Marshall 1, Strachan 1, Wright 1, own goal 1.
League Cup: (1): Dalziel 1 (pen).
Scottish Cup: (1): Dalziel 1.

Record Defeat: 2-11 v Morton, Division II; 18 Mar, 1936.
Most Capped Player: Dave Morris, 6, Scotland.
Most League Appearances: 387: Donald Urquhart.
Most League Goals in Season (Individual): 38: Norman Haywood, Division II; 1937–38.
Most Goals Overall (Individual): —.

Honours
League Champions: Division II 1907–08, 1909–10 (shared), 1937–38, 1948–49; *Runners-up:* Division II 1908–09, 1926–27, 1966–67. Second Division 1975–76, 1977–78, 1986–87.
Scottish Runners-up: 1913.
League Cup Runners-up: 1948–49.
Club colours: Shirt: Navy with white pinstripe front, plain navy back, white sleeves. Shorts: White shadow stripe with two navy stripes on sides. Stockings: Red.

Arthur, G	McStay, J	Murray, D	Coyle, R	Dennis, S	Gibson, I	Simpson, S	Wright, J	Ferguson, I	Dalziel, G	Sweeney, P	Spence, W	Strachan, A	Archibald, E	Logan, A	Romaines, S	Ferguson, E	Buchanan, N	Fraser, C	Brash, A	Marshall, J	Glennie, R	Nelson, M	Burn, P	Match No.
1	2	3	4	5	6	7	8	9*	10	11	12													1
1	2	3	4	5	6	7	8†	9*	10	11	12		14											2
1	8	3	4	5	6	7		9	10*	11			2	12										3
1	2	3	4		6	7†	8	9*	10	11		14	5	12										4
1	2	3	4		6	7			10*	11			5	12	8	9								5
1	11	3	4	5	6	7	14		10				2†	12	8	9*								6
1	2	3	4		6		8†		10			11	5	9*	7	12	14							7
1	2	3	6			7			10	11*		12			8	9		4	5					8
1	2	3			6	7			10	11					8	9		4	5					9
1	2	3	6			7	12		10†	11				14	8	9		4*	5					10
1	2	3	8†		6	7		9*	12	11				10				4	5	14				11
1	2	3	8		6	7		9	12	11				10*				4	5†	14				12
1	2	3	8		6	14		9	10*	11				12				4	5	7†				13
1	2	3	8		6	12		9	10	11					14			4	5*	7†				14
1	2	3	5		6	7		9	10	11								4		8				15
1	2	3	10	5	6	7		9†	8*	11				14	12			4						16
1	2	3		5	6	7*			8†	11				9	10	14		4		12				17
1	2	3		5	6	12		9†	8	11				14	10*			4		7				18
1	2	3	10	5	6	7			8	11*				9	12			4						19
1	2	3	10		6	14				11				8	7*	9†		4	5	12				20
1	2	3	10		6	7†			8	11				9*	12			4	5	14				21
1	2	3	10		6			14	8†	11				9	12			4*	5	7				22
1	2	3	4		6		14	12	8†	10		11		9*	7				5					23
1	2	3	4		6			12	8	11		9*			10					7	5			24
1	2	3	4		6	12	14	9†		11		10*			8					7	5			25
1	2	3	10		6	7*		9	8	11†				12	14			4			5			26
1	2	3	10		6			7	8	11*		14		9†	12			4			5			27
1			10		6	7*		12	8	3				9				4	5	11	2			28
1		3	10		6*	7†		14	8	11				9				4	5	12	2			29
1	2	3	10		6	7*		12	8	11				9				4			5			30
1	2	3	10		6	7†		14	8					9	12					4*	5	11		31
1	2	3	10		6	7†		14	8					9	12					4*	5	11		32
1	2	3	10		6	7*		12	8					9	4						5	11		33
1	2	3	10	5	6	11†		9	8			14			7*						4	12		34
1	2	3	10		6	7		9*	8									4		12	5	11		35
1	2	3	10		6	7*		9	8						14			4		12	5	11†		36
1	2	3	10		6	7*		9	8									4			5	11	12	37
1	4	3	10	12	6	7†		9									2			14	5*	11	8	38
1	2	3	4		6	7			10*						12					9	5	11	8	39
39	37	38	36	9 + 1s	37	29 + 5s	4 + 4s	19 + 9s	34 + 2s	28	— + 2s	4 + 4s	5 + 1s	16 + 9s	14 + 11s	6 + 2s	1 + 1s	23	13	11 + 9s	16	8 + 1s	2 + 1s	

RANGERS — Premier Division

Year Formed: 1873. *Ground & Address:* Ibrox Stadium, Edminston Drive, Glasgow G51 2XD. *Telephone:* 041 427 5232/041 427 1117 (Information Service).
Ground Capacity: total: 44,500 seated: 36,500. *Size of Pitch:* 115yd×75yd.
Chairman: David S. Holmes. *Secretary:* R. C. Ogilvie. *Commercial Manager:* Bob Reilly.
Manager: Graeme Souness. *Assistant Manager:* Walter Smith. *Physio:* Phil Boersma. *Coach:* Phil Boersma, Peter McCloy.
Managers since 1975: Jock Wallace; John Greig; Jock Wallace; Graeme Souness.
Club Nickname(s): The Gers. *Previous Grounds:* None.
Record Attendance: 118,567 v Celtic, Division I; 2 Jan, 1939.
Record Transfer Fee received: £580,000 for Robert Fleck to Norwich C (Dec. 1987).
Record Transfer Fee paid: £1,100,000 for Richard Gough from Tottenham H (Oct 1987).
Record Victory: 14-2 v Blairgowrie, Scottish Cup 1st rd; 20 Jan, 1934.
Record Defeat: 2-10 v Airdrieonians, 1886.
Most Capped Player: George Young, 53, Scotland.

1988–89 LEAGUE RECORD

Match No.	Date		Venue	Opponents	Result		H/T Score	Lg. Pos.	Goalscorers	Attendance
1	Aug	13	A	Hamilton A	W	2-0	1-0	—	Stevens, McCoist	10,500
2		20	H	Hibernian	D	0-0	0-0	2		41,955
3		27	H	Celtic	W	5-1	2-1	1	McCoist, Wilkins, Drinkell 2, Walters	42,858
4	Sept	3	A	Motherwell	W	2-0	2-0	1	Drinkell, Durrant	20,112
5		17	A	Hearts	W	2-1	0-0	1	Durrant (pen), Nisbet	25,401
6		24	H	St Mirren	W	2-1	0-1	1	Cooper D (pen), Walters	35,523
7		27	A	Dundee U	W	1-0	0-0	—	Ferguson I	20,071
8	Oct	1	H	Dundee	W	2-0	1-0	1	Drinkell, Walters	40,768
9		8	A	Aberdeen	L	1-2	1-0	1	Cooper N	22,370
10		12	A	Hibernian	W	1-0	1-0	—	McCoist	25,000
11		29	A	St Mirren	D	1-1	0-0	1	Gray	20,490
12	Nov	1	H	Hearts	W	3-0	0-0	—	Gough, Walters (pen), Gray	36,505
13		5	H	Motherwell	W	2-1	1-1	1	Brown, Drinkell	35,060
14		12	A	Celtic	L	1-3	1-3	1	Walters (pen)	60,113
15		16	H	Hamilton A	W	3-1	1-1	—	Gray, Ferguson I, Drinkell	33,864
16		19	A	Dundee	D	0-0	0-0	1		16,514
17		26	H	Aberdeen	W	1-0	1-0	1	Gough	42,239
18	Dec	3	H	Dundee U	L	0-1	0-0	1		39,123
19		10	A	Hearts	L	0-2	0-1	1		26,424
20		17	H	Hibernian	W	1-0	0-0	1	McCall	36,472
21		31	A	Hamilton A	W	1-0	0-0	1	Ferguson D	10,500
22	Jan	3	H	Celtic	W	4-1	3-1	—	Butcher, Walters 2 (1 pen), Gough	42,515
23		7	A	Motherwell	L	1-2	1-0	1	Drinkell	19,275
24		14	A	Aberdeen	W	2-1	2-1	1	Ferguson D, Munro	22,000
25		21	H	Dundee	W	3-1	1-1	1	Ferguson I, Butcher, McCoist	43,202
26	Feb	11	A	Dundee U	D	1-1	1-0	1	Munro	22,019
27		25	H	St Mirren	W	3-1	1-1	1	Ferguson I, McCoist, Walters	39,021
28	Mar	11	H	Hamilton A	W	3-0	0-0	1	Ferguson I, Sterland, Gough	34,112
29		25	A	Hibernian	W	1-0	1-0	1	Drinkell	22,000
30	Apr	1	A	Celtic	W	2-1	2-0	1	Drinkell, McCoist	60,800
31		8	H	Motherwell	W	1-0	0-0	1	McCoist	37,782
32		22	A	St Mirren	W	2-0	1-0	1	Ferguson I, McCoist	22,096
33		29	H	Hearts	W	4-0	2-0	1	Sterland 2, Drinkell 2	42,856
34	May	2	H	Dundee U	W	2-0	2-0	—	Drinkell, McCoist	39,058
35		6	A	Dundee	W	2-1	0-1	1	Gray 2	14,889
36		13	H	Aberdeen	L	0-3	0-1	1		42,480

Final League Position: 1

GOALSCORERS

League: (62): Drinkell 12, McCoist 9, Walters 8 (3 pens), Ferguson I 6, Gray 5, Gough 4, Sterland 3, Butcher 2, Durrant 2 (1 pen), Ferguson D 2, Munro 2, Brown 1, Cooper D 1 (pen), Cooper N 1, McCall 1, Nisbet 1, Stevens 1, Wilkins 1.
League Cup: (19): Walters 5, McCoist 4 (2 pens), Drinkell 2, Ferguson I 2, Durrant 1, Ferguson D 1, Gough 1, Nisbet 1, Wilkins 1, own goal 1.
Scottish Cup: (19): Drinkell 5, McCoist 5 (1 pen), Walters 3, Brown 2, Ferguson I 2, Stevens 1, own goal 1.

Most League Appearances: 496: John Greig, 1962–78.
Most League Goals in Season (Individual): 44: Sam English, Division I; 1931–32.
Most Goals Overall (Individual): 233: Bob McPhail; 1927–39.

Honours
League Champions: (38 times) Division I 1890–91 (shared), 1898–99, 1899–1900, 1900–01, 1901–02, 1910–11, 1911–12, 1912–13, 1917–18, 1919–20, 1920–21, 1922–23, 1923–24, 1924–25, 1926–27, 1927–28, 1928–29, 1929–30, 1930–31, 1932–33, 1933–34, 1934–35, 1936–37, 1938–39, 1946–47, 1948–49, 1949–50, 1952–53, 1955–56, 1956–57, 1958–59, 1960–61, 1962–63, 1963–64, 1974–75. Premier Division 1975–76, 1977–78, 1986–87, 1988–89; *Runners-up:* 23 times.
Scottish Cup Winners: (24 times) 1894, 1897, 1898, 1903, 1928, 1930, 1932, 1934, 1935, 1936, 1948, 1949, 1950, 1953, 1960, 1962, 1963, 1964, 1966, 1973, 1976, 1978, 1979, 1981; *Runners-up:* 15 times.
League Cup Winners: (15 times) 1946–47, 1948–49, 1960–61, 1961–62, 1963–64, 1964–65, 1970–71, 1975–76, 1977–78, 1978–79, 1981–82, 1983–84, 1984–85, 1986–87, 1987–88, 1988–89; *Runners-up:* 6 times.
European: *European Cup:* 49 matches (1956–57, 1957–58, 1959–60 semi-finals, 1961–62, 1963–64, 1964–65, 1975–76, 1976–77, 1978–79, 1987–88).
Cup Winners Cup Winners: 1971–72. 50 matches (1960–61 runners-up, 1962–63, 1966–67 runners-up, 1969–70, 1971–72 winners, 1973–74, 1977–78, 1979–80, 1981–82, 1983–84). *UEFA Cup:* 34 matches (1967–68, 1968–69 semi-finals, 1970–71 *Fairs Cup*; 1982–83, 1984–85, 1985–86, 1986–87).
Club colours: Shirt: Royal blue with red and white trim. Shorts: White. Stockings: Red.

Woods, C	Stevens, G	Munro, S	Gough, R	Wilkins, R	Butcher, T	Drinkell, K	Brown, J	McCoist, A	Durrant, I	Walters, M	Ferguson, D	Cooper, D	Souness, G	Ferguson, I	Nisbet, S	Gray, A	Cooper, N	Walker, N	MacDonald, K	McCall, I	McSwegan, S	Cowan, T	Sterland, M	Nicholl, J	Kirkwood, D	Robertson, A	Match No.
1	2	3	4	5	6	7	8*	9†	10	11	12	14															1
1	2		4	5*	6	7	3	9	10†	11	8	14	12														2
1	2		4	5	6	7	3	9	10*	11†		14	12	8													3
1	2		4	5	6	7	3		10	11		9		8													4
1	2		4	5*	6	7†	3		10	11		9	12	8	14												5
1	2		4	5	6		3*		10	11		9	12	8	7†	14											6
1	2	3	4	5	6			9	10	11		12		8	7*												7
1	2	3	4	5	6	7†	10	9*		11		12		8		14											8
1	2	12	4		6	7	3	9	10*	11†		14		8			5										9
1	2		4	5	6	7	3	9		11*		12		8			10										10
1	2	3†	4	5	6	7	11	9*		12				8		14	10										11
1	2		4	5	6	7	3			11				8	9*	12	10										12
1	2		4	5	6	7	3			11	12			8	9†	14	10*										13
1	2		4	5	6	7	3			11	9			8		12	10*										14
	2	3	4	5	6	7				11*		14		8	12	9	10†	1									15
	2	3	4	5	6	7	10					11		8	9			1									16
	2		4	5	6	7	3			11*		9		8			10	1	12								17
	2		4	5	6	7	3					9		8		12	10	1	11*								18
	2		4	5	6	7	3			11		9		8		12		1	10*								19
	2	3	4	5	6	7	9*					11	12	8				1		10							20
	2	3	4	5	6	7					12			8		9†	11*	1		10	14						21
	2	3	4	5*	6	7	10†			11	9			8			12	1		14							22
	2	3	4	5	6	7	10*			11	9			8				1		12							23
	2	3	4	5*	6	7	10			11	9			8			12	1									24
	2	3†		5*	6	7	10	14		11	9			8			12	1						4			25
	2	3	4	5	6	7	10			11	9			8				1									26
1	2	3	4	5*	6			9		10	11†	14		8		12	7										27
1	2		4		6	7		9		10	11			8								3	5				28
1	2	3	4	12	6	7		9		10	11*			8									5				29
1	2	3	4	5	6	7	10*	9		11†		14		8									12				30
1	2	3	4	5	6	7	10*	9		11	12												8				31
1	2		4	5*	6	7	3	9		10	11	14		8†									12				32
1	2	3	4	5*	6	7		9†		10	11	14										12	8				33
1	2	3†	4			7	6	9		11*		14	12									10	8		5		34
1	2	3*	4				6	9				11				7				14		10	8		5†	12	35
1		3	4		6	7	10	9†		11		12		8		14							2			5*	36
24	35	21 + 1s	35	30 + 1s	34	32	29	18 + 1s	8	30 + 1s	12 + 4s	9 + 14s	— + 6s	30	5 + 2s	3 + 10s	11 + 3s	12	2 + 1s	2 + 3s	— + 1s	3 + 1s	7 + 2s	1	2	1 + 1s	

ST JOHNSTONE First Division

Year Formed: 1884. *Ground & Address:* McDiarmid Park, Crieff Road, Perth PH1 2SJ. *Telephone:* 0738 26961.
Ground Capacity: total: 10,169 seated: all. *Size of Pitch:* 115yd×75yd.
Chairman: G. S. Brown. *Secretary:* S. Duff. *Commercial Manager:* —.
Manager: Alex Totten. *Assistant Manager:* Bert Paton. *Physio:* J. Peacock. *Coach:* T. Campbell.
Managers since 1975: J. Stewart, J. Storrie; A. Stuart; A. Rennie; I. Gibson; A. Totten.
Club Nickname(s): Saints. *Previous Grounds:* Recreation Grounds, Muirton Park.
Record Attendance: 29,972 v Dundee, Scottish Cup 2nd rd; 10 Feb, 1952.
Record Transfer Fee received: £400,000 for Ally McCoist to Sunderland (1982).
Record Transfer Fee paid: £50,000 for Derek Addison from Hearts (1982).
Record Victory: 8-1 v Partick Th, League Cup; 16 Aug, 1969.

1988–89 LEAGUE RECORD

Match No.	Date	Venue	Opponents	Result	H/T Score	Lg. Pos.	Goalscorers	Attendance
1	Aug 13	H	Raith R	W 3-1	2-1	—	Watters, Maskrey, McVicar (pen)	2635
2	20	A	Dunfermline Ath	L 0-1	0-1	5		5534
3	27	A	Forfar Ath	D 1-1	0-0	7	Heddle	1321
4	Sept 3	H	Airdrieonians	W 2-1	0-0	5	Jenkins 2	2222
5	10	A	Morton	D 1-1	0-1	4	Watters (pen)	2500
6	17	H	Meadowbank T	D 0-0	0-0	5		1694
7	24	A	Ayr U	L 1-2	0-2	10	Sorbie	3543
8	Oct 1	H	Partick T	W 2-1	1-0	6	McVicar (pen), Spittal (og)	1961
9	8	A	Falkirk	L 1-2	0-0	9	Johnston	3779
10	15	H	Queen of the S	W 3-1	2-0	7	McVicar, Maskrey, Sorbie	1689
11	22	A	Clyde	W 4-2	2-0	5	Jenkins, Grant, Maskrey, Sorbie	1050
12	29	H	Kilmarnock	W 2-0	0-0	3	Jenkins, Maskrey	2328
13	Nov 5	A	Clydebank	L 0-2	0-2	6		1278
14	12	H	Morton	W 4-2	2-0	5	Maskrey, Cherry, Sorbie, Watters	3469
15	19	A	Meadowbank T	D 1-1	0-1	5	Heddle	750
16	26	H	Ayr U	W 2-0	2-0	5	Maskrey, Johnston	2813
17	Dec 3	H	Dunfermline Ath	L 0-1	0-1	6		4146
18	10	A	Kilmarnock	W 3-0	1-0	5	Coyle, Watters, Jenkins	2601
19	17	H	Clyde	D 0-0	0-0	5		1959
20	24	A	Queen of the S	D 1-1	0-1	5	Maskrey	1200
21	31	A	Airdrieonians	L 0-1	0-0	6		2400
22	Jan 2	H	Forfar Ath	W 2-1	1-0	—	Jenkins, Cherry	1400
23	7	H	Clydebank	W 2-0	1-0	4	Maskrey 2	2338
24	14	A	Raith R	D 1-1	1-1	4	Maskrey	4500
25	21	H	Falkirk	W 2-1	1-0	5	Jenkins, Maskrey	5091
26	Feb 8	A	Partick T	L 0-2	0-1	—		2131
27	11	A	Dunfermline Ath	L 0-1	0-0	5		6902
28	25	H	Kilmarnock	D 2-2	1-0	5	Grant 2	2993
29	Mar 4	A	Forfar Ath	D 1-1	1-0	5	Maskrey	1350
30	11	H	Morton	L 0-1	0-0	6		2525
31	25	H	Queen of the S	W 3-1	3-0	5	Sorbie 2, Grant	1575
32	Apr 1	A	Clydebank	D 2-2	1-1	5	Auld (og), Jenkins	1332
33	5	A	Raith R	W 2-0	1-0	—	Coyle (pen), Johnson	1550
34	8	H	Partick T	D 1-1	1-1	5	Grant	3788
35	22	H	Falkirk	L 0-1	0-0	5		4611
36	24	A	Airdrieonians	D 1-1	1-0	—	Jenkins	800
37	29	H	Ayr U	L 0-1	0-1	5		6728
38	May 6	A	Meadowbank T	L 1-2	0-0	5	Sorbie	800
39	13	A	Clyde	L 0-2	0-0	6		1381

Final League Position: 6

GOALSCORERS

League: (51): Maskrey 12, Jenkins 9, Sorbie 7, Grant 5, Watters 4 (1 pen), Johnston 3, McVicar 3 (2 pens), Cherry 2, Coyle 2 (1 pen), Heddle 2, own goals 2.
League Cup: (0).
Scottish Cup: (9): Maskrey 4, Coyle 1 (pen), Grant 1, Heddle 1, Jenkins 1, Sorbie 1.

Record Defeat: 1-10 v Third Lanark, Scottish Cup 1st rd; 24 Jan, 1903.
Most Capped Player: Sandy McLaren, 5, Scotland.
Most League Appearances: 298: Drew Rutherford.
Most League Goals in Season (Individual): 36: Jimmy Benson, Division II; 1931–32.
Most Goals Overall (Individual): 140: John Brogan, 1977–83.

Honours
League Champions: First Division 1982–83. Division II 1923–24, 1959–60, 1962–63; *Runners-up:* Division II 1931–32. Second Division 1987–88.
Scottish Cup: Semi-finals 1934, 1968.
League Cup Runners-up: 1969.
European: *European Cup—. Cup Winners Cup—. UEFA Cup:* 1971–72.
Club colours: Shirt: Royal blue with white semi-circular chest panel. Shorts: Royal blue. Stockings: Royal blue.

Balavage, J	Thomson, K	McVicar, D	Barron, D	McKillop, A	Thompson, G	Sorbie, S	Coyle, T	Maskrey, S	Watters, W	Heddle, I	Cherry, P	Johnston, S	Smith, M	Jenkins, G	Spence, W	Grant, R	Irvine, J	Murray, M	Newbigging, W	Maher, G	Treanor, M	Martin, D	Nicolson, K	*Match No.*
1	2	3	4	5	6	7	8*	9	10†	11	12	14												1
1	2†	3	4	5	6*	7	8	9	10	11	12	14												2
1	2	3	4	5†	6	12	8*	9	10	11	14	7												3
1	2		4			7	8	9	10*	11	5	6	3	12										4
1	2	3	4		6	7	8*	9	12	11	5			10										5
1	2	3	4		6	8	14	9	10	11†	5	12		7*										6
1	2	3	4		6*	14	12	9		11	5	7		10†	8									7
1	2	3	4		6*	8	12	9	10†	11	5	7			14									8
1	2	3	4		6*	12	8	9		11	5	7			14	10†								9
1	2	3	4		6	7	8	9		11*	5			12		10								10
1	2	3	4			7	8	9	12	11†	5	14		6		10*								11
1	2	3	4			7	8	9		11*	5	12		6		10								12
1	2	3	4			7	8	9	14	12	5	11		6†		10*								13
1	2	3	4			7	8†	9	14	11	5	6		12		10*								14
1	2		4		3	7	8	9†	14	11	5	6*		12		10								15
1	2		4		3	7†	8	9	12	11	5	6				10*	14							16
1	2		4		3	7†	8	9	12	11†	5	6		14		10								17
1	2	3	4		6	12	8	9	7*	11	5			14		10†								18
1	2	3	4		6	7†	8*	9		11	5			12		10	14							19
1	2		4		6	7	11*	9		3	5	12		8		10†	14							20
1	2	3	4		6	12		9		11	5			8		10*	7							21
1	2	3	4		6	7				10	5	12		8*	14	9	11†							22
1	2	3	4		6	12	14	7		10	5			8*		9†	11							23
1	2	3	4		6			7		10*	5			8	12	9	11							24
1	2	3	4		6*		12	7		10	5			8	14	9	11†							25
1	2	3	4		6	11	8	7			5	14		10†		9*	12							26
1		3	4		6*	14	8	7			5		11†	10		9	12	2						27
1	2	3	4		6*		8†	7		11	5	10	14	12		9								28
1	2		4*		6	14	12	7†		10	5	9	3	8			11							29
1	2	4			6		8*	7		11†	5	10	3	12		9	14							30
1		3	4			10					5	7†	11	8	14	9*	12		2	6				31
1	2		4		6*	9	8	7		3	5	10†	12	11			14							32
1		3	4			12	8	7*		11†	5	10	14	6		9					2			33
1	2	3	4			7	8			11*	5	10	12	6	14	9†								34
1			4		6	7				3	5	10	11†	8*		9	12				2	14		35
1			4		6	12				3	8	14		7		9†	11			10*	2		5	36
1	2		4		6	7†				3	8	10		9	14		11*			12			5	37
1	2		4		6†	12				3	8	7	11*	10		9						14	5	38
1	2	3	4			10				11*	5	7	12	6		9						8		39
39	34	28	38	3	30	24	24	31	7	35	36	21	7	24	1	28	8	1	1	2	3	1	3	
						+	+		+	+	+	+	+	+	+		+			+		+		
						11s	6s		7s	1s	3s	9s	5s	9s	8s		9s			1s		2s		

ST MIRREN

Premier Division

Year Formed: 1877. *Ground & Address:* St Mirren Park, Love St, Paisley PA3 2EJ. *Telephone:* 041 889 2558/041 840 1337.
Ground Capacity: total: 25,344 seated: 1344. *Size of Pitch:* 111yd×78yd.
Chairman: Lewis Kane. *Secretary:* George N. Pratt. *Commercial Manager:* Jack Copland.
Manager: Tony Fitzpatrick. *Assistant Manager:* —. *Physio:* Bobby Holmes. *Coach:* —.
Managers since 1975: Alex Ferguson; Jim Clunie; Rikki MacFarlane; Alex Miller; Alex Smith; Tony Fitzpatrick.
Club Nickname(s): The Buddies or The Paisley Saints. *Previous Grounds:* Short Roods 1877–79, Thistle Park Greenhill 1879–83, Westmarch 1883–94.
Record Attendance: 47,428 v Celtic, Scottish Cup 4th rd; 7 Mar, 1925.
Record Transfer Fee received: £850,000 for Ian Ferguson to Rangers (1988).
Record Transfer Fee paid: £150,000 for Frank McDougall from Clydebank; Tony Fitzpatrick from Bristol C.
Record Victory: 15-0 v Glasgow University, Scottish Cup 1st rd; 30 Jan, 1960.

1988–89 LEAGUE RECORD

Match No.	*Date*	*Venue*	*Opponents*	*Result*	*H/T Score*	*Lg. Pos.*	*Goalscorers*	*Attendance*
1	Aug 13	H	Dundee U	L 0-1	0-0	—		5852
2	20	A	Aberdeen	D 1-1	0-0	9	Godfrey	12,046
3	27	H	Dundee	D 0-0	0-0	7		3801
4	Sept 3	A	Hearts	W 2-1	2-0	5	Chalmers, Hamilton B	11,386
5	17	H	Motherwell	W 1-0	0-0	4	Martin	4045
6	24	A	Rangers	L 1-2	1-0	5	Davies	35,523
7	28	H	Hibernian	L 0-1	0-1	—		5384
8	Oct 1	H	Hamilton A	W 2-0	1-0	5	Davies, Chalmers	3349
9	8	A	Celtic	L 1-7	1-4	7	Chalmers	26,091
10	12	H	Aberdeen	D 1-1	0-1	—	Martin	4284
11	22	A	Dundee U	W 1-0	1-0	6	McWalter	7618
12	29	H	Rangers	D 1-1	0-0	6	McWalter	20,490
13	Nov 1	A	Motherwell	W 2-1	1-0	—	Davies, McGarvey	3773
14	5	H	Hearts	D 1-1	0-0	6	McWalter	7563
15	12	A	Dundee	W 1-0	1-0	6	Chalmers	4657
16	19	A	Hamilton A	W 4-2	2-1	5	Weir, Chalmers 2, Davies	3710
17	26	H	Celtic	L 2-3	0-1	6	Weir (pen), McWalter	21,266
18	Dec 3	A	Hibernian	L 0-2	0-1	6		8500
19	10	H	Motherwell	W 2-1	0-1	6	Cameron, Chalmers	4496
20	17	A	Aberdeen	L 1-3	0-1	6	McWalter	8500
21	31	H	Dundee U	L 0-1	0-1	6		7768
22	Jan 3	H	Dundee	D 1-1	1-1	—	Weir	4920
23	7	A	Hearts	L 0-2	0-1	6		11,961
24	14	A	Celtic	L 1-2	0-2	6	Lambert	26,796
25	21	H	Hamilton A	W 1-0	1-0	6	Weir (pen)	3330
26	Feb 21	H	Hibernian	W 3-1	1-1	—	Lambert, McGarvey, Cameron	4960
27	25	A	Rangers	L 1-3	1-1	6	Chalmers	39,021
28	Mar 11	A	Dundee U	W 4-1	1-1	6	Hegarty (og), Shaw,Chalmers, Walker	8320
29	25	H	Aberdeen	L 1-3	1-1	6	Chalmers	7541
30	Apr 1	A	Dundee	L 1-2	1-0	6	Chalmers	3824
31	8	H	Hearts	D 1-1	1-0	6	Weir	6970
32	19	A	Hibernian	L 0-1	0-1	—		7500
33	22	H	Rangers	L 0-2	0-1	7		22,096
34	29	A	Motherwell	L 0-4	0-2	7		2702
35	May 6	A	Hamilton A	L 1-2	1-1	7	Weir (pen)	1643
36	13	H	Celtic	L 0-1	0-0	7		13,057

Final League Position: 7

GOALSCORERS

League: (39): Chalmers 11, Weir 6 (4 pens), McWalter 5, Davies 4, Cameron 2, Lambert 2, McGarvey 2, Martin 2, Godfrey 1, Hamilton B 1, Shaw 1, Walker 1, own goal.
League Cup: (4): Cameron 1, Chalmers 1, Hamilton B 1, McGarvey 1.
Scottish Cup: (1): Weir 1 (pen).

Record Defeat: 0-9 v Rangers, Division I; 4 Dec, 1897.
Most Capped Player: Iain Munro & Billy Thomson, 7, Scotland.
Most League Appearances: —.
Most League Goals in Season (Individual): 45: Dunky Walker, Division I; 1921–22.
Most Goals Overall (Individual): —.

Honours
League Champions: First Division 1976–77. Division II 1967–68; *Runners-up* 1935–36.
Scottish Cup Winners: 1926, 1959, 1987; *Runners-up:* 1908, 1934, 1962.
League Cup Runners-up: 1955–56.
Victory Cup: 1919–20.
Summer Cup: 1943–44.
Anglo-Scottish Cup: 1979–80.
European: *European Cup*—. *Cup Winners Cup:* 1987–88. *UEFA Cup:* 1980–81, 1983–84, 1985–86.
Club colours: Shirt: Narrow black and white striped with white chest panel. Shorts: Black. Stockings: Black. Change colours: All red.

Money, C	Wilson, T	Hamilton, D	Hamilton, B	Godfrey, P	Cooper, N	Cameron, I	Martin, B	Lambert, P	McDowall, K	Chalmers, P	McGarvey, F	McWhirter, N	Fridge, L	Winnie, D	McWalter, M	Davies, W	Fitzpatrick, A	Weir, P	Shaw, G	Galloway, S	Walker, K	Dawson, R	Kinnaird, P	McIntosh, M	*Match No.*
1	2	3†	4	5	6	7	8	9	10*	11	12	14													1
	2		4	5	6	7	8	12		11	9		1	3	10*										2
1	2		4†	5	6	7	8			11*	9	14		3	12	10									3
1	2		4	5	6	7*	8			11	9	12		3		10									4
1	2		4*	5		7	8	12		11	9†	6		3	14	10									5
1	2		4	5	6	7	8			11	9*			3	12	10									6
1	12	2		5	6*	7	8	4		11	9†			3	14	10									7
1	2		4	5	6	7	8			11				3	9	10*	12								8
1	2		4	5	6	7*	8			11	12			3	9	10									9
1	2		4	5	6	7	8		12	11	9*			3		10									10
1	2			5	6	7	4			11	8			3	9	10									11
1	2		4	5	6	7	8			11				3	9	10									12
1	2		4†	5	6	7	8		14	11*	12			3	9	10									13
1	2		4	5	6†		8		14	7*	12			3	9	10		11							14
1	2		4		6		5		8	7*	12			3	9	10		11							15
1	2		4	5	6	14	3		8†	7	12				9*	10		11							16
1	2		4	5	6	8†	3			7*	12				9	10		11	14						17
1	2		7	5	6		4				12			3	9	10		11		8*					18
1	2		4		6	14	5			10	12			3	9*			11	7	8†					19
1*	2		4	5	6	12	8			10	7†			3	9			11	14						20
	2		4	5		7†	6	12		8			1	3	9*	10		11		14					21
	2		4	5		7*	6	12		8†			1	3	9	10		11		14					22
	2		4	5			6	12	14		7†		1	3	9	10		11			8*				23
	2			5	6		8	14	7†		12		1	3	9	10		11*			4				24
	2			5	6		8	4		7	12		1	3	9*	10†		11			14				25
				5	6	11	3	8*	12	10	9		1						7		4	2			26
				5	6	11	3	8†		10	9*		1		12				7		4	2	14		27
					6	11	5	8†		10	9*		1	3	12				7		4	2	14		28
					6	11	5	8†		10	9*		1	3	12				7		4	2	14		29
1				5	6	11	3	8†		10	9*				12				7		4	2	14		30
1	3				6		8			10	9*			5	12	7		11			4	2			31
	3				6	7	8			10	9*		1	5	12	14		11†			4	2			32
	3		8		6		2			10*	12		1	5	9	7					4		11		33
	3		8†		6		2	14		10	9		1	5		7*		12			4		11		34
	3*			5				12		8			1	6	9	10		11†	7		4	2		14	35
	3					11				8	12		1	6	9*	10			7		4	2		5	36
21	30 + 1s	2	23	27	30	23 + 3s	34	8 + 8s	4 + 5s	33	18 + 13s	1 + 3s	15	30	21 + 10s	26 + 1s	— + 1s	15 + 1s	8 + 2s	2 + 2s	13 + 1s	9	2 + 4s	1 + 1s	

STENHOUSEMUIR Second Division

Year Formed: 1884. *Ground & Address:* Ochilview Park, Gladstone Rd, Stenhousemuir FK5 5QL. *Telephone:* 0324 562992.
Ground Capacity: total: 4000 seated: 350. *Size of Pitch:* 113yd×78yd.
Chairman: John Cook. *Secretary:* A. T. Bulloch. *Commercial Manager:* John Young.
Manager: James Meakin. *Assistant Manager:* —. *Physio:* B. Porteous. *Coach:* H. Nicol.
Managers since 1975: H. Glasgow; J. Black; A. Rose; W. Henderson; A. Rennie; J. Meakin.
Club Nickname(s): The Warriors. *Previous Grounds:* Tryst Ground 1884–86, Goschen Park 1886–90.
Record Attendance: 12,500 v East Fife, Scottish Cup 4th rd; 11 Mar, 1950.
Record Transfer Fee received: £25,000 for Lindsay Hamilton to Rangers.
Record Transfer Fee paid: —.

1988–89 LEAGUE RECORD

Match No.	Date	Venue	Opponents	Result	H/T Score	Lg. Pos.	Goalscorers	Attendance
1	Aug 13	A	Stirling Albion	L 0-2	0-1	—		831
2	20	H	Dumbarton	W 3-1	0-1	8	Beaton 2 (1 pen), Elliott	477
3	27	H	East Stirling	D 1-1	0-1	9	Walker C	350
4	Sept 3	A	Alloa	W 2-1	0-1	6	Condie, Walker C	672
5	10	H	Cowdenbeath	D 0-0	0-0	8		200
6	17	A	Arbroath	L 1-5	0-3	9	Loppas	470
7	24	H	Berwick R	W 3-2	1-1	8	Condie 2, Loppas	200
8	Oct 1	A	Montrose	L 1-3	0-0	9	Elliott	479
9	8	H	Queen's Park	D 0-0	0-0	10		400
10	15	A	East Fife	L 1-2	0-0	12	Beaton (pen)	502
11	22	H	Brechin C	L 0-2	0-0	12		250
12	29	A	Stranraer	L 1-2	0-1	12	Sexton	700
13	Nov 5	H	Albion R	L 2-2	0-2	12	Sexton, McIntosh	300
14	12	A	Dumbarton	W 2-0	1-0	12	Sexton 2	500
15	19	H	Stirling Albion	D 1-1	0-0	12	Walker C	750
16	26	A	Cowdenbeath	L 0-2	0-1	12		450
17	Dec 10	H	Arbroath	D 0-0	0-0	12		300
18	17	A	Berwick R	L 0-1	0-0	12		278
19	24	A	Albion R	L 0-1	0-0	12		663
20	31	H	Stranraer	L 3-4	1-0	12	Erwin 2, Beaton	400
21	Jan 3	A	East Stirling	W 3-0	0-0	—	Walker C, Sexton, Erwin (pen)	200
22	21	H	East Fife	D 1-1	1-1	12	Bell	300
23	24	H	Alloa	W 2-0	1-0	—	Moore, Erwin	460
24	Feb 1	A	Brechin C	L 1-3	1-1	—	Sexton	429
25	4	A	Queen's Park	D 1-1	0-1	12	Bell	705
26	18	A	Cowdenbeath	L 1-2	1-0	13	Bell	300
27	Mar 1	H	Montrose	L 0-1	0-1	—		200
28	4	A	Alloa	L 0-4	0-1	13		726
29	6	H	East Stirling	W 1-0	1-0	—	Beaton	350
30	11	H	Berwick R	D 0-0	0-0	13		350
31	18	A	Brechin C	D 1-1	0-0	13	Walker C	350
32	25	H	Albion R	L 1-2	1-0	14	Walker C	700
33	Apr 1	H	Montrose	L 2-3	1-1	14	Walker C, Gavin	300
34	8	A	Arbroath	L 1-2	0-1	14	McDonald S	280
35	15	A	East Fife	D 1-1	0-0	14	Robinson	547
36	22	H	Stirling Albion	W 4-2	1-1	14	Erwin, Walker C, Beaton, Tennent (og)	450
37	29	H	Stranraer	W 2-0	1-0	14	Cairney, Walker C	300
38	May 6	A	Dumbarton	L 0-2	0-1	14		600
39	13	H	Queen's Park	D 1-1	0-1	14	Condie	386

Final League Position: 14

GOALSCORERS

League: (44): Walker C 9, Beaton 6 (2 pens), Sexton 6, Erwin 5 (1 pen), Condie 4, Bell 3, Elliott 2, Loppas 2, Cairney 1, Gavin 1, McDonald S 1, McIntosh 1, Moore 1, Robinson 1, own goal 1.
League Cup: (3): Sexton 2, McCafferty 1.
Scottish Cup: (4): Erwin 2 (1 pen), Beaton 1, Sexton 1.

Record Victory: 9-2 v Dundee U, Division II; 19 Apr, 1937.
Record Defeat: 2-11 v Dunfermline Ath, Division II; 27 Sept, 1930.
Most Capped Player: —.
Most League Appearances: 189: T. Mullen.
Most League Goals in Season (Individual): 31: Evelyn Morrison, Division II; 1927–28: Robert Murray, Division II; 1936–37.
Most Goals Overall (Individual): —.

Honours
League Champions:—.
Scottish Cup: Semi-finals 1902–03.
League Cup:—.
Club colours: Shirt: Maroon with white pinstripe. Shorts: White. Stockings: Maroon with three white hoops.

Robertson, S	Robinson, B	Gillen, J	Cairney, H	Beaton, D	Erwin, H	Maitland, A	McCafferty, T	Walker, C	Sexton, P	Condie, T	Elliott, A	Loppas, C	Hamill, S	Keith, A	McIntosh, G	Sinclair, D	Barrie, S	Bell, A	Philliben, R	Moore, C	Buchanan, G	McBride, A	McConville, R	Sharp, R	Pelosi, J	Clouston, B	Walker, D	Match No.
1	2	3	4	5	6	7*	8†	9	10	11	12	14																1
1	2	3	4	5	6		8	9	10	11	7																	2
1	2	3	4	5	6	12	8	9	10*	11	7																	3
1	2	3	4	5	6	12	8	9	10†	11	7*		14															4
1	2	3	4	5	10	7*	8	9	6	11			12															5
1	2*	3	4	5	6		8	9	10†	11	7	14	12															6
	12	3	4	5	6		8*	9	14	11	7	10†	2	1														7
		3	4	5	6		8*	9	10	11	7	12	2	1														8
		3	4	5	6			9	10	8	7*	11	2	1	12													9
		3	4	5			8	9	10	6	7	11*	2	1	12													10
1	2	3	4	5					10	11	9	12	8		7*	6												11
1		3	4	5					10	8	11*	9	2		12		6	7										12
1		3	4	5	8			9*	10	11†		14	2		12		6	7										13
1		3	4	5	6			9	10	8	11*		2		12		14	7†										14
1		3	4	5	6			9	10	8			2		11			7*	12									15
1		3	4	5	11		14	9	10	8					12		2†	7*	6									16
1		3	4*	5	11		8	9	10	7			2					12	6									17
1		3	4	5	11		8*	9	10	7			2				14	12	6†									18
1		3	4	5	10		8	9	11	7			6*				12		2									19
1		3	4	5	10		8*	9	6	11†					14			7	2	12								20
1	3		4†	5	10		8	9	6	12								7	2	11*	14							21
1	3		4	5	10		8*	9†	6	11								7	2	12		14						22
1	11	3*	4	5	10				6	9								7	2	8			12					23
1	11		4	5	10				6	9*	12		3					7	2	8†		14						24
1	3		4		10†				6	9	12						14	7	2	8*				5	11			25
1	3†		4		10			12	6	9	11							7*	2					5	8	14		26
1	6*				10				3	14	11						4	7†	8	12				5		2	9	27
1	3*			5	10		14		6	12	9						4		2	8†				11		7		28
1	2			5	4		10		3	11	9													6		8		29
1	2		4	5	10				6	11	9								3	7						8		30
	2		4	5	10			9	6	7	12			1					3							8		31
	2		4	5	10			9	6	7	12			1					3							8		32
1			4	5	10			9		7	12								3							2		33
1	3		4	5	10			9		7†									2	14						8		34
1	12		4	5	10			9		8†							11*		3	14						2		35
1	12		4	5	10†			9		7	14						6		3*							8		36
1			4	5	10			9		7							6		3							8		37
1	12		4	5	10			9		7†							6*		3	14						8		38
1	6*		4	5	10†			9		7							12	14	3							8		39
33	21 + 4s	21	36	36	36	2 + 2s	16 + 2s	29 + 1s	31 + 1s	36 + 3s	16 + 7s	4 + 5s	13 + 3s	6	2 + 7s	1	9 + 5s	13 + 3s	23 + 1s	6 + 6s	— + 1s	— + 2s	— + 1s	5	2	13 + 1s	1	

Also played: Kennedy D – Match 29 (7), Spiers A – Match 31 (11*), McDonald A – Match 32 (11*), Gavin S – Match 33 (6), 34 (6), 35 (6), 36 (11), 37 (11), 38 (11), 39 (11), McKay J – Match 33 (8), McKenna – Match 33 (11*), 34 (12), McDonald – Match 34 (11*), Clark R – Match 35 (7), 36 (2), 37 (2), 38 (2), 39 (2).

STIRLING ALBION Second Division

Year Formed: 1945. *Ground & Address:* Annfield Park, St Ninians Rd, Stirling FK8 2HE. *Telephone:* 0786 50399.
Ground Capacity: total: 4000 seated: 500. *Size of Pitch:* 110yd×74yd.
Chairman: Peter Gardiner C.A. *Secretary:* Duncan McCallum. *Commercial Manager:* —.
Manager: John Brogan. *Assistant Manager:* Frank Coulston. *Physio:* George Cameron. *Coach:* Jim McSherry.
Managers since 1975: A. Smith; G. Peebles; J. Brogan.
Club Nickname(s): The Albion. *Previous Grounds:* None.
Record Attendance: 26,400 v Celtic, Scottish Cup 4th rd; 14 Mar, 1959.
Record Transfer Fee received: £70,000 for John Philliben to Doncaster R (Mar 1984).
Record Transfer Fee paid: £12,500 for David Thompson from Stenhousemuir (Sept 1984).

1988–89 LEAGUE RECORD

Match No.	Date	Venue	Opponents	Result	H/T Score	Lg. Pos.	Goalscorers	Attendance
1	Aug 13	H	Stenhousemuir	W 2-0	1-0	—	Gibson C, Kemp	831
2	20	A	Montrose	L 2-3	2-1	4	Thompson, Gibson C	450
3	27	H	Berwick R	W 2-1	1-1	4	Gibson C, Mitchell	476
4	Sept 3	A	Brechin C	W 3-2	2-0	2	Kemp, Tennant, Gibson C	600
5	10	H	Queen's Park	W 3-2	1-0	1	Gibson, Brogan, Kemp	1208
6	17	A	Stranraer	D 1-1	0-0	2	Kemp	1000
7	24	H	Cowdenbeath	L 2-3	1-1	3	Brogan, Thompson	691
8	Oct 1	A	Arbroath	L 1-2	0-0	4	Brogan	849
9	8	H	Alloa	W 3-1	1-0	4	Brogan 2, Gibson C	730
10	15	A	Dumbarton	W 2-1	0-1	2	Brogan 2	700
11	22	H	Albion R	W 4-2	1-0	2	Brogan 2, Gibson C 2	962
12	29	H	East Fife	W 3-1	2-0	1	Gibson C, Gibson A, George	837
13	Nov 5	A	East Stirling	D 2-2	0-1	1	Brogan, Gibson C	462
14	12	H	Montrose	W 2-0	0-0	1	Brogan 2	741
15	19	A	Stenhousemuir	D 1-1	0-0	1	Gibson C	750
16	26	A	Queen's Park	L 0-2	0-0	2		710
17	Dec 14	H	Stranraer	L 0-3	0-1	—		717
18	17	A	Cowdenbeath	D 1-1	0-0	3	McTeague	450
19	24	H	East Stirling	W 1-0	0-0	2	Brogan	750
20	31	A	East Fife	L 0-2	0-1	4		886
21	Jan 7	A	Berwick R	D 0-0	0-0	5		530
22	18	H	Brechin C	D 2-2	1-0	—	Gibson C, Kemp	476
23	21	H	Dumbarton	D 1-1	1-0	4	Gibson C	620
24	31	A	Albion R	L 0-1	0-0	—		756
25	Feb 4	A	Alloa	L 2-3	0-1	5	Hughes, Given	895
26	11	H	Arbroath	D 1-1	0-1	5	Moore	447
27	18	A	Berwick R	D 2-2	1-1	5	Thompson, Brogan	506
28	27	H	Queen's Park	D 0-0	0-0	—		419
29	Mar 4	A	Stranraer	W 4-1	1-1	4	Given (pen), George, Gibson C, Thompson	800
30	11	H	Brechin C	D 0-0	0-0	4		547
31	18	H	East Stirling	W 2-1	2-0	3	Gibson C, George	497
32	25	A	East Fife	L 0-3	0-0	5		1041
33	Apr 1	H	Dumbarton	W 3-1	3-0	3	Gibson C, Moore, Tennant	634
34	8	A	Alloa	L 0-4	0-0	5		1357
35	15	H	Albion R	D 0-0	0-0	5		861
36	22	A	Stenhousemuir	L 2-4	1-1	6	Moore (pen), Barrie (og)	450
37	29	A	Montrose	W 6-0	4-0	5	Moore, Brogan, George 2, Hughes, Gibson C	409
38	May 6	H	Cowdenbeath	L 0-1	0-1	5		394
39	13	A	Arbroath	W 4-0	1-0	4	Conway, Gilmour, Walsh, Gibson C	400

Final League Position: 4

GOALSCORERS

League: (64): Gibson C 18, Brogan 15, George 5, Kemp 5, Moore 4 (1 pen), Thompson 4, Given 2 (1 pen), Hughes 2, Tennant 2, Conway 1, Gibson A 1, Gilmour 1, McTeague 1, Mitchell 1, Walsh 1, own goal.
League Cup: (5): Brogan 2, Gibson C 1, Kemp 1, Thompson 1.
Scottish Cup: (2): Brogan 2.

Record Victory: 20-0 v Selkirk, Scottish Cup, 1st rd; 8 Dec, 1984.
Record Defeat: 0-9 v Dundee U, Division I; 30 Dec, 1967.
Most Capped Player: —.
Most League Appearances: 504: Matt McPhee, 1967–81.
Most League Goals in Season (Individual): 29: Joe Hughes, Division II; 1969–70.
Most Goals Overall (Individual): 129: Billy Steele, 1971–83.

Honours
League Champions: Division II 1952–53, 1957–58, 1960–61, 1964–65. Second Division 1976–77; *Runners-up:* Division II 1948–49, 1950–51.
Scottish Cup—.
League Cup—.
Club colours: Shirt: Red with white sleeves. Shorts: White. Stockings: White.

Graham, A	Wilson, K	Smith, G	Given, J	Mitchell, C	McTeague, G	Thompson, D	George, D	Gibson, C	Kemp, B	Brogan, J	Gibson, A	Tennant, S	Aitchison, T	Miller, B	Walsh, M	Maxwell, S	Hughes, M	Gilmour, J	Conway, M	Sinclair, J	McConville, R	Moore, V	McKeown, K	Match No.
1	2	3	4	5	6	7*	8	9	10	11	12													1
1		8	4	5	6*	7	12	9	10	11		3	2											2
1		8†	4	5	6	7*	3	9	11	10	12		2	14	3									3
1	14		4	5	6	7*	8	9	10	11	12	3	2†											4
1			4	5	6	7	8	9	10*	11		3	2	12										5
1	12		4	5	6	7	8*	9	10	11		3	2											6
1	12		4	5	6	7		9	10	11	8†	3	2*		14									7
1			4	5	6	7	8	9	10	11		3	2											8
1	2		4	5†	6	7*	8	9	10	11	12	3	14											9
1	2		4	5*	6	7	8	9	10	11		12				3								10
1	2		4	14	6	7	8†	9	10	11	12	3*				5								11
1	2		4	14	6	7*	8	9	10		11	3†		12		5								12
1	2		4	5	6		8	9	10*	11	7	12				3								13
1	2		4	12	6		8*	9	10	11	7	3†		14		5								14
1	2		4	5	6	7*	8	9	10	11	12					3								15
1	2		3*	6†			8	9	10	11	14	12	5	7		4								16
1	2		3				7	9		8	12	10*	5			6	4	11						17
1	2				5	7*	10	9		8		3	12			6	4	11						18
1			12	2	5		7†	9		8		3	10			6	4*	11	14					19
1			7	2	5			9†	12	8		3	10		14	6		11	4*					20
1	2†			14	5		7*	9	10	8		3	4		12	6		11						21
1	2		14	4			7†	9	10	8*		3	5		12	6		11						22
1	2		7	4†			14	9	10	8*		3	5		12	6		11						23
1			6				7*	9	10	8		3	5		12		4	11		2				24
1			6			12		9*	10	8		3†	5			14	4	11		2	7			25
1	2		6			7		9	10*	11†		3	5				12	14			4	8		26
1	2*		6			7†		9	10	11		3	5		14		12				4	8		27
			6		5	7*	11	9†	10	14		3					4	12			2	8	1	28
			6	2	5	7*	11	9	10†	12		3				14	4					8	1	29
			6	2	5	7*	11	9	10	12		3					4					8	1	30
			6	2	5		11	9	10			3		14	7†	12	4*					8	1	31
			6	2	5		7†	9	10			3			14	12	4*	11				8	1	32
1			6	2	5		7	9	10	11*		3					4				12	8		33
1			6*	2	5		7	9	10	11†		3				12	4				14	8		34
1				2	5	14	7*	9	10	12		3				6		11†			4	8		35
1				2	5	11*	7	9	10†	12		3				6	4				14	8		36
1			6	2			7	9		11*		3†			12	14	4		10		8	5		37
1			6	2			7	9		11*		3			12	14	4		10		8†	5		38
1			6	2				9	12			3			7		10*	11	8		4	5		39
34	16 + 3s	3	33 + 2s	28 + 4s	28	20 + 2s	31 + 2s	39	32 + 2s	30 + 5s	4 + 8s	33 + 3s	18 + 2s	1 + 5s	2 + 10s	16 + 7s	16 + 2s	12 + 2s	4 + 1s	2	8 + 3s	14	5	

STRANRAER Second Division

Year Formed: 1870. *Ground & Address:* Stair Park, London Rd, Stranraer DG9 8BS. *Telephone:* 0776 3271.
Ground Capacity: total: 4000 seated: 250. *Size of Pitch:* 110×70yd.
Chairman: T. Rice. *Secretary:* Graham Rodgers. *Commercial Manager:* —.
Manager: Alex McAnespie. *Assistant Manager:* —. *Physio:* —. *Coach:* —.
Managers since 1975: J. Hughes; N. Hood; G. Hamilton; D. Sneddon; J. Clark; R. Clark; A. McAnespie.
Club Nickname(s): The Blues. *Previous Grounds:* None.
Record Attendance: 6500 v Rangers, Scottish Cup 1st rd; 24 Jan, 1948.
Record Transfer Fee received: —.
Record Transfer Fee paid: —.

1988–89 LEAGUE RECORD

Match No.	Date		Venue	Opponents	Result		H/T Score	Lg. Pos.	Goalscorers	Attendance
1	Aug	13	H	Arbroath	L	0-1	0-1	—		714
2		20	A	Berwick R	W	1-0	0-0	11	McMillan	406
3		27	H	Albion R	W	3-1	1-1	5	Frye, McMillan, McQueen	550
	Sept	3	A	Cowdenbeath	L	0-1	0-1	8		150
5		10	A	Dumbarton	W	2-0	1-0	6	Lloyd, McNiven	450
6		17	H	Stirling Albion	D	1-1	0-0	6	McCutcheon (pen)	1000
7		24	A	Montrose	L	2-4	1-3	9	McCutcheon 2 (2 pens)	312
8	Oct	1	H	East Fife	D	2-2	1-1	8	Frye, Watt	700
9		8	A	East Stirling	W	2-1	1-1	6	Lloyd, Henderson	250
10		15	A	Brechin C	D	2-2	1-0	6	Donnelly, Arthur	400
11		22	H	Queen's Park	W	3-1	0-1	4	Lloyd, Arthur, McInnes	800
12		29	H	Stenhousemuir	W	2-1	1-0	3	Arthur, Henderson	700
13	Nov	5	A	Alloa	D	1-1	0-0	4	McCutcheon (pen)	418
14		12	H	Berwick R	D	2-2	0-1	4	McInnes, McMillan	750
15		19	A	Arbroath	L	0-1	0-0	6		550
16		26	H	Dumbarton	D	2-2	1-1	6	Lloyd, McMillan	850
17	Dec	14	A	Stirling Albion	W	3-0	1-0	—	Henderson 2, McInnes	717
18		17	H	Montrose	W	1-0	0-0	2	McMillan	750
19		24	H	Alloa	D	2-2	0-2	3	Lloyd, McNiven	550
20		31	A	Stenhousemuir	W	4-3	0-1	2	McMillan, Frye 3	400
21	Jan	3	A	Albion R	L	0-3	0-1	—		845
22		21	H	Brechin C	L	0-1	0-0	6		850
23		25	H	Cowdenbeath	W	2-0	0-0	—	McCutcheon, Henderson	600
24	Feb	4	H	East Stirling	L	1-2	0-0	4	Cuthbertson	750
25		7	A	Queen's Park	L	3-4	1-2	—	McCutcheon 2 (2 pens), Cuthbertson	623
26		11	A	East Fife	W	2-1	1-0	4	Doherty, Cuthbertson	434
27		22	A	Montrose	L	0-1	0-0	—		250
28		25	H	Dumbarton	D	1-1	1-0	4	McIntyre (pen)	850
29	Mar	4	H	Stirling Albion	L	1-4	1-1	6	Henderson	800
30		11	A	Arbroath	L	3-4	0-2	7	Doherty, Lloyd 2	296
31		18	A	Albion R	D	2-2	2-1	7	McInnes, Lloyd	634
32		25	H	Berwick R	L	1-2	1-2	8	McMillan	600
33	Apr	1	H	Alloa	L	1-4	1-2	10	Lloyd	850
34		8	A	East Fife	L	1-2	0-1	10	McCutcheon	498
35		15	H	Queen's Park	D	3-3	2-2	11	Henderson, McMillan, McCutcheon (pen)	750
36		22	A	Cowdenbeath	D	1-1	0-0	11	Lloyd	200
37		29	A	Stenhousemuir	L	0-2	0-1	11		300
38	May	6	H	East Stirling	D	0-0	0-0	11		450
39		13	H	Brechin C	W	2-1	1-0	11	Lindsay, Lloyd	788

Final League Position: 11

GOALSCORERS

League: (59): Lloyd 11, McCutcheon 9 (7 pens), McMillan 8, Henderson 7, Frye 5, McInnes 4, Arthur 3, Cuthbertson 3, Doherty 2, McNiven 2, Donnelly 1, Lindsay 1, McIntyre 1 (pen), McQueen 1, Watt 1.
League Cup: (2): McCutcheon 1 (pen), McMillan 1.
Scottish Cup: (6): Ewing 2, McMillan 2, Lloyd 1, McInnes 1.

Record Victory: 7-0 v Brechin C, Division II; 6 Feb, 1965.
Record Defeat: 1-11 v Queen of the South, Scottish Cup 1st rd; 16 Jan, 1932.
Most Capped Player: —.
Most League Appearances: 256: Dan McDonald.
Most League Goals in Season (Individual): 27: Derek Frye, Second Division; 1977–78.
Most Goals Overall (Individual): —.

Honours
League Champions:—.
Scottish Cup:—.
League Cup:—.
Club colours: Shirt: Royal blue with amber chest band. Shorts: Royal blue. Stockings: Royal blue.

Duffy, B	Lowe, L	Hay, G	McCutcheon, D	Rogers, J	Watt, N	McQueen, E	Frye, JF	Arthur, J	Donnelly, J	Henderson, D	McNiven, J	McMillan, G	Armour, N	Lloyd, D	Day, R	Gallagher, A	McInnes, I	Cuthbertson, S	Houston, H	Ewing, A	Doherty, J	McIntyre, B	Spittal, I	McDonald, I	Lindsay, C	*Match No.*
1	2	3	4	5	6	7	8†	9	10*	11	12	14														1
1	12	3	6	5	2	7	10†			11	8	14	4*	9												2
1		3	6	5	2	8	10*	12		11		7	4	9												3
1		3	6†	5	2	7	11*			10	14	8	4	9	12											4
1		3	6	5	2	7		14	11*	12	8	10†	4	9												5
1	2*	3	6		4	7	14	12	11		8	10†	5	9												6
1	2	3	6		4	7†		8*	10	14	11	12		9		5										7
1	2	3			6	7	8*	14	11	10		12	5	9†		4										8
1	12	3			2			8*	11	10	6	7	5	9		4										9
1	2	3	6				12	8*	11	10	7†	14	5	9		4										10
1	2	3	6				14	12		10†		8	5	9		4	7	11*								11
1	2*	3	6		12			8		10		11	4	9		5	7									12
1	2	3	6		4			8*		10	11	12		9		5	7									13
1	2†	3	6		4		14	11*		10	8	12		9		5	7									14
1	2*	3	6		4				11	10	8†	12		9		5	7		14							15
1	2	3	6		4		12		11†	10*	5	8		9			7		14							16
1		3	6		2				11	10	4	8	5	9			7									17
1	12	3	6		2		14		11	10*	4	8†	5	9			7									18
1	12	3	6		2					10	4	8†	5	9			7		11*	14						19
1	14	3	6		2*		12			10	4	8	5	9†			7			11						20
1		3	6		2†		14			10	4	8	5	9		12	7			11*						21
1	2	3	6							10	4		5			12	7	8*		11	9					22
1	2*	3	6		14		9†		12	11	8		5			4	7				10					23
1	2*	3	6				14		11	10	4		5	9†			7	8		12						24
1		3	6						11	10	2		5	9		4	7	8*		12						25
1			6				14		11*	10	8		5			4	7	3†		12	9	2				26
1		12					3†		11		8		5	10		4	7	6		14	9*	2				27
1		3							10*		6	7	5	9†		4	12	14	8	11		2				28
1		3								10	4*	8		14		5	7	12	6	11	9	2†				29
1	2†	3								11	4	8		12			7	10	5	14	9*		6			30
1	2	3					14			11		12	5	8			6†	9			10*		4	7		31
1	2†	3								10	4	8	5	11			7*	12		14			6	9		32
1		10	6							12	4	7		9		5*	14			8			2†	11	3	33
1	2	3	6							11	4*	8†		9		14	12			5				7	10	34
1	2	3	6							11		9		12		5†	7		14	8*			4		10	35
1	2	3	6							10	4*	9		12			7†		5	14			8		11	36
1		3	6							10	4	9		8		5	7						2		11	37
1	3		6				9			10*	4			8			7†	12	14	5			2		11	38
1	2		6				8				4			10		12	7	9*		5			3		11	39
39	22 + 5s	35 + 1s	31	5	18 + 2s	8	9 + 11s	7 + 5s	16 + 1s	32 + 3s	31 + 2s	22 + 9s	24	31 + 4s	— + 1s	18 + 4s	26 + 3s	9 + 4s	5 + 4s	10 + 8s	7	4	9	4	7	

B & Q SCOTTISH LEAGUE FINAL TABLES 1988–89

PREMIER DIVISION

			Home			*Goals*		*Away*			*Goals*			
		P	*W*	*D*	*L*	*F*	*A*	*W*	*D*	*L*	*F*	*A*	*GD*	*Pts*
1	Rangers	36	15	1	2	39	11	11	3	4	23	15	+36	56
2	Aberdeen	36	10	7	1	26	10	8	7	3	25	15	+26	50
3	Celtic	36	13	1	4	35	18	8	3	7	31	26	+22	46
4	Dundee U	36	6	8	4	20	16	10	4	4	24	10	+18	44
5	Hibernian	36	8	4	6	20	16	5	5	8	17	20	+1	35
6	Hearts	36	7	6	5	22	17	2	7	9	13	25	−7	31
7	St Mirren	36	5	6	7	17	19	6	1	11	22	36	−16	29
8	Dundee	36	8	4	6	22	21	1	6	11	12	27	−14	28
9	Motherwell	36	5	7	6	21	21	2	6	10	14	23	−9	27
10	Hamilton Acad	36	5	0	13	9	42	1	2	15	10	34	−57	14

DIVISION 1

			Home			*Goals*		*Away*			*Goals*			
		P	*W*	*D*	*L*	*F*	*A*	*W*	*D*	*L*	*F*	*A*	*GD*	*Pts*
1	Dunfermline Ath	39	13	5	2	37	17	9	5	5	23	19	+24	54
2	Falkirk	39	13	3	3	38	10	9	5	6	33	27	+34	52
3	Clydebank	39	12	6	2	50	29	6	6	7	30	26	+25	48
4	Airdrieonians	39	11	6	2	36	16	6	7	7	30	28	+22	47
5	Morton	39	8	5	6	20	20	8	4	8	26	26	0	41
6	St Johnstone	39	11	4	4	30	16	3	8	9	21	26	+9	40
7	Raith Rovers	39	8	6	6	29	25	7	4	8	21	27	−2	40
8	Partick Th	39	7	6	6	26	24	6	5	9	31	34	−1	37
9	Forfar Ath	39	6	9	5	24	24	4	7	8	28	32	−4	36
10	Meadowbank Th	39	8	4	7	26	26	5	6	9	19	24	−5	36
11	Ayr U	39	8	6	6	39	37	5	3	11	17	35	−16	35
12	Clyde	39	7	6	7	23	26	2	10	7	17	26	−12	34
13	Kilmarnock	39	5	7	7	19	25	5	7	8	28	35	−13	34
14	Queen of the S*	39	1	6	13	20	47	1	2	16	18	52	−61	10

DIVISION 2

			Home			*Goals*		*Away*			*Goals*			
		P	*W*	*D*	*L*	*F*	*A*	*W*	*D*	*L*	*F*	*A*	*GD*	*Pts*
1	Albion R	39	14	5	1	39	19	7	3	9	26	29	+17	50
2	Alloa	39	12	6	1	42	20	5	5	10	24	28	+18	45
3	Brechin C	39	8	5	6	27	24	7	8	5	31	25	+9	43
4	Stirling Albion	39	10	6	3	31	20	5	6	9	33	35	+9	42
5	East Fife	39	9	8	3	30	20	5	5	9	25	34	+1	41
6	Montrose	39	10	4	5	25	25	5	7	8	29	30	−1	41
7	Queen's Park	39	8	7	4	26	20	2	11	7	24	29	+1	38
8	Cowdenbeath*	39	6	11	2	30	27	7	3	10	18	25	−4	38
9	East Stirling	39	10	3	7	31	31	3	8	8	23	27	−4	37
10	Arbroath	39	5	6	9	29	40	6	9	4	27	23	−7	37
11	Stranraer	39	6	8	6	30	31	6	4	9	28	32	−5	36
12	Dumbarton	39	10	2	8	28	27	2	8	9	17	28	−10	34
13	Berwick R	39	5	7	7	18	26	5	6	9	32	33	−9	33
14	Stenhousemuir	39	6	8	6	27	24	3	3	13	17	35	−15	29

** 2 points deducted for breach of rules.*

SCOTTISH LEAGUE 1890–91 to 1988–89

*On goal average/difference. †Held jointly after indecisive play-off. ‡Won on deciding match.
††Held jointly. ¶Two points deducted for fielding ineligible player.
Competition suspended 1940–45 during war. ‡‡Two points deducted for registration irregularities.

PREMIER DIVISION

Maximum points: 72

	First	*Pts*	*Second*	*Pts*	*Third*	*Pts*
1975–76	Rangers	54	Celtic	48	Hibernian	43
1976–77	Celtic	55	Rangers	46	Aberdeen	43
1977–78	Rangers	55	Aberdeen	53	Dundee U	40
1978–79	Celtic	48	Rangers	45	Dundee U	44
1979–80	Aberdeen	48	Celtic	47	St Mirren	42
1980–81	Celtic	56	Aberdeen	49	Rangers*	44
1981–82	Celtic	55	Aberdeen	53	Rangers	43
1982–83	Dundee U	56	Celtic*	55	Aberdeen	55
1983–84	Aberdeen	57	Celtic	50	Dundee U	47
1984–85	Aberdeen	59	Celtic	52	Dundee U	47
1985–86	Celtic*	50	Hearts	50	Dundee U	47
			Maximum points: 88			
1986–87	Rangers	69	Celtic	63	Dundee U	60
1987–88	Celtic	72	Hearts	62	Rangers	60
			Maximum points: 72			
1988–89	Rangers	56	Aberdeen	50	Celtic	46

FIRST DIVISION

			Maximum points: 52			
1975–76	Partick Th	41	Kilmarnock	35	Montrose	30
			Maximum points: 78			
1976–77	St Mirren	62	Clydebank	58	Dundee	51
1977–78	Morton*	58	Hearts	58	Dundee	57
1978–79	Dundee	55	Kilmarnock*	54	Clydebank	54
1979–80	Hearts	53	Airdrieonians	51	Ayr U	44
1980–81	Hibernian	57	Dundee	52	St Johnstone	51
1981–82	Motherwell	61	Kilmarnock	51	Hearts	50
1982–83	St Johnstone	55	Hearts	54	Clydebank	50
1983–84	Morton	54	Dumbarton	51	Partick Th	46
1984–85	Motherwell	50	Clydebank	48	Falkirk	45
1985–86	Hamilton A	56	Falkirk	45	Kilmarnock	44
			Maximum points: 88			
1986–87	Morton	57	Dunfermline Ath	56	Dumbarton	53
1987–88	Hamilton A	56	Meadowbank Th	52	Clydebank	49
			Maximum points: 78			
1988–89	Dunfermline Ath	54	Falkirk	52	Clydebank	48

SECOND DIVISION

			Maximum points: 52			
1975–76	Clydebank*	40	Raith R	40	Alloa	35
			Maximum points: 78			
1976–77	Stirling A	55	Alloa	51	Dunfermline Ath	50
1977–78	Clyde*	53	Raith R	53	Dunfermline Ath	48
1978–79	Berwick R	54	Dunfermline Ath	52	Falkirk	50
1979–80	Falkirk	50	East Stirling	49	Forfar Ath	46
1980–81	Queen's Park	50	Queen of the S	46	Cowdenbeath	45
1981–82	Clyde	59	Alloa*	50	Arbroath	50
1982–83	Brechin C	55	Meadowbank Th	54	Arbroath	49
1983–84	Forfar Ath	63	East Fife	47	Berwick R	43
1984–85	Montrose	53	Alloa	50	Dunfermline Ath	49
1985–86	Dunfermline Ath	57	Queen of the South	55	Meadowbank Th	49
1986–87	Meadowbank Th	55	Raith R*	52	Stirling A	52
1987–88	Ayr U	61	St Johnstone	59	Queen's Park	51
1988–89	Albion R	50	Alloa	45	Brechin C	43

FIRST DIVISION to 1974–75

Maximum points: a 36; *b* 44; *c* 40; *d* 52; *e* 60; *f* 68; *g* 76; *h* 84.

	First	*Pts*	*Second*	*Pts*	*Third*	*Pts*
1890–91*a*††	Dumbarton	29	Rangers	29	Celtic	24
1891–92*b*	Dumbarton	37	Celtic	35	Hearts	30
1892–93*a*	Celtic	29	Rangers	28	St Mirren	23
1893–94*a*	Celtic	29	Hearts	26	St Bernard's	22
1894–95*a*	Hearts	31	Celtic	26	Rangers	21
1895–96*a*	Celtic	30	Rangers	26	Hibernian	24
1896–97*a*	Hearts	28	Hibernian	26	Rangers	25
1897–98*a*	Celtic	33	Rangers	29	Hibernian	22
1898–99*a*	Rangers	36	Hearts	26	Celtic	24
1899–1900*a*	Rangers	32	Celtic	25	Hibernian	24
1900–01*c*	Rangers	35	Celtic	29	Hibernian	25
1901–02*a*	Rangers	28	Celtic	26	Hearts	22
1902–03*b*	Hibernian	37	Dundee	31	Rangers	29
1903–04*d*	Third Lanark	43	Hearts	39	Rangers*	38
1904–05*d*	Celtic‡	41	Rangers	41	Third Lanark	35
1905–06*e*	Celtic	49	Hearts	43	Airdrieonians	38
1906–07*f*	Celtic	55	Dundee	48	Rangers	45
1907–08*f*	Celtic	55	Falkirk	51	Rangers	50
1908–09*f*	Celtic	51	Dundee	50	Clyde	48
1909–10*f*	Celtic	54	Falkirk	52	Rangers	46
1910–11*f*	Rangers	52	Aberdeen	48	Falkirk	44
1911–12*f*	Rangers	51	Celtic	45	Clyde	42
1912–13*f*	Rangers	53	Celtic	49	Hearts*	41
1913–14*g*	Celtic	65	Rangers	59	Hearts*	54
1914–15*g*	Celtic	65	Hearts	61	Rangers	50
1915–16*g*	Celtic	67	Rangers	56	Morton	51
1916–17*g*	Celtic	64	Morton	54	Rangers	53
1917–18*f*	Rangers	56	Celtic	55	Kilmarnock	43
1918–19*f*	Celtic	58	Rangers	57	Morton	47
1919–20*h*	Rangers	71	Celtic	68	Motherwell	57
1920–21*h*	Rangers	76	Celtic	66	Hearts	56
1921–22*h*	Celtic	67	Rangers	66	Raith R	56
1922–23*g*	Rangers	55	Airdrieonians	50	Celtic	46
1923–24*g*	Rangers	59	Airdrieonians	50	Celtic	41
1924–25*g*	Rangers	60	Airdrieonians	57	Hibernian	52
1925–26*g*	Celtic	58	Airdrieonians*	50	Hearts	50
1926–27*g*	Rangers	56	Motherwell	51	Celtic	49
1927–28*g*	Rangers	60	Celtic*	55	Motherwell	55
1928–29*g*	Rangers	67	Celtic	51	Motherwell	50
1929–30*g*	Rangers	60	Motherwell	55	Aberdeen	53
1930–31*g*	Rangers	60	Celtic	58	Motherwell	56
1931–32*g*	Motherwell	66	Rangers	61	Celtic	48
1932–33*g*	Rangers	62	Motherwell	59	Hearts	50
1933–34*g*	Rangers	66	Motherwell	62	Celtic	47
1934–35*g*	Rangers	55	Celtic	52	Hearts	50
1935–36*g*	Celtic	66	Rangers*	61	Aberdeen	61
1936–37*g*	Rangers	61	Aberdeen	54	Celtic	52
1937–38*g*	Celtic	61	Hearts	58	Rangers	49
1938–39*g*	Rangers	59	Celtic	48	Aberdeen	46
1946–47*e*	Rangers	46	Hibernian	44	Aberdeen	39
1947–48*e*	Hibernian	48	Rangers	46	Partick Th	36
1948–49*e*	Rangers	46	Dundee	45	Hibernian	39
1949–50*e*	Rangers	50	Hibernian	49	Hearts	43
1950–51*e*	Hibernian	48	Rangers*	38	Dundee	38
1951–52*e*	Hibernian	45	Rangers	41	East Fife	37
1952–53*e*	Rangers*	43	Hibernian	43	East Fife	39
1953–54*e*	Celtic	43	Hearts	38	Partick Th	35
1954–55*e*	Aberdeen	49	Celtic	46	Rangers	41
1955–56*f*	Rangers	52	Aberdeen	46	Hearts*	45
1956–57*f*	Rangers	55	Hearts	53	Kilmarnock	42
1957–58*f*	Hearts	62	Rangers	49	Celtic	46
1958–59*f*	Rangers	50	Hearts	48	Motherwell	44
1959–60*f*	Hearts	54	Kilmarnock	50	Rangers*	42
1960–61*f*	Rangers	51	Kilmarnock	50	Third Lanark	42
1961–62*f*	Dundee	54	Rangers	51	Celtic	46
1962–63*f*	Rangers	57	Kilmarnock	48	Partick Th	46
1963–64*f*	Rangers	55	Kilmarnock	49	Celtic*	47
1964–65*f*	Kilmarnock*	50	Hearts	50	Dunfermline Ath	49
1965–66*f*	Celtic	57	Rangers	55	Kilmarnock	45
1966–67*f*	Celtic	58	Rangers	55	Clyde	46

	First	Pts	Second	Pts	Third	Pts
1967–68*f*	Celtic	63	Rangers	61	Hibernian	45
1968–69*f*	Celtic	54	Rangers	49	Dunfermline Ath	45
1969–70*f*	Celtic	57	Rangers	45	Hibernian	44
1970–71*f*	Celtic	56	Aberdeen	54	St Johnstone	44
1971–72*f*	Celtic	60	Aberdeen	50	Rangers	44
1972–73*f*	Celtic	57	Rangers	56	Hibernian	45
1973–74*f*	Celtic	53	Hibernian	49	Rangers	48
1974–75*f*	Rangers	56	Hibernian	49	Celtic	45

SECOND DIVISION to 1974–75

Maximum points: a 76; *b* 72; *c* 68; *d* 52; *e* 60; *f* 36; *g* 44; *h* 52.

	First	Pts	Second	Pts	Third	Pts
1893–94*f*	Hibernian	29	Cowlairs	27	Clyde	24
1894–95*f*	Hibernian	30	Motherwell	22	Port Glasgow	20
1895–96*f*	Abercorn	27	Leith Ath	23	Renton	21
1896–97*f*	Partick Th	31	Leith Ath	27	Kilmarnock	21
1897–98*f*	Kilmarnock	29	Port Glasgow	25	Morton	22
1898–99*f*	Kilmarnock	32	Leith Ath	27	Port Glasgow	25
1899–1900*f*	Partick Th	29	Morton	26	Port Glasgow	20
1900–01*f*	St Bernard's	26	Airdrieonians	23	Abercorn	21
1901–02*g*	Port Glasgow	32	Partick Th	31	Motherwell	26
1902–03*g*	Airdrieonians	35	Motherwell	28	Ayr U	27
1903–04*g*	Hamilton A	37	Clyde	29	Ayr U	28
1904–05*g*	Clyde	32	Falkirk	28	Hamilton A	27
1905–06*g*	Leith Ath	34	Clyde	31	Albion R	27
1906–07*g*	St Bernard's	32	Vale of Leven*	27	Arthurlie	27
1907–08*g*	Raith R	30	Dumbarton	‡‡27	Ayr U	27
1908–09*g*	Abercorn	31	Raith R*	28	Vale of Leven	28
1909–10*g*‡	Leith Ath	33	Raith R	33	St Bernard's	27
1910–11*g*	Dumbarton	31	Ayr U	27	Albion R	25
1911–12*g*	Ayr U	35	Abercorn	30	Dumbarton	27
1912–13*h*	Ayr U	34	Dunfermline Ath	33	East Stirling	32
1913–14*g*	Cowdenbeath	31	Albion R	27	Dunfermline Ath	26
1914–15*h*	Cowdenbeath*	37	St Bernard's*	37	Leith Ath	37
1921–22*a*	Alloa	60	Cowdenbeath	47	Armadale	45
1922–23*a*	Queen's Park	57	Clydebank	¶50	St Johnstone	¶45
1923–24*a*	St Johnstone	56	Cowdenbeath	55	Bathgate	44
1924–25*a*	Dundee U	50	Clydebank	48	Clyde	47
1925–26*a*	Dunfermline Ath	59	Clyde	53	Ayr U	52
1926–27*a*	Bo'ness	56	Raith R	49	Clydebank	45
1927–28*a*	Ayr U	54	Third Lanark	45	King's Park	44
1928–29*b*	Dundee U	51	Morton	50	Arbroath	47
1929–30*a*	Leith Ath*	57	East Fife	57	Albion R	54
1930–31*a*	Third Lanark	61	Dundee U	50	Dunfermline Ath	47
1931–32*a*	East Stirling*	55	St Johnstone	55	Raith Rovers*	46
1932–33*c*	Hibernian	54	Queen of the S	49	Dunfermline Ath	47
1933–34*c*	Albion R	45	Dunfermline Ath*	44	Arbroath	44
1934–35*c*	Third Lanark	52	Arbroath	50	St Bernard's	47
1935–36*c*	Falkirk	59	St Mirren	52	Morton	48
1936–37*c*	Ayr U	54	Morton	51	St Bernard's	48
1937–38*c*	Raith R	59	Albion R	48	Airdrieonians	47
1938–39*c*	Cowdenbeath	60	Alloa*	48	East Fife	48
1946–47*d*	Dundee	45	Airdrieonians	42	East Fife	31
1947–48*e*	East Fife	53	Albion R	42	Hamilton A	40
1948–49*e*	Raith R*	42	Stirling Albion	42	Airdrieonians*	41
1949–50*e*	Morton	47	Airdrieonians	44	St Johnstone*	36
1950–51*e*	Queen of the S*	45	Stirling Albion	45	Ayr U*	36
1951–52*e*	Clyde	44	Falkirk	43	Ayr U	39
1952–53*e*	Stirling Albion	44	Hamilton A	43	Queen's Park	37
1953–54*e*	Motherwell	45	Kilmarnock	42	Third Lanark*	36
1954–55*e*	Airdrieonians	46	Dunfermline Ath	42	Hamilton A	39
1955–56*b*	Queen's Park	54	Ayr U	51	St Johnstone	49
1956–57*b*	Clyde	64	Third Lanark	51	Cowdenbeath	45
1957–58*b*	Stirling Albion	55	Dunfermline Ath	53	Arbroath	47
1958–59*b*	Ayr U	60	Arbroath	51	Stenhousemuir	40
1959–60*b*	St Johnstone	53	Dundee U	50	Queen of the S	49
1960–61*b*	Stirling Albion	55	Falkirk	54	Stenhousemuir	50
1961–62*b*	Clyde	54	Queen of the S	53	Morton	44
1962–63*b*	St Johnstone	55	East Stirling	49	Morton	48
1963–64*b*	Morton	67	Clyde	53	Arbroath	46
1964–65*b*	Stirling Albion	59	Hamilton A	50	Queen of the S	45
1965–66*b*	Ayr U	53	Airdrieonians	50	Queen of the S	49
1966–67*b*	Morton	69	Raith R	58	Arbroath	57

1967–68*b*	St Mirren	62	Arbroath	53	East Fife	40
1968–69*b*	Motherwell	64	Ayr U	53	East Fife*	47
1969–70*b*	Falkirk	56	Cowdenbeath	55	Queen of the S	50
1970–71*b*	Partick Th	56	East Fife	51	Arbroath	46
1971–72*b*	Dumbarton*	52	Arbroath	52	Stirling Albion	50
1972–73*b*	Clyde	56	Dunfermline Ath	52	Raith R*	47
1973–74*b*	Airdrieonians	60	Kilmarnock	59	Hamilton A	55
1974–75*a*	Falkirk	54	Queen of the S	53	Montrose	53

Elected to First Division: 1894 Clyde; 1897 Partick Th; 1899 Kilmarnock; 1900 Partick Th; 1902 Partick Th; 1903 Airdrieonians; 1905 Falkirk, Aberdeen and Hamilton A; 1906 Clyde; 1910 Raith R; 1913 Ayr U.

RELEGATED FROM PREMIER DIVISION

1975–76 Dundee, St Johnstone
1976–77 Hearts, Kilmarnock
1977–78 Ayr U, Clydebank
1978–79 Hearts, Motherwell
1979–80 Dundee, Hibernian
1980–81 Kilmarnock, Hearts
1981–82 Partick Th, Airdrieonians
1982–83 Morton, Kilmarnock
1983–84 St Johnstone, Motherwell
1984–85 Dumbarton, Morton
1985–86 *No relegation due to League reorganisation*
1986–87 Clydebank, Hamilton A
1987–88 Falkirk, Dunfermline Ath, Morton
1988–89 Hamilton A

RELEGATED FROM DIVISION 1

1975–76 Dunfermline Ath, Clyde
1976–77 Raith R, Falkirk
1977–78 Alloa Ath, East Fife
1978–79 Montrose, Queen of the S
1979–80 Arbroath, Clyde
1980–81 Stirling A, Berwick R
1981–82 East Stirling, Queen of the S
1982–83 Dunfermline Ath, Queen's Park
1983–84 Raith R, Alloa
1984–85 Meadowbank Th, St Johnstone
1985–86 Ayr U, Alloa
1986–87 Brechin C, Montrose
1987–88 East Fife, Dumbarton
1988–89 Kilmarnock, Queen of the S

RELEGATED FROM DIVISION 1 (to 1973–74)

1921–22 *Queen's Park, Dumbarton, Clydebank
1922–23 Albion R, Alloa Ath
1923–24 Clyde, Clydebank
1924–25 Third Lanark, Ayr U
1925–26 Raith R, Clydebank
1926–27 Morton, Dundee U
1927–28 Dunfermline Ath, Bo'ness
1928–29 Third Lanark, Raith R
1929–30 St Johnstone, Dundee U
1930–31 Hibernian, East Fife
1931–32 Dundee U, Leith Ath
1932–33 Morton, East Stirling
1933–34 Third Lanark, Cowdenbeath
1934–35 St Mirren, Falkirk
1935–36 Aidrieonians, Ayr U
1936–37 Dunfermline Ath, Albion R
1937–38 Dundee, Morton
1938–39 Queen's Park, Raith R
1946–47 Kilmarnock, Hamilton A
1947–48 Airdrieonians, Queen's Park
1948–49 Morton, Albion R
1949–50 Queen of the S, Stirling Albion
1950–51 Clyde, Falkirk
1951–52 Morton, Stirling Albion
1952–53 Motherwell, Third Lanark
1953–54 Airdrieonians, Hamilton A
1954–55 No clubs relegated
1955–56 Stirling Albion, Clyde
1956–57 Dunfermline Ath, Ayr U
1957–58 East Fife, Queen's Park
1958–59 Queen of the S, Falkirk
1959–60 Arbroath, Stirling Albion
1960–61 Ayr U, Clyde
1961–62 St Johnstone, Stirling Albion
1962–63 Clyde, Raith R
1963–64 Queen of the S, East Stirling
1964–65 Airdrieonians, Third Lanark
1965–66 Morton, Hamilton A
1966–67 St Mirren, Ayr U
1967–68 Motherwell, Stirling Albion
1968–69 Falkirk, Arbroath
1969–70 Raith R, Partick Th
1970–71 St Mirren, Cowdenbeath
1971–72 Clyde, Dunfermline Ath
1972–73 Kilmarnock, Airdrieonians
1973–74 East Fife, Falkirk

*Season 1921–22 – only 1 club promoted, 3 clubs relegated.

The Scottish Football League was reconstructed into three divisions at the end of the 1974–75 season, so the usual relegation statistics do not apply. Further reorganisation took place at the end of the 1985–86 season. From 1986–87, the Premier and First Division had 12 teams each. The Second Division remains at 14. From 1988–89, the Premier Division reverted to 10 teams, and the First Division to 14 teams.

SCOTTISH LEAGUE SKOL CUP FINALS 1946–89

Season	*Winners*	*Runners-up*	*Score*
1946–47	Rangers	Aberdeen	4-0
1947–48	East Fife	Falkirk	4-1 after 0-0 draw
1948–49	Rangers	Raith R	2-0
1949–50	East Fife	Dunfermline Ath	3-0
1950–51	Motherwell	Hibernian	3-0
1951–52	Dundee	Rangers	3-2
1952–53	Dundee	Kilmarnock	2-0
1953–54	East Fife	Partick T	3-2
1954–55	Hearts	Motherwell	4-2
1955–56	Aberdeen	St Mirren	2-1
1956–57	Celtic	Partick T	3-0 after 0-0 draw
1957–58	Celtic	Rangers	7-1
1958–59	Hearts	Partick T	5-1
1959–60	Hearts	Third Lanark	2-1
1960–61	Rangers	Kilmarnock	2-0
1961–62	Rangers	Hearts	3-1 after 1-1 draw
1962–63	Hearts	Kilmarnock	1-0
1963–64	Rangers	Morton	5-0
1964–65	Rangers	Celtic	2-1
1965–66	Celtic	Rangers	2-1
1966–67	Celtic	Rangers	1-0
1967–68	Celtic	Dundee	5-3
1968–69	Celtic	Hibernian	6-2
1969–70	Celtic	St Johnstone	1-0
1970–71	Rangers	Celtic	1-0
1971–72	Partick T	Celtic	4-1
1972–73	Hibernian	Celtic	2-1
1973–74	Dundee	Celtic	1-0
1974–75	Celtic	Hibernian	6-3
1975–76	Rangers	Celtic	1-0
1976–77	Aberdeen	Celtic	2-1
1977–78	Rangers	Celtic	2-1
1978–79	Rangers	Aberdeen	2-1
1979–80	Dundee U	Aberdeen	3-0 after 0-0 draw
1980–81	Dundee U	Dundee	3-0
1981–82	Rangers	Dundee U	2-1
1982–83	Celtic	Rangers	2-1
1983–84	Rangers	Celtic	3-2
1984–85	Rangers	Dundee U	1-0
1985–86	Aberdeen	Hibernian	3-0
1986–87	Rangers	Celtic	2-1
1987–88	Rangers	Aberdeen *(Rangers won 5-3 on penalties)*	3-3
1988–89	Rangers	Aberdeen	3-2

SCOTTISH LEAGUE CUP WINS

Rangers 16, Celtic 9, Hearts 4, Aberdeen 3, Dundee 3, East Fife 3, Dundee U 2, Hibernian 1, Motherwell 1, Partick Th 1.

APPEARANCES IN FINALS

Rangers 21, Celtic 19, Aberdeen 8, Dundee 5, Hearts 5, Hibernian 5, Dundee U 4, Partick Th 4, East Fife 3, Kilmarnock 3, Motherwell 2, Dunfermline Ath 1, Falkirk 1, Morton 1, Raith R 1, St Johnstone 1, St Mirren 1, Third Lanark 1.

SKOL CUP 1988–89

FIRST ROUND

10 AUG

Alloa (0) 2 *(Lytwyn, Rutherford (pen))*

Stirling Albion (3) 4 *(Brogan, Thompson, Gibson C, Kemp)* 1400

Alloa: Lowrie; Haggart, Lee, Robertson (Shiels), McCulloch, Bateman, Gibson, McGurn, Rutherford, Ramsay (Smith), Lytwyn.
Stirling Albion: Graham; Wilson, Tennant, Given, Mitchell, McTeague, Thompson (Gibson A), George, Gibson C, Kemp, Brogan.

Brechin C (2) 3 *(Adam, Buckley, Lees)*

Montrose (1) 1 *(Paterson)* 500

Brechin C: Lawrie; Hamilton, Watt, Inglis, Taylor, Adam, Gallacher, Hill, Wardell, Lees, Buckley.
Montrose: Larter; Barr, King, Paterson, Brown K, Forbes, Maver, Lyons, Mackay, Robertson (Brown S), Murray.

Cowdenbeath (0) 0

Albion R (0) 0 600

Cowdenbeath: Allan; Redpath, Baillie, McGovern, Young, Muir L, Malone, Herd (Leetion), Grant, McGonigal, Taylor (Kerr).
Albion R: McCulloch; Edgar, McGowan, Cadden, Oliver, Clark, Houston, Chapman, Graham, Rodgers, Teevan (Cougan).
aet; Albion R won 4-3 on penalties

Queen's Park (0) 1 *(Lennox)*

Stranraer (2) 2 *(McCutcheon (pen), McMillan)* 350

Queen's Park: Monaghan; Boyle, McLaughlin, McLean S, Jack, Hendry (McEntegart), McLean P, Armstrong, Lennox, Caven, Crooks.
Stranraer: Duffy; Lowe (Edgar), Hay, McCutcheon, Rogers, Watt, McMillan, McNiven, Arthur, Donnelly (Day), Henderson.

Stenhousemuir (1) 3 *(Sexton 2, McCafferty)*

Berwick R (0) 0 400

Stenhousemuir: Robertson; Robinson, Gillen, Cairney, Beaton, Erwin, Maitland, McCafferty, Walker (Elliott), Sexton, Condie.
Berwick R: Donaldson; Leitch, Fleming, Douglas, Wood, Shell, Graham, Hughes (Neil), Bickmore, Porteous, Kirkhope (Oliver).

11 AUG *(after 1-1 on 10 Aug, match abandoned – floodlight failure)*

East Stirling (0) 0

Arbroath (0) 1 *(Forrest)* 600

East Stirling: Kelly C; Gilchrist, Russell, McCann (Feeney), Kelly P, Woods, Grant A, Wilson (Lauchlan), Ward, McNeill, Irvine.
Arbroath: McAlpine; Mitchell, Tindal, McEwan, Anderson P, Jack, Forrest, Stewart, Fotheringham (McKenna), Brand (Dewar), Richardson.

SECOND ROUND

16 AUG

Albion R (1) 2 *(Rodgers, Chapman (pen))*

Hamilton A (1) 4 *(Collins, Cadden (og), McNauught, McDonald)* 847

Albion R: McCulloch; Edgar, McGowan, Cadden, Oliver, Clark, Houston (Cougan), Chapman, Graham, Rodgers (McDonald D), Teevan.
Hamilton A: Ferguson; McKee, Kerr, McNaught, Jamieson, Collins (Speirs), Faiirlie, Gordon (McCabe), Harris, Roseburgh, McDonald.

Dumbarton (0) 1 *(McQuade)*

St Mirren (1) 3 *(Hamilton B, Chalmers, McGarvey) (aet)* 3800

Dumbarton: Stevenson; Callan, Cranmer, Doyle, McCahill, Martin, Duncan (McQuade), Fulton, Coyle, Docherty, Cairns (McDougall).
St Mirren: Fridge; Wilson, Winnie, Hamilton B, Godfrey, Cooper, Cameron, Martin, McGarvey, McDowall (Lambert), Chalmers.

Meadowbank Th (2) 2 *(Prentice, Irvine)*

Stirling Albion (1) 1 *(Brogan)* 600

Meadowbank Th: McQueen; Hendrie, Armstrong, Boyd, Tierney, Prentice, Logan, Irvine, Walker, Sprott, McGachie.
Stirling Albion: Graham; Wilson, Mitchell, Given, Smith, McTeague (Gibson A), Gibson C, George, Thompson, Brogan, Kemp.

Partick Th (0) 0

Dundee U (0) 2 *(Paatelainan 2)* 5420

Partick Th: MacLean; Dinnie, Workman, Purdie, McGhie, Dempsey, Kelly, Mitchell, Flood (Thompson), Docherty, Watson (McGinley).
Dundee U: Thomson W; Bowman (McPhee), Malpas, Clark, Hegarty, Narey, French (McGinnis), McKinlay, Paatelainan, Gallacher, Redford.

17 AUG

Aberdeen (2) 4 *(Bett, Hewitt, Miller 2)*

Arbroath (0) 0 9139

Aberdeen: Snelders; McKimmie, Robertson D (Mason), Simpson, McLeish, Miller, Gray (Irvine), Bett, Dodds, Connor, Hewitt.
Arbroath: McAlpine; Mitchell, Jack, McEwan, Anderson P, Todd, Forrest (Tindal), Stewart, Brand, Fotheringham (McKenna), Richardson.

Airdrieonians (0) 0

Motherwell (0) 1 *(Farningham)* 4500

Airdrieonians: Walsh; MacKinnon, Black, McKeown, Grant, Nelson (Lawrie), Butler, Conn, MacCabe, Macdonald K (Campbell), MacDonald I.
Motherwell: Duncan; Wishart, Boyd, Paterson, McCart, Kirk, Smith, Farningham, Cowan, Russell (Philliben), Kinnaird (Mair).

Brechin C (0) 0

Morton (2) 2 *(Alexander, McNeil)* 1100

Brechin C: Lawrie; Hamilton, Watt, Brown, Taylor, Adam, Wardell, Gallacher, Lees (Paterson), Hill (Scott), Buckley.
Morton: Wylie; Collins, Hunter, John Boag, MacDonald, Clinging, Ronald (Roberts), McInnes, Alexander, Turner, McNeil (Fowler).

Celtic (2) 4 *(Burns, Walker 2, McAvennie)*

Ayr U (0) 1 *(Templeton)* 25,044

Celtic: Rough; Morris, Rogan, Whyte, McCarthy, Grant, Miller (McGhee), McStay, McAvennie, Walker, Burns (Stark).
Ayr U: Watson; McIntyre, Love, Furphy, McAllister, Evans, Templeton (McCracken), Wilson, Walker, Sludden, Cowell.

Clyde (0) 0

Rangers (2) 3 *(Drinkell, Walters, Ferguson D)* 14,699

Clyde: Ross; McFarlane, Napier, Anderson, Donnelly, Clark, Willcock (Miller), Rooney, McGlashan, Knox, Mailer (Quinn).
Rangers: Woods; Stevens, Munro, Gough, Wilkins, Butcher, Drinkell, Brown (Ferguson D), McCoist, Durrant, Walters (Cooper D).

Clydebank (0) 2 *(Eadie, Charnley)*

Stenhousemuir (0) 0 1000

Clydebank: Brodie; Treanor, Rodger, Maher (Dickson) (Caffrey), Auld, Harvey, Davies, Wright, Eadie, Bryce, Charnley.
Stenhousemuir: Robertson; Robinson, Gillen, Cairney, Beaton, Erwin, Maitland (Elliott), McCafferty, Walker, Sexton (Loppas), Condie.

Dundee (4) 5 *(McGeachie, Harvey 3, Wright)*

Queen of the S (0) 1 *(Doherty)* 3846

Dundee: Geddes; Forsyth, McKinlay, Chisholm, Smith, Saunders, Lawrence, McGeachie (Kirkwood), Wright, Harvey (Coyne), Campbell S.
Queen of the S: Cunningham; Sinclair, Sim, Johnston, Mackin, Mills, Robertson (Shanks), Hughes, Moore, Hetherington, Doherty (Telfer).

East Fife (1) 1 *(Hunter)*

Dunfermline Ath (1) 1 *(Smith T)* 2396

East Fife: Banner; Connor, Harrow, McCafferty, Reid, McLaren, Hope (Thorpe), Graham (Ogston), Hunter, McNaughton, Scott.
Dunfermline Ath: Westwater; Robertson G, Smith R, Riddell, Williamson, Irons, Smith M, Morrison (Davidson), Jack, Robertson C, Smith T (Callaghan).
aet; Dunfermline Ath won 4-3 on penalties

Falkirk (1) 1 *(Burgess (pen))*

Raith R (1) 1 *(Dalziel (pen))* 3500

Falkirk: Marshall; McIntyre, Holmes, Manley, Burgess, Houston (McVeigh), Romaines, Nicol, McWilliams (McNair), McGivern, Rae.
Raith R: Arthur; McStay, Murray, Coyle, Dennis, Gibson, Simpson, Wright, Ferguson (Strachan), Dalziel (Spence), Sweeney.
aet; Falkirk won 9-8 on penalties.

Hearts (3) 5 *(Ferguson 3 (1 pen), Mackay, Jardine I)*

St Johnstone (0) 0 10,474

Hearts: Smith; Galloway, Murray, Whittaker, Berry, McPherson, Colquhoun, Mackay, Clark, Ferguson, Bannon (Jardine I).
St Johnstone: Balavage; Thompson K, McVicar, Barron, McKillop, Thompson G, Sorbie, Coyle, Maskrey, Watters (Johnston), Heddle (Cherry).

Hibernian (2) 4 *(Kane, Evans, Archibald 2)*

Stranraer (0) 0 8100

Hibernian: Goram; Hunter, Sneddon, Orr (Tortolano), Rae, McIntyre, Weir, Archibald, Kane, Collins, Evans (McCluskey).
Stranraer: Duffy; Lowe, Hay, Watt, Rogers, McCutcheon, McQueen, McNiven (McMillan), Arthur (Lloyd), Frye, Henderson.

Kilmarnock (0) 1 *(Gilmour (pen))*

Forfar Ath (0) 0 1523

Kilmarnock: McCulloch; Montgomerie, Robertson, Davidson, Martin, Marshall (Cook), McConville (Cuthbertson), Gilmour, Bourke, McDonald T, McGuire.
Forfar Ath: Kennedy; Lorimer (Brazil), Hamill, Morris, Smith, Morton, Ormond (Taylor), Clarke S, Brown, Brewster, Clark J.

THIRD ROUND

23 AUG

Hibernian (1) 1 *(Kane)*

Kilmarnock (0) 0 8000

Hibernian: Goram; Hunter, Sneddon, Orr, Rae, McIntyre, Weir, Archibald, Kane (McCluskey), Collins, Evans.
Kilmarnock: McCulloch; Montgomerie, Robertson, Davidson (Harkness), Martin, Marshall, McConville, Gilmour, Bourke (Cook), McDonald T, McGuire.

Meadowbank Th (0) 0 *(at Brockville Park)*

Hearts (1) 2 *(Black, Murray)* 8000

Meadowbank Th: McQueen; Hendrie, Armstrong, Boyd, Tierney, Prentice, Logan, Irvine, Walker, Sprott, McGachie (Reilly).
Hearts: Smith; Galloway, Murray, Whittaker, Berry, McPherson, Colquhoun, Black, Clark (Foster), Mackay, Ferguson (Bannon).

Morton (1) 1 *(Alexander)*

Aberdeen (1) 2 *(Bett 2)* 3131

Morton: Wylie; Collins, Hunter, John Boag, MacDonald, Clinging, Ronald, McInnes, Alexander, Turner (Fowler), Roberts (Robertson D).
Aberdeen: Snelders; McKimmie, Robertson D, Simpson, McLeish, Miller, Irvine, Bett, Dodds, Connor, Hewitt (Wright).

Celtic (3) 7 *(Walker 2, McAvennie 2, Burns, Stark, Archdeacon)*

Hamilton A (0) 2 *(Fairlie 2)* 23,109

Celtic: Andrews; Morris, Rogan, Aitken, McCarthy, Grant, Miller, McStay (Stark), McAvennie, Walker (Archdeacon), Burns.
Hamilton A: Ferguson; McKee, Kerr, McNaught, Jamieson (Speirs), Collins, Fairlie, Harris, Scott (McCabe), Roseburgh, McDonald.

Dundee (0) 2 *(Wright, Lawrence)*

Falkirk (0) 1 *(Rae)* 4962

Dundee: Geddes; Forsyth, McKinlay, Chisholm, Smith, Saunders, Campbell S (Lawrence), Kirkwood, Coyne, Harvey, Wright.
Falkirk: Marshall; McIntyre, Holmes, Manley, Burgess, Nicol, Rae, McVeigh (Romaines), McGivern, Houston, McWilliams.

Dunfermline Ath (2) 2 *(Irons, Watson)*

Motherwell (0) 1 *(Kirk (pen))* 6500

Dunfermline Ath: Westwater; Robertson G, Smith R, Holt, Riddell, Beedie, Smith M (Callaghan), Robertson C, Watson, Smith T, Irons.
Motherwell: Duncan; Wishart, Philliben, Paterson, McAdam (Arnott), Boyd, McBride, Kirk, Cowan, Russell, Kinnaird.

Rangers (3) 6 *(McCoist, Gough, Walters, Wilkins, Drinkell, Durrant)*

Clydebank (0) 0 34,376

Rangers: Woods; Stevens, Munro (Souness), Gough, Wilkins, Butcher, Drinkell, Brown, McCoist, Durrant, Walters (Cooper D).
Clydebank: Brodie; Dickson, Rodger, Treanor, Auld, Maher (Murdoch), Davies, Wright, Eadie, Bryce (Caffrey), Charnley.

St Mirren (0) 1 *(Cameron)*

Dundee U (1) 3 *(Gallacher, Paatelainan, Meade)* 5970

St Mirren: Fridge; Wilson, Winnie, Callagan (McWhirter), Godfrey, Cooper, Cameron, Martin, McGarvey (Lambert), McWalter, Chalmers.
Dundee U: Thomson W; Bowman, Malpas, Beaumont, Clark, Narey, Irvine (Meade), McKinlay, Paatelainan, Gallacher, Redford.

SEMI-FINALS

20 SEPT *(at Dens Park)*

Aberdeen (1) 2 *(Hewitt, Dodds)*

Dundee U (0) 0 18,491

Aberdeen: Snelders; McKimmie, Robertson D (Mason), Simpson, McLeish, Miller, Nicholas, Bett, Dodds, Connor, Hewitt (Grant).
Dundee U: Thomson W; Bowman, Malpas, McInally (Krivopacic), Hegarty, Narey, Paatelainan, McKinlay, Cleland, Gallacher, Meade (French).

21 SEPT *(at Hampden Park)*

Hearts (0) 0

Rangers (1) 3 *(Walters 2, Nisbet)* 53,623

Hearts: Smith; Kidd, Berry, Whittaker, Galloway, McPherson (Murray), Colquhoun, Mackay, Foster (Ferguson), Black, Bannon.
Rangers: Woods; Stevens, Brown, Gough, Wilkins, Butcher, Nisbet (Gray), Ferguson I, Cooper D (Souness), Durrant, Walters.

FINAL

23 OCT *(at Hampden Park)*

Aberdeen (1) 2 *(Dodds 2)*

Rangers (1) 3 *(McCoist 2 (1 pen), Ferguson I)* 72,122

Aberdeen: Snelders; McKimmie, Robertson D, Simpson (Irvine), McLeish, Miller, Nicholas, Bett, Dodds, Connor, Hewitt.
Rangers: Woods; Stevens, Brown, Gough, Wilkins, Butcher, Drinkell, Ferguson I, McCoist, Cooper N, Walters.
Referee: G. B. Smith (Edinburgh).

Ally McCoist (9) scores Rangers winner in the Skol Cup Final against Aberdeen.

SCOTTISH CUP FINALS 1874–1989

Year	*Winners*	*Runners-up*	*Score*
1874	Queen's Park	Clydesdale	2-0
1875	Queen's Park	Renton	3-0
1876	Queen's Park	Third Lanark	2-0 after 1-1 draw
1877	Vale of Leven	Rangers	3-2 after 0-0 and 1-1 draws
1878	Vale of Leven	Third Lanark	1-0
1879	Vale of Leven*	Rangers	
1880	Queen's Park	Thornlibank	3-0
1881	Queen's Park†	Dumbarton	3-1
1882	Queen's Park	Dumbarton	4-1 after 2-2 draw
1883	Dumbarton	Vale of Leven	2-1 after 2-2 draw
1884	Queen's Park‡	Vale of Leven	
1885	Renton	Vale of Leven	3-1 after 0-0 draw
1886	Queen's Park	Renton	3-1
1887	Hibernian	Dumbarton	2-1
1888	Renton	Cambuslang	6-1
1889	Third Lanark§	Celtic	2-1
1890	Queen's Park	Vale of Leven	2-1 after 1-1 draw
1891	Hearts	Dumbarton	1-0
1892	Celtic¶	Queen's Park	5-1
1893	Queen's Park	Celtic	2-1
1894	Rangers	Celtic	3-1
1895	St Bernard's	Renton	2-1
1896	Hearts	Hibernian	3-1
1897	Rangers	Dumbarton	5-1
1898	Rangers	Kilmarnock	2-0
1899	Celtic	Rangers	2-0
1900	Celtic	Queen's Park	4-3
1901	Hearts	Celtic	4-3
1902	Hibernian	Celtic	1-0
1903	Rangers	Hearts	2-0 after 1-1 and 0-0 draws
1904	Celtic	Rangers	3-2
1905	Third Lanark	Rangers	3-1 after 0-0 draw
1906	Hearts	Third Lanark	1-0
1907	Celtic	Hearts	3-0
1908	Celtic	St Mirren	5-1
1909	••		
1910	Dundee	Clyde	2-1 after 2-2 and 0-0 draws
1911	Celtic	Hamilton A	2-0 after 0-0 draw
1912	Celtic	Clyde	2-0
1913	Falkirk	Raith R	2-0
1914	Celtic	Hibernian	4-1 after 0-0 draw
1920	Kilmarnock	Albion R	3-2
1921	Partick T	Rangers	1-0
1922	Morton	Rangers	1-0
1923	Celtic	Hibernian	1-0
1924	Airdrieonians	Hibernian	2-0
1925	Celtic	Dundee	2-1
1926	St Mirren	Celtic	2-0
1927	Celtic	East Fife	3-1
1928	Rangers	Celtic	4-0
1929	Kilmarnock	Rangers	2-0
1930	Rangers	Partick T	2-1 after 0-0 draw
1931	Celtic	Motherwell	4-2 after 2-2 draw
1932	Rangers	Kilmarnock	3-0 after 1-1 draw
1933	Celtic	Motherwell	1-0
1934	Rangers	St Mirren	5-0
1935	Rangers	Hamilton A	2-1
1936	Rangers	Third Lanark	1-0
1937	Celtic	Aberdeen	2-1
1938	East Fife	Kilmarnock	4-2 after 1-1 draw
1939	Clyde	Motherwell	4-0
1947	Aberdeen	Hibernian	2-1
1948	Rangers	Morton	1-0 after 1-1 draw
1949	Rangers	Clyde	4-1
1950	Rangers	East Fife	3-0
1951	Celtic	Motherwell	1-0
1952	Motherwell	Dundee	4-0

Year	*Winners*	*Runners-up*	*Score*
1953	Rangers	Aberdeen	1-0 after 1-1 draw
1954	Celtic	Aberdeen	2-1
1955	Clyde	Celtic	1-0 after 1-1 draw
1956	Hearts	Celtic	3-1
1957	Falkirk	Kilmarnock	2-1 after 1-1 draw
1958	Clyde	Hibernian	1-0
1959	St Mirren	Aberdeen	3-1
1960	Rangers	Kilmarnock	2-0
1961	Dunfermline Ath	Celtic	2-0 after 0-0 draw
1962	Rangers	St Mirren	2-0
1963	Rangers	Celtic	3-0 after 1-1 draw
1964	Rangers	Dundee	3-1
1965	Celtic	Dunfermline Ath	3-2
1966	Rangers	Celtic	1-0 after 0-0 draw
1967	Celtic	Aberdeen	2-0
1968	Dunfermline Ath	Hearts	3-1
1969	Celtic	Rangers	4-0
1970	Aberdeen	Celtic	3-1
1971	Celtic	Rangers	2-1 after 1-1 draw
1972	Celtic	Hibernian	6-1
1973	Rangers	Celtic	3-2
1974	Celtic	Dundee U	3-0
1975	Celtic	Airdrieonians	3-1
1976	Rangers	Hearts	3-1
1977	Celtic	Rangers	1-0
1978	Rangers	Aberdeen	2-1
1979	Rangers	Hibernian	3-2 after 0-0 and 0-0 draws
1980	Celtic	Rangers	1-0
1981	Rangers	Dundee U	4-1 after 0-0 draw
1982	Aberdeen	Rangers	4-1 (aet)
1983	Aberdeen	Rangers	1-0 (aet)
1984	Aberdeen	Celtic	2-1 (aet)
1985	Celtic	Dundee U	2-1
1986	Aberdeen	Hearts	3-0
1987	St Mirren	Dundee U	1-0 (aet)
1988	Celtic	Dundee U	2-1
1989	Celtic	Rangers	1-0

*Vale of Leven awarded cup, Rangers failed to appear for replay after 1-1 draw.
†After Dumbarton protested the first game, which Queen's Park won 2-1.
‡Queen's Park awarded cup, Vale of Leven failing to appear.
§Replay by order of Scottish FA because of playing conditions in first match, won 3-0 by Third Lanark.
¶After mutual protested game which Celtic won 1-0.
•• Owing to riot, the cup was withheld after two drawn games – Celtic 2-1, Rangers 2-1.

SCOTTISH CUP WINS

Celtic 29, Rangers 24, Queen's Park 10, Aberdeen 6, Hearts 5, Clyde 3, St Mirren 3, Vale of Leven 3, Dunfermline Ath 2, Falkirk 2, Hibernian 2, Kilmarnock 2, Renton 2, Third Lanark 2, Airdrieonians 1, Dumbarton 1, Dundee 1, East Fife 1, Morton 1, Motherwell 1, Partick Th 1, St Bernard's 1.

APPEARANCES IN FINAL

Celtic 45, Rangers 40, Aberdeen 12, Queen's Park 12, Hearts 10, Hibernian 10, Kilmarnock 7, Vale of Leven 7, Clyde 6, Dumbarton 6, St Mirren 6, Third Lanark 6, Dundee U 5, Motherwell 5, Renton 5, Dundee 4, Dunfermline Ath 3, East Fife 3, Airdrieonians 2, Falkirk 2, Hamilton A 2, Morton 2, Partick Th 2, Albion R 2, Cambuslang 1, Clydesdale 1, Raith R 1, St Bernard's 1, Thornlibank 1.

SCOTTISH CUP 1989

FIRST ROUND
3 DEC

Berwick R (0) 1 *(Sloan)*

Alloa (0) 1 *(Lytwyn)* 395

Berwick R: Donaldson; Oliver, McLaren, Leetion (Porteous), Locke, Muir, Sloan, Thorpe, Bickmore (Graham), Hughes, Callachan.
Alloa: Lowrie; Rodgers, Haggart, Millen, Lee R, Gibson, Smith A, (Smith S), Bateman, Lytwyn, Lee I, Lamont.

East Fife (1) 4 *(Hunter, Pittman, Hope, Bardsley)*

Spartans (1) 1 *(Campbell)* 606

East Fife: Charles; Hall, Pittman, McCafferty, Reid, Deas, Mitchell (Hope), Scott, Hunter, Harrow, McNaughton (Bardsley).
Spartans: Rennie; Carney, Macdonald, Reid, Lennox, Campbell, Egan, Smith, Hardie, Graham, Grant.

East Stirling (0) 1 *(Wilcox D)*

Gala Fairydean (0) 300

East Stirling: Kelly C; Russell, Feeney, Wilcox D, McCann, Woods, Grant A, Wilson, McNeill, Lauchlan, McGraw (O'Brien).
Gala Fairydean: Ramage; Henry, Thomson, Collins, Anderson, Loughran, Frizzel R, Renwick (Malone), Smith, Frizzel I, Ainslie.

Inverness T (0) 0

Dumbarton (0) 0 900

Inverness T: Calder; Skinner, Stevenson, Wilson, Macdonald D, Christie, Macdonald A, Clark (Morrison), Taylor, Robertson, Noble.
Dumbarton: Stevenson (Douglas); Doyle G, Gow, McCahill, Cairney, McGowan, MacIver, Elliott, Duncan, McQuade, Docherty.

Montrose (1) 2 *(Lyons, Maver)*

Arbroath (0) 0 1000

Montrose: Larter; Morrison, King, Brown K, Paterson, Forbes, Maver, Lyons, MacKay, McGlashan, Powell.
Arbroath: McGuinness; Tindal, Fleming, McEwan, Anderson P, Jack, Forrest, Stewart, Brand, Fotheringham, Richardson.

Stranraer (1) 2 *(McMillan, Lloyd)*

Stirling Albion (0) 2 *(Brogan 2)* 800

Stranraer: Duffy; Lowe, Hay, McNiven, Armour, McCutcheon, McInnes, McMillan, Lloyd, Henderson, Donnelly.
Stirling Albion: Graham; Wilson, Tennant, Aitchison, McTeague, Maxwell, George (Given), Mitchell (Gibson A), Gibson C, Kemp, Brogan.

FIRST ROUND REPLAYS
7 DEC

Alloa (1) 2 *(Lamont 2)*

Berwick R (0) 1 *(Hughes)* 538

Alloa: Lowrie; Robertson, Haggart, Millen, Lee R, Gibson, Smith S (Smith A), Rodgers, Lytwyn, Lee I (Bateman), Lamont.
Berwick R: Donaldson; Oliver, McLaren (Graham), Leetion (Porteous), Locke, Muir, Sloan, Thorpe, Bickmore, Hughes, Callachan.

10 DEC

Dumbarton (1) 2 *(Cairney, MacIver)*

Inverness T (0) 1 *(Christie)* 1000

Dumbarton: Strachan; Doyle G, Gow, McCahill, Cairney, McGowan, MacIver, Elliott, Duncan (Cairns), McQuade, Docherty.
Inverness T: Calder; Skinner, Stevenson, Wilson, Macdonald D, Christie, Macdonald A, Morrison (Rees), Taylor, Clark, Noble.

Stirling Albion (0) 0

Stranraer (1) 1 *(McMillan)* 547

Stirling Albion: Graham; Wilson, Tennant, Aitchison (Given), McTeague, Maxwell, George, Mitchell (Gibson A), Gibson C, Kemp, Brogan.
Stranraer: Duffy; Lowe, Hay, McNiven, Armour, McCutcheon, McInnes, McMillan, Lloyd, Henderson, Donnelly (Watt).

SECOND ROUND

7 JAN

Annan Ath (0) 1 *(Elliot (pen))*

Queen's Park (3) 5 *(Elliot 2, Brown 2, McLaughlin)* 1124

Annan Ath: Walker; Dalgleish (Middlemiss), Anderson, Rome, White, Findlay (Clark), Dick, Elliot,Proudfoot, Rayson, Learmont.
Queen's Park: Monaghan; Boyle, McLaughlin, McLean P, Elder, Hendry, Armstrong, Morton (Lennox), Elliot, Brown, Crooks (O'Brien).

Caledonian (0) 1 *(Lisle)*

Brechin C (0) 1 *(Adam)* 1800

Caledonian: Morrison; Davidson, Mann (Bell), Hercher, Bellshaw, Andrew, Hill, Lisle, Polwarth, Duff, Robertson.
Brechin C: Lawrie; Hamilton, Candlish, Wilkie, Stevens, Hill (Gillespie), Wardell, Adam, Paterson I A, Scott, Buckley (Lees).

Coldstream (1) 1 *(Davidson)*

Albion R (1) 1 *(McGowan)* 700

Coldstream: Kerr; Middlemiss (Herbert), Notman, Fleming, Mitchell, Hunter, Wilson (Ritchie), Hume, Byrne, Jack, Davidson.
Albion R: McCulloch; McDonald, McGowan, Chapman (Watson), Oliver, Clark, Diver, Cadden, Graham, Granger, Teevan (Cougan).

Cowdenbeath (0) 1 *(Kerr)*

Stenhousemuir (0) 1 *(Erwin (pen))* 463

Cowdenbeath: Allan; Baillie, Burnside, Malone, Douglas, Kerr, McGonigal, McGovern, Mackenzie, Reid, Hoggan (Young).
Stenhousemuir: Robertson; Philliben, Robinson,

Cairney, Beaton, Sexton, Bell, McCafferty, Walker, Erwin, Moore.

East Stirling (0) 1 *(Wilson)*

Montrose (0) 2 *(Murray, Mackay)* 300

East Stirling: Kelly C; Gilchrist (McGraw), Russell, Wilcox, McCann, Scott, Grant A, Drew, McNeill, Lauchlan, Wilson.
Montrose: Larter; Morrison, Barr, Brown K, Paterson, Forbes, Allan (Mackay), Lyons (Halley), Maver, McGlashan, Murray.

Elgin C (1) 2 *(McGinlay D, McGinlay J)*

Dumbarton (1) 2 *(McQuade, McGowan)* 2074

Elgin C: Gunn; McLennan, Slavin, Mone, Cran (Bennett), Mackay, Teasdale, McGinlay D, Jappy, McGinlay J, Paul (Bowie).
Dumbarton: Strachan; Doyle G, Wharton, McCahill, Cairney, McGowan, MacIver (Docherty), Doyle J, Spence, Robertson, McQuade.

Forres Mechanics (0) 1 *(Grant)*

Alloa (1) 1 *(Gibson)* 1010

Forres M: Gray; Forsyth, Milne, McCulloch, Walker, Mackay (Davidson M), Grant, Mulholland (Winton), Dunbar, Davidson G, Minty.
Alloa: Lowrie; Robertson, Lee R, Millen, McCulloch, Gibson, Blackie (Bateman), Rodgers (Smith A), Lytwyn, Lee I, Ramsay.

Stranraer (2) 2 *(Ewing 2)*

East Fife (0) 1 *(Mitchell)* 1250

Stranraer: Duffy; Watt, Hay, Gallagher, Armour, McCutcheon, McInnes, McNiven, Frye, Cuthbertson, Ewing.
East Fife: Charles; Connor, Pittman, McCafferty (Harrow), Reid, Deas, Mitchell, Hall, Hunter, Gallacher, Bardsley (McNaughton).

SECOND ROUND REPLAYS

14 JAN

Albion R (0) 1 *(Diver)*

Coldstream (0) 0 617

Albion R: McCulloch; McDonald, McGowan, Cadden, Oliver, Clark, Teevan, Chapman (Watson), Graham, Granger, Diver (Bishop).
Coldstream: Kerr; Middlemiss, Notman, Fleming, Mitchell, Hunter (Herbert), Wilson, Hume, Byrne, Jack (Ritchie), Davidson.

Alloa (1) 2 *(Lytwyn, Smith A)*

Forres Mechanics (0) 0 884

Alloa: Lowrie; Robertson, Lee R, Millen, McCulloch, Gibson, Smith A, Bateman (Findlay), Lytwyn, Lee I, Ramsay (West).
Forres M: Gray; Forsyth (Winton), Milne, McCulloch, Walker, Mackay, Grant (Davidson M), Mulholland, Dunbar, Davidson G, Minty.

Brechin C (1) 2 *(Adam, Scott)*

Caledonian (1) 1 *(Hercher (pen))* 450

Brechin C: Lawrie; Hamilton, Candlish, Brown R, Stevens, Paterson I G, Wardell, Adam, Paterson I A, Scott, Ritchie (Lees).
Caledonian: Morrison; Davidson, Mann, Hercher, Hill, Andrew, Hay (Docherty), Lisle, Duff (Mackay), Bell, Robertson.

Dumbarton (1) 4 *(Cairney, MacIver 2, McQuade)*

Elgin C (0) 0 1000

Dumbarton: Strachan; Doyle G, Wharton, McCahill, Cairney, Doyle J, MacIver (Docherty), McGowan, Spence, Robertson (Elliott), McQuade.
Elgin C: Gunn; McArthur (Bennett), McLennan, Mone, Slavin, Mackay, Teasdale, Bowie, Jappy, McGinlay J, McGinlay D (Paul).

Stenhousemuir (2) 3 *(Beaton, Erwin, Sexton)*

Cowdenbeath (0) 2 *(Mackenzie, Young)* 550

Stenhousemuir: Robertson; Philliben, Gillen (Buchanan), Cairney, Beaton, Sexton, Bell (Condie), Moore, Walker, Erwin, Robinson.
Cowdenbeath: Allan; Watt, Baillie, Malone, Young, Kerr, Burnside (Hoggan), Douglas (Reid), Mackenzie, McGonigal, McGovern.

THIRD ROUND
28 JAN

Alloa (1) 3 *(Smith A 2, Gibson)*

Albion R (0) 1 *(McDonald)* 923

Alloa: Lowrie; Haggart, Lee R, Millen, McCulloch, Gibson, Conlin (West), Ramsay, Lytwyn, Lee I, Smith A (Bateman).
Albion R: McCulloch; McDonald, McGowan, Watson (Diver), Oliver, Clark, Bishop, Cadden, Graham, Granger (Edgar), Teevan.

Celtic (0) 2 *(Walker, Burns)*

Dumbarton (0) 0 24,844

Celtic: Bonner; Morris, Rogan, Whyte (Stark), McCarthy, Grant, Miller (Baillie), McStay, Walker, McGhee, Burns.
Dumbarton: Strachan; Doyle G, Wharton, McCahill, Cairney (Docherty), McGowan, McQuade A, Doyle J (Robertson), Spence, MacIver, McQuade J.

Clydebank (0) 2 *(Eadie, Coyle)*

Montrose (0) 1 *(Murray)* 1054

Clydebank: Gallacher; Treanor, Dickson, Maher, Auld, Harvey (Hughes), Davies, Wright, Eadie, Bryce, Coyle.
Montrose: Larter; Morrison, McLelland (Barr), Brown, Paterson, Forbes, Allan, Lyons, Murray (Mackay), McGlashan, Maver.

Dundee (0) 1 *(Angus)*

Dundee U (1) 2 *(Bowman, Meade)* 18,117

Dundee: Geddes; Holt, Kirkwood (Smith), Chisholm, Forsyth, Saunders, Frail, Angus, Wright, Coyne, McBride (Rafferty).
Dundee U: Thomson W; Bowman, Malpas, McInally, Hegarty, Narey, French, Krivokapic, Gallacher, Meade (Sturrock), Paatelainan.

Dunfermline Ath (0) 0

Aberdeen (0) 0 16,656

Dunfermline Ath: Westwater; Robertson G, Smith R, Riddell, Tierney, Beedie, Burns, Smith P, Jack, Watson, Irons.

Aberdeen: Snelders; McKimmie, Robertson I, Simpson, McLeish, Irvine, Nicholas, Bett, Dodds, Connor, Mason (Grant).

Falkirk (1) 1 *(Burgess (pen))*

Motherwell (0) 1 *(Kirk (pen))* 7500

Falkirk: Marshall; McNair, Holmes, Manley, Burgess, Nicol, Rutherford, Mennie, Rae, Hetherston, McWilliams.
Motherwell: Maxwell; Wishart, Boyd, Paterson, McAdam, McCart, Russell, O'Neill, MacCabe (Cowan), Kirk, Kinnaird (McBride).

Forfar Ath (1) 1 *(Clark J)*

Clyde (0) 1 *(Mailer)* 971

Forfar Ath: Kennedy; Bennett, Morton, Brazil, Smith, Clarke S, Ward (Hamill), Lorimer, Brown (Whyte), Brewster, Clark J.
Clyde: Atkins; McFarlane, Cowan, Tait, Speirs, Clark, Willock, Nolan, McGlashan, Rooney, Quinn (Mailer).

Hearts (2) 4 *(McIntyre (og), Galloway, Colquhoun, McPherson)*

Ayr U (1) 1 *(Templeton)* 15,916

Hearts: Smith; McLaren, McKinlay, McPherson, Berry, Levein (Sandison), Galloway, Mackay, Colquhoun, Robertson, Bannon.
Ayr U: Watson; McIntyre, Hughes, Furphy, Kennedy, Evans, Templeton, Wilson (Walker), Scott, Sludden, Cowell.

Hibernian (0) 1 *(Collins)*

Brechin C (0) 0 7746

Hibernian: Goram; Hunter, Tortolano, Orr, Rae, Mitchell, McCluskey (Findlay), Archibald, Kane, Collins, Evans.
Brechin C: Lawrie; Healy, Candlish, Brown, Ritchie, Wilkie, Wardell (Buckley), Paterson I G, Paterson I A (Kennedy), Scott, Lees.

Morton (0) 0

Airdrieonians (0) 0 3400

Morton: Wylie; Collins, Pickering, Hunter, John Boag, O'Hara, Ronald (Robertson D), Fowler, Alexander, McInnes, Turner.
Airdrieonians: Martin; MacKinnon (Lawrie), Black, Nelson, Grant, McLeod, Conn, McPhee, Butler, Macdonald K, MacDonald I.

Partick T (0) 0

St Mirren (0) 0 8700

Partick T: Brough; Dinnie, Kerr, Law, Dempsey, Collins, Mitchell, Abercromby (McDonald), Flood, McCoy, Charnley.
St Mirren: Fridge; Martin, Winnie, Lambert, Godfrey, Cooper, Chalmers, Walker, McWalter, Davies, Weir.

Queen of the S (1) 2 *(McGuire, Sloan)*

Kilmarnock (1) 2 *(Davidson, Speirs)* 2941

Queen of the S: Ferguson; Shanks (Sim), McDonald, Gray, Mills, Bain, Reid, Sloan, Cook, Hetherington, McGuire (Gamble).
Kilmarnock: McCulloch; Millar, McLean, Montgomerie, MacFarlane, Davidson (Lindsay), Reilly, Watters, Faulds (Harkness), Walker, Speirs.

Queen's Park (0) 0

Stranraer (0) 0 1737

Queen's Park: Monaghan; Boyle, McLaughlin, McLean P, McNamee, Lennox, Caven, Armstrong, O'Brien (Elliot), Brown, Crooks.
Stranraer: Duffy; Doherty (Cuthbertson), Hay, Gallagher, Armour, McCutcheon, McInnes, McNiven, Frye, Henderson, Donnelly (Ewing).

Raith R (0) 1 *(Dalziel)*

Rangers (0) 1 *(Ferguson I)* 10,000

Raith R: Arthur; McStay, Murray, Fraser, Glennie, Gibson, Ferguson, Dalziel (Marshall), Logan (Romaines), Coyle, Sweeney.
Rangers: Walker; Stevens, Munro, Nicholl, Wilkins (McCoist), Butcher, Drinkell, Ferguson I, Ferguson D, Brown, Walters.

St Johnstone (1) 2 *(Heddle, Sorbie)*

Stenhousemuir (0) 0 2490

St Johnstone: Balavage; Thomson K, McVicar, Barron, Cherry, Coyle, Maskrey, Jenkins, Grant (Sorbie), Heddle, Irvine (Spence).
Stenhousemuir: Robertson; Philliben, Hamill (Elliott), Cairney, Beaton, Sexton, Bell (Barrie), Moore, Condie, Erwin, Robinson.

29 JAN

Meadowbank T (0) 2 *(Lawrence, Logan)*

Hamilton A (0) 0 1895

Meadowbank T: McQueen; McCormack, Armstrong, Boyd, Williamson, Prentice, Logan, Irvine, Lawrence, Sprott, Perry (Scott).
Hamilton A: Rough; McKee, Napier, Miller, Jamieson, Nelson (Fraser), Gordon, Roseburgh, Harris (Gallagher), Weir, McDonald.

THIRD ROUND REPLAYS

31 JAN

Clyde (0) 0

Forfar Ath (1) 1 *(Brewster)* 600

Clyde: Atkins; McFarlane, Cowan, Tait (McCabe), Speirs, Clark, Willock, Nolan, McGlashan, Rooney (Millar), Mailer.
Forfar Ath: Kennedy; Bennett, Hamill, Brazil, Smith, Morton, Clarke S, Lorimer, Brown, Brewster, Whyte.

St Mirren (0) 1 *(Weir (pen))*

Partick T (2) 3 *(McCoy 2, Mitchell)* 8426

St Mirren: Fridge; Wilson (McGarvey), Winnie, Lambert, Godfrey, Cooper, Chalmers, Martin, McWalter, Davies, Weir.
Partick T: Brough; Dinnie, Kerr, Law, Dempsey, Collins, Mitchell, Workman, Flood, McCoy, Charnley.

1 FEB

Aberdeen (1) 3 *(Wright 2, Nicholas)*

Dunfermline Ath (0) 1 *(Smith T)* 21,500

Aberdeen: Snelders; McKimmie, Robertson I, Simpson (Robertson C), McLeish, Irvine, Nicholas, Bett, Dodds, Connor, Wright.

Dunfermline Ath: Westwater; Robertson G, Smith R, Riddell, Tierney, Beedie, Burns, Smith P, Jack, Watson (Smith T), Irons (Smith M).

Airdrieonians (0) 0

Morton (1) 1 *(John Boag)* 4500

Airdrieonians: Martin; Lawrie, Black, Nelson, Grant, McLeod, Conn, McPhee, Campbell, Macdonald K, MacDonald I, [Butler] [Thomson].
Morton: Wylie; Collins, Pickering, Hunter, John Boag, O'Hara, Ronald, Fowler, Alexander, McInnes, Turner.

Kilmarnock (0) 0

Queen of the S (1) 1 *(McGuire)* 5600

Kilmarnock: McCulloch; Montgomerie, McLean, MacFarlane, Marshall, Davidson, Reilly, Watters, Faulds, Derek Walker (Harkness), Speirs (Lindsay).
Queen of the S: Ferguson; Johnston, McDonald, Gray, Mills, Bain, Reid, Sloan, Cook, Hetherington (Gamble), McGuire (Sim).

Motherwell (0) 2 *(Kirk 2)*

Falkirk (0) 1 *(Rutherford)* 7029

Motherwell: Maxwell; Wishart, Boyd, Paterson, McAdam, McCart, McBride (Gahagan), O'Neill, Cowan (Bryce), Kirk, Kinnaird.
Falkirk: Marshall; McNair (Gallacher), Holmes, Manley, Burgess, Nicol, Rutherford, Hetherston, McGivern, Mennie (Rae), McWilliams.

Rangers (1) 3 *(Walters, Drinkell, Fraser (og))*

Raith R (0) 0 40,307

Rangers: Walker; Stevens, Brown, Gough, Cooper N, Butcher, Drinkell, Ferguson I, McCoist, Walters, Ferguson D (Munro).
Raith R: Arthur; McStay, Murray, Fraser, Glennie, Gibson, Ferguson (Marshall), Dalziel (Romaines), Logan, Coyle, Sweeney.

Stranraer (1) 1 *(McInnes)*

Queen's Park (0) 0 2500

Stranraer: Duffy; McNiven, Hay, Gallagher, Armour, McCutcheon, McInnes, Cuthbertson, Lloyd, Henderson (Ewing), Donnelly (Frye).
Queen's Park: Monaghan; Boyle, McLaughlin, McLean P, McNamee, Lennox, Caven, Armstrong, O'Brien, Hendry (Elliot), Crooks (Brown).

FOURTH ROUND

18 FEB

Aberdeen (1) 1 *(Connor)*

Dundee U (0) 1 *(Paatelainan (pen))* 23,000

Aberdeen: Snelders; McKimmie, Robertson I, Simpson, McLeish, Irvine, Nicholas, Bett, Wright, Connor, Van der Ark (Hewitt).
Dundee U: Thomson W; Clark, Malpas, McInally, Hegarty, Narey, French (Meade), Krivokapic, Gallacher, Bowman, Paatelainan.

Celtic (2) 4 *(Burns 2, Stark, McAvennie)*

Clydebank (1) 1 *(Treanor (pen))* 23,141

Celtic: Bonner; Morris, Rogan, Aitken, McCarthy, Grant, Stark, McStay, McAvennie, McGhee, Burns.
Clydebank: Gallacher; Treanor, Spence, Dickson, Auld, Harvey, Davies, Murdoch, Eadie, Bryce (Hughes), Coyle.

Hearts (0) 2 *(Bannon, Colquhoun)*

Partick T (0) 0 18,350

Hearts: Smith; McLaren, McKinlay, McPherson, Kidd, Berry, Galloway, Mackay (Black), Colquhoun, Robertson (Ferguson), Bannon.
Partick T: Brough; Dinnie, Kerr, Law, Dempsey, Collins, Mitchell, Peebles, Flood, McCoy, Charnley.

Hibernian (1) 2 *(Collins, May)*

Motherwell (0) 1 *(Bryce)* 12,000

Hibernian: Goram; Hunter, Tortolano, May, McIntyre, Mitchell, Orr, Archibald, Kane, Collins, Evans.
Motherwell: Maxwell; Wishart, Boyd (Mair), Paterson, McAdam, McCart, Shanks (Bryce), O'Neill, Kinnaird, Kirk, Gahagan.

Meadowbank T (0) 0

Morton (1) 1 *(Turner)* 750

Meadowbank T: McQueen; McCormack, Armstrong, Boyd, Williamson, Prentice, Logan, Irvine, Park, Sprott, Hendrie (Perry).
Morton: Wylie; Collins, Pickering, Hunter, MacDonald, O'Hara, Ronald, Fowler, Robertson J, McInnes, Turner.

Queen of the S (0) 0

Alloa (0) 0 1800

Queen of the S: Holland; Shanks, Gray, McDonald (Telfer), Gamble (Sim), Fraser, Reid, Sloan, Cook, Hetherington, McGuire.
Alloa: Lowrie; Haggart, Lee R (Rodgers), Millen, McCulloch, Gibson, Blackie (Smith A), Ramsay, McCallum, Lee I, Lytwyn.

Rangers (6) 8 *(Ferguson I, Drinkell 2, Brown 2, McCoist 2 (1 pen), Walters)*

Stranraer (0) 0 41,198

Rangers: Woods; Stevens, Brown, Gough, Wilkins, Butcher, Drinkell, Ferguson I (McCall), McCoist, Walters, Ferguson D (Munro).
Stranraer: Duffy; McNiven, Hay, Gallacher, Armour, McCutcheon (Ewing), McInnes, Lloyd, Doherty (Cuthbertson), Henderson, Donnelly.

St Johnstone (0) 2 *(Maskrey 2)*

Forfar Ath (1) 1 *(Ward)* 4060

St Johnstone: Balavage; Thomson K, McVicar, Barron, Cherry, Thompson G, Maskrey, Coyle, Grant, Jenkins (Sorbie), Irvine (Johnston).
Forfar Ath: Kennedy; Bennett (Brewster), Hamill, Morris, Smith, Morton, Ward, Lorimer, Brown, Clark S (Clark J), Whyte.

FOURTH ROUND REPLAYS

22 FEB

Alloa (1) 4 *(Ramsay, Lytwyn, Smith A 2)*

Queen of the S (1) 2 *(Hetherington, McDonald)* 2642

Alloa: Lowrie; Robertson, Haggart, Millen, McCulloch, Gibson, Blackie, Ramsay, Lytwyn, Lee I, McCallum (Smith A).

Queen of the S: Holland; Johnston, Gray, McDonald, Mills, Fraser, Reid, Sloan, Cook, Hetherington, McGuire.

Dundee U (0) 1 *(Paatelainan (pen))*

Aberdeen (0) 1 *(Grant)*
after extra time (0-0 full time) 18,756

Dundee U: Thomson W; Clark, Malpas, McInally, Hegarty, Narey, Meade (Sturrock), McGinnis, Gallacher, McKinlay (Krivokapic), Paatelainan.
Aberdeen: Snelders; McKimmie, Robertson I (Dodds), Simpson, McLeish, Irvine, Irvine, Nicholas, Bett, Wright, Connor (Grant), Hewitt.

FOURTH ROUND, SECOND REPLAY

27 FEB

Dundee U (0) 1 *(Paatelainan)*

Aberdeen (0) 0 21,095

Dundee U: Thomson W; Clark, Malpas, McInally, Hegarty, Narey, Meade (McLeod), Krivokapic, McKinlay, Sturrock, Paatelainan.
Aberdeen: Snelders; McKimmie, Robertson I, Simpson (Dodds), McLeish, Irvine, Nicholas, Bett, Wright, Connor, Grant.

QUARTER-FINALS

18 MAR

Celtic (2) 2 *(McGhee, Aitken (pen))*

Hearts (0) 1 *(Bannon)* 46,348

Celtic: Bonner; Morris, Rogan, Aitken, McCarthy, Grant, Stark, McStay, McAvennie, McGhee, Burns.
Hearts: Smith; McLaren, McKinlay, Levein (Kidd), Berry, McPherson, Colquhoun, MacKay, Galloway, Ferguson (Robertson), Bannon.

Hibernian (1) 1 *(Kane)*

Alloa (0) 0 10,500

Hibernian: Goram; Sneddon, Tortolano, Orr, Rae, Hunter (McIntyre), Findlay (McCluskey), Archibald, Kane, Collins, Evans.
Alloa: Lowrie; Haggart (Rodgers), Lee R, Millen, McCulloch, Gibson, Blackie, Ramsay, McCallum, Lee I, Lytwyn (Smith A).

21 MAR

Rangers (0) 2 *(Drinkell, McCoist)*

Dundee U (1) 2 *(Gallacher, Paatelainan)* 42,177

Rangers: Woods; Stevens, Munro, Gough, Sterland, Butcher, Drinkell, Ferguson I, McCoist, Cooper N (Wilkins), Walters.
Dundee U: Thomson; McGinnis, Malpas, McInally, Hegarty, Narey, McKinlay, Krivokapic (Bowman), Paatelainan, Sturrock (Irvine), Gallacher.

22 MAR

Morton (1) 2 *(Turner, Robertson D)*

St Johnstone (2) 2 *(Coyle (pen), Grant)* 6300

Morton: Wylie; Collins (McNeil), Pickering, O'Hara, John Boag, Clinging, Spencer, McInnes (Robertson D), Alexander, Fowler, Turner.
St Johnstone: Balavage; Thomson K, McVicar, Barron, Cherry, Thompson G (Jenkins), Maskrey, Coyle, Grant, Johnston (Sorbie), Heddle.

QUARTER-FINALS REPLAYS

27 MAR

Dundee U (0) 0

Rangers (0) 1 *(McCoist)* 21,872

Dundee U: Thomson; Clark, Malpas, McInally, Hegarty, Narey, McKinlay, McGinnis, Paatelainan (Krivokapic), Sturrock, Gallacher (McLeod J).
Rangers: Woods; Stevens, Munro, Gough, Wilkins, Butcher, Drinkell, Ferguson I, McCoist, Sterland (Brown), Walters.

St Johnstone (2) 3 *(Maskrey 2, Jenkins)*

Morton (1) 2 *(Robertson D, Alexander)* 8337

St Johnstone: Balavage; Thomson K, McVicar, Barron, Cherry, Thompson G (Jenkins), Maskrey, Coyle, Grant, Johnston (Sorbie), Heddle.
Morton: Wylie; John Boag, Pickering, Hunter, MacDonald, Clinging, Robertson D, McInnes (McNeil), Alexander, Spencer, Turner (O'Hara).

SEMI-FINALS

15 APR *at Celtic Park*

Rangers (0) 0

St Johnstone (0) 0 47,374

Rangers: Woods; Stevens, Munro, Gough, Wilkins, Butcher, Drinkell, Sterland (Cooper D), McCoist, Brown, Walters.
St Johnstone: Balavage; Thomson K, McVicar, Barron, Cherry, Jenkins, Sorbie, Coyle (Irvine), Grant, Johnston, Heddle (Smith).

16 APR *at Hampden Park*

Celtic (3) 3 *(McCarthy, McGhee, Walker)*

Hibernian (0) 1 *(Archibald)* 42,160

Celtic: Bonner; Grant, Burns, Aitken, McCarthy, Fulton, Stark, McStay, Walker, McGhee, Miller.
Hibernian: Goram; Hunter, Tortolano, Orr, Rae, McIntyre (Mitchell), Houchen, Archibald, Kane, Collins, Evans.

SEMI-FINAL REPLAY

18 APR *at Celtic Park*

Rangers (2) 4 *(Walters, Stevens, Drinkell, McCoist)*

St Johnstone (0) 0 44,205

Rangers: Woods; Stevens, Munro, Gough, Wilkins (Cooper D), Butcher, Drinkell (Gray), Ferguson D, McCoist, Brown, Walters.
St Johnstone: Balavage; Thomson K, McVicar, Barron, Cherry, Jenkins, Maskrey (Irvine), Sorbie (Smith), Grant, Johnston, Heddle.

FINAL

20 MAY *at Hampden Park*

Celtic (1) 1 *(Miller)*

Rangers (0) 0 72,069

Celtic: Bonner; Morris, Rogan, Aitken, McCarthy, Whyte, Grant, McStay, Miller, McGhee, Burns.
Rangers: Woods; Stevens, Munro (Souness), Gough, Sterland (Cooper D), Butcher, Drinkell, Ferguson I, McCoist, Brown, Walters.

Referee: Mr R B Valentine (Dundee).

20 YEARS OF SPORT AND THE LAW

Twenty Years ago on February 7, 1969, after Pele had been brutally assaulted on English soccer fields out of the 1966 World Cup by Portuguese and Bulgarian players named in *My Life and the Beautiful Game*, written with Robert L. Fish, I wrote my first-ever article on the criminal elements in Sport and the Law under the title *Crimes of Soccer Violence* in the *Police Review* journal. It was triggered when a non-league footballer in an Essex local match killed an opponent on the field with a punch, was prosecuted for manslaughter at the old Maidstone Assizes, and mercifully given a suspended prison sentence. I suggested that if the game could not control its own villany, at a time *before* the dam of sustained brutality burst on and off the field, then the law of the land should plug the gap.

Immediately it appeared a famous columnist wrote in the *News of the World* under the headline

STARS BEHIND BARS –
IT'S JUST CRAZY

and concluded

"The day the police take over from referees will be the day sport dies."

Since then, of course, professional footballers have been prosecuted in the criminal courts for violent behaviour during play, and others have escaped the dock. Substantial damages have been awarded to victims of foul play; the state run Criminal Injuries Compensation Board has recorded twice during the 1980's how its services have been required.

"In the last few years, the Board has received an increasing number of applications from violence among players, particularly during rugby or football matches."

Off the field, many consider that the Hillsborough tragedy can be traced back to the time when the FA failed to attend the Home Office enquiry along the lines of the Taylor investigation into that famous first ever Wembley Cup Final in 1923. The 1924 Report laid down a blueprint for crowd control valid unto this day. Fifty years later, the FA compounded this neglect when it failed to take the chance it had to get a grip on crowd violence during the 6th Round of the FA Cup. At St. James' Park, Newcastle United were losing 3-1 to Nottingham Forest when the referee dismissed Pat Howard, the Magpies centre-half. Immediately, the crowd stopped the match. When it resumed, after an interval of nearly ten minutes when the players were taken off the field by the referee, United won 4-3. As Geoffrey Green wrote in *The Times* for Monday, 11th March, 1974, Forest

"were hounded out of the Cup by the criminal behaviour of an undisciplined horde who think that they own football. Unfortunately they can certainly influence it. The real punishment for the Tyneside hooligans would have been for the match to be abandoned and awarded to Nottingham Forest."

Instead, the FA ordered a replay. United won 1-0 and progressed to lose the Final 3-0 to Liverpool. The Rule of Law was abandoned instead; because the police did *not* take over from the referee.

EDWARD GRAYSON

The Football Trust continued from Page 613

DIVISION FOUR: WINNER: CREWE ALEXANDRA: Exceptional efforts to involve all sections of local community, especially elderly and women. Enthusiastic backing of club officers at all levels. Social club and artificial surface receive extensive local use. *TRUST AWARD £20,000. COMMENDATIONS: COLCHESTER UNITED:* Involvement with families and young through the Sporting U's. *DONCASTER ROVERS:* Coaching and match day activities. *GRIMSBY TOWN:* Outreach activities and match day visits for home and visiting fans. *TRANMERE ROVERS:* Catering for all age groups in an area of high unemployment and providing new image for football in Birkenhead. Number of applications: 12 (50%).

WELSH and NORTHERN IRISH FOOTBALL

LEAGUE TABLES, CUP WINNERS
AND HONOURS PAST AND PRESENT

WELSH FOOTBALL 1988–89

THE ABACUS WELSH FOOTBALL LEAGUE

National Division	*P*	*W*	*D*	*L*	*F*	*A*	*W*	*D*	*L*	*F*	*A*	*Pts*
Barry Town	32	15	1	0	59	9	13	3	0	37	11	88
Aberystwyth	32	11	4	1	41	16	13	0	3	44	21	76
Haverfordwest	32	11	3	2	43	13	8	3	5	28	19	63
Ebbw Vale	32	9	0	7	32	27	9	2	5	28	20	56
Brecon Corries	32	9	2	5	30	24	7	5	4	24	20	55
Bridgend Town	32	7	4	5	23	23	7	3	6	26	23	49
Abergavenny	32	9	3	4	30	20	4	5	7	22	33	47
Ton Pentre	32	6	0	10	28	27	7	4	5	23	21	43
Pembroke	32	6	4	6	18	19	5	3	8	20	22	40
Maesteg Park	32	3	5	8	15	22	7	1	8	24	26	36
Port Talbot	32	6	4	6	20	24	4	2	10	18	40	36
A.F.C. Cardiff	32	3	4	9	18	36	5	6	5	19	24	34
Cwmbran Town	32	4	3	9	20	30	5	3	8	23	29	33
Pontllanfraith	32	3	4	9	24	34	4	1	11	15	37	26
Caerleon	32	3	5	8	20	36	3	2	11	20	32	25
Milford	32	4	2	10	17	28	3	1	12	20	48	24

Premier Division	*P*	*W*	*D*	*L*	*F*	*A*	*W*	*D*	*L*	*F*	*A*	*Pts*
Afan Lido	32	12	5	0	3	9	11	2	4	37	20	76
Sully	34	10	5	2	53	20	12	3	2	43	21	74
Ammanford	34	13	1	3	39	15	9	6	2	33	21	73
Cardiff Corries	34	9	3	5	30	12	8	5	4	34	24	59
Panteg	34	11	2	4	38	23	4	8	5	26	26	55
Ferndale	34	9	4	4	35	17	7	1	9	18	28	53
Llanelli	34	9	2	6	39	30	5	5	7	35	45	49
Clydach	34	7	3	7	24	24	8	1	8	24	30	†46
Newport Y.M.C.A.	34	7	3	7	21	22	5	4	8	22	31	43
Llanwern	34	6	6	5	30	29	4	4	9	20	30	40
B.P.	34	7	5	5	23	22	3	4	10	14	27	39
Morriston	34	5	6	6	34	33	5	2	10	15	28	38
Tonyrefail	34	3	6	8	18	23	7	2	8	22	30	38
Blaenrhondda	34	5	5	7	22	32	3	8	6	25	36	37
Trelewis	34	7	4	6	29	21	2	4	11	18	41	35
Merthyr Tydfil	34	6	4	7	29	29	3	2	12	19	34	33
South Wales Police	34	4	5	8	28	41	3	5	9	23	42	31
Abercynon	34	5	2	10	27	38	1	5	11	12	38	25

† 3 points deducted

Divison One	*P*	*W*	*D*	*L*	*F*	*A*	*W*	*D*	*L*	*F*	*A*	*Pts*
Garw	34	12	3	2	40	19	11	3	3	38	13	75
Ynysybwl	34	9	4	39	23	12	12	2	3	43	20	69
Seven Sisters	34	11	4	2	56	24	8	6	3	33	24	67
Pontyclun	34	12	3	2	34	23	6	7	4	23	16	64
Carmarthen	34	12	3	2	37	18	7	3	7	25	20	63
Treharris	34	11	2	4	37	18	7	2	8	28	32	58
Aberaman	34	8	4	5	29	22	7	5	5	36	21	54
Caldicot	34	9	4	4	19	13	7	2	8	20	19	54
Skewen	34	7	4	6	26	19	7	5	5	32	31	51
Pontlottyn	34	11	1	5	28	19	5	2	10	21	34	51
Taffs Well	34	8	3	6	35	25	7	2	8	31	29	50
Tondu Robins	34	5	7	5	27	23	4	7	6	30	26	41
Blaenavon	34	4	6	7	22	45	4	5	8	23	41	35
Caerau	34	7	5	5	24	20	1	5	11	15	35	34
South Glam. Inst.	34	5	3	9	18	32	4	3	10	22	42	33
Pontardawe	34	3	4	10	23	34	3	4	10	17	32	26
Tynte Rovers	34	3	2	12	22	37	1	2	14	18	45	16
Blaina	34	1	4	12	19	52	1	1	15	11	55	11

S. A. Brain Challenge Cup – Winners, Haverfordwest County; Finalists, Barry Town.
Abacus Youth Trophy – Winners, Cardiff Corinthians; Finalists, Merthyr Tydfil.

MANWEB LEAGUE

	P	*W*	*D*	*L*	*F*	*A*	*Pts*
Caersws	28	23	3	2	81	16	49
Newtown	28	21	3	4	70	37	45
Knighton	28	18	5	5	71	27	41
Morda	28	15	8	5	56	29	38
Llanidloes	28	16	2	10	50	37	34
Penrhyncoch	28	12	9	7	54	35	33
Welshpool	28	12	7	9	55	48	31
Machynlleth	28	12	4	12	47	47	28
Bryncrug	28	9	5	14	49	53	23
Preseigne	28	9	4	15	41	60	22
Llandrindod	28	8	4	16	40	67	20
Builth Wells	28	4	10	14	34	52	18
Carno	28	5	7	16	46	71	17
Rhayader	28	3	5	20	19	66	11
UCW	28	4	2	22	20	87	10

League Cup – Winners, Knighton; Finalist, Caersws.
Youth Cup – Winners, Newtown Youth; Finalist, Penrhyncoch Youth.

Central Wales Football Competitions

Challenge Cup – Winners, Caersws; Finalist, Knighton.
J. E. Morgan Cup – Winners, Vale of Arrow; Finalist, Penparcau.
Youth Cup – Winners, Newtown Youth; Finalist, Crickhowell Youth.
Under 12 – Winners, Blacon.
Under 14 – Winners, Llangefni.
Under 16 – Winners, Menai Bridge.
Youth Cup – Winners, Hawarden Rangers.
Junior Cup – Winners, Llanfairfechan
Sunday Challenge Cup – Winners, Welsh Harp.
Challenge Cup – Winners, Mostyn.

THE WELSH ALLIANCE FOOTBALL LEAGUE

	P	W	D	L	F	A	Pts
Flint Town Utd	32	23	4	5	72	26	73
Rhyl Res	32	22	4	6	67	36	70
Nantlle Vale	32	20	6	6	85	42	66
Porthmanog	32	16	10	6	85	60	58
Holywell Town	32	16	3	13	65	64	51
Connhas Quay Nomads	32	15	5	12	58	42	50
Llanfairpwll	32	15	4	13	54	51	49
Bethesda Athletic	32	12	10	10	57	56	46
Y Felinheli	32	12	8	12	48	55	44
Conwy Utd	32	11	10	11	58	55	43
*Bangor City	32	12	6	14	57	57	40
Llanrwst Utd	32	12	3	17	55	69	39
Caernarfon Town Res	32	10	7	15	47	49	37
Mochdre	32	9	8	15	50	66	35
Llandudno Town	32	7	2	23	35	68	23
Pilkingtons	32	4	9	19	37	76	21
Colwyn Bay Res	32	5	3	24	42	100	18

*Denotes two points deducted for non fulfilment of fixture.
Rhos Utd withdrew from the League after playing only 7 fixtures.

Gwent Senior Cup – Albion Rovers A.F.C.

Gwent Amateur Cup – Newport Corinthians A.F.C.

League Champions – Flint Town Utd.

Tyn Lon Volvo Garage Barritt Cup – Winners, Mold Alex.

Cookson Cup – Winners, Flint Town Utd.

Alves Cup – Caernarfon Town.

WELSH INTERMEDIATE CUP 1988–89

First Round

Bala Town v Harlech Town	1-2
Blaenau Amateurs v Bryncrug	3-2
Machynlleth v Llanrug United	4-2
Overton Athletic v Bradley S. C.	1-2
Rhyl Victory Club (withdrew)	
Hawkesbury Villa v Mostyn	0-8
Carno v Welshpool Rangers	2-2, 2-1
Llanfair Caerenion v Builth Wells	3-1
Croesyceiliog v Ammanford Town	2-1
Treorchy Athletic v B. S. C. (Port Talbot)	0-3
Carw v Morriston Town	3-1
Trelewis v Pontyclun	1-0
Abertillery Town v Bryntirion Athletic	1-2

Second Round

Corwen Amateurs v Harlech Town	4-1
Blaenau Amateurs v Machynlleth	1-5
Rhyl Victory Club v Rhydymwyn	3-1
Bradley S. C. v Mostyn	0-1
Holywell Town v Hawarden Rangers	2-0
Carno or Welshpool Rangers v Llanfyllin Town	5-2
Llandrindod Wells v Llanfaircaereinion	3-2
South Gower v Tynte Rovers	3-3
Trelewis v Garw	1-5
Llanwern v Albion Rovers	1-0
Croesyceiliog v Bryntirion Athletic	0-3
BSC (Port Talbot) v Treharris Athletic	2-1
Llantwit Fardre v Hirwaun Welfare	1-3
Fields Park Athletic v Llanfrechfa Grange	4-3

Third Round

Locomotive Llanberis v CP Y Felinheli	1-1, 2-2, 2-0
Conwy United v Llandudno	3-1
Porthmadog v Bethesda Athletic	2-2
Holywell Town v Denbigh Town	2-0
Connah's Quay Nomads v Pilkington's	1-2
Rhyl Victory Club v Shotton Westminster	1-0
Flint Town United v Rhos United	7-0
Llanfairpwll v Llanrwst United	4-1
Llay Royal British Legion v Ruthin Town	4-1
Mostyn v Rhos Aelwyd	1-1, 3-1
Brymbo Steelworks v Cefn Albion	4-2
Penycae v Rhostyllen Villa	2-6
Gresford Athletic v Llay Welfare	3-0
Corwen Amateurs v Chirk AAA	1-4
Buckley v Mold Alexandra	0-2
Presteigne St. Andrews v Llanidloes Town	3-3,3-5
Penrhyncoch v Landrindod Wells	4-1
Carno v Machynlleth	0-3
Rhayader Town v Caersws	0-9
Welshpool v Knighton Town	2-2, 1-0
Aberystwyth Town v Brecon Corinthians	3-0
Tynte Rovers v Clydach United	0-4
Bryntirion Athletic Disqualified.	
Hirwaun Welfare v Ragged School	3-1
Kenfig Hill v BSC (Port Talbot)	2-2, 0-1
Afan Lido v Carmarthen Town	1-0
Newport YMCA v Risca United	0-2
Cardiff Corinthians v Caldicot Town	0-2
South Glamorgan Institute v Abergavenny Thursdays	0-9
Cardiff Civil Service v Newport Corinthians	1-1, 2-1
Llanwern v Fields Park Athletic	0-2

Fourth Round

Conwy United v Llanfairpwll	3-2
Rhyl Victory Club v Flint Town United	0-5
Holywell Town v Locomotive Llanberis	1-0
Porthmadog v Pilkington's	2-0
Machynlleth v Chirk AAA	6-1
Llay Royal British Legion v Penrhyncoch	2-0
Mostyn v Gresford Athletic	2-1
Caersws v Welshpool	3-1
Aberystwyth Town v Rhostyllen Villa	3-0
Llanidloes Town v Brymbo Steelworks	0-0
Mold Alexandra v Lex X1	4-1
Caldicot Town v Bryntirion Athletic	1-1, 0-1
BSC (Port Talbot) v Clydach United	4-1
Risca United v Hirwaun Welfare	1-3
Cardiff Civil Service v Afan Lido	0-3
Fields Park Athletic v Abergavenny Thursdays	1-4

Fifth Round

Afan Lido v Brymbo Steelworks	2-0
Bryntirion Athletic v Porthmadog	1-1, 0-1
Caersws v Mostyn	3-0
Aberystwyth Town v BSC (Port Talbot)	6-0
Abergavenny Thursdays v Llay Royal British Legion	1-0
Flint Town United v Holywell Town	4-0
Machynlleth v Conwy United	5-2
Hirwaun Welfare v Mold Alexandra	1-3

Sixth Round

Abergavenny Thursdays v Flint Town United	2-1
Caersws v Machynlleth	1-1, 2-1
Aberystwyth Town v Porthmadog	3-0
Afan Lido v Mold Alexandra	2-2, 0-1

Semi-finals

Caersws v Abergavenny Thursdays	3-2
Aberystwyth Town v Mold Alexandra	3-0

Final

Aberystwyth Town v Caersws	2-3

(at Llandloes Town)

WELSH CUP 1988–89

First Round
Conway United v Rhydymwyn 2-0
Llanfairpwll v Rhos United 2-0
Porthmadog v Mold Alexandra 2-0
Bethesda Athletic v Lanrwst United 4-1
Llandudno v Flint Town United 0-1
Hawarden Rangers v Shotton Westminster 1-3
Connah's Quay Nomads v Mostyn 0-1, 1-1, 1-2
Pilkingtons v Holywell Town 1-3
Ruthin Town v Corwen Amateurs 3-0
Lex XI v Buckley 2-2
(Lex XI awarded tie – Buckley fielded ineligible player)
Overton Athletic v Llay Welfare 0-2
Cefn Albion v Penycae 3-2
Chirk AAA v Bala Town 9-0
Llay Royal British Legion v Gresford Athletic 3-3, 0-1
Rhos Aelywd v Bradley S. C. 4-1
Builth Wells v Brecon Corinthians 0-4
Caersws v Llandrindod Wells 6-1
Presteigne St. Andrews v Machynleth 2-0
Knighton Town v Rhayader Town 0-0, 2-1
Carno v Llandidloes Town 0-2
Tonyrefail Welfaire v Sully 3-2
Abercynon Athletic v Abergavenny Thursdays 1-4
South Glamorgan Institute v Llanwern 0-9
Trelewis v Ferndale 0-3
Barry Town v Briton Ferry Athletic 2-1
Afan Lido v Maesteg Park Athletic 2-2, 3-2
Risca United v Pontllanfraith 1-1, 1-1, 4-1
Cwbran Town v AFC Cardiff 0-3
Caerleon v Newport YMCA 0-1, 1-0
Caldicot Town v Cardiff Corinthians 3-0
Clydach United v Port Talbot Athletic 2-0
Skewen Athletic v South Wales Police 5-2
Carmarthen Town v Llanelli 1-0
BP Llandarcy v Caerau 0-1
Milford United v Bridgend Town 2-5
Pontardawe Athletic v Haverfordwest County 0-5
Pembroke Borough v Ammanford Town 2-0
Forest Green Rovers v Bath City 1-1, 1-2
Cheltenham Town v Worcester City 0-2

Second Round
Colwyn Bay v Bangor City 1-1, 0-2
Llanfairpwll v Conwy United 2-1
Holywell Town v Porthmadog 1-3
Flint Town United v Rhyl 2-2, 1-2
Bethesda Athletic v Mostyn 3-1
Brymbo Steelworks v Chirk AAA 0-1
Newtown v Cresford Athletic 4-4, 4-1
Lex XI v Cefn Albion 2-0
Rhos Aelwyd v Ruthin Town 2-1
Caersws v Llandidloes Town 4-1
Llay Welfare v Shotton Westminster 3-3, 0-6
Skewen Athletic v Bath City 0-3
Haverfordwest County v Pembroke Borough 2-0
Worcester City v Carmarthen Town 3-0
Ferndale Athletic v Risca United 0-2
Abergavenny Thursdays v Caldicot Town 1-1, 2-0
AFC Cardiss v Merthyr Tydfil 0-6
Ton Pentre v Barry Town 0-3
Presteigne St Andres v Clydach United 1-3
Caerau v Newport YMCA 0-1
Aberystwyth Town v Afan Lido 1-0
Ebbw Vale v Brecon Corinthians 1-0
Tonyrefail Welfare v Knighton Town 3-1
Llanwern v Bridgend Town 0-2

Third Round
Shrewsbury Town v Caernarfon Town 2-0
(Shrewsbury Town forfeit match)
Porthmadog v Bangor City 0-2
Rhos Aelwyd v Hereford United 0-4
Lex XI v Wrexham 0-8
Newtown v Shotton Westminster 5-0
Rhyl v Caersws 2-2, 0-1
Chirk AAA v Bethesda Athletic 0-1
Kidderminster Harriers v Llanfairpwll 3-0
Merthyr Tydfil v Swansea City 0-3
Cardiff City v Bath City 3-0
Berry Town v Clydach United 5-1
Haverfordwest County v Newport YMCA 2-0
Newport County v Bridgend Town 6-1
Tonyrefail Welfare v Worcester City 0-2
Abergavenny Thursdays v Risca United 2-1
Ebbw Vale v Abertystwyth Town 2-1

Fourth Round
Worcester City v Cardiff City 0-1
Barry Town v Haverfordwest County 2-0
Newport County v Caernarfon Town 3-0
Newtown v Bangor City 0-1
Swansea City v Caersws 0-0, 2-0
Bethesda Athletic v Hereford United 0-2
Abergavenny Thursdays v Kidderminster Harriers 1-2
Ebbw Vale v Wrexham 1-2

Fourth Round
Newport County v Hereford United 0-1
Wrexham v Swansea City 1-3
Barry Town v Bangor City 1-0
Kidderminster Harriers v Cardiff City 3-1

Semi-finals
Kidderminster Harriers v Hereford United 1-0, 1-0
Barry Town v Swansea City 1-3

Final: Swansea City 5, Kidderminster Harriers 0

(At Vetch Field, Swansea, 21 May 1989). Att.: 5100.

Swansea C: Bracey; Melville, Colman, Lewis, Knill, Thornber, James, Davies, Raynor, Wade (Legg), Hutchison (Hough).

Kidderminster: Jones P.; Pearson, Barton, Brazier, Weir, Bancroft (Mackenzie), Dearlove (Howell), Casey, Davies, Tuouy, Jones R.

Scorers: Wade, James, Raynor, Hutchison, Thornber.

WELSH YOUTH CUP 1988–89

First Round
Mynydd Isa v Rhos United 1-3
Llanrwst United v Blaenau Ffestiniog
(Bleanau Ffestiniog withdrew)
Rhyl Victory Clun v Mill Tavern Youth 2-1
Abergavenny Thursdays v Aberaman 6-1
Cardiff Corinthians v Croesyceiliog
(Cardiff Corinthians withdrew)
Treorchy Athletic v Newport County
(Newport County withdrew)
Llantwit Fardre v Brecon Corinthians
(Brecon Corinthians withdrew)
Caerau v Garw
(Caerau withdrew)
Afan Lido v Carmarthen Town 3-1
Tregaron Turfs v Skewen Athletic 1-3
Briton Ferry Athletic v Bridgend Town 1-4
Machynlleth v Bala Town 0-4

Second Round
Bangor City v Colwyn Bay 2-0
Trearddur Bay v Llanrwst United 2-1
Locomotive Llanberis v Holyhead United Juniors 0-1
Mold Alexandra v Rhos United 5-1
Bala Town v Hawarden Rangers 1-11
Wrexham Schools v Wrexham 1-5
Aberystwyth Town v Newton 4-6
Caersws v Welshpool 0-2

Cardiff City v Croesyceiliog	5-1
Cwmbran Town v Caldicot Town	2-0
Abergavenny Thursdays v Cogan Coronation	1-2
Garw v Afan Lido *(Garw withdrew)*	
Skewen Athletic v Bridgend Town	0-4
Llantwit Fardre v Swansea City	1-3
Treorchy Athletic v Merthyr Tydfil	1-2
Rhyl Victory Club *(Bye to Round 3)*	

Third Round

Trearddur Bay v Holyhead United Juniors	1-4
Bangor City v Rhyl Victory Club	2-2
Welshpool v Wrexham	1-4
Hawarden Rangers v Mold Alexandra	3-2
Cwmbran Town v Merthyr Tydfil	1-4
Newtown v Cogan Coronation	6-1
Bridgend Town v Cardiff City	0-6
Afan Lido v Swansea City	1-6

Fourth Round

Hawarden Rangers v Holyhead United Juniors	2-3
Wrexham v Bangor City	9-1
Newtown v Swansea City	0-3
Merthyr Tydfil v Cardiff City	0-3

Semi-finals

Holyhead United Juniors v Wrexham *(at Bethesda Athletic)*	1-9
Cardiff City v Swansea City *(at Cardiff City)*	3-0

Final

Cardiff City v Wrexham *(at Rhayader Town)*	2-1

TIB WELSH NATIONAL LEAGUE (WREXHAM AREA)

Premier Division

	P	*W*	*D*	*L*	*F*	*A*	*Pts*
Lex XI	30	21	7	2	77	18	70
Wrexham Res	30	21	4	5	89	36	67
Chirk AAA	30	21	4	5	79	34	67
Mold Alex	30	20	7	3	67	28	67
Llay RBL	30	17	8	5	64	32	59
Ruthin Town	30	14	6	10	52	37	48
Rhos Aelwyd	30	13	6	11	45	42	45
Bradley	30	12	6	12	52	58	42
Corwen Am	30	12	5	13	49	52	41
Brymbo Steel Wks	30	13	0	17	62	56	39
Penycae	30	11	5	14	47	58	38
Cefn Albion	30	8	6	16	45	67	30
Buckley	30	5	6	19	22	68	21
Gresford Ath	30	4	8	18	29	52	20
Llay Welfare	30	5	1	24	32	102	16
Overton Ath	30	2	2	26	37	108	8

Division 1

	P	*W*	*D*	*L*	*F*	*A*	*Pts*
Rhostyllen Villa	26	23	3	0	119	22	72
Smithfield Ath	26	20	2	4	92	43	62
Penley	26	17	2	7	90	36	53
Lex XI Res	26	14	4	8	76	60	46
Ruthin Town Res	26	13	4	9	75	52	43
Johnstown Ath	26	13	3	10	61	66	42
Bala Town	26	11	6	9	49	58	39
Cefn Albion Res	26	10	4	12	55	57	34
Coedpoeth	26	11	2	13	61	66	32
Druids Utd	26	7	7	12	39	57	28
Mynydd-Isa	26	5	6	15	45	68	21
Brymbo SW Res	26	5	5	16	33	66	20
Hawkesbury Villa	26	5	1	20	25	87	16
Penycae Res*	26	2	3	21	25	107	3

Division 2

	P	*W*	*D*	*L*	*F*	*A*	*Pts*
Marchwiel Villa	28	22	2	4	118	39	68
Rubery Owen R'll	28	18	7	3	86	46	61
New Brighton V	28	18	5	5	97	43	59
Flint Town Utd Res	28	17	7	4	81	33	58
New Broughton	28	15	11	2	80	32	56
Treuddyn Villa	28	15	8	5	111	60	53
Chirk AAA Res	28	13	8	7	86	42	47
Rhos Aelwyd Res	28	13	2	13	86	61	41
Castell Alun O's	28	8	6	14	67	87	30
Minera	28	7	6	15	74	91	27
Druids Utd Res*	28	6	5	17	45	103	20
Llay RBL Res*	28	7	2	19	44	128	20
Bala Town Res	28	4	4	20	46	134	16
Glynceiriog*	28	4	4	20	56	103	13
Gresford Ath Res**	28	3	3	21	37	102	3

Division 3

	P	*W*	*D*	*L*	*F*	*A*	*Pts*
Kelloggs	22	17	0	5	72	45	51
Corwen Res	22	15	4	3	78	33	49
Ruthin Colts	22	14	6	2	83	29	48
Penyffordd	22	12	4	6	66	38	40
JCB Transm's	22	8	6	8	50	48	30
Penley Res	22	7	6	9	47	45	27
New Broughton Res	22	7	6	9	42	48	27
Kinnerton	22	6	8	8	36	40	26
Oveerton Ath Res	22	5	5	12	28	48	20
Llay Welfare Res	22	6	2	14	36	68	20
Johnstown Ath Res	22	5	4	17	33	78	19
Coedpoeth Res*	22	3	3	16	36	87	9

*Indicates team withdrew from competition.
**Points deducted for unfulfilled fixtures.

Divisional Cups

Premier Division – Chirk AAA beat Llay RBL 5-3 at Stansty Park in a replay following a 2-2 draw after extra time.
Division 1 – Lex XI Res beat Johnstown Ath 2-1 at Druids.
Division 2 – Marchwiel Villa beat Gresford Ath Res 2-0 at Brymbo.
Division 3 – Ruthin Colts beat Corwen Res 4-0 at Mold.

Caerses won the Challenge Cup.
Vale of Arrow won J. Emrys Morgan Cup.
Newtown won Youth Cup.

NORTHERN IRISH FOOTBALL 1988–89

The long, arduous rebuilding process started by Northern Ireland manager Billy Bingham after Mexico 86 continues with his sights now firmly fixed on the European championships 1992. The World Cup Group Six qualifying series proved a much too formidable challenge for the young team. "It's a pity the World Cup didn't come a year later for we are now showing signs of settling into a pattern," he said.

An unfortunate last-minute 1-0 defeat by Hungary in Budapest, and, then losing home and away to Spain, clearly revealed the immaturity of the side. Gradually, however, there are signs Bingham is getting it right while there are quite a few youngsters emerging from the schools, youth and B Division sides; in fact, the under-18 youth team won the prestigious Venice Cup in June in a 5-4 penalty shoot-out over Italy.

Attendance figures for matches at Windsor Park have caused the Irish FA much concern. Even for competitive fixtures they have dropped alarmingly, due primarily to the performance of the team, while for the friendly with Chile in late May only 3000 went through the turnstiles although, admittedly, it clashed with the live televising of the Liverpool-Arsenal League championship decider.

It has meant a big loss to the Irish FA who, however, have been compensated by the Football Association and the Football League for the live televising of internationals, Cup ties and league games in Northern Ireland. Sponsorship, too, has improved with the international side being commercially backed along with every domestic competition.

Linfield, who won the Smirnoff Irish League championship, released their two Continental players Tony Coly and Sammy Khammal, signed on a year's loan from the Belgian side FC Brugge; they had given a new dimension to the Irish game but faded towards the end of the season.

Bangor's John Flanagan was named Manager of the Year, steering his side to the Cawoods County Antrim Shield win over Glentoran. Biggest surprise of all was Glenavon's 5-1 Budweiser Cup Final replay triumph against Linfield, a tremendous boost for the Lurgan club as it embarks on its centenary celebrations. Ballymena United won the Bass Irish Cup to complete a spread of the trophies.

To sum up – internationally a disappointing year, domestically a reasonably satisfactory one.

MALCOLM BRODIE

SMIRNOFF IRISH LEAGUE CHAMPIONSHIP FINAL TABLE

	P	*W*	*D*	*L*	*F*	*A*	*Pts*
Linfield	26	21	2	3	58	19	65
Glentoran	26	17	4	5	60	29	55
Coleraine	26	15	5	6	42	23	50
Bangor	26	12	9	5	42	30	45
Glenavon	26	13	5	8	47	34	44
Portadown	26	10	9	7	39	19	39
Cliftonville	26	9	9	8	42	31	36
Carrick	26	11	3	12	29	40	36
Ballymena	26	6	11	9	33	41	29
Larne	26	6	10	10	38	38	28
Newry	26	7	5	14	33	43	26
Crusaders	26	5	5	16	22	47	20
Ards	26	4	6	16	25	54	18
Distillery	26	3	3	20	20	73	12

BUDWEISER CUP

Final

(The Oval, Belfast, 22 March 1989)

Linfield 1 *(McGaughey)*

Glenavon 1 *(Coyle) (aet)*

Linfield: Dunlop; Coyle, Dornan, Doherty, Jeffrey, McKeown, Coly (Khammal), Baxter, McGaughey, O'Boyle, Burrows.
Glenavon: Beck; McKeown, Dennison, McLoughlin, Byrne, Scappiticci, Conville, Ferris, Blackledge (McBride), McConville, McCann.
Referee: A. Snoddy (Carryduff).

Replay *(The Oval, Belfast, 25 April 1989)*

Glenavon 6 *(Ferris 3, McBride, Blackledge, Lowry)*

Linfield 1 *(Knell)*

Glenavon: Beck, McKeown, Scappiticci, McCann, Byrne, Lowry, Conville (McLoughlin), Ferris, Blackledge (Dennison), McConville, McBride.
Linfield: Dunlop; Coyle, Dornan, Doherty, Jeffrey, McKeown, Mooney, Knell, Baxter (Khammal), McGaughey, O'Boyle.
Referee: A. Snoddy (Carryduff).

IRISH LEAGUE CHAMPIONSHIP WINNERS

1891	Linfield	1896	Distillery
1892	Linfield	1897	Glentoran
1893	Linfield	1898	Linfield
1894	Glentoran	1899	Distillery
1895	Linfield	1900	Belfast Celtic
1901	Distillery	1951	Glentoran
1902	Linfield	1952	Glenavon
1903	Distillery	1953	Glentoran
1904	Linfield	1954	Linfield
1905	Glentoran	1955	Linfield
1906	Cliftonville/Dist	1956	Linfield
1907	Linfield	1957	Glentoran
1908	Linfield	1958	Ards
1909	Linfield	1959	Linfield
1910	Cliftonville	1960	Glenavon
1911	Linfield	1961	Linfield
1912	Glentoran	1962	Linfield
1913	Glentoran	1963	Distillery
1914	Linfield	1964	Glentoran
1915	Belfast Celtic	1965	Derry City
1920	Belfast Celtic	1966	Linfield
1921	Glentoran	1967	Glentoran
1922	Linfield	1968	Glentoran
1923	Linfield	1969	Linfield
1924	Queen's Island	1970	Glentoran
1925	Glentoran	1971	Linfield
1926	Belfast Celtic	1972	Glentoran
1927	Belfast Celtic	1973	Crusaders
1928	Belfast Celtic	1974	Coleraine
1929	Belfast Celtic	1975	Linfield
1930	Linfield	1976	Crusaders
1931	Glentoran	1977	Glentoran
1932	Linfield	1978	Linfield
1933	Belfast Celtic	1979	Linfield
1934	Linfield	1980	Linfield
1935	Linfield	1981	Glentoran
1936	Belfast Celtic	1982	Linfield
1937	Belfast Celtic	1983	Linfield
1938	Belfast Celtic	1984	Linfield
1939	Belfast Celtic	1985	Linfield
1940	Belfast Celtic	1986	Linfield
1948	Belfast Celtic	1987	Linfield
1949	Linfield	1988	Glentoran
1950	Linfield	1989	Linfield

LOMBARD ULSTER CUP

		P	W	D	L	F	A	Pts
Group A	Glentoran	3	2	1	0	7	1	7
	Larne	3	2	1	0	7	4	7
	Crusaders	3	1	0	2	2	5	3
	Carrick R	3	0	0	3	2	8	0
Group B	Glenavon	3	2	0	1	5	4	6
	Cliftonville	3	1	1	1	8	8	4
	Distillery	3	1	1	1	5	6	4
	Linfield	3	1	0	2	4	4	3
Group C	Coleraine	3	3	0	0	10	3	9
	Ballyclare	3	1	1	1	1	4	4
	Ballymena	3	1	0	2	4	6	3
	Ards	3	0	1	2	4	6	1
Group D	Portadown	3	2	1	0	7	1	7
	Omagh T	3	0	3	0	2	2	3
	Bangor	3	0	2	1	1	4	2
	Newry T	3	0	2	1	2	5	2

Quarter-finals
Glentoran 3, Cliftonville 0
Coleraine 3, Omagh T 1
Glenavon 1, Larne 2
Portadown 1, Ballyclare 0

Semi-finals
Glentoran 2, Coleraine 0 *(Windsor Park, Belfast)*
Larne 2, Portadown 1 (aet) *(The Oval, Belfast)*

Final *(at Windsor Park, Belfast, September 28, 1988)*

Glentoran 5 *(Manley 3, Bowers, Cleary (pen))*

Larne 2 *(D Smyth 2)*

Glentoran: Paterson; Neill, Kennedy, Bowers, Moore, Cleary, Totten, Caskey, McCartney, Manley, Morrison.
Larne: McConnell; McMullan, Huston, Kernohan, Spiers, Bustard, Sloan (F Smith), McDonald, O'Kane, Frazer, D Smyth.
Referee: A. Snoddy (Carryduff).

Winners

1949	Linfield	1959	Glenavon	1969	Coleraine	1979	Linfield
1950	Larne	1960	Linfield	1970	Linfield	1980	Ballymena U
1951	Glentoran	1961	Ballymena U	1971	Linfield	1981	Glentoran
1952		1962	Linfield	1972	Coleraine	1982	Glentoran
1953	Glentoran	1963	Crusaders	1973	Ards	1983	Glentoran
1954	Crusaders	1964	Linfield	1974	Linfield	1984	Linfield
1955	Glenavon	1965	Coleraine	1975	Coleraine	1985	Coleraine
1956	Linfield	1966	Glentoran	1976	Glentoran	1986	Coleraine
1957	Linfield	1967	Linfield	1977	Linfield	1987	Larne
1958	Distillery	1968	Coleraine	1978	Linfield	1988	Glentoran

TNT GOLD CUP

FINAL SECTIONAL TABLES

Section A	P	W	D	L	F	A	Pts
Linfield	6	6	0	0	15	5	18
Coleraine	6	3	0	3	11	9	9
Portadown	6	2	3	1	7	7	9
Ballymena	6	2	1	3	9	8	8
Crusaders	6	2	0	4	5	8	6
Larne	6	1	2	3	6	8	5
Carrick	6	1	0	5	4	11	3

Section B	P	W	D	L	F	A	Pts
Glentoran	6	5	1	0	15	3	16
Newry	6	5	0	1	18	7	15
Glenavon	6	2	3	1	11	9	9
Bangor	6	2	0	4	6	13	6
Distillery	6	2	0	6	7	9	6
Cliftonville	6	1	2	3	6	9	5
Ards	6	1	1	4	7	13	4

Semi-finals
Linfield 2, Newry Town 0 *(at Portadown)*
Glentoran 2, Portadown 2 (aet) *(at Seaview)*
(Portadown won 3-0 on penalties)

Final

(The Oval, Belfast, 1 November 1988, attendance 8000)

Linfield 1 *(McKeown 50 (pen))*

Portadown 0

Linfield: Dunlop; Coyle, Dornan, Doherty, Jeffrey, McKeown, Khammal, Burrows, Baxter (MacLeod), O'Boyle, Coly.
Portadown: Keenan; Major, Curliss, Connell, Strain, Stewart, McCann, McKeever (Tully), Magee (Williamson), Millar, Davidson.
Referee: L. Irvine (Limavady).

Winners (from 1946)

1946	Celtic	1957	Linfield	1968	Linfield	1979	Portadown
1947	Celtic	1958	Coleraine	1969	Coleraine	1980	Linfield
1948	Linfield	1959	Linfield	1970	Linfield	1981	Cliftonville
1949	Linfield	1960	Glentoran	1971	Linfield	1982	Linfield
1950	Linfield	1961	Linfield	1972	Portadown	1983	Glentoran
1951	Glentoran	1962	Glentoran	1973	Linfield	1984	Linfield
1952	Portadown	1963	Linfield	1974	Ards	1985	Linfield
1953	Ards	1964	Derry City	1975	Ballymena U	1986	Crusaders
1954	Glenavon	1965	Linfield	1976	Coleraine	1987	Glentoran
1955	Linfield	1966	Glentoran	1977	Glentoran	1988	Linfield
1956	Glenavon	1967	Linfield	1978	Glentoran	1989	Linfield

OTHER IRISH COMPETITIONS AND TROPHIES

	Winners	*Runners-up*
Roadferry Cup	Glentoran	Linfield
Cawoods Co Antrim Shield	Bangor	Glentoran
Irish League 'B' Division		
Section I	Ballyclare Coms	Dundela
Section II	Linfield Swifts	Glentoran II
Irish FA Youth Cup	Linfield Rangers	
Irish Junior Cup	Oxford Utd	Enniskillen Rangers
Co Antrim Junior Shield	Maghera	Fords
IFA Intermediate Cup	Dundela	Donegal Celtic
George Wilson Cup	Linfield Swifts	Crusaders Res
Cawoods Steel Cup Final	Dundela	Glentoran II
North West Cup	Coleraine	Tobermore Utd
Budweiser Cup	Glenavon	Linfield

BASS IRISH CUP 1988–89

First Round

Ballynahinch v Civil Service	2-2
(Civil Service won 3-2 on penalties)	
Institute v Ards Rangers	0-1
Comber Rec v H and W Sports	0-4
H and W Welders v UUC	3-0
Crewe U v Cullybackey	6-1
Limavady v STC	2-1
Star of the Sea v UUJ	5-1
Killyleagh v Armagh Town	6-1
Islandmagee v Kilmore	2-1
Dundela v Ballymoney	6-2
Cromac Albion v Annagh Utd	2-0
POSC v AFC	2-1
GEC v Loughgall	2-1
Armoy v Dromara	3-1
Moyola v Oxford Utd	4-0
Macosquin v Saintfield	4-0
Shorts v Sirocco	2-1
Portstewart v 1st Bangor	0-1
Bangor Amateurs v Larne Tech	3-1
Armagh City v Orangefield	0-1
Rathfriland v Newtownabbey	2-2
(Rathfriland won 6-3 on penalties)	
Barn Utd v Park	0-2
Tandragee v Roe Valley	2-5

Second Round

Moyola Park v H and W Sports	1-2
Islandmagee v POSC	2-1
Dundela v Killyleagh	4-3
Roe Valley v Blue Circle	5-1
GEC Larne v Ards Rangers	2-4
H and W Welders v Crewe Utd	5-0
Macosquin v Armoy Utd	0-1
Queen's University v Civil Service	3-0
Downshire v Rathfriland Rangers	1-2
Bangor Amateurs v Orangefield OB	1-0
RUC v Star of the Sea	(aet) 2-2
(RUC won 6-5 on penalties)	
Cromac Albion Youth v Shorts	2-1
Annalong Swifts v Limavady Utd	1-2
Park v 1st Bangor	3-0

Third Round

Dundela v Islandmagee	6-0
Limavady Utd v Ards Rangers	2-1
Park v H and W Sports	(aet) 0-0
(Park won 4-3 on penalties)	
Cromac Albion Youth v Bangor Amateurs	2-1
H and W Welders v Queen's University	1-0
Roe Valley v RUC	3-1
Armoy Utd v Rathfriland Rangers	3-1

Fourth Round

Glentoran v Armoy Utd	5-1
Omagh Town v Brantwood	2-0
Park v H and W Welders	2-0
Banbridge Town v Roe Valley	3-0
Cookstown v Ballyclare Comrades	1-4
Tobermore Utd v Limavady Utd	3-0
Dunmurry Rec v Donegal Celtic	0-1
Distillery v Ballymena Utd	1-4
Carrick Rangers v Bangor	1-0
Newry Town v Cliftonville	1-2
Crusaders v Dungannon Swifts	2-0
Larne v Chimney Corner	3-0
Portadown v Coagh Utd	1-0
Glenavon v Dundela	4-2
Ards v Cromac Albion Youth	0-1

Fifth Round

Ballyclare Comrades v Ballymena Utd	2-2, 2-0 *(abandoned 32 mins., snow)*, 5-1
Carrick Rangers v Portadown	2-1
Cliftonville v Park	1-0
Crusaders v Banbridge	1-0
Glenavon v Linfield	0-3
Omagh Town v Glentoran	2-3
Larne v Donegall Celtic	6-1
Tobermore v Cromac Albion	1-1, 1-0

Quarter-finals

Cliftonville v Tobermore	0-0
Crusaders v Ballymena Utd	2-3
Glentoran v Linfield	0-3
Larne v Carrick Rangers	0-0, 3-2

Semi-finals

Cliftonville v Larne	1-1, (aet) 1-2
Linfield v Ballymena Utd	1-1, 1-2

Final

(The Oval, Belfast, 6 May 1989, attendance 5000)

Ballymena Utd 1 *(Hardy)*
Larne 0

Ballymena Utd: Grant; Scott, M Smyth, Garrett, Heron, Young, McKee, Curry, Pyper, Hardy, Doherty (Simpson).

Larne: Magee; McMullan, Huston, Carland, Spiers, Bustard, Murphy, Kernohan, Smith (McDonald), Sloan, D Smyth (Hannan).

Referee: A. Ritchie (Carrickfergus).

IRISH CUP FINALS (from 1946–47)

1946–47	Belfast Celtic 1, Glentoran 0
1947–48	Linfield 3, Coleraine 0
1948–49	Derry City 3, Glentoran 1
1949–50	Linfield 2, Distillery 1
1950–51	Glentoran 3, Ballymena U 1
1951–52	Ards 1, Glentoran 0
1952–53	Linfield 5, Coleraine 0
1953–54	Derry City 1, Glentoran 0
1954–55	Dundela 3, Glenavon 0
1955–56	Distillery 1, Glentoran 0
1956–57	Glenavon 2, Derry City 0
1957–58	Ballymena U 2, Linfield 0
1958–59	Glenavon 2, Ballymena U 0
1959–60	Linfield 5, Ards 1
1960–61	Glenavon 5, Linfield 1
1961–62	Linfield 4, Portadown 0
1962–63	Linfield 2, Distillery 1
1963–64	Derry City 2, Glentoran 0
1964–65	Coleraine 2, Glenavon 1
1965–66	Glentoran 2, Linfield 0
1966–67	Crusaders 3, Glentoran 1
1967–68	Crusaders 2, Linfield 0
1968–69	Ards 4, Distillery 2
1969–70	Linfield 2, Ballymena U 1
1970–71	Distillery 3, Derry City 0
1971–72	Coleraine 2, Portadown 1
1972–73	Glentoran 3, Linfield 2
1973–74	Ards 2, Ballymena U 1
1974–75	Coleraine 1:0:1, Linfield 1:0:0
1975–76	Carrick Rangers 2, Linfield 1
1976–77	Coleraine 4, Linfield 1
1977–78	Linfield 3, Ballymena U 1
1978–79	Cliftonville 3, Portadown 2
1979–80	Linfield 2, Crusaders 0
1980–81	Ballymena U 1, Glenavon 0
1981–82	Linfield 2, Coleraine 1
1982–83	Glentoran 1:2, Linfield 1:1
1983–84	Ballymena U 4, Carrick Rangers 1
1984–85	Glentoran 2, Coleraine 1
1984–85	Glentoran 1,1, Linfield 1, 0
1985–86	Glentoran 2, Coleraine 1
1986–87	Glentoran 1, Larne 0
1987–88	Glenavon 0, Glentoran 1
1988–89	Ballymena U 1, Larne 0

INTERNATIONAL FOOTBALL

[INTERNATIONAL DIRECTORY]

EUROPEAN CHAMPIONSHIP

EUROPEAN CLUB RESULTS

WORLD CUP

BRITISH AND IRISH INTERNATIONAL RESULTS AND APPEARANCES

UNDER-21, UNDER-18 AND UNDER-16

SCHOOLS AND YOUTH FOOTBALL

SOUTH AMERICA AND OTHER INTERNATIONAL FOOTBALL

OLYMPICS

INTERNATIONAL DIRECTORY SECTION

The latest available information has been given regarding numbers of clubs and players registered with FIFA, the world governing body. Where known, official colours are listed. With European countries, League tables show a number of signs. * indicates relegated teams, + play-offs, *+ relegated after play-offs. In Hungary and Yugoslavia, drawn matches result in penalty shoot-outs, the winners receiving more points than the losers. In South America, the 1988 international results for Argentina and Brazil include Olympic Games tournament matches.

There are 166 FIFA members. These include the four home countries, England, Scotland, Northern Ireland and Wales, dealt with elsewhere in the Yearbook.

EUROPE

ALBANIA

Founded: 1932.
Number of Clubs: 49.
Number of Players: 3757.
National Colours: Red shirts, black shorts, red stockings.

International matches 1988

6 Aug, Beirat: v Cuba (h) drew 0-0
20 Sept, Constantza: v Rumania (a) lost 0-3
19 Oct, Chorzow: v Poland (a) lost 0-1
5 Nov, Tirana: v Sweden (h) lost 1-2 (*Shehu*)

League Championship wins (1945–89)

Dinamo Tirana 14; Partizan Tirana 14; 17 Nentori 8; Vlaznia 6; Labinoti 1.

Cup wins (1948–89)

Dinamo Tirana 11; Partizan Tirana 11; 17 Nentori 6; Vlaznia 5; Flamurtari 2; Labinoti 1.

Final League Table 1988–89

	P	*W*	*D*	*L*	*F*	*A*	*Pts*
17 Nentori	22	14	4	4	39	13	32
Partizani	22	13	4	5	33	17	30
Dinamo	22	12	6	4	29	19	30
Apolonia	22	10	7	5	29	10	27
Beselidhja	22	10	4	8	28	24	24
Labinoti	22	9	5	8	27	25	23
Vllaznia	22	9	4	9	28	26	22
Flamurtari	22	9	2	11	26	30	20
Lokomotiva	22	5	6	11	16	31	16
Besa	22	7	1	14	27	36	15
Skenderbeu*	22	4	6	12	14	30	14
Traktori*	22	3	5	14	12	42	11

Final placings after play-offs: 1. 17 Nentori 48 pts; 2. Partizari 45; 3. Dinamo 42; 4. Apolonia 33; 5. Labinoti 31; 6. Beselidhja 27.
Relegation: 7. Vllaznia 37; 8. Flamurtari 32; 9. Besa 26; 10. Lokomotiva 25; 11. Skenderbeu 21; 12. Traktori 17.
Cup Final: Dinamo 3, Partizani 1 (after 0-0 draw).
Top scorer: Kola (17 Nentori) 19

AUSTRIA

Founded: 1904.
Number of Clubs: 1992.
Number of Players: 253,576.
National Colours: White shirts, black shorts, black stockings.

International matches 1988

2 Feb, Tolosa: v Morocco (a) lost 1-3 (*Ogris*)
5 Feb, Monaco: v Switzerland (n) lost 1-2 (*Geiger own goal*)
6 April, Athens: v Greece (a) drew 2-2 (*Zsak, Willfurth*)
27 April, Vienna: v Denmark (h) won 1-0 (*Berggreen own goal*)
17 May, Budapest: v Hungary (a) won 4-0 (*Marko 3, Hasenhuettl*)
3 Aug, Vienna: v Brazil (h) lost 0-2
31 Aug, Linz: v Hungary (h) drew 0-0
20 Sept, Prague: v Czechoslovakia (a) lost 2-4 (*Pacult, Willfurth*)
19 Oct, Kiev: v USSR (a) lost 0-2
2 Nov, Vienna: v Turkey (h) won 3-2 (*Polster, Herzog, Ogris*)

League Championship wins (1912–89)

Rapid Vienna 28; Austria/Vienna (prev. Austria/WAC, FK Austria and WAC) 19; Admira-Energie-Wacker (prev. Sportklub Admira & Admira-Energie) 8; First Vienna 6; Tirol-Svarowski-Innsbruck (prev. Wacker Innsbruck) 6; Wiener Sportklub 3; FAC 1; Hakoah 1; Linz ASK 1; Wacker Vienna 1; WAF 1; Voest Linz 1.

Cup wins (1919–89)

Austria/WAC 22; Rapid Vienna 13; TS Innsbruck (prev. Wacker Innsbruck) 6; Admira-Energie-Wacker (prev. Sportklub Admira & Admira-Energie) 5; First Vienna 3; Linz ASK 1; Wacker Vienna 1; WAF 1; Wiener Sportklub 1, Graz AK 1.

Final League Table 1988–89

	P	*W*	*D*	*L*	*F*	*A*	*Pts*
Tirol	22	15	3	4	52	26	33
Admira Wacker	22	13	5	4	45	27	31
FK Austria	22	12	6	4	54	26	30
St Polten	22	10	5	7	33	32	25
Rapid	22	10	4	8	35	26	24
Vienna	22	6	10	6	31	34	22
Graz	22	7	8	7	27	37	22
Wiener SC	22	8	4	10	38	43	20
Vorwaerts Steyr	22	5	8	9	21	31	18
Austria Klagenfurt	22	5	6	11	30	47	16
Sturm Graz	22	3	6	13	22	37	12
Linz	22	3	5	14	21	43	11

Final Round

	P	*W*	*D*	*L*	*F*	*A*	*Pts*
Tirol	36	24	7	5	78	38	39
Admira Wacker	36	20	8	8	78	52	33
FK Austria	36	18	10	8	76	44	31
Rapid	36	17	7	12	67	40	29
Vienna	36	12	13	11	59	59	26
Wiener SC	36	13	6	17	60	70	22
Graz	36	11	9	16	37	64	20
St Polten	36	10	9	17	44	68	17

Relegation pool

1. Sturm Graz† P 14/21 pts; 2. Vorwaerts Steyr† 19; 3. Austria Salzburg† 17; 4. Kremser† 16; 5. Linz 14; 6. Austria Klagenfurt 13; 7. Flavia Solva 9; 8. Kufstein 3.
Cup Final: Tirol 0, 6, Admira Wacker 2, 2
Top scorer: Pacult (Tirol)

BELGIUM

Founded: 1895.
Number of Clubs: 3362.
Number of Players: 289,770.
National Colours: Red shirts with tri-coloured trim, red shorts, red stockings with trim.

International matches 1988

19 Jan, Tel Aviv: v Israel (a) won 3-2(*De Gryse, Vanderlinden, Grun*)
26 March, Brussels: v Hungary (h) won 3-0 (*Ceulemans, Fitosautorete, Severeyns*)
5 June, Odense: v Denmark (a) lost 1-3 (*Ceulemans*)
12 Oct, Antwerp: v Brazil (h) lost 1-2 (*Clijsters*)
19 Oct, Brussels: v Switzerland (h) won 1-0 (*Vervoort*)
16 Nov, Bratislava: v Czechoslovakia (a) drew 0-0

League Championship wins (1896–89)

Anderlecht 20; Union St Gilloise 11; Standard Liège 8; Beerschot 7; FC Bruges 6; RC Brussels 6; FC Liège 5; Daring Brussels 5; Antwerp 4; Mechelen 4; Lierse SK 3; SV Brugge 3; Beveren 2; RWD Molenbeek 1.

Cup wins (1954–89)

Anderlecht 7; Standard Liège 4; FC Brugge 4; Beerschot 2; Waterschei 2; Beveren 2; Gent 2; Antwerp 1; Lierse SK 1; Tournai 1; Waregem 1; SV Brugge 1; Mechelen 1.

Final League Table 1988–89

	P	*W*	*D*	*L*	*F*	*A*	*Pts*
Mechelen	34	25	7	2	64	20	57
Anderlecht	34	22	9	3	83	36	53
Liege	34	17	12	5	64	22	46
FC Brugge	34	17	9	8	67	44	43
Antwerp	34	16	10	8	61	38	42
Standard	34	14	8	12	46	43	36
Kortrijk	34	9	17	8	53	44	35
St Truiden	34	12	11	11	39	44	35
Waregem	34	11	8	15	48	52	30
Lierse	34	10	9	15	29	46	29
Charleroi	34	6	17	11	31	49	29
Beveren	34	10	8	16	40	50	28
Lokeren	34	9	10	15	42	56	28
Racing Mechelen	34	10	8	16	37	55	28
Beerschot	34	8	11	15	40	61	27
CS Brugge	34	9	8	17	39	54	26
Molenbeek*	34	10	5	19	36	59	25
Genk*	34	2	11	21	20	66	15

Cup Final: Anderlecht 2, Standard 0
Top scorer: Krncevic (Anderlecht) 23

BULGARIA

Founded: 1923.
Number of Clubs: 4328.
Number of Players: 442,829.
National Colours: White shirts, green shorts, red stockings.

International matches 1988

22 Jan, Doha: v Qatar (a) won 3-2 (*Kirov, Alexandrov, Stoichkov*)
26 Jan, Doha: v United Arab Emirates (a) won 3-0 (*Iliev, Kolev, Sadkov*)
30 Jan, Doha: v United Arab Emirates (a) won 3-1 (*Sadkov, Kolev, Alexandrov*)
3 Feb, Cairo: v Egypt (a) lost 0-1
23 March, Sofia: v Czechoslovakia (h) won 2-0 (*Sirakov, Penev*)
13 April, Burges: v East Germany (h) drew 1-1 (*Ivanov*)
24 May, Rotterdam: v Holland (a) won 2-1 *Iliev, Penev*)
4 Aug, Helsinki: v Finland (a) drew 1-1 (*Pashev*)
7 Aug, Reykjavik: v Iceland (a) won 3-2 (*Iordanov, Mladenov, Alexandrov*)
9 Aug, Oslo: v Norway (a) drew 1-1 (*Stoichkov*)
24 Aug, Bialystok: v Poland (a) lost 2-3 (*Stoichov, Penev*)
19 Oct, Sofia: v Rumania (h) lost 1-3 (*Kolev*)
2 Nov, Copenhagen: v Denmark (a) drew 1-1 (*Sadkov*)

League Championship wins (1925–89)

CFKA Sredets (prev. CSKA Sofia, CDNA) 25; Levski Spartak(prev. Levski Sofia) 14; Slavia Sofia 6; Vladislav Varna 3; Lokomotiv Sofia 3; Trakia Plovdiv 2; AS 23 Sofia 1; Botev Plovdiv 1; SC Sofia 1; Sokol Varna 1; Spartak Plovdiv 1; Tichka Varan 1; ZSK Sofia 1; Beroe Stara Zagora 1; Sredets 1.

Cup wins (1946–89)

Levski Spartak (prev. Levski Sofia) 14; CFKA Sredets (prev.CSKA Sofia, CDNA) 11; Slavia Sofia 6; Lokomotiv Sofia 3; Sredets 2; Botev Plovdiv 1; Spartak Plovdiv 1; Spartak Sofia 1; Marek Stanke 1; Trakia Plovdiv 1; Spartak Varna 1; Vitosha 1.

Final League Table 1988–89

	P	*W*	*D*	*L*	*F*	*A*	*Pts*
CFKA Sredets	30	20	8	2	85	25	48
Vitosha	30	17	5	8	63	38	39
Etur	30	13	8	9	48	30	34
Trakia	30	12	9	9	49	36	33
Beroe	30	13	7	10	41	46	33
Dounav	30	12	7	11	29	32	31
Chernomore	30	10	10	10	33	43	30
Lokomotiv Sofia	30	12	4	14	36	34	28
Pirin	30	12	3	15	34	33	27
Sliven	30	11	5	14	38	39	27
Lokomotiv Plovdiv	30	11	5	14	31	54	27
Slavia Sofia	30	8	10	12	32	36	26
Gorna	30	11	4	15	26	45	26
Vratza	30	9	8	13	32	53	26
Varna*	30	7	9	14	37	54	23
Mineur*	30	8	6	16	27	43	22

Cup Final: CFKA Sredets 3, Chernomore 0
Top scorer: Stoichkov (Sredets) 23

CYPRUS

Founded: 1934.
Number of Clubs: 87.
Number of Players: 23,000.
National Colours: Sky blue shirts, white shorts, blue and white stockings.

International matches 1988

12 Oct, Limassol: v Malta (h) lost 0-1
22 Oct, Nicosia: v France (h) drew 1-1 (*Pittas*)
2 Nov, Limassol: v Norway (h) lost 0-3
23 Nov, Valetta: v Malta (a) drew 1-1 (*Ioannou*)
11 Dec, Belgrade: v Yugoslavia (a) lost 0-4

League Championship wins (1935–89)

Omonia 16; Apoel 13; Anorthosis 6; AEL 5; EPA 3; Olympiakos 3; Pezoporikos 2; Chetin Kayal 1; Trast 1.

Cup wins (1935–89)

Apoel 11; Omonia 7; EPA 5; EL 5; Apollon 3; Trast 3; ChetinKaya 2; Pezoporikos 2; Anorthosis 2; Paralimni 1; Olympiakos 1, AEL 1.

Final League Table 1988–89

	P	*W*	*D*	*L*	*F*	*A*	*Pts*
Omonia	28	17	9	2	60	22	43
Apollon	28	15	10	3	61	26	40
Apoel	28	15	4	9	48	37	34
Salamine	28	11	11	6	51	35	33
AEL	28	10	10	8	50	40	30
Anortosi	28	10	10	8	31	30	30
Pezoporikos	28	7	14	7	35	34	28
Apop	28	9	10	9	36	40	28
Olympiakos	28	7	13	8	43	42	27
Ethnikos	28	10	7	11	34	43	27
Paralimni	28	7	13	8	35	47	27
Aris	28	8	10	10	42	39	26
EPA*	28	6	9	13	32	41	21
Keravnos*	28	6	9	13	27	39	21
Aradippu*	28	1	3	24	11	81	5

Cup Final: AEL 3, Aris 2
Top scorer: Maknil (Salamine) 19

CZECHOSLOVAKIA

Founded: 1906.
Number of Clubs: 5972.
Number of Players: 374,421.
National Colours: Red shirts, white shorts, blue stockings.

International matches 1988

12 Jan, Las Palmas: v Finland (n) lost 0-2
15 Jan, Las Palmas: v East Germany (n) won 1-0 (*Hasek*)
24 Feb, Malaga: v Spain (a) won 2-1 (*Knoflicek, Kubik*)
23 March, Sofia: v Bulgaria (a) lost 0-2
27 April, Trnava: v USSR (h) drew 1-1 (*Vlk*)
1 June, Copenhagen: v Denmark (a) won 1-0 (*Kubik*)
24 Aug, Paris: v France (a) drew 1-1 (*Danek*)
20 Sept, Prague: v Austria (h) won 4-2 (*Luhovy, Bilek, Danek 2*)
18 Oct, Eschs'Alzette: v Luxembourg (a) won 2-0 (*Hasek, Chovanek*)
4 Nov, Bratislava: v Norway (h) won 3-2 (*Griga, Weiss, Luhovy*
16 Nov, Bratislava: Belgium (h) drew 0-0

League Championship wins (1926–89)

Sparta Prague 18; Slavia Prague 12; Dukla Prague (prev.UDA) 11; Slovan Bratislava 6; Spartak Trnava 5; Banik Ostrava 3; Inter-Bratislava 1; Spartak Hradec Kralove 1; Viktoria Zizkov 1; Zbrojovka Brno 1; Bohemians 1; Vitkovice 1.

Cup wins (1961–89)

Dukla Prague 7; Sparta Prague 7; Slovan Bratislava 5; Spartak Trnava 4; Banik Ostrava 2; Lokomotiv Kosice 2; TJ Gottwaldov 1; Dunajska Streda 1.

Final League Table 1988–89

	P	*W*	*D*	*L*	*F*	*A*	*Pts*
Sparta Prague	30	19	7	4	73	26	45
Banik Ostrava	30	19	4	7	54	34	42
Nitra	30	15	4	11	38	40	34
Slavia Prague	30	15	3	12	55	49	33
Dukla Prague	30	13	6	11	50	42	32
Dunasjska	30	13	5	12	37	41	31
Slovan	30	13	4	13	41	39	30
Banska Bystrica	30	13	4	13	50	57	30
Inter	30	11	7	12	53	56	29
Olomouc	30	12	5	13	42	47	29
Vitkovice	30	13	2	15	53	40	28
Trnava	30	10	7	13	36	46	27
Cheb	30	10	4	16	38	53	24
Bohemians	30	10	4	16	40	56	24
Skoda Pilsen*	30	10	3	17	40	48	23
Hradec Kralove*	30	6	7	17	32	58	19

Cup Final: Sparta Prague 3, Slovan 0
Top scorer: Luhovy (Dukla Prague) 25

DENMARK

Founded: 1889.
Number of Clubs: 1510.
Number of Players: 323,605.
National Colours: Red shirts, white shorts, red stockings.

International matches 1988

27 April, Vienna: v Austria (a) lost 0-1
10 May, Budapest: v Hungary (a) drew 2-2 (*Frimann, Eriksen*)
1 June, Copenhagen: v Czechoslovakia (h) lost 0-1
5 June, Odense: v Belgium (h) won 3-1 (*M. Olsen, Eriksen 2*)
11 June, Hannover: v Spain (n) lost 2-3 (*Laudrup, Povlsen*)
14 June, Gelsenkirchen: v West Germany (n) lost 0-2
17 June, Cologne: v Italy (n) lost 0-2
31 Aug, Stockholm: v Sweden (a) won 2-1 (*Elstrup 2*)
14 Sept, Wembley: v England (a) lost 0-1
28 Sept, Copenhagen: v Iceland (h) won 1-0 (*Bartram*)
19 Oct, Athens: v Greece (a) drew 1-1 (*Povlsen*)
2 Nov, Copenhagen: v Bulgaria (h) drew 1-1 (*Elstrup*)

League Championship wins (1913–88)

KB Copenhagen 15; B 93 Copenhagen 9; AB (Akademisk) 9; B 1903 Copenhagen 7; Frem 6; Esbjergs BK 5; Vejle BK 5; AGF Aarhus 5; Hvidovre 3; Brondby 3; B 1909 Odense 2; Koge BK 2; Odense BK 2; Lyngby 1.

Cup wins (1955–88)

Aarhus GF 7; Vejle BK 6; BK 09 Odense 3; Randers Freja 3; Aalborg BK 2; Esbjerg BK 2; Frem 2; B93 Copenhagen 2; B 1903 Copenhagen 2; KB Copenhagen 1; Vanlose 1; Hvidovre 1; Odense Bk 1; Lyngby 1.

Final League Table 1988–89

	P	*W*	*D*	*L*	*F*	*A*	*Pts*
Brondby	26	17	6	3	57	22	40
Naestved	26	14	7	5	38	25	35
Lyngby	26	15	5	6	41	27	35
B 1903	26	12	8	6	44	27	32
Vejle	26	10	10	6	38	23	30
Herfolge	26	11	7	8	30	30	29
Odense	26	12	5	9	47	36	29
Aarhus	26	10	6	10	37	29	26
Silkeborg	26	11	4	11	39	35	26
Ikast	26	8	6	12	35	39	22
Bronshoj	26	9	4	13	39	46	22
Aalborg	26	8	6	12	33	50	22
Randers Freja*	26	2	4	20	27	75	8
KB Copenhagen*	26	3	2	21	27	66	8

Cup Final: Aarhus 2, Brondby 1
Top scorer: Christensen (Brondby) 19

FAEROE ISLANDS

Founded: 1979.
Number of Clubs: 22.
Number of Players: 3500.

International matches 1988

24 Aug, Akranes: v Iceland (a) lost 0-1

Final League Table 1988–89

	P	W	D	L	F	A	Pts
HB	18	11	3	4	36	19	25
B68	18	11	2	5	31	14	24
B36	18	8	5	5	29	20	21
IF	18	6	6	6	23	25	18
GI	18	8	1	9	21	25	17
VB	18	6	4	8	24	27	16
LIF	18	6	4	8	26	31	16
KI	18	6	3	9	29	43	15
TB*	18	4	6	8	16	23	14
NSI*	18	4	6	8	15	23	14

Cup Final: HB 1, NSI 0
Top scorer: Morkore (LIF) 13

FINLAND

Founded: 1907.
Number of Clubs: 1140.
Number of Players: 57,732.
National Colours: White shirts, blue shorts, white stockings.

International matches 1988

12 Jan, Las Palmas: v Czechoslovakia (n) won2-0 (*Paatelainen, Alatensio*)
15 Jan, Las Palmas: v Sweden (n) lost 0-1
7 Feb, Valetta: v Malta (a) lost 0-2
13 Feb, Valetta: v Tunisia (n) won 3-0 (*Lipponen 3*)
19 May, Helsinki: v Colombia (h) lost 1-3 (*Rantanen*)
4 Aug, Helsinki: v Bulgaria (h) drew 1-1 (*Myyry*)
17 Aug, Turku: v USSR (h) drew 0-0
31 Aug, Helsinki: v West Germany (h) lost 0-4
19 Oct, Swansea: v Wales (a) drew 2-2 (*Ukkonen, Paatelainen*)
3 Nov, Kuwait: v Kuwait (a) drew 0-0
6 Nov, Kuwait: v Kuwait (a) drew 0-0

Championship wins (1949–88)

Helsinki JK 7; Turun Palloseura 5; Kupion Palloseura 5; Valkeakosken Haka 4; Lahden Reipas 3; Ilves-Kissat 2; IF Kamraterna 2; Kotkan TP 2; OPS Oulu 2; Kuusysi 2; Turun Pyrkivä 1; IF Kronohagens 1; Helsinki PS 1; Kokkolan PV 1; IF Kamraterna 1; Vasa 1.

Cup wins (1955–88)

Valkeakosken Haka 9; Lahden Reipas 7; Kotkan TP 4; Helsinki JK 3; Mikkelin 2; Kuusysi 2; IFK Abo 1; Drott 1; Helsinki PS 1; Kuopion Palloseura 1; Pallo-Peikot 1; Ilves Tampere 1; Rovaniemi PS 1.

Final League Table 1988–89

	P	W	D	L	F	A	Pts
HJK	27	20	3	4	55	28	43
Kuusysi	27	14	6	7	57	30	34
Rovaniemi	27	10	11	6	37	29	31
Reipas Lahti	27	10	10	7	47	39	30
TPS Turku	27	10	10	7	29	27	30
Kemi	27	9	10	8	29	38	28
Haka	27	10	7	10	41	37	27
Mikkeli	27	8	10	9	24	33	26
Ilves	27	8	9	10	40	47	25
Oulu	27	7	9	11	32	36	23
Kups	27	4	12	11	24	34	20
Pori*	27	0	7	20	26	63	7

Cup Final: Haka 1, Oulu 0
Top scorer: Lius (Kuusysi) 22

FRANCE

Founded: 1919.
Number of Clubs: 22,829.
Number of Players: 1,608,470.
National Colours: Blue shirts, white shorts, red stockings.

International matches 1988

27 Jan, Tel Aviv: v Israel (a) drew 1-1 (*Stopyra*)
2 Feb, Toulouse: v Switzerland (h) won 2-1 (*Passi, Fargeon*)
5 Feb, Monaco: v Morocco (h) won 2-1 (*Lamriss own goal, Stopyra*)
23 March, Paris: v Spain (h) won 2-1 (*Passi, Fernandez*)
27 Apirl, Belfast: v Northern Ireland (a) drew 0-0
24 Aug, Paris: v Czechoslovakia (h) drew 1-1 (*Paille*)
28 Sept, Paris: v Norway (h) won 1-0 (*Papin*)
22 Oct, Nicosia: v Cyprus (a) drew 1-1 (*Xuereb*)
19 Nov, Belgrade: v Yugoslavia (a) lost 2-3 (*Perez, Sauzee*)

League Championship wins (1933–89)

Saint Etienne 10; Stade de Reims 6; Nantes 6; AS Monaco 5; Olympique Marseille 5; OGC Nice 4; Girondins Bordeaux 4; Lille OSC 3; FC Sete 2; Sochaux 2; Racing Club Paris 1; Roubaix-Tourcoing 1; Strasbourg 1; Paris St Germain 1.

Cup wins (1918–89)

Olympique Marseille 10; Saint Etienne 6; Lille OSC 5; Racing Club Paris 5; Red Star 5; AS Monaco 4; Olympique Lyon 3; Girondins Bordeaux 3; CAS Genereaux 2; Nancy 2; OGC Nice 2; Racing Club Strasbourg 2; Sedan 2; FC Sete 2; Stade de Reims 2; Stade Rennes 2; Paris St Germain 2; AS Cannes 1; Club Français 1; Excelsior Roubaix 1; Le Havre 1; SO Montpelier 1; Olympique de Pantin 1; CA Paris 1; Sochaux 1; Toulouse 1; Bastia 1; Nantes 1; Metz 1.

Final League Table 1988–89

	P	W	D	L	F	A	Pts
Marseille	38	20	13	5	56	35	73
Paris St Germain	38	19	13	6	45	26	70
Monaco	38	18	14	6	62	38	68
Sochaux	38	19	11	8	50	28	68
Auxerre	38	18	9	11	41	32	63
Nice	38	16	9	13	45	40	57
Nantes	38	15	12	11	41	40	57
Lille	38	15	11	12	50	38	56
Montpellier	38	14	10	14	51	53	52
Toulouse	38	12	15	11	44	46	51
Toulon	38	12	14	12	30	29	50
Cannes	38	14	8	16	45	47	50
Bordeaux	38	12	13	13	54	46	49
St Etienne	38	12	12	14	39	50	48
Metz	38	12	11	15	47	49	47
Caen	38	10	10	18	39	60	40
Matra Racing	38	10	9	19	49	56	39
Strasbourg†	38	10	9	19	47	59	39
Laval*	38	8	11	19	33	55	35
Lens*	38	3	8	27	32	73	17

Cup Final: Marseille 4, Monaco 3
Top scorer: Papin (Marseille) 22

EAST GERMANY

Founded: 1948.
Number of Clubs: 5771.
Number of Players: 577,700.
National Colours: White shirts, blue shorts, white stockings.

International matches 1988

13 Jan, Las Palmas: v Sweden (n) lost 1-4 (*Thom*)
15 Jan, Las Palmas: v Czechoslovakia (n) lost 0-1
27 Jan, Valencia: v Spain (a) drew 0-0
1 March, Mohammedia: v Morocco (a) lost 1-2 (*Ernst*)
30 March, Halle: v Rumania (h) drew 3-3 (*Ernst, Zotzsche, Stahmann*)
13 April, Burgas: v Bulgaria (a) drew 1-1 (*Stubner*)
31 Aug, East Berlin: v Greece (h) won 1-0 (*Sammer*)
21 Sept, Cottbus: v Poland (h) lost 1-2 (*Ernst*)
19 Oct, East Berlin: v Iceland (h) won 2-0 (*Thom 2*)
30 Nov, Istanbul: v Turkey (a) lost 1-3 (*Thom*)

League Championship wins (1950–89)

Dynamo Berlin 10; ASK Vorwaerts 6; Dynamo Dresden 6; Wismut Karl-Marx-Stadt 4; FC Magdeburg 4; Carl Jena (prev. Motor Jena) 3; Chemie Leipzig 2; Turbine Erfurt 2; Turbine Halle 1; Zwickau Horch 1; Empor Rostock 1; ZSG Halle 1; Planitz 1.

Cup wins (1949–89)

Dynamo Dresden 6; Carl Zeiss Jena (prev. Motor Jena) 5; Lokomotiv Leipzig 5; FC Magdeburg 4; Dynamo Berlin 3; Chemie Leipzig 2; Magdeburg Aufbau 2; Motor Zwickau 2; ASK Vorwaerts 2; Dresden Einheit SC 1; Dresden VP 1; Halle Chemie SC 1; North Dessau Waggonworks 1; Thale EHW 1; Union East Berlin 1; Wismut Karl-Marx-Stadt 1; Sachsenring Zwickau 1.

Final League Table 1988–89

	P	*W*	*D*	*L*	*F*	*A*	*Pts*
Dynamo Dresden	26	16	8	2	61	26	40
Dynamo Berlin	26	12	8	6	51	32	32
Karl-Marx-Stadt	26	12	6	8	38	36	30
Hansa Rostock	26	12	5	9	34	31	29
Lokomotiv Leipzig	26	11	6	9	39	26	28
Magdeburg	26	11	6	9	35	30	28
Wismut Aue	26	10	8	8	35	35	28
Carl Zeiss Jena	26	11	5	10	35	24	27
Chemie Halle	26	8	9	9	36	38	25
Cottbus	26	9	5	12	29	41	23
Brandenburg	26	9	4	13	36	43	22
Rot-Weiss Erfurt	26	9	3	14	27	39	21
Zwickau*	26	6	4	16	25	49	16
Union Berlin*	26	5	5	16	22	53	15

Cup Final: Dynamo Berlin 1, Karl-Marx-Stadt 0
Top scorer: Gutchow (Dynamo Dresden) 17

WEST GERMANY

Founded: 1900.
Number of Clubs: 21,510.
Number of Players: 4,765,146.
National Colours: White shirts, black shorts, white stockings.

International matches 1988

31 March, West Berlin: v Sweden (h) drew 1-1 (*K Allofs*) (*Sweden won 5-3 on penalties*)
2 April, West Berlin: v Argentina (h) won 1-0 (*Matthaus*)
27 April, Kaiserslauten: v Switzerland (h) won 1-0 (*Klinsmann*)
4 June, Bremen: v Yugoslavia (h) drew 1-1 (*Matthaus*)
10 June, Dusseldorf: v Italy (h) drew 1-1 (*Brehme*)
14 June, Gelsenkirchen: v Denmark (h) won 2-0 (*Klinsmann, Thon*)
17 June, Munich: v Spain (h) won 2-0 (*Voller 2*)
21 June, Hamburg: v Holland (h) lost 1-2 (*Matthaus*)
31 Aug, Helsinki: v Finland (a) won 4-0 (*Voller 2, Europaeus own goal, Riedle*)
21 Sept, Dusseldorf: v USSR (h) won 1-0 (*Smatowalenko own goal*)
19 Oct, Munich: v Holland (h) drew 0-0

League Championship wins (1903–89)

Bayern Munich 11; IFC Nuremberg 9; Schalke 04 7; SV Hamburg 6; Borussia Moenchengladbach 5; VfB Leipzig 3; VfB Stuttgart 3; Sp Vgg Furth 3; Borussia Dortmund 3; IFC Cologne 3; Viktoria Berlin 2; Hertha Berlin 2; Hanover 96 2; Dresden SC 2; IFC Kaiserslautern 2; SV Werder Bremen 2; Munich 1860 1; Union Berlin 1; FC Freibourg 1; Phoenix Karlsruhe 1; Karlsruher FV 1; Holstein Kiel 1; Fortuna Dusseldorf 1; Rapid Vienna 1; VfR Mannheim 1; Rot-Weiss Essen 1; Eintracht Frankfurt 1; Eintracht Brunswick 1.

Cup wins (1935–89)

Bayern Munich 8; IFC Cologne 4; Eintracht Frankfurt 4; IFC Nuremberg 3; SV Hamburg 3; Dresden SC 2; Fortuna Dusseldorf 2; Karlsruhe SC 2; Munich 1860 2; Schalke 04 2; VfB Stuttgart 2; Borussia Moenchengladbach 2; Borussia Dortmund 2; First Vienna 1; VfB Leipzig 1; Kickers Offenbach 1; Rapid Vienna 1; Rot-Weiss Essen 1; SW Essen 1; Werder Bremen 1; Bayer Verdingen 1.

Final League Table 1988–89

	P	*W*	*D*	*L*	*F*	*A*	*Pts*
Bayern Munich	34	19	12	3	67	26	50
Cologne	34	18	9	7	58	30	45
Werder Bremen	34	18	8	8	55	32	44
Hamburg	34	17	9	8	60	36	43
Stuttgart	34	16	7	11	58	49	39
Moenchengladbach	34	12	14	8	44	43	38
Borussia Dortmund	34	12	13	9	56	40	37
Leverkusen	34	10	14	10	45	44	34
Kaiserslautern	34	10	13	11	47	44	33
St Pauli	34	9	14	11	41	42	32
Karlsruhe	34	12	8	14	48	51	32
Mannheim	34	10	11	13	43	52	31
Uerdingen	34	10	11	13	50	60	31
Nuremberg	34	8	10	16	36	54	26
Bochum	34	9	8	17	37	57	26
Eintracht Frankfurt†	34	8	10	16	30	53	26
Stuttgart Kickers*	34	10	6	18	41	68	26
Hannover 96*	34	4	11	19	36	71	19

Cup Final: Borussia Dortmund 4, Werder Bremen 1
Top scorers: Allofs (Cologne) 17
Wohlfahrt (Bayern Munich) 17

GREECE

Founded: 1926.
Number of Clubs: 3678.
Number of Players: 282,550.
National Colours: White shirts, blue shorts, white stockings.

International matches 1988

17 Feb, Athens: v Northern Ireland (h) won 3-2 (*Manolas 2, Mitropoulos*)
23 March, Athens: v USSR (h) Lost 0-4
6 April, Athens: v Austria (h) drew 2-2 (*Saravakos, Skartados*)
19 May, Montreal: v Canada (a) won 1-0 (*Tsiolis*)
21 May, Toronto: v Canada (a) won 3-0 (*Mitropoulos, Anatopoulos 2*)
23 May, Toronto: v Chile (n) won 1-0 (*Anastopoulos*)
25 May, Toronto: v Canada (a) drew 0-0
31 Aug, East Berlin: v East Germany (a) lost 0-1
21 Sept, Istanbul: v Turkey (a) lost 1-3 (*Anastopoulos*)
19 Oct, Athens: v Denmark (h) drew 1-1 (*Mitropoulos*)
2 Nov, Bucharest: v Rumania (a) lost 0-3

15 Nov, Athens: v Hungary (h) won 3-0 (*Lagonikis, Tsalochidis* 2)

League Championship wins (1928–89)

Olympiakos 25; Panathinaikos 14; AEK Athens 8; Aris Salonika 3; PAOK Salonika 2; Larissa 1.

Cup wins (1932–89)

Olympiakos 18; Panathinaikos 11; AEK Athens 9; PAOK Salonika 2; Aris Salonika 1; Ethnikos 1; Iraklis 1; Panionios 1; Kastoria 1; Larissa 1; Ofi Crete 1.

Final League Table 1988–89

	P	*W*	*D*	*L*	*F*	*A*	*Pts*
AEK Athens	30	19	6	5	46	21	44
Olympiakos	30	16	9	5	54	25	41
Panathinaikos	30	14	9	7	45	25	37
Iraklis	30	13	10	7	44	28	36
Ofi Crete	30	13	8	9	45	36	34
Larissa	30	10	14	6	37	34	34
Aris	30	11	11	8	31	26	33
PAOK	30	11	10	9	34	30	32
Doxa	30	10	8	12	26	28	28
Panionios	30	10	7	13	32	36	27
Volos	30	6	14	10	36	45	26
Levadiakos	30	9	7	14	33	47	25
Apollon	30	7	9	14	29	38	23
Ethnikos*	30	6	11	13	31	49	23
Diagoras*	30	4	12	14	21	43	20
Kalamaria*	30	4	9	17	24	57	17

Cup Final: Panathinaikos 3, Panionios 1
Top scorer: Bota (Volos) 20

HOLLAND

Founded: 1889.
Number of Clubs: 7912.
Number of Players: 978,324.
National Colours: Orange shirts, white shorts, orange stockings.

International matches 1988

23 March, Wembley: v England (a) drew 2-2 (*Adams own goal, Bosman*)
24 May, Rotterdam: v Bulgaria (h) lost 1-2 (*Wouters*)
1 June, Amsterdam: v Rumania (h) won 2-0 (*Bosman, Kieft*)
12 June, Cologne: v USSR (n) lost 0-1
15 June, Dusseldorf: v England (n) won 3-1 (*Van Basten 3*)
18 June, Gelsenkirchen: v Eire (n) won 1-0 (*Kieft*)
21 June, Hamburg: v West Germany (n) won 2-1 (*R. Koeman, Van Basten*)
25 June, Munich: v USSR (n) won 2-0 (*Gullit, Van Basten*)
14 Sept, Amsterdam: v Wales (h) 1-0 (*Gullit*)
19 Oct, Munich: v West Germany (a) drew 0-0
16 Nov, Rome: v Italy (a) lost 0-1

League Championship wins (1898–1989)

Ajax Amsterdam 22; Feyenoord 13; PSV Eindhoven 11; HVV The Hague 8; Sparta Rotterdam 6; Go Ahead Deventer 4; HBS The Hague 3; Willem II Tilburg 3; RCH Haarlem 2; RAP 2; Heracles 2; ADO The Hague 2; Quick The Hague 1; BVV Scheidam 1; NAC Breda 1; Eindhoven 1; Enschede 1; Volewijckers Amsterdam 1; Limburgia 1; Rapid JC Haarlem 1; DOS Utrecht 1; DWS Amsterdam 1; Haarlem 1; Be Quick Groningen 1; SVV Scheidam 1; AZ 67 Alkmaar 1.

Cup wins (1899–1989)

Ajax Amsterdam 11; Feyenoord 6; PSV Eindhoven 6; Quick The Hague 4; AZ 67 Alkmaar 3; HEC 3; Sparta Rotterdam 3; DFC 2; Fortuna Geleen 2; Haarlem 2; HBS The Hague 2; RCH 2; VOC 2; Wageningen 2; Willem II Tilburg 2; FC Den Haag 2; Concordia Rotterdam 1; CVV 1; Eindhoven 1; HVV The Hague 1; Longa 1; Quick Njimegen 1; RAP 1; Roermond 1; Schoten 1; Velocitas Breda 1; Velocitas Groningen 1; VSV 1; VUC 1; VVV Groningen 1; ZFC 1; NAC Breda 1; Twente Enschede 1; Utrecht 1.

Final League Table 1988–89

	P	*W*	*D*	*L*	*F*	*A*	*Pts*
PSV Eindhoven	34	24	5	5	78	31	53
Ajax	34	22	6	6	74	32	50
Twente	34	11	18	5	47	25	40
Feyenoord	34	15	10	9	66	52	40
Roda	34	13	12	9	52	38	38
Groningen	34	14	8	12	62	51	36
Den Bosch	34	15	6	13	48	53	36
Fortuna Sittard	34	11	12	11	40	37	34
Volendam	34	13	7	14	42	51	33
Haarlem	34	11	11	12	37	50	33
RKC	34	11	9	14	53	61	31
Sparta	34	9	12	13	42	50	30
Utrecht	34	11	7	16	49	57	29
Maastricht	34	10	9	15	40	58	29
Willem II	34	8	11	15	50	68	27
PEC Zwolle*	34	8	9	17	48	70	25
VVV Venlo*	34	5	14	15	40	62	24
Veendam*	34	8	8	18	37	59	24

Cup Final: PSV Eindhoven 4, Groningen 1
Top scorer: Romario (PSV Eindhoven) 19

HUNGARY

Founded: 1901.
Number of Clubs: 2503.
Number of Players: 129,087.
National Colours: Red shirts, white shorts, green stockings.

International matches 1989

16 March, Budapest: v Turkey (h) won 1-0 (*Kiprich*)
26 March, Brussels: v Belgium (a) lost 0-3
27 April, Budapest: v England (h) drew 0-0
4 May, Budapest: v Iceland (h) won 3-0 (*Vincze, Sallai, K. Kovacs*)
10 May, Budapest: v Denmark (h) drew 2-2 (*Kiprich, Bognar*)
17 May, Budapest: v Austria (h) lost 0-4
31 Aug, Linz: v Austria (a) drew 0-0
21 Sept, Reykjavik: v Iceland (a) won 3-0 (*Kiprich, Vincze*)
19 Oct, Budapest: v Northern Ireland (h) won 1-0 (*Vincze*)
15 Nov, Athens: v Greece (a) lost 0-3
11 Dec, Valetta: v Malta (a) drew 2-2 (*Vincze, Kiprich*)

League Championship wins (1901–89)

Ferencvaros (prev. FTC) 23; MTK-VM Budapest (prev. Hungaria, Bastay and Vörös Lobogo) 19; Ujpest Dozsa 18; Honved 11; Vasas Budapest 6; Csepel 4; Raba Györ (prev. Vasas Györ) 3; BTC 2; Nagyvarad 1.

Cup wins (1910–89)*

Ferencvaros (prev. FTC) 14; MTK-VM Budapest (prev. Hungaria, Bastya and Vörös Lobogo) 9; Ujpest Dozsa 7; Raba Györ (prev.Vasas Györ) 4; Vasas Budapest 3; Honved 3; Diösgyör 2; Bocskai 1; III Ker 1; Kispesti AC 1; Soroksar 1; Szolnoki MAV 1; Siofok Banyasz 1; Bekescsabal 1.

* *Cup not held regularly until 1964*

Final League Table 1988–89

	P	W	DW	DL	L	F	A	Pts
Honved	30	16	6	1	7	44	28	61
Ferencvaros	30	16	4	3	7	49	30	59
MTK VM	30	13	8	3	6	41	34	59
Videoton	30	17	1	4	8	57	32	57
Raba Eto	30	16	3	2	9	44	30	56
Tatabanya	30	13	2	6	9	41	35	49
Bekescsaba	30	12	4	2	12	40	36	46
Vac	30	10	5	5	10	33	34	45
Ujpest Dozsa	30	11	2	4	13	36	35	41
Pecs	30	9	4	6	11	35	37	41
Veszprem	30	9	5	2	14	23	37	39
Siofok	30	8	4	6	12	34	41	38
Haladas	30	7	5	4	14	31	44	35
Vasas	30	8	2	7	13	35	58	35
Zalaegerszeg*	30	7	3	6	14	37	44	33
Dunaujvaros*	30	3	7	4	16	28	53	26

Cup Final: Honved 1, Ferencvaros 0
Top scorer: Petres (Videoton) 19

ICELAND

Founded: 1929.
Number of Clubs: 82.
Number of Players: 19,400.
National Colours: Blue shirts, white shorts, blue stockings.

International matches 1988

4 May, Reykjavik: v Hungary (a) lost 0-3
7 Aug, Reykjavik: v Bulgaria (h) lost 2-3 (*Ormslev 2*)
31 Aug, Reykjavik: v USSR (h) drew 1-1 (*Gretarson*)
21 Sept, Reykjavik: v Hungary (h) lost 0-3
28 Sept, Copenhagen: v Denmark (a) lost 0-1
12 Oct, Istanbul: v Turkey (a) drew 1-1 (*Tordarsson*)
19 Oct, East Berlin: v East Germany (a) lost 0-2

League Championship wins (1912–88)

KR 20; Valur 19; Fram 17; IA Akranes 12; Vikingur 4; IBK Keflavik 3; IBV Vestmann 2.

Cup wins (1960–88)

KR 7; Fram 6; IA Akranes 5; Valur 5; IBV Vestmann 3; IBA Akureyri 1; Vikingur 1; IBK Keflavik 1.

Final League Table 1988–89

	P	W	D	L	F	A	Pts
Fram	18	16	1	1	38	8	49
Valur	18	13	2	3	36	15	41
IA Akranes	18	9	5	4	32	25	32
KA Akureyri	18	8	3	7	31	29	27
KR Reykjavik	18	7	3	8	26	25	24
Thor	18	6	6	6	25	28	24
IB Keflavik	18	4	6	8	22	32	18
Vikingur	18	5	3	10	20	31	18
Leiftur*	18	1	6	11	12	26	9
Volfunger*	18	2	3	13	13	36	9

Cup Final: Valur 1, IB Keflavik 0
Top scorer: Kristjansson (Valur) 13

REPUBLIC OF IRELAND

Founded: 1921.
Number of Clubs: 3503.
Number of Players: 33,028.
National Colours: Green shirts, white shorts, green stockings.

International matches 1988

23 Match, Dublin: v Rumania (h) won 2-0 (*Moran, Kelly*)
27 April, Dublin: v Yugoslavia (h) won 2-0 (*Lekovic own goal, Moran*)
22 May, Dublin: v Poland (h) won 3-1 (*Sheedy, Cascarino, Sheridan*)
1 June, Oslo: v Norway (a) drew 0-0
12 June, Stuttgart: v England (n) won 1-0 (*Houghton*)
15 June, Hannover: v USSR (n) drew 1-1 (*Whelan*)
18 June, Gelsenkirchen: v Holland (n) lost 0-1
14 Sept, Belfast: v Northern Ireland (a) drew 0-0
19 Oct, Dublin: v Tunisia (h) won 4-0 (*Cascarino 2, Aldridge, Sheedy*)
16 Nov, Seville: v Spain (a) lost 0-2

League Championship wins (1922–89)

Shamrock Rovers 24; Shelbourne 7; Bohemians 7; Dundalk 7; Waterford 6; Cork United 5; Drumcondra 5; St Patrick's Athletic 3; St James's Gate 2; Cork Athletic 2; Sligo Rovers 2; Limerick 2; Athlone Town 2; Dolphin 1; Cork Hibernians 1; Cork Celtic 1, Derry City 1.

Cup wins (1922–89)

Shamrock Rovers 23; Dundalk 8; Drumcondra 5; Bohemians 4; Shelbourne 3; Cork Athletic 2; Cork United 2; St James's Gate 2; St Patrick's Athletic 2; Cork Hibernians 2; Limerick 2; Waterford 2; Alton United 1; Athlone Town 1; Cork 1; Fordsons 1; Transport 1; Finn Harps 1; Home Farm 1; Sligo 1; UCD 1; Derry City 1.

Final League Table 1988–89

	P	W	D	L	F	A	Pts
Derry City	33	24	5	4	70	20	53
Dundalk	33	20	11	2	55	27	51
Limerick	33	18	9	6	57	37	45
St. Patrick's	33	16	11	6	40	19	43
Bohemians	33	12	6	15	40	43	30
Athlone Town	33	11	7	15	30	33	29
Shamrock Rovers	33	8	13	12	34	42	29
Cork City	33	8	10	15	29	36	26
Shelbourne	33	8	10	15	26	40	26
Galway United	33	8	9	16	34	56	25
Cobh Ramblers*	33	6	9	18	29	54	21
Waterford*	33	6	6	21	21	58	18

Cup Final: Derry City 1, Cork City 0 (after 0-0 draw)
Top scorer: Hamilton (Limerick) 21

ITALY

Founded: 1898.
Number of Clubs: 20,117.
Number of Players: 1,129,667.
National Colours: Blue shirts, white shorts, blue stockings, white trim.

International matches 1988

20 Feb, Bari: v USSR (h) won 4-1 (*F. Baresi, Vialli 2,* Bergomi)
31 March, Split: v Yugoslavia (a) drew 1-1 (*Vialli*)
27 April, Luxembourg: v Luxembourg (a) won 3-0 (*Ferri, Bergomi, De Agostini*)
4 June, Brescia: v Wales (h) lost 0-1
10 June, Dusseldorf: v West Germany (n) drew 1-1 (*Mancini*)
14 June, Frankfurt: v Spain (n) won 1-0 (*Vialli*)
17 June, Cologne: v Denmark (h) won 2-0 (*Altobelli, De Agostini*)
22 June, Stuttgart: v USSR (a) lost 0-2
19 Oct, Pescara: v Norway (h) won 2-1 (*Giannini, Ferri*)

16 Nov, Rome: v Holland (h) won 1-0 (*Vialli*)
22 Dec, Perugia: v Scotland (h) won 2-0 (*Giannini*, *Berti*)

League Championship wins (1898–1989)

Juventus 22; Inter-Milan 13; AC Milan 11; Genoa 9; Torino 8; Pro Vercelli 7; Bologna 7; Fiorentina 2; AS Roma 2; Casale 1; Novese 1; Cagliari 1; Lazio 1; Verona 1; Napoli 1.

Cup wins (1922–89)

Juventus 7; AS Roma 6; Torino 4; Fiorentina 4; AC Milan 4; Inter-Milan 3; Napoli 3; Sampdoria 3; Bologna 2; Atalanta 1; Genoa 1; Lazio 1; Vado 1; Venezia 1.

Final League Table 1987–88

	P	*W*	*D*	*L*	*F*	*A*	*Pts*
AC Milan	30	17	11	2	43	14	45
Napoli	30	18	6	6	55	27	42
Roma	30	15	8	7	39	26	38
Sampdoria	30	13	11	6	41	30	37
Internazionale	30	11	10	9	42	35	32
Juventus	30	11	9	10	35	30	31
Torino	30	8	15	7	33	30	31
Fiorentina	30	9	10	11	29	33	28
Cesena	30	7	12	11	23	32	26
Verona	30	7	11	12	23	30	25
Como	30	6	13	11	22	37	25
Ascoli	30	6	12	12	30	37	24
Pisa	30	6	12	12	23	30	24
Pescara	30	8	8	14	27	44	24
Avellino*	30	5	13	12	19	39	23
Empoli*	30	6	13	11	20	30	20

(Empoli minus 5 points.)

Top scorer: Maradona (Napoli) 15
Cup Final: Sampdoria 2,1, Torino 0,2

LIECHTENSTEIN

Founded: 1933.
Number of Clubs: 7.
Number of Players: 1300.
National Colours: Blue & red shirts, red shorts, blue stockings.

No international matches 1988

Liechtenstein has no national league. Teams compete in Swiss regional leagues.

LUXEMBOURG

Founded: 1908.
Number of Clubs: 199.
Number of Players: 23,252.
National Colours: Red shirts, white shorts, blue stockings.

International matches 1988

27 April, Luxembourg: v Italy (h) lost 0-3
21 Sept, Luxembourg: v Switzerland (h) lost 1-4
18 Oct, Esch s'Alzette: v Czechoslovakia (h) lost 0-2 (*Langers*)
19 Nov, Oporto: v Portugal (a) lost 1-0

League Championship wins (1910–89)

Jeunesse Esch 21; Spora Luxembourg 11; Stade Dudelange 10; Red Boys Differdange 6; US Hollerich-Bonnevoie 5; Fola Esch 5; Avenir Beggen 4; US Luxembourg 3; Aris Bonnevoie 3; Progres Niedercorn 3; Sporting Luxembourg 2; Racing Luxembourg 1; National Schiffige 1.

Cup wins (1922–89)

Red Boys Differdange 16; Jeunnesse Esch 9; Spora Luxembourg 8; US Luxembourg 8; Stade Dudelange 4; Progres Niedercorn 4; Fola Esch 3; Avenir Beggen 3; Alliance Dudelange 2; US Rumelange 2; Aris Bonnevoie 1; US Dudelange 1; Jeunesse Hautcharage 1; National Schiffige 1; Racing Luxembourg 1; SC Tetange 1.

Final League Table 1988–89

Qualifying

	P	*W*	*D*	*L*	*F*	*A*	*Pts*
Jeunesse Esch	18	14	1	3	44	6	29
Red Boys	18	11	5	2	31	13	27
Union	18	12	2	4	45	15	26
Spora	18	9	6	3	35	17	24
Avenir Beggen	18	8	6	4	34	20	22
Grevenmacher	18	6	3	9	27	37	15
Hesperange	18	5	3	10	20	36	13
Niedecorn*	18	4	1	13	18	44	9
Eischen*	18	2	4	12	17	48	8
Petange*	18	2	3	13	14	49	7

Final placings after play-offs involving top six: Spora 29 pts; Jeunesse Esch 25.5; Union 24; Avenir Beggen 22; Red Boys 21.5; Grevenmacher 19.5.

Promotion/relegation play-offs
Group A Promotion placings:
Hesperance 16 pts; Aris 14; Mertzig 12; Wiltz 8; Eischen, Diekilch 5.
Group B Promotion placings:
Fola 16 pts; Alliance 13; Niedercorn 12; Vormeldange 10; Obercorn 6; Petange 3.

Top scorer: Krahen (Avenir Beggen) 21
Krings (Avenir Beggen) 21
Scholten (Jeunesse Esch) 21

Cup Final: Avenir Beggen 0, Union 2

MALTA

Founded: 1900.
Number of Clubs: 242.
Number of Players: 4024.
National Colours: Red shirts, white shorts, red stockings.

International matches 1988

7 Feb, Valetta: v Finland (h) won 2-0 (*Busuttil*, 2)
10 Feb, Valetta: v Tunisia (h) won 2-1 (*Vella*, *Busuttil*)
22 March, Valetta: v Scotland (h) drew 1-1 (*Busuttil*)
21 May, Belfast: v Northern Ireland (a) lost 0-3
1 June, Valetta: v Wales (h) lost 2-3 (*Busuttil 2*)
12 Oct, Limassol: v Cyprus (a) won 1-0 (*Busuttil*)
18 Oct, Tel Aviv: v Israel (a) lost 0-2
23 Nov, Valetta: v Cyprus (h) drew 1-1 (*Carabott*)
11 Dec, Valetta: v Hungary (h) drew 2-2 (*Busuttil 2*)

League Championship wins (1910–89)

Floriana 24; Sliema Wanderers 22; Valletta 12; Hibernians 6; Hamrun Spartans 5; Rabat Ajax 2; St George's 1; KOMR 1.

Cup wins (1935–89)

Sliema Wanderers 16; Floriana 15; Valletta 5; Hibernians 5; Hamrun Spartans 5; Gzira United 1; Melita 1; Zurrieq 1; Rabat Ajax 1.

Final League Table 1988–89

	P	W	D	L	F	A	Pts
Sliema Wanderers	16	11	4	1	32	16	26
Valetta	16	9	5	2	24	9	23
Hamrun	16	8	4	4	31	15	20
Floriana	16	6	6	4	20	15	18
Zurrieq	16	5	4	7	14	21	14
Hibernians	16	2	8	6	16	21	12
Rabat Ajax†	16	2	8	6	14	26	12
Naxxar Lions	16	3	6	7	10	22	12
Birikara*	16	1	5	10	14	30	7

Cup Final: Hamrun 1, Floriana 0
Top scorer: Zarb (Valetta) 11

NORWAY

Founded: 1902.
Number of Clubs: 3449.
Number of Players: 298,400.
National Colours: Red shirts, white shorts, blue & white stockings.

International matches 1988

1 June, Oslo: v Eire (h) drew 0-0
28 July, Oslo: v Brazil (h) drew 1-1 (Fjortoft)
9 Aug, Oslo: v Bulgaria (h) drew 1-1 (*Sorloth*)
14 Sept, Oslo: v Scotland (h) lost 1-2 (*Fjortoft*)
28 Sept, Paris: v France (a) lost 0-1
19 Oct, Pescara: v Italy (a) lost 1-2 (*Brandhaug*)
2 Nov, Limassol: v Cyprus (a) won 3-0 (*Sorloth 2, Osvold*)
4 Nov, Bratislava: v Czechoslovakia (a) lost 2-3 (*Sorloth, Adgestein*)

League Championship wins (1938–88)

Fredrikstad 9; Viking Stavanger 7; Rosenborg Trondheim 5; Valerengen 4; Lillestroem 4; Larvik Turn 3; Brann Bergen 2; Lyn Oslo 2; IK Start 2; Friedig 1; Fram 1; Skeid Odo 1; Střomgodset Drammen 1; Moss 1.

Cup wins (1902–88)

Odds Bk, Skien 11; Fredrikstad 10; Lyn Oslo 8; Skeid Oslo 8; Sarpsborg FK 6; Brann Bergen 5; Orn F Horten 4; Mjondalens F 4; Lillestroem 4; Rosenborg Trondheim 4; Střomgodset Drammen 3; Viking Stavanger 3; Mercantile 2; Grane Nordstrand 1; Kvik Halden 1; Sparta 1; Gjovik 1; Bodo-Glimt 1; Valerengen 1; Moss 1; Tromso 1; Bryne 1.
(*Until* 1937 *the cup-winners were regarded as champions.*)

Final League Table 1988–89

	P	W	D	L	F	A	Pts
Rosenborg	22	13	6	3	49	23	45
Lillestrom	22	11	7	4	38	18	40
Molde	22	10	9	3	35	18	39
Moss	22	11	4	7	30	19	37
Tromso	22	9	6	7	27	22	33
Sogndal	22	8	7	7	27	27	31
Valerengen	22	8	6	8	26	32	30
Kongsvinger	22	7	7	8	23	23	28
Brann	22	7	4	11	16	30	25
Bryne	22	5	6	11	29	39	21
Strommen*	22	4	5	13	16	34	17
Djerv 1919*	22	3	5	14	17	54	14

Cup Final: Rosenborg 2, Brann 0
*Top scorer:*Fjortoft (Lillestrom) 14

POLAND

Founded: 1923.
Number of Clubs: 5881.
Number of Players: 317,442.
National Colours: White shirts, red shorts, white & red stockings.

International matches 1988

7 Feb, Haifa: v Rumania (n) drew 2-2 (*Cisek 2*)
10 Feb, Tel Aviv: v Israel (a) won 3-1 (*Kubicki, Prusk, Kosecki*)
23 March, Belfast: v Northern Ireland (a) drew 1-1 (*Dziekanowski*)
22 May, Dublin: v Eire (a) lost 1-3 (*K. Warzycha*)
1 June, Moscow: v USSR (a) lost 1-2 (*Dziekanowski*)
13 July, New Britain v USA (a) won 2-0 (*Kosecki 2*)
15 July, Toronto: v Canada (a) won 2-1 (*Rudy, Taraziewicz*)
24 Aug, Bialystok: v Bulgaria (h) won 3-2 (*Ivanov own goal, Furtok, Rudy*)
21 Sept, Cottbus: v East Germany (a) won 2-1 (*Furtok 2*)
19 Oct, Chorzow: v Albania (h) won 1-0 (*K. Warzycha*)

League Championship wins (1921–89)

Gornik Zabrze 14; Ruch Chorzow 13; Wisla Krakow 6; Cracovia 5; Pogon Lwow 4; Legia Warsaw 4; Warta Poznan 2; Polonia Bytom 2; Stal Mielec 2; Widzew Lodz 2; Lech Poznan 2; Garbarnia Krakow 1; Polonia Warsaw 1; LKS Lodz 1; Slask Wroclaw 1; Szombierki Bytom 1.

Cup wins (1951–89)

Legia Warsaw 8; Gornik Zabrze 6; Zaglebie Sosnowiec 4; Lech Poznan 3; Ruch Chorzow 2; Slask Wroclaw 2; Gwardia Warsaw 1; LKS Lodz 1; Polonia Warsaw 1; Wisla Krakow 1; Stal Rzeszow 1; 1; Arka Gdynia 1; Lechia Gdansk 1; Widzew Lodz 1; GKS Katowice 1.

Final League Table 1988–89

	P	W	D	L	F	A	Pts
Ruch Chorzow	30	19	8	3	48	18	52
Katowice	30	17	8	5	50	24	47
Gornik Zabrze	30	17	5	8	55	29	45
Legia Warsaw	30	14	9	7	41	18	43
Stal Mielec	30	13	7	10	35	27	33
Lech Poznan	30	11	10	9	39	32	33
Widzew Lodz	30	9	12	9	27	27	29
Jagiellonia	30	9	12	9	22	27	29
Slask Wroclaw	30	7	14	9	34	35	28
LKS Lodz	30	8	11	11	34	45	26
Olimpia	30	9	9	12	33	41	25
Wisla Krakow	30	10	6	14	35	48	23
Pogon Stettin	30	7	9	14	34	50	20
Jastrzebie	30	8	8	14	24	43	19
Walbrzych	30	7	5	18	22	44	15
Szombierki	30	4	9	17	33	57	13

One extra point for victories over three goals; one deducted for defeats conceding over three goals.
Top scorer: Warzycha K (Ruch Chorzow) 24
Cup Final: Legia Warsaw 5, Jagiellonia 2

PORTUGAL

Founded: 1914.
Number of Clubs: 1605.
Number of Players: 55,499.
National Colours: Red shirts, white shorts, red stockings.

International matches 1988

12 Oct, Gothenburg: v Sweden (a) drew 0-0
19 Nov, Oporto: v Luxembourg (h) won 1-0 (*Gomes*)

League Championship wins (1935–89)

Benfica 28; Sporting Lisbon 16; FC Porto 10; Belenenses 1.

Cup wins (1939–89)

Benfica 21; Sporting Lisbon 10; FC Porto 5; Boavista 3; Belenenses 3; Vitoria Setubal 2; Academica Coimbra 1; Leixoes Porto 1; Sporting Braga 1.

Final League Table 1988–89

	P	*W*	*D*	*L*	*F*	*A*	*Pts*
Benfica	38	27	9	2	60	15	63
FC Porto	38	21	14	3	52	17	56
Boavista	38	9	11	8	56	29	49
Sporting	38	18	9	11	50	33	45
Setubal	38	15	12	11	44	37	42
Belenenses	38	13	14	11	44	35	40
Braga	38	14	12	12	42	37	40
Amadora	38	13	13	12	33	41	39
Guimaraes	38	14	10	14	39	33	38
Nacional	38	12	12	14	43	49	36
Maritimo	38	10	15	13	40	41	35
Portimonense	38	12	11	15	34	37	35
Chaves	38	12	10	16	37	41	34
Beira Mar	38	10	13	15	29	36	33
Penafiel	38	10	13	15	31	39	33
Espinho*	38	12	8	18	45	57	32
Fafe*	38	9	14	15	29	47	32
Farense*	38	10	11	17	34	51	31
Leixoes*	38	7	14	17	29	46	28
Viseu*	38	5	9	24	20	70	19

Cup Final: Belenenses 2, Benfica 1
Top scorer: Vata (Benfica) 16

RUMANIA

Founded: 1908.
Number of Clubs: 5453.
Number of Players: 179,987.
National Colours: Yellow shirts, blue shorts, red stockings.

International matches 1988

3 Feb, Haifa: v Israel (a) won 2-0 (*Boloni, Ciuca*)
7 Feb, Haifa: v Poland (n) drew 2-2 (*Mateut, Sabau*)
23 March, Dublin: v Eire (a) lost 0-2
30 March, Halle: v East Germany (a) drew 3-3 (*Muller own goal, Andone, Geolgau*)
1 June, Amsterdam: v Holland (a) lost 0-2
20 Sept, Constanza: v Albania (h) won 3-0 (*Belodedici, Hagi, Camataru*)
19 Oct, Sofia: v Bulgaria (a) won 3-1 (*Mateut, Camataru*)
2 Nov, Bucharest: v Greece (h) won 3-0 (*Mateut, Hagi, Sabau*)
23 Nov, Sibiu: v Israel (h) won 3-0 (*Camataru, Mateut 2*)

League Championship wins (1910–89)

Steaua Bucharest (prev.CCA) 14; Dinamo Bucharest 12; Venus Bucharest 7; CSC Temesvar 6; UT Arad 6; Rapid Bucharest 4; Uni Craiova 3; Ripensia Temesvar 3; Petrolul Ploesti 3; Olimpia Bucharest 2; CAC Bucharest 2; Arges Pitesti 2; Soc RA Bucharest 1; Prahova Ploesti 1; CSC Brasov 1; Juventius Bucharest 1; SSUD Reita 1; Craiova Bucharest 1; Progresul 1; Ploesti United 1.

Cup wins (1934–89)

Steaua Bucharest (prev. CCA) 17; Rapid Bucharest 7; Dynamo Bucharest 6; Uni Craiova 4; UT Arad 2; CFR Bucharest 2; Progresul 2; RIP Timisoara 2; ICO Oradeo 1; Metal Ochimia Resita 1; Petrolul Ploesti 1; Stinta Cluj 1; Stinta Timisoara 1; Turnu Severin 1; Chimia Ramnicu 1; Jiul Petroseni 1; Poli Timisoara 1.

Final League Table 1988–89

	P	*W*	*D*	*L*	*F*	*A*	*Pts*
Steaua	34	31	3	0	121	28	65
Dinamo	34	30	2	2	130	30	62
Victoria	34	20	5	2	81	60	45
Flacara	34	16	4	14	63	47	36
Uni. Craiova	34	15	6	13	52	52	36
Sportul	34	15	4	15	52	59	34
Bihor	34	13	6	15	40	46	32
Olt	34	12	8	14	38	47	32
Constantza	34	14	4	16	36	48	32
Brasov	34	12	7	15	46	52	31
Sibiu	34	13	5	16	45	57	31
Bacau	34	13	4	17	49	55	30
Arges	34	13	4	17	49	55	30
Uni. Cluj	34	11	8	15	43	55	30
Corvinul	34	13	3	18	47	68	29
Otelul*	34	11	6	17	36	59	28
Rapid*	34	10	3	21	39	67	23
Tirgu Mures*	34	2	2	30	23	101	6

Cup Final: Steaua 1, Dinamo 0
Top scorer: Mateut (Dinamo) 43

SAN MARINO

Founded: 1931.
Number of Clubs: 17.
Number of Players: 920.
Colours: Blue and white.

No International results 1988

SPAIN

Founded: 1913.
Number of Clubs: 30,920.
Number of Players: 343,657.
National Colours: Red shirts, dark blue shorts, black stockings, yellow trim.

International matches 1988

27 Jan, Valencia: v East Germany (h) drew 0-0
24 Feb, Malaga: v Czechoslovakia (h) lost 1-2 (*Julio Salinas*)
23 March, Paris: v France (a) lost 1-2 (*Caldere*)
27 April, Madrid: v Scotland (h) drew 0-0
1 June, Salamanca: v Sweden (h) lost 1-3 (*Butragueno*)
5 June, Basle: v Switzerland (a) drew 1-1 (*Andrinua*)
11 June, Hannover v Denmark (h) won 3-2 (*Michel, Butragueno, Gordillo*)
14 June, Frankfurt: v Italy (n) lost 0-1
17 June, Munich: v West Germany (n) lost 0-2
14 Sept, Oviedo: v Yugoslavia (h) lost 1-2 (*Michel*)
12 Oct, Seville: v Argentina (h) drew 1-1 (*Butragueno*)
16 Nov, Seville: v Eire (h) won 2-0 (*Manolo, Butragueno*)
21 Dec, Seville: v Northern Ireland (h) won 4-0 (*Rogan own goal, Butragueno, Michel, McClelland own goal*)

League Championship wins (1929–89)

Real Madrid 24; Barcelona 10; Atletico Madrid 8;

Athletic Bilbao 8; Valencia 4; Real Sociedad 2; Real Betis 1; Seville 1.

Cup wins (1902–89)

Athletic Bilbao 23; Barcelona 21; Real Madrid 16; Atletico Madrid 6; Valencia 5; Real Union de Irun 3; Seville 3; Real Zaragoza 3; Espanol 2; Arenas 1; Ciclista Sebastian 1; Racing de Irun 1; Vizcaya Bilbao 1; Real Betis 1; Real Sociedad 1.

Final League Table 1988–89

	P	*W*	*D*	*L*	*F*	*A*	*Pts*
Real Madrid	38	25	12	1	91	37	62
Barcelona	38	23	11	4	80	26	57
Valencia	38	18	13	7	39	26	49
Atletico Madrid	38	19	8	11	69	45	46
Zaragoza	38	15	13	10	48	42	43
Valladolid	38	18	7	13	40	31	43
Athletic Bilbao	38	15	12	11	45	35	42
Celta	38	14	11	13	42	48	39
Sevilla	38	13	12	13	39	37	38
Osasuna	38	13	11	14	39	43	37
Real Sociedad	38	11	14	13	38	47	36
Oviedo	38	12	11	15	44	45	35
Gijon	38	13	9	16	42	42	35
Logrones	38	9	16	13	25	37	34
Malaga	38	12	9	17	39	53	33
Cadiz	38	9	15	14	31	41	33
Espanol†*	38	7	16	15	29	44	30
Betis†*	38	9	11	18	36	55	29
Murcia*	38	9	6	23	27	58	24
Elche*	38	4	7	27	29	71	15

Cup Final: Real Madrid 1, Valladolid 0
Top scorer: Baltazar (Atletico Madrid) 35

SWEDEN

Founded: 1904.
Number of Clubs: 3400.
Number of Players: 437,000.
National Colours: Yellow shirts, blue shorts, yellow and blue stockings.

International matches 1988

13 Jan, Stockholm: v East Germany (h) won 4-1 (*Trudsson 2, Thern, Rehn*)
15 Jan, Las Palmas v Finland (n) won 1-0 (*Thern*)
31 March, West Berlin: v West Germany (n) drew 1-1 (*Trudsson*) Sweden won 5-3 on penalties
2 April, West Berlin: v USSR (n) won 2-0 (*Eskilsson, Rodionov own goal*)
27 April, Stockholm: v Wales (h) won 4-1 (*Holmqvist 2, Stromberg, Eskilsson*)
1 June, Salamanca: v Spain (a) won 3-1 (*J. Nilsson, Hysen, Magnusson*)
31 July, Stockholm: v Brazil (h) drew 1-1 (*Hellstrom*)
31 Aug, Stockholm: v Denmark (h) lost 1-2 (*Pettersson*)
12 Oct, Gothenburg: v Portugal (h) drew 0-0
19 Oct, Wembley: v England (a) drew 0-0
5 Nov, Tirana: v Albania (a) won 2-1 (*Holmqvist, Ekstrom*)

League Championship wins (1896–1988)

Oergryte IS Gothenburg 14; Malmö FF 14; IFK Norrköping 11; IFK Gothenburg 11; Djurgaarden 8; AIK Stockholm 8; GAIS Gothenburg 4; Boras IF Elfsborg 4; Oster Vaxjo 4; IF Halsingborg 3; Halmstad 2; Atvidaberg 2; IFK Ekilstune 1; IF Gavle Brynas 1; IF Gothenburg 1; Fassbergs 1; Norrköping IK Sleipner 1.

Cup wins (1941–88)

Malmö FF 13; AIK Stockholm 4; IFK Norrköping 4; IFK Gothenburg 3; Atvidaberg 2; Kalmar 2; GAIS Gothenburg 1; IFK Halsingborg 1; Raa 1; Landskrona 1; Oster Vaxjo 1.

Final League Table 1988–89

	P	*W*	*D*	*L*	*F*	*A*	*Pts*
Malmo	22	15	2	5	45	26	32
IFK Gothenburg	22	13	5	4	37	18	31
Djurgaarden	22	9	9	4	38	22	27
Orgryte	22	9	5	8	27	23	23
Sundsvall	22	8	7	7	26	26	23
Norrkoping	22	9	3	10	39	29	21
Brage	22	7	7	8	23	30	21
GAIS Gothenburg	22	8	4	10	25	31	20
AIK Stockholm	22	6	6	10	19	30	18
Vastra Frolund	22	6	6	10	24	34	18
Oster Vaxjo*	22	4	9	9	20	33	17
Hammarby*	22	5	3	14	19	40	13

Play-offs: semi-final: Djurgaarden 2, 0, IFK Gothenburg 0, 1; Orgryte 0, 1 Malmo 1, 2; final: Djurgaarden 0, 3, Malmo 0, 7
Cup Final: Norrkoping 3, Orebro 1
Top scorer: Dahli (Malmo) 17

SWITZERLAND

Founded: 1895.
Number of Clubs: 1480.
Number of Players: 182,953.
National Colours: Red shirts, white shorts, red stockings.

International matches 1988

2 Feb, Toulouse: v France (a) lost 1-2 (*B. Sutter*)
5 Feb, Monaco: v Austria (n) won 2-1 (*Koller, B. Sutter*)
27 April, Kaiserslauten: v West Germany (a) lost 0-1
28 May, Lausanne: v England (h) lost 0-1
5 June, Basle: v Spain (h) drew 1-1 (*B. Sutter*)
24 Aug, Lucerne: v Yugoslavia (h) lost 0-2
21 Sept, Luxembourg: v Luxembourg (a) won 4-1 (*A. Sutter, Turkyilmaz 2, B. Sutter*)
19 Oct, Brussels: v Belgium (a) lost 0-1
114 Dec, Cairo: v Egypt (a) won 3-1 (*Zuffi 2, Hermann*)

League Championship wins (1898–1989)

Grasshoppers 20; Servette 15; Young Boys Berne 11; FC Zurich 9; FC Basle 8; Lausanne 7; La Chaux-de-Fonds 3; FC Lugano 3; Winterthur 3; FC Aarau 2; Neuchatel Xamax 2; FC Anglo-Americans 1; St Gallen 1; FC Brühl 1; Cantonal-Neuchatel 1; Biel 1; Bellinzona 1; FC Etoile La Chaux-de-Fonds 1.

Cup wins (1926–89)

Grasshoppers 15; Lausanne 7; La Chaux-de-Fonds 6; Young Boys Berne 6; Servette 6; FC Basle 5; FC Zurich 5; FC Sion 5; FC Lugano 2; FC Granges 1; Lucerne 1; St Gallen 1; Urania Geneva 1; Young Fellows Zurich 1; Aarau 1.

Final League Table 1988–89

	P	*W*	*D*	*L*	*F*	*A*	*Pts*
Lucerne	22	10	8	4	27	25	28
Grasshoppers	22	10	7	5	41	29	27
Bellinzona	22	9	7	6	34	27	25
Sion	22	8	8	6	25	21	24
Wettingen	22	5	14	3	23	21	24
Young Boys	22	8	7	7	45	36	23
Neuchatel Xamax	22	7	9	6	39	33	23
Servette	22	8	6	8	39	34	22
Aarau	22	5	8	9	27	29	18
Lausanne	22	5	8	9	27	34	18
St Gallen	22	5	6	11	29	44	16
Lugano	22	3	10	9	23	46	16

Championship final round

	P	W	D	L	F	A	Q	F	T
Lucerne	14	7	5	2	17	11	14	19	33
Grasshoppers	14	7	2	5	20	18	14	16	30
Sion	14	6	5	3	22	15	12	17	29
Wettingen	14	7	2	5	22	14	12	16	28
Young Boys	14	6	3	5	36	22	12	15	27
Neuchatel Xamax	14	4	3	7	23	26	12	11	23
Bellinzona	14	2	4	8	9	26	13	8	21
Servette	14	3	4	7	25	42	11	10	21

Promotion/relegation

Group 1

	P	W	D	L	F	A	Pts
Lugano	14	10	3	1	29	10	23
Aarau	14	11	1	2	24	9	23
Locarno	14	6	3	5	22	16	15
Baden	14	6	3	5	22	24	15
Yverdon	14	4	6	4	9	9	14
Bulle	14	3	3	8	19	28	9
Chiasso	14	0	7	7	15	30	7
Etoile Carouge	14	1	4	9	8	22	6

Group 2

	P	W	D	L	F	A	Pts
Lausanne	14	9	4	1	42	8	22
St Gallen	14	9	3	2	29	14	21
Basle	14	5	6	3	20	20	16
Zurich	14	6	2	6	29	23	14
Chenois	14	4	4	6	22	29	12
Grenchen	14	3	4	7	17	26	10
Malley	14	2	6	6	15	29	10
Old Boys	14	3	1	10	13	38	7

Cup Final: Grasshoppers 2, Aarau 1
Top scorer: Rummenigge (Servette) 24

TURKEY

Founded: 1923.
Number of Clubs: 3754.
Number of Players: 87,200.
National Colours: White shirts, white shorts, red and white stockings.

International matches 1988

16 March, Budapest: v Hungary (a) lost 0-1
21 Sept, Istanbul: v Greece (h) won 3-1 (*Tanju, Oguz, Ridvan*)
12 Oct, Istanbul: v Iceland (h) drew 1-1 (*Unal*)
2 Nov, Vienna: v Austria (a) lost 2-3 (*Feyyaz, Tanju*)
30 Nov, Istanbul: v East Germany (h) won 3-1 (*Tanju 2, Oguz*)

League Championship wins (1960–1989)

Fenerbahce 11; Galatasaray 7; Trabzonspor 6; Besiktas 5.

Cup wins (1963–89)

Galatasaray 8; Fenerbahce 4; Besiktas 2; Trabzonspor 2; Goztepe Izmir 2; Altay Izmir 2; Ankaragücü 2; Eskisehirspor 1; Bursaspor 1; Genclerbirligi 1; Sakaryaspor 1.

Final League Table 1988–89

	P	W	D	L	F	A	Pts
Fenerbahce	35	28	6	1	100	27	90
Besiktas	35	24	8	3	78	21	80
Galatasaray	34	19	9	6	71	29	66
Sariyer	35	19	5	11	66	45	62
Trabzonspor	35	18	7	10	56	38	61
Ankaragucu	35	17	9	9	50	39	60
Boluspor	35	14	7	14	45	43	49
Konyaspor	35	13	4	18	40	59	43
Bursaspor	35	11	8	16	39	51	41
Sakarya	34	11	8	15	39	55	41
Malatya	35	10	10	15	56	69	40
Adana	35	10	9	16	48	56	39
Altay Izmir	34	10	8	16	43	54	38
Karsiyaka	34	9	10	15	45	53	37
Adanademir	34	10	6	18	45	72	36
Eskisehir*	35	9	8	18	33	57	35
Rizespor*	35	8	8	19	33	65	32
Maras*	34	3	11	20	18	68	20
Samsunspor‡	18	4	7	7	12	16	19

‡Withdrew from championship after coach crash in which two players died and ten were seriously injured.
Cup Final: Besiktas 1, 2, Fenerbahce 0, 1
Top scorer: Aykut (Fenerbahce) 29

USSR

Founded: 1912.
Number of Clubs: 50,198.
Number of Players: 4,800,300.
National Colours: Red shirts, white shorts, red stockings.

International matches 1988

20 Feb, Bari: v Italy (a) lost 1-4 (*Litovchenco*)
23 March, Athens: v Greece (a) won 4-0 (*Protasov 3, Litovchenko*)
31 March, West Berlin: v Argentina (n) won 4-2 (*Zavarov, Litovchenko, Protasov 2*)
2 April, West Berlin: v Sweden (n) lost 0-2
27 April, Trnava: v Czechoslovakia (a) drew 1-1 (*Protasov*)
1 June, Moscow: v Poland (h) won 2-1 (*Litovchenko, Protasov*)
12 June, Cologne: v Holland (n) won 1-0 (*Rats*)
15 June, Hannover: v Eire (n) drew 1-1 (*Protasov*)
18 June, Frankfurt: v England (n) won 3-1 (*Aleinikov, Mikhailchenko, Pasulko*)
22 June, Stuttgart: v Italy (n) won 2-0 (*Litovchenko, Protasov*)
25 June, Munich: v Holland (a) lost 0-2
17 Aug, Turku: v Finland (a) drew 0-0
31 Aug, Reykjavik: v Iceland (a) drew 1-1 (*Litovchenko*)
21 Sept, Dusseldorf: v West Germany (a) lost 0-1
19 Oct, Kiev: v Austria (h) won 2-0 (*Mikhailichenko, Zavarov*)
23 Nov, Kuwait: v Kuwait (a) won 1-0 (*Mikhailichenko*)

League Championship wins (1936–88)

Dynamo Kiev 12; Dynamo Moscow 11; Spartak Moscow 11; CSKA Moscow 6; Torpedo Moscow 3; Dynamo Tbilisi 2; Dnepr Dnepropetrovsk 2; Saria Voroshilovgrad 1; Ararat Erevan 1; Dynamo Minsk 1; Zenit Leningrad 1.

Cup wins (1936–88)

Spartak Moscow 9; Dynamo Kiev 7; Torpedo Moscow 7; Dynamo Moscow 6; CSKA Moscow 4; Donets Shaktyor 4; Lokomotiv Moscow 2; Dynamo Tbilisi 2; Ararat Erevan 2; Karpaty Lvov 1; SKA Rostov 1; Zenit Leningrad 1; Metallist Kharkov 1.

Final League Table 1988–89

	P	*W*	*D*	*L*	*F*	*A*	*Pts*
Dnepr	30	18	10	2	49	23	46
Dynamo Kiev	30	17	9	4	43	19	43
Moscow Torpedo	30	17	8	5	39	23	42
Spartak Moscow	30	14	11	5	40	26	39
Jalgiris	30	14	7	9	39	35	35
Zenit	30	11	9	10	35	34	31
Lokomotiv Moscow	30	10	12	8	35	29	30
Shakhtyor	30	9	10	11	30	28	28
Ararat	30	9	9	12	21	28	27
Moscow Dynamo	30	9	8	13	32	38	26
Metallist	30	8	10	12	29	36	26
Dynamo Minsk	30	7	11	12	29	34	25
Chernomorets	30	9	6	15	24	37	24
Dynamo Tbilisi	30	9	5	16	28	37	23
Neftschi	30	5	7	18	28	46	17
Kairat	30	6	4	20	25	53	16

Cup Final: Metallist 2, Moscow Torpedo 0
Top scorers: Shakhov (Dnepr) 16
Boroduk (Dynamo Moscow) 16

YUGOSLAVIA

Founded: 1919.
Number of Clubs: 7455.
Number of Players: 270,229.
National Colours: Blue shirts, white shorts, red stockings.

International matches 1988

23 March, Swansea: v Wales (a) won 2-1 (*Stojkovic, Jakovlievic*)
31 March, Split: v Italy (h) drew 1-1 (*Jakovlievic*)
27 April, Dublin: v Eire (a) lost 0-2
4 June, Bremen: v West Germany (a) drew 1-1 (*Immel own goal*)
24 Aug, Lucerne: v Switzerland (a) won 2-0 (*Mihajlovic, Djukic*)
14 Sept, Oviedo: v Spain (a) won 2-1 (*Bazdarevic, Cvetkovic*)
19 Oct, Glasgow: v Scotland (a) drew 1-1 (*Katanec*)
19 Nov, Belgrade: v France (h) won 3-2 (*Spasic, Susic, Stojkovic*)
11 Dec, Belgrade: v Cyprus (h) won 4-0 (*Savicevic 3, Hadzibegic*)

League Championship wins (1923–89)

Red Star Belgrade 16; Partizan Belgrade 11; Hajduk Split 9; Gradjanski Zagreb 5; BSK Belgrade 5; Dynamo Zagreb 4; Jugoslavija Belgrade 2; Concordia Zagreb 2; FC Sarajevo 2; Vojvodina Novi Sad 2; HASK Zagreb 1; Zeljeznicar 1.

Cup wins (1947–89)

Red Star Belgrade 11; Dynamo Zagreb 8; Hajduk Split 8; Partizan Belgrade 5; BSK Belgrade 2; OFK Belgrade 2; Rijeka 2; Velez Mostar 2; Vardar Skopje 1; Borac Banjaluka 1.

Final League Table 1988–89

	P	*W*	*DW*	*DL*	*L*	*F*	*A*	*Pts*
Vojvodina	34	18	5	1	10	50	38	41
Red Star	34	18	2	5	9	54	30	38
Hajduk Split	34	15	6	4	9	50	29	36
Rad	34	13	9	2	10	46	38	35
Dinamo Zagreb	34	16	2	7	9	42	29	34
Partizan	34	15	3	4	12	52	37	33
Radnicki	34	14	3	4	13	43	35	31
Osijek	34	13	5	2	14	49	50	31
Vardar	34	13	3	4	14	46	51	29
Rijeka	34	14	0	7	13	35	35	28
Velez	34	13	2	2	17	42	43	28
Sloboda	34	11	6	6	11	35	42	28
Sarajevo	34	11	6	4	13	35	42	28
Buducnost	34	12	4	3	15	32	43	28
Spartak	34	11	4	3	16	30	38	26
Zeljeznicar	34	12	1	3	18	34	49	25
Napredak*	34	11	1	4	18	42	59	23
Celik*	34	9	5	2	18	31	60	17

(Celik penalised 6 pts for previous season's breaches of rules)

Cup Final: Partizan 6, Velez 1
Top scorer: Suker (Osijek) 18

SOUTH AMERICA

ARGENTINA

Founded: 1893.
Number of Clubs: 3,035.
Number of Players: 306,365.
National Colours: Blue and white shirts, black shorts, white stockings.

1988 International results

31 March, West Berlin: v Russia (n) lost 2-4 (*Troglio, Baltacha, own goal*)
2 April, West Berlin: v West Germany (a) lost 0-1
6 July, Adelaide: v Saudi Arabia (n) drew 2-2 (*Hernan Diaz 2*)
10 July, Melbourne: v Brazil (n) drew 0-0
14 July, Sydney: v Australia (n) lost 1-4 (*Ruggeri*)
16 July, Canberra: v Saudi Arabia (n) won 2-0 (*Simeone, Dertycia*)
18 Sept, Taegu: v USA (n) drew 1-1 (*Alfaro Moreno*)
20 Sept, Taegu: v Russia (n) lost 1-2 (*Alfaro Moreno*)
22 Sept, Pusan: v South Korea (n) won 2-1 (*Alfar Moreno, Fabbri*)
25 Sept, Seoul: v Brazil (n) lost 0-1
12 Oct, Seville: v Spain (a) drew 1-1 (*Caniggia*)

BOLIVIA

Founded: 1925.
Number of Clubs: 305.
Number of Players: 15,290.
National Colours: Green shirts, white shorts, green stockings.

No 1988 International results

BRAZIL

Founded: 1914.
Number of Clubs: 12,9877.
Number of Players: 551,358.
National Colours: Yellow shirts, blue shorts, white stockings, green trim.

1988 International results

7 July, Melbourne: v Australia (n) won 1-0 (*Romario*)
10 July, Melbourne: v Argentina (n) drew 0-0
13 July, Melbourne: v Saudia Arabia (n) won 4-1 (*Geovani 2, Jorginho, Edmar*)

17 July, Sydney: v Australia (n) won 2-0 (*Romario, Muller*)
28 July, Oslo: v Norway (a) drew 1-1 (*Edmar*)
31 July, Stockholm: v Sweden (a) drew 1-1 (*Jorginho*)
3 Aug, Vienna: v Austria (a) won 2-0 (*Edmar, Andrade*)
18 Sept, Taejon: v Nigeria (h) won 4-0 (*Romario 2, Edmar, Bebeto*)
20 Sept, Seoul: v Australia (h) won 3-0 (*Romario 3*)
22 Sept, Taejon: v Jugoslavia (h) won 2-1 (*Andree-Cruz, Bebeto*)
25 Sept, Seoul: v Argentina (h) won 1-0 (*Geovani*)
27 Sept, Seoul: v West Germany (h) drew aet, Brazil won 4-3 on penalties (*Romario*)
1 Oct, Seoul: v USSR (a) lost 1-2 aet (*Romario*)
12 Oct, Antwerp: v Belgium (a) won 2-1 (*Geovani 2*)

CHILE

Founded: 1895.
Number of Clubs: 4,598.
Number of Players: 609,724
National Colours: Red shirts, blue shorts, white stockings.

1988 International results

23 May, Toronto: v Greece (a) lost 0-1
25 May, Toronto: v Canada (a) lost 0-1
3 June, San Diego: v USA (a) won 3-1 (*Hurtado, Salgado, Orojas*)
13 Sept, La Serena: v Ecuador (h) won 3-1 (*Salgado, Alvarez, Rodriguez*)
27 Sept, Asuncion: v Paraguay (a) lost 0-2
29 Sept, Asuncion: v Equador (n) drew 0-0
2 Nov, Santiago: v Uruguay (h) drew 1-1 (*Espinosa*)
9 Nov, Montevideo: v Uruguay (a) lost 1-3 (*Espinosa*)
23 Nov, Lima: v Peru (a) drew 1-1 (*Mardones*)
25 Oct, Santiago: v Peru (h) won 2-0 (*Espinosa, H. Gonzalez*)

COLOMBIA

Founded: 1925.
Number of Clubs: 3685.
Number of Players: 188,050
National Colours: Red shirts, blue shorts, tricolour stockings.

International results

30 March, Armenia: v Canada (h) won 3-0 (*Perea, Valderrama, Trellez*)
14 May, Miami: v USA (a) won 2-0 (*Iguaran 2*)
17 May, Glasgow: v Scotland (a) drew 0-0
19 May, Helsinki: v Finland (a) won 3-1 (*Arango, Higuita, Iguaran*)
24 May, Wembley: v England (a) drew 1-1 (*Escobar*)
7 Aug, Bogota: v Uruguay (h) won 2-1 (*Iguaran, Redin*)

ECUADOR

Founded: 1925.
Number of Clubs: 170.
Number of Players: 15,700.
National Colours: Yellow shirts, blue shorts, red stockings.

1988 International results

12 June, Dallas: v USA (a) drew 0-0
16 June, Tegucigalpa: v Honduras (a) drew 1-1 (*Capurro*)
27 Aug, Asuncion: v Uruguay (a) lost 1-2 (*Izquierdo*)
7 Sept, Guayaquil: v Paraguay (h) lost 5-1 (*Cuvi*)
13 Sept, La Serena: v Chile (a) lost 1-3 (*Cuvi*)
29 Sept, Asuncion: v Chile (h) drew 0-0

PARAGUAY

Founded: 1906.
Number of Clubs: 1500.
Number of Players: 140,000
National Colours: Red and white shirts, blue shorts, blue stockings.

1988 International results

7 Sept, Guayaquil: v Ecuador (a) won 5-1 (*Britez, Roman, Almiron, Rivarda Roman, Ferreyra*)
27 Sept, Asuncion: v Chile (h) won 2-0 (*Roman, Reyes own goal*)
29 Sept, Asuncion: v Uruguay (h) won 3-1 (*Palacios. Franco, Jacket*)
12 Oct, Montevideo: v Uruguay (a) lost 0-2
10 Sept, Tegucigalpa: v Honduras (a) drew 0-0
13 Sept, Tegucigalpa: v Honduras (a) won 2-0
16 Sept, San Salvador: v El Salvador (a) won 1-0 (*Roman*)
21 Sept, Lima: v Peru (a) won 1-0

PERU

Founded: 1922.
Number of Clubs: 10,000.
Number of Players: 325,650
National Colours: White shirts, red trim, white shorts, white stockings.

1988 International results

25 Oct, Santiago: v Chile (a) lost 0-2
23 Nov, Lima: v Chile (h) drew 1-1 (*Farfan*)
14 Dec, Montevideo: v Uruguay (a) lost 0-3
21 Sept, Lima: v Paraguay (h) lost 0-1

URUGUAY

Founded: 1900.
Number of Clubs: 1091.
Number of Players: 134,310.
National Colours: Light blue shirts, black shorts, black stockings.

1988 International results

16 March, Guatemala City: v Guatemala (a) lost 0-1
7 Aug, Bogota: v Colombia (a) lost 1-2 (*Herrera*)
27 Sept, Asuncion: v Ecuador (h) won 2-1 (*Dalto, Herrera*)
29 Sept, Asuncion: v Paraguay (h) lost 1-3 (*Da Silva*)
12 Oct, Montevideo: v Paraquay (h) won 2-0 (*da Silva*, Pereira)
2 Nov, Santiago: v Chile (a) drew 1-1 (*Vidal*)
9 Nov, Montevideo: v Chile (h) won 3-1 (*Da Silva, Baez, Martinez*)
14 Dec, Montevideo: v Peru (h) won 3-0 (*Francescoli 2, Ruben Sosa*)

VENEZUELA

Founded: 1926.
Number of Clubs: 1753.
Number of Players: 63,175
National Colours: Magenta shirts, white shorts, white stockings.

International result

26 Sept, Curacao: v Netherlands Antilles (a) drew 0-0

ASIA

AFGHANISTAN

Founded: 1922.
Number of Clubs: 30.
Number of Players: 3,300.
National Colours: White shirts, white shorts, white stockings.

BAHRAIN

Founded: 1951.
Number of Clubs: 25.
Number of Players: 2,030.
National Colours: White shirts, red shorts, white stockings.

BANGLADESH

Founded: 1972.
Number of Clubs: 1,265.
Number of Players: 30,385.
National Colours: Orange shirts, white shorts, green stockings.

BRUNEI

Founded: 1959.
Number of Clubs: 22.
Number of Players: 830.
National Colours: Gold shirts, black shorts, gold stockings.

BURMA

Founded: 1947.
Number of Clubs: 600.
Number of Players: 21,000.
National Colours: Red shirts, white shorts, red stockings.

CHINA

Founded: 1924.
Number of Clubs: 1,045.
Number of Players: 2,250,200.
National Colours: Red shirts, white shorts, red stockings.

HONG KONG

Founded: 1914.
Number of Clubs: 69.
Number of Players: 3,274.
National Colours: Red shirts, white shorts, red stockings.

INDIA

Founded: 1937.
Number of Clubs: 2,000.
Number of Players: 56,000.
National Colours: Light blue shirts, white shorts, dark blue stockings.

INDONESIA

Founded: 1930.
Number of Clubs: 2,880.
Number of Players: 97,000.
National Colours: Red shirts, white shorts, red stockings.

IRAN

Founded: 1920.
Number of Clubs: 6,326.
Number of Players: 306,000.
National Colours: Green shirts, white shorts, red stockings.

IRAQ

Founded: 1948.
Number of Clubs: 155.
Number of Players: 4,400.
National Colours: White shirts, white shorts, white stockings.

ISRAEL

Founded: 1928.
Number of Clubs: 544.
Number of Players: 30,449.
National Colours: White shirts, blue shorts, white stockings.

Final League Table 1988–89

	P	*W*	*D*	*L*	*F*	*A*	*Pts*	*Pos*
Maccabi Natanya	26	14	7	5	35	25	49	3
Maccabi Haifa**	26	12	13	1	41	16	47	1
Hapoel Petah Tikva**	26	12	9	5	28	19	43	2
Beitar Tel Aviv	26	10	9	7	24	22	39	4
Hapoel Beer Sheva	26	10	9	7	19	18	39	5
Shimshon Tel Aviv	26	8	12	6	25	30	36	6
Hapoel Jerusalem*	26	9	9	8	20	19	35	7
Beitar Jerusalem	26	9	5	12	28	31	32	9
Maccabi Tel Aviv**	26	7	10	9	30	34	29	8
Hapoel Kfar Saba	26	6	10	10	21	29	28	10
Tsafririm Hollon**	26	6	9	11	27	28	25	13
Bnei Yehuda Tel Aviv	26	4	13	9	21	23	25	11
Hapoel Tel Aviv****	26	6	8	12	24	37	22	14
Hapoel Tiberias	26	5	5	16	20	42	20	12

* one point deducted for breaking payment regulations, ** two points, **** four points. Top six entered championship play-offs, bottom eight relegation play-offs. Final positions, last column (thus). Teams finishing 12, 13 and 14 relegated.

JAPAN

Founded: 1921.
Number of Clubs: 13,047.
Number of Players: 358,989.
National Colours: Blue shirts, white shorts, blue stockings.

Final League Table 1988–89

	P	*W*	*D*	*L*	*F*	*A*	*Pts*
Yamaha	22	12	10	0	27	10	34
Nippon Kokan	22	13	4	5	25	13	30
Mitsubishi	22	12	5	5	27	15	29
Nissan Motors	22	10	5	7	27	20	25
Yoniuri	22	8	8	6	23	17	24
Yanmar Diesel	22	7	10	5	22	19	24
Furukawa	22	6	9	7	17	16	21
Honda	22	6	8	8	19	22	20
Fulita	22	6	6	10	16	20	18
Sumitomo	22	5	5	12	17	32	15
Mazda	22	2	9	11	8	18	13
Toyota	22	3	5	14	10	36	11

JORDAN

Founded: 1949.
Number of Clubs: 98.
Number of Players: 4,305.
National Colours: White shirts, white shorts, white stockings.

KAMPUCHEA

Founded: 1933.
Number of Clubs: 30.
Number of Players: 650.
National Colours: Blue shirts, white shorts, red stockings.

KOREA, NORTH

Founded: 1945.
Number of Clubs: 90.
Number of Players: 3,420.
National Colours: Red shirts, white shorts, red stockings.

KOREA, SOUTH

Founded: 1928.
Number of Clubs: 476.
Number of Players: 2,047.
National Colours: Red shirts, red shorts, red stockings.

KUWAIT

Founded: 1952.
Number of Clubs: 14 (senior).
Number of Players: 1,526.
National Colours: Blue shirts, white shorts, blue stockings.

LAOS

Founded: 1951.
Number of Clubs: 76.
Number of Players: 2,060.
National Colours: Red shirts, white shorts, blue stockings.

LEBANON

Founded: 1933.
Number of Clubs: 105.
Number of Players: 8,125.
National Colours: Red shirts, white shorts, red stockings.

MACAO

Founded: 1939.
Number of Clubs: 52.
Number of Players: 800.
National Colours: Green shirts, white shorts, green and white stockings.

MALDIVES

Founded: 1986.
National Colours: Green shirts, white shorts, red stockings.

MALAYSIA

Founded: 1933.
Number of Clubs: 450.
Number of Players: Players 11,250.
National Colours: Black and gold shirts, white shorts, black and gold stockings.

NEPAL

Founded: 1951.
Number of Clubs: 85.
Number of Players: 2,550.
National Colours: Red shirts, blue shorts, blue and white stockings.

OMAN

Founded: 1978.
Number of Clubs: 47.
Number of Players: 2,340.
National Colours: White shirts, red shorts, white stockings.

PAKISTAN

Founded: 1948.
Number of Clubs: 882.
Number of Players: 21,000.
National Colours: Green shirts, white shorts, green stockings.

PHILLIPPINES

Founded: 1907.
Number of Clubs: 650.
Number of Players: 45,000.
National Colours: Blue shirts, white shorts, blue stockings.

QATAR

Founded: 1960.
Number of Clubs: 8 (senior).
Number of Players: 1,380.
National Colours: White shirts, maroon shorts, white stockings.

SAUDI ARABIA

Founded: 1959.
Number of Clubs: 120.
Number of Players: 9,600.
National Colours: White shirts, white shorts, white stockings.

SINGAPORE

Founded: 1892.
Number of Clubs: 250.
Number of Players: 8,000.
National Colours: Sky blue shirts, sky blue shorts, sky blue stockings.

SRI LANKA

Founded: 1939.
Number of Clubs: 600.
Number of Players: 18,825.
National Colours: Maroon shirts, white shorts, white stockings.

SYRIA

Founded: 1936.
Number of Clubs: 102.
Number of Players: 30,600.
National Colours: White shirts, white shorts, white stockings.

THAILAND

Founded: 1916.
Number of Clubs: 168.
Number of Players: 15,000.
National Colours: Crimson shirts, white shorts, crimson stockings.

UNITED ARAB EMIRATES

Founded: 1971.
Number of Clubs: Clubs 23 (senior).
Number of Players: 1,787.
National Colours: White shirts, white shorts, white stockings.

VIETNAM

Founded: 1962.
Number of Clubs: 55 (senior).
Number of Players: 16,000.
National Colours: Red shirts, white shorts, red stockings.

YEMEN, ARAB REPUBLIC

Founded: 1962.
Number of Clubs: 61 (senior).
Number of Players: 22,600.
National Colours: Green shirts, green shorts, green stockings.

YEMEN, PDR

Founded: 1940.
Number of Clubs: 36.
Number of Players: 1,700.
National Colours: Light blue shirts, white shorts, light blue stockings.

CONCACAF

ANTIGUA

Founded: 1928.
Number of Clubs: 60.
Number of Players: 1,008.
National Colours: Gold shirts, black shorts, black stockings.

BAHAMAS

Founded: 1967.
Number of Clubs: 14.
Number of Players: 700.
National Colours: Yellow shirts, black shorts, yellow stockings.

BARBADOS

Founded: 1910.
Number of Clubs: 92.
Number of Players: 1,100.
National Colours: Royal blue shirts, gold shorts, royal blue stockings.

BELIZE

Founded: 1986.
National Colours: Blue shirts, red and white trim, white shorts, blue stockings.

BERMUDA.

Founded: 1928.
Number of Clubs: 30.
Number of Players: 1,947
National Colours: Blue shirts, white shorts, white stockings.

CANADA

Founded: 1912.
Number of Clubs: 1,600.
Number of Players: 224,290.
National Colours: Red shirts, red shorts, red stockings.

COSTA RICA

Founded: 1921.
Number of Clubs: 431.
Number of Players: 12,429.
National Colours: Red shirts, blue shorts, white stockings.

CUBA

Founded: 1924.
Number of Clubs: 70.
Number of Players: 12,900.
National Colours: White shirts, blue shorts, white stockings.

DOMINICAN REPUBLIC

Founded: 1953.
Number of Clubs: 128.
Number of Players: 10,706
National Colours: Blue shirts, white shorts, red stockings.

EL SALVADOR

Founded: 1936.
Number of Clubs: 944.
Number of Players: 21,294.
National Colours: Blue shirts, blue shorts, blue stockings.

GRENADA

Founded: 1924.
Number of Clubs: 15.
Number of Players: 200.
National Colours: Green and yellow shirts, red shorts, green and yellow stockings.

GUATEMALA

Founded: 1933.
Number of Clubs: 1,611.
Number of Players: 43,516.
National Colours: Blue shirts, white shorts, blue stockings.

GUYANA

Founded: 1902.
Number of Clubs: 103.
Number of Players: 1,665.
National Colours: Green and yellow shirts, black shorts, white and green stockings.

HAITI

Founded: 1904.
Number of Clubs: 40.
Number of Players: 4,000.
National Colours: Red shirts, black shorts, red stockings.

HONDURAS

Founded: 1951.
Number of Clubs: 1,050.
Number of Players: 15,300.
National Colours: Blue shirts, blue shorts, blue stockings.

JAMAICA

Founded: 1910.
Number of Clubs: 266.
Number of Players: 45,200.
National Colours: Green shirts, black shorts, green and gold stockings.

MEXICO

Founded: 1927.
Number of Clubs: 77 (senior).
Number of Players: 14,022,700.
National Colours: Green shirts, white shorts, green stockings.

NETHERLANDS ANTILLES

Founded: 1921.
Number of Clubs: 85.
Number of Players: 4,500.
National Colours: White shirts, white shorts, red stockings.

NICARAGUA

Founded: 1968.
Number of Clubs: 31.
Number of Players: 160 (senior).
National Colours: Blue shirts, blue shorts, blue stockings.

PANAMA

Founded: 1937.
Number of Clubs: 65.
Number of Players: 4,225.
National Colours: Red and white shirts, blue shorts, red stockings.

PUERTO RICO

Founded: 1940.
Number of Clubs: 175.
Number of Players: 4,200.
National Colours: White and red shirts, blue shorts, white and blue stockings.

SURINAM

Founded: 1920.
Number of Clubs: 168.
Number of Players: 4,430.
National Colours: Red shirts, white shorts, white stockings.

TRINIDAD AND TOBAGO

Founded: 1906.
Number of Clubs: 124.
Number of Players: 5,050.
National Colours: Red shirts, black shorts, red stockings.

USA

Founded: 1913.
Number of Clubs: 7,000.
Number of Players: 1,411,500.
National Colours: White shirts, blue shorts, red stockings.

Recent additions: ARUBA, SANTA LUCIA, ST. VINCENT and the GRENADINES. Aruba is an island in the Caribbean with 1,500 registered players. St. Lucia is another island in the same area with 4,000 players. St Vincent and the Grenadines is similarly situated and has 5,000 players.

OCEANIA

AUSTRALIA

Founded: 1961.
Number of Clubs: 6,816.
Number of Players: 433,957.
National Colours: Gold shirts, green shorts, white stockings.

Final League Table 1988–89

	P	*W*	*D*	*L*	*F*	*A*	*Pts*
Woolongong	26	13	8	5	44	32	34
Sydney Croatia	26	15	4	7	38	30	34
South Melbourne	26	13	8	5	36	29	34
Marconi	26	12	8	6	46	26	32
Sydney Olympic	26	9	9	8	28	22	27
Adelaide City	26	10	7	9	36	35	27
Sunshine George	26	11	5	10	38	39	27
Saint George	26	10	6	10	41	35	26
Melbourne Croatia	26	9	6	11	28	33	24
Footscray	26	7	9	10	34	32	23
Leichhardt	26	8	7	11	28	35	23
Preston	26	5	12	9	29	35	22
Brunswick	26	7	5	14	31	43	19
Brisbane Lions	26	4	4	18	28	59	12

Grand Final: Marconi 2, Sydney Croatia 2 (Marconi won 5-4 on penalties)

FIJI

Founded: 1946.
Number of Clubs: 140.
Number of Players: 21,500.
National Colours: White shirts, black shorts, black stockings.

NEW ZEALAND

Founded: 1891.
Number of Clubs: 312.
Number of Players: 52,969.
National Colours: White shirts, black shorts, white stockings.

PAPUA-NEW GUINEA

Founded: 1962.
Number of Clubs: 350.
Number of Players: 8,250.
National Colours: Red shirts, black shorts, red stockings.

TAIPEI

Founded: 1936.
Number of Clubs: 53.
Number of Players: 17,350.
National Colours: Blue shirts, white shorts, red stockings.

WESTERN SAMOA

Founded: 1986.
National Colours: Blue shirts, white shorts, blue and white stockings.

Recent additions: SOLOMON ISLANDS, VANUATA
The Solomon Islands are situated in the South Pacific to the south-east of Papua New Guinea. There are 4,000 registered players. Vanuatu was formerly known as the New Hebrides and is a double chain of islands to the south-east of the Solomons.

AFRICA

ALGERIA

Founded: 1962.
Number of Clubs: 780.
Number of Players: 58,567
National Colours: Green shirts, white shorts, red stockings.

Final League Table 1988–89

	P	*W*	*D*	*L*	*F*	*A*	*Pts*
Tizi-Ouzou	30	14	9	7	36	22	37
Moul. Alger	30	14	8	8	26	21	36
Relizane	30	12	10	8	31	28	34
Sidi Bel Abbes	30	12	8	10	37	30	32
Assoc. Oran	30	12	6	12	33	28	30
Bordj Menaiel	30	12	6	12	34	32	30
Moul. Oran	30	11	7	12	35	31	29
Annaba	30	10	9	11	29	28	29
Tiaret	30	11	7	12	36	38	29
El Harrach	30	10	9	11	20	28	29
Kouba	30	11	7	12	27	37	29
Ain M'Lila	30	8	12	10	24	23	28
Union Alger	30	9	10	11	27	34	28
Constantine	30	9	9	12	35	33	27
Ain Beida*	30	11	5	14	35	41	27
Collo*	30	8	10	12	27	36	26

Top scorer: Bentayeb (Ain Beida) 19

BURKINA FASO

Founded: 1960.
Number of Clubs: 57.
Number of Players: 4,672.
National Colours: Black shirts, white shorts, red stockings.

ANGOLA

Founded: 1977.
Number of Clubs: 276.
Number of Players: 4,269.
National Colours: Red shirts, black shorts, red stockings.

BENIN

Founded: 1968.
Number of Clubs: 117.
Number of Players: 6,700.
National Colours: Green shirts, green shorts, green stockings.

BOTSWANA

Founded: 1976.
National Colours: Sky blue shirts, white shorts, sky blue stockings.

BURUNDI

Founded: 1948.
Number of Clubs: 132.
Number of Players: 3,930.
National Colours: Red shirts, white shorts, green stockings.

CAMEROON

Founded: 1960.
Number of Clubs: 200.
Number of Players: 9,328.
National Colours: Green shirts, red shorts, yellow stockings.

Final League Table 1988–89

	P	*W*	*D*	*L*	*F*	*A*	*Pts*
Racing	30	18	9	3	43	13	63
Tonnerre	30	18	8	4	35	14	62
Prevoyance	30	11	14	5	35	23	47
Canon	30	12	9	9	34	27	45
Unisport	30	11	10	9	32	25	43
Diamant	30	10	12	8	33	27	42
Panthers	30	12	7	11	25	30	42
Union Douala	30	10	11	9	40	35	41
Canmark	30	12	4	14	29	31	40
PWD Kumba	30	10	10	10	19	24	40
Dinamo Douala	30	10	8	12	27	30	38
Colombe	30	9	11	10	22	27	38
Caiman	30	9	9	12	36	42	36
Federal	30	4	12	11	26	32	33
Aigle	30	3	13	14	20	34	22
Entente	30	2	6	22	20	62	12

Top scorer: Paneberg (Racing) 20

CAPE VERDE ISLANDS

Founded: 1986.
National Colours: Green shirts, green shorts, green stockings.

CENTRAL AFRICA

Founded: 1937.
Number of Clubs: 256.
Number of Players: 7,200.
National Colours: Grey and blue shirts, white shorts, red stockings.

CONGO

Founded: 1962.
Number of Clubs: 250.
Number of Players: 5,940.
National Colours: Red shirts, red shorts, white stockings.

EGYPT

Founded: 1921.
Number of Clubs: 168.
Number of Players: 11,695.
National Colours: Red shirts, white shorts, black stockings.

Final League Table 1988–89

	P	*W*	*D*	*L*	*F*	*A*	*Pts*
National	22	17	3	2	35	9	54
Zamalek	22	15	4	3	42	18	49
Mehalla	22	10	8	4	29	20	38
Ismaeli	22	9	7	6	37	32	34
Arsenal	22	10	2	10	25	25	32
Masri	22	6	8	8	15	16	26
Union Recreation	22	6	7	9	17	20	25
Arab Contractor	22	5	9	8	15	22	24
Suez	22	5	9	8	11	21	24
Olympic	22	5	8	9	22	26	23
Menieh*	22	5	8	9	21	26	23
Merrikh*	22	0	5	17	9	43	5

Cup Final: National 3, Masri 0
Top scorer: Mahmoud El-Machaqi (Mehalla) 11

ETHIOPIA

Founded: 1943.
Number of Clubs: 767.
Number of Players: 20,594.
National Colours: Green shirts, yellow shorts, red stockings.

GABON

Founded: 1962.
Number of Clubs: 320.
Number of Players: 10,000.
National Colours: Blue shirts, white shorts, white stockings.

GAMBIA

Founded: 1952.
Number of Clubs: 30.
Number of Players: 860.
National Colours: White and red shirts, white shorts, white stockings.

GHANA

Founded: 1957.
Number of Clubs: 347.
Number of Players: 11,275.
National Colours: White shirts, white shorts, white stockings.

GUINEA

Founded: 1959.
Number of Clubs: 351.
Number of Players: 10,000
National Colours: Red shirts, yellow shorts, green stockings.

GUINEA-BISSAU

Founded: 1986.
National Colours: Green shirts, green shorts, green stockings.

GUINEA, EQUATORIAL

Founded: 1986.

IVORY COAST

Founded: 1960.
Number of Clubs: 84 (senior).
Number of Players: 3,655.
National Colours: Orange shirts, white shorts, green stockings.

KENYA

Founded: 1960.
Number of Clubs: 351.
Number of Players: 8,800.
National Colours: Red shirts, red shorts, red stockings.

LESOTHO

Founded: 1932.
Number of Clubs: 88.
Number of Players: 2,076.
National Colours: White shirts, blue shorts, white stockings.

LIBERIA

Founded: 1962.
National Colours: Blue and white shirts, white shorts, blue and white stockings.

LIBYA

Founded: 1963.
Number of Clubs: 89.
Number of Players: 2,941.
National Colours: Green shirts, white shorts, green stockings.

MADAGASCAR

Founded: 1961.
Number of Clubs: 775.
Number of Players: 23,536.
National Colours: Red shirts, white shorts, green stockings.

MALAWI

Founded: 1966.
Number of Clubs: 465.
Number of Players: 12,500.
National Colours: Red shirts, red shorts, red stockings.

MALI

Founded: 1960.
Number of Clubs: 128.
Number of Players: 5,480.
National Colours: Green shirts, yellow shorts, red stockings.

MAURITANIA

Founded: 1961.
Number of Clubs: 59.
Number of Players: 1,930.
National Colours: Green and yellow shirts, blue shorts, green stockings.

MAURITIUS

Founded: 1952.
Number of Clubs: 397.
Number of Players: 29,375.
National Colours: Red shirts, white shorts, red stockings.

MOROCCO

Founded: 1955.
Number of Clubs: 350.
Number of Players: 19,768.
National Colours: Red shirts, green shorts, red stockings.
Championship Table 1988

MOZAMBIQUE

Founded: 1978.
Number of Clubs: 144.
National Colours: Red shirts, red shorts, red stockings.

NIGER

Founded: 1967.
Number of Clubs: 64.
Number of Players: 1,525.
National Colours: Orange shirts, white shorts, green stockings.

NIGERIA

Founded: 1945.
Number of Clubs: 326.
Number of Players: 80,190.
National Colours: Green shirts, white shorts, green stockings.

RWANDA

Founded: 1972.
Number of Clubs: 167
National Colours: Red shirts, red shorts, red stockings.

SENEGAL

Founded: 1960.
Number of Clubs: 75 (senior).
Number of Players: 3,977.
National Colours: Green shirts, yellow shorts, red stockings.

SEYCHELLES

Founded: 1986.
National Colours: Green shirts, yellow shorts, red stockings.

ST. THOMAS AND PRINCIPE

Founded: 1986.
National Colours: Green shirts, green shorts, green stockings.

SIERRA LEONE

Founded: 1967.
Number of Clubs: 104.
Number of Players: 8,120.
National Colours: Green shirts, white shorts, blue stockings.

SOMALIA

Founded: 1951.
Number of Clubs: 46 (senior).
Number of Players: 1,150.
National Colours: Sky blue shirts, white shorts, white stockings.

SUDAN

Founded: 1936.
Number of Clubs: 750.
Number of Players: 42,200.
National Colours: White shirts, white shorts, white stockings.

SWAZILAND

Founded: 1976.
Number of Clubs: 136.
National Colours: Blue and gold shirts, white shorts, blue and gold stockings.

TANZANIA

Founded: 1930.
Number of Clubs: 51.
National Colours: Yellow shirts, yellow shorts, yellow stockings.

TOGO

Founded: 1960.
Number of Clubs: 144.
Number of Players: 4,346.
National Colours: Red shirts, white shorts, red stockings.

TUNISIA

Founded: 1957.

Number of Clubs: 215.
Number of Players: 18,300.
National Colours: Red shirts, white shorts, red stockings.

Final League Table 1988–89

	P	*W*	*D*	*L*	*F*	*A*	*Pts*
ES Tunis	26	18	5	3	46	19	85
Club Africain	26	13	7	6	40	28	72
El Sahel	26	12	8	6	37	22	70
Stade Tunisien	26	10	9	7	34	28	65
Sfax RS	26	10	8	8	33	29	64
CS Sfaxien	26	8	11	7	22	26	61
AS Kasserine	26	9	7	10	24	39	60
CO Transports	26	9	6	11	27	26	59
Ol. Beja	26	10	3	13	22	29	59
AS Marsa	26	8	8	10	33	31	58
US Monastir	26	6	13	7	19	29	57
CA Bizerte	26	7	10	9	20	21	57
JS Kairouan	26	6	6	14	19	28	50
OC Kerkennah	26	2	7	17	12	38	39

Top scorers: Touati (Club Africain) 15
Hergal (Stade Tunisien) 15

UGANDA

Founded: 1924.
Number of Clubs: 400.
Number of Players: 1,518.
National Colours: Yellow shirts, black shorts, yellow stockings.

ZAIRE

Founded: 1919.
Number of Clubs: 3,800.
Number of Players: 64,627.
National Colours: Green shirts, yellow shorts, yellow stockings.

ZAMBIA

Founded: 1929.
Number of Clubs: 20 (senior).
Number of Players: 4,100.
National Colours: Green shirts, white shorts, black stockings.

ZIMBABWE

Founded: 1965.
National Colours: White shirts, black shorts, black stockings.

Recent addition: CHAD (readmitted). This landlocked country was once a FIFA member up to 1974 and has now been reaffiliated.

EUROPEAN FOOTBALL CHAMPIONSHIP

(formerly EUROPEAN NATIONS' CUP)

Year	Winners	Runners-up	Venue	Attendance	Referee
1960	USSR 2 *(after extra time)*	Yugoslavia 1	Paris	17,966	Ellis (E)
1964	Spain 2	USSR 1	Madrid	120,000	Holland (E)
1968	Italy 2 *(after extra time; after 1-1 draw)*	Yugoslavia 0	Rome	60,000 75,000	Dienst (Sw)
1972	West Germany 3	USSR 0	Brussels	43,437	Marschall (A)
1976	Czechoslovakia 2 *(Czechoslovakia won 5-3 on penalties)*	West Germany 2	Belgrade	45,000	Gonella (I)
1980	West Germany 2	Belgium 1	Rome	47,864	Rainea (R)
1984	France 2	Spain 0	Paris	80,000	Christov (Cz)
1988	Holland 2	USSR 0	Munich	72,308	Vautrot (F)

FINAL SERIES DATA

Year	*Venue*	*Matches*	*Attendances*	*Average*
1960	France	4	78,958	19,739
1964	Spain	4	156,253	39,063
1968	Italy	5	192,119	38,424
1972	Belgium	4	106,949	26,737
1976	Yugoslavia	4	106,087	26,522
1980	Italy	14	389,838	27,845
1984	France	15	603,977	40,266
1988	West Germany	15	938,541	62,569

EUROPEAN CLUB RESULTS 1988–89

BELGIUM — FRANCE — WEST GERMANY — HOLLAND — ITALY — PORTUGAL — SPAIN — USSR

BELGIUM – LEAGUE RESULTS 1988–89

	Anderlecht	Antwerp	Beerschot	Beveren	CS Brugge	FC Brugge	Charleroi	Kortrijk	Genk	Liege	Lierse	Lokeren	Mechelen	Racing Mechelen	Molenbeek	St Truiden	Standard	Waregem
Anderlecht	—	1-1	3-3	2-0	4-2	1-0	2-0	2-2	6-1	1-0	4-2	5-1	0-0	6-3	4-1	2-2	2-0	2-0
Antwerp	2-1	—	4-1	2-2	3-0	1-2	5-0	0-0	4-0	2-2	1-2	3-0	0-2	2-1	0-1	0-1	2-0	1-1
Beerschot	1-4	5-1	—	3-1	1-0	0-0	0-2	1-1	3-2	1-0	0-1	2-2	1-3	2-0	1-3	1-0	1-1	1-1
Beveren	2-4	1-1	0-0	—	2-0	3-2	1-1	4-2	2-1	0-0	2-2	0-2	1-1	3-0	0-1	2-1	1-0	2-1
CS Brugge	1-3	1-2	1-1	0-1	—	3-1	2-0	2-0	2-2	1-1	0-1	2-2	0-2	0-0	2-0	2-1	2-0	3-0
FC Brugge	1-1	3-1	1-0	3-1	4-2	—	6-1	1-1	3-0	2-2	3-1	2-2	0-1	2-0	4-3	4-0	2-0	2-3
Charleroi	0-0	1-4	2-2	2-0	1-2	1-1	—	2-1	0-0	1-1	1-1	0-0	1-3	2-2	0-0	0-0	0-0	3-0
Kortrijk	2-0	1-2	0-0	1-1	3-1	3-4	2-2	—	6-2	0-0	4-1	1-1	0-0	1-1	3-1	2-2	3-1	2-0
Genk	0-3	1-1	2-2	1-0	1-1	0-1	0-2	0-2	—	0-1	0-0	2-1	1-1	1-1	0-0	0-1	1-2	0-1
Liege	2-0	0-1	6-1	1-0	4-0	0-0	3-0	1-1	2-1	—	0-1	2-0	1-1	7-1	1-1	4-0	1-0	3-1
Lierse	1-4	0-1	3-0	0-2	1-1	0-3	1-1	1-1	1-0	1-4	—	1-2	0-2	0-1	3-1	1-1	0-3	0-0
Lokeren	2-4	2-2	4-0	3-0	2-1	1-2	1-1	0-0	0-0	0-3	0-1	—	0-3	2-3	1-1	4-2	0-2	2-1
Mechelen	1-2	2-1	4-3	2-1	4-0	1-0	3-0	3-1	2-0	1-0	1-0	2-1	—	3-0	2-0	3-0	2-0	0-0
Racing Mechelen	0-4	0-2	1-0	1-3	0-1	1-1	2-0	0-0	4-0	1-1	1-0	3-0	0-1	—	2-0	1-3	1-3	2-2
Molenbeek	0-2	0-2	3-0	3-2	2-1	1-4	2-1	1-0	3-0	1-3	0-1	1-2	0-4	1-0	—	1-2	2-2	1-4
St.Truiden	1-1	0-0	2-1	1-0	2-1	5-1	0-0	3-0	0-0	0-4	0-0	1-0	0-0	0-2	3-0	—	3-1	2-2
Standard	2-2	3-3	2-0	1-0	1-0	0-0	1-1	2-2	5-0	0-3	2-0	2-0	3-4	2-1	2-1	1-0	—	2-1
Waregem	0-1	1-4	1-2	4-1	2-2	4-2	1-2	2-5	3-1	1-1	0-1	1-2	3-0	0-1	1-0	3-0	2-0	—

FRANCE – LEAGUE RESULTS 1988–89

	Auxerre	Bordeaux	Caen	Cannes	Laval	Lens	Lille	Marseille	Matra Racing	Metz	Monaco	Montpellier	Nantes	Nice	Paris-St Germain	St Etienne	Sochaux	Strasbourg	Toulon	Toulouse
Auxerre	—	1-1	3-0	0-0	2-1	1-0	1-0	1-0	1-1	2-1	0-0	1-0	1-0	1-0	0-0	2-0	2-1	2-1	3-0	0-0
Bordeaux	2-0	—	2-3	0-0	2-1	4-1	0-0	0-0	3-2	4-1	1-1	2-1	5-0	2-0	0-1	5-0	1-2	2-0	1-1	1-1
Caen	1-0	3-0	—	3-0	1-1	1-0	2-1	0-0	1-1	0-0	0-3	0-1	2-3	2-1	0-1	2-3	0-0	3-3	2-1	3-0
Cannes	3-0	1-1	2-0	—	3-2	3-0	1-0	3-1	2-1	1-1	3-2	0-1	1-2	2-0	0-3	1-0	2-0	4-1	1-0	5-1
Laval	0-1	1-0	1-1	2-0	—	2-1	1-2	0-1	4-2	3-0	0-0	0-1	0-2	1-2	1-2	1-1	1-1	1-0	0-0	2-0
Lens	0-1	0-2	5-0	2-2	0-2	—	1-2	0-1	1-1	0-2	1-1	0-0	0-0	2-0	0-0	1-3	2-2	1-3	0-1	1-1
Lille	1-0	0-1	1-1	1-0	8-0	1-0	—	2-1	3-0	1-1	2-4	3-1	0-1	2-0	2-1	2-2	2-0	1-1	0-0	0-0
Marseille	2-1	2-2	4-2	2-1	1-0	5-2	1-1	—	2-0	3-2	2-2	1-1	1-0	3-2	1-0	2-0	0-0	3-1	1-0	3-1
Matra Racing	1-2	4-1	3-1	1-0	2-2	3-0	1-0	0-2	—	1-4	3-0	4-0	2-0	1-1	0-2	3-1	0-2	2-1	1-1	0-1
Metz	2-1	3-0	1-0	2-1	0-0	4-0	3-1	1-3	1-1	—	0-3	1-2	0-0	1-0	0-1	1-2	1-0	1-1	1-2	1-1
Monaco	1-2	4-2	3-1	2-0	1-0	1-0	1-1	3-0	1-0	1-1	—	4-2	4-1	1-1	1-0	2-2	0-0	4-1	2-2	1-0
Montpellier	1-0	2-2	1-0	0-0	6-2	2-0	2-3	1-0	0-0	5-2	4-2	—	1-4	1-1	0-0	2-0	1-2	1-0	0-1	1-0
Nantes	3-2	1-0	3-1	1-1	1-1	3-1	1-0	1-1	1-0	1-0	1-1	2-1	—	0-1	1-1	1-1	0-0	2-2	0-0	1-2
Nice	1-0	1-0	5-0	2-1	1-0	3-0	0-1	2-2	3-2	1-1	1-1	3-3	1-0	—	3-1	1-0	3-2	1-0	1-0	2-0
Paris St. Germain	2-2	1-1	3-0	1-0	3-0	3-2	1-1	0-0	2-1	2-2	0-2	3-2	1-0	1-0	—	3-1	1-0	1-0	0-0	2-1
St-Etienne	1-1	1-0	1-1	1-0	1-0	2-4	2-0	0-0	4-3	0-1	0-1	1-0	1-1	0-0	0-0	—	1-2	0-0	2-1	3-2
Sochaux	3-2	1-1	1-0	4-0	3-0	2-1	2-0	0-0	2-0	1-0	0-0	2-0	0-1	1-0	2-1	1-0	—	3-0	2-1	2-2
Strasbourg	1-0	3-2	1-2	0-0	3-0	4-1	1-3	2-3	1-1	1-2	1-2	3-1	2-0	3-0	0-0	0-1	0-3	—	2-1	4-1
Toulon	1-2	1-0	1-0	3-0	0-0	3-1	2-1	1-2	1-0	1-0	1-0	1-1	1-0	0-0	0-1	0-0	0-0	0-0	—	1-1
Toulouse	0-0	1-1	0-0	4-1	0-0	2-1	1-1	0-0	2-1	2-1	2-0	2-2	1-2	2-1	0-0	3-1	2-1	4-0	1-0	—

WEST GERMANY – LEAGUE RESULTS 1988–89

	Bayern Munich	Bochum	Cologne	Borussia Dortmund	Eintracht Frankfurt	Hamburg	Hannover	Kaiserslautern	Karlsruhe	Leverkusen	Mannheim	Moenchengladbach	Nuremberg	St. Pauli	Kickers Stuttgart	Stuttgart	Uerdingen	Werder Bremen
Bayern Munich	—	5-0	2-0	1-1	3-0	1-0	4-0	5-1	3-2	2-0	1-0	3-0	1-0	2-1	3-0	3-3	5-0	0-0
Bochum	0-0	—	1-3	2-2	1-0	2-1	1-3	2-0	2-0	2-4	2-2	1-2	1-0	0-0	2-1	1-0	1-1	0-1
Cologne	1-3	1-0	—	2-0	3-2	1-2	1-0	2-2	6-1	3-0	1-0	3-1	1-1	4-2	5-1	3-0	1-1	2-0
Borussia Dortmund	1-1	2-1	0-4	—	6-0	2-2	4-0	1-1	3-2	2-1	1-2	0-0	4-0	0-0	0-1	1-2	4-2	3-1
Eintracht Frankfurt	2-2	1-1	1-0	2-1	—	0-1	1-0	3-2	1-0	1-1	0-0	1-1	1-0	1-1	1-2	1-3	0-2	0-0
Hamburg	0-1	0-1	0-1	0-0	2-1	—	4-1	1-1	1-1	1-1	5-1	1-2	3-2	1-1	3-0	2-1	3-0	2-0
Hannover	1-1	3-2	2-2	1-5	1-1	2-3	—	0-0	2-3	2-2	0-2	0-1	2-2	2-2	3-4	2-0	0-5	2-2
Kaiserslautern	1-1	3-0	1-1	3-2	3-0	0-0	0-0	—	1-2	0-0	0-3	0-0	2-1	1-0	6-0	6-1	2-0	0-0
Karlsruhe	2-2	1-3	0-0	0-0	1-3	2-2	2-0	4-1	—	2-3	1-0	2-2	1-1	3-1	1-0	2-0	1-1	1-0
Leverkusen	1-1	1-1	0-0	2-0	2-2	1-2	3-1	0-1	1-0	—	3-0	3-1	3-0	2-2	1-3	0-0	2-2	1-0
Mannheim	0-3	2-2	2-1	0-3	1-0	0-0	1-1	0-4	2-0	1-1	—	4-1	2-1	2-1	2-2	3-4	3-3	1-1
Moenchengladbach	2-1	2-0	1-2	1-1	2-1	0-4	2-0	4-1	1-1	2-0	1-1	—	1-1	2-2	1-1	2-2	3-0	4-1
Nuremberg	2-1	3-1	0-2	1-1	1-1	1-4	1-0	1-1	1-3	1-1	1-0	0-0	—	5-3	3-3	1-0	1-0	0-1
St. Pauli	0-0	1-0	0-1	1-0	2-0	1-2	1-1	1-1	1-0	2-0	2-1	1-1	0-1	—	1-0	2-1	5-1	1-3
Kickers Stuttgart	2-0	1-2	0-0	1-2	0-1	2-0	0-1	2-0	1-3	1-3	1-3	3-0	2-1	2-2	—	0-2	3-1	[illegible]
Stuttgart	1-2	3-1	2-0	1-3	4-1	4-2	2-1	3-1	2-0	0-0	2-0	2-1	4-0	2-1	4-0	—	2-2	3-3
Uerdingen	1-3	3-1	1-1	0-0	4-1	0-2	7-3	3-1	0-3	3-1	0-0	0-0	3-2	0-0	1-3	0-0	—	2-1
Werder Bremen	2-2	2-0	1-2	2-0	2-0	2-1	1-0	1-0	3-1	3-1	2-1	2-0	2-1	0-3	4-0	3-0	3-1	—

HOLLAND – LEAGUE RESULTS 1988–89

	Ajax	Den Bosch	Feyenoord	Fortuna Sittard	Groningen	Haarlem	Maastricht	PSV Eindhoven	Roda	Sparta	Twente	Utrecht	Veendam	Venlo	Volendam	RKC	Willem II	PEC Zwolle
Ajax	—	5-1	4-1	2-0	3-0	5-0	4-0	2-0	3-3	2-1	1-1	2-0	4-0	1-0	2-0	3-2	1-0	0-0
Den Bosch	0-3	—	2-0	0-3	1-1	2-5	3-0	2-2	0-1	2-1	1-1	1-0	1-1	1-4	0-1	1-0	5-1	4-0
Feyenoord	1-2	3-0	—	4-2	2-1	3-0	5-2	2-2	2-1	3-2	1-1	3-3	2-2	2-2	4-0	0-0	5-0	1-1
Fortuna Sittard	2-1	0-1	1-0	—	0-0	1-1	1-1	1-0	1-1	3-0	0-0	1-2	1-2	1-0	1-1	2-0	2-2	1-0
Groningen	1-4	4-0	1-1	2-2	—	2-0	4-1	1-2	1-0	2-1	2-0	4-2	1-3	7-3	4-0	1-2	5-3	3-0
Haarlem	0-1	0-0	1-2	2-2	2-1	—	0-4	2-0	1-0	2-0	2-1	2-1	1-0	2-0	3-0	1-1	2-2	0-0
Maastricht	1-1	0-2	1-0	2-1	3-1	1-1	—	1-3	2-1	2-0	0-1	0-2	1-2	2-0	1-3	1-0	0-2	4-2
PSV Eindhoven	1-4	5-2	1-0	1-0	1-0	3-0	3-1	—	4-2	0-1	3-0	3-0	3-1	5-2	2-0	5-2	7-0	2-0
Roda	0-0	3-2	3-1	1-1	1-1	4-1	1-1	0-1	—	4-0	1-1	0-0	2-0	2-1	0-0	3-1	2-0	2-1
Sparta	3-2	1-1	1-3	1-0	1-1	0-0	1-1	0-2	0-1	—	1-1	3-0	3-1	1-1	3-0	2-2	1-1	3-1
Twente	2-1	0-1	6-1	0-0	4-0	0-0	0-0	1-1	0-0	2-0	—	0-0	3-0	1-0	3-0	7-1	0-0	3-1
Utrecht	1-1	1-2	3-1	3-1	3-2	2-1	2-2	1-3	3-2	2-2	2-0	—	3-0	0-0	2-0	1-2	0-2	5-1
Veendam	0-1	1-3	1-2	1-1	0-0	2-0	4-1	1-2	4-4	0-1	0-3	1-0	—	0-0	0-2	2-0	1-1	1-2
Venlo	1-2	1-0	1-1	1-2	1-1	1-1	1-1	0-2	2-2	0-2	1-1	2-1	2-1	—	1-2	1-1	1-1	6-2
Volendam	1-0	2-0	1-3	0-2	0-1	4-0	1-2	1-1	1-0	3-1	1-1	4-0	3-1	1-1	—	4-2	0-2	1-1
RKC	3-1	0-1	1-1	3-2	2-1	3-1	1-0	0-0	1-4	2-2	1-1	5-3	0-1	6-0	5-1	—	3-1	1-1
Willem II	2-5	1-3	1-2	0-2	2-3	1-1	2-2	1-3	1-0	2-2	0-0	2-0	1-1	5-1	2-4	3-0	—	4-1
PEC Zwolle	4-1	2-3	2-4	2-0	1-3	1-2	3-0	0-5	0-1	1-1	2-2	2-1	6-2	2-2	0-0	3-0	3-2	—

ITALY – LEAGUE RESULTS 1988–89

	Ascoli	Atalanta	Bologna	Cesena	Como	Fiorentina	Internazionale	Juventus	Lazio	Lecce	AC Milan	Napoli	Pescara	Pisa	Roma	Sampdoria	Torino	Verona
Ascoli	—	3-1	1-0	1-1	2-0	1-1	1-3	1-1	0-0	1-1	0-2	2-0	0-1	0-1	0-3	2-2	1-0	3-0
Atalanta	1-0	—	2-0	5-1	1-1	0-1	1-1	0-0	3-1	-	1-2	1-1	0-0	1-0	2-2	1-0	1-0	2-2
Bologna	1-0	1-1	—	2-2	1-0	1-0	0-6	3-4	0-0	2-1	1-4	1-1	1-0	1-0	0-1	0-0	2-0	0-0
Cesena	2-1	0-0	2-0	—	-	0-3	1-2	1-2	0-0	3-2	1-0	0-1	1-0	1-0	1-1	0-0	3-2	0-0
Como	0-1	1-0	1-0	0-0	—	3-2	1-2	0-3	2-1	2-1	1-1	0-1	1-0	1-1	0-1	0-2	2-3	1-1
Fiorentina	2-1	1-1	-	4-1	3-1	—	4-3	2-1	3-0	1-1	0-2	1-3	3-2	3-0	2-2	0-2	2-1	1-1
Internazionale	3-1	4-2	1-0	1-0	4-0	2-0	—	1-1	1-0	2-0	0-0	2-1	2-0	4-1	2-0	1-0	2-0	1-0
Juventus	2-0	0-1	2-0	2-2	0-0	1-1	1-1	—	4-2	1-0	0-0	3-5	1-1	3-1	2-1	0-0	1-0	3-0
Lazio	0-0	0-1	0-0	0-0	1-1	1-0	1-3	0-0	—	0-0	1-1	1-1	2-2	1-0	1-0	-	1-1	3-1
Lecce	1-2	2-1	1-1	0-0	0-0	0-0	0-3	2-0	1-0	—	1-1	1-0	1-0	1-0	0-0	1-0	3-1	0-0
AC Milan	-	1-2	1-1	0-0	4-0	4-0	0-1	4-0	0-0	2-0	—	0-0	6-1	0-0	4-1	0-0	2-1	1-1
Napoli	4-1	1-0	3-1	1-0	3-2	2-0	0-0	2-4	1-1	4-0	4-1	—	8-2	-	1-1	1-1	4-1	1-0
Pescara	0-0	1-1	3-1	3-0	-	0-0	0-2	-	0-0	1-1	1-3	0-0	—	0-0	0-0	0-1	2-0	0-0
Pisa	0-0	0-1	0-2	1-0	3-1	0-0	0-3	1-4	1-1	1-1	0-2	0-1	1-1	—	1-0	1-1	1-0	1-0
Roma	1-1	2-1	1-1	1-0	1-0	2-1	0-3	1-3	0-0	1-1	1-3	1-0	1-3	2-1	—	1-0	1-3	0-0
Sampdoria	1-0	1-1	4-1	2-0	2-0	1-2	0-1	1-2	1-0	3-0	1-1	0-0	4-1	2-0	0-2	—	5-1	2-1
Torino	1-1	1-1	1-1	2-0	2-1	1-0	-	0-0	4-3	0-0	2-2	0-1	1-1	0-0	3-1	2-3	—	1-1
Verona	0-1	1-0	0-0	0-0	0-0	2-1	0-0	2-0	0-0	2-1	1-2	0-1	0-0	1-0	-	1-1	0-0	—

PORTUGAL – LEAGUE RESULTS 1988–89

	Amadora	Beira Mar	Belenenscs	Benfica	Boavista	Braga	Chaves	Espinho	Fafe	Farense	Guimaraes	Leixoes	Maritimo	Nacional	Penafiel	Portimonense	FC Porto	Setubal	Sporting	Viseu
Amadora	—	0-0	2-1	1-2	1-1	1-3	1-1	0-0	0-0	1-0	1-0	0-3	1-1	4-1	2-1	1-0	2-2	1-1	0-0	2-1
Beira Mar	1-0	—	1-0	0-1	0-2	3-0	2-0	1-0	1-1	2-2	1-2	1-0	3-2	0-0	2-1	2-0	0-0	0-0	1-2	2-1
Belenenses	1-0	3-0	—	0-1	0-3	1-1	4-2	2-0	1-1	2-0	1-1	2-0	2-2	1-1	2-1	4-0	1-1	0-0	0-3	3-0
Benfica	3-0	0-0	1-0	—	2-2	1-0	2-1	1-0	4-0	3-0	0-0	2-1	2-0	1-0	1-1	3-0	0-0	2-0	2-0	4-0
Boavista	2-0	1-0	0-1	2-1	—	2-0	4-0	1-0	3-1	1-1	0-1	2-2	5-1	0-2	1-0	1-0	4-1	2-0	2-0	2-0
Braga	1-0	1-0	2-0	0-0	0-2	—	0-0	3-1	2-2	4-2	2-0	1-0	2-1	1-1	0-0	1-1	0-1	0-0	0-0	0-1
Chaves	3-0	0-0	0-0	0-2	1-0	1-1	—	3-0	1-1	0-0	1-0	2-2	0-1	0-0	4-1	0-0	2-0	0-1	2-1	5-0
Espinho	2-1	2-1	1-1	2-2	2-2	4-1	2-1	—	1-1	3-1	1-2	2-0	2-1	4-0	1-1	1-0	1-2	1-5	0-2	1-0
Fafe	0-1	2-1	1-1	0-2	1-1	1-4	2-0	2-1	—	1-0	1-0	0-0	2-1	2-0	0-0	2-1	0-0	0-0	0-1	0-0
Farense	2-0	1-1	2-1	0-2	1-1	1-2	0-2	1-3	1-1	—	1-0	3-1	0-0	5-0	0-0	0-0	1-1	2-1	1-0	1-0
Guimaraes	0-2	1-0	0-1	1-2	2-3	2-0	2-1	2-1	2-0	3-0	—	2-0	1-1	1-1	1-1	0-0	1-1	1-0	1-0	5-0
Leixoes	0-0	1-1	0-2	0-2	0-0	0-0	0-0	4-0	1-1	1-0	2-1	—	0-0	2-2	1-1	1-2	0-3	1-0	0-2	2-0
Maritimo	1-2	3-1	1-0	1-1	1-0	0-0	0-1	1-1	3-0	2-1	2-0	0-1	—	0-0	2-0	2-1	0-0	0-1	1-1	4-0
Nacional	0-1	0-0	0-1	0-1	2-0	2-1	3-1	3-0	2-0	3-0	1-1	2-0	1-1	—	3-4	0-0	0-1	4-4	0-1	5-2
Penafiel	0-0	2-0	1-1	1-0	1-2	0-1	1-0	2-0	1-0	0-1	0-1	1-1	1-1	2-0	—	1-0	0-1	2-0	0-0	2-1
Portimonense	0-1	1-0	2-2	0-1	2-1	1-0	3-1	0-0	2-1	0-0	2-1	3-0	2-0	0-1	1-1	—	1-1	3-0	3-1	1-1
FC Porto	4-0	2-0	1-0	0-0	1-1	1-0	1-0	2-1	1-0	5-0	0-0	1-0	3-1	3-0	2-0	1-0	—	0-1	3-0	5-0
Setubal	1-1	2-1	2-1	2-2	1-0	1-3	2-0	2-1	4-0	0-2	0-0	2-2	1-0	0-1	0-0	3-0	0-0	—	1-0	2-0
Sporting	0-1	0-0	0-0	0-2	1-1	2-0	4-1	3-1	3-1	1-0	1-0	2-0	2-2	4-0	4-1	1-0	1-2	4-3	—	2-0
Viseu	2-2	0-0	1-1	0-1	0-0	1-5	0-1	0-2	0-2	3-1	2-1	1-0	0-0	0-2	1-0	0-1	0-0	0-1	2-2	—

SPAIN – LEAGUE RESULTS 1988–89

	Espanol	Barcelona	Athletic Bilbao	Cadiz	Celta	Elche	Gijon	Logrones	Atletico Madrid	Real Madrid	Malaga	Murcia	Osasuna	Oviedo	Real Sociedad	Zaragoza	Betis	Seville	Valencia	Valladolid
Espanol	—	2-2	1-0	0-2	1-1	1-1	2-1	2-0	1-0	1-4	0-1	3-0	1-1	1-2	1-1	2-2	0-0	1-1	0-1	0-1
Barcelona	2-0	—	3-0	3-0	3-1	2-0	4-0	2-1	3-0	0-0	4-0	3-1	1-2	7-1	4-1	1-0	3-0	4-0	1-1	0-0
Athletic Bilbao	1-0	3-2	—	1-0	2-0	2-0	1-4	3-1	1-1	1-1	3-1	3-0	0-0	1-0	2-3	1-1	1-1	3-0	1-2	2-0
Cadiz	0-0	1-1	0-0	—	1-1	2-1	0-3	0-1	2-0	0-2	0-1	0-2	1-1	1-1	1-1	1-1	4-0	0-0	1-1	1-1
Celta	0-0	0-3	1-2	3-2	—	3-0	2-1	1-0	0-3	2-0	2-0	0-0	1-0	1-2	2-2	1-1	0-0	1-0	2-0	1-1
Elche	1-1	0-3	2-0	2-2	0-1	—	0-0	1-2	1-3	1-3	0-2	3-0	0-1	0-1	1-1	1-4	0-0	1-2	0-1	1-0
Gijon	2-1	0-2	0-1	1-0	1-2	2-0	—	3-0	2-2	2-2	1-2	0-1	2-1	0-0	4-2	1-2	0-0	0-0	1-0	2-1
Logrones	0-0	0-2	1-1	1-0	1-1	2-1	1-0	—	1-0	0-1	1-0	0-0	1-1	1-1	1-1	0-2	3-1	0-0	0-1	1-1
Atletico Madrid	6-1	1-3	0-1	3-0	0-0	3-1	0-0	2-0	—	3-3	3-0	3-0	4-1	2-2	3-0	3-1	6-2	2-0	2-0	3-2
Real Madrid	3-0	3-2	3-3	4-0	4-1	4-2	5-1	1-0	2-1	—	2-1	3-0	2-2	1-0	2-2	4-0	5-1	3-0	2-1	3-2
Malaga	1-0	2-2	1-1	0-2	2-2	2-1	1-0	1-0	1-2	2-2	—	1-3	1-2	1-1	1-0	1-3	2-2	1-0	0-1	0-0
Murcia	1-0	2-0	1-1	0-1	1-2	0-1	0-3	0-0	1-1	0-3	1-0	—	6-1	0-0	0-1	0-3	0-2	1-2	0-1	2-1
Osasuna	0-0	1-1	1-0	0-1	1-0	1-1	0-0	0-0	2-0	1-1	1-0	1-0	—	3-1	1-0	3-0	3-1	1-3	0-1	0-2
Oviedo	0-1	1-2	0-3	1-0	4-0	3-0	1-0	1-1	5-2	1-3	2-3	2-0	3-2	—	1-0	1-1	0-3	0-0	0-0	0-1
Real Sociedad	0-1	0-1	1-0	0-0	4-2	1-0	2-1	2-2	1-2	1-1	2-2	0-2	2-1	0-0	—	2-1	2-1	1-0	0-0	1-0
Zaragoza	2-1	0-0	1-0	0-1	2-1	3-1	1-1	1-1	0-0	1-4	2-1	2-1	0-1	3-1	0-0	—	2-1	0-0	0-0	2-0
Betis	2-2	0-2	2-0	1-1	2-0	3-1	0-1	0-0	0-1	0-2	1-2	3-0	1-0	1-0	1-1	2-1	—	1-3	0-0	0-1
Seville	0-0	1-1	0-0	1-1	1-3	4-1	1-0	0-1	4-1	1-1	1-1	3-0	1-0	2-1	2-0	0-1	1-0	—	1-0	2-4
Valencia	1-1	1-1	0-0	1-2	1-0	3-2	2-1	0-0	1-0	1-1	2-1	3-0	3-2	0-1	1-0	2-2	3-0	1-0	—	1-0
Valladolid	1-0	0-0	1-0	1-2	0-1	3-0	0-1	3-1	0-1	0-1	1-0	2-1	1-0	1-0	2-0	1-0	2-1	2-1	1-1	—

USSR – LEAGUE RESULTS 1988–89

	Ararat	Shakhtyor	Dnepr	Dynamo Kiev	Dynamo Minsk	Dynamo Moscow	Dynamo Tbilisi	Jalgiris	Kairat	Lokomotiv Moscow	Metallist	Neftschi	Spartak Moscow	Chernomorets	Torpedo Moscow	Zenit
Ararat	—	1-0	0-0	1-2	0-0	0-1	3-1	1-0	1-0	0-0	2-0	0-0	1-0	1-1	0-2	1-0
Shakhtyor	2-0	—	0-0	1-1	0-1	2-0	3-1	5-1	2-0	0-1	3-0	0-2	0-0	0-1	0-0	1-0
Dnepr	3-0	4-2	—	0-0	4-3	2-0	0-0	3-1	3-0	0-0	1-1	3-2	0-0	2-1	2-0	1-1
Dynamo Kiev	2-0	0-0	2-0	—	1-1	2-1	1-0	3-1	1-0	1-0	3-0	2-1	1-2	1-0	3-0	2-0
Dynamo Minsk	0-0	1-0	0-1	1-2	—	0-0	0-0	0-1	3-1	3-2	1-1	3-1	0-2	2-0	2-1	1-1
Dynamo Moscow	1-0	1-1	1-2	1-2	2-1	—	0-0	0-0	4-3	2-0	1-1	1-0	1-2	1-3	2-0	3-2
Dynamo Tbilisi	1-2	2-0	0-1	1-1	2-1	3-1	—	2-1	3-1	0-0	1-2	2-0	1-0	2-0	0-1	0-1
Jalgiris	1-0	1-0	2-2	0-0	1-0	2-1	0-1	—	2-0	1-2	2-1	2-0	2-0	2-1	2-2	2-0
Kairat	1-0	0-1	0-2	0-1	1-2	2-1	2-0	1-2	—	1-1	1-0	2-1	1-3	1-1	2-1	1-1
Lokomotiv Moscow	1-0	2-0	0-1	1-1	0-0	2-2	2-1	2-2	3-0	—	1-1	1-0	2-2	2-0	1-1	2-0
Metallist	1-2	1-2	0-2	1-1	3-1	1-0	2-0	2-1	1-1	1-0	—	1-1	2-0	0-1	1-1	1-1
Neftschi	1-1	2-2	2-2	0-3	1-0	0-1	1-0	1-2	4-2	1-1	0-1	—	1-2	2-0	1-1	1-2
Spartak Moscow	1-1	2-2	2-2	1-0	4-2	1-0	3-0	1-1	2-0	1-1	2-1	2-0	—	3-1	0-0	1-1
Chernomorets	2-1	1-0	1-3	2-1	0-0	1-1	2-0	1-0	1-0	0-1	1-1	1-0	0-1	—	0-2	1-2
Torpedo Moscow	2-0	2-0	1-0	2-0	1-0	2-1	1-0	2-2	1-2	2-1	1-0	3-1	2-0	2-0	—	2-1
Zenit	2-1	0-0	0-1	1-1	0-0	0-1	5-4	1-2	2-1	3-2	2-1	2-0	0-0	2-0	2-0	—

1990 FIFA WORLD CUP

EUROPE

Group 1 *(Denmark, Bulgaria, Rumania, Greece)*

19 October, Sofia, 52,000

Bulgaria (1) 1 *(Kolev 31)*

Rumania (1) 3 *(Mateut 25, Camataru 79, 89)*

Bulgaria: Mikhailov; Nikolov, Rankov, Vasev (Kiryakov 55), Iliev, Stoichkov, Sadkov, Yordanov, Getov, Alexandrov (Kolev 30), Penev.
Rumania: Lung; Iovan, Andone, Belodedici, Rotariu, Mateut (Klein 55), Sabau, Hagi, Popescu, Lacatus (Vaiscovici 66), Camataru.

19 October, Athens, 45,000

Greece (1) 1 *Mitropoulos 41)*

Denmark (0) 1 *(Povlsen 56)*

Greece: Talikariadis; Hatziathanassiu, Manolas, Mavridis, Kolomitrousis, Skartados (Karapialis 74), Tsalouhidis, Bonovas, Mitropoulos (Georgamlis 56), Saravakos, Anastopoulos.
Denmark: Schmeichel; Heintze, Nielsen I, Olsen L, Sivebaek (Kristensen 46), Bartram, Helt, Jensen J, Povlsen, Laudrup, Brylle (Elstrup 75).

2 November, Copenhagen, 34,600

Denmark (1) 1 *(Elstrup 8)*

Bulgaria (1) 1 *(Sadkov 38)*

Denmark: Schmeichel; Olsen L, Sivebaek, Nielsen K, Kristensen, Heintze (Brylle 76), Helt (Bartram 65), Jensen J, Laudrup, Elstrup, Povlsen.
Bulgaria: Valov; Iliev, Kiryakov, Dochev, Ivanov, Penev, Sadkov, Kirov, Yordanov (Rakov 86), Stoichkov (Balkov 88), Bezinski.

2 November, Bucharest, 22,500

Rumania (2) 3 *(Mateut 26, Hagi 40 (pen), Sabau 84)*

Greece (0) 0

Rumania: Lung; Iovan, Belodedici, Andone, Ungureanu, Popescu, Hagi, Sabau (Klein 85), Mateut, Lacatus (Vaiscovici 77), Camataru.
Greece: Talikariadis; Hatziathanassiu, Kolomitroussis, Manolas, Mavridis, Tsalouhidis, Saravakos, Bonovas, Anastopoulos, Mitropoulos (Kutulas 46), Tsiantakis (Nioblias 68).

26 April, Athens, 30,000

Greece (0) 0

Rumania (0) 0

Greece: Economopoulos; Apostolakis, Hatziathanasiu, Manolas, Mavridis, Tsalouhidis, Saravakos, Papadopoulos (Bonovas 65), Samaras, Savidis, Tsiantakis.
Rumania: Lung; Iovan, Bumbescu, Klein, Rednic, Mateut, Lucescu, Sabau, Camataru (Vaiscovici 89), Hagi, Jupescu (Dumitrescu 78).

26 April, Sofia, 45,000

Bulgaria (0) 0

Denmark (1) 2 *(Povlsen 41, Laudrup B 89)*

Bulgaria: Valov (Donev 55); Kiryakov, Dochev, Bezinski, Iliev, Rakov, Kirov, Sadkov (Simeonov 46), Stoichkov, Mikhtarski, Getov.
Denmark: Schmeichel; Heintze, Nielsen K, Olsen L, Sivebaek, Larsen J, Olsen M (Vilfort 74), Jensen J (Helt 84), Bartram, Povlsen, Laudrup B.

17 May, Copenhagen, 38,500

Denmark (1) 7 *(Laudrup B 24, Bartram 47, Nielsen K 55, Povlsen 56, Vilfort 79, Andersen H 85, Laudrup M 89 (pen))*

Greece (1) 1 *(Samaras 39)*

Denmark: Schmeichel; Sivebaek (Vilfort 30), Olsen L, Nielsen K, Larsen J, Bartram (Andersen H), Olsen M, Jensen J, Laudrup M, Povlsen, Laudrup B.
Greece: Economopoulos; Hatziathanasiu, Mavridis, Manolas, Apostolakis, Tsalouhidis, Tsiantakis, Mitropoulos (Kalitzakis 50), Papadopoulos, Saravakos, Samaras.

17 May, Bucharest, 20,000

Rumania (1) 1 *(Popescu 35)*

Bulgaria (0) 0

Rumania: Stelea; Iovan, Bumbescu, Rednic (Balint 64), Mateut, Sabau (Dumitrescu 85), Popescu, Rotariu, Hagi, Lacatus, Camataru.
Bulgaria: Valov (Donev 46); Dochev, Ivanov, Vasev, Mladenov D, Tinchev, Kestadinov E, Stoichkov, Mladenov S, Bakalov, Balekov.

	P	*W*	*D*	*L*	*F*	*A*	*Pts*
Rumania	4	3	1	0	7	1	7
Denmark	4	2	2	0	11	3	6
Greece	4	0	2	2	2	11	2
Bulgaria	4	0	1	3	2	7	1

Remaining fixtures: 11.10.89 Bulgaria v Greece; Denmark v Rumania; 15.11.89 Greece v Bulgaria; Rumania v Denmark.

Group 2 *(England, Poland, Sweden, Albania)*

19 October, Wembley, 65,628

England (0) 0

Sweden (0) 0

England: Shilton; Stevens, Pearce, Webb, Adams (Walker 64), Butcher, Robson, Beardsley, Waddle, Lineker, Barnes (Cottee 79).
Sweden: Ravelli; Nilsson R (Schiller 77), Hysen, Larsson P, Ljung, Thern, Stromberg, Prytz, Nilsson J, Holmqvist (Ekstrom 63), Pettersson.

19 October, Chorzow, 30,000

Poland (0) 1 *(Warzycha K 78)*

Albania (0) 0

Poland: Wandzik; Warzycha R, Wojcicki, Lukasik, Wdowczyk, Matsik (Ziober 46), Warzycha K, Urban, Furtok (Komornicki 73), Rudy, Smolarek.
Albania: Mersini; Alimehmeti, Josa, Hodja, Gega, Iera, Shehu (Stoia 70), Lekbello, Millo, Minga, Demollari.

5 November, Tirana, 11,500

Albania (1) 1 *(Shehu 33)*

Sweden (0) 2 *(Holmqvist 68, Ekstrom 71)*

Albania: Mersini; Alimehmeti, Hodja, Lekbello, Stoia, Josa, Gega, Demollari, Millo, Shehu, Minga.
Sweden: Ravelli; Nilsson R, Larsson P, Hysen, Ljung, Thern, Prytz (Holmqvist 66), Stromberg, Nilsson J, Pettersson, Ekstrom.

8 March, Tirana, 30,000

Albania (0) 0

England (1) 2 *(Barnes 16, Robson 63)*

Albania: Mersini; Zmijani, Josa, Hodja, Gega, Jera, Shehu, Lekbello, Millo (Majaci 75), Minga, Demollari.
England: Shilton; Stevens, Pearce, Webb, Walker, Butcher, Robson, Rocastle, Waddle (Beardsley 79), Lineker (Smith 79), Barnes.

26 April, Wembley, 60,602

England (2) 5 *(Lineker 5, Beardsley 12, 64, Waddle 72, Gascoigne 88)*

Albania (0) 0

England: Shilton; Stevens (Parker 77), Pearce, Webb, Walker, Butcher, Robson, Rocastle (Gascoigne 67), Beardsley, Lineker, Waddle.
Albania: Nallbani; Zmijani, Bubeqi, Hodja, Gega, Jera, Shehu, Lekbello, Millo, Hasanpapa (Noga 31), Demollari.

7 May, Stockholm, 35,021

Sweden (0) 2 *(Ljung 76, Larsson N 89)*

Poland (0) 1 *(Tarasiewicz 86)*

Sweden: Ravelli T; Nilsson R, Lonn (Ravelli A 80), Ljung, Schiller, Limpar, Prytz, Thern, Nilsson J (Larsson N 58), Ekstrom, Magnusson.
Poland: Bako; Soczynski, Lukasik, Wojcicki, Wdowczyk (Tarasiewicz 15), Prusik, Matysik, Urban, Dziekanowski (Kosecki 60), Furtok, Warzycha K.

3 June, Wembley, 69,203

England (1) 3 *(Lineker 24, Barnes 69, Webb 82)*

Poland (0) 0

England: Shilton; Stevens, Pearce, Webb, Walker, Butcher, Robson, Waddle (Rocastle 75), Beardsley (Smith 75), Lineker, Barnes.
Poland: Bako; Wijas, Wojcicki, Wdowczyk, Lukasik, Matysik, Prusik, Urban (Tarasiewicz 70), Furtok, Warzycha K, Lesniak (Kosecki 58).

	P	*W*	*D*	*L*	*F*	*A*	*Pts*
England	4	3	1	0	10	0	7
Sweden	3	2	1	0	4	2	5
Poland	3	1	0	2	2	5	2
Albania	4	0	0	4	1	10	0

Remaining fixtures: 6.9.89 Sweden v England; 8.10.89 Sweden v Albania; 11.10.89 Poland v England; 25.10.89 Poland v Sweden; 15.11.89 Albania v Poland.

Group 3 *(USSR, East Germany, Austria, Iceland, Turkey)*

31 August, Reykjavik, 8300

Iceland (1) 1 *(Gretarsson 11)*

USSR (0) 1 *(Litovchenko 75)*

Iceland: Sigurdsson; Bergsson, Saevar Jonsson, Edvaldsson, Thordarsson, Gislason, Ormslev, Siggi Jonsson, Sigurvinsson, Gudjohnsen, Gretarsson (Torfasson G 82).
USSR: Dasayev; Bessonov (Dobrovolski 65), Khidiatulin, Kuznetsov, Demianenko, Aleinikov, Litovchenko, Zavarov, Rats, Protasov, Mikhailichenko.

12 October, Istanbul, 25,680

Turkey (0) 1 *(Onal 73)*

Iceland (0) 1 *(Torfasson O 62)*

Turkey: Fatih; Recep (Feyyaz 57), Semih, Cuneyt, Mucahit, Gokhan G, Oguz, Ridvan, Onal, Tanju, Savas K.
Iceland: Fridriksson; Gislason, Edvaldsson, Arnthorsson (Askelsson 79), Bergsson, Siggi Jonsson, Margeirsson, Torfasson O, Torfasson G, Gudjohnsen, Thordarsson.

19 October, East Berlin, 12,000

East Germany (1) 2 *(Thom 34, 88)*

Iceland (0) 0

East Germany: Weissflog; Kreer, Schossler, Stahmann, Lindner, Doschner, Raab, Ernst, Stubner (Sammer 34), Kirsten, Thom.
Iceland: Sigurdsson; Saevar Jonsson, Bergsson, Edvaldsson, Gislason, Thordarsson, Torfasson O, Gudjohnsen, Sigurvinsson, Gretarsson, Torfasson G (Margeirsson 77).

19 October, Kiev, 100,000

USSR (0) 2 *(Mikhailichenko 47, Zavarov 69)*

Austria (0) 0

USSR: Dasayev; Ivanauskas (Gorlukovich), Khidiatulin, Zigmantovich, Demianenko, Aleinikov, Litovchenko, Zavarov, Rats, Mikhailichenko, Protasov (Savichev 83).
Austria: Lindenberger; Russ, Degeorgi, Pfeffer, Weber H, Zsak, Keglevits, Artner, Polster, Hormann (Herzog 63), Willfurth.

2 November, Vienna, 25,000

Austria (2) 3 *(Polster 38, Herzog 42, 54)*

Turkey (0) 2 *(Feyyaz 61, Tanju 81)*

Austria: Lindenberger, Weber G, Russ, Pfeffer, Artner, Willfurth (Pacult 55), Prohaska, Herzog (Glatzmayer 68), Degeorgi, Ogris, Polster.
Turkey: Fatih; Cuneyt, Recep, Gokhan G (Savas K), Semih, Mustafa, Unal, Oguz, Gokhan K, Ridvan, Feyyaz (Tanju).

30 November, Istanbul, 39,000

Turkey (1) 3 *(Tanju 23, 63, Oguz 69)*

East Germany (0) 1 *(Thom 75)*

Turkey: Fatih; Recep, Semih, Cuneyt, Gokhan G, Onal, Ugur, Ridvan, Oguz (Hassan 88), Tanju (Metin 78), Feyyaz.

East Germany: Weissflog; Kreer (Schossler 66), Stahmann, Lindner, Doschner, Pilz, Stubner, Steinmann, Kirsten, Ernst (Doll 46), Thom.

12 April, Magdeburg, 23,000

East Germany (0) 0

Turkey (1) 2 *(Tanju 21, Ridvan 88)*

East Germany: Muller; Hauptmann, Rohde, Trautmann, Lindner, Stubner (Wuckel 64), Sammer, Pilz (Doll 19), Kirsten, Minge, Thom.
Turkey: Engin; Recep, Cuneyt, Gokhan B, Semih, Yusuf, Ugur (Erdal 65), Oguz (Gokhan G 80), Unal, Ridvan, Tanju.

26 April, Kiev, 100,000

USSR (3) 3 *(Dobrovolski 3, Litovchenko 22, Protasov 40)*

East Germany (0) 0

USSR: Dasayev; Luzhny, Gorlukovich, Kuznetsov, Dobrovolski (Savichev 75), Aleinikov (Kulkov 80), Litovchenko, Mikhailichenko, Protasov, Rats, Zavarov.
East Germany: Weissflog; Hauptmann (Mertz 46), Lieberam, Kohler, Trautmann, Doschner, Sammer, Wosz, Scholz (Kirsten 55), Doll, Thom.

10 May, Istanbul, 42,500

Turkey (0) 0

USSR (1) 1 *(Mikhailichenko 40)*

Turkey: Engin; Recep, Cuneyt, Gokhan B, Semih, Yusuf, Ugur (Hasan Vezir 46) (Feyyez 60), Unal, Mustafa, Ridvan, Tanju.
USSR: Dasayev; Luzhny, Gorlukovich, Kuznetsov, Aleinikov (Ketaschvili 89), Rats, Mikhailichenko, Litovchenko, Zavarov, Protasov (Borodyuk 86), Dobrovolski.

20 May, Leipzig, 22,000

East Germany (0) 1 *(Kirsten 86)*

Austria (1) 1 *(Polster 3)*

East Germany: Weissflog; Stahmann, Lindner, Trautmann (Doll 46), Kreer, Rohde, Stubner, Sammer (Weidemann 68), Steinmann, Kirsten, Thom.
Austria: Lindenberger; Weber G, Russ, Pfeffer, Pecl, Rodax (Ogris 68), Prohaska, Zsak, Artner, Herzog (Stoger 60), Polster.

31 May, Moscow, 50,000

USSR (0) 1 *(Dobrovolski 62)*

Iceland (0) 1 *(Askelsson 86)*

USSR: Dasayev; Luzhny, Gorlukovich, Kuznetsov, Rats, Aleinikov, Bessonov (Ketaschvili 82), Dobrovolski, Litovchenko, Protasov (Savichev 82), Zavarov.
Iceland: Sigurdsson; Edvaldsson, Jonsson A, Bergsson, Gislason, Jonsson S, Thordarsson, Torfason O (Kristiansson 82), Arnthorsson, Gretarsson, Torfason G (Askelsson 69).

14 June, Reykjavik, 15,000

Iceland (0) 0

Austria (0) 0

Iceland: Sigurdsson; Edvaldsson, Bergsson, Gislason (Thorkelsson 65), Siggi Jonsson, Thordarsson, Saevar Jonsson, Arnthorsson, Sigurvinsson, Gretarsson, Torfason G.
Austria: Lindenberger; Pecl, Weber, Pfeffer, Hortnagl (Herzog 36), Russ, Zsak, Artner, Prohaska, Polster, Rodax (Ogris 46).

	P	*W*	*D*	*L*	*F*	*A*	*Pts*
USSR	5	3	2	0	8	2	8
Turkey	5	2	1	2	8	6	5
Austria	4	1	2	1	4	5	4
Iceland	5	0	4	1	3	5	4
East Germany	5	1	1	3	4	9	3

Group 4 *(West Germany, Holland, Wales, Finland)*

31 August, Helsinki, 31,693

Finland (0) 0

West Germany (2) 4 *(Voller 6, 15, Matthaus 52, Riedle 86)*

Finland: Laukkanen; Europaeus, Hannikainen (Lipponen 43), Lahtinen, Petaja, Myyry, Pekonen, Ukkonen (Alatensio 62), Hjelm, Rantanen, Paatelainen.
West Germany: Illgner; Brehme, Gortz, Kohler, Fach, Buchwald (Rolff 26), Littbarski, Hassler, Voller, Matthaus, Eckstein (Riedle 75).

14 September, Amsterdam, 58,000

Holland (0) 1 *(Gullit 82)*

Wales (0) 0

Holland: Van Breukelen; Van Aerle, Rijkaard, Koeman R, Van Tiggelen, Vanenburg (Kieft 66), Wouters, Koeman E, Kruzen, Gullit, Van Basten.
Wales: Southall; Hall, Blackmore, Williams, Knill, Davies, Horne, Nicholas, Rush, Hughes (Saunders 76), Aizlewood.

19 October, Swansea, 9603

Wales (2) 2 *(Saunders (pen) 16, Lahtinen (og) 40)*

Finland (2) 2 *(Ukkonen 8, Paatelainen 45)*

Wales: Southall; Hall (Bowen 59), Blackmore, Nicholas, Van Den Hauwe, Ratcliffe, Horne, Saunders, Rush, Hughes, Pascoe.
Finland: Huttunen; Pekonen, Lahtinen, Europaeus, Kanerva, Myyry (Lipponen 86), Holmgren, Ukkonen, Petaja (Rantanen 61), Paatelainen, Hjelm.

19 October, Munich, 73,000

West Germany (0) 0

Holland (0) 0

West Germany: Illgner; Fach, Kohler, Buchwald, Berthold, Hassler, Matthaus, Thon, Brehme, Klinsmann (Mill 67), Voller.
Holland: Van Breukelen; Van Tiggelen, Koeman R, Rijkaard, Vanenburg, Van Aerle (Winter 20), Wouters, Koeman E, Silooy, Van Basten, Bosman.

26 April, Rotterdam, 53,000

Holland (0) 1 *(Van Basten 87)*

West Germany (0) 1 *(Riedle 68)*

Holland: Hiele; Van Aerle, Van Tiggelen, Koeman R, Rijkaard, Hofkens (Rutjes 84), Vanenburg, Koeman E, Van Basten, Winter, Huistra (Eykelkamp 75).
West Germany: Illgner; Berthold, Brehme, Kohler (Rolff 75), Reuter, Buchwald, Riedle, Moller, Voller (Klinsmann 33), Matthaus, Hassler.

31 May, Cardiff, 25,000

Wales (0) 0

West Germany (0) 0

Wales: Southall; Phillips, Blackmore (Bowen 82), Ratcliffe, Aizlewood, Nicholas, Saunders, Horne, Rush, Hughes, Williams (Pascoe 82).
West Germany: Illgner; Berthold, Reinhardt, Buchwald, Reuter, Fach, Hassler, Moller, Brehme, Riedle (Klinsmann 77), Voller.

31 May, Helsinki, 48,000

Finland (0) 0

Holland (0) 1 *(Kieft 87)*

Finland: Laukkanen; Kanerva, Europaeus, Heikkinen, Ikalainen, Holmgren, Ukkonen (Tornvall 68), Hjelm (Petaja 83), Lipponen, Paatelainen, Myyry.
Holland: Van Breukelen; Koeman R, Van Tiggelen, Rutjes, Van Aerle, Vanenburg (Huistra 83), Rijkaard, Koeman E, Ellerman (Gullit 66), Van Basten, Kieft.

	P	*W*	*D*	*L*	*F*	*A*	*Pts*
Holland	4	2	2	0	3	1	6
West Germany	4	1	3	0	5	1	5
Wales	3	0	2	1	2	3	2
Finland	3	0	1	2	2	7	1

Remaining fixtures: 6.9.89 Finland v Wales; 4.10.89 West Germany v Finland; 11.10.89 Wales v Holland; 15.11.89 West Germany v Wales; Holland v Finland.

Group 5 *(France, Scotland, Yugoslavia, Norway, Cyprus)*

14 September, Oslo, 22,769

Norway (1) 1 *(Fjortoft 44)*

Scotland (1) 2 *(McStay 14, Johnston 62)*

Norway: Thorstvedt; Henriksen, Johnsen, Bratseth, Giske, Osvold, Brandhaug, Loken, Sorloth, Sundby (Berg 2, Jakobsen 84), Fjortoft.
Scotland: Leighton; Nicol, Malpas, Gillespie, McLeish, Miller, Aitken (Durrant 55), McStay, Johnston, McClair, Gallacher.

28 September, Paris, 25,000

France (0) 1 *(Papin 84 (pen))*

Norway (0) 0

France: Bats; Amoros, Boli (Kastendeuch 63), Casoni, Sonor, Sauzee, Bravo, Dib, Passi (Paille 76), Papin, Xuereb.
Norway: Thorstvedt; Henriksen (Halle), Johnsen, Kojedal, Giske, Osvold (Gulbrandsen 81), Brandhaug, Bratseth, Berg, Sorloth, Jakobsen.

19 October, Hampden Park, 42,771

Scotland (1) 1 *(Johnston 17)*

Yugoslavia (1) 1 *(Katanec 36)*

Scotland: Goram; Gough, Malpas, Nicol, McLeish, Miller, Aitken (Speedie 70), McStay, Johnston, McClair, Bett (McCoist 55).
Yugoslavia: Ivkovic; Stanojkovic, Spasic (Sabanadzovic 83), Jozic, Hadzibegic, Radanovic, Stojkovic, Katanec, Cvetkovic (Jankovic M 89), Bazdarevic, Zlatko Vujovic.

22 October, Nicosia, 3000

Cyprus (0) 1 *(Pittas (pen) 78)*

France (1) 1 *(Xuereb 44)*

Cyprus: Pantzarias; Christodolu, Stavru, Miamiliotis, Pittas, Petsas, Yiangudakis, Nikolau, Kantilos, Savva, Christofi (Ioannu 77).
France: Bats; Sonor, Casoni, Boli, Amoros, Bravo (Paille 80), Dib, Sauzee, Passi (Vercruysse 72), Papin, Xuereb.

2 November, Limassol, 7767

Cyprus (0) 0

Norway (0) 3 *(Sorloth 56, 78, Osvold 89)*

Cyprus: Pantzarias; Pittas, Miamiliotis, Christodolu (Kastanis 25), Stavrou, Yiangudakis, Kantilos (Koliandris 31), Savva, Savvides, Nikolau, Christofi.
Norway: Thorstvedt; Lokken, Kojedal, Bratseth, Halle, Osvold, Brandhaug, Halvorsen, Gulbrandsen, Sorloth, Agdestein.

19 November, Belgrade, 16,000

Yugoslavia (1) 3 *(Spasic 11, Susic 76, Stojkovic 82)*

France (1) 2 *(Perez 3, Sauzee 68)*

Yugoslavia: Ivkovic; Stanojkovic, Spasic (Juric 55), Hadzibegic, Jozic, Stojkovic, Susic, Bazdarevic, Katanec, Cvetkovic (Savicevic 70), Zlatko Vujovic.
France: Bats; Roche, Boli, Kastendeuch, Amoros, Ferreri (Papin 78), Dib, Sauzee, Tigana, Paille, Perez (Bravo 69).

11 December, Rijeka, 9000

Yugoslavia (3) 4 *(Savicevic 13, 33, 82, Hadzibegic 44 (pen))*

Cyprus (0) 0

Yugoslavia: Ivkovic; Stanojkovic, Spasic (Juric 46), Brnovic, Hadzibegic, Josic, Stojkovic, Susic, Savicevic, Bazdarevic, Zlatko Vujovic.
Cyprus: Pantzarias; Antonionios, Pittas, Papacoats, Stavrou, Yiangudakis, Savva, Nikolau, Christodolu (Kastanas 65), Ioannu (Petsas 77), Tsingis.

8 February, Limassol, 25,000

Cyprus (1) 2 *(Koliandris 14, Ioannu 47)*

Scotland (1) 3 *(Johnston 9, Gough 54, 96 – injury time)*

Cyprus: Pantzarias, Pittas, Miamiliotis, Christodolu, Socratous, Yiangudakis, Koliandris, Savva (Petsas 36), Savvides, Nikolau, Ioannu.
Scotland: Leighton; Gough, Malpas, Aitken, McLeish, Narey, Nicol (Ferguson I 9), McStay, McClair, Speedie (McInally 68), Johnston.

8 March, Hampden Park, 65,204

Scotland (1) 2 *(Johnston 28, 52)*

France (0) 0

Scotland: Leighton; Gough, Malpas, Aitken, McLeish, Gillespie, Nicol, McStay, McCoist (McClair 69), Ferguson (Strachan 56), Johnston.
France: Bats; Amoros, Silvestre, Sonor, Battiston, Sauzee, Durand (Paille 57), Laurey, Papin, Blanc, Xuereb (Perez 70).

26 April, Hampden Park, 50,081

Scotland (1) 2 *(Johnston 26, McCoist 63)*

Cyprus (0) 1 *(Nicolau 62)*

Scotland: Leighton; Gough, Malpas, Aitken, McLeish, McPherson, Nevin (Nicholas 74), McStay, Johnston, McCoist, Durie (Speedie 59).
Cyprus: Charitou; Castanas, Pittas (Elia 64), Christodolou, Michael, Yiangudakis, Petsas, Nicolau, Savvides, Ioannou Y, Kollandris.

29 April, Paris, 39,469

France (0) 0

Yugoslavia (0) 0

France: Bats; Amoros, Sonor, Boli, Battison, Sauzee, Xuereb (Deschamps 76), Durand (Cocard 46), Paille, Blanc, Perez.
Yugoslavia: Ivkovic; Stanojkovic, Spasic, Katanec, Hadzibegic, Josic, Zoran Vujovic, Susic, Bazdarevic, Stojkovic, Zlatko Vujovic (Brnovic 85).

21 May, Oslo, 10,273

Norway (3) 3 *(Osvold 17, Sorloth 34, Bratseth 35)*

Cyprus (1) 1 *(Kollandris 44)*

Norway: Thorstvedt; Halle, Kojedal, Bratseth, Giske, Lokken, Serkh (Gulbrandsen 82), Osvold, Jakobsen, Sorloth (Agdestein 61), Fjortoft.
Cyprus: Charitou; Kastanas, Pittas, Christodolou, Socratous, Yiangudakis, Kollandris (Andrelis 69), Nicolau, Savvides (Orfanides 87), Petsas, Ioannou.

14 June, Oslo, 22,740

Norway (0) 1 *(Fjortoft 90)*

Yugoslavia (1) 2 *(Stojkovic 22, Zlatko Vujovic 88)*

Norway: Ole By Rise; Halle, Bratseth, Kojedal, Giske, Lokken, Berg (Gulbrandsen 83), Osvold, Jakobsen, Sorloth (Agdestein 63), Fjortoft.
Yugoslavia: Ivkovic; Spasic, Stanojkovic, Jozic, Katanec, Hadzibegic, Zoran Vujovic, Susic (Vujavic 73), Bazdarevic, Stojkovic, Zlatko Vujovic.

	P	*W*	*D*	*L*	*F*	*A*	*Pts*
Scotland	5	4	1	0	10	5	9
Yugoslavia	5	3	2	0	10	4	8
Norway	5	2	0	3	8	6	4
France	5	1	2	2	4	6	4
Cyprus	6	0	1	5	5	16	1

Remaining fixtures: 5.9.89 Norway v France; 6.9.89 Yugoslavia v Scotland; 11.10.89 Yugoslavia v Norway; France v Scotland; 28.10.89 Cyprus v Yugoslavia; 15.11.89 Scotland v Norway; 18.11.89 France v Cyprus.

Group 6 *(Spain, Hungary, Northern Ireland, Eire, Malta)*

21 May, Belfast, 9000

Northern Ireland (3) 3 *(Quinn 14, Penney 23, Clarke 25)*

Malta (0) 0

Northern Ireland: McKnight; Donaghy, Worthington, McClelland, McDonald, O'Neill, Penney (McNally 81), Wilson D, Clarke, Quinn, Dennison (Black).
Malta: Cluett; Camilleri E (Refalo 46), Azzopardi, Galea, Brincat, Buttigieg, Busuttil, Scerri, Carabott, Scicluna, Di Giorgio (Caruana 60).

14 September, Belfast, 19,873

Northern Ireland (0) 0

Eire (0) 0

Northern Ireland: McKnight; Donaghy (Rogan), Worthington, McClelland, McDonald, O'Neill, Penney, Wilson D, Clarke, Quinn, Black.
Eire: Peyton; Morris, Hughton, McGrath, McCarthy, Moran, Houghton, Whelan, Aldridge, Cascarino, Sheedy.

19 October, Budapest, 18,000

Hungary (0) 1 *(Vincze 84)*

Northern Ireland (0) 0

Hungary: Disztl P; Sallai, Nagy, Sass, Meszoly (Dajka 46), Garaba, Kiprich, Kozma, Bognar, Detari, Hajszan (Vincze 81).
Northern Ireland: McKnight; Rogan, Worthington, McClelland, McDonald, Donaghy, Dennison, Wilson D, Clarke (Quinn 81), O'Neill (Wilson K 58), Black.

16 November, Seville, 50,000

Spain (0) 2 *(Manolo 52, Butragueno 66)*

Eire (0) 0

Spain: Zubizarreta; Quique Flores (Solana 84), Jimenez, Andrinua, Sanchis, Gorriz, Michel, Roberto, Martin Vazquez, Manolo (Ramon 67), Butrageuno.
Eire: Bonner; Morris, McCarthy, Staunton, O'Leary, Moran, Houghton, Sheridan (O'Brien 82), Aldridge (Quinn 65), Cascarino, Galvin.

11 December, Valletta, 12,000

Malta (0) 2 *(Busuttil 46, 90)*

Hungary (1) 2 *(Vincze 5, Kiprich 56)*

Malta: Cluett; Camilleri E (Saliba 53), Azzopardi, Galea, Camilleri S, (Vella S 70), Busuttil, Vella R, Carabott, Gregory, De Giorgio, Woods.
Hungary: Disztl P; Kozma, Disztl L, Keller, Kekesi, Csuhay, Kiprich (Pinter 85), Kovacs, Czucsansky, Vincze (Fischer 70), Balog.

21 December, Seville, 70,000

Spain (1) 4 *(Rogan (og) 30, Butragueno 55, Michel 60 (pen), Roberto (64)*

Northern Ireland (0) 0

Spain: Zubizarreta; Quique Flores, Jimenez, Andrinua, Gorriz, Roberto, Manolo (Julio Salinas 78), Michel, Butragueno, Martin Vazquez, Beguiristain (Serna 65).

Northern Ireland: McKnight; Rogan, Worthington, McCreery (Quinn 54), McDonald, McClelland, Donaghy (O'Neill 72), Penney, Clarke, Wilson K, Black.

22 January, Valletta, 23,000

Malta (0) 0

Spain (1) 2 *(Michel (pen) 16, Beguiristain 51)*

Malta: Cluett; Camilleri S (Camilleri E 55), Galea, Buttigieg, Azzopardi, Brincat (Scerri 46), Vella R, Gregory, Carabott, De Giorgio, Busuttil.
Spain: Zubizarreta; Quique Flores, Sanchis, Andrinua, Jimenez, Michel, Roberto, Martin Vazquez, Manolo, Butragueno (Gorriz 76), Beguiristain (Eusebio 66).

8 February, Belfast, 20,000

Northern Ireland (0) 0

Spain (1) 2 *(Andrinua 3, Manolo 84)*

Northern Ireland: McKnight; Ramsey, Rogan, Donaghy, McClelland, Wilson D (Clarke 68), Dennison (O'Neill 63), Sanchez, Quinn, Wilson K, Black.
Spain: Zubizarreta; Chendo (Eusebio 44), Jimenez, Andrinua, Serna, Gorriz, Bakero (Manolo 75), Michel, Butragueno, Roberto, Martin Vazquez.

8 March, Budapest, 20,000

Hungary (0) 0

Eire (0) 0

Hungary: Disztl P; Kozma, Disztl L, Bognar Z, Sass, Kovacs E, Detari, Hajszan, Gregor (Boda 77), Kiprich, Meszaros (Bognar G 46).
Eire: Bonner; Morris, Hughton, McGrath, McCarthy, Moran, Whelan, Houghton, Aldridge (Brady 80), Cascarino (Quinn 80), Sheedy.

23 March, Seville, 50,000

Spain (1) 4 *(Michel 38, 68 (pen), Manolo 71, 80)*

Malta (0) 0

Spain: Zubizarreta; Quique Sanchez, Jimenez, Andrinua, Roberto, Sanchis, Michel, Butragueno, Martin Vazquez (Eusebio 68), Beguiristain (Eloy 68), Manolo.
Malta: Cluett; Camilleri E, Azzopardi A (Cauchi 30), Buttigieg, Galea, Vella R, De Giorgio, Scerri C, Carabott, Gregory, Busuttil.

12 April, Budapest, 15,000

Hungary (0) 1 *(Boda 49)*

Malta (1) 1 *(Busuttil 7)*

Hungary: Disztl P; Kozma (Kiprich 57), Keller, Disztl L, Kovacs E, Bognar Z, Boda, Bognar G, Sass (Fischer 46), Detari, Hajszan.
Malta: Cluett; Camilleri E, Azzopardi A, Galea, Cauchi (Vella S 46), Buttigieg, Busuttil, Vella R, Carabott, Scerri, Gregory.

26 April, Valletta, 15,000

Malta (0) 0

Northern Ireland (0) 2 *(Clarke 55, O'Neill 73)*

Malta: Cluett; Buttigieg, Camilleri E, Cauchi (Vella S 62), Galea, De Giorgio, Scerri, Vella R, Busuttil, Gregory, Carabott (Delia 78).

Northern Ireland: Wright; Donaghy, Worthington (Rogan 86), McCreery, McClelland, Dennison, Wilson D, Quinn, Clarke, Sanchez (O'Neill 70), Wilson K.

26 April, Dublin, 49,160

Eire (1) 1 *(Michel (og) 15)*

Spain (0) 0

Eire: Bonner; Hughton, Staunton, McCarthy, Moran, Whelan, McGrath, Houghton, Stapleton (Townsend 69), Cascarino, Sheedy.
Spain: Zubizarreta; Quique Sanchez (Eusebio 69), Jimenez, Serna, Sanchis, Gorriz, Manolo, Michel, Butragueno (Julio Salinas 70), Roberto, Martin Vazquez.

28 May, Dublin, 49,000

Eire (1) 2 *(Houghton 32, Moran 55)*

Malta (0) 0

Eire: Bonner; Hughton, Staunton, O'Leary, Moran, Whelan, McGrath, Houghton (Townsend 70), Stapleton (Aldridge 27), Cascarino, Sheedy.
Malta: Cluett; Camilleri E, Azzopardi (Carabott 65), Galea, Vella S, Buttigieg, Busuttil, Vella R, Scerri, De Giorgio, Gregory.

4 June, Dublin, 49,000

Eire (1) 2 *(McGrath 33, Cascarino 80)*

Hungary (0) 0

Eire: Bonner; Hughton, Staunton, O'Leary, McGrath (Morris 80), Moran, Houghton, Townsend, Aldridge (Brady 74), Cascarino, Sheedy.
Hungary: Disztl P; Bognar Z, Fitos, Disztl L, Garaba, Kozma, Meszaros (Vincze 71), Detari, Czehi (Bognar G 66), Keller, Boda.

	P	*W*	*D*	*L*	*F*	*A*	*Pts*
Spain	6	5	0	1	14	1	10
Eire	6	3	2	1	5	2	8
Northern Ireland	6	2	1	3	5	7	5
Hungary	5	1	3	1	4	5	5
Malta	6	0	2	4	3	14	2

Remaining fixtures: 6.9.89 Northern Ireland v Hungary; 11.10.89 Hungary v Spain; Eire v Northern Ireland; 15.11.89 Spain v Hungary; Malta v Eire.

Group 7 *(Belgium, Portugal, Czechoslovakia, Switzerland, Luxemborg)*

21 September, Luxembourg, 2500

Luxembourg (0) 1 *(Langers 80)*

Switzerland (3) 4 *(Sutter A 15 sec, Turkyilmaz 21 (pen), 53, Sutter B 28)*

Luxembourg: Van Rijswijk; Meunier, Bossi, Weis, Petry, Girres (Scuto 63), Hellers, Jeitz, Scholten, Langers, Krings (Morocutti 73).
Switzerland: Corminboeuf; Geiger, Tschuppert, Martin Weber, Mottiez, Andermatt (Lei-Ravello 70), Hermann, Favre, Sutter B, Turkyilmaz, Sutter A (Bonvin 79).

19 October, Brussels, 14,450

Belgium (1) 1 *(Vervoort 30)*

Switzerland (0) 0

Belgium: Bodart; Grun, Clijsters, Demol, Versavel, Emmers, Van der Elst F, Scifo, Vervoort, Ceulemans, Nilis (Severeyns 76).

Switzerland: Corminboeuf; Mottiez, Geiger, Weber, Schallibaum, Andermatt (Bonvin 76), Hermann, Favre, Zuffi, Sutter B, Turkyilmaz.

18 October, Esch-sur-Alzette, 2500

Luxembourg (0) 0

Czechoslovakia (2) 2 *(Hasek 25, Chovanec 35)*

Luxembourg: Van Rijswijk; Meunier, Scheuer, Petry, Bossi, Jeitz (Girres 82), Hellers, Weis, Scholten, Langers, Krings (Morocutti 61).
Czechoslovakia: Stejskal; Bielik, Kadlec, Hasek, Bilek, Nemecek, Fieber, Chovanec, Griga (Danek 81), Skuhravy, Weiss (Hyravy 75).

16 November, Bratislava, 48,000

Czechoslovakia (0) 0

Belgium (0) 0

Czechoslovakia: Stejskal; Bielik, Nemecek (Danek 87), Chovanec, Kadlec, Vlk, Weiss (Moravcik 80), Hasek, Bilek, Griga, Luhovy.
Belgium: Preud'homme; Demol, Gerets, Grun, Albert, Dewolf, Emmers, Veyt, Van der Elst F, Scifo (Van den Linden 75), Christiaens (Nilis 82).

16 November, Oporto, 29,000

Portugal (1) 1 *(Gomes 31)*

Luxembourg (0) 0

Portugal: Silvino; Jaime, Sobrinho, Morato, Alvaro, Rui Barros, Vitor Paneira, Nunes, Futre, Jordao (Jaime Magalhaes 46), Gomes.
Luxembourg: Van Rijswijk; Meunier, Scheuer, Petry, Bossi, Girres, Jeitz, Weis, Scholten (Thome 82), Krings (Malget 60), Langers.

15 February, Lisbon, 70,000

Portugal (0) 1 *(Paneira)*

Belgium (0) 1 *(Gerets)*

Portugal: Silvino; Joao Pinto, Oliveira, Sobrinho, Veloso, Nunes, Vitor Paneira (Cesar Brito 86), Sousa, Rui Barros, Futre (Pacheco 61), Semedo.
Belgium: Preud'homme; Gerets, Grun, De Wolf, Versavel, Emmers, Demol (Van der Linden 77), Scifo, Van der Elst, Ceulemans, De Grijse.

26 April, Lisbon, 15,000

Portugal (0) 3 *(Joao Pinto 48, Frederico 56, Vitor Paneira 69)*

Switzerland (0) 1 *(Zuffi 64)*

Portugal: Silvano; Joao Pinto, Sobrinho, Frederico (Oliveira 87), Veloso, Nunes, Andre, Vitor Paneira, Rui Barros, Sousa (Jorge Silva 46), Cesar Brito.
Switzerland: Brunner; Mottiez, Birrel (Ryf 73), Weber M, Koller, Marini, Sutter B, Hermann, Favre, Zuffi, Sutter A (Turkyilmaz 86).

29 April, Brussels, 21,000

Belgium (1) 2 *(Degryse 29, 77)*

Czechoslovakia (1) 1 *(Luhovy 41)*

Belgium: Preud'homme; Gerets, Demol, Grun, Albert, Versavel, Van der Elst F, Emmers, Ceulemans, Degryse, Nilis (Van der Linden 65).
Czechoslovakia: Stejskal; Bilek (Weiss 85), Chovanec, Kovan, Straka, Kadlec, Moravcik, Vik (Nemecek 83), Hasek, Griga, Luhovy.

9 May, Prague, 16,350

Czechoslovakia (1) 4 *(Griga 6, Skuhravy 76, 84, Bilek 81)*

Luxembourg (0) 0

Czechoslovakia: Stejskal; Bilek, Kadlec (Bielik 46), Hasek, Kocian, Nemecek (Weiss 71), Straka, Chovanec, Griga, Skuhravy, Moravcik.
Luxembourg: Van Rijswijk; Meunier, Scheuer, Petry, Bossi, Girres, Birsens, Weis, Jeitz (Salbene 76), Hellers, Krings (Malget 89).

7 June, Berne, 30,000

Switzerland (0) 0

Czechoslovakia (1) 1 *(Skuhravy 21)*

Switzerland: Brunner; Koller, Marini, Schepull, Weber, Hermann, Sutter R (Turkyilmaz 58), Geiger, Sutter A, Sutter B (Zuffi 71), Halter.
Czechoslovakia: Stejskal; Bielik, Kadlec, Kouan, Straka, Hasek, Chovanec (Nemecek 83), Moravcik, Bilek, Griga,Skuhravy (Danek 56).

1 June, Lille, 10,000

Luxembourg (0) 0

Belgium (1) 5 *(Van der Linden 13, 52, 62 (pen), 90, Vervoort 64)*

Luxembourg: Van Rijswijk; Meunier, Scheuer, Petry, Bossi, Girres, Birsens, Jeitz (Salbene 75), Scholten (Malget 83), Langers, Krings.
Belgium: Preud'homme; Gerets, Sanders, Versavel, Van der Elst F (Scifo 73), Emmers, Demol, Vervoort, De Gryse, Van der Linden, Ceulemans.

	P	*W*	*D*	*L*	*F*	*A*	*Pts*
Belgium	5	3	2	0	9	2	8
Czechoslovakia	5	3	1	1	8	2	7
Portugal	3	2	1	0	5	2	5
Switzerland	4	1	0	3	5	6	2
Luxembourg	5	0	0	5	1	16	0

Remaining fixtures: 6.9.89 Belgium v Portugal; 20.9.89 Switzerland v Portugal; 6.10.89 Czechoslovakia v Portugal; 11.10.89 Switzerland v Belgium; Luxembourg v Portugal; 25.10.89 Czechoslovakia v Switzerland; Belgium v Luxembourg; 15.11.89 Portugal v Czechoslovakia; Switzerland v Luxembourg.

ASIA

First Round

Group 1

6.1.89 Qatar (1) 1 Jordan (0) 0
6.1.89 Oman (1) 1 Iraq (1) 1
13.1.89 Oman (0) 0 Qatar (0) 0
13.1.89 Jordan (0) 0 Iraq (0) 1
20.1.89 Jordan (2) 2 Oman (0) 0
20.1.89 Qatar (0) 1 Iraq (0) 0
27.1.89 Jordan (0) 1 Qatar (0) 1
27.1.89 Iraq (1) 3 Oman (0) 1
3.2.89 Qatar (1) 3 Oman (0) 0
3.2.89 Iraq (2) 4 Jordan (0) 0
10.2.89 Oman (0) 0 Jordan (0) 2
10.2.89 Iraq (1) 2 Qatar (1) 2

Group 2 *(Bahrain withdrew)*

10.3.89 Yemen AR (0) 0 Syria (1) 1
15.3.89 Saudi Arabia (2) 5 Syria (1) 4
20.3.89 Yemen AR (0) 0 Saudi Arabia (0) 1
25.3.89 Syria (1) 2 Yemen AR (0) 0
30.3.89 Syria (0) 0 Saudi Arabia (0) 0
5.4.89 Saudi Arabia (1) 1 Yemen AR (0) 0

Group 3 *(Yemen PDR withdrew)*

6.1.89 Pakistan (0) 0 Kuwait (0) 1
13.1.89 Kuwait (1) 3 UAE (0) 2
20.1.89 UAE (2) 5 Pakistan (0) 0
27.1.89 Kuwait (1) 2 Pakistan (0) 0
3.2.89 UAE (0) 1 Kuwait (0) 0
10.2.89 Pakistan (0) 1 UAE (3) 4

Group 4 *(India withdrew)*

23.5.89 Malaysia (0) 2 Nepal (0) 0
23.5.89 Singapore (0) 0 Korea Rep (2) 3
25.5.89 Malaysia (0) 1 Singapore (0) 0
25.5.89 Nepal (0) 0 Korea Rep (5) 9
27.5.89 Singapore (2) 3 Nepal (0) 0
27.5.89 Korea Rep (1) 3 Malaysia (0) 0
3.6.89 Singapore (2) 2 Malayasia (1) 2
3.6.89 Korea Rep (3) 4 Nepal (0) 0
5.6.89 Malaysia (0) 0 Korea Rep (0) 3
5.6.89 Nepal (0) 0 Singapore (4) 7
7.6.89 Singapore (0) 0 Korea Rep (1) 3
7.6.89 Malaysia (1) 3 Nepal (0) 0

Group 5

19.2.89 Thailand (0) 1 Bangladesh (0) 0
23.2.89 China (0) 2 Bangladesh (0) 0
23.2.89 Thailand (0) 0 Iran (2) 3
27.2.89 Bangladesh (0) 1 Iran (1) 2
28.2.89 Thailand (0) 0 China (0) 3
4.3.89 Bangladesh (0) 0 China (1) 2
8.3.89 Bangladesh (2) 3 Thailand (0) 1
17.3.89 Iran (0) 1 Bangladesh (0) 0
30.5.89 Iran (2) 3 Thailand (0) 0
15.7.89 China (0) 2 Iran (0) 0
22.7.89 Iran (2) 3 China (0) 0
29.7.89 China 2 Thailand 0

Group 6

21.5.89 Indonesia (0) 0 Korea DPR (0) 0
22.5.89 Hong Kong (0) 0 Japan (0) 0
27.5.89 Hong Kong (0) 1 Korea DPR (2) 2
28.5.89 Indonesia (0) 0 Japan (0) 0
4.6.89 Hong Kong (1) 1 Indonesia (0) 1
4.6.89 Japan (0) 2 Korea DPR (0) 1
11.6.89 Japan (4) 5 Indonesia (0) 0
18.6.89 Japan (0) 0 Hong Kong (0) 0
25.6.89 Indonesia (0) 3 Hong Kong (1) 2
25.6.89 Korea DPR (1) 2 Japan (0) 0
2.7.89 Korea DPR (2) 4 Hong Kong (1) 1
9.7.89 Korea DPR 2 Indonesia 1

AFRICA

First Round

Group 1

7.8.88 Angola (0) 0 Sudan (0) 0
11.11.88 Sudan (1) 1 Angola (0) 2
Lesotho withdrew; Zimbabwe walked over
Zambia walked over; Rwanda withdrew
16.7.88 Uganda (0) 1 Malawi (0) 0
30.7.88 Malawi (2) 3 Uganda (0) 1

Group 2

3.6.88 Libya (3) 3 Burkina Faso (0) 0
3.7.88 Burkina Faso (0) 2 Libya (0) 0
7.8.88 Ghana (0) 0 Liberia (0) 0
21.8.88 Liberia (1) 2 Ghana (0) 0
5.8.88 Tunisia (2) 5 Guinea (0) 0
21.8.88 Guinea (1) 3 Tunisia (0) 0
Togo withdrew; Gabon walked over

Second Round

Group A

6.1.89 Algeria (2) 3 Zimbabwe (0) 0
8.1.89 Ivory Coast (0) 1 Libya (0) 0
20.1.89 Libya v Algeria; *Libya refused to play on the grounds that a state of war existed with the USA. Algeria were awarded the game 2-0. Libya withdrew.*
22.1.89 Zimbabwe (0) 0 Ivory Coast (0) 0
11.6.89 Ivory Coast (0) 0 Algeria (0) 0
25.6.89 Zimbabwe (0) 1 Algeria (1) 2

Group B

6.1.89 Egypt (2) 2 Liberia (0) 0
7.1.89 Kenya (0) 1 Malawi (1) 1
21.1.89 Malawi (0) 1 Egypt (0) 1
22.1.89 Liberia (0) 0 Kenya (0) 0
10.6.89 Kenya (0) 0 Egypt (0) 0
11.6.89 Liberia (1) 1 Malawi (0) 0
24.6.89 Malawi (0) 1 Kenya (0) 0
25.6.89 Liberia (1) 1 Egypt (0) 0

Group C

7.1.89 Nigeria (1) 1 Gabon (0) 0
8.1.89 Cameroon (0) 1 Angola (1) 1
22.1.89 Gabon (1) 1 Cameroon (2) 3
22.1.89 Angola (1) 2 Nigeria (0) 2
10.6.89 Nigeria (1) 2 Cameroon (0) 0
11.6.89 Angola (2) 2 Gabon (0) 0
25.6.89 Angola (1) 1 Cameroon (0) 2
25.6.89 Gabon (2) 2 Nigeria (0) 1

Group D

8.1.89 Morocco (1) 1 Zambia (0) 0
8.1.89 Zaire (2) 3 Tunisia (1) 1
22.1.89 Tunisia (2) 2 Morocco (1) 1
22.1.89 Zambia (2) 4 Zaire (1) 2
11.6.89 Zaire (0) 0 Morocco (0) 0
11.6.89 Zambia (0) 1 Tunisia (0) 0
25.6.89 Tunisia (0) 1 Zaire (0) 0
25.6.89 Zambia (1) 2 Morocco (0) 1

OCEANIA

First Round

11.12.88 Chinese Taipei (0) 0 New Zealand (2) 4
15.12.88 New Zealand (3) 4 Chinese Taipei (0) 1
(both matches played in New Zealand)
26.11.88 Fiji (0) 1 Australia (0) 0
3.12.88 Australia (2) 5 Fiji (0) 1

Second Round

5.3.89 Israel (1) 1 New Zealand (0) 0
12.3.89 Australia (2) 4 New Zealand (0) 1
19.3.89 Israel (0) 1 Australia (0) 1
2.4.89 New Zealand (1) 2 Australia (0) 0
9.4.89 New Zealand (2) 2 Israel (2) 2
16.4.89 Australia (0) 1 Israel (1) 1

Israel qualified for matches against the winner of South American Group 2.

CONCACAF

First Round

17.4.88 Guyana (0) 0 Trinidad/Tobago (2) 4
8.5.88 Trinidad/Tobago (1) 1 Guyana (0) 0
30.4.88 Cuba (0) 0 Guatemala (1) 1
15.5.88 Guatemala (0) 1 Cuba (1) 1
12.5.88 Jamaica (1) 1 Puerto Rico (0) 0
29.5.88 Puerto Rico (0) 1 Jamaica (1) 2
19.6.88 Antigua (0) 0 Netherlands Antilles (0) 1
29.7.88 Netherlands Antilles (0) 0 Antigua (1) 1
(Netherlands Antilles won 3-1 on penalties after extra time)
17.7.88 Costa Rica (1) 1 Panama (1) 1
31.7.88 Panama (0) 0 Costa Rica (1) 2

Second Round

1.10.88 Netherlands Antilles (0) 0 El Salvador (0) 1
16.10.88 El Salvador (2) 5 Netherlands Antilles (0) 0
24.7.88 Jamaica (0) 0 USA (0) 0
13.8.88 USA (1) 5 Jamaica (0) 1
30.10.88 Trinidad/Tobago (0) 0 Honduras (0) 0
13.11.88 Honduras (1) 1 Trinidad/Tobago (0) 1
Costa Rica walked over; Mexico disqualified
9.10.88 Guatemala (1) 1 Canada (0) 0
15.10.88 Canada (0) 3 Guatemala (2) 2

Third Round

19.3.89 Guatemala (1) 1 Costa Rica (0) 0
2.4.89 Costa Rica (1) 2 Guatemala (0) 1
16.4.89 Costa Rica (1) 1 USA (0) 0
30.4.89 USA (0) 1 Costa Rica (0) 0
13.5.89 USA (0) 1 Trinidad/Tobago (0) 1
28.5.89 Trinidad/Tobago (0) 1 Costa Rica (0) 1
11.6.89 Costa Rica (1) 1 Trinidad/Tobago (0) 0
17.6.89 USA (1) 2 Guatemala (1) 1
25.6.89 El Salvador 2 Costa Rica 4
(abandoned 84 mins: score stands)
16.7.89 Costa Rica (0) 1 El Salvador (0) 0

SOUTH AMERICA

(Members: 10; Entries 10); 3 or 4 teams qualify (incl. Argentina as World Champions 1986). (Argentina (World Champions 1986), Bolivia, Brazil, Chile, Colombia, Ecuador, Paraguay, Peru, Uruguay, Venezuela).

Group 1

Uruguay
Peru
Bolivia

Group 2

Paraguay
Colombia
Ecuador

Group 3

Brazil
Chile
Venezuela

The winner of Group 2 will play against the winner of Oceania/Israel

THE WORLD CUP 1930–1986

Year	Winners	Runners-up	Venue	Attendance	Referee
1930	Uruguay 4	Argentina 2	Montevideo	90,000	Langenus (B)
1934	Italy 2 *(after extra time)*	Czechoslovakia 1	Rome	50,000	Eklind (Se)
1938	Italy 4	Hungary 2	Paris	45,000	Capdeville (F)
1950	Uruguay 2	Brazil 1	Rio de Janeiro	199,854	Reader (E)
1954	West Germany 3	Hungary 2	Berne	60,000	Ling (E)
1958	Brazil 5	Sweden 2	Stockholm	49,737	Guigue (F)
1962	Brazil 3	Czechoslovakia 1	Santiago	68,679	Latychev (USSR)
1966	England 4 *(after extra time)*	West Germany 2	Wembley	93,802	Dienst (Sw)
1970	Brazil 4	Italy 1	Mexico City	107,412	Glockner (EG)
1974	West Germany 2	Holland 1	Munich	77,833	Taylor (E)
1978	Argentina 3 *(after extra time)*	Holland 1	Buenos Aires	77,000	Gonella (I)
1982	Italy 3	West Germany 1	Madrid	90,080	Coelho (Br)
1986	Argentina 3	West Germany 2	Mexico City	114,580	Filho (Br)

GOALSCORING AND ATTENDANCES IN WORLD CUP FINAL ROUNDS

	Matches	*Goals (avge)*	*Attendance (avge)*
1930, Uruguay	18	70 (3.8)	434,500 (24,138)
1934, Italy	17	70 (4.1)	395,000 (23,235)
1938, France	18	84 (4.6)	483,000 (26,833)
1950, Brazil	22	88 (4.0)	1,337,000 (60,772)
1954, Switzerland	26	140 (5.3)	943,000 (36,270)
1958, Sweden	35	126 (3.6)	868,000 (24,800)
1962, Chile	32	89 (2.7)	776,000 (24,250)
1966, England	32	89 (2.7)	1,614,677 (50,458)
1970, Mexico	32	95 (2.9)	1,673,975 (52,311)
1974, West Germany	38	97 (2.5)	1,774,022 (46,684)
1978, Argentina	38	102 (2.6)	1,610,215 (42,374)
1982, Spain	52	146 (2.8)	1,766,277 (33,967)
1986, Mexico	52	132 (2.5)	2,199,941 (42,307)

1990 FIFA WORLD CUP — FINAL COMPETITION — MATCH SCHEDULE

8.6. — 8.7. 1990

ITALIA '90

Group	Venue	FIRST PHASE: Group Matches: Friday 8 June	Saturday 9 June	Sunday 10 June	Monday 11 June	Tuesday 12 June	Wednesday 13 June	Thursday 14 June	Friday 15 June	Saturday 16 June	Sunday 17 June	Monday 18 June	Tuesday 19 June	Wednesday 20 June	Thursday 21 June	Rest Day: Friday 22 June	SECOND PHASE: Eight Finals: Saturday 23 June	Sunday 24 June	Monday 25 June	Tuesday 26 June	Rest Days: Wednesday 27 June	Thursday 28 June	Friday 29 June	Quarter Finals: Saturday 30 June	Sunday 1 July	Rest Day: Monday 2 July	THIRD PHASE: Semi-Finals: Tuesday 3 July	Wednesday 4 July	Rest Days: Thursday 5 July	Friday 6 July	3rd/4th Place: Saturday 7 July	Final: Sunday 8 July	Matches/Stadium
A	Rome, Stadio Olimpico		1 v 2					1 v 3					1 v 4			Rest Day			A1 v C3/D3/E3		Rest Day	Rest Day	Rest Day	w41 v w42		Rest Day			Rest Day	Rest Day		w49 v w50	6
A	Florence, Stadio Comunale			3 v 4					2 v 4				2 v 3			Rest Day					Rest Day	Rest Day	Rest Day	w39 v w43		Rest Day			Rest Day	Rest Day			4
B	Naples, Stadio San Paolo						5 v 7					5 v 8				Rest Day	B1 v A3/C3/D3				Rest Day	Rest Day	Rest Day		w37 v w44	Rest Day	w45 v w46		Rest Day	Rest Day			5
B	Bari, Stadio Della Vittoria		7 v 8					6 v 8				6 v 7				Rest Day	A2 v C2				Rest Day	Rest Day	Rest Day			Rest Day			Rest Day	Rest Day	l49 v l50		5
C	Turin, Stadio Comunale			9 v 10						9 v 11				9 v 12		Rest Day		C1 v A3/B3/F3			Rest Day	Rest Day	Rest Day			Rest Day		w47 v w48	Rest Day	Rest Day			5
C	Genoa, Stadio Luigi Ferraris				11 v 12					10 v 12				10 v 11		Rest Day			F2 v B2		Rest Day	Rest Day	Rest Day			Rest Day			Rest Day	Rest Day			4
D	Milan, Stadio Giuseppe Meazza	Opening Match Group B: 5 v 6		13 v 14					13 v 15				13 v 16			Rest Day		D1 v B3/E3/F3			Rest Day	Rest Day	Rest Day		w38 v w40	Rest Day			Rest Day	Rest Day			6
D	Bologna, Stadio Renato Dall' Ara		15 v 16					14 v 16					14 v 15			Rest Day				F1 v E2	Rest Day	Rest Day	Rest Day			Rest Day			Rest Day	Rest Day			4
E	Verona, Stadio Comunale Marc' Antonio Bentegodi					17 v 18					17 v 19				17 v 20	Rest Day				E1 v D2	Rest Day	Rest Day	Rest Day			Rest Day			Rest Day	Rest Day			4
E	Udine, Stadio Friuli						19 v 20				18 v 20				18 v 19	Rest Day					Rest Day	Rest Day	Rest Day			Rest Day			Rest Day	Rest Day			3
F	Cagliari, Stadio Sant' Elia				21 v 22					21 v 23					21 v 24	Rest Day					Rest Day	Rest Day	Rest Day			Rest Day			Rest Day	Rest Day			3
F	Palermo, Stadio Della Favorita					23 v 24					22 v 24				22 v 23	Rest Day					Rest Day	Rest Day	Rest Day			Rest Day			Rest Day	Rest Day			3
	Matches/Day	1	3	3	2	2	2	3	2	3	3	2	4	2	4		2	2	2	2				2	2		1	1			1	1	52

OTHER BRITISH AND IRISH INTERNATIONAL MATCHES 1988–89

Wembley, 14 September 1988, 25,837

England (1) 1 *(Webb 28)*

Denmark (0) 0

England: Shilton (Woods 46); Stevens, Pearce, Rocastle, Adams (Walker 65), Butcher, Robson, Webb, Harford (Cottee 70), Beardsley (Gascoigne 85), Hodge.
Denmark: Rasmussen; Jensen (Heintze 65), Nielsen K, Olsen L, Bartram (Jorgensen 85), Molby, Helt, Hansen, Vilfort (Kristensen 85), Elstrup, Laudrup.

Dublin, 19 October 1988, 13,000

Eire (3) 4 *(Cascarino 27, 43, Aldridge 44, Sheedy 87)*

Tunisia (0) 0

Eire: Peyton; Morris (Scully 46), McCarthy, Anderson, Staunton, Houghton (Kelly D 46), O'Brien, Sheedy, Kelly M, Cascarino (De Mange 76), Aldridge (Quinn 76).
Tunisia: Chouchane; Ouachi, Bousina, Ali Mahjoubi, Benyahia, Taoufik, Nabil, Baoueb, Mizouri, Rannane, Yahmadi.

Riyadh, 16 November 1988, 18,000

Saudi Arabia (1) 1 *(Majid Abdullah 15)*

England (0) 1 *(Adams 54)*

Saudi Arabia: Al Diaye (Al Subiani 44); Saleh, Al Nuaimah, Jameel, Jawad, Al Mutlaq, Al Mussaibeeh, Al Suwayed (Al Thinnayan 75), Majid Abdullah, Mubarak, Al Jamaan (Masa'ad 79).
England: Seaman; Sterland, Pearce, Thomas (Marwood 80), Pallister, Adams, Robson, Rocastle, Beardsley (Smith 68), Lineker, Waddle (Gascoigne 80).

Perugia, 22 December 1988, 25,600

Italy (0) 2 *(Giannini 49 (pen), Berti 70)*

Scotland (0) 0

Italy: Zenga (Tacconi 50); Bergomi (Ferrara 50), Maldini, Baresi F, Ferri,Marocchi, Crippa, Berti, Vialli, Giannini, Serena.
Scotland: Goram; Gough (Speedie 86), Malpas, Aitken, Narey, McLeish, Ferguson (Durie 75), McStay (McClair 56), MacLeod, Gallacher, Johnston.

Dublin, 7 February 1989, 22,000

Eire (0) 0

France (0) 0

Eire: Bonner; Morris, Hughton, McCarthy, McGrath, Brady, Whelan, Houghton, Stapleton (Aldridge 76), Cascarino, Townsend.
France: Bats; Amoros, Kastendeuch, Sonor,Battiston, Silvestre (Roche 74), Durand, Sauzee, Paille (Toure 46), Papin, Blanc (Vercruysse 68).

Athens, 8 February 1989, 6000

Greece (1) 1 *(Saravakos 2 (pen))*

England (1) 2 *(Barnes 9, Robson 79)*

Greece: Economopoulos; Hatzithanasiu (Manolas 72), Kutulas, Kalitzakis, Mavridis, Tsalouhides, Saravakos, Lagonidis (Borbokis 39), Samaras (Kalogeropoulos 46), Nioblias, Tsiantakis.
England: Shilton; Stevens, Pearce, Webb, Walker, Butcher, Robson, Rocastle, Smith (Beardsley 78), Lineker, Barnes.

Tel Aviv, 8 February 1989, 6000

Israel (2) 3 *Klinger 6, Alon 7, Drieks 73)*

Wales (1) 3 *(Horne 11, Aharoni (og), Allen 87)*

Israel: Gilardi; Amar, Aharoni, Klinger, Davidi, Alon, Sinai, Pizanti, Levin (Atar 79), Rosenthal, Menahem (Drieks 46).
Wales: Dibble; Hall (Slatter 68), Bowen, Nicholas, Ratcliffe, Williams (Allen M 68), Horne, Blackmore, Hughes, Saunders, Pascoe.

Wrexham, 26 April 1989, 8000

Wales (0) 0

Sweden (1) 2 *(Schiller 30, Ratcliffe (og) 56)*

Wales: Southall; Phillips, Bowen, Ratcliffe, Van den Hauwe, Nicholas (Aizlewood 67), Saunders, Horne, Rush, Hughes, Williams.
Sweden: Ravelli T; Nilsson R, Lonn, Ljung, Schiller, Limpar, Prytz, Thern, Pettersson, Magnusson (Elkstrom 50), Nilsson B.

Wembley, 23 May 1989, 15,628 (Rous Cup)

England (0) 0

Chile (0) 0

England: Shilton; Parker, Pearce, Webb, Walker, Butcher, Robson, Gascoigne, Clough, Fashanu (Cottee 71), Waddle.
Chile: Rojas; Reyes, Hurtado (Vera 60), Contreras, Gonzalez, Pizarro, Rubio, Ormeno, Espinoza, Covarrubias (Letelier 46), Astengo.

Belfast, 26 May 1989, 2500

Northern Ireland (0) 0

Chile (1) 1 *(Astengo 43)*

Northern Ireland: Wright; Fleming, Rogan, Donaghy, McDonald, McCreery (O'Neill C 75), Wilson D (Dennison 75), O'Neill, Clarke, Quinn (Black 64), Wilson K (Coyle 64).
Chile: Rojas; Astengo (Olmos 46), Espinoza, Gonzalez, Contreras, Reyes, Vera, Pizarro, Hisis, Hurtado (Covarrubias 46), Letelier (Perez 85).

Hampden Park, 27 May 1989, 63,282 (Rous Cup)

Scotland (0) 0

England (1) 2 *(Waddle 20, Bull 80)*

Scotland: Leighton; McKimmie, McLeish, McPherson, Malpas, Nevin, Aitken, McStay, Connor (Grant 59), McCoist, Johnston.
England: Shilton; Stevens, Pearce, Webb, Walker, Butcher, Robson, Steven, Fashanu (Bull 31), Cottee (Gascoigne 78), Waddle.

Hampden Park, 30 May 1989, 9006 (Rous Cup)

Scotland (1) 2 *(McInally 5, MacLeod 53)*

Chile (0) 0

Scotland: Leighton; McKimmie, Malpas, Aitken, Mcleish, Gillespie (Whyte 70), Speedie (Johnston 46), Grant, MacLeod, McStay, McInally.
Chile: Rojas; Reyes, Contreras, Gonzalez, Pizarro, Rubio, Covarrubias (Letelier 46), Vera, Olmos, Hisis, Puebla.
(England won Rous Cup)

BRITISH INTERNATIONAL RESULTS 1872–1989

BRITISH INTERNATIONAL CHAMPIONSHIP 1883–1984

Year	*Champions*	*Pts*
1883–84	Scotland	6
1884–85	Scotland	5
1885–86	England	5
	Scotland	5
1886–87	Scotland	6
1887–88	England	6
1888–89	Scotland	5
1889–90	Scotland	5
	England	5
1890–91	England	6
1891–92	England	6
1892–93	England	6
1893–94	Scotland	5
1894–95	England	5
1895–96	Scotland	5
1896–97	Scotland	5
1897–98	England	6
1898–99	England	6
1899–1900	Scotland	6
1900–01	England	5
1901–02	Scotland	5
1902–03	England	4
	Ireland	4
	Scotland	4
1903–04	England	5
1904–05	England	5
1905–06	England	4
	Scotland	4
1906–07	Wales	5
1907–08	Scotland	5
	England	5
1908–09	England	6
1909–10	Scotland	4
1910–11	England	5
1911–12	England	5
	Scotland	5
1912–13	England	4
1913–14	Ireland	5
1919–20	Wales	4
1920–21	Scotland	6
1921–22	Scotland	4
1922–23	Scotland	5
1923–24	Wales	6
1924–25	Scotland	6
1925–26	Scotland	6
1926–27	Scotland	4
	England	4
1927–28	Wales	5
1928–29	Scotland	6
1929–30	England	6
1930–31	Scotland	4
	England	4
1931–32	England	6
1932–33	Wales	5
1933–34	Wales	5
1934–35	England	4
	Scotland	4
1935–36	Scotland	4
1936–37	Wales	6
1937–38	England	4
1938–39	England	4
	Scotland	4
	Wales	4
1946–47	England	5
1947–48	England	5
1948–49	Scotland	6
1949–50	England	6
1950–51	Scotland	6
1951–52	Wales	5
	England	5
1952–53	England	4
	Scotland	4
1953–54	England	6
1954–55	England	6
1955–56	England	3
	Scotland	3
	Wales	3
	N. Ireland	3
1956–57	England	5
1957–58	England	4
	N. Ireland	4
1958–59	N. Ireland	4
	England	4
1959–60	England	4
	Scotland	4
	Wales	4
1960–61	England	6
1961–62	Scotland	6
1962–63	Scotland	6
1963–64	Scotland	4
	England	4
	N. Ireland	4
1964–65	England	5
1965–66	England	5
1966–67	Scotland	5
1967–68	England	5
1968–69	England	6
1969–70	England	4
	Scotland	4
	Wales	4
1970–71	England	5
1971–72	England	4
	Scotland	4
1972–73	England	6
1973–74	England	4
	Scotland	4
1974–75	England	4
1975–76	Scotland	6
1976–77	Scotland	5
1977–78	England	6
1978–79	England	5
1979–80	N. Ireland	5
1980–81	*Not completed*	
1981–82	England	6
1982–83	England	5
1983–84	N. Ireland	3

Note: In the results that follow, WC = World Cup, EC = European Championship. For Ireland, read Northern Ireland from 1921.

ENGLAND v SCOTLAND

Played: 107; England won 43, Scotland won 40, Drawn 24. *Goals:* England 188, Scotland 168.

	E	*S*
1872 Glasgow	0	0
1873 Kennington Oval	4	2
1874 Glasgow	1	2
1875 Kennington Oval	2	2
1876 Glasgow	0	3
1877 Kennington Oval	1	3
1878 Glasgow	2	7
1879 Kennington Oval	5	4
1880 Glasgow	4	5
1881 Kennington Oval	1	6
1882 Glasgow	1	5
1883 Sheffield	2	3
1884 Glasgow	0	1
1885 Kennington Oval	1	1
1886 Glasgow	1	1
1887 Blackburn	2	3
1888 Glasgow	5	0
1889 Kennington Oval	2	3
1890 Glasgow	1	1
1891 Blackburn	2	1
1892 Glasgow	4	1
1893 Richmond	5	2
1894 Glasgow	2	2
1895 Everton	3	0
1896 Glasgow	1	2
1897 Crystal Palace	1	2
1898 Glasgow	3	1
1899 Birmingham	2	1
1900 Glasgow	1	4
1901 Crystal Palace	2	2
1902 Birmingham	2	2
1903 Sheffield	1	2
1904 Glasgow	1	0
1905 Crystal Palace	1	0
1906 Glasgow	1	2
1907 Newcastle	1	1
1908 Glasgow	1	1
1909 Crystal Palace	2	0
1910 Glasgow	0	2
1911 Everton	1	1
1912 Glasgow	1	1
1913 Chelsea	1	0
1914 Glasgow	1	3
1920 Sheffield	5	4
1921 Glasgow	0	3

1922	Aston Villa	0	1	wc1950	Glasgow	1	0	1971	Wembley	3	1
1923	Glasgow	2	2	1951	Wembley	2	3	1972	Glasgow	1	0
1924	Wembley	1	1	1952	Glasgow	2	1	1973	Glasgow	5	0
1925	Glasgow	0	2	1953	Wembley	2	2	1973	Wembley	1	0
1926	Manchester	0	1	wc1954	Glasgow	4	2	1974	Glasgow	0	2
1927	Glasgow	2	1	1955	Wembley	7	2	1975	Wembley	5	1
1928	Wembley	1	5	1956	Glasgow	1	1	1976	Glasgow	1	2
1929	Glasgow	0	1	1957	Wembley	2	1	1977	Wembley	1	2
1930	Wembley	5	2	1958	Glasgow	4	0	1978	Glasgow	1	0
1931	Glasgow	0	2	1959	Wembley	1	0	1979	Wembley	3	1
1932	Wembley	3	0	1960	Glasgow	1	1	1980	Glasgow	2	0
1933	Glasgow	1	2	1961	Wembley	9	3	1981	Wembley	0	1
1934	Wembley	3	0	1962	Glasgow	0	2	1982	Glasgow	1	0
1935	Glasgow	0	2	1963	Wembley	1	2	1983	Wembley	2	0
1936	Wembley	1	1	1964	Glasgow	0	1	1984	Glasgow	1	1
1937	Glasgow	1	3	1965	Wembley	2	2	1985	Glasgow	0	1
1938	Wembley	0	1	1966	Glasgow	4	3	1986	Wembley	2	1
1939	Glasgow	2	1	EC1967	Wembley	2	3	1987	Glasgow	0	0
1947	Wembley	1	1	EC1968	Glasgow	1	1	1988	Wembley	1	0
1948	Glasgow	2	0	1969	Wembley	4	1	1989	Glasgow	2	0
1949	Wembley	1	3	1970	Glasgow	0	0				

ENGLAND v WALES

Played: 97; England won 62, Wales won 14, Drawn 21. *Goals:* England 239, Wales 90.

		E	*W*			*E*	*W*			*E*	*W*
1879	Kennington Oval	2	1	1911	Millwall	3	0	1955	Cardiff	1	2
1880	Wrexham	3	2	1912	Wrexham	2	0	1956	Wembley	3	1
1881	Blackburn	0	1	1913	Bristol	4	3	1957	Cardiff	4	0
1882	Wrexham	3	5	1914	Cardiff	2	0	1958	Aston Villa	2	2
1883	Kennington Oval	5	0	1920	Highbury	1	2	1959	Cardiff	1	1
1884	Wrexham	4	0	1921	Cardiff	0	0	1960	Wembley	5	1
1885	Blackburn	1	1	1922	Liverpool	1	0	1961	Cardiff	1	1
1886	Wrexham	3	1	1923	Cardiff	2	2	1962	Wembley	4	0
1887	Kennington Oval	4	0	1924	Blackburn	1	2	1963	Cardiff	4	0
1888	Crewe	5	1	1925	Swansea	2	1	1964	Wembley	2	1
1889	Stoke	4	1	1926	Crystal Palace	1	3	1965	Cardiff	0	0
1890	Wrexham	3	1	1927	Wrexham	3	3	EC1966	Wembley	5	1
1891	Sunderland	4	1	1927	Burnley	1	2	EC1967	Cardiff	3	0
1892	Wrexham	2	0	1928	Swansea	3	2	1969	Wembley	2	1
1893	Stoke	6	0	1929	Chelsea	6	0	1970	Cardiff	1	1
1894	Wrexham	5	1	1930	Wrexham	4	0	1971	Wembley	0	0
1894	Queen's Club,			1931	Liverpool	3	1	1972	Cardiff	3	0
	Kensington	1	1	1932	Wrexham	0	0	wc1972	Cardiff	1	0
1896	Cardiff	9	1	1933	Newcastle	1	2	wc1973	Wembley	1	1
1897	Sheffield	4	0	1934	Cardiff	4	0	1973	Wembley	3	0
1898	Wrexham	3	0	1935	Wolverhampton	1	2	1974	Cardiff	2	0
1899	Bristol	4	0	1936	Cardiff	1	2	1975	Wembley	2	2
1900	Cardiff	1	1	1937	Middlesbrough	2	1	1976	Wrexham	2	1
1901	Newcastle	6	0	1938	Cardiff	2	4	1976	Cardiff	1	0
1902	Wrexham	0	0	1946	Manchester	3	0	1977	Wembley	0	1
1903	Portsmouth	2	1	1947	Cardiff	3	0	1978	Cardiff	3	1
1904	Wrexham	2	2	1948	Aston Villa	1	0	1979	Wembley	0	0
1905	Liverpool	3	1	wc1949	Cardiff	4	1	1980	Wrexham	1	4
1906	Cardiff	1	0	1950	Sunderland	4	2	1981	Wembley	0	0
1907	Fulham	1	1	1951	Cardiff	1	1	1982	Cardiff	1	0
1908	Wrexham	7	1	1952	Wembley	5	2	1983	Wembley	2	1
1909	Nottingham	2	0	wc1953	Cardiff	4	1	1984	Wrexham	0	1
1910	Cardiff	1	0	1954	Wembley	3	2				

ENGLAND v IRELAND

Played: 96; England won 74, Ireland won 6, Drawn 16. *Goals:* England 319, Ireland 80.

	E	*I*
1882 Belfast	13	0
1883 Liverpool	7	0
1884 Belfast	8	1
1885 Manchester	4	0
1886 Belfast	6	1
1887 Sheffield	7	0
1888 Belfast	5	1
1889 Everton	6	1
1890 Belfast	9	1
1891 Wolverhampton	6	1
1892 Belfast	2	0
1893 Birmingham	6	1
1894 Belfast	2	2
1895 Derby	9	0
1896 Belfast	2	0
1897 Nottingham	6	0
1898 Belfast	3	2
1899 Sunderland	13	2
1900 Dublin	2	0
1901 Southampton	3	0
1902 Belfast	1	0
1903 Wolverhampton	4	0
1904 Belfast	3	1
1905 Middlesbrough	1	1
1906 Belfast	5	0
1907 Everton	1	0
1908 Belfast	3	1
1909 Bradford	4	0
1910 Belfast	1	1
1911 Derby	2	1
1912 Dublin	6	1
1913 Belfast	1	2
1914 Middlesbrough	0	3
1919 Belfast	1	1
1920 Sunderland	2	0
1921 Belfast	1	1
1922 West Bromwich	2	0
1923 Belfast	1	2
1924 Everton	3	1
1925 Belfast	0	0
1926 Liverpool	3	3
1927 Belfast	0	2
1928 Everton	2	1
1929 Belfast	3	0
1930 Sheffield	5	1
1931 Belfast	6	2
1932 Blackpool	1	0
1933 Belfast	3	0
1935 Everton	2	1
1935 Belfast	3	1
1936 Stoke	3	1
1937 Belfast	5	1
1938 Manchester	7	0
1946 Belfast	7	2
1947 Everton	2	2
1948 Belfast	6	2
wc1949 Manchester	9	2
1950 Belfast	4	1
1951 Aston Villa	2	0
1952 Belfast	2	2
wc1953 Everton	3	1
1954 Belfast	2	0
1955 Wembley	3	0
1956 Belfast	1	1
1957 Wembley	2	3
1958 Belfast	3	3
1959 Wembley	2	1
1960 Belfast	5	2
1961 Wembley	1	1
1962 Belfast	3	1
1963 Wembley	8	3
1964 Belfast	4	3
1965 Wembley	2	1
EC1966 Belfast	2	0
EC1967 Wembley	2	0
1969 Belfast	3	1
1970 Wembley	3	1
1971 Belfast	1	0
1972 Wembley	0	1
1973 Everton	2	1
1974 Wembley	1	0
1975 Belfast	0	0
1976 Wembley	4	0
1977 Belfast	2	1
1978 Wembley	1	0
EC1979 Wembley	4	0
1979 Belfast	2	0
EC1979 Belfast	5	1
1980 Wembley	1	1
1982 Wembley	4	0
1983 Belfast	0	0
1984 Wembley	1	0
wc1985 Belfast	1	0
wc1985 Wembley	0	0
EC1986 Wembley	3	0
EC1987 Belfast	2	0

SCOTLAND v WALES

Played: 101; Scotland won 60, Wales won 18, Drawn 23. *Goals:* Scotland 238, Wales 111.

	S	*W*
1876 Glasgow	4	0
1877 Wrexham	2	0
1878 Glasgow	9	0
1879 Wrexham	3	0
1880 Glasgow	5	1
1881 Wrexham	5	1
1882 Glasgow	5	0
1883 Wrexham	4	1
1884 Glasgow	4	1
1885 Wrexham	8	1
1886 Glasgow	4	1
1887 Wrexham	2	0
1888 Edinburgh	5	1
1889 Wrexham	0	0
1890 Paisley	5	0
1891 Wrexham	4	3
1892 Edinburgh	6	1
1893 Wrexham	8	0
1894 Kilmarnock	5	2
1895 Wrexham	2	2
1896 Dundee	4	0
1897 Wrexham	2	2
1898 Motherwell	5	2
1899 Wrexham	6	0
1900 Aberdeen	5	2
1901 Wrexham	1	1
1902 Greenock	5	1
1903 Cardiff	1	0
1904 Dundee	1	1
1905 Wrexham	1	3
1906 Edinburgh	0	2
1907 Wrexham	0	1
1908 Dundee	2	1
1909 Wrexham	2	3
1910 Kilmarnock	1	0
1911 Cardiff	2	2
1912 Tynecastle	1	0
1913 Wrexham	0	0
1914 Glasgow	0	0
1920 Cardiff	1	1
1921 Aberdeen	2	1
1922 Wrexham	1	2
1923 Paisley	2	0
1924 Cardiff	0	2
1925 Tynecastle	3	1
1926 Cardiff	3	0
1927 Glasgow	3	0
1928 Wrexham	2	2
1929 Glasgow	4	2
1930 Cardiff	4	2
1931 Glasgow	1	1
1932 Wrexham	3	2
1933 Edinburgh	2	5
1934 Cardiff	2	3
1935 Aberdeen	3	2
1936 Cardiff	1	1
1937 Dundee	1	2
1938 Cardiff	1	2
1939 Edinburgh	3	2
1946 Wrexham	1	3
1947 Glasgow	1	2
wc1948 Cardiff	3	1
1949 Glasgow	2	0
1950 Cardiff	3	1
1951 Glasgow	0	1
wc1952 Cardiff	2	1
1953 Glasgow	3	3
1954 Cardiff	1	0
1955 Glasgow	2	0
1956 Cardiff	2	2
1957 Glasgow	1	1
1958 Cardiff	3	0
1959 Glasgow	1	1
1960 Cardiff	0	2
1961 Glasgow	2	0
1962 Cardiff	3	2
1963 Glasgow	2	1
1964 Cardiff	2	3
EC1965 Glasgow	4	1
EC1966 Cardiff	1	1
1967 Glasgow	3	2
1969 Wrexham	5	3
1970 Glasgow	0	0
1971 Cardiff	0	0
1972 Glasgow	1	0
1973 Wrexham	2	0
1974 Glasgow	2	0
1975 Cardiff	2	2
1976 Glasgow	3	1
wc1977 Glasgow	1	0
1977 Wrexham	0	0
wc1977 Liverpool	2	0
1978 Glasgow	1	1
1979 Cardiff	0	3
1980 Glasgow	1	0
1981 Swansea	0	2
1982 Glasgow	1	0
1983 Cardiff	2	0
1984 Glasgow	2	1
wc1985 Glasgow	0	1
wc1985 Cardiff	1	1

SCOTLAND v IRELAND

Played: 91; Scotland won 60, Ireland won 15, Drawn 16. *Goals:* Scotland 253, Ireland 81.

	S	*I*
1884 Belfast	5	0
1885 Glasgow	8	2
1886 Belfast	7	2
1887 Glasgow	4	1
1888 Belfast	10	2
1889 Glasgow	7	0
1890 Belfast	4	1
1891 Glasgow	2	1
1892 Belfast	3	2
1893 Glasgow	6	1
1894 Belfast	2	1
1895 Glasgow	3	1
1896 Belfast	3	3
1897 Glasgow	5	1
1898 Belfast	3	0
1899 Glasgow	9	1
1900 Belfast	3	0
1901 Glasgow	11	0
1902 Belfast	5	1
1903 Glasgow	0	2
1904 Dublin	1	1
1905 Glasgow	4	0
1906 Dublin	1	0
1907 Glasgow	3	0
1908 Dublin	5	0
1909 Glasgow	5	0
1910 Belfast	0	1
1911 Glasgow	2	0
1912 Belfast	4	1
1913 Dublin	2	1
1914 Belfast	1	1
1920 Glasgow	3	0
1921 Belfast	2	0
1922 Glasgow	2	1
1923 Belfast	1	0
1924 Glasgow	2	0
1925 Belfast	3	0
1926 Glasgow	4	0
1927 Belfast	2	0
1928 Glasgow	0	1
1929 Belfast	7	3
1930 Glasgow	3	1
1931 Belfast	0	0
1932 Glasgow	3	1
1933 Belfast	4	0
1934 Glasgow	1	2
1935 Belfast	1	2
1936 Edinburgh	2	1
1937 Belfast	3	1
1938 Aberdeen	1	1
1939 Belfast	2	0
1946 Glasgow	0	0
1947 Belfast	0	2
1948 Glasgow	3	2
1949 Belfast	8	2
1950 Glasgow	6	1
1951 Belfast	3	0
1952 Glasgow	1	1
1953 Belfast	3	1
1954 Glasgow	2	2
1955 Belfast	1	2
1956 Glasgow	1	0
1957 Belfast	1	1
1958 Glasgow	2	2
1959 Belfast	4	0
1960 Glasgow	5	2
1961 Belfast	6	1
1962 Glasgow	5	1
1963 Belfast	1	2
1964 Glasgow	3	2
1965 Belfast	2	3
1966 Glasgow	2	1
1967 Belfast	0	1
1969 Glasgow	1	1
1970 Belfast	1	0
1971 Glasgow	0	1
1972 Glasgow	2	0
1973 Glasgow	1	2
1974 Glasgow	0	1
1975 Glasgow	3	0
1976 Glasgow	3	0
1977 Glasgow	3	0
1978 Glasgow	1	1
1979 Glasgow	1	0
1980 Belfast	0	1
wc1981 Glasgow	1	1
1981 Glasgow	2	0
wc1981 Belfast	0	0
1982 Belfast	1	1
1983 Glasgow	0	0
1984 Belfast	0	2

WALES v IRELAND

Played: 90; Wales won 42, Ireland won 27, Drawn 21. *Goals:* Wales 181, Ireland 126.

	W	*I*
1882 Wrexham	7	1
1883 Belfast	1	1
1884 Wrexham	6	0
1885 Belfast	8	2
1886 Wrexham	5	0
1887 Belfast	1	4
1888 Wrexham	11	0
1889 Belfast	3	1
1890 Shrewsbury	5	2
1891 Belfast	2	7
1892 Bangor	1	1
1893 Belfast	3	4
1894 Swansea	4	1
1895 Belfast	2	2
1896 Wrexham	6	1
1897 Belfast	3	4
1898 Llandudno	0	1
1899 Belfast	0	1
1900 Llandudno	2	0
1901 Belfast	1	0
1902 Cardiff	0	3
1903 Belfast	0	2
1904 Bangor	0	1
1905 Belfast	2	2
1906 Wrexham	4	4
1907 Belfast	3	2
1908 Aberdare	0	1
1909 Belfast	3	2
1910 Wrexham	4	1
1911 Belfast	2	1
1912 Cardiff	2	3
1913 Belfast	1	0
1914 Wrexham	1	2
1920 Belfast	2	2
1921 Swansea	2	1
1922 Belfast	1	1
1923 Wrexham	0	3
1924 Belfast	1	0
1925 Wrexham	0	0
1926 Belfast	0	3
1927 Cardiff	2	2
1928 Belfast	2	1
1929 Wrexham	2	2
1930 Belfast	0	7
1931 Wrexham	3	2
1932 Belfast	0	4
1933 Wrexham	4	1
1934 Belfast	1	1
1935 Wrexham	3	1
1936 Belfast	2	3
1937 Wrexham	4	1
1938 Belfast	0	1
1939 Wrexham	3	1
1947 Belfast	1	2
1948 Wrexham	2	0
1949 Belfast	2	0
wc1950 Wrexham	0	0
1951 Belfast	2	1
1952 Swansea	3	0
1953 Belfast	3	2
wc1954 Wrexham	1	2
1955 Belfast	3	2
1956 Cardiff	1	1
1957 Belfast	0	0
1958 Cardiff	1	1
1959 Belfast	1	4
1960 Wrexham	3	2
1961 Belfast	5	1
1962 Cardiff	4	0
1963 Belfast	4	1
1964 Cardiff	2	3
1965 Belfast	5	0
1966 Cardiff	1	4
EC1967 Belfast	0	0
EC1968 Wrexham	2	0
1969 Belfast	0	0
1970 Swansea	1	0
1971 Belfast	0	1
1972 Wrexham	0	0
1973 Everton	0	1
1974 Wrexham	1	0
1975 Belfast	0	1
1976 Swansea	1	0
1977 Belfast	1	1
1978 Wrexham	1	0
1979 Belfast	1	1
1980 Cardiff	0	1
1982 Wrexham	3	0
1983 Belfast	1	0
1984 Swansea	1	1

OTHER BRITISH INTERNATIONAL RESULTS 1908–1988

ENGLAND

v ALBANIA

			E	*A*
WC1989	8 Mar	Tirana	2	0
WC1989	26 Apr	Wembley	5	0

v ARGENTINA

			E	*A*
1951	9 May	Wembley	2	1
1953	17 May	Buenos Aires	0	0
(abandoned after 21 mins)				
WC1962	2 June	Rancagua	3	1
1964	6 June	Rio de Janeiro	0	1
WC1966	23 July	Wembley	1	0
1974	22 May	Wembley	2	2
1977	12 June	Buenos Aires	1	1
1980	13 May	Wembley	3	1
WC1986	22 June	Mexico City	1	2

v AUSTRALIA

			E	*A*
1980	31 May	Sydney	2	1
1983	11 June	Sydney	0	0
1983	15 June	Brisbane	1	0
1983	18 June	Melbourne	1	1

v AUSTRIA

			E	*A*
1908	6 June	Vienna	6	1
1908	8 June	Vienna	11	1
1909	1 June	Vienna	8	1
1930	14 May	Vienna	0	0
1932	7 Dec	Chelsea	4	3
1936	6 May	Vienna	1	2
1951	28 Nov	Wembley	2	2
1952	25 May	Vienna	3	2
WC1958	15 June	Boras	2	2
1961	27 May	Vienna	1	3
1962	4 Apr	Wembley	3	1
1965	20 Oct	Wembley	2	3
1967	27 May	Vienna	1	0
1973	26 Sept	Wembley	7	0
1979	13 June	Vienna	3	4

v BELGIUM

			E	*B*
1921	21 May	Brussels	2	0
1923	19 Mar	Highbury	6	1
1923	1 Nov	Antwerp	2	2
1924	8 Dec	West Bromwich	4	0
1926	24 May	Antwerp	5	3
1927	11 May	Brussels	9	1
1928	19 May	Antwerp	3	1
1929	11 May	Brussels	5	1
1931	16 May	Brussels	4	1
1936	9 May	Brussels	2	3
1947	21 Sept	Brussels	5	2
1950	18 May	Brussels	4	1
1952	26 Nov	Wembley	5	0
WC1954	17 June	Basle	4	4*
1964	21 Oct	Wembley	2	2
1970	25 Feb	Brussels	3	1
EC1980	12 June	Turin	1	1

**After extra time*

v BOHEMIA

			E	*B*
1908	13 June	Prague	4	0

v BRAZIL

			E	*B*
1956	9 May	Wembley	4	2
WC1958	11 June	Gothenburg	0	0
1959	13 May	Rio de Janeiro	0	2
WC1962	10 June	Vina del Mar	1	3
1963	8 May	Wembley	1	1
1964	30 May	Rio de Janeiro	1	5
1969	12 June	Rio de Janeiro	1	2
WC1970	7 June	Guadalajara	0	1
1976	23 May	Los Angeles	0	1
1977	8 June	Rio de Janeiro	0	0
1978	19 Apr	Wembley	1	1
1981	12 May	Wembley	0	1
1984	10 June	Rio de Janeiro	2	0
1987	19 May	Wembley	1	1

v BULGARIA

			E	*B*
WC1962	7 June	Rancagua	0	0
1968	11 Dec	Wembley	1	1
1974	1 June	Sofia	1	0
EC1979	6 June	Sofia	3	0
EC1979	22 Nov	Wembley	2	0

v CANADA

			E	*C*
1986	24 May	Burnaby	1	0

v CHILE

			E	*C*
WC1950	25 June	Rio de Janeiro	2	0
1953	24 May	Santiago	2	1
1984	17 June	Santiago	0	0
1989	23 May	Wembley	0	0

v COLOMBIA

			E	*C*
1970	20 May	Bogota	4	0
1988	24 May	Wembley	1	1

v CYPRUS

			E	*C*
EC1975	16 Apr	Wembley	5	0
EC1975	11 May	Limassol	1	0

v CZECHOSLOVAKIA

			E	*C*
1934	16 May	Prague	1	2
1937	1 Dec	Tottenham	5	4
1963	29 May	Bratislava	4	2
1966	2 Nov	Wembley	0	0
WC1970	11 June	Guadalajara	1	0
1973	27 May	Prague	1	1
EC1974	30 Oct	Wembley	3	0
EC1975	30 Oct	Bratislava	1	2
1978	29 Nov	Wembley	1	0
WC1982	20 June	Bilbao	2	0

v DENMARK

			E	*D*
1948	26 Sept	Copenhagen	0	0
1955	2 Oct	Copenhagen	5	1
WC1956	5 Dec	Wolverhampton	5	2
WC1957	15 May	Copenhagen	4	1
1966	3 July	Copenhagen	2	0
EC1978	20 Sept	Copenhagen	4	3
EC1979	12 Sept	Wembley	1	0
EC1982	22 Sept	Copenhagen	2	2
EC1983	21 Sept	Wembley	0	1
1988	14 Sept	Wembley	1	0
1989	7 June	Copenhagen	1	1

v ECUADOR

			E	*Ec*
1970	24 May	Quito	2	0

v EGYPT

			E	*Eg*
1986	29 Jan	Cairo	4	0

v FIFA

			E	*FIFA*
1938	26 Oct	Highbury	3	0
1953	21 Oct	Wembley	4	4
1963	23 Oct	Wembley	2	1

v FINLAND

			E	*F*
1937	20 May	Helsinki	8	0
1956	20 May	Helsinki	5	1
1966	26 June	Helsinki	3	0
WC1976	13 June	Helsinki	4	1
WC1976	13 Oct	Wembley	2	1
1982	3 June	Helsinki	4	1
WC1984	17 Oct	Wembley	5	0
WC1985	22 May	Helsinki	1	1

v FRANCE

			E	F
1923	10 May	Paris	4	1
1924	17 May	Paris	3	1
1925	21 May	Paris	3	2
1927	26 May	Paris	6	0
1928	17 May	Paris	5	1
1929	9 May	Paris	4	1
1931	14 May	Paris	2	5
1933	6 Dec	Tottenham	4	1
1938	26 May	Paris	4	2
1947	3 May	Highbury	3	0
1949	22 May	Paris	3	1
1951	3 Oct	Highbury	2	2
1955	15 May	Paris	0	1
1957	27 Nov	Wembley	4	0
EC1962	3 Oct	Sheffield	1	1
EC1963	27 Feb	Paris	2	5
WC1966	20 July	Wembley	2	0
1969	12 Mar	Wembley	5	0
WC1982	16 June	Bilbao	3	1
1984	29 Feb	Paris	0	2

v GERMANY

			E	G
1930	10 May	Berlin	3	3
1935	4 Dec	Tottenham	3	0
1938	14 May	Berlin	6	3

v EAST GERMANY

			E	EG
1963	2 June	Leipzig	2	1
1970	25 Nov	Wembley	3	1
1974	29 May	Leipzig	1	1
1984	12 Sept	Wembley	1	0

WEST GERMANY

			E	WG
1954	1 Dec	Wembley	3	1
1956	26 May	Berlin	3	1
1965	12 May	Nuremberg	1	0
1966	23 Feb	Wembley	1	0
WC1966	30 July	Wembley	4	2*
1968	1 June	Hanover	0	1
WC1970	14 June	Leon	2	3*
EC1972	29 Apr	Wembley	1	3
EC1972	13 May	Berlin	0	0
1975	12 Mar	Wembley	2	0
1978	22 Feb	Munich	1	2
WC1982	29 June	Madrid	0	0
1982	13 Oct	Wembley	1	2
1985	12 June	Mexico City	3	0
1987	9 Sept	Dusseldorf	1	3

*After extra time

v GREECE

			E	G
EC1971	21 Apr	Wembley	3	0
EC1971	1 Dec	Athens	2	0
EC1982	17 Nov	Athens	3	0
EC1983	30 Mar	Wembley	0	0
1989	8 Feb	Athens	2	1

v HOLLAND

			E	N
1935	18 May	Amsterdam	1	0
1946	27 Nov	Huddersfield	8	2
1964	9 Dec	Amsterdam	1	1
1969	5 Nov	Amsterdam	1	0
1970	14 Jan	Wembley	0	0
1977	9 Feb	Wembley	0	2
1982	25 May	Wembley	2	0
1988	23 Mar	Wembley	2	2
EC1988	15 June	Dusseldorf	1	3

v HUNGARY

			E	H
1908	10 June	Budapest	7	0
1909	29 May	Budapest	4	2
1909	31 May	Budapest	8	2
1934	10 May	Budapest	1	2
1936	2 Dec	Highbury	6	2
1953	25 Nov	Wembley	3	6
1954	23 May	Budapest	1	7
1960	22 May	Budapest	0	2
WC1962	31 May	Rancagua	1	2
1965	5 May	Wembley	1	0
1978	24 May	Wembley	4	1
WC1981	6 June	Budapest	3	1
WC1982	18 Nov	Wembley	1	0
EC1983	27 Apr	Wembley	2	0
EC1983	12 Oct	Budapest	3	0
1988	27 Apr	Budapest	0	0

v ICELAND

			E	I
1982	2 June	Reykjavik	1	1

v REPUBLIC OF IRELAND

			E	RI
1946	30 Sept	Dublin	1	0
1949	21 Sept	Everton	0	2
WC1957	8 May	Wembley	5	1
WC1957	19 May	Dublin	1	1
1964	24 May	Dublin	3	1
1976	8 Sept	Wembley	1	1
EC1978	25 Oct	Dublin	1	1
EC1980	6 Feb	Wembley	2	0
1985	26 Mar	Wembley	2	1
EC1988	12 June	Stuttgart	0	1

v ISRAEL

			E	Is
1986	26 Feb	Ramat Gan	2	1
1988	17 Feb	Tel Aviv	0	0

v ITALY

			E	I
1933	13 May	Rome	1	1
1934	14 Nov	Highbury	3	2
1939	13 May	Milan	2	2
1948	16 May	Turin	4	0
1949	30 Nov	Tottenham	2	0
1952	18 May	Florence	1	1
1959	6 May	Wembley	2	2
1961	24 May	Rome	3	2
1973	14 June	Turin	0	2
1973	14 Nov	Wembley	0	1
1976	28 May	New York	3	2
WC1976	17 Nov	Rome	0	2
WC1977	16 Nov	Wembley	2	0
EC1980	15 June	Turin	0	1
1985	6 June	Mexico City	1	2

v KUWAIT

			E	K
WC1982	25 June	Bilbao	1	0

v LUXEMBOURG

			E	L
1927	21 May	Luxembourg	5	2
WC1960	19 Oct	Luxembourg	9	0
WC1961	28 Sept	Highbury	4	1
WC1977	30 Mar	Wembley	5	0
WC1977	12 Oct	Luxembourg	2	0
EC1982	15 Dec	Wembley	9	0
EC1983	16 Nov	Luxembourg	4	0

v MALTA

			E	M
EC1971	3 Feb	Valletta	1	0
EC1971	12 May	Wembley	5	0

v MEXICO

			E	M
1959	24 May	Mexico City	1	2
1961	10 May	Wembley	8	0
WC1966	16 July	Wembley	2	0
1969	1 June	Mexico City	0	0
1985	9 June	Mexico City	0	1
1986	17 May	Los Angeles	3	0

v MOROCCO

			E	Mo
WC1986	6 June	Monterrey	0	0

v NORWAY

			E	N
1937	14 May	Oslo	6	0
1938	9 Nov	Newcastle	4	0
1949	18 May	Oslo	4	1
1966	29 June	Oslo	6	1
wc1980	10 Sept	Wembley	4	0
wc1981	9 Sept	Oslo	1	2

v PARAGUAY

			E	Pa
wc1986	18 June	Mexico City	3	0

v PERU

			E	P
1959	17 May	Lima	1	4
1962	20 May	Lima	4	0

v POLAND

			E	P
1966	5 Jan	Everton	1	1
1966	5 July	Chorzow	1	0
wc1973	6 June	Chorzow	0	2
wc1973	17 Oct	Wembley	1	1
wc1986	11 June	Monterrey	3	0
wc1989	3 June	Wembley	3	0

v PORTUGAL

			E	P
1947	25 May	Lisbon	10	0
1950	14 May	Lisbon	5	3
1951	19 May	Everton	5	2
1955	22 May	Oporto	1	3
1958	7 May	Wembley	2	1
wc1961	21 May	Lisbon	1	1
wc1961	25 Oct	Wembley	2	0
1964	17 May	Lisbon	4	3
1964	4 June	São Paulo	1	1
wc1966	26 July	Wembley	2	1
1969	10 Dec	Wembley	1	0
1974	3 Apr	Lisbon	0	0
EC1974	20 Nov	Wembley	0	0
EC1975	19 Nov	Lisbon	1	1
wc1986	3 June	Monterrey	0	1

v RUMANIA

			E	R
1939	24 May	Bucharest	2	0
1968	6 Nov	Bucharest	0	0
1969	15 Jan	Wembley	1	1
wc1970	2 June	Guadalajara	1	0
wc1980	15 Oct	Bucharest	1	2
wc1981	29 April	Wembley	0	0
wc1985	1 May	Bucharest	0	0
wc1985	11 Sept	Wembley	1	1

v SAUDI ARABIA

			E	SA
1988	16 Nov	Riyadh	1	1

v SPAIN

			E	S
1929	15 May	Madrid	3	4
1931	9 Dec	Highbury	7	1
wc1950	2 July	Rio de Janeiro	0	1
1955	18 May	Madrid	1	1
1955	30 Nov	Wembley	4	1
1960	15 May	Madrid	0	3
1960	26 Oct	Wembley	4	2
1965	8 Dec	Madrid	2	0
1967	24 May	Wembley	2	0
EC1968	3 Apr	Wembley	1	0
EC1968	8 May	Madrid	2	1
1980	26 Mar	Barcelona	2	0
EC1980	18 June	Naples	2	1
1981	25 Mar	Wembley	1	2
wc1982	5 July	Madrid	0	0
1987	18 Feb	Madrid	4	2

v SWEDEN

			E	S
1923	21 May	Stockholm	4	2
1923	24 May	Stockholm	3	1
1937	17 May	Stockholm	4	0
1947	19 Nov	Highbury	4	2
1949	13 May	Stockholm	1	3
1956	16 May	Stockholm	0	0
1959	28 Oct	Wembley	2	3
1965	16 May	Gothenburg	2	1
1968	22 May	Wembley	3	1
1979	10 June	Stockholm	0	0
1986	10 Sept	Stockholm	0	1
wc1988	19 Oct	Wembley	0	0

v SWITZERLAND

			E	S
1933	20 May	Berne	4	0
1938	21 May	Zurich	1	2
1947	18 May	Zurich	0	1
1948	2 Dec	Highbury	6	0
1952	28 May	Zurich	3	0
wc1954	20 June	Berne	2	0
1962	9 May	Wembley	3	1
1963	5 June	Basle	8	1
EC1971	13 Oct	Basle	3	2
EC1971	10 Nov	Wembley	1	1
1975	3 Sept	Basle	2	1
1977	7 Sept	Wembley	0	0
wc1980	19 Nov	Wembley	2	1
wc1981	30 May	Basle	1	2
1988	28 May	Lausanne	1	0

v TURKEY

			E	T
wc1984	14 Nov	Istanbul	8	0
wc1985	16 Oct	Wembley	5	0
EC1987	29 Apr	Izmir	0	0
EC1987	14 Oct	Wembley	8	0

v USA

			E	USA
wc1950	29 June	Belo Horizonte	0	1
1953	8 June	New York	6	3
1959	28 May	Los Angeles	8	1
1964	27 May	New York	10	0
1985	16 June	Los Angeles	5	0

v URUGUAY

			E	U
1953	31 May	Montevideo	1	2
wc1954	26 June	Basle	2	4
1964	6 May	Wembley	2	1
wc1966	11 July	Wembley	0	0
1969	8 June	Montevideo	2	1
1977	15 June	Montevideo	0	0
1984	13 June	Montevideo	0	2

v USSR

			E	USSR
1958	18 May	Moscow	1	1
wc1958	8 June	Gothenburg	2	2
wc1958	17 June	Gothenburg	0	1
1958	22 Oct	Wembley	5	0
1967	6 Dec	Wembley	2	2
EC1968	8 June	Rome	2	0
1973	10 June	Moscow	2	1
1984	2 June	Wembley	0	2
1986	26 Mar	Tbilisi	1	0
EC1988	18 June	Frankfurt	1	3

v YUGOSLAVIA

			E	Y
1939	18 May	Belgrade	1	2
1950	22 Nov	Highbury	2	2
1954	16 May	Belgrade	0	1
1956	28 Nov	Wembley	3	0
1958	11 May	Belgrade	0	5
1960	11 May	Wembley	3	3
1965	9 May	Belgrade	1	1
1966	4 May	Wembley	2	0
EC1968	5 June	Florence	0	1
1972	11 Oct	Wembley	1	1
1974	5 June	Belgrade	2	2
EC1986	12 Nov	Wembley	2	0
EC1988	11 Nov	Belgrade	4	1

SCOTLAND

v ARGENTINA

			S	A
1977	18 June	Buenos Aires	1	1
1979	2 June	Glasgow	1	3

v AUSTRIA

			S	A
1931	16 May	Vienna	0	5
1933	29 Nov	Glasgow	2	2
1937	9 May	Vienna	1	1
1950	13 Dec	Glasgow	0	1
1951	27 May	Vienna	0	4
wc1954	16 June	Zurich	0	1
1955	19 May	Vienna	4	1
1956	2 May	Glasgow	1	1
1960	29 May	Vienna	1	4
1963	8 May	Glasgow	4	1
		(abandoned after 79 mins)		
wc1968	6 Nov	Glasgow	2	1
wc1969	5 Nov	Vienna	0	2
EC1978	20 Sept	Vienna	2	3
EC1979	17 Oct	Glasgow	1	1

v AUSTRALIA

			S	Au
wc1985	20 Nov	Glasgow	2	0
wc1985	4 Dec	Melbourne	0	0

v BELGIUM

			S	B
1947	18 May	Brussels	1	2
1948	28 Apr	Glasgow	2	0
1951	20 May	Brussels	5	0
EC1971	3 Feb	Liège	0	3
EC1971	10 Nov	Aberdeen	1	0
1974	2 June	Brussels	1	2
EC1979	21 Nov	Brussels	0	2
EC1979	19 Dec	Glasgow	1	3
EC1982	15 Dec	Brussels	2	3
EC1983	12 Oct	Glasgow	1	1
EC1987	1 Apr	Brussels	1	4
EC1987	14 Oct	Glasgow	2	0

v BRAZIL

			S	B
1966	25 June	Glasgow	1	1
1972	5 July	Rio de Janeiro	0	1
1973	30 June	Glasgow	0	1
wc1974	18 June	Frankfurt	0	0
1977	23 June	Rio de Janeiro	0	2
wc1982	18 June	Seville	1	4
1987	26 May	Glasgow	0	2

v BULGARIA

			S	B
1978	22 Feb	Glasgow	2	1
EC1986	10 Sept	Glasgow	0	0
EC1987	11 Nov	Sofia	1	0

v CANADA

			S	C
1983	12 June	Vancouver	2	0
1983	16 June	Edmonton	3	0
1983	20 June	Toronto	2	0

v CHILE

			S	C
1977	15 June	Santiago	4	2
1989	30 May	Glasgow	2	0

v COLOMBIA

			S	C
1988	17 May	Glasgow	0	0

v CYPRUS

			S	C
wc1968	17 Dec	Nicosia	5	0
wc1969	11 May	Glasgow	8	0
wc1989	8 Feb	Limassol	3	2
wc1989	26 Apr	Glasgow	2	1

v CZECHOSLOVAKIA

			S	C
1937	22 May	Prague	3	1
1937	8 Dec	Glasgow	5	0
wc1961	14 May	Bratislava	0	4
wc1961	26 Sept	Glasgow	3	2
wc1961	29 Nov	Brussels	2	4*
1972	2 July	Porto Alegre	0	0
wc1973	26 Sept	Glasgow	2	1
wc1973	17 Oct	Prague	0	1
wc1976	13 Oct	Prague	0	2
wc1977	21 Sept	Glasgow	3	1

**After extra time.*

v DENMARK

			S	D
1951	12 May	Glasgow	3	1
1952	25 May	Copenhagen	2	1
1968	16 Oct	Copenhagen	1	0
EC1970	11 Nov	Glasgow	1	0
EC1971	9 June	Copenhagen	0	1
wc1972	18 Oct	Copenhagen	4	1
wc1972	15 Nov	Glasgow	2	0
EC1975	3 Sept	Copenhagen	1	0
EC1975	29 Oct	Glasgow	3	1
wc1986	4 June	Nezahualcayotl	0	1

v FINLAND

			S	F
1954	25 May	Helsinki	2	1
wc1964	21 Oct	Glasgow	3	1
wc1965	27 May	Helsinki	2	1
1976	8 Sept	Glasgow	6	0

v FRANCE

			S	F
1930	18 May	Paris	2	0
1932	8 May	Paris	3	1
1948	23 May	Paris	0	3
1949	27 Apr	Glasgow	2	0
1950	27 May	Paris	1	0
1951	16 May	Glasgow	1	0
wc1958	15 June	Orebro	1	2
1984	1 June	Marseilles	0	2
wc1989	8 Mar	Glasgow	2	0

v GERMANY

			S	G
1929	1 June	Berlin	1	1
1936	14 Oct	Glasgow	2	0

v EAST GERMANY

			S	EG
1974	30 Oct	Glasgow	3	0
1977	7 Sept	East Berlin	0	1
EC1982	13 Oct	Glasgow	2	0
EC1983	16 Nov	Halle	1	2
1985	16 Oct	Glasgow	0	0

v WEST GERMANY

			S	WG
1957	22 May	Stuttgart	3	1
1959	6 May	Glasgow	3	2
1964	12 May	Hanover	2	2
wc1969	16 Apr	Glasgow	1	1
wc1969	22 Oct	Hamburg	2	3
1973	14 Nov	Glasgow	1	1
1974	27 Mar	Frankfurt	1	2
1986	8 June	Queretaro	1	2

v HOLLAND

			S	N
1929	4 June	Amsterdam	2	0
1938	21 May	Amsterdam	3	1
1959	27 May	Amsterdam	2	1
1966	11 May	Glasgow	0	3
1968	30 May	Amsterdam	0	0
1971	1 Dec	Rotterdam	1	2
wc1978	11 June	Mendoza	3	2
1982	23 Mar	Glasgow	2	1
1986	29 Apr	Eindhoven	0	0

v HUNGARY

			S	H
1938	7 Dec	Glasgow	3	1
1954	8 Dec	Glasgow	2	4
1955	29 May	Budapest	1	3
1958	7 May	Glasgow	1	1
1960	5 June	Budapest	3	3
1980	31 May	Budapest	1	3
1987	9 Sept	Glasgow	2	0

v ICELAND

			S	I
wc1984	17 Oct	Glasgow	3	0
wc1985	28 May	Reykjavik	1	0

v IRAN

			S	I
wc1978	7 June	Cordoba	1	1

v REPUBLIC OF IRELAND

			S	RI
wc1961	3 May	Glasgow	4	1
wc1961	7 May	Dublin	3	0
1963	9 June	Dublin	0	1
1969	21 Sept	Dublin	1	1
EC1986	15 Oct	Dublin	0	0
EC1987	18 Feb	Glasgow	0	1

v ISRAEL

			S	I
wc1981	25 Feb	Tel Aviv	1	0
wc1981	28 Apr	Glasgow	3	1
1986	28 Jan	Tel Aviv	1	0

v ITALY

			S	I
1931	20 May	Rome	0	3
wc1965	9 Nov	Glasgow	1	0
wc1965	7 Dec	Naples	0	3
1988	22 Dec	Perugia	0	2

v LUXEMBOURG

			S	L
1947	24 May	Luxembourg	6	0
EC1986	12 Nov	Glasgow	3	0
1987	2 Dec	Esch	0	0

v MALTA

			S	M
1988	22 Mar	Valletta	1	1

v NEW ZEALAND

			S	NZ
wc1982	15 June	Malaga	5	2

v NORWAY

			S	N
1929	28 May	Oslo	7	3
1954	5 May	Glasgow	1	0
1954	19 May	Oslo	1	1
1963	4 June	Bergen	3	4
1963	7 Nov	Glasgow	6	1
1974	6 June	Oslo	2	1
EC1978	25 Oct	Glasgow	3	2
EC1979	7 June	Oslo	4	0
wc1988	14 Sept	Oslo	2	1

v PARAGUAY

			S	P
wc1958	11 June	Norrkoping	2	3

v PERU

			S	P
1972	26 Apr	Glasgow	2	0
wc1978	3 June	Cordoba	1	3
1979	12 Sept	Glasgow	1	1

v POLAND

			S	P
1958	1 June	Warsaw	2	1
1960	4 May	Glasgow	2	3
wc1965	23 May	Chorzow	1	1
wc1965	13 Oct	Glasgow	1	2
1980	28 May	Poznan	0	1

v PORTUGAL

			S	P
1950	21 May	Lisbon	2	2
1955	4 May	Glasgow	3	0
1959	3 June	Lisbon	0	1
1966	18 June	Glasgow	0	1
EC1971	21 Apr	Lisbon	0	2
EC1971	13 Oct	Glasgow	2	1
1975	13 May	Glasgow	1	0
EC1978	29 Nov	Lisbon	0	1
EC1980	26 Mar	Glasgow	4	1
wc1980	15 Oct	Glasgow	0	0
wc1981	18 Nov	Lisbon	1	2

v RUMANIA

			S	R
EC1975	1 June	Bucharest	1	1
EC1975	17 Dec	Glasgow	1	1
1986	26 Mar	Glasgow	3	0

v SAUDI ARABIA

			S	SA
1988	17 Feb	Riyadh	2	2

v SPAIN

			S	Sp
wc1957	8 May	Glasgow	4	2
wc1957	26 May	Madrid	1	4
1963	13 June	Madrid	6	2
1965	8 May	Glasgow	0	0
EC1974	20 Nov	Glasgow	1	2
EC1975	5 Feb	Valencia	1	1
1982	24 Feb	Valencia	0	3
wc1984	14 Nov	Glasgow	3	1
wc1985	27 Feb	Seville	0	1
1988	27 Apr	Madrid	0	0

v SWEDEN

			S	Sw
1952	30 May	Stockholm	1	3
1953	6 May	Glasgow	1	2
1975	16 Apr	Gothenburg	1	1
1977	27 Apr	Glasgow	3	1
wc1980	10 Sept	Stockholm	1	0
wc1981	9 Sept	Glasgow	2	0

v SWITZERLAND

			S	Sw
1931	24 May	Geneva	3	2
1948	17 May	Berne	1	2
1950	26 Apr	Glasgow	3	1
wc1957	19 May	Basle	2	1
wc1957	6 Nov	Glasgow	3	2
1973	22 June	Berne	0	1
1976	7 Apr	Glasgow	1	0
EC1982	17 Nov	Berne	0	2
EC1983	30 May	Glasgow	2	2

v TURKEY

			S	T
1960	8 June	Ankara	2	4

v URUGUAY

			S	U
wc1954	19 June	Basle	0	7
1962	2 May	Glasgow	2	3
1983	21 Sept	Glasgow	2	0
wc1986	13 June	Nezahualcoyotl	0	0

v USA

			S	USA
1952	30 Apr	Glasgow	6	0

v USSR

			S	USSR
1967	10 May	Glasgow	0	2
1971	14 June	Moscow	0	1
wc1982	22 June	Malaga	2	2

v YUGOSLAVIA

			S	Y
1955	15 May	Belgrade	2	2
1956	21 Nov	Glasgow	2	0
wc1958	8 June	Vasteras	1	1
1972	29 June	Belo Horizonte	2	2
wc1974	22 June	Frankfurt	1	1
1984	12 Sept	Glasgow	6	1
wc1988	19 Oct	Glasgow	1	1

v ZAIRE

			S	Z
wc1974	14 June	Dortmund	2	0

WALES

v AUSTRIA

			W	A
1954	9 May	Vienna	0	2
EC1955	23 Nov	Wrexham	1	2
EC1974	4 Sept	Vienna	1	2
1975	19 Nov	Wrexham	1	0

v BELGIUM

			W	B
1949	22 May	Liège	1	3
1949	23 Nov	Cardiff	5	1

v BULGARIA

			W	B
EC1983	27 Apr	Wrexham	1	0
EC1983	16 Nov	Sofia	0	1

v BRAZIL

			W	B
WC1958	19 June	Gothenburg	0	1
1962	12 May	Rio de Janeiro	1	3
1962	16 May	São Paulo	1	3
1966	14 May	Rio de Janeiro	1	3
1966	18 May	Belo Horizonte	0	1
1983	12 June	Cardiff	1	1

v CANADA

			W	Ca
1986	10 May	Toronto	0	2
1986	20 May	Vancouver	3	0

v CHILE

			W	C
1966	22 May	Santiago	0	2

v CZECHOSLOVAKIA

			W	C
WC1957	1 May	Cardiff	1	0
WC1957	26 May	Prague	0	2
EC1971	21 Apr	Swansea	1	3
EC1971	27 Oct	Prague	0	1
WC1977	30 Mar	Wrexham	3	0
WC1977	16 Nov	Prague	0	1
WC1980	19 Nov	Cardiff	1	0
WC1981	9 Sept	Prague	0	2
EC1987	29 Apr	Wrexham	1	1
EC1987	11 Nov	Prague	0	2

v DENMARK

			W	D
WC1964	21 Oct	Copenhagen	0	1
WC1965	1 Dec	Wrexham	4	2
EC1987	9 Sept	Cardiff	1	0
EC1987	14 Oct	Copenhagen	0	1

v FINLAND

			W	F
EC1971	26 May	Helsinki	1	0
EC1971	13 Oct	Swansea	3	0
EC1987	10 Sept	Helsinki	1	1
EC1987	1 Apr	Wrexham	4	0
WC1988	19 Oct	Swansea	2	2

v FRANCE

			W	F
1933	25 May	Paris	1	1
1939	20 May	Paris	1	2
1953	14 May	Paris	1	6
1982	2 June	Toulouse	1	0

v EAST GERMANY

			W	EG
WC1957	19 May	Leipzig	1	2
WC1957	25 Sept	Cardiff	4	1
WC1969	16 Apr	Dresden	1	2
WC1969	22 Oct	Cardiff	1	3

v WEST GERMANY

			W	WG
1968	8 May	Cardiff	1	1
1969	26 Mar	Frankfurt	1	1
1976	6 Oct	Cardiff	0	2
1977	14 Dec	Dortmund	1	1
EC1979	2 May	Wrexham	0	2
EC1979	17 Oct	Cologne	1	5
WC1939	31 May	Cardiff	0	0

v GREECE

			W	G
WC1964	9 Dec	Athens	0	2
WC1965	17 Mar	Cardiff	4	1

v HOLLAND

			W	H
WC1988	14 Sept	Amsterdam	0	1

v HUNGARY

			W	H
WC1958	8 June	Sanviken	1	1
WC1958	17 June	Stockholm	2	1
1961	28 May	Budapest	2	3
EC1962	7 Nov	Budapest	1	3
EC1963	20 Mar	Cardiff	1	1
EC1974	30 Oct	Cardiff	2	0
EC1975	16 Apr	Budapest	2	1
1985	16 Oct	Cardiff	0	3

v ICELAND

			W	I
WC1980	2 June	Reykjavik	4	0
WC1981	14 Oct	Swansea	2	2
WC1984	12 Sept	Reykjavik	0	1
WC1984	14 Nov	Cardiff	2	1

v IRAN

			W	I
1978	18 Apr	Teheran	1	0

v REPUBLIC OF IRELAND

			W	RI
1960	28 Sept	Dublin	3	2
1979	11 Sept	Swansea	2	1
1981	24 Feb	Dublin	3	1
1986	26 Mar	Dublin	1	0

v ISRAEL

			W	I
WC1958	15 Jan	Tel Aviv	2	0
WC1958	5 Feb	Cardiff	2	0
1984	10 June	Tel Aviv	0	0
1989	8 Feb	Tel Aviv	3	3

v ITALY

			W	I
1965	1 May	Florence	1	4
WC1968	23 Oct	Cardiff	0	1
WC1969	4 Nov	Rome	1	4
1988	4 June	Brescia	1	0

v KUWAIT

			W	K
1977	6 Sept	Wrexham	0	0
1977	20 Sept	Kuwait	0	0

v LUXEMBOURG

			W	L
EC1974	20 Nov	Swansea	5	0
EC1975	1 May	Luxembourg	3	1

v MALTA

			W	M
EC1978	25 Oct	Wrexham	7	0
EC1979	2 June	Valletta	2	0
1988	1 June	Valletta	3	2

v MEXICO

			W	M
WC1958	11 June	Stockholm	1	1
1962	22 May	Mexico City	1	2

NORWAY

			W	M
EC1982	22 Sept	Swansea	1	0
EC1983	21 Sept	Oslo	0	0
1984	6 June	Trondheim	0	1
1985	26 Feb	Wrexham	1	1
1985	5 June	Bergen	2	4

v POLAND

			W	P
WC1973	28 Mar	Cardiff	2	0
WC1973	26 Sept	Katowice	0	3

v PORTUGAL

			W	P
1949	15 May	Lisbon	2	3
1951	12 May	Cardiff	2	1

v RUMANIA

			W	R
EC1970	11 Nov	Cardiff	0	0
EC1971	24 Nov	Bucharest	0	2
1983	12 Oct	Wrexham	5	0

v SAUDI ARABIA

			W	SA
1986	25 Feb	Dahran	2	1

v SPAIN

			W	S
WC1961	19 Apr	Cardiff	1	2
WC1961	18 May	Madrid	1	1
1982	24 Mar	Valencia	1	1
WC1984	17 Oct	Seville	0	3
WC1985	30 Apr	Wrexham	3	0

v SWEDEN

			W	S
WC1958	15 June	Stockholm	0	0
1988	27 Apr	Stockholm	1	4
1989	26 Apr	Wrexham	0	2

v SWITZERLAND

			W	S
1949	26 May	Berne	0	4
1951	16 May	Wrexham	3	2

v TURKEY

			W	T
EC1978	29 Nov	Wrexham	1	0
EC1979	21 Nov	Izmir	0	1
WC1980	15 Oct	Cardiff	4	0
WC1981	25 Mar	Ankara	1	0

v REST OF UNITED KINGDOM

			W	UK
1951	5 Dec	Cardiff	3	2
1969	28 July	Cardiff	0	1

v URUGUAY

			W	U
1986	21 Apr	Wrexham	0	0

v USSR

			W	USSR
WC1965	30 May	Moscow	1	2
WC1965	27 Oct	Cardiff	2	1
WC1981	30 May	Wrexham	0	0
WC1981	18 Nov	Tbilisi	0	3
1987	18 Feb	Swansea	0	0

v YUGOSLAVIA

			W	Y
1953	21 May	Belgrade	2	5
1954	22 Nov	Cardiff	1	3
EC1976	24 Apr	Zagreb	0	2
EC1976	22 May	Cardiff	1	1
EC1982	15 Dec	Titograd	4	4
EC1983	14 Dec	Cardiff	1	1
1988	23 Mar	Swansea	1	2

NORTHERN IRELAND

v ALBANIA

			NI	A
WC1965	7 May	Belfast	4	1
WC1965	24 Nov	Tirana	1	1
EC1982	15 Dec	Tirana	0	0
EC1983	27 Apr	Belfast	1	0

v ALGERIA

			NI	A
WC1986	3 June	Guadalajara	1	1

v ARGENTINA

			NI	A
WC1958	11 June	Halmstad	1	3

v AUSTRIA

			NI	A
WC1982	1 July	Madrid	2	2
EC1982	13 Oct	Vienna	0	2
EC1983	21 Sept	Belfast	3	1

v AUSTRALIA

			NI	A
1980	11 June	Sydney	2	1
1980	15 June	Melbourne	1	1
1980	18 June	Adelaide	2	1

v BELGIUM

			NI	B
WC1976	10 Nov	Liège	0	2
WC1977	16 Nov	Belfast	3	0

v BRAZIL

			NI	B
WC1986	12 June	Guadalajara	0	3

v BULGARIA

			NI	B
WC1972	18 Oct	Sofia	0	3
WC1973	26 Sept	Sheffield	0	0
EC1978	29 Nov	Sofia	2	0
EC1979	2 May	Belfast	2	0

v CHILE

			NI	C
1989	26 May	Belfast	0	1

v CYPRUS

			NI	C
EC1971	3 Feb	Nicosia	3	0
EC1971	21 Apr	Belfast	5	0
WC1973	14 Feb	Nicosia	0	1
WC1973	8 May	London	3	0

v CZECHOSLOVAKIA

			NI	C
WC1958	8 June	Halmstad	1	0
WC1958	17 June	Malmo	2	1*

**After extra time*

v DENMARK

			NI	D
EC1978	25 Oct	Belfast	2	1
EC1979	6 June	Copenhagen	0	4
1986	26 Mar	Belfast	1	1

v FINLAND

			NI	F
WC1984	27 May	Pori	0	1
WC1984	14 Nov	Belfast	2	1

v FRANCE

			NI	F
1951	12 May	Belfast	2	2
1952	11 Nov	Paris	1	3
WC1958	19 June	Norrkoping	0	4
1982	24 Mar	Paris	0	4
WC1982	4 July	Madrid	1	4
1986	26 Feb	Paris	0	0
1988	27 Apr	Belfast	0	0

v WEST GERMANY

			NI	WG
WC1958	15 June	Malmo	2	2
WC1960	26 Oct	Belfast	3	4
WC1961	10 May	Hamburg	1	2
1966	7 May	Belfast	0	2
1977	27 Apr	Cologne	0	5
EC1982	17 Nov	Belfast	1	0
EC1983	16 Nov	Hamburg	1	0

v GREECE

			NI	G
wc1961	3 May	Athens	1	2
wc1961	17 Oct	Belfast	2	0
1988	17 Feb	Athens	2	3

v HOLLAND

			NI	N
1962	9 May	Rotterdam	0	4
wc1965	17 Mar	Belfast	2	1
wc1965	7 Apr	Rotterdam	0	0
wc1976	13 Oct	Rotterdam	2	2
wc1977	12 Oct	Belfast	0	1

v HONDURAS

			NI	H
wc1982	21 June	Zaragoza	1	1

v HUNGARY

			NI	H
wc1988	19 Oct	Budapest	0	1

v ICELAND

			NI	I
wc1977	11 June	Reykjavik	0	1
wc1977	21 Sept	Belfast	2	0

v REPUBLIC OF IRELAND

			NI	RI
EC1978	20 Sept	Dublin	0	0
EC1979	21 Nov	Belfast	1	0
wc1988	14 Sept	Belfast	0	0

v ISRAEL

			NI	I
1968	10 Sept	Jaffa	3	2
1976	3 Mar	Tel Aviv	1	1
wc1980	26 Mar	Tel Aviv	0	0
wc1981	18 Nov	Belfast	1	0
1984	16 Oct	Belfast	3	0
1987	18 Feb	Tel Aviv	1	1

v ITALY

			NI	I
wc1957	25 Apr	Rome	0	1
1957	4 Dec	Belfast	2	2
wc1958	15 Jan	Belfast	2	1
1961	25 Apr	Bologna	2	3

v MALTA

			NI	M
1988	21 May	Belfast	3	0
wc1989	26 Apr	Valetta	2	0

v MEXICO

			NI	M
1966	22 June	Belfast	4	1

v MOROCCO

			NI	Mo
1986	23 Apr	Belfast	2	1

v NORWAY

			NI	N
EC1974	4 Sept	Oslo	1	2
EC1975	29 Oct	Belfast	3	0

v POLAND

			NI	P
EC1962	10 Oct	Katowice	2	0
EC1962	28 Nov	Belfast	2	0
1988	23 Mar	Belfast	1	1

v PORTUGAL

			NI	P
wc1957	16 Jan	Lisbon	1	1
wc1957	1 May	Belfast	3	0
wc1973	28 Mar	Coventry	1	1
wc1973	14 Nov	Lisbon	1	1
wc1980	19 Nov	Lisbon	0	1
wc1981	29 Apr	Belfast	1	0

v RUMANIA

			NI	R
wc1984	12 Sept	Belfast	3	2
wc1985	16 Oct	Bucharest	1	0

v SPAIN

			NI	S
1958	15 Oct	Madrid	2	6
1963	30 May	Bilbao	1	1
1963	30 Oct	Belfast	0	1
EC1970	11 Nov	Seville	0	3
EC1972	16 Feb	Hull	1	1
wc1982	25 June	Valencia	1	0
1985	27 Mar	Palma	0	0
wc1986	7 June	Guadalajara	1	2
wc1988	21 Dec	Seville	0	4
wc1989	8 Feb	Belfast	0	2

v SWEDEN

			NI	S
EC1974	30 Oct	Solna	2	0
EC1975	3 Sept	Belfast	1	2
wc1980	15 Oct	Belfast	3	0
wc1981	3 June	Solna	0	1

v SWITZERLAND

			NI	S
wc1964	14 Oct	Belfast	1	0
wc1964	14 Nov	Lausanne	1	2

v TURKEY

			NI	T
wc1968	23 Oct	Belfast	4	1
wc1968	11 Dec	Istanbul	3	0
EC1983	30 Mar	Belfast	2	1
EC1983	12 Oct	Ankara	0	1
wc1985	1 May	Belfast	2	0
wc1985	11 Sept	Izmir	0	0
EC1986	12 Nov	Izmir	0	0
EC1987	11 Nov	Belfast	1	0

v URUGUAY

			NI	U
1964	29 Apr	Belfast	3	0

v USSR

			NI	USSR
wc1969	10 Sept	Belfast	0	0
wc1969	22 Oct	Moscow	0	2
EC1971	22 Sept	Moscow	0	1
EC1971	13 Oct	Belfast	1	1

v YUGOSLAVIA

			NI	Y
EC1975	16 Mar	Belfast	1	0
EC1975	19 Nov	Belgrade	0	1
wc1982	17 June	Zaragoza	0	0
EC1987	29 Apr	Belfast	1	2
EC1987	14 Oct	Sarajevo	0	3

REPUBLIC OF IRELAND

v ALGERIA

			RI	A
1982	28 Apr	Algiers	0	2

v ARGENTINA

			RI	A
1951	13 May	Dublin	0	1
1979	29 May	Dublin	0	0*
1980	16 May	Dublin	0	1

v AUSTRIA

			RI	A
1952	7 May	Vienna	0	6
1953	25 Mar	Dublin	4	0
1958	14 Mar	Vienna	1	3
1962	8 Apr	Dublin	2	3
EC1963	25 Sept	Vienna	0	0
EC1963	13 Oct	Dublin	3	2
1966	22 May	Vienna	0	1
1968	10 Nov	Dublin	2	2
EC1971	30 May	Dublin	1	4
EC1971	10 Oct	Linz	0	6

* Not considered a full international

v BELGIUM

			RI	B
1928	12 Feb	Liège	4	2
1929	30 Apr	Dublin	4	0
1930	11 May	Brussels	3	1
wc1934	25 Feb	Dublin	4	4

1949	24 Apr	Dublin	0	2
1950	10 May	Brussels	1	5
1965	24 Mar	Dublin	0	2
1966	25 May	Liège	3	2
wc1980	15 Oct	Dublin	1	1
wc1981	25 Mar	Brussels	0	1
EC1986	10 Sept	Brussels	2	2
EC1987	29 Apr	Dublin	0	0

v BRAZIL

			RI	B
1974	5 May	Rio de Janeiro	1	2
1982	27 May	Uberlandia	0	7
1987	23 May	Dublin	1	0

v BULGARIA

			RI	B
wc1977	1 June	Sofia	1	2
wc1977	12 Oct	Dublin	0	0
EC1979	19 May	Sofia	0	1
EC1979	17 Oct	Dublin	3	0
EC1987	1 Apr	Sofia	1	2
EC1987	14 Oct	Dublin	2	0

v CHILE

			RI	C
1960	30 Mar	Dublin	2	0
1972	21 June	Recife	1	2
1974	12 May	Santiago	2	1
1982	22 May	Santiago	0	1

v CYPRUS

			RI	C
wc1980	26 Mar	Nicosia	3	2
wc1980	19 Nov	Dublin	6	0

v CZECHOSLOVAKIA

			RI	C
1938	18 May	Prague	2	2
EC1959	5 Apr	Dublin	2	0
EC1959	10 May	Bratislava	0	4
wc1961	8 Oct	Dublin	1	3
1979	26 Sept	Prague	1	4
wc1961	29 Oct	Prague	1	7
EC1967	21 May	Dublin	0	2
EC1967	22 Nov	Prague	2	1
wc1969	4 May	Dublin	1	2
wc1969	7 Oct	Prague	0	3
1981	29 Apr	Dublin	3	1
1986	27 May	Reykjavik	1	0

v DENMARK

			RI	D
wc1956	3 Oct	Dublin	2	1
wc1957	2 Oct	Copenhagen	2	0
wc1968	4 Dec	Dublin	1	1
(*abandoned after 51 mins*)				
wc1969	27 May	Copenhagen	0	2
wc1969	15 Oct	Dublin	1	1
EC1978	24 May	Copenhagen	3	3
EC1979	2 May	Dublin	2	0
wc1984	14 Nov	Copenhagen	0	3
wc1985	13 Nov	Dublin	1	4

v ECUADOR

			RI	E
1972	19 June	Natal	3	2

v FINLAND

			RI	F
wc1949	8 Sept	Dublin	3	0
wc1949	9 Oct	Helsinki	1	1

v FRANCE

			RI	F
1937	23 May	Paris	2	0
1952	16 Nov	Dublin	1	1
wc1953	4 Oct	Dublin	3	5
wc1953	25 Nov	Paris	0	1
wc1972	15 Nov	Dublin	2	1
wc1973	19 May	Paris	1	1
wc1976	17 Nov	Paris	0	2
wc1977	30 Mar	Dublin	1	0
wc1980	28 Oct	Paris	0	2
wc1981	14 Oct	Dublin	3	2
1989	7 Feb	Dublin	0	0

v GERMANY

			RI	G
1935	8 May	Dortmund	1	3
1936	17 Oct	Dublin	5	2
1939	23 May	Bremen	1	1

v WEST GERMANY

			RI	WG
1951	17 Oct	Dublin	3	2
1952	4 May	Cologne	0	3
1955	28 May	Hamburg	1	2
1956	25 Nov	Dublin	3	0
1960	11 May	Dusseldorf	1	0
1966	4 May	Dublin	0	4
1970	9 May	Berlin	1	2
1975	1 Mar	Dublin	1	0†
1979	22 May	Dublin	1	3
1981	21 May	Bremen	0	3†

†*v West Germany 'B'*

v NETHERLANDS

			RI	N
1932	8 May	Amsterdam	2	0
1934	8 Apr	Amsterdam	2	5
1935	8 Dec	Dublin	3	5
1955	1 May	Dublin	1	0
1956	10 May	Rotterdam	4	1
wc1980	10 Sept	Dublin	2	1
wc1981	9 Sept	Rotterdam	2	2
EC1982	22 Sept	Rotterdam	1	2
EC1983	12 Oct	Dublin	2	3
EC1988	18 June	Gelsenkirchen	0	1

v HUNGARY

			RI	H
1934	15 Dec	Dublin	2	4
1936	3 May	Budapest	3	3
1936	6 Dec	Dublin	2	3
1939	19 Mar	Cork	2	2
1939	18 May	Budapest	2	2
wc1969	8 June	Dublin	1	2
wc1969	5 Nov	Budapest	0	4
wc1989	8 Mar	Budapest	0	2
wc1989	4 June	Dublin	2	0

v ICELAND

			RI	I
EC1962	12 Aug	Dublin	4	2
EC1962	2 Sept	Reykjavik	1	1
EC1982	13 Oct	Dublin	2	0
EC1983	21 Sept	Reykjavik	3	0
1986	25 May	Rekjavik	2	1

v IRAN

			RI	I
1972	18 June	Recife	2	1

v N. IRELAND

			RI	NI
EC1978	20 Sept	Dublin	0	0
EC1979	21 Nov	Belfast	0	1
wc1988	14 Sept	Belfast	0	0

v ISRAEL

			RI	I
1984	4 Apr	Tel Aviv	0	3
1985	27 May	Tel Aviv	0	0
1987	10 Nov	Dublin	5	0

v ITALY

			RI	I
1926	21 Mar	Turin	0	3
1927	23 Apr	Dublin	1	2
EC1970	8 Dec	Rome	0	3
EC1971	10 May	Dublin	1	2
1985	5 Feb	Dublin	1	2

v LUXEMBOURG

			RI	L
1936	9 May	Luxembourg	5	1
wc1953	28 Oct	Dublin	4	0
wc1954	7 Mar	Luxembourg	1	0
EC1987	28 May	Luxembourg	2	0
EC1987	9 Sept	Dublin	2	1

v MALTA

			RI	M
EC1983	30 Mar	Valletta	1	0
EC1983	16 Nov	Dublin	8	0
WC1989	28 May	Dublin	2	0

v MEXICO

			RI	M
1984	8 Aug	Dublin	0	0

v NORWAY

			RI	N
WC1937	10 Oct	Oslo	2	3
WC1937	7 Nov	Dublin	3	3
1950	26 Nov	Dublin	2	2
1951	30 May	Oslo	3	2
1954	8 Nov	Dublin	2	1
1955	25 May	Oslo	3	1
1960	6 Nov	Dublin	3	1
1964	13 May	Oslo	4	1
1973	6 June	Oslo	1	1
1976	24 Mar	Dublin	3	0
1978	21 May	Oslo	0	0
WC1984	17 Oct	Oslo	0	1
WC1985	1 May	Dublin	0	0
1988	1 June	Oslo	0	0

v POLAND

			RI	P
1938	22 May	Warsaw	0	6
1938	13 Nov	Dublin	3	2
1958	11 May	Katowice	2	2
1958	5 Oct	Dublin	2	2
1964	10 May	Cracow	1	3
1964	25 Oct	Dublin	3	2
1968	15 May	Dublin	2	2
1968	30 Oct	Katowice	0	1
1970	6 May	Dublin	1	2
1970	23 Sept	Dublin	0	2
1973	16 May	Wroclaw	0	2
1973	21 Oct	Dublin	1	0
1976	26 May	Posnan	2	0
1977	24 Apr	Dublin	0	0
1978	12 Apr	Lodz	0	3
1981	23 May	Bydgoszcz	0	3
1984	23 May	Dublin	0	0
1986	12 Nov	Warsaw	0	1
1988	22 May	Dublin	3	1

v PORTUGAL

			RI	P
1946	16 June	Lisbon	1	3
1947	4 May	Dublin	0	2
1948	23 May	Lisbon	0	2
1949	22 May	Dublin	1	0
1972	25 June	Recife	1	2

v RUMANIA

			RI	R
1988	23 Mar	Dublin	2	0

v SCOTLAND

			RI	S
WC1961	3 May	Glasgow	1	4
WC1961	7 May	Dublin	0	3
1963	9 June	Dublin	1	0
1969	21 Sept	Dublin	1	1
EC1986	15 Oct	Dublin	0	0
EC1987	18 Feb	Glasgow	1	0

v SPAIN

			RI	S
1931	26 Apr	Barcelona	1	1
1931	13 Dec	Dublin	0	5
1946	23 June	Madrid	1	0
1947	2 Mar	Dublin	3	2
1948	30 May	Barcelona	1	2
1949	12 June	Dublin	1	4
1952	1 June	Madrid	0	6
1955	27 Nov	Dublin	2	2
EC1964	11 Mar	Seville	1	5
EC1964	8 Apr	Dublin	0	2
WC1965	5 May	Dublin	1	0
WC1965	27 Oct	Seville	1	4
WC1965	10 Nov	Paris	0	1
EC1966	23 Oct	Dublin	0	0
EC1966	7 Dec	Valencia	0	2
1977	9 Feb	Dublin	0	1
EC1982	17 Nov	Dublin	3	3
EC1983	27 Apr	Zaragosa	0	2
WC1985	26 May	Cork	0	0
WC1988	16 Nov	Seville	0	2
WC1989	26 Apr	Dublin	1	0

v SWEDEN

			RI	S
WC1949	2 June	Stockholm	1	3
WC1949	13 Nov	Dublin	1	3
1959	1 Nov	Dublin	3	2
1960	18 May	Malmo	1	4
EC1970	14 Oct	Dublin	1	1
EC1970	28 Oct	Malmo	0	1

v SWITZERLAND

			RI	S
1935	5 May	Basle	0	1
1936	17 Mar	Dublin	1	0
1937	17 May	Berne	1	0
1938	18 Sept	Dublin	4	0
1948	5 Dec	Dublin	0	1
EC1975	11 May	Dublin	2	1
EC1975	21 May	Berne	0	1
1980	30 Apr	Dublin	2	0
WC1985	2 June	Dublin	3	0
WC1985	11 Sept	Berne	0	0

v TRINIDAD & TOBAGO

			RI	TT
1982	30 May	Port of Spain	1	2

v TUNISIA

			RI	TU
1988	19 Oct	Dublin	4	0

v TURKEY

			RI	T
EC1966	16 Nov	Dublin	2	1
EC1967	22 Feb	Ankara	1	2
EC1974	20 Nov	Izmir	1	1
EC1975	29 Oct	Dublin	4	0
1976	13 Oct	Ankara	3	3
1978	5 Apr	Dublin	4	2

v URUGUAY

			RI	U
1974	8 May	Montevideo	0	2
1986	23 Apr	Dublin	1	1

v USA

			RI	USA
1979	29 Oct	Dublin	3	2

v USSR

			RI	USSR
WC1972	18 Oct	Dublin	1	2
WC1973	13 May	Moscow	0	1
EC1974	30 Oct	Dublin	3	0
EC1975	18 May	Kiev	1	2
WC1984	12 Sept	Dublin	1	0
WC1985	16 Oct	Moscow	0	2
EC1988	15 June	Hanover	1	1

v WALES

			RI	W
1960	28 Sept	Dublin	2	3
1979	11 Sept	Swansea	1	2
1981	24 Feb	Dublin	1	3
1986	26 Mar	Dublin	0	1

v YUGOSLAVIA

			RI	Y
1955	19 Sept	Dublin	1	4
1988	27 Apr	Dublin	2	0

INTERNATIONAL APPEARANCES

This is a list of full international appearances by Englishmen, Irishmen, Scotsmen and Welshmen in matches against the Home Countries and against foreign nations. It does not include unofficial matches against Commonwealth and Empire countries. The year indicated refers to the season; ie 1989 is the 1988-89 season.

Explanatory code for matches played by all five countries: A represents Austria; Alb, Albania; Alg, Algeria; Arg, Argentina; Aus, Australia; B, Bohemia; Bel, Belgium; Br, Brazil; Bul, Bulgaria; Ca, Canada; Ch, Chile; Chn, China; Co, Colombia; Cy, Cyprus; Cz, Czechoslovakia; D, Denmark; E, England; Ec, Ecuador; Ei, Eire; EG, East Germany; Eg, Egypt; F, France; Fi, Finland; G, Germany (pre-war); Gr, Greece; H, Hungary; Ho, Holland; Hon, Honduras; I, Italy; Ic, Iceland; Ir, Iran; Is, Israel; K, Kuwait; L, Luxembourg; M, Mexico; Ma, Malta; Mor, Morocco; N, Norway; Ni, Northern Ireland; Nz, New Zealand; P, Portugal; Par, Paraguay; Pe, Peru; Pol, Poland; R, Rumania; R of E, Rest of Europe; R of W, Rest of World; S.Ar, Saudi Arabia; S, Scotland; Se, Sweden; Sp, Spain; Sw, Switzerland; T, Turkey; Tr, Trinidad & Tobago; Tun, Tunisia; U, Uruguay; UK, Rest of United Kingdom; US, United States of America; USSR; W, Wales; WG, West Germany; Y, Yugoslavia.

As at 30 June 1989.

ENGLAND

Abbott, W. (Everton), 1902 v W (1)

A'Court, A. (Liverpool), 1958 v Ni, Br, A, USSR; 1959 v W (5)

Adams, T. A. (Arsenal), 1987 v Sp, T, Br; 1988 v WG, T, Y, Ho, H, S, Co, Sw, Ei, Ho, USSR ; 1989 v D, Se, S.Ar. (17)

Adcock, H. (Leicester C), 1929 v F, Bel, Sp; 1930 v Ni, W (5)

Alcock, C. W. (Wanderers), 1875 v S (1)

Alderson, J. T. (C Palace), 1923 v F (1)

Aldridge, A. (WBA), 1888 v Ni; (with Walsall Town Swifts), 1889 v Ni (2)

Allen, A. (Stoke C) 1960 v Se, W, Ni (3)

Allen, A. (Aston Villa), 1888 v Ni (1)

Allen, C. (QPR), 1984 v Br (sub), U, Ch; (with Tottenham H), 1987 v T; 1988 v Is (5)

Allen, H. (Wolverhampton W), 1888 v S, W, Ni; 1889 v S; 1890 v S (5)

Allen, J. P. (Portsmouth), 1934 v Ni, W (2)

Allen, R. (WBA), 1952 v Sw; 1954 v Y, S; 1955 v WG, W (5)

Alsford, W. J. (Tottenham H), 1935 v S (1)

Amos, A. (Old Carthusians), 1885 v S; 1886 v W (2)

Anderson, R. D. (Old Etonians), 1879 v W (1)

Anderson, S. (Sunderland), 1962, v A, S (2)

Anderson, V. (Nottingham F), 1979 v Cz, Se; 1980 v Bul, Sp; 1981 v N, R, W, S; 1982 v Ni, Ic; 1984 v Ni; (with Arsenal), 1985 v T, Ni, Ei, R, Fi, S, M, US; 1986 v USSR, M; 1987 v Se, Ni (2), Y, Sp, T; (with Manchester U), 1988 v WG, H, Co (30)

Angus, J. (Burnley), 1961 v A (1)

Armfield, J. C. (Blackpool), 1959 v Br, Pe, M, US; 1960 v Y, Sp, H, S; 1961 v L, P, Sp, M, I, A, W, Ni, S; 1962 v A, Sw, Pe, W, Ni, S, L, P, H, Arg, Bul, Br; 1963 v F (2), Br, EG, Sw, Ni, W, S; 1964 v R of W, W, Ni, S; 1966 v Y, Fi (43)

Armitage, G. H. (Charlton Ath), 1926 v Ni (1)

Armstrong, D. (Middlesbrough), 1980 v Aus; (with Southampton), 1983 v WG; 1984 v W (3)

Armstrong, K. (Chelsea), 1955 v S (1)

Arnold, J. (Fulham), 1933 v S (1)

Arthur, J. W. H. (Blackburn R), 1885 v S, W, Ni; 1886 v S, W; 1887 v W, Ni (7)

Ashcroft, J. (Woolwich Arsenal), 1906 v Ni, W, S (3)

Ashmore, G. S. (WBA), 1926 v Bel (1)

Ashton, C. T. (Corinthians), 1926 v Ni (1)

Ashurst, W. (Notts Co), 1923 v Se (2); 1925 v S, W, Bel (5)

Astall, G. (Birmingham C), 1956 v Fi, WG (2)

Astle, J. (WBA), 1969 v W; 1970 v S, P, Br (sub), Cz (5)

Aston, J. (Manchester U), 1949 v S, W, D, Sw, Se, N, F; 1950 v S, W, Ni, Ei, I, P, Bel, Ch, US; 1951 v Ni (17)

Athersmith, W. C. (Aston Villa), 1892 v Ni, 1897 v S, W, Ni; 1898 v S, W, Ni; 1899 v S, W, Ni; 1900 v S, W (12)

Atyeo, P. J. W. (Bristol C), 1956 v Br, Se, Sp; 1957 v D, Ei (2) (6)

Austin, S. W. (Manchester C), 1926 v Ni (1)

Bach, P. (Sunderland), 1899 v Ni (1)

Bache, J. W. (Aston Villa), 1903 v W; 1904 v W, Ni; 1905 v S; 1907 v Ni; 1910 v Ni; 1911 v S (7)

Baddeley, T. (Wolverhampton W), 1903 v S, Ni; 1904 v S, W, Ni (5)

Bagshaw, J. J. (Derby Co), 1920 v Ni (1)

Bailey, G. R. (Manchester U), 1985 v Ei, M (2)

Bailey, H. P. (Leicester Fosse), 1908 v W, A (2), H, B (5)

Bailey, M. A. (Charlton Ath), 1964 v US; 1965 v W (2)

Bailey, N. C. (Clapham Rovers), 1878 v S; 1879 v S, W; 1880 v S; 1881 v S; 1882 v S, W; 1883 v S, W; 1884 v S, W, Ni; 1885 v S, W, Ni; 1886 v S, W; 1887 v S, W (19)

Baily, E. F. (Tottenham H), 1950 v Sp; 1951 v Y, Ni, W; 1952 v A (2), Sw, W; 1953 v Ni (9)

Bain, J. (Oxford University), 1887 v S (1)

Baker, A. (Arsenal), 1928 v W (1)

Baker, B. H. (Everton), 1921 v Bel; (with Chelsea), 1926 v Ni (2)

Baker, J. H. (Hibernian), 1960 v Y, Sp, H, Ni, S; (with Arsenal) 1966 v Sp, Pol, Ni (8)

Ball, A. J. (Blackpool), 1965 v Y, WG, Se; 1966 v S, Sp, Fi, D, U, Arg, P, WG (2), Pol (2); (with Everton), 1967 v W, S, Ni, A, Cz, Sp; 1968 v W, S, USSR, Sp (2), Y, WG; 1969 v Ni, W, S, R (2), M, Br, U; 1970 v P, Co, Ec, R, Br, Cz (sub), WG, W, S, Bel; 1971 v Ma, EG, Gr, Ma (sub), Ni, S; 1972 v Sw, Gr; (with Arsenal) WG (2), S; 1973 v W (3), Y, S (2), Cz, Ni, Pol; 1974 v P (sub); 1975 v WG, Cy (2), Ni, W, S (72)

Ball, J. (Bury), 1928 v Ni (1)

Balmer, W. (Everton), 1905 v Ni (1)

Bamber, J. (Liverpool), 1921 v W (1)

Bambridge, A. L. (Swifts), 1881 v W; 1883 v W; 1884 v Ni (3)

Bambridge, E. C. (Swifts), 1879 v S; 1880 v S; 1881 v S; 1882 v S, W, Ni; 1883 v W; 1884 v S, W, Ni; 1885 v S, W, Ni; 1886 v S, W; 1887 v S, W, Ni (18)

Bambridge, E. H. (Swifts), 1876 v S (1)

Banks, G. (Leicester C), 1963 v S, Br, Cz, EG; 1964 v W, Ni, S, R of W, U, P (2), US, Arg; 1965 v Ni, S, H, Y, WG, Se; 1966 v Ni, S, Sp, Pol (2), WG (2), Y, Fi, U, M, F, Arg, P; 1967 v Ni, W, S, Cz; (with Stoke C), 1968 v W, Ni, S, USSR (2), Sp, WG, Y; 1969 v Ni, S, R (2), F, U, Br; 1970 v W, Ni, S, Ho, Bel, Co, Ec, R, Br, Cz; 1971 v Gr, Ma (2), Ni, S; 1972 v Sw, Gr, WG (2), W, S (73)

Banks, H. E. (Millwall), 1901 v Ni (1)

Banks, T. (Bolton W), 1958 v USSR (3), Br, A; 1959 v Ni (6)
Bannister, W. (Burnley), 1901 v W; (with Bolton W), 1902 v Ni (2)
Barclay, R. (Sheffield W), 1932 v S; 1933 v Ni; 1936 v S (3)
Barham, M. (Norwich C), 1983 v Aus (2) (2)
Barkas, S. (Manchester C), 1936 v Bel; 1937 v S; 1938 v W, Ni, Cz (5)
Barker, J. (Derby Co), 1935 v I, Ho, S, W, Ni; 1936 v G, A, S, W, Ni; 1937 v W (11)
Barker, R. (Herts Rangers), 1872 v S (1)
Barker, R. R. (Casuals), 1895 v W (1)
Barlow, R. J. (WBA), 1955 v Ni (1)
Barnes, J. (Watford), 1983 v Ni (sub), Aus (sub), Aus (2); 1984 v D, L (sub), F (sub), S, USSR, Br, U, Ch; 1985 v EG, Fi, T, Ni, R, Fi, S, I (sub), M, WG (sub), US (sub); 1986 v R (sub), Is (sub), M (sub), Ca (sub), Arg (sub); 1987 v Se, T (sub), Br; (with Liverpool), 1988 v WG, T, Y, Is, Ho, S, Co, Sw, Ei, Ho, USSR; 1989 v Se, Gr, Alb, Pol, D (47)
Barnes, P. S. (Manchester C), 1978 v I, WG, Br, W, S, H; 1979 v D, Ei, Cz, Ni (2), S, Bul, A; (with WBA), 1980 v D, W; 1981 v Sp (sub), Br, W, Sw (sub); (with Leeds U), 1982 v N (sub), Ho (sub) (22)
Barnet, H. H. (Royal Engineers), 1882 v Ni (1)
Barrass, M. W. (Bolton W), 1952 v W, Ni; 1953 v S (3)
Barrett, A. F. (Fulham), 1930 v Ni (1)
Barrett, J. W. (West Ham U), 1929 v Ni (1)
Barry, L. (Leicester C), 1928 v F, Bel; 1929 v F, Bel, Sp (5)
Barson, F. (Aston Villa), 1920 v W (1)
Barton, J. (Blackburn R), 1890 v Ni (1)
Barton, P. H. (Birmingham), 1921 v Bel; 1922 v Ni; 1923 v F; 1924 v Bel, S, W; 1925 v Ni (7)
Bassett, W. I. (WBA), 1888 v Ni, 1889 v S, W; 1890 v S, W; 1891 v S, Ni; 1892 v S; 1893 v S, W; 1894 v S; 1895 v S, Ni; 1896 v S, W, Ni (16)
Bastard, S. R. (Upton Park), 1880 v S (1)
Bastin, C. S. (Arsenal), 1932 v W; 1933 v I, Sw; 1934 v S, Ni, W, H, Cz; 1935 v S, Ni, I; 1936 v S, W, G, A; 1937 v W, Ni; 1938 v S, G, Sw, F (21)
Baugh, R. (Stafford Road), 1886 v Ni; (with Wolverhampton W) 1890 v Ni (2)
Bayliss, A. E. J. M. (WBA), 1891 v Ni (1)
Baynham, R. L. (Luton T), 1956 v Ni, D, Sp (3)
Beardsley, P. A. (Newcastle U), 1986 v Eg (sub), Is, USSR, M, Ca (sub), P (sub), Pol, Para, Arg; 1987 v Ni (2), Y, Sp, Br, S; (with Liverpool), 1988 v WG, T, Y, Is, Ho, H, S, Co, Sw, Ei, Ho; 1989 v D, Se, S.Ar, Gr (sub), Alb (sub), Alb, Pol, D (34)
Beasley, A. (Huddersfield T), 1939 v S (1)
Beats, W. E. (Wolverhampton W), 1901 v W; 1902 v S (2)
Beattie, T. K. (Ipswich T), 1975 v Cy (2), S; 1976 v Sw, P; 1977 v Fi, I (sub), Ho; 1978 v L (sub) (9)
Becton, F. (Preston NE), 1895 v Ni; (with Liverpool), 1897 v W (2)
Bedford, H. (Blackpool), 1923 v Se; 1925 v Ni (2)
Bell, C. (Manchester C), 1968 v Se, WG; 1969 v W, Bul, F, U, Br; 1970 v Ni (sub), Ho (2), P, Br (sub), Cz, WG (sub); 1972 v Gr, WG (2), W, Ni, S; 1973 v W (3), Y, S (2), Ni, Cz, Pol; 1974 v A, Pol, I, W, Ni, S, Arg, EG, Bul, Y; 1975 v Cz, P, WG, Cy (2), Ni, S; 1976 v Sw, Cy (48)
Bennett, W. (Sheffield U), 1901 v S, W (2)
Benson, R. W. (Sheffield U), 1913 v Ni (1)
Bentley, R. T. F. (Chelsea), 1949 v Se; 1950 v S, P, Bel, Ch, USA; 1953 v W, Bel; 1955 v W, WG, Sp, P (12)
Beresford, J. (Aston Villa), 1934 v Cz (1)
Berry, A. (Oxford University), 1909 v Ni (1)
Berry, J. J. (Manchester U), 1953 v Arg, Ch, U; 1956 v Se (4)
Bestall, J. G. (Grimsby T), 1935 v Ni (1)
Betmead, H. A. (Grimsby T), 1937 v Fi (1)
Betts, M. P. (Old Harrovians), 1877 v S (1)
Betts, W. (Sheffield W), 1889 v W (1)
Beverley, J. (Blackburn R), 1884 v S, W, Ni (3)
Birkett, R. H. (Clapham Rovers), 1879 v S (1)
Birkett, R. J. E. (Middlesbrough), 1936 v Ni (1)
Birley, F. H. (Oxford University), 1874 v S; (with Wanderers), 1875 v S (2)
Birtles, G. (Nottingham F), 1980 v Arg (sub), I; 1981 v R (3)
Bishop, S. M. (Leicester C), 1927 v S, Bel, L, F (4)
Blackburn, F. (Blackburn R), 1901 v S; 1902 v Ni; 1904 v S (3)
Blackburn, G. F. (Aston Villa), 1924 v F (1)
Blenkinsop, E. (Sheffield W), 1928 v F, Bel; 1929 v S, W, Ni, F, Bel, Sp; 1930 v S, W, Ni, G, A; 1931 v S, W, Ni, F, Bel; 1932 v S, W, Ni, Sp; 1933 v S, W, Ni, A (26)
Bliss, H. (Tottenham H), 1921 v S (1)
Blissett, L. (Watford), 1983 v WG (sub), L, W, Gr (sub), H, Ni, S (sub), Aus (1+sub); 1984 v D (sub), H, W (sub), S, USSR (14)
Blockley, J. P. (Arsenal), 1973 v Y (1)
Bloomer, S. (Derby Co), 1895 v S, Ni; 1896 v W, Ni; 1897 v S, W, Ni; 1898 v S; 1899 v S, W, Ni; 1900 v S; 1901 v S, W; 1902 v S, W, Ni; 1904 v S; 1905 v S, W, Ni; (with Middlesbrough), 1907 v S, W (23)
Blunstone, F. (Chelsea), 1955 v W, S, F, P; 1957 v Y (5)
Bond, R. (Preston NE), 1905 v Ni, W; 1906 v S, W, Ni; (with Bradford C), 1910 v S, W, Ni (8)
Bonetti, P. P. (Chelsea), 1966 v D; 1967 v Sp, A; 1968 v Sp; 1970 v Ho, P, WG (7)
Bonsor, A. G. (Wanderers), 1873 v S; 1875 v S (2)
Booth, F. (Manchester C), 1905 v Ni (1)
Booth, T. (Blackburn R.), 1898 v W; (with Everton), 1903 v S (2)
Bowden, E. R. (Arsenal), 1935 v W, I; 1936 v W, Ni, A; 1937 v H (6)
Bower, A. G. (Corinthians), 1924 v Ni, Bel; 1925 v W, Bel; 1927 v W (5)
Bowers, J. W. (Derby Co), 1934 v S, Ni, W (3)
Bowles, S. (QPR), 1974 v P, W, Ni; 1977 v I, Ho (5)
Bowser, S. (WBA), 1920 v Ni (1)
Boyer, P. J. (Norwich C), 1976 v W (1)
Boyes, W. (WBA), 1935 v Ho; (with Everton), 1939 v W, R of E (3)
Boyle, T. W. (Burnley), 1913 v Ni (1)
Brabrook, P. (Chelsea), 1958 v USSR; 1959 v Ni; 1960 v Sp (3)
Bracewell, P. W. (Everton), 1985 v WG (sub), US; 1986 v Ni (3)
Bradford, G. R. W. (Bristol R), 1956 v D (1)
Bradford, J. (Birmingham), 1924 v Ni; 1925 v Bel; 1928 v S; 1929 v Ni, W, F, Sp; 1930 v S, Ni, G, A; 1931 v W (12)
Bradley, W. (Manchester U), 1959 v I, US, M (sub) (3)
Bradshaw, F. (Sheffield W), 1908 v A (1)
Bradshaw, T. H. (Liverpool), 1897 v Ni (1)
Bradshaw, W. (Blackburn R), 1910 v W, Ni; 1912 v Ni; 1913 v W (4)
Brann, G. (Swifts), 1886 v S, W; 1891 v W (3)
Brawn, W. F. (Aston Villa), 1904 v W, Ni (2)
Bray, J. (Manchester C), 1935 v W; 1936 v S, W, Ni, G; 1937 v S (6)
Brayshaw, E. (Sheffield W), 1887 v Ni (1)
Bridges, B. J. (Chelsea), 1965 v S, H, Y; 1966 v A (4)
Bridgett, A. (Sunderland), 1905 v S; 1908 v S, A (2), H, B; 1909 v Ni, W, H (2), A (11)
Brindle, T. (Darwen), 1880 v S, W (2)
Brittleton, J. T. (Sheffield W), 1912 v S, W, Ni; 1913 v S; 1914 v W (5)
Britton, C. S. (Everton), 1935 v S, W, Ni, I; 1937 v S, Ni, H, N, Se (9)
Broadbent, P. F. (Wolverhampton W), 1958 v USSR; 1959 v S, W, Ni, I, Br; 1960 v S (7)

Broadis, I. A. (Manchester C), 1952 v S, A, I; 1953 v S, Arg, Ch, U, US; (with Newcastle U), 1954 v S, H, Y, Bel, Sw, U (14)
Brockbank, J. (Cambridge University), 1872 v S (1)
Brodie, J. B. (Wolverhampton W), 1889 v S, Ni; 1891 v Ni (3)
Bromilow, T. G. (Liverpool), 1921 v W; 1922 v S, W; 1923 v Bel; 1926 v Ni (5)
Bromley-Davenport, W. E. (Oxford University), 1884 v S, W (2)
Brook, E. F. (Manchester C), 1930 v Ni; 1933 v Sw: 1934 v S, W, Ni, F, H, Cz; 1935 v S, W, Ni, I; 1936 v S, W, Ni; 1937 v H; 1938 v W, Ni (18)
Brooking, T. D. (West Ham U), 1974 v P, Arg, EG, Bul, Y; 1975 v Cz (sub), P; 1976 v P, W, Br, I, Fi; 1977 v Ei, Fi, I, Ho, Ni, W; 1978 v I, WG, W, S (sub), H; 1979 v D, Ei, Ni, W (sub), S, Bul, Se (sub), A; 1980 v D, Ni, Arg (sub), W, Ni, S, Bel, Sp; 1981 v Sw, Sp, R, H; 1982 v H, S, Fi, Sp (sub) (47)
Brooks, J. (Tottenham H), 1957 v W, Y, D (3)
Broome, F. H. (Aston Villa), 1938 v G, Sw, F; 1939 v N, I, R, Y (7)
Brown, A. (Aston Villa), 1882 v S, W, Ni (3)
Brown, A. S. (Sheffield U), 1904 v W; 1906 v Ni (2)
Brown, A. (WBA), 1971 v W (1)
Brown, G. (Huddersfield T), 1927 v S, W, Ni, Bel, L, F; 1928 v W; 1929 v S; (with Aston Villa), 1933 v W (9)
Brown, J. (Blackburn R), 1881 v W; 1882 v Ni; 1885 v S, W, Ni (5)
Brown, J. H. (Sheffield W), 1927 v S, W, Bel, L, F; 1930 v Ni (6)
Brown, K. (West Ham U), 1960 v Ni (1)
Brown, W. (West Ham U), 1924 v Bel (1)
Bruton, J. (Burnley), 1928 v F, Bel; 1929 v S (3)
Bryant, W. I. (Clapton), 1925 v F (1)
Buchan, C. M. (Sunderland), 1913 v Ni; 1920 v W; 1921 v W, Bel; 1923 v F; 1924 v S (6)
Buchanan, W. S. (Clapham R), 1876 v S (1)
Buckley, F. C. (Derby Co), 1914 v Ni (1)
Bull, S. G. (Wolverhampton W), 1989 v S (sub), D (sub) (2)
Bullock, F. E. (Huddersfield T), 1921 v Ni (1)
Bullock, N. (Bury), 1923 v Bel; 1926 v W; 1927 v Ni (3)
Burgess, H. (Manchester C), 1904 v S, W, Ni; 1906 v S (4)
Burgess, H. (Sheffield W), 1931 v S, Ni, F, Bel (4)
Burnup, C. J. (Cambridge University), 1896 v S (1)
Burrows, H. (Sheffield W), 1934 v H, Cz; 1935 v Ho (3)
Burton, F. E. (Nottingham F), 1889 v Ni (1)
Bury, L. (Cambridge University), 1877 v S; (with Old Etonians), 1879 v W (2)
Butcher, T. (Ipswich T), 1980 v Aus; 1981 v Sp; 1982 v W, S, F, Cz, WG, Sp; 1983 v D, WG, L, W, Gr, H, Ni, S, Aus (3); 1984 v D, H, L, F, Ni; 1985 v EG, Fi, T, Ni, Ei, R, Fi, S, I, WG, US; 1986 v Is, USSR, S, M, Ca, P, Mor, Pol, Para, Arg; (with Rangers) 1987 v Se, Ni (2), Y, Sp, Br, S; 1988 v T, Y; 1989 v D, Se, Gr, Alb, Alb, Ch, S, Pol, D (63)
Butler, J. D. (Arsenal), 1925 v Bel (1)
Butler, W. (Bolton W), 1924 v S (1)
Byrne, G. (Liverpool), 1963 v S; 1966 v N (2)
Byrne, J. J. (C Palace), 1962 v Ni; (with West Ham U), 1963 v Sw; 1964 v S, U, P (2), Ei, Br, Arg; 1965 v W, S (11)
Byrne, R. W. (Manchester U), 1954 v S, H, Y, Bel, Sw, U; 1955 v S, W, Ni, WG, F, Sp, P; 1956 v S, W, Ni, Br, Se, Fi, WG, D, Sp; 1957 v S, W, Ni, Y, D (2), Ei (2); 1958 v W, Ni, F (33)

Callaghan, I. R. (Liverpool), 1966 v Fi, F; 1978 v Sw, L (4)
Calvey, J. (Nottingham F), 1902 v Ni (1)
Campbell, A. F. (Blackburn R), 1929 v W, Ni; (with Huddersfield T), 1931 v W, S, Ni; 1932 v W, Ni, Sp (8)
Camsell, G. H. (Middlesbrough), 1929 v F, Bel; 1930 v Ni, W; 1934 v F; 1936 v S, G, A, Bel (9)
Capes, A. J. (Stoke C), 1903 v S (1)
Carr, J. (Middlesbrough), 1920 v Ni; 1923 v W (2)
Carr, J. (Newcastle U), 1905 v Ni; 1907 v Ni (2)
Carr, W. H. (Owlerton, Sheffield), 1875 v S (1)
Carter, H. S. (Sunderland), 1934 v S, H; 1936 v G; 1937 v S, Ni, H; (with Derby Co), 1947 v S, W, Ni, Ei, Ho, F, Sw (13)
Carter, J. H. (WBA), 1926 v Bel; 1929 v Bel, Sp (3)
Catlin, A. E. (Sheffield W), 1937 v W, Ni, H, N, Se (5)
Chadwick, A. (Southampton), 1900 v S, W (2)
Chadwick, E. (Everton), 1891 v S, W; 1892 v S; 1893 v S; 1894 v S; 1896 v Ni; 1897 v S (7)
Chamberlain, M (Stoke C), 1983 v L (sub); 1984 v D (sub), S, USSR, Br, U, Ch; 1985 v Fi (sub) (8)
Chambers, H. (Liverpool), 1921 v S, W, Bel; 1923 v S, W, Ni, Bel; 1924 v Ni (8)
Channon, M. R. (Southampton), 1973 v Y, S (2), Ni, W, Cz, USSR, I; 1974 v A, Pol, I, P, W, Ni, S, Arg, EG, Bul, Y; 1975 v Cz, P, WG, Cy (2), Ni (sub), W, S; 1976 v Sw, Cz, P, W, Ni, S, Br, I, Fi; 1977 v Fi, I, L, Ni, W, S, Br (sub), Arg, U; (with Manchester C), 1978 v Sw (46)
Charlton, J. (Leeds U), 1965 v S, H, Y, WG, Se; 1966 v W, Ni, S, A, Sp, Pol (2), WG (2), Y, Fi, D, U, M, F, Arg, P; 1967 v W, S, Ni, Cz; 1968 v W, Sp; 1969 v W, R, F; 1970 v Ho (2), P, Cz (35)
Charlton, R. (Manchester U), 1958 v S, P, Y; 1959 v S, W, Ni, USSR, I, Br, Pe, M, US; 1960 v W, S, Se, Y, Sp, H; 1961 v Ni, W, S, L, P, Sp, M, I, A; 1962 v W, Ni, S, A, Sw, Pe, L, P, H, Arg, Bul, Br; 1963 v S, F, Br, Cz, EG, Sw; 1964 v S, W, Ni, R of W, U, P, Ei, Br, Arg, US (sub); 1965 v Ni, S, Ho; 1966 v W, Ni, S, A, Sp, WG (2), Y, Fi, N, Pol, U, M, F, Arg, P; 1967 v Ni, W, S, Cz; 1968 v W, Ni, S, USSR (2), Sp (2), Se, Y; 1969 v S, W, Ni, R (2), Bul, M, Br; 1970 v W, Ni, Ho (2), P, Co, Ec, Cz, R, Br, WG (106)
Charnley, R. O. (Blackpool), 1963 v F (1)
Charsley, C. C. (Small Heath), 1893 v Ni (1)
Chedgzoy, S. (Everton), 1920 v W; 1921 v W, S, Ni; 1922 v Ni; 1923 v S; 1924 v W; 1925 v Ni (8)
Chenery, C. J. (C Palace), 1872 v S; 1873 v S; 1874 v S (3)
Cherry, T. J. (Leeds U), 1976 v W, S (sub), Br, Fi; 1977 v Ei, I, L, Ni, S (sub), Br, Arg, U; 1978 v Sw, L, I, Br, W; 1979 v Cz, W, Se; 1980 v Ei, Arg (sub), W, Ni, S, Aus, Sp (sub) (27)
Chilton, A. (Manchester U), 1951 v Ni; 1952 v F (2)
Chippendale, H. (Blackburn R), 1894 v Ni (1)
Chivers, M. (Tottenham H), 1971 v Ma (2), Gr, Ni, S; 1972 v Sw (1+1 sub), Gr, WG (2), Ni (sub), S; 1973 v W (3), S (2), Ni, Cz, Pol, USSR, I; 1974 v A, Pol (24)
Christian, E. (Old Etonians), 1879 v S (1)
Clamp, E. (Wolverhampton W), 1958 v USSR (2), Br, A (4)
Clapton, D. R. (Arsenal), 1959 v W (1)
Clare, T. (Stoke C), 1889 v Ni; 1892 v Ni; 1893 v W; 1894 v S (4)
Clarke, A. J. (Leeds U), 1970 v Cz; 1971 v EG, Ma, Ni, W (sub), S (sub); 1973 v S (2), W, Cz, Pol, USSR, I; 1974 v A, Pol, I; 1975 v P; 1976 v Cz, P (sub) (19)
Clarke, H. A. (Tottenham H), 1954 v S (1)
Clay, T. (Tottenham H), 1920 v W; 1922 v W, S, Ni (4)
Clayton, R. (Blackburn R), 1956 v Ni, Br, Se, Fi, WG, Sp; 1957 v S, W, Ni, Y, D (2), Ei (2); 1958 v S, W, Ni, F, P, Y, USSR; 1959 v S, W, Ni, USSR, I, Br, Pe, M, US; 1960 v W, Ni, S, Se, Y (35)
Clegg, J. C. (Sheffield W), 1872 v S (1)
Clegg, W. E. (Sheffield W), 1873 v S; (with Sheffield Albion), 1879 v W (2)
Clemence, R. N. (Liverpool), 1973 v W (2); 1974 v EG, Bul, Y; 1975 v Cz, P, WG, Cy, Ni, W, S; 1976 v Sw, Cz, P, W (2), Ni, S, Br, Fi; 1977 v Ei, Fi, I, Ho, L, S, Br,

Arg, U; 1978 v Sw, L, I, WG, Ni, S; 1979 v D, Ei, Ni (2), S, Bul, A (sub); 1980 v D, Bul, Ei, Arg, W, S, Bel, Sp; 1981 v R, Sp, Br, Sw, H; (with Tottenham H), 1982 v N, Ni, Fi; 1983 v L; 1984 v L (61)
Clement, D. T. (QPR), 1976 v W (sub), W, I; 1977 v I, Ho (5)
Clough, B. H. (Middlesbrough), 1960 v W, Se (2)
Clough, N. H. (Nottingham F), 1989 v Ch (1)
Coates, R. (Burnley), 1970 v Ni; 1971 v Gr (sub); (with Tottenham H), Ma, W (4)
Cobbold, W. N. (Cambridge University), 1883 v S, Ni; 1885 v S, Ni; 1886 v S, W; (with Old Carthusians), 1887 v S, W, Ni (9)
Cock, J. G. (Huddersfield T), 1920 v Ni; (with Chelsea), v S (2)
Cockburn, H. (Manchester U), 1947 v W, Ni, Ei; 1948 v S, I; 1949 v S, Ni, D, Sw, Se; 1951 v Arg, P; 1952 v F (13)
Cohen, G. R. (Fulham), 1964 v U, P, Ei, US, Br; 1965 v W, S, Ni, Bel, H, Ho, Y, WG, Se; 1966 v W, S, Ni, A, Sp, Pol (2), WG (2), N, D, U, M, F, Arg, P; 1967 v W, S, Ni, Cz, Sp; 1968 v W, Ni (37)
Coleclough, H. (C Palace), 1914 v W (1)
Coleman, E. H. (Dulwich Hamlet), 1921 v W (1)
Coleman, J. (Woolwich Arsenal), 1907 v Ni (1)
Common, A. (Sheffield U), 1904 v W, Ni; (with Middlesbrough), 1906 v W (3)
Compton, L. H. (Arsenal), 1951 v W, Y (2)
Conlin, J. (Bradford C), 1906 v S (1)
Connelly, J. M. (Burnley), 1960 v W, N, S, Se; 1962 v W, A, Sw, P; 1963 v W, F; (with Manchester U), 1965 v H, Y, Se; 1966 v W, Ni, S, A, N, D, U (20)
Cook, T. E. R. (Brighton), 1925 v W (1)
Cooper, N. C. (Cambridge University), 1893 v Ni (1)
Cooper, T. (Derby Co), 1928 v Ni; 1929 v W, Ni, S, F, Bel, Sp; 1931 v F; 1932 v W, Sp; 1933 v S; 1934 v S, H, Cz; 1935 v W (15)
Cooper, T. (Leeds U), 1969 v W, S, F, M; 1970 v Ho, Bel, Co, Ec, R, Cz, Br, WG; 1971 v EG, Ma, Ni, W, S; 1972 v Sw (2); 1975 v P (20)
Coppell, S. J. (Manchester U), 1978 v I, WG, Br, W, Ni, S, H; 1979 v D, Ei, Cz, Ni (2), W (sub), S, Bul, A; 1980 v D, Ni, Ei (sub), Sp, Arg, W, S, Bel, I; 1981 v R (sub), Sw, R, Br, W, S, Sw, H; 1982 v H, S, Fi, F, Cz, K, WG; 1983 v L, Gr (42)
Copping, W. (Leeds U), 1933 v I, Sw; 1934 v S, Ni, W, F; (with Arsenal), 1935 v Ni, I; 1936 v A, Bel; 1937 v N, Se, Fi; 1938 v S, W, Ni, Cz; 1939 v W, R of E; (with Leeds U), R (20)
Corbett, B. O. (Corinthians), 1901 v W (1)
Corbett, R. (Old Malvernians), 1903 v W (1)
Corbett, W. S. (Birmingham), 1908 v A, H, B (3)
Corrigan, J. T. (Manchester C), 1976 v I (sub), Br; 1979 v W; 1980 v Ni, Aus; 1981 v W, S; 1982 v W, Ic (9)
Cottee, A. R. (West Ham U), 1987 v Se (sub), Ni (sub); 1988 v H (sub); (with Everton) 1989 v D (sub), Se (sub), Ch (sub), S (7)
Cotterill, G. H. (Cambridge University), 1891 v Ni; (with Old Brightonians), 1892 v W; 1893 v S, Ni (4)
Cottle, J. R. (Bristol C), 1909 v Ni (1)
Cowan, S. (Manchester C), 1926 v Bel; 1930 v A; 1931 v Bel (3)
Cowans, G. (Aston Villa), 1983 v W, H, Ni, S, Aus (3); (with Bari), 1986 v Eg, USSR (9)
Cowell, A. (Blackburn R), 1910 v Ni (1)
Cox, J. (Liverpool), 1901 v Ni; 1902 v S; 1903 v S (3)
Cox, J. D. (Derby Co), 1892 v Ni (1)
Crabtree, J. W. (Burnley), 1894 v Ni; 1895 v Ni, S; (with Aston Villa), 1896 v W, S, Ni; 1899 v S, W, Ni; 1900 v S, W, Ni; 1901 v W; 1902 v W (14)
Crawford, J. F. (Chelsea), 1931 v S (1)
Crawford, R. (Ipswich T), 1962 v Ni, A (2)
Crawshaw, T. H. (Sheffield W), 1895 v Ni; 1896 v S, W, Ni; 1897 v S, W, Ni; 1901 v Ni; 1904 v W, Ni (10)
Crayston, W. J. (Arsenal), 1936 v S, W, G, A, Bel; 1938 v W, Ni, Cz (8)
Creek, F. N. S. (Corinthians), 1923 v F (1)
Cresswell, W. (South Shields), 1921 v W; (with Sunderland), 1923 v F; 1924 v Bel; 1925 v Ni; 1926 v W; 1927 v Ni; (with Everton), 1930 v Ni (7)
Crompton, R. (Blackburn R), 1902 v S, W, Ni; 1903 v S, W; 1904 v S, W, Ni; 1906 v S, W, Ni; 1907 v S, W, Ni; 1908 v S, W, Ni, A (2), H, B; 1909 v S, W, Ni, H (2), A; 1910 v S, W; 1911 v S, W, Ni; 1912 v S, W, Ni; 1913 v S, W, Ni; 1914 v S, W, Ni (41)
Crooks, S. D. (Derby Co), 1930 v S, G, A; 1931 v S, W, Ni, F, Bel; 1932 v S, W, Ni, Sp; 1933 v Ni, W, A; 1934 v S, Ni, W, F, H, Cz; 1935 v Ni; 1936 v S, W; 1937 v W, H (26)
Crowe, C. (Wolverhampton W), 1963 v F (1)
Cuggy, F. (Sunderland), 1913 v Ni; 1914 v Ni (2)
Cullis, S. (Wolverhampton W), 1938 v S, W, Ni, F, Cz; 1939 v S, Ni, R of E, N, I, R, Y (12)
Cunliffe, A. (Blackburn R), 1933 v Ni, W (2)
Cunliffe, D. (Portsmouth), 1900 v Ni (1)
Cunliffe, J. N. (Everton), 1936 v Bel (1)
Cunningham, L. (WBA), 1979 v W, Se, A (sub); (with Real Madrid), 1980 v Ei, Sp (sub); 1981 v R (sub) (6)
Currey, E. S. (Oxford University), 1890 v S, W (2)
Currie, A. W. (Sheffield U), 1972 v Ni; 1973 v USSR, I; 1974 v A, Pol, I; 1976 v Sw; (with Leeds U), 1978 v Br, W (sub), Ni, S, H (sub); 1979 v Cz, Ni (2), W, Se (17)
Cursham, A. W. (Notts Co), 1876 v S; 1877 v S; 1878 v S; 1879 v W; 1883 v S, W (6)
Cursham, H. A. (Notts Co), 1880 v W; 1882 v S, W, Ni; 1883 v S, W, Ni; 1884 v Ni (8)

Daft, H. B. (Notts Co), 1889 v Ni; 1890 v S, W; 1891 v Ni; 1892 v Ni (5)
Danks, T. (Nottingham F), 1885 v S (1)
Davenport, P. (Nottingham F), 1985 v Ei (sub) (1)
Davenport, J. K. (Bolton W), 1885 v W; 1890 v Ni (2)
Davis, G. (Derby Co), 1904 v W, Ni (2)
Davis, H. (Sheffield W), 1903 v S, W, Ni (3)
Davison, J. E. (Sheffield W), 1922 v W (1)
Dawson, J. (Burnley), 1922 v S, Ni (2)
Day, S. H. (Old Malvernians), 1906 v Ni, W, S (3)
Dean, W. R. (Everton), 1927 v S, W, F, Bel, L; 1928 v S, W, Ni, F, Bel; 1929 v S, W, Ni; 1931 v S; 1932 v Sp; 1933 v Ni (16)
Deeley, N. V. (Wolverhampton W), 1959 v Br, Pe (2)
Devey, J. H. G. (Aston Villa), 1892 v Ni; 1894 v Ni (2)
Devonshire, A. (West Ham U), 1980 v Aus (sub), Ni; 1982 v Ho, Ic; 1983 v WG, W, Gr; 1984 v L (8)
Dewhurst, F. (Preston NE), 1886 v W, Ni; 1887 v S, W, Ni; 1888 v S, W, Ni; 1889 v W (9)
Dewhurst, G. P. (Liverpool Ramblers), 1895 v W (1)
Dickinson, J. W. (Portsmouth), 1949 v N, F; 1950 v S, W, Ei, P, Bel, Ch, US, Sp; 1951 v Ni, W, Y; 1952 v W, Ni, S, A (2), I, Sw; 1953 v W, Ni, S, Bel, Arg, Ch, U, US; 1954 v W, Ni, S, R of E, H (2), Y, Bel, Sw, U; 1955 v Sp, P; 1956 v W, Ni, S, D, Sp; 1957 v W, Y, D (48)
Dimmock, J. H. (Tottenham H), 1921 v S; 1926 v W, Bel (3)
Ditchburn, E. G. (Tottenham H), 1949 v Sw, Se; 1953 v US; 1957 v W, Y, D (6)
Dix, R. W. (Derby Co), 1939 v N (1)
Dixon, J. A. (Notts Co), 1885 v W (1)
Dixon, K. M. (Chelsea), 1985 v M (sub), WG, US; 1986 v Ni, Is, M (sub), Pol (sub); 1987 v Se (8)
Dobson, A. T. C. (Notts Co), 1882 v Ni; 1884 v S, W, Ni (4)
Dobson, C. F. (Notts Co), 1886 v Ni (1)
Dobson, J. M. (Burnley), 1974 v P, EG, Bul, Y; (with Everton), 1975 v Cz (5)
Doggart, A. G. (Corinthians), 1924 v Bel (1)

Dorrell, A. R. (Aston Villa), 1925 v W, Bel, F; 1926 v Ni (4)
Douglas, B. (Blackburn R), 1958 v S, W, Ni, F, P, Y, USSR (2), Br, A; 1959 v S, USSR; 1960 v Y, H; 1961 v Ni, W, S, L, P, Sp, M, I, A; 1962 v W, Ni, S, Pe, L, P, H, Arg, Bul, Br; 1963 v S, Br, Sw (36)
Downs, R. W. (Everton), 1921 v Ni (1)
Doyle, M. (Manchester C), 1976 v W, S (sub), Br, I; 1977 v Ho (5)
Drake, E. J. (Arsenal), 1935 v Ni, I; 1936 v W; 1937 v H; 1938 v F (5)
Ducat, A. (Woolwich Arsenal), 1910 v S, W, Ni; (with Aston Villa), 1920 v S, W; 1921 v Ni (6)
Dunn, A. T. B. (Cambridge University), 1883 v Ni; 1884 v Ni; (with Old Etonians), 1892 v S, W (4)
Duxbury, M. (Manchester U), 1984 v L, F, W, S, USSR, Br, U, Ch; 1985 v EG, Fi (10)

Earle, S. G. J. (Clapton), 1924 v F; (with West Ham U), 1928 v Ni (2)
Eastham, G. (Arsenal), 1963 v Br, Cz, EG; 1964 v W, Ni, S, R of W, U, P, Ei, US, Br, Arg; 1965 v H, WG, Se; 1966 v Sp, Pol, D (19)
Eastham, G. R. (Bolton W), 1935 v Ho (1)
Eckersley, W. (Blackburn R), 1950 v Sp; 1951 v S, Y, Arg, P; 1952 v A (2), Sw; 1953 v Ni, Arg, Ch, U, US; 1954 v W, Ni, R of E, H (17)
Edwards, D. (Manchester U), 1955 v S, F, Sp, P; 1956 v S, Br, Se, Fi, WG; 1957 v S, Ni, Ei (2), D (2); 1958 v W, Ni, F (18)
Edwards, J. H. (Shropshire Wanderers), 1874 v S (1)
Edwards, W. (Leeds U), 1926 v S, W; 1927 v W, Ni, S, F, Bel, L; 1928 v S, F, Bel; 1929 v S, W, Ni; 1930 v W, Ni (16)
Ellerington, W. (Southampton), 1949 v N, F (2)
Elliott, G. W. (Middlesbrough), 1913 v Ni; 1914 v Ni; 1920 v W (3)
Elliott, W. H. (Burnley), 1952 v I, A; 1953 v Ni, W, Bel (5)
Evans, R. E. (Sheffield U), 1911 v S, W, Ni; 1912 v W (4)
Ewer, F. H. (Casuals), 1924 v F; 1925 v Bel (2)

Fairclough, P. (Old Foresters), 1878 v S (1)
Fairhurst, D. (Newcastle U), 1934 v F (1)
Fantham, J. (Sheffield W), 1962 v L (1)
Fashanu, J. (Wimbledon), 1989 v Ch, S (2)
Felton, W. (Sheffield W), 1925 v F (1)
Fenton, M. (Middlesbrough), 1938 v S (1)
Fenwick, T. (QPR), 1984 v W (sub), S, USSR, Br, U, Ch; 1985 v Fi, S, M, US; 1986 v R, T, Ni, Eg, M, P, Mor, Pol, Arg; (with Tottenham H), 1988 v Is (sub) (20)
Field, E. (Clapham Rovers), 1876 v S; 1881 v S (2)
Finney, T. (Preston NE), 1947 v W, Ni, Ei, Ho, F, P; 1948 v S, W, Ni, Bel, Se, I; 1949 v S, W, Ni, Se, N, F; 1950 v S, W, Ni, Ei, I, P, Bel, Ch, US, Sp; 1951 v W, S, Arg, P; 1952 v W, Ni, S, F, I, Sw, A; 1953 v W, Ni, S, Bel, Arg, Ch, U, US; 1954 v W, S, Bel, Sw, U, H, Y; 1955 v WG; 1956 v S, W, Ni, D, Sp; 1957 v S, W, Y, D (2), Ei (2); 1958 v W, S, F, P, Y, USSR (2); 1959 v Ni, USSR (76)
Fleming, H. J. (Swindon T), 1909 v S, H (2); 1910 v W, Ni; 1911 v W, Ni; 1912 v Ni; 1913 v S, W; 1914 v S (11)
Fletcher, A. (Wolverhampton W), 1889 v W; 1890 v W (2)
Flowers, R. (Wolverhampton W), 1955 v F; 1959 v S, W, I, Br, Pe, US, M (sub); 1960 v W, Ni, S, Se, Y, Sp, H; 1961 v Ni, W, S, L, P, Sp, M, I, A; 1962 v W, Ni, S, A, Sw, Pe, L, P, H, Arg, Bul, Br; 1963 v Ni, W, S, F (2), Sw; 1964 v Ei, US, P; 1965 v W, Ho, WG; 1966 v N (49)
Forman, Frank (Nottingham F), 1898 v S, Ni; 1899 v S, W, Ni; 1901 v S; 1902 v S, Ni; 1903 v W (9)
Forman, F. R. (Nottingham F), 1899 v S, W, Ni (3)
Forrest, J. H. (Blackburn R), 1884 v W; 1885 v S, W, Ni; 1886 v S, W; 1887 v S, W, Ni; 1889 v S; 1890 v Ni (11)
Fort, J. (Millwall), 1921 v Bel (1)
Foster, R. E. (Oxford University), 1900 v W; (with Corinthians), 1901 v W, Ni, S; 1902 v W (5)
Foster, S. (Brighton & HA), 1982 v Ni, Ho, K (3)
Foulke, W. J. (Sheffield U), 1897 v W (1)
Foulkes, W. A. (Manchester U), 1955 v Ni (1)
Fox, F. S. (Gillingham), 1925 v F (1)
Francis, G. C. J. (QPR), 1975 v Cz, P, W, S; 1976 v Sw, Cz, P, W, Ni, S, Br, Fi (12)
Francis, T. (Birmingham C), 1977 v Ho, L, S, Br; 1978 v Sw, L, I (sub), WG (sub), Br, W, S, H; (with Nottingham F), 1979 v Bul (sub), Se, A (sub); 1980 v Ni, Bul, Sp; 1981 v Sp, R, S (sub), Sw; (with Manchester C), 1982 v N, Ni, W, S (sub), Fi (sub), F, Cz, K, WG, Sp; (with Sampdoria), 1983 v D, Gr, H, Ni, S, Aus (3); 1984 v D, Ni, USSR; 1985 v EG (sub), T (sub), Ni (sub), R, Fi, S, I, M; 1986 v S (52)
Franklin, C. F. (Stoke C), 1947 v S, W, Ni, Ei, Ho, F, Sw, P; 1948 v S, W, Ni, Bel, Se, I; 1949 v S, W, Ni, D, Sw, N, F, Se; 1950 v W, S, Ni, Ei, I (27)
Freeman, B. C. (Everton), 1909 v S, W; (with Burnley), 1912 v S, W, Ni (5)
Froggatt, J. (Portsmouth), 1950 v Ni, I; 1951 v S; 1952 v S, A (2), I, Sw; 1953 v Ni, W, S, Bel, US (13)
Froggatt, R. (Sheffield W), 1953 v W, S, Bel, US (4)
Fry, C. B. (Corinthians), 1901 v Ni (1)
Furness, W. I. (Leeds U), 1933 v I (1)

Galley, T. (Wolverhampton W), 1937 v N, Se (2)
Gardner, T. (Aston Villa), 1934 v Cz; 1935 v Ho (2)
Garfield, B. (WBA), 1898 v Ni (1)
Garratty, W. (Aston Villa), 1903 v W (1)
Garrett, T. (Blackpool), 1952 v S, I; 1954 v W (3)
Gascoigne, P. J. (Tottenham H), 1989 v D (sub), S.Ar (sub), Alb (sub), Ch, S (sub) (5)
Gates, E. (Ipswich T), 1981 v N, R (2)
Gay, L. H. (Cambridge University), 1893 v S; (with Old Brightonians), 1894 v S, W (3)
Geary, F. (Everton), 1890 v Ni; 1891 v S (2)
Geaves, R. L. (Clapham Rovers), 1875 v S (1)
Gee, C. W. (Everton), 1932 v W, Sp; 1937 v Ni (3)
Geldard, A. (Everton), 1933 v I, Sw; 1935 v S; 1938 v Ni (4)
George, C. (Derby Co), 1977 v Ei (1)
George, W. (Aston Villa), 1902 v S, W, Ni (3)
Gibbins, W. V. T. (Clapton), 1924 v F; 1925 v F (2)
Gidman, J. (Aston Villa), 1977 v L (1)
Gillard, I. T. (QPR), 1975 v WG, W; 1976 v Cz (3)
Gilliat, W. E. (Old Carthusians), 1893 v Ni (1)
Goddard, P. (West Ham U), 1982 v Ic (sub) (1)
Goodall, F. R. (Huddersfield T), 1926 v S; 1927 v S, F, Bel, L; 1928 v S, W, F, Bel; 1930 v S, G, A; 1931 v S, W, Ni, Bel; 1932 v Ni; 1933 v W, Ni, A, I, Sw; 1934 v W, Ni, F (25)
Goodall, J. (Preston NE), 1888 v S, W; 1889 v S, W; (with Derby Co), 1891 v S, W; 1892 v S; 1893 v W; 1894 v S; 1895 v S, Ni; 1896 v S, W; 1898 v W (14)
Goodhart, H. C. (Old Etonians), 1883 v S, W, Ni (3)
Goodwyn, A. G. (Royal Engineers), 1873 v S (1)
Goodyer, A. C.(Nottingham F), 1879 v S (1)
Gosling, R. C. (Old Etonians), 1892 v W; 1893 v S; 1894 v W; 1895 v W, S (5)
Gosnell, A. A. (Newcastle U), 1906 v Ni (1)
Gough, H. C. (Sheffield U), 1921 v S (1)
Goulden, L. A. (West Ham U), 1937 v Se, N; 1938 v W, Ni, Cz, G, Sw, F; 1939 v S, W, R of E, I, R, Y (14)
Graham, L. (Millwall), 1925 v S, W (2)
Graham, T. (Nottingham F), 1931 v F; 1932 v Ni (2)
Grainger, C. (Sheffield U), 1956 v Br, Se, Fi, WG; 1957 v W, Ni; (with Sunderland), 1957 v S (7)
Greaves, J. (Chelsea), 1959 v Pe, M, US; 1960 v W, Se, Y, Sp; 1961 v Ni, W, S, L, P, Sp, I, A; (with Tottenham H), 1962 v S, Sw, Pe, H, Arg, Bul, Br; 1963 v Ni, W, S,

F (2), Br, Cz, Sw; 1964 v W, Ni, R of W, P (2), Ei, Br, U, Arg; 1965 v Ni, S, Bel, Ho, H, Y; 1966 v W, A, Y, N, D, Pol, U, M, F; 1967 v S, Sp, A (57)
Green, F. T. (Wanderers), 1876 v S (1)
Green, G. H. (Sheffield U), 1925 v F; 1926 v S, Bel, W; 1927 v W, Ni; 1928 v F, Bel (8)
Greenhalgh, E. H. (Notts Co), 1872 v S; 1873 v S (2)
Greenhoff, B. (Manchester U), 1976 v W, Ni; 1977 v Ei, Fi, I, Ho, Ni, W, S, Br, Arg, U; 1978 v Br, W, Ni, S (sub), H (sub); (with Leeds U), 1980 v Aus (sub) (18)
Greenwood, D. H. (Blackburn R), 1882 v S, Ni (2)
Gregory, J. (QPR), 1983 v Aus (3); 1984 v D, H, W (6)
Grimsdell, A. (Tottenham H), 1920 v S, W; 1921 v S, Ni; 1923 v W, Ni (6)
Grosvenor, A. T. (Birmingham), 1934 v Ni, W, F (3)
Gunn, W. (Notts Co), 1884 v S, W (2)
Gurney, R. (Sunderland), 1935 v S (1)

Hacking, J. (Oldham Ath), 1929 v S, W, Ni (3)
Hadley, N. (WBA), 1903 v Ni (1)
Hagan, J. (Sheffield U), 1949 v D (1)
Haines, J. T. W. (WBA), 1949 v Sw (1)
Hall, A. E. (Aston Villa), 1910 v Ni (1)
Hall, G. W. (Tottenham H), 1934 v F; 1938 v S, W, Ni, Cz; 1939 v S, Ni, R of E, I, Y (10)
Hall, J. (Birmingham C), 1956 v S, W, Ni, Br, Se, Fi, WG, D, Sp; 1957 v S, W, Ni, Y, D (2), Ei (2) (17)
Halse, H. J. (Manchester U), 1909 v A (1)
Hammond, H. E. D. (Oxford University), 1889 v S (1)
Hampson, J. (Blackpool), 1931 v Ni, W; 1933 v A (3)
Hampton, H. (Aston Villa), 1913 v S, W; 1914 v S, W (4)
Hancocks, J. Wolverhampton W), 1949 v Sw; 1950 v W; 1951 v Y (3)
Hapgood, E. (Arsenal), 1933 v I, Sw; 1934 v S, Ni, W, H, Cz; 1935 v S, Ni, W, I, Ho; 1936 v S, Ni, W, G, A, Bel; 1937 v Fi; 1938 v S, G, Sw, F; 1939 v S, W, Ni, R of E, N, I, Y (30)
Hardinge, H. T. W. (Sheffield U), 1910 v S (1)
Hardman, H. P. (Everton), 1905 v W; 1907 v S, Ni; 1908 v W (4)
Hardwick, G. F. M. (Middlesbrough), 1947 v S, W, Ni, Ei, Ho, F, Sw, P; 1948 v S, W, Ni, Bel, Se (13)
Hardy, H. (Stockport Co), 1925 v Bel (1)
Hardy, S. (Liverpool), 1907 v S, W, Ni; 1908 v S; 1909 v S, W, Ni, H (2), A; 1910 v S, W, Ni; 1912 v Ni; (with Aston Villa), 1913 v S; 1914 v Ni, W, S; 1920 v S, W, Ni (21)
Harford, M. G. (Luton T), 1988 v Is (sub); 1989 v D (2)
Hargreaves, F. W. (Blackburn R), 1880 v W; 1881 v W; 1882 v Ni (3)
Hargreaves, J. (Blackburn R), 1881 v S, W (2)
Harper, E. C. (Blackburn R), 1926 v S (1)
Harris, G. (Burnley), 1966 v Pol (1)
Harris, P. P. (Portsmouth), 1950 v Ei; 1954 v H (2)
Harris, S. S. (Cambridge University), 1904 v S; (with Old Westminsters), 1905 v Ni, W; 1906 v S, W, Ni (6)
Harrison, A. H. (Old Westminsters), 1893 v S, Ni (2)
Harrison, G. (Everton), 1921 v Bel; 1922 v Ni (2)
Harrow, J. H. (Chelsea), 1923 v Ni, Se (2)
Hart, E. (Leeds U), 1929 v W; 1930 v W, Ni; 1933 v S, A; 1934 v S, H, Cz (8)
Hartley, F. (Oxford C), 1923 v F (1)
Harvey, A. (Wednesbury Strollers), 1881 v W (1)
Harvey, J. C. (Everton), 1971 v Ma (1)
Hassall, H. W. (Huddersfield T), 1951 v S, Arg, P; 1952 v F; (with Bolton W), 1954 v Ni (5)
Hateley, M. (Portsmouth), 1984 v USSR (sub), Br, U, Ch; (with AC Milan), 1985 v EG (sub), Fi, Ni, Ei, Fi, S, I, M; 1986 v R, T, Eg, S, M, Ca, P, Mor, Para (sub); 1987 v T (sub), Br (sub), S; (with Monaco), 1988 v WG (sub), Ho (sub), H (sub), Co (sub), Ei (sub), Ho (sub), USSR (sub) (31)
Haworth, G. (Accrington), 1887 v Ni, W, S; 1888 v S; 1890 v S (5)
Hawtrey, J. P. (Old Etonians), 1881 v S, W (2)
Hawkes, R. M. (Luton T), 1907 v Ni; 1908 v A (2), H, B (5)
Haygarth, E. B. (Swifts), 1875 v S (1)
Haynes, J. N. (Fulham), 1955 v Ni; 1956 v S, Ni, Br, Se, Fi, WG, Sp; 1957 v W, Y, D, Ei (2); 1958 v W, Ni, S, F, P, Y, USSR (3), Br, A; 1959 v S, Ni, USSR, I, Br, Pe, M, US; 1960 v Ni, Y, Sp, H; 1961 v Ni, W, S, L, P, Sp, M, I, A; 1962 v W, Ni, S, A, Sw, Pe, P, H, Arg, Bul, Br (56)
Healless, H. (Blackburn R), 1925 v Ni; 1928 v S (2)
Hector, K. J. (Derby Co), 1974 v Pol (sub), I (sub), (2)
Hedley, G. A. (Sheffield U), 1901 v Ni (1)
Hegan, K. E. (Corinthians), 1923 v Bel, F; 1924 v Ni, Bel (4)
Hellawell, M. S. (Birmingham C), 1963 v Ni, F (2)
Henfrey, A. G. (Cambridge University), 1891 v Ni; (with Corinthians), 1892 v W; 1895 v W; 1896 v S, W (5)
Henry, R. P. (Tottenham H), 1963 v F (1)
Heron, F. (Wanderers), 1876 v S (1)
Heron, G. H. H. (Uxbridge), 1873 v S; 1874 v S; (with Wanderers), 1875 v S; 1876 v S; 1878 v S (5)
Hibbert, W. (Bury), 1910 v S (1)
Hibbs, H. E. (Birmingham), 1930 v S, W, A, G; 1931 v S, W, Ni; 1932 v W, Ni, Sp; 1933 v S, W, Ni, A, I, Sw; 1934 v Ni, W, F; 1935 v S, W, Ni, Ho; 1936 v G, W (25)
Hill, F. (Bolton W), 1963 v Ni, W (2)
Hill, J. H. (Burnley), 1925 v W; 1926 v S; 1927 v S, Ni, Bel, F; 1928 v Ni, W; 1929 v F, Bel, Sp (11)
Hill, G. A. (Manchester U), 1976 v I; 1977 v Ei (sub), Fi (sub), L; 1978 v Sw (sub), L (6)
Hill, R. (Luton T), 1983 v D (sub), WG; 1986 v Eg (sub) (3)
Hill, R. H. (Millwall), 1926 v Bel (1)
Hillman, J. (Burnley), 1899 v Ni (1)
Hills, A. F. (Old Harrovians), 1879 v S (1)
Hilsdon, G. R. (Chelsea), 1907 v Ni; 1908 v S, W, Ni, A, H, B; 1909 v Ni (8)
Hine, E. W. (Leicester C), 1929 v W, Ni; 1930 v W, Ni; 1932 v W, Ni (6)
Hinton, A. T. (Wolverhampton W), 1963 v F; (with Nottingham F), 1965 v W, Bel (3)
Hitchens, G. A. (Aston Villa), 1961 v M, I, A; (with Inter-Milan), 1962 v Sw, Pe, H, Br (7)
Hobbis, H. H. F. (Charlton Ath), 1936 v A, Bel (2)
Hoddle, G. (Tottenham H), 1980 v Bul, W, Aus, Sp; 1981 v Sp, W, S; 1982 v N, Ni, W, Ic, Cz (sub), K; 1983 v L (sub), Ni, S; 1984 v H, L, F; 1985 v Ei (sub), S, I (sub), M, WG, US; 1986 v R, T, Ni, Is, USSR, S, M, Ca, P, Mor, Pol, Para, Arg; 1987 v Se Ni, Y, Sp, T, S; (with Monaco), 1988 v WG, T (sub), Y (sub), Ho (sub), H (sub), Co (sub), Ei (sub), Ho, USSR (53)
Hodge, S. B. (Aston Villa), 1986 v USSR (sub), S, Ca, P (sub), Mor (sub), Pol, Para, Arg; 1987 v Se, Ni, Y (with Tottenham H), Sp. Ni, T, S; 1989 (with Nottingham F) v D (16)
Hodgetts, D. (Aston Villa), 1888 v S, W, Ni; 1892 v S, Ni; 1894 v Ni (6)
Hodgkinson, A. (Sheffield U), 1957 v S, Ei (2), D; 1961 v W (5)
Hodgson, G. (Liverpool), 1931 v S, Ni, W (3)
Hodkinson, J. (Blackburn R), 1913 v W, S; 1920 v Ni (3)
Hogg, W. (Sunderland), 1902 v S, W, Ni (3)
Holdcroft, G. H. (Preston NE), 1937 v W, Ni (2)
Holden, A. D. (Bolton W), 1959 v S, I, Br, Pe, M (5)
Holden, G. H. (Wednesday OA), 1881 v S; 1884 v S, W, Ni (4)
Holden-White, C. (Corinthians), 1888 v W, S (2)
Holford, T. (Stoke), 1903 v Ni (1)
Holley, G. H. (Sunderland), 1909 v S, W, H (2), A; 1910 v W; 1912 v S, W, NI; 1913 v S (10)

Holliday, E. (Middlesbrough), 1960 v W, Ni, Se (3)
Hollins, J. W. (Chelsea), 1967 v Sp (1)
Holmes, R. (Preston NE), 1888 v Ni; 1891 v S; 1892 v S; 1893 v S, W; 1894 v Ni; 1895 v Ni (7)
Holt, J. (Everton), 1890 v W; 1891 v S, W; 1892 v S, Ni; 1893 v S; 1894 v S, Ni; 1895 v S; (with Reading), 1900 v Ni (10)
Hopkinson, E. (Bolton W), 1958 v W, Ni, S, F, P, Y; 1959 v S, I, Br, Pe, M, US; 1960 v W, Se (14)
Hossack, A. H. (Corinthians), 1892 v W; 1894 v W (2)
Houghton, W. E. (Aston Villa), 1931 v Ni, W, F, Bel; 1932 v S, Ni; 1933 v A (7)
Houlker, A. E. (Blackburn R), 1902 v S; (with Portsmouth), 1903 v S, W; (with Southampton), 1906 v W, Ni (5)
Howarth, R. H. (Preston NE), 1887 v Ni; 1888 v S, W; 1891 v S; (with Everton), 1894 v Ni (5)
Howe, D. (WBA), 1958 v S, W, Ni, F, P, Y, USSR (3), Br, A; 1959 v S, W, Ni, USSR, I, Br, Pe, M, US; 1960 v W, Ni, Se (23)
Howe, J. R. (Derby Co), 1948 v I; 1949 v S, Ni (3)
Howell, L. S. (Wanderers), 1873 v S (1)
Howell, R. (Sheffield U), 1895 v Ni; (with Liverpool) 1899 v S (2)
Hudson, A. A. (Stoke C), 1975 v WG, Cy (2)
Hudson, J. (Sheffield), 1883 v Ni (1)
Hudspeth, F. C. (Newcastle U), 1926 v Ni (1)
Hufton, A. E. (West Ham U), 1924 v Bel; 1928 v S, Ni; 1929 v F, Bel, Sp (6)
Hughes, E. W. (Liverpool), 1970 v W, Ni, S, Ho, P, Bel; 1971 v EG, Ma (2), Gr, W; 1972 v Sw, Gr, Wg (2), W, Ni, S; 1973 v W (3), S (2), Pol, USSR, I; 1974 v A, Pol, I, W, Ni, S, Arg, EG, Bul, Y; 1975 v Cz, P, Cy (sub), Ni; 1977 v I, L, W, S, Br, Arg, U; 1978 v Sw, L, I, WG, Ni, S, H; 1979 v D, Ei, Ni, W, Se; (with Wolverhampton W), 1980 v Sp (sub), Ni, S (sub) (62)
Hughes, L. (Liverpool), 1950 v Ch, US, Sp (3)
Hulme, J. H. A. (Arsenal), 1927 v S, Bel, F; 1928 v S, Ni, W; 1929 v Ni, W; 1933 v S (9)
Humphreys, P. (Notts Co), 1903 v S (1)
Hunt, G. S. (Tottenham H), 1933 v I, Sw, S (3)
Hunt, Rev K. R. G. (Leyton), 1911 v S, W (2)
Hunt, R. (Liverpool), 1962 v A; 1963 v EG; 1964 v S, US, P; 1965 v W; 1966 v S, Sp, Pol (2), WG (2), Fi, N, U, M, F, Arg, P; 1967 v Ni, W, Cz, Sp, A; 1968 v W, Ni, USSR (2), Sp (2), Se, Y; 1969 v R (2) (34)
Hunt, S. (WBA), 1984 v S (sub), USSR (sub) (2)
Hunter, J. (Sheffield Heeley), 1878 v S; 1880 v S, W; 1881 v S, W; 1882 v S, W (7)
Hunter, N. (Leeds U), 1966 v WG, Y, Fi, Sp (sub); 1967 v A; 1968 v Sp, Se, Y, WG, USSR; 1969 v R, W; 1970 v Ho, WG (sub); 1971 v Ma; 1972 v WG (2), W, Ni, S; 1973 v W (2) USSR (sub); 1974 v A, Pol, Ni (sub), S; 1975 v Cz (28)
Hurst, G. C. (West Ham U), 1966 v S, WG (2), Y, Fi, D, Arg, P; 1967 v Ni, W, S, Cz, Sp, A; 1968 v W, Ni, S, Se (sub), WG, USSR (2); 1969 v Ni, S, R (2), Bul, F, M, U, Br; 1970 v W, Ni, S, Ho (1+1 sub), Bel, Co, Ec, R, Br, WG; 1971 v EG, Gr, W, S; 1972 v Sw (2), Gr, WG (49)

Iremonger, J. (Nottingham F), 1901 v S; 1902 v Ni (2)

Jack, D. N. B. (Bolton W), 1924 v S, W; 1928 v F, Bel; (with Arsenal), 1930 v S, G, A; 1933 v W, A (9)
Jackson, E. (Oxford University), 1891 v W (1)
Jarrett, B. G. (Cambridge University), 1876 v S; 1877 v S; 1878 v S (3)
Jefferis, F. (Everton), 1912 v S, W (2)
Jezzard, B. A. G. (Fulham), 1954 v H; 1956 v Ni (2)
Johnson, D. E. (Ipswich T), 1975 v W, S; 1976 v Sw; (with Liverpool), 1980 v Ei, Arg, Ni, S, Bel (8)
Johnson, E. (Saltley College), 1880 v W; (with Stoke C), 1884 v Ni (2)
Johnson, J. A. (Stoke C), 1937 v N, Se, Fi, S, Ni (5)
Johnson, T. C. F. (Manchester C), 1926 v Bel; 1930 v W; (with Everton), 1932 v S, Sp; 1933 v Ni (5)
Johnson, W. H. (Sheffield U), 1900 v S, W, Ni; 1903 v S, W, Ni (6)
Johnston, H. (Blackpool), 1947 v S, Ho; 1951 v S; 1953 v Arg, Ch, U, US; 1954 v W, Ni, H (10)
Jones, A. (Walsall Town Swifts), 1882 v S, W; (with Great Lever), 1883 v S (3)
Jones, H. (Blackburn R), 1927 v S, Bel, L, F; 1928 v S, Ni (6)
Jones, H. (Nottingham F), 1923 v F (1)
Jones, M. D. (Sheffield U), 1965 v WG, Se; (with Leeds U), 1970 v Ho (3)
Jones, W. (Bristol C), 1901 v Ni (1)
Jones, W. H. (Liverpool), 1950 v P, Bel (2)
Joy, B. (Casuals), 1936 v Bel (1)

Kail, E. I. L. (Dulwich Hamlet), 1929 v F, Bel, Sp (3)
Kay, A. H. (Everton), 1963 v Sw (1)
Kean, F. W. (Sheffield W), 1923 v S, Bel; 1924 v W; 1925 v Ni; 1926 v Ni, Bel; 1927 v L; (with Bolton W), 1929 v F, Sp (9)
Keegan, J. K. (Liverpool), 1973 v W (2); 1974 v W, Ni, Arg, EG, Bul, Y; 1975 v Cz, WG, Cy (2), Ni, S; 1976 v Sw, Cz, P, W (2), Ni, S, Br, Fi; 1977 v Ei, Fi, I, Ho, L; (with SV Hamburg), W, Br, Arg, U; 1978 v Sw, I, WG, Br, H; 1979 v D, Ei, Cz, Ni, W, S, Bul, Se, A; 1980 v D, Ni, Ei, Sp (2), Arg, Bel, I; (with Southampton), 1981 v Sp, Sw, H; 1982 v N, H, Ni, S, Fi, Sp (sub) (63)
Keen, E. R. L. (Derby Co), 1933 v A; 1937 v W, Ni, H (4)
Kelly, R. (Burnley), 1920 v S; 1921 v S, W, Ni; 1922 v S, W; 1923 v S; 1924 v Ni; 1925 v W, Ni, S; (with Sunderland), 1926 v W; (with Huddersfield T), 1927 v L; 1928 v S (14)
Kennedy, A. (Liverpool), 1984 v Ni, W (2)
Kennedy, R. (Liverpool), 1976 v W (2), Ni, S; 1977 v L, W, S, Br (sub), Arg (sub); 1978 v Sw, L; 1980 v Bul, Sp, Arg, W, Bel (sub), I (17)
Kenyon-Slaney, W. S. (Wanderers), 1873 v S (1)
Kevan, D. T. (WBA), 1957 v S; 1958 v W, Ni, S, P. Y, USSR (3), Br, A; 1959 v M, US; 1961 v M (14)
Kidd, B. (Manchester U), 1970 v Ni, Ec (sub) (2)
King, R. S. (Oxford University), 1882 v Ni (1)
Kingsford, R. K. (Wanderers), 1874 v S (1)
Kingsley, M. (Newcastle U), 1901 v W (1)
Kinsey, G. (Wolverhampton W), 1892 v W; 1893 v S; (with Derby Co), 1896 v W, Ni (4)
Kirchen, A. J. (Arsenal), 1937 v N, Se, Fi (3)
Kirton, W. J. (Aston Villa), 1922 v Ni (1)
Knight, A. E. (Portsmouth), 1920 v Ni (1)
Knowles, C. (Tottenham H), 1968 v USSR, Sp, Se, WG (4)

Labone, B. L. (Everton), 1963 v Ni, W, F; 1967 v Sp, A; 1968 v S, Sp, Se, Y, USSR, Wg; 1969 v Ni, S, R, Bul, M, U, Br; 1970 v S, W, Bel, Co, Ec, R, Br, WG (26)
Lampard, F. R. G. (West Ham U), 1973 v Y; 1980 v Aus (2)
Langley, E. J. (Fulham), 1958 v S, P, Y (3)
Langton, R. (Blackburn R), 1947 v W, Ni, Ei, Ho, F, Sw; 1948 v Se; (with Preston NE), 1949 v D, Se; (with Bolton W), 1950 v S; 1951 v Ni (11)
Latchford, R. D. (Everton), 1978 v I, Br, W; 1979 v D, Ei, Cz (sub), Ni (2), W, S, Bul, A (12)
Latheron, E. G. (Blackburn R), 1913 v W; 1914 v Ni (2)
Lawler, C. (Liverpool), 1971 v Ma, W, S; 1972 v Sw (4)
Lawton, T. (Everton), 1939 v S, W, Ni, R of E, N, I, R, Y; (with Chelsea), 1947 v S, W, Ni, Ei, Ho, F, Sw, P;

1948 v W, Ni, Bel; (with Notts Co), 1948 v S, Se, I; 1949 v D (23)

Leach, T. (Sheffield W), 1931 v W, Ni (2)

Leake, A. (Aston Villa), 1904 v S, Ni; 1905 v S, W, Ni (5)

Lee, E. A. (Southampton), 1904 v W (1)

Lee, F. H. (Manchester C), 1969 v Ni, W, S, Bul, F, M, U; 1970 v W, Ho (2), P, Bel, Co, Ec, R, Br, WG; 1971 v EG, Gr, Ma, Ni, W, S; 1972 v Sw (2), Gr, WG (27)

Lee, J. (Derby Co), 1951 v Ni (1)

Lee, S. (Liverpool), 1983 v Gr, L, W, Gr, H, S, Aus; 1984 v D, H, L, F, Ni, W, Ch (sub) (14)

Leighton, J. E. (Nottingham F), 1886 v Ni (1)

Lilley, H. E. (Sheffield U), 1892 v W (1)

Linacre, H. J. (Nottingham F), 1905 v W, S (2)

Lindley, T. (Cambridge University), 1886 v S, W, Ni, 1887 v S, W, Ni; 1888 v S, W, Ni; (with Nottingham F), 1889 v S; 1890 v S, W; 1891 v Ni (13)

Lindsay, A. (Liverpool), 1974 v Arg, EG, Bul, Y (4)

Lindsay, W. (Wanderers), 1877 v S (1)

Lineker, G. (Leicester C), 1984 v S (sub); 1985 v Ei, R (sub), S (sub), I (sub), WG, US; (with Everton), 1986 v R, T, Ni, Eg, USSR, Ca, P, Mor, Pol, Para, Arg; (with Barcelona), 1987 v Ni (2), Y, Sp, T, Br; 1988 v WG, T, Y, Ho, H, S, Co, Sw, Ei, Ho, USSR; 1989 v Se, S.Ar, Gr, Alb, Alb, Pol, D (42)

Lintott, E. H. (QPR), 1908 v S, W, Ni; (with Bradford C), 1909 v S, Ni, H (2) (7)

Lipsham, H. B. (Sheffield U), 1902 v W (1)

Little, B. (Aston Villa), 1975 v W (sub) (1)

Lloyd, L. V. (Liverpool), 1971 v W; 1972 v Sw, Ni; (with Nottingham F), 1980 v W (4)

Lockett, A. (Stoke C), 1903 v Ni (1)

Lodge, L. V. (Cambridge University), 1894 v W; 1895 v S, W; (with Corinthians), 1896 v S, Ni (5)

Lofthouse, J. M. (Blackburn R), 1885 v S, W, Ni; 1887 v S, W; (with Accrington), 1889 v Ni; (with Blackburn R), 1890 v Ni (7)

Lofthouse, N. (Bolton W), 1951 v Y; 1952 v W, Ni, S, A (2), I, Sw; 1953 v W, Ni, S, Bel, Arg, Ch, U, US; 1954 v W, Ni, R of E, Bel, U; 1955 v Ni, S, F, Sp, P; 1956 v W, S, Sp, D, Fi (sub); 1959 v W, USSR (33)

Longworth, E. (Liverpool), 1920 v S; 1921 v Bel; 1923 v S, W, Bel (5)

Lowder, A. (Wolverhampton W), 1889 v W (1)

Lowe, E. (Aston Villa), 1947 v F, Sw, P (3)

Lucas, T. (Liverpool), 1922 v Ni; 1924 v F; 1926 v Bel (3)

Luntley, E. (Nottingham F), 1880 v S, W (2)

Lyttelton, Hon. A. (Cambridge University), 1877 v S (1)

Lyttelton, Hon. E. (Cambridge University), 1878 v S (1)

McCall, J. (Preston NE), 1913 v S, W; 1914 v S; 1920 v S; 1921 v Ni (5)

McDermott, T. (Liverpool), 1978 v Sw, L; 1979 v Ni, W, Se; 1980 v D, Ni (sub), Ei, Ni, S, Bel (sub), Sp; 1981 v N, R, Sw, R (sub), Br, Sw (sub), H; 1982 v N, H, W (sub), Ho, S (sub), Ic (25)

McDonald, C. A. (Burnley), 1958 v USSR (3), Br, A; 1959 v W, Ni, USSR (8)

McFarland, R. L. (Derby Co), 1971 v Gr, Ma (2), Ni, S; 1972 v Sw, Gr, WG, W, S; 1973 v W (3), Ni, S, Cz, Pol, USSR, I; 1974 v A, Pol, I, W, Ni; 1976 v Cz, S; 1977 v Ei, I (28)

McGarry, W. H. (Huddersfield T), 1954 v Sw, U; 1956 v W, D (4)

McGuinness, W. (Manchester U), 1959 v Ni, M (2)

McInroy, A. (Sunderland), 1927 v Ni (1)

McMahon, S. (Liverpool), 1988 v Is, H, Co, USSR; 1989 v D (sub) (5)

McNab, R. (Arsenal), 1969 v Ni, Bul, R (1+1 sub) (4)

McNeal, R. (WBA), 1914 v S, W (2)

McNeil, M. (Middlesbrough), 1961 v W, Ni, S, L, P, Sp, M, I; 1962 v L (9)

Mabbutt, G. (Tottenham H), 1983 v WG, Gr, L, W, Gr, H, Ni, S (sub); 1984 v H; 1987 v Y, Ni, T; 1988 v WG (13)

Macaulay, R. H. (Cambridge University), 1881 v S (1)

Macdonald, M. (Newcastle U), 1972 v W, Ni, S (sub); 1973 v USSR (sub); 1974 v P, S (sub), Y (sub); 1975 v WG, Cy (2), Ni; 1976 v Sw (sub), Cz, P (14)

Macrae, S. (Notts Co), 1883 v S, W, Ni; 1884 v S, W, Ni (6)

Maddison, F. B. (Oxford University), 1872 v S (1)

Madeley, P. E. (Leeds U), 1971 v Ni; 1972 v Sw (2), Gr, WG (2), W, S; 1973 v S, Cz, Pol, USSR, I; 1974 v A, Pol, I; 1975 v Cz, P, Cy; 1976 v Cz, P, Fi; 1977 v Ei, Ho (24)

Magee, T. P. (WBA), 1923 v W, Se; 1925 v S, Bel, F (5)

Makepeace, H. (Everton), 1906 v S; 1910 v S; 1912 v S, W (4)

Male, C. G. (Arsenal), 1935 v S, Ni, I, Ho; 1936 v S, W, Ni, G, A, Bel; 1937 v S, Ni, H, N, Se, Fi; 1939 v I, R, Y (19)

Mannion, W. J. (Middlesbrough), 1947 v S, W, Ni, Ei, Ho, F, Sw, P; 1948 v W, Ni, Bel, Se, I; 1949 v N, F; 1950 v S, Ei, P, Bel, Ch, US; 1951 v Ni, W, S, Y; 1952 v F (26)

Mariner, P. (Ipswich T), 1977 v L (sub), Ni; 1978 v L, W (sub), S; 1980 v W, Ni (sub), S, Aus, I (sub), Sp (sub); 1981 v N, Sw, Sp, Sw, H; 1982 v N, H, Ho, S, Fi, F, Cz, K, WG, Sp; 1983 v D, WG, Gr, W; 1984 v D, H, L; (with Arsenal), 1985 v EG, R (35)

Marsden, J. T. (Darwen), 1891 v Ni (1)

Marsden, W. (Sheffield W), 1930 v W, S, G (3)

Marsh, R. W. (QPR), 1972 v Sw (sub); (with Manchester C), WG (sub+1), W, Ni, S; 1973 v W (2), Y (9)

Marshall, T. (Darwen), 1880 v W; 1881 v W (2)

Martin, A. (West Ham U), 1981 v Br, S (sub); 1982 v H, Fi; 1983 v Gr, L, W, Gr, H; 1984 v H, L, W; 1985 v Ni; 1986 v Is, Ca, Para; 1987 v Se (17)

Martin, H. (Sunderland), 1914 v Ni (1)

Marwood, B. (Arsenal), 1989 v S.Ar (sub) (1)

Maskrey, H. M. (Derby Co), 1908 v Ni (1)

Mason, C. (Wolverhampton W), 1887 v Ni; 1888 v W; 1890 v Ni (3)

Matthews, R. D. (Coventry C), 1956 v S, Br, Se, WG; 1957 v Ni (5)

Matthews, S. (Stoke C), 1935 v W, I; 1936 v G; 1937 v S; 1938 v S, W, Cz, G, Sw, F; 1939 v S, W, Ni, R of E, N, I, Y; 1947 v S; (with Blackpool), 1947 v Sw, P; 1948 v S, W, Ni, Bel, I; 1949 v S, W, Ni, D, Sw; 1950 v Sp; 1951 v Ni, S; 1954 v Ni, R of E, H, Bel, U; 1955 v Ni, W, S, F, WG, Sp, P; 1956 v W, Br; 1957 v S, W, Ni, Y, D (2) Ei (54)

Matthews, V. (Sheffield U), 1928 v F, Bel (2)

Maynard, W. J. (1st Surrey Rifles), 1872 v S; 1876 v S (2)

Meadows, J. (Manchester C), 1955 v S (1)

Medley, L. D. (Tottenham H), 1951 v Y, W; 1952 v F, A, W, Ni (6)

Meehan, T. (Chelsea), 1924 v Ni (1)

Melia, J. (Liverpool), 1963 v S, Sw (2)

Mercer, D. W. (Sheffield U), 1923 v Ni, Bel (2)

Mercer, J. (Everton), 1939 v S, Ni, I, R, Y (5)

Merrick, G. H. (Birmingham C), 1952 v Ni, S, A (2), I, Sw; 1953 v Ni, W, S, Bel, Arg, Ch, U; 1954 v W, Ni, S, R of E, H (2), Y, Bel, Sw, U (23)

Metcalfe V. (Huddersfield T), 1951 v Arg, P (2)

Mew, J. W. (Manchester U), 1921 v Ni (1)

Middleditch, B. (Corinthians), 1897 v Ni (1)

Milburn, J. E. T. (Newcastle U), 1949 v S, W, Ni, Sw; 1950 v W, P, Bel, Sp; 1951 v W, Arg, P; 1952 v F; 1956 v D (13)

Miller, B. G. (Burnley), 1961 v A (1)

Miller, H. S. (Charlton Ath), 1923 v Se (1)

Mills, G. R. (Chelsea), 1938 v W, Ni, Cz (3)

Mills, M. D. (Ipswich T), 1973 v Y; 1976 v W (2), Ni, S, Br, I (sub), Fi; 1977 v Fi (sub), I, Ni, W, S; 1978 v WG, Br, W, Ni, S, H; 1979 v D, Ei, Ni (2), S, Bul, A; 1980

v D, Ni, Sp (2); 1981 v Sw (2), H; 1982 v N, H, S, Fi, F, Cz, K, WG, Sp (42)
Milne, G. (Liverpool), 1963 v Br, Cz, EG; 1964 v W, Ni, S, R of W, U, P, Ei, Br, Arg; 1965 v Ni, Bel (14)
Milton, C. A. (Arsenal), 1952 v A (1)
Milward, A. (Everton), 1891 v S, W; 1897 v S, W (4)
Mitchell, C. (Upton Park), 1880 v W; 1881 v S; 1883 v S, W; 1885 v W (5)
Mitchell, J. F. (Manchester C), 1925 v Ni (1)
Moffat, H. (Oldham Ath), 1913 v W (1)
Molyneux, G. (Southampton), 1902 v S; 1903 v S, W, Ni (4)
Moon, W. R. (Old Westminsters), 1888 v S, W; 1889 v S, W; 1890 v S, W; 1891 v S (7)
Moore, H. T. (Notts Co), 1883 v Ni; 1885 v W (2)
Moore, J. (Derby Co), 1923 v Se (1)
Moore, R. F. (West Ham U), 1962 v Pe, H, Arg, Bul, Br; 1963 v W, Ni, S, F (2), Br, Cz, EG, Sw; 1964 v W, Ni, S, R of W, U, P (2), Ei, Br, Arg; 1965 v Ni, S, Bel, H, Y, WG, Se; 1966 v W, Ni, S, A, Sp, Pol (2), WG (2), N, D, U, M, F, Arg, P; 1967 v W, Ni, S, Cz, Sp, A; 1968 v W, Ni, S, USSR (2), Sp (2), Se, Y, WG; 1969 v Ni, W, S, R, Bul, F, M, U, Br; 1970 v W, Ni, S, Ho, P, Bel, Co, Ec, R, Br, Cz, WG; 1971 v EG, Gr, Ma, Ni, S; 1972 v Sw (2), Gr, WG (2), W, S; 1973 v W (3), Y, S (2), Ni, Cz, Pol, USSR, I; 1974 v I (108)
Moore, W. G. B. (West Ham U), 1923 v Se (1)
Mordue, J. (Sunderland), 1912 v Ni; 1913 v Ni (2)
Morice, C. J. (Barnes), 1872 v S (1)
Morley, A. (Aston Villa), 1982 v H (sub), Ni, W, Ic; 1983 v D, Gr (6)
Morley, H. (Notts Co), 1910 v Ni (1)
Morren, T. (Sheffield U), 1898 v Ni (1)
Morris, F. (WBA), 1920 v S; 1921 v Ni (2)
Morris, J. (Derby Co), 1949 v N, F; 1950 v Ei (3)
Morris, W. W. (Wolverhampton W), 1939 v S, Ni, R (3)
Morse, H. (Notts Co), 1879 v S (1)
Mort, T. (Aston Villa), 1924 v W, F; 1926 v S (3)
Morten, A. (C Palace), 1873 v S (1)
Mortensen, S. H. (Blackpool), 1947 v P; 1948 v W, S, Ni, Bel, Se, I; 1949 v S, W, Ni, Se, N; 1950 v S, W, Ni, I, P, Bel, Ch, US, Sp; 1951 v S, Arg; 1954 v R of E, H (25)
Morton, J. R. (West Ham U), 1938 v Cz (1)
Mosforth, W. (Sheffield W), 1877 v S; (with Sheffield Albion), 1878 v S; 1879 v S, W; 1880 v S, W; (with Sheffield W), 1881 v W; 1882 v S, W (9)
Moss, F. (Arsenal), 1934 v S, H, Cz; 1935 v I (4)
Moss, F. (Aston Villa), 1922 v S, Ni; 1923 v Ni; 1924 v S, Bel (5)
Mosscrop, E. (Burnley), 1914 v S, W (2)
Mozley, B. (Derby Co), 1950 v W, Ni, Ei (3)
Mullen, J. (Wolverhampton W), 1947 v S; 1949 v N, F; 1950 v Bel (sub), Ch, US; 1954 v W, Ni, S, R of E, Y, Sw (12)
Mullery, A. P. (Tottenham H), 1965 v Ho; 1967 v Sp, A; 1968 v W, Ni, S, USSR, Sp (2), Se, Y; 1969 v Ni, S, R, Bul, F, M, U, Br; 1970 v W, Ni, S (sub), Ho (sub), Bel, P, Co, Ec, R, Cz, WG, Br; 1971 v Ma, EG, Gr; 1972 v Sw (35)

Neal, P. G. (Liverpool), 1976 v W, I; 1977 v W, S, Br, Arg, U; 1978 v Sw, I, WG, Ni, S, H; 1979 v D, Ei, Ni (2), S, Bul, A; 1980 v D, Ni, Sp, Arg, W, Bel, I; 1981 v R, Sw, Sp, Br, H; 1982 v N, H, W, Ho, Ic, F (sub), K; 1983 v D, Gr, L, W, Gr, H, Ni, S, Aus (2); 1984 v D (50)
Needham, E. (Sheffield U), 1894 v S; 1895 v S; 1897 v S, W, Ni; 1898 v S, W; 1899 v S, W, Ni; 1900 v S, Ni; 1901 v S, W, Ni; 1902 v W (16)
Newton, K. R. (Blackburn R), 1966 v S, WG; 1967 v Sp, A; 1968 v W, S, Sp, Se, Y, WG; 1969 v Ni, W, S, R, Bul, M, U, Br, F; (with Everton), 1970 v Ni, S, Ho, Co, Ec, R, Cz, WG (27)
Nicholls, J. (WBA), 1954 v S, Y (2)
Nicholson, W. E. (Tottenham H), 1951 v P (1)
Nish, D. J. (Derby Co), 1973 v Ni; 1974 v P, W, Ni, S (5)
Norman, M. (Tottenham H), 1962 v Pe, H, Arg, Bul, Br; 1963 v S, F, Br, Cz, EG; 1964 v W, Ni, S, R of W, U, P (2), US, Br, Arg; 1965 v Ni, Bel, Ho (23)
Nuttall, H. (Bolton W), 1928 v W, Ni; 1929 v S (3)

Oakley, W. J. (Oxford University), 1895 v W; 1896 v S, W, Ni; (with Corinthians), 1897 v S, W, Ni; 1898 v S, W, Ni; 1900 v S, W, Ni; 1901 v S, W, Ni (16)
O'Dowd, J. P. (Chelsea), 1932 v S; 1933 v Ni, Sw (3)
O'Grady, M. (Huddersfield T), 1963 v Ni; (with Leeds U), 1969 v F (2)
Ogilvie, R. A. M. M. (Clapham R), 1874 v S (1)
Oliver, L. F. (Fulham), 1929 v Bel (1)
Olney, B. A. (Aston Villa), 1928 v F, Bel (2)
Osborne, F. R. (Fulham), 1923 v Ni, F; (with Tottenham H), 1925 v Bel; 1926 v Bel (4)
Osborne, R. (Leicester C), 1928 v W (1)
Osgood, P. L. (Chelsea), 1970 v Bel, R (sub), Cz (sub), 1974 v I (4)
Osman, R. (Ipswich T), 1980 v Aus; 1981 v Sp, R, Sw; 1982 v N, Ic; 1983 v D, Aus (3); 1984 v D (11)
Ottaway, C. J. (Oxford University), 1872 v S; 1874 v S (2)
Owen, J. R. B. (Sheffield), 1874 v S (1)
Owen, S. W. (Luton T), 1954 v H, Y, Bel (3)

Page, L. A. (Burnley), 1927 v S, W, Bel, L, F; 1928 v W, Ni (7)
Paine, T. L. (Southampton), 1963 v Cz, EG; 1964 v W, Ni, S, R of W, U, US, P; 1965 v Ni, H, Y, WG, Se; 1966 v W, A, Y, N, M (19)
Pallister, G. A. (Middlesbrough), 1988 v H; 1989 v S.Ar (2)
Pantling, H. H. (Sheffield U), 1924 v Ni (1)
Paravacini, P. J. de (Cambridge University), 1883 v S, W, Ni (3)
Parker, P. A. (QPR), 1989 v Alb (sub), Ch, D (3)
Parker, T. R. (Southampton), 1925 v F (1)
Parkes, P. B. (QPR), 1974 v P (1)
Parkinson, J. (Liverpool), 1910 v S, W (2)
Parr, P. C. (Oxford University), 1882 v W (1)
Parry, E. H. (Old Carthusians), 1879 v W; 1882 v W, S (3)
Parry, R. A. (Bolton W), 1960 v Ni, S (2)
Patchitt, B. C. A. (Corinthians), 1923 v Se (2) (2)
Pawson, F. W. (Cambridge University), 1883 v Ni; (with Swifts), 1885 v Ni (2)
Payne, J. (Luton T), 1937 v Fi (1)
Peacock, A. (Middlesbrough), 1962 v Arg, Bul; 1963 v Ni, W; (with Leeds U), 1966 v W, Ni (6)
Peacock, J. (Middlesbrough), 1929 v F, Bel, Sp (3)
Pearce, S. (Nottingham F), 1987 v Br, S; 1988 v WG (sub), Is, H; 1989 v D, Se, S.Ar., Gr, Alb, Alb, Ch, S, Pol, D (15)
Pearson, H. F. (WBA), 1932 v S (1)
Pearson, J. H. (Crewe Alex), 1892 v Ni (1)
Pearson, J. S. (Manchester U), 1976 v W, Ni, S, Br, Fi; 1977 v Ei, Ho (sub), W, S, Br, Arg, U; 1978 v I (sub), WG, Ni (15)
Pearson, S. C. (Manchester U), 1948 v S; 1949 v S, Ni; 1950 v Ni, I; 1951 v P; 1952 v S, I (8)
Pease, W. H. (Middlesbrough), 1927 v W (1)
Pegg, D. (Manchester U), 1957 v Ei (1)
Pejic, M. (Stoke C), 1974 v P, W, Ni, S (4)
Pelly, F. R. (Old Foresters), 1893 v Ni; 1894 v S, W (3)
Pennington, J. (WBA), 1907 v S, W; 1908 v S, W, Ni, A; 1909 v S, W, H (2), A; 1910 v S, W; 1911 v S, W, Ni; 1912 v S, W, Ni; 1913 v S, W; 1914 v S, Ni; 1920 v S, W (25)
Pentland, F. B. (Middlesbrough), 1909 v S, W, H (2), A (5)
Perry, C. (WBA), 1890 v Ni; 1891 v Ni; 1893 v W (3)

Perry, T. (WBA), 1898 v W (1)
Perry, W. (Blackpool), 1956 v Ni, S, Sp (3)
Perryman, S. (Tottenham H), 1982 v Ic (sub) (1)
Peters, M. (West Ham U), 1966 v Y, Fi, Pol, M, F, Arg, P, WG; 1967 v Ni, W, S, Cz; 1968 v W, Ni, S, USSR (2), Sp (2), Se, Y; 1969 v Ni, S, R, Bul, F, M, U, Br; 1970 v Ho (2), P (sub), Bel; (with Tottenham H), W, Ni, S, Co, Ec, R, Br, Cz, WG; 1971 v EG, Gr, Ma (2), Ni, W, S; 1972 v Sw, Gr, WG (1+1 sub) Ni (sub) 1973 v S (2), Ni, W, Cz, Pol, USSR, I; 1974 v A, Pol, I, P, S (67)
Phillips, L. H. (Portsmouth), 1952 v Ni; 1955 v W, WG (3)
Pickering, F. (Everton), 1964 v US; 1965 v Ni, Bel (3)
Pickering, N. (Sunderland), 1983 v Aus (1)
Pickering, J. (Sheffield U), 1933 v S (1)
Pike, T. M. (Cambridge University), 1886 v Ni (1)
Pilkington, B. (Burnley), 1955 v Ni (1)
Plant, J. (Bury), 1900 v S (1)
Plum, S. L. (Charlton Ath), 1923 v F (1)
Pointer, R. (Burnley), 1962 v W, L, P (3)
Porteous, T. S. (Sunderland), 1891 v W (1)
Priest, A. E. (Sheffield U), 1900 v Ni (1)
Prinsep, J. F. M. (Clapham Rovers), 1879 v S (1)
Puddefoot, S. C. (Blackburn R), 1926 v S, Ni (2)
Pye, J. (Wolverhampton W), 1950 v Ei (1)
Pym, R. H. (Bolton W), 1925 v S, W; 1926 v W (3)

Quantrill, A. (Derby Co), 1920 v S, W; 1921 v W, Ni (4)
Quixall, A. (Sheffield W), 1954 v W, Ni, R of E; 1955 v Sp, P (sub) (5)

Radford, J. (Arsenal), 1969 v R; 1972 v Sw (sub) (2)
Raikes, G. B. (Oxford University), 1895 v W; 1896 v W, Ni, S (4)
Ramsey, A. E. (Southampton), 1949 v Sw; (with Tottenham H), 1950 v S, I, P, Bel, Ch, US, Sp; 1951 v S, Ni, W, Y, Arg, P; 1952 v S, W, Ni, F, A (2), I, Sw; 1953 v Ni, W, S, Bel, Arg, Ch, U, US; 1954 v R of E, H (32)
Rawlings, A. (Preston NE), 1921 v Bel (1)
Rawlings, W. E. (Southampton), 1922 v S, W (2)
Rawlinson, J. F. P. (Cambridge University), 1882 v Ni (1)
Rawson, H. E. (Royal Engineers), 1875 v S (1)
Rawson, W. S. (Oxford University), 1875 v S; 1877 v S (2)
Read, A. (Tufnell Park), 1921 v Bel (1)
Reader, J. (WBA), 1894 v Ni (1)
Reaney, P. (Leeds U), 1969 v Bul (sub); 1970 v P; 1971 v Ma (3)
Reeves, K. (Norwich C), 1980 v Bul; (with Manchester C), Ni (2)
Regis, C. (WBA), 1982 v Ni (sub), W (sub), Ic; 1983 v WG; (with Coventry C), 1988 v T (sub) (5)
Reid, P. (Everton), 1985 v M (sub), WG, US (sub); 1986 v R, S (sub), Ca (sub), Pol, Para, Arg; 1987 v Br; 1988 v WG, Y (sub), Sw (sub) (13)
Revie, D. G. (Manchester C), 1955 v Ni, S, F; 1956 v W, D; 1957 v Ni (6)
Reynolds, J. (WBA), 1892 v S; 1893 v S, W; (with Aston Villa), 1894 v S, Ni; 1895 v S; 1897 v S, W (8)
Richards, C. H. (Nottingham F), 1898 v Ni (1)
Richards, G. H. (Derby Co), 1909 v A (1)
Richards, J. P. (Wolverhampton W), 1973 v Ni (1)
Richardson, J. R. (Newcastle U), 1933 v I, Sw (2)
Richardson, W. G. (WBA), 1935 v Ho (1)
Rickaby, S, (WBA), 1954 v Ni (1)
Rigby, A. (Blackburn R), 1927 v S, Bel, L, F; 1928 v W (5)
Rimmer, E. J. (Sheffield W), 1930 v S, G, A; 1932 v Sp (4)
Rimmer, J. J. (Arsenal), 1976 v I (1)
Rix, G. (Arsenal), 1981 v N, R, Sw (sub), Br, W, S; 1982 v Ho (sub), Fi (sub), F, Cz, K, WG, Sp; 1983 v D, WG (sub), Gr (sub); 1984 v Ni (17)
Robb, G. (Tottenham H), 1954 v H (1)
Roberts, C. (Manchester U), 1905 v Ni, W, S (3)
Roberts, F. (Manchester C), 1925 v S, W, Bel, F (4)
Roberts, G. (Tottenham H), 1983 v Ni, S; 1984 v F, Ni, S, USSR (6)
Roberts, H. (Arsenal), 1931 v S (1)
Roberts, H. (Millwall), 1931 v Bel (1)
Roberts, R. (WBA), 1887 v S; 1888 v Ni; 1890 v Ni (3)
Roberts, W. T. (Preston NE), 1924 v W, Bel (2)
Robinson, J. (Sheffield W), 1937 v Fi; 1938 v G, Sw; 1939 v W (4)
Robinson, J. W. (Derby Co), 1897 v S, Ni; (with New Brighton Tower), 1898 v S, W, Ni; (with Southampton), 1899 v W, S; 1900 v S, W, Ni; 1901 v Ni (11)
Robson, B. (WBA), 1980 v Ei, Aus; 1981 v N, R, Sw, Sp, R, Br, W, S, Sw, H; 1982 v N (with Manchester U), H, Ni, W, Ho, S, Fi, F, Cz, WG, Sp; 1983 v D, Gr, L, S; 1984 v H, L, F, Ni, S, USSR, Br, U, Ch; 1985 v EG, FI, T, Ei, R, Fi, S, M, I, WG, US; 1986 v R, T, Is, M, P, Mor; 1987 v Ni (2), Sp, T, Br, 5; 1988 v T, Y, Ho, H, S, Co, Sw, Ei, Ho, USSR; 1989 v S, Se, S.Ar, Gr, Alb, Alb, Ch, S, Pol, D (79)
Robson, R. (WBA), 1958 v F, USSR (2), Br, A; 1960 v Sp, H; 1961 v Ni, W, S, L, P, Sp, M, I; 1962 v W, Ni, Sw, L, P (20)
Rocastle, D. (Arsenal), 1989 v D, S.Ar., Gr, Alb, Alb, Pol (sub), D (7)
Rose, W. C. (Wolverhampton W), 1884 v S, W, Ni; (with Preston NE), 1886 v Ni; (with Wolverhampton W), 1891 v Ni (5)
Rostron, T. (Darwen), 1881 v S, W (2)
Rowe, A. (Tottenham H), 1934 v F (1)
Rowley, J. F. (Manchester U), 1949 v Sw, Se, F; 1950 v Ni, I; 1952 v S (6)
Rowley, W. (Stoke C), 1889 v Ni; 1892 v Ni (2)
Royle, J. (Everton), 1971 v Ma; 1973 v Y; (with Manchester C), 1976 v Ni (sub), I; 1977 v Fi, L (6)
Ruddlesdin, H. (Sheffield W), 1904 v W, Ni; 1905 v S (3)
Ruffell, J. W. (West Ham U), 1926 v S; 1927 v Ni; 1929 v S, W, Ni; 1930 v W (6)
Russell, B. B. (Royal Engineers), 1883 v W (1)
Rutherford, J. (Newcastle U), 1904 v S; 1907 v S, Ni, W; 1908 v S, Ni, W, A (2), H, B (11)

Sadler, D. (Manchester U), 1968 v Ni, USSR; 1970 v Ec (sub); 1971 v EG (4)
Sagar, C. (Bury), 1900 v Ni; 1902 v W (2)
Sagar, E. (Everton), 1936 v S, Ni, A, Bel (4)
Sandford, E. A. (WBA), 1933 v W (1)
Sandilands, R. R. (Old Westminsters), 1892 v W; 1893 v Ni; 1894 v W; 1895 v W; 1896 v W (5)
Sands, J. (Nottingham F), 1880 v W (1)
Sansom, K. (C Palace), 1979 v W; 1980 v Bul, Ei, Arg, W (sub), Ni, S, Bel, I; (with Arsenal), 1981 v N, R, Sw, Sp, R, Br, W, S, Sw; 1982 v Ni, W, Ho, S, Fi, F, Cz, WG, Sp; 1983 v D, WG, Gr, L, Gr, H, Ni, S; 1984 v D, H, L, F, S, USSR, Br, U, Ch; 1985 v EG, Fi, T, Ni, Ei, R, Fi, S, I, M, WG, US; 1986 v R, T, Ni, Eg, Is, USSR, S, M, Ca, P, Mor, Pol, Para, Arg; 1987 v Se, Ni (2), Y, Sp, T; 1988 v WG, T, Y, Ho, S, Co, Sw, Ei, Ho, USSR (86)
Saunders, F. E. (Swifts), 1888 v W (1)
Savage, A. H. (C Palace), 1876 v S (1)
Sayer, J. (Stoke C), 1887 v Ni (1)
Scattergood, E. (Derby Co), 1913 v W (1)
Schofield, J. (Stoke C), 1892 v W; 1893 v W; 1895 v Ni (3)
Scott, L. (Arsenal), 1947 v S, W, Ni, Ei, Ho, F, Sw, P; 1948 v S, W, Ni, Bel, Se, I; 1949 v W, Ni, D (17)
Scott, W. R. (Brentford), 1937 v W (1)
Seaman, D. A. (QPR), 1989 v S.Ar., D (sub) (2)
Seddon, J. (Bolton W), 1923 v F, Se (2); 1924 v Bel; 1927 v W; 1929 v S (6)

Seed, J. M. (Tottenham H), 1921 v Bel: 1923 v W, Ni, Bel; 1925 v S (5)
Settle, J. (Bury), 1899 v S, W, Ni; (with Everton), 1902 v S, Ni; 1903 v Ni (6)
Sewell, J. (Sheffield W), 1952 v Ni, A, Sw; 1953 v Ni; 1954 v H (2) (6)
Sewell, W. R. (Blackburn R), 1924 v W (1)
Shackleton, L. F. (Sunderland), 1949 v W, D; 1950 v W; 1955 v W, WG (5)
Sharp, J. (Everton), 1903 v Ni; 1905 v S (2)
Shaw, G. E. (WBA), 1932 v S (1)
Shaw, G. L. (Sheffield U), 1959 v S, W, USSR, I; 1963 v W (5)
Shea, D. (Blackburn R), 1914 v W, Ni (2)
Shellito, K. J. (Chelsea), 1963 v Cz (1)
Shelton A. (Notts Co), 1889 v Ni; 1890 v S, W; 1891 v S, W; 1892 v S (6)
Shelton, C. (Notts Rangers), 1888 v Ni (1)
Shepherd, A. (Bolton W), 1906 v S; (with Newcastle U), 1911 v Ni (2)
Shilton, P. L. (Leicester C), 1971 v EG, W; 1972 v Sw, Ni; 1973 v Y, S (2), Ni, W, Cz, Pol, USSR, I; 1974 v A, Pol, I, W, Ni, S, Arg; (with Stoke C), 1975 v Cy; 1977 v Ni, W; (with Nottingham F), 1978 v W, H; 1979 v Cz, Se, A; 1980 v Ni, Sp, I; 1981 v N, Sw, R; 1982 v H, Ho, S, F, Cz, K, WG, Sp; (with Southampton), 1983 v D, WG, Gr, W, Gr, H, Ni, S, Aus (3); 1984 v D, H, F, Ni, W, S, USSR, Br, U, Ch; 1985 v EG, Fi, T, Ni, R, Fi, S, I, WG; 1986 v R, T, Ni, Eg, Is, USSR, S, M, Ca, P, Mor, Pol, Para, Arg; 1987 v Se, Ni (2), Sp, Br; (with Derby Co), 1988 v WG, T, Y, Ho, S, Co, Sw, Ei, Ho; 1989 v D, Se, Gr, Alb, Alb, Ch, S, Pol, D (109)
Shimwell, E. (Blackpool), 1949 v Se (1)
Shutt, G. (Stoke C), 1886 v Ni (1)
Silcock, J. (Manchester U), 1921 v S, W; 1923 v Se (3)
Sillett, R. P. (Chelsea), 1955 v F, Sp, P (3)
Simms, E. (Luton T), 1922 v Ni (1)
Simpson, J. (Blackburn R), 1911 v S, W, Ni; 1912 v S, W, Ni; 1913 v S; 1914 v W (8)
Slater, W. J. (Wolverhampton W), 1955 v W, WG; 1958 v S, P, Y, USSR (3), Br, A; 1959 v USSR; 1960 v S (12)
Smalley, T. (Wolverhampton W), 1937 v W (1)
Smart, T. (Aston Villa), 1921 v S; 1924 v S, W; 1926 v Ni; 1930 v W (5)
Smith, A. M. (Arsenal), 1989 v S.Ar. (sub), Gr, Alb (sub), Pol (sub) (4)
Smith, A. (Nottingham F), 1891 v S, W; 1893 v Ni (3)
Smith, A. K. (Oxford University), 1872 v S (1)
Smith, B. (Tottenham H), 1921 v S; 1922 v W (2)
Smith, C. E. (C Palace), 1876 v S (1)
Smith, G. O. (Oxford University), 1893 v Ni; 1894 v W, S; 1895 v W; 1896 v Ni, W, S; (with Old Carthusians), 1897 v Ni, W, S; 1898 v Ni, W, S; (with Corinthians), 1899 v Ni, W, S; 1899 v Ni, W, S; 1901 v S (20)
Smith, H. (Reading), 1905 v W, S; 1906 v W, Ni (4)
Smith, J. (WBA), 1920 v Ni; 1923 v Ni (2)
Smith, Joe (Bolton W), 1913 v Ni; 1914 v S, W; 1920 v W, Ni (5)
Smith, J. C. R. (Millwall), 1939 v Ni, N (2)
Smith, J. W. (Portsmouth), 1932 v Ni, W, Sp (3)
Smith, Leslie (Brentford), 1939 v R (1)
Smith, Lionel (Arsenal), 1951 v W; 1952 v W, Ni; 1953 v W, S, Bel (6)
Smith, R. A. (Tottenham H), 1961 v Ni, W, S, L, P, Sp; 1962 v S; 1963 v S, F, Br, Cz, EG; 1964 v W, Ni, R of W (15)
Smith, S. (Aston Villa), 1895 v S (1)
Smith, S. C. (Leicester C), 1936 v Ni (1)
Smith, T. (Birmingham C), 1960 v W, Se (2)
Smith, T. (Liverpool), 1971 v W (1)
Smith, W. H. (Huddersfield T), 1922 v W, S; 1928 v S (3)
Sorby, T. H. (Thursday Wanderers, Sheffield), 1879 v W (1)
Southworth, J. (Blackburn R), 1889 v W; 1891 v W; 1892 v S (3)
Sparks, F. J. (Herts Rangers), 1879 v S; (with Clapham Rovers), 1880 v S, W (3)
Spence, J. W. (Manchester U), 1926 v Bel; 1927 v Ni (2)
Spence, R. (Chelsea), 1936 v A, Bel (2)
Spencer, C. W. (Newcastle U), 1924 v S; 1925 v W (2)
Spencer, H. (Aston Villa), 1897 v S, W; 1900 v W; 1903 v Ni; 1905 v W, S (6)
Spiksley, F. (Sheffield W), 1893 v S, W; 1894 v S, Ni; 1896 v Ni; 1898 v S, W (7)
Spilsbury, B. W. (Cambridge University), 1885 v Ni; 1886 v Ni, S (3)
Spink, N. (Aston Villa), 1983 v Aus (sub) (1)
Spouncer, W. A. (Nottingham F), 1900 v W (1)
Springett, R. D. G. (Sheffield W), 1960 v Ni, S, Y, Sp, H; 1961 v Ni, S, L, P, Sp, M, I, A; 1962 v W, Ni, S, A, Sw, Pe, L, P, H, Arg, Bul, Br; 1963 v Ni, W, F (2), Sw; 1966 v W, A, N (33)
Sproston, B. (Leeds U), 1937 v W; 1938 v S, W, Ni, Cz, G, Sw, F; (with Tottenham H), 1939 v W, R of E; (with Manchester C), N (11)
Squire, R. T. (Cambridge University), 1886 v S, W, Ni (3)
Stanbrough, M. H. (Old Carthusians), 1895 v W (1)
Staniforth, R. (Huddersfield T), 1954 v S, H, Y, Bel, Sw, U; 1955 v W, WG (8)
Starling, R. W. (Sheffield W), 1933 v S; (with Aston Villa), 1937 v S (2)
Statham, D. (WBA), 1983 v W, Aus (2) (3)
Steele, F. C. (Stoke C), 1937 v S, W, Ni, N, Se, Fi (6)
Stein, B. (Luton T), 1984 v F (1)
Stephenson, C. (Huddersfield T), 1924 v W (1)
Stephenson, G. T. (Derby Co), 1928 v F, Bel; (with Sheffield W), 1931 v F (3)
Stephenson, J. E. (Leeds U), 1938 v S; 1939 v Ni (2)
Stepney, A. C. (Manchester U), 1968 v Se (1)
Sterland, M. (Sheffield W), 1989 v S.Ar. (1)
Steven, T. M. (Everton), 1985 v Ni, Ei, R, Fi, I, US (sub); 1986 v T (sub), Eg, USSR (sub), M (sub), Pol, Para, Arg; 1987 v Se, Y (sub), Sp (sub); 1988 v T, Y, Ho, H, S, Sw, Ho, USSR; 1989 v S (25)
Stevens, G. A. (Tottenham H), 1985 v Fi (sub), T (sub), Ni; 1986 v S (sub), M (sub), Mor (sub), Para (sub) (7)
Stevens, M. G. (Everton), 1985 v I, WG; 1986 v R, T, Ni, Eg, Is, S, Ca, P, Mor, Pol, Para, Arg; 1987 v Br, S; 1988 v T, Y, Is, Ho, H (sub), S, Sw, Ei, Ho, USSR; (with Rangers), 1989 D, Se, Gr, Alb, Alb, S, Pol (33)
Stewart, J. (Sheffield W), 1907 v S, W; (with Newcastle U), 1911 v S (3)
Stiles, N. P. (Manchester U), 1965 v S, H, Y, Se; 1966 v W, Ni, S, A, Sp, Pol (2), WG (2), N, D, U, M, F, Arg, P; 1967 v Ni, W, S, Cz; 1968 v USSR; 1969 v R; 1970 v Ni, S (28)
Stoker, J. (Birmingham), 1933 v W; 1934 v S, H (3)
Storer, H. (Derby Co), 1924 v F; 1928 v Ni (2)
Storey, P. E. (Arsenal), 1971 v Gr, Ni, S; 1972 v Sw, WG, W, Ni, S; 1973 v W (3), Y, S (2), Ni, Cz, Pol, USSR, I (19)
Storey-Moore, I. (Nottingham F), 1970 v Ho (1)
Strange, A. H. (Sheffield W), 1930 v S, A, G; 1931 v S, W, Ni, F, Bel; 1932 v S, W, Ni, Sp; 1933 v S, Ni, A, I, Sw; 1934 v Ni, W, F (20)
Stratford, A. H. (Wanderers), 1874 v S (1)
Streten, B. (Luton T), 1950 v Ni (1)
Sturgess, A. (Sheffield U), 1911 v Ni; 1914 v S (2)
Summerbee, M. G. (Manchester C), 1968 v S, Sp, WG; 1972 v Sw, WG (sub), W, Ni; 1973 v USSR (sub) (8)
Sunderland, A. (Arsenal), 1980 v Aus (1)
Sutcliffe, J. W. (Bolton W), 1893 v W; 1895 v S, Ni; 1901 v S; (with Millwall), 1903 v W (5)
Swan, P. (Sheffield W), 1960 v Y, Sp, H; 1961 v Ni, W, S, L, P, Sp, M, I, A; 1962 v W, Ni, S, A, Sw, L, P (19)

Swepstone, H. A. (Pilgrims), 1880 v S; 1882 v S, W; 1883 v S, W, Ni (6)
Swift, F. V. (Manchester C), 1947, v S, W, Ni, Ei, Ho, F, Sw, P; 1948 v S, W, Ni, Bel, Se, I; 1949 v S, W, Ni, D, N (19)

Tait, G. (Birmingham Excelsior), 1881 v W (1)
Talbot, B. (Ipswich T), 1977 v Ni (sub), S, Br, Arg, U; (with Arsenal), 1980 v Aus (6)
Tambling, R. V. (Chelsea), 1963 v W, F; 1966 v Y (3)
Tate, J. T. (Aston Villa), 1931 v F, Bel; 1933 v W (3)
Taylor, E. (Blackpool), 1954 v H (1)
Taylor, E. H. (Huddersfield T), 1923 v S, W, Ni, Bel; 1924 v S, Ni, F; 1926 v S (8)
Taylor, J. G. (Fulham), 1951 v Arg, P (2)
Taylor, P. J. (C Palace), 1976 v W (sub), W, Ni, S (4)
Taylor, P. H. (Liverpool), 1948 v W, Ni, Se (3)
Taylor, T. (Manchester U), 1953 v Arg, Ch, U; 1954 v Bel, Sw; 1956 v S, Br, Se, Fi, WG; 1957 v Ni, Y (sub), D (2), Ei (2); 1958 v W, Ni, F (19)
Temple, D. W. (Everton), 1965 v WG (1)
Thickett, H. (Sheffield U), 1899 v S, W (2)
Thomas, D. (Coventry C), 1983 v Aus (1+1 sub) (2)
Thomas, D. (QPR), 1975 v Cz (sub), P, Cy (sub+1), W, S (sub); 1976 v Cz (sub), P (sub) (8)
Thomas, M. L. (Arsenal), 1989 v S.Ar (1)
Thompson, P. (Liverpool), 1964 v P (2), Ei, US, Br, Arg; 1965 v Ni, W, S, Bel, Ho; 1966 v Ni; 1968 v Ni, WG; 1970 v S, Ho (sub) (16)
Thompson, P. B. (Liverpool), 1976 v W (2), Ni, S, Br, I, Fi; 1977 v Fi; 1979 v Ei (sub), Cz, Ni, S, Bul, Se (sub), A; 1980 v D, Ni, Bul, Ei, Sp (2), Arg, W, S, Bel, I; 1981 v N, R, H; 1982 v N, H, W, Ho, S, Fi, F, Cz, K, WG, Sp; 1983 v WG, Gr (42)
Thompson, T. (Aston Villa), 1952 v W; (with Preston NE), 1957 v S (2)
Thomson, R. A. (Wolverhampton W), 1964 v Ni, US, P, Arg; 1965 v Bel, Ho, Ni, W (8)
Thornewell, G. (Derby Co), 1923 v Se (2); 1924 v F; 1925 v F (4)
Thornley, I. (Manchester C), 1907 v W (1)
Tilson, S. F. (Manchester C), 1934 v H, Cz; 1935 v W; 1936 v Ni (4)
Titmuss, F. (Southampton), 1922 v W; 1923 v W (2)
Todd, C. (Derby Co), 1972 v Ni; 1974 v P, W, Ni, S, Arg, EG, Bul, Y; 1975 v P (sub), WG, Cy (2), Ni, W, S; 1976 v Sw, Cz, P, Ni, S, Br, Fi; 1977 v Ei, Fi, Ho (sub), Ni (27)
Toone, G. (Notts Co), 1892 v S, W (2)
Topham, A. G. (Casuals), 1894 v W (1)
Topham, R. (Wolverhampton W), 1893 v Ni; (with Casuals) 1894 v W (2)
Towers, M. A. (Sunderland), 1976 v W, Ni (sub), I (3)
Townley, W. J. (Blackburn R), 1889 v W; 1890 v Ni (2)
Townrow, J. E. (Clapton Orient), 1925 v S; 1926 v W (2)
Tremelling, D. R. (Birmingham), 1928 v W (1)
Tresadern, J. (West Ham U), 1923 v S, Se (2)
Tueart, D. (Manchester C), 1975 v Cy (sub), Ni; 1977 v Fi, Ni, W (sub), S (sub) (6)
Tunstall, F. E. (Sheffield U), 1923 v S; 1924 v S, W, Ni, F; 1925 v Ni, S (7)
Turnbull, R. J. (Bradford), 1920 v Ni (1)
Turner, A. (Southampton), 1900 v Ni; 1901 v Ni (2)
Turner, H. (Huddersfield T), 1931 v F, Bel (2)
Turner, J. A. (Bolton W), 1893 v W; (with Stoke C) 1895 v Ni; (with Derby Co) 1898 v Ni (3)
Tweedy, G. J. (Grimsby T), 1937 v H (1)

Ufton, D. G. (Charlton Ath), 1954 v R of E (1)
Underwood A. (Stoke C), 1891 v Ni; 1892 v Ni (2)
Urwin, T. (Middlesbrough), 1923 v Se (2); (with Newcastle U) 1924 v Bel; 1926 v W (4)
Utley, G. (Barnsley), 1913 v Ni (1)

Vaughton, O. H. (Aston Villa), 1882 v S, W, Ni; 1884 v S, W (5)
Veitch, C. C. M. (Newcastle U), 1906 v S, W, Ni; 1907 v S, W; 1909 v W (6)
Veitch, J. G. (Old Westminsters), 1894 v W (1)
Venables, T. F. (Chelsea), 1965 v Ho, Bel (2)
Vidal, R. W. S. (Oxford University), 1873 v S (1)
Viljoen, C. (Ipswich T), 1975 v Ni, W (2)
Viollet, D. S. (Manchester U), 1960 v H; 1962 v L (2)
Von Donop (Royal Engineers), 1873 v S; 1875 v S (2)

Wace, H. (Wanderers), 1878 v S; 1879 v S, W (3)
Waddle, C. R. (Newcastle U), 1985 v Ei, R (sub), Fi (sub), S (sub), I, M (sub), WG, US; (with Tottenham H), 1986 v R, T, Ni, Is, USSR, S, M, Ca, P, Mor, Pol (sub), Arg (sub); 1987 v Se (sub), Ni (2), Y, Sp, T, Br, S; 1988 v WG, Is, H, S (sub), Co, Sw (sub), Ei, Ho (sub); 1989 v Se, S.Ar., Alb, Alb, Ch, S, Pol, D (sub) (44)
Wadsworth, S. J. (Huddersfield T), 1922 v S; 1923 v S, Bel; 1924 v S, Ni; 1925 v S, Ni; 1926 v W; 1927 v Ni (9)
Wainscoat, W. R. (Leeds U), 1929 v S (1)
Waiters, A. K. (Blackpool), 1964 v Ei, Br; 1965 v W, Bel, Ho (5)
Walker, D. S. (Nottingham F), 1989 v D (sub), Se (sub), Gr, Alb, Alb, Ch, S, Pol, D (9)
Walden, F. I. (Tottenham H), 1914 v S; 1922 v W (2)
Walker, W. H. (Aston Villa), 1921 v Ni; 1922 v Ni, W, S; 1923 v Se (2); 1924 v S; 1925 v Ni, W, S, Bel, F; 1926 v Ni, W, S; 1927 v Ni, W; 1933 v A (18)
Wall, G. (Manchester U), 1907 v W; 1908 v Ni; 1909 v S; 1910 v W, S; 1912 v S; 1913 v Ni (7)
Wallace, C. W. (Aston Villa), 1913 v W; 1914 v Ni; 1920 v S (3)
Wallace, D. L. (Southampton), 1986 v Eg (1)
Walsh, P. (Luton T), 1983 v Aus (2+1 sub) (3)
Walters, A. M. (Cambridge University), 1885 v S, N; 1886 v S; 1887 v S, W; (with Old Carthusians) 1889 v S, W; 1890 v S, W (9)
Walters, P. M. (Oxford University), 1885 v S, Ni; (with Old Carthusians), 1886 v S, W, Ni; 1887 v S, W; 1888 v S, Ni; 1889 v S, W; 1890 v S, W (13)
Walton, N. (Blackburn R) 1890 v Ni (1)
Ward, J. T. (Blackburn Olympic), 1885 v W (1)
Ward, P. (Brighton & HA), 1980 v Aus (sub) (1)
Ward, T. V. (Derby Co), 1948 v Bel; 1949 v W (2)
Waring, T. (Aston Villa), 1931 v F, Bel; 1932 v S, W, Ni (5)
Warner, C. (Upton Park), 1878 v S (1)
Warren, B. (Derby Co), 1906 v S, W, Ni; 1907 v S, W, Ni; 1908 v S, W, Ni, A (2), H, B; (with Chelsea), 1909 v S, Ni, W, H (2), A; 1911 v S, Ni, W (22)
Waterfield, G. S. (Burnley), 1927 v W (1)
Watson, D. (Norwich C), 1984 v Br, U, Ch; 1985 v M, US (sub); 1986 v S; (with Everton), 1987 v Ni; 1988 v Is, Ho, S, Sw (sub), USSR (12)
Watson, D. V. (Sunderland), 1974 v P, S (sub), Arg, EG, Bul, Y; 1975 v Cz, P, WG, Cy (2), Ni, W, S; (with Manchester C) 1976 v Sw, Cz (sub), P; 1977 v Ho, L, Ni, W, S, Br, Arg, U; 1978 v Sw, L, I, WG, Br, W, Ni, S, H; 1979 v D, Ei, Cz, Ni (2), W, S, Bul, Se, A; (with Werder Bremen), 1980 v D; (with Southampton) Ni, Bul, Ei, Sp (2), Arg, Ni, S, Bel, I; 1981 v N, R, Sw, R, W, S, Sw, H; (with Stoke C), 1982 v Ni, Ic (65)
Watson, V. M. (West Ham U), 1923 v W, S; 1930 v S, G, A (5)
Watson, W. (Burnley), 1913 v S; 1914 v Ni; 1920 v Ni (3)
Watson, W. (Sunderland), 1950 v Ni, I; 1951 v W, Y (4)
Weaver, S. (Newcastle U), 1932 v S, 1933 v S, Ni (3)
Webb, G. W. (West Ham U), 1911 v S, W (2)
Webb, N. J. (Nottingham F), 1988 v WG (sub), T, Y, Is, Ho, S, Sw, Ei, USSR (sub); 1989 v D, Se, Gr, Alb, Alb, Ch, S, Pol, D (18)
Webster, M. (Middlesbrough), 1930 v S, A, G (3)

Wedlock, W. J. (Bristol C), 1907 v S, Ni, W; 1908 v S, Ni, W, A (2), H, B; 1909 v S, W, Ni, H (2), A; 1910 v S, W, Ni; 1911 v S, W, Ni; 1912 v S, W, Ni; 1914 v W (26)
Weir, D. (Bolton W), 1889 v S, Ni (2)
Welch, R. de C. (Wanderers), 1872 v S; (with Harrow Chequers) 1874 v S (2)
Weller, K. (Leicester C), 1974 v W, Ni, S, Arg (4)
Welsh, D. (Charlton Ath), 1938 v G, Sw; 1939 v R (3)
West, G. (Everton), 1969 v W, Bul, M (3)
Westwood, R. W. (Bolton W), 1935 v S, W, Ho; 1936 v Ni, G; 1937 v W (6)
Whateley, O. (Aston Villa), 1883 v S, Ni (2)
Wheeler, J. E. (Bolton W), 1955 v Ni (1)
Wheldon, G. F. (Aston Villa), 1897 v Ni; 1898 v S, W, Ni (4)
White, T. A. (Everton), 1933 v I (1)
Whitehead, J. (Accrington), 1893 v W; (with Blackburn R) 1894 v Ni (2)
Whitfeld, H. (Old Etonians), 1879 v W (1)
Whitham, M. (Sheffield U), 1892 v Ni (1)
Whitworth, S. (Leicester C), 1975 v WG, Cy, Ni, W, S; 1976 v Sw, P (7)
Whymark, T. J. (Ipswich T), 1978 v L (sub) (1)
Widdowson, S. W. (Nottingham F), 1880 v S (1)
Wignall, F. (Nottingham F), 1965 v W, Ho (2)
Wilkes, A. (Aston Villa), 1901 v S, W; 1902 v S, W, Ni (5)
Wilkins, R. G. (Chelsea), 1976 v I; 1977 v Ei, Fi, Ni, Br, Arg, U; 1978 v Sw (sub), L, I, WG, W, Ni, S, H; 1979 v D, Ei, Cz, Ni, W, S, Bul, Se (sub), A; (with Manchester U) 1980 v D, Ni, Bul, Sp (2), Arg, W (sub), Ni, S, Bel, I; 1981 v Sp (sub), R, Br, W, S, Sw, H (sub); 1982 v Ni, W, Ho, S, Fi, F, Cz, K, WG, Sp; 1983 v D, WG; 1984 v D, Ni, W, S, USSR, Br, U, Ch; (with AC Milan), 1985 v EG, Fi, T, Ni, Ei, R, Fi, S, I, M; 1986 v T, Ni, Is, Eg, USSR, S, M, Ca, P, Mor; 1987 v Se, Y (sub) (84)
Wilkinson, B. (Sheffield U), 1904 v S (1)
Wilkinson, L. R. (Oxford University), 1891 v W (1)
Williams, B. F. (Wolverhampton W), 1949 v F; 1950 v S, W, Ei, I, P, Bel, Ch, US, Sp; 1951 v Ni, W, S, Y, Arg, P; 1952 v W, F; 1955 v S, WG, F, Sp, P; 1956 v W (24)
Williams, O. (Clapton Orient), 1923 v W, Ni (2)
Williams, S. (Southampton), 1983 v Aus (1+1 sub); 1984 v F; 1985 v EG, Fi, T (6)
Williams, W. (WBA), 1897 v Ni; 1898 v W, Ni, S; 1899 v W, Ni (6)
Williamson, E. C. (Arsenal), 1923 v Se (2) (2)
Williamson, R. G. (Middlesbrough), 1905 v Ni; 1911 v Ni, S, W; 1912 v S, W; 1913 v Ni (7)
Willingham, C. K. (Huddersfield T), 1937 v Fi; 1938 v S, G, Sw, F; 1939 v S, W, Ni, R of E, N, I, Y (12)
Willis, A. (Tottenham H), 1952 v F (1)
Wilshaw, D. J. (Wolverhampton W), 1954 v W, Sw, U; 1955 v S, F, Sp, P; 1956 v W, Ni, Fi, WG; 1957 v Ni (12)
Wilson, C. P. (Hendon), 1884 v S, W (2)
Wilson, C. W. (Oxford University), 1879 v W; 1881 v S (2)
Wilson, G. (Sheffield W), 1921 v S, W, Bel; 1922 v S, Ni; 1923 v S, W, Ni, Bel; 1924 v W, Ni, F (12)
Wilson, G. P. (Corinthians), 1900 v S, W (2)
Wilson, R. (Huddersfield T), 1960 v S, Y, Sp, H; 1962 v W, Ni, S, A, Sw, Pe, P, H, Arg, Bul, Br; 1963 v Ni, F, Br, Cz, EG, Sw; 1964 v W, S, R of W, U, P (2), Ei, Br, Arg; (with Everton), 1965 v S, H, Y, WG, Se; 1966 v WG (sub), W, Ni, A, Sp, Pol (2), Y, Fi, D, U, M, F, Arg, P, WG; 1967 v Ni, W, S, Cz, A; 1968 v Ni, S, USSR (2), Sp (2), Y (63)
Wilson, T. (Huddersfield T), 1928 v S (1)
Winckworth, W. N. (Old Westminsters), 1892 v W; 1893 v Ni (2)
Windridge, J. E. (Chelsea), 1908 v S, W, Ni, A (2), H, B; 1909 v Ni (8)
Wingfield-Stratford, C. V. (Royal Engineers), 1877 v S (1)
Withe, P. (Aston Villa), 1981 v Br, W, S; 1982 v N (sub), W, Ic; 1983 v H, Ni, S; 1984 v H (sub); 1985 v T (11)
Wollaston, C. H. R. (Wanderers), 1874 v S; 1875 v S; 1877 v S; 1880 v S (4)
Wolstenholme, S. (Everton), 1904 v S; (with Blackburn R), 1905 v W, Ni (3)
Wood, H. (Wolverhampton W), 1890 v S, W; 1896 v S (3)
Wood, R. E. (Manchester U), 1955 v Ni, W; 1956 v Fi (3)
Woodcock, A. S. (Nottingham F), 1978 v Ni; 1979 v Ei (sub), Cz, Bul (sub), Se; 1980 v Ni; (with Cologne), Bul, Ei, Sp (2), Arg, Bel, I; 1981 v N, R, Sw, R, W (sub), S; 1982 v Ni (sub), Ho, Fi (sub), WG (sub), Sp; (with Arsenal), 1983 v WG (sub), Gr, L, Gr; 1984 v L, F (sub), Ni, W, S, Br, U (sub); 1985 v EG, Fi, T, Ni; 1986 v R (sub), T (sub), Is (sub) (42)
Woodger, G. (Oldham Ath), 1911 v Ni (1)
Woodhall, G. (WBA), 1888 v S, W (2)
Woodley, V. R. (Chelsea), 1937 v S, N, Se, Fi; 1938 v S, W, Ni, Cz, G, Sw, F; 1939 v S, W, Ni, R of E, N, I, R, Y (19)
Woods, C. C. E. (Norwich C), 1985 v US; 1986 v Eg (sub), Is (sub), Ca (sub); (with Rangers), 1987 v Y, Sp (sub), Ni (sub), T, S; 1988 v Is, H, Sw (sub), USSR; 1989 v D (sub) (14)
Woodward, V. J. (Tottenham H), 1903 v S, W, Ni; 1904 v S, Ni; 1905 v S, W, Ni; 1907 v S; 1908 v S, W, Ni, A (2), H, B; 1909 v W, Ni, H (2), A; (with Chelsea), 1910 v Ni; 1911 v W (23)
Woosnam, M. (Manchester C), 1922 v W (1)
Worrall, F. (Portsmouth), 1935 v Ho; 1937 v Ni (2)
Worthington, F. S. (Leicester C), 1974 v Ni (sub), S, Arg, EG, Bul, Y; 1975 v Cz, P (sub) (8)
Wreford-Brown, C. (Oxford University), 1889 v Ni; (with Old Carthusians), 1894 v W; 1895 v W; 1898 v S (4)
Wright, E, G. D. (Cambridge University), 1906 v W (1)
Wright, J. D. (Newcastle U), 1939 v N (1)
Wright, M. (Southampton), 1984 v W; 1985 v EG, Fi, T, Ei, R, I, WG; 1986 v R, T, Ni, Eg, USSR; 1987 v Y, Ni, S; (with Derby Co), 1988 v Is, Ho (sub), Co, Sw, Ei, Ho (22)
Wright, T. J. (Everton), 1968 v USSR; 1969 v R (2), M (sub), U, Br; 1970 v W, Ho, Bel, R (sub), Br (11)
Wright, W. A. (Wolverhampton W), 1947 v S, W, Ni, Ei, Ho, F, Sw, P; 1948 v S, W, Ni, Bel, Se, I; 1949 v S, W, Ni, D, Sw, Se, N, F; 1950 v S, W, Ni, Ei, I, P, Bel, Ch, US, Sp; 1951 v Ni, S, Arg; 1952 v W, Ni, S, F, A (2), I, Sw; 1953 v Ni, W, S, Bel, Arg, Ch, U, US; 1954 v W, Ni, S, R of E, H (2), Y, Bel, Sw, U; 1955 v W, Ni, S, WG, F, Sp, P; 1956 v Ni, W, S, Br, Se, Fi, WG, D, Sp; 1957 v S, W, Ni, Y, D (2), Ei (2); 1958 v W, Ni, S, P, Y, USSR (3), Br, A, F; 1959 v W, Ni, S, USSR, I, Br, Pe, M, US (105)
Wylie, J. G. (Wanderers), 1878 v S (1)

Yates, J. (Burnley), 1889 v Ni (1)
York, R. E. (Aston Villa), 1922 v S; 1926 v S (2)
Young, A. (Huddersfield T), 1933 v W; 1937 v S, H, N, Se; 1938 v G, Sw, F; 1939 v W (9)
Young, G. M. (Sheffield W), 1965 v W (1)

R. E. Evans also played for Wales against E, Ni, S; J. Reynolds also played for Ireland against E, W, S.

NORTHERN IRELAND

Aherne, T. (Belfast C), 1947 v E; 1948 v S; 1949 v W; (with Luton T), 1950 v W (4)
Alexander, A. (Cliftonville), 1895 v S (1)
Allen, C. A. (Cliftonville), 1936 v E (1)
Allen, J. (Limavady), 1887 v E (1)
Anderson, T. (Manchester U), 1973 v Cy, E, S, W; 1974 v Bul, P; (with Swindon T), 1975 v S (sub); 1976 v Is; 1977 v Ho, Bel, WG, E, S, W, Ic; 1978 v Ic, Ho, Bel; (with Peterborough U), S, E, W; 1979 v D (22)
Anderson, W. (Linfield), 1898 v W, E, S; 1899 v S (4)
Andrews, W. (Glentoran), 1908 v S; (with Grimsby T), 1913 v E, S (3)
Armstrong, G. (Tottenham H), 1977 v WG, E, W (sub), Ic (sub); 1978 v Bel, S, E, W; 1979 v Ei, D, Bul, E, Bul, E, S, W, D; 1980 v E, Ei, Is, S, E, W, Aus (3); 1981 v Se; (with Watford), P, S, P, S, Se; 1982 v S, Is, E, F, W, Y, Hon, Sp, A, F; 1983 v A, T, Alb, S, E, W; (with Real Mallorca), 1984 v A, WG, E, W, Fi; 1985 v R, Fi, E, Sp; (with WBA), 1986 v T, R (sub), E (sub), F (sub); (with Chesterfield), D (sub), Br (sub) (63)

Baird, G. (Distillery), 1896 v S, E, W (3)
Baird, H. (Huddersfield T), 1939 v E (1)
Balfe, J. (Shelbourne), 1909 v E; 1910 v W (2)
Bambrick, J. (Linfield), 1929 v W, S, E; 1930 v W, S, E; 1932 v W; (with Chelsea), 1935 v W; 1936 v E, S; 1938 v W (11)
Banks, S. J. (Cliftonville), 1937 v W (1)
Barr, H. H. (Linfield), 1962 v E; (with Coventry C), 1963 v E, Pol (3)
Barron, H. (Cliftonville), 1894 v E, W, S; 1895 v S; 1896 v S; 1897 v E, W (7)
Barry, H. (Bohemians), 1900 v S (1)
Baxter, R. A. (Cliftonville), 1887 v S, W (2)
Bennett, L. V. (Dublin University), 1889 v W (1)
Berry, J. (Cliftonville), 1888 v S, W; 1889 v E (3)
Best, G. (Manchester U), 1964 v W, U; 1965 v E, Ho (2), S, Sw (2), Alb; 1966 v S, E, Alb; 1967 v E; 1968 v S; 1969 v E, S, W, T; 1970 v S, E, W, USSR; 1971 v Cy (2), Sp, E, S, W; 1972 v USSR, Sp; 1973 v Bul; 1974 v P; (with Fulham), 1977 v Ho, Bel, WG; 1978 v Ic, Ho (37)
Bingham, W. L. (Sunderland), 1951 v F; 1952 v E, S, W; 1953 v E, S, F, W; 1954 v E, S, W; 1955 v E, S, W; 1956 v E, S, W; 1957 v E, S, W, P (2), I; 1958 v S, E, W, I (2), Arg, Cz (2), WG, F; (with Luton T), 1959 v E, S, W, Sp; 1960 v S, E, W; (with Everton), 1961 v E, S, WG (2), Gr, I; 1962 v E, Gr; 1963 v E, S, Pol (2), Sp; (with Port Vale), 1964 v S, E, Sp (56)
Black, J. (Glentoran), 1901 v E (1)
Black, K. (Luton T), 1988 v Fr (sub), Ma (sub); 1989 v Ei, H, Sp, Sp, Ch (sub) (7)
Blair, H. (Portadown), 1931 v S; 1932 v S; (with Swansea), 1934 v S (3)
Blair, J. (Cliftonville), 1907 v W, E, S; 1908 v E, S (5)
Blair, R. V. (Oldham Ath), 1975 v Se (sub), S (sub), W; 1976 v Se, Is (5)
Blanchflower, R. D. (Barnsley), 1950 v S, W; 1951 v E, S; (with Aston Villa), F; 1952 v W; 1953 v E, S, W, F; 1954 v E, S, W; (with Tottenham H), 1955 v E, S, W; 1956 v E, S, W; 1957 v E, S, W, I, P (2); 1958 v E, S, W, I (2), Cz (2), Arg, F, WG; 1959 v E, S, W, Sp; 1960 v E, S, W; 1961 v E, S, W, WG (2); 1962 v E, S, W, Gr, Ho; 1963 v E, S, Pol (2) (56)
Blanchflower, J. (Manchester U), 1954 v W; 1955 v E, S; 1956 v S, W; 1957 v S, E, P; 1958 v S, E, I (2) (12)
Bookman, L. O. (Bradford C), 1914 v W; (with Luton T), 1921 v S, W; 1922 v E (4)
Bothwell, A. W. (Ards), 1926 v S, E, W; 1927 v E, W (5)
Bowler, G. C. (Hull C), 1950 v E, S, W (3)
Boyle, P. (Sheffield U), 1901 v E; 1902 v E; 1903 v S, W; 1904 v E (5)
Braithwaite, R. S. (Linfield), 1962 v W; 1963 v P, Sp; (with Middlesbrough), 1964 v W, U; 1965 v E, S, Sw (2), Ho (10)
Breen, T. (Belfast C), 1935 v E, W; 1937 v E, S; (with Manchester U), 1937 v W; 1938 v E, S; 1939 v W, S (9)
Brennan, B. (Bohemians), 1912 v W (1)
Brennan, R. A. (Luton T), 1949 v W; (with Birmingham C), 1950 v E, S, W; (with Fulham), 1951 v E (5)
Briggs, W. R. (Manchester U), 1962 v W; (with Swansea T), 1965 v Ho (2)
Brisby, D. (Distillery), 1891 v S (1)
Brolly, T. (Millwall), 1937 v W; 1938 v W; 1939 v E, W (4)
Brookes, E. A. (Shelbourne), 1920 v S (1)
Brotherston, N. (Blackburn R), 1980 v S, E, W, Aus (3); 1981 v Se, P; 1982 v S, Is, E, F, S, W, Hon (sub), A (sub); 1983 v A (sub), WG, Alb, T, Alb, S (sub), E (sub), W; 1984 v T; 1985 v Is (sub), T (27)
Brown, J. (Glenavon), 1921 v W; (with Tranmere R), 1924 v E, W (3)
Brown, J. (Wolverhampton W), 1935 v E, W; 1936 v E; (with Coventry C), 1937 v E, W; 1938 v S, W; (with Birmingham C), 1939 v E, S, W (10)
Brown, W. G. (Glenavon), 1926 v W (1)
Brown, W. M. (Limavady), 1887 v E (1)
Browne, F. (Cliftonville), 1887 v E, S, W; 1888 v E, S (5)
Browne, R. J. (Leeds U), 1936 v E, W; 1938 v E, W; 1939 v E, S (6)
Bruce, W. (Glentoran), 1961 v S; 1967 v W (2)
Buckle, H. (Cliftonville), 1882 v E (1)
Buckle, H. R. (Sunderland), 1904 v E; (with Bristol R), 1908 v W (2)
Burnett, J. (Distillery), 1894 v E, W, S; (with Glentoran), 1895 v E, W (5)
Burnison, J. (Distillery), 1901 v E, W (2)
Burnison, S. (Distillery), 1908 v E; 1910 v E, S; (with Bradford), 1911 v E, S, W; (with Distillery), 1912 v E; 1913 v W (8)
Burns, J. (Glenavon), 1923 v E (1)
Butler, M. P. (Blackpool), 1939 v W (1)

Campbell, A. C. (Crusaders), 1963 v W; 1965 v Sw (2)
Campbell, D. A. (Nottingham F), 1986 v Mor (sub), Br; 1987 v E (2), T, Y; 1988 v Y (with Charlton Ath), T (sub), Gr (sub), Pol (sub) (10)
Campbell, J. (Cliftonville), 1896 v W; 1897 v E, S, W; (with Distillery), 1898 v E, S, W; (with Cliftonville), 1899 v E; 1900 v E, S; 1901 v S, W; 1902 v S; 1903 v E; 1904 v S (15)
Campbell, J. P. (Fulham), 1951 v E, S (2)
Campbell, R. (Bradford C), 1982 v S, W (sub) (2)
Campbell, W. G. (Dundee), 1968 v S, E; 1969 v T; 1970 v S, W, USSR (6)
Carey, J. J. (Manchester U), 1947 v E, S, W; 1948 v E; 1949 v E, S, W (7)
Carroll, E. (Glenavon), 1925 v S (1)
Casey, T. (Newcastle U), 1955 v W; 1956 v W; 1957 v E, S, W, I, P (2); 1958 v WG, F; (with Portsmouth), 1959 v E, Sp (12)
Cashin, M. (Cliftonville), 1898 v S (1)
Caskey, W. (Derby Co), 1979 v Bul, E, Bul, E, D (sub); 1980 v E (sub); (with Tulsa R), 1982 v F (sub) (7)
Cassidy, T. (Newcastle U), 1971 v E (sub); 1972 v USSR (sub); 1974 v Bul (sub), S, E, W; 1975 v N; 1976 v S, E, W; 1977 v WG (sub); 1980 v E, Ei (sub), Is, S, E, W, Aus (3); (with Burnley), 1981 v Se, P; 1982 v Is, Sp (sub) (24)
Caughey, M. (Linfield), 1986 v F (sub), D (sub) (2)

Chambers, J. (Distillery), 1921 v W; (with Bury), 1928 v E, S, W; 1929 v E, S, W; 1930 v S, W; (with Nottingham F), 1932 v E, S, W (12)
Chatton, H. A. (Partick T), 1925 v E, S; 1926 v E (3)
Christian, J. (Linfield), 1889 v S (1)
Clarke, C. J. (Bournemouth), 1986 v F, D, Mor, Alg (sub), Sp, Br; (with Southampton), 1987, v E, T, Y; 1988 v Y, T, Gr, Pol, F, Ma; 1989 v Ei, H, Sp, Sp (sub) (with QPR) Ma, Ch (21)
Clarke, R. (Belfast C), 1901 v E, S (2)
Cleary, J. (Glentoran), 1982 v S, W; 1983 v W (sub); 1984 v T (sub); 1985 v Is (5)
Clements, D. (Coventry C), 1965 v W, Ho; 1966 v M; 1967 v S, W; 1968 v S, E; 1969 v T (2), S, W; 1970 v S, E, W, USSR (2); 1971 v Sp, E, S, W, Cy; (with Sheffield W), 1972 v USSR (2), Sp, E, S, W; 1973 v Bul, Cy (2), P, E, S, W; (with Everton), 1974 v Bul, P, S, E, W; 1975 v N, Y, E, S, W; 1976 v Se, Y; (with New York Cosmos), E, W (48)
Clugston, J. (Cliftonville), 1888 v W; 1889 v W, S, E; 1890 v E, S; 1891 v E, W; 1892 v E, S, W; 1893 v E, S, W (14)
Cochrane, D. (Leeds U), 1939 v E, W; 1947 v E, S, W; 1948 v E, S, W; 1949 v S, W; 1950 v S, E (12)
Cochrane, M. (Distillery), 1898 v S, W, E; 1899 v E; 1900 v E, S, W; (with Leicester Fosse), 1901 v S (8)
Cochrane, T. (Coleraine), 1976 v N; (with Burnley), 1978 v S (sub), E (sub), W (sub); 1979 v Ei (sub); (with Middlesbrough), D, Bul, E, Bul, E; 1980 v Is, E (sub), W (sub), Aus (1+2 sub); 1981 v Se (sub), P (sub), S, P, S, Se; 1982 v E (sub), F; (with Gillingham), 1984 v S, Fi (sub) (26)
Collins, F. (Glasgow C), 1922 v S (1)
Condy, J. (Distillery), 1882 v W; 1886 v E, S (3)
Connell, T. (Coleraine), 1978 v W (sub) (1)
Connor, J. (Glentoran), 1901 v S, E; (with Belfast C), 1905 v E, S, W; 1907 v E, S; 1908 v E, S; 1909 v W; 1911 v S, E, W (13)
Connor, M. J. (Brentford), 1903 v S, W; (with Fulham), 1904 v E (3)
Cook, W. (Celtic), 1933 v E, W, S; (with Everton), 1935 v E; 1936 v S, W; 1937 v E, S, W; 1938 v E, S, W; 1939 v E, S, W (15)
Cooke, S. (Belfast YMCA), 1889 v E; (with Cliftonville), 1890 v E, S (3)
Coulter, J. (Belfast C), 1934 v E, S, W; (with Everton), 1935 v E, S, W; 1937 v S, W; (with Grimsby T), 1938 v S, W; (with Chelmsford C), 1939 v S (11)
Cowan, J. (Newcastle U), 1970 v E (sub) (1)
Cowan, T. S. (Queen's Island), 1925 v W (1)
Coyle, F. (Coleraine), 1956 v E, S; 1957 v P (with Nottingham F), 1958 v Arg (4)
Coyle, L. (Derry C), 1989 v Ch (sub) (1)
Coyle, R. I. (Sheffield W), 1973 v P, Cy (sub), W (sub); 1974 v Bul (sub), P (sub) (5)
Craig, A. B. (Rangers), 1908 v E, S, W; 1909 v S; (with Morton), 1912 v S, W; 1914 v E, S, W (9)
Craig, D. J. (Newcastle U), 1967 v W; 1968 v W; 1969 v T (2), E, S, W; 1970 v E, S, W, USSR; 1971 v Cy (2), S, S (sub); 1972 v USSR, S (sub); 1973 v Cy (2), E, S, W; 1974 v Bul, P; 1975 v N (25)
Crawford, S. (Distillery), 1889 v E, W; (with Cliftonville), 1891 v E, S, W; 1893 v E, W (7)
Croft, T. (Queen's Island), 1924 v E (1)
Crone, R. (Distillery), 1889 v S; 1890 v E, S, W (4)
Crone, W. (Distillery), 1882 v W; 1884 v E, S, W; 1886 v E, S, W; 1887 v E; 1888 v E, W; 1889 v S; 1890 v W (12)
Crooks, W. (Manchester U), 1922 v W (1)
Crossan, E. (Blackburn R), 1950 v S; 1951 v E; 1955 v W (3)
Crossan, J. A. (Sparta-Rotterdam), 1960 v E; (with Sunderland), 1963 v W, P, Sp; 1964 v E, S, W, U, Sp; 1965 v E, S, Sw (2); (with Manchester C), W, Ho (2), Alb; 1966 v S, E, Alb, WG; 1967 v E, S; (with Middlesbrough), 1968 v S (24)
Crothers, C. (Distillery), 1907 v W (1)
Cumming, L. (Huddersfield T), 1929 v W, S; (with Oldham Ath), 1930 v E (3)
Cunningham, R. (Ulster), 1892 v S, E, W; 1893 v E (4)
Cunningham, W. E. (St Mirren), 1951 v W; 1953 v E; 1954 v S; 1955 v S; (with Leicester C), 1956 v E, S, W; 1957 v E, S, W, I, P (2); 1958 v S, W, I, Cz (2), Arg, WG, F; 1959 v E, S, W; 1960 v E, S, W; (with Dunfermline Ath), 1961 v W; 1962 v W, Ho (30)
Curran, S. (Belfast C), 1926 v S, W; 1928 v S (3)
Curran, J. J. (Glenavon), 1922 v W; (with Pontypridd), 1923 v E, S; (with Glenavon), 1924 v E (4)
Cush, W. W. (Glenavon), 1951 v E, S; 1954 v S, E; 1957 v W, I, P (2); (with Leeds U), 1958 v I (2), W, Cz (2), Arg, WG, F; 1959 v E, S, W, Sp; 1960 v E, S, W; (with Portadown), 1961 v WG, Gr; 1962 v Gr (26)

Dalton, W. (YMCA), 1888 v S; (with Linfield), 1890 v S, W; 1891 v S, W; 1892 v E, S, W; 1894 v E, S, W (11)
D'Arcy, S. D. (Chelsea), 1952 v W; 1953 v E; (with Brentford), 1953 v S, W, F (5)
Darling, J. (Linfield), 1897 v E, S; 1900 v S; 1902 v E, S, W; 1903 v E, S, W; 1905 v E, S, W; 1906 v E, S, W; 1908 v W; 1909 v E; 1910 v E, S, W; 1912 v S (21)
Davey, H. H. (Reading), 1926 v E; 1927 v E, S; 1928 v E; (with Portsmouth), 1928 v W (5)
Davis, T. L. (Oldham Ath), 1937 v E (1)
Davison, J. R. (Cliftonville), 1882 v E, W; 1883 v E, W; 1884 v E, W, S; 1885 v E (8)
Dennison, R. (Wolverhampton W), 1988 v F, Ma; 1989 v H, Sp, Ch (sub) (5)
Devine, W. (Limavady), 1886 v E, W; 1887 v W; 1888 v W (4)
Dickson, D. (Coleraine), 1970 v S (sub), W; 1973 v Cy, P (4)
Dickson, T. A. (Linfield), 1957 v S (1)
Dickson, W. (Chelsea), 1951 v W, F; 1952 v E, S, W; 1953 v E, S, W, F; (with Arsenal), 1954 v E, W; 1955 v E (12)
Diffin, W. (Belfast C), 1931 v W (1)
Dill, A. H. (Knock and Down Ath), 1882 v E, W; (with Cliftonville), 1883 v W; 1884 v E, S, W; 1885 v E, S, W (9)
Doherty, I. (Belfast C), 1901 v E (1)
Doherty, J. (Cliftonville), 1933 v E, W (2)
Doherty, L. (Linfield), 1985 v Is; 1988 v T (sub) (2)
Doherty, M. (Derry C), 1938 v S (1)
Doherty, P. D. (Blackpool), 1935 v E, W; 1936 v E, S; (with Manchester C), 1937 v E, W; 1938 v E, S; 1939 v E, W; (with Derby Co), 1947 v E; (with Huddersfield T), 1947 v W; 1948 v E, W; 1949 v S; (with Doncaster R), 1951 v S (16)
Donaghy, M. (Luton T), 1980 v S, E, W; 1981 v Se, P, S (sub); 1982 v S, Is, E, F, S, W, Y, Hon, Sp, F; 1983 v A, WG, Alb, T, Alb, S, E, W; 1984 v A, T, WG, S, E, W, Fi; 1985 v R, Fi, E, Sp, T; 1986 v T, R, E, F, D, Mor, Alg, Sp, Br; 1987 v E (2), T, Is, Y; 1988 v Y, T, Gr, Pol, F, Ma; 1989 v Ei, H (with Manchester U), Sp, Sp, Ma, Ch (62)
Donnelly, L. (Distillery), 1913 v W (1)
Doran, J. F. (Brighton), 1921 v E; 1922 v E, W (3)
Dougan, A. D. (Portsmouth), 1958 v Cz; (with Blackburn R), 1960 v S; 1961 v E, W, I, Gr; (with Aston Villa), 1963 v S, P (2); (with Leicester C), 1966 v S, E, W, M, Alb, WG; 1967 v E, S; (with Wolverhampton W), 1967 v W; 1968 v S, W, Is; 1969 v T (2), E, S, W; 1970 v S, E, USSR (2); 1971 v Cy (2), Sp, E, S, W; 1972 v USSR (2), E, S, W; 1973 v Bul, Cy (43)
Douglas, J. P. (Belfast C), 1947 v E (1)
Dowd, H. O. (Glenavon), 1974 v W; 1975 v N (sub), Se (3)

Duggan, H. A. (Leeds U), 1930 v E; 1931 v E, W; 1933 v E; 1934 v E; 1935 v S, W; 1936 v S (8)
Dunlop, G. (Linfield), 1985 v Is; 1987 v E, Y (3)
Dunne, J. (Sheffield U), 1928 v W; 1931 v W, E; 1932 v E, S; 1933 v E, W (7)

Eames, W. L. E. (Dublin U), 1885 v E, S, W (3)
Eglington, T. J. (Everton), 1947 v S, W; 1948 v E, S, W; 1949 v E (6)
Elder, A. R. (Burnley), 1960 v W; 1961 v S, E, W, WG (2), Gr; 1962 v E, S, Gr; 1963 v E, S, W, P (2), Sp; 1964 v W, U; 1965 v E, S, W, Sw (2), Ho (2), Alb; 1966 v E, S, W, M, Alb; 1967 v E, S, W; (with Stoke C), 1968 v E, W; 1969 v E (sub), S, W; 1970 v USSR (40)
Elleman, A. R. (Cliftonville), 1889 v W; 1890 v E (2)
Elwood, J. H. (Bradford), 1929 v W; 1930 v E (2)
Emerson, W. (Glentoran), 1920 v E, S, W; 1921 v E; 1922 v E, S; (with Burnley), 1922 v W; 1923 v E, S, W; 1924 v E (11)
English, S. (Glasgow R), 1933 v W, S (2)
Enright, J. (Leeds C), 1912 v S (1)

Falloon, E. (Aberdeen), 1931 v S; 1933 v S (2)
Farquharson, T. G. (Cardiff C), 1923 v S, W; 1924 v E, S, W; 1925 v E, S (7)
Farrell, P. (Distillery), 1901 v S, W (2)
Farrell, P. (Hibernian), 1938 v W (1)
Farrell, P. D. (Everton), 1947 v S, W; 1948 v E, S, W; 1949 v E, W (7)
Feeney, J. M. (Linfield), 1947 v S; (with Swansea T), 1950 v E (2)
Feeney, W. (Glentoran), 1976 v Is (1)
Ferguson, W. (Linfield), 1966 v M; 1967 v E (2)
Ferris, J. (Belfast Celtic), 1920 v E, W; (with Chelsea), 1921 v S, E; (with Belfast C), 1928 v S (5)
Ferris, R. O. (Birmingham), 1950 v S; 1951 v F; 1952 v S (3)
Finney, T. (Sunderland), 1975 v N, E (sub), S, W; 1976 v N, Y, S; (with Cambridge U), 1980 v E, Is, S, E, W, Aus (2) (14)
Fitzpatrick, J. C. (Bohemians), 1896 v E, S (2)
Flack, H. (Burnley), 1929 v S (1)
Fleming, J. G. (Nottingham F), 1987 v E (2), Is, Y; 1988 v T, Gr, Pol; 1989 v Ma, Ch (9)
Forbes, G. (Limavady), 1888 v W; (with Distillery), 1891 v E, S (3)
Forde, J. T. (Ards), 1959 v Sp; 1961 v E, S, WG (4)
Foreman, T. A. (Cliftonville), 1899 v S (1)
Forsyth, J. (YMCA), 1888 v E, S (2)
Fox, W. (Ulster), 1887 v E, S (2)
Fulton, R. P. (Belfast C), 1930 v W; 1931 v E, S, W; 1932 v W, E; 1933 v E, S; 1934 v E, W, S; 1935 v E, W, S; 1936 v S, W; 1937 v E, S, W; 1938 v W (20)

Gaffikin, J. (Linfield Ath), 1890 v S, W; 1891 v S, W; 1892 v E, S, W; 1893 v E, S, W; 1894 v E, S, W; 1895 v E, W (15)
Galbraith, W. (Distillery), 1890 v W (1)
Gallagher, P. (Celtic), 1920 v E, S; 1922 v S; 1923 v S, W; 1924 v S, W; 1925 v S, W, E; (with Falkirk), 1927 v S (11)
Gallogly, C. (Huddersfield T), 1951 v E, S (2)
Gara, A. (Preston NE), 1902 v E, S, W (3)
Gardiner, A. (Cliftonville), 1930 v S, W; 1931 v S; 1932 v E, S (5)
Garrett, J. (Distillery), 1925 v W (1)
Gaston, R. (Oxford U), 1969 v Is (sub) (1)
Gaukrodger, G. (Linfield), 1895 v W (1)
Gaussen, A. W. (Moyola Park), 1884 v E, S; 1888 v E, W; 1889 v E, W (6)
Geary, J. (Glentoran), 1931 v S; 1932 v S (2)
Gibb, J. T. (Wellington Park) 1884 v S, W; 1885 v S, E, W; 1886 v S; 1887 v S, E, W; 1889 v S (10)
Gibb, T. J. (Cliftonville), 1936 v W (1)
Gibson W. K. (Cliftonville), 1894 v S, W, E; 1895 v S; 1897 v W; 1898 v S, W, E; 1901 v S, W, E; 1902 v S, W (13)
Gillespie, R. (Hertford), 1886 v E, S, W; 1887 v E, S, W (6)
Gillespie, W. (Sheffield U), 1913 v E, S; 1914 v E, W; 1920 v S, W; 1921 v E; 1922 v E, S, W; 1923 v E, S, W; 1924 v E, S, W; 1925 v E, S; 1926 v S, W; 1927 v E, W; 1928 v E; 1929 v E; 1931 v E (25)
Gillespie, W. (West Down), 1889 v W (1)
Goodall, A. L. (Derby Co), 1899 v S, W; 1900 v E, W; 1901 v E; 1902 v S; 1903 v E, W; (with Glossop), 1904 v E, W (10)
Goodbody, M. F. (Dublin University), 1889 v E; 1891 v W (2)
Gordon, H. (Linfield), 1891 v S; 1892 v E, S, W; 1893 v E, S, W; 1895 v E, W; 1896 v E, S (11)
Gordon, T. (Linfield), 1894 v W; 1895 v E (2)
Gorman, W. C. (Brentford), 1947 v E, S, W; 1948 v W (4)
Gowdy, J. (Glentoran), 1920 v E; (with Queen's Island), 1924 v W; (with Falkirk), 1926 v E, S; 1927 v E, S (6)
Gowdy, W. A. (Hull C), 1932 v S; (with Sheffield W), 1933 v S; (with Linfield), 1935 v E, S, W; (with Hibernian), 1936 v W (6)
Graham, W. G. L. (Doncaster R), 1951 v W, F; 1952 v E, S, W; 1953 v S, F; 1954 v E, W; 1955 v S, W; 1956 v E, S; 1959 v E (14)
Greer, W. (QPR), 1909 v E, S, W (3)
Gregg, H. (Doncaster R), 1954 v W; 1957 v E, S, W, I, P (2); 1958 v E, I; (with Manchester U), 1958 v Cz, Arg, WG, F, W; 1959 v E, W; 1960 v S, E, W; 1961 v E, S; 1962 v S, Gr; 1964 v S, E (25)

Hall, G. (Distillery), 1897 v E (1)
Halligan, W. (Derby Co), 1911 v W; (with Wolverhampton W), 1912 v E (2)
Hamill, M. (Manchester U), 1912 v E; 1914 v E, S; (with Belfast C), 1920 v E, S, W; (with Manchester C), 1921 v S (7)
Hamilton, B. (Linfield), 1969 v T; 1971 v Cy (2), E, S, W; (with Ipswich T), 1972 v USSR (1+1 sub), Sp; 1973 v Bul, Cy (2), P, E, S, W; 1974 v Bul, S, E, W; 1975 v N, Se, Y, E; 1976 v Se, N, Y; (with Everton), Is, S, E, W; 1977 v Ho, Bel, WG, E, S, W, Ic; (with Millwall), 1978 v S, E, W; 1979 v Ei (sub); (with Swindon T), Bul (2), E, S, W, D; 1980 v Aus (2 sub) (50)
Hamilton, J. (Knock), 1882 v E, W (2)
Hamilton, R. (Distillery), 1908 v W (1)
Hamilton, R. (Glasgow R), 1928 v S; 1929 v E; 1930 v S, E; 1932 v S (5)
Hamilton, W. (QPR), 1978 v S (sub); (with Burnley), 1980 v S, E, W, Aus (2); 1981 v Se, P, S, P, S, Se; 1982 v S, Is, E, W, Y, Hon, Sp, A, F; 1983 v A, WG, Alb, Alb, S, E, W; 1984 v A, T, WG, S, E, W, Fi; (with Oxford U), 1985 v R, Sp; 1986 v Mor (sub), Alg, Sp (sub), Br (sub), (41)
Hamilton, W. D. (Dublin Association), 1885 v W (1)
Hamilton, W. J. (Dublin Association), 1885 v W (1)
Hampton, H. (Bradford C), 1911 v E, S, W; 1912 v E, W; 1913 v E, S, W; 1914 v E (9)
Hanna, D. R. A. (Portsmouth), 1899 v W (1)
Hanna, J. (Nottingham F), 1912 v S, W (2)
Hannon, D. J. (Bohemian), 1908 v E, S; 1911 v E, S; 1912 v W; 1913 v E (6)
Harkin, J. T. (Southport), 1968 v W; 1969 v T; (with Shrewsbury T), W (sub); 1970 v USSR; 1971 v Sp (5)
Harland, A. I. (Linfield), 1923 v E (1)
Harris, J. (Cliftonville), 1921 v W (1)
Harris, V. (Shelbourne), 1906 v E; 1907 v E, W; 1908 v E, W, S; (with Everton), 1909 v E, W, S; 1910 v E, S, W; 1911 v E, S, W; 1912 v E; 1913 v E, S; 1914 v S, W (20)
Harvey, M. (Sunderland), 1961 v I; 1962 v Ho; 1963 v W,

Sp; 1964 v S, E, W, U, Sp; 1965 v E, S, W, Sw (2), Ho (2), Alb; 1966 v S, E, W, M, Alb, WG; 1967 v E, S; 1968 v E, W; 1969 v Is, T (2), E; 1970 v USSR; 1971 v Cy, W (sub) (34)
Hastings, J. (Knock), 1882 v E, W; (with Ulster), 1883 v W; 1884 v E, S; 1886 v E, S (7)
Hatton, S. (Linfield), 1963 v S, Pol (2)
Hayes, W. E. (Huddersfield T), 1938 v E, S; 1939 v E, S (4)
Healy, F. (Coleraine), 1982 v S, W, Hon (sub); (with Glentoran), 1983 v A (sub) (4)
Hegan, D. (WBA), 1970 v USSR; (with Wolverhampton W), 1972 v USSR, E, S, W; 1973 v Bul, Cy (7)
Henderson, A. W. (Ulster), 1885 v E, S, W (3)
Hewison, G. (Moyola Park), 1885 v E, S (2)
Hill, M. J. (Norwich C), 1959 v W; 1960 v W; 1961 v WG; 1962 v S; (with Everton), 1964 v S, E, Sp (7)
Hinton, E. (Fulham), 1947 v S, W; 1948 v S, E, W; (with Millwall), 1951 v W, F (7)
Hopkins, J. (Brighton), 1926 v E (1)
Houston, J. (Linfield), 1912 v S, W; 1913 v W; (with Everton), 1913 v E, S; 1914 v S (6)
Houston, W. (Linfield), 1933 v W (1)
Houston, W. G. (Moyola Park), 1885 v E, S (2)
Hughes, P. (Bury), 1987 v E, T, Is (3)
Hughes, W. (Bolton W), 1951 v W (1)
Humphries, W. (Ards), 1962 v W; (with Coventry C), 1962 v Ho; 1963 v E, S, W, Pol, Sp; 1964 v S, E, Sp; 1965 v S; (with Swansea T), 1965 v W, Ho, Alb (14)
Hunter, A. (Blackburn R), 1970 v USSR; 1971 v Cy (2), E, S, W; (with Ipswich T), 1972 v USSR (2), Sp, E, S, W; 1973 v Bul, Cy (2), P, E, S, W; 1974 v Bul, S, E, W; 1975 v N, Se, Y, E, S, W; 1976 v Se, N, Y, Is, S, E, W; 1977 v Ho, Bel, WG, E, S, W, Ic; 1978 v Ic, Ho, Bel; 1979 v Ei, D, S, W, D; 1980 v E, Ei (53)
Hunter, A. (Distillery), 1905 v W; 1906 v W, E, S; (with Belfast C), 1908 v W; 1909 v W, E, S (8)
Hunter, R. J. (Cliftonville), 1884 v E, S, W (3)
Hunter, V. (Coleraine), 1962 v E; 1964 v Sp (2)

Irvine, R. J. (Linfield), 1962 v Ho; 1963 v E, S, W, Pol (2), Sp; (with Stoke C), 1965 v W (8)
Irvine, R. W. (Everton), 1922 v S; 1923 v E, W; 1924 v E, S; 1925 v E; 1926 v E; 1927 v E, W; 1928 v E, S; (with Portsmouth), 1929 v E; 1930 v S; (with Connah's Quay), 1931 v E; (with Derry C), 1932 v W (15)
Irvine, W. J. (Burnley), 1963 v W, Sp; 1965 v S, W, Sw, Ho (2), Alb; 1966 v S, E, W, M, Alb; 1967 v E, S; 1968 v E, W; (with Preston NE), 1969 v Is, T, E; (with Brighton), 1972 v E, S, W (23)
Irving, S, J. (Dundee), 1923 v S, W; 1924 v S, E, W; 1925 v S, E, W; 1926 v S, W; (with Cardiff C), 1927 v S, E, W; 1928 v S, E, W; (with Chelsea), 1929 v E; 1931 v W (18)

Jackson, T. (Everton), 1969 v Is, E, S, W; 1970 v USSR (1+1 sub); (with Nottingham F), 1971 v Sp; 1972 v E, S, W; 1973 v Cy, E, S, W; 1974 v Bul, P, S (sub), E (sub), W (sub); 1975 v N (sub), Se, Y, E, S, W; (with Manchester U); 1976 v Se, N, Y; 1977 v Ho, Bel, WG, E, S, W, Ic (35)
Jamison, J. (Glentoran), 1976 v N (1)
Jennings, P. A. (Watford), 1964 v W, U; (with Tottenham H), 1965 v E, S, Sw (2), Ho, Alb; 1966 v S, E, W, Alb, WG; 1967 v E, S; 1968 v S, E, W; 1969 v Is, T (2), E, S, W; 1970 v S, E, USSR (2); 1971 v Cy (2), E, S, W; 1972 v USSR, Sp, S, E, W; 1973 v Bul, Cy, P, E, S, W; 1974 v P, S, E, W; 1975 v N, Se, Y, E, S, W; 1976 v Se, N, Y, Is, S, E, W; 1977 v Ho, Bel, WG, E, S, W, Ic; (with Arsenal), 1978 v Ic, Ho, Bel; 1979 v Ei, D, Bul, E, Bul, E, S, W, D; 1980 v E, Ei, Is; 1981 v S, P, S, Se; 1982 v S, Is, E, W, Y, Hon, Sp, F; 1983 v Alb, S, E, W; 1984 v A, T, WG, S, W, Fi; 1985 v R, Fi, E, Sp, T; (with Tottenham H), 1986 v T, R, E, F, D, Mor, Alg, Sp, Br (119)
Johnston, H. (Portadown), 1927 v W (1)
Johnston, R. (Old Park), 1885 v S, W (2)
Johnston, S. (Distillery), 1882 v W; 1884 v E; 1886 v E, S (4)
Johnston, S. (Linfield), 1890 v W; 1893 v S, W; 1894 v E (4)
Johnston, S. (Distillery), 1905 v W (1)
Johnston, W. C. (Glenavon), 1962 v W; (with Oldham Ath), 1966 v M (sub) (2)
Jones, J. (Linfield), 1930 v S, W; 1931 v S, W, E; 1932 v S, E; 1933 v S, E, W; 1934 v S, E, W; 1935 v S, E, W; 1936 v E, S; (with Hibernian), 1936 v W; 1937 v E, W, S; (with Glenavon), 1938 v E (23)
Jones, J. (Glenavon), 1956 v W; 1957 v E, W (3)
Jones, S. (Distillery), 1934 v E; (with Blackpool), 1934 v W (2)
Jordan, T. (Linfield), 1895 v E, W (2)

Kavanagh, P. J. (Glasgow C), 1930 v E (1)
Keane, T. R. (Swansea T), 1949 v S (1)
Kearns, A. (Distillery), 1900 v E, S, W; 1902 v E, S, W (6)
Keith, R, M. (Newcastle U), 1958 v E, W, Cz (2), Arg, I, WG, F; 1959 v E, S, W, Sp; 1960 v S, E; 1961 v S, E, W, I, WG (2), Gr; 1962 v W, Ho (23)
Kelly, H. R. (Fulham), 1950 v E, W; (with Southampton), 1951 v E, S (4)
Kelly, J. (Glentoran), 1896 v E (1)
Kelly, J. (Derry C), 1932 v E, W; 1933 v E, W, S; 1934 v W; 1936 v E, S, W; 1937 v S, E (11)
Kelly, P. (Manchester C), 1921 v E (1)
Kelly, P. M. (Barnsley), 1950 v S (1)
Kennedy, A. L. (Arsenal), 1923 v W; 1925 v E (2)
Kernaghan, N. (Belfast C), 1936 v W; 1937 v S; 1938 v E (3)
Kirkwood, H. (Cliftonville), 1904 v W (1)
Kirwan, J. (Tottenham H), 1900 v W; 1902 v E, W; 1903 v E, S, W; 1904 v E, S, W; 1905 v E, S, W; (with Chelsea), 1906 v E, S, W; 1907 v W; (with Clyde), 1909 v S (17)

Lacey, W. (Everton), 1909 v E, S, W; 1910 v E, S, W; 1911 v E, S, W; 1912 v E; (with Liverpool), 1913 v W; 1914 v E, S, W; 1920 v E, S, W; 1921 v E, S, W; 1922 v E, S; (with New Brighton), 1925 v E (23)
Lawther, W. I. (Sunderland), 1960 v W; 1961 v I; (with Blackburn R), 1962 v S, Ho (4)
Leatham, J. (Belfast C), 1939 v W (1)
Ledwidge, J. J. (Shelbourne), 1906 v S, W (2)
Lemon, J. (Glentoran), 1886 v W; 1888 v S; (with Belfast YMCA), 1889 v W (3)
Leslie, W. (YMCA), 1887 v E (1)
Lewis, J. (Glentoran), 1899 v S, E, W; (with Distillery), 1900 v S (4)
Little, J. (Glentoran), 1898 v W (1)
Lockhart, H. (Rossall School), 1884 v W (1)
Lockhart, N. (Linfield), 1947 v E; (with Coventry C), 1950 v W; 1951 v W; 1952 v W; (with Aston Villa), 1954 v S, E; 1955 v W; 1956 v W (8)
Lowther, R. (Glentoran), 1888 v E, S (2)
Loyal, J. (Clarence), 1891 v S (1)
Lutton, R. J. (Wolverhampton W), 1970 v S, E; (with West Ham U), 1973 v Cy (sub), S (sub), W (sub); 1974 v P (6)
Lyner, D. (Glentoran), 1920 v E, W; 1922 v S, W; (with Manchester U), 1923 v E; (with Kilmarnock), 1923 v W (6)

McAdams, W. J. (Manchester C), 1954 v W; 1955 v S; 1957 v E; 1958 v S, I; (with Bolton W), 1961 v E, S, W, I, WG (2), Gr; 1962 v E, Gr; (with Leeds U), Ho (15)

McAlery, J. M. (Cliftonville), 1882 v E, W (2)
McAlinden, J. (Belfast C), 1938 v S; 1939 v S; (with Portsmouth), 1947 v E; (with Southend U), 1949 v E (4)
McAllen, J. (Linfield), 1898 v E; 1899 v E, S, W; 1900 v E, S, W; 1901 v W; 1902 v S (9)
McAlpine, W. J. (Cliftonville), 1901 v S (1)
McArthur, A. (Distillery), 1886 v W (1)
McAuley, J. L. (Huddersfield T), 1911 v E, W; 1912 v E, S; 1913 v E, S (6)
McAuley, P. (Belfast C), 1900 v S (1)
McCabe, J. J. (Leeds U), 1949 v S, W; 1950 v E; 1951 v W; 1953 v W; 1954 v S (6)
McCabe, W. (Ulster), 1891 v E (1)
McCambridge, J. (Ballymena), 1930 v S, W; (with Cardiff C), 1931 v W; 1932 v E (4)
McCandless, J. (Bradford), 1912 v W; 1913 v W; 1920 v W, S; 1921 v E (5)
McCandless, W. (Linfield), 1920 v E, W; 1921 v E; (with Rangers), 1921 v W; 1922 v S; 1924 v W, S; 1925 v S; 1929 v W (9)
McCann, P. (Belfast C), 1910 v E, S, W; 1911 v E; (with Glentoran), 1911 v S; 1912 v E; 1913 v W (7)
McCashin, J. (Cliftonville), 1896 v W; 1898 v S, W; 1899 v S (4)
McCavana, W. T. (Coleraine), 1955 v S; 1956 v E, S (3)
McCaw, D. (Distillery), 1882 v E (1)
McCaw, J. H. (Linfield), 1927 v W; 1930 v S; 1931 v E, S, W (5)
McClatchey, J. (Distillery), 1886 v E, S, W (3)
McClatchey, R. (Distillery), 1895 v S (1)
McCleary, J. W. (Cliftonville), 1955 v W (1)
McCleery, W. (Cliftonville), 1922 v N; 1930 v E, W; 1931 v E, S, W; 1932 v S, W; 1933 v E, W (10)
McClelland, J. (Arsenal), 1961 v W, I, WG (2), Gr; (with Fulham), 1967 v M (6)
McClelland, J. (Mansfield T), 1980 v S (sub), Aus (3); 1981 v Se, S, (with Rangers), S, Se; 1982 v S, W, Y, Hon, Sp, A, F; 1983 v A, WG, Alb, T, Alb, S, E, W; 1984 v A, T, WG, S, E, W, Fi; 1985 v R, (with Watford), Fi, Is, E, Sp, T; 1986 v T, F (sub); 1987 v E (2), T, Is, Y; 1988 v T, Gr, F, Ma; 1989 v Ei, H, Sp, Sp, Ma (52)
McCluggage, A. (Bradford), 1924 v E; (with Burnley), 1927 v S, W; 1928 v S, E, W; 1929 v S, E, W; 1930 v W; 1931 v E, W (12)
McClure, G. (Cliftonville), 1907 v S, W; 1908 v E; (with Distillery), 1909 v E (4)
McConnell, E. (Cliftonville), 1904 v S, W; (with Glentoran), 1905 v S; (with Sunderland), 1906 v E; 1907 v E; 1908 v S, W; (with Sheffield W), 1909 v S, W; 1910 v S, W, E (12)
McConnell, P. (Doncaster R), 1928 v W; (with Southport), 1932 v E (2)
McConnell, W. G. (Bohemians), 1912 v W; 1913 v E, S; 1914 v E, S, W (6)
McConnell, W. H. (Reading), 1925 v W; 1926 v E, W; 1927 v E, S, W; 1928 v E, W (8)
McCourt, F. J. (Manchester C), 1952 v E, W; 1953 v E, S, W, F (6)
McCoy, J. (Distillery), 1896 v W (1)
McCoy, R. (Coleraine), 1987 v Y (sub) (1)
McCracken, R. (C Palace), 1921 v E; 1922 v E, S, W (4)
McCracken, W. (Distillery), 1902 v E, W; 1903 v E; 1904 v E, S, W; (with Newcastle U), 1905 v E, S, W; 1907 v E; 1920 v E; 1922 v E, S, W; (with Hull C), 1923 v S (15)
McCreery, D. (Manchester U), 1976 v S (sub), E, W; 1977 v Ho, Bel, WG, E, S, W, Ic; 1978 v Ic, Ho, Bel, S, E, W; 1979 v Ei, D, Bul, E, Bul, W, D; (with QPR), 1980 v E, Ei, S (sub), E (sub), W (sub), Aus (1+sub); 1981 v Se (sub), P (sub); (with Tulsa R), S, P, Se; 1982 v S, Is, E (sub), F, Y, Hon, Sp, A, F; (with Newcastle U), v A; 1984 v T (sub); 1985 v R, Sp (sub); 1986 v T (sub), R, E, F, D, Alg, Sp, Br; 1987 v T, E, Y; 1988 v Y; 1989 v Sp, Ma, Ch (63)
McCrory, S. (Southend U), 1958 v E (1)
McCullough, K. (Belfast C), 1935 v W; 1936 v E; (with Manchester C), 1936 v S; 1937 v E, S (5)
McCullough, W. J. (Arsenal), 1961 v I; 1963 v Sp; 1964 v S, E, W, U, Sp; 1965 v E, Sw; (with Millwall), 1967 v E (10)
McCurdy, C. (Linfield), 1980 v Aus (sub) (1)
McDonald, A. (QPR), 1986 v R, E, F, D, Mor, Alg, Sp, Br; 1987 v E (2), T, Is, Y; 1988 v Y, T, Pol, F, Ma; 1989 v Ei, H, Sp, Ch (22)
McDonald, R. (Glasgow R), 1930 v S; 1932 v E (2)
McDonnell, J. (Bohemians), 1911 v E, S; 1912 v W; 1913 v W (4)
McElhinney, G. (Bolton W), 1984 v WG, S, E, W, Fi; 1985 v R (6)
McFaul, W. S. (Linfield), 1967 v E (sub); (with Newcastle U), 1970 v W; 1971 v Sp; 1972 v USSR; 1973 v Cy; 1974 v Bul (6)
McGarry, J. K. (Cliftonville), 1951 v W, F, S (3)
McGaughey, M. (Linfield), 1985 v Is (sub) (1)
McGee, G. (Wellington Park), 1885 v E, S, W (3)
McGrath, R. C. (Tottenham H), 1974 v S, E, W; 1975 v N; 1976 v Is (sub); 1977 v Ho (with Manchester U), Bel, WG, E, S, W, Ic; 1978 v Ic, Ho, Bel, S, E, W; 1979 v Bul (sub), E (sub), E (sub) (21)
McGregor, S. (Glentoran), 1921 v S (1)
McGrillen, J. (Clyde), 1924 v S; (with Belfast C), 1927 v S (2)
McGuire, E. (Distillery), 1907 v S (1)
McIlroy, H. (Cliftonville), 1906 v E (1)
McIlroy, J. (Burnley), 1952 v E, S, W; 1953 v E, S, W; 1954 v E, S, W; 1955 v E, S, W; 1956 v E, S, W; 1957 v E, S, W, I, P (2); 1958 v E, S, W, I (2), Cz (2), Arg, WG, F; 1959 v E, S, W, Sp; 1960 v E, S, W; 1961 v E, W, WG (2), Gr; 1962 v E, S, Gr, Ho; 1963 v E, S, Pol (2); (with Stoke C), 1963 v W; 1966 v S, E, Alb (55)
McIlroy, S. B. (Manchester U), 1972 v Sp, S (sub); 1974 v S, E, W; 1975 v N, Se, Y, E, S, W; 1976 v Se, N, Y, S, E, W; 1977 v Ho, Bel, E, S, W, Ic; 1978 v Ic, Ho, Bel, S, E, W; 1979 v Ei, D, Bul, E, Bul, E, S, W, D; 1980 v E, Ei, Is, S, E, W; 1981 v Se, P, S, P, S, Se; 1982 v S, Is; (with Stoke C), E, F, S, W, Y, Hon, Sp, A, F; 1983 v A, WG, Alb, T, Alb, S, E, W; 1984 v A, T, S, E, W, Fi; 1985 v Fi, E, T; (with Manchester C), 1986 v T, R, E, F, D, Mor, Alg, Sp, Br; 1987 v E (sub) (88)
McIlvenny, J. (Distillery), 1890 v E; 1891 v E (2)
McIlvenny, P. (Distillery), 1924 v W (1)
McKeag, W. (Glentoran), 1968 v S, W (2)
McKee, F. W. (Cliftonville), 1906 v S, W; (with Belfast C), 1914 v E, S, W (5)
McKelvie, H. (Glentoran), 1901 v W (1)
McKenna, J. (Huddersfield), 1950 v E, S, W; 1951 v E, S, F; 1952 v E (7)
McKenzie, H. (Distillery), 1923 v S (1)
McKenzie, R. (Airdrie), 1967 v W (1)
McKeown, H. (Linfield), 1892 v E, S, W; 1893 v S, W; 1894 v S, W (7)
McKie, H. (Cliftonville), 1895 v E, S, W (3)
McKinney, D. (Hull C), 1921 v S; (with Bradford C), 1924 v S (2)
McKinney, V. J. (Falkirk), 1966 v WG (1)
McKnight, A. (Celtic), 1988 v Y, T, Gr, Pol, F, Ma; 1989 (with West Ham U) v Ei, H, Sp, Sp (10)
McKnight, J. (Preston NE), 1912 v S; (with Glentoran), 1913 v S (2)
McLaughlin, J. C. (Shrewsbury T), 1962 v E, S, W, Gr; 1963 v W; (with Swansea T), 1964 v W, U; 1965 v E, W, Sw (2); 1966 v W (12)
McLean, T. (Limavady), 1885 v S (1)
McMahon, J. (Bohemians), 1934 v S (1)
McMaster, G. (Glentoran), 1897 v E, S, W (3)
McMichael, A. (Newcastle U), 1950 v E, S; 1951 v E, S,

F; 1952 v E, S, W; 1953 v E, S, W, F; 1954 v E, S, W; 1955 v E, W; 1956 v W; 1957 v E, S, W, I, P (2); 1958 v E, S, W, I (2), Cz (2), Arg, WG, F; 1959 v S, W, Sp; 1960 v E, S, W (40)
McMillan, G. (Distillery), 1903 v E; 1905 v W (2)
McMillan, S. (Manchester U), 1963 v E, S (2)
McMillen, W. S. (Manchester U), 1934 v E; 1935 v S; 1937 v S; (with Chesterfield), 1938 v S, W; 1939 v E, S (7)
McMordie, A. S. (Middlesbrough), 1969 v Is, T (2), E, S, W; 1970 v E, S, W, USSR; 1971 v Cy (2), E, S, W; 1972 v USSR, Sp, E, S, W; 1973 v Bul (21)
McMorran, E. J. (Belfast C), 1947 v E; (with Barnsley), 1951 v E, S, W; 1952 v E, S, W; 1953 v E, S, F; (with Doncaster R), 1953 v W; 1954 v E; 1956 v W; 1957 v I, P (15)
McMullan, D. (Liverpool), 1926 v E, W; 1927 v S (3)
McNally, B. A. (Shrewsbury T), 1986 v Mor; 1987 v T (sub); 1988 v Y, Gr, Ma (sub) (5)
McNinch, J. (Ballymena), 1931 v S; 1932 v S, W (3)
McParland, P. J. (Aston Villa), 1954 v W; 1955 v E, S; 1956 v E, S; 1957 v E, S, W, P; 1958 v E, S, W, I (2), Cz (2), Arg, WG, F; 1959 v E, S, W, Sp; 1960 v E, S, W; 1961 v E, S, W, I, WG (2), Gr; (with Wolverhampton W), 1962 v Ho (34)
McShane, J. (Cliftonville), 1899 v S; 1900 v E, S, W (4)
McVickers, J. (Glentoran), 1888 v E; 1889 v S (2)
McWha, W. B. R. (Knock), 1882 v E, W; (with Cliftonville), 1883 v E, W; 1884 v E; 1885 v E, W (7)
Macartney, A. (Ulster), 1903 v S, W; (with Linfield), 1904 v S, W; (with Everton), 1905 v E, S; (with Belfast C), 1907 v E, S, W; 1908 v E, S, W; (with Glentoran), 1909 v E, S, W (15)
Mackie, J. (Arsenal), 1923 v W; (with Portsmouth), 1935 v S, W (3)
Madden, O. (Norwich C), 1938 v E (1)
Magill, E. J. (Arsenal), 1962 v E, S, Gr; 1963 v E, S, W, Pol (2), Sp; 1964 v E, S, W, U, Sp; 1965 v E, S, Sw (2), Ho, Alb; 1966 v S, E; (with Brighton), 1966 v Alb, W, WG, M (26)
Maginnis, H. (Linfield), 1900 v E, S, W; 1903 v S, W; 1904 v E, S, W (8)
Maguire, E. (Distillery), 1907 v S (1)
Mahood, J. (Belfast C), 1926 v S; 1928 v E, S, W; 1929 v E, S, W; 1930 v W; (with Ballymena), 1934 v S (9)
Manderson, R. (Glasgow R), 1920 v W, S; 1925 v S, E; 1926 v S (5)
Mansfield, J. (Dublin Freebooters), 1901 v E (1)
Martin, C. J. (Glentoran), 1947 v S; (with Leeds U), 1948 v E, S, W; (with Aston Villa), 1949 v E; 1950 v W (6)
Martin, D. (Bo'ness), 1925 v S (1)
Martin, D. C. (Cliftonville), 1882 v E, W; 1883 v E (3)
Martin, D. K. (Belfast C), 1934 v E, S, W; 1935 v S; (with Wolverhampton W), 1935 v E; 1936 v W; (with Nottingham F), 1937 v S; 1938 v E, S; 1939 v S (10)
Mathieson, A. (Luton T), 1921 v W; 1922 v E (2)
Maxwell, J. (Linfield), 1902 v W; 1903 v W, E; (with Glentoran), 1905 v W, S; (with Belfast C), 1906 v W; 1907 v S (7)
Meek, H. L. (Glentoran), 1925 v W (1)
Mehaffy, J. A. C. (Queen's Island), 1922 v W (1)
Meldon, J. (Dublin Freebooters), 1899 v S, W (2)
Mercer, H. V. A. (Linfield), 1908 v E (1)
Mercer, J. T. (Distillery), 1898 v E, S, W; 1899 v E; (with Linfield), 1902 v E, W; (with Distillery), 1903 v S, W; (with Derby Co), 1904 v E, W; 1905 v S (11)
Millar, W. (Barrow), 1932 v W; 1933 v S (2)
Miller, J. (Middlesbrough), 1929 v W, S; 1930 v E (3)
Milligan, D. (Chesterfield), 1939 v W (1)
Milne, R. G. (Linfield), 1894 v E, S, W; 1895 v E, W; 1896 v E, S, W; 1897 v E, S; 1898 v E, S, W; 1899 v E, W; 1901 v W; 1902 v E, S, W; 1903 v E, S; 1904 v E, S, W; 1906 v E, S, W (27)
Mitchell, C. (Glentoran), 1934 v W (1)
Mitchell, E. J. (Cliftonville), 1933 v S (1)
Mitchell, W. (Distillery), 1932 v E, W; 1933 v E, W; (with Chelsea), 1934 v W, S; 1935 v S, E; 1936 v S, E; 1937 v E, S, W; 1938 v E, S (15)
Molyneux, T. B. (Ligoniel), 1883 v E, W; (with Cliftonville), 1884 v E, W, S; 1885 v E, W; 1886 v E, W, S; 1888 v S (11)
Montgomery, F. J. (Coleraine), 1955 v E (1)
Moore, C. (Glentoran), 1949 v W (1)
Moore, J. (Linfield Ath), 1891 v E, S, W (3)
Moore, P. (Aberdeen), 1933 v E (1)
Moore, T. (Ulster), 1887 v S, W (2)
Moore, W. (Falkirk), 1923 v S (1)
Moorhead, F. W. (Dublin University), 1885 v E (1)
Moorhead, G. (Linfield), 1923 v S; 1928 v S; 1929 v S (3)
Moran, J. (Leeds C), 1912 v S (1)
Moreland, V. (Derby Co), 1979 v Bul (sub), Bul (sub), E, S; 1980 v E, Ei (6)
Morgan, F. G. (Linfield), 1923 v E; (with Nottingham F), 1924 v S; 1927 v E; 1928 v E, S, W; 1929 v E (7)
Morgan, S. (Port Vale), 1972 v Sp; 1973 v Bul (sub), P, Cy, E, S, W; (with Aston Villa), 1974 v Bul, P, S, E; 1975 v Se; 1976 v Se (sub), N, Y; (with Brighton & HA), S, W (sub); (with Sparta Rotterdam), 1979 v D (18)
Morrison, J. (Linfield Ath), 1891 v E, W (2)
Morrison, T. (Glentoran), 1895 v E, S, W; (with Burnley), 1899 v W; 1900 v W; 1902 v E, S (7)
Morrogh, E. (Bohemians), 1896 v S (1)
Morrow, W. J. (Moyola Park), 1883 v E, W; 1884 v S (3)
Muir, R. (Oldpark), 1885 v S, W (2)
Mullan, G. (Glentoran), 1983 v S, E, W, Alb (sub) (4)
Mulholland, S. (Celtic), 1906 v S, E (2)
Mulligan, J. (Manchester C), 1921 v S (1)
Murphy, J. (Bradford C), 1910 v E, S, W (3)
Murphy, N. (QPR), 1905 v E, S, W (3)
Murray, J. M. (Motherwell), 1910 v E, S; (with Sheffield W), 1910 v W (3)

Napier, R. J. (Bolton W), 1966 v WG (1)
Neill, W. J. T. (Arsenal), 1961 v I, Gr, WG; 1962 v E, S, W, Gr; 1963 v E, W, Pol, Sp; 1964 v S, E, W, U, Sp; 1965 v E, S, W, Sw, Ho (2), Alb; 1966 v S, E, W, Alb, WG, M; 1967 v S, W; 1968 v S, E; 1969 v E, S, W, Is, T (2); 1970 v S, E, W, USSR (2); (with Hull C), 1971 v Cy, Sp; 1972 v USSR (2), Sp, S, E, W; 1973 v Bul, Cy (2), P, E, S, W (59)
Nelis, P. (Nottingham F), 1923 v E (1)
Nelson, S. (Arsenal), 1970 v W, E (sub); 1971 v Cy, Sp, E, S, W; 1972 v USSR (2), Sp, E, S, W; 1973 v Bul, Cy, P; 1974 v S, E; 1975 v Se, Y; 1976 v Se, N, Is, E; 1977 v Bel (sub), WG, W, Ic; 1978 v Ic, Ho, Bel; 1979 v Ei, D, Bul, E, Bul, E, S, W, D; 1980 v E, Ei, Is; 1981 v S, P, S, Se; (with Brighton & HA), 1982 v E, S, Sp (sub), A (51)
Nicholl, C. J. (Aston Villa), 1975 v Se, Y, E, S, W; 1976 v Se, N, Y, S, E, W; 1977 v W; (with Southampton), 1978 v Bel (sub), S, E, W; 1979 v Ei, Bul, E, Bul, E, W; 1980 v Ei, Is, S, E, W, Aus (3); 1981 v Se, P, S, P, S, Se; 1982 v S, Is, E, F, W, Y, Hon, Sp, A, F; 1983 v S (sub), E, W; (with Grimsby T), 1984 v A, T (51)
Nicholl, H. (Belfast C), 1902 v E, W; 1905 v E (3)
Nicholl, J. M. (Manchester U), 1976 v Is, W (sub); 1977 v Ho, Bel, E, S, W, Ic; 1978 v Ic, Ho, Bel, S, E, W; 1979 v Ei, D, Bul, E, Bul, E, S, W, D; 1980 v E, Ei, Is, S, E, W, Aus (3); 1981 v Se, P, S, P, S, Se; 1982 v S, Is, E; (with Toronto B), F, W, Y, Hon, Sp, A, F; (with Sunderland), 1983 v A, WG, Alb, T, Alb, (with Toronto B), S, E, W; (with Rangers), 1984 v T, WG, S, E, (with Toronto B), Fi; 1985 v R, (with WBA) Fi, E, Sp, T; 1986 v T, R, E, F, Alg, Sp, Br (73)
Nicholson, J. J. (Manchester U), 1961 v S, W; 1962 v E, W, Gr, Ho; 1963 v E, S, Pol (2); (with Huddersfield T), 1965 v W, Ho (2), Alb; 1966 v S, E, W, Alb, M; 1967 v

S, W; 1968 v S, E, W; 1969 v S, E, W, T (2); 1970 v S, E, W, USSR (2); 1971 v Cy (2), E, S, W; 1972 v USSR (2) (41)

Nixon, R. (Linfield), 1914 v S (1)

Nolan-Whelan, J. V. (Dublin Freebooters), 1901 v E, W; 1902 v S, W (4)

O'Brien, M. T. (QPR), 1921 v S; (with Leicester C), 1922 v S, W; 1924 v S, W; (with Hull C), 1925 v S, E, W; 1926 v W; (with Derby Co), 1927 v W (10)

O'Connell, P. (Sheffield W), 1912 v E, S; (with Hull C), 1914 v E, S, W (5)

O'Doherty, A. (Coleraine), 1970 v E, W (sub) (2)

O'Driscoll, J. F. (Swansea T), 1949 v E, S, W (3)

O'Hagan, C. (Tottenham H), 1905 v S, W; 1906 v S, W, E; (with Aberdeen), 1907 v E, S, W; 1908 v S, W; 1909 v E (11)

O'Hagan, W. (St Mirren), 1920 v E, W (2)

O'Hehir, J. C. (Bohemians), 1910 v W (1)

O'Kane, W. J. (Nottingham F), 1970 v E, W, S (sub); 1971 v Sp, E, S, W; 1972 v USSR (2); 1973 v P, Cy; 1974 v Bul, P, S, E, W; 1975 v N, Se, E, S (20)

O'Mahoney, M. T. (Bristol R), 1939 v S (1)

O'Neill, C. (Motherwell), 1989 Ch (sub) (1)

O'Neill, J. (Leicester C), 1980 v Is, S, E, W, Aus (3); 1981 v P, S, P, S, Se; 1982 v S, Is, E, F, S, F (sub); 1983 v A, WG, Alb, T, Alb, S; 1984 v S (sub); 1985 v Is, Fi, E, Sp, T; 1986 v T, R, E, F, D, Mor, Alg, Sp, Br (39)

O'Neill, J. (Sunderland), 1962 v W (1)

O'Neill, M. A. (Newcastle U), 1988 v Gr, Pol, F, Ma; 1989 v Ei, H, Sp (sub), Sp (sub), Ma (sub), Ch (10)

O'Neill, M. H. (Distillery), 1972 v USSR (sub), (with Nottingham F), Sp (sub), W (sub); 1973 v P, Cy, E, S, W; 1974 v Bul, P, E (sub), W; 1975 v Se, Y, E, S; 1976 v Y; 1977 v E (sub), S; 1978 v Ic, Ho, S, E, W; 1979 v Ei, D, Bul, E, Bul, D; 1980 v Ei, Is, Aus (3); 1981 v Se, P (with Norwich C), P, S, Se; (with Manchester C), 1982 v S (with Norwich C), E, F, S, Y, Hon, Sp, A, F; 1983 v A, WG, Alb, T, Alb, S, E; (with Notts Co), 1984 v A, T, WG, E, W, Fi; 1985 v R, Fi (64)

O'Reilly, H. (Dublin Freebooters), 1901 v S, W; 1904 v S (3)

Parke, J. (Linfield), 1964 v S; (with Hibernian), 1964 v E, Sp; (with Sunderland), 1965 v Sw, S, W, Ho (2), Alb; 1966 v WG; 1967 v E, S; 1968 v S, E (14)

Peacock, R. (Celtic), 1952 v S; 1953 v F; 1954 v W; 1955 v E, S; 1956 v E, S; 1957 v W, I, P; 1958 v S, E, W, I (2), Arg, Cz (2), WG; 1959 v E, S, W; 1960 v S, E; 1961 v E, S, I, WG (2), Gr; (with Coleraine), 1962 v S (31)

Peden, J. (Linfield), 1887 v S, W; 1888 v W, E; 1889 v S, E; 1890 v W, S; 1891 v W, E; 1892 v W, E; 1893 v E, S, W; (with Distillery), 1896 v W, E, S; 1897 v W, S; 1898 v W, E, S; (with Linfield), 1899 v W (24)

Penney, S. (Brighton & HA), 1985 v Is; 1986 v T, R, E, F, D, Mor, Alg, Sp; 1987 v E, T, Is; 1988 v Pol, F, Ma; 1989 v Ei, Sp (17)

Percy, J. C. (Belfast YMCA), 1889 v W (1)

Platt, J. A. (Middlesbrough), 1976 v Is (sub); 1978 v S, E, W; 1980 v S, E, W, Aus (3); 1981 v Se, P; 1982 v F, S, W (sub), A; 1983 v A, WG, Alb, T; (with Ballymena U), 1984 v E, W (sub); (with Coleraine), 1986 v Mor (sub) (23)

Ponsonby, J. (Distillery), 1895 v S; 1896 v E, S, W; 1897 v E, S, W; 1899 v E (8)

Potts, R. M. C. (Cliftonville), 1883 v E, W (2)

Priestley, T. J. (Coleraine), 1933 v S; (with Chelsea), 1934 v E (2)

Pyper, Jas. (Cliftonville), 1897 v S, W; 1898 v S, E, W; 1899 v S; 1900 v E (7)

Pyper, John (Cliftonville), 1897 v E, S, W; 1899 v E, W; 1900 v E, W, S; 1902 v S (9)

Pyper, M. (Linfield), 1932 v W (1)

Quinn, J. M. (Blackburn R), 1985 v Is, Fi, E, Sp, T; 1986 v T, R, E, F, D (sub), Mor (sub); 1987 v E (sub), T; (with Swindon T), 1988 v Y (sub), T, Gr, Pol, F (sub), Ma; 1989 (with Leicester C) v Ei, H (sub), Sp (sub), Sp (with Bradford C), Ma, Ch (25)

Rafferty, P. (Linfield), 1980 v E (sub) (1)

Ramsey, P. (Leicester C), 1984 v A, WG, S; 1985 v Is, E, Sp, T; 1986 v T, Mor; 1987 v Is, E, Y (sub); 1988 v Y; 1989 v Sp (14)

Rankine, J. (Alexander), 1883 v E, W (2)

Raper, E. O. (Dublin University), 1886 v W (1)

Rattray, D. (Avoniel), 1882 v E; 1883 v E, W (3)

Rea, B. (Glentoran), 1901 v E (1)

Redmond, J. (Cliftonville), 1884 v W (1)

Reid, G. H. (Cardiff C), 1923 v S (1)

Reid, J. (Ulster), 1883 v E; 1884 v W; 1887 v S; 1889 v W; 1890 v S, W (6)

Reid, S. E. (Derby Co), 1934 v E, W; 1936 v E (3)

Reid, W. (Hearts), 1931 v E (1)

Reilly, J. (Portsmouth), 1900 v E; 1902 v E (2)

Renneville, W. T. (Leyton), 1910 v S, E, W; (with Aston Villa), 1911 v W (4)

Reynolds, J. (Distillery), 1890 v E, W; (with Ulster), 1891 v E, S, W (5)

Reynolds, R. (Bohemians), 1905 v W (1)

Rice, P. J. (Arsenal), 1969 v Is; 1970 v USSR; 1971 v E, S, W; 1972 v USSR, Sp, E, S, W; 1973 v Bul, Cy, E, S, W; 1974 v Bul, P, S, E, W; 1975 v N, Y, E, S, W; 1976 v Se, N, Y, Is, S, E, W; 1977 v Ho, Bel, WG, E, S, Ic; 1978 v Ic, Ho, Bel; 1979 v Ei, D, E (2), S, W, D; 1980 v E (49)

Roberts, F. C. (Glentoran), 1931 v S (1)

Robinson, P. (Distillery), 1920 v S; (with Blackburn R), 1921 v W (2)

Rogan, A. (Celtic), 1988 v Y (sub), Gr, Pol (sub); 1989 v Ei (sub), H, Sp, Sp, Ma **(sub)**, Ch (9)

Rollo, D. (Linfield), 1912 v W; 1913 v W; 1914 v W, E; (with Blackburn R), 1920 v S, W; 1921 v E, S, W; 1922 v E; 1923 v E; 1924 v S, W; 1925 v W; 1926 v E; 1927 v E (16)

Rosbotham, A. (Cliftonville), 1887 v E, S, W; 1888 v E, S, W; 1889 v E (7)

Ross, W. E. (Newcastle U), 1969 v Is (1)

Rowley, R. W. M. (Southampton), 1929 v S, W; 1930 v W, E; (with Tottenham H), 1931 v W; 1932 v S (6)

Russell, A. (Linfield), 1947 v E (1)

Russell, S. R. (Bradford C), 1930 v E, S; (with Derry C), 1932 v E (3)

Ryan, R. A. (WBA), 1950 v W (1)

Sanchez, L. P. (Wimbledon), 1987 v T (sub); 1989 v Sp, Ma (3)

Scott, E. (Liverpool), 1920 v S; 1921 v E, S, W; 1922 v E; 1925 v W; 1926 v E, S, W; 1927 v E, S, W; 1928 v E, S, W; 1929 v E, S, W; 1930 v E; 1931 v E; 1932 v W; 1933 v E, S, W; 1934 v E, S, W; (with Belfast C), 1935 v S; 1936 v E, S, W (31)

Scott, J. (Grimsby), 1958 v Cz, F (2)

Scott, J. E. (Cliftonville), 1901 v S (1)

Scott, L. J. (Dublin University), 1895 v S, W (2)

Scott, P. W. (Everton), 1975 v W; 1976 v Y; (with York C), Is, S, E (sub), W; 1978 v S, E, W; (with Aldershot), 1979 v S (sub) (10)

Scott, T. (Cliftonville), 1894 v E, S; 1895 v S, W; 1896 v S, E, W; 1897 v E, W; 1898 v E, S, W; 1900 v W (13)

Scott, W. (Linfield), 1903 v E, S, W; 1904 v E, S, W; (with Everton), 1905 v E, S; 1907 v E, S; 1908 v E, S, W; 1909 v E, S, W; 1910 v E, S; 1911 v E, S, W; 1912 v E; (with Leeds City), 1913 v E, S, W (25)

Scraggs, M. J. (Glentoran), 1921 v W; 1922 v E (2)

Seymour, H. C. (Bohemians), 1914 v W (1)

Seymour, J. (Cliftonville), 1907 v W; 1909 v W (2)

Shanks, T. (Woolwich Arsenal), 1903 v S; 1904 v W; (with Brentford), 1905 v E (3)
Sharkey, P. (Ipswich T), 1976 v S (1)
Sheehan, Dr G. (Bohemians), 1899 v S; 1900 v E, W (3)
Sheridan, J. (Everton), 1903 v W, E, S; 1904 v E, S; (with Stoke C), 1905 v E (6)
Sherrard, J. (Limavady), 1885 v S; 1887 v W; 1888 v W (3)
Sherrard, W. (Cliftonville), 1895 v E, W, S (3)
Sherry, J. J. (Bohemians), 1906 v E; 1907 v W (2)
Shields, J. (Southampton), 1957 v S (1)
Silo, M. (Belfast YMCA), 1888 v E (1)
Simpson, W. J. (Glasgow R), 1951 v W, F; 1954 v E, S; 1955 v E; 1957 v I, P; 1958 v S, E, W, I; 1959 v S (12)
Sinclair, J. (Knock), 1882 v E, W (2)
Slemin, J. C. (Bohemians), 1909 v W (1)
Sloan, A. S. (London Caledonians), 1925 v W (1)
Sloan, D. (Oxford U), 1969 v Is; 1971 v Sp (2)
Sloan, H. A. de B. (Bohemians), 1903 v E; 1904 v S; 1905 v E; 1906 v W; 1907 v E, W; 1908 v W; 1909 v S (8)
Sloan, J. W. (Arsenal), 1947 v W (1)
Sloan, T. (Cardiff C), 1926 v S, W, E; 1927 v W, S; 1928 v E, W; 1929 v E; (with Linfield), 1930 v W, S; 1931 v S (11)
Sloan, T. (Manchester U), 1979 v S, W (sub), D (sub) (3)
Small, J. (Clarence), 1887 v E (1)
Small, J. M. (Cliftonville), 1893 v E, S, W (3)
Smith, E. E. (Cardiff C), 1921 v S; 1923 v W, E; 1924 v E (4)
Smith, J. (Distillery), 1901 v S, W (2)
Smyth, R. H. (Dublin University), 1886 v W (1)
Smyth, S. (Wolverhampton W), 1948 v E, S, W; 1949 v S, W; 1950 v E, S, W; (with Stoke C), 1952 v E (9)
Smyth, W. (Distillery), 1949 v E, S; 1954 v S, E (4)
Snape, A. (Airdrie), 1920 v E (1)
Spence, D. W. (Bury), 1975 v Y, E, S, W; 1976 v Se, Is, E, W, S (sub); (with Blackpool), 1977 v Ho (sub), WG (sub), E (sub), S (sub), W (sub), Ic (sub); 1979 v Ei, D (sub), E (sub), Bul (sub), E (sub), S, W, D; 1980 v Ei; (with Southend U), Is (sub), Aus (sub); 1981 v S (sub), Se (sub); 1982 v F (sub) (29)
Spencer, S. (Distillery), 1890 v E, S; 1892 v E, S, W; 1893 v E (6)
Spiller, E. A. (Cliftonville), 1883 v E, W; 1884 v E, W, S (5)
Stanfield, O. M. (Distillery), 1887 v E, S, W; 1888 v E, S, W; 1889 v E, S, W; 1890 v E, S; 1891 v E, S, W; 1892 v E, S, W; 1893 v E, W; 1894 v E, S, W; 1895 v E, S; 1896 v E, S, W; 1897 v E, S, W (30)
Steele, A. (Charlton Ath), 1926 v W, S; (with Fulham), 1929 v W, S (4)
Stevenson, A. E. (Rangers), 1934 v E, S, W; (with Everton), 1935 v E, S; 1936 v S, W; 1937 v E, W; 1938 v E, W; 1939 v E, S, W; 1947 v S, W; 1948 v S (17)
Stewart, A. (Glentoran), 1967 v W; 1968 v S, E; (with Derby Co), 1968 v W; 1969 v Is, T (1+1 sub) (7)
Stewart, D. C. (Hull C), 1978 v Bel (1)
Stewart, I. (QPR), 1982 v F (sub); 1983 v A, WG, Alb, T, Alb, S, E, W; 1984 v A, T, WG, S, E, W, Fi; 1985 v R, Fi, Is, E, Sp, T; (with Newcastle U), 1986 v R, E, D, Mor, Alg (sub), Sp (sub), Br; 1987 v E, Is (sub) (31)
Stewart, R. H. (St Columb's Court), 1890 v E, S, W; (with Cliftonville), 1892 v E, S, W; 1893 v E, W; 1894 v E, S, W (11)
Stewart, T. C. (Linfield), 1961 v W (1)
Swan, S. (Linfield), 1899 v S (1)

Taggart, J. (Walsall), 1899 v W (1)
Thompson, F. W. (Cliftonville), 1910 v E, S, W; (with Bradford C), 1911 v E; (with Linfield), v W; 1912 v E, W; 1913 v E, S, W; (with Clyde), 1914 v E, S (12)
Thompson, J. (Distillery), 1897 v S (1)
Thompson, J. (Belfast Ath), 1889 v S (1)
Thunder, P. J. (Bohemians), 1911 v W (1)

Todd, S. J. (Burnley), 1966 v M (sub); 1967 v E; 1968 v W; 1969 v E, S, W; 1970 v S, USSR; (with Sheffield W), 1971 v Cy (2), Sp (sub) (11)
Toner, J. (Arsenal), 1922 v W; 1923 v W; 1924 v W, E; 1925 v E, S; (with St Johnstone), 1927 v E, S (8)
Torrans, R. (Linfield), 1893 v S (1)
Torrans, S. (Linfield), 1889 v S; 1890 v S, W; 1891 v S, W; 1892 v E, S, W; 1893 v E, S; 1894 v E, S, W; 1895 v E; 1896 v E, S, W; 1897 v E, S, W; 1898 v E, S; 1899 v E, W; 1901 v S, W (26)
Trainor, D. (Crusaders), 1967 v W (1)
Tully, C. P. (Glasgow C), 1949 v E; 1950 v E; 1952 v S; 1953 v E, S, W, F; 1954 v S; 1956 v E; 1959 v Sp (10)
Turner, E. (Cliftonville), 1896 v E, W (2)
Turner, W. (Cliftonville), 1886 v E; 1886 v S; 1888 v S (3)
Twoomey, J. F. (Leeds U), 1938 v W; 1939 v E (2)

Uprichard, W. N. M. C. (Swindon T), 1952 v E, S, W; 1953 v E, S; (with Portsmouth), 1953 v W, F; 1955 v E, S, W; 1956 v E, S, W; 1958 v S, I, Cz; 1959 v S, Sp (18)

Vernon, J. (Belfast C), 1947 v E, S; (with WBA), 1947 v W; 1948 v E, S, W; 1949 v E, S, W; 1950 v E, S; 1951 v E, S, W, F; 1952 v S, E (17)

Waddell, T. M. R. (Cliftonville), 1906 v S (1)
Walker, J. (Doncaster R), 1955 v W (1)
Walker, T. (Bury), 1911 v S (1)
Walsh, D. J. (WBA), 1947 v S, W; 1948 v E, S, W; 1949 v E, S, W; 1950 v W (9)
Walsh, W. (Manchester C), 1948 v E, S, W; 1949 v E, S (5)
Waring, R. (Distillery), 1899 v E (1)
Warren, P. (Shelbourne), 1913 v E, S (2)
Watson, J. (Ulster), 1883 v E, W; 1886 v E, S, W; 1887 v S, W; 1889 v E, W (9)
Watson, P. (Distillery), 1971 v Cy (sub) (1)
Watson, T. (Cardiff C), 1926 v S (1)
Wattle, J. (Distillery), 1899 v E (1)
Webb, C. G. (Brighton), 1909 v S, W; 1911 v S (3)
Weir, E. (Clyde), 1939 v W (1)
Welsh, E. (Carlisle U), 1966 v W, WG, M; 1967 v W (4)
Whiteside, N. (Manchester U), 1982 v Y, Hon, Sp, A, F; 1983 v WG, Alb, T; 1984 v A, T, WG, S, E, W, Fi; 1985 v R, Fi, Is, E, Sp, T; 1986 v R, E, F, D, Mor, Alg, Sp, Br; 1987 v E (2), Is, Y; 1988 v T, Pol, F (36)
Whiteside, T. (Distillery), 1891 v E (1)
Whitfield, E. R. (Dublin University), 1886 v W (1)
Williams, J. R. (Ulster), 1886 v E, S (2)
Williamson, J. (Cliftonville), 1890 v E; 1892 v S; 1893 v S (3)
Willigham, T. (Burnley), 1933 v W; 1934 v S (2)
Willis, G. (Linfield), 1906 v S, W; 1907 v S; 1912 v S (4)
Wilson, D. J. (Brighton & HA), 1987 v T, Is, E (sub); (with Luton T), 1988 v Y, T, Gr, Pol, F, Ma; 1989 v Ei, H, Sp, Ma, Ch (14)
Wilson, H. (Linfield), 1925 v W (1)
Wilson, K. J. (Ipswich T), 1987 v Is, E, Y; (with Chelsea), 1988 v Y, T, Gr (sub), Pol (sub), F (sub); 1989 v H (sub), Sp, Sp, Ma, Ch (13)
Wilson, M. (Distillery), 1884 v E, S, W (3)
Wilson, R. (Cliftonville), 1888 v S (1)
Wilson, S. J. (Glenavon), 1962 v S; 1964 v S; (with Falkirk), 1964 v E, W, U, Sp; 1965 v E, Sw; (with Dundee), 1966 v W, WG; 1967 v S; 1968 v E (12)
Wilton, J. M. (St Columb's Court), 1888 v E, W; 1889 v S, E; (with Cliftonville), 1890 v E; (with St Columb's Court), 1892 v W; 1893 v S (7)
Worthington, N. (Sheffield W), 1984 v W, Fi (sub); 1985 v Is, Sp (sub); 1986 v T, R (sub), E (sub), D, Alg, Sp; 1987 v E (2), T, Is, Y; 1988 v Y, T, Gr, Pol, F, Ma; 1989 v Ei, H, Sp, Ma (25)

Wright, J. (Cliftonville), 1906 v E, S, W; 1907 v E, S, W (6)
Wright, T. J. (Newcastle U), 1989 v Ma, Ch (2)
Young, S. (Linfield), 1907 v E, S; 1908 v E, S; (with Airdrie), 1909 v E; 1912 v S; (with Linfield), 1914 v E, S, W (9)

SCOTLAND

Adams, J. (Hearts), 1889 v Ni; 1892 v W; 1893 v Ni (3)
Agnew, W. B. (Kilmarnock), 1907 v Ni; 1908 v W, Ni (3)
Aird, J. (Burnley), 1954 v N (2), A, U (4)
Aitken, A. (Newcastle U), 1901 v E; 1902 v E; 1903 v E, W; 1904 v E; 1905 v E, W; 1906 v E; (with Middlesbrough), 1907 v E, W; 1908 v E; (with Leicester Fosse), 1910 v E; 1911 v E, Ni (14)
Aitken, G. G. (East Fife), 1949 v E, F; 1950 v W, Ni, Sw; (with Sunderland), 1953 v W, Ni; 1954 v E (8)
Aitken, R. (Dumbarton), 1886 v E; 1888 v Ni (2)
Aitken, R. (Celtic), 1980 v Pe (sub), Bel, W (sub), E, Pol; 1983 v Bel, Ca (1+1 sub); 1984 v Bel (sub), Ni, W (sub); 1985 v E, Ic; 1986 v W, EG, Aus (2), Is, R, E, D, WG, U; 1987 v Bul, Ei (2), L, Bel, E, Br; 1988 v H, Bel, Bul, L, S, Ar, Ma, Sp, Co, E; 1989 v N, Y, I, Cy, F, Cy, E, Ch (47)
Aitkenhead, W. A. C. (Blackburn R), 1912 v Ni (1)
Albiston, A. (Manchester U), 1982 v Ni; 1984 v U, Bel, EG, W, E; 1985 v Y, Ic, Sp (2), W; 1986 v EG, Ho, U (14)
Alexander, D. (East Stirlingshire), 1894 v W, Ni (2)
Allan, D. S. (Queen's Park), 1885 v E, W; 1886 v W (3)
Allan, G. (Liverpool), 1897 v E (1)
Allan, H. (Hearts), 1902 v W (1)
Allan, J. (Queen's Park), 1887 v E, W (2)
Allan, T. (Dundee), 1974 v WG, N (2)
Ancell, R. F. D. (Newcastle U), 1937 v W, Ni (2)
Anderson, A. (Hearts), 1933 v E; 1934 v A, E, W, Ni; 1935 v E, W, Ni; 1936 v E, W, Ni; 1937 v G, E, W, Ni, A; 1938 v E, W, Ni, Cz, Ho; 1939 v W, H (23)
Anderson, F. (Clydesdale), 1874 v E (1)
Anderson, G. (Kilmarnock), 1901 v Ni (1)
Anderson, H. A. (Raith R), 1914 v W (1)
Anderson, J. (Leicester C), 1954 v Fi (1)
Anderson, K. (Queen's Park), 1896 v Ni; 1898 v E, Ni (3)
Anderson, W. (Queen's Park), 1882 v E; 1883 v E, W; 1884 v E; 1885 v E, W (6)
Andrews, P. (Eastern), 1875 v E (1)
Archibald, A. (Rangers), 1921 v W; 1922 v W, E; 1923 v Ni; 1924 v E, W; 1931 v E; 1932 v E (8)
Archibald, S. (Aberdeen), 1980 v P (sub); (with Tottenham H), Ni, Pol, H; 1981 v Se (sub), Is, Ni, Is, Ni, E; 1982 v Ni, P, Sp (sub), Ho, Nz (sub), Br, USSR; 1983 v EG, Sw (sub), Bel; 1984 v EG, E, F; (with Barcelona), 1985 v Sp, E, Ic (sub); 1986 v WG (27)
Armstrong, M. W. (Aberdeen), 1936 v W, Ni; 1937 v G (3)
Arnott, W. (Queen's Park), 1883 v W; 1884 v E, Ni; 1885 v E, W; 1886 v E; 1887 v E, W; 1888 v E; 1889 v E; 1890 v E; 1891 v E; 1892 v E; 1893 v E (14)
Auld, J. R. (Third Lanark), 1887 v E, W; 1889 v W (3)
Auld, R. (Celtic), 1959 v H, P; 1960 v W (3)

Baird, A. (Queen's Park), 1892 v Ni; 1894 v W (2)
Baird, D. (Hearts), 1890 v Ni; 1891 v E; 1892 v W (3)
Baird, H. (Airdrie), 1956 v A (1)
Baird, J. C. (Vale of Leven), 1876 v E; 1878 v W; 1880 v E (3)
Baird, S. (Rangers), 1957 v Y, Sp (2), Sw, WG; 1958 v F, Ni (7)
Baird, W. U. (St Bernard), 1897 v Ni (1)
Bannon, E. (Dundee U), 1980 v Bel; 1983 v Ni, W, E, Ca; 1984 v EG; 1986 v Is, R, E, D (sub), WG (11)
Barbour, A. (Renton), 1885 v Ni (1)
Barker, J. B. (Rangers), 1893 v W; 1894 v W (2)
Barrett, F. (Dundee), 1894 v Ni; 1895 v W (2)
Battles, B. (Celtic), 1901 v E, W, Ni (3)
Battles, B. jun. (Hearts), 1931 v W (1)
Bauld, W. (Hearts), 1950 v E, Sw, P (3)
Baxter, J. C. (Rangers), 1961 v Ni, Ei (2), Cz; 1962 v Ni, W, E, Cz (2), U; 1963 v W, Ni, E, A, N, Ei, Sp; 1964 v W, E, N, WG; 1965 v W, Ni, Fi; (with Sunderland), 1966 v P, Br, Ni, W, E, I; 1967 v W, E, USSR; 1968 v W (34)
Baxter, R. D. (Middlesbrough), 1939 v E, W, H (3)
Beattie, A. (Preston NE), 1937 v E, A, Cz; 1938 v E; 1939 v W, Ni, H (7)
Beattie, R. (Preston NE), 1939 v W (1)
Begbie, I. (Hearts), 1890 v Ni; 1891 v E; 1892 v W; 1894 v E (4)
Bell, A. (Manchester U), 1912 v Ni (1)
Bell, J. (Dumbarton), 1890 v Ni; 1892 v E; (with Everton), 1896 v E; 1897 v E; 1898 v E; (with Celtic), 1899 v E, W, Ni; 1900 v E, W (10)
Bell, M. (Hearts), 1901 v W (1)
Bell, W. J. (Leeds U), 1966 v P, Br (2)
Bennett, A. (Celtic), 1904 v W; 1907 v Ni; 1908 v W; (with Rangers), 1909 v W, Ni, E; 1910 v E, W; 1911 v E, W; 1913 v Ni (11)
Bennie, R. (Airdrieonians), 1925 v W, Ni; 1926 v Ni (3)
Berry, D. (Queen's Park), 1894 v W; 1899 v W, Ni (3)
Berry, W. H. (Queen's Park), 1888 v E; 1889 v E; 1890 v E; 1891 v E (4)
Bett, J. (Rangers), 1982 v Ho; 1983 v Bel; (with Lokeren), 1984 v Bel, W, E, F; 1985 v Y, Ic, Sp (2), W, E, Ic; (with Aberdeen), 1986 v W, Is, Ho; 1987 v Bel; 1988 v H (sub); 1989 v Y (19)
Beveridge, W. W. (Glasgow University), 1879 v E, W; 1880 v W (3)
Black, A. (Hearts), 1938 v Cz, Ho; 1939 v H (3)
Black, D. (Hurlford), 1889 v Ni (1)
Black, E. (Metz), 1988 v H (sub), L (sub) (2)
Black, I. H. (Southampton), 1948 v E (1)
Blackburn, J. E. (Royal Engineers), 1873 v E (1)
Blacklaw, A. S. (Burnley), 1963 v N, Sp; 1966 v I (3)
Blackley, J. (Hibernian), 1974 v Cz, E, Bel, Z; 1976 v Sw; 1977 v W, Se (7)
Blair, D. (Clyde), 1929 v W, Ni; 1931 v E, A, I; 1932 v W, Ni; (with Aston Villa), 1933 v W (8)
Blair, J. (Sheffield W), 1920 v E, Ni; (with Cardiff C), 1921 v E; 1922 v E; 1923 v E, W, Ni; 1924 v W (8)
Blair, J. (Motherwell), 1934 v W (1)
Blair, J. A. (Blackpool), 1947 v W (1)
Blair, W. (Third Lanark), 1896 v W (1)
Blessington J. (Celtic), 1894 v E, Ni; 1896 v E, Ni (4)
Blyth, J. A. (Coventry C), 1978 v Bul, W (2)
Bone, J. (Norwich C), 1972 v Y (sub); 1973 v D (2)
Bowie, J. (Rangers), 1920 v E, Ni (2)
Bowie, W. (Linthouse), 1891 v Ni (1)
Bowman, G. A. (Montrose), 1892 v Ni (1)
Boyd, J. M. (Newcastle U), 1934 v Ni (1)
Boyd, R. (Mossend Swifts), 1889 v Ni; 1891 v W (2)
Boyd, W. G. (Clyde), 1931 v I, Sw (2)
Brackenbridge, T. (Hearts), 1888 v Ni (1)
Bradshaw, T. (Bury), 1928 v E (1)
Brand, R. (Rangers), 1961 v Ni, Cz, Ei (2); 1962 v Ni, W, Cz, U (8)
Branden, T. (Blackburn R), 1896 v E (1)
Brazil, A. (Ipswich T), 1980 v Pol (sub), H; 1982 v Sp, Ho (sub), Ni, W, E, Nz, USSR (sub); 1983 v EG, Sw, W, E (sub) (13)
Bremner, D. (Hibernian), 1976 v Sw (sub) (1)

Bremner, W. J. (Leeds U), 1965 v Sp; 1966 v E, Pol, P, Br, I (2); 1967 v W, Ni, E; 1968 v W, E; 1969 v W, E, Ni, D, A, WG, Cy (2); 1970 v Ei, WG, A; 1971 v W, E; 1972 v P, Bel, Ho, Ni, W, E, Y, Cz, Br; 1973 v D (2), E (2), Ni (sub), Sw, Br; 1974 v Cz, WG, Ni, W, E, Bel, N, Z, Br, Y; 1975 v Sp (2); 1976 v D (54)
Brennan, F. (Newcastle U), 1947 v W, Ni; 1953 v W, Ni, E; 1954 v Ni, E (7)
Breslin, B. (Hibernian), 1897 v W (1)
Brewster, G. (Everton), 1921 v E (1)
Brogan, J. (Celtic), 1971 v W, Ni, P, E (4)
Brown, A. (Middlesbrough), 1904 v E (1)
Brown, A. (St Mirren), 1890 v W; 1891 v W (2)
Brown, A. D. (East Fife), 1950 v Sw, P, F; (with Blackpool), 1952 v USA, D, Se; 1953 v W; 1954 v W, E, N (2), Fi, A, U (14)
Brown, G. C. P. (Rangers), 1931 v W; 1932 v E, W, Ni; 1933 v E; 1935 v A, E, W; 1936 v E, W; 1937 v G, E, W, Ni, Cz; 1938 v E, W, Cz, Ho (19)
Brown, H. (Partick T), 1947 v W, Bel, L (3)
Brown, J. (Cambuslang), 1890 v W (1)
Brown, J. B. (Clyde), 1939 v W (1)
Brown, J. G. (Sheffield U), 1975 v R (1)
Brown, R. (Dumbarton), 1884 v W, Ni (2)
Brown, R. (Rangers), 1947 v Ni; 1949 v Ni; 1952 v E (3)
Brown, R. jun. (Dumbarton), 1885 v W (1)
Brown, W. D. F. (Dundee), 1958 v F; 1959 v E, W, Ni; (with Tottenham H), 1960 v W, Ni, Pol, A, H, T; 1962 v Ni, W, E, Cz; 1963 v W, Ni, E, A; 1964 v Ni, W, N; 1965 v E, Fi, Pol, Sp; 1966 v Ni, Pol, I (28)
Browning, J. (Celtic), 1914 v W (1)
Brownlie, J. (Hibernian), 1971 v USSR; 1972 v Pe, Ni, E; 1973 v D (2); 1976 v R (7)
Brownlie, J. (Third Lanark), 1909 v E, Ni; 1910 v E, W, Ni; 1911 v W, Ni; 1912 v W, Ni, E; 1913 v W, Ni, E; 1914 v W, Ni, E (16)
Bruce, D. (Vale of Leven), 1890 v W (1)
Bruce, R. F. (Middlesbrough), 1934 v A (1)
Buchan, M. M. (Aberdeen), 1972 v P (sub), Bel; (with Manchester U), W, Y, Cz, Br; 1973 v D (2), E; 1974 v WG, Ni, W, N, Br, Y; 1975 v EG, Sp, P; 1976 v D, R; 1977 v Fi, Cz, Ch, Arg, Br; 1978 v EG, W (sub), Ni, Pe, Ir, Ho; 1979 v A, N, P (34)
Buchanan, J. (Cambuslang), 1889 v Ni (1)
Buchanan, J. (Rangers), 1929 v E; 1930 v E (2)
Buchanan, P. S. (Chelsea), 1938 v Cz (1)
Buchanan, R. (Abercorn), 1891 v W (1)
Buckley, P. (Aberdeen), 1954 v N; 1955 v W, Ni (3)
Buick, A. (Hearts), 1902 v W, Ni (2)
Burley, G. (Ipswich T), 1979 v W, Ni, E, Arg, N; 1980 v P, Ni, E (sub), Pol; 1982 v W (sub), E (11)
Burns, F. (Manchester U), 1970 v A (1)
Burns, K. (Birmingham C), 1974 v WG; 1975 v EG (sub), Sp (2); 1977 v Cz (sub), W, Se, W (sub); (with Nottingham F), 1978 v Ni (sub), W, E, Pe, Ir; 1979 v N; 1980 v Pe, A, Bel; 1981 v Is, Ni, W (20)
Burns, T. (Celtic), 1981 v Ni; 1982 v Ho (sub), W; 1983 v Bel (sub), Ni, Ca (1 + 1 sub); 1988 v E (sub) (8)
Busby, M. W. (Manchester C), 1934 v W (1)

Cairns, T. (Rangers), 1920 v W; 1922 v E; 1923 v E, W; 1924 v Ni; 1925 v W, E, Ni (8)
Calderhead, D. (Queen of the South), 1889 v Ni (1)
Calderwood, R. (Cartvale), 1885 v Ni, E, W (3)
Caldow, E. (Rangers), 1957 v Sp (2), Sw, WG, E; 1958 v Ni, W, Sw, Par, H, Pol, Y, F; 1959 v E, W, Ni, WG, Ho, P; 1960 v E, W, Ni, A, H, T; 1961 v E, W, Ni, Ei (2), Cz; 1962 v Ni, W, E, Cz (2), U; 1963 v W, Ni, E (40)
Callaghan, P. (Hibernian), 1900 v Ni (1)
Callaghan, W. (Dunfermline Ath), 1970 v Ei (sub), W (2)
Cameron, J. (St Mirren), 1904 v Ni; (with Chelsea), 1909 v E (2)
Cameron, J. (Queen's Park), 1896 v Ni (1)
Cameron, J. (Rangers), 1886 v Ni (1)
Campbell, C. (Queen's Park), 1874 v E; 1876 v W; 1877 v E, W; 1878 v E; 1879 v E; 1880 v E; 1881 v E; 1882 v E, W; 1884 v E; 1885 v E; 1886 v E (13)
Campbell, H. (Renton), 1889 v W (1)
Campbell, Jas. (Sheffield W), 1913 v W (1)
Campbell, J. (South Western), 1880 v W (1)
Campbell, J. (Kilmarnock), 1891 v Ni; 1892 v W (2)
Campbell, John (Celtic), 1893 v E, Ni; 1898 v E, Ni; 1900 v E, Ni; 1901 v E, W, Ni; 1902 v W, Ni; 1903 v W (12)
Campbell, John (Rangers), 1899 v E, W, Ni; 1901 v Ni (4)
Campbell, K. (Liverpool), 1920 v E, W, Ni; (with Partick T), 1921 v W, Ni; 1922 v W, Ni, E (8)
Campbell, P. (Rangers), 1878 v W; 1879 v W (2)
Campbell, P. (Morton), 1898 v W (1)
Campbell, R. (Falkirk), 1947 v Bel, L; (with Chelsea), 1950 v Sw, P, F (5)
Campbell, W. (Morton), 1947 v Ni; 1948 v E, Bel, Sw, F (5)
Carabine, J. (Third Lanark), 1938 v Ho; 1939 v E, Ni (3)
Carr, W. M. (Coventry C), 1970 v Ni, W, E; 1971 v D; 1972 v Pe; 1973 v D (sub) (6)
Cassidy, J. (Celtic), 1921 v W, Ni; 1923 v Ni; 1924 v W (4)
Chalmers, S. (Celtic), 1965 v W, Fi; 1966 v P (sub), Br; 1967 v Ni (5)
Chalmers, W. (Rangers), 1885 v Ni (1)
Chalmers, W. S. (Queen's Park), 1929 v Ni (1)
Chambers, T. (Hearts), 1894 v W (1)
Chaplin, G. D. (Dundee), 1908 v W (1)
Cheyne, A. G. (Aberdeen), 1929 v E, N, G, Ho; 1930 v F (5)
Christie, A. J. (Queen's Park), 1898 v W; 1899 v E, Ni (3)
Christie, R. M. (Queen's Park), 1884 v E (1)
Clark, J. (Celtic), 1966 v Br; 1967 v W, Ni, USSR (4)
Clark, R. B. (Aberdeen), 1968 v W, Ho; 1970 v Ni; 1971 v W, Ni, E, D, P, USSR; 1972 v Bel, Ni, W, E, Cz, Br; 1973 v D, E (17)
Clarke, S. (Chelsea), 1988 v H, Bel, Bul, S.Ar, Ma (5)
Cleland, J. (Royal Albert), 1891 v Ni (1)
Clements, R. (Leith Ath), 1891 v Ni (1)
Clunas, W. L. (Sunderland), 1924 v E; 1926 v W (2)
Collier, W. (Raith R), 1922 v W (1)
Collins, J. (Hibernian), 1988 v S.Ar (1)
Collins, R. Y. (Celtic), 1951 v W, Ni, A; 1955 v Y, A, H; 1956 v Ni, W; 1957 v E, W, Sp (2), Sw, WG; 1958 v Ni, W, Sw, H, Pol, Y, F, Par; (with Everton), 1959 v E, W, Ni, WG, Ho, P; (with Leeds U), 1965 v E, Pol, Sp (31)
Collins, T. (Hearts), 1909 v W (1)
Colman, D. (Aberdeen), 1911 v E, W, Ni; 1913 v Ni (4)
Colquhoun, E. P. (Sheffield U), 1972 v P, Ho, Pe, Y, Cz, Br; 1973 v D (2), E (9)
Colquhoun, J. (Hearts), 1988 v S.Ar (sub) (1)
Combe, J. R. (Hibernian), 1948 v E, Bel, Sw (3)
Conn, A. (Hearts), 1956 v A (1)
Conn, A. (Tottenham H), 1975 v Ni (sub), E (2)
Connachan, E. D. (Dunfermline Ath), 1962 v Cz, U (2)
Connelly, G. (Celtic), 1974 v Cz, WG (2)
Connolly, J. (Everton), 1973 v Sw (1)
Connor, J. (Airdrieonians), 1886 v Ni (1)
Connor, J. (Sunderland), 1930 v F; 1932 v Ni; 1934 v E; 1935 v Ni (4)
Connor, R. (Dundee), 1986 v Ho; (with Aberdeen), 1988 v S.Ar (sub); 1989 v E (3)
Cook, W. L. (Bolton W), 1934 v E; 1935 v W, Ni (3)
Cooke, C. (Dundee), 1966 v W, I; (with Chelsea), P, Br; 1968 v E, Ho; 1969 v W, Ni, A, WG (sub), Cy (2); 1970 v A; 1971 v Bel; 1975 v Sp, P (16)
Cooper, D. (Rangers), 1980 v Pe, A (sub); 1984 v W, E; 1985 v Y, Ic, Sp (2), W; 1986 v W (sub), EG, Aus (2), Ho, WG (sub), U (sub); 1987 v Bul, L, Ei, Br (20)
Cormack, P. B. (Hibernian), 1966 v Br; 1969 v D (sub); 1970 v Ei, WG; (with Nottingham F), 1971 v D (sub),

W, P, E; 1972 v Ho (sub) (9)
Cowan, J. (Aston Villa), 1896 v E; 1897 v E; 1898 v E (3)
Cowan, J. (Morton), 1948 v Bel, Sw; F; 1949 v E, W, F; 1950 v E, W, Ni, Sw, P, F; 1951 v E, W, Ni, A (2), D, F, Bel; 1952 v Ni, W, USA, D, Se (25)
Cowan, W, D. (Newcastle U), 1924 v E (1)
Cowie, D. (Dundee), 1953 v E, Se; 1954 v Ni, W, Fi, N, A, U; 1955 v W, Ni, A, H; 1956 v W, A; 1957 v Ni, W; 1958 v H, Pol, Y, Par (20)
Cox, C. J. (Hearts), 1948 v F (1)
Cox, S. (Rangers), 1948 v F; 1949 v E, F; 1950 v E, F, W, Ni, Sw, P; 1951 v E, D, F, Bel, A; 1952 v Ni, W, USA, D, Se; 1953 v W, Ni, E; 1954 v W, Ni, E (25)
Craig, A. (Motherwell), 1929 v N, Ho; 1932 v E (3)
Craig, J. (Celtic), 1977 v Se (sub) (1)
Craig, J. P. (Celtic), 1968 v W (1)
Craig, T. (Rangers), 1927 v Ni; 1928 v Ni; 1929 v N, G, Ho; 1930 v Ni, E, W (8)
Craig, T. B. (Newcastle U), 1976 v Sw (1)
Crapnell, J. (Airdrieonians), 1929 v E, N, G; 1930 v F; 1931 v Ni, Sw; 1932 v E, F; 1933 v Ni (9)
Crawford, D. (St Mirren), 1894 v W, Ni; 1900 v W (3)
Crawford, J. (Queen's Park), 1932 v F, Ni; 1933 v E, W, Ni (5)
Crerand, P. T. (Celtic), 1961 v Ei (2), Cz; 1962 v Ni, W, E, Cz (2), U; 1963 v W, Ni; (with Manchester U), 1964 v Ni; 1965 v E, Pol, Fi; 1966 v Pol (16)
Cringan, W. (Celtic), 1920 v W; 1922 v E, Ni; 1923 v W, E (5)
Crosbie, J. A. (Ayr U), 1920 v W; (with Birmingham), 1922 v E (2)
Croal, J. A. (Falkirk), 1913 v Ni; 1914 v E, W (3)
Cropley, A. J. (Hibernian), 1972 v P, Bel (2)
Cross, J. H. (Third Lanark), 1903 v Ni (1)
Cruickshank, J. (Hearts), 1964 v WG; 1970 v W, E; 1971 v D, Bel; 1976 v R (6)
Crum, J. (Celtic), 1936 v E; 1939 v Ni (2)
Cullen, M. J. (Luton T), 1956 v A (1)
Cumming, D. S. (Middlesbrough), 1938 v E (1)
Cumming, J. (Hearts), 1955 v E, H, P, Y; 1960 v E, Pol, A, H, T (9)
Cummings, G. (Partick T), 1935 v E; 1936 v W, Ni; (with Aston Villa), E; 1937 v G; 1938 v W, Ni, Cz; 1939 v E (9)
Cunningham, A. N. (Rangers), 1920 v Ni; 1921 v W, E; 1922 v Ni; 1923 v E, W; 1924 v E, Ni; 1926 v E, Ni; 1927 v E, W (12)
Cunningham, W. C. (Preston NE), 1954 v N (2), U, Fi, A; 1955 v W, E, H (8)
Curran, H. P. (Wolverhampton W), 1970 v A; 1971 v Ni, E, D, USSR (sub) (5)

Dalglish, K. (Celtic), 1972 v Bel (sub), Ho; 1973 v D (1+1 sub), E (2), W, Ni, Sw, Br; 1974 v Cz (2), WG (2), Ni, W, E, Bel, N (sub), Z, Br, Y; 1975 v EG, Sp (sub+1), Se, P, W, Ni, E, R; 1976 v D (2), R, Sw, Ni, E; 1977 v Fi, Cz, W (2), Se, Ni, E, Ch, Arg, Br; (with Liverpool), 1978 v EG, Cz, W, Bul, Ni (sub), W, E, Pe, Ir, Ho; 1979 v A, N, P, W, Ni, E, Arg, N; 1980 v Pe, A, Bel (2), P, Ni, W, E, Pol, H; 1981 v Se, P, Is; 1982 v Se, Ni, P (sub), Sp, Ho, Ni, W, E, Nz, Br (sub); 1983 v Bel, Sw; 1984 v U, Bel, EG; 1985 v Y, Ic, Sp, W; 1986 v EG, Aus, R; 1987 v Bul (sub), L (102)
Davidson, D. (Queen's Park), 1878 v W; 1879 v W; 1880 v W; 1881 v E, W (5)
Davidson, J. A. (Partick T), 1954 v N (2), A, U; 1955 v W, Ni, E, H (8)
Davidson, S. (Middlesbrough), 1921 v E (1)
Dawson, A. (Rangers), 1980 v Pol (sub), H; 1983 v Ni, Ca (2) (5)
Dawson, J. (Rangers), 1935 v Ni; 1936 v E; 1937 v G, E, W, Ni, A, Cz; 1938 v W, Ho, Ni; 1939 v E, Ni, H (14)
Deans, J. (Celtic), 1975 v EG, Sp (2)
Delaney, J. (Celtic), 1936 v W, Ni; 1937 v G, E, A, Cz; 1938 v Ni; 1939 v W, Ni; (with Manchester U), 1947 v E; 1948 v E, W, Ni (13)
Devine, A. (Falkirk), 1910 v W (1)
Dewar, G. (Dumbarton), 1888 v Ni; 1889 v E (2)
Dewar, N. (Third Lanark), 1932 v E, F; 1933 v W (3)
Dick, J. (West Ham U), 1959 v E (1)
Dickie, M. (Rangers), 1897 v Ni; 1899 v Ni; 1900 v W (3)
Dickson, W. (Kilmarnock), 1970 v Ni, W, E; 1971 v D, USSR (5)
Dickson, W. (Dumbarton), 1888 v Ni (1)
Divers, J. (Celtic), 1895 v W (1)
Divers, J. (Celtic), 1939 v Ni (1)
Docherty, T. H, (Preston NE), 1952 v W; 1953 v E, Se; 1954 v N (2), A, U; 1955 v W, E, H (2), A; 1957 v E, Y, Sp (2), Sw, WG; 1958 v Ni, W, E, Sw; (with Arsenal), 1959 v W, E, Ni (25)
Dodds, D. (Dundee U), 1984 v U (sub), Ni (2)
Dodds, J. (Celtic), 1914 v E, W, Ni (3)
Doig, J. E. (Arbroath), 1887 v Ni; 1889 v Ni; (with Sunderland), 1896 v E; 1899 v E; 1903 v E (5)
Donachie, W. (Manchester C), 1972 v Pe, Ni, E, Y, Cz, Br; 1973 v D, E, W, Ni; 1974 v Ni; 1976 v R, Ni, W, E; 1977 v Fi, Cz, W (2), Se, Ni, E, Ch, Arg, Br; 1978 v EG, W, Bul, W, E, Ir, Ho; 1979 v A, N, P (sub) (35)
Donaldson, A. (Bolton W), 1914 v E, Ni, W; 1920 v E, Ni; 1922 v Ni (6)
Donnachie, J. (Oldham Ath), 1913 v E; 1914 v E, Ni (3)
Dougall, C. (Birmingham C), 1947 v W (1)
Dougall, J. (Preston NE), 1939 v E (1)
Dougan, R. (Hearts), 1950 v Sw (1)
Douglas, A. (Chelsea), 1911 v Ni (1)
Douglas, J. (Renfrew), 1880 v W (1)
Dowds, P. (Celtic), 1892 v Ni (1)
Downie, R. (Third Lanark), 1892 v W (1)
Doyle, D. (Celtic), 1892 v E; 1893 v W; 1894 v E; 1895 v E, Ni; 1897 v E; 1898 v E, Ni (8)
Doyle, J. (Ayr U), 1976 v R (1)
Drummond, J. (Falkirk), 1892 v Ni; (with Rangers), 1894 v Ni; 1895 v Ni, E; 1896 v E, Ni; 1897 v Ni; 1898 v E; 1900 v E; 1901 v E; 1902 v E, W, Ni; 1903 v Ni (14)
Dunbar, M. (Cartvale), 1886 v Ni (1)
Duncan, A. (Hibernian), 1975 v P (sub), W, Ni, E, R; 1976 v D (6)
Duncan, D. (Derby Co), 1933 v E, W; 1934 v A, W; 1935 v E, W; 1936 v E, W, Ni; 1937 v G, E, W, Ni; 1938 v W (14)
Duncan, D. M. (East Fife), 1948 v Bel, Sw, F (3)
Duncan, J. (Alexandra Ath), 1878 v W; 1882 v W (2)
Duncan, J. (Leicester C), 1926 v W (1)
Duncanson, J. (Rangers), 1947 v Ni (1)
Dunlop, J. (St Mirren), 1890 v W (1)
Dunlop, W. (Liverpool), 1906 v E (1)
Dunn, J. (Hibernian), 1925 v W, Ni; 1927 v Ni; 1928 v Ni, E; (with Everton), 1929 v W (6)
Durie, G. S. (Chelsea), 1988 v Bul (sub); 1989 v I (sub), Cy (3)
Durrant, I. (Rangers), 1988 v H, Bel, Ma, Sp; 1989 v N (sub) (5)
Dykes, J. (Hearts), 1938 v Ho; 1939 v Ni (2)

Easson, J. F. (Portsmouth), 1931 v A, Sw; 1934 v W (3)
Ellis, J. (Mossend Swifts), 1892 v Ni (1)
Evans, A. (Aston Villa), 1982 v Ho, Ni, E, Nz (4)
Evans, R. (Celtic), 1949 v E, W, Ni, F; 1950 v W, Ni, Sw, P; 1951 v E, A; 1952 v Ni; 1953 v Se; 1954 v Ni, W, E, N, Fi; 1955 v Ni, P, Y, A, H; 1956 v E, Ni, W, A; 1957 v WG, Sp; 1958 v Ni, W, E, Sw, H, Pol, Y, Par, F; 1959 v E, WG, Ho, P; 1960 v E, Ni, W, Pol; (with Chelsea), 1960 v A, H, T (48)
Ewart, J. (Bradford C), 1921 v E (1)
Ewing, T. (Partick T), 1958 v W, E (2)

Farm, G. N. (Blackpool), 1953 v W, Ni, E, Se; 1954 v Ni, W, E; 1959 v WG, Ho, P (10)
Ferguson, D. (Rangers), 1988 v Ma, Co (sub) (2)
Ferguson, I. (Rangers), 1989 v I, Cy (sub), F (3)
Ferguson, J. (Vale of Leven), 1874 v E; 1876 v E, W; 1877 v E, W; 1878 v W (6)
Ferguson, R. (Kilmarnock), 1966 v W, E, Ho, P, Br; 1967 v W, Ni (7)
Fernie, W. (Celtic), 1954 v Fi, A, U; 1955 v W, Ni; 1957 v E, Ni, W, Y; 1958 v W, Sw, Par (12)
Findlay, R. (Kilmarnock), 1898 v W (1)
Fitchie, T. T. (Woolwich Arsenal), 1905 v W; 1906 v W, Ni; (with Queen's Park), 1907 v W (4)
Flavell, R. (Airdrieonians), 1947 v Bel, L (2)
Fleming, C. (East Fife), 1954 v Ni (1)
Fleming, J. W. (Rangers), 1929 v G, Ho; 1930 v E (3)
Fleming, R. (Morton), 1886 v Ni (1)
Forbes, A. R. (Sheffield U), 1947 v Bel, L, E; 1948 v W, Ni; (with Arsenal), 1950 v E, P, F; 1951 v W, Ni, A; 1952 v W, D, Se (14)
Forbes, J. (Vale of Leven), 1884 v E, W, Ni; 1887 v W, E (5)
Ford, D. (Hearts), 1974 v Cz (sub), WG (sub), W (3)
Forrest, J. (Rangers), 1966 v W, I; (with Aberdeen), 1971 v Bel (sub), D, USSR (5)
Forrest, J. (Motherwell), 1958 v E (1)
Forsyth, A. (Partick T), 1972 v Y, Cz, Br; 1973 v D; (with Manchester U), E; 1975 v Sp, Ni (sub), R, EG; 1976 v D (10)
Forsyth, C. (Kilmarnock), 1964 v E; 1965 v W, Ni, Fi (4)
Forsyth, T. (Motherwell), 1971 v D; (with Rangers), 1974 v Cz; 1976 v Sw, Ni, W, E; 1977 v Fi, Se, W, Ni, E, Ch, Arg, Br; 1978 v Cz, W, Ni, W (sub), E, Pe, Ir (sub), Ho (22)
Foyers, R. (St Bernards), 1893 v W; 1894 v W (2)
Fraser, D. M. (WBA), 1968 v Ho; 1969 v Cy (2)
Fraser, J. (Moffat), 1891 v Ni (1)
Fraser, M. J. E. (Queen's Park), 1880 v W; 1882 v W, E; 1883 v W, E (5)
Fraser, J. (Dundee), 1907 v Ni (1)
Fraser, W. (Sunderland), 1955 v W, Ni (2)
Fulton, W. (Abercorn), 1884 v Ni (1)
Fyfe, J. H. (Third Lanark), 1895 v W (1)

Gabriel, J. (Everton), 1961 v W; 1964 v N (sub) (2)
Gallacher, H. K. (Airdrieonians), 1924 v Ni; 1925 v E, W, Ni; 1926 v W; (with Newcastle U), 1926 v E, Ni; 1927 v E, W, Ni; 1928 v E, W; 1929 v E, W, Ni; 1930 v W, Ni, F; (with Chelsea), 1934 v E; (with Derby Co), 1935 v E (20)
Gallacher, K. W. (Dundee U), 1988 v Co, E (sub); 1989 v N, I (4)
Gallacher, P. (Sunderland), 1935 v Ni (1)
Galt, J. H. (Rangers), 1908 v W, Ni (2)
Gardiner, I. (Motherwell), 1958 v W (1)
Gardner, D. R. (Third Lanark), 1897 v W (1)
Gardner, R. (Queen's Park), 1872 v E; 1873 v E; (with Clydesdale), 1874 v E; 1875 v E; 1878 v E (5)
Gemmell, T. (St Mirren), 1955 v P, Y (2)
Gemmell, T. (Celtic), 1966 v E; 1967 v W, Ni, E, USSR; 1968 v Ni, E; 1969 v W, Ni, E, D, A, WG, Cy; 1970 v E, Ei, WG; 1971 v Bel (18)
Gemmill, A. (Derby Co), 1971 v Bel; 1972 v P, Ho, Pe, Ni, W, E; 1976 v D, R, Ni, W, E; 1977 v Fi, Cz, W (2), Ni (sub), E (sub), Ch (sub), Arg, Br; 1978 v EG (sub); (with Nottingham F), Bul, Ni, W, E (sub), Pe (sub), Ir, Ho; 1979 v A, N, P, N; (with Birmingham C), 1980 v A, P, Ni, W, E, H; 1981 v Se, P, Is, Ni (43)
Gibb, W. (Clydesdale), 1873 v E (1)
Gibson, D. W. (Leicester C), 1963 v A, N, Ei, Sp; 1964 v Ni; 1965 v W, Fi (7)
Gibson, J. D. (Partick T), 1926 v E; 1927 v E, W, Ni; (with Aston Villa), 1928 v E, W; 1930 v W, Ni (8)
Gibson, N. (Rangers), 1895 v E, Ni; 1896 v E, Ni; 1897 v E, Ni; 1898 v E; 1899 v E, W, Ni; 1900 v E, Ni; 1901 v W; (with Partick T), 1905 v Ni (14)
Gilchrist, J. E. (Celtic), 1922 v E (1)
Gilhooley, M. (Hull C), 1922 v W (1)
Gillespie, G. (Rangers), 1880 v W; 1881 v E, W; 1882 v E; (with Queen's Park), 1886 v W; 1890 v W; 1891 v Ni (7)
Gillespie, G. T. (Liverpool), 1988 v Bel, Bul, Sp; 1989 v N, F, Ch (6)
Gillespie, Jas. (Third Lanark), 1898 v W (1)
Gillespie, John. (Queen's Park), 1896 v W (1)
Gillespie, R. (Queen's Park), 1927 v W; 1931 v W; 1932 v F; 1933 v E (4)
Gillick, T. (Everton), 1937 v A, Cz; 1939 v W, Ni, H (5)
Gilmour, J. (Dundee), 1931 v W (1)
Gilzean, A. J. (Dundee), 1964 v W, E, N, WG; 1965 v Ni, (with Tottenham H), Sp; 1966 v Ni, W, Pol, I; 1968 v W; 1969 v W, E, WG, Cy (2), A (sub); 1970 v Ni, E (sub), WG, A; 1971 v P (22)
Glavin, R. (Celtic), 1977 v Se (1)
Glen, A. (Aberdeen), 1956 v E, Ni (2)
Glen, R. (Renton), 1895 v W; 1896 v W; (with Hibernian), 1900 v Ni (3)
Goram, A. L. (Oldham Ath), 1986 v EG (sub), R, Ho; 1987 v Br; (with Hibernian) 1989 v Y,I (6)
Gordon, J. E. (Rangers), 1912 v E, Ni; 1913 v E, Ni, W; 1914 v E, Ni; 1920 v W, E, Ni (10)
Gossland, J. (Rangers), 1884 v Ni (1)
Goudle, J. (Abercorn), 1884 v Ni (1)
Gough, C. R. (Dundee U), 1983 v Sw, Ni, W, E, Ca (3); 1984 v U, Bel, EG, Ni, W, E, F; 1985 v Sp, E, Ic; 1986 v W, EG, Aus, Is, R, E, D, WG, U; (with Tottenham H), 1987, Bul, L, Ei (2), Bel, E, Br; 1988 v H (with Rangers), S.Ar, Sp, Co, E; 1989 v Y, I, Cy, F, Cy (43)
Gourlay, J. (Cambuslang), 1886 v Ni; 1888 v W (2)
Govan, J. (Hibernian), 1948 v E, W, Bel, Sw, F; 1949 v Ni (6)
Gow, D. R. (Rangers), 1888 v E (1)
Gow, J. J. (Queen's Park), 1885 v E (1)
Gow, J. R. (Rangers), 1888 v Ni (1)
Graham, A. (Leeds U), 1978 v EG (sub); 1979 v A (sub), N, W, Ni, E, Arg, N; 1980 v A; 1981 v W (10)
Graham, G. (Arsenal), 1972 v P, Ho, Ni, Y, Cz, Br; 1973 v D (2); (with Manchester U), E, W, Ni, Br (sub) (12)
Graham, J. (Annbank), 1884 v Ni (1)
Graham, J. A. (Arsenal), 1921 v Ni (1)
Grant, J. (Hibernian), 1959 v W, Ni (2)
Grant, P. (Celtic), 1989 v E (sub), Ch (2)
Gray, A. (Hibernian), 1903 v Ni (1)
Gray, A. M. (Aston Villa), 1976 v R, Sw; 1977 v Fi, Cz; 1979 v A, N; (with Wolverhampton W), 1980 v P, E (sub); 1981 v Se, P, Is (sub), Ni; 1982 v Se (sub), Ni (sub); 1983 v Ni, W, E, Ca (1+1); (with Everton), 1985 v Ic (20)
Gray, D. (Rangers), 1929 v W, Ni, G, Ho; 1930 v W, E, Ni; 1931 v W; 1933 v W, Ni (10)
Gray, E. (Leeds U), 1969 v E, Cy; 1970 v WG, A; 1971 v W, Ni; 1972 v Bel, Ho; 1976 v W, E; 1977 v Fi, W (12)
Gray, F. T. (Leeds U), 1976 v Sw; 1979 v N, P, W, Ni, E, Arg (sub); (with Nottingham F) 1980 v Bel (sub); 1981 v Se, P, Is, Ni, Is, W, (with Leeds U) Ni, E; 1982 v Se, Ni, P, Sp, Ho, W, Nz, Br, USSR; 1983 v EG, Sw, Bel, Sw, W, E, Ca (32)
Gray, W. (Pollokshields Ath), 1886 v E (1)
Green, A. (Blackpool), 1971 v Bel (sub), P (sub), Ni, E; 1972 v W, E (sub) (6)
Greig, J. (Rangers), 1964 v E, WG; 1965 v W, Ni, E, Fi (2), Sp, Pol; 1966 v Ni, W, E, Pol, I (2), P, Ho, Br; 1967 v W, Ni, E; 1968 v Ni, W, E, Ho; 1969 v W, Ni, E, D, A, WG, Cy (2); 1970 v W, E, Ei, WG, A; 1971 v D, Bel, W (sub), Ni, E; 1976 v D (44)
Groves, W. (Hibernian), 1888 v W; (with Celtic), 1889 v

Ni; 1890 v E (3)
Guilliland, W. (Queen's Park), 1891 v W; 1892 v Ni; 1894 v E; 1895 v E (4)

Haddock, H. (Clyde), 1955 v E, H (2), P, Y; 1958 v E (6)
Haddow, D. (Rangers), 1894 v E (1)
Haffey, F. (Celtic), 1960 v E; 1961 v E (2)
Hamilton, A. (Queen's Park), 1885 v E, W; 1886 v E; 1888 v E (4)
Hamilton, A. W. (Dundee), 1962 v Cz, U, W, E; 1963 v W, Ni, E, A, N, Ei; 1964 v Ni, W, E, N, WG; 1965 v Ni, W, E, Fi (2), Pol, Sp; 1966 v Pol, Ni (24)
Hamilton, G. (Aberdeen), 1947 v Ni; 1951 v Bel, A; 1954 v N (2) (5)
Hamilton, G. (Port Glasgow Ath), 1906 v Ni (1)
Hamilton, J. (Queen's Park), 1892 v W; 1893 v E, Ni (3)
Hamilton, J. (St Mirren), 1924 v Ni (1)
Hamilton, R. C. (Rangers), 1899 v E, W, Ni; 1900 v W; 1901 v E, Ni; 1902 v W, Ni; 1903 v E; 1904 v Ni; (with Dundee), 1911 v W (11)
Hamilton, T. (Hurlford), 1891 v Ni (1)
Hamilton, T. (Rangers), 1932 v E (1)
Hamilton, W. M. (Hibernian), 1965 v Fi (1)
Hannah, A. B. (Renton), 1888 v W (1)
Hannah, J. (Third Lanark), 1889 v W (1)
Hansen, A. D. (Liverpool), 1979 v W, Arg; 1980 v Bel, P; 1981 v Se, P, Is; 1982 v Se, Ni, P, Sp, Ni (sub), W, E, Nz, Br, USSR; 1983 v EG, Sw, Bel, Sw; 1985 v W (sub); 1986 v R (sub); 1987 v Ei (2), L (26)
Hansen, J. (Partick T), 1972 v Bel (sub), Y (sub) (2)
Harkness, J. D. (Queen's Park), 1927 v E, Ni; 1928 v E; (with Hearts), 1929 v W, E, Ni; 1930 v E, W; 1932 v W, F; 1934 v Ni (11)
Harper, J. M. (Aberdeen), 1973 v D (1+1 sub); (with Hibernian), 1976 v D; (with Aberdeen), 1978 v Ir (sub) (4)
Harper, W. (Hibernian), 1923 v E, Ni, W; 1924 v E, Ni, W; 1925 v E, Ni, W; (with Arsenal), 1926 v E, Ni (11)
Harris, J. (Partick T), 1921 v W, Ni (2)
Harris, N. (Newcastle U), 1924 v E (1)
Harrower, W. (Queen's Park), 1882 v E; 1884 v Ni; 1886 v W (3)
Hartford, R. A. (WBA), 1972 v Pe, W (sub), E, Y, Cz, Br; (with Manchester C), 1976 v D, R, Ni (sub); 1977 v Cz (sub), W (sub), Se, W, Ni, E, Ch, Arg, Br; 1978 v EG, Cz, W, Bul, W, E, Pe, Ir, Ho; 1979 v A, N, P, W, Ni, E, Arg, N; (with Everton), 1980 v Pe, Bel; 1981 v Ni (sub), Is, W, Ni, E; 1982 v Se; (with Manchester C), Ni, P, Sp, Ni, W, E, Br (50)
Harvey, D. (Leeds U), 1973 v D; 1974 v Cz, WG, Ni, W, E, Bel, Z, Br, Y; 1975 v EG, Sp (2); 1976 v D (2); 1977 v Fi (sub) (16)
Hastings, A. C. (Sunderland), 1936 v Ni; 1938 v Ni (2)
Haughney, M. (Celtic), 1954 v E (1)
Hay, D. (Celtic), 1970 v Ni, W, E; 1971 v D, Bel, W, P, Ni; 1972 v P, Bel, Ho; 1973 v W, Ni, E, Sw, Br; 1974 v Cz (2), WG, Ni, W, E, Bel, N, Z, Br, Y (27)
Hay, J. (Celtic), 1905 v Ni; 1909 v Ni; 1910 v W, Ni, E; 1911 v Ni, E; (with Newcastle U), 1912 v E, W; 1914 v E, Ni (11)
Hegarty, P. (Dundee U), 1979 v W, Ni, E, Arg, N (sub); 1980 v W, E; 1983 v Ni (8)
Heggie, C. (Rangers), 1886 v Ni (1)
Henderson, G. H. (Rangers), 1904 v Ni (1)
Henderson, J. G. (Portsmouth), 1953 v Se; 1954 v Ni, E, N; 1956 v W; (with Arsenal), 1959 v W, Ni (7)
Henderson, W. (Rangers), 1963 v W, Ni, E, A, N, Ei, Sp; 1964 v W, Ni, E, N, WG; 1965 v Fi, Pol, E, Sp; 1966 v Ni, W, Pol, I, Ho; 1967 v W, Ni; 1968 v Ho; 1969 v Ni, E, Cy; 1970 v Ei; 1971 v P (29)
Hepburn, J. (Alloa Ath), 1891 v W (1)
Hepburn, R. (Ayr U), 1932 v Ni (1)
Herd, A. C. (Hearts), 1935 v Ni (1)
Herd, D. G. (Arsenal), 1959 v E, W, Ni; 1961 v E, Cz (5)
Herd, G. (Clyde), 1958 v E; 1960 v H, T; 1961 v W, Ni (5)
Herriot, J. (Birmingham C), 1969 v Ni, E, D, Cy (2), W (sub); 1970 v Ei (sub), WG (8)
Hewie, J. D. (Charlton Ath), 1956 v E, A; 1957 v E, Ni, W, Y, Sp (2), Sw, WG; 1958 v H, Pol, Y, F; 1959 v Ho, P; 1960 v Ni, W, Pol (19)
Higgins, A. (Kilmarnock), 1885 v Ni (1)
Higgins, A. (Newcastle U), 1910 v E, Ni; 1911 v E, Ni (4)
Highet, T. C. (Queen's Park), 1875 v E; 1876 v E, W; 1878 v E (4)
Hill, D. (Rangers), 1881 v E, W; 1882 v W (3)
Hill, D. A. (Third Lanark), 1906 v Ni (1)
Hill, F. R. (Aberdeen), 1930 v F; 1931 v W, Ni (3)
Hill, J. (Hearts), 1891 v E; 1892 v W (2)
Hogg, G (Hearts), 1896 v E, Ni (2)
Hogg, J. (Ayr U), 1922 v Ni (1)
Hogg, R. M. (Celtic), 1937 v Cz (1)
Holm, A. H. (Queen's Park), 1882 v W; 1883 v E, W (3)
Holt, D. D. (Hearts), 1963 v A, N, Ei, Sp; 1964 v WG (sub) (5)
Holton, J. A. (Manchester U), 1973 v W, Ni, E, Sw, Br; 1974 v Cz, WG, Ni, W, E, N, Z, Br, Y; 1975 v EG (15)
Hope, R. (WBA), 1968 v Ho; 1969 v D (2)
Houliston, W. (Queen of the South), 1949 v E, Ni, F (3)
Houston, S. M. (Manchester U), 1976 v D (1)
Howden, W. (Partick T), 1905 v Ni (1)
Howe, R. (Hamilton A), 1929 v N, Ho (2)
Howie, J. (Newcastle U), 1905 v E; 1906 v E; 1908 v E (3)
Howie, H. (Hibernian), 1949 v W (1)
Howieson, J. (St Mirren), 1927 v Ni (1)
Hughes, J. (Celtic), 1965 v Pol, Sp; 1966 v Ni, I (2); 1968 v E; 1969 v A; 1970 v Ei (8)
Hughes, W. (Sunderland), 1975 v Se (sub) (1)
Humphries, W. (Motherwell), 1952 v Se (1)
Hunter, A. (Kilmarnock), 1972 v Pe, Y; (with Celtic), 1973 v E; 1974 v Cz (4)
Hunter, J. (Dundee), 1909 v W (1)
Hunter, J. (Third Lanark), 1874 v E; (with Eastern), 1875 v E; (with Third Lanark), 1876 v E; 1877 v W (4)
Hunter, R. (St Mirren), 1890 v Ni (1)
Hunter, W. (Motherwell), 1960 v H, T; 1961 v W (3)
Husband, J. (Partick T), 1947 v W (1)
Hutchison, T. (Coventry C), 1974 v Cz (2), WG (2), Ni, W, Bel (sub), N, Z (sub), Y (sub); 1975 v EG, Sp (2), P, E (sub), R (sub); 1976 v D (17)
Hutton, J. (Aberdeen), 1923 v E, W, Ni; 1924 v Ni; 1926 v W, E, Ni; (with Blackburn R), 1927 v Ni; 1928 v W, Ni (10)
Hutton, J. (St Bernards), 1887 v Ni (1)
Hyslop, T. (Stoke C), 1896 v E; (with Rangers), 1897 v E (2)

Imlach, J. J. S. (Nottingham F), 1958 v H, Pol, Y, F (4)
Imrie, W. N. (St Johnstone), 1929 v N, G (2)
Inglis, J. (Kilmarnock Ath), 1884 v Ni (1)
Inglis, J. (Rangers), 1883 v E, W (2)
Irons, J. H. (Queen's Park), 1900 v W (1)

Jackson, A. (Cambuslang), 1886 v W; 1888 v Ni (2)
Jackson, A. (Aberdeen), 1925 v E, W, Ni; (with Huddersfield T), 1926 v E, W, Ni; 1927 v W, Ni; 1928 v E, W; 1929 v E, W, Ni; 1930 v E, W, Ni, F (17)
Jackson, C. (Rangers), 1975 v Se, P (sub), W; 1976 v D, R, Ni, W, E (8)
Jackson, J. (Partick T), 1931 v A, I, Sw; 1933 v E; (with Chelsea), 1934 v E; 1935 v E; 1936 v W, Ni (8)
Jackson, T. A. (St Mirren), 1904 v W, E, Ni; 1905 v W; 1907 v W, Ni (6)
James, A. W. (Preston NE), 1926 v W; 1928 v E; 1929 v E, Ni; (with Arsenal), 1930 v E, W, Ni; 1933 v W (8)
Jardine, A. (Rangers), 1971 v D (sub); 1972 v P, Bel, Ho; 1973 v E, Sw, Br; 1974 v Cz (2), WG (2), Ni, W, E, Bel,

N, Z, Br, Y; 1975 v EG, Sp (2), Se, P, W, Ni, E; 1977 v Se (sub), Ch (sub), Br (sub); 1978 v Cz, W, Ni, Ir; 1980 v Pe, A, Bel (2) (38)
Jarvie, A. (Airdrieonians), 1971 v P (sub), Ni (sub), E (sub) (3)
Jenkinson, T. (Hearts), 1887 v Ni (1)
Johnston, L. H. (Clyde), 1948 v Bel, Sw (2)
Johnston, M. (Watford), 1984 v W (sub), E (sub), F; (with Celtic), 1985 v Y, Ic, Sp (2), W; 1986 v EG; 1987 v Bul, Ei (2), L; (with Nantes), 1988 v H, Bel, L, S.Ar, Sp, Co, E; 1989 v N, Y, I, Cy, F, Cy, E, Ch (sub) (28)
Johnston, R. (Sunderland), 1938 v Cz (1)
Johnston, W. (Rangers), 1966 v W, E, Pol, Ho; 1968 v W, E; 1969 v Ni (sub); 1970 v Ni; 1971 v D; (with WBA), 1977 v Se, W (sub), Ni, E, Ch, Arg, Br; 1978 v EG, Cz, W, W, E, Pe (22)
Johnstone, D. (Rangers), 1973 v W, Ni, E, Sw, Br; 1975 v EG (sub), Se (sub); 1976 v Sw, Ni (sub), E (sub); 1978 v Bul (sub), Ni, W; 1980 v Bel (14)
Johnstone, J. (Abercorn), 1888 v W (1)
Johnstone, J. (Celtic), 1965 v W, Fi; 1966 v E; 1967 v W, USSR; 1968 v W; 1969 v A, WG; 1970 v E, WG; 1971 v D, E; 1972 v P, Bel, Ho, Ni, E (sub); 1974 v W, E, Bel, N; 1975 v EG, Sp (23)
Johnstone, Jas (Kilmarnock), 1894 v W (1)
Johnstone, J. A. (Hearts), 1930 v W; 1933 v W, Ni (3)
Johnstone, R. (Hibernian), 1951 v E, D, F; 1952 v Ni, E; 1953 v E, Se; 1954 v W, E, N, Fi; 1955 v Ni, H; (with Manchester C), 1955 v E; 1956 v E, Ni, W (17)
Johnstone, W. (Third Lanark), 1887 v Ni; 1889 v W; 1890 v E (3)
Jordan, J. (Leeds U), 1973 v E (sub), Sw (sub), Br; 1974 v Cz (sub+1), WG (sub), Ni (sub), W, E, Bel, N, Z, Br, Y; 1975 v EG, Sp (2); 1976 v Ni, W, E; 1977 v Cz, W, Ni, E; 1978 v EG, Cz, W; (with Manchester U), Bul, Ni, E, Pe, Ir, Ho; 1979 v A, P, W (sub), Ni, E, N; 1980 v Bel, Ni (sub), W, E, Pol; 1981 v Is, W, E; (with AC Milan), 1982 v Se, Ho, W, E, USSR (52)

Kay, J. L. (Queen's Park), 1880 v E; 1882 v E, W; 1883 v E, W; 1884 v W (6)
Keillor, A. (Montrose), 1891 v W; 1892 v Ni; (with Dundee), 1894 v Ni; 1895 v W; 1896 v W; 1897 v W (6)
Keir, L. (Dumbarton), 1885 v W; 1886 v Ni; 1887 v E, W; 1888 v E (5)
Kelly, H. T. (Blackpool), 1952 v USA (1)
Kelly, J. (Renton), 1888 v E; (with Celtic), 1889 v E; 1890 v E; 1892 v E; 1893 v E, Ni; 1894 v W; 1896 v Ni (8)
Kelly, J. C. (Barnsley), 1949 v W, Ni (2)
Kelso, R. (Renton), 1885 v W, Ni; 1886 v W; 1887 v E, W; 1888 v E, Ni; (with Dundee), 1898 v Ni (8)
Kelso, T. (Dundee), 1914 v W (1)
Kennaway, J. (Celtic), 1934 v A, W (2)
Kennedy, A. (Eastern), 1875 v E; 1876 v E, W; (with Third Lanark), 1878 v E; 1882 v W; 1884 v W (6)
Kennedy, J. (Celtic), 1964 v W, E, WG; 1965 v W, Ni, Fi (6)
Kennedy, J. (Hibernian), 1897 v W (1)
Kennedy, S. (Aberdeen), 1978 v Bul, W, E, Pe, Ho; 1979 v A, P; 1982 v P (sub) (8)
Kennedy, S. (Partick T), 1905 v W (1)
Kennedy, S. (Rangers), 1975 v Se, P, W, Ni, E (5)
Ker, G. (Queen's Park), 1880 v E; 1881 v E, W; 1882 v W, E (5)
Ker, W. (Granville), 1872 v E; (with Queen's Park), 1873 v E (2)
Kerr, A. (Partick T), 1955 v A, H (2)
Kerr, P. (Hibernian), 1924 v Ni (1)
Key, G. (Hearts), 1902 v Ni (1)
Key, W. (Queen's Park), 1907 v Ni (1)
King, A. (Hearts), 1896 v E, W; (with Celtic), 1897 v Ni; 1898 v Ni; 1899 v Ni, W (6)
King, J. (Hamilton A), 1933 v Ni; 1934 v Ni (2)
King, W. S. (Queen's Park), 1929 v W (1)
Kinloch, J. D. (Partick T), 1922 v Ni (1)
Kinnaird, A. F. (Wanderers), 1873 v E (1)
Kinnear, D. (Rangers), 1938 v Cz (1)

Lambie, J. A. (Queen's Park), 1886 v Ni; 1887 v Ni; 1888 v E (3)
Lambie, W. A. (Queen's Park), 1892 v Ni; 1893 v W; 1894 v E; 1895 v E, Ni; 1896 v E, Ni; 1897 v E, Ni (9)
Lamont, D. (Pilgrims), 1885 v Ni (1)
Lang, A. (Dumbarton), 1880 v W (1)
Lang, J. J. (Clydesdale), 1876 v W; (with Third Lanark), 1878 v W (2)
Latta, A. (Dumbarton), 1888 v W; 1889 v E (2)
Law, D. (Huddersfield T), 1959 v W, Ni, Ho, P; 1960 v Ni, W; (with Manchester C), 1960 v E, Pol, A; 1961 v E, Ni; (with Torino), 1962 v Cz (2) E; (with Manchester U), 1963 v W, Ni, E, A, N, Ei, Sp; 1964 v W, E, N, WG; 1965 v W, Ni, E, Fi (2), Pol, Sp; 1966 v Ni, E, Pol; 1967 v W, E, USSR; 1968 v Ni; 1969 v Ni, A, WG; 1972 v Pe, Ni, W, E, Y, Cz, Br; (with Manchester C), 1974 v Cz (2), WG (2), Ni, Z (55)
Law, G. (Rangers), 1910 v E, Ni, W (3)
Law, T. (Chelsea), 1928 v E; 1930 v E (2)
Lawrence, J. (Newcastle U), 1911 v E (1)
Lawrence, T. (Liverpool), 1963 v Ei; 1969 v W, WG (3)
Lawson, D. (St Mirren), 1923 v E (1)
Leckie, R. (Queen's Park), 1872 v E (1)
Leggat, G. (Aberdeen), 1956 v E; 1957 v W; 1958 v Ni, H, Pol, Y, Par; (with Fulham), 1959 v E, W, Ni, WG, Ho; 1960 v E, Ni, W, Pol, A, H (18)
Leighton, J. (Aberdeen), 1983 v EG, Sw, Bel, Sw, W, E, Ca (2); 1984 v U, Bel, Ni, W, E, F; 1985 v Y, Ic, Sp (2), W, E, Ic; 1986 v W, EG, Aus (2), Is, D, WG, U; 1987 v Bul, Ei (2), L, Bel, E; 1988 v H, Bel, Bul, L, S.Ar, Ma, Sp, (with Manchester U), Co, E; 1989 v N, Cy, F, Cy, E, Ch (50)
Lennie, W. (Aberdeen), 1908 v W, Ni (2)
Lennox, R. (Celtic), 1967 v Ni, E, USSR; 1968 v W, L; 1969 v D, A, WG, Cy (sub); 1970 v W (sub) (10)
Leslie, L. G. (Airdrieonians), 1961 v W, Ni, Ei (2), Cz (5)
Liddell, W. (Liverpool), 1947 v W, Ni; 1948 v E, W, Ni; 1950 v E, W, P, F; 1951 v W, Ni, E, A; 1952 v W, Ni, E, USA, D, Se; 1953 v W, Ni, E; 1954 v W; 1955 v P, Y, A, H; 1956 v Ni (28)
Liddle, D. (East Fife), 1931 v A, I, Sw (3)
Lindsay, D. (St Mirren), 1903 v Ni (1)
Lindsay, J. (Dumbarton), 1880 v W; 1881 v W, E; 1884 v W, E; 1885 v W, E; 1886 v E (8)
Lindsay, J. (Renton), 1888 v E; 1893 v E, Ni (3)
Linwood, A. B. (Clyde), 1950 v W (1)
Little, R. J. (Rangers), 1953 v Se (1)
Livingstone, G. T. (Manchester C), 1906 v E; (with Rangers), 1907 v W (2)
Lochhead, A. (Third Lanark), 1889 v W (1)
Logan, J. (Ayr U), 1891 v W (1)
Logan, T. (Falkirk), 1913 v Ni (1)
Logie, J. T. (Arsenal), 1953 v Ni (1)
Loney, W. (Celtic), 1910 v W, Ni (2)
Long, H. (Clyde), 1947 v Ni (1)
Longair, W. (Dundee), 1894 v Ni (1)
Lorimer, P. (Leeds U), 1970 v A (sub); 1971 v W, Ni; 1972 v Ni (sub), W, E; 1973 v D (2), E (2); 1974 v WG (sub), E, Bel, N, Z, Br, Y; 1975 v Sp (sub); 1976 v D (2), R (sub) (21)
Love, A. (Aberdeen), 1931 v A, I, Sw (3)
Low, A. (Falkirk), 1934 v Ni (1)
Low, T. P. (Rangers), 1897 v Ni (1)
Low, W. L. (Newcastle U), 1911 v E, W; 1912 v Ni; 1920 v E, Ni (5)
Lowe, J. (Cambuslang), 1891 v Ni (1)
Lowe, J. (St Bernards), 1887 v Ni (1)
Lundie, J. (Hibernian), 1886 v W (1)

Lyall, J. (Sheffield W), 1905 v E (1)

McAdam, J. (Third Lanark), 1880 v W (1)
McArthur, D. (Celtic), 1895 v E, Ni; 1899 v W (3)
McAtee, A. (Celtic), 1913 v W (1)
McAulay, J. (Dumbarton), 1882 v W; (with Arthurlie), 1884 v Ni (2)
McAulay, J. (Dumbarton), 1883 v E, W; 1884 v E; 1885 v E, W; 1886 v E; 1887 v E, W (8)
McAuley, R. (Rangers), 1932 v Ni, W (2)
McAvennie, F. (West Ham U), 1986 v Aus (2), D (sub), WG (sub); (with Celtic), 1988 v S.Ar (5)
McBain, E. (St Mirren), 1894 v W (1)
McBain, N. (Manchester U), 1922 v E; (with Everton), 1923 v Ni; 1924 v W (3)
McBride, J. (Celtic), 1967 v W, Ni (2)
McBride, P. (Preston NE), 1904 v E; 1906 v E; 1907 v E, W; 1908 v E; 1909 v W (6)
McCall, J. (Renton), 1886 v W; 1887 v E, W; 1888 v E; 1890 v E (5)
McCalliog, J. (Sheffield W), 1967 v E, USSR; 1968 v Ni; 1969 v D; (with Wolverhampton W), 1971 v P (5)
McCallum, N. (Renton), 1888 v Ni (1)
McCann, R. J. (Motherwell), 1959 v WG; 1960 v E, Ni, W; 1961 v E (5)
McCartney, W. (Hibernian), 1902 v Ni (1)
McClair, B. (Celtic), 1987 v L, Ei, E, Br (sub); (with Manchester U), 1988 v Bul, Ma (sub), Sp (sub); 1989 v N, Y, I (sub), Cy, F (sub) (12)
McClory, A. (Motherwell), 1927 v W; 1928 v Ni; 1935 v W (3)
McCloy, P. (Ayr U), 1924 v E; 1925 v E (2)
McCloy, P. (Rangers), 1973 v W, Ni, Sw, Br (4)
McCoist, A. (Rangers), 1986 v Ho; 1987 v L (sub), Ei (sub), Bel, E, Br; 1988 v H, Bel, Ma, Sp, Co, E; 1989 v Y (sub), F, Cy, E (16)
McColl, A. (Renton), 1888 v Ni (1)
McColl, I. M. (Rangers), 1950 v E, F; 1951 v W, Ni, Bel; 1957 v E, Ni, W, Y, Sp, Sw, WG; 1958 v Ni, E (14)
McColl, R. S. (Queen's Park), 1896 v W, Ni; 1897 v Ni; 1898 v Ni; 1899 v Ni, E, W; 1900 v E, W; 1901 v E, W; (with Newcastle U), 1902 v E; (with Queen's Park), 1908 v Ni (13)
McColl, W. (Renton), 1895 v W (1)
McCombie, A. (Sunderland), 1903 v E, W; (with Newcastle U), 1905 v E, W (4)
McCorkindale, J. (Partick T), 1891 v W (1)
McCormick, R. (Abercorn), 1886 v W (1)
McCrae, D. (St Mirren), 1929 v N, G (2)
McCreadie, A. (Rangers), 1893 v W; 1894 v E (2)
McCreadie, E. G. (Chelsea), 1965 v E, Sp, Fi, Pol; 1966 v P, Ni, W, Pol, I; 1967 v E, USSR; 1968 v Ni, W, E, Ho; 1969 v W, Ni, E, D, A, WG, Cy (2) (23)
McCulloch, D. (Hearts), 1935 v W; (with Brentford), 1936 v E; 1937 v W, Ni; 1938 v Cz; (with Derby Co), 1939 v H, W (7)
MacDonald, A. (Rangers), 1976 v Sw (1)
McDonald, J. (Edinburgh University), 1886 v E (1)
McDonald, J. (Sunderland), 1956 v W, Ni (2)
MacDougall, E. J. (Norwich C) 1975 v Se, P, W, Ni, E; 1976 v D, R (7)
McDougall, J. (Liverpool), 1931 v I, A (2)
McDougall, J. (Airdrieonians), 1926 v Ni (1)
McDougall, J. (Vale of Leven), 1877 v E, W; 1878 v E; 1879 v E, W (5)
McFadyen, W. (Motherwell), 1934 v A, W (2)
Macfarlane, A. (Dundee), 1904 v W; 1906 v W; 1908 v W; 1909 v Ni; 1911 v W (5)
McFarlane, R. (Greenock Morton), 1896 v W (1)
Macfarlane, W. (Hearts), 1947 v L (1)
McGarr, E. (Aberdeen), 1970 v Ei, A (2)
McGarvey, F. P. (Liverpool), 1979 v Ni (sub), Arg; (with Celtic), 1984 v U, Bel (sub), EG (sub), Ni, W (7)
McGeoch, A. (Dumbreck), 1876 v E, W; 1877 v E, W (4)
McGhee, J. (Hibernian), 1886 v W (1)
McGhee, M. (Aberdeen), 1983 v Ca (1+1 sub); 1984 v Ni (sub), E (4)
McGonagle, W. (Celtic), 1933 v E; 1934 v A, E, Ni; 1935 v Ni, W (6)
McGrain, D. (Celtic), 1973 v W, Ni, E, Sw, Br; 1974 v Cz (2), WG, W (sub), E, Bel, N, Z, Br, Y; 1975 v Sp, Se, P, W, Ni, E, R; 1976 v D (2), Sw, Ni, W, E; 1977 v Fi, Cz, W (2), Se, Ni, E, Ch, Arg, Br; 1978 v EG, Cz; 1980 v Bel, P, Ni, W, E, Pol, H; 1981 v Se, P, Is, Ni, Is, W (sub), Ni, E; 1982 v Se, Sp, Ho, Ni, E, Nz, USSR (sub) (62)
McGregor, J. C. (Vale of Leven), 1877 v E, W; 1878 v E; 1880 v E (4)
McGrory, J. E. (Kilmarnock), 1965 v Ni, Fi; 1966 v P (3)
McGrory, J. (Celtic), 1928 v Ni; 1931 v E; 1932 v Ni, W; 1933 v E, Ni; 1934 v Ni (7)
McGuire, W. (Beith), 1881 v E, W (2)
McGurk, F. (Birmingham), 1934 v W (1)
McHardy, H. (Rangers), 1885 v Ni (1)
McInally, A. (Aston Villa), 1989 v Cy (sub), Ch (2)
McInally, J. (Dundee U), 1987 v Bel, Br; 1988 v Ma (sub) (3)
McInally, T. B. (Celtic), 1926 v Ni; 1927 v W (2)
McInnes, T. (Cowlairs), 1889 v Ni (1)
McIntosh, W. (Third Lanark), 1905 v Ni (1)
McIntyre, A. (Vale of Leven), 1878 v E; 1882 v E (2)
McIntyre, H. (Rangers), 1880 v W (1)
McIntyre, J. (Rangers), 1884 v W (1)
McKay, D. (Celtic), 1959 v E, WG, Ho, P; 1960 v E, Pol, A, H, T; 1961 v W, Ni; 1962 v Ni, Cz, U (sub) (14)
Mackay, D. C. (Hearts), 1957 v Sp; 1958 v F; 1959 v W, Ni; (with Tottenham H), 1959 v WG, E; 1960 v W, Ni, A, Pol, H, T; 1961 v W, Ni, E; 1963 v E, A, N; 1964 v Ni, W, N; 1966 v Ni (22)
Mackay, G. (Hearts), 1988 v Bul (sub), L (sub), S.Ar (sub), Ma (4)
McKay, J. (Blackburn R), 1924 v W (1)
McKay, R. (Newcastle U), 1928 v W (1)
McKean, R. (Rangers), 1976 v Sw (1)
McKenzie, D. (Brentford), 1938 v Ni (1)
Mackenzie, J. A. (Partick T), 1954 v W, E, N, Fi, A, U; 1955 v E, H; 1956 v A (9)
McKeown, M. (Celtic), 1889 v Ni; 1890 v E (2)
McKie, J. (East Stirling), 1898 v W (1)
McKillop, T. R. (Rangers), 1938 v Ho (1)
McKimmie, S. (Aberdeen), 1989 v E, Ch (2)
McKinlay, D. (Liverpool), 1922 v W, Ni (2)
McKinnon, A. (Queen's Park), 1874 v E (1)
McKinnon, R. (Rangers), 1966 v W, E, I (2), Ho, Br; 1967 v W, Ni, E; 1968 v Ni, W, E, Ho; 1969 v D, A, WG, Cy; 1970 v Ni, W, E, Ei, WG, A; 1971 v D, Bel, P, USSR, D (28)
MacKinnon, W. (Dumbarton), 1883 v E, W; 1884 v E, W (4)
McKinnon, W. W. (Queen's Park), 1872 v E; 1873 v E; 1874 v E; 1875 v E; 1876 v E, W; 1877 v E; 1878 v E; 1879 v E (9)
McLaren, A. (St Johnstone), 1929 v N, G, Ho; 1933 v W, Ni (5)
McLaren, A. (Preston NE), 1947 v E, Bel, L; 1948 v W (4)
McLaren, J. (Hibernian), 1888 v W; (with Celtic), 1889 v E; 1890 v E (3)
McLean, A. (Celtic), 1926 v W, Ni; 1927 v W, E (4)
McLean, D. (St Bernards), 1896 v W; 1897 v Ni (2)
McLean, D. (Sheffield W), 1912 v E (1)
McLean, G. (Dundee), 1968 v Ho (1)
McLean, T. (Kilmarnock), 1969 v D, Cy, W; 1970 v Ni, W; 1971 v D (6)
McLeish, A. (Aberdeen), 1980 v F, Ni, W, E, Pol, H; 1981 v Se, Is, Ni, Is, Ni, E; 1982 v Se, Sp, Ni, Br (sub); 1983

v Bel, Sw (sub), W, E, Ca (3); 1984 v U, Bel, EG, Ni, W, E, F; 1985 v Y, Ic, Sp (2), W, E, Ic; 1986 v W, EG, Aus (2), E, Ho, D; 1987 v Bel, E, Br; 1988 v Bel, Bul, L, S.Ar (sub), Ma, Sp, Co, E; 1989 v N, Y, I, Cy, Fr, Cy, E, Ch (63)
McLeod, D. (Celtic), 1905 v Ni; 1906 v E, W, Ni (4)
McLeod, J. (Dumbarton), 1888 v Ni; 1889 v W; 1890 v Ni; 1892 v E; 1893 v W (5)
MacLeod, J. M. (Hibernian), 1961 v E, Ei (2), Cz (4)
MacLeod, M. (Celtic), 1985 v E (sub); 1987 v Ei, L, E, Br; (with Borussia Dortmund), 1988 v Co, E; 1989 v I, Ch (9)
McLeod, W. (Cowlairs), 1886 v Ni (1)
McLintock, A. (Vale of Leven), 1875 v E; 1876 v E; 1880 v E (3)
McLintock, F. (Leicester C), 1963 v N (sub), Ei, Sp; (with Arsenal), 1965 v Ni; 1967 v USSR; 1970 v Ni; 1971 v W, Ni, E (9)
McLuckie, J. S. (Manchester C), 1934 v W (1)
McMahon, A. (Celtic), 1892 v E; 1893 v E, Ni; 1894 v E; 1901 v Ni; 1902 v W (6)
McMenemy, J. (Celtic), 1905 v Ni; 1909 v Ni; 1910 v E, W; 1911 v Ni, W, E; 1912 v W; 1914 v W, Ni, E; 1920 v Ni (12)
McMenemy, J. (Motherwell), 1934 v W (1)
McMillan, J. (St Bernards), 1897 v W (1)
McMillan, I. L. (Airdrieonians), 1952 v E, USA, D; 1955 v E; 1956 v E; (with Rangers), 1961 v Cz (6)
McMillan, T. (Dumbarton), 1887 v Ni (1)
McMullan, J. (Partick T), 1920 v W; 1921 v W, Ni, E; 1924 v E, Ni; 1925 v E; 1926 v W; (with Manchester C), 1926 v E; 1927 v E, W; 1928 v E, W; 1929 v W, E, Ni (16)
McNab, A. (Morton), 1921 v E, Ni (2)
McNab, A. (Sunderland), 1937 v A; (with WBA), 1939 v E (2)
McNab, C. D. (Dundee), 1931 v E, W, A, I, Sw; 1932 v E (6)
McNab, J. S. (Liverpool), 1923 v W (1)
McNair, A. (Celtic), 1906 v W; 1907 v Ni; 1908 v E, W; 1909 v E; 1910 v W; 1912 v E, W, Ni; 1913 v E; 1914 v E, Ni; 1920 v E, W, Ni (15)
McNaught, W. (Raith R), 1951 v A, W, Ni; 1952 v E; 1955 v Ni (5)
McNeil, H. (Queen's Park), 1874 v E; 1875 v E; 1876 v E, W; 1877 v W; 1878 v E; 1879 v E, W; 1881 v E, W (10)
McNeil, M. (Rangers), 1876 v W; 1880 v E (2)
McNeill, W. (Celtic), 1961 v E, Ei (2), Cz; 1962 v Ni, E, Cz, U; 1963 v Ei, Sp; 1964 v W, E, WG; 1965 v E, Fi, Pol, Sp; 1966 v Ni, Pol; 1967 v USSR; 1968 v E; 1969 v Cy, W, E, Cy (sub); 1970 v WG; 1972 v Ni, W, E (29)
McPhail, J. (Celtic), 1950 v W; 1951 v W, Ni, A; 1954 v Ni (5)
McPhail, R. (Airdrieonians), 1927 v E; (with Rangers), 1929 v W; 1931 v E, Ni; 1932 v W, Ni, F; 1933 v E, Ni; 1934 v A, Ni; 1935 v E; 1937 v G, E, Cz; 1938 v W, Ni (17)
McPherson, D. (Kilmarnock), 1892 v Ni (1)
McPherson, D. (Hearts), 1989 v Cy, E (2)
McPherson, J. (Kilmarnock), 1888 v W; (with Cowlairs), 1889 v E; 1890 v Ni, E; (with Rangers), 1892 v W; 1894 v E; 1895 v E, Ni; 1897 v Ni (9)
McPherson, J. (Clydesdale), 1875 v E (1)
McPherson, J. (Vale of Leven), 1879 v E, W; 1880 v E; 1881 v W; 1883 v E, W; 1884 v E; 1885 v N (8)
McPherson, J. (Hearts), 1891 v E (1)
McPherson, R. (Arthurlie), 1882 v E (1)
McQueen, G. (Leeds U), 1974 v Bel; 1975 v Sp (2), P, W, Ni, E, R; 1976 v D; 1977 v Cz, W (2), Ni, E; 1978 v EG, Cz, W; (with Manchester U), Bul, Ni, W; 1979 v A, N, P, Ni, E, N; 1980 v Pe, A, Bel; 1981 v W (30)
McQueen, M. (Leith Ath), 1890 v W; 1891 v W (2)
McRorie, D. M. (Morton), 1931 v W (1)
McSpadyen, A. (Partick T), 1939 v E, H (2)
McStay, P. (Celtic), 1984 v U, Bel, EG, Ni, W, E (sub); 1985 v Ic, Sp (2), W; 1986 v EG (sub), Aus, Is, U; 1987 v Bul, Ei (2, 1 sub), L (sub), Bel, E, Br; 1988 v H, Bel, Bul, L, S.Ar, Sp, Co, E; 1989 v N, Y, I, Cy, F, Cy, E, Ch (37)
McStay, W. (Celtic), 1921 v W, Ni; 1925 v E, Ni, W; 1926 v E, Ni, W; 1927 v E, Ni, W; 1928 v W, Ni (13)
McTavish, J. (Falkirk), 1910 v Ni (1)
McWhattie, G. C. (Queen's Park), 1901 v W, Ni (2)
McWilliam, P. (Newcastle U) 1905 v E; 1906 v E; 1907 v E, W; 1909 v E, W; 1910 v E; 1911 v W (8)
Macari, L. (Celtic), 1972 v W (sub), E, Y, Cz, Br; 1973 v D; (with Manchester U), E (2), W (sub), Ni (sub); 1975 v Se, P (sub), W, E (sub), R; 1977 v Ni (sub), E (sub), Ch, Arg; 1978 v EG, W, Bul, Pe (sub), Ir (24)
Macauley, A. R. (Brentford), 1947 v E; (with Arsenal), 1948 v E, W, Ni, Bel, Sw, F (7)
Madden, J. (Celtic), 1893 v W; 1895 v W (2)
Main, F. R. (Rangers), 1938 v W (1)
Main, J. (Hibernian), 1909 v Ni (1)
Maley, W. (Celtic), 1893 v E, Ni (2)
Malpas, M. (Dundee U), 1984 v F; 1985 v E, Ic; 1986 v W, Aus (2), Is, R, E, Ho, D, WG; 1987 v Bul, Ei, Bel; 1988 v Bel, Bul, L, S.Ar, Ma; 1989 v N, Y, I, Cy, F, Cy, E, Ch (28)
Marshall, H. (Celtic), 1899 v W; 1900 v Ni (2)
Marshall, J. (Rangers), 1932 v E; 1933 v E; 1934 v E (3)
Marshall, J. (Middlesbrough), 1921 v E, W, Ni; 1922 v E, W, Ni; (with Llanelly), 1924 v W (7)
Marshall, J. (Third Lanark), 1885 v Ni; 1886 v W; 1887 v E, W (4)
Marshall, R. W. (Rangers), 1892 v Ni; 1894 v Ni (2)
Martin, F. (Aberdeen), 1954 v N (2), A, U; 1955 v E, H (6)
Martin, N. (Hibernian), 1965 v Fi, Pol; (with Sunderland), 1966 v I (3)
Martis, J. (Motherwell), 1961 v W (1)
Mason, J. (Third Lanark), 1949 v E, W, Ni; 1950 v Ni; 1951 v Ni, Bel, A (7)
Massie, A. (Hearts), 1932 v Ni, W, F; 1933 v Ni; 1934 v E, Ni; 1935 v E, Ni, W; 1936 v W, Ni; (with Aston Villa), 1936 v E; 1937 v G, E, W, Ni, A; 1938 v W (18)
Masson, D. S. (QPR), 1976 v Ni, W, E; 1977 v Fi, Cz, W, Ni, E, Ch, Arg, Br; 1978 v EG, Cz, W; (with Derby Co), Ni, E, Pe (17)
Mathers, D. (Partick T), 1954 v Fi (1)
Maxwell, W. S. (Stoke C), 1898 v E (1)
May, J. (Rangers), 1906 v W, Ni; 1908 v E, Ni; 1909 v W (5)
Meechan, P. (Celtic), 1896 v Ni (1)
Meiklejohn, D. D. (Rangers), 1922 v W; 1924 v W; 1925 v W, Ni, E; 1928 v W, Ni; 1929 v E, Ni; 1930 v E, Ni; 1931 v E; 1932 v W, Ni; 1934 v A (15)
Menzies, A. (Hearts), 1906 v E (1)
Mercer, R. (Hearts), 1912 v W; 1913 v Ni (2)
Middleton, R. (Cowdenbeath), 1930 v Ni (1)
Millar, J. (Rangers), 1897 v E; 1898 v E, W (3)
Millar, J. (Rangers), 1963 v A, Ei (2)
Millar, A. (Hearts), 1939 v W (1)
Miller, J. (St Mirren), 1931 v E, I, Sw; 1932 v F; 1934 v E (5)
Miller, P. (Dumbarton), 1882 v E; 1883 v E, W (3)
Miller, T. (Liverpool), 1920 v E; (with Manchester U), 1921 v E, Ni (3)
Miller, W. (Third Lanark), 1876 v E (1)
Miller, W. (Celtic), 1947 v E, W, Bel, L; 1948 v W, Ni (6)
Miller, W. (Aberdeen), 1975 v R; 1978 v Bul; 1980 v Bel, W, E, Pol, H; 1981 v Se, P, Is (sub), Ni, W, Ni, E; 1982 v Ni, P, Ho, Br, USSR; 1983 v EG, Sw, Sw, W, E, Ca (3); 1984 v U, Bel, EG, W, E, F; 1985 v Y, Ic, Sp (2), W, E, Ic; 1986 v W, EG, Aus (2), Is, R, E, Ho, D, WG, U; 1987 v Bul, E, Br; 1988 v H, L, S.Ar, Ma, Sp, Co, E; 1989 v N, Y (63)

Mills, W. (Aberdeen), 1936 v W, Ni; 1937 v W (3)
Milne, J. V. (Middlesbrough), 1938 v E; 1939 v E (2)
Mitchell, D. (Rangers), 1890 v Ni; 1892 v E; 1893 v E, Ni; 1894 v E (5)
Mitchell, J. (Kilmarnock), 1908 v Ni; 1910 v Ni, W (3)
Mitchell, R. C. (Newcastle U), 1951 v D, F (2)
Mochan, N. (Celtic), 1954 v N, A, U (3)
Moir, W. (Bolton W), 1950 v E (1)
Moncur, R. (Newcastle U), 1968 v Ho; 1970 v Ni, W, E, Ei; 1971 v D, Bel, W, P, Ni, E, D; 1972 v Pe, Ni, W, E (16)
Morgan, H. (St Mirren), 1898 v W; (with Liverpool), 1899 v E (2)
Morgan, W. (Burnley), 1968 v Ni; (with Manchester U) 1972 v Pe, Y, Cz, Br; 1973 v D (2), E (2), W, Ni, Sw, Br; 1974 v Cz (2), WG (2), Ni, Bel (sub), Br, Y (21)
Morris, D. (Raith R), 1923 v Ni; 1924 v E, Ni; 1925 v E, W, Ni (6)
Morris, H. (East Fife), 1950 v Ni (1)
Morrison, T. (St Mirren), 1927 v E (1)
Morton, A. L. (Queen's Park), 1920 v W, Ni; (with Rangers), 1921 v E; 1922 v E, W; 1923 v E, W, Ni; 1924 v E, W, Ni; 1925 v E, W, Ni; 1927 v E, Ni; 1928 v E, W, Ni; 1929 v E, W, Ni; 1930 v E, W, Ni; 1931 v E, W, Ni; 1932 v E, W, F (31)
Morton, H. A. (Kilmarnock), 1929 v G, Ho (2)
Mudie, J. K. (Blackpool), 1957 v W, Ni, E, Y, Sw, Sp (2), WG; 1958 v Ni, E, W, Sw, H, Pol, Y, Par, F (17)
Muir, W. (Dundee), 1907 v Ni (1)
Muirhead, T. A. (Rangers), 1922 v Ni; 1923 v E; 1924 v W; 1927 v Ni; 1928 v Ni; 1929 v W, Ni; 1930 v W (8)
Mulhall, G. (Aberdeen), 1960 v Ni; (with Sunderland), 1963 v Ni; 1964 v Ni (3)
Munro, A. D. (Hearts), 1937 v W, Ni; (with Blackpool), 1938 v Ho (3)
Munro, F. M. (Wolverhampton W), 1971 v Ni (sub), E (sub), D, USSR; 1975 v Se, W (sub), Ni, E, R (9)
Munro, I. (St Mirren), 1979 v Arg, N; 1980 v Pe, A, Bel, W, E (7)
Munro, N. (Abercorn), 1888 v W; 1889 v E (2)
Murdoch, J. (Motherwell), 1931 v Ni (1)
Murdoch, R. (Celtic), 1966 v W, E, I (2); 1967 v Ni; 1968 v Ni; 1969 v W, Ni, E, WG, Cy; 1970 v A (12)
Murphy, F. (Celtic), 1938 v Ho (1)
Murray, J. (Renton), 1895 v W (1)
Murray, J. (Hearts), 1958 v E, H, Pol, Y, F (5)
Murray, J. W. (Vale of Leven), 1890 v W (1)
Murray, P. (Hibernian), 1896 v Ni; 1897 v W (2)
Murray, S. (Aberdeen), 1972 v Bel (1)
Mutch, G. (Preston NE), 1938 v E (1)

Napier, C. E. (Celtic), 1932 v E; 1935 v E, W; (with Derby Co), 1937 v Ni, A (5)
Narey, D. (Dundee U), 1977 v Se (sub); 1979 v P, Ni (sub), Arg; 1980 v P, Ni, Pol, H; 1981 v W, E (sub); 1982 v Ho, W, E, Nz (sub), Br, USSR; 1983 v EG, Sw, Bel, Ni, W, E, Ca (3); 1986 v Is, R, Ho, WG, U; 1987 v Bul, E; Bel; 1989 v I, Cy (35)
Neil, R. G. (Hibernian), 1896 v W; (with Rangers), 1900 v W (2)
Neill, R. W. (Queen's Park), 1876 v W; 1877 v E, W; 1878 v W; 1880 v E (5)
Neilles, P. (Hearts), 1914 v W, Ni (2)
Nelson, J. (Cardiff C), 1925 v W, Ni; 1928 v E; 1930 v F (4)
Nevin, P. K. F. (Chelsea), 1986 v R (sub), E (sub); 1987 v L. Ei, Bel (sub); 1988 v L; (with Everton), 1989 v Cy, E (8)
Niblo, T. D. (Aston Villa), 1904 v E (1)
Nibloe, J. (Kilmarnock), 1929 v E, N, Ho; 1930 v W; 1931 v E, Ni, A, I, Sw; 1932 v E, F (11)
Nicholas, C. (Celtic), 1983 v Sw, Ni, E, Ca (3); (with Arsenal), 1984 v Bel, F (sub); 1985 v Y (sub), Ic (sub), Sp (sub), W (sub); 1986 v Is, R (sub), E, D, U (sub); 1987 v Bul, E (sub); (with Aberdeen), 1989 v Cy (sub) (20)
Nicol, S. (Liverpool), 1985 v Y, Ic, Sp, W; 1986 v W, EG, Aus, E, D, WG, U; 1988 v H, Bul, S.Ar, Sp, Co, E; 1989 v N, Y, Cy, F (21)
Nisbet, J. (Ayr U), 1929 v N, G, Ho (3)
Niven, J. B. (Moffatt), 1885 v Ni (1)

O'Donnell, F. (Preston NE), 1937 v E, A, Cz; 1938 v E, W; (with Blackpool), Ho (6)
Ogilvie, D. H. (Motherwell), 1934 v A (1)
O'Hare, J. (Derby Co), 1970 v W, Ni, E; 1971 v D, Bel, W, Ni; 1972 v P, Bel, Ho (sub), Pe, Ni, W (13)
Ormond, W. E. (Hibernian), 1954 v E, N, Fi, A, U; 1959 v E (6)
O'Rourke, F. (Airdrieonians), 1907 v Ni (1)
Orr, J. (Kilmarnock), 1892 v W (1)
Orr, R. (Newcastle U), 1902 v E; 1904 v E (2)
Orr, T. (Morton), 1952 v Ni, W (2)
Orr, W. (Celtic), 1900 v Ni; 1903 v Ni; 1904 v W (3)
Orrock, R. (Falkirk), 1913 v W (1)
Oswald, J. (Third Lanark), 1889 v E; (with St Bernards), 1895 v E; (with Rangers), 1897 v W (3)

Parker, A. H. (Falkirk), 1955 v P, Y, A; 1956 v E, Ni, W, A; 1957 v Ni, W, Y; 1958 v Ni, W, E, Sw; (with Everton), Par (15)
Parlane, D. (Rangers), 1973 v W, Sw, Br; 1975 v Sp (sub), Se, P, W, Ni, E, R; 1976 v D (sub); 1977 v W (12)
Parlane, R. (Vale of Leven), 1878 v W; 1879 v E, W (3)
Paterson, G. D. (Celtic), 1939 v Ni (1)
Paterson, J. (Leicester C), 1920 v E (1)
Paterson, J. (Cowdenbeath), 1931 v A, I, Sw (3)
Paton, A. (Motherwell), 1952 v D, Se (2)
Paton, D. (St Bernards), 1896 v W (1)
Paton, M. (Dumbarton), 1883 v E; 1884 v W; 1885 v W, E; 1886 v E (5)
Paton, R. (Vale of Leven), 1879 v E, W (2)
Patrick, J. (St Mirren), 1897 v E, W (2)
Paul, H. McD. (Queen's Park), 1909 v E, W, Ni (3)
Paul, W. (Partick T), 1888 v W; 1889 v W; 1890 v W (3)
Paul, W. (Dykebar), 1891 v Ni (1)
Pearson, T. (Newcastle U), 1947 v E, Bel (2)
Penman, A. (Dundee), 1966 v Ho (1)
Pettigrew, W. (Motherwell), 1976 v Sw, Ni, W; 1977 v W (sub), Se (5)
Phillips, J. (Queen's Park), 1877 v E, W; 1878 v W (3)
Plenderleith, J. B. (Manchester C), 1961 v Ni (1)
Porteous, W. (Hearts), 1903 v Ni (1)
Pringle, C. (St Mirren), 1921 v W (1)
Provan, D. (Rangers), 1964 v Ni, N; 1966 v I (2), Ho (5)
Provan, D. (Celtic), 1980 v Bel (2 sub), P (sub), Ni (sub); 1981 v Is, W, E; 1982 v Se, P, Ni (10)
Pursell, P. (Queen's Park), 1914 v W (1)

Quinn, J. (Celtic), 1905 v Ni; 1906 v Ni, W; 1908 v Ni, E; 1909 v E; 1910 v E, Ni, W; 1912 v E, W (11)
Quinn, P. (Motherwell), 1961 v E, Ei (2); 1962 v U (4)

Rae, J. (Third Lanark), 1889 v W; 1890 v Ni (2)
Raeside, J. S. (Third Lanark), 1906 v W (1)
Raisbeck, A. G. (Liverpool), 1900 v E; 1901 v E; 1902 v E; 1903 v E, W; 1904 v E; 1906 v E; 1907 v E (8)
Rankin, G. (Vale of Leven), 1890 v Ni; 1891 v E (2)
Rankin, R. (St Mirren), 1929 v N, G, Ho (3)
Redpath, W. (Motherwell), 1949 v W, Ni; 1951 v E, D, F, Bel, A; 1952 v Ni, E (9)
Reid, J. G. (Airdrieonians), 1914 v W; 1920 v W; 1924 v Ni (3)
Reid, R. (Brentford), 1938 v E, Ni (2)
Reid, W. (Rangers), 1911 v E, W, Ni; 1912 v Ni; 1913 v E, W, Ni; 1914 v E, Ni (9)

Reilly, L. (Hibernian), 1949 v E, W, F; 1950 v W, Ni, Sw, F; 1951 v W, E, D, F, Bel, A; 1952 v Ni, W, E, USA, D, Se; 1953 v Ni, W, E, Se; 1954 v W; 1955 v H (2), P, Y, A, E; 1956 v E, W, Ni, A; 1957 v E, Ni, W, Y (38)
Rennie, H. G. (Hearts), 1900 v E, Ni; (with Hibernian), 1901 v E; 1902 v E, Ni, W; 1903 v Ni, W; 1904 v Ni; 1905 v W; 1906 v Ni; 1908 v Ni, W (13)
Renny-Tailyour, H. W. (Royal Engineers), 1873 v E (1)
Rhind, A. (Queen's Park), 1872 v E (1)
Richmond, A. (Queen's Park), 1906 v W (1)
Richmond, J. T. (Clydesdale), 1877 v E; (with Queen's Park), 1878 v E; 1882 v W (3)
Ring, T. (Clyde), 1953 v Se; 1955 v W, Ni, E, H; 1957 v E, Sp (2), Sw, WG; 1958 v Ni, Sw (12)
Rioch, B. D. (Derby Co), 1975 v P, W, Ni, E, R; 1976 v D (2), R, Ni, W, E; 1977 v Fi, Cz, W; (with Everton), W, Ni, E, Ch, Br; 1978 v Cz; (with Derby Co), Ni, E, Pe, Ho (24)
Ritchie, A. (East Stirlingshire), 1891 v W (1)
Ritchie, H. (Hibernian), 1923 v W; 1928 v Ni (2)
Ritchie, J. (Queen's Park), 1897 v W (1)
Ritchie, W. (Rangers), 1962 v U (sub) (1)
Robb, D. T. (Aberdeen), 1971 v W, E, P, D (sub), USSR (5)
Robb, W. (Rangers), 1926 v W; (with Hibernian), 1928 v W (2)
Robertson, A. (Clyde), 1955 v P, A, H; 1958 v Sw, Par (5)
Robertson, G. (Motherwell), 1910 v W; (with Sheffield W), 1912 v W; 1913 v E, Ni (4)
Robertson, G. (Kilmarnock), 1938 v Cz (1)
Robertson, H. (Dundee), 1962 v Cz (1)
Robertson, J. (Dundee), 1931 v A, I (2)
Robertson, J. N. (Nottingham F), 1978 v Ni, W (sub), Ir; 1979 v P, N; 1980 v Pe, A, Bel (2), P; 1981 v Se, P, Is, Ni, Is, Ni, E; 1982 v Se, Ni (2), E (sub), Nz, Br, USSR; 1983 v EG, Sw; (with Derby Co), 1984 v U, Bel (28)
Robertson, J. G. (Tottenham H), 1965 v W (1)
Robertson, J. T. (Everton), 1898 v E; (with Southampton), 1899 v E; (with Rangers), 1900 v E, W; 1901 v W, Ni, E; 1902 v W, Ni, E; 1903 v E, W; 1904 v E, W, Ni; 1905 v W (16)
Robertson, P. (Dundee), 1903 v Ni (1)
Robertson, T. (Queen's Park), 1889 v Ni; 1890 v E; 1891 v W; 1892 v Ni (4)
Robertson, T. (Hearts), 1898 v Ni (1)
Robertson, W. (Dumbarton), 1887 v E, W (2)
Robinson, R. (Dundee), 1974 v WG (sub); 1975 v Se, Ni, R (sub) (4)
Rough, A. (Partick T), 1976 v Sw, Ni, W, E; 1977 v Fi, Cz, W (2), Se, Ni, E, Ch, Arg, Br; 1978 v Cz, W, Ni, E, Pe, Ir, Ho; 1979 v A, P, W, Arg, N; 1980 v Pe, A, Bel (2), P, W, E, Pol, H; 1981 v Se, P, Is, Ni, Is, W, E; 1982 v Se, Ni, Sp, Ho, W, E, Nz, Br, USSR; (with Hibernian), 1986 v W (sub), E (53)
Rougvie, D. (Aberdeen), 1984 v Ni (1)
Rowan, A. (Caledonian), 1880 v E; (with Queen's Park), 1882 v W (2)
Russell, D. (Hearts), 1895 v E, Ni; (with Celtic), 1897 v W; 1898 v Ni; 1901 v W, Ni (6)
Russell, J. (Cambuslang), 1890 v Ni (1)
Russell, W. F. (Airdrieonians), 1924 v W; 1925 v E (2)
Rutherford, E. (Rangers), 1948 v F (1)

St John, I. (Motherwell), 1959 v WG; 1960 v E, Ni, W, Pol, A; 1961 v E; (with Liverpool), 1962 v Ni, W, E, Cz (2), U; 1963 v W, Ni, E, N, Ei (sub), Sp; 1964 v Ni; 1965 v E (21)
Sawers, W. (Dundee), 1895 v W (1)
Scarff, P. (Celtic), 1931 v Ni (1)
Schaedler, E. (Hibernian), 1974 v WG (1)
Scott, A. S. (Rangers), 1957 v Ni, Y, WG; 1958 v W, Sw; 1959 v P; 1962 v Ni, W, E, Cz, U; (with Everton), 1964 v W, N; 1965 v Fi; 1966 v P, Br (16)
Scott, J. (Hibernian), 1966 v Ho (1)
Scott, J. (Dundee), 1971 v D (sub), USSR (2)
Scott, M. (Airdrieonians), 1898 v W (1)
Scott, R. (Airdrieonians), 1894 v Ni (1)
Scoular, J. (Portsmouth), 1951 v D, F, A; 1952 v E, USA, D, Se; 1953 v W, Ni (9)
Sellar, W. (Battlefield), 1885 v E; 1886 v E; 1887 v E, W; 1888 v E; (with Queen's Park), 1891 v E; 1892 v E; 1893 v E, Ni (9)
Semple, W. (Cambuslang), 1886 v W (1)
Shankly, W. (Preston NE), 1938 v E; 1939 v E, W, Ni, H (5)
Sharp, G. M. (Everton), 1985 v Ic; 1986 v W, Aus (sub + sub), Is, R, U; 1987 v Ei; 1988 v Bel (sub), Bul, L, Ma (12)
Sharp, J. (Dundee), 1904 v W; (with Woolwich Arsenal), 1907 v W, E; 1908 v E; (with Fulham), 1909 v W (5)
Shaw, D. (Hibernian), 1947 v W, Ni; 1948 v E, Bel, Sw, F; 1949 v W, Ni (8)
Shaw, F. W. (Pollokshields Ath), 1884 v E, W (2)
Shaw, J. (Rangers), 1947 v E, Bel, L; 1948 v Ni (4)
Shearer, R. (Rangers), 1961 v E, Ei (2), Cz (4)
Sillars, D. C. (Queen's Park), 1891 v Ni; 1892 v E; 1893 v W; 1894 v E; 1895 v W (5)
Simpson, J. (Third Lanark), 1895 v E, W, Ni (3)
Simpson, J. (Rangers), 1935 v E, W, Ni; 1936 v E, W, Ni; 1937 v G, E, W, Ni, A, Cz; 1938 v W, Ni (14)
Simpson, N. (Aberdeen), 1983 v Ni; 1984 v F (sub); 1987 v E; 1988 v E (4)
Simpson, R. C. (Celtic), 1967 v E, USSR; 1968 v Ni, E; 1969 v A (5)
Sinclair, G. L. (Hearts), 1910 v Ni; 1912 v W, Ni (3)
Sinclair, J. W. E. (Leicester C), 1966 v P (1)
Skene, L. H. (Queen's Park), 1904 v W (1)
Sloan, T. (Third Lanark), 1904 v W (1)
Smellie, R. (Queen's Park), 1887 v Ni; 1888 v W; 1889 v E; 1891 v E; 1893 v E, Ni (6)
Smith, A. (Rangers), 1898 v E; 1900 v E, Ni, W; 1901 v E, Ni, W; 1902 v E, Ni, W; 1903 v E, Ni, W; 1904 v Ni; 1905 v W; 1906 v E, Ni; 1907 v W; 1911 v E, Ni (20)
Smith, D. (Aberdeen), 1966 v Ho; (with Rangers), 1968 v Ho (2)
Smith, G. (Hibernian), 1947 v E, Ni; 1948 v W, Bel, Sw, F; 1952 v E, USA; 1955 v P, Y, A, H; 1956 v E, Ni, W; 1957 v Sp (2), Sw (18)
Smith, H. G. (Hearts), 1988 v S.Ar (sub) (1)
Smith, J. (Rangers), 1935 v Ni; 1938 v Ni (2)
Smith, J. (Ayr U), 1924 v E (1)
Smith, J. (Aberdeen), 1968 v Ho (sub); (with Newcastle U), 1974 v WG, Ni (sub), W (sub) (4)
Smith, J. E. (Celtic), 1959 v H, P (2)
Smith, Jas. (Queen's Park), 1872 v E (1)
Smith, John. (Mauchline), 1877 v E, W; 1879 v E, W; (with Edinburgh University), 1880 v E; (with Queen's Park), 1881 v W, E; 1883 v E, W; 1884 v E (10)
Smith, N. (Rangers), 1897 v E; 1898 v W; 1899 v E, W, Ni; 1900 v E, W, Ni; 1901 v Ni, W; 1902 v E, Ni (12)
Smith, R. (Queen's Park), 1872 v E; 1873 v E (2)
Smith, T. M. (Kilmarnock), 1934 v E; (with Preston NE), 1938 v E (2)
Somers, P. (Celtic), 1905 v E, Ni; 1907 v Ni; 1909 v W (4)
Somers, W. S. (Third Lanark), 1879 v E, W; (with Queen's Park), 1880 v W (3)
Somerville, G. (Queen's Park), 1886 v E (1)
Souness, G. J. (Middlesbrough), 1975 v EG, Sp, Se; (with Liverpool), 1978 v Bul, W, E (sub), Ho; 1979 v A, N, W, Ni, E; 1980 v Pe, A, Bel, P, Ni; 1981 v P, Is (2); 1982 v Ni, P, Sp, W, E, Nz, Br, USSR; 1983 v EG, Sw, Bel, Sw, W, E, Ca (2 + 1 sub); 1984 v U, Ni, W; (with Sampdoria), 1985 v Y, Ic, Sp (2), W, E, Ic; 1986 v EG, Aus (2), R, E, D, WG (54)
Speedie, D. R. (Chelsea), 1985 v E; 1986 v W, EG (sub),

Aus, E; (with Coventry), 1989 v Y (sub), I (sub), Cy, Cy (sub), Ch (10)
Speedie, F. (Rangers), 1903 v E, W, Ni (3)
Speirs, J. H. (Rangers), 1908 v W (1)
Stanton, P. (Hibernian), 1966 v Ho; 1969 v Ni; 1970 v Ei, A; 1971 v D, Bel, P, USSR, D; 1972 v P, Bel, Ho, W; 1973 v W, Ni; 1974 v WG (16)
Stark, J. (Rangers), 1909 v E, Ni (2)
Steel, W. (Morton), 1947 v E, Bel, L; (with Derby Co), 1948 v F, E, W, Ni; 1949 v E, W, Ni, F; 1950 v E, W, Ni, Sw, P, F; (with Dundee), 1951 v W, Ni, E, A (2), D, F, Bel; 1952 v W; 1953 v W, E, Ni, Se (30)
Steele, D. M. (Huddersfield), 1923 v E, W, Ni (3)
Stein, C. (Rangers), 1969 v W, Ni, D, E, Cy (2); 1970 v A (sub), Ni (sub), W, E, Ei, WG; 1971 v D, USSR, Bel, D; 1972 v Cz (sub); (with Coventry C), 1973 v E (2 sub), W (sub), Ni (21)
Stephen, J. F. (Bradford), 1947 v W; 1948 v W (2)
Stevenson, G. (Motherwell), 1928 v W, Ni; 1930 v Ni, E, F; 1931 v E, W; 1932 v W, Ni; 1933 v Ni; 1934 v E; 1935 v Ni (12)
Stewart, A. (Queen's Park), 1888 v Ni; 1889 v W (2)
Stewart, A. (Third Lanark), 1894 v W (1)
Stewart, D. (Dumbarton), 1888 v Ni (1)
Stewart, D. (Queen's Park), 1893 v W; 1894 v Ni; 1897 v Ni (3)
Stewart, D. S. (Leeds U), 1978 v EG (1)
Stewart, G. (Hibernian), 1906 v W, E; (with Manchester C), 1907 v E, W (4)
Stewart, J. (Kilmarnock), 1977 v Ch (sub); (with Middlesbrough), 1979 v N (2)
Stewart, R. (West Ham U), 1981 v W, Ni, E; 1982 v Ni, P, W; 1984 v F; 1987 v Ei (2), L (10)
Stewart, W. E. (Queen's Park), 1898 v Ni; 1900 v Ni (2)
Storrier, D. (Celtic), 1899 v E, W, Ni (3)
Strachan, G. (Aberdeen), 1980 v Ni, W, E, Pol, H (sub); 1981 v Se, P; 1982 v Ni, P, Sp, Ho (sub), Nz, Br, USSR; 1983 v EG, Sw, Bel, Sw, Ni (sub), W, E, Ca (2+1 sub); 1984 v EG, Ni, E, F; (with Manchester U), 1985 v Sp (sub), E, Ic; 1986 v W, Aus, R, D, WG, U; 1987 v Bul, Ei (2); 1988 v H; 1989 v F (sub) (42)
Sturrock, P. (Dundee U), 1981 v W (sub), Ni, E (sub); 1982 v P, Ni (sub), W (sub), E (sub); 1983 v EG (sub), Sw, Bel (sub), Ca (3); 1984 v W; 1985 v Y (sub); 1986 v Is (sub), Ho, D, U; 1987 v Bel (20)
Summers, W. (St Mirren), 1926 v E (1)
Symon, J. S. (Rangers), 1939 v H (1)

Tait, T. S. (Sunderland), 1911 v W (1)
Taylor, J. (Queen's Park), 1872 v E; 1873 v E; 1874 v E; 1875 v E; 1876 v E, W (6)
Taylor, J. D. (Dumbarton), 1892 v W; 1893 v W; 1894 v Ni; (with St Mirren), 1895 v Ni (4)
Taylor, W. (Hearts), 1892 v E (1)
Telfer, W. (Motherwell), 1933 v Ni; 1934 v Ni (2)
Telfer, W. D. (St Mirren), 1954 v W (1)
Templeton, R. (Aston Villa), 1902 v E; (with Newcastle U), 1903 v E, W; 1904 v E; (with Woolwich Arsenal), 1905 v W; (with Kilmarnock), 1908 v Ni; 1910 v E, Ni; 1912 v E, Ni; 1913 v W (11)
Thomson, A. (Arthurlie), 1886 v Ni (1)
Thomson, A. (Airdrieonians), 1909 v Ni (1)
Thomson, A. (Celtic), 1926 v E; 1932 v F; 1933 v W (3)
Thomson, A. (Third Lanark), 1889 v W (1)
Thomson, C. (Hearts), 1904 v Ni; 1905 v E, Ni, W; 1906 v W, Ni; 1907 v E, W, Ni; 1908 v E, W, Ni; (with Sunderland), 1909 v W; 1910 v E; 1911 v Ni; 1912 v E, W; 1913 v E, W; 1914 v E, Ni (21)
Thomson, C. (Sunderland), 1937 v Cz (1)
Thomson, D. (Dundee), 1920 v W (1)
Thomson, J. (Celtic), 1930 v F; 1931 v E, W, Ni (4)
Thomson, J. J. (Queen's Park), 1872 v E; 1873 v E; 1874 v E (3)
Thomson, J. R. (Everton), 1933 v W (1)
Thomson, R. (Celtic), 1932 v W (1)
Thomson, R. W. (Falkirk), 1927 v E (1)
Thomson, S. (Rangers), 1884 v W, Ni (2)
Thomson, W. (Dumbarton), 1892 v W; 1893 v W; 1898 v Ni, W (4)
Thomson, W. (Dundee), 1896 v W (1)
Thornton, W. (Rangers), 1947 v W, Ni; 1948 v E, Ni; 1949 v F; 1952 v D, Se (7)
Thomson, W. (St Mirren), 1980 v Ni; 1981 v Ni (sub), Ni; 1982 v P; 1983 v Ni, Ca; 1984 v EG (7)
Toner, W. (Kilmarnock), 1959 v W, Ni (2)
Townsley, T. (Falkirk), 1926 v W (1)
Troup, A. (Dundee), 1920 v E; 1921 v W, Ni; 1922 v Ni; (with Everton), 1926 v E (5)
Turnbull, E. (Hibernian), 1948 v Bel, Sw; 1951 v A; 1958 v H, Pol, Y, Par, F (8)
Turner, T. (Arthurlie), 1884 v W (1)
Turner, W. (Pollokshields), 1885 v Ni; 1886 v Ni (2)

Ure, J. F. (Dundee), 1962 v W, Cz; 1963 v W, Ni, E, A, N, Sp; (with Arsenal), 1964 v Ni, N; 1968 v Ni (11)
Urquhart, D. (Hibernian), 1934 v W (1)

Vallance, T. (Rangers), 1877 v E, W; 1878 v E; 1879 v E, W; 1881 v E, W (7)
Venters, A. (Cowdenbeath), 1934 v Ni; (with Rangers), 1936 v E; 1939 v E (3)

Waddell, T. S. (Queen's Park), 1891 v Ni; 1892 v E; 1893 v E, Ni; 1895 v E, Ni (6)
Waddell, W. (Rangers), 1947 v W; 1949 v E, W, Ni, F; 1950 v E, Ni; 1951 v E, D, F, Bel, A; 1952 v Ni, W; 1954 v Ni; 1955 v W, Ni (17)
Wales, H. M. (Motherwell), 1933 v W (1)
Walker, A. (Celtic), 1988 v Co (sub) (1)
Walker, F. (Third Lanark), 1922 v W (1)
Walker, G. (St Mirren), 1930 v F; 1931 v Ni, A, Sw (4)
Walker, J. (Hearts), 1895 v Ni; 1897 v W; 1898 v Ni; (with Rangers), 1904 v W, Ni (5)
Walker, J. (Swindon T), 1911 v E, W, Ni; 1912 v E, W, Ni; 1913 v E, W, Ni (9)
Walker, R. (Hearts), 1900 v E, Ni; 1901 v E, W; 1902 v E, W, Ni; 1903 v E, W, Ni; 1904 v E, W, Ni; 1905 v E, W, Ni; 1906 v Ni; 1907 v E, Ni; 1908 v E, W, Ni; 1909 v E, W; 1912 v E, W, Ni; 1913 v E, W (29)
Walker, T. (Hearts), 1935 v E, W; 1936 v E, W, Ni; 1937 v G, E, W, Ni, A, Cz; 1938 v E, W, Ni, Cz, Ho; 1939 v E, W, Ni, H (20)
Walker, W. (Clyde), 1909 v Ni; 1910 v Ni (2)
Wallace, I. A. (Coventry C), 1978 v Bul (sub); 1979 v P (sub), W (3)
Wallace, W. S. B. (Hearts), 1965 v Ni; 1966 v E, Ho; (with Celtic), 1967 v E, USSR (sub); 1968 v Ni; 1969 v E (sub) (7)
Wardhaugh, J. (Hearts), 1955 v H; 1957 v Ni (2)
Wark, J. (Ipswich T), 1979 v W, Ni, E, Arg, N (sub); 1980 v Pe, A, Bel (2); 1981 v Is, Ni; 1982 v Se, Sp, Ho, Ni, Nz, Br, USSR; 1983 v EG, Sw, Sw, Ni, E (sub); 1984 v U, Bel, EG; (with Liverpool), E, F; 1985 v Y (29)
Watson, A. (Queen's Park), 1881 v E, W; 1882 v E (3)
Watson, J. (Sunderland), 1903 v E, W; 1904 v E; 1905 v E; (with Middlesbrough), 1909 v E, Ni (6)
Watson, J. (Motherwell), 1948 v Ni; (with Huddersfield T), 1954 v Ni (2)
Watson, J. A. K. (Rangers), 1878 v W (1)
Watson, P. R. (Blackpool), 1934 v A (1)
Watson, R. (Motherwell), 1971 v USSR (1)
Watson, W. (Falkirk), 1898 v W (1)
Watt, F. (Kilbirnie), 1889 v W, Ni; 1890 v W; 1891 v E (4)
Watt, W. W. (Queen's Park), 1887 v Ni (1)
Waugh, W. (Hearts), 1938 v Cz (1)
Weir, A. (Motherwell), 1959 v WG; 1960 v E, P, A, H, T (6)

Weir, J. (Third Lanark), 1887 v Ni (1)
Weir, J. B. (Queen's Park), 1872 v E; 1874 v E; 1875 v E; 1878 v W (4)
Weir, P. (St Mirren), 1980 v N (sub), W, Pol (sub), H; (with Aberdeen), 1983 v Sw; 1984 v Ni (6)
White, John (Albion R), 1922 v W; (with Hearts), 1923 v Ni (2)
White, J. A. (Falkirk), 1959 v WG, Ho, P; 1960 v Ni; (with Tottenham H), 1960 v W, Pol, A, T; 1961 v W; 1962 v Ni, W, E, Cz (2); 1963 v W, Ni, E; 1964 v Ni, W, E, N, WG (22)
White, W. (Bolton W), 1907 v E; 1908 v E (2)
Whitelaw, A. (Vale of Leven), 1887 v Ni; 1890 v W (2)
Whyte, D. (Celtic), 1988 v Bel (sub), L; 1989 v Ch (sub) (3)
Wilson, A. (Sheffield W), 1907 v E; 1908 v E; 1912 v E; 1913 v E, W; 1914 v Ni (6)
Wilson, A. (Portsmouth), 1954 v Fi (1)
Wilson, A. N. (Dunfermline), 1920 v E, W, Ni; 1921 v E, W, Ni; (with Middlesbrough), 1922 v E, W, Ni; 1923 v E, W, Ni (12)
Wilson, D. (Queen's Park), 1900 v W (1)
Wilson, D. (Oldham Ath), 1913 v E (1)
Wilson, D. (Rangers), 1961 v E, W, Ni, Ei (2), Cz; 1962 v Ni, W, E, Cz, U; 1963 v W, E, A, N, Ei, Sp; 1964 v E, WG; 1965 v Ni, E, Fi (22)
Wilson, G. W. (Hearts), 1904 v W; 1905 v E, Ni; 1906 v W; (with Everton), 1907 v E; (with Newcastle U), 1909 v E (6)
Wilson, Hugh, (Newmilns), 1890 v W; (with Sunderland), 1897 v E; (with Third Lanark), 1902 v W; 1904 v Ni (4)
Wilson, I. A. (Leicester C), 1987 v E, Br; (with Everton), 1988 v Bel, Bul, L (5)
Wilson, J. (Vale of Leven), 1888 v W; 1889 v E; 1890 v E; 1891 v E (4)
Wilson, P. (Celtic), 1926 v Ni; 1930 v F; 1931 v Ni; 1933 v E (4)
Wilson, P. (Celtic), 1975 v Sp (sub) (1)
Wilson, R. P. (Arsenal), 1972 v P, Ho (2)
Wiseman, W. (Queen's Park), 1927 v W; 1930 v Ni (2)
Wood, G. (Everton), 1979 v Ni, E, Arg (sub); (with Arsenal), 1982 v Ni (4)
Woodburn, W. A. (Rangers), 1947 v E, Bel, L; 1948 v W, Ni; 1949 v E, F; 1950 v E, W, Ni, P, F; 1951 v E, W, Ni, A (2), D, F, Bel; 1952 v E, W, Ni, USA (24)
Wotherspoon, D. N. (Queen's Park), 1872 v E; 1873 v E (2)
Wright, T. (Sunderland), 1953 v W, Ni, E (3)
Wylie, T. G. (Rangers), 1890 v Ni (1)

Yeats, R. (Liverpool), 1965 v W; 1966 v I (2)
Yorston, B. C. (Aberdeen), 1931 v Ni (1)
Yorston, H. (Aberdeen), 1955 v W (1)
Young, A. (Hearts), 1960 v E, A (sub), H, T; 1961 v W, Ni; (with Everton), Ei; 1966 v P (8)
Young, A. (Everton), 1905 v E; 1907 v W (2)
Young, G. L. (Rangers), 1947 v E, Ni, Bel, L; 1948 v E, Ni, Bel, Sw, F; 1949 v E, W, Ni, F; 1950 v E, W, Ni, Sw, P, F; 1951 v E, W, Ni, A (2), D, F, Bel; 1952 v E, W, Ni, USA, D, Se; 1953 v W, E, Ni, Se; 1954 v Ni, W; 1955 v W, Ni, P, Y; 1956 v Ni, W, E, A; 1957 v E, Ni, W, Y, Sp, Sw (53)
Young, J. (Celtic), 1906 v Ni (1)
Younger, T. (Hibernian), 1955 v P, Y, A, H; 1956 v E, Ni, W, A; (with Liverpool), 1957 v E, Ni, W, Y, Sp (2), Sw, WG; 1958 v Ni, W, E, Sw, H, Pol, Y, Par (24)

WALES

Adams, H. (Berwyn R), 1882 v Ni, E; (with Druids), 1883 v Ni, E (4)
Aizlewood, M. (Charlton Ath), 1986 v S.Ar, Ca (2); 1987 v Fi (with Leeds U), USSR, Fi (sub); 1988 v D (sub), Se, Ma, I; 1989 v Ho, Se (sub), WG (13)
Allchurch, I. J. (Swansea T), 1951 v E, Ni, P, Sw; 1952 v E, S, Ni, R of UK; 1953 v S, E, Ni, F, Y; 1954 v S, E, Ni, A; 1955 v S, E, Ni, Y; 1956 v E, S, Ni, A; 1957 v E, S; 1958 v Ni, Is (2), H (2), M, Sw, Br; (with Newcastle U), 1959 v E, S, Ni; 1960 v E, S; 1961 v Ni, H, Sp (2); 1962 v E, S, Br (2), M; (with Cardiff C), 1963 v S, E, Ni, H (2); 1964 v E; 1965 v S, E, Ni, Gr, I, USSR; 1966 (with Swansea T), v USSR, E, S, D, Br (2), Ch (68)
Allchurch, L. (Swansea T), 1955 v Ni; 1956 v A; 1958 v S, Ni, EG, Is; 1959 v S; (with Sheffield U), 1962 v S, Ni, Br; 1964 v E (11)
Allen, B. W. (Coventry C), 1951 v S, E (2)
Allen, M. (Watford), 1986 v S.Ar (sub), Ca (1 + sub) (with Norwich C);1989 v Is (sub) (4)
Arridge, S. (Bootle), 1892 v S, Ni; (with Everton), 1894 v Ni; 1895 v Ni; 1896 v E; (with New Brighton Tower), 1898 v E, Ni; 1899 v E (8)
Astley, D. J. (Charlton Ath), 1931 v Ni; (with Aston Villa), 1932 v E; 1933 v E, S, Ni; 1934 v E, S; 1935 v S; 1936 v E, Ni; (with Derby Co), 1939 v E, S; (with Blackpool), F (13)
Atherton, R. W. (Hibernian), 1899 v E, Ni; 1903 v E, S, Ni; (with Middlesbrough), 1904 v E, S, Ni; 1905 v Ni (9)

Bailiff, W. E. (Llanelly), 1913 v E, S, Ni; 1920 v Ni (4)
Baker, C. W. (Cardiff C), 1958 v M; 1960 v S, Ni; 1961 v S, E, Ei; 1962 v S (7)
Baker, W. G. (Cardiff C), 1948 v Ni (1)
Bamford, T. (Wrexham), 1931 v E, S, Ni; 1932 v Ni; 1933 v F (5)
Barnes, W. (Arsenal), 1948 v E, S, Ni; 1949 v E, S, Ni; 1950 v E, S, Ni, Bel; 1951 v E, S, Ni, P; 1952 v E, S, Ni, R of UK; 1954 v E, S; 1955 v S, Y (22)
Bartley, T. (Glossop NE), 1898 v E (1)
Beadles, G. H. (Cardiff C), 1925 v E, S (2)
Bell, W. S. (Shrewsbury Engineers), 1881 v E, S; (with Crewe Alex), 1886 v E, S, Ni (5)
Bennion, S. R. (Manchester U), 1926 v S; 1927 v S; 1928 v S, E, Ni; 1929 v S, E, Ni; 1930 v S; 1932 v Ni (10)
Berry, G. F. (Wolverhampton W), 1979 v WG; 1980 v Ei, WG (sub), T; (with Stoke C), 1983 v E (sub) (5)
Blackmore, C. G. (Manchester U), 1985 v N (sub); 1986 v S (sub), H (sub), S.Ar, Ei, U; 1987 v Fi (2), USSR, Cz; 1988 v D (2), Cz, Y, Se, Ma, I; 1989 v Ho, Fi, Is, WG (21)
Blew, H. (Wrexham), 1899 v E, S, Ni; 1902 v S, Ni; 1903 v E, S; 1904 v E, S, Ni; 1905 v S, Ni; 1906 v E, S, Ni; 1907 v S; 1908 v E, S, Ni; 1909 v E, S; 1910 v E (22)
Boden, T. (Wrexham), 1880 v E (1)
Bostock, A. M. (Shrewsbury), 1892 v Ni (1)
Boulter, L. M. (Brentford), 1939 v Ni (1)
Bowdler, H. E. (Shrewsbury), 1893 v S (1)
Bowdler, J. C. H. (Shrewsbury), 1890 v Ni; (with Wolverhampton W), 1891 v S; 1892 v Ni; (with Shrewsbury), 1894 v E (4)
Bowen, D. L. (Arsenal), 1955 v S, Y; 1957 v Ni, Cz, EG; 1958 v E, S, Ni, EG, Is (2), H (2), M, Se, Br; 1959 v E, S, Ni (19)
Bowen, E. (Druids), 1880 v S; 1883 v S (2)
Bowen, M. R. (Tottenham H), 1986 v Ca (sub + sub); (with Norwich C), 1988 v Y (sub); 1989 v Fi (sub), Is,

Se, WG (sub) (7)
Bowsher, S. J. (Burnley), 1929 v Ni (1)
Boyle, T. (C Palace), 1981 v Ei, S (sub) (2)
Britten, T. J. (Parkgrove), 1878 v S; (with Presteigne), 1880 v S (2)
Brookes, S. J. (Llandudno), 1900 v E, Ni (2)
Brown, A. I. (Aberdare Ath), 1926 v Ni (1)
Bryan, T. (Oswestry), 1886 v E, Ni (2)
Buckland, T. (Bangor), 1899 v E (1)
Burgess, W. A. R. (Tottenham H), 1947 v E, S, Ni; 1948 v E, S; 1949 v E, S, Ni, P, Bel, Sw; 1950 v E, S, Ni, Bel; 1951 v S, Ni, P, Sw; 1952 v E, S, Ni, R of UK; 1953 v S, E, Ni, F, Y; 1954 v S, E, Ni, A (32)
Burke, T. (Wrexham), 1883 v E; 1884 v S; 1885 v E, S, Ni; (with Newton Heath), 1887 v E, S; 1888 v S (8)
Burnett, T. B. (Ruabon), 1877 v S (1)
Burton, A. D. (Norwich C), 1963 v Ni, H; (with Newcastle U), 1964 v E; 1969 v S, E, Ni, I, EG; 1972 v Cz (9)
Butler, A. (Druids), 1900 v S, Ni (2)
Butler, J. (Chirk), 1893 v E, S, Ni (3)

Cartwright, L. (Coventry C), 1974 v E (sub), S, Ni; 1976 v S (sub); 1977 v WG (sub); (with Wrexham), 1978 v Ir (sub); 1979 v Ma (7)
Carty, T. (Wrexham), 1889 v Ni (1)
Challen, J. B. (Corinthians), 1887 v E, S; 1888 v E; (with Wellingborough GS), 1890 v E (4)
Chapman, T. (Newtown), 1894 v E, S, Ni; 1895 v S, Ni; (with Manchester C), 1896 v E; 1897 v E (7)
Charles, J. M. (Swansea C), 1981 v Cz, T (sub), S (sub), USSR (sub); 1982 v Ic; 1983 v N (sub), Y (sub), Bul (sub), S, Ni, Br; 1984 v Bul (sub), (with QPR), Y (sub), S; (with Oxford U), 1985 v Ic (sub), Sp, Ic; 1986 v Ei; 1987 v Fi (19)
Charles, M. (Swansea T), 1955 v Ni; 1956 v E, S, A; 1957 v E, Ni, Cz (2), EG; 1958 v E, S, EG, Is (2), H (2), M, Se, Br; 1959 v E, S; (with Arsenal), 1961 v Ni, H, Sp (2); 1962 v E, S; (with Cardiff C), 1962 v Br, Ni; 1963 v S, H (31)
Charles, W. J. (Leeds U), 1950 v Ni; 1951 v Sw; 1953 v Ni, F, Y; 1954 v E, S, Ni, A; 1955 v S, E, Ni, Y; 1956 v E, S, A, Ni; 1957 v E, S, Ni, Cz (2), EG; (with Juventus), 1958 v Is (2), H (2) M, Se; 1960 v S; 1962 v E, Br (2), M; (with Leeds U), 1963 v S; (with Cardiff C), 1964 v S; 1965 v S, USSR (38)
Clarke, R. J. (Manchester C), 1949 v E; 1950 v S, Ni, Bel; 1951 v E, S, Ni, P, Sw; 1952 v S, E, Ni, R of UK; 1953 v S, E; 1954 v E, S, Ni; 1955 v Y, S, E; 1956 v Ni (22)
Collier, D. J. (Grimsby T), 1921 v S (1)
Collins, W. S. (Llanelly), 1931 v S (1)
Conde, C. (Chirk), 1884 v E, S, Ni (3)
Cook, F. C. (Newport Co), 1925 v E, S; (with Portsmouth), 1928 v E, S; 1930 v E, S, Ni; 1932 v E (8)
Crompton, W. (Wrexham), 1931 v E, S, Ni (3)
Cross, E. A. (Wrexham), 1876 v S; 1877 v S (2)
Cross, K. (Druids), 1879 v S; 1881 v E, S (3)
Crowe, V. H. (Aston Villa), 1959 v E, Ni; 1960 v E, Ni; 1961 v S, E, Ni, Ei, H, Sp (2); 1962 v E, S, Br, M; 1963 v H (16)
Cumner, R. H. (Arsenal), 1939 v E, S, Ni (3)
Curtis, A. (Swansea C), 1976 v E, Y (sub), S, Ni, Y (sub), E; 1977 v WG, S (sub), Ni (sub); 1978 v WG, E, S; 1979 v WG, S; (with Leeds U), E, Ni, Ma; 1980 v Ei, WG, T; (with Swansea C), 1982 v Cz, Ic, USSR, Sp, E, S, Ni; 1983 v N; 1984 v R (sub), (with Southampton), S; 1985 v Sp, N (1 + 1 sub); 1986 v H; 1987 (with Cardiff C) v USSR (35)
Curtis, E. R. (Cardiff C), 1928 v S; (with Birmingham), 1932 v S; 1934 v Ni (3)

Daniel, R. W. (Arsenal), 1951 v E, Ni, P; 1952 v E, S, Ni, R of UK; 1953 v S, E, Ni, F, Y; (with Sunderland), 1954 v E, S, Ni; 1955 v E, Ni; 1957 v S, E, Ni, Cz (21)
Darvell, S. (Oxford University), 1897 v S, Ni (2)
Davies, A. (Manchester U), 1983 v Ni, Br; 1984 v E, Ni; 1985 v Ic; (with Newcastle U), 1986 v H; (with Swansea C), 1988 v Ma, I; 1989 v Ho (9)
Davies, A. (Wrexham), 1876 v S; 1877 v S (2)
Davies, A. (Shrewsbury), 1891 v Ni (1)
Davies, A. (Druids), 1904 v S; (with Middlesbrough), 1905 v S (2)
Davies, A. O. (Barmouth), 1885 v Ni; 1886 v E, S; (with Swifts), 1887 v E, S; 1888 v E, Ni; (with Wrexham), 1889 v S; (with Crewe Alex), 1890 v E (9)
Davies, C. (Brecon), 1899 v Ni; (with Hereford), 1900 v Ni (2)
Davies, C. (Charlton Ath), 1972 v R (sub) (1)
Davies, D. (Bolton W), 1904 v S, Ni; 1908 v E (sub) (3)
Davies, D. W. (Treharris), 1912 v Ni; (with Oldham Ath), 1913 v Ni (2)
Davies, E. Lloyd, (Stoke C), 1904 v E; 1907 v E, S, Ni; (with Northampton T), 1908 v S; 1909 v Ni; 1910 v Ni; 1911 v E, S; 1912 v E, S; 1913 v E, S; 1914 v Ni, E, S (16)
Davies, E. R. (Newcastle U), 1953 v S, E; 1954 v E, S; 1958 v E, EG (6)
Davies, G. (Fulham), 1980 v T, Ic; 1982 v Sp (sub), F (sub); 1983 v E, Bul, S, Ni, Br; 1984 v R (sub), S (sub), E, Ni; 1985 v Ic (2) (with Chelsea), N; (with Manchester C), 1986 v S.Ar, Ei (18)
Davies, Rev. H. (Wrexham), 1928 v Ni (1)
Davies, Idwal (Liverpool Marine), 1923 v S (1)
Davies, J. E. (Oswestry), 1885 v E (1)
Davies, Jas. (Wrexham), 1878 v S (1)
Davies, John. (Wrexham), 1879 v S (1)
Davies, Jos. (Everton), 1889 v S, Ni; (with Chirk), 1891 v Ni; (with Ardwick), v E, S; (with Sheffield U), 1895 v E, S, Ni; (with Manchester C), 1896 v E; (with Millwall), 1897 v E; (with Reading), 1900 v E (11)
Davies, Jos. (Newton Heath), 1888 v E, S, Ni; 1889 v S; 1890 v E; (with Wolverhampton W), 1892 v E; 1893 v E (7)
Davies, J. P. (Druids), 1883 v E, Ni (2)
Davies, Ll. (Wrexham), 1907 v Ni; 1910 v Ni, S, E; (with Everton), 1911 v S, Ni; 1912 v Ni, S, E; 1913 v Ni, S, E; 1914 v Ni (13)
Davies, L. S. (Cardiff C), 1922 v E, S, Ni; 1923 v E, S, Ni; 1924 v E, S, Ni; 1925 v S, Ni; 1926 v E, Ni; 1927 v E, Ni; 1928 v S, Ni, E; 1929 v S, Ni, E; 1930 v E, S (23)
Davies, O. (Wrexham), 1890 v S (1)
Davies, R. (Wrexham), 1883 v Ni; 1884 v Ni; 1885 v Ni (3)
Davies, R. (Druids), 1885 v E (1)
Davies, R. O. (Wrexham), 1892 v Ni, E (2)
Davies, R. T. (Norwich C), 1964 v Ni; 1965 v E; 1966 v Br (2), Ch; (with Southampton), 1967 v S, E, Ni; 1968 v S, Ni, WG; 1969 v S, E, Ni, I, WG, R of UK; 1970 v E, S, Ni; 1971 v Cz, S, E, Ni; 1972 v R, E, S, N; (with Portsmouth), 1974 v E (29)
Davies, R. W. (Bolton W), 1964 v E; 1965 v E, S, Ni, D, Gr, USSR; 1966 v E, S, Ni, USSR, D, Br (2), Ch (sub); 1967 v S; (with Newcastle U), E; 1968 v S, Ni, WG; 1969 v S, E, Ni, I; 1970 v EG; 1971 v R, Cz; (with Manchester C), 1972 v E, S, Ni; (with Manchester U), 1973 v E, S (sub), Ni; (with Blackpool), 1974 v Pol (34)
Davies, Stanley (Preston NE), 1920 v E, S, Ni; (with Everton), 1921 v E, S, Ni; (with WBA), 1922 v E, S, Ni; 1923 v S; 1925 v S, Ni; 1926 v S, E, Ni; 1927 v S; 1928 v S; (with Rotherham U), 1930 v Ni (18)
Davies, T. (Oswestry), 1886 v E (1)
Davies, T. (Druids), 1903 v E, Ni, S; 1904 v S (4)
Davies, W. (Swansea T), 1924 v E, S, Ni; (with Cardiff C), 1925 v E, S, Ni; 1926 v E, S, Ni; 1927 v S; 1928 v Ni; (with Notts Co), 1929 v E, S, Ni; 1930 v E, S, Ni (17)
Davies, W. (Wrexham), 1884 v Ni (1)
Davies, William (Wrexham), 1903 v Ni; 1905 v Ni; (with

Blackburn R), 1908 v E, S; 1909 v E, S, Ni; 1911 v E, S, Ni; 1912 v Ni (11)

Davies, W. C. (C Palace), 1908 v S; (with WBA), 1909 v E; 1910 v S; (with C Palace), 1914 v E (4)

Davies, W. D. (Everton), 1975 v H, L, S, E, Ni; 1976 v Y (2), E, Ni; 1977 v WG, S (2), Cz, E, Ni; 1978 v K; (with Wrexham), S, Cz, WG, Ir, E, S, Ni; 1979 v Ma, T, WG S, E, Ni, Ma; 1980 v Ei, WG, T, E, S, Ni, Ic; 1981 v T, Cz, Ei, T, S, E, USSR; (with Swansea C), 1982 v Cz, Ic, USSR, Sp, E, S, F; 1983 v Y (52)

Davies, W. H. (Oswestry), 1876 v S; 1877 v S; 1879 v E; 1880 v E (4)

Davies, W. O. (Millwall Ath), 1913 v E, S, Ni; 1914 v S, Ni (5)

Davis, G. (Wrexham), 1978 v Ir, E (sub), Ni (3)

Day, A. (Tottenham H), 1934 v Ni (1)

Deacy, N. (PSV Eindhoven), 1977 v Cz, S, E, Ni; 1978 v K (sub), S (sub), Cz (sub), WG, Ir, S (sub), Ni; (with Beringen), 1979 v T (12)

Dearson, D. J. (Birmingham), 1939 v S, Ni, F (3)

Derrett, S. C. (Cardiff C), 1969 v S, WG; 1970 v I; 1971 v Fi (4)

Dewey, F. T. (Cardiff Corinthians), 1931 v E, S (2)

Dibble, A. (Luton T), 1986 v Ca (1 + sub); (with Manchester C) 1989 v Is (3)

Doughty, J. (Druids), 1886 v S; (with Newton Heath), 1887 v S, Ni; 1888 v E, S, Ni; 1889 v S; 1890 v E (8)

Doughty, R. (Newton Heath and Druids), 1888 v S, Ni; 1890 v E (3)

Durban, A. (Derby Co), 1966 v Br (sub); 1967 v Ni; 1968 v E, S, Ni, WG; 1969 v EG, S, E, Ni, WG; 1970 v E, S, Ni, EG, I; 1971 v R, S, E, Ni, Cz, Fi; 1972 v Fi, Cz, E, S, Ni (27)

Dwyer, P. (Cardiff C), 1978 v Ir, E, S, Ni; 1979 v T, S, E, Ni, Ma (sub); 1980 v WG (10)

Edwards, C. (Wrexham), 1878 v S (1)

Edwards, G. (Birmingham C), 1947 v E, S, Ni; 1948 v E, S, Ni; (with Cardiff C), 1949 v Ni, P, Bel, Sw; 1950 v E, S (12)

Edwards, H. (Wrexham Civil Service), 1878 v S; 1880 v E; 1882 v E, S; 1883 v S; 1884 v Ni; 1887 v Ni (7)

Edwards, R. I. (Chester), 1978 v K (sub); 1979 v Ma, WG; (with Wrexham), 1980 v T (sub) (4)

Edwards, J. H. (Oswestry), 1895 v Ni; 1897 v E, Ni; (with Aberystwyth), 1898 v Ni (4)

Edwards, J. H. (Wanderers), 1876 v S (1)

Edwards, L. T. (Charlton Ath), 1957 v Ni, EG (2)

Edwards, T. (Linfield), 1932 v S (1)

Egan, W. (Chirk), 1892 v S (1)

Ellis, B. (Motherwell), 1932 v E; 1933 v E, S; 1934 v S; 1936 v E; 1937 v S (6)

Ellis, E. (Nunhead), 1931 v E; (with Oswestry), S; 1932 v Ni (3)

Emanuel, W. J. (Bristol C), 1973 v E (sub), Ni (sub) (2)

England, H. M. (Blackburn R), 1962 v Ni, Br, M; 1963 v Ni, H; 1964 v E, S, Ni; 1965 v E, D, Gr (2), USSR, Ni, I; 1966 v E, S, Ni, USSR, D; (with Tottenham H), 1967 v S, E; 1968 v E, Ni, WG; 1969 v EG; 1970 v R of UK, EG, E, S, Ni, I; 1971 v R; 1972 v Fi, E, S, Ni; 1973 v E (3), S; 1974 v Pol; 1975 v H, L (44)

Evans, B. C. (Swansea C), 1972 v Fi, Cz; 1973 v E (2), Pol, S; (with Hereford U), 1974 v Pol (7)

Evans, D. G. (Reading), 1926 v Ni; 1927 v Ni, E; (with Huddersfield T), 1929 v S (4)

Evans, H. P. (Cardiff C), 1922 v E, S, Ni; 1924 v E, S, Ni (6)

Evans, I. (Crystal Palace), 1976 v A, E, Y (2), E, Ni; 1977 v WG, S (2), Cz, E, Ni; 1978 v K (13)

Evans, J. (Cardiff C), 1912 v Ni; 1913 v Ni; 1914 v S; 1920 v S, Ni; 1922 v Ni; 1923 v E, Ni (8)

Evans, J. (Oswestry), 1893 v Ni; 1894 v E, Ni (3)

Evans, J. H. (Southend U), 1922 v E, S, Ni; 1923 v S (4)

Evans, Len (Cardiff C), 1931 v E, S; (with Birmingham), 1934 v Ni (3)

Evans, L. H. (Aberdare Ath), 1927 v Ni (1)

Evans, M. (Oswestry), 1884 v E (1)

Evans, R. (Clapton), 1902 v Ni (1)

Evans, R. E. (Wrexham), 1906 v E, S; (with Aston Villa), Ni; 1907 v E; 1908 v E, S; (with Sheffield U), 1909 v S; 1910 v E, S, Ni (10)

Evans, R. O. (Wrexham), 1902 v Ni; 1903 v E, S, Ni; (with Blackburn R), 1908 v Ni; (with Coventry C), 1911 v E, Ni; 1912 v E, S, Ni (10)

Evans, R. S. (Swansea T), 1964 v Ni (1)

Evans T. J. (Clapton Orient), 1927 v S; 1928 v E, S; (with Newcastle U), Ni (4)

Evans, W. (Tottenham H), 1933 v Ni; 1934 v E, S; 1935 v E; 1936 v E, Ni (6)

Evans, W. A. W. (Oxford University), 1876 v S; 1877 v S (2)

Evans, W. G. (Bootle), 1890 v E; 1891 v E; (with Aston Villa), 1892 v E (3)

Evelyn, E. C. (Crusaders), 1887 v E (1)

Eyton-Jones, J. A. (Wrexham), 1883 v Ni; 1884 v Ni, E, S (4)

Farmer, G. (Oswestry), 1885 v E, S (2)

Felgate, D. (Lincoln C), 1984 v R (sub) (1)

Finnigan, R. J. (Wrexham), 1930 v Ni (1)

Flynn, B. (Burnley), 1975 v L (2 sub), H (sub), S, E, Ni; 1976 v A, E, Y (2), E, Ni; 1977 v WG (sub), S (2), Cz, E, Ni; 1978 v K (2), S; (with Leeds U), Cz, WG, Ir (sub), E, S, Ni; 1979 v Ma, T, S, E, Ni, Ma; 1980 v Ei, WG, E, S, Ni, Ic; 1981 v T, Cz, Ei, T, S, E, USSR; 1982 v Cz, USSR, E, S, Ni, F; 1983 v N, (with Burnley), v Y, E, Bul, S, Ni, Br; 1984 v N, R, Bul, Y, S, N, Is (66)

Ford, T. (Swansea T), 1947 v S; (with Aston Villa), 1947 v Ni; 1948 v S, Ni; 1949 v E, S, Ni, P, Bel, Sw; 1950 v E, S, Ni, Bel; 1951 v S; (with Sunderland), 1951 v E, Ni, P, Sw; 1952 v E, S, Ni, R of UK; 1953 v S, E, Ni, F, Y; (with Cardiff C), 1954 v A; 1955 v S, E, Ni, Y; 1956 v S, Ni, E, A; 1957 v S (38)

Foulkes, H. E. (WBA), 1932 v Ni (1)

Foulkes, W. I. (Newcastle U), 1952 v E, S, Ni, R of UK; 1953 v E, S, F, Y; 1954 v E, S, Ni (11)

Foulkes, W. T. (Oswestry), 1884 v Ni; 1885 v S (2)

Fowler, J. (Swansea T), 1925 v E; 1926 v E, Ni; 1927 v S; 1928 v S; 1929 v E (6)

Garner, J. (Aberystwyth), 1896 v S (1)

Giles, D. (Swansea C), 1980 v E, S, Ni, Ic; 1981 v T, Cz, T (sub), E (sub), USSR (sub); (with C Palace), 1982 v Sp (sub); 1983 v Ni (sub), Br (12)

Gillam, S. G. (Wrexham), 1889 v S, Ni; (with Shrewsbury), 1890 v E, Ni; (with Clapton), 1894 v S (5)

Glascodine, G. (Wrexham), 1879 v E (1)

Glover, E. M. (Grimsby T), 1932 v S; 1934 v Ni; 1936 v S; 1937 v E, S, Ni; 1939 v Ni (7)

Godding, G. (Wrexham), 1923 v S, Ni (2)

Godfrey, B. C. (Preston NE), 1964 v Ni; 1965 v D, I (3)

Goodwin, U. (Ruthin), 1881 v E (1)

Gough, R. T. (Oswestry White Star), 1883 v S (1)

Gray, A. (Oldham Ath), 1924 v E, S, Ni; 1925 v E, S, Ni; 1926 v E, S; 1927 v S; (with Manchester C), 1928 v E, S; 1929 v E, S, Ni; (with Manchester Central), 1930 v S; (with Tranmere R), 1932 v E, S, Ni; (with Chester), 1937 v E, S, Ni; 1938 v E, S, Ni (24)

Green, A. W. (Aston Villa), 1901 v Ni; (with Notts Co), 1903 v E; 1904 v S, Ni; 1906 v Ni, E; (with Nottingham F), 1907 v E; 1908 v S (8)

Green, C. R. (Birmingham C), 1965 v USSR, I; 1966 v E, S, USSR, Br (2); 1967 v E; 1968 v E, S, Ni, WG; 1969 v S, I, Ni (sub) (15)

Green, G. H. (Charlton Ath), 1938 v Ni; 1939 v E, Ni, F (4)

Grey, Dr W. (Druids), 1876 v S; 1878 v S (2)

Griffiths, A. T. (Wrexham), 1971 v Cz (sub); 1975 v A, H (2), L (2), E, Ni; 1976 v A, E, S, E (sub), Ni, Y (2); 1977 v WG, S (17)
Griffiths, F. J. (Blackpool), 1900 v E, S (2)
Griffiths, G. (Chirk), 1887 v Ni (1)
Griffiths, J. H. (Swansea T), 1953 v Ni (1)
Griffiths, M. W. (Leicester C), 1947 v Ni; 1949 v P, Bel; 1950 v E, S, Bel; 1951 v E, Ni, P, Sw; 1954 v A (11)
Griffiths, P. (Chirk), 1884 v E, Ni; 1888 v E; 1890 v S, Ni; 1891 v Ni (6)
Griffiths, S. (Wrexham), 1902 v S (1)
Griffiths, T. P. (Everton), 1927 v E, Ni; 1929 v E; 1930 v E; 1931 v Ni; 1932 v Ni, S, E; (with Bolton W), 1933 v F, E, S, Ni; (with Middlesbrough), 1934 v E, S; 1935 v E, Ni; 1936 v S; (with Aston Villa), Ni; 1937 v E, S, Ni (21)

Hall, G. D. (Chelsea), 1988 v Y (sub), Ma, I; 1989 v Ho, Fi, Is (6)
Hallam, J. (Oswestry), 1889 v E (1)
Hanford, H. (Swansea T), 1934 v Ni; 1935 v S; 1936 v E; (with Sheffield W), 1936 v Ni; 1938 v E, S; 1939 v F (7)
Harrington, A. C. (Cardiff C), 1956 v Ni; 1957 v E, S; 1958 v S, Ni, Is (2); 1961 v S, E; 1962 v E, S (11)
Harris, C. S. (Leeds U), 1976 v E, S; 1978 v WG, Ir, E, S, Ni; 1979 v Ma, T, WG, E (sub), Ma; 1980 v Ni (sub), Ic (sub); 1981 v T, Cz (sub), Ei, T, S, E, USSR; 1982 v Cz, Ic, E (sub) (24)
Harris, W. C. (Middlesbrough), 1954 v A; 1957 v EG, Cz; 1958 v E, S, EG (6)
Harrison, W. C. (Wrexham), 1899 v E; 1900 v E, S, Ni; 1901 v Ni (5)
Hayes, A. (Wrexham), 1890 v Ni; 1894 v Ni (2)
Hennessey, W. T. (Birmingham C), 1962 v Ni, Br (2); 1963 v S, E, H (2); 1964 v E, S; 1965 v S, E, D, Gr, USSR; 1966 v E, USSR; (with Nottingham F), 1966 v S, Ni, D, Br (2), Ch; 1967 v S, E; 1968 v E, S, Ni; 1969 v WG, EG, R of UK, EG; (with Derby Co), 1970 v E, S, Ni; 1972 v Fi, Cz, E, S; 1973 v E (39)
Hersee, A. M. (Bangor), 1886 v S, Ni (2)
Hersee, R. (Llandudno), 1886 v Ni (1)
Hewitt, R. (Cardiff C), 1958 v Ni, Is, Se, H, Br (5)
Hewitt, T. J. (Wrexham), 1911 v E, S, Ni; (with Chelsea), 1913 v E, S, Ni; (with South Liverpool), 1914 v E, S (8)
Heywood, D. (Druids), 1879 v E (1)
Hibbott, H. (Newtown Excelsior), 1880 v E, S (2)
Hibbott, R. (Newtown), 1885 v S (1)
Higham, G. G. (Oswestry), 1878 v S; 1879 v E (2)
Hill, M. R. (Ipswich T), 1972 v Cz, R (2)
Hockey, T. (Sheffield U), 1972 v Fi, R; 1973 v E (2); (with Norwich C), Pol, S, E, Ni; (with Aston Villa), 1974 v Pol (9)
Hoddinott, T. F. (Watford), 1921 v E, S (2)
Hodges, G. (Wimbledon), 1984 v N (sub), Is (sub); 1987 v USSR, Fi, Cz; (with Newcastle U), 1988 v D (with Watford), D (sub), Cz (sub), Se, Ma (sub), I (sub) (11)
Hodgkinson, A. V. (Southampton), 1908 v Ni (1)
Holden, A. (Chester C), 1984 v Is (sub) (1)
Hole, B. G. (Cardiff C), 1963 v Ni; 1964 v Ni; 1965 v S, E, Ni, D, Gr (2), USSR, I; 1966 v E, S, Ni, USSR, D, Br (2), Ch; (with Blackburn R), 1967 v S, E, Ni; 1968 v E, S, Ni, WG; (with Aston Villa), 1969 v I, WG, EG; 1970 v I; (with Swansea C), 1971 v R (30)
Hole, W. J. (Swansea T), 1921 v Ni; 1922 v E; 1923 v E, Ni; 1928 v E, S, Ni; 1929 v E, S (9)
Hollins, D. M. (Newcastle U), 1962 v Br (sub), M; 1963 v Ni, H; 1964 v E; 1965 v Ni, Gr, I; 1966 v S, D, Br (11)
Hopkins, I. J. (Brentford), 1935 v S, Ni; 1936 v E, Ni; 1937 v E, S, Ni; 1938 v E, Ni; 1939 v E, S, Ni (12)
Hopkins, J. (Fulham), 1983 v Ni, Br; 1984 v N, R, Bul, Y, S, E, Ni, N, Is; 1985 v Ic (1 + 1 sub), N (14)
Hopkins, M. (Tottenham H), 1956 v Ni; 1957 v Ni, S, E, Cz (2), EG; 1958 v E, S, Ni, EG, Is (2), H (2), M, Se, Br; 1959 v E, S, Ni; 1960 v E, S; 1961 v Ni, H, Sp (2); 1962 v Ni, Br (2), M; 1963 v S, Ni, H (34)
Horne, B. (Portsmouth), 1988 v D (sub), Y, Se (sub), Ma, I; 1989 v Ho, Fi, Is (with Southampton), Se,WG (10)
Howell, E. G. (Builth), 1888 v Ni; 1890 v E; 1891 v E (3)
Howells, R. G. (Cardiff C), 1954 v E, S (2)
Hugh, A. R. (Newport Co), 1930 v Ni (1)
Hughes, A. (Rhos), 1894 v E, S (2)
Hughes, A. (Chirk), 1907 v Ni (1)
Hughes, A. J. (Aberystwyth), 1879 v S (1)
Hughes, E. (Everton), 1899 v S, Ni; (with Tottenham H), 1901 v E, S; 1902 v Ni; 1904 v E, Ni, S; 1905 v E, Ni, S; 1906 v E, Ni; 1907 v E (14)
Hughes, E. (Wrexham), 1906 v S; (with Nottingham F), 1906 v Ni; 1908 v S, E; 1910 v Ni, E, S; 1911 v Ni, E, S; (with Wrexham), 1912 v Ni, E, S; (with Manchester C), 1913 v E, S; 1914 v N (16)
Hughes, F. W. (Northwich Victoria), 1882 v E, Ni; 1883 v E, Ni, S; 1884 v S (6)
Hughes, I. (Luton T), 1951 v E, Ni, P, Sw (4)
Hughes, J. (Cambridge University), 1877 v S (1)
Hughes, J. (Liverpool), 1905 v E, S, Ni (3)
Hughes, J. I. (Blackburn R), 1935 v Ni (1)
Hughes, L. M. (Manchester U), 1984 v E, Ni; 1985 v Ic, Sp, Ic, N, S, Sp, N; 1986 v S, H, U; (with Barcelona), 1987 v USSR, Cz; 1988 v D (2), Cz, Se, Ma, I; (with Manchester U) 1989 v Ho, Fi, Is, Se, WG (25)
Hughes, P. W. (Bangor), 1887 v Ni; 1889 v Ni, E (3)
Hughes, W. (Bootle), 1891 v E; 1892 v S, Ni (3)
Hughes, W. A. (Blackburn R), 1949 v E, Ni, P, Bel, Sw (5)
Hughes, W. M. (Birmingham), 1938 v E, Ni, S; 1939 v E, Ni, S, F; 1947 v E, S, Ni (10)
Humphreys, J. V. (Everton), 1947 v Ni (1)
Humphreys, R. (Druids), 1888 v Ni (1)
Hunter, W. H. (North End, Belfast), 1887 v Ni (1)

Jackett, K. (Watford), 1983 v N, Y, E, Bul, S; 1984 v N, R, Y, S, Ni, N, Is; 1985 v Ic, Sp, Ic, N, S, Sp, N; 1986 v S, H, S.Ar, Ei, Ca (2); 1987 v Fi (2); 1988 v D, Cz, Y, Se (31)
Jackson, W. (St Helens Rec), 1899 v Ni (1)
James, E. (Chirk), 1893 v E, Ni; 1894 v E, S, Ni; 1898 v E; 1899 v Ni (7)
James, E. G. (Blackpool), 1966 v Br (2), Ch; 1967 v Ni; 1968 v S; 1971 v Cz, S, E, Ni (9)
James, L. (Burnley), 1972 v Cz, R, S (sub); 1973 v E (3), Pol, S, Ni; 1974 v Pol, E, S, Ni; 1975 v A, H (2), L (2), S, E, Ni; 1976 v A; (with Derby Co), S, E, Y (2), Ni; 1977 v WG, S (2), Cz, E, Ni; 1978 v K (2); (with QPR), WG; (with Burnley) 1979 v T; 1980 (with Swansea C), v E, S, Ni, Ic; 1981 v T, Ei, T, S, E; 1982 v Cz, Ic, USSR, E (sub), S, Ni, F; (with Sunderland), 1983 v E (sub) (54)
James, R. M. (Swansea C), 1979 v Ma, WG (sub), S, E, Ni, Ma; 1980 v WG; 1982 v Cz (sub), Ic, Sp, E, S, Ni, F; 1983 v N, Y, E, Bul; (with Stoke C), 1984 v N, R, Bul, Y, S, E, Ni, N, Is; 1985 v Ic, Sp, Ic, (with QPR), N, S, Sp, N; 1986 v S, S.Ar, Ei, U, Ca (2); 1987 v Fi (2), USSR, Cz; (with Leicester C), 1988 v D (2), (with Swansea C), Y (47)
James, W. (West Ham U), 1931 v Ni; 1932 v Ni (2)
Jarrett, R. H. (Ruthin), 1889 v Ni; 1890 v S (2)
Jarvis, A. L. (Hull C), 1967 v S, E, Ni (3)
Jenkins, E. (Lovell's Ath), 1925 v E (1)
Jenkins, J. (Brighton), 1924 v Ni, E, S; 1925 v S, Ni; 1926 v E, S; 1927 v S (8)
Jenkins, R. W. (Rhyl), 1902 v Ni (1)
Jenkyns, C. A. L. (Small Heath), 1892 v E, S, Ni; 1895 v E; (with Woolwich Arsenal), 1896 v S; (with Newton Heath), 1897 v Ni; (with Walsall), 1898 v S, E (8)
Jennings, W. (Bolton W), 1914 v E, S; 1920 v S; 1923 v Ni, E; 1924 v E, S, Ni; 1927 v S, Ni; 1929 v S (11)
John, R. F. (Arsenal), 1923 v S, Ni; 1925 v Ni; 1926 v E;

1927 v E; 1928 v E, Ni; 1930 v E, S; 1932 v E; 1933 v F, Ni; 1935 v Ni; 1936 v S; 1937 v E (15)

John, W. R. (Walsall), 1931 v Ni; (with Stoke C), 1933 v E, S, Ni, F; 1934 v E, S; (with Preston NE), 1935 v E, S; (with Sheffield U), 1936 v E, S, Ni; (with Swansea T), 1939 v E, S (14)

Johnson, M. G. (Swansea T), 1964 v Ni (1)

Jones, A. (Port Vale), 1987 v Fi, Cz (sub); 1988 v D, (with Charlton Ath), D (sub), Cz (sub) (5)

Jones, A. F. (Oxford University), 1877 v S (1)

Jones, A. T. (Nottingham F), 1905 v E; (with Notts Co), 1906 v E (2)

Jones, Bryn (Wolverhampton W), 1935 v Ni; 1936 v E, S, Ni; 1937 v E, S, Ni; 1938 v E, S, Ni; (with Arsenal), 1939 v E, S, Ni; 1947 v S, Ni; 1948 v E; 1949 v S (17)

Jones, B. S. (Swansea T), 1963 v S, E, Ni, H (2); 1964 v S, Ni; (with Plymouth Arg), 1965 v D; (with Cardiff C), 1969 v S, E, Ni, I (sub), WG, EG, R of UK (15)

Jones, Charlie (Nottingham F), 1926 v E; 1927 v S, Ni; 1928 v E; (with Arsenal), 1930 v E, S; 1932 v E; 1933 v F (8)

Jones, Cliff (Swansea T), 1954 v A; 1956 v E, Ni, S, A; 1957 v E, S, Ni, Cz (2), EG; 1958 v EG, E, S, Is (2); (with Tottenham H), 1958 v Ni, H (2), M, Se, Br; 1959 v Ni; 1960 v E, S, Ni; 1961 v S, E, Ni, Sp, H, Ei; 1962 v E, Ni, S, Br (2), M; 1963 v S, Ni, H; 1964 v E, S, Ni; 1965 v E, S, Ni, D, Gr (2), USSR, I; 1967 v S, E; 1968 v E, S, WG; (with Fulham), 1969 v I, R of UK (59)

Jones, C. W. (Birmingham), 1935 v Ni; 1939 v F (2)

Jones, D. (Chirk), 1888 v S, Ni; (with Bolton W), 1889 v E, S, Ni; 1890 v E, Ni; 1891 v S; 1892 v Ni; 1893 v E; 1894 v E; 1895 v E; 1898 v S; (with Manchester C), 1900 v E, Ni (15)

Jones, D. E. (Norwich C), 1976 v S, E (sub); 1978 v S, Cz, WG, Ir, E; 1980 v E (8)

Jones, D. O. (Leicester C), 1934 v E, Ni; 1935 v E, S; 1936 v E, Ni; 1937 v Ni (7)

Jones, Evan (Chelsea), 1910 v S, Ni; (with Oldham Ath), 1911 v E, S; 1912 v E, S; (with Bolton W), 1914 v Ni (7)

Jones, F. R. (Bangor), 1885 v E, Ni; 1886 v S (3)

Jones, F. W. (Small Heath), 1893 v S (1)

Jones, G. P. (Wrexham), 1907 v S, Ni (2)

Jones, H. (Aberaman), 1902 v Ni (1)

Jones, Humphrey (Bangor), 1885 v E, Ni, S; 1886 v E, Ni, S; (with Queen's Park), 1887 v E; (with East Stirlingshire), 1889 v E, Ni; 1890 v E, S, Ni; (with Queen's Park), 1891 v E, S (14)

Jones, Ivor (Swansea T), 1920 v S, Ni; 1921 v Ni, E; 1922 v S, Ni; (with WBA), 1923 v E, Ni; 1924 v S; 1926 v Ni (10)

Jones, J. (Druids), 1876 v S (1)

Jones, J. (Berwyn Rangers), 1883 v S, Ni; 1884 v S (3)

Jones, J. (Wrexham), 1925 v Ni (1)

Jones, Jeffrey (Llandrindod Wells), 1908 v Ni; 1909 v Ni; 1910 v S (3)

Jones, J. L. (Sheffield U), 1895 v E, S, Ni; 1896 v Ni, S, E; 1897 v Ni, S, E; (with Tottenham H), 1898 v Ni, E, S; 1899 v S, Ni; 1900 v S; 1902 v E, S, Ni; 1904 v E, S, Ni (21)

Jones, J. Love (Stoke C), 1906 v S; (with Middlesbrough), 1910 v Ni (2)

Jones, J. O. (Bangor), 1901 v S, Ni (2)

Jones, J. P. (Liverpool), 1976 v A, E, S; 1977 v WG, S (2), Cz, E, Ni; 1978 v K (2), S, Cz, WG, Ir, E, S, Ni; (with Wrexham), 1979 v Ma, T, WG, S, E, Ni, Ma; 1980 v Ei, WG, T, E, S, Ni, Ic; 1981 v T, Ei, T, S, E, USSR; 1982 v Cz, Ic, USSR, Sp, E, S, Ni, F; 1983 v N, (with Chelsea), v Y, E, Bul, S, Ni, Br; 1984 v N, R, Bul, Y, S, E, Ni, N, Is; 1985 v Ic, N, S, N; (with Huddersfield T), 1986 v S, H, Ei, U, Ca (2) (72)

Jones, J. T. (Stoke C), 1912 v E, S, Ni; 1913 v E, Ni; 1914 v S, Ni; 1920 v E, S, Ni; (with C Palace), 1921 v E, S; 1922 v E, S, Ni (15)

Jones, K. (Aston Villa), 1950 v S (1)

Jones, Leslie J. (Cardiff C), 1933 v F; (with Coventry C), 1935 v Ni; 1936 v S; 1937 v E, S, Ni; (with Arsenal), 1938 v E, S, Ni; 1939 v E, S (11)

Jones, P. W. (Bristol R), 1971 v Fi (1)

Jones, R. (Bangor), 1887 v S; 1889 v E; (with Crewe Alex), 1890 v E (3)

Jones, R. (Bangor), 1900 v S, Ni (2)

Jones, R. (Druids), 1899 v S; (with Millwall), 1906 v S, Ni (3)

Jones, R. A. (Druids), 1884 v E, Ni, S; 1885 v S (4)

Jones, R. S. (Everton), 1894 v Ni; (with Leicester Fosse), 1898 v S (2)

Jones, S. (Wrexham), 1887 v Ni; (with Chester), 1890 v S (2)

Jones, S. (Wrexham), 1893 v S, Ni; (with Burton Swifts), 1895 v S; 1896 v E, Ni (5)

Jones, T. (Manchester U), 1926 v Ni; 1927 v E, Ni; 1930 v Ni (4)

Jones, T. D. (Aberdare), 1908 v Ni (1)

Jones, T. G. (Everton), 1938 v Ni; 1939 v E, S, Ni; 1947 v E, S; 1948 v E, S, Ni; 1949 v E, Ni, P, Bel, Sw; 1950 v E, S, Bel (17)

Jones, T. J. Sheffield W), 1932 v Ni; 1933 v F (2)

Jones, W. (Druids), 1899 v E (1)

Jones, W. E. A. (Swansea T), 1947 v E, S; (with Tottenham H), 1949 v E, S (4)

Jones, W. J. (Aberdare), 1901 v E, S; (with West Ham U), 1902 v E, S (4)

Jones, W. Lot (Manchester C), 1905 v E, Ni; 1906 v E, S, Ni; 1907 v E, S, Ni; 1908 v S; 1909 v E, S, Ni; 1910 v E; 1911 v E; 1913 v E, S; 1914 v S, Ni; (with Southend U), 1920 v E, Ni (20)

Jones, W. P. (Druids), 1889 v E, Ni; (with Wynstay), 1890 v S, Ni (4)

Jones, W. R. (Aberystwyth), 1897 v S (1)

Keenor, F. C. (Cardiff C), 1920 v E, Ni; 1921 v E, Ni, S; 1922 v Ni; 1923 v E, Ni, S; 1924 v E, Ni, S; 1925 v E, Ni, S; 1926 v S; 1927 v E, Ni, S; 1928 v E, Ni, S; 1929 v E, Ni, S; 1930 v E, Ni, S; 1931 v E, Ni, S; (with Crewe Alex), 1933 v S (32)

Kelly, F. C. (Wrexham), 1899 v S, Ni; (with Druids), 1902 v Ni (3)

Kelsey, A. J. (Arsenal), 1954 v Ni, A; 1955 v S, Ni, Y; 1956 v E, Ni, S, A; 1957 v E, Ni, S, Cz (2), EG; 1958 v E, S, Ni, Is (2), H (2), M, Se, Br; 1959 v E, S; 1960 v E, Ni, S; 1961 v E, Ni, S, H, Sp (2); 1962 v E, S, Ni, Br (2) (41)

Kenrick, S. L. (Druids), 1876 v S; 1877 v S; (with Oswestry), 1879 v E, S; (with Shropshire Wanderers), 1881 v E (5)

Ketley, C. F. (Druids), 1882 v Ni (1)

King, J. (Swansea T), 1955 v E (1)

Kinsey, N. (Norwich C), 1951 v Ni, P, Sw; 1952 v E; (with Birmingham C), 1954 v Ni; 1956 v E, S (7)

Knill, A. R. (Swansea C), 1989 v Ho (1)

Krzywicki, R. L. (Huddersfield T), 1970 v E, S; (with WBA), Ni, EG, I; 1971 v R, Fi; 1972 v Cz (sub) (8)

Lambert, R. (Liverpool), 1947 v S; 1948 v E; 1949 v P, Bel, Sw (5)

Lathom, G. (Liverpool), 1905 v E, S; 1906 v S; 1907 v E, S, Ni; 1908 v E; 1909 v Ni; (with Southport Central), 1910 v E; (with Cardiff C), 1913 v Ni (10)

Lawrence, E. (Clapton Orient), 1930 v Ni; (with Notts Co), 1932 v S (2)

Lawrence, S. (Swansea T), 1932 v Ni; 1933 v F; 1934 v S, E, Ni; 1935 v E, S; 1936 v S (8)

Lea, A. (Wrexham), 1889 v E; 1891 v S, Ni; 1893 v Ni (4)

Lea, C. (Ipswich T), 1965 v Ni, I (2)

Leary, P. (Bangor), 1889 v Ni (1)

Leek, K. (Leicester C), 1961 v S, E, Ni, H, Sp (2); (with

Newcastle U), 1962 v S; (with Birmingham C), v Br (sub), M; 1963 v E; 1965 v S, Gr; (with Northampton T), 1965 v Gr (13)

Lever, A. R. (Leicester C), 1953 v S (1)

Lewis, B. (Wrexham), 1891 v Ni; 1892 v S, E, Ni; (with Middlesbrough), 1893 v S, E; (with Wrexham), 1894 v S, E, Ni; 1895 v S (10)

Lewis, D. (Arsenal), 1927 v E; 1928 v Ni; 1930 v E (3)

Lewis, D. J. (Swansea T), 1933 v E, S (2)

Lewis, D. (Swansea C), 1983 v Br (sub) (1)

Lewis, J. (Bristol R), 1906 v E (1)

Lewis, J. (Cardiff C), 1926 v S (1)

Lewis, T. (Wrexham), 1881 v E, S (2)

Lewis, W. L. (Swansea T), 1927 v E, Ni; 1928 v E, Ni; 1929 v S; (with Huddersfield T), 1930 v E (6)

Lewis, W. (Bangor), 1885 v E; 1886 v E, S; 1887 v E, S; 1888 v E; 1889 v E, Ni, S; (with Crewe Alex), 1890 v E, Ni, S; 1891 v E, Ni, S; 1892 v E, S, Ni; 1894 v E, S, Ni; (with Chester), 1895 v S, Ni, E; 1896 v E, S, Ni; (with Manchester C), 1897 v E, S; (with Chester), 1898 v Ni (30)

Lloyd, B. W. (Wrexham), 1976 v A, E, S (3)

Lloyd, J. W. (Wrexham), 1879 v S; (with Newtown), 1885 v S (2)

Lloyd, R. A. (Ruthin), 1891 v Ni; 1895 v S (2)

Lockley, A. (Chirk), 1898 v Ni (1)

Lovell, S. (C Palace), 1982 v USSR (sub); (with Millwall), 1985 v N; 1986 v S (sub), H (sub), Ca (1 + sub) (6)

Lowrie, G. (Coventry C), 1948 v E, S, Ni; (with Newcastle U), 1949 v P (4)

Lowndes, S. (Newport Co), 1983 v S (sub), Br (sub); (with Millwall), 1985 v N (sub); 1986 v S.Ar (sub), Ei, U, Ca (2); (with Barnsley), 1987 v Fi (sub); 1988 v Se (sub) (10)

Lucas, P. M. (Leyton Orient), 1962 v Ni, M; 1963 v S, E (4)

Lucas, W. H. (Swansea T), 1949 v S, Ni, P, Bel, Sw; 1950 v E; 1951 v E (7)

Lumberg, A. (Wrexham), 1929 v Ni; 1930 v E, S; (with Wolverhampton W), 1932 v S (4)

McMillan, R. (Shrewsbury Engineers), 1881 v E, S (2)

Mahoney, J. F. (Stoke C), 1968 v E; 1969 v EG; 1971 v Cz; 1973 v E (3), Pol, S, Ni; 1974 v Pol, E, S, Ni; 1975 v A, H (2), L (2), S, E, Ni; 1976 v A, Y (2), E, Ni; 1977 v WG, Cz, S, E, Ni; (with Middlesbrough), 1978 v K (2), S, Cz, Ir, E (sub), S, Ni; 1979 v WG, S, E, Ni, Ma; (with Swansea C), 1980 v Ei, WG, T (sub); 1982 v Ic, USSR; 1983 v Y, E (51)

Martin, T. J. (Newport Co), 1930 v Ni (1)

Marustik, C. (Swansea C), 1982 v Sp, E, S, Ni, F; 1983 v N (6)

Mates, J. (Chirk), 1891 v Ni; 1897 v E, S (3)

Mathews, R. W. (Liverpool), 1921 v Ni; (with Bristol C), 1923 v E; (with Bradford), 1926 v Ni (3)

Matthews, W. (Chester), 1905 v Ni; 1908 v E (2)

Matthias, J. S. (Brymbo), 1896 v S, Ni; (with Shrewsbury), 1897 v E, S; (with Wolverhampton W), 1899 v S (5)

Matthias, T. J. (Wrexham), 1914 v S, E; 1920 v Ni, S, E; 1921 v S, E, Ni; 1922 v S, E, Ni; 1923 v S (12)

Mays, A. W. (Wrexham), 1929 v Ni (1)

Medwin, T. C. (Swansea T), 1953 v Ni, F, Y; (with Tottenham H), 1957 v E, S, Ni, Cz (2), EG; 1958 v E, S, Ni, Is (2), H (2), M, Br; 1959 v E, S, Ni; 1960 v E, S, Ni; 1961 v S, Ei, Sp; 1963 v E, H (29)

Meredith, S. (Chirk), 1900 v S; 1901 v S, E, Ni; (with Stoke C), 1902 v E; 1903 v Ni; 1904 v E; (with Leyton), 1907 v E (8)

Meredith, W. H. (Manchester C), 1895 v E, Ni; 1896 v E, Ni; 1897 v E, Ni, S; 1898 v E, Ni; 1899 v E; 1900 v E, Ni; 1901 v E, Ni; 1902 v E, S; 1903 v E, S, Ni; 1904 v E; 1905 v E, S; (with Manchester U), 1907 v E, S, Ni; 1908 v E, Ni; 1909 v E, S, Ni; 1910 v E, S, Ni; 1911 v E, S, Ni; 1912 v E, S, Ni; 1913 v E, S, Ni; 1914 v E, S, Ni; 1920 v E, S, Ni (48)

Mielczarek, R. (Rotherham U), 1971 v Fi (1)

Millership, H. (Rotherham Co), 1920 v E, S, Ni; 1921 v E, S, Ni (6)

Millington, A. H. (WBA), 1963 v S, E, H; (with C Palace), 1965 v E, USSR; (with Peterborough U), 1966 v Ch, Br; 1967 v E, Ni; 1968 v Ni, WG; 1969 v I, EG; (with Swansea) 1970 v E, S, Ni; 1971 v Cz, Fi; 1972 v Fi (sub), Cz, R (21)

Mills, T. J. (Clapton Orient), 1934 v E, Ni; (with Leicester C), 1935 v E, S (4)

Mills-Roberts, R. H. (St Thomas' Hospital), 1885 v E, S, Ni; 1886 v E; 1887 v E; (with Preston NE), 1888 v E, Ni; (with Llanberis), 1892 v E (8)

Moore, G. (Cardiff C), 1960 v E, S, Ni; 1961 v Ei, Sp; (with Chelsea), 1962 v Br; 1963 v Ni, H; (with Manchester U), 1964 v S, Ni; (with Northampton T), 1966 v Ni, Ch; (with Charlton Ath), 1969 v S, E, Ni, R of UK; 1970 v E, S, Ni, I; 1971 v R (21)

Morgan, J. R. (Cambridge University), 1877 v S; (with Swansea), 1879 v S; (with Derby School Staff), 1880 v E, S; 1881 v E, S; 1882 v E, S, Ni; (with Swansea), 1883 v E (10)

Morgan, J. T. (Wrexham), 1905 v Ni (1)

Morgan-Owen, H. (Oxford University), 1901 v E, S; 1902 v S; 1906 v E, Ni; (with Welshpool), 1907 v S (6)

Morgan-Owen, M. M. (Oxford University), 1897 v S, Ni; 1898 v E, S; 1899 v S; 1900 v E; (with Corinthians), 1903 v S; 1906 v S, E, Ni; 1907 v E (11)

Morley, E. J. (Swansea T), 1925 v E; (with Clapton Orient), 1929 v E, S, Ni (4)

Morris, A. G. (Aberystwyth), 1896 v E, Ni, S; (with Swindon T), 1897 v E; 1898 v S; (with Nottingham F), 1899 v E, S; 1903 v E, S; 1905 v E, S; 1907 v E, S; 1908 v E; 1910 v E, S, Ni; 1911 v E, S, Ni; 1912 v E (21)

Morris, C. (Chirk), 1900 v E, S, Ni; (with Derby Co), 1901 v E, S, Ni; 1902 v E, S; 1903 v E, S, Ni; 1904 v Ni; 1905 v E, S, NI; 1906 v S; 1907 v S; 1908 v E, S; 1909 v E, S, Ni; 1910 v E, S, Ni; (with Huddersfield T), 1911 v E, S, Ni (28)

Morris, E. (Chirk), 1893 v E, S, Ni (3)

Morris, H. (Sheffield U), 1894 v S; (with Manchester C), 1896 v E; (with Grimsby T), 1897 v E (3)

Morris, J. (Oswestry), 1887 v S (1)

Morris, J. (Chirk), 1898 v Ni (1)

Morris, R. (Chirk), 1900 v E, Ni; 1901 v Ni; 1902 v S; (with Shrewsbury T), 1903 v E, Ni (6)

Morris, R. (Druids), 1902 v E, S; (with Newtown), 1902 v Ni; (with Liverpool), 1903 v S, Ni; 1904 v E, S, Ni; (with Leeds C), 1906 v S; (with Grimsby T), 1907 v Ni; (with Plymouth Arg), 1908 v Ni (11)

Morris, S. (Birmingham), 1937 v E, S; 1938 v E, S; 1939 v F (5)

Morris, W. (Burnley), 1947 v Ni; 1949 v E; 1952 v S, Ni, R of UK (5)

Moulsdale, J. R. B. (Corinthians), 1925 v Ni (1)

Murphy, J. P. (WBA), 1933 v F, E, Ni; 1934 v E, S; 1935 v E, S, Ni; 1936 v E, S, Ni; 1937 v S, Ni; 1938 v E, S (15)

Nardiello, D. (Coventry C), 1978 v Cz, WG (sub) (2)

Neal, J. E. (Colwyn Bay), 1931 v E, S (2)

Newnes, J. (Nelson), 1926 v Ni (1)

Newton, L. F. (Cardiff Corinthians), 1912 v Ni (1)

Nicholas, D. S. (Stoke C), 1923 v S; (with Swansea T), 1927 v E, Ni (3)

Nicholas, P. (C Palace), 1979 v S (sub), Ni (sub), Ma; 1980 v Ei, WG, T, E, S, Ni, Ic; 1981 v T, Cz, E; (with Arsenal), T, S, E, USSR; 1982 v Cz, Ic, USSR, Sp, E, S, Ni, F; 1983 v Y, Bul, S (sub), Ni; 1984 v N, Bul, N, Is; (with C Palace), 1985 v Sp; (with Luton T), N, S, Sp, N; 1986 v S, H, S.Ar, Ei, U, Ca (2); 1987 v Fi (2) USSR,

Cz; (with Aberdeen), 1988 v D (2), Cz, Y, Se; (with Chelsea), 1989 v Ho, Fi, Is, Se, WG (59)

Nicholls, J. (Newport Co), 1924 v E, Ni; (with Cardiff C), 1925 v E, S (4)

Niedzwiecki, E. A. (Chelsea), 1985 v N (sub); 1988 v D (2)

Nock, W. (Newtown), 1897 v Ni (1)

Norman, A. J. (Hull C), 1986 v Ei (sub), U, Ca; 1988 v Ma, I (5)

Nurse, M. T. G. (Swansea T), 1960 v E, Ni; 1961 v S, E, H, Ni, Ei, Sp (2); (with Middlesbrough), 1963 v E, H; 1964 v S (12)

O'Callaghan, E. (Tottenham H), 1929 v Ni; 1930 v S; 1932 v S, E; 1933 v Ni, S, E; 1934 v Ni, S, E; 1935 v E (11)

Oliver, A. (Blackburn R), 1905 v E; (with Bangor), S (2)

O'Sullivan, P. A. (Brighton), 1973 v S (sub); 1976 v S; 1979 v Ma (sub) (3)

Owen, D. (Oswestry), 1879 v E (1)

Owen, E. (Ruthin Grammar School), 1884 v E, Ni, S (3)

Owen, G. (Chirk), 1888 v S; (with Newton Heath), 1889 v S, Ni; 1892 v E; 1893 v Ni (5)

Owen, T (Oswestry), 1879 v E (1)

Owen, Trevor (Crewe Alex), 1899 v E, S (2)

Owen, W. (Chirk), 1884 v E; 1885 v Ni; 1887 v E; 1888 v E; 1889 v E, Ni, S; 1890 v S, Ni; 1891 v E, S, Ni; 1892 v E, S; 1893 v S, Ni (16)

Owen, W. P. (Ruthin), 1880 v E, S; 1881 v E, S; 1882 v E, S, Ni; 1883 v E, S; 1884 v E, S, Ni (12)

Owens, J. (Wrexham), 1902 v S (1)

Page, M. E. (Birmingham C), 1971 v Fi; 1972 v S, Ni; 1973 v E (1+1 sub), Ni; 1974 v S, Ni; 1975 v H, L, S, E, Ni; 1976 v E, Y (2), E, Ni; 1977 v WG, S; 1978 v K (sub+1), WG, Ir, E, S; 1979 v Ma, WG (28)

Palmer, D. (Swansea T), 1957 v Cz; 1958 v E, EG (3)

Parris, J. E. (Bradford), 1932 v Ni (1)

Parry, B. J. (Swansea T), 1951 v S (1)

Parry, C. (Everton), 1891 v E, S; 1893 v E; 1894 v E; 1895 v E, S; (with Newtown), 1896 v E, S, Ni; 1897 v Ni; 1898 v E, S, Ni (13)

Parry, E. (Liverpool), 1922 v S; 1923 v E, Ni; 1925 v Ni; 1926 v Ni (5)

Parry, H. (Newtown), 1895 v Ni (1)

Parry, M. (Liverpool), 1901 v E, S, Ni; 1902 v E, S, Ni; 1903 v E, S; 1904 v E, Ni; 1906 v E; 1908 v E, S, Ni; 1909 v E, S (16)

Parry, T. D. (Oswestry), 1900 v E, S, Ni; 1901 v E, S, Ni; 1902 v E (7)

Pascoe, C. (Swansea C), 1984 v N, Is; (with Sunderland) 1989 v Fi, Is, WG (sub) (5)

Paul, R. (Swansea T), 1949 v E, S, Ni, P, Sw; 1950 v E, S, Ni, Bel; (with Manchester C), 1951 v S, E, Ni, P, Sw; 1952 v E, S, Ni, R of UK; 1953 v S, E, Ni, F, Y; 1954 v E, S, Ni; 1955 v S, E, Y; 1956 v E, Ni, S, A (33)

Peake, E. (Aberystwyth), 1908 v Ni; (with Liverpool), 1909 v Ni, S, E; 1910 v S, Ni; 1911 v Ni; 1912 v E; 1913 v E, Ni; 1914 v Ni (11)

Peers, E. J. (Wolverhampton W), 1914 v Ni, S, E; 1920 v E, S; 1921 v S, Ni, E; (with Port Vale), 1922 v E, S, Ni; 1923 v E (12)

Perry, E. (Doncaster R), 1938 v E, S, Ni (3)

Phennah, E. (Civil Service), 1878 v S (1)

Phillips, C. (Wolverhampton W), 1931 v Ni; 1932 v E; 1933 v S; 1934 v E, S, Ni; 1935 v E, S, Ni; 1936 v S; (with Aston Villa), 1936 v E, Ni; 1938 v S (13)

Phillips, D. (Plymouth Arg), 1984 v E, Ni, N; (with Manchester C), 1985 v Sp, Ic, S, Sp, N; 1986 v S, H, S.Ar, Ei, U; (with Coventry C) 1987 v Fi, Cz; 1988 v D (2), Cz, Y, Se; 1989 v Se, WG (22)

Phillips, L. (Cardiff C), 1971 v Cz, S, E, Ni; 1972 v Cz, R, S, Ni; 1973 v E; 1974 v Pol (sub), Ni; 1975 v A; (with Aston Villa), H (2), L (2), S, E, Ni; 1976 v A, E, Y (2), E, Ni; 1977 v WG, S (2), Cz, E; 1978 v K (2), S, Cz, WG, E, S; 1979 v Ma; (Swansea C), T, WG, S, E, Ni, Ma; 1980 v Ei, WG, T, S (sub), Ni, Ic; 1981 v T, Cz, T, S, E, USSR; (with Charlton Ath), 1982 v Cz, USSR (58)

Phillips, T. J. S. (Chelsea), 1973 v E; 1974 v E; 1975 v H (sub); 1978 v K (4)

Phoenix, H. (Wrexham), 1882 v S (1)

Poland, G. (Wrexham), 1939 v Ni, F (2)

Pontin, K. (Cardiff C), 1980 v E (sub), S (2)

Powell, A. (Leeds U), 1947 v E, S; 1948 v E, S, Ni; (with Everton), 1949 v E; 1950 v Bel; (with Birmingham C), 1951 v S (8)

Powell, D. (Wrexham), 1968 v WG; (with Sheffield U), 1969 v S, E, Ni, I, WG; 1970 v E, S, Ni, EG; 1971 v R (11)

Powell, I. V. (QPR), 1947 v E; 1948 v E, S, Ni; (with Aston Villa), 1949 v Bel; 1950 v S, Bel; 1951 v S (8)

Powell, J. (Druids), 1878 v S; 1880 v E, S; 1882 v E, S, Ni; 1883 v E, S, Ni; (with Bolton W), 1884 v E; (with Newton Heath), 1887 v E, S; 1888 v E, S, Ni (15)

Powell, Seth (WBA), 1885 v S; 1886 v E, Ni; 1891 v E, S; 1892 v E, S (7)

Price, H. (Aston Villa), 1907 v S; (with Burton U), 1908 v Ni; (with Wrexham), 1909 v S, E, Ni (5)

Price, J. (Wrexham), 1877 v S; 1878 v S; 1879 v E; 1880 v E, S; 1881 v E, S; (with Druids), 1882 v S, E, Ni; 1883 v S, Ni (12)

Price, P. (Luton T), 1980 v E, S, Ni, Ic; 1981 v T, Cz, Ei, T, S, E, USSR; (with Tottenham H), 1982 v USSR, Sp, F; 1983 v N, Y, E, Bul, S, Ni; 1984 v N, R, Bul, Y, S (sub) (25)

Pring, K. D. (Rotherham U), 1966 v Ch, D; 1967 v Ni (3)

Pritchard, H. K. (Bristol C), 1985 v N (sub) (1)

Pryce-Jones, A. W. (Newtown), 1895 v E (1)

Pryce-Jones, W. E. (Cambridge University), 1887 v S; 1888 v S, E, Ni; 1890 v Ni (5)

Pugh, A. (Rhostyllen), 1889 v S (sub) (1)

Pugh, D. H. (Wrexham), 1896 v S, Ni; 1897 v S, Ni; (with Lincoln C), 1900 v S; 1901 v S, E (7)

Pugsley, J. (Charlton Ath), 1930 v Ni (1)

Pullen, W. J. (Plymouth Arg), 1926 v E (1)

Rankmore, F. E. J. (Peterborough), 1966 v Ch (sub) (1)

Ratcliffe, K. (Everton), 1981 v Cz, Ei, T, S, E, USSR; 1982 v Cz, Ic, USSR, Sp, E; 1983 v Y, E, Bul, S, Ni, Br; 1984 v N, R, Bul, Y, S, E, Ni, N, Is; 1985 v Ic, Sp, Ic, N, S, Sp; 1986 v S, H, S.Ar, U; 1987 v Fi (2), USSR, Cz; 1988 v D (2), Cz; 1989 v Fi, Is, Se, WG (47)

Rea, J. C. (Aberystwyth), 1894 v Ni, S, E; 1895 v S; 1896 v S, Ni; 1897 v S, Ni; 1898 v Ni (9)

Reece, G. I. (Sheffield U), 1966 v E, S, Ni, USSR; 1967 v S; 1969 v R of UK (sub); 1970 v I (sub); 1971 v S, E, Ni, Fi; 1972 v Fi, R, E (sub), S, Ni; (with Cardiff C), 1973 v E (sub), Ni; 1974 v Pol (sub), E, S, Ni; 1975 v A, H (2), L (2), S, Ni (29)

Reed, W. G. (Ipswich T), 1955 v S, Y (2)

Rees, A. (Birmingham C), 1984 v N (sub) (1)

Rees, R. R. (Coventry C), 1965 v S, E, Ni, D, Gr (2), I, R; 1966 v E, S, Ni, R, D, Br (2), Ch; 1967 v E, Ni; 1968 v E, S, Ni; (with WBA), WG; 1969 v I; (with Nottingham F), 1969 v WG, EG, S (sub), R of UK; 1970 v E, S, Ni, EG, I; 1971 v Cz, R, E (sub), Ni (sub), Fi; 1972 v Cz (sub), R (39)

Rees, W. (Cardiff C), 1949 v Ni, Bel, Sw; (with Tottenham H), 1950 v Ni (4)

Richards, A. (Barnsley), 1932 v S (1)

Richards, D. (Wolverhampton W), 1931 v Ni; 1933 v E, S, Ni; 1934 v E, S, Ni; 1935 v E, S, Ni; 1936 v S; (with Brentford), 1936 v E, Ni; 1937 v S, E; (with Birmingham), 1937 v Ni; 1938 v E, S, Ni; 1939 v E, S (21)

Richards, G. (Druids), 1899 v E, S, Ni; (with Oswestry), 1903 v Ni; (with Shrewsbury), 1904 v S; 1905 v Ni (6)

Richards, R. W. (Wolverhampton W), 1920 v E, S; 1921

v Ni; 1922 v E, S; (with West Ham U), 1924 v E, S, Ni; (with Mold), 1926 v S (9)
Richards, S. V. (Cardiff C), 1947 v E (1)
Richards, W. E. (Fulham), 1933 v Ni (1)
Roach, J. (Oswestry), 1885 v Ni (1)
Robbins, W. W. (Cardiff C), 1931 v E, S; 1932 v Ni, E, S; (with WBA), 1933 v F, E, S, Ni; 1934 v S; 1936 v S (11)
Roberts, D. F. (Oxford U), 1973 v Pol, E (sub), Ni; 1974 v E, S; 1975 v A; (with Hull C), L, Ni; 1976 v S, Ni, Y; 1977 v E (sub), Ni; 1978 v K (1+sub), S, Ni (17)
Roberts, J. G. (Arsenal), 1971 v S, E, Ni, Fi; 1972 v Fi, E, Ni; (with Birmingham C), 1973 v E (2), Pol, S, Ni; 1974 v Pol, E, S, Ni; 1975 v A, H, S, E; 1976 v E, S (22)
Roberts, J. H. (Bolton), 1949 v Bel (1)
Roberts, J. (Corwen), 1879 v S; 1880 v E, S; 1882 v E, S, Ni; (with Berwyn R), 1883 v E (7)
Roberts, J. (Ruthin), 1881 v S; 1882 v S (2)
Roberts, J. (Bradford C), 1906 v Ni; 1907 v Ni (2)
Roberts, Jas. (Chirk), 1898 v S (1)
Roberts, Jas (Wrexham), 1913 v S, Ni (2)
Roberts, P. S. (Portsmouth), 1974 v E; 1975 v A, H, L (4)
Roberts, R. (Rhos), 1891 v Ni; (with Crewe Alex), 1893 v E (2)
Roberts, R. (Druids), 1884 v S; (with Bolton W), 1887 v S; 1888 v S, E; 1889 v S, E; 1890 v S; 1892 v Ni; (with PNE), S (9)
Roberts, R. (Wrexham), 1886 v Ni; 1887 v Ni; 1891 v Ni (3)
Roberts, W. (Llangollen), 1879 v E, S; 1880 v E, S; (with Berwyn R), 1881 v S; 1883 v E, S (7)
Roberts, W. (Wrexham), 1886 v E, S, Ni; 1887 v Ni (4)
Roberts, W. H. (Ruthin), 1882 v E, S; 1883 v E, S, Ni; (with Rhyl), 1884 v S (6)
Rodrigues, P. J. (Cardiff C), 1965 v Ni, Gr (2); 1966 v USSR, E, S, D; (with Leicester C), v Ni, Br (2), Ch; 1967 v S; 1968 v E, S, Ni; 1969 v E, Ni, EG, R of UK; 1970 v E, S, Ni, EG; (with Sheffield W), 1971 v R, E, S, Cz, Ni; 1972 v Fi, Cz, R, E, Ni (sub); 1973 v E (3), Pol, S, Ni; 1974 v Pol (40)
Rogers, J. P. (Wrexham), 1896 v E, S, Ni (3)
Rogers, W. (Wrexham), 1931 v E, S (2)
Roose, L. R. (Aberystwyth), 1900 v Ni; (with London Welsh), 1901 v E, S, Ni; (with Stoke C), 1902 v E, S; 1904 v E; (with Everton), 1905 v S, E; (with Stoke C), 1906 v E, S, Ni; 1907 v E, S, Ni; (with Sunderland), 1908 v E, S; 1909 v E, S, Ni; 1910 v E, S, Ni; 1911 v S (24)
Rouse, R. V. (C Palace), 1959 v Ni (1)
Rowlands, A. C. (Tranmere R), 1914 v E (1)
Rowley, T. (Tranmere R), 1959 v Ni (1)
Rush, I. (Liverpool), 1980 v S (sub), Ni; 1981 v E (sub); 1982 v Ic (sub), USSR, E, S, Ni, F; 1983 v N, Y, E, Bul; 1984 v N, R, Bul, Y, S, E, Ni; 1985 v Ic, N, S, Sp; 1986 v S, S.Ar, Ei, U; 1987 v Fi (2), USSR, Cz; (with Juventus), 1988 v D, Cz, Y, Se, Ma, I; (with Liverpool) 1989 v Ho, Fi, Se, WG (42)
Russell, M. R. (Merthyr T), 1912 v S, Ni; 1914 v E; (with Plymouth Arg), 1920 v E, S, Ni; 1921 v E, S, Ni; 1922 v E, Ni; 1923 v E, S, Ni; 1924 v E, S, Ni; 1925 v E, S; 1926 v E, S; 1928 v S; 1929 v E (23)

Sabine, H. W. (Oswestry), 1887 v Ni (1)
Saunders, D. (Brighton & HA), 1986 v Ei (sub), Ca (2); 1987 v Fi, USSR (sub); (with Oxford U), 1988 v Y, Se, Ma, I (sub); 1989 v Ho (sub), Fi, Is (with Derby Co) Se, WG (14)
Savin, G. (Oswestry), 1878 v S (1)
Sayer, P. (Cardiff C), 1977 v Cz, S, E, Ni; 1978 v K (2), S (7)
Scrine, F. H. (Swansea T), 1950 v E, Ni (2)
Sear, C. R. (Manchester C), 1963 v E (1)
Shaw, E. G. (Oswestry), 1882 v Ni; 1884 v S, Ni (3)
Sherwood, A. T. (Cardiff C), 1947 v E, Ni; 1948 v S, Ni; 1949 v E, S, Ni, P, Sw; 1950 v E, S, Ni, Bel; 1951 v E, S, Ni, P, Sw; 1952 v E, S, Ni, R of UK; 1953 v S, E, Ni, F, Y; 1954 v E, S, Ni, A; 1955 v S, E, Y, Ni; 1956 v E, S, Ni, A; (with Newport Co), 1957 v E, S (41)
Shone, W. W. (Oswestry), 1879 v E (1)
Shortt, W. W. (Plymouth Arg), 1947 v Ni; 1950 v Ni, Bel; 1952 v E, S, Ni, R of UK; 1953 v S, E, Ni, F, Y (12)
Showers, D. (Cardiff C), 1975 v E (sub), Ni (2)
Sidlow, C. (Liverpool), 1947 v E, S; 1948 v E, S, Ni; 1949 v S; 1950 v E (7)
Sisson, H. (Wrexham Olympic), 1885 v Ni; 1886 v S, Ni (3)
Slatter, N. (Bristol R), 1983 v S; 1984 v N (sub), Is; 1985 v Ic, Sp, Ic, N, S, Sp, N; (with Oxford U), 1986 v H (sub), S.Ar, Ca (2); 1987 v Fi (sub), Cz; 1988 v D (2), Cz, Ma, I; 1989 v Is (sub) (22)
Smallman, D. P. (Wrexham), 1974 v E (sub), S (sub), Ni; (with Everton), 1975 v H (sub), E, Ni (sub); 1976 v A (7)
Southall, N. (Everton), 1982 v Ni; 1983 v N, E, Bul, S, Ni, Br; 1984 v N, R, Bul, Y, S, E, Ni, N, Is; 1985 v Ic, Sp, Ic, N, S, Sp, N; 1986 v S, H, S.Ar, Ei; 1987 v USSR, Fi, Cz; 1988 v D, Cz, Y, Se; 1989 v Ho, Fi, Se, WG (38)
Sprake, G. (Leeds U), 1964 v S, Ni; 1965 v S, D, Gr; 1966 v E, Ni, USSR; 1967 v S; 1968 v E, S; 1969 v S, E, Ni, WG, R of UK; 1970 v EG, I; 1971 v R, S, E, Ni; 1972 v Fi, E, S, Ni; 1973 v E (2), Pol, S, Ni; 1974 v Pol; (with Birmingham C), S, Ni; 1975 v A, H, L (37)
Stansfield, F. (Cardiff C), 1949 v S (1)
Stevenson, B. (Leeds U), 1978 v Ni; 1979 v Ma, T, S, E, Ni, Ma; 1980 v WG, T, Ic (sub); 1982 v Cz; (with Birmingham C), Sp, S, Ni, F (15)
Stevenson, N. (Swansea C), 1982 v E, S, Ni; 1983 v N (4)
Stitfall, R. F. (Cardiff C), 1953 v E; 1957 v Cz(2)
Sullivan, D. (Cardiff C), 1953 v Ni, F, Y; 1954 v Ni; 1955 v E, Ni; 1957 v E, S; 1958 v Ni, H (2), Se, Br; 1959 v S, Ni; 1960 v E, S (17)

Tapscott, D. R. (Arsenal), 1954 v A; 1955 v S, E, Ni, Y; 1956 v E, Ni, S, A; 1957 v Ni, Cz, EG; (with Cardiff C), 1959 v E, Ni (14)
Taylor, J. (Wrexham), 1898 v E (1)
Taylor, O. D. S. (Newtown), 1893 v S, Ni; 1894 v S, Ni (4)
Thomas, C. (Druids), 1899 v Ni; 1900 v S (2)
Thomas, D. A. (Swansea T), 1957 v Cz; 1958 v EG (2)
Thomas, D. S. (Fulham), 1948 v E, S, Ni; 1949 v S (4)
Thomas, E. (Cardiff Corinthians), 1925 v E (1)
Thomas, G. (Wrexham), 1885 v E, S (2)
Thomas, H. (Manchester U), 1927 v E (1)
Thomas, M. (Wrexham), 1977 v WG, S (1+1 sub), Ni (sub); 1978 v K (sub), S, Cz, Ir, E, Ni (sub); 1979 v Ma; (with Manchester U), T, WG, Ma (sub); 1980 v Ei, WG (sub), T, E, S, Ni; 1981 v Cz, S, E, USSR; (with Everton), 1982 v Cz; (with Brighton & HA), USSR (sub), Sp, E, S (sub), Ni (sub); 1983 (with Stoke C), v N, Y, E, Bul, S, Ni, Br; 1984 v R, Bul, Y; (with Chelsea), S, E; 1985 v Ic, Sp, Ic, S, Sp, N; 1986 v S; (with WBA), H, S.Ar (sub) (51)
Thomas, M. R. (Newcastle U), 1987 v Fi (1)
Thomas, R. J. (Swindon T), 1967 v Ni; 1968 v WG; 1969 v E, Ni, I, WG, R of UK; 1970 v E, S, Ni, EG, I; 1971 v S, E, Ni, R, Cz; 1972 v Fi, Cz, R, E, S, Ni; 1973 v E (3), Pol, S, Ni; 1974 v Pol; (with Derby Co), E, S, Ni; 1975 v H (2), L (2), S, E, Ni; 1976 v A, Y, E; 1977 v Cz, S, E, Ni; 1978 v K, S; (with Cardiff C), Cz (50)
Thomas, T. (Bangor), 1898 v S, Ni (2)
Thomas, W. R. (Newport Co), 1931 v E, S (2)
Thomson, D. (Druids), 1876 v S (1)
Thomson, G. F. (Druids), 1876 v S; 1877 v S (2)
Toshack, J. B. (Cardiff C), 1969 v S, E, Ni, WG, EG, R of UK; 1970 v EG, I; (with Liverpool), 1971 v S, E, Ni, Fi; 1972 v Fi, E; 1973 v E (3), Pol, S; 1975 v A, H (2), L (2), S, E; 1976 v Y (2), E; 1977 v S; 1978 v K (2), S,

Cz; (Swansea C), 1979 v WG (sub), S, E, Ni, Ma; 1980 v WG (40)
Townsend, W. (Newtown), 1887 v Ni; 1893 v Ni (2)
Trainer, H. (Wrexham), 1895 v E, S, Ni (3)
Trainer, J. (Bolton W), 1887 v S; (with Preston NE), 1888 v S; 1889 v E; 1890 v S; 1891 v S; 1892 v Ni, S; 1893 v E; 1894 v Ni, E; 1895 v Ni, E; 1896 v S; 1897 v Ni, S, E; 1898 v S, E; 1899 v Ni, S (20)
Turner, H. G. (Charlton Ath), 1937 v E, S, Ni; 1938 v E, S, Ni; 1939 v Ni, F (8)
Turner, J. (Wrexham), 1892 v E (1)
Turner, R. E. (Wrexham), 1891 v E, Ni (2)
Turner, W. H. (Wrexham), 1887 v E, Ni; 1890 v S; 1891 v E, S (5)

Van Den Hauwe, P. W. R. (Everton), 1985 v Sp; 1986 v S, H; 1987 v USSR, Fi, Cz; 1988 v D (2), Cz, Y, I; 1989 v Fi, Se (13)
Vaughan, Jas (Druids), 1893 v E, S, Ni; 1899 v E (4)
Vaughan, John (Oswestry), 1879 v S; 1880 v S; 1881 v E, S; 1882 v E, S, Ni; 1883 v E, S, Ni; (with Bolton W), 1884 v E (11)
Vaughan, J. O. (Rhyl), 1885 v Ni; 1886 v Ni, E, S (4)
Vaughan N. (Newport Co), 1983 v Y (sub), Br; 1984 v N; (with Cardiff C), R, Bul, Y, Ni (sub), N, Is; 1985 v Sp (sub) (10)
Vaughan, T. (Rhyl), 1885 v E (1)
Vearncombe, G. (Cardiff C), 1958 v EG; 1961 v Ei (2)
Vernon, T. R. (Blackburn R), 1957 v Ni, Cz (2), EG; 1958 v E, S, EG, Se; 1959 v S; (with Everton), 1960 v Ni; 1961 v S, E, Ei; 1962 v Ni, Br (2), M; 1963 v S, E, H; 1964 v E, S; (with Stoke C), 1965 v Ni, Gr, I; 1966 v E, S, Ni, USSR, D; 1967 v Ni; 1968 v E (32)
Villars, A. K. (Cardiff C), 1974 v E, S, Ni (sub) (3)
Vizard, E. T. (Bolton W), 1911 v E, S, Ni; 1912 v E, S; 1913 v S; 1914 v E, Ni; 1920 v E; 1921 v E, S, Ni; 1922 v E, S; 1923 v E, Ni; 1924 v E, S, Ni; 1926 v E, S; 1927 v S (22)

Walley, J. T. (Watford), 1971 v Cz (1)
Walsh, I. (C Palace), 1980 v Ei, T, E, S, Ic; 1981 v T, Cz, Ei, T, S, E, USSR; 1982 v Cz (sub), Ic; (with Swansea C), Sp, S (sub), Ni (sub), F (18)
Ward, D. (Bristol R), 1959 v E; (with Cardiff C), 1962 v E (2)
Warner, J. (Swansea T), 1937 v E; (with Manchester U), 1939 v F (2)
Warren, F. W. (Cardiff C), 1929 v Ni; (with Middlesbrough), 1931 v Ni; 1933 v F, E; (with Hearts), 1937 v Ni; 1938 v Ni (6)
Watkins, A. E. (Leicester Fosse), 1898 v E, S; (with Aston Villa), 1900 v E, S; (with Millwall), 1904 v Ni (5)
Watkins, W. M. (Stoke C), 1902 v E; 1903 v E, S; (with Aston Villa); 1904 v E, S, Ni; (with Sunderland), 1905 v E, S, Ni; (with Stoke C), 1908 v Ni (10)
Webster, C (Manchester U), 1957 v Cz; 1958 v H, M, Br (4)
Whatley, W. J. (Tottenham H), 1939 v E, S (2)
White, P. F. (London Welsh), 1896 v Ni (1)
Wilcocks, A. R. (Oswestry), 1890 v Ni (1)
Wilding, J. (Wrexham O), 1885 v E, S, Ni; 1886 v E, Ni; (with Bootle), 1887 v E; 1888 v S, Ni; (with Wrexham), 1892 v S (9)
Williams, A. L. (Wrexham), 1931 v E (1)
Williams, B. (Bristol C), 1930 v Ni (1)
Williams, B. D. (Swansea T), 1928 v Ni, E; 1930 v E, S; (with Everton), 1931 v Ni; 1932 v E; 1933 v E, S, Ni; 1935 v Ni (10)
Williams, D. G. (Derby Co), 1988 v Cz, Y, Se, Ma, I; 1989 v Ho, Is, Se, WG (9)
Williams, D. M. (Norwich C), 1986 v S.Ar (sub), U, Ca (2); 1987 v Fi (5)
Williams, D. R. (Merthyr T), 1921 v E, S; (with Sheffield W), 1923 v S; 1926 v S; 1927 v E, Ni; (with Manchester U), 1929 v E, S (8)
Williams, E. (Crewe Alex), 1893 v E, S (2)
Williams, E. (Druids), 1901 v E, Ni, S; 1902 v E, Ni (5)
Williams, G. (Chirk), 1893 v S; 1894 v S; 1895 v E, S, Ni; 1898 v Ni (6)
Williams, G. E. (WBA), 1960 v Ni; 1961 v S, E, Ei; 1963 v Ni, H; 1964 v E, S, Ni; 1965 v S, E, Ni, D, Gr (2), USSR, I; 1966 v Ni, Br (2), Ch; 1967 v S, E, Ni; 1968 v Ni; 1969 v I (26)
Williams, G. G. (Swansea T), 1961 v Ni, H, Sp (2); 1962 v E (5)
Williams, G. J. J. (Cardiff C), 1951 v Sw (1)
Williams, G. O. (Wrexham), 1907 v Ni (1)
Williams, H. J. (Swansea), 1965 v Gr (2); 1972 v R (3)
Williams, H. T. (Newport Co), 1949 v Ni, Sw; (with Leeds U), 1950 v Ni; 1951 v S (4)
Williams, J. H. (Oswestry), 1884 v E (1)
Williams, J. T. (Wrexham), 1939 v F (1)
Williams, J. T. (Middlesbrough), 1925 v Ni (1)
Williams, J. W. (C Palace), 1912 v S, Ni (2)
Williams, R. (Newcastle U), 1935 v S, E (2)
Williams, R. P. (Caernarvon), 1886 v S (1)
Williams, S. G. (WBA), 1954 v A; 1955 v E, Ni; 1956 v E, S, A; 1958 v E, S, Ni, Is (2), H (2), M, Se, Br; 1959 v E, S, Ni; 1960 v E, S, Ni; 1961 v Ni, Ei, H, Sp (2); 1962 v E, S, Ni, Br (2), M; (with Southampton), 1963 v S, E, H (2); 1964 v E, S; 1965 v S, E, D; 1966 v D (43)
Williams, W. (Druids), 1876 v S; 1878 v S; (with Oswestry), 1879 v E, S; (with Druids), 1880 v E, S; 1881 v E, S; 1882 v E, S, Ni; 1883 v Ni (12)
Williams, W. (Northampton T), 1925 v S (1)
Witcomb, D. F. (WBA), 1947 v E, S; (with Sheffield W), 1947 v Ni (3)
Woosnam, A. P. (Leyton Orient), 1959 v S; (with West Ham U), v E; 1960 v E, S, Ni; 1961 v S, E, Ni, Ei, Sp, H; 1962 v E, S, Ni, Br; (with Aston Villa), 1963 v Ni, H (17)
Woosnam, G. (Newton White Star), 1879 v S (1)
Worthington, T. (Newtown), 1894 v S (1)
Wynn, G. A. (Chirk), 1903 v Ni; (with Wrexham), 1909 v E, S, Ni; (with Manchester C), 1910 v E; 1911 v Ni; 1912 v E, S; 1913 v E, S; 1914 v E, S (12)

Yorath, T. C. (Leeds U), 1970 v I; 1971 v S, E, Ni; 1972 v Cz, E, S, Ni; 1973 v E, Pol, S; 1974 v Pol, E, S, Ni; 1975 v A, H (2), L (2), S; 1976 v A, E, S, Y (2), E, Ni; (with Coventry C), 1977 v WG, S (2), Cz, E, Ni; 1978 v K (2), S, Cz, WG, Ir, E, S, Ni; 1979 v T, WG, S, E, Ni; (with Tottenham H), 1980 v Ei, T, E, S, Ni, Ic; 1981 v T, Cz; (with Vancouver W), Ei, T, USSR (59)

REPUBLIC OF IRELAND

Aherne, T. (Belfast Celtic), 1946 v P, Sp; (with Luton T), 1950 v Fi, E, Fi, Se, Bel; 1951 v N, Arg, N; 1952 v WG (2), A, Sp; 1953 v F; 1954 v F (16)
Aldridge, J. W. (Oxford U), 1986 v W, U, Ic, Cz; 1987 v Bel, S, Pol (with Liverpool), S, Bul, Bel, Br, L; 1988 v Bul, Pol, N, E, USSR, Ho; 1989 v Ni, Tun, Sp, F, H, Ma (sub), H (25)
Ambrose, P. (Shamrock R), 1955 v N, Ho; 1964 v Pol, N, E (5)
Anderson, J. (Preston NE), 1980 v Cz (sub), US (sub);

1982 v Ch, Br, Tr; (with Newcastle U), 1984 v Chn; 1986 v W, Ic, Cz; 1987 v Bul, Bel, Br, L; 1988 v R (sub), Y (sub); 1989 v Tun (16)
Andrews, P. (Bohemians), 1936 v Ho (1)
Arrigan, T. (Waterford), 1938 v N (1)

Bailham, E. (Shamrock R), 1964 v E (1)
Barber, E. (Shelbourne), 1966 v Sp; (with Birmingham C), 1966 v Bel (2)
Barry, P. (Fordsons), 1928 v Bel; 1929 v Bel (2)
Beglin, J. (Liverpool), 1984 v Chn; 1985 v M, D, I, Is, E, N, Sw; 1986 v Sw, USSR, D, W; 1987 v Bel (sub), S, Pol (15)
Bermingham, J. (Bohemians), 1929 v Bel (1)
Bermingham, P. (St James' Gate), 1935 v H (1)
Braddish, S. (Dundalk), 1978 v Pol (1)
Bonner, P. (Celtic), 1981 v Pol; 1982 v Alg; 1984 v Ma, Is, Chn; 1985 v I, Is, E, N; 1986 v U, Ic; 1987 v Bel (2), S (2), Pol, Bul, Br, L; 1988 v Bul, R, Y, N, E, USSR, Ho; 1989 v Sp, F, H, Sp, Ma, H (32)
Bradshaw, P. (St James' Gate), 1939 v Sw, Pol, H (2), G (5)
Brady, F. (Fordsons), 1926 v I; 1927 v I (2)
Brady, T. R. (QPR), 1964 v A (2), Sp (2), Pol, N (6)
Brady, W. L. (Arsenal), 1975 v USSR, T, Sw, USSR, Sw, WG; 1976 v T, N, Pol; 1977 v E, T, F (2), Sp, Bul; 1978 v Bul, N; 1979 v Ni, E, D, Bul, WG; 1980 v W, Bul, E, Cy; (with Juventus), 1981 v Ho, Bel, F, Cy, Bel; 1982 v Ho, F, Ch, Br, Tr; 1983 (with Sampdoria), v Ho, Sp, Ic, Ma; 1984 v Ic, Ho, Ma, Pol, Is; (with Internazionale), 1985 v USSR, N, D, I, E, N, Sp, Sw; 1986 v Sw, USSR, D, W; (with Ascoli), 1987 v Bel, S (2), Pol, (with West Ham U), Bul, Bel, Br, L; 1988 v L, Bul (67); 1989 v F, H (sub), H (sub) (70)
Breen, T. (Manchester U), 1937 v Sw, F; (with Shamrock R), 1947 v E, Sp, P (5)
Brennan, F. (Drumcondra), 1965 v Bel (1)
Brennan, S. A. (Manchester U), 1965 v Sp; 1966 v Sp, A, Bel; 1967 v Sp, T, Sp; 1969 v Cz, D, H; 1970 v S, Cz, D, H, Pol (sub), WG; (with Waterford), 1971 v Pol, Se, I (19)
Brown, J. (Coventry C), 1937 v Sw, F (2)
Browne, W. (Bohemians), 1964 v A, Sp, E (3)
Buckley, L. (Shamrock R), 1984 v Pol (sub); (with Waregem), 1985 v M (2)
Burke, F. (Cork), 1934 v Bel (1)
Burke, F. (Cork Ath), 1952 v WG (1)
Burke, J. (Shamrock R), 1929 v Bel (1)
Byrne, A. B. (Southampton), 1970 v D, Pol, WG; 1971 v Pol, Se (2), I (2), A; 1973 v F, USSR (sub), F, N; 1974 v Pol (14)
Byrne, D. (Shelbourne), 1929 v Bel; (with Shamrock R), 1932 v Sp; (with Coleraine), 1934 v Bel (3)
Byrne, J. (Bray Unknowns), 1928 v Bel (1)
Byrne, J. (QPR), 1985 v I, Is (sub), E (sub), Sp (sub); 1987 v S (sub), Bel (sub), Br, L (sub); 1988 v L, Bul (sub), Is, R, Y (sub), Pol (sub) (14)
Byrne, P. (Shamrock R), 1984 v Pol, Chn; 1985 v M, I; 1986 v D (sub), W (sub), U (sub), Ic (sub), Cz (9)
Byrne, P. (Shelbourne), 1931 v Sp; 1932 v Ho; (with Drumcondra), 1934 v Ho (3)
Byrne, S. (Bohemians), 1931 v Sp (1)

Campbell, A. (Santander), 1985 v I (sub), Is, Sp (3)
Campbell, N. (St Patrick's Ath), 1971 v A (sub); (with Fortuna, Cologne), 1972 v Ir, Ec, Ch, P; 1973 v USSR, F (sub); 1975 v WG; 1976 v N; 1977 v Sp, Bul (sub) (11)
Cannon, H. (Bohemians), 1926 v I; 1928 v Bel (2)
Cantwell, N. (West Ham U), 1954 v L; 1956 v Sp, Ho; 1957 v D, WG, E (2); 1958 v D, Pol, A; 1959 v Pol, Cz (2); 1960 v Se, Ch, Se; 1961 v N; (with Manchester U), 1961 v S (2); 1962 v Cz (2), A; 1963 v Ic (2), S; 1964 v A, Sp, E; 1965 v Pol, Sp; 1966 v Sp (2), A, Bel; 1967 v Sp, T (36)
Carey, J. J. (Manchester U), 1938 v N, Cz, Pol; 1939 v Sw, Pol, H (2), G; 1946 v P, Sp; 1947 v E, Sp, P; 1948 v P, Sp; 1949 v Sw, Bel, P, Se, Sp; 1950 v Fi, E, Fi, Se; 1951 v N, Arg, N; 1953 v F, A (29)
Carolan, J. (Manchester U), 1960 v Se, Ch (2)
Carroll, B. (Shelbourne), 1949 v Bel; 1950 v Fi (2)
Carroll, T. R. (Ipswich T), 1968 v Pol; 1969 v Pol, A, D; 1970 v Cz, Pol, WG; 1971 v Se; (with Birmingham C), 1972 v Ir, Ec, Ch, P; 1973 v USSR (2), Pol, F, N (17)
Cascarino, A. G. (Gillingham), 1986 v Sw, USSR, D; (with Millwall), 1988 v Pol, N (sub), USSR (sub), Ho (sub); 1989 v Ni, Tun, Sp, F, H, Sp, Ma, H (15)
Chandler, J. (Leeds U), 1980 v Cz (sub), US (2)
Chatton, H. A. (Shelbourne), 1931 v Sp; (with Dumbarton), 1932 v Sp; (with Cork), 1934 v Ho (3)
Clarke, J. (Drogheda U), 1978 v Pol (sub) (1)
Clarke, K. (Drumcondra), 1948 v P, Sp (2)
Clarke, M. (Shamrock R), 1950 v Bel (1)
Clinton, T. J. (Everton), 1951 v N; 1954 v F, L (3)
Coad, P. (Shamrock R), 1947 v E, Sp, P; 1948 v P, Sp; 1949 v Sw, Bel, P, Se; 1951 v N (sub); 1952 v Sp (11)
Coffey, T. (Drumcondra), 1950 v Fi (1)
Colfer, M. D. (Shelbourne), 1950 v Bel; 1951 v N (2)
Collins, F. (Jacobs), 1927 v I (1)
Conmy, O. M. (Peterborough U), 1965 v Bel; 1967 v Cz; 1968 v Cz, Pol; 1970 v Cz (5)
Connolly, J. (Fordsons), 1926 v I (1)
Connolly, N. (Cork), 1937 v G (1)
Conroy, G. A. (Stoke C), 1970 v Cz, D, H, Pol, WG; 1971 v Pol, Se (2), I; 1973 v USSR, F, USSR, N; 1974 v Pol, Br, U, Ch; 1975 v T, Sw, USSR, Sw, WG; 1976 v T (sub), Pol; 1977 v E, T, Pol (27)
Conway, J. P. (Fulham), 1967 v Sp, T, Sp; 1968 v Cz; 1969 v A (sub), H; 1970 v S, Cz, D, H, Pol, WG; 1971 v I, A; 1974 v U, Ch; 1975 v WG (sub); 1976 v N, Pol; (with Manchester C), 1977 v Pol (20)
Corr, P. J. (Everton), 1949 v P, Sp; 1950 v E, Se (4)
Courtney, E. (Cork U), 1946 v P (1)
Cummins, G. P. (Luton T), 1954 v L (2); 1955 v N (2), WG; 1956 v Y, Sp; 1958 v D, Pol, A; 1959 v Pol, Cz (2); 1960 v Se, Ch, WG, Se; 1961 v S (2) (19)
Cuneen, T. (Limerick), 1951 v N (1)
Curtis, D. P. (Shelbourne), 1957 v D, WG; (with Bristol C), 1957 v E (2); 1958 v D, Pol, A; (with Ipswich T), 1959 v Pol; 1960 v Se, Ch, WG, Se; 1961 v N, S; 1962 v A; 1963 v Ic (with Exeter C), 1964 v A (17)
Cusack, S. (Limerick), 1953 v F (1)

Daly, G. A. (Manchester U), 1973 v Pol (sub), N; 1974 v Br (sub), U (sub); 1975 v Sw (sub), WG; 1977 v E, T, F; (with Derby Co), F, Bul; 1978 v Bul, T, D; 1979 v Ni, E, D, Bul; 1980 v Ni, E, Cy, Sw, Arg; (with Coventry C), 1981 v Ho, Bel, Cy, W, Bel, Cz, Pol (sub); 1982 v Alg, Ch, Br, Tr; 1983 v Ho, Sp (sub), Ma; 1984 v Is (sub); (with Birmingham C), 1985 v M (sub), N, Sp, Sw; 1986 v Sw; (with Shrewsbury T), U, Ic (sub), Cz (sub); 1987 v S (sub) (47)
Daly, J. (Shamrock R), 1932 v Ho; 1935 v Sw (2)
Daly, M. (Wolverhampton W), 1978 v T, Pol (2)
Daly, P. Shamrock R), 1950 v Fi (sub) (1)
Davis, T. L. (Oldham Ath), 1937 v G, H; (with Tranmere R), 1938 v Cz, Pol (4)
Deacy, E. (Aston Villa), 1982 v Alg (sub), Ch, Br, Tr (4)
De Mange, K. J. P. P. (Liverpool), 1987 v Br (sub); (with Hull C) 1989 v Tun (sub) (2)
Dempsey, J. T. (Fulham), 1967 v Sp, Cz; 1968 v Cz, Pol; 1969 v Pol, A, D; (with Chelsea), 1969 v Cz, D; 1970 v H, WG; 1971 v Pol, Se (2), I; 1972 v Ir, Ec, Ch, P (19)
Dennehy, J. (Cork Hibernians), 1972 v Ec (sub), Ch; (with Nottingham F), 1973 v USSR (sub), Pol, F, N; 1974 v

Pol (sub); 1975 v T (sub), WG (sub); (with Walsall), 1976 v Pol (sub); 1977 v Pol (sub) (11)
Desmond, P. (Middlesbrough), 1950 v Fi, E, Fi, Se (4)
Devine, J. (Arsenal), 1980 v Cz, Ni; 1981 v Cz; 1982 v Ho, Alg; 1983 v Sp, Ma; (with Norwich C), 1984 v Ic, Ho, Is; 1985 v USSR, N (12)
Donnelly, J. (Dundalk), 1935 v H, Sw, G; 1936 v Ho, Sw, H, L; 1937 v G, H; 1938 v N (10)
Donnelly, T. (Drumcondra), 1938 v N; (Shamrock R), 1939 v Sw (2)
Donovan, D. C. (Everton), 1955 v N, Ho, N, WG; 1957 v E (5)
Donovan, T. (Aston Villa), 1980 v Cz (1)
Dowdall, C. (Fordsons), 1928 v Bel; (with Barnsley), 1929 v Bel; (with Cork), 1931 v Sp (3)
Doyle, C. (Shelbourne), 1959 v Cz (1)
Doyle, D. (Shamrock R), 1926 v I (1)
Doyle, L. (Dolphin), 1932 v Sp (1)
Duffy, B. (Shamrock R), 1950 v Bel (1)
Duggan, H. A. (Leeds U), 1927 v I; 1930 v Bel; 1936 v H, L; (with Newport Co), 1938 v N (5)
Dunne, A. P. (Manchester U), 1962 v A; 1963 v Ic, S; 1964 v A, Sp, Pol, N, E; 1965 v Pol, Sp; 1966 v Sp (2), A, Bel; 1967 v Sp, T, Sp; 1969 v Pol, D, H; 1970 v H; 1971 v Se, I, A; (with Bolton W), 1974 v Br (sub), U, Ch; 1975 v T, Sw, USSR, Sw, WG; 1976 v T (33)
Dunne, J. (Sheffield U), 1930 v Bel; (with Arsenal), 1936 v Sw, H, L; (with Southampton), 1937 v Sw, F; (with Shamrock R), 1938 v N (2), Cz, Pol; 1939 v Sw, Pol, H (2), G (15)
Dunne, J. C. (Fulham), 1971 v A (1)
Dunne, L. (Manchester C), 1935 v Sw, G (2)
Dunne, P. A. J. (Manchester U), 1965 v Sp; 1966 v Sp (2), WG; 1967 v T (5)
Dunne, S. (Luton T), 1953 v F, A; 1954 v F, L; 1956 v Sp, Ho; 1957 v D, WG, E; 1958 v D, Pol, A; 1959 v Pol; 1960 v WG, Se (15)
Dunne, T. (St Patrick's Ath), 1956 v Ho; 1957 v D, WG (3)
Dunning, P. (Shelbourne), 1971 v Se, I (2)
Dunphy, E. M. (York C), 1966 v Sp; (with Millwall), 1966 v WG; 1967 v T, Sp, T, Cz; 1968 v Cz, Pol; 1969 v Pol, A, D (2), H; 1970 v D, H, Pol, WG (sub); 1971 v Pol, Se (2), I (2), A (23)
Dwyer, N. M. (West Ham U), 1960 v Se, Ch, WG, Se; (with Swansea T), 1961 v W, N, S (2); 1962 v Cz (2); 1964 v Pol (sub), N, E; 1965 v Pol (14)

Eccles, P. (Shamrock R), 1986 v U (sub) (1)
Egan, R. (Dundalk), 1929 v Bel (1)
Eglington, T. J. (Shamrock R), 1946 v P, Sp; (with Everton), 1947 v E, Sp, P; 1948 v P; 1949 v Sw, P, Se; 1951 v N, Arg; 1952 v WG (2), A, Sp; 1953 v F, A; 1954 v F, L, F; 1955 v N, Ho, WG; 1956 v Sp (24)
Ellis, P. (Bohemians), 1935 v Sw, G; 1936 v Ho, Sw, L; 1937 v G, H (7)

Fagan, E. (Shamrock R), 1973 v N (sub) (1)
Fagan, F. (Manchester C), 1955 v N; 1960 v Se; (with Derby Co), 1960 v Ch, WG, Se; 1961 v W, N, S (8)
Fagan, K. (Shamrock R), 1926 v I (1)
Fairclough, M. (Dundalk), 1982 v Ch (sub), Tr (sub) (2)
Fallon, S. (Celtic), 1951 v N; 1952 v WG (2), A, Sp; 1953 v F; 1955 v N, WG (8)
Fallon, W. J. (Notts Co), 1935 v H; 1936 v H; 1937 v H, Sw, F; 1939 v Sw, Pol; (with Sheffield W), 1939 v H, G (9)
Farquharson, T. G. (Cardiff C), 1929 v Bel; 1930 v Bel; 1931 v Sp; 1932 v Sp (4)
Farrell, P. (Hibernian), 1937 v Sw, F (2)
Farrell, P. D. (Shamrock R), 1946 v P, Sp; (with Everton), 1947 v Sp, P; 1948 v P, Sp; 1949 v Sw, P (sub), Sp; 1950 v E, Fi, Se; 1951 v Arg, N; 1952 v WG (2), A, Sp; 1953 v F, A; 1954 v F (2); 1955 v N, Ho, WG; 1956 v Y, Sp; 1957 v E (28)
Feenan, J. J. (Sunderland), 1937 v Sw, F (2)
Finucane, A. (Limerick), 1967 v T, Cz; 1969 v Cz, D, H; 1970 v S, Cz; 1971 v Se, I, I (sub); 1972 v A (11)
Fitzgerald, F. J. (Waterford), 1955 v Ho; 1956 v Ho (2)
Fitzgerald, P. J. (Leeds U), 1961 v W, N, S; 1962 v Cz (2) (5)
Fitzpatrick, K. (Limerick), 1970 v Cz (1)
Fitzsimons, A. G. (Middlesbrough), 1950 v Fi, Bel; 1952 v WG (2), A, Sp; 1953 v F, A; 1954 v F, L, F; 1955 v Ho, N, WG; 1956 v Y, Sp, Ho; 1957 v D, WG, E (2); 1958 v D, Pol, A; 1959 v Pol; (with Lincoln C), 1959 v Cz (26)
Flood, J. J. (Shamrock R), 1926 v I; 1929 v Bel; 1930 v Bel; 1931 v Sp; 1932 v Sp (5)
Fogarty, A. (Sunderland), 1960 v WG, Se; 1961 v S; 1962 v Cz (2); 1963 v Ic (2), S (sub); 1964 v A (2); (with Hartlepools U), Sp (11)
Foley, J. (Cork), 1934 v Bel, Ho; (with Celtic), 1935 v H, Sw, G; 1937 v G, H (7)
Foley, M. (Shelbourne), 1926 v I (1)
Foley, T. C. (Northampton T), 1964 v Sp, Pol, N; 1965 v Pol, Bel; 1966 v Sp (2), WG; 1967 v Cz (9)
Foy, T. (Shamrock R), 1938 v N; 1939 v H (2)
Fullam, J. (Preston NE), 1961 v N; (with Shamrock R), 1964 v Sp, Pol, N; 1966 v A, Bel; 1968 v Pol; 1969 v Pol, A, D; 1970 v Cz (sub) (11)
Fullam, R. (Shamrock R), 1926 v I; 1927 v I (2)

Gallagher, C. (Celtic), 1967 v T, Cz (2)
Gallagher, M. (Hibernian), 1954 v L (1)
Gallagher, P. (Falkirk), 1932 v Sp (1)
Galvin, A. (Tottenham H), 1983 v Ho, Ma; 1984 v Ho (sub), Is (sub); 1985 v M, USSR, N, D, I, N, Sp; 1986 v U, Ic, Cz; 1987 v Bel (2), S, Bul, L; (with Sheffield W), 1988 v L, Bul, R, Pol, N, E, USSR, Ho; 1989 v Sp (28)
Gannon, E. (Notts Co), 1949 v Sw; (with Sheffield W), 1949 v Bel, P, Se, Sp; 1950 v Fi; 1951 v N; 1952 v G, A; 1954 v L, F; 1955 v N; (with Shelbourne), 1955 v N, WG (14)
Gannon, M. (Shelbourne), 1972 v A (1)
Gaskins, P. (Shamrock R), 1934 v Bel, Ho; 1935 v H, Sw, G; (with St James' Gate), 1938 v Cz, Pol (7)
Gavin, J. T. (Norwich C), 1950 v Fi (2); 1953 v F; 1954 v L; (with Tottenham H), 1955 v Ho, WG; (with Norwich C), 1957 v D (7)
Geoghegan, M. (St James' Gate), 1937 v G; 1938 v N (2)
Gibbons, A. (St Patrick's Ath), 1952 v WG; 1954 v L; 1956 v Y, Sp (4)
Gilbert, R. (Shamrock R), 1966 v WG (1)
Giles, C. (Doncaster R), 1951 v N (1)
Giles, M. J. (Manchester U), 1960 v Se, Ch; 1961 v W, N, S (2); 1962 v Cz (2), A; 1963 v Ic, S; (with Leeds U), 1964 v A (2), Sp (2), Pol, N, E; 1965 v Sp; 1966 v Sp (2), A, Bel; 1967 v Sp, T (2); 1969 v A, D, Cz; 1970 v S, Pol, WG; 1971 v I; 1973 v F, USSR; 1974 v Br, U, Ch; 1975 v USSR, T, Sw, USSR, Sw; (with WBA), 1976 v T; 1977 v E, T, F (2), Pol, Bul; (with Shamrock R), 1978 v Bul, T, Pol, N, D; 1979 v Ni, D, Bul, WG, (60)
Givens, D. J. (Manchester U), 1969 v D, H; 1970 v S, Cz, D, H; (with Luton T), 1970 v Pol, WG; 1971 v Se, I (2), A; 1972 v Ir, Ec, P; (with QPR), 1973 v F, USSR, Pol, F, N; 1974 v Pol, Br, U, Ch; 1975 v USSR, T, Sw, USSR, Sw, WG; 1976 v T, N, Pol; 1977 v E, T, F (2), Sp, Bul; 1978 v Bul, N, D; (with Birmingham C), 1979 v Ni (sub), E, D, Bul, WG; 1980 v US (sub), Ni (sub), Sw, Arg; 1981 v Ho, Bel, Cy (sub), W; (with Neuchatel X), 1982 v F (sub) (56)
Glen, W. (Shamrock R), 1927 v I; 1929 v Bel; 1930 v Bel; 1932 v Sp; 1936 v Ho, Sw, H, L (8)
Glynn, D. (Drumcondra), 1952 v WG; 1955 v N (2)

Godwin, T. F. (Shamrock R), 1949 v P, Se, Sp; 1950 v Fi, E; (with Leicester C), 1950 v Fi, Se, Bel; 1951 v N; (with Bournemouth), 1956 v Ho; 1957 v E; 1958 v D, Pol (13)
Golding, L. (Shamrock R), 1928 v Bel; 1930 v Bel (2)
Gorman, W. C. (Bury), 1936 v Sw, H, L; 1937 v G, H; 1938 v N, Cz, Pol; 1939 v Sw, Pol, H; (with Brentford), 1947 v E, P (13)
Grace, J. (Drumcondra), 1926 v I (1)
Grealish, A. (Orient), 1976 v N, Pol, D; 1979 v Ni, E, WG; (with Luton T), 1980 v W, Cz, Bul, US, Ni, E, Cy, Sw, Arg; 1981 v Ho, Bel, F, Cy, W, Bel, Pol; (with Brighton & HA), 1982 v Ho, Alg, Ch, Br, Tr; 1983 v Ho, Sp, Ic, Sp; 1984 v Ic, Ho (with WBA), Pol, Chn; 1985 v M, USSR, N, D, Sp (sub), Sw; 1986 v USSR, D (44)
Gregg, E. (Bohemians), 1978 v Pol, D (sub); 1979 v E (sub), D, Bul, WG; 1980 v W, Cz (9)
Griffith, R. (Walsall), 1935 v H (1)
Grimes, A. A. (Manchester U), 1978 v T, Pol, N (sub); 1980 v Bul, US, Ni, E, Cy; 1981 v Cz, Pol; 1982 v Alg; 1983 v Sp, Sp; (with Coventry C), 1984 v Pol, Is; (with Luton T), 1988 v L, R (17)

Hale, A. (Aston Villa), 1962 v A; (with Doncaster R), 1963 v Ic; 1964 v Sp (2); (with Waterford), 1967 v Sp; 1968 v Pol (sub); 1969 v Pol, A, D; 1970 v S, Cz; 1971 v Pol (sub); 1972 v A (sub) (13)
Hamilton, T. (Shamrock R), 1959 v Cz (2) (2)
Hand, E. K. (Portsmouth), 1969 v Cz (sub); 1970 v Pol, WG; 1971 v Pol, A; 1973 v USSR, F, USSR, Pol, F; 1974 v Pol, Br, U, Ch; 1975 v T, Sw, USSR, Sw, WG; 1976 v T (20)
Harrington, W. (Cork), 1936 v Ho, Sw, H, L (4)
Hartnett, J. B. (Middlesbrough), 1949 v Sp; 1954 v L (2)
Haverty, J. (Arsenal), 1956 v Ho; 1957 v D, WG, E (2); 1958 v D, Pol, A; 1959 v Pol; 1960 v Se, Ch; 1961 v W, N, S (2); (with Blackburn R), 1962 v Cz (2); (with Millwall), 1963 v S; 1964 v A, Sp, Pol, N, E; (with Celtic), 1965 v Pol; (with Bristol R), 1965 v Sp; (with Shelbourne), 1966 v Sp (2), WG, A, Bel; 1967 v T, Sp (32)
Hayes, A. W. P. (Southampton), 1979 v D (1)
Hayes, W. E. (Huddersfield T), 1947 v E, P (2)
Hayes, W. J. (Limerick), 1949 v Bel (1)
Healey, R. (Cardiff C), 1977 v Pol; 1980 v E (sub) (2)
Heighway, S. D. (Liverpool), 1971 v Pol, Se (2), I, A; 1973 v USSR; 1975 v USSR, T, USSR, WG; 1976 v T, N; 1977 v E, F (2), Sp, Bul; 1978 v Bul, N, D; 1979 v Ni, Bul; 1980 v Bul, US, Ni, E, Cy, Arg; 1981 v Bel, F, Cy, W, Bel; (with Minnesota K), 1982 v Ho (34)
Henderson, B. (Drumcondra), 1948 v P, Sp (2)
Hennessy, J. (Shelbourne), 1956 v Pol, B, Sp; 1966 v WG; (with St Patrick's Ath), 1969 v A (5)
Herrick, J. (Cork Hibernians), 1972 v A, Ch (sub); (with Shamrock R), 1973 v F (sub) (3)
Higgins, J. (Birmingham C), 1951 v Arg (1)
Holmes, J. (Coventry C), 1971 v A (sub); 1973 v F, USSR, Pol, F, N; 1974 v Pol, Br; 1975 v USSR, Sw; 1976 v T, N, Pol; 1977 v E, T, F, Sp; (with Tottenham H), F, Pol, Bul; 1978 v Bul, T, Pol, N, D; 1979 v Ni, E, D, Bul; 1981 (with Vancouver W), v W (30)
Horlecher, A. F. (Bohemians), 1930 v Bel; 1932 v Sp, Ho; 1935 v H; 1936 v Ho, Sw (6)
Houghton, R. J. (Oxford U), 1986 v W, U, Ic, Cz; 1987 v Bel (2), S (2), Pol, L; 1988 v L, Bul, (with Liverpool), Is, Y, N, E, USSR, Ho; 1989 v Ni, Tun, Sp, F, H, Sp, Ma, H (26)
Howlett, G. (Brighton & HA), 1984 v Chn (sub) (1)
Hoy, M. (Dundalk), 1938 v N; 1939 v Sw, Pol, H (2), G (6)
Hughton, C. (Tottenham H), 1980 v US, E, Sw, Arg; 1981 v Ho, Bel, F, Cy, W, Bel, Pol; 1982 v F; 1983 v Ho, Sp, Ma, Sp; 1984 v Ic, Ho, Ma; 1985 v M (sub), USSR, N, I, Is, E, Sp; 1986 v Sw, USSR, U, Ic; 1987 v Bel, Bul; 1988 v Is, Y, Pol, N, E, USSR, Ho; 1989 v Ni, F, H, Sp, Ma, H (45)
Hurley, C. J. (Millwall), 1957 v E; 1958 v D, Pol, A; (with Sunderland), 1959 v Cz (2); 1960 v Se, Ch,WG, Se; 1961 v W, N, S (2); 1962 v Cz (2), A; 1963 v Ic (2), S; 1964 v A (2), Sp (2), Pol, N; 1965 v Sp; 1966 v WG, A, Bel; 1967 v T, Sp, T, Cz; 1968 v Cz, Pol (2); (with Bolton W), 1969 v D, Cz, H (40)
Hutchinson, F. (Drumcondra), 1935 v Sw, G (2)

Jordan, D. (Wolverhampton W), 1937 v Sw, F (2)
Jordan, W. (Bohemians), 1934 v Ho; 1938 v N (2)

Kavanagh, P. J. (Celtic), 1931 v Sp; 1932 v Sp (2)
Keane, T. R. (Swansea T), 1949 v Sw, P, Se, Sp (4)
Kearin, M. (Shamrock R), 1972 v A (1)
Kearns, F. T. (West Ham U), 1954 v L (1)
Kearns, M. (Oxford U), 1970 v Pol (sub); (with Walsall), 1974 v Pol (sub), U, Ch; 1976 v N, Pol; 1977 v E, T, F (2), Sp, Bul; 1978 v N, D; 1979 v Ni, E; (with Wolverhampton W), 1980 v US, Ni (18)
Kelly, D. T. (Walsall), 1988 v Is, R, Y; (with West Ham U), 1989 v Tun (sub) (4)
Kelly, J. (Derry C), 1932 v Ho; 1934 v Bel; 1936 v Sw, L (4)
Kelly, J. A. (Drumcondra), 1957 v WG, E; (with Preston NE), 1962 v A; 1963 v Ic (2), S; 1964 v A (2), Sp (2), Pol; 1965 v Bel; 1966 v A, Bel; 1967 v Sp (2), T, Cz (2), Pol; 1968 v Pol, A, D, Cz, D, H; 1970 v S, D, H, Pol, WG; 1971 v Pol, Se (2), I (2), A; 1972 v Ir, Ec, Ch, P; 1973 v USSR, F, USSR, Pol, F, N (47)
Kelly, J. P. V. (Wolverhampton W), 1961 v W, N, S; 1962 v Cz (2) (5)
Kelly, M. J. (Portsmouth), 1988 v Y, Pol (sub); 1989 v Tun (32)
Kelly, N. (Nottingham F), 1954 v L (1)
Kendrick, J. (Everton), 1927 v I; 1934 v Bel, Ho; 1936 v Ho (4)
Kennedy, M. F. (Portsmouth), 1986 v Ic, Cz (sub) (2)
Kennedy, W. (St James' Gate), 1932 v Ho; 1934 v Bel, Ho (3)
Keogh, J. (Shamrock R), 1966 v WG (sub) (1)
Keogh, S. (Shamrock R), 1959 v Pol (1)
Kiernan, F. W. (Shamrock R), 1951 v Arg, N; (with Southampton), 1952 v WG (2), A (5)
Kinnear, J. P. (Tottenham H), 1967 v T; 1968 v Cz, Pol; 1969 v A; 1970 v Cz, D, H, Pol; 1971 v Se (sub), I; 1972 v Ir, Ec, Ch, P; 1973 v USSR, F; 1974 v Pol, Br, U, Ch; 1975 v USSR, T, Sw, USSR, WG; (with Brighton), 1976 v T (sub) (26)
Kinsella, J. (Shelbourne), 1928 v Bel (1)
Kinsella, P. (Shamrock R), 1932 v Ho; 1938 v N (2)
Kirkland, A. (Shamrock R), 1927 v I (1)

Lacey, W. (Shelbourne), 1927 v I; 1928 v Bel; 1930 v Bel (3)
Langan, D. (Derby Co), 1978 v T, N; 1980 v Sw, Arg; (with Birmingham C), 1981 v Ho, Bel, F, Cy, W, Bel, Cz, Pol; 1982 v Ho, F; (with Oxford U), 1985 v N, Sp, Sw; 1986 v W, U; 1987 v Bel, S, Pol, Br (sub), L (sub); 1988 v L (25)
Lawler, J. F. (Fulham), 1953 v A; 1954 v L, F; 1955 v N, H, N, WG; 1956 v Y (8)
Lawlor, J. C. (Drumcondra), 1949 v Bel; (with Doncaster R), 1951 v N, Arg (3)
Lawlor, M. (Shamrock R), 1971 v Pol, Se (2), I (sub); 1973 v Pol (5)
Lawrenson, M. (Preston NE), 1977 v Pol; (with Brighton), 1978 v Bul, Pol, N (sub); 1979 v Ni, E; 1980 v E, Cy, Sw; 1981 v Ho, Bel, F, Cy, Pol; (with Liverpool), 1982 v Ho, F; 1983 v Ho, Sp, Ic, Ma, Sp; 1984 v Ic, Ho, Ma,

Is; 1985 v USSR, N, D, I, E, N; 1986 v Sw, USSR, D; 1987 v Bel, S; 1988 v Bul, Is (38)
Leech, M. (Shamrock R), 1969 v Cz, D, H; 1972 v A, Ir, Ec, P; 1973 v USSR (sub) (8)
Lennon, C. (St James' Gate), 1935 v H, Sw, G (3)
Lennox, G. (Dolphin), 1931 v Sp; 1932 v Sp (2)
Lowry, D. (St Patrick's Ath), 1962 v A (sub) (1)
Lunn, R. (Dundalk), 1939 v Sw, Pol (2)
Lynch, J. (Cork Bohemians), 1934 v Bel (1)

McAlinden, J. (Portsmouth), 1946 v P, Sp (2)
McCann, J. (Shamrock R), 1957 v WG (1)
McCarthy, J. (Bohemians), 1926 v I; 1928 v Bel; 1930 v Bel (3)
McCarthy, M. (Manchester C), 1984 v Pol, Chn; 1985 v M, D, I, Is, E, Sp, Sw; 1986 v Sw, USSR, W (sub), U, Ic, Cz; 1987 v S (2), Pol, Bul, Bel, Br, L; (with Celtic) 1988 v Bul, Is, R, Y, N, E, USSR, Ho; 1989 V Ni, Tun, Sp, F, H, Sp (36)
McCarthy, M. (Shamrock R), 1932 v Ho (1)
McConville, T. (Dundalk), 1972 v A; (with Waterford), 1973 v USSR, F, USSR, Pol, F (6)
McDonagh, J. (Everton), 1981 v W, Bel, Cz; (with Bolton W), 1982 v Ho, F, Ch, Br; 1983 v Ho, Sp, Ic, Ma, Sp; (with Notts Co), 1984 v Ic, Ho, Pol; 1985 v M, USSR, N, D, Sp, Sw; 1986 v Sw, USSR, D (24)
McDonagh, Joe (Shamrock R), 1984 v Pol (sub), Ma; 1985 v M (sub) (3)
McEvoy, M. A. (Blackburn R), 1961 v S (2); 1963 v S; 1964 v A, Sp (2), Pol, N, E; 1965 v Pol, Bel, Sp; 1966 v Sp (2); 1967 v Sp, T, Cz (17)
McGee, P. (QPR), 1978 v T, N (sub), D (sub); 1979 v Ni, E, D (sub), Bul (sub); 1980 v Cz, Bul; (with Preston NE), US, Ni, Cy, Sw, Arg; 1981 v Bel (sub) (15)
McGowan, D. (West Ham U), 1949 v P, Se, Sp (3)
McGowan, J. (Cork U), 1947 v Sp (1)
McGrath, M. (Blackburn R), 1958 v A; 1959 v Pol, Cz (2); 1960 v Se, WG, Se; 1961 v W; 1962 v C (2); 1963 v S; 1964 v A (2), E; 1965 v Pol, Bel, Sp; 1966 v Sp; (with Bradford), 1966 v WG, A, Bel; 1967 v T (22)
McGrath, P. (Manchester U), 1985 v I (sub), Is, E, N (sub), Sw (sub); 1986 v Sw (sub), D, W, Ic, Cz; 1987 v Bel (2), S (2), Pol, Bul, Br, L; 1988 v L, Bul, Y, Pol, N, E, Ho; 1989 v Ni, F, H, Sp, Ma, H (31)
McGuire, W. (Bohemians), 1936 v Ho (1)
McKenzie, G. (Southend U), 1938 v N (2), Cz, Pol; 1939 v Sw, Pol, H (2), G (9)
Mackey, G. (Shamrock R), 1957 v D, WG, E (3)
McLoughlin, F. (Fordsons), 1930 v Bel; (with Cork), 1932 v Sp (2)
McMillan, W. (Belfast Celtic), 1946 v P, Sp (2)
McNally, J. B. (Luton T), 1959 v Cz; 1961 v Sp; 1963 v Ic (3)
Macken, A. (Derby Co), 1977 v Sp (1)
Madden, O. (Cork), 1936 v H (1)
Maguire, J. (Shamrock R), 1929 v Bel (1)
Malone, G. (Shelbourne), 1949 v Bel (1)
Mancini, T. J. (QPR), 1974 v Pol, Br, U, Ch; (with Arsenal), 1975 v USSR (5)
Martin, C. (Bo'ness), 1927 v I (1)
Martin, C. J. (Glentoran), 1946 v P (sub), Sp; 1947 v E; (with Leeds U), 1947 v Sp; 1948 v P, Sp; (with Aston Villa), 1949 v Sw, Bel, P, Se, Sp; 1950 v Fi, E, Fi, Se, Bel; 1951 v Arg; 1952 v WG, A, Sp; 1954 v F (2), L; 1955 v N, Ho, N, WG; 1956 v Y, Sp, Ho (30)
Martin, M. P. (Bohemians), 1972 v A, Ir, Ec, Ch, P; 1973 v USSR; (with Manchester U), 1973 v USSR, Pol, F, N; 1974 v Pol, Br, U, Ch; 1975 v USSR, T, Sw, USSR, Sw, WG; (with WBA), 1976 v T, N, Pol; 1977 v E, T, F (2), Sp, Pol, Bul; (with Newcastle U), 1979 v D, Bul, WG; 1980 v W, Cz, Bul, US, Ni; 1981 v F, Bel, Cz; 1982 v Ho, F, Alg, Ch, Br, Tr; 1983 v Ho, Sp, Ma, Sp (51)
Meagan, M. K. (Everton), 1961 v S; 1962 v A; 1963 v Ic; 1964 v Sp; (with Huddersfield T), 1965 v Bel; 1966 v Sp (2), A, Bel; 1967 v Sp, T, Sp, T, Cz; 1968 v Cz, Pol;
Meehan, P. (Drumcondra), 1934 v Ho (1)
Monahan, P. (Sligo R), 1935 v Sw, G (2)
Mooney, J. (Shamrock R), 1965 v Pol, Bel (2)
Moore, P. (Shamrock R), 1931 v Sp; 1932 v Ho; (with Aberdeen), 1934 v Bel, Ho; 1935 v H, G; (with Shamrock R), 1936 v Ho; 1937 v G, H (9)
Moran, K. (Manchester U), 1980 v Sw, Arg; 1981 v Bel, F, Cy, W (sub), Bel, Cz, Pol; 1982 v F, Alg; 1983 v Ic; 1984 v Ic, Ho, Ma, Is; 1985 v M; 1986 v D, Ic, Cz; 1987 v Bel (2), S (2), Pol, Bul, Br, L; 1988 v L, Bul, Is, R, Y, Pol, N, E, USSR, Ho; (with Sporting Gijon) 1989 v Ni, Sp, H, Sp, Ma, H (44)
Moroney, T. (West Ham U), 1948 v Sp; 1949 v P, Se, Sp; 1950 v Fi, E, Fi, Bel; 1951 v N (2); 1952 v WG; 1954 v F (12)
Morris, C. B. (Celtic), 1988 v Is, R, Y, Pol, N, E, USSR, Ho; 1989 v Ni, Tun, Sp, F, H, H (sub) (14)
Moulson, C. (Lincoln C), 1936 v H, L; (with Notts Co), 1937 v H, Sw, F (5)
Moulson, G. B. (Lincoln C), 1948 v P, Sp; 1949 v Sw (3)
Mucklan, C. (Drogheda U), 1978 v Pol (1)
Muldoon, T. (Aston Villa), 1927 v I (1)
Mulligan, P. M. (Shamrock R), 1969 v Cz, D, H; 1970 v S, Cz, D; (with Chelsea), 1970 v H, Pol, WG; 1971 v Pol, Se, I; 1972 v A, Ir, Ec, Ch, P; (with Crystal Palace), 1973 v F, USSR, Pol, F, N; 1974 v Pol, Br, U, Ch; 1975 v USSR, T, Sw, USSR, Sw; (with WBA), 1976 v T, Pol; 1977 v E, T, F (2), Pol, Bul; 1978 v Bul, N, D; 1979 v E, D, Bul (sub), WG; (with Shamrock R) 1980 v W, Cz, Bul, US (sub) (50)
Munroe, L. (Shamrock R), 1954 v L (1)
Murphy, A. (Clyde), 1956 v Y (1)
Murphy, B. (Bohemians), 1986 v U (1)
Murphy, J. (C. Palace), 1980 v W, US, Cy (3)
Murray, T. (Dundalk), 1950 v Bel (1)

Newman, W. (Shelbourne), 1969 v D (1)
Nolan, R. (Shamrock R), 1957 v D, WG, E; 1958 v Pol; 1960 v Ch, WG, Se; 1962 v Cz (2); 1963 v Ic (10)

O'Brien, F. (Philadelphia F), 1980 v Cz, E, Cy (sub), Arg (4)
O'Brien, L. (Shamrock R), 1986 v U; (with Manchester U), 1987 v Br; 1988 v Is (sub), R (sub), Y (sub), Pol (sub); 1989 v Tun (with Newcastle U), Sp (sub) (8)
O'Brien, M. T. (Derby Co), 1927 v I; (with Walsall), 1929 v Bel; (with Norwich C), 1930 v Bel; (with Watford), 1932 v Ho (4)
O'Brien, R. (Notts Co), 1976 v N, Pol; 1977 v Sp, Pol (4)
O'Byrne, L. B. (Shamrock R), 1949 v Bel (1)
O'Callaghan, B. R. (Stoke C), 1979 v WG (sub); 1980 v W, US; 1981 v W; 1982 v Br, Tr (6)
O'Callaghan, K. (Ipswich T), 1981 v Cz, Pol; 1982 v Alg, Ch, Br, Tr (sub); 1983 v Sp, Ic (sub), Ma (sub), Sp (sub); 1984 v Ic, Ho, Ma; 1985 v M (sub), N (sub), D (sub), E (sub); (with Portsmouth), 1986 v Sw (sub), USSR (sub); 1987 v Br (20)
O'Connell, A. (Dundalk), 1967 v Sp; (with Bohemians), 1971 v Pol (sub) (2)
O'Connor, T. (Shamrock R), 1950 v Fi, E, Fi, Se (4)
O'Connor, T. (Fulham), 1968 v Cz; (with Dundalk), 1972 v A, Ir (sub), Ec (sub), Ch; (with Bohemians), 1973 v F (sub), Pol (sub) (7)
O'Driscoll, J. F. (Swansea T), 1949 v Sw, Bel, Se (3)
O'Driscoll, S. (Fulham), 1982 v Ch, Br, Tr (sub) (3)
O'Farrell, F. (West Ham U), 1952 v A; 1953 v A; 1954 v F; 1955 v Ho, N; 1956 v Y, Ho; (with Preston NE), 1958 v D; 1959 v Cz (9)
O'Flanagan, K. P. (Bohemians), 1938 v N, Cz, Pol (2), H (2), G; (with Arsenal), 1947 v E, Sp, P (10)
O'Flanagan, M. (Bohemians), 1947 v E (1)
O'Hanlon, K. G. (Rotherham U), 1988 v Is (1)
O'Kane, P. (Bohemians), 1935 v H, Sw, G (3)
O'Keefe, E. (Everton), 1981 v W; (with Port Vale), 1984 v Chn; 1985 v M, USSR (sub), E (5)
O'Keefe, T. (Cork), 1934 v Bel; (with Waterford), 1938 v

O'Leary, D. (Arsenal), 1977 v E, F (2), Sp, Bul; 1978 v Bul, N, D; 1979 v E, Bul, WG; 1980 v W, Bul, Ni, E, Cy; 1981 v Ho, Cz, Pol; 1982 v Ho, F; 1983 v Ho, Ic, Sp; 1984 v Pol, Is, Chn; 1985 v USSR, N, D, Is, E (sub), N, Sp, Sw; 1986 v Sw, USSR, D, W; 1989 v Sp, Ma, H (42)
O'Leary, P. (Shamrock R), 1980 v Bul, US, NI, E (sub), Cz, Arg; 1981 v Ho (7)
O'Mahoney, M. T. (Bristol R), 1938 v Cz, Pol; 1939 v Sw, Pol, H, G (6)
O'Neill, F. S. (Shamrock R), 1962 v Cz (2); 1965 v Pol, Bel, Sp; 1966 v Sp (2), WG, A; 1967 v Sp, T, Sp, T; 1969 v Pol, A, D, Cz, D (sub), H (sub); 1972 v A (20)
O'Neill, J. (Everton), 1952 v Sp; 1953 v F, A; 1954 v F, L, F; 1955 v N, Ho, N, WG; 1956 v Y, Sp; 1957 v D; 1958 v M; 1959 v Pol, Cz (2) (17)
O'Neill, J. (Preston NE), 1961 v W (1)
O'Neill, W. (Dundalk), 1936 v Ho, Sw, H, L; 1937 v G, H, Sw, F; 1938 v N; 1939 v H, G (11)
O'Regan, K. (Brighton & HA), 1984 v Ma, Pol; 1985 v M, Sp (sub) (4)
O'Reilly, J. (Brideville), 1932 v Ho; (with Aberdeen), 1934 v Bel, Ho; (with Brideville), 1936 v Ho; Sw, H, L; (with St James' Gate), 1937 v G, H, Sw, F; 1938 v N (2), Cz, Pol; 1939 v Sw, Pol, H (2), G (20)
O'Reilly, J. (Cork U), 1946 v P, Sp (2)

Peyton, G. (Fulham), 1977 v Sp (sub); 1978 v Bul, T, Pol; 1979 v D, Bul, WG; 1980 v W, Cz, Bul, E, Cy, Sw, Arg; 1981 v Ho, Bel, F, Cy; 1982 v Tr; 1985 v M (sub); 1986 v W, Cz; (with Bournemouth), 1988 v L, Pol; 1989 v Ni, Tun (26)
Peyton, N. (Shamrock R), 1957 v WG; (with Leeds U), 1960 v WG, Se (sub); 1961 v W; 1963 v Ic, S (6)

Quinn, N. J. (Arsenal), 1986 v Ic (sub), Cz; 1987 v Bul (sub); 1988 v L (sub), Bul (sub), Is, R (sub), Pol (sub), E (sub); 1989 v Tun (sub), Sp (sub), H (sub) (12)

Reid, C. (Brideville), 1931 v Sp (1)
Richardson, D. J. (Shamrock R), 1972 v A (sub); (with Gillingham), 1973 v N (sub); 1980 v Cz (3)
Rigby, A. (St James' Gate), 1935 v H, Sw, G (3)
Ringstead, A. (Sheffield U), 1951 v Arg, N; 1952 v WG (2), A, Sp; 1953 v A; 1954 v F; 1955 v N; 1956 v Y, Sp, Ho; 1957 v E (2); 1958 v D, Pol, A; 1959 v Pol, Cz (2) (20)
Robinson, J. (Bohemians), 1928 v Bel; (with Dolphin), 1931 v Sp (2)
Robinson, M. (Brighton & HA), 1981 v F, Cy, Bel, Pol; 1982 v Ho, F, Alg, Ch; 1983 v Ho, Sp, Ic, Ma; (with Liverpool), 1984 v Ic, Ho, Is; 1985 v USSR, N, (with QPR), N, Sp, Sw; 1986 v D (sub), W, Cz (23)
Roche, P. J. (Shelbourne), 1972 v A; (with Manchester U), 1975 v USSR, T, Sw, USSR, Sw, WG; 1976 v T (8)
Rogers, E. (Blackburn R), 1968 v Cz, Pol; 1969 v Pol, A, D, Cz, D, H; 1970 v S, D, H; 1971 v I (2), A; (with Charlton Ath), 1972 v Ir, Ec, Ch, P; 1973 v USSR (19)
Ryan, G. (Derby Co), 1978 v T; (with Brighton), 1979 v E, WG; 1980 v W, Cy (sub), Sw, Arg (sub); 1981 v F (sub), Pol (sub); 1982 v Ho (sub), Alg (sub), Ch (sub), Tr; 1984 v Pol, Chn; 1985 v M (16)
Ryan, R. A. (WBA), 1950 v Se, Bel; 1951 v N, Arg, N; 1952 v WG (2), A, Sp; 1953 v F, A; 1954 v F, L, F; 1955 v N; (with Derby Co), 1956 v Sp (16)

Saward, P. (Millwall), 1954 v L; (with Aston Villa), 1957 v E (2); 1958 v D, Pol, A; 1959 v Pol, Cz; 1960 v Se, Ch, WG, Se; 1961 v W, N; (with Huddersfield T), 1961 v S; 1962 v A; 1963 v Ic (2) (18)
Scannell, T. (Southend U), 1954 v L (1)
Scully, P. J. (Arsenal), 1989 v Tun (sub) (1)
Sheedy, K. (Everton), 1984 v Ho (sub), Ma; 1985 v D, I, Is, Sw; 1986 v Sw, D; 1987 v S, Pol; 1988 v Is, R, Pol, E (sub), USSR; 1989 v Ni, Tun, H, Sp, Ma, H (21)
Sheridan, J. J. (Leeds U), 1988 v R, Y, Pol, N (sub); 1989 v Sp (5)
Sloan, J. W. (Arsenal), 1946 v P, Sp (2)
Smyth, M. (Shamrock R), 1969 v Pol (sub) (1)
Squires, J. (Shelbourne), 1934 v Ho (1)
Stapleton, F. (Arsenal), 1977 v T, F, Sp, Bul; 1978 v Bul, N, D; 1979 v Ni, E (sub), D, WG; 1980 v W, Bul, Ni, E, Cy; 1981 v Ho, Bel, F, Cy, Bel, Cz, Pol; (with Manchester U), 1982 v Ho, F, Alg; 1983 v Ho, Sp, Ic, Ma, Sp; 1984 v Ic, Ho, Ma, Pol, Is, Chn; 1985 v N, D, I, Is, E, N, Sw; 1986 v Sw, USSR, D, U, Ic, Cz (sub); 1987 v Bel (2), S (2), Pol, Bul, L; (with Ajax), 1988 v L, Bul, R, (with Derby Co), Y, N, E, USSR, Ho; 1989 (with Le Havre) v F, Sp, Ma (68)
Staunton, S. (Liverpool), 1989 v Tun, Sp, Sp, Ma, H (5)
Stevenson, A. E. (Dolphin), 1932 v Ho; (with Everton), 1947 v E, Sp, P; 1948 v P, Sp; 1949 v Sw (7)
Strahan, F. (Shelbourne), 1964 v Pol, N, E; 1965 v Pol; 1966 v WG (5)
Sullivan, J. (Fordsons), 1928 v Bel (1)
Swan, M. M. G. (Drumcondra), 1960 v Se (sub) (1)
Synnott, N. (Shamrock R), 1978 v T, Pol; 1979 v Ni (3)

Thomas, P. (Waterford), 1974 v Pol, Br (2)
Townsend, A. D. (Norwich C) 1989 v F, Sp (sub), Ma (sub), H (4)
Traynor, T. J. (Southampton), 1954 v L; 1962 v A; 1963 v Ic (2), S; 1964 v A (2), Sp (8)
Treacy, R. C. P. (WBA), 1966 v WG; 1967 v Sp, Cz; 1968 v Cz; (with Charlton Ath), 1968 v Pol; 1969 v Pol, Cz, D; 1970 v S, D, H (sub), Pol (sub), WG (sub); 1971 v Pol, Se (sub), Se, I, A; (with Swindon T), 1972 v Ir, Ec, Ch, P; 1973 v USSR, F, USSR, Pol, F, N; 1974 v Pol; (with Preston NE), 1974 v Br; 1975 v USSR, Sw (2), WG; 1976 v T, N (sub), Pol (sub); (with WBA), 1977 v F, Pol; 1978 (with Shamrock R), v T, Pol (2); 1980 v Cz (sub) (43)
Tuohy, L. (Shamrock R), 1956 v Y; 1959 v Cz (2); (with Newcastle U), 1962 v A; 1963 v Ic (2); (with Shamrock R), 1964 v A; 1965 v Bel (8)
Turner, A. (Celtic), 1963 v S; 1964 v Sp (2)
Turner, C. J. (Southend U), 1936 v Sw; 1937 v G, H, Sw, F; (with West Ham U), 1938 v N (2), Cz, Pol; 1939 v H (10)

Vernon, J. (Belfast Celtic), 1946 v P, Sp (2)

Waddock, G. (QPR), 1980 v Sw, Arg; 1981 v W, Pol (sub); 1982 v Alg; 1983 v Ic, Ma, Sp, Ho (sub); 1984 v Ic, Ho, Is; 1985 v I, Is, E, N, Sp; 1986 v USSR (18)
Walsh, D. J. (WBA), 1946 v P, Sp; 1947 v Sp, P; 1948 v P, Sp; 1949 v Sw, P, Se, Sp; 1950 v E, Fi, Se; 1951 v N; (with Aston Villa), v Arg, N; 1952 v Sp; 1953 v A; 1954 v F (2) (20)
Walsh, J. (Limerick), 1982 v Tr (1)
Walsh, M. (Blackpool), 1976 v N, Pol; 1977 v F (sub), Pol; (with Everton), 1979 v Ni (sub); (with QPR), D (sub), Bul, WG (sub); (with Porto), 1981 v Bel (sub), Cz; 1982 v Alg (sub); 1983 v Sp, Ho (sub), Sp (sub); 1984 v Ic (sub), Ma, Pol, Chn; 1985 v USSR, N (sub), D (22)
Walsh, M. (Everton), 1982 v Ch, Br, Tr; 1983 v Sp, (with Norwich C), Ic (5)
Walsh, W. (Manchester C), 1947 v E, Sp, P; 1948 v P, Sp; 1949 v Bel; 1950 v E, Se, Bel (9)
Waters, J. (Grimsby T), 1977 v T; 1980 v Ni (sub) (2)
Watters, F. (Shelbourne), 1926 v I (1)
Weir, E. (Clyde), 1939 v H (2), G (3)
Whelan, R. (St Patrick's Ath), 1964 v A, E (sub) (2)
Whelan, R. (Liverpool), 1981 v Cz (sub); 1982 v Ho (sub), F; 1983 v Ic, Ma, Sp; 1984 v Is; 1985 v USSR, N, I (sub), Is, E, N (sub), Sw (sub); 1986 v USSR (sub), W; 1987 v Bel (sub), S, Bul, Bel, Br, L; 1988 v L, Bul, Pol, N, E, USSR, Ho; 1989 v Ni,F, H, Sp, Ma (34)
Whelan, W. (Manchester U), 1956 v Ho; 1957 v D, E (2) (4)
White, J. J. (Bohemians), 1928 v Bel (1)
Whittaker, R. (Chelsea), 1959 v Cz (1)
Williams, J. (Shamrock R), 1938 v N (1)

BRITISH INTERNATIONAL GOALSCORERS SINCE 1872

Where two players with the same surname and initials have appeared for the same country, and one or both have scored, they have been distinguished by reference to the club which appears *first* against their name in the international appearances section (pages 643–687). Unfortunately, four of the scorers in Scotland's 10-2 victory v Ireland in 1888 are unknown, as is the scorer of one of their nine goals v Wales in March 1878.

ENGLAND

Player	Goals
A'Court, A.	1
Adams, T. A.	4
Adcock, H.	1
Alcock, C. W.	1
Allen, A.	3
Allen, R.	2
Anderson, V.	2
Astall, G.	1
Athersmith, W. C.	3
Atyeo, P. J. W.	5
Bache, J. W.	4
Bailey, N. C.	2
Baily, E. F.	5
Baker, J. H.	3
Ball, A. J.	8
Bambridge, A. L.	1
Bambridge, E. C.	12
Barclay, R.	2
Barnes, J.	9
Barnes, P. S.	4
Barton, J.	1
Bassett, W. I.	7
Bastin, C. S.	12
Beardsley, P. A.	7
Beasley, A.	1
Beattie, T. K.	1
Becton, F.	2
Bedford, H.	1
Bell, C.	9
Bentley, R. T. F.	9
Bishop, S. M.	1
Blackburn, F.	1
Blissett, L.	3
Bloomer, S.	28
Bond, R.	2
Bonsor, A. G.	1
Bowden, E. R.	1
Bowers, J. W.	2
Bowles, S.	1
Bradford, G. R. W.	1
Bradford, J.	7
Bradley, W.	2
Bradshaw, F.	3
Bridges, B. J.	1
Bridgett, A.	3
Brindle, T.	1
Britton, C. S.	1
Broadbent, P. F.	2
Broadis, I. A.	8
Brodie, J. B.	1
Bromley-Davenport,	2
Brook, E. F.	10
Brooking, T. D.	5
Brooks, J.	2
Broome, F. H.	3
Brown, A.	4
Brown, A. S.	1
Brown, G.	5
Brown, J.	3
Brown, W.	1
Buchan, C. M.	4
Bull, S. G.	1
Bullock, N.	2
Burgess, H.	4
Butcher, T.	3
Byrne, J. J.	8
Camsell, G. H.	18
Carter, H. S.	7
Carter, J. H.	4
Chadwick, E.	3
Chamberlain, M.	1
Chambers, H.	5
Channon, M. R.	21
Charlton, J.	6
Charlton, R.	49
Chenery, C. J.	1
Chivers, M.	13
Clarke, A. J.	10
Cobbold, W. N.	7
Cock, J. G.	2
Common, A.	2
Connelly, J. M.	7
Coppell, S. J.	7
Cotterill, G. H.	2
Cowans, G.	2
Crawford, R.	1
Crawshaw, T. H.	1
Crayston, W. J.	1
Creek, F. N. S.	1
Crooks, S. D.	7
Currey, E. S.	2
Currie, A. W.	3
Cursham, A. W.	2
Cursham, H. A.	5
Daft, H. B.	3
Davenport, J. K.	2
Davis, G.	1
Davis, H.	1
Day, S. H.	2
Dean, W. R.	18
Devey, J. H. G.	1
Dewhurst, F.	11
Dix, W. R.	1
Dixon, K. M.	4
Douglas, B.	11
Drake, E. J.	6
Ducat, A.	1
Dunn, A. T. B.	2
Eastham, G.	2
Edwards, D.	5
Elliott, W. H.	3
Evans, R. E.	1
Finney, T.	30
Fleming, H. J.	9
Flowers, R.	10
Forman, Frank	1
Forman, Fred	3
Foster, R. E.	3
Francis, G. C. J.	3
Francis, T.	12
Freeman, B. C.	3
Froggatt, J.	2
Froggatt, R.	2
Galley, T.	1
Gascoigne, P. J.	1
Geary, F.	3
Gibbins, W. V. T.	3
Gilliatt, W. E.	3
Goddard, P.	1
Goodall, J.	12
Goodyer, A. C.	1
Gosling, R. C.	2
Goulden, L. A.	4
Grainger, C.	3
Greaves, J.	44
Grosvenor, A. T.	2
Gunn, W.	1
Haines, J. T. W.	2
Hall, G. W.	9
Halse, H. J.	2
Hampson, J.	5
Hampton, H.	2
Hancocks, J.	2
Hardman, H. P.	1
Harris, S. S.	2
Hassall, H. W.	4
Hateley, M.	9
Haynes, J. N.	18
Hegan, K. E.	4
Henfrey, A. G.	2
Hilsdon, G. R.	14
Hine, E. W.	4
Hitchens, G. A.	5
Hobbis, H. H. F.	1
Hoddle, G.	8
Hodgetts, D.	1
Hodgson, G.	1
Holley, G. H.	8
Houghton, W. E.	5
Howell, R.	1
Hughes, E. W.	1
Hulme, J. H. A.	4
Hunt, G. S.	1
Hunt, R.	18
Hunter, N.	2
Hurst, G. C.	24
Jack, D. N. B.	3
Johnson, D. E.	6
Johnson, E.	2
Johnson, J. A.	2
Johnson, T. C. F.	5
Johnson, W. H.	1
Kail, E. I. L.	2
Kay, A. H.	1
Keegan, J. K.	21
Kelly, R.	8
Kennedy, R.	3
Kenyon-Slaney, W. S.	2
Kevan, D. T.	8
Kidd, B.	1
Kingsford, R. K.	1
Kirchen, A. J.	2
Kirton, W. J.	1
Langton, R.	1
Latchford, R. D.	5
Latheron, E. G.	1
Lawler, C.	1
Lawton, T.	22
Lee, F.	10
Lee, J.	1
Lee, S.	2
Lindley, T.	15
Lineker, G.	29
Lofthouse, J. M.	3
Lofthouse, N.	30
Hon. A. Lyttelton	1
Mabbutt, G	1
Macdonald, M.	6
Mannion, W. J.	11
Mariner, P.	13
Marsh, R. W.	1
Matthews, S.	11
Matthews, V.	1
McCall, J.	1
McDermott, T.	3
Medley, L. D.	1
Melia, J.	1
Mercer, D. W.	1
Milburn, J. E. T.	10
Miller, H. S.	1
Mills, G. R.	3
Milward, A.	3
Mitchell, C.	5
Moore, J.	1
Moore, R. F.	2
Moore, W. G. B.	2
Morren, T.	1
Morris, F.	1
Morris, J.	3
Mortensen, S. H.	23
Morton, J. R.	1
Mosforth, W.	3
Mullen, J.	6
Mullery, A. P.	1
Neal, P. G.	5
Needham, E.	3
Nicholls, J.	1
Nicholson, W. E.	1
O'Grady, M.	3
Osborne, F. R.	3
Own goals	22
Page, L. A.	1
Paine, T. L.	7
Parry, E. H.	1
Parry, R. A.	1
Pawson, F. W.	1
Payne, J.	2
Peacock, A.	3
Pearson, J. S.	5
Pearson, S. C.	5
Perry, W.	2
Peters, M.	20
Pickering, F.	5
Pointer, R.	2
Quantrill, A.	1
Ramsey, A. E.	3
Revie, D. G.	4
Reynolds, J.	3
Richardson, J. R.	2
Rigby, A.	3
Rimmer, E. J.	2
Roberts, H.	1
Roberts, W. T.	4
Robinson, J.	3
Robson, B.	24
Robson, R.	4
Rowley, J. F.	6
Royle, J.	2
Rutherford, J.	3
Sagar, C.	1
Sandilands, R. R.	2
Sansom, K.	1
Schofield, J.	1
Seed, J. M.	1

Settle, J.	6
Sewell, J.	3
Shackleton, L. F.	1
Sharp, J.	1
Shepherd, A.	2
Simpson, J.	1
Smith, G. O.	12
Smith, Joe	1
Smith, J. R.	2
Smith, J. W.	4
Smith, R.	13
Smith, S.	1
Sorby, T. H.	1
Southworth, J.	3
Sparks, F. J.	3
Spence, J. W.	1
Spiksley, F.	5
Spilsbury, B. W.	5
Steele, F. C.	8
Stephenson, G. T.	2
Steven, T. M.	3
Stewart, J.	2
Stiles, N. P.	1
Storer, H.	1
Summerbee, M.G.	1
Tambling, R. V.	1
Taylor, P. J.	2
Taylor, T.	16
Thompson, P. B.	1
Thornewell, G.	1
Tilson, S. F.	6
Townley, W. J.	2
Tueart, D.	2
Vaughton, O. H.	6
Veitch, J. G.	3
Viollet, D. S.	1
Waddle, C. R.	6
Walker, W. H.	9
Wall, G.	2
Wallace, D.	1
Walsh, P.	1
Waring, T.	4
Warren, B.	2
Watson, D. V.	4
Watson, V. M.	4
Webb, G. W.	1
Webb, N.	3
Wedlock, W. J.	2
Weir, D.	2
Weller, K.	1
Welsh, D.	1
Whateley, O.	2
Wheldon, G. F.	6
Whitfield, H.	1
Wignall, F.	2
Wilkes, A.	1
Wilkins, R. G.	3
Willingham, C. K.	1
Wilshaw, D. J.	10
Wilson, D.	1
Wilson, G. P.	1
Winckworth, W. N.	1
Windridge, J. E.	7
Withe, P.	1
Wollaston, C. H. R.	1
Wood, H.	1
Woodcock, T.	16
Woodhall, G.	1
Woodward, V. J.	29
Worrall, F.	2
Worthington, F. S.	2
Wright, W. A.	3
Wylie, J. G.	1
Yates, J.	3

NORTHERN IRELAND

Anderson, T.	3
Armstrong, G.	12
Bambrick, J.	12
Barr, H. H.	1
Barron, H.	3
Best, G.	9
Bingham, W. L.	10
Blanchflower, D.	2
Blanchflower, J.	1
Brennan, B.	1
Brennan, R. A.	1
Brotherston, N.	3
Brown, J.	1
Browne, F.	2
Campbell, J.	1
Campbell, W. G.	1
Casey, T.	2
Caskey, W.	1
Cassidy, T.	1
Chambers, J.	3
Clarke, C. J.	6
Clements, D.	2
Cochrane, T.	1
Condy, J.	1
Connor, M. J.	1
Coulter, J.	1
Croft, T.	1
Crone, W.	1
Crossan, E.	1
Crossan, J. A.	10
Curran, S.	2
Cush, W. W.	5
Dalton, W.	6
D'Arcy, S. D.	1
Darling, J.	1
Davey, H. H.	1
Davis, T. L.	1
Dill, A. H.	1
Doherty, L.	1
Doherty, P. D.	3
Dougan, A. D.	8
Dunne, J.	4
Elder, A. R.	1
Emerson, W.	1
English, S.	1
Ferguson, W.	1
Ferris, J.	1
Ferris, R. O.	1
Finney, T.	2
Gaffikin, J.	5
Gara, A.	3
Gawkrodger, G.	1
Gibb, J. T.	2
Gibb, T. J.	1
Gibson, W. K.	1
Gillespie, W.	12
Goodall, A. L.	2
Halligan, W.	1
Hamill, M.	1
Hamilton, B.	4
Hamilton, W.	5
Hannon, D. J.	1
Harkin, J. T.	2
Harvey, M.	3
Humphries, W.	1
Hunter, A. (*Distillery*)	1
Hunter, A. (*Blackburn R*)	1
Irvine, R. W.	3
Irvine, W. J.	8
Johnston, H.	2
Johnston, S.	2
Johnston, W. C.	1
Jones, S.	1
Jones, J.	1
Kelly, J.	4
Kernaghan, N.	2
Kirwan, J.	2
Lacey, W.	3
Lemon, J.	2
Lockhart, N.	3
Mahood, J.	2
Martin, D. K.	3
Maxwell, J.	2
McAdams, W. J.	7
McAllen, J.	1
McAuley, J. L.	1
McCandless, J.	3
McCaw, J. H.	1
McClelland, J.	1
McCluggage, A.	2
McCracken, W.	1
McCrory, S.	1
McCurdy, C.	1
McDonald, A.	1
McGarry, J. K.	1
McGrath, R. C.	4
McIlroy, J.	10
McIlroy, S. B.	5
McKnight, J.	2
McLaughlin, J. C.	6
McMordie, A. S.	3
McMorran, E. J.	4
McPharland, P. J.	10
McWha, W. B. R.	1
Meldon, J.	1
Mercer, J. T.	1
Millar, W.	1
Milligan, D.	1
Milne, R. G.	2
Molyneux, T. B.	1
Moreland, V.	1
Morgan, S.	3
Morrow, W. J.	1
Murphy, N.	1
Neill, W. J. T.	2
Nelson, S.	1
Nicholl, C. J.	3
Nicholl, J. M.	2
Nicholson, J. J.	6
O'Hagan, C.	2
O'Kane, W. J.	1
O'Neill, J.	1
O Neill, M. A.	1
O'Neill, M. H.	8
Own goals	5
Peacock, R.	2
Peden, J.	7
Penney, S.	2
Pyper, James	2
Pyper, John	1
Quinn, J. M.	5
Reynolds, J.	1
Rowley, R. W. M.	2
Sheridan, J.	2
Sherrard, J.	1
Simpson, W. J.	5
Sloan, H. A. de B.	4
Smyth, S.	5
Spence, D. W.	3
Stanfield, O. M.	9
Stevenson, A. E.	5
Stewart, I.	2
Thompson, F. W.	2
Tully, C. P.	3
Turner, E.	1
Walker, J.	1
Walsh, D. J.	5
Welsh, E.	1
Whiteside, N.	8
Whiteside, T.	1
Williams, J. R.	1
Williamson, J.	1
Wilson, S. J.	7
Wilton, J. M.	2
Young, S.	2

SCOTLAND

Aitken, R.	1
Aitkenhead, W. A. C.	2
Alexander, D.	1
Allan, D. S.	4
Allan, J.	2
Anderson, F.	1
Anderson W.	4
Andrews, P.	1
Archibald, A.	1
Archibald, S.	4
Baird, D.	2
Baird, J. C.	2
Baird, S.	2
Bannon, E.	1
Barbour, A.	1
Barker, J. B.	4
Battles, B. Jr	1
Bauld, W.	2
Baxter, J. C.	3
Bell, J.	5
Bennett, A.	2
Berry, D.	1
Bett, J.	1
Beveridge, W. W.	1
Black, A.	3
Black, D.	1
Bone, J.	1
Boyd, R.	2
Boyd, W. G.	1
Brackenridge, T.	1
Brand, R.	8
Brazil, A.	1
Bremner, W. J.	3
Brown, A. D.	6
Buchanan, P. S.	1
Buchanan, R.	1
Buckley, P.	1
Buick, A.	2
Burns, K.	1
Cairns, T.	1
Calderwood, R.	2
Caldow, E.	4
Campbell, C.	1
Campbell, John (*Celtic*)	5
Campbell, John (*Rangers*)	4
Campbell, P.	2
Campbell, R.	1
Cassidy, J.	1
Chalmers, S.	3
Chambers, T.	1
Cheyne, A. G.	4
Christie, A. J.	1
Clunas, W. L.	1
Collins, J.	1
Collins, R. Y.	10
Combe, J. R.	1
Conn, A.	1
Cooper, D.	6
Craig, J.	1
Craig, T.	1
Cunningham, A. N.	5
Curran, H. P.	1
Dalglish, K.	30
Davidson, D.	1
Davidson, J. A.	1
Delaney, J.	3
Devine, A.	1
Dewar, G.	1
Dewar, N.	4
Dickson, W.	4
Divers, J.	1
Docherty, T. H.	1
Dodds, D.	1
Donaldson, A.	1
Donnachie, J.	1
Dougall, J.	1
Drummond, J.	2
Dunbar, M.	1
Duncan, D.	7
Duncan, D. M.	1
Duncan, J.	1
Dunn, J.	2

Easson, J. F. 1
Ellis, J. 1

Ferguson, J. 6
Fernie, W. 1
Fitchie, T. T. 1
Flavell, R. 2
Fleming, C. 2
Fleming, J. W. 3
Fraser, M. J. E. 4

Gallacher, H. K. 23
Gallacher, P. 1
Galt, J. H. 1
Gemmell, T. (*St Mirren*) 1
Gemmell, T. (*Celtic*) 1
Gemmill, A. 8
Gibb, W. 1
Gibson, D. W. 3
Gibson, J. D. 2
Gibson, N. 1
Gillespie, Jas. 3
Gillick, T. 3
Gilzean, A. J. 10
Gossland, J. 2
Goudie, J. 1
Gough, C. R. 5
Gourlay, J. 1
Graham, A. 2
Graham, G. 3
Gray, A. 7
Gray, E. 3
Gray, F. 1
Greig, J. 3
Groves, W. 5

Hamilton, G. 4
Hamilton, J. (*Queen's Park*) 3
Hamilton, R. C. 14
Harper, J. M. 2
Harrower, W. 5
Hartford, R. A. 3
Heggie, C. 5
Henderson, J. G. 1
Henderson, W. 5
Herd, D. G. 4
Hewie, J. D. 2
Higgins, A. (*Newcastle U*) 1
Higgins, A. (*Kilmarnock*) 4
Highet, T. C. 1
Holton, J. A. 2
Houliston, W. 2
Howie, H. 1
Howie, J. 2
Hughes, J. 1
Hunter, W. 1
Hutchison, T. 1
Hutton, J. 1
Hyslop, T. 1

Imrie, W. N. 1

Jackson, A. 8
Jackson, C. 1
James, A. W. 3
Jardine, A. 1
Jenkinson, T. 1
Johnston, L. H. 1
Johnston, M. 12
Johnstone, D. 2
Johnstone, J. 4
Johnstone, Jas. 1
Johnstone, R. 9
Johnstone, W. 1
Jordan, J. 11

Kay, J. L. 5
Keillor, A. 3
Kelly, J. 1
Kelso, R. 1
Ker, G. 10
King, A. 1
King, J. 1
Kinnear, D. 1

Love, A. 1
Lowe, J. (*Cambuslang*) 1
Lowe, J. (*St Bernards*) 1

Macari, L. 5
MacDougall, E. J. 3
MacLeod, M. 1
Mackay, D. C. 4
Mackay, G. 1
MacKenzie, J. A. 1
Madden, J. 5
Marshall, H. 1
Marshall, J. 1
Mason, J. 4
Massie, A. 1
Masson, D. S. 5
McAdam, J. 1
McAulay, J. 1
McAvennie, F. 1
McCall, J. 1
McCalliog, J. 1
McCallum, N. 1
McCoist, A. 4
McColl, R. S. 13
McCulloch, D. 3
McDougall, J. 4
McFarlane, A. 1
McFayden, W. 2
McGhee, M. 2
McGregor, J. C. 1
McGrory, J. 6
McGuire, W. 1
McInnally, A. 1
McInnes, T. 2
McKie, J. 2
McKinnon, A. 1
McKinnon, R. 1
McKinnon, W. W. 5
McLaren, A. 4
McLaren, J. 1
McLean, A. 1
McLean, T. 1
McLintock, F. 1
McMahon, A. 6
McMenemy, J. 5
McMillan, I. L. 2
McNeil, H. 5
McNeill, W. 3
McPhail, J. 3
McPhail, R. 7
McPherson, J. 8
McPherson, R. 1
McQueen, G. 5
McStay, P. 6
Meiklejohn, D. D. 3
Millar, J. 2
Miller, T. 2
Miller, W. 1
Mitchell, R. C. 1
Morgan, W. 1
Morris, D. 1
Morris, H. 3
Morton, A. L. 5
Mudie, J. K. 9
Mulhall, G. 1
Munro, A. D. 1
Munro, N. 1
Murdoch, R. 5
Murphy, F. 1
Murray, J. 1

Napier, C. E. 3
Narey, D. 1
Neil, R. G. 2
Nicholas, C. 5
Nisbet, J. 2

O'Donnell, F. 2
O'Hare, J. 5
Ormond, W. E. 1
O'Rourke, F. 1
Orr, R. 1
Orr, T. 1
Oswald, J. 1

Own goals 14

Parlane, D. 1
Paul, H. McD. 2
Paul, W. 6
Pettigrew, W. 2
Provan, D. 1

Quinn, J. 7
Quinn, P. 1

Rankin, G. 2
Rankin, R. 2
Reid, W. 4
Reilly, L. 22
Renny-Tailyour, H. W. 1
Richmond, J. T. 1
Ring, T. 2
Rioch, B. D. 6
Ritchie, J. 1
Robertson, A. 2
Robertson, J. 8
Robertson, J. T. 2
Robertson, T. 1
Robertson, W. 1
Russell, D. 1

Scott, A. S. 5
Sellar, W. 4
Sharp, G. 1
Shaw, F. W. 1
Simpson, J. 1
Smith, A. 5
Smith, G. 4
Smith, J. 1
Smith, John 12
Somerville, G. 1
Souness, G. J. 3
Speedie, F. 2
St John, I. 9
Steel, W. 12
Stein, C. 10
Stevenson, G. 4
Stewart, R. 1
Stewart, W. E. 1
Strachan, G. 4
Sturrock, P. 3

Taylor, J. D. 1
Templeton, R. 1
Thomson, A. 1
Thomson, C. 4
Thomson, R. 1
Thomson, W. 1
Thornton, W. 1

Waddell, T. S. 1
Waddell, W. 6
Walker, J. 2
Walker, R. 7
Walker, T. 9
Wallace, I. A. 1
Wark, J. 7
Watson, J. A. K. 1
Watt, F. 2
Watt, W. W. 1
Weir, A. 1
Weir, J. B. 2
White, J. A. 3
Wilson, A. 2
Wilson, A. N. 13
Wilson, D. (*Queen's Park*) 2
Wilson, D. (*Rangers*) 9
Wilson, H. 1
Wylie, T. G. 1

Young, A. 5

WALES

Allchurch, I. J. 23
Allen, M. 2
Astley, D. J. 12
Atherton, R. W. 2

Bamford, T. 1
Barnes, W. 1
Boulter, L. M. 1
Bowdler, J. C. H. 3
Bowen, D. L. 1
Boyle, T. 1
Bryan, T. 1
Burgess, W. A. R. 1
Burke, T. 1
Butler, A. 1

Chapman, T. 2
Charles, J. 1
Charles, M. 6
Charles, W. J. 15
Clarke, R. J. 5
Collier, D. J. 1
Cross, K. 1
Cumner, R. H. 1
Curtis, A. 6
Curtis, E. R. 3

Davies, D. W. 1
Davies, E. Lloyd 1
Davies, G. 2
Davies, L. S. 6
Davies, R. T. 8
Davies, R. W. 7
Davies, S. 5
Davies, W. 6
Davies, W. H. 1
Davies, William 5
Davies, W. O. 1
Deacy, N. 4
Doughty, J. 6
Doughty, R. 2
Durban, A. 2
Dwyer, P. 2

Edwards, G. 2
Edwards, R. I. 5
England, H. M. 3
Evans, I. 1
Evans, J. 1
Evans, R. E. 2
Evans, W. 1
Eyton-Jones, J. A. 1

Flynn, B. 6
Ford, T. 23
Foulkes, W. I. 1
Fowler, J. 3

Giles, D. 2
Glover, E. M. 7
Godfrey, B. C. 2
Green, A. W. 3
Griffiths, A. T. 6
Griffiths, M. W. 2
Griffiths, T. P. 3

Harris, C. S. 1
Hersee, R. 1
Hewitt, R. 1
Hockey, T. 1
Hodges G. 2
Hole, W. J. 1
Hopkins, I. J. 2
Horne, B. 2
Howell, E. G. 3
Hughes, M. 8

James, E. 2
James, L. 10
James, R. 7
Jarrett, R. H. 3
Jenkyns, C. A. 1
Jones, A. 1
Jones, Bryn 6
Jones, B. S. 2
Jones, Cliff 15
Jones, C. W. 1
Jones, D. E. 1
Jones, Evan 1
Jones, H. 1
Jones, I. 1
Jones, J. O. 1
Jones, J. P. 1

Jones, Leslie J.	1
Jones, R. A.	2
Jones, W. L.	6
Keenor, F. C.	2
Krzywicki, R. L.	1
Leek, K.	5
Lewis, B.	3
Lewis, J.	1
Lewis, W.	10
Lewis, W. L.	2
Lovell, S.	1
Lowrie, G.	2
Mahoney, J. F.	1
Mays, A. W.	1
Medwin, T. C.	6
Meredith, W. H.	11
Mills, T. J.	1
Moore, G.	1
Morgan, J. R.	2
Morgan-Owen, H.	1
Morgan-Owen, M. M.	2
Morris, A. G.	9
Morris, H.	2
Morris, R.	1
Nicholas, P.	2
O'Callaghan, E.	3
O'Sullivan, P. A.	1
Owen, G.	2
Owen, W.	4
Owen, W. P.	6
Own goals	12
Palmer, D.	3
Parry, T. D.	3
Paul, R.	1
Peake, E.	1
Perry, E.	1
Phillips, C.	5
Phillips, D.	1
Powell, A.	1
Powell, D.	1
Price, J.	4
Price, P.	1
Pryce-Jones, W. E.	3
Pugh, D. H.	2
Reece, G. I.	2
Rees, R. R.	3
Richards, R. W.	1
Roach, J.	2
Robbins, W. W.	4
Roberts, J. (*Corwen*)	1
Roberts, Jas.	1
Roberts, P. S.	1
Roberts, R. (*Druids*)	1
Roberts, W. (*Llangollen*)	2
Roberts, W. (*Wrexham*)	1
Roberts, W. H.	1
Rush, I.	16
Russell, M. R.	1
Sabine, H. W.	1
Saunders, D.	4
Shaw, E. G.	2
Sisson, H.	4
Slatter, N.	2
Smallman, D. P.	1
Tapscott, D. R.	4
Thomas, M.	4
Thomas, T.	1
Toshack, J. B.	13
Trainer, H.	2
Vaughan, John	2
Vernon, T. R.	8
Vizard, E. T.	1
Walsh, I.	7
Warren, F. W.	3
Watkins, W. M.	4
Wilding, J.	4
Williams, G. E.	2
Williams, W.	1
Woosnam, A. P.	4
Wynn, G. A.	1
Yorath, T. C.	2

EIRE

Aldridge, J.	1
Ambrose, P.	1
Anderson, J.	1
Bermingham, P.	1
Bradshaw, P.	4
Brady, L.	9
Brown, D.	1
Byrne, J. (Bray)	1
Byrne, J. (QPR)	2
Cantwell, J.	14
Carey, J.	3
Carroll, T.	1
Cascarino, A.	4
Coad, P.	3
Conroy, T.	2
Conway, J.	3
Cummings, G.	5
Curtis, D.	8
Daly, G.	13
Davis, T.	4
Dempsey, J.	1
Dennehy, M.	2
Donnelly, J.	3
Donnelly, T.	1
Duffy, B.	1
Duggan, H.	1
Dunne, J.	12
Dunne, L.	1
Eglinton, T.	2
Ellis, P.	1
Fagan, F.	5
Fallon, S.	2
Fallon, W.	2
Farrell, P.	3
Fitzgerald, P.	2
Fitzgerald, J.	1
Fitzsimmons, A.	7
Flood, J. J.	4
Fogarty, A.	3
Fullam, J.	1
Fullam, R.	1
Galvin, A.	1
Gavin, J.	2
Geoghegan, M.	2
Giles, J.	5
Givens, D.	19
Glynn, D.	1
Grealish, T.	8
Grimes, A. A.	1
Hale, A.	2
Hand, E.	2
Haverty, J.	3
Holmes, J.	1
Horlacher, A.	2
Houghton, R.	2
Hughton, C.	1
Hurley, C.	2
Jordan, D.	1
Kelly, D.	4
Kelly, J.	2
Lacey, W.	1
Lawrenson, M.	5
Leech, M.	2
McCann, J.	1
McCarthy, M.	1
McEvoy, A.	6
McGee, P.	4
McGrath, P.	4
Madden, O.	1
Mancini, T.	1
Martin, C.	6
Martin, M.	4
Mooney, J.	1
Moore, P.	7
Moran, K.	6
Moroney, T.	1
Mulligan, P.	1
O'Callaghan, K.	1
O'Connor, T.	2
O'Farrell, F.	2
O'Flannagan, K.	3
O'Keefe, E.	1
O'Neill, F.	1
O'Reilly, J.	2
O'Reilly, J	1
own goals	5
Quinn, N.	1
Ringstead, A.	7
Robinson, M.	4
Rogers, E.	5
Ryan, G.	1
Ryan, R.	3
Sheedy, K.	4
Sheridan, J.	1
Sloan, W.	1
Squires, J.	1
Stapleton, F.	18
Strahan, J.	1
Sullivan, J.	1
Treacy, R.	5
Tuohy, L.	4
Waddock, G.	3
Walsh, D.	5
Walsh, M.	3
Waters, J.	1
White, J. J.	2
Whelan, R.	2

Peter Shilton – most caps for England (109) and Steve Bull – top goalscorer in all senior games 1988–89.

7th UEFA UNDER-21 TOURNAMENT 1988–90

Group 1 *(Bulgaria, Denmark, Greece, Rumania)*

Greece (1) 2, Denmark (1) 2	Viareggio, 18 October 1988
Bulgaria (1) 2, Rumania (1) 1	Sofia, 18 October 1988
Denmark (0) 1, Bulgaria (0) 3	Slagelse, 1 November 1988
Rumania (1) 2, Greece (0) 0	1 November, 1988
Bulgaria (2) 6, Denmark (0) 0	25 April 1989
Greece (0) 1, Rumania (0) 0	25 April 1989
Denmark (0) 3, Greece (0) 0	16 May 1989
Rumania (2) 2, Bulgaria (1) 1	16 May 1989

Remaining fixtures: 10.10.89 Denmark v Rumania; Bulgaria v Greece; 14.11.89 Rumania v Denmark; Greece v Bulgaria.

Group 2 *(Albania, England, Poland, Sweden)*

England (1) 1, Sweden (0) 1	Coventry, 18 October 1988
Poland (0) 0, Albania (0) 0	Opole, 18 October 1988
Albania (0) 0, Sweden (1) 2	Berat, 4 November 1988
Albania (1) 1, England (0) 2	7 March 1989
England (1) 2, Albania (0) 0	25 April 1989
Sweden (1) 4, Poland (0) 0	6 May 1989
England (2) 2, Poland (0) 1	2 June 1989

Remaining fixtures: 5.9.89 Sweden v England; 7.10.89 Sweden v Albania; 10.10.89 Poland v England; 24.10.89 Poland v Sweden; 14.11.89 Albania v Poland.

Group 3 *(Austria, East Germany, Turkey, USSR)*

USSR (1) 2, Austria (2) 2	Kiev, 18 October 1988
Austria (2) 3, Turkey (0) 0	St Polten, 1 November 1988
Turkey (2) 3, East Germany (2) 2	Istanbul, 29 November 1988
East Germany (0) 0, Turkey (0) 0	11 April 1989
USSR (0) 1, East Germany (0) 0	25 April 1989
Turkey (0) 0, USSR (2) 3	9 May 1989
East Germany (0) 2, Austria (0) 0	16 May 1989

Remaining fixtures: 5.9.89 Austria v USSR; 6.10.89 East Germany v USSR; 24.10.89 Turkey v Austria; 7.11.89 USSR v Turkey; 14.11.89 Austria v East Germany.

Group 4 *(Finland, Holland, Iceland, West Germany)*

Finland (0) 0, West Germany (2) 3	Kouvola, 30 August 1988
Iceland (0) 1, Holland (1) 1	Reykjavik, 13 September 1988
Finland (0) 2, Iceland (1) 1	Oulu, 28 September 1988
West Germany (0) 2, Holland (0) 0	Augsburg, 18 October 1988
Holland (0) 0, West Germany (1) 1	25 April 1989
Finland (1) 1, Holland (1) 1	30 May 1989
Iceland (0) 1, West Germany (0) 1	30 May 1989

Remaining fixtures: 5.9.89 Iceland v Finland; 3.10.89 West Germany v Finland; 10.10.89 Holland v Iceland; 25.10.89 West Germany v Iceland; 14.11.89 Holland v Finland.

Group 5 *(France, Norway, Scotland, Yugoslavia)*

Norway (0) 1, Scotland (1) 1	Drammen, 13 September 1988
France (1) 2, Norway (0) 0	Tours, 27 September 1988
Scotland (0) 0, Yugoslavia (0) 2	Edinburgh, 18 October 1988
Yugoslavia (1) 2, France (1) 2	Titov Vrbas, 18 November 1988
Scotland (1) 2, France (0) 3	Dundee, 7 March 1989
France (0) 0, Yugoslavia (0) 1	Le Havre, 28 April 1989
Norway (0) 0, Yugoslavia (0) 1	13 June 1989

Remaining fixtures: 5.9.89 Norway v France; Yugoslavia v Scotland; 10.10.89 Yugoslavia v Norway; France v Scotland; 14.11.89 Scotland v Norway.

Group 6 *(Cyprus, Hungary, Spain)*

Cyprus (0) 0, Hungary (0) 0	Larnaca, 11 December 1988
Cyprus (0) 0, Spain (0) 1	22 March 1989
Hungary (1) 1, Cyprus (0) 0	?2 April 1989
Spain (0) 1, Cyprus (0) 0	31 May 1989

Remaining fixtures: 10.10.89 Hungary v Spain; 14.11.89 Spain v Hungary.

Group 7 *(Belgium, Czechoslovakia, Luxembourg, Portugal)*

Czechoslovakia (0) 0, Belgium (2) 3	Nitra, 15 November 1988
Portugal (0) 1, Belgium (1) 1	14 February 1989
Czechoslovakia (2) 4, Luxembourg (0) 0	5 April 1989
Portugal (0) 1, Luxembourg (0) 0	25 April 1989
Belgium (1) 1, Czechoslovakia (0) 1	29 April 1989
Luxembourg (0) 0, Belgium (0) 0	26 May 1989

Remaining fixtures: 5.9.89 Belgium v Portugal; 5.10.89 Czechoslovakia v Portugal; 9.10.89 Luxembourg v Portugal; 24.10.89 Belgium v Luxembourg; 14.11.89 Portugal v Czechoslovakia; 29.11.89 Luxembourg v Czechoslovakia.

Group 8 *(Italy, San Marino, Switzerland)*

Switzerland (0) 0, Italy (0) 0	26 April 1989
San Marino (0) 0, Switzerland (2) 5	6 June 1989

Remaining fixtures: 4.10.89 San Marino v Italy; 25.10.89 Italy v Switzerland; 14.11.89 Switzerland v San Marino; 29.11.89 Italy v San Marino.

6th UEFA UNDER-21 TOURNAMENT

Final *(second leg)*

France (1) 3, Greece (0) 0	Besancon, 12 October 1988

(France won 3-0 on aggregate)

7th UEFA UNDER-18 CHAMPIONSHIP 1988-90

Group 1 *(Poland, Scotland, Sweden, West Germany)*

Scotland (0) 0, Sweden (0) 0	Ayr, 21 September 1988
Scotland (0) 1, Poland (2) 2	Hampden Park, 23 November 1988
West Germany (0) 0, Poland (0) 0	Heilbronn, 19 April 1989

Group 2 *(Cyprus, Holland, Norway, USSR)*

Norway (1) 2, Holland (0) 2	Stavanger, 12 October 1988
Cyprus (0) 0, Norway (0) 0	Paralimni, 1 November 1988
Holland (2) 2, Cyprus (0) 1	Roosendaal, 12 April 1989

Group 3 *(Czechoslovakia, England, France, Greece)*

England (1) 5, Greece (0) 0	Birkenhead, 20 October 1988
England (0) 1, France (1) 1	Bradford, 15 November 1988
Greece (1) 2, France (3) 3	Indrama, 14 December 1988
Greece (0) 0, England (2) 3	Xanthi, 8 March 1989
Czechoslovakia (0) 0, Greece (0) 0	Trebechovicen, 12 April 1989
Czechoslovakia ( ) 1, England ( ) 0	Piovazska B, 26 April 1989

Group 4 *(Albania, Italy, Portugal, Switzerland)*

Albania (0) 4, Switzerland (0) 0	Shkodra, 12 October 1988
Portugal (2) 2, Albania (0) 1	Lisbon, 15 March 1989
Albania (0) 1, Italy (2) 2	Elbasan, 12 April 1989
Switzerland (0) 0, Portugal (3) 3	Chatel-St. Denis, 19 April 1989
Albania (0) 0, Portugal (1) 2	Tirana, 23 April 1989

Group 5 *(Belgium, Wales, East Germany, Yugoslavia)*

East Germany (0) 0, Yugoslavia (1) 1	Soemmerda, 12 October 1988
Belgium (1) 1, East Germany (1) 1	Seraing, 2 November 1988
Yugoslavia (2) 4, Wales (1) 1	Bijeljina, 9 November 1988
Wales (0) 2, Belgium (0) 0	Newtown, 30 November 1988
Belgium (2) 2, Yugoslavia (0) 1	Roeselare, 29 March 1989
Wales (0) 0, East Germany (0) 0	Aberystwyth, 12 April 1989

Group 6 *(Bulgaria, Eire, Malta, Iceland (withdrew))*

Malta (1) 1, Bulgaria (1) 2	Ta'qali, 12 April 1989

Group 7 *(Austria, Denmark, Rumania, Spain)*

Spain (1) 4, Denmark (0) 2	Las Palmas, 16 November 1988
Austria (0) 1, Spain (0) 2	Lanzendorf, 19 April 1989

Group 8 *(Finland, Hungary, Luxembourg, Turkey)*

Finland (0) 0, Hungary (0) 1	Toijala, 21 September 1988
Luxembourg (0) 0, Finland (3) 5	Esch sur Alzette, 26 October 1988
Turkey (2) 3, Luxembourg (0) 1	Izmir, 29 March 1989

6th UEFA UNDER-18 CHAMPIONSHIP

(Final stages in Czechoslovakia July 1988)

Quarter-finals
Spain 1, Czechoslovakia 0
East Germany 2, Denmark 0
Portugal 3, Holland
USSR 4, Norway 2

Semi-finals
USSR 3, East Germany 0
Portugal 2, Spain 0

Final
USSR 3, Portugal 1 *aet*

Third place
East Germany 2, Spain 0

Fifth place
Czechoslovakia 1, Holland 0
Norway 1, Denmark 1
(Norway won 5-4 on penalties)

Final placings: 1. USSR; 2. Portugal; 3. East Germany; 4. Spain; 5. Czechoslovakia and Norway; 7. Denmark and Holland.

7th UEFA UNDER-16 CHAMPIONSHIP 1989

Group 1: Finland 0, Scotland 1; Scotland 5, Finland 0. Scotland qualified.
Group 2: Northern Ireland 0, East Germany 0; East Germany 3, Northern Ireland 1. East Germany qualified.
Group 3: Iceland 1, Norway 0; Norway 3, Iceland 0. Norway qualified.
Group 4: Liechtenstein 0, Italy 7; Italy 6, Liechtenstein 0. Italy qualified.
Group 5: Israel 1, Holland 1; Holland 2, Israel 0. Holland qualified.
Group 6: Malta 0, Portugal 1; Portugal 6, Malta 0. Portugal qualified.
Group 7: Cyprus 1, Yugoslavia 3; Yugoslavia 2, Cyprus 0. Yugoslavia qualified.
Group 8: Turkey 1, Austria 1; Austria 0, Turkey 0. Austria qualified.
Group 9: Switzerland 0, Eire 0; Eire 0, Switzerland 1. Switzerland qualified.
Group 10: Luxembourg 1, France 3; France 3, Luxembourg 0. France qualified.
Group 11: Rumania 4, Poland 0; Poland 2, Rumania 1. Rumania qualified.
Group 12: Sweden 2, Spain 2; Spain 2, Sweden 0. Spain qualified.
Group 13: Greece 1, Hungary 0; Hungary 2, Belgium 1; Belgium 3, Greece 2; Greece 2, Belgium 0; Belgium 2, Hungary 0; Hungary 1, Greece 1. Greece qualified.
Group 14: Czechoslovakia 0, Bulgaria 1; Bulgaria 2, Czechoslovakia 0. Bulgaria qualified.
Group 15: West Germany 0, USSR 1; USSR 2, West Germany 0. USSR qualified.

FINAL TOURNAMENT IN DENMARK

GROUP A

Portugal (1) 2, Switzerland (0) 0 — Silkeborg, 4 May 1989
Norway (0) 0, Rumania (1) 1 — Arhus Viby, 4 May 1989
Portugal (1) 3, Norway (0) 0 — Spjald, 6 May 1989
Switzerland (0) 0, Rumania (0) 0 — Redding, 6 May 1989
Portugal (2) 4, Rumania (0) 0 — Vejen, 8 May 1989
Switzerland (0) 4, Norway (0) 1 — Fredericia, 8 May 1989

	P	*W*	*D*	*L*	*F*	*A*	*Pts*
Portugal	3	3	0	0	9	0	6
Switzerland	3	1	1	1	4	3	3
Rumania	3	1	1	1	1	4	3
Norway	3	0	0	3	1	8	0

GROUP B

France (0) 0, Yugoslavia (0) 0 — Hedensted, 4 May 1989
Austria (2) 3, Denmark (4) 9 — Vejle, 4 May 1989
France (2) 3, Austria (0) 2 — Arhus-Abyhej, 6 May 1989
Yugoslavia (1) 2, Denmark (0) 0 — Horsens, 6 May 1989
France (1) 4, Denmark (0) 1 — Vejle, 8 May 1989
Yugoslavia (1) 2, Austria (0) 0 — Odder, 8 May 1989

	P	*W*	*D*	*L*	*F*	*A*	*Pts*
France	3	2	1	0	7	3	5
Yugoslavia	3	2	1	0	4	0	5
Denmark	3	1	0	2	10	9	2
Austria	3	0	0	3	5	14	0

GROUP C

Bulgaria (0) 1, Greece (1) 1 — Langeskov, 4 May 1989
Spain (2) 2, Holland (0) 0 — Nyborg, 4 May 1989
Bulgaria (1) 2, Spain (2) 2 — Thur, 6 May 1989
Greece (2) 3, Holland (0) 3 — Odense-Marien, 6 May 1989
Bulgaria (0) 0, Holland (0) 1 — Odense-Dalum, 8 May 1989
Greece (0) 0, Spain (0) 1 — Svendborg, 8 May 1989

	P	*W*	*D*	*L*	*F*	*A*	*Pts*
Spain	3	2	1	0	5	2	5
Holland	3	1	1	1	4	5	3
Greece	3	0	2	1	4	5	2
Bulgaria	3	0	2	1	3	4	2

GROUP D

Scotland (0) 1, USSR (1) 2 — Kolding, 4 May 1989
East Germany (1) 1, Italy (0) 0 — Sender Omme, 4 May 1989
Scotland (1) 2, East Germany (2) 2 — Varde, 6 May 1989
USSR (0) 1, Italy (0) 1 — Holstebro, 6 May 1989
Scotland (0) 1, Italy (0) 1 — Vildbjerg, 8 May 1989
USSR (1) 1, East Germany (0) 1* — Abenra, 8 May 1989

	P	*W*	*D*	*L*	*F*	*A*	*Pts*
East Germany	3	2	1	0	4	3	4
USSR	3	1	2	0	4	3	4
Scotland	3	0	2	1	4	5	2
Italy	3	0	2	1	2	3	2

**East Germany won 5-4 on penalties.*

Semi-finals

Portugal (1) 2, Spain (0) 1 — Kolding, 11 May 1989
France (0) 0, East Germany (1) 3 — Silkeborg, 11 May 1989

Third-place match

France (1) 3, Spain (0) 2 — Brande, 14 May 1989

Final

Portugal (1) 4, East Germany (0) 1 — Vejle, 14 May 1989

England Under-21 Results 1976–89

EC UEFA Competition for Under-21 Teams

v ALBANIA

Year	Date		Venue	Eng	Alb
EC1989	Mar	7	Shkroda	2	1
EC1989	April	25	Ipswich	2	0

v BULGARIA

Year	Date		Venue	Eng	Bulg
EC1979	June	5	Pernik	3	1
EC1979	Nov	20	Leicester	5	0
1989	June	5	Toulon	2	3

v DENMARK

Year	Date		Venue	Eng	Den
EC1978	Sept	19	Hvidovre	2	1
EC1979	Sept	11	Watford	1	0
EC1982	Sept	21	Hvidovre	4	1
EC1983	Sept	20	Norwich	4	1
EC1986	Mar	12	Copenhagen	1	0
EC1986	Mar	26	Manchester	1	1
1988	Sept	13	Watford	0	0

v EAST GERMANY

Year	Date		Venue	Eng	EG
EC1980	April	16	Sheffield	1	2
EC1980	April	23	Jena	0	1

v FINLAND

Year	Date		Venue	Eng	Fin
EC1977	May	26	Helsinki	1	0
EC1977	Oct	12	Hull	8	1
EC1984	Oct	16	Southampton	2	0
EC1985	May	21	Mikkeli	1	3

v FRANCE

Year	Date		Venue	Eng	Fra
EC1984	Feb	28	Sheffield	6	1
EC1984	Mar	28	Rouen	1	0
1987	June	11	Toulon	0	2
EC1988	April	13	Besancon	2	4
EC1988	April	27	Highbury	2	2
1988	June	12	Toulon	2	4

v GREECE

Year	Date		Venue	Eng	Gre
EC1982	Nov	16	Piraeus	0	1
EC1983	Mar	29	Portsmouth	2	1
1989	Feb	7	Patras	0	1

v HUNGARY

Year	Date		Venue	Eng	Hun
EC1981	June	5	Keszthely	2	1
EC1981	Nov	17	Nottingham	2	0
EC1983	April	26	Newcastle	1	0
EC1983	Oct	11	Nyiregyhaza	2	0

v ITALY

Year	Date		Venue	Eng	Italy
EC1978	Mar	8	Manchester	2	1
EC1978	April	5	Rome	0	0
EC1984	April	18	Manchester	3	1
EC1984	May	2	Florence	0	1
EC1986	April	9	Pisa	0	2
EC1986	April	23	Swindon	1	1

v ISRAEL

Year	Date		Venue	Eng	Isr
1985	Feb	27	Tel Aviv	2	1

v MEXICO

Year	Date		Venue	Eng	Mex
1988	June	5	Toulon	2	1

v MOROCCO

Year	Date		Venue	Eng	Mor
1987	June	7	Toulon	2	0
1988	June	9	Toulon	1	0

v NORWAY

Year	Date		Venue	Eng	Nor
EC1977	June	1	Bergen	2	1
EC1977	Sept	6	Brighton	6	0
1980	Sept	9	Southampton	3	0
1981	Sept	8	Drammen	0	0

v POLAND

Year	Date		Venue	Eng	Pol
EC1982	Mar	17	Warsaw	2	1
EC1982	April	7	West Ham	2	2
EC1989	June	2	Plymouth	2	1

v PORTUGAL

Year	Date		Venue	Eng	Por
1987	June	13	Toulon	0	0

v REPUBLIC OF IRELAND

Year	Date		Venue	Eng	Rep of Ire
1981	Feb	25	Liverpool	1	0
1985	Mar	25	Portsmouth	3	2
1989	June	9	Toulon	0	0

v RUMANIA

Year	Date		Venue	Eng	Rum
EC1980	Oct	14	Ploesti	0	4
EC1981	April	28	Swindon	3	0
EC1985	April	30	Brasov	0	0
EC1985	Sept	10	Ipswich	3	0

v SENEGAL

Year	Date		Venue	Eng	Sen
1989	June	7	Toulon	6	1

v SCOTLAND

Year	Date		Venue	Eng	Scot
1977	April	27	Sheffield	1	0
EC1980	Feb	12	Coventry	2	1
EC1980	Mar	4	Aberdeen	0	0
EC1982	April	19	Glasgow	1	0
EC1982	April	28	Manchester	1	1
EC1988	Feb	16	Aberdeen	1	0
EC1988	Mar	22	Nottingham	1	0

v SPAIN

Year	Date		Venue	Eng	Spa
EC1984	May	17	Seville	1	0
EC1984	May	24	Sheffield	2	0
1987	Feb	18	Burgos	2	1

v SWEDEN

Year	Date		Venue	Eng	Swe
1979	June	9	Vasteras	2	1
1986	Sept	9	Ostersund	1	1
EC1988	Oct	18	Coventry	1	1

v SWITZERLAND

Year	Date		Venue	Eng	Swit
EC1980	Nov	18	Ipswich	5	0
EC1981	May	31	Neuenburg	0	0
1988	May	28	Lausanne	1	1

v USA

Year	Date		Venue	Eng	USA
1989	June	11	Toulon	0	2

v TURKEY

Year	Date		Venue	Eng	Tur
EC1984	Nov	13	Bursa	0	0
EC1985	Oct	15	Bristol	3	0
EC1987	April	28	Izmir	0	0
EC1987	Oct	13	Sheffield	1	1

v USSR

Year	Date		Venue	Eng	USSR
1987	June	9	Toulon	0	0
1988	June	7	Toulon	1	0

v WALES

Year	Date		Venue	Eng	Wales
1976	Dec	15	Wolverhampton	0	0
1979	Feb	6	Swansea	1	0

v WEST GERMANY

Year	Date		Venue	Eng	WG
EC1982	Sept	21	Sheffield	3	1
EC1982	Oct	12	Bremen	2	3
1987	Sept	8	Ludenscheid	0	2

v YUGOSLAVIA

Year	Date		Venue	Eng	Yugo
EC1978	April	19	Novi Sad	1	2
EC1978	May	2	Manchester	1	1
EC1986	Nov	11	Peterborough	1	1
EC1987	Nov	10	Zemun	5	1

England Under-21 and B Teams 1988–89

13 Sept (at Watford)

England (0) 0

Denmark (0) 0 3580

England: Martyn (Pressman); Cooper, Hinchcliffe, Lake (Statham), Redmond (Sedgley), Chettle (Yates), Samways, Brightwell, Merson, Hirst, Smith (Ripley)
Denmark: Kjaer; Sorensen, Reiper, Larsen, Christiansen, Molby, Uldbjerg (Nielsen), Risom, Svinggaard, Strudal, Frank

18 Oct (at Coventry)

England (0) 1 *(White)*

Sweden (0) 1 *(Ingesson)* 3988

England: Martyn; Statham (Burrows), Cooper, Sedgley, Redmond, Chettle, White, Ripley, Dozzell (Oldfield), Samways, Smith
Sweden: Eriksson L; Nilsson, Eriksson J, Aattovaara, Kamark, Karlsson, Ingesson, Schwaritz, Jansson J, Dahlin (Eklund), Andersson

7 Feb (at Patras)

Greece (1) 1 *(Moustakdis (pen))*

England (0) 0 2000

Greece: Karkamanis; Kavassis, Hatzinikolaou, Agelinas, Paopulidis, Alexandris, Ouzounidis, Savidis (Marinakis), Nolis, Moustakidis (Tsanas), Vaitsis
England: Martyn (Horne); Cooper (Martin), Burrows, Redmond (Holdsworth David), Chettle, Thomas, Sedgley, Beardsmore (Batty), Sharpe, Merson (Dozzell), Ripley

7 Mar (at Shkodra)

Albania (1) 1 *(Riza)*

England (0) 2 *(Keci (og), Ripley)* 20,000

Albania: Shkurti; Keci (Ziu), Xhumba, Lutaj, Vata, Pashaj, Leskaj, Bilali, Kacaj, Riza, Kalaci (Tahiri)
England: Martyn; Lake, Burrows (Martin) (Beardsmore), Thomas, Redmond, Chettle, Ripley, Ince, Bull, Sedgley, Smith

25 Apr (at Ipswich)

England (1) 2 *(Brightwell, Bull)*

Albania (0) 0 6023

England: Martyn; Lake, Chettle, Redmond, Burrows, Brightwell, Thomas, Sedgley, Bull, Ripley, Smith
Albania: Kela; Reci, Lufi, Paqini, Keci, Pashaj, Xhumba, Bilali, Ziu (Riza), Lutaj, Ismailati

2 June (at Plymouth)

England (2) 2 *(Sedgley, Thomas)*

Poland (0) 1 *(Jegor)* 10,596

England: Horne; Beardsmore, Lake, Redmond, Chettle, Burrows, Sedgley, Thomas, Bull, Mutch (Merson), Smith
Poland: Matysek; Kryger, Jozwiak, Szewczyk, Jegor, Cyzio, Skrzypszak, Gesior, Dziudinski (Szcwczyk), Kubisztal, Trszeciaka (Jelonek)

5 June (in Toulon)

England (1) 2 *(Palmer, Williams)*

Bulgaria (2) 3 *(Mitharski, Beardsmore (og), Trendafilov)* 1000

England: Horne; Wallace Ray, Butters (Ruddock), Yates, Dobson,Beardsmore, Batty, Palmer, Gabbiadini (Hirst), Williams, Wallace Rod
Bulgaria; Stoyanov T; Velkov, Dartilov, Ouroukov, Petkov, Slavtchav, Kalaydjiev, Trendafilov, Tzvetsnov, Mitharski, Stoyanov R

7 June (in Toulon)

England (3) 6 *(Mortimer 2, Williams 2, Hirst, Batty)*

Senegal (1) 1 *(Kome (pen))* 1000

England: Miller; Charles (Wallace Ray), Yates (Butters), Ruddock, Dobson, Ebbrell, Mortimer, Batty, Palmer, Hirst, Williams
Senegal: Diouf; Saar, Clese, Decosta, Kabou, Ndiaye M, Segna, Kome, Diatta, Thiam, Ndiaye S

9 June (in Toulon)

England (0) 0

Eire (0) 0 1000

England: Horne; Wallace Ray, Yates, Ruddock (Butters), Dobson, Ebbrell, Palmer, Batty, Mortimer (Wallace Rod), Hirst, Williams
Eire: Kelly G; Fleming, Scully, Daish, Kenna, Poutch, Brazil, Staunton, McGee, Dolan, Quinn

11 June (in Toulon)

England (0) 0

USA (0) 2 *(Balboa, Gutierrez)* 1000

England: Horne; Charles, Ruddock, Yates, Dobson, Beardsmore (Ebbrell), Batty, Palmer, Gabbiadini (Williams), Hirst, Wallace Rod
USA: Keller; Benedetti (Santel), Balboa, Gosslein, Agoos, Grimes, Covone, Gutierrez, Henderson, Thompson, Wynalda (Palic)

16 May (in Winterthur)

Switzerland (0) 0

England B (0) 2 *(Gascoigne, Schepull (og))* 950

Switzerland: Lehmann; Rey F, Baumann H, Schepull, Fischer, Rey O, Hausemann (Baumann A), Burri, Lorenz, Baumgartner, Nadig
England B: Beasant (Naylor); Mabbutt, Dorigo, Hurlock, Mowbray, Pallister (McLeary), Mutch (Stewart), Gascoigne, Bull (Ford), Platt, Preece

19 May (in Reykjavik)

Iceland (0) 0

England B (0) 2 *(Hurlock, Bull)* 700

Iceland: Sigurosson; Jonsson A, Bergsson, Edvaldsson, Pordarson, Askelsson, Torfason O, Arnporsson (Porkelsson), Gislason, Margeirsson, Torfason G
England B: Naylor (Beasant); Parker, Mabbutt, Pallister, Dorigo, Gascoigne, Hurlock, Platt, Preece, Bull, Stewart (Mutch)

22 May (in Stavanger)

Norway (0) 0

England B (0) 1 *(Bull (pen))* 1500

Norway: Ole By Rise (Olsen); Hansen, Tangen, Bjerkeland (Halvorsen), Bjornebye, Pedersen, Ingebrightsen, Torvanger (Klepp), Fjetland, Amundsen (Pedersen E), Haberg
England B: Naylor (Beasant); Mabbutt, Mowbray (Pallister), McLeary, Dorigo, Ford, Hurlock (Platt), MacKenzie, Preece, Mutch, Stewart (Bull)

UNDER-21 APPEARANCES 1976–1989

ENGLAND

Ablett, G. (Liverpool), 1988 v Fr (1)
Adams, A. (Arsenal), 1985 v Ei, Fi; 1986 v D; 1987 v Se, Y (5)
Adams, N. (Everton), 1987 v Se (1)
Allen, C. (QPR), 1980 v EG (sub); 1981 (C Palace) v N, R (3)
Allen, M. (QPR), 1987 v Se (sub); 1988 v Y (sub) (2)
Allen, P. (West Ham U), 1985 v Ei, R; (with Tottenham H) 1986 v R (3)
Anderson, V. A. (Nottingham F), 1978 v I (1)
Andrews, I. (Leicester C), 1987 v Se (1)

Bailey, G. R. (Manchester U), 1979 v W, Bul; 1980 v D, S (2), EG; 1982 v N; 1983 v D, Gr; 1984 v H, F (2), I, Sp (14)
Baker, G. E. (Southampton), 1981 v N, R (2)
Barker, S. (Blackburn R), 1985 v Is (sub), Ei, R; 1986 v I (4)
Bannister, G. (Sheffield W), 1982 v Pol (1)
Barnes, J. (Watford), 1983 v D, Gr (2)
Barnes, P. S. (Manchester C), 1977 v W (sub), S, Fi, N; 1978 v N, Fi, I (2), Y (9)
Batty, D. (Leeds U), 1988 v Sw (sub); 1989 v Gr (sub), Bul, Sen, Ei, USA (5)
Beagrie, P. (Sheffield U), 1988 v WG, T (2)
Beardsmore, R. (Manchester U), 1989 v Gr, Alb (sub), Pol, Bul, USA (5)
Beeston, C (Stoke C), 1988 v USSR (1)
Bertschin, K. E. (Birmingham C), 1977 v S; 1978 v Y (2) (3)
Birtles, G. (Nottingham F), 1980 v Bul, EG (sub) (2)
Blissett, L. L. (Watford), 1979 v W, Bul (sub), Se; 1980 v D (4)
Bracewell, P. (Stoke C), 1983 v D, Gr (2, one sub), H; 1984 v D, H, F (2), I (2), Sp (2); 1985 v T (13)
Bradshaw, P. W. (Wolverhampton W), 1977 v W, S; 1978 v Fi, Y (4)
Breaker, T. (Luton T), 1986 v I (2) (2)
Brennan, M. (Ipswich T), 1987 v Y, Sp, T, Mo, F (5)
Brightwell, I. (Manchester C), 1989 v D, Alb (2)
Brock, K. (Oxford U), 1984 v I, Sp (2); 1986 v I (4)
Bull, S. G. (Wolverhampton W), 1989 v Alb (2) Pol (3)
Burrows, D. (WBA), 1989 v Se (sub) (with Liverpool), Gr, Alb (2) Pol (5)
Butcher, T. I. (Ipswich T), 1979 v Se; 1980 v D, Bul, S (2), EG (2) (7)
Butters, G. (Tottenham H), 1989 v Bul, Sen (sub), Ei (sub) (3)
Butterworth, I. (Coventry C), 1985 v T, R; 1986 (with Nottingham F) v R, T, D (2), I (2) (8)

Caesar, G. (Arsenal), 1987 v Mo, USSR (sub), F (3)
Callaghan, N. (Watford), 1983 v D, Gr (sub), H (sub); 1984 v D, H, F(2), I, Sp (9)
Carr, C. (Fulham), 1985 v Ei (sub) (1)
Carr, F. (Nottingham F), 1987 v Se, Y, Sp (sub), Mo, USSR; 1988 v WG (sub), T, Y, Fr (9)
Caton, T. (Manchester C), 1982 v N, H (sub), Pol (2), S; 1983 v WG (2), Gr; 1984 v D, H, F (2), I (2) (14)
Chamberlain, M. (Stoke C), 1983 v Gr; 1984 v F (sub), I, Sp (4)
Chapman, L. (Stoke C), 1981 v Ei (1)
Chettle, S. (Nottingham F), 1988 v M, USSR, Mor, Fr; 1989 v D, Se, Gr, Alb (2), Bul (10)
Clough, N. (Nottingham F), 1986 v D (sub); 1987 v Se, Y, T, USSR, F (sub), P; 1988 v WG, T, Y, S (2), M, Mor, Fr (15)
Coney, D. (Fulham), 1985 v T (sub); 1986 v R; 1988 v T, WG (8)
Connor, T. (Brighton & H A), 1987 v Y (1)
Cooke, R. (Tottenham H), 1986 v D (sub) (1)
Cooper, C. (Middlesbrough), 1988 v Fr (2), M, USSR, Mor; 1989 v D, Se, Gr (8)
Corrigan, J. T. (Manchester C), 1978 v I (2), Y (3)
Cottee, A. (West Ham U), 1985 v Fi (sub), Is (sub), Ei, R, Fi; 1987 v Sp, P; 1988 v WG (8)
Cowans, G. S. (Aston Villa), 1979 v W, Se; 1980 v Bul, EG; 1981 v R (5)
Cranson, I. (Ipswich T), 1985 v Fi, Is, R; 1986 v R, I (5)
Crooks, G. (Stoke C), 1980 v Bul, S (2), EG (sub) (4)
Cunningham, L. (WBA), 1977 v S, Fi, N (sub); 1978 v N, Fi, I (6)
Curbishley, L. C. (Birmingham C), 1981 v Sw (1)

Daniel, P. W. (Hull C), 1977 v S, Fi, N; 1978 v Fi, I, Y (2) (7)
Davis, P. (Arsenal), 1982 v Pol, S; 1983 v D, Gr (2, one sub), H (sub); 1987 v T; 1988 v WG, T, Y, Fr (11)
D'Avray, M. (Ipswich T), 1984 v I, Sp (sub) (2)
Deehan, J. M. (Aston Villa), 1977 v N; 1978 v N, Fi, I; 1979 v Bul Se (sub); 1980 v D (7)
Dennis, M. E. (Birmingham C), 1980 v Bul; 1981 v N, R (3)
Dickens, A. (West Ham U), 1985 v Fi (sub) (1)
Dicks, J. (West Ham U), 1988 v Sw (sub), M, Mor, Fr (4)
Digby, F. (Swindon T), 1987 v Sp (sub), USSR, P; 1988 v T (4)
Dillon, K. P. (Birmingham C), 1981 v R (1)
Dixon, K. (Chelsea), 1985 v Fi (1)
Dobson, A. (Coventry C), 1989 v Bul, Sen, Ei, USA (4)
Donowa, L. (Norwich C), 1985 v Is, R (sub), Fi (sub) (3)
Dorigo, A. (Aston Villa), 1987 v Se, Sp, T, Mo, USSR, F, P; 1988 v WG, Y, S (2) (11)
Dozzell, J. (Ipswich T), 1987 v Se, Y (sub), Sp, USSR, F, P; 1989 v Se, Gr (sub) (8)
Duxbury, M. (Manchester U), 1981 v Sw (sub), Ei (sub), R (sub), Sw; 1982 v N; 1983 v WG (2) (7)
Dyson, P. I. (Coventry C), 1981 v N, R, Sw, Ei (4)

Ebbrell, J. (Everton), 1989 v Sen, Ei, USA (sub) (3)
Elliott, P. (Luton T), 1985 v Fi; 1986 v T, D (3)

Fairclough, C. (with Nottingham F), 1985 v T, Is, Ei; 1987 v Sp, T; 1988 (with Tottenham H) v Y, F (7)
Fairclough, D. (Liverpool), 1977 v W (1)
Fashanu, J. (Norwich C), 1980 v EG; 1981 v N (sub), R, Sw, Ei (sub), H; (Nottingham F), 1982 v N, H, Pol, S; 1983 v WG (sub) (11)
Fenwick, T. W. (C Palace), 1981 v N, R, Sw, Ei, (QPR), R; 1982 v N, H, S (2); 1983 v WG (2) (11)
Fereday, W. (QPR), 1985 v T, Ei (sub), Fi; 1986 v T (sub), I (5)
Flowers, T. (Southampton), 1987 v Mo, F; 1988 v WG (sub) (3)
Forsyth, M. (Derby Co), 1988 v Sw (1)
Foster, S. (Brighton & HA), 1980 v EG (sub) (1)
Futcher, P. (Luton T), 1977 v W, S, Fi, N; (with Manchester C), 1978 v N, Fi, I (2), Y (2); 1979 v D (11)

Gabbiadini, M. (Sunderland), 1989 v Bul, USA (2)
Gale, A. (Fulham), 1982 v Pol (1)
Gascoigne, P. (Newcastle U), 1987 v Mo, USSR, P; 1988 v WG, Y, S (2), F (2), Sw, M, USSR (sub), Mor (13)
Gayle, H. (Birmingham C), 1984 v I, Sp (2) (3)
Gernon, T. (Ipswich T), 1983 v Gr (1)
Gibbs, N. (Watford), 1987 v Mo, USSR, F, P; 1988 v T (5)
Gibson, C. (Aston Villa), 1982 v N (1)
Gilbert, W. A. (C Palace), 1979 v W, Bul; 1980 v Bul; 1981 v N, R, Sw, R, Sw, H; 1982 v N (sub), H (11)
Goddard, P. (West Ham U), 1981 v N, Sw, Ei (sub); 1982 v N (sub), Pol, S; 1983 v WG (2) (8)
Gordon, D. (Norwich C), 1987 v T (sub), Mo (sub), F, P (4)
Gray, A. (Aston Villa), 1988 v S, F (2)

Haigh, P. (Hull C), 1977 v N (sub) (1)
Hardyman, P. (Portsmouth), 1985 v Ei; 1986 v D (2)
Hateley, M. (Coventry C), 1982 v Pol, S; 1983 v Gr (2), H; (with Portsmouth), 1984 v F (2), I, Sp (2) (10)
Hayes, M. (Arsenal), 1987 v Sp, T; 1988 v F (sub) (3)
Hazell, R. J. (Wolverhampton W), 1979 v D (1)
Heath, A. (Stoke C), 1981 v R, Sw, H; 1982 v N, H, (with Everton), Pol, S; 1983 v WG (8)
Hesford, I. (Blackpool), 1981 v Ei (sub), Pol (2), S (2); 1983 v WG (2) (7)
Hilaire, V. (C Palace), 1980 v Bul, S (2, one sub), EG (2); 1981 v N, R, Sw (sub); 1982 v Pol (sub) (9)
Hinchcliffe, A. (Manchester C), 1989 v D (1)
Hinshelwood, P. A. (C Palace), 1978 v N; 1980 v EG (2)
Hirst, D. (Sheffield W), 1988 v USSR, F; 1989 v D, Bul (sub), Sen, Ei, USA (7)
Hoddle, G. (Tottenham H), 1977 v W (sub); 1978 v Fi

(sub), I (2), Y; 1979 v D, W, Bul; 1980 v S (2), EG (2) (12)
Hodge, S. (Nottingham F), 1983 v Gr (sub); 1984 v D, F, I, Sp (2); (with Aston Villa), 1986 v R, T (8)
Hodgson, D. J. (Middlesbrough), 1981 v N, R (sub), Sw, Ei; 1982 v Pol; 1983 v WG (6)
Holdsworth, D. (Watford), 1989 v Gr (sub) (1)
Horne, B. (Millwall), 1989 v Gr (sub), Pol, Bul, Ei, USA (5)
Hucker, P. (QPR), 1984 v I, Sp (2)
Ince, P. (West Ham U), 1989 v Alb (1)
Johnston, C. P. (Middlesbrough), 1981 v N, Ei (2)
Jones, D. R. (Everton), 1977 v W (1)
Jones, C. H. (Tottenham H), 1978 v Y (sub) (1)
Keegan, G. A. (Manchester C), 1977 v W (1)
Keown, M. (Aston Villa), 1987 v Sp, Mo, USSR, P; 1988 v T, S, F (2) (8)
Kerslake, D. (QPR), 1986 v T (1)
Kilcline, B. (Notts C), 1983 v D, Gr (2)
King, A. E. (Everton), 1977 v W; 1978 v Y (2)
Knight, A. (Portsmouth), 1983 v Gr, H (2)
Knight, I. (Sheffield W), 1987 v Se (sub), Y (2)
Lake, P. (Manchester C), 1989 v D, Alb (2), Pol (4)
Langley, T. W. (Chelsea), 1978 v I (sub) (1)
Lee, R. (Charlton Ath), 1986 v I (sub); 1987 v Se (sub) (2)
Lee, S. (Liverpool), 1981 v R, Sw, H; 1982 v S; 1983 v WG (2) (6)
Lowe, D. (Ipswich T), 1988 v F, Sw (sub) (2)
Lukic, J. (Leeds U), 1981 v N, R, Ei, R, Sw, H; 1982 v H (7)
Lund, G. (Grimsby T), 1985 v T; 1986 v R, T (3)
Mabbutt, G. (Bristol R), 1982 v Pol (2), S; (with Tottenham H), 1983 v D; 1984 v F; 1986 v D, I (7)
Martyn, N. (Bristol R), 1988 v S (sub), M, USSR, Mor, F; 1989 v D, Se, Gr, Alb (2) (10)
May, A. (Manchester C), 1986 v I (sub) (1)
McCall, S. H. (Ipswich T), 1981 v Sw, H; 1982 v H, S; 1983 v WG (2) (6)
McDonald, N. (Newcastle U), 1987 v Se (sub), Sp, T; 1988 v WG, Y (sub) (5)
McGrath, L. (Coventry C), 1986 v D (1)
MacKenzie, S. (WBA), 1982 v N, S (2) (3)
McLeary, A. (Millwall), 1988 v Sw (1)
McMahon, S. (Everton), 1981 v Ei; 1982 v Pol; 1983 v D, Gr (2); (with Aston Villa), 1984 v H (6)
Martin, L. (Manchester U), 1989 v Gr (sub), Alb (sub) (2)
Merson, P. (Arsenal), 1989 v D, Gr, Pol (sub) (3)
Middleton, J. (Nottingham F), 1977 v Fi, N; (with Derby Co), 1978 v N (3)
Miller, A. (Arsenal), 1988 v Mor (sub); 1989 v Sen (2)
Mills, G. R. (Nottingham F), 1981 v R; 1982 v N (2)
Mimms, R. (Rotherham U), 1985 v Is (sub), Ei (sub); (with Everton), 1986 v I (3)
Moran, S. (Southampton), 1982 v N (sub); 1984 v F (2)
Morgan, S. (Leicester C), 1987 v Se, Y (2)
Mortimer, P. (Charlton Ath), 1989 v Sen, Ei (2)
Moses, R. M. (WBA), 1981 v N (sub), Sw, Ei, R, Sw, H; 1982 v N (sub), (with Manchester U), H (8)
Mountfield, D. (Everton), 1984 v Sp (1)
Mutch, A. (Wolverhampton W), 1989 v Pol (1)
Newell, M. (Luton T), 1986 v D (1 + sub), I (1 + sub) (4)
Oldfield, D. (Luton T), 1989 v Se (1)
Osman, R. C. (Ipswich T), 1979 v W (sub), Se; 1980 v D, S (2), EG (2) (7)
Owen, G. A. (Manchester C), 1977 v S, Fi, N; 1978 v N, Fi, I (2), Y; 1979 v D, W; (with WBA), Bul, Se (sub); 1980 v D, S (2), EG; 1981 v Sw, R; 1982 v N (sub), H; 1983 v WG (2) (22)
Painter, I. (Stoke C) 1986 v I (1)
Palmer, C. (Sheffield W), 1989 v Bul, Sen, Ei, USA (4)
Parker, G. (Hull C), 1986 v I (2); (with Nottingham F) v F; 1987 v Se, Y (sub), Sp (6)
Parker, P. (Fulham), 1985 v Fi, T, Is (sub), Ei, R, Fi; 1986 v T, D (8)
Parkes, P. B. F. (QPR), 1979 v D (1)
Parkin, S (Stoke C), 1987 v Sp (sub); 1988 v WG (sub), T, S (sub), F (6)
Peach, D. S. (Southampton), 1977 v S, Fi, N; 1978 v N, I (2) (6)
Peake, A. (Leicester C), 1982 v Pol (1)
Pearce, S. (Nottingham F), 1987 v Y (1)
Pickering, N. (Sunderland), 1983 v D (sub), Gr, H; 1984 v F (sub), F, I (2), Sp; 1985 v Is, R, Fi; 1986 v R, T, (with Coventry C) D, I (15)
Platt, D. (Aston Villa), 1988 v M, Mor, F (3)
Porter, G. (Watford), 1987 v Sp (sub), T, Mo, USSR, F, P (sub); 1988 v T (sub), Y, S (2), F, Sw (12)
Pressman, K. (Sheffield W), 1989 v D (sub) (1)
Proctor, M. (Middlesbrough), 1981 v Ei (sub), Sw; 1982 (with Nottingham F), v N, Pol (4)
Ranson, R. (Manchester C), 1980 v Bul, EG; 1981 v R (sub), R, Sw, (1 + sub), H, Pol (2), S (10)
Redmond, S. (Manchester C), 1988 v F (2), M, USSR, Mor, Fr; 1989 v D, Se, Gr, Alb (2), Pol (12)
Reeves, K. P. (Norwich C), 1978 v I, Y (2); 1979 v N, W, Bul, Sw; 1980, v D, S; (with Manchester C), EG (10)
Regis, C. (WBA), 1979 v D, Bul, Se; 1980 v S, EG, 1983 v D (6)
Reid, N. S. (Manchester C), 1981 v H (sub); 1982 v H, Pol (2), S (2) (6)
Reid, P. (Bolton W), 1977 v S, Fi, N; 1978 v Fi, I, Y (6)
Richards, J. P. (Wolverhampton W), 1977 v Fi, N (2)
Rideout, P. (Aston Villa), 1985 v Fi, Is, Ei (sub), R; (with Bari), 1986 v D (5)
Ripley, S. (Middlesbrough), 1988 v USSR, F (sub); 1989 v D (sub), Se, Gr, Alb (2) (7)
Ritchie, A. (Brighton & HA), 1982 v Pol (1)
Rix, G. (Arsenal), 1978 v Fi (sub), Y; 1979 v D, Se; 1980 v D (sub), Bul, S (7)
Robson, B. (WBA), 1979 v W, Bul (sub), Se; 1980 v D, Bul, S (2) (7)
Robson, S. (Arsenal), 1984 v I; 1985 v Fi, Is,Fi; 196 v R, I (6)
Robson, S. (West Ham U), 1988 v S, Sw (2)
Rocastle, D. (Arsenal), 1987 v Se, Y, Sp, T; 1988 v WG, T, Y, S (2), F (2 subs), M, USSR, Mor (14)
Rodger, G. (Coventry C), 1987 v USSR, F, P; 1988 v WG (4)
Rosario, R. (Norwich C), 1987 v T (sub), Mo, F, P (sub) (4)
Rowell, G. (Sunderland), 1977 v Fi (1)
Ruddock, N. (Southampton), 1989 v Bul (sub), Sen, Ei, USA (4)
Ryan, J. (Oldham Ath), 1983 v H (1)
Samways, V. (Tottenham H), 1988 v Sw (sub), USSR, F; 1989 v D, Se (5)
Sansom, K. G. (C Palace), 1979 v D, W, Bul, Se; 1980 v S (2), EG (2) (8)
Seaman, D. (Birmingham C), 1985 v Fi, T, Is, Ei, R, Fi; 1986 v R, F, D, I (10)
Sedgley, S. (Coventry C), 1987 v USSR, F (sub), P; 1988 v F; 1989 v D (sub), Se, Gr, Alb (2), Pol (10)
Sellars, S. (Blackburn R), 1988 v S (sub), F, Sw (3)
Sharpe, L. (Manchester U), 1989 v Gr (1)
Shaw, G. R. (Aston Villa), 1981 v Ei, Sw, H; 1982 v H, S; 1983 v WG (2) (7)
Shelton, G. (Sheffield W), 1985 v Fi (1)
Sheringham, T. (Millwall), 1988 v Sw (1)
Simpson, P. (Manchester C), 1986 v D (sub); 1987 v Y, Mo, F, P (5)
Sims, S. (Leicester C), 1977 v W, S, Fi, N; 1978 v N, Fi, I (2), Y (2) (10)
Sinnott, L. (Watford), 1985 v Is (sub) (1)
Smith, D. (Coventry C), 1988 v M, USSR (sub), Mor; 1989 v D, Se, Alb (2), Pol (8)
Smith, M. (Sheffield W), 1981 v Ei, R, Sw, H; 1982 v Pol (sub) (5)
Snodin, I. (Doncaster R), 1985 v T, Is, R, Fi (4)
Statham, B (Tottenham H), 1988 v Sw; 1989 v D (sub), Se (3)
Statham, D. J. (WBA), 1978 v Fi, 1979 v W, Bul, Se; 1980 v D; 1983 v D (6)
Stein, B. (Luton T), 1984 v D, H, I (3)
Sterland, M. (Sheffield W), 1984 v D, H, F (2), I, Sp (2) (7)
Steven, T. (Everton), 1985 v Fi, T (2)
Stewart, P. (Manchester C), 1988 v F (1)
Suckling, P. (Coventry C), 1986 v D; (with Manchester C), 1987 v Se (sub), Y, Sp, T; (with Crystal Palace), 1988 v S (2), F (2), Sw (5)
Sunderland, A. (Wolverhampton W), 1977 v W (1)
Swindlehurst, D. (C Palace), 1977 v W (1)
Stevens, G. (Brighton & HA), 1983 v H; (with Tottenham H), 1984 v H, F (1 + sub), I (sub), Sp (1 + sub); 1986 v I (8)
Talbot, B. (Ipswich T), 1977 v W (1)

Thomas, D. (Coventry C), 1981 v Ei; 1983 v WG (2), Gr, H; (with Tottenham H), v I, Sp (7)
Thomas, M. (Arsenal), 1988 v Y, S, F (2), M, USSR, Mor; 1989 v Gr, Alb (2), Pol (11)
Thomas, M. (Luton T), 1986 v T, D, I (3)
Thompson, G. L. (Coventry C), 1981 v R, Sw, H; 1982 v N, H, S (6)
Thorn, A. (Wimbledon), 1988 v WG (sub), Y, S, F, Sw (5)

Venison, B. (Sunderland), 1983 v D, Gr; 1985 v Fi, T, Is, Fi; 1986 v R, T, D (2) (10)

Waddle, C. (Newcastle U), 1985 v Fi (1)
Wallace, D. (Southampton), 1983 v Gr, H; 1984 v D, H, F (2), I, Sp (sub); 1985 v Fi, T, Is; 1986 v R, D, I (14)
Wallace, Ray (Southampton), 1989 v Bul, Sen (sub), Ei (3)
Wallace, Rod (Southampton), 1989 v Bul, Ei (sub), USA (3)
Walker, D. (Nottingham F), 1985 v Fi; 1987 v Se, T; 1988 v WG, T, S (2) (7)
Walsh, G. (Manchester U), 1988 v WG, Y (2)
Walsh, P. (Luton T), 1983 v D (sub), Gr (2), H (4)
Walters, K. (Aston Villa), 1984 v D (sub), H (sub); 1985 v Is, Ei, R; 1986 v R, T, D, I (sub) (9)
Ward, P. D. (Brighton & HA), 1978 v N; 1980 v EG (2)
Watson, D. (Norwich C), 1984 v D, F (2), I (2), Sp (2) (7)
Webb, N. (Portsmouth), 1985 v Ei; (with Nottinham F), 1986 v D (2) (3)
White, D. (Manchester C), 1988 v S (2), F, USSR; 1989 v Se (5)
Whyte, C. (Arsenal), 1982 v S (1 + sub); 1983 v D, Gr (4)
Wicks, S. (QPR), 1982 v S (1)
Wilkins, R. C. (Chelsea), 1977 v W (1)
Wilkinson, P. (Grimsby T), 1985 v Ei, R (sub); (with Everton), 1986 v R (sub), I (4)
Williams, P. (Charlton Ath), 1989 v Bul, Sen, Ei, USA) (sub) (4)
Williams, S. C. (Southampton), 1977 v S, Fi, N; 1978 v N, I (1 + sub), Y (2); 1979 v D, Bul, Se (sub); 1980 v D, EG (2) (15)
Winterburn, N. (Wimbledon), 1986 v I (1)
Wise, D. (Wimbledon), 1988 v Sw (1)
Woodcock, A. S. (Nottingham F), 1978 v Fi, I (2)
Woods, C. C. E. (Nottingham F), 1979 v W (sub), Se; (with QPR), 1980 v Bul, EG; 1981 v Sw; (with Norwich C), 1984 v D (6)
Wright, M. (Southampton), 1983 v Gr, H; 1984 v D, H (4)
Wright, W. (Everton), 1979 v D, W, Bul; 1980 v D, S (2) (6)

Yates, D. (Notts Co), 1989 v D (sub), Bul, Sen, Ei, USA (5)

SCOTLAND

Aitken, R. (Celtic), 1977 v Cz, W, Sw; 1978 v Cz, W; 1979 v P, N (2); 1980 v B, E; 1984 v EG, Y (2); 1985 v WG, Ic, Sp (16)
Albiston A. (Manchester U), 1977 v Cz, W, Sw; 1978 v Sw, Cz (5)
Archdeacon, O. (Celtic), 1987 v WG (sub) (1)
Archibald, S. (Aberdeen), 1980 v B, E (2), WG; (with Tottenham H), 1981 v D (5)

Bannon, E. J. P. (Hearts), 1979 v US, (with Chelsea), P, N (2); (with Dundee U), 1980 v B, WG, E (7)
Beaumont, D. (Dundee U), 1985 v Ic (1)
Bell, D. (Aberdeen), 1981 v D; 1984 v Y (2)
Bett, J. (Rangers), 1981 v Se, D; 1982 v Se, D, I, E (2) (7)
Black, E. (Aberdeen), 1983 v EG, Sw (2), Bel; 1985 v Ic, Sp (2), Ic (8)
Blair, A. (Coventry C), 1980 v E; 1981 v Se; (with Aston Villa), 1982 v Se, D, I (5)
Bowman, D. (Hearts), 1985 v WG (sub) (1)
Boyd, T. (Motherwell), 1987 v WG. Ei (2), Bel; 1988 v Bel (5)
Brazil, A. (Hibernian), 1978 v W (1)
Brazil, A. (Ipswich T), 1979 v N; 1980 v B (2), E (2), WG; 1981 v Se; 1982 v Se (8)
Brough, J. (Hearts), 1981 v D (1)
Burley, G. E. (Ipswich T), 1977 v Cz, W, Sw; 1978 v Sw, Cz (5)
Burns, H. (Rangers), 1985 v Sp, Ic (sub) (2)
Burns, T. (Celtic), 1977 v Cz, W, E; 1978 v Sw; 1982 v E (5)

Campbell, S. (Dundee), 1989 v N (sub), Y, F (3)
Casey, J. (Celtic), 1978 v W (1)
Clark, R. (Aberdeen), 1977 v Cz, W, Sw (3)
Clarke, S. (St Mirren), 1984 v Bel, EG, Y; 1985 v WG, Ic, Sp (2), Ic (8)
Collins, J. (Hibernian), 1988 v Bel, E; 1989 v N, Y, F (5)
Connor, R. (Ayr U), 1981 v Se; 1982 v Se (2)
Cooper, D. (Clyde), 1977 v Cz, W, Sw, E; (with Rangers), 1978 v Sw, Cz (6)
Cooper, N. (Aberdeen), 1982 v D, E (2); 1983 v Bel, EG, Sw (2); 1984 v Bel, EG, Y; 1985 v Ic, Sp, Ic (13)
Craig, T. (Newcastle U), 1977 v E (1)
Crainie, D. (Celtic), 1983 v Sw (sub) (1)

Dawson, A. (Rangers), 1979 v P, N (2); 1980 v B (2), E (2) WG (8)
Dodds, D. (Dundee U), 1978 v W (1)
Duffy, J. (Dundee), 1987 v Ei (1)
Durie, D. (Chelsea), 1987 v WG, Ei Bel; 1988 v Bel (4)
Durrant, I. (Rangers), 1987 v WG, Ei, Bel; 1988 v E (4)
Doyle, J. (Partick Th), 1981 v D, I (sub) (2)

Ferguson, D. (Rangers), 1987 v WG, Ei, Bel; 1988 v E (4)
Ferguson, I. (Clyde), 1987 v WG (sub), Ei (with St. Mirren), Ei, Bel; 1988 v Bel (with Rangers), E (sub) (6)
Ferguson, I. (Dundee), 1983 v EG (sub), Sw (sub); 1984 v Bel (sub) EG (4)
Ferguson, R. (Hamilton A), 1977 v E (1)
Fitzpatrick, A. (St Mirren), 1977 v W (sub), Sw (sub), E; 1978 v Sw, Cz (5)
Fleck, R. (Rangers), 1987 v WG (sub), Ei, Bel; (with Norwich C), 1988 v E (2); 1989 v Y (6)
Fridge, L. (St Mirren), 1989 v F (1)
Fulton, M. (St Mirren), 1980 v B, WG, E; 1981 v Se, D (sub) (5)

Gallacher, K. (Dundee U), 1987 v WG, Ei (2), Bel (sub); 1988 v E (2) (6)
Galloway, M. (Hearts), 1989 v F (1)
Geddes, R. (Dundee), 1982 v Se, D, E (2); 1988 v E (5)
Gillespie, G. (Coventry C), 1979 v US; 1980 v E; 1981 v D; 1982 v Se, D, I (2), E (8)
Glover, L. (Nottingham F), 1988 v Bel (sub); 1989 v N (2)
Goram, A. (Oldham Ath), 1987 v Ei (1)
Gough, C. R. (Dundee U), 1983 v EG, Sw, Bel; 1984 v Y (2) (5)
Grant, P. (Celtic), 1985 v WG, Ic, Sp; 1987 v WG, Ei (2), Bel; 1988 v Bel, E (2) (10)
Gunn, B. (Aberdeen), 1984 v EG, Y (2); 1985 v WG, Ic, Sp (2), Ic (8)
Gray, S. (Aberdeen), 1987 v WG (1)

Hamilton, B. (St Mirren), 1989 v Y, F (sub) (2)
Hartford, R. A. (Manchester C), 1977 v Sw (1)
Hegarty, P. (Dundee U), 1987 v WG, Bel; 1988 v E (2) (4)
Hewitt, J. (Aberdeen), 1982 v I; 1983 v EG, Sw (2); 1984 v Bel, Y (sub) (6)
Hogg, G. (Manchester U), 1984 v Y; 1985 v WG, Ic, Sp (4)
Hunter, G. (Hibernian), 1987 v Ei (sub); 1988 v Bel, E (3)
Hunter, P. (East Fife), 1989 v N (sub), F (sub) (2)

Jardine, I. (Kilmarnock), 1979 v US (1)
Johnston, M. (Partick Th), 1984 v EG (sub); (with Watford), v Y (2) (3)

Leighton, J. (Aberdeen), 1982 v I (1)
Levein, C. (Hearts), 1985 v Sp, Ic (2)
Lindsey, J. (Motherwell), 1979 v US (1)

McAlpine, H. (Dundee U), 1983 v EG, Sw (2), Bel; 1984 v Bel (5)
McAvennie, F. (St Mirren), 1982 v I, E; 1985 v Is, Ei, R (5)
McBride, J. (Everton), 1981 v D (1)
McCall, S. (Bradford C), 1988 v E (1)
McClair, B. (Celtic), 1984 v Bel (sub), EG, Y (1 + sub); 1985 v WG, Ic, Sp, Ic (8)
McCluskey, G. (Celtic), 1979 v US, P; 1980 v B (2); 1982 v D, I (6)
McCoist, A. (Rangers), 1984 v Bel (1)
McCulloch, A. (Kilmarnock), 1981 v Se (1)
McCulloch, I. (Notts Co), 1982 v E (2)
MacDonald, J. (Rangers), 1980 v WG (sub); 1981 v Se; 1982 v Se (sub), L, I (2), E (2 sub) (8)
McGarvey, F. (St Mirren), 1977 v E; 1978 v Cz; (with Celtic), 1982 v D (3)
McGarvey, S. (Manchester U), 1982 v E (sub); 1983 v Bel, Sw; 1984 v Bel (4)

McGhee, M. (Aberdeen), 1981 v D (1)
McGinnis, G. (Dundee U), 1985 v Sp (1)
McInally, J. (Dundee U), 1989 v F (1)
McKimmie, S. (Aberdeen), 1985 v WG, Ic (2) (3)
McKinlay, T. (Dundee), 1984 v EG (sub); 1985 v WG, Ic, Sp (2), Ic (6)
McKinlay, W. (Dundee U), 1989 v N, Y (sub), F (3)
McLaren, A. (Hearts), 1989 v F (1)
McLaughlin, J. (Morton), 1981 v D; 1982 v Se, D, I, E (2); 1983 v EG, Sw (2), Bel (10)
McLeish, A. (Aberdeen), 1978 v W; 1979 v US; 1980 v B, E (2); 1987 v Ei (6)
MacLeod, A. (Hibernian), 1979 v P, N (2) (3)
McLeod, J. (Dundee U), 1989 v N (1)
MacLeod, M. (Dumbarton), 1979 v US; (with Celtic), P (sub), N (2); 1980 v B (5)
McNab, N. (Tottenham H), 1978 v W (1)
McNichol, J. (Brentford), 1979 v P, N (2); 1980 v B (2), WG, E (7)
McNiven, D. (Leeds U), 1977 v Cz, W (sub), Sw (sub) (3)
McPherson, D. (Rangers), 1984 v Bel; 1985 v Sp; (with Hearts), 1989 v N, Y (4)
McStay, P. (Celtic), 1983 v EG, Sw (2); 1984 v Y (2) (5)
Main, A. (Dundee U), 1988 v E; 1989 v Y (2)
Malpas, M. (Dundee U), 1983 v Bel, Sw (1 + sub); 1984 v Bel, EG, Y (2); 1985 v Sp (8)
May, E. (Hibernian), 1989 v Y (sub), F (2)
Melrose, J. (Partick Th), 1977 v Sw; 1979 v US, P, N (2); 1980 v B (sub), WG, E (8)
Miller J, (Aberdeen), 1987 v Ei (sub); 1988 v Bel (with Celtic) E; 1989 v N, Y (5)
Miller, W. (Aberdeen), 1978 v Sw, Cz (2)
Milne, R. (Dundee U), 1982 v Se (sub); 1984 v Bel, EG (3)
Money, I. C. (St Mirren), 1987 v Ei; 1988 v Bel; 1989 v N (3)
Muir, L. (Hibernian), 1977 v Cz (sub) (1)

Narey, D. (Dundee U), 1977 v Cz, Sw; 1978 v Sw, Cz (4)
Nevin, P. (Chelsea), 1985 v WG, Ic, Sp (2), Ic (5)
Nicholas, C. (Celtic), 1981 v Se; 1982 v Se; 1983 v EG, Sw, Bel; (with Arsenal), 1984 v Y (6)
Nicol, S. (Ayr U), 1981 v Se; 1982 v Se, D; (with Liverpool), 1982 v I (2), E (2); 1983 v EG, Sw (2), Bel; 1984 v Bel, EG, Y (14)
Nisbet, S, (Rangers), 1989 v N, Y, F (3)

Orr, N. (Morton), 1978 v W (sub); 1979 v US, P, N (2); 1980 v B, E (7)

Parlane, D. (Rangers), 1977 v W (1)
Paterson, C. (Hibernian), 1981 v Se; 1982 v I (2)
Payne, G. (Dundee U), 1978 v Sw, Cz, W (3)
Provan, D. (Kilmarnock), 1977 v Cz (sub) (1)

Redford, I. (Rangers), 1981 v Se (sub); 1982 v Se, D, I (2), E (6)
Reid, M. (Celtic), 1982 v E; 1984 v Y (2)
Reid, R. (St Mirren), 1977 v W, Sw, E (3)
Rice, B. (Hibernian), 1985 v WG (1)
Richardson, L. (St Mirren), 1980 v WG, E (sub) (2)
Ritchie, A. (Morton), 1980 v B (1)
Robertson, C. (Rangers), 1977 v E (sub) (1)
Robertson, D. (Aberdeen), 1987 v Ei (sub); 1988 v E (2); 1989 v N, Y (5)
Robertson, J. (Hearts), 1985 v WG, Ic (sub) (2)
Ross, T. W. (Arsenal), 1977 v W (1)
Russell, R. (Rangers), 1978 v W; 1980 v B; 1984 v Y (3)

Shannon, R. (Dundee), 1987 v WG, Ei (2), Bel; 1988 v Bel, E (2) (6)
Sharp, G. (Everton), 1982 v E (1)
Simpson, N. (Aberdeen), 1982 v I (2), E; 1983 v EG, Sw (2), Bel; 1984 v Bel, EG, Y; 1985 v Sp (11)
Sinclair, G. (Dumbarton), 1977 v E (1)
Smith, G. (Rangers), 1978 v W (1)
Smith, H. G. (Hearts), 1987 v WG, Bel (2)
Sneddon, A. (Celtic), 1979 v US (1)
Speedie, D. (Chelsea), 1985 v Sp (1)
Stanton, P. (Hibernian), 1977 v Cz (1)
Stark, W. (Aberdeen), 1985 v Ic (1)
Stephen, R. (Dundee), 1983 v Bel (sub) (1)
Stevens, G. (Motherwell), 1977 v E (1)
Stewart, J. (Kilmarnock), 1978 v Sw, Cz; (with Middlesbrough), 1979 v P (3)
Stewart, R. (Dundee U), 1979 v P, N (2); (with West Ham U), 1980 v B (2), E (2), WG; 1981 v D; 1982 v I (2), E (12)
Strachan, G. (Aberdeen), 1980 v B (1)
Sturrock, P. (Dundee U), 1977 v Cz, W, Sw, E; 1978 v Sw, Cz; 1982 v Se, I, E (9)

Thomson, W. (Partick Th), 1977 v E (sub); 1978 v W; (with St Mirren), 1979 v US, N (2); 1980 v B (2), E (2), WG (10)
Tolmie, J. (Morton), 1980 v B (sub) (1)
Tortolano, J. (Hibernian), 1987 v WG, Ei (2)

Walker, A. (Celtic), 1988 v Bel (1)
Wallace, I. (Coventry C), 1978 v Sw (1)
Walsh, C. (Nottingham F), 1984 v EG, Sw (2), Bel; 1984 v EG (5)
Wark, J. (Ipswich T), 1977 v Cz, W, Sw; 1978 v W; 1979 v P; 1980 v E (2), WG (8)
Watson, A. (Aberdeen), 1981 v Se, D; 1982 v D, I (sub) (4)
Watson, K. (Rangers), 1977 v E; 1978 v Sw (sub) (2)
Winnie, D. (St Mirren), 1988 v Bel (1)
Whyte, D. (Celtic), 1987 v Ei (2), Bel; 1988 v E (2); 1989 v N, Y (7)
Wilson, T. (St Mirren), 1983 v Sw (sub) (1)
Wilson, T. (Nottingham F), 1988 v E; 1989 v N, Y (3)
Wright, P. (Aberdeen), 1989 v Y, F (2)
Wright, T. (Oldham Ath), 1987 v Bel (sub) (1)

WALES

Aizlewood, M. (Luton T), 1979 v E; 1981 v Ho (2)

Balcombe, S. (Leeds U), 1982 v F (sub) (1)
Bater, P. T. (Bristol R), 1977 v E, S (2)
Blackmore, C. (Manchester U), 1984 v N, Bul, Y (3)
Bodin, P. (Cardiff C), 1983 v Y (1)
Bowen, M. (Tottenham H), 1983 v N; 1984 v Bul, Y (3)
Boyle, T. (C Palace), 1982 v F (1)

Cegielski, W. (Wrexham), 1977 v E (sub), S (2)
Charles, J. M. (Swansea C), 1979 v E; 1981 v Ho (2)
Clark, J. (Manchester U), 1978 v S; (with Derby Co), 1979 v E (2)
Curtis, A. T. (Swansea C), 1977 v E (1)

Davies, A. (Manchester U), 1982 v F (2) Ho; 1983 v N, Y, Bul (6)
Davies, I. C. (Norwich C), 1978 v S (sub) (1)
Deacy, N. (PSV Eindhoven), 1977 v S (1)
Dibble, A. (Cardiff C), 1983 v Bul; 1984 v N, Bul (3)
Doyle, S. C. (Preston NE), 1979 v E (sub); 1984 (with Huddersfield T), v N (2)
Dwyer, P. J. (Cardiff C), 1979 v E (1)

Edwards, R. I. (Chester), 1977 v S; 1978 v W (2)
Evans, A. (Bristol R), 1977 v E (1)

Gale, D. (Swansea C), 1983 v Bul; 1984 v N (sub) (2)
Giles, D. C. (Cardiff C), 1977 v S; 1978 v S; 1981 (with Swansea C), v Ho; 1983 (with C. Palace), v Y (4)
Giles, P. (Cardiff C), 1982 v F (2) Ho (3)

Hodges, G. (Wimbledon), 1983 v Y (sub), Bul (sub); 1984 v N, Bul, Y (6)
Holden, A. (Chester C), 1984 v Y (sub) (1)
Hopkins, J. (Fulham), 1982 v F (sub), Ho; 1983 v N, Y, Bul (5)
Hughes, M. (Manchester U), 1983 v N, Y; 1984 v N. Bul, Y (5)
Hughes, W. (WBA), 1977 v E, S; 1978 v S (3)

Jackett, K. (Watford), 1981 v Ho; 1982 v F (2)
James, R. M. (Swansea C), 1977 v E, S; 1978 v S (3)
Jones, F. (Wrexham), 1981 v Ho (1)
Jones, L. (Cardiff C), 1982 v F (2), Ho (3)
Jones, V. (Bristol R), 1979 v E; 1981 v Ho (2)

Kendall, M. (Tottenham H), 1978 v S (1)

Letheran, G. (Leeds U), 1977 v E, S (2)
Lewis, D. (Swansea C), 1982 v F (2), Ho; 1983 v N, Y, Bul; 1984 v N, Bul, Y (9)
Lewis, J. (Cardiff C), 1983 v N (1)
Loveridge, J. (Swansea C), 1982 v Ho; 1983 v N, Bul (3)
Lowndes, S. R. (Newport Co), 1979 v E; 1981 v Ho; 1984 (with Millwall), Bul, Y (4)

Maddy, P. (Cardiff C), 1982 v Ho; 1983 v N (sub) (2)
Marustik, C. (Swansea C), 1982 v F (2); 1983 v Y, Bul; 1984 v N, Bul, Y (7)
Micallef, C. (Cardiff C), 1982 v F, Ho; 1983 v N (3)

Nardiello, D. (Coventry C), 1978 v S (1)
Nicholas, P. (C Palace), 1978 v S; 1979 v E; (with Arsenal), 1982 v F (3)

Pascoe, C. (Swansea C), 1983 v Bul (sub); 1984 v N (sub), Bul, Y (4)
Phillips, D. (Plymouth Arg), 1984 v N, Bul, Y (3)
Phillips, L. (Swansea C), 1979 v E; (with Charlton Ath), 1983 v N (2)
Pontin, K. (Cardiff C), 1978 v S (1)
Price, P. (Luton T), 1981 v Ho (1)
Pugh, D. (Doncaster R), 1982 v F (2) (2)

Ratcliffe, K. (Everton), 1981 v Ho; 1982 v F (2)
Rees, A. (Birmingham C), 1984 v N (1)
Roberts, G. (Hull C), 1983 v Bul (1)
Roberts, J. G. (Wrexham), 1977 v E (1)
Rush, I. (Liverpool), 1981 v Ho; 1982 v F (2)

Sayer, P. A. (Cardiff C), 1977 v E, S (2)
Slatter, N. (Bristol R), 1983 v N, Y, Bul; 1984 v N, Bul, Y (6)
Stevenson, N. (Swansea C), 1982 v F, Ho (2)
Stevenson, W. B. (Leeds U), 1977 v E, S; 1978 v S (3)

Thomas, Martin R. (Bristol R), 1979 v E; 1981 v Ho (2)
Thomas, Mickey R. (Wrexham), 1977 v E; 1978 v S (2)
Thomas, D. G. (Leeds U), 1977 v E; 1979 v E; 1984 v N (3)
Tibbott, L. (Ipswich T), 1977 v E, S (2)

Vaughan, N. (Newport Co), 1982 v F, Ho (2)

Walsh, I. P. (C Palace), 1979 v E; (with Swansea C), 1983 v Bul (2)
Williams, D. (Bristol R), 1983 v Y (1)
Williams, G. (Bristol R), 1983 v Y, Bul (2)
Wilmot, R. (Arsenal), 1982 v F (2), Ho; 1983 v N, Y; 1984 v Y (6)

Scotland Under-21 Teams 1988–89

13 Sept (in Norway)

Norway (0) 1 *(Eftevaag)*

Scotland (0) 1 *(Miller (pen))* 665

Norway: Linn; Hansen, Pedersen T, Bjarmann, Bjornebye, Pedersen J, Haugen (Johansen), Rekdal, Mellomstrand, Dahlum (Eftevaag), Agdestein
Scotland: Money; Nisbet, Robertson, Whyte, McPherson, McKinlay, Miller, Wilson, Glover (Hunter) (Campbell), Collins, McLeod

18 Oct (in Edinburgh)

Scotland (0) 0

Yugoslavia (0) 2 *(Boban, Suker)* 4023

Scotland: Main; Nisbet, Robertson, Hamilton (McKinlay), McPherson, Whyte, Miller (May), Wright, Fleck, Collins, Campbell
*Yugoslavia:*Zitnjak; Brnovic (Babunski), Jarni, Pavlicic, Petric, Stimac, Mijatovic, Pavlovic, Boban (Jankovic), Prosinecki, Suker

7 Mar (in Dundee)

Scotland (1) 2 *(Wright, Galloway)*

France (0) 3 *(Divert 2, Ziteli)* 4187

Scotland: Fridge; McLaren (Hamilton), Cleland, Nisbet, Campbell, May, McInally, McKinaly, Collins, Wright (Hunter), Galloway
France: Sansone; Valery, Cyprien, Wallemme, Gros, Dogon (Dumas), Delpech, Deschamps, Desailly, Divert (Pavon) Zitelli

Paul Gascoigne, who graduated from England's Under-21 squad to full international honours.

FA Schools and Youth Games 1988–89

GM National School (Under-16)
Nordic Championships in Sweden
31 July, Vasteras

England 4 *(Morah 2, Makin, Flatts)*

Finland 0

England: Stanger (Foster); Hancock, Fowler (Schonberger), Reed, Price (Gaunt), Flitcroft, Sinclair, Clements, Morah (Kenton), Joseph (Makin), Flatts.

1 Aug, Vasteras

England 1 *(Price)*

Norway 1

(England won on penalties)

England: Stanger; Fuller, Schonberger, Gaunt (Price), Reed, Clements, Joseph, Flitcroft (Sinclair) (Fowler), Kenton (Morah), Makin, Flatts.

3 Aug, Vasteras

England 2 *(Morah 2)*

Denmark 2

(England won on penalties)
England: Stanger; Hancock, Fowler (Schonberger), Reed, Price (Gaunt), Clements, Makin, Flitcroft (Fuller), Kenton (Morah), Joseph, Flatts.

5 Aug, Vasteras

England 2 *(Flatts, Morah)*

Iceland 0

England: Stanger; Hancock, Schonberger (Makin), Reed, Gaunt (Price), Clements, Fuller, Flitcroft, Kenton (Morah), Joseph, Flatts (Sinclair).

6 Aug, Vasteras

England 4 *(Kenton 2, Morah, Joseph)*

Sweden 0

England: Stanger; Hancock (Makin), Fowler, Price (Gaunt), Reed, Clements, Fuller (Sinclair), Flitcroft, Morah (Kenton), Joseph, Flatts.

Friendly

20 Aug, Wembley

England 1 *(Flitcroft)*

Israel 1

England: Stanger; Hancock (Makin), Fowler (Schonberger), Flicroft, Price (Gaunt), Reed, Fuller (Sinclair), Clements, Morah (Kenton), Joseph, Flatts.

Tournament in Italy
3 Nov, Chiavari

England 0

Spain 2

England: Stanger; Hancock (Makin), Fowler, Reed, Price, Flitcroft, Clements, Joseph, Flatts (Sinclair), Morah, Kenton (Fuller).

4 Nov, Chiavari

England 3 *(Gaunt, Sinclair, Morah)*

West Germany 2

England: Stanger; Reed, Gaunt, Flitcroft, Clements, Fuller, Joseph, Sinclair, Schonberger (Fowler), Makin (Hancock), Morah.

Semi-final, 7 Nov, Carlini
England 2 *(Flitcroft, Fuller)*

Italy 1

England: Stanger; Hancock, Fowler, Reed, Gaunt, Flitcroft, Clements, Fuller, Joseph, Sinclair (Flatts), Morah.

Final, 9 Nov, Carlini

England 0

Spain 2

England: Stanger; Hancock (Makin), Fowler, Reed, Gaunt (Price), Flitcroft, Clements, Fuller, Joseph, Flatts (Sinclair), Morah.

Friendlies
15 Feb, Sohar
Oman 2

England 0

England: Sheppard (Stanger); Makin, Fowler (Schonberger), Fuller, Gaunt, Flitcroft (Reed), Sinclair, Clements, Morah, Kenton (Joseph), Flatts.

17 Feb, Muscat
Oman 3

England 0

England: Sheppard (Stanger); Reed, Fowler (Schonberger), Fuller, Gaunt, Flitcroft, Joseph, Clements (Makin), Morah, Kenton (Sinclair), Flatts.

Under-17, 20 Sept, Dublin
Eire 0

England 2 *(Cole, own goal)*

England: Walker; Towler, McCarthy (Small), Mitchell, Kavanagh, Hendon, Heaney (Halstead), Cole, Newhouse (Allen), Turner, Hartfield.

UEFA Youth Championship qualifiers
26 Oct, Tranmere

England 5 *(Kavanagh, Heaney, Cole, Houghton, Walters)*

Greece 0

England: Walker; Towler, Hartfield, Walters, Kavanagh, Hendon, Heaney, Cole, Newhouse (Allen), Turner, Wright.

15 Nov, Bradford

England 1 *(Cole)*

France 1

England: Walker; Towler, Wright, Walters, Kavanagh, Hendon, Jones (Michell), Cole, Newhouse (Allen), Turner, Small.

8 Mar, Xanthi
Greece 0

England 3 *(Walters, Newhouse, Jones)*

England: Walker; Mitchell, Wright, Kavanagh, Hendon, Hartfield (Turner), Jones, Walters, Cole, Newhouse, Small.

26 April, Povazska Bystrica

Czechoslovakia 1

England 0

England: Walker; Towler, Wright, Kavanagh, Hendon, Walters, Sutch, Newhouse, Cole, Hartfield, Small (Houghton).

ENGLAND YOUTH INTERNATIONAL MATCHES 1947–89

* *Professionals.* † *Abandoned.* UYT *UEFA Youth Tournament.* WYT *World Youth Tournament.*

v SCOTLAND

			E	S
1947	25 Oct	Doncaster	4	2
1948	30 Oct	Aberdeen	1	3
UYT1949	21 Apr	Utrecht	0	1
1950	4 Feb	Carlisle	7	1
1951	3 Feb	Kilmarnock	6	1
1952	15 Mar	Sunderland	3	1
1953	7 Feb	Glasgow	4	3
1954	6 Feb	Middlesbrough	2	1
1955	5 Mar	Kilmarnock	3	4
1956	3 Mar	Preston	2	2
1957	9 Mar	Aberdeen	3	1
1958	1 Mar	Hull	2	0
1959	28 Feb	Aberdeen	1	1
1960	27 Feb	Newcastle	1	1
1961	25 Feb	Elgin	3	2
1962	24 Feb	Peterborough	4	2
UYT1963	19 Apr	White City	1	0
1963	18 May	Dumfries	3	1
1964	22 Feb	Middlesbrough	1	1
1965	27 Feb	Inverness	1	2
1966	5 Feb	Hereford	5	3
1967	4 Feb	Aberdeen	0	1
UYT1967	1 Mar	Southampton	1	0
UYT1967	15 Mar	Dundee	0	0
1968	3 Feb	Walsall	0	5
1969	1 Feb	Stranraer	1	1
1970	31 Jan	Derby	1	2
1971	30 Jan	Greenock	1	2
1972	30 Jan	Bournemouth	2	0
1973	20 Jan	Kilmarnock	3	2
1974	26 Jan	Brighton	2	2
UYT1981	27 May	Aachen	0	1
UYT1982	23 Feb	Glasgow	0	1
UYT1982	23 Mar	Coventry	2	2
UYT1983	15 May	Birmingham	4	2
UI61983	5 Oct	Middlesbrough	3	1
UI61983	19 Oct	Motherwell	4	0
UYT1984	27 Nov	Craven Cottage	1	2
1985	8 Apr	Cannes	1	0
1986	25 Mar	Aberdeen	1	4

v WALES

			E	W
1948	28 Feb	High Wycombe	4	2
UYT1948	15 Apr	Shepherds Bush	4	0
1949	26 Feb	Swansea	0	0
1950	25 Feb	Worcester	1	0
1951	17 Feb	Wrexham	1	1
1952	23 Feb	Plymouth	6	0
1953	21 Feb	Swansea	4	2
1954	20 Feb	Derby	2	1
1955	19 Feb	Milford Haven	7	2
1956	18 Feb	Shrewsbury	5	1
1957	9 Feb	Cardiff	7	1
1958	15 Feb	Reading	8	2
1959	14 Feb	Portmadoc	3	0
1960	19 Mar	Canterbury	1	1
1961	18 Mar	Newtown	4	0
1962	17 Mar	Swindon	4	0
1963	16 Mar	Haverfordwest	1	0
1964	15 Mar	Leeds	2	1
1965	20 Mar	Newport	2	2
1966	19 Mar	Northampton	4	1
1967	18 Mar	Cwmbran	3	3
1968	16 Mar	Watford	2	3
1969	15 Mar	Haverfordwest	3	1
UYT1970	25 Feb	Newport	0	0
UYT1970	18 Mar	Leyton	1	2
1970	20 Apr	Reading	0	0
1971	20 Feb	Aberystwyth	1	2
1972	19 Feb	Swindon	4	0
1973	24 Feb	Portmadoc	4	1
UYT1974	9 Jan	West Bromwich	1	0
1974	2 Mar	Shrewsbury	2	1
UYT1974	13 Mar	Cardiff	0	1
UYT1976	11 Feb	Cardiff	1	0
UYT1976	3 Mar	Maine Rd	2	3
UYT1977	9 Mar	West Bromwich	1	0
UYT1977	23 Mar	Cardiff	1	1

v NORTHERN IRELAND

			E	NI
1948	15 May	Belfast	2	2
UYT1949	18 Apr	Haarlem	3	3
1949	14 May	Hull	4	2
1950	6 May	Belfast	0	1
1951	5 May	Liverpool	5	2
1952	19 Apr	Belfast	0	2
1953	11 Apr	Wolverhampton	0	0
UYT1954	10 Apr	Bruehl	5	0
1954	8 May	Newtownards	2	2
1955	14 May	Watford	3	0
1956	12 May	Belfast	0	1
1957	11 May	Leyton	6	2
1958	10 May	Bangor	2	4
1959	9 May	Liverpool	5	0
1960	14 May	Portadown	5	2
1961	13 May	Manchester	2	0
1962	12 May	Londonderry	1	2
UYT1963	23 Apr	Wembley	4	0
1963	11 May	Oldham	1	1
1964	25 Jan	Belfast	3	1
1965	22 Jan	Birkenhead	2	3
1966	26 Feb	Belfast	4	0
1967	25 Feb	Stockport	3	0
1968	23 Feb	Belfast	0	2
1969	28 Feb	Birkenhead	0	2
1970	28 Feb	Lurgan	1	3
1971	6 Mar	Blackpool	1	1
1972	11 Mar	Chester	1	1
UYT1972	17 May	Sabadell	4	0
1973	24 Mar	Telford	3	0
1974	19 Apr	Birkenhead	1	2
UYT1975	13 May	Kriens	3	0
UYT1980	16 May	Arnstadt	1	0
UYT1981	11 Feb	Walsall	1	0
UYT1981	11 Mar	Belfast	3	0

v ALGERIA

			E	A
1984	22 Apr	Cannes	3	0

v ARGENTINA

			E	A
*WYT1981	5 Oct	Sydney	1	1

v AUSTRIA

			E	A
UYT1949	19 Apr	Zeist	4	2
UYT1952	17 Apr	Barcelona	5	5
UYT1957	16 Apr	Barcelona	0	3
1958	4 Mar	Highbury	3	2
1958	1 June	Graz	4	3
UYT1960	20 Apr	Vienna	0	1
UYT1964	1 Apr	Rotterdam	2	1
1980	6 Sept	Pazin	0	1
UYT1981	29 May	Bonn	7	0
1981	3 Sept	Umag	3	0
1984	6 Sept	Izola	2	2

v AUSTRALIA

			E	A
*WYT1981	8 Oct	Sydney	1	1

v BELGIUM

			E	B
UYT1948	16 Apr	West Ham	3	1
UYT1951	22 Mar	Cannes	1	1
UYT1953	31 Mar	Brussels	2	0
†1956	7 Nov	Brussels	3	2
1957	13 Nov	Sheffield	2	0
UYT1965	15 Apr	Ludwigshafen	3	0
UYT1969	11 Mar	West Ham	1	0
UYT1969	26 Mar	Waregem	2	0
UYT1972	13 May	Palma	0	0
UYT1973	4 June	Viareggio	0	0
UYT1977	19 May	Lokeren	1	0
1979	17 Jan	Brussels	4	0
1980	8 Sept	Labia	6	1
1983	13 Apr	Birmingham	1	1
1988	20 May	Chatel	0	0

v BRAZIL

			E	B
1986	29 mar	Cannes	0	0
1986	13 may	Peking	1	2

v BULGARIA

			E	B
UYT1956	28 Mar	Salgotarjan	1	2
UYT1960	16 Apr	Graz	0	1
UYT1962	24 Apr	Ploesti	0	0
UYT1968	7 Apr	Nimes	0	0
UYT1979	31 May	Vienna	0	1

v CAMEROON

			E	C
*WYT1981	3 Oct	Sydney	2	0

v CHINA

			E	C
1983	31 Mar	Cannes	5	1
1985	26 Aug	Baku	0	2
1986	5 May	Peking	1	0

v CZECHOSLOVAKIA

			E	C
UYT1955	7 Apr	Lucca	0	1
UYT1966	21 May	Rijeka	2	3
UYT1969	20 May	Leipzig	3	1
UYT1979	24 May	Bischofshofen	3	0
1979	8 Sept	Pula	1	2
1982	11 Apr	Cannes	0	1
UYT1983	20 May	Highbury	1	1
UYT1989	26 Apr	Bystrica	0	1

v DENMARK

			E	D
*1955	1 Oct	Plymouth	9	2
1956	20 May	Esbjerg	2	1
UYT1979	31 Oct	Esbjerg	3	1
UYT1980	26 Mar	Coventry	4	0
*1982	15 July	Stjordal	5	2
1983	16 July	Holbeck	0	1
1987	16 Feb	Maine Road	2	1

v EGYPT

			E	Eg
*WYT1981	11 Oct	Sydney	4	2

v FINLAND

			E	F
UYT1975	19 May	Berne	1	1

v FRANCE

			E	F
1957	24 Mar	Fontainebleau	1	0
1958	22 Mar	Eastbourne	0	1
UYT1966	23 May	Rijeka	1	2
UYT1967	11 May	Istanbul	2	0
*1968	25 Jan	Paris	0	1
UYT1978	8 Feb	Selhurst Park	3	1
UYT1978	1 Mar	Paris	0	0
UYT1979	2 June	Vienna	0	0
1982	12 Apr	Cannes	0	1
1983	2 Apr	Cannes	0	2
UI61984	1 Mar	Watford	4	0
UI61984	21 Mar	Bourg en Bresse	1	1
1984	23 Apr	Cannes	1	2
1986	31 Mar	Cannes	1	2
1986	11 May	Peking	1	1
1988	22 May	Monthey	1	2
UYT1988	15 Nov	Bradford	1	1

v EAST GERMANY

			E	EG
UYT1958	7 Apr	Neunkirchen	1	0
1959	8 Mar	Zwickau	3	4
1960	2 Apr	Portsmouth	1	1
UYT1965	25 Apr	Essen	2	3
UYT1969	22 May	Magdeburg	0	4
UYT1973	10 June	Florence	3	2
UYT1984	25 May	Moscow	1	1
1988	21 May	Monthey	1	0

v WEST GERMANY

			E	WG
UYT1953	4 Apr	Boom	3	1
UYT1954	15 Apr	Gelsenkirchen	2	2
UYT1956	1 Apr	Sztalinvaros	2	1
1957	31 Mar	Oberhausen	4	1
1958	12 Mar	Bolton	1	2
1961	12 Mar	Flensberg	0	2
*1962	31 Mar	Northampton	1	0
*1967	14 Feb	Moenchengladbach	1	0
UYT1972	22 May	Barcelona	2	0
1975	25 Jan	Las Palmas	4	2
1976	14 Nov	Monte Carlo	1	1
UYT1979	28 May	Salzburg	2	0
1979	1 Sept	Pula	1	1
1983	5 Sept	Pazin	2	0

v GREECE

			E	G
UYT1957	18 Apr	Barcelona	2	3
UYT1959	2 Apr	Dimitrovo	4	0
UYT1977	23 May	Beveren	1	1
UI61983	28 July	Puspokladany	1	0
UYT1988	26 Oct	Tranmere	5	0
UYT1989	8 Mar	Xanthi	3	0

v HOLLAND

			E	N
UYT1948	17 Apr	Tottenham	3	2
UYT1951	26 Mar	Cannes	2	1
*1954	21 Nov	Arnhem	2	3
*1955	5 Nov	Norwich	3	1
1957	2 Mar	Brentford	5	5
UYT1957	14 Apr	Barcelona	1	2
1957	2 Oct	Amsterdam	3	2
1961	9 Mar	Utrecht	0	1
*1962	31 Jan	Brighton	4	0
UYT1962	22 Apr	Ploesti	0	3
UYT1963	13 Apr	Wimbledon	5	0
UYT1968	9 Apr	Nimes	1	0
UYT1974	13 Feb	West Bromwich	1	1
UYT1974	27 Feb	The Hague	1	0
UYT1979	23 May	Halle	1	0
1982	9 Apr	Cannes	1	0
1985	7 Apr	Cannes	1	3
1987	1 Aug	Wembley	3	1

v HUNGARY

			E	H
UYT1954	11 Apr	Dusseldorf	1	3
UYT1956	31 Mar	Tatabanya	2	4
*1956	23 Oct	Tottenham	2	1
*1956	25 Oct	Sunderland	2	1
UYT1965	21 Apr	Wuppertal	5	0
UYT1975	16 May	Olten	3	1
UYT1977	10 Oct	Las Palmas	3	0
1979	5 Sept	Pula	2	0
1980	11 Sept	Pula	1	2
1981	7 Sept	Porec	4	0
UI61983	29 July	Debrecen	1	2
1983	3 Sept	Umag	3	2
1986	30 Mar	Cannes	2	0

v ICELAND

			E	I
UYT1973	31 May	Viareggio	2	0
UYT1977	21 May	Turnhout	0	0
UI61983	7 Sept	Reykjavik	2	1
UI61983	19 Sept	Blackburn	4	0
1983	12 Oct	Reykjavik	3	0
1983	1 Nov	Selhurst Park	3	0
UYT1984	16 Oct	Maine Road	5	3
1985	11 Sept	Reykjevik	5	0

v REPUBLIC OF IRELAND

			E	RI
UYT1953	5 Apr	Leuven	2	0
UYT1964	30 Mar	Middleburg	6	0
UYT1968	7 Feb	Dublin	0	0
UYT1968	28 Feb	Portsmouth	4	1
UYT1970	14 Jan	Dublin	4	1
UYT1970	4 Feb	Luton	10	0
UYT1975	9 May	Brunnen	1	0
UYT1985	26 Feb	Dublin	1	0
1986	25 Feb	Leeds	2	0
1987	17 Feb	Stoke	2	0
1988	20 Sept	Dublin	2	0

v ISRAEL

			E	I
*1962	20 May	Tel Aviv	3	1
*1962	22 May	Haifa	1	2

v ITALY

			E	I
UYT1958	13 Apr	Luxembourg	0	1
UYT1959	25 Mar	Sofia	0	3
UYT1961	4 Apr	Braga	2	3

UYT1965	23 Apr	Marl-Huels	3	1
UYT1966	25 May	Rijeka	1	1
UYT1967	5 May	Izmir	1	0
1973	14 Feb	Cava dei Tirreni	0	1
1973	14 Mar	Highbury	1	0
UYT1973	6 June	Viareggio	1	0
1978	19 Nov	Monte Carlo	1	2
UYT1979	28 Feb	Rome	1	0
UYT1979	4 Apr	Villa Park	2	0
UYT1983	22 May	Watford	1	1
1983	20 Apr	Cannes	1	0
1985	5 Apr	Cannes	2	2

v LUXEMBOURG

			E	*L*
UYT1950	25 May	Vienna	1	2
UYT1954	17 Apr	Bad Neuenahr	0	2
1957	2 Feb	West Ham	7	1
1957	17 Nov	Luxembourg	3	0
UYT1958	9 Apr	Eschsalzette	5	0
UYT1984	29 May	Moscow	2	0

v MALTA

			E	*M*
UYT1969	18 May	Wolfen	6	0
UYT1979	26 May	Salzburg	3	0

v MEXICO

			E	*M*
1983	18 Apr	Cannes	4	0
1985	29 Aug	Baku	0	1

v NORWAY

			E	*N*
*1982	13 July	Levanger	1	4
1983	14 July	Korsor	1	0

v PARAGUAY

			E	*P*
1985	24 Aug	Baku	2	2

v POLAND

			E	*P*
UYT1960	18 Apr	Graz	4	2
UYT1964	26 Mar	Breda	1	1
UYT1971	26 May	Presov	0	0
UYT1972	20 May	Valencia	1	0
1975	21 Jan	Las Palmas	1	1
UYT1978	9 May	Chorzow	0	2
1979	3 Sept	Porac	0	1
UYT1980	25 May	Leipzig	2	1
*1982	17 July	Steinkver	3	2
1983	12 July	Slagelse	1	0

v PORTUGAL

			E	*P*
UYT1954	18 Apr	Bonn	0	2
UYT1961	2 Apr	Lisbon	0	4
UYT1964	3 Apr	The Hague	4	0
UYT1971	30 May	Prague	3	0
1978	13 Nov	Monte Carlo	2	0
UYT1980	18 May	Rosslau	1	1
1982	7 Apr	Cannes	3	0

v QATAR

			E	*Q*
*WYT1981	14 Oct	Sydney	1	2
1983	4 Apr	Cannes	1	1

v RUMANIA

			E	*R*
1957	15 Oct	Tottenham	4	2
UYT1958	11 Apr	Luxembourg	1	0
UYT1959	31 Mar	Pazardjic	1	2
UYT1963	15 Apr	Highbury	3	0
*WYT1981	17 Oct	Adelaide	0	1

v SAAR

			E	*SAAR*
UYT1954	13 Apr	Dortmund	1	1
UYT1955	9 Apr	Prato	3	1

v SPAIN

			E	*S*
UYT1952	15 Apr	Barcelona	1	4
1957	26 Sept	Birmingham	4	4
UYT1958	5 Apr	Saarbrucken	2	2
*1958	8 Oct	Madrid	4	2
UYT1961	30 Mar	Lisbon	0	0
*1964	27 Feb	Murcia	2	1
UYT1964	5 Apr	Amsterdam	4	0
UYT1965	17 Apr	Heilbronn	0	0
*1966	30 Mar	Swindon	3	0
UYT1967	7 May	Manisa	2	1
*1971	31 Mar	Pamplona	2	3
*1971	20 Apr	Luton	1	1
1972	9 Feb	Alicante	0	0
1972	15 Mar	Sheffield	4	1
UYT1975	25 Feb	Bristol	1	1
UYT1975	18 Mar	Madrid	1	0
1976	12 Nov	Monte Carlo	3	0
UYT1978	7 May	Bukowno	1	0
1978	17 Nov	Monte Carlo	1	1
UYT1981	25 May	Siegen	1	2
UYT1983	13 May	Stoke	1	0

v SWEDEN

			E	*S*
UYT1971	24 May	Poprad	1	0
1981	5 Sept	Pazin	3	2
1984	10 Sept	Rovinj	1	1
1986	10 Nov	West Bromwich	3	3

v SWITZERLAND

			E	*S*
UYT1950	26 May	Stockerau	2	1
UYT1951	27 Mar	Nice	3	1
UYT1952	13 Apr	Barcelona	4	0
UYT1955	11 Apr	Florence	0	0
1956	11 Mar	Schaffhausen	2	0
1956	13 Oct	Brighton	2	2
1958	26 May	Zurich	3	0
*1960	8 Oct	Leyton	4	3
*†1962	22 Nov	Coventry	1	0
*1963	21 Mar	Bienne	7	1
UYT1973	2 June	Forte dei Marim	2	0
UYT1975	11 May	Buochs	4	0
1980	4 Sept	Rovinj	3	0
*1982	6 Sept	Porec	2	0
UI61983	26 July	Hajduboszormeny	4	0
1983	1 Sept	Porec	4	2
1988	19 May	Sion	2	0

v THAILAND

			E	*T*
1986	7 May	Peking	1	2

v TURKEY

			E	*T*
UYT1959	29 Mar	Dimitrovo	1	1
UYT1978	5 May	Wodzislaw	1	1

v URUGUAY

			E	*U*
1977	9 Oct	Las Palmas	1	1

v USSR

			E	*USSR*
UYT1963	17 Apr	Tottenham	2	0
UYT1967	13 May	Istanbul	0	1
UYT1968	11 Apr	Nimes	1	1
UYT1971	28 May	Prague	1	1
1978	10 Oct	Las Palmas	1	0
*1982	4 Sept	Umag	1	0
1983	29 Mar	Cannes	0	0
UYT1983	17 May	Aston Villa	0	2
UI61984	3 May	Ludwigsburg	0	2
UYT1984	27 May	Moscow	1	1
1984	8 Sept	Porec	1	0
1985	3 Apr	Cannes	2	1

v YUGOSLAVIA

			E	*Y*
UYT1953	2 April	Liège	1	1
1958	4 Feb	Chelsea	2	2
UYT1962	20 Apr	Ploesti	0	5
UYT1967	9 May	Izmir	1	1
UYT1971	22 May	Bardejor	1	0
UYT1972	18 May	Barcelona	1	0
1976	16 Nov	Monte Carlo	0	3
1978	15 Nov	Monte Carlo	1	1
UYT1980	20 May	Altenburg	2	0
1981	10 Sept	Pula	5	0
*1982	9 Sept	Pula	1	0
UI61983	25 July	Debrecen	4	4
**1983	8 Sept	Pula	2	2
UI61984	5 May	Boblingen	1	0
1984	12 Sept	Buje	1	4

UEFA YOUTH TOURNAMENT FINALS 1948–86

Year	*Winners*		*Runners-up*		*Venue*
1948	England	3	Netherlands	2	London
1949	France	4	Netherlands	1	Rotterdam
1950	Austria	3	France	2	Vienna
1951	Yugoslavia	3	Austria	2	Cannes
1952	Spain*	0	Belgium	0	Barcelona
1953	Hungary	2	Yugoslavia	0	Brussels
1954	Spain*	2	West Germany	2	Cologne
1955–56 Played in groups only					
1957	Austria	3	Spain	2	Madrid
1958	Italy	1	England	0	Luxembourg
1959	Bulgaria	1	Italy	0	Sofia
1960	Hungary	2	Rumania	1	Vienna
1961	Portugal	4	Poland	0	Lisbon
1962	Rumania	4	Yugoslavia	1	Bucharest
1963	England	4	Northern Ireland	0	London
1964	England	4	Spain	0	Amsterdam
1965	East Germany	3	England	2	Essen
1966	Italy†	0	USSR	0	Belgrade
1967	USSR	1	England	0	Istanbul
1968	Czechoslovakia	2	France	1	Cannes
1969	Bulgaria*	1	East Germany	1	Leipzig
1970	East Germany*	1	Netherlands	1	Glasgow
1971	England	3	Portugal	0	Prague
1972	England	2	West Germany	0	Barcelona
1973	England	3	East Germany	2	Florence
1974	Bulgaria	1	Yugoslavia	0	Malmo
1975	England	1	Finland	0	Berne
1976	USSR	1	Hungary	0	Budapest
1977	Belgium	2	Bulgaria	1	Brussels
1978	USSR	3	Yugoslavia	0	Krakow
1979	Yugoslavia	1	Bulgaria	0	Vienna
1980	England	2	Poland	1	Leipzig
UEFA YOUTH CHAMPIONSHIPS					
1981	West Germany	1	Poland	0	Dusseldorf
1982	Scotland	3	Czechoslovakia	1	Helsinki
1983	France	1	Czechoslovakia	0	London
1984	Hungary**	0	USSR	0	Moscow
1986	East Germany	3	Italy	1	Subotica
1988	USSR	3	Portugal	1	

* *Won on toss of a coin.* † *Joint holders.* ** *Won on penalty kicks.*

3rd WOMEN'S EUROPEAN TOURNAMENT

Group 1
Finland 3, Norway 3; Norway 0, Denmark 1; Finland 1, England 2; England 2, Denmark 1; Denmark 2 England 0; Norway 0, Finland 2; Denmark 3, Finland 1; Norway 2, England 0; Finland 1, Denmark 2; Denmark 3, Norway 2; England 1, Finland 1; England 1, Norway 3.

Group 2
Sweden 0, Holland 0; Holland 4, Scotland 0; Eire 0, Holland 1; Holland 2, Eire 0; Eire 2, Scotland 1; Eire 1, Sweden 1; Sweden 4, Eire 0; Holland 1, Sweden 0. Scotland withdrew.

Group 3
Hungary 0, West Germany 1; West Germany 3, Italy 0; Hungary 7, Switzerland 1; Italy 0, West Germany 0; Italy 5, Hungary 1; West Germany 0, Switzerland 0; Switzerland 3, Hungary 0; Italy 5, Switzerland 0; Switzerland 0, West Germany 10; Hungary 0, Italy 0; West Germany 4, Hungary 0; Switzerland 0, Italy 6.

Group 4
Bulgaria 1, Spain 1; Belgium 1, Czechoslovakia 1; Belgium 0, France 2; Czechoslovakia 1, Spain 0; France 5, Bulgaria 0; Spain 1, Belgium 0; Spain 1, France 3; Spain 1, Bulgaria 0; Czechoslovakia 0, Belgium 0; Bulgaria 0, Belgium 0; France 0, Spain 0; Bulgaria 0, Czechoslovakia 1; France 2, Czechoslovakia 2; Spain 0,Czechoslovakia 2; France 0, Belgium 0; Belgium 5, Bulgaria 0; Czechoslovakia 0, France 0; Czechoslovakia 3, Bulgaria 0; Belgium 1, Spain 0; Bulgaria 0, France 2.

Quarter-finals
Norway 2, Holland 1; Holland 0, Norway 3; Denmark 1, Sweden 5; Sweden 1, Denmark 1; Czechoslovakia 1, West Germany 1; West Germany 2, Czechoslovakia 0; Italy 2, France 0; France 1, Italy 2.

Final tournament in West Germany
Semi-finals
West Germany 1, Italy 1 *aet*; *West Germany won 4-3 on penalties;* Sweden 1, Norway 2.

Final
West Germany 4, Norway 1 (Osnabruck).

Third place match
Italy 1, Sweden 2.

Women's FA Cup Final: Leasowe Pacific (Liverpool) 3, Friends of Fulham 2.

SOUTH AMERICA

SOUTH AMERICAN FOOTBALLER OF THE YEAR 1988

Ruben Paz, the Uruguayan striker from the Argentine club Racing was voted South America's top player in the annual poll organised by the Venezuelan newspaper *El Mundo*. Uruguayan players took second, third and fourth places in the award.

Past winners

1971 **Tostao** (Brazil)
1972 **Cubillas** (Peru)
1973 **Pele** (Brazil)
1974 **Figueroa** (Chile)
1975 **Figueroa** (Chile)
1976 **Figueroa** (Chile)
1977 **Zico** (Brazil)
1978 **Kempes** (Argentina)
1979 **Maradona** (Argentina)
1980 **Maradona** (Argentina)
1981 **Zico** (Brazil)
1982 **Zico** (Brazil)
1983 **Socrates** (Brazil)
1984 **Francescoli** (Uruguay)
1985 **Romero** (Paraguay)
1986 **Alzamendi** (Uruguay)
1987 **Valderrama** (Colombia)

LEAGUE CHAMPIONS 1988

Argentina: Independiente
Bolivia: Bolivar
Brazil: Bahia
Chile: Cobreloa
Colombia: Millonarios
Ecuador: Emelec
Paraguay: Olimpia
Peru: Sporting Cristal
Uruguay: Danubio
Venezuela: Maritimo

SOUTH AMERICAN (Libertadores) CUP 1988

Group 1

	P	*W*	*D*	*L*	*F*	*A*	*Pts*
Univ Catolica (Chi)	6	4	2	0	9	4	10
Colo Colo (Chi)	6	4	1	1	7	3	9
Maritimo (Ven)	6	0	3	3	2	5	3
Atletico Tachira (Ven)	6	0	2	4	2	8	2

Group 2

	P	*W*	*D*	*L*	*F*	*A*	*Pts*
Newell's Old Boys (Arg)	6	2	4	0	5	1	8
San Lorenzo (Arg)	6	3	2	1	6	4	8
Barcelona (Ecu)	6	3	1	2	9	8	7
Filabanco (Ecu)	6	0	1	5	5	12	1

Group 3

	P	*W*	*D*	*L*	*F*	*A*	*Pts*
America (Col)	6	4	1	1	8	6	9
Nacional (Uru)	6	3	2	1	8	7	8
Millonarios (Col)	6	2	0	4	14	12	4
Wanderers (Uru)	6	1	1	4	3	8	3

Group 4

	P	*W*	*D*	*L*	*F*	*A*	*Pts*
Oriente Petrolero (Bol)	6	3	1	2	8	8	7
Bolivar (Bol)	6	3	0	3	12	10	6
Cerro Porteno (Par)	6	2	2	2	6	7	6
Olimpia (Par)	6	2	1	3	6	7	5

Group 5

	P	*W*	*D*	*L*	*F*	*A*	*Pts*
Guarani (Br)	6	3	2	1	9	5	8
Universitario (Per)	6	2	4	0	5	2	8
Sport Recife (Br)	6	2	1	3	7	6	5
Alianza (Per)	6	1	1	4	2	10	3

Second Round First Leg
America 1, Universitario 0
Bolivar 1, Newell's Old Boys 0
San Lorenzo 1, Guarani 1
Univ Catolica 1, Nacional 1
Oriente Petrolero 2, Colo Colo 1

Second Round Second Leg
Newell's Old Boys 1, Bolivar 0
Nacional 0, Univ Catolica 0
Colo Colo 0, Oriente Petrolero 0
Universitario 2, America 2
Guarani 0, San Lorenzo 1

Third Round First Leg
Penarol 0, San Lorenzo 0
Oriente Petrolero 1, America 1
Newell's Old Boys 1, Nacional 1

Third Round Second Leg
Nacional 2, Newell's Old Boys 1
San Lorenzo 1, Penarol 0
America 2, Oriente Petrolero 0

Semi-finals First Leg
Newell's Old Boys 1, San Lorenzo 0
Nacional 1, America 0

Semi-finals Second Leg
San Lorenzo 1, Newell's Old Boys 2
America 1, Nacional 1

Final First Leg

Newell's Old Boys (0) 1, Nacional (0) 0

(Rosario, Argentina, 19 October 1988, 45,000)

Newell's Old Boys: Scoponi; Llop, Theiler, Pautasse, Sensini, Martino (Fullana), Franco, Alfar, Rossi, Batistuta, Almiron (Gabrich).
Nacional: Sere; Pintos Saldanha, Revelez, De Leon, Soca, Lemos, Ostolaza, Cardaccio, Castro, Vargas (Careno), De Lima.
Scorer: Gabrich.

Second Leg

Nacional (2) 3, Newell's Old Boys (0) 0 *aet*

(Montevideo, Uruguay, 26 October 1988, 75,000)

Nacional: Sere; Pintos Saldanha, Revelez, De Leon, Soca, Lemos, Ostolaza, Cardaccio, Castro (Moran), Vargas (Carreno), De Lima.
Newell's Old Boys: Scoponi; Llop (Ramos), Theiler, Pautasso, Sensini, Martino, Alfaro (Almiron), Franco, Rossi, Batistuta, Gabrich.
Scorers: Vargas, Ostolaza, De Leon (pen).

SOUTH AMERICAN (Libertadores) CUP 1989

Group 1

	P	W	D	L	F	A	Pts
Cobreloa (Chi)	6	3	2	1	7	4	8
Sol de America (Para)	6	2	2	2	7	8	6
Olimpia (Para)	6	2	1	3	8	9	5
Colo Colo (Chi)	6	2	1	3	7	8	5

Group 2

	P	W	D	L	F	A	Pts
Bahia (Br)	6	4	2	0	11	4	10
Tachira (Ven)	6	3	1	2	7	8	7
Internacional (Br)	6	2	1	3	8	5	5
Maritimo (Ven)	6	0	2	4	3	10	2

Group 3

	P	W	D	L	F	A	Pts
Millonarios (Col)	6	4	2	0	12	3	10
Nacional (Col)	6	2	3	1	8	6	7
Dep. Quito (Ecu)	6	1	2	3	4	7	4
Emelec (Ecu)	6	1	1	4	6	12	3

Group 4

	P	W	D	L	F	A	Pts
Boca Juniors (Arg)	6	3	1	2	9	7	7
Racing Avellaneda (Arg)	6	3	1	2	9	6	7
Universitario (Peru)	6	3	0	3	7	6	6
Sporting Cristal (Per)	6	2	0	4	6	12	4

Play-off: Boca Juniors 3, Racing 1

Group 5

	P	W	D	L	F	A	Pts
Penarol (Uru)	6	3	1	2	11	9	7
Danubio (Uru)	6	3	0	3	7	7	6
Bolivar (Bol)	6	2	2	2	6	7	6
The Strongest (Bol)	6	1	3	2	3	4	5

Second Round First Leg
Internacional 6, Penarol 2
Olimpia 2, Boca Juniors 0
Dep. Quito 0, Cobreloa 0
Bolivar 1, Millonarios 0
Sol de America 3, Tachira 0
Nacional 2, Racing 0
Danubio 0, Nacional 0 (Uruguay)
Universitario 1, Bahia 1

Second Round Second Leg
Danubio 3, Nacional (Uruguay) 1
Penarol 1, Internacional 2
Tachira 3, Sol de America 0
Boca Juniors 5, Olimpia 3
Cobreloa 1, Dep. Quito 0
Millonarios 3, Bolivar 2
Bahia 2, Universitario 1
Racing 2, Nacional (Colombia) 1

Quarter-finals First Leg
Cobreloa 0, Danubio 2
Nacional (Colombia) 1, Millonarios 0
Internacional 1, Bahia 0
Olimpia 2, Sol de America 0

Quarter-finals Second Leg
Danubio 2, Cobreloa 1
Olimpia 4, Sol de America 4
Bahia 0, Internacional 0
Millonarios 1, Nacional (Colombia) 1

Semi-finals First Leg
Danubio 0, Nacional (Colombia) 0
Olimpia 0, Internacional 1

Semi-finals Second Leg
Internacional 2, Olimpia 3
(aggregrate 3-3; Olimpia won 5-3 on penalties)
Nacional 6, Danubio 0

Final First Leg
Olimpia (1) 2, Nacional (0) 0

(Asuncion, Paraguay, 24 May 1989, 50,000)

Olimpia: Almeida; Mino, Benitez, Chamas, Krausemann, Sanabria (Balbuena), Guasch, Neffa, Bobadilla, Amarilla, Mendoza (Gonzalez).
Nacional: Higuita; Gomez, Perea, Escobar, Vila (Carmona), Perez, Alvarez, Fajardo, Garcia, Arango (Arboleda), Usurriaga.
Scorers: Bobadilla, Sanabria.

Second Leg
Nacional (1) 2, Olimpia (0) 0

(Bogota, Colombia, 31 May 1989, 50,000)

Nacional: Higuita; Carmona, Perea, Escobar, Gomez, Alvarez, Garcia, Fajardo (Arboleda), Arango (Perez), Usurriaga, Trellez.
Olimpia: Almeida; Mino, Benitez, Chamas, Krausemann, Sanabria, Guasch, Bobadilla (Balbuena), Neffa, Amarilla, Mendoza.
Scorers: Chamas (og), Usurriaga.
(Aggregate 2-2; Nacional (Colombia) won 5-4 on penalties)

SOUTH AMERICAN CHAMPIONSHIP 1989 (Copa America)

Group A (Salvador Bahia, Brazil)
Paraguay 5, Peru 2
Brazil 3, Venezuela 1
Colombia 4, Venezuela 2
Brazil 0, Peru 0
Colombia 0, Paraguay 1
Peru 3, Venezuela 0
Paraguay 3, Venezuela 0
Brazil 0, Colombia 0
Colombia 1, Peru 1
Brazil 2, Paraguay 0

	P	W	D	L	F	A	Pts
Paraguay	4	3	0	1	9	4	6
Brazil	4	2	2	0	5	1	6
Colombia	4	1	2	1	5	4	4
Peru	4	0	3	1	6	6	3
Venezuela	4	0	1	4	3	13	1

Group B (Goiania, Brazil)
Ecuador 1, Uruguay 0
Argentina 1, Chile 0
Ecuador 0, Argentina 0
Uruguay 3, Bolivia 0
Chile 0, Uruguay 3
Ecuador 0, Bolivia 0
Argentina 1, Uruguay 0
Chile 5, Bolivia 0
Chile 2, Ecuador 1
Argentina 0, Bolivia 0

	P	W	D	L	F	A	Pts
Argentina	4	2	2	0	2	0	6
Uruguay	4	2	0	2	6	2	4
Chile	4	2	0	2	7	5	4
Ecuador	4	1	2	1	2	2	4
Bolivia	4	0	2	2	0	8	2

Final Round
Brazil 2, Argentina 0
Uruguay 3, Paraguay 0
Brazil 3, Paraguay 0
Uruguay 2, Argentina 0

Third Place match
Argentina 0, Paraguay 0

Final
Brazil (0) 1, Uruguay (0) 0 Rio, 178,000

Brazil: Tafferel; Mazinho, Galvao, Ricardo, Branco, Elvair, Valdo (Josimar), Silas (Alemao), Dunga, Bebeto, Romario.
Uruguay: Zeoli; Herrera, Gutierrez, De Leon, Dominguez, Perdomo, Ostolaza (Correa), Francescoli, Ruben Paz (Da Silva), Alzamendi, Ruben Sosa.
Scorer: Brazil: Romario.

OTHER INTERNATIONAL RESULTS 1988

January
Guatemala 1, Costa Rica 2
Guatemala 1, USA 0
Guatemala 0, USA 1

February
Benin 1, Mali 2
Bahrain 1, Tunisia 0

April
Jamaica 4, Canada 0
El Salvador 0, Guatemala 0
Canada 1, Mexico 0
Canada 1, Mexico 1

May
USA 0, Colombia 4

June
Zambia 3, Zimbabwe 2
USA 1, Costa Rica 0
Canada 0, Costa Rica 1
New Zealand 2, Saudi Arabia 0
Indonesia 0, Korea Rep. 4
New Zealand 3, Saudi Arabia 2
Hong Kong 0, Saudi Arabia 3

July
Netherlands Antilles 1, Costa Rica 1
Netherlands Antilles 1, Costa Rica 0
Malawi 1, Zambia 0
Malawi 0, Zambia 1
Jamaica 0, Barbados 0
Malawi 0, Zambia 0
Burkino Faso 1, Niger 0

August
Trinidad/Tobago 2, Guatemala 2

September
Zambia 4, Malawi 1
El Salvador 0, Honduras 0
Malawi 1, Mozambique 1
Netherlands Antilles 0, Venezuela 0
Malawi 1, Mozambique 0

October
Indonesia 0, Qatar 1
Trinidad/Tobago 1, Canada 2
Singapore 0, Qatar 1
New Zealand 1, Australia 2

November
Tunisia 1, Algeria 0
El Salvador 0, Guatemala 1
Fiji 1, New Zealand 1

December
Central Africa 2, Chad 1
Congo 1, Central Africa 0
Ivory Coast 1, Tunisia 1
Ivory Coast 1, Tunisia 0
Zambia 1, Egypt 2
Morocco 1, Guinea 0

NORTH AND CENTRAL AMERICA INTER-AMERICAN CUP

Final First Leg
Olimpia (Honduras) (0) 1 *(Rivera (pen))*
Nacional (Uruguay) (1) 1 *(Fonseca)* 30,000

Second Leg
Nacional (Uruguay) (2) 4 *(Fonseca, Ostolaza, Noe 2)*
Olimpia (Honduras) (0) 0 30,000
(Nacional won 5-1 on aggregate)

Arab Club Championship
Sa'ad (Qatar) 2, 1, Rasheed (Iraq) 3, 0
(Sa'ad won on away goals)

Arab Cup Final
Iraq 1, Syria 1 *aet*
(Iraq won 4-3 on penalties)

Balkan Cup Final
Slavia Sofia 5, 1, Arges Pitesti 0, 0

World Indoor Cup Final
Brazil 2, Holland 1 (in Holland)

Canadian Soccer League
Vancouver 86ers 4, Hamilton Steelers 1

ASL (USA)
Washington Diplomats 3, Fort Lauderdale Strikers 2

ASIAN CUP (in Qatar)

Group A	*P*	*W*	*D*	*L*	*F*	*A*	*Pts*
South Korea	4	4	0	0	9	2	8
Iran	4	2	1	1	3	3	5
Qatar	4	2	0	2	7	6	4
UAE	4	1	0	3	2	4	2
Japan	4	0	1	3	0	5	1

Group B	*P*	*W*	*D*	*L*	*F*	*A*	*Pts*
Saudi Arabia	4	2	2	0	3	2	6
China	4	2	1	1	6	3	5
Syria	4	2	0	2	2	5	4
Kuwait	4	0	3	1	2	3	3
Bahrain	4	0	2	2	1	3	2

Semi-finals
South Korea 2, China 1 *aet*
Saudi Arabia 1, Iran 0

Third place match
Iran 0, China 0 *aet*
(Iran won 3-0 on penalties)

Final
Saudi Arabia 0, South Korea 0 *aet*
(Saudi Arabia won 4-3 on penalties)

East and Central African Senior Challenge Cup Final
Malawi (0) 3, Zambia (1) 1
(Blantyre, 19 November 1988)

African Champions Cup Final

First Leg
Iwuanyanwu Nationale 1, Entente Setif 0

Second Leg
Entente Setif 4, Iwuanyanwu Nationale 0
(Entente Setif (Algeria) beat Nationale (Nigeria) 4-1 on aggregate)

African Cup Winners Cup Final

First Leg
Ranchers Bees 0, CA Bizerte 0

Second Leg
CA Bizerte 1, Ranchers Bees 0
(CA Bizerte (Tunisia) beat Ranchers Bees (Nigeria) 1-0 on aggregate)

Veterans World Cup (in Brazil)

Final
Brazil 4, Uruguay 2

Nehru Gold Cup (in India)

Final
Hungary 2, USSR 0

WORLD CUP (Under-16) (in Scotland, 10–24 June)

Group A
Scotland 0, Ghana 0
Cuba 0, Bahrain 3
Scotland 3, Cuba 0
Ghana 0, Bahrain 1
Scotland 1, Bahrain 1
Ghana 2, Cuba 2

Group B
East Germany 1, Australia 0
USA 1, Brazil 0
East Germany 5, USA 2
Australia 1, Brazil 3
Brazil 2, East Germany 1
Australia 2, USA 2

Group C
Argentina 0, China 0
Nigeria 4, Canada 0
Argentina 0, Nigeria 0
China 1, Canada 0
Argentina 4, Canada 1
Nigeria 3, China 0

Group D
Guinea 1, Colombia 1
Saudi Arabia 2, Portugal 2
Guinea 2, Saudi Arabia 2
Colombia 2, Portugal 3
Guinea 1, Portugal 1
Saudi Arabia 1, Colombia 0

Quarter-finals
Scotland 1, East Germany 0
Bahrain 0, Brazil 0
(aet; Bahrain won 4-1 on penalties)
Nigeria 0, Saudi Arabia 0
(aet; Saudi Arabia won 2-0 on penalties)
Portugal 2, Argentina 1

Semi-finals
Saudi Arabia 1, Bahrain 0
Scotland 1, Portugal 0

Final at Hampden Park, 24 June 1989, 51,674
Saudi Arabia (0) 2, Scotland (2) 2 *aet*
(Saudi Arabia won 5-4 on penalties)
Scorers: Saudi Arabia: Al-Reshoudi, Al-Terair; Scotland: Downie, Dickov.

5th WORLD YOUTH CHAMPIONSHIP (in Saudi Arabia)

Group A

	P	*W*	*D*	*L*	*F*	*A*	*Pts*
Portugal	3	2	0	1	2	3	4
Nigeria	3	1	1	1	3	3	3
Czechoslovakia	3	1	1	1	2	2	3
Saudi Arabia	3	1	0	2	4	3	2

Group B

	P	*W*	*D*	*L*	*F*	*A*	*Pts*
USSR	3	3	0	0	7	2	6
Colombia	3	1	0	2	3	4	2
Syria	3	1	0	2	4	6	2
Costa Rica	3	1	0	2	2	4	2

Group C

	P	*W*	*D*	*L*	*F*	*A*	*Pts*
Brazil	3	3	0	0	10	1	6
USA	3	1	1	1	4	4	3
East Germany	3	1	0	2	3	4	2
Mali	3	0	1	2	1	9	1

Group D

	P	*W*	*D*	*L*	*F*	*A*	*Pts*
Iraq	3	3	0	0	4	0	6
Argentina	3	1	0	2	3	3	2
Norway	3	1	0	2	4	5	2
Spain	3	1	0	2	4	7	2

Quarter-finals
Portugal 1, Colombia 0
USSR 4, Nigeria 4 *aet*
(Nigeria won 5-3 on penalties)
Brazil 1, Argentina 0
Iraq 2, USA 1 *aet*

Semi-finals
Portugal 1, Brazil 0
Nigeria 2, USA 1 *aet*

Third Place match
Brazil 2, USA 0

Final
Portugal 2, Nigeria 0

South America's outstanding club side in 1988 was Nacional of Uruguay. Picture includes Sere, Gomez, De Leon, Revelez, Pintos Saldanha, Ostolaza, Vargas, Lemos, De Lima, Cardaccio, Castro.

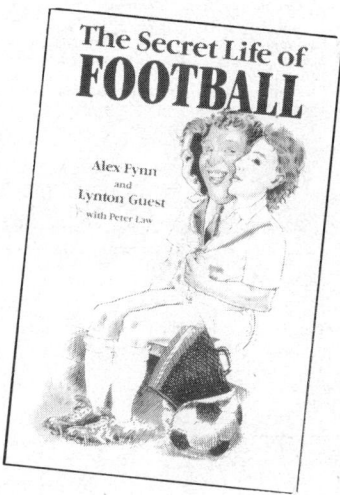

OLYMPIC FOOTBALL TOURNAMENT 1988

FINAL COMPETITION

The Soviet Union won the Olympic Football Tournament for the second time in their history, 32 years after taking their first gold medal in Melbourne. They beat Brazil 2-1 after extra time in Seoul in front of a crowd of 74,000.

Football was again the Number 1 attraction at the Olympics although the final aggregate of spectators was only 743,000, it was more than for any other sport. In Los Angeles in 1984 the figure had been 1.4 million and 1.8 million in the Soviet Union in 1980.

However FIFA and the IOC appear to be on a collision course as far as football in future Olympics is concerned. The IOC want to include all professional players; the world governing body are anxious to limit it to players under the age of 23.

Table of finishing positions:

Gold	**USSR**	9	Iraq
Silver	**Brazil**	10	Yugoslavia
Bronze	**West Germany**	11	Korea Republic
4	Italy	12	USA
5	Zambia	13	Tunisia
6	Sweden	14	China PR
7	Australia	15	Nigeria
8	Argentina	16	Guatemala

Group A *(Sweden, Tunisia, China PR, West Germany)*

17.9.88 Pusan China PR 0, West Germany 3
17.9.88 Taegu Sweden 2, Tunisia 2
19.9.88 Pusan Tunisia 1, West Germany 4
19.9.88 Taegu Sweden 2, China PR 0
21.9.88 Pusan Tunisia 0, China PR 0
21.9.88 Taegu Sweden 2, West Germany 1

	P	*W*	*D*	*L*	*F*	*A*	*Pts*
Sweden	3	2	1	0	6	3	5
West Germany	3	2	0	1	8	3	4
Tunisia	3	0	2	1	3	6	2
China PR	3	0	1	2	0	5	1

Group B *(Zambia, Iraq, Italy, Guatemala)*

17.9.88 Taejon Zambia 2, Iraq 2
17.9.88 Kwangju Italy 5, Guatemala 2
19.9.88 Taejon Iraq 3, Guatemala 0
19.9.88 Kwangju Zambia 4, Italy 0
21.9.88 Kwangju Zambia 4, Guatemala 0
21.9.88 Seoul (Dongdaemon) Iraq 0, Italy 2

	P	*W*	*D*	*L*	*F*	*A*	*Pts*
Zambia	3	2	1	0	10	2	5
Italy	3	2	0	1	7	6	4
Iraq	3	1	1	1	5	4	3
Guatemala	3	0	0	3	2	12	0

Group C *(Korea Rep, USSR, USA, Argentina)*

18.9.88 Pusan Korea Rep 0, USSR 0
18.9.88 Taegu USA 1, Argentina 1
20.9.88 Pusan Korea Rep 0, USA 0
20.9.88 Taegu USSR 2, Argentina 1
22.9.88 Pusan Korea Rep 1, Argentina 2
22.9.88 Taegu USSR 4, USA 2

	P	*W*	*D*	*L*	*F*	*A*	*Pts*
USSR	3	2	1	0	6	3	5
Argentina	3	1	1	1	4	4	3
Korea Rep	3	0	2	1	1	2	2
USA	3	0	2	1	3	5	2

Group D *(Australia, Yugoslavia, Brazil, Nigeria)*

18.9.88 Taejon Brazil 4, Nigeria 0
18.9.88 Kwangju Australia 1, Yugoslavia 0
20.9.88 Taejon Yugoslavia 3, Nigeria 1
20.9.88 Seoul (Dongdaemon) Australia 0, Brazil 3
22.9.88 Taejon Yugoslavia 1, Brazil 2
22.9.88 Seoul (Dongdaemon) Australia 1, Nigeria 0

	P	*W*	*D*	*L*	*F*	*A*	*Pts*
Brazil	3	3	0	0	9	1	6
Australia	3	2	0	1	2	3	4
Yugoslavia	3	1	0	2	4	4	2
Nigeria	3	0	0	3	1	8	0

Quarter-finals

25.9.88 Taegu Sweden 1, Italy 2 *(aet)*
25.9.88 Kwangju Zambia 0, West Germany 4
25.9.88 Pusan USSR 3, Australia 0
25.9.88 Seoul (Dongdaemon) Brazil 1, Argentina 0

Semi-finals

27.9.88 Pusan Italy 2, USSR 3 *(aet)*
27.9.88 Seoul (Main stadium) West Germany 1, Brazil 1 *(aet); Brazil won 3-2 on penalty kicks*

Match for third place

30.9.88 Seoul (Main stadium) Italy 0, West Germany 3

Final

1.10.88 Seoul (Main stadium)

USSR (0) 2 *(Dobrovolski (pen), Savichev)*
Brazil (1) 1 *(Romario) (aet)* 74,000

USSR: Kharin; Gorlukovich, Ketachvili, Yarovenko, Dobrovolski, Kuznetsov, Liutyi (Skliarov), Mikhailichenko, Losev, Narbekovas (Savichev), Tatartchuk.
Brazil: Taffarel; Aloisio, Andre Cruz, Luiz Carlos, Jorginho, Careca, Andrade, Milton, Neto (Edmar), Romario, Bebeto (Joao Paulo).
Referee: G. Biguet (France).

Previous medallists

1896 Athens*	1 Denmark 2 Greece
1900 Paris*	1 Great Britain 2 France
1904 St Louis**	1 Canada 2 USA
1908 London	1 Great Britain 2 Denmark 3 Holland
1912 Stockholm	1 England 2 Denmark 3 Holland
1920 Antwerp	1 Belgium 2 Spain 3 Holland
1924 Paris	1 Uruguay 2 Switzerland 3 Sweden
1928 Amsterdam	1 Uruguay 2 Argentina 3 Italy
1932 Los Angeles	no tournament
1936 Berlin	1 Italy 2 Austria 3 Norway
1948 London	1 Sweden 2 Yugoslavia 3 Denmark
1952 Helsinki	1 Hungary 2 Yugoslavia 3 Sweden
1956 Melbourne	1 USSR 2 Yugoslavia 3 Bulgaria
1960 Rome	1 Yugoslavia 2 Denmark 3 Hungary
1964 Tokyo	1 Hungary 2 Czechoslovakia 3 East Germany
1968 Mexico City	1 Hungary 2 Bulgaria 3 Japan
1972 Munich	1 Poland 2 Hungary 3 E Germany/USSR
1976 Montreal	1 East Germany 2 Poland 3 USSR
1980 Moscow	1 Czechoslovakia 2 East Germany 3 USSR
1984 Los Angeles	1 France 2 Brazil 3 Yugoslavia

* No official tournament
** No official tournament but gold medal later awarded by IOC

EUROPEAN CLUB FOOTBALL

EUROPEAN CHAMPION CLUBS CUP

EUROPEAN CUP-WINNERS' CUP

FAIRS CUP AND UEFA CUP

BRITISH AND IRISH CLUBS IN EUROPE

EUROPEAN CLUB DIRECTORY

EUROPEAN NATIONS SECTION

WORLD CLUB CHAMPIONSHIP

EUROPEAN SUPER CUP

EUROPEAN CUP

EUROPEAN CUP FINALS 1956–88

Year	Winners	Runners-up	Venue	Attendance	Referee
1956	Real Madrid 4	Reims 3	Paris	38,000	Ellis (E)
1957	Real Madrid 2	Fiorentina 0	Madrid	124,000	Horn (Ho)
1958	Real Madrid 3	AC Milan 2 *(aet)*	Brussels	67,000	Alsteen (Bel)
1959	Real Madrid 2	Reims 0	Stuttgart	80,000	Dutsch (WG)
1960	Real Madrid 7	Eintracht Frankfurt 3	Glasgow	135,000	Mowat (S)
1961	Benfica 3	Barcelona 2	Berne	28,000	Dienst (Sw)
1962	Benfica 5	Real Madrid 3	Amsterdam	65,000	Horn (Ho)
1963	AC Milan 2	Benfica 1	Wembley	45,000	Holland (E)
1964	Internazionale 3	Real Madrid 1	Vienna	74,000	Stoll (A)
1965	Internazionale 1	Benfica 0	Milan	80,000	Dienst (Sw)
1966	Real Madrid 2	Partizan Belgrade 1	Brussels	55,000	Kreitlein (WG)
1967	Celtic 2	Internazionale 1	Lisbon	56,000	Tschenscher (WG)
1968	Manchester U 4	Benfica 1 *(aet)*	Wembley	100,000	Lo Bello (I)
1969	AC Milan 4	Ajax 1	Madrid	50,000	Ortiz (Sp)
1970	Feyenoord 2	Celtic 1 *(aet)*	Milan	50,000	Lo Bello (I)
1971	Ajax 2	Panathinaikos 0	Wembley	90,000	Taylor (E)
1972	Ajax 2	Internazionale 0	Rotterdam	67,000	Helies (F)
1973	Ajax 1	Juventus 0	Belgrade	93,500	Guglovic (Y)
1974	Bayern Munich 1	Atletico Madrid 1	Brussels	65,000	Loraux (Bel)
Replay	Bayern Munich 4	Atletico Madrid 0	Brussels	65,000	Delcourt (Bel)
1975	Bayern Munich 2	Leeds U 0	Paris	50,000	Kitabdjian (F)
1976	Bayern Munich 1	St Etienne 0	Glasgow	54,864	Palotai (H)
1977	Liverpool 3	Moenchengladbach 1	Rome	57,000	Wurtz (F)
1978	Liverpool 1	FC Brugge 0	Wembley	92,000	Corver (Ho)
1979	Nottingham F 1	Malmo 0	Munich	57,500	Linemayr (A)
1980	Nottingham F 1	Hamburg 0	Madrid	50,000	Garrido (P)
1981	Liverpool 1	Real Madrid 0	Paris	48,360	Palotai (H)
1982	Aston Villa 1	Bayern Munich 0	Rotterdam	46,000	Konrath (F)
1983	Hamburg 1	Juventus 0	Athens	75,000	Rainea (R)
1984	Liverpool 1	Roma 1	Rome	69,693	Fredriksson (Se)
	(aet; Liverpool won 4-2 on penalties)				
1985	Juventus 1	Liverpool 0	Brussels	58,000	Daina (SW)
1986	Steaua Bucharest 0	Barcelona 0	Seville	70,000	Vautrot (F)
	(aet; Steaua won 2-0 on penalties)				
1987	Porto 2	Bayern Munich 1	Vienna	59,000	Ponnet (Bel)
1988	PSV Eindhoven 0	Benfica 0	Stuttgart	70,000	Agnolin (I)
	(aet; PSV won 6-5 on penalties)				

Ruud Gullit (centre, white shirt) scores for AC Milan in the 1989 European Cup Final against Steaua Bucharest.

EUROPEAN CUP 1988–89

First Round, First Leg

PSV Eindhoven (holders) – Bye.
Brugge (0) 1 (*van Wilk 88*), Brondby (0) 0 20,000
Dundalk (0) 0, Red Star Belgrade (0) 5 (*Mrkela 51, Musemic 61, Stojkovic 65 pen, Stosic 86, Djurovski 88*) 3206
Dynamo Berlin (1) 3 (*Doll 16, Thom 62, Pastor 77*), Werder Bremen (0) 0 22,000
Gornik Zabrze (2) 3 (*R. Warzycha 34, Urban 44, 73*), Jeunesse D'Esch (0) 0 15,000
Hamrun Spartans (0) 2 (*Leo Refalo 46, 89*), Nentori (1) 1 (*Steja 5*) 4500
Honved (1) 1 (*Fodor 8*), Celtic (0) 0 8000
Larissa (1) 2 (*Agorogiannis 5, Mitsibonas 89*), Neuchatel Xamax (0) 1 (*Hermann 59*) 20,000
Moscow Spartak (0) 2 (*Ivanov 53, Shalimov 54*), Glentoran (0) 0 25,000
Pezoporikos (1) 1 (*Livanthinos 20 pen*), IFK Gothenburg (1) 2 (*Ericsson 18, Ravelli 55*) 6000
FC Porto (2) 3 (*Madjer 2, Sousa 22, Rui Aguas 75*), HJK Helsinki (0) 0 45,000
Rapid Vienna (1) 2 (*Kranjcar 33, Kienast 51*), Galatasaray (0) 1 (*B. Savas 81*) 14,500
Real Madrid (3) 3 (*Losada 19, Tendillo 27, Butragueno 30*), Moss (0) 0 65,000
Sparta Prague (1) 1 (*Kukleta 20*), Steaua Bucharest (2) 5 (*Lacatus 29, 44, Hagi 78, 88, Stoica 86*) 22,296
Valur Reykjavik (0) 1 (*Edvaldsson 55*), Monaco (0) 0 4000
Vitosha (0) 0, AC Milan (1) 2 (*Virdis 18, Gullit 75*) 33,000

First Round, Second Leg

Brondby (1) 2 (*Frank 35, Christensen 67*), Brugge (0) 1 (*Brylle 78*) 24,200
Celtic (1) 4 (*Stark 14, Walker 75, McAvennie 80, McGhee 89*), Honved (0) 0 42,763
Galatasaray (0) 2 (*Tanju 53, Cuneyt 65*), Rapid Vienna (0) 0 35,000
Glentoran (0) 1 (*Moore 48*), Moscow Spartak (0) 1 (*Cherenkov 89*), 8000
IFK Gothenburg (4) 5 (*R. Nilsson 5, Zetterlund 7, Holmgren 26, Froberg 44, 54*), Pezoporikos (1) 1 (*Livanthinos 39*) 6442
HJK Helsinki (0) 2 (*Valla 60, Kanerva 85*), FC Porto (0) 0 5640
Jeunesse D'Esch (1) 1 (*Theis 32*), Gornik Zabrze (2) 4 (*Komornicki 6, 30, Urban 66, Zagorski 82*) 960
AC Milan (3) 5 (*van Basten 2, 13, 42, 83, Virdis 62*), Vitosha (1) 2 (*Nachev 29, Iliev 73*), 55,000
Monaco (2) 2 (*Vogel 14, Weah 35*), Valur Reykjavik (0) 0 10,000
Moss (0) 0, Real Madrid (1) (*Butragueno 39*) 5414
Nentori (0) 2 (*Hodja 66, Josa 69*), Hamrun Spartans (0) 0 15,000
Neuchatel Xamax (0) 2 (*Lei-Ravello 61 pen, Luethi 71*), Larissa (0) 1 (*Karapialis 59*), 12,000
Red Star Belgrade (1) 3 (*Sabanadzovic 39, Mrkela 55, Savicevic 77*), Dundalk (0) 0 15,000
Steaua Bucharest (1) 2 (*Hagi 39, Lacatus 78*), Sparta Prague (1) 2 (*Bilek 12, 88*) 30,000
Werder Bremen (1) 5 (*Kutzop 23 pen, Hermann 55, Riedle 63, Burgsmuller 71, Schaaf 89*), Dynamo Berlin (0) 0 23,542

Second Round, First Leg

Brugge (0) 1 (*Mbuyu 47*), Monaco (0) 0 30,000
Celtic (0) 0, Werder Bremen (0) 1 (*Wolter 58*) 50,624
Gornik Zabrze (0) 0, Real Madrid (0) 1 (Hugo, Sanchez 65 pen) 50,000
AC Milan (0) 1 (*Virdis 48*), Red Star Belgrade (0) 1 (*Stojkovic 47*) 66,000
Nentori (0) 0, IFK Gothenburg (2) 3 (*Forsberg 31, Ingesson 35, Lennart Nilsson 82*) 20,000
Neuchatel Xamax (0) 3 (*Leuthi 55, 80, Decastel 90*), Galatasaray (0) 0 23,000
PSV Eindhoven (3) 5 (*Kieft 15, Ellerman 35, R. Koeman 41, 52, Jansson 50*), FC Porto (0) 0 27,000
Steaua Bucharest (1) 3 (*Dumitrescu 33, Hagi 58, 70 pen*), Moscow Spartak (0) 0 35,000

Second Round, Second Leg

Galatasaray (1) 5 (*Ugur Tutuneker 19, 75, Tanju 54, 80, 87*), Neuchatel Xamax (0) 0 35,000
IFK Gothenburg (1) 1 (*Forsberg 30*), Nentori (0) 0 4434
Monaco (5) 6 (*Fofana 6, 27, 74, Sonor 9, Toure 25, 31*), Brugge (0) 1 (*Audoon 63*) 20,000
FC Porto (1) 2 (*Rui Aguas 43, Domingos 82*), PSV Eindhoven (0) 0 30,000
Real Madrid (1) 3 (*Hugo Sanchez 27, 83, Butragueno 76*), Gornik Zabrze (1) 2 (*Jegor 40, Baran 53*) 40,000
Red Star Belgrade (0) 1 (*Savicevic 50*), AC Milan (0) 0 (*abandoned 61 mins – fog*) 90,000
Red Star Belgrade (1) 1 (*Stojkovic 38 pen*), AC Milan (1) 1 (*Van Basten 34*) 65,000
AC Milan won 4-2 on penalties
Spartak Moscow (1) 1 (*Cherenkov 44*), Steaua Bucharest (1) 2 (*Lacatus 11, Balint 89*) 35,000
Werder Bremen (0) 0, Celtic (0) 0 38,980

Quarter-Finals, First Leg

IFK Gothenburg (0) 1 (*Ingesson 55*), Steaua Bucharest (0) 0 16,067
Monaco (0) 0, Galatasaray (1) 1 (*Tanju 20*) 20,000
PSV Eindhoven (0) 1 (*Romario 57*), Real Madrid (1) 1 (*Butrageuno 44*) 28,000
Werder Bremen (0) 0, AC Milan (0) 0 40,000

Quarter-Finals, Second Leg

Galatasaray (0) 1 (*Prekazi 51*), Monaco (0) 1 (*Weah 65*) (*in Cologne*) 60,000
AC Milan (1) 1 (*Van Basten 32 pen*), Werder Bremen (0) 0 71,000
Real Madrid (0) 2 (*Hugo Sanchez 72 pen, Martin Vazquez 105*), PSV Eindhoven (0) 1 (*Romario 84*) *aet* 95,000
Steaua Bucharest (3) 5 (*Lacatus 7, 16, 65, Dumitrescu 39, Balint 89*), IFK Gothenburg (0) 1 (*Zetterlund 53*) 30,000

Semi-Finals, First Leg

Real Madrid (1) 1 (*Hugo Sanchez 41*), AC Milan (0) 1 (*Van Basten 78*) 95,000
Steaua Bucharest (2) 4 (*Dumitrescu 8, Hagi 40 pen, Petrescu 68, Balint 72*), Galatasaray (0) 0 32,000

Semi-Finals, Second Leg

AC Milan (3) 5 (*Ancelotti 18, Rijkaard 25, Gullit 44, Van Basten 49, Donadoni 60*), Real Madrid (0) 0 73,112
Galatasaray (1) 1 (*Cuneyt 36*), Steaua Bucharest (1) 1(*Dumitrescu 39*) (*in Izmir*) 30,000

Final: AC Milan (3) 4, Steaua Bucharest (0) 0

(in Barcelona, 24 May 1989, 97,000)

AC Milan: Galli G; Tassotti, Costacurta (Galli F 74), Baresi, Maldini, Colombo, Rijkaard, Donadoni, Van Basten, Gullit (Virdis 60), Ancellotti. *Scorers:* Gullit 17, 38, Van Basten 26, 46.

Steaua Bucharest: Lung; Petrescu, Iovan, Bumbescu, Ungureanu, Stoica, Lacatus, Minea, Piturca, Hagi, Rotariu (Balaci 46).

Referee: Tritschler (West Germany).

EUROPEAN CUP 1988–89 – BRITISH AND IRISH CLUBS

FIRST ROUND, FIRST LEG

7 SEPT

Dundalk (0) 0

Red Star Belgrade (0) 5 *(Mrkela, Musemic, Stojkovic [pen], Stosic, Djurovski)* 3206

Dundalk: O'Neill; Mackey (Shelley), Lawlor (Gannon), Murray, Cleary, Malone, Wyse, Kehoe, Eviston, Gorman, Lawless.
Red Star: Davidovic; Juric, Vasiliejevic, Sabanadzovic (Desic), Najdoski, Radovanovic, Prosinecki, Djurovski, Musemic, Stojkovic, Mrkela (Stosic).

7 SEPT

Honved (1) 1 *(Fodor)*

Celtic (0) 0 8000

Honved: Disztl P; Sallai, Cseh, Disztl L, Varga, Kovacs, Szijarto (Csehi), Csuhay, Sass, Fodor (Zircher), Gregor.
Celtic: Andrews; Morris, Rogan, Aitken, McCarthy, Whyte, Grant, McStay, McAvennie, Walker, Burns.

7 SEPT

Moscow Spartak (0) 2 *(Ivanov, Shalimov)*

Glentoran (0) 0 25,000

Spartak: Dasayev; Surov, Paveliov, Shalimov (Sparov), Bubnov, Mostovoi, Kuznetsov Y, Pasulko (Ivanov), Kuliev, Cherenkov, Rodionov.
Glentoran: Paterson; Neill, Devine, Moore, Kennedy, Morrison, Caskey (Bowers), Cleary, Patton, Manley (Jameson), McCartney.

FIRST ROUND, SECOND LEG

5 OCT

Celtic (1) 4 *(Stark, Walker, McAvennie, McGhee)*

Honved (0) 0 42,763

Celtic: Rough; Morris, Rogan, Aitken, McCarthy, Whyte, Stark, McStay, McAvennie, Walker, Miller (McGhee).
Honed: Disztl P; Sallai, Cseh, Disztl L, Varga, Csehi (Kovacs), Szijarto (Fule), Csuhay, Sass, Fodor, Gregor.

5 OCT

Glentoran (0) 1 *(Moore)*

Moscow Spartak (0) 1 *(Cherenkov)* 8000

Glentoran: Paterson; Neill, Kennedy, Bowers, Moore, Cleary, Totten (Craig), Caskey, McCartney, Manley (Hillis), Morrison.
Spartak: Dasayev; Glodilento, Paveliov (Rodionov), Shalimov, Bubnov, Mostovoi, Ivanov, Pasulko, Smarov (Kuliev), Cherenkov, Susloparov.

5 OCT

Red Star Belgrade (1) 3 *(Sabanadzovic, Mrkela, Savicevic)*

Dundalk (0) 0 15,000

Red Star: Stojanovic; Juric, Marovic, Sabanadzovic, Radovanovic, Dimitrijevic, Prosinecki (Savicevic), Djurovic, Bursac (Lukic), Stojkovic, Mrkela.
Dundalk: O'Neill; Mackey, Moore, Murray, Cleary, Malone, Wyse, Gannon, Eviston, Gorman (Cousins), Lawless (Shelley).

SECOND ROUND, FIRST LEG

26 OCT

Celtic (0) 0

Werder Bremen (0) 1 *(Wolter)* 50,624

Celtic: Bonner; Morris, Rogan, Aitken, McCarthy, Whyte, Stark (Burns), McStay, McAvennie, McGhee (Walker), Miller.
Werder: Reck; Schaaf, Hermann, Bratseth, Kutzop, Borowka, Wolter, Votava, Riedle, Neubarth (Otten), Ordenewitz.

SECOND ROUND, SECOND LEG

9 NOV

Werder Bremen (0) 0

Celtic (0) 0 38,980

Werder: Reck; Bratseth, Otten, Borowka, Schaaf, Wolter, Votava, Neubarth (Burgsmuller), Hermann, Riedle, Ordenewitz.
Celtic: Bonner; Morris, McCarthy, Whyte, Rogan, Stark, McStay, Aitken, Burns (Miller), McGhee (Archdeacon), McAvennie.

EUROPEAN CUP-WINNERS' CUP

EUROPEAN CUP-WINNERS' CUP FINALS 1961–88

Year	Winners	Runners-up	Venue	Attendance	Referee
1961	Fiorentina 2	Rangers 0 *(1st Leg)*	Glasgow	80,000	Steiner (A)
	Fiorentina 2	Rangers 1 *(2nd Leg)*	Florence	50,000	Hernadi (H)
1962	Atletico Madrid 1	Fiorentina 1	Glasgow	27,389	Wharton (S)
Replay	Atletico Madrid 3	Fiorentina 0	Stuttgart	45,000	Tschenscher (WG)
1963	Tottenham Hotspur 5	Atletico Madrid 1	Rotterdam	25,000	Van Leuwen (Ho)
1964	Sporting Lisbon 3	MTK Budapest 3 *(aet)*	Brussels	9000	Van Nuffel (Bel)
Replay	Sporting Lisbon 1	MTK Budapest 0	Antwerp	18,000	Versyp (Bel)
1965	West Ham U 2	Munich 1860 0	Wembley	100,000	Szolt (H)
1966	Borussia Dortmund 2	Liverpool 1 *(aet)*	Glasgow	41,657	Schwinte (F)
1967	Bayern Munich 1	Rangers 0 *(aet)*	Nuremberg	69,480	Lo Bello (I)
1968	AC Milan 2	Hamburg 0	Rotterdam	60,000	Ortiz (Sp)
1969	Slovan Bratislava 3	Barcelona 2	Basle	40,000	Van Ravens (Ho)
1970	Manchester C 2	Gornik Zabrze 1	Vienna	10,000	Schiller (A)
1971	Chelsea 1	Real Madrid 1 *(aet)*	Athens	42,000	Scheurer (Sw)
Replay	Chelsea 2	Real Madrid 1 *(aet)*	Athens	24,000	Bucheli (Sw)
1972	Rangers 3	Moscow Dynamo 2	Barcelona	35,000	Ortiz (Sp)
1973	AC Milan 1	Leeds U 0	Salonika	45,000	Mihas (Gr)
1974	Magdeburg 2	AC Milan 0	Rotterdam	5000	Van Gemert (Ho)
1975	Dynamo Kiev 3	Ferencvaros 0	Basle	13,000	Davidson (S)
1976	Anderlecht 4	West Ham U 2	Brussels	58,000	Wurtz(F)
1977	Hamburg 2	Anderlecht 0	Amsterdam	65,000	Partridge (E)
1978	Anderlecht 4	Austria/WAC 0	Amsterdam	48,679	Adlinger (WG)
1979	Barcelona 4	Fortuna Dusseldorf 3 *(aet)*	Basle	58,000	Palotai (H)
1980	Valencia 0	Arsenal 0	Brussels	40,000	Christov (Cz)
	(aet; Valencia won 5-4 on penalties)				
1981	Dynamo Tbilisi 2	Carl Zeiss Jena 1	Dusseldorf	9000	Lattanzi (I)
1982	Barcelona 2	Standard Liege 1	Barcelona	100,000	Eschweiler (WG)
1983	Aberdeen 2	Real Madrid 1 *(aet)*	Gothenburg	17,804	Menegali (I)
1984	Juventus 2	Porto 1	Basle	60,000	Prokop (EG)
1985	Everton 3	Rapid Vienna 1	Rotterdam	30,000	Casarin (I)
1986	Dynamo Kiev 3	Atletico Madrid 0	Lyon	39,300	Wohrer (A)
1987	Ajax 1	Lokomotive Leipzig 0	Athens	35,000	Agnolin (I)
1988	Mechelen 1	Ajax 0	Strasbourg	39,446	Pauly (WG)

Julio Salinas leaps high to convert a cross into a goal for Barcelona in the 1989 Cup Winners' Cup Final against Sampdoria.

EUROPEAN CUP-WINNERS' CUP 1988–89

Preliminary Round

Bekescsaba (3) 3 (*Gruborovics 4, 10, Csato 37*), Bryne (0) 0 10,000
Bryne (1) 2 (*Hellvik 44 pen, Meinseth 79 pen*), Bekescsaba (1) 1 (*Kvaszta 35*) 630

First Round, First Leg

Borac Banjaluka (1) 2 (*Lemic 43, Lipovac 89*), Metallist Kharkov (0) 0 25,000
Carl Zeiss Jena (1) 5 (*Weber 19, Strasser 48, 67, Merkel 53, Ludwig 78*), FC Krems (0) 0 9000
Derry (0) 0, Cardiff C (0) 0 14,000
Dinamo Bucharest (1) 3 (*Janti og 12, Andone 72, Vaiscovici 75*), Kuusysi Lahti (0) 0 18,000
Flamurtari (1) 2 (*V. Ruci 40, 76*), Lech Poznan (1) 3 (*Lukasik 32, Araskiewicz 67, Glombiowski 89*) 12,000
Floriana (0) 0, Dundee U (0) 0 2500
Fram Reykjavik (0) 0, Barcelona (1) 2 (*Roberto 33, 62*) 4000
Glenavon (1) 1 (*McCann 17*), AGF Aarhus (1) 4 (*Mortensen 25, Pingel 52, 80, Reeber 67*) 3000
Grasshoppers (0) 0, Eintracht Frankfurt (0) 0 13,600
Inter Bratislava (1) 2 (*Moravec 44, Weiss 58 pen*), CFKA Sredets (2) 3 (*Penev 36, 38 pen, 78*) 4144
Mechelen (0) 5 (*E. Koeman 59, Bosman 61 pen, 84, den Boer 77, Ohana 88 pen*), Avenir Beggen (0) 0 5000
Metz (0) 1 (*Zanon 86*), RSC Anderlecht (2) 3 (*Pfrunner og 1, Krncevic 26, 83*) 24,000
Norrkoping (1) 2 (*Patrik Andersson 9, Jan Hellstrom 86*), Sampdoria (0) 1 (*Amedo Carboni 50*) 14,000
Omonia Nicosia (0) 0, Panathinaikos (1) 1 (*Mavrides 13*) 25,000
Roda JC Kerkrade (1) 2 (*Groenendijk 6, van Loen 87*), Vitoria Guimaraes (0) 0 16,000
Sakaryaspor (1) 2 (*Pesic 35, Yucel Colak 50*), Bekescsaba (0) 0 7000

First Round, Second Leg

AGF Aarhus (1) 3 (*Mortensen 26, B. Kristensen 65, Stampe 87*), Glenavon (0) 1 (*McConville 88*) 2300
RSC Anderlecht (0) 2 (*Krncevic 47, van Tiggelen 73 pen*), Metz (0) 0 16,000
Avenir Beggen (0) 1 (*Krings 65*), Mechelen (1) 3 (*Bosman 34, den Boer 51, Versavel 62*) 2100
Barcelona (2) 5 (*Lineker 9, Beguiristain 23, 63, Roberto 65, Baquero 72*), Fram Reykjavik (0) 0 15,000
Bekescsaba (0) (*Selcuk og 49*), Sakaryaspor (0) 0 13,000
CFKA Sredets (5) 5 (*Penev 1, Stoichkov 3, Kostadinov 12, 38, Getov 21*), Inter Bratislava (0) 0 15,000
Cardiff C (1) 4 (*McDermott 20, Gilligan 47, 65, 76*), Derry (0) 0 6933
Dundee U (0) 1 (*Meade 69*), Floriana (0) 0 9138
Eintracht Frankfurt (1) 1 (*Bakalorz 32*), Grasshoppers (0) 0 13,280
Krems (1) 1 (*Studeny 24*), Carl Zeiss Jena (0) 0 2000
Kuusysi Lahti (0) 0, Dinamo Bucharest (2) 3 (*Vaiscovici 11, 34, Raducioui 71*) 960
Lech Poznan (1) 1 (*Araskiewicz 25*), Flamurtari (0) 0 18,000
Metallis Kharkov (1) 4 (*Tarasov 25, 62, Adzhiev 78 pen, Yesipov 88*), Borac Banjaluka (0) 0 40,000
Panathinaikos (0) 2 (*Dimopulos 57, Nielsen 59*), Omonia Nicosia (0) 0 25,000
Sampdoria (1) 2 (*Salsano 37, Vialli 80*), Norrkoping (0) 0 17,683
Vitoria Guimaraes (1) 1 (*Roldao 27*), Roda JC Kerkrade (0) 0 15,000

Second Round, First Leg

Barcelona (1) 1 (*Roberto 26 pen*), Lech Poznan (0) 1 (*Pachelski 71*) 30,000
CFKA Sredets (1) 2 (*Stoichkov 44, Penev 89 pen*), Panathinaikos (0) 0 22,000
Cardiff C (1) 1 (*Gilligan 41*), AGF Aarhus (1) 2 (*Kristensen 8 73*) 6155
Carl Zeiss Jena (1) 1 (*Weber 38*), Sampdoria (1) 1 (*Vialli 83 pen*) 13,500
Dundee U (0) 0, Dinamo Bucharest (0) 1 (*Mateut 89*) 10,594
Eintracht Frankfurt (3) 3 (*Sievers 9, Balzis 33, Studer 44*), Sakarayaspor (0) 1 (*Kemal 87 pen*) 28,000
Mechelen (0) 1 (*Wilmots 89*), RSC Anderlecht (0) 0 15,000
Roda JC Kerkrade (1) 1 (*van der Luer 43*), Metallist Kharkov (0) 0 10,000

Second Round, Second Leg

AGF Aarhus (2) 4 (*Pingel 15, Andersen 25, 75, Stampe 82 pen*), Cardiff C (0) 0 3700
RSC Anderlecht (0) 0, Mechelen (1) 2 (*E. Koeman 18, Ohana 46*) 33,500
Dinamo Bucharest (0) 1 (*Mateut 83*), Dundee U (0) 1 (*Beaumont 79*) 22,000
Lech Poznan (1) 1 (*Kruszynski 30 pen*), Barcelona (1) 1 (*Roberto 45*) 25,000
Barcelona won 5-4 on penalties
Metallist Kharkov (0) 0, Roda JC Kerkrade (0) 0 40,000
Panathinaikos (0) 0, CFKA Sredets (0) 1 (*Penev 85*) 60,000
Sakaryspor (0) 0, Eintracht Frankfurt (0) 3 (*Sievers 8, 65, Binz 35*) 7000
Sampdoria (1) 3 (*Vierchowod 24, Cerezo 42, Vialli 53*), Carl Zeiss Jena (0) 1 (*Raab 50*) 20,000

Quarter-Finals, First Leg

AGF Aarhus (0) 0, Barcelona (0) 1 (*Lineker 70*) 16,000
CFKA Sredets (1) 2 (*Stoichkov 14, Kostadinov 67*), Roda JC Kerkrade (0) 1 (*Boerebach 84*) 30,000
Dinamo Bucharest (1) 1 (*Vaiscovici 16 pen*), Sampdoria (0) 1 (*Vialli 89*) 15,000
Eintracht Frankfurt (0) 0, Mechelen (0) 0 20,000

Quarter-Finals, Second Leg

Barcelona (0) 0, AGF Aarhus (0) 0 7000
Mechelen (0) 1 (*Wilmots 62*), Eintracht Frankfurt (0) 0 12,000
Roda JC Kerkrade (1) 2 (*Haan 38, Van der Luer 54*), CFKA Sredets (0) 1 (*Stoichkov 77*) 17,500
Sampdoria (0) 0, Dinamo Bucharest (0) 0 (*in Cremona*) 32,500

Semi-Finals, First Leg

Barcelona (2) 4 (*Lineker 36, Amor 37, Baquero 48, Salinas 72*), CFKA Sredets (1) 2 (*Stoichkov 24, 67*) 22,500
Mechelen (1) 2 (*Ohana 11, Deferm 68*), Sampdoria (0) 1 (*Vialli 74*) 14,500

Semi-Finals, Second Leg

CFKA Sredets (0) 1 (*Stoichkov 65*), Barcelona (1) 2 (*Lineker 26, Amor 83*) 55,000
Sampdoria (0) 3 (*Toninho Cerezo 70, Dossena 85, Salsano 88*), Mechelen (0) 0 21,000

Final: Barcelona (1) 2, Sampdoria (0) 0

(Berne, 10 May 1989, 45,000)

Barcelona: Zubizarreta; Aloisio, Alesanco, Milla (Soler 61), Urbano, Amor, Lineker, Eusebio, Julio Salinas, Roberto, Beguiristain (Rekarte 74). *Scorers:* Salinas 4, Rekarte 79.

Sampdoria: Pagliuca; Mannini (S. Pellegrini 27), Salsano, Pari, Lanna, L. Pellegrini (Bonomi 49), Victor, Cerezo, Vialli, Mancini, Dossena.

Referee: Courtney (England).

EUROPEAN CUP-WINNERS' CUP 1988–89 – BRITISH AND IRISH CLUBS

FIRST ROUND, FIRST LEG

7 SEPT

Derry (0) 0

Cardiff C (0) 0 11,000

Derry: Dalton; Vaudequin, Brady, Curran, Neville, Doolin, Hegarty (Carlyle), Larkin, Speak, Gauld, Healy (Keay).
Cardiff C: Wood; Bater, Platnauer, Wimbleton (McDermott), Stevenson, Boyle, Curtis, Walsh (Bartlett), Gilligan, Gummer, Kelly.

7 SEPT

Floriana (0) 0

Dundee U (0) 0 2500

Floriana: Cluett; Cauchi, Xuereb, Holland, Brincat, Briscoe, Miller, Aquilina, Greeno, Spiteri (Licari), Magri.
Dundee U: Thomson; Bowman, Malpas, McInally, Hegarty, Narey, Paatelainen, McKinlay, Cleland, Gallacher, Meade (French).

7 SEPT

Glenavon (1) 1 *(McCann)*

AGF Aarhus (1) 4 *(Mortensen, Pingel 2, Rieper)* 3000

Glenavon: Beck; Dennison, Russell, McCann, Byrne, Lowry, McConville, Ferris, Blackledge (Gardiner), McBride, Woodhead.
Aarhus: Rasmussen; Wachmann, Kristensen B, Stampe, Rieper, Andersen K, Donnerup, Morup (Beck), Kristensen K, Mortensen, Pingel.

FIRST ROUND, SECOND LEG

5 OCT

AGF Aarhus (1) 3 *(Mortensen, Kristensen B, Stampe)*

Glenavon (0) 1 *(McConville)* 2300

Aarhus: Rasmussen; Wachmann, Kristensen B, Stampe, Rieper, Andersen K, Donnerup, Beck, Kristensen K, Pingel (Andersen T), Mortensen.
Glenavon: Beck; Dennison, Russell, McCann D, Byrne, Lowry, Woodhead, Ferris (McConville), Blackledge, McBride, Denver.

5 OCT

Cardiff C (1) 4 *(McDermott, Gilligan 3)*

Derry (0) 0 6933

Cardiff C: Wood; Bater (Perry), Platnauer, Wimbleton (Morgan), Stevenson, Boyle, Curtis, Bartlett, Gilligan, McDermott, Kelly.
Derry: Dalton; Keay, Brady, Curran, Neville, Doolin, Carlyle (Quigg), Larkin, Speak, Cunningham, Healy.

5 OCT

Dundee U (0) 1 *(Meade)*

Floriana (0) 0 9138

Dundee U: Thomson; Bowman, Malpas, McPhee, Clark, Hegarty, Gallacher, McKinlay (French), Paatelainen (Meade), Redford, Preston.
Floriana: Cluett; Cauchi, Darmanin, Delia, Holland, Brincat, Magri (Licari), Aquilina, Miller, Xuereb, Greeno.

SECOND ROUND, FIRST LEG

26 OCT

Cardiff C (1) 1 *(Gilligan)*

AGF Aarhus (1) 2 *(Kristensen K 2)* 6155

Cardiff C: Wood; Platnauer (Rogerson), Baker, Wimbleton, Stevenson, Boyle, McDermott, Bartlett, Gilligan, Kelly, Lynex (Curtis).
Aarhus: Rasmussen; Wachmann, Kristensen B, Stampe, Rieper, Andersen K, Morup (Donnerup), Beck, Kristensen K, Lundkvist, Mortensen.

26 OCT

Dundee U (0) 0

Dinamo Bucharest (0) 1 *(Mateut)* 10,904

Dundee U: Thomson; Bowman, Malpas, McInally (Clark), Hegarty, Narey, Meade, Beaumont, Paatelainen, McPhee (Redford), Gallacher.
Dinamo: Stelea; Mihaescu, Varga, Rednic, Lupescu, Andone, Vaiscovici, Sabau, Camataru, Mateut, Lupu.

SECOND ROUND, SECOND LEG

2 NOV

AGF Aarhus (2) 4 *(Pingel, Andersen 2, Stampe [pen])*

Cardiff C (0) 0 3700

Aarhus: Rasmussen; Wachmann, Stampe, Andersen K, Rieper, Kristensen B, Christensen, Morup, Lundkvist, Mortensen, Pingel.
Cardiff C: Wood; Rodgerson, Boyle, Abraham, Platnauer, Wimbleton, Curtis, Kelly, McDermott, Bartlett, Gilligan.

9 NOV

Dinamo Bucharest (0) 1 *(Mateut)*

Dundee U (0) 1 (Beaumont) 22,000

Dinamo: Stelea; Mihaescu, Andone, Rednic, Varga, Sabau, Lupescu, Mateut, Lupu (Viscreanu), Vaiscovici (Raducioiu), Camataru.
Dundee U: Thomson; Clark (Bowman), Hegarty, Narey, Malpas, McInally (Redford), Beaumont, McKinlay, Meade, Preston, Gallacher.

INTER-CITIES FAIRS & UEFA CUP

FAIRS CUP FINALS 1958–71

(Winners in italics)

Year	First Leg	Attendance	Second Leg	Attendance
1958	London 2 Barcelona 2	45,466	*Barcelona* 6 London 0	62,000
1960	Birmingham C 0 Barcelona 0	40,500	*Barcelona* 4 Birmingham C 1	70,000
1961	Birmingham C 2 Roma 2	21,005	*Roma* 2 Birmingham C 0	60,000
1962	Valencia 6 Barcelona 2	65,000	Barcelona 1 *Valencia* 1	60,000
1963	Dynamo Zagreb 1 Valencia 2	40,000	*Valencia* 2 Dynamo Zagreb 0	55,000
1964	*Zaragoza* 2 Valencia 1	50,000	(in Barcelona)	
1965	*Ferencvaros* 1 Juventus 0	25,000	(in Turin)	
1966	Barcelona 0 Zaragoza 1	70,000	Zaragoza 2 *Barcelona* 4	70,000
1967	Dynamo Zagreb 2 Leeds U 0	40,000	Leeds U 0 *Dynamo Zagreb* 0	35,604
1968	Leeds U 1 Ferencvaros 0	25,368	Ferencvaros 0 *Leeds U* 0	70,000
1969	Newcastle U 3 Ujpest Dozsa 0	60,000	Ujpest Dozsa 2 *Newcastle U* 3	37,000
1970	Anderlecht 3 Arsenal 1	37,000	*Arsenal* 3 Anderlecht 0	51,612
1971	Juventus 0 Leeds U 0 *(abandoned 51 minutes)*			65,000
	Juventus 2 Leeds U 2	65,000	*Leeds U* 1* Juventus 1	42,483

UEFA CUP FINALS 1972–88

(Winners in italics)

Year	First Leg	Attendance	Second Leg	Attendance
1972	Wolverhampton W 1 Tottenham H 2	45,000	*Tottenham H* 1 Wolverhampton W 1	48,000
1973	Liverpool 3 Moenchengladbach 0	41,169	Moenchengladbach 0 *Liverpool* 2	35,000
1974	Tottenham H 2 Feyenoord 2	46,281	*Feyenoord* 2 Tottenham 0	68,000
1975	Moenchengladbach 0 Twente 0	45,000	Twente 1 *Moenchengladbach* 5	24,500
1976	Liverpool 3 FC Brugge 2	56,000	FC Brugge 1 *Liverpool* 1	32,000
1977	Juventus 1 Athletic Bilbao 0	75,000	Athletic Bilbao 2 *Juventus* 1*	43,000
1978	Bastia 0 PSV Eindhoven 0	15,000	*PSV Eindhoven* 3 Bastia 0	27,000
1979	Red Star Belgrade 1 Moenchengladbach 1	87,500	*Moenchengladbach* 1 Red Star Belgrade 0	45,000
1980	Moenchengladbach 3 Eintracht Frankfurt 2	25,000	*Eintracht Frankfurt* 1* Moenchengladbach 0	60,000
1981	Ipswich T 3 AZ 67 0	27,532	AZ 67 4 *Ipswich T* 2	28,500
1982	Gothenburg 1 Hamburg 0	42,548	Hamburg 0 *Gothenburg* 3	60,000
1983	Anderlecht 1 Benfica 0	45,000	Benfica 1 *Anderlecht* 1	80,000
1984	Anderlecht 1 Tottenham H 1	40,000	*Tottenham H* 1[1] Anderlecht 1	46,258
1985	Videoton 0 Real Madrid 3	30,000	*Real Madrid* 0 Videoton 1	98,300
1986	Real Madrid 5 Cologne 1	80,000	Cologne 2 *Real Madrid* 0	15,000
1987	Gothenburg 1 Dundee U 0	50,023	Dundee U 1 *Gothenburg* 1	20,911
1988	Espanol 3 Bayer Leverkusen 0	42,000	*Bayer Leverkusen* 3[2] Espanol 0	22,000

* *won on away goals*
[1] *Tottenham H won 4-3 on penalties aet*
[2] *Bayer Leverkusen won 3-2 on penalties aet*

Diego Maradona (dark shirt) the Napoli captain, is closely watched by two Stuttgart defenders in the 1989 UEFA Cup Final leg in West Germany.

UEFA CUP 1988–89

First Round, First Leg

AEK Athens (1) 1 (*Pittas 24*), Athletic Bilbao (0) 0 23,000
Aarau (0) 0, Lokomotiv Leipzig (2) 3 (*Hobsch 67, 81, Marschall 85*) 6500
Aberdeen (0) 0, Dynamo Dresden (0) 0 14,500
Akranes (0) 0, Ujpest Dozsa (0) 0 1000
Antwerp (2) 2 (*van Rooy 33, Goossens 43*), Cologne (1) 4 (*Keim 3, T. Allofs 47, Povlsen 55, Jenssen 87*) 20,000
Bayer Leverkusen (0) 0, Belenenses (0) 1 (*Mladenov 64*) 10,600
Bayern Munich (2) 3 (*Wegmann 9, Thon 23, 60*), Legia Warsaw (0) 1 (*Iwanicki 57*) 15,000
Besiktas (0) 1 (*Feyyaz 4*), Dinamo Zagreb (0) 0 20,286
Dnepr (0) 1 (*Liuti 49*), Bordeaux (1) 1 (*Roche 24*) 28,250
Groningen (1) 1 (*Groeleken 41*), Atletico Madrid (0) 0 19,000
Inter Milan (1) 2 (*Diaz 44 pen, Matteoli 89*), Brage (0) 1 (*Amberg 64 pen*) 25,000
Malmo (1) 2 (*Dahlin 26, Kovatch og 80*), Moscow Torpedo (0) 0 9505
Molde (0) 0, Waregem (0) 0 3020
Montpellier (0) 0, Benfica (2) 3 (*Hernani 9, Abel 44, Valdo 82*) 12,000
Napoli (0) 1 (*Maradona 58 pen*), PAOK Salonika (0) 0 80,000
Oesters Vaxjo (0) 2 (*Jan Jansson 72, Petaja 77*), Dunajska Streda (0) 0 1141
Otelul Galati (0) 1 (*Profir 59 pen*), Juventus (0) 0 20,000
Partizan Belgrade (2) 5 (*Batrovic 7, 29, V. Dukic 46, Vokrri 68, M. Dukic 89*), Slavia Sofia (0) 0 25,000
Rangers (0) 1 (*Walters 73*), GKS Katowice (0) 0 41,120
Real Sociedad (1) 2 (*Loinaz 38, 47*), Dukla Prague (1) 1 *Bazant 39*) 21,000
Roma (0) 1 (*Desideri 47 pen*), Nuremberg (1) 2 (*Sane 44, Eckstein 58*) 16,000
St Patrick's Athletic (0) 0, Hearts (2) 2 (*Foster 14 pen, Galloway 41*) 8000
Servette (0) 1 (*Grossenbacher 89*), Sturm Graz (0) 0 9800
Sporting Lisbon (3) 4 (*Oceano 6, Pailinho Cascavel 21 pen, Joao Luis 25, Litos 75 pen*), Ajax Amsterdam (1) 2 (*Pettersson 18, 79*) 55,000
Sliema Wanderers (0) 0, Victoria Bucharest (1) 2 (*Culcear 35, Solomon 59 pen*) 1000
Stuttgart (0) 2 (*Gaudino 49, Walter 58*), Tatabanya (0) 0 20,600
TPs Turun (0) 0, Linfield (0) 0 2977
Trakia Plovdiv (0) 1 (*Zaitsev 88 pen*), Dynamo Minsk (1) 2 (*Kondratiev 44, Gotsmanov 80*) 8000
Union Sportive Luxembourg (1) 1 (*Jeitz 3*), FC Liege (2) 7 (*Varga 7, 33, Ernes 54, 59, de Sart 79, Houben 80, Boffin 83*) 2700
Velez Mostar (1) 1 (*Repak 32*), APOEL Nicosia (0) 0 8000
Vienna (1) 1 (*Steinkogler 5*), Ikast (0) 0 3500
Zhalgiris Vilnius (0) 2 (*Fridrikas 59, Baranauskas 78*), FK Austria (0) 0 29,500

First Round, Second Leg

APOEL Nicosia (1) 2 (*Owen 43 pen, Plakitis 63*), Velez Mostar (1) 5 (*Kleanthouse og 35, Gudelj 47, 89, Tuce 50, Rebak 58*) 7000
Ajax Amsterdam (0) 1 (*Verkuyl 80*), Sporting Lisbon (1) 2 (*Silas 22, Maside 87*) 18,000
Athletic Bilbao (2) 2 (*Uralde 3, 6*), AEK Athens (0) 0 35,000
Atletico Madrid (1) 2 (*Baltazar 3 pen, Futre 51*), Groningen (1) 1 (*Ten Caat 19*) 55,000
Groningen won on away goals
Belenenses (0) 1 (*Adao 85*), Bayer Leverkusen (0) 0 15,000
Benfica (1) 3 (*Chalana 22, Ademir 51, Mozer 73*), Montpellier (0) 1 (*Cubaynes 83*) 50,000
Bordeaux (0) 2 (*Stopyra 47, Scifo 66 pen*), Dnepr (1) 1 (*Cherednik 2*) 35,000
Brage (0) 1 (*Hellman 46*), Inter Milan (1) 2 (*Berti 9, Morello 78*) 8652
Cologne (2) 2 (*Littbarski 8, T. Allofs 10*), Antwerp (1) 1 (*Dekenne 3*) 12,000
Dinamo Zagreb (1) 2 (*Mihajlovic 40, 65*), Besiktas (0) 0 30,000
Dukla Prague (1) 3 (*Nemec 17, Foldyna 55, Bittengel 72*), Real Sociedad (0) 2 (*Loren 75, Loinaz 82*) 8000
Real Sociedad won on away goals.
Dunajska Streda (4) 6 (*Liba 8, Takac 14, 22, Pavlik 45, Micinec 46, Soltes 61*), Oesters Vaxjo (0) 0 5000
Dynamo Dresden (1) 2 (*Gutschow 4, Kirsten 66*), Aberdeen (0) 0 36,000
FK Austria (4) 5 (*Pleva 4, 14, Prohaska 5, Sekerlioglu 44, Percudani 73*), Zhalgiris Vilnius (1) 2 (*Baltusnikas 3, Fridrikas 51*) 10,000
GKS Katowice (1) 2 (*Furtok 5, Kubisztal 62*), Rangers (2) 4 (*Butcher 12, 16, Durrant 71, Ferguson 78*) 35,000
Hearts (1) 2 (*Black 24, Galloway 67*), St Patrick's Athletic (0) 0 11,142
Ikast (0) 2 (*Hansen 62, Granlund 75*), Vienna (1) 1 (*Glassmeyer 5*) 3371
Vienna won on away goals.
Juventus (3) 5 (*de Agostini 17, Agiu og 26, Rui Barros 28, 71, Altobelli 49*), Otelul Galati (0) 0 40,000
Legia Warsaw (1) 3 (*Kubicki 36, Robakiewicz 85, 88*), Bayern Munich (4) 7 (*Nachtweih 20, Ekstrom 23, 44, Augenthaler 41, Wegmann 78, 82, Eck 89*) 12,000
FC Liege (2) 4 (Malbasa 8, 56, Veyt 34, 61), Union Sportive Luxembourg (0) 0 3000
Linfield (0) 1 (*O'Boyle 75*), TPs Turun (0) 1 (*Suominen 38*) 904
TPs Turun won on away goals.
Lokomotiv Leipzig (2) 4 (*Zimmerling 21, 28, Halata 59, 83*), Aarau (0) 0 5200
Dynamo Minsk (0) 0, Trakia Plovdiv (0) 0 20,000
Moscow Torpedo (1) 2 (*Grachov 18, Shikinbekov 66*), Malmo (0) 1 (*Ljung 104*) 22,000
Nuremberg (1) 1 (*Eckstein 19*), Roma (2) 3 (*Voller 8, Policano 34, Renato 93*) 20,000
PAOK Salonika (0) 1 (*Skartados 65*), Napoli (1) 1 (*Careca 17*) 45,000
Slavia Sofia (0) 0, Partizan Belgrade (0) 5 (*Vokrri 48, Djordjevic 51, Grekov og 73, M. Djukic 80, V. Djukic 89*) 10,000
Sturm Graz (0) 0, Servette (0) 0 7000
Tatabanya (0) 2 (*Csapo 54, Schmidt 82*), Stuttgart (0) 1 (*Allgower 78 pen*) 8000
Ujpest Dozsa (0) 2 (*Steidl 44, Katona 72*), Akranes (0) 1 (*Thordarsson 68*) 1000
Victoria Bucharest (5) 6 (*Culcear 13, 35, Koras 18, 39, 44, Lais 88*), Sliema Wanderers (0) 1 (*Gauci 90*) 5000
Waregem (1) 5 (*Niederbacher 43, 47, Christiaens 70, 74, Teppers 85*), Molde (0) 1 (*Rekdal 80*) 5000

Second Round, First Leg

Bayern Munich (1) 3 (*Flick 21, Wegmann 53, Thon 75*), Dunajska Streda (0) 1 (*Szaban 77*) 11,000
Cologne (0) 2 (*Jenssen 77, T. Allofs 88*), Rangers (0) 0 42,000
Dinamo Zagreb (0) 1 (*Besek 79*), Stuttgart (1) 3 (*Klinsmann 44, Walter 51, Schroder 63*) 40,000
Dynamo Dresden (3) 4 (*Kirchner 11, Kirsten 23, 39, 64*), Waregem (0) 1 (*Niederbacher 83*) 35,000
Groningen (1) 2 (*Groekelen 9, Meijer 83*), Servette (0) 0 15,000
Hearts (0) 0, FK Austria (0) 0 14,021
Juventus (3) 5 (*Laudrup 3, 51, Galia 23, Mauro 40, Altobelli 46*), Athletic Bilbao (1) 1 (*Uralde 35*) 40,000
FC Liege (0) 2 (*Varga 59, Malbasa 69*), Benfica (0) 1 (*Chalana 48 pen*) 30,000
Lokomotiv Leipzig (0) 1 (*Zimmerling 69*), Napoli (0) 1 (*Francini 75*) 80,000
Malmo (0) 0, Inter Milan (0) 1 (*Serena 82*) 14,203
Dynamo Minsk (1) 2 (*Gurinovich 44, Zigmantovich 78*) Victoria Bucharest (0) 1 (*Kulchar 58*) 35,000
Partizan Belgrade (2) 4 (*Djukic 17, 77, Vermezovic 31, Milojevic 54*), Roma (1) 2 (*Conti 10, 60*) 45,000
Sporting Lisbon (1) 1 (*Cascavel 31 pen*), Real Sociedad (1) 2 (*Iturrino 16, Loren 50*) 50,000
Ujpest Dozsa (0) 0, Bordeaux (1) 1 (*Stopyra 44*) 3000
Velez Mostar (0) 0, Belenenses (0) 0 15,000
Vienna (1) 2 (*Drabits 15, Glatzmayer 61*), TPs Turun (1) 1 (*Jalo 34*) 5000

Second Round, Second Leg

Belenenses (0) 0, Velez Mostar (0) 0 10,000
Velez Mostar won 4-3 on penalties
Bordeaux (0) 1 (Ferreri 73 pen), Ujpest Dozsa (0) 0 22,000
Athletic Bilbao (0) 3 (*Uralde 51, Andrinua 57, 69*), Juventus (1) 2 (*Laudrup 35, Galia 76*) 25,000
Benfica (0) 1 (*Valdo 53*), FC Liege (1) 1 (*Malbasa 18*) 60,000
Dunajska Streda (0) 0, Bayern Munich (2) 2 (*Thon 4 pen, 29*) 19,000
FK Austria (0) 0, Hearts (0) 1 (*Galloway 58*) 15,000
Inter Milan (1) 1 (*Diaz 12*), Malmo (0) 1 (*Nilsson 66*) 45,000
Napoli (1) 2 (*Francini 2, de Napoli 61*), Lokomotiv Leipzig (0) 0 60,000
Rangers (0) 1 (*Drinkell 75*), Cologne (0) 1 (*Jenssen 89*) 42,204
Real Sociedad (0) 0, Sporting Lisbon (0) 0 20,000
Roma (1) 2 (*Voller 20, Giannini 72 pen*), Partizan Belgrade (0) 0 21,000
Roma won on away goals
Servette (1) 1 (*Schallibaum 31*), Groningen (0) 1 (*Meijer 64*) 12,000
Stuttgart (0) 1 (*Walter 48*), Dinamo Zagreb (0) 1 (*Mihajlovic 66*) 17,600
TPs Turun (0) 1 (*Sulonen 69*), Vienna (0) 0 3000
TPs Turun won on away goals
Victoria Bucharest (0) 1 (*Solomon 55*), Dynamo Minsk (0) 0 10,000
Waregem (0) 2 (*Niederbacher 8, van Baekel 47*), Dynamo Dresden (0) 1 (*Pilz 53 pen*) 5000

Third Round, First Leg

Bayern Munich (0) 0, Inter Milan (0) 2 (*Serena 59, Berti 71*) 73,000
Bordeaux (0) 0, Napoli (1) 1 (*Carnevale 6*) 35,000
Dynamo Dresden (1) 2 (*Gutschow 15 pen, Minge 81*), Roma (0) 0 35,000
Groningen (0) 1 (*Meijer 81*), Stuttgart (3) 3 (*Allgower 17, Gaudino 32, 39*) 20,400
Hearts (1) 3 (*Bannon 17, Galloway 55, Colquhoun 89*), Velez Mostar (0) 0 17,417
FC Liege (0) 0, Juventus (1) 1 (*Altobelli 18*) 32,000
Real Sociedad (0) 1 (*Loinaz 76*), Cologne (0) 0 22,500
Victoria Bucharest (1) 1 (*Ursu 4*), TPs Turun (0) 0 10,000

Third Round, Second Leg

Cologne (2) 2 (*Gotz 2, Engels 28*), Real Sociedad (1) 2 (*Giocoechea 35 pen, Fuentes 89*) 38,000
Inter Milan (1) 1 (*Serena 44*), Bayern Munich (3) 3 (*Wohlfarth 33, Augenthaler 37, Wegmann 39*) 75,000
Bayern Munich won on away goals
Juventus (1) 1 (*Altobelli 14*), FC Liege (0) 0 35,000
Napoli (0) 0, Bordeaux (0) 0 62,000
Roma (0) 0, Dynamo Dresden (0) 2 (*Gutschow 69, Kirsten 79*) 30,000
Stuttgart (1) 2 (*Klinsmann 22, 52*), Groningen (0) 0 8500
TPs Turun (1) 3 (*Rajamaki 36, Halonen 51, Jalo 89*), Victoria Bucharest (2) 2 (*Solomon 16, 25*) 3595
Victoria Bucharest won on away goals
Velez Mostar (1) 2 (*Tuce 31, Gudelj 89*), Hearts (0) 1 (*Galloway 53*) 20,000

Quarter-Finals, First Leg

Juventus (2) 2 (*Bruno 13, Corradini og 44*), Napoli (0) 0 46,204
Hearts (0) 1 (*Ferguson 55*), Bayern Munich (0) 0 26,294
Stuttgart (1) 1 (*Walter 34*), Real Sociedad (0) 0 20,000
Victoria Bucharest (0) 1 (*Solomon 48*), Dynamo Dresden (1) 1 (*Gutschow 24*) 15,000

Quarter-Finals, Second Leg

Bayern Munich (1) 2 (*Augenthaler 16, Johnsen 68*, Hearts (0) 0 25,000
Dynamo Dresden (0) 4 (*Minge 47, 77, Gutschow 87, 89 pen*), Victoria Bucharest (0) 0 38,000
Real Sociedad (1) 1 (*Zamora 17*), Stuttgart (0) 0 28,000
Napoli (1) 3 (*Maradona 9 pen, Carnevale 46, Renica 119*), Juventus (0) 0 78,000

Semi-Finals, First Leg

Napoli (1) 2 (*Careca 40, Carnevale 59*), Bayern Munich (0) 0 83,000
Stuttgart (0) 1 (*Allgower 60*), Dynamo Dresden (0) 0 50,000

Semi-Finals, Second Leg

Bayern Munich (0) 2 (*Flick 63, Reuter 81*), Napoli (0) 2 (*Careca 60, 77*) 72,300
Dynamo Dresden (0) 1 (*Lieberam 83*), Stuttgart (0) 1 (*Allgower 64*) 36,000

Final
First Leg: Napoli (0) 2, Stuttgart (1) 1
(in Naples, 3 May 1989, 83,000)

Napoli: Giuliani; Corradini (Crippa 46), Renica, Ferrara, De Napoli, Alemao, Fusi, Francini, Maradona, Careca, Carnevale. *Scorers:* Maradona 68 pen, Careca 87.

Stuttgart: Immel; Buchwald, Schmaler N, Allgower, Hartmann, Schafer, Katanec, Sigurvinsson, Schroder, Walter (Zietsch 70), Gaudino. *Scorer:* Gaudino 17.

Referee: Germanakos (Greece).

Second Leg: Stuttgart (1) 3, Napoli (2) 3
(in Stuttgart, 17 May 1989, 67,000)

Stuttgart: Immel; Schmaler N, Allgower, Schafer, Schroder, Hartmann, Katanec, Sigurvinsson, Klinsmann, Walter (Schmaler O 77), Gaudino. *Scorers:* Klinsmann 27, De Napoli og 70, Schmaler O 89).

Napoli: Giuliani; Corradini, Renica, Ferrara, De Napoli, Alemao (Carannante 30), Fusi, Francini, Maradona, Careca (Bigliardi 70), Carnevale. *Scorers:* Alemao 18, Ferrara 39, Careca 62.

Referee: Sanchez (Spain).

UEFA CUP 1988–89 – BRITISH AND IRISH CLUBS

FIRST ROUND, FIRST LEG

7 SEPT

Aberdeen (0) 0

Dynamo Dresden (0) 0 14,500

Aberdeen: Snelders; McKimmie, Robertson, Simpson, McLeish, Miller, Nicholas, Bett, Dodds, Connor, Hewitt (Mason).
Dynamo Dresden: Teuber, Trautmann, Lieberam, Diebitz, Dotschner, Sammer, Stubner, Pilz, Kirsten, Hauptman, Kirshner.

Rangers (0) 1 *(Walters)*

GKS Katowice (0) 0 41,120

Rangers: Woods; Stevens, Brown, Gough, Wilkins, Butcher, Drinkell, Ferguson I, Cooper, Durrant (Ferguson D), Walters.
GKS Katowice: Jojko; Biegun, Piekarczyk, Kapias, Wijas, Nawrocki, Walczak (Rzezniczek), Rudy, Furtok, Marcinek (Lesniak), Kubisztal.

St Patrick's Ath (0) 0

Hearts (2) 2 *(Foster pen, Galloway)* 8000

St Patrick's Ath: Henderson; Fleming, Kelch, McDonnell, Byrne D, Gaffney, Fenlon, O'Driscoll, Moody (Meagan), Byrne P (Reid), Dennis.
Hearts: Smith (McDermott); Kidd, Berry, Whittaker, Black, McPherson, Colquhoun, Mackay, Ferguson I, Galloway, Foster (Bannon).

TPs Turun (0) 0

Linfield (0) 0 2977

TPs: Eckerman; Heikkinen, Hannikainen, Sulonen, Johansson, Halonen, Jalo, Skants, Lipponen, Suominen, Rajamaki.
Linfield: Dunlop; Coyle, Dornan, Knell (Davies), Jeffrey, McKeown, Khammal, Mooney, McGaughey M, O'Boyle (MacLeod), Burrows.

FIRST ROUND, SECOND LEG

5 OCT

Dynamo Dresden (1) 2 *(Gutschow, Kirsten)*

Aberdeen (0) 0 36,000

Dynamo Dresden: Teuber; Trautmann, Lieberman, Diebitz, Dotschner, Sammer, Stubner, Pilz, Kirsten, Kirschner, Gutschow.
Aberdeen: Snelders; McKimmie, Robertson, Simpson, McLeish, Miller, Mason (Wright P), Bett, Grant, Connor, Dodds.

GKS Katowice (1) 2 *(Furtok, Kubisztal)*

Rangers (2) 4 *(Butcher 2, Durrant, Ferguson)* 35,000

GKS Katowice: Jojko; Biegun, Piekarczyk, Wijas, Marcinek (Lesniak), Nawrocki, Rudy, Kapias, Walczak (Rzezniczek), Furtok, Kubisztal.
Rangers: Woods; Stevens, Gough, Butcher, Munro, Walters, Wilkins, Ferguson I, Cooper, Durrant (McGregor), McCoist.

Hearts (1) 2 *(Black, Galloway)*

St Patrick's Ath (0) 0 8000

Hearts: Smith; Kidd, Berry, Whittaker, Galloway, McPherson, Colquhoun, Mackay, Ferguson, Black, Bannon (Foster).
St Patrick's Ath: Henderson; Fleming, Kelch (Byrne P), McDonnell, Byrne D, Gaffney, O'Driscoll, Treacy (Reid), Moody, Fenlon, Dennis.

Linfield (0) 1 *(O'Boyle)*

TPs Turun (1) 1 *(Suominen) (Played in Wrexham)* 904

Linfield: Dunlop; Coyle, Dornan, Knell, Jeffrey, McKeown, Khammal, Mooney (O'Boyle), McGaughey M, Doherty, Burrows (Coly).
TPs Turun: Eckerman; Heikkinen, Hannikainen, Sulonen, Johansson, Halonen, Jalo, Suominen, Lipponen, Laaksonen, Rajamaki.

SECOND ROUND, FIRST LEG

26 OCT

Cologne (0) 2 *(Jenssen, Allofs T)*

Rangers (0) 0 42,000

Cologne: Illgner; Honerbach (Gotz), Gortz, Kohler, Steiner, Jensen (Jenssen), Allofs T, Engels, Povlsen, Littbarski, Hassler.
Rangers: Woods; Stevens, Munro, Gough, Wilkins, Butcher, Drinkell, Ferguson I, McCoist, Ferguson D, Walters (Nisbet).

Hearts (0) 0

FK Austria (0) 0 14,021

Hearts: Smith; Kidd, Berry, Whittaker, Galloway, McPherson, Colquhoun, Moore, Foster (Mackay), Black, Bannon, (Ferguson).
FK Austria: Wohlfahrt; Sekerlioglu, Obermayer, Degiorgi, Zsak, Pfeffer, Ogris (Pleva), Prohaska, Percudani, Stoger (Frind), Kunast.

SECOND ROUND, SECOND LEG

9 NOV

FK Austria (0) 0

Hearts (0) 1 *(Galloway)* 15,000

FK Austria: Wohlfahrt; Obermayer, Pfeffer, Degiorgi, Zsak, Prohaska, Kunast, Hormann (Sekerlioglu), Ogris, Percudani, Pleva (Furtner).
Hearts: Smith; Kidd, McPherson, Berry, Whittaker, Mackay (Jardine), Sandison, Black, Bannon, Galloway, Foster (Colquhoun).

Rangers (0) 1 *(Drinkell)*

Cologne (0) 1 *(Jenssen)* 42,204

Rangers: Woods; Stevens, Munro, Gough, Nicholl (McCall), Butcher, Cooper (Nisbet), Ferguson I, Drinkell, Ferguson D, Walters.
Cologne: Illgner; Honerbach, Gortz, Kohler, Steiner, Jensen (Keim), Allofs T (Gotz), Jenssen, Povlsen, Littbarski, Hassler.

Continued on Page 894

Summary of Appearances

EUROPEAN CUP (1955–89)

English clubs
12 Liverpool
5 Manchester U
3 Nottingham F
2 Derby Co, Wolverhampton W, Everton, Leeds U, Aston Villa
1 Burnley, Tottenham H, Ipswich T, Manchester C, Arsenal

Scottish clubs
15 Celtic
10 Rangers
3 Aberdeen
2 Hearts
1 Dundee, Dundee U, Kilmarnock, Hibernian

Clubs from Northern Ireland
16 Linfield
7 Glentoran
2 Crusaders
1 Glenavon, Ards, Distillery, Derry C, Coleraine

Clubs from Eire
7 Shamrock R
6 Waterford
6 Dundalk
3 Drumcondra
2 Bohemians, Limerick, Athlone T
1 Shelbourne, Cork Hibs, Cork Celtic, Sligo Rovers

Winners: Celtic 1966–67; Manchester U 1967–68; Liverpool 1976–77, 1977–78, 1980–81, 1983–84; Nottingham F 1978–79, 1979–80; Aston Villa 1981–82

Finalists: Celtic 1969–70; Leeds U 1974–75; Liverpool 1984–85

EUROPEAN CUP-WINNERS' CUP (1960–89)

English Clubs
5 Tottenham H
4 West Ham U
3 Liverpool, Manchester U
2 Chelsea, Everton, Manchester C
1 Wolverhampton W, Leicester C, WBA, Leeds U, Sunderland, Southampton, Ipswich T, Arsenal

Scottish clubs
10 Rangers
6 Celtic, Aberdeen
2 Dunfermline Ath, Dundee U
1 Dundee, Hibernian, Hearts, St Mirren

Welsh clubs
12 Cardiff C
6 Wrexham
5 Swansea C
2 Bangor C
1 Borough U, Newport Co, Merthyr Tydfil

Clubs from Northern Ireland
6 Glentoran
4 Coleraine
3 Ballymena U, Crusaders,
2 Ards, Glenavon, Linfield
1 Derry C, Distillery, Portadown, Carrick Rangers, Cliftonville

Clubs from Eire
6 Shamrock R
3 Limerick, Waterford, Dundalk
2 Cork Hibs, Bohemians
1 Shelbourne, Cork Celtic, St Patrick's Ath, Finn Harps, Home Farm, Sligo Rovers, University College Dublin, Galway U, Derry C

Winners: Tottenham H 1962–63; West Ham U 1964–65; Manchester C 1969–70; Chelsea 1970–71; Rangers 1971–72; Aberdeen 1982–83; Everton 1984–85

Finalists: Liverpool 1965–66; Rangers 1960–61, 1966–67; Leeds U 1972–73; West Ham U 1975–76; Arsenal 1979–80

EUROPEAN FAIRS CUP & UEFA CUP (1955–89)

English clubs
8 Leeds U, Ipswich T
6 Liverpool, Everton, Arsenal
5 Manchester U, Southampton, Tottenham H
4 Manchester C, Birmingham C, Newcastle U, Nottingham F, Wolverhampton W, WBA
3 Aston Villa, Chelsea
2 Sheffield W, Stoke C, Derby Co, QPR
1 Burnley, Coventry C, London Rep XI, Watford

Scottish clubs
14 Dundee U
12 Hibernian
9 Aberdeen
8 Rangers
6 Hearts
5 Dunfermline Ath, Celtic
4 Dundee
3 St Mirren, Kilmarnock
2 Partick Th
1 Morton, St Johnstone

Clubs from Northern Ireland
10 Glentoran
6 Coleraine
4 Linfield
2 Glenavon
1 Ards, Portadown, Ballymena U

Clubs from Eire
7 Bohemians
3 Finn Harps, Dundalk, Shamrock R
2 Shelbourne, Drumcondra, St Patrick's Ath
1 Cork Hibs, Athlone T, Limerick, Drogheda U, Galway U

Winners: Leeds U 1967–68, 1970–71; Newcastle U 1968–69; Arsenal 1969–70; Tottenham H 1971–72, 1983–84; Liverpool 1972–73, 1975–76; Ipswich T 1980–81

Finalists: Birmingham C 1958–60, 1960-61; Leeds U 1966–67; Wolverhampton W 1971–72; Tottenham H 1973–74; Dundee U 1986–87

WORLD CLUB CHAMPIONSHIP

Played annually up to 1974 and intermittently since then between the winners of the European Cup and the winners of the South American Champions Cup – known as the Copa Libertadores. In 1980 the winners were decided by one match arranged in Tokyo in February 1981 and the venue has been the same since.

1960 Real Madrid beat Penarol 0-0, 5-1
1961 Penarol beat Benfica 0-1, 5-0, 2-1
1962 Santos beat Benfica 3-2, 5-2
1963 Santos beat AC Milan 2-4, 4-2, 1-0
1964 Inter-Milan beat Independiente 0-1, 2-0, 1-0
1965 Inter-Milan beat Independiente 3-0, 0-0
1966 Penarol beat Real Madrid 2-0, 2-0
1967 Racing Club beat Celtic 0-1, 2-1, 1-0
1968 Estudiantes beat Manchester United 1-0, 1-1
1969 AC Milan beat Estudiantes 3-0, 1-2
1970 Feyenoord beat Estudiantes 2-2, 1-0
1971 Nacional beat Panathinaikos 1-1, 2-1
1972 Ajax beat Independiente 1-1, 3-0
1973 Independiente beat Juventus 1-0
1974 Atlético Madrid beat Independiente 0-1, 2-0
1975 Independiente and Bayern Munich could not agree dates; no matches.
1976 Bayern Munich beat Cruzeiro 2-0, 0-0
1977 Boca Juniors beat Borussia Moenchengladbach 2-2, 3-0
1978 Not played
1979 Olimpia beat Malmö 1-0, 2-1
1980 Nacional beat Nottingham Forest 1-0
1981 Flamenco beat Liverpool 3-0
1982 Penarol beat Aston Villa 2-0
1983 Gremio Porto Alegre beat SV Hamburg 2-1
1984 Independiente beat Liverpool 1-0
1985 Juventus beat Argentinos Juniors 4-2 on penalties after a 2-2 draw
1986 River Plate beat Steaua Bucharest 1-0
1987 FC Porto beat Penarol 2-1 after extra time

1988

11 December in Tokyo

Nacional (1) 2 *(Ostolaza 2)*

PSV Eindhoven (0) 2 *(Romario, Koeman (pen))* 62,000

aet; 90 min 1-1; Nacional won 7-6 on penalties

Nacional: Sere; Gomez, De Leon, Revelez, Pintos Saldanha, Ostolaza, Vargas (Moran), Lemos, De Lima, Cardaccio (Carreno), Castro.
PSV Eindhoven: Van Breukelen; Gerets, Koot, Koeman, Heintze (Valckx), Lerby, Van Aerle, Vanenburg (Gilhaus), Romario, Kieft, Ellerman.
Referee: Dias Palacio (Colombia).

EUROPEAN SUPER CUP

Played annually between the winners of the European Champions' Cup and the European Cup-Winners' Cup.

Previous Matches

1972 Ajax beat Rangers 3-1, 3-2
1973 Ajax beat AC Milan 0-1, 6-0
1974 Not contested
1975 Dynamo Kiev beat Bayern Munich 1-0, 2-0
1976 Anderlecht beat Bayern Munich 4-1, 1-2
1977 Liverpool beat Hamburg 1-1, 6-0
1978 Anderlecht beat Liverpool 3-1, 1-2
1979 Nottingham F beat Barcelona 1-0, 1-1
1980 Valencia beat Nottingham F 1-0, 1-2
1981 Not contested
1982 Aston Villa beat Barcelona 0-1, 3-0
1983 Aberdeen beat Hamburg 0-0, 2-0
1984 Juventus beat Liverpool 2-0
1985 Juventus v Everton not contested due to UEFA ban on English clubs
1986 Steaua Bucharest beat Dynamo Kiev 1-0
1987 FC Porto beat Ajax 1-0, 1-0

1988

First Leg, 1 February 1989, Mechelen

KV Mechelen (2) 3 *(Bosman 2, De Wilde)*

PSV Eindhoven (0) 0 7000

KV Mechelen: Preud'homme; Emmers, Sanders, Rutjes, Versavel, Hofkens, Koeman E (Deferm), De Wilde, Bosman (Willmots), Den Boer, Demesmaeker.
PSV Eindhoven: Lodewijks; Gerets, Valckx, Koeman R, Veldman, Van Aerle, Lerby, Vanenburg, Romario, Gillhaus, Janssen (Ellerman).
Referee: Kirschen (East Germany).

Second Leg, 8 February 1989, Eindhoven

PSV Eindhoven (0) 1 *(Gillhaus)*

KV Mechelen (0) 0 17,100

PSV Eindhoven: Lodewijks; Gerets, Koeman R, Heintze, Vanenburg, Van Aerle, Linskens (Valckx), Chovanec, Ellerman, Romario, Gillhaus.
KV Mechelen: Preud'homme; Sanders, Rutjes, Emmers (Koeman E), Deferm, Hofkens, Bosman, Versavel, Demesmaeker, De Wilde, Den Boer.
Referee: Frederiksson (Sweden).
KV Mechelen won 3-1 on aggregate.

EUROPEAN CUPS DRAW 1989–90

EUROPEAN CUP
First Round: Spora v Real Madrid; Steaua v Fram; Ruch Chorzow v CFKA Sredets; PSV Eindhoven v Lucerne; Derry City v Benfica; Malmo v Internazionale; Rangers v Bayern Munich; Dynamo Dresden v AEK Athens; Rosenborg v Mechelen; AC Milan v HJK Helsinki; Tirol v Omonia; Marseille v Brondy; Sparta Prague v Fenerbahce; Dnepr v Linfield; Sliema v 17 Nentori; Honved v Vojvodina

CUP WINNERS CUP
Preliminary Round: Chernomorets v Dinamo Tirana.
First Round: Panathinaikos v Swansea C; Anderlecht v Ballymena U: Brann v Sampdoria; Barcelona v Legia; Besiktas v Borussia Dortmund; Union Luxembourg v Djurgaarden; Partizan Belgrade v Celtic; Valur v Dynamo Berlin; Slovan Bratislava v Grasshoppers; Belenenses v Monaco; Valladolid v Hamrun; Dinamo Bucharest v Chernomorets or Dinamo Tirana; Groningen v Ikast; Ferencvaros v Haka; Admira/Wacker v AEL; Torpedo Moscow v Cork City.

UEFA CUP
Preliminary Round: Auxerre v Dinamo Zagreb
First Round: Stuttgart v Feyenoord; Aberdeen v Rapid Vienna; Dynamo Kiev v MTK VM; Wettingen v Dundalk; Twente v FC Brugge; Cologne v Plastika Nitra; Sochaux v Jeunesse Esch; Karl Marx Stadt v Boavista; Gornik Zabrze v Juventus; Hibernian v Videoton; Orgryte v Hamburg; Liege v Akranes; Jalguiris v Gothenburg; Glentoran v Dundee U; Hansa Rostock v Banik Ostrava; Kuusysi v Paris St Germain; FK Austria v Ajax; Lillestrom v Werder Bremen; Rovaniemen v Katowice; Zenit v Naestved; Apollon v Zaragoza; Atalanta v Spartak Moscow; Rad Belgrade v Olympiakos; Vitosha v Antwerp; FC Porto v Flacara Moreni; Atletico Madrid v Fiorentina; PAOK Salonika v Sion; Auxerre or Dinamo Zagreb v Apollonia; Galatasaray v Red Star Belgrade; Sporting Lisbon v Napoli; Valencia v Victoria Bucharest; Valetta v Foto Net.

UEFA Cup – *Continued from Page 891*

THIRD ROUND, FIRST LEG

23 NOV

Hearts (1) 3 *(Bannon, Galloway, Colquhoun)*

Velez Mostar (0) 0 17,417

Hearts: Smith; Kidd (Jardine), Berry, McPherson, Whittaker, Black, Colquhoun, Mackay, Ferguson, Galloway, Bannon (Sandison).
Velez Mostar: Petranovic; Hadziabdic, Gosto (Juric), Rahimic, Jurasovic, Sisic, Repak, Gudelj, Kajtaz, Barbaric, Tuce (Kodro).

THIRD ROUND, SECOND LEG

7 DEC

Velez Mostar (1) 2 *(Tuce, Gudelj)*

Hearts (0) 1 *(Galloway)* 20,000

Velez Mostar: Petranovic; Gosto, Jedvai, Jurasovic, Hadziabdic, Karabeg, Juric S, Gudelj, Tuce, Juric P, Repak (Kodro).
Hearts: Smith; Whittaker, Berry, McPherson, Kidd, Bannon, Black, Mackay, Jardine, Colquhoun, Galloway (Moore).

QUARTER-FINAL, FIRST LEG

28 FEB

Hearts (0) 1 *(Ferguson)*

Bayern Munich (0) 0 26,294

Hearts: Smith; McLaren, McKinlay, McPherson, Berry, Levein, Galloway, Ferguson (Mackay), Colquhoun (Sandison), Black, Bannon.
Bayern Munich: Aumann; Grahammer, Pflugler, Johnsen, Augenthaler, Flick, Kogl (Eck), Reuter, Wohlfarth (Wegmann), Thon, Ekstrom.

QUARTER-FINAL, SECOND LEG

15 MAR

Bayern Munich (1) 2 *(Augenthaler, Johnsen)*

Hearts (0) 0 25,000

Bayern Munich: Aumann; Augenthaler, Johnsen, Pflugler, Nachtweih, Reuter, Flick, Eck (Ekstrom), Kogl, Wohlfarth, Wegmann.
Hearts: Smith; McLaren, Levein, McPherson, McKinlay (Robertson), Mackay, Berry, Black, Bannon (Ferguson), Colquhoun, Galloway.

NON-LEAGUE FOOTBALL

FA CHALLENGE TROPHY

FA CHALLENGE VASE

FA SUNDAY CUP

FA YOUTH CUP AND COUNTY YOUTH CUP

GM VAUXHALL CONFERENCE

HFS LOANS LEAGUE

BEAZER HOMES LEAGUE

VAUXHALL OPEL LEAGUE

AFA, SCHOOLS AND UNIVERSITIES

GM VAUXHALL CONFERENCE 1988–89

Maidstone United won the title by eight points, the largest margin in the competition's history, but only after overhauling Kettering Town in the last weeks of the season, which proved to be the most successful to date. Average attendances rose to a record 1,315.

Despite the withdrawal of Newport County in April with their record expunged from the table, aggregate attendances reached 552,190, the second best figure in the ten years.

Kettering's consolation was that they became only the third Conference club to pass 50,000 attendances, finishing as the best supported club on 50,123 for an average of 2,506. Thirteen clubs attracted four figure gates.

Maidstone, who shared Dartford's ground, replaced Darlington, relegated from the Fourth Division. Barnet defeated Hyde 5-3 on penalties to win the Clubcall Cup and Telford United took the FA Trophy with the only goal against Macclesfield.

GM VAUXHALL CONFERENCE TABLE 1988–89

		Home			*Goals*		*Away*			*Goals*		
	P	*W*	*D*	*L*	*F*	*A*	*W*	*D*	*L*	*F*	*A*	*Pts*
Maidstone United	40	12	5	3	48	22	13	4	3	44	24	84
Kettering Town	40	16	1	3	35	15	7	6	7	21	24	76
Boston United	40	12	3	5	36	28	10	5	5	25	23	74
Wycombe Wanderers	40	9	7	4	34	25	11	4	5	34	27	71
Kidderminster H.	40	10	4	6	32	32	11	2	7	36	25	69
Runcorn	40	11	3	6	39	22	8	5	7	38	31	65
Macclesfield Town	40	9	5	6	31	26	8	5	7	32	31	61
Barnet	40	11	2	7	36	30	7	5	8	28	39	61
Yeovil Town	40	8	5	7	34	30	7	6	7	34	37	56
Northwich Victoria	40	8	5	7	31	30	6	6	8	33	35	53
Welling United	40	8	6	6	27	16	6	5	9	18	30	53
Sutton United	40	10	5	5	43	26	2	10	8	21	28	51
Enfield	40	7	4	9	33	32	7	4	9	29	35	50
Altrincham	40	6	8	6	24	23	7	2	11	27	38	49
Cheltenham Town	40	7	7	6	32	29	5	5	10	23	29	48
Telford United	40	5	5	10	17	24	8	4	8	20	19	48
Chorley	40	6	4	10	26	32	7	2	11	31	39	45
Fisher Athletic	40	6	4	10	31	32	4	7	9	24	33	41
Stafford Rangers	40	7	4	9	27	32	4	3	13	22	42	40
Aylesbury United	40	7	4	9	27	30	2	5	13	16	41	36
Weymouth	40	6	7	7	27	30	1	3	16	10	40	31

* Following Newport County's expulsion only two clubs will be relegated from the GM Vauxhall Conference this season.

GM VAUXHALL CONFERENCE ATTENDANCES 1988–1989

Aggregate 1988–89	Average Gate	% Inc	Gates over 1000	Gates over 2000	Clubs with % Inc
552,190	1315	+ 5	60%	19%	13

GM VAUXHALL CONFERENCE ATTENDANCES BY CLUB 1988–1989

Club	Aggregate Attendance 1988/89	Average Gate 1988/8	% Inc or Dec	Average Gate 1987/88	Gates over 1000
Kettering Town	50,123	2506	+ 81	1381	20
Barnet	48,626	2431	− 8	2644	20
Yeovil Town	47,903	2395	+ 7	2241	20
Wycombe Wanderers	44,967	2248	+ 54	1460	20
Boston U	36,517	1826	+ 18	1546	20
Kidderminster H.	30,089	1504	+ 12	1345	19
Macclesfield Town	28,655	1433	+ 19	1200	18
Cheltenham Town	24,909	1245	− 6	1332	19
Telford United	24,705	1235	− 16	1480	18
Aylesbury United	23,531	1177	+ 24	946	13
Stafford Rangers	22,364	1118	− 9	1231	12
Maidstone United	20,737	1037	+ 6	980	10
Welling United	20,330	1017	+ 16	873	9
Altrincham	18,597	930	− 31	1349	8
Weymouth	18,254	913	− 39	1491	4
Chorley	17,822	891	+ 78	501	9
Sutton United	17,137	857	+ 26	682	5
Runcorn	15,693	785	+ 12	700	2
Enfield	15,594	780	+ 1	776	4
Northwich Victoria	15,060	753	− 4	785	2
Fisher Athletic	10,577	529	− 10	592	0

HIGHEST ATTENDANCES 1988–89

4890	Wycombe Wanderers v Kettering Town	8.4.89	3873	Wycombe Wanderers v Macclesfield Town	27.3.89
4450	Kettering Town v Welling United	1.4.89	3691	Yeovil Town v Weymouth	26.12.88
4377	Kettering Town v Kidderminster H.	25.3.89	3343	Boston United v Kettering Town	2.1.89
4247	Barnet v Enfield	2.1.89	3253	Kettering Town v Macclesfield Town	22.4.89
4239	Wycombe Wanderers v Kidderminster H.	18.2.89			

GM VAUXHALL CONFERENCE LEADING GOALSCORERS

Conf.			FA	Trophy	Club
26	Steve Butler (Maidstone United)	+	—	—	1
	Mark Gall (Maidstone United)	+	2	—	1
23	Chris Camden (Stafford Rangers)	+	9	—	2
	Mark Carter (Runcorn)	+	—	—	1
22	Ken Charlery (Maidstone United)	+	4	—	—
21	Steve Burr (Macclesfield Town)	+	—	5	—
	Don Page (Ex-Runcorn)	+	1	—	3
20	Paul Davies (Kidderminster H.)	+	1	—	4
	Lenny Dennis (Sutton U)	+	3	1	5
	Mark West (Wycombe Wanderers)	+	4	2	—
18	Ronnie Ellis (Altrincham)	+	2	—	—
	Derrick Parker (Northwich Victoria)	+	2	2	—
16	Phil Power (Chorley)	+	1	—	—
	Guy Whittingham (Yeovil Town)	+	—	—	—
15	Chris Cook (Boston United)	+	6	1	1
	Dean Neal (Fisher Athletic)	+	6	—	—
	Paul Wilson (Boston United)	+	5	1	—
14	Frank Murphy (Barnet)	+	2	—	2
	Malcolm O'Connor (Northwich Victoria)	+	6	1	1
13	Gary Abbott (Enfield)	+	4	1	—
	Phil Derbyshire (Macclesfield Town)	+	—	—	—
	Ernie Moss (Kettering Town)	+	1	3	—

GM VAUXHALL CONFERENCE SPONSORSHIP AWARDS 1988–89

	GM Vauxhall Sponsorship	*GM Vauxhall Jackpot*	*Title Award*	*PPA*	*Clubcall Cup*	*Total*
Maidstone United	3000	1000	5000	2000	500	11,500
Barnet	3000	500	—	2000	2500	8000
Kettering Town	3000	—	3000	2000	—	8000
Boston United	3000	—	2000	2000	—	7000
Runcorn	3000	917	—	2000	1000	6917
Yeovil Town	3000	750	—	2000	—	5750
Stafford Rangers	3000	167	—	2000	500	5667
Fisher Athletic	3000	500	—	2000	—	5500
Kidderminster H.	3000	—	—	2000	500	5500
Sutton United	3000	—	—	2000	500	5500
Chorley	3000	167	—	2000	—	5167
Altrincham	3000	—	—	2000	—	5000
Aylesbury United	3000	—	—	2000	—	5000
Cheltenham Town	3000	—	—	2000	—	5000
Enfield	3000	—	—	2000	—	5000
Macclesfield Town	3000	—	—	2000	—	5000
Newport County	3000	—	—	2000	—	5000
Northwich Victoria	3000	—	—	2000	—	5000
Telford United	3000	—	—	2000	—	5000
Welling United	3000	—	—	2000	—	5000
Weymouth	3000	—	—	2000	—	5000
Wycombe Wanderers	3000	—	—	2000	—	5000

HIGHEST SCORERS

4 Mark Boyland Chorley v *CHELTENHAM TOWN*
Conference 11.3.89
Chris Cook *BOSTON UNITED* v Mile Oak
FA Cup 2nd Qualifying 1.10.88
Paul Wilson *BOSTON UNITED* v Coventry Sporting
FA Cup 1st Qualifying 17.9.88

HIGHEST AGGREGATE SCORES

Maidstone United 7-2 Altrincham 27.8.88
Kidderminster H. 3-6 Maidstone United 8.4.88
Stafford Rangers 2-6 Yeovil Town 6.12.88

LARGEST HOME WINS

Maidstone United 7-2 Altrincham 27.8.88
Wycombe Wanderers 6-1 Stafford Rangers 11.2.89
Boston United 5-0 Barnet 29.10.88
Maidstone United 5-0 Yeovil Town 22.10.88
Runcorn 5-0 Aylesbury United 3.12.88
Welling United 5-0 Aylesbury United 12.10.88

LARGEST AWAY WINS

Boston United 0-6 Runcorn 28.9.88
Stafford Rangers 2-6 Yeovil Town 6.12.88
Aylesbury United 1-5 Kidderminster H. 20.9.88
Cheltenham Town 0-4 Maidstone United 20.8.88
Northwich Victoria 0-4 Chorley 18.2.89
Stafford Rangers 0-4 Runcorn 18.2.89

MATCHES WITHOUT DEFEAT

17 Maidstone United
14 Wycombe Wanderers
10 Boston United, Kettering Town

MATCHES WITHOUT A WIN

15 Weymouth
14 Enfield, Stafford Rangers
13 Fisher Athletic
9 Aylesbury United

CONSECUTIVE CONFERENCE VICTORIES

6 Boston United, Chorley, Maidstone United, Runcorn
5 Kettering Town, Kidderminster Harriers, Maidstone United, Runcorn, Wycombe Wanderers
4 Boston United, Enfield, Fisher Athletic, Kidderminster Harriers, Maidstone United, Northwich Victoria *(twice)*, Wycombe Wanderers

CONSECUTIVE CONFERENCE DEFEATS

6 Fisher Athletic
5 Aylesbury United, Boston United, Runcorn
4 Altrincham, Aylesbury United, Fisher Athletic, Stafford Rangers, Welling United, Weymouth *(twice)*

GM VAUXHALL CONFERENCE 1988–89

APPEARANCES AND GOALSCORERS

Altrincham
Baker, M. 25(1); Butcher, J. 9; Byrne, C. 6(4); Cook, N. 14(3); Crerand, D. 3(1); Cuddy, P. 37; Daws, N. 18(5); Doherty, T. 2; Dunn, S. 4(3); Dyson, C. 1(4); Ellis, R. 33; Farrell, T. 15(2); Farrelly, M. 37; Fraser, R. 6; Green, A. 14(2); Hanchard, M. 4; Harris, R. 2(2); Hawkins, K. 9(1); Heesom, D. 31(3); Henshaw, M. 6(1); Iro, L. 5; Johnson, I. 18; Kilner, A. 9(6); Knowles, J. 15; Mountford, K. 12; Parry, W. 5 (3); Phillips, S. 1(1); Rafferty, N. 0(1); Roberts, S. 2; Shaw, N. 19; Smith, O. 6; Stamper, G 0(1); Stewart, G. 25(2); Timmons, J. 19; Vince, J. 0(1); Wealands, J. 28.
Goals (51): Ellis 18, Stewart 8, Shaw 4, Timmons 4, Farrelly 2, Mountford 2, Baker 1, Byrne 1, Daws 1, Dunn 1, Farrell 1, Green 1, Harris 1, Henshaw 1, Kilner 1, Knowles 1, Smith 1, own goals 2.

Aylesbury United
Altenor, A. 5(3); Angol, I. 13; Botterill, D. 7; Boyland, R. 19(1); Coy, R. 25; Day, K. 9; Dodds, R. 6; Duggan, D. 4; Essex, S. 32; Friar, P. 2; Garner, T. 36; Hackett, P. 10(6); Harthill, G. 25(4); Hercules, C. 32(1); Hutter, P. 40; James, K. 12(2); King, A. 2; Lawrence, L. 18(1); Lissaman, J. 27; Mann, A. 12(3); O'Dowd, A. 16; Phillips, B.14(5); Poole, G. 2; Preece, A. 4; Robinson, P. 2(2); Saunders, P. 11; Seasman, J. 15; Smith H. 2(1); Taylor, N. 4; Turner, P. 1; Wilson, J. 33.
Goals (43): Hercules 11, Hutter 6, Lissaman 6, Boyland 4, Botterill 2, Essex 2, Mann 2, O'Dowd 2, Altenor 1, Dodds 1, Duggan 1, Hackett 1, Lawrence 1, Preece 1, Smith 1, own goal 1.

Barnet
Abbott, G. 9(5); Angell, D. 20; Bissett, N. 4; Brown, P. 5(2); Bull, G. 10; Clarke, A. 1; Cox, S. 28; Codner, R. 6; Creaser, G. 2(2); Daish, L. 12; Docker, J. 22(1); Dublin, D. 0(1); Evans, N. 18(3); Fergusson, I. 1(2); Flashman, M. 1; Forde, C. 1; Gormley, E. 2(1); Humphries, S. 3; Iannone, A. 1(1); Ironton, N. 6(1); Jones, D. 2(1); Ketteridge, S. 7(1); Lawrenson, M. 2; Leadbitter, C. 12; Lomas, A. 34; Mann, A. 3(2); Margerrison, J. 6(1); Measham, I. 1; Millett, K. 5; Murphy, F. 27(3); Nugent, R.14(9); Payne, D. 12; Payne, L. 5(2); Phillips, G. 2; Poole, G. 11; Regis, D. 2(5); Reilly, G. 10; Sansom, David. 22(4); Shinners, P. 5(2); Slack, T. 2; Smith, H.2(6); Stacey, P. 19(1); Stein, E. 37(3); Turner, W. 26(1); Wilson, P 20(5); Whitworth, 1.
Goals (64): Murphy 14, Bull 6, Sansom 6, Abbott 5, Docker 5, Evans 5, Stein 4, Shinners 3, Turner 3, Wilson 3, Reilly 2, Angell 1, Clarke 1, Cox 1, Nugent 1, Poole 1, Regis 1, own goals 2.

Boston United
Beattie, A. 2; Beavon, D. 4; Beech, G. 20; Buckley, S. 20(1); Cook, C. 31(4); Creane, G. 6; Crombie, A. 14(7); Cusack, D. 24(8); Duggan, D. 5(8); Grant, D. 6(3); Hamill, S. 32(3); Hardy, M. 35(1); McKenna, J. 40; McLaughlan, S. 2(7); Mell, S. 4; Mossman, D. 26(3); Rawcliffe, P. 15(2); Shirtliff, P. 39; Simpson, G. 28; Vaughan, D. 34(1); Ward, W. 14(7); Wilson, P. 39(1).
Goals (61): Cook 15, Wilson 15, Hamill 12, Mossman 4, Beech 3, Ward 3, Cusack 1, Grant 1, Hardy 1, McLaughlan 1, Mell 1, Rawcliffe 1, Shirtliff 1, Simpson 1, own goal 1.

Cheltenham Town
Baverstock, R. 28(1); Boyland, M. 11; Brooks, S. 28; Brown, K. 3(1); Buckland, M. 40; Burns, C. 29(4); Churchward, A. 12; Collins, R. 0(1); Craig, D. 12(3); Crouch, S. 2(2); Crowley, R. 32(1); Eves, M. 0(1); Fry, C. 0(2); Hewlett, G. 2(3); Jenkins, S. 20(1); Jordan, N. 36(2); Knight, K. 5; Mogg, D. 28; Nuttell, M. 13; Pountain, A. 1(8); Vircavs, A. 28(2); Walsh, I. 3; Whelen, S. 25; Willetts, K. 35(1); Williams, P. 6.
Goals (55): Buckland 9, Boyland 8, Jordan 6, Crowley 5, Brooks 4, Jenkins 4, Shearer 4, Tanner 3, Vircavs 3, Townsend 3, Baverstock 1, Craig 1, Crouch 1, Nuttell 1, Willetts 1, own goal 1.

Chorley
Allen, S. 32; Brady, J. 39; Branagan, J. 13; Buckley, G. 10; Clegg, T. 6; Collins, J. 7(4); Glendon, K. 9(1); Goulding, D. 4; Griffin, P. 2(5); Henshaw, M. 1(1); Hughes, J. 23; Jones, G. 5(5); Lester, M. 10; Lloyd, I. 16(6); Madrick, C. 7(2); Moss, P. 36; Nicholl, J. 3; Pawsey, C. 14; Peters, N. 38; Phillips, S. 7; Power, P. 29(1); Redshaw, R. (6); Ridler, C. 40; Ross, B. 15(6); Russell, M. 8(8); Stephens, G. 27(1); Thomas, D. 0(1); Wardle, C. 33(1); Woods, R. 1; Worthington, F. 3.
Goals (57): Power 16, Brady 10, Moss 9, Ross 8, Allen 2, Griffin 2, Wardle 2, Buckley 1, Clegg 1, Hughes 1, Madrick 1, Pawsey 1, Russell 1, own goals 2.

Enfield
Abbott, G. 12; Bate, F. 3; Benstock, D. 3(14); Canoville, P. 6(3); Cooper, J. 24(8); Cottington, B. 23; Dionsiou, D. 1(1); Edmunds, A. 4; Francis, N. 31; Friar, P. 10(6); Furlong, P. 36(3); Gallagher, J. 0(1); Harding, P. 25; Hazleden, K. 8(7); Howell, D. 38; Hughton, H. 1; Johnson, R. 3; Keen, N. 10; Kelly, N. 2; King, S. 2(1); Lewis, R, 17(9); Pape, A. 40; Parkyn, R. 18; Reeves, J. 16; Schiavi, M. 10(5); Scott, S. 0(2); Smith, G. 31; Smith, P. 6; Sparrow, B. 33(2); Waite, D. 6; Wilkinson, T. 20.
Goals (62): Furlong 11, Francis 10, Abbott 8, Lewis 6, Harding 5, Howell 4, Benstock 3, Reeves 3, Wilkinson 3, Canoville 2, Cooper 2, Bate 1, Friar 1, Keen 1, Schiavi 1, own goal 1.

Fisher Athletic
Ambrose, L. 15(18); Bayram, O. 0(1); Charlery, K. 24; Collins, P. 35; Cooper, G. 12(4); Field, A. 9(5); Fry, D. 23; Gorman, P. 10(1); Harmsworth, L. 7(6); Hiscock, C. 4(1); Little, B. 39; Marston, A. 0(1); Massey, A. 22(11); McClure, D. 29(2); Mehmet, D. 18; Neal, D. 36; Norman, N. 23; Nunes, S. 6(6); Nutton, M. 12; Richardson, D. 17; Shinners, R. 27; Stead, M. 34(1); Towner, T. 38.
Goals (55): Charlery 17, Neal 15, Ambrose 3, Towner 3, Field 2, Gorman 2, Little 2, Mehmet 2, Norman 2, Cooper 1, Harmsworth 1, Massey 1, Nunes 1, Nutton 1, Shinners 1, own goal 1.

Kettering Town
Beasely, A. 8; Beech, G. 6(5); Brown, R. 29; Cooke, R. 31; Creane, G. 24; Edwards, N. 13(7); Fuccillo, L. 37(1); Gallagher, J. 9 (1); Griffith Cohen, 26(8); Heywood, D. 20, Keast, D. 37(1), Lawrence, L. 4(4); Lewis, R. 39; Lim, H. 9; Massey, R. 6(1); Moss, E. 34(2); Nightingale, M. 40; Richardson, P. 22(3); Shoemake, K. 23; Torrance, G. 1 Wright, A. 22(6).
Goals (56): Moss 13, Cooke 12, Griffith 8, Fuccillo 7, Edwards 5, Keast 3, Gallagher 2, Richardson 2, Creane 1, Lawrence 1, Nightingale 1, Wright 1.

Kidderminster Harriers
Bancroft, P. 38; Barton, J. 39; Boxall, C. 8(4); Brazier, C. 32(1); Burton, C. 1; Casey, K. 8(2); Davies, P. 36(1); Dearlove, M. 13(1); Forsyth, R. 1; Howell, p. 30(3); Jones, P. 40; Jones, R. 35(1); Kimberley, S. 3(1); Mackenzie, G. 7(3); Mulders, J. 14(6); Nicholls, A. 0(2); Pearson, J. 35; Shilvock, R. 29; Sugrue, P. 8(2); Tuohy, M. 37(1); Weir, M. 26(1).
Goals (68): Davies 20, Tuohy 10, Howell 9, Shilvock 7, Sugrue 5, Bancroft 4, Casey 3, Jones 2, Weir 2, Boxall 1, Kimberley 1, Pearson 1, own goals 3.

Macclesfield Town
Askey, J. 34(1); Blake, S. 1(1); Burr, S. 29(1); Conner, J. 26(4); Derbyshire, P. 30(1); Edwards, E. 31(1); Grant, D. 3; Hanlon, S. 37; Hardman, M. 19(4); Humphries, G. 1(1); Imrie, J. 13(7); Kendall, P. 37; Lake, M. 34(1); Lodge, P. 2; Mountford, K. 3(4); Parlane, D. 8(18); Roberts, M. 30(2); Shaw, N. 15(3); Shenton, R. 0(1); Timmons, J. 14; Tobin, G. 33; Zelem, A. 40.
Goals (63): Burr 21, Derbyshire 13, Askey 11, Hanlon 4, Lake 3, Imrie 2, Parlane 2, Timmons 2, Kendall 1, Shaw 1, Tobin 1, own goals 2.

Maidstone United
Ashford, N. 27; Beattie, A. 22; Beeney, M. 40; Berry, L. 40; Butler, S. 38; Charlery, K. 10(1); Collins, P. 12(1); Cooper, G. 2; Docker, J. 8(4); Gall, M. 25(9); Golley, M. 40; Goyette, P. 3(2); Hill, M. 31(1); Jacques, D. 24(5); Mehmet, D. 9; Pamphlett, T. 32; Roast, J. 7(8); Rogers, T. 9(8); Scotting, A. 3(3); Sorrell, T. 20(2); Stewart, M. 18(1).
Goals (92): Butler 26, Gall 26, Golley 7, Charlery 5, Ashford 4, Hill 4, Pamphlett 4, Rogers 3, Sorrell 3, Stewart 3, Roast 2, Beattie 1, Berry 1, Collins 1, Docker 1, Mehmet 1.

Northwich Victoria
Bishop, Eddie, 3; Crompton, A. 32(1); Danskin, J. 19(4); Davies, S. 6(1); Eli, R. 10(1); Griffiths, P. 0(4); Healey, J. 3(3); Hill, G. 7; Imrie, J. 1; Jones, M. 38; Keighley, P. 0(1); Kennedy, A. 11; Maguire, P. 37; Malkin, C. 3; McHale, R. 2; McNeilis, S. 36; Morgan, D. 1; Morton, N. 15(1); Murray, E. 2; Nolan, I. 22(7); O;Connor, M. 38(1); Parker, D. 37(1); Parker, J. 28(1); Parker, S. 3(1); Ryan, D. 40; Sayer, P. 7(5); Seasman, J. 7(3); Stimpson, B. 2; Wakenshaw, R. 1; Williams, G. 3; Wilson, A. 0(1); Young, D. 26(2).
Goals (64): Parker D 18, O;Connor 14, Maguire 8, Hill 4, Danskin 3, McNeilis 3, Crompton 2, Malkin 2, Morton 2, Nolan 2, Parker J 2, Bishop 1, Davies 1, Eli 1, Parker S 1.

Runcorn
Anderson, G. 27; Bradley, G. 2(1); Byrne, P. 36(1); Carroll, J. 37; Carter, M. 39; Densmore, P. 26(1); Farrell, T. 8(1); Ferguson, M. 1(2); Galloway, D. 9(3); Haigh, I. 3; Highdale, D. 1(4); Houghton, P. —(14); Jacques, K. 1(2); McBride, R. 37; McMahon, J. 24(2); Miller, T. 36(1); Page, D. 33; Pugh, D. 16(1); Reid, A. 34; Rodwell, A. 37(1); Rooney, A. 26(2); Rowlands, P. 3(1); Williams, D. 4(1).
Goals (77): Carter 23, Page 21, Rodwell 7, Anderson 5, Carroll 4, Galloway 3, McMahon 3, Pugh 3, Reid 3, Byrne 2, Miller 1, Rooney 1, Rowlands 1.

Stafford Rangers
Brown, I. 21(5); Burns, K. 5; Camden, C. 33(2); Campbell, W. 7(2); Cavell, P. 27(2); Chamberlain, N. 12(1); Doyle, M. 1; Eccles, P. 2; Greaves, P. 35(2); Griffiths, P. 9(1); Hignett, C. 12(1); Jones, M. 15(2); Kitchen, D. 9; Knight, T. 16(1); Marsh, E. 22(1); Newton, S. 12(2); Price, R. 38; Ridley, J. 19(1); Salmon, S. 3(5); Saxby, G. 0(1); Simpson, W. 5; Thacker, C. 34; Thornley, M. 2; Titley, P. 10(4); Turley, R. 23(10); Upton, P. 37; Wharton, D. 9(1); Williamson, C. 1(1); Wood, F. 21(2).
Goals (49): Camden 23, Cavell 8, Chamberlain 3, Hignett 3, Turley 3, Newton 2, Salmon 2, Thacker 2, Brown 1, Marsh 1, Upton 1.

Sutton United
Anderson, C. 3(2); Andrews, S. 0(1); Cornwell, M. 12; Dawson, P. 32(3); Dennis, L. 38; Edwards, L. 3(3); Ekoku, E. 14(1); Fowler, S. 6(3); Golding, P. 3; Golley, N. 38; Hanlan, M. 27(2); Hemsley, S. 19; Horner, J. 6(2); Jones, R. 36; Kennedy, J. —(2); McKinnon, P. 26; Morris, G. 9(1); Pratt, V. 29(5); Rains, A. 34; Roffey, T. 33; Rogers, P. 40; Rondeau, I. 2(1); Stephens, M. 18; Turner, S. 3(3); Van Sliedregt Arjan. 2(1); Vincent, J. 7.
Goals (64): Dennis 20, McKinnon 11, Hanlan 5, Pratt 5, Ekoku 4, Stephens 4, Golley 3, Cornwell 2, Dawson 2, Rains 2, Rogers 2, Fowler 1, Jones 1, own goals 2.

Telford United
Alcock, J. 8(2); Biggins, S. 2(1); Brindley, C. 24; Charlton, K. 24; Crawley, I. 24(7); Cunningham, M. 6(2); Grainger, P. 18; Greenough, M. 4; Griffiths, A. 31(4); Hanchard, M. 4(1); Hancock, M. 19; Harrison, M. 16; Joseph, A. 33; Lee, A. 36(1); Lloyd, T. 17(9); Mayman, P. 15(1); McGinty, J. 15(1); McKenna, K. 15(2); Meredith, N. —(1); Nelson, S. 25(6); Sankey, I. 26(6); Stringer, J. 17(1); Storton, T. 27(1); Wiggins, H. 34(2).
Goals (37): Crawley 7, Stringer 5, Lee 4, Lloyd 4, McKenna 4, Griffiths 3, Grainger 2, Greenough 2, Brindley 1, Cunningham 1, Hanchard 1, Hancock 1, Nelson 1, Sankey 1.

Welling United
Barron, P. 39; Battram, P. 13(15); Booker, T. 35(1); Brown, W. 6(1); Buglione, M. 1(8); Burgess, R. 29(2); Clemmence, N. 21(10); Glover, J. 39; Handford, P. 35(1); Haverson, P 0(1); Horton, D. 38; Jones, D. 0(1); Lindsay, D. 13(2); MacDonald, T. 39; Ransom, N. 30; Reynolds, T. 35; Robbins, T. 33; Rossati, J. 0(1); Sawyer, P. 1(1); Walker, R. 1; White, S. 32.
Goals (37): Robbins 12, Booker 10, Burgess 7, Glover 5, White 3, Battram 2, Handford 2, Ransom 2, Lindsay 1, own goal 1.

Weymouth
Baird, S. 9(2); Bunce, P. 8(2); Burman, S. 23(2); Churchill, R. 2; Compton, P. 35; Conning, P. 20(2); Cooper, R. 10; Dawson, T. 18(2); Donegal, G. 3(1); Gibson, W. 30; Gow, G. 1; Grimshaw, M. 12; Gwinnett, M. 14; Holmes, M. 4; Impey, J. 6; Johnson, I. 18; Lewis, M. 17(5); Linney, D. 12(2); McBride, D. 4(1); McCarthy, P. 2(3); Meacham, J. 12(2); Mundee, D. 3; Nardiello, G. 4(4); Oliver, T. 18; Pounder, T. 29(5); Preece, A. 11; Pugh, S. 34(4); Roberts, D. 1(5); Roberts, T. 3; Tanner, M. 11; Taylor, R. 23(5); Smeulders, J. 5; Teale, S. 19; Turrell, P. 19(2).
Goals (37): Turrell 5, Conning 4, Preece 3, Pugh 3, Compton 2, Dawson 2, Meacham 2, Pounder 2, Baird 1, Bunce 1, Cooper 1, Donegal 1, Gibson 1, Grimshaw 1, Holmes 1, Impey 1, McBride 1, Nardiello 1, Roberts D 1, Taylor 1, Teale 1, own goal 1.

Wycombe Wanderers
Abbley, S. 36(2); Barrett, K. 26(1); Blackler, M. 23(4); Boyland, M. 1; Butler, M. 1(4); Carroll, D. 26(1); Creaser, G. 31; Crompton, S. 6; Crossley, M. 15(1); Day, K. 10; Dublin, D. 2; Durham, K. 38(1); Evans, N. 6; Granville, J. 34; Greenaway, B. 1(4); Kerr, A. 21; Kerr, J. 24; Norman, S. 35(3); Osborne, L. 11(4); Regan, J. 3(1); Robinson, A. 39; Roderick, M. —(1); Russell, A. 1(2); Taylor, N. 7; West, M. 37(3); Young, S. 6(5).
Goals (68): West 20, Durham 12, Kerr J 12, Carroll 6, Evans 3, Blackler 2, Kerr A 2, Norman 2, Abbley 1, Creaser 1, Day 1, Osborne 1, Robinson 1, Russell 1, own goals 3.

Yeovil Town
Bond, L. 17; Conning, T. 11; Copeland, P. 1; Cordice, N. 39; Doherty, M. 18; Donellan, G. 24(3); Ferns, P. 1(1); Grimshaw, M. 11(6); Gwinnett, M. 6; Iles, R. 17; Lowe, T. 27(4); McCarthy, P. 5(1); Meare, P. 0(1); Muir, P. 0(1); Mundee, D. 10(1); Pearson, G. 17; Quinn, J. 24(1); Randall, P. 18(11); Ricketts, A. 10(2); Rutter, S. 33; Shail, M. 10; Shepherd, D. 0(2); Sherwood, J. 36; Spencer, M. 12; Stephens, A. 6; Tapley, S. 17(4); Thompson, R. 6(2); Thorpe, P. 8(9); Tonge, K. 1(1); Townsend, C. 1(2); Wallace, A. 33; Whittingham, G. 21.
Goals (68): Whittingham 16, Randall 8, Wallace 8, Doherty 7, Spencer 6, Donellan 4, Cordice 3, Grimshaw 3, Quinn 3, Pearson 2, Tonge 2, Conning 1, Lowe 1, McCarthy 1, Shail 1, Sherwood 1, own goal 1.

Newport County
Abbruzzese, D. 8(3); Andrews, K. 17(2); Banks, C. 15(5); Bennett, S. 0(2); Bickerton, D. 2(1); Bird, T. 29; Brignull, P. 13; Evans, R. 11(2); Foley, W. 7(3); Ford, F. 16(1); Gibbins, R. 1; Giles, D. 3; Gripton, M. 1(1); Hamer, K. 1(1); Jones, G. 2; King, A. 1; King, J. 2; Marustik, C. 14; McLaughlin, J. 2(1); Millett, G. 12(2); Mills, S. 0(1); Morgan, S. 1(1); Nuttell, M. 5; Peacock, D. 14; Preece, R. 0(1); Richards, G. 14; Rogers, G. 4(2); Sanderson, P. 24(1); Sherlock, S. 27; Sugrue, P. 13(1); Taylor, R. 1; Thompson, I. 2(1); Thompson, M. 15; Walker, S. 2(1); Williams, P. 22; Withers, D. 18(2).
Goals (31): Sanderson 5, Withers 4, Marustik 3, Evans 2, Ford 2, Giles 2, Richards 2, Sugrue 2, Williams 2, Andrews 1, Banks 1, Brignull 1, Foley 1, Millett 1, Nuttell 1, Thompson 1.

GM VAUXHALL CONFERENCE: MEMBER CLUBS SEASON 1989–1990

Club: ALTRINCHAM
Colours: Red and black checked shirts, black shorts
Ground: Moss Lane, Altrincham, Cheshire, WA15 8AP
Tel: 061 928 1045
Year Formed: 1903
Record Gate: 10,275 (1925 v Sunderland Boys)
Nickname: The Robins
Manager: John King
Secretary: Jean Baldwin

Club: BARNET
Colours: Amber shirts, black shorts
Ground: Underhill Stadium, Barnet Lane, Herts, EN5 2BE
Tel: 01 440 0277
Year Formed: 1888
Record Gate: 11,026 (1952 v Wycombe Wanderers)
Nickname: The Bees
Manager: Barry Fry
Secretary: Brian Ayres

Club: BARROW
Colours: White shirts, blue shorts
Ground: Holker Street, Barrow-in-Furness, Cumbria
Tel: 0229 23061
Year Formed: 1901
Record Gate: 16,840 (1954 v Swansea City)
Nickname: The Bluebirds
Manager: Ray Wilkie
Secretary: Keith Nelson

Club: BOSTON UNITED
Colours: Wolves gold shirts, black shorts
Ground: York Street Ground, York Street, Boston, Lincs
Tel: 0205 65524/5
Year Formed: 1934
Record Gate: 10,086 (v Corby Town)
Nickname: The Pilgrims
Manager: George Kerr
Secretary: John Blackwell

Club: CHELTENHAM TOWN
Colours: Red and white shirts, white shorts
Ground: Whaddon Road, Cheltenham, Glocs, GL52 5NA
Tel: 0242 513397
Year Formed: 1892
Record Gate: 8326 (1956 v Reading)
Nickname: The Robins
Manager: Jim Barron
Secretary: Ken Turner

Club: CHORLEY
Colours: Black and white shirts, white shorts
Ground: Victory Park, Duke Street, Chorley, PR7 3DU
Tel: 02572 63406
Year Formed: 1883
Record Gate: 15,153 (1986 v Preston NE at Blackburn)
Nickname: The Magpies
Manager: Ken Wright
Secretary: Mick Wearmouth

Club: DARLINGTON
Colours: White shirts, black shorts
Ground: Feethams Ground, Darlington, DL1 5JB
Tel: 0325 465097
Year Formed: 1883
Record Gate: 21,023 (1960 v Bolton Wanderers)
Nickname: The Quakers
Manager: Brian Little
Secretary: Brian Anderson

Club: ENFIELD
Colours: White shirts, blue shorts
Ground: Southbury Road, Enfield, Middlesex, EN1 1YQ
Tel: 01 363 2858
Year Formed: 1893
Record Gate: 35,000 (1981 v Barnsley at Spurs)
Nickname: The E's
Manager: Eddie McCluskey
Secretary: Keith Wortley

Club: FARNBOROUGH TOWN
Colours: All yellow/blue trim
Ground: John Roberts Ground, Cherrywood Road, Farnborough
Tel: 0252 541469
Year Formed: 1967
Record Gate: 3000 (1977 v Billericay Town)
Nickname: The Boro
Manager: Ted Pearce
Secretary: Terry Parr

Club: FISHER ATHLETIC
Colours: Black and white shirts, black shorts
Ground: Surrey Docks Stadium, Salter Road, London, SE16
Tel: 01 237 1432
Year Formed: 1908
Record Gate: 2000 (1984 v Bristol City)
Nickname: The Fish
Manager: Malcolm Allison
Secretary: Les Rowe

Club: KETTERING TOWN
Colours: All red
Ground: Rockingham Road, Kettering, Northants, NN16 9AW
Tel: 0536 83028
Year Formed: 1875
Record Gate: 11,536 (1947 v Peterborough)
Nickname: The Poppies
Manager: Peter Morris
Secretary: George Ellitson

Club: KIDDERMINSTER HARRIERS
Colours: Red/white halves shirts, white shorts
Ground: Aggborough, Hoo Road, Kidderminster
Tel: 0562 823931
Year Formed: 1886
Record Gate: 9155 (1948 v Hereford)
Nickname: The Harriers
Manager: Graham Allner
Secretary: Ray Mercer

Club: MACCLESFIELD TOWN
Colours: Royal blue shirts, white shorts
Ground: Moss Rose Ground, London Road, Macclesfield, Cheshire, SK11 7SP
Tel: 0625 24324
Year Formed: 1875
Record Gate: 8900 (1968 v Stockport County)
Nickname: The Silkmen
Manager: Peter Wragg
Secretary: Barry Lingard

Club: MERTHYR TYDFIL
Colours: White shirts, black shorts
Ground: Penydarren Park, Merthyr Tydfil
Tel: 0685 4102
Year Formed: 1945
Record Gate: 21,000 (1949 v Reading)
Nickname: The Martyrs
Manager: Lyn Jones
Secretary: Phil Dauncey

Club: NORTHWICH VICTORIA
Colours: Green shirts, white shorts
Ground: The Drill Field, Northwich, Cheshire, CW9 5HN
Tel: 0606 41450
Year Formed: 1874
Record Gate: 11,290 (1949 v Witton Albion)
Nickname: The Vics
Manager: Cliff Roberts
Secretary: Derek Nuttall

Club: RUNCORN
Colours: Yellow shirts, green shorts
Ground: Canal Street, Runcorn, Cheshire
Tel: 09285 60076
Year Formed: 1919
Record Gate: 10,011 (1939 v Preston NE)
Nickname: The Linnets
Manager: Barry Whitehead
Secretary: George Worrall

Club: STAFFORD RANGERS
Colours: Black and white shirts, white shorts
Ground: Marston Road, Stafford, ST16 3BX
Tel: 0785 42750
Year Formed: 1876
Record Gate: 8536 (1975 v Rotherham)
Nickname: The Boro
Manager: Ron Reid
Secretary: Angela Meddings

Club: SUTTON UNITED
Colours: Amber shirts, amber shorts
Ground: Boro Sports Ground, Gander Green Lane, Sutton, Surrey
Tel: 01 644 5120
Year Formed: 1898
Record Gate: 14,000 (1970 v Leeds United)
Nickname: The U's
Manager: Barrie Williams
Secretary: Ralph Carr

Club: TELFORD UNITED
Colours: White shirts, blue shorts
Ground: Bucks Head, Watling Street, Telford, TF1 2NJ
Tel: 0952 223838
Year Formed: 1877
Record Gate: 13,000 (1935 v Shrewsbury)
Nickname: The Lillywhites
Manager: Stan Storton
Secretary: Mike Ferriday

Club: WELLING UNITED
Colours: Red shirts, red shorts
Ground: Park View Road Ground, Welling, Kent
Tel: 01 301 1196
Year Formed: 1963
Record Gate: 3850 (1989 v Blackburn)
Nickname: The Wings
Manager: Nicky Brigden
Secretary: Barrie Hobbins

Club: WYCOMBE WANDERERS
Colours: Sky blue shirts, navy blue shorts
Ground: Loakes Park, Queen Alexandra Road, High Wycombe, Bucks, HP11 2JU
Tel: 0494 26567
Year Formed: 1884
Record Gate: 16,000 (1950 v St Albans)
Nickname: The Blues
Manager: Jim Kelman
Secretary: John Goldsworthy

Club: YEOVIL TOWN
Colours: White shirts, green shorts
Ground: The Huish, Yeovil, Somerset, BA20 1AZ
Tel: 0935 23662
Year Formed: 1923
Record Gate: 17,200 (1949 v Sunderland)
Nickname: The Glovers
Manager: Brian Hall
Secretary: Roger Brinsford

GM VAUXHALL CONFERENCE RESULTS 1988–89

	Altrincham	Aylesbury U	Barnet	Boston U	Cheltenham T	Chorley	Enfield	Fisher Ath	Kettering T	Kidderminster H	Macclesfield T	Maidstone U	Northwich Vic	Runcorn	Stafford R	Sutton U	Telford U	Welling U	Weymouth	Wycombe W	Yeovil Town
Altrincham	—	1-0	1-1	0-0	0-1	1-2	0-0	1-1	1-2	3-1	1-3	0-1	2-2	1-2	2-1	1-0	0-0	3-1	2-1	2-2	2-2
Aylesbury U	1-2	—	1-3	1-2	0-0	4-3	2-1	1-1	0-1	1-5	1-2	1-2	2-0	1-2	1-1	1-0	2-0	0-0	4-1	0-2	3-2
Barnet	3-0	1-0	—	0-0	3-1	2-4	2-1	2-3	3-2	0-2	1-4	2-1	2-0	3-2	1-2	1-1	1-3	2-3	4-1	1-0	2-0
Boston U	3-1	2-0	5-0	—	1-1	2-0	3-2	2-4	1-1	0-2	3-2	1-4	2-1	0-6	2-1	3-1	1-0	2-0	2-0	0-1	1-1
Cheltenham T	2-1	0-0	1-2	3-1	—	2-2	3-2	2-2	2-1	4-1	3-0	0-4	2-2	2-1	1-2	2-3	0-1	1-1	1-1	0-1	1-1
Chorley	1-0	1-1	2-3	0-1	1-4	—	1-2	1-1	0-1	1-3	0-1	1-3	3-1	1-3	3-1	2-1	2-0	1-1	0-0	3-2	2-3
Enfield	2-1	2-1	4-0	1-2	3-4	1-2	—	2-1	1-1	1-3	2-1	1-1	1-2	0-3	4-2	1-1	0-1	0-1	3-0	3-4	1-1
Fisher Ath	1-1	0-2	1-2	1-3	2-0	4-0	1-2	—	3-0	2-0	2-2	0-2	2-4	0-1	0-1	1-1	0-1	1-3	3-2	3-3	4-2
Kettering T	0-1	5-2	3-1	1-2	2-0	3-0	0-1	2-1	—	2-1	1-0	3-3	2-1	2-0	1-0	1-0	1-0	2-1	1-0	2-1	1-0
Kidderminster H	2-3	4-3	1-0	0-2	3-2	0-2	1-3	2-1	1-1	—	0-1	3-6	1-1	2-1	3-2	1-0	1-1	2-1	1-0	2-0	2-2
Macclesfield T	1-0	3-1	1-1	0-1	0-0	3-2	1-1	2-2	0-1	1-1	—	4-3	0-2	3-2	2-1	1-3	2-1	3-0	2-0	0-1	2-3
Maidstone U	7-2	1-1	3-2	3-0	2-0	2-0	3-1	1-0	0-0	0-3	3-3	—	4-1	2-2	3-0	1-1	1-3	3-0	3-0	1-3	5-0
Northwich Vic	4-3	1-1	1-1	0-1	1-0	0-4	2-2	3-0	1-1	2-4	3-2	2-0	—	0-1	1-1	4-2	1-0	0-2	2-0	2-3	1-2
Runcorn	3-0	5-0	3-0	1-2	2-1	3-0	1-2	1-1	2-1	1-3	2-2	0-1	3-1	—	4-1	2-1	0-0	1-2	1-0	2-3	2-1
Stafford R	0-2	3-1	1-2	4-1	1-1	3-2	3-1	0-1	2-1	0-1	1-1	0-2	0-1	0-4	—	1-1	1-3	3-0	1-0	1-1	2-6
Sutton U	3-2	5-2	5-1	0-0	1-1	1-2	3-1	2-1	0-2	1-1	1-2	1-1	3-3	3-1	2-0	—	1-2	0-1	3-1	3-0	5-2
Telford U	0-1	0-1	0-3	0-1	2-0	2-1	3-0	1-1	0-1	1-0	1-3	1-2	1-4	1-1	2-2	0-0	—	0-0	1-0	1-2	0-1
Welling U	0-0	5-0	1-1	3-2	0-2	1-0	0-0	3-1	2-1	0-1	2-0	0-0	0-0	4-0	1-3	1-1	0-1	—	4-0	0-1	0-2
Weymouth	1-3	0-0	1-1	2-2	3-2	2-3	2-3	1-0	3-0	3-1	1-2	1-3	2-2	1-1	1-0	2-2	0-0	1-0	—	0-3	0-2
Wycombe W	2-1	1-0	2-3	2-1	1-0	1-1	3-2	3-0	0-1	1-0	1-1	2-3	1-4	3-3	6-1	2-2	1-0	1-1	0-0	—	1-1
Yeovil Town	2-3	1-0	2-1	1-1	1-3	2-1	1-2	1-2	2-2	1-3	2-0	1-2	2-1	2-2	2-0	0-0	4-3	4-0	2-3	1-1	—

THE CLUBCALL CUP
for the Bob Lord Trophy

Qualifying Round
BEAZER HOMES LEAGUE

Bedworth United 1 *(Randle)*
Alvechurch 2 *(Volrath, Crisp)* 203

Crawley Town 2 *(Warrilow, Boyce)*
Waterlooville 1 *(Whittingham)* 435

Dorchester Town *(Morrel 2 (pens))*
Merthyr Tydfil 1 *(French)* 177

Dover Athletic *(Donn)*
Ashford Town 0 660

Gosport Borough 0
Fareham Town 1 *(Carrol)* 383

Leicester United 2 *(Payne, Dakin)*
Corby Town 3 *(Hofbauer, Archer, og)* 192

Moor Green 5 *(P. Davies 2, Fearon 2, Downes)*
VS Rugby 3 *(Webb (pen), McBean 2)* aet 229

Redditch United 1 *(Crawford)*
Burton Albion 2 *(Millard, Whitehouse)* 241

Byes to First Round
Bath City, Bromsgrove Rovers, Cambridge City, Dartford, Wealdstone, Worcester City.

Qualifying Round
HFS LOANS LEAGUE

Buxton 4 *(Nixon, Camilleri 2, O'Malley)*
Gainsborough Trinity 3 *(Dwyer 2, Kay)* 209

Fleetwood Town 3 *(Clarkson, Farnsworth 2)*
Horwich RMI 0 343

Frickley Athletic 2 *(Heaney, Birch)*
Matlock Town 0 265

Mossley 0
Gateshead 2 *(Howey, Harnett)* 251

Rhyl 1 *(Dougherty)*
Stalybridge Celtic 0 446

Shepshed Charterhouse 0
Goole Town 2 *(Shutt, Gauden)* 181

South Liverpool 1 *(Mather)*
Marine 3 142

Witton Albion 3 *(Whitlow, Edwars, Jarvis)*
Southport 1 307

Byes to First Round
Bangor City, Barrow, Caenarfon Town, Hyde United, Morecambe, Worksop Town.

Qualifying Round
VAUXHALL-OPEL LEAGUE

Barking 2 *(Field, Engwell)*
Marlow 0 102

Bishop's Stortford 2 *(Gayle, Zachhau (pen))*
Tooting & Mitcham 1 *(Blackman)* 429

Bognor Regis Town 2 *(Pullen, Guille)*
Hendon 2 *(Dowrie, Mullings)* aet 287

Hendon 2 *(Duffield, Dowie)*
Bognor Regis Town 0 Replay 144

Farnborough Town 2 *(Fielder, Horton)*
Carshalton Athletic 3 *(Russell, Budden, Kane)* aet 297

Grays Athletic 0
Leyton Wingate 2 *(Hamberger, Gordon)* 180

Harrow Borough 1 *(Dicker)*
Croydon 2 *(Daly, Hill)* 160

Kingstonian 0
Dulwich Hamlet 1 *(Gillings)* aet 210

Windsor & Eton 2 *(Woods, Tough)*
St. Albans City 1 *(Oliver)* 202

Byes to First Round
Bromley, Dagenham, Hayes, Leytonstone Ilford, Slough Town, Wokingham Town.

First Round Proper

Alvechurch 2 *(Chappell, Pinnock)*
Buxton 2 *(Bunter, Bartholomew)* aet 161

Buxton 4 *(Dove, Brown, Bartholomew, Bunter)*
Alvechurch 2 *(Whitehouse, Shepherd)* Replay 258

Bangor City 4 *(Edwards, Aspinal, Ferguson, Livens)*
Altrincham 0 375

Barking 3 *(Engwell, Callcut, Wallace)*
Bromley 1 *(Carmichael)* 134

Bromsgrove Rovers 2 *(Rosegreen, Cunningham)*
Boston United 1 *(Cook)* 727

Burton Albion 2 *(Cotterill 2)*
Cambridge City 0 527

Caenarfon Town 3 *(Craven 2, Steel)*
Fleetwood Town 0 Replay 146

Crawley Town 2 *(Boyce, Tiltman)*
Dulwich Hamlet 0 429

Dagenham 1 *(Neal)*
Croydon *(Paterson, Simpson, Dolke)* 253

Dorchester Town 0
Cheltenham Town 3 *(Shearer, Jenkins, og)* 179

Dover Athletic 3 *(Davis, Hare, Kemp)*
Carshalton Athletic 2 *(Russell, Rogers)* aet 546

Enfield 3 *(Reeves, Francis, Furlong)*
Bishops Stortford 4 *(Hoddle, English 3)* aet 430

Fleetwood Town 1 *(Clarkson)*
Caenarfon Town 1 *(Steele)* aet 301

Frickley Athletic 3
Gateshead 0 245

Goole Town 2 *(Ray, Gauden)*
Hyde United 4 *(Edwards, Rudge 2, Harris)* 269

Hayes 5 *(Kelly 2, Graves 2, Walton)*
Slough Town 1 *(Thompson)* Replay 293

Kidderminster Harriers 2 *(Shilvock, Davis)*
Telford United 0 1234

Leytonstone Ilford 1 *(own goal)*
Welling United 0 100

Leyton Wingate 2 *(Campbell, Baker)*
Hendon 1 *(Dowie)* 92

Maidstone United 2 *(Ashford, Rogers)*
Fisher Athletic 0 373

Marine 4 *(Smith, Grant, Ham, Bennett)*
Rhyl 1 *(Crooks)* 149

Moor Green 1 *(Busst)*
Corby Town 6 *(Hofbauer 3, Hines, Johnson, Rayment (pen))* 134

Runcorn 1 *(Anderson)*
Barrow 0 481

Slough Town 2 *(Dodd, Stanley)*
Hayes 2 *(Court, Kelly)* aet 392

Morecambe 0
Chorley 0 518

Chorley 2 *(Hughes, Moss)*
Morecambe 2 *(Stimpson, Pawsey)* Replay 802
(Morecambe won on penalties)

Stafford Rangers 2 *(Thacker, Knight)*
Northwich Victoria 1 *(O'Connor)* 511

Wealdstone 2 *(Olaleye, Lynch)*
Aylesbury United 0 293

Weymouth 1 *(own goal)*
Fareham Town 0 255

Windsor & Eton 1 *(Franks)*
Barnet 4 *(Turner, Sansom 2, Wilson)* 302

Witton Albion 2 *(Lodge, Jarvis)*
Macclesfield Town 0 733

Wokingham Town 1 *(own goal)*
Wycombe Wanderers 2 *(Regan, Young)* aet 695

Worcester City 2 *(Powell 2)*
Bath City 0 548

Worksop Town 0
Kettering Town 3 *(Fuccillo, Keast, Wright)* 348

Yeovil Town 4 *(Stephens, Randall 2, Pearson)*
Newport County 5 *(Abbruzzese, Banks 2, Sanderson 2)* aet 1838

Dartford 1 *(Davidson)*
Sutton United 2 *(Rains, Turner)* 581

Second Round Proper

Bromsgrove Rovers 1 *(Rosegreen)*
Barnet 2 *(Evans, Murphy)* 655

Buxton 3
Newport County 4 *(Saunderson, Sugrue 3)* 429

Continued on Page 916

HFS LOANS LEAGUE 1988–89

HFS LOANS LEAGUE – PREMIER DIVISION

		Home			*Goals*		*Away*			*Goals*		
	P	*W*	*D*	*L*	*F*	*A*	*W*	*D*	*L*	*F*	*A*	*Pts*
Barrow	42	15	2	4	38	17	11	7	3	31	18	87
Hyde United	42	14	4	3	49	17	10	4	7	28	27	80
Witton Albion	42	13	5	3	40	16	9	8	4	27	23	79
Bangor City	42	12	4	5	40	24	10	6	5	37	24	76
Marine	42	12	5	4	39	21	11	2	8	30	27	76
Goole Town	42	14	2	5	49	31	8	5	8	26	29	73
Fleetwood Town	42	12	6	3	28	16	7	10	4	30	28	73
Rhyl	42	10	6	5	43	30	8	4	9	32	35	64
Frickley Ath	42	11	5	5	38	25	6	5	10	26	28	61
Mossley	42	9	6	6	24	19	8	3	10	32	39	60
South Liverpool	42	8	7	6	36	29	7	6	8	29	28	58
Caernarfon Town	42	8	6	7	21	20	7	4	10	29	43	55
Matlock Town	42	12	4	5	47	32	4	1	16	18	41	53
Southport	42	7	6	8	36	22	6	6	9	30	30	51
Buxton	42	6	9	6	35	30	6	5	10	26	33	50
Morecambe*1	42	9	6	6	35	25	4	3	14	20	35	47
Gainsborough T	42	7	5	9	33	35	5	6	10	23	38	47
Shepshed Ch*6	42	8	5	8	27	21	6	3	12	22	39	44
Stalybridge C	42	3	8	10	20	35	6	5	10	26	46	40
Horwich	42	4	6	11	19	35	3	8	10	23	35	35
Gateshead	42	6	5	10	18	24	1	8	12	18	46	34
Worksop Town	42	4	1	16	22	58	2	4	15	20	45	23

* – pts deducted for breaches of rule.

Barrow promoted to GM Vauxhall Conference.
Worksop Town relegated to First Division.
Colne Dynamoes and Bishop Auckland promoted to Premier Division.

Goals scored – 1319 in 462 matches (average 2.854).

Sutton Town relegated to Northern Counties East.
Emley promoted from Northern Counties East.
Rossendale United promoted from North West Counties.

Leading scorers *(HFS Loans League and HFS cups only)*

Premier Division
26 Graham Hoyland (Gainsborough Trinity)
25 Mark Edwards (Witton Albion)
Ian Cain (Fleetwood Town)
22 Colin Cowperthwaite (Barrow)
Jim McCluskie (Mossley)
21 David Eyres (Rhyl)
20 Karl Thomas (South Liverpool)
19 Graham Bennett (Marine)
Paul Crooks (Bangor City, 12 with Rhyl)
18 Bob Gauden (Goole Town)
Malcolm Wagstaffe (Stalybridge Celtic)
17 John Sheppard (Matlock Town)
16 Clint Neysmith (Southport)
Mike Lutkevitch (Hyde United)
15 Mark Ferguson (ex-Bangor City, now Runcorn)
Michael Downing (Frickley Athletic)
13 Barry Diamond (Hyde United)
Malcolm Poskett (Morecambe)

First Division
31 Martin Horsfield (Lancaster City)
29 Dave Lancaster (Colne Dynamoes)
27 Steve Piggett (Congleton Town)
Mike Biddle (Congleton Town)
Graham Millington (Eastwood Town)
25 Kevin Hulme (Radcliffe Borough)
24 Ian Crumplin (Whitley Bay)
Bernard Hughes (Droysden)
17 Martyn Smith (Leek Town)
Rob Grant (Bishop Auckland)
16 Mark Hamilton (Harrogate Town)
Darren Lyone (Droylsden)
Tommy Nicholson (Sutton Town)
15 Gary Messenger (Workington)
Phil Layhe (Irlam Town)
Graeme Nicholson (Workington)
14 Andy Milner (ex-Netherfield, now Man. City)
Peter McCrae (Lancaster City)
Dave Goostrey (Winsford United)
Trevor Russell (Leek Town)
Simon Gate (Penrith)
Garry Haire (Whitley Bay)

HFS LOANS LEAGUE – FIRST DIVISION

		Home			*Goals*		*Away*			*Goals*		
	P	*W*	*D*	*L*	*F*	*A*	*W*	*D*	*L*	*F*	*A*	*Pts*
Colne Dynamoes*3	42	18	3	0	61	5	12	8	1	41	16	98
Bishop Auckland	42	16	2	3	42	11	12	3	6	36	17	89
Leek Town*1	42	12	6	3	36	17	13	5	3	38	24	85
Droylsden	42	14	5	2	49	23	11	4	6	35	25	84
Whitley Bay	42	12	4	5	39	22	11	2	8	38	27	75
Accrington Stan.	42	11	6	4	55	33	10	4	7	26	27	73
Lancaster City	42	13	3	5	39	24	8	5	8	37	30	71
Harrogate Town	42	13	3	5	47	22	6	4	11	21	39	64
Newtown	42	9	8	4	39	24	6	4	11	26	35	57
Congleton Town	42	11	5	5	32	21	4	6	11	30	45	56
Workington	42	13	1	7	41	27	4	2	15	18	47	54
Eastwood Town	42	8	5	8	31	31	6	5	10	24	30	52
Curzon Ashton	42	8	4	9	44	37	5	7	9	30	35	50
Farsley Celtic	42	9	9	3	34	27	3	4	14	18	46	49
Irlam Town	42	7	7	7	30	29	4	7	10	23	34	47
Penrith	42	11	3	7	33	35	3	2	16	28	56	47
Radcliffe Bor	42	10	4	7	38	35	2	6	13	24	51	46
Eastwood Hanley	42	7	7	7	28	28	4	5	12	18	39	45
Winsford United	42	11	4	6	33	23	2	2	17	25	70	45
Alfreton Town	42	5	6	10	25	42	3	5	13	19	50	35
Netherfield*1	42	5	2	14	34	47	3	7	11	23	43	32
Sutton Town*4	42	6	3	12	40	45	1	3	17	30	64	23

* – pts deducted for breaches of rule.

Goals scored – 1458 in 462 matches (average 3.155).

HFS LOANS LEAGUE PREMIER DIVISION RESULTS 1988–89

	Bangor C	Barrow	Buxton	Caernarfon T	Fleetwood T	Frickley Ath	Gainsborough Tr	Gateshead	Goole T	Horwich	Hyde Utd	Marine	Matlock T	Morecambe	Mossley	Rhyl	Shepshed Ch	S Liverpool	Southport	Stalybridge	Witton Alb	Worksop T
Bangor C	—	1-2	0-1	1-1	0-0	1-0	1-1	3-0	2-3	3-2	1-2	3-2	2-0	3-0	3-2	3-1	1-0	2-2	3-0	3-1	2-3	2-1
Barrow	1-0	—	1-0	1-0	2-3	2-0	3-0	2-0	3-2	2-1	1-1	0-2	1-0	3-1	2-2	2-0	1-2	0-2	3-1	4-0	3-0	1-0
Buxton	1-1	5-2	—	1-1	1-0	1-1	1-2	1-1	1-0	0-0	1-2	1-1	4-0	0-3	0-1	0-2	3-3	1-3	3-3	4-1	2-2	4-1
Caernarfon T	0-1	0-1	3-1	—	2-2	0-3	0-1	1-1	0-1	2-2	1-0	2-1	2-0	1-0	0-2	0-1	1-0	2-1	1-1	2-0	0-0	1-1
Fleetwood T.	2-0	2-0	2-1	1-0	—	1-0	1-1	1-1	1-0	2-0	0-2	2-3	4-2	1-0	2-1	1-1	1-1	1-1	1-0	0-0	0-1	2-1
Frickley Ath	0-4	2-1	1-2	2-3	1-1	—	3-0	4-1	2-1	3-3	2-0	2-1	2-0	1-0	5-0	0-3	3-1	2-0	0-0	2-2	0-1	1-1
Gainsborough Tr	2-2	1-2	1-3	1-2	1-1	1-2	—	1-0	1-2	1-1	2-2	1-2	2-1	1-0	3-0	6-1	2-0	0-4	2-1	0-3	3-3	1-3
Gateshead	0-0	1-2	2-1	0-2	0-1	1-1	2-1	—	1-3	1-0	2-0	1-1	0-1	1-0	1-2	1-1	0-2	0-0	1-2	1-2	0-1	2-1
Goole T	3-1	0-2	1-1	6-2	4-3	2-1	2-3	4-2	—	3-1	4-0	0-1	2-1	2-3	1-3	3-2	1-0	2-1	2-1	2-2	3-0	2-1
Horwich	0-3	0-3	0-1	3-0	1-1	1-4	0-4	1-1	1-1	—	0-2	0-1	1-1	1-2	0-1	2-1	0-1	2-0	2-5	1-0	2-2	1-1
Hyde Utd	2-1	0-2	3-2	4-0	1-1	1-0	2-0	5-0	3-0	0-0	—	4-1	3-1	0-1	2-2	4-2	3-0	1-2	2-0	4-0	2-2	3-0
Marine	1-2	0-0	3-1	1-1	4-1	0-1	2-0	1-0	0-2	2-2	3-1	—	3-1	2-0	3-1	3-1	5-2	0-2	2-2	1-1	2-0	1-0
Matlock T	4-2	0-2	5-4	2-3	2-3	2-1	2-2	3-1	3-1	0-0	2-1	2-4	—	3-2	2-0	2-1	1-2	1-0	2-2	3-0	0-0	6-1
Morecambe	1-2	1-1	1-1	3-1	0-2	2-1	5-2	2-0	0-0	1-0	2-2	3-1	1-2	—	3-3	2-0	2-0	2-2	0-1	1-2	0-1	3-1
Mossley	1-2	1-1	1-0	1-1	1-1	2-1	2-0	1-1	2-0	1-0	0-1	0-1	2-1	2-0	—	1-1	2-1	0-1	0-2	1-2	1-1	2-1
Rhyl	2-2	1-1	0-1	1-0	1-1	3-3	1-1	1-1	0-1	6-1	1-2	0-2	2-0	2-1	4-0	—	6-1	4-3	1-0	4-3	1-5	2-1
Shepshed Ch.	1-1	1-1	1-1	0-1	1-2	2-0	2-0	3-1	0-2	1-2	0-3	2-0	2-0	2-2	2-1	1-1	—	3-0	0-1	3-0	0-1	0-1
S Liverpool	1-3	1-2	1-1	5-1	0-2	0-0	4-1	1-1	0-0	4-2	1-2	1-0	1-0	3-1	0-2	1-3	4-1	—	2-1	4-4	1-1	1-1
Southport	0-2	1-1	1-0	5-0	3-1	1-3	0-0	7-0	1-1	0-2	0-2	0-1	4-0	1-1	4-1	1-2	0-0	2-2	—	0-1	0-1	5-1
Stalybridge	2-2	0-4	2-3	0-2	1-1	1-2	1-1	2-2	1-1	1-1	0-1	1-2	1-0	1-1	0-3	0-1	0-3	1-2	2-2	—	1-0	2-1
Witton Alb.	0-1	0-0	1-1	3-0	1-1	1-1	4-0	2-0	3-0	2-1	2-2	1-0	1-3	3-1	1-0	2-3	2-0	1-0	1-0	6-1	—	3-1
Worksop T	0-5	0-1	3-0	2-7	1-2	3-1	0-3	0-4	4-5	0-2	2-0	1-3	1-4	2-1	1-5	0-4	1-2	1-1	0-5	0-1	0-2	—

HFS LOANS LEAGUE – FIRST DIVISION RESULTS 1988–89

	Accrington S	Alfreton T	B. Auckland	Colne Dyn	Congleton T	Curzon Ashton	Droylsden	Eastwood Han	Eastwood T	Farsley C	Harrogate T	Irlam Town	Lancaster C	Leek Town	Netherfield	Newtown	Penrith	Radcliffe Bor	Sutton T	Whitley Bay	Winsford U	Workington
Accrington S	—	2-1	1-2	2-2	1-0	1-3	1-0	3-0	2-2	7-0	1-1	3-2	2-2	0-3	3-1	3-1	7-4	6-1	2-2	1-2	4-1	3-3
Alfreton T	1-1	—	0-3	0-3	1-3	3-3	1-3	0-0	0-1	2-2	1-0	1-1	1-2	2-4	1-4	2-2	1-0	2-1	4-3	0-4	2-1	0-1
B. Auckland	2-0	3-0	—	0-1	1-0	2-0	0-0	3-1	3-0	2-1	0-0	2-0	3-2	0-1	4-0	3-0	1-0	2-1	3-1	1-2	3-1	4-0
Colne Dyn	5-0	6-0	0-0	—	4-0	2-0	2-0	5-0	2-0	2-0	1-0	2-1	1-0	6-0	1-1	0-0	4-0	2-1	5-1	3-0	2-1	6-0
Congleton T	3-3	0-3	1-0	0-0	—	3-3	0-1	2-1	2-0	2-1	0-1	1-1	1-0	0-1	3-1	4-0	1-0	1-1	4-2	0-1	2-0	2-1
Curzon Ashton	3-1	5-1	2-3	0-5	1-1	—	4-2	2-0	0-1	2-2	0-1	0-2	0-1	1-3	2-2	2-2	1-2	2-1	5-0	3-4	6-2	3-1
Droylsden	2-1	2-0	1-0	1-1	3-1	2-3	—	5-0	1-1	4-1	3-1	1-1	3-0	2-2	1-1	2-0	5-4	3-1	1-3	2-1	4-1	1-0
Eastwood Han	0-1	1-1	0-1	1-1	0-0	1-1	0-1	—	2-1	3-4	2-2	3-0	2-7	0-0	0-0	0-1	1-0	2-3	1-0	2-1	5-2	2-1
Eastwood T	2-3	4-2	0-1	0-1	3-1	0-0	1-2	1-1	—	2-1	2-0	1-0	0-1	1-7	1-1	1-3	0-2	2-2	1-0	1-1	4-2	4-0
Farsley C	0-0	1-1	3-2	0-1	2-2	1-1	2-0	2-1	3-3	—	3-0	1-1	0-4	2-2	0-2	2-1	2-0	1-1	3-1	2-1	2-1	2-2
Harrogate	0-1	3-0	0-2	0-1	1-4	2-2	2-2	1-1	2-0	2-0	—	3-0	2-1	3-1	1-2	2-0	2-1	5-1	3-2	1-0	9-1	3-0
Irlam Town	0-4	0-0	0-1	2-2	1-1	3-1	2-2	1-1	1-0	3-1	1-0	—	2-2	1-2	1-1	1-3	5-2	1-0	4-1	0-2	1-2	0-1
Lancaster C	2-1	3-2	1-0	2-3	3-1	0-0	2-3	2-1	2-2	1-0	1-2	1-0	—	0-1	2-0	0-3	4-1	3-1	2-2	1-0	5-1	2-0
Leek Town	0-1	4-0	2-1	1-1	2-2	2-1	0-1	0-1	1-1	0-0	4-1	3-1	2-0	—	2-1	1-0	2-0	2-0	4-2	2-2	1-1	1-0
Netherfield	0-2	1-1	0-5	1-5	1-2	2-1	2-6	1-2	1-2	1-2	1-2	1-2	0-2	0-1	—	4-1	0-0	5-0	7-1	1-5	1-3	4-2
Newtown	0-1	2-2	1-1	0-0	2-0	3-4	1-1	2-2	1-3	0-0	3-1	1-1	4-1	4-2	3-0	—	1-1	2-1	2-1	0-1	4-0	3-1
Penrith	1-3	2-0	0-4	2-2	3-1	1-0	0-3	0-2	0-4	2-1	2-2	2-0	1-4	0-1	3-1	3-2	—	2-2	3-2	2-1	2-0	2-0
Radcliffe Bor	0-2	0-2	1-1	1-4	2-3	3-0	3-2	2-1	2-0	0-1	2-0	2-4	2-2	2-2	2-1	1-0	5-2	—	3-2	2-4	1-1	2-1
Sutton T	4-0	6-0	2-1	1-4	6-6	0-4	1-2	2-3	1-0	4-1	1-3	2-2	0-3	0-1	1-1	2-3	3-5	2-3	—	0-1	2-1	0-1
Whitley Bay	0-0	3-0	1-4	1-2	2-0	2-0	0-2	1-0	3-1	1-0	4-2	1-1	2-2	0-2	4-0	1-0	5-1	2-2	2-0	—	4-2	0-1
Winsford U	0-1	0-2	0-2	1-0	4-2	2-1	0-2	3-0	1-0	2-0	1-2	1-2	2-1	0-0	5-1	1-1	3-1	1-1	1-1	2-1	—	3-2
Workington	2-0	2-1	1-2	0-2	2-0	0-2	1-0	1-0	0-2	4-0	6-0	2-1	0-0	0-2	3-2	0-3	3-2	3-0	4-3	1-4	6-1	—

CUP HONOURS – 1988–89

H.F.S. Challenge Cup – Winners, Mossley; Runners-up, Fleetwood Town.
H.F.S. President's Cup – Winners, Bangor City; Runners-up, South Liverpool.
H.F.S. First Division Cup – Winners, Whitley Bay; Runners-up, Leek Town.

THE BEAZER HOMES LEAGUE 1988–89

PREMIER DIVISION

	P	W	D	L	F	A	Pts
Merthyr Tydfil	42	26	7	9	104	58	85
Dartford	42	25	7	10	79	33	82
VS Rugby	42	24	7	11	64	43	79
Worcester City	42	20	13	9	72	49	73
Cambridge City	42	20	10	12	72	51	70
Dover Athletic	42	19	12	11	65	47	69
Gosport Borough	42	18	12	12	73	57	66
Burton Albion	42	18	10	14	79	68	64
Bath City	42	15	13	14	66	51	58
Bromsgrove Rovers	42	14	16	12	68	56	58
Wealdstone	42	16	10	16	60	53	58
Crawley Town	42	14	16	12	61	56	58
Dorchester Town	42	14	16	12	56	61	58
Alvechurch	42	16	8	18	56	59	56
Moor Green	42	14	13	15	58	70	55
Corby Town	42	14	11	17	55	59	53
Waterlooville	42	13	13	16	61	63	52
Ashford Town	42	13	13	16	59	76	52
Fareham Town	42	15	6	21	43	68	51
Leicester Town	42	6	11	25	46	84	29
Redditch United	42	5	7	30	36	105	22
Bedworth United	42	4	7	31	36	102	19

MIDLAND DIVISION

	P	W	D	L	F	A	Pts
Gloucester City	42	28	8	6	95	37	92
Atherstone United	42	26	9	7	85	38	87
Tamworth	42	26	9	7	85	45	87
Halesowen Town	42	25	10	7	85	42	85
Grantham Town	42	23	11	8	66	37	80
Nuneaton Borough	42	19	9	14	71	58	66
Rushden Town	42	19	8	15	71	50	65
Spalding United	42	17	13	12	72	64	64
Dudley Town	42	16	13	13	73	62	61
Sutton Coldfield Town	42	18	7	17	56	56	61
Willenhall Town	42	16	12	14	65	71	60
Forest Green Rovers	42	12	16	14	64	67	52
Bilston Town	42	15	7	20	63	71	52
Ashtree Highfield	42	12	15	15	57	62	51
Hednesford Town	42	12	15	15	49	57	51
Banbury United	42	10	14	18	53	74	44
Bridgnorth Town	42	12	7	23	59	77	43
Stourbridge	42	11	10	21	37	65	43
King's Lynn	42	7	13	22	31	67	34
Coventry Sporting	42	6	13	23	39	91	31
Wellingborough Town	42	5	15	22	39	72	30
Mile Oak Rovers	42	5	10	27	46	98	25

SOUTHERN DIVISION

	P	W	D	L	F	A	Pts
Chelmsford City	42	30	5	7	106	38	95
Gravesend & Northfleet	42	27	6	9	70	40	87
Poole Town	42	24	11	7	98	48	83
Bury Town	42	25	7	10	75	34	82
Burnham	42	22	13	7	78	47	79
Baldock Town	42	23	5	14	69	40	74
Hastings Town	42	21	11	10	75	48	74
Hounslow	42	21	6	15	75	60	69
Salisbury	42	20	5	17	79	58	65
Trowbridge Town	42	19	7	16	59	52	64
Folkestone	42	17	8	17	62	65	59
Corinthian	42	13	13	16	59	69	52
Canterbury City	42	14	8	20	52	60	50
Witney Town	42	13	11	18	61	71	50
Dunstable	42	11	14	17	42	57	47
Buckingham Town	42	12	10	20	56	79	46
Erith & Belvedere	42	11	10	21	48	63	43
Andover	42	11	9	22	56	90	42
Sheppey United	42	10	8	24	50	90	38
Thanet United	42	7	15	20	47	95	36
Tonbridge AFC	42	7	6	29	50	98	27
Ruislip	42	6	8	28	47	112	26

Westgate Insurance Cup
Dartford 1, Burton Albion 1 att. 925
Burton Albion 0, Dartford 2 att. 1991

Merit Cup Winners *(Most League Goals)*
Chelmsford City

LEADING GOALSCORERS

(League and League Cup)

Premier Division

M. Whitehouse (Burton Albion)	42
D. Webley (Merthyr Tydfil)	37
C. Hanks (Bromsgrove Rovers)	25
K. Wilkin (Cambridge City)	25
A. Canning (Burton Albion)	23
S. Cotterill (Burton Albion)	23
P. Taylor (Dartford)	22
L. Lee (Dover Athletic)	22
D. Arter (Ashford Town)	21
L. Maddocks (Fareham Town)	20

Midland Division

C. Townsend (Gloucester City)	31
J. Muir (Dudley Town)	30
A. Rammell (Atherstone United)	28
P. Joinson (Halesowen Town)	27
S. Penney (Gloucester City)	26
T. Shrieves (Rushden Town)	25
N. Civil (Ashtree Highfield)	23
M. Stanton (Tamworth)	23
M. Richards (Bilston Town)	21
M. Devaney (Tamworth)	20

Southern Division

G. Manson (Poole Town)	28
T. Funnell (Poole Town)	25
M. Springett (Chelmsford City)	23
D. Lansley (Burnham)	20
I. Pickering (Folkestone)	20
D. Platt (Salisbury)	19
I. Chalk (Salisbury)	18
V. Schwartz (Hounslow)	18
K. Alexander (Erith & Belvedere)	17
A. Douglas (Gravesend & Northfleet)	17
M. Freeman (Corinthian)	17

BEAZER HOMES SOUTHERN LEAGUE PREMIER DIVISION RESULTS 1988–89

	Alvechurch	Ashford T	Bath C	Bedworth U	Bromsgrove R	Burton A	Cambridge C	Corby T	Crawley T	Dartford	Dorchester T	Dover Ath	Fareham T	Gosport Bor	Leicester U	Merthyr Tydfil	Moor Green	Redditch U	VS Rugby	Waterlooville	Wealdstone	Worcester C
Alvechurch	—	0-0	1-0	3-0	2-1	3-4	1-1	0-1	2-1	1-0	1-0	2-3	0-2	3-1	0-1	4-3	1-1	3-1	1-2	2-1	2-1	0-2
Ashford T	0-1	—	2-1	4-1	2-1	1-3	3-1	1-1	2-2	0-0	1-1	3-2	1-0	1-1	0-3	1-3	0-0	1-1	0-2	1-1	3-2	1-2
Bath C	1-0	4-0	—	6-0	0-0	5-1	1-1	1-1	0-0	4-2	0-0	2-1	1-1	1-3	2-1	2-3	0-2	5-0	1-1	0-2	1-0	1-1
Bedworth U	1-1	0-3	2-3	—	1-1	1-7	2-0	0-5	1-1	0-6	0-1	0-2	0-2	1-1	1-1	0-2	1-3	4-1	2-5	0-2	1-2	0-1
Bromsgrove R	1-1	2-2	3-1	3-0	—	2-3	6-0	2-1	0-2	0-2	3-0	3-3	2-0	1-1	4-3	1-1	2-1	2-0	1-2	0-0	2-1	2-2
Burton A	2-4	0-2	2-1	3-1	3-0	—	2-2	0-0	1-1	3-2	1-0	2-0	4-0	2-3	2-0	1-1	2-1	4-2	0-2	2-0	2-2	3-2
Cambridge C	3-1	1-1	1-1	3-2	1-1	2-1	—	0-2	2-0	1-0	1-0	0-1	1-2	7-1	4-0	1-2	1-2	5-0	3-0	2-1	2-1	0-2
Corby T	1-1	1-3	1-1	3-1	0-4	3-3	0-2	—	1-1	0-4	1-1	3-0	1-0	3-3	1-0	4-2	1-2	1-0	1-2	3-1	2-0	1-1
Crawley T	4-2	2-3	1-1	2-2	1-1	1-1	2-0	2-1	—	1-3	1-1	2-0	2-4	0-2	3-1	1-1	2-1	2-0	2-4	0-2	1-1	2-0
Dartford	2-1	1-0	1-0	1-0	0-1	3-0	0-0	3-0	1-0	—	4-0	1-1	3-0	4-2	3-0	0-2	5-1	1-0	1-0	1-1	0-1	2-0
Dorchester T	2-1	1-1	1-0	4-2	1-1	1-1	2-2	0-1	2-3	1-5	—	2-2	0-0	3-2	2-1	4-2	1-1	4-1	1-1	2-1	1-3	3-3
Dover Ath	1-0	2-1	0-1	3-0	0-0	3-1	1-3	0-3	1-1	1-0	4-0	—	1-1	1-0	1-1	2-3	3-1	3-2	1-0	2-1	2-0	2-2
Fareham T	3-4	2-1	0-2	1-1	0-1	0-1	0-4	2-0	2-1	1-0	0-1	0-1	—	0-1	1-0	0-3	1-0	2-1	2-1	1-1	2-1	1-1
Gosport Bor	2-0	5-1	4-0	1-0	3-0	2-0	4-2	2-1	2-2	1-2	1-0	0-1	5-0	—	3-0	0-3	1-1	2-0	0-1	1-2	2-2	2-0
Leicester U	1-1	4-0	2-1	1-0	1-1	0-4	1-2	1-3	0-1	3-3	0-1	1-1	2-5	2-2	—	2-1	3-3	0-1	1-2	0-4	0-2	1-1
Merthyr Tydfil	2-1	6-1	3-1	2-0	3-1	3-1	2-3	3-0	3-1	1-2	2-2	2-0	3-1	1-1	3-1	—	6-0	4-2	3-1	5-0	1-1	4-2
Moor Green	1-2	2-2	1-1	3-1	1-1	2-1	2-1	1-0	1-1	1-1	1-3	1-1	2-1	1-1	2-1	2-0	—	2-2	0-2	3-2	3-1	1-3
Redditch U	2-1	1-5	0-6	0-2	2-1	2-2	1-5	0-0	0-2	0-2	1-2	0-6	1-2	0-2	2-1	3-3	1-2	—	1-3	1-1	2-0	0-1
VS Rugby	1-1	2-1	1-2	2-0	2-5	2-0	0-0	1-0	0-2	1-1	3-1	1-0	2-0	1-1	2-2	1-2	2-0	2-0	—	2-1	2-0	0-1
Waterlooville	0-1	1-3	3-2	3-1	3-3	1-1	0-1	3-1	2-1	1-4	1-3	1-1	3-0	2-0	2-2	4-1	3-2	2-2	0-2	—	0-0	1-1
Wealdstone	2-0	4-1	1-2	3-1	3-2	2-1	0-0	2-1	1-3	1-3	0-0	0-0	3-0	3-0	2-1	0-3	4-0	4-0	2-0	1-1	—	0-2
Worcester C	1-0	6-0	1-1	1-3	1-0	3-2	0-1	3-1	1-1	1-0	1-1	0-5	5-1	2-2	5-0	3-1	2-1	3-0	0-1	2-0	1-1	—

BEAZER HOMES SOUTHERN LEAGUE SOUTHERN DIVISION RESULTS 1988–89

	Andover	Baldock T	Buckingham T	Burnham	Bury T	Canterbury C	Chelmsford C	Corinthian	Dunstable	Erith & Belvedere	Folkestone	Gravesend & Northfleet	Hastings T	Hounslow	Poole T	Ruislip M	Salisbury	Sheppey U	Thanet U	Tonbridge T	Trowbridge T	Witney T
Andover	—	1-0	1-3	1-2	1-4	0-1	1-4	0-0	2-1	2-0	1-1	1-4	3-3	1-1	0-2	1-4	2-2	2-3	0-0	2-1	1-2	1-3
Baldock T	0-1	—	3-0	0-1	4-1	2-0	0-2	0-0	1-0	1-0	2-1	0-1	1-2	2-1	0-1	4-0	2-1	3-1	0-0	4-2	1-2	4-0
Buckingham T	1-2	2-0	—	1-3	1-2	0-0	2-2	0-2	0-2	1-1	0-0	0-1	1-1	2-3	0-8	4-2	0-0	0-2	2-2	1-1	3-0	2-0
Burnham	2-2	4-1	2-0	—	1-1	1-0	2-1	3-3	1-2	0-1	2-0	1-1	1-0	3-0	1-1	1-1	4-1	6-1	1-1	3-0	1-3	2-2
Bury Town	2-0	1-0	8-0	0-0	—	0-1	0-1	6-1	0-0	1-0	2-1	1-2	2-0	4-0	1-2	2-0	1-0	2-0	3-0	2-0	2-0	3-0
Canterbury C	3-2	0-0	0-1	0-2	0-0	—	0-1	3-1	0-0	2-3	0-1	1-2	3-1	2-0	3-3	0-1	0-1	2-1	1-2	6-0	2-0	0-1
Chelmsford C	2-0	1-0	2-1	0-3	0-2	1-2	—	4-1	3-0	8-0	5-2	3-0	0-0	2-1	3-2	3-2	4-1	6-0	4-1	5-0	1-0	1-0
Corinthian	5-1	1-0	2-5	3-4	1-3	1-2	0-0	—	0-2	1-1	4-4	0-2	1-4	1-2	0-3	4-0	1-0	0-3	2-2	2-1	0-1	3-2
Dunstable	3-2	0-2	2-0	0-0	2-2	2-1	1-1	0-1	—	1-1	0-3	0-0	1-1	2-2	0-1	5-0	0-5	2-5	1-1	1-0	2-0	0-0
Erith & Belvedere	0-1	1-3	0-1	1-2	5-0	4-2	0-2	1-1	2-1	—	4-2	0-0	0-1	1-3	0-2	2-0	1-2	5-1	2-2	3-1	0-1	1-0
Folkestone	2-0	1-4	4-1	3-2	0-1	1-1	1-2	0-3	2-1	1-1	—	1-2	1-1	1-2	2-0	2-1	1-0	4-0	1-1	2-1	1-0	1-3
Gravesend & Northfleet	3-1	2-1	0-4	1-0	0-3	2-0	0-2	1-1	1-0	1-0	0-1	—	1-0	2-1	1-2	5-1	2-0	0-0	3-0	5-0	3-0	0-1
Hastings T	1-2	1-2	3-1	2-1	1-4	4-0	1-0	0-1	0-0	4-1	3-1	0-3	—	3-2	1-1	2-0	5-2	5-1	1-1	2-1	2-2	2-2
Hounslow	1-1	1-3	2-1	1-2	1-0	1-1	3-0	0-2	0-0	3-0	3-1	1-4	1-3	—	1-0	3-1	1-2	3-0	8-1	1-1	2-0	3-1
Poole T	7-0	2-2	5-4	4-0	4-1	2-2	1-1	2-0	3-2	1-0	4-3	1-1	0-0	3-2	—	5-2	3-0	0-3	1-2	2-2	2-0	4-0
Ruislip M	4-2	1-3	2-2	2-5	0-2	0-1	0-9	0-0	0-3	1-1	0-1	2-4	0-2	0-1	1-5	—	1-5	2-2	2-2	2-2	3-1	1-4
Salisbury	1-1	1-3	0-1	2-3	3-1	3-2	1-2	1-1	4-0	2-1	0-2	5-0	0-2	0-1	2-0	4-1	—	5-0	5-2	3-2	2-0	4-0
Sheppey U	1-3	0-1	3-1	2-3	1-0	2-3	1-5	1-1	1-2	2-0	1-1	0-2	0-2	1-2	1-1	0-3	1-0	—	5-0	1-1	0-2	3-3
Thanet U	0-4	0-2	1-1	0-0	0-2	1-3	3-2	2-2	1-1	1-0	0-1	1-2	0-3	1-2	1-6	3-0	1-3	2-0	—	2-0	1-2	1-1
Tonbridge AFC	6-2	0-2	0-3	1-2	0-2	2-0	2-3	1-3	1-0	1-3	4-2	0-3	2-4	0-4	1-2	1-2	1-3	1-0	6-2	—	0-1	2-2
Trowbridge T	4-3	1-4	4-0	0-0	1-1	6-1	1-3	1-3	2-0	0-0	3-1	1-2	1-0	1-2	0-0	3-1	1-1	0-0	4-1	4-0	—	1-0
Witney T	1-2	2-2	1-3	1-1	0-0	2-1	0-5	1-0	5-0	1-1	0-1	3-1	1-2	4-3	2-0	1-1	1-2	4-0	6-2	0-2	0-3	—

BEAZER HOMES SOUTHERN LEAGUE MIDLAND DIVISION RESULTS 1988–89

	Ashtree Highfield	Atherstone U	Banbury U	Bilston T	Bridgnorth T	Coventry Sp	Dudley T	Forest Green R	Gloucester C	Grantham	Halesowen T	Hednesford T	King's Lynn	Mile Oak R	Nuneaton B	Rushden T	Spalding	Stourbridge	Sutton Coldfield T	Tamworth	Wellingborough T	Willenhall T
Ashtree Highfield	—	0-0	1-1	1-1	2-1	2-0	3-4	1-2	0-0	2-1	0-3	1-1	1-0	3-1	3-1	1-2	0-2	2-1	5-1	3-3	0-0	3-2
Atherstone U	2-2	—	1-1	2-0	2-1	3-0	6-1	1-0	1-1	3-1	2-1	4-0	1-1	1-0	2-1	2-1	2-4	4-1	2-0	2-2	2-1	3-0
Banbury U	0-2	0-4	—	1-3	5-1	2-2	0-0	2-2	1-1	0-1	1-1	4-0	2-0	3-2	1-1	1-0	1-1	1-2	2-1	0-2	1-0	3-1
Bilston T	2-0	0-3	3-1	—	2-6	2-0	1-1	4-0	0-3	2-3	2-5	6-1	3-0	4-2	0-1	1-0	1-1	0-0	3-1	0-2	4-2	2-1
Bridgnorth T	1-1	0-2	1-1	2-0	—	5-1	0-4	1-0	2-4	0-0	0-2	0-3	1-0	1-0	0-1	0-0	3-2	2-1	0-1	3-1	5-2	2-3
Coventry Sp	3-2	3-2	2-4	1-0	3-1	—	1-1	2-1	0-2	0-3	1-5	1-3	1-1	1-2	0-0	0-1	1-4	1-2	1-0	2-4	1-1	0-2
Dudley T	1-0	0-2	3-1	3-2	0-0	4-1	—	5-1	0-2	1-2	0-1	0-3	3-1	4-3	4-2	0-1	3-3	1-0	1-1	1-2	1-1	2-3
Forest Green R	0-1	1-1	3-1	2-1	0-0	1-1	1-1	—	0-2	5-1	0-2	4-2	4-1	3-0	2-4	1-1	0-2	6-1	3-3	0-4	1-1	2-2
Gloucester C	2-0	3-1	4-1	2-1	4-1	7-0	1-1	7-1	—	2-0	1-2	2-1	1-0	8-0	1-2	2-1	0-1	2-1	1-3	1-1	3-1	1-1
Grantham	0-0	1-0	6-0	2-1	2-0	4-0	1-1	0-0	1-1	—	0-1	1-0	1-0	2-1	3-0	3-0	1-0	0-2	2-1	0-0	0-0	2-2
Halesowen T	2-2	3-3	3-1	4-1	3-1	1-1	3-0	0-0	0-0	2-1	—	1-1	6-1	3-1	4-2	1-3	2-2	3-0	1-0	0-1	6-0	2-2
Hednesford T	2-0	0-1	1-1	0-1	2-1	3-1	1-3	1-1	2-1	0-0	2-3	—	0-0	3-0	1-1	1-0	0-1	2-1	0-0	0-2	2-2	0-0
Kings Lynn	2-2	1-1	1-0	0-0	2-1	1-1	0-0	0-2	0-2	0-2	0-0	0-2	—	3-2	0-0	0-0	3-0	0-1	1-0	2-2	1-0	3-1
Mile Oak R	3-2	1-0	2-2	3-1	2-2	5-1	1-3	2-7	0-2	0-2	0-2	1-1	1-1	—	0-1	1-5	1-1	1-1	0-1	0-2	1-1	4-4
Nuneaton B	3-0	3-1	5-0	2-2	2-1	1-0	1-3	1-2	1-2	1-1	3-0	3-1	2-1	1-0	—	1-1	0-3	3-0	1-3	4-3	4-1	2-3
Rushden T	0-0	0-1	4-0	3-1	4-3	2-0	2-1	1-0	2-3	0-3	0-1	2-1	7-0	5-0	2-2	—	3-1	3-1	0-2	3-3	3-1	3-2
Spalding	1-1	0-4	2-1	2-2	4-2	2-2	2-1	1-1	1-4	4-2	1-2	2-0	2-1	3-0	1-3	4-0	—	1-1	0-1	2-2	2-1	3-0
Stourbridge	1-0	1-0	0-3	2-0	0-2	0-0	2-1	1-1	1-2	2-3	2-1	1-1	3-2	0-0	1-1	0-4	0-0	—	0-2	0-1	0-1	0-0
Sutton Coldfield T	2-0	0-2	3-2	3-0	2-1	1-1	1-4	1-1	1-3	1-1	0-2	2-2	2-1	1-0	1-0	2-1	4-0	4-2	—	0-2	1-0	0-1
Tamworth	2-2	2-3	1-0	2-0	4-0	2-0	2-2	3-1	1-2	1-3	3-0	0-1	5-0	3-1	1-0	1-0	3-2	1-0	2-0	—	3-2	2-1
Wellingborough T	1-2	0-4	1-1	0-2	3-0	1-1	0-3	1-1	1-2	1-2	0-1	1-1	1-0	0-0	2-1	1-1	1-1	0-1	2-1	1-2	—	2-2
Willenhall T	5-4	0-2	0-0	1-2	0-5	1-1	1-1	0-1	2-1	0-2	1-0	1-1	1-0	4-2	1-3	1-0	4-1	3-1	3-2	1-0	2-1	—

VAUXHALL-OPEL LEAGUE 1988–89

Premier Division

		Home			*Goals*		*Away*			*Goals*		
	P	*W*	*D*	*L*	*F*	*A*	*W*	*D*	*L*	*F*	*A*	*Pts*
Leytonstone Ilford	42	15	5	1	45	21	11	6	4	31	15	89
Farnborough Town	42	14	2	5	48	29	10	7	4	37	32	81
Slough Town	42	14	2	5	43	20	10	4	7	29	22	78
Carshalton Athletic	42	11	6	4	26	12	8	9	4	33	24	72
Grays Athletic	42	11	6	4	42	26	8	7	6	20	21	70
Kingstonian	42	11	3	7	33	20	8	8	5	21	17	68
Bishop's Stortford	42	11	3	7	34	23	9	3	9	36	33	66
Hayes	42	11	5	5	34	24	7	7	7	27	23	66
Bognor Regis Town	42	10	5	6	21	20	7	6	8	17	29	62
Barking	42	8	8	5	23	16	8	5	8	26	29	61
Wokingham Town	42	7	7	7	31	19	8	4	9	29	35	56
Hendon	42	5	13	3	26	25	8	4	9	25	43	56
Windsor & Eton	42	8	5	8	30	27	6	8	7	22	23	55
Bromley	42	6	8	7	32	24	7	7	7	29	24	54
Leyton-Wingate	42	7	9	5	32	25	6	6	9	23	31	54
Dulwich Hamlet	42	7	7	7	32	29	5	5	11	26	28	48
St. Albans City	42	7	7	7	31	27	5	2	14	20	32	45
Dagenham	42	5	5	11	24	33	6	7	8	29	35	45
Harrow Borough	42	7	3	11	30	36	2	10	9	23	39	40
Marlow	42	3	8	10	26	38	6	3	12	22	45	38
Tooting & Mitcham U	42	8	3	10	25	35	2	3	16	16	46	36
Croydon	42	3	5	13	8	31	1	4	16	19	50	21

Division One

		Home			*Goals*		*Away*			*Goals*		
	P	*W*	*D*	*L*	*F*	*A*	*W*	*D*	*L*	*F*	*A*	*Pts*
Staines Town	40	14	5	1	45	13	12	4	4	34	16	87
Basingstoke Town	40	14	4	2	47	15	11	4	5	38	21	83
Woking	40	9	6	5	29	20	15	4	1	43	10	82
Hitchin Town	40	13	4	3	35	17	8	7	5	25	15	74
Wivenhoe Town	40	11	3	6	34	26	11	3	6	28	18	72
Lewes	40	13	2	5	40	23	8	6	6	32	31	71
Walton & Hersham	40	10	4	6	30	17	11	3	6	26	19	70
Kingsbury Town	40	12	2	6	37	21	8	5	7	28	20	67
Uxbridge	40	8	6	6	27	25	11	1	8	33	29	64
Wembley	40	8	5	7	22	29	10	1	9	23	29	60
Boreham Wood	40	8	5	7	36	28	8	4	8	21	24	57
Leatherhead	40	7	5	8	35	29	7	3	10	21	29	50
Metropolitan Police	40	8	4	8	31	34	5	5	10	21	34	48
Chesham United	40	7	5	8	28	28	5	4	11	26	39	45
Southwick	40	6	5	9	20	25	3	10	7	24	33	42
Chalfont St. Peter	40	7	4	9	33	37	4	5	11	23	45	42
Hampton	40	5	6	9	16	28	2	8	10	21	34	35
Worthing	40	5	5	10	20	31	3	5	12	29	49	*32
Collier Row	40	5	5	10	23	33	3	2	15	14	49	31
Bracknell Town	40	6	2	12	23	27	2	4	14	15	43	30
Basildon United	40	2	4	14	18	35	4	3	13	16	42	25

* 2 pts deducted by League

Division Two South

	P	*W*	*D*	*L*	*F*	*A*	*Pts*
Dorking	40	32	4	4	109	35	100
Whyteleafe	40	25	9	6	86	41	84
Finchley	40	21	9	10	70	45	72
Molesey	40	19	13	8	58	42	70
Harefield United	40	19	7	14	56	45	64
Hungerford Town	40	17	13	10	55	45	64
Ruislip Manor	40	16	9	15	56	43	57
Feltham	40	16	9	15	58	53	57
Epsom & Ewell	40	16	8	16	55	55	56
Egham Town	40	16	7	17	54	58	55
Eastbourne United	40	15	9	16	68	61	54
Chertsey Town	40	13	14	13	55	58	53
Flackwell Heath	40	13	11	16	51	49	50
Camberley Town	40	15	5	20	51	71	50
Yeading	40	13	9	18	47	63	*46
Banstead Athletic	40	12	8	20	50	65	44
Maidenhead United	40	10	13	17	44	61	43
Southall	40	11	10	19	41	73	43
Newbury Town	40	11	8	21	47	65	41
Horsham	40	7	14	19	36	68	35
Petersfield United	40	5	7	28	36	87	22

*2 pts deducted by League

AC Delco Cup: Bishop's Stortford 1, Farnborough T 0

Division Two North

	P	*W*	*D*	*L*	*F*	*A*	*Pts*
Harlow Town	42	27	9	6	83	38	90
Purfleet	42	22	12	8	60	42	78
Tring Town	42	22	10	10	65	44	76
Stevenage Borough	42	20	13	9	84	55	73
Heybridge Swifts	42	21	9	12	64	43	72
Billericay Town	42	19	11	12	65	52	68
Clapton	42	18	11	13	65	56	65
Barton Rovers	42	18	11	13	58	50	65
Aveley	42	18	10	14	54	52	64
Hertford Town	42	16	13	13	62	49	*59
Ware	42	17	8	17	60	65	59
Hemel Hempstead	42	16	10	16	55	58	58
Witham Town	42	16	7	19	69	67	55
Vauxhall Motors	42	15	9	18	53	57	54
Berkhamsted Town	42	14	10	18	57	70	52
Hornchurch	42	11	16	15	59	61	49
Tilbury	42	13	10	19	53	60	49
Royston Town	42	12	7	23	46	72	43
Rainham Town	42	9	15	18	49	62	42
Saffron Walden Town	42	8	16	18	54	72	40
Letchworth Garden C	42	4	18	20	34	71	30
Wolverton Town	42	5	7	30	42	95	**13

*2 pts deducted by League
**9 pts deducted by League

VAUXHALL-OPEL LEAGUE PREMIER DIVISION RESULTS 1988–89

	Barking	Bishop's Stortford	Bognor Regis T	Bromley	Carshalton Ath	Croydon	Dagenham	Dulwich Hamlet	Farnborough T	Grays Ath	Harrow Bor	Hayes	Hendon	Kingstonian	Leytonstone-Ilford	Leyton-Wingate	Marlow	St Albans C	Slough T	Tooting & Mitcham U	Windsor & Eton	Wokingham T
Barking	—	4-0	0-0	2-2	0-1	1-1	0-1	0-0	2-2	1-0	3-1	2-2	0-1	0-0	0-1	1-0	0-0	1-0	1-0	2-1	2-3	1-0
Bishops Stortford	0-1	—	1-3	2-1	0-1	3-0	3-3	1-0	0-1	1-0	2-0	3-2	3-2	0-1	1-0	1-2	1-1	1-1	4-0	2-1	4-1	1-2
Bognor Regis T	1-0	0-4	—	0-3	1-1	1-0	0-1	2-2	3-2	0-1	1-1	2-1	2-0	0-1	0-0	2-0	1-2	1-0	1-0	2-1	0-0	1-0
Bromley	1-2	2-0	1-2	—	1-1	3-2	3-3	1-2	4-0	0-0	1-1	1-1	0-1	1-1	0-2	1-1	6-0	0-1	0-1	3-1	1-1	2-1
Carshalton Ath	0-1	1-2	2-1	1-1	—	1-0	3-1	2-0	1-2	0-1	0-0	1-0	1-0	0-0	0-0	1-0	3-0	5-1	0-0	2-1	1-1	1-0
Croydon	1-2	0-3	0-1	0-3	1-1	—	1-1	1-0	0-1	0-1	0-0	0-2	1-1	0-2	0-3	0-0	1-0	0-2	0-2	0-3	0-3	2-0
Dagenham	1-2	0-2	0-0	0-4	2-1	5-2	—	1-2	1-2	2-3	2-1	0-0	1-2	3-2	1-4	1-1	0-2	1-1	0-1	0-0	0-1	3-0
Dulwich Hamlet	1-1	1-3	2-2	1-1	1-2	2-1	2-1	—	2-4	1-2	2-2	0-0	4-2	0-1	0-2	3-0	1-2	1-0	1-0	1-1	1-1	5-1
Farnborough T	1-0	2-2	3-0	1-0	4-4	5-1	4-1	3-1	—	3-0	2-0	4-1	0-2	0-3	0-2	3-0	4-1	2-1	2-6	1-0	1-0	3-4
Grays Ath	2-2	4-3	5-0	2-2	0-2	1-0	2-0	1-2	1-2	—	5-0	1-2	0-0	2-2	2-2	3-2	4-2	1-0	2-1	2-1	0-0	2-1
Harrow Bor	2-3	1-2	4-0	2-0	0-4	0-3	3-3	2-1	1-1	1-0	—	1-2	1-2	0-3	1-1	1-2	3-2	0-2	1-2	2-1	3-0	1-2
Hayes	3-1	1-1	2-0	2-1	2-0	1-1	0-3	1-0	1-1	3-1	2-4	—	4-2	0-1	1-0	3-1	0-2	2-0	0-1	2-0	2-2	2-2
Hendon	2-2	1-0	1-1	1-1	2-4	2-1	2-2	1-1	0-1	1-1	0-0	1-1	—	0-0	2-2	1-1	4-1	2-1	1-1	1-0	1-1	0-3
Kingstonian	2-0	3-2	1-0	1-0	1-0	3-2	1-1	1-1	1-2	0-0	1-2	0-3	7-0	—	4-1	0-1	2-0	3-0	0-1	0-2	1-0	1-2
Leytonstone-Ilford	2-0	3-2	3-0	4-0	3-1	4-1	2-1	1-0	5-3	1-1	3-1	2-1	1-4	2-0	—	1-1	1-1	1-0	1-0	3-2	0-0	2-2
Leyton-Wingate	3-2	1-0	0-2	0-0	1-1	2-0	1-0	1-1	2-2	2-2	3-3	0-2	9-1	1-1	0-2	—	4-0	1-0	1-1	0-0	0-4	0-1
Marlow	0-0	1-2	0-1	0-1	2-2	3-0	0-2	1-7	3-3	0-2	1-1	0-0	1-1	2-2	1-4	3-1	—	1-2	0-2	3-0	2-3	2-2
St Albans C	1-0	2-2	1-1	1-1	1-1	5-1	0-0	1-4	2-0	0-1	3-2	1-3	0-1	0-0	0-0	2-4	4-0	—	1-4	4-0	1-0	1-2
Slough T	1-0	0-2	3-0	4-1	1-1	4-0	0-2	3-2	0-3	2-0	1-1	2-0	4-0	2-0	2-0	1-3	2-0	4-3	—	4-1	0-1	3-0
Tooting & Mitcham U	1-1	3-2	0-2	0-3	0-3	2-1	2-1	1-0	1-3	1-1	1-1	0-3	1-2	2-0	0-1	0-2	3-2	2-1	2-3	—	2-0	1-3
Windsor & Eton	2-3	1-2	0-1	0-3	0-1	1-1	0-1	1-0	0-0	2-2	3-1	1-1	2-0	2-0	0-3	2-0	1-3	3-2	3-2	5-0	—	1-1
Wokingham T	2-3	2-0	0-0	0-1	1-1	1-1	6-1	2-0	2-2	0-1	3-1	1-0	1-1	0-1	0-1	1-1	0-1	0-2	1-1	7-0	1-0	—

VAUXHALL-OPEL LEAGUE DIVISION ONE RESULTS 1988–89

	Basildon United	Basingstoke Town	Boreham Wood	Bracknell Town	Chalfont St Peter	Chesham United	Collier Row	Hampton	Hitchin Town	Kingsbury Town	Leatherhead	Lewes	Metropolitan Police	Southwick	Staines Town	Uxbridge	Walton & Hersham	Wembley	Wivenhoe Town	Woking	Worthing
Basildon United	—	0-2	0-1	2-3	1-2	2-2	1-0	1-2	1-1	0-3	0-1	2-3	1-1	0-0	0-2	1-0	1-3	1-2	1-2	1-2	2-3
Basingstoke Town	3-0	—	2-0	3-1	2-0	7-0	1-0	4-1	1-1	4-0	2-1	1-2	3-0	2-1	2-2	2-1	0-1	3-0	3-2	1-1	1-1
Boreham Wood	2-0	2-2	—	5-0	3-1	2-1	5-0	1-1	1-2	1-1	1-1	1-3	1-2	3-3	0-2	2-0	2-0	0-4	0-1	2-3	2-1
Bracknell Town	1-1	0-2	0-3	—	3-0	1-0	1-2	3-1	0-1	2-0	0-1	0-2	2-3	1-3	0-1	2-3	1-2	0-1	1-0	0-0	5-1
Chalfont St Peter	2-0	1-4	3-2	4-0	—	2-1	2-2	0-3	0-2	1-4	1-3	4-0	1-1	0-0	0-3	2-4	0-1	3-1	2-2	1-3	4-1
Chesham	2-0	3-4	0-1	4-1	4-4	—	2-0	3-0	0-1	0-0	1-0	2-1	1-4	5-2	0-2	0-0	0-0	0-1	0-1	0-5	1-1
Collier Row	1-0	0-3	2-2	1-0	0-1	1-3	—	2-2	0-3	1-1	1-1	1-3	3-0	3-0	1-1	1-2	0-2	2-3	0-3	0-2	3-1
Hampton	0-0	0-0	0-0	0-0	3-2	1-0	2-1	—	0-3	1-2	1-4	0-0	1-0	3-4	0-2	0-1	1-3	1-0	1-3	0-2	1-1
Hitchin Town	0-3	2-0	2-0	1-1	5-1	2-0	6-1	2-1	—	1-0	3-0	1-0	1-1	2-2	2-1	1-0	2-1	0-1	0-3	1-1	1-0
Kingsbury Town	6-1	0-2	0-2	2-1	2-2	5-1	1-2	2-1	3-1	—	3-0	0-1	1-4	2-0	2-1	2-1	1-2	1-1	1-0	0-1	3-1
Leatherhead	1-2	2-4	3-1	3-0	3-0	6-4	0-2	1-1	1-0	1-2	—	2-2	1-1	1-1	0-1	1-2	0-0	1-0	4-0	0-1	4-5
Lewes	2-1	0-3	2-2	3-1	3-2	2-2	6-0	3-1	1-0	1-4	3-0	—	2-0	1-0	0-1	2-1	2-1	4-1	0-1	0-2	3-0
Metropolitan Police	3-0	0-3	0-1	2-1	1-2	1-0	1-0	3-2	0-0	0-2	2-0	3-3	—	2-2	1-5	5-3	1-3	2-1	1-2	1-2	2-2
Southwick	5-0	0-3	0-1	1-0	1-0	0-4	1-1	1-0	1-4	2-1	0-1	0-0	4-0	—	0-1	0-2	2-2	1-2	0-0	0-2	1-1
Staines Town	4-2	1-1	2-1	3-0	5-0	1-1	5-0	1-1	1-0	0-0	2-0	3-0	3-0	1-1	—	1-2	2-0	2-0	2-1	1-0	5-3
Uxbridge	0-0	0-0	3-0	1-1	0-1	3-1	3-1	1-1	2-2	2-1	0-0	2-1	1-0	2-3	1-2	—	1-3	2-0	1-3	0-4	2-1
Walton & Hersham	2-0	2-1	0-0	1-0	3-1	0-1	3-0	1-1	0-2	0-0	3-0	0-1	3-1	2-0	2-2	1-0	—	5-0	0-2	1-3	1-2
Wembley	0-2	1-0	0-2	3-1	0-0	1-1	2-1	0-0	0-0	2-1	3-2	0-2	1-3	1-1	0-2	2-3	1-0	—	1-0	0-5	4-3
Wivenhoe Town	5-1	4-2	1-0	2-2	2-0	2-0	3-0	2-0	2-1	0-3	0-1	3-3	2-1	1-1	2-1	2-4	0-1	0-2	—	0-3	1-0
Woking	1-0	3-0	4-1	1-2	2-2	0-2	3-1	2-1	1-1	1-0	2-1	2-2	1-1	1-0	1-1	1-2	0-1	0-1	0-0	—	3-1
Worthing	2-3	0-2	0-1	1-0	2-2	0-2	1-0	1-1	0-0	0-3	1-4	4-3	1-2	0-0	2-1	1-2	2-0	1-2	0-2	1-1	—

VAUXHALL-OPEL LEAGUE DIVISION TWO NORTH RESULTS 1988–89

	Aveley	Barton Rovers	Berkhamsted Town	Billericay Town	Clapton	Harlow Town	Hemel Hempstead	Hertford Town	Heybridge Swifts	Hornchurch	Letchworth Garden City	Purfleet	Rainham Town	Royston Town	Saffron Walden Town	Stevenage Borough	Tilbury	Tring Town	Vauxhall Motors	Ware	Witham Town	Wolverton Town
Aveley	—	2-1	3-0	0-3	3-1	0-1	2-1	2-0	2-2	1-1	1-1	0-1	2-1	3-2	1-2	0-0	1-0	1-0	1-2	1-1	1-0	1-1
Barton Rovers	3-1	—	3-0	0-1	2-2	1-1	2-0	2-1	0-1	2-0	1-1	2-2	1-1	2-1	1-0	1-1	1-0	4-1	0-0	2-0	2-1	2-1
Berkhamsted Town	1-1	2-1	—	0-1	3-3	1-1	2-3	2-1	1-3	0-2	2-2	4-0	2-0	3-1	0-2	2-0	1-1	3-3	2-1	1-3	2-0	2-4
Billericay Town	2-0	1-2	6-1	—	1-1	2-1	3-1	1-1	3-2	2-0	1-0	1-2	2-4	3-1	0-3	3-0	0-0	1-2	2-1	1-2	1-1	3-1
Clapton	0-1	0-2	0-1	1-1	—	2-2	1-0	1-0	1-3	3-1	2-0	3-0	4-3	2-1	1-1	1-1	2-1	2-1	2-0	1-0	3-1	3-2
Harlow Town	3-0	4-1	1-4	1-0	3-0	—	3-0	1-2	1-1	3-0	2-2	1-4	0-0	2-1	2-0	3-1	3-2	0-2	3-0	1-1	1-0	1-0
Hemel Hempstead	2-0	1-0	1-2	1-2	1-4	1-4	—	0-0	2-0	2-1	0-0	1-1	2-1	0-1	1-1	2-2	4-1	2-1	3-1	2-1	2-0	1-0
Hertford Town	0-2	3-0	1-1	1-1	2-1	0-0	2-0	—	3-1	2-2	0-0	3-0	1-1	2-0	1-0	1-1	3-0	2-0	4-2	1-3	0-3	2-1
Heybridge Swifts	2-0	1-0	1-0	2-0	1-0	1-3	2-0	2-0	—	2-1	3-0	0-1	1-0	1-0	1-1	1-2	5-0	1-1	2-0	6-0	2-1	2-0
Hornchurch	1-1	2-0	0-0	3-3	1-2	1-3	0-3	2-0	2-2	—	5-0	0-1	0-1	1-1	2-2	1-1	2-2	0-1	1-1	3-2	0-3	1-1
Letchworth Garden City	0-1	1-1	0-1	1-3	2-6	1-4	1-1	2-2	0-0	1-1	—	0-2	0-1	0-1	1-1	1-1	0-3	2-2	0-3	1-2	2-4	0-3
Purfleet	2-0	0-0	1-1	6-1	2-1	2-0	1-2	2-1	3-2	0-0	1-1	—	0-2	2-0	1-1	2-2	3-0	0-0	1-0	3-0	0-1	2-1
Rainham Town	2-3	2-2	3-1	0-0	1-0	1-1	0-1	0-4	0-0	2-4	0-3	1-1	—	2-3	1-1	1-3	1-1	0-1	1-1	1-0	0-0	3-1
Royston Town	0-1	1-3	0-3	2-1	0-1	0-3	1-1	1-0	2-2	2-1	0-0	2-0	2-1	—	1-4	0-4	1-0	0-1	2-1	0-2	2-5	4-0
Saffron Walden Town	1-1	3-1	2-1	0-2	1-1	1-5	3-3	2-2	0-2	1-3	1-1	2-3	2-2	3-3	—	0-0	0-1	2-1	1-2	1-3	2-4	2-3
Stevenage Borough	3-0	3-0	5-1	0-1	2-1	2-3	2-0	3-5	3-0	1-3	2-1	2-3	3-2	2-2	2-0	—	1-1	4-4	3-0	2-1	3-1	3-1
Tilbury	2-3	1-3	0-1	1-0	0-0	0-5	1-0	3-2	2-0	1-2	1-0	0-0	1-1	0-0	1-1	2-3	—	1-2	0-1	2-0	2-1	5-0
Tring Town	0-0	2-1	0-0	0-1	1-1	0-2	2-1	0-1	2-0	1-0	3-0	3-1	2-0	3-1	4-0	1-1	1-0	—	3-2	2-2	1-0	2-0
Vauxhall Motors	2-1	0-0	3-1	3-1	2-1	0-1	2-3	0-0	0-0	1-1	0-1	0-1	1-0	2-1	1-0	1-2	0-3	4-0	—	3-2	3-1	4-1
Ware	1-3	2-1	3-0	2-2	3-0	0-1	1-1	1-0	1-0	0-3	2-3	0-0	2-2	0-1	2-1	0-4	4-3	0-4	2-0	—	4-1	3-0
Witham Town	4-3	1-2	2-1	1-1	2-2	0-1	2-1	2-2	4-2	1-2	1-2	1-2	2-1	2-0	4-1	2-0	2-6	0-1	2-2	1-1	—	3-0
Wolverton Town	0-4	2-3	2-1	1-1	1-2	1-2	2-2	1-4	1-2	3-3	0-0	0-1	1-3	3-2	0-2	0-4	0-2	1-4	1-1	0-1	1-2	—

VAUXHALL-OPEL LEAGUE DIVISION TWO SOUTH RESULTS 1988–89

	Banstead Athletic	Camberley Town	Chertsey Town	Dorking	Eastbourne United	Egham Town	Epsom & Ewell	Feltham	Finchley	Flackwell Heath	Harefield United	Horsham	Hungerford Town	Maidenhead United	Molesey	Newbury Town	Petersfield United	Ruislip Manor	Southall	Whyteleafe	Yeading
Banstead Athletic	—	2-3	2-3	0-2	0-4	4-0	1-2	3-1	1-2	2-0	3-4	0-2	0-0	0-2	0-0	1-0	3-0	2-0	0-0	2-4	0-0
Camberley Town	0-3	—	0-4	2-3	1-3	2-1	2-0	2-1	2-0	0-0	0-2	1-2	2-2	2-2	1-2	3-2	2-0	0-1	0-5	0-3	3-1
Chertsey Town	2-0	0-3	—	1-2	1-1	2-0	1-0	1-2	2-2	0-2	2-2	1-1	1-0	4-4	0-0	4-0	2-0	1-0	1-1	1-6	0-2
Dorking	8-1	5-0	4-2	—	1-1	4-2	3-0	0-2	3-1	1-2	0-1	3-1	1-1	5-1	2-2	5-2	5-1	2-1	5-0	2-0	3-0
Eastbourne United	0-2	2-0	2-0	2-4	—	1-3	5-3	3-1	0-1	1-1	0-1	2-1	2-2	5-2	4-0	1-1	3-1	0-2	7-0	0-1	1-2
Egham Town	1-0	1-2	1-2	1-4	5-1	—	1-2	0-0	0-3	1-0	3-0	1-1	3-2	0-0	1-1	3-0	3-2	1-0	2-3	1-3	3-0
Epsom & Ewell	3-0	3-0	2-1	0-1	0-1	2-1	—	4-0	1-4	0-0	1-0	3-0	1-3	1-1	2-3	1-0	3-3	0-1	0-2	1-1	2-0
Feltham	3-0	3-1	3-0	1-3	2-2	0-1	1-1	—	2-4	5-0	0-0	3-0	4-0	2-3	0-0	1-3	2-1	1-3	2-1	0-0	3-1
Finchley	2-0	1-0	1-1	0-3	3-0	0-3	3-2	0-1	—	2-1	4-3	4-1	1-1	3-0	0-0	3-1	1-1	2-1	3-1	2-1	2-1
Flackwell Heath	1-1	0-1	2-3	0-2	4-1	0-1	3-1	0-1	0-0	—	1-0	1-1	1-1	0-3	1-1	0-3	5-0	1-2	3-0	2-2	1-0
Harefield United	1-2	2-4	2-0	2-3	4-0	3-0	1-2	1-1	1-0	2-0	—	0-0	0-2	2-0	0-0	2-0	2-1	0-3	1-3	0-1	2-0
Horsham	0-2	1-1	0-0	1-2	0-4	2-2	1-3	0-2	2-1	2-2	1-2	—	1-1	1-2	0-2	3-0	2-2	0-2	1-1	0-2	3-1
Hungerford Town	2-0	0-0	4-1	0-1	1-0	2-2	1-1	4-2	2-1	2-3	3-1	1-2	—	1-0	3-1	1-0	2-1	1-1	3-1	0-1	0-2
Maidenhead United	1-2	0-1	0-0	1-4	0-0	3-0	0-1	1-1	0-3	3-2	0-0	2-0	0-2	—	0-0	1-1	2-1	1-0	0-2	3-2	1-1
Molesey	1-0	2-1	0-1	2-1	1-0	3-0	3-1	3-1	2-0	1-1	3-2	0-1	4-0	2-1	—	3-0	2-0	0-0	2-0	1-2	2-1
Newbury Town	2-2	2-0	1-1	0-4	3-3	1-0	0-1	0-3	0-0	1-0	0-1	4-0	0-0	2-0	3-0	—	3-1	1-2	1-4	2-2	1-2
Petersfield	2-1	0-3	0-0	0-1	3-2	1-0	0-1	0-1	0-1	0-4	1-1	1-1	0-1	0-0	2-3	1-4	—	1-2	2-0	2-4	2-4
Ruislip Manor	2-2	2-0	2-2	0-1	0-1	1-3	1-1	3-0	2-2	1-3	0-2	0-0	0-1	2-1	3-3	0-1	6-1	—	4-0	0-0	2-0
Southall	0-2	0-2	0-4	0-3	1-1	1-1	2-0	1-0	0-0	0-2	0-2	2-0	0-3	3-1	1-1	2-1	0-2	0-1	—	2-2	1-1
Whyteleafe	3-2	5-2	2-1	1-1	3-1	0-1	1-1	3-0	3-2	0-2	1-2	4-0	0-0	2-1	2-1	2-1	4-0	2-1	6-0	—	2-0
Yeading	2-2	3-2	2-2	0-2	0-1	0-1	3-2	0-0	0-6	1-0	0-2	1-1	3-0	1-1	4-1	2-0	1-0	3-2	1-1	1-3	—

LEADING GOALSCORERS

Premier Division

		Lge	*AC*	*CC*
41	Simon Read (Farnborough T)	34	7	0
26	Tom English (B Stortford)	18	2	6
24	Neal Stanley (Slough T)	23	0	1
21	Carl Zachhau (B Stortford)	12	4	5
20	Graham Westley (Kingstonian)	17	3	0
19	Steve Thompson (Slough T)	18	0	1
18	Dave Pearce (Wokingham T)	17	1	0
	Jimmy Bolton (Harrow Bor)	17	1	0
	Andy Weddell (B Stortford)	14	2	2
17	Micky Dingwall (L'stone Ilford)	15	1	1
16	Tony Kelly (Hayes)	13	0	3
	Andy Wallace (Barking)	12	2	1
	John Collins (Dulwich H)	16	0	0
	Jimmy Brown (Kingstonian)	16	0	0
15	Iain Dowie (Hendon)	11	1	3
	Murray Jones (Carshalton Ath)	12	3	0
	Joe Simmonds (L'stone Ilford)	15	0	0
	Stone (Marlow)	15	0	0
	Byron Walton (Windsor & Eton)	14	1	0
14	Richard Evans (Windsor & Eton)	13	1	0
	Steve Guille (Bognor Regis T)	12	1	1
	Jon Warden (Carshalton Ath)	13	1	0
13	John Neal (Dagenham)	13	0	0

Division One

		Lge	*AC*
23	Paul Harrison (Wivenhoe T)	23	
21	Mark Deacon (Basingstoke T)	20	1
	Pip Parris (Lewes)	20	1
	Steve Wallace (Chesham U)	21	
	(Includes 6 League Goals for Borehamwood)		
20	Mark Dawber (Staines T)	17	3
19	Mark Reed (Lewes)	18	1

Division Two North

		Lge	*AC*
30	Jeff Wood (Harlow T)	28	2
27	Mark Watkins (Tring T)	27	
20	Martin Gitings (Harlow T)	20	
	(Includes 18 League Goals for Stevenage Bor)		
	Bobby Moyce (Aveley)	20	
	(Includes 4 League Goals for Rainham T)		
	Jason Spiteri (Clapton)	20	
19	Cliff Campbell (Barton R)	18	1

Division Two South

		Lge	*AC*
32	Andy Bushnell (Dorking)	32	
28	Steve Milton (Whyteleafe)	27	1
25	John Daubney (Eastbourne U)	25	
21	Paul Grainger (Dorking)	16	5
	Glen Price (Camberley T)	21	
20	Lee Mooney (Feltham)	18	2

TOP SIX ATTENDANCES

Premier Division

1763	Slough T v Farnborough T	27.12.88
1347	Farnborough T v L'stone Ilford	27.03.89
1046	Windsor & Eton v Slough T	02.01.89
645	Grays Ath v Slough T	07.02.89
608	Barking v Dagenham	18.02.89
596	Marlow v Carshalton Ath	06.05.89

Division One

1432	Woking v Lewes	06.05.89
1122	Staines T v Woking	29.04.89
753	Basingstoke T v Woking	02.01.89
	v Staines T	21.03.89
459	Hitchin T v Wembley	01.04.89
442	Chalfont St Peter v Woking	15.04.89
427	Wivenhoe T v Wembley	25.10.88

Division Two North

512	Stevenage Bor v Harlow T	14.01.89
443	Billericay T v Harlow T	11.02.89
379	Aveley v Tilbury	27.12.88
316	Ware v Stevenage Bor	27.12.88
289	Tring T v Harlow T	18.03.89
281	Royston T v Stevenage Bor	04.03.89

Division Two South

365	Whyteleafe v Dorking	08.04.89
315	Dorking v Eastbourne U	29.10.88
258	Epsom & Ewell v Dorking	21.03.89
236	Ruislip Manor v Yeading	02.01.89
235	Egham Town v Southall	27.12.88
225	Horsham v Dorking	26.10.88

The Clubcall Cup – *Continued from Page 903*

Corby Town 1 *(Richards)*
Bishops Stortford 2 *(Weddell, Zachhau)* 137
Dover Athletic 3 *(Cotter 2, Lee)*
Barking 0 381
Hyde United 2 *(Rudge, Lutkevitch)*
Bangor City 0 527
Frickley Athletic 1 *(Birch)*
Witton Albion 0 277
Kidderminster Harriers 4 *(Howell 2, Davies, Jones)*
Wycombe Wanderers 1 *(Young)* 929
Leytonstone Ilford 3 *(Holmes, Flint, Dingwall)*
Kettering Town 0 206
Maidstone United 3 *(Pamphlett, Rogers, Gall)*
Crawley Town 0 445
Morecambe 5 *(Pawsey 3, Houston, Worrell)*
Marine 1 *(Haw)* 229
Runcorn 3 *(Pugh, Page, Houghton)*
Caenarfon Town 0 379
Stafford Rangers 1 *(Camden)*
Cheltenham Town 0 527
Sutton United 2 *(Dennis, McKinnon)*
Croydon 0 420
Wealdstone 3 *(Morris, Olaleye, own goal)*
Hayes 2 *(Payne, Kelly)* 263
Weymouth 0
Leyton Wingate 1 *(Baker)* 469
Worcester City 3 *(Shail, Musford, Golan)*
Burton Albion 1 *(Cotterill)* 797

Third Round

Barnet 5 *(Shinners, Ironton, Sansom, Evans 2)*
Dover Athletic 1 *(Cotter)* 811
Bishops Stortford 3 *(Jackman, English, Zacchau)*
Leyton Wingate 2 *(Campbell, Baker)* 434
Hyde United 2 *(Nisbett 2)*
Frickley Athletic 0 452
Leytonstone Ilford 1 *(Flint)*
Maidstone United 3 *(Pamphlett 2, Butler)* 241
Newport County 5 *(Saunderson, Sugrue 2, Thompson 2)*
Kidderminster Harriers 6 *(Shilvock, Howell 2, Davies 2, Jones)* aet 895
Runcorn 5 *(Carroll, Pugh, Page 2, Anderson)*
Morecambe 3 *(Houston 2, Poskett)* 428
Stafford Rangers 2 *(Camden, Brown)*
Worcester City 1 *(Mugford)* 437
Wealdstone 0
Sutton United 4 *(Hemsley, Dennis 3)* 255

Fourth Round

Bishops Stortford 4 *(Weddell, English, Zacchau, Gayle)*
Sutton United 3 *(Dennis, McKinnon 2 (1 pen))* 854
Hyde United 1 *(Megram)*
Stafford Rangers 0 aet 681
Kidderminster Harriers 0
Runcorn 1 *(Carter)* 742
Maidstone United 1 *(Rogers)*
Barnet 2 *(Abbott, Shinners)* 492

Semi-finals

Bishops Stortford 1 *(Zacchau)*
Barnet 1 *(Bull)* aet 1020
Barnet 4 *(Poole 2, Ketterage, Murphy)*
Bishops Stortford 1 *(English)* Replay 875
Hyde United 2 *(Megram, Kirkham)*
Runcorn 1 *(Miller)* 818

Final Barnet 3, Hyde United 3 aet (7 May 1989, at Telford, attendance 814) *Barnet won 5–3 on penalties.*

Barnet: Lomas; Wilson, Turner, Millett, Reilly, Poole, Stein, Ketteridge, Sansom, Bull (Regis), Murphy.

Hyde United: Walker; Shepherd, Hooton, Megram, Jackson, Bishop, Edwards, Rudge, Lutkevitch (Harris), Kirkham, Connor (Blackwood). *Scorers:* Barnet – Reilly, Poole, Sansom. Hyde United – Shepherd, Edwards, Kirkham.

FA CHALLENGE TROPHY 1988–89

The following 32 clubs were exempted to the First Round Proper: Altrincham, Aylesbury United, Barnet, Barrow, Bath City, Blyth Spartans, Boston United, Bromley, Bromsgrove Rovers, Burton Albion, Cheltenham Town, Chorley, Dartford, Enfield, Fareham Town, Fisher Athletic, Hyde United, Kettering Town, Kidderminster Harriers, Macclesfield Town, Maidstone United, Marine, Newcastle Blue Star, Newport County, Runcorn, Stafford Rangers, Sutton United, Telford United, Wealdstone, Weymouth, Wokingham Town, Yeovil Town.

The following 32 clubs were exempted to the Third Round Qualifying: Bangor City, Billingham Synthonia, Bishop Auckland, Bishops Stortford, Caernarfon Town, Cambridge City, Corby Town, Crawley Town, Dagenham, Frickley Athletic, Gateshead, Harrow Borough, Hendon, Leytonstone Ilford, Leyton-Wingate, Merthyr Tydfil, Morecambe, Northwich Victoria, Nuneaton Borough, Rhyl, Saltash United, Slough Town, South Bank, Spennymoor United, Tooting & Mitcham United, Welling United, Whitby Town, Whitley Bay, Windsor & Eton, Witton Albion, Worthing, Wycombe Wanderers.

First Round Qualifying

Accrington Stanley v Fleetwood Town	1-1, 1-2
Workington v Worksop Town	0-0, 2-3
Tow Law Town v Stockton	1-3
Alfreton Town v North Shields	2-2, 1-2
Southport v Buxton	3-4
Goole Town v Horwich RMI	3-0
Chester-le-Street Town v Radcliffe Borough	0-0, 0-1
Ryhope CA v Gretna	0-1
Stalybridge Celtic v Shildon	2-0
Seaham Red Star v Guisborough Town	0-2
Ferryhill Athletic v Brandon United	0-3
South Liverpool v Mossley	4-1
Easington Colliery v Crook Town	6-0
Dudley Town v Congleton Town	4-1
Winsford United v Coventry Sporting	1-4
Grantham v Shepshed Charterhouse	2-1
Sutton Coldfield v Colwyn Bay	2-3
Matlock Town v Redditch United	3-1
Moor Green v Eastwood Town	2-4
Gainsborough Trinity v Halesowen Town	1-0
VS Rugby v Atherstone United	1-3
Willenhall Town v Leek Town	4-3
Bedworth United v Stourbridge	1-0
Staines Town v Dunstable	3-0
Farnborough Town v Hampton	2-2, 3-2
Wivenhoe Town v Chalfont St Peter	0-0, 3-1
Uxbridge v Witney Town	4-0
Ashford Town v Burnham	2-0
Basingstoke Town v Folkestone	1-0
Erith & Belvedere v Dover Athletic	0-3
Sheppey United v Banbury United	3-2
Tonbridge AFC v Grays Athletic	0-3
Billericay Town v Kingstonian	1-5
Leatherhead v Kingsbury Town	2-1
Metropolitan Police v Boreham Wood	2-1
Gravesend & Northfleet v Bognor Regis Town	1-1, 1-1, 1-0
Woking v St Albans City	1-1, 4-1
Barking v Basildon United	1-1, 3-2
Wembley v Chelmsford City	2-1
Hayes v Bracknell Town	4-2
Thanet United v Hitchin Town	1-0
Lewes v Dulwich Hamlet	2-2, 1-4
Chesham United v Collier Row	2-0
Croydon v Walton & Hersham	1-0
Bridgend Town v Salisbury	1-6
Frome Town v Cwmbran Town	0-0, 4-2
Barry Town v Bideford	4-1
Taunton Town v Dorchester Town	0-2
Forest Green Rovers v Gloucester City	1-2
Ton Pentre v Andover	3-3, 2-3
Maesteg Park v Weston-super-Mare	0-2
Worcester City v Waterlooville	4-0
Gosport Borough v Trowbridge Town	2-0

Second Round Qualifying

Worksop Town v Goole Town	0-1
Stockton v Penrith	0-0, 5-4
Fleetwood Town v Stalybridge Celtic	2-1
Brandon United v Buxton	1-5
North Shields v South Liverpool	3-3, 2-2, 1-2
Easington Colliery v Radcliffe Borough	2-2, 0-2
Gretna v Guisborough Town	1-0
Coventry Sporting v Eastwood Town	1-4
Grantham v Alvechurch	1-1, 1-0
Dudley Town v Willenhall Town	1-1, 1-0
Wellingborough Town v Matlock Town	0-1
Colwyn Bay v Hednesford Town	2-1
Leicester United v Gainsborough Trinity	0-0, 4-2
Atherstone United v Bedworth United	4-1
Metropolitan Police v Carshalton Athletic	1-2
Barking v Gravesend & Northfleet	0-1
Dover Athletic v Kings Lynn	6-0
Chesham United v Basingstoke Town	1-3
Farnborough Town v Wivenhoe Town	1-2
Sheppey United v Woking	0-2
Oxford City v Hayes *(walkover for Hayes)*	
Southwick v Uxbridge	0-4
Croydon v Staines Town	2-1
Ashford Town v Dulwich Hamlet	2-1
Marlow v Grays Athletic	2-1
Thanet United v Leatherhead	0-3
Kingstonian v Wembley	2-0
Gloucester City v Frome Town	3-2
Weston-super-Mare v Worcester City	0-2
Gosport Borough v Poole Town	4-0
Andover v Salisbury	2-5
Dorchester Town v Barry Town	1-0

Third Round Qualifying

Whitby Town v Stockton	2-2, 0-3
Spennymoor United v Gretna	0-0, 0-3
Morecambe v Fleetwood Town	1-1, 0-4
South Bank v Radcliffe Borough	5-0
Gateshead v South Liverpool	0-1
Whitley Bay v Frickley Athletic	0-1
Billingham Synthonia v Bishop Auckland	1-1, 1-3
Witton Albion v Nuneaton Borough	2-1
Bangor City v Rhyl	2-0
Corby Town v Colwyn Bay	2-2, 1-2
Northwich Victoria v Goole Town	2-0
Dudley Town v Atherstone United	1-2
Grantham v Matlock Town	2-2, 0-3
Eastwood Town v Buxton	1-3
Leicester United v Caernarfon Town	1-0
Ashford Town v Slough Town	0-3
Leyton Wingate v Windsor & Eton	1-1, 0-2
Wivenhoe Town v Kingstonian	2-3
Bishops Stortford v Gravesend & Northfleet	3-3, 1-2
Croydon v Dagenham	2-2, 0-0, 0-1
Carshalton Athletic v Leatherhead	2-1
Leytonstone Ilford v Uxbridge	0-1
Hendon v Hayes	3-3, 2-0
Dover Athletic v Tooting & Mitcham United	3-2
Wycombe Wanderers v Cambridge City	2-0
Merthyr Tydfil v Salisbury	5-0
Saltash United v Gosport Borough	1-2
Worcester City v Marlow	1-0
Dorchester Town v Gloucester City	1-1, 3-1
Worthing v Basingstoke Town	1-2
Crawley Town v Woking	3-4

First Round

Bangor City v South Bank	2-3
Matlock Town v Northwich Victoria	2-6
Boston United v Stafford Rangers	2-0
Stockton v Hyde United	1-4
Telford United v Witton Albion	3-0
Burton Albion v Chorley	4-1
Colwyn Bay v Frickley Athletic	1-1, 0-3
Marine v Macclesfield Town	2-2, 1-4
Buxton v Altrincham	0-2
Leicester United v Blyth Spartans	3-0
Runcorn v Gretna	2-3
Newcastle Blue Star v South Liverpool	1-0
Fleetwood Town v Bishop Auckland	0-0, 1-5
Atherstone United v Barrow	1-4
Fisher Athletic v Cheltenham Town	0-1
Dover Athletic v Worcester City	3-1
Bromsgrove Rovers v Woking	2-3
Fareham Town v Yeovil Town	1-2
Windsor & Eton v Gosport Borough	2-0
Enfield v Hendon	4-1
Barnet v Gravesend & Northfleet	1-1, 1-2
Sutton United v Kingstonian	1-0

Kidderminster Harriers v Maidstone United	2-1
Bath City v Wycombe Wanderers	0-0, 0-4
Dagenham v Aylesbury United	2-2, 0-4
Uxbridge v Carshalton Athletic	1-1, 2-5
Wokingham Town v Merthyr Tydfil	2-2, 0-1
Dartford v Dorchester Town	4-0
Weymouth v Newport County	2-1
Welling United v Slough Town	4-0
Basingstoke Town v Kettering Town	1-1, 3-5
Bromley v Wealdstone	1-2

Second Round

Boston United v Northwich Victoria	3-2
Gravesend & Northfleet v Kettering Town	1-1, 2-1
Kiddermimster Harriers v Burton Albion	1-1, 1-0
Aylesbury United v Merthyr Tydfil	1-3
Sutton United v Bishop Auckland	1-1, 1-2
Wealdstone v Wycombe Wanderers	0-1
Cheltenham Town v Barrow	0-0, 0-0, 0-1
Altrincham v Carshalton Athletic	2-0
Windsor & Eton v Enfield	1-0
Woking v Weymouth	2-1
South Bank v Macclesfield Town	0-3
Hyde United v Gretna	1-1, 3-2
Newcastle Blue Star v Frickley Athletic	3-1
Dover Athletic v Dartford	0-0, 0-2
Yeovil Town v Telford United	1-4
Leicester United v Welling United	1-3

Third Round

Dartford v Bishop Auckland	2-0
Newcastle Blue Star v Woking	2-0
Windsor & Eton v Hyde United	2-2, 0-2
Kidderminster Harriers v Telford United	1-1, 0-2
Welling United v Boston United	0-0, 1-0
Wycombe Wanderers v Merthyr Tydfil	2-0
Altrincham v Barrow	5-3
Macclesfield Town v Gravesend & Northfleet	2-0

Quarter-Finals

Macclesfield Town v Welling United	1-0
Newcastle Blue Star v Telford United	1-4
Hyde United v Wycombe Wanderers	1-0
Dartford v Altrincham	1-0

Semi-Finals *(2 legs)*

Dartford v Macclesfield Town	0-0, 1-4
Hyde United v Telford United	0-1, 0-3

Final (at Wembley, 13 May 1989)

Macclesfield Town 0, Telford United 1 *aet*; *18,106*
Macclesfield Town: Zelem; Roberts, Hardman, Edwards, Tobin, Hanlon, Askey (Derbyshire), Timmons, Lake, Burr, Imrie (Kendall).
Telford United: Charlton; Lee, Wiggins, Mayman (Crawley), Brindley, Hancock, Joseph, Grainger, Stringer, Lloyd (Griffiths), Nelson. Scorer: *Crawley*.
Referee: T. Holbrook.

FA COUNTY YOUTH CUP 1988–89

The following 19 counties received byes to the Second Round: Army, Bedfordshire, Birmingham, East Riding, Essex, Gloucestershire, Hampshire, Herefordshire, Huntingdonshire, Lancashire, London, Middlesex, Northamptonshire, Northumberland, Sheffield & Hallamshire, Shropshire, Sussex, West Riding, Wiltshire.

First Round

Cumberland v Westmorland	2-0
Durham v North Riding	3-1
Liverpool v Manchester	1-0
Cheshire v Nottinghamshire	3-4
Derbyshire v Staffordshire	2-1
Leicestershire & Rutland v Lincolnshire	0-1
Norfolk v Cambridgeshire	3-1
Suffolk v Hertfordshire	2-6
Kent v Surrey	2-3
Berks & Bucks v Royal Navy	1-3
Oxfordshire v Worcestershire	2-0
Devon v Dorset	4-0
Cornwall v Somerset & Avon (South)	1-4

Second Round

Northumberland v East Riding	1-2
Lancashire v Cumberland	1-2
West Riding v Durham	3-1
Sheffield & Hallamshire v Liverpool	1-3
Birmingham v Nottinghamshire	3-1
Shropshire v Derbyshire	0-1
Bedfordshire v Lincolnshire	4-0
Huntingdonshire v Northamptonshire	0-3
Essex v Norfolk	2-0
London v Hertfordshire	1-3
Sussex v Middlesex	0-1
Army v Surrey	2-6
Hampshire v Royal Navy	1-0
Herefordshire v Oxfordshire	2-1
Gloucestershire v Devon	0-1
Wiltshire v Somerset & Avon (South)	2-1

Third Round

West Riding v Cumberland	2-1
East Riding v Liverpool	3-6
Bedfordshire v Derbyshire	0-1
Birmingham v Northamptonshire	1-4
Middlesex v Hertfordshire	0-1
Essex v Surrey	2-1
Devon v Herefordshire	4-1
Hampshire v Wiltshire	2-2, 3-0

Quarter-Finals

Northamptonshire v West Riding	1-0
Derbyshire v Liverpool	1-3
Hampshire v Hertfordshire	1-3
Devon v Essex	3-1

Semi-Finals

Liverpool v Northamptonshire	5-2
Devon v Hertfordshire	1-2

Final

Hertfordshire v Liverpool	?-?

FA CHALLENGE VASE 1988–89

The following 32 clubs were exempted to the Second Round: Abingdon Town, Bashley, Braintree Town, Bridgnorth Town, Chertsey Town, Clevedon Town, Colne Dynamoes, Corinthian, Dawlish Town, Emley, Falmouth Town, Farsley Celtic, Garforth Town, Gresley Rovers, Harefield United, Havant Town, Haverhill Rovers, Horsham, Hungerford Town, Mangotsfield United, Newport IOW, Old Georgians, Rainworth MW, St Helens Town, Sholing Sports, Sudbury Town, Tamworth, Warrington Town, Whyteleafe, Wisbech Twn, Witham Town, Wythenshawe Amateurs.

The following 32 clubs were exempted to the First Round: Barton Rovers, Borrowash Victoria, Bridport, Buckingham Town, Bury Town, Camberley Town, Dorking, Exmouth Town, Guiseley, Harwich & Parkeston, Hatfield Main, Heybridge Swifts, Hounslow, Hucknall Town, Irthingborough Diamonds, Lincoln United, Murton, Northampton Spencer, North Ferriby United, Rocester, Rossendale United, Sharpness, Shortwood United, Stamford, Steyning Town, Thackley, Thatcham Town, Torrington, Vauxhall Motors (Beds), West Allotment Celtic, Whickham, Yeading.

Preliminary Round

South Shields v Eppleton CW	3-1
Esh Winning v Rowntree Mackintosh	0-4
Peterlee Newtown v Harrogate RA	1-3
Alnwick Town v Horden CW	4-3
Darlington CB v Northallerton Town	0-1
Harrogate Town v Durham City	1-0
Dunston FB v Lancaster City	2-0
Norton & Stockton Anc v Seaton Delaval ST	0-1
Ponteland United v Pickering Town	1-0
Clitheroe v Ashington	3-2
West Auckland Town v Annfield Plain	0-2
Leyland Motors v Willington	4-1
Bridlington Town v Wren Rovers	0-0, 3-0
Darwen v Langley Park Welfare	3-2
Cleator Moor Celtic v Shotton Comrades	2-1
Netherfield v Bedlington Terriers	3-1
Billingham Town v Bridlington Trinity	3-0
Consett v Boldon CA	2-0
Hebburn Reyrolls v Evenwood Town	3-0
Burscough v St Dominics	3-1
Poulton Victoria v Newtown	2-0
Merseyside Police v Heswall	3-3, 1-0
Droylsden v Prescot Cables	2-1
Bootle v Waterloo Dock	4-1
Daisy Hill v General Chemicals	1-2
Maine Road v Eastwood Hanley	1-2
Chadderton v Maghull	1-3
Meir KA v Curzon Ashton	1-2
Newcastle Town v Glossop	2-2, 1-0
Atherton LR v Salford	1-2
Knypersley Vic v Vauxhall GM (Cheshire)	1-3
Irlam Town v Skelmersdale United	4-3
Formby v Ashton United	2-3
Armthorpe Welfare v Stapenhill	0-5
Kimberley Town v Belper Town	1-1, 1-1, 0-0, 1-3
Stavely Works v Long Eaton United	2-0
Gainsborough Town v Radford	3-0
Grimethorpe MW v Melton Town	1-3
Louth United v Sheffield	3-0
Yorkshire Amateur v Heanor Town	1-2
Oakham United v Immingham Town	1-1, 0-1
Ilkeston Town v Liversedge	3-2
Boston v Eccleshill United	0-4
Wigston Fields v Ossett Albion	1-2
Derby Prims v Brigg Town *(at Brigg Town)*	0-4
Maltby MW v Sutton Town	1-0
Rossington Main v Denaby United	1-0
Hallam v Ossett Town	0-3
Kiveton Park v Arnold	1-0
Harworth CI v Collingham	1-0
Baker Perkins v Northfield Town	0-2
Racing Club Warwick v Oldbury United	5-2
Tividale v Harrisons	2-3
Wednesfield Social v Walsall Wood	3-2
Paget Rangers v Mile Oak Rovers & Youth	1-1, 2-1
Hinckley Town v Rushall Olympic	2-1
Spalding United v Solihull Borough	1-2
Bilston Town v Anstey Nomads	0-1
Hinckley Athletic v Chasetown	1-2
Desborough Town v Ashtree Highfield	5-4
West Midlands Police v Highgate United	3-0
Lye Town v Evesham United	2-1
Long Buckby v Kings Heath	1-0
Malvern Town v Halesowen Harriers	0-1
Brackley Town v Rushden Town	2-2, 0-3
Boldmere St Michaels v Rothwell Town	1-0
Bourne Town v Eynesbury Rovers	0-0, 1-2
Sawbridgeworth Town v Chatteris Town	0-2
Norwich United v Harlow Town	0-1
Stansted v Downham Town	2-1
LBC Ortonians v Saffron Walden Town	0-2
Histon v Watton United	0-2
Newmarket Town v Gorleston	1-2
Holbeach United v Halstead Town	2-2, 3-0
Great Yarmouth Town v Stowmarket Town	1-0
Clacton Town v Tiptree United	0-1
Thetford Town v Lowestoft Town	3-2
Burnham Ramblers v Brightlingsea United	4-0
St Ives Town v March Town United	1-5
Brantham Athletic v Ely City	5-5, 2-4
Diss Town v Soham Town Rangers	3-2
Wroxham v Canvey Island	4-2
Felixstowe Town v Bowers United	6-2
Hemel Hempstead v Flackwell Heath	0-2
Maidenhead United v Wingate	4-0
Feltham v Wolverton Town (MK)	2-1
London Colney v Baldock Town	0-2
Shillington v Ford United (London)	0-2
Wootton Blue Cross v Cheshunt	2-2, 1-4
Berkhamsted Town v Edgware Town	3-3, 4-1
Hornchurch v The 61	1-2
Ruislip v Leighton Town	3-2
Aveley v Ruislip Manor	0-3
Hertford Town v Hanwell Town	2-1
Totternhoe v Kempston Rovers	3-1
Milton Keynes Borough v Clapton	1-0
Welwyn Garden City v Beckton United	4-0
Northwood v Letchworth Garden City	2-0
Barkingside v Finchley	0-2
Purfleet v Tring Town	0-1
Hoddesdon Town v Pirton	2-0
Selby v Langford	6-2
Amersham Town v Rainham Town	2-0
Arlesey Town v East Thurrock United	0-1
Stotfold v Potton United	2-1
Tilbury v Stevenage Borough	1-0
Royston Town v Rayners Lane	1-1, 1-0
Southgate Athletic v Ware	1-2
Three Bridges v Deal Town	3-1
Bedfont v Faversham Town	3-1
Hythe Town v Sittingbourne	2-0
Eastbourne Town v Egham Town	2-2, 2-1
Corinthian Casuals v Horsham YMCA	3-2
Redhill v Darenth Heathside	0-3
Peacehaven & Telscombe v Ringmer	1-2
Molesey v Hastings Town	1-2
Southwark Borough v Langney Sports *(at Langney Sports)*	4-2
Crockenhill v Banstead Athletic	2-3
Lancing v Whitehawk	0-1
Old Salesians v Wandsworth & Norwood	1-1, 0-2
Cray Wanderers v Farnham Town	2-1
Chipstead v Whitstable Town	0-2
Chobham v Malden Vale	0-2
Chatham Town v Epsom & Ewell	0-5
Oakwood v Haywards Heath	2-1
Burgess Hill Town v Canterbury City	1-0
Pagham v Slade Green	4-1
Beckenham Town v Littlehampton Town	1-0
Herne Bay v Eastbourne United	2-7
Shoreham v Hailsham Town	0-1
Ramsgate v Tunbridge Wells	1-0
West Wickham v Merstham	2-0
Clanfield v Vale Recreation	7-4
Horndean v Portfield	2-1
Bournemouth v Portsmouth RN	2-2, 3-2
Eastleigh v Bosham	3-1
Thame United v Wick	0-2
Chichester City v AFC Totton	3-4
East Cowes Victoria Ath v Petersfield United	1-0

Didcot Town v Arundel 3-0
Newbury Town v Romsey Town 2-3
Brockenhurst v Abingdon United 2-4
Bicester Town v Hertley Wintney 2-0
Barnstaple Town v Odd Down 1-0
DRG(FP) v Calne Town 1-4
Sherborne Town v Paulton Rovers 1-3
Moreton Town v Fairford Town 2-1
Chard Town v Westbury United 1-4
Radstock Town v Penhill 2-1
Welton Rovers v Glastonbury 3-1
St Blazey v Minehead 1-3
Melksham Town v Wellington 1-3
Chippenham Town v Pegasus Junior 2-1
Lawrence Weston Hallen v Swanage Town & Herston 1-1, 2-1
Yate Town v Almondsbury Picksons 2-1
Larkhall Athletic v Tiverton Town 1-3
Harrow Hill v Clandown 4-1
Truro City v Wimborne Town 2-1
Bishops Cleeve v Bristol Manor Farm 1-0
Devizes Town v Brislington 2-1

First Round

Cleator Moor Celtic v Clitheroe 1-2, 0-1
(match ordered to be replayed as Clitheroe fielded an ineligible player)
Rowntree Mackintosh v Northallerton Town 4-1
Annfield Plain v Leyland Motors 1-4
South Shields v Darwen 4-1
Dunston FB v Ponteland United 1-0
Whickham v Seaton Delaval ST 3-0
Bridlington Town v Alnwick Town 3-1
Billingham Town v West Allotment Celtic 0-2
Harrogate RA v Harrogate Town 3-2
Netherfield v Murton 0-2
Hebburn Reyrolls v Consett 1-3
Irlam Town v Newcastle Town 3-2
Eastwood Hanley v Rocester 0-0, 1-0
(first game abandoned 97 mins, fog)
Merseyside Police v Vauxhall GM (Cheshire) 0-1
Burscough v Rossendale United 1-6
Droylsden v Salford 1-1, 2-1
Maghull v Poulton Victoria 2-4
Ashton United v General Chemicals 1-0
Bootle v Curzon Ashton 0-1
North Ferriby United v Melton Town 1-0
Belper Town v Ossett Albion 5-2
Thackley v Guisely 0-3
Kiveton Park v Hatfield Main 0-1
Brigg Town v Lincoln United 0-0, 1-0
Eccleshill United v Rossington Main 0-2
Hucknall Town v Ilkeston Town 1-2
Maltby MW v Borrowash Victoria 3-5
Gainsborough Town v Stapenhill 2-1
(at Harworth CI FC)
Heanor Town v Harworth CI 4-3
Staveley Workis v Lough United 1-2
Ossett Town v Immingham Town 2-1
Rushden Town v Wednesfield Social 4-0
Buckingham Town v Hinckley Town 0-3
Northampton Spencer v Racing Club Warwick 0-1
Long Buckby v Boldmere St Michaels 1-2
Lye Town v Stamford 1-2
Chasetown v West Midlands Police 1-2
Desborough Town v Anstey Nomads 5-0
Harrisons v Paget Rangers 1-4
Solihull Borough v Northfield Town 0-2
Halesowen Harriers v Irthingborough Diamonds 3-0
Wroxham v Saffron Walden Town 2-1
Eynesbury Rovers v Gorleston 3-1
Harwich & Parkston v Harlow Town 0-1
Ely City v Felixstowe Town 3-3, 2-5
March Town United v Heybridge Swifts 2-1
Tiptree United v Burnham Ramblers 0-2
Thetford Town v Great Yarmouth Town 0-5
Stansted v Watton United 5-3
Holbeach United v Chatteris Town 1-0
Diss Town v Bury Town 0-3
Flackwell Heath v Milton Keynes Borough 4-0
Amersham Town v Tilbury 0-1
Totternhoe v East Thurrock United 0-1
Baldock Town v Ruislip 3-3, 4-0
Vauxhall Motors v Selby 1-1, 1-3
Hertford Town v Tring Town 1-3
Welwyn Garden City v Ford United (London) 0-3
Maidenhead United v Royston Town 2-5
Hoddesdon Town v Feltham 2-0
Ware v Berkhamsted Town 1-1, 0-2
Hounslow v Northwood 3-2
Finchley v Stotfold 1-0
The 61 v Ruislip Manor 1-0
Cheshunt v Barton Rovers 2-0
Yeading v Wandsworth & Norwood 2-1
Pagham v Hailsham Town 2-4
Whitehawk v Beckenham Town 0-1
Hythe Town v Hastings Town 4-3
Steyning Town v Burgess Hill Town 2-3
Banstead Athletic v Epsom & Ewell 1-2
Cray Wanderers v Eastbourne Town 3-3, 0-3
Three Bridges v Ramsgate 1-1, 0-0, 2-0
Oakwood v Bedfont 0-2
West Wickham v Darenth Heathside 0-1
Dorking v Whitstable Town 0-1
Malden Vale v Eastbourne United 1-0
Ringmer v Southwark Borough 2-1
Corinthian Casuals v Camberley Town 1-6
Wick v Eastleigh 2-0
AFC Totton v Romsey Town 2-2, 0-3
Abingdon Unied v Clanfield 4-1
Horndean v Thatcham Town 0-1
Didcot Town v East Cowes Victoria Athetic 0-1
Bournemouth v Bicester Town 0-2
Tiverton Town v Minehead 2-0
Torrington v Paulton Rovers 1-2
Wellington v Chippenham Town 1-2
Shortwood United v Yate Town 0-1
Westbury United v Welton Rovers 0-2
Sharpness v Radstock Town 1-4
Lawrence Weston Hallen v Calne Town 4-1
Truro City v Exmouth Town 0-2
Barnstaple Town v Moreton Town 0-1
Harrow Hill v Bridport 0-2
Devizes Town v Bishops Cleve 5-0

Second Round

Harrogate RA v Rossington Main 5-1
Garforth Town v Consett 1-0
Rowntree Mackintosh v Dunston FB 0-1
South Shields v Murton 3-4
Leyland Motors v Bridlington Town 0-1
Rossendale United v Farsley Celtic 3-2
West Allotment Celtic v Ossett Town 0-2
Colne Dynamoes v Emley 1-2
Clitheroe v Whickham 2-4
Brigg Town v Droylsden 4-1
Guiseley v Curzon Ashton 2-1
Gainsborough Town v Borrowash Victoria 1-3
Heanor Town v Hatfield Main 3-1
Ilkeston Town v Belper Town 3-1
Eastwood Hanley v St Helens Town 2-0
Irlam Town v North Ferriby United 0-3
Louth United v Wythenshawe Amateurs 2-2, 2-0
Poulton Victoria v Ashton United 2-1
Vauxhall GM (Cheshire) v Warrington Town 1-0
Hinckley Town v Boldmere St Michaels 0-2
Paget Rangers v Stamford 4-0
Desborough Town v Halesowen Harriers 0-2
West Midlands Police v Gresley Rovers 2-4
Northfield Town v Racing Club Warwick 2-0
Tamworth v Bridgnorth Town 2-1
March Town United v Rainworth MW 5-2
Wisbech Town v Rushden Town 2-1
Hoddesdon Town v Holbeach United 0-2
Braintree Town v Royston Town 3-1
Tring Town v East Thurrock United 2-4
Ford United (London) v Bury Town 0-2
Great Yarmouth Town v Felixstowe Town 1-1, 4-2
Burnham Ramblers v Eynesbury Rovers 3-0
Sudbury Town v Baldock Town 2-0
Stansted v Cheshunt 0-1
Berkhamsted Town v Witham Town 3-2
Harefield United v Harlow Town 1-6
Wroxham v Finchley 0-1
Tilbury v The 61 4-1
Haverhill Rovers v Selby 1-1, 2-0
Abingdon United v Bedfont 1-0
Horsham v Eastbourne Town 1-4
Ringmer v Hailsham Town 0-3
Hounslow v Sholing Sports 4-0

Bicester Town v Chertsey Town	0-3
Romsey Town v Hythe Town	1-0
Whitstable Town v Corinthian	2-3
Havant Town v Flackwell Heath	1-0
East Cowes Victoria Athletic v Thatcham Town	2-5
Beckenham Town v Burgess Hill Town	0-3
Whyteleafe v Hungerford Town	0-2
Yeading v Bashley	1-2
Wick v Abingdon Town	2-0
Malden Vale v Darenth Heathside	1-3
Epsom & Ewell v Three Bridges	6-2
Newport IOW v Camberley Town	1-2
Falmouth Town v Bridport	0-3
Tiverton Town v Exmouth Town	2-0
Welton Rovers v Old Georgians	3-2
Radstock Town v Chippenham Town	3-3, 0-2
Clevedon Town v Devizes Town	2-2, 0-1
Lawrence Weston Hallen v Paulton Rovers	1-4
Mangotsfield United v Yate Town	1-1, 0-3
Moreton Town v Dawlish Town	4-2

Third Round

Harrowgate RA v Borrowash Victoria	6-3
Whickham v Dunston FB	3-0
Ossett Town v Bridlington Town	2-2, 1-0
Emley v Guiseley	4-0
Garforth Town v Rossendale United	1-4
North Ferriby United v Murton	3-0
Ilkeston Town v Northfield Town	4-2
Paget Rangers v Louth United	3-1
Halesowen Harriers v Heanor Town	0-1
Gresley Rovers v Tamworth	1-3
Eastwood Hanley v Poulton Victoria	3-1
Vauxhall GM (Cheshire) v Holbeach United	1-2
Brigg Town v Boldmere St Michaels	2-2, 1-0
Braintree Town v Finchley	0-0, 2-0
Cheshunt v Bury Town	1-3
Berkhamsted Town v Wisbech Town	2-4
Harlow Town v Tilbury	3-3
(tie awarded to Tilbury as Harlow Town failed to fulfil the replay fixture)	
East Thurrock United v Great Yarmouth Town	3-0
Burnham Ramblers v Haverhill Rovers	6-0
March Town United v Sudbury Town	1-2
Hailsham Town v Darenth Heathside	1-0
Burgess Hill Town v Chertsey Town	1-1, 1-3
Hungerford Town v Eastbourne Town	5-1
Wick v Epsom & Ewell	1-1, 2-4
Hounslow v Corinthian	2-0
Havant Town v Camberley Town	1-7
Abingdon United v Thatcham Town	0-1
Bashley v Moreton Town	4-1
Paulton Rovers v Devizes Town	4-3
Welton Rovers v Yate Town	5-1
Romsey Town v Bridport	1-2
Tiverton Town v Chippenham Town	3-0

Fourth Round

Ossett Town v Whickham	1-0
Rossendale United v Emley	3-1
Heanor Town v Eastwood Hanley	1-1, 1-2
North Ferriby United v Harrogate RA	2-2, 3-1
Ilkeston Town v Tamworth	1-2
Brigg Town v Holbeach United	3-5
Braintree Town v Bury Town	0-0, 1-2
Wisbech Town v Paget Rangers	1-0
East Thurrock United v Chertsey Town	2-0
Hounslow v Sudbury Town	0-1
Epsom & Ewell v Hailsham Town	1-2
Tilbury v Burnham Ramblers	0-1
Camberley Town v Hungerford Town	0-1
Bridport v Welton Rovers	3-0
Tiverton Town v Thatcham Town	1-2
Paulton Rovers v Bashley	1-3

Fifth Round

Ossett Town v North Ferriby United	1-2
Eastwood Hanley v Tamworth	0-1
Holbeach United v Wisbech Town	2-4
Rossendale United v Sudbury Town	0-1
Bury Town v Burnham Ramblers	2-0
Hailsham Town v Hungerford Town	2-3
Bridport v Thatcham Town	0-2
East Thurrock United v Bashley	1-4

Quarter-Finals

Bury Town v North Ferriby United	1-2
Sudbury Town v Bashley	2-0
Tamworth v Wisbech Town	1-0
Hungerford Town v Thatcham Town	2-0

Semi-Finals *(2 legs)*

Tamworth v North Ferriby United	1-2, 3-1
Hungerford Town v Sudbury Town	0-0, 0-6

Final *(at Wembley)*

6 MAY

Sudbury Town (1) 1 *(Hubbick)*

Tamworth (0) 1 *(Devaney)* 26,487

Sudbury Town: Garnham; Henry, Thorpe, Barker, Boyland, Barker, Oldfield (Hunt), Klug, Hubbick, Smith, Barton (Money).
Tamworth: Belford; Lockett, McCormack (Heston), Atkins, Cartwright, Devaney, Myers, Finn, Stanton, Gordon, Moores (Rathbone).
Referee: D. Vickers.

Replay at Peterborough

10 MAY

Sudbury Town (0) 0

Tamworth (1) 3 *(Stanton 2, Moores)* 11,201

Sudbury Town: Garnham; Henry, Thorpe, Barker, Boyland, Barker, Oldfield (Money), Klug, Hubbick, Smith, Barton (Hunt).
Tamworth: Belford; Lockett, Finn, Atkins, Cartwright, Devaney, Myers, George, Stanton, Gordon (Heaton), Moores.
Referee: D. Vickers.

FA YOUTH CUP 1988-89

The following 30 clubs were exempted to the Second Round: Arsenal, Birmingham City, Charlton Athletic, Chelsea, Coventry City, Crystal Palace, Doncaster Rovers, Everton, Fulham, Ipswich Town, Leeds United, Leicester City, Leyton Orient, Liverpool, Luton Town, Manchester City, Manchester United, Mansfield Town, Middlesbrough, Newcastle United, Nottingham Forest, Notts County, Sheffield United, Sheffield Wednesday, Southampton, Southend United, Stoke City, Tottenham Hotspur, Watford, Wimbledon.

The following 50 clubs were exempted to the First Round: Aston Villa, Barnsley, Blackpool, AFC Bournemouth, Bradford City, Brighton & Hove Albion, Bristol City, Bristol Rovers, Burnley, Cambridge United, Cardiff City, Chester City, Colchester United, Crewe Alexandra, Croydon, Derby County, Epsom & Ewell, Erith & Belvedere, Exeter City, Gillingham, Grimsby Town, Hartlepool United, Hednesford Town, Hendon, Horndean, Hull City, Millwall, Newport County, Northampton Town, Norwich City, Oldham Athletic, Oxford United, Plymouth Argyle, Portsmouth, Port Vale, Queen's Park Rangers, Reading, Shrewsbury Town, Staines Town, Sunderland, Sutton United, Swansea City, Swindon Town, Walsall, West Bromwich Albion, West Ham United, Wigan Athletic, Wokingham Town, Wolverhampton Wanderers, Wrexham.

Preliminary Round

Stockton v Bedlington Terriers	1-2
(at Bedlington Terriers)	
Billingham Synthonia v Shildon	2-1
Guiseley v Carlisle United	1-2
South Bank v Guisborough Town	0-5
Chester-le-Street Town v Darlington	2-7
Marske United v Billingham Town	2-0
Preston North End v Blackburn Rovers	0-2
South Liverpool v Atherton Collieries	
(walkover for Atherton Collieries)	
Chadderton v Rotherham United	1-10
Marine v Bolton Wanderers	0-3
Thackley v Atherton LR	4-1
Bootle v Rochdale	4-0
Heanor Town v Bury	
(walkover for Bury)	
Formby v Halifax Town	
(walkover for Halifax Town)	
Chesterfield v Tranmere Rovers	0-2
Hinckley Town v Lincoln City	1-2
Radford v Bilston Town	0-8
Burton Albion v Scunthorpe United	0-3
Kettering Town v Walsall Wood	5-1
Nuneaton Borough v Alvechurch	1-1, 3-1
Tamworth v Mile Oak Rovers & Youth	0-3
Rothwell Town v Kidderminster Harriers	0-7
Banbury United v Oldswinford	4-2
Corby Town v Rushall Olympic	4-0
Dunstable v Welwyn Garden City	1-1, 4-2
Wisbech Town v Rushden	1-4
Stevenage Borough v Wellingboro Town	2-0
Ruislip Manor v Bury Town	3-1
Letchworth Garden City v St Albans City	2-6
Vauxhall Motors (Beds) v Clapton	
(walkover for Clapton)	
Billericay Town v Saffron Walden Town	2-2, 4-0
East Ham United v Collier Row	
(walkover for Collier Row)	
Welling United v Canvey Island	0-1
Hampton v Hounslow	3-0
Uxbridge v Boreham Wood	5-0
Brentford v Kingsbury Town	7-0
Walton & Hersham v Burnham	1-0
Slough Town v Maidenhead United	7-2
Worthing v Marlow	1-1, 2-3
Dover Athletic v Chatham Town	
(walkover for Dover Athletic)	
Egham Town v Carshalton Athletic	2-1
Hailsham Town v Sheppey United	3-1
Worthing United v Ringmer	1-1, 3-3, 5-2
Banstead Athletic v Whitehawk	2-2, 0-2
Bognor Regis Town v Hungerford Town	9-0
Basingstoke Town v Newbury Town	1-2
Yate Town v Cheltenham Town	2-4
Weston-super-Mare v Hereford United	0-0, 0-2
Worcester City v Mangotsfield United	0-3
Dorchester Town v Torquay United	0-3
Romsey Town v Weymouth	3-1
Trowbridge Town v Wimborne Town	
(walkover for Trowbridge Town)	

First Round Qualifying

Carlisle United v Billingham Synthonia	3-2
York City v Bedlington Terriers	2-0
Marske United v Darlington	0-5
Spennymoor United v Guisborough Town	1-2
Rotherham United v Atherton Collieries	8-1
Rhyl v Blackburn Rovers	
(walkover for Blackburn Rovers)	
Bootle v Thackley	1-0
Huddersfield Town v Bolton Wanderers	1-1, 2-1
Tranmere Rovers v Halifax Town	5-1
Garforth Town v Bury	1-7
Scunthorpe United v Bilston Town	3-0
Hinckley Athletic v Lincoln City	2-1
Mile Oak Rovers & Youth v Nuneaton Borough	1-0
Witney Town v Kettering Town	1-2
Corby Town v Banbury United	7-0
Lye Town v Kidderminster Harriers	0-3
Stevenage Borough v Rushden Town	1-2
Peterborough United v Dunstable	1-1, 3-2
Clapton v St Albans City	1-3
Loughton v Ruislip Manor	1-5
Canvey Island v Collier Row	0-1
(at Collier Row)	
Royston Town v Billericay Town	3-7
Brentford v Uxbridge	6-2
Feltham v Hampton	1-3
Marlow v Slough Town	1-5
Whyteleafe v Walton & Hersham	1-1, 4-0
Thanet United v Egham Town	
(walkover for Egham Town)	
Southwick v Dover Athletic	1-1, 1-3
Whitehawk v Worthing United	4-2
Horley Town v Hailsham Town	3-2
Aldershot v Newbury Town	0-0, 2-4
Havant Town v Bognor Regis Town	0-3
Mangotsfield United v Hereford United	1-2
Wotton Rovers v Cheltenham Town	3-2
Trowbridge Town v Romsey Town	0-3
Gosport Borough v Torquay United	0-2

Second Round Qualifying

Carlisle United v York City	2-1
Darlington v Guisborough Town	4-0
Rotherham United v Blackburn Rovers	0-1
Bootle v Huddersfield Town	1-0
Tranmere Rovers v Bury	3-1
Scunthorpe United v Hinckley Athletic	4-0
Mile Oak Rovers & Youth v Kettering Town	1-0
Corby Town v Kidderminster Harriers	0-1
Rushden Town v Peterborough United	2-4
St Albans City v Ruislip Manor	3-2
Collier Row v Billericay Town	0-2
Brentford v Hampton	4-0
Slough Town v Whyteleafe	2-2, 3-4
Egham Town v Dover Athletic	4-1
Whitehawk v Horley Town	0-0, 0-6
Newbury Town v Bognor Regis Town	4-0
Hereford United v Wotton Rovers	6-1
Romsey Town v Torquay United	0-4

First Round

Carlisle United v Bootle	2-0
Tranmere Rovers v Hull City	1-1, 1-2
Blackpool v Barnsley	2-0
Hartlepool United v Bury	0-3
Blackburn Rovers v Oldham Athletic	1-1, 0-1
Wigan Athletic v Darlington	1-1, 0-4
Sunderland v Bradford City	1-3
West Bromwich Albion v Scunthorpe United	9-0
Mile Oak Rovers & Youth v Hednesford Town	1-3
Chester City v Aston Villa	0-2
Grimsby Town v Derby County	0-3
Wrexham v Port Vale	0-2
Walsall v Wolverhampton Wanderers	3-2
Shrewsbury Town v Crewe Alexandra	1-6
Cambridge United v St Albans City	3-1
Brentford v Wokingham Town	4-1

Norwich City v Northampton Town 1-2
Peterborough United v Billericay Town 6-0
Hendon v Colchester United 1-4
Kidderminster Harriers v West Ham United 1-2
Millwall v Oxford United 0-0, 4-4, 4-0
Epsom & Ewell v Erith & Belvedere 1-1, 1-0
Horley Town v Queen's Park Rangers 0-5
Brighton & Hove Albion v Sutton United 5-0
Staines Town v Reading 2-6
Whyteleafe v Egham Town 5-1
Newbury Town v Horndean 3-0
Croydon v Gillingham 1-7
AFC Bournemouth v Swansea City 1-1, 2-0
Hereford United v Torquay United 2-0
Exeter City v Cardiff City 0-0, 1-3
Portsmouth v Swindon Town 4-2
Bristol Rovers v Bristol City 1-3
Plymouth Argyle v Newport County 11-0

Second Round
Bradford City v Port Vale 2-1
Liverpool v Carlisle United 3-0
Burnley v Leeds United 1-2
Blackpool v Newcastle United 1-2
Darlington v Manchester United 2-5
Doncaster Rovers v Everton 1-1, 1-4
Middlesbrough v Sheffield Wednesday 2-2, 0-2
Oldham Athletic v Sheffield United 1-2
Mansfield Town v Manchester City 0-1
Crewe Alexandra v Hull City 1-4
Hednesford Town v Birmingham City 0-5
Leicester City v Nottingham Forest 2-1
Aston Villa v Luton Town 1-3
Northampton Town v Walsall 0-3
Colchester United v Southend United 2-3
Derby County v Coventry City 1-1, 1-3
West Bromwich Albion v West Ham United 3-1
Notts County v Ipswich Town 2-2, 1-4
Watford v Leyton Orient 1-1, 0-0, 2-1
Cambridge United v Stoke City 2-2, 1-6
Tottenham Hotspur v Peterborough United 7-1
Epsom & Ewell v Arsenal 0-11
Crystal Palace v Southampton 2-1
Queen's Park Rangers v Fulham 3-1
(at Yeading FC)
Whyteleafe v Reading 1-5
Newbury Town v Cardiff City 0-3
Brighton & Hove Albion v Charlton Athletic 1-7
Millwall v Hereford United 2-0
Wimbledon v Chelsea 0-4
Bristol City v Plymouth Argyle 2-3
AFC Bournemouth v Brentford 2-3
Portsmouth v Gillingham 1-0

Third Round
Everton v Leicester City 0-0, 1-4
Newcastle United v Walsall 4-3
Coventry City v Liverpool 2-4
Leeds United v Birmingham City 0-0, 1-1, 2-4
Sheffield United v Bradford City 0-0, 0-1
Manchester City v Hull City 1-0
Sheffield Wednesday v Manchester United 0-0, 0-2
Chelsea v Ipswich Town 2-2, 1-2
Millwall v Reading 4-2
Plymouth Argyle v Portsmouth 0-6
Charlton Athletic v Tottenham Hotspur 2-2, 0-2
Cardiff City v Stoke City 0-1
Brentford v Crystal Palace 1-0
Watford v Queen's Park Rangers 2-2, 2-0
West Bromwich Albion v Southend United 3-2
Arsenal v Luton Town 3-2

Fourth Round
Brentford v Stoke City 1-1, 2-1
Millwall v Liverpool 0-1
Manchester United v Ipswich Town 4-1
Bradford City v Manchester City 0-5
Leicester City v Newcastle United 1-3
Portsmouth v Watford 1-1, 2-5
Arsenal v West Bromwich Albion 2-0
Tottenham Hotspur v Birmingham City 2-1

Quarter-Finals
Tottenham Hotspur v Manchester City 0-2
Newcastle United v Arsenal 1-0
Watford v Liverpool 3-0
Brentford v Manchester United 2-1

Semi-Finals *(2 legs)*
Watford v Brentford 2-1, 2-2
Manchester City v Newcastle United 2-1, 1-0

Final first leg

2 MAY

Manchester C (1) 1 *(Wallace)*

Watford (0) 0 4900

Manchester C: Margetison; Lennon, Wills, Peters, Taggart, Quigley, Thompstone, Ward, Hasford, Hughes, Wallace.
Watford: James; Towler, Drysdale, Price, Soloman, Ashby, Evans, Gunn, Bennett, Naylor, Meara (Fuller).
Referee: D. Phillips.

Second leg

9 MAY

Watford (0) 2 *(Gunn, Thomas)*

Manchester C (0) 0 *aet; 90 mins 1-0* 5442

Watford: James; Taylor, Drysdale, Price, Soloman, Ashby, Evans (Meara), Thomas, Bennett, Naylor, Gunn.
Manchester C: Margetison; Lennon, Wills, Peters, Taggart, Quigley, Thompstone (Small), Ward, Hasford (Sheron), Hughes, Wallace.
Referee: D. Phillips.

FA SUNDAY CUP 1988–89

The following 23 clubs received byes to the Second Round: Birmingham Celtic, Chuckery WMC, Cleator Moor WMC, Deborah United, Eagle, East Bowling Unity, Fantail, Grosvenor Oark, Halesowen Harriers, Hazel Tennants, Inter Volante, Iron Bridge, Leggatts Athletic, Morrison Sports, Northwood, Railway Hotel, Rolls Royce Sunday, St Josephs (South Oxhey), Sandwell, Santogee 66, Verulam Arms Athletic, Watford Labour Club, Whetley Lane WMC.

The following 15 clubs were exempted to the Second Round: Avenue Victoria Lodge, Broad Plain House, Cabot Towers, Ford Basildon, Lee Chapel North, Leyton Argyle, Lion Rangers, Lodge Cottrell, Newey Goodman, Nexday, Nicosia, Ranelagh Sports, Slade Celtic, Sunderland Humbledon Plains, Woodpecker.

First Round

Dudley & Weetslade v Almethak 1-1, 0-3
Kent v Blackhall WMC 1-3
Blyth Waterloo SC v Nenthead 0-3
Boundary v Royal Oak (Gorton Albion) 1-0
Carnforth v Lynemouth Inn 1-2
Croxteth & Gillmoss RBL v Overpool United 4-2
East Levenshulme v Britannia 2-1
East & West Toxteth v Oakenshaw 0-1
FC Nirvana v Harrows 4-0
AD Bulwell v FC Coachmen 0-3
Hoval Farrar v Rose United 3-0
Brereton Town v Darchem SM 8-1
BRJ v Dereham Hobbies United 3-3, 1-3
Shouldham Sunday v Kettering Odyssey 1-2
Bulmers v Girton Eagles 1-3
Greenlays v Mackintosh 2-1
Colne Hammers v Evergreen 1-0
Trinity v Brimsdown Rovers 0-2
Scott v HSC 0-6
Hallen Sunday v AFC Bishopstoke 3-1
Sheffield House Rangers v Inter Royalle 2-0
Port of Bristol v Horndean 2-3
Chequers v Sanco
(walkover for Chequers)
Sartan United v Dee Roof Vikings 2-1
Oxford Road Social v Sheerness East 4-1
Artois United v Essex Sports 5-2

Second Round

Oakenshaw v Blackhall WMC 1-5
Nenthead v Sunderland Humbledon Plains 1-1, 0-3
Almethak v Eagle 2-1
Morrison Sports v Lynemouth Inn 2-0
East Bowling Unity v Cleator Moor WMC 2-5
Boundary v Croxteth & Gillmoss RBL 1-3
Northwood v Whetley Lane WMC 3-0
Deborah United v Woodpecker 1-4
East Levenshulme v Nicosia 3-2
Hoval Farrar v Railway Hotel 5-1
Fantail v Lodge Cottrell 0-2
Avenue Victoria Lodge v FC Coachman 1-1, 2-1
Iron Bridge v Slade Celtic 0-1
Chuckery WMC v Brereton Town 2-3
Greenleys v Lion Rangers
(walkover for Greenleys)
FC Nirvana v Birmingham Celtic 1-0
Verulam Arms Athletic v Sandwell 4-3
Girton Eagles v Dereham Hobbies United 3-1
Grosvenor Park v Kettering Odyssey 5-1
Hazel Tennants v Leyton Argyle 2-1
Halesowen Harriers v Brimsdown Rovers 4-0
Newey Goodman v Leggatts Athletic 1-0
Inter Volante v HSC 3-2
Ford Basildon v Colne Hammers 3-1
Sheffield House Rangers v Santogee 66 2-3
Nexday v Rolls Royce Sunday 1-0
Hallen Sunday v St Josephs (South Oxhey) 5-4
Oxford Road Social v Lee Chapel North 0-2
Artois United v Chequers 0-1
Cabot Towers v Horndean 4-1
Broad Plain House v Ranelagh Sports 1-0
Sartan United v Watford Labour Club 2-2, 2-1

Third Round

Woodpecker v Cleator Moor WMC 3-0
Avenue Victoria Lodge v Morrison Sports 5-1
Blackhall WMC v Croxteth & Gillmoss RBL 3-1
(Blackhall subsequently disqualified following misconduct by their supporters. Croxteth were not awarded the tie following misconduct by their players)
Almethak v Northwood 2-0
Sunderland Humbledon Plains v East Levenshulme 0-2
Hoval Farrar v Slade Celtic 0-3
Girton Eagles v FC Nirvana 4-1
Lodge Cottrell v Verulam Arms Athletic 1-0
Hazel Tennants v Brereton Town 4-2
Grosvenor Park v Greenleys 0-1
Halesowen Harriers v Broad Plain House 0-8
Newey Goodman v Hallen Sunday 2-0
Chequers v Nexday 0-4
Cabot Towers v Inter Volante 2-2, 1-4
Ford Basildon v Santogee 66 4-1
Sartan United v Lee Chapel North 0-2

Fourth Round

East Levenshulme v Avenue Victoria Lodge 3-2
Blackhall WMC v Woodpecker
(walkover for Woodpecker)
Almethak v Slade Celtic 3-0
Ford Basildon v Hazel Tennants 5-1
Nexday v Girton Eagles 4-0
Greenleys v Lodge Cottrell 0-3
Lee Chapel North v Broad Plain House 2-0
Inter Volante v Newey Goodman 2-2, 1-2

Quarter-Finals

Almethak v Newey Goodman 2-1
Woodpecker v East Levenshulme 0-3
Lee Chapel North v Lodge Cottrell 2-3
Nexday v Ford Basildon 3-2

Semi-Finals

East Levenshulme v Lodge Cottrell 4-1
(at Warrington Town FC)
Nexday v Almethak 0-1
(at Irthlingborough Diamonds FC)

Final

East Levenshulme v Almethak ?-?

FA CHALLENGE TROPHY FINALS 1970–88

Year	Winner		Runner-up	
1970	Macclesfield T	2	Telford U	0
1971	Telford U	3	Hillingdon B	2
1972	Stafford R	3	Barnet	0
1973	Scarborough	2	Wigan Ath	aet 2
1974	Morecambe	2	Dartford	1
1975	Matlock	4	Scarborough	0
1976	Scarborough	3	Stafford R	aet 2
1977	Scarborough	2	Dagenham	1
1978	Altrincham	3	Leatherhead	1
1979	Stafford R	2	Kettering T	0
1980	Dagenham	2	Mossley	1
1981	Bishop's Stortford	1	Sutton U	0
1982	Enfield	1	Altrincham	aet 0
1983	Telford U	2	Northwich V	1
1984	Northwich V	2	Bangor C	1
			(after 1-1 draw)	
1985	Wealdstone	2	Boston U	1
1986	Altrincham	1	Runcorn	0
1987	Kidderminster H	2	Burton A	1
			(after 0-0 draw)	
1988	Enfield	3	Telford U	2
			(after 0-0 draw)	

FA CHALLENGE VASE FINALS 1975–88

Year	Winner		Runner-up	
1975	Hoddesdon T	2	Epsom & Ewell	1
1976	Billericay T	1	Stamford	aet 0
1977	Billericay T	2	Sheffield	1
			(after 1-1 draw)	
1978	Blue Star	2	Barton R	1
1979	Billericay T	4	Almondsbury G	1
1980	Stamford	2	Guisborough	0
1981	Whickham	3	Willenhall T	aet 2
1982	Forest Green R	3	Rainworth MW	0
1983	VS Rugby	1	Halesowen T	0
1984	Stansted	3	Stamford	2
1985	Halesowen T	3	Fleetwood T	1
1986	Halesowen T	3	Southall	0
1987	St Helens T	3	Warrington T	2
1988	Colne D	1	Emley	0

FA YOUTH CHALLENGE CUP FINALS 1953–88 (aggregate scores)

Year	Winner		Runner-up	
1953	Manchester U	9	Wolverhampton W	3
1954	Manchester U	5	Wolverhampton W	4
1955	Manchester U	7	WBA	1
1956	Manchester U	4	Chesterfield	3
1957	Manchester U	8	West Ham U	2
1958	Wolverhampton W	7	Chelsea	6
1959	Blackburn R	2	West Ham U	1
1960	Chelsea	5	Preston N E	2
1961	Chelsea	5	Everton	3
1962	Newcastle U	2	Wolverhampton W	1
1963	West Ham U	6	Liverpool	5
1964	Manchester U	5	West Ham U	2
1965	Everton	3	Arsenal	2
1966	Arsenal	5	Sunderland	3
1967	Sunderland	2	Birmingham C	0
1968	Burnley	3	Coventry C	2
1969	Sunderland	6	WBA	3
1970	Tottenham H	4	Coventry C	3
1971	Arsenal	2	Cardiff C	0
1972	Aston Villa	5	Liverpool	2
1973	Ipswich T	4	Bristol C	1
1974	Tottenham H	2	Huddersfield T	1
1975	Ipswich T	5	West Ham U	1
1976	WBA	5	Wolverhampton W	0
1977	C Palace	1	Everton	0
1978	C Palace	1	Aston Villa	0
			(one game only)	
1979	Millwall	2	Manchester C	0
1980	Aston Villa	3	Manchester C	2
1981	West Ham U	2	Tottenham H	1
1982	Watford	7	Manchester U	6
1983	Norwich C	6	Everton	5
			(including replay)	
1984	Everton	4	Stoke C	2
1985	Newcastle U	4	Watford	1
1986	Manchester C	3	Manchester U	1
1987	Coventry C	2	Charlton Ath	1
1988	Arsenal	6	Doncaster R	1

FA COUNTY YOUTH CHALLENGE CUP FINALS 1945–88 (aggregate scores)

Year	Winner		Runner-up	
1945	Staffordshire	3	Wiltshire	2
1946	Berks & Bucks	4	Durham	3
1947	Durham	4	Essex	2
1948	Essex	5	Liverpool	3
1949	Liverpool	4	Middlesex	3
1950	Essex	4	Middlesex	3
1951	Middlesex	3	Leics. & Rutland	1
1952	Sussex	3	Liverpool	1
1953	Sheffield & Hallam	5	Hampshire	3
1954	Liverpool	4	Gloucestershire	1
1955	Bedfordshire	2	Sheffield & Hallam	0
1956	Middlesex	3	Staffordshire	2
1957	Hampshire	4	Cheshire	3
1958	Staffordshire	8	London	0
1959	Birmingham	7	London	5
1960	London	6	Birmingham	4
1961	Lancashire	6	Nottinghamshire	3
1962	Middlesex	6	Nottinghamshire	3
1963	Durham	3	Essex	2
1964	Sheffield & Hallam	1	Birmingham	0
1965	Northumberland	7	Middlesex	4
1966	Leics. & Rutland	6	London	5
1967	Northamptonshire	5	Hertfordshire	4
1968	North Riding	7	Devon	4
1969	Northumberland	1	Sussex	0
	(one game only from here)			
1970	Hertfordshire	2	Cheshire	1
1971	Lancashire	2	Gloucestershire	0
1972	Middlesex	2	Liverpool	0
1973	Hertfordshire	3	Northumberland	0
1974	Nottinghamshire	2	London	0
1975	Durham	2	Bedfordshire	1
1976	Northamptonshire	7	Surrey	1
1977	Liverpool	3	Surrey	0
1978	Liverpool	3	Kent	1
1979	Hertfordshire	4	Liverpool	1
1980	Liverpool	2	Lancashire	0
1981	Lancashire	3	East Riding	2
1982	Devon	3	Kent	2
			(after 0-0 draw)	
1983	London	3	Gloucestershire	0
1984	Cheshire	2	Manchester	1
1985	East Riding	2	Middlesex	1
1986	Hertfordshire	4	Manchester	0
1987	North Riding	3	Gloucestershire	1
1988	East Riding	5	Middlesex	3
			(after 0-0 draw)	

FA SUNDAY CUP FINALS 1965–88

Year	Winner		Runner-up	
1965	London	6	Staffordshire	2
			(aggregate scores)	
1966	Unique U	1	Aldridge F	0
1967	Carlton U	2	Stoke W	0
1968	Drovers	2	Brook U	0
1969	Leigh Park	3	Loke U	1
1970	Vention U	1	Unique U	0
1971	Beacontree R	2	Saltley U	0
1972	Newton Unity	4	Springfield C	0
1973	Carlton U	2	Wear Valley	aet 1
1974	Newtown Unity	4	Brentford E	0
1975	Fareham T Cent	1	Players Ath E	0
1976	Brandon U	2	Evergreen	1
1977	Langley Park RH	2	Newtown Unity	0
1978	Arras	2	Lion R	1
			(after 2-2 draw)	
1979	Lobster	3	Carlton U	2
1980	Fantail	1	Twin Foxes	0
1981	Fantail	1	Mackintosh	0
1982	Dingle Rail	2	Twin Foxes	1
1983	Eagle	2	Lee Chapel N	1
			(after 1-1 draw)	
1984	Lee Chapel North	4	Eagle	3
1985	Hobbies	2	Avenue	1
			(after 1-1 and 2-2 draws)	
1986	Avenue	1	Glenn Sports	0
1987	Lodge Cottrell	1	Avenue	0
1988	Nexday	2	Sunderland HP	0

OVENDEN PAPERS FOOTBALL COMBINATION

	P	W	D	L	F	A	Pts
Tottenham Hotspur	38	23	10	5	90	37	56
Arsenal	38	20	12	6	83	44	52
Wimbledon	38	22	7	9	77	39	51
Watford	38	20	9	9	90	60	49
Chelsea	38	20	9	9	74	52	49
Millwall	38	19	10	9	79	46	48
Luton Town	38	18	10	10	90	55	46
Swindon Town	38	20	5	13	70	62	45
Oxford United	38	18	7	13	82	66	43
Crystal Palace	38	16	9	13	55	44	41
Ipswich Town	38	18	5	15	63	62	41
Norwich City	38	16	8	14	64	63	40
Southampton	38	15	7	16	66	67	37
West Ham United	38	9	10	19	53	72	28
Brighton & HA	38	7	13	18	43	81	27
Fulham	38	10	7	21	49	96	27
Charlton Athletic	38	8	9	21	59	80	25
Portsmouth	38	8	6	24	33	88	22
Queen's Park Rangers	38	6	5	27	36	79	17
Reading	38	5	6	27	38	101	16

CENTRAL LEAGUE

Division One

	P	W	D	L	F	A	Pts
Nottingham Forest	34	20	6	8	83	45	66
Everton	34	19	7	8	70	35	64
Aston Villa	34	18	7	9	73	50	61
Liverpool	34	16	9	9	64	40	57
Coventry City	34	17	6	11	66	52	57
Derby County	34	15	11	8	44	33	56
Sheffield United	34	14	9	11	67	74	51
Huddersfield Town	34	12	12	10	51	54	48
Leeds United	34	13	7	14	59	59	46
Leicester City	34	13	6	15	65	63	45
Manchester City	34	12	9	13	64	65	45
Blackburn Rovers	34	13	2	19	55	62	41
Manchester United	34	10	10	14	61	62	40
Newcastle United	34	10	10	14	51	58	40
West Bromwich Albion	34	10	8	16	55	76	38
Barnsley	34	8	9	17	46	80	33
Sheffield Wednesday	34	8	8	18	40	70	32
Sunderland	34	6	8	20	40	76	26

Division Two

	P	W	D	L	F	A	Pts
Hull City	34	25	3	6	82	38	78
Notts County	34	20	8	6	77	48	68
Bradford City	34	19	7	8	78	53	64
Oldham Athletic	34	18	8	8	67	39	62
Bolton Wanderers	34	18	8	8	77	52	62
Stoke City	34	17	10	7	60	38	61
Middlesbrough	34	15	7	12	78	61	52
Darlington	34	13	7	14	50	60	46
Rotherham United	34	12	6	16	60	64	42
Grimsby Town	34	12	5	17	47	61	41
Blackpool	34	12	5	17	52	78	41
Preston North End	34	12	4	18	56	63	40
Port Vale	34	11	6	17	44	58	39
York City	34	10	8	16	52	58	38
Mansfield Town	34	9	11	14	59	68	38
Wigan Athletic	34	7	11	16	44	60	32
Scunthorpe United	34	8	7	19	39	68	31
Doncaster Rovers	34	4	7	23	31	86	19

DRYBROUGHS NORTHERN LEAGUE

Division One

	P	W	D	L	F	A	Pts
Billingham Synthonia	38	26	6	6	83	34	84
Tow Law Town	38	23	8	7	74	45	77
Gretna	38	22	7	9	80	37	73
Guisborough Town	38	21	9	8	74	37	72
Billingham Town	38	20	4	14	59	47	64
Newcastle Blue Star	38	17	10	11	61	38	61
Brandon United	38	15	8	15	50	60	53
Ferryhill Athletic	38	15	7	16	72	65	52
Blyth Spartans	38	13	13	12	51	50	52
Stockton	38	15	7	16	58	63	52
Spennymoor United	38	14	9	15	47	60	51
Whitby Town	38	13	9	16	56	52	48
Easington Colliery	38	12	11	15	51	57	47
Durham City	38	11	13	14	41	42	46
South Bank	38	12	10	16	46	58	46
Seaham Red Star	38	12	8	18	50	67	44
Shildon	38	9	11	18	50	88	38
North Shields	38	10	6	22	56	77	36
Chester-le-Street Town	38	6	14	18	35	60	32
Crook Town	38	5	8	25	32	89	*20

Division Two

	P	W	D	L	F	A	Pts
Consett	38	30	3	5	89	32	93
Alnwick Town	38	25	9	4	92	36	84
Whickham	38	26	6	6	88	38	84
Prudhoe East End	38	24	6	8	68	32	78
Ashington	38	21	5	12	79	52	68
Peterlee Newtown	38	20	7	11	70	53	67
Bedlington Terriers	38	16	7	15	63	50	55
Horden Colliery Welfare	38	15	10	13	57	58	55
Northallerton Town	38	13	15	10	62	38	*51
Ryhope Community	38	13	11	14	67	60	50
Murton	38	14	8	16	65	62	50
West Auckland Town	38	12	11	15	66	72	47
Langley Park Welfare	38	13	6	19	58	72	*42
Norton and Stockton Ancients	38	11	7	20	52	72	40
Esh Winning	38	10	8	20	42	68	38
Darlington Cleveland Bridge	38	10	8	20	49	83	38
Evenwood Town	38	8	8	22	53	100	32
Washington	38	8	6	24	50	87	30
Willington	38	8	6	24	43	97	30
Shotton Comrades	38	5	9	24	32	83	24

*Denotes three points deducted.

LINCOLNSHIRE STANDARD GROUP LEAGUE

	P	W	D	L	F	A	Pts
Ruston Sports	28	21	3	4	75	26	66
Grimsby Charltons	28	20	5	3	65	24	65
Crowle United	28	16	8	4	78	31	56
Louth United Reserves	28	16	5	7	66	45	53
Sleaford Town	28	12	9	7	49	37	45
Skegness Town	28	12	6	10	52	41	42
Grimsby Amateurs	28	12	6	10	48	41	41
Bottesford Town	28	11	4	13	54	54	37
Louth Old Boys	28	8	11	9	39	47	*34
Grimsby Athletic	28	9	5	14	57	69	32
BRSA Immingham	28	8	6	14	35	53	30
Nettleham	28	7	6	15	29	65	27
Barton Town	28	7	5	16	50	75	26
Market Rasen Town	28	3	9	16	33	87	18
Eaton Hall College	28	1	7	20	34	80	10

*Point deducted for playing ineligible player.

KEY CONSULTANTS SOUTH MIDLANDS LEAGUE

Premier Division	P	W	D	L	F	A	Pts
Langford	34	26	4	4	73	24	82
Thame United	34	23	6	5	81	32	75
Selby	34	19	9	6	70	38	66
Shillington	34	19	8	7	62	40	65
Hoddesdon Town	34	17	10	7	53	33	61
Welwyn Garden City	34	15	9	10	64	50	54
The 61 F.C. (Luton)	34	15	8	11	50	48	53
Pitstone & Ivinghoe	32	13	10	11	53	49	49
Totternhoe	34	13	9	12	49	46	48
Leighton Town	34	13	7	14	47	60	46
New Bradwell St. Peter	34	12	4	18	56	64	40
Pirton	34	10	10	14	41	52	40
Winslow United	34	9	8	17	46	72	35
Electrolux	34	9	5	20	35	67	32
Biggleswade Town	34	8	6	20	39	66	30
Brache Sparta	34	8	5	21	33	64	29
Shefford Town	34	7	5	22	49	68	26
Milton Keynes Borough	34	4	9	21	37	65	21

Division One	P	W	D	L	F	A	Pts
Welwyn Garden United	22	16	2	4	62	22	50
Buckingham Athletic	22	15	5	2	58	30	50
Caddington	22	13	3	6	50	27	42
Ashcroft	22	12	1	9	42	39	37
Ickleford	22	8	5	9	30	39	29
Walden Rangers	22	7	7	8	32	33	28
Cranfield United	22	8	3	11	30	44	27
Delco Products	22	7	5	10	38	41	26
Tring Athletic	22	7	5	10	35	47	26
Sandy Albion	22	8	2	12	37	51	26
Stony Stratford Town	22	6	3	13	29	49	21
Harpenden Town	22	4	1	17	23	44	13

VAUX WEARSIDE LEAGUE

	P	W	D	L	F	A	Pts
Dunston FB	32	23	7	2	70	23	76
Eppleton CW	32	24	3	5	76	25	75
Vaux Ryhope	32	22	2	8	74	33	68
South Shields	32	19	5	8	67	46	62
Hebburn	32	18	6	8	68	44	60
Marske Utd	32	15	7	10	60	49	52
Newton Aycliffe	32	14	4	14	49	60	46
Boldon CA	32	12	7	13	47	47	43
Herrington CW	32	11	8	13	41	55	41
Hartlepool BWOB	32	12	6	14	66	59	*39
Cleator Moor Celtic	32	11	6	15	44	60	39
Roker	32	9	7	16	32	46	34
Annfield Plain	32	9	5	18	46	66	32
Dawdon CW	32	7	9	16	38	47	30
Coundon TT	32	8	5	19	38	69	29
Gateshead Clarke Chapman	32	7	5	20	45	77	26
Blackhall CW	32	3	4	25	23	78	13

*3 points deducted.

THE JEWSON SOUTH-WESTERN LEAGUE

	P	W	D	L	F	A	Pts
Falmouth Town	34	24	7	3	95	27	55
St. Blazey	34	23	7	4	73	29	53
Bodmin Town	34	22	9	3	69	24	53
Newquay	34	22	8	4	68	24	52
Launceston	34	14	15	5	45	26	43
Truro City	34	16	8	10	60	51	40
Wadebridge Town	34	14	12	8	57	48	40
Torpoint Athletic	34	12	10	12	52	72	34
Tavistock	34	10	10	14	48	57	30
Millbrook	34	12	5	17	48	57	29
Oak Villa	34	10	9	15	47	65	29
St. Austell	34	8	9	17	32	52	25
Newton Abbot	34	10	5	19	41	63	25
Clyst Rovers	34	7	10	17	40	66	24
Bugle	34	7	9	18	34	50	23
Penzance	34	7	8	19	45	72	22
Holsworthy	34	5	10	19	33	66	20
Appledore/BAAC	34	5	5	24	44	76	15

THE BASS NORTH WEST COUNTIES LEAGUE

Division 1	P	W	D	L	F	A	Pts
Rossendale United	34	24	8	2	84	27	56
Knowsley United	34	21	8	5	85	43	50
St. Helens Town	34	20	8	6	60	25	48
Colwyn Bay	34	19	9	6	77	45	47
Darwen	34	19	9	6	64	36	47
Warrington Town	34	16	10	8	47	37	42
Flixton	34	15	8	11	61	44	38
Leyland Motors	34	15	8	11	53	44	38
Bootle	34	14	4	16	49	54	32
Burscough	34	11	10	13	40	51	32
Ellesmere Port	34	9	12	13	36	42	30
Clitheroe	34	8	12	14	38	41	28
Skelmersdale United	34	8	9	17	39	68	25
Atherton LR	34	9	6	19	47	74	24
Prescot Cables	34	7	9	18	36	60	23
Salford	34	7	8	19	33	70	22
Ashton United	34	7	6	21	37	72	*18
Formby	34	3	4	27	24	77	10

*Denotes points deducted for breach of rule.

Division 2	P	W	D	L	F	A	Pts
Vauxhall GM	34	25	8	1	68	17	58
Main Road	34	22	7	5	96	40	51
Chadderton	34	20	9	5	71	29	49
Wren Rovers	34	19	10	5	77	45	48
Nantwich Town	34	20	4	10	66	28	44
Newcastle Town	34	15	10	9	53	37	40
Great Harwood Town	34	16	6	12	52	40	38
Maghull	34	12	13	9	46	44	37
Bacup Borough	34	11	12	11	55	57	34
Daisy Hill	34	12	6	16	36	49	30
Atherton Collieries	34	9	11	14	52	58	29
Padiham	34	9	10	15	39	57	28
Glossop	34	10	7	17	42	60	27
Cheadle Town	34	10	7	17	46	67	27
Oldham Town	34	6	11	17	46	66	23
Blackpool Mechanics	34	9	5	20	46	72	23
Ashton Town	34	4	11	19	31	68	19
Newton	34	1	5	28	23	111	7

NORTHERN COUNTIES EAST LEAGUE

Premier Division	P	W	D	L	F	A	Pts
Emley	32	25	5	2	80	18	80
Hatfield Main	32	21	9	2	67	24	72
Bridlington Town	32	21	5	6	67	26	68
North Ferriby	32	17	9	6	63	31	60
Guiseley	32	16	10	6	50	27	58
Denaby United	32	13	7	12	52	50	46
Pontefract Colls	32	10	11	11	37	34	41
Harrogate Railway	32	10	11	11	41	43	41
Thackley	32	11	6	15	43	59	39
Belper Town	32	9	10	13	45	51	37
Armthorpe Welfare	32	9	9	14	44	60	36
Hallam	32	9	5	18	47	77	32
Long Eaton United	32	8	7	17	32	54	31
Brigg Town	32	8	7	17	43	66	31
Grimethorpe MW	32	8	5	19	38	59	29
Bridlington Trinity	32	6	7	19	40	72	25
Ossett Albion	32	5	9	18	33	71	24

Division 1	P	W	D	L	F	A	Pts
Sheffield	30	21	5	4	76	25	63
Rowntree Mackintosh	30	18	6	6	68	36	60
Woolley MW	30	16	11	3	49	28	59
Maltby MW	30	17	5	8	68	38	56
Pickering Town	30	16	4	10	58	54	52
Garforth Town	30	15	5	10	56	34	50
Eccleshill United	30	15	4	11	47	39	49
Collingham	30	14	5	11	38	30	47
Immingham Town	30	12	10	8	39	31	46
Kiveton Park	30	11	1	18	30	44	34
Mexborough Town	30	8	7	15	28	40	31
Parkgate	30	8	6	16	29	54	30
Frecheville CA	30	6	11	13	31	44	29
York RI	30	6	10	14	25	37	28
Bradley Rangers	30	6	3	21	22	62	21
Pilkington Recs.	30	3	3	24	18	86	12

NENE GROUP UNITED COUNTIES LEAGUE

Premier Division

	P	W	D	L	F	A	Pts
Potton	38	24	6	8	70	37	78
Brackley	38	20	8	10	71	33	68
Holbeach	38	18	10	10	70	46	64
Irthlingborough	38	17	13	8	56	37	64
Rothwell	38	18	8	12	63	55	62
Raunds	38	18	8	12	54	47	62
Stamford	38	17	10	11	55	51	61
Wootton	38	17	8	13	50	46	59
Long Buckby	38	15	8	15	60	55	53
Stotfold	38	14	10	14	59	55	52
Desborough	38	13	10	15	58	65	49
Eynesbury	38	12	12	14	47	44	48
N'ton Spencer	38	13	8	17	56	55	47
Arlesey	38	14	5	19	40	66	47
S & L Corby	38	12	8	18	57	68	44
Cogenhoe	38	12	8	18	53	71	44
Baker Perkins	38	10	11	17	43	62	41
M Blackstone	38	10	8	20	43	58	38
Kempston	38	8	11	19	46	67	35
Bourne	38	8	10	20	39	72	34

Division One

	P	W	D	L	F	A	Pts
Ramsey	36	28	4	4	103	37	88
Burton PW	36	22	10	4	65	27	76
Sharnbrook	36	23	6	7	78	37	75
Blisworth	36	17	11	8	75	46	62
Cottingham	36	18	8	10	65	39	62
Newport Pagnell	36	18	6	12	55	35	60
St. Ives	36	16	11	9	62	44	59
Thrapston	36	16	8	12	69	51	56
Higham	36	15	9	12	43	41	54
Bugbrooke	36	11	12	13	52	50	45
Towcester	36	12	8	16	49	68	44
Timken Duston	36	12	7	17	58	50	43
Ampthill	36	11	10	15	48	69	43
Whitworths	36	12	6	18	57	77	42
Irchester	36	9	10	17	53	61	37
O N Chenecks	36	7	10	19	32	70	31
Olney	36	7	5	24	47	82	26
Ford Sports	36	7	5	24	39	106	26
Timken Athletic	36	4	8	24	33	93	20

WINSTON LEAD KENT LEAGUE

Division One

	P	W	D	L	F	A	Pts
Hythe Town	38	29	3	6	133	41	90
Deal Town	38	24	4	10	80	35	76
Faversham	38	22	7	9	68	36	73
Darenth Heathside	38	20	8	10	69	44	68
Sittingbourne	38	18	12	8	59	43	66
Alma Swanley	38	18	10	10	66	46	64
Cray Wanderers	38	19	7	12	67	53	64
Whitstable Town	38	18	9	11	75	42	63
Ramsgate	38	19	6	13	66	61	63
Slade Green	38	17	10	11	60	59	61
Tunbridge Wells	38	16	8	14	58	57	56
Kent Police	38	16	5	17	61	74	53
Crockenhill	38	11	12	15	52	51	45
Danson	38	12	5	21	55	67	41
Met. Police (Hayes)	38	11	7	20	50	83	40
Greenwich Boro'	38	8	15	12	53	56	*36
Beckenham	38	8	10	20	41	68	34
Thames Poly	38	8	10	20	44	83	34
Chatham Town	38	3	8	27	41	105	17
Herne Bay	38	3	4	31	27	121	13

*Greenwich Boro' – 3 points deducted.

Division Two

	P	W	D	L	F	A	Pts
*Hythe Town	36	27	4	5	112	31	79
Ashford	36	24	4	8	67	32	76
Dover Athletic	36	22	7	7	102	45	73
Hastings Town	36	21	6	9	83	49	69
Sittingbourne	36	18	11	7	84	52	65
Sheppey United	36	19	6	11	89	45	63
Cray Wanderers	36	19	3	14	75	61	60
Ramsgate	36	16	7	13	65	60	55
Faversham	36	14	10	12	62	57	52
Thames Poly	36	12	11	13	50	54	47
*Greenwich Boro'	36	15	5	16	62	72	47
*Snowdown CW	36	14	9	13	54	60	44
Folkestone	36	9	10	17	56	77	37
*Beckenham	36	10	8	18	39	67	35
Deal Town	36	9	7	20	37	99	34
*Thanet United	36	7	9	20	47	79	30
Whitstable Town	36	8	6	22	38	74	30
*Chatham Town	36	6	7	23	42	91	24
Herne Bay	36	4	6	26	29	104	18

*Beckenham – 3 points & 4 goals deducted.
*Chatham Town – 1 point & 1 goal deducted.
*Greenwich Boro' – 3 points & 3 goals deducted.
*Hythe Town – 6 points deducted.
*Snowdon CW – 7 points & 7 goals deducted.
*Thanet United – 1 goal deducted.

BANKS'S BREWERY LEAGUE

Premier Division

	P	W	D	L	F	A	Pts
Blakenall	40	25	11	4	81	31	86
Gresley Rovers	40	24	13	3	100	30	85
Halesowen Harriers	40	23	9	8	74	43	78
Paget Rangers	40	23	8	9	91	41	77
Rushall Olympic	40	22	11	7	73	39	77
Oldbury United	40	22	10	8	89	49	76
Hinckley Town	40	23	6	11	96	38	75
Lye Town	40	20	7	13	61	42	67
Chasetown	40	19	9	12	54	48	66
Malvern Town	40	17	12	11	81	47	63
Rocester	40	14	15	11	67	49	57
Harrisons	40	12	10	18	50	71	46
Tividale	40	10	9	21	65	84	39
Hinckley Athletic	40	9	12	19	50	76	39
Wolverhampton Casuals	40	8	13	19	49	86	37
Wednesfield Social	40	9	8	23	33	82	35
Westfields	40	8	9	23	43	97	33
Millfields	40	9	5	26	42	85	32
Oldswinford	40	8	8	24	42	98	32
Tipton Town	40	8	6	26	30	86	30
Stourport Swifts	40	6	11	23	45	94	29

Division 1

	P	W	D	L	F	A	Pts
Newport Town	34	24	6	4	71	27	78
Donnington Wood	34	22	6	6	79	43	72
Ettingshall HT	34	21	6	7	71	44	69
Darlaston	34	20	8	6	83	42	68
Pelsall Villa	34	19	9	6	64	41	66
Chasetown Reserves	34	16	7	11	68	62	55
Ludlow Town	34	16	6	12	79	50	54
Springvale-Tranco	34	14	5	15	49	49	47
Aero Lucas	34	12	10	12	55	59	46
Hinton	34	13	7	14	56	65	46
Brewood	34	10	11	13	51	60	41
Cradley Town	34	10	8	16	43	61	38
Nuneaton Bor Res	34	9	9	16	50	56	36
Cannock Chase	34	10	6	18	52	72	36
Great Wyrley	34	9	4	21	62	76	31
Gornal Athletic	34	8	7	19	51	78	31
Wolverhampton United	34	6	6	22	42	76	24
Bilston United	34	4	5	25	25	90	17

McEWAN'S NORTHERN ALLIANCE

Premier Division

	P	W	D	L	F	A	Pts
Seaton Terrace	28	22	3	3	72	25	69
West Allotment	28	20	2	6	84	38	62
Seaton Delaval	28	18	4	6	57	31	58
Dunston	28	12	6	10	52	48	42
Newbiggin	28	12	5	11	51	51	41
Heaton Stannington	28	12	5	11	38	42	41
Swalwell	28	11	6	11	61	57	39
Ponteland	28	10	5	13	55	54	35
Morpeth Town	28	9	8	11	54	62	35
Forest Hall	28	11	3	14	47	48	*33
Wark	28	9	7	12	52	56	33
Dudley Welfare	28	8	7	13	57	64	31
Percy Main	28	9	4	15	50	66	31
Wigton	28	6	5	17	46	78	23
Stobswood	28	5	3	20	56	111	*15

* 3 points deducted

GREAT MILLS LEAGUE

Premier Division

	P	W	D	L	F	A	Pts
Saltash United	40	26	10	4	90	35	62
Exmouth Town	40	29	4	7	79	43	62
Taunton Town	40	23	10	7	95	41	56
Liskeard Athletic	40	20	12	8	46	25	52
Plymouth Argyle	40	19	13	8	84	39	51
Bristol Manor Farm	40	20	7	13	72	49	47
Weston Super Mare	40	17	8	15	73	52	42
Paulton Rovers	40	14	14	12	60	53	42
Barnstaple Town	40	17	7	16	61	54	41
Swanage & Herston	40	15	10	15	71	73	40
Clevedon Town	40	16	7	17	63	70	39
Chippenham Town	40	11	14	15	48	52	36
Welton Rovers	40	13	10	17	50	57	36
Radstock Town	40	9	18	13	38	65	36
Chard Town	40	12	11	17	49	78	35
Bideford	40	12	9	19	49	72	33
Frome Town	40	11	10	19	54	80	32
Mangotsfield United	40	10	9	21	53	74	29
Dawlish Town	40	11	7	22	48	69	29
Torrington	40	7	12	21	46	84	26
Minehead	40	5	4	31	30	94	14

First Division

	P	W	D	L	F	A	Pts
Larkhall Athletic	38	25	11	2	88	40	61
Tiverton Town	38	27	6	5	108	33	60
Bridport	38	24	7	7	90	35	55
Calne Town	38	17	14	7	58	34	48
Devizes Town	38	19	9	10	55	39	47
Odd Down	38	17	12	9	57	45	46
Wellington	38	17	11	10	72	56	45
Ilfracombe Town	38	16	13	9	59	47	45
Backwell United	38	15	8	15	49	46	38
Keynsham Town	38	11	13	14	55	55	35
Heavitree United	38	13	9	16	54	58	35
Melksham Town	38	11	13	14	43	49	35
Ottery St Mary	38	12	8	18	46	71	32
Clandown	38	10	11	17	47	63	31
Bath City	38	11	7	20	60	67	29
Westbury United	38	10	9	19	59	66	29
Yeovil Town	38	10	9	19	42	49	29
Warminster Town	38	5	11	22	34	84	21
Glastonbury	38	6	9	23	38	97	21
Elmore	38	8	2	28	38	118	18

ESSEX SENIOR LEAGUE

Senior Section

	P	W	D	L	F	A	Pts
Brightlingsea United	32	21	5	6	68	28	68
East Thurrock United	32	19	8	5	70	38	65
Ford United	32	18	7	7	56	31	61
Burnham Ramblers	32	17	8	7	65	43	59
Stansted	32	15	5	12	53	52	50
Canvey Island	32	14	7	11	62	52	49
Southend Manor	32	13	10	9	46	39	49
Eton Manor	32	12	9	11	46	43	45
Brentwood	32	12	8	12	45	52	44
Woodford Town	32	12	7	13	40	37	43
Sawbridgeworth Town	32	11	7	14	43	43	40
Stambridge	32	10	8	14	45	56	38
Chelmsford C Res	32	7	11	14	41	55	32
Coggeshall Town	32	8	8	16	42	57	32
Bowers United	32	7	10	15	36	55	31
East Ham United	32	7	7	18	42	75	28
Maldon Town	32	3	7	22	28	72	16

JEWSON LEAGUE

Premier Division

	P	W	D	L	F	A	Pts
Sudbury Town	40	29	6	5	117	46	93
Braintree Town	40	26	7	7	106	41	85
Wisbech Town	40	24	12	4	84	40	84
March Town United	40	22	9	9	76	49	*72
Great Yarmouth Town	40	21	9	10	75	50	72
Histon	40	19	7	14	87	57	64
Haverhill Rovers	40	18	8	14	63	63	62
Stowmarket Town	40	17	9	14	69	51	60
Thetford Town	40	17	8	14	79	74	59
Gorleston	40	15	10	15	58	69	55
Felixstowe Town	40	15	11	14	82	67	53
Lowestoft Town	40	15	8	17	68	71	53
Watton United	40	14	7	19	70	82	49
Harwich & Parkeston	40	12	11	17	60	64	47
Tiptree United	40	13	6	20	60	70	45
Newmarket Town	40	10	12	18	39	63	42
Brantham Athletic	40	11	8	21	57	90	41
Clacton Town	40	9	13	18	42	65	40
Chatteris Town	40	9	9	22	44	75	36
Ely City	40	8	6	26	48	108	30
Soham Town Rangers	40	6	4	30	36	125	22

*3 points deducted for failing to fulfil fixture.

First Division

	P	W	D	L	F	A	Pts
Wroxham	26	20	2	4	90	22	62
Halstead Town	26	20	2	4	88	30	62
Diss Town	26	18	5	3	65	31	59
Fakenham Town	26	13	5	8	42	31	44
Downham Town	26	10	8	8	49	46	38
Loadwell Ipswich	26	10	7	9	57	47	37
Long Sutton Ath	26	8	7	11	40	44	31
Bury Town Reserves	26	9	4	13	38	53	31
Huntingdon United	26	8	7	11	30	48	31
Coalite Yaxley	26	8	5	13	38	42	29
King's Lynn Reserves	26	7	8	11	33	39	29
Warboys Town	26	7	5	14	31	57	26
Mildenhall Town	26	2	8	16	23	72	14
Somersham Town	26	3	5	18	24	86	14

FEDERATED HOMES LEAGUE

Premier Division

	P	W	D	L	F	A	Pts
Yate Town	32	26	5	1	75	16	83
Sharpness	32	21	8	3	77	31	71
Abingdon United	32	18	6	8	54	26	60
Fairford Town	32	15	7	10	45	40	52
Pegasus Juniors	32	15	6	11	60	55	51
Bicester Town	32	14	8	10	70	40	50
Moreton Town	32	12	10	10	51	47	46
Didcot Town	32	12	10	10	38	36	46
Penhill	32	13	4	15	41	36	43
Bishops Cleeve	32	12	5	15	32	54	41
Shortwood United	32	11	7	14	40	47	40
Wantage Town	32	9	9	14	42	57	36
Rayners Lane	32	8	7	17	41	60	31
Supermarine	32	8	5	19	29	57	29
Kintbury Rangers	32	6	8	18	24	51	26
Wallingford Town	32	6	8	18	31	64	26
Viking Sports	32	6	7	19	28	61	25

Division One

	P	W	D	L	F	A	Pts
Almondsbury Picksons	28	20	4	4	66	20	64
Headington Amateurs	28	19	5	4	49	19	62
Lambourn Sports	28	14	7	7	53	40	49
Highworth Town	28	12	8	8	52	41	44
Wootton Bassett Town	28	11	7	10	50	41	40
Purton	28	11	7	10	37	42	40
Cheltenham Town Res	28	12	3	13	53	50	39
Easington Sports	28	9	12	7	41	43	39
Chipping Norton Town	28	11	6	11	45	49	39
Clanfield	28	9	8	11	49	55	35
Kidlington	28	10	5	13	41	57	35
Cheltenham Saracens	28	6	10	12	33	45	28
The Herd	28	8	4	16	44	62	28
Carterton Town	28	7	5	16	36	54	26
Cirencester Town	28	3	5	20	28	59	14

CENTRAL MIDLANDS LEAGUE

Supreme Division

	P	W	D	L	F	A	Pts
Boston	32	19	8	5	69	27	65
Arnold	32	17	9	6	67	34	60
Gainsborough Town	32	17	6	9	68	41	57
Heanor Town	32	17	5	10	74	49	56
Harworth CI	32	15	10	7	62	45	55
Oakam United	32	16	7	9	69	54	55
Ilkeston Town	32	14	10	8	47	33	52
Borrowash Victoria	32	12	10	10	59	46	46
Staveley Works	32	13	5	14	42	46	44
Crookes	32	10	13	9	41	42	43
Louth United	32	11	8	13	43	48	41
Lincoln United	32	10	7	15	38	57	37
Stanton	32	7	10	15	38	56	31
Kimberley Town	32	8	6	18	30	48	30
Melton Town	32	7	8	17	35	72	29
Rossington	32	7	7	18	45	72	28
Grimsby (Ross)	32	4	7	21	45	102	19

Premier Division

	P	W	D	L	F	A	Pts
Priory	36	25	8	3	92	26	83
Mickleover RBL	36	23	5	8	85	40	74
Highfield Rangers	36	23	5	8	85	40	74
Station	36	21	7	8	83	45	70
Derby Rolls-Royce	36	19	9	8	57	33	66
Derby Prims	36	20	5	11	71	54	65
Blidworth	36	19	7	10	85	57	64
Blackwell	36	17	9	10	73	55	60
Nettleham United	36	17	6	13	66	66	57
Radford	36	15	11	10	64	56	56
Newhall United	36	13	5	18	65	66	44
Sandiacre Town	36	12	7	17	66	83	43
Kilburn MW	36	12	7	17	49	69	43
Shirebrook	36	8	7	21	29	77	31
Belper Thorntons	36	8	5	23	47	81	29
Slack & Parr	36	8	5	23	43	87	29
Arnold Kingswell	32	7	7	22	51	78	28
Wombwell SA	36	8	3	25	40	93	27
Retford Rail	36	3	5	28	34	98	14

MIDLAND FOOTBALL COMBINATION

Premier Division

	P	W	D	L	F	A	Pts
Bolmere St. Michaels	34	23	9	2	76	22	55
Racing Club Warwick	34	22	8	4	77	31	52
Evesham United	34	21	7	6	82	30	49
Princes End United	34	17	9	8	58	37	43
West Midlands Police	34	18	6	10	66	41	42
Northfield Town	34	15	10	9	55	43	40
Stratford Town	34	14	10	10	60	44	38
Walsall Wood	34	13	10	11	49	52	36
Hinckley FC	34	12	11	11	49	55	35
Highgate United	34	9	15	10	60	61	33
Bolehall Swifts	34	12	8	14	44	55	32
Kings Heath	34	9	11	14	42	52	29
Chelmsley Town	34	10	7	17	37	65	27
Knowle	34	8	10	16	34	58	26
Polesworth North Warwick	34	4	14	16	37	62	22
Coleshill Town	34	8	6	20	46	73	22
Solihull Borough	34	7	6	21	41	72	20
Shirley Town	34	4	3	27	20	80	11

GREENE KING SPARTAN LEAGUE

Premier Division

	P	W	D	L	F	A	Pts
Abingdon Town	38	25	9	4	95	26	84
Wandsworth & Norwood	38	25	9	4	83	34	84
Northwood	38	25	4	9	84	40	79
Edgware Town	38	22	9	7	88	55	75
Barkingside	38	21	11	6	73	41	74
Cheshunt	38	20	11	7	78	44	71
Brimsdown Rovers	38	21	7	10	77	44	70
Southgate Athletic	38	19	11	8	83	37	68
Southwark Borough	38	16	12	10	80	65	60
Walthamstow Pennant	38	17	7	14	57	47	58
Hanwell Town	38	16	9	13	58	48	57
Waltham Abbey	38	16	7	15	65	63	55
Amersham Town	38	10	7	21	49	69	37
North Greenford U	38	11	3	24	44	81	36
Thamesmead Town	38	9	6	23	43	87	33
Corinthian Casuals	38	9	5	24	41	91	32
Bromley Athletic	38	8	6	24	58	84	30
Beaconsfield United	38	5	9	24	32	73	24
Beckton United	38	6	6	26	48	106	24
Crown and Manor	38	4	2	32	37	138	14

Division One

	P	W	D	L	F	A	Pts
Newmont Travel	30	23	5	2	87	25	74
Metrogas	30	19	6	5	71	35	63
Catford Wanderers	30	19	5	6	71	34	62
Walthamstow Trojans	30	18	4	8	70	33	58
Hackney Downs Ath	30	18	4	8	62	33	58
Brook House	30	15	8	7	58	31	53
Old Roan	30	15	8	7	68	43	52
Royal George	30	15	2	13	62	58	47
Swanley Town	30	12	6	12	62	70	42
Phoenix Sports	30	11	4	15	55	63	37
REMA	30	9	7	14	43	67	34
AFC Millwall	30	9	2	19	52	83	29
Ilford	30	8	3	19	53	76	27
Chigwell Police	30	6	5	19	39	74	23
Ulysses	30	4	6	20	32	69	18
Penhill Standard	30	0	4	26	29	120	4

HIGHLAND LEAGUE

	HOME						AWAY					
	P	*W*	*D*	*L*	*F*	*A*	*W*	*D*	*L*	*F*	*A*	*Pts*
Peterhead	34	13	3	1	45	19	9	4	4	34	19	73
Cove Rangers	34	10	5	2	40	20	11	1	5	31	18	69
Huntly	34	11	1	4	47	21	9	5	4	35	19	66
Inverness Thistle	34	11	5	2	39	9	8	4	4	31	20	66
Elgin City	34	10	5	2	32	15	9	4	4	41	22	66
Keith	34	11	4	1	33	15	8	4	6	28	17	65
Forres Mechanics	34	11	6	1	37	16	7	3	6	26	18	63
Ross County	34	9	1	7	35	30	9	2	6	26	21	57
Buckie Thistle	34	8	3	6	33	22	8	3	6	33	31	54
Caledonian	34	7	6	4	38	15	7	5	5	32	27	53
Fraserburgh	34	8	3	5	26	22	7	5	6	26	21	53
Lossiemouth	34	7	1	9	33	33	4	6	7	24	33	40
Deveronvale	34	4	6	7	23	33	4	1	12	21	47	31
Brora Rangers	34	6	0	12	31	38	2	2	12	11	29	26
Clachnacuddin	34	5	0	12	16	41	1	6	10	18	42	24
Nairn County	34	3	5	9	25	45	2	3	12	24	57	23
Rothes	34	4	3	10	22	42	0	1	16	19	62	16
Fort William	34	2	3	12	11	37	1	1	15	13	63	13

LEICESTERSHIRE SENIOR LEAGUE

Premier Division

	P	*W*	*D*	*L*	*F*	*A*	*Pts*
Stapenhill	30	26	1	3	102	26	53
Wigston Town	30	15	8	7	57	33	38
Birstall United	30	16	6	8	62	37	38
Lutterworth Town	30	14	7	9	53	35	35
St Andrews SC	30	15	5	10	69	57	35`
Friar Lane OB	30	13	8	9	52	37	34
Holwell Sports	30	13	7	10	62	51	33
Newfoundpool WMC	30	11	11	8	46	41	33
Oadby Town	30	14	5	11	48	51	33
Anstey Nomads	30	10	12	8	53	50	32
Wigston Fields	30	12	8	10	42	48	*30
Narborough & Litt.	30	11	7	12	48	44	29
Thringstone	30	6	6	18	43	85	18
Syston St Peters	30	5	7	18	38	65	17
Quorn	30	6	3	21	29	66	15
Kirby Muxlow SC	30	1	3	26	21	99	5

Division One

	P	*W*	*D*	*L*	*F*	*A*	*Pts*
Earl Shilton Alb	30	17	8	5	61	38	42
Pedigree Petfoods	30	16	7	7	70	48	39
Hillcroft	30	17	3	10	72	43	37
Barwell Athletic	30	15	7	8	60	54	37
Barlestone St. Giles	30	15	6	9	56	39	36
Houghton Rangers	30	14	7	9	48	41	35
Rolls Royce	30	12	8	10	56	37	32
Anstey Town	30	13	5	12	42	49	31
Downes Sports	30	12	6	12	60	52	30
North Kilworth	30	11	8	11	49	64	30
Sileby Town	30	10	6	14	53	61	26
Whetstone Athletic	30	10	5	15	34	44	25
Ibstock Welfare	30	7	9	14	42	53	23
Harborough Town	30	8	7	15	31	57	23
Barrow Town	30	7	6	17	35	48	20
Leicester YMCA	30	4	6	20	25	66	14

SCHOOLS FOOTBALL 1988–89

Under-15 Victory Shield
Northern Ireland 0, England 5
Scotland 3, Northern Ireland 2
Northern Ireland 2, Wales 2
Scotland 3, Wales 0
England 0, Scotland 1
Wales 0, England 4

Final Table

	P	*W*	*D*	*L*	*F*	*A*	*Pts*
Scotland	3	3	0	0	7	2	6
England	3	2	0	1	9	1	4
Northern Ireland	3	0	1	2	4	10	1
Wales	3	0	1	2	2	9	1

Other Under-15 Results 1988–89
England 3, Belgium 1
France 0, England 1
Holland 1, England 2
England 4, Switzerland 0
England 1, West Germany 3
England 2, West Germany 0

Final Under-15 Playing Record for England
Played 9, Won 7, Drawn 0, Lost 2, For 22, Against 6

Under-18 Centenary Shield
Wales 1, Switzerland 1
England 0, Switzerland 0
England 5, Wales 0

Final Table

	P	*W*	*D*	*L*	*F*	*A*	*Pts*
England	2	1	1	0	5	0	3
Switzerland	2	0	2	0	1	1	2
Wales	2	0	1	1	1	6	1

Other Under-18 results 1988–89
Holland 1, England 1

Final Under-18 playing record for England
Played 3, Won 1, Drawn 2, Lost 0, For 6, Against 1

ESFA NATIONAL COMPETITIONS 1988–89

INTER-ASSOCIATION TROPHY
First Leg St Helens 1, Salford 2
Second Leg Salford 0, St Helens 2
(St Helens won 3-2 on aggregate)

NABISCO GROUP TROPHY
Final
Cheshire B *(Chester RC High)* 1
Essex A *(Emerson Park)* 0

BARCLAYS BANK COMPETITION
Final
West Yorkshire *(St Michael's College)* 2
Hampshire A *(Hill College)* 2

MITRE INTER-COUNTY CHAMPIONSHIP
Final
Lincolnshire 0, West Midlands 1

INER-COUNTY COMPETITION
Final
West Midlands 3, Essex 3

SMITHS CRISPS CUP
Final
Brampton Primary, Bexleyheath 0
Greaseborough Jun., Rotherham 0
(Trophy shared)

AMATEUR FOOTBALL ALLIANCE SEASON 1988–89

CUP COMPETITION FINALS

Senior
Old Stationers v Old Ignatians 1-0

Greenland Memorial
Clifford Chance Royex v Goldsmiths' College 5-2

Essex Senior
Old Parkonians v Old Westhamians 3-0

Middlesex Senior
Enfield Old Grammarians v St Mary's College *2-1

Surrey Senior
Royal Bank of Scotland v Old Wilsonians 2-1

Intermediate
Winchmore Hill 2nd v Albanian 2nd *3-3, 1-2

Essex Intermediate
Old Chigwellians 2nd v Old Fairlopians 2nd 4-0

Kent Intermediate
West Wickham 2nd v Royal Bank of Scotland 2nd 2-0

Middlesex Intermediate
Barclays Bank 2nd v Lensbury 2nd 2-1

Surrey Intermediate
Corinthian Casuals 'A' v Old Suttonians 2nd 5-1

Junior
Southgate Olympic 3rd v Parkfield 3rd 7-0

Minor
Barclays Bank 4th v Norsemen 4th 3-0

Senior Novets
Winchmore Hill 5th v Old Tollingtonians 5th 3-1

Intermediate Novets
Old Bromleians 6th v Old Parmiterians 6th 2-0

Junior Novets
Norsemen 7th v Old Stationers 8th 2-3

Veterans
Ulysses Veterans v Old Salvatorians Veterans *3-2

Open Veterans
Sonning Common & Peppard Veterans v William Fitt Veterans *2-1

*after extra time

AMATEUR FOOTBALL ALLIANCE SENIOR CUP 1988–89

1st Round Proper

Cardinal Manning OB v O. Grammarians	1-0
E. Barnet OG v O. Ignatians	*1-1, 1-2
O. Esthameians v Carshalton	0-3
O. Cholmeleians v O. Westmin. Citz.	4-0
Alleyn OB v Enfield O. Gram'ns	0-3
Bank of England v Mill Hill Village	1-2
John Fisher OB v Strand-Hollington OB	*2-2, 0-1
Lancing OB v O. Bromleians	0-5
Latymer OB v O. Aloysians	2-3
Chertsey O. Salesians v O. Actonians Assn.	*4-4, *2-5
O. Danes v Barclays Bank	3-4
Mayfield Athletic v O. Kingsburians	0-3
Mill County OB v O. Meadonians	0-4
Chace OB v Wake Green	0-3
O. Brentwoods v O. Fincunians	3-4
Pearl Assurance v Midland Bank	1-0
Polytechnic v O. Elizabethans	2-0
Brent v O. Stationers	0-4
Derbyshire Amateurs v O. Woodhouseians	*2-1
O. Vaughanians v O. Tollingtonians	*1-1a, 4-1
Southgate Olympic v O. Parmiterians	3-2
O. Salesians v Parkfield	3-1
O. Monovians v O. Finchleians	*1-1, 1-5
British Petroleum v South Bank Polytechnic	1-2
West Wickham v Winchmore Hill	3-1
Norsemen v Shene O. Grammn	3-0
O. Malvernians v O. Tiffinians	0-3
Kew Association v Merton	*3-4
O. Isleworthians v Alexandra Park	*3-2
Nat. Westmin. Bank v O. Carthusians	4-0
Crouch End Vampires v Albanian	2-1
O. Hamptonians v Broomfield	*0-0

2nd Round Proper

Cardinal Manning OB v O. Ignatians	1-2
Carshalton v O. Cholmeleians	3-1
Enfield O. Gram'ns v Mill Hill Village	4-2
Strand Hollingtonians v O. Bromleians	*3-4
O. Aloysians v O. Actonians Assn.	2-1
Barclays Bank v O. Kingsburians	3-0
O. Meadonians v Wake Green	2-1
O. Fincunians v Pearl Assurance	3-0
Polytechnic v O. Stationers	1-4
Derbyshire Amateurs v O. Vaughanians	6-1
Southgate Olympic v O. Salesians	0-2
O. Finchleians v South Bank Polytechnic	*3-2
West Wickham v Norsemen	4-1
O. Tiffinians v Merton	2-0
O. Isleworthians v Nat. Westmin. Bank	1-4
Crouch End Vampires v Broomfield	3-1

3rd Round Proper

O. Ignatians v Carshalton	3-1
Enfield O. Gram'ns v O. Bromleians	2-1
O. Aloysians v Barclays Bank	7-2
O. Meadonians v O. Fincunians	*3-2
O. Stationers v Derbyshire Amateurs	2-2
O. Salesians v O. Finchleians	1-0
West Wickham v O. Tiffinians	1-0
Nat. Westmin. Bank v Crouch End Vampires	2-1

4th Round Proper

O. Ignatians v Enfield O. Gram'ns	*3-3, 2-1
O. Aloysians v O. Meadonians	3-0
O. Stationers v O. Salesians	1-0
West Wickham v Nat. Westmin. Bank	2-1

Semi-Finals

O. Ignatians v O. Aloysians	1-0
O. Stationers v West Wickham	1-0

Final *(not available at time of going to press)*

REPRESENTATIVE MATCHES

v Army FA	Won 2-1
v Cambridge University	Won 2-1
v Oxford University	Lost 1-2
v Kent County FA	Won 1-0
v Royal Navy	Drawn 0-0
v Royal Air Force	Drawn 1-1
v Football Association XI	Lost 0-3
v Sussex County FA	Lost 1-2
v London University	Drawn 1-1

PLAYERS GAINING REPRESENTATIVE TIES SEASON 1988–89

A. Carr (Old Ignatians), J. McDonagh (Old Josephians), T. Lumme (Norsemen).

ARTHUR DUNN CUP

Final Tie: Old Malvernians v Old Brentwoods *3-1

ARTHURIAN LEAGUE

Premier Division

	P	W	D	L	F	A	Pts
Old Cholmeleians	16	10	4	2	34	19	24
Old Reptonians	16	10	3	3	42	28	23
Old Chigwellians	16	10	1	5	38	26	21
Old Brentwoods	16	6	5	5	33	30	17
Old Malvernians	16	4	6	6	32	29	14
Old Salopians	16	6	2	8	31	41	14
Old Carthusians	16	4	5	7	30	33	13
Lancing Old Boys	16	4	3	9	28	37	11
Old Harrovians	16	1	5	10	12	37	7

Division One

	P	W	D	L	F	A	Pts
Old Foresters	16	14	0	2	62	23	28
Old Etonians	16	9	3	4	40	20	21
Old Aldenhamians	16	10	1	5	46	30	21
Old Wellingburians	16	9	3	4	39	30	21
Old Westminsters	16	5	3	8	35	30	13
Old Wykehamists	16	5	3	8	34	47	13
Old Bradfieldians	16	5	1	10	23	38	11
Old Citizens	16	3	3	10	34	54	9
Old Ardinians	16	2	3	11	20	61	7

Division Two – 9 Teams – won by Old Chigwellians 2nd
Division Three – 9 Teams – won by Old Harrovians 2nd
Division Four – 9 Teams – won by Old Cholmeleians 3rd
Division Five – 7 Teams – won by Old Salopians 3rd

Junior League Cup O. Chigwellians 2nd v O. Cholmeleians 2-0

LONDON LEGAL LEAGUE 1988–89

Division One

	P	W	D	L	F	A	Pts
Gray's Inn	22	19	2	1	103	22	40
Slaughter & May	22	18	1	3	79	14	37
Freshfields	22	17	3	2	77	19	37
Clifford Chance Royex	22	14	3	5	30	22	31
Wilde Sapte	22	11	1	10	45	45	23
Nabarro Nathanson	22	8	4	10	37	48	20
Linklaters & Paines	21	8	2	11	33	35	18
Norton Rose Botterell & Roche	22	6	2	14	17	56	14
Baker McKenzie	22	6	1	15	24	68	13
Macfarlanes	22	6	0	16	34	61	12
Titmuss Sainer & Webb	21	5	0	16	32	16	10
Lovell White Durrant (Holborn)	22	3	1	18	17	74	7

Division Two

	P	W	D	L	F	A	Pts
Joynson Hicks	22	18	4	0	68	13	40
Ingledew Boodles	22	16	2	4	50	21	34
McKenna & Co	22	14	3	5	45	26	31
Allen & Overy	22	13	3	6	52	27	29
Cameron Markby	22	15	4	8	29	25	24
Beachcroft Stanleys	22	10	2	10	35	37	22
D J Freeman	22	6	7	9	37	50	19
Clifford Chance	22	7	4	11	27	33	18
Blackfriars Ashurst Goddard	22	7	3	12	30	36	17
Bristows CC	22	7	3	12	23	37	17
Denton Hall Burgin & Warrens	22	3	2	16	12	49	8
Lovell White Durrant Cheapside	22	2	1	10	15	76	5

LONDON INSURANCE FA 1988–89

Division One

	P	W	D	L	F	A	Pts
Sedgwick	18	12	4	2	55	28	28
Liverpool Victoria	18	11	2	4	64	28	24
Eagle Star	18	11	2	5	47	27	24
Granby	18	8	5	5	59	45	21
Hill Samuel IS	18	8	3	6	42	41	19
Gaflac	18	8	2	8	43	43	18
Sun Alliance	18	6	4	8	29	34	16
Bardhill	18	6	3	9	45	63	15
Temple Bar	18	3	5	10	37	56	11
Bowring	18	1	0	17	31	87	2

Division Two

	P	W	D	L	F	A	Pts
Sun Alliance 2nd	20	15	1	4	59	30	31
Liverpool Victoria 2nd	20	10	4	6	51	41	24
Sedgwick 2nd	20	9	5	6	53	39	23
Eagle Star 2nd	20	7	3	10	46	53	17
Medical Sickness	20	8	1	11	40	44	17
Temple Bar 2nd	20	3	2	15	37	79	8

LONDON BANKS FA 1988–89

Division One

	P	W	D	L	F	A	Pts
Royal Bank of Scotland	18	15	3	0	74	15	33
Samuel Montagu & Co	18	12	3	3	48	25	27
Bankers Trust & Co	18	11	3	4	52	30	25
Coutts & Co	18	11	1	6	45	34	23
Allied Irish	18	7	3	8	25	40	17
Citibank	18	4	5	9	28	39	13
Bank of America	18	5	2	11	33	48	12
National Westminster Bank 'A'	18	4	3	11	35	48	11
Bank of Ireland	18	3	5	10	29	55	11
Standard Chartered Bank	18	4	0	14	26	61	8

Division Two

	P	W	D	L	F	A	Pts
Royal Bank of Scotland 2nd	18	15	1	2	76	21	31
Bank Credit & Commerce Intl	18	12	5	1	53	19	29
Hill Samuel	18	12	3	3	73	33	27
Hong Kong & Shanghai Bank	18	10	4	4	60	33	24
Kleinwort Benson	18	6	3	9	31	50	15
Chase Manhattan Bank	18	6	2	10	32	58	14
National Westminster Bank 'B'	18	6	1	11	34	54	13
Bank of Scotland	18	4	3	11	30	40	11
Morgan Guaranty	18	3	2	13	24	60	8
Polytechnic	18	2	4	12	26	71	*7

Division Three

	P	W	D	L	F	A	Pts
Royal Bank of Scotland 3rd	18	12	3	3	91	30	27
Credit Suisse	18	13	1	4	63	28	27
Banque Nationale de Paris	18	13	1	4	49	38	27
Coutts & Co 2nd	18	9	6	3	45	29	24
Westpac	18	9	1	8	61	43	19
National Westminster Bank 'C'	18	8	2	8	47	40	18
Manufacturers Hanover Trust	18	6	3	9	44	49	15
Austral & N.Z. Banking Corpn	18	6	3	9	34	50	15
C. Hoare & Co	18	3	2	13	33	61	8
Standard Chartered Bank	18	0	0	18	12	167	*–2

Division Four

	P	W	D	L	F	A	Pts
Citibank 2nd	16	13	1	2	54	18	27
Royal Bank of Scotland 3rd	16	11	2	3	50	28	24
Bank of America 2nd	16	10	3	3	49	26	23
Barclays Bank 'A'	16	8	1	7	46	43	17
Trustees Savings Bank	16	6	1	9	43	49	13
Union Bank of Switzerland	16	5	3	8	39	53	13
National Westminster Bank 'D'	16	4	2	10	40	48	10
Australia & N. Zealand Bnk 2nd	16	4	2	10	24	44	10
Bank Credit & Commerce Intl 2nd	16	2	3	11	19	55	7

* pts deducted for breach of rule

Division Five – 10 Teams – won by Samuel Montagu & Co
Division Six – 11 Teams – won by Bankers Trust Co
Challenge Cup – 17 entries – won by Lloyds Bank
Senior Cup – 27 entries – won by Royal Bank of Scotland
Senior Plate – 16 entries – won by Hong Kong & Shanghai Bank
Minor Cup – 40 entries – won by National Westminster Bank
Junior Cup – 42 entries – won by Bank of America
Saunders Shield (VI-a-Side) – won by National Westminster Bank
Sportsmans Cup – won by Credit Suisse

MIDLAND AMATEUR ALLIANCE

Division One

	P	W	D	L	F	A	Pts
Old Elizabethans	22	20	2	0	82	16	42
Derbyshire Amateurs	22	13	5	4	52	41	31
Wollaton	22	12	5	5	51	23	29
Nottinghamshire	22	12	1	9	58	56	25
Brunts Old Boys	22	10	4	8	55	37	24
Tibshelf Old Boys	22	9	2	11	46	56	20
Peoples College	22	8	3	11	46	60	19
Lady Bay	22	6	6	10	32	39	18
Beeston OBA	22	5	6	11	41	59	16
Wilford	22	6	3	13	31	54	15
Chilwell	22	5	4	13	34	54	14
Mapperley Park	22	2	7	13	32	65	11

Division Two

	P	W	D	L	F	A	Pts
Wollaton 2nd	24	19	4	1	76	16	42
Magdala Amateurs	24	18	5	1	87	34	41
Old Elizabethans 2nd	24	18	2	4	82	33	38
Sherwood Amateurs	24	14	2	8	60	40	30
Old Bemrosians	24	10	6	8	38	34	26
Nottinghamshire 2nd	24	10	5	9	61	45	25
Ilkeston Electric	23	10	4	9	48	50	24
W Bridgford Casuals	24	10	2	12	65	67	22
Heanor Amateurs	24	6	5	13	37	68	17
Brunts OB 2nd	24	4	6	14	43	50	14
Nottingham Spartan	24	3	7	14	43	69	13
Old Mundellans	24	4	4	16	41	103	12
Wilford 2nd	23	3	0	20	21	93	6

Division Three – 13 Teams – won by Bassingfield
Division Four – 14 Teams – won by Derbyshire Amateurs 3rd

Senior Cup – Old Elizabethans
Intermediate Cup – Wollaton 2nd
Minor Cup – Old Elizabethans 3rd
Challenge Trophy – Wollaton
H.B. Poole Trophy – Old Elizabethans
Senior Supplementary Cup – Wollaton 2nd
Junior Supplementary Cup – Old Elizabethans 3rd

LONDON OLD BOYS' CUP

Senior Cup (67 Entries)
O. Ignatians v O. Parmiterians 0-1

Intermediate Cup (72)
O. Parmiterians 2nd v Phoenicians 2-0

Junior Cup (68)
O. Buckwellians 3rd v O. Parmiterians 3rd 0-2

Minor Cup (61)
Latymer OB 4th v O. Tenisonians 4th 1-5

Novets Cup (52)
O. Aloysians 5th v O. Parmiterians 5th 0-3

Drummond Cup (32)
O. Parmiterians 6th v O. Salesians 6th 2-1

Nemean Cup (37)
Albanians 7th v O. Parmiterians 7th 0-2

Veterans' Cup (33)
O. Sinjuns Vets v Wm Fitt OB Vets *1-4

THE OLD BOYS' FOOTBALL LEAGUE 1988–89

Premier Division

	P	W	D	L	F	A	Pts
Old Aloysians	18	14	3	1	47	12	31
Old Ignatians	18	12	3	3	42	17	27
Old Meadonians	18	10	1	7	33	25	21
Cardinal Manning OB	18	7	5	6	26	24	19
Enfield Old Grammarians	18	8	3	7	25	27	19
Latymer OB	18	7	2	9	34	35	16
Old Suttonians	18	5	5	8	24	35	15
Old Kingsburians	18	5	2	11	23	35	12
Old Josephians	18	4	3	11	23	36	11
Old Fincunians	18	2	5	11	22	53	9

Senior Division One

	P	W	D	L	F	A	Pts
Old Danes	22	14	6	2	61	26	34
Mill Hill County OB	22	12	9	1	53	33	33
Old Wokingians	22	14	3	5	56	25	31
Old Minchendenians	22	9	8	5	52	35	26
Glyn OB	22	8	6	8	36	33	22
Old Greenfordians	22	7	8	7	40	40	22
Old Sinjuns	22	8	3	11	50	67	19
Old Salvatorians	22	5	8	9	39	47	18
Phoenix OB	22	6	4	12	26	46	16
Clapham O. Xaverians	22	6	4	12	38	66	16
Strand Hollingtonian OB	22	4	6	12	29	44	14
Old Vaughanians	22	3	7	12	31	49	13

Senior Division Two (A)

	P	W	D	L	F	A	Pts
Chertsey O. Salesians	18	12	3	3	57	21	27
Old Tollingtonians	18	10	5	3	41	27	25
Enfield O. Grammarians 2nd	18	9	5	4	45	30	23
Old Sedcopians	18	10	1	7	50	39	21
Shene Old Grammarians	18	8	4	6	43	28	20
Old Ignatians 2nd	18	8	4	6	35	31	20
Leyton County OB	18	6	2	10	52	59	14
Old Buckwellians	18	5	2	11	38	50	12
Wood Green Old Boys	18	4	2	12	29	61	10
Phoenix OB 2nd	18	4	0	14	24	68	8

Senior Division Two (B)

	P	W	D	L	F	A	Pts
Old Tenisonians	20	15	3	2	52	16	33
Old Alpertonians	20	12	4	4	48	21	28
Old Westhamians	20	11	5	4	49	37	27
Old Southallians	20	10	4	6	52	27	24
Old Tiffinians	20	11	2	7	42	26	24
Old Manorians	20	11	2	7	40	25	24
Old Hamptonians	20	8	6	6	44	34	22
Old Dorkinians	20	8	5	7	43	36	*19
Old Uffingtonians	20	2	4	14	19	53	8
Old Paludians	20	1	2	17	24	74	4
Old Addeyans	20	2	1	17	13	77	*3

**indicates points deducted*

Senior Division 3 (NW) – 12 Teams – won by Ravenscroft OB
Senior Division 3 (SW) – 11 Teams – won by John Fisher OB
Intermed. Division North – 12 Teams – won by O. Elysians
Intermed. Division South – 12 Teams – won by O. Meadonians 2nd
Intermed. Division West – 12 Teams – won by O. Camdenians 2nd
Division One North – 10 Teams – won by O. Buckwellians 3rd
One South – 12 Teams – won by O. Meadonians 3rd
One West – 11 Teams – won by O. Paludians 2nd
Two North – 12 Teams – won by Chace OB 2nd
Two South – 12 Teams – won by Glyn OB 4th
Two West – 12 Teams – won by Cardinal Manning OB 3rd
Three North – 12 Teams – won by Leyton County OB 5th
Three South – 12 Teams – won by O. Reigatians 3rd
Three West – 11 Teams – won by O. Meadonians 5th
Four North – 12 Teams – won by O. Grocers 2nd
Four South – 11 Teams – won by Chertsey O. Salesians 4th
Four West – 9 Teams – won by O. Kingsburians 5th
Five North – 11 Teams – won by O. Grocers 3rd
Five South – 10 Teams – won by O. St Marys
Five West – 10 Teams – won by Shene OG 5th
Six South – 9 Teams – won by O. Dorkinians 5th
Six West – 8 Teams – won by O. Paludians 4th

SOUTHERN AMATEUR LEAGUE 1988–89

SENIOR SECTION

Division One	P	W	D	L	F	A	Pts
West Wickham	22	15	5	2	44	9	35
Old Esthameians	22	14	5	3	45	19	33
Old Parkonians	22	10	3	9	34	31	23
Norsemen	22	6	11	5	26	26	23
Old Salesians	22	9	5	8	32	39	23
South Bank Polytechnic	22	8	6	8	34	31	22
Winchmore Hill	22	8	4	10	41	43	20
Crouch End Vampires	22	6	7	9	37	47	19
National Westminster Bank	22	6	6	10	27	39	18
Old Actonians Association	22	7	3	12	44	47	17
Lloyds Bank	22	7	3	12	25	38	17
Lensbury	22	5	4	13	24	44	14

Division Two	P	W	D	L	F	A	Pts
Midland Bank	22	15	3	4	50	20	33
Old Stationers	22	13	5	4	46	30	31
Carshalton	22	13	3	6	40	25	29
Pearl Assurance	22	11	5	6	46	32	27
Polytechnic	22	9	8	5	36	29	26
Old Bromleians	22	10	4	8	44	36	24
Civil Service	22	8	5	9	44	39	21
Merton	22	6	6	10	28	46	18
Barclays Bank	22	4	8	10	30	42	16
Old Lyonians	22	5	5	12	22	40	15
Broomfield	22	4	7	11	35	57	15
Kew Association	22	3	3	16	21	46	9

Division Three	P	W	D	L	F	A	Pts
East Barnet Old Grammarians	22	16	3	3	64	20	35
British Petroleum	22	14	5	3	54	21	33
Southgate Olympic	22	12	6	4	41	20	30
Alleyn Old Boys	22	11	4	7	34	29	26
Ibis	22	11	2	9	40	34	24
Alexandra Park	22	7	8	7	41	36	22
Old Westminster Citizens	22	8	6	8	34	35	22
Bank of England	22	9	4	9	33	34	22
Brentham	22	7	4	11	29	65	18
Old Latymerians	22	2	9	11	22	39	13
Reigate Priory	22	2	7	13	22	39	11
Cuaco	22	3	2	17	23	65	8

Reserve Team Section
Division One – 12 Teams – won by West Wickham 2nd
Division Two – 12 Teams – won by Winchmore Hill 2nd
Division Three – 12 Teams – won by Pearl Assurance 2nd

THIRD TEAM SECTION
Division One – 12 Teams – won by Lensbury 3rd
Division Two – 12 Teams – won by Old Bromleians 3rd
Division Three – 12 Teams – won by Brentham 3rd

FOURTH TEAM SECTION
Division One – 12 Teams – won by National Westminster Bank 4th
Division Two – 12 Teams – won by Southgate Olympic 4th
Division Three – 12 Teams – won by Old Latymerians 4th

FIFTH TEAM SECTION
Division One – 12 Teams – won by Winchmore Hill 5th
Division Two – 11 Teams – won by Crouch End Vampires 5th
Division Three – 10 Teams – won by Old Salesians 5th

SIXTH TEAM SECTION
Division One – 11 Teams – won by Southgate Olympic 6th
Division Two – 10 Teams – won by Polytechnic 6th
Division Three – 9 Teams – won by Old Salesians 6th

SEVENTH TEAM SECTION
Division One – 11 Teams – won by Winchmore Hill 7th
Division Two – 10 Teams – won by Old Bromleians 7th

EIGHTH TEAM SECTION
Division One – 11 Teams – won by Old Stationers 8th
Division Two – 10 Teams – won by Midland Bank 9th

SOUTHERN OLYMPIAN LEAGUE 1988–89

SENIOR SECTION

Division One	P	W	D	L	F	A	Pts
Old Parmiterians	18	12	3	3	63	22	27
St Mary's College	18	11	3	4	26	15	25
Fulham Compton Old Boys	18	9	4	5	40	32	22
Old Grammarians	18	7	6	5	32	29	20
Mill Hill Village	18	7	4	7	39	31	18
Albanian	18	5	7	6	31	36	17
Old Finchleians	18	6	3	9	27	53	15
Old Bealonians	18	4	6	8	20	31	14
Old Fairlopians	18	3	7	8	33	42	13
Witan	18	4	1	13	26	46	9

Division Two	P	W	D	L	F	A	Pts
Southgate County	18	17	1	0	57	14	35
Parkfield	18	12	4	2	58	24	28
Academicals	18	8	4	6	36	31	20
Old Edmontonians	18	5	6	7	36	52	16
Old Wilsonians	18	4	6	8	37	32	14
Old Monovians	18	5	4	9	19	32	14
Wandsworth Borough	18	4	6	8	26	39	14
Inland Revenue	18	5	4	9	30	46	14
Old Colfeians	18	5	3	10	33	34	13
Hale End Athletic	18	5	2	11	26	54	12

Division Three	P	W	D	L	F	A	Pts
Colposa	18	13	3	2	55	30	29
Hadley	18	10	5	3	43	24	25
Pollygons	18	9	2	7	45	41	20
Cent YMCA	18	7	4	7	32	32	18
Hampstead Heathens	18	7	2	9	39	42	16
Old Woodhouseians	18	6	4	8	29	36	16
Ealing Association	18	7	2	9	31	39	16
Misfits	18	5	5	8	32	39	15
Birkbeck College	18	6	2	10	29	34	14
Bourneside	18	4	3	11	35	53	11

Division Four	P	W	D	L	F	A	Pts
Old Owens	20	14	5	1	69	26	33
Tansley	20	14	3	3	72	30	31
Mayfield Athletic	20	10	7	3	54	40	27
Westerns	20	10	4	6	54	43	24
BBC	19	9	5	5	30	20	23
Brent	20	11	0	9	43	37	22
Economicals	20	6	2	12	27	45	14
Charterhouse	20	6	2	12	34	57	14
Distillers	20	6	1	13	29	60	13
Electrosport	19	5	1	13	28	56	11
London Welsh	20	2	2	16	28	54	6

Intermediate Division One – 10 Teams – won by Old Parmiterians 2nd
Intermediate Division Two – 10 Teams – won by Witan 2nd
Intermediate Division Three – 11 Teams – won by London Airways
Intermediate Division Four – 10 Teams – won by Fulham Compton OB 2nd
Junior Division One – 10 Teams – won by Old Parmiterians 3rd
Junior Division Two – 10 Teams – won by Albanian 4th
Junior Division Three – 10 Teams – won by Academicals 3rd
Junior Division Four – 10 Teams – won by Old Parmiterians 6th
Minor Division 'A' – 9 Teams – won by Old Parmiterians 7th
Minor Division 'B' – 10 Teams – won by Old Wilsonians 5th
Minor Division 'C' – 9 Teams – won by Colposa 6th
Minor Division 'D' – 10 Teams – won by Academicals 4th
Minor Division 'E' – 10 Teams – won by Parkfield 6th
Minor Division 'F' – 10 Teams – won by Old Parmiterians 9th
Minor Division 'G' – 8 Teams – won by Mayfield Athletic 4th
Veterans' Section – 6 Teams – won by Wandsworth Borough Vets.
Challenge Bowl – won by Mill Hill Village
Challenge Shield – won by Old Wilsonians
Intermediate Challenge Cup – won by Colposa 2nd
Intermediate Challenge Shield – won by Old Grammarians 2nd

UNIVERSITY FOOTBALL 1988–89

UNIVERSITY OF LONDON INTER-COLLEGIATE LEAGUE

Premier Division

	P	*W*	*D*	*L*	*F*	*A*	*Pts*
Imperial College	16	12	2	2	44	18	26
R. Holloway & Bedford New College	16	11	1	4	47	31	23
London School of Economics	16	9	2	5	37	24	20
University College	16	9	2	5	32	24	20
King's College (KQC)	16	8	2	6	32	22	18
Goldsmith's College	16	6	2	8	24	34	14
Guy's Hospital MS	16	3	4	9	22	37	10
Queen Mary College	16	3	1	12	19	38	7
The London Hospital MC	16	1	4	11	15	44	6

Division 1 – 10 Teams – won by Queen Mary College 2nd
Division 2 – 10 Teams – won by King's College Hospital
Division 3 – 9 Teams – won by School of Pharmacy
Division 4 – 9 Teams – won by St. Georges Hospital 2nd
Division 5 – 9 Teams – won by Imperial College 5th
Division 6 – 9 Teams – won by King's College Hospital 6th

Challenge Cup – Bedford & R. Holloway New College 1
London School of Economics 0

UNIVERSITY MATCH

(14 December 1988, at Highbury

Oxford 3, Cambridge 2 (h-t 1-1)

Oxford: J. Calloway (Yale University and Wadham); K. Ingram (St Cyres CS, Penarth and University), P. Woolner (Wisbech GS and Oriel), C. Evans (Otago University and Worcester), M. Crawley (Manchester GS and Oriel) (capt), R. Morris (Ysgol Dyffryn Conway, Llanrwst and Oriel), I. Falshaw (St Francis Xavier, Liverpool and Pembroke), D. George (Altrincham GS and Hertford), C. Zis (Manchester GS and St Anne's), D. Goldie (Glasgow University and Wadham), A. Mitchell (Sevenoaks and New College). *Scorers:* Mitchell, Evans, Falshaw.
Cambridge: J. Skelton (Shrewsbury and Trinity); S. Hudson (King's, Chester and Christ's), N. Phillips (Millfield and Downing), N. Jenkins (Wootton Upper and Robinson), P. Hales (St Bede's, Manchester and Christ's), B. Palmer (Varndean Sixth Form College and Christ's) (capt), J. Rimmer (Liverpool Collegiate and Queen's), J. Beeby (Pudsey Grangefield and Trinity), M. Lindstrom (Highgate and Caius) (sub: J. Falk [Highgate and St Catharine's]), P. Todd (St Aidan's RC Comprehensive, Sunderland and Sidney Sussex) (sub: G. Luff [Latymer Upper and Downing]), J. Curwen (Tupton Hall and St Catherine's). *Scorers:* Calloway (og), Lindstrom.

DIVISIONAL MATCHES

WALES
Aberystwyth 0, Swansea 3
UWCC 4, Lampeter 3
Lampeter 1, Aberystwyth 4
UWCC 9, Bangor 0
Bangor 1, Lampeter 1
Bangor 0, Aberystwyth 1
Swansea 4, UWCC 0
Swansea 3, Bangor 0
Aberystwyth 0, UWCC 2
Lampeter 1, Swansea 5

	P	*W*	*D*	*L*	*F*	*A*	*Pts*
Swansea	4	4	0	0	15	1	8
UWCC	4	3	1	0	15	7	6
Aberystwyth	4	2	2	0	5	6	4
Lampeter	4	0	4	0	6	14	1
Bangor	4	0	3	1	1	14	1

SOUTH WEST
Bath 1, Bristol 0
Southampton 1, Exeter 1
Reading 4, Bristol 1
Exeter 4, Bath 0
Reading 1, Southampton 4
Bristol 2, Exeter 2
Bristol 1, Southampton 1
Bath 2, Reading 1
Southampton 1, Bath 1
Exeter 7, Reading 1

	P	*W*	*D*	*L*	*F*	*A*	*Pts*
Exeter	4	2	0	2	14	4	6
Bath	4	2	1	1	4	6	5
Southampton	4	1	0	3	7	4	5
Bristol	4	0	2	2	4	8	2
Reading	4	1	3	0	7	14	2

SOUTH-EAST SOUTH
Kent 1, LSE 0
Sussex 2, Imperial 2
RHBNC 0, Surrey 2
Kent 0, Surrey 0
LSE 0, Imperial 3
Sussex 2, RHBNC 2
Surrey 1, Sussex 0
Imperial 3, Kent 3
RHBNC 1, LSE 0
Sussex 0, Kent 1
Surrey 5, LSE 0
Imperial 2, RHBNC 2
LSE 1, Sussex 1
Imperial 0, Surrey 4
Kent 5, RHBNC 0

	P	*W*	*D*	*L*	*F*	*A*	*Pts*
Surrey	5	4	0	1	12	0	9
Kent	5	3	0	2	10	3	8
Imperial	5	1	1	3	10	11	5
RHBNC	5	1	2	2	5	11	4
Sussex	5	0	2	3	5	7	3
LSE	5	0	4	1	1	11	1

SOUTH EAST NORTH
UEA 1, Essex 1
City 2, UCL 8
Brunel 5, UEA 1
Essex 2, UCL 0
Brunel 9, City 0
UCL 2, UEA 1
UEA w/o, City scr
City 0, Essex 12
UCL 2, Brunel 4
Brunel 2, Essex 0

	P	*W*	*D*	*L*	*F*	*A*	*Pts*
Brunel	4	4	0	0	20	3	8
Essex	4	2	1	1	15	3	5
UCL	4	2	2	0	12	9	4
UEA	4	1	2	1	3	8	3
City	4	0	4	0	2	29	0

NORTH EAST
York 2, Leeds 8
Newcastle 0, Durham 2
Hull 4, Leeds 1
York 2, Newcastle 5

Durham 1, Hull 1
Newcastle 0, Leeds 3
Leeds 2, Durham 1
Hull 7, York 2
Durham 1, York 1
Hull 1, Newcastle 1

	P	*W*	*D*	*L*	*F*	*A*	*Pts*
Hull	4	2	0	2	13	5	6
Leeds	4	3	1	0	14	7	6
Durham	4	1	1	2	5	3	4
Newcastle	4	1	2	1	6	8	3
York	4	0	3	1	7	21	1

NORTH WEST
Manchester 3, Salford 3
Lancaster 1, UMIST 2
UMIST 2, Manchester 3
Salford 2, Liverpool 0
Liverpool 1, UMIST 0
Lancaster 4, Manchester 2
Manchester 2, Liverpool 5
Salford 1, Lancaster 3
Liverpool 2, Lancaster 2
UMIST 1, Salford 1

	P	*W*	*D*	*L*	*F*	*A*	*Pts*
Lancaster	4	2	1	1	10	7	5
Liverpool	4	2	1	1	8	6	5
Salford	4	1	1	2	7	7	4
UMIST	4	1	2	1	5	6	3
Manchester	4	1	2	1	10	14	3

WEST MIDLAND
Keele 2, Birmingham 3
Warwick 1, Leicester 2
Birmingham 8, Aston 0
Keele 2, Leicester 5
Aston 1, Warwick 2
Leicester 2, Birmingham 2
Birmingham 1, Warwick 0
Aston 1, Keele 0
Warwick 4, Keele 1
Leicester 1, Aston 2

	P	*W*	*D*	*L*	*F*	*A*	*Pts*
Birmingham	4	3	1	0	14	4	7
Leicester	4	2	1	1	10	7	5
Warwick	4	2	2	0	7	5	4
Aston	4	2	2	0	4	11	4
Keele	4	0	4	0	5	13	0

EAST MIDLAND
Loughborough 5, Nottingham 0
Sheffield 2, Bradford 2
Bradford 1, Loughborough 4
Nottingham 2, Sheffield 1
Bradford 0, Nottingham 0
Sheffield 2, Loughborough 1

	P	*W*	*D*	*L*	*F*	*A*	*Pts*
Loughborough	3	2	1	0	10	3	4
Sheffield	3	1	1	1	5	5	3
Nottingham	3	1	1	1	2	6	3
Bradford	3	0	1	2	3	6	2

Play-offs (North East)/(East Midland)
Nottingham 1, Newcastle 3
Durham 0, Bradford 1

Play-off Round
Sheffield 3, Bradford 1
Leicester 3, Aberystwyth 0
UWCC 3, Warwick 2
Southampton 3, Imperial 4
Leeds 3, Salford 1
Essex 2, Bath 1
Liverpool 2, Newcastle 1
Kent 4, UCL 1

Challenge Round
Lancaster 0, Sheffield 1
Surrey 0, Leicester 1
Hull 6, UWCC 0
Birmingham 2, Imperial 1
Brunel 4, Leeds 0
Exeter 3, Essex 1
Loughborough 3, Liverpool 1 *aet*
Swansea 2, Kent 0

Quarter-finals
Sheffield 1, Leicester 2
Hull 0, Birmingham 4
Brunel 1, Exeter 5
Loughborough 1, Swansea 0

Semi-finals
Leicester 0, Birmingham 3
Exeter 1, Loughborough 3

Final
Loughborough 1, Birmingham 0 *aet*

UNIVERSITY OF LONDON REPRESENTATIVE XI
(75th Anniversary Season)

v Ulysses	Won	1-0
v Arthurian League	Lost	0-2
v Old Boys' League	Lost	0-3
v Southern Amateur League	Lost	2-5
v Cambridge University	Drawn	2-2
v Oxford University	Lost	0-4
v Royal Air Force	Lost	0-4
v London Legal League	Drawn	0-0
v United Banks	Won	3-1
v Army XI	Drawn	1-1
v Kent County FA	Lost	1-3
v Metropolitan Police	Lost	0-1
v Southern Olympian League	Lost	0-1
v British Colleges	Drawn	0-0
v Amateur Football Alliance	Drawn	1-1

Anniversary Tour to USSR

v Moscow Dinamo Reserves	Lost	0-1
v Zamaya Truda Orechevo	Lost	1-3
v Moscow State University	Lost	1-3

BUSF GROUP TOURNAMENT in Bangor

POOL A

England I v Scotland	3-3
Oxford v Cambridge	6-1
Cambridge v England I	2-4
Scotland v Oxford	2-2
Scotland v Cambridge	7-0
England I v Oxford	1-1

POOL B

England II v London	6-0
N Ireland v Wales	3-1
Wales v England II	0-0
London v N Ireland	2-2
London v Wales	1-0
England II v N Ireland	1-1

FINAL
England II v Scotland 2-0

3rd/4th Place
N Ireland v Oxford 1-1
(N Ireland won 5-4 on penalties)

SHERPA VAN TROPHY – *Continued from Page 636*

Wrightson, Hughes, Mooney, Joyce, Ellis, Brazil, Patterson.
Bolton W: Felgate; Brown Cowdrill, Darby, Keeley, Winstanley, Henshaw, Thompson, Morgan, Brookman, Chandler.

Tranmere R (0) 0

Wigan Ath (0) 1 *(Thompson)* 2915

Tranmere R: Nixon; Higgins, McCarrick (Bishop), Martindale (McKenna), Hughes, Vickers, Morrissey, Harvey, Malkin, Muir, Mungall.
Wigan Ath: Adkins; Atherton, Tankard, Parkinson, Hemming, Senior, Thompson, Pilling, Entwistle, Hilditch (Ainscow), Griffiths.

Wrexham (0) 2 *(Bowden, Russell)*

Sheffield U (0) 1 *(Jones (og))* 2653

Wrexham: Morris; Salathiel, Wright, Hunter, Williams, Jones, Bowden, Flynn, Buxton, Russell, Cooper.
Sheffield U: Benstead; Ryan, Whitehouse, Booker, Thompson, Carr, Roberts (Francis), Todd, Agana, Williams (Joseph), Bryson.

Southern Area

Brentford (2) 2 *(Godfrey, Cadette)*

Notts Co (0) 0 3194

Brentford: Roberts; Feeley, Stanislaus, Millen, Evans, Cockram (Ratcliffe), Jones, Sinton, Cadette, Godfrey, Smillie.
Notts Co: Leonard; McStay, Withe, O'Riordan, Yates, Law (Draper), Mills (Thorpe), Rimmer, Lund, Kevan, Fairclough.

Chesterfield (3) 4 *(Waller, McDonald, Morris 2)*

Cambridge U (0) 2 *(Croft, Clayton [pen])* 2726

Chesterfield: Cherry; Hewitt, Prindiville, Arnott, Brien (Hoole), Rogers, Eley, McDonald, Waller (Gibson), Bloomer, Morris.
Cambridge U: Vaughan; Poole, Kimble, Daish, Chapple, Turner, Clayton, Ryan, Dublin, Taylor, Croft.

Colchester U (1) 3 *(Walsh, Allinson, Wilkins)*

Leyton Orient (0) 1 *(Hull)* 1736

Colchester U: Walton; Coleman, Bedford, Kelly, Hicks, Hetzke, Daniels, English, Tempest (Wilkins), Walsh, Allinson.
Leyton Orient: Heald; Howard, Dickenson, O'Shea (Castle), Day, Sitton, Hull, Ward, Baker, Juryeff, Comfort.

Northampton T (0) 2 *(Berry, Westley (og))*

Southend U (0) 1 *(Crown) aet* 2539

Northampton T: Gleasure; Williams, Wilson, Donald, Bodley, McPherson, Sandeman, Culpin (Donegal), Gilbert, Adcock, Berry.
Southend U: Newell; Roberts, Johnson, Butler, Westley, Hall, Clark, Robinson, Crown, McDonough, Ling.

Torquay U (3) 3 *(Pugh [pen], Joyce, Smith)*

Gillingham (0) 0 1844

Torquay: Veysey; Pugh (Holmes), Kelly, McNichol, Leyden, Loram, Smith, Lloyd, Thompson (Edwards), Weston, Joyce.
Gillingham: Kite; Burley, Holmes, Peacock, West, Walker, Haylock, Shipley, Lovell, Docker, Smith.

18 JAN

Reading (1) 2 *(Williams, Senior)*

Hereford U (2) 3 *(Stant 2, Narbett)* 2175

Reading: Phillips; Williams (Gernon), Richardson, Beavon, Hicks, Whitlock, Knight (Conroy), Elsey, Senior, Moran, Gilkes.
Hereford U: Elliott; Jones M, Crane, Pejic, Stevens, Devine, Jones R, Narbett, Stant, Mardenborough, McLoughlin.

24 JAN

Bristol R (1) 2 *(Smith, Reece)*

Cardiff C (0) 1 *(Wimbleton)* 4029

Bristol R: Martyn; Alexander, Twentyman, Yates, Smith, Jones, Holloway, Reece, White, McClean, Purnell.
Cardiff C: Wood; Rodgerson, Platnauer, Wimbleton, Abrahams, Stevenson, Bater, Bartlett, Gilligan, Kelly (Morgan), Lynex.

Wolverhampton W (1) 3 *(Bull 3)*

Bristol C (0) 0 14,216

Wolverhampton W: Kendall; Bellamy, Venus, Streete, Robertson (Downing), Vaughan, Thompson, Gooding (Robinsin), Bull, Mutch, Dennison.
Bristol C: Waugh; Honor, Llewellyn, Newman, Pender, McClaren, Galliers, Shepherd, Shutt (McGarvey), Walsh, Gavin.

QUARTER-FINALS
Southern Area
14 FEB

Colchester U (0) 0

Hereford U (1) 1 *(Stant)* 2059

Colchester U: McAlister; Hicks, Bedford, Barnett (Daniels), Hetzke, Hill, Allinson, English, Wilkins, Walsh, McGee.
Hereford U: Elliott; Jones M, Devine, Stevens, Pejic, Jones R, Benbow, Narbett, Stant, Tester, McLoughlin.

Northern Area
21 FEB

Bolton W (0) 3 *(Winstanley 2, Savage)*

Wrexham (0) 1 *(Jones) aet* 3833

Bolton W: Felgate; Brown, Cowdrill, Savage, Crombie, Winstanley, Storer (Thomas), Thompson, Morgan, Jeffrey, Darby.
Wrexham: Salmon; Salathiel, Wright, Hunter, Williams, Jones, Preece, Flynn (Thackeray), Cooper (Carter), Russell, Bowden.

Halifax T (0) 0

Blackpool (1) 2 *(Walwyn, Methven)* 3281

Halifax T: Sinclair; Barr W, Horner, Pullan, Robinson (Whitehead), Bramhall, Fleming (Broadbent), Watson, McPhillips, Allison, Blain.
Blackpool: O'Keefe; Burgess, Morgan, Coughlin (Davies), Methven, Elliott, Deary, Cunningham, Garner, Thompson, Walwyn.

Huddersfield T (0) 1 *(Maskell (pen))*

Scarborough (1) 2 *(Adams, Brook)* 4665

Huddersfield T: Hardwick; Trevitt, Hutchings, May,

O'Doherty, France, O'Regan, Bent, Cecere, Maskell, Marsden (Withe).
Scarborough: Ironside; Kamara, Thompson, Olsson, Richards, Bennyworth, Adams, Cook, Graham, Brook, Russell.

Wigan Ath (0) 0

Crewe Alex (1) 1 *(Sussex)* 3004

Wigan Ath: Adkins; Atherton, Tankard, Parkinson (Johnson), Beesley, Hemming, Crompton (Ramage), Pilling, Senior, Griffiths, Entwistle.
Crewe Alex: Edwards P; Swain, Edwards P R, Billing, Macowat, Walters, Jasper, Murphy, Sussex (Morton), Gardiner, Fishenden.

Southern Area

Chesterfield (0) 0

Brentford (1) 1 *(Blissett)* 4207

Chesterfield: Astbury; Hewitt, Prindiville, Arnott, Brien, Rogers, Rolph (Hoole), Alleyne (McDonald), Waller, Bloomer, Morris.
Brentford: Parks; Feeley, Stanislaus, Millen, Evans, Ratcliffe, Jones, Sinton, Cadette, Blissett, Smillie (Godfrey).

Wolverhampton W (0) 3 *(Dennison, Gooding, Bull)*

Northampton T (0) 1 *(Streete (og)) aet* 16,815

Wolverhampton W: Kendall; Bellamy, Venus, Streete, Downing, Vaughan, Thompson, Gooding (Robinson), Bull, Mutch, Dennison (Kelly).
Northampton T: Gleasure; Williams, Wilson, Donald (Preece), Bodley, McPherson, Sandeman (Collins), Culpin, Gilbert, Adcock, Berry.

22 FEB

Bristol R (0) 0

Torquay U (1) 1 *(Loram)* 4316

Bristol R: Martyn; Alexander, Twentyman, Yates, McClean, Jones, Holloway, Reece (Mehew), White, Penrice, Purnell.
Torquay U: Veysey; Leyden, Morrison, McNichol, Cole, Loram, Holmes, Lloyd, Edwards, Weston, Joyce.

SEMI-FINALS
Northern Area
21 MAR

Blackpool (0) 1 *(Coughlin (pen))*

Scarborough (0) 0 aet 4300

Blackpool: Siddall; Burgess, Morgan, Coughlin, Methven, Elliott, Deary, Walwyn (Madden), Garner, Thompson (Gore), Davies.
Scarborough: Ironside; Kamara, Thompson, Olsson, Richards, Short Craig, Morris (Cook), Graham, Norris, Brook, Russell.

Crewe Alex (1) 1 *(Sussex)*

Bolton W (0) 2 *(Winstanley, Brown) aet* 5928

Crewe Alex: Edwards P; Swain, Edwards P R, Billing (Macowat), Callaghan, Walters, Jasper, Murphy (Gage), Sussex, Gardiner, Fishenden.
Bolton W: Felgate; Brown, Cowdrill, Savage, Crombie, Winstanley, Storer (Chandler), Thompson, Thomas, Jeffrey, Darby.

Southern Area

Brentford (0) 0

Torquay U (0) 1 *(Lloyd)* 5802

Brentford: Parks; Feeley, Stanislaus, Millen, Evans, Cockram, Bates, Sinton, Cadette, Blissett, Godfrey (Sealy).
Torquay U: Veysey; Holmes, Kelly, McNichol, Leyden, Loram, Smith J (Edwards), Lloyd, Airey, Weston, Bastow (Cole).

22 MAR

Hereford U (0) 0

Wolverhampton W (2) 2 *(Mutch, Bull)* 10,204

Hereford U: Elliott; Jones M, Devine, Bradley, Pejic, Jones R, Crane (Lamb), Narbett, Stant, Tester, McLoughlin.
Wolverhampton W: Hansbury; Bellamy, Venus, Streete, Vaughan, Thompson, Gooding, Bull, Mutch, Dennison.

Northern Area Final First Leg
11 APRIL

Bolton W (0) 1 *(Darby)*

Blackpool (0) 0 10,345

Bolton W: Felgate; Brown, Cowdrill, Savage (Storer), Crombie, Winstanley, Chandler, Thompson, Thomas, Morgan, Darby.
Blackpool: Siddall; Burgess, Morgan (Wright), Coughlin, Methven, Elliott, Davies, Madden, Garner, Deary, Gore.

Southern Area Final First Leg

12 APRIL

Torquay U (1) 1 *(Edwards)*

Wolverhampton W (0) 2 *(Bull 2)* 4612

Torquay U: Veysey; Hirons, Kelly, McNichol, Elliott, Loram (Pugh), Airey, Lloyd, Edwards, Weston, Bastow (Holmes).
Wolverhampton W: Hansbury; Thompson, Venus, Streete, Robertson, Vaughan, Chard (Gooding), Downing, Bull, Mutch, Dennison.

Northern Area Final Second Leg

18 APRIL

Blackpool (0) 1 *(Garner (pen))*

Bolton W (0) 1 *(Thompson (pen)) aet* 9027

Blackpool: Siddall; Burgess, Wright (Thompson), Coughlin, Methven, Elliott, Davies, Walwyn, Garner, Deary, Gore (Madden).
Bolton W: Felgate; Brown, Cowdrill, Savage, Crombie, Winstanley, Chandler, Thompson, Thomas, Morgan, Darby.

Southern Area Final Second Leg

Wolverhampton W (0) 0

Torquay U (2) 2 *(Edwards, Loram)* 22,532

Wolverhampton W: Hansbury; Thompson, Venus (Chard), Bellamy, Robertson, Vaughan, Steele (Downing), Gooding, Bull, Mutch, Dennison.
Torquay U: Allen; Holmes, Kelly, McNichol, Elliott, Loram, Morrison, Lloyd, Edwards, Weston, Smith (Pugh).

FINAL (at Wembley)
28 MAY

Torquay U (1) 1 *(Edwards)* 46,513

Bolton W (1) 4 *(Darby, Chandler, Crombie, Morgan)*

Torquay U: Allen; Pugh, Kelly, McNichol, Elliott, Loram, Airey (Smith), Lloyd, Edwards, Weston (Joyce), Morrison.
Bolton W: Felgate; Brown, Cowdrill, Savage, Crombie, Winstanley, Chandler (Storer), Thompson, Thomas, Morgan, Darby.
Referee: G. Courtney (Spennymoor).

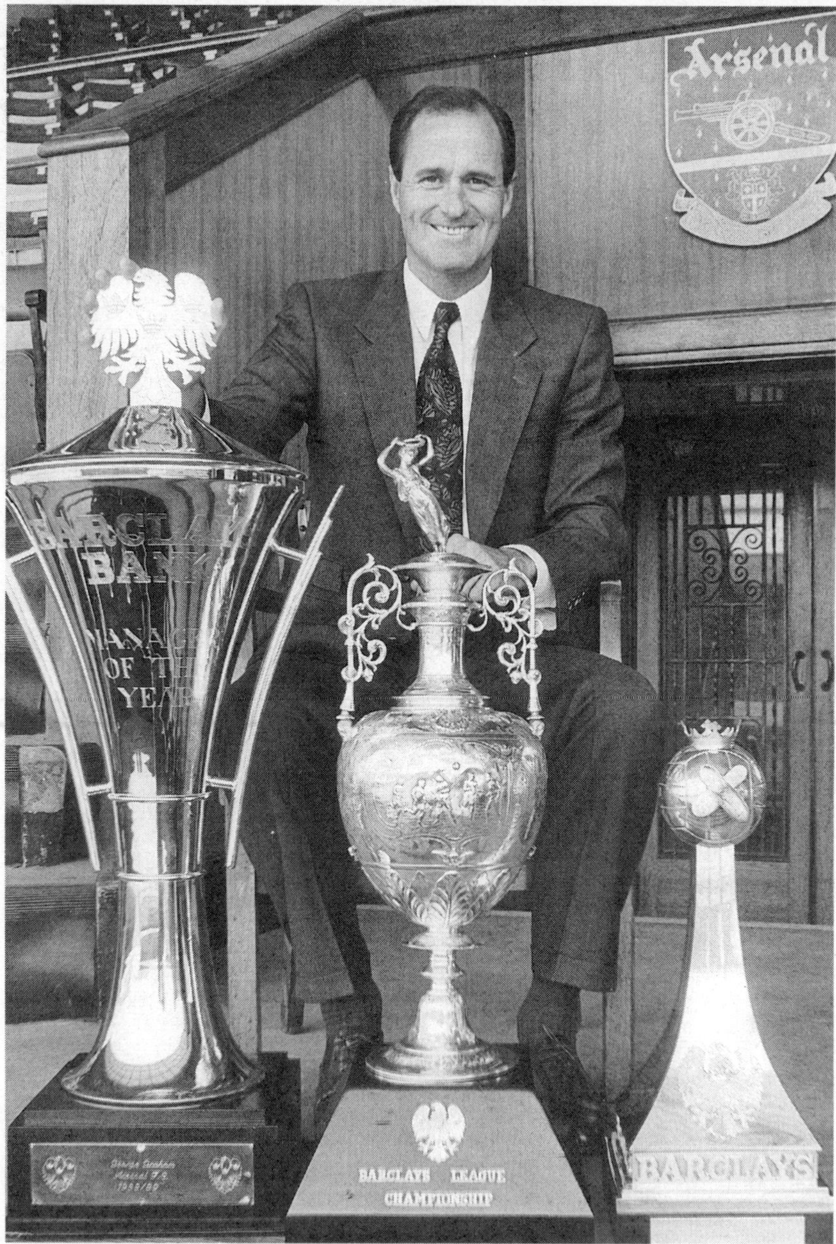

George Graham of Barclays League Champions, Arsenal, became the first London club manager to win the Manager of the Year title in 18 years when he was named the Barclays Bank Manager of the Year by a panel of leading football journalists and commentators. Bertie Mee was the last London manager to land the prize – in 1971, the Gunners "double" year. The award was Graham's 10th managerial accolade in six years – four at Millwall and six at Arsenal.

INFORMATION AND RECORDS

OBITUARIES

Batey, Bob (b. Greenhead 18.10.1912; d. 29.11.1988), was a dependable left-back or left-half with Carlisle United, Preston, Leeds United and Southport from 1932 to 1948. At his peak with Preston where he succeeded Jimmy Milne at left-half and gained an FA Cup-winners' medal in 1938.

Baxter, Mick (b. Birmingham 30.12.1956; d. 16.1.1989), died of cancer at a tragically young age while serving his old club Preston as community relations officer. Joined Preston as an apprentice in 1971 and made over 200 appearances (mostly at centre-half) before his £425,000 transfer to Middlesbrough in 1981. Finished his playing career with Portsmouth before retiring in 1986.

Bell, Bob "Bunny" (b. Birkenhead 1911, d. 25.12.1988). On Boxing Day 1935 this centre-forward created a Football League record (since broken) by scoring nine goals in Tranmere Rovers' 13-4 defeat of Oldham Athletic. He also missed a penalty in the second half of that game. Before the end of that season he was snapped up by Everton but with "Dixie" Dean still leading their attack he had few first-team outings with them although remaining on their books until 1946. However, his total of 104 League goals for Tranmere Rovers is still a record for that club.

Crook, Walter (b. Whittle-le-Woods 28.4.1913; d. December 1988), was one of Blackburn Rovers' most consistent defenders in the immediate pre-war years and made 218 League appearances for them before rounding off his League career in season 1947–48 at Bolton. Managed Ajax (Amsterdam) in the 1950s.

Cunningham, Laurie (b. Archway 8.3.56; d. 15.7.89), died in a car crash in Spain. Apprentice at Orient and developed into an England winger (6 caps) with West Bromwich Albion. Later played for Real Madrid, Manchester United, Marseille, Leicester City, Rayo Vallecano and Wimbledon for whom he appeared as substitute in the 1988 FA Cup Final.

Dobbie, Harold (b. Bishop Auckland 20.2.1923; d. July 1988), began with Middlesbrough in December 1946 and also had a spell with Plymouth Argyle before Torquay United made most consistent use of his services as an inside-forward for three seasons beginning in October 1953.

Edwards, Stanley (b. Dawdon 17.10.1926; d. 14.1.1989), joined Chelsea as a centre-forward from Horden Colliery Welfare in October 1949 but with Roy Bentley in full flow at Stamford Bridge he got his League changes with Colchester 1952–53 and Orient 1953–54.

Harper, Bill (b. Winchburgh, West Lothian, 19.1.1897; d. April 1989), former Scottish international goalkeeper who gave Plymouth Argyle more than 40 years service as player, trainer and groundsman. Arsenal paid Hibernian £4500 for his transfer in 1925, then a record fee for a goalkeeper. Joined Fall Rivers, USA in 1927 but returned to Arsenal 1930 to help them win the League championship. Moved to Plymouth December 1931.

Harris, John (b. Glasgow 30.6.1917, d. 24.7.1988), a Scottish war-time cap who captained Chelsea to the Wembley finals of 1944 and 1945 and helped them win their first Championship in 1954–55. Began with Wolvess and guested for Chelsea before his £5000 transfer in August 1945. After 326 peace-time League appearances as centre-half and later right-back went to Chester as manager in April 1956 and subsequently had 14 years as manager and general manager with Sheffield United.

Harvey, Joe (b. Edlington, Doncaster 11.6.1918, d. February 1989), was one of the North-East's most popular football personalities who captained Newcastle United in consecutive FA Cup wins in 1951 and 1952 as well as helping them win the League Championship three times. A strong defensive wing-half he had signed for United in October 1945 after pre-war spells with Wolves, Bournemouth and Bradford City. After managing Barrow and Workington he returned to manage Newcastle United 1962–75 restoring them to the First Division.

Hastings, Alex (b. Falkirk 17.3.1912; d. December 1988), joined Sunderland from Stenhousemuir in 1930 and remained 15 years captaining them for several seasons including when they won the championship in 1935–36. As a left-half he won two Scottish caps. Managed Kilmarnock 1948–50 and also scouted for Stoke City and Hearts before emigrating to Australia.

Hilton, Billy (b. Oldham 14.4.1911; d. 31.1.1989), a right-back with Oldham Athletic throughout his professional career from 1934 until a knee injury forced his retirement in 1945. Became a town councillor and chairman of Royton Council.

Jack, John (b. Glasgow 1932; d. October 1988), was a centre-half with Celtic from 1951 to 1958 during a period when Jock Stein was favourite for this position. Succeeded the injured Stein for a spell in 1956–57 before moving on to Morton a year later.

Jones, Bob, Snr. (b. Liverpool 9.1.1902; d. December 1988), given very few opportunities to show his paces in Everton's League side from 1924 but succeeded Dick Pym at Bolton in 1930 and kept goal for them in all but one game when they won promotion to the First Division 1934–35. Ended League career with two seasons at Cardiff.

Leary, Stuart (b. Cape Town, South Africa 30.4.1933; d. August 1988), was one of Charlton Athletic's favourite post-war centre-forwards scoring a club record 153 League goals for them 1950 to 1962 when he moved to QPR. An all-round sportsman he was a middle-order Kent batsman 1951–71.

Leslie, Jack (b. Barking 17.8.1901; d. 1988), one of only two black Football League players before the war Jack Leslie joined Plymouth Argyle from Barking Town in 1921 and made 385 League appearances before retiring in 1934. As an inside-left he formed with Sammy Black one of the finest left-wing combinations outside the First Division.

'Wor Jackie' Milburn, the legendary Newcastle United and England forward.

Little, Jack (b. Dunston-on-Tyne 18.9.1904; d. 5.7.1988), was a thoughtful type of full-back who, after signing for Liverpool in January 1927, became a regular first team defender with Southport, Chester, Northampton and Exeter City up to 1939. Also had brief spell as player-coach to Le Havre in France.

Lowrie, George (b. Tonypandy 19.12.1919; d. May 1989), as an inside or centre-forward was especially popular with Coventry City where he had two spells. Made nine war-time appearances for Wales and gained four peace-time caps. After spells with Swansea, Preston North End, and Coventry City his £18,000 transfer to Newcastle United in March 1948 was at that time the third highest British transfer fee. Also had two and a half years with Bristol City.

Milburn, Jackie (b. Ashington 11.5.1924; d. 9.10.1988), a favourite Geordie "Wor Jackie" was one of the fastest of centre-forwards who scored a Newcastle United club record of 178 League goals in a distinguished career with that club. First appeared for them in war-time football in 1943 and remained until June 1957 when he joined Linfield as player-manager. Won three FA Cup winners' medals with Newcastle and one Irish Cup winners' medal with Linfield. He made 13 appearances for England scoring a total of nine goals including a hat-trick against Wales at Cardiff in 1948. Also managed Yiewsley and Ipswich Town before returning to Newcastle as a sporting journalist. Was made a Freeman of the City of Newcastle.

Mills, Steve (b. Portsmouth 9.12.1953; d. 1.8.1988), his promising career as a full-back with Southampton was cut short in 1975 through injury sustained in a car accident and although he attempted a come-back he was forced to retire. Had already gained recognition as an England U-23 international in 1974.

Parker, Johnny (b. Birkenhead 5.7.1925; d. August 1988), a stylish inside-forward who was at his best with Everton in 1953–54 when he struck up a great understanding with Dave Hickson and scored 31 goals in 38 League appearances, helping put Everton back into the First Division. Went to Bury in 1956 and was their leading scorer in his last season of 1957–58.

Pym, Dick (b. Topsham 2.2.1893; d. 29.9.1988), was England's oldest ex-international when he died at his birthplace at the age of 95. "Pincher" Pym has gone down in football history as the goalkeeper who won three FA Cup medals with Bolton Wanderers without conceding a single goal in those Wembley finals. Also capped three times by England in the 1920s. Turned professional with Exeter City in 1911 and his 203 Southern and Football League games with them included a run of 186 consecutive appearances. Transferred to Bolton in 1921 and added 298 League appearances to 1930.

Redpath, Willie (b. Stoneyburn, W. Lothian 8.8.1922; d. 20.1.1989). A wing-half in one of Motherwell's best-ever sides in the 1950s, winning the League Cup in 1951 and the FA Cup the following year. They were also beaten finalists in 1951. A highly skilful player he was capped nine times by Scotland. Made 227 League appearances for Motherwell 1946–56 before joining Third Lanark.

Revie, Don, OBE (b. Middlesbrough 10.7.1927; d. 26.5.1989), died tragically of motor neurone disease, he had enjoyed an outstanding career both as a player and a manager. As the former he had a football plan named after him – "The Revie Plan" – when Manchester City used him as a deep lying centre-forward and goal-maker in the 1950s. Began as a winger with Leicester City during the war; Hull City (£20,000) 1949, Manchester City (£25,000) 1951; Sunderland (£24,000) 1956; Leeds United (£14,000) 1958. Made a total of 474 League appearances. As player-manager and manager of Leeds United he was one of the most successful managers in the game's history including twice League champions and five times runners-up, plus FA Cup, League Cup, Fairs Cup (2) wins, and it was no surprise when he was made England manager in 1974. Left his job for the United Arab Emirates in 1977.

Riddell, Gary (b. Ellon 9.8.1966; d. 11.6.1989), died tragically at the age of 22 a few weeks after helping Dunfermline Athletic win promotion to the Premier Division. Had joined Dunfermline from Aberdeen in 1987.

Rimmer, John (b. Southport 15.3.1910; d. January 1989), an outside-left with Southport 1928–30 and Bolton Wanderers 1930–37. It was Bolton who persuaded him to turn professional after he had won an England amateur cap in 1930.

Robledo, George (b. Chile 14.4.1926; d. April 1989), emigrated to England in 1932 and returned to his homeland to play for Colo-Colo FC in 1953 after a distinguished career as an inside-forward with Huddersfield Town, Barnsley and Newcastle United. He played in the same League side as his brother Ted for most of his career and indeed Newcastle made a £26,500 deal for their joint transfer from Barnsley in January 1949. Stockily built George was outstanding on heavy grounds. He won FA Cup medals in 1951 and 1952.

Underwood, Dave (b. London 15.3.1928; d. January 1989), as a goalkeeper he was especially popular at Watford with whom he had three spells 1952–53, 56–57, 60–63. Also appeared with QPR, Liverpool, Dartford, Fulham and Dunstable in a professional career from 1949 to 1966. Manager of Hastings United 1967 and chairman of Barnet in the 1970s.

Wardle, Billy (b. Houghton-le-Spring 20.1.1918; d. January 1989), a tricky outside-left who turned professional with Southport in 1936 and subsequently served Manchester City, Grimsby Town, Blackpool, Birmingham City, Barnsley and Skegness Town up to 1956. Made 239 peace-time League appearances.

White, Roy (b. Bootle 13.8.1918; d. December 1988), a wing-half with a distinguished war record who made over 150 war-time appearances for Tottenham Hotspur from 1940 and then joined Bradford City PA in May 1946 to add 151 peace-time League appearances up to 1951.

Young, Dick (b. Gateshead 17.4.1918; d. 31.1.1989), a big six-footer who played full-back or centre-half and helped Sheffield United win promotion to the First Division in 1938–39. Joined Lincoln City in March 1949 and retired in 1951. Succeeded Alan Ashman as Carlisle United's manager in November 1975 (having previously been trainer) but remained only 12 months.

Dick Pym, Bolton Wanderers.

Don Revie OBE, Leeds United and England manager.

FOOTBALL LEAGUE CUP 1960–1989

	FOOTBALL LEAGUE CUP																						MILK CUP				LITTLEWOODS CUP			
	1960–61	1961–62	1962–63	1963–64	1964–65	1965–66	1966–67	1967–68	1968–69	1969–70	1970–71	1971–72	1972–73	1973–74	1974–75	1975–76	1976–77	1977–78	1978–79	1979–80	1980–81	1981–82	1982–83	1983–84	1984–85	1985–86	1986–87	1987–88	1988–89	
Accrington S	1	1	–	–	–	–	–	–	–	–	–	–	–	–	–	–	–	–	–	–	–	–	–	–	–	–	–	–	–	Accrington S
Aldershot	2	1	2	2	1	2	2	1	1	1	2	2	1	1	1	1	1	1	1	1	1	2	1	2	3	1	1	1	1	Aldershot
Arsenal	–	–	–	–	–	–	3	F	F	3	4	4	5	2	2	2	5	SF	2	5	4	4	SF	4	3	5	W	F	3	Arsenal
Aston Villa	W	3	F	3	SF	5	2	2	2	2	F	4	3	2	W	3	W	4	4	3	3	5	2	SF	3	SF	4	4	5	Aston Villa
Barnsley	2	2	3	2	2	1	1	1	2	1	1	2	1	1	1	1	2	1	1	2	4	5	4	2	2	2	2	3	2	Barnsley
Barrow	1	1	3	1	1	1	2	3	1	2	1	1	–	–	–	–	–	–	–	–	–	–	–	–	–	–	–	–	–	Barrow
Birmingham C	3	1	W	2	2	2	SF	3	2	2	4	2	4	5	2	3	2	2	2	3	5	2	4	4	3	3	3	1	2	Birmingham C
Blackburn R	4	SF	5	2	3	2	4	4	3	3	2	2	1	2	3	1	2	2	2	2	3	3	2	2	2	2	2	2	3	Blackburn R
Blackpool	2	SF	2	3	3	3	5	3	5	3	3	5	5	2	2	2	3	2	3	2	2	1	3	1	2	1	1	2	3	Blackpool
Bolton W	4	1	2	3	2	3	2	3	2	2	3	4	2	3	2	2	SF	4	3	2	2	1	2	1	3	2	1	1	1	Bolton W
Bournemouth	2	4	2	4	2	1	1	1	1	3	1	2	2	2	2	1	1	2	1	1	1	1	2	1	1	2	1	3	2	Bournemouth
Bradford PA	2	1	3	3	1	2	2	1	1	1	–	–	–	–	–	–	–	–	–	–	–	–	–	–	–	–	–	–	–	Bradford PA
Bradford C	3	1	1	1	5	1	1	1	2	4	1	1	1	1	2	1	2	1	2	2	2	3	3	1	2	2	4	5	5	Bradford C
Brentford	3	1	2	2	1	2	2	1	3	1	1	1	2	1	2	2	1	1	1	1	1	1	4	2	2	2	1	1	2	Brentford
Brighton	3	1	2	2	1	2	4	2	2	3	1	2	2	1	1	1	4	2	5	4	3	3	2	3	2	3	2	1	1	Brighton
Bristol C	3	1	2	1	2	2	2	2	3	2	SF	1	2	3	3	2	2	3	2	4	2	3	2	1	2	1	2	1	SF	Bristol C
Bristol R	3	2	4	3	2	2	1	1	1	1	5	5	4	1	2	3	1	1	1	1	3	2	2	2	2	2	1	1	1	Bristol R
Burnley	SF	–	–	–	–	5	3	5	SF	4	2	3	2	3	4	5	2	3	3	2	2	1	SF	1	2	1	1	2	2	Burnley
Bury	3	2	SF	2	3	2	2	3	1	2	1	1	4	3	3	2	3	5	1	1	3	1	1	2	1	2	2	4	2	Bury
Cambridge U	–	–	–	–	–	–	–	–	–	–	1	1	1	2	1	1	2	1	1	2	4	2	2	2	1	1	4	2	1	Cambridge U
Cardiff C	2	3	3	2	2	SF	2	2	2	2	2	2	1	2	1	1	2	2	1	2	3	1	2	2	2	1	4	1	2	Cardiff C
Carlisle U	1	1	3	2	3	2	5	2	3	SF	4	3	2	3	3	3	2	1	1	1	2	2	1	2	2	1	1	2	1	Carlisle U

	FOOTBALL LEAGUE CUP																						MILK CUP				LITTLEWOODS CUP			
	1960–61	1961–62	1962–63	1963–64	1964–65	1965–66	1966–67	1967–68	1968–69	1969–70	1970–71	1971–72	1972–73	1973–74	1974–75	1975–76	1976–77	1977–78	1978–79	1979–80	1980–81	1981–82	1982–83	1983–84	1984–85	1985–86	1986–87	1987–88	1988–89	
Charlton Ath	1	3	4	2	4	3	2	1	2	2	2	3	3	2	2	3	3	2	4	1	3	2	2	1	2	1	4	3	3	Charlton Ath
Chelsea	4	–	–	2	W	–	3	2	3	4	4	F	SF	2	3	2	4	2	2	2	2	3	3	3	SF	5	3	2	2	Chelsea
Chester C	1	1	3	1	3	1	1	1	1	1	2	1	2	1	SF	1	2	1	3	2	1	1	1	2	1	2	1	1	2	Chester C
Chesterfield	3	1	1	1	4	3	2	1	1	1	1	2	3	3	2	1	1	2	3	3	2	1	1	2	1	1	1	1	1	Chesterfield
Colchester U	2	1	2	4	1	2	1	1	2	2	2	3	1	1	5	1	1	3	1	2	1	3	2	3	1	1	1	1	1	Colchester U
Coventry C	2	1	3	3	5	4	3	2	4	2	5	2	3	5	2	3	4	4	2	3	SF	2	3	3	2	3	4	3	3	Coventry C
Crewe Alex	3	2	1	1	1	2	2	1	2	1	1	1	1	1	3	3	1	1	3	1	1	1	1	2	1	2	1	1	1	Crewe Alex
Crystal Palace	1	1	2	2	4	2	2	2	5	4	5	3	2	2	2	2	2	2	3	3	3	4	3	1	2	2	3	3	3	Crystal Palace
Darlington	3	1	2	1	2	4	2	5	2	2	2	1	1	2	1	3	2	1	3	1	1	1	1	2	1	2	1	2	2	Darlington
Derby Co	3	2	2	2	2	3	2	SF	5	5	4	2	3	2	3	3	5	3	3	2	2	2	3	2	2	3	3	2	3	Derby Co
Doncaster R	3	2	2	1	3	2	3	1	1	2	1	1	1	2	2	5	2	1	1	2	1	2	1	2	1	1	1	2	1	Doncaster R
Everton	5	–	–	–	–	–	–	3	4	4	–	2	2	3	2	4	F	5	4	4	3	4	3	F	4	4	5	SF	4	Everton
Exeter C	1	1	1	2	2	1	3	1	3	1	1	1	1	4	2	2	2	2	4	4	1	2	1	1	1	2	1	1	1	Exeter C
Fulham	1	1	4	2	3	4	4	5	2	2	5	2	2	3	4	3	3	1	2	2	1	4	2	3	3	3	2	2	1	Fulham
Gillingham	2	1	1	4	1	2	2	2	1	2	1	3	2	2	1	2	2	1	1	2	2	1	1	1	2	2	2	2	2	Gillingham
Grimsby T	2	1	2	2	3	5	4	2	2	1	1	4	2	2	1	1	1	2	2	5	1	2	2	2	5	3	2	1	1	Grimsby T
Halifax T	2	1	1	4	1	1	1	2	1	2	2	2	1	2	2	2	1	1	1	1	1	1	1	1	2	1	1	1	2	Halifax T
Hartlepool U	1	1	1	1	1	2	1	2	1	2	1	1	2	1	4	1	1	1	1	1	1	1	2	1	1	1	1	1	1	Hartlepool U
Hereford U	–	–	–	–	–	–	–	–	–	–	–	–	1	1	3	2	1	1	2	1	1	1	1	1	1	2	1	2	1	Hereford U
Huddersfield T	2	2	2	3	2	3	2	SF	2	2	2	2	2	1	2	2	3	2	1	2	1	2	4	3	2	2	2	1	1	Huddersfield T
Hull C	1	3	3	3	2	2	1	2	2	3	2	2	3	4	2	4	2	4	1	1	1	1	1	1	2	2	3	2	2	Hull C
Ipswich T	1	4	–	2	2	5	3	3	2	3	2	2	3	4	5	2	2	4	2	2	4	SF	2	4	SF		53	4	4	Ipswich T
Leeds U	4	4	3	4	3	3	4	W	4	3	2	2	3	4	2	4	3	2	SF	SF	2	2	2	3	3	3	2	3	3	Leeds U
Leyton Orient	2	2	5	2	3	2	1	1	3	1	1	1	2	3	2	2	3	2	2	2	2	1	1	1	2	2	1	1	3	Leyton Orient
Leicester C	2	2	2	W	F	2	4	2	4	5	4	2	2	2	3	4	2	2	2	1	2	3	2	2	3	2	3	3	4	Leicester C

	FOOTBALL LEAGUE CUP																						MILK CUP				LITTLEWOODS CUP			
	1960–61	1961–62	1962–63	1963–64	1964–65	1965–66	1966–67	1967–68	1968–69	1969–70	1970–71	1971–72	1972–73	1973–74	1974–75	1975–76	1976–77	1977–78	1978–79	1979–80	1980–81	1981–82	1982–83	1983–84	1984–85	1985–86	1986–87	1987–88	1988–89	
Lincoln C	1	2	2	3	1	1	3	4	2	1	3	3	1	1	1	3	1	2	1	1	2	3	3	2	1	1	2	–	2	Lincoln C
Liverpool	3	–	–	–	–	–	–	2	4	3	3	4	5	5	4	3	2	F	2	SF	W	W	W	W	3	SF	F	3	4	Liverpool
Luton T	2	2	4	2	2	1	1	2	3	3	3	2	2	4	3	2	2	3	5	1	3	2	4	2	4	3	*	W	F	Luton T
Manchester C	3	1	5	SF	2	3	3	4	3	W	2	3	3	F	3	W	2	5	5	3	SF	4	3	3	4	3	3	5	4	Manchester C
Manchester U	2	–	–	–	–	–	2	–	–	SF	SF	4	3	2	SF	4	5	2	3	3	2	2	F	4	3	4	3	5	3	Manchester U
Mansfield T	1	2	2	2	3	3	2	1	1	2	2	1	2	1	1	5	1	1	1	3	2	2	1	1	1	2	1	2	1	Mansfield T
Middlesbrough	1	3	2	2	2	3	1	3	2	2	3	2	3	3	5	SF	2	3	2	3	2	3	2	1	1	1	2	2	2	Middlesbrough
Millwall	1	1	1	4	2	4	1	4	3	2	3	2	4	5	2	1	5	3	2	1	1	2	1	2	2	2	3	2	3	Millwall
Newcastle U	1	2	2	3	2	2	2	2	3	2	2	3	3	3	5	F	4	2	2	2	2	2	2	2	3	3	2	3	2	Newcastle U
Newport Co	1	1	3	1	1	1	1	2	1	1	2	1	2	1	2	1	1	1	1	1	2	2	2	1	1	1	2	2	–	Newport Co
Northampton T	2	1	3	3	5	3	5	3	1	1	3	1	1	1	2	1	2	2	3	3	1	3	2	1	1	2	1	2	2	Northampton T
Norwich C	4	W	5	5	4	2	2	3	4	2	3	5	F	SF	F	2	3	2	4	5	3	3	4	5	W	4	4	3	3	Norwich C
Nottingham F	4	3	–	–	–	–	2	3	2	4	3	3	2	2	2	3	3	W	W	F	4	5	5	2	3	4	5	3	W	Nottingham F
Notts Co	2	1	4	5	3	1	1	1	1	1	1	2	5	1	2	5	3	3	2	3	4	2	4	3	4	2	1	1	2	Notts Co
Oldham Ath	2	1	2	1	2	2	1	1	1	1	2	2	1	1	1	2	1	3	2	2	2	3	2	3	1	2	3	4	3	Oldham Ath
Oxford U	–	–	1	1	2	1	1	3	1	5	3	3	2	2	1	2	1	2	3	1	3	3	2	5	4	W	4	SF	2	Oxford U
Peterborough U	1	1	2	2	2	SF	2	1	4	1	1	1	1	1	1	4	2	3	4	3	2	1	2	2	1	1	2	3	2	Peterborough U
Plymouth Arg	4	1	2	2	SF	2	2	2	1	1	1	2	1	SF	1	2	1	1	2	3	1	2	1	2	2	1	1	2	2	Plymouth Arg
Portsmouth	5	3	4	4	3	3	2	3	2	1	3	1	2	2	2	2	1	3	1	1	4	2	1	2	2	5	3	2	2	Portsmouth
Port Vale	2	1	2	2	1	1	1	2	1	1	1	1	2	1	1	1	1	1	1	1	1	2	1	2	2	2	2	1	2	Port Vale
Preston NE	3	3	4	2	2	4	3	2	2	1	3	4	1	1	3	2	1	2	2	2	4	2	2	3	2	2	2	1	2	Preston NE
QPR	1	2	2	1	2	1	W	4	2	5	3	4	2	4	3	4	SF	3	4	4	3	4	2	3	5	F	3	3	5	QPR
Reading	2	2	2	1	4	4	2	3	1	1	1	1	1	2	3	1	1	1	4	2	2	1	1	1	1	1	2	4	2	Reading
Rochdale	3	F	1	2	2	2	1	1	1	1	2	1	2	2	1	1	1	2	1	1	1	1	2	1	1	1	2	2	1	Rochdale
Rotherham U	F	5	4	5	3	4	3	2	1	3	2	1	3	2	2	1	2	2	3	2	1	2	3	5	3	1	2	2	2	Rotherham U

* Luton Town expelled from the competition.

	FOOTBALL LEAGUE CUP																						MILK CUP				LITTLEWOODS CUP			
	1960–61	1961–62	1962–63	1963–64	1964–65	1965–66	1966–67	1967–68	1968–69	1969–70	1970–71	1971–72	1972–73	1973–74	1974–75	1975–76	1976–77	1977–78	1978–79	1979–80	1980–81	1981–82	1982–83	1983–84	1984–85	1985–86	1986–87	1987–88	1988–89	
Scarborough	–	–	–	–	–	–	–	–	–	–	–	–	–	–	–	–	–	–	–	–	–	–	–	–	–	–	–	1	3	Scarborough
Scunthorpe U	1	1	3	2	2	1	1	2	3	1	1	1	1	2	2	1	2	2	1	1	1	1	1	1	2	1	2	2	3	Scunthorpe U
Sheffield U	2	5	3	2	2	2	5	2	2	4	3	5	4	2	4	3	2	2	3	1	1	2	3	2	2	2	3	2	3	Sheffield U
Sheffield W	–	–	–	–	–	–	2	4	2	2	2	2	3	3	1	1	4	4	2	2	3	2	5	5	5	3	3	5	2	Sheffield W
Shrewsbury T	SF	2	2	1	2	3	2	1	1	2	1	2	1	1	1	2	1	1	1	2	2	2	2	3	2	3	5	2	1	Shrewsbury T
Southampton	5	1	2	2	3	3	3	2	5	2	2	3	3	4	4	2	2	3	F	3	2	2	4	3	4	4	SF	2	5	Southampton
Southend U	2	1	2	3	3	2	1	2	2	3	1	1	2	1	2	1	1	1	1	3	1	1	1	1	1	1	2	3	2	Southend U
Southport	1	1	2	2	1	1	1	1	2	2	1	2	2	1	1	2	1	2	–	–	–	–	–	–	–	–	–	–	–	Southport
Stockport Co	2	1	1	1	1	1	1	2	2	1	1	2	4	3	1	1	3	1	2	2	3	1	1	2	2	1	2	1	1	Stockport Co
Stoke C	2	2	3	F	4	4	2	5	2	2	2	W	4	4	4	2	3	2	5	3	2	2	2	4	2	3	2	4	2	Stoke C
Sunderland	2	5	SF	2	4	3	2	4	2	2	2	2	2	3	2	2	3	2	2	4	2	3	3	3	F	2	1	1	2	Sunderland
Swansea C	2	2	2	3	4	2	3	1	3	2	2	1	1	1	1	1	4	1	3	2	2	2	3	2	1	2	2	1	1	Swansea C
Swindon T	2	2	3	4	2	2	4	1	W	3	4	2	2	2	1	2	1	4	3	SF	3	1	1	1	1	4	2	3	2	Swindon T
Torquay U	2	1	2	1	2	1	1	3	1	2	2	3	1	1	1	3	3	1	1	2	1	1	1	2	1	1	1	2	1	Torquay U
Tottenham H	–	–	–	–	–	–	2	–	SF	2	W	SF	W	2	2	SF	3	3	2	2	5	F	5	3	4	4	SF	3	4	Tottenham H
Tranmere R	4	1	1	3	2	1	2	2	2	3	2	2	1	3	2	1	2	1	1	2	2	4	2	1	1	1	1	1	4	Tranmere R
Walsall	2	2	2	3	1	2	4	2	2	1	2	1	1	2	1	1	2	3	2	1	1	1	1	SF	3	2	2	2	2	Walsall
Watford	1	3	1	1	2	2	1	2	1	2	2	3	1	1	1	2	3	3	SF	1	5	5	3	2	5	3	3	4	2	Watford
Wimbledon	–	–	–	–	–	–	–	–	–	–	–	–	–	–	–	–	–	2	2	4	2	1	1	4	1	3	2	4	4	Wimbledon
WBA	–	–	–	–	–	W	F	2	3	F	4	2	3	3	3	2	3	4	2	4	5	SF	2	4	4	4	2	1	1	WBA
West Ham U	2	2	3	SF	2	F	SF	4	3	3	3	SF	3	2	3	4	4	2	2	5	F	3	5	4	3	3	5	2	SF	West Ham U
Wigan Ath	–	–	–	–	–	–	–	–	–	–	–	–	–	–	–	–	–	–	2	1	2	4	2	1	2	1	1	2	1	Wigan Ath
Wolverhampton W	–	–	–	–	–	–	3	2	4	4	2	2	SF	W	2	4	2	2	2	W	2	2	2	2	3	1	1	2	1	Wolverhampton W
Workington	2	3	1	5	5	3	3	3	3	1	2	1	2	1	1	1	1	–	–	–	–	–	–	–	–	–	–	–	–	Workington
Wrexham	5	1	1	3	1	2	1	1	2	3	1	1	2	2	1	2	4	5	2	2	1	3	1	1	1	2	2	1	1	Wrexham
York C	1	5	1	2	1	2	3	1	1	1	2	3	1	4	1	2	1	1	1	1	2	1	1	1	2	2	2	2	1	York C

AWARDS 1988–89

FOOTBALLER OF THE YEAR

The Football Writers' Association Award for the Footballer of the Year went to Steve Nicol of Liverpool and Scotland. A consistent and versatile player for the Anfield club he was ever present in League appearances last season.

Past Winners
1947–48 Stanley Matthews (Blackpool), 1948–49 Johnny Carey (Manchester U), 1949–50 Joe Mercer (Arsenal), 1950–51 Harry Johnston (Blackpool), 1951–52 Billy Wright (Wolverhampton W), 1952–53 Nat Lofthouse (Bolton W), 1953–54 Tom Finney (Preston NE), 1954–55 Don Revie (Manchester C), 1955–56 Bert Trautmann (Manchester C), 1956–57 Tom Finney (Preston NE), 1957–58 Danny Blanchflower (Tottenham H), 1958–59 Syd Owen (Luton T), 1959–60 Bill Slater (Wolverhampton W), 1960–61 Danny Blanchflower (Tottenham H), 1961–62 Jimmy Adamson (Burnley), 1962–63 Stanley Matthews (Stoke C), 1963–64 Bobby Moore (West Ham U), 1964–65 Bobby Collins (Leeds U), 1965–66 Bobby Charlton (Manchester U), 1966–67 Jackie Charlton (Leeds U), 1967–68 George Best (Manchester U), 1968–69 Dave Mackay (Derby Co) shared with Tony Book (Manchester C), 1969–70 Billy Bremner (Leeds U), 1970–71 Frank McLintock (Arsenal), 1971–72 Gordon Banks (Stoke C), 1972–73 Pat Jennings (Tottenham H), 1973–74 Ian Callaghan (Liverpool), 1974–75 Alan Mullery (Fulham), 1975–76 Kevin Keegan (Liverpool), 1976–77 Emlyn Hughes (Liverpool), 1977–78 Kenny Burns (Nottingham F), 1978–79 Kenny Dalglish (Liverpool), 1979–80 Terry McDermott (Liverpool), 1980–81 Frans Thijssen (Ipswich T), 1981–82 Steve Perryman (Tottenham H), 1982–83 Kenny Dalglish (Liverpool), 1983–84 Ian Rush (Liverpool), 1984–85 Neville Southall (Everton), 1985–86 Gary Lineker (Everton), 1986–87 Clive Allen (Tottenham H), 1987–88 John Barnes (Liverpool).

THE PFA AWARDS 1989

Player of the Year: Mark Hughes (Manchester U).
Previous Winners: 1974 Norman Hunter (Leeds U); 1975 Colin Todd (Derby Co); 1976 Pat Jennings (Tottenham H); 1977 Andy Gray (Aston Villa); 1978 Peter Shilton (Nottingham F) 1979 Liam Brady (Arsenal); 1980 Terry McDermott (Liverpool); 1981 John Wark (Ipswich T); 1982 Kevin Keegan (Southampton); 1983 Kenny Dalglish (Liverpool); 1984 Ian Rush (Liverpool); 1985 Peter Reid (Everton); 1986 Gary Lineker (Everton); 1987 Clive Allen (Tottenham H); 1988 John Barnes (Liverpool).
Young Player of the Year: Paul Merson (Arsenal).
Previous Winners: 1974 Kevin Beattie (Ipswich T); 1975 Mervyn Day (West Ham U); 1976 Peter Barnes (Manchester C); 1977 Andy Gray (Aston Villa); 1978 Tony Woodcock (Nottingham F); 1979 Cyrille Regis (WBA); 1980 Glenn Hoddle (Tottenham H); 1981 Gary Shaw (Aston Villa); 1982 Steve Moran (Southampton); 1983 Ian Rush (Liverpool); 1984 Paul Walsh (Luton T); 1985 Mark Hughes (Manchester U); 1986 Tony Cottee (West Ham U); 1987 Tony Adams (Arsenal); 1988 Paul Gascoigne (Tottenham H).
Merit Award: Nat Lofthouse.
Previous Winners: 1974 Bobby Charlton CBE, Cliff Lloyd OBE; 1975 Denis Law; 1976 George Eastham OBE; 1977 Jack Taylor OBE; 1978 Bill Shankley OBE; 1979 Tom Finney OBE; 1980 Sir Matt Busby CBE; 1981 John Trollope MBE; 1982 Joe Mercer OBE; 1983 Bob Paisley OBE; 1984 Bill Nicholson; 1985 Ron Greenwood; 1986 The 1966 England World Cup team, Sir Alf Ramsey, Harold Shepherdson; 1987 Sir Stanley Matthews; 1988 Billy Bonds MBE.

BARCLAYS BANK MANAGER OF THE YEAR 1988-89

George Graham of Barclays League Champions, Arsenal, became the first London club manager to win the Manager of the Year title in 18 years when he was named Barclays Bank Manager of the Year by a panel of leading football journalists and commentators. He was presented with the new Barclays trophy and a Barclayshare portfolio valued at £5000 at the FLESA (Football League Executive Staffs' Association) Dinner in London. The presentations were made by Mr Bill Gordon, Barclays UK Corporate Director.

Bertie Mee was the last London manager to land the prize – in 1971, the Gunners' "double" year. Since then, in the 17 years from 1973 when Bill Shankly won the title, the award has gone to Merseyside on twelve occasions: Bob Paisley ('76, '77, '79, '80, '83), Joe Fagan ('84), Howard Kendall ('85 and '87), and Kenny Dalglish ('86 and '88). This award is Graham's 10th managerial accolade in six years – four at Millwall and six at Arsenal.

BARCLAYS BANK SERVICE TO FOOTBALL AWARD

FLESA (The Football League Executive Staffs' Association) named Derek Dooley (59), managing director of Sheffield United, as the first recipient of the Barclays Bank Service to Football Award. He was presented with an inscribed rose bowl and a cheque for £1000 at the FLESA annual dinner in London. With Sheffield Wednesday – whom he joined from Lincoln in June 1947 – Dooley scored 180 goals in 168 matches at all levels. (He scored 64 goals from 63 League matches with Wednesday and Lincoln.) After only two seasons in the first team his promising career was brought to an untimely end when he broke a leg in a collision with the goalkeeper at Preston on St Valentine's Day 1953 and gangrene set in leading to its amputation. Since then he has served football in virtually every capacity: at Sheffield Wednesday, as scout, youth coach, development club manager, commercial manager and club manager when he was sacked on Christmas Eve 1973; and subsequently, from 1974, with Sheffield United, as commercial manager, director and currently managing director and chief executive.

BARCLAYS LEAGUE YOUNG EAGLE AWARD

David Rocastle, Arsenal's home-bred latest full international squad recruit, was named the Barclays Young Eagle of the Year by a panel including Ron Greenwood, Bill Nicholson, Bob Paisley, Jack Charlton, Stan Cullis, Trevor Cherry and Terry Yorath and chaired by England manager Bobby Robson.

Rocastle received the magnificent Barclays Silver Eagle trophy and a Barclayshare portfolio valued at £5000 on the pitch at Highbury prior to Arsenal's Barclays League match against Wimbledon.

Rocastle's (22), nearest rivals for the Barclays accolade were Steve Staunton (Liverpool), Terry Wilson (Nottingham Forest), Paul Ince (West Ham United) – and his club mates Michael Thomas and Paul Merson.

THE SCOTTISH PFA AWARDS 1989

Player of the Year: Theo Snelders (Aberdeen).

Previous Winners: 1978 Derek Johnstone (Rangers); 1979 Paul Hegarty (Dundee U); 1980 Davie Provan (Celtic); 1981 Sandy Clark (Airdrieonians); 1982 Mark McGhee (Aberdeen); 1983 Charlie Nicholas (Celtic); 1984 Willie Miller (Aberdeen); 1985 Jim Duffy (Morton); 1986 Richard Gough (Dundee U); 1987 Brian McClair (Celtic); 1988 Paul McStay (Celtic).

Young Player of the Year: Bill McKinlay (Dundee U).

Previous Winners: 1978 Graeme Payne (Dundee U); 1979 Graham Stewart (Dundee U); 1980 John MacDonald (Rangers); 1981 Francis McAvennie (St Mirren); 1982 Charlie Nicholas (Celtic); 1983 Pat Nevin (Clyde); 1984 John Robertson (Hearts); 1985 Craig Levein (Hearts); 1986 Craig Levein (Hearts); 1987 Robert Fleck (Rangers); 1988 John Collins (Hibernian).

SCOTTISH FOOTBALL WRITERS' ASSOCIATION

Player of the Year 1989 – Richard Gough (Rangers)

1965 **Billy McNeill** (Celtic)
1966 **John Greig** (Rangers)
1967 **Ronnie Simpson** (Celtic)
1968 **Gordon Wallace** (Raith R)
1969 **Bobby Murdoch** (Celtic)
1970 **Pat Stanton** (Hibernian)
1971 **Martin Buchan** (Aberdeen)
1972 **Dave Smith** (Rangers)
1973 **George Connelly** (Celtic)
1974 **Scotland's World Cup Squad**
1975 **Sandy Jardine** (Rangers)
1976 **John Greig** (Rangers)
1977 **Danny McGrain** (Celtic)
1978 **Derek Johnstone** (Rangers)
1979 **Andy Ritchie** (Morton)
1980 **Gordon Strachan** (Aberdeen)
1981 **Alan Rough** (Partick Th)
1982 **Paul Sturrock** (Dundee U)
1983 **Charlie Nicholas** (Celtic)
1984 **Willie Miller** (Aberdeen)
1985 **Hamish McAlpine** (Dundee U)
1986 **Sandy Jardine** (Hearts)
1987 **Brian McClair** (Celtic)
1988 **Paul McStay** (Celtic)

EUROPEAN FOOTBALLER OF THE YEAR 1988

Marco Van Basten was voted European Footballer of the Year for 1988 in the poll carried out by *France Football* magazine. He thus followed his Dutch countryman and AC Milan colleague Ruud Gullit in achieving the honour based on his performances in the 1988 European Championship when he finished top scorer with five goals.

Born on 31 October 1964 in Utrecht he joined Ajax from Elinkwijk as a 17 year old in 1981 and made his debut as substitute for the legendary Johan Cruyff, twice winner of Europe's top award himself. Two years later he broke into the international scene in the World Youth Cup finals in Mexico.

For four seasons he headed the Dutch scorers for Ajax with 28, 22, 37 and 31 goals among 128 goals for the Amsterdam club before being sold to AC Milan for £1.5 million in the summer of 1987. The move came after he captained Ajax to victory in the Cup Winners Cup final against Lokomotiv Leipzig, when inevitably he notched the only goal of the game.

His subsequent achievement in the European Championship was all the more remarkable since he had missed most of his initial term at Milan with injury. Against England he scored a memorable hat-trick having started the tournament on the substitutes' bench against the USSR.

A world class striker his overall work as a target man in attack able to hold on to the ball by sheer ease of control raised him above the normal sharp-shooter's ability. He is probably best remembered for the stunning volley with his right foot some eight yards from the by-line on the edge of England's penalty area, which found the far corner of the net.

Past winners
1956 **Stanley Matthews** (Blackpool)
1957 **Alfredo Di Stefano** (Real Madrid)
1958 **Raymond Kopa** (Real Madrid)
1959 **Alfredo Di Stefano** (Real Madrid)
1960 **Luis Suarez** (Barcelona)
1961 **Omar Sivori** (Juventus)
1962 **Josef Masopust** (Dukla Prague)
1963 **Lev Yashin** (Moscow Dynamo)
1964 **Denis Law** (Manchester United)
1965 **Eusebio** (Benfica)
1966 **Bobby Charlton** (Manchester United)
1967 **Florian Albert** (Ferencvaros)
1968 **George Best** (Manchester United)
1969 **Gianni Rivera** (AC Milan)
1970 **Gerd Muller** (Bayern Munich)
1971 **Johan Cruyff** (Ajax)
1972 **Franz Beckenbauer** (Bayern Munich)
1973 **Johan Cruyff** (Barcelona)
1974 **Johan Cruyff** (Barcelona)
1975 **Oleg Blokhin** (Dynamo Kiev)
1976 **Franz Beckenbauer** (Bayern Munich)
1977 **Allan Simonsen** (Borussia Moenchengladbach)
1978 **Kevin Keegan** (SV Hamburg)
1979 **Kevin Keegan** (SV Hamburg)
1980 **Karl-Heinz Rummenigge** (Bayern Munich)
1981 **Karl-Heinz Rummenigge** (Bayern Munich)
1982 **Paolo Rossi** (Juventus)
1983 **Michel Platini** (Juventus)
1984 **Michel Platini** (Juventus)
1985 **Michel Platini** (Juventus)
1986 **Igor Belanov** (Dynamo Kiev)
1987 **Ruud Gullit** (AC Milan)

BARCLAYS BANK MANAGER AWARDS 1988–89

SEPTEMBER
Division 1 – **Dave Stringer** (Norwich City); *Division 2* – **Don Mackay** (Blackburn Rovers); *Division 3* – **Dave Bassett** (Sheffield United); *Division 4* – **Billy McEwan** (Rotherham United).

OCTOBER
Division 1 – **George Graham** (Arsenal); *Division 2* – **Bobby Campbell** (Chelsea); *Division 3* – **Joe Jordan** (Bristol City); *Division 4* – **Neil Warnock** (Scarborough).

NOVEMBER
Division 1 – **Chris Nicholl** (Southampton); *Division 2* – **Howard Wilkinson** (Leeds United); *Division 3* – **John Rudge** (Port Vale); *Division 4* – **Johnny King** (Tranmere Rovers).

DECEMBER
Division 1 – **George Graham** (Arsenal); *Division 2* – **Brian Talbot** (West Bromwich Albion); *Division 3* – **Harry McNally** (Chester City); *Division 4* – **Dixie McNeill** (Wrexham).

JANUARY
Division 1 – **Alex Ferguson** (Manchester United); *Division 2* – **Steve Harrison** (Watford); *Division 3* – **Steve Perryman** (Brentford); *Division 4* – **Alan Buckley** (Grimsby Town).

FEBRUARY
Division 1 – **Brian Clough** (Nottingham Forest); *Division 2* – **Mel Machin** (Manchester City); *Division 3* – **Graham Turner** (Wolverhampton Wanderers); *Division 4* – **Dario Gradi** (Crewe Alexandra).

MARCH
Division 1 – **Kenny Dalglish** (Liverpool); *Division 2* – **Bobby Campbell** (Chelsea); *Division 3* – **Ray Lewington** (Fulham); *Division 4* – **Billy McEwan** (Rotherham United).

APRIL
Division 1 – **Brian Clough** (Nottingham Forest); *Division 2* – **Steve Harrison** (Watford); *Division 3* – **Phil Neal** (Bolton Wanderers); *Division 4* – **Frank Clark** (Leyton Orient).

Barclays Bank Manager of the Year 1989: George Graham (Arsenal).

Barclays Bank Division Two Manager of the Season: Bobby Campbell (Chelsea).
Barclays Bank Division Three Manager of the Season: Graham Turner (Wolverhampton Wanderers).
Barclays Bank Division Four Manager of the Season: Billy McEwan (Rotherham United).

BARCLAYS YOUNG EAGLES AWARDS 1988–89

September	**Michael Thomas** (Arsenal)
October	**Colin Cooper** (Middlesbrough)
November	**Matthew Le Tissier** (Southampton)
December	**Paul Merson** (Arsenal)
January	**Paul Ince** (West Ham United)
February	**Terry Wilson** (Nottingham Forest)
March	**Steve Staunton** (Liverpool)

BARCLAYS PERFORMANCE OF THE WEEK

Each week a panel of leading managers, chaired by Bobby Robson select the outstanding performance by a League club in the Barclays League or FA Cup competition. The selected club then nominates a local boy's club to receive the Barclays award, from the local Manager on the pitch at the next home match. The award consists of a complete strip in the bank's colours and a cheque for £300, half of which must be spent on a local community project. The club receives an inscribed silver salver. Thirty-three awards were presented last season to clubs from all four divisions – from champions, Arsenal (twice) to Burnley.

1	Aston Villa	12	Derby County	23	Brentford
2	Burnley	13	Wrexham	24	Scunthorpe United
3	Norwich City	14	West Ham United	25	Stoke City
4	Sheffield United	15	Shrewsbury Town	26	Nottingham Forest
5	Newcastle United	16	Southend United	27	Swindon Town
6	Fulham	17	Arsenal	28	Newcastle United
7	Leyton Orient	18	Coventry City	29	Liverpool
8	Halifax Town	19	Bury	30	Chester City
9	West Bromwich Albion	20	Brentford	31	Tottenham Hotspur
10	Chelsea	21	Chelsea	32	Charlton Athletic
11	Arsenal	22	Walsall	33	Liverpool

FROM THE CHAPLAIN

The terrible events at Hillsborough last season and their aftermath sharpened the significance of the chaplain's role at many clubs and several more League clubs are now considering such an appointment. Here, one of the longest serving honorary chaplains writes for Rothmans readers about the work of the chaplain.

When a young couple visited me for a wedding interview, they were surprised to see in my study a Fixture list and calendar of the football club for which I am chaplain. The young man said that he did not think that 'Parsons' were interested in football. Well some are, and I have been pleased to serve as a Football Club Chaplain, with two different clubs, since 1973.

The manager said to me, when I was first appointed, "We hope that we never need you but when we do we hope that you will be there".

Most of the work is 'being there', being there to share with players and staff in their disappointments, for example when a young player is told that he is not going to make it. Or when a player first realises that his playing career is drawing to a close and he has trained for nothing else other than playing football, or when a player is told that he cannot play again because of an injury or an illness.

Being there when a manager is dismissed, and this is never an easy time for the man or the club, after all dismissal is a sign of failure in most cases, and no one likes that.

Being there when a player has a serious injury, visiting him in hospital and then when recovering at home. Being there in times of bereavement or family illness, to listen and give whatever help that one can.

It is also being there when the club has its successes, like promotion to share in their joys.

A football chaplain is not or should not be an expert who can by his advice put right what is wrong on the playing side of the team. The manager nor the players require us to tell them when the team is not playing well. They know! But if we can help a player who has a personal problem, and these do affect their play, then we have done what is expected of us.

The roll of the football club chaplain is a supportive one to the Directors, Managerial Staff, Players, Office Staff and to Supporters. Year by year more clubs are coming to realise the value of having a chaplain and if any reader would like to discuss such a possibility at his club, in strictest confidence of course, he is invited to contact Christians In Sport, PO Box 93, Oxford.

'THE REV'

CHAPLAINS TO FOOTBALL LEAGUE CLUBS

Rev John Smith — Sheffield U
Rev John Bingham — Chesterfield
Rev Richard Chewter — Exeter C
Rev Alan Fisher — Bournemouth
Rev Andrew Taggart — Torquay U
Rev Gordon Wilson — Sheffield W
Rev Nigel Sands — Swindon T, Crystal Palace
Very Rev Alan Warren — Leicester C
Rev Phillip Miller — Ipswich T
Rev Allen Bagshawe — Hull C
Rev Tony Adamson — Newcastle U
Rev Derek Cleave — Bristol C
Rev Brian Rice — Hartlepool U
Rev John Boyers — Watford
Rev Michael Chantry — Oxford U
Rev Dennis Hall — Wigan Ath
Rev William Hall — Middlesbrough
Rev Canon John Hestor — Brighton & HA
Rev Mervyn Terrett — Luton T
Rev Jim Rushton — Carlisle U
Rev Robert de Berry — Queens Park Rangers
Rev Gary Piper — Fulham
Rev Tony Horsfall — Barnsley
Rev Barry Kirk — Reading

OBITUARY

THE REV JOHN JACKSON

The Rev John Jackson, Methodist Minister and formerly the chaplain at Leeds United died late in 1988. He was the first chaplain ever to be appointed at a Football League club and he served at Elland Road in that capacity for 27 years. Greatly missed by his many friends in the game and by his colleagues in chaplaincy, perhaps the epitaph Mr Jackson would most appreciate is that offered by Leeds' former Scottish International captain, Billy Bremner who said: "He was always a good lad to have a chat to".

ADDRESSES

The Football Association: R. H. G. Kelly, F.C.I.S., 16 Lancaster Gate, London W2 3LW

Scotland: Ernie Walker, 6 Park Gardens, Glasgow G3 7YE. *041-332 6372*

Northern Ireland (Irish FA): D. I. Bowen, 20 Windsor Avenue, Belfast BT9 6EG. *0232-669458*

Wales: A. Evans, 3 Westgate Street, Cardiff, South Glamorgan CF1 1JF. *0222-372325*

Republic of Ireland (FA of Ireland): Dr. T. O'Neill, 80 Merrion Square South, Dublin 2. *0001-766864*

International Federation (FIFA): S. Blatter, FIFA House, Hitzigweg 11, CH-8032 Zurich, Switzerland

Union of European Football Associations: G. Aigner, PO Box 16, CH-3000 Berne 15, Switzerland

THE LEAGUES

The Football League: J. D. Dent, F.C.I.S., The Football League, Lytham St Annes, Lancs FY8 1JG. *0253-729421. Telex 67675*

The Scottish League: J. Farry, 188 West Regent Street, Glasgow G2 4RY. *041-248 384415*

The Irish League: M. Brown, 87 University Street, Belfast BT7 1HP. *0232-242888*

Football League of Ireland: E. Morris, 80 Merrion Square South, Dublin. *0001-765120*

GM Vauxhall Conference: P. D. Hunter, 24 Barnehurst Road, Bexleyheath, Kent DA7 6EZ. *0322-521116*

Central League: D. J. Grimshaw, 118 St Stephens Road, Deepdale, Preston, Lancs PR1 6TD. *Preston 55898*

North West Counties League: F. Hunter, Tyrella, 53 Darby Road, Liverpool L19 9BP. *051-4271719*

Eastern Counties League: B. A. Baldock, 12 Dolphin Close, Linton, Cambs CB1 6XA. *0223-317142*

Football Combination: T. P. R. Kirkup, 15 Oulton Rise, Spinney Hill, Northampton NN3 1EW. *0604-47831*

Hellenic League: T. Cuss, 7 Blenheim Road, Kidlington, Oxford OX5 2HP. *08675 5920*

Kent League: D. Baker, 17 Sterling Road, Sittingbourne, Kent. *Sittingbourne 25105*

Lancashire Amateur League: R. G. Bowker, 13 Shores Green Drive, Wincham, Northwich, Cheshire CW9 6EE. *061-480 7723*

Lancashire Football League: J. W. Howarth, 465 Whalley Road, Clapton-le-Moors, Accrington, Lancs BB5 5RP. *0704-79523*

Leicestershire Senior League: P. Henwood, 450 London Road, Leicester LE2 2PP. *Leicester 704121*

London Spartan: D. Cordell, 44 Greenleas, Waltham Abbey, Essex. *Lea Valley 712428*

Manchester League: F. J. Fitzpatrick, 102 Victoria Road, Stretford, Manchester. *061-865 2726*

Midland Combination: L. W. James, 175 Barnet Lane, Kingswinford, Brierley Hill, West Midlands. *Kingswinford 3459*

Mid-Week Football League: N. A. S. Matthews, Cedar Court, Steeple Aston, Oxford. *0869-40347*

Northern Premier: R. D. Bayley, 22 Woburn Drive, Hale, Altrincham, Cheshire WA15. *061-980 7007*

Northern Intermediate League: F. R. Vicary, 12 Holmefield Avenue, Thornes, Wakefield, Yorks WF2 7AF. *Wakefield 75013*

Northern League: G. Nicholson, 99 Watling Road, Bishop Auckland, Co. Durham. *Bishop Auckland 2167*

North Midlands League: G. Thompson, 7 Wren Park Close, Ridgway, Sheffield

Peterborough and District League: M. Starkey, 18 Wisbech Road, Thorney, Peterborough, Cambs. *Peterborough 270836*

Vauxhall League: N. Robinson, 226 Rye Lane, Peckham SE15. *01-653 3903*

Southern Amateur League: S. J. Lucas, 36 Beaufort Close, North Weald Bassett, Epping, Essex CM16 6JZ. *037882-3932*

South-East Counties League: R. A. Bailey, 10 Highlands Road, New Barnet, Herts. EN5 5AB. *01-449 5131*

Southern League: D. J. Strudwick, 11 Welland Close, Durrington, Worthing, West Sussex BN13 3NR. *0903-67788*

South Midlands League: M. Mitchell, 26 Leighton Court, Dunstable, Beds LU6 1EW. *0582-67291*

South Western League: R. Lowe, Panorama, Lamerton, Tavistock, Devon PL19 8SD. *0822 61376*

United Counties League: R. Gamble, 8 Bostock Avenue, Northampton. *0604 37766*

Wearside: B. Robson, 12 Deneside Howdon Lewear, Crook, Co. Durham, DL15 8JR. *0388 762034*

Western League: M. E. Washer, 126 Chessel Street, Bristol BS3 3DQ. *0272-638308*

The Welsh League: K. J. Tucker, 16 The Parade, Merthyr Tydfil, Mid Glamorgan CF47 0ET. *0685 723884*

West Midlands Regional League: K. H. Goodfellow, 11 Emsworth Grove, Kings Heath, Birmingham B14 6HY. *021 444 3056*

West Yorkshire League: W. Keyworth, 2 Hill Court Grove, Branley, Yorks L13 2AP. *Pudsey 74465*

Northern Counties (East): B. Wood, 6 Restmore Avenue, Guiseley, Nr Leeds LS20 9DG. *Guiseley 4558 (home); Bradford 29595 (9 a.m. to 5 p.m.)*

COUNTY FOOTBALL ASSOCIATIONS

Bedfordshire: R. G. Berridge, The Limes, 14 Bedford Road, Sandy, Beds SG19 1EL. *0767-80417*

Berks and Bucks: W. S. Gosling, 15a London Street, Faringdon, Oxon SN7 8AG. *0367 22099*

Birmingham County: M. Pennick, County FA Offices, Rayhall Lane, Great Barr, Birmingham B43 6JE. *021-357 4278*

Cambridgeshire: R. E. Rogers, 20 Aingers Road, Histon, Cambridge CB4 4JP. *022023 2803*

Cheshire: A. Collins, 50 Ash Grove, Timperley, Altrincham WA15 6JX. *061-980 4706*

Cornwall: J. M. Ryder, Penare, 16 Gloweth View, Truro, Cornwall, TR1 3JZ

Cumberland: R. Johnson, 72 Victoria Road, Workington, Cumbria CA14 2QT. *0900-3979*

Derbyshire: K. Compton, King's Chambers, 35 Ocean Street, Derby DE1 3DS. *0332-361422*

Devon County: C. Squirrel, 4 Paradise Road, Teignmouth, Devon TG14 8NR. *06267-2013*

Dorset County: P. Hough, 110 Dorchester Road, Oakdale, Poole, Dorset BH15 3SD. *0202 746244*

Durham: J. R. Walsh, 'Codeslaw', Ferens Park, Durham DH1 1JZ. *0385-48653*

East Riding County: C. Branton, 83 Belvedere Road, Hessel, Hull HU13 9JH. *0482-649294*

Essex County: T. Alexander, 31 Mildmay Road, Chelmsford, Essex CM2 0DN. *0245-357727*

Gloucestershire: E. J. Marsh, 46 Douglas Road, Horfield, Bristol BS7 0JD. *0272-519435*

Guernsey: G. R. Skuse, Ar-Hyd-Y-Nos, Courtil Olivier Castel, Guernsey CI. *0481-26241*

Hampshire: R. G. Barnes, 8 Ashwood Gardens, off Winchester Road, Southampton SO9 2UA. *0703-766884*

Herefordshire: E. R. Prescott, 7 Kirkland Close, Hampton Park, Hereford HR1 1XP. *0432-51134*

Hertfordshire: C. R. Brown, 21 Hawthorn Crescent, Caddington, Luton, Beds LU1 4EQ. *082-423094*

Huntingdonshire: M. M. Armstrong, 1 Chapel End, Great Giddings, Huntingdon. Cambs PE17 5NP. *08323-262*

Isle of Man: Mrs J. F. Shaw, 120 Bucks Road, Douglas, IOM. *0624-6349*

Jersey: B. Ahier, Sunbrayton, Route Orange, St Brelade, Jersey, CI
Kent County: K. T. Masters, 69 Maidstone Road, Chatham, Kent ME4 6DT. *0634-43824*
Lancashire: J. Kenyon, 31a Wellington St, St John's, Blackburn, Lancs BB1 8AU. *0254-64333*
Leicestershire and Rutland: R. E. Barston, Holmes Park, Dog and Gun Lane, Whetstone, Leicester LE8 3LJ. *0533-867828*
Lincolnshire: F. S. Richardson, PO Box 26, 12 Dean Road, Lincoln LN2 4DP. *0522-24917*
Liverpool County: S. A. Rudd, 23 Greenfield Road, Old Swann, Liverpool L13 3EN. *051-526 9515*
London: R. S. Ashford, 4 Aldworth Grove, London SE13 6HY. *01-690-9626*
Manchester County: S. Holliday, 87 Hart Road, Fallowfield, Manchester M14 7AE. *061-224-5185*
Middlesex County: P. J. Clayton, 30 Rowland Avenue, Kenton, Harrow, Middx HA3 9AF.
Norfolk County: R. Kiddell, 39 Beaumont Road, Costessey, Norwich NR5 0HG. *0603-742421*
Northamptonshire: B. Walden, 37 Harding Terrace, Northampton NN1 2PF. *0604-39584*
North Riding County: P. Kirby, 284 Linthorpe Road, Middlesbrough TS1 3QU. *0642-224585*
Northumberland: J. A. Forster, 30 St Mary's Place, Newcastle upon Tyne NE1 7PG. *0632-261 0779.*
Nottinghamshire: W. T. Annable, 7 Clarendon Street, Nottingham NG1 5HS. *0602-418954*
Oxfordshire: P. J. Ladbrook, 3 Wilkins Road, Cowley, Oxford OX4 2HY. *0865-775432*
Sheffield and Hallamshire: G. Thompson, Clegg House, 5 Onslow Road, Sheffield S11 7AF. *0742-670068*
Shropshire: A. W. Brett, High Street Chambers, 10–11 High Street, Shrewsbury SY1 1SG. *0743-56066*
Somerset & Avon (South): L. G. Webb, 32 North Road, Midsomer Norton, Bath BA3 2QQ. *0761-413176*
Staffordshire: G. S. Brookes, 2 Miller Street, Newcastle, Staffs ST5 1HB. *0782-622585*
Suffolk County: W. M. Steward, 2 Millfields, Haughley, Suffolk IP14 3PU. *0449-673481*
Surrey County: L. F. J. Smith, 2 Fairfield Avenue, Horley, Surrey RH6 7PD. *0293-784945*
Sussex County: D. M. Worsfold, County Office, Culver Road, Lancing, Sussex BN15 9AX. *0903-753547*
Westmorland: J. R. Plumbe, 24 Crescent Green, Kendal LA9 6DR. *0539-23227*
West Riding County: R. M. Robin, 77 Great George Street, Leeds LS1 3DR. *0532-452444*
Wiltshire: E. M. Parry, 44 Kennet Avenue, Swindon SN2 3LG. *0793-29036*
Worcestershire: P. Rushton, 84 Windermere Drive, Warndon, Worcester WR4 9IB. *0905-51166*

OTHER USEFUL ADDRESSES

Amateur Football Alliance: W. P. Goss, 55 Islington Park Street, London N1 1QB. *01-359 3493*
English Schools FA: C. S. Allatt, 4a Eastgate Street, Stafford ST16 2NN. *0785-51142*
Oxford University: I. Falshaw, Pembroke College, Oxford OX1 1DW. *0865 276444*
Cambridge University: Dr A. J. Little, St Catherine's College, Cambridge CB2 1RL.
Army: Major T. C. Knight, Clayton Barracks, Aldershot, Hants GU11 2BG. *0252-24431 Ext 3571*
Royal Air Force: Group Capt P. W. Hilton, RAF, 20 Stray Walk, Harrogate, N. Yorks HG2 8DU. *0423-793455*
Royal Navy: Lt-Cdr J. Danks, R.N. Sports Office, H.M.S. Temeraine, Portsmouth, Hants PO1 4QS. *0705-822351 Ext 22671*
Universities Athletic Union: Secretary, U.A.U., 28 Woburn Square, London WC1 0AA. *01-637 4828.*
Central Council of Physical Recreation: General Secretary, 70 Brompton Road, London SW3 1HE. *01-584 6651*
British Olympic Association: 6 John Prince's Street W1M 0DH. *01-408 2029*
National Federation of Football Supporters' Clubs: Chairman: A. M. Kershaw, 87 Brookfield Avenue, Loughborough, Leicestershire LE11 3LN. *0509 267643.*
National Playing Fields Association: Col R. Satterthwaite, O.B.E., 578b Catherine Place, London, SW1.
The Scottish Football Commercial Managers Association: J. E. Hillier (Chairman), c/o Keith FC Promotions Office, 60 Union Street, Keith, Banffshire, Scotland.
Professional Footballers' Association: G. Taylor, 2 Oxford Couret, Bishopsgate, Off Lower Mosley Street, Manchester M2 3W2. *061-236 0575*
Referees' Association: W. J. Taylor, Cross Offices, Summerhill, Kingswinford, West Midlands DY6 9JE. *0384 288386*
Women's Football Association: Miss L. Whitehead, 448/450 Hanging Ditch, The Corn Exchange, Manchester M4 3ES. *061-832 5911*
The Association of Football League Commercial Managers: G. H. Dimbleby, Secretary WBA FC, The Hawthorns, Halford Lane, West Bromwich B71 4LF
The Association of Football Statisticians: R. J. Spiller, 22 Breton, Basildon, Essex. *0268 416020*
The Football Programme Directory: David Stacey, 'The Beeches', 66 Southend Road, Wickford, Essex SS11 8EN.
England Football Supporters Association: Publicity Officer, David Stacey, 66 Southend Road, Wickford, Essex SS11 8EN.
The Football League Executive Staffs Association: PO Box 52, Leamington Spa, Warwickshire.
The Ninety-Two Club: 104 Gilda Crescent, Whitchurch, Bristol BS14 9LD.
The Football Trust: Second Floor, Walkden House, 10 Melton Street, London NW1 2EJ. *01-388 4504.*
Association of Provincial Football Supporters' Clubs in London: Miss Sallyann Watson, Secretary APFSCIL, 6 Bradshaws Close, Kings Road, London SE25 4ES. *01-676 8390 (home).*

LAWS OF THE GAME

The Laws of the Game and Decisions of the International Board that follow are reproduced with the special permission of FIFA, and the text is the official text as published by FIFA.

LAW I

THE FIELD OF PLAY

The Field of Play and appurtenances shall be as shown in the following plan:

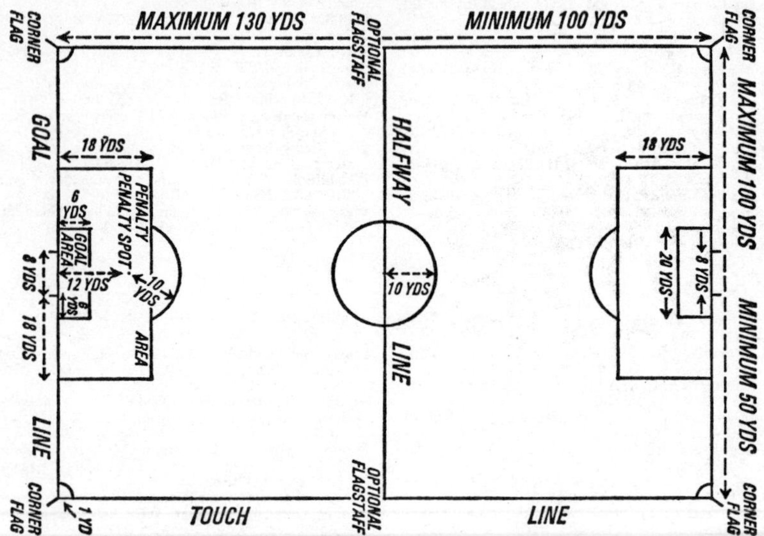

(1) **Dimensions.** The field of play shall be rectangular, its length being not more than 130 yards nor less than 100 yards, and its breadth not more than 100 yards nor less than 50 yards. (In International Matches the length shall be not more than 120 yards nor less than 110 yards and the breadth not more than 80 yards nor less than 70 yards.) The length shall in all cases exceed the breadth.

(2) **Marking.** The field of play shall be marked with distinctive lines, not more than 5 inches in width, not by a V-shaped rut, in accordance with the plan, the longer boundary lines being called the touch-lines and the shorter the goal-lines. A flag on a post not less than 5ft high and having a non-pointed top, shall be placed at each corner; a similar flag-post may be placed opposite the half-way line on each side of the field of play, not less than 1 yard outside the touch-line. A half-way-line shall be marked out across the field of play. The centre of the field of play shall be indicated by a suitable mark and a circle with a 10 yards radius shall be marked round it.

(3) **The Goal-Area.** At each end of the field of play two lines shall be drawn at right-angles to the goal-line, 6 yards from each goal-post. These shall extend into the field of play for a distance of 6 yards and shall be joined by a line drawn parallel with the goal-line. Each of the spaces enclosed by these goal-lines and the goal-line shall be called a goal-area.

(4) **The Penalty-Area.** At each end of the field of play two lines shall be drawn at right angles to the goal-line, 18 yards from each goal-post. These shall extend into the field of play for a distance of 18 yards and shall be joined by a line drawn parallel with the goal-line. Each of the spaces enclosed by these lines and the goal-line shall be called a penalty-area. A suitable mark shall be made within each penalty area. 12 yards from the mid-point of the goal-line, measured along an undrawn line at right-angles thereto. These shall be the penalty-kick marks. From each penalty-kick mark an arc of a circle, having a radius of 10 yards, shall be drawn outside the penalty-area.

(5) **The Corner Area.** From each corner-flag post a quarter circle, having a radius of 1 yard, shall be drawn inside the field of play.

(6) **The Goals.** The goals shall be placed on the centre of each goal-line and shall consist of two upright posts, equidistant from the corner-flags and 8 yards apart (inside measurement), joined by a horizontal cross-bar the lower edge of which shall be 8ft from the ground. The width and depth of the goal-posts and the width and depth of the cross-bars shall not exceed 5 inches (12cm). The goal-posts and the cross-bars shall have the same width.

Nets may be attached to the posts, cross-bars and ground behind the goals. They should be appropriately supported and be so placed as to allow the goal-keeper ample room.

Footnote

Goal nets. The use of nets made of hemp, jute or nylon is permitted. The nylon strings may, however, not be thinner than those made of hemp or jute.

Decisions of the International Board

(1) In International Matches the dimensions of the field of play shall be: maximum 110×75 metres; minimum 100×64 metres.

(2) National Associations must adhere strictly to these dimensions. Each National Association organising an International Match must advise the visiting Association, before the match, of the place and the dimensions of the field of play.

(3) The Board has approved this table of measurements for the laws of the Game:

130 yards	. . . 120metres
120 yards	. . . 110
110 yards	. . . 100
100 yards	. . . 90
80 yards	. . . 75
70 yards	. . . 64
50 yards	. . . 45
18 yards	. . . 16.50
12 yards	. . . 11
10 yards	. . . 9.15
8 yards	. . . 7.32
6 yards	. . . 5.50
1 yard	. . . 1
8 feet	. . . 2.44
5 feet	. . . 1.50
28 inches	. . . 0.71
27 inches	. . . 0.68
9 inches	. . . 0.22
5 inches	. . . 0.12
¾ inch	. . . 0.019
½ inch	. . . 0.0127
⅜ inch	. . . 0.010
14 ounces	. . . 396 grams
16 ounces	. . . 453 grams
15 lb/sq in	. . . 1 kg/cm^2

(4) The goal-line shall be marked the same width as the depth of the goal-posts and the cross-bar, so that the goal-line and goal-post will conform to the same interior and exterior edges.

(5) The 6 yards (for the outline of the goal-area) and the 18 yards (for the outline of the penalty-area) which have to be measured along the goal-line, must start from the inner sides of the goal-posts.

(6) The space within the inside areas of the field of play includes the width of the lines marking these areas.

(7) All Associations shall provide standard equipment, particularly in International Matches, when the laws of the Game must be compiled with in every respect and especially with regard to the size of the ball and other equipment which must conform to the regulations. All cases of failure to provide standard equipment must be reported to FIFA.

(8) In a match played under the Rules of a Competition, if the cross-bar becomes displaced or broken, play shall be stopped and the match abandoned unless the cross-bar has been repaired and replaced in position or a new one provided without such being a danger to the players. A rope is not considered to be a satisfactory substitute for a cross-bar.

In a Friendly Match, by mutual consent, play may be resumed without the cross-bar provided it has been removed and no longer constitutes a danger to the players. In these circumstances, a rope may be used as a substitute for a cross-bar. If a rope is not used and the ball crosses the goal-line at a point which in the opinion of the Referee is below where the cross-bar should have been he shall award a goal.

The game shall be restarted by the Referee dropping the ball at the place where it was when play was stopped.

(9) National Association may specify such maximum and minimum dimensions for the cross-bars and goal-posts, within the limits laid down in Law I, as they consider appropriate.

(10) Goal-posts and cross-bars must be made of wood, metal or other approved material as decided from time to time by the International FA Board. They may be square, rectangular, round, half-round or clliptical in shape. Goal-posts and cross-bars made of other materials and in other shapes are not permitted. The goal-posts must be of white colour.

(11) 'Curtain-raisers' to International Matches should only be played following agreement on the day of the match, and taking into account the condition of the field of play, between representatives of the two Associations and the Referee (of the International Match).

(12) National Associations, particularly in International Matches, should

- restrict the number of photographers around the field of play.
- have a line ('photographers' line') marked behind the goal-lines at least two metres from the corner flag going through a point situated at least 3.5 metres behind the intersection of the goal-line with the line marking the goal area to a point situated at least six metres behind the goal-posts.
- prohibit photographers from passing over these lines.
- forbid the use of artificial lighting in the form of 'flashlights'.

LAW II – THE BALL

The ball shall be spherical; the outer casing shall be of leather or other approved materials. No material shall be used in its construction which might prove dangerous to the players.

The circumference of the ball shall not be more than 28in and not less than 27in. The weight of the ball at the start of the game shall not be more than 16oz nor less than 14oz. The pressure shall be equal to 0.6-1.1 atmosphere (=600-1100gr/cm^2) at sea level. The ball shall not be changed during the game unless authorised by the Referee.

Decisions of the International Board

(1) The ball used in any match shall be considered the property of the Association or Club

on whose ground the match is played, and at the close of play it must be returned to the Referee.

(2) The International Board, from time to time, shall decide what constitutes approved materials. Any approved material shall be certified as such by the International Board.

(3) The Board has approved these equivalents of the weights specified in the Law: 14 to 16 ounces=396 to 453 grammes.

(4) If the ball bursts or becomes deflated during the course of a match, the game shall be stopped and restarted by dropping the new ball at the place where the first ball became defective.

(5) If this happens during a stoppage of the game (place-kick, goal-kick, corner-kick, free-kick, penalty-kick or throw-in) the game shall be restarted accordingly.

LAW III – NUMBER OF PLAYERS

(1) A match shall be played by two teams, each consisting of not more than eleven players, one of whom shall be the goalkeeper.

(2) Substitutes may be used in any match played under the rules of an official competition under the jurisdiction of FIFA, Confederations or National Associations, subject to the following conditions:

(a) that the authority of the international association(s) or national associations(s) concerned, has been obtained.

(b) that, subject to the restriction contained in the following paragraph (c), the rules of a competition shall state how many, if any, substitutes may be nominated and how many of those nominated may be used.

(c) that a team shall not be permitted to use more than two substitutes in any match, who must be chosen from not more than five players whose names may (subject to the rules of the competition) be required to be given to the referee prior to the commencement of the match.

(3) Substitutes may be used in any other match, provided that the two teams concerned reach agreement on a maximum number, not exceeding five, and that the terms of such agreement are intimated to the Referee, before the match. If the Referee is not informed, or if the teams fail to reach agreement, no more than two substitutes shall be permitted. In all cases, the substitutes must be chosen from not more than five players whose names may be required to be given to the referee prior to the commencement of the match.

(4) Any of the other players may change places with the goalkeeper, provided that the Referee is informed before the change is made, and provided also, that the change is made during a stoppage in the game.

(5) When a goalkeeper or any other player is to be replaced by a substitute, the following conditions shall be observed.

(a) the Referee shall be informed of the proposed substitution, before it is made.

(b) the substitute shall not enter the field of play until the player he is replacing has left, and then only after having received a signal from the Referee.

(c) he shall enter the field during a stoppage in the game, and at the half-way line.

(d) a player who has been replaced shall not take any further part in the game.

(e) a substitute shall be subject to the authority and jurisdiction of the Referee whether called upon to play or not.

(f) the substitution is completed when the substitute enters the field of play, from which moment he becomes a player and the player whom he is replacing ceases to be a player.

Punishment:

(a) Play shall not be stopped for an infringement of paragraph 4. The players concerned shall be cautioned immediately the ball goes out of play.

(b) If a substitute enters the field of play without the authority of the Referee, play shall be stopped. The substitute shall be cautioned or sent off according to the circumstances. The game shall be restarted by the Referee dropping the ball at the place where it was when play was stopped, unless it was within the goal area at that time, in which case it shall be dropped on the part of the goal area line which runs parallel to the goal-line, at the point nearest to where the ball was when play was stopped.

(c) For any other infringement of the Law, the player concerned shall be cautioned, and if the game is stopped by the Referee, to administer the caution, it shall be restarted by an indirect free-kick, to be taken by a player of the opposing team from the place where the ball was, when play was stopped. If the free-kick is awarded to a team within its own goal-area, it may be taken from any point within that half of the goal-area in which the ball was when play was stopped.

(d) If a competition's rules require the names of substitutes to be given to the Referee prior to the commencement of the match, then failure to do so will mean no substitutes can be permitted.

Decisions of the International Board

(1) The minimum number of players in a team is left to the discretion of National Associations.

(2) The Board is of the opinion that a match should not be considered valid if there are fewer than seven players in either of the teams.

(3) A player who has been ordered off before play begins may be replaced only by one of the named substitutes. The kick-off must not be delayed to allow the substitute to join his team.

A player who has been ordered off after play has started may not be replaced.

A named substitute who has been ordered off, either before or after play has started, may not be replaced (this decision relates only to players who are ordered off under Law XII. It does not apply to players who have infringed Law IV).

(4) A player who has been replaced shall not take any further part in the game.

(5) For any offence committed on the field of play a substitute shall be subject to the same punishment as any other player whether called upon or not.

LAW IV – PLAYERS' EQUIPMENT

A player shall not wear anything which is dangerous to another player. Footwear must be worn by players and conform to the following standard.

(a) Bars shall be made of leather or rubber and

shall be transverse and flat, not less than half an inch in width and shall extend the total width of the sole and be rounded at the corners.

(b) Studs which are independently mounted on the sole and are replaceable shall be made of leather, rubber, aluminium, plastic or similar material and shall be solid. With the exception of that part of the stud forming the base, which shall not protrude from the sole more than one quarter of an inch, studs shall be round in plan and not less than half an inch in diameter. Where studs are tapered, the minimum diameter of any section of the stud must not be less than half an inch. Where metal seating for the screw type is used, this seating must be embedded in the sole of the footwear and any attachment screw shall be part of the stud. Other than the metal seating for the screw-type of stud, no metal plates even though covered with leather or rubber shall be worn, neither studs which are threaded to allow them to be screwed on to a base screw that is fixed by nails or otherwise to the soles of footwear, nor studs which, apart from the base, have any form of protruding edge rim or relief marking or ornament should be allowed.

(c) Studs which are moulded as an integral part of the sole and are not replaceable shall be made of rubber, plastic, polyurethene or similar soft materials. Provided that there are no fewer than ten studs on the sole, they shall have a minimum diameter of three-eighths of an inch (10mm). Additional supporting material to stabilise studs of soft materials, and ridges which shall not protrude more than 5mm from the sole and moulded to strengthen it, shall be permitted provided that they are in no way dangerous to other players. In all other respects they shall conform to the general requirements of this Law.

(d) Combined bars and studs may be worn, provided the whole conforms to the general requirements of this Law. Neither bars not studs on the soles or heels shall project more than three-quarters of an inch. If nails are used they shall be driven in flush with the surface.

The goalkeeper shall wear colours which distinguish him from the other players and from the Referee.

Punishment: For any infringement of this Law, the player at fault shall be sent off the field of play to adjust his equipment and he shall not return without first reporting to the Referee, who shall satisfy himself that the player's equipment is in order; the player shall only re-enter the game at a moment when the ball has ceased to be in play.

Decisions of the International Board

---

(1) The usual equipment of a player is a jersey or shirt, shorts, stockings, and footwear. In a match played under the rules of a competition, players need not wear boots or shoes, but shall wear jersey or shirt, shorts, or track suit or similar trousers, and stockings.

(2) The Law does not insist that boots or shoes must be worn. However, in competition matches Referees should not allow one or a few players to play without footwear when all the other players are so equipped.

(3) In International Matches, International Competitions, International Club Competitions and friendly matches between clubs of different National Associations, the Referee, prior to the start of the game, shall inspect the players' footwear, and prevent any player whose footwear does not conform to the requirements of the Law from playing until such time as it does comply.

The rules of any competition may include a similar provision.

(4) If the Referee finds that a player is wearing articles not permitted by the Laws and which may constitute a danger to other players, he shall order him to take them off. If he fails to carry out the Referee's instruction, the player shall not take part in the match.

(5) A player who has been prevented from taking part in the game or a player who has been sent off the field for infringing Law IV must report to the Referee during a stoppage of the game and may not enter or re-enter the field of play unless and until the Referee has satisfied himself that the player is no longer infringing Law IV.

(6) A player who has been prevented from taking part in a game or who has been sent off because of an infringement of Law IV, and who enters or re-enters the field of play to join or rejoin his team, in breach of the conditions of Law XII(j), shall be cautioned. If the Referee stops the game to administer the caution, the game shall be restarted by an indirect free-kick, taken by a player of the opposing side, from the place where the ball was when the Referee stopped the game. If the free-kick is awarded to a side within its own goal-area, it may be taken from any point within that half of the goal-area in which the ball was when play was stopped.

LAW V – REFEREES

A Referee shall be appointed to officiate in each game. The authority and the exercise of the powers granted to him by the Laws of the Game commence as soon as he enters the field of play.

His power of penalising shall extend to offences committed when play has been temporarily suspended, or when the ball is out of play. His decision on points of fact connected with the play shall be final, so far as the result of the game is concerned. He shall:

(a) Enforce the Laws.

(b) Refrain from penalising in cases where he is satisfied that, by doing so, he would be giving an advantage to the offending team.

(c) Keep a record of the game, act as timekeeper and allow the full or agreed time, adding thereto all time lost through accident or other cause.

(d) Have discretionary power to stop the game for any infringement of the Laws and to suspend or terminate the game whenever, by reason of the elements, interference by spectators, or other cause, he deems such stoppage necessary. In such a case he shall submit a detailed report to the competent authority, within the stipulated time, and in accordance with the provisions set up by the National Association under whose jurisdiction the match was played. Reports will be deemed to be made when received in the ordinary course of post.

(e) From the time he enters the field of play, caution any player guilty of misconduct or ungentlemanly behaviour and, if he persists, suspend him from further participation in the game. In such cases the Referee shall send the name of the offender to the competent authority, within the stipulated time, and in accordance with the provisions set up by the National Association under whose jurisdiction the match was played. Reports will be deemed to be made when received in the ordinary course of post.

(f) Allow no person other than the players and linesmen to enter the field of play without his permission.

(g) Stop the game if, in his opinion, a player has been seriously injured, have the player removed as soon as possible from the field of play, and immediately resume the game. If a player is slightly injured, the game shall not be stopped until the ball has ceased to be in play. A player who is able to go to the touch or goal-line for attention of any kind, shall not be treated on the field of play.

(h) Send off the field of play, any player who, in his opinion, is guilty of violent conduct, serious foul play, or the use of foul or abusive language.

(i) Signal for recommencement of the game after all stoppages.

(j) Decide that the ball provided for a match meets with the requirements of Law II.

Decisions of the International Board

(1) Referees in International Matches shall wear a blazer or blouse the colour of which is distinct from the colours worn by the contesting teams.

(2) Referees for International Matches will be selected from a neutral country unless the countries concerned agree to appoint their own officials.

(3) The Referee must be chosen from the official list of International Referees. This need not apply to Amateur and Youth International Matches.

(4) The Referee shall report to the appropriate authority misconduct or any misdemeanour on the part of spectators, officials, players, named substitutes or other persons which take place either on the field of play or in its vicinity at any time prior to, during, or after the match in question so that appropriate action can be taken by the authority concerned.

(5) Linesmen are assistants of the Referee. In no case shall the Referee consider the intervention of a Linesman if he himself has seen the incident and from his position on the field, is better able to judge. With this reserve, and the Linesman neutral, the Referee can consider the intervention and if the information of the Linesman applies to that phase of the game immediately before the scoring of a goal, the Referee may act thereon and cancel the goal.

(6) The Referee, however, can only reverse his first decision so long as the game has not been restarted.

(7) If the Referee has decided to apply the advantage clause and to let the game proceed, he cannot revoke his decision if the presumed advantage has not been realised, even though he has not, by any gesture, indicated his decision. This does not exempt the offending player from being dealt with by the Referee.

(8) The Laws of the Game are intended to provide that games should be played with as little interference as possible, and in this view it is the duty of Referees to penalise only deliberate breaches of the Law. Constant whistling for trifling and doubtful breaches produces bad feeling and loss of temper on the part of the players and spoils the pleasure of spectators.

(9) By para. (d) of Law V the Referee is empowered to terminate a match in the event of grave disorder, but he has no power or right to decide, in such event, that either team is disqualified and thereby the loser of the match. He must send a detailed report to the proper authority who alone has power to deal further with the matter.

(10) If a player commits two infringements of a different nature at the same time, the Referee shall punish the more serious offence.

(11) It is the duty of the Referee to act upon the information of neutral Linesmen with regard to incidents that do not come under the personal notice of the Referee.

(12) The Referee shall not allow any person to enter the field until play has stopped, and only then, if he has given him a signal to do so, nor shall he allow coaching from the boundary lines.

LAW VI – LINESMEN

Two Linesmen shall be appointed, whose duty (subject to the decision of the Referee) shall be to indicate when the ball is out of play, which side is entitled to the corner-kick, goal-kick or throw-in, and when a substitute is desired. They shall also assist the Referee to control the game in accordance with the Laws. In the event of undue interference or improper conduct by a Linesman, the Referee shall dispense with his services and arrange a substitute to be appointed. (The matter shall be reported by the Referee to the competent authority.) The Linesmen should be equipped with flags by the Club on whose ground the match is played.

Decisions of the International Board

(1) Linesmen, where neutral, shall draw the Referee's attention to any breach of the Laws of the Game of which they become aware if they consider that the Referee may not have seen it, but the Referee shall always be the judge of the decision to be taken.

(2) National Associations are advised to appoint official Referees of neutral nationality to act as Linesmen in International Matches.

(3) In International Matches, Linesmen's flags shall be of a vivid colour, bright reds and yellows. Such flags are recommended for use in all other matches.

(4) A Linesman may be subject to disciplinary action only upon a report of the Referee for unjustified interference or insufficient assistance.

LAW VII – DURATION OF THE GAME

The duration of the game shall be two equal periods of 45 minutes, unless otherwise mutually agreed upon, subject to the following: (a) Allowance shall be made in either period for all time lost through substitution, the transport from the field of injured players, time-wasting or other cause, the amount of which shall be a matter for the discretion of the Referee; (b) Time shall be extended to permit a penalty-kick being taken at or after the expiration of the normal period in either half.

At half-time the interval shall not exceed five minutes except by consent of the Referee.

Decisions of the International Board

(1) If a match has been stopped by the Referee, before the completion of the time specified in the rules, for any reason stated in Law V it must be replyed in full unless the rules of the competition concerned provide for the result of the match at the time of such stoppage to stand.

(2) Players have a right to an interval at half-time.

LAW VIII – THE START OF PLAY

(a) **At the beginning of the game**, choice of ends and the kick-off shall be decided by the toss of a coin. The team winning the toss shall have the option of choice of ends or the kick-off. The Referee having given a signal, the game shall be started by a player taking a place-kick (i.e. a kick at the ball while it is stationary on the ground in the centre of the field of play) into his opponents' half of the field of play. Every player shall be in his own half of the field and every player of the team opposing that of the kicker shall remain not less than 10 yards from the ball until it is kicked-off; it shall not be deemed in play until it has travelled the distance of its own circumference. The kicker shall not play the ball a second time until it has been touched or played by another player.

(b) **After a goal is scored**, the game shall be restarted in like manner by a player of the team losing the goal.

(c) **After half-time:** when restarting after half-time, ends shall be changed and the kick-off shall be taken by a player of the opposite team to that of the player who started the game.

Punishment: For any infringement of this Law, the kick-off shall be retaken, except in the case of the kicker playing the ball again before it has been toched or played by another player; for this offence, an indirect free-kick shall be taken by a player of the opposing team from the place where the infringement occurred, unless the offence is committed by a player in his opponents' goal-area, in which case the free-kick shall be taken from a point anywhere within that half of the goal-area in which the offence occurred. A goal shall not be scored direct from a kick-off.

(d) **After any other temporary suspension:** when restarting the game after a temporary suspension of play from any cause not mentioned elsewhere in these Laws, provided that immediately prior to the suspension the ball has not passed over the touch or goal-lines, the Referee shall drop the ball at the place where it was when play was suspended, unless it was within the goal area at that time, in which case it shall be dropped on that part of the goal area line which runs parallel to the goal-line, at the point nearest to where the ball was when play was stopped. It shall be deemed in play when it has touched the ground; if, however, it goes over the touch or goal-lines after it has been dropped by the Referee, but before it is touched by a player, the Referee shall again drop it. A player shall not play the ball until it has touched the ground. If this section of the Law is not complied with the Referee shall again drop the ball.

Decisions of the International Board

(1) If, when the Referee drops the ball, a player infringes any of the Laws before the ball has touched the ground, the player concerned shall be cautioned or sent off the field according to the seriousness of the offence, but a free-kick cannot be awarded to the opposing team because the ball was not in play at the time of the offence. The ball shall therefore be again dropped by the Referee.

(2) Kicking-off by persons other than the players competiting in a match is prohibited.

LAW IX – BALL IN AND OUT OF PLAY

The ball is out of play.

(a) When it has wholly crossed the goal-line or touch-line, whether on the ground or in the air.

(b) When the game has been stopped by the Referee.

The ball is in play at all other times from the start of the match to the finish including:

(a) If it rebounds from a goal-post, cross-bar or corner-flag post into the field of play.

(b) If it rebounds off either the Referee or Linesmen when they are in the field of play.

(c) In the event of a supposed infringement of the Laws, until a decision is given.

Decisions of the International Board

(1) The lines belong to the area of which they are the boundaries. In consequence, the touch-lines and the goal-lines belong to the field of play.

LAW X – METHOD OF SCORING

Except as otherwise provided by these Laws, a goal is scored when the whole of the ball has passed over the goal-line, between the goal-posts and under the cross-bar, provided it has not been thrown, carried or intentionally propelled by hand or arm, by a player of the attacking side, except in the case of a goalkeeper, who is within his own penalty area.

The team scoring the greater number of goals during a game shall be the winner; if no goals, or an equal number of goals are scored, the game shall be termed a 'draw'.

Decisions of the International Board

(1) Law X defines the only method according to which a match is won or drawn; no variation whatsoever can be authorised.

(2) A goal cannot in any case be allowed if the ball has been prevented by some outside agent from passing over the goal-line. If this happens in the normal course of play, other than at the taking of a penalty-kick, the game must be stopped and restarted where the ball came into contact with the interference.

(3) If, when the ball is going into goal, a spectator enters the field before it passes wholly over the goal-line, and tries to prevent a score, a goal shall be allowed if the ball goes into goal unless the spectator has made contact with the ball or has interfered with play, in which case the Referee shall stop the game and restart it by dropping the ball at the place where the contact or interference occurred.

LAW XI – OFF-SIDE

(1) A player is in an off-side position if he is nearer to his opponents' goal-line than the ball **unless:**

(a) He is in his own half of the field of play, or

(b) There are at least two of his opponents nearer their own goal-line than he is.

(2) A player shall only be declared off-side and penalised for being in an off-side position, if, at the moment the ball touches, or is played by, one of his team, he is, in the opinion of the Referee

(a) interfering with play or with an opponent, or

(b) seeking to gain an advantage by being in that position.

(3) A player shall not be declared off-side by the Referee

(a) merely because of his being in an off-side position, or

(b) if he receives the ball, direct, from a goal-kick, a corner-kick, a throw-in, or when it has been dropped by the Referee.

(4) If a player is declared off-side, the Referee shall award an indirect free-kick, which shall be taken by a player of the opposing team from the place where the infringement occurred, unless the offence is committed by a player in his opponents' goal-area, in which case, the free-kick shall be taken from a point anywhere within that half of the goal-area in which the offence occurred.

Decisions of the International Board

(1) Off-side shall not be judged at the moment the player in question receives the ball, but at the moment when the ball is passed to him by one of his own side. A player who is not in an off-side position when one of his colleauges passes the ball to him or takes a free-kick, does not therefore become off-side if he goes forward during the flight of the ball.

LAW XII – FOULS AND MISCONDUCT

A player who intentionally commits any of the following nine offences:

(a) Kicks or attempts to kick an opponent;

(b) Trips an opponent, i.e. throwing or attempting to throw him by the use of the legs or by stooping in front of or behind him;

(c) Jumps at an opponent;

(d) Charges an opponent in a violent or dangerous manner;

(e) Charges an opponent from behind unless the latter be obstructing;

(f) Strikes or attempts to strike an opponent;

(g) Holds an opponent;

(h) Pushes an opponent;

(i) Handles the ball, i.e. carries, strikes or propels the ball with his hand or arm. (This does not apply to the goalkeeper within his own penalty-area);

shall be penalised by the award of a direct free-kick to be taken by the opposing side from the place where the offence occurred, unless the offence is committed by a player in his opponents' goal-area in which case, the free-kick shall be taken from a point anywhere within that half of the goal-area in which the offence occurred.

Should a player of the defending side intentionally commit one of the above nine offences within the penalty-area he shall be penalised by a **penalty-kick.**

A penalty-kick can be awarded irrespective of the position of the ball, if in play, at the time an offence within the penalty-area is committed.

A player committing any of the five following offences:

(1) Playing in a manner considered by the Referee to be dangerous, e.g. attempting to kick the ball while held by the goalkeeper.

(2) Charging fairly, i.e. with the shoulder, when the ball is not within playing distance of the players concerned and they are definitely not trying to play it;

(3) When not playing the ball, intentionally obstructing an opponent, i.e. running between the opponent and the ball, or interposing the body so as to form an obstacle to an opponent;

(4) Charging the goalkeeper except when he

(a) is holding the ball;

(b) is obstructing an opponent;

(c) has passed outside the goal-area;

(5) When playing as goalkeeper and within his own penalty area.

(a) from the moment he takes control of the ball with his hands, he takes more than four steps in any direction whilst holding, bouncing or throwing the ball in the air and catching it again, without releasing it into play, or, having released the ball into play before, during or after the four steps, he touches it again with his hands, before it has been touched or played by another player of the same team outside of the penalty area or by a player of the opposing team either inside or outside of the penalty area, or

(b) indulges in tactics which, in the opinion of the Referee, are designed merely to hold up the game and thus waste time and so give an unfair advantage to his own team—shall be penalised by the award of an **indirect free-kick** to be taken by the opposing side from the place where the infringement occurred, unless the offence is committed by a player in his opponents' goal-area, in which case the free-kick shall be taken from a point anywhere within that half of the goal-area in which the offence occurred.

A player shall be **cautioned** if:

(j) he enters or re-enters the field of play to join or rejoin his team after the game has commenced, or leaves the field of play during the progress of the game (except through accident) without, in either case, first having received a signal from the Referee showing him that he may do so. If the Referee stops the game to administer the caution the game shall be restarted by an indirect free-kick taken by a player of the opposing team from the place where the ball was when the Referee stopped the game. If the free-kick is awarded to a side within its own goal-area it may be taken from any point within the half of the goal-area in which the ball was when play was stopped. If, however, the offending player has committed a more serious offence he shall be penalised according to that section of the law he infringed.

(k) he persistently infringes the Laws of the Game;

(l) he shows by word or action, dissent from any decision given by the Referee;

(m) he is guilty of ungentlemanly conduct.

For any of these last three offences, in addition to the caution, an **indirect free-kick** shall also be awarded to the opposing side from the place where the offence occurred unless a more serious infringement of the Laws of the Game was committed. If the offence is committed by a player in his opponents' goal-area, a free-kick shall be taken from a point anywhere, within that half of the goal-area in which the offence occurred.

A player shall be **sent off** the field of play, if:

(a) in the opinion of the Referee he is guilty of violent conduct or serious foul play;

(o) he uses foul or abusive language;

(p) he persists in misconduct after having received a caution.

If play be stopped by reason of a player being ordered from the field for an offence without a separate breach of the Law having been committed, the game shall be resumed by an **indirect free-kick** awarded to the opposing side from the place where the infringement occurred, unless the offence is committed by a player in his opponents' goal-area, in which case, the free-kick shall be taken from a point anywhere within that half of the goal-area in which the offence occurred.

Decisions of the International Board

(1) If the goalkeeper either intentionally strikes an opponent by throwing the ball vigorously at him or pushes him with the ball while holding it, the Referee shall award a penalty-kick, if the offence took place within the penalty-area.

(2) If a player deliberately turns his back to an opponent when he is about to be tackled, he may be charged but not in a dangerous manner.

(3) In case of body-contact in the goal-area between an attacking player and the opposing goalkeeper not in possession of the ball, the Referee, as sole judge of intention, shall stop the game if, in his opinion, the action of the attacking player was intentional, and award an indirect free-kick.

(4) If a player leans on the shoulders of another player of his own team in order to head the ball, the Referee shall stop the game, caution the player for ungentlemanly conduct and award an indirect free-kick to the opposing side.

(5) A player's obligation when joining or rejoining his team after the start of the match to 'report to the Referee' must be interpreted as meaning 'to draw the attention of the Referee from the touch-line'. The signal from the Referee shall be made by a definite gesture which makes the player understand that he may come into the field of play; it is not necessary for the Referee to wait until the game is stopped (this does not apply in respect of an infringement of Law IV), but the Referee is the sole judge of the moment in which he gives his signal of acknowledgement.

(6) The letter and spirit of Law XII do not oblige the Referee to stop a game to administer a caution. He may, if he chooses, apply the advantage. If he does apply the advantage, he shall caution the player when play stops.

(7) If a player covers up the ball without touching it in an endeavour not to have it played by an opponent, he obstructs but does not infringe Law XII para. 3 because he is already in possession of the ball and covers it for tactical reasons whilst the ball remains within playing distance. In fact, he is actually playing the ball and does not commit an infringement; in this case, the player may be charged because he is in fact playing the ball.

(8) If a player intentionally stretches his arms to obstruct an opponent and steps from one side to the other moving his arms up and down to delay his opponent, forcing him to change course, but does not make 'bodily contact' the Referee shall caution the player for ungentlemanly conduct and award an indirect free-kick.

(9) If a player intentionally obstructs the opposing goalkeeper, in an attempt to prevent him from putting the ball into play in accordance with Law XII, 5(a), the Referee shall award an indirect free-kick.

(10) If after a Referee has awarded a free-kick a player protests violently by using abusive or foul language and is sent off the field, the free-kick should not be taken until the player has left the field.

(11) Any player, whether he is within or outside the field of play, whose conduct is ungentlemanly or violent, whether or not it is directed towards an opponent, a colleague, the Referee, a Linesman or other person, or who uses foul or abusive language, is guilty of an offence, and shall be dealt with according to the nature of the offence committed.

(12) If, in the opinion of the Referee a goalkeeper intentionally lies on the ball longer than is necessary, he shall be penalised for ungentlemanly conduct and

(a) be cautioned and an indirect free-kick awarded to the opposing team;

(b) in case of repetition of the offence, be sent off the field.

(13) The offence of spitting at opponents, officials or other persons, or similar unseemly

behaviour shall be considered as violent conduct within the meaning of section (n) of Law XII.

(14) If, when a Referee is about to caution a player, and before he has done so, the player commits another offence which merits a caution, the player shall be sent off the field of play.

LAW XIII – FREE-KICK

Free-kicks shall be classified under two headings:'Direct' (from which a goal can be scored direct against the offending side), and 'Indirect' (from which a goal cannot be scored unless the ball has been played or touched by a player other than the kicker before passing through the goal).

When a player is taking a direct or an indirect free-kick inside his own penalty-area, all of the opposing players shall be at least 10 yards (9.15m) from the ball and shall remain outside the penalty area until the ball has been kicked out of the area. The ball shall be in play immediately it has travelled the distance of its own circumference and is beyond the penalty-area. The goalkeeper shall not receive the ball into his hands, in order that he may thereafter kick it into play. If the ball is not kicked direct into play, beyond the penalty-area, the kick shall be retaken.

When a player is taking a direct or an indirect free-kick outside his own penalty-area, all of the opposing players shall be at least ten yards from the ball, until it is in play, unless they are standing on their own goal-line, between the goal-posts. The ball shall be in play when it has travelled the distance of its own circumference.

If a player of the opposing side encroaches into the penalty-area, or within ten yards of the ball, as the case may be, before a free-kick is taken, the Referee shall delay the taking of the kick, until the Law is complied with.

The ball must be stationary when a free-kick is taken, and the kicker shall not play the ball a second time, until it has been touched or played by another player.

Notwithstanding any other reference in these Laws to the point from which a free-kick is to be taken:

1. Any free kick awarded to the defending team, within its own goal area, may be taken from any point within that half of the goal area in which the free kick has been awarded.

2. Any indirect free kick awarded to the attacking team within its opponents' goal area shall be taken from that part of the goal area line which runs parallel to the goal-line, at the point nearest to where the offence was committed.

Punishment: If the kicker, after taking the free-kick, plays the ball a second time before it has been touched or played by another player an indirect free-kick shall be taken by a player of the opposing team from the spot where the infringement occurred, unless the offence is committed by a player in his opponents' goal area, in which case the free kick shall be taken from a point anywhere within that half of the goal area in which the offence occurred.

Decisions of the International Board

---

(1) In order to distinguish between a direct and indirect free-kick, the Referee, when he awards an indirect free-kick, shall indicate accordingly by raising an arm above his head. He shall keep his arm in that position until the kick has been taken and retain the signal until the ball has been played or touched by another player or goes out of play.

(2) Players who do not retire to the proper distance when a free-kick is taken must be cautioned and on any repetition be ordered off. It is particularly requested of Referees that attempts to delay the taking of a free-kick by encroaching should be treated as serious misconduct.

(3) If, when a free-kick is being taken, any of the players dance about or gesticulate in a way calculated to distract their opponents, it shall be deemed ungentlemanly conduct for which the offender(s) shall be cautioned.

LAW XIV – PENALTY-KICK

A penalty-kick shall be taken from the penalty-mark and, when it is being taken, all players with the exception of the player taking the kick, properly identified, and the opposing goalkeeper, shall be within the field of play but outside the penalty-area, and at least 10 yards from the penalty-mark. The opposing goalkeeper must stand (without moving his feet) on his own goal-line, between the goal-posts, until the ball is kicked. The player taking the kick must kick the ball forward; he shall not play the ball a second time until it has been touched or played by another player. The ball shall be deemed in play directly it is kicked, i.e., when it has travelled the distance of its circumference. A goal may be scored directly from a penalty-kick. When a penalty-kick is being taken during the normal course of play, or when time has been extended at half-time or full-time to allow a penalty-kick to be taken or re-taken, a goal shall not be nullified if, before passing between the posts and under the cross-bar, the ball touches either or both of the goal-posts or the cross-bar, or the goalkeeper, or any combination of these agencies, providing that no other infringement has occurred.

Punishment: For any infringement of this Law:

(a) by the defending team, the kick shall be retaken if a goal has not resulted.

(b) by the attacking team other than by the player taking the kick, if a goal is scored it shall be disallowed and the kick retaken.

(c) by the player taking the penalty-kick, committed after the ball is in play, a player of the opposing team shall take an indirect free-kick from the spot where the infringement occurred. If, in the case of paragraph (c), the offence is committed by the player in his opponents' goal-area, the free-kick shall be taken from a point anywhere within that half of the goal-area in which the offence occurred.

Decisions of the International Board

---

(1) When the Referee has awarded a penalty-kick, he shall not signal for it to be taken, until the players have taken up position in accordance with the Law.

(2) (a) If, after the kick has been taken, the ball

is stopped in its course towards goal, by an outside agent, the kick shall be retaken.

(b) If, after the kick has been taken, the ball rebounds into play, from the goalkeeper, the cross-bar or a goal-post, and is then stopped in its course by an outside agent, the Referee shall stop play and restart it by dropping the ball at the place where it came into contact with the outside agent.

(3) (a) If, after having given the signal for a penalty-kick to be taken, the Referee sees that the goalkeeper is not in his right place on the goal-line, he shall, nevertheless, allow the kick to proceed. it shall be retaken, if a goal is not scored.

(b) If, after the Referee has given the signal for a penalty-kick to be taken, and before the ball has been kicked, the goalkeeper moves his feet, the Referee shall, nevertheless, allow the kick to proceed. It shall be retaken, if a goal is not scored.

(c) If, after the Referee has given the signal for a penalty-kick to be taken, and before the ball is in play, a player of the defending team encroaches into the penalty-area, or within ten yards of the penalty-mark, the Referee shall, nevertheless, allow the kick to proceed. It shall be retaken, if a goal is not scored.

The player concerned shall be cautioned.

(4) (a) If, when a penalty-kick is being taken, the player taking the kick is guilty of ungentlemanly conduct, the kick, if already taken, shall be retaken, if a goal is scored.

The player concerned shall be cautioned.

(b) If, after the Referee has given the signal for a penalty-kick to be taken, and before the ball is in play, a colleague of the player taking the kick encroaches into the penalty-area or within ten yards of the penalty-mark, the Referee shall, nevertheless, allow the kick to proceed. If a goal is scored, it shall be disallowed, and the kick retaken.

The player concerned shall be cautioned.

(c) If, in the circumstances described in the foregoing paragraph, the ball rebounds into play from the goalkeeper, the crossbar or a goal-post and a goal has not been scored, the Referee shall stop the game, caution the player and award an indirect free-kick to the opposing team from the place where the infringement occurred, subject to the over-riding conditions imposed in Law XIII.

(5) (a) If, after the referee has given the signal for a penalty-kick to be taken, and before the ball is in play, the goalkeeper moves from his position on the goal-line, or moves his feet, and a colleague of the kicker encroaches into the penalty-area or within 10 yards of the penalty mark, the kick, if taken, shall be retaken.

The colleague of the kicker shall be cautioned.

(b) If, after the Referee has given the signal for a penalty-kick to be taken, and before the ball is in play, a player of each team encroaches into the penalty area, or within 10 yards of the penalty-mark, the kick, if taken, shall be retaken.

The players concerned shall be cautioned.

(6) When a match is extended, at half-time or full-time, to allow a penalty-kick to be taken or retaken, the extension shall last until the moment that the penalty-kick has been completed, i.e. until the Referee has decided whether or not a goal is scored, and the game shall terminate immediately the referee has made his decision. After the player taking the penalty-kick has put the ball into play, no player other than the defending goalkeeper may play or touch the ball before the kick is completed.

A goal is scored when the ball passes wholly over the goal-line.

(a) direct from the penalty-kick.

(b) having rebounded from either goal-post or the cross-bar, or

(c) having touched or been played by the goalkeeper.

The game shall terminate immediately the Referee has made his decision.

(7) When a penalty-kick is being taken in extended time:

(a) the provisions of all of the foregoing paragraphs, except paragraphs (2)(b) and (4)(c) shall apply in the usual way, and

(b) in the circumstances described in paragraphs (2)(b) and (4)(c) the game shall terminate immediately the ball rebounds from the goalkeeper, the cross-bar or the goal-post.

LAW XV – THROW-IN

When the whole of the ball passes over a touch-line, either on the ground or in the air, it shall be thrown in from the point where it crossed the line, in any direction, by a player of the team opposite to that of the player who last touched it. The thrower at the moment of delivering the ball must face the field of play and part of each foot shall be either on the touch-line or on the ground outside the touch-line. The thrower shall use both hands and shall deliver the ball from behind and over his head. The ball shall be in play immediately it enters the field of play, but the thrower shall not again play the ball until it has been touched or played by another player. A goal shall not be scored direct from a thorw-in.

Punishment:

(a) If the ball is improperly thrown in, the throw-in shall be taken by a player of the opposing team.

(b) If the thrower plays the ball a second time before it has been touched or played by another player, an indirect free-kick shall be taken by a player of the opposing team from the place where the infringement occurred, unless the offence is committed by a player in his opponents' goal-area, in which case, the free-kick shall be taken from a point anywhere within that half of the goal-area in which the offence occurred.

Decisions of the International Board

(1) If a player taking a throw-in, plays the ball a second time by handling it within the field of play before it has been touched or played by another player, the Referee shall award a direct free-kick.

(2) A player taking a throw-in must face the field of play with some part of his body.

(3) If, when a throw-in is being taken, any of the opposing players dance about or gesticulate in a way calculated to distract or impede the thrower,

it shall be deemed ungentlemanly conduct for which the offender(s) shall be cautioned.

(4) A throw-in taken from any position other than the point where the ball passed over the touch-line shall be considered to have been improperly thrown.

Decisions of the International Board

(1) When a goal-kick has been taken and the player who has kicked the ball touches it again before it has left the penalty-area, the kick has not been taken in accordance with the Laws and must be retaken.

LAW XVI – GOAL-KICK

When the whole of the ball passes over the goal-line excluding that portion between the goal-posts, either in the air or on the ground, having last been played by one of the attacking team, it shall be kicked direct into play beyond the penalty-area from a point within that half of the goal-area nearest to where it crossed the line, by a player of the defending team. A goalkeeper shall not receive the ball into his hands from a goal-kick in order that he may thereafter kick it into play. If the ball is not kicked beyond the penalty-area, i.e. direct into play, the kick shall be retaken. The kicker shall not play the ball a second time until it has touched—or been played by—another player. A goal shall not be scored direct from such a kick. Players of the team opposing that of the player taking the goal-kick shall remain outside the penalty-area whilst the kick is being taken.
Punishment: If a player taking a goal-kick plays the ball a second time after it has passed beyond the penalty-area, but before it has touched or been played by another player, an indirect free-kick shall be awarded to the opposing team, to be taken from the place where the infringement occurred, unless the offence is committed by a player in his opponents' goal-area, in which case, the free-kick shall be taken from a point anywhere within that half of the goal-area in which the offence occurred.

LAW XVII – CORNER-KICK

When the whole of the ball passes over the goal-line, excluding that portion between the goal-posts, either in the air or on the ground, having last been played by one of the defending team, a member of the attacking team shall take a corner-kick, i.e. the whole of the ball shall be placed within the quarter circle at the nearest corner-flag post, which must not be moved, and it shall be kicked from that position. A goal may be scored direct from such a kick. Players of the team opposing that of the player taking the corner-kick shall not approach within 10 yards of the ball until it is in play, i.e. it has travelled the distance of its own circumference, nor shall the kicker play the ball a second time until it has been touched or played by another player.
Punishment:
(a) If the player who takes the kick plays the ball a second time before it has been touched or played by another player, the Referee shall award an indirect free-kick to the opposing team, to be taken from the place where the infringement occurred, unless the offence is committed by a player in his opponents' goal-area, in which case the free-kick shall be taken from a point anywhere within that half of the goal-area in which the offence occurred.

(b) For any other infringement the kick shall be retaken.

LEAGUE REFEREES FOR SEASON 1989–90

ALCOCK, P. E. (S. Merstham, Surrey)
ALLISON, D. B. (Lancaster)
APLIN, G. (Kendal)
ASHBY, G. R. (Worcester)
ASHWORTH, J. (Luffenham, Leics.)
AXCELL, D. J. (Southend)
BAILEY, M. C. (Impington, Cambridge)
BARRATT, K. P. (Coventry)
BELL, S. D. (Huddersfield)
BENNETT, A. (Chesterfield)
BIGGER, R. L. (Croydon)
BODENHAM, M. J. (Looe, Cornwall)
BORRETT, I. J. (Harleston, Norfolk)
BREEN, K. J. (Liverpool)
BUKSH, A. N. (London)
BURGE, W. K. (Tonypandy)
BURNS, W. C. (Scarborough)
BUTLER, N. S. (East Grinstead, W. Sussex)
CALLOW, V. G. (Solihull)
CARTER, J. M. (Christchurch)
COOPER, K. (Pontypridd)
COOPER, K. A. (Swindon)
COURTNEY, G. (Spennymoor)
CRUIKSHANKS, I. G. (Hartlepool)
DANSON, P. S. (Leicester)
DAWSON, A. (Jarrow)
DEAKIN, J. C. (Llantwit Major, S. Glam.)
DILKES, L. R. (Mossley, Lancs)
DON, P. (Hanworth Park, Middlesex)
DURKIN, P. A. (Portland, Dorset)
ELLERAY, D. R. (Harrow)
FITZHARRIS, T. (Bolton)
FLOOD, W. A. (Stockport)
FOAKES, P. L. (Clacton-on-Sea)
GIFFORD, R. B. (Llanbradach, Mid. Glam.)
GROVES, R. G. (Weston-Super-Mare)
GUNN, A. (South Chailey, Sussex)
HACKETT, K. S. (Sheffield)
HAMER, R. L. (Bristol)
HARRISON, P. W. (Oldham, Lancs.)
HART, R. A. (Darlington)
HEDGES, D. A. (Oxford)
HEMLEY, I. S. (Ampthill, Beds.)
HENDRICK, I. A. (Preston)
HILL, B. (Kettering)
HOLBROOK, T. J. (Walsall)
HUTCHINSON, D. (Marcham, Oxford)
JAMES, M. L. (Horsham)
JONES, P. (Loughborough)
KEY, J. M. (Sheffield)
KING, H. W. (Merthyr Tydfil)
KIRKBY, J. A. (Sheffield)
LEWIS, R. S. (Gt. Bookham, Surrey)
LLOYD, J. W. (Wrexham)
LODGE S. J. (Barnsley)
LUNT, T. (Ashton-in-Makerfield, Lancs)
LUPTON, K. A. (Stockton-on-Tees)
MARTIN, J. E. (Nr. Alton, Hants.)
MIDGLEY, N. (Bolton)
MILFORD, R. G. (Bristol)
MILLS, T. (Barnsley)
MORTON, K. (Bury St. Edmunds)
MOULES, J. A. (Erith, Kent)
NIXON, R. F. (West Kirkby, Wirral)
PARKER, E. J. (Preston)
PAWLEY, R. K. (Cambridge)
PECK, M. G. (Kendal)
PHILLIPS, D. T. (Barnsley)
PIERCE, M. E. (Portsmouth)
POOLEY, G. R. (Bishop's Stortford)
REDFERN, K. A. (Whitley Bay)
REED, M. D. (Birmingham)
ROBERTS, F. (Prestatyn)
RUSHTON, J. (Stoke-on-Trent)
SCOTT, D. (Burnley)
SEVILLE, A. (Birmingham)
SHAPTER, L. C. (Torquay)
SIMMONS, A. F. (Cheadle Hulme, Cheshire)
SIMPSON, T. (Sowerby Bridge, W. Yorks.)
SINGH, G. (Wolverhampton)
SMITH, A. W. (Rubery, Birmingham)
STEVENS, B. T. (Stonehouse. Glos.)
TRUSSELL, C. C. (Liverpool)
TYLDESLEY, P. A. (Stockport)
TYSON, G. M. (Sunderland)
VANES, P. W. (Warley, West Midlands)
VICKERS, D. S. (Ilford, Essex)
WARD, A. W. (London)
WATSON, J. L. (Whitley Bay)
WEST, T. E. (Hull)
WILKIE, A. B. (Chester-le-Street)
WISEMAN, R. M. (Borehamwood, Herts.)
WORRALL, J. B. (Warrington)
WRIGHT, P. L. (Northwich)

RECORDS

Major British Records

HIGHEST WINS

First-Class Match		Arbroath (*Scottish Cup 1st Round*)	36	Bon Accord	0	12 Sept 1885
International Match		England	13	Ireland	0	18 Feb 1882
FA Cup		Preston NE (*1st Round*)	26	Hyde U	0	15 Oct 1887
League Cup		West Ham U (*2nd Round, 2nd Leg*)	10	Bury	0	25 Oct 1983
		Liverpool (*2nd Round, 1st Leg*)	10	Fulham	0	23 Sept 1986
FOOTBALL LEAGUE						
Division 1	(*Home*)	WBA	12	Darwen	0	4 April 1892
		Nottingham F	12	Leicester Fosse	0	21 April 1909
	(*Away*)	Newcastle U	1	Sunderland	9	5 Dec 1908
		Cardiff C	1	Wolverhampton W	9	3 Sept 1955
Division 2	(*Home*)	Newcastle U	13	Newport Co	0	5 Oct 1946
	(*Away*)	Burslem PV	0	Sheffield U	10	10 Dec 1892
Division 3	(*Home*)	Gillingham	10	Chesterfield	0	5 Sept 1987
	(*Away*)	Halifax T	0	Fulham	8	16 Sept 1969
Division 3(S)	(*Home*)	Luton T	12	Bristol R	0	13 April 1936
	(*Away*)	Northampton T	0	Walsall	8	2 Feb 1947
Division 3(N)	(*Home*)	Stockport Co	13	Halifax T	0	6 Jan 1934
	(*Away*)	Accrington S	0	Barnsley	9	3 Feb 1934
Division 4	(*Home*)	Oldham Ath	11	Southport	0	26 Dec 1962
	(*Away*)	Crewe Alex	1	Rotherham U	8	8 Sept 1973
Aggregate Division 3(N)		Tranmere R	13	Oldham Ath	4	26 Dec 1935
SCOTTISH LEAGUE						
Premier Division	(*Home*)	Aberdeen	8	Motherwell	0	26 March 1979
	(*Away*)	Hamilton A	0	Celtic	8	5 Nov 1988
Division 1	(*Home*)	Celtic	11	Dundee	0	26 Oct 1895
	(*Away*)	Airdrieonians	1	Hibernian	11	24 Oct 1950
Division 2	(*Home*)	East Fife	13	Edinburgh C	2	11 Dec 1937
	(*Away*)	Alloa Ath	0	Dundee	10	8 March 1947

LEAGUE CHAMPIONSHIP HAT-TRICKS

Huddersfield T	1923–24 to 1925–26
Arsenal	1932–33 to 1934–35
Liverpool	1981–82 to 1983–84

MOST GOALS FOR IN A SEASON

FOOTBALL LEAGUE		*Goals*	*Games*	*Season*
Division 1	Aston V	128	42	1930–31
Division 2	Middlesbrough	122	42	1926–27
Division 3(S)	Millwall	127	42	1927–28
Division 3(N)	Bradford C	128	42	1928–29
Division 3	QPR	111	46	1961–62
Division 4	Peterborough U	134	46	1960–61
SCOTTISH LEAGUE				
Premier Division	Dundee U	90	36	1982–83
	Celtic	90	36	1982–83
	Celtic	90	44	1986–87
Division 1	Hearts	132	34	1957–58
Division 2	Raith R	142	34	1937–38

FEWEST GOALS FOR IN A SEASON

FOOTBALL LEAGUE	(minimum 42 games)	*Goals*	*Games*	*Season*
Division 1	Stoke C	24	42	1984–85
Division 2	Watford	24	42	1971–72
Division 3(S)	Crystal Palace	33	42	1950–51
Division 3(N)	Crewe Alex	32	42	1923–24
Division 3	Stockport Co	27	46	1969–70
Division 4	Crewe Alex	29	46	1981–82
SCOTTISH LEAGUE	(minimum 30 games)			
Premier Division	Clydebank	23	36	1977–78
	Kilmarnock	23	36	1980–81
Division 1	Stirling Albion	18	39	1980–81
Division 2	Lochgelly U	20	38	1923–24

MOST GOALS AGAINST IN A SEASON

FOOTBALL LEAGUE		*Goals*	*Games*	*Season*
Division 1	Blackpool	125	42	1930–31
Division 2	Darwen	141	34	1898–99
Division 3(S)	Merthyr T	135	42	1929–30
Division 3(N)	Nelson	136	42	1927–28
Division 3	Accrington S	123	46	1959–60
Division 4	Hartlepools U	109	46	1959–60
SCOTTISH LEAGUE				
Premier Division	Morton	100	36	1984–85
	Morton	100	44	1987–88
Division 1	Leith Ath	137	38	1931–32
Division 2	Edinburgh C	146	38	1931–32

FEWEST GOALS AGAINST IN A SEASON

FOOTBALL LEAGUE	(minimum 42 games)	*Goals*	*Games*	*Season*
Division 1	Liverpool	16	42	1978–79
Division 2	Manchester U	23	42	1924–25
Division 3(S)	Southampton	21	42	1921–22
Division 3(N)	Port Vale	21	46	1953–54
Division 3	Middlesbrough	30	46	1986–87
Division 4	Lincoln C	25	46	1980–81
SCOTTISH LEAGUE	(minimum 30 games)			
Premier Division	Aberdeen	21	36	1983–84
Division 1	Celtic	14	38	1913–14
Division 2	Morton	20	38	1966–67

MOST POINTS IN A SEASON

FOOTBALL LEAGUE	(under old system)	*Points*	*Games*	*Season*
Division 1	Liverpool	68	42	1978–79
Division 2	Tottenham H	70	42	1919–20
Division 3	Aston V	70	46	1971–72
Division 3(S)	Nottingham F	70	46	1950–51
	Bristol C	70	46	1954–55
Division 3(N)	Doncaster R	72	42	1946–47
Division 4	Lincoln C	74	46	1975–76
FOOTBALL LEAGUE	(three points for a win)			
Division 1	Everton	90	42	1984–85
	Liverpool	90	40	1987–88
Division 2	Chelsea	99	46	1988–89
Division 3	Bournemouth	97	46	1986–87
Division 4	Swindon T	102	46	1985–86
SCOTTISH LEAGUE				
Premier Division	Celtic	72	44	1987–88
Division 1	Rangers	76	42	1920–21
Division 2	Morton	69	38	1966–67

FEWEST POINTS IN A SEASON

FOOTBALL LEAGUE	(minimum 34 games)	*Points*	*Games*	*Season*
Division 1	Stoke C	17	42	1984–85
Division 2	Doncaster R	8	34	1904–05
	Loughborough T	8	34	1899–1900
Division 3	Rochdale	21	46	1973–74
	Cambridge U	21	46	1984–85
Division 3(S)	Merthyr T	21	42	1924–25 & 1929–30
	QPR	21	42	1925–26
Division 3(N)	Rochdale	11	40	1931–32
Division 4	Workington	19	46	1976–77
SCOTTISH LEAGUE	(minimum 30 games)			
Premier Division	St Johnstone	11	36	1975–76
Division 1	Stirling Albion	6	30	1954–55
Division 2	Edinburgh C	7	34	1936–37

MOST WINS IN A SEASON

FOOTBALL LEAGUE		*Wins*	*Games*	*Season*
Division 1	Tottenham H	31	42	1960–61
Division 2	Tottenham H	32	42	1919–20
Division 3(S)	Millwall	30	42	1927–28
	Plymouth Arg	30	42	1929–30
	Cardiff C	30	42	1946–47
	Nottingham F	30	46	1950–51
	Bristol C	30	46	1954–55
Division 3(N)	Doncaster R	33	42	1946–47
Division 3	Aston Villa	32	46	1971–72
Division 4	Lincoln C	32	46	1975–76
	Swindon T	32	46	1985–86
SCOTTISH LEAGUE				
Premier Division	Aberdeen	27	36	1984–85
	Rangers	31	44	1986–87
	Celtic	31	44	1987–88
Division 1	Rangers	35	42	1920–21
Division 2	Morton	33	38	1966–67

RECORD HOME WINS IN A SEASON

Brentford won all 21 games in Division 3(S), 1929–30

UNDEFEATED AT HOME

Liverpool 85 games (63 League, 9 League Cup, 7 European, 6 FA Cup), Jan 1978–Jan 1981

RECORD AWAY WINS IN A SEASON

Doncaster R won 18 of 21 games in Division 3(N), 1946–47

FEWEST WINS IN A SEASON

FOOTBALL LEAGUE		*Wins*	*Games*	*Season*
Division 1	Stoke	3	22	1889–90
	Woolwich Arsenal	3	38	1912–13
	Stoke C	3	42	1984–85
Division 2	Loughborough T	1	34	1899–1900
Division 3(S)	Merthyr T	6	42	1929–30
	QPR	6	42	1925–26
Division 3(N)	Rochdale	4	40	1931–32
Division 3	Rochdale	2	46	1973–74
Division 4	Southport	3	46	1976–77
SCOTTISH LEAGUE				
Premier Division	St Johnstone	3	36	1975–76
	Kilmarnock	3	36	1982–83
Division 1	Vale of Leven	0	22	1891–92
Division 2	East Stirlingshire	1	22	1905–06
	Forfar Ath	1	38	1974–75

MOST DEFEATS IN A SEASON

FOOTBALL LEAGUE		Defeats	Games	Season
Division 1	Stoke C	31	42	1984–85
Division 2	Tranmere R	31	42	1938–39
Division 3	Cambridge U	33	46	1984–85
Division 3(S)	Merthyr T	29	42	1924–25
	Walsall	29	46	1952–53
	Walsall	29	46	1953–54
Division 3(N)	Rochdale	33	40	1931–32
Division 4	Newport Co	33	46	1987–88
SCOTTISH LEAGUE				
Premier Division	Morton	29	36	1984–85
Division 1	St Mirren	31	42	1920–21
Division 2	Brechin C	30	36	1962–63
	Lochgelly	30	38	1923–24

HAT-TRICKS

Career 19 Dixie Dean (Tranmere R, Everton, Notts Co, England)
Division 1 (one season post-war) 6 Jimmy Greaves (Chelsea), 1960–61
Three for one team one match
Enoch West, Arthur Spouncer, Billy Hooper, Nottingham F v Leicester Fosse, Division 1, 21 April 1909
Ron Barnes, Roy Ambler, Wynn Davies, Wrexham v Hartlepools U, Division 4, 3 March 1962
Tony Adcock, Paul Stewart, David White, Manchester C v Huddersfield T, Division 2, 7 Nov 1987

FEWEST DEFEATS IN A SEASON
(*Minimum 20 games*)

FOOTBALL LEAGUE		Defeats	Games	Season
Division 1	Preston NE	0	22	1888–89
	Leeds U	2	42	1968–69
Division 2	Liverpool	0	28	1893–94
	Burnley	2	30	1897–98
	Bristol C	2	38	1905–06
	Leeds U	3	42	1963–64
Division 3	QPR	5	46	1966–67
Division 3(S)	Southampton	4	42	1921–22
	Plymouth Arg	4	42	1929–30
Division 3(N)	Port Vale	3	46	1953–54
	Doncaster R	3	42	1946–47
	Wolverhampton W	3	42	1923–24
Division 4	Lincoln C	4	46	1975–76
	Sheffield U	4	46	1981–82
SCOTTISH LEAGUE				
Premier Division	Celtic	3	44	1987–88
Division 1	Rangers	1	42	1920–21
Division 2	Clyde	1	36	1956–57
	Morton	1	36	1962–63
	St Mirren	1	36	1967–68

MOST DRAWN GAMES IN A SEASON

FOOTBALL LEAGUE		Draws	Games	Season
Division 1	Norwich C	23	42	1978–79
Division 4	Exeter C	23	46	1986–87
SCOTTISH LEAGUE				
Premier Division	Hibernian	19	44	1987–88

MOST GOALS IN A GAME

FOOTBALL LEAGUE		
Division 1	Ted Drake (Arsenal) 7 goals v Aston Villa	14 Dec 1935
	James Ross (Preston NE) 7 goals v Stoke	6 Oct 1888
Division 2	Tommy Briggs (Blackburn R) 7 goals v Bristol R	5 Feb 1955
	Neville Coleman (Stoke C) 7 goals v Lincoln C (away)	23 Feb 1957
Division 3(S)	Joe Payne (Luton T) 10 goals v Bristol R	13 April 1936
Division 3(N)	Bunny Bell (Tranmere R) 9 goals v Oldham Ath	26 Dec 1935

Division 3	Steve Earle (Fulham) 5 goals v Halifax T	16 Sept 1969
	Barrie Thomas (Scunthorpe U) 5 goals v Luton T	24 April 1965
	Keith East (Swindon T) 5 goals v Mansfield T	20 Nov 1965
	Alf Wood (Shrewsbury T) 5 goals v Blackburn R	2 Oct 1971
	Tony Caldwell (Bolton W) 5 goals v Walsall	10 Sept 1983
	Andy Jones (Port Vale) 5 goals v Newport Co	4 May 1987
Division 4	Bert Lister (Oldham Ath) 6 goals v Southport	26 Dec 1962
FA CUP	Ted MacDougall (Bournemouth) 9 goals v Margate (*1st Round*)	20 Nov 1971
LEAGUE CUP	Derek Reeves (Southampton) 5 goals v Leeds U	5 Dec 1960
	Alan Wilks (QPR) 5 goals v Oxford U	10 Oct 1967
	Bob Latchford (Everton) 5 goals v Wimbledon	28 Aug 1978
	Cyrille Regis (Coventry C) 5 goals v Chester C	9 Oct 1985
SCOTTISH LEAGUE CUP	Jim Fraser (Ayr U) 5 goals v Dumbarton	13 Aug 1952
SCOTTISH LEAGUE		
Premier Division	Paul Sturrock (Dundee U) 5 goals v Morton	17 Nov 1984
Division 1	Jimmy McGrory (Celtic) 8 goals v Dunfermline Ath	14 Sept 1928
Division 2	Owen McNally (Arthurlie) 8 goals v Armadale	1 Oct 1927
	Jim Dyet (King's Park) 8 goals v Forfar Ath	2 Jan 1930
	John Calder (Morton) 8 goals v Raith R	18 April 1936
	Norman Hayward (Raith R) 8 goals v Brechin C	20 Aug 1937
SCOTTISH CUP	John Petrie (Arbroath) 13 goals v Bon Accord (*1st Round*)	12 Sept 1885

MOST LEAGUE GOALS IN A SEASON

FOOTBALL LEAGUE		*Goals*	*Games*	*Season*
Division 1	Dixie Dean (Everton)	60	39	1927–28
Division 2	George Camsell (Middlesbrough)	59	37	1926–27
Division 3(S)	Joe Payne (Luton T)	55	39	1936–37
Division 3(N)	Ted Harston (Mansfield T)	55	41	1936–37
Division 3	Derek Reeves (Southampton)	39	46	1959–60
Division 4	Terry Bly (Peterborough U)	52	46	1960–61
FA CUP	Albert Brown (Tottenham H)	15		1900–01
LEAGUE CUP	Clive Allen (Tottenham H)	12		1986–87
SCOTTISH LEAGUE				
Division 1	William McFadyen (Motherwell)	52	34	1931–32
Division 2	Jim Smith (Ayr U)	66	38	1927–28

MOST LEAGUE GOALS IN A CAREER

FOOTBALL LEAGUE		*Goals*	*Games*	*Season*
Arthur Rowley	WBA	4	24	1946–48
	Fulham	27	56	1948–50
	Leicester C	251	303	1950–58
	Shrewsbury T	152	236	1958–65
		434	619	
SCOTTISH LEAGUE				
Jimmy McGrory	Celtic	1	3	1922–23
	Clydebank	13	30	1923–24
	Celtic	396	375	1924–38
		410	408	

MOST CUP GOALS IN A CAREER

FA CUP
Denis Law 41 (Huddersfield T, Manchester C, Manchester U)

A CENTURY OF LEAGUE AND CUP GOALS IN CONSECUTIVE SEASONS

George Camsell	Middlesbrough	59 Lge	5 Cup	1926–27
(101 goals)		33	4	1927–28
Steve Bull	Wolverhampton W	34 Lge	18 Cup	1987–88
(102 goals)		37	13	1988–89

(Camsell's cup goals were all scored in the FA Cup; Bull had 12 in the Sherpa Van Trophy, 3 Littlewoods Cup, 3 FA Cup in 1987–88; 11 Sherpa Van Trophy, 2 Littlewoods Cup in 1988–89).

LONGEST WINNING SEQUENCE

FOOTBALL LEAGUE		*Games*		*Season*
Division 1	Everton	12		1893–94 (4)
			and	1894–95 (8)
Division 2	Manchester U	14		1904–05
	Bristol C	14		1905–06
	Preston NE	14		1950–51
Division 3	Reading	13		1985–86
From season's start				
Division 1	Tottenham H	11		1960–61

LONGEST SEQUENCE WITHOUT A WIN FROM SEASON'S START

Division 1	Manchester U	12	1930–31

LONGEST SEQUENCE OF CONSECUTIVE SCORING (Individual)

John Aldridge (Liverpool)	10		1986–87 (1)
		and	1987–88 (9)

LONGEST WINNING SEQUENCE IN A SEASON

FOOTBALL LEAGUE		*Games*	*Season*
Division 1	Tottenham H	11	1960–61
Division 2	Manchester U	14	1904–05
Division 2	Bristol C	14	1905–06
Division 2	Preston NE	14	1950–51
SCOTTISH LEAGUE			
Division 2	Morton	23	1963–64

LONGEST UNBEATEN SEQUENCE

FOOTBALL LEAGUE		*Games*	*Seasons*
Division 1	Nottingham F	42	Nov 1977–Dec 1978

LONGEST UNBEATEN CUP SEQUENCE

Liverpool 25 rounds League/Milk Cup 1980–1984

LONGEST UNBEATEN SEQUENCE IN A SEASON

FOOTBALL LEAGUE		*Games*	*Season*
Division 1	Burnley	30	1920–21

LONGEST UNBEATEN START TO A SEASON

FOOTBALL LEAGUE		*Games*	*Season*
Division 1	Leeds U	29	1973–74
Division 1	Liverpool	29	1987–88

LONGEST SEQUENCE WITHOUT A WIN IN A SEASON

FOOTBALL LEAGUE		*Games*	*Season*
Division 2	Cambridge U	31	1983–84

LONGEST SEQUENCE OF CONSECUTIVE DEFEATS

FOOTBALL LEAGUE		*Games*	*Season*
Division 3N	Rochdale	17	1931–32

GOALKEEPING RECORDS (Without conceding a goal)

British record *(all competitive games)*
Chris Woods, Rangers, in 1196 minutes from 26 November 1986 to 31 January 1987.

Football League
Steve Death, Reading, 1103 minutes from 24 March to 18 August 1979.

PENALTIES

Most in a season (individual)		*Goals*	*Season*
Division 1	Francis Lee (Manchester C)	13	1971–72
Most awarded in one game			
Five	Crystal Palace (4 – 1 scored, three missed) v Brighton & HA (1 scored), Div 2		1988–89
Most saved in a season			
Division 1	Paul Cooper (Ipswich T)	8 (of 10)	1979–80

MOST LEAGUE APPEARANCES

FOOTBALL LEAGUE
864 Peter Shilton (286 Leicester City, 110 Stoke City, 202 Nottingham Forest, 188 Southampton, 78 Derby County) 1966–89
824 Terry Paine (713 Southampton, 111 Hereford United) 1957–77
777 Alan Oakes (565 Manchester City, 211 Chester City, 1 Port Vale) 1959–84
770 John Trollope (all for Swindon Town) 1960–80†
764 Jimmy Dickinson (all for Portsmouth) 1946–65
761 Roy Sproson (all for Port Vale) 1950–72
758 Ray Clemence (48 Scunthorpe United, 470 Liverpool, 240 Tottenham Hotspur) 1966–87
757 Pat Jennings (48 Watford, 472 Tottenham Hotspur, 237 Arsenal) 1963–86
†record for one club

Consecutive
401 Harold Bell (401 Tranmere R; 459 in all games) 1946–55

FA CUP
88 Ian Callaghan (79 Liverpool, 7 Swansea C, 2 Crewe Alex)

Most Senior Matches
1201 Peter Shilton (864 League, 79 FA Cup, 83 League Cup, 109 Internationals, 13 Under-23, 4 Football League XI, 49 others including European Cup, UEFA Cup, World Club Championship, various domestic cup competitions)

MOST CUP WINNERS' MEDALS

FA CUP – 5 medals each

James Forrest (Blackburn R) 1884, 1885, 1886, 1890, 1891.
Hon. A. F. Kinnaird (Wanderers) 1873, 1877, 1878, (Old Etonians) 1879, 1882.
C. H. R. Wollaston (Wanderers) 1872, 1873, 1876, 1877, 1878.

SCOTTISH CUP – 7 medals each

Jimmy McMenemy (Celtic) 1904, 1907, 1908, 1911, 1912, 1914, (Partick Th) 1921.
Bob McPhail (Airdieonians) 1924, (Rangers) 1928, 1930, 1932, 1934, 1935, 1936.
Billy McNeill (Celtic) 1965, 1967, 1969, 1971, 1972, 1974, 1975.

MOST LEAGUE MEDALS

Phil Neal (Liverpool) 8: 1976, 1977, 1979, 1980, 1982, 1983, 1984, 1986

RECORD ATTENDANCES

Football League	83,260	Manchester U v Arsenal, Maine Road	17.1.1948
Scottish League	118,567	Rangers v Celtic, Ibrox Stadium	2.1.1939
FA Cup Final	126,047*	Bolton W v West Ham U, Wembley	28.4.1923
European Cup	135,826	Celtic v Leeds U, semi-final at Hampden Park	15.4.1970
Scottish Cup	146,433	Celtic v Aberdeen, Hampden Park	24.4.37
World Cup	199,854†	Brazil v Uruguay, Maracana, Rio	16.7.50

* It has been estimated that as many as 70,000 more broke in without paying.
† 173,830 paid.

OTHER RECORDS

YOUNGEST PLAYERS

Football League Albert Geldard, 15 years 158 days, Bradford Park Avenue v Millwall, Division 2, 16.9.29; and Ken Roberts, 15 years 158 days, Wrexham v Bradford Park Avenue, Division 3N, 1.9.51

Football League scorer
Ronnie Dix, 15 years 180 days, Bristol Rovers v Norwich City, Division 3S, 3.3.28.

Division 1
Derek Forster, 15 years 185 days, Sunderland v Leicester City, 22.8.84.

Division 1 scorer
Jason Dozzell, 16 years 57 days as substitute Ipswich Town v Coventry City, 4.2.84

Division 1 hat-tricks
Alan Shearer, 17 years 240 days, Southampton v Arsenal, 9.4.88
Jimmy Greaves, 17 years 10 months, Chelsea v Portsmouth, 25.12.57

FA Cup (any round)
Andy Awford, 15 years 88 days as substitute Worcester City v Borehamwood, 3rd Qual. rd, 10.10.87

FA Cup proper
Scott Endersby, 15 years 288 days, Kettering v Tilbury, 1st rd, 26.11.77

FA Cup Final
Paul Allen, 17 years 256 days, West Ham United v Arsenal, 1980

FA Cup Final scorer
Norman Whiteside, 18 years 18 days, Manchester United v Brighton & Hove Albion, 1983

FA Cup Final captain
David Nish, 21 years 212 days, Leicester City v Manchester City, 1969

League Cup Final scorer
Norman Whiteside, 17 years 324 days, Manchester U v Liverpool, 1983

League Cup Final captain
Barry Venison, 20 years, 7 months, 8 days, Sunderland v Norwich C, 1985

INTERNATIONALS

England
Duncan Edwards (Manchester United), 18 years 183 days, v Scotland, 2.4.55

Northern Ireland
Norman Whiteside (Manchester United), 17 years 42 days, v Yugoslavia, 17.6.82

Scotland
Johnny Lambie (Queen's Park), 17 years 92 days, v Ireland, 20.3.1886

Wales
John Charles (Leeds United), 18 years 71 days, v Ireland, 8.3.50

Republic of Ireland
Jimmy Holmes, 17 years 200 days, v Austria, 30.5.71

OLDEST PLAYERS

Football League
Neil McBain, 52 years 4 months, New Brighton v Hartlepools United, Div 3N, 15.3.47 (McBain was New Brighton's manager and had to play in an emergency)

Division 1
Stanley Matthews, 50 years 5 days, Stoke City v Fulham, 6.2.65

FA Cup Final
Walter Hampson, 41 years 8 months, Newcastle United v Aston Villa, 1924

FA Cup
Billy Meredith, 49 years 8 months, Manchester City v Newcastle United, 29.3.24

International debutant
Leslie Compton, 38 years 2 months, England v Wales, 15.11.50

International
Billy Meredith, 45 years 229 days, Wales v England, 15.3.20

SENDINGS-OFF

Season	242 (211 League, 19 FA Cup, 12 Milk Cup)	1982–83
Day	15 (3 League, 12 FA Cup*) **worst overall FA Cup total*	20 Nov 1982
League	13	14 Dec 1985
FA Cup Final	Kevin Moran, Manchester U v Everton	1985
Wembley	Boris Stankovic, Yugoslavia v Sweden (Olympics)	1948
	Antonio Rattin, Argentina v England (World Cup)	1966
	Billy Bremner (Leeds U) and Kevin Keegan (Liverpool), Charity Shield	1974
	Gilbert Dresch, Luxembourg v England (World Cup)	1977
	Mike Henry, Sudbury T v Tamworth (FA Vase)	1989
Quickest	Ambrose Brown, Wrexham v Hull C (away) Div 3N: 20 secs	25 Dec 1936
Division 1	Liam O'Brien, Manchester U v Southampton (away): 85 secs	3 Jan 1987
World Cup	Jose Batista, Uruguay v Scotland, Neza, Mexico (World Cup): 55 secs	13 June 1986
Most one game	Four: Crewe Alex (2) v Bradford PA (2) Div 3N	8 Jan 1955
	Four: Sheffield U (1) v Portsmouth (3) Div 2	13 Dec 1986
	Four: Port Vale (2) v Northampton T (2) Littlewoods Cup	18 Aug 1987
	Four: Brentford (2) v Mansfield T (2) Div 3	12 Dec 1987

TRANSFERS

British players £1 million and over

£4,500,000 Chris Waddle, Tottenham H to Marseille, July 1989
£3,200,000 Ian Rush, Liverpool to Juventus, June 1987
£2,750,000 Gary Lineker, Everton to Barcelona, June 1986
£2,300,000 Mark Hughes, Manchester U to Barcelona, May 1986
£2,200,000 Tony Cottee, West Ham to Everton, July 1988
£2,000,000 Paul Gascoigne, Newcastle U to Tottenham H, July 1988
£1,900,000 Peter Beardsley, Newcastle United to Liverpool, July 1987
£1,500,000 Paul Stewart, Manchester C to Tottenham H, June 1988
£1,500,000 Bryan Robson, WBA to Manchester U, October 1981
£1,500,000 Ray Wilkins, Manchester U to AC Milan, June 1984
£1,500,000 Richard Gough, Tottenham H to Rangers, September 1987
£1,500,000 Mark Hughes, Barcelona to Manchester U, June 1988
£1,500,000 Gary Lineker, Barcelona to Tottenham H, July 1989
£1,500,000 Neil Webb, Nottingham F to Manchester U, July 1989
£1,469,000 Andy Gray, Aston Villa to Wolverhampton W, September 1979
£1,437,500 Steve Daley, Wolverhampton W to Manchester C, September 1979
£1,350,000 Kenny Sansom, Crystal Palace to Arsenal, August 1980
£1,250,000 Kevin Reeves, Norwich C to Manchester C, March 1980
£1,250,000 Ian Wallace, Coventry C to Nottingham F, July 1980
£1,250,000 Clive Allen, Arsenal to Crystal Palace, August 1980
£1,250,000 Garry Birtles, Nottingham F to Manchester U, October 1980
£1,250,000 Frank McAvennie, Celtic to West Ham U, March 1989
£1,200,000 Clive Allen, QPR to Arsenal, June 1980
£1,200,000 Trevor Francis, Nottingham F to Manchester C, September 1981
£1,200,000 Mo Johnston, Nantes to Rangers, July 1989
£1,180,000 Trevor Francis, Birmingham C to Nottingham F, February 1979
£1,150,000 Steve Archibald, Tottenham H to Barcelona, August 1984
£1,100,000 Gary Lineker, Leicester C to Everton, June 1985 (including additional £300,000 when transferred to Barcelona)
£1,100,000 Frank Stapleton, Arsenal to Manchester U, August 1981
£1,100,000 Alan McInally, Aston Villa to Bayern Munich, July 1989
£1,000,000 Mark Hateley, AC Milan to Monaco, June 1987
£1,000,000 Justin Fashanu, Norwich C to Nottingham F, August 1981
£1,000,000 Luther Blissett, Watford to AC Milan, July 1983
£1,000,000 Ian Ferguson, St. Mirren to Glasgow Rangers, February 1988
£1,000,000 Gary Stevens, Everton to Rangers, July 1988
£1,000,000 Clive Allen, Tottenham H to Bordeaux, June 1988
£1,000,000 Dean Saunders, Oxford U to Derby Co, October 1988
£1,000,000 Clive Allen, Bordeaux to Manchester C, July 1989

World records

£6,900,000 Diego Maradona, Barcelona to Napoli, June 1984
£5,500,000 Ruud Gullit, PSV Eindhoven to AC Milan, June 1987
£4,800,000 Diego Maradona, Argentinos Juniors to Barcelona, June 1982
£4,800,000 Lajos Detari, Eintracht Frankfurt to Olympiakos, July 1988
£4,000,000 Rui Barros, Porto to Juventus, July 1988
£3,500,000 Ruggiero Rizzitelli, Cesena to Roma, 1988
£3,000,000 Karl-Heinz Rummenigge, Bayern Munich to Internazionale, July 1984
£2,800,000 Careca, São Paulo to Napoli, May 1987
£2,500,000 Artur Antunes Coimbra (Zico), Flamengo to Udinese, July 1983
£2,500,000 Paulo Futre, Porto to Atletico Madrid, June 1987
£2,500,000 Frank Rijkaard, Sporting Lisbon to AC Milan, June 1988
£2,400,000 Lothar Matthaus, Bayern Munich to Internazionale, April 1988
£2,330,000 Enzo Scifo, Anderlecht to Internazionale, May 1987
£2,300,000 Rudi Voller, Werder Bremen to AS Roma, June 1987

Chris Waddle who became the most expensive British player in the 1989 summer when he was transferred from Tottenham to Marseille for £4.5 million.

International Records

MOST GOALS IN AN INTERNATIONAL

England	Malcolm Macdonald (Newcastle U) 5 goals v Cyprus, at Wembley	16.4.1975
	Willie Hall (Tottenham H) 5 goals v Ireland, at Old Trafford	16.11.1938
	G. O. Smith (Corinthians) 5 goals v Ireland, at Sunderland	18.2.1899
	Steve Bloomer (Derby Co) 5 goals* v Wales, at Cardiff	16.3.1896
	Oliver Vaughton (Aston Villa) 5 goals v Ireland, at Belfast	18.2.82
Scotland	Charles Heggie (Rangers) 5 goals v Ireland, at Belfast	20.3.1886
Ireland	Joe Bambrick (Linfield) 6 goals v Wales, at Belfast	1.2.1930
Wales	James Price (Wrexham) 4 goals v Ireland, at Wrexham	25.2.1882
	Mel Charles (Cardiff C) 4 goals v Ireland, at Cardiff	11.4.1962
	Ian Edwards (Chester) 4 goals v Malta, at Wrexham	25.10.1978

* There are conflicting reports which make it uncertain whether Bloomer scored four or five goals in this game.

MOST GOALS IN AN INTERNATIONAL CAREER

		Goals	*Games*
England	Bobby Charlton (Manchester U)	49	106
Scotland	Denis Law (Huddersfield T, Manchester C, Torino, Manchester U)	30	55
	Kenny Dalglish (Celtic, Liverpool)	30	102
Ireland	Billy Gillespie (Sheffield U)	12	25
	Joe Bambrick (Linfield, Chelsea)	12	11
	Gerry Armstrong (Tottenham H, Watford, Real Mallorca, WBA, Chesterfield)	12	63
Wales	Trevor Ford (Swansea T, Aston Villa, Sunderland, Cardiff C)	23	38
	Ivor Allchurch (Swansea T, Newcastle U, Cardiff C)	23	68
Republic of Ireland	Don Givens (Manchester U, Luton T, QPR, Birmingham C Neuchatel Xamax)	19	56

HIGHEST SCORES

World Cup Match	New Zealand	13	Fiji	0	1981
Olympic Games	Denmark	17	France	1	1908
	Germany	16	USSR	0	1912
International Match	Germany	13	Finland	0	1940
	Spain	13	Bulgaria	0	1933
European Cup	Feyenoord	12	Reykjavik	2	1969
European Cup-Winners' Cup	Sporting Lisbon	16	Apoel Nicosia	1	1963
Fairs & UEFA Cups	Ajax	14	Red Boys	0	1984

GOALSCORING RECORDS

World Cup Final	Geoff Hurst (England) 3 goals v West Germany	1966
World Cup Final tournament	Just Fontaine (France) 13 goals	1958
Major European Cup game	Lothar Emmerich (Borussia Dortmund) v Floriana in Cup-Winners' Cup – 6 goals	1965
Career	Arthur Friedenreich (Brazil) 1329 goals	1910–30
	Pele (Brazil) 1281 goals	*1956–78
	Franz 'Bimbo' Binder (Austria, Germany) 1006 goals	1930–50

**Pelé has since scored two goals in Testimonial matches making his total 1283.*

MOST CAPPED INTERNATIONALS IN BRITISH ISLES

England	Peter Shilton	109 appearances	1970–
Northern Ireland	Pat Jennings	119 appearances	1964–86
Scotland	Kenny Dalglish	102 appearances	1971–86
Wales	Joey Jones	72 appearances	1975–87
Republic of Ireland	Liam Brady	70 appearances	1974–

Milestones in British transfers

£1000 Alf Common, Sunderland to Middlesbrough, 1905
£10,000 David Jack, Bolton Wanderers to Arsenal, 1928
£100,000 Denis Law, Torino to Manchester U, 1962
£200,000 Martin Peters, West Ham U to Tottenham, 1970
£500,000 Kevin Keegan, Liverpool to SV Hamburg, 1977

BARCLAYS LEAGUE FIXTURES 1989–90

Saturday 19 August

Division One
Charlton Ath v Derby Co
Coventry C v Everton
Liverpool v Manchester C
Manchester U v Arsenal
Nottingham F v Aston Villa
QPR v Crystal Palace
Sheffield W v Norwich C
Southampton v Millwall
Tottenham H v Luton T
Wimbledon v Chelsea

Division Two
Blackburn R v Oldham Ath
Bradford C v Port Vale
Brighton & HA v AFC Bournemouth
Hull C v Leicester C
Ipswich T v Barnsley
Middlesbrough v Wolverhampton W
Newcastle U v Leeds U
Plymouth Argyle v Oxford U
Stoke C v West Ham U
Swindon T v Sunderland
Watford v Portsmouth
WBA v Sheffield U

Division Three
Birmingham C v Crewe Alex
Blackpool v Wigan Ath
Bristol R v Brentford
Bury v Bristol C
Cardiff C v Bolton W
Chester C v Mansfield T
Fulham v Tranmere R
Huddersfield T v Swansea C
Leyton O v Notts Co
Reading v Shrewsbury T
Rotherham U v Preston NE
Walsall v Northampton T

Division Four
Chesterfield v Colchester U
Exeter C v Doncaster R
Gillingham v Aldershot
Grimsby T v Cambridge U
Halifax T v Hartlepool U
Hereford U v Carlisle U
Lincoln C v Scunthorpe U
Peterborough U v Maidstone U
Rochdale v Burnley
Scarborough v Wrexham
Southend U v York C
Stockport Co v Torquay U

Tuesday 22 August

Division One
Arsenal v Coventry C
Chelsea v QPR
Crystal Palace v Manchester U
Everton v Tottenham H
Luton T v Sheffield W
Millwall v Charlton Ath

Division Two
AFC Bournemouth v WBA
Barnsley v Stoke C
Oldham Ath v Watford
Sunderland v Ipswich T

Wednesday 23 August

Division One
Aston Villa v Liverpool
Derby Co v Wimbledon
Manchester C v Southampton
Norwich C v Nottingham F

Divisioin Two
Leeds U v Middlesbrough
Leicester C v Blackburn R
West Ham U v Bradford C

Friday 25 August

Division Three
Crewe Alex v Reading

Saturday 26 August

Division One
Arsenal v Wimbledon
Aston Villa v Charlton A
Chelsea v Sheffield W
Crystal Palace v Coventry C
Derby Co v Manchester U
Everton v Southampton
Luton T v Liverpool
Manchester C v Tottenham H
Millwall v Nottingham F
Norwich C v QPR

Division Two
AFC Bournemouth v Hull C
Barnsley v Brighton & HA
Leeds U v Blackburn R
Leicester C v Newcastle U
Oldham Ath v Swindon T
Oxford U v Watford
Port Vale v WBA
Portsmouth v Stoke C
Sheffield U v Ipswich T
Sunderland v Middlesbrough
West Ham U v Plymouth Arg
Wolverhampton W v Bradford C

Division Three
Bolton W v Fulham
Brentford v Chester C
Bristol C v Birmingham C
Mansfield T v Bristol R
Notts Co v Blackpool
Preston NE v Bury
Shrewsbury T v Leyton O
Swansea C v Northampton T
Tranmere R v Cardiff C
Walsall v Huddersfield T
Wigan Ath v Rotherham U

Division Four
Aldershot v Lincoln C
Burnley v Stockport Co
Cambridge U v Hereford U
Carlisle U v Chesterfield
Colchester U v Halifax T
Doncaster R v Gillingham
Hartlepool U v Exeter C
Maidstone U v Scarborough
Scunthorpe U v Rochdale
Torquay U v Grimsby T
Wrexham v Southend U
York C v Peterborough U

Tuesday 29 August

Division One
Charlton Ath v Chelsea
Southampton v Aston Villa
Wimbledon v Millwall

Wednesday 30 August

Division One
Coventry C v Manchester C
Liverpool v Crystal Palace
Manchester U v Norwich C
Nottingham F v Derby Co
QPR v Luton T
Sheffield W v Everton

Friday 1 September

Division Four
Southend U v Hartlepool U
Stockport Co v York C

Saturday 2 September

Division Two
Blackburn R v Oxford U
Bradford C v Portsmouth
Brighton & HA v Port Vale
Hull C v West Ham U
Ipswich T v AFC Bournemouth
Middlesbrough v Sheffield U
Newcastle U v Oldham Ath
Plymouth Arg Barnsley
Stoke C v Leeds U
Watford v Leicester C
WBA v Sunderland

Division Three
Birmingham C v Swansea C
Blackpool v Shrewsbury T
Bristol R v Notts Co
Bury v Wigan Ath
Cardiff C v Brentford
Chester C v Crewe Alex
Huddersfield T v Bolton W
Leyton O v Preston NE
Northampton T v Bristol C
Reading v Tranmere R
Rotherham U v Walsall

Division Four
Chesterfield v Burnley
Exeter C v Carlisle U
Gillingham v Scunthorpe U
Grimsby T v Colchester U
Halifax T v Torquay U
Hereford U v Maidstone U
Linclon C v Doncaster R
Peterborough U v Aldershot
Rochdale v Wrexham
Scarborough v Cambridge U

Sunday 3 September

Division Two
Swindon T v Wolverhampton W

Friday 8 September

Division Four
Colchester U v Hereford U

Saturday 9 September

Division One
Arsenal v Sheffield W
Aston Villa v Tottenham H
Chelsea v Nottingham F
Crystal Palace v Wimbledon
Derby Co v Liverpool

Everton v Manchester U
Luton T v Charlton Ath
Manchester C v QPR
Millwall v Coventry C
Norwich C v Southampton

Division Two
AFC Bournemouth v Newcastle U
Barnsley v Middlesbrough
Leeds U v Ipswich T
Leicester C v WBA
Oldham Ath v Plymouth Arg
Oxford U v Bradford C
Port Vale v Blackburn R
Portsmouth v Hull C
Sheffield U v Brighton & HA
Sunderland v Watford
West Ham U v Swindon T
Wolverhampton W v Stoke C

Division Three
Bolton W v Bristol R
Brentford v Bury
Bristol C v Blackpool
Crewe Alex v Fulham
Mansfield T v Cardiff C
Notts Co v Reading
Preston NE v Huddersfield T
Shrewsbury T v Birmingham C
Swansea C v Chester C
Tranmere R v Rotherham U
Walsall v Leyton O
Wigan Ath v Northampton T

Division Four
Aldershot v Southend U
Burnley v Exeter C
Cambridge U v Chesterfield
Carlisle U v Grimsby T
Doncaster R v Peterborough U
Hartlepool U v Gillingham
Maidstone U v Stockport Co
Scunthorpe U v Scarborough
Torquay U v Lincoln C
Wrexham v Halifax T
York C v Rochdale

Tuesday 12 September

Division Two
Portsmouth v Plymouth Arg
Port Vale v Hull C
Sheffield U v Swindon T
Wolverhampton W v Brighton & HA

Wednesday 13 September

Division Two
Oxford U v Newcastle U

Friday 15 September

Division Three
Chester C v Notts Co

Division Four
Halifax T v Carlisle U
Southend U v Torquay U
Stockport Co v Hartlepool U

Saturday 16 September

Division One
Charlton Ath v Everton
Coventry C v Luton T
Liverpool v Norwich C
Manchester U v Millwall
Nottingham F v Arsenal
QPR v Derby Co
Sheffield W v Aston Villa
Southampton v Crystal Palace
Tottenham H v Chelsea
Wimbledon v Manchester C

Division Two
Blackburn R v Sunderland
Bradford C v Leicester C
Brighton & HA v West Ham U
Hull C v Leeds U
Ipswich T v Wolverhampton W
Middlesbrough v AFC Bournemouth
Newcastle U v Portsmouth
Plymouth Arg v Sheffield U
Stoke C v Oldham Ath
Swindon T v Barnsley
Watford v Port Vale
WBA v Oxford U

Division Three
Birmingham C v Tranmere R
Blackpool v Crewe Alex
Bristol R v Preston NE
Bury v Mansfield T
Cardiff C v Bristol C
Fulham v Swansea C
Huddersfield T v Brentford
Leyton O v Wigan Ath
Northampton T v Shrewsbury T
Reading v Walsall
Rotherham U v Bolton W

Division Four
Chesterfield v Aldershot
Exeter C v Cambridge U
Gillingham v Burnley
Grimsby T v Maidstone U
Hereford U v Wrexham
Lincoln C v York C
Peterborough U v Scunthorpe U
Rochdale v Colchester U
Scarborough v Doncaster R

Friday 22 September

Division Three
Tranmere R v Huddersfield T

Division Four
Cambridge U v Halifax T
Doncaster R v Southend U

Saturday 23 September

Division One
Arsenal v Charlton Ath
Aston Villa v QPR
Chelsea v Coventry C
Crystal Palace v Nottingham F
Derby Co v Southampton
Everton v Liverpool
Luton T v Wimbledon
Manchester C v Manchester U
Millwall v Sheffield W
Norwich C v Tottenham H

Division Two
AFC Bournemouth v Blackburn R
Barnsley v Bradford C
Leeds U v Swindon T
Leicester C v Brighton & HA
Oldham Ath v WBA
Oxford U v Ipswich T
Port Vale v Stoke C
Portsmouth v Middlesbrough
Sheffield U v Hull C
Sunderland v Newcastle U
West Ham U v Watford
Wolverhampton W v Plymouth Arg

Division Three
Bolton W v Leyton O
Brentford v Birmingham C
Bristol C v Bristol R
Crewe Alex v Northampton T
Mansfield T v Blackpool
Notts Co v Rotherham U
Preston NE v Chester C
Shrewsbury T v Bury
Swansea C v Reading
Walsall v Fulham
Wigan Ath v Cardiff C

Division Four
Aldershot v Stockport Co
Burnley v Hereford U
Carlisle U v Gillingham
Colchester U v Scarborough
Hartlepool U v Peterborough U
Maidstone U v Chesterfield
Scunthorpe U v Exeter C
Torquay U v Rochdale
Wrexham v Lincoln C
York C v Grimsby T

Tuesday 26 September

Division Two
AFC Bournemouth v Port Vale
Barnsley v Wolverhampton W
Portsmouth v West Ham U
Sheffield U v Oldham Ath
Stoke C v Bradford C
Swindon T v Plymouth Arg

Division Three
Birmingham C v Walsall
Bristol C v Shrewsbury T
Bury v Rotherham U
Cardiff C v Northampton T
Crewe Alex v Brentford
Fulham v Huddersfield T
Leyton O v Bristol R
Notts Co v Bolton W
Preston NE v Blackpool
Reading v Chester C
Wigan Ath v Tranmere R

Division Four
Burnley v York C
Cambridge U v Carlisle U
Colchester U v Maidstone U
Doncaster R v Aldershot
Gillingham v Southend U
Rochdale v Hartlepool U
Scunthorpe U v Torquay U
Wrexham v Stockport C

Wednesday 27 September

Division Two
Brighton & HA v Ipswich T
Leeds U v Oxford U
Leicester C v Sunderland
Middlesbrough v Hull C
Newcastle U v Watford
WBA v Blackburn R

Division Four
Exeter C v Grimsby T
Hereford U v Chesterfield
Lincoln C v Peterborough U
Scarborough v Halifax T

Friday 29 September

Division Three
Tranmere R v Bristol C

Saturday 30 September

Division One
Aston Villa v Derby Co
Chelsea v Arsenal
Crystal Palace v Everton
Liverpool v Manchester U
Manchester C v Luton T
Millwall v Norwich C
Nottingham F v Charlton Ath
Sheffield W v Coventry C
Southampton v Wimbledon
Tottenham H v QPR

Division Two
Blackburn R v Barnsley
Bradford C v Swindon T
Hull C v Newcastle U
Ipswich T v Stoke C
Oldham Ath v Leicester C
Oxford U v AFC Bournemouth
Plymouth Arg v Brighton & HA
Port Vale v Leeds U
Sunderland v Sheffield U
Watford v Middlesbrough
West Ham U v WBA
Wolverhampton W v Portsmouth

Division Three
Blackpool v Birmingham C
Bolton W v Mansfield T
Brentford v Wigan Ath
Bristol R v Reading
Chester C v Fulham
Huddersfield T v Leyton O
Northampton T v Bury
Rotherham U v Cardiff C
Shrewsbury T v Crewe Alex
Swansea C v Notts Co
Walsall v Preston NE

Division Four
Aldershot v Scunthorpe U
Carlisle U v Colchester U
Chesterfield v Rochdale
Grimsby T v Hereford U
Halifax T v Exeter C
Hartlepool U v Doncaster R
Maidstone U v Cambridge U
Peterborough U v Gillingham
Southend U v Lincoln C
Stockport Co v Scarborough
Torquay U v Burnley
York C v Wrexham

Friday 6 October

Division Three
Blackpool v Reading
Tranmere R v Leyton O

Division Four
Halifax T v Gillingham

Saturday 7 October

Division Two
Blackburn R v Middlesbrough
Bradford C v Brighton & HA
Hull C v Swindon T
Ipswich T v Newcastle U
Oldham Ath v Barnsley
Oxford U v Portsmouth
Plymouth Arg v Stoke C
Port Vale v Leicester C
Sunderland v AFC Bournemouth
Watford v WBA
West Ham U v Leeds U
Wolverhampton W v Sheffield U

Division Three
Bolton W v Wigan Ath
Brentford v Bristol C
Bristol R v Fulham
Chester C v Bury
Huddersfield T v Cardiff C
Northampton T v Preston NE
Rotherham U v Birmingham C
Shrewsbury T v Mansfield T
Swansea C v Crewe Alex
Walsall v Notts Co

Division Four
Aldershot v Colchester U
Carlisle U v Wrexham
Chesterfield v Lincoln C
Grimsby T v Rochdale
Hartlepool U v Scunthorpe U
Maidstone U v Burnley
Peterborough U v Exeter C
Southend U v Scarborough
Stockport Co v Hereford U
Torquay U v Doncaster R
York C v Cambridge U

Friday 13 October

Division Four
Cambridge U v Torquay U
Colchester U v York C

Saturday 14 October

Division One
Arsenal v Manchester C
Charlton Ath v Tottenham H
Coventry C v Nottingham F
Derby Co v Crystal Palace
Everton v Millwall
Luton T v Aston Villa
Manchester U v Sheffield W
Norwich C v Chelsea
QPR v Southampton
Wimbledon v Liverpool

Division Two
AFC Bournemouth v Oldham Ath
Barnsley v Port Vale
Brighton & HA v Watford
Leeds U v Sunderland
Leicester C v Oxford U
Middlesbrough v Plymouth Arg
Newcastle U v Bradford C
Portsmouth v Blackburn R
Sheffield U v West Ham U
Stoke C v Hull C
Swindon T v Ipswich T
WBA v Wolverhampton W

Division Three
Birmingham C v Northampton T
Bristol C v Swansea C
Bury v Bristol R
Cardiff C v Chester C
Crewe Alex v Bolton W
Fulham v Rotherham U
Leyton O v Blackpool
Mansfield T v Walsall
Notts Co v Tranmere R
Preston NE v Brentford
Reading v Huddersfield T
Wigan Ath v Shrewsbury T

Division Four
Burnley v Hartlepool U
Doncaster R v Carlisle U
Exeter C v Chesterfield
Gillingham v Stockport Co
Hereford U v Southend U
Lincoln C v Halifax T
Rochdale v Peterborough U
Scarborough v Grimsby T
Scunthorpe U v Maidstone U
Wrexham v Aldershot

Monday 16 October

Division Three
Tranmere R v Mansfield T

Division Four
Stockport Co v Southend U

Tuesday 17 October

Division Two
Barnsley v Sheffield U
Hull C v Oldham Ath
Plymouth Arg v Leicester C
Portsmouth v Leeds U
Stoke C v WBA
Swindon T v Oxford U
Watford v AFC Bournemouth
Wolverhampton W v Port Vale

Division Three
Brentford v Bolton
Bristol C v Notts Co
Bury v Swansea C
Cardiff C v Bristol R
Chester C v Birmingham C
Huddersfield T v Wigan Ath
Northampton T v Blackpool
Preston NE v Crewe Alex
Reading v Fulham
Rotherham U v Leyton O
Walsall v Shrewsbury T

Division Four
Burnley v Peterborough U
Cambridge U v Doncaster R
Carlisle U v Scunthorpe U
Chesterfield v Halifax T
Colchester U v Wrexham
Grimsby T v Gillingham
Rochdale v Exeter C
Torquay U v Hartlepool U
York C v Aldershot

Wednesday 18 October

Division One
Tottenham H v Arsenal

Division Two
Bradford C v Ipswich T
Middlesbrough v Brighton & HA
Newcastle U v Blackburn R
West Ham U v Sunderland

Division Four
Hereford U v Scarborough
Maidstone U v Lincoln C

Friday 20 October

Division Three
Swansea C v Tranmere R

Saturday 21 October

Division One
Coventry C v Manchester U
Crystal Palace v Millwall
Derby Co v Chelsea
Everton v Arsenal
Luton T v Norwich C
Manchester C v Aston Villa
QPR v Charlton Ath
Southampton v Liverpool
Tottenham H v Sheffield W
Wimbledon v Nottingham F

Division Two
AFC Bournemouth v Portsmouth
Blackburn R v Watford
Brighton & HA v Newcastle U
Ipswich T v Plymouth Arg
Leeds U v Wolverhampton W
Leicester C v Swindon T
Oldham Ath v Middlesbrough
Oxford U v Barnsley
Port Vale v West Ham U
Sheffield U v Stoke C
Sunderland v Bradford C
WBA v Hull C

Division Three
Birmingham C v Huddersfield T
Blackpool v Cardiff C
Bolton W v Chester C
Bristol R v Northampton T
Crewe Alex v Rotherham U
Fulham v Bury
Leyton O v Reading
Mansfield T v Bristol C
Notts Co v Preston NE
Shrewsbury T v Brentford
Wigan Ath v Walsall

Division Four
Aldershot v Torquay U
Doncaster R v Burnley
Exeter C v Hereford U
Gillingham v Chesterfield
Halifax T v Rochdale
Hartlepool U v York C
Lincoln C v Grimsby T
Peterborough U v Stockport Co
Scarborough v Carlisle U
Scunthorpe U v Colchester U
Southend U v Maidstone U
Wrexham v Cambridge U

Tuesday 24 October

Division Three
Mansfield T v Swansea C

Friday 27 October

Division Three
Tranmere R v Crewe Alex

Saturday 28 October

Division One
Arsenal v Derby Co
Aston Villa v Crystal Palace
Charlton Ath v Coventry C
Chelsea v Manchester C
Liverpool v Tottenham H
Manchester U v Southampton
Millwall v Luton T
Norwich C v Everton
Nottingham F v QPR
Sheffield W v Wimbledon

Division Two
Barnsley v Leicester C
Bradford C v Leeds U
Hull C v Brighton & HA
Middlesbrough v WBA
Newcastle U v Port Vale
Plymouth Arg v Blackburn R
Portsmouth v Ipswich T
Stoke C v Sunderland
Swindon T v AFC Bournemouth
Watford v Sheffield U
West Ham U v Oxford U
Wolverhampton W v Oldham Ath

Division Three
Brentford v Fulham
Bristol C v Wigan Ath
Bury v Birmingham C
Cardiff C v Leyton O
Chester C v Bristol R
Huddersfield T v Shrewsbury T
Northampton T v Notts Co
Preston NE v Bolton W
Reading v Mansfield T
Rotherham U v Blackpool
Walsall v Swansea C

Division Four
Burnley v Aldershot
Cambridge U v Scunthorpe U
Carlisle U v Hartlepool U
Chesterfield v Southend U
Colchester U v Peterborough U
Grimsby T v Halifax T
Hereford U v Lincoln C
Maidstone U v Wrexham
Rochdale v Scarborough
Stockport Co v Exeter C
Torquay U v Gillingham
York C v Doncaster R

Monday 30 October

Division Two
Port Vale v Middlesbrough

Tuesday 31 October

Division Two
AFC Bournemouth v West Ham U
Blackburn R v Hull C
Ipswich T v Watford
Oldham Ath v Bradford C
Sheffield U v Portsmouth
Sunderland v Barnsley

Division Three
Birmingham C v Cardiff C
Blackpool v Bury
Bolton W v Walsall
Crewe Alex v Bristol C
Fulhamv v Northampton T
Leyton O v Chester C
Mansfield T v Preston NE
Notts Co v Brentford
Shrewsbury T v Tranmere R
Swansea C v Rotherham U
Wigan Ath v Reading

Division Four
Aldershot v Carlisle U
Doncaster R v Maidstone U
Gillingham v Rochdale
Halifax T v Hereford U
Hartlepool U v Cambridge U
Scunthorpe U v York C
Southend U v Burnley
Wrexham v Torquay U

Wednesday 1 November

Division Two
Brighton & HA v Swindon T
Leeds U v Plymouth Arg
Leicester C v Wolverhampton W
Oxford U v Stoke C
WBA v Newcastle U

Division Three
Bristol R v Huddersfield T

Division Four
Exeter C v Colchester U
Lincoln C v Stockport Co
Peterborough U v Grimsby T
Scarborough v Chesterfield

Friday 3 November

Division Three
Cardiff C v Bury

Division Four
Stockport Co v Halifax T

Saturday 4 November

Division One
Arsenal v Norwich C
Aston Villa v Everton
Charlton Ath v Manchester U
Chelsea v Millwall
Liverpool v Coventry C
Luton T v Derby Co
Manchester C v Crystal Palace
Nottingham F v Sheffield W
Southampton v Tottenham H
Wimbledon v QPR

Division Two
Barnsley v Portsmouth
Brighton & HA v Blackburn R
Hull C v Watford
Ipswich T v WBA
Leeds U v AFC Bournemouth
Newcastle U v Middlesbrough
Oldham Ath v Sunderland
Plymouth Arg v Bradford C
Port Vale v Oxford U
Sheffield U v Leicester C
Swindon T v Stoke C
Wolverhampton W v West Ham U

Division Three
Bolton W v Swansea C
Brentford v Tranmere R
Bristol Rovers v Blackpool
Chester C v Huddersfield T
Leyton O v Fulham
Mansfield T v Notts Co
Northampton T v Rotherham U
Preston NE v Shrewsbury T
Reading v Birmingham C
Walsall v Bristol C
Wigan Ath v Crewe Alex

Division Four
Burnley v Colchester U
Cambridge U v Aldershot
Carlisle U v Maidstone U
Doncaster R v Scunthorpe U
Exeter C v Lincoln C
Gillingham v Scarborough
Grimsby T v Chesterfield
Hartlepool U v Wrexham
Hereford U v Rochdale
Southend U v Peterborough U
York C v Torquay U

Friday 10 November

Division Three
Crewe Alex v Mansfield T
Tranmere R v Walsall

Division Four
Colchester U v Cambridge U
Halifax T v Southend U

Saturday 11 November

Division One
Coventry C v Southampton
Crystal Palace v Luton T
Derby Co v Manchester C
Everton v Chelsea
Manchester U v Nottingham F
Millwall v Arsenal
Norwich C v Aston Villa
QPR v Liverpool
Sheffield W v Charlton Ath
Tottenham H v Wimbledon

Division Two
AFC Bournemouth v Sheffield U
Blackburn R v Ipswich T
Bradford C v Hull C
Leicester C v Leeds U
Middlesbrough v Swindon T
Oxford U v Oldham Ath
Portsmouth v Port Vale
Stoke C v Brighton & HA
Sunderland v Wolverhampton W
Watford v Plymouth Arg
WBA v Barnsley
West Ham U v Newcastle U

Division Three
Birmingham C v Leyton O
Blackpool v Brentford
Bristol C v Bolton W
Bury v Reading
Fulham v Cardiff C
Huddersfield T v Northampton T
Notts Co v Wigan Ath
Rotherham U v Chester C
Shrewsbury T v Bristol R
Swansea C v Preston NE

Division Four
Aldershot v Hartlepool U
Chesterfield v Stockport Co
Lincoln C v Gillingham
Maidstone U v York C
Peterborough U v Hereford U
Rochdale v Doncaster R
Scarborough v Exeter C
Scunthorpe U v Burnley

Torquay U v Carlisle U
Wrexham v Grimsby T

Saturday 18 November

Division One
Arsenal v QPR
Aston Villa v Coventry C
Chelsea v Southampton
Crystal Palace v Tottenham H
Derby Co v Sheffield W
Everton v Wimbledon
Luton T v Manchester U
Manchester C v Nottingham F
Millwall v Liverpool
Norwich C v Charlton Ath

Division Two
AFC Bournemouth v Stoke C
Barnsley v Newcastle U
Leeds U v Watford
Leicester C v Ipswich T
Oldham Ath v Brighton & HA
Oxford U v Hull C
Port Vale v Swindon T
Portsmouth v WBA
Sheffield U v Bradford C
Sunderland v Plymouth Arg
West Ham U v Middlesbrough
Wolverhampton W v Blackburn R

Friday 24 November

Division Three
Chester C v Walsall

Division Four
Gillingham v Colchester U
Scarborough v York C
Southend U v Cambridge U

Saturday 25 November

Division One
Charlton Ath v Manchester C
Coventry C v Norwich C
Liverpool v Arsenal
Manchester U v Chelsea
Nottingham F v Everton
QPR v Millwall
Sheffield W v Crystal Palace
Southampton v Luton T
Tottenham H v Derby Co
Wimbledon v Aston Villa

Division Two
Blackburn R v West Ham U
Bradford C v AFC Bournemouth
Brighton & HA v Sunderland
Hull C v Barnsley
Ipswich T v Oldham Ath
Middlesbrough v Oxford U
Newcastle U v Sheffield U
Plymouth Arg v Port Vale
Stoke C v Leicester C
Watford v Wolverhampton W
WBA v Leeds U

Division Three
Birmingham C v Bolton W
Blackpool v Tranmere R
Bristol R v Swansea C
Bury v Crewe Alex
Cardiff C v Preston NE
Fulham v Wigan Ath
Huddersfield T v Notts Co
Leyton O v Mansfield T
Northampton T v Brentford
Reading v Bristol C
Rotherham U v Shrewsbury T

Division Four
Chesterfield v Hartlepool U
Exeter C v Wrexham
Grimsby T v Aldershot
Halifax T v Maidstone U
Hereford U v Doncaster R
Lincoln C v Burnley
Peterborough U v Torquay U
Rochdale v Carlisle U
Stockport C v Scunthorpe U

Sunday 26 November

Division Two
Swindon T v Portsmouth

Wednesday 29 November

Division One
Sheffield W v Liverpool

Friday 1 December

Division Two
Oldham Ath v Blackburn R

Division Three
Wigan Ath v Birmingham C

Saturday 2 December

Division One
Arsenal v Manchester U
Aston Villa v Nottingham F
Chelsea v Wimbledon
Crystal Palace v QPR
Derby Co v Charlton Ath
Everton v Coventry C
Luton T v Tottenham H
Manchester C v Liverpool
Millwall v Southampton
Norwich C v Sheffield W

Division Two
AFC Bournemouth v Brighton & HA
Barnsley v Ipswich T
Leeds U v Newcastle U
Leicester C v Hull C
Oxford U v Plymouth Arg
Port Vale v Bradford C
Portsmouth v Watford
Sheffield U v WBA
Sunderland v Swindon T
West Ham U v Stoke C
Wolverhampton W v Middlesbrough

Division Three
Bolton W v Northampton T
Bristol C v Rotherham U
Crewe Alex v Cardiff C
Mansfield T v Huddersfield
Notts Co v Fulham
Preston NE v Reading
Shrewsbury T v Chester C
Swansea C v Blackpool
Tranmere R v Bury
Walsall v Bristol R

Division Four
Aldershot v Halifax T
Burnley v Grimsby T
Cambridge U v Rochdale
Carlisle U v Peterborough U
Colchester U v Lincoln C
Doncaster R v Stockport C
Hartlepool U v Hereford U
Maidstone U v Exeter C
Scunthorpe U v Southend U
Torquay U v Scarborough
Wrexham v Chesterfield
York C v Gillingham

Sunday 3 December

Division Three
Brentford v Leyton O

Saturday 9 December

Division One
Charlton Ath v Millwall
Coventry C v Arsenal
Liverpool v Aston Villa
Manchester U v Crystal Palace
Nottingham F v Norwich City
QPR v Chelsea
Sheffield W v Luton T
Southampton v Manchester C
Tottenham H v Everton
Wimbledon v Derby Co

Division Two
Blackburn R v Leicester C
Bradford C v West Ham U
Brighton & HA v Wolverhampton W
Hull C v Port Vale
Ipswich T v Sunderland
Middlesbrough v Leeds U
Newcastle U v Oxford U
Stoke C v Barnsley
Watford v Oldham Ath
WBA v AFC Bournemouth

Sunday 10 December

Division Two
Plymouth Arg v Portsmouth
Swindon T v Sheffield U

Friday 15 December

Division Three
Tranmere R v Chester C

Division Four
Halifax T v Doncaster R

Saturday 16 December

Division One
Arsenal v Luton T
Charlton Ath v Crystal Palace
Chelsea v Liverpool
Coventry C v Wimbledon
Everton v Manchester C
Manchester U v Tottenham H
Millwall v Aston Villa
Norwich C v Derby Co
Sheffield W v QPR

Division Two
AFC Bournemouth v Barnsley
Blackburn R v Stoke C
Hull C v Ipswich T
Leeds U v Brighton & HA
Middlesbrough v Leicester C
Newcastle U v Plymouth Arg
Oxford U v Wolverhampton W
Port Vale v Sheffield U
Portsmouth v Sunderland
Watford v Bradford C
West Ham U v Oldham Ath

Division Three
Birmingham C v Preston NE
Blackpool v Fulham
Bristol C v Leyton O
Bury v Walsall
Cardiff C v Notts Co
Crewe Alex v Bristol R
Rotherham U v Huddersfield T
Shrewsbury T v Bolton W
Wigan Ath v Swansea C

Division Four
Chesterfield v York C
Colchester U v Torquay U
Exeter C v Gillingham
Grimsby T v Southend U
Hereford U v Scunthorpe U
Maidstone U v Hartlepool U
Rochdale v Lincoln C

Scarborough v Aldershot
Wrexham v Burnley

Sunday 17 December

Division One
Nottingham F v Southampton

Division Two
WBA v Swindon T

Division Three
Brentford v Mansfield T
Northampton T v Reading

Division Four
Cambridge U v Peterborough U
Carlisle U v Stockport Co

Tuesday 26 December

Division One
Aston Villa v Manchester U
Crystal Palace v Chelsea
Derby Co v Everton
Liverpool v Sheffield W
Luton T v Nottingham F
Manchester C v Norwich C
QPR v Coventry C
Southampton v Arsenal
Tottenham H v Millwall
Wimbledon v Charlton Ath

Division Two
Barnsley v Watford
Bradford C v Middlesbrough
Brighton & HA v Portsmouth
Ipswich T v West Ham U
Leicester C v AFC Bournemouth
Oldham Ath v Port Vale
Plymouth Arg v WBA
Sheffield U v Leeds U
Stoke C v Newcastle U
Sunderland v Oxford U
Swindon T v Blackburn R
Wolverhampton W v Hull C

Division Three
Bolton W v Blackpool
Bristol R v Birmingham C
Chester C v Wigan Ath
Fulham v Bristol C
Huddersfield T v Bury
Leyton O v Northampton T
Mansfield T v Rotherham U
Notts C v Shrewsbury T
Preston NE v Tranmere R
Reading v Brentford
Swansea C v Cardiff C
Walsall v Crewe Alex

Division Four
Aldershot v Exeter C
Burnley v Carlisle U
Doncaster R v Wrexham
Gillingham v Maidstone U
Hartlepool U v Scarborough
Lincoln C v Cambridge U
Peterborough U v Chesterfield
Scunthorpe U v Grimsby T
Southend U v Colchester U
Stockport Co v Rochdale
Torquay U v Hereford U
York C v Halifax T

Friday 29 December

Division Two
Plymouth Arg v Hull C

Division Four
Stockport Co v Cambridge U

Saturday 30 December

Division One
Aston Villa v Arsenal
Crystal Palace v Norwich C
Derby Co v Coventry C
Liverpool v Charlton Ath
Luton T v Chelsea
Manchester C v Millwall
QPR v Everton
Southampton v Sheffield W
Tottenham H v Nottingham F
Wimbledon v Manchester U

Division Two
Barnsley v Leeds U
Bradford C v WBA
Brighton & HA v Oxford U
Ipswich T v Middlesbrough
Leicester C v West Ham U
Oldham Ath v Portsmouth
Sheffield U v Blackburn R
Stoke C v Watford
Sunderland v Port Vale
Swindon T v Newcastle U
Wolverhampton W v AFC Bournemouth

Division Three
Bolton W v Bury
Bristol R v Tranmere R
Chester C v Blackpool
Fulham v Shrewsbury T
Huddersfield T v Bristol C
Leyton O v Crewe Alex
Mansfield T v Northampton T
Notts Co v Birmingham C
Preston NE v Wigan Ath
Reading v Rotherham U
Swansea C v Brentford
Walsall v Cardiff C

Division Four
Aldershot v Rochdale
Burnley v Halifax T
Doncaster R v Colchester U
Gillingham v Wrexham
Hartlepool U v Grimsby T
Lincoln C v Carlisle U
Peterborough U v Scarborough
Scunthorpe U v Chesterfield
Southend U v Exeter C
Torquay U v Maidstone U
York C v Hereford U

Monday 1 January

Division One
Arsenal v Crystal Palace
Charlton Ath v Southampton
Chelsea v Aston Villa
Coventry C v Tottenham H
Everton v Luton T
Manchester U v QPR
Millwall v Derby Co
Norwich C v Wimbledon
Nottingham F v Liverpool
Sheffield W v Manchester C

Division Two
AFC Bournemouth v Plymouth Arg
Blackburn R v Bradford C
Hull C v Sunderland
Leeds U v Oldham Ath
Middlesbrough v Stoke C
Newcastle U v Wolverhampton W
Oxford U v Sheffield U
Port Vale v Ipswich T
Portsmouth v Leicester C
Watford v Swindon T
WBA v Brighton & HA
West Ham U v Barnsley

Division Three
Birmingham C v Fulham
Blackpool v Huddersfield T
Brentford v Walsall
Bristol C v Preston NE
Bury v Leyton O
Cardiff C v Reading
Crewe Alex v Notts Co
Northampton T v Chester C
Rotherham U v Bristol R
Shrewsbury T v Swansea C
Tranmere R v Bolton W
Wigan Ath v Mansfield T

Division Four
Cambridge U v Burnley
Carlisle U v York C
Chesterfield v Doncaster R
Colchester U v Hartlepool U
Exeter C v Torquay U
Grimsby v Stockport C
Halifax T v Peterborough U
Hereford U v Gillingham
Maidstone U v Aldershot
Rochdale v Southend U
Scarborough v Lincoln C
Wrexham v Scunthorpe U

Friday 5 January

Division Three
Tranmere R v Northampton T

Division Four
Colchester U v Stockport Co

Saturday 6 January

Division Three
Bolton W v Reading
Brentford v Rotherham U
Bristol C v Chester C
Crewe Alex v Huddersfield T
Mansfield T v Birmingham C
Notts Co v Bury
Preston NE v Fulham
Shrewsbury T v Cardiff C
Swansea C v Leyton O
Walsall v Blackpool
Wigan Ath v Bristol R

Division Four
Aldershot v Hereford United
Burnley v Scarborough
Cambridge U v Gillingham
Carlisle U v Southend U
Doncaster R v Grimsby T
Hartlepool U v Lincoln C
Maidstone U v Rochdale
Scunthorpe U v Halifax T
Torquay U v Chesterfield
Wrexham v Peterborough U
York C v Exeter C

Friday 12 January

Division Three
Chester C v Brentford

Division Four
Halifax T v Colchester U
Southend U v Wrexham

Saturday 13 January

Division One
Charlton Ath v Aston Villa
Coventry C v Crystal Palace
Liverpool v Luton T
Manchester U v Derby Co
Nottingham F v Millwall
QPR v Norwich C
Sheffield W v Chelsea
Southampton v Everton
Tottenham H v Manchester C
Wimbledon v Arsenal

Division Two
Blackburn R v Leeds U
Bradford C v Wolverhampton W
Brighton & HA v Barnsley
Hull C v AFC Bournemouth
Ipswich T v Sheffield U
Middlesbrough v Sunderland
Newcastle U v Leicester C
Plymouth Arg v West Ham U
Stoke C v Portsmouth
Swindon T v Oldham Ath
Watford v Oxford U
WBA v Port Vale

Division Three
Birmingham C v Bristol C
Blackpool v Notts Co
Bristol R v Mansfield T
Bury v Preston NE
Cardiff C v Tranmere R
Fulham v Bolton W
Huddersfield T v Walsall
Leyton O v Shrewsbury T
Reading v Crewe Alex
Rotherham U v Wigan Ath

Division Four
Chesterfield v Carlisle U
Exeter C v Hartlepool U
Gillingham v Doncaster R
Grimsby T v Torquay U
Hereford U v Cambridge U
Lincoln C v Aldershot
Peterborough U v York C
Rochdale v Scunthorpe U
Scarborough v Maidstone U
Stockport Co v Burnley

Sunday 14 January

Division Three
Northampton T v Swansea C

Friday 19 January

Division Three
Tranmere R v Fulham

Saturday 20 January

Division One
Arsenal v Tottenham H
Aston Villa v Southampton
Chelsea v Charlton Ath
Crystal Palace v Liverpool
Derby Co v Nottingham F
Everton v Sheffield W
Luton T v QPR
Manchester C v Coventry C
Millwall v Wimbledon
Norwich C v Manchester U

Division Two
AFC Bournemouth v Ipswich T
Barnsley v Plymouth Arg
Leeds U v Stoke C
Leicester C v Watford
Oldham Ath v Newcastle U
Oxford U v Blackburn R
Port Vale v Brighton & HA
Portsmouth v Bradford C
Sheffield U v Middlesbrough
Sunderland v WBA
West Ham U v Hull C
Wolverhampton W v Swindon T

Division Three
Bolton W v Cardiff C
Brentford v Bristol R
Bristol C v Bury
Crewe Alex v Birmingham C
Mansfield T v Chester C
Notts C v Leyton O
Preston NE v Rotherham U
Shrewsbury T v Reading
Wigan Ath v Blackpool

Division Four
Aldershot v Gillingham
Burnley v Rochdale
Cambridge U v Grimsby T
Carlisle U v Hereford U
Colchester U v Chesterfield
Doncaster R v Exeter C
Hartlepool U v Halifax T
Maidstone U v Peterborough U
Scunthorpe U v Lincoln C
Torquay U v Stockport C
Wrexham v Scarborough
York C v Southend U

Sunday 21 January

Division Three
Swansea C v Huddersfield T

Friday 26 January

Division Three
Chester C v Swansea C

Division Four
Halifax v Wrexham

Saturday 27 January

Division Three
Birmingham C v Shrewsbury T
Blackpool v Bristol C
Bristol R v Bolton W
Bury v Brentford
Cardiff C v Mansfield T
Fulham v Crewe Alex
Huddersfield T v Preston NE
Leyton O v Walsall
Reading v Notts Co
Rotherham U v Tranmere R

Division Four
Chesterfield v Cambridge U
Exeter C v Burnley
Gillingham v Hartlepool U
Grimsby v Carlisle U
Hereford U v Colchester U
Lincoln C v Torquay U
Peterborough U v Doncaster R
Rochdale v York C
Scarborough v Scunthorpe U
Southend U v Aldershot
Stockport Co v Maidstone U

Sunday 28 January

Division Three
Northampton T v Wigan Ath

Friday 2 February

Division Four
Halifax T v Cambridge U
Southend U v Doncaster R

Saturday 3 February

Division One
Charlton Ath v Arsenal
Coventry C v Chelsea
Liverpool v Everton
Manchester U v Manchester C
Nottingham F v Crystal Palace
QPR v Aston Villa
Sheffield W v Millwall
Southampton v Derby Co
Tottenham H v Norwich C
Wimbledon v Luton T

Division Two
Blackburn R v AFC Bournemouth
Bradford C v Barnsley
Brighton & HA v Leicester C
Hull C v Sheffield U
Ipswich T v Oxford U
Middlesbrough v Portsmouth
Newcastle U v Sunderland
Plymouth Arg v Wolverhampton W
Stoke C v Port Vale
Watford v West Ham U
WBA v Oldham Ath

Division Three
Birmingham C v Brentford
Blackpool v Mansfield T
Bristol R v Bristol C
Bury v Shrewsbury T
Cardiff C v Wigan Ath
Chester C v Preston NE
Fulham v Walsall
Huddersfield T v Tranmere R
Leyton O v Bolton W
Northampton T v Crewe Alex
Reading v Swansea C
Rotherham U v Notts Co

Division Four
Chesterfield v Maidstone U
Exeter C v Scunthorpe U
Gillingham v Carlisle U
Grimsby T v York C
Hereford U v Burnley
Lincoln C v Wrexham
Peterborough U v Hartlepool U
Rochdale v Torquay U
Scarborough v Colchester U
Stockport Co v Aldershot

Sunday 4 February

Division Two
Swindon T v Leeds U

Friday 9 February

Division Three
Tranmere R v Birmingham C

Saturday 10 February

Division One
Arsenal v Nottingham F
Aston Villa v Sheffield W
Chelsea v Tottenham H
Crystal Palace v Southampton
Derby Co v QPR
Everton v Charlton Athletic
Luton T v Coventry C
Manchester c v Wimbledon
Millwall v Manchester U
Norwich C v Liverpool

Division Two
AFC Bournemouth v Middlesbrough
Barnsley v Swindon T
Leeds U v Hull C
Leicester C v Bradford C
Oldham Ath v Stoke C
Oxford U v WBA
Port Vale v Watford
Portsmouth v Newcastle U
Sheffield U v Plymouth Arg
Sunderland v Blackburn R
West Ham U v Brighton & HA
Wolverhampton W v Ipswich T

Division Three
Bolton W v Rotherham U
Brentford v Huddersfield T
Bristol C v Cardiff C
Crewe Alex v Blackpool
Mansfield T v Bury
Notts Co v Chester C
Preston NE v Bristol R
Shrewsbury T v Northampton T
Swansea C v Fulham
Walsall v Reading
Wigan Ath v Leyton O

Division Four
Aldershot v Chesterfield
Burnley v Gillingham
Cambridge U v Exeter C
Carlisle U v Halifax T
Colchester U v Rochdale
Doncaster R v Scarborough
Hartlepool U v Stockport C
Maidstone U v Grimsby T
Scunthorpe U v Peterborough U
Torquay U v Southend U
Wrexham v Hereford U
York C v Lincoln C

Monday 12 February

Division Three
Tranmere R v Reading

Tuesday 13 February

Division Three
Bolton W v Huddersfield T
Brentford v Cardiff C
Bristol C v Northampton T
Crewe Alex v Chester C
Mansfield T v Fulham
Notts Co v Bristol R
Preston NE v Leyton O
Shrewsbury T v Blackpool
Swansea C v Birmingham C
Walsall v Rotherham U
Wigan Ath v Bury

Division Four
Aldershot v Peterborough U
Burnley v Chesterfield
Cambridge U v Scarborough
Carlisle U v Exeter C
Colchester U v Grimsby T
Doncaster R v Lincoln C
Hartlepool U v Southend U
Scunthorpe U v Gillingham
Torquay U v Halifax T
Wrexham v Rochdale
York C v Stockport C

Wednesday 14 February

Division Four
Maidstone U v Hereford U

Friday 16 February

Division Four
Stockport C v Doncaster R

Saturday 17 February

Division One
Charlton Ath v Luton T
Coventry C v Millwall
Liverpool v Derby Co
Manchester U v Everton
Nottingham F v Chelsea
QPR v Manchester C
Sheffield W v Arsenal
Southampton v Norwich C
Tottenham H v Aston Villa
Wimbledon v Crystal Palace

Division Two
Blackburn R v Port Vale
Bradford C v Oxford U
Brighton & HA v Sheffield U
Hull C v Portsmouth
Ipswich T v Leeds U
Middlesbrough v Barnsley
Newcastle U v AFC Bournemouth
Plymouth Arg v Oldham Ath
Stoke C v Wolverhampton W
Swindon T v West Ham U
Watford v Sunderland
WBA v Leicester C

Division Three
Birmingham C v Wigan Ath
Blackpool v Swansea C
Bristol R v Walsall
Bury v Tranmere R
Cardiff C v Crewe Alex
Chester C v Shrewsbury T
Fulham v Notts Co
Huddersfield T v Mansfield T
Leyton O v Brentford
Northampton T v Bolton W
Reading v Preston NE
Rotherham U v Bristol C

Division Four
Chesterfield v Wrexham
Exeter C v Maidstone U
Gillingham v York C
Grimsby T v Burnley
Halifax T v Aldershot
Hereford U v Hartlepool U
Lincoln C v Colchester U
Peterborough U v Carlisle U
Rochdale v Cambridge U
Scarborough v Torquay U
Southend U v Scunthorpe U

Tuesday 20 February

Division Three
Northampton T v Walsall

Friday 23 February

Division Three
Tranmere R v Blackpool

Division Four
Colchester U v Gillingham

Saturday 24 February

Division One
Arsenal v Liverpool
Aston Villa v Wimbledon
Chelsea v Manchester U
Crystal Palace v Sheffield W
Derby Co v Tottenham H
Everton v Nottingham F
Luton T v Southampton
Manchester C v Charlton Ath
Millwall v QPR
Norwich C v Coventry C

Division Two
AFC Bournemouth v Bradford City
Barnsley v Hull C
Leeds U v WBA
Leicester C v Stoke C
Oldham Ath v Ipswich T
Oxford U v Middlesbrough
Port Vale v Plymouth Arg
Portsmouth v Swindon T
Sheffield U v Newcastle U
Sunderland v Brighton & HA
West Ham U v Blackburn R
Wolverhampton W v Watford

Division Three
Bolton W v Birmingham C
Bristol C v Reading
Crewe Alex v Bury
Mansfield T v Leyton O
Notts Co v Huddersfield T
Preston NE v Cardiff C
Shrewsbury T v Rotherham U
Swansea C v Bristol R
Walsall v Chester C
Wigan Ath v Fulham

Division Four
Aldershot v Grimsby T
Burnley v Lincoln C
Carlisle U v Rochdale
Hartlepool U v Chesterfield
Maidstone U v Halifax T
Scunthorpe v Stockport Co
Torquay U v Peterborough U
Wrexham v Exeter C
York C v Scarborough

Sunday 25 February

Division Three
Brentford v Northampton T

Division Four
Cambridge U v Southend U
Doncaster R v Hereford U

Friday 2 March

Division Three
Cardiff C v Shrewsbury T

Division Four
Stockport Co v Colchester U

Saturday 3 March

Division One
Charlton Ath v Norwich C
Coventry C v Aston Villa
Liverpool v Millwall
Manchester U v Luton T
Nottingham F v Manchester C
QPR v Arsenal
Sheffield W v Derby Co
Southampton v Chelsea
Tottenham H v Crystal Palace
Wimbledon v Everton

Division Two
Blackburn R v Wolverhampton W
Bradford C v Sheffield U
Brighton & HA v Oldham Ath
Hull C v Oxford U
Ipswich T v Leicester C
Middlesbrough v West Ham U
Newcastle U v Barnsley
Plymouth Arg v Sunderland
Stoke C v AFC Bournemouth
Swindon T v Port Vale
Watford v Leeds U
WBA v Portsmouth

Division Three
Birmingham C v Mansfield T
Blackpool v Walsall
Bristol R v Wigan Ath
Bury v Notts Co
Chester C v Bristol C
Fulham v Preston NE
Huddersfield T v Crewe Alex
Leyton O v Swansea C
Northampton T v Tranmere R
Reading v Bolton W
Rotherham U v Brentford

Division Four
Chesterfield v Torquay U
Exeter C v York C
Gillingham v Cambridge U
Grimsby T v Doncaster R
Halifax T v Scunthorpe U
Hereford U v Aldershot
Lincoln C v Hartlepool U
Peterborough U v Wrexham
Rochdale v Maidstone U
Scarborough v Burnley
Southend U v Carlisle U

Tuesday 6 March

Division Two
AFC Bournemouth v Oxford U
Barnsley v Blackburn R
Portsmouth v Wolverhampton W
Sheffield U v Sunderland
Stoke C v Ipswich T
Swindon T v Bradford C

Division Three
Birmingham C v Blackpool
Bristol C v Tranmere R
Bury v Northampton T
Cardiff C v Rotherham U
Crewe Alex v Shrewsbury T
Fulham v Chester C
Leyton O v Huddersfield T
Mansfield T v Bolton W
Notts C v Swansea C
Preston NE v Walsall
Reading v Bristol R
Wigan Ath v Brentford

Division Four
Burnley v Torquay U
Cambridge U v Maidstone U
Colchester U v Carlisle U
Doncaster R v Hartlepool U
Gillingham v Peterborough U
Rochdale v Chesterfield
Scunthorpe U v Aldershot
Wrexham v York C

Wednesday 7 March

Division Two
Brighton & HA v Plymouth Arg
Leeds U v Port Vale
Leicester C v Oldham Ath
Middlesbrough v Watford
Newcastle U v Hull C
WBA v West Ham U

Division Four
Exeter C v Halifax T
Hereford U v Grimsby T
Lincoln C v Southend U
Scarborough v Stockport Co

Friday 9 March

Division Three
Chester C v Reading
Tranmere R v Wigan Ath

Division Four
Southend U v Gillingham
Stockport Co v Wrexham

Saturday 10 March

Division One
Aston Villa v Luton T
Chelsea v Norwich C
Crystal Palace v Derby Co
Liverpool v Wimbledon
Manchester C v Arsenal
Millwall v Everton
Nottingham F v Coventry C
Sheffield W v Manchester U
Southampton v QPR
Tottenham H v Charlton Ath

Division Two
Blackburn R v WBA
Bradford C v Stoke C
Hull C v Middlesbrough
Ipswich T v Brighton & HA
Oldham Ath v Sheffield U
Oxford U v Leeds U
Plymouth Arg v Swindon T
Port Vale v AFC Bournemouth
Sunderland v Leicester C
Watford v Newcastle U
West Ham U v Portsmouth
Wolverhampton W v Barnsley

Division Three
Blackpool v Preston NE
Bolton W v Notts Co
Brentford v Crewe Alex
Bristol R v Leyton O
Huddersfield T v Fulham
Northampton T v Cardiff C
Rotherham U v Bury
Shrewsbury T v Bristol C
Swansea C v Mansfield T
Walsall v Birmingham C

Division Four
Aldershot v Doncaster R
Carlisle U v Cambridge U
Chesterfield v Hereford U
Grimsby T v Exeter C
Halifax T v Scarborough
Hartlepool U v Rochdale
Maidstone U v Colchester U
Peterborough U v Lincoln C
Torquay U v Scunthorpe U
York C v Burnley

Friday 16 March

Division Three
Wigan Ath v Bolton W

Division Four
Cambridge U v York C
Gillingham v Halifax T

Saturday 17 March

Division One
Arsenal v Chelsea
Charlton Ath v Nottingham F
Coventry C v Sheffield W
Derby Co v Aston Villa
Everton v Crystal Palace
Luton T v Manchester C
Manchester U v Liverpool
Norwich C v Millwall
QPR v Tottenham H
Wimbledon v Southampton

Division Two
AFC Bournemouth v Sunderland
Barnsley v Oldham Ath
Brighton & HA v Bradford C
Leeds U v West Ham U
Leicester C v Port Vale
Middlesbrough v Blackburn R
Newcastle U v Ipswich T
Portsmouth v Oxford U
Sheffield U v Wolverhampton W
Stoke C v Plymouth Arg
Swindon T v Hull C
WBA v Watford

Division Three
Birmingham C v Rotherham U
Bristol C v Brentford
Bury v Chester C
Cardiff C v Huddersfield T
Crewe Alex v Swansea C
Fulham v Bristol R
Leyton O v Tranmere R
Mansfield T v Shrewsbury T
Notts Co v Walsall
Preston NE v Northampton T
Reading v Blackpool

Division Four
Burnley v Maidstone U
Colchester U v Aldershot
Doncaster R v Torquay U
Exeter C v Peterborough U
Hereford U v Stockport C
Lincoln C v Chesterfield
Rochdale v Grimsby T
Scarborough v Southend U
Scunthorpe U v Hartlepool U
Wrexham v Carlisle U

Monday 19 March

Division Two
Port Vale v Barnsley

Division Three
Tranmere R v Notts Co

Division Four
Stockport Co v Gillingham

Tuesday 20 March

Division Two
Blackburn R v Portsmouth
Hull C v Stoke C
Ipswich T v Swindon T
Oldham Ath v AFC Bournemouth
Plymouth Arg v Middlesbrough
Sunderland v Leeds U
Watford v Brighton & HA
Wolverhampton W v WBA

Division Three
Blackpool v Leyton O
Bolton W v Crewe Alex
Brentford v Preston NE
Chester C v Cardiff C
Huddersfield T v Reading
Northampton T v Birmingham C
Rotherham U v Fulham
Shrewsbury T v Wigan Ath
Swansea C v Bristol C
Walsall v Mansfield T

Division Four
Aldershot v Wrexham
Carlisle U v Doncaster R
Chesterfield v Exeter C
Grimsby T v Scarborough
Halifax T v Lincoln C
Hartlepool U v Burnley
Southend U v Hereford U
Torquay U v Cambridge U
York C v Colchester U

Wednesday 21 March

Division Two
Bradford C v Newcastle U
Oxford U v Leicester C
West Ham U v Sheffield U

Division Three
Bristol Rv Bury

Division Four
Maidstone U v Scunthorpe U
Peterborough U v Rochdale

Friday 23 March

Division Three
Swansea C v Bury

Division Four
Southend U v Stockport Co

Saturday 24 March

Division One
Coventry C v Charlton Ath
Crystal Palace v Aston Villa
Derby Co v Arsenal
Everton v Norwich C
Luton T v Millwall
Manchester C v Chelsea
QPR v Nottingham F
Southampton v Manchester U
Tottenham H v Liverpool
Wimbledon v Sheffield W

Division Two
AFC Bournemouth v Watford
Blackburn R v Newcastle U
Brighton & HA v Middlesbrough
Ipswich T v Bradford C
Leeds U v Portsmouth
Leicester C v Plymouth Arg
Oldham Ath v Hull C
Oxford U v Swindon T
Port Vale v Wolverhampton W
Sheffield U v Barnsley
Sunderland v West Ham U
WBA v Stoke C

Division Three
Birmingham C v Chester C
Blackpool v Northampton T
Bolton W v Brentford
Bristol R v Cardiff C
Crewe Alex v Preston NE
Fulham v Reading
Leyton O v Rotherham U
Mansfield T v Tranmere R
Notts Co v Bristol C
Shrewsbury T v Walsall
Wigan Ath v Huddersfield T

Division Four
Aldershot v York C
Exeter C v Rochdale
Gillingham v Grimsby T
Halifax T v Chesterfield
Hartlepool U v Torquay U
Peterborough U v Burnley
Scarborough v Hereford U
Scunthorpe U v Carlisle U
Wrexham v Colchester U

Sunday 25 March

Division Four
Doncaster R v Cambridge U
Lincoln C v Maidstone U

Friday 30 March

Division Three
Tranmere R v Swansea C

Division Four
Cambridge U v Wrexham
Stockport Co v Peterborough U

Saturday 31 March

Division One
Arsenal v Everton
Aston Villa v Manchester C
Charlton Ath v QPR
Chelsea v Derby Co
Liverpool v Southampton
Manchester U v Coventry C
Millwall v Crystal Palace
Norwich C v Luton T
Nottingham F v Wimbledon
Sheffield W v Tottenham H

Division Two
Barnsley v Oxford U
Bradford C v Sunderland
Hull C v WBA
Middlesbrough v Oldham Ath
Newcastle U v Brighton & HA
Plymouth Arg v Ipswich T
Portsmouth v AFC Bournemouth
Stoke C v Sheffield U
Swindon T v Leicester C
Watford v Blackburn R
West Ham U v Port Vale
Wolverhampton W v Leeds U

Division Three
Brentford v Shrewsbury T
Bristol C v Mansfield T
Bury v Fulham
Cardiff C v Blackpool
Chester C v Bolton W
Huddersfield T v Birmingham C
Northampton T v Bristol R
Preston NE v Notts Co
Reading v Leyton O
Rotherham U v Crewe Alex
Walsall v Wigan Ath

Division Four
Burnley v Doncaster R
Carlisle U v Scarborough
Chesterfield v Gillingham
Colchester U v Scunthorpe U
Grimsby T v Lincoln C
Hereford U v Exeter C
Maidstone U v Southend U
Rochdale v Halifax T
Torquay U v Aldershot
York C v Hartlepool U

Friday 6 April

Division Two
Brighton & HA v Hull C
Oldham Ath v Wolverhampton W

Division Three
Crewe Alex v Tranmere R

Division Four
Aldershot v Burnley

Saturday 7 April

Division One
Arsenal v Aston Villa
Charlton Ath v Liverpool
Chelsea v Luton T
Coventry C v Derby Co
Everton v QPR
Manchester U v Wimbledon
Millwall v Manchester C
Norwich C v Crystal Palace
Nottingham F v Tottenham H
Sheffield W v Southampton

Division Two
AFC Bournemouth v Swindon T
Blackburn R v Plymouth Arg
Leeds U v Bradford C
Leicester C v Barnsley
Oxford U v West Ham U
Port Vale v Newcastle U
Sunderland v Stoke C
Watford v Ipswich T
WBA v Middlesbrough

Division Three
Birmingham C v Bury
Blackpool v Rotherham U
Bolton W v Preston NE
Brentford v Notts Co
Bristol R v Chester C
Leyton O v Cardiff C
Mansfield T v Reading
Northampton T v Fulham
Shrewsbury T v Huddersfield T
Swansea C v Walsall
Wigan Ath v Bristol C

Division Four
Doncaster R v York C
Exeter C v Stockport Co
Gillingham v Torquay U
Halifax T v Grimsby T
Hartlepool U v Carlisle U
Lincoln C v Hereford U
Peterborough U v Colchester U
Scarborough v Rochdale
Scunthorpe U v Cambridge U
Southend U v Chesterfield
Wrexham v Maidstone U

Monday 9 April

Division Three
Tranmere R v Shrewsbury T

Division Four
Stockport Co v Lincoln C

Tuesday 10 April

Division Two
Barnsley v Sunderland
Bradford C v Oldham Ath
Hull C v Blackburn R
Ipswich T v Portsmouth
Plymouth Arg v Leeds U
Sheffield U v Watford
Stoke C v Oxford U
Swindon T v Brighton & HA
Wolverhampton W v Leicester C

Division Three
Bristol C v Crewe Alex
Bury v Blackpool
Cardiff C v Birmingham C
Chester C v Leyton O
Fulham v Brentford
Huddersfield T v Bristol R
Notts Co v Northampton T
Preston NE v Mansfield T
Reading v Wigan Ath
Rotherham U v Swansea C
Walsall v Bolton W

Division Four
Burnley v Southend U
Cambridge U v Hartlepool U
Carlisle U v Aldershot
Chesterfield v Scarborough
Colchester U v Exeter C
Grimsby T v Peterborough U
Rochdale v Gillingham
Torquay U v Wrexham
York C v Scunthorpe U

Wednesday 11 April

Division Two
Middlesbrough v Port Vale
Newcastle U v WBA
West Ham U v AFC Bournemouth

Division Four
Hereford U v Halifax T
Maidstone U v Doncaster R

Friday 13 April

Division Two
Oldham Ath v Leeds U

Saturday 14 April

Division One
Aston Villa v Chelsea
Crystal Palace v Arsenal
Derby Co v Millwall
Liverpool v Nottingham F
Luton T v Everton
Manchester C v Sheffield W
QPR v Manchester U
Southampton v Charlton Ath
Tottenham H v Coventry C
Wimbledon v Norwich C

Division Two
Barnsley v West Ham U
Bradford C v Blackburn R
Brighton & HA v WBA
Ipswich T v Port Vale
Leicester C v Portsmouth
Plymouth Arg v AFC Bournemouth
Sheffield U v Oxford U
Stoke C v Middlesbrough
Sunderland v Hull C
Swindon T v Watford
Wolverhampton W v Newcastle U

Division Three
Bolton W v Tranmere R
Bristol R v Rotherham U
Chester C v Northampton T
Fulham v Birmingham C
Huddersfield T v Blackpool
Leyton O v Bury
Mansfield T v Wigan Ath
Notts Co v Crewe Alex
Preston NE v Bristol C
Reading v Cardiff C
Swansea C v Shrewsbury T
Walsall v Brentford

Division Four
Aldershot v Maidstone U
Burnley v Cambridge U
Doncaster R v Chesterfield
Gillingham v Hereford U
Hartlepool U v Colchester U
Lincoln C v Scarborough
Peterborough U v Halifax T
Scunthorpe U v Wrexham
Southend U v Rochdale
Stockport Co v Grimsby T
Torquay U v Exeter C
York C v Carlisle U

Monday 16 April

Division One
Arsenal v Southampton
Charlton Ath v Wimbledon
Chelsea v Crystal Palace
Coventry C v QPR
Everton v Derby Co
Millwall v Tottenham H
Norwich C v Manchester C
Nottingham F v Luton T

Division Two
Blackburn R v Swindon T
Hull C v Wolverhampton W
Leeds U v Sheffield U
Middlesbrough v Bradford C
Newcastle U v Stoke C
Oxford U v Sunderland
Port Vale v Oldham Ath
Portsmouth v Brighton & HA
WBA v Plymouth Arg

Division Three
Birmingham C v Bristol R
Blackpool v Bolton W
Brentford v Reading
Bristol C v Fulham
Bury v Huddersfield T
Cardiff C v Swansea C
Crewe Alex v Walsall
Northampton T v Leyton O
Rotherham U v Mansfield T
Tranmere R v Preston NE
Wigan Ath v Chester C

Division Four
Carlisle U v Burnley
Chesterfield v Peterborough U
Colchester U v Southend U
Exeter C v Aldershot
Grimsby v Scunthorpe U
Halifax T v York C
Hereford U v Torquay U
Maidstone U v Gillingham
Rochdale v Stockport Co
Scarborough v Hartlepool U
Wrexham v Doncaster R

Tuesday 17 April

Division One
Manchester U v Aston Villa

Division Two
AFC Bournemouth v Leicester C
Watford v Barnsley
West Ham U v Ipswich T

Division Three
Shrewsbury T v Notts Co

Division Four
Cambridge U v Lincoln C

Friday 20 April

Division Three
Chester C v Tranmere R

Division Four
Southend U v Grimsby T
Stockport Co v Carlisle U

Saturday 21 April

Division One
Aston Villa v Millwall
Crystal Palace v Charlton Ath
Derby Co v Norwich C
Liverpool v Chelsea
Luton T v Arsenal
Manchester C v Everton
QPR v Sheffield W
Southampton v Nottingham F
Tottenham H v Manchester U
Wimbledon v Coventry C

Division Two
Barnsley v AFC Bournemouth
Bradford C v Watford
Brighton & HA v Leeds U
Ipswich T v Hull C
Leicester C v Middlesbrough
Oldham Ath v West Ham U
Plymouth Arg v Newcastle U
Sheffield U v Port Vale
Stoke C v Blackburn R
Sunderland v Portsmouth
Swindon T v WBA
Wolverhampton W v Oxford U

Division Three
Bolton W v Shrewsbury T
Bristol R v Crewe Alex
Fulham v Blackpool
Huddersfield T v Rotherham U
Leyton O v Bristol C
Mansfield T v Brentford
Notts Co v Cardiff C
Preston NE v Birmingham C
Reading v Northampton T
Swansea C v Wigan Ath
Walsall v Bury

Division Four
Aldershot v Scarborough
Burnley v Wrexham
Doncaster R v Halifax T
Gillingham v Exeter C
Hartlepool U v Maidstone U
Lincoln C v Rochdale
Peterborough U v Cambridge U
Scunthorpe U v Hereford U
Torquay U v Colchester U
York C v Chesterfield

Monday 23 April

Division Two
Port Vale v Sunderland

Division Three
Tranmere R v Bristol R

Tuesday 24 April

Division Two
AFC Bournemouth v Wolverhampton W
Blackburn R v Sheffield U
Hull C v Plymouth Arg
Portsmouth v Oldham Ath
Watford v Stoke C

Division Three
Birmingham C v Notts Co
Blackpool v Chester C
Brentford v Swansea C
Bristol C v Huddersfield T
Bury v Bolton W
Cardiff C v Walsall
Crewe Alex v Leyton O
Northampton T v Mansfield T
Rotherham U v Reading
Shrewsbury T v Fulham
Wigan Ath v Preston NE

Division Four
Cambridge U v Stockport Co
Carlisle U v Lincoln C
Chesterfield v Scunthorpe U
Colchester U v Doncaster R
Grimsby T v Hartlepool U
Halifax T v Burnley
Rochdale v Aldershot
Wrexham v Gillingham

Wednesday 25 April

Division Two
Leeds U v Barnsley
Middlesbrough v Ipswich T
Newcastle U v Swindon T
Oxford U v Brighton & HA
WBA v Bradford C
West Ham U v Leicester C

Division Four
Exeter C v Southend U
Hereford U v York C
Maidstone U v Torquay U
Scarborough v Peterborough U

Friday 27 April

Division Four
Southend U v Halifax T

Saturday 28 April

Division One
Arsenal v Millwall
Aston Villa v Norwich C
Charlton Ath v Sheffield W
Chelsea v Everton
Liverpool v QPR
Luton T v Crystal Palace
Manchester C v Derby Co
Nottingham F v Manchester U
Southampton v Coventry C
Wimbledon v Tottenham H

Division Two
Barnsley v WBA
Brighton & HA v Stoke C
Hull C v Bradford C
Ipswich T v Blackburn R
Leeds U v Leicester C
Newcastle U v West Ham U
Oldham Ath v Oxford U
Plymouth Arg v Watford
Port Vale v Portsmouth
Sheffield U v AFC Bournemouth
Swindon Town v Middlesbrough
Wolverhampton W v Sunderland

Division Three
Bolton W v Bristol C
Brentford v Blackpool
Bristol R v Shrewsbury T
Cardiff C v Fulham
Chester C v Rotherham U
Leyton O v Birmingham C
Mansfield T v Crewe Alex
Northampton T v Huddersfield T
Preston NE v Swansea C
Reading v Bury
Walsall v Tranmere R
Wigan Ath v Notts Co

Division Four
Burnley v Scunthorpe U
Carlisle U v Torquay U
Doncaster R v Rochdale
Exeter C v Scarborough
Gillingham v Lincoln C
Grimsby T v Wrexham
Hartlepool U v Aldershot
Hereford U v Peterborough U
Stockport Co v Chesterfield
York C v Maidstone U

Sunday 29 April

Division Four
Cambridge U v Colchester U

Saturday 5 May

Division One
Coventry C v Liverpool
Crystal Palace v Manchester C
Derby Co v Luton T
Everton v Aston Villa
Manchester U v Charlton Ath
Millwall v Chelsea
Norwich C v Arsenal
QPR v Wimbledon
Sheffield W v Nottingham F
Tottenham H v Southampton

Division Two
AFC Bournemouth v Leeds U
Blackburn R v Brighton & HA
Bradford C v Plymouth Arg
Leicester C v Sheffield U
Middlesbrough v Newcastle U
Oxford U v Port Vale
Portsmouth v Barnsley
Stoke C v Swindon T
Sunderland v Oldham Ath
Watford v Hull C
WBA v Ipswich T
West Ham U v Wolverhampton W

Division Three
Birmingham C v Reading
Blackpool v Bristol R
Bristol C v Walsall
Bury v Cardiff C
Crewe Alex v Wigan Ath
Fulham v Leyton O
Huddersfield T v Chester C
Notts Co v Mansfield T
Rotherham U v Northampton T
Shrewsbury T v Preston NE
Swansea C v Bolton W
Tranmere R v Brentford

Division Four
Aldershot v Cambridge U
Chesterfield v Grimsby T
Colchester U v Burnley
Halifax T v Stockport Co
Lincoln C v Exeter C
Maidstone U v Carlisle U
Peterborough U v Southend U
Rochdale v Hereford U
Scarborough v Gillingham
Scunthorpe U v Doncaster R
Torquay U v York C
Wrexham v Hartlepool U

BARCLAYS LEAGUE FIXTURES 1989–90

DIVISION ONE

	Arsenal	Aston Villa	Charlton Ath	Chelsea	Coventry C	Crystal Palace	Derby Co	Everton	Liverpool	Luton T	Manchester C	Manchester U	Millwall	Norwich C	Nottingham F	QPR	Sheffield W	Southampton	Tottenham H	Wimbledon
Arsenal	—	7.4	23.9	17.3	22.8	1.1	28.10	31.3	24.2	16.12	14.10	2.12	28.4	4.11	10.2	18.11	9.9	16.4	20.1	26.8
Aston Villa	30.12	—	26.8	14.4	18.11	28.10	30.9	4.11	23.8	10.3	31.3	26.12	21.4	28.4	2.12	23.9	10.2	20.1	9.9	24.2
Charlton Ath	3.2	13.1	—	29.8	28.10	16.12	19.8	16.9	7.4	17.2	25.11	4.11	9.12	3.3	17.3	31.3	28.4	1.1	14.10	16.4
Chelsea	30.9	1.1	20.1	—	23.9	16.4	31.3	28.4	16.12	7.4	28.10	24.2	4.11	10.3	9.9	22.8	26.8	18.11	10.2	2.12
Coventry C	9.12	3.3	24.3	3.2	—	13.1	7.4	19.8	5.5	16.9	30.8	21.10	17.2	25.11	14.10	16.4	17.3	11.11	1.1	16.12
Crystal Palace	14.4	24.3	21.4	26.12	26.8	—	10.3	30.9	20.1	11.11	5.5	22.8	21.10	30.12	23.9	2.12	24.2	10.2	18.11	9.9
Derby Co.	24.3	17.3	2.12	21.10	30.12	14.10	—	26.12	9.9	5.5	11.11	26.8	14.4	21.4	20.1	10.2	18.11	23.9	24.2	23.8
Everton	21.10	5.5	10.2	11.11	2.12	17.3	16.4	—	23.9	1.1	16.12	9.9	14.10	24.3	24.2	7.4	20.1	26.8	22.8	18.11
Liverpool	25.11	9.12	30.12	21.4	4.11	30.8	17.2	3.2	—	13.1	19.8	30.9	3.3	16.9	14.4	28.4	26.12	31.3	28.10	10.3
Luton T	21.4	14.10	9.9	30.12	10.2	28.4	4.11	14.4	26.8	—	17.3	18.11	24.3	21.10	26.12	20.1	22.8	24.2	2.12	23.9
Manchester C	10.3	21.10	24.2	24.3	20.1	4.11	28.4	21.4	2.12	30.9	—	23.9	30.12	26.12	18.11	9.9	14.4	23.8	26.8	10.2
Manchester U	19.8	17.4	5.5	25.11	31.3	9.12	13.1	17.2	17.3	3.3	3.2	—	16.9	30.8	11.11	1.1	14.10	28.10	16.12	7.4
Millwall	11.11	16.12	22.8	5.5	9.9	31.3	1.1	10.3	18.11	28.10	7.4	10.2	—	30.9	26.8	24.2	23.9	2.12	16.4	20.1
Norwich C	5.5	11.11	18.11	14.10	24.2	7.4	16.12	28.10	10.2	31.3	16.4	20.1	17.3	—	23.8	26.8	2.12	9.9	23.9	1.1
Nottingham F	16.9	19.8	30.9	17.2	10.3	3.2	30.8	25.11	1.1	16.4	3.3	28.4	13.1	9.12	—	28.10	4.11	17.12	7.4	31.3
QPR	3.3	3.2	21.10	9.12	26.12	19.8	16.9	30.12	11.11	30.8	17.2	14.4	25.11	13.1	24.3	—	21.4	14.10	17.3	5.5
Sheffield W	17.2	16.9	11.11	13.1	30.9	25.11	3.3	30.8	29.11	9.12	1.1	10.3	3.1	19.8	5.5	16.12	—	7.4	31.3	28.10
Southampton	26.12	29.8	14.4	3.3	28.4	16.9	3.2	13.1	21.10	25.11	9.12	24.3	19.8	17.2	21.4	10.3	30.12	—	4.11	30.9
Tottenham H	18.10	17.2	10.3	16.9	14.4	3.3	25.11	9.12	24.3	19.8	13.1	21.4	26.12	3.2	30.12	30.9	21.10	5.5	—	11.11
Wimbledon	13.1	25.11	26.12	19.8	21.4	17.2	9.12	3.3	14.10	3.2	16.9	30.12	29.8	14.4	21.10	4.11	24.3	17.3	28.4	—

DIVISION TWO

	Barnsley	Blackburn R	Bournemouth	Bradford C	Brighton & HA	Hull C	Ipswich T	Leeds U	Leicester C	Middlesbrough	Newcastle U	Oldham Ath	Oxford U	Plymouth Arg	Portsmouth	Port Vale	Sheffield U	Stoke C	Sunderland	Swindon T	Watford	WBA	West Ham U	Wolverhampton W
Barnsley	—	6.3	21.4	23.9	26.8	24.2	2.12	30.12	28.10	9.9	18.11	17.3	31.3	20.1	4.11	14.10	17.10	22.8	10.4	10.2	26.12	28.4	14.4	26.9
Blackburn R	30.9	—	3.2	1.1	5.5	31.10	11.11	13.1	9.12	7.10	24.3	19.8	2.9	7.4	20.3	17.2	24.4	16.12	16.9	16.4	21.10	10.3	25.11	3.3
Bournemouth	16.12	23.9	—	24.2	2.12	26.8	20.1	5.5	17.4	10.2	9.9	14.10	6.3	1.1	21.10	26.9	11.11	18.11	17.3	7.4	24.3	22.8	31.10	24.4
Bradford C	3.2	14.4	25.11	—	7.10	11.11	18.10	28.10	16.9	26.12	21.3	10.4	17.2	5.5	2.9	19.8	3.3	10.3	31.3	30.9	21.4	30.12	9.12	13.1
Brighton & HA	13.1	4.11	19.8	17.3	—	6.4	27.9	21.4	3.2	24.3	21.10	3.3	30.12	7.3	26.12	2.9	17.2	28.4	25.11	1.11	14.10	14.4	16.9	9.12
Hull C	25.11	10.4	13.1	28.4	28.10	—	16.12	16.9	19.8	10.3	30.9	17.10	3.3	24.4	17.2	9.12	3.2	20.3	1.1	7.10	4.11	31.3	2.9	16.4
Ipswich T	19.8	28.4	2.9	24.3	10.3	21.4	—	17.2	3.3	30.12	7.10	25.11	3.2	21.10	10.4	14.4	13.1	30.9	9.12	20.3	31.10	4.11	26.12	16.9
Leeds U	25.4	26.8	4.11	7.4	16.12	10.2	9.9	—	28.4	23.8	2.12	1.1	27.9	1.11	24.3	7.3	16.4	20.1	14.10	23.9	18.11	24.2	17.3	21.10
Leicester C	7.4	23.8	26.12	10.2	23.9	2.12	18.11	11.11	—	21.4	26.8	7.3	14.10	24.3	14.4	17.3	5.5	24.2	27.9	21.10	20.1	9.9	30.12	1.11
Middlesbrough	17.2	17.3	16.9	16.4	18.10	27.9	25.4	9.12	16.12	—	5.5	31.3	25.11	14.10	3.2	11.4	2.9	1.1	13.1	11.11	7.3	28.10	3.3	19.8
Newcastle U	3.3	18.10	17.2	14.10	31.3	7.3	17.3	19.8	13.1	4.11	—	2.9	9.12	16.12	16.9	28.10	25.11	16.4	3.2	25.4	27.9	11.4	28.4	1.1
Oldham Ath	7.10	1.12	20.3	31.10	18.11	24.3	24.2	13.4	30.9	21.10	20.1	—	28.4	9.9	30.12	26.12	10.3	10.2	4.11	26.8	22.8	23.9	21.4	6.4
Oxford U	21.10	20.1	30.9	9.9	25.4	18.11	23.9	10.3	21.3	24.2	13.9	11.11	—	2.12	7.10	5.5	1.1	1.11	16.4	24.3	26.8	10.2	7.4	16.12
Plymouth Arg	2.9	28.10	14.4	4.11	30.9	29.12	31.3	10.4	17.10	20.3	21.4	17.2	19.8	—	10.12	25.11	16.9	7.10	3.3	10.3	28.4	26.12	13.1	3.2
Portsmouth	5.5	14.10	31.3	20.1	16.4	9.9	28.10	17.10	1.1	23.9	10.2	24.4	17.3	12.9	—	11.11	7.4	26.8	16.12	24.2	2.12	18.11	26.9	6.3
Port Vale	19.3	9.9	10.3	2.12	20.1	12.9	1.1	30.9	7.10	30.10	7.4	16.4	4.11	24.2	28.4	—	16.12	23.9		18.11	10.2	26.8	21.10	24.3
Sheffield U	24.3	30.12	28.4	18.11	9.9	23.9	26.8	26.12	4.11	20.1	24.2	26.9	14.4	10.2	31.10	21.4	—	21.10	6.3	12.9	10.4	2.12	14.10	17.3
Stoke C	9.12	21.4	3.3	26.9	11.11	14.10	6.3	2.9	25.11	14.4	26.12	16.9	10.4	17.3	13.1	3.2	31.3	—	28.10	5.5	30.12	17.10	19.8	17.2
Sunderland	31.10	10.2	7.10	21.10	24.2	14.4	22.8	20.3	10.3	26.8	23.9	5.5	26.12	18.11	21.4	30.12	30.9	7.4	—	2.12	9.9	20.1	24.3	11.11
Swindon T	16.9	26.12	28.10	6.3	10.4	17.3	14.10	4.2	31.3	28.4	30.12	13.1	17.10	26.9	26.11	3.3	10.12	4.11	19.8	—	14.4	21.4	17.2	3.9
Watford	17.4	31.3	17.10	16.12	20.3	5.5	7.4	3.3	2.9	30.9	10.3	9.12	13.1	11.11	19.8	16.9	28.10	24.4	17.2	1.1	—	7.10	3.2	25.11
WBA	11.11	27.9	9.12	25.4	1.1	21.10	5.5	25.11	17.2	7.4	1.11	3.2	16.9	16.4	3.3	13.1	19.8	24.3	2.9	17.12	17.3	—	7.3	14.10
West Ham U	1.1	24.2	11.4	23.8	10.2	20.1	17.4	7.10	25.4	18.11	11.11	16.12	28.10	26.8	10.3	31.3	21.3	2.12	18.10	9.9	23.9	30.9	—	5.5
Wolverhampton W	10.3	18.11	30.12	26.8	12.9	26.12	10.2	31.3	10.4	2.12	14.4	28.10	21.4	23.9	30.9	17.10	7.10	9.9	28.4	20.1	24.2	20.3	4.11	—

DIVISION THREE

	Birmingham C	Blackpool	Bolton W	Brentford	Bristol C	Bristol R	Bury	Cardiff C	Chester C	Crewe Alex	Fulham	Huddersfield T	Leyton Orient	Mansfield T	Northampton T	Notts Co	Preston NE	Reading	Rotherham U	Shrewsbury T	Swansea C	Tranmere R	Walsall	Wigan Ath
Birmingham C	—	6.3	25.11	3.2	13.1	16.4	7.4	31.10	24.3	19.8	1.1	21.10	11.11	3.3	14.10	24.4	16.12	5.5	17.3	27.1	2.9	16.9	26.9	17.2
Blackpool	30.9	—	16.4	11.11	27.1	5.5	31.10	21.10	24.4	16.9	16.12	1.1	20.3	3.2	24.3	13.1	10.3	6.10	7.4	2.9	17.2	25.11	3.3	19.8
Bolton W	24.2	26.12	—	24.3	28.4	9.9	30.12	20.1	21.10	20.3	26.8	13.2	23.9	30.9	2.12	10.3	7.4	6.1	10.2	21.4	4.11	14.4	31.10	7.10
Brentford	23.9	28.4	17.10	—	7.10	20.1	9.9	13.2	26.8	10.3	28.10	10.2	3.12	17.12	25.2	7.4	20.3	16.4	6.1	31.3	24.4	4.11	1.1	30.9
Bristol C	26.8	9.9	11.11	17.3	—	23.9	20.1	10.2	6.1	10.4	16.4	24.4	16.12	31.3	13.2	17.10	1.1	24.2	2.12	26.9	14.10	6.3	5.5	28.10
Bristol R	26.12	4.11	27.1	19.8	3.2	—	21.3	24.3	7.4	21.4	7.10	1.11	10.3	13.1	21.10	2.9	16.9	30.9	14.4	28.4	25.11	30.12	17.2	3.3
Bury	28.10	10.4	24.4	27.1	19.8	14.10	—	5.5	17.3	25.11	31.3	16.4	1.1	16.9	6.3	3.3	13.1	11.11	26.9	3.2	17.10	17.2	16.12	2.9
Cardiff C	10.4	31.3	19.8	2.9	16.9	17.10	3.11	—	14.10	17.2	28.4	17.3	28.10	27.1	26.9	16.12	25.11	1.1	6.3	2.3	16.4	13.1	24.4	3.2
Chester C	17.10	30.12	31.3	12.1	3.3	28.10	7.10	20.3	—	2.9	30.9	4.11	10.4	19.8	14.4	15.9	3.2	9.3	28.4	17.2	26.1	20.4	24.11	26.12
Crewe Alex	20.1	10.2	14.10	26.9	31.10	16.12	24.2	2.12	13.2	—	9.9	6.1	24.4	10.11	23.9	1.1	24.3	25.8	21.10	6.3	17.3	6.4	16.4	5.5
Fulham	14.4	21.4	13.1	10.4	26.12	17.3	21.10	11.11	6.3	27.1	—	26.9	5.5	2.9	31.10	17.2	3.3	24.3	14.10	30.12	16.9	19.8	3.2	25.11
Huddersfield T	31.3	14.4	2.9	16.9	30.12	10.4	26.12	7.10	5.5	3.3	10.3	—	30.9	17.2	11.11	25.11	27.1	20.3	21.4	28.10	19.8	3.2	13.1	17.10
Leyton Orient	28.4	14.10	3.2	17.2	21.4	26.9	14.4	7.4	31.10	30.12	4.11	6.3	—	25.11	26.12	19.8	2.9	21.10	24.3	13.1	3.3	17.3	27.1	16.9
Mansfield T	6.1	23.9	6.3	21.4	21.10	26.8	10.2	9.9	20.1	28.4	13.2	2.12	24.2	—	30.12	4.11	31.10	7.4	26.12	17.3	24.10	24.3	14.10	14.4
Northampton T	20.3	17.10	17.2	25.11	2.9	31.3	30.9	10.3	1.1	3.2	7.4	28.4	16.4	24.4	—	28.10	7.10	17.12	4.11	16.9	14.1	3.3	20.2	28.1
Notts Co	30.12	26.8	26.9	31.10	24.3	13.2	6.1	21.4	10.2	14.4	2.12	24.2	20.1	5.5	10.4	—	21.10	9.9	23.9	26.12	6.3	14.10	17.3	11.11
Preston NE	21.4	26.9	28.10	14.10	14.4	10.2	26.8	24.2	23.9	17.10	6.1	9.9	13.2	10.4	17.3	31.3	—	2.12	20.1	4.11	28.4	26.12	6.3	30.12
Reading	4.11	17.3	3.3	26.12	25.11	6.3	28.4	14.4	26.9	13.1	17.10	14.10	31.3	28.10	21.4	27.1	17.2	—	30.12	19.8	3.2	2.9	16.9	10.4
Rotherham U	7.10	28.10	16.9	3.3	17.2	1.1	10.3	30.9	11.11	31.3	20.3	16.12	17.10	16.4	5.5	3.2	19.8	24.4	—	25.11	10.4	27.1	2.9	13.1
Shrewsbury T	9.9	13.2	16.12	21.10	10.3	11.11	23.9	6.1	2.12	30.9	24.4	7.4	26.8	7.10	10.2	17.4	5.5	20.1	24.2	—	1.1	31.10	24.3	20.3
Swansea C	13.2	2.12	5.5	30.12	20.3	24.2	23.3	26.12	9.9	7.10	10.2	21.1	6.1	10.3	26.8	30.9	11.11	23.9	31.10	14.4	—	20.10	7.4	21.4
Tranmere R	9.2	23.2	1.1	5.5	29.9	23.4	2.12	26.8	15.12	27.10	19.1	22.9	6.10	16.10	5.1	19.3	16.4	12.2	9.9	9.4	30.3	—	10.11	9.3
Wallsall	10.3	6.1	10.4	14.4	4.11	2.12	21.4	30.12	24.2	26.12	23.9	26.8	9.9	20.3	19.8	7.10	30.9	10.2	13.2	17.10	28.10	28.4	—	31.3
Wigan Ath	1.12	20.1	16.3	6.3	7.4	6.1	13.2	23.9	16.4	4.11	24.2	24.3	10.2	1.1	9.9	28.4	24.4	31.10	26.8	14.10	16.12	26.9	21.10	—

DIVISION FOUR

	Aldershot	Burnley	Cambridge U	Carlisle U	Chesterfield	Colchester U	Doncaster R	Exeter C	Gillingham	Grimsby T	Halifax T	Hartlepool U	Hereford U	Lincoln C	Maidstone U	Peterborough U	Rochdale	Scarborough	Scunthorpe U	Southend U	Stockport Co	Torquay U	Wrexham	York C
Aldershot	—	6.4	5.5	31.10	10.2	7.10	10.3	26.12	20.1	24.2	2.12	11.11	6.1	26.8	14.4	13.2	30.12	21.4	30.9	9.9	23.9	21.10	20.3	24.3
Burnley	28.10	—	14.4	26.12	13.2	4.11	31.3	9.9	10.2	2.12	30.12	14.10	23.9	24.2	17.3	17.10	20.1	6.1	28.4	10.4	26.8	6.3	21.4	26.9
Cambridge	4.11	1.1	—	26.9	9.9	29.4	17.10	10.2	6.1	20.1	22.9	10.4	26.8	17.4	6.3	17.12	2.12	13.2	28.10	25.2	24.4	13.10	30.3	16.3
Carlisle U	10.4	16.4	10.3	—	26.8	30.9	20.3	13.2	23.9	9.9	10.2	28.10	20.1	24.4	4.11	2.12	24.2	31.3	17.10	6.1	17.12	28.4	7.10	1.1
Chesterfield	16.9	2.9	27.1	13.1	—	19.8	1.1	20.3	31.3	5.5	17.10	25.11	10.3	7.10	3.2	16.4	30.9	10.4	24.4	28.10	11.11	3.3	17.2	16.12
Colchester U	17.3	5.5	10.11	6.3	20.1	—	24.4	10.4	23.2	13.2	26.8	1.1	8.9	2.12	26.9	28.10	10.2	23.9	31.3	16.4	5.1	16.12	17.10	13.10
Doncaster R	26.9	21.10	25.3	14.10	14.4	30.12	—	20.1	26.8	6.1	21.4	6.3	25.2	13.2	31.10	9.9	28.4	10.2	4.11	22.9	2.12	17.3	26.12	7.4
Exeter C	16.4	27.1	16.9	2.9	14.10	1.11	19.8	—	16.12	27.9	7.3	13.1	21.10	4.11	17.2	17.3	24.3	28.4	3.2	25.4	7.4	1.1	25.11	3.3
Gillingham	19.8	16.9	3.3	3.2	21.10	24.11	13.1	21.4	—	24.3	16.3	27.1	14.4	28.4	25.12	6.3	31.10	4.11	2.9	26.9	14.10	7.4	30.12	17.2
Grimsby T	25.11	17.2	19.8	27.1	4.11	2.9	3.3	10.3	17.10	—	28.10	24.4	30.9	31.3	15.9	10.4	7.10	20.3	16.4	16.2	1.1	13.1	28.4	3.2
Halifax T	17.2	24.4	2.2	15.9	24.3	12.1	15.12	30.9	6.10	7.4	—	19.8	31.10	20.3	25.11	1.1	21.10	10.3	3.3	10.11	5.5	2.9	26.1	16.4
Hartlepool U	28.4	20.3	31.10	7.4	24.2	14.4	30.9	26.8	9.9	30.12	20.1	—	2.12	6.1	21.4	23.9	10.3	26.12	7.10	13.2	10.2	24.3	4.11	21.10
Hereford U	3.3	3.2	13.1	19.8	27.9	27.1	25.11	31.3	1.1	7.3	11.4	17.2	—	28.10	2.9	28.4	4.11	18.10	16.12	14.10	17.3	16.4	16.9	25.4
Lincoln C	13.1	25.11	26.12	30.12	17.3	17.2	2.9	5.5	11.11	21.10	14.10	3.3	7.4	—	25.3	27.9	21.4	14.4	19.8	7.3	1.11	27.1	3.2	16.9
Maidstone U	1.1	7.10	30.9	5.5	23.9	10.3	11.4	2.12	16.4	10.2	24.2	16.12	14.2	18.10	—	20.1	6.1	26.8	21.3	31.3	9.9	25.4	28.10	11.11
Peterborough U	2.9	24.3	21.4	17.2	26.12	7.4	27.1	7.10	30.9	1.11	14.4	3.2	11.11	10.3	19.8	—	21.3	30.12	16.9	5.5	21.10	25.11	3.3	13.1
Rochdale	24.4	19.8	17.2	25.11	6.3	16.9	11.11	17.10	10.4	17.3	31.3	26.9	5.5	16.12	3.3	14.10	—	28.10	13.1	1.1	16.4	3.2	2.9	27.1
Scarborough	16.12	3.3	2.9	21.10	1.11	3.2	16.9	11.11	5.5	14.10	27.9	16.4	24.3	1.1	13.1	25.4	7.4	—	27.1	17.3	7.3	17.2	19.8	24.11
Scunthorpe U	6.3	11.11	7.4	24.3	30.12	21.10	5.5	23.9	13.2	26.12	6.1	17.3	21.4	20.1	14.10	10.2	26.8	9.9	—	2.12	24.2	26.9	14.4	31.10
Southend U	27.1	31.10	24.11	3.3	7.4	26.12	2.2	30.12	9.3	20.4	27.4	1.9	20.3	30.9	21.10	4.11	14.4	7.10	17.2	—	23.3	15.9	12.1	19.8
Stockport Co	3.2	13.1	29.12	20.4	28.4	2.3	16.2	28.10	19.3	14.4	3.11	15.9	7.10	9.4	27.1	30.3	26.12	30.9	25.11	16.10	—	19.8	9.3	1.9
Torquay U	31.3	30.9	20.3	11.11	6.1	21.4	7.10	14.4	28.10	26.8	13.2	17.10	26.12	9.9	30.12	24.2	23.9	2.12	10.3	10.2	20.1	—	10.4	5.5
Wrexham	14.10	16.12	21.10	17.3	2.12	24.3	16.4	24.2	24.4	11.11	9.9	5.5	10.2	23.9	7.4	6.1	13.2	20.1	1.1	26.8	26.9	31.10	—	6.3
York C	17.10	10.3	7.10	14.4	21.4	20.3	28.10	6.1	2.12	23.9	26.12	31.3	30.12	10.2	28.4	26.8	9.9	24.2	10.4	20.1	13.2	4.11	30.9	—

THE FOOTBALL ASSOCIATION FIXTURE PROGRAMME – SEASON 1989–90

August 1989

Sat 5 Official Opening of Season
Sat 12 FA Charity Shield
Sat 19 Football League season starts
Wed 23 Littlewoods Cup (1) 1st Leg
Wed 30 Littlewoods Cup (1) 2nd Leg

September 1989

Sat 2 FA Cup (P)
Wed 6 Sweden v England (WC)
Finland v Wales (WC)
Yugoslavia v Scotland (WC)
Sat 9 FA Vase (EP)
FA Youth Cup (P)*
Wed 13 European Cups (1) 1st Leg
Sat 16 FA Cup (1Q)
Wed 20 Littlewoods Cup (2) 1st Leg
Sat 23 FA Trophy (1Q)
Wed 27 European Cups (1) 2nd Leg
Sat 30 FA Cup (2Q)
FA Youth Cup (1Q)*

October 1989

Wed 4 Littlewoods Cup (2) 2nd Leg
Sat 7 FA Vase (P)
Sun 8 FA Sunday Cup (1)
Wed 11 Poland v England (WC)
Wales v Holland (WC)
France v Scotland (WC)
Rep of Ireland v N Ireland (WC)
Sat 14 FA Cup (3Q)
FA Youth Cup (2Q)*
Wed 18 European Cups (2) 1st Leg
Sat 21 FA Trophy (2Q)
FA County Youth Cup (1)*
Wed 25 Littlewoods Cup (3)
Sat 28 FA Cup (4Q)

November 1989

Wed 1 European Cups (2) 2nd Leg
Sat 4 FA Vase (1)
Sat 11 FA Youth Cup (1)*
Sun 12 FA Sunday Cup (2)
Wed 15 England v Italy (F)
West Germany v Wales (WC)
Scotland v Norway (WC)
Sat 18 FA Cup (1)
Wed 22 UEFA Cup (3) 1st Leg
Sat 25 FA Vase (2)
Wed 29 Littlewoods Cup (4)

December 1989

Sat 2 FA Trophy (3Q)
FA County Youth Cup (2)*
Wed 6 UEFA Cup (3) 2nd Leg
Sat 9 FA Cup (2)
FA Youth Cup (2)*
Sun 10 FA Sunday Cup (3)
Sat 16 FA Vase (3)

January 1990

Sat 6 FA Cup (3)
Sat 13 FA Trophy (1)
FA Youth Cup (3)*
Wed 17 Littlewoods Cup (5)
Sat 20 FA Vase (4)
FA County Youth Cup (3)*
Sun 21 FA Sunday Cup (4)
Sat 27 FA Cup (4)

February 1990

Sat 3 FA Trophy (2)
Sat 10 FA Vase (5)
FA Youth Cup (4)*
Wed 14 Littlewoods Cup (SF) 1st Leg
Sat 17 FA Cup (5)
Sun 18 FA Sunday Cup (5)
Sat 24 FA Trophy (3)
FA County Youth Cup (4)*
Wed 28 Littlewoods Cup (SF) 2nd Leg

March 1990

Sat 3 FA Vase (6)
FA Youth Cup (5)*
Wed 7 European Cups (QF) 1st Leg
Sat 10 FA Cup, (6)
England v France (Schoolboys)
Sat 17 FA Trophy (4)
Sun 18 FA Sunday Cup (SF)
Wed 21 European Cups (QF) 2nd Leg
Sat 24 FA Vase (SF) 1st Leg
FA County Youth Cup (SF)*
Wed 28 International date
Sat 31 FA Vase (SF) 2nd Leg
FA Youth Cup (SF)*

April 1990

Wed 4 European Cups (SF) 1st Leg
Sat 7 FA Cup (SF)
FA Trophy (SF) 1st Leg
Sat 14 FA Trophy (SF) 2nd Leg
Wed 18 European Cups (SF) 2nd Leg
Wed 25 International date
Sat 28 FA County Youth Cup Final
Sun 29 Littlewoods Cup Final
FA Sunday Cup Final

May 1990

Wed 2 UEFA Cup Final 1st Leg
Sat 5 FA Vase Final
FA Youth Cup Final*
Wed 9 European Cup-Winners' Cup Final
Sat 12 FA Cup Final
Wed 16 UEFA Cup Final 2nd Leg
Sat 19 FA Trophy Final
Wed 23 European Champion Clubs' Cup Final

June 1989

Sat 2 England v Holland (Schoolboys)
Fri 8 World Cup Finals (end 8 July)

P = Preliminary Round
WC = World Cup
EP = Extra Preliminary Round
1Q = First Qualifying Round
F = Friendly
QF = Quarter-Final
SF = Semi-Final
**Closing date for round*